KU-182-060

WATERFORD CITY AND COUNTY
WITHDRAWN
LIBRARIES

Mary Garden as Mélisande in Debussy's Pelléas et Mélisande *(Paris, 1902)*

WATERFORD

No. 199219.

MUNICIPAL LIBRARY

The

VIKING

OPERA

GUIDE

WATERFORD CITY AND COUNTY

WITHDRAWN

LIBRARIES

EDITED BY AMANDA HOLDEN

with

NICHOLAS KENYON

and STEPHEN WALSH

Consultant Editor RODNEY MILNES

Recordings Consultant ALAN BLYTH

With a Preface by SIR COLIN DAVIS

VIKING

VIKING

Published by the Penguin Group
Penguin Books Ltd, 27 Wrights Lane, London W8 5TZ, England
Penguin Books USA Inc., 375 Hudson Street, New York, New York 10014, USA
Penguin Books Australia Ltd, Ringwood, Victoria, Australia
Penguin Books Canada Ltd, 10 Alcorn Avenue, Toronto, Ontario, Canada M4V 3B2
Penguin Books (NZ) Ltd, 182–190 Wairau Road, Auckland 10, New Zealand

Penguin Books Ltd, Registered Offices: Harmondsworth, Middlesex, England

First published 1993
1 3 5 7 9 10 8 6 4 2
First edition

Copyright © Amanda Holden, 1993

The moral right of the editor has been asserted

The extract from W. H. Auden's poem 'Metalogue to The Magic Flute' is
reprinted from *Collected Poems* by kind permission of Faber and Faber Ltd

The picture credits on p.1271 constitute an extension to this copyright page

All rights reserved.
Without limiting the rights under copyright
reserved above, no part of this publication may be
reproduced, stored in or introduced into a retrieval system,
or transmitted, in any form or by any means (electronic, mechanical,
photocopying, recording or otherwise), without the prior
written permission of both the copyright owner
and the above publisher of this book

Printed in Great Britain by Clays Ltd, St Ives plc

A CIP catalogue record for this book is available from the British Library

ISBN 0–670–81292–7

Contents

Preface

BY SIR COLIN DAVIS

The Viking Opera Guide is a wonderful book – practical, entertaining and scholarly. Amanda Holden and her distinguished team of contributors have produced a reference work that is invaluable to anyone with an interest in opera, from the most experienced professional to the person with the slightest curiosity.

Since I began conducting opera I have seen it undergo a remarkable renaissance. The availability of recordings has played an important part; but every year the appetite of audiences grows, not only for perennial favourites and new works, but also for the rediscovery of long-neglected operas from a repertoire that seems inexhaustible.

The great strength of this book is that it provides a more comprehensive guide to that repertoire than any of its predecessors. No other volume gives such detailed coverage to so many composers – and to so many of their operas. If you are hurrying out to a performance a synopsis can be read in a few minutes. Or you can find out what resources are needed (e.g. eight solo sopranos for Rameau's *Platée* – and a chorus of frogs and satyrs as well! – four harps and two guitars for the orchestra of Berlioz's *Benvenuto Cellini*).

This book contains more operas than anyone can appreciate in a lifetime. Everyone who has any interest in opera must buy it.

About this Book

The *Viking Opera Guide* consists of more than 800 articles on opera composers (alphabetically listed by surname). That composer's operatic works follow after an introduction.

The term opera (Italian: literally 'work') is here interpreted in its widest sense as any dramatic work that can be sung (or at times declaimed or spoken) in a place for performance, set to original music for singers (usually in costume) and instrumentalists. We have included not only operas in the strict sense, but also *all* related works, e.g. operettas, singspiels, music-theatre. A viable subtitle for the book could be '400 Years of Musical Entertainment', or 'Opera: From the Masque to the Musical'.

Within each composer entry the operas are examined in detailed entries in order of composition. Those operas that do not have separate entries are listed (chronologically) at the end of the article with dates of premieres (the dates in brackets signify year of completion of composition, if known and significantly earlier than the premiere date). Each composer's *complete* operatic works are included.

Operas have been graded according to how much space they merit.

Every opera that has its own entry includes title (in original language and English translation), genre and duration (for operas under one hour to the nearest five minutes, for operas over one hour to the nearest 15 minutes, if known), librettist and source of libretto (if known) and premiere dates (world premiere, followed by UK and US premieres in chronological order). The paragraphs that follow include some background to the work, full or brief synopsis and

some musical commentary. Recordings (not including reissues), videos and editions end the entry. We are aware that in any work of reference information may not remain completely up to date. In the case of recordings, the explosion of new records and reissues on CD makes the task especially difficult. We have therefore recommended the best at the time of going to press.

Major operas receive a full cast list and orchestration details; works on the edge of the main repertoire receive abbreviated cast and orchestration details.

To look up an opera turn to the index of opera titles. Opera titles are listed there in their original form and in English translation.

Technical terms are listed in the glossary. Very familiar musical terms which have all but entered the English language, such as intermezzo, or singspiel, have been treated as English words – i.e. printed in roman type, and (in the case of German) without initial capital letters. Other less familiar foreign words remain in italics.

Contributors are credited by initial. A full list of contributors is at the back of the book.

Russian dates are New Style. Russian transliteration follows modern usage, except where familiarity seems more important. For example, we have used 'Prokofiev' instead of 'Prokof'yev', and so on. Titles in Czech, Hungarian or Russian are translated both in individual entries and in listings of operas which do not have a full entry. Titles in French, German, Italian or Spanish are translated only in their individual entries.

Acknowledgements

A reference book of this size contains contributions of different kinds from almost as many people as it contains composers. Many of the contributors have themselves consulted colleagues, and many other generous enthusiasts have left no leaf unturned to find a date or a reference I was intent on including. This list, like the book, cannot therefore claim to be completely comprehensive.

My first thanks go to my ex-husband Anthony Holden, for helping me set up the idea, and to our children, Sam, Joe and Ben, for their constant help to, understanding of, and patience with their opera-bound mother.

Apart from all the contributors who wrote the book, I am especially grateful to the following:

Hilary Rubinstein (formerly at A. P. Watt) and Clarissa Rushdie (at A. P. Watt); Nicholas Kenyon and Stephen Walsh who, apart from their role as editors, contributed from the beginning to all decisions regarding the content of the book; Rodney Milnes, the ever sympathetic and wise consultant editor to the project; at Penguin: Peter Carson, Judith Flanders and Ravi Mirchandani, continuously encouraging, understanding and helpful editors; many other members of the Penguin group; Jill Burrows, who patiently and valiantly copy-edited the entire book; Julia Engelhardt, who read every article as part of her quest for the pictures; Alan Blyth and John T. Hughes who shared their vast knowledge of recordings; my assistants and researchers: Mark Audus and Gwen Hughes, also, Catherine Wearing, Gill Vale, Stewart Collins, Chris Wood, Benedict Warren; Stewart Spencer and Professor Michael Talbot, for their translating skills; Marcus Warren for his up-to-date expertise in the Russian language.

For myriad essential details: *Opera* magazine (John Allison, Deirdre Tilley), Boosey and Hawkes (Emma Kerr), Chappells (Alison Nichols), Chester Music, Faber Music, Finnish National Opera (Leena Nivanka), the National Sound Archive (Tim Day, Chris Hill), Novello (Leslie East), The Really Useful Company Ltd (Dave Robinson), Ricordi (Milan: Ilaria Narici; UK: Tim Cowles), Schott (London: Sally Groves, Ulrike Müller; Mainz: Almuth Willing), the Sir Arthur Sullivan Society (Stephen Turnbull), Stainer and Bell, Universal Edition (London: Ben Newing, Bill Colleran; Vienna: Eva Smirzitz), Joseph Weinberger Ltd (Richard Toeman).

Also, for their advice and various contributions: Lisa Agate, Antony Beaumont, Christopher Booker, Henrietta Bredin, Jonathan Burton, Paul Daniel, Sir Colin Davis, John Denny, David Freeman, John Harrison, Linda Hirst, Professor H. C. Robbins Landon, Magnus Linklater, John McMurray, the late William Mann, Penny Neary, David Pountney, Dr Manfred Rätzer, Joan Rodgers, Professor Norman Stone, Stephen Wadsworth.

Finally I thank my parents, Josephine Barnes and Brian Warren, who first took me to the opera, for inspiring my love for music.

Amanda Holden
Highbury, London, 1993

Abbreviations

a	alto		edn	edition
A cl	*see* clarinet		eds	editors
alto sax	alto saxophone		ENO	English National Opera
arr.	arranger; arranged by		fl	flute
			fl.	*floruit* (flourished)
b	bass		f.s.	full score
b	born (composer headings)			
bar	baritone		glock	glockenspiel
basset hn	basset horn		gtr	guitar
b-bar	bass-baritone			
BBC	British Broadcasting		hn	horn
	Corporation		hp	harp
bc	basso continuo		hpd	harpsichord
b cl	bass clarinet			
bd	bass drum		inc.	incomplete
boy s	boy soprano; treble		*IRASM*	*International Review of the*
bsn	bassoon			*Aesthetics and Sociology of*
				Music
ca	cor anglais		ISCM	International Society for
cel	celesta			Contemporary Music
Ch	Choeur, Choir, Chorus, etc.			
cl	clarinet		*JAMS*	*Journal of the American*
cl, A	clarinet in A, etc.			*Musicological Society*
CO	Chamber Orchestra		Jg.	Jahrgang (volume)
coll.	collaborator; collaboration		jnr	junior
cond.	conductor; conducted by			
cont	continuo		kbd	keyboard
ct	counter-tenor			
CUP	Cambridge University Press		lib.	libretto
cym	cymbals		LPO	London Philharmonic
				Orchestra
d	died		LSO	London Symphony Orchestra
db	double-bass			
dbsn	double-bassoon		mand	mandoline
	(contrabassoon)		*MGG*	*Die Musik in Geschichte und*
DDT	Denkmäler deutscher			*Gegenwart*
	Tonkunst		*ML*	*Music and Letters*
dir.	director; directed by		*MMR*	*Monthly Musical Record*
DJbM	*Deutsches Jahrbuch der*		*MQ*	*Musical Quarterly*
	Musikwissenschaft		*MR*	*Music Review*
DTB	Denkmäler der Tonkunst in		*MT*	*Musical Times*
	Bayern			
DTÖ	Denkmäler der Tonkunst in		n.d.	no date
	Österreich		no.	number
			nr	near
ECO	English Chamber Orchestra		*NRMI*	*Nuova rivista musicale italiana*
ed.	editor		NT	National Theatre
EDM	Das Erbe deutscher Musik		*NZM*	*Neue Zeitschrift für Musik*

O	Orchester, Orchestra, Orchestre, etc.	SO	Symphony Orchestra
ob	oboe	*STMf*	*Svensk tidskrift för musikforskning*
orch.	orchestrator; orchestrated by	str	strings
ORTF	Office de Radiodiffusion-Télévision Française	study s.	study score
OUP	Oxford University Press	supp.	supplement
		susp cym	suspended cymbal
perc	percussion	*t*	tenor
pf	piano	tenor d	tenor drum
picc	piccolo	timp	timpani
PM	*Portugaliae musica*	tpt	trumpet
PO	Philharmonic Orchestra	trans.	translator; translated by
PRMA	Proceedings of the Royal Musical Association	trbn	trombone
		t-t	tam-tam
prod.	producer; produced by		
pt	part	va	viola
		vc	cello
RAI	Radio Audizioni Italiane	vg	viola da gamba
rec	recorder	vib	vibraphone
rev.	revised	vn	violin
RIM	*Rivista italiana di musicologia*	vol.	volume
RMI	*Rivista musicale italiana*	v.s.	vocal score
rp	reprint		
RPO	Royal Philharmonic Orchestra	wb	woodblock
RTE	Radio Telefís Eireann	WNO	Welsh National Opera
		ww	woodwind
s	soprano		
satb	soprano, alto, tenor, bass	xyl	xylophone
sax	saxophone		
sd	side drum	*ZMw*	*Zeitschrift für Musikwissenschaft*
SMw	*Studien zur Musikwissenschaft*		
snr	senior		

Glossary

12-note see serial

afterpiece short opera performed after a play or an opera, in 18th-century England

aleatoric involving elements of chance ('with dice')

allegro cheerful, lively: quick

alto the register between soprano and tenor; the alto voice is usually that of a male (falsetto) singer in this register, but the term is also used for choral singers of either sex; also denotes the specific register of a member of an instrumental family (e.g. alto saxophone)

andante 'walking': slow but mobile

aria Italian for 'air', and the standard term for a distinct solo song in an opera

arioso 'like an aria'; an arioso is usually an accompanied recitative in strict time, but the term can also denote a short, informal aria (q.v.)

arpeggio (from *arpa*, Italian for 'harp'): a chord whose notes are played consecutively instead of simultaneously

atonal having no discernible key or tonality (q.v.)

avant garde term describing artists whose techniques and aims are radically different from traditional ones, its common usage dates from the year immediately after the Second World War

azione scenica a part of a play that is set to music

azione teatrale (1) a short one-act opera or piece of musical theatre, with a small cast and orchestra, designed to form part of an evening's entertainment; (2) a staged oratorio

balalaika the Russian peasant lute, with a triangular body and three strings

ballet dance episode in an opera, with or without singing (also the dancers who perform it)

banda a stage band, usually a group of wind instruments, often a feature of Italian 19th-century opera

bandora plucked bass string instrument, often used as continuo (q.v.) instrument in 17th-century opera; it had (usually) six metal strings, and a characteristic scalloped body outline

baritone (1) the male voice in the register between bass and tenor; (2) a euphonium-like valved brass instrument, related to the so-called tenor horn, and found chiefly (in Britain and the US) in brass and wind bands

baryton-Martin a light baritone voice with near-tenor range of the kind often found in French Romantic opera. Named after the singer Jean-Blaise Martin (1768–1837)

Basler Trommel, see Paradetrommel

bass (1) the lowest male voice; (2) the lowest part of a musical texture

bass-baritone bass voice with strong top notes

basset clarinet modern name for the (downward) extended clarinet in A for which Mozart wrote his concerto and other important solo parts in his late works. Anton Stadler, who invented it, called it a bass clarinet, but that term now refers to a later, more autonomous bass-register member of the family

basset horn a low clarinet (in F) much used by Mozart in his late works

basso continuo the instrument or instruments which, in baroque and early-classical music, played the bass line and supporting harmonies; the part was normally notated as a single line of music, with or without figures indicating the chords

bell tree set of tuned bells mounted on a handle and played with a small stick

bombardone Italian name for the largest of the bass tubas

book musical term sometimes used to distinguish a musical with story and continuing characters (i.e. a libretto or book) from a revue (which has neither)

breeches role male part sung by a woman

brindisi drinking song

buffo, buffa Italian for 'comic' (cf. 'buffoon')

bylina traditional Russian epic poem or ballad

cabaletta quick, often brilliant, final section of an aria (q.v.), especially in Italian opera

cadence harmonic formula at the end of a musical phrase (derived from the convention of melodic fall (Latin *cadere*) in plainsong); cf. 'dying fall' *cadenza* free solo (vocal or instrumental) passage originally improvised over the penultimate chord of a cadence (q.v.), later sometimes written in by the composer; any such bravura solo

Camerata name given to the salon, or intellectual circle, of Count Giovanni de' Bardi in Florence in the 1570s and 1580s; it included the composer Giulio Caccini, through whom the term was later also associated with the 'first' experiments in music drama, by Caccini and Peri, in the 1590s

cantilena melody (or 'small song'), usually applied to sustained phrases of vocal melody

canzona originally a verse form of the troubadour period, the term is now freely used to denote a simple song of popular or quasi-folk character

canzonetta literally a small 'canzona'; usually denotes a light-hearted song in simple verse form

castrato the vocal type of the male soprano in 17th- and 18th-century opera, achieved by prepubescent castration

catuba imprecise term probably implying the use of a small group of percussion centred on a bass drum with cymbals, and perhaps including a triangle or other 'Turkish' instrument

cavatina a short aria, distinguished in 18th-century opera from the aria proper by its lack of a *da capo* (q.v.)

chaconne slow baroque dance in triple time, designed as a series of variations over a repeating bass line

chain finale an extended finale in a number of linked sections and without formal (large-scale) reprise (e.g. Act II of Mozart's *Le nozze di Figaro*)

ciaccona Italian for 'chaconne' (q.v.)

cimbasso the deep bass valved trombone of Verdi's opera scores

clarinetto d'amore (clarinette d'amour) late 18th-century clarinet with a pear-shaped bell; used in opera by J. C. Bach among others; obsolete after about 1810

clarino originally a trumpet, later (in the operatic era) the brilliant upper register of the instrument, also the particular instrument allocated to the high baroque trumpet parts

claves a percussion instrument consisting of two short pieces of wood which are struck together, making a dry, clicking noise

colascione rustic long-necked Italian lute

coloratura Italian for 'colouring'; florid vocal ornamentation, and the type of brilliant and agile voice (usually soprano) suited to such music

comprimario in Italian opera, a sub-principal operatic soloist, not qualifying for full-blown solo arias

concertino the soloist of a solo group, as opposed to the ripieno (q.v.), in baroque music

conte French for 'tale'

continuo see *basso continuo*

contralto the female alto (q.v.); originally also a low-voiced castrato (q.v.)

cornamusa (cornemuse) a kind of bagpipe

corna da caccia Italian for 'hunting horn', and the standard word in Italy for the coiled natural horn of the 17th and 18th centuries

counter-tenor the male alto; historically the terms seem to be interchangeable, though there is some support for the idea that the counter-tenor sings without the 'break' into falsetto that characterizes the alto (q.v.; see also *haute-contre*)

csárdás Hungarian dance in two sections: slow (*lassú*) and fast (*friss*)

da capo 'from the beginning'; a *da capo* form (e.g. aria, q.v.) is in three parts, of which the third is a repeat of the first, shown by a *da capo*, or 'D.C.', sign at the end of the second

dal segno 'from the sign'; an instruction to repeat from a point marked by a particular sign (often 'D.S.')

deus ex machina 'god from a machine'; the device in 17th- and 18th-century opera whereby a happy ending is contrived by the sudden appearance of a god or allegorical figure who decrees that all shall be well

development a musical section in which material already presented is subjected to various elaborative processes

divertissement (1) a musical episode, of a light or diversionary character though often with its own narrative, in a large-scale drama; (2) a self-contained theatrical entertainment, involving singing, dance and spectacle, celebrating some grand event; both meanings were standard in 17th- and 18th-century France

dodecaphonic see *serial*

dominant the fifth degree of the major and minor scales (for instance, in the scale of C major, the dominant is G); it has a strong controlling function in the harmonic structure of tonal music

domra Russian peasant plucked stringed instrument

Drama für Musik see *dramma per musica*

dramaturgy the general principles of drama or stage action

drame larmoyant 'tearful drama'; sentimental tragedy

drame lyrique a genre of Romantic opera, without dialogue but less 'public' and ostentatious than grand opera (q.v.) (Massenet's *Werther* is a well-known example)

dramma boschereccio 'sylvan drama'

dramma giocoso comic operatic genre developed by Galuppi and Goldoni, in which serious and comic characters and elements intermingle (the best-known example is Mozart's *Don Giovanni*)

dramma per musica (1) play written specifically for setting to music; (2) term for serious opera in the 18th century, synonymous with opera seria (q.v.)

duodrama a melodrama (q.v.) with two main characters

entr'acte musical interlude between acts of a play or opera; a distinct musical work intended for performance in this way

farsa 'farce'; (1) musical intermezzo or afterpiece (q.v.) to a comic play (18th-century Italy before 1770); (2) a short independent musical play of a farcical character

febiarmonici Italian touring opera companies of the mid-17th century

fiaba Italian for 'fable, fairy-tale'

fioritura 'flourish': vocal embellishment

fisarmonica 'bellows harmonica'; the standard Italian word for an accordion

flageolet small recorder-like flute in which the breath is directed on to a short edge and thus split automatically

flexatone percussion instrument in which a flexible metal strip is vibrated to make a ghostly twanging

fortepiano the modern term for the early wooden-framed piano

galant see *style galant*

gamelan the traditional Indonesian orchestra (Bali and Java) consisting mainly of metal percussion, with one or two melody instruments

géophone sand-machine (q.v.)

Gesamtkunstwerk German for 'total art-work'; in Wagner and others, a work in which all or many art forms are combined

ghazal an Indian (Urdu) poetic genre with associated melody

glass harp instrument invented by Bruno Hoffmann in 1929, consisting of an array of tuned wine glasses played by resonating their rims with the hands

gopak Ukrainian dance in quick duple time

grand opera (1) the large-scale operatic genre of the early 19th century particularly in France, in which epic historical subjects were staged with enormous forces and great spectacle; (2) opera in general, as opposed to operetta or other forms of sung musical theatre

gruppetto a melodic 'turn', in which a rapid group of notes forms round a pivotal note

guerre des bouffons one of the most famous controversies in French musical history, between the adherents of French and Italian opera respectively; it raged in Paris between 1752 and 1754, when an Italian comic opera troupe (the Bouffons in question) performed Pergolesi's *La serva padrona* and triggered off a virulent argument which involved many of the greatest figures of the day, including Rousseau, Diderot and, on the Francophile side, Madame de Pompadour

gusli Russian folk psaltery or zither

habanera ('from Havana') a slow Cuban dance in duple time, with a characteristic dotted rhythm on the first beat

Handlung German for 'plot'

haute-contre the very high tenor voice of French 18th-century opera

head voice a vocal technique resonated in the head (rather than in the chest) for the production of a light sound quality; occasionally called head tone

heitere Oper German term for 'light opera'

Heldentenor German for 'heroic tenor'; the standard term for the powerful tenor voice called for by Wagner

Heldenbariton 'heroic baritone'

Hosenrolle German for 'breeches role' (q.v.)

intermedio (1) 'intermezzo' (q.v.); (2) the normal term for the short staged pieces often interpolated between the acts of Italian serious plays or operas in the 16th–18th centuries; they were typically comic or light in tone, but court intermedi were lavish affairs with elaborate sets and stage machinery; the early intermedio was part of the ancestry of 17th-century opera, while the later intermedio is generally regarded as the forerunner of 18th-century comic opera

intermezzo (1) a musical (usually orchestral) interlude between operatic scenes; (2) intermedio (q.v.)

IRCAM Institut de Recherche et de Coordination Acoustique/Musique; the Parisian Institute for electronic and computer music, opened in 1976 with Pierre Boulez as its director

ISCM International Society for Contemporary Music; founded in 1922, it has an annual festival held each year in a different country

Kapellmeister originally the master of music in a court chapel; later any musical director, whether working at an ecclesiastical or a theatrical establishment

key see *tonal*

keyed trumpet the trumpet with keys was invented about 1770, and was the first reliable form of chromatic trumpet (that is, on which the whole musical scale could be played). It was superseded by the valve trumpet during the first half of the 19th century

khorovod traditional Russian 'round dance'

Klangfarben-melodie 'sound-colour melody'; the term applied to a style of 20th-century composition in which pitch change (i.e. melody) is replaced, or enhanced, by frequent changes of instrumental timbre

Klappentrompet German for 'keyed trumpet'

kobza Ukrainian guitar-like plucked stringed instrument

krakowiak a cheerful dance from the Krakow region of Poland, in duple time with frequent syncopations

Leitmotiv/Leitmotif the 'leading motif' of Wagner's music dramas (though the term was neither invented nor significantly used by him): a theme or musical figure that recurs – altered or unaltered – as a recognizable symbol or reminder of a character or some other element of the plot

Les Six Parisian group of composers brought together by Jean Cocteau at the end of the First World War to promote his idea that art should be practical, anti-earnest, and fun; its members were Auric, Louis Durey, Honegger, Milhaud, Poulenc and Germaine Tailleferre

libretto 'small book' (1) printed or manuscript literary text of an operatic work; (2) the text of an operatic work

Liebestod 'love-death'; term applied to the final scene of Wagner's *Tristan und Isolde*, where love finally carries Isolde beyond life to join Tristan in death, in literal fulfilment of the opera's imagery of love as death to the world

Lied the standard German word for 'song', especially art song

lieto fine 'happy ending', but specifically a contrived one, as with the *deus ex machina* (q.v.) of 17th- or 18th-century opera

Literaturoper an opera set to an existing text as opposed to a specially written libretto

lyric soprano, tenor, etc. voice of comparatively light, fluent quality

lyrics words for singing as distinct from spoken dialogue

Märchenoper 'fairy-tale opera'

masque the hybrid court entertainment of 16th- and 17th-century England, combining music, dance, spoken poetry and elaborate sets and costumes

mazurka Polish dance (from Mazovia, near Warsaw), in triple time with the accent on the second or third beat

melisma a melodic phrase sung to a single syllable

melodrama (1) technique found within opera or as an independent genre in which a text is spoken to musical accompaniment, or in the pauses between musical phrases; (2) exaggerated or sensational drama

mezza voce 'half-voice'; a direction to sing with soft, withdrawn tone

mezzo-soprano the female voice between soprano and contralto

Mighty Handful common English translation of the Russian expression *moguchaya kuchka*: the Russian Five (Balakirev, Borodin, Cui, Musorgsky, Rimsky-Korsakov) who in the 1860s promoted the idea of a national Russian music

minimalism a term borrowed from visual art in the 1960s to describe a kind of music in which a single figure or phrase is made to constitute a long stretch of music through extremely slow tempo or multiple repetition with little or no change

modal modal music confines itself to the notes of a single unchanging scale (or collection), as opposed, for example, to tonal music, which tends to contradict an initial scale by the introduction of foreign (chromatic) notes, often leading to change of key; the effect of modal music is typically rather static. The term is also used, more loosely, to refer to music using the old scales (modes) of church music, or other exotic or ethnic scales, or even unusual invented scales, even where the scales are not rigidly adhered to

modernism the idea that modern art must by necessity be difficult, abrasive, complicated and hard to understand, perhaps because the modern world is those things

modulation the procedure of changing key in tonal (q.v.) music

monodrama a melodrama (q.v.) with only one main character

monody music consisting of only a single melodic line (e.g. plainsong); the vocal music of the early Baroque is 'monody' though accompanied, as distinct from the polyphony (q.v.) of contemporary church music

motif a short, characteristic theme that recurs often as a unifying element; see also *Leitmotiv*

musette (1) a small bagpipe; (2) a dance with a drone accompaniment such as might be provided by the musette

musical apparently short for 'musical comedy' (q.v.), and since the 1920s the normal term for the popular musical play with songs, dances and chorus ensembles

musical comedy see *musical*; now usually applied to the early history of the genre (from about the 1890s), when it diverged from conventional operetta towards the idea of the popular play with music, often with a contemporary bourgeois setting

music drama a highly integrated form of opera in which music, words, stage action and setting work together on an equal footing; the term is often erroneously attributed to Wagner, who in fact rejected it

music-theatre originally a coinage of the 1960s to describe a kind of highly informal opera, often involving speech and dance as well as singing, invariably for a small number of performers, designed to be played in a concert hall, church, or almost anywhere except a theatre; the term soon broadened to include concert works incorporating elements of gesture, and (in the other direction) various kinds of small-scale but otherwise fairly conventional opera. There remains an unstated assumption that music-theatre is somehow more serious and socially/psychologically aware than opera, though the artistic achievement of the genre remains slight

Nachspiel German for 'postlude' (q.v.)

nastro magnetico Italian for 'electronic tape'

neotonality a fashionable tendency in music since the late 1970s, in which certain aspects of tonality (q.v.) are once again accepted by so-called avant-garde (q.v.) composers as part of their musical language

new objectivity ('neue Sachlichkeit') a movement in art of the 1920s, in which commonplace objects and situations are treated in a style emphasizing their ordinariness

nonet a musical work or movement for nine instruments or voices

number opera opera clearly divided into distinct pieces or 'numbers' (so-called because they are in fact numbered in the score

obbligato an important instrumental solo (in opera often forming a duet with the solo voice), so-called because in baroque music such parts were fully written out and had to be played as written, unlike the continuo (q.v.) part, which involved improvisation

ondes martenot an electronic instrument named after its inventor, Maurice Martenot, and popular especially with French composers from Varèse to Messiaen; a melody-only keyboard instrument, it makes a sound like an amorous cat

opera-ballet hybrid genre particularly in the French musical theatre of the 18th century, usually with a number of separate actions illustrating the central idea through singing and dance

opera buffa the genre of Italian comic opera of the 18th and 19th centuries, usually with musical numbers divided by sung recitative

opera semiseria hybrid genre in which a serious or melodramatic subject is moderated by comic or picturesque elements; it often uses spoken dialogue instead of recitative

opera seria a term now applied to the whole range of Italian-language serious or tragic opera of the 18th and early 19th centuries, especially as defined by the somewhat stereotyped librettos of Metastasio (1698–1782)

operetta (also 'opérette') the light romantic opera of the 19th century, usually with spoken dialogue between the musical numbers; in the 20th century it faded almost imperceptibly into musical comedy (q.v.)

organo di legno Italian term for the xylophone

overture (ouverture) 'opening'; an instrumental piece, often in several sections, introducing an operatic work, played before the curtain rises

Paradetrommel a tenor 'marching' drum, also known as Basler Trommel because of its connections with the town of Basle

pasticcio a work consisting mainly or entirely of borrowings from existing works by the same or other composers

pentatonic containing five notes: applied above all to certain scales of folk music. The best-known pentatonic scale is provided by the black notes of the piano

picche (plural of *picca*) small sticks for beating time

polyphony 'many-voiced' music; music made up of several independent vocal (or instrumental) lines

polytonal music is said to be polytonal when two or more key-notes are functioning simultaneously. But from a theoretical point of view the concept is vague, and in practice polytonal harmony is tonal (q.v.) harmony with a lot of added discord, or harmony in which different types of tonal chord are played simultaneously

postlude by extension from prelude, a concluding section usually for instruments alone

post-modernism the 1980s reaction against modernism (q.v.) involving a return to such things as tonality (q.v.), antique styles (often with quotation), and popular aesthetic values

premiere in English usage, the very first performance of a work

prima donna the principal female singer in an operatic cast; in Italian usage it is only one of several such defining terms, including seconda donna, primo uomo (q.v.) and comprimario (q.v.)

primo uomo the principal male singer in an operatic cast

prostonarodni (Russian) relating or belonging to the common people

querelle des bouffons see *guerre des bouffons*

ranz des vaches Swiss mountain cow-call, as originally played on the Alphorn

recapitulation formal repeat of an identifiable musical section

recitative free setting of speech in which the music follows the rhythms and inflexions of the spoken language; in *recitativo secco* the voice is accompanied only by continuo (q.v.) playing a skeleton of chords outlining the harmony; in *recitativo accompagnato* it is accompanied more fully by the orchestra

recitativo accompagnato see *recitative*

recitativo secco see *recitative*

recitativo semplice the original term for what was later dubbed *recitativo secco* (see *recitative*)

reggae West Indian urban popular music (specifically Jamaican)

relative major/minor the pair of keys – one major, the other minor – with the same number of sharps or flats in the key signature: for instance, F major/D minor (one flat); relative keys are always the same interval (a minor third) apart

répétiteur musician in an opera company with responsibility for rehearsing/coaching singers (at the piano)

rescue opera genre of opera in the French Revolutionary period in which the hero or heroine is rescued in the nick of time from some tyrant or natural disaster through the agency of human self-sacrifice or heroism. Beethoven's *Fidelio* is the best-known example

ripieno the main body of the orchestra (as opposed to the *concertino* (q.v.)) in baroque music

rock music term used to embrace most types of popular music since the early 1970s

rondeau form based on a simple alternation of a repeating refrain and changing verses (couplets); also the French version of the more general rondo form (q.v.)

rondo any form based on the alternation of a repeating main section with contrasting episodes; it includes the simple French rondeau (q.v.), but also the more elaborate form often found in symphonic finales

Rührtrommel German name for the tenor drum

rusalka Russian word for a mermaid or water sprite

Rute German for 'birch'; birch brush used as a stick on the bass drum

sand-machine a sand-box, shaken to produce (e.g.) the sound of shuffling feet

Sax Belgian family of wind-instrument makers of which Adolphe (1814–1894) was the most remarkable innovator. The saxhorn, saxophone and saxotromba are named after him

scale repertoire of notes arranged in ascending or descending order; the steps of a musical scale are normally close together, but in some ethnic or non-European scales slightly larger steps are found. The scale is strictly speaking an abstraction which is thought of as defining the basic 'field' of operation of a piece of music, but it materializes in vocal and instrumental exercises, and also frequently as a melodic feature

scena Italian for 'scene', but with various other connotations as well: (1) the stage itself; (2) the stage setting; (3) an informal episode as opposed to a formal set piece; also such an episode designed as a separate concert piece

Schauspiel German for a stage play

Second Viennese School group of composers led by Arnold Schoenberg, and including above all his two greatest pupils, Alban Berg and Anton Webern (the First Viennese School being understood as the classical group of composers Haydn, Mozart and Beethoven)

semantron metal bar used as a bell in the Orthodox Church

semi-opera a late 17th- or early 18th-century English work combining spoken dialogue and through-composed operatic scenes, usually having elaborate sets

semiseria see *opera semiseria*

serenata Italian for 'serenade', but usually denoting a ceremonial vocal work of a courtly kind, with quasi-dramatic elements

serial based on a series, or ordered note-row; serial music originally always meant the music of Schoenberg and his school, in which all 12 notes are included in the serial ordering that governs the music; but any music that uses a fixed order, of whatever number of notes, can properly be described as serial

serpent a keyed wind instrument with a cupped mouthpiece, named after its coiled shape; it was gradually displaced in orchestras and bands by the more versatile valved brass instruments

sinfonia Italian for 'symphony'; a name used as a description of the instrumental preludes and interludes of early operas (since these were the only sections where all the instruments 'sounded together'), though it had also a wider currency for instrumental works and became a strict generic term only with the appearance of the classical symphony

Singspiel the German 'ballad' opera form, with songs and spoken dialogue, which evolved into operas such as Mozart's *Die Zauberflöte* and Weber's *Der Freischütz* and survives in the musical plays of Brecht and Weill

sistrum a U-shaped rattle with metal rods which jingle when shaken

skazka Russian for 'tale'

skočná quick Czech dance in duple time of a light and comic nature

sonata now usually a substantial instrumental work in several movements (or one elaborate one), but earlier applied to any instrumental piece; something sounded (*sonata*) as opposed to sung (*cantata*)

sonata form the standard name for the particular form in which the first (and sometimes later) movements of the classical sonata and symphony were usually cast; in its textbook format a first theme is followed by a second theme in the key of the dominant (q.v.), a development (q.v.) of this material, and a recapitulation (q.v.) with the second theme now in the home, or tonic, key. In practice this form was much varied

soprano the highest female voice

soubrette the stock servant-girl figure of 18th-century opera; she is usually clever, quick and resourceful; the term is sometimes misleadingly extended to describe the kind of voice called for

sousedska Bohemian dance in triple time

Spieloper a form of singspiel (q.v.) with songs and dialogue, but with more emphasis on the 'operatic', less on the idea of popular theatre

spinto Italian for 'pushed' (properly, *lirico spinto*); a lyrical voice with reserves of muscle, as usually called for by the main tenor and soprano roles of late-Romantic Italian opera

Sprechgesang a hybrid vocal delivery, between speech and song, used most famously by Schoenberg and Berg, but developed earlier by Humperdinck in the original version of *Königskinder* (1897). There is no accepted sprechgesang technique, and Schoenberg's account of his requirements is obscure

style galant French for 'gallant style'; the light and elegant 18th-century rococo style, as opposed to the serious and elaborate baroque style

subdominant the fourth degree of the major and minor scales (for instance, in the key of C, the note F)

tableau French for 'scene', in the sense of stage setting and subdivision of an act

taille early French word for 'tenor', both vocal and instrumental

tambour voilé French for 'muffled drum'

tamburello Italian for 'tambourine'

tamburo Italian for 'drum'

tenor the standard high male voice (but see *haute-contre* and *counter-tenor*)

theorbo a large lute with sympathetic (resonating) bass strings, much used in 17th-century continuos (q.v.)

third stream 1960s fusion of the two streams of classical and jazz (later, ethnic) music

thunder-sheet large metal sheet, shaken or struck to simulate the sound of thunder

tinta (vocal) colour

tonal tonal music partakes of the system of keys that dominated music and music theory of the 17th to early 20th centuries, and still dominates much popular music; key = tonality (the key note is known as the tonic)

tragédie-lyrique the epic form of serious French opera from Lully to Gluck

transpose to play a passage of music in a key other than that in which it is written, or in which it was previously heard

trautonium monophonic electronic instrument named after its inventor, Friedrich Trautwein, who first exhibited it in Berlin in 1930

travesti French for 'disguised', especially as someone of the opposite sex; a person or role so disguised

travestito Italian for *travesti* (q.v.)

treble the top (soprano) voice in choral music, and the name of the register it inhabits; the standard term for a child's singing voice

trouser role breeches role (q.v.)

unendliche Melodie 'endless melody': metaphorical description of the extended and more or less informal flow of the music of Wagner and his successors

vaudeville a Parisian street song, of the kind that, in the 18th century, formed the basis of the comic musical plays ('comédies en vaudevilles') which borrowed the name; in the first half of the 20th century, vaudeville meant 'variety' or music-hall; the kind of operatic finale in which a single tune is passed from character to character (as in Mozart's *Die Entführung aus dem Seraglio* and Rossini's *Il barbiere di Siviglia*) is also sometimes known as a vaudeville

verbunkos Hungarian corruption of the German *Werbung* ('recruitment'); *verbunkos* music was originally the recruitment music of the Austrian army, but its style was absorbed into the urban popular and gypsy music of 18th-century Hungary; it also borrowed elements of the ancient Hungarian folk music

verismo 'realism', but specifically as applied to the brutal and earthy dramas of late 19th- and early 20th-century Italian opera

vibrato the rapid fluctuation of pitch (and sometimes loudness) that gives the voice and certain instruments their main expressive quality; it is also a vehicle for control as well as for the disguising of defects, but can itself get out of control, when it is called 'wobble'

viola d'amore a viola-like member of the viol family with sympathetic (resonating) strings in addition to the stopped ones

violetta 18th-century name for the viola or middle-register viola da gamba

violetta marina a viola with sympathetic strings, perhaps close to the viola d'amore (q.v.)

Vorspiel German for prelude

Wagner tuba tuba-like brass instrument, but with horn-like bore and mouthpiece, evolved by Wagner to enrich the choir of orchestral horns; the Wagner tubas are invariably played by the horn-players (never by the tuba-players) *wind-machine* instrument for imitating the sound of wind, traditionally consisting of a barrel turned by a handle so that it rubs against a strip of silk

zarzuela traditional Spanish operetta form combining singing, dialogue and dance

Zauberoper 'magic opera', usually applied to the Viennese singspiel (q.v.) of the late 18th and early 19th centuries, in which complicated stage machinery is used to create spectacular or magical effects

Zeitoper 'topical opera', specifically in 1920s Germany, where there was a fashion for operas of modern life

The Viking Opera Guide

INTRODUCTION

BY NICHOLAS KENYON

'Enter a different world', as a leading London department store used to advertise itself. Opera's unique appeal is its difference, its aesthetic remoteness, its wanton splendour and often wanton expensiveness. It tugs at the irrational in us; it flatters our need to belong to something larger than ourselves without commitment. In opera, with its unique conflation of the visual, verbal and musical arts, we can recognize a piercing clarity of emotion which suddenly makes sense of confused impulses and ambiguous feelings. The art form has changed radically through the centuries, and there are not many attributes that apply equally to the operas of Monteverdi, Handel, Mozart, Verdi, Wagner, Puccini and Berg – but that elemental, emotional directness is one of them.

For all its high appeal and exclusive status, opera has today become a plaything: over the last couple of decades it has become a status symbol for the upwardly mobile and a genuine 'entry point' to the whole world of classical music for many who would never previously have dreamed of sampling it. Sampling is the key here: it is the compilation compact discs of famous arias divorced from their dramatic contexts that reach the bestseller charts, not the recordings of complete operas. The unique 'Three Tenors' concert in Rome in 1990 was a case in point: popular lollipops plus a made-to-measure medley that would not have disgraced a variety show from three decades ago proved to be exactly what the public wanted. Yet that runaway success has so far been impossible for the record companies to repeat.

If there was a moment when opera's popular appeal was encapsulated, then it was surely the decision to use Pavarotti's recording of Puccini's 'Nessun dorma' as the signature tune of the 1990 World Cup Football television broadcasts. At that time more people must have heard that track than had ever, in the entire history of opera, actually attended one: the whole world of opera focused on to a football. Without that, would a commercial entrepreneur have risked putting on the Royal Opera's *Turandot* at Wembley Arena for a potential 8000 people a night? There, inflated spectacle mingled uneasily with the long wait for the famous aria (and when it arrived, it was, disappointingly to some, sung by only one tenor . . .).

Perhaps in the wake of Caruso and Gigli it is absurd to claim that opera has attained cult status only in recent years of mass marketing. But only now is opera potentially big business: 2.7 million attend live performances throughout Britain each year, and a crowded night of arena opera at Earl's Court can net £500,000 (as indeed can a royally attended mega-price gala at Covent Garden). The investment it requires is huge, however, and at the big American houses, especially the Metropolitan in New York (which has its own lavish production of *Turandot* paid for by a single private donor), there is the suspicion that audiences are now paying more and more money for their seats to see more and more money spent on stage. The success of Philip Glass's Columbus epic, *The Voyage*, there in the autumn of 1992 was attributed more to its stage effects than to its music.

Such popularity for opera may be illusory. The enjoyment of one striking aria does not guarantee the survival of an art form long regarded as over-élitist, over-recondite, and over-priced. Recently a leading figure in the world of commercial pop music admitted to me that though he regularly weeps over his cassette of extracts from *La bohème*, he had difficulty sitting through the whole of *Tosca* even with Pavarotti on hand to help. Instant gratification is one thing, but a temporary one; instant understanding is another, and more elusive one. More

Design by Bernardo Buontalenti for Apollo slaying the dragon; a scene from one of the grandest sequences of intermedi ever staged in Florence; the occasion was the wedding of Grand Duke Ferdinando I de Medici to Christine of Lorraine (1589)

durable understanding and enjoyment is what this book hopes to inspire.

Before the beginning, there was speech. Formal speaking – the rhetorical discourse, the poem, the epic – has existed in many ages. And one way of regarding opera is simply as an intensification of that art of dramatic spoken utterance. In our time, which has almost lost the skills of public declamation, this is hard to imagine – even political oratory is now scaled down for television. But for centuries of Western culture from plainchant through the troubadours to Monteverdi, one of music's chief aims was to heighten the impulses of speech.

Indeed when medieval theorists began to write about the differences between poetry and song, one of them called poetry 'musique naturelle', and song 'musique artificielle': a provoking distinction for any operatic composer to ponder. In proto-operas such as the medieval church dramas, liturgical and non-liturgical stories were given extra weight and colour by dramatic action, but it is difficult to trace a direct line between them and the operatic entertainments of later centuries. Far more significant were the intermedi inserted between the acts of plays in late 16th-century court entertainments. Here allegorical and philosophical stories were enacted with the utmost refinement and sumptuousness, and madrigalian music was performed side-by-side with new-style solo virtuoso declamation: opera was nearly born. These intermedi,

of which the grandest were conceived for royal weddings, were staged in specially decorated rooms so that the audience became an integral part of the spectacle. They drew on idealistic neo-Platonic visions of the world and the universe, and portrayed music as a reflection and an agent of universal harmony.

Some of the composers involved in that uniquely fertile Florentine court of the late 16th century, including Emilio de'Cavalieri, and the singers Jacopo Peri and Giulio Caccini, were the musical vessels through which, in collaboration with thinkers and theorists, the 'new art' of opera evolved. Though each vigorously claimed his unique part in the process, it is better to see the process as evolving from the wider cultural and intellectual effort to rediscover the past. As in most such archaeological attempts, the result was to create a radically new future. Monteverdi's *Orfeo*, an extraordinary masterpiece to have been created so early in the life of the form, owes much to the tradition of the intermedi, and its formal use of madrigal-like choruses and formal symmetry marks it out as radically different from the human stories, told largely through narrative drama, which Monteverdi was to write towards the end of his life.

In the often squally relationship between the 'blest pair of sirens' who make up the opera composer's art, words and music have fluctuated in their relative importance. 'Prima la musica' – music first – has been the underlying assumption of so much opera from the central years of the mainstream repertoire that we tend to forget it was ever different. But it is impossible to imagine those 'inventors' of opera in Italy at the start of the 17th century agreeing with such a formulation. The whole function of instrumental music in the dramas of Peri and Caccini and Monteverdi was merely to support the voices – a point forgotten by those who in reviving these works today add elaborate instrumental parts.

Once the first public theatres opened, led by the Teatro San Cassiano in Venice in 1637, operas were often of necessity put on with minimal forces. A few strings in the pit playing the occasional interlude while leaving the accompaniment of recitative to the continuo group of keyboards and lutes was the norm for the public performance of Monteverdi's late operas and many of those by Cavalli and his contemporaries. There were grander spectacles, of course, especially at court. Cesti's *Il pomo d'oro*, written for a royal wedding in Vienna in 1668, went on for some eight hours with numerous changes of elaborate scenery, and Fux's *Costanza e Fortessa* carried on that same Viennese tradition of sumptuousness. The extent to which the scenic spectacle dominated these extravagances cannot be emphasized

enough, and putting them on today as pure music would be as meaningful as doing Lloyd Webber's *Starlight Express* without the roller-skating.

Throughout the turbulent history of opera – where economics, national pride, and the self-aggrandisement of monarchs, patrons, conductors and great singers have been at least as important as artistic considerations – we stumble on forms that in their peculiarity owe little to our stereotyped ideas of the mainstream 19th-century repertoire. What were those curious hybrids, the 'semi-operas' of the later 17th century to which Purcell and others contributed in London? They were not operas with a lot of dialogue but rather plays with a lot of music. The commentator Roger North admitted that some of the audience came for the music and were bored by the play, and vice versa, but the form served its purpose and there is no point in regretting that *The Fairy Queen* or *King Arthur*, with their dazzling wealth of music, do not have the through-composed continuity of *Dido and Aeneas*. They were designed for a different purpose and have different virtues.

There is a link here with the comédies-ballets that were popular at the French court around the same time, and later with the opéra-ballet where

The Dorset Garden Theatre at Blackfriars, London's first opera house. The theatre, designed by Christopher Wren, opened on 19 November 1671 and closed in October 1706 (engraving, c. 1820)

Engraving by William Hogarth of John Rich's entry into Covent Garden, London for the opening of his new Theatre Royal on 7 December 1732; the speech bubble reads 'Rich for ever'

spectacle was everything and content often next to nothing. How one longs to see, in all their scenic splendour, with real dance, the creations of the French baroque from Campra to Marc Antoine Charpentier! Lully's tragédies-lyriques were made of sterner stuff and were, dare one say it, less musically stimulating. It took Rameau to mould that form with his brilliant orchestral skills into a series of operas, from *Hippolyte et Aricie* through to *Les Boréades*, which have been a striking rediscovery of our generation. But how slow these things are to catch on: in spite of John Eliot Gardiner's efforts in Lyons and Aix-en-Provence, and those of Lina Lalandi's English Bach Festival in London, no established British opera company mounted a full-length Rameau opera until the City of Birmingham Touring Opera's *Les Boréades* in April 1993.

Handel is a different matter, and there the tide has decisively turned in recent years, thanks to a flood of superb recordings from Sigiswald Kuijken's *Partenope* and *Alessandro* to René Jacobs's *Flavio* and *Giulio Cesare*, where the art of baroque opera can be studied at its zenith. This is a development of a process that began with the German revivals of the 1920s, and continued with the regular stagings of the Handel Opera Society; in the United States, the New York City Opera had a *Julius Caesar* in its repertoire that became the butt of scholarly complaint for its rewritings and re-orderings. The fate of opere serie whose music

is less magically variegated than that of Handel must remain uncertain, and in this book there are many accounts of composers and operas whose future on the stage must seem bleak. But who knows? The most remote art forms now seem accessible to us, and huge unknown tracts of the 18th and 19th century beckon; perhaps, as another ambition, this book can help to stimulate exploration into little-known corners of the repertoire.

Gluck, whose librettist Calzabigi threw away the restrictions of opera seria and adopted a consciously reformist stance, was more continuously performed in the 19th century than Handel. Gluck's rarefied spirit and simple eloquence were suitable for transposition to the world of Berlioz and the voice of Pauline Viardot, while his evocation of an antique purity rang true in a society that ever more looked to that past for its justification. In their time, though, Gluck's reforms were a way of renewing opera. Comic intermezzi, written within traditions developed by the *commedia dell'arte*, also revitalized the staid conventions of serious opera. Pergolesi's *La serva padrona* of 1733, with its crisp melodies and short-breathed arias, set a new idiom, and when revived in Paris in 1752 created a furious row between the self-styled supporters of high art and those who favoured the emerging opera buffa.

It was left to a leading dramatist to reconcile these opposing factions: Carlo Goldoni, in

Italy, drew together serious and comic strands in his libretti (set first by Galuppi and Piccinni) and created a new synthesis which was enormously influential – particularly since it took root just at the time when Mozart was coming to prominence as an opera composer. The Da Ponte comedies, mixing rank and class and status, are unthinkable without Goldoni, just as Mozart's supremely sophisticated act finales, with their sequence of keys and kaleidoscopic action, are unthinkable without the hectic finales of the 18th-century opere buffe. Mozart, however, goes far beyond his models and defines opera for his time as surely as did Monteverdi for his.

Theorists have argued long and hard about the relationship of music and drama in opera, but there is one formulation on which most of us agree: in all the greatest operas *the composer is the dramatist*. Not that he necessarily writes the words himself, though Wagner, Tippett and others have done so with rewarding and baffling results. One of the many things we would dearly love to know about Mozart's collaboration with his librettist Lorenzo da Ponte is the amount of influence the composer had on the text; scarcely a glimmer of evidence survives. Given the acute and penetrating interest Mozart took in the text of *Idomeneo* (recorded in a series of letters to his father) it is difficult to believe that he was not just as active in moulding Da Ponte's libretti to his own purposes as he composed.

Mozart ensures that the time-scale of events, the pacing of action and reflection, the tiniest twists of motivation, are all created by – not merely reflected in – the music. Where the play of musical motifs begins to originate and control the unfolding drama, this kind of operatic composition is seen at its greatest. When Verdi unifies the first act of *La forza del destino* with a tiny thematic tag that germinates the whole argument of the opera, when Mozart in *Così fan tutte* creates a quasi-symphonic development in the sextet from a series of repetitive, modulatory phrases, then we are passing beyond the mere 'reflection' of the text to something quite different and more musically motivated.

There is one major caveat which must be noted here in connection with opera of the 18th century, which applies also to some 20th-century works, notably musicals. Our dictionary format, with its codified entries and frozen contents, is ideally suited to the kind of opera that attained a single, finished form. For much of

opera's history it was not like that. Rameau's *Dardanus* and Bernstein's *Candide*, to take two examples far apart, went through significant changes of content during their composers' lives. Change, for much of the operatic repertoire, has been of the essence, and this book should be used with that caution in mind.

This has been well put by Reinhard Strohm in his *Essays on Handel and Italian Opera*. Strohm's contention is that it was the individual production that defined the piece, rather than the piece dictating the production. Perpetual adaptation to meet changing circumstances – whether the theatres, the casts available or simply the composer's or patron's whim – was the order of the day. 'If we compare the situation today [in our opera houses] with Italian operatic practice in the 18th century, the first thing that strikes us is how little attention was paid in the theatre of the day to the individual "work". The continuity of planning, composing, rehear sing, performing and reperforming guaranteed artistic standards; even the most successful work could never be repeated unaltered in conditions that were perpetually changing.'

Strohm also outlines how the 'production' of an 18th-century opera would be quite different from one today. It began before the writing of the score and ended, if it ended, after the performance. The libretto, rarely unique and often reused by many different composers, would be the origin: then followed casting, the demands of key singers, the writing and rewriting of arias to suit their skills. Both the essential adaptability of the operatic form and the bold demands of singers lasted far longer than we care to imagine.

Today, it is expected that if a leading singer such as Cleo Laine takes a role in *Show Boat*, as she did in the London revival of 1971, she will have specially written numbers added for her. Paradoxically, singers of the stature of Teresa Stratas and Frederica von Stade now take part in a reconstruction of the 'original' *Show Boat*: the 18th century would have written new arias for them, for, as Strohm puts it, 'The claims of history in the matter of musical performance always collapse in cases where the performer has to become the creator.' The claim of the star singer in opera to run the show has always been strong.

The confusions and contradictions that surround the Prague (1787) and Vienna (1788) versions of Mozart's *Don Giovanni* are evident to any opera-lover who goes to the opera twice and encounters different versions. The later revisions and changes to *Le nozze di Figaro* (1789) are less remarked because they are less frequently performed. But they involve radical rewriting, replacing two of Susanna's arias and changing those of the Count and Countess. Why? Because new singers were to sing the parts. Adriana Ferraresi del Bene, who was to create Fiordiligi in *Così fan tutte* (1790), was not a natural Susanna, and certainly could not act through the light-hearted subtleties of the dressing-up aria in Act II. So that was replaced with a much more static, minuet-type aria, and Susanna's Act IV aria, 'Deh vieni', was replaced with a fine rondo in which Susanna almost seems to become the Countess whom she is impersonating.

This seemingly tiny detail is worth highlighting because recent studies of Mozart's singers have begun to demonstrate to what a remarkable extent the dramatic character of each part was created from the vocal characteristics of the singer cast in that part – even using their favourite tricks of coloratura, for instance. Operas revolved around singers first, décor and machinery second; the composer was lower on the list. This situation can be graphically illustrated in the contract of 1791 between the Bohemian Estates who wanted an opera for the coronation of the new Emperor Leopold II and the impresario who commissioned Mozart to write *La clemenza di Tito* – the librettist, the singers and even the designs were crucial; who wrote the music was, in a sense, the least of the impresario's worries.

Among the myriad operatic developments of the 19th century after Mozart's early death it becomes impossible to pick out a single line, since the demands of public performance and national influences took opera in so many different directions. We shall leap boldly through the mainstream development of opera in the 19th century to see how it was deconstructed in the 20th. But some important themes stand out. One was the expansion of the form to suit the new demands of large public arenas, while another was the reassertion of politics as a germinating force in opera, as it had been in the prologues of French tragédies. Auber's *La muette de Portici* caused a revolutionary uprising, and Beethoven's *Fidelio* argued the cause of freedom in a directly political manner. But now it was not the court or the composer's patron, but the public that was the judge of success, and the grand gesture became ever more important in reaching across the footlights to the audience's affection and loyalty.

The interior of the Palais Garnier (the Paris Opéra) which opened on 5 January 1875; drawing by Ch. Fichot

Rossini developed the lighter side of the Italian idiom and found favour in France. Beneath his florid vocal virtuosity lay a real human penetration: the extrovert flourishes of his characters' voices really do express the depths of their emotions. The worst you can say of Rossini is that this florid, ingratiating melodic brilliance was achieved at the expense of harmonic interest: Berlioz argued just that as he began his new revolution against what he perceived as shallow and superficial operatic writing. Berlioz's sprawling masterpieces, *Les troyens* and *Benvenuto Cellini,* are answers of a kind, imperfect but always stimulating. They were never successful in France even though (or perhaps because) *Les troyens* echoed many elements of the historical French operatic tradition.

Opera with dialogue, inherited from the singspiel tradition in Germany (to which *Die Zauberflöte* as well as countless lesser works belong) continued to flourish, and the works of Weber provide a fascinating bridge between this tradition and the new romanticism. In *Der Freischütz* there is less and less dialogue as the drama builds up. Increasingly, works that originated with spoken dialogue (like Gounod's *Faust* and Bizet's *Carmen*) were dignified with recitative as they aspired to respectability. But other French composers appeared to descend into mere pleasing by-ways; Lalo, Offenbach, Ambroise Thomas and Massenet offered an unchallenging kind of opera, which satisfied most tastes but did little to develop the art form.

Romanticism had already begun to infiltrate the operatic idiom, most famously with Weber's *Der Freischütz.* But it was central to the operatic language of Bellini and Donizetti. Star-crossed lovers, confrontation and tragedy were the stuff of their libretti, and if the idea of 'conventional' opera has an origin it is surely in their melting-pot of veristic action, emotional simplicity and cathartic resolution – features we might these days associate with television soap operas. In Bellini's *La sonnambula* tragedy is avoided in the end, as befitted the emerging form of opera semiseria, and through this whole period of opera a new range of vocal types emerged which suggested a new range of characters: the heroic tenor and the treacherous baritone became stock figures.

In spite of all the efforts of France and Germany, Italian opera swept all before it in the 19th century – at least until Wagner. The towering figure was Verdi, who shines above all 19th-century Italian opera composers with his depth and seriousness. Politics was crucial to him, and he was deeply committed to the uni-fication of Italy. In his early works, with their rum-ti-tum accompaniments and stirring melodies, there is a dangerous crudeness. But the extraordinary aspect of Verdi's achievement is how without ever wholly repressing those direct means, he deepened and coloured his operatic art through a series of masterpieces, until in *Otello* and *Falstaff* he achieved a ripeness and maturity that make these operas almost timeless.

Italy lost its pre-eminence with Wagner, about whom more has been written than of any other musician. One tiny addition will suffice: like every great operatic composer, Wagner creates his own sense of time and space, within which the texts seem merely pretexts for music, almost as Bach used numbers or Messiaen used alphabets. In this symphonic world of massive proportions and endless melody, Wagner's all-encompassing *Gesamtkunstwerk* (his own term) represents one furthest point of development of operatic art. You realize this fully only when you sit in the theatre he created in Bayreuth. This is the art of illusion at its zenith. Everything is concealed behind the proscenium arch, and there is no glimmer of life from the auditorium. The famous curved edge of the pit completely covers the orchestra and conductor; there are no spotlights as in most theatres which shine from the theatre on to the stage. Everything comes from, and remains within, that frame of illusion: artifice is complete. Gone is the cheering, chattering audience, the prominent patron or monarch: the art work is all, and Wagner becomes 'the man who arrogantly pre-empted to himself the very concept of opera' (Joseph Kerman).

As nationalism took root, national legends and myth became a vital subject for opera, and the achievements of Russian opera in the period are vivid testimony to that: Glinka's two operas, Musorgsky's *Boris Godunov,* which has proved the most exportable of these visions of a nation, and Tchaikovsky, less overtly nationalistic (and frankly less successful as a dramatic composer) but shot through with Russian spirit. In other countries there was Moniuszko's *Halka* from Poland, a distant 19th-century ancestor of Karol Szymanowski's blazing *King Roger* in the 20th; and the warmer Bohemian spirit of Smetana, whose *Bartered Bride* is secure at the centre of the repertoire, and Dvořák, whose operas are not, though there is

The Vienna Staatsoper at the end of the 19th century

ravishing music in *Rusalka* and *The Jacobin*. Russian nationalism continued to provide a well-spring of fine opera in the 20th century, notably with Prokofiev's stirring if superficial *War and Peace* and Shostakovich's powerful *Lady Macbeth of the Mtsensk District*.

Where could opera go after Wagner, except into terminal decline? Many believe that it has done just that, and that no 20th-century opera is fully worthy of its predecessors. The notion is challenged most obviously by Puccini, whose operas in essentially traditional form laced with spicings of the new *verismo* have earned him undying popularity with the audience and undying contempt from critics. It was not Joseph Kerman who started the trend with his remark that *Tosca* was a 'shabby little shocker': even so restrained a scholar as E. J. Dent apparently used to talk of Puccini's 'slobbering erotics'. This kind of unwillingness to accept full-blooded vulgarity on its own terms has certainly harmed Puccini's reputation, and the precision with which he re-created natural effects – the *ambientismo* of the start of *Tosca*'s third act, for example – now seems strained. But for forceful emotion and for pathos rather than tragedy he remains unsurpassed.

Wagner's gauntlet was picked up most decisively by Richard Strauss in *Salome* of 1905 and *Elektra* of 1909, but then even he appeared to believe he could go no further in that direction and completely changed course. *Der Rosenkavalier* of 1911 is a totally individual work of genius, but in *Die Frau ohne Schatten* (1914–19) one hears Strauss slipping act by act from the tremendous sounds of sensationalism into a more comfortable, less challenging mode. Straussians loathe the unfavourable comparison of his later works with those of his earlier period. Yet it is difficult to avoid the conclusion that in Strauss the operatic convictions of the late 19th century finally burned themselves out, as indeed they had to if opera was to readjust itself to a new century and new needs.

A more distinctive contribution of our century is the art of text-based, small-scale music-theatre, in which dance, gesture and words (spoken as well as sung) are as important as music. The origins of this genre go back to Stravinsky (*The Soldier's Tale* and *Renard*), Schoenberg's cabaret-based *Pierrot lunaire*, and the Brecht–Weill collaborations of the 1920s. But it only assumed widespread importance after the Second World War, when composers began seriously to question the value of the conventional theatre with its proscenium arch and audience of passive onlookers. The deeper ancestry of music-theatre lies in such popular manifestations as pantomime and the medieval miracle plays. But in our own day it has usually been the mouthpiece for rather sophisticated political, sociological or moral diatribes directed at specialized audiences.

All the same, the return to a concern with text dominates the best 20th-century opera. One of the greatest examples is also one of the first. Debussy's *Pelléas et Mélisande* (1902), with its almost recitative-like treatment of Maeterlinck's play, though Debussy's exquisite, elusive music in itself surely represents the farthest development of opera as programmatic tone poem, where mood and atmosphere are more important than the verbal drama. Significant here is the reliance on symbol, something *Pelléas* shares with another key work of the early 20th century, Bartók's haunting one-act masterpiece *Duke Bluebeard's Castle* (1918), where music again becomes more than text-expression, and encompasses the whole symbolic basis of the libretto to provide a perfect mirror of the arching form of the piece.

Another kind of language-obsessed composer is Janáček, whose operas are now at last receiving the international recognition they deserve. His concern to reflect every nuance of spoken Czech in his musical lines led him to notate the speech he heard around him. An electric sensitivity to speech and its inflexions characterizes the work of Benjamin Britten, who re-created a traditional form of operatic discourse based on real characters and living situations. His operas, inaugurated with the American essay *Paul Bunyan* (1941) but growing from the epoch-making premiere of *Peter Grimes* (1945), are among the most natural of the 20th century, and there is no higher praise than that in this self-conscious age. Britten's great contemporary Michael Tippett has relied more on stereotypes and symbols to create his original visions – for which, mistakenly some think, he has always written his own libretti.

Tippett's eclectic musical style raises the repeated attempt by 20th-century opera composers to integrate popular musical styles into 20th-century opera. The synthesis of Ernst Krenek's *Jonny spielt auf*, a jazz-influenced opera of 1927, now seems intolerably dated, but the stature of Kurt Weill's popular works grows every year. Weill's desire to be useful as a composer links him to Hindemith and Britten, and at different times in his career it dictated whether he wrote pungent Berlin cabaret or

racy American musicals. Of the popular works of this period, Gershwin's *Porgy and Bess* (1935) has been revealed, in recent opera-house revivals and recordings, as far more than a musical, whose weight and substance outweigh a thinness of compositional subtlety which can be attributed to Gershwin's inexperience in form and in orchestration. Of all music's many early deaths, Gershwin's at 38 may well be the most tragic for the cause of truly popular 20th-century opera.

A vital element in our operatic life today is what we might fancily call deconstruction: the sideways look, the critical glance both at the work and its production – opera looks at opera, opera comments on itself. Composers as diverse as Schoenberg, Stravinsky and Pousseur have joined in the clamour of questioning. Luciano Berio's *Opera* is an opera about opera: his more substantial *Un re in ascolto* is an essay in the art of hearing and listening, questioning the extent to which the act of conscious listening is ever more forcibly submerged by the tumult of passive hearing.

Perhaps the most forceful, though not the most recent, 20th-century questioning of our ability to articulate is Schoenberg's *Moses und Aron*, which pits the ever eager communicator against the man of integrity who would prefer to remain silent than to be compromised. One could argue, too, that Stravinsky's *The Rake's Progress*, in its own quirky version of 18th-century style, is not so much an act of homage to Mozart as an admission that in our day we have no real operatic idiom of our own: we live, in opera as elsewhere, in borrowed clothes.

One consequence of this has been that we have found it easier to reinterpret old opera in ever more trendy ways than we have to create new opera: the ingredients of a new opera of our age seem as elusive as ever, and the impact of John Adams's *Nixon in China* (1987) or *The Death of Klinghoffer* (1991) owed much to the dominating collaboration of Peter Sellars as director and Alice Goodman as poet. Berg's indisputable one-off reinvention of the form in *Wozzeck* (1925), whose concision, musical cohesion and dramatic force are surely unparalleled in our century's opera, is an exception. New operas have been created in their hundreds, and have often found favour with local audiences, but with rare exceptions – Judith Weir translated to America, Aribert Reimann to Britain, Peter Maxwell Davies to Europe – they have not yet travelled well.

A scene from the English National Opera production by Jonathan Miller of Rigoletto *(London, 1982), designed by Patrick Robertson and Rosemary Vercoe (photograph by Bill Rafferty of the 1992 revival)*

The most reassuring fact, though, is that contemporary opera is now a fact of life. Major opera houses have their workshops and new-writing ventures and feel that their audiences will accept new work: this extends even to the Metropolitan in New York (which sold out John Corigliano's *The Ghosts of Versailles* (1991), another work obsessed by the past) and the Royal Opera in London, which most recently commissioned and premiered Harrison Birtwistle's *Gawain* (1991). Opera is now so much a part of national life both in Britain and America that it is difficult to remember a time when it was not so and when ramshackle companies toured on a shoestring with what were doubtless often very variable offerings. Opera is now 'in'.

That applies also to writing about opera, which has become an industry in itself. Scholarly thought about opera is currently more subtle and more original than for many a year, and it is another qualification of the dictionary format of the present book that it can reflect only in passing the radical thought about opera taking place in scholarly books and articles. Too often the operatic literature has been content to tell 'great stories' without discussing music or context at all. Of course plots have to be told, as they are in this book, but only against the background of a composer's creative contribution to operatic form. It was Joseph Kerman's *Opera as Drama* some 35 years ago that set the agenda for a new

approach to the art form as integrated music drama, and this has been taken up by a new generation of writers discussing opera from new vantage points.

A couple of random examples might be Philip Brett's work on Britten's *Peter Grimes*, a supremely honest attempt to explore the impulses behind a work of art which revealed much that had been hitherto skated over. Britten's cry in a letter to Pears, 'I'm rather scared of what I'm creating,' could stand as the motto for a whole range of unconscious motivation in opera; and Catherine Clément's *Opera and the Undoing of Women* was a similarly original essay in a neglected aspect of opera: women as victims at the hands of male composers and male librettists. The techniques of semiology and contextual analysis are now used to great effect in discussing opera, but music still has a long way to catch up with literature in this respect.

In our time opera has been deconstructed not only by scholars but also on stage: it is through ironically distanced and self-conscious stagings like Jonathan Miller's Mafioso *Rigoletto* (seen in London and New York) and Peter Sellars's *Così fan tutte* set in Despina's Diner (and now on video), that many audiences today have first encountered opera. German directors from Joachim Herz to Ruth Berghaus and Harry Kupfer have created a new fashion for what one might call oblique stagings which perfectly represents the uncertain standpoint of our age towards its artistic past. And though continual obloquy has been poured on this style of opera production by some critics and commentators (the American professor Alois Nagler wrote a whole book called *Misdirection: Opera Production in the Twentieth Century*, and Henry Pleasants's *Opera in Crisis* includes a chapter detailing with relish the excesses of 'Produceritis') the fact remains that the public responds, and not only out of ignorance. We no longer have the confidence of a single developing tradition, and looking sideways at our art is our way of relating to it.

The death of opera has often been pronounced: most notoriously by Pierre Boulez, who in an interview of 1966 said that no opera worth mentioning had been composed since Berg (of Hans Werner Henze's operas he complained, 'They always make me think of an oily hairdresser subscribing to an entirely superficial modernism'). The central problem rightly identified by Boulez was that 'only with the greatest difficulty can one present modern operas in a theatre in which, predominantly, repertoire pieces are played. It is really unthinkable. The most expensive solution would be to blow the opera houses up. But don't you think that would also be the most elegant?'

The urge to blow opera houses up seems now to have evaporated; Boulez is still attempting to write a piece for the theatre, and complicated new works like Henze's *We Come to the River* (1976) and Birtwistle's *The Mask of Orpheus* (1986) have been successfully staged in repertoire houses. There is a huge wealth of talent among the composers, writers, singers, designers, directors, translators and administrators working in opera today. Yet the crucial tension of our time remains that between reinterpreting old works and inventing new ones. W. H. Auden, writing on the bicentenary of Mozart's birth, in 1956, imagined the audiences of the future listening not to their own new operas but still to those of the past:

> Whether they live in air-borne nylon cubes
> Practise group marriage or are fed through tubes,
> That crowds two centuries from now will press
> (Absurd their hair, ridiculous their dress)
> And pay in currencies, however weird,
> To hear Sarastro booming through his beard,
> Sharp connoisseurs approve if it is clean
> The F *in alt* of the Nocturnal Queen,
> Some uncouth creature from the Bronx amaze
> Park Avenue by knowing all the K's!

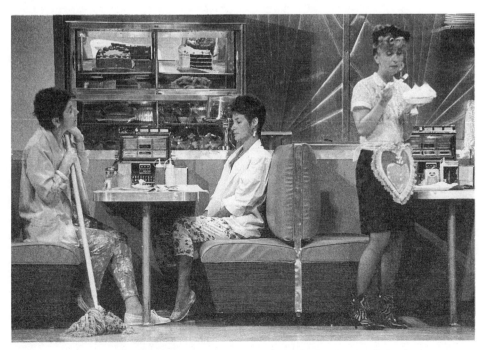

Despina's Diner; a scene from Peter Sellars's production of Così fan tutte *at the PepsiCo Summerfare, Purchase, New York (1986 Peter Krupenye)*

It is a little too early to say what opera in the next millennium may be, but it is clearly far from dead. And the experience of helping to assemble this book has proved above all the unimaginable variety of the operatic experience, from the opéra-ballets of the *ancien régime* to the symphonic fantasies of the 19th century and the tough contemporary dramas of our time: any attempt to confine opera to a single line of tradition or a single aesthetic ideal is doomed to fail in the face of the sheer wealth of material. A different world awaits: enter it.

ANTONIO MARIA ABBATINI

b 1609 or 1610, Città di Castello; *d* ?1679, Città di Castello

From 1626 to 1672 Abbatini was maestro of several important Roman churches, including the Gesù, St John Lateran, S. Maria Maggiore and S. Luigi dei Francesi, though he left Rome for short periods to reside in his native city, and to hold posts in Orvieto and Loreto; a description of his varied career is given in a detailed autobiography in verse. Abbatini wrote a number of collections of small-scale motets, as well as contributing works in the grandiose polychoral idiom characteristic of baroque Rome.

Abbatini's most important stage work is the opera *Dal male il bene*, composed in collaboration with Marazzoli. Towards the end of his life Abbatini wrote two further surviving operas, *Ione*, to a libretto by Antonio Draghi, (?Vienna, 1664; Rome, 1666), and *La comica del cielo, ovvero la Baltasara*, to a libretto by Giulio Rospigliosi (Rome, 1668).

Dal male il bene
From Bad Comes Good

Opera in a prologue and three acts (2h 30m)
Libretto by Giulio and Giacomo Rospigliosi, after Calderón's comedy *La dama duende* (1629)
PREMIERE 1654, Palazzo Barberini, Rome

Abbatini composed Acts I and III of the opera; his collaborator Marazzoli composed Act II. It was first performed at the marriage of Maffeo Barberini, Prince of Palestrina, and Olimpia Giustiniani. The complicated story concludes as two pairs of lovers are finally reunited after a series of mishaps. It is free from the Roman tendency to use opera as a vehicle for a moral message. *Dal male il bene* is the first truly comic opera with real, rather than stock, characters and includes an early example of an ensemble finale. The score is also unusual for its period for the detail of its stage directions.

BIBLIOGRAPHY Margaret Murata, *Operas for the Papal Court 1631–1668*, UMI Research Press, 1981

G.D.

PAUL ÁBRAHÁM

Ábrahám Pál; *b* 2 November 1892, Apatin, Hungary (now Romania); *d* 9 May 1960, Hamburg, Germany

Ábrahám studied (as did his operetta compatriots, Kálmán, Szirmai, and Jacobi) at the Budapest Royal Academy of Music, and had a promising start with serious compositions, including a cello concerto. However, his duties as conductor at the Budapest Municipal Operetta included occasional song interpolations, and he fell under the spell of the then popular dance orchestras and their jazz-inflected arrangements. His first operetta, *Zenebona* (1928), written in collaboration with other composers, showed promise, and he had a triumph two years later in Vienna with *Viktoria und ihr Husar* (1930), which spread across Europe. This was followed by two other international hits, *Die Blume von Hawaii* (1931) and *Ball im Savoy* (1932). Common to all were libretti co-authored by the adept Alfred Grünwald, a touch of foreign flavouring, and a striking use of up-to-date, 'American' popular song-and-dance formats. *Viktoria*, with its spectacular and romantic plot tied to events in the First World War, had a modern appeal despite the formula operetta interruptions of soubrette and buffo. Ábrahám's film scores, which include *Die Privatsekretärin* (1931), hold up brightly, although subsequent stage works, written while fleeing the Nazis in Vienna or Budapest, are forgotten. He spent the war years in Cuba and New York; his mental health deteriorated, although he and his old works reappeared in Germany after the war.

Operettas: *Zenebona*, 1928; *Az utolsó Verebély-lány* (*The Last Verebély Girl*), 1928; *Szeretem a feleségem* (*I Love Wives*), 1919; *Viktoria und ihr Husar*, 1930 (RECORDING Telefunken, 1960s); *Die Blume von Hawaii*, 1931 (RECORDING Decca, 1960s); *Ball im Savoy*, 1932; *Märchen im Grand-Hotel*, 1934; *Történnek még csodák* (*Miracles Still Happen*), 1935; *Dschainah*, 1935; *3:1 szerelem javára* (*Love Wins 3 to 1*), 1936; *Roxy und ihr Wunderteam*, 1937; *Julia*, 1937; *Fehér hattyú* (*The White Swan*), 1938

BIBLIOGRAPHY György Sándor Gál and Vilmos Somogyi, *Operettek Könyve*, Zeneműkiadó, 1976

R.T.

ADOLPHE ADAM

Adolphe-Charles Adam; *b* 24 July 1803, Paris; *d* 3 May 1856, Paris

Adam composed prolifically for the French stage, especially in the sphere of opéra comique. At the Paris Conservatoire he studied composition with Boieldieu, the strongest influence on his music, and assisted him in the preparation of *La dame blanche* in 1825. He was also encouraged in his career by Hérold. His first opera, *Pierre et Marie*, was staged in 1824, and his first success, *Pierre et Cathérine*, was seen at the Opéra-Comique in 1829. After a period spent in London Adam returned to Paris and scored a further success with *Le chalet* in 1834 to a libretto by Scribe, one of his regular collaborators. He was a leading composer for the Opéra-Comique in the succeeding years, with *Le postillon de Longjumeau* staged there in 1836. In 1844 he attempted a grand opera, *Richard en Palestine*, but without success. After a dispute with the Opéra-Comique Adam undertook a disastrously timed venture into theatrical management and lost a considerable fortune with the short-lived Opéra National of 1847–8. Subsequently he took up teaching and writing as subsidiary careers, but resumed composition with his old fertility. *Giralda* appeared in 1850 and a string of successes in the years 1852 and 1853. He was also a skilled composer for the ballet; indeed, *Giselle*, written for Grisi in 1841, is today his best-known score.

Adam's music is light and tuneful, deftly orchestrated, never attempting effects beyond his reach. 'My only ambition', he wrote, 'is to write music that is transparent, easy to understand and amusing to the public. Of course I can write only light music, but I am content to do what I can, and I shall not stop writing until the public tires of my work.'

Le chalet

The Chalet
Opéra comique in one act (1h 30m)
Libretto by Eugène Scribe and Anne-Honoré-Joseph Mélesville, after Goethe's *Jery und Bätely* (1780)
PREMIERES   25 September 1834, Opéra-Comique, Paris; US: 22 September 1836 (as *The Swiss Cottage*); UK: 6 June 1845, Covent Garden, London

The Swiss setting provides an opportunity for local colour (imitating Rossini's *Guillaume Tell*). There are only three characters, thrown into misunderstanding by a hoax letter sent to Daniel (tenor) convincing him that Bettly (soprano) accepts his advances. Her soldier brother Max confuses matters by concealing his own identity. His air 'Arrêtons-nous ici' is the best-known piece in a light and charming score. Boieldieu, with only a month left to live, said he would like to have written the opera himself. In Paris, it was even more popular than *Le postillon de Longjumeau*.

EDITIONS   f.s./v.s., Schonenberger, [*c.* 1834]

Le postillon de Longjumeau

The Postilion of Longjumeau
Opéra comique in three acts (2h)
Libretto by Adolphe de Leuven and Léon-Lévy Brunswick
premieres   13 October 1836, Opéra-Comique, Paris; UK: 13 March 1837, St James's Theatre, London (as *Postilion!*); US: 30 March 1840, New York

Adam's most successful operatic work, Le postillon parodies society manners and operatic mannerisms. Chapelou, a postilion with a high tenor voice, becomes an opera singer, as Wachtel, a later exponent of the role, himself once a postilion, also did. Set in Longjumeau in 1756, the opera traces Chapelou and Madeleine, his wife, in their rise to become 'Saint Phar', a famous tenor, and 'Madame Latour', with many an opportunity for satirical pleasantries.

RECORDINGS   1. Kesteren, Melander, Sardi, Krukowski, Hoppe, RIAS Ch and O, Peters, Eurodisc, date unknown; 2. Anderson, Aler, Le Roux, Lafont, Ottevaere, Ensemble Chorale Jean Laforge, Monte Carlo PO, Fulton, HMV, 1985

EDITION   v.s., Schott, [1837]; *rp*, 1920

Adolphe Adam; caricature silhouette by Jean Pierre Dantan the Younger

Giralda, ou La nouvelle Psyché

Giralda, or The New Psyche
Opéra comique in three acts (2h 15m)
Libretto by Eugène Scribe
PREMIERES   20 July 1850, Opéra-Comique, Paris; UK: 21 September 1876, Lyceum, London; US: 4 March 1885, Boston

Giralda illustrates the perennial taste of French composers for Spanish colour, the overture containing a fandango and a chorus in Act I requiring castanets. It is commonly thought to contain Adam's finest music. Set near Santiago di Compostella, the plot, full of improbable intrigue, tells how Giralda marries not Ginès, the miller to whom she is betrothed, but Don Manoël, a cavalier with whom she is in love.

EDITIONS   f.s., Brandus et Cie, [c. 1850]; v.s., Brandus et Cie, [1850]

Si j'étais roi

If I Was King
Opéra comique in three acts (2h 15m)
Libretto by Adolphe-Philippe Dennery and Jules-Henri Brésil
PREMIERES   4 September 1852, Théâtre-Lyrique, Paris; US: 10 April 1856, New Orleans; UK: 20 February 1893, Newcastle

The story is taken from *The Thousand and One Nights* with the setting changed to Goa. It was staged with the utmost splendour in 1852 and has remained popular ever since. The Goncourts wrote of its production, 'M. Ballue, the designer, piles on precious stones and red garnets. He arrays silk on velvet, gold on gauze with the lavishness of a nabob.'

RECORDING   Berton, Gabriel, Mallabrera, Bianco, Médus, Ch Charles Pernès, unnamed orchestra, Blareau, Decca, 1961
EDITIONS   f.s./v.s., Peschier, [1852]

Le sourd, ou L'auberge pleine

The Deaf Man, or The Full Inn
Opéra comique in three acts
Libretto by Adolphe de Leuven and Joseph-Adolphe-Ferdinand Langlé after the comedy by P.-J.-B. Choudard Desforges (1790)
PREMIERES   2 February 1853, Opéra-Comique, Paris; US: 18 February 1870, New York

The setting in Avignon allows a spirited ensemble in Act II on the tune 'Sur le pont d'Avignon'. The libretto is full of puns and comic word-play arising from the deaf Chevalier d'Orbe's imperfect grasp of everything that is said to him. The music perfectly matches the witty flavour of Desforges's comedy.

EDITION   v.s., Choudens, [c. 1880]

Other operas: *Pierre et Marie, ou Le soldat ménétrier*, 1824; *Le baiser au porteur*, 1824; *Le bal champêtre*, 1824; *La haine d'une femme*, 1824; *L'exilé*, 1825; *La dame jaune*, 1826; *L'oncle d'Amérique*, 1826; *L'anonyme*, 1826; *Le hussard de Felsheim*, 1827; *L'héritière et l'orpheline*, 1827; *Perkin Warbeck*, 1827; *Mon ami Pierre*, 1827; *Monsieur Botte*, 1827; *Le Caleb de Walter Scott*, 1827; *Le mal du pays*, 1827; *Lidda,*

ou La jeune servante, 1828; *La reine de seize ans*, 1828; *Le barbier châtelain*, 1828; *Les comédiens par testament*, 1828; *Les trois cantons*, 1828; *Valentine, ou La chute des feuilles*, 1828; *Le clé*, 1828; *Le jeune propriétaire et le vieux fermier*, 1829; *Pierre et Cathérine*, 1829; *Isaure*, 1829; *Henry V et ses compagnons*, 1830; *Danilowa*, 1830; *Rafaël*, 1830; *Trois jours en une heure*, 1830; *Les trois Catherine*, 1830; *Joséphine, ou Le retour de Wagram*, 1830; *Le morceau d'ensemble*, 1831; *Le grand prix, ou Le voyage à frais communs*, 1831; *Casimir, ou Le premier tête-à-tête*, 1831; *His First Campaign*, 1832; *The Dark Diamond*, 1832; *Le proscrit, ou Le tribunal invisible*, 1833; *Une bonne fortune*, 1834; *La marquise*, 1835; *Micheline, ou L'heure d'esprit*, 1835; *Le fidèle berger*, 1838; *Le brasseur de Preston*, 1838; *Régine, ou Les deux nuits*, 1839; *La reine d'un jour*, 1839; *La rose de Péronne*, 1840; *La main de fer, ou Le mariage secret*, 1841; *Le roi d'Yvetot*, 1842; *Lambert Simnel*, 1843; *Cagliostro*, 1844; *Richard en Palestine*, 1844; *La bouquetière*, 1847; *Les premiers pas*, 1847; *Le toréador, ou L'accord parfait*, 1849 (RECORDING Musidisc, 1963); *Le fanal*, 1849; *La poupée de Nuremberg*, 1852; *Le farfadet*, 1852; *La faridondaine*, 1852; *Le roi des halles*, 1853; *Le bijou perdu*, 1853; *Le muletier de Tolède*, 1854; *A Clichy*, 1854; *Le Houzard de Berchini*, 1855; *Falstaff*, 1856; *Mam'zelle Geneviève*, 1856; *Les pantins de Violette*, 1856
BIBLIOGRAPHY   A. Pougin, *Adolphe Adam: sa vie, sa carrière, ses mémoires artistiques*, Paris, 1868

H.M.

JOHN ADAMS

John Coolidge Adams; *b* 15 February 1947, Worcester, Massachusetts, US

Together with Philip Glass, Adams is a leading composer of the so-called minimalist opera of the late 20th century. But his development owes more to that other well-known American minimalist, Steve Reich; additionally, Adams has moved further away even than Reich from minimalism as previously understood.

While only ten years younger than Glass, Adams could be said to have become the foremost figure in a second generation of composers inspired by the early explorations of repetition, long-held sounds and clearly audible structural processes undertaken by La Monte Young and Terry Riley around 1960. They built their experimental work on a solid conventional training in Western classical music and Adams has allied himself more consistently with this heritage, though he has more recently become more interested in the wide range of other musics – non-Western, jazz, rock – from which the minimalist approach in part derived. Following Adams's move from the East Coast to the West in 1972, his music first became more experimental – notably during the earlier part of his period as a teacher at the San Francisco Conservatory (1972–82) – and then increasingly related to the styles and techniques of a range of 19th- and early 20th-century Romantic composers. His invention in the mid-1980s of an operatic style owing at least as much to earlier operatic and even oratorio traditions as to avant-garde genres of music-theatre and performance art thus appears quite natural. And it is by bringing a new vigour and purpose to composing music for drama that does not avoid a clear narrative basis that Adams has found his full maturity.

Adams's style from as far back as the late 1970s is, in fact, characterized by its individual development of a repetitive idiom in which direct emotional expression is, unusually, not avoided, and in which allusions to – or even direct quotations from – other musics have played an increasingly significant part; *Shaker Loops* for string septet (1978) represents the emergence of this style. An avoidance of extensive reliance on tuned percussion or keyboard instruments (mainstays of at least the earlier Reich and Glass) is significant. Even more important is an increasing concern with melody, harmonic motion and regular metre (which Adams shares with these composers but takes even further).

The development of this approach has taken him naturally to opera. Here he has been aided by the American poet Alice Goodman, who has provided him with texts closely reflecting Adams's own musical approach in their combination of everyday language with references to great literature of the past (particularly in *The Death of Klinghoffer*). But he has also been strongly influenced and assisted by the American director Peter Sellars – who has provided the initial ideas for the two operas Adams has so far composed, as well as directing them using his own particular blend of past and present – and, to a lesser extent, by the American choreographer Mark Morris.

Nixon in China

Opera in three acts (2h 30m)
Libretto by Alice Goodman
PREMIERES 22 October 1987, Brown Theater, Wortham Center, Houston; UK: 1 September 1988, Playhouse Theatre, Edinburgh (Houston Grand Opera)
CAST Chou En-lai *b*, Richard Nixon *b*, Henry Kissinger (also Lao Szu) *b*, Nancy T'sang (First Secretary to Mao) *ms*, Second Secretary to Mao *ms*, Third Secretary to Mao *ms*, Mao Tse-tung *t*, Pat Nixon *s*, Chiang Ch'ing (Madame Mao Tse-tung) *s*, Wu Ching-hua *dancer*, Hung Chang-ching (Party Representative) *silent*; *satb* chorus of Chinese militia, guests at banquet, citizens of Peking, trio of citizens (also singing the roles of participants in *The Red Detachment of Women* and the voice of Ching-hua); dancers in *The Red Detachment of Women*
CHAMBER ORCHESTRA including 4 sax, 4 electric kbd

Peter Sellars's idea of basing an opera on the American President Richard Nixon's visit to the Chinese Chairman Mao Tse-tung in February 1972 resulted in his close collaboration with the librettist Alice Goodman and the choreographer Mark Morris and Adams himself. The original Sellars production toured to New York, Washington, Amsterdam, Edinburgh and Los Angeles and was televised.

SYNOPSIS
Act I Nixon – with an entourage that includes his wife Pat and Dr Henry Kissinger – arrives at Peking airport for his historic visit to China in February 1972. His first audience with Chairman Mao finds the Chinese leader philosophical and inscrutable, but a

banquet the same evening brings the two sides together more successfully.

Act II Pat Nixon goes sightseeing and the Nixons watch a performance of the ballet *The Red Detachment of Women*, presided over by Madame Mao, in the course of which fact and fiction become hopelessly confused; the singer playing Kissinger is required to take a leading role in the ballet's action.

Act III consists of one long scene in which the six main protagonists, on the Americans' last night in Peking, ruminate on the events that have taken place and on their significance for themselves as individuals more than as political figures.

Nixon in China demonstrates, in a more extended form than ever before in Adams's music, the move from stylistic allusion – to Romantic music in particular – to actual quotation. Also notable is the integration of musical and dramatic incident and the related use of music for characterization. As the action develops following the performance of *The Red Detachment* ballet in Act II, for instance, an arpeggio figure is quickly speeded up and soon develops into the perfect complement to the onset of a tropical storm.

The increasing emphasis on the protagonists as real people, in an opera that could easily have developed purely as a political pageant in poster colours, is most clearly demonstrated in the final act. And it is here that another expansion of Adams's style is to be found: the virtual abandonment of minimalist repetition and its replacement by a new, highly lyrical manner, predominantly slow but highly sensitive to the ebb and flow of action and, especially, text. Emphasis is placed firmly on a natural and free-flowing setting of Goodman's libretto, underpinned by a harmonic language of great variety and subtlety.

RECORDING Page, \Sylvan, Hammons, Maddalena, Ch and O of St Luke's, de Waart, Nonesuch, 1988
EDITIONS f.s., Boosey & Hawkes (on hire), 1987; v.s., Boosey & Hawkes, 1993

The Death of Klinghoffer

Opera in a prologue and two acts (2h 30m)
Libretto by Alice Goodman
PREMIERES 19 March 1991, Théâtre de la Monnaie, Brussels; US: 5 September 1991, Brooklyn Academy of Music, New York
CAST Alma Rumor *ms*, Jonathan Rumor *t*, Harry Rumor *b*, Captain *b*, Swiss Grandmother *s*, First Officer *b*, Molqi *t*, Mamoud *b*, Austrian Woman *s*, Leon Klinghoffer *b*, 'Rambo' *b*, British Dancing Girl *s*, Omar *ms*, Marilyn Klinghoffer *a*; dancers (both ensemble and solo, including the doubling of some of the solo singing roles); *satb* chorus
FULL ORCHESTRA including 3 electronic synthesizer-/sampler-players

As with the same team's previous opera, *The Death of Klinghoffer* is based on a recent world event: in this case, the hijacking, in 1985, of the cruise liner *Achille Lauro* by Palestinian terrorists and their eventual murder of a paralysed American Jewish

Nixon in China, *Act I, Scene 1 (Houston, 1987)*

tourist. Goodman drew for her libretto on the Bible and the Koran, as well as on her own personal transmutations of everyday language. The original production by Sellars was shared among opera houses in Lyons, Vienna, New York, Los Angeles, San Francisco and Glyndebourne.

SYNOPSIS

A lengthy prologue portrays a wealthy American family relaxing at home and talking about travel abroad; this is preceded by a Chorus of Exiled Palestinians and followed by a Chorus of Exiled Jews.

Act I   The cruise liner *Achille Lauro* has been hijacked just a few hours out of Alexandria. The purpose of the hijackers is at first unclear. The hostages are rounded up; the ship's Captain is guarded by Mamoud, and both soon start to reflect on their situation.

Act II   The liner awaits permission to enter the Syrian port of Tartus. The passengers have now been moved on deck, but the wheelchair-bound Leon Klinghoffer is forced to remain apart. The Palestinians begin to quarrel. Klinghoffer is shot. The Captain and the hijackers come to an arrangement which will allow the ship to return to Alexandria, where the Palestinians will be able to disembark. Klinghoffer's body is thrown overboard. After their arrival in port, the Captain tells Mrs Klinghoffer of her husband's death.

As in the final act of *Nixon in China*, Klinghoffer takes as its main subject matter the private thoughts and emotions of its characters. The two main acts allow the action to unfold via a libretto consisting mainly of individual statements and meditations. The opera thus falls into a sequence of arias and choruses inspired, according to Sellars, by Bach's Passions. The arias offer reflections of the individual protagonists in the *Achille Lauro* drama, with the Captain of the ship emerging as the character with whom one might most readily sympathize. In this opera, however, unlike *Nixon*, Sellars and his associates deliberately eschew attempts at characterization, in order to focus more strongly on the issues and make the audience question their own preconceptions.

Musically, the opera continues for the most part the approach first observed in the final act of *Nixon*. Occasional use is made of what the composer himself calls his 'trickster' style – the other aspect of Adams's recent development in his non-operatic works – as in the aria for a British Dancing Girl in Act II, which draws on popular styles in a more overtly minimalist way. But, for the most part, the music is more reflective and sometimes more dissonant, responding acutely to the nuances of Goodman's text but still providing virtuosic orchestration, aided in the premiere production by a specially devised sound-distribution system. The use of video to provide close-up views added a further dimension. Even more than *Nixon, The Death of Klinghoffer* suggests that Adams may ultimately remove from his style all traces of minimalism as previously practised.

RECORDING Friedman, Sylvan, Maddalena, Felty, Hammons, Young, Perry, Nadler, English Opera Ch, Opéra de Lyon O, Nagano, Nonesuch, 1992
EDITIONS f.s., Boosey & Hawkes (on hire); v.s., Boosey & Hawkes, 1993

BIBLIOGRAPHY Andrew Porter, '*Nixon in China*: John Adams in Conversation', *Tempo*, no. 167 (December 1988), pp. 25–30; booklet accompanying Nonesuch recording of *The Death of Klinghoffer*

K.P.

RICHARD ADLER

b 3 August 1921, New York

and Jerry Ross

Jerrold Rosenberg; *b* 9 March 1926, Bronx, New York; *d* 11 November 1955, New York

Richard Adler, though intent on a literary career, found himself increasingly attracted to song-writing. In 1950 he met Jerry Ross, an actor in the New York Yiddish theatre and himself a song-writer. The pair commenced a collaboration in which both partners wrote both words and music.

After favourable notices as contributors to a revue in 1953, Adler and Ross had two great successes in the following two years. But the partnership ended almost immediately thereafter when Ross died from a chronic lung ailment. Adler has continued to write for the Broadway stage, and also for the concert hall, ballet, and television.

The Pajama Game

Musical comedy in two acts (1h 45m)
Libretto by George Abbott and Richard Bissel, based on Bissel's novel *7½ Cents*
PREMIERES 13 May 1954, St James Theatre, New York; UK: 13 October 1955, Coliseum, London

Dispute between labour and management in a pyjama factory is brought to a resolution by romance between leaders of the opposing sides. Songs include 'Hey there' and 'Hernando's Hideaway'; the show provided an early indication of the abilities of choreographer Bob Fosse (the dance number 'Steam Heat' displayed many of his trademarks) and producer Harold Prince.

RECORDING Paige, Haney, Raitt, Foy, Hastings, CBS, 1954
FILM Donen (dir.), Warner, 1957
EDITION v.s., Frank Music, 1955

Damn Yankees

Musical comedy in two acts (film: 1h 45m)
Libretto by George Abbott, Douglass Wallop and Richard Bissel, based on the novel *The Year the Yankees Lost the Pennant* by Douglass Wallop
PREMIERES 5 May 1955, 46th Street Theatre, New York; UK: 28 March 1957, Coliseum, London

A humorous variation on the Faust story, in which the Devil entraps Joe, an ageing baseball fan, by turning him into a youthful athlete and allowing him to bring his home team to victory. The demonic seductress Lola, summoned to insure Joe's damnation, instead helps him outwit the Devil in the end and return to his former identity. The score includes 'Heart' and 'Whatever Lola wants'. The original production united most of the *Pajama Game* production team, and enhanced the stardom of Gwen Verdon, perfectly cast as the self-mocking vamp Lola.

RECORDING Verdon, Douglass, Walston, Hastings, RCA, 1955
FILM Donen (dir.), Warner, 1958
EDITION v.s., Frank Music, 1957

Also by Adler (without Ross): *Kwamina*, 1961; *A Mother's Kisses*, 1968; *Music Is*, 1976
BIBLIOGRAPHY Richard Adler with Lee Davis, *You Gotta Have Heart*, D. I. Fine, 1989

J.A.C.

AGOSTINO AGAZZARI

b 2 December 1578, Siena; *d* ?10 April 1640, Siena

Although Agazzari is described as a 'Sienese nobleman' in a number of his publications, he was not above pursuing music professionally. From 1602 to 1603 he was maestro at the German College in Rome, and in 1606 he held a similar position at another Jesuit institution, the Seminario Romano. It seems that he returned to Siena in the following year. His few-voiced motets with continuo were the first to be published in Rome, and a number of his collections reached several editions in different Italian centres. He was also the author of one of the earliest treatises on continuo practice, *Del sonare sopra'l basso con tutti li stromenti e dell'uso loro nel conserto* (Siena, 1607).

Eumelio

Dramma pastorale in a prologue and three acts (1h)
Text by Fr. Torquato de Cupis and Francesco Tirletti
PREMIERE Carnival 1606, Seminario Romano, Rome

Agazzari's only known involvement with a dramatic production was intended for the entertainment of the students of the Seminario Romano; unlike many moralizing Roman operas, it is an allegory based on mythological material.

Eumelio, a boy, is tempted by the Vices to abandon his simple pastoral existence for one of

WATERFORD

No 199219

...LIBRARY

luxury and fame. He soon regrets his decision when he realizes that he has been deceived, and that he is to be offered as a trophy to Pluto. Apollo agrees to descend to Hades to retrieve Eumelio: his mission is successful, and the work ends with a scene of rejoicing.

Following the style of Cavalieri's *La rappresentatione di Anima e di Corpo* (1600), most of the music is for solo voice and continuo, though choruses conclude the acts. Some melodies are used on several occasions: in the preface Agazzari explains that the ancients did not always vary their arias, and that this will make the work more convenient to perform.

EDITION   Rome, 1606

BIBLIOGRAPHY   M. F. Johnson, 'Agazzari's *Eumelio*, a *dramma pastorale*', *MQ*, vol. 57 (1971), p. 419

G.D.

ISAAC ALBÉNIZ

Isaac Manuel Francisco Albéniz; *b* 29 May 1860, Camprodón, Lérida, Spain; *d* 18 May 1909, Cambô-les-Bains, France

Albéniz is best known for his piano music, in particular his *Suite Iberia*, which was influential in shaping a national Spanish idiom in serious music. His stage works – significantly less successful than Albéniz's music in other genres – are today largely neglected.

After early attempts at zarzuela, it was a stay in Britain that led to Albéniz's short ill-suited operatic career. His pseudo-oriental *The Magic Opal* was an attempt to restore the fortunes of London's Lyric Theatre, and a Faustian contract with the banker Francis Money-Coutts, whereby Albéniz agreed to set his libretti in exchange for a pension, resulted in three more operas, of which the mediocre *Merlin* formed part of an unfinished 'Wagnerian' trilogy entirely unsuited to Albéniz's temperament.

Pepita Jiménez

Lyric comedy in two acts (1h 45m)
Libretto by F. B. Money-Coutts, after the novel by Juan Valera (1874)
Composed 1894
PREMIERE   5 January 1896, Teatro Liceo, Barcelona

Albéniz's only successful opera treats the theme of spiritual versus romantic love as represented by the love of father and son for the same woman. The opera is steeped in Spanish rhythms and melodic modes and exudes a heavy Catholic religiosity; one of the highlights is an unaccompanied *Noël* for children.

RECORDING   Rivadineira, Berganza, Molina, Blancas, De Narké, unnamed O, Sorozábal, Spanish Columbia, 1960s
EDITIONS   f.s., Eschig, 1907; v.s., Breitkopf und Härtel, 1896

Zarzuelas: *Cuanto más viejo* (lost), (before 1889); *El canto de salvación* (lost), (before 1889); *Catalanes de gracia* (lost), (before 1889); *San Antonio de la Florida*, 1894, rev. as *L'ermitage fleuri*, 1905
Other operas: *The Magic Opal*, 1893, rev. as *La sortija*, 1894; *Henry Clifford*, 1895; *Merlin*, (1886); *Lancelot* (inc.); additional numbers for Millöcker's *Der arme Jonathan*, 1893
BIBLIOGRAPHY   Gabriel Laplane, *Albéniz: sa vie, son oeuvre*, Editions du Milieu du Monde, 1956

S.J.W.

EUGEN D'ALBERT

Eugen [Eugène] Francis Charles d'Albert; *b* 10 April 1864, Glasgow; *d* 3 March 1932, Riga, Latvia

D'Albert's mother came from Newcastle and his father, a composer and ballet master, was of French nationality though born in Hamburg. He studied composition with Arthur Sullivan and Ebenezer Prout and, having taught himself German, developed an obsession with Germany and its music. He became devoted to Wagner, whose music he heard in London conducted by Hans Richter. Richter recognized d'Albert's talents and brought him to Vienna, where he introduced him to Brahms and, more significantly, to Liszt, who took him on to Weimar as a pupil. Within a few years d'Albert was established as one of the foremost concert pianists of his day, and he travelled throughout Europe and to America. In 1895 he was appointed hofkapellmeister in Weimar and hofpianist to the King of Saxony. Though performance was the mainstay of his life, composition became more important in later years. D'Albert published songs, concertos, a symphony and string quartets. He also edited piano classics and transcribed Bach organ works for piano. Between 1893 and his death in 1932 he composed twenty operas; only the seventh, *Tiefland*, has endured. The first three show the strong influence of Wagner. As a composer he never achieved the fame he had earned as a concert pianist. D'Albert, six times married, had a temperamental personality, and his music is either highly passionate or delightfully humorous.

None of d'Albert's later operas achieved the success of *Tiefland*. Several are based on the theme of confrontation, which underlies *Tiefland*, including *Revolutionshochzeit* (set during the French Revolution) which d'Albert considered to be his finest work.

Die Abreise

The Departure
Comedy in one act (50m)
Libretto by F. von Sporck, after A. von Steigentesch
Composed 1898
PREMIERES   20 October 1898, Frankfurt; UK: 3 September 1925, London; US: 30 October 1973, Provo, Utah

Gilfen has been neglecting his wife Louise. Their friend Trott hopes to profit by their marital problems and woo Louise. Gilfen pretends to depart on a

A scene from the first Czech production of Tiefland *(Vinohrady, 1909)*

journey, but returns to be reunited with his wife and to confound the hopes of Trott who is the one who finally departs.

D'Albert's music for this intermezzo, written in a melodious, Mozartian style, is skilfully orchestrated, and it remains the most successful of his comic operas. An interesting highlight is Louise's aria 'Der Jüngling spricht', a soliloquy accompanied by a spinet, played by Louise.

RECORDING   Moser, Schreier, Prey, Philharmonia Hungarica, Kulka, Electrola, 1978
EDITION   v.s., Brockhaus, 1898

Tiefland

The Lowlands
Musikdrama in a prologue and two acts (2h 15m)
Libretto by Rudolf Lothar, based on the Catalan play *Terra Baixa* by Angel Guimeras
Composed 1902; rev. 1904–5
PREMIERES   15 November 1903, Neue Deutsches Theater, Prague (without prologue); rev. version: 16 January 1905, Stadttheater, Magdeburg; US: 23 November 1908, Metropolitan, New York; UK: 5 October 1910, Covent Garden, London
CAST   Sebastiano *bar*, Tommaso *b*, Moruccio *bar*, Marta *s*, Pepa *s*, Antonia *s*, Rosalia *a*, Nuri *s*, Pedro *t*, Nando *t*, Priest *silent*; *satb* chorus of peasants
FULL ORCHESTRA

Tiefland's opening bears a striking resemblance to Leoncavallo's *Pagliacci*. D'Albert had already been impressed by Mascagni's operas, and the influence of these two composers had changed the flavour of his music from that of the Germanic north to the *verismo* style of the Italianate south.

SYNOPSIS
Prologue Pedro, a simple mountain shepherd, dreams of marriage. The local landowner, Sebastiano, arrives with his mistress, Marta. As he has decided to marry a rich girl, he orders Marta to marry Pedro, who agrees to leave the mountains for life in the village below.

Act I The village girls gossip about Marta's marriage. Sebastiano, meanwhile, tells the unhappy Marta that he expects her to continue as his mistress after her marriage. After the wedding Pedro lovingly gives Marta a silver coin, which he received from Sebastiano when he killed a wolf with his bare hands. Marta, though touched, insists they sleep in separate rooms. But when she sees a signal that Sebastiano is in her room, she stays with Pedro.

Act II The next day Tommaso, the wise old man of the village, advises Marta to tell her husband the truth. Pedro, teased by the village girls who know Sebastiano has made a fool of him, decides to return to the mountains. But Marta, now in love with him, begs him to take her with him and admits that she has been Sebastiano's mistress. When Sebastiano, whose marriage has been called off, returns for Marta he is challenged by Pedro, who strangles him.

The unique success of *Tiefland*, like that of *Carmen*, with which it shares both the sexual antagonism and the thrilling passion of fatal love, lay in its earthy drama. Though the music includes simple melodies which set the rustic and wedding scenes, it is generally thickly orchestrated and overladen with musico-dramatic clichés. Its best qualities are revealed in the two narratives, Marta's dream and Pedro's tale of his fight with the wolf, and at the shattering climax when the shepherd strangles his master. The opera shows how well the Anglo-German d'Albert had assimilated hot-blooded drama through *Pagliacci* and *Cavalleria rusticana*, and how he would in turn influence Puccini's conclusion to *Il tabarro*. In the 36 years between the Prague premiere of *Tiefland* in 1903 and the outbreak of the Second World War the opera was performed in 38 cities, even proving popular with the British occupation forces in Cologne in 1919.

RECORDING Strauss, Schock, Feldhoff, Sardi, RIAS Ch, Berlin SO, Zanotelli, Ariola, 1982
EDITIONS f.s., Bote und Bock, 1903; v.s., Peters, 1935

Other operas: *Der Rubin*, 1893; *Ghismonda*, 1895; *Gernot*, 1897; *Kain*, 1900; *Der Improvisator*, 1902; *Flauto solo*, 1905; *Tragaldabas*, 1907; *Izeyl*, 1909; *Die verschenkte Frau*, 1912; *Liebesketten*, 1912; *Die toten Augen*, 1916; *Der Stier von Olivera*, 1918; *Revolutionschochzeit*, 1919; *Scirocco*, 1921; *Mareike von Nymwegen*, 1923; *Der Golem*, 1926; *Die schwarze Orchidee*, 1928; *Mister Wu* (inc.; completed by Leo Blech), 1932

BIBLIOGRAPHY W. Raupp, *Eugen D'Albert, ein Künstler- und Menschenschicksal*, Leipzig, 1930

C.F.

TOMASO ALBINONI
Tomaso Giovanni Albinoni; *b* 8 June 1671, Venice; *d* 17 January 1751, Venice

Albinoni's 50 or more operas were written mostly for Venetian theatres, where they were heard over a period of almost half a century (1694–1741) – an unusually long time for an age when fashions changed rapidly. The composer was the son of a stationer and manufacturer of playing cards. Trained in his father's profession, he abandoned it in early adulthood for music, having become an accomplished singer and violinist. In 1705 he married the operatic soprano Margherita Raimondi. His essays in composition were divided equally between instrumental music (sonatas and concertos) and vocal music (operas and cantatas). He obtained no official posts but practised as a freelance composer and teacher of singing in his native city until his death.

A superb natural melodist, Albinoni cultivated in his arias a robust, 'popular' style that mostly eschews the contrapuntal complexities found in his instrumental music, whose influence is nevertheless felt in such features as the dancelike rhythms and the idiomatic writing for the violins. The little of his operatic music that survives in complete form shows him to have possessed no exceptional powers of dramatic expression; he was best when conveying mild emotions suited to simple lyrical treatment.

Zenobia, regina de' Palmireni
Zenobia, Queen of the Palmyrans
Dramma per musica in three acts
Libretto by Antonio Marchi
PREMIERE Carnival 1694, Teatro Santi Giovanni e Paolo, Venice; revived as a pasticcio, *Il vinto trionfante del vincitore*, 1717

With this opera Albinoni made his début. Marchi's libretto is historically false and poetically inept but dramatically cogent. It tells how Zenobia, the courageous Queen of Palmyra, is defeated by the Roman Emperor Aureliano through the treachery of Ormonte, the city's governor. When she refuses to reciprocate Aureliano's love, Zenobia is placed under sentence of death – but she impresses her conqueror by spurning a proposal by Ormonte to assassinate him and is finally restored to her throne.
Albinoni's score contains several good arias but betrays its immaturity by the awkwardness of the word-setting in many recitatives. The sinfonia to Act I, a trumpet sonata that survives elsewhere as a separate instrumental composition, offers a very early example of unison writing for strings.

EDITION facsimile, Garland, 1979

Pimpinone
Intermezzi comici musicali in three acts (50m)
Libretto by Pietro Pariati
PREMIERE Autumn 1708, Teatro San Cassiano, Venice

The reform of the Italian opera libretto around 1700 caused the scenes for comic characters that had previously formed part of the opera proper to be replaced by dramatically independent scenes termed intermezzi because they were inserted between the acts of the host work. A set of intermezzi was conceived as a miniature comic opera with a continuous plot. Its separation from the main opera meant that it was now free to tackle contemporary subjects in satirical fashion.
Albinoni's *Pimpinone*, first heard together with his opera *Astarto*, was one of the most successful works of the first generation of Venetian intermezzi. It was revived almost 30 times up to 1740 and travelled as far as Brussels, Ljubljana and Moscow, becoming a mainstay of the repertoire of itinerant pairs of comic singers. Pariati's sparkling libretto has only two characters, both modelled on the stereotypes of 17th-century opera: the cunning young maidservant, Vespetta, and the gullible old bachelor, Pimpinone.

In Intermezzo I Vespetta (alto) entices Pimpinone (bass) into employing her by promising to organize his life more efficiently. In Intermezzo II she persuades him to marry her to avoid scandal, promising to behave as a good wife should. In Intermezzo III she abruptly announces her intention to lead a life of idleness and pleasure; Pimpinone, though appalled, can do nothing since he fears to lose her – and the dowry that he himself earlier provided.

This simple plot touches on one of the most sensitive issues in Venetian society of the time: the adoption by lower social strata of customs that had formerly belonged only to the nobility. The portrayal of Vespetta has a deliberate ambivalence: one can admire her for her resourcefulness or loathe her for her social climbing. By the same token, one may laugh at Pimpinone's credulity while respecting his sense of decorum.

Albinoni's music is attractively tuneful and suitably comic in spirit, though it lacks the variety, sophistication, and feeling for effect of Telemann's later (1725) setting of a version of the same libretto. The best movements are the opening aria for Vespetta ('Chi mi vuol? Son cameriera') which cleverly uses dotted rhythms to express waspishness, and the duets concluding each intermezzo, which differentiate the characters very effectively. The work deserves modern revival and is within the competence of good amateur performers.

RECORDING   Zilio, Trimarchi, I Solisti Veneti, Scimone, Italia, 1980
EDITION   f.s., Michael Talbot (ed.), A-R Editions, 1983

La Statira

Statira
Dramma per musica in three acts
Libretto by Apostolo Zeno and Pietro Pariati
PREMIERE   Carnival 1726, Teatro Capranica, Rome

This opera shows Albinoni in an early stage of his *galant* period, which is marked by florid, rhythmically intricate melodic writing. His recitatives are now metrically accurate and in places very telling, though the main interest centres, as always, on the arias. Act III contains a fine trio that is a rare demonstration in his vocal music of Albinoni's contrapuntal mastery. He was well served by the libretto, which unites Zeno's dramatic gifts and Pariati's flair for versification. The subject is the rivalry of Barsina and Statira for the Persian throne. Barsina is the daughter of deposed King Ciro (Cyrus), while Statira is the daughter of the man who supplanted him, Artaserse. In the end Statira prevails, but Barsina gains the consolation prize of a neighbouring kingdom.

MANUSCRIPT   Österreichische Nationalbibliothek, Musiksammlung, Vienna

Other surviving opera: *Engelberta* (Acts I–III only, coll. with Gasparini), 1709
Surviving short stage works: *Il nascimento dell'aurora*, c. 1710; *Il nome glorioso in terra, santificato in cielo*, 1724 (RECORDING (as *Climène*) Adda, 1988)

Operas with arias surviving: *L'inganno innocente*, 1701, as *Rodrigo in Algeri*, 1702; *Griselda*, 1703, as *L'umiltà esaltata*, 1734; *Astarto*, 1708; *Il tiranno eroe*, 1711; *Eumene* (libretto by Salvi), 1717; *Gli eccessi della gelosia*, 1722; *I veri amici*, 1722; *Eumene* (libretto by Zeno), 1723; *Laodice*, 1724; *L'incostanza schernita*, 1727, as *L'infedeltà delusa*, 1729, as *Filandro*, 1729; *Ardelinda*, 1732; 40 lost operatic works
BIBLIOGRAPHY   Michael Talbot, *Tomaso Albinoni: The Venetian Composer and His World*, The Clarendon Press, 1990

M.T.

GIUSEPPE ALDROVANDINI

Giuseppe Antonio Vincenzo Aldrovandini [Aldovandini, Andervandino]; *b* 8 June 1671, Bologna; *d* 9 February 1707, Bologna

Aldrovandini enjoyed a certain amount of fame in his time, limited perhaps by the excesses of his character – his early death was from drowning while intoxicated. Taught by Perti, maestro di cappella at S. Pietro in Bologna, two of his oratorios were performed in local religious confraternities. He was a member of Bologna's Accademia Filarmonica, becoming its principe in 1701. In the same year he is mentioned in libretti as the honorary maestro di cappella to the Duke of Mantua, and later as the maestro at the Accademia dello Santo Spirito in Ferrara.

Aldrovandini's musical style derives from the late 17th-century Bolognese school of vocal and instrumental composition. His works were performed in Bologna, Turin, Venice, Genoa and Naples. Three of his earliest operas (only libretti survive) are important to the early history of opera buffa; in the Bolognese vernacular, they are independent of the Neapolitan school and reflect the Bolognese taste for dialect humour. Their style can be inferred from the comic episodes in *Cesare in Alessandria*. In his opere serie Aldrovandini adhered to the *da capo* aria form, which he used in conjunction with the motto principle. He was sensitive to the moods of the text, reflected in his harmony, and used melisma for expressive means rather than for mere vocal display.

Surviving operas: *Cesare in Alessandria*, 1699; *Semiramide*, 1701; *Mitridate in Sebastia*, 1701; *L'odio e l'amore* (8 arias only), 1704; *L'incoronazione di Dario*, 1705; 10 lost operas
BIBLIOGRAPHY   James Jackman, 'Giuseppe Antonio Aldrovandini', in *Grove*, Macmillan, 1980

D.S.B.

FELICE ALESSANDRI

b 24 November 1747, Rome; *d* 15 August 1798, Casinalbo, nr Modena

Alessandri was active as a composer in Italy, France, England, Russia and Germany. Trained as a keyboard-player and composer in Naples, by 1770 he had composed operas for Verona and Venice (Carnival, 1767), London (1768–9) and Vienna (1768).

He continued to work in Italy during the early 1770s, mainly in Turin and Venice, but moved to Paris in 1776, where he shared the direction of the Concert Spirituel and composed for the Concerts des Amateurs. He moved to St Petersburg in 1786 in the hope of finding a post as composer to the Russian court, remaining as a singing teacher until 1789, when he moved to Berlin as assistant director of the court opera. His time there (1789–92) was marked by difficulties with colleagues and his employer, King Friedrich Wilhelm II. His operas met at best with mixed success and the last two he wrote for Berlin, *Dario* and *Vasco di Gama*, ended in disaster; he was dismissed in July 1792.

Following his return to Italy in the autumn of 1792, he composed the opera *Virginia* for Venice, while hoping for further commissions from Vienna and Berlin. The greatest successes of his later years were in Padua, with *Zemira* and *Armida*. As well as operas, he composed two oratorios, music for several ballets and some instrumental music. Alessandri's operas are divided equally between serious and comic works. Among the former are four settings of familiar Metastasio texts; among his comic works are those based on Goldoni.

Surviving operas: *Ezio*, 1767; *Il matrimonio per concorso*, 1767; *Creso*, 1774; *La novità*, 1775; *La sposa persiana*, 1775; *Calliroe*, 1778; *Adriano in Siria*, 1779; *Attalo re di Bitinia*, 1780; *Il vecchio geloso*, 1781; *La finta principessa, ossia i due fratelli Pappamosca*, 1782; *Artaserse*, 1783; *Il ritorno di Ulysse a Penelope*, 1790; *L'ouverture du grand opéra italien à Nankin*, 1790; *Dario*, 1791; *Armida*, 1794; 19 lost operas
BIBLIOGRAPHY   Sven Hansell, 'Felice Alessandri', in *Grove*, Macmillan, 1980

D.S.B.

FRANCO ALFANO

b 8 March, 1875, Posillipo, Naples; *d* 27 October 1954, San Remo

Although best known outside Italy as the man who completed Puccini's *Turandot*, Alfano won considerable success south of the Alps with his own works, which were not by any means all operas. Like most leading Italian composers of his generation, he sought a more equal balance between operatic and non-operatic composition, after the long period when opera had dominated his country's musical life. He was also active as a pianist and teacher.

Nevertheless, after studies in Naples and Leipzig, plus short periods of residence in Berlin and Paris, he won his biggest popular success with the relatively traditional opera *Risurrezione*, which had reached its 1000th Italian performance by 1951. Though less favoured by the public, his best subsequent operas – especially *La leggenda di Sakùntala*, commonly regarded as his masterpiece – show greater musical individuality and enterprise: by the time *Sakùntala*

was written, Alfano had absorbed important lessons from Strauss, the Russian nationalists, Ravel and (especially) Debussy. None of his later operas won the popularity of *Risurrezione* or the critical acclaim of *Sakùntala*, although the uneven *Cyrano de Bergerac* contains some eloquent scenes and colourful orchestration, and is still heard occasionally on Italian radio.

Alfano's completion of *Turandot*, based (not altogether satisfactorily) on Puccini's sketches, gives little idea of the quality and character of his own best work. Nevertheless the recent discovery that the usually performed version contains drastic cuts has led critics (notably Mosco Carner) to make forceful pleas for restoring the uncut original, which was first performed at the Barbican Hall, London, on 3 November 1982.

Risurrezione

Resurrection
Opera in four acts (2h)
Libretto by Cesare Hanau, after the novel by Tolstoy (1900)
Composed 1902–3
PREMIERES   30 November 1904, Teatro Vittorio Emanuele II, Turin; US: 31 December 1925, Chicago; UK: 30 November 1967, The Old Town Hall, Fulham Broadway, London (Hammersmith Municipal Opera)

Risurrezione's success owes much to its effective libretto. The heroine Katiusha is seduced and abandoned by Prince Dimitri. Having lost the child born of their union and become a prostitute, she is unjustly condemned for murder and sent to Siberia. The repentant Dimitri follows her there: he obtains a pardon for her, but she refuses his offer of marriage because helping her fellow prisoners has given her a new purpose in life.

The story's Russian setting and the Russian colouring of some of the music recall certain operas by Giordano (especially *Siberia*, with which *Risurrezione* is almost exactly contemporary). But Puccini's influence is also strong, and Alfano's melodic invention cannot quite stand up to the inevitable comparisons. However, the dramatic power of the second act – in which the pregnant Katiusha, in a Ukrainian railway station in winter, vainly awaits a chance to speak to Dimitri again and eventually sees him boarding a train with another woman – is itself sufficient to justify the revivals that the opera still occasionally receives.

RECORDING   Olivero, Gismondo, Boyer, Turin Ch and SO of Italian Radio, Boncompagni, MRF, 1973
EDITION   v.s., Ricordi, 1904

La leggenda di Sakùntala

The Legend of Sakùntala
Opera in three acts (1h 45m)
Libretto by the composer, mainly after Kalidasa's drama *Abhijnana-shakuntala* (*Sakùntala and the Ring of Recognition*, c. 5th century)
Composed 1914–20
PREMIERES   10 December 1921, Teatro Comunale, Bologna; new version (reorch., as *Sakùntala*, after the destruction of the original full score in the Second World

War): 9 January 1952, Teatro dell'Opera, Rome; Ireland: 20 October 1982, Theatre Royal, Wexford

Alfano's adaptation of one of Sanskrit literature's supreme masterpieces sacrifices some of the original's most striking features – e.g. its comic side and its wonderfully moving ending. Yet the libretto serves its purpose, although the total effect is atmospheric rather than urgent. Sakùntala, who has been brought up in a hermitage, wins the love of a king who meets her when out hunting. He gives her a ring before leaving her, but does not return because a curse has removed his memory of their meeting, which can be revived only by his seeing the ring. This goes missing, and is recovered too late to prevent Sakùntala from throwing herself into a pool and being carried off in a cloud of fire. However, she has meanwhile given birth to a child whom, at the end of the opera, the repentant king and his court honour as the future hero of the world.

Sakùntala's most consistently admirable aspect is its sumptuous orchestral textures. The vocal writing, whose methods range freely and flexibly between those of Puccini and those of Pelléas et Mélisande, is only intermittently memorable, but includes notable highlights such as Sakùntala's Act II aria 'O nuvola', addressed to a cloud which she imagines can convey a message to the distant king. In Italy this aria has often been performed separately, as have the flamboyantly colourful dance and finale from Act III.

RECORDING   Casapietra, Didier Gambardella, Molese, Tomicich, Mazzoli, Rome Ch and SO of Italian Radio, Ziino, MRF, 1979
EDITION   v.s., Ricordi, 1921

Other operas: *Miranda*, (1896); *La fonte di Enschir*, 1898; *Il principe Zilah*, 1909; *L'ombra di Don Giovanni*, 1914, rev. as *Don Juan de Manara*, 1941; *Madonna Imperia*, 1927; *L'ultimo lord*, 1930; *Cyrano de Bergerac*, 1936 (RECORDING MRF, 1975); *Il dottor Antonio*, 1949
BIBLIOGRAPHY   Guido M. Gatti, 'Franco Alfano', *MQ*, vol. 9 (1923), pp. 556–77

J.C.G.W.

FRANCISCO ANTÓNIO DE ALMEIDA

b c. 1702; *d* ?1755, Lisbon

Almeida studied in Rome as a Portuguese royal scholar (1722–8 at least). A drawing of him by the caricaturist Pier Leone Ghezzi dated 9 July 1724 is in the Biblioteca Apostolica Vaticana. The legend, in Ghezzi's own hand, refers to him as a young Portuguese student who was already a very fine composer of concertos and church music and who sang superbly.

In April 1728 Almeida's serenata *Il trionfo della virtù* was performed in Lisbon, and at Carnival 1733 his first opera *La pazienza di Socrate*, sung at the royal palace, became the first Italian opera to be performed in Portugal. He wrote two other operas, *La finta pazza* (now lost) and *La Spinalba*, also performed at the royal palace by the court singers, and several serenatas. He also wrote music for the *presépios* (popular Nativity plays) and church music for the royal chapel. He was probably a victim of the Lisbon earthquake of 1755.

La Spinalba, ovvero Il vecchio matto
Spinalba, or The Mad Old Man
Dramma comico da rappresentarsi in musica in three acts
Librettist unknown
PREMIERES   Carnival 1739, Ribeira Palace, Lisbon; 26 May 1965, Teatro Nacional de San Carlos, Lisbon; UK: 28 March 1978, Collegiate Theatre, London (Phoenix Opera)

The action takes place in Rome. Spinalba, the daughter of Arsenio, disguises herself as a man in order to get into the service of her unfaithful Roman lover Ippolito. In doing so she awakens the love of her cousin Elisa, who does not recognize her, and who in turn is wooed by Ippolito. She is also the cause of her father becoming mad with grief at losing her. Arsenio's madness is the pretext for several comic scenes. In the end Arsenio recovers his reason, Ippolito recognizes Spinalba and repents and Elisa reconciles herself with her former lover Leandro.

The musical style of the opera is reminiscent of Pergolesi, whose *La serva padrona* had been written six years earlier. It is both elegant and very expressive, stressing the sentimental rather than the comical character of the opera.

RECORDING   Marimpietri, Righetti, Zanini, Garazioti, Benelli, Serafim, Borgonovo, Rovetta, Gulbenkian CO, Rivoli, Philips, 1969
EDITIONS   f.s./v.s., *Portugaliae musica XII*, Gulbenkian Foundation (Lisbon), 1969

BIBLIOGRAPHY   Manuel Carlos de Brito, *Opera in Portugal in the Eighteenth Century*, CUP, 1989

M.C.B.

WILLIAM ALWYN

b 7 November 1905, Northampton, England; *d* 11 September 1985, Blythburgh, Suffolk, England

Alwyn studied at the Royal Academy of Music, 1920–23, and became a professional flautist. At the age of 21 he became a professor of composition at the RAM. He had a significant career as a composer up to 1939 when, criticizing his earlier technique, he withdrew his works up to that date. He subsequently produced mainly orchestral and instrumental music, including symphonies, many film scores (such as *Desert Victory* (1945), *The History of Mr Polly* (1949) and *The Ship That Died of Shame* (1955)) and much incidental music for the BBC. An early neo-classical style had given way, by 1955, to a more overtly romantic musical language, in which Alwyn imposed his own restrictions of limited modes on his writing.

His independent, non-derivative style was considered unfashionable for much of his life.

A childhood attempt at opera, *The Fairy Fiddler* (1917), is lost. Later, Alwyn orchestrated the missing sections of Wolf's *Der Corregidor* at the request of Sir John Barbirolli. His first mature opera was a BBC commission, *Farewell Companions* (1955), a ballad opera on the life of the Irish nationalist Robert Emmet. His next opera, *Juan or the Libertine* (1965–73), largely after James Elroy Flecker's play, remains unperformed.

Miss Julie

Opera in two acts (2h)
Libretto by the composer, after the play by August Strindberg (1888)
Composed 1973–6
PREMIERES 16 July 1977, BBC (radio broadcast); 4 February 1991, Copenhagen

The composer put his theories about opera to the test in this, his only successful opera, particularly in allowing the music to spring naturally from the words.

In a Swedish country house Miss Julie spends Midsummer night with Jean, her father's valet, who persuades her to steal from her father to finance their elopement. On the return of their master the servants return to their duties and Miss Julie, humiliated and trapped, walks into the night holding an open razor.

RECORDING Gomez, Jones, Mitchinson, Luxon, Philharmonia O, Tausky, Lyrita, 1983

BIBLIOGRAPHY Booklet with Lyrita recording of *Miss Julie* includes articles by Rodney Milnes and Cecil Parrott, extracts from the composer's writings on opera and his own synopsis; William Mann, 'Alwyn's *Miss Julie*', *Opera*, vol. 28 (1977), pp. 641–5

L.F.

JOHANN ANDRÉ

b 28 March 1741, Offenbach; *d* 18 June 1799, Offenbach

In the early 1770s André was engaged to translate the texts of various opéras comiques by Philidor into German at Frankfurt. His elegant writing caught the attention of the impresario Theobald Marchand, at whose suggestion he produced the libretto and music of his first stage composition, a comic singspiel, *Der Töpfer*. Mounted at Hanau in 1773, it was a remarkable success, despite its relatively modest aims. Goethe praised the composer's skill in combining 'correct declamation with light, flowing melody', and subsequently commissioned him to set a singspiel text of his own, *Erwin und Elmire*, which was successfully performed at Frankfurt in 1775.

Later, André was appointed as conductor, in Berlin, to the important theatre troupe of Theophil Doebbelin, and began a period of great productivity. Noteworthy among the singspiels he wrote for Berlin are his settings of Goethe's *Claudine von Villa Bella* (later set by Schubert), of Bretzner's *Die Entführung*

aus dem Serail (a year before Mozart's version of the same libretto, with additions by Gottlob Stephanie) and of his own German translation of de Montenoy's *Le barbier de Baghdad*. Distinguished mainly by the fluent, folksong-like character of the songs contained in them, these works also display a clear grasp of theatrical effects which secured for them instant, but not lasting, acclaim. In his final years André returned to his native Offenbach to oversee the work of his publishing firm, which soon issued well over a thousand prints, including works by Haydn, Pleyel and Gyrowetz; it is for this activity that he is chiefly remembered today.

Singspiels: *Der Töpfer*, 1773; *Erwin und Elmire*, 1775; *Der alte Freyer*, 1776; *Die Bezauberten*, 1777; *Die Schadenfreude*, 1778; *Der Alchymist*, 1778; *Laura Rosetti*, 1778; *Azakia*, 1778; *Claudine von Villa Bella*, 1778; *Das tartarische Gesetz*, 1779; *Alter schütz vor Thorheit nicht*, 1779; *Kurze Thorheit ist die beste*, 1780; *Das wüthende Heer, oder Das Mädchen im Thurme*, 1780; *Die Entführung aus dem Serail*, 1781; *Elmine*, 1782; *Eins wird doch helfen, oder Die Werbung aus Liebe*, 1782; *Der Barbier von Baghdad*, 1783; *Der Bräutigam in der Klemme*, 1796
BIBLIOGRAPHY A. H. André, *Zur Geschichte der Familie André*, Garmisch, 1963

B.S.

GAETANO ANDREOZZI

b 22 May 1755, Aversa; *d* 21 or 24 December 1826, Paris

Andreozzi studied at the Santa Maria di Loreto Conservatory in Naples. From 1779, when his oratorio *Giefte* was performed in Rome, he enjoyed a series of musical successes in Italy. He visited Russia in 1784 but returned to Italy the following year, when he produced operas in Naples, Pisa and Lucca. From 1801 Andreozzi lived in Naples and was active there and in Rome. While his operatic success diminished, he gradually became more famous as a singing teacher. Financial problems forced him to move to Paris in 1825, where he enjoyed the protection of the Duchess of Berry, Maria Carolina, daughter of King Francesco I of Naples.

Andreozzi belongs, with Valentino Fioravanti, to a generation of Neapolitan musicians, slightly younger than that of Paisiello and Cimarosa, whose works are now largely forgotten. However, contemporary sources indicate a highly successful career, no doubt due to his ability to write decorative, if rather hollow, music which flattered the singers and impressed the audience. Andreozzi never strayed far from the tried and tested Neapolitan style, with its emphasis on pleasing lyricism and its characteristic use of instrumental effects. However, there are occasional hints of more imaginative and individual elements, for example in the use of the chorus, in the choice of forms (e.g. cavatina and rondo are used quite prominently in *Amleto*) and in the structuring of these to create larger-scale scenes rather than simply writing a sequence of numbers.

Operas surviving in whole or part: *L'equivoco*, 1781; *L'Arbace*, 1781; *L'Olimpiade*, 1782; *Bajazet*, 1783; *Medonte re d'Epiro*, 1783; *Didone abbandonata*, 1785; *Catone in Utica*, 1786; *Virginia*, 1786; *Agesilao re di Sparta*, 1788; *Sofronia ed Olindo*, 1788; *Giovanna d'Arco, ossia La Pulcella d'Orléans*, 1789; *Artaserse*, 1789; *La morte di Giulio Cesare*, 1789; *Teodolinda*, 1789; *Angelica e Medoro*, 1791; *Amleto*, 1792 (EDITION see BIBLIOGRAPHY below); *Gli amanti in Tempe*, 1792; *Giasone e Medea*, 1793; *La principessa filosofa, ossia Il contraveleno*, 1794; *Il trionfo di Arsace*, 1795; *Arsinoe*, 1795; *La vergine del sole*, 1797; *Pamela nubile*, 1800; *Sesostri*, 1802; *Armida e Rinaldo*, 1802; *Piramo e Tisbe*, 1803; *Il trionfo di Claudia*, 1803; *Sedesclavo*, 1805; *Il trionfo di Tomiri*, 1807; *Tutti i torti son dei mariti*, 1814; *Il trionfo di Alessandro Magno il Macedone*, 1815; 13 lost operas
BIBLIOGRAPHY   Marcello Conati, introductory essay in Gaetano Andreozzi, *Amleto*, facsimile, Ricordi, 1984

D.S.B.

PASQUALE ANFOSSI

b 5 April 1727, Tággia; *d* February 1797, Rome

The facts about Anfossi's early career cannot be fully verified. After training at the Loreto Conservatory in Naples, he apparently worked as an orchestral musician in the city (*c.* 1752–62). His first successes were *La serva spiritosa* (Rome, 1763), and *L'incognita perseguitata* (Rome, 1773). During the 1770s Anfossi was also active in Venice and, from 1782 to 1786, he was music director at the King's Theatre in London. Five of his new comic operas were performed there, but his success declined, and he returned to Venice. A brief revival of his fortunes in Rome, with *Le pazzie e' gelosi* (1787, lost), ended in 1790, when he turned almost exclusively to sacred music.

Anfossi's early style shows the influence of Piccinni, whose pupil he may have been. In his later works, he makes use of lighter textures, and the style is in general less ornate, while his orchestration is enriched by a more imaginative use of wind instruments. The *da capo* aria rules in his early heroic operas, but not in his comic operas and it does not appear in his works after 1770.

It was after seeing Anfossi's *La finta giardiniera* (1774) that Mozart decided to write his opera of the same name. A further link between the two composers came in 1783 when Mozart provided additional arias for the Vienna premiere of Anfossi's *Il curioso indiscreto*. Despite Mozart's comment to his father that the opera 'failed completely with the exception of my . . . arias', the work was among Anfossi's most successful, performed regularly throughout Europe well into the 1790s.

Surviving operas: *La serva spiritosa, ossia I ripieghi della medesima*, 1763; *Lo sposo di tre e marito di nessuna*, 1763; *La clemenza di Tito*, 1769, rev. 1772; *Armida*, 1770; *Cajo Mario*, 1770; *Quinto Fabio*, 1771; *Il barone di Rocca Antica* (coll. with Carlo Franchi), 1771 (RECORDING Bongiovanni, 1988); *Nitteti*, 1771; *Alessandro dell'Indie*, 1772; *L'amante confuso*, 1772; *L'incognita perseguitata*, 1773; *La finta giardiniera*, 1774; *Lucio Silla*, 1774; *Il geloso in cimento*, 1774; *Olimpiade*, 1774; *La contadina incivilita*, 1775; *Didone abbandonata*,

1775; *L'avaro*, 1775; *La vera costanza*, 1776; *Isabella e Rodrigo, o sia La costanza in amore*, 1776; *Il curioso indiscreto*, 1777; *Gengis-Kan*, 1777; *Adriano in Siria*, 1777 (EDITION facsimile, J. Joly (ed.), Ricordi, 1983); *Lo sposo disperato*, 1777; *Ezio*, 1778; *La forza delle donne*, 1778; *L'americana in Olanda*, 1778; *Cleopatra*, 1779; *Il matrimonio per inganno*, 1779; *I viaggiatori felici*, 1780; *Il trionfo d' 'Arianna*, 1781; *L'imbroglio delle tre spose*, 1781; *Gli amanti canuti*, 1781; *Zemira*, 1782; *La maga Circe*, 1788 (RECORDING Bongiovanni, 1989); *Artaserse*, 1788; *Zenobia in Palmira*, 1789; *Gli artigiani*, 1794; 24 lost operas
BIBLIOGRAPHY   Michael F. Robinson, 'Pasquale Anfossi', in *Grove*, Macmillan, 1980

D.S.B.

GEORGE ANTHEIL

George Carl Johan Antheil; *b* 8 July 1900, Trenton, New Jersey, US; *d* 12 February 1959, New York

Antheil was one of the most colourful characters in 20th-century American music; he created a sensation wherever he went. He was of German ancestry and his principal composition teacher, whom he idolized, was Ernest Bloch. Even in his teens Antheil was incorporating aspects of popular music into his compositions. In 1922 he went to Europe to give piano recitals. These included his own works which were controversial both in their violence and dissonance and in their titles, such as *Airplane Sonata* and *Sonatina: Death of the Machines*. Moving from Berlin to Paris in 1923 he was taken up by the avant garde, Ezra Pound being one of his most enthusiastic champions. This period reached its climax with the *succès de scandale* of his *Ballet mécanique*, premiered in Paris in 1926, which carried aspects of Stravinsky's *Les noces* and Satie's *Parade* to almost absurd extremes in a rhythmic and textural context (anticipating the minimalism of the 1980s). Before settling to a more stable American folk style which was to serve him for much of the rest of his career, Antheil, again following Stravinsky, turned briefly to neo-classicism: at this point he moved back to Germany, accepted an appointment at the Berlin Stadttheater and turned to opera.

Transatlantic (1930) followed on from Krenek's popular jazz-inspired *Jonny spielt auf* and some of the successes of Kurt Weill. Antheil told his generous and long-suffering patron, Mary Louise Bok, that it was to be 'the great American opera that America has talked [of] and awaited so eagerly for so many years'. At its Frankfurt premiere the opera – a send-up of an American presidential election campaign – was so well received that the composer's prophecies almost came true, but the lavish production proved too expensive to revive; it has yet to receive its American premiere.

In 1933 Antheil returned to America, to New York. Before *Transatlantic* had been staged, Antheil had planned his next opera, *Helen Retires*, a Classical subject with a poetic libretto by John Erskine, President of the Juilliard School of Music, New York. Even the composer had to describe the production there in 1934 as 'a gigantic flop'. No doubt influenced by this failure, he turned his hand to writing film music, settling in Hollywood in 1935, where he remained for the rest of his life.

In the 1950s Antheil returned to opera with four works, none of which has yet had a fair trial on stage. They reflect the neo-Romantic style he had adopted in the 1940s which aimed at 'a musical language which would be comprehensible to American theatre audiences and easily understood'. The most substantial of these operas is *Volpone* (the other three are each in one act), based on the comedy by Ben Jonson. Originally over four hours long, *Volpone* was reduced by half by Antheil and his librettist Albert Perry: it is a light work, with hints of Broadway, and enjoyed some success.

Antheil published a vividly entertaining auto-biography and wrote regularly on topics other than music.

Operas: *Transatlantic*, 1930; *Helen Retires*, 1931; *Volpone*, 1952; *The Brothers*, 1954; *Venus in Africa*, 1954; *The Wish*, 1955
BIBLIOGRAPHY   George Antheil, *Bad Boy of Music*, Doubleday, 1945; Linda Whitesitt, *The Life and Music of George Antheil 1900–1959*, UMI Research Press, 1983

P.D.

FRANCESCO ARAIA

Francesco Araia [Araja]; *b* 25 June 1709, Naples; *d* after 1762, ?Bologna

For 20 years Araia was maestro di cappella to the Russian empresses Anne and Elizabeth, writing operas and cantatas for the court in St Petersburg and Moscow. Most of the former were opere serie and the most famous, *Cephal i Prokris*, to a text by Alexandr Sumarokov, is the first opera known to have been sung in Russian.

Araia was clearly precocious, winning acclaim at 14 as the director of a concert in Naples. He is said to have written a Neapolitan comic opera, *Lo matremmonejo pe' mennetta*, but most of his early operas (1729–35) were serious. They were performed in Pratolino (near Florence), Rome, Milan and Venice.

Araia went, with an Italian troupe, to Russia in 1735. His *La forza dell'amore e dell'odio*, previously presented in Milan, was produced in St Petersburg in March 1736, and although not – as often stated – the first Italian opera to be staged in Russia (an honour that probably belongs to Tommaso Ristori's *Calandro*, 1731), the work helped to establish an Italian operatic tradition at the Russian court. He wrote two new operas before the Empress Anne's death in 1740, when he returned to Italy to recruit new personnel for the opera. In the service of the Empress Elizabeth from 1742, he continued to write operas, many of them to libretti by Giuseppe Bonecchi, whom he had brought back from Italy. In deference to his patrons, however, he occasionally included Russian folk tunes. Having left in 1759,

Araia returned in 1762 to write music for the coronation of Tsar Peter III; but after the tsar's deposition and his subsequent assassination in July 1762, Araia retired to Bologna.

Surviving operas: *La forza dell'amore e dell'odio*, 1734; *Il finto Nino, overo La Semiramide riconosciuto*, 1737; *Cephal i Prokris*, 1755; 14 lost operas
BIBLIOGRAPHY   U. Prota-Giurleo, 'Francesco Araja', in *Dizionario biografico degli italiani*, vol. 3, Istituto della Enciclopedia Italiana, 1961

D.S.B.

ANTON ARENSKY

Anton Stepanovich Arensky; *b* 12 July 1861, Novgorod, Russia; *d* 25 February 1906, Terioki, Finland

Arensky was a pupil of Rimsky-Korsakov, who was sufficiently impressed to entrust him with the preparation of the vocal score of *The Snow Maiden* in 1880–81. After graduation, Arensky went to the Moscow Conservatory as a professor of harmony and counterpoint. His pupils there included Rakhmaninov, Skryabin and Glier, and he became a friend of Tchaikovsky. A successful pianist and conductor, he was by all accounts work-obsessed, an inveterate drinker and a gambler. This undermined his health and he succumbed to tuberculosis. His first opera, *A Dream on the Volga* (1891) (using the same libretto set by Tchaikovsky in *The Voyevoda*), was a success that his later operas never matched. The music, some of which was written when he was a student, has both a vigour and an original approach to folksong which he was never to develop. *Raphael* (1894) is indebted to Tchaikovsky, and *Nal and Damayanti* (1904), picturesque in places, shows a belated and undigested influence of Wagner. Always an eclectic composer, Arensky was rebuked by Tchaikovsky for appropriating 'his' unusual metre of 5/4 in many works, and a rather brutal obituary of him appeared in Rimsky-Korsakov's memoirs, *My Musical Life*, ranking him below Rubinstein as a composer and predicting that he would be totally forgotten.

RECORDING   *Raphael*, Melodiya, 1957
BIBLIOGRAPHY   Rosa Newmarch, *Russian Opera*, Herbert Jenkins, 1914

J.G.

DOMINICK ARGENTO

b 27 October 1927, York, Pennsylvania, US

Argento is one of the most successful American opera composers of his generation. His parents came from Italy and his music has its roots in the tradition of Italian opera. He has said, 'I want my work to have emotional impact: I want it to communicate, not obfuscate.'

At first self-taught, in 1947 Argento went to the Peabody Conservatory in Baltimore and, in 1951, to Florence where he studied with Dallapiccola and encountered serial techniques. Soon after his return to the US Argento's first opera, *Sicilian Lines*, was produced; this was later withdrawn.

From 1955 to 1957 Argento studied at the Eastman School, Rochester, with Hanson, Rogers and Hovhaness. Here his second opera, *The Boor* – based on Chekhov – was premiered in the 1957 Festival of American Music. It was praised for its idiomatic handling of traditional operatic techniques of aria, ensemble and dramatic pacing and has been widely performed throughout the US and abroad. Back in Florence on a Guggenheim Fellowship, Argento began *Colonel Jonathan the Saint*, which was a failure when it was eventually premiered at Denver (1971).

In 1958 Argento took a teaching post at Minnesota University. Here, along with his librettist and director John Olon-Scrymgeour, he founded Center Opera (later called Minnesota Opera) which was launched with Argento's *The Masque of Angels*. In the mid-1960s Argento worked with Tyrone Guthrie and Douglas Campbell, writing incidental music for several plays. His most popular work came in 1971 – the chamber extravaganza, *Postcard from Morocco*.

The Voyage of Edgar Allan Poe was an American Bicentennial commission, to a libretto by C. M. Nolte, based on the later years of Poe's madness. Minnesota Opera gave the premiere, then took its production to Baltimore. The plot was felt to be confused, but Andrew Porter wrote of 'touching lyrical passages' and found the opera 'intelligent, accomplished, imaginative'.

Generally melodious and harmonious, Argento's music belongs to no particular contemporary trend. It has enjoyed considerable success in America, but apart from isolated performances in Britain (especially at the Aldeburgh Festival) it has made little impact abroad.

Postcard from Morocco

Opera in one act (1h 30m)
Libretto by John Donahue
Composed 1971
PREMIERES 14 October 1971, Center Opera Company, Minneapolis; UK: 28 July 1976, King's College, London (Contemporary Opera Company)

Postcard from Morocco is set in 1914 at a railway station in Morocco, where a group of travellers is stranded. After various deceptively light-hearted incidents, one of the travellers is tricked into revealing himself when he opens his suitcase. Matching the episodic nature of the libretto, with its sequence of dreams and reminiscences, Argento's music – scored for seven singers and eight instrumentalists – is eclectic, with hints of Stravinsky and Britten.

RECORDING Brandt, Roche, Hardy, Marshall, Sutton, Busse, Foreman, Center Opera of Minnesota Instrumental Ensemble, Brunelle, Desto, 1972

A scene from Postcard from Morocco *(Minnesota, 1971)*

EDITION v.s., Boosey & Hawkes, 1972

Other operatic works: *Sicilian Lines* (withdrawn), 1954; *The Boor*, 1957; *Colonel Jonathan the Saint*, (1958–60), 1971; *Christopher Sly*, 1963; *The Masque of Angels*, 1964; *The Shoemaker's Holiday*, 1967; *A Waterbird Talk*, (1974–6), 1977; *The Voyage of Edgar Allan Poe*, 1976; *Miss Havisham's Fire*, 1979; *Miss Havisham's Wedding Night*, 1981; *Casanova's Homecoming*, 1985; *The Aspern Papers*, 1987
BIBLIOGRAPHY David Ewen, *American Composers: A Biographical Dictionary*, Hall, 1983; *New Grove Dictionary of American Music*, Macmillan, 1986

P.D.

ATTILIO ARIOSTI

Attilio Malachia Clemente (Frate Ottavio) Ariosti;
b 5 November 1666, Bologna; *d* summer 1729, London

Ariosti is remembered mainly for a volume of six cantatas and six lessons for the viola d'amore (1724), but he was active as an opera composer in his native Italy, and in Berlin, Vienna and London, where he became a leading member of the Royal Academy of Music and was a major rival of Handel.

Nothing is known of Ariosti's musical training. A Servite monk, he sang, and played several instruments as well as being a composer. In 1696 he entered the service of the Duke of Mantua, for whom he wrote operas performed in Venice at Carnival time. A move to Berlin followed a request from the Electress Sophie Charlotte for a good musician. Ariosti's withdrawal from the Protestant Berlin court, after a controversy over his position there as a Catholic monk, was followed by a period in Vienna, where he wrote an opera and was also active in a diplomatic role.

By 1716 Ariosti was playing the viola d'amore in the Haymarket opera orchestra in London, where he soon established himself as a performer and composer, making his operatic début in 1717 as the composer of *Tito Manlio*, a highly individual work, with nine long accompanied recitatives, many unusual arias and five duets. In the 1720s Ariosti was engaged, with Handel and Giovanni Bononcini, to compose operas for the recently formed Royal Academy. His first, and most successful, opera for the company was *Coriolano* (1723); also a considerable success was *La Vespasiano*, which was performed in 1724 with a cast that included some of the foremost singers of the day – Francesca Cuzzoni, Anastasia Robinson and the castrato Senesino. Later works were less successful and Ariosti is said to have died in poverty.

Ariosti's opera for the Royal Academy, though generally popular, failed to display the originality that makes *Tito Manlio* so unusual. Arias are mostly in conventional *da capo* form and scored only for continuo accompaniment (i.e. none of the interesting obbligato woodwind parts that Handel was writing); many show a tendency towards the simple, affecting style at which Bononcini excelled, but this was going out of fashion by the mid-1720s.

Operatic works: *La festa del Himeneo*, 1700; *La fede ne' tradimenti*, 1701; *La più gloriosa fatica d'Ercole*, 1703; *Il bene dal male*, 1704; *I glorioso presagi di Scipione Africano*, 1704; *Marte placato*, 1707; *La gara delle antiche eroine ne' Campi Elisi*, 1707; *Amor tra nemici*, 1708; *La Placidia*, 1709; *Tito Manlio*, 1717; *Coriolano*, 1723; *Vespasiano*, 1724 (EDITION facsimile, Garland, 1977); *Teuzzone*, 1727; 10 lost operas
BIBLIOGRAPHY   Lowell Lindgren, 'Ariosti's London Years, 1716–1729', *ML*, vol. 62 (1981), pp. 331–51

D.S.B.

HAROLD ARLEN
Hyman Arluck; *b* 15 February 1905, Buffalo, New York; *d* 23 April 1986, New York

Harold Arlen worked in his teens as a pianist, arranger and singer. First associated with revues and nightclub shows, including famously those at Harlem's Cotton Club (1930–34), he later turned to Broadway and to film work. His stage musicals – usually memorable musically but often hampered by problematic libretti – benefited from his unique jazz-influenced melodic and harmonic gift as well as his willingness to experiment with song structure.

The Wizard of Oz
Musical fantasy in two acts (film: 1h 45m)
Film screenplay by Noel Langley, Florence Ryerson and Edgar Allan Woolf, based on the book by L. Frank Baum; 1987 stage libretto adapted by John Kane
PREMIERES   16 August 1939, MGM film premiere; 10 August 1942, Municipal Opera, St Louis; UK: rev. version: 12 December 1987, Barbican Theatre, London

Baum's classic story received its definitive musical treatment in the 1939 film. Wishing for a more colourful world than her home in Kansas ('Over the Rainbow'), Dorothy finds herself transported to the magical land of Oz. There she finds new friends – a scarecrow, a tin woodman and a cowardly lion ('If I

only had a brain/a heart/the nerve') – with whom she finds the great Wizard of Oz and defeats the Wicked Witch of the West before happily returning home. In its stage version this is the most performed of Arlen's musicals. The 1942 St Louis Municipal Opera production was allowed to use the MGM orchestrations, but not the script; the 1987 version (the first with official permission to make use of the screenplay) will probably become the standard performing version, establishing a definitive stage libretto for the first time.

RECORDING   Bevan, Edwards, Royal Shakespeare Company, TER, 1989
FILM   Fleming (dir.), MGM, 1939
EDITION   v.s., Leo Feist, 1964

Other stage works: *You Said It*, 1931; *Hooray for What?*, 1937; *Bloomer Girl*, 1944; *St Louis Woman*, 1946, rev. as *Free and Easy*, 1959; *House of Flowers*, 1954; *Jamaica*, 1957; *Saratoga*, 1959
BIBLIOGRAPHY   John Fricke, Jay Scarfone, and William Stillman, *The Wizard of Oz: The Official 50th Anniversary Pictorial History*, Warner, 1989; Edward Jablonski, *Harold Arlen, Happy with the Blues*, Doubleday, 1961; rev. edn, Da Capo, 1986

J.A.C.

MICHAEL ARNE
b ?1740; *d* 14 January 1786, Lambeth, London

A natural son of Thomas Arne, Michael was an actor, singer, harpsichordist and composer who started his career as a child prodigy. As 'The Lass with the Delicate Air' demonstrates, he was an able if facile melodist, whose songs were much in demand at Vauxhall and Ranelagh. Most of his work for the theatre consisted of occasional contributions to the compositions of others and much of his music has been lost. Two works deserve mention, *Almena* (1764) and *Cymon* (1767). *Almena*, composed in conjunction with Jonathan Battishill to a libretto by Richard Rolt, was an ambitious attempt at an all-sung opera. Arne's contributions are elaborate and Italianate; indeed two Italians took part in the production, and in this, as in much else, the opera resembles his father's *Artaxerxes*. It was modestly successful. *Cymon*, by contrast, was enormously popular. Garrick's five-act libretto is based on Dryden's fable *Cymon and Iphigenia* and was intended as a vehicle for a lavish production set in the 'Arthurian' Middle Ages. The music is banal; such life as it has derives from the fact that Garrick's lyrics exploit the kind of simple situations on which the pleasure-garden songs depended. Michael Arne made a tour of Germany and latterly lived in Dublin; he abandoned music for alchemy and died in poverty.

Operatic works: *Edgar and Emmeline*, 1761; *Hymen*, 1764; *Almena* (coll. with Battishill), 1764; *Cymon*, 1767; *The Artifice*, 1780

BIBLIOGRAPHY Roger Fiske, *English Theatre Music in the Eighteenth Century*, OUP, 1973; 2nd edn, 1986; John A. Parkinson, *An Index to the Vocal Works of Thomas Augustine Arne and Michael Arne*, Information Co-ordinators (Detroit), 1972

R.Lu.

THOMAS ARNE

Thomas Augustine Arne; *baptized* 28 May 1710, London; *d* 5 March 1778, London

Thomas Arne, by Francesco Bartolozzi

Arne was the pre-eminent English theatrical composer of the 18th century; his whole professional and private life revolved around the playhouses. He was also the leading English composer of opera, but his bread and butter was ensured by providing incidental music for straight drama. It is his misfortune that a number of his works, including several much admired by his contemporaries, are lost, and those that survive are mostly incomplete. His work is notably uneven, the case against probably most forcibly stated by Fanny Burney: 'Thoughtless, dissipated, and careless, he neglected or rather scoffed at all other but musical reputation. [Even so], so happy was his self-complacency in the fertility of his invention and the ease of his compositions, and so dazzled by the brilliancy of his success in his powers of melody – which, in truth, for the English stage were in sweetness and variety unrivalled – that . . . he had no ambition, or rather, no thought, concerning the theory of his art.' Throughout his life he returned to the problem of English opera and its two most likely solutions: the one Italianate, the other Purcellian.

His father was a well-to-do upholsterer (in the 18th-century sense: he provided furnishings and funerals). Arne was sent to Eton and destined for the law, but obstinately pursued his passion for music. Eventually the son's wishes prevailed, in that his father permitted him to teach singing to his sister Susanna and brother Richard and went on to back a production of Handel's *Acis and Galatea* at the Haymarket (1732) in which all three took part. In 1733 Arne launched out as a composer with a setting of *Rosamond*, to the libretto by Joseph Addison with which Thomas Clayton had so notably failed in 1707. It achieved success only when rewritten as an afterpiece in 1740. For the next five years Arne was a successful composer of stage masques and incidental music, being retained by the Drury Lane Theatre. In 1736 he married Cecilia Young, daughter of a church organist and thought by many to be the finest English soprano of her time.

In 1742 Arne, following Handel's example, investigated the possibilities of Dublin, where Susanna had gone after separating from her husband, Theophilus Cibber. It was his main field of operation until he returned to Drury Lane early in 1745. His next attempt at full-scale opera was not until 1754, when he put on *Eliza* at the Little Theatre. Once again a feeble libretto, by Richard Rolt, demonstrated that the fundamental fault of English opera

was literary, not musical. The subject is the threat of the Armada, which finally arrives onstage as a fleet of model ships.

In his final years Arne's work for the stage, with one exception, consisted of incidental music and short afterpieces. The exception was *The Fairy Prince*, done at Covent Garden in 1771 to mark the investiture of the Duke of York as a Knight of the Garter. It was derived by George Colman the elder from Ben Jonson's *Masque of Oberon*, thus reviving the recipe for *Comus*. The work includes surprising borrowings from other 17th-century texts, though it remains virtually plotless. Oberon and his fairy court come to pay homage to the monarch in whose realm they live, but of course they have to vanish at the coming of the morning star. The music reveals that Arne, in returning to his old territory, did not wholly discard the innovations of *Artaxerxes* (1762): the element of overt vocal display is still much to the fore, appropriately in a work that so greatly depended on spectacle and dance. The orchestration, however, is witty rather than profound.

It is sentiment, rather than profundity, that distinguishes *The Cooper* (1772), the most ample of the afterpieces to survive, although in a vocal score only. It has, rather surprisingly, received the accolade of a modern edition (Schott, 1965), in which it has been rendered still less complete. Arne translated his own libretto from that written by Audinot and Quétant for Gossec's *Le tonnelier* (1765): the cooper of the title is frustrated in his attempt to seduce his ward.

When Arne died he had spent 45 years working in the theatre; if his early compositions were advanced for their time his later ones still continue to sound up to date. What is remarkable is that his style in fact changed very little. He remained throughout his life a melodist, but this gift did not enable him to achieve the emancipation of the English lyric stage at which he undoubtedly (if haphazardly) aimed.

Comus

Masque in three acts (3h)
Libretto by the Revd John Dalton, after the masque by Milton (1637)
PREMIERE 4 March 1738, Drury Lane, London

Arne achieved national celebrity with the production of *Comus* at Drury Lane. Dalton turned Milton's masque into a three-act play, enlivened the dialogue and provided the occasion for almost two hours of music (in its original form it had less music in proportion to text than any other Stuart masque). The production was sumptuous; the singers included Handel's tenor, John Beard, Mrs Arne and Susanna Cibber.

Two noble brothers, somewhat carelessly, lose the Lady, their sister, in the wild wood, where she falls into the power of Comus, who holds his voluptuous revels there. The brothers are told of her fate by the Spirit, in the guise of a shepherd; he leads them to where she is held captive and invokes the river goddess, Sabrina, whose touch releases her from the chair to which Comus' enchantments bind her. The music has a charm and vitality of its own, sometimes reminiscent of Purcell or Handel (Giovanni Bononcini is also a perceptible influence) but breathing an individual air: cleanly constructed, crisply orchestrated, often using dance rhythms (there was much dancing in the production) yet able to cope with the element of moral seriousness that survives from the original. The invocation of Sabrina is particularly effective in this respect.

RECORDING Ritchie, Morison, Herbert, St Anthony Singers, L'Ensemble Orchestral de l'Oiseau-Lyre, Lewis, Oiseau-Lyre, 1954
EDITIONS William Smith, [c. 1740]; Julian Herbage (ed.), *Musica Britannica III*, Stainer and Bell, 1951

Alfred

Masque in three acts (2h 15m)
Libretto by James Thomson and David Mallet
PREMIERES 1 August 1740, Cliveden House (private); 20 March 1745, Drury Lane, London

In 1740 Arne followed *Comus* with *Alfred*, variously described as a 'masque', a 'drama for music' and an 'English opera'. The libretto tells of the 'British' King Alfred's flight from the Danes under their king, Hubba, of the shelter afforded him by a peasant couple and a hermit, the master plan for the defeat of the Danes devised by the Earl of Devon, the reunion of Alfred with his queen, Eltruda, and an offstage British victory of overwhelming proportions ('The valiant Hubba bites the bloody field'), the festivities to celebrate this concluding with the 'Grand Ode', 'Rule Britannia'.

Although *Alfred* was first given at Cliveden, the country residence of Frederick, Prince of Wales, to celebrate the birthday of his daughter Augusta, it seems originally to have been intended for Drury Lane, to which it eventually made its way in 1745, after much tinkering by Mallet and Arne. Besides 'Rule Britannia', the original version contained Eltruda's exquisite 'O Peace, thou fairest child of Heaven'. 'The Shepherd's plain life' is equally fine in a different, robust way, the use of obbligato horns typical of Arne's deft orchestration throughout the piece. But Mallet and Thomson could not contrive that balance of the pastoral, the heroic and the patriotic which Dryden achieved in *King Arthur* and no amount of reorganization or additional music could make the work cohere even when David Garrick turned his hand to the job.

EDITIONS Walsh, 1757; Alexander Scott (ed.), *Musica Britannica MLVII*, Stainer and Bell, 1981

The Judgement of Paris

Masque in one act (1h 15m)
Libretto by William Congreve
PREMIERE 12 March 1742, Drury Lane, London

Congreve's poem was written for the 'Musick Prize' that five composers, Thomas Arne, John Eccles, Godfrey Finger, Daniel Purcell and John Weldon competed for at the Dorset Garden Theatre in the spring of 1701. In the 1730s and early 1740s, there was a revival of interest in the libretti that Dryden and Congreve had provided for composers at the turn of the century: Handel reset *Alexander's Feast* (Dryden, 1697) and *A Song for St Cecilia's Day* (Dryden, 1687). *The Judgement of Paris* was an obvious further candidate and provided, as Paris chose between the three goddesses, just the kind of static but at the same time dramatic tableau that the form favoured. Arne's wife, Cecilia Young, sang Venus; Mrs Clive, Pallas, and Miss Edwards, Juno. John Beard, Handel's oratorio tenor, was Paris, and Thomas Lowe, Mercury. When Arne moved to Dublin in June 1742 *The Judgement of Paris* proved a particularly effective companion piece in a double-bill with *Alfred*.

EDITION Ian Spink (ed.), *Musica Britannica XLII*, Stainer and Bell, 1978

Thomas and Sally, or The Sailor's Return

Afterpiece in two acts (1h)
Libretto by Isaac Bickerstaffe
PREMIERES 28 November 1761, Covent Garden, London; US: 14 November 1766, Philadelphia

It was not until 1761 that Arne miraculously managed to find, in Bickerstaffe, a natural comic librettist. The consequence was the all-sung miniature *Thomas and Sally*. Sally, a village maiden, is pursued by the wicked squire, who is aided by a lady of doubtful morals. In the nick of time Thomas, Sally's sailor sweetheart, returns from sea to snatch her from ruin and take her to the altar. That the plot is hackneyed is part of the comedy; the characterization is humorously neat; the element of generic parody perfectly judged. The music strikes just the right light-hearted note, and its felicities (which include the first use of the clarinet in the English opera house and some ingenious rhythmic tricks) are never permitted to draw attention to themselves.

Two years later Bickerstaffe and Arne turned to another form, ballad opera, and proved in *Love in a Village* (a pasticcio, but mainly Arne's) that they could repeat their success. But there was no chance for further collaboration after Bickerstaffe fled to France in 1772.

RECORDING   Holt, Temperley, Taylor, Langridge, Northern Sinfonia, Preston, Pye, 1970
EDITION   f.s., for the author, 1761; *reissue*, J. Walsh, 1765

Artaxerxes

Opera, all sung, in three acts (3h)
Libretto: Pietro Metastasio's *Artaserse* (1730), translated into English by the composer
PREMIERE   2 February 1762, Covent Garden, London; US: 31 January 1828, New York

With *Artaxerxes*, Arne made his penultimate assault on the London operatic stage. Metastasio's text had already been set by Hasse, Vinci, Gluck, Graun and Jommelli. It takes place in Persepolis in the 5th century BC. Xerxes is the king, Artabanes his chief general. Prince Artaxerxes is in love with Artabanes' daughter, Semira, and Princess Mandane with Artabanes' son, Arbaces. Xerxes disapproves of his daughter's choice and banishes Arbaces, whereupon the ambitious and vengeful Artabanes promptly murders Xerxes. Xerxes' elder son, the Crown Prince Darius, is suspected of the crime, and promptly also murdered by Artabanes. But it is Arbaces who is suspected of the second crime, and sent by the new king, Artaxerxes, his close friend, to be tried by his father since he cannot trust himself to sit as judge. Artabanes condemns Arbaces to death. Artaxerxes, doubtful of Arbaces' guilt, helps him to escape from prison. In his flight Arbaces falls in with a rebel army and kills their leader. Artaxerxes learns of this from Semira and is convinced of Arbaces' innocence. Artabanes attempts to poison Artaxerxes; the plot is discovered; all is revealed, and the conventional Metastasian happy ending extends to the pardoning of Artabanes.

The plot is not entirely simple; nor is the music. Arne forsook English naturalness (however contrived) for overt Italianate artifice, even going so far as to cast two castrati, Peretti and Tenducci, as Artaxerxes and Arbaces. To what even Dr Burney described as 'Italian divisions and difficulties' Arne added what was, for England, unusually ambitious orchestration. But the experiment worked; the opera was much liked; it held the stage until 1839 and in due course excited the admiration of Haydn (and the disapprobation of Jane Austen). 'Water parted from the sea', 'The Soldier tir'd of war's alarms', 'In

infancy our hopes and fears' and 'Adieu fair youth' became concert and parlour pieces. It has been suggested, by Arne's only biographer, that the word-setting is often inappropriate and that to succeed it needs translating back into Italian. (Arne's last opera *L'Olimpiade* (lost) was a setting of Metastasio in the original language, but it survived only two performances.) The idiom of *Artaxerxes* is unusual, but so was its object, a wholly serious one. It is the one work, outside his oratorios, in which Arne achieves a degree of personal characterization.

EDITIONS   f.s. (minus recitatives most of which are in manuscript in the Royal College of Music), for J. Johnson, [1762]; v.s. (minus recitatives), arr. John Barnett, Chappell, 1834

Other surviving operatic works: *Rosamond*, 1733; *Love in a Village*, 1762; *The Guardian Outwitted*, 1764; *The Fairy Prince*, 1771; *The Cooper*, 1772 (RECORDING Saga, 1959); Lost opera: *L'Olimpiade*
BIBLIOGRAPHY   Roger Fiske, *English Theatre Music in the Eighteenth Century*, OUP, 1973; 2nd edn, 1986; Hubert Langley, *Dr Arne*, CUP, 1938; John A. Parkinson, *An Index to the Vocal Works of Thomas Augustine Arne and Michael Arne*, Information Co-ordinators (Detroit), 1972

R.Lu.

MALCOLM ARNOLD

Malcolm Henry Arnold; *b* 21 October 1921, Northampton, England

Arnold's reputation rests on his orchestral music, and particularly on his many film scores, which include *The Bridge on the River Kwai* (for which he won an Oscar) and *The Inn of the Sixth Happiness*. His two one-act operas and a short musical play for television, *Parasol*, have been almost completely ignored.

Arnold was first a trumpet-player in the London Philharmonic Orchestra; his reputation as a composer grew during the 1950s, and his five successful ballets later demonstrated his practical feel for the stage. After two incomplete operas (*Henri Christophe*, 1949, and *Up at the Villa*, 1951) Arnold and his librettist, Joe Mendoza, produced *The Dancing Master* (1951), a delightful comedy after the Restoration play by William Wycherley, making use of the popular rhythms familiar from his lighter music. It has never been professionally performed. His second opera, *The Open Window* (1956), is a slight but tuneful setting, for television, of a ghost story by Saki.

BIBLIOGRAPHY   Hugo Cole, *Malcolm Arnold: An Introduction to his Music*, Faber Music, 1989

L.F.

SAMUEL ARNOLD

b 10 August 1740, London; *d* 22 October 1802, London

Arnold received his musical education as a chorister at the Chapel Royal. In 1764 he became harpsichordist at Covent Garden, which also involved acting as house composer and répétiteur. From 1769 to 1776 he ran Marylebone Gardens, where comic operas formed part of the entertainment; from 1777 until his death he composed for the Colmans' Little Theatre. In 1783 he became organist of the Chapel Royal, and in 1793 of Westminster Abbey. His output, which included editing the first collected edition of Handel, was prodigious, but despite energy and musical ability he never succeeded in writing an opera with a distinct musical and dramatic identity, and most of his operas, along with virtually all those by his English contemporaries were pasticcios.

Arnold's first stage work, *The Maid of the Mill* (1765), to a good libretto by Isaac Bickerstaffe, demonstrates that pasticcios were not of their nature contemptible; moreover Arnold's serious interest in folksong led him to good tunes, but he was never to equal this initial success. His two most significant works, *The Castle of Andalucia* (1782) and *Inkle and Yarico* (1787), owed more to their plots and settings than to any musical virtues. *The Castle of Andalucia*, to a libretto by John O'Keeffe, is Gothic–Romantic in its scenery, its cast of brigands, and its hair-raising plot. *Inkle and Yarico*, by George Colman the younger and based on Steele's *Spectator* No. 11, is the story of the young Indian girl who shelters a fugitive English trader and falls in love with him. The music is, at best, tuneful, but the opera, intensely topical because of the movement to abolish the slave trade, was deservedly popular.

Surviving operatic works: *The Maid of the Mill*, 1765; *Tom Jones*, 1769; *Polly* (arr. from Gay), 1777; *The Castle of Andalucia* (rev. of *The Banditti*, 1781), 1782; *Two to One*, 1784; *Inkle and Yarico*, 1787; *The Battle of Hexham*, 1789; *New Spain, or Love in Mexico*, 1790; *The Mountaineers*, 1793; *Zorinski*, 1795; *Cambro-Britons*, 1798
BIBLIOGRAPHY   Roger Fiske, *English Theatre Music in the Eighteenth Century*, OUP, 1973; 2nd edn, 1986; J. O'Keeffe, *Recollections of His Life*, London, 1826

R.Lu.

EMILIO ARRIETA

(Don) Pascual Juan Emilio Arrieta [Arriete] y Corera; *b* 21 October 1823, Puente la Reina, Navarra, Spain; *d* 11 February 1894, Madrid

Arrieta was an exact contemporary of Francisco Barbieri and, like him, was an important figure in the development of the zarzuela in the 19th century. His works were the first to be sung in Spanish at the Spanish court, the one for which he is still remembered today being *Marina*. In addition to composing over fifty zarzuelas, Arrieta, who studied with Ponchielli in Milan, wrote a number of Italian operas early in his career which have libretti by Verdi's librettist Solera.

Marina

Zarzuela in two acts (1h 30m)
Libretto by Francisco Camprodon
PREMIERE   21 September 1855, Teatro del Circo, Madrid

Revised as opera española three acts (1h 30m)
Libretto by M. Ramos Carrion
PREMIERES   16 March 1871, Teatro Real, Madrid: US: 20 December 1916, New York

While zarzuela dominated the Spanish operatic stage in the mid-19th century, Arrieta felt that by the replacement of its spoken dialogue by recitative, and by an expansion of the traditional two acts to three, a real Spanish operatic form would emerge. This he did with *Marina*. However, this transformation made little difference to the work's original spirit, which is essentially Italianate pastiche, skilfully written and attractive, but having little connection – apart from its setting – with Spain.

Marina loves Jorge, a ship's captain. Uncertain of his feelings she persuades Pascual to tell Jorge that he himself plans to marry Marina. The plan goes awry and Marina finds herself betrothed to Pascual. He breaks off the engagement, suspecting Marina of unfaithfulness with another sailor, leaving her free to marry Jorge.

RECORDINGS (of opera)   1. Alvarez, A. Kraus, F. Kraus, Yebra, Agrupación Coral Magerit, Madrid SO, Olmedo, Carillon, 1970s; 2. Canale, Aragall, Blancas, De Narké, Orfeón Donostiarra Chamber Ch, Spanish PO, Frühbeck de Burgos, Spanish Columbia, *c.* 1967
EDITION   v.ss., Madrid, [*c.* 1865]; rev. version: Unión musical española, 1946

Other zarzuelas include: *El grumete*, 1853; *La estrella de Madrid*, 1853; *La Caceria real*, 1854; *Guerra a muerte*, 1855; *La dama del rey*, 1855; *La bija de la Providencia*, 1856; *El Sonambulo*, 1856; *El planeta Venus*, 1858; *Azon Visconti*, 1859; *Quien manda manda*, 1859; *Llamada y tropa*, 1861; *Dos coronas*, 1861; *El agente de Matrimonio*, 1862; *La vuelta del corsario*, 1863; *De tal palo tal astilla*, 1864; *Cadenas de oro*, 1864; *La insula barataria*, 1864; *El capitan negrero*, 1865; *Un sarao y una soiree*, 1866; *La suegra del diablo*, 1867; *Los novios de Teruel*, 1867; *Los misterios del parnaso*, 1868; *Las fuentes del Prado*, 1870; *El potosi submarino*, 1870; *El motin contra Esquilache*, 1871; *La sota de espadas*, 1871; *Las manzanas de oro*, 1873; *Entre el alcalde y el rey*, 1875; *La guerra Santa*, 1879; *San Franco de Sena*, 1883
BIBLIOGRAPHY   Gilbert Chase, *The Music of Spain*, Dover, 1959

S.J.W.

ROBERT ASHLEY

Robert Reynolds Ashley; *b* 28 March 1930, Ann Arbor, Michigan, US

Ashley's work is characterized by mixed media, electronics and an open definition of what constitutes music. He began training as a concert pianist but the repertoire failed to interest him. Then, at the University of Michigan, he studied with conventional composers but became absorbed with psychoacoustics and speech research. Rejecting the mechanisms of composer, publisher and performing institution, he created his own electronic studio emphasizing live performance. As he said, 'The only people I've ever been affected or influenced by are people who make their own music.'

The principal expression of Ashley's creative instincts was the ONCE group, which specialized in avant-garde mixed-media performances (1958–66). The group included artists, writers and film-makers as well as other composers. Their activities were informal, lacking notation, owing their indeterminacy and theatrical dimension to John Cage. ONCE pioneered a type of what was later called performance art.

Ashley's operas can be loosely described as music-theatre pieces. His first work so described is *That Morning Thing*, for five principal voices, eight dancers, women's chorus and tapes (1968). Most of his dramatic works presented during the 1970s and 1980s were for television, but he later made some adaptations for the stage. Outstanding was the uniquely original *Perfect Lives (Private Parts)*, characterized by Ashley's own drawling narration. Ashley's works remain in a special category since they still exist only through his own performances and recordings. He uses his own texts.

By comparison with the publicity achieved by minimalist composers such as Glass and Adams in the opera house, Ashley seems deliberately indulgent, private and obscure. But like Cage he aims to change our frame of reference and has succeeded in being provocative.

Atalanta (Acts of God)

Rev. in three separate episodes as *Max*, *Willard* and *Bud* (2h each)
PREMIERES 5 November 1982, Centre Georges Pompidou, Paris; US: 5 January 1983, Marymount Manhattan Theater, New York; rev. version: UK: 8, 10 and 11 April 1987 (*Max*, *Willard* and *Bud* separately), Bloomsbury Theatre, London

Based loosely on the Greek myth in which Atalanta is won by Hippomenes, who uses three golden apples to distract her during a race for her hand, Ashley's opera is essentially non-narrative. The composer describes it as a 'proto-populist, pre-post-modernist interpretation of the myth', explaining that 'The music and texts are composed in the form of anecdotes, or moral fables. Three principal anecdotes are given to the solo voice in the section called "Anecdote". This is the core of the opera and can be performed separately as a concert work (*Songs from Atalanta*). The principal anecdotes are surrounded by minor anecdotes recorded on tape and/or performed live in different versions of the work.'

Atalanta is the first part of a planned trilogy of operas by Ashley, of which *Perfect Lives (Private Parts)* is the second.

EDITION Visibility Music Publishers

Other operatic works: *In Memoriam . . . Kit Carson*, 1963; *That Morning Thing*, 1968; *Music with Roots in the Aether* (television opera), 1976; *Title Withdrawn*, 1976; *The Lessons*, 1981; *Atalanta Strategy*, 1984; *Perfect Lives (Private Parts)* (television opera), 1984 (RECORDING Lovely Music/Impetus, 1987); 4 short operas entitled *Now Eleanor's Idea*: 1 *Improvement (Don Leaves Linda)*, 1991 (RECORDING Nonesuch/Elektra, 1992); 2 *Foreign Experiences (Persuasion)*; 3 *Now Eleanor's Idea (Declamation)*; 4 *eL/Aficionado*, 1991

BIBLIOGRAPHY Cole Gagne and Tracy Caras, *Soundpieces: Interviews with American Composers*, Scarecrow, 1982; J. Rockwell, *All American Music*, Kahn and Averill, 1985

P.D.

FRANZ ASPELMAYR

Franz Aspelmayr [Aspelmayer]; *baptized* 2 April 1728, Linz; *d* 29 July 1786, Vienna

Trained as a violinist, Aspelmayr was essentially self-taught as a composer. In 1761, however, he was appointed composer at the Kärntnertortheater in Vienna, a post he held for probably two years; this involved the composition of ballet and incidental music. He later collaborated with the dancer and choreographer Noverre, whose reforms in ballet anticipated those of Gluck in opera.

As well as several ballet scores for Noverre, Aspelmayr wrote a number of singspiels (now lost) and is credited, for his *Pygmalion* (1772), with being the first composer to introduce the new genre of melodrama, originated by Jean-Jacques Rousseau, to the German-speaking countries.

BIBLIOGRAPHY Gayle A. Henrotte, 'Franz Aspelmayr', in *Grove*, Macmillan, 1980

G.H.

GEORGI ATHANASSOV

Georgi Athanassov [Atanasov]; *b* 18 May 1882, Plovdiv, Bulgaria; *d* 17 November 1931, Lake Garda, Italy

Athanassov was the first Bulgarian composer to devote himself almost entirely to opera composition. Encouraged by Panayot Pipkov, he first went to study in Bucharest in 1897, where he also worked as a trombonist in the orchestra of the Bucharest Opera . From 1901 to 1903 he studied in Pesaro with Mascagni, then returned to an uncertain future in Bulgaria. After working as a bandmaster he settled in Sofia, and continued to work as a conductor while composing operas. Athanassov died in Italy while undergoing treatment for tuberculosis.

Athanassov's music combines elements of Italian Romanticism with a feel for Bulgarian folk heritage, as exemplified in his most popular opera, *Gergana*. Here, as in *Tsveta*, the historic domination of

Bulgaria by the Turks is recalled. In his last two operas, Athanassov experimented with the use of leitmotif.

Operatic works: *Borislav*, 1911; *Moralisti*, 1916; *Gergana*, 1917 (RECORDING Balkanton, 1960s); *Sapustjalata wodeniza* (*The Deserted Watermill*), 1923; *Tsveta*, 1925; *Kossara*, 1929; *Altzek*, 1930; 5 children's operettas
BIBLIOGRAPHY Venelin Krustev, trans. Jean Patterson-Alexieva, *Bulgarian Music*, Sofia Press, 1978, pp. 86–90

E.A.

KURT ATTERBERG
Kurt Magnus Atterberg, *b* 12 December 1887, Gothenburg, Sweden; *d* 15 February 1974, Stockholm

Atterberg was a leading neo-Romantic nationalist Swedish composer, writing in a post-Sibelian–Straussian style. He is best known for the so-called 'Dollar' Symphony, his Sixth, which won the Columbia Graphophone Company's Schubert Centenary Prize in 1928 and was conducted by Toscanini, Beecham, who recorded it, and others.

Like his father, he trained first as an engineer, but the success of his First Symphony (1910–12) encouraged him to take lessons from Andreas Hallén in Stockholm and Max von Schillings in Berlin. He was conductor of the Royal Dramatic Theatre in Stockholm (1913–22). He composed five operas, much incidental music, nine symphonies and as many orchestral suites. He wrote criticism in *Stockholms-Tidning* (1919–57), and acted as Secretary of the Royal Swedish Academy of Music (1940–53). Throughout his working life he also served as engineer to the Swedish Patent Office (1912–68). His music enjoyed much success in Germany between the wars and most of his operas were also produced in the German-speaking countries; they have now fallen out of the repertoire.

Operas: *Härvard Harpolekare* (*Hereward the Harpist*) 1919, rev. as *Härvard der Harfner* (1936), rev. as *Härvards Hemkomst* (*Hereward's Homecoming*), 1954; *Bäckahästen* (*The River Horse*), 1925; *Fanal* (*The Burning Land*), 1934 (RECORDING Act III, closing scene, EMI, 1934); *Aladdin*, 1941 (RECORDING Laila's aria, Act I, EMI, 1941); *Stormen* (*The Tempest*), 1948

R.La.

THOMAS ATTWOOD
b November 1765, London; *d* 24 March 1838, London

Attwood ought to have been the outstanding English theatrical composer of his time. The son of a musician, he became a child chorister at the Chapel Royal, and in 1783 was sent by the Prince of Wales to study music first in Naples, then in Vienna, where he had composition lessons from Mozart, who took great pains with his English pupil. On returning to England he became music teacher to the Duchess of

York and, in 1795, to the Princess of Wales. In 1796 he was appointed organist of St Paul's and composer to the Chapel Royal. From 1792 he worked for the London theatres, first the Haymarket, then Drury Lane and, finally, Covent Garden.

The Prisoner (his first work, 1792), *The Old Clothesman* (1799) and *Il Bondocani* (1800) are his only surviving full-length stage pieces; all had spoken dialogue and none was entirely his own work. The rest of his productions were afterpieces and frequently introduced songs by other composers, including Mozart. Of these *The Smugglers* (1796) had a lively libretto by Samuel Birch, to which Attwood responded, as to a certain extent he would to Thomas Holcroft's book for *The Old Clothesman*. Thus this favoured pupil of Mozart and future intimate of Mendelssohn, a man who composed anthems and chamber music of real worth, provided only musical pap for the English stage. Yet it should be recollected that Mozart's operas made no impact in England at this time; Attwood could hardly succeed in a climate in which such a master was ignored.

BIBLIOGRAPHY C. B. Oldman, 'Thomas Attwood's Dramatic Works', *MT*, vol. 107 (1966), p. 23

R.Lu.

DANIEL AUBER
Daniel-François-Esprit Auber; *b* 29 January 1782, Caen, France; *d* 12 May 1871, Paris

In his long life Auber composed fluently and prolifically for the French operatic stage, especially in the field of opéra comique. With Adam, he took on the mantle of Boieldieu and Hérold, and passed it on in turn to Thomas and Offenbach.

His first efforts in composition were Italian airs, French romances and concertos for violin and cello. He studied with Cherubini, whom he was later to succeed as Director of the Paris Conservatoire. From 1811 for 60 years he was engaged in operatic enterprises, his first success being *Le séjour militaire*, a one-act comedy played at the Opéra-Comique in 1813. *Leicester*, in 1823, began a long collaboration with Scribe, whose versatility and fecundity brought a stream of successes in the coming years. Their most impressive work is *La muette de Portici*, a grand opera that served as a model for the Meyerbeerian genre. Yet Auber made few later attempts at serious opera and confined himself principally to the lighter forms. *Fra Diavolo*, *Le domino noir*, *Les diamants de la couronne*, and many others, held the stage throughout the century. His melodies are attractive and popular, his orchestral textures piquant and simple. He never explored the harmonic avenues suggested in *La muette de Portici*; he eschewed the sentimental. In his later years he reached his peak with *Haydée*, based on a story by Mérimée, and in *Manon Lescaut*, in which he anticipated the better-known settings of Prévost's novel by Massenet and Puccini.

Le maçon

The Mason
Opéra comique in three acts (2h)
Libretto by Eugène Scribe and Germain Delavigne, based on
an English report of a true story
PREMIERES 3 May 1825, Opéra-Comique, Paris; US:
8 January 1857, New York; UK: 13 March 1850, St James's
Theatre, London

The most successful of Auber's early collaborations
with Scribe, *Le maçon* was seen on French and
German stages for at least a hundred years. On his
wedding night, Roger, a mason, is held captive in a
château by some marauding Turks, escapes and
saves a nobleman who is also a prisoner. A late
specimen of 'rescue opera', *Le maçon* has a melody,
Roger's *ronde*, which recurs throughout the opera.

EDITIONS f.s., Pleyel, [1825]; v.s., Sollinger, 1827

Masaniello, ou La muette de Portici

Masaniello, or The Dumb Girl of Portici
Opera in five acts (2h 30m)
Libretto by Eugène Scribe and Germain Delavigne, after
Raimond de Moirmoiron's *Mémoires sur la révolution de
Naples de 1647*
PREMIERES 29 February 1828, Opéra, Paris; UK: 4 May
1829, Drury Lane, London; US: 15 August 1831, New York
CAST Elvire *s*, Masaniello *t*, Alphonse *t*, Lorenzo *t*, Pietro *b*,
Borello *b*, Moreno *b*, Selva *b*, *ms*, *dancer*; *satb* chorus of
fishermen, soldiers, the court, Neapolitans
FULL ORCHESTRA including ophicleide, t-t; onstage: fl, 2 cl,
2 bsn, 2 hn, bells

La muette de Portici was one of the earliest and most
influential specimens of French grand opera, even
though its composer's *métier* was truly in opéra
comique. It preceded Rossini's *Guillaume Tell* by a
year and had a pronounced influence on both
Meyerbeer and Wagner. It set Scribe on the course
of his later career more clearly perhaps than Auber,
for the libretto contains many of the elements that
became standard at the Opéra in the next 30 years,
notably a foreground of personal dilemma against a
background of political tension in a specified
historical and geographical setting. The five acts
contain ample ensembles, choruses and ballets.

SYNOPSIS
The opera is set in Naples in 1647 at the time of
Masaniello's revolt against Spanish rule.
    Act I As Alfonso, the son of the Spanish viceroy,
marries Elvira, a Spanish princess, he is denounced
by Fenella, a dumb girl, as her seducer.
    Act II At Portici, Masaniello, Fenella's brother,
gives the signal for insurrection.
    Act III They take the rebellion to Naples.
    Act IV In their flight Alfonso and Elvira are
unknowingly sheltered by Masaniello himself.
    Act V Masaniello is eventually killed after saving
his royal guests. At the final curtain Fenella leaps
into the crater of Vesuvius.

Apart from the vivacity and ingenuity of the music,
the opera's strength lies in its touching treatment of
the dumb heroine, whose thoughts are transmitted
throughout in mime with expressive orchestral
accompaniment. There is much Neapolitan colour in
the music, and the chorus is prominently featured,
especially in the big ensembles. The opera was
successful in the 19th century, although little more
than the overture (with its tremendous opening on a
diminished seventh) has been played in the
twentieth. When played in Brussels in 1830 it is said
to have sparked off the revolt that led to Belgian
independence.

RECORDING Anderson, Kraus, Aler, Munier, Lafont,
Courtis, Ensemble Chorale Jean Laforge, unnamed
orchestra, Fulton, EMI, 1986
EDITIONS f.s., Troupenas, [1828]; facsimile *rp*, Garland,
1980; v.s., Brandus et Cie, [c. 1850]

Fra Diavolo, ou L'Hôtellerie de Terracine

Fra Diavolo, or The Inn at Terracina
Opéra comique in three acts (2h)
Libretto by Eugène Scribe, based on a historical character of
c. 1810
PREMIERES 28 January 1830, Opéra-Comique, Paris; UK:
1 February 1831, Drury Lane, London; US: 17 October 1831,
New York
CAST Fra Diavolo *t*, Lord Cokbourg *b* (or *t*), Lady Pamela
ms, Lorenzo *t*, Mathéo *b*, Zerline *s*, Beppo *t*, Giacomo *b*; *satb*
chorus of inhabitants of Terracina, servants, soldiers
FULL ORCHESTRA onstage: 4 hn, 2 tpt, 2 trbn, bells

The most successful of Auber's many opéras
comiques, *Fra Diavolo* uses a historical Italian bandit
(Michele Pezza) as a model for a comic character
who masquerades as a marquis and preys on
travellers around Naples. His victims are an English
milord and lady named Cockburn (rendered by
Scribe as 'Cokbourg') staying at an inn at Terracina.

SYNOPSIS
Act I Zerline, daughter of the innkeeper Mathéo, is
to marry a rich peasant, Francesco, but really she
loves Lorenzo, a poor soldier. Lorenzo has
instructions to find the bandit Fra Diavolo. Lord and
Lady Cokbourg arrive at the inn, having been
robbed. A mysterious marquis (in fact Fra Diavolo)
steals Lady Pamela's diamonds from around her
neck. Lorenzo retrieves some of the missing goods
and is rewarded with enough money to enable him to
marry Zerline.
    Act II The 'marquis' steals into Zerline's
bedroom and there confronts Lorenzo, who takes
him for a rival in love.
    Act III A trap is set for Fra Diavolo and his two
clumsy henchmen. The English travellers realize that
the 'marquis' was a bandit after all. Zerline is able to
marry Lorenzo.

The dashing bandit was a winning operatic idea and
the two subsidiary bandits, Giacomo and Beppo,
provided characters for Laurel and Hardy's *Fra
Diavolo* in 1933.
    The music has a lively spring, with Auber's
abundant melodic gift always in evidence. The
military music is plain, too dependent on the
percussion, but there are some excellent individual

Set design for Act III of Fra Diavolo *(Paris, 1830)*

numbers. The duet for the milord and his lady is a neat adaptation of the traditional 'couplets' formula, and the quintet that follows in Act I is original and witty, with an enchanting 'oompah' effect in the voices. Diavolo's recitative and aria at the beginning of Act III is a *tour de force*, offering scope for vocal antics of every kind. While Rossini's mannerisms are to be heard here and there, there are also chromatic touches that anticipate Smetana.

RECORDING   Mesplé, Berbié, Gedda, Dran, Corazza, Bastin, Monte-Carlo PO, Soustrot, EMI, 1984
EDITIONS   f.s., Troupenas, [1830]; v.s., Brandus, Dufour et Cie, [1855]

Gustave III, ou Le bal masqué

Gustave III, or The Masked Ball
Opéra in five acts (3h)
Libretto by Eugène Scribe
PREMIERES   27 February 1833, Opéra, Paris; UK: 13 November 1833, Covent Garden, London; US: 21 July 1834, New York

The libretto supposes that Gustav III of Sweden was assassinated by a jealous husband, Ankastrom, whose wife Amélie returns the king's love. The opera

offers a magnificent ball in the last act, the scene of the assassination, and a sinister midnight setting for Act III. The role of Oscar the page was a striking novelty. The same libretto was later set much more successfully by Verdi, as *Un ballo in maschera*.

EDITIONS   f.s., Troupenas, [1833]; facsimile *rp*, Garland, 1980; v.s., Brandus, Dufour et Cie, [1855]

Le cheval de bronze

The Bronze Horse
Opéra comique in three acts (2h)
Libretto by Eugène Scribe
PREMIERES   23 March 1835, Opéra-Comique, Paris; UK: 14 December 1835, Covent Garden, London; US: 15 April 1836, New Orleans

The opera concerns a bronze horse that transports unsuspecting victims to the planet Venus where they are at the mercy of the goddess of love. It arrives with a group of Chinese. The men of the party are of course susceptible, but a young girl, Péki, dressed as a man, naturally resists seduction, and is thus able to bring the beautiful princess Stella back to China so that she may become the bride of the Prince Yang.

The music is more concerned with picturesque and fairy effects than with *chinoiserie*. The ballad 'Là-bas, sur ce rocher sauvage' became popular, and the mandarin's sleep scene had some effective orchestral effects. The overture long outlived the opera in the repertoire. In 1857 the work was transformed into an opéra-ballet and put on at the Opéra, although the general view was that the music was too lightweight for the larger house.

RECORDING Garcisanz, Rodde, Nigoghossian, Pezzino, Cold, New Philharmonic Ch and O of French Radio, Marty, MRF, 1970s
EDITIONS f.s., Dépôt central de musique de libraire, [c. 1835]; v.s., Brandus, Dufour et Cie, [1855]

Le domino noir
The Black Domino
Opéra comique in three acts (1h 30m)
Libretto by Eugène Scribe
PREMIERES 2 December 1837, Opéra-Comique, Paris; UK: 16 February 1838, Covent Garden, London; US: November 1839, New Orleans

This was one of Auber's most successful opéras comiques despite its large cast and a complicated plot conducted largely in dialogue. Since the setting is Spain, the music offers some touches of an Andalusian flavour. The opera recounts how Angèle, confined to a nunnery against her wishes, decides to escape with her confidante Brigitte to taste the true pleasures of life for a brief period. In the course of a series of adventures she finds herself at a ball, dressed in a black domino, a costume that finally reveals her identity when it is seen by her lover Horace at the nunnery. She also has a scene disguised as a lady's maid. The role of Angèle was one of Mme Cinti-Damoreau's greatest parts. Auber's music is, in Berlioz's words, 'light, brilliant, gay, full of piquant flashes and coquettish gestures', and it ensured the enormous success of the opera throughout the 19th century.

RECORDING abridged: Lubin, Dachary, Capderou, Stiôt, Mallabrera, Lyric O of French Radio, Hartemann, UORC, 1960s
EDITIONS f.s., Troupenas, [1837]; v.s., Brandus et Cie, [1850]

Les diamants de la couronne
The Crown Diamonds
Opéra comique in three acts (2h)
Libretto by Eugène Scribe and Vernoy de St Georges
PREMIERES 6 March 1841, Opéra-Comique, Paris; US: 31 March 1842, New Orleans; UK: 2 May 1844, Princess's Theatre, London

The crown diamonds of the title belong to a Portuguese princess who, forced by straitened circumstances to sell them, disguises herself (as Catarina) and mingles with bandits who can supply her with counterfeit jewels to put in their place. She falls in love with Don Henrique, leader of the bandits. Disguised as monks and smoking cigarettes, the bandits provide many comic situations and a number of anticipations of *Il trovatore* and *Carmen*.

EDITIONS f.s., Troupenas, [1841]; v.s., Brandus et Cie, [1850]

Haydée, ou Le secret
Haidée, or The Secret
Opéra comique in three acts (2h)
Libretto by Eugène Scribe
PREMIERE 28 December 1847, Opéra-Comique, Paris

Based on a story by Mérimée, *La partie de trictrac* (1830), and perhaps on Dumas *père*'s *Le comte de Monte Cristo* (1845), with the title taken from Byron's poem *Haidée*, Scribe's libretto is set in the wars between Venice and the Turks in the 16th century. Lorédan, a Venetian admiral, is tormented by guilt at having once cheated at dice. His action ruined a friend Donato, who took his own life. Donato's son is, unknown to Lorédan, a member of his company. Meanwhile Haydée, a captured Cypriot slave, tries to protect Lorédan from the machinations of Malipieri, the villain of the piece, who has discovered Lorédan's secret. Malipieri is killed in a duel, Haydée turns out to have royal blood, and Lorédan becomes doge.

The plot has many of the usual Scribe complexities and improbabilities but still supports some convincing dramatic action. Auber's score is powerfully dramatic at times, but with many lighter moments, as was expected of an opéra comique. There are two barcarolles in the score, one of his favourite genres. The role of Lorédan was one of Roger's greatest successes, and the opera remained firmly in the repertoire until 1894.

EDITIONS f.s., Troupenas, [1847]; v.s., Troupenas et Cie, [1845]

Manon Lescaut
Opéra comique in three acts (2h)
Libretto by Eugène Scribe, after the novel by Prévost *Histoire du Chevalier Des Grieux et de Manon Lescaut* (1731)
PREMIERE 23 February 1856, Opéra-Comique, Paris

Although overshadowed by Massenet's and Puccini's operas on the same subject, Auber's opéra comique has many fine qualities, not least its treatment of a serious, or at least sentimental, subject in closing with Manon's death. The subject provoked criticism for its 'immorality', but Scribe had made extensive modifications to the original, retaining only three characters from the novel: Manon, Des Grieux, and Lescaut, who is Manon's cousin, not her brother. He also put more emphasis on Manon's underlying faithfulness to Des Grieux, despite her frequent lapses, than did either of the later libretti. The remaining characters and most of their actions are of Scribe's invention.

For the work of a man of 73, the opera is attractively light and youthful, but it enjoyed little success and passed quite quickly out of the repertoire.

RECORDING Mesplé, Greger, Orliac, Bisson, Runge, Ch and Lyric O of French Radio, Marty, Voix de son Maître, 1976

EDITIONS f.s./v.s., Boieldieu, [1856]

Other operas: *L'erreur d'un moment*, 1811; *Jean de Couvin*, 1812; *Le séjour militaire*, 1813; *Le testament et les billets-doux*, 1819; *La bergère châtelaine*, 1820; *Emma, ou La promesse imprudente*, 1821; *Leicester, ou Le château de Kenilworth*, 1823; *La neige, ou Le nouvel Eginard*, 1823; *Vendôme en Espagne*, 1823; *Les trois genres*, 1824; *Le concert à la cour, ou La débutante*, 1824; *Léocadie*, 1824; *Le timide, ou Le nouvel séducteur*, 1826; *Fiorella*, 1826; *La fiancée*, 1829; *Le Dieu et la bayadère*, 1830; *Le philtre*, 1831; *La Marquise de Brinvilliers*, 1831; *Le serment, ou Les faux-monnayeurs*, 1832; *Lestocq, ou L'intrigue et l'amour*, 1834; *Actéon*, 1836; *Les chaperons blancs*, 1836; *L'ambassadrice*, 1836; *Le lac des fées*, 1839; *Zanetta, ou Jouer avec le feu*, 1840; *Le Duc d'Olonne*, 1842; *La part du diable*, 1843; *La sirène*, 1844; *La barcarolle, ou L'amour et la musique*, 1845; *Les premiers pas*, 1847; *L'enfant prodigue*, 1850; *Zerline, ou La corbeille d'oranges*, 1851; *Marco Spada*, 1852; *Jenny Bell*, 1855; *La circassienne*, 1861; *La fiancée du Roi de Garbe*, 1864; *Le premier jour de bonheur*, 1868; *Rêve d'amour*, 1869
BIBLIOGRAPHY R. Longyear, 'La muette de Portici', *MR*, vol. 19 (1958), pp. 37–46; C. Malherbe, *Auber*, Paris, 1911; K. Pendle, *Eugène Scribe and French Opera of the 19th Century*, UMI, 1979

H.M.

EDMOND AUDRAN

b 12 April 1840, Lyons, France; *d* 17 August 1901, Tierceville, Oise, France

Audran, the son\ of an Opéra-Comique tenor, attended Paris's Ecole Niedermeyer and became organist at St Joseph's Church, Marseilles. After composing some religious music and Provençal dialect songs, he turned his attention to the stage, and his first short operettas were first performed in Marseilles. *Le grand Mogol* (1877), his first work in three acts, was performed at the Théâtre Gymnase there, leading to a Paris commission for the Bouffes-Parisiens. This was *Les noces d'Olivette* (1879), which did fairly well in Paris, but had a happier career in London, where it ran for 466 performances in its initial engagement, as *Olivette*, at the Strand Theatre.

The follow-up was Audran's best work, *La mascotte* (1880) which enjoyed a run of nearly 500 performances at the Bouffes-Parisiens and which by 1885 had reached its thousandth, plus tours and many revivals. This saucy tale of a farm girl bringing luck to whoever possessed her (providing she remained a virgin) is chock-full of racy rhythms and enchanting melodies, most famously a farmyard duet with yodelled animal sounds in praise of sheep and turkeys which was encored all over Europe and America.

The pleasantly Provençal *Gillette de Narbonne* (1882) consolidated Audran's hold on the Bouffes-Parisiens, and the Paris public stayed with him when he switched to the Gaieté for an amplification of *Le grand Mogol* and a new work, *La cigale et la fourmi* (1886). This did quite well in London as *La cigale*.

Miss Helyett (1890) was a huge hit at the Bouffes, another *risqué* situation elaborated into an operetta. The show's period flavour and sprightly score have kept it on the boards in France. Audran's final work of quality was *La poupée* (1896), the story of an automaton that again pleased London and other cities on the Continent far more than Paris. While not revealing any great subtlety, Audran's basically cheerful tunes endeared him to a large public a hundred years ago; whether his works will appeal in the 21st century is open to question.

Operettas (selective list): *Le grand Mogol*, 1877 (RECORDING Musidisc (French Radio, 1960s/70s), in preparation); *Les noces d'Olivette*, 1879; *La mascotte*, 1880 (RECORDINGS Clio, 1964; London International, *c.* 1956); *Gillette de Narbonne*, 1882 (RECORDING Musidisc (French Radio, 1960s/70s), in preparation); *Les pommes d'or*, 1883; *La dormeuse éveillée*, 1883; *Serment d'amour*, 1886; *La cigale et la fourmi*, 1886; *Miss Helyett*, 1890 (RECORDING Musidisc (French Radio, 1960s/70s), in preparation); *L'enlèvement de la Toledad*, 1894; *La poupée*, 1896 (RECORDING Musidisc (French Radio, 1960s/70s), in preparation)
BIBLIOGRAPHY F. Bruyas, *Histoire de l'opérette en France*, Vitte, 1974; Richard Traubner, *Operetta: A Theatrical History*, Gollancz, 1984

R.T.

PIETRO AULETTA

b 1693 or 1694, San Angelo a Scala, Avellino; *d* September 1771, Naples

After serving his apprenticeship at the Neapolitan conservatory of S. Onofrio, where Porpora was one of his teachers, Auletta made his début in 1725 with a comic opera for Naples. *L'Orazio* (Naples, 1737), his greatest success in the genre, suffered a strange fate, for at each performance (in London, 1748) it was subjected to changes that finally turned it into a virtual pasticcio retaining only a few pieces by its original composer. A condensed version of the original opera, given in Paris in 1752 under the title *Il maestro di musica*, was attributed to Pergolesi, though four of the 34 numbers are by Auletta. Another success was *La locandiera*, a 'double intermezzo' performed in Naples in July 1738 to celebrate the wedding of Princess Maria Amalia to King Charles III.

Auletta was a serious rival of Pergolesi in his ability to characterize a role through very modest means – simple, attractive tunes and discreet, effective orchestral accompaniments.

Surviving operas: *Il trionfo dell'amore, ovvero Le nozze tra nemici*, 1725; *L'Orazio*, 1737, many rev. versions under various titles; *L'impresario* (1748); *L'impresario abbandonato* (1748); *El maestro de capilla* (1750); *Il maestro di musica* (1752); *La locandiera*, 1738; *Didone*, 1759; 9 lost operas
BIBLIOGRAPHY Michael F. Robinson, *Naples and Neapolitan Opera*, OUP, 1972

D.A.D'A.

GEORGES AURIC

b 15 February 1899, Lodève, France; *d* 24 July 1983, Paris

Auric is one of the most diverse figures in the history of French 20th-century music. A product of the deeply conservative Schola Cantorum (a composition pupil of d'Indy), he became involved with Cocteau during the First World War, and was one of Les Six. Later, moving away from the anti-earnest philosophy of that group, he began to write instrumental music of a more serious-minded modernism. Later still, he became something of an Establishment figure. He was director of the Opéra and Opéra-Comique (1962– 8). After draining that well-known poisoned chalice, he returned to instrumental composition and wrote works with up-to-date titles such as *Imaginées I–IV* and *Double-jeux I–III*.

In the 1920s Auric was best known for his ballets, of which he composed three for Diaghilev's Ballets Russes. Subsequently he provided scores for several Cocteau and René Clair films; the title song of John Huston's *Le moulin rouge* (1952) became a popular hit. His operatic work was confined to operetta: *Sous le masque*, a lyrical one-act comedy to a libretto by Louis Laloy (written, according to Richard Traubner, in 1923); and *Les oiseaux* (based on Aristophanes; 1928). A third operetta, *Sans façon* (1929), is said by Florian Bruyas (in *Histoire de l'opérette en France*) to have had music by Auric. In addition Riemann's *Musik-Lexikon* lists another 1920s piece, *La reine de coeur*, as belonging to this genre. Such speculations are curiously hard to confirm in the soap-bubble world of light opera. But it is clear that none of Auric's operetta scores enjoyed much success, possibly because his satirical bent imposed too much on this ephemeral genre.

BIBLIOGRAPHY   Paul Landormy, *La musique française après Debussy*, Gallimard, 1943, pp. 165–9

S.W.

JOHANN CHRISTIAN BACH
b 5 September 1735, Leipzig; *d* 1 January 1782, London

J. C. Bach, often known as the 'London' or 'Milan' Bach, was the youngest son of Johann Sebastian and effectively the only member of his family to write operas (an opera, *Lausus und Lydie*, begun by Wilhelm Friedemann Bach in his later years, was never finished). Thus he broke away from the church-centred tradition of his forebears, and followed instead in the footsteps of his two great Saxon predecessors, Handel and Hasse, whose operas were in the Italian tradition.

Christian's early training was evidently supervised by his father and, after Sebastian's death, by his half-brother Carl Philipp Emanuel in Berlin. His stay in Italy (1755–62) transformed his musical outlook and introduced him to Italian opera in Milan and Naples.

The first three of Bach's eleven operas (ten Italian opere serie and one French tragédie lyrique) were written in Italy. Their success attracted attention elsewhere and Bach was invited to compose two works for the King's Theatre, London, in 1762. In fact Bach settled in London from that year and established himself, not only as the most important composer and musician in the city, but also as a master of international renown.

He composed five full-scale Italian operas for London, a fine serenata, *Endimione*, an oratorio, *Gioas, re di Giuda* (both performed at the King's Theatre), and contributed to many Italian and English pasticcios, including *Tom Jones* and *The Summer's Tale*. With Pietro Guglielmi, he also wrote additional numbers for a version of Gluck's *Orfeo ed Euridice* (1770). He received two commissions for operas for the electoral court at Mannheim (*Temistocle*, 1772, and *Lucio Silla*, 1775) and apparently two for Paris, although only *Amadis de Gaule* (1779) was completed.

It was Bach's misfortune to produce some of his finest music for opera seria, a form that was in terminal decline in the 1760s and 1770s. On the whole, Bach conformed to the stereotyped Metastasian conventions, though he reduced the amount of recitative. In his London operas he practically abandoned the *da capo* aria, preferring sonata-like or rondo patterns, and in several operas gave greater prominence to the chorus.

Bach was no operatic innovator, however. In the one opportunity that he had to compose a reform opera, *Amadis*, written for Paris in 1779, the year of the premiere of Gluck's *Iphigénie en Tauride*, he chose to set in a relatively traditional style a revised version of the libretto composed by Quinault for Lully almost a century earlier.

Bach's operas received a somewhat mixed reception: on the whole, they did not hold the stage for more than a few performances and were seldom revived. After his death, only one operatic production (*La clemenza di Scipione*, in 1805, revived in the following season) is documented until the present century, when, with the current revival of interest in Bach's music, most have received concert or broadcast performances and their true worth has been revealed. The only music from Bach's operas performed with any regularity today are the splendid three-movement overtures, a number of which were published to be performed separately as symphonies.

Orione, ossia Diana vendicata
Orion, or Diana's Revenge
Opera seria in three acts
Libretto by Giovanni Gualberto Bottarelli
PREMIERE 19 February 1763, King's Theatre, London

The plot of Bach's fourth opera, his first for London, revised in 1777, concerns Orion's love for the Princess Candiope, the enmity of the goddess Diana, her vengeance on the hero and his metamorphosis as a constellation. Bach, like Handel before him in *Rinaldo*, evidently intended making his mark on the London public with a lavish production, tailored to English taste, which preferred a more spectacular type of opera to the aria-dominated style of Bach's three early operas written for Italy. *Orione* has large-scale choruses, a relatively unusual feature in contemporary opera seria, an expanded orchestra, with a woodwind section including clarinets and cor anglais, and dances by the celebrated Giovanni Gallini and others. Bach varied the formal patterns of the arias, severely curtailing the *da capo* type, a trend continued throughout his London operas. The great success of *Orione* was reported by Burney, who wrote: 'Every judge of Music perceived the emanations of genius throughout the whole performance.'

Memorial print of J. C. Bach by Francesco Bartolozzi

Most of the opera survives in two manuscripts in the Bodleian Library, Oxford, and the British Library; eight numbers were published in a set of *Favourite Songs*; several arias and choruses are missing.

EDITION   E. Warburton (ed.), *The Collected Works of J. C. Bach*, vol. 4, Garland, 1989

Zanaida

Opera seria in three acts
Libretto by Giovanni Gualberto Bottarelli, after Metastasio's *Siface*
PREMIERE   7 May 1763, King's Theatre, London

Orione was followed by *Zanaida*, which was equally lavish in orchestration and spectacular effects. The plot deals with love and intrigue in Persia in the aftermath of war between the Emperor of the Turks and Tamasses Sophi of Persia. The aria 'Se spiego le prime vele' was known to the young Mozart, who visited London in 1764–5. The eight-year-old impressed the musician William Jackson by his ability to read the score upside down and point out a wrong note.

EDITION   (of *Favourite Songs*), E. Warburton (ed.), *The Collected Works of J. C. Bach*, vol. 4, Garland, 1989

Adriano in Siria

Hadrian in Syria
Opera seria in three acts (2h 15m)
Libretto anonymous, after Pietro Metastasio
PREMIERE   26 January 1765, King's Theatre, Haymarket, London; modern revival: 20 March 1982, Logan Hall, London (concert)

Bach's third work for London marked a return to the aria-dominated type of opera, is without chorus. The Emperor Hadrian, though betrothed to Sabina, is enamoured of Emirena, a recently captured Parthian princess, whose father, Osroa, attempts to rescue his daughter and kill the emperor. The plot is resolved in the usual Metastasian way, with Hadrian demonstrating his magnanimity, restoring Osroa to his kingdom, Emirena to her former betrothed Farnaspe and Sabina to himself.

Despite the singing of the two famous castrati Ferdinando Tenducci and Giovanni Manzuoli, *Adriano in Siria* was unsuccessful. Burney, with some justice, found the arias 'as detached airs, excellent, though they had been unfortunate in their totality', a criticism that applies to many of Bach's operas. Among the finest numbers are the *mezza di voce* 'Cara la dolce fiamma' and the superb, fiery 'Disperato in mar' turbato'.

EDITION   E. Warburton (ed.), *The Collected Works of J. C. Bach*, vol. 5, Garland, 1985

Carattaco

Caractacus
Opera seria in three acts
Libretto by Giovanni Gualberto Bottarelli, after Tacitus, *Annals*, xii
PREMIERE   14 February 1767, King's Theatre, Haymarket, London

After abandoning the chorus in *Adriano*, Bach returned to lavish spectacular opera, with ballets and choruses in his fourth London opera, *Carattaco*, which was the last opera he wrote for London for over ten years. His use of chorus caused one contemporary critic to refer to Bach as 'a second Handel' (though it was the Handel of the oratorios rather than the operas the critic had in mind). The patriotic subject, with the British hero Caractacus engaged in revolt against the Romans, also found favour with critics and audiences alike.

There are some splendid arias in *Carattaco*, notably Pratusago's vivid 'Sfida il ciel' and Carattaco's 'Se amico mi chiami'. 'Non e ver' also survived as a song written for Vauxhall Gardens, with the words 'Tender virgins shun deceivers'.

EDITIONS   Facsimile of the autograph manuscript, introduction by E. Weimer, Garland, 1982; E. Warburton (ed.), *The Collected Works of J. C. Bach*, vol. 6, Garland, 1986

Temistocle

Themistocles
Opera seria in three acts (3h)
Libretto by Mattia Verazi, after Pietro Metastasio
PREMIERES 4 or 5 November 1772, Hoftheater, Mannheim;
UK: 21 August 1972, BBC Radio 3 (broadcast)

Temistocle, which deals with the exile from Greece of
Themistocles and the magnanimity of the Persian
King Xerxes, was composed for the electoral court at
Mannheim, whose superb orchestra was highly
regarded for the precision of its string playing and
the virtuosity of the woodwind. Bach makes much of
these features here and includes music for the rare
clarinetto d'amore. In line, presumably, with
Mannheim taste, the chorus is relegated to the
sidelines and the *da capo* aria predominates. Many
resemble long concerto-like movements, demonstrating the virtuosity of both instrumentalists and
singers, such as Themistocles' aria 'Non m'alletta quel
riso', with its elaborate bassoon obbligato. The court
librettist Verazi's adaptation of Metastasio's libretto
allows for extended finales at the ends of Acts II
and III. The singers in the first production included
Anton Raaff, then aged 58, for whom Mozart
later composed the role of Idomeneo. *Temistocle*
was highly successful and was revived at Mannheim
in 1773.

RECORDING Fusco, Gamberucci, Carral, Handt, Cesari;
RAI Chamber Ch, RAI Alessandro Scarlatti O of Naples,
Delman, Voce, 1976
EDITIONS E. Warburton (ed.), *The Collected Works of J. C.
Bach*, vol. 7, Garland, 1987; v.s., edited and adapted by
Edward Downes and H. C. Robbins Landon, Universal, 1965

Lucio Silla

Opera seria in three acts (2h 45m)
Libretto by Mattia Verazi, after Giovanni de Gamerra
PREMIERE 5 November 1775, Hoftheater, Mannheim;
modern revival: 22 March 1929, Kiel

Bach's second commission for Mannheim, an
adaptation by Verazi of the libretto set by Mozart in
Milan in 1772, concerns the love of Silla, dictator of
Rome, for Giunia, who is betrothed to Cecilio, a
banished senator conspiring against Silla. The plot is
discovered, Cecilio arrested and condemned to
death; Giunia is prepared to share her beloved's fate.
In the face of such devotion, Silla relents, resigns his
dictatorship and restores the lovers to each other.

Bach's setting again makes use of elaborate
orchestration, including clarinetti d'amore, but this
time severely reduces the number of *da capo* arias
and makes greater use of the chorus. As in
Temistocle, Anton Raaff sang the title role. The
opera was less successful than its predecessor.

RECORDING Varady, Geszty, Zeumer, Gaifa, Hermann;
South German Radio Ch, Cappella Coloniensis, Kehr, Voce,
1974
EDITION E. Warburton (ed.), *The Collected Works of J. C.
Bach*, vol. 8, Garland, 1986

La clemenza di Scipione

The Clemency of Scipio
Opera seria in three acts
Libretto anonymous
PREMIERES 4 April 1778, King's Theatre, Haymarket,
London; modern revival: 3 May 1972, Queen Elizabeth Hall,
London (concert)

The text for Bach's last London opera was, according
to a contemporary account, the work of a foreign
ambassador to the English court. It deals with love
and intrigue in Cartagena, recently besieged and
captured by Scipio. Luceius fails in an attempt to
rescue two princesses, one of whom is his lover, held
by Scipio, but the clemency of the hero prevails,
allowing the lovers to be united.

Da capo arias are banished and there are
important choruses in all three acts. Interestingly,
Bach makes an attempt to integrate the overture into
the opera: motifs from it appear in the final chorus of
Act III. But the finest numbers are the arias and
ensembles. 'Infelice in van m'affano' is often cited as
a precursor of Mozart's 'Martern aller Arten' from
Die Entführung aus dem Serail, both being concerto-
like movements with the same four obbligato
instruments. Mozart met Bach again in Paris in the
summer of 1778 and it is possible that he may have
become acquainted with the score on that occasion.
(Valentin Adamberger, the first Scipio, was also the
first Belmonte in *Die Entführung*.) Perhaps Mozart
also had the opening of the trio 'Tu mi dividi altero'
from *Scipione* in mind when he wrote Donna Elvira's
'Ah! chi mi dice mai' in *Don Giovanni*; both are in
the key of E♭.

Bach took the highly unusual step of having the
work published in full score (without the *secco*
recitatives) around 1778.

EDITIONS facsimile of the 1st edn, introduction by Denis
Arnold, Gregg International, 1972; E. Warburton (ed.), *The
Collected Works of J. C. Bach*, vol. 8, Garland, 1987

Amadis de Gaule

Amadis of Gaul
Tragédie lyrique in three acts (1h 45m)
Libretto by Alphonse-Denis-Marie de Vismes, after Quinault
PREMIERES 14 December 1779, Académie Royale de
Musique, Paris; modern revival: 30 January 1983, Staatsoper,
Hamburg

The libretto of *Amadis*, a somewhat botched
condensing of Quinault's five-act drama, is unlike
anything Bach had previously set. The neat, classical,
Metastasian texts, with their historical settings,
complex amatory entanglements and somewhat
simplistic resolutions are here replaced by a larger,
more vivid plot set in chivalric times, a tale of love
(Amadis for Oriane), jealousy, and attempted
revenge, with frequent interventions of the
supernatural (ghosts, demons, etc.) and nature
(thunder and lightning, enveloping clouds, etc.). The
chorus, in various guises as prisoners or demons, is a
main protagonist and ballet and divertissements are
important elements. Bach met these new challenges
successfully, making vivid use of the large Paris

orchestra, creating sumptuous and occasionally extraordinary effects: the ghost music of Act II (foreshadowed in the overture) employs a dramatic crescendo and diminuendo on a diminished seventh chord, scored for trombones, bassoons and woodwind; it is used again in Act III when Arcabonne recalls the ghost's prophecy, and can be seen as an early use of leitmotif technique.

The opera, while attracting praise from some quarters, was derided by others (it was Bach's misfortune to become unwittingly embroiled in the Gluck–Piccinni controversies), and it was not revived. There is an important and fascinating manuscript score of Acts I and II marked for performance in the Bibliothèque de l'Opéra, Paris. The full score was published by Sieber in 1779.

RECORDING Sonntag, Höbarth, Verebics, Wagner, Schöne, Stuttgart Gächinger Kantorei, Stuttgart Bach Collegium, Rilling, Hänssler, 1991
EDITION Facsimile of the 1st edn, introduction by Anthony Ford, Gregg International, 1972

Other operas: *Artaserse*, 1760; *Catone in Utica*, 1761; *Alessandro nell'Indie*, 1762
Bach contributed to the following operas and pasticcios for which music has survived: Ferradini's *Demofoonte*, 1758; Cafaro's *Ipermestra*, 1761; *Il tutore a la pupilla*, 1762; *Astarto, rè di Tiro*, 1762; *La cascina*, 1763; Galuppi's *La calamita de cuori*, 1763; *Issipile*, 1763; *Ezio*, 1764; *The Maid of the Mill*, 1765; *Berenice*, 1765; *The Summer's Tale*, 1765; *Sifari*, 1767; *Tom Jones*, 1769; Piccinni's *Le contadine bizzarre*, 1769; *L'olimpiade*, 1769; Gluck's *Orfeo ed Euridice*, 1770; *The Flitch of Bacon*, 1778
BIBLIOGRAPHY Charles Sanford Terry, *John Christian Bach*, OUP, 1929, rev. H. C. Robbins Landon, 1967

S.R.

CARLO AGOSTINO BADIA
b 1672, ?Venice; *d* 23 September 1738, Vienna

Badia's first operas were performed in Rome during 1692. That year he moved to Innsbruck to become court composer to the Imperial Princess Eleonora Maria, whom he followed to Vienna a year later. In 1694 he was appointed as court composer to the imperial court, where over the next 18 years he produced at least a dozen operas and over 30 oratorios, some of which were performed regularly outside Vienna, especially in Italy. In 1709 he wrote *Gli amori di Circe con Ulisse* for a visit of the King of Denmark to Dresden. He was employed at the imperial court for a total of 44 years, but after the accession in 1711 of Charles VI, who preferred more up-to-date music, he produced little.

Badia injected new ideas into Viennese dramatic music, at a time when Antonio Draghi had firmly established a highly successful but rather unadventurous style. A gift for idiomatic string-writing, including the use of concerto grosso contrasts, and imaginative vocal ensembles are among his Viennese legacy.

Surviving operas: *Bacco, vincitore dell'India*, 1697; *La costanza d'Ulisse*, 1700; *Il Telemacco, ovvero Il valore coronato*, 1702; *Ercole, vincitore di Gerione*, 1708; *Gli amori di Circe con Ulisse*, 1709; 19 other stage works
BIBLIOGRAPHY Lawrence E. Bennett, 'Carlo Agostino 34Badia', in *Grove*, Macmillan, 1980

T.T.C.

CARLOS BAGUER
Carlos Baguer ['Carlets']; *b* March 1768, Barcelona; *d* 1 March 1808, Barcelona

Organist at Barcelona Cathedral from 1786 until his death, Baguer seems to have been well known as a composer of organ and sacred vocal music in his native Catalonia and in Spain generally, judging from the spread of his manuscripts. His only opera, *La princesa filósofa, o sea El desdén con el desdén* (*The Philosophical Princess, or Disdain Cured by Disdain*), was highly regarded. There are records of five performances in 1797 and at least a sixth in 1798 in the Teatro Santa Cruz in Barcelona, rubbing shoulders with successful works by Haydn and Sors. The libretto is based on a reworking by Count Carlo Gozzi (1720–1806) of an influential comedy, *El desdén con el desdén*, by the Spanish playwright Agustín Moreto.

BIBLIOGRAPHY Antonio Martín Moreno, *Historia de la música española*, vol. 4: *Siglo XVIII*, Alianza, 1985

J.W.S.

TADEUSZ BAIRD
b 26 July 1928, Grodzisk Mazowiecki, Poland; *d* 2 September 1981, Warsaw

Baird, whose grandfather was Scottish (hence the name), matured early, and composed several piano and orchestral works while still a student. Later his interest shifted and in addition to orchestral and chamber music he wrote much for voices, as well as incidental and film music. There is, however, only one opera, *Tomorrow*, composed at a time when Baird's style combined the influences of Berg and Varèse with a lyrical melodic style.

Tomorrow
Jutro
Music drama in one act (1h)
Libretto by Jerzy S. Sito, after Joseph Conrad's story
PREMIERE 18 September 1966, Wielki Theatre, Warsaw

An old man and a girl, Jessica, the daughter of a blind carpenter, are awaiting the return of the old man's son (who ran away to sea years ago), believing that when he comes back life will change for the better. But when the son (Harry) returns, he proves to be a bad lot. To protect his dream, the father refuses to recognize Harry and throws him out, and then, when Harry tries to rape Jessica, kills him. The old man can now go on awaiting his son's return.

Tomorrow is a music drama in which leitmotifs represent psychological states rather than people or concepts, and specific colourings are used to characterize emotions. Harry is a spoken role, a device that highlights the gulf between his world and that of the other characters.

RECORDING Szostek-Radkowa, Artysz, Pawlak, Ostrowski, Poznan SO, Czajkowski, Polskie Nagrania/Disco, 1973
EDITION v.s., PWM/Chester-Hansen, 1967

BIBLIOGRAPHY M. de Manziarly, '*Tomorrow*. Musical Drama in One Act', *Polish Music*, 1966, no. 3, pp. 11–13

Z.C.

SÁNDOR BALASSA

b 20 January 1935, Budapest

Balassa took up music late after seeing a film of Verdi's *Il trovatore*, when he was a fitter in a Budapest factory. He left his job and became a music student, studying with Endre Szervánszky at the Budapest Academy, then worked as a music producer for Hungarian Radio. He has composed in almost every medium: there are major orchestral works (including several British and American commissions), and much vocal and choral music, with and without orchestra. Balassa has written two operas: *Az ajtón kívül* and *A harmadik bólygo* (*The Third Planet*), composed 1986–7. He is at work (1991) on a third, *Karl und Anna* (after the novel by Leonhard Frank).

The Man Outside

Az ajtón kívül

Opera in five movements (1h 15m)
Libretto by Géza Fodor, after Wolfgang Borchert's play *Draussen vor der Tür*
Composed 1973–7
PREMIERES 28 December 1977 (broadcast); 20 October 1978, Budapest; UK: 1 March 1980, BBC Radio 3 (broadcast)

The work is dominated by choral writing and a didactic manner, which at times gives it the character of oratorio. The hero is a guilt-racked soldier cast adrift by demobilization, and an epic, symbolic tone predominates in spite of all Balassa's attempts to individualize his characters. Much of the writing is dense, multi-stranded and beautifully wrought, a quality Balassa has cultivated also in his concert works. The dramatic pacing is less sure.

RECORDING Palcsó, Tokody, Polgár, Fülöp, Gregor, Nagy, Bordás, Hungarian Radio and Television Ch, Budapest SO, Lehel, Hungaroton, 1980
EDITION v.s., Editio Musica Budapest, 1978

BIBLIOGRAPHY Stephen Walsh, review of *Az ajtón kívül*, *Opera*, vol. 30 (January 1979), pp. 28–30

S.W.

MICHAEL BALFE

Michael William Balfe; *b* 15 May 1808, Dublin; *d* 20 October 1870, Rowney Abbey, Hertfordshire, England

Balfe was the most prolific British opera composer of his generation and arguably the most popular of the 19th century. His works enjoyed great success both in Britain and widely abroad.

After early training in Dublin and London Balfe spent some years in Italy and Paris, gaining the support of Rossini and Cherubini as he developed his career as an opera singer and composer. In 1833 he came to London and in 1835 achieved an overnight success with his first English opera, *The Siege of Rochelle*. His subsequent commissions included *Falstaff* for Her Majesty's Theatre, then among the most prestigious Italian opera houses in Europe. Balfe made an attempt as a manager himself, but after the venture's failure transferred his attention to Paris. Drury Lane reopened as the English Opera House in 1843 and that autumn saw the premiere there of Balfe's best-known opera, *The Bohemian Girl*. Its popularity outstripped that of all other English works of the period. Balfe continued to divide his time between London and Paris; in 1843, 1844 and 1845 he produced a new opera in each capital, including *L'Étoile de Séville* for the Paris Opéra, the Continental Mecca for opera composers – a unique achievement for a British musician. In *The Daughter of St Mark*, Balfe made his second attempt to overcome the traditional national prejudice against all-sung opera (*Catherine Grey*, of 1837, also excluded spoken dialogue), but this did not score a success.

In addition to composing and continuing to sing – he was London's first Papageno in 1838 – Balfe became conductor at Her Majesty's in 1846, working with Verdi when he came to prepare *I masnadieri* the following year. Renewed managerial failure brought English opera virtually to a halt and Balfe again sought his fortunes abroad, travelling to Berlin, Vienna, St Petersburg, and Trieste, where *Pittore e duca* appeared in 1854. Its libretto was by Piave, Verdi's librettist. In 1856 Balfe returned to London after four years' absence. The final phase of his composing career lasted from 1857 until 1864. Written with a new management and superior singers in mind, the operas of this period are more expansive, though not free from the carelessness over word-setting and dramatic effect that mars his earlier work. He emerged from his retirement in 1868 for a Parisian revival of *The Bohemian Girl*.

Balfe may have lacked the dramatic imagination of great opera composers, but he nevertheless led the attempt to institute English opera as a substantial musical form, and his international reputation served to raise the status of British composers. His talent was primarily melodic, and stylistically he was essentially Italianate. Having been the source of his rise to fame, these features also contributed to his decline. Within a few years of his death, the increasing support for Wagner led to an altered view

The finale of The Bohemian Girl, *from a contemporary piano score*

of Balfe's operas, from which they have yet to recover.

The Bohemian Girl

Opera in three acts (3h)
Libretto by Alfred Bunn after St Georges's and Mazillier's ballet *The Gypsy* (1839), based in turn on Cervantes's novel *La gitanilla* (1614)
PREMIERES 27 November 1843, Drury Lane, London; US: 25 November 1844, New York
CAST Count Arnheim *bar*, Thaddeus *t*, Florestein *t*, Devilshoof *b*, Arline *s*, Queen of the Gypsies *s*, 3 other solo parts, *s, t, b*; *satb* chorus of Austrians and gypsies

Like many English operas of the period, *The Bohemian Girl* was based by Bunn, the manager of Drury Lane, on a French source, in this case a ballet.

SYNOPSIS
The opera is set near Pressburg at the end of the 18th century.

Act I Following festivities in praise of the Austrian emperor, Arline, the six-year-old daughter of Count Arnheim, is kidnapped.

Act II Twelve years later. Arline has been brought up in a gypsy camp. Here she falls in love with Thaddeus, a proscribed Polish soldier who has been forced to take refuge in the camp. But this enrages the Gypsy Queen, who herself loves Thaddeus, and she engineers a trumped-up charge in order to remove her rival. At her trial Arline is recognized by her father, the judge.

Act III The thwarted Gypsy Queen plans Thaddeus's death, but is herself killed. The hero is accepted by the Austrians, and general rejoicing brings the opera to an end.

True to the English tradition, the opera includes spoken dialogue, and there is little recitative. The music is characteristic of Balfe and, stylistically, owes much to Rossini. Its effect derives not from dramatic intensity but from melodic charm. This emerges strongly in the ballads, the simple songs typical of English opera of the period. 'I dreamt that I dwelt in marble halls' and 'When other lips and other hearts', for the heroine and hero respectively, are two of Balfe's best-known examples. Their apparent effortlessness belies the time and concern he lavished on them – far more, clearly, than he devoted to details of word-setting and dramatic impact. However, it should be remembered that the sales of such ballads provided an important source of income for the composer.

RECORDING Thomas, Cullen, Power, Summers, del Carlo, Radio Telefis Eireann Philharmonic Choir, National SO of Ireland, Bonynge, Argo, 1991
EDITION v.ss., Boosey & Co., 1872; Novello, [n.d.]

The Daughter of St Mark

Opera in three acts (3h)
Libretto by Alfred Bunn, after St Georges
PREMIERES   27 November 1844, Drury Lane, London; US:
18 June 1855, New York

For the text of this work Bunn again drew on a recent Parisian work, in this instance the opera *La reine de Chypre* (1841), whose libretto, by St Georges, had been set by Halévy, and was also set by the German composer Lachner (1841), Donizetti (as *Caterina Cornaro*, of 1844), and Pacini (1846) – unmistakable testimony to the powerful influence of the French librettist. Set in the 15th century, the plot concerns the vicissitudes facing Caterina and her beloved Adolphe when she is used as a pawn in Venetian politics.

Doubtless buoyant with the continuing success of *The Bohemian Girl*, Balfe decided to challenge the traditional English concept of opera as a form that included speech. This is, then, one of the relatively few national operas written before the 20th century in which all the text was sung. Its *éclat* was limited. Bunn's poetry was weak, but Balfe himself was also to blame. The word-setting, not least in the recitatives, is sometimes very cavalier, and even the composer's *forte*, melodic inspiration, seems to have diminished. The circumstances under which the work was composed must have taken their toll: Balfe produced the opera swiftly, taxing even his unusual ability to compose at great pace.

RECORDING   Black, Shovelton, Beavan, King, Gala Opera
Group Ch and O, Jones, RRE, 1973
EDITION   v.s., London, 1845

The Rose of Castille

Opera in three acts (3h)
Libretto by Augustus Harris and Edmund Falconer
(pseudonym for Edmund O'Rourke), after the libretto by
Adolphe Philippe d'Ennery and 'Clairville' (Louis François
Nicolaie) for Adolphe Adam's *Le muletier de Tolède* (1854)
Composed 19 September–11 October 1857
PREMIERES   29 October 1857, Lyceum, London; US: 27 July
1864, New York

The plot concerns the machinations of the Spanish aristocrat Don Pedro, who conspires to seize power from Elvira, the beautiful young Queen of León. In order to create confusion, Pedro brings to the court a country girl who bears a striking resemblance to the queen. But this is the queen herself, travelling incognito. Assisted by Manuel, a brave muletier with whom she is in love, she thwarts Don Pedro's intrigues. Once aware of her identity, Pedro contrives the queen's marriage to Manuel, hoping such an alliance will enforce her abdication. But – as Elvira has long realized – 'Manuel' is actually the Infant of Castille, also travelling in disguise. With Don Pedro's ambitions in ruins, Elvira is both Queen of León and Rose of Castille.

Tailored for the newly formed opera company of Louisa Pyne and William Harrison, *The Rose of Castille* marked Balfe's return to the London stage after a five-year absence. Doubtless meeting Pyne's wishes he wrote virtuosic Italianate solos for Elvira. This would have been a congenial task as Balfe had composed an Italian opera, *Pittore e duca*, for Trieste in 1854. The Italian flavour is strengthened by the use of characteristic forms and orchestral rhythms. Balfe also had to accommodate English taste, specifically for the ballad. Inserted with little concern for the drama, their stylized texts, slow pace and strophic form are often at odds with the characterization. The speed with which the work was composed testifies to Balfe's extraordinary facility, even allowing for the incorporation of an aria originally written for his French opera *L'Étoile de Séville* (1845).

RECORDING   Springer, O'Connor, Cuthbert, Dickie,
unnamed Ch and O, RRE, date not known
EDITIONS   v.ss., Cramer, Beale and Chappell, 1858; Boosey
& Co., 1901

Satanella, or The Power of Love

Opera in four acts (3h)
Libretto by Augustus Glossop Harris and Edmund
Falconer (O'Rourke), after the ballet *Le diable amoureux* by
St Georges and Mazillier
PREMIERES   20 December 1858, Covent Garden, London;
US: 23 February 1863, New York

Satanella is ordered by the devil to help Count Rupert recover the fortune he has lost in gambling, and thereby to gain his soul. When the bond is due Leila, Rupert's foster-sister and his new love, declares that she will accompany him to hell. Satanella, also in love with Rupert, is overcome by Leila's devotion and destroys the bond. A timely gift of a rosary saves her from the devil's clutches.

Balfe took advantage of the presence in the company of a better soprano, Louisa Pyne, than had been available in previous years, and gave her part – the title role – material of a more virtuosic order than would formerly have been possible. Though the standard of craftsmanship is variable, the opera is written on a grander scale than Balfe's earlier works. There is a more serious sense of purpose, with more attention paid to characterization. Thematic recall is used more schematically than elsewhere in the composer's work, emphasizing the underlying theme of the redemptive power of love. Even the conventions of that cornerstone of Balfe's style, the ballad, show signs of being loosened, with more flexible forms emerging.

RECORDING   Debret, Lea, Flint, Donert, Addison,
Galloway, RRE, 1970s
EDITION   v.s., Boosey & Co., 1876

Other operas: *I rivali di se stessi*, 1829; *Un avertimento ai gelosi*, 1830; *Enrico IV al passo della Marno*, 1833; *The Siege of Rochelle*, 1835; *The Maid of Artois*, 1836; *Catherine Grey*, 1837; *Joan of Arc*, 1837; *Diadesté*, 1838; *Falstaff*, 1838; *Keolanthe*, 1841; *Le puits d'amour*, 1843; *Les quatre fils Aymon*, 1844; *The Enchantress*, 1845; *L'Étoile de Séville*, 1845; *The Bondman*, 1846; *The Maid of Honour*, 1847; *The Sicilian Bride*, 1852; *The Devil's In It*, 1852; *Pittore e duca*,

1854; *Bianca, or The Bravo's Bride*, 1860; *The Puritan's Daughter*, 1861; *Blanche de Nevers*, 1862; *The Armourer of Nantes*, 1863; *The Sleeping Queen*, 1864; *The Knight of the Leopard* (inc.; completed Costa), 1874
BIBLIOGRAPHY   Charles Lamb Kenney, *A Memoir of Michael William Balfe*, Tinsley Brothers, 1875; *rp*, Da Capo, 1978

G.B.

ADRIANO BANCHIERI

Adriano Tomaso Banchieri; *b* 3 September 1568, Bologna; *d* 1634, Bologna

With Orazio Vecchi, Banchieri was a chief exponent of the new madrigal comedy. An Olivetan monk, he spent his life in Bologna, although he travelled widely around northern Italy. As an organist, composer and distinguished theorist, Banchieri was the leading musician in the city. He also founded the musical Accademia dei Floridi (later, dei Filomusi) in 1614, with which Claudio Monteverdi was briefly associated.

His numerous secular publications include three madrigal comedies: *La pazzia senile* (1598), *Il metamorfosi musicale* (1601) and *Prudenza giovenile* (1607). Following Vecchi's *L'Amfiparnaso*, they take the stock characters and scenarios of the *commedia dell'arte* and sketch out a more or less coherent dramatic action. These three-part works were not necessarily intended to be acted or mimed, although Banchieri recommended that a narrator keep track of the plot.

T.C.

JOHN BANISTER

b 1624 or 1625, London; *d* 3 October 1679, London

John Banister came to public attention in 1656 as a violinist in the distinguished ensemble that accompanied Davenant's *The Siege of Rhodes* with music by Locke and others, long thought of as the first English opera. After the Restoration in 1660 he soon became an important court musician, a member of the Twenty-four Violins and, in 1662, director of a newly formed select violin band; Charles II had sent him to France in 1661 to study the French orchestral style. He was probably the first English composer to use French idioms such as the overture and the branle, and his music was influential in its day. His part-writing often seems incompetent to us, though this may be the result of corrupt sources.

Masque-like plays and semi-operas to which Banister contributed: *The Slighted Maid*, 1663; *The Queen's Masque*, 1671; *Beauty's Triumph*, 1676; *The Parley of Instruments*, 1676; *Circe*, 1677
BIBLIOGRAPHY   Curtis Price, *Music in the Restoration Theatre*, UMI, 1979

P.H.

GRANVILLE BANTOCK

(Sir) Granville Ransome Bantock; *b* 7 August 1868, London; *d* 11 October 1946, London

Bantock's father was a celebrated surgeon who initially opposed his son's aspiration to be a composer. After abortive training for chemical engineering and for the Indian Civil Service, Bantock arrived at the Royal Academy of Music in 1888. In the mid-1890s he became musical director of one of George Edwardes's touring companies. Later he was conductor at The Tower, New Brighton (a Merseyside resort) and, from 1900, principal of the Midland Institute School of Music in Birmingham. In 1908 he succeeded Elgar as Peyton Professor of Music at Birmingham University.

During the decade before the First World War Bantock emerged as a composer with an inclination for working on the largest scale, perhaps most celebrated for his huge choral work *Omar Khayyám*, which sets the whole of Fitzgerald's poem. He forged a personal style from what was new in the 1890s – largely Wagner, Tchaikovsky and Strauss – and developed little in later years. Always tremendously fluent, he was often content to let his first thoughts be his last. From a very large corpus of music there is much that has not lasted; nevertheless there is also some fine music, especially his larger-scale works.

Bantock's operas are divided almost equally between musical comedies, inspired by his adventures on tour, and more substantial fare, at first broadly Wagnerian, but including one highly individual score, *The Seal-Woman*.

The Seal-Woman

Celtic folk opera in two acts (2h)
Libretto by Marjory Kennedy-Fraser, after a Hebridean folktale
PREMIERE   27 September 1924, Birmingham Repertory Theatre

An Isleman marries a 'seal-woman'. In human form she lives happily with her husband for seven years, bearing him a son. Eventually she can no longer resist the call of the sea, and leaves to return to her true home. Twenty Hebridean tunes are used and these, with Bantock's idiosyncratic Straussian harmony and the tiny orchestra (16 players), give this atmospheric work a unique fascination.

EDITION   v.s., Boosey & Hawkes, 1924

Other operatic works: *Comalla*, (n.d.); *Caedmar*, 1892 (concert); *The Pearl of Iran*, (1894); *Eugene Aram*, (inc.; 1896); *ABC, or Flossie the Frivolour*, (1898); *Sweet Briar*, (1898); *Harlequinade, or Only a Clown*, (1899)
BIBLIOGRAPHY   Lewis Foreman, 'Bantock Revival [Seal-Woman]', *Music & Musicians*, May 1975, pp. 10 and 12

L.F.

SAMUEL BARBER

b 9 March 1910, West Chester, Pennsylvania, US;
d 23 January 1981, New York

Barber was one of the most successful American composers of the mid-20th century. Confidently conservative in style, his romantic music has stood its ground through changes of fashion and seems as enduring as that of Copland or Gershwin, although it is less distinctively American in style.

Barber's family background was conducive to his musical development. His mother was a good pianist and his aunt, the opera singer Louise Homer, was married to a composer. Barber began composing when he was seven and his first attempts at an opera date from three years later. In 1924 Barber became a student of singing, piano and conducting as well as composition at the newly founded Curtis Institute in Philadelphia. There he met Gian Carlo Menotti who became an essential colleague, librettist and near-lifelong companion. After graduating Barber went to study singing in Vienna, gave recitals and radio broadcasts and recorded his own song, *Dover Beach* (composed 1931), for voice and string quartet.

At Curtis, Barber received a thorough traditional grounding in composition from Rosario Scalero. His student works were polished and well received, enabling him to gain awards for European travel. He soon attracted the attention of major conductors such as Rodzinski and Toscanini. The latter conducted the first performance of the famous *Adagio* for strings (arranged from the String Quartet, 1936) which has become a classic.

All this augured well for Barber's progression to opera, as did his early orchestral pieces related to dramatic subjects, such as the *School for Scandal* overture and the *Music for a Scene from Shelley*, as well as his ballets, *Medea* (1946) and *Souvenirs* (1952). Barber was concerned to communicate directly. In a late interview he said, 'There's no reason music should be difficult for an audience to understand, is there?'

Vanessa

Opera in four acts, Op. 32 (2h)
Libretto by Gian Carlo Menotti, based on a story in *Seven Gothic Tales* by Isak Dinesen (1934)
Composed 1956–7, rev. 1964
PREMIERES 15 January 1958, Metropolitan, New York; rev. version: 3 March 1964, Metropolitan, New York
CAST Vanessa *s*, Erika *ms*, The Old Baroness *a*, Anatol *t*, The Old Doctor *bar*, Nicholas *b*, Footman *b*; *satb* chorus of servants, guests, peasants, children, musicians
LARGE ORCHESTRA onstage: fl, ob, 2 cl, 2 bsn, 2 hn, 2 tpt, accordion, bells, organ, str

Menotti, as a seasoned man of the theatre, contributed significantly as both librettist and director of *Vanessa*. Elegant sets and costumes were designed by Cecil Beaton and the casting – as can readily be confirmed in the original recording – was superb. Barber had written *Knoxville: Summer of 1915* (1948) for Eleanor Steber and she was chosen for the title role (Callas had refused it on the grounds that the work had no melody and she could not be expected to fall in love with a man who had slept with the mezzo-soprano). Menotti's plot has overtones of Ibsen, which suited Barber's nostalgic side and inspired arias, dances and dramatic moments in his strongest vein.

Remarkably for a first opera, *Vanessa* was a resounding success. Winthrop Sargeant considered it a 'near masterpiece in the genre' and Paul Henry Lang predicted that its impeccable vocal writing and sumptuous orchestration would be an 'eye-opener for Europeans'. Although there were reservations about its derivative nature when it was performed at the Salzburg Festival later in 1958, *Vanessa* seems likely to survive.

SYNOPSIS
The action takes place at Vanessa's country house in an unspecified northern country, *c.* 1905.

Act I Vanessa, her mother the Baroness and her niece Erika are waiting for the return of Vanessa's lover, Anatol, who left 20 years ago. When he arrives he turns out to be the son of her lover, and also called Anatol; his father is dead.

Act II Anatol and Vanessa are becoming increasingly attached although Anatol had seduced Erika on the night of his arrival. Erika decides to give him up.

Act III At a splendid ball Anatol and Vanessa pledge their love in public: Erika collapses.

Act IV Erika, pregnant by Anatol, is recovering after attempting suicide. Vanessa and Anatol, married, prepare to leave for Paris. Erika settles down to wait for Anatol indefinitely, as had Vanessa at the start of the opera.

Although Barber sticks to the traditional forms of opera (arias, duets, ensembles, etc.) his musical language is far-ranging, encompassing folklike and parodistic elements within the predominantly lyrical whole. Barber and Menotti revised the opera to a three-act version in 1964, but the original version is more commonly performed.

RECORDING Steber, Elias, Resnik, Gedda, Tozzi, Metropolitan Opera Ch and O, Mitropoulos, RCA, 1958
EDITIONS f.s./v.s., Schirmer, 1957; rev. version: f.s./v.s., Schirmer, 1964

A Hand of Bridge

Miniature opera, Op. 35 (9m)
Libretto by Gian Carlo Menotti
Composed 1953
PREMIERES 17 June 1959, Spoleto, Italy; UK: 1 August 1986, Buxton Festival
CAST David *bar*, Geraldine *s*, Bill *t*, Sally *a*
CHAMBER ORCHESTRA

A Hand of Bridge, which predates *Vanessa* (although it was produced afterwards), can be regarded as a study in levels of consciousness. Two couples are playing bridge and during the game the thoughts of one character or another are amusingly brought to the surface. Less has been said by many longer operas.

RECORDING   Neway, Alberts, Lewis, Maero, Symphony of the Air, Golschmann, Vanguard, 1960
EDITION   v.s., Schirmer, 1960

Antony and Cleopatra

Opera in three acts, Op. 40 (2h)
Libretto by Franco Zeffirelli, after the play by Shakespeare (1606–7)
Composed 1966, rev. 1975
PREMIERES   16 September 1966, Metropolitan, New York; rev. version: 6 February 1975, Julliard School of Music, New York; UK: 27 March 1982, Logan Hall, London (Abbey Opera; concert)
CAST   Cleopatra *s*, Octavia *spoken role*, Charmian *ms*, Iras *a*, Antony *bar*, Caesar *t*, Agrippa *b*, Enobarbus *b*, Eros *t* or *bar*, Dolabella *bar*, Thidias *t* or *bar*, Maecenas *spoken role*, Caesar's Soldier *bar*, Rustic *bar* or *b*, Messenger *t*, Soothsayer *b*, Eunuch *spoken role*, Alexas *b*, 4 Guards *t*, *bar*, 2 *b*, 2 soldiers 2 *b*, Watchman *spoken role*; *satb* chorus; dancers

Barber's *Antony and Cleopatra* was commissioned for the opening of the new Metropolitan Opera House at Lincoln Center – a public ordeal that proved as damaging to the work's future as the Coronation gala performance in 1953 was to Britten's *Gloriana*. Although the singers were much admired, Zeffirelli's production was felt to be over-elaborate. Desmond Shawe-Taylor reported that Barber's music, 'rich in substance and sometimes very engaging, was being submerged beneath the glitter and complexity of the spectacle', on- and offstage. The opera was regarded as a failure. Even after the 1975 revival produced by Menotti, Andrew Porter pointed out the difficulties of word-for-word Shakespeare setting and thought that the music 'did not rise to the size of the subject'. The impact of this apparent failure on Barber was disastrous and may have contributed to the decline of his health. But the recording by Leontyne Price and more recent radio broadcasts suggest that there is unrealized potential in *Antony and Cleopatra*.

RECORDINGS   1. Hinds, Wells, Halfvarson, Westminster Ch, Spoleto Festival O, Badea, New World, 1984; 2. excerpt: Price, New Philharmonia O, Schippers, RCA, 1969
EDITION   v.s., Schirmer, 1966; *rp*, 1976

BIBLIOGRAPHY   N. Broder, *Samuel Barber*, Schirmer, 1954; D. A. Hennessee, *Samuel Barber: a Bio-bibliography*, Greenwood, 1985; Barbara Heyman, *Samuel Barber*, OUP, 1992

P.D.

FRANCISCO BARBIERI

Francisco Asenjo Barbieri; *b* 3 August 1823, Madrid; *d* 19 February 1894, Madrid

Barbieri is the most important figure in the history of zarzuela. His early medical career was abandoned in favour of studies at the Madrid Conservatory, after which he led a varied and Bohemian musical life, centred mainly around opera houses and orchestras in Madrid.

In 1850 he collaborated with various other musicians to take over the Teatro del Circo, for which he wrote the first three-act zarzuela, *Jugar con fuego*. This was the first of more than 70 works by him in the genre – all of them immensely popular. Barbieri was also the most eminent Spanish musicologist of his time and his erudition infiltrated an authentic national flavour, both in subject matter and in music, into his stage works. *Pan y toros* (1864), set in his native Madrid, for example, portrays bullfighters, beggars and churchmen, and its introduction of Goya as the major character foreshadows Granados.

His masterpiece is *El barberillo de Lavapiés* (1874), which tells of the exploits of Lamparilla, a barber, factotum, and dentist, and his flirtations with and eventual marriage to the dressmaker Paloma. Set at the time of Carlos III, the plot is of political intrigue, disguise, imprisonment and escape. Barbieri's later compatriot Roberto Gerhard was so taken with the work that he made two adaptations and arrangements of it (1954, 1955).

Zarzuelas: *Gloria y peluca*, 1850; *Tramoya*, 1850; *Escenas de Chamberi*, 1850; *La Picaresca*, 1851; *Jugar con fuego*, 1851 (RECORDING abridged: London International, *c*. 1955); *Por seguir a una mujer*, 1851; *La Hechicera*, 1852; *El Manzanares*, 1852; *Gracias a Dios que está puesta la mesa*, 1852; *La espada de Bernardo*, 1853; *El Marqués de Caravaca*, 1853; *Don Simplicio de Bobadilla*, 1853; *Galanteos en Venecia*, 1853; *Un día de Reinado*, 1854; *Aventuras de un cantante*, 1854; *Los diamantes de la corona*, 1854 (RECORDING abridged: Alhambra, ?1960s); *Mis dos mujeres*, 1855; *Los dos ciegos*, 1855; *El vizconde*, 1855; *El sargento Federico*, 1855; *Entre dos aguas*, 1856; *Gato per liebre*, 1856; *El diablo en el poder*, 1856; *El relámpago*, 1857; *Por conquista*, 1858; *Amar sin conocer*, 1858; *Un caballero particular*, 1858; *El robo de las Sabinas*, 1859; *El niño*, 1859; *Compromisos del no ver*, 1859; *Entre mi mujer y el negro*, 1859; *Un tesoro escondido*, 1861; *Los Herederos*, 1861; *El secreto de una dama*, 1862; *Dos pichones del Turia*, 1863; *Pan y toros*, 1864; *Gibraltar en 1890*, 1865; *El rábano por las hojas*, 1866; *Revista de un muerto*, 1866; *De tejas arriba*, 1866; *El pavo de Navidad*, 1866; *El pan de la boda*, 1868; *El soprano*, 1869; *Robinsón*, 1870; *Los holgazanes*, 1871; *Don Pacifico*, 1871; *El hombre es débil*, 1871; *El tributo de las cien doncellas*, 1872; *Sueños de oro*, 1872; *El proceso del can-can*, 1873; *Los comediantes de antaño*, 1874; *El domador de fieras*, 1874; *El testamento azul*, 1874; *El barberillo de Lavapiés*, 1874 (RECORDING Alhambra, 1950s); *La vuelta al mundo*, 1875; *Chorizos y polacos*, 1876; *Juan de Urbina*, 1876; *La confitera*, 1876; *Artistas para la Habana*, 1877; *Los carboneros*, 1877; *El loro y la lechuza*, 1877; *El triste Chactas*, 1878; *El diablo cojuelo*, 1878; *Los chichones*, 1879; *¡Ojo a la ninera!*, 1879; *¡A Sevilla por todo!*, 1880; *¡Anda, valiente!*, 1880; *La filoxera*, 1882; *De Getafe al paraíso*, 1883; *¡Hoy sale, hoy!*, 1884; *Novillos en Polvoranca*, 1885; *El señor Luis el tumbón*, 1891
BIBLIOGRAPHY   A. Martinez Olmedilla, *El maestro Barbieri y su tiempo*, Ediciones Españolas, 1941

S.J.W.

PAUL BARKER

Paul Alan Barker; *b* 1 July 1956, Cambridge, England

Barker studied at the Guildhall School of Music (1974–8); he was then visiting lecturer at the City University, London (1978–83) and at Durham University (1983–5). He has been active with a number of performing groups, musical director of Dancers Anonymous and, since 1985, of the Modern Music Theatre Troupe, which has premiered four of his operas to date.

Barker has written extensively for the theatre, with a number of dance scores and children's operas to his credit. In the mid-1980s he came to prominence with a series of small-scale operas at a time when that sub-genre had largely become the province of modernists. Barker's music, which combines tonal elements with an inventive approach to instrumental combinations and timbres and a rewarding vocal style, won over audiences at a crucial time.

His first opera, *The Marriages Between Zones 3, 4 and 5*, based on a story by Doris Lessing, for four soloists, children's chorus and nine-piece ensemble, makes use of conventional set pieces, the vocal writing challenging but gratifying. This was followed by *Phantastes*, 'a faerie romance for men and women' after the novel (1858) by George MacDonald, unusually scored for keyboards, percussion and Irish bagpipes.

The Pillow Song, the personal diary of a Japanese emperor's concubine, makes formidable demands on a solo soprano, accompanied by four other sopranos and percussionist (played by the composer himself at the premiere). *La Malinche* is just as bold in its treatment of Cortés's conquest of the Aztecs: the text is set partly in Nahuatl, Spanish and Latin, with accompaniment from percussion and two trumpets doubling on conches. *Albergo Empedocle* is based on a short story by E. M. Forster in which a young Englishman about to marry into a middle-class family undergoes a mystical experience when they all travel to Italy. Again, Barker's scoring is inventive: just a string quartet.

Operatic works: *Wall* (music theatre), 1983; *The Marriages Between Zones 3, 4 and 5*, 1985; *Phantastes*, 1986; *The Pillow Song*, 1988; *La Malinche*, 1989; *Albergo Empedocle*, 1990

M.A.

JOHN BARNETT

b 15 July 1802, Bedford, England; *d* 16 April 1890, Leckhampton, England

Barnett was articled to the theatre manager Samuel Arnold as a boy alto. He also studied the piano with Ferdinand Ries, a German composer who spent several years in London. Barnett's early work was limited to incidental music for theatrical works, but in 1834 Arnold gave him the opportunity to produce *The Mountain Sylph*, which initiated the 19th-century

development of English opera as a dramatic medium in which music is an integral, not an ancillary, element.

Two further operas, *Fair Rosamond* and *Farinelli*, were given in 1837 and 1839. These are of a different cut: longer (*Fair Rosamond* lasted four and a half hours), and with a mixture of styles accommodating not only Weber's influence but that of Auber, Rossini, and Beethoven as well as the national elements of ballads, madrigal-type choruses and spoken dialogue. This catch-all stylistic variety reflects the unstable circumstances then bedevilling native opera. Barnett exacerbated his own position by antagonizing many in the theatrical and musical world. He made an unsuccessful attempt at managing a London theatre (St James's), aiming to make it a base for an English national opera, before settling in Cheltenham in 1841. Three more operas were undertaken, but probably none was performed. The loss to English opera is difficult to assess: certainly Barnett was gifted with unusual powers of invention.

The Mountain Sylph

Romantic grand opera in two acts (3h 30m)
Libretto by Thomas James Thackeray
PREMIERE   25 August 1834, Lyceum, London

Set on the Isle of Skye, the plot was derived from the Romantic ballet, *La Sylphide*, performed in Paris two years earlier. The frequent description of the work as the first all-sung 19th-century opera is incorrect, and derives from Barnett's own rather ambiguous statement in the preface to the vocal score. However, the opera does include, alongside the traditional British features of spoken dialogue and simple songs, extended solos, concerted pieces, and finales that far exceed the norm. The musical style is strongly influenced by Weber, exemplified by the Act I finale, whose harmonic style, scoring, melodrama (speech accompanied by orchestral music), and dramatic effect were modelled on the Wolf's Glen scene in *Der Freischütz*.

EDITION   v.s., Boosey & Co., [*c.* 1880]

Other operas and operettas: *The Deuce is in Her*, 1830; *The Picturesque*, 1831; *The Convent, or The Pet of the Petticoats*, 1832; *Win Her and Wear Her*, 1832; *Fair Rosamond*, 1837; *Farinelli*, 1839; *Kathleen*, (1840); *Queen Mab*, (n.d.); *Marie* (inc.); many stage works with music
BIBLIOGRAPHY   Bruce Carr, 'The First All-sung English 19th-century Opera', *MT*, vol. 115 (1974), pp. 125–6; Eric Walter White, *A History of English Opera*, Faber, 1983

G.B.

HENRY BARRAUD

b 23 April 1900, Bordeaux, France

A pupil of Dukas and Louis Aubert, Barraud has been one of the most eclectic, least aesthetically partisan of modern French composers. During the Second World War he was prominent in Resistance broadcasting, and for 20 years after the war he was in charge of the music broadcasts of French Radio. His own music reflects the breadth of sympathy necessary in such a post. At one time he actually gave up composing in order to take time absorbing the significance of avant-garde developments in the 1960s. But though his subsequent music has serial and other progressive elements, they are really no more than extensions of an idiom based on the traditional French preoccupations of extended tonal/modal harmony combined with an austere formal grandeur more redolent of the organ loft than the *café-concert*.

Despite this, however, Barraud has composed successfully for the stage, mostly on subjects of an antique or quasi-medieval cast. His five operas range widely between the one-act *Farce de maître Pathelin*, the workmanlike opéra bouffe *Lavinia* (based on a novel by Félicien Marceau: an ironic choice, since Marceau had worked for the pre-Resistance Nazi radio in France), and the chamber opera *Le Roi Gordogane*, to tragedies in the grand manner: *Numance*, a substantial and sometimes violent one-act opera based on Cervantes's account of the siege of Numantia in 133BC, staged at the Paris Opéra in 1955, and *Tête d'or*, after the tragedy by Claudel.

Operas: *La farce de maître Pathelin*, (1938), 1948; *Numance*, (1952), 1955; *Lavinia*, (1959), 1961; *Le Roi Gordogane*, (1974), 1979; *Tête d'or*, (1980)
BIBLIOGRAPHY C. Rostand, *French Music Today*, Da Capo, 1973, pp. 101–5

S.W.

LIONEL BART

Lionel Begleiter; *b* 1 August 1930, London

Bart, from an East End London-Jewish background, rose to the top of the British pop charts in the 1950s with songs for Tommy Steele and Cliff Richard. An early theatre-club offering, *Wally Pone* (1958, after the play *Volpone*) led to the musical *Fings Ain't Wot They Used T'Be* (1959), directed by Joan Littlewood at the Theatre Royal, Stratford East, which transferred to the West End with great success. Similarly popular the same season was *Lock Up Your Daughters*, based on Fielding's *Rape upon Rape*, for which Bart wrote the lyrics.

But Bart made British theatre history with *Oliver!* which originally ran for 2,618 performances. He followed it with *Blitz!* (1962), a musical pageant of the East End during the German air raids, and *Maggie May* (1964), its story, of a legendary Liverpool prostitute, not geared to the *Oliver!* family audience. *Twang!!* (1965), a Robin Hood burlesque, was a notorious fiasco.

Oliver!

Musical in two acts (2h 30m)
Book and lyrics by the composer, after *Oliver Twist* (1837–9) by Charles Dickens

PREMIERES 30 June 1960, New (now Albery) Theatre, London; US: 6 January 1963, Imperial Theater, New York

This enormous hit had a fortuitous blend of a brilliant and rousingly tuneful score, a superb production and sets and admirable performances by its original cast in a comparatively intimate theatre. Yet the show has proved popular all over the world, so effective is its Dickensian aura. Among its catchy songs are 'Food, glorious food', 'Consider yourself', 'You've got to pick a pocket or two' and 'As long as he needs me', which became a chart hit in 1960. (The 1968 film version won an Academy Award as Best Picture.)

RECORDING original cast, including Moody, Brown, Decca, 1960
FILM Carol Reed (dir.), Columbia, 1968
EDITION v.s., Lakeview Music Co. Ltd, 1960

BIBLIOGRAPHY Kurt Gänzl, *The British Musical Theatre*, vol. 2: *1915–1984*, Macmillan, 1986

R.T.

FRANÇOIS-HIPPOLYTE BARTHÉLÉMON

b 27 July 1741, Bordeaux, France; *d* 20 July 1808, London

The son of a French officer and an Irish lady, Barthélémon seemed destined for a military career. But by 1755 he was already playing the violin in the orchestra of the Comédie-Italienne in Paris. He gave one of his first London appearances on 5 June 1764 at the same concert in which the young Mozart and his sister made their English public début. Soon he was engaged as music master to the Dukes of Cumberland and Brunswick and enjoyed the patronage of the Prince of Wales.

Active as a composer, player of violin, viola d'amore and harp (for which he wrote an early tutor), he was especially in demand as the foremost orchestral leader of his age. His serious opera *Pelopida*, though supported by J. C. Bach and Abel, was but a moderate success when it was produced at the King's Theatre, Haymarket, in 1766. Of his many lighter works *Orpheus* (1767), inserted into Garrick's farce *A New Rehearsal, or A Peep Behind the Curtain*, was especially well received, leading to a string of similar English burlettas.

During a tour of the Continent in 1776–7 the oratorio or sacred opera *Jefte in Masfa* was commissioned by the Grand Duke of Tuscany; Barthélémon completed the work in ten days, and it was well received in Florence and in Rome.

Barthélémon's later fame rested largely on his extraordinary talents on the violin. On his death in 1808, Salomon proclaimed, 'We have lost our Corelli.'

Operatic works: *Pelopida*, 1766; *Love in the City* (coll.), 1767; *La fleuve Scamandre*, 1768; *The Maid of the Oaks* (coll.), 1774; *Jefte in Masfa*, 1776; *Belphegor, or The Wishes*, 1778; *c.* 12 other stage works
BIBLIOGRAPHY   Roger Fiske, *English Theatre Music in the Eighteenth Century*, OUP, 1973; 2nd edn, 1986; Cecilia Maria Henslowe (*née* Barthélémon, *b c.* 1770), biography of her father in the preface to the 1827 edition of extracts from *Jefte in Masfa*

T.T.C.

BÉLA BARTÓK

Béla Viktor János Bartók; *b* 25 March 1881, Nagyszentmiklós (now Sînnicolau Mare, Romania); *d* 26 September 1945, New York

Bartók wrote only one opera, but it is the major work of his early maturity. *Duke Bluebeard's Castle* would doubtless have had successors but for the obstacles it encountered; these not only deterred him from writing for the stage but for a time blocked his creative faculty altogether. In 1911, at the time of its composition, Bartók was becoming established as a leading figure in Hungarian music, albeit through performance of early works which were no longer representative of his current style. In 1910 the first performance of his String Quartet No. 1, together with the experimental Bagatelles and the First Romanian Dance, Op. 8a, for piano, had been greeted with incomprehension verging on hostility, and when he entered his new opera for a competition sponsored by the Budapest Lipótvarós Club, it was rejected as unperformable and denied a prize.

The opera is nevertheless the most integrated of all Bartók's works written before the First World War and the first to show a completely personal synthesis of the various strains in his music up to that time. Seven years earlier he had been writing chamber works in a post-Brahmsian manner. Then, in about 1905, he made his first contact with the ancient peasant music of Hungary, a music remote from the Hungarian style copied by Brahms, Liszt and others; and a year or two later he came across the latest piano music of Debussy (the *Estampes* and *Images*). The Bagatelles of 1908 show in rather anecdotal form some of the effects of these encounters. Folktunes with drumming accompaniments alternate with pieces using streams of common chords or series of irregular scale patterns that seem to mimic the modal scales of peasant music. In the first Bagatelle the left and right hands play in different keys, a semitone apart. But the String Quartet No. 1, written at about the same time, sticks to a lyrical manner not wholly remote from the Expressionism of contemporary Viennese music, though with folksong ingredients too. In the opera, which was Bartók's first work for voices, these apparently incompatible elements fused to create a unique masterpiece of Hungarian Symbolism.

Duke Bluebeard's Castle

A kékszakállú herceg vára
Opera in one act, Op. 11 (1h)
Libretto by Béla Balázs, after the story by Charles Perrault
Composed March–September 1911; ending rev. 1912, 1918, 1921
PREMIERES   24 May 1918, Budapest Opera; US: 2 October 1952, City Opera, New York; UK: 16 January 1957, Sadler's Wells, London
CAST   Prologue (The Bard) *speaker*, Judith *s*, Duke Bluebeard *bar*, Bluebeard's 3 former wives *silent*
ORCHESTRATION   4 fl/2 picc, 2 ob, ca, 2 cl/E♭cl, cl/b cl, 4 bsn/dbsn, 4 hn, 4 tpt, 4 trbn, tuba, 2 hp, cel, organ, timp, perc (sd, bd, cym, susp cym, t-t, triangle, 2 xyl (originally xyl a tastiera (kbd), 1 player); str; onstage: 4 tpt, 4 alto trbn

Balázs's play owes a good deal to Maeterlinck's *Ariane et Barbe-bleu*, set by Dukas in 1907, and was apparently written in the same spirit as that play – that is, without commission but in the conscious hope that it would be set as an opera: 'I wrote [it] for Béla Bartók and Zoltán Kodály because I wanted to give them an opportunity to write works for the stage.' It treats the well-known legend of Bluebeard in Symbolistic fashion as an allegory of the incommunicable privacy of our inmost selves, and hence as a tragedy of Expressionism well adapted to the dying years of Romanticism. It must have had special resonance for Bartók, an intensely withdrawn but passionate man who had, moreover, recently married (the opera is dedicated to his wife, Mártá Ziegler).

Duke Bluebeard's Castle had to wait until after the success of Bartók's ballet *The Wooden Prince* (1917) for its first production, and after 1918 there were no further Hungarian productions for nearly 20 years because the reactionary regime of Admiral Horthy would not allow the socialist Balázs's name to be credited, and Bartók would not allow performances if it were not. Recent revivals have shown, however, that the work's supposed untheatricality is a myth; static it may be, but the strong visual imagery more than compensates.

SYNOPSIS

The short spoken Prologue (often omitted in performance) hints that the well-known tale is to be retold as a parable of the inner self; the curtain then rises on a 'vast, circular Gothic hall' with seven large doors. When Bluebeard and Judith enter through another door at the top of the stairs, the 'dazzling white opening' is the only light in the darkened hall.

A short orchestral introduction sets the gloomy scene. Judith, who is still in her wedding dress, has married Bluebeard against her family's wishes. She finds his castle cold and dark and the walls ooze moisture. Bluebeard reminds her that she could have married into a 'brighter castle, girt with roses', but she insists that she will bring brightness to his castle. An orchestral transition clearly supports Bluebeard's denial of this possibility.

Judith now notices the seven doors and demands that they be unlocked. She hammers on the first door, and as she does so a deep sigh is heard from behind it 'like the wind in a long, low corridor'. As

Miklós Bánffy's set design for Duke Bluebeard's Castle *(Budapest, 1918)*

the door swings open to reveal Bluebeard's torture chamber a blood-red light glares on to the stage. Undeterred, Judith insists on opening the second door. This time Bluebeard's armoury is revealed in 'a lurid reddish-yellow light'. Once again the 'blood' motif intrudes, as Judith sees blood on the weapons. But as she presses Bluebeard for the remaining keys, he senses the joy of release from oppressive secrets. He allows her three more keys. The doors open to display first his treasury and then his garden, bathed in a blue-green light. Yet again, the image of blood returns as Judith sees spots of red on the flowers. Finally the fifth door opens on to Bluebeard's vast and beautiful domains, portrayed in the grandest and loudest music in the whole work.

This is the architectural centre of the opera, and its climax of light. The mood now returns gradually to the gloom and darkness of the start. Bluebeard tries to distract Judith from the remaining two doors, but she persists. She sees blood even on the lands that for him are radiant with light. Reluctantly he yields the sixth key, and as she turns it in the lock another deep sigh warns of sinister revelations, and a shadow passes over the hall. The door conceals a silent lake of tears. Judith now exerts her feminine guile to coax the final key out of Bluebeard. She questions him about his past lovers and suddenly guesses that the blood on his possessions signifies that he has murdered them all. Bluebeard gives her the key. The seventh door opens (at this point doors five and six should swing shut), and his three former wives, richly adorned, process slowly out. The first, he says, he

met in the morning, the second at midday, the third in the evening. 'You', he tells Judith as the three women vanish back through the door, 'I met at night.' He dresses her in the crown, mantle and jewels she herself brought from the treasury (the third door closes as he does so), and she slowly follows the other wives through the seventh door, which closes behind her. 'The darkness of night creeps back across the stage, and engulfs Bluebeard.'

In musical style, *Duke Bluebeard's Castle* is still an early work which shows Bartók's debt to German and Austrian late-Romanticism. But it also reveals influences that were to help turn him into an abrasive modernist. Debussy is an obvious model for passages such as the massive parallel chords at the opening of the fifth door (cf. *La cathédrale engloutie* in the first book of *Préludes*, published in 1909), while echoes of Strauss's *Ein Heldenleben*, a work Bartók had once transcribed for piano, are unmistakable in the biting semitone clashes of the 'blood' motif. Yet *Bluebeard* is hardly a derivative score. It has an individuality that comes partly, perhaps, from Bartók's study of Hungarian folk music, with its strange modal scales, which seem to rub off on the opera's harmony as well as on its melody. The sharpened fourth note, which produces the interval C–F♯, is a common feature of the folksongs Bartók was collecting at this time, as is the descending perfect fourth, and both leave their mark on the very opening of the opera. Also typical of Hungarian peasant music are rhythmic details such as the decorated first beat, which produces the characteristic 'snap' or 'turn', and the so-called *parlando rubato* style of word-setting, which ensures that the incessant Hungarian accent on the first syllable rarely becomes monotonous, though it makes translation hard. Balázs himself modelled his regular octosyllabic lines on peasant verse.

Balázs's imagery, on the other hand, aligns him with modern Expressionism, with its strong colour symbolism, and with the German *art nouveau*, or *Jugendstil*, of which images of blood, flowers, castles and crowns were the stock in trade. Bartók adapts the gentle colourings of Debussian Impressionism to provide vivid but not-so-gentle musical equivalents of this imagery. In this respect *Bluebeard* is a kind of stage tone poem. It also has a strong built-in symbolism of its own, based on the opposition of keys and tonal centres. The score follows the arch form of the libretto. The darkness–light–darkness cycle is exactly matched by the tonal scheme, F♯–C–F♯, with its centre at the opening of the fifth door, and its ending in the 'darkness' music of the start. Bartók's later instrumental music offers many more instances of this type of plan: the first movement of the *Music for Strings, Percussion and Celesta* (A–E♭–A), its third movement, and the larger arch structures of the Third and Fourth String Quartets. The actual key symbolism of *Bluebeard*, however, is unique in Bartók. F♯ stands for Bluebeard's world, while the outside world represented by Judith inhabits the region of F and C. But the symbolism is made ambiguous. For example, the C major of the fifth door is Bluebeard's pretence at normality, while Judith sees the shadow of blood on it (F♯). Bluebeard's first note is F♯; Judith's is F, but the wives are in C minor, though now belonging exclusively to his world. Bluebeard's last two notes are F♯ and C, and the last orchestral note C♯. The same ambiguity is constantly present in the harmony, which achieves psychological depth by mixing elements rather than segregating them.

RECORDINGS   1. Sass, Kováts, LPO, Solti, Decca, 1979: idiomatic and above all superbly played; includes prologue; 2. Marton, Ramey, Hungarian State SO, Fischer, CBS/Hungaroton, 1987: the most modern recording, brilliantly sung; 3. Troyanos, Nimsgern, BBC SO, Boulez, CBS, 1976: perhaps all-round best sung of all the modern versions, but less intense than 1 and 2, and sometimes slow
EDITIONS   f.s., Universal, 1925; rev. edn, 1963; v.s., Universal, 1921

BIBLIOGRAPHY   Paul Griffiths, *Bartók*, Dent (Master Musicians Series), 1984; G. Kroó, *A Guide to Bartók*, Corvina, 1974; H. Stevens, *The Life and Music of Béla Bartók*, OUP, 1953; rev. edn, 1964

S.W.

WILLIAM BATES

b ?1726, ?London; *d* ?1779, ?London

Bates is a puzzle: no secure biographical details have been established. Roger Fiske writes of his *Pharnaces* that its 'merits are considerable . . . the most competently written and the most inventive of the three Drury Lane "English Operas".' But of his successful ballad opera, *The Jovial Crew*, composed in the ensuing year, Fiske remarks that 'Bates had not yet learned how to write instrumental music.' The popularity of his pleasure-garden songs shows that his facile talent was much appreciated. His instrumental music after 1765 shows that he had a real, if unrealized, ability.

Surviving operatic works: *The Jovial Crew, or The Merry Beggars*, 1760, rev. as *The Ladies' Frolick* in coll. with T. A. Arne, 1770; *Pharnaces*, 1765; *Flora, or Hob in the Well*, 1770; *The Theatrical Candidates*, 1775
BIBLIOGRAPHY   Roger Fiske, *English Theatre Music in the Eighteenth Century*, OUP, 1973; 2nd edn, 1986

R.Lu.

ALISON BAULD

Alison Margaret Bauld; *b* 7 May 1944, Sydney, Australia

The high proportion of music-theatre works in Bauld's output reflects her early training as an actor. After studying at the National Institute of Dramatic Art in Sydney, she performed in radio, television and live theatre. She then studied music at the University of Sydney, and in England with Hans Keller and Elisabeth Lutyens. Studies at the University of York led to the performance of her first chamber opera, *In a Dead Brown Land*, which has also been performed in Australia in a double-bill with another music-theatre work, *Exiles*. Her works include monodramas (many premiered by Jane Manning), a choral fantasy, chamber and larger-scale operas. *Nell* was premiered at the London International Opera Festival in 1988.

A strong concern for creating works that communicate has led Alison Bauld to include elements of speech, mime and dance in her music-theatre works, alongside song and episodes for the small instrumental ensembles she favours.

Operatic works: *In a Dead Brown Land*, 1973; *Exiles*, 1975; *Once Upon a Time*, 1986; *Nell*, 1988

A.I.G.

GILBERT BÉCAUD

François Silly; *b* 24 October 1927, Toulon, France

Best known as a popular singer in the French *chansonnier* manner, Bécaud has written a large number of his own songs, of which at least one ('Et maintenant') was a commercial hit (as 'What now, my love?' in English-speaking countries), and another, 'Je t'ai dans la peau', was sung by Edith Piaf. He is also the author of shows, film scores, and a single opera, *L'opéra d'Aran* (1962), written, he said at the time, 'for the man in the street who dances the twist and has never been to the Opéra'. The libretto, based by Jacques Emmanuel on an original script for a film by Robert Flaherty, tells of an Italian seaman washed up on an Irish island who falls for a local girl abandoned by her Irish lover. When the Irishman returns the girl is blinded in a fight. But the Italian remains true to her, and they sail away together. Despite, or perhaps because of, its direct, uncomplicated style, the work enjoyed a *succès fou*, ran for three months in Paris and was later revived and recorded (Pathé, 1972). Doubtless Bécaud's notoriety ensured this in any case.

BIBLIOGRAPHY   Elliott Stein, review in *Opera*, vol. 14 (1963), pp. 103–6

S.W.

DAVID BEDFORD
David Vickerman Bedford; *b* 4 August 1937, London

Bedford studied at the Royal Academy of Music with Lennox Berkeley (1958–61), and with Nono in Venice. He also worked in the electronic studio of RAI, Milan. His music, though tonal, makes use of aleatoric techniques and unconventional instruments. His operas – all written for young people – reflect his wide experience in both popular and educational music. *The Rime of the Ancient Mariner* was followed by the 'Baldur' trilogy, written for Gordonstoun School. Based on the Norse Elder and Prose Eddas, it comprises *The Death of Baldur* (1980), *The Ragnarok* (1983) and *Fridiof's Saga* (1981) and contains characters familiar from Wagner's *Ring*. In 1988 he wrote *The Return of Odysseus* for W11 Children's Opera.

The Rime of the Ancient Mariner
Opera for young people in one act (55m)
Libretto adapted by the composer from Samuel Taylor Coleridge's poem (1798)
PREMIERE   14 February 1979, Queen Elizabeth Hall, London

Bedford's first opera has also been his most successful, combining elements of popular and ballad music. The overture incorporates a *basse* dance by the 16th-century composer Tylman Susato, which recurs at points throughout the opera. A large cast is called for, including a chorus of sailors and wedding guests. Kazoos, warblers and a wordless choir depict the sound of the wind, and tuned wine glasses and bottles effectively evoke an arctic seascape. There are four set-piece sea shanties, two of which are heard simultaneously at the work's apotheosis.

EDITION   v.s., Universal, 1979

BIBLIOGRAPHY   Hugo Cole, 'David Bedford', in *Grove*, Macmillan, 1981

M.A.

JACK BEESON
Jack Hamilton Beeson; *b* 15 July 1921, Muncie, Indiana, US

Beeson has continued the tradition of Douglas Moore in writing accessible operas on American subjects. He studied at the Eastman School and, most unusually, had some private lessons with Bartók in the last year of his life, 1944–5. From then onwards Beeson taught at Columbia University and became MacDowell Professor there in 1967.

Beeson's first opera, *Jonah*, was not produced but *Hello, Out There* was staged and recorded. *The Sweet Bye and Bye* is replete with marches, hymns and dances, but it was *Lizzie Borden* – a thriller in which the heroine is accused of murdering her father and his second wife but finally acquitted – which brought Beeson his greatest acclaim. Virgil Thomson found 'unquestionably an operatic gift, a sense of the stage, and some expressivity in the vocal line'. Eschewing contemporary trends, Beeson's music is traditional in style. His aim, nevertheless, is to redress the stagnation and atavistic behaviour he sees in most American opera houses, providing accessible and enjoyable new works.

Operatic works: *Jonah*, (1950); *Hello, Out There*, 1954 (RECORDING Desto, 1950s); *The Sweet Bye and Bye*, 1957 (RECORDING Desto, c. 1972); *Lizzie Borden*, 1965 (RECORDING Desto, 1966); *My Heart's in the Highlands*, 1969; *Captain Jinks of the Horse Marines*, 1975 (RECORDING Desto, 1970s); *Dr Heidegger's Fountain of Youth*, 1978 (RECORDING CRI, 1978)

P.D.

LUDWIG VAN BEETHOVEN
b 16 December 1770, Bonn; *d* 26 March 1827, Vienna

Amid the abundance and supreme self-confidence of Beethoven's *oeuvre*, his solitary opera cuts a strangely isolated and equivocal figure. In large-scale instrumental forms, Beethoven wrote prolifically and with a mastery surpassed by none. Yet he achieved only one opera – and this not from any lack of interest in writing for the theatre. (Music for the stage forms a surprisingly large part of his output – *Egmont* and the *Prometheus* ballet music are only the most obvious examples – and at intervals throughout his career we find him searching for a congenial opera libretto.) Moreover, that one opera took more than ten years to reach its final shape and went through three separate versions and no fewer than four overtures. Compared with the speed and assurance with which he wrote the 'Eroica' Symphony, the Violin Concerto, the Razumovsky quartets, this degree of uncertainty suggests a clear distinction between a composer in his element in the symphonic medium and out of it in the operatic one.

So the argument frequently goes. *Fidelio* has regularly fallen foul of academic commentators. It is as if the work's detractors needed to free themselves of the burden of Beethoven's greatness by finding some field of composition in which he was not a master but could, on the contrary, be criticized and even patronized with impunity. Yet looked at without prejudice (including the prejudice against opera with spoken dialogue), *Fidelio* in its final form is as characteristic and as powerfully wrought as anything Beethoven wrote. It took him longer to get right, not only because to begin with he lacked experience of the operatic medium but also because the subject – the unjustly imprisoned man, the fearless, dedicated woman – moved him too much and struck such resounding chords in the depth of his being. But he got it right in the end.

Fidelio, oder Die eheliche Liebe

Fidelio, or Married Love
Opera in two acts (19 scenes), Op. 72 (2h 15m)
Libretto by Joseph Sonnleithner and Georg Friedrich Treitschke, after Jean Nicolas Bouilly's libretto *Léonore ou L'amour conjugal* for Pierre Gaveaux (1789)
Composed 1804–5, rev. 1806 and 1814
PREMIERES original three act version: 20 November 1805, Theater an der Wien, Vienna; first rev. version, in two acts: 29 March 1806, Theater an der Wien; second rev. version: 23 May 1814, Kärntnertortheater, Vienna; UK: 18 May 1832, King's Theatre, Haymarket, London; US: 9 September 1839, Park Theater, New York
CAST Leonore (Fidelio) *s*, Florestan *t*, Rocco *b*, Marzelline *s*, Jaquino *t*, Don Pizarro *bar*, Don Fernando *b-bar*, first prisoner *t*, second prisoner *bar*; *satb* chorus of officers, soldiers, state prisoners, people
ORCHESTRATION picc, 2 fl, 2 ob, 2 cl, 2 bsn, dbsn, 4 hn, 2 tpt, 2 trbn, timp, str; offstage tpt

Vienna first heard the rescue operas of the French Revolution school in the spring of 1802. These opéras comiques – i.e. operas with spoken dialogue, of which Cherubini's *Lodoïska* and *Les deux journées* were the prime examples – startled the Viennese by their dramatic force, realism and topicality and, for the next few years, dominated the Viennese stage. They made a profound impression on Beethoven, whose orchestral style, not only in *Fidelio* but generally, shows clear signs of the influence of Cherubini's massive, driving tuttis, insistent rhythms, incisive accents and cross-accents, and strong dynamic contrasts. By early 1803 he had signed a contract with the Theater an der Wien.

For some reason it was for a work not after the current French model but on an ancient Roman subject, entitled *Vestas Feuer*, the libretto by Emanuel Schikaneder (perhaps Beethoven accepted it because of his admiration for *The Magic Flute*). He composed a couple of scenes – musical material from one of them was later used for the *Fidelio* duet 'O namenlose Freude!' – but by the end of 1803 he had abandoned it and turned to a French libretto by J. N. Bouilly (librettist of *Les deux journées*), which had been set a few years earlier by the French composer Pierre Gaveaux (and which both Paer and Mayr set at about the same time as Beethoven).

The plot was based on an actual event that had happened not long before in France during the Terror: a woman disguising herself as a man in order to free her husband from a gaol where he was being held as a political prisoner. The poet Joseph Sonnleithner made a German version, and Beethoven worked on it during 1804 and the first half of 1805. Composition coincided with his abortive love affair with Josephine von Brunswick, and there is little doubt that his longing for a woman who would commit herself unreservedly to him gave added intensity to his portrait of Leonore, just as his self-identification with the lonely, persecuted Florestan – immured in the darkness of his cell, as Beethoven felt himself imprisoned in his growing deafness – contributed to the extraordinary force and vividness of the dungeon scene.

Despite its many beauties the first version of *Fidelio* (usually known as *Leonore*, the title Beethoven wanted to give the work) was not a success when it was performed in November 1805. Vienna was occupied by Napoleon's army. Most of Beethoven's supporters were absent, having fled the city, and by the time they came back the opera had been taken off. But it was also felt that the work had failed because it was too long, in particular because the early scenes dragged. For the revival in March–April 1806 Beethoven was persuaded, by Stephan von Breuning and others, to make cuts, some of them quite drastic. In this form (in two acts instead of three) it was more successful, but Beethoven, in dispute with the management, withdrew his score after only two performances.

It was not heard again for eight years. (A Prague production planned for 1807 came to nothing. It was probably for this production that Beethoven wrote the overture known as *Leonore No. 1*.) In 1814 when his fame (thanks to the enormously popular orchestral extravaganza *Wellington's Victory*) was at its height in Vienna, the Kärntnertortheater asked permission to revive *Fidelio*. He agreed, but insisted on a thorough revision. This time the opera was a triumphant success. The remodelling of the libretto was carried out by G. F. Treitschke, the theatre's stage manager and resident poet, in close collaboration with the composer. Treitschke removed several numbers from Act I and provided texts for a new final scene for the act, a new recitative ('Abscheulicher!') before the great aria 'Komm, Hoffnung' in which Leonore reasserts her faith in her heroic mission, a new final section for Florestan's scena, and a rewritten opening to the final scene of the opera (which was moved to the castle parade ground). It is to this revision that we owe two of the most exalted passages in the work: the farewell to the light of day sung by the prisoners as they return to their cells at the end of Act I (replacing the blustering, conventional original number) and Florestan's radiant vision of his wife.

In addition, the whole score was subjected to minute overhaul. *Fidelio* is a shorter opera than *Leonore*, not only because there are fewer numbers but because of a general tightening up. The excessive repetitions that marred the original score, especially in the domestic scenes of Act I, were stripped away. (Its prolixity is one reason why *Leonore*, though sometimes revived, cannot seriously be regarded as a valid alternative to *Fidelio*.) But the changes go deeper than simple abbreviation. Again and again Beethoven altered the declamation or the rhythmic emphasis, so that the voice part made its point more tellingly and the rhythms became more varied and vital. To take only the most striking example, the dungeon quartet was transformed; though most alterations may be small, the cumulative effect is crucial. Already a very powerful piece of dramatic music in 1805, it becomes overwhelming in its final form.

A few changes made in 1806 were retained; but some of the most extreme were rejected. In particular, both the dungeon trio and the great ensemble of thanksgiving in the final scene were reshaped, ending up the same length as in the hurriedly cut version of 1806 but now perfectly formed, no longer mutilated.

The work's key structure was also changed. In *Leonore* C major, the key of freedom and salvation, was established at the outset as the home key; in *Fidelio* it emerges gradually. The new overture (*Fidelio*) is in E (the key of Leonore's aria). During the first act B♭, the prison key, becomes increasingly prominent, and the second act begins in its dominant minor, F. C is touched on from time to time, but as a foreign key, though often at moments of transcendent meaning (the sacrament of bread in the dungeon trio, Leonore's holy resolve to save the prisoner even if he is not her husband). It is only in the final scene that its triumph is finally achieved. This new evolutionary treatment of tonality is an aspect of the more flexible and dramatic conception of opera that Beethoven had acquired by the time he revised his score.

Even more important, he reduced the weight of his orchestration. The original version is much more thickly scored, less epic in sound, more lyrical, more Romantic. For example, in *Leonore* the introduction to the dungeon scene makes an almost Wagnerian effect. Beethoven's revision, which also shortened it by nine bars, altered its character profoundly. The texture was thinned out: string tremolos were confined to four bars, the trombones were removed altogether. So were the trumpets; they were now kept back until the quartet, to blaze forth the more brilliantly at the moment when the prisoner defies his assassin. Horns and timpani were left on their own to evoke a far more awesome sense of cold, vaulted darkness; in this austerer texture, too, the melodic cries in octave doublings on the woodwind which sound from the surrounding gloom stand out more sharply. This leaner, starker but also more glowing sonority is characteristic of the final version as a whole; it is true to the original idea behind the opera as the luxuriance of 1805 was not. The grief and passion and heroism of the drama, the sense of feelings stretched almost to breaking point, the central concept of human suffering in the context of divine providence, achieved their destined sound in 1814.

SYNOPSIS

Florestan, who disappeared two years ago and is believed dead, has been incarcerated secretly by his

Wilhelmine Schröder-Devrient as Leonore in Fidelio *(Dresden, 1822)*

political enemy Don Pizarro. Florestan's wife, Leonore, in search of him, disguises herself as a young man and, under the name Fidelio, enters the service of the prison where Pizarro is governor.

Act I The prison courtyard on a fine spring morning. Marzelline, the gaoler's daughter, is ironing. Jaquino the turnkey, in the intervals of dealing with packages arriving at the postern gate, tries to get her to name a day for their wedding, but she rebuffs him ('Jetzt, Schätzchen, jetzt sind wir allein'). She used to like Jaquino, but everything has changed; now her dream is of married bliss with Fidelio ('O wär ich schon mit dir vereint'). Rocco, the gaoler, enters, followed by Fidelio (Leonore) who is carrying heavy chains from the blacksmith. Rocco praises Fidelio's zeal, and hints broadly that he understands the reason for it. They all reflect on what this new turn of events means for them ('Mir ist so wunderbar'). Rocco offers Fidelio his daughter's hand, but points out that a sound marriage depends as much on money as on love ('Hat man nicht auch Gold beineben'). Leonore begs Rocco, as a mark of trust, to let her help him in the cells. Rocco agrees to ask the governor, though there is one cell, occupied by a prisoner on starvation rations, where he will never be allowed to take Fidelio. Pizarro arrives with an armed escort. One of the letters he is given warns him that the Minister, Don Fernando, has heard rumours of injustice and is coming to inspect the gaol. Pizarro decides to kill Florestan ('Ha! welch' ein Augenblick!'). He posts a trumpeter on the tower overlooking the road from Seville, and orders Rocco to prepare the unnamed prisoner's grave. Leonore overhears their conversation. Appalled by Pizarro's inhuman cruelty, she reaffirms her faith in the power of love ('Abscheulicher! . . . Komm, Hoffnung'). Leonore persuades Rocco to let the prisoners out into the garden. With Jaquino she unlocks the cell doors, and the prisoners emerge wonderingly into the light of day ('O welche Lust!'). Rocco returns with the news that Fidelio is to be allowed to help dig the grave of the mysterious prisoner. Leonore weeps at the thought that it may be her husband's, but convinces Rocco that it is her duty to go with him. Pizarro, discovering that the prisoners have been let out, angrily orders them back, and they return to their cells ('Leb' wohl, du warmes Sonnenlicht').

Act II   A deep dungeon. Florestan sits in darkness lit by a small lamp; he is chained to a stone, but his spirit is unbroken. Half delirious with hunger, he has a vision of an angel in the likeness of Leonore, surrounded by bright light and leading him to freedom ('Gott! welch' Dunkel hier! . . . In des Lebens Frühlingstagen'). He rises to follow it but the chain drags him back and he collapses unconscious. Rocco and Leonore enter the dungeon and, while the prisoner sleeps (his face invisible), clear the opening of a disused cistern. Leonore resolves to save the man whoever he is. When Florestan wakes, she recognizes him. Rocco gives him a little wine, and is persuaded by Leonore to overlook orders and let her give him some bread ('Euch werde Lohn'). At a signal from Rocco, Pizarro appears. He is about to stab Florestan when Leonore springs forward and shields him, crying 'Töt' erst sein Weib!' ('First kill his wife!'). She draws a pistol. At that moment, far above, a trumpet sounds. It sounds a second time, louder, as Jaquino calls out from the top of the steps that the Minister has arrived. Alone, Leonore and Florestan, reunited, thank God for their deliverance ('O namenlose Freude!'). The parade ground of the fortress. The Minister addresses the people: he has come to free them from tyranny. Pizarro is taken away by guards. Leonore unlocks Florestan's chains and all give thanks to God who did not forsake them ('O Gott! welch' ein Augenblick!'). Led by Florestan, the released prisoners and the people join in a hymn of praise to the noble woman who saved her husband's life ('Wer ein holdes Weib errungen').

The mixture of domestic comedy and heroic melodrama, which Beethoven took from Cherubini and which remains central to the work even in the shortened final version, has worried many commentators. But it is fundamental to the whole conception, which is that love, devotion, courage, faith are not exclusively 'operatic' qualities, to be presented only in lofty romantic settings, but human attributes that may flower in the most humdrum surroundings. It is right that *Fidelio* should begin with Marzelline ironing, that Leonore's first words – spoken, not sung – should concern the cost of repairs carried out by the blacksmith, and that we learn of her perilous quest only by degrees. The process by which the singspiel atmosphere of the early scenes is gradually left behind and the musical language deepens and intensifies in preparation for the great dungeon scene – a process that culminates in the mysterious final bars of Act I – is the work of a master of music drama, however heterodox.

For the same reasons the two huge *Leonore* overtures of 1805 (*No. 2*) and 1806 (*No. 3*), virtual symphonic poems that anticipate the heroic issues of the opera, make way for a much shorter piece, a true prelude to the action – to quote Tovey, 'dramatic,

brilliant, terse, and with an indication of some formidable force in the background'. The practice of playing the *Leonore No. 3* overture between the dungeon scene and the finale – a practice, still not uncommon, that goes back at least to the middle of the 19th century and therefore antedates Mahler, who is often said to have originated it – is wrong on at least two counts. It imposes an alien sound on *Fidelio* – the heavier 1805–6 orchestration that Beethoven deliberately changed in 1814 – and it destroys the effect that is created by going straight from the sublimities of the Leonore–Florestan duet to the festive, breezy march that begins the finale.

To bring us back to earth again in the final scene of the opera, after the torrential force of the dungeon quartet and the incandescence of the ensuing duet, is a stroke of the highest realism. But realism cannot have the last word. The opera ends in a mighty hymn to liberty and the noble, all-enduring woman, sung by the whole company, soloists and chorus, in a blazing C major that dissolves the personal drama into a vision of universal love. This conclusion has been criticized as being more cantata than opera. But *Fidelio* could not end in any other way. That has been the message of the work from the moment that Leonore's aria was followed immediately by the prisoners' chorus. The final progression from the particular to the universal is the natural and logical conclusion. It brings to flower the seed of selfless love planted in the darkness of the dungeon (and in the key of C major) at the most apparently hopeless point of Leonore's quest, as she digs the grave of the man who may be her husband – the discovery that ultimately it does not matter who he is: even if he is not Florestan and her journey has been in vain, 'I will loose your chains whoever you are, unhappy man, by God I will save you and set you free.'

RECORDINGS   1. *Leonore* (1805): Moser, Donath, Büchner, Cassilly, Adam, Ridderbusch, Polster, Leipzig Radio Ch, Dresden Staatskapelle, Blomstedt, EMI, 1977: worthy reading of first version; 2. Ludwig, Hallstein, Unger, Vickers, Berry, Frick, Crass, Philharmonia Ch and O, Klemperer, EMI, 1962: classic version, grandly conducted, movingly sung; 3. Janowitz, Popp, Dallapozza, Kollo, Fischer-Dieskau, Jungwirth, Sotin, Vienna State Opera Ch, Vienna PO, Bernstein, DG, 1978: a more subjective reading than Klemperer's, vivid, free and exciting [A.B.]

EDITIONS   *Leonore*: f.s., Willy Hess (ed.), supplement to complete works, vols xi and xii, Breitkopf und Härtel, 1967; v.s., Breitkopf und Härtel, 1905; 2nd version: f.s., Willy Hess (ed.), supplement to complete works, vol. xiii, Breitkopf und Härtel, 1970; v.s., Breitkopf und Härtel, [1810]; *Fidelio*: f.s.s., complete works, vol. xxvi (series 20, no. 206), Breitkopf und Härtel, [1865]; *rp*, Kalmus, [1973]; *rp*, Dover, 1984; v.s.s., Artaria, 1814; Peters, 1888; study s., Eulenberg, [1960]

BIBLIOGRAPHY   David Cairns, '*Fidelio*' in *Responses*, Secker and Warburg, 1973; *rp*, Da Capo, 1980, pp. [3]–21; Winton Dean, 'Beethoven and Opera' in Denis Arnold and Nigel Fortune (eds), *The Beethoven Companion*, Faber, 1971, pp. 331–86; Willy Hess, *Das Fidelio-Buch*, Amadeus, 1986; Thomas Love Peacock, *Memoirs of Shelley and Other Essays and Reviews*, Howard Mills (ed.), Rupert Hart-Davis, 1970; Maynard Solomon, *Beethoven*, Cassell, 1977; Donald Francis

Tovey, 'Dungeon Scene from *Fidelio*' in *Essays in Musical Analysis*, vol. 5, OUP, 1937, pp.185–93

D.A.C.

VINCENZO BELLINI

Vincenzo Salvatore Carmelo Francesco Bellini;
b 3 November 1801, Catania, Sicily; *d* 23 September 1835,
Puteaux, Paris

Vincenzo Bellini, tempera portrait (c. 1825)

Together with Rossini, Donizetti and Verdi, Bellini is one of the four great figures of Italian Romantic opera whose work remains fundamental to the repertoire of all Italian and most international opera houses. Less prolific and less versatile than the other three, he nevertheless produced in the late 1820s a group of operas that were seminal in establishing in Italy a distinctively Romantic musical language; and in the masterpieces of the early 1830s – *La sonnambula* (1831), *Norma* (1831) and *I puritani* (1835) – he brought the art of *bel canto* opera to its apogee.

Bellini's early musical education was at the hands of his father Rosario and his grandfather Vincenzo Tobia, both professional musicians in Catania. In 1819, he was enrolled as a pupil at the Conservatorio di San Sebastiano in Naples, where, from 1822, the teaching of Nicola Zingarelli, the director, exerted a lasting influence. Zingarelli introduced Bellini to the best of the Neapolitan masters of the past, and to the instrumental music of Haydn and Mozart, but his shrewdest pedagogical stroke was to invite him to put away his contrapuntal studies and concentrate on refining his skills as a melodist, listening to the dictates of his heart, and striving to express them in pure and simple song. Zingarelli apparently felt it necessary to 'protect' his students from Rossini, whose music dominated the repertoire in the public theatres of the city, and it was only as a final-year student, in 1824, that Bellini first heard a Rossini opera (*Semiramide*). Nevertheless, relations between Bellini and Zingarelli remained exceptionally affectionate: the old maestro followed his young protégé's career with pride, and in due course was thanked in princely fashion with the dedication of *Norma*.

It was customary each year to give one of the outstanding students the experience of composing a short opera and staging it in the conservatory theatre. Bellini's début, *Adelson e Salvini*, came early in 1825, and was so successful that he was commissioned to compose a full-length opera (*Bianca e Gernando*) for the Teatro San Carlo the following year. The impresario there, Domenico Barbaja, was also involved in the running of La Scala in Milan. Inevitably therefore, Bellini's success in Naples led to his being invited to go north and compose his third opera, *Il pirata* (1827), for La Scala, to a libretto by Felice Romani, the most admired theatre poet of the age. The two men got along famously, and their partnership was to prove one of the most remarkable

in operatic history: all seven of the remaining operas Bellini composed in Italy had Romani libretti, and all but *Zaira* (1829) and *Beatrice di Tenda* (1833) triumphed gloriously. Their first works together, *Il pirata* and *La straniera* (1829), bizarre and violent in plot and set to music of matching emotional abandon, marked the beginning of full-blooded Romanticism in Italian opera. But tragedy in the most elevated Classical style also came within their range (*Norma*); and so did sentimental tenderness (*La sonnambula*).

Until the early months of 1833, Bellini had enjoyed a prodigiously successful Italian career, and by now his fame had spread throughout Europe and reached America. From an early date he could and did demand high fees for his operas, not simply out of greed, but because he was, for Italy, a new kind of composer, one who felt a need for a greater measure of independence than did most of his predecessors; he liked to work slowly, and was disinclined to assume the kind of official teaching or administrative posts they had virtually always filled. The fiasco of *Beatrice di Tenda* in March 1833 and the attendant breakdown of his partnership with Romani was a severe blow. At the same time his personal life was in a state of upheaval; a longstanding love affair with Giuditta Turina, having been discovered by her husband, had become a source of embarrassment and inconvenience. An invitation to visit London to help produce three of his operas was probably doubly welcome therefore. After a successful trip, he made no hasty return to Italy, but lingered in Paris, traditionally a Mecca for Italian composers.

Bellini's last opera, *I puritani*, was composed for the Théâtre-Italien. Like so many Italians before him, he found it enormously stimulating to compose for Paris: the scope of his work seemed to expand, its manner to become more urbane and cosmopolitan. During the composition he was often with Rossini, who, though he no longer held an official position at the Théâtre-Italien, remained the presiding genius of operatic life in Paris. A relationship that began, as far as Bellini was concerned, out of calculated self-interest developed into one of genuine mutual respect, and Bellini benefited much from the older composer's advice. But working on the opera showed him more clearly than ever how badly he needed a librettist of Romani's calibre, and in the last year of his life he made energetic attempts to re-establish a working relationship with his old comrade-in-arms. The success of *I puritani* gave Bellini a position in Parisian musical life 'second only to Rossini' (letter to Francesco Florimo, 21 September 1834); but there is no reason to doubt that, but for an untimely and wretched death from acute gastro-enteritis, complicated by an abscess of the liver, he would soon have returned to Italy.

Adelson e Salvini
Adelson and Salvini

Dramma semiserio in three acts; rev. version in two acts
Libretto by Andrea Leone Tottola, ?after Prospère Delamare's drama (?1803), or directly from Thomas-Marie de Baculard d'Arnaud's novel (1772); rev. libretto possibly by Felice Romani
Composed 1824–5; rev. probably 1826 and 1828
PREMIERES 12 or 13 February 1825, Teatrino del Conservatorio di S. Sebastiano, Naples (private); 6 November 1985, Teatro Metropolitan, Catania
CAST rev. version: Nelly *s*, Fanny *a*, Salvini *t*, Adelson *bar*, Struley *b*, Bonifacio *b comico*, *ms*, *b*; *tb* chorus of vassals and peasants

The opera, a setting of an old libretto first used by Fioravanti in 1816, was written for the students of the Naples Conservatorio di San Sebastiano (all roles were taken by male voices). The 1826/8 revision was made with a view to professional staging, but was never performed.

SYNOPSIS
Seventeenth-century Ireland. Salvini, a painter befriended by Lord Adelson, falls in love with Adelson's fiancée, Nelly. Her uncle Struley (a bitter enemy of Adelson outlawed from Ireland for some political offence) returns home in disguise, and plans to exploit Salvini's passion as a means to be revenged on Adelson; but Salvini sees through his treachery and foils him. The opera ends with Adelson marrying Nelly, while Salvini departs for his native Italy; after a year has elapsed he will return to marry his young pupil, Fanny.

In its original form the opera had spoken dialogue, not recitatives, and the part of the comic servant Bonifacio was in Neapolitan dialect. The influence of Rossini is pronounced in Bonifacio's scenes and, more generally, in the verve of much of the orchestral writing. But in the lyrical episodes Bellini's tone of voice is already distinctive: ecstatic, sensuous, and with an expressive directness that has often been associated with his sympathy for Sicilian and Neapolitan popular song. The romanza 'Dopo l'oscuro nembo' was masterly enough to be taken up essentially unchanged in *I Capuleti e i Montecchi* five years later.

EDITIONS rev. version only: v.ss. (without recitatives and with overture borrowed from *Il pirata*), Schonenberger, [1843–75]; Ricordi, [1903], and *rp*s
MANUSCRIPTS original version: Museo Belliniano, Catania; rev. version (fragments): Conservatorio di Musica S. Pietro a Majella, Naples; Accademia filarmonica, Bologna, and Bibliothèque Nationale, Paris

Bianca e Fernando
Bianca and Fernando

Melodramma serio in two acts (3h)
Libretto by Domenico Gilardoni, after Carlo Roti's drama *Bianca e Fernando alla tomba di Carlo IV, Duca di Agrigento* (1825); rev. libretto (1828) by Felice Romani
Composed 1825–6, rev. February–April 1828
PREMIERES 30 May 1826, Teatro San Carlo, Naples; rev. version: 7 April 1828, Teatro Carlo Felice, Genoa
CAST Bianca *s*, Fernando *t*, Carlo *b*, Filippo *b*, 2 *ms*, *t*, *b*
FULL ORCHESTRA and stage band

Adelson e Salvini created so favourable an impression that Bellini was commissioned to compose an opera for the great San Carlo theatre the following year. The proper title of the opera, changed by the censor to *Bianca e Gernando* out of respect for the late King Ferdinando, was restored only in 1828 when Bellini made a revised version for the inauguration of the new Carlo Felice theatre at Genoa.

SYNOPSIS
While his son Fernando is abroad, Carlo, Duke of Agrigento, is deposed and imprisoned by the usurper Filippo, who, the better to secure his position, gives it out that the duke is dead, and seeks the hand in marriage of his daughter Bianca. Eager to avenge his father, Fernando returns home in disguise; he wins his way into Filippo's confidences, and is entrusted with the task of murdering Carlo. Having persuaded Bianca that she must repulse Filippo's advances, Fernando takes her with him to Carlo's dungeon, where the three are joyfully reunited. Filippo's attempts at blackmail are unavailing, and the opera ends with general rejoicing.

Together with *Il pirata* and *La straniera*, the revised *Bianca e Fernando* was one of a group of operas through which, in the late 1820s, Bellini transformed the face of Italian opera. The excitement and perplexity they occasioned is nicely illustrated by the reaction of Adelaide Tosi, Bianca in the Genoa premiere, who at first dismissed her music as fit only for children to sing; at the same time the leader of the orchestra, Serra, found it 'full of philosophy', by which he meant that its very simplicity was a means of achieving a more deeply expressive relationship between poetry and music.

Two movements from the 1828 version, Bianca's *cabaletta* 'Contenta appien' and the chorus 'Tutti siam? Si, tutti uniti' – its orchestral accompaniment famously reminiscent of the opening of Beethoven's 'Moonlight' Sonata – recur in revised form in *Norma*.

RECORDING Hayashi, Savastano, Machí, Fissore, Michalopoulos, Turin Ch and SO of RAI, Ferro, MRF, 1976
EDITIONS v.ss.: original version, Girard, [1826]); rev. version, Ricordi, [1837], [1900], later edn and *rps*
MANUSCRIPT original version: Conservatorio Musica S. Pietro a Majella, Naples

Il pirata
The Pirate

Melodramma (opera seria) in two acts (2h 30m)
Libretto by Felice Romani, after the melodrama *Bertram, ou Le pirate* (1826) by Raimond (Isidore J. S. Taylor), itself a translation of Charles Robert Maturin's drama *Bertram, or The Castle of Saint Aldobrand* (1816)
Composed April and May–October 1827
PREMIERES 27 October 1827, La Scala, Milan; UK: 17 April 1830, His Majesty's Theatre, London; US: 5 December 1832, Richmond Hill Theater, New York
CAST Ernesto *b*, Imogene *s*, Gualtiero *t*, *s*, *t*, *b*; *satb* chorus of fisherfolk, pirates, courtiers, ladies and maidens
FULL ORCHESTRA and stage band

The first of seven operas composed by Bellini in collaboration with Felice Romani, *Il pirata* has good claim to be regarded as the earliest full-bloodedly Romantic opera to appear in Italy. It was by now clear that Bellini's was the most individual voice among the post-Rossinian generation of composers, and the huge success enjoyed by *Il pirata* laid the foundation for his international fame. The part of Gualtiero was written for Giovanni Battista Rubini who, like many of the great singers of the period, was at first disconcerted by the apparent simplicity of Bellini's music, but soon became a passionate admirer and one of the composer's most trusted collaborators.

SYNOPSIS
Thirteenth-century Sicily. Gualtiero, Count of Montaldo, and Ernesto, Duke of Caldora, both love Imogene, but are supporters of rival factions in the power struggle for the Sicilian throne between Manfred and Charles of Anjou. After the death of Manfred and the Angevin victory, Gualtiero is driven into exile, where he resorts to a life of piracy, while Ernesto blackmails Imogene into marrying him by threatening the life of her father – like Gualtiero a supporter of Manfred.

Act I After some years of buccaneering, Gualtiero's ships are pursued by a punitive expedition led by Ernesto; they are scattered and, during a storm, shipwrecked on the coast near Ernesto's castle. In accordance with Caldoran custom Imogene offers hospitality to the shipwrecked mariners; she recognizes Gualtiero.

Act II Though long absence has done nothing to lessen their love, the pirate chieftain is unable to persuade Imogene to abandon her lawful husband

and the child she has borne him. Discovered by Ernesto, Gualtiero kills him in a duel and then surrenders himself. Imogene despairs. (In the libretto there follows a final scene which Bellini did set, but cut again, apparently before it was performed: Gualtiero's pirate band attempts to rescue him; but he refuses to rejoin them and kills himself.)

Giovanni Battista Rubini as Gualtieri, his wife Adele Comelli as Imogene, in Il pirata, *Act I, Scene 6 (Vienna, 1828)*

Contemporaries particularly admired the way in which Bellini resisted the temptation to emulate Rossini's brilliant style, cultivating instead a type of melody that was sometimes so simple, and followed the inflexions of the text so closely, that it seemed almost to 'speak'. The coloratura that Rossini had scattered so prodigally is now reserved for specific points of expression, such as the lacerating despair of Imogene's final *cabaletta* ('O sole! ti vela'). Bellini's simpler melodic style is matched by a fondness for symmetrically balanced aria forms, with a clearly audible reprise at the point of climax; the pattern he preferred in *Il pirata* (AA'BA') remained the favourite of Italian composers until the 1850s. Bellini's and Romani's genius for extracting dramatic capital from the theatrical conventions within which they worked is clearest in their handling of the chorus, which is never used merely decoratively: it serves either as a means of creating dramatic atmosphere (the opening storm scene has often been seen as a precursor of that in Verdi's *Otello*), or to make explicit the dramatic context within which the soloists find themselves. It is a remarkable fact that all the arias involve the chorus.

RECORDING Caballé, Martí, Cappuccilli, Raimondi, Rome Ch and O of Italian Radio, Gavazzeni, HMV, 1971
EDITIONS facsimile of original autograph manuscript (2 vols) in Philip Gosset (ed.), *Early Romantic Opera*, Garland, 1983; v.s., Ricordi, [1827–8], [*c*. 1905], later edn and *rps*

La straniera

The Stranger

Melodramma in two acts (3h)

Libretto by Felice Romani, after Charles-Victor Prévost d'Arlincourt's novel *L'étrangère* (1825)

Composed September 1828–February 1829

PREMIERES 14 February 1829, La Scala, Milan; UK: 23 June 1832, King's Theatre, London; US: 10 November 1834, Italian Opera House, New York

CAST Alaide (*la straniera*) *s*, Isoletta *ms*, Arturo, Count of Ravenstel *t*, Baron Valdeburgo *bar*, *t*, 2 *b*; *satb* chorus of ladies, knights, fishermen, gondoliers, monks, hunters, guards and vassals

FULL ORCHESTRA and stage band

Bellini's first experience of Milan audiences had persuaded him that nothing suited the city so well as originality and boldness. *La straniera*, a setting of a libretto he rightly described as 'abounding in novel situations', accordingly became his most radically Romantic opera, demanding new types of skill from the performers. 'In this opera it is not just a matter of singing,' wrote Romani. 'It is a matter of passion, of soul, of imagination: here is love in all its transports, sorrow with all its sighs, disaster in all its pallor.' Unable to have Rubini – whose singing had contributed so much to the success of *Il pirata* – in his cast, Bellini wrote the tenor part for the young Domenico Reina; towards the end of the year he revised it for a revival in Naples in which Rubini was to sing, but it enjoyed little success in this form.

SYNOPSIS

The action is set in Brittany, the castle of Montolino and its vicinity, in *c.* 1300. Agnese, Queen of France (disguised as Alaide), has been banished to Brittany under the guardianship of her brother Leopoldo (disguised as Valdeburgo), because of the Pope's insistence that the king honour an earlier marriage contract.

Act I Alaide has escaped, and lives in solitude on the shores of Lake Montolino as *la straniera*, a mysterious recluse, suspected of witchcraft by the local people. But Arturo, shortly to be married to Isoletta, daughter of the Lord of Montolino, has fallen in love with her. Witnessing a secret meeting between Alaide and Valdeburgo, he challenges the latter to a duel. Valdeburgo slips, apparently drowning, and Alaide is accused of his murder.

Act II Arturo is prepared to take the blame for the death of Valdeburgo, who however now appears. On the death of the new queen, Alaide/Agnese is summoned back to take her place as rightful wife of the King of France, but not before Arturo, maddened by his passion and the revelation of Alaide's true identity, has stabbed himself to death in the middle of his own wedding to Isoletta.

The premiere of *La straniera*, hugely successful with the public, prompted much debate over the dilemma posed by one critic of the time: 'We do not know whether we should describe the style he has adopted as sung declamation or declamatory song.' For while the melodies in aria and ensemble are even plainer than in *Il pirata*, the recitatives are now full of passages of expressive *cantabile* singing. As it happened, the contrast with Rossini's florid song was highlighted at the premiere, since the new opera had been preceded by a run of Rossini performances.

The number of arias is small in relation to the ensembles: Arturo himself – and Bellini explained this in terms of the violent instability of his character – has no aria at all. But Valdeburgo's music, composed for Antonio Tamburini, introduces a warmly *cantabile* quality into Bellini's writing for the baritone voice that had no precedent in Italian opera. The imaginative handling of the chorus and the frequent boldness of modulation testify to Bellini's readiness to explore sonority, texture and colour as means of dramatic expression.

RECORDINGS 1. Caballé, Casoni, Zambon, Sardinero, American Opera Society Ch and O, Guadagno, MRF, 1969; 2. Scotto, Zillo, Cioni, Campi, Ch and O of Teatro Massimo, Palermo, Sanzogno, Hunt, 1968: both sets were recorded live: choice depends on preference for Caballé or Scotto. [A.B.]

EDITIONS facsimile of a contemporary manuscript (2 vols) in Philip Gosset (ed.), *Early Romantic Opera*, Garland, 1982; v.s., Ricordi, [1829], [*c.* 1905], later edn and *rp*s

Zaira

Tragedia lirica (opera seria) in two acts (3h)

Libretto by Felice Romani, after Voltaire's tragedy *Zaïre* (1732)

Composed March–May 1829

PREMIERES 16 May 1829, Nuovo Teatro Ducale, Parma

The remarkable impact the young Bellini had made on his contemporaries is demonstrated by the fact that in *Zaira* he was already for the second time composing an opera for the inauguration of a new theatre in one of Italy's leading operatic centres. But, despite an outstanding cast, the Parma premiere of *Zaira* was very coolly received; it was the first serious setback of a hitherto brilliant career. Parma audiences were particularly fervent in their admiration of Rossini, and were not favourably disposed towards a young innovator who, some tactless remarks by Romani in the printed libretto seemed to imply, had written his new opera in undue haste.

SYNOPSIS

Zaira, daughter of Lusignano, the last French King of Jerusalem, is enslaved in childhood by the Turkish sultan Orosmane, brought up a Muslim, falls in love with Orosmane, and is about to marry him. When her father and her brother Nerestano are discovered among Orosmane's prisoners and persuade Zaira to return to the Christian faith, catastrophe is precipitated. The opera ends with the deaths of Zaira and Orosmane.

Zaira had only eight performances at Parma; save for one revival in Florence in 1836, it was not heard again until 1975, nor was it ever published. The composer reused virtually all its music in later operas, chiefly *I Capuleti e i Montecchi*.

RECORDING Scotto, Nave, Lamberti, Roni, Rinaudo, Ch and O of Teatro Massimo Bellini, Catania, Belardinelli, Unique Opera, 1976
MANUSCRIPT Conservatorio di Musica S. Pietro a Majella, Naples

I Capuleti e i Montecchi
The Capulets and the Montagues
Tragedia lirica in two acts (four parts) (2h 15m)
Libretto by Felice Romani (a reworking of his libretto, *Giulietta e Romeo*, written for Vaccai in 1825), after Matteo Bandello's 16th-century novella *Giulietta e Romeo* and a play of the same name by Luigi Sceola (1818)
Composed January–March 1830
PREMIERES 11 March 1830, La Fenice, Venice; UK: 20 July 1833, King's Theatre, London; US: 4 April 1837, St Charles Theater, New Orleans
CAST Capellio *b*, Giulietta *s*, Romeo *ms*, Tebaldo *t*, Lorenzo *bar* or *b*; *satb* chorus of Capulets, Montagues, maidens, soldiers, squires
FULL ORCHESTRA and stage band

At the end of 1829, while Bellini was in Venice to supervise a revival of *Il pirata*, Giovanni Pacini withdrew from a contract to write an opera for the same 1829–30 Carnival season. The impresario Lanari persuaded Bellini to come to his rescue by composing a new opera in considerable haste – something he was normally most reluctant to do. The task proved possible partly because Romani was able quickly to rework to Bellini's satisfaction a libretto originally set by Nicola Vaccai four years earlier, and partly because, having written off *Zaira*, Bellini had a store of good music waiting to find a more congenial dramatic home. Eight movements are based on material from the ill-fated Parma opera, and a further one is a revision of 'Dopo l'oscuro nembo' from *Adelson e Salvini*. The opera was ecstatically received: in Bellini's own words, '*Zaira* was revenged in *I Capuleti e i Montecchi*.' At a revival in Paris in 1832, Maria Malibran, apparently at Rossini's suggestion, replaced the final scene of the opera with the corresponding scene from Vaccai's setting, a piece of high-handedness that was long imitated. Despite its theme, Bellini's opera is only tenuously linked to Shakespeare: Romani made some use of Jean-François Ducis's then fashionable French adaptation of Shakespeare, but his primary sources were Bandello's novella and Sceola's play.

SYNOPSIS
Act I Thirteenth-century Verona. As warfare threatens again between Guelphs and Ghibellines, Capellio, chief of the Capulets, scorns the offer of a pact, to be sealed by the marriage of his daughter Giulietta with Romeo, and agrees that her wedding with Tebaldo should take place without delay. Having failed to persuade Giulietta to elope with him, Romeo and his supporters enter the city in disguise and interrupt the festivities. Romeo reveals himself as Tebaldo's rival.
Act II Giulietta is persuaded by the family doctor Lorenzo that her only chance of escaping marriage with Tebaldo is to take a sleeping draught so powerful that she will be taken for dead; when she revives in the family burial vault, he and Romeo will

be waiting for her. But Lorenzo's plan goes wrong: he himself is arrested, and Romeo, believing Giulietta to be really dead, comes to her tomb and takes poison. She awakes as he is dying, and when Capellio and Lorenzo rush in in a desperate bid to avert catastrophe they find her, broken-hearted and lifeless, lying on Romeo's body.

Though so much of *I Capuleti e i Montecchi* consists of 'parody' (the reworking of pre-existent music to fit a new text and a new dramatic context) – and parody was doubtless a labour-saving device – Bellini took infinite trouble over the procedure, scrupulously reassessing every detail of the original in the light of its new purpose. After the 'philosophical' austerity of *Il pirata* and *La straniera*, Bellini's lyricism begins to relax and smile a little once more: the swaying 9/8 and 12/8 rhythms, the charming ornamental flourishes at cadences, the many dulcet passages where voices and instruments move in parallel thirds, are all characteristic of his full maturity. The orchestration was much admired by contemporary critics: a striking feature is the several instrumental preludes built around a 'song-without-words' type of instrumental solo. The *stretto* of the Act I finale ('Se ogni speme è a noi rapita'), where the lovers sing a long ecstatic *cantabile* melody in unison is one of the earliest and most eloquent examples of what was soon to become a hackneyed device; when Berlioz heard a performance of the opera in Florence in 1831 he was, despite his impatience with what he mistakenly took to be a travesty of his beloved Shakespeare, bowled over by the 'wonderful *élan* and intensity' of this passage. Wagner, for whom the performance of Wilhelmine Schröder-Devrient as Romeo had been one of the great artistic experiences of his youth, acknowledged the influence of Bellini's opera on the second act of *Tristan und Isolde*.

RECORDINGS 1. Gruberova, Baltsa, Raffanti, Howell, Tomlinson, Covent Garden Ch and O, Muti, HMV, 1985; 2. Ricciarelli, Montague, Rafforti, Lippi, Salvadori, Ch and O of La Fenice, Campanella, Nuova Era, 1991: these are both live performances, nicely complementing each other's virtues [A.B.]
EDITIONS facsimile of original autograph manuscript in Philip Gosset (ed.), *Early Romantic Opera*, Garland, 1981; v.s., Ricordi, [1831], rev. edn and *rps*

La sonnambula
The Sleepwalker
Melodramma in two acts (3h)
Libretto by Felice Romani, after Scribe's scenario for Jean-Pierre Aumer's ballet *La somnambule, ou L'arrivée d'un nouveau seigneur* (1827) (music by Ferdinand Hérold)
Composed January–March 1831
PREMIERES 6 March 1831, Teatro Carcano, Milan; UK: 28 July 1831, King's Theatre, London; US: 13 November 1835, Park Theater, New York
CAST Count Rodolfo *b*, Teresa *ms*, Amina *s*, Elvino *t*, Lisa *s*, Alessio *b*, Notary *t*; *satb* chorus of peasants
ORCHESTRATION picc, 2 fl, 2 ob, 2 cl, 2 bsn, 4 hn, 2 tpt, 3 trbn, timp, bd, cym, str; stage band

At the end of February 1830, while Bellini was preparing the Venetian premiere of *I Capuleti e i*

Montecchi, Victor Hugo's *Hernani* had been performed amid clamorous controversy at the Comédie-Française in Paris. Echoes of *Hernani*'s triumph, which signalled the taking over of the French theatre by the representatives of Romanticism and Liberalism, were heard all over Europe, and in the late summer and autumn Bellini and Romani worked on an operatic adaptation. But in the wake of the series of political insurrections that had occurred during the year, Italian theatre censorship was tightened up, *Ernani* was abandoned, and the two colleagues turned from a revolutionary subject to what was ostensibly the most socially reactionary of all their operas. *La sonnambula* is an Arcadian idyll in which a group of simple Swiss villagers are saved from the consequences of their folly by the benign protection of Count Rodolfo, the 'signor del villaggio'. With its pastoral setting, its Utopian vision of a harmoniously ordered society, and a happy ending reached by way of situations of great poignancy, rather than by the intrigues of comedy, *La sonnambula* is close in spirit to the first classic of the semiseria genre, Paisiello's *Nina* of 1789.

The principal role in *La sonnambula* was composed for Giuditta Pasta, one of the very greatest of the many remarkable sopranos of that era, a consummate artist with whom Bellini established a working relationship as fruitful as that he enjoyed with Rubini (who took the role of Elvino). He once paid tribute to her 'encyclopaedic' artistry, and proved the point by composing for her not only the gracefully tender Amina, but the more austere and powerfully dramatic roles of Norma and Beatrice di Tenda. Thanks to the combination of the exquisite lyricism of Bellini's full maturity and the incomparable vocal arts of Pasta and Rubini the early performances of *La sonnambula* provided some of the most blissful evenings in the annals of Italian opera. The Russian composer Glinka, who witnessed them, left in his *Memoirs* a vivid account of the scenes in the theatre and of the 'tears of emotion and ecstasy' that were continually shed.

Detail from song-sheet showing Jenny Lind in the title role of La sonnambula *(London, 1847)*

SYNOPSIS

Act I The scene is set in a Swiss village. Scene 1: Outside Teresa's mill the village is celebrating the approaching marriage of the orphan Amina to the wealthy farmer Elvino; only the jealous Lisa, hostess of the local inn, finds it difficult to join in ('Tutto è gioia, tutto è festa'). Amina thanks her friends, especially Teresa, who has loved her like a mother ('Come per me sereno . . . Sovra il sen la man mi posa'). Elvino, who has been praying at his mother's tomb, arrives a little late. But now the civil wedding can proceed ('Prendi: l'anel ti dono'); tomorrow it will be solemnized in church. A stranger enters; though the villagers do not know him, he is in fact Rodolfo, their feudal lord, who, on the death of his father, is returning home after a long absence during which he was himself mourned for dead. Learning that the castle is far off, he decides to stay overnight in Lisa's inn. The village scene brings youthful memories flooding back ('Vi ravviso, o luoghi ameni'); and the sight of the young bride reminds

him of his own lost love ('Tu non sai con quei begli occhi'). Evening falls; before making their way home, the villagers tell the sceptical Rodolfo of a ghost that has been haunting the vicinity. Elvino is jealous at the attention Rodolfo was paying his bride, but left alone with Amina he is soon reassured ('Son geloso del zefiro errante'). Scene 2: In a room in the inn, Rodolfo is enjoying his homecoming, and when Lisa comes to inquire after his comfort, he flirts with her. They are interrupted when the window opens and Amina enters. Lisa hides, dropping a handkerchief; then, believing that Amina has come for an assignation with the Count, she hurries out to alert Elvino. Meanwhile Rodolfo realizes that Amina is sleep-walking; tempted as he is to take advantage of her, he is touched by the words she utters in her dream and goes out, leaving her asleep on the sofa. Villagers come to pay homage to the noble guest, and are perplexed to find no one but a sleeping woman. When Lisa returns with Elvino, the sleeper is revealed as Amina; she awakes, to find herself denounced for her shamelessness. Though she protests her innocence ('D'un pensiero a d'un accento'), Elvino declares that there can now be no wedding; only Teresa is moved by Amina's plight.

Act II Scene 1: A wood. The villagers' affection for Amina has revived, and they set out to the castle to ask Rodolfo to clear up the mystery. Amina and Teresa are also going there, but as they pass Elvino's farm Amina's strength fails her. They meet Elvino, who repulses her again and takes back his ring; even the joyful return of the villagers, and their assurances of Amina's innocence, cannot soften his bitterness ('Tutto è sciolto'– 'Ah! perchè non posso odiarti?'). Scene 2: The village. The unhappy Alessio, a peasant who loves Lisa, learns that Elvino has decided to marry her instead of Amina; Lisa exults in her good fortune ('De' lieti auguri a voi son grata'). Rodolfo explains to Elvino the phenomenon of som-nambulism; but neither he nor the villagers credit such unlikely tales. When Teresa produces the hand-kerchief Lisa dropped in Rodolfo's room, Elvino is ready to despair of womankind; but now they are all astonished to see Amina indeed sleep-walking across the roof of the mill. When she reaches the ground she can be heard praying for Elvino and lamenting the loss of his love ('Ah! non credea mirarti'). Rodolfo prompts Elvino to replace the ring he took from Amina's finger. When she wakes, she finds Elvino kneeling at her feet and her friends rejoicing. The lovers are escorted away to church for the wedding ('Ah! non giunge uman pensiero').

La sonnambula is Bellini's first mature masterpiece: the little world of Amina and Elvino is embodied in music of a rare unity of spirit, yet within that unity the melodic invention is of a prodigal richness. Nothing is lost of the expressive directness his music had gained during his 'philosophical' years; but it is now combined with a new elegance and sensibility, heard at its most beguiling in the duet 'Son geloso del zefiro errante'. Aria forms have become more varied, with less dependence on the tight, symmetrical A–A'–B–A' design of the previous years. Bellini's determination to make even the most conventional and formal parts of the opera dramatically meaningful is vividly shown in the introduction to Elvino's 'Tutto è sciolto', where a recitative sung by Amina – a commentary on Elvino's emotional state – is superimposed on the orchestral melody, a device used again with powerful effect in *Norma*. The sense that the leading characters are part of a close-knit community is conveyed musically by the continual interaction of soloists and chorus: in the majority of the arias and ensembles, the solo voices are at some stage or other set in high relief against a background in which colour and harmony are due as much to the chorus as to the orchestra. In writing for Pasta, Bellini was stimulated to extend the expressive range of his lyricism. The magnificent amplitude of Amina's opening cavatina – which embraces ecstatic introspection, tender recitative-like musings and exuberant virtuosity – is new in his work; and in the closing scene her heart-broken 'Ah! non credea mirarti' has good claims to be regarded as the supreme example of those 'long, long, long melodies' that Verdi so much admired.

RECORDINGS 1. Callas, Valletti, Modesti, La Scala Ch and O, Bernstein, Cetra, 1955: Callas's 'unofficial' set is preferable to her EMI recording because of Bernstein's superior conducting; 2. Scotto, Kraus, Vinco, La Fenice Ch and O, Santi, HRE, 1961: Scotto's 'unofficial' set is in the Callas mould; 3. Sutherland, Pavarotti, Ghiaurov, London Opera Ch, National PO, Bonynge, Decca, 1980: this second of Sutherland's recordings is preferable to her first, mainly because of Pavarotti's contribution – it is also the most accurate and authentic performance – though not as moving as the Callas. [A.B.]

EDITIONS f.s., Cottran-Ricordi, [c. 1895]; facsimile of autograph manuscript: Reale Accademia d'Italia, 1934; v.s., Ricordi, [1831], [1875], new edn and rps

Norma

Tragedia lirica in two acts (3h)
Libretto by Felice Romani, after Alexandre Soumet's tragedy *Norma* (1831), and drawing on Chateaubriand's *Les martyrs*
Composed September–December 1831
PREMIERES 26 December 1831, La Scala, Milan; UK: 20 June 1833, King's Theater, London; US: 1 April 1836, St Charles Theater, New Orleans
CAST Pollione *t*, Oroveso *b*, Norma *s*, Adalgisa *s*, Clotilde *ms*, Flavio *t*, 2 children (sons of Norma and Pollione) *silent*; *satb* chorus of druids, bards, eubages, priestesses, virgins, warriors, soldiers
ORCHESTRATION picc, 2 fl, 2 ob, 2 cl, 2 bsn, 4 hn, 2 tpt, 3 trbn, cimbasso, hp, timp, perc (bd, cym, t-t); str; stage band

Of all Bellini's operas *Norma* is the one whose reputation has been least affected by changes in fashion. For his librettist, Felice Romani, it was 'the most beautiful rose in the garland'; and this view was shared by Richard Wagner, who, in his Riga years (1837–9), wrote an eloquent essay on what he called 'indisputably Bellini's most successful composition' (as well as an insert aria for Oroveso, 'Norma il predesse'). He went on to praise Romani's libretto, 'which soars to the tragic heights of the ancient Greeks . . . all the passions, so characteristically ennobled by Bellini's melodies, are thereby given a majestic foundation and support, [and] form themselves into grandiose and distinct pictures, that remind us involuntarily of the creations of Gluck and Spontini'. The mastery of Romani's text was not lightly achieved. Bellini, now at the height of his powers and self-confidence, was exacting in his demands, and many sections of the libretto were written over and over again before they satisfied him.

The role of Norma was designed for Giuditta Pasta. It would be ideal, Bellini told her, for a singer with her 'encyclopaedic' range of expression; and he encouraged her, once she had read Romani's text, to let him know if she had any thoughts on the part which he ought to bear in mind when he was composing. A well-authenticated anecdote reports that she at first disliked 'Casta Diva', finding it ill-suited to her voice; that Bellini promised he would rewrite it, if she practised it faithfully every day for a week and still felt the same; that Pasta agreed, was slowly won over by the splendour of the music and, having sent Bellini a charming gift as an expression of contrition, went on to make her performance of it one of the highlights of the score.

Norma enjoyed a less instantaneous success than most of Bellini's operas; the composer blamed hostile factions in the audience for what he felt had been 'a solemn fiasco'. But it rapidly overcame that initial coolness, enjoying 34 performances before the end of the season, and conquering the whole of Europe in the space of a few years. In view of the reputation the opera now enjoys as one of the most demanding in the repertoire, it is astonishing to see the central position it held in popular music-making in the mid-19th century. When Glinka was in Murcia, southern Spain, in 1845, he witnessed a performance given by a local children's theatre; at much the same time Charles Dickens visited Carrara, where he heard an act of the opera performed in the local theatre with a chorus provided by labourers from the marble quarries. On several occasions during the Risorgimento we hear of music from *Norma* serving as the focus for patriotic demonstrations. In 1848, for example, at a service in the cathedral at Palermo to celebrate the liberation of Sicily from the Bourbons, the blessing of the tricolour was accompanied by a performance of 'Guerra, guerra!', the 'war hymn' from Act II of the opera.

Giuditta Pasta as Norma, Giulia Grisi as Adalgisa and Domenico Donzelli as Pollione in Norma *(Milan, 1831)*

SYNOPSIS

Act I Gaul during the Roman Occupation, *c.* 50 BC. Scene 1: the sacred forest of the druids; night. Gaulish warriors and druids, led by the chief druid, Oroveso, process to the oak of Irminsul; at moonrise they expect the druidess Norma, Oroveso's daughter, to signal a revolt against the Romans ('Ite sul colle').

Pollione, the Roman pro-consul, and Flavio enter. Pollione's love for Norma has been quenched by a new passion for Adalgisa, an acolyte in the temple of Irminsul; and, despite an ominous dream, he is determined to take her to Rome and marry her ('Meco all'altar di Venere'). Summoned by a gong, the Gauls reassemble. Norma is angered by their impatience, for all will be lost if they strike too soon; then, while priestesses gather the sacred mistletoe, she invokes the moon ('Casta Diva, che inargenti'). But in reality she still longs to win back Pollione's love ('Ah! bello a me ritorna'). Left alone, Adalgisa prays for relief from the emotions that torment her; but when Pollione appears, urging her to abandon the cruel gods of the North, she agrees to elope the following night ('Va crudele . . . Vieni in Roma'). Scene 2: Norma's dwelling. Pollione has been recalled to Rome, and Norma is troubled by the sight of the children she has secretly borne him. Adalgisa comes to confess her love and seek Norma's guidance; Norma, oblivious of the object of Adalgisa's passion, and touched by the story, readily releases her from her vows ('Sola, furtiva, al tempio . . . Ah sì! fa core, abbracciami'). But when Pollione arrives, the truth is clear. Adalgisa is appalled to learn that he is Norma's seducer, and swears she would rather die than let him abandon Norma. As they argue the temple gong sounds; Pollione is warned that for him it signifies death ('Oh! di qual sei tu vittima . . . Vanne, sì, mi lascia, indegno').

Act II Scene 1: The same. Norma watches over her sleeping children, dagger in hand; would it not be better to kill them than to have them carried off to Rome as slaves ('Dormono entrambi')? Since she must die to atone for her guilt, she solemnly entrusts the children to Adalgisa. But in a long, emotional dialogue she is persuaded that all may yet be well: Adalgisa vows to love Pollione no more, but to bring him back to Norma ('Deh! con te, con te li prendi . . . Mira, o Norma . . . Sì, fino all'ore estreme'). Scene 2: A desolate spot close to the druids' forest. The Gauls eagerly await Pollione's departure, but are dismayed to hear from Oroveso that an even harsher pro-consul has been appointed to succeed him; they must be patient a little longer ('Ah! del Tebro al giogo indegno'). Scene 3: The temple of Irminsul. Learning that Adalgisa's mission to Pollione failed, Norma strikes the sacred shield to summon the Gauls. The hour has come for the Romans to be destroyed ('Guerra, guerra!'); all that is wanting is a victim to sacrifice to the god. Pollione is reported captured while sacrilegiously breaking into the virgins' temple enclosure. Norma insists that she be left alone to question him: unafraid of death, he refuses to renounce Adalgisa ('In mia man alfin tu sei'). Norma calls back the Gauls, orders a pyre to be prepared, and reveals that she is herself the sacrificial victim. Her nobility revives Pollione's love; but Oroveso is deeply ashamed, and only Norma's most eloquent prayers can persuade him to accept guardianship of her children. She is stripped of her sacred insignia, veiled in black, anathematized and led off with Pollione to the flames ('Qual cor tradisti . . . Deh! non volerli vittime').

The greatest Bellini is not necessarily the most sophisticated. The noblest pages of *Norma* tend to be sustained by a harmonic vocabulary of no more than three or four basic chords; and it is the dissonant tensions set up between this 'primitive', impassive harmony and the singing voices that soar above that give the music its weight of expressiveness (the arioso 'Teneri figli' encapsulates the style in a few bars). Similarly, Bellini makes no attempt with his orchestra to emulate the verve and wit of Rossini, let alone to explore the new worlds of sound opened up by his French and German contemporaries. There are some beautifully apt orchestral colours in the score – the cool, sacral flute in 'Casta Diva', for example, or the combination of pure string tone and ominously rumbling timpani in 'Qual cor tradisti' – but Bellini's most astonishing achievement in *Norma* is, amid all the more obvious excitements of musical Romanticism, to have asserted his belief that the true magic of opera depended on a kind of incantation in which dramatic poetry and song are perfectly fused.

'In mia man' – a duet without ensemble singing, in which the melody passes dialogue-like from voice to voice – is an ideal place to observe Bellini's art of conjuring poetry, character and drama into song. For 26 bars, as Norma and Pollione are stalemated in a conflict of wills, the music remains virtually motionless, using a vocabulary of three chords, and giving not the slightest hint of a modulation; a glimpse of possible freedom has the music opening up to the relative C major; and when Pollione declines the proffered bargain, it returns inexorably to the home key; the music turns to the minor, and the delivery of the text accelerates nervously as Norma begins to realize that she has no chance of conquering Pollione's will. And all the time, the melody is exquisitely sculpted around the words, highlighting crucial phrases by tessitura, rhetorical word-repetition or 'madrigalisms'. Such perfect fusion of music with dramatic meaning is to be found everywhere in Bellini's mature works.

Norma follows *I Capuleti e i Montecchi* in discarding the popular convention of an aria finale, complete with *cabaletta*, for the prima donna. In fashioning the closing scene to match the dramatic catastrophe, Bellini apparently had to overcome the resistence of a nervous impresario. But, in his own words, 'these last two pieces ('Qual cor tradisti' and 'Deh! non volerli vittime') are of so original a type and so effective, that they have silenced any enemies I might have had . . . I think they are the best pieces I have composed so far.'

RECORDINGS 1. Callas, Stignani, Filippeschi, Rossi-Lemeni, La Scala Ch and O, Serafin, EMI, 1954; 2. Callas, Ludwig, Corelli, Zaccaria, La Scala Ch and O, EMI, 1960; 3. Sutherland, Horne, Alexander, Cross, London Symphony Ch and O, Bonynge, Decca, 1964: neither Callas performance is quite complete and both involve traditional transpositions, but both have in Callas the supreme Norma of modern times. The second of her sets, in stereo, has the better support and recording, the first shows Callas in firmer form but less subtle than in 1960. The Sutherland version is both complete and in the original keys. The more recent Sutherland set is to be avoided. [A.B.]

EDITIONS f.s., Ricordi, 1915; facsimile of original autograph manuscript (2 vols) in Philip Gosset (ed.), *Early Romantic Opera*, Garland, 1983; v.s., Ricordi, [1832], [1859], [1869], later edns and *rps*

Beatrice di Tenda

Tragedia lirica (opera seria) in two acts (2h 45m)
Libretto by Felice Romani, after Antonio Monticini's ballet (1832), which was in turn modelled on Carlo Tedaldi-Fores's tragedy (1825)
Composed January–March 1833
PREMIERES 16 March 1833, La Fenice, Venice; UK: 22 March 1836, King's Theater, London; US: 5 March 1842, St Charles Theater, New Orleans
CAST Filippo Maria Visconti, Duke of Milan *bar*, Beatrice di Tenda *s*, Agnese del Maino *ms*, Orombello, Lord of Ventimiglia *t, t, b*; *satb* chorus of courtiers, ladies-in-waiting, judges, soldiers
FULL ORCHESTRA and stage band

The subject of the opera was chosen by the composer in consultation with Giuditta Pasta (they had seen the ballet together in Milan), against the better judgement of Romani and despite the recognized similarities with Donizetti's *Anna Bolena*. After a tormented and protracted gestation, it proved impossible to complete the finale in time for the premiere, and Beatrice's final *cabaletta* was borrowed from *Bianca e Fernando*; Bellini's sketches for the final scene were realized by Vittorio Gui for a series of influential revivals, beginning in the late 1960s. Romani's distaste for the subject and his exasperation with Bellini prompted him to include in the printed libretto a tactless apology for the imperfections of his text. This led to bitter recriminations with the composer and a complete breakdown of their glorious, if often difficult, collaboration. Contemporary reports suggest that Pasta's dignified stage behaviour and magnificent artistry came close to overcoming the audience's hostility; despite a fiasco, Bellini had no doubt that Beatrice was 'not unworthy of her sisters' and it was the only one of his operas to be published in full score during his life.

SYNOPSIS
Act I The castle of Binasco in 1418. Filippo finds marriage with Beatrice irksome and has fallen in love with Agnese, while Beatrice regrets the blind passion which, after the death of her first husband, has delivered her and her people into Filippo's tyrannical hands. Agnese, jealous of Orombello's adoration of Beatrice, encourages Filippo to believe that his wife is unfaithful. Because of these malicious rumours Beatrice is unwilling to allow Orombello to lead an uprising of her subjects; as they argue, they are surprised by Filippo, who sees in their *tête-à-tête* confirmation of his suspicions, and orders them both to be clapped in prison.

Act II Under torture, Orombello has compromised Beatrice; but when brought to trial he makes handsome amends, avowing her innocent of all charges. The judges order further torture for him and Beatrice, but by now the consciences of Agnese and Filippo are troubling them, and when it is reported that Beatrice has steadfastly refused to admit to any crime, Filippo's rigour wavers. Enraged, however, to find his castle besieged by people clamouring for Beatrice's release, he signs the death warrant. As Beatrice is led to execution, she forgives the now penitent Agnese, and urges her friends to pray for Filippo.

Bellini felt that he had 'corrected' the horror of the story by his music, which would dispel any sense of disgust by exciting fearful and sorrowful emotions. The opera is notable for the part played by the chorus, which, even more than in Bellini's earlier operas, comments on the action, and advises and comforts the protagonists, altogether in the manner of the choruses of Classical Greek tragedy. The relationship of chorus and protagonist is sometimes underlined musically, as in the opening scene, where a theme from the first chorus recurs in varied forms during Filippo's 'cavatina', creating a large-scale, thematically unified scene of a kind that is generally associated with Spontini's and Rossini's 'grand operas', but which was becoming increasingly typical of Bellini's work too. Many solo arias return to the formal A–A'–B–A', scheme of pre-*Sonnambula* days, but they are typical of Bellini's ripest style in their fusion of declamatory and coloratura elements, and in the way he draws out their length by the continuous overlapping of phrases.

RECORDINGS 1. Sutherland, Veasey, Pavarotti, Opthof, Ambrosian Opera Ch, LSO, Bonynge, Decca, 1966; 2. Gruberova, Kasarova, Bernardini, Morozov, Wiener Jeunesse-Chor, Austrian Radio SO, Steinberg, Nightingale, 1992: the 1992 performance is less well sung than that of 1966 but has the advantage of a vivid, live event [A.B.]
EDITIONS f.s., Pittarelli, [*c.*1833]; facsimile of the contemporary printed score in Philip Gosset (ed.), *Early Romantic Opera*, Garland, 1980; v.s., Ricordi, [*c.* 1833], [*c.* 1860–70], [1877/8], new edn and *rps*;

I puritani

The Puritans
Opera seria (melodramma serio) in three parts (2h 45m)
Libretto by Count Carlo Pepoli, after the historical drama *Têtes rondes et cavaliers* (1833) by Jacques-Arsène Polycarpe François Ancelot and Joseph-Xavier Boniface ('Xavier Saintine'), in turn derived from Sir Walter Scott's novel *Old Mortality* (1816)
Composed April 1834–January 1835; rev. December 1834–January 1835
PREMIERES 25 January 1835, Théâtre-Italien, Paris; UK: 21 May 1835, King's Theatre, London; US: 22 July 1843, Chestnut St Theater, Philadelphia; rev. version: 14 December 1985, Barbican Centre, London (concert); 1 April 1986, Teatro Petruzzelli, Bari
CAST Lord Gualtiero Valton *b*, Sir Giorgio *b*, Lord Arturo Talbo *t*, Sir Riccardo Forth *bar*, Sir Bruno Roberton *t*, Enrichetta di Francia *s*, Elvira *s*; *satb* chorus of soldiers of Cromwell, heralds and armigers of Lords Talbo and Valton, Puritans, lords and ladies, ladies-in-waiting, pages, servants
ORCHESTRATION 2 fl/picc, 2 ob, 2 cl, 2 bsn, 4 hn, 2 tpt, 3 trbn, hp, timp, perc (bd, cym, triangle), str; onstage: 2 sd, bell, *acciarini* (pistols/muskets), 2 cl, 2 bsn, 4 hn, organ (optional, may be replaced by muted strings), hp

When Bellini settled in Paris in August 1833, he was besieged by inquiries about possible new operas; the only project that came to fruition, however, was a commission from the Théâtre-Italien. Bellini began work on *I puritani* in April 1834, 'after a year of real solid rest'; and he composed it at a more leisurely pace than any of his earlier operas, 'orchestrating it with such indescribable care that I feel very great satisfaction on looking at every piece I complete'. During the composition he consulted Rossini continually; one of Rossini's several services was to persuade the Théâtre-Italien to instal an organ for the Act I quartet.

Bellini met Count Carlo Pepoli at the Paris salon of Princess Belgioioso. A political exile from Italy, he was a fluent versifier who had written poems for Rossini's *Soirées musicales*. But Bellini soon found he was no Romani; his exasperation with Pepoli was to lead to a memorable outburst in which he explained his philosophy in drastic terms: 'Carve in your head in letters of adamant: the music drama must draw tears, inspire terror, make people die, through singing.' Even after the unqualified triumph of the opera he continued to deplore the way in which the strong theatrical situations were undermined by the poor dialogue, the 'repetitive, commonplace and sometimes stupid turns of phrase'.

The four principal singers – Giulia Grisi (Elvira), Giovanni Battista Rubini (Arturo), Antonio Tamburini (Riccardo) and Luigi Lablache (Giorgio) – formed as fine an ensemble as has ever been assembled in an opera house; they are remembered to this day as the '*Puritani* Quartet' because none of the other operas they sang together was so beautifully tailored to match their peculiar gifts, or occasioned so delirious a triumph. Such was the enthusiasm at the premiere and so insistent the demand for encores, especially of the duet 'Suoni la tromba', that immediately afterwards Bellini had to make a number of substantial cuts to prevent the opera over-running. Already at rehearsals the effect of the duet 'Suoni la tromba' had been so great that it was decided to turn it into a finale: the original second act was subdivided into two, and Elvira's 'mad scene' – the *scena ed aria* 'O rendetemi la speme' – which had followed the duet, was moved to its present position lest it fell flat after the frenzy that 'Suoni la tromba' seemed bound to provoke.

While in Paris, Bellini was asked by the San Carlo in Naples for a new opera for Maria Malibran, who had just enjoyed a spectacular triumph there in *Norma*. Short of time, Bellini agreed to make an alternative version of *I puritani*, in which Elvira became a mezzo-soprano and Riccardo a tenor. He worked on this in December and January of 1834–5; but the revised score arrived in Naples too late to be fitted into the season, and was not performed anywhere until 1985. It includes music cut from the Paris version after the encore-protracted premiere, but not 'Suoni la tromba', on which Bellini was still working in January 1835.

SYNOPSIS
Part I A fortress near Plymouth. Scene 1: A

I puritani: *the scene in the armoury (Paris, 1835)*

spacious glacis outside the fortress. Day breaks, reveille sounds, the guard is changed and the soldiers look forward to victory over the Stuarts ('Quando la tromba squilla'); a morning hymn is heard from the fortress, and all rejoice at the thought of the forthcoming marriage of Elvira, daughter of the Puritan governor-general Sir Gualtiero Valton. Riccardo, a colonel in the Puritan army, confides his sorrows to Bruno, a fellow officer: Elvira had been promised to him; but returning to Plymouth after years of soldiering, he finds that she loves Lord Arturo Talbo, a Cavalier, and that her father is unwilling to force his own wishes on her ('Ah! per sempre io ti perdei . . . Bel sogno beato'). Scene 2: Elvira's apartment. Giorgio, Elvira's uncle, turns her melancholy into joy by telling how he has persuaded her father to allow her to marry Arturo ('Sorgea la notte folta'). Cries from the courtyard announce Arturo's arrival. Scene 3: The armoury. The chorus acclaims the bridal pair; Arturo compares his present happiness with the time he had to woo Elvira secretly ('A te, o cara, amor talora'). Valton has been commanded to escort a lady – a suspected Stuart spy – to appear before Parliament. Arturo speaks with her. She proves to be Enrichetta, the widowed

queen, and Arturo vows to save her. Elvira now reappears, in part adorned for the wedding, but carrying her veil. Singing of her happiness, she playfully drapes the veil round Enrichetta ('Son vergin vezzosa'). This gives Arturo an idea of how the queen might be rescued, and as soon as Elvira and her companions have left, he veils her and hurries her away. When they are challenged by the jealous Riccardo, Enrichetta, fearing bloodshed, reveals herself; Riccardo allows them to make their escape. The wedding party reappears and Valton sounds the alarm and organizes the pursuit. Shock and grief strike Elvira senseless, and in a dreamlike delirium she imagines herself being married to Arturo ('Oh, vieni al tempio, fedele Arturo').

Part II The fortress. A room with an outlook over the English camp. As Giorgio is describing Elvira's ravings ('Cinta di fiori') Riccardo brings news that Parliament has condemned Arturo to the scaffold. The mad Elvira enters, dreaming still of her lost love ('Qui la voce sua soave . . . Vien, diletto, è in ciel la luna'). Giorgio urges Riccardo to save Arturo; otherwise he will have Elvira's death on his conscience ('Il rival salvar tu dei'). Finally Riccardo agrees; but if Arturo is in the Royalist ranks fighting against them on the morrow, he must die ('Suoni la tromba').

Part III Countryside close to the fortress. A loggia in a garden shrubbery; nightfall. Three months have elapsed. While a storm rages and sounds of distant gunfire are heard, Arturo enters and hears Elvira singing. Despite the danger from passing groups of soldiers, he takes up the song ('A una fonte afflitto e solo'). When she appears he falls at her feet, begging forgiveness, and explaining what has happened. The lovers embrace ecstatically ('Vieni fra le mie braccie'). But Elvira's mind darkens once more: she imagines that Arturo is again leaving her, and her screams bring Riccardo, Giorgio and the rest hurrying in. Riccardo announces the sentence passed on Arturo, the word 'death' so shocking Elvira that she recovers her senses. In the face of death the lovers stand united, and even Riccardo is moved to compassion ('Credeasi, misera'). The Puritan soldiery are demanding summary execution when a messenger arrives: the Civil War is over; the Stuarts have been defeated, and a general pardon is issued.

Giulia Grisi was a superb singer, but she lacked the 'encyclopaedic' talents of Pasta, and Bellini had no thought of composing for her a tragedy in the grand manner of *Norma*. In *I puritani* all his old sweetness and pathos return; he himself described the opera as 'fundamentally in the style of *La sonnambula* or Paisiello's *Nina*, with a dash of military robustness, and something of Puritan severity'. It derives the robust and severe qualities from the pervasive march rhythm and from the ever-present sound of brass and drums.

The music that Bellini heard in Paris convinced him that, though the French were almost as skilful as the Germans in their use of the orchestra, they had 'little understanding of what real song was'. Certainly a more sumptuous feast of song than *I puritani* can hardly be imagined. It ranges in style from the sparkling coloratura of 'Son vergin vezzosa' (which may well have been inspired more by the idea of Malibran's voice than of Grisi's) to such ecstatically long-drawn *cantabiles* as 'A te, o cara'; from the plangent nostalgia of 'Ah! per sempre' to the blood-stirring fervour of 'Suoni la tromba'. Rubini's part in particular is one of the truly fabulous tenor roles, demanding a high C♯ at his first appearance on stage, and moving into the vocal stratosphere in the final scene, with a D in his duet with Elvira, and an F in the last finale.

But Bellini also relished showing the Parisians that he too was capable of orchestral and harmonic finesse. French taste encouraged him to go further than before in breaking down the frontiers between lyrical numbers and recitatives and between solos and ensembles. In the *Introduzione*, he seems to attempt to match French rhythmic sophistication: there are as many changes of metre in this single piece as in whole acts of some Bellini operas. All these elements contribute to make *I puritani* the most sophisticated and brilliant of Bellini's operas. No wonder Rossini, who had once found *Il pirata* 'a little bit lacking in brilliance', was impressed, and

regarded this last opera as being, along with *Norma*, the most unmistakable proof of Bellini's greatness.

The *Largo maestoso* from the Act III finale ('Credeasi, misera'), adapted by August-Mathieu Panseron to the text of the Lachrymosa, was sung at Bellini's funeral in Les Invalides on 2 October 1835.

RECORDINGS 1. Callas, Di Stefano, Panerai, Rossi-Lemeni, La Scala Ch and O, Serafin, EMI, 1955; 2. Tucci, Pavarotti, Protti, Raimondi, Ch and O of Teatro Massimo, Catania, Quadri, Butterfly, 1969; 3. Sutherland, Pavarotti, Cappuccilli, Ghiaurov, Royal Opera House Ch, LSO, Bonynge, Decca, 1975; 4. Caballé, Kraus, Manuguerra, Ferrin, Ambrosian Opera Ch, Philharmonia, Muti, EMI, 1979: Callas, as ever, is unique and has rewarding support, but the Caballé set is the more authentic and superbly conducted by Muti. Both versions are essential listening. The live Catania performance is sensational as regards Tucci's and Pavarotti's singing; the Sutherland preserves a notable reading of Elvira's role. [A.B.]

EDITIONS f.s., Cottram-Ricordi, [c. 1895]; facsimile of original autograph manuscript (including Naples variants) (2 vols) in Philip Gosset (ed.), *Early Romantic Opera*, Garland, 1983; v.s., Ricordi, [1836], [c. 1875], later edns and *rps*

BIBLIOGRAPHY M. R. Adamo and Friedrich Lippmann, *Vincenzo Bellini*, Edizioni RAI Radiotelevisione, 1981; Friedrich Lippmann, 'Vincenzo Bellini und die italienische Opera seria seiner Zeit', *Analecta musicologica* VI, 1969; Friedrich Lippmann, 'Bellini', *The New Grove Masters of Italian Opera*, Macmillan, 1983; Leslie Orrey, *Bellini*, Dent, 1969; Friedrich Pastura, *Bellini seconda la storia*, Guanda, 1959; H. Weinstock, *Vincenzo Bellini, His Life and His Operas*, Weidenfeld and Nicolson, 1971

D.K.

RALPH BENATZKY

Rudolf Josef František Benatzky; *b* 5 June 1884, Mährisch-Budweis, Moravia (now Moravské Budějovice); *d* 16 October 1957, Zurich, Switzerland

Benatzky began his career in the military world, but switched to university studies, including music, in Vienna. His facility and felicity with cabaret songs attracted early attention, and by the First World War he was contributing to revues, farces, and operettas in Munich and Vienna. Moving to Berlin, he was instrumental in the creation of the large-scale revue–operetta. *Casanova* (1928), based on melodies by Johann Strauss II, is a pasticcio; *Drei Musketiere* (1928) and the very popular *Im weissen Rössl* (1930) are basically original, although the latter has interpolations by other hands.

These spectacles were intended to compete with the film musicals, which were rapidly gaining popularity in the 1930s; similarly, Benatzky's clever *Meine Schwester und Ich* (*c.* 1930) was an intimate, Parisian-styled reaction to these overblown extravaganzas. Benatzky wrote music for over 100 stage works, many film scores, and some 5000 songs, for which he often wrote the lyrics. He is buried, appropriately, near the site of the White Horse Inn in St Wolfgang, Austria.

Im weissen Rössl
At the White Horse Inn
Revue–operetta in three acts (2h 30m)
Libretto by Hans Müller and Erik Charell
Composed 1930
PREMIERES   8 November 1930, Grosses Schauspielhaus,
Berlin; UK: 8 April 1931, Coliseum, London; US: 1 October
1936, Center Theater, New York

One of the most spectacular of all operettas, *White Horse Inn* seemed to Depression audiences like a holiday in the Tyrol at the turn of the century. The story of the innkeeper Josepha and her headwaiter Leopold – which had previously been a popular stage comedy – now became a convenient peg for lavish scenes involving an enormous company: tourists arriving by lake steamer, a rainstorm, the arrival of Kaiser Franz Joseph, plus yodellers, Austrian clog dancers, cowhands, etc.

Benatzky's most famous numbers are 'Es muss was wunderbares sein' and the title song, heard as a march and a waltz. But other hands supplied some of the other hits: Robert Stolz – 'Die ganze Welt ist himmelblau' and 'Mein Liebeslied muss ein Walzer sein'; Bruno Granichstaedten – 'Zuschau'n kann i' net'; and Robert Gilbert – 'Was kann der Sigismund dafür'.

RECORDING   Rothenberger, Minich, Bavarian Radio Ch
and O, Mattes, EMI, 1979
FILM   Lamac (dir.), 1935
EDITION   v.s., Charivari, 1930

Other operatic works: *Laridon*, 1912; *Cherchez la femme*, 1913; *Der lachende Dreibund*, 1913; *Prinzesschens Frühlingserwachen*, 1914; *Anno 14*, 1914; *Das Scheckbuch des Teufels*, 1914; *Fräulein Don Juan*, 1915; *Liebe im Schnee*, 1916; *Du goldige Frau*, 1916; *Die Schmiedin v. Kent*, 1916; *Die tanzende Maske*, 1918; *Liebesreigen*, 1919; *Die Verliebten*, 1919; *Graf Chevreaux*, 1919; *Yu-Shi tanz t*, 1920; *Apachen*, 1920; *Pipsi*, 1921; *Ein Märchen aus Florenz*, 1923; *Adieu Mimi!*, 1926; *Die Nacht von San Sebastian*, 1926; *Die Blinde*, 1927; *Casanova*, 1928; *Mit Dir allein auf einer einsamen Insel*, 1929; *Meine Schwester und Ich*, 1930; *Cocktail*, 1930; *Zur goldenen Liebe, c.* 1931; *Morgen gehts uns gut*, 1931; *Zirkus Aimée*, 1932; *Bezauberndes Fräulein*, 1933; *Deux sous les fleurs*, 1933; *Das kleine Café*, 1934; *Die Prinzessin auf der Leiter*, 1934; *Büxl*, 1934; *Der König mit der Regenschirm*, 1935; *Axel an der Himmelstür*, 1936; *Herzen im Schnee*, 1937; *Maajestät – privat*, 1937; *Landrinette*, 1939; *Angielina*, 1940; *Kleinstadtzauber*, 1947; *Liebesschule*, 1950
BIBLIOGRAPHY   Richard Traubner: *Operetta: A Theatrical History*, Doubleday, 1983

R.T.

FRIEDRICH BENDA
›Friedrich Ludwig Benda; *baptized* 4 September 1752, Gotha;
d 20 or 27 March 1792, Hamburg

The eldest of five musician children of Georg Benda, Friedrich began his career with the Seyler company at Gotha. For them he composed his most important work, the singspiel *Der Barbier von Sevilla*, to a

German text by Grossman, based on Beaumarchais. Performed at Leipzig only a year after the French play's original production, it appears to have been the earliest operatic version of the story, predating Paisiello's by six years. Benda later held theatrical posts at Berlin and Hamburg, undertook concert tours and worked at Ludwigslust as chamber composer to the Duke of Mecklenburg-Schwerin. In 1788 he moved to Königsberg where he wrote three more singspiels.

Singspiels: *Der Barbier von Sevilla*, 1776; *Der Verlobung*, 1790; *Louise*, 1791; *Mariechen*, 1792
BIBLIOGRAPHY   H. Wirth, 'Friedrich Benda', in *MGG*

B.S.

GEORG BENDA
Georg Anton [Jiří Antonín] Benda; *baptized* 30 June 1722,
Staré Benátky, nr Prague; *d* 6 November 1795, Köstritz (now
Kostrzyn, Poland)

Georg was the third son of Jan Jiří Benda, father and grandfather to a large Bohemian family of professional musicians active in Germany during the late 18th century. Georg's career was spent mainly at the ducal court of Saxe-Gotha, where he was successively kapellmeister and kapelldirektor. Though his operatic ambitions were initially hampered by opposition from the local clergy, he gained valuable experience while on paid leave in Italy during 1765, where he met Hasse among others. This led to the composition of his only Italian opera, *Xindo riconnosciuto*, to a text by J. A. Galletti. A visit to Gotha in 1774 by the Seyler theatrical company inspired him to write German works for the stage, and in the following year there appeared his German duodramas, *Ariadne auf Naxos* and *Medea*, on which his reputation mainly rests. Subsequently a happy partnership with the court archivist at Gotha, Friedrich Wilhelm Gotter, provided him with libretti for his four singspiels, of which *Der Jahrmarkt* and *Romeo und Julie* were particularly successful.

Ariadne auf Naxos
Melodrama in one act (40m)
Libretto by Johann Christian Brandes
PREMIERES   27 January 1775, Gotha; UK: 1975, Edinburgh
(concert); 8 December 1991, Queen Elizabeth Hall, London

Based on the principles established by Rousseau in his scène lyrique *Pygmalion* (1770), this was the first of Benda's influential melodramas, in which the spoken word and mime are combined with orchestral music. Because it involves two characters, Ariadne and Bacchus, the work is rightly designated a duodrama. It was not, however, the earliest of its type in Germany since both Aspelmayr and Schweitzer are known to have produced similar settings in 1772, in German translation, of Rousseau's *Pygmalion*. A further German version of the Rousseau scene, probably by Gotter, was set by Benda himself in 1779. Mozart (in a letter of

Charlotte Brandes, wife of the librettist of Georg Benda's
Ariadne auf Naxos, *in the title role (Gotha, 1776)*

November 1778) expressed warm admiration for
Ariadne and its companion piece *Medea*: '. . . of all
the Lutheran kapellmeisters', he wrote, 'Benda has
always been my favourite, and I like these two works
so much that I carry them about with me.' In later
operatic history the influence of Benda's melodrama
style is apparent, for example in Mozart's *Zaïde*, the
grave-digging scene in Beethoven's *Fidelio* and the
Wolf's Glen scene in Weber's *Der Freischütz*.

EDITION   A. Einstein (ed.), Leipzig, 1920

Der Jahrmarkt

(*Der Dorfjahrmarkt: Lucas und Bärbchen*)
The Village Fair: Lucas and Barbie
Singspiel in one act
Libretto by Friedrich Wilhelm Gotter
PREMIERE   10 February 1775, Gotha

This is the first of Benda's singspiels; it is typical in
the richness of its orchestration and variety of its
styles, embracing recitatives and arias, as well as
other features drawn from buffa and seria traditions.
In 1776 it was recast in two acts, with additional
music by J. A. Hiller.

RECORDING   one-act version: Kramer, Hoff, Rotzsch, Leib,
Czech Singers' Ch, Prague CO, von Benda, Archiv, 1968
EDITION   Theodor Werner (ed.), *DDT*, vol. 64, Breitkopf
und Härtel, *rp*, 1930

Medea

Melodrama in one act (45m)
Libretto by Friedrich Wilhelm Gotter
PREMIERE   1 May 1775, Rannstädtler Tor, Leipzig

The success of *Ariadne auf Naxos* led almost
immediately to the production of Benda's second
duodrama. Broadly based on Euripides, Gotter's
German text portrays Medea's passionate reaction to
Jason's desertion of her and her children in order to
marry Glauce, the daughter of Creon, King of Crete.

EDITION   f.s., Jan Trojan (ed.), *Musica antiqua bohemica*,
series 2, no. 8, Supraphon, 1976

Other operatic works: *Xindo riconnosciuto*, 1765; *Walder*,
1776; *Romeo und Julie*, 1776; *Die Holzhauer, oder Die drey
Wünsche*, 1778; *Pygmalion*, 1779; *Das tartarische Gesetz*,
1787; *Das Findelkind, oder Unverhoft kommt oft* (children's
operetta), 1787
BIBLIOGRAPHY   Edith Vogl Garrett, 'Georg Benda, the
Pioneer of Melodrama', *Studies in Eighteenth-century Music:
A Tribute to Karl Geiringer*, George Allen and Unwin, 1970

B.S.

KAREL BENDL

b 16 April 1838, Prague; *d* 20 September 1897, Prague

Bendl graduated from the Prague Organ School in
1858 and pursued a varied career both in Bohemia
and abroad; his longest and most successful post was
as chorus master of the Prague Hlahol Choral
Society (1865–77). He was one of the most prolific
Czech opera composers of his generation, with 11
completed operas to his credit. Blessed with a fluent
technique, he was equally cursed with a versatility
that excluded any distinctive musical personality. He
moved with equal grace from the grand-opera clichés
of his first operas to the melodramatics of his one-act
verismo opera, *Mother Míla*. His most successful vein
was a gentle lyricism, reminiscent of Gounod, which
informs some of his lighter numbers.

Lejla

Grand opera in five acts
Libretto by Eliška Krásnohorská, after Edward Bulwer-
Lytton's novel *Leila, or The Siege of Granada*
Composed 1867, rev. 1874
PREMIERES   original version (four acts): 4 January 1868,
Provisional Theatre, Prague; rev. version (five acts):
24 September 1874, Provisional Theatre, Prague

Bendl's first opera was in many ways his most
successful. Written as the first Czech 'grand opera',
its exotic setting and enormous cast of historical
characters (including King Ferdinand of Spain, the
Grand Inquisitor, and the last Moorish King of
Granada) proved popular with audiences, and the
opera continued to be revived into the 1890s. It was
the first Czech opera to be published after *The
Bartered Bride*. Despite the many spectacular and
dramatic moments, it is the lyrical numbers
(especially those for the Moorish slave Zorajda) that

are the most memorable and are still occasionally heard.

EDITION v.s., Hudební matice, 1874 (Acts I and II) and 1880 (Acts III–V)

The Elderly Suitor

(originally *Mr Franc*)
Starý ženich (originally *Pan Franc*)
Folk opera in three acts
Libretto by Karel Sabina, rev. Gustav Eim and V. J. Novotný
Composed 1871–4
PREMIERE 4 February 1882, Chrudim, Bohemia

Apart from one operetta, *The Elderly Suitor* was Bendl's only Czech comic opera. Shaped in the mould of *The Bartered Bride* but first performed almost 20 years later, it was old-fashioned for its time and, as Janáček complained, kept to no ethnographical models. Its easy charm and modest demands have prompted occasional revivals in the 20th century.

EDITION v.s., Hudební matice, 1883

Other operas: *Břetislav a Jitka* (*Břetislav and Jitka*), (1869), as *Břetislav*, 1870; *Die Wunderblume*, (1876); *Indická princezna* (*The Indian Princess*), 1877; *Černohorci* (*The Montenegrins*), (1877), 1881; *Karel Škreta*, 1883; *Gina*, (1884); *Dítě Tábora* (*The Child of Tábor*), (1888), 1892; *Máti Míla* [*Matka Míla*] (*Mother Míla*), 1895; *Švanda dudák* (*Švanda the Bagpiper*), (1896), 1907

BIBLIOGRAPHY John Tyrrell, *Czech Opera*, CUP, 1988

J.T.

JULIUS BENEDICT

(Sir) Julius Benedict; *b* 27 November 1804, Stuttgart, Germany; *d* 5 June 1885, London

As a pupil of Hummel and Weber (in whose company he met Beethoven in 1823), Benedict would have been well placed to further Austro-German opera, but his career proved cosmopolitan and took him to Britain, where he helped establish English Romantic opera. He was conductor of the Kärntnertortheater in Vienna in 1824 and of the San Carlo and Fondo theatres in Naples, for which his first three operas were written, from 1825 to 1834. He arrived in London via Paris in 1835 and became conductor successively at the Lyceum (1836), Drury Lane (1838–48), and Her Majesty's theatres (from 1852). He accompanied Jenny Lind on her American tour in 1850 conducting many of her concerts. He was naturalized, and was knighted in 1871.

The Lily of Killarney

Opera in three acts (1h 30m)
Libretto by John Oxenford and Dion Boucicault, after Boucicault's play *The Colleen Bawn* (1859)

PREMIERE 8 February 1862, Covent Garden, London

The Lily of Killarney is one of a trio of successful works that purveyed a British operatic Romanticism (though it failed to develop further). The other two were Balfe's *The Bohemian Girl* (1843) and Wallace's *Maritana* (1845), both premiered by Benedict under Alfred Bunn's management at Drury Lane. *The Lily of Killarney* revels in the vernacular appeal and social mythology of Ireland, its cast replete with grasping landlord, impecunious gentry, priest as confidant, fanatically loyal boatman, and simple peasant girl (the Colleen Bawn) whose love for a social superior eventually triumphs. The musical style, less Italianate and harmonically much more sophisticated than Balfe's, is none the less unfailingly melodious and transferred well to the Victorian drawing room in such numbers as 'The moon has rais'd her lamp above'. There are touches of Irish folk idiom and some Gaelic in the libretto.

EDITION v.s., Boosey, 1862

Other operas: *Giacinta ed Ernesto*, *c.* 1827; *I portoghesi in Goa*, 1830; *Un anno ed un giorno*, 1836; *The Gypsy's Warning*, 1838; *The Brides of Venice*, 1844; *The Crusaders*, 1846; *The Bride of Song*, 1864
BIBLIOGRAPHY Nicholas Temperley (ed.), *The Athlone History of Music in Britain*, vol. 5: *The Romantic Age: 1800–1914*, Athlone, 1981

S.B.

ARTHUR BENJAMIN

b 18 September 1893, Brisbane, Australia; *d* 10 April 1960, London

A fluent pianist at an early age, Benjamin came to study at the Royal College of Music in London, where he formed lifelong friendships with Ivor Gurney and Herbert Howells. After war service Benjamin returned to Australia to teach at the Sydney Conservatory, but soon returned to London. An examining trip to the West Indies made a profound impression, and many of his works are imbued with Latin American dance rhythms, including his most famous work, *Jamaican Rumba*, originally for two pianos, and later orchestrated.

His first opera, *The Devil Take Her*, a comedy in a prologue and one act, was produced at the Royal College of Music (1931). This tale of a romantic poet, who finds he prefers the Devil's company when his formerly dumb wife is revealed a shrew, is perhaps stronger in its romantic invention than its farce. Two years later he wrote *Prima Donna*, which unaccountably was not produced until 1949. The pace and wit of this Italian comedy reveal a true grasp of the stage.

Many talented composers submitted entries for the Festival of Britain Opera Competition in 1951, and of the four winning works the best was possibly Benjamin's *A Tale of Two Cities*, produced in 1957. A practical and well-constructed libretto (by Cedric

Cliffe after Dickens), a good pace and sweeping choral writing distinguish it from most other British operas of the period.

Other operas: *Mañana*, 1956; *Tartuffe* (orch. Alan Boustead), 1964

BIBLIOGRAPHY   Alan Boustead, *A Tale of Two Cities*, *Opera*, vol. 8 (1957), pp. 413–6; Cedric Cliffe, *Benjamin's Tartuffe*, *MT*, vol. 105 (1964), pp. 819–20

L.F.

RICHARD RODNEY BENNETT

b 29 March 1936, Broadstairs, Kent, England

Born into a musical family, Bennett from an early age showed signs of the talent that has made him one of the most prolific British composers of his generation. In 1953 he won a scholarship to the Royal Academy of Music, studying with Lennox Berkeley and Howard Ferguson, and in 1957 a French government award enabled him to study with Pierre Boulez in Paris for two years. More important influences have been Berg, Britten, Dallapiccola and Henze. Bennett's own music mixes 12-note technique with a quasi-tonal palette, resisting both the dogmatism of strict serialism and the passing fads of modern musical taste. He has been active in educational music, has written a number of film scores and is an accomplished pianist in both serious music and jazz. Since 1970 his output has included a dozen concertos and a full-length ballet, *Isadora*, for Covent Garden (1981).

In the 1960s Bennett wrote a series of five operas, exploring various sub-genres: after the early short work *The Ledge* came three full-length pieces and a children's opera, *All the King's Men*. All aroused considerable interest and for a while Bennett was seen as a potential new champion of British opera. But largely because of an apparent reluctance to allow the music to dominate dramatic events, and also perhaps because of their too well-crafted surface, these works failed fully to match such expectation. Bennett's own view was philosophical: 'I would not have the presumption to try to change the face of opera as it is known – opera will, after all, get on very nicely without me.'

The Ledge

Chamber opera in one act (30m)
Libretto by Adrian Mitchell
PREMIERE   12 September 1961, Sadler's Wells, London

Bennett's first opera is a modern-day tale of a man about to throw himself from a high building. First another man who has been through the same experience attempts to persuade him down. Then, the following morning, his wife tries, and eventually succeeds: in trying to make him laugh she begins to do so herself, and since she is unable to repeat this when he asks, he determines to come down and make her laugh again. Neither drama nor music attempts to look at the anonymous characters'

motivations and for much of the time the music takes a back seat to the action. However, the central interlude, as night falls, is highly effective, as is the peaceful, slow epilogue for all three characters as the man finally begins his descent.

EDITIONS   f.s., Belwin-Mills/Central Music Library, [1975]; v.s., Mills Music Ltd, 1963

The Mines of Sulphur

Opera in three acts (1h 45m)
Libretto by Beverley Cross
Composed April–November 1963
PREMIERE   24 February 1965, Sadler's Wells, London
CAST   Braxton/Sherrin/the Count *b-bar*, Rosalind *ms*, Boconnion *t*, Tovey *bar*, Jenny/Haidee *s*, Leda/Mrs Traxel *a*, Fenney/Hugo *t*, Tooley/a flunkey *bar*, Trim *silent*
LARGE ORCHESTRA including pf, harpsichord, cel; offstage: hn

Cross's text started life as an opera libretto in 1961. He was about to adapt it as a play when the producer Colin Graham recommended it to Bennett for his Sadler's Wells commission. The initial idea for the work came when Cross, on military service on Salisbury Plain, read an account of a winter plague. This, coupled with his interest in post-Restoration touring theatre troupes, resulted in this Grand Guignol of murder in a country house and its gruesome exposure. The work's title (a quotation from Shakespeare's *Othello*, Act III, Scene 3) is also that of the central play-within-a-play – another Shakespearean device.

SYNOPSIS

Act I   A run-down West Country manor house, the home of Braxton, a rich landowner: a winter's night, *c.* 1760. Braxton berates his maid Rosalind for staying out on the moor. Unobserved, her companions enter: the deserter Boconnion and the vagabond Tovey. Rosalind then eggs Boconnion on to murder Braxton. The three are trying on their ill-gotten finery when Sherrin, the manager of a troupe of touring players, enters seeking shelter. Dismissing Tovey's suspicions, Boconnion invites the players in, in return for entertainment.

Act II   The actors perform their play, *The Mines of Sulphur*, about a wealthy count (Sherrin) whose young wife (Haidee) and valet (Hugo) conspire to murder him. The 'hosts' interrupt the play when it comes uncomfortably near the knuckle, whereupon one of the actors, Tooley, exposes the impostors.

Act III   Boconnion defiantly holds the actors prisoner and plans to burn them in the house while he and his accomplices escape to a new life. But the actors escape from the windowless, doorless cellar, leaving one of their number, Jenny, to reveal that they are ghosts carrying the plague – and now Boconnion is infected. The three conspirators are left alone to ask God's mercy.

For his first full-scale opera Bennett produced one of his most assured scores, successfully conjuring up an atmosphere of oppressive gloom. Though serial, it contains tonal elements, and the use of ballads

Alix Stone's set for The Mines of Sulphur *(London, 1965)*

(including a haunting setting of 'The Unquiet Grave' sung by Jenny) and recurrent motifs (such as the actors' horn motif) make for an easily graspable musical idiom. Fluent orchestral writing and arioso vocal style help sustain the overall momentum, while in the play-within-a-play the three nocturnes create an appropriate sense of tension. The opera – dedicated to Benjamin Britten – was a considerable success when it first appeared, with performances in Cologne, Zagreb, Marseilles and Stockholm, as well as at La Scala, Milan (1966), where it created a furore. Though the score indicates that the roles of Braxton and Sherrin/the Count should be doubled, they are commonly split.

EDITION v.s., Universal, 1966

A Penny for a Song

Opera in two acts (1h 45m)
Libretto by Colin Graham, based on the play by John Whiting (1950, rev. 1962)
Composed 1966
PREMIERE 2 November 1967, Sadler's Wells, London

Even before the premiere of *The Mines of Sulphur* Bennett was contemplating a comic opera for his next Sadler's Wells commission. His choice of subject fell on John Whiting's Napoleonic satire cum farce,

adapted by the opera's producer Colin Graham. Set on the Dorset coast, it centres on the antics of two eccentric brothers, Sir Timothy and Lamprett Bellboys, one summer's day. Sir Timothy is convinced of an imminent French invasion, his brother has a fixation about fire and keeps a fire-engine constantly at the ready. When the local home guard goes on manoeuvres the brothers believe it to be the real thing: Sir Timothy disguises himself as Napoleon to confuse the 'enemy' troops, while Lamprett extinguishes every signal fire in sight. Meanwhile the daughter of the house, Dorcas, has fallen in love with a young mercenary returned from the real battleground and now a passionate radical. This brings him into conflict with the world-weary house guest, Hallam Matthews. In the words of the composer, 'Many lives and loves are changed by the end of the day.'

The characterization is more successful here than in Bennett's earlier works, with each character given his or her own musical mannerisms. If the opera fails to capture either the hectic comedy of the original or its satirical undertones, it contains some fine lyrical writing in the Henze mould, notably for the two lovers and at the end of the opera as the long day draws to its close. It enjoyed some success abroad, with performances in Munich and Osijek (1968).

EDITION v.s., Universal, 1967

All the King's Men

Opera in one act for young people (40m)
Libretto by Beverley Cross
Composed 1968
PREMIERE 28 March 1969, Coventry Technical College, Coventry

Commissioned by the Coventry Schools' Music Association, *All the King's Men* is based on the historical events behind the popular rhyme 'Humpty Dumpty'. Set in August 1643 during the Civil War, it recounts how Royalist forces tried to take the Roundhead garrison of Gloucester with a siege machine that would breach the river Severn and the city walls. During the night, the citizens of Gloucester widened the river, so that the machine ('Humpty-Dumpty') collapsed into the Severn. The work calls for modest but accomplished forces including three solo singing parts and small orchestra with percussion. In contrast to Bennett's previous operas, it makes extensive use of pastiche, some of it appropriate (including a lullaby sung by the queen's entourage), some (echoes of Weill; a Latin American number during the machine building) less so.

RECORDING Trinity Boys' Choir, Squibb, Abbey, 1971
EDITIONS f.s./v.s., Universal, 1968

Victory

Opera in three acts (1h 45m)
Libretto by Beverley Cross, based on the novel *Victory* by Joseph Conrad (1914)
Composed 1968–9
PREMIERE 13 April 1970, Covent Garden, London

Bennett's fifth opera was written to a commission from Covent Garden. In many ways it is his most ambitious. The action is on a broader time scale than that of his earlier works, and takes place over the course of some weeks rather than a single day/night. Nevertheless, Cross's libretto necessarily greatly condenses Conrad's East Indian tale of a sceptical recluse (Heyst) drawn into contact with the 'real' world through his compassion and ultimate love for an unhappy chorus girl (Lena). As such, it is unable to do more than hint at the complex motivations of the various characters, and this puts the onus on the music itself, in which Bennett returned to a 12-note idiom. The emotions of the two central characters led him to tap a vein of lyricism that recalls Henze (the work's dedicatee), notably in the first scene of Act III for Heyst and Lena. He also captures well the oppressive seediness of the bar on Surabaya and of the three gamblers who precipitate Heyst's downfall. The exotic setting prompts the use of some colourful though not obtrusive percussion, while the palm-court-style ladies' orchestra in Act I allows Bennett to indulge once again his gift for pastiche. However, the work has a constricted expressive range, which can be ascribed only partly to the emotional reticence of the central character, and the tragic *dénouement* is less powerful than it might be. As a result, the opera has failed to match the success of its full-length predecessors.

EDITION v.s., Universal, 1970

BIBLIOGRAPHY Susan Bradshaw, 'Victory' (interview with Bennett), *MT*, vol. 111 (1970), pp. 370–72; Noël Goodwin, 'The Mines of Sulphur' (interview with Bennett), *Opera*, vol. 16 (1965), pp. 85–8; Christopher Palmer and Lewis Foreman, 'Richard Rodney Bennett', in Lewis Foreman (ed.), *British Music Now*, Paul Elek, 1975

M.A.

FRANÇOIS BENOIST

b 10 September 1794, Nantes, France; *d* 6 May 1878, Paris

Benoist was a well-known French organist and teacher who ventured occasionally on to the operatic stage. He attended the Paris Conservatoire as a pupil of Catel from 1811 to 1815, when he won the Prix de Rome. In 1819, after returning from Italy, he became professor of organ at the Conservatoire and remained there for many years; his pupils included Adam, Bizet and Saint-Saëns. In 1840 he became premier chef de chant at the Opéra where he was responsible for overseeing the current repertoire. His first opera, *Léonore et Félix*, a one-act opéra comique to a libretto by Saint-Marcellin, was played at the Feydeau on 27 November 1821. His second, *L'apparition*, was played at the Opéra (then known as the Théâtre de la Nation) during his employment there, on 16 June 1848. Its libretto by Germain Delavigne concerns a Spanish girl, Clara, who takes on ghostly form to haunt a French army officer who has deserted her. Its short run was blamed more on the political turbulence of the day than on any lack of merit. The disturbances that broke out in Paris soon after its opening closed all theatres and deprived the opera of any chance of success. Its best-known number is the *quatuor de l'apparition*: 'Quoi! c'est Clara; c'est elle!'. Benoist's score was praised for its instrumentation and integral ballets. He also composed four full ballet scores.

BIBLIOGRAPHY F. Clément and P. Larrouse, *Dictionnaire lyrique*, Paris, 1869

H.M.

NIELS VIGGO BENTZON

b 24 August 1919, Copenhagen

Bentzon comes from a Danish family with strong musical traditions; he is descended from J. P. E. Hartmann, and Jørgen Bentzon (1897–1951) was his cousin. In his youth he was a formidable pianist and a keen advocate not only of his own keyboard works but also those of Schoenberg. He is enormously prolific: his published compositions ran to 429 opus numbers in 1980, and have now increased further to include three complete operas, 20 symphonies, 22 concertos, and no fewer than 20 piano sonatas. His neo-classical style is broadly derived from Nielsen,

Stravinsky and Hindemith. Since 1960 his compositions have embraced more avant-garde styles,
including 'happenings' and graphic notation. The
operas are based on Kafka (*Faust III*), Hoffmann's
Märche und Erzählungen (*Die Automaten*), Goethe
and Joyce.

Operas: *Faust III*, 1964; *Die Automaten*, 1974; *Jardin des
Plantes* (inc.), (1969); *Bankchefen* (*The Bank Manager*),
(1974)

R.La.

ALBAN BERG

Alban Maria Johannes Berg; *b* 9 February 1885, Vienna; *d* 24
December 1935, Vienna

Although Schoenberg also wrote operas, Berg is the
only member of the so-called Second Viennese
School whose music can regularly be heard in the
opera house. True, his personality was warmer and
more outgoing and his style more naturally lyrical
than Schoenberg's or Webern's. But one might just
as well say that he was simply more interested in the
theatre and the voice. From the start, he wrote songs.
Some 50 survive from before his 20th birthday, and
he wrote another 40-odd during and just after his
years of study with Schoenberg. Song-writing was
displaced by the long drawn-out composition of his
first opera, *Wozzeck* (1914–22); and *Lulu* occupied
him from 1928 until his death in 1935, with
interruptions for the cantata *Der Wein* (1929) and the
Violin Concerto (1935).

Berg came from a cultivated, well-to-do bourgeois
Viennese family where reading and plays were part
of normal life. He read widely, knew the best writing
of his day, and kept up with the theatre. Both his
libretti are direct adaptations of successful stage
plays: Büchner's *Woyzeck*, whose Viennese premiere
Berg attended in May 1914; and Wedekind's 'Lulu'
plays, the first of which Berg had read in 1904, while
he saw the second performed the following May. This
is in marked contrast with Schoenberg, whose stage
works are mostly musical enactments of
psychological states or abstract concepts. Yet Berg
was strongly under Schoenberg's influence from their
first meeting in 1905 until his death 30 years later.
Schoenberg claimed it was through his teaching that
Berg learned how to write extended instrumental
movements, and it was certainly under his tutelage
that Berg composed his Piano Sonata, Op. 1, and the
String Quartet, Op. 3. He seems to have opposed
Wozzeck as an operatic subject. And in general the
relationship between master and pupil preserved
hidden tensions, which come out in Berg's
sycophantic letters that still give little ground on
creative matters.

Musically Berg was certainly indebted to
Schoenberg's classically based teaching, with its
insistence on good formal models and coherent
musical argument. But his style owes more to the

*Alban Berg at the window of his Vienna flat (in 1935) with
Schoenberg's portrait of him (1920)*

pluralism of Mahler, with its rich strata of
association, than to the tortured intellectualism of
Schoenberg. Later, in adopting Schoenberg's serial
method (*Lyric Suite*, 1925–6), he adapted it to the
point where it loses its strict cohesive function in
Schoenberg's music of the time, and takes on a quasi-
secret quality that links it with the hidden ciphers in
the music of Schumann, as well as with other features
of Berg's own music such as the large-scale
palindromes and symmetries in the *Chamber
Concerto*, *Lyric Suite* and *Lulu*, the Baudelaire
subtext of the finale of the *Lyric Suite*, and the
cryptic numbers (10 and 23) which play a part in this
latter work. Of course, Berg's serialism has a
cohesive function too. But it is typical of him that, in
the *Lyric Suite* and *Lulu*, he derives a succession of
note rows from the original one, whereas
Schoenberg, no less typically, always confined
himself to a single row in any one work. These

derivatives often have a strong tonal feeling, as indeed do the original rows; Berg never shared the view that a tonal focus was something to avoid in music that was truly progressive (whether serial or not).

For all the free-sounding Romanticism and natural sweep of his best music, Berg composed slowly and with great effort. Work on *Wozzeck* was constantly interrupted, first by the First World War, in which he served as an officer cadet and later as an official in the War Ministry, then by the heavy demands of Schoenberg's Society for Private Musical Performance (1918–21), as well as administrative duties in connection with the Berg family estate. Later, while at work on *Lulu*, he suffered poor health (he was a severe asthmatic), and like most Viennese had to endure a drastic decline in his living standards as a result of the hyper-inflation of the mid-1920s. Finally, after the accession of the Nazis to power in January 1933, his music was branded decadent and excluded from performance in Germany, as well as, increasingly, in Austria, which deprived him of any strong practical incentive to finish *Lulu*. The opera was nevertheless virtually complete when, on Christmas Eve 1935, he died of blood poisoning after a short illness resulting from an abscess on his back. It seems certain that, if penicillin had been available (it came into use in 1941), Berg's life could have been saved.

Wozzeck

Opera in three acts (15 scenes), Op. 7 (1h 30m)
Libretto by the composer, from Georg Büchner's play, *Woyzeck* (1837)
Composed 1914–22
PREMIERES 14 December 1925, Staatsoper, Berlin; US: 19 March 1931, Philadelphia (Philadelphia Grand Opera Company); UK: 14 March 1934, Queen's Hall, London (concert); 22 January 1952, Covent Garden, London
CAST Wozzeck *bar*, Drum-Major *Helden-t*, Andres *lyric t*, Captain *buffo t*, Doctor *buffo b*, 2 Apprentices *deep b*, *high bar*, Idiot *high t*, Marie *s*, Margret *a*, Marie's son *treble*, Soldier *t*; *satb* chorus of girls, wenches, youths and soldiers and children
ORCHESTRATION 4 fl/picc, 4 ob/1 ca, 4 cl/2 E♭cl, b cl, 3 bsn, dbsn, 4 hn, 4 tpt, 4 trbn, db tuba, timp, perc (triangle, sds, *Rute*, cym, bd, t-ts, xyl, cel) hp, str; onstage: sds; military band: picc, 2 fl, 2 ob, 2 E♭cl, 2 bsn, 2 hn, 2 tpt, 3 trbn, db tuba, perc (triangle, sds, bd with cym); tavern music: 2 fiddles, C cl, accordion, gtr, bombardon; out-of-tune pianino; chamber orchestra (as in Schoenberg's Chamber Symphony No. 1, Op. 9): fl/picc, ob, ca, E♭cl, cl, b cl, bsn, dbsn, 2 hn, 2 vn, va, vc, db (also reduced version for triple woodwind, arr. Erwin Stein with Berg's approval)

The composition of *Wozzeck* took almost eight years, but Berg worked on it for only a fraction of that time. After seeing the play in 1914, he made some musical sketches and set about adapting Büchner's text, but was then interrupted by the war, and returned to the opera only during 1917 and 1918. Act I was finished by summer 1919, Act II in August 1921, and the final act during the following two months (the orchestration took a further six). During this whole period Berg wrote nothing else, except to complete the *Three Orchestral Pieces* (1913–15), with

whose final movement (*Marsch*) the opera shares its style and even some material. The first performance was conducted by Erich Kleiber, who programmed it on his own initiative, with no fewer than 34 orchestral and 14 full rehearsals. It was a *succès de scandale*, with disturbances during the performance and a mixed press afterwards, but it led to a stream of productions in Germany and Austria, before the Nazis consigned it to the dustbin of 'decadent art' after 1933.

For its time, *Wozzeck* now seems a highly modern and topical subject. But the play was in fact some 77 years old when Berg saw it in Vienna (its world premiere was in Munich the previous year). Its author, Georg Büchner, had died of typhus in 1837 at the age of 23, leaving *Woyzeck* unfinished and in an unclear and disorganized state. It was first edited into a coherent text by Karl Emil Franzos in 1879, and this edition was further reorganized by Paul Landau for a 1909 publication which formed the basis of the stage premieres and of Berg's libretto. In adapting this text, Berg cut out a few scenes and conflated two or three others, but he retained the essential character of the play, with its many short scenes, its abrupt and sometimes brutal language, and its stark, if haunted, realism – so unusual for its day, but reflecting the fact that Büchner's source was an actual incident (of 1824) in which an ex-soldier had been executed for the murder of his unfaithful mistress.

Büchner, a post-1830 revolutionary thinker, made his Woyzeck a representative of the downtrodden proletariat; a soldier, because soldiers have always been slaves to a cruel and mindless system, but also the helpless victim of modern social experimentation which is more general and insidious in its effects. It is this aspect of the character that Berg portrays most movingly. Wozzeck's fumbling attempts to articulate his thoughts, and to comprehend and control his passions, reverberate in the music, while the social 'machine', with its fads and statistics masking an essential unconcern for the individual, rolls on in the fugues, rhythmic mechanisms and ostinato effects that Berg also loved.

SYNOPSIS

The square-bracketed designations are from a chart drawn up by Berg's pupil Fritz Mahler; they are not included in the score.

Act I [Five Character Pieces] Scene 1 [Suite]: The Captain's room: Wozzeck is shaving him. The Captain, a high, yapping, grotesque tenor, philosophizes about eternity. Wozzeck acquiesces to everything in a flat monotone, but when the Captain impugns his morality, Wozzeck quotes the Bible and adds: 'We poor folk ... I could be virtuous if I were a gentleman with a hat and a watch and an eye-glass, and could talk posh.' Scene 2 [Rhapsody]: An open field outside the town. Wozzeck and Andres, another soldier, are cutting sticks. Wozzeck senses mysterious forces around them, and sees in the sunset 'a fire rising from earth to heaven, and an uproar descending like the last trump'. Andres pooh-poohs him, and sings a hunting song. Scene 3 [Military

Set designs by Panos Aravantinos for Wozzeck *(Berlin, 1925)*

March and Lullaby]: Marie's room. In the street, Margret comments on Marie's candid admiration for the Drum-Major. Marie turns angrily back into the house and sings her child a bitter lullaby. Wozzeck looks in through the window and tries to describe his experience in the field, but will not look at his child, and hurries off to barracks. Scene 4 [Passacaglia]: The Doctor's study. The Doctor, a caricature of scientific positivism, uses Wozzeck as guinea-pig for dietary experiments. When Wozzeck tries to explain his visions, the Doctor is delighted with his 'aberratio mentalis partialis, second species' and gives him a rise of one groschen. Scene 5 [Rondo]: The street outside Marie's door. Marie is again admiring the Drum-Major. After token resistance, she takes him into her house.

Act II [Symphony in Five Movements]   Scene 1 [Sonata Movement]: Marie's room. She is admiring a pair of ear-rings given her by the Drum-Major. When the child wakes up, she sings him a song about a gypsy. Wozzeck comes in and is at once suspicious of the ear-rings, but gives Marie his pay, leaving her guilt-stricken. Scene 2 [Fantasia and Fugue]: A street in the town. The Captain and Doctor meet and talk, the Doctor pretending to see in the Captain's florid complexion and bloated physique signs of fatal illness. Wozzeck arrives and they torment him by hinting at Marie's infidelity. Scene 3 [Largo]: The street outside Marie's door. Wozzeck confronts her, obliquely and apocalyptically, with her infidelity. As obliquely, she denies it, defying him to hit her: 'Rather a knife in my body than a hand on me.' Scene 4 [Scherzo]: The garden of an inn. A band

plays a ländler to which the customers dance, and two apprentices sing drunkenly. Marie dances with the Drum-Major, watched jealously by Wozzeck. There is a hunting chorus and a song for Andres with guitar. Finally an idiot, reading the future, smells blood on Wozzeck. Scene 5 [Rondo con introduzione]: Guardroom in the barracks. Wozzeck, unable to sleep, complains to Andres of inner voices and a vision of a flashing knife blade. The Drum-Major arrives drunk and boasts of his success with Marie. The two men fight, and Wozzeck is knocked down.

Act III [Six Inventions]   Scene 1 [Invention on a Theme]: Marie's room. Marie reads from the Bible about the woman taken in adultery, and Mary Magdalene. In between, the child presses against her, and she tells him a story about a hungry orphan. Scene 2 [Invention on a Note]: A woodland path by a pond. Marie and Wozzeck walk past. Wozzeck kisses her menacingly, then as the moon rises he stabs her in the throat. Scene 3 [Invention on a Rhythm]: A tavern. A frenzied polka on an out-of-tune piano. Wozzeck is drowning his guilt and sings a folksong. Margret draws attention to the blood on his hand, and he rushes out in a panic. Scene 4 [Invention on a Six-note Chord]: Woodland path by the pond. Wozzeck returns for the knife, which he throws into the pond. Then, frightened by the moon, he decides to throw the knife in farther, wades in and drowns. The Captain and Doctor pass, comment on the eerie scene, and hurry away. [Orchestral Interlude: Invention on a Key.] Scene 5 [Invention on a Regular Quaver Motion]: The street outside Marie's door. Her child is playing with other children. A child announces that Marie's body has been found, and they all run off, followed by Marie's child.

Though technically 'atonal' (no key signatures and few definite key centres), *Wozzeck* is really ambivalent in this respect. Its musical world is Viennese Expressionism, with its violently dissonant gestures, dense textures and steep dynamic gradients. Schoenberg's sprechgesang technique – a kind of haunted half speech, half singing – figures prominently. But the music also hints at a simpler, more homely tonal language, which stands for normal life, or elusive happiness, or other concepts opposed to the excess, misery and inhumanity we witness on the stage. Marie's lullaby, Andres's hunting song, and above all the great D minor interlude in Act III, all have this quality. Berg also uses conventional music – ländler, march, out-of-tune polka – ironically, in Mahler fashion (the inn scene in Act I is perhaps the most Mahlerian music Berg ever wrote). In the same way he uses background forms for both structure and irony. It is an open question whether the sonata form of Act II Scene 1 or the rondo of Act II Scene 5 could ever be heard as such, but there is no mistaking the sarcasm of the fugue in Act II Scene 2 or the obsessiveness of the passacaglia in Act I Scene 4, with its 21 variations on a ground (a patent influence on Britten's *Peter Grimes*). Meanwhile the demoniac repeated Bs in the murder scene and the wild ostinato rhythms in the tavern scene following are obviously straight dramatic devices dignified by formal tags.

A unique feature is the cinematic time flow. Not only do the short scenes intercut like a film montage, but this even leads in Act III to an experimental handling of actual clock time. By cutting from the murder to the tavern (where Wozzeck is already drinking) back to the murder scene (where he is just arriving to look for the knife), Berg both speeds up the action and seems to override the physical limitations of the medium (how can Wozzeck already be in the tavern?). This is in fact an adaptation of a real ambiguity of sequence in the play (which admittedly Büchner might have got rid of in due course), and it influenced later operas like Zimmermann's *Die Soldaten*, where cinematic devices are used to suggest multiple layers of action.

In other ways *Wozzeck* is an authentic renewal of the German tradition of symphonic drama. The five scenes in each act play continuously, linked by interludes, and organized by leitmotifs and recurrent harmonies. And while Berg perfected the hyper-modern idea of symbolic characterization ('Captain', 'Doctor', 'Drum-Major', etc.), his musical portraiture is as fine and precise as anything in German opera since Mozart. The humanizing of the potentially subhuman Wozzeck and Marie through the music they sing is one of the great miracles of 20th-century theatre.

RECORDINGS 1. Behrens, Zednik, Grundheber, Haugland, Vienna State Opera, Vienna PO, Abbado, DG, 1988 (also available on Pioneer Laserdisc): brilliantly exciting live recording from the Vienna Opera (1987), but suffers from poor vocal/orchestral balance; 2. Silja, Zednik, Waechter, Malta, Vienna State Opera Ch, Vienna PO, Dohnányi, Decca, 1981: sound studio recording, with a superb Marie (but poor sprechgesang) and magnificent orchestral playing; 3. Lear, Stolze, Fischer-Dieskau, Kohn, Ch and O of the Deutsche Oper Berlin, Böhm, DG, 1965: the most moving and emotionally rich recording, though not the most accurate EDITIONS f.s., Universal, 1926; v.s., composer, now Universal, 1922; study s., Universal, 1955

Lulu

Opera in three acts (2h 45m)
Libretto by the composer from two plays, *Erdgeist* (1895) and *Die Büchse der Pandora* (1903; first performed 1918), by Frank Wedekind
Composed 1928–35; Act III ed. and orch. by Friedrich Cerha, 1974
PREMIERES Acts I and II, plus fragments of Act III: 2 June 1937, Zurich; UK: 1 October 1962, Sadler's Wells, London (Hamburg State Opera); US: 7 August 1963, Santa Fe; complete version: 24 February 1979, Opéra, Paris; UK: 16 February 1981, Covent Garden, London; US: 28 July 1979, Santa Fe
CAST [Perle, 1985] Lulu *high s*, Countess Geschwitz *dramatic ms*, Wardrobe Mistress/Schoolboy/Groom *a*, Medical Specialist/Banker/Professor *high b*, Painter/Negro *lyric t*, Dr Schön/Jack the Ripper *heroic bar*, Alwa *youthful heroic t*, Schigolch *high character b*, Animal Tamer/Acrobat *heroic b with buffo flavour*, Prince/Manservant/Marquis *buffo t*, Stage Manager *low buffo b*, Clown *silent*, Stagehand *silent*, Police Commissioner *spoken role*, 15-year-old Girl *opera soubrette*, Her Mother *a*, Designer *ms*, Journalist *high bar*, Servant *deep bar*; pianist, attendants to the Prince,

policemen, nurses, wardresses, dancers, party guests, servants, workers *silent*
ORCHESTRATION 3 fl/2 picc, 3 ob/ca, 3 cl/2 E♭cl, b cl, alto sax, 3 bsn/dbsn, 4 hn, 3 tpt, 3 trbn, tuba, timp, perc (triangle, tambourine, sd, jazz d, bd, cym, *Rute*, t-t, gong, xyl, vib), hp, pf, str; onstage: picc, fl, 3 cl/tenor sax, b cl, alto sax, dbsn, 2 jazz tpt, 2 jazz trbn, sousaphone, jazz perc (sd, bd, cym, temple-blocks, steel brush, vib, triangle, fairground d with cym), banjo, pf, 3 vln (with jazz horn), db

After the premiere of *Wozzeck* Berg was soon on the look-out for another libretto. He made abortive sketches for an opera called *Und Pippa tanzt* (1928, based on a play by Gerhart Hauptmann), but then decided on an adaptation of Wedekind's 'Lulu' plays. As before, he himself carried out the textual surgery, which had to be much more extensive than with Büchner; and this time he adapted as he composed. The opera was complete in short score by April 1934, apart from a few passages in Act II (87 bars in all) where accompanying detail was implicit rather than explicit. He then started work on the full score, beginning with what was to be the symphonic suite – the only music from *Lulu* he ever heard performed (11 December 1935; Kleiber had previously conducted it in Berlin, 30 November 1934), and which included the *Variations* and *Adagio* from Act III. Finally he scored the opera from the start, and had reached bar 268 of Act III (out of 1,326) at the time of his final illness.

To complete *Lulu* therefore involved mainly orchestration, plus a small amount of added harmony and counterpoint, much of it facilitated by the large amount of musical recapitulation involved. A vocal score of Act III (by Erwin Stein) was actually ready for press in 1936, by which time the composer's widow, Helene, had asked Schoenberg and Webern (in vain) to finish and edit the full score. Only later did she adopt the obstructive attitude that kept the material of Act III virtually unavailable until after her death in August 1976. Meanwhile *Lulu* was performed as a torso, normally with only the end of Act III, mimed to the music of the *Adagio* from the suite (the procedure adopted in Zurich in 1937). Cerha's completion was ready by 1974, but not heard until 1979 in Paris (conducted by Pierre Boulez), since when the full version has been widely produced.

SYNOPSIS
Prologue The Animal Tamer introduces the beasts in his menagerie (identified by the music as characters in the opera). Lulu, the snake, 'created to make trouble', is carried on and presented in person.

Act I Scene 1: The Painter's studio. Lulu is having her portrait painted, watched by Dr Schön (an 'editor-in-chief') and his son Alwa (a composer). The dialogue makes clear the men's interest in Lulu, or hers in them. She offers sarcastic respects to Schön's fiancée. When he and Alwa leave, the Painter makes a heavy pass at Lulu, chasing her round the studio. There is a bang on the door, which collapses to admit her husband, the Medical Specialist. Seeing the two together, he has a stroke and dies. Lulu, seemingly detached from events, allows herself to be taken over by the Painter. Scene 2:

Nuri Hadzig in Lulu *(Zurich, 1937)*

A very elegant drawing room. The Painter, now married to Lulu, is rich from the sale of pictures (fixed, it transpires, by Schön). News of Schön's engagement arrives in the post. The doorbell rings, and the asthmatic old tramp Schigolch comes in as the Painter retires to his studio. Lulu's father figure, Schigolch, is delighted to see her living in luxury. He soon leaves, as Schön arrives. Schön wants to end their affair and live respectably with his wife-to-be. They are interrupted by the Painter, to whom, as Lulu exits, Schön obliquely explains the true situation. Shocked, the Painter goes out, ostensibly to confront Lulu, in reality to cut his own throat. Alwa arrives and they break down the door to reach the body. Seeing his own engagement 'bleeding to death', Schön calls the police, as Lulu insists, 'You'll marry me all the same.' Scene 3: A theatre dressing room. Lulu is dancing in Alwa's latest work. They drink champagne and discuss Schön, their own first meeting, and the Prince who wants to marry Lulu and take her to Africa. As she returns to the stage, Alwa ponders writing an opera about her. Cheering is heard from the auditorium as the Prince enters, soon followed by Lulu, who has seen Schön in the audience with his fiancée and has shammed a fainting fit. Left alone with Schön, she threatens to go to Africa with the Prince, and taunts Schön over his engagement. At last Schön realizes he cannot leave her. She forces him to write a letter to his fiancée breaking off their engagement.

Act II   Scene 1: A magnificent room (in Schön's house). Lulu and Schön are now married. The lesbian Countess Geschwitz has come to invite Lulu to the lady artists' ball, but quickly leaves in the face of Schön's disapproval. Schön and Lulu go out together. The Countess returns and hides. Schigolch and two other admirers, the Acrobat and the Schoolboy, come in from the balcony; Lulu also comes back in, and they talk. Next Alwa is announced and the admirers hide, as Alwa declares his love for her. Schön overhears and also notices the Acrobat, at whom he points a revolver; he then takes Alwa out, while the Acrobat finds a new hiding-place. Schön returns and gives Lulu the gun to shoot herself as the Acrobat makes his escape. Schön now discovers the Countess and locks her in the next room. Continuing his argument with Lulu he again tries to force her to shoot herself, but as the Schoolboy intervenes she shoots Schön instead. As Lulu implores Alwa to save her, the police arrive. Interlude: A silent film depicts Lulu's arrest, trial and imprisonment, her deliberate infection with cholera, and her escape from the isolation hospital disguised as the Countess. Scene 2: The same room, shuttered and dusty. Alwa, the Countess and the Acrobat await Schigolch, who is to take the Countess to the hospital to change places with Lulu. The Acrobat is to marry Lulu and take her to Paris as his performing partner. Alwa offers the Countess money, Schigolch arrives and leaves with the Countess, after which the Acrobat himself demands money from Alwa. Next the Schoolboy arrives, but is sent packing in the belief that Lulu is dead. Schigolch then returns with Lulu, who is so physically spoilt by illness that the Acrobat abandons the plan and goes off to the police. Schigolch departs to collect train tickets. Left alone, Alwa and Lulu declare their love.

Act III   Scene 1: A spacious salon (in a Paris casino). A gambling party is in progress. As the company exit to the gaming room, talk is mainly of their booming Jungfrau shares. The Marquis threatens to expose Lulu unless she agrees to be sold to a Cairo brothel. The company returns from the gaming room, all having won. The Acrobat also tries to blackmail Lulu, who meanwhile abuses Countess Geschwitz as a pervert. A telegram informs the Banker of the collapse of the Jungfrau shares. Schigolch now arrives, also asking for money; but he agrees to lure the Acrobat to his hotel and murder him. After a brief exchange with the Acrobat, the Marquis goes for the police. Lulu contrives that the Acrobat and the Countess go off together to Schigolch's hotel. As the company learns of the share collapse, Lulu changes clothes with the Groom and leaves with Alwa just before the police arrive. Scene 2: An attic room (in London). Alwa and Schigolch await the return of Lulu, now a prostitute, with a client. They hide as she comes in with a Professor, and while they are in her room Schigolch goes through his pockets. When the Professor has gone, Countess Geschwitz arrives with the portrait of Lulu (which has featured in every scene). Alwa nails it up, and Lulu goes back out, followed by the Countess. Alwa tells Schigolch that Lulu has infected him with a disease to which she herself is immune. She returns with a second client, a Negro. There is an altercation about payment and the Negro kills Alwa. Schigolch goes off to the pub, the Countess returns, contemplating suicide. Lulu comes in with her third client, Jack the Ripper. They go into her room, where he murders her. On the way out he stabs the Countess, who dies as the curtain falls.

Wedekind's ramshackle and contrived narrative was a challenge to Berg that he was partly, but not wholly, successful in meeting. Too many characters have to be accommodated, and at times (Act II Scene 1; Act III Scene 1) they get in each other's way. There are too many stock dramatic devices: the doorbell, the telegram, the exchange of garments, not all strictly germane (the Jungfrau shares). And Berg's use of hidden structural process is incredibly elaborate: a treasure trove for analysts but of mixed significance in the theatre. Unlike the abstract forms in *Wozzeck*, those in *Lulu* are deployed sectionally over large spans of music, intercutting with other processes: for instance, Lulu's conversations with Schön about his engagement (Act I Scenes 2 and 3) form a large sonata movement whose exposition and development are separated by well over 500 bars of music; similarly Alwa's declarations of love in Act II Scenes 1 and 2 comprise a rondo, and there are two large sets of variations in Act III. In between come shorter, self-contained units with such titles as 'Chorale', 'English Waltz', 'Cavatina', or vague generic names like 'Chamber Music I', 'Ensemble I'. Some of them employ strict technical devices such as canon, or isorhythm ('Monoritmica', like the 'Invention on a Rhythm' in *Wozzeck*). The somewhat modish film sequence in Act II is a musical palindrome, marking the high point from which Lulu begins her descent to degradation. Embracing everything is a complex scheme of 'leading sections', in which recapitulation serves to remind us of previous incident, while at the same time giving structure. This comes to a head in the final scene, which is substantially built on such reminiscence, reflecting Berg's idea that Lulu's clients should be the avenging spirits of her former husbands.

Berg's serial technique is another aspect of this plurality of formal procedures. Unlike Schoenberg in *Moses und Aron* (1932–4), he uses several 12-note rows, as well as smaller unordered sets, derived from each other by a variety of more or less convoluted operations. They not only bind the music harmonically and thematically, but also act as leitmotifs: each character has his or her own set or series. But the serial treatment itself is extremely free (as in *Der Wein* and the Violin Concerto); and there is a strong tonal emphasis built into the basic ('Lulu') series, brought out in the derivatives, and dwelt on by the music's harmony and texture.

Whatever the importance of this apparatus, *Lulu* works in the end because of its direct musical beauty and richness of portraiture. As a universal morality about the power of sensual experience, it depends on a broad range of characterization: Lulu has to conquer all sorts and conditions of men. And for this Berg, with his emotional breadth and intellectual focus, was brilliantly equipped. As with the best operas of Strauss, there is a cornucopian feeling about the work as a whole, and an endless fascination in its detail (not least orchestral: the *Lulu* sound is unique). Whether Berg would have significantly tightened or revised the score remains an open question. It would surely have remained an essentially diverse experience, with all the virtues and defects of its genre.

RECORDINGS 1. Stratas, Minton, Riegel, Mazura, Blankenheim, Paris Opera O, Boulez, DG, 1979: the first complete recording, and takes full measure of the work; 2. Lear, Johnson, Grobe, Fischer-Dieskau, Deutsche Oper O, Berlin, Böhm, DG, 1968: Acts I and II only (plus the *Variations* and *Adagio*). Unequal cast, but supreme musical naturalness and warmth from Böhm
EDITIONS f.ss.: Acts I and II (plus *Variations* and *Adagio*), Universal, 1964, 1975; 2nd edn, 1983; complete (2 vols), Universal, 1985; v.ss.: Acts I and II, Universal, 1936; complete, Erwin Stein and Friedrich Cerha (eds), Universal, 1977/8

BIBLIOGRAPHY Julian Brand, Christopher Hailey and Donald Harris (eds), *The Berg–Schoenberg Correspondence*, Macmillan, 1987; Mosco Carner, *Alban Berg*, Duckworth, rev. edn, 1983; Douglas Jarman (ed.), *The Berg Companion*, Macmillan, 1989; Douglas Jarman, *Alban Berg: Wozzeck*, CUP, 1989; Douglas Jarman, *Alban Berg: Lulu*, CUP, 1991; Nicholas John (ed.), *Wozzeck*, John Calder (ENO Opera Guide), 1990; George Perle, *The Operas of Alban Berg: Wozzeck*, University of California Press, 1980; George Perle, *Lulu*, University of California Press, 1985

S.W.

JOSEF BERG

b 8 March 1927, Brno, Czechoslovakia; *d* 26 February 1971, Brno

Berg studied in Brno at the conservatory under Janáček's pupil Vilém Petrželka, and at the university. He worked briefly as a music editor at Brno radio and as a critic, before devoting himself entirely to composition. He was a leading force in the Brno 'Creative Team A', which pioneered the use of avant-garde techniques among Czech composers. Apart from cultivating a contemporary language, the team favoured a music-theatre approach, which coloured Berg's conception of opera. Except for his last opera, *Johannes Doctor Faust*, all his stage works are short 'mini-operas', some lasting only 15 minutes. Forces are equally modest. *The Return of Odysseus* is written for eight performers: actor, soprano, baritone, dancer, violin, trumpet, bass clarinet and piano; *Euphrides at the Gates of Tymen* requires an actor, a tenor, two dancers, tuba and tape. Musically the works are eclectic, drawing on Weill-like idioms (in *European Tourism*) or operatic parodies, placed in an ironic perspective by the use of avant-garde techniques. Berg had considerable talent as a writer and created or adapted his own texts. Their subject matter ranges from Greek mythology (as in the case of *Euphrides*, a modern spoof), to old Czech puppet plays (*Breakfast at Šlankenvald Castle*; *Faust*) and an account of German 'tourists' in France: Nazi soldiers incognito exploring the terrain on the eve of the Second World War (*European Tourism*). Berg's death from cancer at the age of 44 cut short a promising and distinctive career. At the time he had virtually completed a full version of *Faust* (for seven soloists, chorus and full orchestra), and had partly sketched a parallel chamber version.

Operas: *The Return of Odysseus* (*Odysseův návrat*), (1962), 1967; *European Tourism* (*Evropská turistika*), (1963), 1967; *Euphrides at the Gates of Tymen* (*Eufrides před branami Tymén*), 1967; *Breakfast at Šlankenvald Castle* (*Snídaně na hradě Šlankenvaldě*), (1966), 1969; *Johannes Doctor Faust* (*Johannes Doktor Faust*), (1966), 1982

BIBLIOGRAPHY Ladislav Šíp, *Česká opera a jeho tvůrci* (*Czech Opera and Its Creators*), Supraphon, 1983

J.T.

NATANAEL BERG
[Carl] Natanael [Rexroth-]Berg; *b* 9 February 1879, Stockholm; *d* 14 October 1957, Stockholm

Berg grew up in a musical family and was a cousin of the famous opera singer, John Forsell. He trained as a veterinary surgeon, first in civilian life and then in the Swedish army. After encouragement from Stenhammar, he studied first in Stockholm and later in Berlin, where he fell under the spell of Richard Strauss whose *Salome* he heard on the evening of his arrival in 1907. His musical language has strong Expressionist, neo-Romantic overtones and his first major work, a symphonic poem, *Traumgewalten* (after Lenau), is powerful and imaginative. His five operas (all to his own libretti) were performed during his lifetime but for the most part his music suffered (and still suffers) neglect.

Operas: *Leila*, 1912; *Engelbrekt*, 1929; *Judith*, 1936; *Brigitta*, 1942; *Genoveva*, 1947

R.La.

LUCIANO BERIO
b 24 October 1925, Oneglia, Italy

Born into a family of professional musicians, Berio was trained from an early age by both grandfather and father, and entered the Milan Conservatory in 1945. His strong sense of the potential of the human voice, first instilled in childhood as he listened to his father giving singing lessons, was fortified during his six years of study at the conservatory by work as an accompanist and as a conductor in provincial opera houses, and above all by his marriage, in 1950, to the singer Cathy Berberian, who was to become so notable an interpreter of his works.

Berio began work for Italian Radio and Television (RAI) in 1952, and there developed an electronic studio. The experience, first encountered at this time, of counterpointing dense layers of sound was to have far-reaching consequences in all aspects of his work. He left the RAI in 1961 to take up a series of teaching appointments, first on the West then the East Coast of the United States. A decade later he returned to Italy, but from 1974 to 1980 established a second base in Paris, where he directed the electro-acoustic section of IRCAM. Since 1987 he has directed his own institute, Tempo Reale, in Florence.

It is a reflection of the vivid, gestural nature of Berio's music in the 1950s that his first work for the stage was for mimes. In 1952–3 he had written two pieces, one orchestral, the other electronic, both entitled *Mimusique*. Having received a commission from the 1955 Teatro delle Novità festival in Bergamo he asked Roberto Leydi to devise a scenario around the orchestral *Mimusique*, adding further music where appropriate. The result, *Tre modi per sopportare la vita*, was a rather wooden Brechtian parable. When the 1959 Venice Biennale requested a mime piece, Berio dusted off his composite score, and requested a new scenario from Italo Calvino. This, the final version, was entitled *Allez Hop* – the cry of a travelling showman, one of whose performing fleas escapes and provokes instructive mayhem.

This first series of ventures established a way of working that was to be repeated in most of Berio's future work in the theatre: only once he had established a general musico-dramatic conception – and indeed often composed a good deal of the music for it – would he turn to a collaborator to find specific images that would give it theatrical focus. Although both of the mime pieces mentioned above told stories, they were the last of Berio's theatrical works to do so. Thereafter, a more complex, 'musical' proliferation of visual and verbal materials that found their theoretical counterpart in Umberto Eco's discussions of the 'open work' became the hallmark of his theatre.

The gradual unfolding of Cathy Berberian's extraordinary gifts as a performer had a profound impact on the development of Berio's sense of theatre. The electronic works that he produced with her – *Thema (Omaggio a Joyce)* in 1958, and above all *Visage* in 1960–61 – revealed a complex theatre of the voice that was independent of narrative and, in the case of *Visage*, of words. Furthermore the theatricalization of the concert hall in *Circles*, where circular processes proliferate not just within the music, but also visually, on stage, pointed directly onwards to his first piece of vocal theatre, *Passaggio*.

Indeed, many of Berio's works of the mid-1960s underline the theatrical aspect of concert-hall performance: notably *Sequenza III* for voice, and *Sequenza V* for trombone. More significant in developing a 'theatre of the mind' was *Laborintus II* (1965). This multi-layered homage to Dante, in which Berio and Sanguineti were able to experiment richly with the fragmentation and counterpointing of texts, was in principle 'open' to theatrical realization, but in the main has proved more effective in the concert hall.

Laborintus II and *Sinfonia* were the essential stepping-stones from *Passaggio* to Berio's next theatrical work, *Opera* (1969–70). Precisely because of its rich, multi-layered nature, *Opera* has also proved a challenge to effective theatrical realization – yet the difficulties that Berio encountered with it enabled him to see his way towards a form of large-scale theatre in which skeletal narrative structures and proliferating imagery are held in fruitful tension. In consequence, between 1977 and 1984 he was able to produce two full-scale operatic works, *La vera storia* and *Un re in ascolto*, which have held the stage with conviction.

Passaggio

Messa in scena (a punning description: both 'something put on stage' and 'Mass on stage') (35m)
Text by Edoardo Sanguineti
Composed 1961–2
PREMIERE   6 May 1963, Piccola Scala, Milan

Berio's initial conception was of the utmost simplicity: a woman slowly tracing a 'passage' from one side of the stage to the other, stopping at various points along the way to sing texts that would reflect the tortuous relationship described in Kafka's *Letters to Milena*. Looking for a congenial collaborator, he approached the radical young poet, Edoardo Sanguineti, who readily accepted.

Sanguineti brought to the project both an enriching of subject matter, and a poetic style predisposed to musico-theatrical elaboration. The exclamatory, fragmented style of his poems richly evoked the speaking voice; the counterpoint of images (enhanced by using different languages) suggested simultaneous, but interacting, layers that could be literally realized in the theatre. To Berio's Kafkaesque point of departure, he added images inspired by Rosa Luxembourg's prison diaries. The female protagonist, 'She' (the only solo vocal part), now enacts at each of her stopping-points, or 'Stations' (by analogy with those of the Cross), a skeletal story of being hunted down, arrested, brutally interrogated, and finally released into the squalor of an urban bedsit awash with a tangled jumble of possessions. Most of this we infer from visual clues, and from the reactions of two choruses: it is confirmed when, at the end, the singer puts acting behind her, and revisits each site, acknowledging what was represented there. 'She' herself is absorbed in an interior monologue devoted to more intimate memories: of search and sexual arousal, of an idyll in a garden relapsing into nightmare, etc. – the latter in particular echoing Berio's original conception.

But the essence of the drama lies in the tension between what happens on stage, and what happens beyond it. In the pit, alongside the instrumental ensemble, is an eight-part singing chorus that assumes its traditional role as commentator, amplifying the action. More crucial, however, are five speaking groups dispersed around the auditorium giving brutally revealing voice to the reactions of a bourgeois audience. In a counterpoint of Italian, French, English, German and Latin (the latter pointedly reserved for moments of self-confirming gravitas), they invoke social order; abuse, lust after, and cheer on the torture of the protagonist; offer bids for the auction of a 'perfectly domesticated woman'; and chant lists of consumer goods that metamorphose into a catalogue of weapons.

The overtly confrontational element in *Passaggio* was to re-emerge from time to time in Berio's work. But while capitalizing on the technical experiments of *Passaggio*, Berio's theatre was from now on to move into more complex dimensions.

EDITIONS   f.s., Universal, 1963

Opera

Music-theatre piece in three acts (1h 30m)
Libretto by the composer, Furio Colombo, Umberto Eco, Alessandro Striggio and Susan Yankowitz with the Open Theater of New York
Composed 1969–70, rev. 1977
PREMIERES   12 August 1970, Santa Fe; revised version: 26 May 1977, Teatro della Pergola, Florence

Opera is intended as the plural of *opus*, for three different musico-theatrical projects and a number of autonomous musical pieces are here combined. The three projects are united by the theme of death. The first sets fragments from Striggio's libretto for Monteverdi's *Orfeo*. The second takes up materials from a project devised in 1956 by Berio, Umberto Eco and Furio Colombo around the sinking of the *Titanic*: a parable of misplaced trust in technical achievement. The third derives from a then current production by Jo Chakin's Open Theater of New York, *Terminal*, that denounced contemporary attitudes towards the terminally ill.

These three layers are so counterpointed that moments of congruence allow one to dissolve into another. This dreamlike ebb and flow is subjected to a formalized structure that makes full use of Berio's passion for reworking pre-established materials. Each of three acts opens with a setting of Striggio, *Air*, at first in rehearsal, then in a more developed form, and finally with full orchestra. In Act I there follows a complex *Concerto*, and a further setting of Striggio, *Memoria*, using the text of the Messagera from *Orfeo*, but setting it for baritone. In Act II there follows a reworking of *Memoria* and a series of other numbers. Act III then establishes a symmetry with Act I by permutation: *Air* is followed by a final reworking of *Memoria*, and by a *Concerto II* that richly develops the materials of *Concerto I* and *Air*.

This complex exercise in 'open theatre' entirely baffled the opera-lovers of Santa Fe. The work was a fiasco: the first of Berio's career. He reworked it in 1977, giving it a new sense of *dénouement* by building around two subsequently composed works, *Agnus* and *E vo'*. Two terrified children are hunted down by searchlights. *Agnus* is sung. A mezzo-soprano enters, and snatching up one of the children's dolls, sings *E vo'* as a lament. In this form, *Opera* has achieved several subsequent productions, but for all its individual musical felicities, has never proved fully convincing theatrically.

EDITIONS   f.s., Universal (on hire), 1977; rev. version: v.s., Universal (on hire), 1977

La vera storia
The True Story
Opera in two parts ('a full evening')
Libretto by Italo Calvino
Composed 1977–81
PREMIERE   9 March 1982, La Scala, Milan
CAST   Leonora *s*, Luca *t*, Ada *ms*, Ivo/Commandant *bar*, The Condemned Man *b*, Ugo/Priest *t*, at least 2 street-singers, passers-by I, II and IV, Passer-by III *s*, 3 voices in the street; *satb* chorus of at least 60 voices; speakers, mimes, dancers, acrobats
ORCHESTRATION   4 fl/2 picc, 2 ob/ca, E♭cl, 2 cl, b cl, 3 bsn, alto sax, tenor sax, 3 hn, 3 tpt, 3 trbn, bass tuba, electric organ, hp, 2 pf/cel, timp, perc (3 players), str

Berio started with his own musico-dramatic conception, and indeed had already begun work on the music before he invited Calvino to fine down the project into a concrete libretto. Part I, like *Opera*, is built from three interacting, but now closely related levels. The first of these concerns the popular feast, or *festa*, embodied in four large choral sections that show collective life in all its ambivalence: anarchic ebullience, sadism in the face of a public execution, rebellion against an oppressive regime, and when that rebellion is crushed by the authorities, stoic resignation.

Within this framework, Berio and Calvino use individual protagonists to operate what is in effect a structural analysis of the conventions of 19th-century opera. Individual protagonists have names, but little more. They act out a series of stock situations whose emotional urgency is taken entirely seriously, but unembellished by narrative detail. Clearly *Il trovatore* lies in the background: a baby is stolen in an act of revenge, two brothers – one powerful, one not – fight for the love of a passive heroine. The music abets the analytical process: characters wedded to action sing clean, urgent lines, while those to whom circumstance denies the chance of action proliferate into melismatic settings of richly poetic texts. A third level of commentary, some of it decidedly ironic, is provided by a series of six popular ballads, of which the last two, both reflecting Berio's studies of folk music, acquire remarkable intensity.

Part II synthesizes the disjunct verbal and musical material of Part I into a powerful and continuous flow. It reinterprets the framework of Part I in grimly contemporary terms. But in the urban police state of Part II the power of the authorities is omnipresent: the popular solidarity of the Part I *feste* has been silenced; the chorus on stage is almost mute (their powers of articulation being transferred to disembodied voices in the orchestra, as in *Passaggio*), and where individuals dare to raise their voice, they are no longer 'characters from an opera', but nameless 'passers-by'. The same story of police brutality and revenge, of revolt and suppression is enacted, but now under circumstances where, if the voice of stoic resignation that ended Part I is to be heard at all, it behoves the creatures of operatic fiction from Part I to re-enter at the end of Part II and sing on behalf of a silent and utterly crushed chorus. It is one of Berio's bleakest and most powerful conceptions.

EDITIONS   f.s./v.s., Universal (on hire)

Un re in ascolto
A King Listens
'Musical action' in two parts (1h 30m)
Libretto by the composer, after Italo Calvino, W. H. Auden and Friedrich Gotter
Composed 1979–84
PREMIERES   7 August 1984, Kleines Festspielhaus, Salzburg; UK: 9 February 1989, Covent Garden, London
CAST   Prospero *bar*, Producer *t*, Friday *actor*, Female Protagonist *s*, Soprano I (with her Pianist), Soprano II, Mezzo-Soprano, 3 singers *t*, *bar*, *b*, Nurse *s*, Wife *ms*, Doctor *t*, Lawyer *b*, Singing Pianist; *satb* chorus; Mime (Ariel), Messenger, Stage Designer and Assistants, Seamstress, A Lady to Saw in Half, Acrobats, Clown, 3 Dancers and others, *silent*; Accordion-player
ORCHESTRATION   3 fl/picc, 2 ob, ca, E♭cl, 2 cl, b cl, 2 bsn, dbsn, tenor sax, 3 hn, 3 tpt, 3 trbn, bass tuba, cel, electric organ, perc, str; onstage: pf, accordion

Un re in ascolto started life as a parable, proposed by Calvino, about a king who deciphers the collapse of his kingdom and the infidelity of his queen from what he hears listening in his palace. Berio transmuted this figure into an elderly theatrical impresario, so closely at one with his latest project – a search for 'another theatre' for which *The Tempest* is to serve as a vehicle – that he himself is called Prospero, and his theatre becomes his island. Prospero listens because he is auditioning a series of three singers in the hope of finding the ideal female protagonist for his production. But his hopes of finding his fantasies made flesh are confounded – indeed each woman addresses to him the same disturbingly personal message. He can never hope to capture the essential 'otherness' of a desired woman within his own world.

Meanwhile his new project is slipping from his control. An ambitious producer is turning it into an extravaganza quite alien to his own aspirations. In desperate revolt he finally starts to tear down some of the producer's scenery, but collapses.

At the start of Part II he is found where he fell (Berio originally intended the whole musical action to be continuous). Realizing that he is dying, those nearest to him react with predictable self-interest, but his players initiate a ragged ceremony of watching with the dying man. Prospero, by now wholly absorbed in his own dreams, takes on the role of the 'listening king' from which Berio and Calvino started – but does so recognizing that his kingdom is

Part II of Un re in ascolto *(Salzburg, 1984)*

not essentially that of lights and scenery, but rather that of 'the sea of music'. Thus fortified, he can now confront one final apparition: the female Protagonist for whom he was searching enters to confront him with a summation of all that he has heard during the three auditions: the distance between them is immutable. His players bid him farewell, and left alone on the island of his theatre, Prospero dies.

Recurrent musical threads run through *Un re in ascolto*. The female Protagonist's aria sums up the musical, as well as the verbal materials of *Auditions I* and *II*. Three of the four *Concertati* for Prospero's players share common materials. Above all, Prospero's five arias on listening (settings of monologues by Calvino that survived from the original project) all use the same restricted pitch field, and in consequence abound in similar melodic gestures. But it is above all the subtlety of Berio's mature harmonic language, accommodating as it does many echoes from previous generations, that gives *Un re in ascolto* its singular expressive power.

EDITIONS   f.s., Universal (on hire), 1984; v.s., Universal (on hire), 1983; lib., Universal, 1984

BIBLIOGRAPHY   David Osmond-Smith, *Berio*, OUP, 1991, pp. 90–118

D.O.-S.

LENNOX BERKELEY
(Sir) Lennox Randal Francis Berkeley; *b* 12 May 1903, Sunningwell Plains, Oxford, England; *d* 26 December 1989, London

Berkeley studied French and philology at Oxford, and only after 1927, when Ravel had seen some of his early scores and recommended him to Nadia Boulanger, did he begin a course of musical education, spending five years in Paris as her pupil and becoming acquainted with most of the young French composers of the day, including Poulenc, a lifelong friend. Another friend was Benjamin Britten, with whom he (jointly) composed the suite of Catalan dances, *Mont Juic*, in 1936.

Berkeley composed four symphonies and many vocal and chamber works. In the 1930s he wrote the oratorio *Jonah* and the ballet *The Judgement of Paris*. Later came commissions for wartime films and BBC features and after the war he orchestrated piano music by Fauré for the ballet *La fête étrange*. When he eventually came to opera he already had varied experience of writing for the stage. This is apparent in *Nelson* and *A Dinner Engagement*, less so in the oratorio-like *Ruth* to a libretto by Eric Crozier (1956). Fragments of a last opera, *Faldon Park*, to a libretto by Winton Dean, remain in short score since the composer had to abandon its composition in 1982 owing to ill-health.

Nelson

Opera in three acts, Op. 41 (2h 30m)
Libretto by Alan Pryce-Jones
Composed 1949–54
PREMIERE 22 September 1954, Sadler's Wells, London

Berkeley's first opera is also his most substantial one. The chronological treatment starts at a party in Naples for Nelson's 40th birthday, after the Battle of the Nile, and ends in the garden at Merton where Hardy tells Emma of Nelson's death and she consoles herself with thoughts of her role in the making of history. Revivals in concert performance have suggested that the work's failure to establish itself in 1954 may have been as much the fault of the production as any intrinsic lack of drama or lyricism on the part of the composer, both strong points of the opera. Though it has a certain static quality, it is alive to character, with memorable arias, a powerful quartet for the lovers and their respective spouses, and a brilliant birthday party set piece (one of several).

A Dinner Engagement

Opera in one act, Op. 45 (1h)
Libretto by Paul Dehn
PREMIERE 17 June 1954, Jubilee Hall, Aldeburgh

Berkeley's most successful opera was first seen at the Aldeburgh Festival in a double-bill with Arthur Oldham's version of the ballad opera *Love in a Village*. In a Chelsea kitchen the impoverished Earl and Countess of Dunmow are preparing a dinner with the help of their daughter Susan. The royal party arrives by accident at the kitchen door. In the second scene the Grand Duchess's son falls in love with Susan and the opera ends with a humorous septet. As in the later *Castaway*, the character of the music is set by the orchestra, though the vocal writing is memorably witty and lyrical.

EDITION v.s., Chester, 1955

A Dinner Engagement *(Aldeburgh, 1954)*

Castaway

Opera in one act, Op. 68 (55m)
Libretto by Paul Dehn
PREMIERE 3 June 1967, Jubilee Hall, Aldeburgh

This was intended as a companion to *A Dinner Engagement*, though at its premiere it was paired with Walton's *The Bear*. On his ten-year journey home to Ithaca Odysseus is shipwrecked on Scheria (now Ischia) where Princess Nausicaa falls in love with him. When he sails from the island he calls his wife Penelope's name to the same four haunting notes with which he had addressed Nausicaa. *Castaway* is more through-composed than his earlier operas and though the colourful orchestral writing holds the attention more strongly than the vocal writing, the word-setting is remarkably skilful.

EDITION v.s., Chester, 1970

Other operatic works: *Ruth*, 1956; *Faldon Park* (inc.), (1982)
BIBLIOGRAPHY Peter Dickinson, *The Music of Lennox Berkeley*, Thames Publishing, 1989

L.F.

IRVING BERLIN

Israel Baline; *b* 11 May 1888, Tyumen', Russia;
d 22 September 1989, New York

Having moved with his family to New York at the age of five, Irving Berlin worked at an early age as song-plugger, chorister, singing waiter and ultimately song-writer. Despite his lack of formal musical training, he was always able to write songs – both music and lyrics – seemingly effortlessly, in any idiom desired. Whether ragtime ditties, sentimental waltzes, suave 1930s dance tunes, patriotic rousers, blues or up-to-date 1940s show tunes, Berlin's songs always have a persuasive rightness about them, sounding deceptively like the sort of simple songs his listeners imagine they could write themselves – until they try it.

Annie Get Your Gun

Musical comedy in two acts (film: 1h 45m)
Libretto by Herbert and Dorothy Fields; lyrics by Irving Berlin
PREMIERES 16 May 1946, Imperial Theater, New York; UK: 7 June 1947, Coliseum, London; rev. version: 31 May 1966, New York State Theater, New York

A fanciful version of the life of Wild West Show sharp-shooting star Annie Oakley and her love for fellow performer Frank Butler, the show was originally planned for Jerome Kern. Berlin took over the project after Kern's death, and it has held the stage for decades. The score comprises an amazing collection of Broadway classics, the best known of which include 'You Can't Get a Man with a Gun', 'The Girl That I Marry', 'They Say It's Wonderful', 'Moonshine Lullaby', 'Sun in the Morning', 'Anything You Can Do' and 'There's No Business

Like Show Business'. A revision made for a 1966 revival with the original star, Ethel Merman, added one new song and eliminated a sub-plot with its two songs.

Ethel Merman in the title role of Annie Get Your Gun *(New York, 1946)*

RECORDINGS 1. Merman, Yarnell, Allers, RCA, 1966: features the original Annie in the rev. version; 2. Criswell, Hampson, London Sinfonietta, McGlinn, EMI, 1990: the only complete recording of the original version
FILM Sidney (dir.), MGM, 1950
EDITIONS v.ss., Irving Berlin, 1947; rev. edn, 1967

Other musicals include: *Watch Your Step*, 1914; *Stop! Look! Listen!*, 1915; *The Cocoanuts*, 1925; *Face the Music*, 1932; *Louisiana Purchase*, 1940; *Miss Liberty*, 1949; *Call Me Madam*, 1950; *Mr President*, 1962
BIBLIOGRAPHY Laurence Bergreen, *As Thousands Cheer*, Viking, 1990; Michael Freedland, *Irving Berlin*, Stein and Day, 1974

J.A.C.

HECTOR BERLIOZ

Louis Hector Berlioz; *b* 11 December 1803, La Côte St André, Isère, France; *d* 8 March 1869, Paris

Opera should have been at the centre of Berlioz's composing career, as it was of his life. The musical culture in which he grew to maturity was dominated by it. Once he had decided to be a composer (against the will of his doctor father, who wanted him to take up medicine), opera became his goal. Everything conspired to make him see music – requiem mass, secular cantata, above all opera – as a dramatic, expressive art: his own instincts; the precepts of his teacher Jean-François Le Sueur; the example of Gluck and Spontini and also of Salieri, Sacchini, Méhul and Cherubini, whose works he immersed himself in from his first arrival in Paris in 1821 and whose cause he defended against the, to him,

frivolous, undramatic values of Rossini; and, in the mid-1820s, the discovery of Weber through the performances of *Der Freischütz* at the Odéon. A large part of Berlioz's apprenticeship was practically lived in the opera house (and in the library, where he pored over and analysed the scores he had heard). Even the revelation of Beethoven at the Conservatoire Concerts from 1828 onwards – the crucial event in the evolution of his musical personality and the catalyst that precipitated the *Symphonie fantastique* – did not alter the fundamentally dramatic bias of his outlook. Symphony became a branch of dramatic music, to be developed in the direction opened up by Beethoven's Fifth, Sixth and Ninth. But opera remained a major preoccupation.

Yet it was symphonic and choral, non-operatic music that, in the event, absorbed the greater part of his compositional energies. Though the *Symphonie fantastique* and its successors, *Harold en Italie*, *Roméo et Juliette* and the *Symphonie funèbre et triomphale*, may contain quasi-theatrical elements, as do – even more – the 'dramatic legend' *La damnation de Faust* and the oratorio *L'enfance du Christ*, they were all conceived as concert works. In a career of 40 years Berlioz completed only four operas (five, if we count the lost ballad opera *Estelle et Némorin* of 1823): the first version of *Les francs-juges* (a medieval drama of tyranny and intrigue composed in 1824–6 and musically influenced by Méhul), *Benvenuto Cellini*, *Les troyens* and *Béatrice et Bénédict*.

It was certainly not for want of trying that he did not write more. Throughout his career there was usually some operatic project or other under consideration. Subjects he actively contemplated included *Antony and Cleopatra*, *Romeo and Juliet* (many years after the composition of his symphony on the play) and Scott's *The Talisman*. Undoubtedly Berlioz was more choosy than most of his contemporaries (in the end he became, like Wagner, his own librettist), and also more idealistic and demanding in his attitude to performance. The low standards that his work as music critic brought him daily into contact with may at times have discouraged him from writing operas. But the chief reason was simply the hostility and scepticism of the Paris operatic establishment. In the age of Auber, Meyerbeer and Halévy, Berlioz was not regarded as a good commercial investment: he was an eccentric, and besides – in the pigeonholing way of musical opinion in Paris – he was a 'symphonist' and therefore unfitted for writing opera.

The failure of *Benvenuto Cellini*, which was due to a combination of factors, among them the extreme technical difficulty of the score and the unfashionably colloquial style of the libretto, effectively ended Berlioz's hopes of establishing himself as an opera composer in Paris. He never had another commission there. As a brilliant and widely read critic, and as protégé of the influential daily newspaper the *Journal des débats*, he could not be entirely ignored; and for a few years, during the 1840s, he was in negotiation with the Opéra to set a

Scribe libretto, *La nonne sanglante* ('The Bleeding Nun') based on M. G. Lewis's Gothic novel *The Monk*. The surviving numbers show him making some effort to accommodate his style to the tastes of the Opéra. But neither party had much belief in the collaboration; the project languished, and the libretto was eventually set by Gounod.

In the last 25 years of his career Berlioz's only direct involvement with the Opéra was as musical consultant to productions of operas by Weber and Gluck. In 1841 he composed recitatives for *Der Freischütz* (spoken dialogue being forbidden at the Opéra) and orchestrated Weber's piano rondo *Invitation to the Dance* for the obligatory ballet; and in 1861 he supervised a revival of *Alceste* (repeated in 1866). This followed the Théâtre-Lyrique's immensely successful revival, in 1859, of *Orphée*, with Pauline Viardot, in an edition by Berlioz which adapted Gluck's Paris revision of the score to the title role's original alto pitch. It is in this edition that the opera is still usually given.

Berlioz's most regular operatic activity consisted in reviewing the endless succession of mostly ephemeral works that came and went on the Paris stage. The theatrical adaptation of *La damnation de Faust* which he planned to give (under the title *Méphistophélès*) in London in the late 1840s, during his period as musical director of Adolphe Jullien's Grand English Opera at Drury Lane, remained only an idea: Jullien went bankrupt before work could begin on it or on another unspecified opera intended for Jullien. Of Berlioz's last two operas, *Béatrice et Bénédict* was commissioned by a foreign theatre. *Les troyens* he wrote, in the first place, for himself. Then, having completed libretto and score in two years, he spent five years trying to get it put on, and in the end had to settle for performances of Acts III to V only, themselves in truncated form, by an opera house whose resources were inadequate.

Berliozian opera does not lend itself to generalization. In his output as a whole each major work inhabits its own poetic world, with an atmosphere and a style unique to it. The three completed operas of his maturity are quite unlike each other. *Béatrice et Bénédict*, outwardly, is a conventional opéra comique, breaking no new ground. *Benvenuto Cellini* is a most unconventional combination of comedy and grand opera and musically a work of great originality – in terms of rhythm especially, years ahead of its time. *Les troyens* harks back to classical tragédie lyrique and its successor, Spontinian grand opera, but it fuses them with the expressive language of Berliozian musical Romanticism at its most fully developed and highly charged. It has taken the musical world a good hundred years to realize that the work which resulted from this idiosyncratic mixture is among the supreme achievements of the 19th century – in Tovey's words, 'one of the most gigantic and convincing masterpieces of music-drama'.

Benvenuto Cellini

Opera semi-seria in two acts (2h 45m)
Libretto by Léon de Wailly and Auguste Barbier, after Cellini's *Memoirs* (1558–66; published 1728)
Composed 1836–8, rev. 1851–3
PREMIERES 10 September 1838, Académie Royale de Musique (Opéra), Paris; rev. version: 20 March 1852, Hoftheater, Weimar; UK: 25 June 1853, Covent Garden, London (Royal Italian Opera); US: 3 May 1975, Boston
CAST Benvenuto Cellini *t*, Giacomo Balducci *b*, Teresa *s*, Ascanio *ms*, Fieramosca *bar*, Pope Clement VII *b*, Francesco *t*, Bernardino *bar*, Pompeo *bar*, inn-keeper *t*; *satb* chorus of metalworkers, foundrymen, maskers, guards, monks, the Pope's retinue, Balducci's female servants and neighbours, people of Rome; dancers
ORCHESTRATION 2 fl/picc, 2 ob/ca, 2 cl/b cl, 4 bsn, 4 hn, 2 tpt, 2 cornet, 3 trbn, ophicleide, 3 timp, perc, 4 hp, 2 gtr, str; onstage: 2 tpt, 2 gtr, tambourine, cym

Berlioz apparently did not read the *Memoirs* of Benvenuto Cellini ('that bandit of genius', as he called him) until after his return from Italy in 1832. Yet in an important sense the opera springs from the 15 months he spent there as winner of the Prix de Rome. It celebrates Italy – not the Italy he experienced during his time in Rome (like Mendelssohn, who was there at the same time, he found contemporary Italian culture depressingly decadent and lethargic) but its Renaissance counterpart, an ideal Italy where art is proud and vital and held in high public esteem. The Renaissance artist–hero was a cult among the Romantics (cf. Delacroix's *Michelangelo in his Studio*). The libretto freely adapted by Barbier and Wailly from Cellini's *Memoirs* (with *commedia dell'arte* additions), showed the triumph of the unorthodox, embattled artist over obstructive officialdom and conventional, academic art – a subject with which Berlioz could identify strongly – in a setting that evoked the colour and energy of 16th-century Rome.

In its original form (1834), that of an opéra comique (i.e. with spoken dialogue), it was turned

Berlioz in 1856

down by the director of the Opéra-Comique. The following year a revised version, in which Alfred de Vigny had a hand, was accepted by the Opéra, and the work was given there three years later (with Pope Clement VII replaced, at the insistence of the censor, by a cardinal). It had a stormy reception and ran for only four performances (followed by three of Act I only plus a ballet). The opera remained unperformed for 13 years and in 1844 Berlioz used material from it for his concert overture *Le carnaval romain*. On becoming kapellmeister at Weimar, Liszt, a great admirer of the work, chose it as his second major production (the first was Wagner's *Lohengrin*). For the first Weimar performances, in March 1852, Berlioz revised the score, shortening it slightly, simplifying some of its technical difficulties and, with German taste in mind, removing or toning down its more burlesque elements. Before it was given again, in November 1852, Liszt suggested more drastic surgery in the form of a large cut in the final act, removing many scenes so as to achieve a much swifter *dénouement*. Berlioz concurred; but in order to save a few of the numbers involved he placed them earlier in the action.

This shorter, three-act 'Weimar version' was the one in which the work was generally known and performed for the next hundred years. Recently, however, there has been a return to the fuller two-act form and more logical scene order of the Paris *Cellini* of 1838 (as well as to the Pope) and even, beyond that, to spoken dialogue, as in the original opéra-comique conception. (In this connection it is significant that for a production proposed by the Théâtre-Lyrique in 1856, the opera was to have been given with spoken dialogue instead of recitatives.) The Paris version plus spoken dialogue and the Pope was the form in which Covent Garden presented the opera in 1966; and most subsequent performances, as well as the complete recording based on Covent Garden material, have done the same. So does the following synopsis.

SYNOPSIS

Act I Tableau 1: Shrove Monday, Rome; Balducci's house, evening. Balducci, the Papal Treasurer, is unhappy because the Pope has commissioned the Florentine metalworker Cellini, instead of the official papal sculptor, Balducci's prospective son-in-law Fieramosca, to make a statue of Perseus. Maskers, Cellini among them, annoy Balducci by singing a Carnival song under his window. He goes off angrily and Cellini and Teresa, Balducci's daughter, decide to elope the following night. Fieramosca overhears their plan ('Demain soir, mardi gras'). When Balducci returns, Cellini gets away, but Fieramosca is given a drubbing. Tableau 2: Shrove Tuesday evening; Piazza Colonna, with tavern courtyard and, opposite, Cassandro's open-air theatre. Cellini and his metalworkers sing to the glory of their art ('Honneur aux maîtres ciseleurs'). They plot public revenge on the Papal Treasurer for the meagre advance payment for Perseus: one of Cassandro's actors will impersonate him in the satirical pantomime about to be performed. Fieramosca and

his friend Pompeo plan to foil the abduction of Teresa. Fieramosca brags of his fencing skill ('Ah! qui pourrait me résister'). The revellers have gathered for Cassandro's show, *King Midas with the Ass's Ears*. Among them are Balducci, Teresa, Cellini, Ascanio (Cellini's apprentice), Fieramosca and Pompeo – the last four dressed as monks. Balducci is furious and a fight breaks out between the 'monks'. Cellini kills Pompeo. He is seized and about to be taken away when the Sant'Angelo cannon proclaims the end of Carnival. All lights are extinguished and in the confusion Cellini escapes.

Act II Tableau 3: Ash Wednesday; Cellini's studio, dawn. As a religious procession passes, Teresa and Ascanio pray for Cellini's safety ('Sainte Vierge Marie'). A moment later he appears: they must get away to Florence immediately. Before they can leave, Balducci enters with Fieramosca and denounces Cellini ('Ah! je te trouve enfin'). Their quarrel is interrupted by the arrival of the Pope, impatient to see if his Perseus is finished. He grants general absolution ('A tous péchés pleine indulgence') but gives Cellini an ultimatum: pardon and Teresa if the statue is cast that day. If not, he will hang. Tableau 4: That evening, in Cellini's foundry in the Colosseum, Ascanio looks forward to their 'bronze offspring's baptism of fire' ('Tra la la, mais qu'ai-je donc?'). Cellini gives way to weariness and longs for the simple life ('Seul pour lutter – sur les monts'). Fresh setbacks now threaten him. Fieramosca insists on their fighting a duel. In Cellini's absence the men down tools. But their mood changes when Fieramosca reappears and tries to bribe them to leave Cellini's service; Fieramosca is forced to help in the foundry. The Pope arrives and commands the casting to begin. Suddenly Fieramosca announces that they are running out of metal. But Cellini orders his men to throw all his finished works of art into the crucible. The metal fills the waiting mould and the statue is cast. The Pope acknowledges divine sanction for Cellini's labours, and all praise the art of the master metalworkers.

Berlioz's own verdict on *Benvenuto Cellini* – 'a variety of ideas, a vitality and zest and a brilliance of musical colour such as I shall perhaps never find again' – hardly seems excessive when the work is performed well. These qualities were, of course, its undoing. The music's rhythmic complexity, its constantly changing pulse and syncopation of orchestral colour, and the sheer pace at which things happen – the means by which the composer evokes the agitated, exuberant life and times of his hero – made it exceptionally difficult to perform. The final section of Fieramosca's fencing aria, to take one example, is metred successively in 7, 6 and 5 – this long before conductors were taught to deal with such irregularities.

Even now it is a virtuoso score, for chorus (male chorus especially) as well as orchestra. The best numbers are also among the most demanding: notably the huge, and hugely vivacious, tumultuous Carnival scene (in which, as Liszt said 'for the first time in opera the crowd speaks with its great roaring

The Carnival scene costume for Gilbert Duprez, who created the title role of Benvenuto Cellini *(Paris, 1838)*

voice') and the swift-moving yet lyrically expansive Act I trio 'Demain soir, mardi gras', music as scintillating as anything by Berlioz. Other striking numbers or passages include the E major prayer sung by Teresa and Ascanio against a background of liturgical chanting, with its softly glowing woodwind scoring; the firecracker finale of the sextet (the whole ensemble shows Berlioz's gift for comic music); the pungent Musorgsky-like recital of the innkeeper's bill for wine; the graphically evocative rhythms and colours of the forging scene; Harlequin's beautiful love song (cor anglais, harp, cello, with comments from the crowd) contrasted with Pasquarello's parody cavatina on ophicleide (tuba) and thumping bass drum, complete with ludicrously prolonged final cadence. The opera's characteristic blend of grandeur and levity is epitomized in the dramatic and musical treatment of the Pope – a personage at once awesome and profoundly cynical who, however, places supreme value on art.

RECORDING Eda-Pierre, Berbié, Gedda, Massard, Bastin, Soyer, Covent Garden Ch, BBC SO, C. Davis, Philips, 1973
EDITIONS f.ss., Hugh Macdonald (ed.), *New Berlioz Edition*, Bärenreiter, vols 1a and 1b, 1993; vols 1c and 1d, 1944; v.s., Choudens, 1963; study s. (Weimar version), Kalmus, 1974

La damnation de Faust

The Damnation of Faust
Légende dramatique in four parts (2h 15m)

Text by Gérard de Nerval, Almire Gandonniere and the composer, based on Part 1 of the play *Faust* by Goethe (1806) Gandonniere]]
Composed 1845–6
PREMIERES 6 December 1846, Opéra-Comique, Paris (concert); UK: 7 February 1848, Drury Lane, London (Parts I and II; concert); 18 February 1893, Monte Carlo; UK: 3 February 1894, Liverpool; US: 17 February 1894, New Orleans (concert)

Of all Berlioz's dramatic concert works from the *Symphonie fantastique* (1830) to *L'enfance du Christ* (1854), *La damnation de Faust* is closest to the opera house. (For long its popularity eclipsed his actual operas.) Berlioz himself at one time planned to adapt it to the stage; the project, however, came to nothing when the company for which it was intended, Jullien's English Grand Opera at Drury Lane, collapsed in bankruptcy. The appeal of its brilliantly evocative scenes to theatre directors is easy to understand. Yet in its existing form *La damnation* is an opera of the mind's eye, not of the stage. As John Warrack has said, 'The pace is different, the arena impalpable and too varied, the dramatic logic not that of the theatre but of a listener with an imagination able to free itself from physical surroundings and to course with the composer in a flash of thought from scene to scene or dwell upon a held mood of hilarity or tenderness or terror.' If the work suggests any visual medium, it is the cinema that its dramatic technique anticipates.

Berlioz originally composed eight disparate 'Scenes from *Faust*', settings of songs and ballads taken from Nerval's translation of *Faust Part 1*, which he read in 1828. By the time he embarked on a full-scale work, 17 years later, *Part 2* – the redemption of Faust – had been published; but it was *Part 1* (which had ended with the clear implication that the hero will be damned) that he chose to set. The Nerval numbers, revised, were incorporated into a structure which, though episodic, is no more so than Goethe's play. The central idea that governs and binds Berlioz's scenes is Faust's progress towards a deeper and deeper isolation and emptiness of soul – urged on by a Mephistopheles who is the dramatization of his own dark self – as, one by one, all his aspirations turn to dust.

RECORDINGS 1. Danco, Poleri, Singher, Harvard Glee Club, Radcliffe Choral Society, Boston SO, Munch, RCA, 1954; 2. Veasey, Gedda, Bastin, Van Allan, Ambrosian Singers, Wandsworth School Boys' Ch, London Symphony Ch and O, C. Davis, Philips, 1973; 3. Von Otter, Myers, Lafont, Schirrer, Edinburgh Festival Ch, Lyons Opera O, Gardiner, Philips, 1989: all three versions are conducted by experienced Berliozians [A.B.]
EDITIONS f.ss., Richaut, 1854; Julian Rushton (ed.), *New Berlioz Edition*, vol. 8a, Bärenreiter, 1979; v.s., Schott, 1968; study s., Eulenberg, 1964

Les troyens

The Trojans
Grand opera in five acts (3h 45m)
Libretto by the composer, based on Books 1, 2 and 4 of the *Aeneid* by Virgil (*c.* 19 BC)
Composed 1856–8, rev. 1859–60
PREMIERES Acts III–V, *Les troyens à Carthage*: 4 November 1863, Théâtre-Lyrique, Paris; Acts I–II, *La prise*

de Troie: 6 December 1890, Grossherzogliches Hoftheater, Karlsruhe; Acts I–V, condensed: 18 May 1913, Königliches Hoftheater, Stuttgart; US: Acts I–V, condensed: 27 March 1955, New England Opera Theater, Boston; UK: Acts I–II, *La prise de Troie*: 18 March 1935, Acts III–V, *Les troyens à Carthage*: 19 March 1935, Theatre Royal, Glasgow; Acts I–V, with a few cuts: 6 June 1957, Covent Garden, London; complete: 3 May 1969, King's Theatre, Glasgow; US: complete: 26 September 1983, Metropolitan, New York
CAST Cassandre *ms*, Chorèbe *bar*, Enée *t*, Ascagne *s*, Panthée *b*, Priam *b*, Ghost of Hector *b*, Hécube *s*, Hélénus *t*, Polyxène *s*, Andromache *silent*, Astyanax *silent*, Greek captain *b*, Didon *ms*, Anna *a*, Iopas *t*, Narbal *b*, Hylas *t*, Mercure *bar* or *b*, 2 Trojan soldiers 2 *b*, priest of Pluto *b*; *satb* chorus of Trojans, Greeks, Tyrians, Carthaginians, nymphs, satyrs, fauns, sylvans, invisible spirits
ORCHESTRATION picc, 2 fl/picc, 2 ob/ca, 2 cl/b cl, 4 bsn, 4 hn, 2 tpt, 2 cornet, 3 trbn, ophicleide or tuba, timp, perc, 6 or 8 hp, str; onstage: 3 ob, 3 trbn, high saxhorn, 2 soprano saxhorn (or 2 tpt), 2 alto saxhorn (or 2 tpt), 2 tenor saxhorn (or 2 hn), 2 bass saxhorn (or 2 tuba), 2 timp, perc

The roots of Berlioz's culminating masterpiece lie far back in his boyhood, in the passion for Virgil's *Aeneid* that he conceived while studying Latin under his father's tuition. The characters of the *Aeneid* became familiar inhabitants of his inner world; they were so real to him, he later wrote, that 'I imagine they knew me, so well do I know them.' Though the idea of basing an opera on the fall of Troy and the founding of Rome must have often been in his mind in the intervening years, it was not until the early 1850s that he began to think really seriously of doing so. At first he resisted it, knowing that in the climate of the time the likelihood of the Paris Opéra accepting such a work, by a composer of his dubious reputation, let alone performing it adequately, was practically nil. But in 1856, prompted by the recent unexpected success of his oratorio *L'enfance du Christ* and by the urgings of Princess Carolyne Sayn-Wittgenstein, Liszt's mistress, with whom he had discussed the project on his visits to Weimar (and who made it her mission to get the work written), he changed his mind. Beginning in May 1856, he wrote *Les troyens*, poem and score, in less than two years.

In structure and language the libretto is influenced by the example of Berlioz's beloved Gluck. At the same time it borrows important features (though not its ancient-world subject) from Parisian grand opera: among them the five-act form, the central role of the chorus, the spectacular crowd scenes and the large forces, including stage bands. A further influence is Shakespeare – not only in the Act IV love duet, whose text is inspired by Lorenzo's and Jessica's 'In such a night' in *The Merchant of Venice*, but, generally, in the mixture of genres and juxtaposition of sharply contrasted scenes and in the wide geographical scope of the action. Berlioz described the work as 'Virgil Shakespeareanized'. Reshaped with great skill, the *Aeneid* – chiefly Books 1, 2 and 4, but other parts of the epic as well – provides the material for most of the text, part of which is a direct translation from the Latin.

If the libretto of *Les troyens* contains elements that were old-fashioned by the standards of the day, the music is Berlioz at his most audacious and richly expressive; it is both a summing up – a merging of the two main streams of his compositional life, the operatic and the dramatic–symphonic – and a reaching out into new territory.

Despite its grand scale *Les troyens* is not an exceptionally long opera. But before a note had been heard it had acquired the reputation of being so; and that reputation seemed confirmed when Berlioz subsequently made two operas of it, *La prise de Troie* and *Les troyens à Carthage*. The Théâtre-Lyrique, whose offer he had accepted when the Opéra continued to make no serious move to put on *Les troyens*, decided that the work's demands were too great for its resources, and insisted on his dividing it in two; and, so that he could hear it before he died, he reluctantly agreed. In the event only *Les troyens à Carthage* was given and, even then, extensive cuts were made during the run of 21 performances. For nearly a century *Les troyens*, when it was played in the theatre, was given mostly as a two-part work on successive evenings, or if on one evening, in drastically shortened form. It was not until the near-complete *Troyens* at Covent Garden in 1957 that Berlioz's original conception was vindicated: that of a single epic of the destiny of a people and its tragic consequences in the lives of individual human beings.

SYNOPSIS
Act I Troy: the abandoned Greek camp outside the walls. The Trojans celebrate their deliverance from ten years of siege. They hurry off to look at the huge wooden horse left by the Greeks, many believe, as an offering to Pallas Athene. Cassandra, the Trojan prophetess and daughter of King Priam, foresees the fate of Troy – the people, led by the king, going blindly to their doom, and with them her betrothed, the young Asian prince Corebus, whom she will not live to marry ('Malheureux roi'). When Corebus appears she rejects his soothing words and, as her vision takes shape, prophesies the destruction of Troy. She urges Corebus to save his life by leaving at once. He dismisses her terrors ('Quitte-nous dès ce soir'). Trojan leaders lay thank offerings at a field altar but their rejoicing breaks off at the arrival of Andromache, widow of Hector, the Trojan hero and son of Priam. Aeneas rushes in and describes the appalling death of the priest Laocoon, devoured by sea serpents as he was inciting the people to burn the wooden horse. The whole assembly is struck with horror ('Châtiment effroyable'). Aeneas interprets the portent as Athene's anger at the sacrilege. Priam orders the horse to be placed beside the temple of the goddess. Cassandra's warning cries are ignored. The torchlit procession draws near, chanting the sacred hymn of Troy ('Du roi des dieux, ô fille aimée'). Suddenly it halts: from within the horse has come a sound like the clash of arms. But the people, possessed, take it as a happy omen. Cassandra hears the procession pass into the city.

Act II Tableau 1: a room in Aeneas' palace. The ghost of Hector appears to Aeneas and tells him that he must escape and found a new Troy in Italy ('Ah! fuis, fils de Vénus'). Corebus enters at the head of a

Projected design by A. Casse for Act II, Tableau 2, of Les troyens *(Paris, 1863)*

band of armed men. He reports that the citadel is holding out. They resolve to defend it to the death. Tableau 2: a hall in Priam's palace; at the back a high colonnade. Women pray before an altar to Vesta ('Ha! puissante Cybèle'). Cassandra prophesies that Aeneas will found a new Troy in Italy. But now Corebus is dead, and she would rather take her own life than fall into the hands of the Greeks. Those women too frightened to face death are driven out. The rest, in growing exaltation, vow to die with Cassandra ('Complices de sa gloire'). Cassandra stabs herself. Greek soldiers announce that Aeneas has escaped with the treasure of Troy. With a last cry of 'Italie!', some of the women throw themselves from the colonnade, others stab or strangle themselves. Fire engulfs the palace.

Act III Carthage (the city founded by Dido after she fled from Tyre and her brother Pygmalion, murderer of her husband Sychaeus); a hall in Dido's palace, decorated for a festival, on a brilliant day after storms. The people celebrate their city and their queen ('Gloire à Didon') and promise to defend her against the Numidian king, Iarbas. Builders, sailors and farmworkers are presented with symbolic gifts. Alone with her sister Anna, Dido confesses to a mysterious sadness. She denies she is pining for love,

and resists her sister's argument that she should marry again. But to herself she admits the appeal of Anna's words ('Sa voix fait naître dans mon sein'). Iopas, the court poet, announces the arrival of an unknown fleet, driven ashore by the storm. Dido, recalling her own wanderings ('Errante sur les mers'), gives the strangers audience. Trojan chiefs enter, and Ascanius, Aeneas' son, presents trophies from Troy. Panthus explains Aeneas' mission: to found a new Troy in Italy. Narbal rushes in with the news that Iarbas and his hordes have attacked. Aeneas, till now disguised, offers the dazzled queen an alliance and, after entrusting Ascanius to her care, leads Trojans and Carthaginians to battle.

Act IV Tableau 1 (*Royal Hunt and Storm*): A forest near Carthage. Naiads bathing in a stream take fright at the sound of hunting horns and vanish as huntsmen enter the clearing. A storm breaks. Dido and Aeneas, separated from the rest, take refuge in a cave and there acknowledge and consummate their love, while satyrs and wood nymphs utter cries of 'Italie!'. The storm passes. Tableau 2: Dido's garden by the sea; night. Narbal and Anna discuss the situation, he full of foreboding, she optimistic: 'Fate calls Aeneas to Italy' – 'Love is the greatest of the gods'. Dido, Aeneas and the court watch dances performed to celebrate victory over the Numidians. Iopas, to soothe the queen's restless mood, sings of the fruits of the earth ('O blonde Cérès'). Dido learns from Aeneas that Andromache has married Pyrrhus, son of Achilles the slayer of her husband Hector. She feels absolved ('Tout conspire à vaincre mes remords'). All contemplate the beauty of the night ('Tout n'est que paix et charme'). Alone, Dido and Aeneas pour out their love ('Nuit d'ivresse et d'extase infinie'). As they leave, Mercury appears by a column on which Aeneas' arms are hung and, striking the shield, calls three times 'Italie!'.

Act V Tableau 1: The harbour of Carthage; night. Hylas, a young Phrygian sailor, sings of his longing for the forests of Mount Ida ('Vallon sonore'). Panthus and the Trojan chiefs agree they must delay their departure for Italy no longer. Two Trojan sentries fail to see why they should go. Aeneas enters, determined to leave but torn by love and remorse ('Inutiles regrets'). The ghosts of dead Trojan heroes appear and urge him to be gone. He rouses the sleeping army. Dido, distraught, confronts him. But her entreaties and her curses are equally vain. Tableau 2: A room in the royal palace. The Trojan fleet is seen setting sail. Dido orders a pyre, on which she will burn all memorials of Aeneas. Alone, she resolves on her death and takes farewell of life, friends and city ('Je vais mourir – Adieu, fière cité'). Tableau 3: A terrace overlooking the sea. Narbal and Anna pronounce a ritual curse on Aeneas. Dido ascends the pyre. To the horror of all she stabs herself with Aeneas' sword. Before doing so, she has prophesied the coming of a great conqueror – Hannibal – who will avenge her wrongs. But her final vision is of Eternal Rome.

As a musical epic and a dramatization of Virgil, *Les troyens* necessarily encompasses a wide variety of scenes and atmospheres. It is Berlioz's richest, most eventful score, embracing at one extreme the panoply of the *Royal Hunt and Storm* and the procession of the wooden horse and at the other the chamber-music intimacy of Dido's 'Adieu, fière cité'. But the composer is at great pains to unify its wealth of incident, not only by large-scale tonal design but also by means of innumerable recurring motifs, melodic, harmonic and rhythmic, of which the *Trojan March*, the fateful hymn heard in Acts I, III and V, is only the most obvious. Musically as well as verbally, the central idea of Roman destiny is a constant presence.

At the same time, contrast is a fundamental principle governing the musico-dramatic structure of the work. There is, first and most striking, the contrast between the musical idioms of Acts I and II (Troy) and III and IV (Carthage) – the one harsh, jagged, possessed, rhythmically on a knife edge; the other warm, expansive, sensuous. Then there is the contrast between one act and the next: Act I spacious and, for much of its course, static, followed by the violent, highly compressed Act II – Troy on its final fatal night – itself giving way to the Arcadian picture of peaceful Carthage in Act III, which, however, like Act I ends with a fast-moving, highly dramatic and

martial finale. Act IV is a sustained lyrical interlude, a time out of war, but ending with a grim reminder of the great questions of fate and war which will come to a head in Act V, the act that draws together and completes the preceding four.

There are also continual smaller-scale contrasts of musical character and dramatic perspective: the Trojans' rejoicing interrupted by the mime scene for the grieving Andromache, with its long clarinet melody, classical as a Grecian frieze, itself followed abruptly by Aeneas' brief, hectic narration of the death of Laocoon and the horror-struck ensemble it provokes; the sudden shift of focus from high romance and affairs of state to the feelings of ordinary people caught up in the tides of history, as Hylas the young sailor sings of his longing for his lost homeland; the Trojans chiefs' earnest discussion of policy giving way to the low-life grumbling of two sentries, for whom 'Italy' means nothing more significant than danger and discomfort, and whose homely dialogue in turn yields to the anguished, exalted mood of Aeneas' monologue, with its extended melodic lines, panting rhythms and heroic orchestration.

The central theme of the work is embodied in music of truly heroic temper. Yet Berlioz has no illusions about great 'causes' and what they can do to the lives of individuals. The juggernaut of Roman destiny marches across the personal fates of two contrasted but complementary tragic heroines, Cassandra and Dido. Cassandra is virtually Berlioz's own creation, developed from a few glimpses in the *Aeneid* into the fiery protagonist of the opera's first two acts; she is the personification of Troy's doom, which she foresees but is powerless to prevent. The role of Dido is the composer's tribute – a tribute of extraordinary radiance, tenderness and expressive intensity – to the mythical but to him totally real person who had first possessed his imagination 40 years before.

RECORDINGS   1. Lindholm, Veasey, Begg, Vickers, Glossop, Soyer, Covent Garden Ch and O, C. Davis, Philips, 1970; 2. Act V, Scenes 2 and 3: Baker, Greevy, Erwen, Howell, Ambrosian Opera Ch, LSO, Gibson, EMI, 1970
EDITIONS   f.s., Hugh Macdonald (ed.), *New Berlioz Edition*, vols. 2a and 2b, Bärenreiter, 1969; v.s., Choudens, 1863; study s. (photographic reduction of f.s.), Eulenburg, [1974]

Béatrice et Bénédict

Opéra comique in two acts (1h 30m)
Libretto by the composer, after Shakespeare's play *Much Ado About Nothing* (1598–9)
Composed 1860–62, rev. 1863
PREMIERES   9 August 1862, Neues Theater, Baden-Baden; 4 June 1890, Opéra-Comique, Paris; UK: 24 March 1936, Glasgow; US: 3 June 1964, Washington DC
CAST   Béatrice *s*, Bénédict *t*, Héro *s*, Claudio *bar*, Don Pedro *b*, Léonato *spoken role*, Ursule *ms*, Somarone *b*; *satb* chorus of people of Sicily, musicians, choristers, lords and ladies at the governor's court; dancers
STANDARD ORCHESTRA plus cornet, gtr, 2 hp

As early as 1833 Berlioz had contemplated composing an opera on *Much Ado About Nothing*. In the event it was to be his last major work, written nearly 30 years later to inaugurate the new opera house at the fashionable spa town of Baden-Baden in Germany. Since the mid-1850s the manager of the casino, Edouard Bénazet, had engaged Berlioz to give an annual gala concert at the height of the season, with an élite orchestra assembled for the occasion and rehearsed for as long as was necessary. In 1858 Bénazet commissioned an opera from him. The libretto, by Edouard Plouvier, concerned an episode from the Thirty Years War. Berlioz, however, felt little enthusiasm for it, and persuaded Bénazet to release him from his contract (Plouvier's libretto was set by Henry Litolff) and to agree instead to an opera, with spoken dialogue, on *Much Ado*.

Béatrice et Bénédict ('Bénédict' was the standard French form of Shakespeare's 'Benedick') was composed to a text by Berlioz himself, closely based, for the most part, on the play. The Baden-Baden performances of August 1862 were followed by a production, in German, at Weimar in the spring of 1863, with two numbers added to the second act (the women's trio and the distant chorus). In this form the opera was revived at Baden-Baden the following August.

Berlioz had first thought in terms of a one-act opera. Even at its full length *Béatrice* contains only 15 numbers, separated by mostly very short dialogue scenes. The work is a divertissement on one aspect of the play. Composing it, he said, was 'a relaxation after *Les troyens*' – 'I have taken as my text part of Shakespeare's tragi-comedy.' There is no Don John, no sinister sub-plot, no Dogberry and the watch; and Claudio remains a shadowy figure. The drama consists in 'persuading Beatrice and Benedick that they love each other', and in contrasting with their complex but ultimately more rewarding relationship the conventionally starry-eyed romance of the 'sentimental couple', Hero and Claudio. Somarone, the portrait of a pedantic, fussily conscientious court musician of the old school, is Berlioz's invention, derived from Shakespeare's Balthasar, whose song 'Sigh no more, ladies' comes at the same point in the action as Somarone's *Epithalame grotesque*, and prompts the same comment from Benedick: 'An he had been a dog that should have howled thus, they would have hanged him.'

SYNOPSIS

Act I In the park of the governor, Leonato, the inhabitants of Messina joyfully await the return of the victorious army from the Moorish wars. Hero, Leonato's daughter, learns that Claudio has come back loaded with honours. Beatrice inquires about 'Signor Mountanto' – that is, Benedick, between whom and Beatrice (Leonato explains) 'there is a kind of merry war – they never meet but there's a skirmish of wits'. After a *sicilienne*, the people disperse. Hero reflects on the happiness of being reunited with Claudio ('Je vais le voir'). Beatrice and Benedick mock each other in a duet whose teasing manner does not conceal an exasperated mutual interest ('Comment le dédain'). Don Pedro congratulates Claudio. Does the example not tempt

Benedick? But Benedick is impervious to their jests; he will die a bachelor ('Me marier'). Don Pedro and Claudio decide to find a way of tricking Beatrice and Benedick into loving one another. Court musicians rehearse the epithalamium which the choirmaster Somarone has written for the bridal couple. Benedick overhears an apparently serious discussion between Don Pedro, Leonato and Claudio about the wonderful behaviour of Beatrice, who has actually fallen in love with him. Benedick, astonished but impressed, resolves to requite her ('Ah! je vais l'aimer'). Hero and Ursula, too, laugh about the deception practised on Beatrice, who has been made to overhear that Benedick has fallen hopelessly in love with her. The two girls sink into a sweetly melancholy reverie on the beauty of the night and the impending wedding ('Nuit paisible et sereine').

Entr'acte   reprise of the *sicilienne*.

Act II A room in the governor's palace. From near by come the shouts of soldiers calling for drink, and Somarone's voice improvising a song in honour of Sicilian wines ('Le vin de Syracuse'). Beatrice enters, in great agitation. She recalls her unexpected sadness when Benedick left for the wars, and her dreams of him during his absence ('Il m'en souvient'). Then, with sudden decision, she faces her feelings: 'Contempt, farewell and maiden pride, adieu: Benedick, love on – I will requite you.' Hero and Ursula affect astonishment to see Beatrice at once agitated and strangely softened. With her they sing of the happiness of a bride about to marry the man she loves ('Je vais d'un coeur aimant'). Alone, Beatrice listens to a distant chorus summoning the bride. Benedick enters, and the two skirmish in a new key. Their embarrassed exchange is cut short by the wedding march. Claudio and Hero sign the contract. The scrivener produces a second one. 'Who else is marrying?' asks Don Pedro. Beatrice and Benedick confront each other. Each denies loving the other 'more than reason'. Avowals of love in their own hands are produced to confound them. A sign is brought in with the words, 'Here you may see Benedick the married man', which all sing to the music to which Benedick (trio, Act I) swore he'd never marry. Unabashed, Benedick ripostes by acknowledging the power of love and the giddiness of mankind ('L'amour est un flambeau').

Berlioz described *Béatrice et Bénédict* as 'a caprice written with the point of a needle'. It is his most light-fingered score, echoing in a gentler vein the rhythmic high spirits and wit of *Benvenuto Cellini*, and bathed in a kind of late-afternoon glow. The woodwind-writing is piquant and luminous. Prominent also are *pizzicato* strings and finely shaped violin lines of the utmost delicacy. Trombones play only in the latter part of the overture, the middle section of Beatrice's aria, the 13-bar *enseigne* (No. 14) and the final tutti. Tambourines and guitar add a touch of exotic colour. The exuberant overture alludes to half-a-dozen different numbers. Its angular, lilting theme in triplets, full of cross-rhythms, reappears in the final number, in which Benedick and Beatrice, declaring a temporary truce, sing of love as a 'will o' the wisp', a brief but enchanting gleam that 'comes from nowhere and then vanishes, to the distraction of our souls'. The other best numbers include the men's trio 'Me marier', with its nimble musical repartee; the charming women's trio 'Je vais d'un coeur aimant' in Berlioz's favourite slow 6/8 time; also in 6/8, the nocturne sung by Hero and Ursula, music of great economy used to evoke a mood of deep enchantment; and the noble, long-breathed *andante* (interrupted by martial sounds reminiscent of *Les troyens*) in which Beatrice recalls her sadness when Benedick left for the wars.

RECORDINGS 1. Veasey, Cantelo, Watts, Mitchinson, Cameron, Shilling, St Anthony Singers, LSO, C. Davis, Oiseau-Lyre, 1962; 2. Baker, Eda-Pierre, Watts, Tear, Allen, Lloyd, Bastin, Van Allan, John Alldis Ch, LSO, C. Davis, Philips, 1978; 3. Graham, McNair, Robbin, Viala, Cachemaille, Bacquier, Lyon Opéra Ch and O, Nelson, Erato, 1991
EDITIONS f.s., Hugh Macdonald (ed.), *New Berlioz Edition*, vol. 3, Bärenreiter, 1980; v.s., Brandis et Dufour, 1863

BIBLIOGRAPHY Jacques Barzun, *Berlioz and the Romantic Century*, 2 vols, Columbia University Press, 1969; Hector Berlioz, *Correspondence générale*: vol. 2 (1832–1842), Frédéric Robert (ed.), Flammarion, 1975; vol. 4 (1851–1855), Pierre Citron, Yves Gérard and Hugh Macdonald (eds), Flammarion, 1983; vol. 5 (1855–1859), Hugh Macdonald and François Lesure (eds), Flammarion, 1989; Hector Berlioz, *Memoirs*, trans. David Cairns, Cardinal, 1990; David Cairns, 'The Romantic Cult of the Artist–Hero', in booklet of complete recording of *Benvenuto Cellini*, Philips, 1973; David Cairns, *Berlioz: The Making of an Artist*, Deutsch, 1989; Ian Kemp (ed.), *Les troyens*, CUP (Cambridge Opera Handbooks), 1988; D. Kern Holman, *Berlioz*, Harvard University Press, 1989; Hugh Macdonald, *Berlioz*, Dent (Master Musicians Series), 1982

D.A.C.

MARCELLO BERNARDINI

[Marcello da Capua]; *b ?c.* 1740, ?Capua, Italy; *d* after 1799

Although his nickname suggests that he came from Capua, Bernardini is sometimes referred to as a Roman in libretti. Most of his operas were produced in Rome, though he certainly visited Munich and Turin (1768–9), Naples (1790–91) and Venice (1798–9) in a professional capacity. During the last decade of the century he seems to have been in the service of the Polish Princess Lubomirski. Almost all of his known operas are comic, and even in their own time they were criticized for being full of what we would now term slapstick humour. This certainly drew the crowds, and some of the works, such as *Li tre Orfei*, *Le donne bisbetiche* and *La donna di spirito*, were performed even into the 19th century. Perhaps this says more about the taste of the Roman audiences than about the quality of the operas. Bernadini also seems to have written a number of his own libretti.

Surviving operas: *Amore in musica* or *L'amore della musica*, 1773; *L'isola incantata* or *L'isola d'Alcina*, 1778, rev. 1784; *Il basso generoso*, 1780; *Li tre Orfei*, 1784; *Le donne bisbetiche*,

1785, rev. as *La finta Galatea*, 1788; *La donna di spirito*, *La donna bizzarra* or *Le quattro nazioni*, 1787; *L'amore per incanto* or *L'amore per magia*, 1791; *La statua per puntiglio*, 1792; *Don Simoncino, ossia Furberia e puntiglio*, 1798; *c.* 21 lost operas
BIBLIOGRAPHY Alessandro Ademollo, *I teatri di Roma nel secondo decimosettimo*, Rome, 1888

G.D.

ANDREA BERNASCONI

b ?1706 or ?1712, ?Marseilles, France; *d* ?27 January 1784, Munich

Bernasconi was the son of a French officer of Italian descent, who settled in Parma after relinquishing his commission. Up to 1753, he lived and worked mainly in Italy, where he produced a number of opere serie in the standard Neapolitan style of the period, many of them to libretti by Metastasio, such as *Didone abbandonata*, *Temistocle* and *Demofoonte*. Though generally conventional in manner, his operas are distinguished by the effectiveness of their declamatory writing, with carefully fashioned recitatives comparable to those of Hasse. In 1747, at Parma, Bernasconi married the widow of a *valet de chambre* of the Duke of Württemberg, and acquired a stepdaughter, Antonia, who became a fine opera singer, notably in the title role of Gluck's *Alceste*, which the composer is said to have written especially for her. From August 1753, Bernasconi was assistant kapellmeister to the electoral court at Munich, becoming full kapellmeister two years later. After the opening of the new Residenztheater in Munich in 1753, several of his earlier operas were revived there with much acclaim, and a number of new ones introduced, including versions of Metastasio's *Semiramide*, *La clemenza di Tito* and *Demetrio*. During the last 12 years of his life he devoted himself to the composition of sacred music, including 34 masses, all of which are now lost.

Opere serie: *Flavio Anicio Olibrio*, 1737; *Didone abbandonata*, 1738; *Alessandro Severo*, 1738; *Temistocle*, 1740; *Demofoonte*, 1741; *Il Bajazet*, 1742; *Germanico*, 1744; *Antigono*, 1745; *Artaserse*, 1746; *Ezio*, 1749; *Adriano in Siria*, 1755; *Agelmondo*, 1760; *Olimpiade*, 1764; *Semiramide*, 1765; *La clemenza di Tito*, 1768; *Demetrio*, 1772; 4 other secular dramatic works
Contributions to pasticcios: *Ixion*, 1746; *Andromeda*, 1749/50; *Euridice*, 1750, with additional arias by Hasse, Galuppi, Holzbauer, Handel, Jommelli, Wagenseil and others
BIBLIOGRAPHY E. J. Weiss, *Andrea Bernasconi als Opernkomponist*, dissertation, University of Munich, 1923

B.S.

LORD BERNERS

(Sir) Gerald Hugh Tyrwhitt-Wilson; *b* 18 September 1883, Bridgnorth, Shropshire, England; *d* 19 April 1950, Faringdon House, Berkshire, England

Berners was an accomplished writer and painter as well as a composer; he was also self-consciously an English eccentric. A member of the Diplomatic Service during the First World War, he knew Stravinsky and Casella and was considered by them a leading avant-garde figure. His five ballets include *The Triumph of Neptune*, written for Diaghilev in 1926.

Le Carrosse du Saint-Sacrement

The Carriage of the Blessed Sacrament
Opéra comique in one act (1hr 15m)
Libretto by the composer, after the comedy by Prosper Mérimée
Composed 1920, rev. 1926
PREMIERES 24 April 1924, Théâtre des Champs-Elysées, Paris; UK: 18 September 1983, BBC broadcast (in English)

The Viceroy of Peru is persuaded to part with his new status symbol, a coach, to the actress La Périchole, who in turn gives it to the Church in order to escape the law. The headlong action and witty conversational style is set to music indebted to Les Six and the popular music of the day. Most of the thematic interest is in the orchestral music, some of which reappeared, rearranged by Constant Lambert, in the orchestral *Caprice Péruvien*.

EDITIONS v.ss., J. & W. Chester, 1923; rev. version, 1926

BIBLIOGRAPHY G. Jean-Aubry, '*Le Carrosse du Saint-Sacrement*', *Chesterian*, June 1923, pp. 244–51

L.F.

LEONARD BERNSTEIN

b 25 August 1918, Lawrence, Massachusetts, US; *d* 14 October 1990, New York

Bernstein worked with huge success in the fields of both classical music and the Broadway musical theatre. He wrote ballets, musicals and later in life returned to opera. Some of his works, such as *Candide*, have been performed both in theatres and in opera houses. One of his most distinctive contributions was the development of a new direction for popular music theatre in *West Side Story*.

He first achieved fame as a conductor (studying with Reiner and serving as assistant to Koussevitzky and Rodzinski). A last-minute substitution for Bruno Walter with the New York Philharmonic in November 1943 led to a huge demand for Bernstein as both conductor and composer. Within months, he had composed the highly successful one-act ballet *Fancy Free*, and he followed it with an impressive series of concert pieces over the following years. His position as principal conductor of the New York Philharmonic from 1956 to 1966 (the first American-born conductor to hold that post), and his television appearances as a commentator on music, made him one of the most familiar faces in American music. In the years following his departure from the

Leonard Bernstein in the 1950s

Philharmonic, he became one of the most prominent international conductors of his time.

At the same time, Bernstein involved himself with musical theatre on an ever-increasing level of musical complexity and sophistication. He achieved success in many genres, and all but one of his stage works (an unsuccessful collaboration with Alan Jay Lerner) have retained an active stage life. He several times expressed the belief that a living American opera literature can evolve only from its popular musical theatre, and his own efforts contributed to that development. He ranks among the handful of popular composers who had the ability to orchestrate their own musicals (though he in fact delegated part, sometimes all, of this work to others). His first efforts for the Broadway stage aspired to be little more than well-crafted entertainments, but beginning with *Candide* he took pains to unify his theatre scores motivically and to find opportunities for extended musical development. The essay 'Why Don't You Run Upstairs and Write a Nice Gershwin Tune?' from his book *The Joy of Music* reveals his disappointment that after two musicals he had not produced a truly popular song, but *West Side Story* (in particular, its film version) changed that. Unfortunately, thereafter he composed only sporadically for the musical stage.

On the Town

Musical comedy in two acts (film: 1h 45m)
Libretto by Betty Comden and Adolph Green, based on an idea by Jerome Robbins
PREMIERES 28 December 1944, Adelphi Theater, New York; UK: 30 May 1963, Prince of Wales Theatre, London

Suggested by the ballet *Fancy Free*, this light-hearted show tells of three sailors on 24-hour shore leave in New York City, finding adventure and love. In addition to its tuneful songs (most familiarly 'New York, New York') it features extended dance sequences originally choreographed by Jerome Robbins.

RECORDING Walker, Comden, Green, Reardon, unnamed O, Bernstein, CBS, 1960: Walker, Comden and Green were in the original cast; reissues have added two songs omitted from the first release
FILM Kelly (dir.), Donen, MGM, 1949: most of score omitted, other songs added
EDITIONS facsimile of manuscript, Boosey & Hawkes (on hire)

Trouble in Tahiti

Opera in seven scenes (45m)
Libretto by the composer
PREMIERE 12 June 1952, Brandeis University, Waltham, Massachusetts
CAST Dinah *ms*, Sam *bar*, jazz trio *s, t, b*
SMALL THEATRE ORCHESTRA with single str

This opera's first presentation, in a double-bill with *The Threepenny Opera* in Blitzstein's translation, initially resulted in unfavourable comparisons with Weill's newly rediscovered masterpiece. It has, however, shown considerable staying power, especially in its reworked version, *A Quiet Place*, and as Bernstein's first true opera shows him in notable command of his resources. If his libretto cannot quite justify its satirical attack on suburban complacency, the unpretentious format and humorous undercurrent minimize the problem. The opera's title is that of a mindless musical film which Dinah describes in the scene 'What a movie!', a solo frequently excerpted for revues and recitals.

The trio croons about the bliss of suburbia, as an introduction to Sam's and Dinah's angry breakfast conversation. We then see Sam engaging in questionable dealings at work, while Dinah tells her (unseen) psychiatrist of her frustration with her life and her longing to escape to a dream garden, a quiet place. She and Sam accidentally meet on the street, and (to their momentary regret) avoid having lunch together by lying about prior engagements. That afternoon he gloats in the locker room over a handball triumph while she goes to see an 'awful' movie; they both avoid seeing their son's school play. That evening the two attempt to communicate about their problems but give it up and go out to the movies instead – to the same movie Dinah had seen earlier that afternoon, an escapist fantasy called *Trouble in Tahiti*.

In this piece, Bernstein darts elusively between comic bravura and deep sadness, ingeniously grafting classical and vocal styles to popular American song forms to do so.

RECORDING see *A Quiet Place*, below
EDITION v.s., Jalni/Boosey & Hawkes, 1953

Wonderful Town

Musical comedy in two acts (2h)
Libretto by Joseph Fields and Jerome Chodorov, based on their play *My Sister Eileen*; lyrics, Betty Comden and Adolph Green
PREMIERES 25 February 1953, Winter Garden, New York; UK: 23 February 1955, Prince's Theatre, London

Sisters Eileen and Ruth have moved from Ohio to Greenwich Village, and in the episodic course of the story find love and success. Conceived as a star vehicle for Rosalind Russell, the score features several novelty turns for her, and attempts a modicum of unification among some of the songs.

RECORDING Russell, Adams, Gaynes, unnamed O, Engel, US Decca, 1953
EDITIONS facsimile of manuscript, Boosey & Hawkes (on hire); lib., Chilton, 1976; vocal selection. Chappells, 1953

Candide

Comic operetta in two acts
Revised version in one act
Libretto by Lillian Hellman (rev. versions, by Hugh Wheeler), based on the novel by Voltaire (1756); lyrics by Richard Wilbur; additional lyrics by John Latouche, Dorothy Parker, Hellman, Bernstein and (in rev. versions) Stephen Sondheim
Composed 1954–6, rev. 1973, 1988–9
PREMIERES 1 December 1956, Martin Beck Theater, New York; UK: 30 April 1959, Saville Theatre, London; US: published rev. version: 18 December 1973, Chelsea Theater Center, Brooklyn, New York

The journey of Voltaire's eponymous hero from naïve optimism to disillusioned knowledge of the world's evil is told in a mock-operetta style. Its music covers a wide range, from allusions to various popular styles (tango, *schottische*, waltz) through mock operetta, to some passages of fully operatic weight. Its most familiar portions are the pseudo-Rossinian overture (probably Bernstein's most performed concert piece) and the coloratura soprano aria, both sincere and parodistic, 'Glitter and Be Gay'.

Far more popular in revival (sometimes by opera companies) than during its brief Broadway run in 1956, *Candide* has undergone sweeping revisions since its troubled conception. The music used in the Broadway premiere (pre-production manuscripts included many songs and lyrics not used in that production) corresponds to that in the published vocal score and, with some sections omitted, to the original-cast recording. For the first London production, Bernstein supplied a new song ('We are Women'). Then, in a series of US West Coast productions, the libretto was revised and different music used, culminating in a full-scale revival which began in San Francisco and ended in Washington DC, closing before its intended Broadway opening.

The 1973 revision, conceived and directed by Harold Prince, moved to Broadway in 1974 and had a successful run there. It became the usual performing version thereafter. Hugh Wheeler supplied a new libretto to replace Hellman's, in one act and with a quite different sequence of events (more faithful to Voltaire in some respects), often more farcical in tone, and with Pangloss and the Governor combined into a single role to be played by Voltaire as narrator. Five numbers were omitted and Stephen Sondheim supplied minor lyric revisions as well as words for three new songs.

The fight between the Jets and the Sharks in West Side Story *(New York, 1957)*

John Mauceri, who had assembled the music for the 1973 production, performed the same service for New York City Opera when it added *Candide* to its repertoire. This was closely based on the 1973 version (Prince was still directing), but in two acts and with the five missing songs restored, mostly in new contexts (sometimes with new lyrics, by Wilbur).

A 1988 Scottish Opera production, with yet another reconsidered libretto (still credited to Hugh Wheeler) and additional restorations, established another new text. This adaptation by John Wells and Mauceri aimed to include as much of Bernstein's music as possible, and was able for the first time since 1971 to use the locations, if not the words, of Hellman's libretto. A 1989 concert and a recording by the composer in London used primarily the Scottish Opera version but introduced revisions and restorations of its own.

RECORDINGS 1. Cook, Petina, Rounseville, Adrian, Krachmalnick, CBS, 1956: still unsurpassed in most respects; 2. Anderson, Hadley, Gedda, Ludwig, Green, London Symphony Ch and O, Bernstein, DG, 1989: contains the most music of any *Candide* recording, and the composer's final thoughts on it
EDITIONS 1956 version: v.s., Jalni/Boosey & Hawkes, 1988; 1973 version: v.s. (including lib.), Schirmer Books, 1976

West Side Story

Musical in two acts
Libretto by Arthur Laurents, based on a concept by Jerome Robbins after Shakespeare's *Romeo and Juliet*; lyrics by Stephen Sondheim
PREMIERES 26 September 1957, Winter Garden, New York; UK: 12 December 1958, Her Majesty's Theatre, London
CAST Maria *s*, Tony *t*, Anita *ms/dancer*, Riff *bar/dancer*, Bernardo *bar/dancer*, 4 adult *spoken roles*, dance chorus of Jets and Sharks (all named roles, with speaking and singing)

ORCHESTRATION (Bernstein, with Sid Ramin and Irwin Kostal) theatre orchestra, ww doubles, gtr, no vlas

West Side Story is now regarded as a classic musical. Among its many important features, it was a landmark in granting dance a central place in the musical, in allowing extended compositional techniques, and in permitting a truly tragic ending. But it was only a moderate success in its first productions. The 1961 film version introduced it to a far wider audience and boosted it to a popularity it has retained ever since. One of the few shows as famous for its dance music (composed by Bernstein rather than relegated to an arranger, and later collected by him in a concert suite) as for its songs, *West Side Story* includes Bernstein's most memorable melodies.

SYNOPSIS
Act I New York's West Side in the 1950s. A dance 'prologue' depicts the growth of the rival gangs, the longer-established Jets (led by Riff) and the Puerto Rican Sharks (led by Bernardo). Tony, a former Jet, meets Maria (Bernardo's sister) at a community dance ('Dance at the Gym'); the two fall in love ('Maria'), not realizing that they are supposed to be enemies. While the two pledge their love ('Tonight'), the Shark women engage in cynical banter about the relative advantages of Puerto Rico and New York ('America') and the Jets prepare for a meeting with the Sharks ('Cool'). Riff and Bernardo arrange a rumble to settle the gang rivalry. Having just exchanged private wedding vows with Maria ('One Hand, One Heart'), Tony interrupts 'The Rumble', trying to make peace, but unintentionally allows his friend Riff to be killed; enraged, he kills Bernardo.

Act II   Happily waiting for Tony's return ('I Feel Pretty') Maria instead hears that he has killed her brother. She manages to forgive him ('Somewhere'), and the two determine to flee together; he goes into hiding for the night with the Jets, who are themselves bewildered by the turn of events ('Gee, Officer Krupke'). Anita tries to carry a message from Maria to Tony, but is so abused by the Jets that she instead tells him that Maria is dead. In despair, Tony allows himself to be killed by the Sharks. Only Maria's intervention, pointing out what everyone has lost by the war, stops the bloodshed and provides a hint of some hope for the future.

RECORDINGS   1. Lawrence, Rivera, Kert, Goberman, CBS, 1957; 2. Te Kanawa, Troyanos, Carreras, Broadway Ch and O, Bernstein, DG, 1984: though the DG studio version is oddly cast, it is the only recording to contain the entire score
FILM   Wise (dir.), Mirisch–7 Arts/UA 1961
EDITION   v.s., Schirmer and Chappell, 1959; study s., Boosey & Hawkes, in preparation

Mass

Theatre piece in one act (1h 45m)
Libretto from the liturgy of the Roman Mass, with additional texts by Stephen Schwartz and the composer
Composed 1971
PREMIERES   8 September 1971, Kennedy Center Opera House, Washington DC; UK: 7 May 1986, Guildhall School of Music and Drama, London

A stylized theatre piece that uses the celebration of a Mass as its framework for an exploration of the sources and nature of faith and love, *Mass* focuses on the figure of a Celebrant and his doubts. The varied social and personal forces surrounding him are appropriately embodied in a musical eclecticism.

RECORDING   Titus, Bernstein, CBS, 1971
EDITION   v.s., Amberson/Schirmer, 1971

1600 Pennsylvania Avenue

Musical in two acts
Libretto by Alan Jay Lerner
PREMIERE   4 May 1976, Mark Hellinger Theater, New York

Bernstein's commercially least successful theatre piece was an attempt to contribute to the US Bicentennial with a historical statement, told through a series of presidencies in the White House, and the continuity of the (predominantly black) domestic staff. Control was taken away from Lerner and Bernstein, and the version that opened in New York did not reflect their wishes. Revivals (the first of which took place in 1992, in Bloomington, Indiana) will undoubtedly make use of earlier versions of the work.

A Quiet Place

Opera in three acts (original version in four scenes) (2h 30m)
Libretto by Stephen Wadsworth
Composed 1980–83, rev. 1983–4
PREMIERES   17 June 1983, Jones Hall, Houston; rev. version: 19 June 1984, La Scala, Milan; rev. version: 22 July 1984, Kennedy Center, Washington DC

As a sequel to *Trouble in Tahiti*, *A Quiet Place* portrays and tentatively resolves the family reactions years later after Dinah's death in a car crash. Friends and family gather at the funeral parlour. Sam's and Dinah's children arrive: Junior and his sister Dede, with her husband François, who was formerly Junior's lover. Sam cannot accept the *ménage à trois* or his son's disturbed behaviour. The two come to blows near the coffin. At home that evening, Sam reads Dinah's diaries – first flashback, *Trouble in Tahiti* Part I – François helps Junior through another psychotic episode and Dede and François reaffirm their love. The second flashback, *Trouble in Tahiti* Part II, completes the act. In the last act Sam accepts François and there is a new sense of unity in the family, Junior being the first to reach through the confusion.

The score is a web of leitmotifs based mostly on themes from *Trouble in Tahiti*. The imagery of the earlier libretto and the core element of jazz are also elaborated in the sequel, most tellingly in the character of Junior, whose madness is portrayed in fragments from *Tahiti*. *A Quiet Place* attempts to capture the broken, searching rhythms of modern American life and language. Bernstein writes virtuosically for a large orchestra, rarely settling for long in a clearly tonal idiom. An orchestral suite from the opera was created posthumously in 1991.

RECORDING   Morgan, White, Ludgin, Brandstetter, Crafts, Austrian Radio O, Bernstein, DG, 1986: the incorporated *Trouble in Tahiti* performance is the preferred recording of that work
EDITION   v.s., Jalni, 1988

BIBLIOGRAPHY   Peter Gradenwitz, *Leonard Bernstein*, Berg, 1987

J.A.C.

FERDINANDO BERTONI

Ferdinando Gasparo Bertoni; *b* 15 August 1725, Salo, nr Bréscia; *d* 1 December 1813, Desenzano, nr Lake Garda

After studying with Padre Martini in Bologna, Bertoni moved to Venice, where the success of his comic opera *La vedova accorta* (1745) led to subsequent performances in other Italian cities and in Spain. In 1752 he became first organist at St Mark's, and subsequently maestro in succession to Galuppi in 1785; in all, his association with the basilica lasted for 55 years. Despite composing an astonishing amount of church music, he also devoted himself energetically to an operatic career, achieving performances throughout Italy. He worked at the King's Theatre in London for four seasons (1778–80 and 1781–3), during which time he directed 14 operas and pasticcios, having been granted leave of absence from St Mark's. His music had already been heard in England; various arias and duets had been included in pasticcios some 20 years earlier.

Burney was not over-impressed; he considered Bertoni's music pleasing but lacking in genius. None the less, Bertoni enjoyed enormous popularity in Italy, and his operas and recreational music were constantly in the repertoire: *Quinto Fabio*, for example, was performed 20 times in Padua with considerable success, due at least in part to the involvement of the castrato Gasparo Paccierotti, who also accompanied Bertoni to England. *Orfeo ed Euridice* (1776) was his most widely disseminated work; Bertoni's preface acknowledges Gluck's 1762 setting of the same text, but an aria in Gluck's 1774 French revision of his opera was said to have been plagiarized from Bertoni's *Tancredi* of 1766.

Surviving operas: *Ipermestra*, 1748; *Le pescatrici*, 1751; *Antigono*, 1752; *La moda*, 1754; *Sesostri*, 1754; *Antigona*, 1756; *Lucio Vero*, 1757; *Il Vologeso*, 1759; *Le vicende amorose*, 1760; *La bella Girometta*, 1761; *Ifigenia in Aulide*, 1762; *Achille in Sciro*, 1764; *L'ingannatore ingannato*, 1764; *Il Bajazetto*, 1765; *Olimpiade*, 1765; *Tancredi*, 1766; *Ezio*, 1767; *Semiramide riconosciuta*, 1767; *Scipione nelle Spagne*, 1768; *Alessandro nell'Indie*, 1769; *Il trionfo di Clelia*, 1769; *L'anello incantato*, 1771; *Andromaca*, 1771; *Narbale*, 1774; *Aristo e Temira*, 1776; *Orfeo ed Euridice*, 1776; *Artaserse*, 1776; *Telemaco ed Eurice nell'isola di Calipso*, 1776; *Medonte*, 1777; *Quinto Fabio*, 1778; *Demofoonte*, 1778; *La governante*, 1779; *Armida abbandonata*, 1780; *Cajo Mario*, 1781; *Il convito, or The Banquet*, 1782; *Eumene*, 1783; *Nitteti*, 1789: 13 lost operas

G.D.

FRANZ BERWALD

Franz Adolf Berwald; *b* 23 July 1796, Stockholm; *d* 3 April 1868, Stockholm

Berwald was the leading Swedish composer of his day and is best known for his four symphonies, composed during the 1840s. In his youth he was a violinist and violist at the Royal Opera in Stockholm. All his life Berwald longed to be accepted as an opera composer; he composed (or planned) more than eleven. His first attempt was *Gustaf Wasa*, also the theme of the Swedish national opera by J. G. Naumann (1786); only a march survives.

In 1829 he went to Berlin, where he founded an enterprising and successful orthopaedic institute, but he finally settled in Sweden in 1849, hoping to succeed his cousin, Johan Fredrik Berwald (1787–1861) as conductor of the Royal Opera.

On his return to Sweden, he wrote two operettas: *Jag går i kloster*, heard first in fragmentary form at a concert in which Jenny Lind took part, and *Modehandlerskan*. His best-known operas are *Estrella di Soria*, thanks in part to its splendid overture, and *Drottningen av Golconda*, whose leading role of Aline was composed for Christina Nilsson, who was enjoying great success at the Paris Opéra. But the promised production came to nothing and the opera was not staged in Stockholm until the centenary of the composer's death. The text was freely adapted from Vial's and Favières's libretto for Henri-Montan Berton's opera (1812): the subject had also been set by Monsigny (1766), Uttini (1776), Boieldieu (1804) and Donizetti (1828).

Berwald's contribution to the operatic repertoire is not comparable with his achievement as a symphonist, but his writing is often distinguished by great inventive fluency and charm. Neither of his major operas has sufficient dramatic flair or feeling for character to hold the stage outside his native Sweden.

Operas: *Gustaf Wasa* (inc.), (1827); *Cecilia* (inc.; lost), (1829); *Leonida* (lib. and fragments survive), (1829); *Der Verräter* (lost), (1830); *Donna Isabella* (inc.; lost), (1830); *Jag går i kloster (I Enter a Convent)*, 1842; *Modehandlerskan (The Modiste)*, (coll.), 1843; *Estrella di Soria*, (1841; rev. 1848 and 1862), 1862; *Slottet Lochleven, or Maria Stuart (Lochleven Castle)*, (inc.; lost), (1863); *Drottningen av Golconda (The Queen of Golconda)* (RECORDING excerpt: Zelie's aria, Act II, Nordin, EMI, 1968), (1864), 1968

BIBLIOGRAPHY Ingmar Bengtsson, Nils Castegren and Erling Lömnäs, *Franz Berwald: die Dokumente seines Lebens*, Bärenreiter, 1979; Robert Layton, *Franz Berwald*, Bonniers, 1956

R.La.

LOUIS BEYDTS

Louis Antoine Hector Désiré Beydts; *b* 29 June 1895, Bordeaux, France; *d* 16 September 1953, Paris

One of the few post-war masters of the operetta, Beydts was a pupil of Messager, and his best works follow closely in his master's footsteps. His first and finest operetta, *Moineau* (1931), a flimsy tale of a promiscuous painter who is surprised into fidelity by the charms of a pretty florist, is candidly indebted to the older composer but brings a new and distinctive edge to the familiar style. Beydts had two other successes in the same year, with his music for Sacha Guitry's *La S.A.D.M.P.* ('Society Anonyme de Messieurs Prudents'), and with an operetta called *Les canards mandarins*; the following year (1932) there was another Guitry piece, *Le voyage de Tchong-Li*, set in legendary China. But when he returned to operetta after the war, with *A l'aimable Sabine*, Beydts found that, while connoisseurs were still willing to admire his mastery of the genre, audiences were less willing to accept its carefree pre-austerity assumptions.

Beydts also wrote concert works, film music, and an orchestral fanfare for the 1936 Olympic Games.

BIBLIOGRAPHY Florian Bruyas, *Histoire de l'opérette en France*, Emmanuel Vitte, 1974

S.W.

GÜNTER BIALAS

b 19 July 1907, Bielschowitz, Upper Silesia (now Poland)

In an autobiographical sketch Bialas wrote, 'I belong to the intermediate generation between the established masters Stravinsky, Bartók and Hindemith and the younger composers Henze, Stockhausen and Klebe.' During his childhood the strongest musical influence was that of Reger. Despite first-hand experience of theatre during his early years in Katowice, Breslau and later Berlin, he first became known as a composer of choral and instrumental music, also as theorist and teacher.

In 1966 the Nationaltheater in Mannheim staged Bialas's first opera, *Hero und Leander*, with a libretto based on Grillparzer and a score that employs a 'complementary 12-note technique in which colour and rhythm dominate'. In *Die Geschichte von Aucassin und Nicolette* (1969) the composer drew on Tankred Dorst's puppet-play adaptation of the 13th-century French *chantefable*. The score is divided into separate musical numbers and calls for a small orchestra. An auspicious premiere in Munich was followed by productions in Berne and Kiel.

Operas: *Hero und Leander*, 1966; *Die Geschichte von Aucassin und Nicolette*, 1969; *Der gestiefelte Kater, oder Wie Man das Spiel spielt*, 1974
BIBLIOGRAPHY G. Pankalla and G. Speer (eds), 'Gunter Bialas. Eine Selbstdarstellung', *Zeitgenössische schlesische Komponisten*, A. Laumannsche Verlagsbuchhandlung, 1972

A.C.W.B.

FRANCESCO BIANCHI

Giuseppe Francesco Bianchi, *b c.* 1752, Cremona; *d* 27 November 1810, London

Bianchi studied with Cafaro and Jommelli in Naples, but his earliest operas were produced in his native Cremona (1772) and in nearby Pavia (1775), after which he went to Paris as harpsichordist at the Théâtre-Italien; while there he also composed comic and serious operas.

Returning to Italy in 1778, Bianchi settled into a prolific rate of opera composition, producing around 50 works within the next 16 years. From 1782 to 1793 he served at Milan Cathedral as vicemaestro, and also as organist at St Mark's in Venice (from 1785 until the fall of the Republic in 1797) and for the 1783–4 season was chorus master at La Scala, Milan. Among the most successful operas of his prodigious output was *La villanella rapita* (Venice, 1783), seen throughout Europe, and for which Mozart composed a quartet and trio for insertion in a performance in Vienna in 1785. *Il disertore francese* (1784) is said to have shocked its audience because of its reform elements, such as the combination of the serious and comic. A production of *La vendetta di Nino* in London in 1794 was followed by 14 other works for the King's Theatre between 1795 and 1802. Bianchi was also successful as a composer of many opéras comiques (now lost) in Paris between 1802 and 1807. He committed suicide in 1810.

Contemporary reports praised his music for its liveliness and grace, for the tenderness and pathos it displayed, rather than for any particularly innovatory or bold elements. Nevertheless Bianchi's original practice of distributing the principal melodic line between more than one voice (in ensembles) or between voice and orchestra – displaying an awareness of orchestral colour lacking in many of his contemporaries – deserves mention. Haydn, who saw *Aci e Galatea* in London in 1795, described the music as 'very rich in parts for the wind instruments', while his comment that 'one could hear the principal melody better if it were not so richly scored' no doubt reflects Bianchi's habit of doubling the vocal line with oboes.

Operas surviving in whole or part: *Demetrio*, 1774; *Castore e Polluce*, 1779; *Arbace*, 1781; *Venere e Adone*, 1781; *La Zemira*, 1781; *Olimpiade*, 1781; *Il trionfo della pace*, 1782; *La Zulima*, 1782; *L'astrologa*, 1782; *Piramo e Tisbe*, 1783; *La villanella rapita*, 1783; *Briseide*, 1783; *Aspardi, principe di Battriano*, 1784; *Cajo Mario*, 1784; *Il disertore francese*, 1784; *Alessandro nell'Indie*, 1785; *La stravagante inglese*, 1785; *Alonso e Cora*, 1786; *Mesenzio, re d'Etruria*, 1786; *L'orfano cinese*, 1787; *Artaserse*, 1787; *Pizzarro*, 1787; *Scipione africano*, 1787; *Il ritratto*, 1787; *Calto*, 1788; *La morte di Cesare*, 1788; *Nitteti*, 1789; *Daliso e Delmita*, 1789; *Il finto astrologo*, 1790; *La vendetta di Nino, o sia Semiramide*, 1790; *Caio Ostilio*, 1791; *La dama bizzarra*, 1791; *Deifile*, 1791; *La sposa in equivoco*, 1791; *Seleuco, re di Siria*, 1791; *Aci e Galatea*, 1792; *Tarara, o sia La virtù premiata*, 1792; *Il cinese in Italia*, 1793; *La secchia rapita*, 1794; *Ines de Castro*, 1794; *La capricciosa ravveduta*, 1794; *Antigona*, 1796; *Il consiglio imprudente*, 1796; *Merope*, 1797; *Cinna*, 1798; *Alzira*, 1801; *La morte di Cleopatra*, 1801; *Armida*, 1802; *Blaisot et Pasquin*, 1804; *Corali, ou La lanterne magique*, 1804; several others, doubtful; 30 others, lost
BIBLIOGRAPHY A. M. Monterosso Vacchelli, 'Francesco Bianchi', *Dizionario biografico degli italiani*, vol. 10, Instituto della Enciclopedia Italiana, 1968

D.S.B.

ANTONIO BIBALO

b 18 January 1922, Trieste, Italy

Antonio Bibalo is of Slovak origin (the name was originally Bibalitsch). He paid for his studies in wartime Trieste by working as a nightclub pianist and a street cleaner before moving to Australia and then London (1953), where he studied with Elisabeth Lutyens. She introduced him to Schoenberg's music and he began to write in a form of 12-note technique. In 1956 he settled in Norway and adopted Norwegian nationality.

Bibalo attracted attention with his first opera in music-theatre style, *The Smile at the Foot of the Ladder*, after a short story by Henry Miller, when it was produced in Hamburg in 1965. *Frøken Julie* (*Miss Julie*), after Strindberg's play, followed in 1975 and shows a more personal and original style than his earlier music. His third opera was *Gespenster* (*Ghosts*) (1981), after Ibsen, and in 1990 he scored a striking success with the premiere, at the National Opera in Oslo, of *Macbeth*.

R.La.

HARRISON BIRTWISTLE

(Sir) Harrison Birtwistle; *b* 15 July 1934, Accrington,
Lancashire, England

Birtwistle has made a more significant contribution
to opera than any other British musician of his
generation. He studied at the Royal Northern
College of Music (1952–5) and was a member of the
New Music Manchester Group along with Alexander
Goehr, Peter Maxwell Davies, John Ogdon and
Elgar Howarth. The Group performed new music, in
line with the preoccupation with Webern characteristic of young Continental composers of the time;
medieval techniques of composition also formed
a strong area of interest. However, the earliest
works Birtwistle himself acknowledges date only
from 1957, and his first operatic work, *Punch and
Judy*, was not written until 1967.

Birtwistle worked as a school teacher until a
Harkness Fellowship in 1965 enabled him to take up
musical studies in America and devote himself to
composition. *Punch and Judy* was followed by *Down
by the Greenwood Side* in 1969 and in 1973 he
embarked on *The Mask of Orpheus*, a project that
would not be completed for another ten years. All
these works exhibit the interests in mythic narration
(whether from Classical or English sources),
ritualistic patterning and different ways of organizing
time that are essential features of Birtwistle's musical
thinking. While the subject matter of all these pieces
includes murder, the violence is tempered by a
melody-based style and by dramatic resolutions
incorporating the idea of regenerative life force.

In 1975 Birtwistle became the first Musical
Director of the National Theatre, composing
incidental music notable for its cohesion with the
accompanied dramatic action. *Bow Down* (1977) is a
piece that sits midway between theatre and opera in
the requirements from its performers. In 1983,
Birtwistle took on the more advisory post of
Associate Director, Music, and has composed
prolifically since then. A television opera, *Yan Tan
Tethera*, was written in 1984; *Gawain and the Green
Knight* was premiered at Covent Garden in 1991, and
a new opera, *King Kong*, has been commissioned for
the first season of the new Glyndebourne opera
house.

The somewhat accidental appearance of three
major scores in 1986 (*The Mask of Orpheus, Yan
Tan Tethera* and *Earth Dances*) was followed by
London festivals of Birtwistle's music in 1987 and
1988; all of which served to establish him at the
forefront of modern composition. Official recognition of his standing came with a knighthood in
June 1988.

Although only one of Birtwistle's pieces to date
bears the title 'opera', his entire output depends on
ideas of musical drama, and the resulting musical
language seems ideally suited to the combination of
narrative, word, movement and music. Several
features are constant throughout Birtwistle's music.
One is the technique of creating textures from a
single line, embellished with adjacent notes and

proliferated via doublings at the octave or fifth. This
gives a firm sense of direction even within very
complex passages, and enables the violence of many
musical gestures to be counterbalanced by an elegiac
melodic style which often moves via semitone or tone
steps. Alongside this, the consistent use of ostinato
patterns enables harmonic, rhythmic and melodic
structures to be followed by the ear. Another
consistent technique is that of presenting fragments
of music again and again, but juxtaposed differently
with each other. This is similar to Varèse's approach
to composition, centred on the use of what he called
'musical objects'; blocks of sound appear alongside,
above or below each other, as if spatially (rather than
harmonically) related. The music is seen from
different angles, distances and perspectives, so to
speak. This in turn involves a distinctive approach to
time: different temporal schemes are explored in
order to exhibit the ceaseless interaction of what has
passed and what is present. This concern for the
'sanctity of the context', in Birtwistle's phrase, has
grown and become ramified in recent years. Thus
different versions of narratives (often traditional
stories) may be presented in a single operatic work,
intercut with each other and with other strands of
narrative. This moves the audience away from the
sense of being told a story, towards considering the
status of the story itself as a lived experience. A
literary parallel might be found in the Bergsonian
exploration of time and memory in Proust's novel *A
la recherche du temps perdu*.

If Stravinsky and Messiaen are two composers for
whom Birtwistle acknowledges great respect, they
also suggest themselves as the nearest comparisons in
this century for a composer who has created a
distinctive voice in working and reworking musical
concepts with clarity and vision as well as extremism.

Punch and Judy

Comical tragedy or tragical comedy in one act (1h 45m)
Scenario and libretto by Stephen Pruslin
Composed 1966–7
PREMIERES 8 June 1968, Jubilee Hall, Aldeburgh
CAST Punch *high bar*, Judy/Fortune Teller *ms*, Pretty
Polly/Witch *high s*, Choregos/Jack Ketch *low bar*, Doctor
basso profundo, Lawyer *high t*, 5 mime dancers
INSTRUMENTALISTS tpt, trbn, hp, perc (2 players),
str quintet; onstage: fl/picc, ob/ca/ob d'amore,
cl/E♭cl/b cl/soprano sax, hn, bsn/dbsn

Birtwistle's first operatic work became something of
a *cause célèbre* when Benjamin Britten and Peter
Pears vacated their box some time before the end of
the premiere. One reviewer remembered the
performance as seeming 'almost gratuitously
offensive'; another described it as 'the baby's
tantrum beneath our civilized sociability'. Birtwistle
himself has referred to it as a central work in his
output, acting as a source for other pieces. The music
has the Expressionistic energy of other music-theatre
pieces from the 1960s (such as Peter Maxwell
Davies's *Eight Songs for a Mad King*), harnessed to a
stylized plot that focuses on elemental and violent
urges. Punch's desire to destroy leads to four
murders (Melodramas), and is linked to the desire to

Punch and Judy *(Aldeburgh, 1968)*

possess by the three Quests for Pretty Polly. These Quests are unsuccessful, and only by escaping from the rules of his own games does Punch eventually win his love.

The work divides into nine sections, plus a prologue and an epilogue. Four sections are Melodramas, and three are Quests. The action opens with Choregos, the Punch-and-Judy man, opening his booth. Melodrama I begins as Punch enters, carrying the baby. He sings a lullaby and then throws the baby into the fire, with the war cry that precedes each of his murders. Judy enters, finds the baby dead, and confronts Punch in a word game. Punch then murders Judy. Punch embarks on his first Quest for Pretty Polly. He journeys east, and serenades her with a gavotte. She rejects his offered sunflower, though, with the words, 'The flaw in this flower is a flicker of flame.'

Melodrama II follows, in which Punch confronts the Lawyer and Doctor in three riddle games. After this legal and medical disputation, Punch murders the Doctor with a hypodermic syringe and the Lawyer with a quill pen. He then sets off again on the second Quest for Pretty Polly, travelling west on a hobby-horse. Pretty Polly dances to his *allemande*. This time she rejects his offer of a gem.

For the third Melodrama, Punch takes on Choregos himself, 'crowning' him by breaking a trumpet, cymbal and drum over his head. He then locks him in his bass-viol case. This time, though, the war cry falters as Punch's creator falls out of the case dead. At this point a Nightmare begins. Punch travels north, where his victims turn on him to exact revenge, Judy appearing as a Fortune-Teller and Pretty Polly as a Witch. He manages to escape from

the Nightmare on the hobby-horse; but on the third Quest for Pretty Polly, journeying south, his pavan fails even to make her appear.

In the final Melodrama, Punch again confronts Choregos, who returns in the guise of Jack Ketch, the legendary hangman. After an interview game, Punch is condemned to death; at the last moment, however, he tricks Jack Ketch into trying the noose on himself; as the hangman is hanged, Pretty Polly appears; the final section, 'Punch Triumphans', sees Punch finally united with his love in a maypole dance.

Despite the violence of both subject matter and musical gesture, there are moments of great lyricism and humour in the work. The repeated prayer, 'Let the winds be gentle, let the seas be calm', and the paradox that precedes each death, 'The sweetness of this moment is unendurably bitter', are examples of 'musical signposts' for the audience, along with the use of sequences of colours, dance forms, games and so forth through the different sections. The incessant verbal playing ('Witness, avenging gods, my Choregos in stringent suffering strung on a violent viol vile,' sings Judy) sometimes suffers in the musical turbulence; but by and large, this first theatre piece shows a musical inventiveness that creates great contrasts within a consistent language.

RECORDING   Bryn-Julson, De Gaetani, Langridge, Roberts, Wilson-Johnson, Tomlinson, London Sinfonietta, Atherton, Decca, 1980
EDITIONS   v.s./lib., Universal, 1968

Down by the Greenwood Side
Dramatic pastoral in one act (30m)
Text by Michael Nyman
Composed 1968–9
PREMIERE   8 May 1969, Festival Pavilion, West Pier, Brighton

There are strong connections between *Down by the Greenwood Side* and *Punch and Judy*. Emblematic figures, traditional narrative, and the image of resurrection and new life provided by the Green Man are common to both works.

Two separate sources provide the dramatic material of this piece: the traditional English Mummers' Play, and the Ballad of the Cruel Mother, the refrain of which provides the title. The action of the play concerns the contest between St George and Bold Slasher, the Black Knight (both spoken roles). Twice St George is defeated, revived first by the doubtful medical attentions of a third speaking character, Dr Blood, and then by the 'Green Man', Jack Finney (played by a mime). It is the earth magic of the latter, the reviving power of spring, that vanquishes the evil opponent. The play is presided over by Father Christmas (another spoken role), with all characters dressed in huge, puppet-like costumes. This drama is intercut with the enigmatic figure of Mrs Green, the Cruel Mother and the only singer in the piece. She sings several different versions of the Ballad, which relates how she murdered her two illegitimate children, 'down by the greenwood side'. Years later, passing near the same place, she meets two naked children. She remarks that were they hers, she would give them clothes; to which they reply, 'When we were yours, you drest us in our own hearts' blood.'

The dramatic connections between the two stories become clear in the final section, when Mrs Green is drawn into a dance with Father Christmas and the other characters that is reminiscent of May festivals. The 'green' life force has overcome death at the last. The scoring is for a chamber ensemble of nine players, and features melodic lines consisting of sustained notes alternating with wide leaps, often in the form of ostinato sections repeated as the accompanied action necessitates.

EDITION f.s., Universal, 1971

Bow Down

Music-theatre in one act (50m)
Text by Tony Harrison, after various versions of a traditional ballad
PREMIERE 5 July 1977, Cottesloe Theatre, National Theatre, London

This piece for five actors and four musicians is based on different forms of the Ballad of the Two Sisters, in a similar manner to the treatment of the Ballad of the Cruel Mother in *Down by the Greenwood Side*. The musical material is integral to the choreographed movement, and uses wind instruments (bamboo flutes and pipes, oboe, penny whistle), percussion instruments and vocal techniques (humming, chanting, etc.).

EDITION f.s., Universal, 1983

The Mask of Orpheus

Lyric tragedy in three acts (nine scenes, *parados* and *exodos*) (3h 30m)
Libretto by Peter Zinovieff
Electronic material realized by Barry Anderson
Composed 1973–5 (Acts I and II), 1981–4 (Act III and electronics)
PREMIERE 21 May 1986, Coliseum, London
CAST Orpheus Man *t*, Orpheus Myth/Hades *t*, Euridice Woman *lyric ms*, Euridice Myth/Persephone *lyric ms*, Aristaeus Man *high bar*, Aristaeus Myth/Charon *high bar*, Oracle of the Dead/Hecate *high s*, The Caller *b-bar*, 3 Furies *s*, *ms*, *a*, 3 Priests *t*, *bar*, *b-bar*; 12-part chorus (in pit); mimes: Orpheus Hero, Euridice Heroine, Aristaeus Hero; troupe of Passing Clouds; 7 mime artists
ORCHESTRATION 4 fl/3 picc/ 2 alto fl/bass fl, 3 ob/ob d'amore/2 ca, bass ob/ca, 3 cl/2 Ebcl/2 b cl, b cl/contrabass cl, 3 bsn/2 dbsn, dbsn, 3 soprano sax/3 conches, 4 hn, 4 tpt, 6 trbn, 2 tubas, 3 hp, electric gtr, electric bass gtr, electric mand, perc (7 players), tape; the work requires two conductors

By far Birtwistle's most ambitious project, *The Mask of Orpheus* brought almost universal acclaim at its premiere, despite reservations concerning the production and major cuts to the final act. The huge forces required to mount the work reflect the scope of the subject matter. The myth of Orpheus, a subject that has fascinated composers since the very birth of opera, is the basis for an exploration of the origins and nature of language, music and myth. The work manages to create its own musical and dramatic form and language, without lapsing either into triviality or pretension. In the words of the librettist, 'The use of the word Mask should suggest a slight connection with Elizabethan English masque which combined music, dance, poetry, scenic decoration and pageantry to express mythological and allegorical subjects.'

The 12 years between its conception and first performance reflect an interrupted compositional history. Birtwistle halted after completing the first two acts, when the possibility of producing such a complex work seemed to have receded (it was intended originally for Glyndebourne). Six years later, in 1981, he picked up the pieces of the project, a creative feat which he described as 'the worst period of my life'. Not only was the period of composition extended, *The Mask of Orpheus* is also foreshadowed in a number of other vocal pieces, notably *Nenia: The Death of Orpheus* and *On the Sheer Threshold of the Night*.

The work is intricately patterned throughout, dividing its three hours' length into units constituting comprehensible, single gestures. The bulk of the score is made up of 42 'trinities of action': three Magic Formulae, three Orphic Hymns, three Hysterical Arias and so on. These 'trinities' often overlap or occur simultaneously. Although this does entail some exact repetitions of musical material (giving 'reference points' for the audience), recurrent events (such as Orpheus' suicide) are nearly always altered or distorted in some way, often according to whether they are being predicted, observed or remembered. While the musical style is generally more dense and complex than in the other stage works, it ranges from moments of tenderness or pathos to those of sheer horror (as in the Oracle of the Dead's screams as she attempts to learn singing from Orpheus).

Throughout the action, three different versions of each of the three central characters are present. Each version represents a different aspect of time: the Man self represents the past, the Hero the possible, and the Myth the eternal. Thus the 'reliving' of events explores the interweaving of memory, hope and time. For instance, two different versions of Aristaeus' advances to Euridice are seen simultaneously: she is willingly seduced in one, and raped in the other. Her death is then seen as respectively retribution and deliverance. Later, Orpheus 'remembers' the scene, as Aristaeus' Man self shows him only Euridice's seduction by Orpheus' Hero self. Depths of interpretation are constantly opened up by this sort of treatment of events.

It is difficult to provide a synopsis of the work precisely because of its multi-faceted approach to the Orpheus myth. Different versions of episodes are presented and re-presented in varying perspectives, in a culmination of the techniques familiar from Birtwistle's other works. Each act is built around a different narrative: Euridice's marriage and death in the first, Orpheus' descent to the Underworld in the second, and the invention of language and the birth of the cultic myth in the third.

SYNOPSIS

Act I The sun rises as Apollo gives Orpheus the gifts of speech, poetry and music. His first attempts at words are intercut with his first act of memory, recalling the voyage of Jason's ship the *Argos* (on which Orpheus sailed). The act then divides into three scenes. In the first, Orpheus falls in love with Euridice and woos her. Their wedding is marred by bad omens, despite Orpheus' love song. The second scene shows the two simultaneous versions of Euridice's death (from a snakebite). The third contains Euridice's funeral, seen from Orpheus' point of view, after which he consults the Oracle of the Dead in order to pursue her to the Underworld.

Act II Orpheus journeys through 17 arches of the Underworld, each with a symbolic name ('Countryside', 'Crowds', 'Evening', and so forth), and leading to his encounter with Hades, Persephone and the Goddess of Witches (grotesque mythic reincarnations of Orpheus, Euridice and the Oracle of the Dead) and back. He crosses the Styx by singing to Charon, brings tears to the eyes of the Furies, has his death foretold by the Judges of the Dead, and passes the dead in torment before standing before the three rulers of the Underworld. He escapes them and begins his journey back, believing Euridice to be following him; but it is only her substitutes, Persephone and Euridice's Heroine self, who are there. Orpheus crosses the Styx again to find Euridice unable to do likewise. Realizing that he has lost her for ever, he hangs himself. (Though the continuous dramatic sweep of this act has led to its being presented as a concert piece, even here the story-telling is not conventional; the act opens with yet another version of Euridice's death, and the narration of the action by Orpheus Man makes it clear that the journey, with its visions and phantoms of Euridice, is all taking place in his sleeping mind, exhausted and traumatized by his bereavement. As Charon carries the last of the three different embodiments of Euridice backwards for ever, Orpheus wakes up.)

Act III consists of nine 'episodes', linked by the image of the tide: in the first three, time flows backwards, so that Orpheus' return from the Underworld, then his descent, and then Euridice's death are re-enacted. Then the tide turns; time flows forwards and the journey out of the Underworld (with the addition of Orpheus' song to the animals) is followed by Aristaeus' punishment by his own bees; finally Orpheus Hero is killed by Zeus' thunderbolt, and Orpheus Myth is dismembered by the Dionysiac women. Time continues into the future as Orpheus becomes a cultic figure: his head sings as it floats down the river, and Orpheus Myth becomes an oracle, finally silenced by Apollo, Orpheus' spiritual father. In the last episode, time begins to flow backwards once more, as the Dionysiac women again sacrifice Orpheus and eat his flesh. The final *exodos* shows the decay of the myth.

Electronic techniques provide three of the most striking components of the work. In each act, the prevailing seasonal metaphor is indicated by a sound veil (or 'aura') of electronic sounds that acts rather like an aural backdrop to the music. Secondly, there are about 70 points at which Apollo speaks. This vast, deep, voicelike sound was created at the Parisian electronic music institute IRCAM in collaboration with Barry Anderson, and employs an invented language in which the words contain only syllables drawn from the names Orpheus and Euridice (for example, 'RUFÌ AS-RÌ DÌ' means 'Love did it'). Lastly, there are six points at which the action halts in order for a Greek myth to be acted out by the mime troupe, to the accompaniment of short electronic pieces. Three of these mime interludes are entitled 'Allegorical Flowers of Reason' (Adonis, Hyacinth and Lotus representing the Apollonian impulse) and three 'Passing Clouds of Abandon' (Dionysus, Lycurgus and Pentheus representing the Dionysian impulse). The music for these interludes is based on plucked harp notes (recalling Orpheus), resynthesized and greatly altered by computer.

Only the enormous complexity involved in producing this work threatens its recognition as one of the most striking pieces of operatic theatre written this century.

EDITIONS f.s./v.s./lib., Universal, 1986

Yan Tan Tethera

Mechanical pastoral (1h 30m)
Text by Tony Harrison, after a northern folktale
Composed 1984
PREMIERES 7 August 1986, Queen Elizabeth Hall, London; 19 April 1987, Channel 4/Radio 3 (broadcast)

Commissioned for television by the BBC, this work takes its title from a traditional northern numbering system used for counting sheep.

The story concerns two shepherds. Alan, from the north, has come south with his two sheep. He marries; his flock increases, and his wife Hannah gives birth to twins. All this arouses the jealousy of the local shepherd Caleb Raven, who enlists the help of the Bad'un (a devil figure who also appears as a Pan-like piper) to imprison Hannah and the twins. Only after seven years are they liberated, and Caleb Raven swallowed up by the Wiltshire hills. The whole drama is taken up with counting and number magic; Alan's initial prosperity, along with Hannah and the boys' preservation and eventual release from evil, is accomplished with the aid of the incantation, 'Yan Tan Tethera / One Two Three / Sweet Trinity / Keep us and our sheep.'

Yan Tan Tethera returns to the traditional sources and resurrection parables of *Down by the Greenwood Side*. In addition, Birtwistle's handling of disjunct time schemes has become more subtle. The music and the drama remain distinct from each other, but converge at various culminatory points. Both musical and dramatic events are repeated in different perspectives: for instance, Alan's attempt to befriend

Caleb by waving to him is seen from both shepherds' viewpoints, while the 'music of the hill' which introduces each section is constantly varied on each occurrence. A reviewer of the premiere commented on the 'softening of idiom' in this work, in which strongly characterized, lyrical melodic fragments (the piping of the Bad'un, the 'Yan Tan Tethera' incantation) recur unaltered time and again, providing easily recognized landmarks in the musical texture.

EDITIONS   f.s./v.s., Universal, 1986

Gawain

Opera in two acts (3h)
Libretto by David Harsent, after the anonymous
14th-century poem *Sir Gawain and the Green Knight*
Composed 1989–91
PREMIERE   30 May 1991, Covent Garden, London
CAST   Gawain *bar*, The Green Knight/Sir Bertilak de Hautdesert *b*, Morgan le Fay *s*, Lady de Hautdesert *ms*, Arthur *t*, Guinevere *s*, A Fool *bar*, Agravain *b-bar*, Ywain *t*, Bishop Baldwin *ct*, Bedevere *actor; satb* chorus of clerics; offstage: *satb* chorus
LARGE ORCHESTRA including extended perc, hp, cimbalom; amplification and special effects for offstage voices

The first work by Birtwistle to bear the title 'opera' is a massive work that represents the culmination of his interest in the folklore of the Green Man. The first of his works to be produced at Covent Garden, its premiere was broadcast by radio and recorded for television.

David Harsent's libretto is strikingly faithful to the medievalism of the original poem, though it presents the whole action as controlled by Morgan le Fay, who is on stage but invisible to the other characters for almost the whole opera.

SYNOPSIS
Act I   Arthur's court is celebrating New Year when the Green Knight enters. He issues a challenge for someone to strike a blow at his neck with his axe, and to receive a return blow a year later. Eventually Gawain accepts, and strikes the Knight's head from his body. The Knight himself picks the head up, tells Gawain to meet him at the Green Chapel, and leaves. During a long representation of the changing seasons, Gawain is prepared for his quest.

Act II   Gawain's journey. He eventually reaches the castle of Sir Bertilak and Lady de Hautdesert, who tell him that the Green Chapel is near by. For three days he is entertained: Bertilak hunts all day while his wife attempts, unsuccessfully, to seduce Gawain. Each evening, fulfilling a pact between them, the two men exchange the day's winnings: a stag, a boar and a fox, for one, two and then three kisses. However, on the third day Gawain also secretly accepts a protective girdle from Lady de Hautdesert. Gawain then goes to the Green Chapel. The Green Knight feigns two blows, and cuts Gawain only slightly with the third. The Knight is then revealed to be Bertilak, and the cut is retribution for keeping the girdle. Gawain returns to Arthur's court,

convinced of his cowardice and refusing to be seen as 'that hero' who was sent out.

There are points of contact between the medieval and contemporary verse. The alliteration of the original is occasionally echoed, as in Gawain's words to the Green Knight, 'My life is light – easier to lift than the axe', and the overall effect of the libretto derives from the features of the original that must have drawn Birtwistle to it: the mixture of mythic figures (the Green Man; the 'magic site' of the Chapel, a barrow; the Christian symbolism and the repetitions and parallelisms of the text) and the equivocal *dénouement*, which is preserved without any attempt at more modern didactic point-making.

The half-hour masque that concludes Act I aroused much comment at the premiere, and some found it tedious. Emblematic figures, including Father Time and nature spirits, process carrying symbols of seasonal growth, harvest and death, while the Fool and the knights strip, wash and arm Gawain for his journey. Birtwistle has indicated that he may revise this section for future performances, although the difficulties it gave critics seemed to stem from its deliberate adoption of ritually repeated blocks of time in the context of an otherwise straightforward narrative, rather than a misjudgement of its length.

The opera is at first sight much more conservative in form than earlier Birtwistle works. There are none of the alternative narratives of *The Mask of Orpheus*, and no repetition of blocks of action, except for the masque of the seasons and the beheading itself, where the Green Knight enters for a second time to expedite the special effect. The music accompanies the action in a fairly direct manner, with the moments of violence or tenderness set alongside

François le Roux in Gawain *(London, 1991)*

onomatopoeia (the Green Knight's horse's clip-clopping shoes, or, in the hunting scenes, abundant horn calls; these last are used leitmotivically elsewhere, for instance slowed down in the texture of the overture). But if the opera lacks the experimental form of *The Mask of Orpheus*, it should not be assumed that this is a retrograde stylistic step. Birtwistle's gritty and consistent harmonic language owes much to the techniques of *Earth Dances* (1986), frequently proliferating melodic lines stratified into separate layers of orchestral texture; this consistency allows great diversity of rhythm and sonority without falling into the bathos that any treatment of myth and metaphor courts. There are moments of parody (Gawain's first kiss is accompanied by a sugary cello phrase), stylistic reference (notably to Stravinsky's *The Rite of Spring*), and occasional rhythmic relaxation (for instance in Morgan le Fay's and Lady de Hautdesert's dance). The typical Birtwistle interest in altered repetitions of material follows the parallelisms of the text itself, and melodic repetition is skilfully deployed, for instance for Morgan le Fay's recurring lines, 'This is the hour of legacy or loss. / This is the hour of vanity or choice.'

EDITIONS   f.s./v.s./lib., Universal, 1991

BIBLIOGRAPHY   A. Bye, 'Harrison Birtwistle, *Gawain*', *MT*, vol. 132 (1991); Michael Hall, *Harrison Birtwistle*, Robson, 1984; Michael Hall, 'The Sanctity of the Context: Birtwistle's Recent Music', *MT*, vol. 129 (1988)

R.J.S.

GEORGES BIZET

Alexandre-César-Léopold [Georges] Bizet; *b* 25 October 1838, Paris; *d* 3 June 1875, Le Bougival, nr Paris

Bizet began and ended his career with operas, though he also wrote orchestral music, piano pieces, songs, choral and incidental music. None of his operas was immediately successful in Paris, but from the start his work was original enough to be taken seriously. The faith placed in Bizet by a few contemporaries has been amply justified by the brilliant posthumous triumph of his operatic masterpiece, *Carmen* (1875), an enduring place in the repertoire for *Les pêcheurs de perles* (1863), and a growing appreciation for several of his other operas.

Bizet achieved a vibrant and original amalgam of memorable melody, piquant harmony, vivid orchestration, and on occasion a realistic, dramatic power that has rarely been equalled in opera. Though contemporary critics frequently applied the label 'Wagnerian' to Bizet's operas, the composer kept his distance from Wagner's theories and chose to work within the number- and scene-opera tradition; however, his orchestra plays a more active role in presenting melody and countermelody than that of earlier French composers, and its tone colours are essential to the varying of motifs for dramatic ends.

Like most French composers, Bizet formed his skills largely at the Conservatoire (1847–57), where he studied composition with F. Halévy; Gounod, perhaps the most potent single influence on his development, came to know Bizet outside that institution. The connection involved not only some composition lessons, but also arrangements of Gounod's works. Bizet's delightful Symphony in C, composed at this time (1855), is clearly modelled on Gounod's Symphony in D.

Bizet's early operas are charming, comic Italianate works, where the models of Rossini and Donizetti show through clearly. As he expanded his range in the 1860s to more dramatic and serious topics, his scores show the influence of others, notably Gounod, F. David, Meyerbeer, Halévy, Verdi and Weber. Although they are generally more uneven, these scores teem with ideas. Abandoned or lost projects from the period 1868–71 obscure the route by which Bizet achieved true artistic maturity. From the 1870s there are just two mature opéras comiques (*Djamileh* and *Carmen*) and an abandoned grand opera *Don Rodrigue*, which remains largely unscored; since rehearsal revisions were normally an essential stage in Bizet's creative process, it is difficult to speculate on the final form this torso might have taken.

Bizet's first two completed operas were written while he was still a student at the Conservatoire. *La maison du docteur* (*c.* 1855) was probably composed for private performance with his fellow students, but *Le Docteur Miracle* (1856) was given at the Bouffes-Parisiens theatre as one of the prizewinners in a competition conducted by Offenbach to promote opéra comique. A few months later Bizet capped a brilliant student career by winning the Prix de Rome with his cantata *Clovis et Clotilde* (1857). This enabled him to spend nearly three years in Rome, from January 1858 to July 1860. During this time he worked on *Don Procopio*, which he submitted as his first *envoi* as a Prix de Rome winner (officially this should have been a sacred work). He considered further operatic projects and began some, but completed none until the one-act opéra comique *La Guzla de l'Emir* (1862, now lost) which, as a Prix de Rome *envoi* (his last), was due to be performed at the Opéra-Comique, though it was never produced. Instead Bizet turned his attention to *Les pêcheurs de perles*, which in late March or early April 1863 was commissioned by Leon Carvalho, the influential director of the Théâtre-Lyrique.

Bizet wrote most of the three-act score in only four months, presumably incorporating large parts of *La Guzla de l'Emir*. Treated severely by the critics (with the notable exception of Berlioz), *Les pêcheurs de perles* enjoyed little public support. It did not hold the stage for long, and was virtually forgotten until the 1880s; however, Carvalho immediately encouraged Bizet to complete *Ivan IV*. At the outset this grand opera, modelled largely on Meyerbeer, was apparently intended for Baden-Baden (as was, perhaps, the mysterious fragment, *La prêtresse* (*c.* ?1860), whose florid vocal lines are akin to Léïla's in *Les pêcheurs de perles*). To Bizet's great disappointment and eventual bitterness, *Ivan* was

Bizet, aged 25

from his score, much as he had earlier begun to recycle material from *Ivan IV*. In 1870–71 he sketched two opéras comiques, *Grisélidis* and *Clarisse Harlowe*, but abandoned both when the Opéra-Comique and its new co-director, Camille du Locle, withdrew from an earlier commitment to produce a new full-length work.

Bizet's fortunes in the 1870s were tied largely to du Locle and the Opéra-Comique. He was delighted at the prospect of changing a genre he regarded as old-fashioned and insipid. His one-act opéra comique *Djamileh* (1871–2) is rich in beautiful scoring and dramatic subtlety but was attacked by Parisian critics as 'Wagnerian' and had little success. Du Locle immediately asked Bizet, none the less, to collaborate with the experienced team of Henri Meilhac and Ludovic Halévy on a full-length work; Bizet soon proposed Mérimée's novella *Carmen*. That summer, however, Bizet turned his attention to providing incidental music and mélodrames for Daudet's Provençal tragedy, *L'arlésienne* (1872) at Carvalho's new theatre, the Vaudeville. Though the play failed, Bizet's exquisite suite soon became popular with Parisian concert audiences.

A grand opera, *Don Rodrigue* (1873, based on the Cid legend) was abandoned prior to orchestration, partly because the Opéra was destroyed by a fire (October) and partly because the Opéra administration chose to mount Membrée's *L'esclave* instead. Bizet had continued to work on *Carmen*, and orchestrated it quickly in the summer of 1874. He knew certain critics were prejudiced against him, but had thought this score would finally convert them: 'They make out that I am obscure, complicated, tedious, more fettered by technical skill than lit by inspiration. Well, this time I have written a work that is all clarity and vivacity, full of colour and melody.' After the premiere in March 1875 the more even-handed critics praised individual pieces, but even they often predicted that the work would not attract the public. Bizet fell ill with an attack of quinsy shortly afterwards and never completely regained his health; obsessed by thoughts of death, suffering from rheumatism and an ear infection, he none the less continued planning an oratorio, *Geneviève de Paris*. Three months later, after two heart attacks, he died aged 36, just before *Carmen* began to conquer the entire operatic world. Its enormous popularity encouraged revival of other Bizet operas in the 1880s and 1890s. *Carmen* remains one of the greatest operas ever written; in an era dominated by Verdi and Wagner, Bizet achieved, within the traditional frame of the number opera, an original and vital solution to the balance of music and drama.

never staged owing both to Carvalho's budget problems and to the Opéra's unwillingness to open its doors to a beginner. Carvalho's substitute project, *La jolie fille de Perth* (1866–7), took shape while Bizet was crushed by hackwork for publishers. Critics reacted more favourably to it than to *Les pêcheurs de perles*, for here Bizet turned to a style more natural to him, and aimed for charm rather than power.

In 1868 Bizet wrote to a friend that an extraordinary artistic change was taking place in him, but unfortunately no complete original opera score survives from the period 1868–71. The Franco-Prussian War disrupted all artistic activities, but with his marriage to Halévy's daughter, Geneviève, in June 1869, Bizet had new responsibilities that took time and emotional energy away from composition. The responsibility of his beautiful but neurotic wife, and a mother-in-law who suffered at times from attacks of insanity, though it matured and deepened him, was hardly an ideal situation. Furthermore, the considerable financial advantages he anticipated from a generous marriage contract did not materialize. Both to show loyalty to his former teacher and to increase family income, therefore, Bizet completed and orchestrated Halévy's opera *Noé* (1868–9). At this time Bizet also looked at or began work on a half-dozen libretti, but he completed only *La coupe du roi de Thule* for a competition at the Opéra; there were rumours of corruption as the jury passed over scores by Bizet, Guiraud, Massenet and others for the effort of an amateur. Bizet soon reused some of the best ideas

La maison du docteur

The Doctor's House

Opéra comique in one act (1h)

Libretto by Henry Boisseaux (previously set by Paul Xavier Désiré, Marquis d'Ivry, 1854; texts greatly altered, apparently by Bizet)

Composed c. 1855

PREMIERE 23 February 1989, University of Texas Opera Theater, Austin

Bizet probably knew d'Ivry's earlier amateurish setting of this libretto, either through one of its salon performances in 1854 or through the vocal score, published early in 1855 and dedicated to Gounod. Bizet's work consists of seven solo and ensemble numbers for four soloists with piano accompaniment only. Set in London, the plot centres around the middle-aged and wealthy hypochondriac Lord Harley who decides to marry 18-year-old Eva, at her father's urging, as a cure for his incapacitating boredom. The music, indebted to the Italian comic style, is sometimes naïve, but has lyric charm and rhythmic verve. *La maison du docteur* may have been intended as a salon opera and performed privately. Annotations on the manuscript include names of his friends, teachers and fellow students at the Conservatoire as well as a fugue subject Bizet worked on during his studies with Halévy.

MANUSCRIPT   Bibliothèque nationale, fonds du Conservatoire, Paris

Le Docteur Miracle

Doctor Miracle
Opérette in one act (1h)
Libretto by Léon Battu and Ludovic Halévy, after Richard Brinsley Sheridan's farce *St Patrick's Day* (1775)
PREMIERES   9 April 1857, Bouffes-Parisiens, Paris; UK: 18 January 1953, BBC broadcast; winter 1956/7, West Riding Opera Circle, Leeds; US: 24 March 1971, Mannes Opera workshop, Kaufman Concert Hall, New York
CAST   Laurette *s*, Le Podestat *bar*, Véronique *s*, Capitaine Silvio/Pasquin/ Dr Miracle *t*
CHAMBER ORCHESTRA   offstage: cl, trbn, bd, cym

In July 1856 Offenbach advertised a comic-opera competition for composers who had not yet been presented at the Opéra or Opéra-Comique. Six finalists, selected by an eminent jury from 78 entrants, were given the Halévy–Battu libretto. The young composers turned in their scores on this stereotypical comedy just three months later, in December. Bizet and Charles Lecocq (who composed operettas throughout his career), came equal first, and had their respective works played 11 times each at Offenbach's theatre.

SYNOPSIS
The Magistrate (Podestat) of Padua suspects his daughter Laurette's suitor, Captain Silvio, of making the early-morning racket in the town square, but discovers it actually comes from the booth of a visiting charlatan, Dr Miracle. After chasing him off, the Magistrate hires a new servant, Pasquin, who claims to hate all soldiers; Pasquin will therefore be the ideal guardian for Laurette until she is married off to the town pharmacist. The new servant prepares an omelette which tastes and smells so horrible that only the Magistrate can force himself to eat it. While he and his wife Véronique take a stroll, 'Pasquin' reveals to Laurette that he is Silvio in disguise. They decide to elope, but the Magistrate returns, recognizes Silvio and banishes him. Almost immediately a soldier delivers a letter which reveals that the omelette had been poisoned. Luckily Dr Miracle is still in town, and the family sends for him. The bearded, Latin-speaking doctor agrees to treat the poisoned Magistrate but demands Laurette's hand as payment. The Magistrate and Laurette agree, and Silvio reveals his identity once more, explaining that the poisoning was a hoax. Véronique persuades the Magistrate that he should put up with what he cannot prevent; all four praise Dr Miracle and the miracle of love.

At 18 Bizet was already in fine control of the comic French and Italian styles and had mastered an excellent, though conservative, orchestral technique. Clear Rossinian sonorities appear in the overture. By far the finest of the six numbers is the 'omelette' quartet, encored at the premiere. After an ostentatious introduction, Bizet delights in playing with the rhythm of the words, 'Voici l'omelette'. Other effective comic touches in this extended piece include the rocking, accelerating figure in close harmony to illustrate the beating of the eggs and the use of diminished seventh chords to underline both the horror of the first tasting and the confirmation that the flavour is indeed awful. Little of the score could be called original, but it sparkles with lyricism and provides a first glimpse of Bizet's rare gift for true musical wit.

RECORDING   Eda-Pierre, Guitton, Corazza, Massard, O of French Radio, Amaducci, MRF, 1975
EDITION   v.s., Editions françaises de musique, 1962
MANUSCRIPT   Bibliothèque nationale, fonds du Conservatoire, Paris

Don Procopio

Opera buffa in two acts (1h 15m)
Libretto by Carlo Cambiaggio, after Luigi Prividali's libretto *I pretendenti delusi* adapted by the composer
Composed 1858–9
PREMIERES   Malherbe's version: 10 March 1906, Monte Carlo; original version: UK: 2 February 1955, University College, London; France: 6 February 1958, Théâtre Municipal, Strasburg
CAST   Eufemia *ms*, Andronico *b*, Pasquino *b*, Bettina *s*, Odoardo *t*, Ernesto *bar*, Don Procopio *b*; *satb* chorus of servants, countryfolk, musicians
FULL ORCHESTRA including mand, gtr

For his first *envoi de Rome* Bizet searched the bookshops of Rome and found an Italian farce in the style of *Don Pasquale*. This score, his longest work to that date, matches the Italian libretto (previously set by Vincenzo Fioravanti *et al.*, 1844) with music that he called 'purely Italian, like rejuvenated Cimarosa'. The Institute's official report praised eight of the twelve pieces and pointed to Bizet's marked propensity for comedy. During his lifetime, however, the work was never performed, and the manuscript remained among Daniel Auber's papers instead of being deposited at the Conservatoire library. After the manuscript's rediscovery in 1894, Charles Malherbe added recitatives and a potpourri *entr'acte*; he also made other alterations in preparing the published score. His more modern-sounding music does not blend well with Bizet's charmingly mid-19th century Italianate score.

SYNOPSIS

Act I Don Andronico has arranged for his niece Bettina to marry Don Procopio, a rich old miser. Bettina bemoans her fate, for she loves a young colonel, Don Odoardo. Her brother Don Ernesto, Odoardo and she hatch a plan: Bettina will pretend she is delighted to marry Don Procopio, but will also make it clear that she has every intention of living in high style. Don Procopio, uneasy at the prospect of marriage anyhow, and Bettina are presented to one another.

Act II Bettina hints strongly that she will be neither docile nor thrifty, and Don Procopio becomes so frightened that he flees even though the family presses him to keep his word. Don Andronico bows to the inevitable and consents to the marriage of the young lovers.

The tuneful and vivacious score skilfully imitates Donizetti. The introduction quickly establishes the Italianate vocal textures that dominate 'the ensembles: detached chords (for the chorus) support Eufemia's soaring lines while Andronico, the bass, splutters comically as his authority is challenged. One of the few passages to reveal Bizet's personality is Odoardo's charming entrance march: Bizet borrowed the idea from the fourth movement of his Symphony in C. Act I is stronger than Act II, but the latter opens with the most appealing number, Odoardo's 6/8 serenade, accompanied by mandoline, guitar and cors anglais. Bizet had learned a great deal about pacing within the comic style from his experience in Offenbach's theatre, for though he never heard this work in rehearsal or reworked it, the musical numbers never lose their momentum.

RECORDING Mesplé, Berton, Vanzo, Massard, Blanc, Bastin, Soumagnac, French Radio Ch and O, Amaducci, MRF, 1975
EDITIONS edited and adapted by Charles Malherbe: v.s., Choudens, 1905; with further changes by Charles Malherbe: f.s./v.s., Choudens, 1906
MANUSCRIPT Bibliothèque nationale, fonds du Conservatoire, Paris

Ivan IV

Opera in five acts (2h 45m)
Libretto by François-Hippolyte Leroy and Henri Trianon
Composed ?1862–3, rev. 1864–5
PREMIERES winter 1943, Théâtre des Capucines, Paris (concert with pf) 1946, Möhringen Castle, nr Tübingen, West Germany, as Ivan le Terrible (private, in German); 12 October 1951, Grand-Théâtre, Bordeaux (after suppression of the German score, music completed and altered by Henri Busser); UK: 21 October 1955, Liverpool Amateur Opera Company, Liverpool; 5 October 1975, BBC Radio 3 (broadcast; complete authentic version)
CAST Marie s, Le Jeune Bulgare ms, Ivan IV bar, Temrouk b, Igor t, Yorloff b, Olga ms, Circassian t, Caucasian t, Officer t, Herald t, Sentinel b; satb chorus of Caucasian women, Caucasian old men and hunters, victims, boyars, nuns, Russian people, courtiers

LARGE ORCHESTRA including organ and expanded perc; onstage: 2 cornets, 2 tpt, 3 trbn, 3 saxhorn, tambour, t-t

Bizet may have begun work on his grand opera Ivan IV in 1862, after conferring with Bénazet, director of the Baden-Baden theatre. Gounod had already given up on his own setting of the libretto and probably gave the book to Bizet. It contains a generous sampling of grand-opera clichés. Since the last two of the 21 numbers are not orchestrated in the manuscript that now survives, Bizet must have prepared another score (now lost) which was submitted to the Théâtre-Lyrique's copyist in the autumn of 1865. Postponements and budget problems over 18 months made him despair of Ivan ever reaching Carvalho's stage. To the director's chagrin, Bizet withdrew his score and submitted it to the Opéra, where he was summarily rebuffed; according to his first biographer, Pigot, he eventually burned the manuscript of Ivan.

SYNOPSIS

Act I Marie, Princess of the Caucasus, rescues a young Bulgarian, lost and separated from his master in the mountain fog. His master (Ivan IV) enters, and Marie notices his noble bearing. Shortly after the two leave, the Russians attack and demand Marie as a hostage. She nobly sacrifices herself to prevent devastating bloodshed. When Igor, her brother, and his retainers return from hunting, Igor is chosen as the Caucasians' instrument of vengeance.

Act II The boyars in Ivan's palace celebrate their victory while merciless executions take place outside. Ivan has decided to take a wife, and Yorloff, an ambitious boyar, expects the choice to fall on his daughter. To his astonishment and dismay Ivan selects the beautiful Marie. When she proudly refuses him, he threatens to rape her, but his sister Olga protects Marie.

Act III The people celebrate the impending marriage of Ivan and Marie. Igor and Temrouk, his father, have separately made their way to the Kremlin, and, after a reunion, they encounter Yorloff who enlists their aid in his plot to assassinate the tsar.

Act IV Yorloff tries to make Ivan suspicious of Marie with an anonymous note of warning. He sneaks Igor into the royal chambers, and there an astonished brother and sister are reunited. Scarcely has Igor renounced vengeance, when Yorloff brings in Ivan and denounces brother and sister for an assassination conspiracy. A heartbroken Ivan condemns them; he falls to the ground in a seizure as the Kremlin burns.

Act V Ivan recovers his senses, kills his guards, and, with his own death knell sounding, rushes into the Kremlin just as the new tsar, Yorloff, is having the crown removed from Marie's head in preparation for her execution. He greets Marie lovingly and sentences Yorloff to the scaffold; all praise the royal couple.

Bizet made every effort to be impressive and original in this, his first grand opera; as a result, Ivan IV is heavily scored and uneven. Moments of brilliant originality sometimes follow passages strongly indebted to other composers (most often Meyerbeer, but sometimes Verdi, Gounod or even Wagner). Bizet sometimes expands material that is too weak to withstand a grand climax. Though the orchestra often depends on an array of familiar accompaniment figures, here, too, are the first uses of recurring motifs, the most striking among them the sinuous, chromatic, minor-mode idea that represents the scheming Yorloff. (It is probably indebted to Verdi's motif for Sparafucile, for Bizet much admired Act IV of *Rigoletto*.) The grand climaxes are unconvincing, but a fine 12/8 idea in E minor for Ivan's heartbreak in Act IV and the choral climax built on that idea have some of Verdi's power. The surging trombone theme at the very close of Act I, on the other hand, strongly resembles the Act III prelude of Wagner's *Lohengrin* in both opening gesture and continuation. A delightful vignette, quite typical of Bizet, opens Act V: the original B minor version of *Trompette et tambour* (*Jeux d'enfants*, 1871) is presented as a meeting of two sentinels by the Kremlin wall, the orchestra coloured by snare drum and piccolo. Though there are some original numbers, *Ivan IV* is basically an eclectic and grandiose score, in which only the secondary characters, like Yorloff and the Young Bulgarian, begin to come alive.

RECORDING Scovotti, Kern, Robotham, Brecknock, Noble, Taylor, Angas, BBC Northern Ch and O, Thomson, MRF, 1975
EDITION v.s., edited and completed by Henri Busser, Choudens, 1951
MANUSCRIPT 1862–3, Bibliothèque nationale, fonds du Conservatoire, Paris

Les pêcheurs de perles

The Pearlfishers
Opera in three acts (four tableaux) (1h 45m)
Libretto by Eugène Cormon and Michel Carré
Composed and rev. April–September 1863
PREMIERES 30 September 1863, Théâtre-Lyrique, Paris; UK: 22 April 1887, Covent Garden, London (as *Leïla*); US: 25 August 1893, Hinrichs, Philadelphia
CAST Zurga *bar*, Nadir *t*, Leïla *s*, Nourabad *b*; *satb* chorus of pearlfishers, Indians and Brahmins
ORCHESTRATION 2 fl/picc, 2 ob/ca, 2 cl, 2 bsn, 4 hn, 2 cornets, 3 trbn, timps, perc (bd, cym, tambourine, triangle, t-t, tambour), 2 hp, str; offstage: 2 picc, tambourine, hp

Bizet signed a contract with Carvalho in late March or early April 1863 to complete a three-act opera that would go into rehearsal in August, with an anticipated premiere in mid-September. He responded imaginatively to the setting (originally Mexico, but changed to Ceylon [Sri Lanka]), but to meet the tight schedule had to borrow from several earlier works (including *Ivan IV*) and probably cannibalized most of his last *envoi de Rome*, the one-act opéra comique, *La Guzla de l'Emir*. Until the rehearsals were under way the opera apparently contained spoken dialogue for several scenes in the first two acts. Other rehearsal revisions centred on the Act II love duet and, in particular, the problematic final scene.

The critical reception of the premiere was largely negative, but Berlioz, writing his last review for the *Journal des débats*, found 'a considerable number of beautiful, expressive pieces filled with fire and rich colouring'. *Les pêcheurs de perles* had 18 performances (respectable for a début work) but was not revived until 1886. At about that time the publisher Choudens began tampering with the score. The wonderful Act I tenor–baritone duet lost its triple-metre closing *allegro* for a dramatically nonsensical return to the more attractive opening *andante* (some audiences are still loathe to give up this posthumous version). To compensate for various cuts Godard wrote a new, but extremely weak Act III trio, 'O lumière sainte'. Editors also altered both stage action and music in the final scene: first they had Zurga being burned at the stake; later he was stabbed in the back by an Indian. The 1975 edition returns largely to the 1863 vocal score, with orchestration by Arthur Hammond for restored portions (since the autograph manuscript has been missing since the 1890s); however, recent discovery of an 1863 short score has made reconstruction of Bizet's orchestration possible.

Les pêcheurs de perles: *the first vocal score*

SYNOPSIS

Act I On a wild beach in Ceylon the pearlfishers are preparing for the fishing season. Zurga reminds them that it is time to elect a chief. They unanimously choose him and swear absolute obedience. His old friend Nadir the hunter suddenly appears, and Zurga invites him to stay. They recall their last trip, where at the temple in Kandi both had seen and fallen in love with a beautiful young woman leading a religious ceremony ('Au fond du temple saint'); both had sworn never to approach her so that nothing would trouble their friendship ('Amitié sainte'). A canoe arrives bringing that year's unknown, veiled, virgin priestess (Léïla), who will sing and pray for the safety of the pearlfishers during this season. They all welcome her and attend the initiation ritual where Léïla swears to give up friend, husband and lover, even though at the last minute she has recognized Nadir. Nourabad, the high priest, conducts Léïla to the temple as the sun is setting. Left alone, Nadir admits that despite his oath he had returned to hear Léïla's songs; he remembers the magic of the experience ('Je crois entendre encore') and falls asleep. Léïla now appears on the crag that looks out to sea and begins her prayers ('O Dieu Brahma, O maître souverain'), but her thoughts turn to Nadir, who wakes, comes closer, and recognizes his beloved.

Act II Léïla's forbidden ruined temple. Léïla tells Nourabad how, still a child, she had risked her life to protect a fugitive; this man had given her a necklace as a memento. Left alone, Léïla rejoices that Nadir is again watching over her ('Comme autrefois, dans la nuit sombre'). Nadir arrives and in their happiness the couple forget the danger they risk ('Ton coeur n'a pas compris le mien'). As a storm rumbles in the distance, Nourabad and the guards discover the lovers and catch Nadir as he attempts to flee. Zurga plans to allow the guilty couple to leave – until he recognizes Léïla. Blind with jealousy, he too cries for vengeance. All pray to Brahma, and Nadir and Léïla are led away.

Act III Scene 1: Zurga, alone in his tent, regrets his rage against his old friend ('O Nadir, tendre ami de mon jeune âge') and recalls Léïla's radiant beauty. She comes to beg for mercy for Nadir ('Je frémis, je chancelle, de son âme cruelle'), but succeeds only in reigniting Zurga's jealous anger when she reveals her love for Nadir. As Léïla is led away she asks a young pearlfisher to give her necklace to her mother; Zurga then recognizes this as the gift he had presented to the brave young girl who saved his life many years earlier. Scene 2: Nadir watches preparations for the execution ('Dès que le soleil'). Léïla and Nadir prepare to face death in each other's arms. Suddenly Zurga enters, hatchet in hand, and announces a fire in the camp. After the Indians have left, he releases Nadir and Léïla and reveals that he started the fire to aid their escape and repay his debt to Léïla. The lovers flee, and Zurga leans against an idol of Brahma while frightened Indians escape through the forest, their children in their arms.

In early 1867 Bizet modestly referred to his début work as 'an opera much discussed, attacked, defended . . . in all, an honourable, brilliant failure . . .' He correctly assessed his first two acts as stronger than the third and his lyric passages and exotic numbers (usually quite imaginatively scored) as more successful than the uneven dramatic portions.

Each of the major soloists has at least one strong solo number, usually indebted to Gounod in style. Among them, Nadir's Act I romance is perhaps the loveliest, not only for its melody but also for its poetic orchestration (cor anglais, muted violins and two solo cellos). The depth of Nadir's obsession is brought out by understatement – high Bs taken *pianissimo* for his 'mad rapture' much as a high *pianissimo* Bb later illustrated Don José's obsession with Carmen.

That Bizet had already developed a fine sense of the grand moment is demonstrated by his preparation for the famous tenor–baritone melody in Act I. He moves from Nadir's eloquent recitative evoking their experience in Kandi to a chromatic descent as Zurga describes that evening, through shimmering muted strings and murmured vocal lines to the tune itself, in flute and harp on the long-delayed tonic. Most wonderfully, however, a chromatic section with shorter phrases maintains tension until the men finally present the marvellous, Gounod-indebted melody, gloriously harmonized. The 'goddess' motif, though rather long for its purpose, recurs frequently, rescored and often doubled in speed, whenever the two men's friendship is influenced by Léïla.

Portions of the work are indebted to other composers; critics in 1863 cited Gounod, David, Halévy and Verdi, among others. But despite the score's unevenness, its lyric beauty and unforgettable moments have won *Les pêcheurs de perles* a place in the standard repertoire.

RECORDINGS 1. 1893 version: Micheau, Gedda, Blanc, Mars, Ch and O of Opéra-Comique, Dervaux, EMI, 1960; 2. 1863 version: Cotrubas, Vanzo, Sarabia, Soyer, Ch and O of Paris Opéra, Prêtre, EMI, 1977; 3. 1863 version: Hendricks, Aler, Quilico, Courtis, Ch and O of Capitole Toulouse, Plasson, EMI, 1989; all three are recommendable, but the latest has the best all-round cast; it is also complete [A.B.]
EDITIONS original version: v.ss., Choudens, 1863, 1975; rev. version: v.s., Choudens, [1885]; 2nd rev. version: f.s./v.s., Choudens, [1893]; version based on the 1863 v.s., with orchestration for posthumous cuts supplied by Arthur Hammond: f.s., Choudens, 1975

La jolie fille de Perth

The Fair Maid of Perth
Opera in four acts (five tableaux) (2h)
Libretto by Jules-Henry Vernoy, Marquis de Saint-Georges and Jules Adenis, freely adapted from Sir Walter Scott's *The Fair Maid of Perth* (1828)
PREMIERES 26 December 1867, Théâtre-Lyrique, Paris; UK: 4 May 1917, Manchester
CAST Henri Smith *t*, Mab *s*, Catherine *s*, Ralph *b* or *bar*, Glover *b*, Duc de Rothsay *bar* or *t*, worker/majordomo *b*, an aristocrat *t*; *tb* chorus of armourers, bourgeois Perth residents, the Duke of Rothsay's friends, artisans; *satb* chorus of carnival celebrants, young people
FULL ORCHESTRA including tambourine, tambour, bd; onstage: anvil (Act I); offstage: chimes (Act II); fl, ob, 2 cornets, trbn, triangle, hp, 2 vn (Act III)

Having reconciled his differences with Carvalho over the latter's failure to stage *Ivan IV*, Bizet agreed in July 1866 to write *La jolie fille de Perth*. He completed it by the end of the year, and claimed that he had ignored Saint-Georges's trite verse and forced rhymes. The libretto, perhaps the worst he ever set, consists largely of operatic clichés and unbelievable coincidences and bears very little relation to Scott's novel. When the work finally came to the stage, the press was relatively complimentary, but it nevertheless closed after only 18 performances. Bizet regretted his concession to public taste in the coloratura title role, including a mad scene, originally intended for Christine Nilsson (though not sung by her at the first performance); thereafter he avoided such a florid style.

SYNOPSIS
Act I As the carnival evening begins, Smith persuades Catherine, a beautiful coquette, to become his valentine, but her subsequent flirtation with the Duke of Rothsay angers him. Mab, the gypsy queen, prevents him from striking the duke, and Catherine is in turn jealous, thinking that Smith has a mistress.

Act II Catherine has spurned the duke, but he turns to Mab (herself a former mistress) to ask for help in getting her to come to the carnival ball. However, Mab disguises herself and she is the 'Catherine' Ralph, a rather tipsy apprentice, sees driven away in the duke's litter. He alerts Smith, who has been singing a serenade to Catherine (lifted from Bizet's earlier *Don Procopio*) beneath her window. He hurries off immediately but Ralph remains long enough to see the real Catherine appear at the window.

Act III The duke woos the false Catherine (Mab). When the real Catherine and her father arrive to announce her engagement to Smith, Smith denounces her publicly.

Act IV Ralph, to prove Catherine's innocence, accepts Smith's challenge to a duel. Smith and Catherine sing a second love duet before he goes off intending to die to restore her honour. Alerted by Mab, the duke stops the duel, but Catherine has already gone mad from the stress. When Mab impersonates Catherine once more while Smith sings his earlier serenade, Catherine's sanity returns and all rejoice.

With *La jolie fille* Bizet returned to a lighter style that has much in common with the opéras comiques of Gounod and Ambroise Thomas (though without spoken dialogue). Filled with delightful scoring and lyric beauty, a surprising number of passages anticipate *Carmen*. The relationship between voice and orchestra has become more supple, the orchestration clearer and subtler. Act II contains Bizet's most sustained inspiration to that date, and Act III includes an offstage minuet, better known, but less effective, in the second suite from *L'arlésienne* (arr. Guiraud). Unfortunately the improbable action of Act IV did not inspire Bizet, and the work ends lamely. Had Bizet written a final act as strong as the second, the charming score, regardless of the painfully contrived plot, would have qualified *La jolie fille* for a place in the repertoire as a minor masterpiece.

RECORDING Anderson, Zimmermann, Kraus, Quilico, Bacquier, Van Dam, Ch of Radio France, Nouvel O Philharmonique, Prêtre, EMI, 1985
EDITIONS v.s., Choudens, 1868; versions 2a/b/c: Choudens, [c. 1883]; version 2d: f.s., Choudens, [c. 1886]; version 3: v.s., Choudens, [c. 1891], rp, 1964

Djamileh
Opéra comique in one act (1h)
Libretto by Louis Gallet, after Alfred de Musset's poem *Namouna* (1832)
Composed summer 1871, orch. winter 1871–2, rev. during rehearsals April–May 1872
PREMIERES 22 May 1872, Opéra-Comique, Paris; UK: 22 September 1892, Manchester; US: 24 February 1913, Boston Opera House
CAST Haroun *t*, Splendiano *t* (or *bar*), Djamileh *ms*, slave trader *spoken role*, L'Almée *dancer*, Arakel *silent*; *sa* chorus of slaves and musicians; *tb* chorus of Haroun's friends; offstage: *stb* chorus of boatmen
ORCHESTRATION 2 fl/picc, 2 ob/ca, 2 cl, 2 bsn, 4 hn, 2 cornets, 3 trbn, timps, perc (cym, tambour, triangle), hp, str; offstage: 2 ob, tambour de basque, pf

In 1871 Camille du Locle offered Bizet the book of *Namouna*, renamed *Djamileh* at the director's suggestion. Bizet found the work charming but very difficult to set; however, within two months he had drafted enough of the score to be concerned about eventual casting, which would determine questions of range and key. The effect of a sumptuous production was spoilt by the Djamileh, a beautiful baroness who could not sing. Most critics condemned Bizet's score as bizarre and Wagnerian, and in June 1872 Bizet admitted to a friend that the work was not a success, partly because the poem was untheatrical. He took some comfort in the fact that a one-act opera had been taken so seriously. 'What satisfies me more than the opinions of all these gentlemen is the absolute certainty of having found my way. I know what I am doing.'

SYNOPSIS
Haroun lives in luxury in his Cairo palace, spending his money on gambling and on buying a new slave girl each month. Djamileh's month is coming to an end and Splendiano, Haroun's servant and former tutor, proposes himself as her next protector. However, she has fallen in love with Haroun and persuades Splendiano to let her return as Haroun's 'new' slave on condition that she will become his if Haroun rejects her. Djamileh returns and conceals her identity as Haroun tries to conquer her. A ray of moonlight reveals her, and Haroun is surprised at his feelings. Djamileh swears that she loves Haroun more than her liberty. Haroun at first rejects her, but then capitulates before true love. The pair sing a paean to romantic love.

In this mature and original score Bizet created an atmosphere with greater subtlety and skill than in his *Pearlfishers*, but more important as a sign of his maturity as an opera composer, in Djamileh he drew a sympathetic, multi-dimensional central character. Bizet deliberately contrasts her dramatically intense music with the more diatonic, Gounod-like style

Costume sketch for Djamileh *(Paris, 1872)*

of the self-indulgent Haroun and the light opéra-comique couplets of Splendiano (much as he would later use different styles to dramatic effect in *Carmen*). Unfortunately Haroun's last-minute conversion to true love leaves the audience wondering whether this, too, is a whim that will pass with the next full moon.

Bizet had suggested Priola or Galli-Marié (later the first Carmen) for the role of Djamileh. Had one of them sung the part, the work might have had a more successful premiere, for despite magically effective orchestration and a perfumed atmosphere *Djamileh* disappeared after 11 performances and was ignored until the 1890s. The excellent score has never received the attention it merits.

RECORDING Popp, Bonisolli, Lafont, Ch of Bavarian Radio, O of Munich Radio, Gardelli, Orfeo, 1988: omits spoken dialogue
EDITIONS f.s., Choudens, 1892; v.s., Choudens, 1872, *rp*, 1962

Carmen

Opéra comique in four acts (2h 45m)
Libretto by Henri Meilhac and Ludovic Halévy, after the novella by Prosper Mérimée (1845, rev. 1846)
Composed 1873–5; recitatives by Ernest Guiraud, 1875; ballets from *L'arlésienne* (farandole and chorus) and *La jolie fille de Perth* (*Danse bohémienne*) inserted by Guiraud
PREMIERES 3 March 1875, Opéra-Comique, Paris; UK: 22 June 1878, Her Majesty's Theatre, London; US: 23 October 1878, Mapleson Academy of Music, New York
CAST Moralès *bar*, Micaëla *s*, Don José *t*, Zuniga *b*, Carmen *ms*, Frasquita *s*, Mercédès *s* (or *ms*), Lillas Pastia *spoken role*, Escamillo *bar*, Le Remendado *t*, Le Dancaïre *t* (or *bar*), guide *spoken role*, soldier *spoken role*; *satb* chorus of soldiers, men

and women of Seville, cigarette-factory girls, gypsies, street vendors; street urchins *trebles*
ORCHESTRATION 2 fl/2 picc, 2 ob/ca, 2 cl, 2 bsn, 4 hn, 2 cornets, 3 trbn, timps, perc (triangle, cym, bd, tambour, tambourine, castanets), 2 hp, str; offstage: 2 cornets, 3 trbn

Bizet himself seems to have proposed Mérimée's *Carmen* as the source for his librettists. The experienced team, Meilhac and L. Halévy, made numerous astute changes to the narrative and provided the necessary opportunities for a variety of musical numbers. They invented the episodic, messenger role of Micaëla (the pure, bourgeois opéra-comique heroine) to serve as a foil to Carmen, the gypsy, an unrepentant sinner who prizes the freedom to control her own life over all else. Escamillo's role was greatly expanded, and Don José, after his gradual descent from dutiful corporal/son to deserter/smuggler, commits only one murder, the final crime of jealous rage (in Mérimée's novella he commits at least three). The extent of Bizet's involvement in shaping the libretto is unknown (though he certainly contributed much of the *habanera* text and Carmen's death song in the Card Trio). The novella itself was widely admired, but placing such a subject on the Opéra-Comique stage was a bold step in a theatre that depended on a bourgeois clientele. Furthermore, in his quest to renovate the genre, Bizet wrote a score rich in ensembles and choruses, more demanding and complex than his performers and audience were used to. Not surprisingly the chorus (asked to smoke, quarrel, or enter by twos and threes instead of marching in *en masse* to sing simple tunes) threatened to strike after two months of rehearsal; even the orchestra claimed certain passages were unplayable. Some revisions during rehearsals accommodated the performers' limitations; but most of them also refined and sharpened the dramatic impact of each scene. The soloists came to believe strongly in the work, particularly Galli-Marié (Carmen) and Lhérie (Don José), and with Bizet they resisted the director's and librettists' attempts to tone down their performance.

At the premiere audience response cooled as drama and music moved further away from the traditional opéra comique. Most of the press condemned the plot as too immoral to be staged and, though they praised certain pieces (like the Act II entr'acte and Micaëla's air), they found Bizet's score both overlong and 'scientific'. *Carmen* was not the great success Bizet had hoped for, but there were 35 performances that spring and 13 more the next season, many more than any of his other operas. *Carmen* had succeeded in 18 other countries before the Opéra-Comique revived the work in 1883; yet by 1905 there had been 1000 performances in that house alone. In most other theatres, *Carmen* was performed with competent recitatives by Bizet's good friend Ernest Guiraud to texts supplied by Halévy; Bizet himself apparently intended to write such recitatives to make the work more widely performable. Ever since the publication of a flawed critical edition in 1964, however, which made a great many passages that Bizet removed during rehearsals more accessible than the final versions themselves and which reinstated the original orchestration for Moralès's couplets and the Act III duel (cuts that date back to 1875), most music directors have opted for a performing version which includes some of the rejected passages alongside Bizet's final text.

SYNOPSIS

Act I Outside the tobacco factory in Seville soldiers amuse themselves by watching the passers-by ('Sur la place chacun passe'). Micaëla approaches looking for Don José; when she is told he will arrive with the changing of the guard, she flees their assiduous gallantry. The soldiers then return to their initial pastime. Children imitate the guard as they enter ('Avec la garde montante'); this group includes Don José and his new superior officer Zuniga. The bell sounds and the women factory-workers come outside to take their break, smoking cigarettes ('La cloche a sonné, nous, des ouvrières'); their arrival delights the men who apparently wait for them each day. When the gypsy Carmen finally makes her grand entrance, she describes the fickle nature of her love to her many admirers (*habanera*: 'L'amour est un oiseau rebelle'). She speaks provocatively to Don José, and throws a flower at him before she and the others are summoned inside by the factory bell. José is disturbed by her effrontery, but picks up the flower. Micaëla returns to bring a kiss from José's mother ('Parle-moi de ma mère'), as well as a letter which suggests Micaëla as a suitable wife. José is about to throw away Carmen's flower, but the women suddenly rush out of the factory arguing ('Au secours! n'entendez-vous pas'); Carmen has cut another worker's face. When she refuses to answer Zuniga ('Coupe-moi, brûle-moi, je ne te dirai rien'), he orders José to take her to prison. Left alone with José, she uses all her practised wiles on him. He can no longer resist when she tempts him with the prospect of becoming her next lover (*seguedilla*: 'Près des remparts de Séville'), and helps her to escape.

Act II Carmen and her gypsy friends, Frasquita and Mercédès, entertain officers in Lillas Pastia's tavern ('Les tringles des sistres tintaient'). Zuniga tells Carmen that José has been released after a month in prison; she is delighted. The toreador Escamillo enters with his entourage and drinks with the patrons ('Votre toast . . . je peux vous le rendre'). Though Carmen does not encourage Escamillo's attentions, she tells him that it is always pleasant to hope. When all but the three gypsy women and Pastia have left, Le Remendado and Le Dancaïre enter and describe their plan for that night ('Nous avons en tête une affaire'). They are all astonished when Carmen refuses to participate because she is 'in love'. They urge her to recruit her new lover and leave as they hear José approaching ('Halte-là!'). To celebrate his release Carmen orders a feast and then dances for José ('Je vais danser en votre honneur'), but her joy quickly turns to fury when José announces he must leave because the call to barracks is sounding; she is unmoved when he shows her the flower he has saved ('La fleur que tu m'avais jetée)

Célestine Galli-Marié as the first Carmen (Paris, 1875)

and claims that if he loved her, he would follow her to the mountains ('Là-bas, là-bas dans la montagne'). José is about to leave when Zuniga returns, hoping to find Carmen alone. When ordered to get out, José, blind with jealousy, attacks his superior officer. He now has no choice but to leave the army and reluctantly throws in his lot with the gypsies.

Act III The smugglers gather in the mountains ('Ecoute, écoute, compagnon, écoute'). Carmen and José argue again. Mercédès and Frasquita pass the time by telling their fortunes with cards ('Mêlons! Coupons!'); when Carmen joins in, she reads death again and again, first for herself, then for José. The smugglers depart to set about their task while the women distract the customs officials ('Quant au douanier, c'est notre affaire'). José stays behind on guard. A guide brings in a frightened but determined Micaëla ('Je dis que rien ne m'épouvante'); she hides when José fires a shot and Escamillo enters, calmly examining the bullet hole in his hat. He has heard that Carmen has tired of her latest lover and has come to seek her out ('Je suis Escamillo, toréro de Grenade'). Drawing his knife, the furious José challenges the toreador. Escamillo spares him, but falls in the second round. José is ready to kill him, but Carmen arrives with Le Dancaïre and stops the fight. Escamillo invites her to his next bullfight in Seville and leaves. Micaëla is discovered and tells José that his mother is dying. He leaves with her after threatening Carmen.

Act IV Outside the bullring in Seville merchants hock their wares ('A deux cuartos'). The participants in the bullfight march past ('Les voici! Voici la quadrille!'), and Escamillo arrives with a radiantly happy and beautifully dressed Carmen. Frasquita and Mercédès warn her that José is hiding in the crowd, but Carmen is determined to face him. The crowd follows the procession into the bullring leaving Carmen alone. José confronts Carmen and implores her to leave with him, but she says she no longer loves him; she would rather die than give up her freedom. She is eager to witness Escamillo's triumph, but José blocks her path. When she furiously throws away his ring, José draws his knife and stabs her while Escamillo is fêted in the bullring. As everyone comes out José, confessing his crime, throws himself on the body of his beloved Carmen.

Bizet's ability to create effective local colour is vividly represented in this score. The accelerating gypsy dance that opens Act II is an orchestral *tour de force* in which dissonance and sliding harmonies paint the scene of Lillas Pastia's underworld tavern as surely as any set design. Carmen's mesmerizing entrance piece, the *habanera*, winds sensually and chromatically above a pedal that provides tonal stability and symbolizes her irresistible sexuality. The *seguidilla* was Bizet's own invention, but its combination of guitar-like accompaniment, dance rhythm and remarkably ambiguous tonality seem just as 'Spanish' as the borrowed tunes. For Escamillo's entrance aria, Bizet adopted a deliberately popular manner as overstated as the toreador himself. In contrast, the susceptible Don José sings very little in Act I; his first solo is the simple, unaccompanied soldier's march in Act II, sung backstage.

Bizet's orchestration had been quite distinctive in his earlier works, but Richard Strauss regarded *Carmen* as sheer perfection: 'If you want to learn how to orchestrate, don't study Wagner's scores, study the score of *Carmen* . . . What wonderful economy, and how every note and every rest is in its proper place.' Woodwind instruments receive particular attention: the flute is associated with Carmen in the *seguidilla* and elsewhere and has the famous solo in the lovely *entr'acte* preceding Act III. The cor anglais makes a rare appearance as José shows Carmen the flower he has kept with him through his month in prison, and flutes and bassoons play a delicate counterpoint to Mercédès's and Frasquita's warning to Carmen just before the final tragedy.

As in earlier operas Bizet imaginatively rescores his motifs for dramatic effect. The flickering 'Carmen' motif (with an augmented second) and its alternate form, the 'fate' motif (with a slower tempo) are used economically. (The 'fate' motif itself appears only at the end of the prelude and in one number of each act.) Unexpected harmonies and modulations advance the drama in virtually every number. The featherlight Act II quintet moves effortlessly from a distant G major back to the tonic refrain in D♭ major. Bizet's contemporaries were shocked by the cadential harmonies of the Flower Song, which are unrelated to the key that surrounds them; after the seamless beauty of the melody itself and Don José's *pianissimo* high B♭, this harmonic gesture (to the words 'je t'aime') underlines how utterly José is bewitched by Carmen.

Though Bizet's final scenes had often previously fallen short, those in *Carmen* contain his most

dramatic and original inspiration (he revised three of the four repeatedly during rehearsals). Certainly the idea for offstage trumpets (duty) playing in counterpoint to Carmen's sensual dance (love) in Act II is a brilliant stroke, but even more powerful is the combination of different styles and recurring motifs in the finale of Act III. Escamillo's suavely popular refrain, Micaëla's Gounod-like message from José's mother, Don José's impassioned threats, and the 'fate' motif build to a climax of great intensity. In the Act IV duet Bizet achieved a dramatic potency that has rarely been equalled in any opera and in the final section the regular phrasing and diatonic harmonies of the joyful, backstage choruses contrast starkly with the rapid, uncontrolled phrases of the protagonists. The bright F♯major of the 'Toreador' refrain, celebrating the death of the bull, forms a supremely ironic commentary on the murder outside the bullring. The realism and tragic power that so shocked Bizet's Parisian contemporaries had a profound influence on the *verismo* composers just a few years later, and has moved countless others ever since. 'I do not know any other instance where tragic humour, which constitutes the essence of love, is expressed . . . in a more shattering phrase than in Don José's last words . . .' (Nietzsche, *Randglossen zu Carmen*, 1912).

RECORDINGS   1. Te Kanawa, Troyanos, Domingo, Van Dam, John Alldis Ch, LPO, Solti, Decca, 1976; 2. Guiot, Callas, Gedda, Massard, René-Duclos Ch, Paris Opéra O, Prêtre, EMI, 1964; 3. Cotrubas, Berganza, Domingo, Milnes, Ambrosian Singers, LSO, Abbado, DG, 1977; 4. Esham, Migenes, Domingo, Raimondi, French Radio Ch, French National O, Maazel, Erato, 1984. The Maazel version, very well cast, uses dialogue of Opéra-Comique version; so does the Solti, which is a carefully edited version (Dean–Solti) adding very few of Oeser's 'discoveries'. Abbado's taut, eloquent reading (using too much Oeser) has Berganza's serious, tragic Carmen. The EMI set, with Callas's unique contribution, is traditional Choudens. [A.B.]

VIDEOS   1. Esham, Migenes-Johnson, Domingo, Raimondi, French Radio Ch, French National O, Maazel, Triumph Films (RCA/Columbia Pictures Home Video), 1984; 2. McLaughlin, Ewing, McCauley, Holloway, Glyndebourne Festival Ch and O, Haitink, Castle, 1985; 3. Vaduva, Ewing, Lima, Quitico, Ch and O of Covent Garden, Mehta, Pioneer (Laserdisc only), 1990: the first is a genuine film, directed by Rosi; the second is a recording of Sir Peter Hall's intelligent staging; the third enshrines a more ordinary performance, interestingly sung [A.B.]

EDITIONS   v.s., Choudens, 1875; with Guiraud recitatives: f.s., Choudens, [1877]; v.s., Choudens, [1877], *rp*, 1980; F. Oeser (ed.) (extremely problematic critical edn): f.s./v.s., Alkor-Edition, 1964

Other operatic works: *L'amour peintre* (inc.; lost), (1860); *La prêtresse* (inc.), (?1860); *La Guzla de l'Emir* (lost), (1862); *Malbrough s'en va-t-en guerre* (operetta, Act I by Bizet, coll. with Legouix, Jonas, Delibes; lost), 1867; *La coupe du roi de Thule* (inc.; manuscript now largely missing), (1868–9), 1955 (BBC broadcast of fragments); *Noé* (completion of F. Halévy's opera), (1869); *Clarisse Harlowe*, (sketched, 1870–71); *Grisélidis*, (sketched, 1870–71); *Sol-si-re-pif-pan* (operetta; lost), 1872; *Don Rodrigue* (inc.), (1873)

BIBLIOGRAPHY   Mina Curtiss, *Bizet and his World*, Knopf, 1958; Winton Dean, *Bizet*, Dent (Master Musicians Series), 2nd edn, 1975; Winton Dean, 'The True Carmen', *MT*, vol.

106 (1965), p. 846, *rp* in Winton Dean, *Essays on Opera*, Clarendon Press, 1990; Nicholas John (ed.), *Carmen* (ENO Opera Guides 13), Calder, 1982, *rp*, 1990; Lesley Wright, 'A New Source for *Carmen*', *19th-Century Music*, vol. 2 (1978), p. 61; Lesley Wright, '*Les pêcheurs de perles*: Before the premiere', *Studies in Music*, vol. 20 (1986), p. 27

L.A.W.

BORIS BLACHER
b 3 January 1903, Newchang, China; *d* 30 January 1975, Berlin

It is not altogether surprising that Blacher, who was born in China and spent his early years in Siberia and Manchuria, should occupy a strikingly individual position among modern German composers. In 1922 he settled in Berlin to read architecture but soon changed to music; in 1939 he was obliged to relinquish a teaching post in Dresden owing to differences with the Nazi authorities. After the Second World War he exerted a strong influence on the younger generation of German composers.

Blacher's work bears witness to unfailing originality, an 'intellectual *leggierezza* that has no parallel in German music' (Oehlmann). Instrumental virtuosity, jazz influence and cool, dry textures place his music close to Stravinsky and Milhaud. From 1950 he also made use of dodecaphonic techniques, extending serial principles to evolve a rhythmic language of 'variable metre'.

The *Abstract Opera No. 1* (it had no successor), inspired by an idea of Werner Egk's, uses phonemes, nonsense syllables and isolated phrases of Russian and English to depict feelings of fear, love, pain, etc. *Zwischenfälle bei einer Notlandung* ('Incidents at an Emergency Landing'), described by Blacher as a 'reportage', uses electronic effects to highlight a nightmarish sequence of absurd and terrifying events. Blacher's more conventional stage works, such as the chamber operas *Romeo und Julia* and *Die Flut*, demonstrate that he possessed sure dramatic instinct, a pleasing lyric gift and unflagging imagination.

Preussisches Märchen
Prussian Fairy-tales
Ballet-opera in five scenes (2h 30m)
Libretto by Heinz von Cramer
Composed 1949
PREMIERE   23 September 1952, Berlin

Blacher chose preponderantly serious subjects for his operas. *Preussisches Märchen*, which crosses the lines dividing opera from operetta and ballet, comes closer to the playful spirit of his instrumental works and is his most widely performed opera. The opening scene plays in the office of the municipal cashier, while the climax is enacted at the annual ball of a fire insurance company. The hero, a clerk by the name of Wilhelm Fadenkreuz, disguises himself as a Prussian army officer. He soon discovers that his uniform endows him with almost unlimited powers. When he commandeers a troop of soldiers and occupies the town hall, the chaos is complete. The libretto, inspired by the Hauptmann von Köpenick saga, includes elements of zeitoper (cf. Hindemith's *Neues vom Tage*), dream sequences and dance interludes. The score, which comprises 20 linked musical numbers, features moments of virtuosic pastiche.

EDITION   v.s., Bote und Bock, 1952

Other operatic works: *Habemeajaja* (lost), (1929); *Fürstin Tarakanowa*, 1941; *Romeo und Julia*, 1947; *Die Flut*, 1946; *Die Nachtschwalbe*, 1948; *Abstrakte Oper No. 1*, 1953; *Rosamunde Floris*, 1960; *Zwischenfälle bei einer Notlandung*, 1966; *200,000 Taler*, 1969; *Yvonne, Prinzessin von Burgund*, 1973; *Das Geheimnis des entwendeten Briefes*, 1975

BIBLIOGRAPHY   Werner Oehlmann, 'Zum Werk Boris Blachers', *Musica*, 1967, p. 54

A.C.W.B.

DAVID BLAKE
David Leonard Blake; *b* 2 September 1936, London

David Blake's decision to study in East Berlin with Hanns Eisler, one of Schoenberg's most influential pupils and at the same time one of the most politicized, swept Blake's music into a distinctive channel. His first job on returning to England was as a schoolmaster, which led to his school opera *It's a Small War* (1962). This used a variety of popular styles including 1930s musicals, a Weillesque march and even an anticipation of Lennon and McCartney. Blake began a long association with York University at its inception in 1964, and the climax of his early maturity, the large-scale cantata *Lumina*, setting the *Cantos* of Ezra Pound, suggested that the lyric stage might be his natural *métier*.

Toussaint, or The Aristocracy of the Skin
Opera in three acts (22 scenes) (3h)
Libretto by Anthony Ward
Composed 1973–6, rev. 1982
PREMIERES   28 September 1977, Coliseum, London; rev. version: 6 September 1983, Coliseum, London

This vast historical fresco tells the story of Toussaint Breda, subsequently Toussaint L'Ouverture the black slave, who led the Haitian slave rebellion of 1791–1803, but died in a French prison at its moment of triumph. Blake's vivid setting juxtaposes intimate vignettes with epic battles and vivid local colour (like the voodoo drumming at the outset) with French quadrilles. The underlying style is basically Bergian, but the excellent music fails in the opera house because of slow dramatic pace and an unsubtle political message. Yet there are many memorable moments, strong lyricism and splendid crowd scenes within the series of sprawling many-peopled tableaux (in the manner of Prokofiev's *War and Peace*). A revised and much shortened version (2h 30m) was produced by ENO in 1983.

EDITION   v.s., Novello, 1977

The Plumber's Gift

Opera in two acts
Libretto by John Birtwistle
Composed 1986–8
PREMIERE   25 May 1989, Coliseum, London (English National Opera)

Blake's second opera is in marked contrast to its epic predecessor. Set in a guest house on the south coast of England 'last year', it is a kind of group-therapy conversation piece between a childless middle-class couple, and a plumber and his lover. There are delightful incidental moments. But the opera as a whole lacks fire and dramatic pacing, though it might be successful in a small house.

BIBLIOGRAPHY   Andrew Clements, '*Toussaint*: Exotic Epic with a Relevant Message', *ENO and Friends*, summer 1983, pp. 6–8; Gerald Larner and David Blake, '*Toussaint*', *MT*, vol. 118 (1977), pp. 721–3

L.F.

MICHEL BLAVET

baptized 13 March 1700, Besançon, France; *d* 28 October 1768, Paris

As the greatest French flautist of his day, Blavet devoted most of his compositions to his own instrument. He did, however, provide four stage works for the private theatre of his employer, the Comte de Clermont.

Le jaloux corrigé

The Man Cured of Jealousy
Intermède with divertissement in one act
Libretto by Charles Collé
PREMIERE   18 November 1752, Château de Berny

Four months after its private premiere *Le jaloux corrigé* was given at the Paris Opéra on the same bill as Rousseau's *Le devin du village*. There it played a small but important part in the establishment of a new type of opéra comique – the Italianate, all-sung variety that evolved in the wake of the *querelle des bouffons*, which had been sparked off the previous year by the performance of intermezzi by Pergolesi and others. The overture, arias and accompanied recitative are taken from those same intermezzi; Blavet merely added a final divertissement and provided linking recitatives. The latter nevertheless broke new ground, being written not in the traditional declamatory French manner but in a style modelled (somewhat crudely) on the Italian *secco* recitative.

RECORDING   Monteil, Prudhon, Vessières, Jean-Marie Leclair Instrumental Ensemble, Paillard, Erato, *c.* 1954
EDITION   Paris, 1753

Other stage works: *Floriane, ou La grotte des spectacles* (comédie-ballet), 1752; *Les jeux olympiques* (ballet-héroïque), 1753; *La fête de Cythère* (opera), 1753
BIBLIOGRAPHY   L. de La Laurencie, 'Deux imitateurs français des bouffons: Blavet et Dauvergne', *Année musicale*, vol. 2 (1912), pp. 65–125

G.S.

ARTHUR BLISS

(Sir) Arthur Edward Drummond Bliss; *b* 2 August 1891, London; *d* 27 March 1975, London

Bliss's education, at Cambridge and the Royal College of Music under Stanford, was interrupted by the First World War during which he was on active service in France. After the war Bliss repudiated his earlier works and developed an interest in the avant-garde of Les Six, Stravinsky, Bartók, and British composers such as van Dieren. But his *Colour Symphony* (1922) showed that his heart lay close to the English tradition. A two-year interlude followed in California (1923–5) before two choral works, the *Pastoral: Lie Strewn the White Flocks* (1929) and the choral symphony *Morning Heroes* (1930), proclaimed his sympathy with the English vocal tradition. He was a pioneer composer of film music, and his score for *Things To Come* (1935) was a popular success, while his ballets demonstrated his feeling for the stage. He became Master of the Queen's Music in 1953, a role he discharged with flair and panache.

Bliss wrote a stage opera, *The Olympians*, and a television opera, *Tobias and the Angel* (1960, libretto by Christopher Hassall), which has never had a stage production. He also prepared a version of *The Beggar's Opera* for the Imperadio Pictures film directed by Peter Brook (1952–3).

The Olympians

Opera in three acts, Op. 69 (2h 30m)
Libretto by J. B. Priestley
Composed 1945–8
PREMIERE   29 September 1949, Covent Garden, London

With its distinguished and thoughtful libretto, *The Olympians* was a short-lived success when first produced. Set in the south of France in 1836, the story concerns a group of poor players who, on midsummer night, assume their true forms of gods and goddesses for a few hours. A semi-professional performance in Edinburgh in 1985 was a triumphant reassertion of Bliss's grasp of the stage and of the virile quality of his invention.

EDITION   v.s., Novello, 1950

BIBLIOGRAPHY   Sir Arthur Bliss, *As I Remember*, Thames Publishing, rev. edn, 1989

L.F.

MARC BLITZSTEIN

b 2 March 1905, Philadelphia, US; *d* 22 January 1964, Fort-de-France, Martinique

Marc Blitzstein appeared as a piano soloist with the Philadelphia Orchestra at 15 and went on to study composition with Nadia Boulanger and Arnold Schoenberg. His theatrical sympathies tended strongly toward the confrontational, experimental approach typified by Bertolt Brecht and Kurt Weill; probably his most performed work is the English translation he made of *The Threepenny Opera*. His efforts in musical theatre are each unique experiments, generally to his own texts. His dramatic compositions also include ballets, a great deal of incidental music for the stage, and film and radio music. His music constitutes one of the most successful examples of a meeting of popular and 'serious' idioms in American music. Tuneful, subtle, and sometimes unexpectedly evocative, Blitzstein's music remains individual and important.

The Cradle Will Rock

Play in music in ten scenes
Libretto by the composer
Composed 1936
PREMIERE   16 June 1937, Venice Theater, New York

A musical presenting a plea for industrial unionization in deliberately cartoon-like terms, *The Cradle Will Rock* was further stylized by a catchy score designed to be available to untrained actors' voices. The circumstances of its original production are even more memorable than its intrinsic quality. Originally to be produced by the Federal Theater Project, the controversial nature of the work led both to its being taken on as an independent production by Orson Welles and John Houseman and also to the company being shut out of their theatre and forbidden to perform the play on any other stage. They outwitted the law by buying tickets to an unused theatre, to which the audience was directed, and delivering their roles from their seats while Blitzstein accompanied them onstage at the piano. It was performed exactly the same way for 19 performances before beginning a more regular run elsewhere.

RECORDING   Stanton, Da Silva, Blitzstein, MGM, 1937: the first complete recording of a Broadway score with its original cast
EDITIONS   v.s., Tams-Witmark (on hire); lib., Random House, 1938

Regina

Opera in three acts (2h 30m)
Libretto by the composer, based on Lillian Hellman's play
The Little Foxes (1939)
Composed 1946–9, rev. 1953, 1958
PREMIERES   31 October 1949, 46th Street Theater, New York; UK: 16 May 1991, Theatre Royal, Glasgow

The machinations of the greedy Hubbard family, conniving for power in the post-Civil-War South, had made for a highly theatrical and effective play, and provided a solid basis for Blitzstein's only real operatic success. The through-composed score encompasses a variety of vocal textures and frequent period flavourings. Like Weill's *Street Scene* and Menotti's early successes, it was presented in a Broadway theatre, and seemed to herald the arrival of an American operatic literature that could be both popular and sophisticated – an arrival that never quite took place. The revisions Blitzstein made for later productions (to be heard on the 1959 recording) are not reflected in the published score and are not to be taken as definitive. The edition prepared by Tommy Krasker and John Mauceri for Scottish Opera is based on a re-examination of available materials, even restoring some music cut before the premiere.

RECORDINGS   1. B. Lewis, Carron, Brice, Hecht, Irving, Driscoll, NY City Opera, Krachmalnick, CBS, 1959; 2. Katherine Ciesinski, Réaux, Kuebler, Noble, Maddalena, Scottish Opera Ch and O, Mauceri, Decca, 1992: Mauceri's reconstructed 'original' version (2h 30m)
EDITION   v.s., Chappell, 1954

Other stage works include: *Triple-Sec*, 1929; *Parabola and Circula*, 1929; *The Harpies*, 1931; *The Condemned*, 1932; *No for an Answer*, 1941; *Reuben, Reuben*, 1955; *Juno*, 1959; *Sacco and Vanzetti* (inc.), (1964); *The Magic Barrel* (inc.), (1964); *Idiots First* (inc.), (1964), completed by Leonard J. Lehman, 1974
BIBLIOGRAPHY   Eric A. Gordon, *Mark the Music: The Life and Work of Marc Blitzstein*, St Martin's Press, 1989

J.A.C.

ERNEST BLOCH

b 24 July 1880, Geneva; *d* 15 July 1959, Portland, Oregon, US

Bloch, of Jewish background, grew up in Switzerland, then studied composition in Brussels where he was also a violin pupil of Ysaÿe. After spells in Frankfurt, as a pupil of Ivan Knorr, and Munich he spent a year in Paris where he met Debussy, a significant influence on his early work. On returning to Switzerland he took up conducting and first went to the US in 1916 as a conductor for Maud Allan's dance company. He returned enthusiastically to New York to teach there the following year. Bloch became an American citizen in 1924.

Bloch's only completed opera, *Macbeth*, was written early in his career. It was premiered at the Opéra-Comique in Paris (1910), considered *outré* although deriving from Wagner, Debussy and Musorgsky, and not revived until 1938. But it was a significant step in the evolution of Bloch's highly individual style, which, with its repeated note patterns, rhythmic fluidity and distinctive intervals, came to be identified as particularly Jewish, although not directly derived from Hebrew music.

In 1927 Roger Sessions, one of several distinguished American composers to come under Bloch's guidance at a formative stage, claimed, 'It is difficult at some moments to resist the temptation to regard *Macbeth* as Bloch's masterpiece. One is aware of a new personality, full-blooded, uninhibited, and conscious of its own strength.' A second opera, on the biblical subject of Jezebel, was not completed.

BIBLIOGRAPHY S. Bloch and I. Heskes, *Ernest Bloch, Creative Spirit: A Programme Source Book*, Jewish Music Council (New York), 1976; R. Strassburg, *Ernest Bloch, Voice in the Wilderness: A Biographical Study*, California State University Press, 1977

P.D.

VILÉM BLODEK

b 3 October 1834, Prague; *d* 1 May 1874, Prague

Blodek studied at the Prague Conservatory (composition under Kittl) 1846–52 and in 1860 succeeded his flute teacher Eiser as professor of flute at the conservatory. His Flute Concerto is still occasionally played, but his reputation today rests almost entirely on his one completed opera, *In the Well*. An early German opera, *Clarissa*, was abandoned; his mental breakdown in 1870 through overwork and his early death in a mental home meant that he left his last opera *Zítek* unfinished. The surviving fragments of *Zítek* are most attractive and indicate the makings of a much more ambitious work than *In the Well*. Though he did not work in the theatre like other Czech opera composers such as Smetana and Šebor, Blodek gained a useful insight into dramatic music by composing incidental music for about 60 plays.

In the Well

V studni

Comic opera in one act (1h 15m)
Libretto by Karel Sabina
Composed 1866–7
PREMIERE 17 November 1867, Provisional Theatre, Prague

Sabina's libretto is part of a group of village-opera libretti he wrote for different Czech opera composers (Smetana's *The Bartered Bride*, Rozkošný's *Mikuláš*, Bendl's *The Elderly Suitor*) based on a young couple's happiness being threatened by the girl's enforced marriage to an unsuitable bridegroom. The plot depends on the comic removal of this obstruction. *In the Well* makes use of the belief that a girl's future husband will be magically revealed on midsummer's eve should she look into the village well. Janek, the rich but elderly farmer that Lidunka's mother has in mind for her, attempts to further his suit by climbing a tree overlooking the well so that his reflection will appear there. Instead he falls in, makes a fool of himself, and Lidunka is allowed to marry her lover Vojtěch. There is only one other character, Veruna, the village 'witch' whom Lidunka consults, and the opera consists of a simple succession of short numbers, including one quartet, two duets and a couple of choruses. Unusually for a Czech comic opera of the time, it

links the numbers with simple recitatives rather than spoken dialogue. Blodek's pleasing melodic gifts resulted in a work of great charm, and the modest demands of the opera made it an immediate favourite, especially in the less well-equipped venues outside Prague. It is the only Czech opera of the 1860s apart from those of Smetana that has never quite lost its place in the repertoire.

RECORDINGS 1. Šounová, Márová, Kocián, Berman, Prague NT Ch and O, Stych, Supraphon, 1981: includes recording of the *Zítek* fragment; 2. Šubrtová, Štěpánová, Žídek, Kroupa, Prague NT Ch and O, Škvor, Supraphon, 1959
EDITION v.s., Starý, 1878; 13th edn, 1946

Other operas: *Clarissa* (inc.; ?lost), (1861); *Zítek* (inc.), (1869), 1934
BIBLIOGRAPHY John Tyrrell, *Czech Opera*, CUP, 1988

J.T.

KARL-BIRGER BLOMDAHL

b 19 October 1916, Växjö, Småland, Sweden; *d* 14 June 1968, Kungsängen, nr Stockholm

Blomdahl was probably the most influential single figure in 20th-century Swedish music. In the later 1930s he founded the Monday Group of young musicians to analyse and discuss modern works and after the Second World War ran several important promotional and concert-giving agencies including the Swedish branch of the ISCM and the Music Department of Swedish Radio. His music encompasses a diversity of styles: Hindemith's neoclassicism was the major influence on his wartime works (*Concerto Grosso* (1944), String Trio (1945)); later serialism, as practised by Berg and theorized about by Krenek, took over as a compositional principle, spiced up by a rhythmic vitality in the manner of folk-inspired composers such as Mátyás Seiber. Later still he embraced jazz and electronics. He tended to reflect styles, rather than pioneer them; so it is not altogether surprising that his major international success, the 'space opera' *Aniara*, is musically wildly eclectic. His second opera, *Herr von Hancken*, did not achieve comparable recognition, but the ballet scores *Sisyphos* (1954) and *Minotaurus* (1957) have been staged fairly frequently. A third opera, *Sagan om den Stora Datan* (*The Story of the Big Computer*), was incomplete at the time of Blomdahl's death.

Aniara: A revue of men in time and space

En revy om människan i tid och rum

Opera in two acts (seven scenes) (1h 45m)
Libretto by Erik Johan Lindegren, adapted from Harry Edmund Martinson's epic poem *Aniara* (1956)
Composed 1957–9
PREMIERES 31 May 1959, Royal Opera, Stockholm; UK: 3 September 1959, King's Theatre, Edinburgh, (Royal Opera, Stockholm)
CAST Blind Poet *high s*, First Engineer *high lyric t*, Captain *bar*, Mimarobe *b-bar, s, high t buffo, t, bar*; 9 dancers, dance

troupe, mime artists; *satb* chorus of space cadets, passengers on the *Aniara*, people, etc.

FULL ORCHESTRA including alto sax, perc (4 players); 3 pre-recorded electronic tapes

SYNOPSIS
Act I   *Aniara* is a spaceship regularly shuttling 8000 human passengers to Mars after Earth's nuclear devastation. During a celebration of Midsummer Day *Aniara* is disabled by an asteroid; its fate is to continue its journey for ever into outer space. The captain is reassuring: 'We have our lives before us.' The celebrations resume. Seven years later the ship's near-human computer, Mima, depicts Earth's total destruction.

Act II   Mima's usefulness is over and it dies. More years pass and religious cults spring up, developing from primitive erotic celebrations to a more elevated belief in Light (although the spaceship is travelling in darkness). Gradually the passengers die, leaving *Aniara* hurtling on through space.

These events are interspersed with grander, more universal reflections: the emigrants' voices bewailing the ravaged Earth combining with the hopes of the youthful space cadets, the First Engineer's aria observing the insignificance of *Aniara* in the greater scheme of things, a lament for Earth by the spaceship's pilot and two visionary vocalises of a blind poet, the leader of the cult of Light. There is a parody of Beethoven's 'Ode to Joy', 'Be embraced O ye space-millions', as the body of the deceased Chief Engineer is fired off into space, and several large-scale dance numbers. There are three pre-recorded electronic tapes: the first, crystalline and gamelan-like, depicts the immensity of outer space; the second, closing Act I, is the last communication from Earth to the spaceship before the planet's total destruction, and the third, opening Act II, depicts the death of Mima.

Far from being the operatic equivalent of a disaster movie, *Aniara* is a modern opera on a totally post-war subject whose significance, in terms of man's relationship with his fellows and his destiny, is greater than the sum of its parts.

RECORDING   Hoel, Arvidson, Haugan, Swedish Radio Ch and SO, Westerberg, Caprice, 1983
EDITIONS   f.s./v.s., Schott, 1959

Herr von Hancken
Opera in three acts (2h 30m)
Libretto by Erik Johan Lindegren, after the novel by Hjalmar Bergman
Completed 1963
PREMIERE   5 September 1965, Royal Opera, Stockholm

The story of the landlocked adventures of an eccentric Swedish sea captain, Herr von Hancken, whose contact with people (who might be Death, the Devil or God) ends with his being stripped of his pretensions and dying at peace. The music is rich in allusions to other composers' works, but its basic grammar is that of atonal serialism.

EDITION   v.s., Schott, 1965

BIBLIOGRAPHY   R. K. Inglefield, 'Karl-Birger Blomdahl: A Portrait', *MQ*, vol. 58 (1972), pp. 67–81

C.B.

JOHN BLOW
b ?1649, Newark, Nottinghamshire, England; *d* 1 October 1708, London

In 1660 Blow was among the first choristers of the restored Chapel Royal, recruited (in effect press-ganged) by Captain Henry Cooke, Master of the Children of the Chapel Royal. By the age of 13 he had written three anthems. In 1665 he was given his 'retirement livery' from the Chapel, his voice having broken; two years later he was auditioned by Samuel Pepys, on the look-out for a musical servant, who noted his 'extraordinary skill' but thought his inability to keep in tune would 'make a man mad, so bad it was'. His skill brought him through; in 1668 he was appointed organist of Westminster Abbey and was playing the harpsichord in the King's Private Musick. In 1674 he succeeded Pelham Humfrey as Master of the Children of the Chapel Royal and Composer in Ordinary to the King. He was Henry Purcell's teacher, and stepped down from his job at the Abbey to allow Purcell to take over in 1680. After Purcell's death in 1695 he resumed the posts he had passed to his pupil; his book of songs, *Amphion Anglicus* (1700) is a conscious imitation of Purcell's posthumous *Orpheus Britannicus*. The dedication, to the Princess (subsequently Queen) Anne, is a defence of sacred music; however, the contents are entirely secular. By that time, Blow's energies were devoted entirely to sacred music and that is probably what he is most remembered for today. It is remarkable that few of his surviving songs appear to have a theatrical context. *Venus and Adonis* is his one work for the stage, the first surviving through-composed opera in English, and was a decisive influence on Purcell's *Dido and Aeneas* (1689). Besides anthems, songs, and *Venus and Adonis* Blow wrote court and Cecilian odes, harpsichord suites and string sonatas. Since the 18th century there has been a tendency to sweeten the acerbities of his harmonic writing, but there is no doubt that these are deliberate and considered.

Venus and Adonis
A Masque for the Entertainment of the King in three acts (1h)
Librettist unknown
Date of composition unknown
PREMIERE   at court, date unknown
CAST   Venus *s*, Adonis *b*, Cupid *s*; *satb* chorus of shepherds, shepherdesses, huntsmen, graces and little cupids

We cannot tell when *Venus and Adonis* was first performed, though we know it was a 'Masque for the Entertainment of the King' and that Venus was played by the actress Mary Davies, once the king's mistress, and Cupid by Lady Mary Tudor, their natural daughter. The little cupids were the boys of the Chapel Royal. The second performance is more substantially documented, since we have an annotated libretto; it took place on 17 April 1684 at Josias Priest's boarding school for young gentlewomen at Chelsea, which is where, in due course, *Dido* was given. The writer of the libretto is unknown, though it has been attributed to Aphra Behn and (more plausibly) to James Allestree, a dissolute fellow of Christ Church, Oxford, whose collaboration with Blow is documented.

The plot follows Shakespeare and Ovid, but the imitation of Lullian tragédie lyrique in miniature demands an allegorical prologue. This wittily satirizes its portentous models; it reflects, ambivalently but accurately, on the morals of Charles's court, where constancy is equated with ugliness.

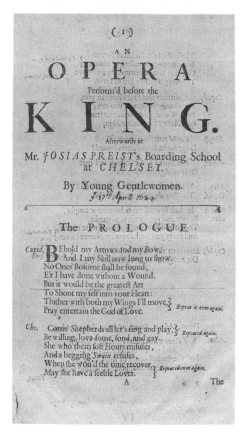

Part 1 of the annotated libretto for Venus and Adonis *(1684)*

SYNOPSIS

Act I 'The Curtain opens and discovers Venus and Adonis sitting together upon a Couch, embracing each other.' A hunting party is heard offstage; Venus attempts to persuade a reluctant Adonis to join it since 'Absence kindles new desire, / I would not have my lover tire.' The huntsmen arrive and Adonis leaves with them.

Act II 'Venus and Cupid are seen standing with Little Cupids round about them.' Cupid asks Venus how to 'destroy / All such as scorn your wanton boy'. She answers that he must match the foolish to the foolish, and Cupid amplifies the lesson to the little cupids who repeat after him a list of love's enemies: 'the insolent, the arrogant, the mercenary, the vain and silly'. Then the cupids play at hide-and-seek until Cupid frightens them away. Venus commands Cupid to call the graces, who sing in her praise and in anticipation of 'this joyful night'. The act ends with a sequence of dances; the last is a ground which prefigures the utterly different mood of what is to come.

Act III Venus is standing 'in a melancholy posture'. A mourning Cupid shakes an arrow at her. She repents that she has let Adonis leave and calls on him to return. Adonis is led in, but fatally wounded, gored by the 'Aedalian boar'. Venus in vain implores the gods to save him, and the scene of love and death culminates in her passionate cries of 'Ah Adonis my love, ah, Adonis'. The mourning cupids lament the 'mighty huntsman', the 'wretched Queen of Love', and their 'forsaken grove'.

The subtlety of Blow's treatment lies in the way in which he negotiates the transition from the public world of the court (in the music of the prologue) to the private world of Venus' ultimate desolation – a move from the social to the tragic and elegiac. The intensity of the opera develops through an increasingly intense use of chromaticism, notably in Venus' impassioned opening arioso in Act III, and in the duet and lament that follow Adonis' entry; indeed in the best manuscript several of Venus' exclamations of 'Ah' are not notated and demonstrate the way the declamation threatens to break all constraints of musical form.

RECORDINGS 1. Ritchie, Field-Hyde, Clinton, L'Ensemble Orchestral de L'Oiseau Lyre, Lewis, L'Oiseau Lyre, 1953; 2. Argenta, L. Dawson, Varcoe, Covey-Crump, London Baroque Ch and O, Medlam, Harmonia Mundi, 1987
EDITIONS f.ss., Arkwright (ed.), *The Old English Edition XXV*, London, 1902; Lewis (ed.), *Editions de l'Oiseau Lyre*, 1939

BIBLIOGRAPHY Edward J. Dent, *Foundations of English Opera*, CUP, 1928; Wilfrid Mellers, *Harmonious Meeting*, Dobson, 1965; Ian Spink, *English Song: Dowland to Purcell*, Batsford, 1974

R.Lu.

NICOLAS BOCHSA

Robert-Nicolas-Charles Bochsa; *b* 9 August 1789, Montmédy, France; *d* 6 January 1856, Sydney, Australia

Noted for his brilliant harp-playing and for his colourful financial and private affairs, Bochsa also composed briefly for the Paris and London stages. Between 1813 and 1816, when he was forced to flee France to avoid imprisonment for forgery, he wrote a series of seven works for the Opéra-Comique and might have developed a successful operatic career if he had been able to stay. In London, where he became director of the King's Theatre, he had to face a charge of bigamy, and he later eloped with a third lady to Naples, where he was musical director of the San Carlo theatre for two years. His later stage works were ballets. His final wanderings took him to America and to Australia.

His French opéras comiques were produced in very quick succession: seven works within 25 months, and although they appealed to the public of those unsettled years, they inevitably attracted Fétis's criticism that even in his most inspired pieces haste and carelessness were evident; they were not revived.

Operas: *Le retour de Trajan, ou Rome triomphante*, 1805; *L'héritier de Paimpol*, 1813; *Les héritiers Michau*, 1814; *Alphonse de Aragon*, 1814; *Le roi et la ligue, ou La ville assiégée*, 1815; *Les noces de Gamache*, 1815; *La lettre de change*, 1815; *Un mari pour étrenne*, 1816
BIBLIOGRAPHY   Fétis, *Biographie universelle de musiciens*, 1st and rev. edns and supp., Brussels, 1835–4; 2nd edn, 1860–65; *rp*, 1963

H.M.

JERRY BOCK

Jerrold Lewis Bock; *b* 23 November 1928, New Haven, Connecticut, US

Jerry Bock discovered his musical ability early, and wrote words and music for shows while in high school and college. With lyricist Larry Holofcener he contributed to a revue and wrote *Mr Wonderful*; shortly after the latter opened, he met Sheldon Harnick, with whom he maintained a collaboration until 1970. Since that date Harnick has continued to write (including opera libretti) but no further work by Bock has been seen on Broadway.

The team's body of work coincides almost exactly with the 1960s and therefore seems to typify the style of that decade, showing great attention to precision of character and locale, as well as a considerable variety of approach. Of the three musicals described below, the first is rousingly entertaining, the second charmingly intimate, the third deeply emotional; all seem equally characteristic of Bock and Harnick.

Fiorello!

Musical in two acts
Libretto by Jerome Weidman and George Abbott; lyrics by Sheldon Harnick
PREMIERES   23 November 1959, Broadhurst Theater, New York; UK: 8 October 1962, Piccadilly Theatre, London

The team's first widely successful show presented a biography of the beloved former mayor of New York City, Fiorello La Guardia. It is most remembered for Tom Bosley's engaging performance, for its production numbers satirically dramatizing politics-as-usual, and as the third of the six musicals to have won the Pulitzer Prize for drama.

RECORDING   Bosley, Wilson, Hanley, Da Silva, Hastings, Capitol, 1959
EDITIONS   v.s., Tams-Witmark (on hire); lib., Random House, 1960; vocal selection, Times Square Music, 1959

She Loves Me

Musical in two acts
Libretto by Joe Masteroff, based on the play *Parfumerie* by Miklos Laszlo; lyrics by Sheldon Harnick
PREMIERES   23 April 1963, Eugene O'Neill Theater, New York; UK: 29 April 1964, Lyric Theatre, London

A man and a woman who bicker constantly at work discover that they have been carrying on a romance by mail. The subtle score combines with an exceptionally well-crafted libretto to give this musical a lasting appeal, a short initial run notwithstanding.

RECORDING   Cook, Bosley, Massey, Cassidy, Hastings, MGM, 1963
EDITIONS   v.s., Tams-Witmark (on hire); lib., Dodd, Mead, 1964

Fiddler on the Roof

Musical play in two acts (film: 3h)
Libretto by Joseph Stein, based on stories by Sholom Aleichem; lyrics by Sheldon Harnick
PREMIERES   22 September 1964, Imperial Theater, New York; UK: 16 February 1967, Her Majesty's Theatre, London
CAST   Tevye *bar*, Golde *a*, Tzeitel *ms*, Hodel *s*, Chava *a*, Yente *ms*, Motel *bar*, Perchik *t*, Lazar Wolf *bar*; other solo parts from *satb* chorus of villagers
ORCHESTRATION (Don Walker)   theatre orchestra, including accordion, gtr/mand

With a story whose appeal might have been seen as limited (its authors were constantly worried during its creation that it would become 'too heavy and too Jewish'), Bock and Harnick achieved far and away their biggest success, an international phenomenon that enthralled audiences everywhere it played. In addition to the appeal of the story, whose theme was the response of tradition to changing times, *Fiddler* owed much of its strength to the direction of Jerome Robbins, whose judgement influenced every element of the original production. The score served its purpose perfectly, without providing many detachable excerpts except for the wedding song, 'Sunrise, Sunset'.

SYNOPSIS
Act I   The action takes place in the Jewish section of the Russian village Anatevka in the late 19th century. The milkman Tevye chooses a husband for his oldest daughter Tzeitel, only to find that she and the tailor Motel have already given each other a pledge. At first disturbed by this break with tradition, Tevye finally tricks his wife Golde into agreeing to it. The act ends with the wedding – interrupted by a raid from the Gentile town authorities.

Act II   The challenge to tradition continues. Tevye's second daughter Hodel wishes to marry a travelling scholar who questions the old ways; Tevye reluctantly gives his blessing. But there can be no blessing when the next daughter, Chava, chooses to

Herschel Bernardi as Tevye in Fiddler on the Roof *(New York, 1964)*

marry a Gentile; she is to have no further share in the community – a community which itself is ended when all Jews are ordered to leave Anatevka. The final image is of the circle of tradition joining hands a final time, then dissolving as all the characters (including the symbolically precarious fiddler of the title) go their separate ways.

RECORDING Mostel, Karnilova, Migenes, Pendleton, Convy, RCA, 1964: the CD reissue adds two songs cut from the original release
FILM Jewison (dir.), UA, 1971
EDITION v.s., Charles Hansen, 1965

Other musicals include: *Mr Wonderful*, 1956; *The Body Beautiful*, 1958; *Tenderloin*, 1960; *The Apple Tree*, 1966; *The Rothschilds*, 1970
BIBLIOGRAPHY Richard Altman and Mervyn D. Kaufman, *The Making of a Musical: Fiddler on the Roof*, Crown, 1971; Christopher Davis, *The Producer*, Harper and Row, 1972

J.A.C.

FELIPE BOERO
b 1 May 1884, Buenos Aires; *d* 9 August 1958, Buenos Aires

The Argentinian Boero was an almost exact contemporary of the Brazilian Heitor Villa-Lobos, and in many ways their careers ran in parallel, each epitomizing the rise and fall of fervent nationalism in their respective Latin American nations. Like Villa-

Lobos, Boero resided as a young man in Paris, where he studied with Fauré. On his return to Argentina he undertook administrative duties with teacher-training institutes in Buenos Aires; his position on the National Fine Arts Committee resulted in him organizing large-scale choral concerts in the 1930s, again similar to those put on by Villa-Lobos.

Boero's compositions, and particularly his operas, seized on the nationalist *gauchesco* trend already taken up by earlier Argentinian composers. The operas all take Latin American folk legends as their base, and employ actual folk melodies. In *Raquela* these make up almost half the score. *Tucumán* was the first Argentinian opera to a libretto in Spanish (rather than in the all-pervasive Italian), and *El matrero*, a *verismo*-type opera styled a leyenda dramatica, is set deep in the pampas. It was hugely successful at its 1929 Buenos Aires premiere and has retained a regular place in the repertoire.

Operatic works: *Tucumán*, 1918; *Ariana y Dionysos* (ópera-ballet), 1920; *Raquela*, 1923; *El matrero*, 1929; *Siripo*, 1937; *Zincalí*, 1954
BIBLIOGRAPHY Gerard Béhague, *Music in Latin America: An Introduction*, Prentice-Hall, 1979

S.J.W.

PHILIPPE BOESMANS
b 17 May 1936, Tongres, Belgium

Boesmans had lessons with Froidebise and Pousseur, and attended the Darmstadt summer school, but considers himself a self-taught composer. Berio would seem to have been his most important model. Like Berio's, his music is richly allusive, offering manifold glimpses of the past (or of present notions of the past) in its variety of styles, forms, textures and ideas over a range from Machaut to yesterday. Like Berio too, he is an expert orchestrator, and his scores sometimes evoke the finish of Strauss, Berg or Debussy. Most of his works have been for instrumental formations, but he has also written a music-theatre piece, *Attitudes* (1977), as well as two operas, *La passion de Gilles* and *Reigen* (Brussels, 1993).

La Passion de Gilles
The Passion of Gilles
Opera in three acts (2h)
Libretto by Pierre Mertens
Composed 1982
PREMIERE 18 October 1983, Théâtre de la Monnaie, Brussels
INSTRUMENTATION 4 fl, 2 ob, 4 cl, 2 bsn, 4 tpt, 4 hn, 3 trbn, tuba, timp, perc (6 players), hp, cel, str

The central characters are Gilles de Rais (baritone) and Jeanne d'Arc (soprano), comrades who attained diametrically opposed states of sainthood. In Act I, set at the siege of Paris in 1429, Gilles and Jeanne recognize each other as mirror images, both distanced from their surroundings, destined to pursue journeys inwards into excess (much in the same way, the opera itself is uncomfortable with the conditions of historical epic it has set up for itself, wanting something more). Act II is set ten years later. Jeanne has died at the stake; Gilles, in his castle, abandons himself to sorcery and sadism, though the appetites he tries to assuage are not sensual but metaphysical: hence his detachment, despair and disgust. A false Jeanne arrives (the meeting of the two is similarly placed in each act), and he welcomes her to his table before being arrested. In Act III he is tried as a heretic and himself condemned to the stake, where once again he encounters his contrary and eternal partner.

RECORDING Farley, Gottlieb, Ch et O Symphonique de l'Opéra National, Bartholomée, Ricercar, 1983
EDITION f.s./v.s., Jobert, 1983

BIBLIOGRAPHY Célestin Deliège, Bernard Foccroulle and Claude Ledoux, *Philippe Boesmans*, Opéra Nationale de Belgique, 1983

P.A.G.

ADRIEN BOIELDIEU

François-Adrien Boieldieu; *b* 16 December 1775, Rouen, France; *d* 3 October 1834, Jarcy, France

After making his operatic début in Rouen, Boieldieu moved to Paris in 1796 to develop his career. Having been much impressed in his youth by the opéras comiques of Monsigny, Grétry and Dalayrac, it was to this genre that he was principally attracted.

During the second half of the 18th century the opéra comique had grown to comprise a wide variety of styles and subject matter. Some works retained the charming sentimentality and comic intrigues of the early opéra comique, while others acquired more sombre overtones and evolved into the drame lyrique. This genre, first suggested by Monsigny's *Le déserteur*, eschewed simple elegance in favour of a more passionate lyricism. By the Revolutionary period, composers such as Cherubini, Méhul and Lesueur were writing opéras comiques of a highly dramatic character. Although several of Boieldieu's works approach this style, they rarely achieve a comparable depth of expression. He specialized in light but sophisticated comedy, but within this style the tone and content of his operas were exceptionally diverse.

Boieldieu composed two opéras comiques to libretti by his father while still in Rouen and followed these with three one-act *works* in Paris which explored both comic and *larmoyant* styles. His first major success was *Zoraïme et Zulnar* (1798), a dramatic oriental tale, and he secured a European reputation two years later with another drame lyrique, *Béniowski*. *Le calife de Bagdad* (also 1800) is, in contrast, a lively comic work which was a great success; it remained in the repertoire for 75 years.

In 1803 Boieldieu became director of the French Opéra at the Russian court of Tsar Alexander I. He remained there for eight years, composing several light opéras comiques, the most highly acclaimed of which was *Les voitures versées* (later admired by Berlioz). On his return to Paris he had successes with *Jean de Paris* and *Le nouveau seigneur de village* and followed these with a number of collaborations celebrating various contemporary events. Boieldieu's most important works were composed towards the end of his career: *Le petit chaperon rouge* (1818), an opéra féerie with a richly inventive score, *La dame blanche* (1825), which affirmed the popularity of the French opéra comique during a period of widespread support for Rossini's works, and *Les deux nuits* (1829), whose complex orchestration and harmonies added depth to Boieldieu's style.

Boieldieu's operas are characterized primarily by the fluency and wealth of their melodic inspiration. Their melodies are graceful yet full of vitality and often contain much virtuosic display. The harmonic language remains within a secure diatonic framework, but is embellished by frequent appoggiaturas and passing notes. Modulations are thus used sparingly and rarely broach the depths explored by Cherubini, Méhul and, later, by Berlioz. Boieldieu's skilful treatment of the orchestra, however, does much to mask these limitations. His dexterous grouping of instruments and vivid sense of colour – muted horn and trumpet solos in *Béniowski*, a piccolo duet in *Le calife de Bagdad* – result in many distinct and original effects.

La dame blanche

The White Lady
Opéra comique in three acts (2h)
Libretto by Eugène Scribe, based loosely on the novels *Guy Mannering* (1815) and *The Monastery* (1820) by Walter Scott
PREMIERES 10 December 1825, Opéra-Comique, Paris; UK: 9 October 1826, Drury Lane, London; US: 24 August 1827, Park Theater, New York
CAST Gaveston *b*, Anna *s*, Georges *t*, Dikson *t*, Jenny *s*, Marguerite *s*, Gabriel *s*, MacIrton *b*; *satb* chorus of tenants and their wives, country men and women
CHAMBER ORCHESTRA

SYNOPSIS
Act I George Brown, recently returned to Scotland from war, is intrigued by the nearby castle of Avenel. He learns that it houses a beneficent ghost, known as the 'White Lady'. When Dikson, a tenant on the castle estate, shows reluctance to meet her (as he has been summoned) George readily offers to take his place.

Act II Since the heir to the estate is absent (possibly due to the machinations of Gaveston, steward to the late Count of Avenel) the castle is to be auctioned. Gaveston wants it but Anna, his ward, opposes the plan. When George arrives at the castle the 'White Lady' appears: he promises to follow her instructions. At the auction Gaveston is outbid by George. The 'White Lady', he says, has promised to provide the money.

Act III Anna, who is the 'White Lady', finds the means to pay for the castle in a treasure chest belonging to the Avenel family. But it emerges that

George is in fact the true heir. He takes his place as the rightful laird, with Anna as his wife.

La dame blanche was one of the most popular opéras comiques of the 19th century. It was translated into many European languages and by 1874 had received its 1,500th performance in Paris. The score is rich in melodic invention; the vocal and instrumental writing is characterized by fluent, yet elaborate, lines. The mysterious and Romantic atmosphere of the opera opened up new avenues for the genre, yet the synthesis of comedy and drama showed that it could treat serious subjects while preserving its characteristic charm and simplicity.

The White Lady appears: La dame blanche *(Paris, 1825)*

RECORDING Louvay, Berbié, Sénéchal, Doniat, Legros, Ch and O of Raymond Saint-Paul, Stoll, Ace of Diamonds, 1964, *reissue*, 1990
EDITIONS f.s., Janet et Cotelle, 1826; v.s., Janet et Cotelle, 1850

Other operas: *La fille coupable*, 1793; *La famille suisse*, 1797; *Zoraïme et Zulnar*, 1798; *La dot de Suzette*, 1798; *Emma, ou La prisonnière* (coll. with Cherubini; one fragment survives), 1799; *Béniowski, ou Les exilés du Kamtchatka*, 1800; *Le calife de Bagdad*, 1800 (RECORDING Musidisc, 1960s); *Ma tante Aurore, ou Le roman impromptu*, 1803 (RECORDING Fontana, 1960s); *Le baiser et la quittance* (coll. with R. Kreutzer, Méhul, Isouard), 1803; *Aline, reine de Golconde*, 1804; *Abderkan*, 1805; *La jeune femme colère*, 1805; *Un tour de soubrette*, 1806; *Télémaque dans l'île de calypso, ou Le triomphe de la sagesse*, 1806; *Les voitures versées*, 1808, (rev. 1820) (RECORDING Musidisc, 1971); *Rien de trop, ou Les deux paravents*, 1811; *Jean de Paris*, 1812 (RECORDING Musidisc, 1966); *Le nouveau seigneur de village*, 1813 (RECORDING Musidisc, ?1960s); *Bayard à Méz ières* (coll. with Catel, Cherubini, Isouard), 1814; *Angéla, ou L'atelier de Jean Cousin* (coll. with S. Gail), 1814; *La fête du village voisin*, 1816; *Charles de France, ou Amour et Gloire* (coll. with Hérold), 1816; *Le petit chaperon rouge*, 1818; *Blanche de Provence, ou La cour des fées* (coll. with Berton, Cherubini, R. Kreutzer, Paer), 1821; *Les trois genres* (coll. with Auber), 1824; *Pharamond* (coll. with Berton, R. Kreutzer), 1825; *Les*

deux nuits, 1829; *La marquise de Brinvilliers* (coll. with Auber, Batton, Berton, Blangini, Carafa, Cherubini, Hérold, Paer), 1831; *Marguerite* (inc.); *Les jeux floraux* (inc.); 8 lost operas
BIBLIOGRAPHY G. Favre, *Boieldieu: sa vie, son oeuvre*, vols 1–2, E. Droz, 1944–5; B. Gibson, 'Boieldieu (1775–1834)', *Music and Musicians*, vol. 24 (1975–6), no. 4, pp. 26–30; J. Mitchell, *The Walter Scott Operas*, The University of Alabama Press, 1977

E.C.

JOSEPH BODIN DE BOISMORTIER

b 23 December 1689, Thionville, France; *d* 28 October 1755, Roissy-en-Brie, France

In Boismortier's prolific output (over a hundred publications, many of them comprising six or more compositions) opera plays only a small part. Of his three works presented at the Paris Opéra, only the pastorale *Daphnis et Chloé* (1747) enjoyed any real success. *Les voyages de l'Amour* (1736) and *Don Quichote chez la Duchesse* (1743; revived London, 1973), though not outright failures, were never revived there. The latter is one of the very few comedies staged at the Opéra before the 1750s.

The music of Boismortier's operas, though lightweight and sometimes rather obvious, possesses considerable charm. In style it represents a skilful blending of French and Italian elements, the former predominating in the vocal music, the latter in the instrumental. By the time of *Daphnis et Chloé*, the influence of Rameau is clear both in the substance of the music and in its colourful orchestration.

G.S.

ARRIGO BOITO

Enrico Arrigo Boito; *b* 24 February 1842, Padua; *d* 10 June 1918, Milan

Boito's reputation rests on three distinct achievements: first, his contribution as Verdi's librettist for *Otello* and *Falstaff*, as well as for the revised *Simon Boccanegra*; second, his own two operas (*Mefistofele* and *Nerone*); and third, to a lesser extent, his books of poems, *Libro dei versi* and *Re Orso*. Educated at the Milan Conservatory, where he studied composition with Alberto Mazzucato, he and his lifelong friend Franco Faccio, the composer–conductor, won scholarships for study abroad. In Paris, Boito met both Rossini and Verdi, and for the latter he supplied the text for the cantata *Inno delle naz ioni*. Returning to Milan, he wrote musical journalism and continued work on his *Faust* opera, a project he had begun as a student in Milan.

It was at a dinner following the premiere of Faccio's first opera, *I profughi fiamminghi* (1863), that the idealistic young Boito made the notorious comment comparing the defiled altars of Italian opera to the splattered walls of a brothel. Verdi assumed Boito included him among the defilers (in fact he was just being over-enthusiastic about Faccio's opera) and took umbrage. That he was deeply offended by it is proved by his allusions to this sentiment, never getting the words quite right, in a number of his letters over the succeeding years. Boito's faith in his friend's skill continued and in 1865 he wrote his first opera libretto, significantly on a Shakespearean subject, *Hamlet*, for Faccio.

Three years later the opportunity arose for Boito himself to demonstrate his hopes for the future of Italian music drama with his *Mefistofele*. The work precipitated a historic fiasco at La Scala, and was withdrawn after two rowdy performances. Proudly hiding his humiliation, Boito spent the next years writing libretti for others (including, as 'Tobia Gorrio', *La gioconda* for Ponchielli) and supplying a number of translations of songs and operas, including Wagner's *Rienzi* and *Tristan*. At Bologna in 1875, the drastically revised *Mefistofele* proved successful.

Arrigo Boito (Il teatro illustrato, July 1881)

Through Faccio and the music publisher Giulio Ricordi, a *rapprochement* was arranged with Verdi in 1879, with the agreement that Boito would provide a text for *Otello* without any firm commitment on the part of the composer. As a test, Boito was invited to prepare a revision of Piave's text for *Simon Boccanegra*. That task successfully accomplished, work progressed on *Otello*, but not without some crises. However, by the time *Otello* had its triumphant premiere at La Scala in 1887, Boito had forged a firm friendship with Verdi and their collaboration on *Falstaff* (1893) went much more smoothly. Boito proposed *King Lear* as their next project and began a libretto, but, though he had

planned for decades to write an opera on the play (he got as far as sketching a complete scenario in 1850) Verdi finally realized that, at past 80, such an undertaking was beyond him. Boito's relationship with Verdi remained close, and he was present when Verdi died.

As early as 1862, Boito had sketched plans for an opera on the subject of Nero but other commissions had always prevented his working on it consistently. Shortly after Verdi's death, he published his five-act libretto for *Nerone*, which was hailed as a major literary achievement. With the passage of time, Boito suffered from increasing difficulty in concentration, and diminished confidence in his ability to compose this work. When he died, *Nerone* was still incomplete, 56 years after its conception. Although much of the score existed, including sketches for the discarded fifth act, the work required considerable preparation. This was supervised by Toscanini, who conducted the posthumous premiere at La Scala in 1924.

Mefistofele
Mephistopheles

Opera in a prologue, four acts and an epilogue (originally a prologue and five acts) (2h 15m)
Libretto by the composer, after Goethe's *Faust* (1808, 1832)
Composed 1860–67, rev. 1871, 1875, 1881
PREMIERES 5 March 1868, La Scala, Milan; rev. version: 4 October 1875, Bologna; UK: 6 July 1880, Her Majesty's Theatre, London; US: 16 November 1880, Boston; definitive version: 25 May 1881, Milan
CAST Mefistofele *b*, Faust *t*, Margherita *s*, Elena *s*, Marta *a*, Pantalis *a*, Wagner *t*, Nerèo *t*; *satb* chorus of heavenly host, burghers, witches, sirens; ballet
FULL ORCHESTRA including serpent, organ, thunder-machine

Boito's revisions, after the failure of the 1868 version of *Mefistofele* (which he conducted himself), included omitting a scene at the emperor's court and an intermezzo sinfonico. Although most of the changes were made for an 1875 production at Bologna, the score did not emerge in its final form until 1881. The opera includes the prologue in heaven and the Helen of Troy scene from the second part of Goethe's *Faust* (both ignored by Gounod in his *Faust*, 1859).

SYNOPSIS
Prologue The devil, Mefistofele, wagers with God that he can win the soul of Faust, while the chorus praises the Lord.

Act I In Kermesse, the aged scholar Faust and his disciple Wagner first see Mefistofele, disguised as a grey friar. Later, in his study, Faust contemplates nature, but Mefistofele appears, introduces himself as the spirit of negation, rejuvenates Faust, and persuades him to sign the fatal pact.

Act II While Mefistofele flirts with Marta, Faust woos her friend Margherita and wins the promise of a later assignation. He gives her a narcotic for her mother so that they won't be disturbed. Mefistofele brings Faust to the Brocken mountains to witness the orgiastic Walpurgis Night.

Act III Margherita languishes in prison, condemned for the death of her mother, who was poisoned by Faust's sleeping draught, and for drowning the child she bore Faust. Faust comes to her cell, hoping to save her, but the appearance of Mefistofele fills her with dread. Dying, she remains constant in her Christian faith.

Act IV In Classical Greece, whither Mefistofele has transported Faust, Elena (Helen of Troy) has a vision of the destruction of Troy. Faust woos her, anticipating a fusion of the Classic and Romantic spirits.

The epilogue shows the aged Faust longing for death. Despite Mefistofele's warnings, he invokes divine forgiveness and dies redeemed.

The projected plan for the work was without equal in Italian opera in the latter half of the 19th century, but, unfortunately, Boito's incapacity as a composer (his frequent inability to develop musical ideas) prevented him from realizing his ambition fully. Boito's revisions, gigantic in scope, brought *Mefistofele* far closer to the conventional operatic forms of the time, emphasizing the romance of Faust and Margherita and the conflict of good and evil. The success the opera enjoyed in its less overtly 'futuristic' version reassured Boito after its initial failure. The music, although at times inspired, on the whole lacks spontaneity – particularly the rhythm. *Mefistofele* survives today, principally in Italy and the United States, as a vehicle for star basses.

RECORDINGS 1. Tebaldi, Cavalli, Del Monaco, Siepi, Accademia di Santa Cecilia Ch and O, Serafin, Decca, 1958; 2. Caballé, Ligi, Domingo, Treigle, Ambrosian Opera Ch, LSO, Rudel, EMI, 1974; 3. Freni, Caballé, Pavarotti, Ghiaurov, London Opera Ch, National PO, De Fabritiis, Decca, 1984
EDITIONS f.s., Ricordi, 1881; v.ss., Ricordi, 1875 (first version), 1880; final version: f.s., Ricordi, 1895; v.ss., Ricordi, 1892

Nerone

Nero

Tragedia in four acts (2h 45m)
Libretto by the composer
Composed 1862–1918 (inc.; completed by Vincenzo Tommasini, Arturo Toscanini and (Act I only) Antonio Smareglia)
PREMIERES 1 May 1924, La Scala, Milan; UK: 26 March 1985, Logan Hall, London (Abbey Opera); US: 12 April 1982, Carnegie Hall, New York (concert)

This work, revised and completed by others after Boito's death, was intended to be his masterpiece and proved to be his nemesis. The opera had been scheduled for production more than once (including a performance at the Metropolitan Opera in New York with Caruso and Toscanini) but was repeatedly withdrawn by the composer. Though the result is powerful but heavy-going, *Nerone* proves to be a fascinating, if episodic, testament to Late Romanticism, requiring vast spectacle on stage.

In a series of pictures, the opera depicts Ancient Rome at the time of Nero. At the centre of the action lies the contrast between evil and good, between the debauched life-style of the pagan Romans (represented by the priest–conjurer Simon Mago) and the purity and simplicity of the new Christians (principally represented by Fanuèl and the vestal virgin Rubria). The opera ends with a moving scene of Rubria's death and also includes the burning of Rome.

Nerone points to the pathetic discrepancy between Boito's vision and his ability to realize it. In the score, the composer tries to invoke contrasting *tinte* for the forces he presents in conflict; most nearly successful is the diatonicism of the Christians, particularly in such moments as Fanuèl's recitation of the Beatitudes and the death of Rubria.

RECORDING Tokody, Takács, Nagy, Miller, Hungarian Radio and TV Ch, Hungarian State Opera O, Queler, Hungaroton, 1983
EDITIONS f.s., Ricordi, 1925; v.s., Ricordi, 1924
BIBLIOGRAPHY William Ashbrook, 'Boito and the 1868 *Mefistofele* Libretto as a Reform Text', in Roger Parker and A. Groos (eds), *Reading Opera*, Princeton University Press, 1988; Jay Nicolaisen, 'The First *Mefistofele*', *19th-Century Music*, vol. 2 (1978), p. 221; G. Tintori (ed.), *Arrigo Boito: musicista e letterato*, Nuove Edizioni, 1986

W.A.

GIUSEPPE BONNO

Giuseppe Giovanni Battista Bonno [Bono]; *b* 29 January 1711, Vienna; *d* 15 April 1788, Vienna

Bonno, the son of an Italian servant in the Viennese imperial household, was sent to Naples in 1726 at the expense of Charles VI and studied composition with Durante and Leo. After his return in 1736 he received several commissions for operas from the emperor and his family, although he was not appointed court composer for another three years. For just over a decade, until 1761, Bonno worked as kapellmeister to the Prince of Sachsen-Hildburghausen together with Gluck and Dittersdorf. In 1774 he became imperial kapellmeister, his assistant being Salieri; he was also for many years an official and chief conductor of the important Tonkünstlersocietät. He was impressed by Mozart's prodigious talents, and remained friendly with the family.

Bonno's musical style was essentially conservative, but highly accomplished. In his operas he often worked with the influential court poet Metastasio until he gave up stage works and concentrated on sacred music. Among his pupils were the composer Dittersdorf and many leading singers.

Surviving operas: *Il re pastore*, 1751; *L'eroe cinese*, 1752; 22 other stage works; 3 lost operas
BIBLIOGRAPHY R. Angermüller, 'Giuseppe Bonno', in *Grove*, Macmillan, 1980

T.T.C.

ANTONIO MARIA BONONCINI

b 18 June 1677, Modena; *d* 8 July 1726, Modena

Antonio Bononcini is best known by the persisting misattribution to him of *Il trionfo di Camilla*, a score by his elder brother, Giovanni. This is doubly unfortunate, because the lightly accompanied tunes in *Camilla* are far removed from Antonio's basic style, which features counterpoint similar to that of Corelli's church sonatas. Antonio's most complex textures are found in his best-known work, the *Stabat Mater*. Besides a few liturgical works, he is known to have written eleven operas, four oratorios, and several serenatas and cantatas.

Antonio followed in the footsteps of his elder brother until Giovanni went to London in 1720: he studied with G. B. Colonna in Bologna, and became a proficient cellist; he was in Rome by 1696; Vienna and Berlin by 1702; and back in Italy after 1711. At first, he was active mainly as a performer, then, from 1705 to 1711, he was employed (undoubtedly through his brother's influence) to write dramatic works for the Viennese court, one of which was the opera, *Tigrane, re d'Armenia*. Antonio's other operas were composed for cities ruled or dominated by Austria: Naples, Milan, Reggio Emilia and Modena. In his operas of 1715–21, his style became much more *galant à la* Vivaldi. Perhaps because of their light-hearted liveliness, they pleased patrons and public, and he continued to receive commissions until he was appointed maestro di cappella to the Duke of Modena in 1721. During the remaining five years of his life he composed no opera, but he arranged at least one, *Mitridate Eupatore*, first set by Alessandro Scarlatti for Venice in 1707. None of his works received a production in a second city.

Operas: *Tigrane, re d'Armenia*, 1710; *Il tiranno eroe*, 1715; *Sesostri re d'Egitto*, 1716; *La conquista del vello d'oro*, 1717; *Astianatte*, 1718; *Griselda*, 1718 (EDITION facsimile, Garland, 1977); *Merope*, 1721; *Endimione*, 1721; *Rosiclea in Dania*, 1721; 2 lost operas
BIBLIOGRAPHY   Lowell Lindgren, *A Bibliographic Scrutiny of Dramatic Works set by Giovanni and His Brother Antonio Maria Bononcini*, University Microfilms (Ann Arbor), 1974; Lowell Lindgren, 'Antonio Maria Bononcini e *La conquista del vello d'oro*, (Reggio Emilia, 1717)', in Susi Davoli (ed.), *Civiltà teatrale e Settecento emiliano*, Mulino, 1986

L.L.

GIOVANNI BONONCINI

b 18 July 1670, Modena; *d* 9 July 1747, Vienna

Giovanni Bononcini is often remembered by a satirical epigram of 1725, in which John Byrom ridiculed the ardent operatic partisans of Bononcini and Handel, then concluded: 'Strange all this Difference should be/'Twixt Tweedle-dum and Tweedle-dee!' But most musicians would agree with the composer John Ernest Galliard, who in 1716 labelled Bononcini's style 'agreeable and easie'.

Largely because of its uncomplicated melodic grace, his music was highly prized throughout Europe during his prime; he was arguably the most sought-after Italian opera composer of the day. He wrote many dramatic vocal works, comprising 32 operas, 7 oratorios, 25 serenatas and nearly 300 cantatas.

Wealthy patrons supported Bononcini throughout his career. After the death of Bononcini's father Giovanni Maria (the composer and theorist) in 1678, the Duke of Modena sent him to study under G. P. Colonna in Bologna. In 1692, his first opera was written in Rome, where both he and his librettist, Silvio Stampiglia, served the family of the Spanish ambassador, Luigi della Cerda. When the ambassador became viceroy of Naples, he commissioned *Il trionfo di Camilla* from Bononcini and Stampiglia. It became the greatest operatic success of the age: there were 23 Italian productions between 1696 and 1719, probably using Bononcini's score (though alterations may have been made by other hands), and it was presented in London 111 times between 1706 and 1728. Its astonishing success there, five years before Handel's arrival, was largely responsible for establishing completely sung operas on the London stage.

After the accession of Joseph I in 1705, Bononcini became the principal opera composer in Vienna until the death of the emperor in 1711. Bononcini went to Rome in 1714, where he served the Viennese ambassador, Count Gallas. After Gallas's death Bononcini returned to London, and was employed by the Royal Academy of Music. His operas dominated the London stage during the 1720–22 seasons and he was considered to be Handel's greatest rival. Losing favour because of his association with Jacobites

Anonymous portrait of Giovanni Bononcini

implicated in anti-government plots, he would have left England for good in 1724 had the Duchess of Marlborough not employed him to direct her chamber concerts. But by 1732 he had left her employ and returned to the Continent, where he occupied himself with various musical ventures until a pension awarded him by the Empress Maria Theresa in 1742 enabled him to retire.

Operas: *Eraclea* (?Act II only), 1692; *Xerse*, 1694 (EDITION facsimile, Garland, 1986); *Tullo Ostilio*, 1694; *Muzio Scevola*, 1695, rev. 1710; *Il trionfo di Camilla*, 1696, rev. 1698 (EDITION facsimile, Garland, 1978); *La clemenza d'Augusto* (Act III only), 1697; *Temistocle in Bando*, 1698; *La fede publica*, 1699; *Gli affetti più grandi vinti dal più giusto*, 1701; *Cefalo*, 1702; *Polifemo*, 1702; ?*Feraspe, c.* 1704; *Pastorella* (Act III only), 1705; *La regina creduta re*, 1706; *Endimione*, 1706; *Etearco*, 1707, rev. 1719; *Turno Aricino*, 1707; *Mario fuggitivo*, 1708; *Abdolomino*, 1709; *Caio Gracco*, 1710; *Astarto*, 1715, rev. 1720; *Erminia*, 1719, rev. 1723; *Crispo*, 1721, rev. 1722; *Muzio Scevola* (Act II only), 1721; *L'odio e l'amore*, 1721; *Griselda*, 1722 (RECORDING excerpts: Sutherland, Bonynge, Decca, 1968); *Farnace*, 1723; *Calfurnia*, 1724; *Astianatte*, 1727; *Alessandro in Sidone*, 1737; 2 lost operas

BIBLIOGRAPHY   A. Ford, 'Music and Drama in the Operas of Giovanni Bononcini', *PRMA*, vol. 101 (1974–5), pp. 107–20; P. H. Lang, *George Frideric Handel*, Faber, 1966; Lowell Lindgren, *A Bibliographic Scrutiny of Dramatic Works Set by Giovanni and His Brother Antonio Maria Bononcini*, University Microfilms (Ann Arbor), 1974

L.L.

GIOVANNI BORETTI

Giovanni Antonio Boretti; *b c.* 1640, Rome; *d* 17 December 1672, Venice

Boretti was a composer who had the rare distinction of singing in his own opera, *Alessandro amante* (1668). He seems to have had considerable promise, and was appointed vicemaestro to the Duke of Parma only months before his death. His stage works were widely performed, not only in Venice where most received their premieres: *La Zenobia* was perhaps heard even in Vienna in November 1662. If one can rely on the evidence of the surviving scores, it would seem that Boretti concentrated on opera to the virtual exclusion of other genres.

Boretti's operas seem to have conformed to Venetian taste of the 1660s and 1670s. It is clear from the stage directions that his *Marcello in Siracuso* (1670) demanded a prodigious quantity of scenery, including fountains and flowing waters, royal halls and balconies, and a complete ballo given by the pupils of Archimedes. Boretti also seems to have responded to the vogue for constant arias: his librettist for *Claudio Cesare* (1672) mentions the need to include as many as possible in the opera, to satisfy the whims of the public, as well as the singers themselves.

Surviving operas: *Eliogabalo*, 1668; *Marcello in Siracusa*, 1670; *Ercole in Tebe*, 1671 (EDITION facsimile, H. M. Brown (ed.), Garland, 1977); *Claudio Cesare*, 1672: 4 lost operas

G.D.

ALEKSANDR BORODIN

Aleksandr Porfiryevich Borodin; *b* 12 November 1833, St Petersburg, Russia; *d* 27 February 1887, St Petersburg

Borodin, whose mere handful of mainly instrumental compositions are regularly performed in the concert hall and whose only opera, *Prince Igor*, is a household name, was an untrained spare-time composer and proud of the fact. Despite the repeated reproaches of his musical friends for not devoting more time to fulfilling his outstanding musical gifts, he resolutely maintained that he was essentially a 'Sunday composer' and that his professional work obliged him to consider composition simply as a relaxation and indulgence.

Borodin trained as a chemist and at the age of 31 became Professor of Organic Chemistry at the Medico-Surgical Academy in St Petersburg. An exceptionally genial and attractive man, he took his professional duties very seriously and spent most of his time in research, teaching, committee work and looking after the well-being of his students. These biographical details are particularly relevant to *Prince Igor* for they largely explain the otherwise incomprehensible fact that he failed to complete the opera after 17 years of sporadic work on it. At his sudden death aged 53, the overture had been improvised but not written down, some of the numbers were in a very sketchy form, quite a lot remained unorchestrated and, worst of all, the third act had large chunks missing, including the libretto itself. For this reason *Igor* will always be a problem opera; its extended, diffuse dramatic shape is far from satisfactory and the libretto sometimes lapses into banality. Nevertheless it is packed with magnificent music, wonderful opportunities for solo and choral singing, and the *Polovtsian Dances* that conclude Act II undoubtedly constitute one of the most overwhelming scenes in all opera.

Prince Igor

Knyaz' Igor'
Opera in four acts with a prologue (3h 30m)
Libretto by the composer, based on a scenario by V. V. Stassov
Composed 1869–70, 1874–87
PREMIERES   4 November 1890, Mariinsky Theatre, St Petersburg; UK: 8 June 1914, Drury Lane, London; US: 30 December 1915, Metropolitan, New York
CAST   Prince Igor *bar*, Yaroslavna *s*, Vladimir *t*, Prince Vladimir Galitsky *high b*, Khan Konchak *b*, Khan Gzak *silent*, Konchakovna *a*, Ovlur *t*, Skula *b*, Eroshka *t*, Nurse *s*, Polovtsian Girl *s*; *satb* chorus of Russian princes and princesses, boyars and their wives, elders, Russian warriors, attendant girls, the people, Polovtsian Khans, Konchakovna's friends, Konchak's slaves, Russian prisoners-of-war, Polovtsian guards

ORCHESTRATION 3 fl, 2 ob, 3 cl, 2 bsn, 4 hn, 2 tpt, 3 trbn, tuba, timp, perc, hp, pf, str; onstage (Act III): cornets, hns, tubas, sds

In 1869 Borodin asked Vladimir Stassov, art historian and literary mentor to the 'Mighty Handful' composers, to suggest a suitable subject for an opera. Stassov recognized Borodin's qualities as an essentially lyrical composer who had inherited Glinka's sympathy with Russia's epic past and astutely prepared a detailed scenario based on the 12th-century national epic *The Lay of Igor's Army.* In this Prince Igor of Seversk (now in the Ukraine) decides to make a show of strength by leading his army against the Polovtsi, a nomadic tribe of Turkish origin which habitually ravaged southern Russia. A battle takes place in which the army is all but annihilated and Igor and his son captured. Eventually he escapes and is reunited with his wife Yaroslavna. The original purpose of the epic was to use the campaign to underline the political and spiritual disunity of the separate principalities of Kiev and to show the need for a united Russia. Borodin was delighted with the idea, but unfortunately decided to write the libretto himself and instead of finalizing the text before beginning composition, wrote it piecemeal as he went along. In the process the original intention of the epic was watered down and Igor himself, because of his courageous, impulsive but essentially weak character, becomes almost an anti-hero.

Leonid Yakovlev as the first Prince Igor (St Petersburg, 1890)

SYNOPSIS

Prologue The town square in Putivl, 1185. Igor, with his son Vladimir, prepares to set out with his army, despite the entreaties of his wife Yaroslavna and an ill-omened eclipse of the sun.

Act I Scene 1: Skula and Eroshka, deserters from Igor's army, ingratiate themselves with Yaroslavna's dissolute brother, Prince Galitsky, who boasts of his hedonistic life, 'Greshno taits ya skuki nye lyublyu' ('I hate a dreary life'). Scene 2: In a touchingly expressive arioso, Yaroslavna describes her loneliness, fear of civil strife and troubled dreams. Boyars enter and solemnly inform her of Igor's defeat and captivity; at the same time the Polovtsi begin to attack Putivl.

Act II Khan Konchak's camp in the eastern steppe. Vladimir has already fallen in love with Konchak's daughter, Konchakovna, and apostrophizes her in a beautifully lyrical aria, 'Medlenno dyen ugasal' ('Slowly the daylight faded'). Igor's thoughts are filled with remorse and longing for Yaroslavna, 'Ni sna, ni otdykha' ('No rest, no sleep'). The barbaric but magnanimous Khan Konchak cannot understand his captive's depression, 'Zdorov li, knyaz?' ('Unhappy, Prince?'), and, in order to entertain him, arranges for his slaves to dance and sing for him (*Polovtsian Dances*).

Act III After hearing of the attack on Putivl, Igor decides to escape, although Vladimir is reluctant to leave Konchakovna and is captured. Konchak admires Igor for his audacity and unites the two lovers.

Act IV Yaroslavna laments Igor's captivity and the devastation of Putivl (vividly described in a hauntingly elegiac unaccompanied chorus), but is overjoyed when he arrives back safely to general rejoicing.

The great strength of *Prince Igor* lies in the distinguished and noble quality of its music rather than its emotional force or sense of dramatic involvement. Act II in particular consists of one outstanding number after another (the arias of Konchakovna, Vladimir, Igor, Konchak), culminating in the barbaric splendour of the *Polovtsian Dances*. The music has a richly lyrical quality that never becomes cloying, and the writing for solo voices, chorus and orchestra is always freshly minted. Although constructed very much as a series of set tableaux, the opera is generally successful in putting over the big-boned, epic quality of the story, and the characters of Yaroslavna and Konchak in particular are finely delineated in their text and music.

After Borodin's death his self-appointed musical executors, Rimsky-Korsakov and Glazunov, were faced with the task of putting the noble torso of *Igor* into performable shape. With Glazunov filling in most of the empty gaps (including writing out the overture from memory), while Rimsky undertook the equally onerous task of editing and orchestrating the rest, they soon produced the only edition of the opera that has ever been published. Although it includes Borodin's Polovtsian March and Trio (featuring the second subject of the overture), Glazunov's bravely attempted reconstruction of Act III is frequently cut in performance, resulting in the omission of the all-important dramatic episode of Igor's escape.

RECORDINGS 1. Smolenskaya, Borisenko, Lemeshev, Ivanov, Pirogov, Reizen, Bolshoi Opera Ch and O, Melik-Pashayev, Melodiya, 1950s; 2. Wiener, Penkova, Todorov, Christoff, Sofia National Opera Ch and O, Semkov, EMI, 1967; 3. Evstatieva, Milcheva, Kaludov, Martinovich, Ghiaurov, Ghiuselev, Sofia National Opera Ch and Festival O, Tchakarov, Sony, 1990: the Sony set is the only one to include the often omitted Act III. The older sets also make other cuts, but they have some superb singers, particularly the old Bolshoi version [A.B.]
EDITIONS f.ss., Belyayev, 1890; four excerpts from Act I, three not included in the Belyayev edition, edited from Borodin's manuscripts by A. Nefedov, Muzyka, 1977; v.s., Belyayev, 1888

Other operatic works: *The Valiant Knights* (*Bogatyry*) (pastiche opera–farce), 1867; *Mlada* (composite opera–ballet), 1872, sketches for Act IV only (see Rimsky-Korsakov *et al.*)
BIBLIOGRAPHY Gerald Abraham, 'The History of Prince Igor', in *On Russian Music*, W. Reeves, n.d.; Sergei Dianin, *Borodin*, OUP, 1963

D.L.-J.

DMITRI BORTNYANSKY
Dmitri Stepanovich Bortnyansky: *b* 1751, Glukhov, Ukraine; *d* 10 October 1825, St Petersburg, Russia

At the age of eight, Bortnyansky was admitted to the imperial chapel choir, where he was a pupil of Galuppi. He gained a scholarship from Catherine II to study in Italy, and his first operatic successes were there. He returned to Russia in 1779 as kapellmeister to the imperial court, and composed at least four further operas for the court, to French texts. His stage works never deviate from the popular formulae of the time. His Italian works are in opera-seria mould and his French works, lighter in tone for courtly tastes, are number operas with spoken dialogue, similar in form to those of Grétry, which were favourites at the court. His operatic work is overshadowed by his sacred music, still a staple of the repertoire of the Russian Orthodox Church, which influenced 19th- and early 20th-century composers, particularly Tchaikovsky, who edited a complete edition of his sacred music (1881).

Operas: *Quinto Fabio*, 1778; *Alcide*, 1778; *Le Faucon*, 1786 (RECORDING Melodiya, 1970s); *Le fête du Seigneur*, 1786; *Le fils-rival, ou La moderne Stratonice*, 1787; 2 lost operas
BIBLIOGRAPHY B. Dobrokhotov, *D. S. Bortnyansky*, Moscow State Publishing House, 1950

J.G.

GIOVANNI BOTTESINI
b 22 December 1821, Crema, Italy; *d* 7 July 1889, Parma, Italy

Although Bottesini's reputation is based primarily on his fame as a double-bass virtuoso, he was also well known as a conductor and a composer; among his works are 13 operas and he conducted the premiere of Verdi's *Aida* in Cairo (1871). Bottesini wrote both tragic and comic operas, notable for a strain of parody, but his conservative adherence to closed forms was old-fashioned. He persisted in writing operas because, for an Italian composer of his generation, that was the surest path to fame and prosperity.

Bottesini's only successful opera was *Ero e Leandro*, to a libretto by Boito, premiered at the Teatro Regio, Turin, in 1879. Boito had originally planned to use this text himself; after Bottesini's death, it was set again by Luigi Mancinelli (1896).

Operas: *Cristoforo Colombo*, 1847; *L'assedio di Firenze*, 1856; *Il diavolo della notte*, 1858; *Marion Delorme*, 1862; *Vinciguerra il bandito*, 1870; *Ali Baba*, 1871; *Ero e Leandro*, 1879; *Cedar*, (1880); *La regina di Nepal*, 1880; also: *Azeale*; *Graziella*; *La torre di Babele*; *La figlia dell Angelo* (all unperformed)
BIBLIOGRAPHY G. Vetro (ed.), *Giovanni Bottesini*, 1989

W.A.

RUTLAND BOUGHTON
b 23 January 1878, Aylesbury, Buckinghamshire, England; *d* 25 January 1960, London

The son of a grocer, Boughton was apprenticed early to a London concert agent. In his teens he published several works and even had a piano concerto performed in London. This early music came to the attention of Fuller Maitland, who showed it to Stanford, who in turn found a patron to pay for Boughton to study at the Royal College of Music. This formal study was short-lived, however, and after a few terms poverty forced him to leave to make his living. He became a protégé of Bantock, who employed him on the staff of the Midland Institute of Music (1904–11).

Two influences combined to shape his art: Wagnerian music drama (he went to Bayreuth in 1911) and socialism. Boughton, later a member of the Communist Party, was a musical manifestation of the Arts and Crafts Movement of William Morris. His ideas were developed with Reginald Buckley in *Music Drama of the Future* (1911), a book containing Boughton's essay on choral drama, 'Drama of the Future', the proposed scheme for the Temple Theatre (in which Boughton envisaged a theatre run as part of an agricultural commune, primarily for the local community but with an annual national festival), and finally the collaborative text of the choral drama *Uther and Igrane*, which became his first opera, *The Birth of Arthur* (1908–9). This was the beginning of a five-part Arthurian cycle which occupied Boughton for almost 40 years.

He established his theatrical base at Glastonbury in an unpropitious year, 1914. But though only a village-hall affair with piano accompaniment, it attracted the support of celebrities such as Shaw and Elgar. It lasted for 12 years and, while Boughton's own music was featured, many other operas were also produced. The first festival included the premiere of his second opera, *The Immortal Hour*, and this was followed by the second of the Arthurian dramas, *The Round Table* (1916), *Alkestis* (1922), a setting of Euripides in Gilbert Murray's verse translation and Boughton's only opera to be produced at Covent Garden (1924), and finally *The Queen of Cornwall*, which was put on at the penultimate Glastonbury Festival of 1926. In between he set the Coventry Nativity Play in the manner of a folk opera, *Bethlehem*, with choruses based on early English carols (1915). Later he completed the Arthurian cycle with *The Lily Maid* and, during the Second World War, the last two, *Galahad* and *Avalon*, but only the first three of the cycle have ever been produced.

Boughton wrote choral music, part-songs and orchestral works throughout his life, but his non-operatic music was almost completely forgotten until the revival of the Third Symphony (1938) by Edward Downes in 1983. With the revival of his orchestral music, the complete recording of *The Immortal Hour*, and the support of the Boughton Trust, his achievement may yet produce a living performance tradition.

The Immortal Hour

Music drama in two acts (2h)
Libretto by the composer, after the play and poems of 'Fiona Macleod' (William Sharp)
Composed 1910–12
PREMIERES 26 August 1914, Glastonbury (with pf); 7 January 1915, Bournemouth (with orchestra); US: 6 April 1926, Grove Street Theater, New York
CAST Dalua *bar*, Etain *s*, Eochaidh *bar*, Manus *b-bar*, Maive *a*, Old Bard *b-bar*, Midir *t*, 2 Spirit Voices *s*, *a*; *satb* chorus of druids, bards, warriors, maidens, elemental spirits
STANDARD ORCHESTRA

After its early success in the West Country, *The Immortal Hour* was accepted by the Carnegie publication scheme in 1921, and proceeded to make Boughton a huge reputation in the 1920s. Barry Jackson's production opened at the Repertory Theatre, Birmingham, on 23 June 1921, and moved to London on 13 October 1922 where it ran for a total of 216 consecutive performances, and subsequently for nearly 1000 performances in all. Throughout, Gwen Ffrangcon-Davies was celebrated in the role of Etain. It was one of those interwar excursions into escapism whose magic defied revival. After the Second World War it failed to rekindle the same magic until the BBC broadcast the closing scene in 1978 and received so many letters that it quickly scheduled a Radio 3 revival, which in turn led to the Hyperion recording.

Gwen Ffrangcon-Davies as Etain in The Immortal Hour *(Glastonbury, 1914)*

SYNOPSIS
Act I Etain is of the faery folk, but as a mortal becomes Eochaidh's queen, an event manipulated by Dalua, the shadow of whose hand brings forgetfulness, and whose touch is death.

Act II A year later Midir, a prince of faery, comes to the king's court and sings the celebrated 'Faery Song' ('How beautiful they are', which alone kept Boughton's name before the musical public for many years). It reminds Etain of her past, and as she leaves with the stranger, Dalua touches Eochaidh, who falls dead as the faery chorus fades into the distance.

Boughton maintained music drama to be an expression of a 'living religious experience' which enabled him 'to express the mystery of spiritual drama with conviction. In the music drama the lyric comes as the culmination of passion.' Here atmosphere is all-important, and *The Immortal Hour* succeeds, not by virtue of epic qualities as Boughton had at first envisaged, but through its personal voice, folk-generated melody, somewhat homespun individuality and its memorable choral writing.

RECORDING abridged: Ffrangcon-Davies, Johnstone-Douglas, Cranmer, Queen's Theatre Ch and O, Ervine, Columbia, 1932; complete: Dawson, Davies, Kennedy, Wilson-Johnson, Geoffrey Mitchell Ch, ECO, Melville, Hyperion, 1983
EDITIONS f.s., Stainer and Bell, 1923; v.s., Stainer and Bell, 1920

The Queen of Cornwall

Music drama in two acts (1h 30m)
Libretto by the composer, adapted from Thomas Hardy's verse play *The Famous Tragedy of the Queen of Cornwall* (1923)
Composed 1923–4

PREMIERES 26 August 1924, Glastonbury (with pf);
October 1963, St Pancras Festival, London (with orchestra)

Hardy's version of the Tristan legend was first staged
in November 1923, by which time Boughton had
already begun to set it to music. He also inserted six
of Hardy's poems, including memorable settings of
'When I set out for Lyonesse' and 'If it's ever spring
again'. The work is rounded out by vivid 'storm'
choruses and at each step of the action the chorus
commentates, telling the audience of past events or
the characters' thoughts.

EDITION v.s., Joseph Williams, 1926

Other operas: *The Birth of Arthur*, (1908–9), 1920;
Bethlehem, 1915; *The Round Table*, 1916; *Alkestis*, (1920–22),
1922; *The Ever Young*, (1928–9), 1935; *The Lily Maid*, 1934;
Galahad, (1943–4); *Avalon*, (1944–5)
BIBLIOGRAPHY Rutland Boughton and Reginald H.
Buckley, *Music-Drama of the Future*, William Reeves, 1911;
Michael Hurd, *Immortal Hour: The Life and Period of
Rutland Boughton*, Routledge and Kegan Paul, 1962; Eric
Walter White, *A History of English Opera*, Faber, 1983,
pp. 392–402

L.F.

WILLIAM BOYCE

b September 1711, London; *d* 7 February 1779, Kensington,
London

Boyce was the son of a cabinet-maker; he began his
musical career as a chorister at St Paul's, where he
became an articled pupil of the organist, Maurice
Greene. He also studied with Pepusch; in 1734 he
became organist at the Earl of Oxford's Chapel,
Vere Street, and in 1736 was appointed composer to
the Chapel Royal. From 1737 he conducted the
Three Choirs Festival; he composed songs for
Vauxhall Gardens, and in about 1736 set *Peleus and
Thetis*, a masque by Lord Lansdowne. From then
until 1759 he composed incidental music and short
stage works. In 1757 he became Master of the King's
Music in succession to Greene; his last years,
inhibited by growing deafness, were taken up with
his court duties and work on his historical anthology
Cathedral Music. He was a fine contrapuntalist with a
command of fugato that approached Handel's;
compared with the music of his near contemporary
and rival Thomas Arne his work is more studied,
masculine and compressed, though he lacked Arne's
melodic fluency.

Peleus and Thetis

Dramatic masque (40m)
Libretto by George Granville, Lord Lansdowne
PREMIERE Unknown; modern revival: early 1970s,
St John's, Smith Square, London (Opera da Camera)

The masque, originally interpolated into Lansdowne's 1701 version of *The Merchant of Venice*,
is set on Mount Caucasus, where Prometheus is

chained to a rock while a vulture gnaws at his
breast. The libretto is vivid and taut. Boyce begins
with a remarkably dramatic and pathetic overture,
and creates a convincing and godlike Jupiter, whose
aria of Renunciation, 'Shall then the Son of Saturn
be undone' is infused with what Fiske justly calls
'tragic feeling'.

MANUSCRIPT f.s., Bodleian Library, Oxford

The Secular Masque

Dramatic masque (40m)
Libretto by John Dryden (1700)
PREMIERE 1749, Cambridge; however, an earlier
performance is possible

Dryden's remarkable commemoration of the turn
of the century was originally the conclusion of
Vanbrugh's adaptation of Fletcher's *The Pilgrim* and
set by David Purcell and Finger. Boyce again
demonstrates his capacity to match a good economical text. Dryden's sardonic presentation of a
world-weary Chronos, who appears on the stage
bowed beneath the weight of the globe that rests on
his shoulders and avers that hunting (Diana), war
(Mars) and love (Venus) have been the bane of the
last century, is pointed up by the quiet acerbities of
Boyce's score.

MANUSCRIPT f.s., Royal College of Music, London

Musical entertainments: *The Chaplet*, 1749; *The Shepherd's
Lottery*, 1751
BIBLIOGRAPHY Roger Fiske, *English Theatre Music in the
Eighteenth Century*, OUP, 1973; 2nd edn, 1986; E. Taylor,
'William Boyce and the Theatre', *MR*, vol. 14 (1953), pp. 75ff.

R.Lu.

ATTILA BOZAY

b 11 August 1939, Balatonfüzfö, Hungary

A pupil of Ferenc Farkas in Budapest, Bozay is
known outside Hungary almost exclusively for his
instrumental works. An early string quartet was
played at the ISCM Festival in Prague in 1967, and
since then chamber and solo instrumental music has
taken up much of his time (though he destroyed an
early opera). This includes virtuoso works for
recorder and zither, instruments he taught himself to
play.
  As a young composer, Bozay used serial method,
underpinning a lean, economical style with hints of
Webernian severity. Later instrumental works
explore some of the consequences of Bartók's 'night
music' style (Bozay's interest in the zither goes back
to this time). But in the opera *Csongor and Tünde* he
took a step towards a more sumptuous and accessible
neo-Romanticism.

Csongor and Tünde

Csongor és Tünde

Opera in three acts (2h 15m)
Libretto by the composer, after the play by Mihály Vörösmarty
Composed 1979–84
PREMIERE 20 January 1985, Opera House, Budapest

The story, of the love of a mortal for a fairy, and the trials they have to endure before they are united, has overtones of Mozart's *Die Zauberflöte* and the early German Romantics, Wieland and Fouqué. Divided into numbers, the opera preserves some serial elements but is basically tonal and melodious, ending in a succulent A major. The first performance was the first operatic premiere in the lavishly restored Budapest Opera House.

RECORDING Molnár, Csavlek, Kalmár, Jablonkay, Gáti, Lukács, Hungarian State Opera Ch and O, Mihály, Hungaroton, 1985
EDITION v.s., Editio Musica Budapest, 1984

BIBLIOGRAPHY András Fodor, 'A New Hungarian Opera', *New Hungarian Quarterly*, no. 99 (autumn 1985), pp. 183–7

S.W.

EDVARD BRAEIN

Edvard Fliflet Braein; *b* 23 August 1924, Kristiansund, Norway; *d* 30 April, 1976, Oslo

After studies in Oslo, Braein became a pupil of Jean Rivier in Paris. He was a composer of great natural talent and a strong melodic gift that is heard to striking effect in his Concert Overture, Op. 2 (1948). His first opera, *Anne Pedersdotter*, was successfully produced in Oslo in 1971. It is based on the play by Hans-Wiers-Jensen (1866–1925), which draws on the best-known trial for sorcery in Norwegian history, that of Anne Pedersdotter, who was burned at the stake at Bergen in 1590. Braein's second opera, *Den Studenlöse* (1975), based on a comedy by Holberg, is written in a tuneful, but somewhat old-fashioned, style.

RECORDING *Anne Pedersdotter* (excerpts): Norwegian Opera, Philips, 1974

R.La.

MAX BRAND

Maximilian Brand; *b* 26 April 1896, Lemberg (now Lviv, Ukraine); *d* 5 April 1980, Langenzersdorf, nr Vienna

Brand's opera *Maschinist Hopkins* made his name and reputation. It was awarded first prize in the 1929 Allgemeine Deutsche Musikverein festival and within a year it had received over 100 performances in 37 different German opera houses. Before that this onetime pupil of Schreker, Haba and Erwin Stein was virtually unknown. He was a modernist, one of

the first composers outside the Schoenberg circle to write 12-note music – his set of *Five Biblical Ballads* for soprano and ensemble (1927) post-dates Schoenberg's first serial work by only three years. Brand's second opera, *Requiem*, was in rehearsal at the Berlin State Opera when the Nazi party banned his music in February 1933. The score and parts were lost in Czechoslovakia during the Second World War.

He moved to Vienna, where he worked at an experimental film studio with Hanns Eisler. In 1938 he fled via Prague, Switzerland and Brazil to the United States where he lived until he returned to Vienna in 1975. In the US he did some pioneering work with electronic music (he wrote a hymn, 'The Astronauts', to celebrate John Glenn's achievements) and continued this after his return to Europe. But neither these nor his non-electronic pieces, which include a 'scenic oratorio', *The Gate* (1940), performed at the Metropolitan, New York, in 1944, and an orchestral work, *The Wonderful One-Hoss-Shay*, premiered by Ormandy and the Philadelphia Orchestra in 1959, have won recognition.

Maschinist Hopkins

Hopkins the Factory Worker

Opera in a prologue and three acts (12 scenes), Op. 11 (2h 15m)
Libretto by the composer
Composed 1928
PREMIERES 13 April 1929, Stadttheater, Duisburg; January 1984, Bielefeld (with many cuts and some reordering of scenes); UK: 9 February 1986, BBC Radio 3 (broadcast; in English)
CAST Hopkins *bar*, Bill *t*, Nell *s*, *s*, *bar*, 6 *b*, male close-harmony group (2 *t*, 2 *bar*, 2 *b*), 2 spoken roles; offstage: *s*, *a*, *bar*; *satb* chorus of machines (with soloists), workers, bar customers
FULL ORCHESTRA including 3 sax and perc (11 players); onstage: jazz band, pianino

Maschinist Hopkins was one of the greatest musical successes of the Weimar Republic; within a year of its premiere all the major German houses and many minor ones had staged it; by 1933 it had also been heard in Prague (in Czech), Stockholm (in Swedish), Kharkov (in Ukrainian), Zurich and Leningrad. It epitomizes Weimar Germany's progressive art: its urban setting, its realism, its concern with the morality and humanitarian aspects of industrialized society are combined with music that exhilaratingly brings together all that was most modern and chic – neo-classicism, serial technique, jazz, popular dance and melodies in the style of Puccini. The plot asks awkward sociological questions; the music's intensity sharpens them.

SYNOPSIS

Prologue Bill and his mistress, Nell, steal a secret production formula from a factory. The theft is disturbed by Nell's husband, who is accidentally crushed to death when the factory machines roar into life.

Act I Seven years have passed; with his stolen knowledge Bill has opened his own factory and Nell is about to be a nightclub star. During the party to

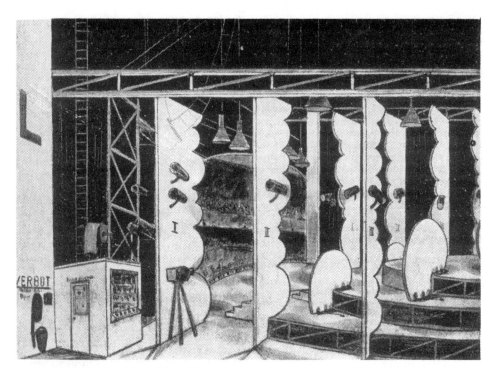

Set design for Maschinist Hopkins *(Duisburg, 1929)*

celebrate her new contract, Bill buys the factory from which he stole the formula; he will close it, unconcerned at the resultant unemployment, to bury his misdeeds.

Act II One of the workers, Hopkins, hears a rumour about Bill's past and blackmails first Nell and then Bill.

Act III Nell's and Bill's world collapses. She is forced into prostitution and he decides to wreck the factory. He murders his prostitute wife while she is with a client but before he can destroy the machines Hopkins stops him. They fight. Bill falls into the machinery, just as Nell's husband did in the prologue. The people, their jobs saved, take their place on the production line.

The music's almost self-conscious eclecticism brought the work a short-lived notoriety which masked its symphonic seriousness but underlined its dramatic effectiveness; its two jazz sections (a black-bottom and a tango) are colouristic passages in a sophisticated restaurant setting; a bawdy song performs the same function for a working-class bar; crisp neo-classicism depicts the ruthless efficiency of Bill's new factory; gestures subsequently purloined by the film industry illustrate the viciousness of Hopkins's blackmail. But the music also indicates that the plot is only one level of the piece. The opera's last 20 minutes are a reprise of the opening 20, with the same music, slightly varied, but with the motivation of the action reversed. The music to which Nell steals the master key (the key to their

future) in the prologue returns in Act III as Bill kills her (their future destroyed). Subsequently the lines sung in the prologue by the master switch, the source of energy-giving power (Brand makes his machines sing in surreal, unearthly voices), are reprised by Nell's voice; clearly Nell, not just lust for power, was the driving force in Bill's life. The reprise of the machines' music suggests that they and not man are now the rulers. The closing pages, with 11 percussion-players at full tilt and the workers mechanistically yelling 'Arbeit' ('Work'), is an overwhelming evocation of the new machine age.

EDITIONS   f.s., Universal, 1929; v.s./lib., Universal, 1928

BIBLIOGRAPHY   Clive Bennett, '*Maschinist Hopkins*: A Father for *Lulu*?', *MT*, vol. 127 (1986), pp. 481–4

C.B.

TOMÁS BRETÓN

b 29 December 1850, Salamanca, Spain; *d* 2 December 1923, Madrid

Although Bretón, who received his musical grounding in zarzuela and theatre orchestras, campaigned throughout his life for the cause of Spanish opera and against the use of the Italian language for Spanish opera libretti, his own stage works met with little success in his lifetime. He eventually became composition professor at the Madrid Conservatory, where he taught Pablo Casals. *Los amantes de Teruel* and *La Dolores* were his most colourful and successful operas, while *La verbena de la paloma* was the outstandingly popular work among Bretón's zarzuelas. The tale, about the amorous activities of an elderly apothecary, is set against the dazzling street life of Madrid, during the 14 August nocturnal celebrations for the annual Festival of the Virgin of the Dove.

Operas: *Guzmán el Bueno*, 1875; *Los amantes de Teruel*, 1889; *Garín*, 1892; *La Dolores*, 1895; *Raquel*, 1900; *Farinelli*, 1903; *El certamen de Cremona*, 1906; *Tabaré*, 1913; *Don Gil*, 1914
Zarzuelas: in three acts: *El campanero de Begoña*, 1878; *El barberillo de Oran* 1879; *Corona contra corona*, 1879; *Los amores de un principe*, 1881; *El clavel rojo*, 1899; *Covadonga*, 1901; *Las cortes de amor*, 1916; in two acts: *El alma en un hilo y El viaje de Europa*, 1874; *María*, 1875; *Los 2 leones y Huyendo de ellas*, 1877; *El bautizo de Pepín* (coll. with Chueca y Valverde); *Bonito país*; in one act: *Los dos caminos*, 1874; *El 93 y El inválido*, 1875; *Un chaparrón de maridos y Vista y sentencia*, 1876; *¡Cuidado con los estudiantes!*, 1877; *Las señoritas de Conil*, 1881; *El grito en el cielo*, 1886; *El domingo de Ramos*, 1894; *La Nieves*, 1895; *El guardia de Corps y La verbena de la Paloma*, 1897 (RECORDING London International, 1950s); *El puente del diablo y El reloj de cuco*, 1898; *La Cariñosa*, 1899; *El caballo del señorito*, 1901; *Botín de guerra y La bien plantá*, 1902; *La generosa y Piel de oso*, 1909; *Al alcance de la mano y Las percheleras*, 1911; *Los husares del Czar*, 1914
BIBLIOGRAPHY Angel Sanchez Salcedo, *Tomás Bretón: su vida y sus obras*, Imprenta Clasica Española, 1924

S.J.W.

HAVERGAL BRIAN
William Havergal Brian; *b* 19 January 1876, Dresden, Staffordshire, England; *d* 28 November 1972, Shoreham, Sussex, England

Self-taught and from a working-class Potteries background, Brian began to establish himself as a composer before the First World War, making a reputation that did not survive after 1918. However, he continued to compose, producing scores on the largest scale, including the epic *Gothic Symphony* (composed 1919–27, premiered 1960), the first of his 32 symphonies.

The Tigers
Opera in a prologue and three acts (3h)
Libretto by the composer
Composed 1916–30
PREMIERE 3 May 1983, BBC Radio 3 (broadcast)

The Tigers, originally entitled *The Grotesques*, tells of a regiment of recruits whose unheroic escapades provided the composer with an outlet from his experience of wartime military incompetence and horror. Negotiations for a performance in Dresden ended with the arrival of the Nazis and although it was published in vocal score, the full score disappeared during the Second World War and was not rediscovered until 1977.

In *The Tigers*, Brian draws on his experience of operas by Richard Strauss, Borodin and Wagner given at Covent Garden immediately before the First World War. Deliberate pastiche rubs shoulders with his developing symphonic style. The resulting, remarkably integrated, score has enormous gusto.

EDITION v.s., Cranz, 1932

Other operas: *Turandot*, (1950–51); *The Cenci*, (1952); *Faust*, (1956); *Agamemnon*, (1957), 1971
BIBLIOGRAPHY Reginald Nettel, *Havergal Brian and His Music*, Dobson, 1976

L.F.

FRANK BRIDGE
b 26 February 1879, Brighton, Sussex, England; *d* 10 January 1941, Eastbourne, Sussex

A pupil of Stanford at the Royal College of Music, Bridge first made his name writing Brahmsian chamber music, and as a viola-player and conductor. His Impressionistic suite *The Sea* (1910–11) was his most lasting orchestral success. The First World War affected his music profoundly and after 1918 he gradually assumed a more radical style which antagonized many of his previous admirers. For years after his death he was remembered mainly as the teacher of Benjamin Britten, and for some songs and chamber works. After Britten's performance, in 1967, of his orchestral tone poem *Enter Spring*, his true stature became apparent with revivals of his later works.

The Christmas Rose
Nativity opera in three scenes (50m)
Libretto by the composer, after the children's play by Margaret Kemp-Welch and Constance Cotterell
Composed 1919–29
PREMIERE 8 December 1931, Royal College of Music, London

The composition of Bridge's only opera straddled the period during which his style changed. Two shepherd children journey to Bethlehem. Their tears at having no present for the infant Jesus cause roses to spring up in the snow; these they take as their offering. The music does not echo the sentimentality of the story; both lyrical and orchestrally colourful, its harmony reflects Bridge's then quickly developing vocabulary.

RECORDING Eathorne, James, Davies, Herford, Wilson-Johnson, Chelsea Opera Group Ch and O, Williams, Pearl, 1983
EDITION v.s., Augener, 1931

BIBLIOGRAPHY Anthony Payne, *Frank Bridge – Radical and Conservative*, Thames Publishing, 1984

L.F.

GEORGE FREDERICK BRISTOW

b 19 December 1825, Brooklyn, New York; *d* 13 December 1898, New York

Best remembered as the composer of *Rip Van Winkle*, the first grand opera on an American subject, Bristow was also influential as a performer, conductor and teacher. He played the violin in the New York Philharmonic Society Orchestra from 1843 to 1879, directed major choral groups in the city and held organist posts.

Rip Van Winkle, to a libretto by J. H. Wainwright after Washington Irving's story, was produced at Niblo's Garden, New York, on 27 September 1855, and later revised. Despite his patriotic choice of subjects and his efforts to create a specifically American style, Bristow's music is unoriginal, reminiscent of contemporary European composers. A second opera, *King of the Mountains* (1894), was unfinished.

P.D.

BENJAMIN BRITTEN

Edward Benjamin, Lord Britten of Aldeburgh; *b* 22 November 1913, Lowestoft, Suffolk, England; *d* 4 December 1976, Aldeburgh, Suffolk

Britten was the first major composer to be born in England for 300 years who was first and foremost an opera composer. The premiere of *Peter Grimes* at Sadler's Wells Theatre on 7 June 1945 is generally accounted a watershed in the history of British music. Although there had been hostility to its production among members of the company, the opera's impact on the public and on most of the critics was likened to a fresh, invigorating storm and it was immediately recognized as the start of a new dawn for British opera as well as of a brilliant dramatic career for its composer. Within three years it had been produced in the major opera houses of Europe, including Milan, where Tullio Serafin conducted it, and in the United States, where its first conductor was Leonard Bernstein.

There was general astonishment in 1945 that Britten's first opera should be so stageworthy and show such theatrical and dramatic flair. It was then not widely known that during his sojourn in North America from 1939 to 1942 he had composed what he called an 'operetta', *Paul Bunyan*, to a libretto by his friend W. H. Auden. This was performed by university students and was remarkable for its assimilation of the American idiom, so that it had both the zip and immediate melodic appeal of a Broadway musical and also absorbed other elements from spirituals, folk ballads and choral music. *Paul Bunyan* marked out its creator as a 'natural' for stage subjects. With hindsight it can be seen that there was a nascent opera composer in some of the concert works by which his name first became known to British audiences before the Second World War; for

example, the symphonic cycle *Our Hunting Fathers* (1936), for voice and orchestra, also to a text compiled and partly written by Auden, is intensely dramatic.

Although *Peter Grimes* was staged at the Royal Opera House, Covent Garden, in 1947, Britten's immediate operatic future was not to be in large opera houses. He was first associated with Glyndebourne, Sussex, where *The Rape of Lucretia* was first performed in July 1946. A second chamber opera, *Albert Herring*, followed a year later, but by then a provincial tour of *The Rape of Lucretia* had been a financial disaster and although John Christie, the owner of Glyndebourne, stood the loss, he stated that this was as far as he would go. Early in 1947, the English Opera Group, with Britten, Eric Crozier and the artist John Piper as artistic directors, was launched as a non-profit-making company.

Touring again proved costly and in 1948 Britten, Pears and Crozier founded a festival at Aldeburgh, Suffolk, where they lived. Thereafter many of Britten's works were written specifically for this festival, held in June each year. But as it happened, Britten's next three major operas were not composed for Aldeburgh. For the 1951 Festival of Britain he wrote *Billy Budd* for Covent Garden, a return to the large orchestra and chorus of *Peter Grimes*. With its all-male cast and grim story, it was not at first a popular success, but revivals in the 1970s and 1980s established it, in the opinion of many, as Britten's greatest opera. It was followed by *Gloriana*, commissioned by Covent Garden for the Coronation of Elizabeth II in 1953. This, too, was a relative failure, the first-night audience being offended by the supposed *lèse-majesté* of the treatment of Queen Elizabeth I and her relationship with the Earl of Essex. Wounded, Britten returned to chamber opera, and composed *The Turn of the Screw*, based on Henry James's ghost story, for the Venice Biennale in 1954.

In 1956 Britten visited Bali, where he was profoundly impressed by the sounds of the gamelan. These were not entirely strange to him, since he had been introduced to them in 1939 by Colin McPhee. Henceforward, however, exotic Eastern sounds became a feature of his orchestration, giving rise even to such a homely invention as the 'slung mugs' representing rain in *Noye's Fludde* (1957). Memories of the gamelan lend a supernatural glitter to the score of *A Midsummer Night's Dream* (1960), but find full expression in the three church parables, *Curlew River*, *The Burning Fiery Furnace* and *The Prodigal Son*, composed between 1964 and 1968. Another major influence here was Britten's first encounter with the art of the Noh play in Japan in 1956. In these three works, highly sophisticated as they are musically, Britten achieved his ideal of providing operas that could be performed almost by improvisation in the surroundings of a village church or hall.

Britten's deep pacifist convictions, fuelled by the Vietnam War, led him to select an antimilitaristic short story by Henry James – *Owen Wingrave* – for his next opera, written for television but soon

Britten and Auden in 1941

transferred to Covent Garden. His last opera – composed in a grim race against time when his doctors diagnosed a serious heart condition for which surgery was essential – was based on Thomas Mann's *Death in Venice*. This was produced at Snape Maltings, the Aldeburgh Festival's concert hall and opera house, although the composer was too ill to attend the rehearsals and first performance.

Paul Bunyan

Operetta in two acts and a prologue, Op. 17 (2h)
Libretto by W. H. Auden
Composed 1939–41; rev., with new instrumental introduction, 1974–5
PREMIERES 5 May 1941, Brander Matthews Hall, Columbia University, New York; rev. version: UK: 1 February 1976, Manchester (radio studio production); 4 June 1976, The Maltings, Snape, Suffolk
CAST in the Prologue: *satb* chorus of Old Trees; 4 Young Trees 2 *s*, 2 *t*; 3 Wild Geese 2 *ms*, 1 *s*; Narrator in the Ballad Interludes *bar* or *t*, Voice of Paul Bunyan *spoken role*, Johnny Inkslinger *t*, Tiny *s*, Hot Biscuit Slim *t*, Sam Sharkey *t*, Ben Benny *b*, Hel Helson *bar*, Andy Anderson *t*, Pete Peterson *t*, Jen Jenson *b*, Cross Crosshaulson *b*, John Shears *bar*, Western Union boy *t*, Fido *high s*, Moppet *ms*, Poppet *ms*, Quartet of the Defeated (Blues) *a*, *t*, *bar*, *b*; 4 cronies of Hel Helson 4 *bar*; Heron, Moon, Wind, Beetle, Squirrel *spoken roles*; *satb* chorus of lumberjacks, farmers and frontier women
ORCHESTRATION 2 fl/picc, ob, 2 cl/alto sax, b cl, bsn, 2 hn, 2 tpt, 2 trbn, tuba, timp, perc (triangle, cym, sd, bd, wb, tenor d, xyl, glock, tambourine, gong, vib), hp, pf/cel, gtr, str

Paul Bunyan has its origins in the music Britten composed for short documentary films in the mid-1930s and his incidental music for stage plays by Auden, J. B. Priestley, Montagu Slater and others. This apprenticeship sharpened his musical wits and made him a master of improvised effects. In 1939, when Britten was living in America, his American publisher, Hans Heinsheimer, suggested that he and Auden should write something that could be performed by an American high school. They chose the giant logger of American folklore, Paul Bunyan (who grew as tall as the Empire State Building) and used the subject as the vehicle for Auden's indictment of aspects of modern American society. His libretto follows America from virgin forest to settlement and cultivation, when 'the human task is now a different one, of how to live well in a country that the pioneers have made it possible to live in'.

The June 1939 idea of 'an operetta for children' had four months later become 'a Broadway opera', with Paul Bunyan as the probable subject. By 21 November 1939 the first act was completed. Work continued in the early part of 1940, but was suspended because of Britten's illness, followed by his need to complete several commissions, including the *Sinfonia da Requiem*. The opera was completed by April 1941 and given seven performances conducted by Hugh Ross and produced by Milton Smith, who had been convinced at a private playthrough that the music was 'incredibly tremendous'. In spite of cool reviews, other performances were mooted although they did not materialize. Britten and Auden planned a thorough revision, but after Britten's return to England in 1942, *Paul Bunyan* was put into a drawer, where it remained until 1974, the year after his major heart operation. To encourage him to compose again, Donald Mitchell suggested he should reconsider the 33-year-old work. Some extracts were performed at the 1974 Aldeburgh Festival, after which Britten made further revisions for a radio production. The first European stage performance was at the 1976 Aldeburgh Festival.

SYNOPSIS
After a brief prologue and a narrator's ballad describing Paul Bunyan's giant dimensions, Act I shows Bunyan's loggers at work. A Swede, Hel Helson, is their foreman and Johnny Inkslinger, an intellectual, becomes Bunyan's aide-de-camp. When the two male cooks are sacked, a cowboy, Slim, takes over. He is helped in the kitchen by Tiny, Bunyan's daughter. Inkslinger warns Bunyan that Helson could be a bad influence and that some of the loggers want to become farmers.

Act II Bunyan leads some of the men to be farmers at Topsy Turvy mountain, 1000 miles away. In his absence Helson is encouraged to usurp Bunyan's leadership and when Paul returns they fight. Helson loses, admits his folly and is forgiven ('Great day of discovery'). Tiny and Slim have meanwhile declared their love. In the last scene, on Christmas Eve, the camp is breaking up as new jobs are offered to its leaders. Tiny and Slim are to manage a Manhattan hotel, Inkslinger goes to Hollywood, and Helson to Washington. Finally Bunyan bids farewell, telling them that America is what they choose to make it.

The emphasis in *Paul Bunyan* is on ensemble rather than 'star' roles and Britten's use of the chorus as a dramatic force clearly anticipates *Peter Grimes*. His keen ear for parody and pastiche is here at its most finely tuned, and the score indicates how rapidly he had absorbed the American idiom – though in his cabaret songs of 1937 he had already shown his penchant for composing blues and for writing in the style of George Gershwin and Cole Porter. Some of the 'arias' sound like hit songs from *Oklahoma!*, which *Paul Bunyan* predates by two years, and the ballad interludes are in 'Country and Western' style. Although Britten himself said he had problems with Auden's self-consciously wordy libretto, the text is in itself a brilliant piece of work and must have stimulated Britten to rival its wit and its extraordinary encapsulation of the spirit of Roosevelt's New Deal. The spirit of Kurt Weill's American musicals also flavours *Paul Bunyan*.

Britten's principal changes in 1974–5 were: the composition of the new introduction, in place of the original overture (not used in 1941); revision of the middle section of Slim's Song and the addition of a woodblock to imitate his horse's hoofs; revision of the coda of Tiny's Song; provision of an accompaniment to Bunyan's Goodnight at the end of Act I, Scene 2 (the text was spoken unaccompanied in 1941); revision of 'Heron, heron, winging by' by providing Helson with something to sing (the 1941 Helson could not sing and the original version was for two sopranos, speaker and chorus). Britten composed a Love Song for Inkslinger which was sung in 1941, but he omitted it from the 1975 revision because he was still unhappy with the dazzling complexity of Auden's text.

RECORDING Nelson, Lawless, Dressen, Bohn, Ch and O of the Plymouth Music Series, Minnesota, Brunelle, Virgin Classics, 1987: a brilliant performance and recording, with the American voices a distinct asset
EDITION v.s., Faber Music, 1978

Peter Grimes
Opera in a prologue and three acts, Op. 33 (2h 15m)
Libretto by Montagu Slater, after George Crabbe's poem *The Borough* (1810); rev. version published 1961
Composed January 1944 – 10 February 1945
PREMIERES 7 June 1945, Sadler's Wells, London; US: 6 August 1946, Berkshire Music Center, Lenox, Massachusetts (Tanglewood)
CAST Peter Grimes *t*, Boy (John) *silent*, Ellen Orford *s*, Captain Balstrode *bar*, Auntie *a*, Niece 1 *s*, Niece 2 *s*, Bob Boles *t*, Swallow *b*, Mrs Sedley *ms*, Revd Horace Adams *t*, Ned Keene *bar*, Hobson *b*, Dr Crabbe *silent*; *satb* chorus of townspeople and fisherfolk
ORCHESTRATION 2 fl/2 picc, 2 ob/ca, B♭cl, A cl/E♭cl, 2 bsn, dbsn, 4 hn, 3 tpt, 3 trbn, tuba, timp, perc (2 players: bd, susp cym, gong, sd, xyl, tambourine, triangle, whip, cym, tenor d, rattle), cel, hp, str; organ (offstage); dance band: 2 cl, vn, db, perc (cym, sd, bd), optional pf

The plan for an opera on the subject of Peter Grimes originated when Britten and Pears, staying on the West Coast of America, read an article by E. M. Forster about George Crabbe in the *Listener* (29 May 1941). It made them homesick for Aldeburgh, the subject of Crabbe's poem *The Borough*, and anxious to read his poetry. Pears found an edition in San Diego and Britten at once saw the operatic possibilities of the section dealing with the sadistic fisherman Peter Grimes, accused of ill-treating and murdering his apprentices. Grimes appealed to Britten as an outsider in society, the first of several of his operatic heroes (or anti-heroes) who embody this experience: a reflection of Britten's own position as a homosexual and conscientious objector.

When Britten was offered a commission of $1000 from the Koussevitzky Music Foundation for a full-length opera, he and Pears began to sketch a scenario before they sailed back to Britain in March 1942. There he approached the playwright Montagu Slater, with whom he had worked on left-wing plays in the 1930s. This was a prickly collaboration, since Slater worked slowly and did not always meet Britten's wishes. Some of the libretto was rewritten during rehearsals by Eric Crozier (who produced the first performance), Britten and Pears.

In 1944 Britten played parts of the opera to the soprano Joan Cross, who was managing the Sadler's Wells opera company during its arduous wartime tours. She became 'possessive' (her own word) about the work and decided it was the ideal opera to reopen Sadler's Wells Theatre in London when the war ended. But she encountered fierce hostility from within the company. Tired and bored by four years of provincial touring of a limited repertoire, they found this modern score unattractive and, some of them claimed, unsingable and unplayable. Nevertheless, Cross had her way. Pears sang the title role; Cross sang Ellen Orford; the designs were by Kenneth Green, and Reginald Goodall conducted. Tension backstage on the first night was high. However, most of the reviews were ecstatic, like the public's response, and *Peter Grimes* was launched on its international career. Pears's Grimes was one of his strongest characterizations, never losing sight of Britten's interpretation of the character as a romantic figure. Another major assumption of the role, rougher and harsher, was that of the Canadian tenor Jon Vickers. Tyrone Guthrie's Covent Garden production in 1947 was outstanding for its handling of the crowd scenes and powerful creation of the atmosphere of a witch hunt. *Peter Grimes* has remained the most popular of Britten's operas.

Costume design by Kenneth Green for the title role of Peter Grimes *(London, 1945)*

SYNOPSIS

Prologue An inquest is held in the Moot Hall of the Borough into the death of the young apprentice of the fisherman Peter Grimes, who explains that on the way to London to sell a huge catch they were blown off course and ran out of drinking water. After three days the boy died. The coroner, Mr Swallow, returns a verdict of accidental death but advises Grimes not to get another apprentice. After the court has been cleared, Ellen Orford, who has befriended Grimes, pleads with him, in vain, to leave the Borough with her.

Act I

Interlude I [Dawn]

Scene 1: Morning by the sea, in a street outside the Moot Hall and the Boar public house. Women are mending the nets ('Oh, hang at open doors the nets'). Borough personalities arrive: the Methodist fisherman Bob Boles, the Boar's landlady Auntie and her two 'nieces' (as they are euphemistically called), Mrs Sedley, widow of an East India Company employee, the Rector, and Balstrode, a retired merchant sea captain. When Grimes calls for help to haul up a boat, only Balstrode and Ned Keene, the apothecary, go to his aid. Keene tells Grimes he has found another apprentice at the workhouse. Hobson the carrier will fetch him. Ellen agrees to accompany Hobson to look after the boy. She rebukes those who criticize her ('Let her among you without fault cast the first stone'). The entire cast sings together of the approaching storm which 'will eat the land'. Balstrode advises Grimes to join the merchant fleet, but Grimes says he is rooted in the Borough. He describes the boy's death ('Picture what the day was like') and says his ambition is to make enough money from fishing to buy a shop and marry Ellen ('They listen to money'). Grimes sings of Ellen ('What harbour shelters peace?').

Interlude II [Storm]

Scene 2: Inside the Boar, Mrs Sedley awaits Hobson's return with her consignment of laudanum. Each new arrival tells of storm damage along the coast. Quarrels break out, quietened by Balstrode ('We live and let live, and look, we keep our hands to ourselves'). Grimes enters, wet and dishevelled, and begins a soliloquy ('Now the Great Bear and Pleiades'). Boles, drunk, tries to attack him, but Balstrode intervenes and Keene starts up a catch ('Old Joe has gone fishing'). Hobson, Ellen and the boy (John) arrive and Grimes immediately takes the boy to his hut on the cliff.

Act II

Interlude III [Sunday Morning]

Scene 1: In the street again, on a Sunday morning some weeks later, Ellen and the boy sit watching the church-goers and listening to the hymns ('Glitter of waves'). Ellen notices a tear in the boy's coat and a bruise on his neck. Grimes comes to collect the boy – he has seen a shoal. Ellen pleads for the boy to have a day's rest and tells Grimes the Borough's gossips will never be silenced – their own dreams were a mistake. In anguish, he strikes her and runs after the boy. This scene has been observed by Keene, Boles and others, who stir up anger against Grimes

('Grimes is at his exercise'). Ellen explains her compassion, but is shouted down. The Rector proposes a visit to Grimes's hut by the men alone, but the crowd follows ('Now is gossip put on trial'). Only Auntie, the nieces and Ellen remain ('From the gutter, why should we trouble at their ribaldries?').

Interlude IV: Passacaglia

Scene 2: In his hut, Grimes dresses the boy to go to sea. He thinks of the life he had planned with Ellen ('In dreams I've built myself some kindlier home'). But he also imagines he can see his dead former apprentice staring at him. He sees the Rector's procession coming up the hill and blames the boy and Ellen for gossiping. He opens the cliff door and the boy scrambles out and falls. Grimes goes after him. The Rector and his companions find an empty tidy hut. Looking out of the open door they comment on the landslide. They leave, saying they have misjudged Grimes.

Act III

Interlude V [Moonlight]

Scene 1: A few days later, on a summer evening in the village street, sounds of a dance are heard. The nieces run from the hall, followed by Swallow ('Assign your prettiness to me'). Mrs Sedley tackles Keene about the missing Grimes and his apprentice ('Murder most foul it is'). He dismisses her but she hides and hears Balstrode tell Ellen that Grimes's boat has returned, although there is no sign of him or the boy. Ellen has found the boy's jersey, on which she had embroidered an anchor ('Embroidery in childhood'). They vow to help Grimes. Mrs Sedley has overheard this conversation and summons Swallow to tell him Grimes's boat is back. Shouting 'Peter Grimes!' the crowd sets off on a manhunt.

Interlude VI

Scene 2: To the distant sounds of a foghorn and the voices of the mob, Grimes enters, weary and demented. Ellen and Balstrode approach him. Balstrode tells him to take his boat out of sight of shore and sink it. Next morning the Borough resumes normal life. Swallow says the coastguard has reported a boat sinking. 'One of these rumours,' Auntie says.

The principal character in *Peter Grimes* is the Borough. Although the opera has a major central figure in Grimes, it repeats the pattern of *Paul Bunyan* in having a number of smaller, vividly drawn parts. Grimes is probably the least well drawn, for while he is given magnificent music, the romanticizing of Crabbe's brutal fisherman into a misjudged victim of society is at odds with the plot. But such is the power and conviction of Britten's score that this in no way lessens the opera's impact.

In many respects, *Grimes* is less 'original' than *Paul Bunyan*. It is a brilliant synthesis – as is *Bunyan* – of the influences that made Britten the composer he was. It sounds fresh and 'different', but on closer acquaintance one realizes that the novelty is really Britten's ability, also displayed in works such as *Les Illuminations* (1939) and the *Serenade* (1943), to present old forms and musical devices as if they were new. *Peter Grimes* is an opera in the great tradition –

with a storm and a mad scene – but it owes something also to Berg's *Wozzeck*.

Britten unified the opera symphonically through six extended orchestral interludes. The pre-act interludes are atmospheric pieces, describing the scene and mood to follow, while those between the scenes are psychological commentaries on the plot and in particular on Grimes himself. The storm (Interlude II), for instance, is not only a wonderful depiction of an east-coast gale, but a penetrating analysis of the conflicts in Grimes's mind as he moves towards madness. The finest interlude is the Passacaglia, a favourite form of Britten's. His word-setting is one of the opera's great features – the Prologue, for example, with its naturalistic recitative contrasted with Grimes's arioso.

RECORDINGS 1. C. Watson, J. Watson, Elms, Pears, Pease, Ch and O of the Royal Opera House, Covent Garden, Britten, Decca, 1958: as near to a definitive version as it is possible to come; fine recording; 2. Harper, Bainbridge, Payne, Vickers, Summers, Dobson, Ch and O of the Royal Opera House, Covent Garden, C. Davis, Philips, 1978: Vickers's idiosyncratic way with the title role will not please all listeners, but Heather Harper's sympathetic Ellen and Davis's highly dramatic interpretation make this an important alternative
VIDEO Harper, Vickers, Bailey, Ch and O of Royal Opera House, Covent Garden, C. Davis, Castle, 1980s
EDITIONS f.s., Boosey & Hawkes, 1945; 2nd edn, 1963; v.s., Boosey & Hawkes, 1945

The Rape of Lucretia

Opera in two acts, Op. 37 (1h 45m)
Libretto by Ronald Duncan, based on André Obey's play *Le viol de Lucrèce* (1931)
Composed 1945–6; rev. 1947
PREMIERES 12 July 1946, Glyndebourne, Sussex; US: 1 June 1947, Shubert Theater of Chicago Opera, Chicago
CAST Male Chorus *t*, Female Chorus *s*, Collatinus *b*, Junius *bar*, Tarquinius *bar*, Lucretia *a*, Bianca *ms*, Lucia *s*
ORCHESTRATION fl/picc/alto fl, ob/ca, cl/b cl, hn, perc (sd, cym, gong, bd, tenor d, triangle, whip, tambourine), hp, 2 vn, va, vc, db, pf (played by the conductor in recitatives)

In March 1946, when the team that had championed *Peter Grimes* in 1945 resigned from Sadler's Wells – among them the soprano Joan Cross, the producer Eric Crozier, and Britten's lifelong friend and interpreter Peter Pears – Britten joined them in forming a new company to perform new works at the least possible expense, implying chamber operas. At first the company was called the Glyndebourne English Opera Company and *The Rape of Lucretia* was premiered at Glyndebourne, which itself had been closed during the war. Its general manager, Rudolf Bing, persuaded its owner, John Christie, that an association with Britten and his colleagues would be worthwhile. Britten agreed to compose an opera for eight singers and twelve musicians for a limited Glyndebourne season in the summer of 1946. Crozier suggested the subject of the rape of Lucretia and Britten chose as his librettist his friend Ronald Duncan, for whose verse play *This Way to the Tomb* he had composed incidental music in 1945. For the first performances at Glyndebourne, the opera was produced by Crozier and the designer was John Piper, who was later to design several other Britten operas. Two casts were assembled, with Kathleen Ferrier and Nancy Evans alternating as Lucretia, and Ernest Ansermet and Reginald Goodall as conductors. The company then took the opera on tour in the provinces and to Holland. For the 1947 Glyndebourne performances of *The Rape of Lucretia*, the libretto was revised and a substitute aria was composed for Collatinus in Act I. After Ferrier's death in 1953, the outstanding Lucretia was Janet Baker, who sang the role on stage and recorded it in 1970. Like *Peter Grimes*, *The Rape of Lucretia* was performed widely in Europe and North America.

SYNOPSIS
Act I Scene 1: The Male and Female Choruses recount how 'the Etruscan upstart' Tarquinius Superbus seized power in Rome and how his son Tarquinius Sextus has become a warrior leader and 'treats the proud city as if it were his whore'. Their perspective on the action of the opera is in relation to an event still 500 years in the future – Christ's birth and death. The curtain rises to show an army camp outside Rome. In the generals' tent, Collatinus, Junius and Tarquinius are drinking and talking about women. On the previous night, six generals had ridden back to Rome to check on their wives' fidelity. The only wife found virtuously at home was Collatinus' wife, Lucretia. Junius, whose wife was found with a Negro, quarrels violently with the unmarried Tarquinius. Collatinus parts them and proposes a toast to Lucretia. Junius rushes from the tent. He is sick of hearing Lucretia's name because Collatinus will win over political supporters from him on the strength of her chastity. Collatinus joins Junius and rebukes him for his attitude to Lucretia. They shake hands, at which point a drunken Tarquinius leaves the tent and mocks Junius as a cuckold. Collatinus brings them together, leaving the two generals to discuss women and power. Women are whores by nature, Junius says. Not Lucretia, Tarquinius retorts, adding 'I'll prove her chaste' and calling for his horse. In an interlude, the Male Chorus describes Tarquinius' ride to Rome ('Tarquinius does not wait'). Scene 2: In Lucretia's house in Rome that evening she is sewing while her servants Bianca and Lucia are spinning. She thinks she hears a knock at the gate, but Lucia finds no one there. Before folding the linen, Lucretia sings, 'How cruel men are to teach us love!' The three women prepare to go to bed while the Male and Female Choruses describe Tarquinius' arrival in Rome and his violent knock on Lucretia's door. He asks Lucretia for wine and says his horse is lame. She shows him to a room for the night.
Act II Scene 1: A short introduction by the Choruses and offstage voices describes the Etruscan domination of Rome. Then Lucretia is seen asleep in her bedroom with Tarquinius approaching the bed (Male Chorus: 'When Tarquin desires, then Tarquin will dare'). Tarquinius kisses her and she, dreaming

of her husband, draws him to her. She wakes and repulses him ('How could I give, Tarquinius, since I have given to Collatinus?'). They struggle until he draws his sword and rapes her. The Choruses, in an interlude, invoke Christ's compassion. Scene 2: In the hall of Lucretia's home, Lucia and Bianca extol the beauty of the morning and arrange flowers ('Oh, Lucia, please help me fill my vase with laughing daffodils'). Bianca has heard Tarquinius gallop away before dawn. Lucretia enters in a trancelike state. She says she hates the flowers and gives an orchid to Lucia for a messenger to take to Collatinus with a message that a Roman harlot has sent it. She makes a wreath from the remaining orchids ('Flowers bring to every year the same perfection'). Bianca tries to stop the messenger, but Collatinus has already arrived with Junius, who alerted him after seeing Tarquinius leave the camp and return at dawn. Lucretia enters in purple mourning ('Now there is no sea deep enough to drown my shame'). She tells Collatinus what has happened. He forgives her, but she stabs herself to death. In an epilogue the Choruses ask, 'Is it all?' and conclude that Jesus Christ is all.

Britten unifies the score by two motifs, one for Tarquinius, the other for Lucretia, constructed from a diminished fourth. These dominate the work in various subtle guises. The Male and Female Choruses have a chorale-like motif, which establishes their credentials as Christian commentators. The scoring for the small orchestra is a masterpiece of colour and imaginative sonority, with the harp's contribution a major feature. Like several Britten scores, *The Rape of Lucretia* is full of nocturnal imagery and onomatopoeic sounds – the chirp of crickets, the croaking of bullfrogs. When the Female Chorus describes the sleeping Lucretia, the evocative instrumentation is alto flute, bass clarinet and muted horn.

The full sound of the chamber orchestra is deployed to brilliant effect in the accompaniment to the Male Chorus's description of Tarquinius' Ride, a remarkable piece of graphic scoring. Lyrical passages abound in the opera: the sensuous trio for the women as they fold the linen and the music, full of summer morning heat, of 'O what a lovely day' at the start of the tragic final scene. Here Britten again employs one of his favourite devices, the passacaglia.

RECORDINGS 1. Ferrier, Cross, Pears, Kraus, Brannigan, English Opera Group O, Britten (various labels): excerpts from live performance recorded in Holland, 4 October 1946, i.e. within 3 months of Glyndebourne first performance (complete performance exists but has never been issued), Ferrier is deeply moving as Lucretia; 2. Baker, Harper, Pears, Luxon, Shirley-Quirk, ECO, Britten, Decca, 1970: a compelling central performance by Janet Baker, fine singing from the rest of the cast and, of course, superb direction by the composer
VIDEO Rigby, Harries, Rolfe Johnson, Van Allan, ENO O, Friend, Virgin, 1980s: film of Graham Vick's imaginative staging
EDITIONS f.s., rev. version, Boosey & Hawkes, 1949; 2nd edn, 1958; v.s., Boosey & Hawkes, 1946; rev. version, 1947

Albert Herring

Comic opera in three acts, Op. 39 (2h 15m)
Libretto by Eric Crozier, after Guy de Maupassant's short story *Le rosier de Madame Husson* (1888)
Composed 1946–7
PREMIERES 20 June 1947, Glyndebourne, Sussex; US: 8 August 1949, Berkshire Music Center, Lenox, Massachusetts (Tanglewood)
CAST Albert *t*, Lady Billows *s*, Mrs Herring *ms*, Florence Pike *a*, Vicar (Mr Gedge) *bar*, The Mayor (Mr Upfold) *t*, Miss Wordsworth *s*, Superintendent Budd *b*, Sid *bar*, Nancy *ms*, Emmie *s*, Cis *s*, Harry *treble*
ORCHESTRATION fl/picc/alto fl, ob, cl/b cl, bsn, hn, perc (timp, sd, tenor d, bd, triangle, cym, castanets, tambourine, gong, bells in F, B♭, D, glock, whip, wb), hp, pf, 2 vn, va, vc, db

Albert Herring was written as a companion piece to *The Rape of Lucretia* for performance by the same vocal and instrumental forces of the English Opera Group. It was first performed at Glyndebourne, whose owner John Christie disliked it intensely and is said to have greeted members of the first-night audience with the words: 'This isn't our kind of thing, you know.' Nevertheless, nearly 40 years later, in 1985, the Glyndebourne production by Peter Hall was one of the most successful the opera has had. Having shown the tragic aspects of Aldeburgh life in the early years of the 19th century in *Peter Grimes*,

Britten now showed its comic side, taking the opportunity to poke fun at a lady bountiful, moral hypocrisy, village fêtes, mayors, vicars, schoolmarms and policemen. The gift for parody, which he had exhibited in *Paul Bunyan* and in several of his instrumental compositions, was again to the fore in *Albert Herring* and ranged from the Sullivanesque to self-quotation. In spite of criticism in Britten's own country that the opera was 'cosily provincial' in its treatment of stock characters, *Albert Herring* has proved popular in translation in several European and Scandinavian countries. Like the best comedies, it has a dark side.

SYNOPSIS
Act I Scene 1: The Mayor and Vicar of Loxford, the schoolmistress Miss Wordsworth and Police Superintendent Budd are meeting Lady Billows in her breakfast room on 10 April 1900 to select a May Queen. Lady Billows announces that she is putting up a prize of 25 sovereigns. Each member of the committee puts forward a candidate, but each name is torpedoed by Florence Pike, Lady Billows's housekeeper, who knows something disreputable about them all. Budd suggests a King of the May and nominates Albert Herring, who works for his mother in her greengrocer's. Encouraged by the vicar and by a general chorus of 'Albert is virtuous', Lady Billows

John Piper's design for the marquee at the vicarage in Albert Herring *(Glyndebourne, 1947)*

agrees. Scene 2: Mrs Herring's shop. Sid the butcher's assistant taunts Albert for being under his mother's thumb and tells him of delights in store if he breaks the apron strings – 'Courting a girl is the king of all sports'. Nancy from the bakery joins them and Sid makes an assignation with her for that night ('Meet me at quarter past eight'). Left alone, Albert muses that Sid might be right that he misses all the fun. Lady Billows, with the rest of the committee, arrives ('We bring great news to you upon this happy day!'). Albert regards his election as May King as 'daft' and tells his mother he will refuse. But Mrs Herring has heard about the 25-sovereign prize.

Act II Scene 1: Inside the marquee near the vicarage. A trestle table has been set for eleven places. Sid tells Nancy that he plans to put a generous tot of rum into Albert's lemonade ('Just loosen him up and make him feel bright'). The bigwigs now arrive with Albert, who is wearing a straw hat crowned with a wreath of orange blossom. The children sing their welcome to him and present flowers to Lady Billows, Albert and Mrs Herring. Lady Billows orates about the evils of carnal indulgence, gambling and the havoc wrought by gin. After receiving various prizes, Albert calls for three cheers for Lady Billows, drains his glass and promptly has hiccups. Scene 2: The shop. Albert, tipsy rather than drunk, recalls the feast he has just eaten – 'but oh! the taste of that lemonade'. He has been disturbed by Nancy – 'why did she stare each time I looked towards her?' He then hears Sid whistle in the street outside. Nancy joins Sid and Albert overhears them discussing him, saying he'll be all right once he's sown a few wild oats. They kiss and go off to the common. Albert tosses a coin and decides to leave. His mother returns, calls him and gets no reply. 'Fast asleep, poor kid. Worn out by all this fuss.'

Act III The shop, the following afternoon. Albert is missing and the whole town is searching for him. Nancy, who has a guilty conscience, quarrels with Sid, who doesn't think Albert is dead. Superintendent Budd asks Mrs Herring for a photograph of Albert to send round the police stations. She gives him one in a frame ('It was took on the pier at Felixstowe'). Lady Billows demands that Scotland Yard and Conan Doyle should be called in. The Mayor solemnly carries in a tray. Underneath a cloth cover is Albert's orange-blossom wreath, found on a road crushed by a cart. All now assume Albert is dead and sing a threnody 'In the midst of life is death'. As it ends a dishevelled and mud-stained Albert returns. They turn on him and cross-examine him. He has spent three of his 25 pounds and has been with girls; he got drunk in one pub, until he was ejected, and started a fight in another. He turns on his mother – 'you squashed me down and reined me in'. Lady Billows prophesies he will pay for his sins of the flesh. Albert is left with Sid and Nancy and the village children, who now see him in a new light.

Albert Herring is a brilliantly successful comic opera, almost Rossinian in the speed and dexterity of Britten's treatment of recitatives. Contrapuntal treatment of certain episodes – fugal and canonic – is also extremely adept. The orchestral interludes are as racy, witty and illustrative as anything Britten wrote, and his use of parody and quotation is inspired. The children's street-game song, the hymnlike 'Albert the Good' and the zany patriotism of Lady Billows's speech in the marquee are superb examples of Britten's fertile melodic invention. The committee meeting in Act I is a notable example of Britten's gift for characterization. Each character is given an apposite aria, from the Vicar's quasi-ecclesiastical vocalizing to Miss Wordsworth's ballad-like twitterings. When Albert's lemonade is laced with rum and when he drinks it, the love-potion motif from Wagner's *Tristan* coils upwards and when Budd the policeman confides to Sid that he'd find 'a criminal case of rape' preferable to a manhunt, the orchestra quotes Lucretia's motif.

The musical climax is the nine-part threnody in Act III. This begins as a parody of a chant, but it quickly becomes a deeply felt lament, with each of the characters making an individual contribution and, towards the end, joining together in an elaborate piece of polyphonic writing over a pedal B♭. It is at this moment, when the opera turns serious, that one experiences it most strongly as a nostalgic re-creation of a vanished England.

RECORDING Fisher, Wilson, Cantelo, Rex, Pears, Brannigan, Ward, ECO, Britten, Decca, 1964: recorded in the Jubilee Hall, Aldeburgh: superbly characterful performance with stage cast of contemporary revival [A.B.]
VIDEO P. Johnson, Palmer, Rigby, Graham-Hall, Opie, etc., Glyndebourne Ch, LPO, Haitink, Castle, 1985: the Glyndebourne production, brilliantly sung, characterized and designed
EDITIONS f.s., Boosey & Hawkes, 1969; v.s., Boosey & Hawkes, 1948

The Little Sweep

A children's opera in three scenes, Op. 45 (45m)
Libretto by Eric Crozier
Composed 1949
PREMIERES 14 June 1949, Jubilee Hall, Aldeburgh; US: 22 March 1950, Music Educators' National Conference, Kiel Auditorium, St Louis, Missouri
CAST Black Bob *b*, Clem *t*, Sam *treble*, Miss Baggott *a*, Juliet Brook *s*, Gay Brook *treble*, Sophie Brook *s*, Rowan *s*, Jonny Crome *treble*, Hugh Crome *treble*, Tina Crome *s*, Tom *b*, Alfred *t*
INSTRUMENTATION 2 vn, va, vc, perc (bd, sd, gong, cym, triangle, castanets, wbs), pf (4 hands)

The Little Sweep was the first opera Britten wrote for the Aldeburgh Festival, which he had founded in 1948. It formed part of an entertainment called *Let's Make an Opera!* This was a play (with incidental music) in which adults and children are shown preparing to perform the opera they have written. Part of its purpose was to enable the conductor to rehearse the audience in their contribution. Later the librettist, Eric Crozier, revised the play by enlarging it to two acts. In 1965 he condensed the two acts into one, but he then decided the play did not wear well and it was not reprinted. Ideally, it should be rewritten to suit the circumstances and personalities of any group performing *The Little Sweep*.

Britten suggested the subject of the young boys who were used to sweep the more difficult and dangerous chimney flues, a practice not abolished until late in the 19th century. He took the idea from Blake's two poems entitled 'The Chimney Sweeper'; and Crozier and he set the opera in Suffolk in 1810. They both knew Iken Hall, a farmhouse on the river Alde, and based the children on those of friends who lived at Great Glemham. It is another of Britten's operas concerned with the betrayal of innocence and cruelty to children, a subject already explored in *Peter Grimes* through the fisherman's apprentice.

SYNOPSIS

Scene 1: Black Bob, the sweepmaster, and his son Clem bring Sam, aged eight, to sweep the nursery chimney at Iken Hall, supervised by Miss Baggott the housekeeper and watched sympathetically by Rowan, the nursery maid, who pleads in vain for Sam not to be sent up the chimney. Sam gets stuck and is rescued by the children of the house and their guests, who hide him and make it appear he has run away. The sweep and Miss Baggott leave to search for him, but Rowan sings, 'Run, poor sweepboy!' The children welcome her as an ally and reveal Sam's hiding place. Scene 2: The children and Rowan have given Sam a bath. They plan to hide him in the toy cupboard for the night and smuggle him out next day. When Miss Baggott returns and is about to open the cupboard, Juliet 'faints' as a distraction. Scene 3: The next morning. Juliet gives Sam three half-crowns as a gift from her friends who are going home. Sam is packed into a trunk which the coachman and gardener refuse to lift because of its weight. The children help them and wave Sam to freedom.

Britten's skill in writing for children was never better exemplified than in this ingenious little work. As an introduction to opera, it must be unrivalled in its seductive charm. The use of choruses involving the audience, instead of orchestral interludes, is a clever device. The Night Song divides the participants into four groups – owls, herons, doves and chaffinches. Simple and direct effects are obtained by sophisticated musical means. Thus in the opening chorus, each cry of 'Sweep!' has a different harmonization. Juliet's feigned faint leads to an elaborate ensemble in Britten's favourite passacaglia form; elsewhere much use is made of ostinati. Spoken dialogue takes the place of recitative.

RECORDINGS 1. Vyvyan, Cantelo, Thomas, Hemmings, Pears, Anthony, English Opera Group, Britten, Decca, 1955, mono; 2. Wells, Benson, Begg, Monck, Tear, Lloyd, Medici Quartet, Ledger, EMI, 1978
EDITIONS f.s., Boosey & Hawkes, 1965; v.ss.: voice and pf duet, Boosey & Hawkes, 1950; voice and pf (2 hands), Boosey & Hawkes, 1968

Billy Budd

Opera in four acts, Op. 50; rev. as two acts, 1960 (2h 45m)
Libretto by E. M. Forster and Eric Crozier, adapted from the story *Billy Budd, Foretopman* by Herman Melville (1891)

Composed 1950–51, rev. 1960
PREMIERES four-act version: 1 December 1951, Covent Garden, London; US: 19 October 1952, NBC Television Opera Workshop, New York (excerpts); 7 December 1952, Indiana University Opera Theater, Bloomington, Indiana; two-act version: 13 November 1960 (BBC broadcast); 9 January 1964, Covent Garden; US: 4 January 1966, Carnegie Hall, New York (American Opera Society; concert); 6 November 1970, Civic Opera House, Chicago
CAST Captain Vere *t*, Billy Budd *bar*, Claggart *b*, Mr Redburn *bar*, Mr Flint *b-bar*, Lieutenant Ratcliffe *b*, Red Whiskers *t*, Dansker *b*, Donald *bar*, Novice *t*, Squeak *t*, Novice's friend *bar*, Captain's cabin boy *spoken role*, Bosun *bar*, 1st mate *bar*, 2nd mate *bar*, Maintop *t*, Arthur Jones *bar*, 4 midshipmen *boys' voices*; *tb* chorus of officers, sailors, powder monkeys, drummers, marines
ORCHESTRATION 4 fl/4 picc, 2 ob, ca, 2 cl/E♭cl/b cl, alto sax, 2 bsn, dbsn, 4 hn, 4 tpt, 3 trbn, tuba, timp, perc (6 players: sd, tenor d, bd, tambourine, cym, triangle, gong, wb, whip, whistles, xyl, glock), hp, str; onstage: 4 tpt

Britten himself suggested the subject of Billy Budd to Crozier and Forster, who began work on the text in 1949; Crozier was responsible for the technical scenes and the dialogue, Forster for the 'big slabs of narrative'. The libretto is almost wholly in prose, since Forster could not write poetry, though some verses from Melville were interpolated, such as the ballad 'Billy in the Darbies', which is appended to the original story. Melville's first draft (1888) was a short story, *Baby Budd, Sailor*. This was expanded to a novella, *Billy Budd, Foretopman* and completed in April 1891, a few months before the author's death. Melville was moved to write the story by events in 1842 aboard the United States brig-of-war *Somers* (and known as the Mackenzie Case), but he transferred the action to the Royal Navy just after the mutinies at Spithead and The Nore in 1797. Britten was attracted by this tale of innocence destroyed, of good crushed by evil and of an 'outsider' against society.

Britten's relationship with both librettists underwent crises during composition of the opera, which is certainly a masterpiece born of creative tensions. The fourth draft was finished at the end of 1949. Britten began to compose the music in earnest six months later. The first performance at Covent Garden was to have been conducted by Josef Krips but he withdrew at a late stage and Britten himself took over. Although the opera was fully appreciated by a handful of critics, it was generally received with a cold respect and it was not until nearly 20 years later that it became a real success with the public.

Billy Budd had been planned in two acts, but for reasons Britten himself could not remember, it was made into four. Three interruptions of the action for intervals weakened the dramatic flow, and in 1960 Britten reverted to the two-act format. In doing so, he deleted a scene at the end of Act I, when Captain Vere addresses his crew with a rousing death-or-glory speech. In the revised version, the crew discuss Vere – 'he cares for us, he wishes us well' – and Billy sings, 'Star of the morning . . . I'd die to save you.'

SYNOPSIS

Act I The action takes place on board the *Indomitable*, a seventy-four, during the French wars of 1797. Prologue: Captain Vere, as an old man, looks back over his life. He has found 'always some flaw' in the good that has come his way, 'some stammer in the divine speech'. Scene 1: The main deck and quarter-deck. A cutter returns to the ship with three press-ganged recruits. One is Billy Budd, a foundling and an able seaman, whose answers reveal that he stammers. But Claggart, the master-at-arms, calls him 'the jewel of great price'. He is placed in the foretop and is exultant ('Billy Budd, king of the birds!'). During this aria he sings farewell to the merchantman, 'Farewell, old *Rights o' Man*'. This disturbs the officers, who associate the phrase 'Rights of Man' with Thomas Paine's seditious book, a sensitive issue after the mutinies. Claggart calls Squeak, the ship's corporal, and orders him to keep an eye on Billy and to 'tangle up his hammock, mess his kit, spill his grog'. Dansker, an old seaman, warns Billy to beware of Claggart, known as Jemmy Legs. Scene 2: Captain Vere's cabin, a week later. Vere sends for the officers Redburn and Flint to take wine with him. They look forward to being in action ('Don't like the French') and mention Billy's shout of 'Rights o' Man'. Vere dismisses their fears: 'No danger there.' Scene 3: The berth deck. The seamen are singing ('Blow her away'). Billy and Red Whiskers try to persuade Dansker to join in, but he says he's too old. All he misses is tobacco. Billy offers to lend him some and goes to his kitbag. He begins to stammer as he finds Squeak there. Squeak draws a knife. Billy knocks him down just as Claggart appears. Dansker tells him what happened and Claggart has no option but to have Squeak put in irons. Left alone, Claggart sings his evil Credo about Billy: 'Would that I never encountered you . . . I have you in my power and I will destroy you.' The Novice joins him and, after some hesitation, agrees to tempt Billy with money to lead a mutiny. Furious, Billy strikes out. The scene has been witnessed by Dansker, who tells him, 'Jemmy Legs is down on you.'

Act II Scene 1: The main deck and quarter-deck some days later. Claggart asks to see Vere, who is visibly irritated by his sycophantic and long-winded manner of presenting his complaint. He still has not reached the point when they are interrupted by a shout of 'Enemy sail on starboard bow'. The crew goes to action stations ('This is the moment'), but the French ship escapes in a mist. Claggart returns to his charge and tells how the Novice was offered gold by Billy to join a mutiny. Vere ridicules him, but agrees to see Billy. Scene 2: Vere's cabin. Vere calls in Claggart, who formally accuses Billy of mutiny. Billy is aghast, stammers, and shoots out his right fist which strikes Claggart's forehead. Claggart falls dead. Vere calls in the three officers to hold a drumhead court martial. Billy pleads with Vere to save him, but Vere stays silent. Scene 3: A bay of the gun deck, shortly before dawn. Billy, in irons, sings his ballad, 'Look! Through the port comes the moonshine astray!' Dansker brings him food. The

Claggart interrupts the fight between Billy and Squeak in Billy Budd *(London, 1964)*

whole ship is seething, he says, and some of the crew plan to rescue Billy. Billy says they must not or they will hang too. Alone, he sings, 'I've sighted a sail in the storm, the far-shining sail.' Scene 4: The main deck and quarter-deck at 4 a.m. The crew assembles in silence. Billy cries, 'Starry Vere, God bless you!' As he is hanged, an ugly muttering from the crew grows louder. The officers order, 'Down all hands.' Epilogue: Vere as an old man describes the trial of Billy and laments, 'I could have saved him. He knew it. But he has saved me. I was lost in the infinite sea, but I've sighted a sail in the storm, the far-shining sail . . .'

Billy Budd is among Britten's greatest achievements (some are tempted to rank it the greatest). The struggle between good and evil, Billy and Claggart, is symbolized by the opposition of the chords of B♭ major and B minor which is heard in the strings that accompany Vere's musings at the start of the opera. This opposition permeates the whole score. The tonal ambiguity stands, too, for the moral uncertainty that is a feature of the opera, particularly affecting the character of Vere. Yet the music is firmly tonal, with certain keys acting almost as leitmotifs for the characters concerned. Claggart's key is F minor, for example. The opera's harmonic range is extraordinarily wide and its structure is taut and tense, the themes often similar in melodic outline as if to stress the obsessive nature of the piece.

The atmosphere is claustrophobic, but there is no sense of monotony because of the richness and variety of the orchestral score. *Billy Budd* has the largest orchestra of any of Britten's operas; it requires, for example, six percussionists. Claggart's evil is represented by the darker, lower sonorities – trombones, tuba, double bassoon. Billy's stammer is brilliantly depicted by a trill on a muted trumpet and a roll on the block. Potent use is made of the saxophone, while the large wind band is associated with the sea itself and with the harsh life aboard a man-of-war. For deeper human qualities, the strings are used with poignant effect, and Britten's writing for the chorus in the shanties is powerfully moving. Not the least skilful feature of the score is the most obvious – that it is for male voices only, without any sense of limitation or monotony.

The opera is Verdian in its juxtaposition of the public and the private – the external life of the ship and the personal dramas of Vere, Billy and Claggart. Each is given a solo aria of outstanding beauty and memorability. Yet perhaps the most compelling episode in the score is the celebrated passage when Vere tells Billy of his sentence: the stage is empty and the orchestra plays 34 slow chords, each varying in colour and dynamics and eventually reaching an F major that seems to wipe away Claggart's vile influence.

RECORDING   Pears, Tear, Glossop, Luxon, Langdon, Ambrosian Singers, LSO, Britten, Decca, 1968
VIDEO   Langridge, Allen, van Allan, ENO Ch and O, Atherton, Virgin, 1990
EDITIONS   f.s., Boosey & Hawkes, 1954; 2nd edn, 1985; v.ss.: 4-act version, Boosey & Hawkes, 1952; 2-act version, Boosey & Hawkes, 1961

Gloriana

Opera in three acts, Op. 53 (2h 30m)
Libretto by William Plomer, based on Lytton Strachey's *Elizabeth and Essex* (1928)
Composed 1952–3
PREMIERES   8 June 1953, Covent Garden, London; US: 8 May 1955, Music Hall, Cincinnati, Ohio (concert); 6 June 1984, Lila Cockrell Theater, San Antonio, Texas (English National Opera)
CAST   Queen Elizabeth I *s*, Earl of Essex *t*, Countess of Essex *ms*, Lord Mountjoy *bar*, Penelope, Lady Rich *s*, Sir Robert Cecil *bar*, Sir Walter Raleigh *b*, Henry Cuffe *bar*, Lady-in-Waiting *s*, Blind ballad singer *b*, Recorder of Norwich *b*, Housewife *ms*, Spirit of the Masque *t*, Master of Ceremonies *t*, City Crier *bar*; *satb* chorus of citizens, maids of honour, ladies and gentlemen of the household, courtiers, masquers, old men, men and boys of Essex's following, councillors; Time *male dancer*, Concord *female dancer*; country girls, rustics, fishermen, morris dancer, *dancers*; pages, ballad singer's runner, Sir John Harington, French ambassador, Archbishop of Canterbury, phantom kings and queens, *actors*
ORCHESTRATION   3 fl/2 picc, 2 ob, ca, 2 cl, b cl, 2 bsn, dbsn, 4 hn, 3 tpt, 3 trbn, tuba, timp, perc (3 players: sd, tenor d, bd, cym, tambourine, glock, gong, wb, triangle, whip, bells), hp, str; onstage: tpts, 5 str and/or 5 ww, pipe, fl, tabor, gittern, sd, cym, bd, wind-machine, hp

When Princess Elizabeth became Queen in February 1952 her cousin the Earl of Harewood, founder editor of *Opera* magazine (and later director of the Edinburgh Festival and managing director of English

National Opera), suggested to Britten that he should compose an opera on the subject of Queen Elizabeth I and the Earl of Essex to mark the Coronation the following year. Royal permission was obtained and Britten laid aside all other creative work in order to complete the opera in time for the premiere on 8 June 1953 when Joan Cross sang the role of Elizabeth I and Peter Pears that of Essex.

Gloriana came at an unfortunate moment in Britten's career. Because of his success and his acceptance by a wide public, there was intense jealousy of him in musical circles (heightened by his appointment as a Companion of Honour at the age of 39) and enmity because of his homosexuality, which was then still a criminal offence. These were undoubtedly factors in the cool reception of *Gloriana*, but the gala audience comprised mainly diplomats and civil servants for many of whom any opera, let alone one by a 20th-century composer, would have been an alien and tedious experience. Because the character of Elizabeth I was not sycophantically treated in the opera, it was said that *Gloriana* was a tasteless choice for the occasion. Later performances were warmly received, but the work had been given a bad name and was soon dropped from the Covent Garden repertoire. When it was revived, in a slightly revised version, by the Sadler's Wells company in 1966 (with Sylvia Fisher in the title role) it enjoyed a popular success. But for many years after its first performance, *Gloriana* remained the only Britten opera not to have been recorded in full.

SYNOPSIS
Act I Scene 1: The Earl of Essex and Lord Mountjoy, rivals for the Queen's favour, quarrel at a tournament. The Queen rebukes them and they are uneasily reconciled. Scene 2: Sir Robert Cecil warns the Queen against Essex's lack of restraint. Essex sings two lute songs to the Queen and urges his claim to be made Viceroy of Ireland.

Act II Scene 1: Essex, Mountjoy, Cecil and others attend the Queen who is in Norwich on a royal progress. They watch a rustic masque. Scene 2: At Essex House in the Strand, Mountjoy awaits his lover, Essex's sister Lady Rich. They are joined by Essex and his wife. Essex complains of delay over the Ireland decision and all four agree that when the Queen dies they will decide her successor. Scene 3: At a dance in the Palace of Whitehall, the Queen humiliates the gorgeously gowned Lady Essex by ordering the ladies to change their linen and herself returning in Lady Essex's dress, which does not fit her. But a moment later she appoints Essex Lord Deputy of Ireland.

Act III Scene 1: Essex's Irish campaign has failed. He bursts in on the Queen while she is dressing and is without her wig. She orders him to be kept under guard. Scene 2: Essex is proclaimed a traitor after trying to persuade the citizens of London to rebel. Scene 3: Essex has been condemned to death but the Queen does not sign the warrant for his execution until she is angered by Lady Rich's haughty demeanour. The opera ends with the Queen speaking, not singing, while six brief episodes of her life pass before her.

Gloriana is a succession of tableaux and brilliantly succeeds in giving a dignified and touching portrait of the Queen both as a public and a private individual. All the other characters are subsidiary, even Essex himself. The music is often subtle, as when the first lute song, 'Quick music is best', is undermined in the bass by the motif that stands for the Queen's cares of state. The sedition scene (Act II, Scene 2) is Verdian in its dramatic effectiveness, and there is no denying the impact of the Queen's spoken epilogue, unorthodox as it may be. In the ceremonial music – the Norwich masque and at the Palace ball – Britten evokes the Tudor age without a trace of pastiche.

RECORDING   Barstow, Langridge, WNO Ch and O, Mackerras, Decca, 1993
VIDEO   Walker, Vaughan, Rigby, Rolfe Johnson, Donnelly, Howlett, Van Allan, ENO Ch and O, Elder, Virgin, 1984
EDITION   v.s., Boosey & Hawkes, 1953; 2nd edn, 1968

The Turn of the Screw

Opera in a prologue and two acts, Op. 54 (1h 45m)
Libretto by Myfanwy Piper, after the story by Henry James (1898)
Composed 1954
PREMIERES   14 September 1954, La Fenice, Venice (English Opera Group); UK: 6 October 1954, Sadler's Wells, London; US: 19 March 1958, New York College of Music, New York
CAST   Prologue *t*, Governess *s*, Flora *s*, Mrs Grose *s*, Quint *t*, Miss Jessel *s*, Miles *treble*
ORCHESTRATION   fl/picc/b fl, ob/ca, cl/b cl, bsn, hn, timp, perc (bd, sd, tenor d, tomtom, gong, cym, triangle, wb, glock, tubular bells), 2 vn, va, vc, db, hp, pf/cel

The idea for an opera based on Henry James's ghost story was given to Britten by Myfanwy Piper, wife of the artist John Piper, who had been a friend of Britten since 1935 and had provided designs for several of the operas. The theme of *The Turn of the Screw* appealed particularly to Britten – corruption and innocence. It tells of two orphaned Victorian children, brother and sister, living in an Essex country house, who come under the evil influence of the ghosts of their guardian's former valet and the governess he seduced. A new governess discovers what is happening and tries to counteract it, with disastrous consequences. James never states what happens between haunters and haunted. But the story and the opera imply some sexual or erotic relationship, and the impression of evil is all the greater for remaining unspecified. In James the ghosts never speak; Mrs Piper's outstandingly skilful libretto provides words for them to sing and Britten directed that the audience should see them. The reader of the story is left to decide whether the ghosts exist or are figments of the distraught Governess (Britten's finest soprano role). James himself said he did not know. The dialogue between the ghosts at the beginning of Act II is an invention of Mrs Piper. She quotes a line from W. B. Yeats, 'The ceremony of

innocence is drowned'. For Britten this was the heart of the matter.

The opera was written to a commission from the 1954 Venice Biennale. Beginning to write the music in February 1954, Britten had composed the first three scenes when he decided there should be a prologue. Another late insertion was the letter scene, one of the finest in the work. Britten worked on the opera very fast: Imogen Holst, who copied the vocal score several pages at a time and posted them to the publisher, was amazed by Britten's confidence in parting with the start of a scene before he had composed the end of it. He conducted the English Opera Group in the first performance in Venice with a fine cast fortunately preserved in a recording.

Peter Pears (Quint) and Jennifer Vyvyan (the Governess in The Turn of the Screw *(Venice, 1954)*

SYNOPSIS

Prologue (to be played in front of a drop curtain)   A male narrator relates 'a curious story' written 'long ago' by a woman: it tells how she agreed to become governess to two orphaned children in the country on condition that she would never write to their handsome young guardian because he was so busy.
Act I
Theme
Scene 1: The Journey. The Governess is in a coach travelling to Bly ('Nearly there. Very soon I shall know'). How will the old housekeeper welcome her?
Variation I
Scene 2: The Welcome. On the porch at Bly Mrs Grose, the housekeeper, and the excited children, Flora and Miles, await the Governess ('Mrs Grose! Mrs Grose! Will she be nice?'). They practise curtseying and bowing. The Governess finds them charming and beautiful.
Variation II
Scene 3: The Letter. News comes that Miles has been expelled from school. Mrs Grose tells the Governess that she has known him to be wild, but not bad. They

watch the children innocently singing 'Lavender's blue' and decided the school has erred. The Governess says she will not tell the guardian.

Variation III

Scene 4: The Tower, 'evening, sweet summer'. The Governess is strolling in the grounds of Bly ('How beautiful it is'). She is enchanted more each day by her 'darling children'. Yet she has heard a cry in the night and a footstep outside her door. Suddenly she sees a man on the tower ('Who is it, who?').

Variation IV

Scene 5: The Window. In the hall Flora and Miles are riding a hobby-horse ('Tom, Tom, the piper's son'). The Governess again sees the man in the window. She describes the apparition to Mrs Grose, whose reaction is 'Quint! Peter Quint! Is there no end to his dreadful ways?' She explains that Quint was the master's former valet. He was 'free with everyone', spent hours with Miles, and 'had his will' with the lovely Miss Jessel, the children's previous governess, who left when pregnant and died. Quint also died when he fell on an icy road. The Governess, horrified, vows to protect the children.

Variation V

Scene 6: The Lesson. The Governess is giving Miles a Latin lesson in the schoolroom. He sings her a plaintive rhyme ('Malo I would rather be. Malo in an apple tree').

Variation VI

Scene 7: The Lake. On a sunny morning the Governess, with a book, and Flora, with a doll, sit by the lake in the park. Flora names the seas she knows, ending with the Dead Sea. She sings to her doll ('Go to sleep, my dolly dear') while the Governess reads. The Governess sees the ghost of Miss Jessel on the other side of the lake and realizes Flora has seen her too ('They are lost! Lost!').

Variation VII

Scene 8: At Night. Miles, in his nightgown, is in the garden near the tower. Quint's voice calls to him ('I'm all things strange and bold'). Later Miss Jessel, by the lake, calls to Flora. The colloquy between the ghosts and children is interrupted by the Governess and Mrs Grose. Miles tells the Governess, 'You see, I am bad.'

Act II

Variation VIII

Scene 1: Colloquy and Soliloquy (The setting is 'nowhere'). Quint and Miss Jessel reproach each other and sing that 'The ceremony of innocence is drowned.' They disappear, and the Governess sings ('Lost in my labyrinth') of the evil she fears.

Variation IX

Scene 2: The Bells. In the churchyard, Flora and Miles sing a mock-Benedicite. Mrs Grose is reassured by 'how sweet they are together', but the Governess tells her 'they are not playing, they are talking horrors' and are 'with the others'. Mrs Grose urges her to write to their guardian, but she refuses. As Flora goes into the church, Miles hangs back ('Do you like the bells? I do!'). He asks the Governess when he is returning to school. He mentions 'the others' to her. She knows she has been challenged and decides to leave Bly.

Variation X

Scene 3: Miss Jessel. The Governess enters the schoolroom to find Miss Jessel sitting at the desk and bemoaning her suffering ('Here my tragedy began'). The Governess defies her and she vanishes. The Governess decides to stay, but writes to the guardian ('Sir – dear Sir – my dear Sir').

Variation XI

Scene 4: The Bedroom. Miles is singing 'Malo'. The Governess tells him she has written to his guardian. Quint's voice calls to the boy, who shrieks and the candle goes out. ''Twas I who blew it,' Miles tells the alarmed Governess.

Variation XII, in which Quint is seen hovering ('So! She has written . . . It is there on the desk . . . Easy to take.').

Scene 5: Quint. Quint tempts Miles to steal the letter. Miles creeps into the schoolroom and takes the letter back to his bedroom.

Variation XIII

Scene 6: The Piano. In the schoolroom the Governess and Mrs Grose listen admiringly to Miles playing the piano ('O what a clever boy') while Flora makes a cat's cradle. Flora slips away and the two women set off to find her while Miles, his ruse successful, plays triumphantly.

Variation XIV

Scene 7: Flora. Flora is found by the lake. Miss Jessel appears ('Flora! Do not fail me!') and is seen by the Governess but not by Mrs Grose and Flora, or so they say ('I can't see anybody'). Flora, shouting abuse at the Governess, is led away by Mrs Grose. The Governess bewails Mrs Grose's desertion.

Variation XV

Scene 8: Miles. Mrs Grose is taking Flora away from Bly after a night listening to her outpourings of 'things I never knew or hope to know'. She reveals that Miles took the Governess's letter. The Governess is left behind ('O Miles – I cannot bear to lose you!'). The boy saunters in ('So, my dear, we are alone'). 'I stay as your friend,' she tells him. But he is listening for Quint. As the Governess questions Miles, Quint tells him not to betray their secrets. The boy becomes hysterical and admits he took the letter. 'Say the name of him who made you take it,' she says, 'and he will go for ever.' Miles screams, 'Peter Quint, you devil!' Quint disappears. The Governess realizes Miles is dead in her arms. She lays him on the ground and sings his 'Malo' tune as a requiem.

The title of James's story gave Britten the clue for the musical plan of the opera. The tension is maintained and heightened by turns of the musical screw, i.e. by the use of variation form. The prologue and 15 scenes are linked by 16 orchestral interludes – the theme and 15 variations – which are as vocal as any words in creating atmosphere. The theme (the 'screw') is 12-note, but it is not a Schoenbergian note row and is not treated as such. The opera's tonal conflict 'turns' between A minor and A♭major – a conflict similar to that in *Billy Budd*. The first seven scenes are in the white-note keys of the octave. Only in the last scene of Act I, when the two ghosts are heard for the first time, does the first black-note key appear.

Britten's scoring for chamber orchestra in this opera is as beautiful and imaginative as he ever achieved. The use of harp and low woodwind is especially striking, while his obsession with bells contributes powerfully to the opera's potent spell. Britten's employment of children's nursery rhymes, the lyrical writing of the letter by the Governess, her ecstatic aria as she strolls through the grounds of Bly, the mock-Benedicite, the brilliant pastiche Mozart that Miles (originally performed by David Hemmings, later a film actor) plays at the piano and his poignant 'Malo' song are among the highlights.

RECORDINGS   1. Vyvyan, Cross, Mandikian, Dyer, Pears, Hemmings, English Opera Group, Britten, Decca, 1955: the original cast and instrumentalists, unsurpassed; 2. Donath, June, Harper, Watson, Ginn, Langridge, Tear, O of Royal Opera House, Covent Garden, C. Davis, Philips, 1981: also very fine, with a second tenor used to sing the Prologue instead of the usual doubling with Quint (also available as the soundtrack for Peter Weigl's video, Philips)
EDITIONS   f.s., Boosey & Hawkes, 1958; 2nd edn, 1966; v.s., Boosey & Hawkes, 1955

Noye's Fludde

Chester miracle play in one act, Op. 59 (50m)
Text taken from A. W. Pollard (ed.), *English Miracle Plays, Moralities and Interludes*
Composed 1957
PREMIERES   18 June 1958, Orford Church, Suffolk; US: 31 July 1958, New York (radio broadcast); 16 March 1959, School of Sacred Music, Union Theological Seminary, New York
CAST   The Voice of God *spoken role*, Noye *b-bar*, Mrs Noye *a*, Sem *treble*, Ham *treble*, Jaffett *treble*, Mrs Sem *girl s*, Mrs Ham *girl s*, Mrs Jaffett *girl s*, Mrs Noye's Gossips *girl s*; *satb* children's chorus of animals and birds; congregation
ORCHESTRATION   professional: 2 vn, va, vc, db, treble rec, pf (4 hands), organ, timp; children or amateurs: vns I, II, III; vas; vcs I, II; dbs; descant recs I, II; treble recs, bugles in B♭ (in 4 parts), 12 handbells in E♭, bd, tenor d, sd, tambourine, cyms, triangle, whip, gong, Chinese blocks, wind-machine, sandpaper, slung mugs

Britten's written introduction to the full score of *Noye's Fludde* is lengthy and precise. He liked to involve children and amateurs in music-making and was anxious to compose a dramatic work that could be staged in Orford Church during the Aldeburgh Festival. He found the subject of the Flood vividly dealt with in one of the Chester miracle plays which in medieval times were performed by local craftsmen and tradesmen with the church choir. Each guild performed one play from the cycle on a cart that moved around the town. *Noye's Fludde*, Britten wrote, is 'intended for the same style of presentation – though not necessarily on a cart. Some big building should be used, preferably a church – but not a theatre – large enough to accommodate actors and orchestra, with the action raised on rostra, but not a stage removed from the congregation.' He specified that though the 16th-century spelling of the text is retained it should be pronounced in modern English (including the name Noye as Noah) except for the nouns ending in e, as in *shippe*.

At the first performance 35 pairs of 'animals' were used, divided into seven groups. But 'the more animals the better' was Britten's wish; and part of the charm and fun of the work is the devising of costumes and headgear for lions, goats, dogs, wolves, rats, mice, herons, owls, curlews and many more. Britten also stipulated 'as many recorder-players as possible'. He wanted a professional to play the timpani, with at least six amateurs to play the other percussion instruments. 'The slung mugs and sandpaper can be concocted at home.' The mugs were Britten's inspired idea for the depiction of raindrops – 'mugs (or cups) of varying thickness and size – so as to make a kind of scale – slung on string by the handles from a wooden stand and hit with a wooden spoon (by one player)'. As in his cantata *Saint Nicolas* (1948), Britten makes use of familiar hymn tunes in which the audience join. Ideally, the orchestra for *Noye's Fludde* numbers a minimum of 67 players, of whom 57 are amateurs. The total cast comprises three adults and 90 children.

SYNOPSIS

While the congregation sings 'Lord Jesus, think on me', Noye has walked through the church to the empty stage, where he kneels. The Voice of God, from high up and away from the stage, tells of his intention to flood the earth and destroy all upon it except Noye and his family. He instructs Noye to build a ship. The sons and their wives fall to with a will, but Noye's wife derides the venture and prefers to drink with her Gossips (cronies). The Ark is built and God's voice tells Noye to enter it with his family, the beasts and the birds. The rain begins and the animals, heralded by bugle calls, march through the congregation and into the Ark, singing 'Kyrie eleison'. Mrs Noye continues drinking with her cronies. Eventually her three sons pick her up and carry her struggling into the Ark, while the Gossips run off screaming. The storm begins in earnest and the inhabitants of the Ark sing 'Eternal Father, strong to save', joined by the congregation for the second and third verses. The storm subsides; the creatures go to sleep, and Noye looks out of the window. Forty days have passed, so he sends a raven to see if there is a dry place anywhere. If it does not return, somewhere is dry. It does not return. He then sends a dove, which returns with an olive branch. God's Voice tells Noye to step ashore; the animals leave the Ark, singing 'Alleluia'. God promises that he will never again wreak vengeance on mankind and creates a rainbow as a token of this promise. All the cast, joined in the last verse by the congregation, sing 'The spacious firmament on high', to Tallis's tune, during which the sun, then the moon and stars appear. The animals walk slowly out in procession. Noye is left alone. The Voice of God tenderly blesses him.

Noye's Fludde is Britten's most lovable work, infinitely touching in its emotional impact. Every device, every piece of compositional artifice, is brilliantly imagined and skilfully organized. The raw sound of the bugles, the fluttering of recorders, the chimes of handbells, the characterization of the animals as they chant their Kyrie on their way to the Ark, the comedy of Mrs Noye's drunken refusal to join her husband, and the storm itself (a passacaglia) – all these are infallibly effective, the work of a master of theatrical effect.

RECORDINGS 1. Rex, Brannigan, Anthony, ECO, Del Mar, Argo, 1961: historic cast, recorded under Britten's supervision; 2. A. Harwood, Salisbury and Chester School Ch, Endymion Ensemble, Hickox, Virgin, 1990
EDITIONS f.s., Boosey & Hawkes, 1959; 2nd edn, 1965; v.s., Boosey & Hawkes, 1958

A Midsummer Night's Dream
Opera in three acts, Op. 64 (2h 30m)
Libretto by Benjamin Britten and Peter Pears, adapted from the play by William Shakespeare (c. 1593–4)
Composed October 1959–April 1960
PREMIERES 11 June 1960, Jubilee Hall, Aldeburgh; US: 10 October 1961, War Memorial Opera House, San Francisco
CAST Oberon ct or a, Tytania coloratura s, Puck boy acrobat, spoken role, Theseus b, Hippolyta a, Lysander t, Demetrius bar, Hermia ms, Helena s, Bottom b-bar, Quince b, Flute t, Snug b, Snout t, Starveling bar, Cobweb treble, Peaseblossom treble, Mustardseed treble, Moth treble; treble or s chorus of fairies
ORCHESTRATION 2 fl/picc, ob/ca, 2 cl, bsn, 2 hn, tpt, tenor trbn, perc (2 players: triangle, cym, tambourine, gong, 2 wbs, vib, glock, xyl, drum in F♯, sd, tenor d, bd, timp, 2 bells) 2 hp, hpd/cel, str; onstage: sopranino recs, small cyms, 2 wbs

Design by Carl Toms for Oberon in A Midsummer Night's Dream *(Aldeburgh, 1960)*

For the 1960 Aldeburgh Festival, the stage and pit of the Jubilee Hall were enlarged and other improvements were made. Britten wanted to compose a new opera as a celebration but in the time left it was impossible to commission a libretto. So he and Pears adapted Shakespeare's *A Midsummer Night's Dream*, cutting the play by about half and simplifying the action. Some of Puck's lines are given to the chorus of fairies and other lines are reallocated among the singers. Britten said he did not feel in the least guilty about the cuts: 'The original Shakespeare will survive.' The whole project was completed in seven months, during part of which Britten was ill, though he conducted the first performance.

SYNOPSIS
Act I The wood, deepening twilight. Oberon, King of the Fairies, has quarrelled with his Queen, Tytania, because she has 'a lovely boy' as attendant, stolen from an Indian king, and Oberon wants him. Tytania defies him and Oberon plans his revenge, ordering Puck to fetch him a herb of which the juice, sprinkled on a sleeping human's eyelids, will make the sleeper 'madly dote upon the next live creature that it sees'. Hermia, in love with Lysander, has been ordered by her father to marry Demetrius, who loves her. She and Lysander plan to flee outside Athens where the ruling will not apply. As they leave, Demetrius and Helena enter. Demetrius tells Helena he does not love her; he is looking for Lysander and Hermia – 'The one I'll slay, the other slayeth me.' Puck returns with the herb. Oberon, who has been eavesdropping, tells of his plan for Tytania ('I know a bank where the wild thyme blows') and orders Puck to find Demetrius – 'Thou shalt know the man by the Athenian garments he hath on' – and to anoint his eyes when he can ensure that 'the next thing he espies' will be Helena. The rustics arrive to rehearse a play, *Pyramus and Thisbe*, to be performed before Duke Theseus of Athens on the occasion of his marriage to Hippolyta. Parts are allotted – Bottom the weaver is to be Pyramus – and they agree to rehearse later. Lysander and Hermia are lost and settle to sleep. Puck sprinkles Lysander's eyelids with juice. When Demetrius and Helena arrive, Helena awakens Lysander who declares his love for her and follows her. Hermia finds herself alone and goes in search of Lysander. Tytania and her retinue arrive. When she is asleep, Oberon squeezes the juice on her eyes.
    Act II The wood, dark night. The rustics arrive for their rehearsal. Bottom leaves the clearing (followed by Puck) and returns wearing the head of an ass. Tytania awakes and falls in love with him. When Hermia and Demetrius return, it is obvious that Puck has bewitched the wrong man. Oberon orders him to search for Helena. As Demetrius lies down to sleep, Oberon squeezes juice on his eyes. Lysander is still protesting his sincerity to Helena when Demetrius awakes, declaring passion for Helena, who thinks everyone is playing a joke on her. Hermia returns and the women, formerly close friends, mock and insult each other. Oberon orders Puck to lead the four astray in the wood and to put

the juice on Lysander's eyes to restore the status quo.

Act III Scene 1: The wood, early next morning. Oberon, now that he has acquired Tytania's boy attendant, frees her and Bottom from the spell. Bottom rejoins his companions. The four lovers awaken and are reconciled, Lysander with Hermia and Demetrius with Helena. Scene 2: Theseus' palace. The Duke tells Hermia he will overrule her father and allow her to marry Lysander. The rustics' play is enacted, after which the couples retire. The fairies and Puck occupy the room ('Now the hungry lion roars'). Oberon and Tytania enter and, with the fairies, sing, 'Now until the break of day, through this house each fairy stray.' They leave the stage to Puck, who addresses the audience: 'Give me your hands, if we be friends, and Robin shall restore amends.'

In *A Midsummer Night's Dream*, Britten found themes congenial to him: night and sleep, the juxtaposition of the natural and the supernatural, marvellous lyric poetry, and the opportunity for a rich display of musical parody. He responded with some of his most inventive, enchanting and evocative music. Each of the three strata of beings in the opera – fairies, lovers and rustics – has its own sound-world, each with distinctive instrumental timbres – harps, celesta, harpsichord and percussion for the fairies, strings and woodwind for the lovers, bassoon and deep brass for the rustics. Two other inspirations contribute to the opera's success: Puck is a spoken role, accompanied by trumpet cadenzas and drums, and Oberon is assigned to a counter-tenor, an otherworldly sound that is both sinister and beguiling. The fairies' music has an acerbic quality. Britten said he had 'always been struck by a kind of sharpness in Shakespeare's fairies'. *A Midsummer Night's Dream* is as melodious a score as he ever wrote. His setting of 'I know a bank' is exquisite, as is the love music for Tytania and Bottom. The rustics' play is a closely organized opera buffa, notable for its witty parodies of Italian opera. And over the whole score lies the magic of the wood, brought before our eyes in the opera's first bars, with its slow portamento sighs depicting the rustling leaves and creaking branches. Although Britten never used serial method as such, the series of major triads, connected by glissandi on the strings, which so vividly depict the wood, covers all 12 notes of the chromatic scale. As they are in false relation to one another, Britten again (as in *Billy Budd*) creates a tonal ambiguity which is continued in the music given to the fairies on their first appearance, Lydian G major spiced with D major and F♯ major. At the end of the opera, in the haunting 'Now until the break of day', a radiant Mahlerian F♯ major is achieved. On the journey to that magical moment, Britten creates a Shakespearean opera to rank with Verdi's masterpieces.

RECORDING Harwood, Harper, Veasey, Watts, Deller, Pears, Hemsley, Shirley-Quirk, Brannigan, Terry, Children's Choirs, LSO, Britten, Decca, 1966: a marvellous cast that does full justice to the work's poetry and humour

VIDEO Lott, Cotrubas, Powell, Bowman, Davies, Duesing, Applegren, Glyndebourne Festival Ch and O, Haitink, Castle, 1981
EDITIONS f.s., Boosey & Hawkes, 1961; v.s., Boosey & Hawkes, 1960

Curlew River

Parable for church performance, Op. 71 (1h 15m)
Libretto by William Plomer, based on the medieval Japanese Noh play *Sumidagawa* by Juro Motomasa (1395–1431)
Composed February–2 April 1964
PREMIERES 12 June 1964, Orford Church, Suffolk; US: 26 June 1966, Spanish Courtyard, Caramoor Festival, Katonah, New York
CAST Madwoman *t*, Ferryman *bar*, Traveller *bar*, Spirit of the Boy *treble*, Abbot *b*, 3 assistants (acolytes); chorus of pilgrims 3 *t*, 3 *bar*, 2 *b*
INSTRUMENTALISTS (lay brothers) fl/picc, hn, va, db, hp, chamber organ, perc (5 small untuned drums, 5 small bells, large tuned gong)

On a visit to Tokyo early in 1956, Britten saw two performances of the Japanese Noh play *Sumidagawa* (*The Sumida River*). They made an enormous impression on him, haunting him for some years afterwards. Seeking a means of bringing operatic entertainment into the church without involving amateurs and the audience, as *Noye's Fludde* had, he remembered the Japanese play and asked William Plomer to transpose it from a Japanese and Buddhist milieu to the framework of a medieval English religious drama. So the Sumida river became the Curlew river in the East Anglia Britten knew so well. Instead of ancient Japanese music, the opera, or church parable, grew from the plainsong hymn 'Te lucis ante terminum' which is chanted by the Abbot and a group of monks and acolytes as they walk to the acting area where the monks who are to play the Madwoman, Ferryman and Traveller are robed for their parts.

Britten had been particularly impressed by the stylized ritual of the play's presentation in Japan: 'the intense slowness of the action . . . the beautiful costumes, the mixture of chanting, speech and singing which, with the three instruments, made up the strange music'. Plomer's adaptation retained some of this stylization. Britten increased the number of percussion instruments in order to achieve the effect of a gamelan and wrote a major part for the flute. He also decided that no conductor was necessary, and in order to specify which vocal or instrumental part had precedence, he invented a new flexible pause mark, the 'curlew'.

The producer of the first performance, Colin Graham, devised a simple setting of a raised and raked circle, approached from two directions by a spiralling ramp, and placed at one end of the church. At the foot of the ramp were the instrumentalists (lay brothers). The actors wore masks. Peter Pears sang the Madwoman and John Shirley-Quirk the Ferryman.

SYNOPSIS

In a church by a Fenland river in medieval times the Abbot tells the congregation they will witness a mystery: 'How in sad mischance a sign was given of God's grace, not far away, where, in our reedy Fens, the Curlew River runs.' The Ferryman explains it is the day on which people use the ferry to cross to the other bank to pray before a grave where they believe 'some special grace' heals the sick. He hears a strange noise. A Traveller says it is a woman who seems to be crazy and is making the people on the road laugh. The Madwoman enters ('Let me in! Let me out! Tell me the way!'). She is seeking her child, who was seized as slave by a foreigner, at her home in the Black Mountains. The Ferryman refuses to take her across the river unless she entertains the passengers with her singing. She rebukes him and watches the flight of some birds. 'Common gulls,' says the Ferryman, but she calls them 'Curlews of the Fenland'. They sail the river ('Curlew river, smoothly flowing') and he tells the Traveller that a year ago to the day a heathen stranger ('a big man arm'd with a sword and cudgel') came aboard the ferry with a 12-year-old Christian boy whom he said he had bought as a slave. The boy looked ill and when they reached the other side he lay on the grass near the chapel. The heathen threatened him, but abandoned him. The river people cared for the boy but he grew weaker. He told them his dead father had been a nobleman and that his mother brought him up near the Black Mountains until the day he was seized while walking alone. He asked to be buried by the path to the chapel so that 'if travellers from my dear country pass this way, their shadows will fall on my grave'. Then he died. The river people believe he was a saint. The boat arrives. The Madwoman has been weeping at the story and from her questions everyone realizes that the child was hers. The Ferryman leads her to the grave where she tells of her search ('Hoping, I wander'd on'). As she prays for the child his voice is heard and finally his spirit appears, freeing her from her madness before returning to the tomb ('Go your way in peace, mother').

Although the orchestral score of *Curlew River* seems on first acquaintance to represent a new departure for Britten, it develops the strand of orientalism – through gamelan sounds – that can be found in earlier works, most obviously in the three-act ballet *The Prince of the Pagodas* (1956). Britten here joins a number of 20th-century composers, from Debussy to Boulez (*Le marteau sans maître*), in inflecting Western music with Eastern procedures. Not far away, too, is the influence of Holst, another composer who was preoccupied with orientalism in his work. The Madwoman is one of the finest parts he wrote for Pears, the disordered mind poignantly depicted by the use of unequal fourths in the cries of 'You mock me', while 'Hoping, I wander'd on' sung in duet with the flute, is an inspired invention. The score is marked by supremacy of melodic line, derived from the use of plainsong. The melodies create the harmonies. As Eric Walter White noted, in this work Britten replaced polyphony with heterophony (the simultaneous variation of a melody, particularly as found in much Eastern music for voice and instrument).

RECORDING Pears, Shirley-Quirk, Blackburn, Drake, instrumental ensemble, Britten, Decca, 1965: virtually the original cast and therefore a historic document
EDITIONS f.s., Faber Music, 1983; v.s. (rehearsal score), Faber Music, 1964

The Burning Fiery Furnace

Second parable for church performance, Op. 77 (1h)
Libretto by William Plomer, based on the Book of Daniel, Chapter 3
Composed autumn 1965–5 April 1966
PREMIERES 9 June 1966, Orford Church, Suffolk; US: 25 June 1967, Spanish Courtyard, Caramoor Festival, Katonah, New York
CAST Nebuchadnezzar *t*, Astrologer (Abbot) *bar*, Ananias *bar*, Misael *t*, Azarias *b*, Herald and Leader of the Courtiers *bar*; chorus of courtiers 3 *t*, 2 *bar*, 2 *b*; 5 attendants *trebles*
INSTRUMENTALISTS (lay brothers) fl/picc, hn, trbn, va, db/Babylonian drum, hp/little harp, chamber organ/small cym, perc (5 small untuned drums, anvil (small untuned steel plate), 2 tuned wbs, lyra glock, Babylonian drum, multiple whip)

Encouraged by the success of *Curlew River*, Britten and Plomer devised a second church parable based on a familiar biblical episode, 'something much less sombre, an altogether gayer affair', as Britten said. The idea came to him on holiday in France when he was impressed by the colours of Chartres Cathedral and a sculpture of Nebuchadnezzar and the Fiery Furnace. Plomer intended that Nebuchadnezzar, the cult of the 'god of gold', and the 'resistance movement' of the three Jewish exiles should be relevant 'to our own times'.

SYNOPSIS

Babylon, the 6th century BC. A herald welcomes Ananias, Misael and Azarias, 'three young men . . . chosen out of all the world for knowledge and skill to

Peter Pears as the Madwoman in Curlew River *(Aldeburgh, 1964)*

take high rank in Babylon' as rulers over three provinces. King Nebuchadnezzar is giving a feast in their honour. He orders the Astrologer to tell them their Babylonian names, Shadrach, Meschach and Abednego. The feast begins, but the three refuse the food handed to them. Entertainers dance and sing ('The waters of Babylon . . . all ran dry. Do you know why?'). The Astrologer tells the King this is what comes of taking on foreigners. Nebuchadnezzar leaves the banquet in panic, declaring that the stars are against him. The three see that they have enemies, but vow to continue as children of Israel. The herald proclaims that a huge golden image of Merodak, the great god of Babylon, is to be erected and that whenever a fanfare is played everyone must bow down and worship it or be thrown into a burning fiery furnace. When the image arises the three Israelites refuse to kneel and are put into the furnace, heated 'seven times hotter than it ever was before'. They stand unharmed, a fourth figure with them, singing the Benedicite. Nebuchadnezzar says the fourth figure is like the Son of God. He approaches the furnace and orders the three out and the fourth figure disappears. Seeing they are unharmed Nebuchadnezzar turns on the Astrologer ('Where is your wisdom now?') and dismisses him. The King acknowledges that there is no god except the God of Shadrach, Meshach and Abednego ('Down with the god of gold'). He joins the three in a hymn of peace.

The fount of the opera's thematic material is the plainsong chant with which it opens. The alto trombone supplies the distinctive instrumental timbre of the score, and there is more humour and direct action than in *Curlew River*. The role of Nebuchadnezzar, originally sung by Pears, is richly drawn, his conversion from paganism being effected musically by the transference to him of the plainchant-inspired idiom of the angel within the furnace. During the feast, the entertainment, with its recurring 'Do you know why? And so do I', recalls the humour of *A Midsummer Night's Dream*, while the golden image is erected to a march with sonorities more oriental than any in *Curlew River*. This is the most dramatic and perhaps the most appealing of the parables.

RECORDING Pears, Tear, Drake, Shirley-Quirk, Dean, English Opera Group, Britten, Decca, 1967: four of the original cast in a definitive performance
EDITIONS f.s., Faber Music, 1983; v.s., Faber Music, 1966; rehearsal s., Faber Music, 1968

The Prodigal Son

Third parable for church performance, Op. 81 (1h 15m)
Libretto by William Plomer, based on the New Testament parable (Luke 15:11–32)
Composed January 1968–22 April 1968
PREMIERES 10 June 1968, Orford Church, Suffolk; US: 29 June 1969, Spanish Courtyard, Caramoor Festival, Katonah, New York
CAST Tempter (Abbot) *t*, Father *b-bar*, Elder Son *bar*, Younger Son *t*; chorus of servants, parasites and beggars 3 *t*, 3 *bar*, 2 *b*; 5 young servants and distant voices *trebles*

INSTRUMENTALISTS alto fl/picc, tpt, hn, va, db, hp, chamber organ, perc (5 small untuned drums, small Chinese cym, conical gourd rattle, large tuned gong, 2 tuned wbs, high-pitched wb); onstage: small drum (tambour), small cym, tambourine, sistrum (jungle rattle), small bell-lyra

To complete their triptych, Britten and Plomer went to the New Testament for what Plomer called a story that 'seems to bring into the clearest possible focus the Christian view of life', the triumph of forgiveness.

SYNOPSIS
Disguised as the Tempter, the Abbot mocks the Amen from the opposite end of the church ('What I bring you is evil'). He sets the scene: a country patriarch, a worthy family, a dull life. 'See how I break it up.' After the actors have robed, the chorus gathers round the Father, who extols the work ethic. The Tempter waylays the Younger Son and describes the delights he is missing through keeping himself 'locked up in this desert here of stupid family life'. The Younger Son confesses his discontent to his father and asks for his portion of the inheritance. The Father grants this request, to the disgust of the Elder Son, and he and the servants bid him farewell. The Tempter accompanies the Younger Son to the city where he introduces him to the pleasures of wine, women and gambling. The Younger Son loses all his money and is deserted by his drinking friends. 'Now you must pay,' the Tempter tells him and advises him to join a band of beggars and to work as a swineherd. The Younger Son decides to return home and asks his father to let him be one of the servants. But the Father welcomes him and orders the killing of the fatted calf to celebrate his return. The Elder Son objects, but at the Father's prompting is reconciled with his brother. The Tempter disrobes and, as the Abbot, points out the moral. He joins the monks and leads them out.

The chorus plays a larger part in this parable than in its predecessors. The trumpet in D and the alto flute are the dominant instruments, with a solo viola representing the Younger Son's uncorrupted nature. Another striking effect is the use of a conical gourd to suggest trudging through desert sand. Britten fails in his depiction of the temptations of the flesh, but the music for the reconciliation between father and son is both moving and ravishingly scored.

RECORDING Tear, Pears, Shirley-Quirk, Drake, English Opera Group, Britten, Decca, 1969: the original cast and, like the first two parables, the original venue, Orford Church, with its remarkable acoustic
EDITIONS f.s., Faber Music, 1986; v.s. (rehearsal score), Faber Music, 1971

Owen Wingrave

Opera in two acts, Op. 85 (1h 45m)
Libretto by Myfanwy Piper, based on Henry James's short story (1892)
Composed May 1969–August 1970
PREMIERES 16 May 1971, BBC2 Television (recorded at The Maltings, Snape, 22–30 November 1970); 10 May 1973, Covent Garden, London; US: 9 August 1973, Santa Fe

CAST   Owen Wingrave *bar*, Spencer Coyle *b-bar*, Lechmere *t*, Miss Wingrave *dramatic s*, Mrs Coyle *s*, Mrs Julian *s*, Kate *ms*, General Sir Philip Wingrave *t*, Narrator *t*, distant chorus, trebles

ORCHESTRATION   2 fl/2 picc, 2 ob, 2 cl/E♭cl/b cl, 2 bsn/dbsn, 2 hn, 2 tpt, 2 trbn, tuba, timp, perc (3 players: sd, tenor d, bd, wb, whip, susp cym, cym, bells, 2 gongs, tomtom, vib, xyl, glock), str, hp, pf

In November 1967 Britten received a commission from the BBC for a television opera. He had read Henry James's short story *Owen Wingrave* in the 1950s and admired it because it coincided with his own strong pacifist sympathies. He had discussed the possibility of making an opera from it with Myfanwy Piper before 1962. Now the Vietnam War, and in particular the shooting of American students demonstrating against it on the campus of Kent State University, refocused his attention on it. While not particularly interested in television, he accepted the challenge posed by the medium, though there is no doubt that he always intended that *Owen Wingrave* should ultimately be a stage work. Each part was written with a particular singer in mind. The opera was first shown on British television, but within a week it had also been screened in the United States and on 12 European networks. Although its music is admired by many, it has failed to appeal to the public.

SYNOPSIS
Act I   Late 19th century. An instrumental prelude describes the ten Wingrave family portraits at their country seat Paramore (the fifth is a double portrait). Each portrait – of a military man – is depicted by a cadenza for a solo instrument. Scene 1: The study at Coyle's military establishment in Bayswater. Coyle is lecturing Owen and his friend Lechmere about battle tactics. Lechmere is anxious to be in the thick of war, but Owen hates it. He tells Coyle he can't go through with becoming a soldier whatever his family may say. Coyle soliloquizes that Owen was his most gifted pupil. Scene 2: Hyde Park/Miss Wingrave's lodgings in Baker Street. Owen, in the park, thinks about death in battle and how its 'glory' is an illusion. Owen's aunt, Miss Wingrave, extols to Coyle the Wingraves' past military feats and says Owen's 'fancy' must be stopped. Scene 3: A room at the Coyles'. Owen tells Coyle and his wife nothing will change his mind. They drink to Owen's future 'wherever that may lie'. Owen tells Lechmere he dreads going to Paramore: his grandfather knows no life but war, his father was killed in battle, countless other Wingraves had died for their country. Scene 4: At Paramore Owen's aunt is awaiting his arrival, together with Mrs Julian, a widow and dependant, and her daughter Kate, who says, 'He reckons without me . . . he shall not carry out so infamous a plan.' Owen, alone, addresses the portraits, particularly that of his father. His grandfather, Sir Philip, emerges from his study: 'Sirrah! How dare you!' Scene 5: In this abstract scene, spread over a week, the voices of Sir Philip, Miss Wingrave, Kate and Mrs Julian taunt and insult Owen – 'dragging our name in the dirt', 'insulting your Queen and country',

'you are no gentleman', 'I'll court-martial you', 'you're not worthy of Paramore'. Scene 6: The hall at Paramore. The Coyles arrive. Coyle hints at a Paramore ghost and points out the double portrait, Colonel Wingrave and a boy. Owen tells Coyle his encounter with his family has been worse than he thought possible. Scene 7: The dinner table at Paramore. Owen praises Coyle's brilliance as a teacher and this leads to Sir Philip's open attack on Owen. When Mrs Coyle interposes that Owen has his scruples, the others seize on this word for a concerted attack on Owen. He retorts that he would make it a crime to draw a sword for one's country. Sir Philip leaves in a fury.

Act II   As a prologue a ballad singer tells of a young Wingrave who refuses a school friend's challenge to fight after they have quarrelled over boasts about their fathers' property. The Wingrave's father accuses him of cowardice and kills him in an upstairs room at Paramore. On the day of the funeral, the father is found dead 'without a wound' in the same room. Scene 1: The gallery at Paramore. Coyle and Owen are looking at the double portrait of the father and son in the ballad. Owen says the father would not have died from remorse: Sir Philip disinherits Owen. Mrs Julian collapses at this blow to Kate's future. Lechmere immediately begins to flatter Kate, to the Coyles' disgust. Owen bids the portraits farewell. He is joined by Kate and they sing of former days at Paramore ('Why did you spoil it all?'). He rebukes her for flirting with Lechmere and she calls him a coward, challenging him to sleep in the haunted room. He orders her to lock him in it. Scene 2: The Coyles' bedroom, later that evening. Mrs Coyle is still indignant about Kate and Lechmere. Lechmere knocks at their door having overheard Kate's challenge to Owen. They go to the haunted room but at that moment hear Kate crying 'Ah, Owen, Owen, you've gone.' Sir Philip opens the door to find Owen dead.

Britten's use of military music is a feature of the opera. In the *marziale* prelude with which it begins, each Wingrave family portrait is assigned a particular obbligato instrument or instruments, rather as in the linking passages of the *Nocturne* (1958). Trombone and piccolo feature in the double portrait of the father and son in the ballad. Each cadenza passage is in some respect grotesque, for Britten has no admiration for these military ancestors, and they resolve into the memorable horn solo that represents Owen's nobler character.

The three chords forming the basis of a three-bar martial motif in the prelude, which represents the Wingrave army tradition, are evolved from a 12-note series. As in *The Turn of the Screw* and *A Midsummer Night's Dream*, Britten here makes use of note rows but not in any systematic way. Each row is constructed from diminished triads. There are three different 12-note sets in the prelude – the figure already mentioned, the double portrait (trombone and piccolo) and Owen's father. Owen's portrait, by juxtaposition of perfect and diminished triads, brings out the conflict in Owen's mind through a conflict of major and minor. Subtle references to the material of this prelude honeycomb the rest of the score in the form of diminished triads.

The refining process of the church parables is evident in the orchestral writing. It may be felt that Britten's invention failed him at climactic moments in the opera, where it suffers alongside comparable episodes in the earlier operas. But neither the television screen nor the large stage of Covent Garden was an ideal setting for *Owen Wingrave*, which still awaits a production to do justice to its remarkable qualities and probably to reveal several as yet unrecognized.

RECORDING   Baker, Fisher, Harper, Vyvyan, Douglas, Pears, Luxon, Shirley-Quirk, Wandsworth School Choir, ECO, Britten, Decca, 1970: the original television cast, recorded in the Maltings, Snape
EDITIONS   f.s., Faber Music, 1972; v.s., Faber Music, 1973

Death in Venice

Opera in two acts, Op. 88 (2h 30m)
Libretto by Myfanwy Piper, based on Thomas Mann's novella *Der Tod in Venedig* (1912)
Composed spring 1971–March 1973; rev. 27 August 1973 and early 1974
PREMIERES   16 June 1973, The Maltings, Snape; US: 18 October 1974, Metropolitan, New York
CAST   Gustav von Aschenbach *t*, Traveller/Elderly Fop/Old Gondolier/Hotel Manager/Hotel Barber/Leader of the Players/Voice of Dionysus *b-bar*, Voice of Apollo *ct*; *satb* chorus of youths and girls, hotel guests and waiters, gondoliers and boatmen, street vendors, touts and beggars, citizens of Venice, choir in St Mark's, tourists, followers of Dionysus; chorus includes (*s*) Danish lady, Russian mother, English lady, French girl, strawberry seller, lace seller, newspaper seller, strolling player; (*a*) French mother, German mother, Russian nanny, beggar woman; (*t*) hotel porter, 2 Americans, 2 gondoliers, glass maker, strolling player; (*bar* and *b*) ship's steward, lido boatman, Polish father, German father, Russian father, hotel waiter, guide in Venice, restaurant waiter, gondolier, priest in St Mark's, English clerk in the travel bureau; Polish mother, Tadzio, 2 daughters, governess, Jaschiu, boys and girls, strolling players, beach attendants, *dancers*
ORCHESTRATION   2 fl/2 picc, 2 ob, 2 cl/b cl, 2 bsn, 2 hn, 2 tpt, 2 trbn, tuba, hp, pf, timp, perc (5 players): 2 sd, 2 tenor d, 2 bd (1 large), 3 tomtoms, 3 Chinese drums, small drum, tuned drum, pair cym, 2 susp cyms, pair small cym, tambourine, wb, triangle, 2 whips (large and small), 2 tuned gongs, 2 t-t (large and small), wind-machine, bells, bell-tree, crotales, vib, 2 glock, 2 xyl (1 small), marimba, str

The idea of an opera based on Mann's *Death in Venice* had been in Britten's mind for some years. In November 1970 he approached Myfanwy Piper for a libretto and began work on the music in the spring of 1971. He completed the short score just before Christmas 1972. For most of the time he was ill, and in the autumn of 1972 his doctors decreed that he needed an operation to replace a deficient heart valve. He made a bargain with them – he would have the operation provided they allowed him to finish *Death in Venice* first. The full score was completed in March 1973. The opera had become an obsession. Not only was it a subject with which he was

passionately involved, but he wanted to complete it as a tribute to Peter Pears.

During the operation (in May 1973), Britten had a slight stroke which permanently affected his right hand. He was not well enough to supervise rehearsals of the opera, conducted by Steuart Bedford, nor to attend the first performance at the Maltings. He first saw it at a special, semi-private performance on 12 September and later attended the first London performance at Covent Garden on 18 October. He attended the recording sessions in spring 1974 although very ill, and saw the opera again at the 1975 Aldeburgh Festival and at Covent Garden on 7 July 1975. Thus he heard Pears give the performance of his life in the long, taxing and testing role of Aschenbach and John Shirley-Quirk, equally impressive, in the seven baritone roles.

SYNOPSIS
Act I Scene 1: Munich. Aschenbach, a famous novelist and now a widower, is walking in a Munich suburb and musing on the apparent drying up of his creativity ('My mind beats on and no words come'). He enters a cemetery and reads the texts on the façade of the chapel. He becomes aware of a Traveller, who sings of exotic sights in far-off lands ('Marvels unfold! . . . Go, travel to the South'). Aschenbach decides to have a holiday in the sun. Scene 2: On the boat to Venice. Youths are leaning over the rail shouting to their girls on shore. An Elderly Fop joins the youths as they sing 'Serenissima' and starts a popular song, 'We'll meet in the Piazza'. Aschenbach comes on to the deck and is disgusted by the rouged 'young–old horror'. Arrival in Venice is described in an overture based on the Serenissima theme. Scene 3: The journey to the Lido. Aschenbach is in a gondola and sings his own praise of Serenissima. The Old Gondolier is not rowing him the way he wants to go. They pass a boatload of boys and girls singing 'Serenissima . . . Bride of the sea'. On arrival at the quayside, Aschenbach is met by a Boatman and the Hotel Porter. The Old Gondolier has disappeared, without payment. Aschenbach soliloquizes ('Mysterious gondola . . . black, coffin black, a vision of death itself'). Scene 4: The first evening at the hotel. The Manager shows Aschenbach his room with its superb view of the lagoon. He watches the other guests assemble for dinner – French, American, German, Polish, Danish, English and Russian. The Polish family enters, with the boy Tadzio, whose beauty is immediately noticed by Aschenbach ('Surely the soul of Greece lies in that bright perfection'). Scene 5: On the beach. Aschenbach watches children playing games and buys some strawberries. Tadzio arrives and joins the games. Scene 6: The foiled departure. Aschenbach crosses to Venice from the Lido. The city is hot and crowded and the sirocco is blowing. Back at the hotel, he decides to leave. Just before he goes, Tadzio walks through the hall. Aschenbach learns that his luggage has been sent on to the wrong destination, so he returns to the hotel. The Manager has kept his room and reminds him that the wind is now blowing from a healthier quarter. Through the

window Aschenbach sees Tadzio playing on the beach ('That's what made it hard to leave. So be it'). Scene 7: The Games of Apollo. On the Lido beach, Aschenbach watches the boys' beach games as if they were in an Olympian world. The Voice of Apollo is heard ('He who loves beauty worships me'). Competing in a variety of games, Tadzio wins each time. Aschenbach, excited, wants but fails to speak to the boy, who passes him and smiles ('Ah, don't smile like that! No one should be smiled at like that'). On an empty stage, Aschenbach exclaims 'I love you.'

Act II Aschenbach analyses his outburst. Scene 8: The Hotel Barber's shop. While trimming Aschenbach's hair, the garrulous barber mentions 'the sickness'. Scene 9: The pursuit. Aschenbach crosses to Venice where people are reading notices advising precautions against infection. In a newspaper he reads denials of rumours of cholera in Venice. He follows the Polish family into St Mark's and later in a gondola ('They must not leave . . .'). He is in thrall to Tadzio. Scene 10: The Strolling Players. At the hotel, Aschenbach attends an entertainment by strolling players. He taxes their leader about the plague, but is rebuffed. Scene 11: The Travel Bureau. An English clerk is frank with Aschenbach: there is cholera and he should leave. Scene 12: The Lady of the Pearls. Aschenbach decides to warn Tadzio's mother, but he cannot bring himself to speak. Scene 13: The dream. In his sleep he hears the voices of Apollo and Dionysus, who depict the struggle in his mind. Scene 14: The empty beach. Aschenbach watches Tadzio and his friends as they play games desultorily. Scene 15: The Hotel Barber's shop. Aschenbach has his hair dyed and his face made up. Scene 16: The last visit to Venice. Rejuvenated, Aschenbach takes a gondola to Venice, jauntily singing the youths' song from Scene 2. He again trails the Polish family but loses them. Buying strawberries, he finds them musty. In a soliloquy he recalls Socrates ('Does beauty lead to wisdom, Phaedrus?'). Scene 17: The departure. The guests are leaving the hotel. Aschenbach goes to the deserted beach where Tadzio loses a fight with one of his friends. Aschenbach calls out and Tadzio beckons him, but the writer slumps dead in his chair.

Death in Venice is a *tour de force* of Britten's compositional skill. The long role of Aschenbach combines a Monteverdi-like recitative with Schoenbergian *Sprechstimme* and Mahlerian melody. The atmosphere of decay and decadence is as uncannily evoked as are the sounds of Venice itself. Britten again employs three strata of sound: piano accompaniment for the recitatives, a gamelan percussion for Tadzio and his friends, and the full orchestra for Venice and for the other characters. The silent Polish family are dancers. For the Voice of Apollo a counter-tenor is used. Thus the fantasy of *A Midsummer Night's Dream* and the austerity of the parables are tributaries flowing into this rich and compelling elegy.

RECORDING Bowman, Pears, Shirley-Quirk, English Opera Group, ECO, Bedford, Decca, 1974: the original cast, but with some cuts in the score which Britten later restored
VIDEO Chance, Tear, Opie, Glyndebourne Touring Ch and O, Jenkins, Virgin, 1989
EDITIONS f.s., Faber Music, 1979; v.s., Faber Music, 1974

BIBLIOGRAPHY Humphrey Carpenter, *Benjamin Britten: A Biography*, Faber, 1992; John Evans, Philip Reed and Paul Wilson (eds), *A Britten Source Book*, Britten–Pears Library, 1987; Peter Evans, *The Music of Benjamin Britten*, Dent, 1979; David Herbert (ed.), *The Operas of Benjamin Britten*, Hamish Hamilton, 1979; Eric Walter White, *Benjamin Britten, His Life and Operas*; 2nd edn, John Evans (ed.), Faber, 1983; Christopher Palmer (ed.), *The Britten Companion*, Faber, 1984

M.K.

MAX BRUCH

Max Christian Friedrich Bruch; *b* 6 January 1838, Cologne; *d* 2 October 1920, Berlin

As a boy Bruch studied with Ferdinand Hiller, whose influence and musical taste were to dominate him throughout his life. At a time when choices were being made and sides taken, Bruch allied himself firmly with the classical camp that favoured the music of Spohr, Weber, Mendelssohn and Schumann, rather than the New German School of Wagner and Liszt. He believed in the beauty of melody (in particular folksong) and rejected progressive harmony and the destruction of tonality. He was famous during his lifetime as a composer of secular oratorios and works for violin and orchestra, earning his living as a conductor to courts (Koblenz, Sondershausen) and cities (Liverpool, Breslau) and only occasionally freelancing as a composer. His fame rests almost entirely on his First Violin Concerto in G minor (1867), together with the *Scottish Fantasy* and *Kol nidrei*. He ended his career as a respected teacher of composition at the Musikhochschule in Berlin. His three operas failed because of poor libretti, a weak sense of drama and his own uncompromising resistance to contemporary developments in musical form and harmony, though there is much to admire in the music of *Die Loreley*.

Die Loreley
The Loreley
Romantic opera in four acts, Op. 16 (2h 30m)
Libretto by Emanuel Geibel
Composed 1862, rev. 1887
PREMIERES 14 June 1863, Mannheim; UK: 18 February 1986, Collegiate Theatre, London
FULL ORCHESTRA including hp

Bruch's second opera is set in the wine-producing heartlands of the river Rhine. It is based on the legend of a jilted peasant girl who sells her soul to the spirits of the river in exchange for the power to exact murderous revenge on her lover by her seductive singing. Geibel's libretto was intended for Mendelssohn, who completed only three fragments before his death. Bruch had to convince Geibel of the worth of his opera, for the poet, in spite of publishing the libretto, had forbidden any attempt by other composers (including Marschner) to set it.

The opera comprises a succession of set numbers of arias and ensembles with occasional orchestrally accompanied recitative, much in the style of Weber. The short second act, during which Lenore, the Loreley, makes her pact with the river spirits, is reminiscent of Weber's Wolf's Glen scene in *Der Freischütz*, and reveals Bruch's gift for instrumental colour and melodic invention. The successful premiere did much for Bruch's reputation, but although the opera was performed in many German cities and abroad it soon disappeared from the repertoire. In 1887 the young Gustav Mahler conducted the revised version in Leipzig; the original version was revived in 1916 by Pfitzner in Strasburg.

EDITIONS   f.s./v.s., F. E. C. Leuckart, 1862

Other operas: *Scherz, List und Rache*, 1858; *Hermione*, 1872

BIBLIOGRAPHY   Christopher Fifield, *Max Bruch, His Life and Works*, Gollancz, 1988

C.F.

ALFRED BRUNEAU

Louis Charles Bonaventure Alfred Bruneau; *b* 3 March 1857, Paris; *d* 15 June 1934, Paris

At the Paris Conservatoire, Bruneau studied with Massenet. Following his mentor's example, Bruneau wrote mainly stage works. Of paramount influence was the work of Emile Zola, who became a close friend and collaborator, the literary inspiration of *Le rêve* and of eight further stage works. Of these, the most famous was *L'attaque du moulin* (1893) which reached 13 opera houses in addition to the Paris Opéra-Comique before the end of 1917. The libretto was based on a story in Zola's *Soirées de Medan*. Zola himself suggested the subject to Bruneau and also introduced a new character, the servant Marcelline, who, having had two sons killed by the enemy, curses war, horrible war, 'in a powerful appeal to reason and humanity'. The libretto was versified by Louis Gallet.

The Zola–Bruneau partnership was fruitful, but none of their later ventures proved comparably successful, not least because they had taken sides in the Dreyfus affair and made enemies. An unashamedly tonal musical realist himself, Bruneau branded the realism of Italian musical *verismo* as vulgar and without symbolism. He preferred to express nature – 'the truth, but illuminating it by thought, philosophy and a great love of humanity'. For 43 years he was, consecutively, music critic of *Gil Blas*, *Le Figaro* and *Le Matin*.

Operatic works: *Kérim*, 1886; *Le rêve*, 1891; *L'attaque du moulin*, 1893; *Messidor*, 1897; *L'Ouragan*, 1901; *Lazare*, (1902); *L'enfant roi*, 1905; *Naïs Micoulin*, 1907; *Les quatre*
journées, 1916; *Le roi Candaule*, 1920; *Le jardin du paradis*, 1921; *Angelo, tyran de Padoue*, 1928; *Virginie*, 1931

BIBLIOGRAPHY   Arthur Hervey, *Alfred Bruneau*, John Lane, 1907; Paul Landormy, *La musique française après Debussy*, Gallimard, 1943

F.A.

VALENTINO BUCCHI

b 29 November 1916, Florence; *d* 9 May 1976, Rome

Bucchi was a versatile, independent-minded composer, who refused to align himself consistently either with conservative orthodoxies or with avant-garde fashions. In his stage works he steered a distinctive and enterprising zigzag course between the worlds of opera and music theatre; he already showed an interest in the latter in the late 1930s, before he had finished his studies at the Florence Conservatory (where his teachers included Frazzi and Dallapiccola). The first fruit of this interest was *Il giuoco del barone* (1937–9) – a capriciously original *jeu d'esprit* based on a traditional Tuscan dice game, with pungent, playfully grotesque music.

In Bucchi's most widely known stage piece, *Il contrabbasso*, he reverted to a more straightforwardly operatic approach, while continuing to cultivate a personal vein of grotesque humour with melancholy undercurrents. But his interest in more experimental relationships between music and drama reasserted itself in the 'cantafavola' *Una notte in Paradiso* (1959–60), whose rapid 'montage' techniques reflect the work's origin as a radio opera. A culminating point of music-theatrical non-conformity was reached in the boldly controversial *Il coccodrillo* (1969–70): here Dostoevsky's famous satire about a man swallowed alive by a crocodile provides the nucleus for an episodic extravaganza in which song, speech, dance, mime, film projections, note clusters, quarter-tones and electronic means all play their parts.

Bucchi also wrote much for the concert hall, and was active as a critic, music administrator and teacher. His highly 'unauthentic' arrangements of early music – which include an exceedingly free adaptation (1951–3) of *Li gieus de Robin et de Marion* by the 13th-century *trouvère* Adam de la Halle – inevitably now seem dated, although one might legitimately regard some of them as, in effect, original compositions.

Il contrabbasso

The Double-bass

Grottesco in one act (three scenes) (50m)
Libretto by Mario Mattolini and Mauro Pezzati, after Chekhov's short story *Roman s kontrabasom* ('Romance with a Double-bass')
Composed 1953–4
PREMIERES   20 May 1954, Teatro della Pergola, Florence; UK: 27 April 1970, BBC Radio 3 (broadcast)

Chekhov's amusing, mildly *risqué* tale admirably suited Bucchi's special brand of humour. A double-bass player, on whom life is weighing rather heavily, sees a princess bathing in a lake. He is tempted to bathe there too: they both have their clothes stolen. Gallantly he lets the princess take refuge in his double-bass case, while he hides in the bushes. His fellow musicians, unaware of the seemingly abandoned case's new contents, take it to the castle where they are all to play at the princess's betrothal party. General puzzlement at her apparent disappearance changes to astonished outrage when the case is opened before the assembled company. Meanwhile the double-bass player, left alone with his instrument, seeks refuge in melancholy music under the cover of darkness: the local inhabitants think they hear the voice of an evil spirit or a soul in torment.

The music of *Il contrabbasso* ingeniously combines touches of neo-medieval semi-pastiche with a tonally ambiguous chromaticism making some use of modes of limited transposition (with results that are not, however, at all like Messiaen). There is, of course, a *concertante* double-bass part.

EDITION   v.s., Suvini Zerboni, 1954

Other operas and music-theatre works: *Il giuoco del barone* (music-theatre), 1939, (rev. 1955), 1958; *Laudes Evangelii* (choral ballet), 1952, (rev.), 1959; *Li gieus de Robin et de Marion*, 1953 (RAI broadcast), 1974; *Una notte in Paradiso* (radio opera), 1960 (RAI broadcast and stage), *Il coccodrillo*, 1970; edn of Monteverdi's *Orfeo*, 1967 (RAI broadcast), 1968 (RAI televised)
BIBLIOGRAPHY   Liliana Pannella, *Valentino Bucchi: anticonformismo e politica musicale italiana*, La nuova Italia, 1976

J.C.G.W.

JOHN BULLER
b 7 February 1927, London

Although Buller was trained as a chorister, he initially followed a career as an architectural surveyor, beginning to compose seriously only in the 1960s. In 1965 he attended a summer school led by Maxwell Davies, Birtwistle and Goehr, who provided him with much inspiration. Another influence is the writing of James Joyce. Among Joyce-inspired works is the theatre piece *The Mime of Mick, Nick and the Magpies* (1978), derived from *Finnegans Wake*, a piece Buller described at the time as 'my kind of opera'.

The Bacchae (1992) is Buller's first conventional opera, though it is unconventional in that most of the text is in ancient Greek. Based on the tragedy by Euripides, it recounts how Dionysus persuades Pentheus, King of Thebes, to spy on the activities of the Bacchae. He is discovered and savaged by the women. In a tense final scene Pentheus' mother realizes that it is not a lion's head she has borne home in triumph but her son's.

Buller's decision to preserve the Greek text was inspired by the natural rhythm and metre of the language, which he has aimed to echo in his music. This results in a score that is necessarily fragmentary, but that varies from states of violent energy to extreme stillness. Contrasting sound-worlds are used to represent opposing characters: brass instruments for Pentheus, more ethereal sounds for Dionysus.

BIBLIOGRAPHY   Stephen Pettitt, 'Digesting Buller's *Bakxai*', *Opera*, vol. 43 (1992), pp. 532–5

G.H.

EMIL BURIAN
Emil František Burian; *b* 11 June 1904, Plzen, Bohemia; *d* 9 August 1959, Prague

Emil Burian came from a musical family (his uncle was the tenor Karel Burian, known as Carl Burrian) and trained at the Prague Conservatory, graduating from Foerster's composition masterclasses in 1927. At the same time he was active in theatrical circles, as actor, dramaturg and most prominently as founder of the ensemble Voice Band, which performed at the ISCM festival in Siena in 1928. The mixed-media approach (the group combined music and recitation) and a committed political stance were characteristic of Burian's pre-war activities, which included music for films and his founding of Theatre D (1933). In 1941 Theatre D was disbanded for its political activities and Burian imprisoned. After the war Burian played an enthusiastic part in the new socialist state, as a Communist delegate to parliament and a writer of mass songs.

Burian established a reputation in many cultural fields: as playwright, poet, film and theatre director, designer and singer. His compositions included seven operas, incidental music, film music, ballets and songs. Most were ephemera written for fringe groups, though the most substantial, his opera *Maryša*, has proved surprisingly durable.

Maryša
Opera in five scenes (1h 45m)
Libretto by the composer, after the play by Alois and Vilém Mrštík
Composed 1938–9
PREMIERE   10 May 1939, Brno

The libretto is based on one of the best-known plays in the Moravian Realism movement (which produced Preissová's plays and thus the operas *Jenůfa* and *Eva*). Janáček himself considered the play as a possible operatic text, and Burian's opera is much nearer *Jenůfa* in its effective combination of folk elements and drama than the modernistic, satirical and lightweight pieces that make up the bulk of his stage works.

RECORDING   excerpts: Míková, Procházková, Mixová, Štěpánová, Votova, Otava, Jedlička, Smetana Theatre Ch and O, Krombholc, Supraphon, 1961

EDITION v.s., Státní hudební vydavatelství, 1964

Other operas: *Alladina and Palomid* (*Alladina a Palomid*), (1923), 1959; *Before the Going Down of the Sun* (*Před slunce východem*), (1923), 1925; *Master Ipokras*; *The Quack* (*Mistr Ipokras*; *Mastičkař*), 1926; *Bubu from Montparnasse* (*Bubu z Montparnassu*), (1927); *Opera from the Fair* (*Opera z pouti*), 1956; *I Beg Your Pardon* (*Račte odpustit*), 1956
BIBLIOGRAPHY Ladislav Šíp, *Česká opera a jeho tvůrci* (*Czech Opera and Its Creators*), Supraphon, 1983

J.T.

CHARLES BURNEY

b 7 April 1726, Shrewsbury, England; *d* 12 April 1814, Chelsea, London

Burney came to London in 1744, when Thomas Arne, *en route* from Dublin, took him as his apprentice. In 1746 the young aristocrat Fulke Greville engaged him as his music teacher and introduced him to society; he developed his connections with the Norfolk gentry during a spell as organist at King's Lynn in the 1750s. In 1760 he returned to London and set up as a fashionable music teacher, though he subsequently became more interested in literature; in 1770 and 1772 he undertook two extensive foreign tours to collect material for the massive *General History of Music* for which he is remembered today; this was published in instalments in 1776, 1782 and 1789. Burney was a friend of David Garrick and wrote for the theatre; his

Pen and ink drawing by John Nixon of Dr Charles Burney

Cunning Man, an adaptation of Rousseau's *Le devin du village*, was influential in its day.

Masques and operas Burney wrote or to which he contributed: *Robin Hood*, 1750; *Alfred*, 1751; *A Fairy Tale*, 1763; *The Cunning Man*, 1766
BIBLIOGRAPHY Percy A. Scholes, *The Great Dr Burney*, OUP, 1948; *rp*, Greenwood Press, 1971

P.H.

ALAN BUSH

Alan Dudley Bush; *b* 22 December 1900, London

Bush was a pupil of the composer Frederick Corder at the Royal Academy of Music; he also studied with John Ireland (1921–7). His early compositions were in an advanced idiom, abreast of the latest trends, but by the time he wrote his operas he had adopted a less complex, self-consciously national style. Bush embraced communism during the 1930s and his espousal of the People's Convention at the outbreak of war resulted in his proscription by the BBC, and in Vaughan Williams's much publicized support of him. If his political beliefs impeded his acceptance in the West, they certainly resulted in his operas being given lavish productions in East Germany and the USSR.

Before the war Bush composed the music for a succession of political pageants as well as an operatic setting, later destroyed, of Bulwer Lytton's *Last Days of Pompeii*. There are four mature operas and three children's operettas, all to libretti by his wife Nancy. All are on historical themes viewed from his particular political viewpoint: themes of exploitation and of working-class heroism.

Men of Blackmoor is about a pit strike in the 1820s, while *The Sugar Reapers* moves to a contemporary setting, in British Guyana at the time of the first elections and state of emergency in 1953. In his fourth opera, *Joe Hill – the man who never died*, Bush told the story of the militant American trade unionist whose principal weapon was his rousing songs. Hill was eventually framed in a murder charge and executed in 1915.

Wat Tyler

Opera in a prologue and two acts (2h 45m)
Libretto by Nancy Bush
Composed 1948–50
PREMIERES December 1950, London (extracts; with pf); 3 April 1952, East German Radio (broadcast); 6 September 1953, Leipzig; 19 June 1974, Sadler's Wells, London (Keynote Opera)

Wat Tyler was one of the four winners of the Arts Council's Festival of Britain Opera competition (1951), none of which were produced at the time. The opera tells the story of the Peasants' Revolt of 1381, and largely concerns their refusal to pay the poll tax. Bush initially promoted it himself but its productions in Germany set the pattern for his three

later operas, all written for East German opera
houses.

EDITION   v.ss., Henscherverlag, 1954; Novello, 1959

Other operatic works: *The Press-gang*, 1947; *The Spell
Unbound*, 1955; *Men of Blackmoor*, 1956; *The Ferryman's
Daughter*, 1964; *The Sugar Reapers, or Guayana Johnny*,
1966; *Joe Hill – the man who never died*, 1970
BIBLIOGRAPHY   Alan Bush, 'Problems of Opera', *Music*,
October 1952; Ronald Stevenson (ed.), *Alan Bush: An 80th
Birthday Symposium*, Bravura Publications, 1981

L.F.

GEOFFREY BUSH
b 23 March 1920, London

Bush's musical roots were five years as a choirboy at
Salisbury Cathedral and lessons in his teens with
John Ireland. After Oxford University, his professional career was as a teacher, at Oxford, London
and Aberystwyth universities. Simultaneously he
developed as a composer, pianist and a scholar,
undertaking pioneering research into British music
of the 19th century.

He is best known for his songs, but has also written
operas, choral, orchestral and church music. Bush has
said his passion is for the theatre, but laments that he
is prevented from writing for it by the inflexible
conditions of English operatic life.

Bush's first opera, *The Spanish Rivals*, after
Sheridan, was produced for puppets in Brighton
(1948) and at the Festival of Britain in 1951. The
composer subsequently withdrew it but the overture
survives as a concert piece. His later operas are also
intimate in character and for small forces. They
maintain a consistently swift pace, with an inventive
mixture of *parlando* and arioso in the voice-writing,
memorable turns of phrase, colourful orchestration
and effective set pieces.

Operas: *The Blind Beggar's Daughter*, 1952, rev. 1964; *If the
Cap Fits*, 1956; *The Equation*, 1968; *Lord Arthur Savile's
Crime*, 1972; *The Cat who went to Heaven*, 1974; *Love's
Labours Lost*, (1988)
BIBLIOGRAPHY   Geoffrey Bush, 'Librettist *malgré lui*', in
Left, Right and Centre, Thames Publishing, 1983, pp. 141–8

L.F.

FERRUCCIO BUSONI
Ferruccio Dante Michelangelo Benvenuto Busoni; *b* 1 April
1866, Empoli, Italy; *d* 27 July 1924, Berlin

Busoni enjoyed no regular schooling and matured
young. Although born in Italy, he grew up in a
central European cultural environment and spent
most of his adult life in German-speaking countries.
He acquired a specialist's knowledge of Bach and
Liszt, adored Mozart and felt a growing antipathy
towards Wagner. Schoenberg and many other
contemporary composers interested him intensely yet
he remained independent of all schools and 'isms',
hence acquiring a reputation for aloofness. During
his lifetime his worldwide reputation as a virtuoso
pianist completely eclipsed his activities as a
composer. In recent years a growing familiarity with
his works has helped penetrate the barrier of his
alleged intellectualism and established him as an
important figure in 20th-century music.

His first operatic project, based on Hertz's *King
René's Daughter*, dates from 1883; it came to nothing.
In 1884 Busoni negotiated unsuccessfully for a stage
adaptation of G. Keller's *A Village Romeo and Juliet*
(later set by Delius). During a period of study at
Leipzig, he began to compose his first opera, *Sigune,
oder Das stille Dorf*. He completed the short score
but orchestrated only the prelude before abandoning
the work in about 1892. Some of the music was
salvaged in the *Konzertstück*, Op. 31a, for piano and
orchestra, while an important motif, connected with
the building of a cathedral, appears in the *Pezzo
serioso* of the monumental Piano Concerto, Op. 39
(1904). The Piano Concerto closes with a chorus of
offstage male voices to a text from Oehlenschlaeger's
play *Aladdin*. This too is the remains of a theatrical
plan, a setting of *Aladdin*, 'not as an opera but as a
Gesamtkunstwerk with drama, music, dance [and]
magic'.

During the 1890s Busoni composed relatively
little, expending much energy on perfecting his piano
technique and widening his repertoire. The world
premiere of Verdi's *Falstaff* in 1893 revived his belief
in the future of Italian music and influenced his
developing style. During this period he worked on
the libretto for an opera about the Wandering Jew,
Ahasver. Although he later abandoned the plan, he
was to vary the central theme – the profoundly gifted
outsider who strives for immortality – in several
subsequent operatic projects, arriving at a definitive
version in *Doktor Faust*. Variants of the same idea
are to be found in *Der mächtige Zauberer*, *Leonardo
da Vinci* and *Dante*. Libretti or sketches for these
have survived; several further ideas for opera
subjects are mentioned in Busoni's copious
correspondence. Although Busoni made sporadic
approaches to writers such as G. B. Shaw,
D'Annunzio and Hofmannsthal, he actually wrote all
his opera texts himself, in German.

In 1907 Busoni published his controversial *Outline
of a New Aesthetic of Music* together with the libretto
of *Die Brautwahl*. Although *Die Brautwahl*
ultimately failed, Busoni was convinced that opera
was the 'universal domain' of contemporary music
and that his own musical language was intrinsically
theatrical. In the revised edition of the *New Aesthetic*
(1916) he elaborates on his idea of opera as a multi-
media spectacle which should 'rely on the incredible,
untrue or unlikely'. The opera of the future, he
writes, should use music only where it is
indispensable, particularly for the portrayal of the
supernatural or the unnatural, hence as a magic
mirror (opera seria) or a distorting mirror (opera
buffa). These theories, coupled with his earliest
memories of Italian puppet theatre, form the

Busoni with his masterclass – Kurt Weill, Walther Geiser, Luc Balmer and Vladimir Vogel (Berlin, 1922)

foundation of his three remaining operas, *Arlecchino*, a one-act 'musical caprice', its companion piece, *Turandot*, and *Doktor Faust*. *Turandot* and *Arlecchino* are grouped together as *la nuova commedia dell'arte*, while *Doktor Faust* is based largely on the early German puppet play of *Faust*.

During the years immediately preceding the First World War Busoni came into contact with progressive artists in various fields – the Viennese Secessionists, the Italian Futurists, D'Annunzio, Rilke, Schoenberg and Varèse, to name but a few – and himself entered on a period of experiment. The earliest studies for *Doktor Faust*, the *Sonatina seconda* for piano and *Nocturne symphonique*, Op. 43, for orchestra, date from this time. Apart from their dense, brooding textures, these works are notable for a new harmonic and rhythmic boldness and a distinctive instrumental chiaroscuro. The war effected a gradual change of direction, which finally led Busoni in 1918 to proclaim *Junge Klassizität* ('Young Classicality') as his artistic aim. 'Many experiments have been made in this young century,' he wrote. 'Now . . . it is time to form something durable again.' *Arlecchino* was his first brilliant essay in the new style.

Junge Klassizität is a concept that embraces many possibilities, for Busoni believed that the achievements of past generations could be combined with all new developments, and that a full flowering of Western music would hence lie in the distant future. The libretto of *Doktor Faust* expresses this belief in allegorical form and can be interpreted as the composer's definitive artistic and philosophical statement.

Die Brautwahl

The Bridal Choice
Musikalisch-fantastische Komödie in three acts and an epilogue (2h 30m)
Libretto: an adaptation by the composer of the novella by E. T. A. Hoffmann (1820)
Composed 1905–11
PREMIERE   13 April 1912, Stadttheater, Hamburg

Hoffmann's short story is an unlikely choice for an opera, for the plot is complex, the language verbose and the ending inconclusive. Busoni appears to have ignored the difficulties of adapting such a work for the stage. Composed soon after publication of the *New Aesthetic*, *Die Brautwahl* marks a significant turning-point in Busoni's musical development. Tonality is at no point abandoned, but the harmony is exploratory with frequent use of modes and unusual scales. A distinguishing feature of the score is Busoni's subtle integration of diverse extraneous elements (phrases of Carissimi or Rossini, folk music, synagogal chant, etc.). In weaker moments the musical language seems contrived and lacks convincing melodic invention; at its best it is imbued with an inimitably Busonian mysticism.

Edmund, a young painter, falls in love with Albertine, daughter of a wealthy Berlin merchant. Leonhard, a goldsmith and 'white' magician, is Edmund's protector, supporting him in his wooing of

Albertine while deploring his resultant lack of application to art. Both he and his rival, the Jew Manasse, are 'revenants', superhumans who have lived for over 300 years. Further rivals for Albertine's hand are Manasse's son Baron Bensch and Thusman, a pedantic minor official. The bridal choice is eventually decided, as in Shakespeare's *The Merchant of Venice*, by a trial with three caskets. Manasse is disgraced; Edmund wins Albertine and immediately sets off, at Leonhard's command, to study in Rome.

Busoni's brilliant score is almost overburdened with buffo scenes but also includes characteristically Hoffmannesque moments in which reality dissolves into pure fantasy. The vision of Albertine at a tower window and the climactic church vision in Act III, where Edmund is seen painting a great altarpiece, are the finest instances.

RECORDING Sukis, Handt, English, Fourié, Nimsgern, Ariè, Turin Ch and SO of Italian Radio, Previtali, Voce, 1975: in German, substantially cut
EDITIONS f.s./v.s. Harmonie, 1912

Arlecchino, oder Die Fenster

Arlecchino, or The Windows
Theatralisches capriccio in one act, Op. 50 (1h)
Libretto by the composer
Composed 1913–16
PREMIERES 11 May 1917, Stadttheater, Zurich; UK: 25 June 1954, Glyndebourne, Sussex

In the first draft libretto for *Doktor Faust* (1910), the serious action was intended to be interspersed with comic Casperle episodes, as in the 16th-century puppet plays. Busoni decided to write these in advance – a few loosely connected scenes in the spirit of a baroque operatic intermezzo, with Harlequin, the Italian equivalent to Casperle, as the leading figure and in a spoken role. Inspired by a visit to Bergamo, Harlequin's birthplace, and by hearing Schoenberg's *Pierrot lunaire*, he drafted a libretto during the summer of 1913. Work on the score was begun in December 1914 but abandoned three weeks later. In 1915 the extant musical material of *Arlecchino* was transformed into an orchestral work, the *Rondò arlecchinesco*, Op. 46. The first performance of the *Rondò* (5 March 1916, Rome) and a visit to a Rossini opera performed by marionettes encouraged Busoni to resume work on *Arlecchino*, which he completed in August 1916.

SYNOPSIS
The action is divided into four 'movements' and plays in Bergamo.

(1) Arlecchino as rogue. The hero dallies with the lovely Annunziata while her ageing husband, the tailor Ser Matteo, reads Dante. Arlecchino persuades him that the town is surrounded by barbarians, hurries him into the house, locks the door and pockets the key. The Abbate and Dottore pass by on their evening stroll. They are alarmed at Matteo's news and set off in haste to inform the mayor, but vanish instead into a nearby tavern.

(2) Arlecchino as warrior. Ser Matteo is called up for military service; Arlecchino, vaunting his military powers, allows him to take his copy of *La divina commedia* into battle.

(3) Arlecchino as husband: the hero's confrontation with his wife, Colombina. She scolds him for his infidelity, but he, feigning reconciliation, sneaks away. Leandro, cavalier and wandering minstrel, regales Colombina with extravagant, operatic advances. His wooing is interrupted by Arlecchino who challenges him to a duel. Colombina is escorted to safety; Leandro falls.

(4) Arlecchino as victor. The Abbate and Dottore, emerging from the inn with Colombina, stumble over Leandro's inert body. They hoist the wounded cavalier into a cart drawn by a donkey and set off for the infirmary. The coast is clear, and Arlecchino enters triumphantly to elope with Annunziata. Ser Matteo returns to his sewing table, deserted and baffled. The curtain falls and Arlecchino steps out to the footlights to outline his mocking philosophy of marriage.

The score bridges the stylistic gap between Busoni's experimental pre-war compositions and the later works written in the spirit of *Young Classicality*. The element of operatic parody in the score gives rise to quotations and allusions ranging from Gluck to Wagner, from *bel canto* to ragtime. These are unified through harmonic cunning and brilliant use of a modestly sized orchestra. Arlecchino's speech (rhythmically notated but unpitched) etches his role against the singing of the other characters, stylizing him into an *Übermarionette*, a comic mask whose counterpart is Faust, the tragic mask and *Übermensch*. The opera has enjoyed a certain enduring popularity, although the extreme rapidity of the action and the hard, brilliant effect of the music serve, even today, to alienate.

RECORDING Malbin, Dickie, Evans, Gester, Ollendorff, Wallace, Glyndebourne Festival O, Pritchard, HMV, 1954
EDITIONS f.s., Breitkopf und Härtel, 1918; v.s., Breitkopf und Härtel, 1917

Turandot

Chinesische fabel in two acts (1h 30m)
Libretto by the composer, after the play by Gozzi (1761)
Composed 1917
PREMIERES 11 May 1917, Stadttheater, Zurich; UK: 19 April 1966, BBC (radio broadcast); Ireland: 22 October 1988, Wexford Festival

In 1905 Busoni composed incidental music for Gozzi's *Turandot*; in 1911 Max Reinhardt staged a successful production of the play at the Deutsches Theater, Berlin, using Busoni's complete score. After one further production in London, which was by all accounts a travesty, Busoni resolved to rework his score into an opera. He put this plan into effect in 1917, reducing the orchestration and adding several new sections including arias for Kalaf, Turandot and Altoum, thus devising an apt companion piece for *Arlecchino*. The two works have little in common however, apart from the participation of *commedia dell'arte* characters.

After his father's defeat in battle, Kalaf flees to Peking in search of adventure. He is recognized by his former servant, Barak. The latter tells him of the emperor's daughter Turandot and of the cruel trials imposed on her suitors. Kalaf sees her portrait, is fired with love and storms off to the imperial palace. Truffaldino, chief eunuch, prepares the great hall for the new trial. Neither the Emperor Altoum nor his ministers, Pantalone and Tartaglia, are able to dissuade Kalaf, who steadfastly refuses to reveal his identity and insists on 'death or Turandot'. Turandot's confidante Adelma recognizes him as the man she once vainly loved. The riddle ceremony begins: before the third riddle, Turandot unveils herself, nearly dazzling Kalaf with her beauty. However he triumphs and, when Turandot refuses to fulfil her pledge of marriage, he counters with the riddle of his name. Nothing can soothe Turandot's rage until Altoum informs her that a messenger has brought him the coveted information; the treacherous Adelma, hoping to win Kalaf for herself, then whispers the name to her mistress. Turandot, dressed in mourning, reveals Kalaf's name to the assembled throng. But she also surprises and delights them by declaring her love for Kalaf and proclaims her wedding. The opera ends with a jubilant choral dance in praise of Buddha.

Much of the thematic material in Busoni's score, based on Chinese, Arabic, Byzantine, Indian and Nubian melodies, is taken from the *Geschichte der Musik* by the Austrian musicologist Ambros. As the notation of these melodies often implies a superficial similarity to Western music, Busoni detected in them a cultural link which evidently supported his theory of 'the Oneness of music'. In the same spirit, Busoni works the melody of 'Greensleeves' into his score in a delicate, harmonically ambiguous arrangement for female voices.

RECORDING Muszely, Geissler, Uhl, Gillig, Fehr, Ch and O of Swiss Radio, Ackermann, MR, 1959
EDITIONS v.s., Breitkopf und Härtel, 1917

Doktor Faust

Opera in two preludes, two intermezzi and three scenes (2h 30m)
Libretto by the composer
Composed 1916–24 (inc.); completed by Philipp Jarnach (1925) and Antony Beaumont (1984)
PREMIERES Jarnach version: 21 May 1925, Dresden, Sachsisches Staatstheater; UK: 17 March 1937, Queen's Hall, London (concert); US: 1974, Nevada (Opera Guild); Beaumont version: 2 April 1985, Teatro Comunale, Bologna; UK: 25 April 1986, Coliseum, London
CAST Faust *bar*, Mephistopheles *t*, Wagner *b*, Duke of Parma *t*, Duchess of Parma *s*, Master of Ceremonies *b*, Gretchen's Brother *bar*, Lieutenant *t*, 3 Students from Cracow *t*, 2 *bar*, Theology Student *bar*, Law Student *b*, Student of Natural Philosophy *bar*, Beelzebub *t*, Megaeros *t*, Gravis *b*, Levis *bar*, Asmodus *bar*, Student *t*, Poet *spoken role*, Helen of Troy *silent*, Boy *silent*; offstage: 3 *s*; *satb* chorus of churchgoers, soldiers, courtiers, huntsmen, Catholic and Lutheran students, countryfolk; dancers
LARGE ORCHESTRA including 2 hp, cel, solo organ

Busoni consciously conceived *Doktor Faust* as his most significant work and his life's crowning achievement. Before finally deciding on *Faust* he had actively considered several alternatives, including the Wandering Jew, Leonardo da Vinci and Don Juan. He wrote the libretto between 1910 and 1915, the major portion coming to him impulsively during Christmas of 1914. Work on the score was begun in 1916, although the first musical studies for the opera date from 1912. Ill health began to impede Busoni's progress from 1921 onwards and when he died in 1924 two substantial passages were still incomplete, the apparition of Helen of Troy to Faust in Scene 2 and the closing monologue of the final scene. In 1974, hitherto unknown sketches for these missing sections were bequeathed to the Prussian State Library in Berlin by Philipp Jarnach. Antony Beaumont's completion, based on this material, comes closer to Busoni's own concept than Jarnach's hastily written interpretation.

SYNOPSIS

The opera opens with an orchestral introduction (*Symphonia*), in which invisible voices chime out the word 'Pax' like bells, and a spoken prologue in which the poet outlines the genesis of the libretto and stresses its puppet origins. The opening scenes take place in Faust's study at Wittenberg. Wagner, his factotum, admits three students from Cracow, who bring a magic book, *Clavis Astartis Magica*. Following the instructions of the book, Faust summons the servants of Lucifer; they appear to him as six tongues of fire. Mephistopheles, the highest of them, claims to be 'swifter than the thoughts of man'. He draws up a pact which Faust signs with his own blood, against an offstage chorus of Eastertide churchgoers. Faust collapses. The scene changes to a Romanesque chapel (scenic intermezzo), where Gretchen's brother vows to revenge himself on Faust. Mephistopheles engineers his brutal murder.

For the main body of the work the scene changes to the ducal park in Parma. As climax to the duke's wedding celebrations, Faust is presented as a celebrity and astonishes the guests with magic tricks. He conjures up three visions from antiquity (Samson and Delilah, Solomon and the Queen of Sheba, Salome and John the Baptist) which express his love for the duchess. With the aid of Mephistopheles he soon succeeds in winning her. The duchess sings her infatuation for Faust and flees with him. Disguised as court chaplain, Mephistopheles advises the duke to remarry, raising his clawed hand in ghastly benediction. A sombre orchestral sarabande marks the turning-point in the drama (symphonic intermezzo). In a tavern in Wittenberg, Faust mediates in an argument between Catholic and Protestant students, but his words lead only to uproar and dissent. Mephistopheles, disguised as a courier, brings the dead body of the duchess's child. He sets it alight and out of the flames emerges Helen of Troy. Faust tries in vain to grasp the visionary figure. Again he is confronted by the students from Cracow, who tell him that he is to die at midnight. The scene changes to Wittenberg town

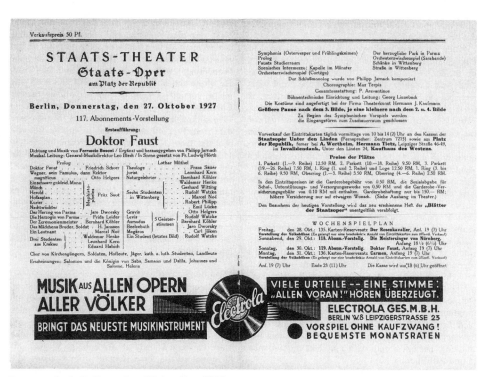

Programme for the Berlin premiere of Doktor Faust *(1927)*

square, snow is falling. Mephistopheles, as night-watchman, calls the hour: it is ten o'clock. Students skittishly serenade Wagner, who has succeeded Faust as rector of the university. Faust gives alms to a beggarwoman but she is revealed as the ghost of the duchess, who urges him to 'finish the work before midnight'. Faust transfers his soul to the dead child, dying as midnight strikes. The child arises in his place and strides out into the night. Mephistopheles is defeated.

The score is assembled from numerous musical studies, ranging from unfinished fragments (lieder, piano pieces, etc.) to substantial published works. Diverse as the sources are, they are unified by a 'Faustian' musical vocabulary: tonal music of extreme harmonic subtlety, with predominantly polyphonic textures and clear, sophisticated orchestral sonorities.

Busoni distinguished between Wagnerian music drama and his own (epic) theatre, in which words and music are intended to fulfil their own, separate functions. In 1922 he published his essay 'Outline of a Preface to the Score of *Doktor Faust*', in which he stressed that each section of his score is shaped into an organic, if unorthodox symphonic form: the festivities at Parma are formed into a dance suite, the tavern scene features a scherzo, chorale and fugue. The introspective, Faustian element is countered in each main scene by lighter, extrovert episodes; hence

the work can be understood as a mystery play, part folk festival, part Passion. Among those rarified stage works concerned with artistic creativity and higher philosophical questions (such as Wagner's *Die Meistersinger*, Schoenberg's *Moses und Aron*, Pfitzner's *Palestrina*) it occupies a prominent place.

RECORDING Jarnach version: Hillebrecht, Cochran, de Ridder, Fischer-Dieskau, Grundheber, Kohn, Bavarian Radio Ch and SO, Leitner, DG, 1969: substantially cut
EDITIONS v.s., Breitkopf und Härtel, 1925; Beaumont version: v.s., Breitkopf und Härtel, 1984

Other operatic work: *Sigune oder Das stille Dorf* (not orch.), (1892)
BIBLIOGRAPHY Antony Beaumont, *Busoni the Composer*, Faber, 1985; Antony Beaumont, 'Busoni and the Theatre', *Opera*, vol. 37 (1986), pp. 384–91; Antony Beaumont, 'Busoni's *Doctor Faust*. A Reconstruction and its Problems', *MT*, vol. 127 (1986), pp. 196–9; Edward J. Dent, *Ferruccio Busoni*, Eulenberg, 1933; 2nd edn, 1974; Edward J. Dent, 'Busoni and His Operas', *Opera*, vol. 5 (1954), pp. 391–7

A.C.W.B.

SYLVANO BUSSOTTI
b 1 October 1931, Florence, Italy

Bussotti emerged with precocious talents from a family background widely devoted to the arts (his brother and uncle were both painters), and a sense of theatre runs deep in his work. His scores are visual events in themselves, and insistently assert an idiosyncratic mixture of aestheticism and eroticism. Despite some experiments with marionette theatre in the mid-1950s, his first incursion into musical theatre in the strict sense was *La Passion selon Sade* (1965–6). During the next decade, this concern became so central to his work that since 1976 all of his projects have been grouped together under the title of BUSSOTTIOPERABALLET. As this term implies, Bussotti's concerns are all-embracing: he directs, designs, even on occasion choreographs. These talents are exercised both on his own compositions, and on the traditional operatic repertoire.

Because it is conceived as part of a total theatrical experience, Bussotti's music embraces at one extreme the concentrated sophistication of the post-war avant-garde, and at the other entirely pragmatic musical narration, or background. Although he exploits the voice's full exclamatory potential, his love of the Italian lyric tradition, and particularly of Puccini, lends a telling warmth to his melodic writing.

A fair proportion of BUSSOTTIOPERABALLET is, or can be theatrically presented as, dance work. Included here, therefore, are all those projects that involve singing actors.

La Passion selon Sade
(The) Passion According to Sade
Mystère de chambre in one act (1h 15m)
Text by the composer, after a sonnet by Louise Labe (1555)
Composed 1965–6
PREMIERE   5 September 1965, Teatro Biondo, Palermo

The cruel pun of the title provides warning enough. There is no plot as such. The mezzo-soprano part, written for Cathy Berberian, incorporates the contrasting characteristics of Sade's two heroines, Justine and Juliette, but does so through the words of the 16th-century poetess of erotic suffering, Louise Labe. Instrumentalists are drawn into the ambiguous, ritualistic action (presided over, in the original productions, by Bussotti himself as an 18th-century *maestro di cappella*).

The materials of the work, and of other concert pieces derived from it, were taken up by Bussotti in 1990 and developed to form *Intégrale Sade*, a film that constitutes the first of his *Tredici Trame* (see below).

RECORDING   concert extracts: Ross, Panni, Dischi Ricordi, 1979
EDITION   f.s., Ricordi, 1966, *rp*, 1975

Lorenzaccio
Melodramma romantico danzato in five acts (3h 15m)
Text assembled by the composer from multiple sources as an *hommage* to the drama by Alfred de Musset (1834)
Composed 1968–72
PREMIERE   7 September 1972, La Fenice, Venice

After completing *La Passion selon Sade*, Bussotti had planned a further exercise in the theatre of ritual gesture: a large-scale project dedicated to Italy, of which various portions survive as concert pieces. Subsequently, he veered towards a more narrative form of theatre, and with it embraced for the first time what has since proved an obsessive theme: the relation between the artist and his creations.

Here the artist is Alfred de Musset, travelling in Italy with George Sand, and through his imagination investing with new life a story of treachery and wild living in early 16th-century Florence. Throughout the complex succession of episodes, centring around the reprobate Lorenzino dei Medici (a mimed role), dialogue continues between the 19th and the 16th century, and as Bussotti populates the stage with the denizens of his own erotic fantasy world, the 20th century impinges in the form of bike boys in full regalia.

Much of the action is confined to dancers, mimes and actors – thus allowing the singers, who in terms of plot take minor roles, to expand lyrically on what unfolds around them. The score is one of Bussotti's richest, and has yielded two concert suites (*Lorenzaccio Symphonies I and II*, as well as embracing the pre-existent *Rara Requiem*).

EDITIONS   f.s./v.s., Ricordi, 1972; v.s., K. D. Grawe (ed.), Ricordi, 1973

Nottetempo
Night Time
Dramma lirico in a fragment (1h 50m)
Text by the composer and Romano Amidei, after Jacobus a Varagine, Michelangelo and Sophocles
Composed 1975–6
PREMIERE   7 April 1976, Teatro Lirico, Milan

A further essay on the inner world of the creative artist – in this case Michelangelo Buonarroti. Michelangelo is visited by apparitions from his past: Julius II, Tomaso Cavalieri, Vittoria Colonna. To illuminate Michelangelo's relations to those around him, Bussotti and Amidei suggest an astute parallel with Sophocles' *Philoctetes*: in delirium, Michelangelo becomes Philoctetes, cursed with an incurable wound; Julius II becomes Ulysses, who uses both deceit and force to get from him the bow and arrows of Hercules, and Antonio Mini becomes Neoptolemus, the confederate of Ulysses, finally overcome by conscience. The Sophoclean dimension also allows for one of Bussotti's happiest musical inventions in the work, the chorus of sailors – underlining the powerful presence of the chorus throughout the opera.

EDITION   f.s., Ricordi, 1977

Le Racine, pianobar pour Phèdre
Racine, Pianobar for Phaedra
A prologue, three acts and an *intermezzo* (1h 45m)
Text by the composer, after Jean Racine's tragedy *Phèdre* (1677)
Composed 1980
PREMIERE   9 December 1980, Piccola Scala, Milan

A first version of one of Bussotti's most remarkable ventures. Having fallen in love with Racine's play when he first saw it at the age of 20 in Paris, Bussotti had long intended to find his own musical and theatrical response to this disturbingly sympathetic presentation of an 'impossible' passion. Scored for voice, piano duet and bells, it is set in a sordid Parisian pianobar, in which those in the front row of the audience take their seats at tables and are served drinks. An old actress, who has played Phèdre so many times that she cannot get it out of her head, sees in every local gigolo another Hippolyte. Fragments of Racine echo provocatively among the bar's louche patrons, but it is the great monologues, set with deliberately 'psychoanalytic' intensity either for solo voice, or voice and piano, that focus the attention.

EDITION   f.s., Ricordi, 1980

Phèdre

Phaedra
Tragédie lyrique en trois actes avec un 'intermezzo' d'après Jean Racine (1h 30m)
Text: Italian adaptation by the composer
Composed 1980–88
PREMIERE   19 April 1988, Teatro dell'Opera, Rome

In transforming his *Pianobar* into a grand opera, Bussotti chose to play on cultural memory. The cast of characters remains constant throughout the work's three acts, but the historical setting changes. Acknowledging the Euripidean origins of Racine's tragedy, Act I is set in 'ancient Greece' – specifically taking its inspiration from a spectacular painting by Schinkel of the building of the Parthenon. Act II moves to the Hôtel de Bourgogne in 1677, for the first performance, before king and court, of *Phèdre*. Act III returns to Paris, and this century – in principle we are in 1931 (the year of Bussotti's birth), but as dawn breaks over Paris and over the dying Phèdre the Beaubourg Centre rises against the skyline. Contexts change: basic human passions do not.

Bussotti places Racine on stage throughout, singing phrases from his own drama underlining the ambiguities inherent in the fact that Phèdre's passion for her beautiful stepson is the product of a male imagination: at the end of Act II he sings, 'I cannot without horror look at myself in these mirrors.' A rich orchestration of the original piano part nevertheless leaves room for declamatory singing lines of exemplary clarity. In its synthesis of discipline (everything in the opera derives from a single series whose 12 notes echo Racine's Alexandrines) and fantasy, *Phèdre* constitutes one of Bussotti's most formidable achievements.

EDITION   f.s./v.s., Ricordi, 1988

L'ispirazione

Inspiration
Melodramma in three acts, after Ernst Bloch's story *Die gutmachende Muse* from *Spuren* (1930) (2h)
Text by the composer incorporating poems by Foscolo, Joyce, and Trakl

Composed 1986–8
PREMIERE   26 May 1988, Teatro Communale, Florence

The outlines of Bloch's story, faithfully respected by Bussotti, are simple: an old, hen-pecked, increasingly alcoholic violinist in an 18th-century court orchestra is both mocked and pitied by his colleagues. At home he quarrels with his wife, shouts at his daughter, and locks himself away to compose music too challenging for hope of recognition. Thrown out of the orchestra for obstructive behaviour, he locks himself away again; his daughter meanwhile meets success as a singer. One day the theatre director sends round his carriage. Arriving at the theatre, the old violinist recognizes the music: it is his own opera, secretly copied by his loving daughter, and now presented with her in the leading role.

Bussotti projects this story into a science-fiction framework: a future where all pasts and futures are available (for time is circular, and human behaviour does not change) presided over by Harno Lupo, Master of Music and Time, and Futura, Mistress of Theatre and Space. A visually kaleidoscopic, almost cinematographic style of production is demanded.

EDITIONS   f.s./v.s., Ricordi, 1988

Bozzetto siciliano

Sicilian Sketch
Opera in one act
Text adapted by the composer from the novella *Amore e morte*, from *Storielle siciliane* by Emanuele Navarro della Miraglia
Composed 1989
PREMIERE   18 April 1990, Teatro Massimo Bellini, Catania

The ninth in a series of *Tredici Trame* (*Thirteen Plots*), a series of works planned by Bussotti to embrace a variety of forms of spectacle (see *La Passion selon Sade* and *Intégrale Sade* above), and in each to sketch out concisely and graphically a plot. In this instance the story is as old as the hills. Martino, a peasant, married but jealous, meets an old friend on the road. He invites him home. Friend and wife are irresistibly attracted. Discovering their infidelity, Martino shoots both. The *hommage* to *verismo* extends beyond choice of plot to the score, with its echoes of late 19th-century emotional fervour.

EDITION   f.s., Ricordi, 1990

Other operatic work: *Le rarità, Potente*, 1979

BIBLIOGRAPHY   Jürgen Maehder, 'Bussottioperaballet: sviluppi della drammaturgia musicale Bussottiana', *NRMI*, vol. 18 (1984), no. 3, pp. 441–68

D.O.-S.

NIGEL BUTTERLEY

Nigel Henry Butterley; *b* 13 May 1935, Sydney, Australia

As well as being a composer Butterley is an accomplished pianist, with a particular affinity with

20th-century works. He studied at the New South Wales Conservatorium and joined the Australian Broadcasting Commission in 1952, while still a student. In 1961 he went overseas, where study with Priaulx Rainier in England and travel in Italy had a profound effect on his compositional style. In 1966 he won the Italia Prize for his oratorio *In the Head the Fire*. He now teaches composition at the Newcastle (NSW) Conservatorium.

Butterley has written many vocal works and a music-theatre piece, *The Owl* (1983), which is a dramatic monologue for soprano and small ensemble. His two-act opera *Laurence Hargrave Flying Alone*, inspired by a sculpture of the Australian aviation pioneer, was commissioned and produced (24 September 1988, Sydney) by the NSW Conservatorium for the Australian Bicentenary. In keeping with the introspective nature of much of Butterley's work, his opera concentrates on the aspirations and inner life of the hero, using puppets and a dancer, among other devices, to achieve this effect.

BIBLIOGRAPHY   Essay by David Swale in Frank Callaway and David Tunley (eds), *Australian Composition in the 20th Century*, OUP, 1987

A.I.G.

FRANCESCA CACCINI

b 18 September 1587, Florence; *d* after 1637

Francesca Caccini, daughter of Giulio, performed in her father's *concerto di donne* and took part in the festivities for the wedding of Maria de' Medici and Henry IV of France in October 1600. She made her début as a theatrical composer with a tournament, *La stiava*, to a text by Michelangelo Buonarroti *il giovane*, staged before the Medici court in Pisa in early 1607.

Francesca entered court employment on 15 November 1607, despite attempts to lure her from Florence by Prince Ferdinando Gonzaga of Mantua and Cardinal Montalto. She later toured widely as a singer and was regularly compared favourably with the best sopranos in Italy: her talents are apparent in her collection of solo songs printed in 1618. She also provided music for several Florentine court entertainments, often to texts by Buonarroti, whose letters and poetry to her suggest that he acted as her patron. But despite her reputation, the death of her husband, the musician Giovanni Battista Signorini, in December 1626 and increasing squabbles among the court musicians led her to retire from service by May 1627.

La liberazione di Ruggiero dall'isola d'Alcina

The Liberation of Ruggiero from Alcina's Island
Balletto rappresento in musica (2h)
Libretto by Ferdinando Saracinelli, after Canto VI of the epic poem *Orlando furioso* by Ariosto (1516)
PREMIERE 3 February 1625, Villa Poggio Imperiale, Florence

La liberazione was staged for the visit of Prince Władisław of Poland (it may have been performed in Warsaw in 1628), and the plot is a thinly veiled allegory of his recent notable victory over the Turks. It is set entirely to music, combining drama and dance, and reflects a shift away from the mythological subject matter of early Florentine opera towards themes drawn from epic poetry; Ariosto's epic became a standard source for later baroque operas (most notably in Handel's *Alcina*).

Ruggiero is freed from his enchantment with the wicked sorceress, Alcina, who is revealed as a monster. Her former lovers, turned into plants and trees, are also liberated, and all rejoice in the victory of good over evil. The entertainment concluded with a grand balletto a cavallo, a cavalry ballet of a type popular in Florence from the mid-1610s onwards.

Caccini's music is clearly Florentine in orientation, and her recitatives follow the lyrical manner of her father. However, arias are more predominant, with tuneful melodies, particularly in triple time, characteristic of the newer operatic style.

EDITIONS   D. Silbert (ed.), *Smith College Music Archives*, vol. 7, Northampton, Massachusetts, 1945

7 other stage works lost
BIBLIOGRAPHY   A. Solerti, *Musica, ballo e drammatica alla corte medicea dal 1600 al 1637*, Florence, 1905; *rp*, New York, 1968

T.C.

GIULIO CACCINI

b 8 October 1551, Tivoli; *buried* 10 December 1618, Florence

Caccini was closely associated with the 'invention' of opera in Florence over the 1600s, competing for precedence with his colleague Jacopo Peri. Although his family was from Tuscany, he was born near Rome and trained as a choirboy in the Cappella Giulia (in St Peter's). In November 1565 he was recruited by the Medici ambassador in Rome to sing the role of Psyche in the intermedi accompanying Francesco d'Ambra's comedy *La cofanaria*, performed at the wedding of Prince Francesco de' Medici and Johanna of Austria (Florence, 1565–6). By all accounts Caccini was a great success, and he stayed in Florence for the rest of his life, employed by the court as a tenor, instrumentalist and composer. He also directed his concerto di donne, a female vocal group modelled on the more famous Ferrarese ensemble and including his second wife, Margherita, and his two daughters, Settimia and Francesca.

Caccini participated in the magnificent festivities celebrating the marriage of Grand Duke Ferdinando I de' Medici and Christine of Lorraine in 1589 (a solo song for the fourth intermedio of Girolamo

Bargagli's comedy *La pellegrina* survives in manuscript). But in the 1590s he was dismissed from service because of court intrigue. He sought positions in Rome, Ferrara and Genoa, but never, it seems, left Florence. Caccini took advantage of the festivities for the wedding of Maria de' Medici and Henri IV of France in October 1600 to regain favour at the court. He provided the bulk of the music for the grand musico-dramatic spectacle forming the climax of the festivities, *Il rapimento di Cefalo* (performed in the Uffizi theatre), and he insinuated his music into the performance of Peri's *Euridice*. He also raced Peri to the press, completing his own setting of *Euridice* and publishing it some six weeks before Peri's score appeared.

Il rapimento di Cefalo, to a libretto by Gabriello Chiabrera, is one of those curious mixed genres typical of early opera. Its five-part structure, mythological subject matter and grandiose scenic effects are characteristic of the court intermedi, and as with the intermedi the music was a collaborative effort (Caccini, with the lion's share, was joined by Stefano Venturi del Nibbio, Luca Bati and Piero Strozzi). Moreover, and unlike *Euridice*, the emphasis was less on the drama than on a spectacular display of pro-Medici propaganda. But the work was sung throughout, and clearly Caccini made use of the new recitative style. He planned to publish the score but only the final chorus (alternating solo voices and six-part choir) survives. The audience at the first performance praised the scenic effects but, as with Peri's *Euridice*, they found the new recitative somewhat tedious.

Caccini was reinstated in court service shortly after the 1600 wedding, and in 1602 he issued an important collection of songs for solo voice and basso continuo, one of the first to be printed, called *Le nuove musiche*. Its important preface outlines Caccini's claim to have developed a new style of vocal declamation which 'moved the affect of the soul'. His setting of *Euridice* was performed complete later that year. It made no great impression, although the performers were rewarded with a roasted boar. Nevertheless, Caccini played an increasingly dominant role in the court music, taking advantage of Peri's apparently declining popularity, and he consolidated his reputation by a successful tour to Paris with his family from 1604 to 1605. He then had charge of the music for the festivities for the wedding of Prince Cosimo de' Medici and Maria Magdalena of Austria in October 1608: he produced a number of settings (now lost) reminiscent, it seems, of the music for the 1589 festivities. Caccini continued to be associated with music at court during the reign of Grand Duke Cosimo II (1609–21), but he left court entertainment to Marco da Gagliano and Jacopo Peri. Ill-health and waning fortunes eventually forced him into retirement.

Caccini was evidently both cantankerous and litigious, and his polemical prefaces help document the squabbles between himself, Peri and Emilio de' Cavalieri over precedence in creating the new opera and solo song. Certainly his role in early opera is less significant than Peri's, despite the enthusiastic claims

of his pupils and supporters (notably Severo Bonini). However, the graceful songs in his *Le nuove musiche* gave an important impetus to the stylistic changes occurring during the 1600s.

Euridice

Favola in musica in a prologue and one act (2h)
Libretto by Ottavio Rinuccini, after Book VIII of Ovid's *Metamorphoses*
PREMIERES 6 October 1600 (music mainly by Peri) and 5 December 1602, Palazzo Pitti, Florence; UK: 20 March 1985, Nereid Gallery, British Museum, London (New London Consort)

Title page of the first edition of Caccini's Euridice *(Florence, 1600)*

Caccini was understandably anxious to associate himself with the latest musico-dramatic experiments in Florence. Like Peri, he was supported by Jacopo Corsi, the leading music patron in Florence, although he does not seem to have been a direct party to Corsi's, Peri's and Rinuccini's earliest attempts at opera (his claim to have composed a setting of Rinuccini's *Dafne*, made in the preface to his *Nuove musiche e nuova maniera di scriverle* of 1614, is almost certainly false). In his own setting of *Euridice*, Caccini followed the text provided by Rinuccini for Peri, and he imitated Peri's new recitative. However, he was temperamentally more suited to an elegant lyricism than to exploiting emotional and dramatic intensity, and although Caccini's ornate score may be appealing, Peri's setting is undoubtedly more effective.

RECORDING Dietschy, Foronda, Instrumental Ensemble, Zayas, Arion, 1980
EDITIONS L'Euridice... composta in musica, Florence, 1600; facsimile, Bologna, 1968; A. Coan (ed.), Florence, 1980

Other surviving stage works: 'Io che dal ciel farei cader la luna' (song from Intermedio IV for G. Bargagli's La pellegrina), 1589; Il rapimento di Cefalo, 1600 (one chorus in Caccini's Le nuove musiche, 1602); music for the intermedi for M. Buonarroti's Il giudiz io di Paride (lost), 1608
BIBLIOGRAPHY Tim Carter, 'A Florentine Wedding of 1608', Acta musicologica, vol. 55 (1983), pp. 89–107; Tim Carter, 'Giulio Caccini (1551–1618): New Facts, New Music', Studi musicali, vol. 16 (1987), pp. 13–31; B. R. Hanning, Of Poetry and Music's Power: Humanism and the Creation of Opera, UMI Research Press, 1980; H. W. Hitchcock (ed.), 'Giulio Caccini: Le nuove musiche (1602)', Recent Researches in the Music of the Baroque Era, vol. 9, Madison, 1970

T.C.

CHARLES WAKEFIELD CADMAN

b 24 December 1881, Johnstown, Pennsylvania, US; d 30 December 1946, Los Angeles, US

Cadman's significance lies in his introduction of indigenous American music into his works, pursuing a tradition of self-consciously national American opera in the first quarter of the 20th century.

His first American-Indian work was the set of four American Indian Songs (1907), one of which, 'From the land of the sky-blue water', was a particular success, selling over 2 million copies. However, his serious interest in the music of the American Indians began with a visit in 1909 to the Omaha tribe, when he recorded their ceremonial songs and flute music on a primitive phonograph. This led directly to the composition of his first opera, The Land of the Misty Water, and to piano and orchestral works (notably the Thunderbird Suite, 1914) which cited actual Indian motifs and melodies rather than simply simulated their mood.

Cadman's most important opera is Shanewis, or The Robin Woman (1918) which traces the story of an Indian girl who goes to New York to study music and falls in love with a white man; he follows her back to her reservation but is shot by her brother with a poisoned arrow. The opera quotes several Indian songs and was a great success, securing an unprecedented second staging at the Metropolitan Opera in 1919. From A Witch of Salem (1926) onwards Cadman's interest in Indian music waned. His later works remain recognizably American – as founder of the Hollywood Bowl summer concerts and organizer of the Congress for the

Encouragement of American Music, Cadman was an important force in American music. His last performed opera, The Willow Tree (1933), was written for radio – a fact that makes the highly conservative musical style at which the composer had arrived seem all the more outmoded.

Operas and operettas: The Land of the Misty Water, (1912), rev. as Ramala (n.d.); Shanewis, or The Robin Woman, 1918; The Garden of Mystery, (1916), 1925; The Ghost of Lollypop Bay, 1926; Lelawala, 1926; A Witch of Salem, 1926; The Belle of Havana, 1928; South in Sonora, 1932; The Willow Tree, 1933
BIBLIOGRAPHY David Ewen, 'Charles Wakefield Cadman', in American Composers: A Biographical Dictionary, Hale, 1982

G.H.

JOHN CAGE

John Milton Cage; b 5 September 1912, Los Angeles, US; d 12 August 1992, New York

John Cage was a magnetic influence as an avant-garde figure since the 1950s. He combined the careers of composer, writer, graphic artist and philosopher in his own inimitable way. His father was an inventor and Arnold Schoenberg categorized the son as 'an inventor of genius'.

Cage's first compositions were exquisite miniatures, often related to dance, for piano or percussion. His invention of the prepared piano was crowned with the Sonatas and Interludes (1946–8), a classic of unorthodox keyboard music which already revealed oriental influences. These became more marked when Cage became involved with Zen Buddhism which caused him to give up responsibility for controlling many aspects of his compositions. Through using chance operations based on the I Ching, he regarded himself as 'the maker of a camera who allows someone else to take the picture'.

Cage's contribution to opera grew out of his interest in dramatic happenings, both in concert and elsewhere. In 1952 Cage arrived at his silent piece, 4' 33", in which no sounds are intentionally made by any performers taking part for that length of time; also in 1952 at Black Mountain College he initiated a happening, involving all kinds of artists in simultaneous, uncoordinated activity.

Cage's Theatre Piece (1960) confirmed his notion that a musical performance implies theatre. So did environmental assemblies such as HPSCHD (1967–9) and Musicircus (1967). Cage's literary interests were always important – at first Gertrude Stein and later Henry Thoreau and James Joyce. When Cage was commissioned by Westdeutscher Rundfunk to write a multi-media piece he produced Roaratorio, an Irish Circus on Finnegans Wake (1979), originally called a 'radio play'. This consisted of several superimposed events related to each other only in the sense that they take place at the same time.

The need for the spectator to be able to accept anything, select for himself and adjust to it had been

John Cage in the early 1970s

established through Cage's other work for more than a generation before he wrote his operatic works, although this idea has remained controversial. The Austrian composer Kurt Schwertsik said that 'You have to be in good shape to listen to Cage!' It is possible to trace the influence of Cage in various types of what Philip Glass calls 'non-narrative' opera as well as in the other arts singly or combined. He explained part of the reasoning behind his anarchic compositions: 'The Europeans have been sending Americans their operas for the past 150 years, and now I'm sending them all back!'

Europeras 1 and 2

Two operas in one act (1h 30m; 45m)
Text selected by the composer from the operatic repertoire
Composed 1985–7
PREMIERES 12 December 1987, Schauspielhaus, Frankfurt; US: 14 July 1988, State University of New York, Purchase (Pepsico Summerfare)

Cage called *Europeras 1 and 2* 'a circus of independent elements: music, programme notes, lights, costume, décors, action'. His desire to keep each element discrete led Cage to select pre-existing music so that the process of composition would be separate from the content. The singers (ten in *Europera 1*, nine in 2) are consequently given arias from over 60 (non-copyright) operas ranging from Gluck to Puccini. They perform these at random regardless of each other, controlled only by a stopwatch which determines when each extract should start and finish. Similar principles are applied to the dancing – although collisions must be avoided – and to the décor, sets and projected images.

EDITION Peters, 1987

Europeras 3 and 4

(1h 15m; 30m)
Composed 1990
PREMIERE 17 June 1990, Almeida Theatre, London

Europeras 3 and 4 are, like *Europeras 1 and 2*, aleatoric pieces made up of fragments from the standard opera repertoire. *Europera 3* requires six singers, twelve record-players playing '78s and two pianists; *Europera 4* requires two singers, one wind-up gramophone and a pianist. Cage called *Europera 3* 'thick, dramatic and Wagnerian' whereas *Europera 4* is 'simple and pleasant, though (after *Europera 3*) elaborate and Mozartian'.

EDITION Peters, 1990

Europera 5

Opera in one act (1h)
Composed 1991
PREMIERES 1991, SUNY, Buffalo Department of Music, Buffalo; UK: 9 October 1992, Blackheath Concert Halls, London

To the forces of *Europera 4* this work adds a local radio station. The stage area is divided into 68 squares. The singers each select five operatic arias which they perform (unaccompanied) at times and on squares specified by Cage. The pianist plays operatic transcriptions, the gramophone old opera recordings (Gigli, etc.). The singers are each required to wear an animal mask once at precise points while remaining silent. Though *Europera 5* can be staged anywhere – from a small room to a whole town – the setting always assumes great importance: a typically Cageian paradox.

EDITION Peters, 1991

BIBLIOGRAPHY Cage's own writings: *Empty Words*, 1979; *Themes and Variations*, 1982; *X*, 1983, Wesleyan University Press; *I–VI: The Charles Eliot Norton Lectures*, Harvard University Press, 1990; *Muzik-Konzepte Sonderband: John Cage*, vol. 2, Edition text kritik, 1990

P.D.

ANTONIO CAGNONI

b 8 February 1828, Godiasco, nr Voghera; *d* 30 April 1896, Bergamo, Italy

Cagnoni was one of the less obviously talented members of Verdi's generation. Of his first three stage works written while he was still a student at the Milan Conservatory, one, *Don Bucefalo*, proved to be one of the last fruitful sprigs of Italian opera buffa, supplying comic basses with a favoured role for several years. None of his later comedies was as successful. Since a livelihood in the theatre continued to elude him, he accepted a number of positions with ecclesiastical institutions not far from Milan. He continued to write operas, however, until a few years before his death, the last five to texts by Ghislanzoni, the librettist of Verdi's *Aida*. Of this final group, only *Papà Martin* managed to circulate beyond Italy, reaching London and New York.

Cagnoni began as an imitator of the fluent comic style of Donizetti's *L'elisir d'amore* and *Don Pasquale*, but he lacked the firm grasp of dramatic values crucial to an opera composer. For a while, he sought to find his niche by imitating French *opéra comique*. The serious works are, for the most part, laborious and strained, while his efforts to stay abreast of the times – for instance, his increasing reliance on 'reminiscence' motifs – are rarely apposite or convincing. Boito wrote a devastatingly satirical review of Cagnoni's *Il vecchio della montagna* after its La Scala premiere in 1863. Cagnoni also wrote a number of sacred compositions, including the 'Quid sum miser' for the *Messa per Rossini* proposed by Verdi in 1868.

Operas: *Rosalia di San Miniato*, 1845; *I due savoiardi*, 1846; *Don Bucefalo*, 1847; *Il testamento di Figaro*, 1848; *Amori e trappole*, 1850; *Il sindaco babbeo*, 1851; *La valle d'Andorra*, 1851; *Giralda*, 1852; *La fioraia*, 1853; *La figlia di Don Liborio*, 1856; *Il vecchio della montagna*, 1860; *Michele Perin*, 1864; *Claudia*, 1866; *La tombola*, 1867; *Gli amori di Cleopatra*, (1870); *Un capriccio di donna*, 1870; *Papà Martin*, 1871; *Il duca di Tapigliano*, 1874; *Francesca da Rimini*, 1878; *Il re Lear*, (1893)
BIBLIOGRAPHY Carlo Schmidl, *Dizonario universale dei musicisti*, vol. 1, Casa Editrice Sonzogno, 1937

W.A.

ANTONIO CALDARA
b c. 1670, Venice; *d* 28 December 1736, Vienna

The fact that Caldara's life led him away from his native Venice to the northern imperial centre of Vienna says a good deal about the close cultural relationship the two cities enjoyed in the early 18th century. Vienna in this period was one of the greatest centres of Italian opera, and after his arrival there, Caldara's contribution to opera became prolific. As a boy Caldara sang in the choir at St Mark's in Venice, and learned a number of instruments; he probably studied with Legrenzi. His operatic activity had begun in Venice as early as 1689 with *L'Argene* to a libretto by Badi. During the late 1690s he collaborated on composite operas with Lotti, Ariosti and C.F. Pollarolo. In 1699 he left for Mantua, where he became maestro da chiesa e da teatro to the last duke, Ferdinando Carlo Gonzaga; here, too, he was responsible for a small number of stage works. Shortly before the duke's death in 1708, Caldara moved to Rome, where he had contacts developed from previous visits.

Caldara quickly won a place in the flourishing musical life of Rome – along with the Scarlattis, Handel and Corelli – but he soon departed when an invasion by the imperial forces threatened. He spent a short while in Barcelona at the Habsburg court of

Engraving of a scene from Metastasio's L'Olimpiade, *set by Caldara in 1733*

Charles III, where a number of his chamber operas were given. In 1709 Caldara returned to Rome to join the household of the Prince Ruspoli, who had earlier been Handel's patron. In the seven years he was associated with Ruspoli, Caldara composed large numbers of cantatas, operas and oratorios, not only for the prince but for other leading Roman patrons. In 1711 he travelled to Milan to greet his former patron, on his way to claim the imperial throne as Charles VI; he went on to Vienna, only to find that his hopes of a permanent appointment there were not – on this occasion – fulfilled. He returned to Rome to Prince Ruspoli for a few years, finally leaving for Vienna in 1716 on his appointment as vice-Kapellmeister at the Viennese court in succession to Fux. He was to remain there for the remainder of his exceptionally productive life.

About 60 dramatic works, mostly full-scale operas, date from Caldara's period in Vienna. The court demanded a constant flow of stage works to celebrate birthdays and name days, as well as Carnival each year. These works – most of which survive – were performed in Salzburg and Graz as well as in the imperial capital. Caldara was well rewarded for his industry, being paid larger sums than Fux, who was the actual Kapellmeister.

Caldara arrived in Vienna at a fortuitous moment: not only was the court actively encouraging operatic activity, but another Venetian settled in Vienna some two years later, Apostolo Zeno. Zeno was part of a movement to reform the operatic libretto, which he saw as a literary genre in its own right. He collaborated with Caldara over almost two decades, and it was probably this working relationship that established Caldara's originality as an operatic composer. Essentially, this reform of the libretto involved a greater concentration on realistic situations and characters, abandoning the artificially complex plots, full of bizarre happenings, expressed in magnificent machines, vacuous spectacle and showy arias, that had prevailed in earlier opera. The libretti used by Caldara in Vienna encourage the development of real characters, resulting in a decrease in the number of arias, in favour of lengthy recitatives; where the aria occurs, it is increasingly used at moments of reflection, while the majority of the dramatic action is borne by the recitatives. The number of characters is also restricted by the concern to portray each as a coherent personality, rather than a means to a dramatic end. Zeno's successor in these reforms was the poet Pietro Metastasio, who arrived in Vienna in 1730, and continued to develop the concept of opera as drama.

During Caldara's two decades in Vienna he was responsible for the original settings of 23 of the 25 opere serie written by both librettists. Although his operas failed to hold the stage after his death, some of the simpler songs from his works remained popular. His reputation today is dominated by the outstanding librettists with whom he worked, yet the esteem in which he was held at the Habsburg court indicates that Caldara was regarded as one of the most competent opera composers of his generation.

Operatic works (many ?lost): *L'Argene*, 1689; *Il Tirsi* (coll. with Lotti, Ariosti *et al.*), 1696; *La promessa serbata al primo*, 1697; *L'oracolo in sogno* (coll. with Quintavalle and C. F. Pollaroli), 1699; *Opera pastorale*, 1701, rev. as *La costanza in amore vince l'inganno*, 1710; *La Partenope*, 1701; *Gli equivoci del sembiante*, 1703; *Farnace*, 1703; *Paride sull'Ida, ovvero Gli amori di Paride con Enone* (coll. with Quintavalle), 1704; *L'Arminio*, 1705; *Il selvaggio eroe*, 1707; *Il più bel nome*, 1708; *L'Imeneo*, 1708; *Sofonisba*, 1708; *L'ingratitudine gastigata*, ?1709; *L'inimico generoso*, 1709; *L'Atenaide* (coll. with Fiore and Gasparini), 1709; *Il nome più glorioso*, 1709; *L'Anagilda*, 1711; *Pimpinone e Vespetta*, 1711; *Astrobolo e Lisetta*, 1711; *Giunio Bruto, ovvero La caduta de' Tarquini* (coll. with Cesarini and A. Scarlatti), 1711; *L'Atenaide* (coll. with M. A. Ziani and Negri), 1714; *Tito e Berenice*, 1714; *La dulcinea e cuoco*, 1715; *Il giubilo della salza*, 1716; *Il Costantino* (coll. with Lotti and Fux), 1716; *Caio Marzio Coriolano*, 1717; *Il Tiridata, ossia La verità nell'inganno*, 1717; *Ifigenia in Aulide*, 1718; *Teodosio* (coll. with Fux and Gasparini), 1718; *Dafne*, 1719 (EDITION C. Schneider (ed.), Vienna, 1955); *Sirita*, 1719; *Zaira*, 1719; *Lucio Papirio dittatore*, 1719; *Gli eccessi dell'infedeltà*, 1720; *L'inganno tradito dall'amore*, 1720; *Apollo in cielo*, 1720; *Psiche*, 1720; *Atamo huomo vecchio e Palancha giovine*, 1720; *Dorina e Grullo*, 1721; *Il germanico Marte*, 1721; *Grespilla e Fanfarone*, 1721; *Ormisda rè di Persia*, 1721; *Camaide, imperatore della China*, 1722; *La Marchesina di Nanchin*, 1722; *Nitocri*, 1722; *Scipione nelle Spagne*, 1722; *La contesa d'numi*, 1723; *La concordia de'planeti*, 1723; *Euristeo*, 1724; *Il finto Policare*, 1724; *Andromaca*, 1724; *Madame ed il cuoco*, 1724; *Gianguir*, 1724; *Astarto*, 1725; *Semiramide in Ascalona*, 1725; *Il Venceslao*, 1725; *Amalasunta*, 1726; *Nigella e Tirsi*, 1726; *I due dittatori*, 1726; *Ghirlande di fiori*, 1726; *L'Etearco*, 1726; *Don*

Chisciotte in corte della duchessa, 1727; *La verità nell'inganno, ossia Arsinoe*, 1727; *Imeneo*, 1727; *Ornospade*, 1727; *La forza dell'amicizia, ossia Pilade ed Oreste* (coll. with Reutter), 1728; *Mitridate*, 1728; *Ciro riconosciuto*, 1728; *Amor no ha legge*, 1728; *I disingannati*, 1729; *Caio Fabbrizio*, 1729; *Enone*, 1729; *Dialogo tra la vera disciplina ed il genio*, 1720; *Lisetta ed Astrobolo*, 1730; *La pazienza di Socrate con due mogli* (coll. with Reutter), 1731; *Il Demetrio*, 1731; *Livia*, 1731; *L'asilo d'amore*, 1732; *Adriano in Siria*, 1732; *Demofoonte*, 1733; *L'Olimpiade*, 1733 (EDITION facsimile, H. M. Brown (ed.), Garland, 1979); *Sancio Pansa governatore dell'isola Barattaria*, 1730; *Le lodi d'Augusto*, 1734; *La clemenza di Tito*, 1734; *Le Cinesi*, 1735; *Il natale di Minerva Tritonia*, 1735; *Scipione Africano il maggiore*, 1735; *Le grazie vendicate*, 1735; *Achille in Sciro*, 1736; *Il Temistocle*, 1736; *La selva illustrata dal merito*, (n.d.)

BIBLIOGRAPHY   Robert S. Freeman, *Opera without Drama: Currents of Change in Italian Opera 1675–1725*, UMI Research Press, 1981

G.D.

ROBERT CAMBERT

b c. 1627, Paris; *d* February or March 1677, London

Cambert played a key role in the establishment of opera in France. In 1659 he produced his *Pastorale d'Issy* – not quite, as it claims, 'the first French play set to music' (that honour goes to Charles de Beys's

Engraving for Cambert's pastoral Pomone *(from* Recueil général des opéra, *1703)*

and Michel de La Guerre's *Le triomphe de l'Amour* of 1655, the music for which, like that of Cambert's *Pastorale* and his *Ariane, ou Le mariage de Bacchus* (1699), is now lost).

In 1669 the poet Pierre Perrin received a royal privilege to establish 'Académies d'Opéra' in Paris and elsewhere. Two years later, with himself as composer, Cambert inaugurated his Parisian Académie with the pastorale *Pomone*, effectively the first French opera. Another pastorale, *Les peines et les plaisirs de l'Amour*, followed in 1672. That year, however, Lully took advantage of Perrin's financial difficulties to secure the privilege for himself. Cambert's promising career as an opera composer in France thus came to an abrupt end. He fled to London, where some earlier compositions, notably *Ariane* and *Pomone*, were performed in versions that now contained music by a former pupil, Louis Grabu.

Only fragments of Cambert's two operas survive. These reveal a composer less sensitive to French prosody than Lully, but are more adventurous in their use of affective melodic leaps, expressive melisma and chromatic harmony.

BIBLIOGRAPHY   J. R. Anthony, *French Baroque Music from Beaujoyeulx to Rameau*, Batsford, 1973; rev. 2nd edn, 1978; R. M. Isherwood, *Music in the Service of the King: France in the Seventeenth Century*, Cornell University Press, 1973

G.S.

THOMAS CAMPION

Thomas Campion [Campian]; *baptized* 12 February 1567, London; *buried* 1 March 1620, London

Unlike most of those who composed music for Jacobean masques, Campion was not a court musician: he studied law at Gray's Inn and medicine at the University of Caen; he was also a distinguished poet. He worked in legal circles and the fringes of the court; his patrons apparently included the Earl of Essex, the Clifford family and Sir Thomas Monson, Master of the Armoury. Through his connection with the Monson family he was involved in the scandal surrounding the murder of Sir Thomas Overbury in 1613, though he was later exonerated. Campion's music was a by-product of his literary activities. His songs all appear to be settings of his own poetry, and he was the only person to contribute both words and music to court masques; he used his double role as author and composer to experiment with polychoral effects, but his surviving masque music is relatively unadventurous.

Campion wrote words and/or music for the following court masques: *Lord Hay's Masque*, 1607; *The Lords' Masque*, 1613; *The Masque of Squires*, 1613; songs (lost) for *Gesta Grayorum*, 1594.

EDITIONS   W. R. Davis (ed.), *The Works of Thomas Campion: Complete Songs, Masques and Treatises, with a Selection of the Latin Verse*, Faber, 1967; A. J. Sabol (ed.), *Four Hundred Songs and Dances from the Stuart Masque*, Brown University Press, 1978
BIBLIOGRAPHY   E. Lowbury, T. Salter and A. Young, *Thomas Campion: Poet, Composer, Physician*, Chatto and Windus, 1970

P.H.

ANDRÉ CAMPRA

baptized 4 December 1660, Aix-en-Provence, France; *d* 29 June 1744, Versailles, France

André Campra was an important figure in the history of French opera between Lully and Rameau. His early appointments were as a church musician and he studied for holy orders. He continued to write church music, securing an appointment at the royal chapel in 1723. However, an interest in the theatre drew him more and more into this field. Mindful of the church's views, he published his first stage works anonymously or under his brother's name, but by the end of 1700 Campra was able to relinquish his Notre Dame appointment and have his first tragédie en musique, *Hésione*, published under his own name. While continuing to write operas in the Lullian mould, Campra's most original contribution to French theatre was the creation of the opéra-ballet. Like the tragédie en musique, this harnessed the French passions for vocal music and ballet, but in minimizing the role of the intrigue and finding substitutes for gods and mythological characters, the new genre gained in immediacy and freshness. In his opéra-ballets as well as his serious operas and

André Campra

cantatas, Campra was responsible for introducing Italianate elements such as the *da capo* air and ariette, with their more ornate vocal lines – a trend deplored by conservative French critics – and he also developed the descriptive use of the orchestra.

L'Europe galante
Europe in Love
Opéra-ballet in a prologue and four entrées (1h 30m)
Libretto by Antoine Houdar de la Motte
PREMIERE   24 October 1697, Opéra, Paris

L'Europe galante marked both the début of its librettist and the creation of a new genre, the opéra-ballet. A contemporary writer described opéras-ballets as 'pretty Watteaus, piquant miniatures'.

The pretext for *L'Europe galante* is established in an argument between Venus and Discord over the conflict between war and love in the personality of the king (i.e. Louis XIV). In the entrées, four nations are in turn characterized by vignettes which supposedly demonstrate their differing attitudes to love. The French scene shows the participants as 'fickle, indiscreet and coquettish'; the Spaniards are 'faithful and romantic', the Italians 'jealous and violent'. More exotically, the last entrée portrays the sultans and sultanas of Turkey. In an epilogue, Venus and Discord reappear, and the latter is forced to concede that love has triumphed.

Musically, and in the emphasis of the decorative elements, *L'Europe galante* resembles the divertissements of the Lullian tragédie en musique: simple airs and ensembles, with plenty of dances, are infused with Campra's particular gift for melody.

RECORDING   Yakar, Kweksilber, Jacobs, La Petite Bande, Leonhardt, Harmonia Mundi, 1978
EDITIONS   f.s., Ballard, 1724; v.s., *Chefs-d'oeuvre*, vol. 4, [1880]; *rp*, Broude Bros, 1971; facsimile, Gregg, 1967

Tancrède
Tancredi
Tragédie en musique in a prologue and five acts (2h 30m)
Libretto by Antoine Danchet, after Tasso's epic poem *Gerusalemme liberata* (1581)
PREMIERES   7 November 1702, Opéra, Paris; modern revival: 15 July 1986, Aix-en-Provence

Tancrède was Campra's most successful serious opera, enjoying revivals and performances up to 1764. Tancrède has fallen in love with his prisoner, Clorinde, the Saracen princess. The jealous Herminie, who loves Tancrède, and Argant, who loves Clorinde, conspire with the sorcerer Isménor to lure Tancrède to the enchanted forest. At night Tancrède fights with an opponent whom he believes to be Argant but is in reality Clorinde, wearing Argant's armour. The opera ends with Tancrède's suicidal despair.

The plot gave Campra plenty of scope for descriptive writing and effects; for example, the use of flutes to evoke the sounds made by the trees in the enchanted forest. The opera is unusual for its time in not casting the hero as an *haute-contre* voice, and in

giving all three major roles (Tancrède, Argant and Isménor) to basses.

RECORDINGS   1. excerpts: Dussaut, Bona, Arapian, Ensemble Vocal et Instrumental de Provence, Pianissime, 1987; 2. Dubosc, Evangelatos, Le Roux, Le Maigat, Reinhart, The Sixteen, Grand Ecurie, J.-C. Malgoire, Erato, 1990
EDITIONS   f.s., facsimile, *French Opera in the 17th and 18th Centuries*, vol. 18, Pendragon, forthcoming; v.s., *Chefs-d'oeuvre*, vol. 6, [1882]; *rp*, Broude Bros, 1971

Iphigénie en Tauride
Iphigenia in Tauris
Tragédie en musique in a prologue and five acts
Libretto by Jean-François Duche de Vancy, after Euripides' tragedy (prologue by Antoine Danchet)
Composed 1695–1704
PREMIERE   6 May 1704, Opéra, Paris

This opera was left unfinished by Henri Desmarets when he fled the country in 1699 to avoid a scandal. Campra composed the prologue, five other scenes and some airs to complete the opera. This was the first libretto to be based on Euripides' *Iphigenia in Tauris*, but is greatly inferior to the one written by Guillard for Gluck. It was, nevertheless, a considerable success, and enjoyed several revivals.

EDITION   facsimile, *French Opera in the 17th and 18th Centuries*, vol. 21, Pendragon, forthcoming

Les fêtes vénitiennes
Venetian Festivities
Opéra-ballet in a prologue and three entrées; final version in five entrées (1710)
Libretto by Antoine Danchet
PREMIERES   17 June 1710, Opéra, Paris; modern revival: 14 May 1970, Schwetzingen (Wuppertal Oper)

This was probably Campra's greatest success, capitalizing on a vogue for things Venetian in the theatre, and demonstrating most clearly the Italian influences on his music. In the course of its first run of more than 60 performances, and in subsequent revivals, the order of the entrées was changed several times; new entrées were substituted for some of the originals. Each is in effect a one-act comedy drawing on Venetian settings and characters.

In its original form, *Les fêtes vénitiennes* consists of a prologue (*Le triomphe de la Folie sur la Raison dans le temps du Carnaval*) and three entrées (*La fête des Barquerolles*, *Les Sérénades et les Joueurs*, *L'Amour saltimbanque*). Perhaps the most striking feature of the music is the great variety of airs, ranging from the most simple binary-form *petit air*, often a sung version of one of the dances, to the more elaborate ariette.

EDITIONS   1710 version: f.s., Lutolf (ed.), Heugel, 1972; v.s., *Chefs-d'oeuvre*, vol. 5, [1883]; *rp*, Broude Bros, 1971

Idomenée
Idomeneo
Tragédie en musique in a prologue and five acts (2h 15m)
Libretto by Antoine Danchet, after the tragedy *Idomenée* by Crébillon *père* (1703)

PREMIERE   12 January 1712, Opéra, Paris

Idomenée is a much embroidered version of the story of the king who buys his deliverance from a storm at sea by promising to sacrifice to the gods the first thing he sees on his return, which is his son, Idamante. Crébillon had invented rivalry between father and son for the love of the same woman; Danchet further complicates matters by introducing the character of Electre, who has no associations with this story in any source, in love with Idamante.

With a shipwreck, a further storm and the apparition of a monster, Campra has ample opportunity for vivid orchestral description, and uses the chorus to react to these events most effectively. The opera is particularly rich in soliloquy scenes for the major protagonists.

Danchet's libretto for *Idomenée* was adapted by Varesco for Mozart's *Idomeneo* in 1780.

EDITION   facsimile, *French Opera of the 17th and 18th Centuries*, vol. 19, Pendragon, forthcoming

Ballet des âges

Opéra-ballet in a prologue and three entrées
Libretto by Louis Fuzelier
PREMIERE   9 October 1718, Opéra, Paris

This was Campra's last success in the theatre. It depicts the course of love in youth, adulthood and old age. Campra seems to some extent to hark back 20 years to the musical style of *L'Europe galante*, with less reliance on the vocal display of the ariette. Graceful, elegant melodies, less subservient to the demands of the versification than their models in serious opera, anticipate the opéra comique of a later generation.

EDITION   facsimile, *French Opera of the 17th and 18th Centuries*, vol. 20, Pendragon, forthcoming

Other works: *Le carnaval de Venise*, 1699 (EDITION facsimile, Pendragon, 1990); *Hésione*, 1700; *Aréthuse, ou La vengeance de l'amour*, 1701; *Les fragments de Monsieur de Lully* (arr. Campra), 1702, rev. 1731; *Les muses*, 1703; *Télémaque, fragment des modernes* (arr. Campra), 1704; *Alcine*, 1705; *Hippodamie*, 1708; *Les amours de Vénus et de Mars*, 1712; *Télèphe*, 1713; *Camille, reine des volsques*, 1717; *Achille et Déidamie*, 1735
BIBLIOGRAPHY   J. R. Anthony, *French Baroque Music from Beaujoyeulx to Rameau*, Batsford, 1973; rev. edn, 1978; M. Barthélemy, *André Campra, sa vie et son oeuvre*, Picard, 1957

C.W.

HENRY CAREY

b ?1689, ?Yorkshire, England; *d* 5 October 1743, London

Poet, librettist and song-writer, Carey is believed to have been an illegitimate son of Lord Eland, the younger son of the Marquis of Halifax, the Restoration politician and wit. In 1713 he published his first volume of poems, and in 1715 a comedy, *The*

Contrivances. He also wrote a tune, which proved immensely popular, to his own 'Sally in our Alley', a ballad that won the approbation of Addison. He subsequently took music lessons and numbered the composers Galliard, Pepusch and Geminiani among his friends. His compositions, usually collaborative or composite, include pantomimes, ballad operas, dramatic masques, and a notable burlesque, *Chrononhotonthologos* (1734); he also provided three libretti, including *Teraminta* for John Christopher Smith (1732) and *The Dragon of Wantley*, for John Frederick Lampe (1737). Of these works only a couple of the ballad operas are recoverable, though enough survives of *Britannia, or The Royal Lovers* (1734) to show why it achieved a remarkable run. Carey was a witty writer of lyrics and contriver of farcical situations with a gift for facile and catchy melody; many of his songs outlived the pieces for which they were written. His last work, the interlude *Nancy*, for which there is a vocal score, was the direct ancestor of Dibdin's afterpieces about the British tar and his long-suffering lass ashore. It was revived as *The Press Gang* in 1755.

Surviving operatic works: *The Quaker's Opera*, 1728; *Love in a Riddle*, 1729; *Chrononhotonthologos*, 1734; *Britannia, or The Royal Lovers* (rev. of *The Happy Nuptials*, 1733), 1734; *Nancy, or The Parting Lovers*, 1739 (RECORDING as *True Blue*, Decca, 1950)
BIBLIOGRAPHY   Roger Fiske, *English Theatre Music in the Eighteenth Century*, OUP, 1973; 2nd edn, 1986; Frederick T. Wood (ed.), *The Poems of Henry Carey*, The Scholartis Press, 1930

R.Lu.

JOÃO DE SOUSA CARVALHO

b 22 February 1745, Estremoz, Portugal; *d* 1799, Lisbon

Carvalho attended the Colégio dos Santos Reis in Vila Viçosa, Portugal, and went in 1761 to the Conservatorio di S. Onofrio in Naples, where Paisiello was among his fellow students; he may have studied with Piccinni. During Carnival 1766 his opera *La Nittetti* (now lost) was performed at the Teatro delle Dame in Rome. On his return to Portugal he joined the Lisbon musicians' guild, the Irmandade de S. Cecília, and began to teach at the Seminário de Patriarcal, where Marcos Portugal was one of his students. In 1778 he became music teacher to the Portuguese princes and probably unofficial court music director.

For the Lisbon court he composed *L'amore industrioso*, *Eumene*, *Testoride argonauta* and *Nettuno ed Egle*, as well as church music and several serenatas. *L'amore industrioso* (his only dramma giocoso) and *Testoride argonauto* have had modern revivals. The quality of his music confirms him as the leading Portuguese composer of the second half of the 18th century. Having married a wealthy woman, he retired to his estates in the Alentejo during the last years of his life.

Operas surviving in manuscript: *L'amore industrioso*, 1769; *Eumene*, 1773; *Testoride argonauta*, 1780, *Nettuno ed Egle*, 1785
BIBLIOGRAPHY   M. C. de Brito, *Opera in Portugal in the Eighteenth Century*, CUP, 1989

M.C.B.

ALFREDO CASELLA
b 25 July 1883, Turin, Italy; *d* 5 March 1947, Rome

Among the leading Italian composers in the generation born around 1880 (the *generazione dell'Ottanta*), Casella was the most passionately committed to the modernization of Italian musical life. A born organizer, he returned to Italy in 1915 after 19 years in France, where he had attended Fauré's composition class, had become a close friend of Ravel, and had enthusiastically studied the most radical musical trends of the time. Inevitably the Italian musical scene, which was still dominated largely by the established opera tradition, seemed to him provincial by comparison: consequently he for a time developed a rooted prejudice against most Italian opera (even Verdi), and did not try to write an opera himself until he was 45. Meanwhile his boldly dissonant non-operatic music of the First World War period had influenced, among others, Puccini.

Casella's only two stage pieces composed before 1928 were ballets, and his one full-length opera, *La donna serpente*, was planned originally as a choral ballet. Although it was a failure at first and had to wait many years for recognition, the work can now be seen as centrally important among his compositions of the period. Casella's two one-act operas are less interesting, although the eclectic, slightly academic *La favola d'Orfeo* (1932) has been relatively often performed. *Il deserto tentato* (1936–7) has not been staged since 1943, but remains notorious in Italy for its overt celebration of Mussolini's Ethiopian campaign. Casella's well-known (and essentially simple-minded) support for the more culturally developed aspects of fascism has harmed his music's reputation since his death in a way that has little to do with its artistic qualities.

La donna serpente
The Snake Woman (or *Lady into Serpent*)
Opera-fiaba in a prologue and three acts (seven scenes)
(2h 45m)
Libretto by Cesare Lodovici, after the play by Carlo Gozzi
(1762)
Composed 1928–31
PREMIERES   17 March 1932, Teatro Reale dell'Opera, Rome; UK: 13 March 1966, BBC Third Programme (radio broadcast)

Gozzi's bizarre fairy-tale drama – also used by Wagner for his first opera *Die Feen* – provided Casella with a wildly fantastic sequence of events which needs careful handling if it is to convince in the theatre (Prokofiev's equally eccentric Gozzi opera *The Love for Three Oranges* is a comparable case). Altidor, King of Tiflis, marries the fairy princess Miranda against her father's will. Unable to stop the marriage, her father nevertheless imposes stringent conditions: for the first nine years and a day after the wedding she must conceal her true identity, and after that she must put Altidor's devotion through a series of atrocious tests. If at the end of these tribulations the king has still not cursed her, then she can go on living with him as a mortal; otherwise he will lose her – she will turn into a snake for 200 years and eventually return to the fairy world. Unfortunately Miranda's tests – which include having their children burnt to death and appearing to lead an army of Tartars against his kingdom – prove too strong for Altidor: he curses her and she turns into a snake. However, the supernatural forces in favour of the marriage win in the end, when the king has boldly defied fire and three monsters among the high peaks of the Caucasus.

By the time he wrote *La donna serpente* Casella's 'modernist' convictions had mellowed somewhat: there are even signs of Puccini's influence in King Altidor's more poignant monologues. A neo-Rossinian lightness pervades the music associated with the *commedia dell'arte* characters (thinly disguised by 'Caucasian' names: cf. Ping, Pang, and Pong in Puccini's *Turandot*), and whose presence – as usual in Gozzian dramas – is unexplained. The music of the 'magic' scenes can trace its lineage, via early Stravinsky, back to the fairy-tale operas of Rimsky-Korsakov; a tough, driving neo-classicism runs through the more pugnacious episodes; and there are some radiantly beautiful choruses, notably the unaccompanied, neo-madrigalian lament at the beginning of Act III.

Though often broadcast in Italy, and well known there through its two orchestral suites, *La donna serpente* has seldom been staged. However, its theatrical potential was triumphantly confirmed in a delightful production at Palermo in 1982.

EDITION   v.s., Ricordi, 1932

Other operas: *La favola d'Orfeo*, 1932; *Il deserto tentato* (one-act *mistero*), 1937
BIBLIOGRAPHY   Alfredo Casella, *Music in My Time* (Italian version, 1939), University of Oklahoma Press, 1955

J.C.G.W.

JOHN CASKEN
John Arthur Casken; *b* 15 July 1949, Barnsley, Yorkshire, England

Casken studied at Birmingham University, and later in Poland with Andrzej Dobrowolski and, privately, with Witold Lutosławski. He himself has held academic posts – most recently at Manchester

University, where he became professor in October 1992. Until his late thirties Casken composed nothing for the stage, though he showed in vocal/instrumental works a strong feeling for the dramatic content of language and poetry, under influences as diverse as Lutoslawski and Berio. He had also experimented with various approaches to sound and texture. But his first opera, *Golem*, was also perhaps the first work in which all these different resources fused into a single integrated and completely personal expression.

Golem

Chamber opera in two acts (1h 45m)
Libretto by the composer and Pierre Audi
Composed 1986–8
PREMIERES 28 June 1989, Almeida Theatre, London; US: 15 September 1990, Joslyn Art Museum, Omaha, Nebraska

Casken's collaborator on the libretto was the Almeida Festival's director, who also commissioned and directed the first production. The work won the first Britten Award for composition in 1990.

The Jewish/East European legend on which it is based is that of the clay man created by a rabbi in 16th-century Prague to protect the community, which gradually develops feelings and a will of its own, kills one of the townspeople, and has to be destroyed.

The score shows the value of Casken's experience as a vocal writer. He commands a vast range of vocal expression, from the lyrical to the very violent and disjointed, and handles his 12-piece orchestra with virtuosity and a powerful sense of colour. There is also highly effective use of pre-recorded tape. But though theatrical in feeling, *Golem* is probably too remorselessly earnest, austere and painful ever to be much loved by opera-goers.

RECORDING Clarke, Hall, Rozario, C. Robson, Music Projects/London, Bernas, Virgin Classics, 1991
EDITION v.s., Schott, 1990

BIBLIOGRAPHY Paul Griffiths, *New Sounds, New Personalities: British Composers of the 1980s in Conversation*, Faber, 1985

S.W.

MARIO CASTELNUOVO-TEDESCO

b 3 April 1895, Florence, Italy; *d* 17 March 1968, Los Angeles, US

Castelnuovo-Tedesco's career falls into two parts, separated by his emigration to the US in 1939 as a Jewish refugee. He made his name early, as a prolific composer of elegantly atmospheric, sometimes rather facile, miniatures. Of his pre-American stage works only *La mandragola* (1920–23), adapted from Machiavelli's bawdy comedy, can truly be called an opera. The music contains ingratiating ideas and appropriate touches of colour, but cannot match the characterization and sardonic humour of the original.

During his American years – when he wrote most of the guitar pieces for which he is now best remembered – Castelnuovo also wrote several operas, which have won little success: most remain unpublished, and two had not been performed by 1991. *The Merchant of Venice* (1956), however, was published and staged (Florence and Los Angeles). Using Shakespeare's own words, the work too often merely underlines the familiar text with fluent, unmemorable music. *The Importance of Being Earnest* (1961–2; unpublished) is said to make amusing use of musical quotations.

But Castelnuovo's best compositions for the stage probably remain two relatively brief and unpretentious pieces dating from the interwar years. The 'ditirambo' *Bacco in Toscana*, in effect a choral ballet in one act with two solo voices, has a sustained verve which neither of the published operas can match; while the unpublished *Aucassin et Nicolette* (a 'chant-fable du XII siècle pour une voix, quelques instruments et quelques marionettes') has been described by Nick Rossi as 'a work many consider to be [the composer's] finest'.

Operatic works: *La mandragola*, (1923), 1926, rev. 1928; *Bacco in Toscana*, (1926), 1931; *Aucassin et Nicolette*, (1938), 1952, rev. 1964; *The Song of Songs* ('rustic wedding idyll'), (1955), 1963; *The Merchant of Venice*, (1956), 1961; *All's Well That Ends Well*, (1958), 1960; *Saul*, (1960); *The Importance of Being Earnest*, (1962), 1972 (RAI broadcast), 1975; *Tobias and the Angel* ('scenic oratorio'), (1965), 1975
BIBLIOGRAPHY Nick Rossi, *Catalogue of Works by Mario Castelnuovo-Tedesco*, The International Castelnuovo-Tedesco Society (New York), 1977

J.C.G.W.

CASTIL-BLAZE

François-Henri-Joseph Blaze; *b* 1 December 1784, Cavaillon, France; *d* 11 December 1857, Paris

Castil-Blaze was an influential French critic from 1820 until his death, and he played a considerable part in the formation of operatic taste in those years. He admired Rossini and Meyerbeer for their focus on vocal technique and decried Beethoven and Berlioz for their tendency, as he saw it, to draw French composers away from the lyric stage towards instrumental music. From 1824 to 1829 he was director of the Odéon, where he produced adaptations of works by Mozart, Weber and others. *Der Freischütz* appeared as *Robin des bois*, and *Die Zauberflöte* as *Les mystères d'Isis*. He was bitterly castigated by Berlioz for his free treatment of these works, for inserting his own music and that of other composers and for the abundant liberties he took with both libretti and scores. He mounted a number of successful pastiches, using other composers' music to set plays by Destouches, Molière and others. His own operas were three in number, only one of which,

Pigeon vole, was staged in Paris (1843). *Belzébuth, ou Les jeux du roi René*, was played in Montpellier in 1841, but the comic opera *Choriste et liquoriste* was never performed.

BIBLIOGRAPHY   Fétis, *Biographie universelle de musiciens*, Brussels, 1835–44; 2nd edn, 1860–65; *rp*, 1963

H.M.

ALFREDO CATALANI

b 19 June 1854, Lucca, Italy; *d* 7 August 1893, Milan, Italy

Catalani is an isolated figure in late 19th-century Italian opera. Eschewing both the Verdian vein of French-influenced international opera and the melodramatic excesses of the emerging *verismo* school, he pursued a brand of Germanic Romanticism, yet endowed it with an authentic Italian flavour. He was just coming into his own when he died of tuberculosis at 39.

His first musical studies, in Lucca with Puccini's uncle, Fortunato Magi, were followed by further lessons in Paris under Bazin. Later, he settled in Milan, where he continued his studies in composition at the conservatory with Antonio Bazzini. In 1875 he wrote an eclogue (in effect a one-act opera), *La falce* (to a text by Boito), as his graduation exercise, which won him the support of the publisher Giovannina Lucca, who then underwrote his career for several years.

Encouraged by a modest monthly stipend from Lucca, he embarked on an opera, *Elda*, finishing the first version in 1876, but continuing to revise it until it was premiered in Turin in 1880. Next came *Dejanice* (1883) and *Edmea* (1886); the latter won him favourable critical attention, despite one of Ghislanzoni's more implausible libretti. *Edmea* is the first of Catalani's scores to hint at his natural inclination towards idiosyncratic Romanticism. The same year he was appointed professor of composition at the Milan Conservatory on the death of Ponchielli, but because of his ill-health he was granted the post only on a year's probation.

When Lucca's publishing house was merged with that of Ricordi in 1888, Catalani failed to find favour with the new regime, and his final works were brought to fruition largely through his own efforts. He embarked on a full-scale revision of *Elda*. Retitled *Loreley*, it was introduced at the Teatro Regio, Turin, early in 1890. It subsequently became the first of Catalani's works to be widely performed outside Italy. His last opera, *La Wally* (1892), to a text by Illica (commissioned and paid for by Catalani himself), was even more successful. With *La Wally*, he finally earned the good will of Giulio Ricordi, but by then it was too late.

Catalani struggled to find himself at a time when Italian stages were dominated by the final works of Verdi and by the emergence of the *veristi*. He laboured by trial and error to achieve what came more easily to other opera composers with a stronger instinct for the stage. His ability to create poetically atmospheric orchestral music, as in the 'Dance of the Ondine' in Act III of *Loreley* and the prelude to Act III of *La Wally*, compensates to some extent for his difficulty in projecting clearly individualized personalities for his characters.

Dejanice

Dramma lirico in four acts (2h 30m)
Libretto by Angelo Zanardini, after a suggestion by Boito
Composed 1882
PREMIERE   17 March 1883, La Scala, Milan

Determined to achieve an operatic success after the rather indifferent response to *Elda*, Catalani asked Boito – then regarded as one of the foremost librettists of the day – to provide him with a text. He declined but suggested the Classical theme used by Zanardini.

The action takes place in Syracuse in the 4th century BC. The lovers Argelia and Admeto are separated because of their different social classes. The villain Dardano tempts the courtesan Dejanice with a ruse to redeem her respectability if she will help him to destroy Admeto's and Argelia's relationship. Herself in love with Admeto and jealous of Argelia, Dejanice unwillingly agrees. Admeto awaits the arrival of Argelia, but it is Dejanice who confronts her, intending to drag her away and kill her. However, moved by the sincerity of the love of Argelia and Admeto, Dejanice sacrifices herself instead, first stabbing Dardano and then herself.

An opera on a large scale, *Dejanice* betrays an obvious debt to Ponchielli's *La gioconda*, particularly in Act II. The work shows Catalani's attempts to work through Ponchielli's style to discover his own. Although much of the score is bombastic, the orchestral passages are on a higher level, and Act IV has a musico-dramatic tautness that anticipates *La Wally*. *Dejanice* was tepidly received at its La Scala premiere, but went on to enjoy modest success in other Italian theatres.

RECORDINGS   1. Colli, Novielli, Frusoni, Gatti, Tomicich, Ch and O of Italian Radio, Guarnieri, UORC, 1975; 2. Basto, Garbato, Garaventa, Massis, Zardo, Ch and O of Teatro Giglio di Lucca, Latham-Koenig, Bongiovanni, 1985: the latter is more readily available, but cut [A.B.]
EDITION   v.s., F. Lucca, 1883

Loreley

Azione romantica in three acts (2h 15m)
Libretto by Carlo d'Ormeville, based on the Lorelei legend; rev. by Angelo Zanardini and Giuseppe Depanis
Composed 1876–9 (as *Elda*, in four acts), rev. 1889
PREMIERES   as *Elda*: 31 January 1880, Teatro Regio, Turin; as *Loreley*: 16 February 1890, Teatro Regio, Turin; UK: 12 July 1907, Covent Garden, London; US: 17 January 1919, Auditorium, Chicago

An uncommon example of an Italian opera based on a German myth, *Loreley* enjoyed a greater success than any of Catalani's previous operas. *Elda*, in four acts and with comparatively little dramatic action, had generally been considered too long. Catalani pruned the opera to three acts, tightening its dramatic structure but retaining much of the refined orchestral episodes which remain its strongest feature.

Lord Walter is betrothed to Anna di Rehburg, but has fallen for a strange girl he met on the banks of the Rhine. He confesses his dilemma to his friend Hermann who, though himself in love with Anna, advises him to go through with the marriage. When Walter tells the strange girl that he will marry Anna, she leaps into the river in despair. Suddenly, the river halts in its course, and she reappears as Loreley, seated on a rock, combing her golden hair. Walter, she says, will atone for jilting her. Just before the wedding, Hermann warns Anna of Walter's inconstancy, but she remains determined. As the procession starts, Loreley's siren song is heard. Walter follows it to the riverbank and stands transfixed as the Loreley vanishes into the water. Later, Anna dies of a broken heart and Walter is filled with such remorse that he falls unconscious beside the Rhine. When the Loreley appears holding out her arms to him, he regains his senses and rushes towards her; she disappears and Walter follows her into the river.

Loreley is an uneven opera, but it contains some outstanding passages, especially set pieces such as Anna's funeral procession and the 'Dance of the Ondine' (both retained from the earlier *Elda*). A fine example of Catalani's original melodic vein is Anna's aria in Act II, 'Amor, celeste ebbrezza'.

RECORDINGS 1. Suliotis, Talarico, Cappuccilli, Ferrin, Ch and O of La Scala, Gavazzeni, MRF, 1968; 2. Colalillo, Garbato, Visconti, Cassis, Monici, Ch and O of Teatro Giglio di Lucca, Annovazzi, Bongiovanni, 1982
EDITIONS *Elda*: v.s., F. Lucca, 1880; *Loreley*: v.s., Ricordi, 1890

La Wally

Dramma musicale in four acts (2h)
Libretto by Luigi Illica, after the novel *Die Geyer-Wally* by Wilhelmine von Hillern (1875)
Composed 1890–91
PREMIERES 20 January 1892, La Scala, Milan; US: 6 January 1909, Metropolitan, New York; UK: 27 March 1919, Manchester
CAST Wally *s*, Stromminger *b*, Afra *ms*, Walter *s*, Giuseppe Hagenbach *t*, Vincenzo Gellner *bar*, messenger *t* or *b*; *satb* chorus of Tyroleans, shepherds, peasants, hunters, old women, village children
LARGE ORCHESTRA onstage: 6 hn, 2 tpt, t-t, bells; offstage: organ

Premiered within months of Verdi's *Falstaff* and Puccini's *Manon Lescaut, La Wally* is the clearest example of the 'alternative' direction Italian opera might have taken had not Catalani's death intervened. It is the composer's most successful opera and – initially thanks to the championing of Toscanini, who conducted its premiere (and named his daughter Wally) – has become an established, if infrequently performed, part of the repertoire.

Set design by Hohenstein for the premiere of La Wally *(Milan, 1892)*

SYNOPSIS

Act I   The setting is the Tyrolean Alps, and the plot turns on the triangle of the independent but vulnerable Wally, Gellner, whom her father, Stromminger, wants her to marry, and Hagenbach, whom she loves. At Stromminger's 70th birthday party, Wally rejects Gellner and her father turns her out.

Act II   After her father's death, Wally, now wealthy, comes to a festival at Sölden. There, Gellner urges her to accept him, but Wally is still fascinated by Hagenbach, with whom she dances a *valzer del bacio*. Wally confesses she loves him, but Hagenbach's kiss is derisive, whereupon she orders Gellner to kill him.

Act III   That night Wally wishes she could take back her words. Hagenbach comes to ask pardon, but Gellner intercepts him, and hurls him down a ravine. Wally clambers down and saves Hagenbach. Once more she retreats to the heights, leaving her possessions to the woman she believes Hagenbach loves.

Act IV   High in the Alps, Hagenbach comes to Wally and, their mutual misunderstanding resolved, they rejoice in their love. An ominous storm has gathered and they both perish in an avalanche.

Catalani took advantage of the setting to introduce some local colour into his music, for example, the 'Edelweiss' song sung by Walter, a village boy, in Act I, and the Tyrolean dances in Act II; Wally's 'Ebben? Ne andro lontan', the best known of all Catalani's arias, is an adaptation of the melody of Catalani's *Chanson groënlandaise*, but its nordic character is not so pronounced as to make it seem out of place here. While these individual set numbers may be singled out, one of the most significant features of the score is its continuity. Catalani abandoned the number-opera structure of his earlier operas and, no doubt influenced by Wagner and perhaps by Verdi's *Otello*, created instead an opera where the music flows seamlessly, incorporating and then developing motifs of dramatic significance.

RECORDINGS   1. Tebaldi, Del Monaco, Cappuccilli, Diaz, Monte Carlo Opera Ch and O, Cleva, Decca, 1968;
2. Marton, Araiza, Titus, d'Argenta, Bavarian Radio Ch, Munich Radio O, P. Steinberg, Eurodisc, 1990: the 1968 set is the better sung and conducted [A.B.]
EDITIONS   f.s., Ricordi, 1946; v.ss., Ricordi, 1892, 1945

Other operas: *La falce*, 1875; *Elda*, 1880; *Edmea*, 1886
BIBLIOGRAPHY   Carlo Gatti, *Alfredo Catalani, la vita e le opere*, Garanti, 1953; J. Nicolaisen, *Italian Opera in Transition: 1871–1893*, UMI Research Press, 1980, pp. 153–85

W.A.

CHARLES CATEL

Charles-Simon Catel; *b* 10 June 1773, Laigle, Normandy, France; *d* 29 November 1830, Paris

Catel rose to some prominence as a composer of Revolution festival music, and as the author of the textbook *Traité d'harmonie* (1802). The tragic opera *Sémiramis* had some success, but Catel subsequently chose to exploit different genres; his ballet *Alexandre chez Apelles* (1808) contained an unusual quantity of original music, and – like *Les bayadères* – used the then rare cor anglais. Of his comic works, *L'auberge de Bagnières* was Catel's most long-lasting success. The 'Scottish' opéra comique about William Wallace contained little that we recognize as folk-influenced music, and was hampered by a static plot. On its revival in 1844, it was spoiled by too many additions by other hands.

Sémiramis

Tragédie-lyrique in three acts (3h)
Libretto by Philippe Desriaux, after Voltaire's tragedy (1748)
PREMIERES   4 May 1802, Opéra, Paris; rev. version:
8 November 1803, Paris

The overture, which is performed occasionally in concert, is a powerful F minor piece, resembling Beethoven's overture to *Egmont*. The doom-laden atmosphere of the plot is well captured throughout the score; there is a strong leading role for the tragic queen, perhaps influenced by Cherubini's *Médée*. Azéma's Act II aria 'Que l'éclat' was once a popular single number.

RECORDING   Overture: Dresden PO, Masur, Eterna, 1969
EDITIONS   f.s./v.s. (extracts), Magasin de Musique du Conservatoire, 1802; rev. version: f.s., Magasin de Musique du Conservatoire, 1804

Les bayadères

Opera in three acts (2h 30m)
Libretto by Victor-Joseph Etienne de Jouy, after Voltaire's story *L'éducation d'un prince* (1764)
PREMIERES   8 August 1810, Paris; rev. version in two acts:
21 June 1814, Paris

The subject of this, Catel's most successful work for the Paris Opéra, is related to Goethe's poem *Der Gott und die Bajadere*. The opera anticipates later 'Indian' operas such as *Les pêcheurs de perles*, but ends happily. Démaly, Raja of Benares (where the action takes place) loves the *bayadère*, or temple-dancer, Laméa. Proving to be the only female willing to die with Démaly after his supposed poisoning, Laméa is permitted to marry him. The aria 'Chère Démaly pour toi' was popular.

EDITIONS   f.s., Magasin de Musique du Conservatoire, [c. 1810]; v.s., Michaelis, 1883; facsimile, Boude Bros, 1971

Other operatic works: *Les artistes par occasion*, 1807; *L'auberge de Bagnières*, 1807; *Les aubergistes de qualité*, 1812; *Bayard à Méz ières* (coll. with Boieldieu, Cherubini, Isouard), 1814; *Le premier en date*, 1814; *Wallace, ou Le ménestrel écossais*, 1817; *Zirphile et Fleur de Myrte*, 1818; *L'officier enlevé*, 1819
BIBLIOGRAPHY   F. Hellouin and J. Picard, *Un musicien oublié: Catel*, Librairie Fischbacher, 1910

D.P.C.

EMILIO DE' CAVALIERI

b c. 1550, Rome; *d* 11 March 1602, Rome

Cavalieri was born into a noble Roman family, and gained his first musical experience in his birthplace. He was in charge of organizing the Lenten music of the Oratorio del SS. Crocifisso (1578–84), and also seems to have been associated with Cardinal Ferdinando de' Medici. When Ferdinando became Grand Duke of Tuscany in 1587, Cavalieri was appointed director of the artists and musicians of the Florentine court.

In 1589 he took charge of one of the most elaborate stage presentations ever conceived, the intermezzi for the wedding of Ferdinando with Christine of Lorraine. Cavalieri also composed part of the music for the entertainment along with Malvezzi, Marenzio, Caccini and Peri; the designer Bernardo Buontalenti and the poets Ottavio Rinuccini, Giovanni Battista Strozzi and Laura de' Guidiccioni Lucchesini were also involved. The overall allegorical plan was devised by Giovanni de' Bardi.

The 1590s were an important decade for Florence. The fundamental principles of monodic composition had been determined, and musicians such as Peri and Caccini were beginning to experiment with the musical implications of the current desire to revive the theatrical style that had been used by the Greeks in their tragedies. Much controversy has centred around which of the Florentine composers first developed the new recitative style, but it seems most likely that although Cavalieri claimed precedence, it emerged communally in the years before 1600.

In 1600 another marriage was the pretext for displaying the latest dramatic achievements of the Florentine musicians. Cavalieri directed the performance of Rinuccini's *Euridice* with music by Peri and Caccini, and for a banquet on 5 October Cavalieri set Guarini's *La contesa fra Giuone e Minerva*.

Cavalieri felt his role in the celebrations had been undervalued, and returned to Rome in 1600. During the 1590s he had kept close contact with the city: he had acted diplomatically on behalf of the Florentine court in Rome and had maintained his association with both the Oratorio del SS. Crocifisso and the Roman Oratorians. It was Philip Neri's Congregazione dell'Oratorio that gave Cavalieri the opportunity of producing the single work for which he is remembered, *La rappresentatione di Anima et di Corpo.*

La rappresentatione di Anima et di Corpo

The Portrayal of the Soul and the Body
Sacred drama in three acts (1h 30m)
Libretto by Agostino Manni, with Dorisio Isorelli
PREMIERES   February 1600, Oratorio of S. Maria in Vallicella (Chiesa Nuova), Rome; UK: June 1949, Girton College, Cambridge; US: 23 February 1966, University of North Dakota

The circumstances of the original performances suggest that *La rappresentatione* could be termed an oratorio, yet it cannot be classed as such since it was a staged drama. It is perhaps more appropriate to see it as a forerunner of the spiritual operas that were to become part of Roman musical life under the patronage of the Barberini and other powerful families.

This basically monodic work (though it includes madrigals, songs and dance songs) was performed twice in Rome during Carnival, 1600, and was well received on both occasions. Those who had also heard Peri's and Caccini's *Euridice* in Florence were said (by Cavalieri) to prefer *La rappresentatione* 'since the music moved them to tears and laughter and pleased them greatly, unlike the music of Florence, which did not move them at all, unless to boredom and irritation'. It also has the distinction of being the earliest printed opera, and the first printed score with a figured bass.

RAPPRESENTATIONE
DI ANIMA, ET DI CORPO
Nuouamente pofta in Mufica dal Sig. Emilio del Cauallicre,
per recitar Cantando.

Data in luce da Aleffandro Guidotti Bolognefe.

Con Licenza de' Superiori.

IN ROMA
Appreffo Nicolò Mutij l'Anno del Iubileo. M. D C.

The title page of La rappresentatione di Anima e di Corpo *(Rome, 1600)*

The crucial part of *La rappresentatione* occurs in Act I, where a *lauda* text of 1577 is set as a dialogue beween the Body and the Soul. Most of the remainder of Act I and Act II develop the tension between the world and sensual pleasure on one hand, and the joys of heaven on the other. Towards the end of Act II, the Guardian Angel and the Body show the poverty of the world and worldly life by stripping them of their superficially beautiful raiment. Body and Soul choose to reject the world. Act III contrasts the suffering of the Damned with the joys of the Blessed Souls. The stage was divided into three areas representing earth, heaven and hell, and it was suggested that the performance conclude with a ballo.

RECORDING   Zylis-Gara, Geszty, Moser, Troyanos, Esswood, Equiluz, Prey, Adam, Vienna Chamber Ch, Ensemble Wolfgang von Karajan, Mackerras, DG Archiv, 1970
EDITIONS   Mutii, 1600; facsimile, Gregg Press, 1967

Other stage works: two madrigals and one ballo for 1589 intermedi; four lost pastorales
BIBLIOGRAPHY   W. Kirkendale, 'Emilio de Cavalieri, a Roman Gentleman at the Florentine Court', *Quadrivium*, vol. 12, no. 2 (1971), pp. 9–21; H. E. Smither, *A History of the Oratorio*, vol. 1: *The Oratorio in the Baroque Era: Italy, Vienna, Paris*, Chapel Hill, 1977, pp. 79–91

G.D.

FRANCESCO CAVALLI

Pietro [Pier] Francesco Caletti [Caletto, Caletti-Bruni, Caletti di Bruno] detto il Cavalli; *b* 14 February 1602, Crema; *d* 14 January 1676, Venice

One of the major composers of the 17th century, Cavalli played a crucial role in establishing opera as a genre. Although opera had been 'invented' in the 1590s, performances had largely been isolated events mounted for special court occasions. In 1637, however, the concept of public opera, with regular seasons financed by ticket sales, emerged in Venice. This idea stimulated a wave of creativity that quickly won opera a permanent place in the musical world, with Venice as its centre. After the death of Monteverdi (1643), Cavalli became the leading opera composer in Venice; he wrote 32 between 1639 and 1673. Unlike those of his contemporaries, most of his works survive: the Biblioteca Marciana, Venice, preserves 28 manuscript scores from Cavalli's own collection, some autograph, and many bearing his corrections. Moreover, as opera spread throughout Italy in the 1640s and 1650s, Cavalli's works played a vital part in initiating the tradition of opera performance in numerous cities (including Naples). His fame reached beyond Italy to England, Austria, and particularly France, and in 1660 he was commissioned to write an opera, *Ercole amante*, for the wedding of Louis XIV. In an era that constantly demanded new operas, Cavalli's were unusual for their sustained popularity; today many have been revived with considerable success.

Cavalli received his first musical training from his father, G. B. Caletti, maestro di cappella of the Crema Cathedral. In 1616, the boy was brought to Venice by Federico Cavalli, Governor of Crema; Francesco later adopted his patron's name. Shortly after his arrival in Venice, Francesco joined the choir at St Mark's, where Monteverdi was the new maestro

di cappella. This was the beginning of a lifelong association with St Mark's in which Cavalli rose from soprano to tenor to second organist (1639) to first organist (*c.* 1645), and finally maestro di cappella (1668).

Cavalli's opera career began in 1639, when he signed a contract with Venice's first opera theatre, S. Cassiano; besides composing, he initially helped finance and manage the company. In 1641 Cavalli teamed up with Giovanni Faustini, librettist and later impresario, with whom he collaborated (on ten operas) until the latter's death in 1651; he subsequently worked for Faustini's brother Marco, who took over as impresario. He composed seven operas to libretti by Nicolò Minato, and three to works by G. F. Busenello, author of *L'incoronazione di Poppea*. Cavalli apparently helped revise Monteverdi's music to *Poppea*: the Marciana collection includes a score with his annotations.

In 1660 Cavalli accepted Mazarin's invitation to Paris. This journey was ill-fated from the start: preparations for the celebration were over budget and behind schedule, and Mazarin died before they were completed. *Ercole amante*'s premiere was delayed until 1662; in the meantime, a revival of *Xerse* was staged. Both were adapted to French taste by Lully, who added long ballet entrées. Cavalli's music received little comment, and he departed vowing never to write another opera. He did ultimately finish six more, but two of the last three fell victim to the fickle tastes of the Venetian public. Even so, as maestro of St Mark's, he died in 1676 the most respected musician in Venice. The expressive quality of his music and his gift for dramatic portrayal mark him as a worthy successor to Monteverdi.

Gli amori d'Apollo e di Dafne

The Loves of Apollo and Daphne
[Dramma per musica] in a prologue and three acts (2h)
Libretto by Giovanni Francesco Busenello, after Ovid's *Metamorphoses*
Composed 1640
PREMIERE   Carnival 1640, Teatro S. Cassiano, Venice

In Busenello's mythological libretto, Cupid causes Apollo to fall in love with the nymph Daphne. Although she rejects him, Apollo pursues her. In despair, Daphne invokes the aid of her father, who changes her into a laurel tree. A sub-plot involves the loves of Aurora and Cefalo.

At the musical climax, Apollo laments Daphne's transformation. To reflect Apollo's own metamorphosis from grief to resolution, Cavalli progresses through poignant dissonances and restless descending ostinati to an energetic duple metre. This lament shifts between recitative and aria, following the mood of the text more closely than its structure.

EDITIONS   f.ss., Bernhard Klebel (ed.), Boosey & Hawkes, 1982; facsimile, Howard M. Brown (ed.), in *Italian Opera 1640–1770*, Garland (series 1), 1978

The destruction of Argos in Cavalli's Hipermestra *(Florence, 1658)*

L'Egisto

Favola drammatica musicale in a prologue and three acts
(abridged Leppard version: 2h 15m)
Libretto by Giovanni Faustini
Composed 1643
PREMIERES Carnival 1643, Teatro S. Cassiano, Venice; US:
1 August 1974, Santa Fe (rev. Raymond Leppard)

Despite his death at the age of 31, Faustini was the
most influential librettist of his generation: countless
later operas were modelled on his new type of
libretto. A Faustini plot is typically 'newly invented'
rather than based on well-known stories; each one
features two pairs of lovers whose relationships
become tangled – due to divine interference, misunderstandings, disguises, etc. – but are eventually resolved.

In *Egisto*, one of each pair (Egisto and Climene) is
captured by pirates and presumed dead. They
escape, only to find that their partners (Clori and
Lidio) have fallen in love with each other. In scenes
already typical of operatic convention, Climene is
reconciled to Lidio when she raises her sword and
cannot bring herself to kill him; Clori takes pity on
Egisto, who has gone mad with despair.

The most famous scenes in this opera are those
depicting Egisto's madness – despite Faustini's
complaint that he was forced to add them to please
the singer. The musical setting emphasizes contrast:
as Egisto's mind flits between subjects, Cavalli
changes tempo, register, harmony, and style,

juxtaposing meandering recitative, strict fanfares,
and simple tunes.

RECORDINGS 1. Sukis, Schmidt, Wohlers, Hopfner,
Hillebrand, Kammerensemble des Bayerischen
Staatsorchesters, Hirsch, Ariola-Eurodisc, 1973; 2. Talarico,
Dominguez, Alva, I Virtuosi di Roma, Collegium Musicum
Italicum, Fassano, MRF, 1970
EDITION v.s., Raymond Leppard (ed.), Faber Music, 1977:
heavily revised
MANUSCRIPTS f.ss., Österreichische Nationalbibliothek,
Vienna, formerly part of Cavalli's collection, copied by Maria
Cavalli; Biblioteca Marciana, Venice

L'Ormindo

Favola regia per musica in a prologue and three acts
(abridged Leppard version: 2h 15m)
Libretto by Giovanni Faustini
Composed 1644
PREMIERES Carnival 1644, Teatro S. Cassiano, Venice;
UK: 16 June 1967, Glyndebourne, Sussex (rev. Raymond
Leppard)
CAST Ormindo *a*, Amida *t*, Hariadeno *b*, Erisbe *s*, Sicle *s*. 4
s, 3 *ms*, *a*, 3 *t*; *ttb* chorus of winds
INSTRUMENTATION chamber ensemble à 5: 2 vn, 2 va and
bc (hpds, theorbos, violone, etc.)

Since 1967, when Leppard's Glyndebourne revival
prompted the rediscovery of Cavalli, *Ormindo* has
been one of the most popular baroque operas. In the
17th century, however, it was just one of many works

that entertained audiences for one season, never to be revived. None the less, its libretto and music are typical of the period, and became models for later operas – notably Aureli/Cavalli's *Erismena* (1656), which borrowed *Ormindo*'s plot outline, as well as the prison scene.

SYNOPSIS

Act I Ormindo and his friend Amida discover they both love Erisbe, wife of King Hariadeno. Erisbe declares she loves both equally; she cannot love her husband because he is too old. Amida's jilted lover, Sicle, arrives disguised as a gypsy.

Act II Sicle reads Amida's palm, revealing to Erisbe his past infidelity. Disenchanted with Amida, Erisbe runs away with Ormindo.

Act III Sicle's nurse Erice lures Amida to a cave, promising a magic spell to reunite him with his beloved. In a fake incantation scene, Erice instead summons the 'ghost' of Sicle, telling Amida that she committed suicide because he left her. When Amida is overcome with remorse, Sicle reveals herself and they are reunited. Hariadeno, furious, orders the arrest of Ormindo and Erisbe, and commands Osman to poison them. They drink the potion, sing a lament, and pass out. On seeing the bodies, however, Hariadeno weeps bitterly, especially after learning from a letter that Ormindo was his own son. Osman finally reveals that he had substituted a sleeping potion for the poison. Ormindo and Erisbe awaken and are forgiven by Hariadeno, who bestows on Ormindo both his wife and his kingdom.

Cavalli's music, compared with that of later, more familiar composers, is distinguished by the rich, varied nature of its recitative, and the high proportion of recitative to arias. During his lifetime, however, arias slowly gained ground, growing in number if not in size. Cavalli's operas also contain frequent, short 'arioso' passages that exhibit some features of aria style: for example, *Ormindo* has several instances where melodious refrains (typical of arias) surround recitative passages.

The arias in *Ormindo* are suave and lyrical, often cast in a lilting triple metre. The expressive details, however, are carefully tailored to the dramatic context: Erisbe's youth is conveyed by sweet thirds and ebullient runs; Ormindo's despair by poignant suspensions and unusual leaps. Arias are short, but tightly constructed; Cavalli uses just enough repetition to give the piece shape without belabouring its message. Many have strophic texts, and individual strophes often repeat the last phrase (ABB') or the first (ABA'); the latter is a prototype of the da capo aria, the form that eventually dominated opera for a century (e.g. Erisbe's 'Fortunato mio core'). Many of the arias are framed by short instrumental sections; only the most important ones have orchestral accompaniment.

Cavalli is particularly renowned for his treatment of the lament. His favourite scheme involves a descending tetrachord ground bass, usually in the minor with chromatic inflexions; over this is woven a melody whose flexibility contrasts with the rigidity of the bass. A famous example is the prison scene in *Ormindo*.

RECORDING Van Bork, Howells, Garcisanz, Berbié, Cuenod, Wakefield, Runge, Davia, Glyndebourne Festival Ch, LPO, Leppard, Argo, 1968: a popular recording, fine modern-style performance, though substantially cut and rewritten, several roles transposed, modern instruments in thick orchestration
EDITION v.s., Raymond Leppard (ed.), Faber Music, 1969; heavily revised (not recommended for serious study of Cavalli's music)
MANUSCRIPT f.s., Biblioteca Marciana, Venice

Giasone

Jason

Dramma musicale in a prologue and three acts (4h)
Libretto by Giacinto Andrea Cicognini
Composed 1649
PREMIERES Carnival 1649, Teatro S. Cassiano, Venice; UK: 3 August 1984, Opera House, Buxton
CAST Giasone *a*, Medea *ms*, Isifile *s*, Egeo *t*, 4 *s*, 2 *a*, 2 *t*, 4 *b*; *attb* chorus of spirits, winds
INSTRUMENTATION chamber ensemble à 3: 2 vn, bc (harpsichords, theorbos, violone, etc.); à 5 in a few passages (add. 2 va)

Giasone was the single most popular opera of the 17th century. Along with *Egisto*, *Erismena*, *Xerse*, and Cesti–Cicognini's *Orontea*, it toured Italy in the repertoire of travelling companies, helping opera take root throughout the peninsula. *Giasone*'s widespread appeal was due partly to Cicognini's complex, fast-moving plot and the profusion of cleverly delineated characters. Particularly noteworth is Cicognini's blend of comedy and tragedy: the ludicrous escapades and libertine attitudes of the comic characters provide a perfect foil for the tragic predicaments and moral conflicts of their noble counterparts. Ostensibly based on mythology, Cicognini's libretto contains rather more amorous intrigue than myth – in typical mid-17th-century style.

SYNOPSIS

Act I At Hercules' urging, Jason has abandoned Hypsipyle to continue his search for the Golden Fleece. At the start of the opera, the quest has run aground for a second time in Colchis, where Jason falls in love with Medea. Medea, enchanted with her new lover, scorns her betrothed, Aegeus. In a remarkable incantation scene, she employs her supernatural arts to help the quest. She invokes Pluto, who sends Jason a magic ring.

Act II Helped by the ring's power, Jason slays the monsters and carries off the Fleece. To ensure that he marries Hypsipyle, the gods create a storm that shipwrecks Jason and Medea near Hypsipyle's home.

Act III The suspicious Medea demands that Jason kill Hypsipyle. He agrees, and dispatches Besso to do the deed. But the plan backfires, and Medea is thrown into the sea instead. This mishap brings about the reunion of Medea and Aegeus: Aegeus rescues her, which makes her recognize the value of his constancy. Jason, meanwhile, is tormented by visions of the 'drowned' Hypsipyle on the one hand, and the jealous Medea on the other. When Hypsipyle appears alive, and Medea enters with Aegeus, Jason first refuses to give up Medea. He finally capitulates after Hypsipyle sings a moving lament.

Medea's incantation is one of Cavalli's most celebrated numbers. To create a stark, unnatural mood, he uses four chords, often with bare fifths, repeated incessantly. Medea's forceful arpeggios, compassing the extremes of her range, aptly convey the terrible power she is unleashing. In marked contrast stands Jason's first aria, sung as he staggers from Medea's bed. The mellifluous vocal line and rich, sweet harmonies immediately explain why Jason's heroic quest has stalled: Mars has been vanquished by Venus.

Hypsipyle, like many tragic heroines in Cavalli's early works, sings primarily in passionate recitative and arioso. In her final lament, she explores various emotions as she offers herself to Jason's sword. The central portion is set in aria style over a tetrachord bass; at the climax it erupts into recitative. The lament concludes with a heart-rending farewell, reminiscent of Ottavia's from *Poppea*.

Cavalli's treatment of comedy is vital to the success of this work. Comic arias tend to be sectional and unpredictable; patter style is common.

RECORDING Mellon, Dubosc, Banditelli, Chance, Visse, de Mey, Concerto Vocale, Jacobs, Harmonia Mundi, 1988: a first-class performance, with baroque instruments and original voice registers; minor changes include instrumental accompaniment to a few numbers, the addition of two viola parts to all orchestral music, some cuts
EDITIONS f.ss., prologue and Act I, abridged (based on the Vienna manuscript): Robert Eitner (ed.), *Die Oper von ihren ersten Anfängen bis zur Mitte des 18. Jahrhunderts*, in *Publikation älterer praktischer und theoretischer Musikwerke*, vol. 12, Gesellschaft für Musikforschung, [1883]; facsimile (with article by L. Bianconi), in *Drammaturgia Musicale Veneta*, Ricordi, forthcoming
MANUSCRIPTS f.ss., Österreichische Nationalbibliothek, Vienna; Biblioteca Marciano, Venice; seven others

L'Oristeo

Dramma per musica in a prologue and three acts (3h)
Libretto by Giovanni Faustini
Composed 1651
PREMIERE Carnival 1651, Teatro S. Apollinare, Venice

Besides inaugurating Venice's seventh opera theatre, the premiere of *Oristeo* marked Faustini's impresarial début. In this typical Faustini story, Diomeda breaks her engagement to Oristeo when he accidentally kills her father; Oristeo hides in shame. Trasimede courts Diomeda; his jilted fiancée, Corinta, pursues him in disguise. When Corinta and Oristeo reveal their identities to save their loved ones, Diomeda and Trasimede realize their errors.

In Act I, Corinta and Oristeo debate the value of love. In a duet that prefigures later opera buffa traditions, Cavalli skilfully characterizes their

opposing viewpoints, and conveys the animation of the dispute with motifs that chase and interrupt each other.

EDITION facsimile, Howard M. Brown (ed.), in *Italian Opera 1640–1770*, Garland (series 2), 1982
MANUSCRIPT autograph f.s., Biblioteca Marciana, Venice

La Calisto

Callisto
Dramma per musica in a prologue and three acts (2h 30m)
Libretto by Giovanni Faustini
Composed 1651
PREMIERES 28 November 1651, Teatro S. Apollinare, Venice; UK: 25 May 1970, Glyndebourne, Sussex (rev. Raymond Leppard)
CAST Callisto *s*, Jove *bar*, Diana *s*, Endymion *a*, Mercury *t*, 7 *s*, 2 *a*, *bar*; satb chorus of celestial spirits
INSTRUMENTATION chamber ensemble à 3: 2 vn and bc (hpd, theorbo, violone)

Calisto is probably Cavalli's best-loved opera today, thanks to Leppard's 1970 revival. In its day, however, it was one of Cavalli's least successful works: attendance at the premiere was meagre, and the opera was shelved after 11 performances. Moreover, Faustini – who was serving as both librettist and impresario – died suddenly in the middle of the run. Whatever the reasons for the opera's initial failure, however, the overall quality of the work is extremely high: as Cavalli's fifteenth opera and his ninth collaboration with Faustini, *Calisto* reveals both men working at the peak of their creative powers.

The libretto fuses together the myth of Jove's seduction of Callisto with that of Diana's affair with Endymion. Although mythological plots were out of fashion at the time, these two stories are laden with potential for love intrigue in the contemporary style: Faustini portrays the gods and goddesses as more or less real humans, with plenty of human flaws.

SYNOPSIS
Act I As a follower of the virgin goddess Diana, the nymph Callisto is sworn to chastity. To win her, Jove cleverly turns himself into Diana (a deceit devised by Mercury); the naïve Callisto is then obedient to his every command, and overwhelmed by the delight of their encounter. Diana, meanwhile, has fallen in love with the shepherd Endymion, despite her own vows of chastity.

Act II Juno, suspecting her errant husband is up to his usual tricks, quickly discovers the truth. Diana's secret affair is discovered by Pan, who had long adored her. Pan and his band of satyrs torment Endymion.

Act III Juno, in revenge, turns Callisto into a bear. In the end, Endymion is rescued by his beloved goddess, and Jove reveals his true identity to Callisto. Although he cannot undo Juno's spell, he elevates Callisto to the stars as the constellation Ursa Major.

Cavalli clearly designed Endymion to be the star of this show: he is awarded some of the most beautiful and substantial numbers (including three out of four accompanied arias) as well as the most moving recitative. Particularly fine is 'Lucidissima face', his salute to the moon goddess Diana. Callisto is another character given to lyricism: as she moves between prim defiance, exultation, despair, confusion, and humble adoration of her great lover, Cavalli captures each moment with a beautifully wrought aria. The final *Poppea*-like duet between Jove and Callisto is one of many delightful ensembles in this work.

The wood deities Pan, Sylvan, and the Young Satyr provide *Calisto* with an unusual flavour. These are wild, passionate creatures, yet the Satyr is comic as well. Following a tradition for rustic poetry, Faustini concluded each line with a dactyl. Cavalli followed this rhythm, and intensified the strangeness of these 'half-beasts' by eschewing recitative, writing entirely in melodious arioso style.

RECORDINGS 1. Piscitelli, Mantovani, Bandera, Pertusi, Sonatori de la Gioiosa Marca, Moretti, Stradivarius, 1988: 'first complete recording' (with some cuts), uses original voice registers and baroque instruments; 2. Cotrubas, Kubiak, Baker, Bowman, Cuenod, Gottlieb, Davià, Trama, Glyndebourne Festival Ch, LPO, Leppard, Argo, 1971: a splendid modern-style performance, though substantially cut and rewritten with several transposed roles, modern instruments in thick orchestration
EDITIONS f.ss., Paul Daniel (ed.), 1984; Jennifer Williams Brown and Maria Archetto (eds), 1987; Bruno Moretti (ed.), 1988, available through Sonzongo, Milan; v.s., Raymond Leppard (ed.), Faber Music, 1975 (heavily revised), not recommended for serious study of Cavalli's music
MANUSCRIPT f.s., Biblioteca Marciana, Venice: copied by Cavalli's wife Maria with his annotations, including the transposition of Endymion's role up a fifth

Xerse

Xerxes
Dramma per musica in a prologue and three acts (3h 45m)
Libretto by Nicolò Minato, after Herodotus
Composed 1654
PREMIERE 12 January [1655], Teatro SS. Giovanni e Paolo, Venice

Xerse was one of Cavalli's most successful works. Moreover, a revision of Minato's libretto was later set by both Bononcini and Handel; many seemingly unusual features of Handel's version – the integration of comic and noble characters, rapid-fire comic dialogue, flexible scene structures, unconventional aria forms – can be attributed to the 17th-century libretto.

Although primarily a comedy, *Xerse* reveals the enthusiasm for semi-historical plots that arose around 1650. King Xerxes decides to marry Romilda, his brother Arsamene's girlfriend, despite a previous attachment to Amastre. Similarly, Romilda's sister Atalanta loves Arsamene. After lengthy quarrels caused by Atalanta's mischief, Romilda and Arsamene make up, and Romilda rejects Xerxes. Furious, Xerxes orders Arsamene's execution. Romilda's father, however, misunderstanding a cryptic decree from Xerxes, marries Romilda to

Arsamene. Xerxes goes wild, but is checked by the appearance of Amastre; smitten with sudden remorse, he marries her.

The opera opens with a grand aria, 'Ombra mai fù', Xerxes' famous apostrophe to a tree. Cavalli's music portrays the noble side of Xerxes' ambiguous character, and helps make his capitulation believable. One of several ABA' forms in *Xerse*, 'Ombra mai fù' is more clear cut formally than many others: the central section is itself a two-strophe aria.

RECORDING Nelson, Poulenard, Jacobs, Gall, Elwes, de Mey, Concerto Vocale, Jacobs, Harmonia Mundi, 1985: superb recording, virtually complete, using baroque instruments; some minor revisions
EDITION f.s. in Martha Novak Clinkscale, 'Pier Francesco Cavalli's *Xerse*', Ph.D. dissertation, University of Minnesota, 1970, vol. 2
MANUSCRIPTS f.ss., Biblioteca Marciana, Venice; Bibliothèque Nationale, Paris; Vatican Library, Rome

L'Erismena

Dramma per musica in a prologue and three acts (2h)
Libretto by Aurelio Aureli
Composed 1656
PREMIERES Carnival 1656, Teatro S. Apollinare, Venice; UK: 1967, BBC Radio 3 (broadcast; ed. Lionel Salter); US: 17 May 1968, Berkeley

A box office success in 1656, *Erismena* was revived repeatedly in the 17th century. It was known even in England, where a score with translation was prepared, possibly for a performance. Like all 17th-century operas, *Erismena* acquired numerous changes on the road.

Even more than Faustini, Aureli built his literary career on constructing complicated networks of impossible situations, then wriggling out of them with astonishing (and often unlikely) plot twists. In this variation on *Ormindo*, Aldimira, unwilling mistress of the old King Erimante, loves two men – Orimeno and Idraspe, Erismena's former lover. When Erismena arrives disguised as a soldier, Aldimira falls in love with 'him', sparking Erimante's jealousy. The king, frightened by a prophetic dream, imprisons Erismena, and orders Idraspe to poison her. Ultimately, Erismena and Idraspe are reunited, Idraspe revealed to be Aldimira's brother, and Erismena the long-lost daughter of Erimante.

In the mid-17th century, entrance arias were frequently weightier than exit arias; *Erismena* has some particularly fine examples. Aldimira's first aria, sung while admiring her lovers' portraits, is perhaps one of Cavalli's most beautiful compositions. As the voice lingers dreamily over individual notes, Aldimira gazes on the features of each face. The refrain is written in an exquisitely high tessitura, accompanied by a rocking, passacaglia-like bass.

RECORDING Hafenrichter, Bogard, Esswood, Jameson, Brown, Matthes, Oakland SO, Curtis, Vox, 1968: sung in 17th-century English translation
MANUSCRIPTS f.ss., Biblioteca Marciana, Venice: two different versions (1656 and 1670); private collection

L'Ercole amante

Hercules in Love

Tragedia in a prologue and five acts (Corboz recording: 2h 45m)

Libretto by Francesco Buti

Composed 1662

PREMIERES 7 February 1662, Théâtre des Tuileries, Paris; modern revival: 4 May 1979, Lyons Opéra

Since *Ercole* was written for a French court wedding, it differs considerably from Cavalli's Venetian operas. Conceived on a vast scale, this production involved more performers and stage machinery than any public theatre could afford. Cavalli's most remarkable numbers are the many large ensembles (rare in Venetian operas), which range in style from magnificent Venetian polychoral to continuo madrigal. Although Italian operas normally contained dance music by other composers, Lully's ballets were apparently more elaborate than Italian balli. Cavalli's music may have been ignored at the time, but its influence was felt a decade later, when French opera was born: Lully's expressive recitatives, frequent ariosi, and laments often seem to echo Cavalli.

In accordance with French literary custom, Buti's five-act libretto describes a detailed mythological allegory. Hercules (i.e. Louis XIV), the mightiest hero of all, is yet a slave to love: in pursuit of his son's fiancée, he kills her father, betrays his wife, and drives his son to suicide. After Iole accidentally poisons Hercules with the centaur's shirt, Jupiter elevates him to Olympus, where he marries Beauty (i.e. Maria Theresa); as a god freed of human passion, Hercules can finally devote himself to duty and morality.

RECORDING Sgrizzi edn: Cold, Palmer, Lewis, Miller, English Bach Festival Ch and O, Corboz, Erato, 1981

EDITION f.s., Luciano Sgrizzi (ed.), 1981, available through Costellat, Paris

MANUSCRIPT f.s., Biblioteca Nazionale Marciana, Venice

Scipione Affricano

Scipio the African

Dramma per musica in a [prologue and] three acts (4h)

Libretto by Nicolò Minato

Composed 1664

PREMIERE 9 February 1664, Teatro SS. Giovanni e Paolo, Venice; modern revival: Drottningholm

After returning to Venice, Cavalli wrote three successful operas with Minato. All were based on Roman history; throughout the second half of the 17th century, the Venetians were at war with the Turks, hence patriotic themes implicitly equating Venice with ancient Rome were popular. In *Scipione*, naturally, the history is richly embroidered with intrigue, disguises, misplaced letters and overheard conversations.

Scipione is more obviously aria-laden than Cavalli's earlier works, due partly to Minato's clear distinction between aria and recitative verse, and partly to changing fashions. Eventually, however, Cavalli could not keep pace with the growing

demand for arias: two of his last three operas were rejected because their 'ariette' failed to please.

EDITION facsimile, Howard M. Brown (ed.), in *Italian Opera 1640–1770*, Garland (series 1), 1978

MANUSCRIPTS f.ss., Biblioteca Marciana, Venice; Vatican Library, Rome; Biblioteca Comunale, Siena

Other operatic works: *Le nozze di Teti e di Peleo*, 1639; *Didone*, 1641; *La virtù de'strali d'Amore*, 1642; *Doriclea*, 1645; *Orimonte*, 1650; *Rosinda* (Jane Glover (ed.), 1973), 1651; *Eritrea* (Jane Glover (ed.), 1975), 1652; *Veremonda l'amazzone di Aragona*, 1652/3; *Orione*, 1653; *Ciro*, 1654 (rev. by Cavalli and Aureli of work by F. Provenzale and G. C. Sorrentino); *Statira principessa di Persia*, 1655/?6; *Artemesia*, 1656/?7; *Hipermestra*, (1654), 1658; *Elena*, 1659/60; *Mutio Scevola*, 1665; *Pompeo magno*, 1666; *Eliogabalo*, (1667/8); 6 other operas, music lost

BIBLIOGRAPHY Jane Glover, *Cavalli*, St Martin's Press, 1978; Ellen Rosand, *Opera in Seventeenth-Century Venice: The Creation of a Genre*, University of California Press, 1991; Thomas Walker, 'Francesco Cavalli', in *Grove*, Macmillan, 1980; *rp* in *The New Grove Italian Baroque Masters*, Macmillan, 1984

J.W.B.

FRIEDRICH CERHA

b 17 February 1926, Vienna

Best known to the musical public for his completion of the final act of Alban Berg's *Lulu*, Cerha is also a considerable composer in his own right, and the author of four dramatic works, including two operas, *Baal* and *Der Rattenfänger*. In the 1950s and 1960s, Cerha was active in new Austrian music. He attended the Darmstadt summer schools in Germany, and in 1958 he founded, with Kurt Schwertsik, the Viennese chamber ensemble die reihe: he has also run an electronic studio and taught composition at the Vienna Hochschule. Despite this background his own music is eclectic. Orthodox serial pieces (with titles like *Relazioni fragili*) give way to a more broadly based and humanistic music in the Austrian tradition of Bruckner, Mahler and Berg. This tendency culminates in *Baal*.

Baal

Opera in two acts (25 scenes) (3h 15m)

Libretto by the composer, from the play by Bertolt Brecht (1923)

Composed 1974–9

PREMIERE 7 August 1981, Kleines Festspielhaus, Salzburg

Baal was Brecht's first stage work. Written when Marxism still seemed (to some) to hold out hope for the individual against the bourgeoisie, the play offers a rather disagreeable picture of the selfish hedonist in open conflict with organized society.

The poet Baal is lionized at a *soirée*, but is himself interested only in drinking and womanizing. He seduces and mistreats a succession of women, one of whom commits suicide. After more unsavoury adventures he abandons his pregnant mistress for

Ekart, a homosexual. They have a vision of a futuristic landscape built entirely of steel. Eventually, after he has murdered Ekart in a fit of jealousy, Baal, on the run but anxious to find friends, is beaten up in a tavern. He retires to the forest where he dies unmourned.

The debt to Berg is evident in Cerha's score. The short scenes are linked by reflective or intensifying interludes, and the orchestral texture is broken up by ballad settings in the Brecht manner. Viennese-type serial music rubs shoulders with idioms borrowed from popular music (including reggae). And as in both Berg's operas, *Wozzeck* and *Lulu*, set forms such as fugue and passacaglia are used to offset the anti-hero's disordered life-style. Though the music is consistently arresting, it cannot be said that Cerha emulates Berg in making his outcast sympathetic.

EDITION v.s., Universal, 1981

Other operatic works: *Netzwerk* (music-theatre), 1981; *Der Rattenfänger*, 1987
BIBLIOGRAPHY Articles by Friedrich Cerha, Lothar Knessl and György Ligeti in *Tempo*, no. 161/2 (June and September 1987), pp. 3–10

S.W.

ANTONIO CESTI

(Pietro) Antonio Cesti; *baptized* 5 August 1623, Arezzo; *d* 14 October 1669, Florence

Cesti was the most important Italian opera composer of the generation following Monteverdi and Cavalli. The given name Marc' Antonio, often associated with Cesti, has no basis in fact. He was baptized Pietro and took the name Antonio when he joined the Franciscan order in 1637. Because of the success of many of his operas in Venice, Cesti has often been associated with that city. He was, however, born a Tuscan, probably received some of his early musical training in Rome, spent some time in monasteries in Volterra and Arezzo, and held posts in Innsbruck, Vienna and, finally, Florence.

In 1643 Cesti was elected organist at the cathedral in Volterra, a position he held until 1645. From then until the end of the decade, he held musical posts at the Franciscan seminary at Volterra and at the cathedral there. In 1647 he sang as a tenor in an operatic production in Siena. It was during this period that he made the acquaintance of a group of Florentine men of letters, among whom were two of his future librettists, G. A. Cicognini and G. F. Apolloni, and the painter–writer Salvator Rosa, who became a close personal friend. Rosa's letters are, in fact, a major source of biographical information about the composer.

Cesti apparently was irresistibly drawn to the operatic stage, so much so that in 1650 the superior-general of his order issued a rebuke, calling attention to Cesti's 'dishonourable and irregular life' as a performer. Although there is disagreement over the place and date of Cesti's setting of Cicognini's *Orontea* (Venice 1649 or Innsbruck 1656), his extraordinarily successful career as a composer of operas began in Venice. Two of his operas, *Alessandro vincitor di se stesso* and *Il Cesare amante* appeared there in 1651. In 1652 Cesti was appointed to a position in the court of Archduke Ferdinand Karl at Innsbruck, where he remained for a number of years. In 1654, *La Cleopatra*, a revised version of *Il Cesare amante*, was performed there, and in 1655 he composed *L'Argia* especially to honour the visit of the recently abdicated Queen Christina of Sweden, who was on her way to Rome. *La Dori*, one of Cesti's most enduring works, was first performed at Innsbruck in 1657. In 1658, the composer made a trip to Rome, apparently to obtain release from his monastic vows. This done, he remained there as a singer in the papal choir. In 1661, Cesti was in Florence where *La Dori* was performed. After his return to Innsbruck, his *La magnanimità d'Alessandro* was performed there in 1662. In 1666 he transferred to the imperial court in Vienna and was awarded the title 'intendant of theatrical music'. In the same year his opera *Il Tito* appeared in Venice. Cesti's years in Vienna were very productive and include the operas *Nettuno e Flora*, *Le disgrazie d'Amore*, *La Semirami* – composed earlier in Innsbruck – and *Il pomo d'oro*. In 1669, the last year of his life, Cesti was in Florence in the employ of the Tuscan court. He died there, according to unsubstantiated rumour poisoned by his rivals.

Cesti's operas differ significantly from the late works of Monteverdi and the earlier works of Cesti's older contemporary Cavalli. There are few violent contrasts in mood and little harmonic experimentation. Instead, in the arias in Cesti's Venetian operas particularly, there is an emphasis on languid melody. The arias are often strophic and in triple metre with the formal scheme ABA' or ABB'. The size of the orchestra is modest, frequently comprising only two upper voices (violins) and continuo. Many of the arias are accompanied by continuo only, although the orchestra may occasionally accompany the entire aria or supply ritornellos before or after stanzas. Solo arias predominate, and rarely do ensembles appear. At key dramatic moments, Cesti's recitative tellingly reflects the situation, but in normal conversation it is less dramatic and presages the later *secco* recitative. Cesti's operas for the courts in Austria are another matter. Composed as private court spectacles, the musical forces, orchestral and vocal, are larger. *L'Argia*, for example, has many choruses and *Il pomo d'oro* employs a large number of solo roles and a greatly expanded orchestra. These later works contain more ensembles and, generally, more florid vocal writing.

Orontea

Dramma musicale in a prologue and three acts (3h)
Libretto by Giacinto Andrea Cicognini
PREMIERE November/December 1649, Teatro di SS. Apostoli, Venice; or 1656, Teatro Sala, Innsbruck

If the contested date of 1649 is to be accepted, *Orontea* is Cesti's first opera. It was enormously successful and had at least 22 productions in Italy between 1649 and 1686. Cicognini's masterful libretto is a romantic comedy. Orontea, Queen of Egypt, is taken with a young commoner, a foreigner, Alidoro, who appears accompanied by his 'mother' Aristea. Orontea's conflicting emotions, love for Alidoro on the one hand and a sense of regal duty on the other, torment her throughout the opera. Creonte, her adviser, is aghast at the thought of the queen's marrying a commoner. There are sub-plots: the love affair of the courtiers Corindo and Silandra is threatened by Silandra's attraction to Alidoro, and a former confidante of Orontea, Giacinta, masquerading as a boy, 'Ismero', must fend off the amorous advances of old Aristea. These many complications are observed by the young page, Tibrino, and the brilliantly drawn drunken comic servant, Gelone. Through a series of discoveries and coincidences, all is set right. Alidoro is identified as a once kidnapped prince, who had been reared by Aristea as her own child. Orontea decrees that she shall marry him and that there will be a double wedding as Silandra and Corindo have been reunited.

Despite its popularity, the music of *Orontea* disappeared for centuries, with the exception of Orontea's famous aria 'Intorno all'idol mio' (Act II, Scene 17) printed in Dr Burney in his *A General History of Music* (1789). In the 1950s, however, three scores of the opera were discovered in Italy and a fourth at Magdalene College, Cambridge.

RECORDING   Molinari, Poulenard, Cadelo, Feldman, Bierbaum, Jacobs, James, de Mey, Sarti, Reinhart, Baroque Instrumental Ensemble, Jacobs, Harmonia Mundi, 1982; this recording is based on the manuscript source at Cambridge University and differs considerably from the Italian sources
EDITION   William C. Holmes (ed.), *The Wellesley Edition*, no. 11, Wellesley (Massachusetts), 1974

La Dori, ò vero La schiava fedele
Dori, or The Faithful Slave
Dramma musicale in a prologue and three acts
Libretto by Giovanni Filippo Apolloni
PREMIERES   1657, Ertzfürstlichen Hof Saal, Innsbruck (only a printed scenario remains to testify to this performance); ?October 1661, Teatro in via del Cocomero, Florence

La Dori, like *Orontea* and Cavalli's *Giasone*, was among the most performed operas in the second half of the 17th century. Splendid as its music is, its libretto is absurdly complicated and confused.

Some time before the opera begins, the King of Nicea had promised his daughter Dori in marriage to Oronte, son of the King of Persia. Dori was kidnapped and presumed dead. On a trip to Egypt, Oronte fell in love with the daughter of the king, also called Dori. Confused identities and various disguises cause innumerable complications (two of the principal characters are travesti roles). At the dénouement it is revealed that the real Dori of Egypt had died accidentally, and that her guardian Arsete had captured another child, Dori of Nicea, and reared her as the Egyptian princess. Therefore, the original marriage contract between the kings of Nicea and Persia can be honoured. Two of Cesti's finest comic characters, the nurse Dirce and the servant Golo, weave in and out of the various plot lines to afford needed comic relief.

EDITIONS   prologue and sections of Act I: Robert Eitner (ed.), in *Publikationen älterer praktischer und theoretischer Musikwerke*, vol. 12, Berlin, 1883, pp. 86–177; Viennese score, which follows almost exactly the Florentine libretto of 1661: Howard Mayer Brown (ed.), facsimile, in *Italian Opera: 1640–1770*, Garland, series 2, no. 63, 1981; 1661 Florentine libretto: facsimile in *Italian Opera Librettos: 1640–1770*, Garland, series 2, vol. 14, no. 95, 1981

Il pomo d'oro
The Golden Apple
Festa teatrale in a prologue and five acts
Libretto by Francesco Sbarra, after the Greek myth, The Judgement of Paris
PREMIERES   Prologue, Acts I and II: 12 July 1668; Acts III, IV and V: 14 July 1668; in the specially constructed court theatre, Vienna

Il pomo d'oro, with its prologue and five acts, its 47 sung roles, its large orchestral forces, its 24 extravagant sets by Ludovico Burnacini, and its complicated stage machinery, was among the most lavish court spectacles of the 17th century. The work was originally to be performed in late 1666 as part of the wedding celebrations of the Infanta Margarita of Spain and Emperor Leopold I, who himself composed some of the opera's music. For a number of reasons its first performances were delayed until July 1668 and the occasion of Margarita's birthday. Sbarra's sprawling libretto is based on the well-known Greek myth with a number of embellishments and sub-plots. In addition to Jupiter, Paris, and the goddesses Juno, Athena, and Venus, there are three new major characters: Momo, a comic character in the Venetian style; Filaura, a sympathetic nurse, and Aurindo, a shepherd in love with Ennone, who, in turn, is in love with Paris. Helen of Troy, the object of Paris's affection, does not appear in the opera. Most of the action concerns the machinations of the three goddesses to obtain the golden apple. The libretto is constructed so that each act affords ample opportunities for spectacular stage effects such as storms, battles and shipwrecks. There are also ballets, three in the last act alone. Sbarra concludes the opera with an original departure from the myth: Jupiter bestows the golden apple on the Empress Margarita.

EDITIONS   music for the Prologue and Acts I, II and IV: Guido Adler (ed.), in *DTÖ*, Jg. iii/2 (Band 6) and Jg. iv/2 (Band 9), Vienna, 1896–7; *rp*, Graz, 1959; music for Acts III and V: Carl B. Schmidt (ed.), in *Recent Researches in the Music of the Baroque Era*, vol. 42, A-R Editions (Madison), 1982

Other operatic works: *Alessandro vincitor di se stesso*, 1651; *Il Cesare amante*, 1651; *La Cleopatra* (*Il Cesare amante* with

The Vienna court theatre during a performance of Il pomo d'oro *(1668)*

additions), 1654; *L'Argia*, 1655; *La magnanimità d'Alessandro*, 1662; *Il Tito*, 1666; *Nettuno e Flora festeggianti*, 1666; *Le disgrazie d'Amore*, 1667; *Genserico* (doubtful), 1669
BIBLIOGRAPHY William C. Holmes, 'Giacinto Andrea Cicognini's and Antonio Cesti's *Oronteas*', in William Austin (ed.), *New Looks at Italian Opera: Essays in Honor of Donald J. Grout*, Cornell University Press, 1968, pp. 108–32; Carl B. Schmidt, 'Antonio Cesti's *La Dori*: A Study of Sources, Performance Traditions and Musical Style', *RIM*: 'in onore di Nino Pirrotta', vol. 10 (1975), pp. 455–98; Carl B. Schmidt, 'Antonio Cesti's *Il pomo d'oro*: A Re-examination of a Famous Habsburg Court Spectacle', *JAMS*, vol. 29 (fall 1976), pp. 381–412; Egon Wellesz, trans. Patricia Kean, 'A Festival Opera of the Seventeenth Century', in *Essays on Opera*, Dobson, 1950, pp. 54–81

W.C.H.

EMMANUEL CHABRIER
Alexis-Emmanuel Chabrier; *b* 18 January 1841, Ambert, Puy-de-Dôme, France; *d* 13 September 1894, Paris

Despite early evidence of his musicality, Chabrier's family insisted on a legal training for him. After graduation he took a civil-service post in Paris but continued to compose. Cultivated and gregarious, his circle was more Bohemian than bureaucratic. As well as musicians, he enjoyed the friendship of painters, including Manet (Chabrier was the first owner of his painting, *The Bar aux Folies-Bergères*), and poets,

including Verlaine with whom he collaborated in the early 1860s on two uncompleted operettas: *Fisch-Ton-Kan* and *Vaucochard et fils 1er*. A grand opera, *Jean Hunyard*, followed in 1867 and was also left unfinished.

His particular musical character began to focus in the late 1870s with a pair of further comic pieces – *L'étoile* (1877) and *Une éducation manquée* (1879). Their apparent frivolity was compatible with a passion for Wagner: indeed the experience of hearing *Tristan* in Munich (1879) precipitated (as well as the wicked set of piano-duet quadrilles on its principal motifs) the decision to resign his civil-service post and devote himself entirely to composition. A trip to Spain in 1882 seems almost purposely to have realized Nietzsche's call to purge Bayreuth with the Mediterranean. Its most famous result came the following year with the orchestral rhapsody, *España*.

Other highlights from his brief maturity include the *Dix pièces pittoresque* (1881) for solo piano and the *Trois valses romantiques* for two pianos (1883); the orchestral *Joyeuse marche* (1888); two ravishing works for women's voices and orchestra, *La Sulamite* (1884) (seminal to Debussy's *Damoiselle élue*) and the *Ode à la musique* (1890), as well as a handful of songs to which Ravel and Poulenc were the appreciative heirs. His later operatic ventures, serious as well as comic, run alongside this small but choice output – *Gwendoline*, *Le roi malgré lui* and the unfinished *Briséïs*. He undoubtedly pinned his most ardent hopes on them and gave them his all – his love was unreciprocated. From the early 1890s his

Henri Fantin-Latour's group portrait of the principal French Wagnerians; Chabrier is at the piano and d'Indy is standing far right

health deteriorated rapidly, and he died aged 53 of general paralysis of the insane.

Chabrier's operatic career shows that, though the comic muse came to him with greater naturalness, there is real substance in his musical make-up to justify his ambition in tackling exalted subjects. And though only *L'étoile* can be called even marginally a repertoire piece, all five add, in different ways, to the range and stature of this mixed-up composer who is so much more significant than he seems.

L'étoile

The Star
Opéra bouffe in three acts (1h 30m)
Libretto by Eugène Leterrier and Albert Vanloo
Composed 1877
PREMIERES 28 November 1877, Théâtre des Bouffes-Parisiens, Paris; US: 18 August 1890, Broadway Theater, New York (arr. Sousa); UK: 7 January 1899, Savoy Theatre, London (arr. Sousa as *The Merry Monarch*); 14 April 1970, John Lewis Theatre, London (as *The Lucky Star*)
CAST Ouf *t*, Siroco *b*, Hérisson de Porc-Epic *bar*, Aloès *ms*, Tapioca *t*, Lazuli *s* (*travesti* role), Princess Laoula *s*, maids of honour (Oasis, Asphodèle, Youca, Adza, Zinnia, Koukouli) 6 *s*, Mayor and Chief of Police *spoken roles*; *satb* chorus of people, watchmen, courtiers
STANDARD ORCHESTRA

For all the (to us) charm of Chabrier's first completed opera, it was at first regarded as excessively

complicated for an opéra bouffe. It was accused of Wagnerian orchestration (Henri Duparc, who admired it, later called it 'a French *Meistersinger*'), and both the orchestra and the chorus had difficulty preparing their music. Its original run of 40 performances at the Bouffes-Parisiens was regarded as disappointing, and it was not seen again in Paris until 1941.

SYNOPSIS

Act I Ouf the First roams his city in disguise to find a suitable subject to execute as a 39th birthday treat. Enter, also disguised, Hérisson, his wife Aloès, secretary Tapioca, and Laoula, daughter of the neighbouring monarch. Their mission, of which she is unaware, is to marry Laoula to Ouf. The pedlar Lazuli has already fallen for her. Scolded for flirting with the two ladies (who are disguised as each other) he insults Ouf, who thus finds the desired candidate for death by impalement. Just in time Siroco, the king's astrologer, reveals that Ouf's fate and Lazuli's are inextricably linked. Lazuli is escorted with honour into the palace.

Act II Lazuli longs to escape and join Laoula. Ouf, still unaware of the two women's exchange, furthers the lovers' marriage by having the superfluous husband, Hérisson, imprisoned. Lazuli and Laoula depart happily together, leaving Aloès and Ouf in friendly contact, to the discomposure of Hérisson who has now escaped. This confusion is resolved and Hérisson orders the pedlar to be shot. Gunfire is heard from the lake. Laoula is brought in, but no Lazuli, so Ouf and Siroco accept that this day will be their last.

Act III Lazuli, who has swum to safety, returns to overhear Ouf and his astrologer drowning their sorrows in green chartreuse and then, when Hérisson enters, an explanation. The men leave; the girls return. Their sadness is dispelled when Lazuli reveals himself, suffering only from a sneeze. A second elopement is planned. But Ouf returns, anxious to implant an heir without delay (an earlier prediction said he would lose his throne if his successor was not sired before he turned 40). Functionaries arrive to perform the marriage. Then when Siroco's latest erratic stargazing tells Ouf that his death is imminent, he releases Laoula and declares the pedlar his heir. His disappointment is lost in the general rejoicing.

Danburay (Ouf), Scipion (Siroco) and Jolly (Hérisson) in L'étoile *(Paris, 1877)*

The attractions of this charming piece include the tender *romance de l'étoile* where Lazuli first declares his love (its words possibly by Verlaine) and the delicious Tickling trio which follows. The words for the gruesome punishment which gives the otherwise kindly king such pleasure can surely be attributed in all their salacious innuendo to Verlaine: 'Le Pal / Est de tous les supplices / Le principal / Et le plus fécond en délices.' (The official librettists changed the last line to 'le moins rempli de délices'.) The note of tenderness is struck again in Act III with Laoula's *couplets de la rose* (at the moment when all hope of Lazuli has abandoned her for the second time). Parody of Donizetti/Bellini, lurking everywhere, surfaces in the Green Chartreuse duet a little earlier. But the music's main language is French, the accent unmistakably Chabrier's.

RECORDING Alliot-Lugaz, Raphanel, Damonte, Gautier, Le Roux, Bacquier, David, Lyons Opéra Ch and O, Gardiner, HMV, 1984
EDITION v.s., Enoch, 1877

Une éducation manquée
An Unsuccessful Education
Opérette in one act (40m)
Libretto by Eugène Leterrier and Albert Vanloo
Composed 1879
PREMIERES 1 May 1879, Cercle de La Presse, Paris (with pf); 9 January 1913, Théâtre des Arts, Paris; US: 3 August 1953, Tanglewood, Massachusetts; UK: 22 May 1955, Fortune Theatre, London
CAST Gontran de Boismassif *s* (*travesti* role), Hélène de la Cerisaie *s*, Maître Pausanias *b*
CHAMBER ORCHESTRA

The period is Louis XVI. Gontran and Hélène, newly married, don't know what happens next. The boy's tutor, Pausanias, lives in a world of textbooks; a letter from his grandfather is unspecific; the girl's aunt merely counsels obedience. They kiss, and Hélène departs sadly for bed. Gontran, alone after a blast of useless information from his tutor, gazes moodily out at the rain. It grows thundery. Hélène rushes back in terrified. They huddle together, and nature takes its course.

This charming miniature is worthy of Bizet both in amorous tenderness and sparkling wit. They combine in its best number, the duet for the lovers when their knowledge is still confined to kissing. And surely the Maître's babbling list of classic authors and off-putting subjects was remembered by Ravel for the fiendish maths problems in *L'enfant et les sortilèges*.

RECORDING Castelli, Collart, Depraz, unnamed O, Bruck, Chant du Monde, 1954
EDITION v.s., Enoch, 1879

Gwendoline
Opera in three acts (2h 45m)
Libretto by Catulle Mendès
Composed 1885
PREMIERES 10 April 1886, Théâtre de la Monnaie, Brussels; US: 2 October 1982, San Diego; UK: 23 February 1983, Bloomsbury Theatre, London

The opera is set on the English coast in the eighth century. Gwendoline, daughter of the Saxon chief Armel, while recounting her dream of being carried off to sea by a marauding Dane, is interrupted by a real invasion. Harald, the Danish leader, has never seen a living woman before and is overwhelmed by her beauty. He tells her his dream of a Valkyrie maiden. Soon he is eating out of her hand, and the wedding is fixed for the very same day. But Armel plans to massacre the enemy. Gwendoline must herself stab her new husband. Horrified, she urges him to escape, without telling him why. He comforts her; they sing an ardent duet, then he rushes out with the dagger. In combat with Armel it breaks, and Harald is easily struck down by the father's sword. Gwendoline, seeing him dying, snatches the broken dagger and stabs herself. The crowd gathers round while the lovers together await their assumption into Valhalla.

This absurd story invites obvious Wagnerism, but Chabrier's music, including the rampaging overture, is entirely his own. Especially good is the celebratory music early in Act II, culminating in the gorgeous *Epithalame* for the three principals with double five-part chorus. Chabrier would no doubt have been a non-starter as a tragic–melodramatic composer even with a better plot: one loves the piece for the musical richness he could not help devoting even to such a sinking ship.

RECORDING Miranda, Garazzi, Angot, Meloni, Ch and O of French Radio, Gallois, MRF, 1977
EDITION v.s. Enoch, 1886

Le roi malgré lui

The Reluctant King
Opéra comique in three acts (2h 45m)
Libretto by Emile de Najac, Paul Burani (pseudonym for Urbain Roucoux) and the composer, after the play by Ancelot (1836)
Composed 1886
PREMIERES 18 May 1887, Opéra-Comique, Paris; US: 18 November 1976, Juilliard School, New York; UK: 7 November 1992, Queen Elizabeth Hall, London (concert)
CAST The French: Henri de Valois *bar*, Comte de Nangis *t*, 5 Seigneurs (Liancourt *t*, Elbeuf *t*, Maugiron *bar*, Caylus *bar*, Villequier *b*); The Poles: Count Laski *b*, Basile (innkeeper) *t*, soldier *b*, Duc de Fritelli (a Venetian) *bar-bouffe*; The Ladies: Minka (Laski's servant) *s*, Alexina, Duchesse de Fritelli *s*; *satb* chorus of pages, French and Polish Lords, Polish ladies, soldiers, populace
LARGE ORCHESTRA

The plot of *Le roi malgré lui*, which centres around the election in 1574 of Henri de Valois to the Polish throne, must be among the most complicated ever undertaken by an opera composer. As Harry Halbreich says, 'It is a negative *tour de force* to invent such a confusing story with so few characters in it.'

SYNOPSIS
Act I Henry of Valois has been elected King of Poland. But he and his nobles would rather be in France, while Count Laski is drumming up local support for a rival, the Archduke of Austria. Henry – disguised – learns of a plot to kidnap him and escort him out of Poland. He secretly wishes it success, but decides to attend a ball in disguise as his friend Nangis, whom he meanwhile arrests.

Act II At the ball, Henry meets Laski, who lets slip that Alexina (a former love of Henry's) is now the wife of Fritelli, Henry's chamberlain. After a *tête-à-tête* with Alexina (who knows him only as her

Venice lover) he takes the conspiracy oath. He summons Nangis and presents him to the conspirators as the king. Nangis grasps Henry's intention, and plays along. But when Laski announces that the 'king' is to die, Henry tries in vain to reveal his true identity. The conspirators draw lots to decide the assassin, and Henry himself is chosen. Nangis escapes with the help of his beloved Minka, a Polish slave.

Act III Henry (still as Nangis) arrives at a wayside inn, proclaiming the Archduke of Austria, but hides as Alexina announces that the archduke has fled, believing the plot discovered. Minka arrives looking for the 'king' and, persuaded by Alexina that he is dead, is about to stab herself when the real Nangis appears. Alexina and Henry leave for the frontier, but are accosted by Nangis and the French guard. Henry decides to be king after all.

Even if the music were as transparent as Offenbach or Sullivan it would be difficult to imagine the complex plot coming over clearly. But Chabrier has lavished upon it enough invention for a lifetime of operetta. The forms are large ('cette opérette colossale' said Reynaldo Hahn) and the richness of detail is extravagant. Size is shown above all in the finales of the first two acts and in the piece's only well-known section, the *Fête polonais* (in its full form, with voices, the ballroom scene to end all ballroom scenes) that opens Act II. Detail is shown at its most precious in such numbers as the quintet where one heroine, Minka, is rescued from a soldier; the duet she sings in Act III with the other heroine Alexina (a delectable next step from the duet in Berlioz's *Béatrice et Bénédict*); above all in the Act II barcarolle where Alexina and the reluctant king recall their former *amour*. These are some of the highlights in a score that contains nothing inferior. The waste of music so good is, in artistic terms, tragic. *Le roi malgré lui* and Weber's *Euryanthe* are the two greatest casualties in the history of the musical stage.

After some initial success in Germany, *Le roi* has languished between infrequent attempts at revival, adored by every lover of its composer. It remains to be seen whether it could be made to work on the modern stage.

RECORDING Hendricks, Garcisanz, Jeffes, Quilico, Lafont, De Moor, Ch and New PO of French Radio, Dutoit, Erato, 1984
EDITION f.s., Enoch et Costallat, 1887; new text, Enoch, 1929

Briséis

Drame lyrique in three acts (inc.)
Libretto by Catulle Mendès and Ephraim Mikhael, after Goethe's ballad *The Bride of Corinth* (1797)
Composed 1888–91
PREMIERES 31 January 1897, Concerts Lamoureux, Paris (concert); 14 January 1899, Königliche Oper, Berlin; US: 3 March 1911 (concert)

Only Act I was completed. At the time of the Emperor Hadrian, Hylas is setting out from Corinth on a voyage: he and his lover, Briséïs, exchange vows. Thanasto, her mother, subject to demonic possession, invokes Jesus and vows to devote herself to the new gospel. A hymn to the Saviour Apollo is heard, then the Christian preacher appears with his story of the True Saviour. Stratokles, head man of Thanasto's household, mocks and blasphemes. The preacher rebukes him and swears that Thanasto will be cured if her daughter embraces the new religion. Briséïs is torn between familial piety and her love for Hylas. Thanasto reappears, vowing her daughter's life to Jesus. Briséïs submits, and the act ends with her mother's hymn of Christian victory.

The other two acts remained fragmentary at Chabrier's death. The first was published post-humously, and given in concert performances and even stage productions. As with *Gwendoline* one puzzles over such an intelligent man going for such an obvious dead duck. Yet the music it elicited from him is in his ripest and boldest manner, whose richness of invention will be properly recognized one of these days.

EDITION v.s., Enoch, 1897

Other operas: *Fisch-Ton-Kan* (inc.), (1864), 1941; *Vaucochard et fils 1er* (inc.), (1864), 1941; *Jean Hunyade* (inc.), (1867); *Le sabbat* (inc.), (1877); *Les muscadins* (inc.), (1880)

BIBLIOGRAPHY   Roger Delage (ed.), *Emmanuel Chabrier, Iconographie Musicale*, Editions Minkoff et Luttes, 1982; Edward Lockspeiser (ed.), *The Literary Clef*, Calder, 1958; Rollo Myers, *Emmanuel Chabrier and His Circle*, Dent, 1969

R.H.

GEORGE CHADWICK
George Whitfield Chadwick; *b* 13 November 1854, Lowell, Massachusetts, US; *d* 4 April 1931, Boston, US

Chadwick was one of the most influential figures in later 19th-century American music as composer, performer and educator. Like many American composers of his generation and later, including his pupil Horatio Parker, Chadwick spent some years studying in Germany where his teachers included Rheinberger. Chadwick's first stage works, *The Peer and the Pauper*, *A Quiet Lodging* (both now lost) and *Tabasco* were modelled on the operettas of Gilbert and Sullivan, then in vogue in New York. Although the last enjoyed considerable success, it was many years before he wrote his next opera, *Judith*, a large-scale biblical drama, composed for the Worcester Festival (Massachusetts) but never performed. A decade later Chadwick sought to consolidate his important position in American musical life with a modern, native-set *verismo* opera, *The Padrone*, a story of Mafia control of poor Italian immigrants. However, the opera was rejected by the Metropolitan Opera and subsequent neglect of it and Chadwick's other works has meant that an important part of the history of American opera is missing.

Surviving operatic works: *Tabasco*, 1894; *Judith*, 1901; *Everywoman: Her Pilgrimage in Quest of Love*, 1911; *The Padrone*, (1913); *Love's Sacrifice*, 1923

BIBLIOGRAPHY   V. F. Yellin, *Chadwick: Yankee Composer*, Smithsonian Institution Press, 1990

P.D.

STANISLAS CHAMPEIN
b 19 November 1753, Marseilles, France; *d* 19 September 1830, Paris

Champein arrived in Paris in 1776. He made his début three years later with *Le soldat français*, and thereafter wrote principally for the Comédie-Italienne (from 1793 the Opéra-Comique). Admin-istrative duties as a civil servant took him away from composition and from Paris (1794–1804), and after his return he composed less intensely. However, he wrote 30 light operas and numerous other stage works.

Although Champein's gift for melody made him a natural successor of Monsigny, the light and vivacious character of his works owed much to Italian composers. Certain compositions, however – *Isabelle et Fernand*, *Menzikoff et Foedor* – approached the more serious and Romantic style of opéra comique cultivated by Cherubini, Méhul and Lesueur.

Champein's earliest works were his most successful. *La mélomanie* (1781) remained in the repertoire until 1829 and was performed extensively abroad. *Le nouveau Don Quichotte* (1789) was considered a masterpiece in its skilful blend of French taste and Italian spirit. In addition to his abundant melodic talents, contemporaries praised Champein's generally sound technique and charming humour, but found his accompaniments at times cumbersome and his inspiration occasionally limited. The poor literary quality of some libretti was also criticized.

Operas: *Le soldat français*, 1779; *Mina*, 1780; *La mélomanie*, 1781; *Léonore, ou L'heureuse épreuve*, 1781; *Le baiser, ou La bonne fée*, 1781; *Le poète supposé, ou Les préparatifs de fête*, 1782; *Isabelle et Fernand, ou L'alcade de Zaláméa*, 1783; *Les amours de Colombine, ou Cassandre pleurer*, 1785; *Les amours de Bayard, ou Le chevalier sans peur et sans reproche*, 1786; *Les fausses nouvelles, ou Les noces cauchoises*, 1786; *Le manteau, ou Les deux nièces rivales*, 1786; *Les dettes*, 1787; *Florette et Colin*, 1787; *Lanval et Viviane, ou Les fées et les chevaliers*, 1788; *Les déguisements amoureux*, 1789; *Le nouveau Don Quichotte*, 1789; *Le portrait, ou La divinité du sauvage*, 1790; *Les ruses de Frontin*, 1790; *Bayard dans Bresse*, 1791; *Les espiègleries de garnison*, 1791; *Les deux prisonniers, ou La fameuse journée*, 1794; *Le cannonier convalescent* (coll. with J. F. Guichard), 1794; *Les épreuves du républicain, ou L'amour de la patrie*, 1794; *Les trois Hussards*, 1804; *Valmier, ou Le salut du roi*, 1805; *Laurette*, (1807); *Menzikoff et Foedor, ou Le fou de Bérézoff*, 1808; *La ferme du Mont-Cénis*, 1809; *Les rivaux d'un moment*, 1812; *Le mariage extravagant*, 1812; *Les Hussards en cantonnement*, 1817

BIBLIOGRAPHY   Louis Petit de Bachaumont *et al.*, *Mémoires secrets*, 36 vols, J. Adamson, 1777–89

E.C.

RUPERTO CHAPÍ

Ruperto Chapí y Lorente; *b* 27 March 1851, Villena, Spain; *d* 25 March 1909, Madrid

Chapí, dubbed the Spanish Massenet, was one of Spain's leading zarzuela composers, with over 150 successful works to his credit, including *La revoltosa* (1897) which Saint-Saëns admired. He also wrote religious and chamber music, songs and military music.

The success of Chapí's early one-act opera *Las naves de Cortés* in 1874 won him a government scholarship to Italy and France, where he wrote the bulk of his operas. His last, *Margarita la Tornera*, was hailed by Chapí's friends as the definitive Spanish opera when it was premiered shortly before his death. However, the mere suppression of the spoken dialogue of zarzuela did not automatically produce great opera, and Chapí's superficial characterization and inability to project drama on a large scale resulted in his operas slipping quickly from public view.

Operas: *Las naves de Cortés*, 1874; *La hija de Jefté*, 1876; *La muerte de Garcilaso*, (1876); *Roger de Flor*, 1878; *Circe*, 1902; *Margarita la Tornera*, 1909
Zarzuelas, in three or more acts: *Las dos huerfanas*, 1880; *La calle de Carretas*, 1880; *Adiós Madrid*, 1880; *El hijo de la Nieve*, 1881; *La tempestad*, 1882 (RECORDING London International, 1950s); *El milagro de la Virgen*, 1884; *El gerrillero*, 1885; *La Bruja*, 1887 (RECORDING Alhambra, 1970); *El Rey que rabió*, 1891 (RECORDING London International, 1950s); *La bala del rifle*, 1892; *Los Mostenses*, 1893; *El Duqe de Gandia*, 1894; *Mujer y Reina*, 1895; *Los hijos del batallón*, 1898; *Curro Vargas*, 1899; *La Cara de Dios*, 1899; *La cortijera*, 1900; *Don Juan de Austria*, 1902; *Juan Francisco*, 1904; *Las mil maravillas*, 1908; in two acts: *Abel y Cain*, 1873; *Madrid y sus afueras*, 1880; *El Domingo Gordo*, 1886; *Juan Matias el barbero*, 1887; *El fantasma de los aires*, 1887; *Los lobos marinos*, 1887; *El esclavo o la venida del Mesias*, 1887; *Las hijas del Zebedeo*, 1889; *El Cocodrilo*, 1889; *Todo por ella*, 1890; *El mismo demonio*, 1891; *Blasones y talegas*, 1901; in one act: *Música clásica*, 1880; *La calandria*, 1880; *Nada entre dos platos*, 1881; *La Serenata*, 1881; *La flor de lis*, 1884; *El país del abanico*, 1885; *Ya pican ya pican*, 1885; *Los quintos de mí pueblo*, 1885; *Término medio*, 1885; *El figon de las desdichas*, 1887; *Playeras*, 1887; *Felipe*, 1887; *Noche de feria*, 1888; *Exposicion Universal; Ortografía*, 1888; *El país de los insectos*, 1889; *Las doce y media y sereno*, 1890; *Los nuestros*, 1890; *Nocturno*, 1890; *Pan de flor*, 1890; *La tentaciones de San Antonio*, 1890; *Para hombres solos*, 1890; *Los trabajadores*, 1891; *La raposa*, 1892; *Las campanadas*, 1892; *La Cranna*, 1892; *El organista*, 1892; *Via libre*, 1893; *Los gendarmes*, 1893; *El reclamo*, 1893; *El moro Muza*, 1894; *El tambor de granaderos*, 1894; *El cura del regimiento*, 1895; *El señor corregidor*, 1895; *El bajo de arriba*, 1895; *El cortejo de la Irene*, 1896; *La gitanilla*, 1896; *Los golfos*, 1896; *Las peluconas*, 1896; *Las bravias*, 1896; *Los charlatanes*, 1896; *El si natural*, 1897; *El paso a nivel*, 1897; *La niña del estanquero*, 1897; *La revoltosa*, 1897 (RECORDING Spanish HMV, 1968); *La piel del diablo*, 1897; *Pepe Gallardo*, 1898; *El fonógrafo*

ambulante, 1898; *La señá Frasquita*, 1899; *Los buenos mozos*, 1899; *El galope de los siglos*, 1900; *Maria de los Angeles*, 1900; *El estreno*, 1900; *El barquillero*, 1900 (RECORDING London International, 1950s); *Tierra por medio*, 1901; *Academia militar*, 1901; *La Guajira*, 1901; *¿Quo vadis?*, 1901; *El sombrero de plumas*, 1902; *Plus ultra*, 1902; *El tio Juan*, 1902; *Abanicos y panderetas*, 1902; *El puñao de rosas*, 1902 (RECORDING excerpts: London International, 1950s); *Cuadros vivos*, 1902; *La venta de Don Quijote*, 1902; *El rey mago*, 1902; *La leyenda dorada*, 1903; *El equipaje del Rey José*, 1903; *La chica del maestro*, 1903; *La cruz del abuelo*, 1903; *Género chico*, 1904; *Aves de paso*, 1904; *Sesión pública*, 1904; *La punalado*, 1904; *Mam'zelle Margot*, 1904; *Juan Francisco*, 1904; *El cisne de Lohengrin*, 1905; *Guardia de honor*, 1905; *Miss Full*, 1905; *El seductor*, 1905; *La inocente Virginia*, 1905; *La peseta enferma*, 1905; *El alma del pueblo*, 1905; *Calabazas*, 1905; *El hijo de Daño Urraca*, 1905; *El amor en solfa*, 1905; *Angelitos al cielo*, 1905; *La reina*, 1905; *Alma Gitana*, 1905; *Le sobresalienta*, 1905; *La joroba*, 1906; *Dos contrahechos*, 1906; *El maldito dinero*, 1906; *El rey del petróleo*, 1906; *El triunfo de Venus*, 1906; *La frugua de Vulcano*, 1906; *La pesadilla*, 1906; *Los bárbaros del Norte*, 1906; *El pino del norte*, 1906; *Ninón*, 1907; *Los veteranos*, 1907; *La pátria chica*, 1907; *La dama Roja*, 1908; *El merendero de la alegria*, 1908; *Los madrileños*, 1908; *Entre rocas*, 1908; *La carabina de Ambrosio*, 1908; *Sábado blanco*, 1908; *La eterna revista*, 1908; *El amor en capilla*, 1908; *Las calderas de Pedro botero*, 1908; *Aqui hase farta un hombre*, 1909; *El diablo con faldas*, 1909; *Los majos de plante*, 1909
BIBLIOGRAPHY   Angel S. Salcedo, *Ruperto Chapí: su vida y sus obras*, Editora Nacional Edinal (Madrid), 1929; *rp*, Mexico City, 1958

S.J.W.

GUSTAVE CHARPENTIER

b 25 June 1860, Dieuze, Meurthe, France; *d* 18 February 1956, Paris

The son of a baker who had moved with his family from his native Lorraine to Tourcoing at the time of the Franco-Prussian War, Charpentier entered the Lille Conservatoire at the age of 15. Success there led to a municipal scholarship to the Paris Conservatoire in 1881. He studied composition with Massenet, and in 1887 won the prestigious Prix de Rome. During his three-year stay in Rome he produced a colourful orchestral suite, *Impressions d'Italie*, which won widespread notice, and a symphonie-drame in four movements, *La vie du poète*, for solo voices, chorus and orchestra, set to his own text. He also began work on the libretto and score for an opera set in working-class Paris and in the village of Montmartre, where he had lived as a student.

After his return to Paris Charpentier's affinities with the poets gave birth to four Baudelaire settings for voice and piano, and three songs for voice and orchestra on texts by Verlaine. Fashionable interest in the 18th century found expression in a *Sérénade à Watteau*, for solo voices, chorus and orchestra. The manuscript score of a second orchestral suite was accidentally destroyed and the work was lost. His *Fête du couronnement de la Muse*, intended for an open-air ceremony in Montmartre organized by the

Gustave Charpentier's Louise *(Paris, 1900)*

composer himself, was performed in Lille and Paris in 1898. In the meantime Charpentier continued work on his opera, in collaboration with some literary friends, including the writer Saint Pol-Roux. He incorporated the music of the *Fête du couronnement* as the central scene of the third act. After some delay attributable to its unusual nature, the completed work, now named *Louise*, was accepted by the Opéra-Comique, and at its premiere in February 1900 was an immediate success, attracting enthusiastic audiences from all social classes. It made its way round the opera houses of the world, and was conducted by Mahler, in both Vienna and New York. It also launched the career of the young Scottish singer Mary Garden, who stepped into the leading role in the course of the eighth performance.

In 1902, in accordance with his philosophy and interests, Charpentier founded the Conservatoire populaire Mimi Pinson, designed to provide a free education in the arts for the working girls of Paris. Thereafter the cultivation of his image as an artist became a substitute for creative production: the only other work of significance that he wrote was *Julien*, a poème lyrique in four acts and a prologue, again to his own libretto. *Julien*, conceived as a sequel to *Louise*, was performed at the Opéra-Comique in June 1913. The score was largely a reworking of the earlier *Vie du poète*, with additional material borrowed from *Louise*. The later work, which

substituted fantasy for realism, shared the limitations but lacked the strengths of its predecessor. In 1913 it was already a relic of a bygone age, and it did not survive its initial productions in Paris, Prague and New York. It may have been some consolation for the composer that in the previous year he was elected to succeed his friend and teacher Massenet as a member of the Académie des Beaux Arts. Other stage projects came to nothing, and the rest of his life was uneventful.

Louise

Roman musical in four acts (five tableaux) (2h 15m)
Libretto by the composer
Composed *c.* 1889–96
PREMIERES 2 February 1900, Opéra-Comique, Paris; UK: 18 June 1909, Covent Garden, London; US: 3 January 1908, Manhattan Opera, New York
CAST Louise *s*, Her Mother *ms*, Julien *t*, Louise's Father *bar*, 19 female soloists, 20 male soloists; *satb* chorus of Paris citizens, street sellers, workmen, dressmakers, beggars, street urchins, people of Montmartre, Bohemians, etc.
LARGE ORCHESTRA including 2 hp, cel, gtr

SYNOPSIS
Act I The action is set in Paris in 1900. Louise, a young dressmaker, is torn between her love for the poet Julien and her attraction to his Bohemian way of life, and her loyalty to her devoted but narrow-minded working-class parents.

Act II At first Julien fails to persuade Louise to abandon her family for freedom and happiness, but she eventually runs away with him.

Act III In a carnival atmosphere Louise is crowned Queen of Bohemia and Muse of Montmartre. But her mother interrupts the celebrations and persuades her to return to see her father, who is dangerously ill.

Act IV Although her father recovers, he is broken by disappointment and bitterness, and her parents use all means to prevent Louise from leaving. But the freedom and pleasures of the life she has tasted are too compelling. After a violent dispute her father orders her from the home. She flees to her lover and his world, and her despairing parent curses the city that has taken her from him.

The attraction of *Louise* lies in its unique amalgam of disparate elements and influences. It owes something to the late 19th-century French school of social realism, as exemplified in the novels of Zola: the portrayal of the bleak existence of the poor and deprived is unadorned. At the same time the pill is sweetened by the romantic portrayal of the Bohemian life of Montmartre, and by the heroine's proclaimed desire, daring in its day, for sensual pleasure. The musical style too is eclectic, with influences ranging from Berlioz and Wagner to Gounod and Massenet, and incorporating a naturalistic treatment of Paris street cries. Some aspects of the work, in particular the Symbolist elements, are undoubtedly dated. But at his best, as in the well-known air 'Depuis le jour' and in the crowd scenes, Charpentier displays a genuine melodic gift and a lively theatrical sense, which have ensured for *Louise* a distinctive place in the repertoire of French opera.

RECORDINGS 1. Vallin, Lecouvreur, Thill, Pernet, Raugel Ch and O, Bigot, Columbia, 1936; 2. Cotrubas, Berbié, Domingo, Bacquier, Ambrosian Opera Ch, New Philharmonia O, Prêtre, CBS, 1975; 3. Lott, Pruett, Gorr, Blanc, Ch and O de l'Opéra National de Belgique, Cambreling, Erato, 1982: the early version houses classic performances by Ninon Vallin and Georges Thill and suggests an authentic French style. The modern sets are both acceptable, with lovely sopranos in the title role. [A.B.]
EDITION v.s., Heugel, 1900

Other operatic works: *L'amour au faubourg*, (c. 1913); *Orphée* (inc.), (1913)
BIBLIOGRAPHY K. O'Donnell Hoover, 'Gustave Charpentier', *MQ*, vol. 25 (1939), pp. 334–50

B.D.

MARC-ANTOINE CHARPENTIER

b 1643, Paris; *d* 24 February 1704, Paris

Though best known today mainly for his sacred works, Charpentier occupied himself on numerous occasions with music for the stage. Indeed, his first datable compositions after his youthful studies with Carissimi in Rome consist of incidental music

for Molière's plays: an overture for *La Comtesse d'Escarbagnas* was given on 8 July 1672 together with his brief intermèdes for a revival of *Le mariage forcé*, the latter replacing those provided by Lully for the original in 1664. More ambitious was Charpentier's contribution to Molière's *Le malade imaginaire* (1673), the music of which lasts well over an hour.

Charpentier's association with what was soon to become the Comédie-Française continued for some 12 years after Molière's death in 1673. His scope there, however, was increasingly limited by a series of crippling legal restrictions introduced by Lully to stifle competition with the Académie Royale de Musique, his newly established opera company. These restrictions forced Charpentier to reduce both the quantity of music and the number of performers at the Comédie-Française.

Lully's monopoly also effectively prevented French composers from presenting all-sung dramatic works, at least in public. It was thus not until after Lully's death in 1687 that Charpentier had the chance to compose a full-scale opera. In the meantime he had to content himself, as far as dramatic music was concerned, with short pastorales and similar entertainments for private patrons. Most of those that survive were written for his employer Mlle de Guise, among them *Les arts florissants*, *La descente d'Orphée aux Enfers*, *Actéon* and two Christmas *pastorales*. Two others are courtly works: *La fête de Rueil*, commissioned to mark the unveiling of a statue of Louis XIV in the Duc de Richelieu's chateau at Rueil, and *Les plaisirs de Versailles*, a remarkably unbuttoned comic divertissement said to have been performed in the Sun King's private *appartements*. Slight though they are, all these works contain fine music and demonstrate Charpentier's gift for capturing a wide range of dramatic moods.

Far grander in scale are *Celse martyr* (1687) and *David et Jonathas* (1688), tragedies that Charpentier wrote for the Jesuit College Louis-le-Grand, the most prestigious school in France. Jesuit colleges had quickly latched on to the popular appeal of opera: within little more than a decade of the emergence of Lully's tragédie en musique we find the first adaptations of the genre to the Jesuits' own ends. Why, they would argue, should the Académie Royale de Musique have all the good tunes? Jesuit productions characteristically involved large performing forces and elaborate staging, as *David et Jonathas* amply demonstrates. (*Only the libretto of* Celse martyr *survives.*)

Charpentier's one work for the Académie Royale de Musique, *Médée*, was not particularly successful. There is evidence of 'a cabal of the envious and the ignorant' (Brossard). Too powerful and disturbing for those accustomed to the blandness and optimism of Lully, the opera was taken off after nine or ten performances. Nevertheless, it is arguably the finest French opera of the 17th century, Lully's *Armide* notwithstanding.

H. numbers refer to the Hitchcock catalogue, see BIBLIOGRAPHY

Le malade imaginaire

Comédie-ballet in a prologue and three acts, H. 495 (1h 15m)
Libretto by Molière
PREMIERE   10 February 1673, Théâtre du Palais-Royal

Like Molière's other comédies-ballets, this satire on contemporary medicine is a spoken play incorporating self-contained musical episodes or intermèdes. *Le malade imaginaire* includes three of these, together with a prologue and other music. Apart from the final intermède (the famous burlesque *cérémonie des médecins*), none of the music is more than tangentially related to the plot. It ranges from the pastoral allegory of the prologuev (only slightly tongue-in-cheek since it was addressed to Louis XIV) and the exoticism of the second intermède (a 'Moorish' entertainment in which gypsies with monkeys try to cheer up the eponymous hypochondriac) to the uninhibited buffoonery of the first intermède (Polichinelle's ludicrous serenade and his mugging by the night watch) and the cruel satire of the final cérémonie. This last includes percussion parts for apothecaries' mortars and pestles.

RECORDINGS   1. Poulenard, Feldman, Laurens, Ragon, Verschaeve, Deletré, Les Musiciens du Louvre, Minkowski, Erato Musifrance, 1988; 2. Zanetti, Rime, Brua, Visse, Crook, Gardeil, Les Arts Florissants, Christie, Harmonia Mundi, 1990
EDITIONS   f.s., H. Wiley Hitchcock (ed.), Minkoff, 1973; v.s. G. Marie (ed.), Durand, 1894
AUTOGRAPH MANUSCRIPT   Bibliothèque Nationale, Paris

Actéon

Pastorale en musique in one act, H. 481 (40m)
Libretto anonymous, after Ovid's *Metamorphoses*, Book III
PREMIERE   *c.* 1683–5, private performance at the Hôtel de Guise

The huntsman Acteon, having spied on Diana bathing naked, is transformed by the goddess into a stag and is savaged by his own hounds. Charpentier's treatment of the familiar legend, despite its brevity and economy of means (only two principal roles, a one-to-a-part chorus and a chamber ensemble of recorders, treble viols and continuo), generates an unusual degree of pathos, notably in Acteon's *plainte* (marked *obscur et triste*) as he catches sight of his metamorphosed reflection and in the powerful final chorus of hunters, 'Hélas, est-il possible'.

RECORDING   Feldman, Laurens, Mellon, Paut, Visse, Les Arts Florissants, Christie, Harmonia Mundi, 1982
AUTOGRAPH MANUSCRIPT   Bibliothèque Nationale, Paris

Les arts florissants

Opéra (or 'idylle en musique') in one act, H. 487 (40m)
Libretto anonymous
PREMIERE   *c.* 1685–6, private performance at the Hôtel de Guise

Charpentier's 'opéra' resembles the allegorical prologues of contemporary tragédie en musique.

With a group of demobilized warriors, the arts of Music, Poetry, Painting and Architecture pay homage to Louis XIV, who has established the peace that allows them to flourish. Their eulogy is interrupted by Discord and the Furies, jealous of Louis's achievements. The goddess Peace, invoking Jupiter's aid, restores order, and the arts join in a celebration of the joys she brings. For all the dramatic sterility of the libretto, Charpentier responds with music of extraordinary beauty, notable for its vivid contrasts, especially where the chorus is involved. The performing forces are similar to those required for *Actéon*.

RECORDING   Feldman, Mellon, Laurens, Dussaut, Visse, Reinhart, Cantor, Les Arts Florissants, Christie, Harmonia Mundi, 1982
AUTOGRAPH MANUSCRIPT   Bibliothèque Nationale, Paris

David et Jonathas

Tragédie en musique in a prologue and five acts, H. 490 (2h)
Libretto by Père François de Paule Bretonneau after Kings I (RC Bible)/Samuel I (Hebrew and Protestant Bibles)
PREMIERE   25 February 1688, Collège Louis-le-Grand, Paris
CAST   David *haute-contre*, Jonathas s, Saul b, Achis b, Joabel t, La Pythonisse (The Witch of Endor), L'Ombre de Samuel (The Ghost of Samuel) b, 3 Shepherds 3 s, 2 Warriors t, b, 2 Captives 2 s, a follower of David *haute-contre*, a follower of Jonathas b; satb chorus of people, warriors, captives, followers of David and Jonathan, shepherds, Philistines, Israelites, guards
ORCHESTRATION   largely unspecified but requiring 4- and 5-pt str (respectively with 2 or 3 va parts and with bass vns rather than vc and db), obs, recs, probably tpts and timp, and bc (hpd, theorbo[es], bass viols)

As with other Jesuit opéras de collège, *David et Jonathas* was originally performed in a manner that now seems extraordinary: sandwiched between the prologue and each of the five acts was a Latin spoken tragedy, *Saul*, also in five acts and with its own self-contained but complementary action. (The text of *Saul* is lost, though a detailed synopsis survives.) Since the music alone lasts two hours, the resulting spectacle must have been extremely long.

Like *Saul*, *David et Jonathas* deals with events surrounding the battle between the Israelites and Philistines, during which Saul and his son Jonathan are killed. It is preceded by a prologue in which Saul causes the Witch of Endor to summon up the ghost of Samuel and in so doing learns of Jonathan's and his own impending death.

Because the action of the spoken tragedy anticipates, act by act, that of the opera (albeit from a different perspective), the latter contains far less expository recitative than any contemporary tragédie en musique. It is consequently richer in set pieces, particularly ensembles and choruses. Some of these are remarkably long: the rondo-like sequence of numbers that make up Act I Scene 1, in which warriors and shepherds welcome the victorious David, lasts almost ten minutes.

While *David et Jonathas* never quite reaches the astonishing power of *Médée*, its musical and dramatic interest is more evenly distributed. Charpentier brings extraordinary poignancy to the scenes involving the parting of David and Jonathan and, later, the deaths of Saul and Jonathan. In depicting the Witch of Endor he establishes an eerie atmosphere, her music unfolding as a manic succession of shifting moods involving keys as remote as G flat major; this prepares especially well for the apparition of the ghost of Samuel, to the sepulchral accompaniment of four unspecified bass instruments (cf. *Médée*, Act IV Scene 9). It is indeed fascinating to see how easily the language, both musical and poetic, of the Lullian tragédie could be adapted to the sacred setting. Only the ballet, too lubricious for the Reverend Fathers, is missing, though Charpentier manages to sneak in a few isolated dance movements, just as he does in his histoires sacrées.

RECORDINGS   1. Zanetti, Lesne, Visse, Gardeil, Deletré, Fouchécourt, Les Arts Florissants, Christie, Harmonia Mundi, 1988: a stylish if at times quirky performance; 2. Alliot-Lugaz, Esswood, Jacobs, David, Huttenlocher, Soyer, Marinov, English Bach Festival Baroque Orchestra, Maitrise de l'Opéra de Lyon, Corboz, Erato, 1981: less secure in its grasp of style or dramatic pace, but still quite serviceable.
EDITION   f.s., J. Duron (ed.), Editions du Centre National de la Recherche Scientifique, 1981

Médée

Tragédie en musique in a prologue and five acts, H. 491 (3h)
Libretto by Thomas Corneille
PREMIERE   4 December 1693, Paris Opéra (Académie Royale de Musique)
CAST   Médée *s*, Créon *b*, Créuse *s*, Jason *haute-contre*, Oronte *b*, Nérine *s*; 7 *s*, 2 *haute-contre*, 2 *t*, 2 *b* soloists; *satb* chorus of shepherds and country folk, Corinthians, Argians, Cupid's captives, Italians, demons and phantoms
ORCHESTRATION   5-pt str (with 3 va parts and bass vns rather than vc and db), obs, recs, fls, tpts and timp; bc (hpd, theorbo[es], bass viols)

SYNOPSIS

Act I   With her husband Jason, the sorceress Medea has taken refuge in Corinth, which is now under threat from the Thessalians who wish to avenge Medea's earlier crimes. In self-defence the Corinthian king Creon has allied himself with Orontes, prince of Argos, by promising him the hand of his daughter Creusa. Medea, though grateful for the Corinthians' support, begins to suspect that Jason loves Creusa despite his feigned innocence. The citizens celebrate the arrival of Orontes and the Argians.

Act II   Creon requests Medea to leave Corinth during the impending battle, since his people are worried that her presence will bring misfortune. For his own ends, Creon encourages the blossoming love between Jason and Creusa, whom Orontes meanwhile vainly tries to woo.

Set design by Jean Bérain for Marc-Antoine Charpentier's Médée *(Paris, 1693)*

Act III Medea warns Orontes of her suspicions about Jason, and they form an alliance. Her fears are confirmed when she learns that Creon has consented to the marriage of Jason and Creusa. Summoning her demons, Medea poisons a robe that she had promised to Creusa.

Act IV Creusa appears wearing the robe, its poison not yet active. Assuring Orontes that Jason's wedding will not take place, Medea gives Creon an ultimatum: she will not leave Corinth unless Creusa marries Orontes. When the king tries to arrest her, the sorceress uses her powers to force the guards to fight each other, and then drives the king insane.

Act V Reluctantly Medea resolves to kill her children by Jason. Creusa implores her to calm Creon's madness. Medea agrees, on condition that the princess marry Orontes. For her father's sake Creusa reluctantly agrees, but too late: news arrives that the demented king has killed Orontes. Confronted by Creusa, Medea causes the robe's poison to take effect. Jason, finding the princess dying in agony, resolves vengeance. But the triumphant Medea tells him of the murder of their children. As she disappears on a dragon, her palace collapses.

Although Thomas Corneille borrows lines from his brother Pierre's *Médée* (1635), his libretto differs both from the earlier play and from those of Euripides and Seneca in beginning the action well before Medea has proof of her husband's infidelity. In so doing, he deprives the first two acts of dramatic tension. At the same time he allows scope for his central character to develop with greater psychological depth: Medea's proud, vengeful nature is softened by the compassion she reveals as wife and mother, while her dreadful retribution acquires some justification from Jason's false assurances. To this flawed but psychologically subtle libretto Charpentier responds magnificently. His music, though outwardly following the Lullian model, is shot through with Italian influence and develops with an intensity unparalleled in 17th-century France: its harmonic richness and audacity would remain without equal at the Opéra until the appearance of Rameau 40 years later, while its use of orchestral colour to delineate mood and character is especially imaginative.

RECORDING Feldman, Mellon, Boulin, Ragon, Bona, Cantor, Les Arts Florissants, Christie, Harmonia Mundi, 1984: occasionally tentative and understated, but generally a dramatic and moving account

EDITIONS Ballard, Paris, 1694; facsimile, Gregg, 1968; f.s., Lemaître (ed.), Editions du Centre National de la Recherche Scientifique, 1987

Other operatic works: *Petite pastorale*, ?mid-1670s; *Les plaisirs de Versailles*, early 1680s; *Actéon changé en biche*, 1683–5 (rev. of *Actéon*); *Sur la naissance de N[otre] S[eigneur] J[ésus] C[hrist]: pastorale*, 1683–5; *Pastorale sur la naissance de N[otre] S[eigneur] J[ésus] C[hrist]*, 1683–5; *Il faut rire et chanter: dispute de bergers*, 1684–5; *La fête de Rueil*, 1685; *La couronne de fleurs: Pastorale*, 1685; *La descente d'Orphée aux enfers*, ?mid-1680s (inc.); *Idyle sur le*

retour de la santé du Roi, 1686–7; *Amor vince ogni cosa*, [n.d.]; *Pastoraletta italiana*, [n.d.]

BIBLIOGRAPHY H. Wiley Hitchcock, *The Works of Marc-Antoine Charpentier. Catalogue raisonné*, Picard, 1982; H. Wiley Hitchcock, *Marc-Antoine Charpentier*, OUP, 1990; J. S. Powell, 'Charpentier's Music for Molière's *Le malade imaginaire* and its Revisions', *JAMS*, vol. 39 (1986), pp. 87–142; P. Ranum, 'A Sweet Servitude: a musician's life at the court of Mlle de Guise', *Early Music*, vol. 15 (1987), pp. 347–60

G.S.

ERNEST CHAUSSON

Amédée-Ernest Chausson; *b* 20 January 1855, Paris; *d* 10 June 1899, Limay, Yvelines, France

Unlike his younger contemporary Debussy, Chausson came from a well-to-do middle-class family – his father was a building contractor who made a fortune in Haussmann's reconstruction of Paris. Chausson developed late. After qualifying as a lawyer, he began his formal musical studies with Massenet when he was almost 25, before passing on to the more congenial César Franck. Between then and his death in a cycling accident 20 years later he wrote a small number of densely composed instrumental works including a symphony in B♭, a 'concerto' for piano, violin and string quartet, a piano trio and a piano quartet, the famous *Poème* for violin and orchestra, songs (including the Maeterlinck settings, *Serres chaudes*), and music for the theatre.

Like so many French composers of his generation, Chausson fell under the influence of Wagner in the 1870s, travelling to Munich in 1879 to see *The Ring* and later to Bayreuth. Wagnerian harmonic traits crop up even in his early concert works, mixed with the melodic chromaticisms of Franck, but his theatre music is never systematically Wagnerian, and in *Le roi Arthus*, the only opera he completed, leitmotifs play no more than a limited part.

Chausson's stage works include more or less fragmentary incidental music for Musset's *Les caprices de Marianne* (1882–4), Shakespeare's *The Tempest* (1888), Aristophanes' *The Birds* (1889) and a more substantial score for Bouchor's *La légende de Sainte-Cécile* (1891). He also planned at least ten operas, but apart from *Le roi Arthus* he appears to have composed fragments of only one, *Hélène* (1883–6), based on a poem by Leconte de Lisle, and the libretto for *La vie est un songe*, after the drama by the Spanish playwright Calderón.

Le roi Arthus
King Arthur
Drame lyrique in three acts (six tableaux), Op. 23 (2h 45m)
Libretto by the composer
Composed 1886–95
PREMIERE 30 November 1903, Théâtre de la Monnaie, Brussels

Chausson's version of the legend of King Arthur and the Round Table centres on the adulterous love of Lancelot for Queen Guinevere. The lovers are betrayed by the knight Mordred, but Arthur refuses to believe in Lancelot's guilt until Merlin, the wizard, tacitly confirms it. Guinevere strangles herself with her own hair, but Lancelot fights in a final battle against Mordred who has usurped Arthur's throne. Lancelot is killed, and Arthur is carried to Avalon on a skiff crewed by maidens, one of whom 'extends her wings to act as sails'.

While the plot bears an obvious resemblance to that of *Tristan und Isolde*, the music shows few parallels with Wagner's organic chromaticism and large-scale harmonic structures. Chromaticism of that kind is most marked in the love duet in Act I, where the 'Tristan' chord is prominent, but elsewhere the music makes use of the more decorative chromatic technique of Franck. The opera ends, like *Parsifal*, with a huge choral apotheosis in C major.

RECORDING Zylis-Gara, Winbergh, Quilico, French Radio Ch, French Radio New PO, Jordan, Erato, 1986: the first complete recording
EDITIONS v.s., Edition Salabert, 1900; v.s., Choudens, 1900

BIBLIOGRAPHY Ralph Scott Grover, *Ernest Chausson: The Man and His Music*, Athlone, 1980

S.W.

ALEKSANDR CHEREPNIN
See Tcherepnin, Aleksandr

NIKOLAY CHEREPNIN
See Tcherepnin, Nikolay

LUIGI CHERUBINI
Maria Luigi Carlo Zenobi Salvatore Cherubini;
b 14 September 1760, Florence; *d* 15 March 1842, Paris

Cherubini's background was typical of that of a talented young Italian musician of his time. The son of a harpsichordist at the Teatro della Pergola in Florence, he showed precocious talent. His intermezzo *Il giuocatore* (1775) demonstrates a thorough mastery of the idiom made popular by Pergolesi's *La serva padrona*. Cherubini came to the attention of the Grand Duke of Tuscany who, in 1778, sent him to study with Giuseppe Sarti, one of the leading composers of the day. In 1780 Cherubini received a commission for a full-length opera seria, *Il Quinto Fabio*, and other operas followed. His early works, generally, show a competence without any particular originality or promise of greater things to come. Like many of his contemporaries he sought fortune abroad and in 1784 accepted an invitation to London where an opera buffa, *La finta principesse*

(1785), and an opera seria, *Il Giulio Sabino* (1786), were presented at the King's Theatre in the Haymarket. Neither was successful, due, at least in part, to inadequate performances. So in 1787 Cherubini, encouraged by his compatriot, the violinist and composer Viotti, a leading figure on the French musical scene, took up residence in Paris, which was to become his permanent home.

When Cherubini arrived in the French capital the battle for supremacy at the Opéra between the supporters of Piccinni and Gluck, representing traditional and reform opera respectively, was still raging. Cherubini was engaged by Marmontel, a leading traditionalist, to set his libretto on the theme of Demophoon, a typically classic theme of love, conflict, and sacrifice and rescue already familiar in a version by Metastasio. Cherubini's work was weighed against a rival treatment of the same plot by Vogel, a dedicated follower of Gluck, and was found wanting. Not for the last time Cherubini was saddled with an incompetent libretto, and his imperfect understanding of the French language attracted critical condemnation. But despite its uncertainties *Démophoön* foreshadows Cherubini's mature style in its richly orchestrated accompaniments, its effective choral writing, and the sustained power of the dramatic conclusion.

Cherubini's association with Viotti and the queen's perfumer, Léonard, in forming a new opera company at the Théâtre de Monsieur, intended principally for the promotion of imported Italian opera buffa, established his position as an important influence in the musical life of Paris. The new theatre opened to acclaim in January 1789. With the advent of the Revolution the directors of the company realized that a change of name and of artistic policy was desirable. They commissioned a new building in the rue Feydeau, and the Théâtre Feydeau, as it came to be known, played a prominent role in the theatrical life of Paris throughout the turbulent final decade of the century. The new politically minded audiences rejected traditional opera on Classical themes (unless the themes were consonant with the principles of Republicanism), looking instead for subjects of contemporary relevance, with heroic deeds, highly charged action, exotic settings, cataclysmic climaxes. A vehicle for the new style was to hand in opéra comique, a medium combining music with spoken dialogue, whose flexible possibilities had already been explored by Grétry and his contemporaries in the preceding decades. Cherubini adapted his style at once to this genre. His solidly grounded musical training (not always matched by that of his French contemporaries), a symphonic mode of thinking, and an imaginative command of orchestral colour and texture served him well. His first attempt, *Lodoïska*, a rescue opera set in Poland, won instant acclaim. First performed in 1791 it remained the longest-running opera of the decade. Its successor, *Eliza*, written at the height of the Terror in 1794, is a romantic story set in the Swiss Alps. Cherubini's next work, *Médée*, of 1797, took up in the more liberal post-revolutionary period a central Classical legend, in a score of almost unparalleled intensity. In *Les deux journées*, which opened the new century in January 1800, the composer adopted a simpler idiom to proclaim a message of social and political reconciliation.

This opera, though not his last, marked the apogee of Cherubini's theatrical career. In 1803 his opéra-ballet *Anacréon* was staged at the Opéra. Its failure was attributed by the composer to a cabal; but it suffers from an inane plot, which was not rescued by some excellent dance music, a dramatic storm, and a sparkling overture much admired by Weber. However, an extended season of his earlier works performed in Vienna the previous year had won him the admiration and applause of the Viennese public, not least among them Beethoven, and Cherubini wrote his next opera, *Faniska* (1806), to a commission for Vienna. This was a rescue opera in the tradition of *Lodoïska* on a text by Beethoven's librettist Sonnleithner. It was initially well received by all, including the aged Haydn, who warmly embraced the composer at the premiere; but the opera did not establish itself. Nor did his next fulllength opera, *Les abencérages* (1813), based on a medieval Spanish theme, despite the colour and opulence of the score.

The anachronistic *Ali-Baba*, performed 20 years later, was a reworking of much earlier material. It was a total failure, exciting the gleeful derision of Berlioz. Meanwhile the disillusioned Cherubini had turned to church music; the two settings of the Requiem Mass are among his best works. He had been associated with the National Conservatoire since its creation in 1795, and in 1822 was appointed director. Thereafter administrative and public duties limited his musical output. By the time of his death in 1842 his operas had long since disappeared from the French stage, as the young Wagner, writing from Paris in the previous year, remarked with caustic disapproval.

Cherubini's influence on the course of opera in his adopted country after 1800 was slight. But in the German-speaking countries it was more important. *Lodoïska* and *Les deux journées* were widely performed in Europe in the early years of the new century. A season of the four principal operas staged in Vienna in 1802 had a profound effect on Beethoven, who regarded Cherubini as his greatest contemporary – one not confined to his obvious indebtedness to Cherubini in *Fidelio*. Weber, another great admirer, also drew inspiration from him, notably in *Der Freischütz*. It is difficult, however, to arrive at an overall assessment of Cherubini's operatic achievement because of the comparative neglect from which his work has suffered.

Lodoïska

Comédie héroïque in three acts (2h 30m)
Libretto by Claude-François Fillette Loraux, after *Les amours du chevalier de Faublas* by Jean Baptiste Louvet de Couvray (1790)
PREMIERES 18 July 1791, Théâtre Feydeau, Paris; US: 4 December 1826, New York (music arr. R. Honey); UK: [pasticcio version (in English) by Stephen Storace, including adaptations of music from the Cherubini and Kreutzer settings: 9 June 1794, Drury Lane, London]; 6 February 1962, Collegiate Theatre, London

The interest in rescue opera, dating from Grétry's *Richard Coeur de Lion* of 1784, was greatly stimulated by the storming of the Bastille in 1789. Cherubini's *Lodoïska* established the genre as a major operatic subspecies. Another operatic treatment of the theme by the violinist–composer Rodolphe Kreutzer was produced at the rival Théâtre Favart 12 days after the Cherubini premiere.

The action is set in Poland around 1600, near the castle of the tyrant Dourlinski, who is holding prisoner Lodoïska, beloved of Count Floreski. Floreski and his servant, who are searching for Lodoïska, fall into dispute with a band of Tartars. A combat ensues between the Tartar leader Titzikan and Floreski. Floreski overcomes his opponent and spares his life. They swear eternal friendship, and the Tartars depart. Floreski discovers Lodoïska's presence in the castle. In disguise he and his servant penetrate the fortress. They are taken prisoner; but at the crucial moment the Tartars successfully storm and burn down the castle, rescue the lovers and capture the tyrant.

Lodoïska set new standards in scale and complexity for French operatic writing. A notable feature (characteristic of the composer's subsequent works) is the symphonic treatment of motivic development in the orchestra, which allows for a full working out of individual scenes, especially in the ensembles and finales. The finale of Act III in particular sweeps powerfully forward to its dramatic

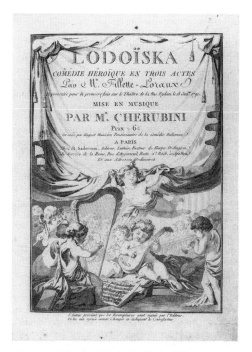

Title page of Cherubini's Lodoïska *(Paris, 1791)*

climax, the conflagration of the castle. It was above all the musical and visual treatment of this culmination that impressed audiences of the time.

RECORDINGS 1. Ligabue, Prandelli, Bruscantini, Monachesi, Cava, Rome Ch and SO of Italian Radio, De Fabritiis, MRF, 1961; 2. Devia, Lombardo, Corbelli, Shimell, Luperi, Ch and O of La Scala, Muti, Sony, 1991
EDITIONS f.s., Naderman, [1791]; facsimile, Garland (Early Romantic Opera 33), 1978

Eliza, ou Le voyage aux glaciers du Mont St Bernard

Eliza, or The Journey to the Glaciers of Mont St Bernard
Opera in two acts
Libretto by Jacques-Antoine de Reveroni de Saint Cyr
PREMIERE 13 December 1794, Théâtre Feydeau, Paris

Eliza has a claim to be the first Romantic opera centred on nature. The scene is set near the snow-covered heights of Mont St Bernard. The prior of a nearby hospice and his attendants are engaged on their daily task of searching for lost travellers. They discover Florindo, a young Genoese painter escaping from an unhappy love affair to find solace in the mountains. A letter arrives telling him that his beloved Eliza is now betrothed to another. Florindo in despair is led off by the prior. Eliza arrives, seeking Florindo, to assure him of her continued love. In the meantime Florindo has gone to find death on a treacherous glacier, leaving a farewell message. The others hasten after him. A raging storm precipitates an avalanche, apparently engulfing the hero. He is however rescued, and all misunderstandings are cleared up, amid general rejoicing.

The subject of the Swiss Alps as a background to the solitude of the individual had been a popular theme since Rousseau. Grétry, for example, had used it in his *Guillaume Tell* of 1791. And the portrayal of the natives of Savoy with their simple virtues and customs also appealed to the Parisian public. *Eliza* combines these two elements with a hero who, a landscape painter himself, has a special relationship with nature. The dramatic development of the opera is restricted by the poor libretto, the exiguous action, and the unheroic personality of the leading role. But the music has an evocative and picturesque quality unique in its day. Leitmotif plays its part: the introduction to the overture is a *ranz de vaches*, which reappears in the following *allegro*, and at a crucial point in the later action. The sounds of the tolling monastery bell and the tinkling bells of the mule train are integrated into the score. The Savoyards' songs provide more local colour.

The slow steps of the rescuers and the mysterious stillness of a mountain dawn are movingly evoked in the opening choral scene, which may well have influenced the prisoners' chorus in *Fidelio*. It is in striking contrast to the turbulence of the opera's climax, the Alpine storm. Each scene has its own special atmosphere, and together they form a series of nature tableaux, which excited and inspired Weber.

RECORDING Tucci, Raimondi, Zanasi, Washington, Ch and O of Maggio Musicale Fiorentino, Capuana, Melodram, 1960
EDITIONS f.s., Imprimerie du Conservatoire (Paris), [1794]; facsimile, Garland (Early Romantic Opera 34), 1979

Médée

Medea
Opera in three acts (2h 15m)
Libretto by François Benoit Hoffmann, after the tragedy by Pierre Corneille (1635)
PREMIERES 13 March 1797, Théâtre Feydeau, Paris; UK: 6 June 1865, Her Majesty's Theatre, London (in Italian, with recitatives by Luigi Arditi); US: 8 November 1955, New York (concert); 7 July 1973, City Opera, New York; UK: original version: 28 July 1984, Opera House, Buxton
CAST Médée *s*, Dircé *s*, Néris *ms*, Jason *t*, Créon *b*, Captain of the Guard *bar*, 2 servants *s*, *ms*; 2 children *silent*; *satb* chorus of servants of Dircé, Argonauts, priests, warriors, people of Corinth
STANDARD ORCHESTRA onstage: wind band including trbns and thunder-machine

Médée, by virtue of its dramatic and musical range and intensity, is Cherubini's masterpiece. It is also the only work out of the two thousand or so theatrical productions during the revolutionary decade in France to maintain a place in the repertoire, albeit until recently in a bowdlerized version. It has links with the pre-revolutionary classical opera of Gluck and his contemporaries and immediate successors. But in other respects it anticipates the 19th-century conception of tragic opera. The libretto focuses throughout on the personality and situation of the tormented sorceress, torn between her hatred of Jason, who has deserted and betrayed her, and her love for her children, who have been taken from her. The symphonic treatment of the accompaniment heightens the emotional tension, as do the enormous demands on the technique and stamina of the leading role. The obligatory final catastrophe, the immolation of the children and the destruction of the temple, remains unsurpassed in its dramatic and psychological power. Although coolly received at its premiere, *Médée* later won the admiration of Beethoven, Weber, Schumann, Wagner and Brahms.

SYNOPSIS

Act I The action takes place at Corinth. Outside the palace of King Créon, preparations are in train for the wedding of the king's daughter Dircé to Jason, who stole the Golden Fleece from Colchis, with the aid of the sorceress Médée. Médée betrayed her family and people to help him, and subsequently bore him two children, before he abandoned her. Dircé is fearful of Médée's wrath. Médée appears, demands that Jason return to her, and is rebuffed. She curses Jason and swears a terrible vengeance.

Act II Inside the palace Médée is in despair. Her servant Néris urges her to leave. Créon appears and banishes her from the city. Médée, whose schemes of vengeance are taking shape, begs to be allowed to spend a last day with her children. Créon grants her request. Apparently more calm, she asks Néris to take to Dircé two wedding gifts, a cloak and a diadem given to her by Apollo.

Act III Between the palace and a temple. Néris brings the children out of the palace to Médée, who embraces them. Sounds of lamentation come from the palace. The bride is dead, poisoned by Médée's gifts. The enraged populace storms out, seeking revenge. Médée, Néris, and the children take refuge in the temple. Soon a horrified Néris re-emerges, followed by Médée, brandishing the bloodstained knife with which she has slain her sons, and attended by Furies. Jason dies, to her imprecations. The temple is consumed by fire, and Médée and her Furies disappear in the flames.

Act III of Médée, *title page of the score*

The role of Médée was written for a singer of quite exceptional gifts, Mme Scio, principal soprano at the Théâtre Feydeau. The range and sustained power necessary to fulfil the requirements of the part ensure that the singer increasingly dominates the action, from her anticipated first appearance in the middle of Act I, to her virtually continuous presence in the final act, in which the interruption of spoken dialogue is reduced to a minimum. The other principals are perceived in relation to the sorceress, and have limited scope; they are none the less clearly delineated in musical terms. The marches in the first two acts are fine examples of their type. The mood of each act is established by the preceding orchestral music. The turbulent one-section overture, in F minor, bears some striking resemblances to the later *Egmont* overture of Beethoven (1810).

RECORDINGS 1. Callas, Scotto, Pirazzini, Picchi, Modesti, Ch and O of La Scala, Serafin, EMI, 1957: the only 'official' set with Callas; other versions from live performances exist with Callas in better voice; 2. Sass, Kalmár, Takács, Luchetti, Kováts, Hungarian Radio and TV Ch, Budapest SO, Gardelli, Hungaroton, 1978; no recording of the French original with dialogue [A.B.]
EDITIONS original version: f.s., Le Duc, [1797]; facsimile, Gregg International, 1971; v.s., Breitkopf und Härtel, [1855]

Les deux journées, ou Le porteur d'eau

The Watercarrier
Opera in three acts (1h 30m)
Libretto by Jean Nicolas Bouilly
PREMIERES 16 January 1800, Théâtre Feydeau, Paris; US: 12 March 1811, Théâtre St Phillippe, New Orleans; UK: [an adaptation entitled *The Escapes, or The Water Carrier*, containing some of Cherubini's music, as well as items by other composers, arranged by Thomas Attwood, 14 October 1801, Covent Garden, London]; 27 October 1875, Princess's Theatre, London (Carl Rosa Company)
CAST Constance *s*, Angelina *s*, Marcellina *s*, Village Girl *s*, Armand *t*, Antonio *t*, Mikeli *bar*, 2 *s*, *t*, 6 *b*; *satb* chorus of inhabitants of Gonesse, guards, soldiers
STANDARD ORCHESTRA including trbns

By the turn of the century, after the years of revolutionary unrest and excess, the taste of the Parisian theatre-going public was moving away from themes of violence towards those of peace and social reconciliation. Bouilly had already distinguished himself as an opera librettist with the rescue text *Léonore*, set by Pierre Gaveaux in 1798 (and destined to be the source of Beethoven's *Fidelio* a few years later). He now produced a new libretto, based (he later imaginatively claimed) on a real incident which had occurred in the early days of the Revolution. His theme of a rescue transcending class boundaries appealed at once to the public. Bouilly's libretto is, by the standards of the time, of exceptional quality. Concise, well structured, it was cited as a model of excellence by both Goethe and Mendelssohn. Cherubini's score did Bouilly full justice. The composer simplified his usual style (which was regarded by many of his French critics as too complex and learned) and wrote music of sparkling freshness and instant appeal. The opera was immediately successful, and quickly established itself in the German-speaking countries, where it maintained its place in the repertoire into the 20th century. There, and in England, it is known by the original alternative title, *The Watercarrier*.

SYNOPSIS
Act I The action is set in 1647, when Cardinal Mazarin, adviser to the Queen Regent, was effectively ruler of France. The Parliament of Paris has refused to endorse some new and unjust edicts. It has been dissolved, and its members are fugitives from arrest and imprisonment. A price has been put on the head of their outspoken leader, Count Armand. All the exits from the city are guarded by Mazarin's troops. Armand and his wife Countess Constance are offered shelter by Mikeli, a humble but generous and noble-minded watercarrier.

Mikeli's son, Antonio, recognizes in the count the stranger who rescued him from death some years earlier in Switzerland. Mikeli resolves to save the life of his family's benefactor at all costs. He devises a plan to enable the couple to escape from the city. Antonio is to be married the following day at the village of Gonesse outside Paris. The countess will pass through the barriers with him, disguised as his sister, and Mikeli himself will smuggle the count to safety.

Act II At the city barriers the guards are suspicious about the identity of the disguised countess. Mikeli arrives with his watercart and persuades them to let her through. While he distracts the attention of the guards, Armand, concealed in a compartment of the cart, slips out and escapes. Mikeli goes off down the side streets with his cart. Thus ends the first day.

Act III In the village preparations for the wedding are interrupted by the arrival of soldiers. Armand hides in a tree, but comes out and declares his identity when his wife is arrested. He too is taken prisoner. At this crucial moment Mikeli arrives with news of a free pardon from the queen for all the Parliamentarians. The count and countess are reunited. Antonio and his bride are married. Mikeli's courage and devotion are rewarded by the general rejoicing which ends the second day.

The appeal of the opera derives both from its direct and tuneful idiom and from the colourful blending of many different elements: solo numbers and ensembles of varying character, picturesque elements such as a Savoyard *romanza*, a village chorus, soldiers' marches. There are two instances of melodrama (spoken dialogue with orchestral accompaniment), a technique that reached its full potential in in *Fidelio*. Another noteworthy feature is Cherubini's use of two themes as reminiscence motifs in the orchestral accompaniment.

RECORDING Micheau, Giannotti, Regnier, Paul, BBC Theatre Ch, RPO, Beecham, Fonit Cetra, 1947
EDITIONS f.s., Frères Gaveaux, [1800]; facsimile, Garland (Early Romantic Opera 35), 1980

Other surviving operatic works: *Il giuocatore* (*intermezzo*), (1775) (RECORDING Europa, 1990); untitled *intermezzo*, 1778; *Il Quinto Fabio* (original lost), 1779, rev. 1783; *Armida abbandonata*, 1782; *Mesenzio re d'Etruria*, 1782; *Lo sposo di tre e marito di nessuna*, 1783; *Olimpiade*, (*c.* 1783); *L'Alessandro nell'Indie*, 1784; *L'Idalide*, 1784; *Demetrio*, 1785; *Il Giulio Sabino*, 1786; *Ifigenia in Aulide*, 1788; *Démophoön*, 1788 (EDITION facsimile, Garland, Early Romantic Opera 32, 1978); *La Molinarella*, 1789; *L'hôtellerie portugaise*, 1798 (RECORDING Melodram, 1952); *La punition*, 1799; *La prisonnière*, 1799; *Epicure*, 1800; *Anacréon, ou L'amour fugitif*, 1803 (RECORDING MRF, 1971); *Achille à Scyros*, 1804; *Faniska*, 1806; *Pigmalione*, 1809 (RECORDING MRF, 1955); *Il crescendo*, 1810 (RECORDING MRF, 1966); *Les abencérages, ou L'étendard de Grenade*, 1813 (RECORDINGS Cetra, 1956; MRF, 1975); *Ali-Baba, ou Les quarante voleurs*, 1833 (RECORDING Nuova Era, 1963); 6 others lost

BIBLIOGRAPHY Winton Dean, 'French Opera', *New Oxford History of Music*, vol. 8: *The Age of Beethoven 1790–1830*, OUP, 1982, pp. 37–46; Basil Deane, *Cherubini*, OUP, 1965; Basil Deane, 'Cherubini and opéra comique', *Opera*, vol. 40 (1989), pp. 1305–10; D. Galliver, 'Jean-Nicolas Bouilly (1763–1842), Successor of Sédaine', *Studies in Music*, vol. 13 (1979); A. Ringer, 'Cherubini's *Médée* and the Spirit of French Revolutionary Opera', *Essays in Musicology, in Honour of Dragan Plamenac*, Pittsburgh, 1969

B.D.

HENRI CHRISTINÉ

b 27 December 1867, Geneva; *d* 23 November 1941, Paris

Christiné, the son of a Swiss watchmaker, began his musical career writing songs for popular *café-concert* stars. His initial operettas were performed in Brussels, among them *Service d'amour* (1903) and *Les vierges du harem* (1907). But his greatest success came two days after the end of the First World War with *Phi-Phi* (1918), which revitalized the Offenbachian *opéra bouffe* of Classical antiquity, making it racier, more streamlined (in its elimination of heavy ensembles) and more dependent on the American dances that were sweeping Europe. *Dédé* (1921) was a comédie musicale about an amorous Parisian shoe salesman, memorably played by Maurice Chevalier. None of Christiné's later works, including two spectacles written for the Châtelet in the 1930s, has proved as enduring as *Phi-Phi* and *Dédé*, both of which have been revived fairly regularly.

Operettas (selective): *Service d'amour*, 1903; *Les vierges du harem*, 1907; *Phi-Phi*, 1918 (RECORDING Decca, 1960s); *Dédé*, 1921 (RECORDING Decca, 1960s); *Madame*, 1923; *J'adore ça*, 1925; *P.L.M.*, 1925; *Arthur*, 1929; *Au temps des merveilleuses*, 1934; *Yana*, 1936
BIBLIOGRAPHY Richard Traubner, *Operetta: A Theatrical History*, Gollancz, 1984

R.T.

JANI CHRISTOU

b 9 January 1926, Heliopolis, Egypt; *d* 8 January 1970, Athens

Brought up in Alexandria, the Greek composer Christou was from his earliest days imbued with the ancient Egyptian obsession with life after death. He studied philosophy at King's College, Cambridge, with Russell and Wittgenstein, and had private music lessons with Hans Redlich. His musical style developed rapidly from atonality, through serial techniques, to his own system, creating works through preparing, as it were, libraries of sound patterns that were subsequently ordered and selected by the composer into large-scale forms. Having secured his technique, Christou then, in the 1960s, expanded his palette to include all the performing arts in his works, using symbolic and often pictorial notation in his scores. Most of the works of his last decade are musico-theatrical and operatic in conception, including even the 'oratorio' *Mysterion*, based on texts from the ancient Egyptian *Book of the Dead*, and his final, culminating and most ambitious work, the opera *Oresteia*, left incomplete at his death. Among his later works were sketches for 130 *Anaparastasis* ('Re-enactments'), of which 33 were completed: they are short scenarios in which musicians and actors are required to improvise within carefully prescribed and defined situations, responding to each other's psychic stimulation.

Operatic works: *La ruota della vita* (cycle of 3 operas; lost), (1957); *Gilgamesh* (opera–oratorio; lost), (1958); *The Breakdown* (lost), (1964); *Oresteia* (inc.), (1970); many music-theatre works including: *The Strychnine Lady*, 1967; *Epicycle*, 1968; 33 *Anaparastasis* (1966–8)

BIBLIOGRAPHY   John G. Papaioannou, *Jani Christou and the Metaphysics of Music*, Chester, 1970

G.C.P.

FEDERICO CHUECA

b 5 May 1846, Madrid; *d* 20 July 1908, Madrid

Although his musical gifts were unrefined – many of his works were orchestrated by Joaquin Valverde – Chueca's innate lyricism enabled him to characterize the diverse Spanish scene with great success. His dozens of zarzuelas depicted Spanish life with realism and fervour, and became a part of the national musical fabric to the extent that Falla boldly alluded to a melody from one of them, *La canción de la Lola* (1880), at the policeman's entry in his *El sombrero de tres picos* (1917). Chueca's greatest success was the revue-like zarzuela *La gran vía* (1886), which ran for over 1000 consecutive performances, and whose material was adapted and purloined by imitators in several countries. Its plot tells of the concern in Madrid's streets and squares at plans to construct a huge highway through them all on the following 30 February. This was but an excuse to introduce sparkling and pointed social comment through the words of sea cadets, soldiers, guards, a serving girl, and three rats. The work became crucial in establishing the popularity of the one-act 'genero chico' zarzuela during the 1880s.

Operatic works include: *Las ferías* (coll. with Valverde), 1878; *La canción de la Lola*, 1880; *Luces y sombras* (coll. with Valverde), 1882; *De la noche à la mañana* (coll. with Valverde), 1883; *¡Hoy sale, hoy!* (coll. with Barbieri), 1884; *Vivitos y coleando*, 1884; *Fiesta nacional* (coll. with Valverde), 1884; *Caramelo* (coll. with Valverde), 1884; *La gran vía* (coll. with Valverde), 1886 (RECORDING London International, 1953); *Cádiz* (coll. with Valverde), 1886; *El año pasado por agua* (collab. Valverde), 1889; *De Madrid à Paris* (coll. with Valverde), 1889; *El arca de Noé*, 1890, as *Fotografías animadas*, 1897; *El chaleco blanco*, 1890; *La caza del oso, ó El tendero de comestibles*, 1891; *Los descamisados*, 1893; *Las zapatillas*, 1895; *El coche correo*, 1896; *Agua, azucarillos y aguardiente*, 1897 (RECORDING Alhambra,

1960s); *El mantón de Manila*, 1898; *Los arrastraos* 1899, as *El capote de paseo*, 1901; *La alegría de la huerta*, 1900 (RECORDING London International, 1954); *El bateo*, 1901; *La borracha*, 1904; *Chinita* (coll. with P. Córdoba), 1907; *El estudiante* (coll. with L. Fontanals), 1907; *Las mocitas del barrio*, 1909

BIBLIOGRAPHY   Kurt Gänzl and Andrew Lamb, *Gänzl's Book of the Musical Theatre*, The Bodley Head, 1988, pp. 1207–9, 1214–16

S.J.W.

VINCENZO CIAMPI

Vincenzo Legrenzio Ciampi; *b* ?1719, Piacenza; *d* 30 March 1762, Venice

A student of Leo and Durante in Naples, Ciampi made his early reputation there with six comic operas between 1737 and 1745. After a brief period in Palermo, he moved to Venice in 1748, where he produced *L'Adriano*, his second opera seria, for the Teatro S. Cassiano in 1748, and four more comic operas for the Teatro S. Moisè by autumn 1749. From 1749 Ciampi acted as music director for an Italian company that had been brought to London, expressly to perform a season of opera buffa at the King's Theatre – the first such season. As Burney's comments show, English taste remained loyal to the opera seria it was accustomed to from Handel and, with the exception of *Gli tre cicisbei ridicoli*, Ciampi had only moderate success. However, his operas were performed successfully in Brussels and in Paris where he achieved his greatest success with the pasticcio *Bertoldo, Bertoldino e Cacasenno* (1748). Such was its popularity that the dramatist Favart made a French adaptation, *Ninette à la cour*, which retained most of Ciampi's music. In this form the opera is recognized as a significant landmark in the development of opéra comique (and its German translation, *Lottschen am Hofe*, with new music by Hiller, in the development of the singspiel). Ciampi returned to Venice, probably in 1756, and ended his days as maestro del coro at the Ospedale degli Incurabili.

Ciampi stood between the baroque and the *galant* in style, imposing fashionable frills and flounces on traditional forms. Burney considered the buffo works to be his best, but was somewhat grudging in his praise as a whole: 'He had fire and abilities, but there seems something wanting, or redundant, in all his compositions.'

Surviving operatic works: *Bertoldo, Bertoldino e Cacasenno*, 1748; *La favola de' tre gobbi*, 1749; *Il negligente*, 1749; *Il trionfo di Camilla*, 1750; *Didone abbandonata*, 1754; *Catone in Utica*, 1756; *La clemenza di Tito*, 1756/7; *Il chimico*, 1756/7; *Arsinoe*, 1758; *Amore in caricatura*, 1761; 11 lost operas

D.S.B.

JÁN CIKKER

b 29 July 1911, Banská Bystrica, Slovakia; *d* 21 December 1989, Bratislava, Czechoslovakia

Cikker is probably the best-known modern Slovak opera composer. He studied at the Prague Conservatory (1930–36; composition with Křička and Novák) and with Weingartner in Vienna (1936–7). He taught at the Bratislava Conservatory (1939–44) and from 1951 at the Academy; he also worked as opera dramaturg at the Bratislava National Theatre (1945–8).

Like Suchoň, three years his senior, Cikker received a large number of performances outside his native Slovakia; but whereas Suchoň's fame rests largely on one work, all but the two most recent of Cikker's operas have been heard abroad; two, *Mr Scrooge* and *The Play of Love and Death*, received their premieres outside Czechoslovakia, in Kassel and Munich respectively.

Cikker's earliest operas are based on figures from Slovak history. Juro Jánošík was a legendary Robin Hood-type hero of Slovak folklore, executed in the early 18th century for his courageous stand against authority; Beg Bajazid was a Slovak child kidnapped and brought up as a Turk during the 16th century, when Slovakia was under Turkish rule, who returned to his native country as a Turkish commander. After two works based on these figures, Cikker chose his subjects increasingly widely, himself adapting international authors such as Tolstoy, Dickens, Rolland, Shakespeare and Kleist with considerable skill. Most of these operas have a background of dramatic events (for instance the French Revolution in *The Play of Love and Death*) against which characters grapple, often with tragic conclusions, though *Mr Scrooge* and *The Siege of Bystrica* have comic and grotesque elements. In *Mr Scrooge* however, the ethical character of the work rather than the sentimental is stressed.

Cikker first established himself as a symphonic composer, and his operas have been characterized as 'magnificent symphonic poems'. The musical language of the earlier works is tonal, though with modal and chromatic inflexions (e.g. to characterize, respectively, the Slovaks and the Turks in *Beg Bajazid*). *Mr Scrooge* employs a more extended tonality; *Resurrection* uses chords based on intervals other than thirds. Ostinato structures dominate, sounding occasionally, for instance in *The Play of Love and Death*, like Janáček. Cikker's first six operas employ a full symphony orchestra, to which voice parts can sometimes seem extraneous. There is an important dance element in all his works, not only in the obvious folkloric opportunities offered by the two nationalist operas, but more surprisingly in the later works as well, for instance at the dramatic climax of *The Earthquake in Chile*. From *Coriolanus* onwards, the chorus plays a large role. The most striking single feature of Cikker's operas is the care for large-scale structure. Elements return to give cohesion (for instance the opening of *The Play of Love and Death* returns abridged in the finale).

An 'intermezzo' technique, chiefly for reflective soliloquies, allows for both contrast in dramatic intensity and the manipulation of theatrical time, for instance in visionary scenes in *The Earthquake in Chile*, in which the past, the present and the hypothetical future are presented.

Resurrection

Vzkriesenie
Opera in three acts (2h 30m)
Libretto by the composer, after the novel by Tolstoy
Composed 1960–61
PREMIERES 18 May 1962, National Theatre, Prague; UK: 18 August 1964, King's Theatre, Edinburgh (Prague National Theatre)

Cikker's fourth opera, *Resurrection*, was brought to the Edinburgh Festival in 1964, in a production especially memorable for the spacious designs by Zbyněk Kolář. The music was heard as being closest (in the British experience) to that of *Wozzeck*: an Expressionist score, strongest in theatrical verve, centred on an elaborately architectonic scheme. Each of the three acts is itself divided into three parts, each consisting of two scenes flanking a central intermezzo. These 'intermezzi' are, however, sung: soliloquies or dialogues in which the two central characters (Katusha, a prostitute charged with murder, and Prince Nekhludov, once her lover, now her judge) review their past lives.

RECORDING Miková, Šrubař, Ovčačíková, Blachut, Veverka, Ch and O of the Prague NT, Krombholc, Supraphon, 1964

Set design by Zbyněk Kolář for Resurrection *(Prague, 1962)*

EDITION v.s., Slovenský hudobný fond, 1961

Other operas: *Juro Jánošík*, 1954, rev. 1956; *Beg Bajazid*, 1957; *Mr Scrooge*, (1959), 1963; *The Play of Love and Death* (*Hra o láske a smrti*), 1969; *Coriolanus*, (1971), 1974 (RECORDING Supraphon, 1970s); *Judgment/The Earthquake in Chile* (*Rozsudok/Zemetrasenie v Chile*), 1979; *The Siege of Bystrica* (*Obliehanie Bystrice*), 1983; *The Insect Play* (*Zo života hmyzu*), 1987

BIBLIOGRAPHY Igor Vajda, *Slovenská Opera*, Opus, 1988

J.T.

FRANCESCO CILEA

b 23 July 1866, Palmi, Italy; *d* 20 November 1950, Varazze, Italy

Cilea is remembered principally for his opera *Adriana Lecouvreur* and certain arias from *L'arlesiana*. Continued success in the opera house eluded him, and he devoted much of his time to teaching, finally becoming the director of the Naples Conservatory, where he had been a student (1881–9). His first opera, *Gina*, was premiered when he was still enrolled there and received enough attention to win him a contract with the publishing house of Sonzogno. His second, *La Tilda* (1892), an over-wrought work seeking to capitalize on the vogue for *verismo* subjects, was a setback.

Better fortune attended *L'arlesiana* (1897), where Caruso's success with Federico's 'Lament' helped establish Cilea as a relatively prominent member of his generation of Italian composers. Yet when this opera failed to maintain its initial success, Cilea began to rework it and over the next 40 years he made a number of modifications.

Cilea reached the high point of his career with *Adriana Lecouvreur* (1902), but failed to repeat its success with his remaining operas. Of these *Gloria* was premiered at La Scala under Toscanini (1907), but survived for only two performances. In 1932 Cilea revised it for Naples, but without happier results. His last opera, *Il matrimonio selvaggio*, was not performed.

Cilea possessed an undeniable melodic gift, as 'Io sono l'umile ancella' from *Adriana Lecouvreur* shows, but his powers of invention were limited. Brief motivic ideas recur, but are rarely developed into a cohesive musical fabric. His operas give the overall impression that the musical materials have been stretched perilously thin.

L'arlesiana

The Woman from Arles
Dramma lirico in three (originally four) acts (1h 30m)
Libretto by Leopoldo Marenco, after Daudet's play *L'Arlésienne* (1872)
Composed 1896–7, condensed 1898, further adjustments 1910–37
PREMIERES 27 November 1897, Teatro Lirico, Milan; three-act version: 22 October 1898, Teatro Lirico, Milan; US: 11 January 1962, Society Hill Playhouse, Philadelphia; UK: 15 May 1968, International Students' House, London

A Provençal mother, Rosa Mammai, is concerned for the happiness of her son Federico, who has lost his heart to a disreputable woman from Arles (the title character who never appears on stage). To help him get over his bitter disillusionment once he learns the truth about the woman, Rosa advises a young girl, Vivetta, who loves Federico in her timid way, on how to win him. She is apparently successful, but just before their wedding Federico is reminded of his former passion by news that the local ostler, Metifio, has been having an affair with the woman from Arles. His torment is so great that he kills himself.

Cilea was attracted by the subject of Daudet's play (for the premiere of which Bizet had composed his popular incidental music) which enabled him to combine pastoral and veristic elements. The best music is contained in three arias: the sympathetic old shepherd Baldassare's 'Come due tizzi accesi' (Act I), Federico's 'Lament' (Act II) and Rosa's prayer, 'Esser madre è un inferno' (Act III).

RECORDINGS 1. Galli, Tassinari, Tagliavini, Silveri, Turin Ch and SO of Italian Radio, Basile, Cetra, 1955; 2. Spacagna, Zilio, Kelen, Anderson, Poka, Hungarian State Ch and O, Rosekrans, Quintana, 1991: this last version, vividly recorded, brings out the drama and pathos of the score, with fine all-round singing, but each version has something to offer [J.T.H.]
EDITIONS three-act version: f.s./v.s., Sonzogno, 1899; final version: f.s./v.s. Sonzogno, 1937

Adriana Lecouvreur

Opera in four acts (2h 15m)
Libretto by Arturo Colautti, after Scribe's and Legouve's play *Adrienne Lecouvreur* (1849)
Composed 1901–2
PREMIERES 6 November 1902, Teatro Lirico, Milan; UK: 8 November 1904, Covent Garden, London; US: 5 January 1907, French Opera House, New Orleans
CAST Adriana Lecouvreur *s*, Maurizio *t*, Prince de Bouillon *b*, L'abate di Chazeuil *bar*, Quinault *b*, Poisson *t*, Princess de Bouillon *ms*, Mlla Jouvenot *s*, Mlla Dangeville *ms*, Michonnet *bar*, Major Domo *t*; 4 acted roles; *satb* chorus of ladies, gentlemen, stagehands, servants; ballet
FULL ORCHESTRA including hp, cel

The plot is melodramatic fiction, but the title character (and some of the others) were real people: Adrienne Lecouvreur (1692–1730) was a star actress at the Comédie Française in Paris. The libretto is quite condensed and rife with unexplained allusions. During the rehearsal period, Cilea had tightened up the score, omitting some episodes that would have rendered the complex plot easier to follow.

SYNOPSIS
Act I In the green room of the Comédie, Adriana tells the stage manager Michonnet, who loves her faithfully, that she is enamoured of Maurizio (who is, unknown to her, Comte de Saxe and pretender to the throne of Poland). Adriana and Maurizio meet briefly and, before she leaves to perform onstage, she gives him a bouquet of violets as a memento. Later, the Prince de Bouillon intercepts a note asking

Maurizio for a meeting; he assumes the note is from Maurizio's mistress, the actress Duclos, but it is in fact written by his own wife. The Prince invites the whole company to his house for a post-theatre party.

Act II In a fever of jealous anticipation the princess awaits her rendezvous with Maurizio. When he arrives, she is obsessed with the idea that he loves another woman; to placate her Maurizio gives her the violets. When the guests are heard arriving, the princess hides in an inner room. Later, Adriana, at Maurizio's request, helps her to leave under cover of darkness, but, while neither is aware of the other's identity, each suspects the other of being her rival.

Act III At a sumptuous party given by the princess, she identifies Adriana's voice as that of her suspected rival and shows her the fading bouquet. In retaliation, the actress recites a scene from Racine's *Phèdre*, thereby making pointed allusions to the princess's promiscuity, an insult the princess vows to avenge.

Act IV It is Adriana's name day, and among the presents she receives is a mysterious box containing violets, which she mistakenly assumes is a token of farewell from Maurizio. He arrives, delighted to see her, but she is dying, killed by the violets that the princess has soaked in poison.

Though not consistently strong musically, *Adriana* continues to maintain itself on the fringes of the repertoire principally because it contains a challenging dramatic soprano role that is not particularly taxing on the upper register.

RECORDINGS 1. Tebaldi, Simionato, Del Monaco, Fioravanti, Ch and O of the Accademia di Santa Cecilia, Capuana, Decca, 1962; 2. Scotto, Obraztsova, Domingo, Milnes, Ambrosian Opera Ch, Philharmonia O, Levine, CBS, 1977; 3. Sutherland, Ciurca, Bergonzi, Nucci, Welsh National Opera Ch and O, Bonynge, Decca, 1988; 4. Gavazzi, Truccato Pace, Prandelli, Meletti, Ch and O of RAI, Simonetto, Cetra, 1952; 5. Olivero, Simionato, Corelli, Bastianini, Ch and O of San Carlo, Rossi, MRF, 1959 (live): the choice really depends on which prima donna you prefer. Non-commercial performances with Magda Olivero, *the* Adriana, are worth looking for. [A.B.]
EDITIONS f.s., Sonzogno, 1902; v.s., Sonzogno, 1903

Other operas: *Gina*, 1889; *La Tilda*, 1892; *Gloria*, 1907 (RECORDING MRF, 1969); *Il matrimonio selvaggio*, (1909)
BIBLIOGRAPHY T. d'Amico, *Francesco Cilea*, Edizioni Curci, 1960; John W. Klein, 'Cilea – A Centenary Tribute', *Opera*, vol. 17 (1966), pp. 527–33

W.A.

DOMENICO CIMAROSA

Domenico Nicola Cimarosa [Cimmarosa]; *b* 17 December 1749, Aversa; *d* 11 January 1801, Venice

Together with Paisiello, Cimarosa was the most popular opera composer in the late 18th century. He produced some 60 opere buffe and 20 opere serie,

many of which quickly entered the repertoire of opera houses throughout Europe.

Cimarosa studied with Pietro Antonio Gallo in Naples at the Conservatorio di S. Maria di Loreto, and later with the leading opera composer Niccolò Piccinni. His first opera, *Le stravaganze del conte*, was premiered in Naples in Carnival 1772, and he produced a number of comic operas for the Teatro dei Fiorentini, Naples, and (from 1778) for Rome; his first major triumph was *L'italiana in Londra* (1778). He was appointed supernumerary organist of the Neapolitan royal chamber in November 1779, and by the early 1780s he was also a visiting maestro at the Ospedaletto di SS. Giovanni e Paolo, Venice. In 1787, Cimarosa moved to St Petersburg to replace Giuseppe Sarti as maestro di cappella to Empress Catherine II (a post held earlier by Paisiello). His period in Russia was an unhappy one – the court theatre was under severe financial difficulties and Catherine seems to have disliked Cimarosa's music – and when his contract expired in 1791 he moved to Vienna. Emperor Leopold II (whom Cimarosa had known as Grand Duke Leopold of Tuscany) appointed him kapellmeister in place of Antonio Salieri, and Cimarosa's most successful opera, *Il matrimonio segreto*, was staged at the court theatre on 7 February 1792.

The death of Leopold II some three weeks later left Cimarosa unemployed, and he returned to Italy. In 1796, he was appointed first organist to Ferdinand IV, King of Naples, and he continued to write operas for Naples, Rome and Venice. In 1799, the composer came under a political cloud for espousing the libertarian cause of the short-lived 'Parthenopean Republic'. He was arrested and threatened with execution, although after four months in prison the sentence was commuted to exile. Cimarosa moved to

Cimarosa; engraving by Luigi Rados after a drawing by Roberto Focosi

Venice, where he died of stomach cancer perhaps contracted during his imprisonment (although some suspected poison). His last opera, *Artemisia*, was left incomplete on his death.

Cimarosa's output includes instrumental works, sacred music, oratorios and cantatas, but operas predominate. His facility as a composer was legendary, but doubtless he also made extensive reuse of material (which has not yet been fully studied) and relied on assistants (for example, to compose recitatives). His first Neapolitan period focused on opera buffa – Cimarosa's first opera seria, *Cajo Mario*, dates from 1780 – and, with some notable exceptions (including *Gli Orazi ed i Curiazi*, 1796), he remained most sympathetic to the comic style. His opere buffe (encompassing intermezzi, farse, commedie per musica and dramme giocose) gradually adopted a standard two-act format, balancing tuneful arias with action ensembles. Their popularity is documented by the large number of performances and adaptations: the resulting spread of manuscript and printed sources remains a scholarly minefield. Cimarosa's style was much admired by Goethe, Stendhal (who noted his 'glittering array of comic verve, of passion, strength and gaiety'), and Hanslick; many compared him (often favourably) with Mozart. But the two composers came from very different operatic traditions, and Cimarosa's significance lies in his development of a Neapolitan tradition following on from Piccinni that eventually led, through Paisiello, to Rossini.

L'italiana in Londra

The Italian Girl in London
Intermezzo in two parts (2h)
Libretto by Giuseppe Petrosellini
PREMIERES 28 December 1778, Teatro alla Valle, Rome; UK: 15 January 1788, King's Theatre, Haymarket, London (as *La locandiera*, with duet 'Con quelle tue manine' from *L'amor costante*, 1782); US: 25 May 1955, Hunter College Playhouse, New York (in one act as *Love Triumphant*); UK modern revival: 27 July 1989, Buxton

Cimarosa's first success, with a witty plot and sparkling music.

Livia, from Genoa, comes to London in pursuit of Milord Arespingh and eventually gains his hand, but only after comic confusion (a Neapolitan who thinks he can make himself invisible) and jokes at the expense of the English. Cimarosa exploits arias mingling humour and pathos, and extended multi-part finales. The first milord was Francesco Bussani (who later sang for Mozart, including Don Alfonso in *Così fan tutte*).

Haydn revised the score for performance at Eszterháza in 1783–4; Cherubini added arias and a trio for a performance in Paris, 1790; Cimarosa added a quartet and two arias for revival in Naples in 1794; the opera was revised as *La virtù premiata* in Genoa (1794), and as a three-act opéra comique in Paris (1801).

RECORDING Orciani, Peters, Comencini, Ariostini, Praticò, Piacenza SO, Rizzi, Bongiovanni, 1986
EDITION v.s., Ricordi, 1979

Giannina e Bernardone

Dramma giocoso in two acts
Libretto by Filippo Livigni
PREMIERES November 1781, Teatro San Samuele, Venice; UK: 9 January 1787, King's Theatre, Haymarket, London

Another highly successful opera, both in Italy and elsewhere. A jealous husband torments his wife: Bernardone's aria 'Maritati poverelli' invokes the misogynist tendencies that were a staple of opera buffa, while both finales develop extensive multi-sectional plans. Francesco Bussani again took part in the first performance, and by 1788 the opera had been performed very widely around Europe. In 1786, it was revived in Venice as *Il villano geloso*.

RECORDING Jurinac, Sciutti, De Cecco, Bruscantini, Milan Ch and SO of RAI, Sanzogno, Myto, 1953
EDITION v.s., Ricordi, [c. 1870]

I due baroni di Rocca Azzurra

The Two Barons of Rocca Azurra
Intermezzo in two parts (1h 30m)
Libretto by Giuseppe Palomba
PREMIERES February 1783, Teatro alla Valle, Rome; UK: 1 January, 1803, King's Theatre, Haymarket, London

Two ridiculous noblemen, Barone Totaro and his uncle Don Demofonte, are outwitted by the servant Franchetto, who marries his sister to the baron and the baron's intended bride himself. The first Don Demofonte was Francesco Benucci (Mozart's first Figaro and Guglielmo). For the Vienna premiere (1789) Mozart composed an additional aria ('Alma grande e nobil core', K. 578). It was revised and enlarged as a commedia by Palomba and Cimarosa for Naples in 1793, and appeared as *La sposa in contrasto* in Modena, 1802, and as *Il barone deluso* in Paris, 1805. Cimarosa's 'Con quelle tue manine' (*L'amor costante*, 1782; also used in the London version of *L'italiana in Londra*, see above) became a popular addition.

EDITION v.s., Corsi, 1970

L'impresario in angustie

The Impresario in Distress
Farsa per musica in one (sometimes two) act(s) (1h 30m)
Libretto by Giuseppe Maria Diodati
PREMIERES October 1786, Teatro Nuovo, Naples; UK: 1 March 1794, King's Theatre, Haymarket, London (arr. Lorenzo da Ponte as *Il capriccio drammatico*)

Cimarosa's most widely performed opera in the late 18th and early 19th centuries. The first version was a one-act farsa (performed with Cimarosa's *Il credulo*) poking fun at opera itself (compare Mozart's *Der Schauspieldirektor*, also premiered in 1786), with an impresario trying to cope with recalcitrant singers. Later versions survive in two and three acts, although the one-act version continued to be paired with other works, often arrangements of *Il convitato di pietra* (i.e. *Don Giovanni*), in versions by Lorenzi–Tritto or Bertati–Gazzaniga. Its companion at the London premiere was Da Ponte's *Il Don Giovanni* with music by Gazzaniga, Sarti, Federici and Guglielmi. Goethe produced a version as *Die theatralischen Abenteuer* in Weimar (1791), which was revived in 1797 with additional music from Mozart's *Der Schauspieldirektor*.

The opera displays many of the usual opera buffa characteristics (e.g. the imitation of instrumental sounds was a popular element) which Cimarosa uses to foster the mood of light sentimentality which pervades the work. Among the most successful numbers is the duet 'Senti, senti l'augellino' in which, contributing to the evocation of a spring morning, a solo violin represents a bird in flight with its trills and glides.

RECORDING Gatti, Galli, Bottazzo, Bruscantini, Tajo, Alessandro Scarlatti O of Naples, Colonna, UORC, 1963
EDITION f.s., Sieber, 1802 (with French words)
MANUSCRIPT Conservatorio di Musica S. Pietro a Majella, Naples

Il matrimonio segreto

The Secret Marriage
Dramma giocoso in two acts (3h)
Libretto by Giovanni Bertati, after Colman's and Garrick's *The Clandestine Marriage* (1766)
PREMIERES 7 February 1792, Burgtheater, Vienna; UK: 11 January 1794, King's Theatre, Haymarket, London (libretto rev. Lorenzo da Ponte); US: 4 January 1834, Italian Opera House, New York; UK: 17 March 1959, St Pancras Town Hall, London (Impresario Society)
CAST Geronimo *b*, Elisetta *ms*, Carolina *s*, Fidalma *a*, Count Robinson *b*, Paolino *t*

Title page of the libretto of Il matrimonio segreto *(Florence, 1793)*

Cimarosa's best-known opera, so popular that, at its premiere, Emperor Leopold II reputedly ordered that a second performance take place after dinner – the longest encore in operatic history. In the two years after its premiere, the opera was widely performed in Europe and translated into several languages. Cimarosa later claimed that it was not his best work: he preferred *Artemisia regina di Caria*. But Verdi called it a 'true musical comedy, which has everything an opera buffa should', and Hanslick proclaimed it 'full of sunshine'.

SYNOPSIS

Act I Geronimo, a wealthy, albeit deaf, Bolognese merchant, has two daughters, Elisetta and Carolina: their household is run by his sister, Fidalma. Carolina is secretly married to Paolino, who is loved by Fidalma. Count Robinson arrives to wed Elisetta but falls for Carolina, who fails to convince him of her many faults. Geronimo, delighted at the count's supposed interest in Elisetta, organizes a banquet in his honour, but remains confused by the shenanigans.

Act II Geronimo and the count agree a marriage with Carolina; Paolino goes to Fidalma for help but she misinterprets his words as a proposal of marriage, and he faints into her arms. Carolina enters inopportunely and takes some convincing of Paolino's love for her. The count seeks to estrange Elisetta by painting himself as an ogre; she and Fidalma respond by trying to send Carolina to a

convent. Paolino and Carolina decide to run away but are caught by Elisetta, who summons the household. The assumption is that the man with Carolina is the count, but he makes a surprise entrance from another room (shades here of the Countess in Act IV of *Le nozze di Figaro*), and Paolino and Carolina eventually confess. The count agrees to marry Elisetta, and all ends happily.

While some elements of the opera's music are Mozartian, others anticipate the works of Rossini, for instance the patter of fast words sung on a repeated note, comic nonsense sounds ('ba ba ba') and the overall structure of the work, which, in keeping with the latest developments in Italian opera, contains an extended finale and numerous ensembles. The first performance included Mozart's 'Al desio di chi t'adora' (K. 577; written for the 1789 revival of *Figaro*) and a *Scena Livornese*, alluding to Cimarosa's meeting with Leopold II as Grand Duke of Tuscany when the composer was *en route* to St Petersburg. Both are now omitted.

RECORDINGS 1. Sciutti, Ratti, Stignani, Alva, Badioli, Calabrese, O of La Piccola Scala, Sanzogno, Columbia, 1955; 2. Noni, Rovero, Simionato, Valletti, Bruscantini, Cassinelli, O of Maggio Musicale Fiorentino, Wolf-Ferrari, Cetra, 1950: though these recordings are elderly, no more recent version has matched such singers as Sciutti, Valletti or Bruscantini. [J.T.H.]
EDITION v.s., Ricordi, [c. 1930]

Le astuzie femminili

Feminine Wiles

Commedia per musica in two (in some sources, three or four) acts (2h 30m)
Libretto by Giuseppe Palomba, after Bertati's libretto *Amor rende sagace*
PREMIERES   26 August 1794, Teatro dei Fiorentini, Naples; UK: 21 February 1804, King's Theatre, Haymarket, London

This opera about a young girl threatened with an arranged marriage and escaping to marry her beloved was not the most popular of Cimarosa's operas: on its first performance in London, *The Times* reported, 'There is indeed nothing to astonish but there is scarcely any air that does not please.' However, it later achieved some recognition: a version as *La Cimarosiana*, freely arranged by Respighi, with choreography by Massine and produced by Diaghilev, was produced at the Paris Opéra in May 1920. Diaghilev was no doubt drawn to the opera by its finale, a Russian ball scene, which shows the influence of Cimarosa's time in St Petersburg.

EDITIONS   f.s., Respighi (ed.), Ricordi, 1941; v.ss., Cottrau, 1871; Escudier, 1874; Respighi (ed.), Ricordi, 1939

Gli Orazi ed i Curiazi

The Horatii and the Curiatii

Tragedia per musica in three acts (2h 30m)
Libretto by Antonio Simcone Sografi, after Corneille's tragedy *Horace* (1640)
PREMIERES   26 December 1796, La Fenice, Venice; UK: 2 May 1805, King's Theatre, Haymarket, London

Cimarosa's most successful serious opera, *Gli Orazi ed i Curiazi* has a strong plot – Orazia has conflicting loyalties to her husband, Curiazio, and her family, and is eventually murdered by her brother – and the music deserves performance, at least to judge from the surviving material (the composer's autograph is lost). Selected arias were rapidly circulated in printed and manuscript copies. The English premiere was a great success for Josephina Grassini (in whose benefit it was staged), and on 18 January 1810 it received a private performance for Napoleon.

Thanks to the structure of Sografi's libretto, *Gli Orazi ed i Curiazi* is formally one of the most 'modern' of opere serie. Multi-partite arias and complex scene structures combine with a flexible use of chorus (there are several *arie con coro* and an unusual number of ensembles which take the opera far away from its stylized, rigid predecessors). Material from *Gli Orazi ed i Curiazi* was reused in Cimarosa's next opera seria, *Achille all'assedio di Troia*; it was revised as an oratorio, *La morte di Asalone*, and excerpts were used in the pasticcio oratorio *La riedificazione di Gerusalemme* (1804).

RECORDING   Dessì, Angeloni, Pozzi, Bolognesi, Fallisi, Alaimo, Ch di Teatro dell'Opera Giocosa, O Sinfonica di San Remo, De Bernart, Bongiovanni, 1983

EDITIONS   f.s., Carli, 1820; v.s., Simrock, n.d.
Other operas: *Le stravaganze del conte*, 1772 (Act III also

given separately as *Le magie di Merlina e Zoroastro*); *La finta parigina*, 1773; *I sdegni per amore*, 1776; *I matrimoni in ballo*, 1776 (rev. as Act III of *Il credulo*, 1786); *La frascatana nobile* (*La finta frascatana*), 1776; *I tre amanti*, 1777 (rev. as *Le gare degl'amanti*, 1783); *Il fanatico per gli antichi romani*, 1777; *L'Armida immaginaria*, 1777; *Gli amanti comici, o sia La famiglia in scompiglio*, ?1778 (rev. 1796; as *Il matrimonio in commedia*, 1797; as *La famiglia stravagante, ovvero Gli amanti comici*, 1798); *Il ritorno di Don Calandrino*, 1778 (rev. as *Armidoro e Laurina*, 1783); *Le stravaganze d'amore*, 1778; *Il matrimonio per raggiro* (*La donna bizzarra*), ?1779 (rev. 1802), related to *L'apprensivo raggirato*, 1798; *L'infedeltà fedele*, 1779; *Le donne rivali*, 1780 (rev. as *Le due rivali*, 1791); *Caio Mario*, 1780; *I finti nobili*, 1780; *Il falegname*, 1780 (rev. as *L'artista*, 1789); *Il capriccio drammatico*, ?1781, related to *L'impresario in angustie*, 1786 (rev. da Ponte, 1794); *Il pittor parigino*, 1781 (rev. as *Il barone burlato*, 1784; as *Le brame deluse*, 1787 (RECORDING Hungaroton, 1988); as *Der Onkel aus Amsterdam*, 1796); *Alessandro nell'Indie*, 1781; *L'amante combattuto dalle donne di punto*, 1781 (rev. as *La biondolina*, 1781, as *La giardiniera fortunata*, 1805); *Giunio Bruto*, 1781; *Il convito*, 1782, (rev. as *Der Schmaus*, 1784); *L'amor costante*, 1782, (rev. as *Giulietta ed Armidoro*, 1790); *L'eroe cinese*, 1782; *La ballerina amante*, 1782, (rev. as *L'amante ridicolo*, 1789); *La Circe*, 1783; *La villana riconosciuta*, 1783, (rev. as *La villanella rapita*, 1793); *Oreste*, 1783; *Chi dell'altrui si veste presto si spoglia*, 1783

(RECORDING Nuova Era, 1968), (rev. as *Nina e Martuffo*, 1825); *I matrimoni impensati* (*La bella greca*), 1784; *L'apparenza inganna, o sia La villeggiatura*, 1784; *La vanità delusa* (*Il mercato di Malmantile*), 1784; *L'Olimpiade*, 1784; *I due supposti conti, ossia Lo sposo senza moglie*, 1784, (rev. as *Lo sposo ridicolo*, 1786); *Artaserse*, 1784; *Il marito disperato* (*Il marito geloso*), 1785, (rev. as *Die bestrafte Eifersucht*, 1794; as *L'amante disperato*, 1795) (RECORDING Unique Opera, 1975); *La donna sempre al suo peggior s'appiglia*, 1785; *Il credulo*, 1786, (see *I matrimoni in ballo*, 1776; rev. as *Il credulo deluso*, 1786); *Le trame deluse*, 1786, (rev. as *L'amor contrastato*, 1788; as *Li raggiri scoperti*, 1799); *Volodimiro*, 1787; *Il fanatico burlato*, 1787 (RECORDING Hunt, 1988), (rev. as *Der adelsüchtige Bürger*, 1791); *La felicità inaspettata*, 1788; *La vergine del sole*, ?1788; *La Cleopatra*, 1789; *Amor rende sagace*, 1793, related to *Le astuzie femminili*, 1794; *I traci amanti*, 1793, (rev. as *Il padre alla moda, ossia Lo sbarco di Mustanzir Bassà*, 1795; as *Gli turchi amanti*, 1796); *Penelope*, 1795; *Le nozze in garbuglio*, 1795; *L'impegno superato*, 1795; *La finta ammalata*, 1796; *I nemici generosi*, 1796, (rev. as *Il duello per complimento*, 1797); *Achille all'assedio di Troia*, 1797, related to *Gli Orazi ed i Curiazi*, 1797; *L'imprudente fortunato*, 1797; *Artemisia regina di Caria*, 1797; *L'apprensivo raggirato*, 1798; *Il secreto*, 1798; *L'intrigo della lettera*, 1798; *Artemisia* (inc.), 1801; 26 other undated or doubtful operas

BIBLIOGRAPHY   Winton Dean, 'The Libretto of *The Secret Marriage*', *Music Survey*, vol. 3 (1950), p. 33–8; C. Engel, 'A Note on Domenico Cimarosa's *Il matrimonio segreto*', *MQ*, vol. 33 (1947), p. 201–6; J. E. Johnson, *Domenico Cimarosa (1749–1801)*, Ph.D. dissertation, University College, Cardiff, 1976; David Kimbell, *Italian Opera*, CUP, 1991; Stendhal, *Vie de Rossini*, Paris, 1824; English trans., 1956, rev. 2nd edn, 1970

T.C.

JEREMIAH CLARKE

d 1 December 1707, London

Not much is known about Clarke's origins, except that he may have come from a family of musicians at

Windsor; he was successively a chorister in the Chapel Royal and organist of Winchester College before coming to London around 1695. His first major work, composed in his early twenties, was a remarkable ode in memory of Henry Purcell. Subsequently he was in demand for theatre music and odes; for St Cecilia's Day 1697 he produced the original setting of Dryden's *Alexander's Feast*. In 1699 and 1700 respectively he joined the choirs of St Paul's Cathedral and the Chapel Royal, eventually becoming almoner, master of the choristers and organist of the former and joint organist of the latter.

Clarke was one of the most talented followers of Purcell, and his sudden death (he supposedly shot himself as the result of an unhappy love affair) significantly weakened England's musical life. Jeremiah Clarke's most famous work is *The Prince of Denmark's March*, formerly known as Purcell's Trumpet Voluntary.

The Island Princess
Collaboration with Daniel Purcell, Richard Leveridge and others
Semi-opera
Text by John Fletcher, adapted by Nahum Tate and Peter Motteux
PREMIERE ?7 February 1699, Drury Lane, London

The Island Princess was the most successful and important post-1695 semi-opera – the type of spectacular play mixed with operatic scenes popularized by Purcell. Unusually for the period, it survives in its entirety. Set in the East Indies, it concerns the unjust imprisonment and threatened execution of the Portuguese hero, Armusia, and the native heroine, Quisara. Clarke's major contribution, an all-sung comic *Masque of the Four Seasons* at the end of the play, was written originally as an independent interlude, probably for Drury Lane in 1696.

EDITION Curtis Price and Robert Hume (eds), *Music in London Entertainment*, series C, vol. 2, facsimile, Macnutt, 1985

Other semi-operas: *Cinthia and Endymion* (?coll. with Daniel Purcell; one song survives), 1697; *The World in the Moon* (coll. with Daniel Purcell), 1697; numerous songs for stage works
BIBLIOGRAPHY Roger Fiske, *English Theatre Music in the Eighteenth Century*, OUP, 1973; 2nd edn, 1986

P.H.

THOMAS CLAYTON
b ?1661; *d* ?1720

Clayton was the son of a member of the King's Musick, in which he in due course became a violinist.

He studied in Italy and in January 1705 his *Arsinoe, Queen of Cyprus*, an 'opera after the Italian manner', was staged at Drury Lane. It was a great popular success, despite its absurd plot and a translation so feeble that Clayton had to excuse it in his preface. About a third of the music was borrowed. The real achievement was the presentation of an all-sung opera on the English public stage. In 1707 Clayton attempted to follow this up with a setting of Joseph Addison's *Rosamond*, an original libretto on the theme of King Henry, Queen Elinor and Fair Rosamond. But despite the good intentions of the librettist ('Britannia's learned theatre disdains/ Melodious trifles, and enervate strains') this proved a resounding failure, a result of Clayton's incompetence as a composer, of which his more musical contemporaries were fully aware.

BIBLIOGRAPHY Roger Fiske, *English Theatre Music in the Eighteenth Century*, OUP, 1973; 2nd edn, 1986

R.Lu.

ALDO CLEMENTI
b 25 May 1925, Catania, Sicily

Clementi is one of several Italian composers of the post-war generation who had seemed to turn their backs on opera lirica. Until 1980, he devoted himself exclusively to concert-hall works, most of them instrumental, constructed from interweaving, canonic lines rotating quietly upon themselves like a complex mobile. Initially he worked with atonal materials, but from 1970 on he submitted borrowed tonal fragments to the same procedure, transposing them so as to produce densely chromatic textures amid which familiar gestures momentarily appear. He has put this technique to unexpectedly effective use in his one theatre work to date, *ES*. Another, *Carillon*, is in preparation.

ES
Rondeau in one act (50m)
Libretto drawn by the composer from Nello Saito's play *Es*
Composed 1980–81
PREMIERE 28 April 1981, La Fenice, Venice

Three sopranos (all representing different characteristics of Tuni, a secretary), three mezzo-sopranos (Rica, a housewife) and three altos (Mina, an artist), are trapped within identical offices, kitchens or studios, and within a circular and unresolvable situation. They wait in vain for an absent Don Juan, singing and speaking fragments of Saito's text, or dissolving into hysterical laughter. Their compulsive self-torture recalls the myth of Sisyphus, which they re-enact, constantly righting a falling object within their environment. Each nine-part ensemble is followed by a dance collage to which the performers gyrate mechanically, and the

Sketch by James Thornhill for Clayton's Arsinoe, Queen of Cyprus *(London, 1705)*

austere consolation of an orchestral *berceuse*. Finally, the recorded voice of an old woman intervenes to spell out the protagonists' all too familiar folly.

RECORDING   O Sinfonica della RAI di Milano, Peško, Fonit-Cetra, 1980s
EDITION   f.s., Suvini Zerboni, 1981

BIBLIOGRAPHY   David Osmond-Smith, '*Au creux néant musicien*: Recent Work by Aldo Clementi', *Contact*, no. 23 (winter 1981), pp. 5–9

D.O.-S.

ALBERT COATES
b 23 April 1882, St Petersburg, Russia; *d* 11 December 1953, Cape Town, South Africa

Coates's parents were English and he went to school in Liverpool at the age of 12. But his musical education was in Leipzig where he became Nikisch's assistant. He first made a successful career in Russia, where he knew the leading composers of the day, before settling in England in 1919 and subsequently enjoying an international reputation as a conductor.

Pickwick
Opera in three acts (12 scenes) (2h 15m)
Libretto by the composer, after *The Pickwick Papers* by Charles Dickens
PREMIERE   20 November 1936, Covent Garden, London (British Music Drama Opera Company)

Though the subject matter of *Pickwick* is uniquely English, Coates's approach to the musical theatre

exemplifies a somewhat rootless internationalism. It was composed while Coates was preparing Shostakovich's *Lady Macbeth of Mtsensk* for its BBC premiere (March 1936), and the orchestral writing reflects its influence. *Pickwick* has a large cast and orchestra and its stage demands are considerable, including film or shadowplay. It was the first opera to appear on BBC Television; excerpts were shown prior to the premiere. Two orchestral interludes, the *Pickwick Scherzo* and the *Cricket Fugue*, achieved life independently.

EDITION   v.s., Universal, 1936

Other operas: *Assurnabipal*, (1915); *Sardanapalus*, (1916); *The Myth Beautiful*, (1917); *Samuel Pepys*, 1929; *Gainsborough's Duchess*, (1939); *The Boy David*, (1948); *The Duel*, (1950); *Van Hunks and the Devil*, 1952
BIBLIOGRAPHY   *South African Music Encyclopedia*, vol. 1, Cape Town, 1979

L.F.

GIOACCHINO COCCHI
b c. 1720, ?Naples; *d* after 1788, ?Venice

Cocchi was trained at the Neapolitan Conservatory of S. Maria di Loreto. His apprenticeship there and his repeated claim to be a Neapolitan caused him to be accepted as such. His first steps in a long and prolific operatic career were taken in Naples and Rome. He followed this with work in Venice and northern Italy (1750–57); he then went to London, where he remained until the early 1770s.

Cocchi was the musical director of the King's Theatre in the Haymarket until 1762. In addition to overseeing operatic productions, he composed serious operas and contributions to pasticcios. Burney appreciated Cocchi's careful preparation and professionalism but found that 'his invention was very inconsiderable, and even what he used from others became languid in passing through his hands'. When his post at the King's Theatre lapsed, Cocchi turned to private teaching and directed the concerts promoted by Mrs Cornelys in Carlisle House, Soho Square, where he met Mozart in 1764 or 1765. He subsequently returned to Venice and probably remained in the city for the rest of his life.

Cocchi's greatest success remained *La maestra*, one of his earliest comic operas. First performed in Naples in 1747, it was staged under various titles all over Italy and abroad. It fulfils Cocchi's artistic goal, stated by the composer 16 years later in 1763, of achieving 'that naturalness and facility that characterizes truth'.

Surviving operatic works: *Adelaide*, 1743; *La maestra*, 1747 (EDITION facsimile, Ricordi (*Drammaturgia Musicale Veneto*, vol. 19), 1987); *Merope*, 1748; *Siface*, 1749; *Arminio*, 1749; *Siroe*, 1750; *Semiramide riconosciuta*, 1753, rev. 1771; *La Rosmira fedele*, 1753; *Li matti per amore*, 1754; *Zenobia*, 1758; *Issipile*, 1758; *Il Ciro reconosciuto*, 1759; *La clemenza di Tito*, 1760; *Tito Manlio*, 1761; 37 lost operas
BIBLIOGRAPHY   C. Burney, *A General History of Music*, vol. 4, London, 1789, pp. 468ff.

D.A.D'A.

CARLO COCCIA
b 14 April 1782, Naples; *d* 13 April 1873, Novara

Coccia studied in Naples, first at the Loreto Conservatory and later with Paisiello. His first opera in 1807 was a failure but, encouraged by his teacher, he persevered and produced operas all over Italy during the next 11 years. The most successful was *Clotilde* (1815), especially notable for its dramatic treatment of the chorus on the model of Mayr. In 1820, perhaps apprehensive of Rossini's triumphant progress in Italy, Coccia transferred his activities to Lisbon, and in 1823 to London where he taught harmony and singing at the newly formed Royal Academy of Music and produced *Maria Stuart* with success. This work marked a change in style: back in Italy from 1827, he dedicated himself mainly to serious operas, among them his best work, *Caterina di Guisa* (1833). His last opera was produced in 1841, and the remaining 32 years of his life were devoted to church music and teaching.

In his younger days Coccia wrote with phenomenal speed and was generally regarded as a brilliant but unreliable purveyor of opera. From 1828 there is more evidence of care in harmony, orchestration and dramatic style but, partly perhaps because of this, his later works never achieved the popularity of the earlier ones.

Operas: *Il matrimonio per lettera di cambio*, 1807; *Il poeta fortunato, ossia Tutto il mal vien dal mantello*, 1808; *L'equivoco, o Le vicende di Martinaccio*, 1809; *Voglia di dote e non di moglie*, 1809; *La verità nella bugia*, 1809; *Una fatale supposizione, ovvero Amore e dovere* (also as *Matilde*), ?1810; *I solitari*, ?1811; *Il sogno verificato*, 1812; *Arrighetto*, 1813; *La donna selvaggia*, 1813 (rev. 1841); *Il crescendo*, 1813–14; *Carlotta e Werther*, 1814; *Evelina*, 1814–15; *Euristèa, o L'amore generoso*, 1815; *Clotilde*, 1815 (also as *La foresta d'Hermannstadt*, 1817); *I begli'usi di citta*, 1815; *Medea e Giasone*, 1815; *Rinaldo d'Asti*, 1816; *Etelinda*, 1816; *Claudina in Torino*, 1817; *Fajello*, 1817 (rev. as *Gabriella di Vergy*, 1818); *Donna Caritea, regina di Spagna*, 1818; *Elena e Virginio*, 1818; *Atar*, 1820; *La festa della rosa*, 1821; *Mandane, regina di Persia*, 1821; *Elena e Costantino*, 1821; *Maria Stuart, regina di Scozia*, 1827; *L'orfano della selva*, 1828; *Rosmonda* (also as *Rosmunda d'Inghilterra*), 1829; *Edoardo Stuart re in Iscozia*, 1831; *Enrico di Monfort*, 1831; *Caterina di Guisa*, 1833 (rev. 1836); *La figlia dell'arciere*, 1834; *Marfa*, 1835; *La solitaria delle Asturie*, 1838 (rev. 1839 as *La Spagna ricuperata*); *Giovanna II regina di Napoli*, 1840; *Il lago delle fate*, 1841
BIBLIOGRAPHY   Franco Schlitzer, 'Carlo Coccia', in *Enciclopedia dello Spettacolo*, G. C. Sansoni, 1956

M.R.

CY COLEMAN
Seymour Kaufman; *b* 14 June 1929, Bronx, New York

Coleman studied the piano from an early age, and has retained an active performing career as a pianist alongside his composing work. A successful creator of independent popular tunes in the 1950s, he went on to become one of the ablest and most fertile writers to continue the tradition of creating theatre scores full of catchy 32-bar songs ready to be taken up by solo performers. Yet Coleman often springs structural and harmonic surprises even in these songs, and he has shown that his gifts can encompass other idioms such as the mock-operatic, the circus-flavoured, and the big-band sound.

Sweet Charity
Musical in two acts (2h)
Libretto by Neil Simon, based on the film *Nights of Cabiria* by Federico Fellini, Tullio Pinelli and Ennio Fliano; lyrics by Dorothy Fields
PREMIERES   29 January 1966, Palace Theater, New York; UK: 11 October 1967, Prince of Wales Theatre, London

The modest aspirations and tribulations of a dance-hall hostess are told in episodic stylized terms, with plenty of opportunity for dancing. Perhaps the most characteristic combination of the talents of Bob Fosse and Gwen Verdon, *Sweet Charity* also provided such standards as 'Big Spender' and 'If They Could See Me Now'.

RECORDING   Verdon, Gallagher, Oliver, McMartin, Werner, CBS, 1966

FILM   Fosse (dir.), Universal, 1969
EDITION   v.s., Notable Music, 1983

On the Twentieth Century

Musical comedy in two acts
Libretto by Betty Comden and Adolph Green, based on
plays by Ben Hecht, Charles MacArthur and Bruce
Millholland
PREMIERES   19 February 1978, St James Theater, New
York; UK: 19 March 1980, Her Majesty's Theatre, London

This farce follows some typical 1930s theatrical types
through a transcontinental train ride. Rather than
emphasizing the period, Coleman unexpectedly
chose to emphasize the self-dramatizing nature of the
characters by writing most of the score in a mock-
operetta style.

RECORDING   Kahn, Coca, Cullum, Kline, Gemignani, CBS,
1978
EDITIONS   v.s., Samuel French (on hire); lib., Drama Book
Specialists, 1981; vocal selections, Belwin Mills

Barnum

Musical comedy in two acts (1h 45m)
Libretto by Mark Bramble; lyrics by Michael Stewart
PREMIERES   30 April 1980, St James Theater, New York;
UK: 11 June 1981, London Palladium

The life of showman P. T. Barnum is presented in
extravagantly unrealistic theatrical terms, evoking the
attractions of the circuses he helped originate.

RECORDING   Dale, Close, Howard, CBS, 1980
VIDEO   Crawford, BBC Video, 1989
EDITION   v.s., Belwin, 1989

City of Angels

Musical comedy in two acts (2h 15m)
Libretto by Larry Gelbart; lyrics by David Zippel

PREMIERES   11 December 1989, Virginia Theater, New York;
UK: 30 March 1993, Prince of Wales Theatre, London

A double story of novelist Stine working in Hollywood in the 1940s and the *film noir* he is writing
about detective Stone takes unexpected turns when
the two stories interact. The former is shown in
colour, the latter in black and white, and the whole is
given a distinctive flavour by one of Broadway's
surprisingly few jazz-influenced scores.

RECORDING   Naughton, Edelman, Hoty, Graff,
McClelland, Harrell, Columbia, 1990
EDITION   v.s., Tams-Witmark (on hire); lib., Applause
Musical Library, 1990; vocal selections, Belwin Mills

Other musicals include: *Wildcat*, 1960; *Little Me*, 1962;
Seesaw, 1973; *I Love My Wife*, 1977; *Home Again*, 1979;
Welcome to the Club, 1989; *The Will Rogers Follies*, 1991
BIBLIOGRAPHY   David Ewen, *American Songwriters*, H. W.
Wilson, 1987

J.A.C.

PASCAL COLLASSE

baptized 22 January 1649, Rheims, France; *d* 17 July 1709,
Versailles, France

When Lully died in 1687 and his much resented
monopoly over French opera was broken, Collasse
was better prepared than most to take the advantage:
for ten years he had been both batteur de mesure
(conductor) at the Paris Opéra and one of Lully's
secretaries, charged with writing inner parts for his
master's works. Within a few months of Lully's
death, he completed and staged *Achille et Polyxène*,
adding four new acts to Lully's one. There followed a
succession of operas, of which only *Thétis et Pélée*
and the *Ballet des saisons* were really successful. He
was granted a privilege in 1696 to found an opera
company in Lille, but when fire destroyed the theatre
in 1700 he was saddled with large debts.

Collasse's style is often indistinguishable from
Lully's, and he was frequently accused of plagiarism,
though he made no secret of his many borrowings
from Lully. He was, however, innovative in several
respects, notably in developing the much imitated
tempête (first found in *Thétis et Pélée*) and in his
more colourful use of the orchestra. Moreover, his
Ballet des saisons became a model for the new opéra-
ballet, taken up by Campra and others during the
following decade.

Operatic works: *Achille et Polyxène*, 1687; *Divertissement, ou
Impromptu de Livry*, 1688; *Thétis et Pélée*, 1689; *Sigalion*,
1689; *Amarillis*, 1689; *Enée et Lavinie*, 1690; *Astrée et
Celadon*, 1690; *Ballet de Villeneuve St-Georges*, 1692; *Ballet
des saisons*, 1695; *La naissance de Vénus*, 1696; *Jason, ou La
toison d'or*, 1696; *Canente, ou Picus et Canente*, 1700;
Polyxène et Pyrrhus, 1706
BIBLIOGRAPHY   J. R. Anthony, *French Baroque Music
from Beaujoyeulx to Rameau*, Batsford, 1973, rev. 2nd edn,
1978; Caroline Wood, 'Orchestra and Spectacle in the
tragédie en musique 1673–1715; *oracle, sommeil* and *tempête*',
PRMA, vol. 108, (1981–2), pp. 25–46

G.S.

CARLO CONTI

b 14 October 1796, Arpino, Frosinone; *d* 10 July 1868, Arpino

Conti studied in Naples with both Zingarelli and
Mayr, and produced his first opera there while he
was still a student. This won praise from Rossini (on
whose style it was largely modelled) and Conti's
fame increased rapidly: his greatest successes came
with *Gli aragonesi in Napoli* in 1827 and especially
L'Olimpia in 1829. But in that year, to please his
father, he gave up operatic composition and devoted
the rest of his life mainly to teaching and academic
work. His operas, though now forgotten, display a
degree of technical and contrapuntal refinement that
is exceptional among the followers of Rossini – as
Rossini was himself the first to point out.

Operas: *Le truppe in Franconia*, 1819; *La pace desiderata*, 1820; *Il trionfo della giustizia*, 1823; *Misantropia e pentimento*, 1823; *L'audacia fortunata*, 1827; *Bartolomeo della Cavalla, ovvero L'innocente in periglio*, 1827; *I finti sposi*, 1827; *Gli aragonesi in Napoli*, 1827; *Alexi* (coll. with Vaccai), 1828; *L'Olimpia*, 1829; *Giovanna Shore*, 1829
BIBLIOGRAPHY Franco Schlitzer, 'Carlo Conti', in *Enciclopedia dello spettacolo*, G. C. Sansoni, 1956

M.R.

FRANCESCO BARTOLOMEO CONTI
b 20 January 1681, Florence; *d* 20 July 1732, Vienna

Conti is known today as a composer, but his first appointment to the Habsburg court in 1701 was as a theorbo-player, in which capacity he achieved a high reputation. In 1711, when Fux was promoted to vice-kapellmeister, Conti became the official court composer, holding this post for the rest of his life. His first opera, *Clotilde*, was probably composed for the 1706 Carnival, but only songs remain from a later production in London (published in 1709). Between 1714 and 1725 Conti contributed all but one of the scores for the Carnival opera, always the high point of the theatrical season. His comic operas, in particular *Don Chisciotte in Sierra Morena*, became popular outside Vienna, and were occasionally adapted or revised by contemporary composers, most notably by Telemann in Hamburg.

Conti is an important figure in the history of opera in Vienna, but his works are overshadowed by those of his better-known contemporaries Fux and Caldara. His style was experimental and individualistic, and he had a real dramatic talent, responding with great originality to the text he was setting. Critics have praised his mastery in depicting characters, the variety of his orchestration and the fine fugal writing of the choruses in his oratorios.

Surviving operas: *Il trionfo dell'amicizia e dell'amore*, 1711, rev. 1723; *Circe fatta saggia*, 1713; *Alba Cornelia*, 1714; *I Sattiri in Arcadia*, 1714; *intermezzi* and *licenzo* to *Atenaide* (coll. with Ziani, Negni and Caldara), 1714; *Ciro*, 1715; *Teseo in Creta*, 1715; *Il finto Policare*, 1716; *Sesostri, re di Egitto*, 1717; *Amore in Tessaglia*, 1718; *Astarto*, 1718; *Don Chisciotte in Sierra Morena*, 1719 (EDITION facsimile, Garland, 1982); *Galatea vendicata*, 1719, rev. 1724; *Cloris und Thyrsis*, 1719; *Alessandro in Sidone*, 1721; *La via del saggio*, 1721; *Archelao, re di Cappadocia*, 1722; *Pallade trionfante*, 1722; *Creso*, 1723; *Il trionfo della fama*, 1723; *Penelope*, 1724; *Meleagro*, 1724; *Griselda*, 1725; *Il contrasto della Bellezza e del Tempo*, 1726; *Issicratea*, 1726; *Issipile*, 1732; 3 lost operatic works
BIBLIOGRAPHY Hermine Williams, 'Francesco Bartolomeo Conti', in *Grove*, Macmillan, 1980

T.T.C.

FREDERICK CONVERSE
Frederick Shepherd Converse; *b* 5 January 1871, Newton, Massachusetts, US; *d* 8 June 1940, Westwood, Massachusetts

Converse studied at Harvard with John Knowles Paine then rejected a business career before going, like Chadwick and Parker before him, to study with Rheinberger in Munich. Converse's Germanic fluency gained him a considerable reputation, although he later became overtly American with a tone poem to celebrate the 10 millionth Model-T Ford car produced – *Flivver Ten Million* (1926).

The Pipe of Desire (1906), was described as 'a tragic little fairy-tale, vividly portrayed by the music'. It was the first American opera to be produced at the Metropolitan in New York (1910). *The Sacrifice* (1911), mounted in Boston, was better received, but Converse's last two operas, *Beauty and the Beast* (1913) and *The Immigrants* (1914) apparently remain unperformed.

BIBLIOGRAPHY David Ewen, *American Composers: A Biographical Dictionary*, Hall, 1983

P.D.

BARRY CONYNGHAM
b 27 August 1944, Sydney, Australia

Conyngham's early musical interest was jazz and he studied law before switching to composition in 1965 at the University of Sydney under Peter Sculthorpe and Raymond Hanson. In 1970, on a Churchill Fellowship, he studied in Japan with Takemitsu. There then followed periods in the US (1972–4) and in France. In 1975 he was appointed lecturer in music at the University of Melbourne, and in 1990 Head of the School of Creative Arts at the University of Wollongong (New South Wales). Opera and music-theatre feature prominently in his output, much of which has been recorded. In 1988, he was commissioned to write a music-theatre piece, *Bennelong* (using singers and puppets) and a ballet, *Vast* (for choreographer Graeme Murphy) for the Australian Bicentenary.

Edward John Eyre
Opera in one act
Libretto: poems by Meredith Oakes and extracts from Edward John Eyre's *Journals of Expedition and Discovery*
PREMIERES 1 May 1971, Science Theatre, University of New South Wales, Sydney; rev. version: 31 July 1973, Concert Hall, New Sydney Opera House, Sydney

Eyre explored much of South Australia and opened it up for settlement. He made a difficult first crossing to Western Australia, finally being left with only one companion, the Aborigine Wylie. The original version of the opera was for solo contralto, wind quintet and string orchestra; in the revised version a part for the explorer Eyre himself and extracts from his diaries were added. The work is in a mixture of styles with choral passages, lyrical solos and spoken narration.

RECORDING Bruce, Brown, Ferris, Coad, Carroll, University of New South Wales Opera, Covell, EMI, 1974
EDITION f.s., Universal (on hire), 1971

Fly

Opera in two acts (1h 15m)
Libretto by Murray Copland, based on the life of the Australian aviation pioneer Lawrence Hargrave
PREMIERE 25 August 1984, State Theatre, Victorian Arts Centre, Melbourne

Conyngham's major work for the theatre was commissioned and performed by the Victoria State Opera. The composer and librettist aimed for closeness to real life with imitation of speech rhythms which fit the narrative approach to the subject. The score is melodious and lyrical, particularly in the set aria-type pieces.

RECORDING Haggart, Mills, Roden, Ferraro, Wood, Victoria State Opera O, Hopkins, MOVE, 1987
EDITION f.s., Universal (on hire), 1984

Other operas: *Ned*, 1978; *The Apology of Bony Anderson*, 1978
BIBLIOGRAPHY David Symons, 'Barry Conyngham', in Frank Callaway and David Tunley (eds), *Australian Composition in the 20th Century*, OUP, 1978, pp. 212–17

A.I.G.

HENRY COOKE
b c. 1615; *d* 13 July 1672, Hampton Court, Surrey, England

Henry Cooke seems to have been a choirboy in Charles I's Chapel, and he certainly served in the Royalist army during the Civil War. He was one of the consortium who provided the music for Davenant's masque-like *First Day's Entertainment at Rutland House* of 1656, and that year he wrote the music for the second and third entries of *The Siege of Rhodes* and played the part of Solyman. None of this music has survived, but Cooke was an admired exponent of the Italian manner of singing, so his recitatives for the all-sung *Siege of Rhodes* were probably as Italianate as anything by a contemporary English composer; to judge from his surviving music, their quality probably left something to be desired. He became Master of the Children of the Chapel Royal after the Restoration in 1660, and was probably too busy training his choirboys – including Pelham Humfrey, John Blow and Henry Purcell – to continue working in the theatre.

BIBLIOGRAPHY Edward J. Dent, *Foundations of English Opera*, CUP, 1928; *rp*, Da Capo, 1965

P.H.

AARON COPLAND
b 14 November 1900, Brooklyn, New York; *d* 2 December 1990, N. Tarrytown, New York

Aaron Copland is often regarded as the quintessentially American composer of the mid-20th century. Like Stravinsky, he gained access to a large public through a triptych of ballets – *Billy the Kid* (1938); *Rodeo* (1942); and *Appalachian Spring* (1944) – couched in a national musical idiom. These stage works, and his film scores, show Copland's rare ability to communicate through using the simplest materials in a recognisable and personal way. Copland's more severe side came to the fore in some exploratory works for his own instrument, the piano – the *Variations* (1930), *Sonata* (1941), and *Fantasy* (1957) – as well as some early and late orchestral and chamber works.

Copland's two operas were both written for young performers. When he was a student in Paris, working with Nadia Boulanger, he felt that opera was not part of new music. Composers, for him, fell into two categories: 'those who were "hopelessly" opera composers – such as Rossini, Wagner and Puccini – and those who debate whether and when to write an opera'. Copland, like Debussy, was one of the latter and it is no surprise that his operas fall into the middle period when he became involved with folk subjects which allowed him to cultivate 'a kind of musical naturalness'. That was Copland's *métier*.

Aaron Copland in the 1930s

The Second Hurricane

A play opera in two acts (1h)
Libretto by Edwin Denby
Composed 1936
PREMIERES 21 April 1937, Henry Street Settlement Music School, New York; UK: 8 June 1990, The Maltings, Snape

Copland's opera for high-school students came about through the initiative of Lehman Engel, who conducted the premiere. The composer relished the idea of 'musical contact with an entirely new audience – the youth of America' and approached the poet and dance critic Edwin Denby for a libretto. The work's final form, with three spoken parts as well as seven soloists, owed something to the *Gebrauchsmusik* of Hindemith and Weill and exhibits the liveliness of the American musical theatre. *The Second Hurricane* may well have influenced Britten since he admired it when Copland played it through to him in 1938 before Britten had written an opera.

Edwin Denby has summarized the plot: 'An aviator comes to the principal of a high school for volunteers to help in flood relief. The principal chooses six pupils, four boys and two girls, and off they go in the airplane. It falters and is forced down in a deserted spot near a great river. They unload, and the plane leaves for help. The young people begin to quarrel when they are left to fend for themselves. A small boy appears. He is afraid and lonely. The students fight over the food, while a chorus of parents on stage comments and a chorus of pupils replies. The six students decide to leave in different directions in search of the nearest town. It is then that the hurricane hits hard. They gratefully find each other again and are rescued by a search plane.' The moral of the story, stated in an epilogue, is that working together on an equal basis brings happiness and freedom.

The director was the young Orson Welles but *The Second Hurricane* had a mixed reception. Virgil Thomson admired it but rightly found the ending inconclusive, a problem that was to recur in *The Tender Land*. The opera falls down in its linking dialogue, which is highly unrealistic.

RECORDING in preparation
EDITIONS f.s., Birchard & Co., 1959; v.s., Birchard & Co., 1958

The Tender Land

Opera in three acts (1h 45m)
Libretto by Horace Everett (Erik Johns) inspired by James Agee's book *Let Us Now Praise Famous Men*
Composed 1952–4 (in two acts), rev. (in three acts) 1955
PREMIERES 1 April 1954, New York City Center; rev. version: 20 May 1955, Oberlin Conservatory Opera Laboratory, Ohio; UK: 26 February 1962, Arts Theatre, Cambridge (Cambridge University Opera Group)

In the early 1950s Copland cast around widely for an opera plot and met a number of writers. In 1952 he was commissioned by Richard Rodgers and Oscar Hammerstein II, through the League of Composers, to write an opera for television. NBC foolishly rejected *The Tender Land*, which would film particularly well, and the New York City Center took it on, to be staged by Jerome Robbins and conducted by Thomas Schippers.

Like Copland's ballet *Appalachian Spring*, *The Tender Land* is concerned with rural America: it quotes two folksongs included in Copland's arrangements, *Old American Songs*. The story is set on a Midwest farm in the 1930s at harvest time. The family consists of the grandfather, the mother and her daughter, Laurie, who is about to graduate from high school. Two itinerant workers, Martin and Top, arrive looking for odd jobs and are accepted with some suspicion. Laurie falls for Martin and plans to go away with him to freedom. The grandfather has given the men their notice and Martin, realizing that attachment to Laurie would mean having to settle down, steals off with his companion before she wakes. When Laurie finds that she has been jilted she decides to leave anyway: 'I'm ready for leaving like this harvest is ready to be gathered in.'

Like *The Second Hurricane*, *The Tender Land* had an uneasy reception. Both composer and librettist felt they had made mistakes and there was considerable revision – the work became three instead of two acts. In 1965 a concert version of *The Tender Land* was the basis for the recording of excerpts which made it more widely known; it was televised, as originally intended, in 1975; in 1987 a revival in Newhaven using a reduced orchestration ran for over 50 performances. It was revived and recorded by the Plymouth Music Group in 1989, a performance that went to Aldeburgh (1990). The result was again inconclusive; problems with the libretto remain and the ending fails to convince, in spite of some vintage Copland *en route*.

RECORDING Comeaux, Hardy, Jette, Dressen, Bohn, Lehr, Plymouth Music Series Ch and O, Brunelle, Virgin Classics, 1990
EDITION v.s., Boosey & Hawkes, 1956

BIBLIOGRAPHY Aaron Copland and Vivian Perlis, *Copland*, vol. i: *1900–1942*, Faber, 1984; Aaron Copland and Vivian Perlis, *Copland since 1943*, Marion Boyars, 1992; notes and libretto with recording of *The Tender Land*, Virgin Classics, 1990

P.D.

PIETRO ANTONIO COPPOLA

b 11 December 1793, Castrogiovanni, Sicily; *d* 13 November 1877, Catania, Sicily

Born into a musical family and largely self-taught, Coppola was from 1810 an assistant conductor at Catania. His first operas had little success, but in 1832 a revival of *Achille in Sciro* in Naples won him high praise from both Donizetti and Rossini, and as a result the directorship of the Teatro San Carlo. His greatest triumph came in Rome in 1835 with *La pazza per amore* (to a revised version of the libretto of Paisiello's *Nina*), which is generally regarded as his best work and made his publisher a million lire in its first year. Its success was followed up immediately by *Gli Illinesi*, and by *La festa della rosa* in Vienna in the following year. At this stage of his career Coppola was seen as the successor of Bellini, but he never came anywhere near his model and in his later operas was left behind by the development of Italian melodrama. From 1839 to 1843 and again from 1850 to 1871 he was director of the opera at Lisbon.

Operas: *Il figlio del bandito*, 1816; *Artale d'Aragona*, ?1816; *Il destino*, 1825; *Achille in Sciro*, ?1825/?1828; *Il gondoliere di Venezia*, ?1833; *La pazza per amore* (also as *Nina*), 1835; *Gli Illinesi*, 1835; *Enrichetta di Baienfeld, ossia La festa della rosa*, 1836; *La bella celeste degli Spadari*, 1837; *Il postiglione di Longjumeau*, 1838; *Giovanna I, regina di Napoli*, 1840; *Ines de Castro*, 1841; *Il folletto*, 1842; *L'orfana guelfa*, 1846, rev. as *Stefanella*, 1852; *Fingal*, 1847; *Oaunel de Salamão* (*The Ring of Solomon*), 1853

BIBLIOGRAPHY Emilia Zanetti, 'Pietro Antonio Coppola', in *Enciclopedia dello Spettacolo*, G. C. Sansoni, 1956

M.R.

JOHN COPRARIO
d c. June 1626, ?London

Coprario was, in the words of Roger North, 'plain Cooper but affected an Itallian termination'. Anthony Wood first suggested that he changed his name in Italy, though there is evidence only for a trip to the Netherlands in 1603 on behalf of Robert Cecil, his patron. After Cecil's death in 1612, Coprario became increasingly involved with the court. He wrote music for at least one of the masques given for Princess Elizabeth's marriage to the Elector Palatine in 1613, and was a member of the retinue that accompanied them to Heidelberg. In 1616 and 1617 he made further trips abroad, and in 1622 became associated with the household of Prince Charles; a good deal of Coprario's innovative music for varied combinations of violins and viols was written for the prince's musicians. When Charles became king in 1625 Coprario was appointed royal composer, though he died soon after.

Court masques to which Coprario contributed songs: *The Lords' Masque*, 1613; *The Masque of Squires*, 1613

BIBLIOGRAPHY R. Charteris, *John Coprario: A Thematic Catalogue of his Music with a Biographical Introduction*, Pendragon, 1977

P.H.

JOHN CORIGLIANO
John Paul Corigliano; *b* 16 February 1938, New York

Corigliano was born into a musical family – his father was leader of the New York Philharmonic. A pupil of Luening, Gianini and Creston, Corigliano worked for radio, record companies and television as writer, producer and arranger and gained valuable experience composing incidental music. Of his series of concertos, the Clarinet Concerto (1977) was acclaimed for its vivid theatrical impact based on a technique of style modulation between and during movements. Corigliano has written fluently for films, and his scores have gained several awards. His first theatre work, *The Naked Carmen* (1970), a mixed-media opera after Bizet, was undertaken for Mercury Records. His first full-scale opera, *The Ghosts of Versailles*, was commissioned by the Metropolitan Opera in 1983.

The Ghosts of Versailles
Grand opera buffa in two acts (3h)
Libretto by William M. Hoffman, after the play *La mère coupable* by Beaumarchais (1792)
Composed 1980–91
PREMIERE 19 December 1991, Metropolitan, New York

Taking the final part of Beaumarchais's 'Figaro' trilogy, *La mère coupable*, as their starting point, Corigliano and his librettist have created a work in which past meets present. The ghost of Beaumarchais helps the ghost of Marie Antoinette come to terms with her execution and to exorcize the bitterness she feels, by rerunning history with Figaro and the Almaviva family as central characters. Echoes of historical fact are mirrored in the music by pastiche elements including regular quotations from Mozart's and Rossini's 'Figaro' operas and more oblique references to styles ranging from Richard Strauss to Gilbert and Sullivan.

EDITIONS f.s., G. Schirmer (on hire); v.s., G. Schirmer, 1993

P.D.

PETER CORNELIUS
Carl August Peter Cornelius; *b* 24 December 1824, Mainz; *d* 26 October 1874, Mainz

Cornelius wrote mainly small-scale vocal compositions; his only large-scale works are his three operas, and it is for the first of these, *Der Barbier von Bagdad*, together with some of his lieder, that he is remembered.

Cornelius's parents were both actors and, though he was given a sound musical education, they initially intended him for a theatrical career. However, after his father's death in 1843 he went to live with his uncle Peter von Cornelius in Berlin, where he studied music with Siegfried Dehn. Through his cousin, a noted painter and sculptor, he also made many contacts in Berlin literary and intellectual circles, and began to develop his skill as a writer and poet. In addition to writing his own libretti, he later translated those of other composers' operas (including four by Gluck) and wrote music criticism, essays and poetry.

In 1852 he was drawn into Liszt's circle in Weimar and Liszt became, as Cornelius described him in the autograph score of *Der Barbier von Bagdad*, his 'master, friend and benefactor'. Cornelius at first concentrated on lieder, but, encouraged by Liszt, began his opera *Der Barbier von Bagdad* in 1855. Its premiere in 1858 provoked extraordinary opposition, aimed at the artistic creed that Liszt and Cornelius were seen to represent, and it was withdrawn after a single performance, which Liszt conducted. This fiasco precipitated Liszt's resignation as court conductor at Weimar: both he and Cornelius left the city shortly afterwards.

Cornelius spent the next six years in Vienna, where he came under Wagner's direct influence in 1861. There was genuine mutual admiration between the two men; Wagner acknowledged Cornelius as the only one of his adherents 'whom one could rightly call a genius'. Cornelius, though profoundly affected by his connection with Wagner and committed to his cause, did not allow his own artistic personality to be completely overwhelmed. The major work of Cornelius's Vienna years was his second opera, *Der Cid*, which was given a gratifyingly successful premiere in Weimar in 1865.

In the same year he moved to Munich at Wagner's invitation and became reader to King Ludwig II. Two years later he was appointed Professor of Music Theory and Rhetoric at the Königliche Musikhochschule. During his time in Munich, though he wrote a number of fine lieder, duets and choruses, he failed to complete any major works. After 1866 he worked sporadically on a third opera, *Gunlöd*, based on the legends of the Edda, in which the influence of Wagner's *Ring* is close to the surface. By the time of his death, substantial portions of the opera had been sketched and a few numbers were essentially finished, though none had been orchestrated. The opera was premiered, in a completion by Karl Hoffbauer and Ernst Lassen, in 1891; another version, completed by Waldemar von Bausznern, is included in the complete edition of Cornelius's works, but neither version has entered the repertoire.

H. numbers refer to M. Hasse (ed.), *P. Cornelius: Musikalische Werke*, Leipzig, 1905–6.

Der Barbier von Bagdad

The Barber of Baghdad
Comic opera in two acts, H. iii (2h)
Libretto by the composer, after *The Tailor's Tale* and *The Barber's Stories of His Six Brothers* from *The Arabian Nights*
Composed 1855–8
PREMIERES 15 December 1858, Hoftheater, Weimar; rev. version: 1 February 1884, Karlsruhe; US: 3 January 1890, New York; UK: 9 December 1891, Savoy Theatre, London
CAST Nureddin *t*, Bostana *ms*, Abdul Hassan Ali Ebn Bekar (the Barber) *b*, Margiana *s*, The Cadi, Baba Mustapha *t*, The Caliph *bar*, a slave *t*, 3 muezzins 2 *t*, *b*, 4 armed men 2 *t*, 2 *b*; *satb* chorus of servants of Nureddin, friends of the Cadi, people of Baghdad, mourning women, followers of the Caliph
FULL ORCHESTRA including hp

Originally planned in one act, the libretto was – on Liszt's advice – expanded to two. Liszt also recommended changes in orchestration which Cor-

nelius executed. The premiere was a fiasco, and *Der Barbier von Bagdad* was not staged again until after Cornelius's death. Two versions made during the late 19th century – one by Felix Mottl, reworking the opera in one act and orchestrated in highly Wagnerian colours, the other by Hermann Levi, restoring some of Mottl's cuts, but using passages in Cornelius's scoring – have now generally been discredited in favour of the original version.

SYNOPSIS
Act I Nureddin is lovesick for Margiana, daughter of the Cadi. Bostana, an old relative of the Cadi, tells Nureddin that Margiana is expecting him at midday. She advises him to bath and shave, promising to send him a good barber. When the barber arrives he seems more interested in talking than working, and when he learns about Nureddin's assignation he insists on helping him. With great difficulty Nureddin gets his shave and escapes from the barber.

Act II In the women's quarters of the Cadi's house Margiana waits for Nureddin. The delighted Cadi comes in, having received an offer for her hand and a chest of gifts from his old rich friend Selim. When the Cadi leaves for the mosque Nureddin enters and begins his courtship. The barber, who has arrived outside the house, hears the shrieks of a slave being punished and, thinking they are Nureddin's cries, breaks in. Meanwhile Nureddin has been hidden in the chest. Thinking the chest contains Nureddin's corpse, the servants and the barber are about to carry it off when the Cadi returns; he thinks they are stealing his treasure. After much confusion the caliph arrives. The unconscious Nureddin is let out and everything ends happily with his revival and his betrothal to Margiana.

Despite Cornelius's connection with the New German School of Liszt and Wagner, *Der Barbier von Bagdad* is closer in style and in spirit to the earlier German Romantic operas of Weber, Lortzing and Nicolai. Cornelius deviated from previous comic models, however, in writing an opera with continuous music, rather than keeping the traditional structure of individual numbers interspersed with spoken dialogue. Elements such as the use of reminiscence motif, which might be termed Wagnerian, were already established elements in German Romantic opera. Much of the best music is written for the strongly characterized title role, including a buffo patter song ('Bin Akademiker'), in which the barber lists his many accomplishments.

RECORDING Schwarzkopf, Hoffman, Gedda, Prey, Czerwenka, Philharmonia Ch and O, Leinsdorf, EMI, 1956
EDITIONS f.s., Breitkopf und Härtel (vol. 3 of complete works), 1904; v.s., Breitkopf und Härtel, 1905

Der Cid

The Cid
Lyric drama in three acts, H. iv (1h 45m)
Libretto by the composer, after the plays *Las mocedades del Cid* (1618) by Guillén de Castro y Bevis, *Le Cid* (1636) by

Pierre Corneille and *Der Cid* (1804) by Johann Gottfried von Herder
Composed 1860–64; rev. Levi, 1891
PREMIERES 21 May 1865, ?Hoftheater, Weimar; rev. version: 21 April 1891, Munich

Composed in Vienna, when Cornelius was in constant contact with Wagner, then hard at work on *Lohengrin*, *Der Cid* shows more pronounced Wagnerian traits, notably its more fluid, continuous structure, which emphasizes a declamatory type of writing at the expense of closed-form melodies. Nevertheless, the opera is far from being a slavish emulation and displays many original touches which demonstrate Cornelius's concern to retain an individual voice. The libretto, relating the 11th-century struggles of Christians and Moors in Spain, was, however, weaker than that of *Der Barbier von Bagdad*, and *Der Cid* has never enjoyed the same success. After its premiere in Weimar, it was not staged again until 1891, in a revision by Hermann Levi. The original version was revived in 1904 by Max Hasse and has been occasionally produced in Germany since then.

EDITIONS original version: f.s./v.s., Breitkopf und Härtel, 1905; Levi rev. version: f.s., Hofmusikalienverlag, 1895; v.s., Universal, 1891

Other opera: *Gunlöd* (inc.), (1874)
BIBLIOGRAPHY Hellmut Federhofer and Kurt Oehl (eds), *Peter Cornelius als Komponist, Dichter, Kritiker und Essayist*, Gustav Bosse Verlag, 1977

C.Br.

FRANCESCO CORRADINI

Francesco Corradini [Coradigni, Coradini]; *b c.* 1700, Venice; *d* 14 October 1769, Madrid

Corradini was the first Italian composer to dominate the Spanish musical scene in the 18th century. After launching his career in Naples with *Lo 'ngiegno de le femmine* (1724) and two other comic operas in dialect, he moved to Spain in 1725. He worked first in Valencia, then in Madrid (from 1731) and for 15 years enjoyed great success. In 1747 he was appointed director of the orchestra at the new royal theatre in the palace of Buen Ritiro, Madrid, managed by Farinelli. With Farinelli and Francesco Corselli, the primo maestro, Corradini collaborated on settings of Metastasio's *La clemenza di Tito* and Rolli's *Polifemo* (translated into Spanish) for the Carnival seasons in 1747 and 1748 respectively. In the final 20 years of his life he acted as maestro de musica de camera of the queen dowager, Isabella Farnese, retiring in 1766.

While Corradini's zarzuelas reflected the native Spanish tradition and taste, his operas (almost all of which are lost) remained firmly rooted in the Italian style. This deliberate decision of the Spanish court is exemplified by the choice of Italian rather than indigenous texts.

BIBLIOGRAPHY P. Caraba, 'Francesco Corradini', in *Diz ionario biografico degli italiani*, vol. 29, Istituto della Enciclopedia Italiana, 1983

D.S.B.

DOMENICO CORRI
b 4 October 1746, Rome; *d* 22 May 1825, London

The son of Cardinal Portacarero's confectioner, Domenico Corri was already to be found playing the violin in opera orchestras in Rome at the age of ten. He was taken into the cardinal's household, and the cardinal tried to persuade him to enter the Church against the wishes of his family. Corri studied with Nicolò Porpora in Naples until the great teacher's death in 1767. His first opera, *La raminga fedele*, was given in Rome in 1770, and Burney's praise of Corri published in the following year led to the Musical Society of Edinburgh's invitation to direct a series of concerts. In 1774 *Alessandro nel Indie* was put on at London's King's Theatre. Corri also became manager of Vauxhall Gardens for a time and, less successfully, took over the Theatre Royal in Edinburgh which failed in 1779.

Corri's most successful opera was *The Travellers* (1806). Otherwise his music was much in demand for lighter theatrical genres; he provided music for several stage pieces by Thomas Dibdin. One of his last works was a musical version of Garrick's dramatic romance for children, *Lilliput* (1817). In his treatise *The Singer's Preceptor* (1810), Corri wrote extravagant decorations for some of Mozart's arias.

Operatic works: *La raminga fedele* (music lost), 1770; *Alessandro nel Indie*, 1774; *The Wives Revenged*, 1778; *The Cabinet* (coll.), 1802; *The Travellers, or Music's Fascination*, 1806; *In and Out of Tune*, 1808; *Lilliput*, 1817

T.T.C.

NOËL COWARD
[Sir] Noël Pierce Coward; *b* 16 December 1899, Teddington, Middlesex, England; *d* 26 March 1973, Blue Harbour, Jamaica

It is difficult to find a parallel for Coward's career, for he was a playwright, screen and stage actor, film director, novelist, singer, cabaret entertainer and ballet composer as well as a song-writer. He grew up in a theatrical environment, and his initial success, after the First World War, was in the writing of plays, notably *Hay Fever* (1925), and revues. He then undertook the music, book, lyrics and production of *Bitter Sweet*, which won universal acclaim, and it could be argued that he was the only English composer–lyricist for the musical theatre between the Edwardian era and the 1960s fully equal to his great American contemporaries. However, he did not sustain his activities in this field and is scarcely regarded as a nodal figure in the history of the musical.

Naturally his prodigious talent thrived on his personality, attuned to the elegant yet biting social comedy of Oscar Wilde and to traditions of sentimentality and breeziness in operetta and music-hall. But his critical wit, verbal and musical, could none the less cover a broad range of contemporary allusion, and in his songs, as in his writing and acting, he epitomized several successive phases of British cultural history, from 1920s frivolity to post-war *Angst*.

Bitter Sweet

Opérette in three acts (1h 30m)
Book, music and lyrics by Noël Coward
PREMIERES   2 July 1929, Palace Theatre, Manchester; US: 5 November 1929, Ziegfeld Theater, New York

Bitter Sweet, not unlike Kern's *Show Boat* in its chronological perspective, provided the perfect vehicle for Coward's style. Its scenario is framed by the jazz age while its central action looks back to *fin-de-siècle* Belgravia and Vienna (the action concerns an upper-class English girl's elopement with her Austrian music teacher around 1875, their Bohemian happiness, his death in a duel, and her return to England and aristocracy). This affords a double perspective on the nostalgia of the best-known number, the waltz song 'I'll see you again', which the youngest generation turns into a foxtrot as the action ends.

RECORDING   excerpts: original cast, EMI, 1973 (re-released World Record Club)
FILMS   1. Herbert Wilcox (dir.), British and Dominion, 1933; 2. W. S. Van Dyke (dir.), MGM, 1940
EDITION   v.s., Chappell, 1929

Other operettas: *Conversation Piece*, 1934; *Operette*, 1938
Musicals: *Pacific 1860*, 1946; *Ace of Clubs*, 1950; *After the Ball*, 1954; *Sail Away*, 1961; *The Girl Who Came to Supper*, 1963; revues and plays with music not listed
BIBLIOGRAPHY   Cole Lesley, *The Life of Noël Coward*, Cape, 1976

S.B.

EDWARD COWIE

b 17 August 1943, Birmingham, England

In addition to his activities as a composer and teacher, Cowie is an accomplished painter and ornithologist, and these interests have stimulated much of his music. He studied privately with Alexander Goehr (1964–8) and later worked with Lutosławski. Other influences include Tippett and Messiaen. In 1973 he was appointed composer-in-residence at the University of Lancaster, and since 1983 has been Professor of Creative Arts at the University of Wollongong, New South Wales. Cowie's eclectic style produces multi-layered textures often of great beauty. His first stage work was the 'fantasy opera' *Commedia* (Kassel, 1979; London, 1982). This transported stock figures and forms of the Italian *commedia dell'arte* into the timeless realm of nature. The four acts represent the four seasons, and the work examines man's relationship with the natural world. His second opera, *Ned Kelly*, is a treatment of the life of the Australian folk hero, inspired by the paintings of Sir Sidney Nolan and conceived before Cowie's own move to Australia. Originally commissioned by the Royal Opera, Covent Garden, it remains unperformed, although – as with *Commedia* – the composer has written a series of 'satellite' works around the same subject including the music-theatre piece *Kate Kelly's Road Show* (1983), which follows the vaudeville adventures of Kelly's sister.

BIBLIOGRAPHY   Edward Cowie, 'Commedia', *Opera*, vol. 30 (1979), pp. 534–5

M.A.

GORDON CROSSE

b 1 December 1937, Bury, Lancashire, England

A pupil of Wellesz in Oxford and later of Petrassi in Rome, Crosse briefly espoused the avant-garde tendencies of the early 1960s, but then settled down to evolve a more personal and less abrasive style with its roots in the music of Britten. Like Britten, he has usually been at his best in vocal music, finding a ready escape from the threat of intellectualism in verbal declamation and lyrical melody, while preserving elements of a more sinewy modernism in his instrumental writing. Above all, Crosse is one of the sharpest-eared British composers of his generation, and his virtual eclipse in the late 1970s and 1980s is hard to account for except in terms of musical politics.

Crosse has written four operas, plus several works that straddle the border between opera and choral entertainment, including several excellent works for children. Of these *The Demon of Adachigahara* (1967) is a cantata with narrator and mime; *Wheel of the World* (1972) is an 'entertainment' for children and a small orchestra, based on Chaucer's *Canterbury Tales*, and *Holly from the Bongs* (1974) is a nativity opera designed to be played in church.

Purgatory

Opera in one act (40m)
Libretto by the composer, an abridgement of the play by W. B. Yeats (1939)
Composed 1965
PREMIERES   7 July 1966, Everyman Theatre, Cheltenham; US: 30 January 1970, Dallas, Texas
CAST   Old Man *bar*, Boy *t*; offstage: *sa* chorus (wordless)
CHAMBER ORCHESTRA

Crosse's first opera, an almost straight setting with only minor abridgements of a late play by Yeats, was jointly commissioned by Cheltenham Festival and the BBC (the first television production, in a slightly modified version, was screened later in July 1966). The choice of play, Crosse wrote later, was 'a matter of playing safe'. It provided a 'copperbottomed' theatrical text and no collaborator to argue with. It had only two characters, on stage throughout and singing entirely in monologue, and the action was largely in the Old Man's memory, so there were no problems of timing or characterization. All this makes *Purgatory* sound like a concert work (it does in fact resemble a later concert score by Crosse, *Memories of Morning: Night*, in genre). But production has shown that the work's intensity of atmosphere and psychology are best realized on stage, where the lurking threat of violence has physical reality.

An old man brings his son to a large ruined house in the Irish countryside. The story emerges gradually. His mother was a rich woman who married a drunken groom, then died in childbirth. The father squandered all her money, then in a drunken stupor burned the house down and died mysteriously in the ruins. The old man now confesses to having murdered his father. Since that day, his parents have been doomed to relive their deeds in purgatory. The old man and his son quarrel, and the old man stabs the boy. He imagines he has broken the cycle of tragedy 'because I finished all that consequence'. But the purgatory continues, and the old man ends up praying to God to 'appease the misery of the living and the remorse of the dead'.

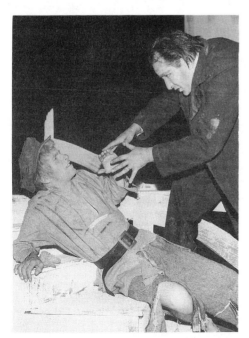

Purgatory *(Cheltenham, 1966)*

The rather abstract verse play permitted a setting tightly controlled by music, rather like a symphonic poem. Crosse studiously avoids dramatizing the one piece of action (the murder of the boy). Drama is projected through musical imagery, like the sinister hoof-beats that open the work and then return near the end when it becomes clear that the murder has solved nothing; or, more unusually, by contrasting the music's 'normal' atonal style with the unearthly radiance of simple old-fashioned tonal harmonies like the C major that ends the work or the haunting triads sung by the offstage choir. The music clearly owes something to Berg's *Wozzeck* and perhaps also to Britten's *Peter Grimes*. Yet its touch is personal. *Purgatory*, for all its recent neglect, remains one of the best one-act operas by a British composer since the war.

RECORDING   Bodenham, Hargreaves, Royal Northern
College O, Lankester, Argo, 1975
EDITION   v.s., OUP, 1968

The Grace of Todd

Comedy in one act (three scenes) (1h 15m)
Libretto by David Rudkin
Composed 1967–8, rev. 1974
PREMIERE   7 June 1969, Jubilee Hall, Aldeburgh

Written as a companion piece for *Purgatory*, *The Grace of Todd* followed that work in a double-bill at its early performances.

Rudkin's libretto is a slightly uneasy mixture of old-fashioned army farce, and allegory in the manner of Eric Crozier's text for Britten's *Albert Herring*. Todd (a tenor role sung originally by Robert Tear) is a categorically hopeless army private – fat, short-sighted, untalented, incapable of almost any physical co-ordination. He is mercilessly victimized by a stock-comedy drill sergeant and an officious lieutenant, but – in a quasi-fantasy central scene – discovers with the help of a Lady Bountiful figure that he has one talent, the ability to make people laugh. In the final scene, after the lieutenant has fallen into the river, Todd is marched off to the cooler, but his triumphant spirit remains at large.

Crosse responds well to the farcical elements in this plot, and *The Grace of Todd* is that rare thing, an uproariously funny comic opera. But the allegorical episodes are much less effective. The musical pacing is erratic, and the resulting work much too long.

EDITION   v.s., OUP, 1969

The Story of Vasco

Opera in three acts (2h 15m)
Libretto by Ted Hughes, after George Schehadé's play
L'histoire de Vasco
Composed 1968–73, rev. 1977
PREMIERE   13 March 1974, Coliseum, London

Crosse's only full-length opera, commissioned by Sadler's Wells Opera, is a tragi-comedy based on a play that ridicules war through a highly personal brand of goonish humour. Vasco is an innocent village barber who is seconded to the war effort because the general believes that fear is a more effective weapon than heroism. He is pursued by a mad scholar and his daughter Marguérite, who has a vision of herself as 'a Madonna, and bride to a little barber'. Unfortunately her vision is heroic, and she fails to recognize Vasco when she meets him. Later he himself suddenly realizes the truth, becomes heroic, and is killed.

The Story of Vasco is notable for its lyricism, gentle humanity and grateful treatment of the voices, virtues that increasingly mark Crosse out as a successor to Britten. The music is (very extendedly) tonal; melody is a feature, and the orchestration is masterly. But pacing remains a problem. Unimportant episodes are blown up, so that the work is too long for its weight, and some of the characterization is bland. Crosse himself later acknowledged the work's 'dramatic shortcomings' and substantially revised it, especially shortening Act I. But the revised version still awaits production.

EDITION   v.s., OUP, 1975

Potter Thompson

Music drama in one act (1h 45m)
Libretto by Alan Garner
Composed 1972–3
PREMIERE   9 January 1975, St Mary Magdalene, Munster Square, London

Potter Thompson, though ponderously billed as a 'music drama', is a children's opera, commissioned by the Finchley Children's Music Group. The story is a quest. The morose and embittered Potter Thompson is goaded by the villagers to set off in search of the Sleeping Hero under the Hill. After many adventures, he finds the Hero but at the last moment declines to wake him, and instead returns to the village healed and able to confront the present.

Though long and at times obscure, the work is well written, effective and moving. It has a single adult singer in the title role, and a seven-piece orchestra, but also 'noise orchestra' and a large supporting cast of children, who have excellent music to sing. That the composer of such a work in his thirties should have written no further operas is a terrible indictment of the state of opera in Britain in the late 20th century.

BIBLIOGRAPHY   Gordon Crosse, 'A Setting of W. B. Yeats', *Opera*, vol. 17 (1966), pp. 534–7; Gordon Crosse, '*Potter Thompson* – an Introduction', *Opera*, vol. 26 (1975), p. 22; Stephen Walsh, '*The Story of Vasco*', *Music and Musicians*, March 1974, pp. 26–8

S.W.

CESAR CUI

César Antonovich Cui; *b* 18 January 1835, Vilnius, Lithuania; *d* 26 March 1918, Petrograd [St Petersburg], Russia

Cui, a Russian composer, engineer and expert on fortifications, was born of French and Lithuanian parents. He was the chief spokesman of the so-called Mighty Handful group of nationalist Russian composers, writing regularly for the *Sanktpeterburgskiye vedomosti* where his partisan views managed to antagonize most people; as if to prove impartiality, he would occasionally trounce his friends and colleagues. His usually wrong-headed denunciations of Musorgsky, Rimsky-Korsakov and Tchaikovsky make amusing reading today. The gulf between the nationalist ideals of his writing and his composition is marked, his abiding musical influences being Auber, Schumann and Chopin. He is at his best as a miniaturist, with some songs well worth investigating.

Of Cui's 15 operas, none is still heard, though in the case of *William Ratcliff*, this is unjust. Cui was drawn to French subjects, Victor Hugo (*Angelo* – the same source that inspired Ponchielli's *La gioconda*), Maupassant (*Mademoiselle Fifi*), and even set an opéra-comique text by Richepin (*Le Flibustier*) that was premiered in Paris. This later music can be redolent of a tired Massenet, the harmonic refinement is undoubtable, but the lack of energy cloying. His Pushkin operas – *The Prisoner of the Caucasus*, *A Feast in Time of Plague* and *The Captain's Daughter* – do not differ greatly in style from his settings of French subjects. Cui's first act of the Mighty Handful's collective opera-ballet project *Mlada* is published and this dates from his most self-consciously nationalist period (1872). It is saturated with folksong idioms and has some advanced harmony, but cannot bear comparison with Rimsky-Korsakov's vivid setting, using an almost identical text, of 1889. At the end of his life, Cui wrote several children's operas and a completion of Musorgsky's unfinished *Sorochintsy Fair*.

William Ratcliff

Vil'yam Ratclif
Opera in three acts (2h 45m)
Libretto by Aleksey Nikolayovich Pleshcheyev, after the tragedy by Heine (1823)
Composed 1861–8
PREMIERE   26 February 1869, Mariinsky Theatre, St Petersburg

One of the many settings of Heine's early Romantic tragedy, this opera was the flagship of the Mighty Handful, the first opera by the nationalists to appear, and became a self-styled source book for their ideals of dramatic truth, faithful declamation in recitative and an authentic use of folk material. *Ratcliff* bends these ideals somewhat; a Scottish subject is a strange début for a Russian nationalist.

The complex family saga concerns a past liaison between Edward Ratcliff and 'Beautiful Betty' who was betrothed to a Scottish lord, MacGregor, who before the actions starts has murdered Edward. William Ratcliff was betrothed to Maria, MacGregor's daughter, but has abandoned her, so she marries Count Douglas. Ratcliff returns and challenges Douglas to a duel at the haunted Black Rock. Douglas wins, but spares Ratcliff, who dispatches Maria, MacGregor and then himself in the last act, leaving the maid, Margaret, to lament the fate of children who suffer through the fault of their parents.

The recitative in *Ratcliff* usually turns into songlike arioso and shades of Auber and Gounod occasionally appear. Though there are grave dramatic weaknesses, such as four narratives placed together, Cui was never again to write music of such dramatic power. The supernatural scene at the Black Rock, MacGregor's monologue and the last-act duet and finale have a vitality and inspiration that belie Cui's limp reputation. It survived only seven performances, though it did have a successful revival in Moscow in 1900.

EDITION v.s., Roder, 1874

Other operatic works: *Kavkazskii plennik* (*A Prisoner in the Caucasus*), (1857–8, 1881), 1883; *Syn mandarina* (*The Mandarin's Son*), (1859), 1878; *Angelo*, 1876; *Mlada* (Act I), (1872); *Le Flibustier*, (1889), 1894; *Saratsin* (*The Saracen*), 1899; *Pir vo vremya chumy* (*A Feast in Time of Plague*), 1900; *Mam'selle Fifi*, (1900), 1903; *Matteo Falcone*, (1901), 1907; *Kapitanskaya dochka* (*The Captain's Daughter*), (1909), 1911 Children's operas: *Snezhnyi Bogatyr'* (*The Snow Prince*), 1906; *Kot v sapogakh* (*Puss in Boots*), (c. 1900), 1915; *Red Riding Hood*, 1911; *Ivan the Idiot*, 1913

BIBLIOGRAPHY Gerald Abraham, 'Heine, Cui and *William Ratcliff*', in *Essays on Russian and East European Music*, Clarendon Press, 1985; Richard Taruskin, *Opera and Drama in Russia*, UMI Research Press, 1981

J.G.

D

NICOLAS DALAYRAC

Nicolas-Marie Dalayrac; *b* 8 June 1753, Muret, Haute
Garonne, France; *d* 26 November 1809, Paris

Dalayrac worked almost exclusively in opéra
comique, writing for the Comédie-Italienne (later
Opéra-Comique) in Paris. He became the most
prolific and successful exponent of this genre. But
whereas the best works by his contemporary Grétry
were revived well into the 19th century, Dalayrac's
were not.

He came from a well-to-do background and
studied law. In Paris, he became an informal pupil of
Grétry's, but his main teacher was Honoré Langlé, a
minor composer of opera. Dalayrac wrote little
Revolution music for state use, but campaigned
actively for the rights of opera composers to receive
performance fees. His patriotism was displayed in *La
prise de Toulon* and other works.

Dalayrac's music covered the range of styles
prevalent in opéra comique: from sentimental
romances to tense large-scale ensembles, taking in
virtuoso Italianate arias on the way. In some works
he employed the systematic reuse of musical material; *Léon* and *Léhéman* are outstanding examples,
and the latter was favourably reviewed by Weber.
Dalayrac's operas were widely appreciated outside
France, and his skill in planning them was praised
by several librettists.

L'amant statue

The Lover as Statue
Comédie in one act (50m)
Libretto by Desfontaines (François-Georges Fouques)
PREMIERE 4 August 1785, Comédie-Italienne, Paris

Dorval, a young officer, sends love letters every day
to the coy Célimène. To bring matters to a happy
conclusion, he first disguises himself as a seller of
chansons and almanacs. With the help of Frontin and
Rosette (Célimène's maid) he contrives to leave a
message for his beloved. Finally, Dorval pretends to
be a new garden statue, but one fitted with an
interior mechanism; such is Célimène's attraction to
this 'statue' (which plays the flute too) that she
affirms her love for it, whereupon Dorval reveals
himself.

Dalayrac's ensembles capture the ephemeral wit of
the text, but most memorable are Célimène's two
virtuoso Italianate arias, the second of which ascends
to top E.

RECORDING Dudziak, Chevalier, Launay, Vidal, M. Cook,
Scalen' Disc, *c.* 1985
EDITION f.s., Le Duc, 1785

Nina, ou La folle par amour

Nina, or The Woman Crazed through Love
Comédie in one act (1h)
Libretto by Benoît-Joseph Marsollier des Vivetières, after
F. Thomas de Baculard d'Arnaud's short story *La nouvelle
Clémentine* (1783) and other sources
PREMIERES 15 May 1786, Comédie-Italienne, Paris; UK:
24 April 1787, Covent Garden, London; US: 23 July 1794,
Charleston, South Carolina

Dalayrac's range, both musically and dramatically,
expanded over his first decade of production. *Nina*
had no dramatic precedent in French opera, and it is
hard to imagine, say, Grétry setting this text.
However, the 'correction' of parental error (in
having forced a daughter into marriage) was also the
theme of Dezède's popular *Julie* (1772) and Paisiello
scored a success with a setting of the same story
(*Nina*, 1789).

Nina's father, a count, has insisted she marry a
wealthy suitor rather than Germeuil, her childhood
sweetheart. After a duel with the suitor, in which it is
believed Germeuil has died, Nina loses her reason.
Each day, nursed by assorted villagers, she goes
distractedly into her garden to wait for her lover. She
no longer recognizes her father. After Germeuil's
return and acceptance by the count, Nina's reason
returns and the couple are married.

Dalayrac's approach was, necessarily, careful and
lyrical, not shocking and melodramatic. Nina's theme
song, 'Quand le bien-aimé reviendra', is a 6/8
strophic ditty that became long familiar in France;
Berlioz referred to it in his *Mémoires* as his 'first
musical experience'.

EDITIONS f.s., Chez le Duc, Paris, 1786; v.s., Schott, *c.* 1787;
facsimile, Herbert Schneider (ed.), *French Opera in the 17th
and 18th Centuries*, Pendragon, forthcoming

Azémia, ou Les sauvages

Azémia, or The Savages
Comédie in three acts (2h)

Louise Dugazon as Azémia (Paris, 1786)

Libretto by Ange Etienne Xavier Poisson de Lachabeaussière
PREMIERES first version: 17 October 1786, Court Theatre, Fontainebleau; second version: 3 May 1787, Comédie-Italienne, Paris; US: 20 September 1827, Park Theater, New York

The title role of *Azémia*, like that of *Nina*, was destined for the dramatic soprano Louise-Rosalie Dugazon (1755–1821). The plot was inspired partially by *The Tempest*. The libretto's preface argues staunchly for 'romanesque situations' and 'picturesque effects' in opéra comique, thus anticipating 19th-century tendencies. The whole opera takes place on an unknown desert island, and was intended to have highly realistic natural stage settings. Dalayrac's music is markedly varied, with both Italianate coloratura and his more typical sentimental themes. There is some chorus work, and a mimed overture in which the native islanders are seen in their boats.

EDITION f.s., Chez le Duc, 1786

Les deux petits Savoyards
The Two Little Savoyard Boys
Comédie in one act (1h)
Libretto by Benoît-Joseph Marsollier des Vivetières
PREMIERES 14 January 1789, Comédie-Italienne, Paris; UK: 29 June 1789, Sadler's Wells, London; US: 16 January 1797, Philadelphia

With this exceedingly popular little opera, Dalayrac reached the point where real folk melody entered the armoury of local colour. Dalayrac's heroes are two boys (sung by sopranos in *travesti*) in national costume who, following the depression of the late 1780s, eke out a living by travelling to Lyons to sell spiced cakes, sing, and exhibit a live marmot. Near the opening, they have to protest in order to gain admission to Verseuil's castle and so earn a crust. Verseuil is an elderly bachelor who has made a fortune in the Americas, and whose brother has now died. He takes an interest in the Savoyard boys and considers adopting them. He talks to them individually and, because they are less than keen to oblige, leaves them to think it over. They escape from their respective rooms, but are then discovered to be carrying a portrait of their father, who turns out to be Verseuil's late brother.

With its appeal to a united nation of all classes and people of good will, this work typified the France of 1789. The opera's most popular tune was the traditional 'Escouto d'Jeannetto'.

EDITIONS f.s., Chez le Duc, 1789; v.s., Schott, n.d.

Léon, ou Le château de Monténéro
Leon, or The Castle of Montenero
Drame in three acts (2h 30m)
Libretto by François-Benoît Hoffman, after the romance by Ann Radcliffe, *The Mysteries of Udolfo* (1794)
PREMIERE 15 October 1798, Opéra-Comique, Paris

Léon is one of Dalayrac's several 'Gothic' operas, which include *Raoul sire de Créqui* and *Camille*, both also involving imprisonment in a castle. *Léon* expands the genre in order to explore the ambiguities between appearance and reality.

The background is a warring feud between the *seigneurs* of Monténéro (Léon) and Fondi (Romualde). Romualde's daughter Laure, her bethrothed, Louis, and her nurse Vénérande, are captured by Léon's men. Held separately in his castle, they are threatened by Léon, who is stopped from forcibly marrying Laure only by her threatened suicide. With the help of the disaffected steward Ferrant, Louis overcomes Léon and delivers him to justice.

Dalayrac's music uses five different motifs, which are recollected in various dramatic ways. In some cases, the use of the motifs in the orchestra conveys defined emotions and thoughts. The score is strong in ensemble writing and in the unity of its solo style, which avoids coloratura.

EDITION facsimile, Sherwood Dudley (ed.), *French Opera in the 17th and 18th Centuries*, Pendragon, forthcoming

Gulistan, ou Le hulla de Samarcande
Gulistan, or The Hulla of Samarkand
Opéra comique in three acts (2h 30m)
Libretto by Charles-Guillaume Etienne and Ange Etienne Xavier Poisson de Lachabeaussière
PREMIERES 30 September 1805, Opéra-Comique, Paris; US: 1 August 1827, New York

This is one of a new generation of 'oriental' operas seen in Paris, which included Boieldieu's *Zoraïme et Zulnar* and *Le calife de Bagdad*. The accent in *Gulistan* was more on exotic staging and ceremonial than wit, and a camel was demanded in the Act III procession. Gulistan is a musician, a former royal favourite, fallen from grace. He is poor but happy, save for the disappearance of his beloved, Dilara. A rich merchant, Taher, wishes to separate from his wife. The law demands that before this may occur, she must marry a *hulla* (or temporary husband) for one night. Gulistan is selected, installed in the house with great ceremony, and 'married' to Taher's wife, who of course turns out to be Dilara. The score contains triangle, cymbals and piccolos, and prefigures the 'oriental' music of Weber's *Oberon*.

Other operas: *Le petit souper*, 1781; *L'éclipse totale*, 1782; *Le corsair*, 1783; *Les deux tuteurs*, 1784; *La dot*, 1785; *Renaud d'Ast*, 1787; *Sargines*, 1788; *Raoul, sire de Créqui*, 1789; *La soirée orageuse*, 1790; *Camille, ou Le souterrain*, 1791; *Philippe et Georgette*, 1791; *Tout pour l'amour, ou Roméo et Juliette*, 1792; *Ambroise*, 1793; *La prise de Toulon*, 1794; *La pauvre femme*, 1795; *Adèle et Dorsan*, 1795; *La famille américaine*, 1796; *Marianne, ou L'amour maternelle*, 1796; *La leçon, ou La tasse de glaces*, 1797; *La maison isolée*, 1797; *Gulnare, ou L'esclave persanne*, 1797; *Alexis, ou L'erreur d'un bon père*, 1798; *Adolphe et Clara, ou Les deux prisonniers*, 1799; *Maison à vendre*, 1800; *Une matinée de Catinat*, 1800; *Léhéman, ou La tour de Neustadt*, 1801; *La boucle de cheveux*, 1802; *Picaros et Diégo, ou La folle soirée*, 1803; *La jeune prude, ou Les femmes entre elles*, 1804; *Une heure de mariage*, 1804; *Le pavillon du calife*, 1804; *Deux mots, ou Une nuit dans la forêt*, 1806; *Koulouf, ou Les chinois*, 1806; *Lina, ou Le mystère*, 1807; *Elise-Hortense*, 1809; *Le poète et le musicien, ou Je cherche un sujet*, 1811; *c.* 13 lost operas

BIBLIOGRAPHY David Charlton, 'Motif and Recollection in Four Operas of Dalayrac', *Soundings*, vol. 7 (1978), p. 38; K. Pendle, 'A Working Friendship: Marsollier and Dalayrac', *ML*, vol. 64 (1983), pp. 44–57

D.P.C.

LUIGI DALLAPICCOLA

b 3 February 1904, Pisino d'Istria, Slovenija; *d* 19 February 1975, Florence, Italy

Dallapiccola was the son of an Istrian schoolmaster, and his teenage education was disrupted when his father's school was closed by the Austrian authorities, and the family was interned at Graz. Only at the close of the First World War, when Istria was ceded to Italy, was the family able to return to Pisino. In 1922 Dallapiccola moved to Florence, which was to be his home for the rest of his life. He studied at the conservatory there, where in 1934 he became professor of piano as a second study – a post that he held until his retirement. His compositions of the late 1930s and 1940s showed first a tentative, and then an increasingly convinced use of serial techniques, and after the Second World War Dallapiccola emerged as the most authoritative advocate of that tradition in Italy.

In his theatrical work, Dallapiccola was heir to a theatre of philosophical challenge perhaps most strikingly exemplified in Busoni's *Doktor Faust*. He sought to infuse the Italian lyric tradition with a distinctive complexity of musical and dramatic thought and, in so doing, markedly influenced a younger generation of post-war composers, particularly with *Il prigioniero*, whose first performances in 1949 and 1950 were an important index of reviving cultural fortunes in Italy.

Volo di notte
Night Flight
[Opera in] one act (1h)
Libretto by the composer, after Antoine de Saint-Exupéry's short novel *Vol de nuit* (1931)
Composed 1937–9
PREMIERES 18 May 1940, Teatro della Pergola, Florence; US: 1 March 1962, Stanford University, California; UK: 29 May 1963, King's Theatre, Glasgow

Although much of his previous work had shown a strong sense of identity with medieval and renaissance Italian culture, Dallapiccola's first viable theatrical project broke entirely out of this framework to confront a modern subject. Based on the aviator–writer Saint-Exupéry's own experience when working for the Latécoère company, it chronicles the tenacity of purpose of those who pioneered airmail services in South America. Its protagonist, Rivière, is a portrait of Didier Daurat, the director of those services.

Rivière seeks to maximize the potential of his project through as yet unexplored techniques of night flying: the mail is brought into Buenos Aires, and there transferred to another plane, which will set off for Europe in the middle of the night. The pilot of the flight from Chile, Pellerin, is caught up in a fearful Pacific cyclone while crossing the Andes, yet survives. But that same cyclone engulfs the plane flying up from Patagonia (the route that Saint-Exupéry had himself pioneered). The pilot, Fabien, defying his radiographer's warnings of bad weather, battles on in the darkness. About to run out of petrol, he decides on a crash landing, but throwing out a flare, discovers that he has been blown out to sea. He glimpses the stars through a gap in the clouds, and knowing that there is now no hope of safety, directs his plane upwards towards them, and rides above the storm in a new and revelatory realm until his petrol runs out. When it becomes clear that Fabien has been lost, the company staff expect Rivière to abandon his project. But the plane from Paraguay arrives safely: Rivière musters his strength, and orders the pilot for Europe on to the tarmac.

Dallapiccola locates the action entirely within Rivière's office: Fabien's final moment of revelation is relayed through a radio telegraphist. The opera's six scenes are constructed as autonomous musical structures. A good deal of their material derives from the *Tre laudi* that Dallapiccola had composed in 1936–7: the most important instance being the music that opens the opera, and recurs at its climax, as Fabien climbs towards the stars. In its coupling of serial melody with a harmony still rooted in tonal associations, and its rhythmic vitality, *Volo di notte* remains a child of its time – but an interesting and accessible one.

EDITIONS f.s., Universal, 1940; v.s., Universal, 1952, 1964

Il prigionero
The Prisoner

[Opera in] a prologue and one act (55m)
Libretto by the composer, after Count Philippe Auguste Villiers de l'Isle-Adam's story *La torture par l'espérance* from *Nouveaux contes cruels* (1888), with additions after Charles de Coster's novel *La légende d'Ulenspiegel* (1868), and other sources
Composed 1944–8
PREMIERES 1 December 1949, RAI broadcast; 20 May 1950, Teatro Comunale, Florence; US: 15 March 1951, Juilliard School of Music, New York; UK: 27 July 1959, Sadler's Wells, London

Dallapiccola first considered the theatrical potential of Villiers de l'Isle-Adam's story in 1939, at the instigation of his Jewish wife, Laura. That story is a more specific study of anti-Semitic persecution than is the libretto that Dallapiccola derived from it, for it centred on a rabbi tortured by the Inquisition in Saragossa. Drawing his imagery from de Coster's extraordinary epic of Flemish defiance to Spanish rule, *La légende d'Ulenspiegel*, Dallapiccola substituted for the rabbi an imprisoned Flemish freedom fighter, simply designated the Prisoner. Introducing two new figures, the Mother and the Gaoler, he fleshed out the spare simplicity of Villiers de l'Isle-Adam's narration so as to emphasize the theme of resistance to tyranny (embodied in the opera in the brooding but unseen presence of Philip II).

Dallapiccola's ground plan is symmetrical. The Prisoner's Mother enters before the curtain to sing a prologue, recounting her nightly dream of Philip II (derived from de Coster and from Victor Hugo's portrait of Philip in *La légende des siècles*). She is engulfed by the first choral intermezzo, symbolizing the power of the Inquisition. The three main scenes follow: the Mother visits the Prisoner – as she rightly guesses – for the last time. Next comes the central scene of the Prisoner's temptation by the 'Gaoler' (Dallapiccola's point of departure when setting to work on the music). The Gaoler addresses him as *fratello* ('brother'), urges him to hope, and tells of a Flemish uprising. He departs, leaving the Prisoner's door unlocked. The third scene charts his fearful progress as, taking advantage of this opportunity, he makes his way along seemingly endless subterranean corridors: miraculously, two passing monks fail to notice him. A second choral intermezzo reasserts the presence of the Inquisition with thunderous force. Finally, in a scene that balances the first of the opera, the Prisoner emerges into a nocturnal garden. Ecstatic beneath the night sky, as was Fabien in *Volo di notte*, the Prisoner advances to embrace a great cedar tree. Arms shoot out from the tree, and a familiar voice intones 'fratello': it is the Grand Inquisitor who, posing as a gaoler, has put the Prisoner to the ultimate torture: that of hope. As a

fire begins to flicker in the background, he leads him towards it.

The work is knit together by three different note rows, each used thematically, and by short motifs in part derived from them. The first is associated with the Prisoner's prayer, 'Signore, aiutarmi a camminare' ('Lord, help me to walk'), the second with hope, and thus with the 'fratello' motif that announces the insidious presence of the 'Gaoler'. The third row, rich in tonal associations, is that of freedom on which the Gaoler's 'aria in three strophes' depicting the revolt in Flanders is based. A further motif depicts Roelandt, the great bell of Ghent (destroyed by Philip II's father, Charles V), which the Prisoner is induced to believe may yet ring again. As he makes his way down the corridor, Dallapiccola summarizes his mental state by three ricercars: one on the prayer note row, one on the 'fratello' motif and one on the 'Roelandt' motif. Such associations and interactions are typical of the opera: in consequence, the score repays repeated listening.

RECORDING Barrera, Emili, Mazzieri, University of Maryland Ch, National SO of Washington, Dorati, Decca, 1974
EDITIONS f.s., Suvini Zerboni, 1948; v.s., Suvini Zerboni, 1947

Job
Sacra rappresentazione (35m)
Libretto by the composer, after the Book of Job
Composed 1950
PREMIERES 30 October 1950, Teatro Elisio, Rome; US: 13 December 1970, University of Southern California Opera Theater, Los Angeles

Asked by the Associazione Amfiparnasso in Rome for a short stage work, Dallapiccola, again prompted by his wife, turned to the story of Job. The symmetrical discipline that he liked to impose on narrative structures is clearly in evidence. This time there are seven sections. At the outer extremes are parallel narrations of Job's good fortune before and after his faith is put to the test. At the centre stands the debate between Job and his three friends as to how a just God can visit suffering and destruction on an upright man. The second movement, a quartet of messengers bringing news of Satan's destruction of Job's family and possessions, is balanced by the sixth in which the Voice of God (the singing chorus) speaks out of the whirlwind and puts an end to Job's doubts.

The parallel battles of words between God and his errant son Satan in movements 1 and 3 are set for two speaking choruses, and they alternate with the multi-voiced, often canonical, writing of movements 2 (the messengers) and 4 (the friends). Along with the shorter *Tre poemi* of the previous year, *Job* was the first of Dallapiccola's works to derive from a single row, and the first to experiment with row permutations. Dallapiccola thus had to hand the essential technical procedures that would in due course allow him to start work on *Ulisse*.

EDITIONS f.s./v.s., Suvini Zerboni, 1951

Ulisse

Ulysses

Opera in a prologue and two acts (2h 15m)
Libretto by the composer, after Homer and others
Composed 1960–68
PREMIERES   29 September 1968, Deutsche Oper, Berlin (as *Odysseus*); UK: 20 September 1969, BBC Radio 3 (radio broadcast; studio performance)

Dallapiccola had already immersed himself in the Ulysses story when he had prepared a new version of Monteverdi's *Il ritorno d'Ulisse* for the Maggio Musicale in Florence in 1942. Intended as a summation of Dallapiccola's work, rather as *Doktor Faust* had been for Busoni, his own *Ulisse*'s combination of a richly worked libretto and a rather austere, unbending musical idiom have denied it as yet any clear-cut place within the operatic repertoire. The figure of Ulysses as conceived by Dallapiccola owes as much to Dante as to Homer: a man plunging into all aspects of human experience in search of a spiritual centre of gravity, to whom Dallapiccola (but not Homer or Dante) eventually accords an answer not in his homecoming and revenge on Penelope's suitors, but alone at sea in a boat – and needless to say beneath an epiphanic night sky.

Like *Job*, but more explicitly so, *Ulisse* is structured as a palindrome in 13 sections at whose centre lies his descent to the underworld. At either extreme stand Calypso alone on the seashore meditating on Ulysses' insatiable search, and Ulysses alone in his boat. To section 2, an orchestral representation of Poseidon's rage against Ulysses, corresponds section 12, an orchestral representation of the love of Ulysses and Penelope. To Nausicaa's danced ball game on the beach (3), corresponds the whore Melantho's dance of death (11); to Ulysses' arrival at the palace of King Alcinous (4) corresponds that of Ulysses at his own home in Ithaca (10). And so forth. Unity is achieved by grouping together a selection of Ulysses' adventures (up to and including the descent to the underworld) as a narration to King Alcinous and his court (Act I), and the *dénouement* at Ithaca with Ulysses' solitary epilogue (Act II).

Ulysses is also conceived as a *summa* of the feminine spirit. As a young man Dallapiccola believed he had found in the *Odyssey* archetypes for five essential aspects of womanhood. Moving from woman to woman through the opera, Ulysses completes a survey of the intractable 'otherness' of femininity. But tellingly, his own masculine identity is a negative, not a positive, counter-pole. In Dallapiccola's version, the revenge of Poseidon is not the constant threat of annihilation by shipwreck, but a more subtle deliquescence. Ulysses becomes unsure of his own self: he hesitates to use his own name, even the word 'I'. Despite the moment of self-assertion needed to kill Penelope's suitors, it is the fragmented Ulysses that returns to the ocean – unaware until the very last moment of the opera that

A scene, designed by Fernando Farulli, from Ulisse *(Berlin, 1968)*

this scattering of self is the path through which an awareness of God can penetrate.

The sea is an ubiquitous symbol in *Ulisse*. It is therefore appropriate that the basic series from which all else derives is in the form of a wave. An extraordinary range of transformational processes yields all the other series, used motivically in association with specific characters (particularly the various women) or places (Ithaca, the underworld). In view of what was said above, it comes as no surprise that Ulysses does not have a character series as such – but mention of him consistently evokes one of the sea series. It is a solution of which Freud would have approved.

RECORDING   Ruk-Fočić, BakoÄević, Bottion, English, Cesari, Rome Ch and SO of Italian Radio, Pesko, RAI (presentation copies only), 1972
EDITION   f.s., Suvini Zerboni, 1971; v.s., Suvini Zerboni, 1968

BIBLIOGRAPHY   Luigi Dallapiccola, ed. and trans. Rudy Shackelford, *Dallapiccola on Opera*, Toccata Press, 1987

D.O.-S.

JEAN-MICHEL DAMASE
b 27 January 1928, Bordeaux

Damase, a star pupil of the Paris Conservatoire in the 1940s, enjoyed early success both as a virtuoso pianist and as a composer. He won the Prix de Rome in 1947. That accolade has rarely been any indication of avant-garde tendencies, and Damase was at that time and has remained a traditionalist, his music a continuation of the post-tonal line of Debussy and Ravel without the modish interest in their deeper-seated implications.

His theatre music is consistently fluent, effective, and well made. It includes several ballets and seven operas, some of them with libretti by his close friend and fellow Bordelais, Jean Anouilh. In their way the best of these are as theatrically telling as Anouilh's own plays. *Madame de . . .* (1970) is as sumptuously evocative as the novel by Louise de Vilmorin on which Anouilh based his libretto, while *Eurydice* (1972) is a strong neo-*verismo* setting of Anouilh's wartime Orpheus update (known in English as *Point of Departure*). Damase's last opera to date, *L'héritière* (1974), sets a libretto based on Henry James's *Washington Square* in a style described by one critic as 'latter-day Messager'. The composer has conducted most of his own operatic premieres.

Operas: *La tendre Eleonore*, (1958); *Colombe*, 1961; *Eugène le mystérieux*, 1964; *Le matin de Faust*, (1965); *Madame de . . .*, 1970; *Eurydice*, 1972; *L'héritière*, 1974
BIBLIOGRAPHY   D. Pistone (ed.), 'Quarante ans de créations françaises à Monte-Carlo', *Le théâtre lyrique français 1947–85*, Paris, 1987, pp. 339–46

S.W.

DANIEL-LESUR
Daniel Jean Yves Lesur; *b* 19 November 1908, Paris

Daniel-Lesur is best known as one of the four composers (with Messiaen, Jolivet and Baudrier) of the so-called La Jeune France group, which presented itself in 1936 as in reaction against the mechanical and anti-emotional tendencies in French music of the 1920s and early 1930s. Daniel-Lesur's own music, which – with its roots in d'Indy, Debussy and Tournemire (who taught him for a time) – is more conventional than Messiaen's, is mostly for the concert hall. But he has written three operas, all substantial. *Andrea del Sarto* (1969) is based on Alfred de Musset's dramatization of the life of the 16th-century Florentine painter, while *Ondine* (1982) derives from Jean Giraudoux's treatment (1939) of the myth of the water sprite who marries a mortal. The third opera, a reportedly powerful adaptation of Montherlant's *La reine morte*, still awaits performance. The two earlier operas are unashamedly post-Debussian; *Ondine*, especially, seems to descend directly from Debussy's *Pelléas et Mélisande*.

RECORDING   *Andrea del Sarto* (abridged), Barclay, 1970s
BIBLIOGRAPHY   Andrew Thomson, 'Daniel-Lesur: the Athenian of Paris', *MT*, vol. 132 (July 1991), pp. 333–6

S.W.

FRANZ DANZI
Franz Ignaz Danzi; *b* 15 June 1763, Schwetzingen; *d* 13 April 1826, Karlsruhe

Although known today mainly for his chamber music for wind instruments, Danzi also made important contributions to German theatre music. In a career that straddled the operatic worlds of Mozart and Weber, he produced numerous stage works, including singspiels, melodramas, incidental music, and one full-length, through-composed grand opera, *Iphigenie in Aulis*, now unfortunately lost. In his youth he studied in Mannheim with the Abbé Vogler at his renowned Tonschule; and while serving at the National Theatre, where he was a cellist with the orchestra, produced his earliest incidental music. After transferring to Munich in 1783, he achieved his first major theatrical success with his comic opera *Die Mitternachtsstunde*, eventually published by Simrock. In 1807 he settled in Stuttgart as hof-kapellmeister and during the succeeding years he formed a close friendship with Weber. Later, as kapellmeister at the court of Karlsruhe, the works he produced included his own *Turandot* (one of the earliest known settings of Gozzi's drama (1762)) and several of Weber's operas including *Der Freischütz* and *Euryanthe*. Danzi's highly competent theatrical scores reflect the influence of Mozart together with modernist elements in harmony and orchestration clearly prompted by his links with Weber.

Operatic works: *Cleopatra*, 1780; *Die Mitternachtsstunde*, 1788; *Der Sylphe*, 1788; *Deucalion et Pirrha* (?doubtful), *c.* 1795; *Camilla und Eugen, oder Der Gartenschlüssel*, 1812; *Rübezahl*, 1813; *Malvina*, 1814; *Turandot*, 1817; *Die Probe*, 1817; *L'Abbé de l'Attaignant, oder Die Theaterprobe*, 1820; 3 lost

BIBLIOGRAPHY   F. Walter, *Geschichte des Theaters und der Musik am kurpfälzischen Hofe*, Leipzig, 1898; *rp*, 1968

B.S.

ALEKSANDR DARGOMYZHSKY

Aleksandr Sergeyevich Dargomyzhsky; *b* 14 February 1813, Troitskoye, Tula District, Russia; *d* 17 January 1869, St Petersburg, Russia

As a follower of Glinka, Dargomyzhsky helped establish the tradition of national opera that was brought to fruition by the so-called Mighty Handful and Tchaikovsky. He is of great historical importance in the development of Russian music, but is not widely performed in the West.

His father, the illegitimate son of a nobleman, had eloped with Princess Kozlovskaya, a poetess, whose fascination with French culture was passed on to their six children. Dargomyzhsky showed great promise as a pianist and composer from an early age, and became a noted singing teacher in later life, though his own voice was notoriously high-pitched. His first piano teacher, Danilevsky, did not consider composing a suitable occupation for an aristocrat and tried to discourage him. In 1833, Dargomyzhsky met Glinka, who lent him notebooks of counterpoint exercises from his studies in Berlin with Siegfried Dehn; this was Dargomyzhsky's first thorough theoretical training.

Glinka and Dargomyzhsky organized concerts together. Playing piano duets and constant attendance during the preparations of Glinka's *A Life for the Tsar* inspired Dargomyzhsky to write an opera of his own. He toyed with Victor Hugo's *Lucrèce Borgia*, but then discovered a libretto Hugo himself had prepared for *Notre Dame de Paris*, which he translated – by 1841 *Esmeralda* was complete. Its style, that of French grand opera, was unfashionable in the Italian-dominated Russian operatic world, and it was not premiered until 1847. Discouraged by this, and by Glinka's huge success, he went to Paris (1844–5) where he met Auber, Meyerbeer and Halévy, his erstwhile idols. Curiously, like Glinka before him, absence from the homeland made him appreciate the richness of his native folk tradition, which was, as yet, relatively untapped. His songs from the mid-1840s onwards, perhaps his most significant compositions, demonstrate a striving for truth and realism in declamation, favouring dramatic scenes rather than lyric outpourings of emotion, and often show a racy sense of humour. The opera-ballet, *The Triumph of Bacchus* (completed in 1848, but premiered disastrously in 1867), is a retrograde step, favouring French models, though a harmonic quirkiness, which flavours all of his later work, lifts some of the music above the banal. *Rusalka* shows the most extensive

use of folksong in his work, and was the first significant Russian opera to appear after Glinka's *Ruslan and Lyudmila*; but it did not become popular until the late 1860s, and its initial neglect precipitated another trip to Europe. On this trip he was cordially received by Liszt, and scored a great success in Brussels with two orchestral pieces and excerpts from *Rusalka*. By now, his reputation was growing. He had been elected to the Russian Musical Society Committee and was involved with Balakirev's new circle of composers, the Mighty Handful. From this period date two opera fragments, a duet from a setting of Pushkin's *Poltava* and five numbers from a fairy-tale opera *Rogdana* – a hermits' chorus from the latter showing great grandeur and advanced harmonic thinking.

In the last years of his life, beset with chronic illness and even more chronic hypochondria, Dargomyzhsky worked on a setting of Pushkin's *The Stone Guest*, a controversial work that has become a legend, but is very rarely heard. His is a curious case, a composer whose ideals and theories were often more fecund than his musical ideas; he lacked the inspiration and ability to carry his conceptions through, but left an indelible mark on the next generation, particularly on Musorgsky.

Rusalka

Opera in four acts (2h 15m)
Libretto by the composer after the dramatic poem by Pushkin (1837)
Composed 1848–55
PREMIERES   16 May 1856, Circus Theatre, St Petersburg; UK: 18 May 1931, Lyceum (English Opera House), London; US: 8 May 1922, New York

A repertoire piece in Russia, *Rusalka* is Dargomyzhsky's only opera strongly grounded in folk music, and his nascent realist and dramatic gifts are detectable. It is based on an unfinished verse play of Pushkin, one of many versions of the ancient *Rusalka* – or Undine, Wilis, Lorelei – legend, concerning dishonoured girls who drown themselves and are transformed into water nymphs who revenge themselves on men. Natasha, a miller's daughter, has been wooed by a prince in disguise, who abandons her, not knowing she is pregnant. To the horror of her father, she throws herself into the river Dnieper. The prince's marriage ceremony to a princess is disrupted by Natasha's voice. The princess is abandoned by her husband who is constantly drawn to the riverbank, where he meets the miller, now totally insane, and learns the truth. Natasha is now Queen of the Rusalki, and with her child, she plans revenge. The water baby meets the prince. Pushkin's version breaks off here, but in Dargomyzhsky's conclusion, Natasha appears to the prince and he jumps into the river.

The role of the miller is the most notable character Dargomyzhsky ever created, starting as a worldly-wise, humorous old codger and ending up insane; a detailed and histrionic portrait that became one of Chaliapin's favourite roles. Some of the folk-inspired material is first rate, particularly a melancholy aria for the princess, but the rest of the opera is inconsistent. The prince is pallidly drawn, his lyrical music is weak – Dargomyzhsky was never a melodist of distinction – and the fantastic scenes were beyond his range, despite some fanciful harp-writing.

RECORDINGS 1. Smolenskaya, Borisenko, Kozlovsky, Krivchenya, Ch and O of Bolshoi Theatre, Svetlanov, Melodiya, c. 1955; 2. Mikhailova, Terentieva, Pluzhnikov, Vedernikov, USSR TV and Radio Ch and O, Fedoseyev, Melodiya, 1983
EDITIONS f.s., State Music Publishing House (Moscow), 1949; v.s., A. Gutheil, 1857

The Stone Guest
Kamennyi Gost'
Opera in three acts (1h 15m)
Libretto by Alexander Pushkin (1830)
Composed 1860–69 (unfinished); completed by César Cui and orchestrated by Nikolay Rimsky-Korsakov
PREMIERES 20 February 1872, Mariinsky Theatre, St Petersburg; US: 25 February 1986, Marymount Manhattan Theater, New York; UK: 23 April 1987, Coliseum, London
CAST Don Juan *t*, Leporello *b*, Donna Anna *s*, Laura *ms*, Don Carlo *bar*, Monk *b*, the statue *b*, 2 guests *t*, *b*; *satb* chorus of Laura's guests
FULL ORCHESTRA

In this work, Dargomyzhsky took the unprecedented step of taking one of Pushkin's 'Little Tragedies' and setting it practically word for word, disregarding all operatic conventions and musical closed forms, allowing the words to dictate both structure and musical argument. Thus, there are no arias (except two songs that are called for in the original play) and the opera consists of continuous recitative. It was composed under the eyes of the Mighty Handful and Dargomyzhsky, when he realized his health was failing, bequeathed its completion to Cui, then the most experienced opera composer in the circle, and its orchestration to Rimsky-Korsakov.

Pushkin kept a detailed list of all the women he had possessed, and his version of the Don Juan legend has an amoral lightness of touch that is ambivalent and disturbing.

SYNOPSIS
Act I Don Juan has returned to Madrid with his servant, Leporello, illegally breaking his exile, which he had incurred for murdering the Commander in a duel. He catches sight of Donna Anna, the Commander's widow, being escorted to her husband's grave by a monk, and vows to woo her. (Pushkin's version is unique in making Donna Anna the wife of the Commander, rather than his daughter.) In Scene 2 Laura, a seductress, is having a supper party. She sings and dismisses her guests, detaining Don Carlo, whose fiery temper reminds her of her old flame, Don Juan. He appears in person, interrupting their love-making, dispatches Don Carlo in a duel and seduces Laura.

Act II Don Juan, disguised as a monk, waits for Donna Anna by the statue of the Commander. He woos her, and eventually she agrees to an assignation. Leporello later appears and is frightened by the statue. Don Juan forces him to invite the

statue to Donna Anna's house, and it bows. They flee.

Act III Don Juan reveals his identity to Donna Anna and swears he loves her. The statue appears and pulls Don Juan into the earth.

F. P. Kommissarzhevsky as Don Juan in The Stone Guest *(St Petersburg, 1872)*

The immediate influence of *The Stone Guest* was far-reaching. Cui referred to it as 'the Gospel, which Russian composers will consult on matters of declamation and of faithful word-setting'. Musorgsky completed his own experiment in declamation alongside Dargomyzhsky's in his setting of the first act of Gogol's *The Marriage* (1868) – though these ideas bear greater musical fruit in the inn scene in *Boris Godunov* – and Rimsky-Korsakov took *The Stone Guest* as a model for parts of his first opera, *The Maid of Pskov*. It may seem that Dargomyzhsky's operatic reforms owe something to Wagner's ideas, well publicized by Serov in the 1860s, but this is not apparent in the light of any musical analysis and, anyway, Dargomyzhsky was unsympathetic to the Wagner he heard (*Lohengrin* and *Tannhäuser*), considering it musically forced and undramatic, the texts overburdened with too much musical significance at the expense of pace.

The Stone Guest goes to the other extreme, containing long expanses of bare recitative with chordal support. One might suppose that the logical end to these reforms would be to omit music altogether. The pace is unvaried, excepting the conclusions of the last two acts, the melodic shapes are often anonymous, with more than a whiff of routine French or Italian recitative about them. Leitmotifs are attached to certain characters, but these are all-purpose labels, expressing neither emotion nor character. Occasional passages are vivid: the irruption of Don Juan and the duel in the first act, as well as the music for the statue. The latter has excited a great deal of comment, being based extensively on the whole-tone scale. Dargomyzhsky uses it with a boldness that suspends tonality for long stretches, quite unlike Glinka's fleeting use to portray supernatural events in *Ruslan and Lyudmila*, though obviously indebted to it: this music does convey genuine unease and terror.

The opera as a whole has many bold harmonic surprises, conceived empirically at the piano, though the wildest of these were ironed out by Rimsky-Korsakov in his well-meant but misguided edition of 1906. It has never been a repertoire piece, even in Russia, though its UK premiere by English National Opera was well received and showed the work, despite its manifold limitations on the page, to have a surprisingly theatrical impact.

RECORDING Milashkina, Sinyavskaya, Atlantov, Valaitis, Vedernikov, Vernigora, Ch and O of Bolshoi Theatre, Ermler, Chant du Monde, 1979
EDITIONS f.s., Leningrad [St Petersburg], 1929; v.ss., W. Bessel, 1871; new edn, 1906; Leningrad Music, 1982; study s., Boosey & Hawkes (on hire)

Other operatic works: *Esmeralda*, (1841), 1847; *Torzhestvo Vakha* (*The Triumph of Bacchus*), (1848), 1867; *Mazepa* (inc.), (1860s); *Rogdana* (inc.), (1860s)
BIBLIOGRAPHY Gerald Abraham, *Studies in Russian Music*, Reeves, 1935; Richard Taruskin, *Opera and Drama in Russia*, UMI Research Press, 1981

J.G.

ANTOINE DAUVERGNE
b 3 October 1713, Moulins, France; *d* 11 February 1797, Lyons, France

A pupil of Rameau and Leclair, Dauvergne was associated with the Paris Opéra from 1744 until 1790, as violinist, composer and eventually director. Among his works for the Opéra are four *tragédies* (*Enée et Lavinie*, *Canente*, *Hercule mourant* and *Polyxène*), indicative of a renewed interest in this genre during Rameau's last years. The first two use existing libretti set by Collasse in 1690 and 1700; this was a practice unknown in France before Rameau's *Pigmalion* (1748), and Dauvergne was indeed the first to follow Rameau's lead. These operas contain some powerful and imaginative music, rather old-fashioned for its date but none the worse for that.

Dauvergne's works for the Opéra and the French court have been overshadowed by his one contribution to Jean Monnet's revitalized Opéra-Comique:

Les troqueurs (1753), produced at the height of the *querelle des bouffons*, was deliberately modelled on opera buffa. The combination of Dauvergne's fashionably Italianate, memorable, witty music with Jean-Joseph Vadé's simple plot and lifelike peasant characters was immediately successful, and did much to establish a style of opéra comique in which newly composed music replaced traditional melodies.

Operatic works: *Les amours de Tempé*, 1752; *Les troqueurs*, 1753 (RECORDING Ace of Diamonds, *c.* 1966); *La coquette trompée*, 1753 (RECORDING Decca, 1976); *Enée et Lavinie*, 1758; *Les fêtes d'Euterpe*, 1758; *Canente*, 1760; *Hercule mourant*, 1761; *Polyxène*, 1763; *La vénitienne*, 1768
BIBLIOGRAPHY Martin Cooper, *Opéra comique*, Max Parrish, 1949; L. de La Laurencie, 'Deux imitateurs français des bouffons: Blavet et Dauvergne', *Année musicale*, vol. 2 (1912), pp. 65–125

G.S.

FÉLICIEN DAVID
Félicien-César David; *b* 13 April 1810, Cadenet, Vaucluse, France; *d* 29 August 1876, St Germain-en-Laye, France

Though chiefly (if at all) remembered today as the composer of the oratorio-like *Le désert* (sometimes rather fancifully dubbed 'the first symphonic poem'), David was also in his day a successful composer for the stage. When he first came to Paris from his native Vaucluse in 1830, he was briefly involved with the millennialist Saint-Simon movement, while at the same time studying at the Conservatoire. After the suppression of Saint-Simon in 1833, he embarked with the surviving faithful on a Middle Eastern voyage in quest of the so-called 'free woman', who, (according to Saint-Simon) would fulfil human destiny. There is no evidence that David found 'la femme libre', but he did return to France with a good deal of 'oriental' musical material, which he proceeded to incorporate into a series of 'odes-symphoniques', starting with *Le désert* (1844), and continuing with *Christophe Colombe* (1846) and the quasi-theatrical *L'Eden* (1848).

David's true operas are all later works. They too flirt with exotic subjects, but in a more conventional style. *La perle du Brésil* is a grand opera in the manner of Meyerbeer's *L'africaine*, with spectacular scenes on board ship and on the Brazilian coast, while *Herculaneum* is a Christians-and-barbarians tragedy in which the lovers die in each other's arms during a volcanic eruption. There is also a strong vein of the exotic in *Lalla-Rookh*, which evokes well the saturated 'Persian' atmosphere of Thomas Moore's poem, but handles its action woodenly. *Le saphir* is a somewhat stilted comedy based on Shakespeare's *All's Well That Ends Well*.

David's music is a curious amalgam of evocative originality and off-the-peg ordinariness. Its orientalism is up to a point authentic (more so than Meyerbeer's, or perhaps Bizet's), if insufficiently absorbed. But David could also too easily fall into routine. Berlioz thought *Herculaneum* excessively feeble, and Auber memorably enjoined David to come down off his camel. It is easy to mock, but David does historically come at the start of a trend towards the exotic that embraced the Russian Nationalists and many later French composers, as well as the Wagner of *Parsifal* and the Verdi of *Aida*.

Operatic works: *La perle du Brésil*, 1851, (rev. 1861); *Le fermier de Franconville*, (*c.* 1857); *Herculaneum*, 1859; *Lalla-Rookh*, 1862; *La captive*, (*c.* 1864); *Le saphir*, 1865

S.W.

PETER MAXWELL DAVIES
(Sir) Peter Maxwell Davies; *b* 8 September 1934, Manchester, England

Davies has said that he was set on the path to becoming a composer when, at the age of four, he was taken to a Gilbert and Sullivan operetta, and he has written more for the theatre than any other leading composer of his generation: operas, ballets, school operas, and small-scale works of 'music theatre', a genre he helped establish in the late 1960s. Perhaps the importance to him of the stage springs out of his concern with hypocrisy and betrayal, both intellectual and moral: each of his major dramatic works is concerned with an individual's search for personal authenticity in a mirror world of truth and falsehood, and the theatre – where real people assume roles, where musical thought can be traduced by stage action and vice versa – provides the ideal location for his questioning, ironical imagination.

The musical roots of that imagination lie in the great Austro-German tradition, which Davies absorbed as a boy, and in the alternatives of medieval, Indian and modern music which he encountered as a student in Manchester, where he was part of an extraordinary group of young musicians who interested themselves in the latest music of Boulez, Stockhausen and Nono (other members of the group included Birtwistle and Goehr). In essence his musical world was established by the mid-1950s. It depended on an equivalence between medieval and serial techniques, on a Schoenbergian reverence for developing form, and on a keenness to upset convention by means of complex rhythms, wild sonorities and harmonic double-thought. The idea for the opera *Taverner* came while he was still a student, though he did not begin the score until 1962, meanwhile concerning himself mostly with instrumental pieces and with school music (associated with his time as music master at Cirencester Grammar School, 1959–62).

While working on *Taverner* he found his music becoming more and more extravagant, its ironies exploding into manifest parody: plainsong themes could be converted into Victorian hymns or foxtrots; any and every musical intention could be mocked and guyed. It was out of this deeply unsettled and unsettling time that offshoots from the opera began to appear as pieces of music theatre, extending the debate about how a man can separate himself (or how a musical idea can separate itself) from masquerades, imitations, forced roles and madness. In order to put on their music-theatre pieces, Davies and Birtwistle founded the Pierrot Players in 1967 (the group continued, after Birtwistle's departure, as The Fires of London, 1970–87), and for that ensemble – consisting of the forces of Schoenberg's *Pierrot lunaire* together with a percussionist – Davies produced a host of dramatic works, chamber pieces and arrangements (or in some cases travesties).

In the early 1970s he settled in an isolated croft on the island of Hoy, and began a new period when the seascapes and tranquillity of Orkney started to wash over the puzzles and hysteria. Then, with his First Symphony (1973–6), he turned his attention more to the orchestra than to chamber groupings, though the operas that have followed *Taverner* have tended to be for reduced forces and have profited from the composer's experience of writing for The Fires.

Eight Songs for a Mad King
Music-theatre piece (30m)
Libretto by Randolph Stow
Composed 1969
PREMIERE 22 April 1969, Queen Elizabeth Hall, London

The work is scored for a male vocalist, ranging extravagantly in pitch and colour, with flautist, clarinettist, violinist, cellist, percussionist and keyboard-player who sometimes participate in the action. The soloist purports to be King George III, who was indeed mad, and there are references to 18th-century music and to the king's life, especially his attempts at training birds to sing tunes from a musical box.

RECORDING Eastman, Fires of London, Maxwell Davies, Unicorn-Kanchana, 1970
EDITION f.s., Boosey & Hawkes, 1971

Taverner
Opera in two acts (eight scenes) (2h 15m)
Libretto by the composer, after 16th-century documents/sources
Composed 1962–8, partly reconstructed 1970
PREMIERES 12 July 1972, Covent Garden, London; US: 12 March 1986, Opera Company of Boston
CAST John Taverner *t*, White Abbot *bar*, King *b*, Cardinal *t*, Jester *bar*, Richard Taverner *bar*, Rose Parrowe *s*, Priest-Confessor *ct*, Boy *treble*, Captain *b*, Antichrist *speaking t*, Archangel Gabriel *high t*, Archangel Michael *low b*, 2 monks 2 *t*; *satb* and *boy treble* chorus
FULL ORCHESTRA and stage bands of 16th-century instruments

The opera depends on a misreading of the documents (a misreading that was general at the time the work was begun) which suggested that Taverner, after writing some of the most glorious masses and motets in Henrican England, abandoned his art to become a zealous persecutor of the old faith. But though this may be false history, as fiction it touches important truth: in turning his back on music, the Taverner of the opera rejects what is best in himself,

Peter Maxwell Davies's Taverner *(London, 1972)*

and becomes a vessel of hatred and negation. He becomes a crude caricature, a parody of himself, and the opera discloses this on the largest scale by making its second act a parody of the first: there is a parallel with Liszt's *Faust-Symphonie*, Taverner being a Faust who sells his soul not for power and knowledge but for the security of blind certainty. Like Liszt, Davies deflates and counters his own music's pretensions by means of speed, drastic simplification of melody, and rhythmic crudity, so that the second act is almost a cartoon-strip version of the first. This effect is, however, slightly modified by the fact that parody is at work all through the score: parody in the musicological sense, in that the original Taverner's music provides the basic material for symphonic elaboration, and parody in the more common sense, in that certain scenes (especially Act I, Scene 4) are full of wild musical and dramatic exaggerations. The essential substance of the music, which in depth, inwardness and intensity recalls Schoenberg and Mahler, is thus under a double threat: that of relapse into Renaissance pastiche, and that of hysterical over-emphasis. Taverner's search for the way to save his soul is the music's search for integrity.

SYNOPSIS

Act I The opera opens with a courtroom scene: Taverner is being tried by the White Abbot for Protestant heresy, but at the last moment he is pardoned by the Cardinal, to whom he is too valuable as a musician. Then, in chapel, the composer considers his religious duty while monks seem to be chanting the office, though in fact their words relate the protagonist's past and future. The orchestra then falls silent, to be replaced by a stage band of viols and lute for the first council scene: the King wants a break with Rome; the Cardinal temporizes and the Jester exposes the self-seeking motives of both parties. The Jester remains on stage, reveals himself as Death, and calls up Taverner in order to lead him through a treacherous, nightmare catechism, at the end of which the composer disavows his music and takes up the sword on behalf of a manifestly false Jesus. Death shrieks a salutation.

Act II also opens with a courtroom scene, but at frenetic speed, and this time with the White Abbot at the mercy of Taverner. The Abbot is sentenced to the stake, and now when the Cardinal appears he has no face. Instead Death is seen controlling a huge wheel of fortune. The second council scene, accompanied like the first by Renaissance instruments, portrays the progress of the Reformation, and the second chapel scene shows a moment in it: the White Abbot and monks are saying Mass when Taverner and soldiers enter to dispossess them. Finally, in a big choral tableau, the townspeople of Boston are gathered to watch the burning of the White Abbot, though the man who is really destroyed is Taverner.

RECORDING   *Second Taverner Fantasia* (essentially a *Taverner* symphony) and *Points and Dances* from the throne-room scenes, Argo, 1973
EDITIONS   v.s./f.s./lib., Boosey & Hawkes, 1972

Blind Man's Buff

Masque (20m)
Libretto by the composer, after Georg Büchner's play *Leonce und Lena* (1836) and nonsense rhymes
Composed 1972
PREMIERE   29 May 1972, Round House, London

The work is a game of shadow dances and echo arias on themes of identity, scored for two singers (soprano or treble and mezzo-soprano), two mutes (mime and dancer), a stage septet of wind and plucked strings, and a small string orchestra. A reduced version (also 1972) exists for soprano, mime and seven instrumentalists.

EDITION   f.s., Chester Music, 1972

Miss Donnithorne's Maggot

Music-theatre piece (36m)
Libretto by Randolph Stow
Composed 1974
PREMIERE   9 March 1974, Adelaide

This is a female counterpart to *Eight Songs*: a mad scene for a jilted spinster (the historical Australian prototype for Dickens's Miss Havisham), sung by a mezzo-soprano with the same instrumental sextet.

RECORDING   Thomas, Fires of London, Peter Maxwell Davies, Unicorn-Kanchana, 1984
EDITION   f.s., Boosey & Hawkes, 1977

The Martyrdom of St Magnus

Chamber opera in nine scenes (1h 15m)
Libretto by the composer, after the novel *Magnus* by George Mackay Brown (1973)
Composed 1976
PREMIERES   18 June 1977, St Magnus's Cathedral, Orkney; US: 29 July 1978, Aspen Music Festival, Colorado
CAST   Earl Magnus *t*, Norse Herald/The Keeper of the Loom *bar*, Welsh Herald/The Tempter *bar*, Earl Hakon *b*, Blind Mary *ms*; each singer takes several roles: only the main ones are indicated
INSTRUMENTATION   fl/picc/alto fl, cl/b cl, hn, 2 tpt, kbds, perc, gtr, va, vc, db

Magnus was Earl of Orkney in the 12th century, and by repute a Viking unusual for his pacifism. The opera is staged hagiography, devised to be performed in a quite simple, stylized setting, whether in a church or a small theatre (the composer's own preference is for performance in the round). Magnus is to some extent a reincarnation of Taverner, though his path is made easier, and correspondingly there is a musical softening, attributable to the folk-modal flavour that entered Davies's music in the 1970s: only the penultimate scene has the savagery of his immediately pre-Orcadian scores, including *Taverner*.

The instrumentation shows Davies's resourcefulness in using the Fires sextet, to which he adds brass for tones of eruption and nobility, and a guitar to bring out the ethnic roots of Blind Mary's songs.

Blind Mary, the opera's chorus figure, introduces the first of the nine scenes, in which Magnus is present at a sea battle between the Norsemen and the Welsh. He prefers to fight with the words of Psalm 23 rather than with arms, and his side is victorious. In Scene 2 the Keeper of the Loom, the guardian of Magnus's soul, introduces the Tempter, who tries to seduce Magnus with promises of fame, marriage, sovereignty, monastic retirement and the sword. But he refuses them all. Blind Mary then returns to lament the condition of Orkney, torn by civil war between Magnus and Hakon. Heralds of the rival earls meet the bishop to arrange a peace conference on the island of Egilsay (Scene 4); Magnus sings an aria of resolution on his way to the island (Scene 5). The musical style then becomes much fiercer as Hakon orders Magnus's execution and in Scene 7 both action and music zoom forward to the present, the cast becoming reporters who comment on the developing tension. Scene 8 is fully in the present, or the recent past: Hakon is a hysterical Military Officer, and Magnus a nameless Prisoner who quietly goes to meet his fate. The last scene is Blind Mary's: she prays to Magnus for the return of her sight, and gains it, while the rest of the cast as monks add Magnus's name to the litany of northern saints.

EDITIONS   f.s. (with pf reduction)/lib., Boosey & Hawkes, 1977

Le jongleur de Notre-Dame

Masque (55m)
Libretto by the composer, after the traditional tale
Composed 1978
PREMIERE   18 June 1978, Stromness, Orkney

Written, like *Eight Songs* and *Miss Donnithorne*, for Davies's own ensemble, this work differs from them in being an unpretentious comedy. There is an *intrada* for children's wind band, intended to bring the performers into the hall in procession. The Jongleur (mime) is accepted into a monastery by the Abbot (baritone) and given various tasks, which he fails to fulfil: the flautist, clarinettist and percussionist offer musical rebukes. But then he starts to juggle, and this gift is accepted by the Virgin Mary (violinist).

EDITION   f.s., Chester Music, 1978

The Lighthouse

Chamber opera in one act with prologue (1h 15m)
Libretto by the composer
Composed 1979
PREMIERES   2 September 1980, Moray House Gymnasium, Edinburgh; US: 1 November 1983, Boston Shakespeare Company, Boston
CAST   Officer 1/Sandy *t*, Officer 2/Blazes *bar*, Officer 3/Arthur *b*

INSTRUMENTATION fl/picc/alto fl, A cl/b cl, hn, tpt, trbn, keyboards, perc, gtr/banjo, vn, va, vc, db; some str also play perc

The work is scored for very similar forces to those used in *St Magnus*, but the pageantry of that work is replaced by atmospheric grimness, by evocations of the cold Northern sea at night, and by parodies that heighten the passions and nightmares of the characters.

The prologue is set at a court of inquiry into the disappearance of three lighthouse keepers from their station. Questions are posed by solo horn, which may sound from the audience, and three officers give answer. Gradually they move from straight testimony into fantastical imaginings of evil during a flashback to the lighthouse; but then we snap back to the courtroom.

In the main act the three singers become the vanished keepers. They have been together for months, long enough to know each other well, and to know how to taunt each other: their relationship is highly unstable. To reduce the tension they sing songs. Blazes begins with a rough ballad of street violence, accompanied by violin and banjo; Sandy, with cello and upright piano, sings of making love; and Arthur, with brass and clarinet, belts out a hymn. But the songs serve only to resurrect in their minds ghosts from the past, and as fog descends each of them becomes convinced that he is being claimed by the Beast. They prepare to meet its dazzling eyes, which become the lights of the relief vessel, and the three men reappear as officers, finding at the lighthouse only an infestation of rats. They leave, and at the end the last hours of the three keepers begin to play over again.

EDITIONS f.s./v.s./lib., Chester Music, 1982

Resurrection

Opera in one act with a prologue (1h 20m)
Libretto by the composer
Composed 1986
PREMIERE 18 September 1988, Staatsoper, Darmstadt
CAST Mam *ct*, Headmaster *t*, Dad *bar*, Younger Brother *bar*, Doctor *b*, Vicar *t*, Elder Sister *ms*, Cat *pop vocalist*; each singer takes several roles: only the main ones are indicated
SMALL ORCHESTRA plus pop group, and amplified *satb* quartet

Like *The Lighthouse*, *Resurrection* proceeds continuously through a prologue and one act. In the prologue the hero, a life-size dummy with his back to the audience, is berated by the seven principal singers (other than the Cat), representing the social pressures of family and professionals acting on a young man. Their tirades are intercut both with pop songs and with television commercials, and at the end of all this the hero explodes. The subsequent act, somewhat disguised as a post-mortem, is an examination of his political, religious and sexual irregularities, which are duly eradicated so that he may be resurrected as Antichrist.

EDITION f.s., Chester Music, 1987

Music-theatre works: *Eight Songs for a Mad King*, 1969; *Vesalii icones*, 1969; *Miss Donnithorne's Maggot*, 1974; *Le jongleur de Notre Dame*, 1978; *The No. 11 Bus*, 1984
Children's operas: *The Two Fiddlers*, 1978; *Cinderella*, 1980
Children's music-theatre pieces: *The Rainbow*, 1981; *Jupiter Landing*, 1990; *The Great Bank Robbery*, 1990; *Dinosaur at Large*, 1990; *Dangerous Errand*, 1990; *Computer Chaos*, 1991

BIBLIOGRAPHY Paul Griffiths, *Peter Maxwell Davies*, Robson, 1981; Stephen Pruslin (ed.), *Peter Maxwell Davies*, Boosey & Hawkes, 1979

P.A.G.

ANTHONY DAVIS
b 20 February 1951, Paterson, New Jersey, US

Davis is an American jazz pianist and composer whose work fuses black and white traditions from an Afro-American starting point. He studied at Yale University where he co-founded a free-jazz group, Advent, in 1973 and then worked with New Delta Ahkri and various other groups in New York. Davis's style has been described as an amalgam of Ellington, Bartók and Balinese gamelan. The ostinato-type multiple repetitions of the last, in particular, are a prominent feature of his first opera, *X: The Life and Times of Malcolm X*. The composer's brother suggested the subject of the controversial black leader; the libretto was written by their cousin, the poet Thulani Davis, and it enabled the composer to explore a range of racial and political issues. Davis developed *X* in workshops at the American Music Theater Festivals in Philadelphia and Brooklyn before the New York City Opera premiered it in 1986, where it was well received.

With *Under the Double Moon* (1989), based on a novel and libretto by Deborah Anderson, Davis produced a more intimate work – a combination of science fiction and puppet theatre. The structure of the opera is based on Davis's long series of pieces called *Wayang*, after the repetitive Indonesian gamelan music used for shadow-puppet plays.

BIBLIOGRAPHY D. Wright, *Anthony Davis* (catalogue), Schirmer, 1990

P.D.

JOHN DAVY
b 23 December 1763, Upton Hellions, Devon, England; *d* 22 February 1824, London

An illegitimate child, Davy was brought up by his uncle, a blacksmith. The local rector noted his natural musical gift, and he was sent for lessons to William Jackson of Exeter. The violin became his strongest instrument, and it was as a violinist that he joined the Covent Garden orchestra. From 1796 he was active as a theatrical composer, chiefly of incidental music and pantomimes.

His operas survive only in vocal scores, though full scores existed in the 19th century. All have spoken dialogue. The most successful was *What a Blunder!* (Little Theatre, 1800) to a libretto with a Spanish setting by Joseph Holman, who played Count Alphonso d'Esparza. The only other consequential work is *Rob Roy Macgregor, or Auld Lang Syne* (Covent Garden, 1818), to a libretto by Isaac Pocock after Scott. Its merit is a good narrative line and scenic and musical local colour. Davy was a better instrumental than vocal composer; his best works are his overtures and his pieces for harp. The finest moment in *Rob Roy* is a chorus actually contributed by Sir Henry Bishop, and Davy's most famous song, 'The Bay of Biscay, O!' ('Loud roared the dreadful thunder . . .'), from a short afterpiece, was simply a harmonization of a genuine shanty, with new words by Andrew Perry. Davy died destitute.

BIBLIOGRAPHY   Roger Fiske, *English Theatre Music in the Eighteenth Century*, OUP, 1973; 2nd edn, 1986

R.Lu.

CLAUDE DEBUSSY

Achille-Claude Debussy; *b* 22 August 1862, St Germain-en-Laye, nr Paris; *d* 25 March 1918, Paris

The son of a suburban Parisian shopkeeper who was imprisoned for his part in the Commune of 1871, Debussy studied piano (with Verlaine's mother-in-law, Mme Mauté, and later at the Conservatoire) and turned seriously to composition only when hopes of a virtuoso career receded in the late 1870s. Though to this day best known for his piano and orchestral music, and even though he completed only one opera, he was almost continuously preoccupied with music for the theatre in some form from the early 1880s until shortly before he died. Very few of these projects came to fruition, but they show that Debussy was fascinated by musical theatre and, under favourable conditions, a brilliant exponent of it. His single opera and the one purpose-made ballet of which he composed and orchestrated every note, *Jeux* (1912–13), are both masterpieces. Many other projects, on the other hand, were never even sketched, partly because he perhaps had no real intention of composing them, partly because of his intense self-criticism and partly because other work intervened or circumstances changed. For French composers, the theatre has always been a much stronger presence than for their German or British colleagues, and to some extent Debussy's involvement was an automatic reaction to context. But it was also a genuine creative preoccupation, connected with an early enthusiasm for Wagner, and then with his interest in Symbolist literature and his friendship with some of its best-known exponents (including Mallarmé). It was this literary connection which gave rise to the two abortive Edgar Allan Poe projects of the years following *Pelléas et Mélisande*.

Debussy's earliest proper theatre score is *Rodrigue et Chimène*, which was substantially composed in short score between 1888 and 1892, when it gave way to the first version of the orchestral *Nocturnes*, the *Prélude à l'après-midi d'un faune*, and soon *Pelléas et Mélisande*. Before this, Debussy's most successful works had been songs, including the compact and atmospheric Verlaine settings of the *Ariettes oubliées* (1885–8), and the more elaborate *Cinq poèmes de Baudelaire* (1887–9), with their Wagnerian turn of phrase. *Rodrigue et Chimène* is the sort of first opera one might expect of the composer of the Baudelaire songs. Its conventionally heroic subject suggests many other post-Wagner French operas, and while its harmonic language is that of mature early Debussy, its gesture often lacks the finesse and restraint of the composer at his subtlest. It was in about 1890 that Debussy described to his former composition teacher Ernest Guiraud the sort of operatic text he would like to set: 'The ideal would be two associated dreams. No place, no time. No big scene. No compulsion on the musician, who must complete and give body to the work of the poet. Music in opera is far too predominant. Too much singing and the musical settings are too cumbersome. The blossoming of the voice into true singing should occur only when required . . . My idea is of a short libretto with mobile scenes. No discussion or arguments between the characters whom I see at the mercy of life or destiny.' This is remarkably prescient of Maeterlinck's *Pelléas* (as yet neither published nor performed), and a direct rebuttal of the *Rodrigue* kind of opera.

The composition, revision and orchestration of *Pelléas* preoccupied Debussy from 1893 until its first performance in April 1902, and during this period he started no other significant new works except the

Debussy (with stick) at Eragny (1902) with (left to right) Pierre Lalo, Paul Dukas, Debussy's first wife, Lily, and Paul Poujaud

Chansons de Bilitis (1897–8) and *Pour le piano* (1894–1901). But once *Pelléas* reached the stage, he entered a completely new phase of mainly instrumental composition, in which he explored the formal and imaginative possibilities of innovations that had first been prompted, in song or opera, by words. This is the time of the great piano collections, the *Estampes* (1903), *Images* (1905, 1907) and *Préludes* (1910, 1912–13), *L'isle joyeuse* (1904), and the orchestral masterpieces *La mer* (1903–5) and *Images* (1905–12). Yet for much of the same period, Debussy tinkered with a one-act opera on Poe's *The Devil in the Belfry*, somewhat later turning to *The Fall of the House of Usher*, sketches for which occupied him, on and off, for the last decade of his life. It is hard to imagine what Debussy could have made of Poe's absurd tale about the devil who makes the midday chimes strike thirteen and thereby brings chaos to the well-ordered life of the Dutch village of Vondervotteimittis. But *Usher*, as a subject, is a direct descendant of Debussy's early Symbolist obsessions. (Poe was a hero of the French Symbolist movement, and was translated by Baudelaire.) It might have made a superbly mysterious successor to *Pelléas*, if Debussy had solved its problems before the rectal cancer that tormented him from 1909 onwards finally made sustained creative concentration impossible.

Rodrigue et Chimène

Opera in three acts
Libretto by Catulle Mendès, based on Giullén de Castro y Beris's *Las mocedades del Cid* (1618) and Corneille's tragedy *Le Cid* (1637)
Composed (fragmentary short score only) 1888–92/?1893

Mendès (a sometime close friend of Wagner) centred his libretto on the love of Don Rodrigue de Bivar (El Cid) for the daughter of a count whom he is unfortunately obliged to kill in revenge for an insult to his father. She in turn swears vengeance against her lover, but the situation is saved by the King's decree that Rodrigue must take the field as his commander against the Moors.

Debussy's score, through-composed in the Wagnerian manner, is incomplete and, like most Debussy drafts, often inconclusive about accidentals, speeds and dynamics. The libretto itself survives only as part of this defective short score. Nevertheless, the work was apparently in essence fully composed, and Debussy poured into it much first-rate invention, even if he was never wholly at ease with the conventionally heroic aspects of the subject. Some of it must have pleased him, since he played it through to Paul Dukas in the summer of 1893. The surviving music was given three concert performances with piano, in a realization by Richard Langham Smith, in London and Manchester in February 1988.

MANUSCRIPT Pierpont Morgan Library, New York

Pelléas et Mélisande

Drame lyrique in five acts (12 tableaux) (3h 15m)

Libretto by the composer; abridgement of the play by Maurice Maeterlinck
Composed ?September 1893–17 August 1895; rev. January 1900 (or earlier)–1902 (orch. ?November 1901–January 1902; interludes composed March–April 1902)
PREMIERES 30 April 1902, Opéra-Comique, Paris; US: 19 February 1908, Manhattan Opera Company, New York; UK: 21 May 1909, Covent Garden, London
CAST Mélisande *s*, Pelléas *t*, Golaud *bar*, Arkel *b*, Geneviève *ms*, Yniold *s*, Doctor *b*, Shepherd *bar*, 3 poor men *silent*, servants *silent*; (offstage) *atb* chorus of sailors
ORCHESTRATION 3 fl/picc, 2 ob, ca, 2 cl, 3 bsn, 4 hn, 3 tpt, 3 trbn, tuba, timp, perc (cym, triangle), 2 hp, str

Debussy attended the first performance of Maeterlinck's play at the Théâtre des Bouffes-Parisiens on 17 May 1893. But he had probably already read it (it had been published a year before) and considered setting it to music, having even before that (1891) applied unsuccessfully to Maeterlinck for permission to set his earlier play *La Princesse Maleine*. Over *Pelléas*, the playwright was more accommodating. Debussy set to work initially on the big final scene of Act IV, setting the text as it stood, without cuts. Then, finding his music too Wagnerian, he at once revised the scene, before returning to the start of the drama and composing it through roughly in sequence, omitting four of Maeterlinck's scenes and making extensive cuts to the remainder. At this stage he was seeking a new way of rendering into music Maeterlinck's curious mixture of high-sounding realism and interior symbolism, and finally came up, as he wrote to Ernest Chausson on 2 October 1893, 'with a technique which seems to me quite extraordinary, that is to say, Silence (don't laugh!) as a means of expression!'

Early proposals for performance came to nothing, and even though the new director of the Opéra-Comique, Albert Carré, accepted the work in principle in the spring of 1898, it was another three years before it was firmly scheduled for production. During this time Debussy made substantial revisions, especially to Act IV, and after the work's acceptance he again revised that act, as well as at last carrying out the orchestration. Also, during the rehearsal period, he composed the somewhat Wagnerian orchestral interludes to cover the numerous scene changes (performance is still possible, though unusual, without them). At this stage a row blew up with Maeterlinck over the casting of Mélisande, for whom the Scottish soprano Mary Garden was announced in December 1901. Maeterlinck's determination that his mistress Georgette Leblanc should have the part drove him to the extremes of a formal complaint to the Société des Auteurs, an open letter to *Le Figaro* expressing the hope that the opera would fail, and the printing of a satirical 'synopsis', which was distributed to the audience at the public dress rehearsal on 28 April 1902, which may well have fuelled the near riot at that performance.

Despite these troubles and the work's unusual character, the official premiere passed off well, and *Pelléas* quickly entered the repertoire of the Opéra-Comique. Debussy himself supervised the rehearsals, and even had a hand in the beautiful pre-Raphaelite designs of Lucien Jusseaume and Eugène Ronsin. The first cast was generally strong, and the music sympathetically conducted by André Messager. But casting nevertheless has remained problematic; Pelléas has been sung variously by tenors and baritones (the first Pelléas, Jean Périer, was a 'baryton Martin', a voice like Debussy's own in which the lighter head tone is prominent). But later there was even talk of playing Pelléas as a *travesti* role for soprano. The original Yniold was a boy treble named Blondin, but his performance prompted such hilarity at the public dress rehearsal that a number of cuts were made in his part for the official premiere. (His scene with the sheep in Act IV, however, had probably already been omitted, and was first performed in public only in autumn 1902, when the part was sung by a woman, Suzanne Dumesnil.)

SYNOPSIS

Arkel is King of Allemonde, Geneviève his daughter, and Golaud and Pelléas her sons by different marriages. Yniold is Golaud's son by his first wife, who is now dead.

Act I Scene 1: Golaud, lost in the forest while out hunting, comes upon the frail Mélisande, who is lost too and crying. She recoils from him, evades his questions, and refuses to let him retrieve her crown, which he sees glistening in the pool. Eventually she tells him her name, and he persuades her to go with him. Scene 2: Golaud has written to Pelléas about Mélisande, whom he married six months ago. Golaud fears Arkel (who wished a political remarriage for him). But Arkel, when Geneviève reads him the letter, accepts the will of fate. Pelléas asks to visit a dying friend, but Arkel insists he await Golaud's return. Scene 3: Mélisande is walking in the grounds with Geneviève. They remark on the darkness of the surrounding forests. Pelléas joins them, and they turn their attention to the sea (where the ship that brought Mélisande can be seen and heard departing). Pelléas announces that he is going away the next day.

Act II Scene 1: Pelléas and Mélisande are by a fountain in the park. Mélisande leans over and tries to touch the water, but only her long hair can reach it. Playing with the ring Golaud gave her, she drops it into the water as a harp softly sounds the distant chime of noon. Scene 2: Golaud has been thrown by his horse on the stroke of noon. Nursing him that night, Mélisande complains of being unhappy in the castle, and Golaud tries to find out why. He notices that her ring is missing, and furiously orders her to find it, taking Pelléas with her. Scene 3: Pelléas and Mélisande pretend to look for the ring in a sea cave, but they are scared when they find three starving beggars asleep on the ground.

Act III Scene 1: Mélisande is combing her hair at a tower window. Pelléas appears and persuades her to lean out so far that her hair tumbles down the wall. He makes passionate simulated love to it, winding her hair round himself and then tying it to the branches of a willow. As he does so Mélisande's white doves fly out of the tower. Golaud appears and chides them for their 'childishness'. Scene 2: Golaud takes Pelléas into the vaults. But the air is stifling, and they climb back out – Scene 3 – emerging into the fresh midday air. Golaud lectures Pelléas about his behaviour with Mélisande, who is pregnant. Scene 4: Below Mélisande's window Golaud questions Yniold roughly about her and Pelléas. To each question Yniold replies with a child's elusiveness. A lamp is lit in Mélisande's room and Golaud lifts Yniold to spy on her. Pelléas is with her, but they are merely gazing silently at the lamp.

Act IV Scene 1: Pelléas and Mélisande agree to meet by the fountain. He is going away. His father (who never appears in the opera) has been ill but is now recovering and has ordered him to travel. Scene 2: Arkel expects the recovery of Pelléas's father to revitalize the castle, he tells Mélisande. But Golaud appears and picks a quarrel with her, accusing her of deception. He takes her by the hair and drags her from side to side, despite Arkel's protests. Scene 3: At the fountain, Yniold is looking for his ball. A shepherd passes with his flock, Yniold asks him why the sheep have stopped bleating. 'Because this isn't the way to the stable.' Scene 4: Pelléas and Mélisande meet for the last time. Passionately they declare their love. But in the distance the castle gates clang shut, and Mélisande realizes that Golaud has followed her in the darkness and is watching them from behind a tree. As they kiss with utter abandon, Golaud runs out and kills Pelléas with his sword.

Act V Mélisande, having given birth to a daughter, lies dying, attended by the doctor and Arkel. Golaud is stricken with remorse, but asks her in desperation if her and Pelléas's love was guilty. It was not, she says; but Golaud accuses her of lying and remains uncertain to the end. The serving women file silently in and, at the moment of Mélisande's death, fall to their knees.

The most celebrated feature of *Pelléas* is its unique vocal declamation, which carries the text on a continuous, fluid cantilena, somewhere between chant and recitative, a note to a syllable. There are no arias or set pieces. Debussy consciously avoided both the broad formal and gestural clichés of French and Italian Romantic opera, and the heavy arioso style of Wagner, though he was certainly influenced by the 'endless melody' of *Tristan*. The refinement and subtlety of the word-setting come partly from the French language, with its discreet and flexible accentuation, and are a natural extension of Debussy's Verlaine and Baudelaire songs. But they are also a response to the dreamlike world of Maeterlinck's play, a world of doomed children at the mercy of passions they only dimly apprehend. The play's 'tableau' design, so different from the purposeful symphonic structures of Wagner, must also have appealed to Debussy. His own style was moving towards a kind of suspended-animation harmony in which gentle discords are relished for their sensual beauty rather than their grammar (just as in Proust individual words and phrases take on an almost magical significance while the sentence structure fades into the background). The fact that

Lucien Jusseaume's design for the last act of Pelléas et Mélisande *(Paris, 1902)*

many of Debussy's favourite chords are Wagnerian in type merely emphasizes the restraint with which he uses them.

In fact *Pelléas* deploys an incredibly small number of harmonic and melodic ideas for such a long work. Leitmotifs are used sparingly. There are motifs for the main characters (some of them distinctly Wagnerian in cut) and for aspects of the drama, like the spirit of remote antiquity conveyed by the solemn modal chords of the prelude; and there are one-off musical ideas for Maeterlinck's symbols, like the crown in Act I or the white doves in Act III. Harmony is used to fix or intensify atmosphere, almost like a kind of musical scenery or lighting. So the menacing scene in the vaults is entirely in whole tones, while the sparkling sunlight and water of the next scene are conveyed throughout in pentatonic harmony which looks forward to piano pieces like *Reflets dans l'eau* or *Cloches à travers les feuilles*. The 'static' character of this kind of writing is tempered by some of the most exquisitely varied orchestration in any opera. The sound is soft and restrained, but the texture mobile and vividly graphic, and the music rises to dramatic climaxes that are all the more effective for their rarity.

Pelléas is a key work for the 20th century. Musically, it established an approach to form, harmony and texture which profoundly influenced composers as various as Stravinsky, Messiaen (who was given the score at the age of nine), and Puccini,

who was fascinated by its 'extraordinary harmonic qualities and . . . transparent instrumental texture'. Operatically, it was a shot across the bows of stage realism, as represented by works such as Gustave Charpentier's *Louise* or Massenet's *Werther*. The play's strangeness, admittedly, is a matter more of style than of content, and hidden meanings are less important than the evasive treatment of the commonplace: it is really a bourgeois tragedy slowed down, with a few poetic *non sequiturs* and a strong atmosphere. But these are qualities that lend themselves to musical treatment. It is significant that Maeterlinck's play also attracted avant-garde composers outside France and Belgium: Schoenberg's tone poem was written in 1902–3, and the link with Expressionism comes out in his *Erwartung* (1909). But where Maeterlinck's play has dated, the music it inspired has not, which is only fitting, as Symbolism in France began as an imitation of music, and specifically that of Wagner.

RECORDINGS 1. Joachim, Jansen, Etcheverry, Cabanel, Paris Conservatoire O, Désormière, Pathé-Marconi, 1942: classic wartime recording (now on CD) with the cast that later performed the work internationally; 2. Spoorenberg, Maurane, London, Hoekman, Suisse Romande O, Ansermet, Decca, 1964: the later and more polished of Ansermet's two recordings; 3. Söderström, Shirley, McIntyre, Ward, Covent Garden O, Boulez, CBS, 1970: immaculate and beautifully recorded, with perhaps the most intelligent recorded cast, and a boy Yniold

EDITIONS v.s., Fromont, 1902, lacks extended interludes; v.s., Durand, 1907, with interludes; study s., Durand, 1902, reduced from f.s., Fromont, 1904

La chute de la maison Usher

The Fall of the House of Usher
Drame lyrique in one act
Libretto by the composer, after the tale by Edgar Allan Poe (1839), trans. Charles Baudelaire
Composed (fragments only) 1908–17

Debussy's next definite operatic project after *Pelléas* was a comic opera on Poe's *The Devil in the Belfry*, but this got no further than a scenario and a few sketches. Surviving material for *The Fall of the House of Usher* is more extensive, but it never reached anything like a definitive state, perhaps because Debussy, though haunted by the tale's atmosphere of gloom and terror, was unable to find a satisfactory music-theatrical form for it. He constantly interrupted it to compose other works such as the *Images* for orchestra, incidental music to d'Annunzio's *Le martyre de Saint-Sébastien*, and the ballet *Jeux*. The sketches suggest a continued exploration of harmonic and textural refinements, though as always with Debussy's drafts some of their ambiguity may come from vagueness of notation.

At least two musicians have made performing editions full enough to support some kind of stage production. Carolyn Abbate's version was staged at Yale University in 1977; a version by Juan Allende-Blin was broadcast by the Hessischer Rundfunk, Frankfurt, also in 1977, and staged in Berlin in October 1979. Moreover the Allende-Blin version has been published (v.s., Editions Jobert, 1979) and commercially recorded (EMI, 1984). A glance at the sketches published in Edward Lockspeiser's *Debussy et Edgar Poe* (Editions du Rocher, 1962) will give some idea of the fragmentary and ambiguous character of the material on which these scholars had to base their all too concrete realizations.

BIBLIOGRAPHY David A. Grayson, *The Genesis of Debussy's 'Pelléas et Mélisande'*, UMI Research Press, 1986; Robin Holloway, *Debussy and Wagner*, Eulenburg, 1979; Nicholas John (ed.), *Pelléas et Mélisande*, John Calder (ENO Opera Guide), 1982; François Lesure and Roger Nichols (eds; trans. Nichols), *Debussy Letters*, Faber, 1987; Robert Orledge, *Debussy and the Theatre*, CUP, 1982; Richard Langham Smith (ed. and trans.), *Debussy on Music*, Secker and Warburg, 1977

S.W.

LÉO DELIBES

Clément Philibert Léo Delibes; *b* 21 February 1836, St Germain du Val, France; *d* 16 January 1891, Paris

Delibes came to Paris from the provinces at the age of 12 after the death of his father. Musical on his mother's side, he studied at the Conservatoire, though his evident melodic gift gained him no outstanding distinctions there. His teachers included the organist–composer Benoist and the stage composer Adam. His own career was divided between church, as chorister and organist, and stage, as ballet and opera composer. Among about 30 stage works his four most important scores are *Le roi l'a dit*, *Lakmé* and the ballets *Coppélia* (1870) and *Sylvia* (1876).

If these four works survive, the remainder testifies more to his industry than to his genius as a composer. Adam's interest in his pupil, a boy chorister at La Madeleine and at the Opéra (he sang in the cathedral scene at the premiere of Meyerbeer's *Le prophète* in 1849), saw Delibes, at the age of 17, appointed organist at Saint-Pierre de Chaillot and accompanist at the Théâtre-Lyrique, a modest establishment directed by Hervé, who supplied all its music. These posts brought Delibes into contact with some of the popular composers of the day, notably Victor Massé, who, late with his work on *La Reine-Topaze*, employed the youth as copyist. With the amused blessing of Adam, Delibes also took over from Hervé the setting of *Deux sous de charbon*, completing it within a few days. Delibes was 19 when this first work was given at the Folies-Nouvelles in 1856. Fourteen others followed in as many years.

However, between *Le roi l'a dit* (1873) and *Sylvia* (1876), the only notable composition was the song 'Les filles de Cadix'. His music for the theatre was engendered by the need to earn a living and support his widowed mother. His musical ambitions were restricted by these considerations, for after a good start his academic career at the Conservatoire had been disappointing. It seems that he never even thought of competing for the Prix de Rome. Yet the initial success of *Le roi l'a dit* spread his fame abroad and official honours came his way. Finally, in 1881, he succeeded Reber as a professor at the Conservatoire at the instance of the director, Ambroise Thomas, to whom Delibes disclaimed any knowledge of fugue and counterpoint. Urged to practise those skills, he did, and became an unusually conscientious and dedicated teacher. Essentially ebullient yet shy and unsure, Delibes had a need to be loved that was gratified. The successes of *Jean de Nivelle* (1880) and *Lakmé* (1883) were conclusive; the posthumous performance (1893) of *Kassya* (completed by Massenet) proved an anti-climax.

Le roi l'a dit

The King Says So
Comic opera in three acts (2h)
Libretto by Edmond Gondinet
Composed 1873
PREMIERES 24 May 1873, Opéra-Comique, Paris; UK: 1 December 1894, Prince of Wales's Theatre, London; US: 29 April 1967, University of Iowa

Delibes's very successful comic opera is a comedy of errors set at the court of Louis XIV. The obscure Marquis de Montecontour has four daughters but no son. Finding himself at court, he is befuddled into telling the monarch that he has one, and then commanded to present him. Montecontour adopts, as son, Benoît, a childhood friend of his housemaid,

Scenes from Lakmé *(L'Illustration, April 1883)*

Javotte. Benoît plays his role too well, taking sides with his supposed sisters in opposing their father's ideas of convenient marriages, setting fire to the convent to which they are sent, ruining the marquis, before pretending to be killed in a duel. The king's condolences include a dukedom for Montecontour, who counters Benoît's return to life with the observation that he is well and truly dead, as 'The king says so!', and sends him off happily with Javotte and a dowry.

Le roi l'a dit follows the conventions of 18th-century opéra comique in its simple harmonies and *parlando*-style vocal writing. The musical style, in keeping with the opera's setting, seems deliberately backward-looking, with its traditional rondos and

ensembles. It was, nevertheless, well received and was performed frequently until the First World War.

RECORDING Pleydell/Kelly, Barstow/Rhys Thomas, Gurner/Te Kanawa, Bateman/Williams, Lufton/Neal, London Opera Centre O, Robertson, RRE, 1966 (2 recordings, with different casts)
EDITIONS f.s., Heugel, 1890; v.ss., Escudier, 1873; Heugel, 1885

Lakmé
Opera in three acts (2h 15m)
Libretto by Edmond Gondinet and Philippe Gille, after Pierre Loti's novel *Le mariage de Loti* (1882)
Composed 1883
PREMIERES 14 April 1883, Opéra-Comique, Paris;

US: 4 October 1883, Grand Opera House, Chicago;
UK: 6 June 1885, Gaiety Theatre, London
CAST   Lakmé s, Mallika ms or a, Mistress Bentson ms, Ellen
s, Rose ms, Gerald t, Nilakantha b, Frederic bar, Hadji t,
Gypsy t, Chinese merchant t, pickpocket bar; satb chorus of
Indians, Brahmins, Chinese merchants; ballet
LARGE ORCHESTRA   onstage band

In *Lakmé*, Delibes, already successful as a composer
of memorably tuneful ballets, fulfilled his ambition
to produce a successful serious opera. Its title role
attracted the finest sopranos of the time, such as
Patti, and Tetrazzini, and its survival is due largely to
the vehicle it provides for the coloratura soprano
voice.

SYNOPSIS
The plot centres around the fanatical hatred of the
Brahmin priests in 19th-century India for the English
invaders, who forbid them to practise their religion.
    Act I   Gerald and Frederic, two English officers,
find themselves in a sacred grove. Catching sight of
Lakmé, daughter of the Brahmin priest Nilakantha,
Gerald falls in love with her. He is seen by
Nilakantha, who swears vengeance on the intruder
who has desecrated holy ground.
    Act II   Gerald and Frederic meet in a crowded
marketplace, whence Gerald has been shadowed by
Nilakantha. He commands Lakmé to sing an old
Brahmin song ('The Bell Song') so that the intruder
will again be drawn to her and Nilakantha will be
able to identify him. At the sight of Gerald, Lakmé
faints, but she later manages to warn him of her
father's plans for vengeance. Nevertheless, during a
procession, Gerald is stabbed and slightly injured.
    Act III   Lakmé is nursing Gerald in a forest hut,
where Frederic finds him and calls him back to duty.
Lakmé, realizing that she will lose Gerald, takes
poison, and dies just as her father rushes in to find
her.

Delibes's desire to please caused him to conform
without question to procedures already well worn in
the field of opéra comique. *Lakmé* is composed of
separate numbers, devoid of musical links between
them, with a contrived symmetry of form in each and
a subordinate, purely accompanimental role for the
orchestra throughout. It has, on the other hand, a
melodic fluency that has proved irresistible to singers
and listeners alike, a transparency of texture and a
French elegance that places it poles apart from the
Wagnerian influences of the time to which Delibes's
more forward-looking compatriots were prone.

RECORDINGS   1. Sutherland, Berbié, Vanzo, Bacquier,
Ch and O of Monte Carlo Opera, Bonynge, Decca, 1968;
2. Mesplé, Millet, Burles, Soyer, Ch and O of Paris Opéra-
Comique, Lombard, EMI, 1971
EDITIONS   f.s./v.s., Heugel, 1883

Other operatic works: *Deux sous de charbon, ou Le suicide
de Bigorneau*, 1856; *Deux vieilles gardes, ou Double garde, ou
Un malade qui se porte bien*, 1856; *Six demoiselles à marier*,
1856; *Maître Griffard, ou Les deux procureurs*, 1857; *La fille
du golfe*, (1859); *L'omelette à la Follembuche*, 1859

(RECORDING Musidisc, ?1960s); *Monsieur de Bonne-Etoile*,
1860; *Les musiciens de l'orchestre* (coll. with Offenbach,
Erlanger, Hignard), 1861; *Les eaux d'Ems*, 1861; *Mon ami
Pierrot, ou L'enfance de Pierrot*, 1862; *Le jardinier et son
seigneur* (*Le lièvre*), 1863; *La tradition*, 1864; *Grande
nouvelle*, 1864; *Le serpent à plumes*, 1864 (RECORDING
Musidisc, ?1960s); *Le boeuf Apis*, 1865; *Malbrough s'en va-t-
en guerre* (Act IV of coll.), 1868; *L'écossais de Chatou, ou
Montagnards écossais*, 1869 (RECORDING Musidisc, ?1960s);
La cour du roi Pétaud, 1869; *Jean de Nivelle*, 1880; *Kassya*
(inc.; orch. by Massenet), 1893; 2 lost *opéras bouffes*
BIBLIOGRAPHY   André Coquis, *Léo Delibes, sa vie et son
oeuvre (1836–1891)*, Richard-Masse, 1957; Henri de Curzon,
Léo Delibes, sa vie et ses oeuvres (1836–1892), Legouix, 1926;
Joseph Loisel, *Lakmé de Léo Delibes, étude historique et
critique, analyse musicale*, Delaplane, 1924

F.A.

FREDERICK DELIUS

Frederick (originally Fritz) Theodor Albert Delius;
b 29 January 1862, Bradford, Yorkshire; *d* 10 June 1934, Grez-
sur-Loing, France

Although Delius's music is regarded by many
listeners as quintessentially English, his parents were
German and he lived most of his life outside
England. His works were appreciated first in
Germany and most of them were inspired by the
orange groves of Florida, the mountains and fjords of
Norway and his garden in France. His father settled
in Bradford from Germany to build up a wool
business; although a lover and patron of music, he
was implacably opposed to music as a career for his
son, who quickly demonstrated that he had no
aptitude for commerce.
    In 1884 Delius went to Florida to manage an
orange plantation at Solana Grove. The oranges
were left to manage themselves while Delius studied
music with the local organist and taught the violin.
The Negro melodies he heard there influenced
several of his works, particularly the choral–
orchestral *Appalachia* and the opera *Koanga*. By
1886 he had persuaded his father grudgingly to pay
for him to enter the Leipzig Conservatory, where he
heard concerts and operas conducted by Nikisch and
Mahler and formed friendships with the Norwegian
composers Sinding and Grieg as well as with Busoni.
In 1888 he settled in Paris. Between 1890 and 1902 he
composed five operas. This passion for the stage
undoubtedly derived from his admiration for
Wagner. He wrote to a friend in 1894: 'I want to
tread in Wagner's footsteps . . . For me dramatic art
is almost taking the place of religion.'
    From 1897, Delius lived at Grez-sur-Loing, near
Fontainebleau, with the German artist Jelka Rosen,
who became his wife in 1903. A concert of his music
was given in London in 1899, but it was in Elberfeld
after 1901, where the conductors Hans Haym and
Fritz Cassirer became his champions, that his music
came to the fore. Thomas Beecham and Henry Wood
championed his music and both conducted works by
him in London from 1907 onwards. Of his six operas,
Delius saw only three staged during his lifetime.

In the early 1920s Delius developed the first signs of progressive paralysis, the legacy of syphilis contracted in his Bohemian youth in Paris, or perhaps earlier in Florida. By the end of 1925 he was blind and helpless, but in 1928 a young British musician, Eric Fenby, offered his services as amanuensis and during the next few years laboriously took down from Delius's dictation the scores of half-a-dozen works.

Delius's chromatic harmonies are in the post-Wagnerian idiom of Chausson and Strauss, spiced with the Nordic flavour of Grieg. He was essentially the poet of regret for the vanished hour and hedonistic delight, epitomized in such orchestral and choral works as *Sea Drift*, *Song of the High Hills*, *In a Summer Garden*, *Brigg Fair*, and the *Songs of Sunset*. It is strange that so ruminative a composer should have been drawn to the operatic stage, but at least in *A Village Romeo and Juliet* he demonstrated that a bucolic *Tristan und Isolde* was feasible and stageworthy and in all six operas some of his most attractive and characteristic music is enshrined. Curiously, in 1903 Delius negotiated with Oscar Wilde's executors for the rights to make an opera from *Salome*.

Edvard Munch's portrait lithograph of Delius at an outdoor concert in Wiesbaden (1922)

Irmelin

Opera in three acts (2h 15m)
Libretto by the composer, based on the legend of Princess Irmelin and Hans Christian Andersen's *The Princess and the Swineherd*
Composed 1890–92
PREMIERE 4 May 1953, New Theatre, Oxford
CAST Irmelin *s*, Nils *t*, King *b*, Rolf *b-bar*, 2 *s*, *ms*, *t*, 2 *bar*, *b*; *satb* chorus of robbers, knights, guests, women, wood nymphs, etc.
MEDIUM ORCHESTRA

Irmelin was the first and longest of Delius's operatic scores. He had considered a variety of subjects before embarking on this medieval story based on a conflation of two tales. After failing to decide on a librettist, Delius wrote the text himself. The score aroused the interest of André Messager, conductor

at the Opéra-Comique in Paris, but did not reach the stage, although the French composer Florent Schmitt was commissioned by Delius to prepare a vocal score.

SYNOPSIS
Act I In her room in the castle, the Princess Irmelin rejects the three latest in a series of a hundred knightly suitors, old, young and middle-aged, whom her father the king has found for her. She awaits her 'dream lover'. The king threatens to impose a husband on her.

Act II Nils, a prince disguised as a swineherd, employed by an elderly outlaw named Rolf, bewails his failure to follow the silver stream that would have led him to his dream princess. Rolf agrees that he can go, but encourages the women in his entourage to try to seduce Nils. They fail. Nils finds the stream and determines to follow it to its source.

Act III Six months later, the disconsolate Irmelin's enforced betrothal to a middle-aged (warlike) knight is being celebrated. Nils arrives and he and Irmelin immediately recognize each other as their dream lovers. They declare their love and wander off together through the forest.

Irmelin shares the late 19th century's preoccupation with medievalism as reflected by the Pre-Raphaelites and, in music, by such works as Elgar's *The Black Knight*, Debussy's *Pelléas et Mélisande*, and Schoenberg's *Gurrelieder*. The tale of young innocents forsaking the world for love is characteristic Delius and, in spite of the stilted libretto, the music succeeds. It is a pastoral idyll, melodically fresh, well written for the voices (especially for Irmelin herself) and beautifully scored. The characterization of the three suitors is operatically effective.

RECORDING Hannan, Mitchinson, Rippon, Rayner Cook, BBC Singers and Concert O, Del Mar, BBC (recording of studio performance broadcast 18 December 1984), 1985
EDITIONS f.s., Boosey & Hawkes, 1992; v.s., Boosey & Hawkes, 1953

The Magic Fountain

Opera in three acts (1h 45m)
Libretto by the composer and Jutta Bell
Composed 1894–June 1895, minor rev. 1898
PREMIERE 20 November 1977, BBC broadcast (recorded July 1977)
CAST Solano *t*, Watawa *s*, Wapanacki *b*, Talum Hadjo *b*, Spanish sailor *b*; *satb* chorus of sailors, Indian warriors, Indian women, night mists and invisible spirits of the fountain
MEDIUM ORCHESTRA including sarrusophone

The Magic Fountain was the first of a trilogy planned by Delius on 'the Indians, the Gypsies and the Negroes and quadroons'. *The Magic Fountain* is the 'Indian' work, *Koanga* the Negro, and the Gypsies became the vagabonds of *A Village Romeo and Juliet*. Again, Florent Schmitt prepared the vocal score and during 1896 the opera was sent to Felix Mottl at Karlsruhe, Stavenhagen at Weimar and Alfred Hertz at Elberfeld, but all rejected it. A proposed Prague performance also fell through.

A German translation was made by Emma Klingenfeld.

SYNOPSIS

Act I It is the early 16th century. On board a becalmed ship in the tropics, Solano (based on Juan Ponce de Leon, who discovered Florida) tells of his quest for the fountain of eternal youth. A storm breaks the calm and wrecks the ship off the coast of Florida. Solano is found unconscious by the American Indian Princess Watawa, who takes him to the Indians' camp.

Act II At the camp he tells the chief, Wapanacki, of his quest. Wapanacki advises him to visit the seer, Talum Hadjo, who lives in the swamps. Watawa, who hates the white race, offers to lead him there, after the Indians have performed a war dance. When they reach Hadjo's hut in the Everglades she asks Hadjo if she should kill Solano. He tells her this is unnecessary because the waters of the magic fountain mean death.

Act III On the way to the fountain, Watawa softens towards Solano and they kiss. She confesses her plot to kill him, but 'love, my treason, saves thy life'. As they fall asleep in each other's arms, the spirits of the fountain perform a ballet. At the fountain Watawa implores Solano not to drink. He scorns the legend, so she drinks and falls dead. Solano follows her example.

The Magic Fountain represents little advance on Irmelin where stagecraft is concerned and it is scarcely surprising that it has not yet been staged. But the music is entrancing, although not as continuously beautiful as that of Irmelin. The score borrows from the earlier orchestral suite Florida (1886–7, rev. 1889), and the first two bars of the motif for Watawa recur in Delius's Whitman setting Sea Drift (1903–4) at the words 'O past, O happy life'. Wagner's influence may be traced in the complex system of leitmotifs.

RECORDING Pring, Mitchinson, Welsby, Angas, BBC Singers and Concert O, Del Mar, BBC, 1980
EDITIONS f.s., Boosey & Hawkes, 1990; v.s., Delius Trust/Boosey & Hawkes, 1979

Koanga

Opera in a prologue, three acts and an epilogue (1h 45m)
Libretto by Charles F. Keary (1848–1917), from draft by the composer and Jutta Bell, after G. W. Cable's novel The Grandissimes: A Story of Creole Life (1880)
Composed 1895–7, rev. April 1898
PREMIERES 30 March 1904, Stadttheater, Elberfeld; UK: 23 September 1935, Covent Garden, London; US: 18 December 1970, Lisner Auditorium, Washington, DC
CAST Uncle Joe b, Don José Martinez b, Simon Perez t, Koanga bar, Rangwan b, Palmyra s, Clotilda a, planters' daughters 4 s, 4 a; satb chorus of slaves, dancers, servants
LARGE ORCHESTRA

Koanga derives from Delius's time in Florida, when he had been entranced by the Negroes' songs. He had hoped for a production in London in 1899, but only concert extracts were performed in St James's Hall on 30 May 1899, under Alfred Hertz. Beecham planned to stage it at Covent Garden in 1910 but it was not until 1935 that he did so. For this Beecham and Edward Agate revised the libretto, which Jelka Delius had translated back into English from her German version. For a 1972 performance in London, a further revision (later published) was made by Douglas Craig (who produced the revival) and Andrew Page.

SYNOPSIS

In a prologue, Uncle Joe, an old slave, tells the planters' eight daughters their favourite story of Koanga and Palmyra.

Act I On a sugar-cane plantation in Louisiana, a mulatto slave girl, Palmyra, rejects the advances of Simon Perez, foreman of the plantation. The plantation owner, Don José Martinez, tells of a new batch of slaves which includes Koanga, a West African prince and voodoo priest. Palmyra at once falls in love with the new arrival, who refuses to submit to slavery. Noticing this attraction, Martinez offers Palmyra to Koanga if he will work. But Clotilda, Martinez's wife, protests at losing Palmyra's services as her maid.

Act II On the wedding day of Koanga and Palmyra, Clotilda tells Perez that Palmyra is her half-sister and promises her to him if he will stop the marriage. Palmyra is abducted by Perez's servants. Koanga strikes Martinez and calls down a voodoo curse on the plantation, which is stricken with plague.

Act III Koanga returns to rescue Palmyra from Perez, whom he kills. He is pursued into the swamps and brought back mortally wounded. After he dies, Palmyra stabs herself.

The epilogue returns to the planters' daughters listening to Uncle Joe.

Koanga is the most dramatic and powerful of Delius's operas. The score is brilliant and colourful, with Negro spirituals and working songs as background to the start of Act I and an elaborate ensemble for five principals and chorus to end the act. The banjo-accompanied distant voices in the wedding scene are Delius magic and Act II also contains the well-known Creole choral-dance episode, La Calinda, originally a movement in the Florida suite and a favourite concert item in the 1931 orchestral arrangement by Eric Fenby. At some stage before the first performance of Koanga, Delius substituted the prelude to Act II of The Magic Fountain for the music he had written to introduce Act III of Koanga. In the 1935 Covent Garden performances, Beecham adapted the original Florida suite version of La Calinda as the prelude to Act II and included the Irmelin prelude as an interlude in Act III (its first performance). Palmyra's lovely Act II aria, 'The hour is near', was composed during the Elberfeld rehearsals, apparently to appease the soprano because she disliked the costume Jelka Delius had designed for her. All the principals have splendid music, Palmyra's final 'Liebestod' being particularly eloquent.

RECORDING Lindsey, Allister, Holmes, Herincx, Estes, Groves, HMV, 1974
EDITIONS f.s., Boosey & Hawkes, 1980; v.s., Boosey & Hawkes, 1935

A Village Romeo and Juliet

Opera in six tableaux (1h 45m)
Libretto by the composer, based on the short story *Romeo und Juliet auf dem Dorfe* from the collection *Die Leute von Seldwyla* (1856) by Gottfried Keller (1819–1890)
Composed November 1899–1901
PREMIERES 21 February 1907, Komische Oper, Berlin; UK: 22 February 1910, Covent Garden, London; US: 26 April 1972, Kennedy Center, Washington, DC
CAST Manz *bar*, Marti *bar*, Sali (as a boy) *s*, Sali (as a man) *t*, Vreli *s*, Dark Fiddler *bar*, 5 *s*, 3 *a*, 3 *t*, 5 *bar*, 2 *b*; *satb* chorus of vagabonds, peasants, bargees
LARGE ORCHESTRA

Work on the libretto started in 1897. Delius asked C. F. Keary to write it, but was dissatisfied with the first draft. He then commissioned Karl-August Gerhardi, who produced a German draft in 1898. This still did not please Delius, who turned again to Keary, but finally wrote his own English libretto in 1899. When the opera had its Berlin premiere in 1907, it was sung in a German translation by Jelka Delius. The most famous music in the opera, the *entr'acte* between Scenes 5 and 6 known as *The Walk to the Paradise Garden*, was expanded in 1906 to cover a scene change.

SYNOPSIS
Scene 1 At Seldwyla, Switzerland, in the mid-19th century, two farmers, Manz and Marti, plough their fields, which are separated by a strip of overgrown land, now up for sale since its owner, the Dark Fiddler, has no legal claim to it because he is a bastard. Their children, Sali and Vreli, play happily together in the woods and there meet the Dark Fiddler, who knows that the farmers are each surreptitiously taking an extra furrow out of his land. When it is all ploughed and no longer a haunt of birds and animals, then beware, he tells them. The farmers quarrel and forbid the children to play together.
Scene 2 Six years later, Sali and Vreli – now grown up – agree to resume their friendship. Both their homes have been impoverished by their fathers' lawsuit.
Scene 3 They meet in the wild land; the Dark Fiddler appears and invites them to share his vagabond life. Marti comes looking for his daughter and is dragging her away when Sali knocks him down.
Scene 4 Vreli is spending her last night in her old home. Her father has lost his mind as a result of Sali's blow and is in an asylum. Sali joins her and they fall asleep in each other's arms, dreaming that they are being married. On awakening they decide to go to the fair in Berghald.
Scene 5 At the fair they are happy until they are recognized and made to feel uncomfortable. They walk to the Paradise Garden, to a dilapidated riverside inn where they can dance.

Scene 6 The Dark Fiddler is there with four vagabonds. They try to persuade the two lovers to join them, but mock them for their 'respectability'. Sali and Vreli hear bargemen singing on the river. They take a hay barge moored near the inn and decide to 'drift away for ever'. Sali withdraws the plug from the bottom of the barge and the village Romeo and Juliet clasp each other closely as the boat sinks.

The *Village Romeo* contains some of Delius's most inspired nature music and is on his favourite theme of the world well lost for love. The duets for Sali and Vreli are passionate and lyrical and the role of the Dark Fiddler is a fine one for a baritone. In Keller's story the Fiddler is a sinister presence: in Delius he represents freedom from conventional family ties and identification with nature – in other words, Delius himself. The fair scene (inspired by *Die Meistersinger*) provides a lively contrast to the ruminative mood of much of the opera. But, as so often in Delius, it is the offstage chorus of distant voices – the vagabonds and bargees – that creates his special brand of theatrical magic.

RECORDINGS 1. Dyer, Soames, Dowling, Sharp, Clinton, Royal Philharmonic Ch and O, Beecham, HMV, 1948: of historical significance being the only Delius opera recorded by Beecham; 2. Harwood, Tear, Luxon, Shirley-Quirk, Mangin, John Alldis Ch, RPO, M. Davies, HMV, 1972; 3. Field, Davies, Mora, Hampson, Dean, Arnold Schönberg Ch, Austrian Radio SO, Mackerras, Argo, 1989: the second is less well recorded but better cast than the third [A.B.]
VIDEO Field, Davies, Mora, Hampson, Dean, Arnold Schönberg Ch, Austrian Radio SO, Mackerras: imaginative version in Peter Weigl's film [A.B.]
EDITIONS f.s./v.s., Harmonie (now Boosey & Hawkes), 1910

Margot-la-Rouge

(*A Night in Paris*)
Opera in one act (45m)
Libretto by 'Rosenval' (Berthe Gaston-Danville)
Composed April 1901 – June 1902
PREMIERES 9 December 1981, BBC recording (broadcast 21 February 1982; Fenby orch.); 28 March 1984, Collegiate Theatre, London (original orch.); US: 8 June 1983, Opera Theatre of St Louis, St Louis, Missouri (original orch.)
CAST Margot *s*, Lili Béguin *s*, La Patronne *a*, Thibault *t*, 3 *s*, *a*, 7 *bar*, 3 *b*; *satb* chorus of girls, bar customers, policemen
SMALL ORCHESTRA

This uncharacteristically melodramatic subject was composed for a prize competition – the Concorso Melodrammatico – organized by the Italian publisher Sonzogno. (The 1889 competition had been won by Mascagni's *Cavalleria rusticana*. The prize in 1902 went to Lorenzo Filiasi's *Manuel Menendez*.) A vocal score was prepared in 1902 by Maurice Ravel and published in Paris in 1905. No performance materialized and, although the work was considered by the Komische Oper in Berlin in 1904, the conductor Fritz Cassirer told Delius he disliked it 'on account of the tearful ending and the *violettes blanches*'. In 1932, when working with Eric Fenby, Delius resurrected the central love scene and converted it into a concert work to words by

Whitman: *Idyll: Once I passed through a populous city*. In 1979–80, the Delius Trust, believing the original manuscript to be lost, commissioned Fenby to provide a performing score for a BBC broadcast. After the broadcast, the original score was found.

SYNOPSIS

Soldiers and other clientele of a Paris café are discussing Margot-la-Rouge's latest love affair. The sergeant, Thibault, does not join in because he realizes that Margot is his former mistress. When she arrives they sing a passionate duet (the music of the *Idyll*) until interrupted by her new lover, whom Margot says she hates. He tries to stab her, but Thibault intervenes and is himself fatally stabbed. Margot kills her lover with Thibault's bayonet and is arrested.

Delius as a *verismo* composer is unconvincing, but *Margot-la-Rouge*, followed as it was by a plan to compose *Salome*, suggests that the success of Charpentier's *Louise* and Puccini's *La bohème* had spurred him to emulate them. The best part of the score is the love music.

RECORDING   McDonall, Andrew, Woollam, Donnelly, BBC Concert O, Del Mar, BBC, 1982
EDITIONS   f.s., Boosey & Hawkes, 1988; v.s., Delius Trust/Boosey & Hawkes, 1990

Fennimore and Gerda

Opera in 11 pictures (1h 15m)
Libretto by the composer, after the novel *Niels Lyhne* (1880) by J. P. Jacobsen (1847–1885)
Composed 1908–10, rev. 1912–13
PREMIERES   21 October 1919, Opernhaus, Frankfurt; UK: 23 May 1968, Old Town Hall, Hammersmith, London; US: 3 June 1981, Opera Theater of St Louis, St Louis, Missouri
CAST   Niels Lyhne *bar*, Fennimore *ms*, Consul *b*, Gerda *s*, 3 *s*, 3 *ms*, *a*, 2 *t*, 3 *bar*, 2 *b*; *satb* chorus of maidservants, girls, farmhands
LARGE ORCHESTRA

In his last opera – which he said was an inappropriate word for what he called 'two episodes . . . in 11 pictures' – Delius returned to the Scandinavian poet and novelist Jens Peter Jacobsen, whose verses he had set in the 1890s. (Jacobsen's *Gurrelieder* were set by Schoenberg.) Originally he set nine scenes from the novel, completing this version in the spring of 1911. Later he added three (eventually two) scenes relating to Gerda. A proposed premiere in Cologne was scuppered by the war and the successful first performance was given in Frankfurt five years later under Gustav Brecher.

SYNOPSIS

The writer Niels Lyhne and his friend the painter Erik Refstrup are staying with Niels's uncle, the Consul, and are both in love with his daughter Fennimore, who marries Erik. After three years the marriage is on the rocks and Erik invites Niels to visit them. Niels discovers that Erik is experiencing a 'creative block' and is drinking heavily. He and Fennimore have a passionate affair. Erik is killed in

an accident and the guilt-stricken Fennimore sends Niels away. After wandering abroad for three years, he returns to his childhood home where he meets and marries his neighbour's teenage daughter Gerda.

Delius regarded *Fennimore and Gerda* as his best and most advanced stage work – a psychological drama in which text and music sprang from the same source. Beecham, on the other hand, disliked it and wrote of 'three rather dreary people who have nothing to sing'. The opera's origins lie somewhere in Delius's friendship with the Norwegian painter Edvard Munch, but it lacks Munch's sense of brooding terror – Delius even substituted a happy ending for the novel's final tragedy. The opera is uncomfortably short, unless it is part of a double-bill, even with Delius's ill-advised afterthought of adding the Gerda episode. Musically, the score is of interest as marking a change of style towards the more astringent harmonies of the *Requiem* (1913–16). He intended to apply a similar approach – i.e. 'pictures' and 'episodes' – to *Wuthering Heights*, but he wrote no more operas.

RECORDING   Söderström, Tear, Rayner Cook, Danish Radio Ch and SO, M. Davies, HMV, 1976
EDITIONS   f.s., Universal (now Boosey & Hawkes), 1926; v.s., Universal (now Boosey & Hawkes), 1919

BIBLIOGRAPHY   Thomas Beecham, *Frederick Delius*, Hutchinson, 1959; *rp*, Severn House, 1975; Lionel Carley, *Delius, A Life in Letters*, vol. 1: *1862–1908*, Scolar Press, 1983; vol. 2: *1909–1934*, Scolar Press, 1988; Eric Fenby, *Delius As I Knew Him*, Bell, 1936; rev. edn, Icon, 1966; 2nd rev. edn, Faber, 1981

M.K.

DOMENICO DELLA-MARIA

Pierre-Antoine Dominique Della-Maria; *b* 14 June 1769, Marseilles, France; *d* 9 March 1800, Paris

The brief but meteoric career of Della-Maria bears the signs of a typically Parisian fashion craze. It was launched on a wave of five opéras comiques produced within a single year, 1798. The public was ready to welcome light, fresh new melodic talent: Dalayrac's idiom had long been familiar, and Boieldieu was only just beginning his career in the capital.

Della-Maria seems to have had Italian parentage, and was something of a child prodigy. At 18, he had an opera produced in Marseilles, then studied in Italy before arriving in Paris in 1796. The key work here was *Le prisonnier*, a romantic comedy of intrigue initially designed as a play by its expert librettist, Duval, who later reported that the score was composed in a week. Audiences responded very like the veteran German composer and writer, Reichardt, who saw it in 1802: 'What ensemble! What naturalness and charm! I haven't enjoyed such an evening for a century!' *Le prisonnier* was adapted for London as *The Castle of Sorrento* in 1799.

Operatic works: *Il maestro di cappella*, 1792; *Chi vuol non puole*, 1795; *Il matrimonio per scommessa*, 1795; *Le prisonnier, ou La ressemblance*, 1798; *Le vieux château, ou La rencontre*, 1798; *Jacquot, ou L'école des mères*, 1798; *L'opéra comique*, 1798; *L'oncle valet*, 1798; *La maison du Marais*, 1799; *La fausse duègne*, 1802

D.P.C.

EDISON DENISOV
Edison Vasil'evich Denisov; *b* 6 April 1929, Tomsk, Siberia

Denisov first studied mathematics and physics, but sent some early compositions to Shostakovich to resolve his indecision about his career. Shostakovich encouraged him to enter the Moscow Conservatory, where he studied with Shebalin until 1959 and later became professor of orchestration. Unusually among the post-Shostakovich generation of Soviet composers, Denisov has more affinity with the Western avant-garde, and is often dubbed 'The Russian Boulez'. His latest opera, a setting of Picasso's play *The Four Young Girls*, has yet to be performed in the West for copyright reasons.

L'écume des jours
Froth on the Daydream
Lyric drama in three acts (2h 45m)
Libretto by the composer, after the novel by Boris Vian (1947)
Composed 1977–80
PREMIERE 15 March 1986, Salle Favart, Paris

Boris Vian (1920–1959), jazz trumpeter, impresario and a sort of French literary James Dean, is best remembered for his singing and his surrealist novels (though he also himself composed an opera). In *L'écume des jours*, Colin has fallen in love with Chloe, though on their honeymoon a water-lily lodges in her lungs and she becomes ill. The environment turns against them; Colin loses his money; his room shrinks, and a 'mouse', a pathetic double of Chloe, appears. The music contains quotations from Duke Ellington, and a chamber group, including saxophones and electric guitar, is effectively pitted against a huge orchestra that unleashes climaxes of great density as the lovers' world turns sour.

EDITION f.s., Boosey & Hawkes, [1980]

Other operatic works: *Ivan-Soldat*, 1959; *The Four Young Girls*, 1986
BIBLIOGRAPHY Edison Denisov, 'The Foam of Days: Denisov', *Music in the USSR*, winter 1984

J.G.

HENRY DESMARETS
Henry Desmarets [Desmarest]; *b* February 1661, Paris; *d* 7 September 1741, Lunéville, France

To escape the death sentence unjustly passed on him in 1699 after a bizarre incident involving a tax inspector's daughter, Desmarets spent most of his last 42 years in exile, eventually settling in the Duchy of Lorraine as surintendant de la musique to Duke Leopold I. The episode stunted a modestly promising operatic career: after 1699 he produced little more than occasional pieces. Of his dramatic works, however, only *Didon* was immediately successful, though *Iphigénie en Tauride* (completed by Campra during Desmarets's exile) was belatedly recognized as his masterpiece; it was revived five times, the last as late as 1762.

In most of his operas Desmarets reveals himself to be an unadventurous follower of Lully. Several works show signs of haste, and most suffer from poor libretti. There are, however, sporadic passages of considerable originality, notably a number of invocation scenes using low-lying textures and dark sonorities. Most of Desmarets's works for the Opéra are tragédies, though *Les amours de Momus* has the distinction of being the first musical comedy staged there.

Surviving operatic works: *Plutus, ou Le triomphe des richesses* (attrib. Desmarets), 1682; *La Diane de Fontainebleau*, 1686; *Didon*, 1693; *Circe*, 1694; *Théagène et Cariclée*, 1695; *Les amours de Momus*, 1695; *Vénus et Adonis*, 1697; *Les festes galantes*, 1698; *Iphigénie en Tauride* (completed by Campra), 1704; *Renaud, ou La suite d'Armide*, 1722
BIBLIOGRAPHY J. R. Anthony, *French Baroque Music from Beaujoyeulx to Rameau*, Batsford, 1973, rev. edn, 1978

G.S.

PAUL DESSAU
b 19 December 1894, Hamburg; *d* 28 June 1979, Zeuten, nr Berlin

Dessau enjoyed a thorough grounding in classical repertoire, learning the violin from the age of six and composing from the age of 12. He continued violin studies in Berlin, later turning to conducting, piano and composition. During his student years (1910–12) he began to compose an opera, *Giuditta*, but this never progressed beyond a piano sketch. The strongest influences on his early development were, as he recalled, Schoenberg and Strauss, Nikisch and Weingartner. For some ten years his career followed the characteristic pattern of a German Kapellmeister: after initial experience as répétiteur in Hamburg he worked as conductor in Bremen, Cologne (under Klemperer), Mainz and Berlin. Here disagreement with Bruno Walter caused him to relinquish his post and he was obliged to earn his living by writing music for silent movies. This hack work committed him to composing a new score every week, but Dessau thus acquired an enviable discipline and remarkable technical fluency. His fondness for quotations – whether of his own or of other composers' music – dates from this period of enforced productivity. With the advent of sound film he composed five scores for Richard Tauber.

In 1933 Dessau left Nazi Germany and settled in Paris. He studied 12-note technique with René Leibowitz and composed music for the French premiere of Brecht's *Furcht und Elend des dritten Reiches*. In 1939 he moved to New York where he met Brecht for the first time, subsequently spending the remaining war years in California as a ghost-writer of Hollywood movie scores. In 1948 it became clear that his communist sympathies were unwelcome in the US and he returned to Germany. There, although never an official member of the Communist Party, he played a leading role (together with Hanns Eisler) in the musical and ideological development of the newly founded GDR. His best-known score is probably the incidental music to Brecht's *Mother Courage*, composed in 1948. With *The Trial of Lucullus*, first performed in 1951, Dessau aroused international interest. He married Ruth Berghaus, who staged his later world premieres and became renowned for her controversial opera productions.

Dessau was a brilliant propagandist, an eloquent public speaker and a committed interpreter of his own music – as conductor and even as singer. His concern to bring his music into line with Marxist–Leninist dialectic was offset by an individual artistic standpoint which was progressive and anti-popular. He was not prepared to renounce Schoenberg, even at a time when Western avant-garde tendencies were officially denounced as 'formalist', and he responded to criticisms of harshness in his own music in typically harsh tones: 'We have many discomforting tasks ahead of us. They may take an effort but we shall achieve them. Therefore I favour discomfort.' In this sense he exerted a strong influence on younger GDR composers such as Siegfried Matthus and Udo Zimmermann. With the collapse of the Communist regime Dessau's reputation suffered a major setback. Time alone can tell whether his theatre scores will acquire new relevance.

Die Verurteilung des Lukullus
The Trial of Lucullus
Opera in 12 scenes (1h 30m)
Libretto by Bertolt Brecht (1939)
Composed and rev. 1951
PREMIERES 17 March 1951, Staatsoper, Berlin; rev. version: 12 October 1951, Staatsoper, Berlin; UK: 20 March 1953, BBC broadcast; 28 January 1970, Guildhall, Cambridge
CAST Lukullus *t*, frieze figures: King *b*, Queen *s*, Lasus *t*; court of shades: Fishwife *a*, Courtesan *ms*, Teacher *t*, Baker *t*, Peasant *b*, numerous smaller parts; *satb* chorus of soldiers, slaves, shades; children's chorus
ORCHESTRATION 3 fl, 3 tpt, 3 trbn, tuba, perc (8 players), accordion, trautonium, 2 pf, hp, 6 vc, 4 db

Trial scene from Der Verurteilung des Lukullus *(East Berlin, 1951)*

Brecht's *Verhör des Lukullus* was written as a radio play soon after Hitler's invasion of Poland and first broadcast from Berne the following year. An operatic version by Roger Sessions (1947) flopped and, after Stravinsky turned the subject down, Brecht offered it to Dessau. The score was completed in three weeks and the premiere (subsequently classified as a 'preliminary performance'), in a production designed by Caspar Neher, was conducted by Hermann Scherchen before an invited audience. Brecht was requested to bring the anti-militarism of the text into line with the defensive strategical role envisaged by the government of the recently founded GDR. The new version, now entitled *Die Verurteilung des Lukullus*, was performed by the same forces in October 1951 (in the West Scherchen conducted and published the original version). Dessau made several further substantial revisions to the score before it was published in its definitive form in 1961.

SYNOPSIS
The opening scene depicts Lucullus' funeral procession interspersed with isolated comments from the crowd, after which Rome returns to work. Schoolchildren visit the mausoleum and their teacher reels off a list of the dead general's great battles. The scene changes to the realm of shades, where Lucullus is called for trial before a jury composed of a peasant, a teacher, a baker, a fishwife and a courtesan. The general demands that his triumphal frieze be presented in his defence but the jury questions the persons depicted upon it – a conquered king, a ravished queen, two children carrying a tablet inscribed with the names of destroyed cities, all of whom bring damning evidence against the accused. Only Lucullus' cook speaks well of his master and the general is also praised by the peasant for having introduced the cherry tree to Italy. But this could have been achieved without loss of life the jury concludes, while Lucullus is responsible for the death of 80,000. He is cast into the eternal void.

Dessau's score is remarkable for its use of massed percussion, brilliantly worked crowd scenes (including speaking chorus) and instrumental colours ranging from aggressive brass interjections (accompanying the general's Heldentenor outbursts) to a small ensemble of flutes and alto flute (in a scene where the fishwife laments the loss of her son). Rarer instruments are tellingly introduced: an accordion for the peasant, two prepared pianos and, in the final chorus, a trautonium. The opera has been frequently performed in Germany.

RECORDING Breul, Pawlik, Burmeister, Melchert, Schreier, Rotsch, Leipzig Radio Ch and O, Kegel, Telefunken, 1965
EDITIONS v.s., Ars Nova (Zurich), 1952; final rev. version: f.s./v.s., Henschel, 1961

Puntila

Opera in 13 scenes, a prologue and an epilogue (2h 45m)
Libretto by Peter Palitzsch and Manfred Wekwerth, after the play *Herr Puntila und sein Knecht Matti* by Bertolt Brecht (1940)

Composed 1956–9
PREMIERE 15 November 1966, Staatsoper, Berlin

While *Lucullus* was composed in direct collaboration with Brecht, the score of *Puntila* was not begun until after his death. Dessau's librettists abbreviated the original text while adhering faithfully to its structure.

The theme of the opera is class hatred, expressed as comedy. Puntila, a wealthy and tyrannic land-owner, behaves decently only when drunk. In search of a dowry for his daughter Eva he finds himself in a dilemma: whether to sell a valuable forest or marry the wealthy Frau Klinkmann, a singularly unattractive woman (who in the opera never appears on stage). While sober, Puntila resolves to engage his daughter to Frau Klinkmann's gormless nephew Eino; but, drunk again, he instead conceives a wild plan to marry her off to his chauffeur, Matti. The latter is horrified. Eva takes flight and Puntila decides to destroy his alcohol supply, but he does so by consuming it. Overcome by renewed feelings of warm-heartedness, he rids himself of the luckless Eino and summons the wedding guests. This time Matti does not wait for his master to sober up and departs in haste: class consciousness, as he well knows, is a permanent state, while drunkenness passes.

The score is extravagantly written for a large orchestra (including guitar, accordions and prepared piano), in a wide range of musical styles and complex vocal lines. The domain of Puntila and his fellow capitalists is represented by 12-note technique while a more popular tonal vein is adopted for the simple people, Matti, the peasants and the servants. These contrasting elements are superimposed and unified by brittle, clear declamation and a consciously stilted, incisive rhythmic language – also apparent in *Lucullus* – which can be recognized as Dessau's hallmark.

RECORDING Arnold, Pawlik, Burmeister, Ritzmann, Rehm, Süss, Ch and O of Staatsoper Berlin, Dessau, DG, 1970
EDITIONS f.s./v.s., Henschel, 1959

Lanzelot

Opera in 15 scenes (2h 30m)
Libretto by Heiner Müller and Ginka Tsholakova, after motifs by Hans Christian Andersen and *The Dragon* by Jevgeni Schwarz
Composed 1967–9
PREMIERE 19 December 1969, Staatsoper, Berlin

Heiner Müller is one of the finest dramatists in post-war Germany and it was logical that Dessau should choose him as successor to Brecht. Müller provided a libretto that is witty, economical and politically astute.

In a Stone-Age village cholera rages. The medicine man declares that the dragon from the golden pool can save the situation. The latter answers the villagers' appeal for help by boiling the water in the lake with his fiery breath; as his reward he demands the annual sacrifice of a virgin. Lanzelot appears with a mission to kill the dragon and free Elsa, the next victim. Initially the people regard him with suspicion but he fulfils his task, helped by workers, children and animals. Meanwhile a corrupt burgomaster takes control of the community and demands Elsa's hand. Lanzelot, wounded by the dragon, returns healed and frees the people. A new era is born.

Dessau's fondness for large-scale effects is developed further than in *Puntila*, with a large cast, an immense orchestra, *musique concrète* and additional music on tape, and a flamboyant range of compositional techniques. The vocal writing, particularly for Elsa and the dragon, makes frequent use of wide intervals and extreme tessituras, yet the most effective moment is probably Lanzelot's brief monologue (Scene 14), accompanied by a single cello.

EDITIONS f.s./v.s., Henschel, 1970

Einstein

Opera in three acts, a prologue, two intermezzi and an epilogue (2h)
Libretto by Karl Mickel
Composed 1971–3
PREMIERE 16 February 1974, Staatsoper, Berlin

Originally this was to be a further collaboration with Brecht and plans date back to 1955. Karl Mickel based his libretto on sketches made at that time, but the text itself is entirely his own work, as was his idea of introducing the traditional German comic figure of Hans Wurst.

The plot follows Einstein's life story from 1933 until shortly before his death. In Nazi Germany his writings are burned, SA thugs vandalize his house and the Führer declares total war; in America he is forced to help construct the atom bomb and experiences the fearful destruction it causes; aged and disillusioned, he destroys a new, significant discovery in order to prevent this too from being abused. The opera also features two other scientists, one of whom eventually joins the German Communist Party, and there are scenes in which Einstein converses with Galileo, Giordano Bruno and Leonardo. Hans Wurst, who represents the man in the street, is eventually gobbled up by a crocodile, symbol of fascist imperialism.

Dessau's music reflects the avant-garde influence of Lutosławski and Penderecki, combining many of their notational innovations with his own characteristic hard-edged sonorities and complex rhythms. He also incorporates lengthy quotations, particularly of Bach, e.g. in the scene of SA terror which is accompanied by the D minor ('Doric') organ prelude and dissonant interjections of the chorale 'Vom Himmel hoch'.

RECORDING Schreier, Adam, Süss, Dessau, Dresden State Opera Ch, Staatskapelle Dresden, Suitner, Nova, 1977
EDITIONS f.s./v.s., Henschel, 1973

Leonce und Lena

Opera in a prelude and two acts (1h 15m)
Libretto by Thomas Körner, after the play by Georg Büchner (1836)

Composed 1976–8
PREMIERE 24 November 1979, Staatsoper, Berlin

Although Büchner's comedy can be interpreted as anti-Romantic satire and a subtle jibe at the ruling classes, Dessau's last work represents an aesthetic change of direction. He spoke of *Leonce und Lena* as his *Così fan tutte* and his score is a model of economy and clarity. Körner's libretto changes the sequence of Büchner's scenes and adds a symmetrical outer frame to the action, in which Leonce and Valerio question the meaning of *la fama* (fame) and *la fame* (hunger). The plot, influenced by Shakespeare's *As You Like It*, tells of a prince and a princess who are betrothed but have never met. Unaware of each other's identity, they fall deeply in love. They attend the dreaded marriage ceremony wearing masks: the ensuing recognition scene is a moment of utopian bliss.

RECORDING Nossek, Schaller, Büchner, Süss, Ch of Deutsche Staatsoper, Berlin, Staatskapelle Berlin, Suitner, Nova, 1980
EDITION f.s./v.s., Henschel, 1978

Other operas: *Giuditta* (inc.), (1912); *Die Reisen des Glücksgotts* (inc.), (1945)
BIBLIOGRAPHY Paul Dessau, *Aus Gesprächen*, VEB Deutscher Verlag für Musik, 1974; Fritz Hennenberg, *Paul Dessau*, VEB Deutscher Verlag für Musik, 1965

A.C.W.B.

ANDRÉ CARDINAL DESTOUCHES

baptized 6 April 1672, Paris; d 7 February 1749, Paris

Destouches was one of the leading French composers of the early 18th century. It appears that he did not show any precocious talent for music, and joined the Mousquetaires du Roi in 1692. It was claimed that he left the army to devote himself to music; Lecerf de la Viéville says that, seized with a passion for opera, Destouches began to compose without knowing how to read or write music.

His social position and connections were undoubtedly a help. One of his teachers was André Campra, to whose opéra-ballet *L'Europe galante* (1697) Destouches was said to have contributed three airs. Destouches's probably greatest success came with his first work, the pastorale heroïque *Issé*, a three-act opera on a pastoral theme. Saying that no music had given him so much pleasure since Lully's, Louis XIV gave the composer 200 louis. Destouches then composed a series of five-act operas in which, like Campra, he continued developments that were to culminate in the work of Rameau: the expansion of the role of the orchestra and of dance and divertissement, and a less severe and restricted harmonic palette. Destouches's operas enjoyed mixed fortunes; however, he secured successively more important positions in the musical

Establishment. He was inspector general of the Académie (1713) and later its director (1728), and surintendant (1718), and maître de musique de la chambre (1727); he directed many concerts in the queen's apartments at Versailles.

In a period when the Académie and its composers were in difficulties, Destouches, although criticized like his contemporaries for cultivating 'novelty' and deviating from the 'purity' of the Lullian model of opera, achieved some success and much royal approbation.

Issé

Pastorale heroïque in a prologue and three acts
Libretto by Antoine Houdar de la Motte
Composed 1697, rev. (two acts added) 1708 (2h 45m)
PREMIERES   7 October 1697, Fontainebleau (concert);
30 December 1697, Opéra, Paris; rev. version: 14 October 1708, Opéra, Paris

In the prologue, set in the grounds of the Hesperides, Jupiter congratulates Hercules (who was understood to represent Louis XIV) on restoring peace by his many conquests. The pastorale then relates one of the many legends about Apollo, in which he disguises himself as a shepherd, Philemon, in order to win the

Design by Jean Bérain for Issé *(Receuil général des opéra, 1703)*

nymph Issé. Having fallen in love with 'Philemon', she is horrified to hear from an oracle that Apollo wants her. Apollo, delighted that Issé wishes to remain true to her simple shepherd, reveals himself and all ends happily.

The character of Issé herself is particularly well drawn, through such devices as her soliloquy 'Funeste amour' (Act IV, Scene 1, in 1708 version). *Flûtes* (recorders) and strings, to which are added in the middle section a solo *flûte allemande* (flute), are used in combination and in alternation to reflect her changes of mood.

EDITIONS   f.s., facsimile, Barry Brook (ed.), *French Opera in the 17th and 18th Centuries*, vol. 14, Pendragon, 1984; v.s., *Chefs-d'oeuvre*, vol. 1, [1883]; *rp*, Broude Bros, 1971

Amadis de Grèce
Amadis of Greece
Tragédie en musique in a prologue and five acts
Libretto by Antoine Houdar de la Motte, after the Spanish chivalric poem *Amadis de Gaula*, Book IX, by ?Juan Diaz, translated (Book VII) by Herberay des Essarts (1546)

PREMIERE   26 March 1699, Opéra, Paris

The prologue identifies Amadis with Louis XIV. The main plot concerns the rivalry of Amadis and the Prince de Thrace for Niquée, daughter of the king of Thebes. The popular supernatural element is provided by the involvement of an enchantress, Mélisse, and by the return of the spirit of the prince which, summoned by Mélisse to her aid, brings instead a message from the underworld that the gods are on the side of Amadis and Niquée, the faithful lovers.

Mélisse and her entourage evoke the most vivid music, as Destouches strives to convey the supernatural by means of irregular rhythms and low scoring. La Motte's libretto was remodelled for Handel's *Amadigi*, 1715.

EDITION   f.s., facsimile (3rd version, 1712), Gregg, 1967

Omphale
Tragédie en musique in a prologue and five acts (2h 30m)
Libretto by Antoine Houdar de la Motte
PREMIERE   10 November 1701, Opéra, Paris

This opera (sometimes listed as *Hercule et Omphale*) was one of Destouches's most successful, enjoying several revivals during the following 50 years. The prologue eschews the usual panegyric of the king and sets up the main action by having Juno request the god of love to wound Alcide (Hercules). The action is set in Sardis, capital of Lydia; both Alcide and his friend Iphis are in love with the queen, Omphale. Alcide is unaware of the identity of his rival. A further complication in the shape of the sorceress Argine again offers plenty of scope for scenes of magic and spectacle. Eventually, Iphis and Omphale are able to declare their love, whereupon Alcide generously concedes and gives them his blessing.

Act III opens with a particularly fine soliloquy air for Omphale, 'Digne objet d'une flamme éternelle', unusually over an eight-bar descending ground bass. An equally fine air of Iphis in Act IV, 'Quoi! je vis, malheureux!' is modelled on the same chaconne, perhaps surprisingly in view of the vehemence of the sentiments expressed.

The title of this opera is best known through Grimm's *Lettre sur Omphale* (1752), one of the most powerful salvoes in the perpetual wars between supporters of French and Italian music which raged in the 18th century. Grimm used a revival of *Omphale* as an excuse to write scathing criticism of the old order (i.e. tragédie en musique in the mould of Lully) and heap fulsome praise on the head of Rameau.

EDITION v.s., *Chefs-d'oeuvre*, vol. 11, [1883]; *rp*, Broude Bros, 1971

Callirhoé

Tragédie en musique in a prologue and five acts
Libretto by Pierre-Charles Roy, after Pausanias and La Fosse
PREMIERE 27 December 1712, Opéra, Paris

The action of *Callirhoé* centres on an oracle which tells Coresus, high priest of Bacchus, that he can save his people only by sacrificing either Callirhoé, the woman he loves, or someone willing to take her place. He decides to save her by sacrificing himself.

There are two good examples of the popular temple scene. In the first (Act II), Coresus calls down the vengeance of Bacchus; effective use is made of a four-part male chorus of priests. The second (Act III) invokes the oracle of Pan, and is appropriately pastoral in character and instrumentation.

EDITION facsimile, Barry Brook (ed.), *French Opera in the 17th and 18th Centuries*, vol. 15, Pendragon, forthcoming

Les éléments

The Elements
Opéra-ballet in a prologue and four entrées
Libretto by Pierre-Charles Roy
Composed 1721, rev. 1725
PREMIERES 31 December 1721, Tuileries, Paris; rev. version: 29 May 1725, Opéra, Paris

This work was a collaboration between Michel-Richard de Lalande, nearing the end of his career, and his former pupil, Destouches. It is clear that the greater part of the music was written by the younger man, and that Lalande probably contributed no more than the overture and a few numbers in the prologue and first act.

In the prologue, Destiny summons the gods who represent the elements to appear in place of chaos. *L'air* relates the story of Ixion, a mortal who falls in love with Juno, goddess of air and winds, and is punished for his temerity. *L'eau* is set in Neptune's palace; *Le feu* brings to the stage the Vestal virgins, and *La terre* celebrates the fruits of the earth.

EDITIONS v.s., *Chefs-d'oeuvre*, vol. 14, [1883]; *rp*, Broude Bros, 1971; facsimile, Barry Brook (ed.), *French Opera in the*

17th and 18th Centuries, vol. 16, Pendragon, forthcoming
Other stage works: *Marthésie, reine des Amazones*, 1699; *Le carnaval et la folie*, 1703; *Télémaque/Télémaque et Calypso*, 1714; *Semiramis*, 1718; *Les stratagèmes de l'amour*, 1726
BIBLIOGRAPHY J. R. Anthony, *French Baroque Music from Beaujoyeaulx to Rameau*, Batsford, 1973; rev. edn, 1978

C.W.

FRANÇOIS DEVIENNE

b 31 January 1759, Joinville, Haute-Marne, France; *d* 5 September 1803, Paris

As a celebrated flautist and bassoonist, Devienne composed many chamber and orchestral works before writing for the stage. Due to an early death, his theatrical career spanned less than a decade, although his operas were popular and a number remained in the repertoire for several decades.

Devienne specialized in the light and humorous type of opéra comique established by Duni, Monsigny and Philidor in the 1760s. Although a contemporary of Cherubini, Méhul and Lesueur, who popularized a more serious style of opéra comique, the drame lyrique, Devienne's works rarely exchanged amusing and sentimental intrigues for more passionate and sombre subject matter.

From 1790 to 1801 Devienne was employed as principal bassoonist at the Théâtre de Monsieur (later the Théâtre Feydeau), for which he also wrote the majority of his operas. This theatre was established in 1789 as a rival to the official Opéra-Comique (then known as the Comédie-Italienne). The abolition of theatrical privileges in 1791 encouraged further competition among Parisian theatres and, until its closure in 1801, the Feydeau was particularly renowned for the high standard of its orchestral playing.

Devienne's musical style made use of the Feydeau's talented instrumentalists. His orchestration was rich and sonorous, at times brilliant, but carefully conceived so as to blend skilfully with voices. As a melodist he successfully combined simplicity and grace with vocal display. His greatest asset, however, was his imaginative sense of staging, a quality enhanced by the elegance of his musical style and its capacity for natural and direct expression.

Les visitandines

The Nuns of the Order of the Visitation
Opéra comique in two acts (2h)
Libretto by Louis-Benoît Picard
Composed 1792, rev. 1793 in three acts
PREMIERES 7 July 1792, Théâtre Feydeau, Paris; rev. version: 5 June 1793

Les visitandines is the tale of a valet and his master who, lost in a storm, mistake a convent for a hotel. They gain admission through disguise and chance upon the hero's long-lost love, rescuing her as she is about to take her vows. It was one of the most popular stage works of the Revolution period, partly because of its broad humour and musical charm, and partly because of its anti-clerical sentiments – a heroine saved from religious life and the mockery of religious figures through transvestite disguise. An earlier opéra comique by Berton, *Les rigueurs du cloître* (1790) had been the first to exploit such subject matter, but *Les visitandines*, performed in Paris as late as 1920, enjoyed greater success. The work was also famous for the ariette 'Enfant chéri des dames' in Act I, a parody of Papageno's aria 'Ein Mädchen oder Weibchen' from *Die Zauberflöte*.

EDITIONS f.ss., Cousineau, 1792; facsimile, Sherwood Dudley (ed.), *French Opera in the 17th and 18th Centuries*, vol. 71, Pendragon Press, 1992; v.s., Brandus et Cie, [c. 1875]

Other operas: *Le mariage clandestin*, 1790; *Les précieuses ridicules*, 1791; *Encore des Savoyards, ou L'école des parvenus*, 1792; *L'enlèvement des Sabines* (doubtful), 1792; *Les quiproquos espagnols*, 1792; *Le congrès des rois* (coll. with 11 others, including Méhul and Grétry), 1794; *Rose et Aurèle*, 1794; *Agnès et Félix, ou Les deux espiègles*, 1795; *Volécour, ou Un tour de page*, 1797; *Les comédiens ambulans*, 1798; *Le valet de deux maîtres*, 1799
BIBLIOGRAPHY A. Pougin, *Musiciens français du XVIIIe siècle: Devienne*, N. Chaix, 1864; serialized in *Revue et gazette musicale de Paris*, vol. 31 (1864)

E.C.

NICOLAS DEZÈDE

Nicolas ?Alexandre Dezède [Dezèdes, Dezaides, Desaides, Desede, De Zède]; *b* ?1740–45; *d* 11 September 1792, Paris

Details of Dezède's birth and parentage remain a mystery. Suggestions that he was the illegitimate son of Frederick II of Prussia cannot be corroborated, although he was certainly of noble extraction. By attempting to ascertain his ancestry he forfeited his entitlement to a generous annual allowance and turned to opera composition to earn his living.

Alongside Grétry and, later, Dalayrac and Berton, Dezède developed the light, sentimental style of opéra comique. Many of his works, written for the Comédie-Italienne, paint the charm and simplicity of rural life. Dezède's musical style mirrors this atmosphere: his melodies have a natural grace and freshness – many are formed as romances and vaudevilles – and his harmonic language is beguilingly simple. However, his works do not lack strong dramatic intrigue or comedy and there are colourful touches in his instrumentation.

Attempts at a more serious style of composition met with little success. *Péronne sauvée* and *Alcindor*, produced at the Opéra, were both failures, and two similar works were left unfinished at Dezède's death. His most popular opéras comiques – *L'erreur d'un moment*, *Les trois fermiers* and *Blaise et Babet* (which remained in the repertoire for over 40 years) – owed much of their success to their skilful libretti, by Jacques-Marie de Monvel.

Operas: *Julie*, 1772; *L'erreur d'un moment, ou La suite de Julie*, 1773; *Le stratagème découvert*, 1773; *Les trois fermiers*, 1777; *Fatmé, ou Le langage des fleurs*, 1777; *Zulima, ou L'art*

et la nature, 1778; *Le porteur de chaise*, 1778, rev. as *Jérôme et Champagne*, 1781; *Cécile*, 1780; *A trompeur, trompeur et demi, ou Les torts du sentiment*, 1780; *Péronne sauvée*, 1783; *Blaise et Babet, ou La suite des trois fermiers*, 1783; *Le véritable Figaro*, (1784); *Alexis et Justine*, 1785; *Alcindor*, 1787; *Auguste et Théodore, ou Les deux pages*, 1789; *Les trois noces*, 1790; *Ferdinand, ou La suite des deux pages*, 1790; *Paulin et Clairette, ou Les deux espiègles*, 1792; *La fête de la cinquantaine*, (1796); *Amadis* (inc.); *Inez de Castro* (inc.);
BIBLIOGRAPHY A. Pougin, *Musiciens français du XVIIIe siècle: Dezède*, N. Chaix, 1862; serialized in *Revue et gazette musicale de Paris*, vol. 29 (1862)

E.C.

CHARLES DIBDIN

baptized 15 March 1745, Southampton, England; *d* 25 July 1814, London

Dibdin, now remembered mainly as the composer of the song 'Tom Bowling', was something of a youthful prodigy, and was more or less self-taught as a composer. By the age of 15 he was in London, singing in the chorus at Covent Garden, and his first opera, the all-sung pastoral *The Shepherd's Artifice*, was produced there in 1764 when he was just 19; he wrote the words and the music, and sang the leading role. He became famous, however, when he played the farmer's boy Ralph in the pastiche opera *The Maid of the Mill* (1765), and the black servant Mungo in his own afterpiece *The Padlock* (1768). The words of both were by Isaac Bickerstaffe, who collaborated with Dibdin in a string of successful and forward-looking comic operas until 1772, when a homosexual scandal forced Bickerstaffe to leave England.

With such an auspicious start, it was not surprising that Dibdin's later career was a disappointment, particularly since he had a chaotic private life, was careless with money, and tended to quarrel with colleagues. Sooner or later he fell out with most of London's theatre managers, and was forced to write for fringe venues such as Sadler's Wells, where his 'dialogues' (miniature all-sung operas) were popular. Things came to a head in 1776, when he fled to France to escape his debts; he ended up in a debtor's prison when his involvement in the Royal Circus theatre came to grief in 1784. After an abortive attempt to emigrate to India in 1787 (the ship ran aground at Torbay), Dibdin found success once more in the 1790s with his 'table entertainments' or one-man variety shows, which featured his topical, comic and patriotic songs. Somehow he also found time to paint, to publish several music journals, and to write a number of books, including three novels. He died in poverty in 1814.

Dibdin's talents as a composer were limited to comedy. He was out of his depth in serious opera; his overtures and other instrumental pieces are mostly poor, and he was frequently hasty and careless. But at his best, in his early works, he was unsurpassed at setting ordinary speech and down-to-earth situations to vivid music. Most of his later operas were not published, though portions of some survive in his chaotic and scattered autograph manuscripts.

The Ephesian Matron

All-sung opera (45m)
Text by Isaac Bickerstaffe, after Petronius' *Satyricon* (1st century AD)
PREMIERE 12 May 1769, Ranelagh Gardens

The Ephesian Matron is a black comedy; it is probably the only opera set entirely in a tomb. The matron, a young widow, has resolved to stay with her husband's body for ever, despite the attempts of her father and maid to console her. She sings a delicious parody of an opera-seria mad aria, but cheers up when a handsome centurion (originally played by Dibdin himself) appears; he has been guarding the bodies of executed criminals, and when one disappears in his absence she offers her husband instead. The work survives complete with recitatives (spoken dialogue was not allowed outside the main London theatres) but only in vocal score; several modern revivals have used an unpublished orchestration by Roger Fiske.

RECORDING Mills, Streeton, Padmore, Knight, Opera Restor'd, Holman, Hyperion, 1992
EDITION v.s., I. Johnston, [1769]

Other operatic works surviving substantially complete: *Love in the City*, 1767; *Lionel and Clarissa*, 1768; *The Padlock*, 1768; *Damon and Phillida*, 1768; *The Captive*, 1769; *The Jubilee*, 1769; *The Recruiting Sergeant*, 1770; *The Institution of the Garter*, 1771; *The Palace of Mirth*, 1772; *The Brickdust Man*, 1772 (RECORDING Hyperion, 1992); *The Wedding Ring*, 1773; *The Ladle*, 1773; *The Grenadier*, 1773 (RECORDING Hyperion, 1992); *The Trip to Portsmouth* (coll. with Thomas Arne), 1773; *The Deserter* (after Monsigny and Philidor), 1773; *The Christmas Tale*, 1773; *The Waterman*, 1774; *The Cobler*, 1774; *The Mischance*, ?1774; *The Quaker*, 1775; *The Seraglio* (coll. with Samuel Arnold), 1776; *Poor Vulcan*, 1778; *The Cestus*, 1783; *Liberty Hall*, 1785; *Harvest Home*, 1787; *The Round Robin*, 1811; c. 30 works largely or completely lost
BIBLIOGRAPHY Roger Fiske, *English Theatre Music in the Eighteenth Century*, OUP, 1973; 2nd edn, 1986

P.H.

CHRISTIAN LUDWIG DIETER

b 13 June 1757, Ludwigsburg; *d* 15 May 1822, Stuttgart

Dieter's significance in German operatic history rests on his popularization of the singspiel; he wrote 12 works in the genre for Stuttgart. *Belmonte und Konstanze, oder Die Entführung aus dem Serail* (1784 – two years after Mozart's setting) is of special interest. Dieter's version, like those of André (1781) and Knecht (1790), follows closely in the tradition of Hiller and, its shared subject apart, has little in common with Mozart's masterpiece. Concerned chiefly with the addition to the play of Italianate arias and simple, often folk-style, songs, it makes little attempt at sophisticated character delineation in a truly operatic manner. Nevertheless in this work, as in his only other surviving stage piece, Dieter uses orchestral colour skilfully to depict dramatic situations, probably basing his methods on those of his great predecessor at Stuttgart, Jommelli.

Operatic works: *Der Irrwisch, oder Endlich fand er sie*, 1779; *Belmonte und Konstanze, oder Die Entführung aus dem Serail*, 1784; 11 lost
BIBLIOGRAPHY G. Reichart, 'Christian Ludwig Dieter', in *MGG*

B.S.

KARL DITTERS VON DITTERSDORF

b 2 November 1739, Vienna; *d* 24 October 1799, Schloss Rothlhotta, nr Nové Dvory, Bohemia

Dittersdorf is best remembered for his singspiels which, in the 1780s, rivalled and even exceeded the popularity of Mozart's operas in Vienna. Dittersdorf played the violin in the orchestra of the Prince of Sachsen-Hildburghausen in Vienna from 1751 and was taught composition by Bonno, who was in charge of the orchestra until its dissolution in 1761. He then worked at the opera and at the court, playing the Italian repertoire and witnessing the evolution of Gluck's reform operas. Disagreements with the opera administrator led him to leave Vienna in 1765 to become Kapellmeister to the Bishop of Grosswarden in Hungary. Between 1771 and 1795 he was employed by Count Schaffgotsch, the Prince-Bishop of Breslau, who kept a private orchestra in Johannisberg, and there Dittersdorf composed his first 11 comic operas. In 1774 he rejected an offer to succeed Gassmann as imperial court Kapellmeister in Vienna.

Following the spectacular success of his *Doktor und Apotheker* in 1786, Dittersdorf was commissioned to write two more singspiels, *Betrug durch Aberglauben* and *Die Liebe im Narrenhause*, and one Italian opera, *Democrito corretto* (which became popular in a German adaptation). He wrote further highly successful singspiels for Vienna, and a final group of 11 works for the court of Brunswick-Oels.

Dittersdorf's stage works are almost all comedies. While the spoken dialogue of his singspiels inevitably arrested the flow of drama, he usually employed fast-paced, *parlando*-style melodies and a syllabic text-setting to enliven those pieces which, by virtue of their slow tempo, might suggest a more reflective mood. The arias are often songlike with the orchestral accompaniment restricted to supporting the harmony. Dittersdorf was particularly successful in presenting burlesque characters, and he was also fond of using onomatopoeic motifs to represent animals, cannons, bells, thunder, etc. (for example Filz's aria 'Ich hör den Donner brummen' in *Hieronymus Knicker*). Indeed, short phrases and

Caricature of Sander and Nitsche in Dittersdorf's Das rote Käppchen, *published in 1792*

repeated motifs are startling features of his music, but although they animate his compositions they also deprive them of musical development. This is particularly noticeable in the finales – sometimes even longer than those of Mozart – which are constructed of many short sections. The music of these ensembles does not attempt to capture the emotional development of the characters; consequently they are more like opera choruses.

In 1791 a critic of the *Berliner Wochenblatt* praised Dittersdorf's *Liebe im Narrenhause* by saying that 'Nothing makes a real effect on stage that is not simple and comprehensible.' Indeed, though this simplicity ensured Dittersdorf's success in the 1780s, it also prompted his downfall once the public appreciated the more complex musical language of his contemporaries. He stated in his autobiography that he considered his whole life a failure. He had remained a court composer who aimed to give immediate pleasure to his patron and public.

Doktor und Apotheker

Doctor and Pharmacist
Singspiel in two acts (2h 30m)
Libretto by Johann Gottlieb Stephanie der Jüngere, after the drama *L'apothicaire de Murcie* by 'Le Comte N.'
PREMIERES 11 July 1786, Kärntnertortheater, Vienna; UK: 25 October 1788, Drury Lane, London (with additions by Storace); US: 1795, Boston

Doktor und Apotheker made a success of the Emperor Joseph II's second attempt to found a German National singspiel company after the first endeavour, launched in 1778, had been abandoned in 1783. Mozart's *Figaro*, premiered two months earlier, had to give way to Dittersdorf's opera, which was

subsequently performed all over the world and is still occasionally revived.

Leonore is in love with Gotthold Krautmann, the local doctor's son. Yet her father, the quack Stoessel, hates the doctor and makes arrangements for Leonore to marry the drunkard and invalid soldier Sturmwald. At first the lovers fail to extricate themselves from the approaching disaster, despite being helped by a second, sympathetic couple. But finally everybody is happy except for the ridiculed suitor and Stoessel.

Like Mozart's *Die Entführung aus dem Serail*, premiered in Vienna four years earlier, *Doktor und Apotheker* combines traditional singspiel elements (spoken dialogue, simple folklike songs, including the almost ubiquitous drinking song) with ornate arias in opera-seria style and with features drawn from opera buffa (e.g. *parlando* writing). The work contains one of the earliest examples in singspiel of the multi-sectional finale, no doubt influenced by that of Act II of Mozart's *Le nozze di Figaro* (which Dittersdorf saw in 1786), whose length it rivals.

RECORDING Uhrmacher, Woodward, Stamm, Meier, Schöne, Lang, Finke, Unger, Staatsorchester Rheinische Philharmonie, Lockhard, RBM, 1981
EDITION v.s., Heinrich Burkhard (ed.), Universal, 1935

Surviving operatic works: *L'amore disprezzato*, 1771; *Il finto pazzo per amore*, 1772; *Il tutore e la pupilla*, 1773; *Lo sposo burlato*, 1773; *Il tribunale di Giove*, 1774; *Il maniscalco*, 1775; *La contadina fedele*, 1776; *La moda, o sia Gli scompigli domestici*, 1776; *L'Arcifanfano, re de' matti*, 1776 (RECORDING Voce); *Il barone di Rocca antica*, 1776; *Betrug durch Aberglauben, oder Die Schatzgräber*, 1786; *Democrito corretto*, 1786; *Die Liebe im Narrenhause*, 1787 (EDITION facsimile, Garland, 1986); *Das rote Käppchen, oder Hilft's nicht so schadt's nicht*, 1788; *Im dunkeln ist nicht gut munkeln, oder Irrung über Irrung*, 1789; *Hieronymus Knicker*, 1789; *Der Schiffspatron, oder Der neue Gutsherr*, 1789; *Hokus-Pokus*, 1790; *Der Teufel ein Hydraulikus*, 1790; *Das Gespenst mit der Trommel*, 1794; *Don Quixote der Zweyte*, 1795; *Gott Mars und der Hauptmann von Bärenzahn*, 1795; *Der Durchmarsch*, 1795; *Der Schach von Schiras*, 1795; *Die befreyten Gwelfen*, 1795; *Ugolino*, 1796; *Die lustigen Weiber von Windsor*, 1796; *Der schöne Herbsttag*, 1796; *Der Ternengewinst, oder Der gedemütigte Stolz*, 1797; *Der Mädchenmarkt*, 1797; *Die opera buffa*, 1798; *Don Coribaldi*, 1798; 3 lost singspiels including *Die Hochzeit des Figaro*, 1789
BIBLIOGRAPHY Karl von Dittersdorf, *Karl von Dittersdorfs Lebensbeschreibung, seinem Sohne in die Feder diktiert*, Leipzig, 1801; English trans. (1896), *rp*, Da Capo, 1970; L. Riedinger, 'Karl Ditters von Dittersdorf als Opernkomponist', *SMw*, vol. 2 (1914), pp. 212–349; H. Unverricht (ed.), *Carl Ditters von Dittersdorf 1733–1799*, 1990

M.F.

ERNÖ DOHNÁNYI

b 27 July 1877, Pozsony (now Bratislava, Slovakia); *d* 9 February 1960, New York

Although famous in his day as an outstanding virtuoso pianist and conductor, and remembered now mainly for his dazzling *Variations on a Nursery Song* (1914), Dohnányi was a versatile composer who achieved equal success in chamber music, orchestral music (his First Piano Concerto (1898) was once popular and his Suite in F♯ minor (1909) is still sometimes played) and opera. From 1905 to 1915 he taught at the Berlin Hochschule, and his first opera, the comic *Tante Simona*, was first staged in German (Dresden, 1913). Its two successors were premiered in Budapest, where Dohnányi settled in 1915, the more melodramatic *A Vajda Tornya* (*The Voyevoda's Tower*), in 1922, and *Der Tenor*, a comedy about a stand-in singer who makes advances to the daughter of the local bass, in 1929. German influences, especially Brahms and Strauss, remained paramount with Dohnányi (*Der Tenor* contains actual parodies of German music), and the operas are tuneful, polished and effective, but not outstandingly individual. Dohnányi was in trouble with the Nazis before and during the war and with the communists after it, and in 1949 he settled in the US.

BIBLIOGRAPHY 'Ernö Dohnányi: A Picture Biography', *Clavier*, February 1977, pp. 12–15; Bálint Vázsonyi, *Ernö Dohnányi*, Corvina, 1971

S.W.

Donizetti first established himself as a potential talent with *Zoraide di Grenata* (Rome, 1822), which was successful enough to win him a contract with the impresario Barbaja, who brought him to Naples. The next eight years have been described as his 'apprenticeship', a period of experimentation and unflagging productivity. The turning point of his career was the great success of *Anna Bolena* (Milan, 1830), which won him commissions from all the leading Italian opera houses. Although he never totally renounced comedy (two of his greatest opere buffe, *L'elisir d'amore* (1832) and *Don Pasquale* (1843) were written after *Anna Bolena*), he now chiefly confined himself to tragedy. Some of these works, among them *Lucrezia Borgia* and *Lucia di Lammermoor*, soon made him a household name.

In 1838, Donizetti left Naples for Paris, drawn there not only by the possibility of prestige and larger fees, but also by the greater freedom of subject matter permitted there. In 1842, he was named Hofkapellmeister to the Habsburg court in Vienna and for the next three years divided his time between the French and Austrian capitals, with occasional trips to Italy. In 1846, signs of mental deterioration forced his confinement to a sanatorium at Ivry, but later, paralysed and almost totally bereft of speech, he was brought home to Bergamo, where he was nursed by friends until his death.

As a man, Donizetti was gregarious, good-humoured, and well disposed toward his fellow

GAETANO DONIZETTI

Gaetano Domenico Maria Donizetti; *b* 29 November 1797, Bergamo; *d* 8 April 1848, Bergamo

Although a handful of Donizetti's 65 operas have always maintained a place in the international repertoire, his reputation has undergone some profound changes. From a position of dominance at the time of his death, when one in every four Italian operas performed in Italy was one of his, his standing declined seriously in the last decades of the 19th century, when his music was often dismissed as facile and imitative. Since the Second World War, however, an extraordinarily widespread re-examination of most of his output has established his importance as a vital link in the development of Italian opera.

To see Donizetti at his true value, it is essential to understand him in terms of his period. Coming from poor parents, he was fortunate to have his talent recognized early, and to acquire as good a musical training (at the hands of Simon Mayr and Padre Mattei) as was then available in Italy. To support himself he had to accept every possible commission offered him. Writing sometimes as many as four operas a year and confronted with the exigencies of an audience that insisted on freshness without eccentricity, he deliberately set out to attain a mastery over the range of operatic types and genres then current in Italy. Not least of Donizetti's attributes as an opera composer was the effectiveness of his writing for every range of voice.

Pastel portrait of Donizetti attributed to Girolamo Induno

composers, whom he recognized as working against the obstacles of the censors and the court-controlled theatres. His letters are filled with his spontaneous reactions to his increasingly tragic life. None of his three children lived more than a few days, and his beloved wife Virginia died at the age of 29 in 1837 in the midst of a horrifying outbreak of cholera; he never remarried. Thereafter, a morbid streak in his character became more pronounced. His death was ultimately caused by a long-standing syphilitic infection.

It was Donizetti more than anyone else who raised the temperature of drama in Italian opera. Throughout his career, but particularly after 1830, he engaged in as near open warfare with the censors as he dared without losing his livelihood as an opera composer. He protested against the niggling restrictions that long forbade religious topics on the stage. He wanted to show rulers as human beings with human failings and not as mere benign figureheads. His many operas on English subjects, particularly those dealing with the Tudors, were able to pass muster with the Italian censors because they dealt with Protestant, rather than Catholic, kings and queens. *La favorite*, with its scenes of convent life and the delivery of a Papal Bull, was first given in Italy in mutilated form, as was *Dom Sébastien*, which included a funeral procession with a great catafalque on stage. Parisian authorities were more tolerant; for instance, *Poliuto*, banned in Naples for showing the martyrdom of a Christian saint, was given at the Opéra as *Les martyrs*.

Working within the conventions of his day, Donizetti found a variety of ways to adapt them to his manifold dramatic purposes: as in his fondness for elegiac *cabalettas*, sometimes slower in tempo than the arias they follow, or in his knack of creating ambiguity between the major and minor modes, and in his way of heightening an emotion by smoothly modulating into an unexpected key (as in Lucia's 'Spargi d'amaro pianto' or Norina's 'E' duretta la lezione' in Act III of *Don Pasquale*). In his late works Donizetti felt freer to foreshorten or even dismember the conventional structures; for instance, in these works he often abandoned the tradition of the aria-finale.

It is difficult to conceive of the phenomenon of Verdi without the foundation stone of Donizetti's works. Verdi's exploitation of the possibilities of the baritone persona finds its antecedents in such powerful roles as Cardenio in *Il furioso*, and in the title roles of *Tasso* and *Belisario*. In such scores as *Lucia*, *La favorite* and *Maria di Rohan* one discovers foreshadowing of the concept of *tinta* that Verdi came to insist on. While not suggesting that there is any conscious imitation, one can scarcely exaggerate the centrality of Donizetti to the tradition of Italian melodramma from which Verdi sprang and which he carried to loftier heights.

Il Pigmalione
Pygmalion
Scena lirica in one act (30m)
Libretto anonymous, based on Sografi's libretto for

Cimadoro's *Pimmaglione* (1790), ultimately derived from Ovid, *Metamorphoses*, Book X
Composed 1816
PREMIERE 13 October 1960, Teatro Donizetti, Bergamo

Composed in the latter half of September 1816, during Donizetti's student days in Bologna, the plot concerns Pigmalione, who, despairing of ever finding his ideal of feminine beauty, turns sculptor to create it for himself. He falls in love with his statue and prays to Venus, who thoughtfully brings his carved Galatea to life. Musically slender, the score, nevertheless, reveals the fledgling composer's flair for melody.

RECORDING Santunione, Antonioli, O of the Teatro Donizetti, Bergamo, Gatto, Melodram, 1960
MANUSCRIPT Bibliothèque Nationale, Paris

La lettera anonima
The Anonymous Letter
Farsa (with spoken dialogue) in one act (1h)
Libretto by Giulio Genoino, after Pierre Corneille's *Mélite, ou Les fausses lettres* (1630)
Composed 1822
PREMIERE 29 June 1822, Teatro del Fondo, Naples

Melita has written an anonymous letter to the Countess, in which she charges the Count with infidelity. The letter, however, is picked up by Rosina, who takes it to imply that her own fiancé, Filinto, has been untrue. The servant Lauretta is accused of having written the trouble-making missive but, when she demonstrates she can neither read nor write, she is absolved, whereupon Melita confesses her naughtiness, and is forgiven by the Countess. The score contains an attractive speciality number for the dancing master, Flageolet, and an extended quartet, the one number of the work to be praised by the critics after the premiere.

RECORDING Virgili, Pecchioli, Laghezza, Bottazzo, Panerai, Coro 'Amici della Polifonia', Naples SO of RAI, Caracciolo, UORC, 1972
EDITION v.s., Schonenberger, 1856

L'ajo nell'imbarazzo, o Don Gregorio
The Tutor in Trouble
Opera buffa in two acts (1h 45m)
Libretto by Jacopo Ferretti, after Giraud's comedy *L'ajo nell'imbarazzo* (1807)
Composed 1823–4, rev. 1826
PREMIERES 4 February 1824, Teatro Valle, Rome; rev. as *Don Gregorio*, 11 June 1826, Teatro Nuovo, Naples; UK: 28 July 1846, Her Majesty's Theatre, Haymarket, London (as *Don Gregorio*); US: January 1980, New York
CAST Gilda *s*, Leonarda *ms*, Enrico *t*, Marchese *bar*, Don Gregorio *buffo*, Pipetto *t*, Simone *b*; *satb* chorus of servants
SMALL ORCHESTRA

The earliest of Donizetti's operas to circulate widely outside Italy, *L'ajo* gives a clear foretaste of Donizetti's comic flair. The genuinely amusing plot concerns a father who is determined to bring up his two sons without knowledge of women. The result is that the younger son falls hopelessly in love with their superannuated servant Leonarda, the only woman he has ever seen, while the more enterprising Enrico is secretly married to Gilda, the daughter of a neighbour, by whom he has already had one son. Through Gilda's skilful manoeuvres, the Marchese is brought to see the impracticality of his educational system and blesses the marriage of his heir.

Donizetti's indebtedness to Rossinian comedy is apparent, but there are several moments, the *larghetto* of the Gilda–Don Gregorio duet for instance, where his characteristic humanity shines through The richly embellished aria for the Marchese (designed for Tamburini) in Act II is a baritone's golden opportunity, and the sparkling *rondò* for Gilda at the end, a set of three variations describing woman's true role, points the moral of the piece.

RECORDING Fusco, Benelli, Clabassi, Rome PO, Ferrari, RCA Italiana, [*c.* 1965]: some cuts

EDITIONS v.ss. Schonenberger, 1856; Ricordi, 1872, 1913; Belwin-Mills, *c.* 1980

Emilia di Liverpool

Opera semiseria in two acts (1h 30m)
Libretto anonymous, rev. by Giuseppe Checcherini, but after Scatizzi's *Emilia di Liverpaut*, derived in turn from August von Kotzebue's drama, trans. as *Emilia, o la benediz ione paterna* (1788)
Composed 1824, rev. 1828 as *L'ermitaggio di Liverpool*
PREMIERES 28 July 1824, Teatro Nuovo, Naples; rev. version: 8 March 1828, Teatro Nuovo, Naples; UK: 12 June 1957, Philharmonic Hall, Liverpool

Emilia is a girl from Naples who, as penance for having been seduced, tends a hospice in the mountains above Liverpool. A carriage accident and the arrival of a stranger serve to introduce both her seducer and her father into the action. The father had been captured by the Barbary pirates and escaped after 20 years' imprisonment. Emilia's father challenges the seducer to a duel, revealing his true identity as they raise their pistols, but Emilia and others rush in, she to announce both her conviction that the seducer is reformed and her determination to marry him. General rejoicing.

A not very plausible example of period Neapolitan opera semiseria (with spoken dialogue), the plot contains some Romantic elements (storms, a duel among tombs) but the score shows more evidence of tasteful craftsmanship than deeply felt inspiration. The 1828 revision involved the suppression of seven numbers, the addition of three, the borrowing of the aria-finale from *Alahor in Granata*, and the reshuffling of the seven that are common to both versions.

RECORDINGS 1. Kenny, Merritt, Bruscantini, Dolton, Geoffrey Mitchell Ch, Philharmonia O, Parry, Opera Rara, 1986: this presents both versions (without dialogue), booklet contains a fine essay by Jeremy Commons; 2. 1828 revision: Sutherland, Cantelo, McAlpine, Dowling, Liverpool Music Group Ch, Royal Liverpool PO, Pritchard, Voce, 1957: condensed, narrative replaces the spoken dialogue

EDITION 1828 rev. version: v.s., Schonenberger, [*c.* 1855]

Gabriella di Vergy

Opera seria in three (originally two) acts (2h 15m)
Libretto by Andrea Leone Tottola, after Dormont de Belloy's play *Gabrielle de Vergy* (1770), itself based on two 14th-century French tales, rev. possibly by the composer and others
Composed 1826, rev. 1838
PREMIERES 29 November 1869, Teatro San Carlo, Naples (as *Gabriella*); UK: 9 November 1978, Whitla Hall, Belfast (rev. version)

The history of *Gabriella* is unique among Donizetti's stage works. It was originally composed for his own experience and without a commission, the composer making his own version of the libretto Tottola wrote for Carafa's once famous *Gabriella di Vergy* (1816). It is significant as Donizetti's first attempt to set a tragic plot and write a death scene, giving thereby a striking premonition of something he was later to make one of his great specialities. In its original form the opera was never performed, though Donizetti borrowed several passages for inclusion in later operas. The work premiered posthumously in 1869 was based on Donizetti's opera but was, in effect, a pastiche, with alterations by other hands. The existence of the 1838 revision had scarcely been hinted at until the autograph was found at the Sterling Library, and this discovery formed the basis for the Belfast production and the recording.

Believing her beloved Raoul dead, Gabriella has married Fayel. When Raoul unexpectedly arrives as the king's emissary, Gabriella is much upset. Fayel's suspicions become sufficiently aroused for him to challenge Raoul to a duel and incarcerate his wife. To her cell, he brings an urn containing Raoul's still warm heart. Gabriella dies of the shock.

RECORDING Andrew, Arthur, Du Plessis, Tomlinson, Geoffrey Mitchell Ch, RPO, Francis, Opera Rara, 1978: the 1838 version, but contains excerpts of the 1826 original
MANUSCRIPTS original 1826 version: Civico Instituto Musicale Gaetano Donizetti; 1869 revision: Biblioteca S. Pietro a Maiella, Naples; 1838 revision: Sterling Library, London

Olivo e Pasquale

Opera buffa in two acts (2h)
Libretto by Jacopo Ferretti after Sografi's comedy *Olivo e Pasquale* (1794) with some material drawn from Sografi's *Il più bel giorno della Westfalia*
Composed 1826, rev. 1827
PREMIERE 7 January 1827, Teatro Valle, Rome; 1827 version: 1 September 1827, Teatro Nuovo, Naples; UK: 31 March 1832, King's Theatre, Haymarket, London

Isabella, the daughter of Olivo, a Lisbon merchant, loves the good-hearted Camillo, a shop boy, but her father has plans for her to marry Le Bross, a wealthy trader from Cadiz. When Le Bross arrives, Isabella confesses that she loves another, but she pretends that her beloved is a vain old fellow, Columella. Discovering that Isabella is intent on disobeying him, Olivo becomes enraged. Seeing the girl's despair, Le Bross gallantly offers to help her win her heart's desire. Following his plan, Isabella and Camillo threaten to kill themselves. They hurry out, whereupon shots are heard from offstage. Olivo's tender-hearted brother Pasquale faints, while Olivo is filled with remorse. When Isabella and Camillo re-enter, wreathed in smiles, Olivo gives them his blessing. There is a fine quartet and an engaging duet for Isabella and Le Bross.

RECORDING   Gibbs, Bizzo, Mastino, Bonelli, Sarti, Del Carlo, Ch della 'Polifonia lucchese', O of Opera Barga, Rigacci, Bongiovanni, 1980
EDITION   v.s., Schonenberger, 1856

Il borgomastro di Saardam
The Burgomaster of Saardam
Opera buffa in two acts (2h)
Libretto by Domenico Gilardoni, derived from the *livret* by Mélesville, Merle and de Boirie for Schaffner's *Le bourgmestre de Sardam, ou Les deux pierres* (1818)
Composed 1827
PREMIERE   19 August 1827, Teatro Nuovo, Naples

Disguised as Pietro Mikailoff, Tsar Peter (i.e. Peter the Great, who actually worked incognito in Holland and Deptford, London, 1697–8) is working as a lowly carpenter in the shipyards of Saardam. He has made friends with Pietro Flimann, also a Russian, who has deserted the army and is also employed as a carpenter. Flimann has fallen in love with the mayor's daughter Marietta, but his lowly status gives him few expectations of winning her, even though Mikailoff has offered to help. The mayor has learned that the tsar of Russia is working in disguise in the shipyard and comes to identify him. Receiving ambiguous answers from both Russians, who are both named Pietro, the mayor begins to wonder whether he has a pair of tsars on his hands. A messenger from Russia arrives to summon the tsar back to his duties. Before he leaves, the tsar confers a patent of nobility on Flimann, an honour that allows him to wed Marietta.

Donizetti's score has plenty of graceful facility, but little to engage one's interest for long. The same story was later set by Lortzing, as *Zar und Zimmerman* (1837).

RECORDING   Philippo, Langridge, Capecchi, van den Berg, Ch and O of Zaandam Opera, Schaap, MRF, 1973
EDITION   v.s., Schonenberger, 1856

Le convenienze ed inconvenienze teatrali
Theatrical Customs: Good and Bad
Farsa in one act (1h), later expanded to two acts (1h 40m)
Libretto by the composer, after two comedies by Antonio Simone Sografi, *Le convenienze teatrali* (1794), and *Le inconvenienze teatrali* (1800)
Composed 1827
PREMIERES   21 November 1827, Teatro Nuovo, Naples (in one act as *Le convenienze teatrali*); 20 April 1831, Milan (in two acts); US: 2 April 1966, Terre Haute, Indiana (as *An Unconventional Rehearsal*); UK: 9 October 1969, BBC broadcast (as *Upstage and Downstage*); 16 May 1972, Collegiate Theatre, London (Opera Rara; as *The Prima Donna's Mother is a Drag*)

Since its first 20th-century revival, this has been the most frequently performed of Donizetti's operas before *Anna Bolena*. A broad farce, it pokes fun at a rehearsal of an opera seria by a provincial Italian touring company. Its chief *clou* is presenting the seconda donna's mother as a baritone *en travesti*. (The idea for this impersonation came from Donizetti's memory of the night Tamburini assumed the indisposed prima donna's role in a performance of Mercadante's *Elisa e Claudio* in Palermo in 1825.) The characters include the harried impresario, the victimized composer, the capricious prima donna, her pretentious father (the *basso* of the troupe), as well as the formidable Mamm'Agata. The most amusing segments of the score include a hair-pulling duet for the prima donna and Mamm'Agata, the latter's 'audition' piece (a harrowingly misremembered version of the 'Willow Song' from Rossini's *Otello*), and part of the actual rehearsal. The two-act version strengthens the work by replacing the weaker pieces, including a lame *finaletto*, with stronger ones, and adding a new character in the person of a German tenor with a dim grasp of Italian.

RECORDINGS   two-act version: 1. Dessì, Perasso, Matteuzzi, Sioli, Alaimo, Ch del Teatro dell'Opera Giocosa, O Sinfonico Estense, Allemandi, Ars Nova, 1981; 2. Adani, Handt, Capecchi, Tadeo, Montarsolo, Cantori pisani, O of Milan Angelicum, Rigacci, Voce, 1963
EDITIONS   one-act version: v.s., Schonenberger, 1856; two-act version (with the inclusion of an aria from *Pia de' Tolomei*), Otos, [c. 1980]

L'esule di Roma, ossia Il proscritto (Settemio il proscritto)
The Exile from Rome
Opera seria in two acts (1h 30m)
Libretto by Domenico Gilardoni, after Luigi Marchionni's play *Il proscritto romano, ossia il leone del Caucaso* (c. 1820), derived from the play *Androcles, ou Le lion reconnaissant* by Louis Charles Caignez and Debotière (1804)
Composed 1827
PREMIERES   1 January 1828, Teatro San Carlo, Naples; UK: 2 February 1832, King's Theatre, Haymarket, London

L'esule di Roma enjoyed a vogue for about a decade, and it is one of the stronger scores of the pre-*Anna Bolena* phase of Donizetti's career. The plot concerns Settimio, who has been exiled from Rome, on false charges brought against him by Murena. Settimio loves Argelia, Murena's daughter, and defies death to return secretly to Rome to be with her. Murena's conscience is deeply troubled as Settimio can prove the falsity of the charges against him, and refrains from doing so only for his beloved Argelia's sake. Settimio is arrested and sentenced to be thrown to the lions. Murena is haunted by visions of Settimio's death in the jaws of the beasts. Word comes that one of the lions has recognized Settimio as one who had befriended him in the wilds and spared him. Settimio's release is ordered and Murena is pardoned; whereupon Settimio and Argelia are happily reunited.

Emotions are communicated with something close to vividness, and there is not a truly weak number in the score. Particularly notable are the trio that concludes Act I, Murena's 'mad' scene in Act II, 'Entra nel Circo', and Argelia's touching aria-finale, 'Morte! ah, pria che l'una uccidi'.

RECORDING Gasdia, Palacio, Alaimo, Ch dell'Opera Giocosa, Piacenza SO, De Bernart, Bongiovanni, 1986
EDITIONS v.ss., Ricordi, 1840; Egret House, 1982

Alina, regina di Golconda
Alina, Queen of Golconda
Opera buffa in two acts (2h 30m)
Libretto by Felice Romani, after Sedaine's text for Monsigny's *Aline, reine de Golconde* (1766), in turn after the story *La Reine de Golconde* by Stanislas-Jean de Bouffler (1761)
Composed 1828, rev. 1829
PREMIERES 12 May 1828, Teatro Carlo Felice, Genoa; rev. version: 10 December 1829, Teatro Valle, Rome

Until recently this engaging opera buffa had been neglected by the Donizetti revival. Endowed with a graceful libretto and containing much effective (though demanding) music, it is difficult to understand why this should be so.

The action takes place in French India during the 18th century. Alina, the Queen of Golconda, is being forced to accept the hand of Seide, when cannon shots reveal a French ship approaching the anchorage. Aboard it are Volmar and Belfiore, the long-separated husbands of Alina and her maid, Fiorina. These ladies in disguise visit the Frenchmen. Upset by this turn of events, Seide tries to rouse the people to revolt. Later, with the help of a sleeping potion, Alina and Fiorina deceive their husbands into believing they are back in France where first they met. When Seide has Alina imprisoned, she tries to give up her throne, but Seide insists she continue to reign as his consort. The French attack the palace, free Alina, capture Seide, and restore Alina to her royal status.

Donizetti revised the score for its Roman production in 1829, and this version was widely performed over the next 40 years. The finest music is in the exquisite quartet in Act I, but it also has a well-wrought mid-point finale. Besides, there is a stirring aria for Seide in Act I and an ingratiating aria-finale.

RECORDING Dessì, Tabiadon, Blake, Coni, Ch of Teatro Regio, Parma, Arturo Toscanini O of Emilia Romagna, Allemandi, Nuova Era, 1987
EDITIONS v.ss., Ricordi, 1842; Kalmus 1984

Il giovedì grasso
(*Il nuovo Pourceaugnac*)
Carnival Thursday
Farsa in one act (1h)
Libretto by Domenico Gilardoni, after a vaudeville by Eugène Scribe and Charles Gaspard Delestre-Poirson, *Le nouveau Pourceaugnac* (1817)
Composed 1828–9
PREMIERES 26 February 1829, Teatro del Fondo, Naples; Ireland: 23 October 1970, Theatre Royal, Wexford

Nina is in love with Teodoro, but her father, the Colonel, wants her to marry Ernesto. Monsieur and Madame Piquet resolve to help her, and plan a trick, based on Molière's *Monsieur de Pourceaugnac*, in which a city slicker is outwitted by resourceful country folk. When Ernesto arrives, Monsieur Piquet, claiming himself to be Sigismondo, hails the newcomer as an old friend, but Ernesto outwits him, by pretending to recognize Madame Piquet, now calling herself Camilla, as an old flame and hints at their supposed rendezvous, a disclosure that infuriates Piquet–Sigismondo. Eventually, Ernesto persuades the Colonel to permit Nina to marry Teodoro; the Piquets are also reconciled.

A genuinely engaging comedy of character, *Il giovedì grasso* has much to recommend it: the *introduzione* develops into a charming quintet; Piquet as Sigismondo sings a tarantella; Nina's aria-finale turns into a neat vaudeville praising Carnival.

RECORDING Rizzoli, Oncina, Catalani, Loomis, Ch and O of Swiss Radio, Loehrer, UORC, 1963
EDITION v.s., Schonenberger, 1856

Elisabetta al castello di Kenilworth
(*Il castello di Kenilworth*)
Elizabeth at Kenilworth Castle (*Kenilworth Castle*)
Opera seria in three acts (2h 15m)
Libretto by Andrea Leone Tottola, based on Gaetano Barbieri's play *Elisabetta al castello di Kenilworth* (1824), in turn adapted from Scribe's text for Auber's *Leicester, ou Le château de Kenilworth* (1823), derived in turn from Sir Walter Scott's *Kenilworth* (1821)
Composed 1829, rev. 1830 as *Il castello di Kenilworth*
PREMIERES 6 July 1829, Teatro San Carlo, Naples; rev. version: 24 June 1830, Teatro San Carlo, Naples; UK: 30 April 1818, King's Theatre, Haymarket, London
CAST Elisabetta *s*, Amelia *s*, Leicester *t*, Warney originally *t*, rev. as *bar*, Fanny *s*; *satb* chorus of courtiers
FULL ORCHESTRA

The twenty-sixth of Donizetti's operas, *Il castello di Kenilworth*, as this work has been referred to since the composer revised it in 1830, is the first of Donizetti's operas to have two important female roles.

SYNOPSIS
The plot deals with Leicester's secret marriage to Amelia (Amy Robsart) and Warney's villainous attempts, first to seduce her and, later, to murder her. Act I As the queen's current favourite, Leicester is anxious to conceal his true relationship to Amelia. Amelia confronts Leicester to protest at his keeping her in seclusion, declaring she would prefer him to kill her rather than deprive her of his love.

Act II When Elizabeth discovers the pair are, in fact, married, she is at first furious and demands vengeance. Leicester offers himself as the queen's victim, but Elisabetta insists that Amelia should be punished.

Act III Warney comes to the cell where Amelia is confined, intending to poison her, but the timely arrival of Leicester spares her. When the queen is apprised of these developments (as befits a traditional opera seria with a happy ending) she finally relents, ordering the imprisonment of Warney and bestowing her gracious blessing on Leicester and Amelia.

One of his most compact scores, *Il castello di Kenilworth* contains effective arias for the two women and a powerful quartet at the end of Act II. The chorus that greets the queen's arrival in Act I was later adapted by Donizetti to anticipate the entrance of Dr Dulcamara in *L'elisir d'amore*.

RECORDINGS 1. J. Price, Kenny, Arthur, Du Plessis, Opera Rara Ch, Philomusica of London, Francis, MRF, 1977; 2. Nevia, Mazzola, Kundlak, B. Anderson, Striuli, Fotti, Milan Ch and O of RAI, Ricordi, 1989
EDITION v.s., Schonenberger, 1856

I pazzi per progetto
Madmen by Design

Farsa in one act (1h 15m)
Libretto by Domenico Gilardoni, after the play by Giovanni Carlo di Cozzenza (1824), derived in turn from Eugène Scribe's and Charles-Gaspard Delestre-Poirson's *Une visite à Bedlam* (1818) via the libretto to Bertini's *Una visita a Bedlam* (1824)
Composed 1829–30
PREMIERE 7 February 1830, Teatro del Fondo, Naples

The slender plot takes place in Darlemont's Parisian mental hospital. Norina and her husband Colonel Blinval, who have been separated by his military service, arrive there; each in turn pretends to be mad in their efforts to test one another's faithfulness. There are others: Frank, a comic servant; Eustachio, an ex-trumpeter in Blinval's regiment, now posing as an alienist; and Cristina, who had been in love with the Colonel, but whose guardian, Venanziano, is now threatening to have her committed so that he can get his hands on her money. Everything turns out for the best, with Blinval and Cristina reconciled.

RECORDING Rigacci, Cicogna, Polidori, Monreale, Fissore, Arturo Toscanini SO of Emilia Romagna, Rigacci, Bongiovanni, 1988
EDITIONS v.ss., Schonenberger, 1856; Otos, 1977

Il diluvio universale
The Great Flood

Azione tragica-sacra in three acts (2h 30m)
Libretto by Domenico Gilardoni derived from Francesco Ringhieri's play *Il diluvio universale* (1788), Lord Byron's drama *Heaven and Earth* (1822) and Thomas Moore's poem *The Loves of the Angels* (1823)
Composed 1829–30, rev. 1833
PREMIERES 28 February 1830, Teatro San Carlo, Naples; rev. version: 17 January 1834, Teatro Carlo Felice, Genoa

Cadmo, Satrap of Senaar, becomes enraged when his wife Sela tries to protect Noah and his sons, who are building the ark. Ada, Sela's treacherous confidante, aspiring to supplant her as Cadmo's wife, tells him that Sela is enamoured of Jafet, one of Noah's sons. Ada rejoices when Cadmo renounces his wife and condemns her and Noah's family to death. Noah warns Cadmo not to provoke Jehovah's wrath, predicting a great flood. Sela interrupts Cadmo's marriage to Ada, desperate because she cannot give

up her son. Cadmo offers to take her back if she will renounce Jehovah. Terrified, Sela does so and falls dead. A furious storm breaks, and all flee to save themselves. In the final scene, Noah's ark is seen riding the waves, unscathed.

The score contains a number of self-borrowings. Noah's prayer is an early version of the regimental song from *La fille du régiment*. Its main interest, however, is that it shows Donizetti's attempt to absorb the lessons of Rossini's *Moïse*.

RECORDING Hayashi, Dupuy, Garaventa, Giaiotti, Ch and O of Teatro Comunale, Genoa, Latham-Koenig, Voce, 1973
EDITION v.s., Schonenberger, 1856

Imelda de' Lambertazzi

Opera seria in two acts (2h)
Libretto by Andrea Leone Tottola, after Sperduti's five-act tragedy *Imelda* (1825)
Composed 1830
PREMIERE 23 August 1830, Teatro San Carlo, Naples

The Lambertazzi and Geremei families of Bologna are on opposite sides of the Guelf–Ghibelline feud. Imelda Lambertazzi loves Bonifacio, the heir of the Geremei. When he proposes peace, sealed by his marriage to Imelda, her father and brother are enraged. Bonifacio makes a last effort to see Imelda, but is stabbed by her brother with a poisoned dagger. Begging her father's forgiveness, Imelda too dies.

Imelda is one of Donizetti's early settings of a story fraught with tragic violence; Imelda's death scene is truly poignant. The role of Bonifacio was written for the baritone Tamburini, for whom the composer provided an elaborate aria.

RECORDING Sovilla, D'Auria, Tenzi, Martin, Swiss Italian Radiotelevision Ch and O, Andreae, Nuova Era, 1989

Anna Bolena
Anne Boleyn

Tragedia lirica in two acts (3h 15m)
Libretto by Felice Romani, after Ippolito Pindemonte's translation (1816) of Marie-Joseph de Chenier's play *Henri VIII* (1791) and Alessandro Pepoli's play *Anna Bolena* (1788)
Composed 1830
PREMIERES 26 December 1830, Teatro Carcano, Milan; UK: 8 July 1831, King's Theatre, Haymarket, London; US: 12 November 1839, Théâtre d'Orléans, New Orleans
CAST Anna Bolena *s*, Giovanna Seymour *ms*, Smeton *ms*, Percy *t*, Enrico VIII *b*, Rochefort *b*, Hervey *t*; *satb* chorus of courtiers
FULL ORCHESTRA including hp; onstage: 2 hn, banda, drums

Anna Bolena established Donizetti among the leading composers of his day and introduced him to the audiences of Paris and London. It used to be a critical commonplace that this work marked a watershed in Donizetti's *oeuvre* and that here, in his thirtieth opera, he found at long last his personal style. Today, however, as more and more of his earlier works have been revived, *Anna Bolena* appears, rather, to be the logical culmination of tendencies implicit in his development. The critical factor seems to have been that Donizetti had at his disposal a superior libretto, one that moved him

Set design by Alessandro Sanquirico for Anna Bolena *(Milan, 1830)*

deeply. He also had the incentive of striving to win over the Milanese, till then unimpressed by successes won elsewhere. The element of consistency in Donizetti's development can be demonstrated by his having adapted an aria from his first opera, *Enrico di Borgogna*, as the basis of Anna's famous *larghetto* in the Tower scene ('Al dolce guidami'). The work retained its currency for nearly 50 years and then lapsed into oblivion, until its successful revival at La Scala with Maria Callas provided the incentive for performances elsewhere.

SYNOPSIS
Act I Scene 1: The courtiers suspect that the king's fickleness bodes ill for Anna, an impression strengthened by the conscience-stricken Giovanna Seymour. Anna enters and bids her musician Smeton sing, but he, infatuated with Anna, offers an amorous ditty, reminding her of Percy, her first love ('Come innocente, giovane'). Anna retires, leaving Seymour alone; soon she is joined by the king. She wants this to be their last meeting, declaring that honour forbids the continuation of their relationship. Accused of being more in love with the throne than with him, Seymour begs the king to free her conscience ('Ah! qual sia cercar non oso'). Scene 2: Unknown to Anna, the king has laid her a trap, by arranging a hunting party at which she will unexpectedly encounter Percy, returned from exile.

Percy questions Anna's brother, Lord Rochefort, about the rumours of Anna's unhappiness ('Da quel diche, lei perduta'). When the hunt appears, Percy approaches to thank the king, but he withdraws his hand; when Percy kisses Anna's hand, she feels his tears of gratitude on it ('Io sentii sulla mia mano'). As the hunt moves on, all hail this auspicious day. Enrico is happy too; but he has been hunting a different prey. Scene 3: Smeton surreptitiously enters the queen's apartment, carrying her miniature in a locket. Hearing someone approach, Smeton hides. Rochefort asks Anna to grant Percy a brief interview. When Percy appears, Anna's admission that the king now hates her prompts him to declare his love ('S'ei t'abborre, io t'amo ancora'). Frightened, Anna firmly refuses his request to see her again. Percy draws his sword, and Smeton, misinterpreting Percy's intentions, rushes out, drawing his. Anna faints. The king arrives, enraged, and summons guards. Smeton offers to die as proof of the compromised queen's innocence, and when he tears open his jacket, Anna's miniature falls out at the king's feet. Anna begins an eloquent sextet ('In quegli sguardi impresso'); she wants to explain, but the king declares she must defend herself in court. Anna is shocked ('Anna! ai giudici!') and realizes that her fate is already sealed.

Act II Scene 1: In Anna's apartment in the Tower, her ladies comment on Anna's plight ('Oh!

dove mai ne andarono'). Anna appears and prays for consolation. Seymour enters to inform her that the king has promised to spare her life if she will acknowledge her guilt. Anna's astonishment turns to fury when she hears Seymour beg it not only in the king's name but in that of the woman who will succeed her on the throne. Anna calls on heaven to punish her rival. When Seymour tearfully prostrates herself, Anna realizes the identity of her rival and orders her to leave, but Seymour cannot contain her remorse ('Dal mio cor punita io sono'). Scene 2: Hervey announces that Smeton has confessed to adultery with Anna, having been told that such a declaration would spare her life. Anna and Percy are led in. When Enrico tells her of Smeton's confession, Anna turns the charge of adultery back on him. Percy is willing to die to spare her life, reminding her that she was once married to him. They are led off, leaving Enrico furious. Seymour comes to beg him to forget her and be merciful. Scene 3: In the Tower, Percy tells Rochefort that he should live to defend Anna's memory ('Vivi tu'). Anna longs for her childhood home and first love ('Al dolce guidami'). Summoned to the scaffold, Anna sings a prayer ('Cielo, a' miei lunghi spasimi'). Cannon announce the king's marriage to Seymour, and Anna calls for heaven's mercy on the guilty couple ('Coppia iniqua!').

Romani clearly outlined the conflicts between the characters, giving Donizetti many opportunities for psychologically apposite expressiveness. This is particularly true in the great duet for Seymour and Enrico in Act I and in that for Anna and Seymour in the opening scene of Act II. The contrast between the devious menace of Enrico and the straightforward remorse of Seymour is reinforced by the unusual device of having Seymour repeat one of her melodies from the *larghetto* section in the *cabaletta*, a convincing expression of her failure to be convinced by Enrico's arguments. In the scene between the women, the emotional range is even greater, each shift of feeling being persuasively characterized as this pair, who have every reason to distrust each other, come to a *rapprochement*.

From the start of his career, Donizetti had demonstrated a considerable flair for writing ensembles, more persuasive in the slow movements than in the rapid pendants, where he was as yet restricted by the conventional *settinari* (seven-syllable verses). Especially effective is the canonic quintet, 'Io sentii sulla mia mano' (adapted from the score of *Otto mesi in due ore*, 1827) near the close of Act I, Scene 2. Even more so is the sextet 'In quegli sguardi impresso' in the next scene on Anna's regaining consciousness, where the interweaving of the parts creates a mood of welling intensity. On almost as high a level is the trio for Anna, Percy and Enrico in Act II, Scene 2, 'Fin dall'età più tenera', where the indignation of Anna, the nostalgia of Percy, and the fury of the king are neatly contrasted.

The musical climax of the work comes in the Tower scene, which consists primarily of two full-scale arie-finali. Percy's 'Vivi tu' is full of pathos, but

that mood is given even deeper expression in Anna's 'Al dolce guidami', with its purling cor anglais obbligato and yearning figurations. The *tempo di mezzo* of her scena flowers into a lyrical outpouring at 'Cielo, a' miei lunghi spasimi' (a variant of the melody of 'Home, Sweet Home'), with the solo voice supported by three other voices and a chamber-size accompaniment. The *cabaletta*, 'Coppia iniqua!', conveys with its driving rhythms and succession of trills the emotional delirium that brings Anna to the point of death.

RECORDINGS 1. Sills, Verrett, Burrows, Plishka, John Alldis Ch, LSO, Rudel, ABC, 1972: an uncut recording with strong contributions by the women, particularly Verrett; 2. Sutherland, Mentzer, Hadley, Ramey, WNO Ch and O, Bonynge, London, 1987: although Sutherland is past her prime, she is stylistically sound, but Ramey is the star
EDITION v.s., Ricordi, [c. 1957]; rp, 1986

Gianni di Parigi
Opera comica in two acts (1h 45m)
Libretto by Felice Romani, after Claude de St-Just's text for Boieldieu's *Jean de Paris* (1812)
Composed 1831
PREMIERE 10 September 1839, La Scala, Milan

The page Oliviero arrives at an inn to order a fine dinner for his master, Gianni of Paris. When the innkeeper explains that the inn has been booked by the the Princess of Navarre, Oliviero insists that his hostelry should be open to all travellers. Gianni arrives and orders his page not to reveal his true identity. By offering to double the sum the princess has put down, Gianni is accepted as a guest. When the princess arrives, her seneschal is outraged to find her quarters already occupied. The princess, however, graciously accepts Gianni's invitation to share his dinner, later confessing that she had guessed his true identity as the Dauphin of France and her betrothed.

Gianni di Parigi contains some melodies redolent of youthful romance. The aria-finale for the princess is delightful.

RECORDING Serra, Zilio, Morino, Romero, Fissore, O of Teatro Donizetti, Bergamo, Cillario, Nuova Era (live), 1988
EDITION v.s., Ricordi, 1843

Fausta
Opera seria in two acts (2h 30m)
Libretto by Domenico Gilardoni (inc.), completed by the composer
Composed 1831, rev. 1832
PREMIERES 12 January 1832, Teatro San Carlo, Naples; rev. version: 28 December 1833, La Fenice, Venice; UK: 29 May 1841, London

The plot, though set in imperial Rome, resembles that of Racine's *Phèdre*. Fausta, the second wife of the Emperor Costantino, has developed a passion for her stepson, Crispo. She confesses her feelings to the innocent young man. Interrupted by Costantino, Crispo is speechless when Fausta accuses him of lusting after her. Fausta's father, the deposed Emperor Massimiano, plots to undo Costantino.

Knowing this, Crispo sets out sword in hand after the conspirators, only to find himself face to face with Costantino, whereupon before the whole Roman Senate Massimiano charges the young man with attempted parricide. Costantino's heart breaks as he is forced to sign his son's death sentence, which Massimiano snatches up to carry out at once. Seeing no way to stop the execution, Fausta takes poison. Learning of Massimiano's plot, the emperor is too late to save his son. The dying Fausta confesses her lie to Costantino.

Fausta is on a grander scale than any previous Donizetti opera. The work opens with an extended multi-sectioned *introduzione*. Fausta's finely expressive aria-finale (the composer's contribution to the text) is the first great number he created for his favourite prima donna, Ronzi De Begnis.

RECORDING Kabaivanska, Giacomini, Bruson, Roni, Ch and O of Rome Opera, Oren, UORC, 1981
EDITION v.s., Ricordi, [c. 1832]

Ugo, Conte di Parigi

Opera seria in two acts (3h)
Libretto by Felice Romani, after Hippolyte Bis's play *Blanche d'Aquitaine, ou Le dernier des Carlovingiens* (1827)
Composed 1831–2
PREMIERE 13 March 1832, La Scala, Milan

Ugo was altered by the censors to such an extent that Romani refused to put his name to the libretto. The plot concerns the machinations of Bianca, betrothed to Louis V, but in love with Ugo (Hugues Capet). She is consumed by jealousy when she learns that her sister Adelia loves Ugo and by fury when she discovers the king sanctions their marriage. In front of the king, Bianca declares her love for Ugo and demands he confirm it. Ugo remains silent, but Louis orders that he be imprisoned. Ugo's partisans rebel, but Ugo suppresses the revolt and acknowledges that he has designs upon neither the throne nor the royal fiancée. While Ugo is being married to Adelia in a nearby chapel, Bianca takes the poison she had originally intended for the king and dies, declaring herself avenged.

Because of the delay caused by revising the libretto, the premiere of *Ugo* came late in the season at La Scala that had opened with the premiere of Bellini's *Norma*. Although sung by the same cast, including Pasta and Giulia Grisi, that had triumphed in *Norma*, *Ugo* made only a dim impression with its obscurely motivated plot, but Donizetti's music won a *succès d'estime*. *Ugo* is unusual in that it is dominated by ensembles rather than solo arias. These ensembles reveal clearly Donizetti's unflagging melodic gift and his skill at developing musical ideas with increasing intensity. Donizetti inserted several passages from it into later scores, among them *Sancia di Castiglia*, *Il furioso*, *Parisina*, and the 1838 *Gabriella di Vergy*, when he became convinced that *Ugo* had a scant future on the stage.

RECORDING J. Price, Jones, Arthur, Du Plessis, Geoffrey Mitchell Ch, Philharmonia O, Francis, Opera Rara, 1977

EDITION v.s., Ricordi, [1832]

L'elisir d'amore

The Love Potion
Opera comica in two acts (2h)
Libretto by Felice Romani, after Scribe's text for Auber's *Le philtre* (1831), in turn after Silvio Malaperta's *Il filtro*
Composed 1832
PREMIERES 12 May 1832, Teatro Canobbiana, Milan; UK: 10 December 1836, Lyceum, London; US: 18 June 1838, Park Theater, New York
CAST Adina *s*, Nemorino *t*, Sergeant Belcore *bar*, Dr Dulcamara *buffo*, Giannetta *s*
ORCHESTRATION 2 fl/picc, 2 ob, 2 cl, 2 bsn, 2 hn, 2 tpt, 3 trbn, timp, bd, hp, str; offstage: sd; onstage: cornet, banda

L'elisir d'amore is the earliest of Donizetti's operas never to have left the standard repertoire and during his lifetime it was the most frequently performed of his works. Although Romani's libretto is at times a literal translation of Scribe's text for Auber's *Le philtre*, it contains a number of significant passages that have no counterpart in the French libretto: the Adina–Nemorino duet, 'Chiedi all'aura', the tenor's 'Adina, credimi', and his famous 'Una furtiva lagrima'. All of these additions contribute an element of pathos that Donizetti believed to be a necessary constituent of truly satisfying comedy. Another modification was moving the setting of Scribe's plot from the Basque countryside to rural northern Italy, Donizetti's native soil.

SYNOPSIS
Act I The gentle Nemorino is hopelessly in love with Adina, who amuses the harvesters by reading to them the story of Queen Iseult and the love potion ('Della crudele Isotta'). Sergeant Belcore and his platoon enter and he gallantly presents Adina with a

Fanny Persiani (Adina) and Antonio Tamburini (Belcore) in L'elisir d'amore *(London, 1847)*

nosegay ('Come Paride vezzoso'). Nemorino is upset by Adina's apparent susceptibility to Belcore. She tells a disconsolate Nemorino that she will never love him ('Chiedi all'aura'); he protests that he would die for her. The quack Dr Dulcamara arrives to peddle his nostrums ('Udite, udite, o rustici!'). Nemorino, remembering the story of Iseult, buys a bottle of love potion, which he is assured will work in 24 hours ('Obbligato, ah! si obbligato'). Tipsy from the elixir, which in reality is Bordeaux, Nemorino gains in confidence ('Esulti pur la barbara'), but his spirits are crushed when he hears Adina agree to marry Belcore that very evening ('Adina, credimi').

Act II The wedding feast is under way, and Dulcamara sings a mock barcarolle with the bride-to-be ('Io son ricco, tu sei bella'). Adina forestalls the notary, however, since Nemorino is not present to witness the ceremony. Penniless, Nemorino is desperate to buy more elixir, and on impulse he allows Belcore to enlist him into the army, because an enrollee receives a bounty ('Venti scudi'). Giannetta and the village girls have heard that Nemorino's rich uncle has died, leaving him his heir, and they fawn over him, a response that Nemorino attributes to the elixir. The sight of these attentions astonishes Adina. From Dulcamara she learns the story of Nemorino and the potion, but she assures him her own charms are a more potent weapon in winning a man ('Quanto amore'). Nemorino has observed that Adina has been affected by seeing him with the girls, but he would rather die than live without her ('Una furtiva lagrima'). Adina tells him that she has bought back his enlistment ('Prendi: per me sei libero') and at last confesses that she loves him. The village turns out to celebrate their betrothal, while Dulcamara takes his leave, firmly convinced that his potion has unexpected powers.

Donizetti's score alternates sparkling tunes with emotional melodies. There is not a weak number in the whole opera. The patter song for Dulcamara has an orotund garrulity about it that is irresistible. The scene between Nemorino and the village girls can seem a comic anticipation of that between Parsifal and the Flower Maidens. Donizetti's gift for pungent characterization animates the duet between the smarmy Dulcamara and Adina, confident of her own female wiles. The tenderness of the first Adina–Nemorino duet and their successive arias in Act II, particularly Nemorino's 'Una furtiva lagrima', with its haunting bassoon obbligato and climactic shifts from minor to major mode, are the jewels of this delightful score. Unlike most opere buffe, L'elisir presents us with two characters that develop before our eyes. Nemorino learns to assert himself, and Adina comes to see that a constant heart is preferable to the fickle one of a practised womanizer in uniform.

RECORDINGS 1. Sutherland, Pavarotti, Cossa, Malas, Ambrosian Singers, ECO, Bonynge, Decca, 1970; including a cabaletta, 'Nel dolce incanto', written for Malibran, which did not form a permanent part of the score; 2. Cotrubas, Domingo, Wixell, G. Evans, Ch and O of Royal Opera,

Covent Garden, Pritchard, CBS, 1977: Pritchard's is the more lively theatrical show, Bonynge's the more idiomatically sung [A.B.]
EDITIONS f.s., Ricordi, 1916; v.ss., Ricordi, 1832; 1869; Schirmer, 1941; study s., Ricordi, 1962; rp, 1974; 1980

Sancia di Castiglia

Opera seria in two acts (2h)
Libretto by Pietro Salatino
Composed 1832
PREMIERE 4 November 1832, Teatro San Carlo, Naples

The ambitious Moor Ircano hopes to marry Sancia, as recompense for his military assistance. Receiving word that her son and heir Garzia has died in battle, Sancia is eager to console herself, even though her counsellors are unanimously opposed to the match. Garzia arrives after a narrow escape from death and demands that his regent mother restore the throne to him. Fearing his own designs on Castille are about to be thwarted, Ircano urges the impressionable Sancia to poison Garzia. When he raises the chalice of poison to his lips, the remorseful Sancia snatches it away and drains it.

Sancia was intended by Donizetti as another vehicle for the soprano Ronzi De Begnis. Working with an uninspired librettist, he found himself hampered, but there are moments in the score that attest to his vivid sense of musical theatre. The musical high point is a grandiose aria-finale.

RECORDING Bandelli, Cicogna, Costanzo, De Grandis, Ch and O of Teatro Donizetti, Bergamo, R. Abbado, Voce, 1984
EDITION v.s., Ricordi, 1833

Il furioso all'isola di San Domingo
The Madman on the Island of San Domingo

Opera semiseria in three acts (2h 30m)
Libretto by Jacopo Ferretti, after an Italian play (author unknown), Il furioso all'isola di S. Domingo (1820), but ultimately derived from Cervantes's Don Quixote, Book 1, chapters 23–7 (1605)
Composed 1832
PREMIERES 2 January 1833, Teatro Valle, Rome; UK: 17 December 1836, Lyceum, London; US: 4 June 1978, Dock Street Theater, Charleston; 7 August 1979, Kennedy Center, Washington DC

Along with Linda di Chamonix this is the most successful of Donizetti's semiseria operas. It includes a buffo role, Kaidama, who provides a tragi-comic dimension to the action. The entrance aria of the title character, Cardenio (the first of Donizetti's parts written for Ronconi), 'Raggio d'amor parea', has an ensemble for its cabaletta. The slow section of the first finale, 'Ah! un mar di lagrime' is comparable with the famous example in Lucia di Lammermoor.

The mad Cardenio is on a Caribbean island, where he has fled believing his wife Eleonora to have been unfaithful to him. A shipwreck in a tropical hurricane brings her to the shore. After many vicissitudes, including his trying to stab Eleonora in a jealous rage and later, when he has recognized her, leaping into the sea (a shock that restores his reason), Cardenio proposes that they should shoot one another. When people come carrying torches, Cardenio sees that

Eleonora aims her pistol at her own heart. Finally persuaded that she truly loves him, he embraces her. The element of pathos that ran so deep in Donizetti finds memorable expression in this score.

RECORDINGS   1. Serra, Canonici, Antonucci, Coviello, Francesco Cilea Ch, Piacenza SO, Rizzi, Bongiovanni, 1987; 2. Talarico, Reyes, Colmagro, Luchetti, Borgato, C. Williams, Ch and O Teatro Verdi, Trieste, Bruno Campanella, Music Heritage, 1973
EDITIONS   v.ss., Ricordi, 1833; Latte, c. 1845; Otos, c. 1980

Parisina

Opera seria in three acts (2h 15m)
Libretto by Felice Romani, after Byron's *Parisina* (1815)
Composed 1833
PREMIERES   17 March 1833, Teatro Pergola, Florence; US: 4 June 1837, Charles Street Theater, New Orleans; UK: 1 June 1838, Her Majesty's Theatre, Haymarket, London

Azzo, Duke of Ferrara, is consumed by jealousy; this has already led to the death of his first wife, Matilde. His second wife, Parisina, had lost her heart to Ugo before her father forced her into a loveless marriage with Azzo. Without the duke's consent, Ugo returns from exile to participate in a tourney and, seeing Parisina again, feels all the former attraction. That night Azzo overhears Parisina murmur Ugo's name in her sleep. Furiously he awakens her and forces her to confess that she loves Ugo. Azzo condemns Ugo to death, and even the revelation by Ernesto, who has brought up Ugo as his own son, that the young man is Azzo's son by Matilde cannot soften the duke's heart. Forced by her cruel husband to see Ugo's lifeless body, Parisina dies of grief.

In *Parisina* there are not only vocally grateful arias and duets, but the quartet in the first finale is a major achievement. The high point of the score, however, is Parisina's *romanza* before she goes to bed and the ferocious duet with Azzo that ensues.

RECORDING   Caballé, Pruett, L. Quilico, Morris, Opera O of New York, Queler, Bongiovanni, 1974
EDITIONS   f.s., facsimile of autograph manuscript, Philip Gossett and Charles Rosen (eds), Garland (*Early Romantic Opera*, vol. 25), 1981; v.ss., Ricordi, 1833, 1911; *rp*, Belwin-Mills, [c. 1979]

Torquato Tasso

Opera semiseria in three acts (3h)
Libretto by Jacopo Ferretti, after Giovanni Rossini's *Torquato Tasso* (1832), and secondarily from the plays *Torquato Tasso* by Goldoni (1755) and *Tasso* by Goethe (1809)
Composed 1833
PREMIERES   9 September 1833, Teatro Valle, Rome; UK: 3 March 1840, Her Majesty's Theatre, Haymarket, London

Tasso is the second of the roles Donizetti composed for the baritone Giorgio Ronconi. Long having wanted to pay homage to Tasso, the famous Italian poet who had connections with his native Bergamo, Donizetti suggested the subject to his librettist.

Tasso is in love with the Duchess Eleonora d'Este, but the course of his passion is hampered by the difference in their stations and by the fact she is married. Tasso is betrayed by a rival, who arranges an interview between the lovers that is overheard by the duke. The duke declares that Tasso must be mad and should be put away. Seven years later, courtiers come to tell Tasso that he is free and is to be crowned poet laureate. He inquires after Eleonora and is grief-stricken to discover that she has died. Deranged by grief, Tasso imagines he can see her, while the bystanders tell him to think of his approaching honour and glory.

The brief final act, for baritone and chorus, is the apex of the score. It was often performed as a concert item.

RECORDING   Serra, Palacio, Coviello, Alaimo, Ch and O of Teatro Comunale, Genoa, De Bernart, Bongiovanni, 1985
EDITION   v.ss., Ricordi, c. 1835

Lucrezia Borgia

Opera seria in a prologue and two acts (2h 15m)
Libretto by Felice Romani, after Victor Hugo's play *Lucrèce Borgia* (1832)
Composed 1833; ending rev. 1839 and 1841/2
PREMIERES   26 December 1833, La Scala, Milan; UK: 6 June 1839, Her Majesty's Theatre, Haymarket, London; first rev. version: 11 January 1840, La Scala, Milan; 31 October 1840, Théâtre-Italien, Paris (original version trans. as *La rinnegata*); 31 March 1842, Théâtre de Versailles, Paris (rev. as *Nizza di Grenade*); US: 11 May 1843, American Theater, New Orleans
CAST   Lucrezia Borgia s, Gennaro t, Maffio Orsini ms, Alfonso b, 3 t, 4 b; satb chorus of maskers, spies, guards, nobles
FULL ORCHESTRA   offstage: bells, banda

Because of its sensational plot, *Lucrezia Borgia* made its way slowly in Italy at first, but by 1840 it had established itself as one of Donizetti's most durable scores. After the opera's Paris premiere in October 1840, Hugo sued successfully for plagiarism against the French translation of Romani's libretto. For several seasons, first on 16 January 1843, *Lucrezia* was performed at the Théâtre-Italien in a revised version as *La rinnegata*, the action transferred to Turkey.

SYNOPSIS
Prologue   In Venice Gennaro is enjoying Carnival with Maffio and his other friends. Gennaro is attracted by the tender concern of a beautiful woman, but when his friends unmask her he is dismayed to learn that she is the infamous Lucrezia Borgia.

Act I   In Ferrara, Duke Alfonso suspects that his wife Lucrezia is having an affair with a young man who is, in fact, her son by a previous marriage. Gennaro lops off the initial letter of her last name from the crest on the façade of her *palazzo*, leaving the word 'orgia' – an orgy. Unaware who has so insulted her, Lucrezia insists her honour be avenged. Gennaro, brought in as the culprit, is administered poison by Alfonso, but Lucrezia gives him an antidote and urges him to leave Ferrara.

Act II   Maffio and his friends look forward to a ball at Princess Negroni's. He sings a *brindisi*, but then sinister voices sing of death. The young men seek to escape, but Lucrezia appears, announcing she has poisoned them all for their insults. Horrified to see Gennaro among them, she has the others led away. She swears she never meant her vengeance to extend to him, but he refuses her antidote and dies, horrified in turn when she tells him she is his mother.

Donizetti was unhappy at ending his opera with a *cabaletta* for Lucrezia, sung over the corpse of the son she has herself poisoned; but Méric-Lalande, the original Lucrezia, insisted on her prerogatives as a prima donna, which included a complete aria-finale. For La Scala in 1840, he removed the offending *cabaletta* and supplied a touching arioso for the dying Gennaro. For Grisi in Paris, he added a *cabaletta* to her (formerly) one-movement aria in the prologue, and an aria for the tenor in Act II, Scene 1, and cut the concluding *cabaletta* to a single statement.

There is much fine music in *Lucrezia*. The septet of the unmasking at the close of the prologue works up to a powerful climax. The Act I trio for Lucrezia, Gennaro and Alfonso was to remain in the back of Verdi's memory and the extended dialogue for Astolfo and Rustighello over an orchestral melody is the prototype of the episode between Rigoletto and Sparafucile. The best-known number in the score is Orsini's bumptious *brindisi* in Act II, 'Il segreto per esser felice', but greater intensity is to be found in the anguished figurations of Lucrezia's exquisitely wrought 'M'odi, ah m'odi' in the final scene. With Gennaro's final arioso, 'Madre, se ognor lontano', Donizetti found the idiom to express the tragic persona of the tenor.

RECORDINGS   1. Caballé, Verrett, Kraus, Flagello, RCA Italiana Opera Ch and O, Perlea, Victor, 1966: this includes Lucrezia's *cabaletta* added to the prologue and uses the original version of the aria-finale; 2. Sutherland, Horne, Aragall, Wixell, London Opera Ch, National PO, Bonynge, Decca, 1977: this recording includes an aria, 'T'amo quel dama un angelo', inserted for the tenor Ivanov before the Gennaro–Maffio duet in Act II, and inserts Gennaro's dying arioso into the original version of the finale
EDITIONS   f.s., Ricordi, [c. 1895]; v.ss., Ricordi, 1834, 1859; Latte, [c. 1840]

Rosmonda d'Inghilterra
Rosamund of England

Opera seria in two acts (1h 45m)
Libretto by Felice Romani, a revision of that set by Coccia (1829)
Composed 1834, partly rev. 1837, as *Eleonora di Gujenna*
PREMIERES   27 February 1834, Teatro Pergola, Florence; UK: 11 October 1975, Queen Elizabeth Hall, London (concert)

Enrico II, King of England, returns from the Irish wars, eager to see Rosmonda Clifford, whom he has wooed under the alias of Edegardo, tired of the jealous shrewishness of his wife, Eleanora of Aquitaine. The queen, however, learns the identity of her rival from the page Arturo, himself enamoured of Rosmonda. The king determines to divorce Eleanora and marry Rosmonda, in spite of the opposition of various lords, including Clifford,

Rosmonda's father and Enrico's former tutor. Rosmonda, who has been kept in seclusion at Woodstock, receives a visit from Eleanora, and the queen stabs her rival, who expires in her father's arms.

Some of the most effective vocal writing in this score is found in Rosmonda's brilliant *sortita*, a brace of arias that Donizetti transferred in 1839 to the heroine's entrance in the French version of *Lucia*. The musico-dramatic climax of the work is the supercharged duet for Rosmonda and Eleonora in Act II.

RECORDING   Kenny, Andrew, Greager, Du Plessis, Opera Rara Ch, Ulster O, Francis, MRF, 1975
EDITION   excerpts: v.s., Ricordi, 1851

Maria Stuarda
Mary Stuart

Opera seria in two acts (2h 30m)
Libretto by Giuseppe Badari, after Maffei's translation of the tragedy by Friedrich von Schiller (1800)
Composed 1834
PREMIERES   18 October 1834, Teatro San Carlo, Naples (as *Buondelmonte*; libretto adapted by the composer and Pietro Salatino); original version: 30 December 1835, La Scala, Milan; 15 October 1958, Bergamo; UK: 1 March 1966, St Pancras Town Hall, London; US: 16 November 1964, Carnegie Hall, New York (concert); 7 March 1972, City Opera, New York
CAST   Maria *s*, Elisabetta *s*, Leicester *t*, Talbot *bar*, Anna *ms*, Lord Cecil *bar*; *satb* chorus of courtiers, huntsmen, soldiers, servants
FULL ORCHESTRA   offstage: 2 tpt, 2 hn, 3 trbn, cannons

After *Maria Stuarda* was banned in Naples by the king while in rehearsal in 1834, Donizetti used most of the score as *Buondelmonte*, but this version has never been revived. Malibran sang the premiere of the original version at La Scala but, as she did not follow the censor's changes, the opera was soon prohibited. In 1865, after Donizetti's death, it was performed in Naples with two substitute numbers taken from Donizetti's lesser works. In contrast to its limited performance history in the 19th century, *Maria Stuarda* has entered the repertoire since its revival at Bergamo in 1958. The discovery of the autograph in a Swedish collection in 1987 has made possible the preparation of an authentic edition.

SYNOPSIS

Act I   Scene 1: At Westminster, Elisabetta suspects Leicester's affections are elsewhere engaged. Talbot shows Leicester a portrait and letter from Maria, who is imprisoned at Fotheringay, begging for an interview with the queen. When Leicester asks Elisabetta to grant Maria's request, her jealousy cannot be disguised, but she does not refuse. Scene 2: At Fotheringay, Maria envies the clouds their freedom to sail towards France. Leicester comes to prepare her for the queen's visit. Elisabetta enters and regards her young rival with ill-concealed hostility. When Elisabetta insults Maria, she is stung in turn, declaring that Elisabetta is a 'vile bastard' whose 'foot sullies the English throne'. Furious, Elisabetta orders Maria seized.

Act II Elisabetta debates whether to sign Maria's death warrant, urged on to it by Cecil. When Leicester comes to beg clemency, he is told that he is to witness Maria's execution. Scene 2: At Fotheringay, Maria does not flinch when Cecil delivers the fatal warrant. She turns to Talbot, who wears a cassock beneath his cloak, and confesses her sins. Maria asks her friends to join her in a prayer for all those who have wronged her. Leicester watches helplessly while Maria is led to the block.

Maria Stuarda, which used to have a reputation as an opera that even Malibran could not save, has proved a grateful vehicle for a number of recent singers. Today, it stands as a clear example of Donizetti's eagerness, in the face of the increasingly repressive censors of the 1830s, to expand the range of powerful subject matter for the opera stage. The explosive scene between the two queens, which has no basis in history, is unparalleled in operas of the period for its dramatic immediacy. The hushed, elegiac aria of Maria to the clouds, 'Oh! nube che lieve', is both a masterly piece of tone-painting and a shrewdly low-key anticipation of the fireworks that follow. Donizetti's skill at combining features of the solo aria with a duet, keeping within the conventions but using them in unpredictable ways, is shown in Leicester's aria in the opening scene and in Maria's 'Lascio contento al carcere' as she confesses herself to Talbot. The prayer for Maria with chorus, a magnificent reworking of a musical idea from the early *Il paria*, builds to a fine climax. The whole final scene, including Maria's aria-finale with its unexpected modulations, is one of the composer's major achievements.

RECORDINGS 1. Sills, Farrell, Burrows, L. Quilico, John Alldis Ch, LPO, Ceccato, HMV, 1971; 2. Plowright, Baker, Rendall, Tomlinson, ENO Ch and O, Mackerras, EMI (in English), 1982; 3. Sutherland, Tourangeau, Pavarotti, Soyer, Ch and O of the Teatro Comunale, Bologna, Bonynge, Decca, 1974/5; 4. Gruberova, Baltsa, Araiza, D'Artegna, Ch of Bavarian Radio, Munich Radio O, Patanè, Philips, 1989; all versions use different texts and varying transpositions. None is ideal, each has its virtues [A.B.]
VIDEO Plowright, Baker, Rendall, Tomlinson, ENO Ch and O, MacKerras, Castle, 1982 (in English)
EDITIONS v.ss. Gerard, 1866; Ricordi, 1990

Gemma di Vergy

Opera seria in two acts (2h 30m)
Libretto by Giovanni Emmanuele Bidera, after the play *Charles VII chez les grands vassaux* by Alexandre Dumas *père* (1831)
Composed 1834
PREMIERES 26 December 1834, La Scala, Milan; UK: 12 March 1842, London; US: 2 October 1843, New York

The plot concerns the tribulations resulting from Gemma's discovery that her husband has had their union dissolved as she has borne him no children and that he is planning a second marriage. Distraught at this news, she wants vengeance, which is carried out by an Arab slave, Tamas, who stabs Count di Vergy during his second wedding. Gemma has cursed the count and tried to pray, but when she learns that Tamas has stabbed first the count and then himself, she realizes how much she loved her late husband and longs for the release of death.

Gemma di Vergy enjoyed a period of great popularity in its early years and then gradually disappeared from sight by the end of the century; its 20th-century revival came about when Caballé undertook the daunting role of the heroine. Particularly noteworthy are Tamas's Act I aria, 'Mi toglieste a un sole ardente', and Gemma's powerful aria-finale.

RECORDING Caballé, Lima, L. Quilico, Schola Cantorum, Opera O of New York, Queler, CBS, 1976
EDITION v.s., Ricordi, *c.* 1870

Marino Faliero

Opera seria in three acts (2h 15m)
Libretto by Giovanni Emmanuele Bidera and Agostino Ruffini (who revised Bidera's text in Paris), after the tragedy by Delavigne (1829), in turn after the play *Marino Faliero* by Byron (1821)
Composed 1834–5
PREMIERES 12 March 1835, Théâtre-Italien, Paris; UK: 14 May 1835, Covent Garden, London; US: 22 February 1842, Charles Street Theater, New Orleans

Composed for the Italian company in Paris, and Donizetti's first premiere there, *Marino Faliero*'s plot deals with a Venetian conspiracy against the venerable Doge Faliero. The doge's enemy Steno has accused Faliero's wife Elena of adultery with Fernando, her husband's young nephew. At a ball, Elena complains of the insulting attentions of a masker, whom Fernando recognizes as Steno, whereupon he challenges him to a duel in which Fernando is mortally wounded. Faliero swears vengeance, but his plan is betrayed. As the doge informs Elena of Fernando's death, the guards of the Council arrive to arrest Faliero. Condemned to death, he requests a final meeting with Elena, at which she confesses to having loved Fernando. The doge pardons her and is himself led off to be executed. Elena faints as the axe falls.

Marino Faliero suffered from being found inferior to Bellini's *I puritani*, the other novelty of the same season, and performed by the same stellar cast. A sombre work, it nevertheless contains deeply moving music, particularly in the final scene. The role of Fernando, designed for Rubini's high tenor, is very challenging. Donizetti later quoted the gondolier's song that opens Act II in *Il campanello*.

RECORDING Roberti, Mori, Meliciani, Ferrin, Ch and O of Teatro Donizetti, Bergamo, Camozzo, Raritas, 1966
EDITION v.s., Ricordi, 1835; *rp*, Belwin-Mills, [1980s]

Lucia di Lammermoor

Dramma tragico in three acts (2h 30m)
Libretto by Salvatore Cammarano, after Sir Walter Scott's novel *The Bride of Lammermoor* (1819); French version by Alphonse Royer and 'Gustave Vaëz' (Jean Nicolas Gustave van Nieuvenhuysen)
Composed 1835; rev. (in French) 1839
PREMIERES 26 September 1835, Teatro San Carlo, Naples; UK: 5 April 1838, Her Majesty's Theatre, Haymarket,

London; 1839 version: 6 August 1839, Théâtre de la Renaissance, Paris; US: 28 December 1841, Théâtre d'Orléans, New Orleans
CAST Lucia *s*, Edgardo *t*, Enrico *bar*, Raimondo Bide-the-Bent *b*, Arturo *t*, Alisa *ms*, Normanno *t*; *satb* chorus of huntsmen and wedding guests
FULL ORCHESTRA offstage: banda

Lucia has never lost its place in the popular affection, although there has been a change from the days when it was regarded primarily as a vehicle for a coloratura soprano until, in the wake of the impact of Callas, it has come to be appreciated as a compelling Romantic melodrama. Far from being a conventional score, it is filled with original touches. The prevailing orchestral colour, dominated by horns, and the subtle repetition of brief motivic ideas lend the score its distinctive *tinta*. The psychological and dramatic appositeness of its striking contrasts in situation and melody, now idyllic, now propulsively energetic, add to its richness. Clearly, *Lucia* is one of the scores that Verdi knew during his formative years.

When it was new, *Lucia* was regarded as the last word in Romantic sensibility. And as such it was used by Flaubert in the famous episode when Emma Bovary meets Léon again at the theatre in Rouen; he even wove phrases from the French libretto into the narrative.

SYNOPSIS
Act I Scene 1: Enrico Ashton learns from his huntsmen that his sister Lucia has been meeting his hated rival Edgardo Ravenswood and has fallen in love with him. This disclosure sends Enrico into a murderous rage ('Cruda, funesta smania'). Scene 2: Lucia and her old nurse Alisa are waiting by a fountain, where she has a secret rendezvous with Edgardo. Lucia tells Alisa that she has seen the ghost of her ancestress who was murdered by a Ravenswood ('Regnava nel silenzio'). When her lover arrives, she sends Alisa off to keep watch. Edgardo wants to ask Enrico to forget their family feud, but Lucia is terrified of her brother's temper. When Edgardo tells her he must go to France (to aid the Stuart cause), she is desolate, but they exchange rings ('Verranno a te sull' aure').

Act II Scene 1: Enrico and his friend Normanno have forged a letter to convince Lucia of Edgardo's infidelity. When Lucia enters, Enrico tells her of his desperate political position and that only her marrying Arturo can save him ('Il pallor funesto'). Weeping, Lucia protests, but she is badly shaken when Edgardo shows her the forged letter. The chaplain Raimondo further weakens Lucia's resolution by reminding her of her obligations to her family. Scene 2: The guests greet Arturo on his arrival for the wedding ('Per te l'immenso giubilo'). Half fainting, Lucia has just signed the wedding contract when Edgardo unexpectedly returns to claim her ('Chi mi frena in tal momento'). When Enrico shows him the signed contract, Edgardo curses Lucia, whereupon Enrico demands vengeance.

Act III Scene 1: During a storm, Enrico comes to Edgardo's ruined hall to challenge him to a duel.

Scene 2: The wedding festivities are interrupted by Raimondo's disclosure that Lucia has murdered Arturo. Crazed, she appears, blood-stained dagger in hand, believing that she is about to marry Edgardo ('Alfin son tua'), and collapses. Scene 3: Edgardo comes to his family tombs to meet Enrico. Waiting, he thinks he no longer wants to live since Lucia has proved faithless ('Fra poco a me ricovero'). Learning of her death, he looks forward to their reunion in heaven ('Tu che a Dio spiegasti l'ali') and stabs himself.

Illustration from the title page of the first French vocal score of Lucia di Lammermoor, *showing Fanny Persiani, the original Lucia*

Lucia is filled with memorable melodies, but it is easy to overlook their dramatic appositeness and psychological depth. For instance, during the accompanied recitative preceding the famous mad scene, Lucia's mental confusion is underscored by the recurrence of earlier themes in altered form; the one tune she manages to keep straight is that of her Act I duet with Edgardo: 'Verranno a te'. A striking contrast is afforded by the merry chorus at the beginning of Act III, Scene 2, followed by Raimondo's grim narrative, 'Dalle stanze ove Lucia', with its uneasy modulations. It is followed by the elegiac chorus in E major, 'Oh, qual funesto avvenimento', which, like Edgardo's final aria, testifies to Donizetti's unusual skill in expressing grief in the major mode. Although much of the score of Lucia uses conventional compound structures, the dramatic propulsiveness of the plot, combined with Donizetti's melodic inventiveness, endows the work with surprising strength.

RECORDINGS 1. Callas, Di Stefano, Gobbi, Ch and O of Maggio Musicale Fiorentino, Serafin, EMI, 1953: makes old-fashioned cuts, but Callas's interpretation is riveting;

2. Sutherland, Pavarotti, Milnes, Ch and O of Royal Opera, Covent Garden, Bonynge, Decca, 1971: complete; 3. Caballé, Carreras, Sardinero, Ambrosian Opera Ch, New Philharmonia O, Lopez-Cobos, Philips, c. 1976: follows the autograph scrupulously, without added embellishments and restores the original higher keys to Lucia's Act I arias, her duet with Enrico, and the mad scene
VIDEO Sutherland, Greagor, Donnelly, Grant, Australian O Ch, Sydney Eliz O, Bonynge, Virgin, 1986
EDITIONS f.ss., Ricordi, 1910; facsimile of autograph manuscript, Bestetti, 1941; Kalmus, [c. 1965]; v.s., Gerard, c. 1835; Ricordi, 1960; rp, 1983; French version: v.s., Latte, Paris, 1839

Belisario

Opera seria in three acts (1h 45m)
Libretto by Salvatore Cammarano, based on Jean-François Marmontel's drama *Belisaire* (1776)
Composed 1835–6
PREMIERES 4 February 1836, La Fenice, Venice; UK: 1 April 1837, London; US: April 1842, French Opera House, Philadelphia

Belisario returns to Byzantium with his victorious army and asks the Emperor Giustiniano to liberate his prisoners, among whom is Alamiro, who has formed a strong attachment to his captor. Belisario is accused by his wife Antonina of having murdered their young son, for which he is sentenced to be blinded and exiled. Alamiro swears to avenge him. Belisario's daughter, Irene, leads her blind father away from the scene of his disgrace. In a desolate landscape, Irene and Belisario encounter Alamiro, who has allied himself with an army of Bulgars and Alani against Byzantium. Belisario accuses Alamiro of betrayal, but Irene recognizes him as her long-lost brother. Alamiro dissolves his alliance with the invaders and joins Belisario in the defence of Byzantium. In the ensuing conflict, Belisario is mortally wounded. Filled with remorse at having falsely accused her husband, Antonina begs for pardon, but Belisario dies.

Belisario is a compact score with much to recommend it. The highpoints include an expansive *larghetto* to the first finale, Alamiro's stirring 'Trema, Bisanzio', the tenderly pathetic duet for Irene and her father at the prison gates, and Antonina's emotional aria-finale. It is one of the few Donizetti operas without the motif of romantic love.

RECORDINGS 1. Gencer, Grilli, Taddei, Zaccaria, La Fenice Ch and O, Gavazzeni, BJR, 1969; 2. Zampieri, Toczyska, Terranova, Bruson, Meneghetti, Ch and O of Teatro Colón, Masini, HRE, 1981
EDITIONS v.ss., Ricordi, 1836, 1870

Il campanello di notte

(*Il campanello dello speziale*)
The Night Bell
(*The Chemist's Bell*)
Farsa (with recitatives) in one act (1h)
Libretto by the composer, after a vaudeville, *La sonnette de la nuit*, by Brunswick, Troin and Lhérie (1836)
Composed 1836
PREMIERES 1 June 1836, Teatro Nuovo, Naples; UK: 30 September 1837, Lyceum, London; US: 7 May 1917, Lyceum, New York

Serafina has married the aged pharmacist Don Annibale. Her rejected suitor Enrico takes advantage of the law that requires a chemist to answer his bell at any hour to disrupt their wedding night by appearing in a number of disguises (a French dandy, an opera singer who has lost his voice, and as an old codger with an endless prescription to fill). This virtuoso role was created by the baritone Giorgio Ronconi. Donizetti's inventive score and the amusing plot have kept *Il campanello* a favourite among his short operas.

RECORDING Baltsa, Romero, Dara, Vienna State Opera Ch, Vienna SO, Bertini, CBS, 1981
EDITION v.s., Ricordi, 1971

Betly, ossia La campanna svizzera

Betly, or The Swiss Campaign
Opera giocosa in one act (1h), rev. in two acts (1h 30m)
Libretto by the composer after Eugène Scribe's and Anne-Honoré-Joseph Mélesville's libretto for Adam's *Le chalet* (1834), in turn after Goethe's singspiel text *Jery und Bätely* (1780)
Composed 1836, rev. 1837
PREMIERES 24 August 1836, Teatro Nuovo, Naples; in two acts: 29 October 1837, Teatro Carolino, Palermo; UK: 9 January 1838, Lyceum, London; US: 25 October 1861, Philadelphia

The unassertive Daniele has been fooled by his fellow villagers into believing that his beloved Betly will become his bride. When Daniele eagerly confronts her, she disillusions him by asserting her love of independence. Betly's brother, Corporal Max, unexpectedly turns up with his platoon of soldiers after years of absence. Learning of Daniele's plight, he resolves to assist him without revealing his identity to his sister. He has his troops billeted in Betly's chalet, where their disorderly behaviour causes consternation. Max even challenges the timid Daniele to a duel, but when Daniele stoutly prepares to defend Betly from the intruders, Max reveals his identity and his ruse, thereby forcing Betly to realize that although her single state gives her a measure of independence, she still needs protection. She sees the merit of accepting Daniele as her husband.

The character of Daniele is a pendant to Nemorino (in *L'elisir*), that of a timid soul who learns to stand on his own. The score contains some charming music, particularly Betly's *sortita*, 'In questo semplice, modesto asilo' with its yodelling refrain, a beguiling example of Donizetti's deft arias of self-introduction, and a duet, 'Dolce instante inaspettato', for Betly and Daniele, who is determined to protect her from the intruders; it ends with her singing a cadenza, while he, desperately trying to remain awake, utters notated yawns.

RECORDING one-act version: Tuccari, Gentile, Catalani, Ch and O of Teatro dell'Opera Comica, Rome, Morelli, Nixa, [c. 1952]
EDITIONS v.ss., Ricordi, 1836, 1877; Belwin-Mills, [c. 1980]

L'assedio di Calais

The Siege of Calais
Opera seria in three acts (2h)

Libretto by Salvatore Cammarano, after Luigi Marichionni's Italian adaptation of Philippe-Jacques Laroche's play *Eustache de Saint-Pierre, ou Le siège de Calais* (1822)
Composed 1836
PREMIERES 19 November 1836, Teatro San Carlo, Naples; Ireland: 24 October 1991, Theatre Royal, Wexford; UK: 3 March 1993, Guildhall School of Music and Drama, London

This is Donizetti's first explicit attempt to approach the genre of French grand opera; the work includes a ballet divertissement – then an unusual feature in Italy as operas were characteristically performed in conjunction with a separate full-length ballet. Some details may have been suggested by Luigi Henry's ballet, *L'assedio di Calais*, which had been revived at the Teatro San Carlo in 1835. Because of the lack of an adequate leading tenor, Donizetti wrote the important male role of Aurelio for a mezzo-soprano *en travesti*.

The plot deals with the incident of the burghers of Calais, prepared to sacrifice themselves to lift the English siege of their city, their lives being spared through the intercession of the English queen. The score contains a notable and unusually elaborate final ensemble to Act I, but the Act II scene in the council chamber, at which both the mayor, Eustacio de Saint-Pierre, and his son Aurelio volunteer to serve as hostages, must rank among the most powerful pages in all of Donizetti's *oeuvre*. Probably in 1837, Donizetti added an attractive aria-finale for Aurelio's wife Eleonora to strengthen Act III.

RECORDING Focile, D. Jones, Serbo, Du Plessis, Geoffrey Mitchell Ch, Philharmonia O, Parry, Opera Rara, 1988: includes the aria-finale as an appendix
EDITION v.s., Ricordi, 1836

Pia de' Tolomei

Opera seria in two acts (1h 45m)
Libretto by Salvatore Cammarano, based on the verse novella by Bartolomeo Sestini (1822); Pia is mentioned in Book V of Dante's *Purgatorio*
Composed 1835–7, rev. 1837
PREMIERES 18 February 1837, Teatro Apollo, Venice; rev. version: 31 July 1837, Sinigaglia; 2nd rev. version (to appease local censors): 30 September 1838, Teatro San Carlo, Naples

The Ghibelline Ghino is insanely in love with Pia, the young bride of his brother Nello. When Pia spurns Ghino's advances, he accuses her of adultery, suspecting from an intercepted letter that she has a lover. In fact, the letter was from her brother Rodrigo, a Guelf, begging for a secret meeting. Nello and Ghino hide to surprise the nocturnal visitor. When Rodrigo escapes, Pia refuses to reveal her visitor's identity. Convinced that her refusal is an admission of guilt, Nello orders her to be imprisoned. Ghino comes to her cell and offers to win her release if she will make love to him, but she tells her untrustworthy brother-in-law that it was only Rodrigo who visited her and begs him to reveal this to Nello. Meanwhile Pia's gaoler Ubaldo has received orders from Nello to kill her if he should die in the coming battle with the Guelfs. Nello survives the engagement, in which he is defeated, but Ghino is mortally wounded. Dying, he confesses his

treachery toward Pia. Nello goes at once to the prison, but Ubaldo has already administered poison to Pia. Rodrigo appears, having won the battle, just in time to hear the dying Pia beg him and Nello to resolve their differences and live in peace.

The most effective music in the score is that for the tenor, Ghino. His Act I arioso, 'O Pia mendace!', is an unexpected anticipation of Violetta's 'Amami, Alfredo' (Verdi's *La traviata*, Act II). The tenor–baritone duet in Act I, Scene 1, in which Ghino rouses his brother to murderous rage, is rousing indeed. Ghino's death scene is vivid both dramatically and musically. Unfortunately, the music for Pia (the last of the three parts Donizetti wrote for Fanny Persiani) is of a lower order, which dislocates the intended centre of interest in this score.

RECORDING Cuberli, Pecchioli, Casellato, Fioravanti, Milan Ch and SO of RAI, Rigacci, MRF, 1976
EDITION excerpts: v.s., Ricordi, [c. 1837]; *rp*, Belwin Mills, 1982

Roberto Devereux

Opera seria in three acts (2h)
Libretto by Salvatore Cammarano, after François Ancelot's play *Elisabeth d'Angleterre* (1832) and with some indebtedness to Felice Romani's text for Mercadante's *Il conte d'Essex* (1833), also derived from Ancelot's play
Composed 1837, rev. 1838
PREMIERES 29 October 1837, Teatro San Carlo, Naples; rev. version: 27 December 1838, Théâtre-Italien, Paris; UK: 24 June 1841, London; US: 15 January 1849, Astor Place Opera House, New York
CAST Elisabetta *s*, Sara, Duchess of Nottingham *ms*, Roberto Devereux (Essex) *t*, Nottingham *bar*, Cecil *t*, Gualtiero (Walter Raleigh) *b*, Page *b*, Nottingham's confidant *b*; *satb* chorus of courtiers
FULL ORCHESTRA

Composed at the time of his wife's death, *Roberto Devereux* reflects Donizetti's effort to assuage his grief by losing himself in a work of great power. Twentieth-century revivals of this opera have proved that its dramatic intensity can still grip audiences. For its demands on a potent singing actress, the role of Elisabetta is worthy of mention alongside Bellini's Norma. The score also shows Donizetti's growing avoidance of lengthy sections of chordally accompanied recitative.

SYNOPSIS
Act I At Westminster, Roberto is threatened with arrest for treason for his recent débâcle in Ireland, but Elisabetta loves him and is determined to save him, giving him a ring that will guarantee his freedom. Unknown to the queen, however, Roberto is deeply in love with Sara, who during his absence has been forced into a loveless union with his friend Nottingham. Later, Roberto visits Sara to say farewell, and he entrusts her with Elisabetta's ring, while she gives him a scarf in return.

Act II The ministers of the queen are meeting to decide Roberto's fate. They have searched his apartments and bring the queen the scarf. When Nottingham sees it, remembering that he has observed his wife working on it, he bursts into a jealous rage. Deeply offended herself at this apparent evidence of Roberto's infidelity, the queen is furious. Roberto is sent to the Tower.

Act III Nottingham confronts his wife, ordering her seclusion at home, thereby making it impossible for her to send the ring to Elisabetta. In the Tower, Roberto hopes he can restore Sara's reputation before he is executed. At Westminster, Elisabetta is miserable, wondering why she has not received the ring, wanting Roberto to be spared. As a cannon shot announces Roberto's execution, Sara rushes in with the ring, followed by Nottingham, who declares he detained Sara so that he might have his revenge. The queen orders their arrest and then, haunted by visions of Roberto's ghost and her own demise, announces her abdication.

Although the plot plays fast and loose with history, the opera carries its own brand of dramatic conviction. The overture, added for Paris, capitalizes on the tune of 'God Save the Queen'. The terse second act develops considerable tension, exploding at the end into an impulsive trio-finale. Act III opens with a powerful asymmetrical duet for Sara and Nottingham. Roberto's fine aria in the Tower scene, preceded by an almost Beethovenesque prelude, exemplifies Donizetti's canny writing for the tenor voice. Even more wonderful is Elisabetta's aria-finale, 'Vivi, ingrato', which expands in a long arc of restrained emotion, capped by a propulsive *cabaletta*.

RECORDINGS 1. Sills, Wolff, Ilosfalvy, Glossop, Ambrosian Opera Ch, RPO, Mackerras, HMV, 1970; 2. Caballé, Marsee, Carreras, Sardinero, unnamed Ch and O, Rudel, HRE, 1977
EDITIONS f.s., facsimile, Garland, 1982; v.ss., Ricordi, 1838; Egret House, 1975

Maria de Rudenz

Opera seria in three acts (2h)
Libretto by Salvatore Cammarano, derived from the play *La nonne sanglante* (1835) by Bourgeois, Cuvelier and Mallian
Composed 1837
PREMIERES 30 January 1838, La Fenice, Venice; UK: 27 October 1974, Queen Elizabeth Hall, London (concert)

Perhaps the darkest of Donizetti's tragedies, *Maria de Rudenz* presents the tragic story of Maria's love for the villainous Corrado. Her jealousy at his determination to marry Mathilde causes her to feign her death, murder Mathilde, and then, as she really is dying from stab wounds sustained earlier, to proclaim her obsession with Corrado. The score contains a fine *larghetto* ensemble in the Act I finale, later rearranged for Poliuto; a seething soprano–baritone duet in Act II ('Fonte d'amare lagrime'), and an unusually extended aria-finale for Maria. Its most surprising feature is a lengthy bass clarinet solo in the prelude to Act II. A baritone *romanza* for Corrado, 'Ah! non avea più lagrime', remained a popular concert item throughout the 19th century.

RECORDING Ricciarelli, Cupido, Nucci, Ch and O of La Fenice, Inbal, CBS, 1981

EDITION v.s., Ricordi, [*c.* 1840]

Poliuto

Opera seria in three acts (1h 45m)
Rev. as *Les martyrs*, grand opera in four acts (2h 45m)
Libretto by Salvatore Cammarano, after the tragedy *Polyeucte* by Corneille (1640); libretto for *Les martyrs* by Eugène Scribe
Composed 1838, rev. 1839
PREMIERES *Poliuto*: 30 November 1848, Teatro San Carlo, Naples; US: 25 May 1859, New York; *Les martyrs*: 10 April 1840, Opéra, Paris; US: 24 March 1846, Théâtre d'Orléans, New Orleans; UK: 20 April 1852, Covent Garden, London
CAST Paolina s, Poliuto t, Severo bar, Callistene b, Nearco t, Felice b, a Christian t; satb chorus of Christians, Romans, priests, people
FULL ORCHESTRA including 4 bsn, hp

Poliuto was banned by the censors when already in rehearsal because it showed on stage the martyrdom of a Christian saint. After Donizetti moved to Paris in the autumn of 1838, he rearranged and expanded the score to a French text, as the first of his three works for the Paris Opéra. Though Donizetti retained 80 per cent of the score of *Poliuto*, these expansions included a full-length overture (one section to be sung by a chorus behind the curtain), some choruses, arias, and the obligatory ballet divertissement. The work was not performed in its original form until after Donizetti's death.

SYNOPSIS (*Poliuto*)
Act I In the Roman province of Armenia, Poliuto has decided to be baptized by Nearco, but this rite is overheard by his wife Paolina, the daughter of the governor Felix. The news that Severo will shortly arrive upsets her because she was once betrothed to him but had believed the false rumour of his death in battle.

Act II Severo reproaches Paolina, but she is steadfast in her loyalty to Poliuto, who has been brought to overhear their conversation by the evil priest Callistene. Poliuto's jealous outburst is interrupted by news that his Christian sponsor Nearco has been seized and is to be tried in the temple of Jupiter. There, Poliuto publicly confesses that he is a Christian neophyte and overturns the altar of Jupiter.

Act III Paolina comes to him in prison and is so persuaded by the steadfastness of his new faith that she declares herself ready to adopt his new religion. Together they enter the arena with their fellow Christians to meet their martyrdom.

Poliuto is more compact and lacks the extraneous elements that make *Les martyrs* seem bloated in comparison. In both versions, Donizetti employed a number of melodies thematically as reminiscence motifs: the Christian hymn from Act I, the pagan chorus at the beginning of the temple scene, and the *cabaletta* of the conversion duet, opposing the last two contrapuntally in the final ensemble. The whole temple scene is a fine example of the enlarged scope of Donizetti's musical dramaturgy and clearly looks forward in some of its details to the triumphal scene

Gilbert Duprez (Polyeucte) in Les martyrs *(Paris, 1840)*

of Verdi's *Aida*. Today, the work is usually performed in its original form, sometimes (as in the Callas revival of 1960) with the inclusion of the Act I trio from *Les martyrs*.

RECORDINGS   1. Callas, Corelli, Bastianini, Zaccaria, Ch and O of La Scala, Votto, Replica, 1960; 2. Connell, Martinucci, Bruson, Federici, Rome Opera Ch and O, Latham-Koenig, Nuova Era, 1988; 3. Ricciarelli, Carreras, Pons, Polgár, Vienna Singakademie Ch, Vienna SO, Caetani, CBS, 1986; 4. *Les martyrs*: Gencer, Garaventa, Bruson, Ch and O of La Fenice, Venice, Gelmetti, Voce, 1978: the Callas version is easily the most thrilling [A.B.]
EDITIONS   *Poliuto*: v.s., Ricordi, 1988; *Les martyrs*: f.s., facsimile (2 vols), Garland, 1978; v.s., Egret House, 1975

Il duca d'Alba
The Duke of Alba
Grand opera in four acts (Acts I and II only by Donizetti) (2h 30m)
Libretto (French) by Eugène Scribe and Charles Duveyrier from an unidentified source; Scribe's text translated into Italian and amended by Angelo Zanardini
Composed (two acts orchestrated, plus a few sketches, to a French text) 1839; completed, in an Italian translation, 1881–2 by Matteo Salvi; Salvi's version rev. 1959 by Thomas Schippers
PREMIERES   Salvi version: 22 March 1882, Teatro Apollo, Rome; Schippers version: 9 July 1959, Teatro Nuovo, Spoleto; US: 20 October 1959, Carnegie Hall, New York (concert)

When Donizetti died in 1848, among the materials he left was the incomplete score of *Le duc d'Albe*. In September 1881 the existing material was acquired by the resourceful music publisher Giovannina Lucca, who hired Donizetti's only pupil, Matteo Salvi, to complete the opera, under the aegis of a commission consisting of maestri on the faculty of the Milan Conservatory, one of whom was Ponchielli. Only a few were aware in 1881 that Scribe's text was the original form of what he later adapted, transferring the action to Palermo, as the text for Verdi's *Les vêpres siciliennes* (1855). After its Roman premiere, Salvi's version survived for only three additional productions, until it was revived by RAI in 1952.

The disinterment reawakened interest in this semi-Donizetti score. Thomas Schippers determined to revise Salvi's work, bringing the orchestration more into line with the practice of the 1840s. Additionally, he restored the tenor aria 'Ange si pur' (better known as 'Spirto gentil'), which Donizetti had transferred to the last act of *La favorite* to be sung by Duprez, to whose vocal measurements he had tailored it. This aria is the one part of Donizetti's original score for *Le duc d'Albe* that had been performed prior to 1882. The aria that was substituted for it by Salvi, 'Angelo casto e bel', familiar through a number of recordings, is not by Donizetti.

The work is set in the period of the Spanish occupation of the Low Countries. The rebellious Amelia, the daughter of Egmont, rouses the Flemings against the Spaniards, but a rising is prevented by the timely arrival of the Duke of Alba. Amelia's co-conspirator is her beloved Marcello, who turns out to be the long-lost love-child of the duke. When the rebels are arrested, all but Marcello are detained, a situation that convinces Amelia that he has betrayed the cause. Amelia is determined to assassinate the duke, but at the last minute Marcello throws himself between them, receiving a fatal wound. Dying, he begs his father to forgive Amelia.

RECORDINGS   1. Salvi version: Mancini, Berdini, G. Guelfi, Rome Ch and SO of RAI, Previtali, Voce, 1952; 2. Schippers version: Krilovici, Garaventa, Carroli, Ch and O of Théâtre de la Monnaie, Brussels, De Fabritiis, MRF, 1979
EDITIONS   Salvi version: v.s., Massa, 1882; *rp*, Belwin-Mills, [*c.* 1982]

La fille du régiment
The Daughter of the Regiment
Opéra comique (with spoken dialogue) in two acts (1h 30m)
Libretto by J. F. A. Bayard and J. H. Vernoy de Saint-Georges
Composed 1839; Italian opera buffa version (with recitatives) 1840
PREMIERES   11 February 1840, Opéra-Comique, Paris; as an opera buffa: 3 October 1840, La Scala, Milan; US: 2 March 1843, Théâtre d'Orléans, New Orleans; UK: 27 May 1847, Her Majesty's Theatre, Haymarket, London
CAST   Marie *s*, Marquise *ms*, Tonio *t*, Sergeant Sulpice *b*, Hortensius *b*, Corporal *b*, Farmer *t*; *spoken roles*: Duchesse de Crakentorp, Notary; *satb* chorus of soldiers, peasants, guests of the Marquise

FULL ORCHESTRA   onstage: 2 small tpt, pf; offstage: hn, cornet, banda

One of the most popular of Donizetti's comedies, *La fille* shows no signs of weakening its hold on the public's affections. It is a tribute to the composer's grasp of the Gallic spirit that this opera became a staple of the French repertoire and that Marie's *cabaletta* in Act II, 'Salut à la France!', attained the status of a patriotic song. Although in the summer of 1840 Donizetti adapted the work as an Italian opera buffa with sung recitatives, dropping the typically French couplets and inserting some other material, including an aria from *Gianni di Calais* (1828), this variant has never seriously challenged the appeal of the original opéra-comique version, in which the work is almost always performed today.

SYNOPSIS

Act I   Brought up by the soldiers of the 21st Regiment of the French Army and adopted by them as their 'daughter', the *vivandière* Marie confesses to gruff old Sulpice that she is much taken with a strapping Tyrolean, Tonio, who saved her life when she nearly fell off a precipice. The attraction is mutual, for Tonio has been lurking around the encampment hoping to talk to Marie. Seized as a spy, the young fellow is claimed by Marie as her personal prisoner, and in their ensuing duet ('De cet aveu si tendre') their true feelings for one another emerge. Hoping to marry Marie, Tonio is surprised to learn that her husband must be a member of the regiment, tidings that cause him promptly to enlist. The regiment celebrates his decision, calling on Marie to sing the regimental song ('Chacun le sait, chacun le dit'). The aged Marquise de Birkenfeld, strangely discomfited by the presence of the campaigning so near her château, learns from Sulpice that a certain Captain Robert had been a member of this very regiment. On the strength of this information, she claims to be Marie's aunt and insists on removing the girl from what in her eyes is a very unsuitable environment. Now in uniform, Tonio has come to claim his bride, but Marie is forced to leave by the marquise's intervention ('Il faut partir, mes bons compagnons d'armes').

Act II   At the château, Marie is bored by lessons in dancing and in singing vapid romances, her reluctance strengthened by the presence of Sulpice, whom the marquise has taken in to recover from a wound. Longing for her old freedom and harassed by her aunt's insistence on respectability and that she marry a silly young duke, Marie is overjoyed when the 21st Regiment arrives at the château. Tonio, who has been promoted on the battlefield, pleads with the marquise for Marie's hand. He has been investigating her true parentage and now demands an explanation. During the reception to announce Marie's engagement to the duke, the marquise suffers a change of heart and confesses to the startled company that Marie is in fact her own daughter and consents to her marriage to Tonio. Amid general rejoicing, the opera ends with a patriotic chorus, 'Salut à la France'.

The score is filled with effective numbers. Particularly noteworthy are Marie's regimental song, 'Chacun le sait' (surprisingly adapted from an ensemble in *Il diluvio universale*, 1830), and her farewell to Tonio, 'Il faut partir', a finely crafted melody with a cor anglais obbligato that serves as the opening movement of the mid-point finale. A prime moment of comedy is provided by her lesson scene, in which the marquise tries to teach her an old tune by Garat, while Sulpice cannot resist teasing her into a reprise of 'Chacun le sait'. Tonio has both 'Pour mon âme' in Act I, with its redoubtable series of high Cs, and his tender plea to the marquise in Act II, 'Pour me rapprocher de Marie'. The character of the intrepid Marie stands squarely behind Verdi's portrait of another *vivandière*, Preziosilla in *La forza del destino*. Far from the least attractive aspect of *La fille du régiment* is Donizetti's skill and economy in contrasting military atmosphere with the tone of polite society, established at once by the charming *tyrolienne* that serves as a prelude to Act II.

RECORDINGS   1. Sutherland, Sinclair, Pavarotti, Malas, Ch and O of Royal Opera, Covent Garden, Bonynge, Decca, 1968; 2. Anderson, T'Hezan, Kraus, Trempont, Paris Opéra Ch and O, Campanella, EMI, 1986
EDITIONS   French: v.ss., Latte, 1840; Joubert, 1916; Italian: v.s., Ricordi, 1840, 1872, 1980

La favorite

Grand opera in four acts (2h 30m, excluding the ballet)
Libretto by Alphonse Royer, Gustave Vaëz and Eugène Scribe after Baculard d'Arnaud's play *Le Comte de Comminge* (1764) among other sources, on which Scribe grafted the story of Leonora de Guzman
Composed 1840
PREMIERES   2 December 1840, Opéra, Paris; US: 9 February 1843, Théâtre d'Orléans, New Orleans; UK: 18 October 1843, Drury Lane, London
CAST   Léonor *ms*, Inès *s*, Fernand *t*, Alphonse *bar*, Balthazar *b*, Don Gaspard *t*; *satb* chorus of monks and courtiers; ballet
ORCHESTRATION   picc, 2 fl, 2 ob, ca, 2 bsn, 4 hn, 3 tpt, 3 trbn, ophicleide, timp, cym, triangle, organ, hp, str

In December 1839, Donizetti had completed a four-act semiseria entitled *L'ange de Nisida* for the Théâtre de la Renaissance, but the management declared bankruptcy before that work could be produced, leaving Donizetti with an unperformed score that, because of the nature of its plot (dealing with a royal mistress of the Bourbons), would offend the Italian censors. In the summer of 1840 when he was in Milan concocting the Italian adaptation of *La fille du régiment*, he was summoned back to Paris to produce a full-length work for the Opéra. Only the existence of *L'ange* and some other unperformed works allowed the resourceful Donizetti to complete *La favorite* and meet his deadline. Most of the major arias were newly composed, being tailored to the vocal characteristics of the cast.

SYNOPSIS

Act I   Castile, 1340. Fernand informs Balthazar, his father and the Superior of a monastic order, that he must renounce his novitiate because he has fallen in love with a beautiful woman without being aware of her identity ('Une ange, une femme inconnue'). Balthazar's austere admonitions serve only to strengthen the young man's resolve. Blindfolded, Fernand is taken to the island of Léon, where he is greeted by Inès and other ladies. Léonor appears and tells Fernand that she appreciates his feelings, but she refuses to tell him who she is and asks him to forget her. As a farewell present she hands him a royal commission and leaves. Alone, Fernand determines to win military glory so that he can ask for her hand.

Act II Alphonse, king of Castile, thinks longingly of Léonor as he walks through the gardens of Alcazar ('Léonor, viens!'). He intends to divorce his wife and make his mistress his queen. Léonor comes to him and sadly begs him to release her from what is an intolerably humiliating position. Alphonse attempts to cheer her up with some dancing (ballet). Balthazar, who is father to the queen as well as to Fernand, arrives at court with a Papal Bull of excommunication that will take effect if the king pursues his intention of putting his consort aside. When Alphonse proudly refuses to heed this injunction, Balthazar pronounces an anathema before the horrified courtiers.

Act III Covered with honour for having defeated the Moors, Fernand comes to make obeisance to the king. Complacently, the king offers to grant any favour that Fernand might request. When the young man asks for Léonor's hand, Alphonse, who cannot believe that Fernand is ignorant of the lady's compromised position, ironically accedes to this happy solution of his dilemma and commands the ceremony be performed at once ('Pour tant d'amour'). Léonor loves the young man's sincerity, but she feels unworthy of him ('O, mon Fernand'). She asks Inès to deliver a note revealing her true position, but one of the courtiers, Don Gaspard, detains Inès so that Fernand goes into the adjacent chapel uninformed. While the ceremony is taking place, the courtiers comment on the dishonourable affair. When Fernand emerges from the chapel, Alphonse confers noble titles on him. The courtiers, however, refuse to acknowledge him as their equal. Balthazar arrives and from him Fernand learns the truth. Fernand confronts the king; refusing the titles given him, and breaking his sword and casting it at the royal feet, he leaves to resume the cloistered life.

Act IV Monks dig the grave of the queen, who has just died. Fernand is still haunted by the memory of Léonor ('Ange si pur'). After he leaves to be received into full membership of the order, Léonor, disguised as a novice, appears, ill and conscience-stricken, hoping for a last glimpse of Fernand. When he returns, he starts to order her away, but then, seeing the genuineness of her contrition, he can think only of being with her. For a time, she shares his vain illusion, but her strength fails her and she dies at his feet.

In spite of its diverse sources, the score of *La favorite* is remarkably cohesive. Unlike most grand operas of its period, it has an almost austere and solemn colour, yet it contains much smouldering feeling, particularly in the final act, much admired by Toscanini. The sensuous, aristocratic nature of Alphonse is admirably depicted. Once one accepts the odd premiss that Fernand, as the queen's brother, should be ignorant of the identity of his brother-in-law's mistress, the plot is convincing. Although this opera has usually been performed in a not very exact Italian translation and in a version inauthentic in a number of details, the publication of the facsimile edition raises hopes that *La favorite* will regain its former pride of place.

RECORDINGS 1. (in French) Lapeyrette, R. Lassalle, Albers, anon. Ch and O, Ruhlmann, Pathé, 1912; Bourg, 1983: primitive sound but the only authentic recording; Albers is the best Alphonse on disc; 2. (in Italian) Cossotto, Pavarotti, Bacquier, Ghiaurov, Ch and O of Teatro Comunale, Bologna, Bonynge, Decca, 1974
EDITIONS in French: f.s., facsimile, Garland, 1982; v.s., Schonenberger, 1841; in Italian: v.s., Ricordi, [c. 1955]

Rita, ou Le mari battu
Rita, or The Beaten Husband
Opéra comique (with spoken dialogue) in one act (50m)
Libretto by Gustave Vaëz
Composed 1841
PREMIERES 7 May 1860, Opéra-Comique, Paris; US: 14 May 1957, Hunter College, New York; UK: 12 December 1962, National School of Opera, London

This engaging little comedy about a meek husband who learns how to stand up to a termagant of a wife boasts a finely crafted score. The conflict is given a humorous dimension when Gasparo, Rita's first husband, returns to collect his marriage contract so that he may be free to marry again. Gasparo and his successor Beppe play a game of chance to see who will end up with the wife neither of them wants. Gasparo tricks Beppe into standing up to gratified Rita, and leaves, having accomplished his mission.

Rita had only a brief stage history in the 19th century, but its revivals since the Second World War have given it a new lease of life. Rita's opening aria establishes her at once, and Beppe's air, 'Je suis joyeux comme un pinson', conveys his joy when he thinks (briefly) that he is a free man. Rita ends with an effective trio.

RECORDINGS 1. Arnaldi, Franzini, Montarsolo, Turin SO of RAI, Cattini, Cetra, 1955; 2. Sciutti, Cestari, Cortis, O della Scuola di Arzignano, Leibowitz, Fonit, 1956
EDITIONS in French: v.s., Paris, 1860; in Italian, v.s., Ricordi, 1957

Maria Padilla
Opera seria in three acts (3h)
Libretto by Gaetano Rossi and the composer, after François Ancelot's play *Maria Padilla* (1838)
Composed 1841
PREMIERES 26 December 1841, La Scala, Milan; UK: 8 April 1973, Queen Elizabeth Hall, London (concert); US: 23 April 1983, Stony Brook, New York (concert); 14 September 1990, Joslyn Art Museum, Omaha, Nebraska

One of Donizetti's most powerful scores, this work has been overshadowed by his more popular works.

Maria Padilla, mistress of King Pedro the Cruel of Castile, extracts a promise from the monarch that he will marry her by threatening to commit suicide if he does not. The plan must, however, remain secret since, for reasons of state, Pedro has to appear to be negotiating a marriage with a Bourbon princess, Blanche. When Blanche arrives at court and is greeted as queen, Maria fears she has been rejected. In anger, she snatches the crown from Blanche's head, placing it on her own. Pedro at last acknowledges publicly his feelings for Maria, and she consequently dies 'of a surfeit of joy'.

The opera was originally intended to end with the frustrated Maria's suicide, but was changed when the censors objected. An alternative version also exists where Maria survives to reign triumphant. Among several strong musical numbers are the Act I duet between Maria and Pedro, 'Core innocente e giovane', when he comes in disguise to abduct her (although she already knows his identity), a duet in Act II for Maria and her sister Ina ('A figlia incauta') which has a particularly brilliant *cabaletta* sung *a due*, and a duet for Maria and her father, 'Padre, padre, oh rio dolore!', in Act III which is among the most moving duets Donizetti ever wrote.

RECORDING McDonall, D. Jones, Davies, Clark, Caley, Du Plessis, Earle, Kennedy, Geoffrey Mitchell Ch, LSO, Francis, Opera Rara, 1980
EDITIONS v.ss., Ricordi, 1842; Schonenberger, [*c.* 1845]; *rp*, Belwin Mills, [*c.* 1980]

Linda di Chamounix

Linda of Chamounix
Opera semiseria in three acts (2h 30m)
Libretto by Gaetano Rossi, after the drama *La grâce de Dieu* by Adolphe d'Ennery and Gustave Lemoine (1841)
Composed and rev. 1842
PREMIERES 19 May 1842, Kärntnertortheater, Vienna; UK: 1 June 1843, Her Majesty's Theatre, Haymarket, London; US: 4 January 1847, Palmo's Opera House, New York
CAST Linda *s*, Carlo *t*, Marquis de Boisfleury *bar*, Antonio *bar*, Pierotto, Maddalena *s*, Prefect *b*, Intendant *t*; *satb* chorus of peasants, Savoyards
FULL ORCHESTRA

One of the major successes of Donizetti's career and arguably his finest achievement in the problematic semiseria genre, *Linda* shows well the refinement and melancholic power of the mature Donizetti.

SYNOPSIS

Act I Linda, a tenant farmer's daughter, has fallen in love with Carlo, unaware that he is the Vicomte de Sirval, believing him just a poor artist. She, however, has caught the roving eye of the lecherous marchese, Carlo's elderly kinsman, and therefore to protect his daughter from possible dishonour, her father Antonio decides, with the village prefect's prompting, to send her to France with a party of Savoyard seasonal workers.

Act II Linda is living in high style in Paris, maintained in all innocence by Carlo, who hopes to persuade his difficult mother to allow him to wed the girl of his dreams, but his mother (who does not appear) has different plans for him. Antonio arrives at Linda's luxurious apartment seeking news of his daughter, whom he does not at first recognize; when he does he suspects the worst and curses her. Linda's friend Pierotto appears with the dreadful news that he has heard that Carlo is going to wed an aristocratic girl. Linda promptly loses her reason.

Act III Linda is persuaded to return to her native village by Pierotto playing a familiar tune on his hurdy-gurdy. There she learns that Carlo managed to evade his mother's scheme for his marriage, and he, full of contrition, cannily restores Linda's sanity by the simple device of singing his love theme to her. All ends with a happy ensemble to celebrate the betrothal of Carlo and Linda.

The work has a fine overture (derived from the first movement of one of Donizetti's string quartets) and a number of effective duets; especially notable is that Act I love duet, the principal theme of which, 'A consolarmi affrettisi', serves to restore Linda's reason in time for the happy ending. The best-known aria, Linda's Act I 'O luce di quest'anima', in which she expresses her love for Carlo, was added along with a number of other revisions for the Paris premiere at the Théâtre-Italien in November 1842. The true merit of *Linda*, however, lies in Donizetti's rich and apposite musical setting of a drama that sometimes stretches credibility to its limits.

RECORDING Stella, Barbieri, Valletti, Taddei, Capecchi, Ch and O of San Carlo, Naples, Serafin, Philips, 1958
EDITIONS v.ss., Vienna, 1842; Ricordi, [*c.* 1872]

Caterina Cornaro

Opera seria in a prologue and two acts (2h)
Libretto by Giacomo Sacchero, after Vernoy de Saint-Georges's libretto for Halévy's *La reine de Chypre* (1841)
Composed 1842–3, rev. 1844–5
PREMIERES 18 January 1844, Teatro San Carlo, Naples; rev. version: 2 February 1845, Teatro Regio, Parma; UK: 10 July 1972, Royal Festival Hall, London (concert); US: 1973, New York (concert)

Although this was the last of Donizetti's operas to be produced in his lifetime, he had begun composing it in late 1842 and finished it the following spring. Rarely performed in the 19th century, *Caterina* has demonstrated itself in its few revivals in this century to be a score worthy of revival. The compression of forms and the raw energy of some pages command attention.

The marriage of Caterina Cornaro to her beloved Gerardo is put off by the intervention of Mocenigo, who announces that Lusignano, king of Cyprus, wishes to marry Caterina – a desirable political union that will eventually win Cyprus for Venice. Knowing that Gerardo's life is in danger, Caterina pretends that she no longer loves him. During an uprising one of Mocenigo's men attempts to kill Gerardo, but he is saved by Lusignano; only later does the king learn that this is the man for whom Caterina has been pining. Mocenigo, who has been poisoning

Lusignano with the ultimate aim of taking power in Cyprus himself, stages a revolt, during which Lusignano is fatally wounded. Dying, he begs Caterina to rule in his stead. She undertakes the role he wished for her, leaving Gerardo to return to the Knights Hospitalliers in Rhodes. (In the 1845 revision of the opera, Donizetti has Gerardo killed in the fighting, thereby focusing final attention on Lusignano and Caterina.)

RECORDING   Caballé, Carreras, Saccomani, London Symphony Ch and O, Cillario, MRF, 1972
EDITION   v.s., Ricordi, 1845; rp, Egret House, 1974

Don Pasquale
Opera buffa in three acts (2h)
Libretto by Giovanni Ruffini and the composer, after Angelo Anelli's libretto for Pavesi's *Ser Marc'Antonio* (1810)
Composed 1843
PREMIERES   3 January 1843, Théâtre-Italien, Paris; UK: 29 June 1843, Her Majesty's Theatre, Haymarket, London; US: 7 January 1845, Théâtre d'Orléans, New Orleans
CAST   Norina *s*, Ernesto *t*, Dr Malatesta *bar*, Don Pasquale *b*; Notary *b*; *satb* chorus of servants
ORCHESTRATION   2 fl/picc, 2 ob, 2 cl, 2 bsn, 4 hn, 2 tpt, 2 trbn, timp, perc, str; onstage: tambourine, 2 gtr

Donizetti's comic masterpiece is the last of the golden tradition of opera buffa of the first half of the 19th century to remain in the international repertoire. Designed for the principal quartet of the

Théâtre-Italien, *Don Pasquale* has a concentration and comic sweep, humanized by touches of Donizettian pathos, that sets it in a class by itself. At this point in his busy, occasionally frantic, career Donizetti had accumulated a background of practical theatrical experience unmatched by that of any of his rivals, and this experience in combination with his musical talent produced a work whose freshness has never faltered. In the light of this achievement, it is difficult to realize that before the year was out the illness that would dim his mental capacities would manifest itself.

SYNOPSIS
Act I   Scene 1: Don Pasquale impatiently awaits his friend and doctor, determined to disinherit his nephew Ernesto, who to his uncle's displeasure has fallen in love with the widow Norina. Pasquale wishes to consult Dr Malatesta about undertaking a marriage himself and siring some more direct heirs. When Malatesta appears, he informs Pasquale that he knows of the perfect bride for him ('Bella siccome un angelo'), whom he claims to be none other than his own sister, though he intends to employ his cousin Norina as the supposed bride. Pasquale confronts his nephew about his refusal to marry the woman his uncle approves of, ordering his nephew out of the house and announcing his own impending marriage ('Prender moglie!'). Realizing that his own hopes of marrying Norina are ruined ('Sogno soave e

The premiere of Don Pasquale *(Leipziger Illustrirte Zeitung, 1843)*

casto'), Ernesto suggests that his uncle should consult Dr Malatesta about this implausible prospect; he is astounded when he learns that the doctor has already given his whole-hearted approval. Scene 2: Norina reads a tale of chivalric love, laughing over its absurdity, and expressing her conviction that real femininity is far more persuasive ('So anch'io la virtù magica'). Dr Malatesta comes to see Norina to enlist her assistance in his plan to bring Pasquale to his senses. She is to pretend to be his sister 'Sofronia', fresh from a convent, and they agree on the details of the impersonation ('Pronta io son').

Act II The disillusioned Ernesto has made his preparations to depart ('Cercherò lontana terra'). In a fever of impatience, Pasquale awaits the bride. The doctor leads in a demure young lady wearing a veil, a spectacle that titillates the susceptible Pasquale ('Sta a vedere'). 'Sofronia' is upset to find herself in a room with a strange man, and, on being questioned, she admits to sewing as her only pastime. Malatesta produces a notary (in reality his nephew Carlino) and a wedding contract is drawn up by which Pasquale endows his bride with half his worldly goods. This arrangement is barely concluded when Ernesto appears to bid his uncle farewell; he is dismayed by Norina's apparent infidelity. No sooner is the contract signed than 'Sofronia' changes character completely, appointing Ernesto her *cavaliere servante*. When Pasquale objects, she insists on having her way. The old man is stunned by this turn of events ('E' rimasto là impietrato'). She demands more servants, carriages, and other extravagances, leaving Pasquale close to apoplexy.

Act III Scene 1: Don Pasquale is dismayed at the accumulation of bills run up by his bride. She appears in evening dress, announcing she is going to the theatre. When he objects, she advises him to go to bed. At the height of the altercation, she slaps his face. Now thoroughly disillusioned, Pasquale contemplates the results of his impulsiveness ('E' finita, Don Pasquale'). Seeing his discomfiture, Norina feels sorry for him and advises him to get a good night's sleep ('Via, caro sposino'). As she leaves, she drops a note, which Pasquale picks up and reads. Horrified to learn that an assignation in the garden is planned for that very evening, Pasquale summons Malatesta. The servants comment on the turmoil of the household ('Che interminabile andirivieni!'). When Malatesta appears, he and the doctor plot how they will catch Norina and unmask her infidelity ('Cheti, cheti, immantinente'). Scene 2: Ernesto serenades his beloved ('Com'è gentil'). Norina steals in, and they sing a tender duet ('Tornami a dir che m'ami'). Pasquale surprises them, but Malatesta resolves the imbroglio by persuading his friend to agree to annul his own marriage and allow Ernesto to marry Norina. Although he feels he has been made a fool of, Pasquale is so relieved to be free of 'Sofronia' that he blesses the young lovers.

Although *Don Pasquale* makes some use of music that had already been used in other contexts, the score seems perfectly homogenous. Written in a relatively short time, the music was carefully worked out, as the compositional sketches testify. The overture sparkles, and quotes several themes that appear later in the opera: notably Ernesto's Act III serenade and Norina's self-analysing aria from Act I. Malatesta's aria in the opening scene, 'Bella siccome un angelo', in which he describes the charms of his mythical sister, is a fine example of *bel canto* irony. The high spirits of the work are neatly epitomized in the duet for Norina and Malatesta that closes Act I, wherein he coaches her in the part she must play to bamboozle Pasquale. Act II, with its unflagging build-up to an hilarious climax, is for many the summit of Donizetti's achievement. Act III contains its own share of riches in three irresistible duets and an apt finale to point the moral of the piece: that December should not tempt fate with May. Instead of the traditional *secco* recitative, the connective passages are string-accompanied. The mid-point finale is a solo quartet without choral reinforcement; indeed, the chorus appears only in the two scenes of Act III.

RECORDINGS 1. Saraceni, Schipa, Poli, Badini, Ch and O of La Scala, Sabajno, EMI, 1932 (CD 1990); 2. Noni, Valletti, Borriello, Bruscantini, Turin Ch and SO of RAI, Rossi, Cetra, 1952; 3. Freni, Winbergh, Nucci, Bruscantini, Ambrosian Opera Ch, Philharmonia O, Muti, EMI, 1983: in terms of style and brio the older performances are both preferable, with the 1952 the more equally cast, but the 1932, refurbished on CD, is notable for Schipa's classic Ernesto [A.B.]
VIDEO Watson, R. Davies, Smythe, G Evans, WNO Ch and O, Armstrong, Pickwick
EDITIONS f.s., Ricordi, [c. 1895]; rp, 1971, 1980; v.s., Ricordi, [c. 1970]

Maria di Rohan

Opera seria in three acts (2h 15m)
Libretto by Salvatore Cammarano (originally for Lillo, 1839) after the play by Lockroy and Edmond Badon, *Un duel sous le Cardinal de Richelieu* (1832)
Composed 1843, rev. 1843
PREMIERES 5 June 1843, Kärntnertortheater, Vienna; rev. version: 14 November 1843, Théâtre-Italien, Paris; UK: 8 May 1847, Covent Garden, London; US: 10 December 1849, New York
CAST Maria s, Riccardo (Chalais) t, Enrico (Chevreuse) bar, Armando di Gondi t (a in rev. version), Visconte di Suze b, De Fiesque b, Aubry t, servant b; satb chorus of courtiers, servants
FULL ORCHESTRA including cimbasso, ophicleide

Maria di Rohan is Donizetti's tautest, most melodramatic opera. Beginning slowly, the action accelerates, punctuated by striking clocks, until it erupts in the devastating final scene. It shows the mature Donizetti in complete control of his musico-dramatic goals. The erroneous notion that so-called *bel canto* operas require only great singing and are devoid of dramatic values is given the emphatic lie by this work.

SYNOPSIS

Act I In Paris during the period of Cardinal Richelieu, Riccardo, count of Chalais, has been

The finale of Maria di Rohan *with Eugenia Tadolini (Maria), Giorgio Ronconi (Chevreuse) and Carlo Guasco (Chalais); (Vienna, 1843)*

Maria's lover, and he still loves her. When she comes to him to implore him to use his influence to save her husband Chevreuse, who has killed the cardinal's nephew in a duel, he, unaware of her secret marriage, obliges. When Gondi, a young gallant, insults Maria, Chalais instantly challenges him. Maria's husband, released from prison through Chalais's intercession, volunteers to be his second.

Act II   Chalais sends a note of farewell to Maria to be delivered only if he falls in the duel with Gondi. Maria arrives, come to warn him that Richelieu is now his enemy, but she conceals herself when Chevreuse appears to accompany Chalais to the duel. Chevreuse leaves first, and Maria emerges from her hiding place to insist that Chalais not risk such danger on her account and admits that she still loves him. When he is informed that Chevreuse is about to fight Gondi in his place, he rushes off.

Act III   Chevreuse has fought in the place of the tardy Chalais and has sustained a wound in his arm. Learning that Richelieu's men have seized compromising documents in his room, Chalais comes to warn Maria that discovery is imminent and urges her to escape with him. Unaware of these developments, Chevreuse shows Chalais a secret passage, and as Chalais enters it he informs Maria that he will return for her when the clock next strikes if she has not come to him by then. One of the cardinal's men sends Maria off and gives Chevreuse the compromising letter. Consumed by murderous jealousy, he confronts Maria, who refuses to deny that she has been Chalais's mistress. The clock strikes and Chalais returns, whereupon Chevreuse challenges him. They rush off into the secret passage, leaving Maria half fainting as a gunshot is heard. Chevreuse returns to inform her that Chalais has turned his pistol on himself. Maria demands that her husband kill her too, but he condemns her to a life of shame.

There are a number of expressive arias, particularly Maria's *larghetto* in Act I ('Cupa, fatal mestizia') and Chalais's single-movement air ('Alma soave e cara') at the beginning of Act II. The duet for Maria and Chalais at the end of Act II ('Ecco l'ora') sounds a genuine note of despair. The interchange between Chevreuse and Maria in Act III, when he confronts her with her guilt, has a conciseness and emotional impact that show Donizetti at the height of his powers.

RECORDING   Nicolesco, Morino, Coni, Slovak Philharmonic Ch of Bratislava, International O of Italian Opera, De Bernart, Nuova Era, 1988
EDITION   v.s., Ricordi, [c. 1872]

Dom Sébastien

Grand opera in five acts
Libretto by Eugène Scribe after Paul Henri Foucher's play
Dom Sébastien de Portugal (1838)
Composed 1843
PREMIERES   13 November 1843, Opéra, Paris;
US: 25 November 1864, New York

The complicated plot deals with the crusade of Dom Sébastien, king of Portugal, against the Moors in Africa. At Lisbon, the Grand Inquisitor plots against him, intending to turn Portugal over to Spain. Having rescued a beautiful Moorish princess Zaïde before he sailed for Africa, the king takes her with him to return her to her father. At Alcazar Kebir, the Portuguese army meets Arab forces in battle; Dom Sébastien is seriously wounded and presumed dead. However, nursed by Zaïde, he survives and returns to Lisbon, where he is horrified to witness a state funeral for the 'late' ruler. When he protests, he is seized as an impostor. Zaïde has also come to Lisbon, with her jealous Moorish fiancé, Abayaldos. She appears at Sébastien's trial by the Inquisition, but when she attempts to reveal the true circumstances of the king's survival, she is charged with treason. In prison, Zaïde has been told that she can save her life and the king's if she can persuade him to sign his approval of Spain's claim to his kingdom. He refuses, and they agree to die together since they cannot live together. Camoëns, the poet and the king's truest friend, opportunely appears at the window of Sébastien's cell ready to help them escape via a rope ladder. In the brief final scene, the lovers are shot by soldiers as they make their way down the ladder, while the Grand Inquisitor pledges his allegiance to Spain, but Camoëns, led in under guard, has the last words: 'Gloire à Dom Sébastien!'

Dom Sébastien is Donizetti's most monumental work, although it is hampered by Scribe's crude dramaturgy. There are many massive ensembles, most notably the eloquent septet in Act IV. Justifiably famous arias are Sébastien's romance at the end of Act II, 'Seul sur la terre', and Camoëns's air at the beginning of Act III, 'O Lisbonne'. The awesome funeral march provided the basis for an evocative piano transcription by Liszt, and Mahler's *Lieder eines fahrenden Gesellen* contains an allusion to this march. *Dom Sébastien* is worthy of rediscovery as it contains some of the mature Donizetti's most highly wrought music, although the score is not of uniformly top quality.

RECORDING   in Italian as *Don Sebastiano*: Barbieri, Poggi, Mascherini, Neri, Ch and O of Maggio Musicale Fiorentino, Giulini, Melodram, 1955
EDITIONS   f.s. (in Italian), facsimile, Garland, 1980; v.ss., (in French), Bureau central de musique, 1843; (in Italian), Ricordi, 1844, 1846, *rp*, Belwin Mills, 1981; (in German), Mechetti, 1844

Other operas: *L'ira d'Achille*, (1817); *Enrico di Borgogna*, 1818; *Una follia*, 1818; *Il falegname di Livonia, o Pietro il grande, czar delle Russie*, 1819; *Le nozze in villa*, 1820/21; *Zoraide di Granata*, 1822; *La zingara*, 1822; *Chiara e Serafina*, 1822; *Alfredo il grande*, 1823; *Il fortunato inganno*, 1823; *Alahor in Granata*, 1826; *Elvida*, 1826; *Otto mesi in due ore*, 1827; *Gianni di Calais*, 1828; *Il paria*, 1829; *Francesca di Foix*, 1831; *La romanziera e l'uomo nero*, 1831; *L'ange de Nisida*, (1839); *Adelia*, 1841
BIBLIOGRAPHY   John Stewart Allitt, *Donizetti and the Tradition of Romantic Love*, The Donizetti Society, 1975; John Stewart Allitt, *Donizetti in the Light of the Romanticism and the Teaching of Johann Simon Mayr*, Element, 1991; William Ashbrook, *Donizetti and His Operas*, CUP, 1982; Philip Gossett, *Anna Bolena and the Artistic Maturity of Donizetti*, OUP, 1985; H. Weinstock, *Donizetti*, Random House, 1963

W.A.

ANTONIO DRAGHI
b c. 1634, Rimini; *d* 16 January 1700, Vienna

Although virtually forgotten today, Antonio Draghi was one of the most influential personalities in the history of Viennese opera. He may have spent his early years in Rome or Mantua, though his music suggests Venice as a more likely training ground. He sang in at least one opera as a bass in Venice before moving to Vienna in 1658. For his first few years in Vienna his main work was as a librettist; in 1666 he wrote both words and music for his first opera, *La Mascherata*. At this time he was in the service of the Empress Dowager, Eleanor, but was also involved with operatic performances at the imperial court, where he was appointed director of dramatic music in 1673. Nine years later he succeeded J. H. Schmelzer as imperial kapellmeister.

Draghi's enormous output included over 120 operas, many to libretti by the court poet Nicolò Minato. For a number of these the Emperor Leopold I, a talented musician, provided several arias and even whole scenes. Draghi's early style is based on that of the Venetian masters Cesti and Cavalli, but in his later works the arias in particular show a development from the earlier strophic form into full-scale *da capo* arias, sometimes with virtuoso passage-work.

Surviving operas: *La Mascherata*, 1666; *Comedia ridicula*, 1667; *Gl'amori di Cefalo e Procri*, 1668; *Chi più sà manco l'intende, overo Gli amori di Clodio e Pompea*, 1669; *Achille in Sciro*, 1669; *Il Perseo*, 1669; *Atalanta*, 1669; *Leonida in*

Tegea, 1670 (EDITION facsimile, Garland, 1982); *Iphide Greca*, 1670; *Penelope*, 1670; *L'avidità di Mida*, 1671; *La prosperità di Elia Seiano*, 1671; *La gara dei genij*, 1671; *Cidippe*, 1671; *Gl'atomi d'Epicuro*, 1672; *Gundeberga*, 1672; *Sulpitia*, 1672; *Il gioir della speranza*, ?1673; *Batto convertito in sasso*, 1673; *Gl'incantesimi disciolti*, 1673; *La lanterna di Diogene*, 1674; *Le staggioni ossequiose*, 1674; *Il ratto delle Sabine*, 1674; *Il trionfatore de' centauri*, 1674; *Il fuoco eterno custodito dalle Vestali*, 1674; *I pazzi Abderiti*, 1675; *Pirro*, 1675; *Turia Lucretia*, 1675; *Scegliere non potendo adoprare*, 1676; *Hercole acquistatore dell'immortalità*, 1677; *Chilonida*, 1677; *Adriano sul Monte Casio*, 1677; *Le maghe di Tessaglia*, 1677; *Rodogone*, 1677; *La fortuna delle corti*, 1677; *La conquista del vello d'oro*, 1678; *Leucippe Festia*, 1678; *Il tempio di Diana in Taurica*, 1678; *Enea in Italia*, 1678; *Li favoriti dalla fortuna*, 1678; *Baldracca*, 1679; *La svogliata*, 1679; prologue, sung parts and epilogue to *Mixtum austriacum*, 1679; *I vaticinij di Tiresia tebano*, 1680; *La patienza di Socrate con due moglie*, 1680; *Temistocle in Persia*, 1681; *L'albero del ramo d'oro*, 1681; *Gli stratagemi di Biante*, 1682; *La chimera*, 1682; *Il tempio d'Apollo in Delfo*, 1682; *Il giardino della virtù*, 1683; *Lo smemorato*, 1683; *La lira d'Orfeo*, 1683; *Gl'elogii*, 1684; intermedio for *Il finto astrologo*, 1684; prologue and intermezzi for *Anfitrione*, 1685; *La più generosa Spartana*, 1685; *Il Palladio in Roma*, 1685; *Il rissarcimento della ruota della Fortuna*, 1685; *Lo studio d'amore*, 1686; *Le scioccagini degli Psilli*, 1686; *Il nodo gordiano*, 1686; *Le ninfe ritrose*, 1686; *Il ritorno di Teseo dal labirinto di Creta*, 1686; *La grotta di Vulcano*, 1686; *La vittoria della fortezza*, 1687; *La fama addormentata e risvegliata*, 1687; *Il marito ama più*, 1688; *Tanisia*, 1688; *La moglie ama meglio*, 1688; *Psiche cercando Amore*, 1688; *Pigmaleone in Cipro*, 1689; *La Rosaura, overo Amore, figlio della gratitudine*, 1689; *Il riposo nelli disturbi*, 1689; *Il Telemacco, overo Il valore coronato*, 1689; *La regina de' Volsci*, 1690; *La chioma di Berenice*, 1695; *Il ringiovenito*, 1691; *Il pelegrinaggio delle Gratie all'oracolo dodoneo*, 1691; *Fedeltà e Generosità*, 1692; *Le varietà di fortuna*, 1692; *Il vincitor magnanimo*, 1692; *L'amore in sogno, overo Le nozze d'Odati, e Zoriadre*, 1693; *La madre degli dei*, 1693; *Pelopida tebano in Tessaglia*, 1694; *L'industrie amorose in Filli di Tracia*, 1695; *La finta cecità di Antioco il Grande*, 1695; *La magnanimità di Marco Fabrizio*, 1695; *Timone misantropo*, 1696; *Le piramidi d'Egitto*, 1697; *L'Adalberto, overo La forza dell'astuzia femminile*, 1697; *L'amare per virtù, overo La tirannide placata*, 1697; *La tirannide abbatuta dalla virtù*, 1697; *L'Arsace, fondatore dell'imperio de' Parthi* (coll. with C. D. Draghi), 1698; *La forza dell'amor filiale* (coll. with C. D. Draghi), 1698; 24 lost operas
BIBLIOGRAPHY   Rudolf Schnitzler and Herbert Seifert, 'Antonio Draghi', in *Grove*, Macmillan, 1980

T.T.C.

GIOVANNI BATTISTA DRAGHI
d 1708, London

If the harpsichordist and organist Giovanni Battista Draghi was the younger brother of the Viennese opera composer Antonio Draghi, as has been suggested, then he was born in Rimini around 1640. He appeared in England in the winter of 1666–7 as a member of an embryonic Italian opera company, and astonished Pepys in February 1667 by singing from memory an act of an Italian opera he had composed for the venture. The operatic venture came to nothing, and the opera has not survived – if it was ever written down. Instead, Draghi became organist of the queen's Catholic chapel, and wrote songs and instrumental music for the London theatres. He collaborated with Matthew Locke in the instrumental music for Shadwell's operatic version of *The Tempest* (1674), and contributed incidental music and dances to Locke's semi-opera *Psyche* (1675), also to a text by Shadwell; virtually all of this is lost. His most important surviving work is his setting of Dryden's 1687 *Ode to St Cecilia*, 'From harmony, from heavenly harmony', which influenced Purcell's subsequent odes, and shows that he could have been a fine opera composer. He served successive monarchs until 1698, when William III gave him a pension 'in consideration of near 30 years service in the royal family [i.e. household] and of his being incapacitated by the gout'.

BIBLIOGRAPHY Introduction to Michael Tilmouth, *Matthew Locke: Dramatic Music*, Stainer and Bell (*Musica Britannica* 51), 1986

P.H.

GEORGE DREYFUS
b 22 July 1928, Wuppertal, Germany

Dreyfus migrated to Australia in 1939. He studied at the Melbourne University Conservatorium (clarinet and bassoon), and later (1955–6) at the Vienna Academy. The experience of playing the bassoon in various opera orchestras led him to compose his first opera, *Garni Sands*, in 1965. He has been involved in the performance of new music, and he formed the New Music Ensemble in 1958. But the advanced style of his early works has given way to a more popular manner in music for children, such as a school opera *The Takeover*, and his successful film and television music.

Operatic works: *Garni Sands*, 1965; *The Takeover*, 1969; *The Gilt-Edged Kid*, 1970; *Rathenau*, 1993
BIBLIOGRAPHY James Murdoch, *Australian Contemporary Composers*, Macmillan, 1972

A.I.G.

PAUL DUKAS
Paul Abraham Dukas; *b* 1 October 1865, Paris; *d* 17 May 1935, Paris

Dukas is still best known – even almost exclusively known – for his brilliant orchestral scherzo *L'apprenti sorcier* (1897). But his major works include two distinguished scores for the theatre; the opera *Ariane et Barbe-Bleue* and the ballet *La Péri* (1911–12), and he started or planned several other operas, including *Horn et Rimenhild* (1892, libretto by Dukas, Act I only drafted), *L'arbre de science* (1899, libretto by Dukas), and possibly a late setting of *The Tempest*, which, if it existed, was probably destroyed by the composer. Two student overtures,

to Shakespeare's *King Lear* (1883) and Goethe's *Goetz von Berlichingen* (1884), survive in manuscript, and there is a published overture based on Corneille's *Polyeucte* (1891).

Dukas studied composition at the Paris Conservatoire with Debussy's teacher Ernest Guiraud (whose own opera, *Frédégonde*, he later helped Saint-Saëns to orchestrate), and he spent much of the 1880s striving without success to emulate Debussy in winning the Prix de Rome, although he was awarded second prize in 1888 for his cantata *Velléda*. Later he published quantities of music criticism (again like Debussy), worked as an editor (of Beethoven, Rameau, Couperin, Domenico Scarlatti) and taught composition: his pupils included Albéniz and Messiaen. But creative work gave him difficulty; he produced only at a very slow pace, and eventually gave up finishing new works altogether, though as with his exact contemporary Sibelius there were always reports of major works in hand. He was a member of the Académie des Beaux-Arts for the last year of his life and it was to his chair that Stravinsky failed to secure election in January 1936.

Ariane et Barbe-Bleue
Ariadne and Bluebeard
Conte musical in three acts (2h)
Libretto by Maurice Maeterlinck
Composed 1899–1906
PREMIERES 10 May 1907, Opéra-Comique, Paris; US: 29 March 1911, Metropolitan Opera, New York; UK: 20 April 1937, Covent Garden, London
CAST Barbe-Bleue *b*, Ariane *ms*, Nurse *a*, Sélysette *ms*; Ygraine *s*, Mélisande *s*, Bellangère *s*, Alladine *silent*, Old Peasant *b*, 2 other peasants *t*, *b*; *satb* chorus of peasants
LARGE ORCHESTRA including 2 hp, cel

Dukas was at work on *L'arbre de science* when, in 1899, the Symbolist Maeterlinck's text was first published. Unlike his earlier *Pelléas et Mélisande*, it was always intended as an operatic libretto, which, it seems, Maeterlinck hoped would be set by Grieg. Dukas was thus able to compose it as it stood, apart from minor cuts and a few verbal changes (which tend, in particular, to dilute the eroticism of Ariadne's relationship with Bluebeard's previous wives).

Perhaps because it was meant as an opera, the libretto has more action than usual in Maeterlinck. The chorus of peasants intrudes into Bluebeard's domain almost like the populace breaking into the prison in Verdi's *Don Carlos*, and there is also a good deal of description, by the wives, of vigorous action offstage. The drama is hence much less private than *Pelléas* or than Balázs's later *Bluebeard* libretto set by Bartók, both of which are plays about the communication of inward states or feelings. *Ariane* seems rather to confront the problem of freedom, on the one hand as a social issue (in the feudal and feminist sense), and on the other as a question of what is psychologically consistent with normal human affections. Ariadne, like her Cretan namesake, shows the way out of prison, though this time it is rejected (Maeterlinck subtitled his play 'La délivrance inutile'). The other wives, incidentally, are named after characters in earlier plays by Maeterlinck, and much of the drama's symbolic apparatus is likewise familiar.

SYNOPSIS
Act I Ariadne, Bluebeard's latest wife, arrives at his castle with her Nurse, to the offstage shouts of peasants hostile to Bluebeard but sympathetic to her. She holds the keys to the seven locked doors, but discards the first six (which she is allowed to use) in favour of the forbidden seventh: 'The permitted teaches us nothing.' The Nurse nevertheless opens the first six in turn; from each cascade precious stones (respectively amethysts, sapphires, pearls, emeralds, rubies, diamonds). But when Ariadne opens the seventh door, it reveals only a shadowy opening, from which surges up the song of the five former wives, based on the folksong 'Les cinq filles d'Orlamonde' (a name that recalls the hidden world of *Pelléas*, Allemonde). Here Bluebeard makes the first of his two brief appearances and tries to prevent Ariadne descending the steps. The crowd breaks into the castle, but she assures them that Bluebeard has not harmed her.

Act II Ariadne does indeed go down into the subterranean hall to find and free her predecessors. Though miserable, they are reluctant to escape against Bluebeard's prohibition. All the same Ariadne leads them joyfully upwards into the light.

Act III The former wives are regaling themselves in fine clothes and jewellery when Bluebeard returns to the castle. But he is attacked by peasants (offstage) and brought in bound. Believing that the wives will kill him, the peasants withdraw. But in fact the women fuss round him, tending his injuries, and stealing furtive kisses. Finally, Ariadne releases him and, after inviting the other wives, one by one, to accompany her, departs alone with the Nurse.

When Dukas started his opera, Debussy's *Pelléas* was substantially composed (though neither completed nor performed until 1902), and Dukas knew much or all of the music, except the interludes, from the private runthroughs Debussy gave for close friends. Dukas's score is more robust than Debussy's (Debussy himself commented, in a letter to Dukas, on 'a certain implacability in the beauty of Ariane . . . [and] the torrent of sound which floods the orchestra'); yet there are many parallels, for instance in the use of the whole-tone scale to suggest subterranean mystery, contrasted with a bright, pentatonic B major for the sunlit sea- and landscape at noon. Dukas even quotes Debussy's opera, at Mélisande's first appearance in Act II, and again when Ariadne unties her hair in Act III. In Act III there are allusions to Debussy's *La mer* (1905).

But Dukas's music seldom actually sounds like Debussy, who indeed later criticized it as un-French. It has a long line which still occasionally recalls Wagner, and which can accommodate lengthy quotations of folksongs such as 'Les cinq filles d'Orlamonde' and 'Au clair de la lune' without incongruity; and there are passages of glittering orchestration, notably in Act III, which suggest a

Léon Rothier as Bluebeard in Ariane et Barbe-Bleue *(New York, 1911)*

Russian influence. The radical elements in Debussy are lacking. Dukas's recitative is more conventional and rhetorical, and the descriptive music (particularly for the first six doors) may suggest Massenet or Fauré. Nevertheless Dukas employs the extended tonal harmony of the day with much subtlety and virtuosity, including scene-setting archaisms, like the sumptuously scored open fifths that frame the work. On the larger scale the work is strongly made, with an incisive key structure (based on F sharp) which occasionally takes on symbolic force but mainly works structurally, as in a three-movement symphony.

Ariane et Barbe-Bleue is exceptionally dependent on the female voice. Ariadne herself is on stage almost throughout, and the Nurse and the four singing wives all have bigger parts than Bluebeard, who sings for only a few minutes at the end of Act I. The chorus male voices and the small parts for male peasants are a slight counterbalance. But since the male characters are as supine and deferential as the former wives, they between them merely draw attention to the dominating life-force of Ariadne herself and the way she controls the action.

RECORDING   Katherine Ciesinski, Paunova, Bacquier, Nouvel O Philharmonique, Jordan, Erato, 1983
EDITIONS   f.s., Durand, 1907; v.s., Durand, 1906

BIBLIOGRAPHY   Booklet with Erato recording of *Ariane et Barbe-Bleue*, which includes English texts of essays by Dukas and Messiaen first published in the Dukas issue of *La revue musicale*, May–June 1936; G. Favre, *L'oeuvre de Paul Dukas*, Durand, 1969

S.W.

ISAAK DUNAYEVSKY
Isaak Iosifovich Dunayevsky; *b* 30 January 1900, Lokhvitsa, Poltava, Russia; *d* 25 July 1955, Moscow

Dunayevsky studied at the Kharkov Conservatory. In the early 1920s, he composed incidental music and ballet scores for the Kharkov Dramatic Theatre, and later for the Moscow Theatre of Satire. This led to a complete operetta, *Zhenikhi* (*The Bridegroom*), in 1927. In 1934 he wrote the score for the first notable Soviet film musical, *Vesyoliye rebyata* (*Merry Fellows*, 1934). By this time, Dunayevsky's style was a cheerful amalgam of Russian folksiness and 1920s proto-American popular jazz. Stage successes included *Zolotoya dolina* (*The Golden Valley*, 1937) and *Belaya akatsia* (*The White Acacia*, 1955) – the latter is still occasionally revived. Dunayevsky's style is direct and patriotic, concentrating on robust marches and sentimental melodies, many of which are remembered today by older Russians.

RECORDINGS   *The Golden Valley* (excerpts), Melodiya, 1960s; *The White Acacia*, Melodiya, 1950s
BIBLIOGRAPHY   Genrikh Orlov, 'Isaac Iosifovich Dunayevsky', in *Grove*, Macmillan, 1981

R.T.

THOMAS DUNHILL
Thomas Frederick Dunhill; *b* 1 February 1877, London *d* 13 March 1946, Scunthorpe, England

Dunhill, who studied at the Royal College of Music in London and later taught there and at Eton College, gained a reputation (which has barely survived) as a minor composer of chamber music and art songs and as an academic author. However, one of his later books was on Sullivan's comic operas, and it shortly preceded his own ventures in this field.

Tantivy Towers
Light opera in three acts
Libretto by A. P. Herbert
PREMIERE   16 January 1931, Lyric Theatre, Hammersmith

Nigel Playfair's management of the Lyric Theatre had resulted in successful revivals of English ballad operas in the 1920s (starting with *The Beggar's Opera*); *Tantivy Towers* inaugurated a further policy of producing new English operas. Its plot concerns what happens when Bohemia and County meet (and fall in love); both worlds can appear ridiculous, and when Hugh the modern artist puts a hunted fox out of its misery he is rejected by the upper-class Ann and returns to Chelsea with his girlfriend Jenny. Herbert and Dunhill were acclaimed by some as the new Gilbert and Sullivan, but the incisive lyrics and well-crafted music showed merit rather than genius.

EDITION   v.s., Cramer, 1930

Other operas: *The Enchanted Garden*, 1928; *Happy Families*, 1933
BIBLIOGRAPHY   Kurt Gänzl, *The British Musical Theatre*, vol. 2: *1915–1984*, Macmillan, 1986

S.B.

EGIDIO DUNI
Egidio Romualdo Duni; *baptized* 11 February 1708, Matera, nr Naples; *d* 11 June 1775, Paris

An important turning-point in Duni's career came in the late 1740s when he was appointed maestro di cappella at the court of Parma. Until then his output had consisted of a dozen fairly conventional opere serie, variously staged in Rome, Milan, London and Florence. At Parma, however, he turned almost exclusively to musical comedy. First he collaborated with the playwright Goldoni on the 'melodramma giocoso' *La buona figliuola* (the music of this, Duni's last Italian opera, is lost). Then, encountering opéra comique for the first time at the francophile Parma court, he set Anseaume's *Le peintre amoureux de son modèle*. For its first performance at the Opéra-Comique in 1757, Duni travelled to Paris and settled there soon afterwards, composing some 20 works for the Comédie-Italienne and other theatres.

With their sensitive treatment of the French language within an Italian musical idiom, Duni's opéras comiques were highly successful. Much imitated both in France and abroad, they helped create a new musical genre: the comédie mêlée d'ariettes. Vaudeville melodies were gradually eliminated, while the Italianate style of the ariettes and recitative was subtly balanced by traditional French elements, notably divertissements and small ensembles.

Surviving operatic works: *Nerone*, 1735; *Demofoonte*, 1737; *Catone in Utica*, 1740; *Demetrio* (doubtful), ?1747; *Olimpiade*, 1755; *Le retour au village*, (1759); *Le peintre amoureux de son modèle*, 1757; *Le docteur Sangrado*, 1758; *La fille mal gardée, ou Le pédant amoureux*, 1758; *Nina et Lindor, ou Les caprices du coeur*, 1758; *La veuve indécise*, 1759; *L'isle des foux*, 1760; *Mazet*, 1761; *Le procès, ou La plaideuse*, 1762; *Le milicien*, 1763; *Les deux chasseurs et la laitière*, 1763; *Le rendez-vous*, 1763; *L'école de la jeunesse, ou Le Barnevelt français*, 1765; *La fée Urgèle, ou Ce qui plaît aux dames*, 1765; *La clochette*, 1766; *Les moissonneurs*, 1768; *Les sabots*, 1768; *Thémire*, 1770

BIBLIOGRAPHY K. M. Smith, *Egidio Duni and the Development of the 'Opéra-Comique' from 1753 to 1770*, dissertation, Cornell University, 1980

G.S.

JOSEP DURÁN

Josep Durán [José Durán]; *b* Barcelona, Spain; *d* after 1791, Barcelona

By 1755, the Catalan composer Durán was serving as music master in the household of the Marqués de los Vélez and later probably became maestro de capilla of Barcelona Cathedral. He wrote two operas, *Antígona* and *Temístocles*, first performed in Barcelona in 1760 and 1762 respectively, not only in unashamed Italian style with libretti by Metastasio but also with Italian singers. These Italianate operas are a corollary to one of the 18th century's most celebrated polemics about music in Spain, centred on a debate during the 1750s between Durán and the maestro de capilla of Toledo Cathedral, Jaime Casellas, about nationalism in sacred music. The importance of *Antígona* and *Temístocles* lies less in their success as operas than in their testimony to Durán's unswerving preference for Italian styles over Catalan or Spanish traditions.

BIBLIOGRAPHY E. Cotarelo y Mori, *Orígenes y establecimiento de la ópera hasta finales del siglo XVIII*, Archivos, 1917

J.W.S.

ZSOLT DURKÓ

b 10 April 1934, Szeged, Hungary

A pupil of Ferenc Farkas in Budapest and Goffredo Petrassi in Rome, Durkó was for some years the most successful, and the most performed abroad, of the new generation of Hungarian composers that emerged in the more liberal climate after the 1956 Revolution. His style appeared as a synthesis of certain modern base ingredients: serial atonality on the one hand, and on the other a kind of historical Impressionism drawing on the music of old Hungary – medieval codices, organum, gypsy music, and a micro-polyphony weaving tiny motifs into dense patterns (as in middle-period Bartók). This was mainly an instrumental style, but there are also important choral works, and an opera.

Moses

Mózes

Music drama in three acts
Libretto by the composer, after the play by Imre Madách
Composed 1972–7
PREMIERES 15 May 1977, Budapest

This is a fairly straight three-act telling of the biblical story, cast, like nearly all Durkó's works, in a number of short sections, or tableaux. Many of the above-noted fingerprints are prominent. The texture is often dense, and there is very full choral writing, using speech, non-synchronized polyphony and clusters to create the feeling of a crowd. Individual tableaux are somewhat static, as in oratorio. Durkó said at the time that 'the drama arises from the interdependence of the leader, a man of superior gifts including that of guiding others, and the community who are incapable of consciously taking their fate into their own hands'.

RECORDING excerpts: Sass, Szönyi, Utö, Hungarian State Opera Ch and O, Kórodi, Hungaroton, 1970s
EDITION v.s., Editio Musica Budapest, 1977

BIBLIOGRAPHY Stephen Walsh, 'Durkó's *Mózes*', *Tempo*, no. 122 (September 1977), pp. 32–3

S.W.

SEBASTIÁN DURÓN

baptized 19 April 1660, Brihuega, Castile, Spain; *d* 3 August 1716, Cambo-les-Bains, Pyrenees, France

Durón's importance lies not only in his crucial role in the development of 18th-century theatre music in Spain but in the controversy stirred up by his music and his political affiliations. Between 1679 and 1691 his fame, thanks to prominent organist positions, grew to the extent that in 1691 he was appointed music master of the royal chapel of Charles II (the last Habsburg monarch) in Madrid. But, with the king's death in 1700, the proclamation of a Bourbon as Philip V of Spain and the War of Succession that followed, Durón found himself forced into exile. He spent most of the remainder of his life in southern France.

Durón was fiercely attacked by the influential Benedictine, Feijoo, allegedly for corrupting Spanish traditions by introducing an Italianate style of composition. Since his operatic style is no more than a logical and sensitive development of the Italian styles introduced half a century earlier by Hidalgo, the most likely explanation of Feijoo's venom is political bias.

Durón wrote at least ten music dramas, eight of which are extant. *La guerra de los gigantes* is specifically an *ópera* (the first recorded use of the word in Spain) and *Apolo y Dafne* is virtually an opera though designated a zarzuela. Acclaimed by fellow composers in his day in the teeth of Feijoo's vitriolic attack, Durón merits the recent revival of interest in his theatre music.

Operatic works: *Salir el Amor del mundo*, 1696; *Muerte en amor es la ausencia*, 1697; possibly *Júpiter y Yoo, Los cielos premian desdenes* ('Anon.'), (fiesta zarzuela), 1699; *Selva encantada de Amor, c. 1700; Deducida de la guerra de los gigantes*, 1700; *Apolo y Dafne* (coll. with Juan de Navas), *c. 1700; El imposible mayor, en amor le vence Amor*, 1710; *Las nuevas armas de Amor*, 1711; *Veneno es de amor la envidia*, 1711

BIBLIOGRAPHY   William M. Bussey, *French and Italian Influence on the Zarzuela, 1700–1770*, UMI Research Press, 1982

J.W.S.

ANTONÍN DVOŘÁK

Antonín Leopold Dvořák; *b* 8 September 1841, Nelahozeves, nr Kralupy; *d* 1 May 1904, Prague

Dvořák's operatic education came largely from playing the viola in the orchestra of the Prague Provisional Theatre from its opening in 1862 until 1871, by which time he had written his first opera, *Alfred*. To say that his operatic career spanned most of his life as a composer is accurate but misleading. *Alfred* was written within five years of his first substantial surviving compositions such as the first two symphonies and the song-cycle *Cypresses* (*Cypřiše*); *Armida* was his last completed composition, premiered only a few weeks before his death. However the pattern of work that spans these two operas is irregular: between 1882, when he completed *Dimitrij*, and 1897, when he wrote *The Devil and Kate*, Dvořák composed only one new opera. During this 15-year period he was at the height of his powers, writing his three last symphonies, the Cello Concerto, the late chamber music and most of his choral music. His turning away from opera was partly a sign of his frustration with the medium and his lack of success in making any mark abroad with it, and perhaps a recognition that his natural talents lay elsewhere. There were also the practical circumstances that some of this time was spent outside Bohemia – his numerous trips to England (where large-scale choral works were preferred to operas), his three-year stint in America (where he went to the opera only twice and even wrote to a friend that he regretted all the time he had spent writing operas). Nor was there much demand for operas from Prague, which preferred to fill its brand new National Theatre, at least in the opening decade, with lavishly produced foreign novelties and ballets rather than native operas.

Therefore Dvořák's opera-writing falls into two distinct halves: at the beginning of his life and at the end, bridged by *The Jacobin* in the middle. Dvořák's earlier operatic period epitomizes many of the trends in contemporary Czech opera. His first opera, *Alfred* (1870), was in German, looking back to earlier German-orientated Prague composers. Its subject matter, like that of *Vanda* (1875), was concerned with national conflicts: English against Danes in *Alfred*; Poles against Germans in *Vanda*. This series of large-scale serious operas reaches a climax with

Dimitrij (1881–2). *Vanda* was written originally in five acts; *Dimitrij* was planned in five acts, though later reduced to four. This, together with their 'political' subject matter, suggests a debt to French grand opera, a model evident in many other aspects of composition, such as the deployment of double choruses and large-scale concerted finales.

Dvořák's three other operas of the 1870s, *King and Charcoal Burner*, *The Stubborn Lovers* and *The Cunning Peasant*, are all instead in the 'village comedy' type of Czech operas of the period. They are all on a smaller scale, the second and third in one and two acts respectively. The musical idiom is lighter and owes more to Lortzing and Nicolai than to Meyerbeer. Uniting both lines of development is an emphasis on instrumental music. All the operas have overtures; most have instrumental dances and recurring motifs to provide unity. It is remarkable that the libretti of these six operas were all by different librettists, in some cases writers completely unknown to Dvořák.

In *Dimitrij* Dvořák had worked closely with the librettist, Marie Červinková-Riegrová, and she provided him with the libretto for his next opera, *The Jacobin* (1887–8). Though Dvořák was not to write another new opera until 1897, the years after *Dimitrij* saw revision of three operas, among them a final version of *King and Charcoal Burner*, and some additions to *The Jacobin*. But the most radical revision was that of *Dimitrij*, rewritten in a sternly 'declamatory' version that jettisoned many of the ensembles. The inspiration behind this was Dvořák's later recognition of Wagnerian music drama: if there are Wagnerian traits in the earlier operas they are a good generation behind the time, the Wagner of *Tannhäuser* and *Lohengrin*.

With this radically changed aesthetic Dvořák approached the three operas written in his final period, which together with a series of tone poems formed the entire output of his final eight years. *The Devil and Kate* avoids duets, though the role of the chorus is undiminished and the piece is studded with recognizable set numbers. Orchestrally there is a great expansion – perhaps too great to accommodate the slender folktale on which it is based. In Dvořák's next opera, *Rusalka*, without doubt his masterpiece, the chorus has less work, but there are a number of real duets, while by the final opera, *Armida*, he had slipped back into an aesthetic not noticeably different from that of his first opera over 30 years earlier.

This is symptomatic of the problems with Dvořák's operas. He inherited a conception of opera that was, by current European standards, out of date, and, despite a flirtation with Wagnerian music drama in the 1890s, it did not really change or develop. Though he used recurring themes, they are those of a symphonist attempting to unify a long complex work rather than those of a musical dramatist using leitmotifs to supply extra-musical information. Dvořák's early operas tend to be hit or miss affairs, over-dependent on the strength of their libretti. His own compositional personality was not sufficiently developed to override this in the way that it does in

Antonín Dvořák (seated left) photographed in 1885 with Karel Bendl, Bohuslav Foerster, Karel Kovařovic (standing), Jindřich Kàan and Zdeněk Fibich

later works. With the exception of the flagging *Armida*, his operas from *Dimitrij* onwards all have distinct and forceful musical personalities which have spoken directly to the Czech public, over the heads of the strongly anti-Dvořák lobby that, in the early years of the century, was keen to promote almost any composer other than Dvořák as 'Smetana's successor'. Some of the results of this official disdain are still evident in the niggardly provision of scores and and recordings of the earlier works.

B. numbers refer to the Burghauser thematic catalogue; see BIBLIOGRAPHY.

Alfred

Heroic opera in three acts, B. 16
Libretto by Karl Theodor Korner (*Alfred der Grosse*)
Composed 1870
PREMIERE   in Czech: 10 December 1938, City Theatre, Olomouc

Dvořák composed his first opera in German to an early 19th-century text (used already by Flotow). Apart from an offhand remark in a German interview, Dvořák himself never referred to it and knowledge of its existence did not come to light until after the composer's death. This, together with the fact that it was written in German, has meant that the work has hardly been regarded as part of the canon

of Dvořák's operas. Nevertheless there are several links with his later operas, especially with *Vanda* (for which Dvořák borrowed music for one number) and, in its choice of operatic conventions, with later works such as *Dimitrij* and *Armida*. Its plot concerns Alfred the Great of England in ultimately successful conflict with the Danes.

King and Charcoal Burner
Král a uhlíř

First version: opera in three acts, B. 21
Second version: opera in three acts, B. 42
Third version: comic opera in three acts, B. 151
Libretto by B. J. Lobeský (pseudonym of Bernard Guldener), after a traditional puppet play; additions (third version) by V. J. Novotny
Composed 1871 (first version); 1874 (second version); rev. 1887
PREMIERES   second version: 24 November 1874, Provisional Theatre, Prague; third version: 15 June 1887, National Theatre, Prague; first version: 28 May 1929, National Theatre, Prague

The first version of Dvořák's first opera in Czech was put into rehearsal in 1873 and withdrawn by the composer because of difficulties it caused the performers. Dvořák then rewrote the opera completely, and in this state it was given in 1874. Dvořák's later revisions concern changes to the second version, especially to Act III, which was extensively rewritten.

SYNOPSIS

The core of the plot is a well-known puppet play. The king and the charcoal burner of the title are both called Matěj (Matthew) – which would date the action (unspecified by Dvořák) to the early 17th century during the rule of King Matyáš (1611–19). Lost in the wood, King Matěj seeks shelter with one of his humblest subjects and the two find that they have more than their name in common. The king's fatherly interest in Matěj's daughter Liduška, however, is misinterpreted by her hot-blooded lover Jeník, who goes off as a soldier. He prospers in the service of the king, who, with a ruse, finds a way of demonstrating Liduška's love for Jeník and uniting the lovers.

Dvořák's individuality in this work is more apparent than in the heroic operas that flank it, possibly because he was working with more familiar locales and more down-to-earth characters. Particularly striking is the long bagpipe episode in Act I, one of the earliest and most developed instances of this particularly distinctive feature of Czech opera of the period.

EDITION final (third) version: v.s., Hudební matice, 1915; 2nd edn, 1929

The Stubborn Lovers
Tvrdé palice
Comic opera in one act, B. 46 (1h)
Libretto by Josef Štolba
Composed 1874
PREMIERE 2 October 1881, New Czech Theatre, Prague

In the same year that Dvořák wrote his second version of *King and Charcoal Burner* he went on enthusiastically to complete a second comic opera. Unlike its predecessor, which had a range of characters from the very poor to the very rich (a feature of several of Dvořák's later operas), the characters of *The Stubborn Lovers* are all villagers: a girl and a boy (Lenka and Toník) destined for one another by their parents and also by inclination. But the couple are *tvrdé palice* (stubborn, pigheaded folk) and it needs the machinations of Řeřicha, their benevolent 'godfather', to bring them together by insinuating that Toník's widowed father was keen to marry Lenka and that Lenka's widowed mother had her eye on Toník. The three central characters bear something of a family resemblance to Mařenka, Jeník and Kecal in *The Bartered Bride*, with the difference that the bass Řeřicha is clearly on the lovers' side.

EDITIONS v.ss., Simrock, 1882; Simrock/Hudební matice, 1913

Vanda
Grand opera in five acts (rev., four acts), B. 55
Libretto by ?Julian Surzycki, Václav Beneš-Šumavský and František Zákrejs

Composed 1875, rev. 1879, 1883
PREMIERES original version: 17 April 1876, Provisional Theatre, Prague; four-act version: 13 February 1880, Provisional Theatre, Prague

The suggestion that a Warsaw professor, Julian Surzycki, provided the original material for the opera which was then translated into Czech by Václav Beneš-Šumavský and adapted for the stage by František Zákrejs, is undermined by the fact that no suitable Surzycki can be found and that his Czech collaborators had little to say about their part in the venture. The 'Polish' origin could perhaps be no more than a diversion to distract the censor from sensitive material about a sister Slav nation successfully repelling German invaders.

Vanda, who has succeeded her father to the Polish throne, promises her life to the gods in order to win a desperate fight against the German invaders. The Poles are successful, and Vanda throws herself into the Vistula, to the dismay of her courtiers and especially of her Polish lover, Slavoj. The parallels with Smetana's opera *Libuše* are limited to a central female ruler who, unlike Libuše, clearly has all her subjects behind her. The music is written on a grand scale, oratorio-like in places, with double choruses, a ballet and an interesting diversion into a black-magic atmosphere around the witch Homena, who is consulted by Roderich, Vanda's German suitor.

RECORDING Tikalová, Petrová, Hanzalíková, Blachut, Bednář, Rujan, Kalaš, Prague Radio Ch and O, Dyk, Supraphon, recorded 1951, issued 1985

The Cunning Peasant
Šelma sedlák
Comic opera in two acts, B. 67 (1h 45m)
Libretto by Josef Otakar Veselý
Composed 1877
PREMIERE 27 January 1878, Provisional Theatre, Prague

The Cunning Peasant was Dvořák's first opera to be played abroad (Dresden, 1882) and is written with considerable assurance and zest. Dvořák's skill in characterizing some of the minor comic parts (e.g. Veruna the village 'fixer'; Martin the rich but ponderous suitor, or Jean the nervous valet of the Prince) is clear and was to prove useful in his later operas. The Czech folkdance basis of some of the music (e.g. a particularly catchy male duet, 'Jsme čeští sedláci') begins to disengage the work from earlier models such as Lortzing. The ensemble-writing is accomplished, and two solos in Act I (for the heroine Bětuška, and for the Prince) impress as two of the most ravishing operatic numbers that Dvořák had written to date. All these considerable charms are however impaired by an over-complicated libretto in which Bětuška, ever faithful to the gormless Jeník, has not only her father's choice (Martin) to fight off as possible suitor, but also both the local Prince and his valet Jean. The philandering Prince, reconciled to his Princess by female stratagems, has often reminded commentators of *Le nozze di Figaro*. More significant, however, was the Czech penchant for action by strong women (the Princess, Veruna and even Bětuška) and the typical Dvořák libretto, with its range of classes, well separated, though living on friendly terms.

RECORDING Děpoltová, Soběhartová, Effenberková, Veselá, Vodička, Kundlák, Kopp, Zítek, Berman, Czech Radio Ch and O, Vajnar, Supraphon, 1987
EDITIONS f.s./v.s., Simrock, 1882; v.s., Simrock/Hudební matice, 1913

Dimitrij
Dimitri

Grand opera in four acts, B. 127; 1894–5 version, B. 186 (3h 15m)
Libretto by Marie Červinková-Riegrová, after Schiller and Mikovec
Composed 1881–2; rev., 1883, 1885, 1894–5
PREMIERES original version: 8 October 1882, New Czech Theatre, Prague; rev. version: 7 November 1894, National Theatre, Prague; UK: 30 January 1979, University Great Hall, Nottingham; US: April 1984, New York (concert)

Scenes from Dmitrij *(Prague, 1882)*

CAST Dimitrij Ivanovič *t*, Marfa Ivanovna *s*, Marina Mníškova *s*, Xenie Borisovna *s*, Petr Fedorovič Basmanov *b*, Prince Vasilij Šujský *bar*, Jov, Patriarch of Moscow *b*, 2 *bar*; *satb* chorus of people of Moscow, boyars and their wives, priests, Polish entourage, soldiers, dancers, pages
FULL ORCHESTRA

The plot of *Dimitrij* is a continuation of the story of Boris Godunov, with four characters in common: Dimitrij (assumed son of Ivan the Terrible who, however, genuinely believes in his claim), the Polish Marina of the princely Sandomír family (now his wife), the Russian Xenie (the daughter of Boris Godunov) and Prince Šujský, surprisingly now a supporter of Boris, and Dimitrij's chief antagonist.

SYNOPSIS
Act I After Boris's death the people of Moscow are confused and factionalized. Some (led by the Patriarch and Šujský) continue to support the Godunov family; others (led by the army general Basmanov) support the victorious Dimitrij. All depends on whether Marfa, the widow of Ivan the Terrible, will recognize Dimitrij as her son. In the crucial confrontation, Marfa realizes that Dimitrij is not her son, but decides to use him as an instrument of her revenge and publicly acknowledges him.
Act II shows Dimitrij in a positive light: quelling the fracas that breaks out between Poles and Russians, rescuing Xenie when she is pursued by drunken Poles, breaking up a conspiracy led by Šujský.
Act III When Šujský is to be executed, Xenie begs Dimitrij for mercy for him, only then realizing the identity of her rescuer. Marina jealously spots the sympathy between Dimitrij and Xenie and in a private scene with Dimitrij plays her most powerful card – revealing that Dimitrij is simply a peasant – only to find that Dimitrij has every intention of remaining tsar. She is crushed by his heroic stance: he repudiates her.
Act IV Dimitrij urges Xenie to marry him, though his intention is thwarted by (1882 version) Marina's having Xenie murdered or (later versions) Xenie's decision to enter a nunnery. Marina now publicly reveals Dimitrij's origins, which leads to a call for Marfa's renewed identification of Dimitrij. As Marfa hesitates, Dimitrij calls to her not to perjure herself, and is shot by Šujský.

For all its resemblance to Meyerbeer's *Le prophète* (the central figure of an impostor, with a crucial mother–son 'recognition' scene in full public gaze, and the generally French grand-opera conventions), there are vital differences between this opera and an actual French opera on the same subject (Joncières's *Dimitri*). In the French opera, there is no Russian–Polish confrontation (most of the plot takes place before Dimitrij gets to Russia); whereas Dvořák uses his double-chorus confrontations to great effect for opposing nationalities, and with surprisingly convincing imitations of Orthodox chant. Joncières's hero is a philandering weakling, a lyric tenor caught between

mistresses; Dvořák's Dimitrij is heroic in voice and action and chooses his consorts politically – the Polish Marina discarded for the Russian Xenie. Dvořák's opera unfolds unevenly, but in its dialectic confrontations, particularly that of Marina and Dimitrij in Act III, and in one of the greatest scenes in all Czech opera, Marfa's hesitation in Act IV, Dvořák shows a handling of dramatic tension that is immensely powerful and unparalleled in his other operas.

RECORDING Ághová, Drobková, Vodička, Czech Philharmonic Ch and O, Albrecht, Supraphon, 1989
EDITIONS v.s., Starý, 1886; f.s./v.s., Milan Pospíšil (ed.), Supraphon, in preparation

The Jacobin
Jakobín
Opera in three acts, B. 159; rev. version, B. 200 (2h 45m)
Libretto by Marie Červinková-Riegrová; additions by F. L. Riger
Composed 1887–8, rev. 1897
PREMIERES original version: 12 February 1889, National Theatre, Prague; rev. version: 19 June 1898, National Theatre, Prague; UK: 22 July 1947, St George's Hall, London (concert); 30 October 1968, Aston University, Birmingham
CAST Count Vilém z Harasova *b*, Bohuš z Harasova *bar*, Adolf z Harasova *bar*, Julie *s*, Filip *b*, Jiří *t*, Benda *t*, Terinka *s*, *contralto*; *satb* chorus of townsfolk, young people, schoolchildren, musicians, musketeers, country folk
FULL ORCHESTRA

SYNOPSIS
Act I Bohuš returns with his wife Julie to his home town in rural Bohemia. It is 1793; they have been abroad in Revolutionary France. Bohuš learns that during his absence his cousin Adolf has contrived to estrange him from his father, Count Vilém, for his 'Jacobin' tendencies and is due to replace him as the count's heir.
Act II Benda, the local teacher, rehearses his choir. He does not recognize his former pupil Bohuš who arrives asking for lodging, but hearing that Bohuš and Julie are musicians, agrees to take them in. Adolf meanwhile has heard of the arrival of the 'Jacobin' and arrests him.
Act III Julie manages to enter the castle secretly where she sings to the count a favourite song of his long-dead wife. The count asks who has been singing, meets Julie and hears about Bohuš's arrest and Adolf's machinations. Father and son are reconciled and at the same time Benda is persuaded to let his daughter marry her lover Jeník and relinquish the advantageous match that he had in mind for her.

Dvořák was at first reluctant to take on this libretto, which had been specially written for him. *The Cunning Peasant* had failed in Vienna; *Dimitrij*, written with an eye to foreign markets, had not been taken up abroad and Červinková-Riegrová's new libretto seemed to him too local – 'Such a teacher–musician [as Benda] exists only here and just wouldn't be understood elsewhere.' In many senses he was right: *The Jacobin* can claim to be one of the most quintessentially Czech operas. Like many of

Smetana's, it is about reconciliation, but this message is less important than the crucial role of music in the Czech national psyche, a notion that is stressed three times in the work. It is music – Julie's lullaby – that effects the reconciliation. Benda's celebrated choir-rehearsal scene, unlike its model in Lortzing's *Zar und Zimmermann*, is touching rather than amusing, and the characterization of Benda himself is an affectionate tribute to generations of Czech teacher-musicians. The most moving number in the opera, however, is Bohuš's and Julie's Act II duet ('My cizinou jsme bloudili' – 'We have wandered through foreign parts') where to poignantly emotional harmony they tell how in their long exile abroad – the fate of so many Bohemians – it was only in music that they found relief.

RECORDING Machotková, Šounová, Přibyl, Blachut, Zítek, Průša, Tuček, Berman, Brno State Philharmonic Ch and O, Pinkas, Supraphon, 1978
EDITIONS f.s., Souborné vydání, 1966, i/10; v.s., Hudební matice, 1911; rev. Kovařovic, Orbis, 1952

The Devil and Kate
Čert a Káča

Opera in three acts, B. 201 (2h 45m)
Libretto by Adolf Wenig, after a folktale
Composed 1898–9
PREMIERES 23 November 1899, National Theatre, Prague; UK: 22 November 1932, Oxford University Opera Club, Oxford; US: May 1988, Berkeley Opera Company
CAST Jirka *t*, Káča *ms*, Marbuel *b*, Lucifer *b*, Princess *s*, *s*, *t*, 3 *b*; *satb* chorus of peasants, young people, musicians, devils, courtiers, offstage populace
FULL ORCHESTRA

SYNOPSIS
Act I Amid the dancing one summer's evening two characters stand out: the shepherd Jirka, reluctantly leaving for work, and the portly and garrulous Káča (Kate). No one wants to dance with her, and in her anger she declares that she would dance even 'with the Devil' which is the cue for the appearance of the devil Marbuel, who is making inquiries about the oppressive local lady of the manor (the Princess) and her steward. Marbuel dances with Káča, who is then only too pleased to accompany him to his 'red castle'. The pair promptly vanish through the floor. Jirka, having lost his job, volunteers to rescue her.
Act II When Marbuel arrives in hell with his burden, he finds he has met his match in Káča. Hell is eager to be rid of her; she, however, is less eager to return. A deal is done: Káča will get money if she leaves; Jirka, who has now arrived in pursuit of her, will 'save' the Princess's steward from Marbuel when he comes for him and the Princess, and claim a reward from him.
Act III The Princess, now living in fear of her life, enlists Jirka's services. In return for her abolishing serfdom he frightens Marbuel away by producing Káča.

The Devil and Kate was written at the height of Dvořák's powers as a symphonist. This shows in the preponderance of purely instrumental music – partly justified by the story with its emphasis on dancing in the Act I pub scene, and in hell. There are also surprisingly long scene-preludes, including a striking descent to a Nibelheim-like hell at the beginning of Act II. Other Wagnerian influences are apparent in the almost total absence of solo ensemble; though not of the chorus, which plays a large part. It is one of the few Czech operas to lack love interest altogether: Act III ends with Káča's seemingly cynical declaration that now she has been richly rewarded for scaring off the Devil, she will be able to afford any bridegroom she likes. For all its oddness, this is one of Dvořák's most popular operas in Czechoslovakia, largely perhaps because it reinforces so many popular national assumptions. Musicians open the proceedings with another of Dvořák's bagpipe imitations, and continue to provide the fare for the dancing. Most Czech devils are comically incompetent; Marbuel is especially so, and is worsted by one of the most assertive of all the strong women depicted in Czech opera. And for all the laborious motivic work, it is the folklike strophic numbers that linger most in the mind: Jirka, with his touching song about losing his sheep, or Marbuel with his haunting and magnificently orchestrated description of his 'red castle'.

RECORDING Barová, Šulcová, Ježil, Horáček, Novák, Brno State Theatre Ch and O, Pinkas, Supraphon, 1980
EDITIONS f.s., Souborné vydání, 1972, i/11; v.ss., Mojmír Urbánek, 1908; Orbis, 4th edn, 1951

Rusalka

Lyric fairy-tale in three acts, B. 203 (3h)
Libretto by Jaroslav Kvapil, after Friedrich Heinrich Carl de la Motte Fouqué's tale *Undine*
Composed 1900
PREMIERES 31 March 1901, National Theatre, Prague; US: 10 November 1935, Sokol Slav Hall, Chicago; UK: 9 May 1950, Peter Jones Theatre, London
CAST Prince *t*, Foreign Princess *s*, Rusalka *s*, Water Goblin *b*, Ježibaba *ms*, 3 *s*, *a*, 2 *t*; *satb* chorus of wood sprites, the Prince's entourage, guests at the castle
FULL ORCHESTRA

SYNOPSIS
Act I Rusalka (a water nymph) wishes to become human to gain the love of the Prince. Ježibaba the witch makes two conditions for her magic: that Rusalka be dumb and that her lover be true – otherwise both will be damned. Despite the warnings of the fearful Water Goblin, Rusalka proceeds on this hazardous path; her Prince is captivated by her appearance, and takes her off with him.
Act II At court the dumb Rusalka is no match for the brilliant and evil Foreign Princess. Rumours circulate about Rusalka's supernatural origins, and the Prince rejects her.
Act III Rusalka, a pale shadow of her former self, mourns her state. Her Prince, now repentant, returns. She is able to speak to him and explain that he will die if she kisses him. He begs her to do so. At her kiss, he perishes, and Rusalka, released from the curse, disappears into the lake.

Ruzena Maturova in the title role of Rusalka

Rusalka stands out clearly above all of Dvořák's operas as his most successful and most popular. Unlike the rather thin tale on which *The Devil and Kate* is based, the Undine legend that lies behind *Rusalka* has a haunting resonance which is magically matched by Dvořák's music. The composer found a vein of melodic poignancy that memorably sets off his heroine: for many years Rusalka's 'Hymn to the moon' was all that was known abroad of Dvořák's vast operatic output. The libretto itself cleverly grafted on to its sources (which include Andersen's *Little Mermaid*) a folk periphery that identifies the work as distinctively Czech. Characters such as the doleful Water Goblin and the malicious witch were by then well known from Erben's ballads and had recently formed the basis of two of Dvořák's tone poems. Kvapil changed the chief characters too, notably Rusalka herself, who is here essentially a suffering Slavonic heroine (rather like Dargomyzhsky's Rusalka), rather than the skittish Undine in Lortzing's opera. Dvořák responded well to all aspects of the libretto with the result that the work has an impressive range of characterization, from its poignant heroine and evocative nature scenes to the brilliant court scenes in Act II, and some surprisingly effective comic relief with the mock-serious witch, a kitchen boy and a gamekeeper. For all the Wagnerian ripeness of the harmony and orchestration, Dvořák discarded some of the Wagnerian aesthetic that lay behind *The Devil and Kate* and

his revision of *Dimitrij*. The duets he now included were some of his most committed and passionate.

RECORDING Beňačková, Drobková, Soukupová, Ochman, Novák, Prague Philharmonic Ch, Czech PO, Neumann, Supraphon, 1984
VIDEO Hannan, Howard, Treleaven, Macann, Ch and O of ENO, Elder, Virgin, 1986
EDITIONS f.s., Souborné vydání, 1960; v.ss., Mojmír Urbánek, 1905; Karel Solc (ed.), Supraphon, 1960; 3rd edn, 1982

Armida

Opera in four acts, B. 206 (3h)
Libretto by Jaroslav Vrchlický, after Tasso's *Gerusalemme liberata* (1575)
Composed 1902–3
PREMIERE 25 March 1904, National Theatre, Prague

After the riches of *Rusalka*, Dvořák's final opera, *Armida*, is a disappointment. Dvořák had found his best form when he could tap Czech roots – the depiction of folk scenes, folk dancing and musicians, or the rich world of Czech folk mythology. With *Armida* he cast adrift from all this and instead looked back to a much earlier self, to the stiffer and less characteristic world of *Alfred* and *Vanda*, surprisingly with many of the same conventions intact. This was perhaps inevitable, given the familiar international plot of the enchantress Armida, who herself falls in love with a man she has deliberately enchanted. Vrchlický's libretto had earlier defeated Kovařovic, who showed good theatrical sense by abandoning the project. Dvořák himself wanted a work for the great Czech soprano Růžena Maturová (his Rusalka), and in a couple of arias he recaptured something of Rusalka's poignancy. There are also some colourful orientalisms to depict the Damascus setting (the muezzin's call dominates the first number). But, surprisingly, the Christians failed to inspire Dvořák – much of their music is unmemorably foursquare – and characterization as a whole relies on conventional formulas.

RECORDING Caballé, Ruesche, Scheibner, Schlott, Bremen City Theatre Ch and O, Albrecht, Voce, recorded 1961: a much truncated live performance in German
EDITION v.s., Dědici Dr. Antonína Dvořáka/Hudební matice, 1941; 2nd edn, 1951

BIBLIOGRAPHY J. Burghauser, *Antonín Dvořák: Thematický katalog, bibliografie, přehled života a díla* (Thematic catalogue, bibliography, survey of life and works), Státní nakladatelst ví krásné literatury hudby a umění, 1960; John Clapham, *Antonín Dvořák: Musician and Craftsman*, Faber, 1966; John Tyrrell, *Czech Opera*, CUP, 1988

J.T.

E

JOHN C. EATON

John Charles Eaton; *b* 30 March 1935, Bryn Mawr,
Pennsylvania, US

Eaton, an American composer whose stylistic
sources are richly eclectic, has made a particular
impact with his operas. He attended Princeton
University, where his teachers were Babbitt, Cone
and Sessions, and went on to win many awards,
including three American Prix de Rome (1959–61)
and two Guggenheim Fellowships (1962 and 1965).
Unlike some of the more conservative American
composers of opera, Eaton has been deeply involved
with electronic music. During the 1960s he wrote for
the SynKet, a synthesizer built by Paolo Ketoff, and
later used electronic sounds in his operas. Since 1970
Eaton has been associated with the University of
Indiana's School of Music in Bloomington. His 3½-
hour long opera, *Heracles*, previously seen in Turin,
was revived to inaugurate the university's Musical
Arts Center in 1972. The following year saw the
premiere of Eaton's television opera *Myshkin*, to a
libretto by Patrick Creagh based on Dostoevsky's
The Idiot.

Three major operas followed inside a decade.
Danton and Robespierre was widely admired and led
to the one-act *The Cry of Clytaemnestra*, also
premiered at Bloomington. Reactions varied, but
among the strongest advocates was Andrew Porter,
who wrote that Eaton was 'the most interesting
opera composer writing in America today'.

Danton and Robespierre

Grand opera in three acts (2h)
Libretto by Patrick Creagh
PREMIERE 21 April 1978, Bloomington, Indiana

Requiring ten soloists, chorus, large orchestra and
electronic tape, the setting is Paris during the French
Revolution and the plot concerns the conflict
between the idealist Danton and the realist
Robespierre, who are both beheaded in the final act.
The score is dense and complex, yet lyrical,
combining traditional tonal arias and duets with
atonal, microtonal and electronic music.

RECORDING Indiana University Opera Theater, Baldner,
CRI, 1980
EDITION G. Schirmer (on hire)

The Tempest

Opera in three acts
Libretto by Andrew Porter, after the play by Shakespeare
(1611)
PREMIERE 27 July 1985, Santa Fe

Porter's enthusiasm for Eaton's operas led to their
collaboration in *The Tempest*, a three-act technological extravaganza. There is a large cast and chorus:
vocal ranges are wide. In addition to the orchestra,
there is a Renaissance ensemble, electronic tape and
a jazz trio – Caliban is a jazz singer – which are
used to create the separate, conflicting worlds of
groups of characters. Prospero stands at the centre,
controlling the alternation and superimposition of
these musical hierarchies.

EDITION v.s., Schirmer, 1992

Other operatic works: *Ma Barker*, 1957; *Heracles*, 1968;
Myshkin, 1973; *The Lion and Androcles*, 1974; *The Cry of
Clytaemnestra*, 1980
BIBLIOGRAPHY John Eaton, *Involvement with Music: New
Music since 1950*, Harper's College Press, 1976; David Ewen,
American Composers: A Biographical Dictionary

P.D.

ANTON EBERL

Anton Franz Josef Eberl; *b* 13 June 1765, Vienna; *d* 11 March
1807, Vienna

Eberl's early studies in piano and composition were
encouraged by Mozart, who possibly taught him. At
19 he gave his first public recital in Vienna and in
February 1787 his first stage work, *Die Marchande
des Modes*, was performed at the Theater in der
Leopoldstadt, apparently earning Gluck's approbation. Eberl produced four more stage works before
his first concert tour of Germany (in 1795–6 with
Constanze Mozart and her sister, Aloysia Lange)
and a visit to the St Petersburg court. Back in Vienna
between 1799 and 1801 before returning to Russia,
he completed his last three operas, the most successful being *Die Königin der schwarzen Insel*
(1801), which has an oriental setting and is also the
only opera by Eberl that survives. It was praised
by Haydn. Like much of Eberl's music, it shows

affinities with early Beethoven. Though canonic ensembles were not unknown at the time, the quartet in the Act I finale, 'O folge nicht den süssen Tönen', bears comparison with 'Mir ist so wunderbar' in Act I of Beethoven's *Fidelio*.

BIBLIOGRAPHY   R. Haas, 'Anton Eberl', *Mozart-Jahrbuch*, Internationalen Stiftung Mozarteum, 1951, Jg. 2, pp. 123ff.

C.Br.

JOHN ECCLES

b ?1668, ?London; *d* 12 January 1735, Hampton Wick, England

The son of a violinist in the King's Musick, of which he himself became a member, Eccles began his career in the theatre as a composer of incidental music. On several occasions he collaborated with Henry Purcell: 'I burn, I burn', from D'Urfey's *Don Quixote*, Part II (1694), is a mad song that stands comparison with those of his colleague. In 1695 the actor Thomas Betterton established a new company of actors at Lincoln's Inn Fields, with Anne Bracegirdle as a principal; Eccles became master of the music. He contributed a series of stage masques for insertion into spoken plays and a full-length dramatic opera, *Rinaldo and Armida* (1698) to a well-constructed libretto by John Dennis, after Tasso. Eccles and Dennis made a conscientious attempt to continue the tradition established by Purcell and Betterton.

To celebrate the Peace of Ryswick in 1697 Eccles provided a musical entertainment for the court, *Europe's Revels*; it is an English approximation of a French comédie-ballet, and the words, appropriately enough, are by Peter Anthony Motteux, a Huguenot who edited England's first literary magazine, the *Gentleman's Journal*; he wrote the libretti of several of Eccles's masques. In 1700 Eccles became Master of the King's Musick.

In March 1700 'several Persons of Quality' headed by Lord Halifax offered very substantial prizes for the best setting of William Congreve's *The Judgment of Paris*. When, in June 1701, the subscribers pronounced their verdict, Eccles came second to John Weldon, from New College, Oxford. Daniel Purcell came third, Gottfried Finger fourth. But it was Eccles's contribution that proved popular and lasting, and the association with Congreve, begun before the 'Musick Prize', when Eccles had provided songs for his plays, was to culminate in the original setting of *Semele* (1707), never staged in his lifetime. Various reasons have been adduced for this: Congreve's withdrawal from theatrical management and Mrs Bracegirdle's retirement from the stage being two. The inevitable comparison with Handel's subsequent setting of the same text is by no means to Eccles's disadvantage: Stoddard Lincoln claimed that 'Had Semele been produced it might have laid the foundations for a national English opera.' The

meticulous scoring is remarkable, the vocal lines expressive and original.

In the previous year Eccles had set the last of the English dramatic operas, George Granville's (Lord Lansdowne's) *The British Enchanters; or, No Magick like Love*; this was a box-office success, but only two songs survive. After 1708 Eccles wrote no more for the stage and devoted himself to composing the required court odes, and to fishing.

The Judgment of Paris

Masque in one act
Libretto by William Congreve
PREMIERE   21 March 1701, Dorset Garden, London

Congreve's elegant poem, written with musical setting in mind, tells the traditional story of Paris, the mortal required to choose the most beautiful of three goddesses, Juno, Athene and Venus, and bribed by Venus, with the promise of Helen, the most beautiful of earthly beings, to give her the golden apple.

Eccles's setting is distinguished by its elaborate and innovative scoring which sets off a restrained vocal style. It is the first English score to call for a flûte d'Almagne (transverse flute), although it also employs recorders. It cunningly begins with an overture for trumpet and strings, only to unmask a further three trumpets, and drums, in Athene's last song and its chorus, though these are self-denyingly *tacet* in the conclusion, where the martial connotations would be inappropriate. Paris's first vision of the goddesses, 'O ravishing delight', aptly conveys a gradual awakening of wonder with the harmonic richness of its string accompaniment, decisively marked 'soft'. Dynamic indications throughout are unusually detailed.

EDITION   f.s., Walsh and Hare, 1702

Other operatic works: *The Rape of Europa*, 1694; *The Loves of Mars and Venus*, 1696; *Europe's Revels for the Peace*, 1697; *Rinaldo and Armida*, 1698; *Acis and Galatea*, 1700; *The British Enchanters*, 1706; *Semele*, (1707), 1972
BIBLIOGRAPHY   Roger Fiske, *English Theatre Music in the Eighteenth Century*, OUP, 1973; 2nd edn, 1986; S. Lincoln, 'The First Setting of Congreve's *Semele*', *ML*, vol. 54 (1963), p. 103

R.Lu.

ARNE EGGEN

b 28 August 1881, Trondheim, Norway; *d* 26 October 1955, Bærum, Norway

Eggen studied in Leipzig and between the wars made extensive tours as an organist in the Scandinavian countries. His musical language is firmly in the national Norwegian tradition of Grieg, Svendsen and Halvorsen and his reputation rests largely on his writing for the voice and, in particular, his two operas. *Olav Liljekrans* (1931–40) is based on Ibsen's youthful drama (1856) of the same name, and was first produced in Oslo in 1940. This was followed by an opera based on Shakespeare's *Cymbeline* (1943–8), first staged in 1951.

R.La.

WERNER EGK

Werner Mayer; *b* 17 May 1901, Auchsesheim, Bavaria; *d* 10 July 1983, Inning am Ammersee, Germany

Egk spent his childhood in Augsburg. Despite this provincial background he became aware at an early age of progressive trends in German art. As his parents were opposed to a musical career he left home in 1920, studying briefly with Orff. However he was largely self-taught, both as composer and conductor. During two years spent in Italy (1925–7), convalescing from a serious illness, he composed fragments of an opera based on Immermann's *Merlin*. A major influence on his later theatrical style was the celebrated Marionettentheater Münchener Künstler, for which his wife occasionally played the violin.

In 1929 Egk settled in Berlin. Here he composed several radio cantatas in the Brechtian Lehrstück manner, followed by a series of children's operas for Bavarian Radio. The first work he later acknowledged was the *Quattro canzoni* for tenor and orchestra, premiered in Dortmund in 1932. A radio opera, *Columbus*, written as a realist reaction to the mystical treatment of the subject by Milhaud and Claudel, was performed in 1933 and twice revised (as 'theatrical reportage' and ballet-oratorio). In 1936 Heinz Tietjen engaged Egk as a conductor at the Berlin Staatsoper.

Egk achieved his first lasting success with the comic opera *Die Zaubergeige*. During the war years he completed a ballet, *Joan von Zarissa*, and an opera, *Circe*, based on Calderón. *Abraxas* (composed 1944–6), a choreographic adaptation of Heine's *Doktor Faust* fragment, caused an outrage in Munich on account of alleged immorality. In 1950 Egk was appointed director of the Musikhochschule in West Berlin. Here he composed two further ballet scores, *Ein Sommertag* and *Die chinesische Nachtigall* (on the same Andersen story as Stravinsky's *The Nightingale*) before returning to his native Bavaria in 1953. He began work on a setting of Molière's *L'école des femmes* but abandoned it on hearing that Rolf Liebermann was setting the same text. A new opera, *Irische Legende*, based on Yeats's *Countess Cathleen*, was premiered in 1955 at the Salzburg Festival. There followed *Der Revisor* (after Gogol) and *Die Verlobung in San Domingo* (after Kleist), inspired by journeys to the Caribbean, North and Central America. *Siebzehn Tage und vier Minuten*, composed in 1966, is a complete reworking of the earlier *Circe*.

Although Egk's role in Nazi Germany was not entirely unambiguous, the darker years of his career were soon forgotten. His sympathy for French music was unusual in a German musician of his generation and is particularly evident in his orchestration. Weill, Stravinsky, Bartók and Schoenberg were palpable influences on his developing musical style.

Die Zaubergeige

The Magic Fiddle
Comic opera in three acts (2h 15m)
Libretto by the composer and Ludwig Andersen (Ludwig Strecker), after Graf Franz von Pocci's play for marionettes (1868)
Composed 1934–5, rev. 1953–4
PREMIERES 22 May 1935, Opernhaus, Frankfurt; rev. version: 2 May 1954, Staatsoper, Stuttgart

Egk knew von Pocci's play from the Marionettentheater Münchener Künstler and wrote his operatic adaptation with the help of Ludwig Strecker, director of Schott Verlag.

Kaspar is dissatisfied with his existence as a lowly serf and, taking a fond farewell of his beloved Gretl, he sets off in search of adventure. On the road he gives his last three coins to a beggar. Revealing himself as the earth spirit Cuperus, the latter presents Kaspar with a fiddle imbued with magic powers which function only if the player renounces love. Kaspar tries the instrument out on the rich swindler Guldensack and forces him to dance until he drops. Inert, he is robbed. Kaspar becomes a celebrated virtuoso, Spagatini. He encounters Guldensack, his old enemy, and Gretl, to whom he remains cold. Gretl's noble mistress, Ninabella, seduces Kaspar so persuasively that he breaks his vow; worse still, he is arrested on a charge of robbery, the fiddle loses its magic powers, and he is sent to the gallows. Cuperus saves the situation, but this time Kaspar refuses the fiddle, opting for Gretl and the quiet life.

With its earthy tunes, diatonic harmonies and thigh-slapping dance rhythms, Egk's music appears to veer towards musical comedy, yet the score is subtly parodistic and spiked with dissonance. Like many German comic operas *Die Zaubergeige* has gone almost unnoticed in the outside world, while theatres from Kiel to Klagenfurt play it to packed houses.

RECORDING excerpts: Köth, Lindermeier, Holm, Cordes, Proebstl, Frick, Bavarian State Opera O, Egk, DG, [*c.* 1958]
EDITIONS v.ss., Schott, 1935; rev. version, Schott, 1954

Peer Gynt

Opera in three acts (2h 15m)
Libretto by the composer, after the dramatic poem by Henrik Ibsen (1866–7)
Composed 1936–8
PREMIERES 24 November 1938, Staatsoper, Berlin; US: 23 February 1966, Hartt College of Music, Hartford, Connecticut

Peer Gynt was commissioned by the Berlin Staatstheater in 1936. As Egk wrote, the fame of Grieg's music to Ibsen's play 'would perhaps scare off a commercial opera hack, while the real problem lies not there but in the dimensions of the drama'. It was the rich blend of Scandinavian saga, Don Juan adventure, Faustian drama and Symbolist labyrinth that attracted Egk to Ibsen. The need for condensation caused him to avoid overtly philosophical passages, however, and to reduce the original five acts to three.

Peer is hated and feared by all; Solveig sympathizes with him but, as she spurns his affection, he abducts Ingrid, only to turn her away. A red-headed woman lures him into the Dovreberg, home of the trolls. A menacing situation develops and he calls Solveig to his aid. The redhead bears Peer an ugly child; he flees. In Central America, 20 years later, Peer has grown rich but is ruined by confidence men. In a bar he meets the redhead, who scorns him. Peer seeks his way home, but a stranger leads him back to the Dovreberg. He begs his mother to forgive him and is finally reunited with Solveig.

The opera contains many allusions to (and indirect criticisms of) fascism. Peer quotes Mussolini: 'I help the strong but not the weak'; the trolls, Nordic powers of evil, are depicted by wild 'Negro' music (charleston, tango, etc.) while their hymn to pleasure is a quasi-Lutheran chorale. Other passages inhabit the world of Brecht and Weill; indeed the score is influenced by many 'decadents' of the 1930s. The opera accordingly had a stormy reception in Berlin and was not often performed. In post-war years it gained ground but failed to establish a secure place in the repertoire.

RECORDING Perry, Sharp, Lovaas, Hopf, Hermann, Munich Radio SO, Wallberg, Orfeo, 1982
EDITION v.s., Schott, 1938

Der Revisor

The Government Inspector

Comic opera in five acts (1h 45m)
Libretto by the composer, after the comedy by Gogol (1836)
Composed 1956–7
PREMIERES 9 May 1957, Schlosstheater Schwetzingen; UK: 25 July 1958, Sadler's Wells, London; US: 19 October 1960, City Opera, New York

The opera was commissioned by South German Radio. Apart from a few cuts, Egk's libretto adheres faithfully to the form and substance of Gogol's comedy. Several shorter scenes are ingeniously telescoped into ensembles.

In a small provincial town in early 19th-century Russia, the town mayor, judge, postmaster and other leading officials – all of them corrupt – are alarmed by the news that an inspector from St Petersburg is planning an incognito visit. Chlestakov, a low-ranking civil servant, is spotted at the local inn by two landowners, Bobchinsky and Dobchinsky. His strange behaviour is taken as a ploy, and he is wined and dined by the town mayor, judiciously bribed by the officials and voluptuously approached by Anna, the mayor's wife – on the assumption that he is the government inspector. Seconded by his servant Ossip, Chlestakov readily falls in with the situation and is particularly taken by Anna's daughter Marja. Having announced their betrothal he departs in haste. The postmaster intercepts a letter which uncovers his mistaken identity. At the height of the resultant hubbub the mayor's servant rushes in to announce the arrival of the real government inspector.

Egk's score brilliantly exploits several possibilities unique to opera: in a dream sequence, for instance, Chlestakov's erotic entanglement with Anna and Marja is depicted by three dancers, and the bribery scenes are enacted as mime, without a word spoken or sung. A light touch is maintained throughout, and Egk misses no opportunity for witty musical parody.

EDITIONS f.s./v.s., Schott, 1957

Other works: *Merlin* (inc.), (1927); *Der Löwe und die Maus*, (1929); *Der Fuchs und der Rabe*, (1929); *Columbus*, radio opera, 1933, rev. for stage, 1942 and 1951; *Circe* (withdrawn 1949), 1948; *Die Schule der Frauen* (inc.), (1951); *Irische Legende*, 1955, rev. 1970; *Die Verlobung in San Domingo*, 1963; *Siebzehn Tage und vier Minuten*, rev. of *Circe*, 1966
BIBLIOGRAPHY B. Kohl and E. Nolle, *Werner Egk: Opern, Ballette, Konzertwerke*, Schott, 1966; E. Krause, *Werner Egk: Oper und Ballett*, Heinrichshofen's Verlag, 1971

A.C.W.B.

GOTTFRIED VON EINEM

b 24 January 1918, Bern

Of Austrian parentage, von Einem was educated in Germany and England. At the age of 20 he became an apprentice répétiteur at the Staatsoper in Berlin and worked in the same capacity at Bayreuth. He fell foul of the Gestapo and spent the war years, like many of his German colleagues, in 'inner emigration'. His closest allies in the musical world at this time were the composers Orff, Egk and Wagner-Régeny. From 1941 to 1944 he studied privately with Boris Blacher, who recalled that von Einem came to him 'already formed' and that his personal style was recognizable even in simple harmony exercises. In 1944 von Einem established his reputation with the world premiere of his ballet *Die Prinzessin Turandot* at the Staatsoper in Dresden. The same institution commissioned his first opera, *Dantons Tod*, but this, by good fortune, was first given in Salzburg and was indeed the first performance of an opera by a living composer ever to be given at the International Festival. Salzburg then commissioned a further work, *Der Prozess*, which was premiered there in 1952. Both operas have since been performed frequently, in Germany and elsewhere, to widespread acclaim.

Von Einem has remained first and foremost a composer of opera and ballet, writing orchestral works almost exclusively to commission. He has occupied a number of high-ranking administrative posts (e.g. director of the Vienna Festival and professor of composition at the Vienna Hochschule für Musik) and sat for some years on the directors' committee of the Salzburg Festival. In 1980 his self-styled mystery play *Jesu Hochzeit* was staged at the Vienna Staatsoper. The libretto, written by von Einem's second wife, Lotte Ingrisch, was denounced by leading members of the Austrian Catholic Church as blasphemous and the world premiere, which was televised live, provoked a major scandal.

Opinions as to the quality of von Einem's music differ widely. Even his teacher, Blacher (also librettist for four of his operas), later classified him as a 'conservative' and there has been criticism of the discrepancy between his choice of authors (particularly Büchner and Kafka) and his musical style, which is largely straightforward and tonal. His admirers regard him as post-war Germany's leading theatre composer.

Dantons Tod
Danton's Death
Opera in two parts (2h 15m)
Libretto by the composer and Boris Blacher, after the play by Georg Büchner (1835)
Composed 1944–6
PREMIERES 6 August 1947, Festspielhaus, Salzburg; US: 9 March 1966, City Opera, New York

Blacher helped his former pupil condense Büchner's original 32 episodes into six scenes, telescoping some of the smaller roles and emphasizing the influence of the chorus – an area where opera offers considerably greater possibilities than spoken drama. Passages from Büchner's letters to his wife are also incorporated into the libretto.

Paris, 1794: Danton and Desmoulins criticize Robespierre for his brutality and arrogance. They are arrested and put on trial. Danton defends himself eloquently before the Tribunal but is no match for his devious opponent. Although no verdict is reached, he and his friends are led to the guillotine.

The score consists of 17 separate musical numbers, some linked by orchestral intermezzi, others running continuously. Themes and motifs are not interlinked, although the opening brass chord sequence reappears in the final bars. Diversity of rhythm and form is the vital differentiating feature of the score, while the polyphonic disposition of brief motivic cells invests the chorus writing with a vivacity akin to the *turba* passages of Bach's Passions. Britten's use of the chorus in *Peter Grimes* (which is a close contemporary of *Dantons Tod*) is strikingly similar.

RECORDING Laki, Hollweg, Hiestermann, Adam, Rydl, Bavarian Radio Ch and O, Zagrosek, Orfeo, 1984
EDITIONS f.s., Universal, 1961; v.s., Universal, 1947

Der Prozess
The Trial
Opera in two parts (nine scenes) (2h 30m)
Libretto by Boris Blacher and Heinz von Cremer, after the novel by Kafka (1925)
Composed 1950–52
PREMIERES 17 August 1953, Festspielhaus, Salzburg; US: 22 October 1953, City Opera, New York; UK: 24 May 1973, Collegiate Theatre, London

Since Gide's dramatization of Kafka's surrealistic novel appeared unsuitable, von Einem again turned to Blacher for a libretto. The latter condensed the action to just six scenes; Heinz von Cramer supplied three further episodes and revised the remainder in close collaboration with the composer. The choice of *The Trial* as subject for an opera reflects the fears of

Nazi harassment that plagued the composer during his formative years. When in 1951 he assisted Brecht in obtaining Austrian citizenship, his friendly gesture was misinterpreted as pro-Communist and provoked considerable hostility. The opera was written under the shadow of this disillusioning experience. It describes the attempts of Josef K., a bank official, to clear his name after he has been accused of a crime he did not commit. He fails, and the opera ends as he is led away to be executed.

Der Prozess is a sturdy, unexceptional score that eschews melodic lines and aims for an 'epic' style in line with post-war Brechtian aesthetics. However, it does serve as an adept vehicle for inspired direction and acting. With Max Lorenz as Josef K., Lisa della Casa in the three female roles and a production team consisting of Karl Böhm, Oskar Fritz Schuh and Caspar Neher, the success of the world premiere was virtually guaranteed.

EDITIONS f.s., Bote und Bock, 1969; v.s., Schott, 1953

Der Besuch der alten Dame
The Visit of the Old Lady
Opera in three acts (2h 15m)
Libretto by Friedrich Dürrenmatt, adapted from his own tragi-comedy (1956)
Composed 1970
PREMIERES 23 May 1971, Staatoper, Vienna; UK: 31 May 1973, Glyndebourne, Sussex; US: 25 October 1972, War Memorial Opera House, San Francisco

Der Besuch der alten Dame was published in 1955 and filmed by Bernhard Vicki (*The Visit*) in 1964. In 1968 Dürrenmatt saw a performance of *Dantons Tod* and immediately agreed to collaborate with von Einem on an operatic adaptation.

Many years before the opera begins, a young girl named Clara Wäscher, pregnant and disgraced by her lover, Alfred Ill, leaves Güllen, a provincial town 'somewhere in Central Europe', for the big wide world. Humiliated and forced into prostitution, she rises from the gutter to become 'the richest woman in the world'. Now she returns as Claire Zachanassian, followed by a grotesque entourage carrying a coffin. In exchange for a gift of a billion to the town council she demands Ill's head. At first – 'in the interests of humanity' – the townspeople refuse, but in the course of time her offer appears irresistible. Ill gradually realizes the inevitability and even the logic of his fate. After some deliberation the citizens accept Zachanassian's deal: Ill is slain, his corpse is lowered into the coffin and the burgomaster takes receipt of the cheque. The people break into a wild dance.

Dürrenmatt's libretto is a skilful job of cutting and pasting. In the opera he also places a stronger accent on Zachanassian, while Ill becomes a lesser figure than in the play. Von Einem's wide vocabulary of rhythmic figures helps to characterize the various strands of the drama. Specific timbres are also used to symbolic effect: strings and wind represent dreams and memories of the couple's youth together, brass episodes of resistance, and the percussion interludes the macabre nature of the situation. The sheer verve of the score compensates to some extent for its lack of melodic distinction. The title role is, however, a *tour de force*; at the world premiere it was sung by Christa Ludwig.

EDITIONS   f.s., Boosey & Hawkes, 1972; v.s., Boosey & Hawkes, 1971

Other works: *Der Zerrissene*, 1964; *Kabale und Liebe*, 1975; *Jesu Hochzeit*, 1980; *Tulifant*, 1990
BIBLIOGRAPHY   H. Hopf and B. Sonntag (eds), *Gottfried von Einem. Ein Komponist unseres Jahrhunderts*, Lit Verlag, 1989

A.C.W.B.

EDWARD ELGAR
(Sir) Edward William Elgar; *b* 2 June 1857, Broadheath, Worcestershire, England; *d* 23 February 1934, Worcester, England

Elgar's exceptional fame as one of England's greatest composers rests securely on his orchestral and choral works. He was Master of the King's Music from 1924 until his death, but he had been the nation's unofficial Laureate since 1897, when his *Imperial March* caught the tone of Queen Victoria's Diamond Jubilee. He contemplated an opera based on Thomas Hardy's novel *A Pair of Blue Eyes*, but no sketches exist. In 1932 he began to compose a two-act opera, *The Spanish Lady*, Op. 89, to a libretto by Sir Barry Jackson based on Ben Jonson's *The Devil is an Ass*. Most of what was written was drawn from old sketchbooks of 50 years earlier. He died leaving it in fragmentary form. Two songs and a suite for strings from it have been published, edited by Percy M. Young.

BIBLIOGRAPHY   Jerrold Northrop Moore, *Edward Elgar, A Creative Life*, OUP, 1984

M.K.

VIVIAN ELLIS
Vivian John Herman Ellis; *b* 29 October 1903, London

Ellis's work remains somewhat in the shadow of Noël Coward's but it has created a niche for itself none the less. His melodic gift, firmly related to that of his predecessor Edward German, was nurtured by classical training at the Royal Academy of Music but also epitomized the catchiness of the novelty hit song.

Mr Cinders
Musical comedy in two acts (1h 30m)
Music by Vivian Ellis and Richard Myers
Book and lyrics by Clifford Grey and Greatrex Newman
PREMIERES   25 September 1928, Opera House, Blackpool; US: 30 April 1986, Forum Theater, Metuchen, New Jersey

A 20th-century version of the Cinderella fairy-tale with gender roles reversed (the poor relation, Jim Lancaster, has ugly brothers). The show's original success was repeated when it was revived 55 years later. Ellis and Newman witnessed this revival and wrote a new song for it. *Mr Cinders* includes Ellis's best-known song, 'Spread a little happiness'.

RECORDING   excerpts: original cast, EMI (re-released World Record Club)
FILM   British Film Institute, 1934
EDITION   vocal selections, Chappell, 1929

Bless the Bride
Musical show in two acts
Book and lyrics by A. P. Herbert
PREMIERE   26 April 1947, Adelphi Theatre, London

An English girl elopes with a handsome Frenchman, Pierre (who has sung 'Ma belle Marguérite' to her), to the resort of Eauville-sur-mer just before the outbreak of the Franco-Prussian War. Humorous business follows when her disguised parents are mistaken for spies. Pierre is called up but the lovers are eventually reunited. A. P. Herbert's libretto may not be his finest, but Ellis's songs are superb, and the show, successfully competing with *Oklahoma!*, ran for two years in London.

RECORDING   excerpts: original (1947) cast, EMI (re-released World Record Club), 1975
EDITION   v.s., Chappell, 1947

Other musical comedies and light operas: *Follow a Star*, 1929; *Jill Darling (Jack and Jill)*, 1933; *Streamline*, 1934; *Under Your Hat*, 1938; *Big Ben*, 1946; *Tough at the Top*, 1949; *And so to Bed*, 1951; *Listen to the Wind*, 1954; *Water Gipsies*, 1955
BIBLIOGRAPHY   Kurt Gänzl, *The British Musical Theatre*, vol. 2: *1915–1984*, Macmillan, 1986

S.B.

JÓZEF ELSNER
Józef Antoni Franciszek Elsner; *b* 1 June, 1769, Grodkow, Germany (now Grotków, Poland); *d* 18 April 1854, Warsaw

Elsner was the foremost Polish opera composer of the early Romantic era. He studied in Grodkow and Wrocław (Breslau) where he also played the violin in the opera orchestra, sang in the chorus and began writing music in many genres. From 1792 to 1799 he was conductor at the theatre in Lvov where his first operas were staged. For 25 years from 1799 Elsner was director of the Opera in Warsaw, which under him reached a high artistic standard; this was the zenith of Elsner's career. In Warsaw he was also an outstanding pedagogue (his pupils included Chopin).

Both his manners-and-morals operas and those based on Polish history were immensely popular. Because he used elements of Polish musical folklore, Elsner is regarded as a precursor of the Polish national style in opera. Many of his works, which included comic operas, melodramas and opere serie, are lost, but the extant ones follow the conventions of early Romantic opera, with obvious influence of classical music. Spoken dialogue is important, while the set pieces include both large-scale coloratura arias and simple strophic songs; there are technically excellent ensembles. In the orchestra, colouristic effects and 'reminiscence' themes play a significant role, especially in the later works. The earlier operas set German texts, the rest Polish.

Operas: *Iskahar, król Guaxary* (*Iskahar, King of Guaxara*), 1797; *Amazonki, czyli Herminia* (*The Amazons, or Herminia*), 1797; *Sydney i Zuma, czyli Moc kochania czarnej niewiasty* (*Sydney and Zuma, or the Power of Love for a Black Woman*), 1798; *Sułtan Wampum, czyli Nieroztropne życzenia* (*Sultan Wampum, or the Rash Wish*), 1800; *Siedem razy jeden* (*Seven Times One*), (1804); *Stary trzpiot i młody mędrzec* (*The Old Fool and the Young Sage*), 1805; *Nurzahad, czyli Nieśmiertelność i bogactwa* (*Nurzahad, or Immortality and Riches*), 1805; *Wieszczka Urzella, czyli To co się damom podoba* (*The Soothsayer Urzella, or What Pleases the Ladies*), 1806; *Sąd Salomona* (*The Judgment of Solomon*), 1806; *Andromeda*, 1807; *Trybunał niewidzialny, czyli Syn występny* (*The Invisible Tribunal, or the Wicked Son*), 1807; *Pospolite ruszenie, czyli Bitwa z kozakami* (*The Levy-en-Masse, or The Battle with the Cossacks*), 1807; *Karol Wielki i Witykind* (*Charlemagne and Wittekind*), 1807; *Chimère et réalité/Urojenie i rzeczywistość*, (c. 1805) 1808; *Echo w lesie* (*The Forest Echo*), 1808 (RECORDING Muza, 1970s); *Leszek Biały, czyli Czarownica z Łysej Góry* (*Leszek the White, or The Witch from the Bare Mountain*), 1809; *Wyspa małżeńska, czyli Żony przez los wybrane* (*The Isle of Matrimony, or Wives Chosen by Fate*), 1811; *Wąwozy Sierra Morena* (*The Ravines of the Sierra Morena*), 1812; *Kabalista* (*The Cabalist*), 1813; *Kochankowie ukryci* (*The Concealed Lovers*), (n.d.); *Król Łokietek, czyli Wiśliczanki* (*King Lokietek, or The Girls of Wiślica*), 1818; *Jagiełło w Tenczynie* (*Jagiello in Tenczyn*), 1820; *Ofiara Abrahama* (*Abraham's Sacrifice*), 1821; *Powstanie narodu* (*The Insurrection of a Nation*), 1831; 10 lost operas

BIBLIOGRAPHY   Alina Nowak-Romanowicz, *Joseph Elsner*, PWM, 1957

J.M.

GEORGE ENESCU

George Enescu [Georges Enesco]; *b* 19 August 1881, Liveni, Romania; *d* 4 May 1955, Paris

The cellist Pablo Casals once called Enescu 'the greatest musical phenomenon since Mozart'. Sadly, the sheer range of Enescu's gifts – as violinist, conductor, pianist and teacher – helped to obscure his achievements as a composer; most concert-goers in the West know only his two early *Romanian Rhapsodies*, and think of his music (wrongly) as merely 'folkloric'.

After his studies in both Vienna and Paris, Enescu's musical language was deeply influenced by Brahms, Wagner (whose *Ring* he memorized) and Fauré (who taught him). To this mixture he added some Romanian folk characteristics: shifting major/minor modal scales, and heterophony (the superimposition of different versions of the same melodic material). The result was, from the 1920s onwards, a very personal idiom, inhabiting the

borderland between richly chromatic late Romanticism and a sparse, elliptical modernism.

Based in both Paris and Romania, Enescu travelled widely as violinist and conductor; time for composing had to be found between concert engagements, and he was a meticulous reviser of his drafts in manuscript. The first sketches of *Oedipe* were written in 1910–14, then lost during the war; a draft of the entire opera was written with great speed during July and August 1921; but it took Enescu another ten years to finish elaborating, revising and orchestrating the work. Though he contemplated another opera in the late 1920s (on the Romanian folk hero Meøterul Manole), *Oedipe* remained his only work in the genre.

George Enescu (aged 70) imitating the actor Mounet-Sully in the role of Oedipus

Oedipe
Oedipus

Tragédie lyrique in four acts, Op. 23 (3h)
Libretto by Edmond Fleg, after Sophocles
Composed 1921–31
PREMIERE   13 March 1936, Opéra, Paris
CAST   Oedipe *b-bar*, Tirésias *b*, Créon *bar*, Jocaste *ms*, Sphinx *a*, Antigone *s*; *a*, *ms*, *t*, *bar*, 3 *b*; *satb* chorus of citizens of Thebes, revellers, Eumenides, Athenian elders; dancers
LARGE ORCHESTRA including 2 hp, pf, harmonium, alto sax, wind machine and saw

The Swiss Jewish author Edmond Fleg originally wrote a huge two-part libretto, for a diptych opera to be performed on two successive nights. Enescu persuaded him to condense it into a unitary work, which still told the full story of Oedipus' life.

SYNOPSIS
Act I presents the joyful baptism of Oedipus, interrupted by Tiresias' prophecy that he will kill his father (Laios) and marry his mother (Jocasta).

Act II shows Oedipus as a young man, first leaving Corinth (where he has been brought up as a foundling), then at a crossroads where he encounters Laios and kills him, and finally at Thebes, where he kills the Sphinx by answering its riddle and is given Jocasta's hand in marriage.

Act III corresponds to Sophocles' *Oedipus Tyrannus*. Oedipus discovers the truth about his past and blinds himself.

Act IV corresponds to Sophocles' *Oedipus at Colonus*. The old, exiled Oedipus is accompanied by his daughter Antigone; they take refuge in a sacred grove, where he argues defiantly in self-justification and is taken up by the gods.

Though presented (in Acts I, III and IV) as a succession of large-scale, dramatically rather static tableaux, *Oedipe* is musically unified and organic. Enescu uses several (at least 21) inter-related leitmotifs, constantly weaving them into a rich, polyphonic score which he himself once described as a 'symphony'.

RECORDINGS   1. Øindilaru, Cernei, Ohanesian, Iordăchescu, Ch and O of Romanian Opera, Bucharest, Brediceanu, Electrecord, 1964 (in Romanian); 2. Hendricks, Fassbaender, Van Dam, Vanaud, Les Petits Chanteurs de Monaco, Orfeon Donostiarra, Monte Carlo Philharmonic, Foster, EMI, 1990 (in French)
EDITION   f.s., Salabert/Editura Muzicală (Bucharest), 1964

BIBLIOGRAPHY   Noel Malcolm, *George Enescu: His Life and Music*, Toccata Press, 1990

N.M.

FERENC ERKEL
b 7 November 1810, Gyula, Hungary; *d* 15 June 1893, Budapest

Erkel is the traditional father figure of Hungarian national opera – one of Budapest's two opera houses is named after him, and he composed the Hungarian national anthem. He made an early reputation as a virtuoso pianist in Budapest in the late 1830s, and started composing operas only when the arrival of Liszt on the Hungarian scene in 1839–40 convinced him that he should not try to compete as a pianist at the highest level. Nevertheless Erkel was by this time an experienced man of the theatre. He had worked as an opera conductor in Kolozsvár (Cluj), had encountered the pioneering operas of Ruzitska, and – arriving in Budapest probably in 1835 – was soon working as conductor of the Hungarian theatre in Buda, a post that led to his appointment as conductor

of the recently founded Hungarian National Theatre in January 1838.

Erkel's own first opera, *Báthori Mária* (staged at the National Theatre in August 1840), already shows him moving away from the singspiels of his predecessors towards a more modern type of through-composed music drama, though still within the stylistic limits of Rossini/Weber coloured by the *verbunkos* style which passed for ethnic Hungarianism throughout the 19th century. This tendency was cemented by *Hunyadi László*, an immense success at its premiere in 1844, and an intermittent repertoire piece in Hungary ever since. But political conditions in Hungary after the revolutionary war of 1848–9, as well as Erkel's own busy life as a concert conductor, seem to have inhibited his operatic work. He contributed an act to the collaborative *Erzsébet* in 1857, but his next solo effort, *Bánk Bán*, was completed only in 1860, at a time when Austria's defeats at Magenta and Solferino (1859) had brought some easing of political pressure in the Empire (a crucial moment also for Smetana in Prague).

Bánk Bán was as successful as *Hunyadi László*. But Erkel's later operas (often written with the collaboration of his sons Gyula and Sándor) failed to build on that success. Again like Smetana he wrote both earnest national music dramas, and comedies with an authentic peasant flavour, and as with Smetana the bigger works show the increasing influence of Wagner. But Erkel's music remained to some extent experimental, and it is clear from the fragment of *Dózsa György* printed in Szabolcsi's book (see BIBLIOGRAPHY) that the *verbunkos* elements in these later works are no mere decoration but a genuine attempt at a radical, individual style with nationalistic connotations. This would help explain their relative lack of success, at a time when popular taste might have been thought ripe to appreciate a local version of epic music drama.

Hunyadi László
Opera in three acts (2h 30m)
Libretto by Béni Egressy, after the play *Two Lászlós* by Lőrinc Tóth (1841)
Composed 1842–4
PREMIERE   27 January 1844, Pest National Theatre, Budapest

Erkel's second most popular work is an epic tragedy on the life and death of the 15th-century Hungarian soldier and politician, László Hunyadi (son of the great János Hunyadi, scourge of the Turks). The format hardly digresses from the conventions of historical grand opera, but the Hungarianisms are strong enough to give the music real individuality. They include use of the peculiar *verbunkos* scale, with its double augmented second, and the snapped rhythmic figure known as the choriamb, familiar from Liszt's F minor Hungarian Rhapsody. Erkel wrote an overture in 1845 (i.e. after the early performances) which is in some ways more individual than the opera itself, and is widely regarded as his best work.

The success of *Hunyadi László* was undoubtedly linked to patriotic feeling against the Austrians, and it established Erkel as the national Hungarian composer. He composed the piece that became the Hungarian national anthem (*Himnusz*) the following year. (The 'second' national anthem, *Szozat*, was composed by Erkel's librettist, Egressy.)

RECORDING   Sass, Dénes, Gulyás, Molnár, Ch and O of Hungarian State Opera, J. Kovács, Hungaroton, 1985
EDITION   v.s., Editio Musica Budapest, 1968

Cover of the first edition of Bánk Bán *(Pest, 1861) with a portrait of the composer*

Bánk Bán

Opera in three acts (2h 15m)
Libretto by Béni Egressy, after the tragedy by József Katona (1814)
Composed 1859–61
PREMIERES   9 March 1861, Pest National Theatre, Budapest; UK: 20 February 1968, Collegiate Theatre, London

Katona's tragedy is one of the best known of all Hungarian 19th-century dramas, and Erkel seems to have envisaged a setting soon after the troubles of 1848–9, at a time when the play was officially banned. The libretto must have been written by 1851, when Egressy died. When the work was finally composed and staged, it soon became the most popular of all Hungarian operas, and it remains a repertoire piece in Hungary to this day, though it is rarely performed abroad.

The plot hinges on the persistent attempts of the Hungarian Queen Gertrude's brother Otto to seduce Melinda, the wife of Bánk Bán – the hero's name is 'Bánk', while 'Bán' is his title as a provincial governor – who is acting as regent while the king campaigns abroad. This situation, of which Bánk is initially unaware, is used by a group of Hungarian patriots to win his support for their cause. When he witnesses one of Otto's attempts, he even turns against Melinda, though she has never encouraged the prince. And when Otto finally rapes her, Bánk curses their child. Later, when Bánk confronts the queen with her brother's misdeeds, she draws a dagger but he seizes it and kills her. Finally, Bánk gives himself up to the king, but as he does so the peasant Tiborc announces that Melinda has thrown herself, with the child, into the river Tisza. The king accepts this as punishment enough for Bánk.

Dramatically the work is both far-fetched and wooden, and its success on the Hungarian stage must be attributed largely to its patriotic associations, and to the strong musical Hungarianisms, backed up by the use of the dulcimer-like cimbalom (perhaps its first appearance in a composed work). The mixture of styles remains disconcerting; the *verbunkos* elements alternate with stock Italianisms and memories of Meyerbeer. But at its best the music is distinctive, with some striking orchestration, including a part for viola d'amore, and the unusual sound of a pair of offstage piccolos.

RECORDING   Ágay, Komlóssy, Simándy, Réti, Melis, Faragó, Hungarian State Opera Ch, Budapest PO, Ferencsik, Hungaroton, 1960s
EDITION   v.s., Editio Musica Budapest, 1957

Other operas: *Báthori Mária*, 1840; *Erzsébet* (Act II by Erkel, the rest by F. and K. Doppler), 1857; *Sarolta*, 1862; *Dózsa György*, 1867; *Brankovics György*, 1874; *Névtelen hösök* (*Unknown Heroes*), 1880; *István Király* (*King Stephen*), 1885
BIBLIOGRAPHY   Bence Szabolcsi, trans. Sára Karig, *A Concise History of Hungarian Music*, Corvina, 1964

S.W.

PABLO ESTEVE

Pablo Esteve y Grimau; *b* ?1734, Barcelona, Spain; *d* 4 June 1794, Madrid

The Catalan Esteve won such acclaim as a composer of tonadillas escénicas (light operas in Spanish popular style) that by 1760 he was installed in Madrid as virtually the leading official composer of theatre music and later as the Duke of Osuna's master of music. From about 1765 he turned to opera, collaborating (as he often had in his tonadillas) with the playwright Ramón de la Cruz in an adaptation of Piccinni's popular opera buffa *La Cecchina, ossia La buona figliuola*, first performed in Madrid in 1765. Though billed as a zarzuela, its operatic nature, like so-called zarzuelas generally in the 17th and 18th century, is unquestionable. He followed this up with other such adaptations, notably

Los portentosos efectos de la gran Naturaleza (1766), after Giuseppe Scarlatti. On 25 December 1768 *Los jardineros de Aranjuez, o También de amor los rigores sacan fruto entre las flores*, to his own libretto, was premiered and published in Madrid with the designation ópera cómico-bufo-dramática.

BIBLIOGRAPHY   William M. Bussey, *French and Italian Influence on the Zarzuela 1700–1770*, UMI Research Press, 1982

J.W.S.

EDMUND EYSLER

Edmund Eysler [Eisler]; *b* 12 March 1874, Vienna; *d* 4 October 1949, Vienna

Eysler attended the Vienna Conservatory along with Leo Fall, and gave piano lessons to support himself. A libretto rejected by Johann Strauss II was set by Eysler, who was later asked to salvage the lighter numbers and build a new operetta around them. The result, *Bruder Straubinger* (1903), was a hit starring Alexander Girardi. More works followed in the local farce-with-songs style, with Girardi as various Viennese characters; some later works crossed the Austrian frontier, such as *Der lachende Ehemann* and *Ein Tag im Paradies* (both 1913), while Eysler's last success, *Die gold'ne Meisterin* (1927) was a throwback to the old, pre-jazz-age Vienna. Though he was fêted after the Second World War as a grand old survivor – he was in hiding and his works were banned after the *Anschluss* – his rather trite scores have not held up as well as the more vibrant, delectable operettas of his contemporaries, Kálmán and Lehár, or Straus and Fall.

Operettas: *Das Gastmahl des Lucullus*, 1901; *Bruder Straubinger*, 1903; *Pufferl*, 1905; *Die Schützenliesl*, 1905; *Phryne*, 1906; *Künstlerblut*, 1906; *Vera Violetta*, 1907; *Ein Tag auf dem Mars*, 1908; *Das Glücksschweinchen*, 1908; *Johann der Zweite*, 1908; *Der junge Papa*, 1909; *Lumpus und Pumpus*, 1910; *Der unsterbliche Lump*, 1910; *Das Zirkuskind*, 1911; *Der Frauenfresser*, 1911; *Der Natursänger*, 1912; *Der lachende Ehemann*, 1913; *Ein Tag im Paradies*, 1913; *Frühling am Rhein*, 1914; *Der Durchgang der Venus*, 1914; *Die oder keine*, 1915; *Wenn sich zwei lieben*, 1915; *Das Zimmer der Pompadour*, 1915; *Warum geht's denn jetzt*, 1916; *Hanni geht tanzen*, 1916; *Der berühmte Gabriel*, 1916; *Graf Toni*, 1917; *Der Aushilfsgatte*, 1917; *Leute von heute*, 1918; *Der dunkle Schatz*, 1918; *Der fidele Geiger*, 1919; *Rund um die Bühne*, 1920; *Der König heiratet*, 1920; *Wer hat's gemacht*, 1920; *La Bella Mammina*, 1921; *Die fromme Helene*, 1921; *Julicka*, 1922; *Fräul'n Sopherl*, 1922; *Drei auf einmal*, 1923; *Der ledige Schwiegersohn*, 1923; *Das Land der Liebe*, 1926; *Die gold'ne Meisterin*, 1927; *Das Strumpfband der Pompadour*, 1930; *Ihr erster Ball*, 1930; *Die schlimme Paulette*, 1931; *Zwei alter Wiener*, 1932; *Die Rakete*, 1932; *Donauliebchen*, 1933; *Das ist die erste Liebe*, 1934; n.d.: *Komm deutscher Bruder; Diana; Der Stern von New York; Meister Florian; Neapel; Im Jahre 3600; Foxtrott & Co.; Das Weib; Casanova's letzte Liebe; Wiener Musik*

Operas: *Der Hexenspiegel*, 1900; *Hochzeitspräludium*, 1946

BIBLIOGRAPHY   Robert Maria Prosl, *Edmund Eysler: Aus Wiens zweiter klassischer Operettenzeit*, Verlag Karl Kuhne, 1947

R.T.

F

LEO FALL

Leopold Fall; *b* 2 February 1873, Olomouc, Moravia;
d 16 September 1925, Vienna

Like Lehár, Fall was the son of a military
bandmaster, and played the violin alongside Lehár in
Lehár senior's 50th Infantry Regiment band. He had
previously received instruction at the Vienna
Conservatory, where Eysler was a fellow student.
Moving to Berlin, Fall played in his father's café
ensemble and other theatre orchestras, which led to
his becoming a theatre conductor.

Fall's second opera, *Irrlicht*, had an inauspicious
Mannheim hearing in 1904, as did his first operetta,
Der Rebell, the following year, in Vienna. But *Der
fidele Bauer*, with its catchy peasant tunes, was a
conspicuous success in Mannheim in a 1907 summer
season. Later that year, the Vienna premiere of *Die
Dollarprinzessin* launched Fall into international
orbit; a huge triumph, cleverly set in rich America,
about a New York 'selfmade Mädel' and a European
nobleman.

Die geschiedene Frau (1908) was just as good, and
nearly as popular, and Fall became, along with Lehár
and Oscar Straus, one of the leading lights of the
'silver' era of Viennese operetta. Many of his
subsequent operettas were snapped up for foreign
consumption, notably *Das Puppenmädel* (1910), *Die
Sirene* (1911), and the superb *Der liebe Augustin*
(1912) – a revision of *Der Rebell*, which owed its
success partially to its Berlin star, Fritzi Massary. The
First World War did not interrupt his output. The
excellent homage to Maria-Theresia, *Die Kaiserin*
(1915), was followed by one of the great successes of
the war period, *Die Rose von Stambul* (1916), which
ran for nearly 500 performances in Vienna and was
later, like many of Fall's works, seen in New York.
This frisky tale of a Turkish harem and the struggle
between Eastern customs and European social ideas
was a triumph in Berlin, with Massary. Fall's greatest
post-war hit was one of his finest operettas, the still
popular *Madame Pompadour* (1922).

For some reason, Fall's mercurial scores – with
their transcendent waltzes and superb ensembles,
have not been fully recorded. Productions are
infrequent, and usually in provincial Austria–
Germany, save for a handsome staging of *Madame
Pompadour* at the Vienna Volksoper in 1986. The
time has come to rediscover these operetta delights,
especially in English, a language in which they were
originally popular.

Die Dollarprinzessin

The Dollar Princess
Operetta in three acts (2h 30m)
Libretto by A. M. Willner and Fritz Grunbaum, after a
comedy by Gatti and Trotha
PREMIERES 2 November 1907, Carltheater, Vienna; UK:
24 December 1908, Prince's Theatre, Manchester; US:
6 September 1909, Knickerbocker Theater, New York

The American millionaire widower John Couder
employs down-at-heel European nobility and teaches
them about American business. One such employee,
Baron Hans von Schlick, is falling for Couder's niece,
Daisy, when his friend Fredy meets Couder's
daughter, Alice. Couder's brother Tom, and nephew,
Dick, return from Europe with 'Countess' Olga.
After dalliances, engagements are announced by
Couder, to Olga, and by Alice, to Fredy. This is a
surprise to Fredy. Hans and Daisy happily elope, but
Couder has to buy himself out of his unsuccessful
marriage to Olga. Fredy eventually becomes as
wealthy as Alice and can therefore marry her without
shame.

This delightful operetta opens with a chorus of
typists tapping away, and displays an impressive
array of fabulous marches, irresistible waltzes,
sophisticated and often touching comic duets, first-
class finales, and glittering orchestration.

RECORDING excerpts: Barabas, Hoppe, etc., EMI, 1964
EDITION v.ss., J. Weinberger, 1907; Harmonie, 1907;
Karczay and Wallner, 1907

Other operatic works: *Paroli* (*Frau Denise*), 1902; *Irrlicht*,
1905; *Der Rebell*, 1905; *Der fidele Bauer*, 1907; *Die
geschiedene Frau*, 1908; *Der Schrei nach der Ohrfeige*, 1909;
Brüderlein fein, 1909; *Das Puppenmädel*, 1910; *Die schöne
Risette*, 1910; *Die Sirene*, 1911; *The Eternal Waltz*, 1911; *Der
liebe Augustin* (rev. of *Der Rebell*), 1912; *Die Studentengräfin*,
1913; *Der Nachtschnellzug*, 1913; *Die Frau Ministerpräsident*,
1914; *Der künstliche Mensch*, 1915; *Die Kaiserin*, 1915;
Die Rose von Stambul, 1916; *Der goldene Vogel*, 1920;
Die spanische Nachtigall, 1920; *Der heilige Ambrosius*, 1921;
Die Strassensängerin, 1922; *Madame Pompadour*, 1922;
Der süsse Kavalier, 1923

BIBLIOGRAPHY Otto Schneidereit, *Operette A–Z*, Henschelverlag, 1971; W. Zimmerli, *Leo Fall*, Schweizer Musik Revue, 1957

MANUEL DE FALLA

Manuel María de los Dolores de Falla y Matheu; *b* 23 November 1876, Cadiz, Spain; *d* 14 November 1946, Alta Gracia de Córdoba, Argentina

Falla was the outstanding Spanish composer of the 20th century. His music evolved from the easy out-pourings of *La vida breve* to the burning economy of the Harpsichord Concerto (1926) and the pungent austerity of *Atlántida*. Meanwhile regionalism made way for a wider view, still intensely Spanish but of supra-national relevance. Falla was born and educated in Cadiz, where, apart from the vital background of Andalusian folksong, there was little but salon music and decent amateur endeavour. When his family moved in 1896 to Madrid, Falla entered the conservatory, completing the seven-year course in two years. The only outlet for an ambitious young composer was the theatre, where light opera in the form of zarzuelas held sway. Unwillingly Falla conformed, writing six zarzuelas, three of them in collaboration with Amadeo Vives. Only *Los amores de la Inés* was performed (1902). Of greater importance was the revelation of the music of Felipe Pedrell (1841–1922), persuaded by Falla to take him as a pupil. In 1904 Falla entered and won two competitions, one a piano contest, the other for one-act operas for which he submitted *La vida breve*. The authorities' failure to implement the promised Madrid production of the winning piece caused Falla much frustration. His dream of going to Paris was not realized until 1907. Once there he met Dukas, Debussy, Ravel and other French musicians as well as his compatriot Albéniz. After a long wait *La vida breve* was performed in Nice, Paris and finally, after Falla had returned there in 1914 on the outbreak of war, in Madrid. He completed *Nights in the Gardens of Spain* for piano and orchestra and wrote the two ballets, *El amor brujo* and *The Three-Cornered Hat*.

After his parents' deaths in 1919 Falla moved to Granada, paradoxically ceasing to write overtly Andalusian music. His strange character intensified: he was a devout Catholic, superstitious, a conservative who abhorred violence and militarism. Since he had many friends of liberal tendencies, in the Civil War he suffered mental agony. His health deteriorated. When he left Spain for Argentina in 1939, *Atlántida*, a score that had already occupied him for more than a decade, was unfinished, and remained incomplete at his death. In Granada Falla wrote some incidental music for two autos sacramentales, Calderón's *El gran teatro del mundo* and Lope de Vega's *La vuelta de Egipto*. Many operatic collaborations with friends, including the poet Lorca and the painter Zuloaga, were discussed but not started. A curious project towards the end of his second Madrid period was a three-act comic opera *Fuego fatuo* (Will-o'-the-wisp) with a libretto

Manuel de Falla (centre) with the choreographer Leonide Massine at the Fountain of Lions in the Alhambra at Granada, Spain (1919)

by María Martinez Sierra and music adapted from Chopin's piano works by Falla. Only the outer acts of the three were finished before the scheme was abandoned. In 1976 Antoni Ros Marbá made an orchestral suite out of the completed acts.

La vida breve

Life is Brief

Lyric drama in two acts (four tableaux) (1h 15m)
Libretto by Carlos Fernández Shaw
Composed 1904
PREMIERES 1 April 1913, Casino Municipal, Nice (in French); US: 6 March 1926, Metropolitan, New York; UK: 9 September 1958, Edinburgh
CAST Salud *s*, La abuela (grandmother) *ms* or *a*, Paco *t*, Uncle Sarvaor *bar* or *b*, Manuel *bar*, Carmela *ms*, Cantaor (singer) *bar*, 3 street-sellers 2*s*, *ms*, 2 offstage voices 2 *t*; *satb* chorus of townsfolk (wedding guests)
FULL ORCHESTRA with onstage gtr

Falla and the zarzuela writer Fernández Shaw had agreed to collaborate and had started work on their project when the one-act opera competition was announced by the Royal Academy of San Fernando in 1904. Even so, *La vida breve* had to be written quickly. The opera won the prize, but the Madrid production held out as an inducement did not materialize. When Falla showed the score to musicians in Paris they (Dukas especially) were favourably impressed, but not until 1913 was the opera accepted. By then Falla had for practical reasons divided the opera into two acts, touched up the orchestration, expanded the second scene and the second dance and, on the advice of Debussy, shortened the ending. The success of the Nice premiere induced the Opéra-Comique to change its mind; the further acclaim in Paris caused Madrid to open its doors at last. The success of the first performance in Spanish, on 14 November 1914 in Madrid, was triumphant.

SYNOPSIS

Act I   Granada, at the turn of the century. Salud lives with her grandmother in the gypsy quarter above the town. She is anxiously awaiting Paco, a local playboy who has seduced her and promised marriage. The grandmother is reassuring but warns Salud against loving too much. Voices of workmen in a nearby forge are heard, lamenting the miserable poor, born to be anvils, not hammers. Salud enlarges on their words in an aria. Paco arrives, protesting love. Unnoticed by the couple, Salvador steals in and confirms to the grandmother the truth of a rumour about Paco's impending marriage to a well-off girl in the town. Paco and Salud arrange to meet next day. The following scene takes place in mime as night falls over Granada. Paco takes leave of Salud. The grandmother restrains Salvador from following him.

Act II   Scene 1: The front of a house in the town. Night. Through the windows the patio can be seen, illuminated for the wedding of Paco to Carmela. A *cantaor* sings in their honour. During the following dance (familiar in transcriptions as 'Spanish Dance No. 1') Salud appears. She sings of her grief at Paco's betrayal and of her wish to die. Her grandmother and Salvador join her. Salud repeats the workmen's hammer-and-anvil comparison. Scene 2: Inside the patio Paco, Carmela and her brother Manuel (the host) are the centre of a throng of wedding guests. There is a second dance, with wordless chorus. Salvador appears leading Salud; she holds back, then suddenly denounces Paco. As she advances towards him she falls dead at his feet.

The libretto veers between passionate feelings violently expressed and another form of *verismo* – a detailed depiction of the sights and sounds of Granada, a remarkable case of empathy (reminiscent of Gustave Charpentier's depiction of Paris in *Louise*) since Falla had not visited the town when he wrote the opera. The music, written in haste when Falla was bursting with invention, is irresistible in spite of stylistic inconsistency. The depiction of Salud, the only character drawn in the round, is highly individual. There is a quality of youthful exuberance in the opera which Falla neither achieved nor sought again.

RECORDINGS 1. De los Angeles, Cossutta, Ch. Orfeón Donostiarra, Nat O of Spain, Frühbeck de Burgos, EMI, 1966; 2. Berganza, Carreras, Ambrosian Opera Ch, LSO, Navarra, DG, 1978: both these sets capture the work's authentic spirit [A.B.]
EDITIONS   v.s., Eschig, 1913

El retablo de Maese Pedro
Master Peter's Puppet Show

Musical and scenic version of an episode from *El Ingenioso Cavallero Don Quixote de la Mancha* in one act (30m)
Libretto by the composer after Cervantes's *Don Quixote* (1605 and 1615)
Composed 1919–22
PREMIERES   23 March 1923, Teatro San Fernando, Seville (concert); 25 June 1923, Paris (private); UK: 13 October 1924, Victoria Rooms, Clifton, Bristol; US: 29 December 1925, New York
CAST   Don Quixote *bar* or *b*, Maese Pedro *t*, El trujaman (the boy) *boy s*, 5 mime roles, several puppets
CHAMBER ORCHESTRA including perc, hpd, harp-lute or pedal harp

In 1919 Princess Edmond de Polignac asked Falla to write a chamber opera for performance in her house in Paris. Falla, who had arranged the music for some private puppet shows in Granada devised by Lorca, suggested a puppet opera based on an episode in *Don Quixote*. The princess gave permission for a concert performance in Seville (conducted by Falla) a few months before the private Paris premiere. On the latter occasion Hector Dufranne sang Don Quixote, the conductor was Wladimir Golschmann, and Wanda Landowska played the harpsichord.

On a trestle table in the yard of a Spanish inn the travelling showman Master Peter presents a puppet play. The boy, interrupted from time to time by pedantic objections from Don Quixote in the audience, intones the narration. The play is set in the time of Charlemagne. The Emperor's daughter Melisendra is a captive of the Moors at Saragossa in Spain. The Emperor rebukes her husband, Don Gayferos, for not going to her rescue. From her prison in a tower Melisendra scans the horizon. A Moor steals a kiss and is sentenced by the King, Marsilius, to punishment, which is duly effected. Gayferos sets out on horseback for Spain. The hills resound with horn- and trumpet-calls. Gayferos reaches Saragossa and reveals himself. Melisendra leaps from her tower into his arms. They ride off towards France. When Quixote sees Moors in pursuit of the Christian couple, he rises in fury. Believing the spectacle to be real, he wrecks the puppets with his sword before declaring himself 'knight errant and captive of the most fair Dulcinea' to whom he sings a prayer. Finally he addresses the public on the virtues of knight-errantry.

The opera can be performed by two sets of puppets (large ones for Quixote, Master Peter, his boy and the onlookers, small ones for the players) with the three singers in the orchestra, or by the singers and mimes for the 'real' characters and small puppets for the players. Another possibility is to use singers and mimes with children in the place of puppets – all masked.

El retablo, in every way a more sophisticated work than *La vida breve*, ranks with Stravinsky's *L'histoire du soldat* as a seminal piece of music theatre. The spontaneity and wide range of expression conceal a carefully prepared synthesis of national, historical and popular elements. Typical are the writing for the boy, whose narrations, delivered in shrill monotone, were based on plainsong and street cries, and the way in which Falla lifts the final scene for Quixote on to a different plane. The scoring, for example in Gayferos's ride through the Pyrenees, shows Falla at his most masterly. So finely calculated are the proportions that the opera feels longer and bigger than it really is.

RECORDINGS 1. Tourné, Lavirgen, Cesari, Madrid Concert O, Freitas Branco, Erato, 1960; 2. Smith, Oliver, Knapp, London Sinfonietta, Rattle, Argo, 1980; 3. Linay, Thompson, Best, Matrix Ensemble, Ziegler, ASV, 1990
EDITIONS f.s., Chester, 1950; v.s., Chester, 1924

Atlántida

Atlantis

Scenic cantata in a prologue and three parts (1h 20m)
Libretto by the composer, adapted from the poem *L'Atlántida* by Jacint Verdaguer
Composed 1928–46, unfinished; realized and completed by Ernesto Halffter
PREMIERES 24 November 1961, Barcelona (concert); 18 June 1962, La Scala, Milan; rev. version: UK: 26 August 1962, Usher Hall, Edinburgh (concert); US: 29 September 1962, Philharmonic Hall, New York (concert); 9 September 1976, Kunsthaus, Lucerne
CAST Isabella *s*, Pyrene *a*, Corifeo (narrator) *b*, the boy Columbus *boy s*, the Pleiades 3 *s*, 2 *ms*, 2 *a*, the three-headed Geryon 2 *t*, *b*, Court Lady *a*, page *boy s*, Alcide (Hercules) *silent*; *satb* chorus, mimes and/or dancers
FULL ORCHESTRA with triple ww, perc and 2 pf

Falla discovered the Catalan writer Verdaguer's epic poem *L'Atlántida* in 1926 and began to set parts of it about two years later. Although he used the Catalan text he chose a Castilian form of the title, *Atlántida*. As he worked the scope of the project widened, difficulties arose and *Atlántida* hung fire. Falla took the incomplete score with him to Argentina and continued to work on it when his health permitted. After Falla's death, Ernesto Halffter was asked to undertake completion. He found the Prologue complete and orchestrated except for a few bars; Part I complete and partly orchestrated, and Part III in an advanced state of composition with some orchestration. Part II, however, was in confusion, with sketches and alternatives to be sorted out and pieced together. In 1961, after years of labour, a concert performance of major extracts was given in Barcelona. Eduardo Toldrá conducted and Victoria de los Angeles and Raimundo Torres were the principal soloists. After *Atlántida* was staged at La Scala, Milan, in the following year, Halffter withdrew the score for further revision. It was not until 1976 that a shortened, 'definitive' version was performed in concert form at the Lucerne Festival. Once again Halffter withdrew the score, briefly this time, restoring another 20 minutes of music. This, the version recorded by EMI, was given in Madrid in 1977, but the Lucerne version was chosen for publication.

SYNOPSIS (Lucerne version)
Prologue A shipwrecked boy (the future Christopher Columbus) learns of the legendary fate of the drowned continent of Atlantis, the one-time garden of the Hesperides. Who protected Spain during the cataclysm? The answer comes with the *Hymnus Hispanicus*: the Almighty saved Spain for future greatness, tying the land to the wall of the Pyrenees.

Part I In mythical times. The roaming Hercules (Alcide) comes to Spain and finds the Queen Pyrene, driven by the three-headed monster Geryon to the northern end of her kingdom. Geryon has set fire to the forests. As she dies she begs Hercules to avenge her. With his club he flattens the mountains and erects a new range, the Pyrenees, then descends to the coast to found a city (the future Barcelona) and sails southwards to confront Geryon.

Part II In a magic boat Hercules reaches Gades (Cadiz) where Geryon awaits him. The monster craftily urges Hercules to sample the delights of the Atlantis gardens. Here the hero finds the seven Pleiades dancing round a tree bearing golden oranges. The foliage conceals a venomous dragon. Hercules slays the beast who, in his agony, destroys the tree. The Pleiades expire in grief and are changed into stars. Hercules returns to Gades. The opulence of Atlantis has attracted divine wrath: through the chorus, Jehovah foretells punishment in the form of a second Flood.

Part III In historical times. Columbus, now grown up, hears prophetic voices foretell a great extension of the world's known boundaries. They direct the mariner to the Catholic Queen Isabella. In her palace at Granada Isabella has dreamed of a dove flying away over the sea carrying her betrothal ring in its beak. The dove drops the ring in the waters, from which arise flowery islands. Isabella offers Columbus her jewels to buy 'winged ships'. The chorus delivers the Lord's command 'to bring together my sons and daughters from the ends of earth'. Three caravels appear, carrying the sons of the regions of Spain in fraternal unity across the sea. Columbus prays, surrounded by his sailors. On the last night of the voyage he watches on deck alone.

The attraction for Falla of the subject, fusing Classical and Christian elements and dealing with sites in Spain (Barcelona and Cadiz) which he loved, is understandable; yet for musical purposes the text proved intractable. There is spectacular drama in some of the chosen sections (the drowning of the continent and the arrival in the New World) but Falla did not complete them: the subjects were alien to his later style. Theatrical, or more precisely operatic, possibilities are few – Hercules is mute; Columbus sings one phrase as a boy in the Prologue, nothing else.

There have been three stage productions, at La Scala (Margherita Wallmann), in Berlin (Franco Zeffirelli) in 1962 and in Buenos Aires (Louis Erlo) in 1963. Some kind of symbolic staging with mimes or dancers, for instance in one of Spain's ancient abbeys (a possibility conceived by Falla), might be feasible but the future of *Atlántida*, which contains some of Falla's finest music in his later, concentrated, interiorized manner, may well lie in the concert hall.

RECORDING Tarrés, Ricci, Sardinero, Spanish National Ch and O, Frühbeck de Burgos, EMI, 1978
EDITIONS f.s./v.s., Ricordi, 1981

Other operas: *El conde de Villamediana* (lost), (1887); *Fuego fatuo* (Acts I and III; Act II, inc.), (1919)
Zarzuelas: *Los amores de la Inés*, 1902; *Prisionero de guerra* (coll. with Vives; inc.), (1904); lost zarzuelas: *La Juana y la Petra*, or *La casa de Tócame Roque* (1902); *Limosna de amor* (?1903); *El cornetín de órdenes* (with Vives), (1903); *La Cruz de Malta* (with Vives), (?1903)
BIBLIOGRAPHY A. Budwig, *Manuel de Falla's 'Atlántida': An Historical and Analytical Study*, dissertation, University of Chicago, 1984; R. Crichton, *Falla*, BBC Music Guides, 1982; B. James, *Manuel de Falla and the Spanish Musical Renaissance*, Gollancz, 1979

R.H.C.

GABRIEL FAURÉ

Gabriel-Urbain Fauré; *b* 12 May 1845, Pamiers, Ariège, France; *d* 4 November 1924, Paris

After a quiet, rather solitary early childhood, Fauré was sent to the Ecole Niedermeyer in Paris at the age of nine. It was a school for budding organists and choirmasters whose founder hoped to propagate a respect for older church music, which he thought grievously neglected. Niedermeyer pupils were therefore instructed thoroughly in the ancient ecclesiastical modes (of which there are traces in Fauré's mature music), and discouraged from investigating modernists such as Schumann and Liszt. When Fauré was 16, however, a new piano teacher was appointed: Saint-Saëns, who introduced him to all that forbidden fruit, and also to the light, polished style of the latest French music. It is not hard to see how the features of the younger composer's style developed from that intensive tuition, at least so far as the songs and the piano and chamber music go. His operatic projects were more unexpected.

Admirers of his songs are often surprised to learn that Fauré wrote an opera at all. In fact he was seeking libretti as early as 1879, and got as far as writing a sextet for *Barnabé*, a one-act *opéra comique*; later he had hopes for a Pushkin project, *Mazeppa*. By the 1890s he was a familiar figure in the artistic salons of Paris, and the Princesse de Scey-Montbéliard (later de Polignac) made plans for him: first an opera to be called *La tentation de Bouddha*, for which poor Albert Samain (whose poems Fauré often turned into songs) wrote 750 stanzas in vain, and then a collaboration with Verlaine on *L'hôpital Watteau* – *commedia dell'arte* personages in a hospital ward – which came to nothing because the poet was already a proven alcoholic. Much earlier, however, Fauré had composed a mythological scene for soloists, chorus and orchestra after Paul Collin, *La naissance de Vénus*, and between 1888 and 1919

he wrote several scores for the theatre: for the *Caligula* of Dumas *père*, for a *Merchant of Venice* adaptation called *Shylock* (thriftily recycled later for *Jules César*), and for the London production of Maeterlinck's *Pelléas et Mélisande*. (The familiar suite from the latter misses out the song composed for Mrs Patrick Campbell's Mélisande; four years later came Debussy's opera.) The year after *Prométhée*, Fauré supplied musical *chinoiserie* for a mock-oriental morality play by Georges Clemenceau, *Le voile du bonheur*; finally, when he was nearly 75, he brought together one new piece and many old ones – two or three of them 40 years old – for a divertissement conceived by his *Pénélope* librettist Fauchois, *Masques et bergamasques*. With the exception of *Le voile du bonheur*, each of these scores included a voice or voices.

It is striking that, though several numbers from those modest theatrical commissions have become staples of the lighter repertoire, not a single extract from the ambitious *Prométhée* or *Pénélope* is familiar to the musical public. That is not evidence that Fauré was unsuccessful on a grander scale – *Prométhée* was designed for exceedingly special circumstances, and *Pénélope* is too smoothly through-composed to permit excerpts. For deeper reasons, however, both works do stand apart from the rest of Fauré's *oeuvre*. They flank his crucial transition period, from late Romantic to post-Romantic. The outward marks of the change, as shown in his other music of those years, were laconic density and stripped-down textures – whereas the operatic projects required sonorous, rhetorical breadth. To secure that for *Prométhée*, he recalled the church style and the Wagnerian leanings of his earlier years; his *Pénélope*, on the other hand, is something like a magnified, more freely constructed version of a chamber score. Neither has any close parallel.

Just before Fauré began *Pénélope*, he had reviewed the Paris premiere of Richard Strauss's *Salome*; he admired many aspects of the score, but repined at 'so many cruel dissonances which defy all explanation'. Though his own harmonic excursions may strike orthodox Teutonic ears as wayward and elusive, Fauré was rigorously faithful to a Gallic ideal of 'logic' in harmony. No gratuitous surprises: every new chord had to stand in a rational relation to the last, however remote. In Fauré, the result demands more sophisticated attention than the Expressionist shocks in the music of his more famously 'radical' Austrian contemporaries.

Prométhée
Prometheus

Tragédie lyrique in three acts, Op. 82
Libretto by Jean Lorrain and André-Ferdinand Hérold after Greek mythology
Composed February–July 1900
PREMIERES first version: 27 August 1900, Arènes de Béziers; 5 December 1907, Paris; second version: 17 May 1917, Opéra, Paris
CAST Prométhée, Pandore, Hermès *spoken roles*; Bia *s*, Gaïa *ms*, Andros *t*, Kratos *t*, Héphaïstos *b*; *satb* chorus of men, women and Oceanides

ORCHESTRATION   first version by the composer and
Charles Eustace (winds), for the local Béziers orchestra plus
2 large wind bands, 30 tpt, 100 str and 15 hp; second version
(1914–16) for symphony orchestra by Jean Roger-Ducasse,
revised in part by the composer

Prométhée was conceived as an epic *pièce d'occasion*,
in terms so special as to discourage revivals. Besides
the audience of 10,000 for its open-air premiere,
there were almost 800 performers – large choruses,
wind bands strategically located at widely separated
points, a 'curtain' of harps stretched across the front
of the playing area. Roger-Ducasse's reduced
version for stagebound production has never found
favour, though it is used for concert extracts. What
is specially awkward about the piece, however, is
its dramatic form, which enlists music only some of
the time, and otherwise requires lofty declamation
of badly dated dialogue. The leading characters,
Prometheus and Pandora, have spoken roles, as does
the messenger Hermes; only the gods, the companions of Prometheus and the Oceanides sing. Fauré's
score, dignified and mostly sombre or gentle or both,
does not represent the whole of the action, and
even counting its several purely instrumental passages it could not stand on its own.

Apart from the wordiness of the text, the plot is
weakly constructed.

SYNOPSIS

Act I   Prometheus, urged on by his fellow humans,
tries to steal Zeus's fire, but is felled by a lightning
bolt and captured by the gods; meanwhile Pandora
expires in shock.

Act II begins with her funeral cortège; later,
however, she is resuscitated and attempts to comfort
Prometheus, whom Hephaestus is chaining to the
Caucasian rock in accordance with Zeus's sentence –
his liver is to be devoured daily by an eagle.

Act III   Pandora seeks help from the Oceanides,
gentle water-nymphs. The gods' sentence on
Prometheus is proclaimed, but Hermes comes to
offer Pandora the famous box (of troubles): against
the heroic victim's anxious warnings, she and the
other humans welcome it – only Pandora's tears will
be able to heal his wound.

Like many another composer of his time, Fauré
employed Wagner's leitmotif method for building his
theatrical score. A few basic themes are associated
with the various characters (even the non-singing
ones), the fire and so forth, and further material is
generated from them. The result combines imposing
gravitas with tenderness; at the premiere Fauré's
fellow musicians were astonished to find that his
idiom, which they had thought too small-scale and
subtle to bear expansion, could be adapted so
successfully to fill a large dramatic space. The
Requiem and many other choral works were already
behind him, of course, so the strength of the choral
writing in *Prométhée* might have been anticipated.
The traces of academic stiffness in some numbers
were as nothing compared to the literary creaking in
the libretto. Since the main characters were confined

to speech, Fauré was not called upon to represent
any psychological development; the solo music
apportioned between the minor figures generally
taps only one vein at a time – grieving or minatory,
lyrical or declamatory. This noble torso of a score
seems likely to remain partly buried, though always
revered by Fauré enthusiasts.

RECORDING   excerpts (the preludes to each act, Act II
Cortège and Interlude, Airs for Gaïa and Bia, Chorus of the
Océanides): Gailland, Orchestre National de l'Opéra de
Monte Carlo and Maîtrise Gabriel Fauré, Norrington, IPG
Q.S., 1976
EDITION   v.s. (first version), Hamelle, 1907

Pénélope

Drame lyrique in three acts (2h)
Libretto by René Fauchois, after the *Odyssey* of Homer
Composed 1907–12
PREMIERES   4 March 1913, Salle Garnier, Monte Carlo;
10 May 1913, Paris; US: 29 November 1945, Cambridge,
Massachusetts; UK: 20 November 1970, Royal Academy of
Music, London
CAST   Ulysse *t*, Eumée *bar*, Antinoüs *t*, Eurymaque *bar*,
Pénélope *s*, Euryclée *ms*, Léodès *t*, Ctésippe *t* or *bar*,
Pisandre *t* or *bar*, un pâtre *t*, Cléone *ms*, Melantho *s*,
Alkandre *ms*, Phylo *s*, Lydie *s*, Eurynome *s* or *ms*; *satb* chorus
of servants and shepherds
LARGE ORCHESTRA including hp, large perc section (latter
parts of Acts II and III orch. by Fernand Pecoud)

Warmly acclaimed at its premiere and still admired
by connoisseurs, *Pénélope* is very rarely performed.
The libretto that Fauchois made for Fauré, much less
'literary' than Lorrain's text for *Prométhée*, keeps the
story simple: there are no gods in surveillance, and

Poster design for Pénélope *(Paris, 1913)*

even Ulysses' son Telemachus is omitted from the action. Though Fauré allows some forceful effect to the climactic slaying of the suitors, the opera is no warrior epic, but at heart a celebration of bourgeois marriage rather as the song-cycle *La bonne chanson* was a celebration of bourgeois engagement – private hopes and doubts resolved at last in secure domestic happiness.

Fauré's own situation was more complicated than that: before his marriage it had been his mistress, the soprano Emma Bardac (later Debussy's wife), who inspired *La bonne chanson*, and it is generally accepted that he had discreet arrangements with other ladies during much of his apparently decorous married life. (There is a soberly moving letter from Fauré to his wife, three weeks before his death, in which he strives to console her for an unrewarding life of family duties.) Fauchois's surprising arrangement of his libretto, with a central act that contains no overt action but is given over to an anxious questioning *rapprochement* between long-neglected wife and still-disguised husband might have been cunningly devised to capture Fauré's interest – the libretto was proposed and accepted at a dinner party, and he discovered only later that Fauchois had yet to write it. In any case, the combination of a drama of inner feelings with the composer's refined, temperately intense score seems to have discouraged opera producers; derring-do and mock-Wagner would have gone down better.

SYNOPSIS

Act I After a measured, thoughtful prelude (based on the themes of Penelope and Ulysses), Ulysses' palace on Ithaca is revealed in gloom. While Penelope's serving maids spin, they discuss her unhappy situation: after ten years her husband has not returned from the Trojan War, and she is beset by rapacious young suitors who are heard carousing in another room. The maids think her patient waiting has become pointless; by now, she should have settled for one of the suitors. They enter, rudely calling for her and angering her nurse Euryclea. Penelope appears, reiterates her devotion to Ulysses and reminds the suitors of her promise to choose one of them only when she has finished weaving a shroud for her father-in-law, Laertes. They are dismayed to see how much weaving is still to be done; she has a dance staged to mollify them and meanwhile yearns after her husband ('Ulysse! fier époux!'). He arrives, in the guise of a humble beggar. The suitors abuse him and return to their feast; Penelope welcomes him kindly – for a moment she thinks she recognizes him, but decides not. The old nurse does, but Ulysses enjoins her to silence before going off with her to be fed. Penelope begins to unpick her day's weaving, as she always does; the suitors catch her in the deception, and declare that her choice can be postponed no longer. She and Euryclea prepare to keep their nightly watch for Ulysses' ship. The 'beggar' agrees to join them, and while they fetch a cloak for him he exults in his wife's fidelity.

Act II On a hilltop the old shepherd Eumaeus muses, and greets passing friends. Arriving with the nurse and Ulysses for their vigil, Penelope recalls how she used to come here with her husband; aside, Euryclea promises to help him rout the suitors. Penelope interrogates the 'beggar', who claims ('O mon hôte, à présent') to be an unlucky Cretan king who recently harboured the storm-tossed Ulysses for twelve days, and assures her that he is on his way. The wife is overjoyed, and the husband deeply moved. Before the women go home to prepare for the suitors tomorrow, the 'beggar' asks Penelope whether any of them has shown himself worthy of her by managing to draw Ulysses' great bow, and she takes the hint. After they depart he reveals himself to the shepherds, who hail him and swear to assist him.

Act III A surging, angry prelude takes us to the royal hall as day breaks. Alone, Ulysses has prowled the palace all night, and now conceals the sword of Hercules beneath the throne in readiness. The nurse tells him that Penelope has been sleepless and despairing, and Eumaeus reports that the suitors have ordered up a wedding banquet, which means that the shepherds will be on hand – with their knives. The suitors assemble, Antinous singing the delights of youth and Eurymachus fretting over an ill omen (a crow seen on his left). There are dances, with flutes. Penelope proclaims that her choice will be fixed by an archery contest with the great bow. As storm clouds gather she describes a foreboding vision, and the jeering suitors become anxious. Servants set up the dozen axes through which the winning arrow must be shot. Not one of the suitors can draw the bow; the 'beggar' steps forward, passes the test and then shoots Eurymachus dead. The shepherds rush forward to assist in the slaughter of all the other suitors. Ulysses and Penelope rejoice in their reunion, and everybody praises Zeus.

Where Fauré had managed to compose *Prométhée* in less than six months, *Pénélope* took him about five years, for in 1905 he had become director of the Paris Conservatoire. Again he adapted the leitmotif method to fix various aspects of the leading roles, as well as the sword, the bow, the shroud. He took great pains to get them right, for each had to be imbued with potent character; there is little room in this score for the picturesque. There is far less 'symphonic' development than in Wagner (once the prelude to Act I is past), but not much straight recitative either, nor any number arias. Only the opening spinning chorus, the little dances and the final eulogy to Zeus are anything like formal set pieces. The vocal writing is eloquent (the principal couple need fairly heroic voices), and all the music follows the sense of the action closely and flexibly. As usual in Fauré's later work, the harmony tends to be 'elliptic': when the music slips into remote tonal areas, as it often does, the intervening steps are implied rather than spelled out. Tonality is stretched hard, without breaking. The conservative Saint-Saëns, who greatly preferred *Prométhée*, was puzzled and disappointed by Fauré's new style; but modern listeners who have learned to appreciate his later non-operatic music will find no difficulty here.

In theatrical terms, the static second act is certainly risky. Fauchois must at least have supposed that the situation would be sufficiently intriguing, with its conjugal duologue carried on as if between strangers. A further hypothesis is possible, however, and even hinted at in the text: perhaps Penelope, who is not only unhappy but aggrieved (like Monteverdi's Penelope), has from the outset recognized her husband in the grizzled wanderer, but maintains a feigned ignorance because she wants reassurance – she quizzes the 'beggar' about Ulysses' women abroad – and time to consider. Perhaps in fact Ulysses understands that, and Penelope knows that he does, in which case the whole central duologue is a game of tender bluff and cautious exploration. One would like to see it played like that, but one has to be lucky to see it played at all.

RECORDINGS 1. Crespin, Gayraud, Jobin, Massard, Vessières, French National Radio Ch and O, Inghelbrecht, Discoreale-INA, 1956; 2. Norman, Taillon, Vanzo, Huttenlocher, van Dam, Jean Laforge Vocal Ensemble, Monte Carlo PO, Dutoit, Erato, 1980: the first is more idiomatic; the second is better recorded [A.B.]
EDITIONS f.s./v.s., Heugel, 1913

BIBLIOGRAPHY Charles Koechlin, trans. Leslie Orrey, *Gabriel Fauré*, Dennis Dobson, 1945; Jean-Michel Nectoux, *Fauré*, Editions du Seuil, 1972; Jean-Michel Nectoux, trans. J. A. Underwood, *Gabriel Fauré: His Life through His Letters*, Marion Boyars, 1984; Robert Orledge, *Gabriel Fauré*, Eulenburg, 1979

D.M.

FRANCESCO FEO
b 1691, Naples; *d* 28 January 1761, Naples

Like 'learned' Cafaro in the following generation, Francesco Feo was a pupil of Nicola Fago at the Neapolitan Conservatory of S. Maria della Pietà dei Turchini, where Leonardo Leo also studied. In order to instil the true operatic tradition into the students, Provenzale had instituted a final examination which required each student to compose and produce a short sacred opera. Feo was raised in this tradition, which he respected and honoured.

Indeed, his first stage works were a dramma per musica (1713) and a dramma sacro entitled *Il martirio di S. Caterina* (1714). His first comic work for Naples was staged in 1719, but after this his career became centred around opera seria, his works reaching the theatres of Rome and Turin. His main activity, however, was always teaching, both privately and in the Neapolitan conservatories. As a theorist, he was considered by Padre Martini worthy of 'esteem and veneration'. He composed his last opera in 1740, thereafter writing only church music.

His interest in the properties of the voice caused him, in his operas, to give increasing prominence to the *da capo* aria, providing opportunities for virtuoso vocal displays against generally simple orchestral accompaniments. Burney considered him 'one of the greatest Neapolitan masters of his time', describing his music as 'full of fire, invention, and force in the melody and expression of the words'.

Surviving operas: *L'amor tirannico, ossia Zenobia*, 1713; *Siface, re di Numidia* (with the comic intermezzo *Morano e Rosina*), 1723; *Ipermestra*, 1728; *Andromaca*, 1730 (EDITION facsimile, Garland, 1977); *Issipile*, 1733 or 1735; *Oreste*, 1738; *Polinice* (inc.), 1738; *Arsace*, 1740; 6 lost operas
BIBLIOGRAPHY H.-B. Dietz, 'Francesco Feo', in *Grove*, Macmillan, 1980

D.A.D'A.

ALFONSO FERRABOSCO II
b c. 1575, ?Greenwich, London; *buried* 11 March 1628, Greenwich

The son of the Bolognese composer Alfonso Ferrabosco I, Ferrabosco II was in effect orphaned when his father returned to Italy in 1578. He

Costume design by Inigo Jones for the Countess of Bedford as Penthesilia in Ferrabosco's The Masque of Queens *(1609)*

subsequently became one of the most favoured English court composers, holding posts as a viol-player (1592), a violinist (1601), music teacher to Prince Henry and Prince Charles (1605) and composer (1626). Thus, in the reign of James I his court activities were divided between the privy chamber of the monarch and the households of his two sons. He married Ellen, the daughter of Nicholas Lanier, and on his death his posts were divided between their two sons Alfonso III and Henry. Ferrabosco contributed to most genres of the day, though he is particularly noted for his viol fantasias and his songs, some of which show the influence of Italian monody. He apparently wrote most of the music for Ben Jonson's court masques, particularly in the first decade of James I's reign; he was commended by Jonson in several masque texts.

Ferrabosco contributed songs and music to the following court masques, all with texts by Ben Jonson: *Masque of Blackness*, 1605; *Hymenai*, 1606; *Masque of Beauty*, 1608; *Haddington Masque*, 1608; *Masque of Queens*, 1609; *Oberon*, 1611; *Love Freed from Ignorance and Folly*, 1611; *The Masque of Augurs*, 1622

EDITIONS   E. Fellowes (ed.), *The English School of Lutenist Song Writers*, second series, vol. 16, Stainer and Bell, 1925–6; A. J. Sabol (ed.), *Four Hundred Songs and Dances from the Stuart Masque*, Brown University Press, 1978
BIBLIOGRAPHY   J. Duffy, *The Songs and Motets of Alfonso Ferrabosco, the Younger (1575–1628)*, UMI, 1979–80

P.H.

GIOVANNI FERRANDINI
Giovanni Battista [Johann Baptist, Zaneto] Ferrandini [Ferandini]; *b c.* 1710, Venice; *d* 25 September 1791, Munich

After early training in Venice, Ferrandini moved to Munich, initially as a court oboist and later as director of chamber music. His first stage work, *Gordio*, to a libretto by Perozzo da Perozzi, was performed at Munich in 1727 when he was not yet 20; and this was followed by an extended sequence of operas, many of them to well-known libretti by Metastasio and Zeno, which appear to have been well received at the Bavarian court. His opera seria, *Catone in Utica*, to a Metastasio text, was mounted in 1753 for the opening of the new Residenztheater built by Cuvilliés in Munich. In later life he retired on a pension to Padua and was visited there in 1771 by the 15-year-old Mozart. His last opera for Munich was written in 1781. Particularly noteworthy among his pupils were the Saxon princess, Maria Antonia Walpurgis, herself an opera composer, and the tenor Anton Raaff, who in 1781 sang the title role in Mozart's *Idomeneo* at its first performance in Munich.

Operatic works: *Gordio*, 1727; *Il sacrificio invalido*, 1729; *Colloquio pastorale*, 1729; *Berenice*, 1730; *Scipio nelle Spagna*, 1732; *Adriano in Siria*, 1737; *Demofoonte*, 1737; *Catone in Utica*, 1753; *Diana placata*, 1755; *Demetrio*, 1756 or 1758; *Talestri*, (n.d.); *L'Amor prigionero*, 1781

BIBLIOGRAPHY   E. J. Luin, 'Giovanni Ferrandini e l'apertura del Teatro Residenziale a Monaco nel 1745', *RMI*, vol. 39 (1932), p. 561

B.S.

BENEDETTO FERRARI
Benedetto Ferrari 'dalla Tiorba'; *b* 1603 or 1604, Reggio Emilia; *d* 22 October 1681, Modena

Ferrari was one of the chief figures involved in the apparent shift to 'public' opera in Venice in the late 1630s: his impressive range of skills – poet, librettist, composer, instrumentalist (he played the theorbo) and impresario – was well suited to the new demands of opera houses now opening their doors to a paying audience. In 1617–18 Ferrari was a singer at the Collegio Germanico in Rome, from 1619 to 1623 he was in court service at Parma, and in the late 1620s and 1630s he may have been associated with the Este court in Modena, which (according to Sigismondo d'India) employed some of the best singers in Europe. In 1637, he provided the libretto for *L'Andromeda* (music by Francesco Manelli), the first 'public' opera staged at the Teatro S. Cassiano in Venice.

Ferrari wrote music for five other operas (four to his own libretti) for Venetian theatres before 1645. In the late 1640s, he may again have been associated with Modena – he provided a ballet, *La vittoria d'Imeneo*, for the wedding of Francesco I d'Este and Vittoria Farnese in 1648. In 1651, he moved to Vienna as instrumentalist and director of court festivities to Emperor Ferdinand III, but returned to Modena as court maestro di cappella in 1653. Economic difficulties led to his dismissal from Modena in 1662, but he was reinstated in December 1674, and stayed there until his death.

His first libretti for Venice adopted the pastoral–mythological subjects and elaborate stage effects typical of court opera, although *La maga fulminata*'s comic governess, Scarabea, established a trend for humorous *travestiti* roles. Only later did he shift to the historical plots often (but wrongly) deemed archetypal of Venetian opera, with *Enone abbandonata* (1651), *Egisto* (1651; Faustini's libretto had already been set by Cavalli), *Gli amori di Alessandro Magno, e di Rossane* (1656), and *L'Erosilda* (1658). His six Venetian libretti were published in his *Poesie drammatiche* (1644): here his skill seems to have lain chiefly in his ability to devise flexible verse structures to cater for the incipient recitative–aria divisions slowly establishing themselves in operatic music. The music for his nine operas is entirely lost, but three books of chamber songs (published in 1633, 1637 and 1641) suggest an awareness of the up-and-coming musical styles in Venice: affective recitative, sensuous triple-time arias, and lengthy ground-bass settings. The libretto of Ferrari's *Il pastor regio* as revived in Bologna in 1641 contains 'Pur ti miro, pur ti godo' as the final duet: the same text (it is not clear whether or not with Ferrari's music) also appears at the end of Monteverdi's *L'incoronazione di Poppea* (1643).

BIBLIOGRAPHY Lorenzo Bianconi and Thomas Walker, 'Production, Consumption and Political Function of Seventeenth-Century Opera', *Early Music History*, vol. 4 (1984), pp. 209–96; A. Magini, 'Le monodie di Benedetto Ferrari e *L'incoronazione di Poppea*: un rilevamento stilistico comparativo', *RIM*, vol. 21 (1986), pp. 266–99

T.C.

LORENZO FERRERO
b 17 November 1951, Turin, Italy

A principal exponent of the neo-tonal tendencies common to a number of Italian composers of his generation, Ferrero has championed a brand of narrative music-theatre that aims to capture a wider audience than that achieved by the heirs of the modernist tradition. His idiom, highly eclectic from the start, has drawn increasingly on popular and neo-romantic idioms.

Rimbaud, ou Le fils du soleil
Rimbaud, or The Son of the Sun
Almost a melodrama in three parts
Libretto by L.-F. Claude
Composed 1974
PREMIERE 24 July 1978, Festival Theatre, Avignon

A series of scenes, half fantastic, half realistic, evoke cardinal points in Rimbaud's turbulent poetic development. Ferrero's acute sense of theatrical opportunity is constantly in evidence even in this, his earliest project. His score juxtaposes the experimental vocalism of the 1960s and 1970s with moments of adroit pastiche.

EDITIONS f.s./v.s., Ricordi, 1978

Marilyn
Scenes from the 1950s in two acts, from documents of American life (1h 30m)
Libretto by Floriana Bossi and the composer
Composed 1978–9
PREMIERE 23 February 1980, Teatro dell'Opera, Rome

The action cuts between scenes from the life of Marilyn Monroe – here a coloratura soprano – and wider perspectives: the Korean War, the McCarthy hearings, the prosecution of Wilhelm Reich, beat poets and Timothy Leary lecturing on the use of LSD. Ferrero's score is more consistently direct and populist than that of *Rimbaud*.

EDITIONS f.s./v.s., Ricordi, 1980

La figlia del mago
The Wizard's Daughter
Children's opera in two acts
Libretto by Marco Ravasini
Composed 1980–81

PREMIERE 31 July 1981, Teatro Poliziano, Montepulciano

Subtitled a *giocodramma melodioso* (as opposed to a *melodramma giocoso*), the element of play (*gioco*) extends to Ravasini's witty libretto, inspired by the analysis of typical situations from opera libretti pursued by Mario Lavagetto in his book, *Quei più modesti romanzi*. Ferrero responds in kind, showing his talents as a *pasticheur* of 19th-century mannerisms in a sequence of closed numbers. Alongside professional singers, children take mime roles. A flexible children's orchestra accompanies.

EDITIONS f.s./v.s., Ricordi, 1981

Mare nostro
Our Sea
Comic opera in two acts
Libretto by Marco Ravasini
Composed 1984–5
PREMIERE 11 September 1985, Teatro Comunale, Alessandria

A cheerful farce, again taking up the conventions of 19th-century opera, but within a contemporary context. A Middle European philosopher, temporarily out of work, deserts negative dialectics for money-making, seeking out a fishing machine being developed on a small Mediterranean island. Duping the machine's owner by a series of ruses, he is about to make off with it, when he is discovered, and condemned to devise nightly entertainments for the new tourist village that is another of the owner's projects. Ferrero juxtaposes Rossini and Bronski Beat in a fine display of post-modern cool.

EDITION f.s., Ricordi, 1985

Night
Opera in one act (divided into three parts) (1h 15m)
Text by the composer, from the *Hymnen an die Nacht* of Novalis
Composed 1985
PREMIERE 8 November 1985, Theater am Marstall, Munich

In direct contrast to *Mare nostro*, the theatrical conception of *Night* grows directly out of contemporary experiment. In the first section, the texts of Novalis are set for a madrigalian ensemble of solo voices, evoking the birth of the son of the night. The second part explodes into metropolitan night life, with Ferrero once again exploring funk and hard rock im what he describes as his *megadisco*. A solo singer concludes this cross between opera and cabaret, to which visual spectacle provides an essential contribution.

EDITION f.s., Ricordi, 1985

Salvatore Giuliano
Opera in one act
Libretto by Giuseppe Di Leva
Composed 1984–5
PREMIERE 25 January 1986, Teatro dell'Opera, Rome

A scene from Ferrero's Night *(Munich, 1985)*

Designed to be played alongside Mascagni's *Cavalleria rusticana, Salvatore Giuliano* is in effect an exercise in 'neo-*verismo*'. Di Leva's libretto outlines in a series of short, graphic scenes the network of intrigue between Sicilian independence activists, Mafia and state that surrounds, and eventually destroys, the bandit hero.

EDITIONS f.s./v.s., Ricordi, 1985

Charlotte Corday

Opera in three acts
Libretto by Giuseppe Di Leva
Composed 1986–8
PREMIERE 21 February 1989, Teatro dell'Opera, Rome

Again, Di Leva provides a clear-cut narration, in this case of Corday's assassination of Marat. Ferrero continues his revitalization of operatic conventions, this time reaching beyond closed numbers to through-composed scenes and a generous use of thematic reminiscence.

EDITIONS f.s./v.s., Ricordi, 1988

BIBLIOGRAPHY Marco Russo, 'Moderno, post-moderno, neoromanticismo: orientamenti di teatro musicale contemporaneo', *Il Verri*, vol. 2 (1988)

D.O.-S.

ZDENĚK FIBICH

Zdeněk [Zdenko] Antonín Václav Fibich; *b* 21 December 1850, Všebořice; *d* 15 October 1900, Prague

Fibich's operatic career started early. While still in his teens, he attempted four operas, one of which, *Kappellmeister in Venedig*, was completed and privately performed. These operas were written in German, reflecting both Fibich's mother's home language and his early education. By the time he left Prague for Leipzig for further musical education (1865–7), Fibich was already a prolific composer with 50 works to his name. He continued his studies in Paris (1868–9) and Mannheim (1869–70) before returning to Bohemia.

Fibich's first professional post was in Vilnius, training school choirs (1873–4). On his return his first extant opera, *Bukovín*, was given in Prague. Three years as chorus master and deputy conductor at the Prague Provisional Theatre (1875–8) were uncongenial to the composer, who preferred to earn his living through composition and private teaching, but it meant an important growth in his understanding of the stage (further encouraged by the large amount of incidental music for the theatre that he composed thoughout his career). His six operas beginning with *Blaník* are all mature, stage-worthy works; all were published, one remains in the Czech repertoire, the others are occasionally revived.

Two factors are worth noting in Fibich's operatic career. One is his fascination with words and their combination with music, attested by his extensive experiments with concert and stage melodrama: of all the Czech composers of the 19th century he showed the greatest mastery of and interest in idiomatic word-setting. The second factor is a more international orientation than that of his Czech contemporaries, partly the result of temperament, but partly also because of his wide cultural background and education. Only two of his operas are set in Bohemia: most of the rest are based on texts from foreign literature – Schiller, Byron and Shakespeare. Fibich also had little sympathy with attempts to cultivate a Czech style based on folksong and dance. When he did quote a Czech folksong (in *Šárka*) it was not a familiar one, but a recently discovered 15th-century song. Because of this there is little in most of his operas to endear them to a Czech public seeking national nourishment. Instead he brought to his work a standard of craftsmanship, competence and awareness of foreign developments far beyond that of most of his Czech contemporaries. Although groomed by powerful figures in the Czech musicological establishment to take over Smetana's mantle, Fibich never achieved the popularity of his contemporary Dvořák and in the 20th century has been further eclipsed by Janáček, only four years his junior.

Blaník

Opera in three acts, Op. 50
Libretto by Eliška Krásnohorská
Composed 1874–7
PREMIERE 25 November 1881, Provisional Theatre, Prague

True to her aesthetic principles, Krásnohorská provided a libretto with large-scale ensembles and other set numbers built into its structure. Its Czech subject matter (celebrated orchestrally by Smetana and Janáček) is based on the bitter religious divide in the Czech nation after its defeat at the Battle of the White Mountain (1620). In losing their political independence, the Czechs also lost their distinctive Hussite religion, which was rapidly suppressed by the now victorious Catholic Habsburgs. Central to the complicated plot, which gestures towards national reconciliation, is the messianic legend by which the defeated Czech warriors (characterized with a fine 7/4 'march') wait on the mountain of Blaník, ready to come to the aid of the nation. Krásnohorská grafted on to this the European legend of the White Lady, a stately alto part written specifically for Fibich's wife, Betty. The melodramatic overture provided a model for Fibich's many such exercises in the genre.

EDITION   v.s., Fr. A. Urbánek, 1897

The Bride of Messina
Nevěsta messinská
Tragic opera in three acts, Op. 18 (2h 15m)
Libretto by Otakar Hostinský, after the tragedy by Schiller
Die Braut von Messina (1803)
Composed 1882–3
PREMIERE   28 March 1884, National Theatre, Prague

The libretto for *The Bride of Messina* was not written by an experienced librettist with a passion for ensembles, but by the leading Czech aesthetician and friend of Fibich, Otakar Hostinský. Believing that Czech opera did not need to rely on patriotic subjects any more, Hostinský provided one of the few Czech libretti of the period based on foreign literature rather than domestic material. A fine prose stylist, Hostinský was not a poet and did not consider his time well spent producing rhymes or contriving duets. His libretto was thus little more than an unrhymed Czech translation of Schiller's play, which as a *Trauerspiel mit Chören* included a quasi-Greek chorus. This provided the foundation for the chorus-based ensembles which, together with the declamatory dialogue, constitute the two principal types of vocal texture in the piece.

After the over-full libretto of *Blaník*, the plot is simple. The ruling Princess of Messina (another dignified part for Betty Fibichová) attempts to reconcile her two warring sons. Both have fallen in love with a young girl confined to a convent who, as it turns out after one son has killed the other and then committed suicide, is their sister. The sombre effect of the piece is heightened by limiting the double chorus (a chorus for the retinue of each son) to male voices, with altos added to one retinue for slight colour differentiation. With its developed leitmotif system, this is Fibich's severest operatic work (its most popular number is a funeral march).

RECORDING   excerpts: Soukupová, Šounová, Novotný, Zítek, Průša, Prague NT Ch and O, Košler, Supraphon, 1984
EDITION   v.s., Hudební matice /Fr. A. Urbánek, 1884; 4th edn, 1950

The Tempest
Bouře
Opera in three acts, Op. 40 (2h)
Libretto by Jaroslav Vrchlický, after the play by Shakespeare (1611–12)
Composed 1893–4

PREMIERE   1 March 1895, National Theatre, Prague

Much had happened to Fibich by the time he wrote another opera. His Wagnerian tendencies, especially that of leaving more and more of the musical argument to the orchestra, had reached their extreme in his melodrama trilogy, *Hippodamia* (1888–91), in which vocal lines were reduced to speech. Furthermore Fibich had fallen in love with a young pupil, Anežka Schulzová (1868–1905). There were no more alto parts for Betty Fibichová but instead a succession of passionate love stories, in which more traditional operatic elements began to reassert themselves. The first of these operas was *The Tempest*, adapted by the Czech poet Jaroslav Vrchlický to make the lovers Miranda and Ferdinand the central figures of the work. Magic elements were emphasized, and Caliban became a comic bass with strophic songs. If this sounds like a number opera, it is hardly surprising since some of the material – for instance the ABA conclusion of Ferdinand's aria at the beginning of Act II – is based on pickings from Fibich's 'erotic diary' to Anežka, a continuing series of short piano pieces celebrating events in their lives or features of Anežka's own person and appearance. *The Tempest* is Fibich's lightest opera, the only surviving one with comic elements.

RECORDING   excerpts: Domanínská, Tattermuschová, Žídek, Šrubař, Berman, Prague NT Ch and O, Bartl, Supraphon, c. 1960
EDITION   v.s., Fr. A. Urbánek, 1895

Hedy
Opera in four acts, Op. 43
Libretto by Anežka Schulzová after Byron's narrative poem *Don Juan* (1824)
Composed 1894–5
PREMIERE   12 February 1896, National Theatre, Prague

Hedy followed closely after *The Tempest*. The scenario was taken from Byron and the passionate love story of Hedy (Haidée), who is wooed by Don Juan while her pirate father (Lambro) is away. Lambro's unexpected return has terrible consequences: he puts a stop to his daughter's wedding with Don Juan, who is sold into slavery. Hedy expires in a *Liebestod*.

The opera was the first of Fibich's operas to a libretto by Anežka Schulzová, who was to remain house librettist for the rest of Fibich's life. For all her blue-stocking background and progressive political and moral views, she took an old-fashioned view of opera, which is reflected in the conventions built into her libretto. Act III has an elaborate *ballabile* crowned with a multi-tempo *concertato* finale. Schulzová herself described the work as a 'Czech *Tristan*', and provided the lovers with a long love duet taking up most of Act II. In the character of Lambro, the fierce pirate father, Fibich wrote for a voice type that, after Smetana, disappeared from Czech opera for a couple of decades: the angry baritone villain.

EDITION   v.s., Fr. A. Urbánek, 1895; 2nd edn, 1912

Šárka

Opera in three acts, Op. 51 (2h)
Libretto by Anežka Schulzová
Composed 1896–7
PREMIERE   28 December 1897, National Theatre, Prague

The next collaboration between Schulzová and Fibich, *Šárka*, was Fibich's most popular opera, and the only one that is still regularly played. Since its musical language and conventions are much the same as those of *Hedy* (though with more chorus, less ensemble and no ballet), it is likely that *Šárka*'s success with the Czech public had much to do with the nationalistic subject, familiar from Smetana's *Má vlast* and from Czech painting and literature. As in Janáček's earlier opera *Šárka*, the plot comes from Czech mythic history: the 'Maidens' War' in which the women vainly take arms against the male rulers in an attempt to regain their former power. Fibich's opera has the bigger cast, with an important part for Vlasta, the leader of the women's band (Šárka is her lieutenant), and by far the more competent libretto – less 'poetic', but with more dramatic opportunities for the composer. Although Act II ends with the same climax, the hatred between Šárka and Ctirad giving way to mutual love, it does not end in Ctirad's death, as Janáček's opera does. Instead it is the women who die in Act III, betrayed by Šárka herself who, driven by pangs of conscience and by the reproaches of her dead comrades, finally takes her own life. Like all of Fibich's operas, *Šárka* has wonderfully paced declamation – no better demonstrated than in the opening monologue for Vlasta. The most memorable part of the work is the central love duet, tracing successive stages of Šárka's dawning love and culminating in what was Fibich's greatest strength, a melodic vein of sweet tenderness.

RECORDING   Děpoltová, Randová, Přibyl, Zítek, Brno State PO, Štych, Supraphon, 1980
EDITION   v.s., Fr. A. Urbánek, 1897; 4th edn, 1950

The Fall of Arkona

Pád Arkuna
Opera; prelude (*Helga*), Op. 55, and opera in three acts (*Dargun*), Op. 60
Libretto by Anežka Schulzová
Composed 1898–9
PREMIERE   9 November 1900, National Theatre, Prague

Fibich did not capitalize on the popularity of *Šárka* by writing a nationalistic successor. Although its origin is not Czech, the subject matter of *The Fall of Arkona* is nevertheless Slavonic – about the Baltic Slavs on the island of Rügen off the northern coast of what was to become East Germany. Their cult of Svantovít was the most developed, or at least best documented, of any of the Slav pagan religions and the opera depicts its conflict with Christianity, which resulted in the destruction of the pagan temples by the Christian Danes in 1168. The two forces are embodied in Absolon, the Christian bishop and Danish chancellor, and Dargun, the high priest of Svantovít. An independent prelude, *Helga*, which is set 20 years earlier, depicts the two men competing for the love of the same woman, thereby establishing the roots of the conflict between them. The dark personality of Dargun is further explored in the three-act opera that follows. Fibich himself died three weeks before the premiere, a fact that may have given rise to the belief that it is an 'unlucky' opera. It has been seldom revived, which is a pity since it contains some of the composer's strongest and most vigorous music and signals an interesting development towards a type of psychological music drama. In this context Fibich's unrealized plans for setting Ibsen's *Lady from the Sea* are all the more tantalizing.

EDITIONS   v.ss., *Helga*, Fr. A. Urbánek, 1899; *Dargun*, Fr. A. Urbánek, 1901

BIBLIOGRAPHY   Jan Smaczny, 'The Operas and Melodramas of Zdeněk Fibich (1850–1900)', *PRMA*, vol. 109 (1982–3), pp. 119–33; John Tyrrell, *Czech Opera*, CUP, 1988

J.T.

MICHAEL FINNISSY

Michael Peter Finnissy; *b* 17 March 1946, London

Finnissy studied in London at the Royal College of Music, and in Italy with Roman Vlad. In 1969 he founded a music department at the London School of Contemporary Dance, where he taught until 1974. In 1988 he began teaching at Sussex University. Though often of extreme complexity, Finnissy's music has a lyrical quality that places him in some respects in the English tradition. His experience in the theatre and passion for opera have resulted in a number of music-theatre works, ranging from *Bouffe* (1975) 'for a person alone on stage' to the larger-scale *Tom Fool's Wooing* (1978) for 14 *a cappella* soloists, and *Vaudeville* (1983). Many of these take traditional theatre forms which are transformed by the musical setting. A good example is *Mr Punch* (1978), in which the music, often violent and Expressionist, personalizes the familiar Punch and Judy story.

The Undivine Comedy

Opera in 17 scenes (1h 45m)
Libretto by the composer, after Zygmunt Krasiński's *Nieboska komedia* (1835) and passages from Hölderlin and De Sade
PREMIERES   11 May 1988, Théâtre de la Bastille, Paris; UK: 3 July 1988, Almeida Theatre, London

Though scored for only five soloists and nine instruments, this is Finnissy's most ambitious music-theatre work to date. Krasiński's pro-Catholic message is changed into a more pessimistic vision: man's dilemma faced with his own spirituality, as seen through the experiences of the Count and the revolutionary Leader. The music makes use of plainchant, Romanian folk music and Middle Eastern intonations. The lack of strong instrumental bass lends a shimmering intensity to the sound, while each of the characters has a strongly defined vocal style.

EDITION f.s./v.s., OUP (on hire), 1988

Other operatic/music-theatre works: *Mysteries* ('The Parting of Darkness', 'The Earthly Paradise', 'Noah and the Great Flood', 'The Prophecy of Daniel', 'The Parliament of Heaven', 'The Annunciation', 'The Betrayal and Crucifixion of Jesus of Nazareth', 'The Deliverance of Souls'), 1972–9; *Circle, Chorus and Formal Act*, 1973; *Bouffe*, 1975; *Commedia dell'incomprensibile potere che alcune donne hanno sugli nomini*, 1977; *Tom Fool's Wooing*, 1978; *Mr Punch*, 1978; *Vaudeville*, 1983

BIBLIOGRAPHY Andrew Clements, 'Finnissy's 'Undivine Comedy'', *MT*, vol. 129 (1988), pp. 330–32; Lynne Williams, 'Finnissy's 'Undivine Comedy'', *Opera*, vol. 39 (1988), pp. 679–82

M.A.

VALENTINO FIORAVANTI

b 11 September 1764, Rome; *d* 16 June 1837, Capua

Fioravanti went to Naples in 1779 for tuition in composition, returning after two years to Rome, where he made his début in 1784 with an intermezzo. He made his name with comic opera and after the success of *Gl'inganni fortunati* (1788), written for the Neapolitan stage, the doors of other Italian theatres immediately opened for him. *Le cantatrici villane* (1799) launched him on the European scene and was the work that secured his posthumous fame.

In 1798 he had established relations with Lisbon, where works already staged successfully in Italy were frequently revived. In 1801, however, he received a commission from Lisbon for a new work, *Camilla*, whose acceptance earned him the directorship of its S. Carlos Theatre. He held this post for five years. On his way back to Italy he stopped in Paris, where his *I virtuosi ambulanti* (1807) was performed with acclaim at the Théâtre-Italien. Back in Italy, Fioravanti continued to compose operas at a prodigious rate. With some sense of irony, he chose to make his last operatic work (his 77th) a setting of Tottola's *Ogni eccesso è vizioso* (*Any Excess is a Vice*) and after 1824 he wrote only sacred music.

The technical and stylistic ingredients used by Fioravanti in his works were neither very refined nor unusual, but he had an undoubted gift for comedy which enabled him to compete for public favour even with Cimarosa, who is reported to have feared coming off worse in comparisons between the two: 'Not on account of musical quality, in which regard . . . I truly believe I am better than him, but on account of those comic escapades of his, his masterly *parlando* sections, and those agitated pieces that he produces . . . whose swiftness, neatness and attractiveness never fail to win plaudits.'

While best remembered for his comic works,

Fioravanti also wrote serious operas, in a number of which he adopted the pathetic-cum-sentimental tendency that the *larmoyant* ('tearful') tradition had introduced to French opera. He scored particular success in Naples with an unusual trio of melodrammas on the subject of Count Comingio, *Adelaide e Comingio* (1817), which intersperses comic parts in local dialect into a sorry tale of love and death.

Surviving operas: *Le avventure di Bertoldino, o sia La dama contadina*, 1784; *Il fabbro parigino, o sia La schiava fortunata*, 1791; *Con i matti il savio la perde, ovvero Le pazzie a vicenda*, 1791; *La famiglia stravagante, ossia Gli amanti comici*, 1792; *L'audacia fortunata*, 1793; *I matrimoni per magia*, 1794; *L'astuta in amore, ossia Il furbo malaccorto*, 1795; *Liretta e Giannino*, 1795; *Il ciabattino incivilito*, 1796; *I puntigli per equivoco*, 1796; *Il furbo contro il furbo*, 1797; *L'amor per interesse*, 1797; *L'innocente ambizione*, 1797; *L'amore a dispetto*, 1798; *Le cantatrici villane*, 1798 (RECORDING Bongiovanni, 1992); *L'avaro*, 1800; *L'ambizione punita*, 1800; *Il villano in angustie*, 1801; *Camilla, ossia La forza del giuramento*, 1801; *La capricciosa pentita*, 1802; *Amore e destrezza, ossia I contrattempi superati dall'arte*, 1802; *L'amore aguzza l'ingegno*, 1802; *L'orgoglio avvilito*, 1803; *La dama soldato*, 1805; *Il bello piace a tutti*, 1806, rev. 1812; *I virtuosi ambulanti*, 1807; *I raggiri ciarlataneschi*, 1808; *La bella carbonara*, 1809; *Semplicità ed astuzia, ossia La serva e il parrucchiere*, 1810; *Le nozze per puntiglio*, 1811; *Raoul signore di Crequi*, 1811; *La foresta di Hermannstadt*, 1812; *Adelaide maritata e Comingio pittore*, 1812; *Nefte*, 1813; *Adelaide e Comingio romiti, ossia La morte di Adelaide*, 1814; *L'africano generoso*, 1814; *Inganni ed amori*, 1814; *Adelson e Salvini*, 1816; *La contessa di Fersen, ossia La moglie di due mariti*, 1817; *Gli amori di Adelaide e Comingio*, 1817; *Paolina e Susetta*, 1819; *La donna di genio bizzarro*, 1823; *Ogni eccesso è vizioso*, 1824; 37 lost operas

BIBLIOGRAPHY A. della Corte, *L'opera comica italiana del '700*, vol. 2, Bari, 1923, pp. 176–98

D.A.D'A.

VINCENZO FIORAVANTI

b 5 April 1799, Rome; *d* 28 March 1877, Naples

The son of the better-known composer Valentino Fioravanti, Vincenzo was intended for the medical profession, and studied music against his father's wishes. His first opera was produced in Naples in 1819, but its successor, given in Rome the following year, had the advantage of advice from Donizetti and was much more successful. A check to his career followed when his father-in-law insisted on his abandoning the theatre, but after only ten months his wife died and in 1828 Fioravanti returned to the operatic stage with *Robinson Crusoè nell'isola deserta* in Naples. Here he continued to produce operas for the next three decades, mostly Neapolitan opere buffe in the by now rather outmoded style of his father: the most popular, *Il ritorno di Pulcinella dagli studi di Padova*, even had some success abroad, and in Italy held the stage until late in the 19th century. After his last opera in 1856 Fioravanti's career declined and he died in poverty.

Operas: *Pulcinella molinaro, spaventato dalla fata Serafinetta*, 1819; *La pastorella rapita*, 1820; *Robinson Crusoè nell'isola deserta*, 1828; *Il supposto sposo*, 1828; *Il sarcofago scozzese*, 1828; *La conquista del Messico*, 1829; *Colombo alla scoperta delle Indie*, 1829; *La scimia brasiliana*, 1830 (also as *La portentosa scimia del Brasile con Pulcinella bersagliato dall'amante e dalla scimia*); *Il folletto innamorato*, 1831; *Il cieco del dolo*, 1834; *I due caporali*, 1835; *Il ritorno di Pulcinella dagli studi di Padova*, 1837 (also as *Columella*, and rev. as *Il ritorno di Columella da Padova*); *La larva, ovvero Gli spaventi di Pulcinella*, 1839; *I vecchi burlati*, 1839; *Mille talleri*, 1839; *La dama e lo zoccolajo, ossia La trasmigrazione di Pulcinella*, 1840 (also as *La trasmigrazione di Tarantella*); *Un matrimonio in prigione*, 1842; *Non tutti i pazzi sono all'ospedale, ovvero Una burla comica*, 1843; *Il notaro d'Ubeda, ovvero Le gelosie di Pulcinella*, 1843; *La lotteria di Vienna*, 1843; *Don Procopio* (coll.), 1844; *Gli zingari, ossia Gli amori di Pulcinella*, 1844; *Chi cenera?*, 1845 (rev. as *Un imbarazzo per la padrona e la cameriera*, 1848); *Una rassegna al campo*, 1845 (also as *Una rivista al campo*; *Il parrucchiere e la crestaja*, 1846; *Un padre comprato*, 1846 (also as *X.Y.Z., ovvero Il riconoscimento*); *Pulcinella e la fortuna*, 1847; *Amore e disinganno*, 1847; *Pulcinella e la sua famiglia*, 1849; *La pirata*, 1849; *La figlia del fabbro, ossia Quattro la chiedono il quinto la sposa*, 1850; *Annella la tavernara di Porta Capuana*, 1854; *Jacopo lo scortichino*, 1855; *Il signor Pipino*, 1856

Unperformed operas (n.d.): *La strega ed il corsaro*; *Il castello degli spiriti*; *La testa di Mercurio*; *Pulcinella erede senza eredità*; *Il ciurmatore*

BIBLIOGRAPHY Franco Schlitzer, 'Vincenzo Fioravanti', in *Enciclopedia dello Spettacolo*, Casa Editrice le Maschere, 1958

M.R.

JAN F. FISCHER

Jan Frank Fischer, *b* 15 September 1921, Louny, Czechoslovakia

After training at the Prague Academy, Fischer gained theatrical experience by working in theatre and in films. His first opera was a reworking of a classic Czech 19th-century comedy, *The Bridegrooms*, already set by Kovařovic. Despite the broader approach evident in his best-known opera, *Romeo, Juliet and Darkness*, or in *Copernicus*, Fischer's preferred *métier* is for small, experimental forms and versatile forces, for instance in the six mini-operas contained in *The Decameron*, or in the chamber opera after Verne, *Oh, Mr Fogg*, in which 71 roles are taken by 11 soloists supported by a 19-piece orchestra, a small chorus and a group of six to eight dancers.

Romeo, Juliet and Darkness

Romeo, Julie a tma
Opera in two parts
Libretto by the composer, after the novel by Jan Otčenášek
Composed 1959–61
PREMIERE 14 September 1962, Brno

Romeo, Juliet and Darkness is a sombre retelling of the familiar story, now translated to wartime Czechoslovakia, with the star-crossed lovers represented by a Czech boy and a Jewish girl who seeks refuge with him from the Nazis. It has been given in many Czech theatres and in Germany, Italy and Yugoslavia.

RECORDING excerpts: Tattermuschová, Jedenáctík, Švehla, Otava, Kalaš, Vonášek, Prague NT O, Tichý, Supraphon, 1965
EDITION v.s., Panton, 1964

Other operas: *The Bridegrooms* (*Ženichové*), 1957; *Oh, Mr Fogg*, 1971; *The Miraculous Theatre* (*Zázračné divadlo*), radio opera, 1970; *The Decameron* (*Dekameron*), 1977; *Copernicus* (*Kopernikus*), (1983); *A Bridge for Clara* (*Most pro Kláru*), television opera, 1988

BIBLIOGRAPHY Ladislav Šíp, *Česká opera a jeho tvůrci* (*Czech Opera and Its Creators*), Supraphon, 1983

J.T.

LUBOŠ FIŠER

b 30 September 1935, Prague

Fišer studied in Prague at the Conservatory (1952–6) and Academy (1956–60). He has earned his living chiefly as a composer (with over 300 film, television and stage scores to his credit), but in 1989 he became director of the publishing firm Panton. His works, mostly for chamber, orchestral and cantata forces, show considerable versatility, and a clarity and intensity of expression, for instance his *Fifteen Prints after Dürer's Apocalypse* (1965), with which he established his international reputation. He has written two chamber operas. *Lancelot*, written as a graduation exercise, has held its position in the Czech repertoire; a televised version by Jaromil Jireš of its much later successor, *Eternal Faust*, won the main prize in the Salzburg International Television Opera Competition in 1986.

Operatic works: *Lancelot*, 1961; *Eternal Faust* (*Věčný Faust*), 1985; *Spring in Paris, or Bloody Henrietta* (*Jedno jaro v Paříže aneb Krvavá Henrietta*), musical for actors, (1987)

BIBLIOGRAPHY Alena Martínková *et al.* (eds), *Čeští skladatelé současnosti* (*Czech Composers of Today*), Panton, 1985

J.T.

FRIEDRICH VON FLOTOW

Friedrich Adolf Ferdinand (Freiherr von) Flotow; *b* 27 April 1812, Teutendorf, Mecklenburg; *d* 24 January 1883, Darmstadt, Germany

Remembered today for just two works, *Martha* and *Alessandro Stradella*, Flotow produced a string of Romantic operas in the mid-19th century which, with varying success, combined elements of French *opéra comique* with the sentimentality and sonorities of German Romanticism and an Italianate melodic style. Born of aristocratic stock, he was originally destined for a diplomatic career. When his musical gifts were recognized, however, he was allowed to study music, and from 1828 to 1830 attended the

Paris Conservatoire, where he studied composition with Reicha. In the French capital he experienced at first hand the works of Adam, Donizetti, Halévy, Meyerbeer and Rossini. Among the most important influences were the opéras comiques of Auber and he later made the acquaintance of Gounod and Offenbach. Work on his first opera was interrupted by the revolution of 1830, and he completed it in Germany. Other early works included a symphony (now lost) and two piano concertos.

Returning to Paris, he wrote a number of operas for private performance before collaboration with the Belgian composer Albert Grisar brought him to prominence. With another collaborator, Auguste Pilati, he wrote Le naufrage de la Méduse (1839). When the score was destroyed by fire before a performance in Hamburg, Flotow rewrote the work to a German libretto by 'W. Friedrich' (Friedrich Wilhelm Riese). This was eventually performed in 1845, a year after the composer and librettist won critical acclaim with Alessandro Stradella. To this triumph they added Martha, performed in Vienna in 1847, which quickly became Flotow's most popular work.

Flotow's later operas failed to live up to these two successes, but he continued to produce work at a prolific rate. In 1852 he wrote the comic opera Rübezahl to a text by his friend Gustav Heinrich Gans zu Pulitz, who also provided the libretto for Indra (1852), a successful reworking of the earlier L'esclave de Camoëns. From 1855 to 1863 Flotow was intendant of the grand ducal court theatre in Schwerin, for which he wrote Herzog Johann Albrecht von Mecklenburg. It was Paris, however, that witnessed three late successes, Zilda (1866), L'ombre (1870) and, above all, La veuve Grapin (1859), a delightful one-act operetta in the Pergolesi–Serva padrona mould. In 1868 Flotow divorced his second wife Anna Theen and married her younger sister, Rose, moving first to Lower Austria, then Teutendorff (where he wrote his last opera) and finally, in 1880, settling in Darmstadt.

Flotow's output included works in a variety of genres, but was dominated by his operas, of which Alessandro Stradella and Martha have long eclipsed the others. His music made no pretensions to profundity, and his achievement was to combine various national traditions in a natural, unforced and charming style that pandered unashamedly to popular taste. As such he may be seen as the bridge between opéra comique and the comic operas of later composers such as Sullivan.

Alessandro Stradella

Romantic opera in three acts (2h)
Libretto by 'W. Friedrich' (Friedrich Wilhelm Riese), after the 'comédie mêlée de chant' Stradella by Paul Duport and Philippe Auguste Pittaud Deforges (1837)
PREMIERES 30 December 1844, Stadttheater, Hamburg; UK: 6 June 1846, Drury Lane, London; US: 29 November 1853, New York

Flotow had already provided some arias for Duport's and Deforges's comédie. The story was based on the life of Alessandro Stradella as found in Pierre and Jacques Bonnet-Bourdelot's Histoire de la musique et de ses effets depuis son origine jusqu'à présent (1715). Riese, who was based in Hamburg, had translated Le naufrage de la Méduse in 1842, and this, together with Alessandro Stradella and Martha, was the brief but fruitful sum of their partnership.

The action is set in Venice and Rome in about 1670. At the Venice Carnival Stradella abducts his beloved Leonore from her guardian Bassi. They flee to Rome, where they are married. Bassi's henchmen catch up with them, but are won over by the composer's singing, as eventually is Bassi himself.

The opera provided obvious showpieces for Stradella (tenor), particularly the Act III hymn 'Jungfrau Maria', as well as a lively Carnival scene. It was the comic assassins Malvolino and Barbarino, however, that prompted Flotow's best music, recalling Giacomo and Beppo in Auber's Fra Diavolo. The work was an immediate success in German opera houses, and two productions in Vienna in 1845 resulted in the commissioning of Martha.

RECORDING Donath, Hollweg, Gruber, Kogel, Malta, Ch and O of Bavarian Radio, Wallberg, Voce, 1977
EDITIONS f.s., Böhme, 1845; v.s., Böhme, 1844

Martha, oder Der Markt zur Richmond

Martha, or Richmond Market
Romantic–comic opera in four acts (2h)
Libretto by 'W. Friedrich' (Friedrich Wilhelm Riese), partly after a scenario by Jules Henri Vernoy, Marquis de Saint-Georges
PREMIERES 25 November 1847, Kärntnertortheater, Vienna; UK: 4 July 1849, Drury Lane, London; US: 1 November 1852, Niblo's Garden, New York
CAST Lady Harriet Durham s, Nancy ms, Lord Tristan Mickleford b, Plumkett b, Lyonel t, 3 s, a, t, 4 b, silent role; satb chorus of maids, servants, huntresses in the queen's retinue, tenants, farmers; silent: pages
FULL ORCHESTRA including ophecleide; onstage: band

As with Alessandro Stradella, this opera had its roots in an earlier project to which Flotow had contributed, in this case Mazilier's ballet-pantomime Lady Harriette, ou La servante de Greenwich (1844), to a scenario by Vernoy de Saint-Georges. Flotow had written Act I (Acts II and III were by Burgmüller and Deldevez). Much of the music for Act I of Martha was taken from the earlier ballet, with Riese providing the text. One of the most celebrated numbers, Lyonel's Act II aria 'Ach so fromm', was actually taken over from Flotow's previous opera L'âme en peine (1846).

SYNOPSIS

Act I The setting is England during the reign of Queen Anne, c. 1710. Lady Harriet, maid of honour to the queen, is bored with court life and longs to escape from the advances of her elderly foppish cousin Lord Tristan. Her maid Nancy vainly suggests diversions until, together with the reluctant Tristan, they decide to join girls on their way to the Richmond hiring fair. There, under the names of

The spinning scene from Martha *(Vienna, 1847)*

Martha and Julia, they are hired by two young farmers, Plumkett and his foster-brother Lyonel.

Act II 'Martha' and 'Julia' find it difficult to adapt to life as working girls. They are rescued by Tristan, but not before Lyonel and Plumkett have fallen in love with them.

Act III On a hunting party with the queen, Lady Harriet and Julia are recognized by their 'employers', but Harriet feigns ignorance.

Act IV Lyonel, it emerges, is the son of the wrongly banished late Earl of Derby: now it is his turn to snub Lady Harriet. In order to win him back, Plumkett and Nancy set up another fair in front of the farmhouse, and there, seeing his 'Martha' again, Lyonel takes her into his arms.

Riese's libretto gave Flotow plenty of scope for what he excelled at: lively choruses, enchanting solos and ensembles. With no dialogue to interrupt the flow, the music is one glorious set piece after another. Two favourites quickly established themselves: 'Letzte Rose', sung originally by 'Martha' at the fair, is a version of the Irish melody 'The Grove of Blarney', better known as Thomas Moore's 'The Last Rose of Summer'. The other is Lyonel's 'Ach so fromm', which became hugely popular in its Italian version as 'M'appari'. But there is much more to enjoy, such as the Act II 'spinning' quartet and 'Gute Nacht' quartet, and Plumkett's Act III aria in praise of 'Porterbier'. It is not difficult to account for *Martha*'s astonishing popularity (it was given by Liszt in Weimar in 1848, and was the subject of a number of parodies). The characters are well drawn and Flotow wastes no opportunity to repeat catchy tunes until the audience cannot avoid humming them. He also succeeds in keeping the action moving, thus balancing sentimentality with exuberance. *Martha* may not be great music, but it deserves more attention than it has latterly received in English-speaking countries – not least for its amusing impressions of 'Englishness'.

RECORDINGS 1. Rothenberger, Fassbaender, Gedda, Prey, Bavarian State Opera Ch and O, Heger, EMI, 1968; 2. Popp, Soffel, Jerusalem, Ridderbusch, Ch of the Bavarian Radio, Munich Radio O, Wallberg, BMG Ariola, 1978
EDITION v.s., Cranz/Peters, [1890]

Other operas: *Pierre et Cathérine*, 1835 (in German); *Die Bergknappen*, n.d.; *Alfred der Grosse*, n.d.; *Rob-Roy*, 1836; *Sérafine*, 1836; *Alice*, 1837; *La lettre du préfet*, 1837; *Le Comte de Saint-Magrin*, 1838, rev. as *Le Duc de Guise*, 1840; *Lady Melvil* (coll. with Grisar), 1838, rev. as *La joaillier de Saint-James*, 1862; *L'eau merveilleuse* (coll. with Grisar), 1839; *Le naufrage de Méduse* (Act I by Pilati, Acts II and III by Flotow), 1839, rewritten as *Die Matrosen*, 1845; *L'esclave de Camoëns*, 1843, rev. as *Indra*, 1852, as *Alma l'incantatrice*, 1878; *L'âme en peine*, 1846; *Sophie Katharina, oder Der Grossfürstin*, 1850; *Rübezahl*, 1852; *Albin, oder Der Pflegesohn*, 1856, rev. as *Der Müller von Meran*, 1859; *Herzog Johann Albrecht von Mecklenburg, oder Andreas Mylius*, 1857; *Pianella*, 1857; *La veuve Grapin*, 1859; *Naida (Le vannier)*, 1865; *La châtelaine (Der Märchensucher)*, 1865; *Zilda, ou La nuit des dupes*, 1866; *Am Runenstein*, 1868; *Die Musikanten (La jeunesse de Mozart)*, (?1869), 1887; *L'ombre*, 1870; *La fleur de Harlem*, 1876 (in Italian); *Rosellana*; *Sakuntala*
BIBLIOGRAPHY Edward J. Dent, 'A Best-seller in Opera', *ML*, vol. 22 (1941), pp. 139–45; Robert Didion, 'Alessandro Stradella' and 'Martha' in 'Friedrich von Flotow', in C. Dahlhaus (ed.), *Pipers Enzyklopädie des Musiktheaters*, Munich, 1986, vol. 2, pp. 215–21

M.A.

CARLISLE FLOYD
Carlisle Sessions Floyd Jnr; b 11 June 1926, Latta, South Carolina, US

Floyd's opera *Susannah* was a major success when it was staged in New York in 1956. It made him the most highly praised American opera composer of his generation and the work entered the standard repertoire with astonishing speed.

His early training was in piano as well as composition. Floyd's first opera, the one-act *Slow Dusk*, was to his own libretto – a practice he continued to follow – and was produced at Syracuse University, where Floyd was a student. His second opera was withdrawn after a single performance at Florida State University, but three years later, at the same venue, *Susannah* was launched on its spectacular career.

After this success, Floyd went on to compose *Wuthering Heights* on a commission from Santa Fe Opera. In its original form it was criticized for its cliché-ridden libretto and for the uneven quality of the music. Floyd made some major revisions and this version was more favourably received. One critic found it 'a profound emotional experience . . . one that leaves both performers and audience shaken with the elemental power of the Brontë story'.

Susannah has remained the most frequently performed of Floyd's operas, though *Of Mice and Men*, based on John Steinbeck's novel, has also had numerous productions in the US and in Europe. For the American Bicentennial in 1976 Floyd wrote *Bilby's Doll*, based on Esther Forbes's novel *A Mirror for Witches*, which deals, as does Arthur Miller's play *The Crucible* (and Robert Ward's opera based on it), with the 17th-century witchcraft trials in Massachusetts, a subject Floyd had been considering since the McCarthy era in the 1950s. He said, 'I believe my opera has a comment to make on our national character and destiny.' He added that the score broke new ground for him in its Romantic lyricism and its use of orchestral colour. The length of the work, however, causes such exuberance to become repetitive and it has not entered the repertoire.

Susannah
A musical drama in two acts (1h 30m)
Libretto by the composer
Composed 1953–4
PREMIERES 24 February 1955, Florida State University, Tallahassee; UK: 27 July 1961, Orpington Civic Hall (Kentish Opera Group)

The production of *Susannah* by the New York Opera Company, on 27 September 1956, conducted by Erich Leinsdorf, made history. The opera was given a New York Music Critics' Circle Award after journalists had reached for superlatives. Winthrop Sargeant regarded *Susannah* as 'probably the most moving and impressive opera to have been written in America – or anywhere else, as far as I am aware – since Gershwin's *Porgy and Bess*'.

The story of *Susannah* is based on that in the Apocrypha (on which Handel based his oratorio *Susanna*) but the action is transferred to a modern-day Tennessee mountain valley and the work ends unhappily. Susannah is caught bathing in a creek used for baptisms and is denounced by the Elders of the Church who denounce her as being 'of the devil'. At a public revivalist meeting conducted by the Reverend Blitch she is urged to confess and repent. She refuses. Blitch, believing the lies about her, follows her home and attempts to seduce her; in doing so he discovers her innocence. He tries to tell the Elders, without incriminating himself, but they are not convinced. Susannah's brother, Sam, finds out what Blitch has done and shoots him at the baptismal creek. The people threaten Susannah and urge her to leave. The experience leaves her embittered and alone.

Much of the force of the opera derives from Floyd's word-setting – a flexible *parlando* style where pitch and rhythm follow the natural inflexions of speech. Alongside this he presents fully-fledged, lyrical Puccinian arias and – to maintain the American flavour – folk-type tunes, hymns and square-dance melodies.

RECORDING Niska, Shuttleworth, Theyard, Treigle, New York City Ch and O, Rudel, MRF, 1971
EDITIONS f.s., Boosey & Hawkes, 1955; v.s., Boosey & Hawkes, 1957

Other operatic works: *Slow Dusk*, 1949; *The Fugitives*, 1951; *Wuthering Heights*, 1958; *The Passion of Jonathan Wade*, 1962; *The Sojourner and Mollie Sinclair*, 1963; *Markheim*, 1966; *Of Mice and Men*, 1970; *Bilby's Doll*, 1976; *Willie Stark*, 1981
BIBLIOGRAPHY David Ewen, *American Composers: A Biographical Dictionary*, Hale, 1983

P.D.

JOSEF BOHUSLAV FOERSTER
b 30 December 1859, Prague; d 29 May 1951, Vestec, nr Stará Boleslav, Czechoslovakia

Foerster had many natural advantages as an opera composer. He came from a musical family (his father, also a composer, taught at Prague Conservatory) and was trained accordingly. But he was also a distinguished writer: from 1884 he worked as a music critic and later published several collections of essays. He showed an early interest in the theatre (he had thought of becoming an actor) and was married to a leading Czech soprano, Berta Lautererová; when she was engaged at the Hamburg Staatsoper (in 1893) and at the Vienna Hofoper (1903), Foerster went with her, serving as music critic in both cities. He returned to Prague on the formation of the Czechoslovak Republic in 1918, teaching at the conservatory and at the university.

His operatic career began promisingly with *Debora*. It had only four performances, but it was well crafted and in its subject matter and general approach provided a dry run for his masterpiece, and most popular opera, *Eva*. But Foerster's subsequent opera career was disappointing. *Jessika*, an adaptation of *The Merchant of Venice*, failed to achieve the same success and Foerster wrote no more operas for over a decade. His last three operas, all to his own libretti and exploring a personal, mystical world, were received with increasing embarrassment, and none has been performed since the war.

Eva

Opera in three acts, Op. 50 (2h 15m)
Libretto by the composer after Gabriela Preissová's play *The Farm Mistress (Gazdina roba)*
Composed 1895–7
PREMIERE 1 January 1899, National Theatre, Prague
CAST Eva *s*, Mánek *t*, Mešjanovka *a*, Samko *bar, ms, b*; *satb* chorus of young men and women, musicians
FULL ORCHESTRA including hp and organ

Preissová's play, *The Farm Mistress*, is the immediate precursor of *Her Stepdaughter*, on which Janáček's *Jenůfa* was based. Both are set in the same ethnographic region of Moravia, Slovácko, with its dialect, costumes and customs. But while Janáček's opera left much of the original play, Foerster smoothed out *The Farm Mistress* by omitting colourful subsidiary characters and turning the regional dialogue into verse.

As in *Debora*, the central couple are of different social classes, and are separated by ambitious parents. Eva is a poor seamstress, Mánek the son of a wealthy widow.

SYNOPSIS

Act I The opera is set in the 1880s. A quarrel breaks out between the couple during a dance at the village festival. The lame Samko, a furrier, also in love with Eva, takes her side and, partly in gratitude, partly in pique at Mánek's inability to stand up to his mother, Mešjanovka, Eva consents to marry him.

Act II Eva's marriage is unhappy. Her daughter has died, partly as a result of Samko's refusal to call a doctor. Eva is susceptible to an invitation from Mánek, now married, to join him as 'mistress' of the farm on a seasonal farm job in Austria. She believes that if he becomes a Lutheran like her, he will be able to divorce his wife and marry her.

Act III Eva's happy life on the farmstead in Austria is upset by word getting round that she is not Mánek's married wife. The arrival of his mother puts an end to the idyll, and after Mánek's weak compliance with his mother's wishes, Eva ends her unhappy life by jumping into the Danube.

Despite the substantial dance and chorus at the beginning of Act III, Foerster's opera has none of the folkloristic ambitions of *Jenůfa*; nor, despite possibilities in the plot, are there the great dramatic moments so characteristic of Janáček's opera. Characters sing to each other not merely in verse but in formal duets, often simultaneously. The result is a somewhat old-fashioned-sounding opera, firmly rooted in 19th-century conventions, formal rather than naturalistic, lyrical rather than dramatic. Its most memorable passage is Eva's farewell as she contemplates her fate with her two final long-held cries of 'Ja vidím raj!' ('I see Paradise!') just before she jumps to her death.

RECORDING Děpoltová, Barová, Vodička, Souček, Prague Radio Ch and O, Vajnar, Supraphon, 1984
EDITIONS v.ss., Hudební matice, 1909; Orbis, 4th edn, 1951

Other operas: *Debora*, 1893; *Jessika*, 1905, rev. 1906; *The Invincible Ones (Nepřemoženi)*, 1918; *The Heart (Srdce)*, 1923; *The Fool (Bloud)*, 1936
BIBLIOGRAPHY John Tyrrell, *Czech Opera*, CUP, 1988

J.T.

WOLFGANG FORTNER

b 12 October 1907, Leipzig; *d* 5 September 1987, Heidelberg, Germany

As was customary for a musician born in Leipzig, Fortner's education, which included organ tuition with Karl Straube, was traditional. However, he also read German literature, philosophy and psychology, and his subsequent development bore witness to an open intellect. He took a lively interest in contemporary musical developments, rapidly establishing his position among the pre-war modernists. In 1929 Hermann Scherchen conducted his chamber cantata *Fragment Mariae* for Austrian Radio; in 1931 he was engaged by the Institute for Church Music in Heidelberg, where he later also founded the Heidelberg Chamber Orchestra. During the years of National Socialism he wrote little, indeed it was not until after the war that he felt free to realize his musical intentions, collaborating with Karl Amadeus Hartmann in organizing Musica Viva concerts and becoming an influential exponent of the 12-note system. His most prominent pupil was Hans Werner Henze.

Fortner's first stage works were a school opera, *Cress ertrinkt*, and incidental music for Aristophanes' *Lysistrata* (1945) and Lorca's *Blood Wedding* (1948). In 1949 he composed a ballet, *Die weisse Rose*, based on Wilde's *Birthday of the Infanta*, which was followed in 1952 by a further dance score, *Die Witwe von Ephesus*. He came to opera relatively late and after some hesitation, writing in 1958, 'I believe that a reform of music-theatre cannot evolve from opera but must be founded on the conquest of spoken drama by musicians and dancers.' In this spirit he composed *Bluthochzeit*, which was an immediate success. There followed a further Lorca setting, *Don Perlimplin*, perhaps his finest opera score, and *Elisabeth Tudor*, an ambitious project which failed. Fortner's last works for the stage were *Carmen*, a Bizet collage composed in 1970 for John Cranko, and a setting of Samuel Beckett's *That Time* (1977) for two singers and speaker, each paired with an instrument (piano, guitar and harpsichord) and optional live electronics. The score reflects the anti-operatic tendencies of the 1970s.

Fortner occupied an isolated position at a considerable remove from such contemporaries as Egk or von Einem, for his musical world was bounded by Reger, Schoenberg and Stravinsky. The classicism of Reger, which reflected his Leipzig origins, was complemented by a sympathy for baroque and renaissance music; the expressiveness of later Schoenberg guided him towards his own unforced treatment of 12-note technique; Stravinsky was a constant inspiration in matters of form and texture.

Bluthochzeit
Blood Wedding

Lyric tragedy in two acts (seven scenes) (2h 30m)
Libretto after the play by Federico García Lorca (1933), trans. Enrique [Heinrich] Beck
Composed 1956
PREMIERES 8 June 1957, Opernhaus, Cologne
CAST The Mother *ms*, the Bride *s*, the Maid *ms*, Leonardo's Wife *a*, Leonardo's Mother-in-law *a*, Beggar-woman *s*, Child *s*, the Moon *t*, Leonardo *bar*, the Bridegroom *spoken role*, the Bride's Father *spoken role*, 15 small parts; *satb* chorus of guests, neighbours, etc.; ballet
LARGE ORCHESTRA including hp, cel, 2 mand, 2 gtr; onstage: small ensemble

Fortner's opera was preceded by his incidental music to Lorca's play and a dramatic scene from the same drama, *Der Wald*, written in 1953. Enrique Beck's German translation is minimally shortened. Lorca relates the fatalistic and mystical tale of a long-standing blood feud, of rivalry between Leonardo and the (unnamed) Bridegroom and of the catastrophe, a duel with knives fought by night in a forest. In the closing scene the Mother bewails the death of both men.

The musical language of Fortner's score, based on the permutations of a 12-note row, is governed by Schoenberg's principle of developing variation, while octaves are liberally employed, creating ephemeral illusions of tonality. Elements of Spanish folk music are ingeniously integrated into the texture and dramatic contrast is provided by an imaginative play between sung and spoken passages. Fortner's vocal lines are distinguished by wide leaps and angular

intervals, yet many passages have a folkloric ring to them and there are some well-organized ensembles. The structure of the seven scenes is symphonic, unified by tautly written orchestral interludes. The orchestra itself is otherwise sparingly used, reduced in the climactic forest scene to unpitched percussion and two offstage violins. In his choice of instruments, Fortner here follows Lorca's original text, stressing that he devised the canonic writing for this scene to evoke 'the forest as spiritual reality'.

The world premiere of *Bluthochzeit* marked the opening of the Cologne Opera in 1957.

EDITIONS f.s. (rev.), Schott, 1963; v.s., Schott, 1957

In seinem Garten liebt Don Perlimplin Belisa
Don Perlimplin's Love of Belisa in his Garden
'Four scenes of an erotic picture book in the style of a chamber play'
Opera in two acts (1h 15m)
Libretto after Federico Garcia Lorca's play *Amor de Don Perlimplin con Belisa en su jardín* (1931), trans. Enrique [Heinrich] Beck
Composed 1961
PREMIERES 10 May 1962, Schlosstheater, Schwetzingen

Lorca's play, which begins as surrealist farce and ends in tragedy, tells of the marriage of a wealthy old man to the beautiful young Belisa, both of whom are urged to the union by Belisa's avaricious mother. After the wedding night five ladders are found leaning against Belisa's balcony and the five doors to her room are wide open; Don Perlimplin enters as cuckold with golden horns. In Act II a mysterious youth (who remains unseen) declares his love for Belisa, which she reciprocates. A rendezvous is arranged in Perlimplin's garden. The youth enters, dressed in a red cape, mortally wounded by a dagger still planted in his breast. He dies in Belisa's arms. She unmasks him: it is Perlimplin himself.

As in *Bluthochzeit*, Fortner alternates freely between sung and spoken passages and introduces elements of Spanish folk music into the score, yet without resorting to literal quotation. The structure is rigorous, with each scene corresponding to a symphonic movement (scherzo, canon, duet, serenade). Archaic contrapuntal techniques are subtly employed to delineate character. Fortner has made much of the role of Belisa's mother, sung by a high coloratura soprano. The iridescent orchestration is dominated by celesta, guitar, vibraphone and harpsichord.

EDITION v.s., Schott, 1962

Elisabeth Tudor
Opera in three acts and an epilogue (3h)
Libretto by Matthias Braun, rev. by the composer
Composed 1968–71
PREMIERE 23 October 1972, Deutsche Oper, Berlin

With a public controversy between Fortner and his librettist, *Elisabeth Tudor* was born under an evil star. The plot is a pseudo-realistic depiction of the circumstances leading to the imprisonment and execution of Mary Stuart, overshadowed by the

A scene from Bluthochzeit *(Cologne, 1957)*

Counter-Reformation and dominated by massive crowd scenes.

Fortner's score features every modern convenience: clusters, glissandi, free and organized improvisation, graphic and spaced notation, taped effects and *musique concrète*, jazz percussion and Ivesian superimpositions of music by Byrd, Morley and Brade, a triple offstage chorus divided into 18 parts, a children's chorus singing 'Come again, sweet love doth now invite' (in English). Complex ensembles alternate with entire scenes spoken without music, Mary Stuart sings a duet with the Duke of Norfolk in French, a barrel organ (in Elizabethan London!) plays 'O du lieber Augustin'. The influence of the Darmstadt school, the Polish avant-garde and Bernd Alois Zimmermann's *Die Soldaten* is palpable on almost every page, while the shrewd simplicity of Fortner's earlier music is smothered by technical luxuriance.

EDITION v.s., Schott, 1972

Other operatic works: *Cress ertrinkt*, 1930; *Der Wald* (withdrawn), (1953); *Corinna*, 1958; *Damals*, 1977
BIBLIOGRAPHY H. Lindlar (ed.), *Wolfgang Fortner, eine Monographie*, P. J. Tonger Musikverlag, 1960; R. U. Ringger, 'Wolfgang Fortner – Musiker der Vielfalt', *NZM*, vol. 10 (1972), p. 573

A.C.W.B.

LUKAS FOSS

Lukas Foss [Fuchs]; *b* 15 August 1922, Berlin

Born into an artistic family in Berlin, Foss moved to Paris in 1933, because of increasing threats of Nazism, and then to the US in 1937. There he studied at the Curtis Institute in Philadelphia at the suggestion of Barber and Menotti. Foss's other teachers included Hindemith and Koussevitzky, who conducted some of his works and gave him the post of orchestra pianist with the Boston Symphony Orchestra.

All Foss's operas to date were written in the earlier part of his career before his espousal of the principles of indeterminacy, collage and improvisation, which have, since the 1960s, affected his compositional methods. His first opera, *The Jumping Frog of Calaveras Country* (1950), demonstrates this traditional classic–romantic style although, as befits a work based on a story by Mark Twain, the music also has a distinctly American flavour and includes a cowboy tune at one point. *Griffelkin*, Foss's next opera, written for television and broadcast in 1955, maintains this straightforward style and, since it is a children's opera, based on a fairy-story by the Brothers Grimm, Foss deliberately included lyrical tunes and some music in pop-music style. He also interpolated an extract from a Mozart piano sonata.

By the time Foss's next opera, the nine-minute *Introductions and Goodbyes*, was composed (1959), he had taken up his post of professor of composition at the University of California (succeeding Schoenberg) and was becoming increasingly involved in the work of the Improvisation Chamber Ensemble, which he had founded in 1957. Nevertheless *Introductions*, written for the Festival of Two Worlds in Spoleto and with a libretto by its director, Gian-Carlo Menotti, displays no experimental methods. Scored for baritone and chorus, it depicts the host of a cocktail party and his guests.

RECORDING *The Jumping Frog of Calaveras Country*, Lyrichord, 1950
BIBLIOGRAPHY C. Gane and T. Caras, *Soundpieces: Interviews with American Composers*, Scarecrow Press, 1982

P.D.

JEAN FRANÇAIX
b 23 May 1912, Le Mans, France

Like many French composers of his generation, Françaix has survived to some extent on a reputation for effortless inconsequentiality in a world dominated by avant-garde 'relevance'. He has shone at light chamber-orchestral music, and on the ballet stage. But his operas show more range, and include at least two works where lightness of touch is applied to material of richer nuance.

The most interesting of these scores are *La main de gloire* (1950), an intriguing setting of a tale by Gérard de Nerval about a knight with a magic right hand, which, like Weber's bullet, eventually leads him astray, and *La Princesse de Clèves* (1965), an ambitious and effective re-creation of the courtly 17th-century world of the novel by Mme de Lafayette, through music of impressive dignity in the neo-classical manner. Françaix's other operas are more in the spirit of his chamber music. *Le diable boiteux* (1937, but first staged after the war and later recorded by Françaix himself with the original tenor, Hugues Cuenod (Véga, 1950s)), is a small-scale comic chamber opera for two male voices and 14 instruments, while *L'apostrophe* (1947) and *Paris à nous deux* (1954) are bitter-sweet comedies, which, as one critic said of *L'apostrophe*, 'combine the sugary, the acid and the frothy'. Many would take this as, in general, an accurate account of Françaix's virtues and limitations.

BIBLIOGRAPHY Marc Lanjean, *Jean Françaix: musicien français*, Contact, 1961

S.W.

ALBERTO FRANCHETTI
b 18 September 1860, Turin, Italy; *d* 4 August 1942, Viareggio, Italy

Now largely neglected, even in Italy, Franchetti enjoyed considerable success around the turn of the century. Some have tried to attribute this merely to his influential position as a rich aristocrat. Yet it was no less a person than Verdi who, impressed by Franchetti's first opera, *Asrael* (1888), suggested he be invited to compose *Cristoforo Colombo* (1892).

These first two Franchetti operas are still the most interesting, though strongly influenced by Meyerbeer and Wagner. Their best qualities can be seen in the big spectacular scenes, for Franchetti had a flair for weaving complex ensembles and manipulating large masses of sound. There is scope for this in *Asrael*, parts of which are set in hell and heaven. But the most impressive single act is the second of *Cristoforo Colombo*, which takes place on board the *Santa Maria* during her epic voyage across the Atlantic. Columbus himself is beginning to be plagued by doubts, and mutiny is boiling up among the crew, while monks pray for their safety – until shouts are heard as the New World appears on the horizon. This exciting dramatic picture is supported by music of genuine power.

Franchetti's most widely performed opera, however, was *Germania* (1902), which was staged in London (1907) and New York (1910). This is set amid the underground resistance to Napoleon's occupation of Germany, and since melodic invention was never Franchetti's strongest point, he was wise to supplement his own ideas with actual German patriotic songs. Although many found *Germania* stirring at the time, there seems no strong case for reviving it today. Franchetti wrote few non-operatic works, but they include a symphony and a symphonic poem.

Operatic works: *Asrael*, 1888; *Cristoforo Colombo*, 1892 (RECORDING Koch-Schwann, 1991); *Fior d'Alpe*, 1894; *Il signor di Pourceaugnac*, 1897; *Germania*, 1902; *La figlia di Iorio*, 1906; *Notte di leggenda*, 1915; *Giove a Pompei* (operetta; coll. with Giordano), 1921; *Glauco*, 1922; 3 unperformed, possibly inc., operas
BIBLIOGRAPHY J. Nicolaisen, *Italian Opera in Transition, 1871–1893*, UMI Research Press, 1980

J.C.G.W.

CÉSAR FRANCK
César-Auguste-Jean-Guillaume-Hubert Franck;
b 10 December 1822, Liège; *d* 8 November 1890, Paris

Although apparently quite ungifted in the field of theatre music, Franck began or completed four operas, not one of which was staged in his lifetime.

A native of the French-speaking Walloon part of what became Belgium when he was seven, Franck attended the Liège Conservatory and gave concerts as a pianist in various Belgian cities before moving with his family to Paris in 1835. With one short Belgian interlude, he spent the rest of his life in the French capital, much of it as a church organist and organ professor at the conservatoire. Franck's improvisations on the new Cavaillé-Coll organ in the church of Ste Clothilde became famous, and they

spawned a long and splendid series of published works for the instrument. Franck also wrote sacred music, including two large-scale oratorios, which now seem hopelessly banal and sentimental. But he matured very late as a creative artist, and nearly all the concert works by which he is remembered were composed in the last decade of his life, as were his last two operas, *Hulda* and *Ghiselle*.

Franck first tried his hand at opera in the 1840s, with an unfinished sketch for a piece called *Stradella* (on the life of the 17th-century Italian composer). A second attempt, *Le valet de ferme*, an opéra comique set in Ireland, was fully composed (1851–3), apparently under the influence of Franck's new in-laws who were actors at the Comédie-Française. But it failed to reach the stage, even when one of the librettists, Alphonse Royer, became director of the Opéra in 1856.

The mature operas, though more ambitious, hardly enjoyed much greater success. Franck seems to have been pressured into writing *Hulda* (1882–5) by his wife and son, hoping for a broader popular success than was open to a composer of organ and chamber music. But this large-scale four-act grand opera about the Viking-like Aslaks of 11th-century Norway (based on a play by Björnstjerne Björnson) is almost wholly lacking in genuine drama, though there are effective orchestral numbers, including a lively ballet. *Ghiselle* (1888–90), set in Merovingian France, has the advantage, for Franck, of some church scenes, but is also dramatically inert. The scoring was unfinished, and was completed by various of Franck's pupils, including d'Indy. Both works were staged in Monte Carlo after the composer's death (*Hulda* in 1894, *Ghiselle* in 1896) but have seldom been revived.

BIBLIOGRAPHY *César Franck and His Circle*, Barrie and Jenkins, 1970

S.W.

JOHANN WOLFGANG FRANCK
baptized 17 June 1644, Unterschwanigen, middle Franconia; *d* ?*c*. 1710

Franck was the first major opera composer in Hamburg; his Hamburg operas were a significant step towards the development of German opera at the turn of the 18th century. Between 1679 and 1686 at least 17 of his works were heard there at the Oper am Gänsemarkt. Little is known about Franck's early life, but he served as a musician and later as 'Director der Comoedia' at the Ansbach court, introducing the French style and discipline of orchestral ensemble playing. In 1679 he fled to Hamburg, accused of assassinating a court musician.

Most of Franck's operas are lost, although a score *Die drey Töchter Cecrops* is extant and aria collections preserve one aria apiece from six other operas. His operatic style combines elements of Venetian opera and some aspects of French music.

His arias are often strophic, based on dance rhythms suggesting folksongs. Others, also strophic, resemble the style of German chorales. Franck also composed many longer arias expressing tragic or other solemn affections with dramatic melodic gestures and strong dissonances. He appears to have been the first Hamburg composer sometimes to accompany arias with orchestra, rather than simply to precede and follow the vocal section with an instrumental ritornello.

Operatic works surviving in whole or in part: *Die errettete Unschuld, oder Andromede und Perseus*, 1675; *Die drey Töchter Cecrops*, 1680, rev. ?1686 (EDITIONS *DTB*, vol. 38 (1838); *EDM*, 2nd series, vol. 2 (1938)); *Aneas der trojanischen Fürsten Ankunft in Italien*, 1680; *Vespasianus*, 1681; *Diocletianus*, 1682; *Semiramis, oder Die allererste regierende Königin*, 1683; *Der glückliche Grossvesier Cara Mustapha, erster Teil, nebenst der grausigen Belagerung und Bestürmung der Kaiserlichen Residenzstadt Wien; andern Teil, nebenst dem freulichen Entsatze der Kaiserlichen Residenzstadt Wien*, 1686; 10 lost operas
BIBLIOGRAPHY   G. J. Buelow, 'Hamburg Opera during Buxtehude's Lifetime: The Works of Johann Wolfgang Franck', in Paul Walker (ed.), *Church, Stage, and Studio: Music in its Contexts in Seventeenth-Century Germany*, UMI Research Press, 1990, pp. 127–41

G.J.B.

FRANÇOIS FRANCOEUR

See Rebel, François

BENJAMIN FRANKEL

b 31 January 1906, London; *d* 12 February 1973, London

Frankel's reputation rests largely on his instrumental music, which includes eight symphonies, though he also wrote over 100 film scores including *The Seventh Veil* and *The Man in the White Suit*. During the 1930s he worked as orchestrator and conductor in London's West End theatres. His serious style, lyrical yet chromatically dissonant, encompasses a personal, tonally inflected serialism, which emerged in the First Symphony (1958), and is also the basis of his only opera, *Marching Song*.

Marching Song

Opera in three acts, Op. 52 (1h 45m)
Libretto by Hans Keller, after the play by John Whiting (1954)
Composed 1972–3; orch. Buxton Orr
PREMIERE   3 October 1983, BBC broadcast

By the time composition was under way Frankel was very sick (and was also trying to complete his Eighth Symphony). At his death only the vocal score was complete. The proposed staging by the English National Opera in 1975 was cancelled because of a financial crisis.

A defeated but fundamentally 'good' general, returning from being a prisoner of war to the house of his mistress, is persuaded to commit suicide by the dictator of the country rather than stand trial. He falls in love and changes his mind, but eventually complies with the dictator's wishes. Militarism eliminates all humanity, a message underlined by Frankel's successful portrayal of character through his natural feel for theatrical pacing.

BIBLIOGRAPHY   Hans Keller, 'The Musician as Librettist', *Opera*, vol. 35 (1984), pp. 1095–9

L.F.

RUDOLF FRIML

Charles Rudolf Friml; *b* 7 December 1879, Prague; *d* 12 November 1972, Los Angeles, US

Having studied with Dvořák in Prague and toured Europe as a pianist, Friml established himself as a performer and composer in New York in 1906. He became involved with the popular musical stage quite unexpectedly. A falling out between Victor Herbert and Emma Trentini, the star of *Naughty Marietta*, made it impossible for Herbert to write her next vehicle, *The Firefly*, as had been previously announced. The well-trained but untried Friml took over the job in 1912, and the result was so successful that he occupied himself with light opera for the rest of his composing career (which he brought to an end in the 1930s).

The Firefly, *The Vagabond King* and *The Three Musketeers* were hits in their time, and some of their music remains familiar; but revivals are seldom attempted. Only *Rose-Marie* is occasionally revived as an example of Friml's old-world, lush and highly appealing style.

Rose-Marie

Collaboration with Herbert Stothart
Musical play in two acts (films: 2h)
Libretto by Otto Harbach and Oscar Hammerstein II
PREMIERES   2 September 1924, Imperial Theater, New York; UK: 20 March 1925, Theatre Royal, Drury Lane, London

Rose-Marie, a singer at a hotel in Saskatchewan, evades the unwelcome attentions of a wealthy suitor and the complications of a murder case to find happiness with the trapper she loves. The best-known excerpts are the title song and the 'Indian Love Call'.

RECORDING   Andrews, Tozzi, Engel, RCA, 1958
FILMS   1. Van Dyke (dir.), MGM, 1935; 2. Le Roy (dir.), MGM, 1954
EDITION   v.s., Harms, 1924

Other musicals: *The Firefly*, 1912; *High Jinks*, 1913; *The Peasant Girl* (with Oskar Nedbal), 1915; *Katinka*, 1915; *You're in Love*, 1917; *Kitty Darlin'*, 1917; *Sometime*, 1918; *Glorianna*, 1918; *Tumble In*, 1919; *The Little Whopper*, 1919; *June Love*, 1921; *The Blue Kitten*, 1922; *Cinders*, 1923; *The Vagabond King*, 1925; *The Wild Rose*, 1926; *The White Eagle*,

1927; *The Three Musketeers*, 1928; *Luana*, 1930; *Music Hath Charms*, 1934
BIBLIOGRAPHY Gerald Bordman, *American Operetta from H.M.S. Pinafore to Sweeney Todd*, OUP, 1981

J.A.C.

GUNNAR DE FRUMERIE

Per Gunnar Fredrik de Frumerie: *b* 20 July 1908, Nacka, Sweden; *d* 9 September 1987, Täby, Sweden

Gunnar de Frumerie belongs to the same generation as Dag Wiren and Lars-Erik Larsson but he is far less well established outside Sweden. In so far as he is known it is for his charming *Pastoral Suite* for flute and strings, and for his cultivated songs – in particular his fastidious settings of Lagerkvist. De Frumerie's style is firmly diatonic with a strong modal flavouring: indeed one could be forgiven for mistaking the opening of his only opera, *Singoalla* (1940), for Kodály or Vaughan Williams. Parts of the score are imaginative, and its simplicity and unpretentiousness made a good impression when it was recently revived by the Royal Swedish Opera.

RECORDING *Singoalla*, Caprice, 1985

R.La.

WILLIAM HENRY FRY

b 19 August 1813, Philadelphia, US; *d* 21 December 1864, Santa Cruz, West Indies

Now remembered as the composer of *Leonora*, the first grand opera by an American composer (though not on an American subject) to be staged in America, Fry was primarily an influential critic, ahead of his time in encouraging American composers to turn to their own national music and literature for inspiration.

Leonora, to a libretto by Fry's brother Joseph, based on E. G. Bulwer-Lytton's novel *The Lady of Lyons*, echoed many features of the operas of Bellini and Donizetti, of which Fry was an ardent admirer. Following its premiere in Philadelphia (1845) critics admired its *bel canto* arias and Italianate choruses, but the work was less enthusiastically received when revived in New York (1858) and it faded from the repertoire. Working as a foreign correspondent in Paris in the 1840s, Fry's attempts to get *Leonora* staged at the Opéra (at his own expense) were rebuffed with the comment 'in Europe we look to America as an industrial country – excellent for electronic railroads but not for art'.

Other operatic works: *Christiani e pagani* (inc.; lost), (c. 1838); *Aurelia the Vestal*, (1841); *Notre Dame de Paris*, 1864
BIBLIOGRAPHY William Treat Upton, *William Henry Fry*, Da Capo Press, 1974

P.D.

JOHANN JOSEPH FUX

b 1660, Hirtenfeld, Styria; *d* 13 February 1741, Vienna

Fux was for a long time remembered only as a theorist. His treatise *Gradus ad Parnassum* was studied by many important composers in the 18th and 19th centuries and had an enormous influence on the preservation of a strict style of composition that could be traced right back to Palestrina in the 16th century (hence Fux's nickname, 'the Austrian Palestrina').

Fux was in fact the most distinguished Austrian composer of his time, and held the highest positions a musician could attain: he was Hofcompositor at the imperial court, then Vice-Hofkapellmeister, and finally, from 1715 onwards, Hofkapellmeister. He wrote a great deal of important church music, some chamber music, and a remarkable succession of operas, most of which were first performed at the Hoftheater in Vienna.

He was born near Graz, of peasant stock, and studied with the Jesuits. He probably visited Italy, where he may have encountered Corelli, or at least may have been influenced by his music. While in the employ of an Austrian archbishop, he was noticed by the Emperor Leopold I, who appointed him over the heads of more likely candidates as Hofcompositor. As well as serving at the court, Fux was also involved in the provision of music for St Stephen's Cathedral in Vienna, becoming Kapellmeister there in 1712. His fame spread far afield: when J. S. Bach's first biographer, Forkel, asked Bach's son Carl Philipp Emanuel which composers his father admired, Fux came first on the list (and there is possibly a more direct homage in the fact that the ascending canons of Bach's *Goldberg Variations* directly echo those of Fux's remarkable *Missa prolationum*).

Fux's contemporary J. A. Scheibe wrote that 'Fux, although he was the most profound contrapuntalist, nevertheless possessed the skill of writing lightly, appealingly and naturally, as his theatrical works show.' His operas are often grand in design, making use of traditional instruments and quasi-ecclesiastical textures, but they are magnificent works, which, in their original productions, must have made a fine impression.

K. numbers refer to the Köchel thematic catalogue; see BIBLIOGRAPHY.

Julo Ascanio, Re d'Alba

Julius Ascanius, King of Alba
Poemetto dramatico in one act, K. 304
Libretto by Pier Antonio Bernardoni, after Livy's story of Ascanius and Ovid's story of Euander in *Fasti*
PREMIERE 19 March 1708, Vienna

Written for the name day of Emperor Joseph I, the opera's plot concerns the marriage of Ascanius to Emilia, sister of the king he conquers, bringing peace and reconciliation. The score includes such unusual features as two violas da gamba and two bassoons; in

The specially built auditorium and stage, designed by Giuseppe Galli-Bibiena, for Costanza e Fortezza *(Prague, 1723)*

style the opera combines features of French and Neapolitan opera.

EDITION f.s., Hellmut Federhofer (ed.), *J. J. Fux Samtliche Werke*, 5/1, Bärenreiter, 1962

Costanza e Fortezza
Constancy and Fortitude
Festa teatrale in three acts, K. 315 (5h 30m)
Libretto by Pietro Pariati
PREMIERES 28 August 1723, Hradschin, Prague; US: 7 May 1938, Northampton, Massachusetts

Fux's most famous opera, presented with unparalleled magnificence to celebrate not only the empress's birthday but also the Coronation festivities of Charles VI. An open-air theatre holding 4000 spectators was specially built for the occasion on the Hradschin next to the Royal Palace in Prague. On the day of the performance, 'Everybody appeared in full court dress at the royal palace to offer the usual compliments. Towards 11 o'clock all went to Mass and afterwards back to the palace, where dinner was served. In the afternoon the emperor, the empress and all their guests went to hear the opera.' (*Wiener Diarium*, 28 August 1723.)

The title was the emperor's motto, and the libretto celebrates his achievements with episodes of Roman constancy and fortitude. The music, which includes parts for eight trumpets and four timpani, is on a very large scale.

Among the many visitors to this performance were the composers Johann Quantz and C. H. Graun, with the lutenist Sylvius Weiss. Quantz described the opera in detail, noting that its slightly ecclesiastical, bold and simple style, 'which on paper may have looked stiff and dry, sounded well in the opera, much better even than melodies with many quick notes would have done'.

EDITION f.s., Egon Wellesz (ed.), *DTÖ*, Jg XVII, vols 34–5, 1910; *rp*, 1959

Other operas: *Pulcheria*, 1708; *Il mese di Marzo*, 1709; *Gli ossequi della notte*, 1709; *La decima fatica d'Ercole*, 1710; *Dafne in Lauro*, 1714; *Orfeo ed Euridice*, 1715 (EDITION facsimile, Garland, 1978); *Diana placata*, 1717; *Elisa*, 1719; *Psiche*, 1720 (coll. with Caldara), 1722 (alone); *Le nozze di Aurora*, 1722; *Giunone placata*, 1725; *La corona d'Arianna*, 1726; *Enea degli Elisi*, 1731; 4 other operas, music lost

BIBLIOGRAPHY Ludwig von Köchel, *Johann Josef Fux* (includes thematic catalogue and list of works), A. Holder, 1872; *rp*, 1974; Egon Wellesz, *Fux*, OUP, 1965

N.K.

DOMENICO GABRIELLI

['Minghino dal violoncello']; *b* 15 April 1651, Bologna;
d 10 July 1690, Bologna

Although remembered mainly as a composer for and
virtuoso on the cello, Gabrielli composed for the
Venetian stage, and this despite his permanent
residence in Bologna, where he was a cellist at the
basilica of S. Petronio. His operatic career conflicted
with the regular nature of his commitment to the
basilica, and after taking frequent periods of absence
he was dismissed – though only temporarily – in 1687.

So consistently was Gabrielli's output associated
with the major theatres of Venice, that Allacci, the
historian, considered him to be of Venetian origin.
His operas generally deal with the heroic deeds of
the rulers of the Classical world, and while most of
them were written for Venice, two were published
initially in his native city. Towards the end of his life
the works were also staged in Bergamo and Turin.
His vocal music includes three surviving oratorios
and a number of cantatas and related secular pieces.

Surviving operas: *Flavio Cuniberto*, 1682; *Il Gige in Lidia*,
1683; *Il Rodoaldo, re d'Italia*, 1685; *Il Clearco in Negroponte*,
1685; *Le generose gare tra Cesare e Pompeo*, 1686;
Il Maurizio, 1687; *Il Gordiano*, 1688; *Carlo il Grande*, 1688;
Silvio, re d'Albani, 1689; 3 lost operas

G.D.

MARCO DA GAGLIANO

b 1 May 1582, Florence; *d* 25 February 1643, Florence

Together with his older colleague Jacopo Peri,
Gagliano was a leading composer of early opera in
Florence. From 1602 he pursued a career in the
Medici church of S. Lorenzo and in the Compagnia
dell'Arcangelo Raffaello. He came into close contact
with the Mantuan patron Prince (later Duke)
Ferdinando Gonzaga, with whom he maintained a
regular correspondence, and in mid-1607 Gagliano
founded the first formal Florentine academy devoted
to music, the Accademia degli Elevati.

In 1607 Ferdinando Gonzaga commissioned
Gagliano to compose a new setting of Ottavio
Rinuccini's *Dafne*, previously set by Jacopo Corsi

and Jacopo Peri in the mid-1590s as the 'first' opera.
Gagliano's version was intended for the festivities
for the wedding of Prince Francesco Gonzaga and
Margherita of Savoy in Mantua, but the wedding
was delayed and the opera was performed instead in
the Carnival of 1608 (and again in Florence on
9 February 1611). Gagliano remained in Mantua to
provide music for the festivities themselves, including
a ballo, *Il sacrificio d'Ifigenia*, and the third
intermedio for Battista Guarini's play *L'Idropica*.
Gagliano's success and financial reward caused much
complaint from the Mantuan director of music,
Claudio Monteverdi.

Back in Florence, Gagliano collaborated on the
music for the intermedi to Michelangelo Buonarroti's
Il giudizio di Paride, performed to celebrate the
wedding of Prince Cosimo de' Medici and Maria
Magdalena of Austria. Later in 1608, again supported by Ferdinando Gonzaga, he succeeded Luca
Bati as director of music of Florence Cathedral, and
in 1609 of the Medici court, a post he held for
nearly 35 years. He became a canon of S. Lorenzo on
26 January 1610, and apostolic protonotary there in
1615. He directed and composed music for a large
number of court and civic entertainments, often
collaborating with Jacopo Peri and the poet Andrea
Salvadori. Some of this music (such as the *Ballo di
donne turche*) is included in his *Musiche* of 1615, but
most of it is lost.

In the 1620s, Gagliano may have visited Innsbruck
and Warsaw, but he provided music for at least two
sacre rappresentazioni by Salvadori, *La regina
Sant'Orsola* (1624) and *L'itoria di Iudit* (1626). He
collaborated with Peri on *La Flora*, for the wedding
in 1628 of Margherita de' Medici and Duke Odoardo
Farnese of Parma, and may have been involved in
the festivities for the wedding of Grand Duke
Ferdinando II and Vittoria della Rovere in 1637. His
madrigals, solo songs, sacred works and music for
theatrical entertainments show him to be among the
most talented and wide-ranging composers of his
generation.

Dafne

Daphne

Favola in musica, in a prologue and one act (six scenes) (1h)
Libretto by Ottavio Rinuccini, after Book I of Ovid's
Metamorphoses
PREMIERE 1608, Mantua

CAST Ovid *t*, Apollo *t*, Dafne *s*, Venus *s*, Cupid/Amore *s*,
Tirsi *a*; *satb* chorus of nymphs and shepherds
INSTRUMENTATION probably 2 rec, cembalo, virginals,
lute, 2 chitarroni, organo di legno, str

Rinuccini revised and expanded his libretto for
Gagliano, but the plot remains substantially the same
as that treated by Corsi and Peri in the 1590s. There
are no scene divisions in the score, although the
strophic choruses divide the work into six sections.

After the prologue delivered by Ovid, nymphs and
shepherds enter, praying for salvation from the
dragon that is attacking their fields. Apollo slays the
monster and, encountering Venus and Cupid, vaunts
his skill. Cupid vows revenge on the haughty
demigod. Apollo meets Daphne and falls in love with
her, despite her resisting his advances. She flees, and
Cupid exalts in his victory. The messenger Tirsi
reports that, to avoid being caught by Apollo,
Daphne has transformed herself into a laurel. The
chorus mourns the fate of the nymph as Apollo
enters to lament his loss and to consecrate himself to
the laurel and to art.

Gagliano clearly owes much to the example of
Peri's *Dafne* and *Euridice*: he adopts Peri's intense,
emotional recitative, enriching it further with his
own experience of the polyphonic madrigal. Here,
however, the choruses, instrumental interludes and
arias (three apparently by Ferdinando Gonzaga) are
much more developed, and Gagliano's score
approaches that of Monteverdi's *Orfeo* (1607) both
in its use of a wide variety of styles and genres and in
the care with which Gagliano specifies directions for
production. According to his preface, and for the first
time, the instrumentalists are to be positioned in
front of the stage in full view of the singers, and
Gagliano gives precise instructions for staging and
interpretation.

RECORDING Schlick, Lerer, Rogers, Partridge, Hamburg
Monteverdi Ch, Hamburg, Camerata Accademia, Jürgens,
Archiv, 1977
EDITIONS Marescotti, Florence, 1608; facsimile, Forni,
1970; J. Erber (ed.) (contains English translation of the
preface), Cathedral Music, 1978

La Flora, ovvero Il natal de' Fiori
Flora, or The Birth of Flowers
Favola in musica in a prologue and five acts
Libretto by Andrea Salvadori
PREMIERE 14 October 1628, Teatro Mediceo degli Uffizi,
Florence

La Flora was written for the wedding of Margherita
de' Medici and Odoardo Farnese: its botanical
imagery plays on the bride's name and on the flowers
associated with Florence and Parma. The plot
concerns the love of Zephyrus and Chlorys. Cupid, at
first reluctant to bless the pair, sows discord, but he
eventually yields to pressure from the gods. The
flowers that result from the union, watered by
Apollo and the Muses, cover the earth and produce
the lilies of Florence and Parma. The acts were
separated by ballets performed by tritons and sea
nymphs, satyrs and wood nymphs, cupids, winds and

Costume sketch by Alfonso Parigi for La Flora *Florence,
1628)*

storms, and breezes. The subject is dominated by its
pro-Medici propaganda, and the music (largely by
Gagliano, although Peri composed the recitatives for
the part of Clori) is somewhat old-fashioned. However, some of the tuneful arias perhaps point in a
new direction away from Florentine recitative.

EDITION Pignoni, 1628; facsimile, Forni, 1969

Other operatic works: *Ovunque irato Marte in terra scende*,
1608; *Mascherata di ninfe di Senna* (partly by Peri), 1611;
Ballo di donne turche, 1615; 10 lost
BIBLIOGRAPHY Alois Maria Nagler, *Theatre Festivals of
the Medici, 1539–1637*, Yale University Press, 1964

T.C.

HANS GÁL
b 5 August 1890, Brunn, nr Vienna; *d* 3 October 1987,
Edinburgh

A widely respected musicologist and teacher, Gál
was also a successful opera composer early in his
career. He studied with Brahms's friend Eusebius
Mandyczewski in Vienna (1908–13). In 1929 he was
appointed director of the Musikhochschule in Mainz,
returning to Vienna in 1933, but in 1938 he left
again in the face of growing Nazism and settled
in Edinburgh. There he became a lecturer at the

university and a leading light in the city's musical life.

Though Gál grew up in the Vienna of Schoenberg and his school, his music remained firmly in the tradition of Brahms and Richard Strauss, as is evident in his operas. Best received was the 'play with gods and humans', *Die heilige Ente* (*The Holy Duckling*), which was widely performed in Germany in the 1920s. This, with *Die beiden Klaas*, formed the comic panels of an operatic triptych to libretti by von Levekov, framing the central 'dramatic ballad' *Das Lied der Nacht*.

Operas: *Der Ärzt der Sobeide*, 1919; *Die heilige Ente*, 1923; *Das Lied der Nacht*, 1926; *Der Zauberspiegel*, 1930; *Die beiden Klaas*, 1933
BIBLIOGRAPHY Wilhelm Waldstein, *Hans Gál*, Verlag Elisabeth Lafite/Österreichischer Bundesverlag, 1965

M.A.

JOHN ERNEST GALLIARD

b ?1687, ?Celle; *d* 1749, London

French by origin but German by birth, Galliard came to London in 1706 as a court musician to the Prince Consort, George of Denmark. A flautist and oboist, he was soon playing in the band of the Queen's Theatre, and became active as a composer, writing instrumental and vocal music, operas, masques and pantomimes. He was a friend of Handel, who wrote obbligato parts for him; most of his dramatic work was commissioned by John Rich, the manager first of the Lincoln's Inn Fields Theatres and subsequently of Covent Garden. Of his three operas only the first, *Calypso and Telemachus* (1712), to a libretto by John Hughes based on Fénelon's didactic novel *Aventures de Télémaque*, survives, though it lacks the recitatives and choruses. Of the four dramatic masques *Pan and Syrinx* (1718) remains intact. *The Rape of Proserpine* (1727) and *Merlin, or The Devil of Stonehenge* (1734) are the only two of his eight pantomimes to survive reasonably intact. *Merlin*, given at Drury Lane, was an unsuccessful attempt to work independently of Rich; the autograph manuscript is in Durham Cathedral Library. The torso of *Calypso and Telemachus* is particularly tantalizing because its libretto (in English) has both form and substance; *Pan and Syrinx* contains a remarkable transformation aria and some interestingly experimental scoring; *The Rape of Proserpine* proved a popular success and alternates serious ballet with a knockabout harlequinade. Rich himself played Harlequin in the pantomimes and Galliard was as adept at providing catchy 'comic tunes' as more solemn music. Elaborate scenes and dancing did much to attract a middle-class public, unlikely to have ventured to the opera, to these shows. However Galliard's scholarly translation of P. F. Tosi's *Observations on the Florid Song* (1742) reveals that his true interests lay elsewhere.

BIBLIOGRAPHY Roger Fiske, *English Theatre Music in the*

Eighteenth Century, OUP, 1973; 2nd edn, 1986; J. M. Knapp, 'A Forgotten Chapter in English Eighteenth-Century Opera', *ML*, vol. 42 (1961), pp. 4ff.

R.Lu.

BALDASSARE GALUPPI

b 18 October 1706, Burano, nr Venice; *d* 3 January 1785, Venice

Galuppi was one of the most popular and successful of 18th-century Venetian opera composers, and some of his works gained a wide international reputation. Such was his predilection for the stage that as early as 1722 he composed an opera, *La fede nell'incostanza*, for an opera house in Chioggia. The failure of the work led him to consult Benedetto Marcello and Antonio Lotti for lessons in composition, and by the late 1720s he had begun to work as an opera composer in Venice. From 1740 Galuppi was maestro at the Ospedale dei Mendicanti, but his operatic reputation was expanding, and in 1741 the Earl of Middlesex invited him to become composer of opera seria at the King's Theatre in Haymarket. During the two years he stayed in London, he wrote four operas for the theatre, and he subsequently remained popular with London audiences for many years. On his return to Venice he began to turn his attention – though not exclusively – to opera buffa, from 1749 in collaboration with Goldoni. But he still maintained a career outside the opera house, being appointed vicemaestro at St Mark's in 1748 and maestro in 1762.

During the 1750s his fame spread widely: he composed operas for Milan, Vienna, Madrid, Naples, Rome, Turin and many other Italian cities. Due to the popularity of his operas in Russia, he was invited in 1765 to work for three years as director of the Russian court chapel in St Petersburg and in Moscow. Though he composed music for the Orthodox liturgy, only one St Petersburg opera seems to have survived. On his return to Venice in 1768 he returned to his post at St Mark's, and took further responsibilities at the Ospedale degli Incurabili. In Venice he was regarded as the most distinguished composer of his generation, as was attested by his legendary wealth.

His output as an opera composer is difficult to assess, since many of his *c.* 100 operas are still scattered throughout the libraries of Europe. The 18th-century opera buffa originated in Naples, but Galuppi was the first non-Neapolitan composer to ensure the popularity of the genre through his close collaboration with Goldoni. It was largely due to the success of Galuppi's works that opera buffa became established as being equal in artistic importance to opera seria. *Il filosofo di campagna* (1754) enjoyed particular success throughout Europe, as is evident from the number of manuscript sources. Such works were the stock in trade of travelling opera companies, ensuring the wide dissemination of the opera buffa. Both plots and music of Galuppi's opere

Galuppi by G. Bernasconi

Galuppi had produced a number of operas in collaboration with Goldoni since 1740, but *Il filosofo di campagna* was their first long-lasting success. In fact, along with Pergolesi's *La serva padrona* and Piccinni's *La buona figliuola*, it was one of the most popular works of the 18th century and still receives occasional revivals.

The plot recounts the amorous intrigues of Don Triternio, who loves Lesbina (his daughter's companion), who loves Nardo (the philosopher of the title), who is betrothed to Eugenia (Triternio's daughter), who loves Rinaldo, who – astonishingly – returns her love. After many typical disguises and confusions, Eugenia and Rinaldo are united, as are Lesbina and Nardo.

That many features of *Il filosofo di campagna* – plot, character types, variety and forms of arias and ensembles, finale structure, etc. – are now regarded as typical of 18th-century opera buffa, indicates the impact of the opera. Galuppi borrowed some elements from opera seria, notably the music of the more 'serious' couple, Eugenia and Rinaldo, juxtaposing exit arias with light canzonettas.

RECORDING   abridged: Moffo, Rizzieri, Andreolli, Panerai, Petri, I Virtuosi di Roma, Fasano, HMV, 1958
EDITIONS   f.ss., Walsh, 1761; Wolf-Ferrari (ed.), Ricordi, 1954; v.ss., Carish, 1938; Wolf-Ferrari (ed.), Ricordi, 1954; *rp*, 1975

buffe tend to reject the stock formulae of earlier comic scenes, and try to present human characters in imaginable situations. To this end, Galuppi paid particular attention to clarity of text, often scoring accompaniments lightly and incorporating short instrumental phrases that depicted the singers' words. He also wrote multi-sectional finales where, over a continuous orchestral background, voices could stop and start in a dramatically realistic manner (the structure known as a chain finale). In his later serious works he was as much concerned with the creation of a coherent drama in music, as were the so-called reformers of the period, and it is interesting to note the changes that had occurred in his opera-seria style since rigid Metastasian structures had dominated his early works. Galuppi, in conversation with Burney who admired him, stated that good music consisted of 'beauty, clarity, and good modulation'. It was his pursuit of these qualities that won him admirers throughout Europe in the mid-18th century, and prompted Burney's own comment that 'Many of the refinements in modern melody, and effects in dramatic music, seem to originate from the genius of Galuppi.'

Il filosofo di campagna

The Country Philosopher
Dramma giocoso per musica in three acts (2h 30m)
Libretto by Carlo Goldoni
PREMIERES   26 October 1754, Teatro di S. Samuele, Venice;
UK: 6 January 1761, King's Theatre, Haymarket, London;
US: 26 February 1960, Conservatory, Boston

Surviving operas: *La fede nell'incostanza, ossia Gli amici rivali* (one aria only), 1722; *Ergilda*, 1736; *Gustavo primo re di Svezia*, 1740; *Scipione in Cartagine*, 1742; *Enrico*, 1743; *Antigono*, 1746; *Evergete*, 1747; *L'Olimpiade*, 1747 (EDITION facsimile, H. M. Brown (ed.), Garland, 1978); *Demetrio*, 1748; *Artaserse*, 1749; *L'Arcadia in Brenta*, 1749 (RECORDING Fonit Cetra, 1980); *Il conte Caramella*, 1749; *Il mondo della luna*, 1750; *Il mondo alla roversa, ossia Le donne che comandano*, 1750 (Leipzig, 1758); *Antigona*, 1751; *Dario*, 1751; *Le virtuose ridicole*, 1752; *La calamità de'cuori*, 1752; *I bagni d'Abano* (coll. with Bertoni), 1753; *L'eroe cinese*, 1753; *Siroe*, 1754; *Attalo*, 1755; *Le nozze*, 1755; *La diavolessa*, 1755 (EDITION facsimile, H. M. Brown (ed.), Garland, 1978); *Idomeneo*, 1756; *Ezio*, 1757; *Sesostri*, 1757; *Ipermestra*, 1758; *Adriano in Siria*, 1758; *Melite riconosciuto*, 1759; *La clemenza di Tito*, 1760; *Solimano*, 1760; *L'amante di tutte*, 1760; *Li tre amanti ridicoli*, 1761; *Il caffè di campagna*, 1761; *La donna di governo*, 1761; *Antigono*, 1762; *Il marchese villano*, 1762; *Viriate*, 1762; *Il Muzio Scevola* (only Act II survives), 1762; *L'uomo femmina*, 1762; *Il puntiglio amoroso*, 1762; *Arianna e Teseo*, 1763; *Il re alla caccia*, 1763; *Sofonisba*, 1764; *Cajo Mario*, 1764;
La partenza il ritorno de'marinari, 1764; *La cameriera spiritosa*, 1766; *Ifigenia in Tauride*, 1768; *Il villano geloso*, 1769; *L'inimico delle donne*, 1771 (EDITION facsimile, H. Geyer-Kiefl (ed.), *Drammaturgia Musicale Veneta*, vol. 21 (3 vols), Ricordi, 1986); *Gl'intrighi amorosi*, 1772; *Montezuma*, 1772; *La serva per amore*, 1773; 10 doubtful; 40 lost operas
BIBLIOGRAPHY   Maria Teresa Muraro and Franco Rossi (eds), *Galuppiana 1985: Studi e Ricerche*, Quaderni della rivista italiana di musicologia società italiana di musicologia 13, Leo S. Olschki, 1986; Reinhard Wiesend, *Studien zur Opera seria von Baldassare Galuppi*, 2 vols, Hans Schneider, 1984

G.D.

JOHN GARDNER

John Linton Gardner; *b* 2 March 1917, Manchester, England

During the 1950s Gardner, a one-time répétiteur at Covent Garden, was seen as one of the most promising composers of the younger generation, his reputation based principally on a well-regarded Symphony in D minor (1951), the first of four. His idiom found less favour during the 1960s, but he continued to compose, his style encompassing a sympathy for jazz, and he fulfilled varied commissions, including works for students and amateur performers.

His opera *The Moon and Sixpence*, after Somerset Maugham's novel, is in a romantic idiom that quickly dropped from favour in the 1960s but is far from *passé*.

Operatic works: *A Nativity Opera*, 1950; *The Moon and Sixpence*, 1957; *Vile Bodies* (musical), 1961; *The Visitors*, 1972; *Bel and the Dragon*, 1973; *Tobermory*, 1976
BIBLIOGRAPHY Noel Goodwin, 'John Gardner's Opera, *The Moon and Sixpence*', *MT*, vol. 98 (1957), pp. 250–51

L.F.

FRANCESCO GASPARINI

b 5 March 1668, Camaiore, nr Lucca; *d* 22 March 1727, Rome

Gasparini may well have studied under Legrenzi in Venice. He was made a member of the Accademia di S. Cecilia in Rome in 1689, which suggests that he was living there by that time. In Rome he would have had the chance to hear music by Corelli, Pasquini and Alessandro Scarlatti. Indeed, when Gasparini had returned to Venice, Alessandro Scarlatti sent Domenico to study with him there. In 1701 when Gasparini was appointed maestro del coro at the Ospedale della Pietà in Venice, he had already produced three operas for performance in Rome and Naples, but his return to Venice, with its flourishing public opera, heralded the beginning of a period of intense involvement with opera at the Teatro S. Cassiano, which lasted until his departure for Rome once again in 1713. Though he was active in Rome as a maestro di cappella, Gasparini continued to produce operas for Rome, Florence, Naples, Turin, Vienna and elsewhere, including a collaboration with Fux and Caldara for Brunswick, *Teodosio ed Eudossa* (1716). Towards the end of his life his health deteriorated, and he wrote little after 1720.

Gasparini's most active period as an opera composer were the two decades between his arrival in Venice and 1720. Altogether he composed some 25 operas for the city, frequently using libretti by Zeno, Pariati and Silvani. His fame clearly spread quickly, since *Il più fedel fra i vassalli* (1703) was one of the earliest Italian operas to be performed in London (as *Antioco*, 1711), and arias from the opera were printed. The following year the same attention was accorded his *Ambleto* (*Hamlet*) of 1705. The

idea that he visited England in this period may be discounted, making these revivals all the more remarkable. Gasparini also contributed to pasticcios performed in London and elsewhere.

Gasparini's comic scenes were well received, and were of such proportions that they were used as independent intermezzi out of context. The best known of these is *Melissa e Serpillo*, which was performed as a separate interlude in *L'amor generoso* (1707). Few of Gasparini's operas have survived, but it is clear that he favoured the continuo aria, while not excluding the use of solo instruments or strings for particular occasions. His many cantatas, more accessible works than the operas, demonstrate that he had a good mastery of vocal writing, and the ability to delineate clearly character and emotion. Burney described these works as 'graceful, elegant, natural and often pathetic'; it is unfortunate that it is impossible to gain anything other than a very partial view.

Michelangelo Gasparini (*c.* 1670–*c.* 1732), probably a brother, also composed a number of operas for the Venetian stage; none survives.

Surviving operatic works: *L'Ajace*, 1697; *Il più fedel fra i vassalli*, 1703; *La fede tradita e vendicata*, 1704; *Ambleto*, 1705; *Anfitrione* (?25 arias survive), 1707; *Friletta e Chilone*, 1707; *Melissa schernita, vendicata, contenta*, 1707; *Engelberta*, 1708; *Atenaide* (coll. with Fiore and Caldara), 1709; *Sesostri Re d'Egitto* (only arias survive), 1709; *La ninfa Apollo* (coll. with Lotti; ?arias survive), 1709; *Tamerlano* (lost), 1710, rev. as *Il Bajazet*, 1719 (EDITION facsimile, H. M. Brown (ed.), Garland, 1978); *Lucio Vero* (only arias survive), 1719; *Astianatte*, 1719; *L'oracolo del fato*, 1719; 43 lost operas

G.D.

FLORIAN LEOPOLD GASSMANN

b 3 May 1729, Brüx (now Most, Czech Republic); *d* 20 January 1774, Vienna

This Bohemian composer is now remembered for his symphonies and chamber music, yet his first successes were in the opera house. Many opera composers travelled north to the imperial centre of Vienna, but Gassmann made the reverse journey to the greatest Italian centre, Venice, against the wishes of his family, in order to study, probably with Padre Martini. Between 1757 and 1762 he enjoyed success with a series of operas written for the Venetian Carnival, and mainly performed at the Teatro S. Moisè. He was called to the Viennese court as ballet composer and successor to Gluck in 1763, though he never entirely severed connections with Venice, returning there in 1766 for the performance of his *Achille in Sciro* to a libretto by Metastasio. In addition to Zeno's and Metastasio's texts, he also frequently set libretti by Goldini, the first of these Goldini operas being *Gli uccellatori* (1759), Gassmann's first opera buffa.

Gassmann's contract in Vienna required the composition of operas: his first, *L'Olimpiade* (1764) to a libretto by Metastasio, was performed at the nearly rebuilt Kärntnertortheater, while in the following year his *Il trionfo d'amore* was performed for the marriage of the future Emperor Joseph II – this was not the only one of his operas performed at a major imperial celebration. His most popular opera, *La contessina* (1770), based on Goldoni, was composed for a meeting between Joseph II and Frederick the Great of Prussia. In 1772 Gassmann became court kapellmeister, and at the same time he founded the Viennese Tonkünstler-Sozietät. He died suddenly in 1774, after falling from a carriage.

One comedy for Vienna is worth mentioning – *L'opera seria* (1769) to a libretto by Calzabigi, a satire on the state of opera seria and the composition of the company required to mount such an event. Despite the number of his comic operas, Gassmann can be closely associated with Gluck in his insistence on the integrity of the dramatic plot. He makes imaginative use of the orchestra, even on occasion allowing it to dominate the voices with its own melodic material.

The scores of most of Gassmann's operas survive in libraries all over Europe: it is a testimony to his popularity that these works were performed in theatres as widely separated as Copenhagen and Lisbon. Opera determined the course of the lives of his two daughters; both studied with Salieri (whom Gassmann had earlier taught himself) and enjoyed a high reputation as singers.

Operas: *Merope* (overture and one aria survive), 1757; *Issipile*, 1758; *Gli uccellatori*, 1759; *Filosofia ed amore*, 1760; *Catone in Utica* (one aria survives), 1761; *Un pazzo ne fa cento*, 1762; *L'Olimpiade*, 1764; *Il trionfo d'amore*, 1765; *Achille in Sciro*, 1766; *Il viaggiatore ridicolo*, 1766; *L'amore artigiano*, 1767; *Amore e Psiche*, 1767; *La notte critica*, 1768; *L'opera seria*, 1769; *Ezio*, 1770; *La contessina*, 1770 (EDITION Robert Haas (ed.), *DTÖ*, vols 42–4, 1914); *Il filosofo inamorato*, 1771; *Le pescatrici*, 1771; *Don Quischott von Mancia*, 1771; *I rovinati*, 1772; *La casa di campagna*, 1773; *Arcifanfano, re dei natti*, 1778
BIBLIOGRAPHY G. Donath, 'Florian Leopold Gassmann als Opernkomponist', *SMw*, vol. 2 (1914), p. 34; R. Strohm, *Die italienische Oper im 18. Jahrhundert*, Wilhelmshaven, 1979

G.D.

PIERRE GAVEAUX

Pierre Gaveaux [Gavaux, Gaveau]; *b* 9 October 1760, Béziers, France; *d* 5 February 1825, Charenton, nr Paris

Gaveaux grew up in the south of France, where he attended Béziers Cathedral choir school. Later he studied composition with the symphonist Franz Beck at Bordeaux, and there began his career as a celebrated operatic tenor. At the Théâtre Feydeau in Paris he took leading roles in the new generation of works by Cherubini (*Lodoïska*, 1791), Steibelt (*Roméo et Juliette*, 1793), and others. In 1795 Gaveaux's anti-Jacobin sentiments surfaced in his song 'Le réveil du peuple', which became a rallying call for the Right, and was eventually banned by the Directoire.

Gaveaux's increased interest in orchestral writing

was seen in *Sophie et Moncars* (1797); its *entr'acte* is in the style of a *seguidilla* (the Andalusian dance, later to feature in Bizet's *Carmen*). There are inventive effects in *Léonore*, and, to a lesser degree, in *Le diable couleur de rose*. Gaveaux continued to sing and compose for the re-formed Opéra-Comique after 1801.

Léonore, ou L'amour conjugal
Leonore, or Married Love
Fait historique in two acts (2h)
Libretto by Jean Nicolas Bouilly
PREMIERE 19 February 1798, Théâtre Feydeau, Paris

Although Gaveaux had limited originality as a composer, his *Léonore* (the first setting of the *Fidelio* story, shortly followed by those by Paer, 1804; Mayr, 1805, and Beethoven, 1805) was popular for some years. Beethoven probably had access to the score, and it contains things he might well have remembered when he tackled the same libretto in German. For example: the eerie sonorities of the dungeon music (horns played bell to bell); the blunt line of Roc's song; gradually swelling figurations as the prisoners emerge into the light; a solo oboe as Florestan looks at his portrait of Léonore (comparable with Beethoven's music at 'Und spür' ich'). These were obviously keenly felt moments for Gaveaux. He himself sang the role of Florestan, and probably identified the tyrant Dom Pizare with the figure of Robespierre, in the volatile years after the end of the Terror (1794).

Bouilly's ingenious libretto combined two traditions in French opera: release from the clutches of a tyrant (e.g. Cherubini's *Lodoïska*), and humanitarian endeavour in the cause of liberty (e.g. Grétry's *Richard Coeur-de-lion*).

EDITION facsimile in Barry S. Brook (series ed.), *French Opera in the 17th and 18th Centuries*, Pendragon, forthcoming

Other operas: *Les deux invalides*, also titled *L'amour filial, ou Les deux Suisses*, 1792; *Les deux ermites*, 1793; *La partie carrée*, 1793; *La famille indigente*, 1794; *Le petit matelot, ou Le mariage impromptu*, 1796; *Lise et Colin*, 1796; *Le traité nul*, 1797; *Sophie et Moncars, ou L'intrigue portugaise*, 1797; *Le diable couleur de rose*, 1798; *Le locataire*, 1800; *Le trompeur trompé*, 1800; *Une quart d'heure de silence*, 1804; *Le bouffe et le tailleur*, 1804; *Avis aux femmes, ou Le mari colère*, 1804; *Le diable en vacances*, 1805; *L'amour à Cythère*, 1805; *Monsieur Des Chalumeaux*, 1806; *L'échelle de soie*, 1808; *La rose blanche et la rose rouge*, 1809; *L'enfant prodigue*, 1811
BIBLIOGRAPHY David Charlton, 'On Redefinitions of "Rescue Opera"', in Malcolm Boyd (ed.), *Music and the French Revolution*, CUP, 1992

D.P.C.

JOHN GAY

b September 1685, Barnstaple, Devon, England; *d* 4 December 1732, London

John Gay is unique among the figures treated in this book in that he is not known to have composed a bar of music in his life; but he invented opera's most significant mutant form. Ballad opera, of which Gay's *The Beggar's Opera* is the first and the best, led to German singspiel, French *opéra bouffon* and the Anglo-American musical. His musical attainments did not extend beyond recorder-playing, but this gave him access to the innumerable songbooks of the day which provided transpositions of the tunes within the compass of that instrument. He went to London as apprentice to a silk mercer; a small legacy enabled him to break the indenture and, in 1708, to embark on a literary career. He became a lifelong friend of Alexander Pope.

From the start Gay's work exploited a deliberate incongruity of form and content; a mordant sense of social reality was given point by being expressed in an effortlessly decorous literary attire. He wrote the libretto for Handel's *Acis and Galatea* (1718), which is notable for its firm and economical construction and for the reanimation of stock material by dint of drastic pruning. At about this time Gay started to explore the possibilities of the broadside ballad: 'Sweet William's Farewell to Black-ey'd Susan' (1720) rapidly acquired tunes by four rival composers. The idea of a 'Newgate Pastoral' had been mooted by Dean Swift, in a letter to Pope, as early as 1715. In 1724 Newgate became especially topical: the highwayman Jack Sheppard was finally captured and hanged and the informer and receiver Jonathan Wild was knifed in court by one of his victims. Gay celebrated this in 'Newgate's Garland', a ballad to be sung to the tune of 'Packington's Pound', which prefigures the method, setting and substance of *The Beggar's Opera*. But whereas 'Newgate's Garland' is a single song, *The Beggar's Opera* is a three-act drama with spoken dialogue and 69 airs all to existing tunes: English, Irish and Scots traditional melodies, and popular songs by recent composers including Purcell, Handel, Henry Carey and Bononcini.

A sequel, *Polly*, in which Macheath is transported to the West Indies, marries Jenny Diver, but is followed by Polly who becomes an honorary member of an Indian tribe and captures him, disguised, is amusing but bland, and Gay seems to have used up his repertoire of good and pointed tunes in *The Beggar's Opera*. It was banned by the Lord Chamberlain and a failure when performed, as was a posthumous ballad opera, on a classical theme, *Achilles*.

There was nothing new about plays with an extensive musical component nor in writing fresh words to existing tunes; Gay's originality lay in seeing how the principle could be extended, making song the predominant element, advancing the action rather than serving merely as its reflection. *The Beggar's Opera* was an immediate success, running for 32 nights consecutively, and 62 in the season altogether. Though there are some contemporary allusions (Lockit as Walpole, the Prime Minister; Polly and Lucy as Faustina and Cuzzoni, the rival prima donnas from the Italian Opera), Gay did not attempt to make them run consistently through the piece. The satire is general: what distinguishes a military hero from a highwayman in uniform, a woman who marries for money from a prostitute, a politician from a venal gaoler, an operatic aria from a good vernacular song? Many of the original words to the tunes would have been familiar to the audience, and the subversion of the sentiments these express is also part of Gay's design.

It has been claimed, improbably, that Gay originally intended the airs to be unaccompanied. In the event Dr Pepusch, harpsichordist at Lincoln's Inn Fields, provided basses for the songs and a lively overture, which has for its *allegro* an anticipation of Lucy's 'I'm like a ship on the ocean tossed'. The songs would probably have been introduced by the orchestra and doubled as appropriate. Dr Burney, no great admirer of Pepusch, thought his basses 'so excellent that no sound contrapuntist will ever attempt to alter them'. Nevertheless, in almost every subsequent generation some such effort has been made. Notable 20th-century versions have been those of Frederick Austin (1920, with text edited by Arnold Bennett, décor by Lovat Fraser, and a brilliant production by Nigel Playfair), and Benjamin Britten (1948). It also inspired the completely rewritten Brecht–Weill collaboration, *Die Dreigroschenoper* (Berlin, 1928). Weill and Britten radically miscomprehended Gay's intentions by giving acerbic accompaniments to pretty tunes and thus upsetting

The Beggar's Opera

Ballad opera in three acts (original version: 3h)
Libretto by John Gay
PREMIERES   29 January 1728, London; 1733, Jamaica;
US: 3 December 1750, New York; UK: Austin arrangement:
5 June 1920, Hammersmith, London; Britten arrangement:
24 May 1948, Cambridge
CAST   Peachum *b*, Lockit *b*, Macheath *t*, Filch *t*, Mrs
Peachum *ms*, Polly Peachum *s*, Lucy Lockit *s*; *sa* chorus of
women of the town; *tb* chorus of Macheath's gang
ORCHESTRATION   2 ob, str, cont; Austin arrangement: fl,
ob, va d'amore, va da gamba, str, hpd; Britten arrangement:
fl/picc, ob/ca, cl, bsn, hn, perc, hp, str quartet

Ticket, believed to be designed by William Hogarth, for The Beggar's Opera *at Covent Garden for the benefit for Thomas Walker, the first Macheath*

the whole ironic balance of words and music in the original. Richard Bonynge and Douglas Gamley, in their 1980 travesty, went to the other extreme by sanitizing the text and tinsellizing the music. Austin did not make either mistake. Jeremy Barlow, in 1980, was the first person to attempt a scholarly historical reconstruction.

SYNOPSIS

In a spoken introduction the Beggar apologizes for failing to make his opera 'throughout, unnatural, like those in vogue; for I have no Recitative'; otherwise it 'must be allowed an Opera in all its Forms'.

Overture.

Act I takes place in the house of Peachum, an informer and receiver of stolen goods. He is anxious to arrange 'a decent Execution against next sessions', and has his eye on Robin of Bagshot, who proves to be a favourite of his wife's. Mrs Peachum voices her suspicion that their daughter, Polly, is involved with the handsome, free-handed highwayman, Captain Macheath. Taxed with this Polly confesses her love and her desire to preserve her honour: 'Virgins are like the fair Flower in its Lustre'. Meanwhile Mrs Peachum has discovered the awful truth: Polly has actually married Macheath, and worse, still loves him. Her parents attempt to make Polly see sense, impeach Macheath and have him hanged. She demurs: 'For on the Rope that hangs my Dear/ Depends poor Polly's life'. Macheath opportunely calls and Polly persuades him he must flee.

Act II commences in a tavern near Newgate. Macheath's gang lay their plans and set out singing 'Let us take the Road' to the march from Handel's *Rinaldo*. Macheath, insatiate for women, summons the ladies of the town. Two favourites, while fondling him, take his pistols and signal for Peachum and the constables to enter and seize him. Macheath is removed to Newgate and the custody of Mr Lockit. He is then confronted by Lucy, Lockit's daughter, whom he has seduced and abandoned. Trapped, he agrees to marry her and they go in search of the chaplain. Peachum and Lockit come to blows over the division of the reward for Macheath's capture, but eventually compose their differences, recognizing their 'Mutual Interest'. Lucy and Macheath return, only to encounter a distracted Polly, resolved to stay with her husband 'till Death'. The quarrel between the girls reaches its climax in 'Why how now, Madam Flirt'; finally Peachum has to tear his daughter away, which gives Macheath the chance to persuade Lucy to help him escape.

Act III begins in Newgate. Lockit berates Lucy for her folly and goes to find Peachum. Macheath meets his gang in a gaming house and is recognized by Diana Trapes, who informs Peachum. In Newgate Lucy, torn by 'Jealousy, Rage, Love and Fear' tries to poison Polly, but when Macheath is brought in, recaptured, Polly drops the laced cordial. Lockit and Peachum hurry him to the Old Bailey. The final scene takes place in the condemned cell where Macheath laments his fate 'O cruel, cruel, cruel Case/Must I suffer this disgrace?'. Other wives arrive: 'Four Women more, Captain, with a Child

apiece'. 'This is too much,' says Macheath and the Player agrees, imploring the Beggar to make the piece end as an opera should, happily. The Beggar agrees, a reprieve is granted and Macheath and Polly lead off the concluding chorus and dance.

RECORDINGS 1. Marquesita, Nelis, Ranalow, Ch and O of Lyric Theatre, Hammersmith, F. Austin, HMV, 1920 and 1922; 2. Prietto, Lipton, Noble, Argo Chamber Ensemble, R. Austin, Argo, 1955; 3. Sutherland, Te Kanawa, Morris, Dean, London Voices, National PO, Bonynge, Decca, 1981; 3. Walker, Thompson, Daniels, Mills, Dawson, Barlow, Hyperion, 1991
EDITIONS J. Watts, 1728; J. Watts (with Pepusch's overture and basses), 1729; Arne arrangement: Longman and Broderip, 1776; Austin arrangement: Boosey & Co., 1920; Britten arrangement: Boosey & Hawkes, 1948; Barlow arrangement: OUP, 1980; Bonynge–Gamley arrangement: Josef Weinberger, 1981
Other works: *Polly*, (1728), 1779; *Achilles*, 1733
BIBLIOGRAPHY Dearing and Beckwith (eds), *John Gay, Poetry and Prose* (2 vols), OUP, 1974; P. F. Gaye, *John Gay*, London, 1938; P. E. Lewis, *John Gay: The Beggar's Opera*, Oliver and Boyd, 1977

R.Lu.

NOEL GAY

Reginald Moxon Armitage; *b* 15 July 1898, Wakefield, Yorkshire, England; *d* 3 March 1954, London

Although Armitage, as he then was, started his musical career as a prodigy at the church organ, an interest in the works of Sullivan led him to the world of the musical theatre. After the success of the *Charlot Show of 1926*, he changed his name to Noel Gay, composing the scores for some 15 shows and producing a string of hugely popular songs: these included 'All the king's horses' (1930), 'The Sun has got his hat on' (1932), 'Leaning on a lamp-post' (1937, immortalized by George Formby) and 'Run, rabbit, run' (1939). Their cheerful optimism led during the war years to their virtual absorption into popular British folk culture. After the war the onset of deafness led him to devote more time to publishing.

Me and My Girl

Musical comedy in two acts (rev. version: 2h)
Book by L. Arthur Rose and Douglas Furber; lyrics by Furber
PREMIERES 16 December 1937, Victoria Palace, London; 4 February 1985, Adelphi Theatre, London (rev. version by Stephen Fry); US: 10 August 1986, Marquis Theater, New York

The rags-to-riches story of a Cockney lad who turns heir to a fortune but hankers after his roots provided British musical comedy with one of its most enduring successes. The original production ran for 1,646 performances, while the number 'The Lambeth Walk' was turned into a popular dance that attained cult status. The revised version of the show, incorporating many popular songs by Gay not in the original, continues to prove that the work has lost none of its popular appeal.

RECORDING Broadway cast, MCA, 1986
EDITION v.s. Cinephonic Music Co., 1953

BIBLIOGRAPHY Kurt Gänzl and Andrew Lamb, *Gänzl's Book of the Musical Theatre*, Bodley Head, 1988, pp. 145–9

M.A.

GIUSEPPE GAZZANIGA

b 5 October 1743, Verona; *d* 1 February 1818, Crema

Gazzaniga was a member of the last generation of Italian buffa composers (which included Paisiello and Cimarosa), before the advent of Rossini. Although intended for the priesthood, he studied music secretly and eventually entered the Conservatorio di Sant'Onofrio a Capuana in Naples thanks to the patronage of Porpora, with whom he had previously studied in Venice. From 1767 he was also taught by Piccinni.

His first stage work, the comic intermezzo *Il barone di Trocchia*, was performed in Naples in 1768; but Gazzaniga returned north in 1770, and during the following 20 years wrote a wide variety of works for cities in north and central Italy. Productions of his works also took place in Dresden (*La contessa di Nuovaluna*, 1778) and Vienna (*Il finto cieco*, 1786, to a libretto by Da Ponte). Gazzaniga's greatest success, for which he is remembered today, was *Don Giovanni Tenorio*. Most of Gazzaniga's operas are comic. Despite a conventional melodic and simple harmonic style, their arias and more especially their ensembles and finales, for example in *Il disertore* and *La dama soldato*, are sensitively written for the voice and express the comic situation adequately.

In 1791 Gazzaniga became maestro di cappella at Crema Cathedral, where he remained for the rest of his life, composing mainly sacred works.

Don Giovanni Tenorio, o sia Il convitato di pietra

Don Giovanni, or The Stone Guest
Dramma giocoso in one act (1h 15m)
Libretto by Giovanni Bertati
PREMIERES 5 February 1787, Teatro S. Moisè, Venice; UK: 1 March 1794, King's Theatre, Haymarket, London; Ireland: 28 October 1988, Theatre Royal, Wexford

During the 1770s and 1780s the story of Don Giovanni was a frequent operatic subject, popular with the crowds if considered somewhat vulgar and bizarre by cognoscenti. At its premiere, Gazzaniga's opera was staged as the second half of a double-bill, the first half of which (*Il capriccio drammatico*) dealt with the troubles of an Italian opera company travelling in Germany when the impresario decided to put on *Don Giovanni*; the second half (i.e. the opera proper) is presented as the company's rehearsal.

Gazzaniga's opera follows the traditional outline of the story: the duel and the death of the Commendatore, the rebuffal of Elvira (with a showpiece list aria), the rural wedding festivities, the graveyard scene, the visit of the statue and Don Giovanni's descent into hell. The names of some characters differ from those in Mozart's later version (Leporello is here Pasquarille; Zerlina is Maturina and Masetto Biagio), there is another deceived mistress and an additional servant.

The music is far less complex (and substantially shorter) than in Mozart's opera; it displays typical Neapolitan traits and is comprised mainly of short arias and straightforward ensembles (the catty duet, 'Per questo ben ti guardo', between Donna Elvira and Maturina is a typical, spirited example). The peasant wedding scene has a choral tarantella, complete with castanets, while the opera ends, after Don Giovanni's descent into hell, in a major key.

Don Giovanni Tenorio was very successful in Italy and was subsequently given in Paris, Lisbon and London; there were 32 editions of the libretto up to 1821. Although Da Ponte was clearly influenced by Bertati's text for his own libretto, it is not clear if Mozart knew Gazzaniga's music. In 1794, when Da Ponte was poet to the King's Theatre in London, he had a version of Gazzaniga's opera performed with music by other composers, including Leporello's catalogue aria from Mozart's opera.

RECORDINGS 1. Steinsky, Coburn, Kinzel, Kaufmann, Aler, Chaignaud, Scharinger, von Kannen, Bavarian Radio Ch, Munich Radio O, Soltesz, Orfeo, 1991; 2. Serra, Szmytka, Johnson, Furlanetto, Allemano, Tafelmusik Baroque O, Weil, Sony Classical, 1991
EDITION f.s., S. Kunze (ed.), Bärenreiter, 1974

Other surviving operas: *Il Calandrino*, 1771; *La locanda*, 1771; *L'isola d'Alcina*, 1772; *Zon Zon*, 1773; *La donna [dama] soldato*, 1774; *La bizzaria degli umori*, 1777; *La vendemmia*, 1778; *Il disertore*, 1779; *Antigono*, 1779; *La moglie [donna] capricciosa*, 1780; *Il serraglio di Osmano*, 1784; *Circe*, 1786; *Gli Argonauti in Colco*, 1790; 33 lost operas
BIBLIOGRAPHY Daniel Heartz, 'Goldoni, *Don Giovanni* and the dramma giocoso', *MT*, vol. 120 (1979), p. 993

D.S.B.

RICHARD GENÉE

Franz Friedrich Richard Genée; *b* 7 February 1823, Danzig (now Gdańsk, Poland); *d* 15 June 1895, Baden bei Wien [nr Vienna]

The son of a theatre conductor at Danzig, Genée studied medicine in Berlin, but switched to music, and became a theatre conductor himself, working in Danzig, Cologne, Düsseldorf, Prague and other cities. His first operetta appeared in 1857, and in 1868, when he was conductor at the Theater an der Wien in Vienna, he supplied his first libretto, for a (lost) work by Flotow. With Camillo Walzel ('F. Zell') he wrote libretti for the most enduring operettas of the 'golden' 19th-century works,

including *Die Fledermaus, Eine Nacht in Venedig*
(Strauss II); *Fatinitza, Boccaccio* (Suppé); *Der
Bettelstudent, Gasparone* (Millöcker). Genée composed two works that were once internationally
popular: *Der Seekadett* (1876) and *Nanon* (1877).
With Zell, he also made superb German translations
of French and British operetta classics, including
several by Offenbach and Gilbert and Sullivan.

Operettas: *Der Geiger aus Tirol*, 1857; *Der Musikfeind*, 1862;
Der Generalprobe, 1862; *Rosita*, 1864; *Der schwarze Prinz*,
1866; *Schwefeles, der Höllenagent*, 1869; *Der Seekadett*, 1876;
Nanon (die Wirtin vom goldenen Lamm), 1877; *Im
Wunderlande der Pyramiden*, 1877; *Die letzten Mohikaner*,
1879; *Nisida*, 1880; *Rosina*, 1881; *Die Zwillinge*, 1885;
Die Dreizehn, 1887
BIBLIOGRAPHY   Richard Traubner: *Operetta: A Theatrical
History*, Doubleday, 1983

R.T.

PIETRO GENERALI
[Pietro Mercandetti]; *b* 23 October 1773, Masserano,
Piedmont; *d* 3 November 1832, Novara

Trained in Rome and Naples, Generali produced his
first opera in 1800, having been active mainly as a
composer of sacred music before then. His first
major success was *Pamela nubile* to a libretto by
Gaetano Rossi after Goldoni, performed in Venice in
1804. This was followed by further opera-buffa
successes, notably *Adelina* (1810), also produced in
Venice. From 1812 to 1816 Generali wrote several
opere serie, including *I baccanali di Roma*, his most
successful work.

Generali's career was adversely affected by the
overwhelming popularity of Rossini, and he moved
to Barcelona in 1817, staying there until 1819. He
then spent some time in Paris, before returning to
work in Naples (1821) and Palermo (as director of
the opera house). From 1827 to his death he was
maestro di cappella at Novara in northern Italy.

Surviving operatic works: *Pamela nubile*, 1804; *Le lagrime
d'una vedova*, 1808; *Adelina*, 1810; *I baccanali di Roma*, 1816
(EDITION facsimile, Garland, forthcoming); *c.* 50 other
operas ?lost
BIBLIOGRAPHY   James Freeman, 'Pietro Generali in Sicily',
MR, vol. 34 (1973), pp. 231–40

D.S.B.

ROBERTO GERHARD
b 25 September 1896, Valls, nr Barcelona, Spain; *d* 5 January
1970, Cambridge, England

Until he was 40 Gerhard was considered a Spanish
composer. A composition pupil of the celebrated
Spanish musician Felipe Pedrell and a piano pupil
of Granados, he also studied composition with

Schoenberg in Vienna and Berlin (1923–8), and in
1931 became professor of music at the Escola
Normal de la Generalitat in Barcelona and subsequently music librarian at the Catalan Library
there. In 1939, finding himself on the losing side at
the end of the Spanish Civil War, he left Spain and
settled in Cambridge.

His first stage works were ballets, the third of
which, *Don Quixote*, was staged at Covent Garden in
1950. The unique flavour of his music reflects the
influence of both Spanish, particularly Catalan, music
and Schoenberg. This is particularly true of his only
opera, *The Duenna*.

The Duenna
Opera in three acts (2h 30m)
Libretto by the composer, after the comedy by Sheridan
(1775)
Composed 1945–7, rev. 1951
PREMIERES   23 February 1949, BBC Home Service
(broadcast); 27 June 1951, Wiesbaden (concert); 21 January
1992, Teatro Lirico Nacional, Madrid; UK: 17 September
1992, Grand Theatre, Leeds

The Duenna appears to have been written in
ignorance of Prokofiev's version (1941). Gerhard
came across a copy of Sheridan's play (in the 1775
setting by the two Thomas Linleys – father and son)
and, without any prospect of performance, set about
the opera's composition. Although it was broadcast
soon after its completion and given a concert
performance, *The Duenna* had to wait 45 years for its
stage premiere. This was given in a version that
adhered largely to Gerhard's 1951 revision of the
work, in which several passages were tightened, with
the aim of improving the opera's dramatic pacing.

The opera follows Sheridan's romantic comedy
closely, recounting the efforts of Louisa, daughter
of a Seville nobleman Don Jerome, to avoid her
planned marriage to the elderly Don Mendoza. Don
Mendoza is eventually tricked into marrying Louisa's
duenna, leaving Louisa free to marry her beloved
Antonio.

While *The Duenna*'s idiom was at first seen as
fairly advanced, its Spanish roots (echoes of the
zarzuela) and a mixture of tonal strophic songs in a
chromatic framework make it more approachable
than its history suggests. Gerhard's skill is in weaving
together 20 more or less independent numbers into a
coherent through-composed form.

EDITION   David Drew (ed.), Boosey & Hawkes (on hire),
1991; v.s. (facsimile of manuscript), Boosey & Hawkes (on
hire)

BIBLIOGRAPHY   David Drew, 'Gerhard's *Duenna* and
Sheridan's', *Opera*, (Dec. 1991), pp. 1,393–8, (Jan. 1992),
pp. 40–47; Roberto Gerhard, '*The Duenna* Revised', *Opera*,
(Feb. 1951), pp. 356–8

L.F.

EDWARD GERMAN

(Sir) German Edward Jones; *b* 17 February 1862,
Whitchurch, Shropshire, England; *d* 11 November 1936,
London

This Edwardian composer of operettas and
incidental music came of organist stock. At the Royal
Academy of Music, his interest turned from the
organ to the violin, which he later taught there. His
first operetta, *The Two Poets*, written for an RAM
opera class, was performed in 1886, and a symphony
followed in 1887. German played in various West
End theatre orchestras, including the Savoy's, and in
1888 became music director of the Globe Theatre.
There began a series of plays with German's incidental scores, including Shakespeare's *Richard III*,
as a result of which Henry Irving commissioned
him to compose music for *Henry VIII*. The published
dances from this became immensely popular, and are
still heard today, along with those from a forgotten
play about Nell Gwyn.

In 1900, German was chosen to complete the score
of *The Emerald Isle* on the death of Arthur Sullivan.
Sullivan was reported to have left the basic outline
for Act I, and sketches for Act II, so German was
responsible for virtually all the orchestration and
several of the tunes. This led to his next, and most
famous, operetta, *Merrie England* (1902), with the
same librettist, Basil Hood. Having entered the
operetta world with Sullivan, he left it with Gilbert,
who wrote the libretto for *Fallen Fairies* (1909), a
wan reheating of *Iolanthe* which led to German's
retirement from the stage.

Merrie England

Comic opera in two acts
Libretto by Basil Hood
PREMIERES 2 April 1902, Savoy Theatre, London;
6 September 1945, Prince's Theatre, London (rev. version by
Edward Knoblock); US: 13 April 1956, Hunter College, New
York (concert)

This is a fictional romance of Elizabethan days, with
historical characters (the Queen herself, Raleigh,
Essex) thrown in. An impressive line-up of
patriotically tinted numbers and the kind of old
English country-dance music at which German
excelled recall his earlier Shakespeare scores, as
well as the Sullivan of *The Yeomen of the Guard*. Less
successful are the comic numbers and Hood's
undistinguished lyrics. On its first run the whole
suffered in comparison with the first revival of
Iolanthe, but although it ran for only 102
performances at the Savoy there were numerous
revivals. Of the many memorable tunes the patriotic
anthem 'The Yeomen of England' for Essex and the
chorus achieved great popularity.

RECORDING Bronhill, Kern, Sinclair, McAlpine, Glossop,
Glynne, The Williams Singers, Michael Collins O, Collins,
EMI, 1960
EDITION v.s., Chappell, 1902

Tom Jones

Comic opera in three acts
Libretto by Alexander M. Thompson and Robert
Courtneidge, after the novel by Henry Fielding (1748), lyrics
by Charles H. Taylor
PREMIERES 17 April 1907, Apollo Theatre, London;
US: 11 November 1907, Astor Theater, New York

German's version of Fielding's *Tom Jones*, with its
highly bowdlerized libretto, is his best operetta. Here
the West Country atmosphere drew forth pleasantly
nationalist solos and ensembles, and some effective
18th-century pastiche, plus a not unwelcome French
strain in several numbers that recalls Messager and
even Gounod.

RECORDING excerpts: Glover, Minty, Harvey, Riley, Nigel
Brooks Ch, Gilbert Vinter O, Vinter, EMI, 1967
EDITION v.s., Chappell, 1907

Other operatic works: *The Two Poets*, 1886; *A Princess of
Kensington*, 1903; *Fallen Fairies*, 1909
BIBLIOGRAPHY Brian Rees, *A Musical Peacemaker: The
Life and Work of Sir Edward German*, Kensal Press, 1986

R.T.

GEORGE GERSHWIN

Jacob Gershvin; *b* 26 September 1898, Brooklyn, New York;
d 11 July 1937, Hollywood, California

Piano and theory studies at an early age led George
Gershwin to work as a pianist at the age of 15. His
compositional studies remained haphazard and short-
lived throughout his life (his longest period of study
with a single teacher was his work with Joseph
Schillinger from 1932 to 1936). From working as a
song-plugger for a publishing house, he quickly
moved to composing songs of his own and getting
them interpolated into musicals written by others. He
soon had the opportunity to supply whole scores for
revues, and for George White's *Scandals of 1922* he
provided a 20-minute 'jazz opera', *Blue Monday*.

Gershwin continued to challenge himself by
writing instrumental music, and established himself
as a leading composer of musicals for the most
popular performers of his day; from 1924 onwards he
almost always wrote to lyrics by his older brother
Ira. His writing for Gertrude Lawrence and the
Astaires conformed to the standard structure of
musicals of the period, rarely going beyond the 32-
bar form. Noteworthy, however, are his harmonic
deftness (often evident at the return to the original
theme) and the exceptional care he devoted to verses.

His first venture beyond Broadway conventions,
Strike Up the Band (1927), was initially a failure, but
it was successfully revived three years later, and was
followed by two other ventures in similar vein (*Of
Thee I Sing*, and *Let 'Em Eat Cake*). The libretti
satirize (in a broadly entertaining way) certain
aspects of American life; Gershwin made the most of
this by creating scores with links to the quick-witted

George Gershwin painting a portrait of Arnold Schoenberg (December 1936)

style of operetta created by Gilbert and Sullivan, as opposed to the more sentimental Viennese-derived strain that had flourished on Broadway. These operettas, though intended for show, rather than operatic, voices, indulged in such luxuries as passages of recitative and ensemble finales that did not reprise the songs (Leonard Bernstein, in *The Joy of Music*, pointed out the parallels between the Act I finales of *The Mikado* and *Of Thee I Sing*), and a greater variety of musical idioms. The use of marches, waltzes, patter, and other styles meant that these musicals contained fewer hits than Gershwin's more conventional efforts. But they constituted more satisfying overall entities, extending to greater care in the construction of overtures.

Other commercial Broadway enterprises were not totally abandoned during this period: *Girl Crazy* launched an extraordinary number of hit songs. But the real culmination of Gershwin's work for the musical stage was his opera *Porgy and Bess*. In some technical respects it reveals (as had his concert and stage work since 1932) the skills he had learned from Schillinger in terms of handling thematic development, transition, and transformation in an efficient way. From another vantage point it reveals Gershwin reconciling his more ambitious theatrical forms with the abundance of memorable melodies that had characterized his earlier shows; few operas or musicals contain as many famous and unforgettable excerpts as *Porgy*. As he had also achieved success in the film musical during the 1930s, future possibilities seemed limitless for Gershwin, but his life ended tragically early when he died of a brain tumour in 1937.

Gershwin's music retains an indelible place in modern culture. He created songs unsurpassed in the fertility of their melodic invention, the variety of their structures, and the perfection of their

craftsmanship. Most of his stage musicals, observing the stage conventions of their time and devised in part as vehicles for distinctive performers, have not borne revival in recent times without extensive alteration – despite the enormous appeal of their music. Perhaps the recent increase in historical performance styles may lead to a revival of Gershwin's musicals on their own terms. Purely on musical grounds, there should always be occasional attempts to bring his earlier shows back to the stage; *Strike Up the Band*, with its merry treatment of an anti-war theme, might well merit first attention. Whether such revivals happen or not, *Porgy and Bess* has secured Gershwin his place as a stage composer of consequence.

Blue Monday

(later retitled *135th Street*)
Opera in one act (20m)
Libretto by E. Ray Goetz and B. G. De Sylva
PREMIERE 28 August 1922, Globe Theater, New York
(as part of George White's *Scandals of 1922*)

This story of misunderstanding, jealousy and murder in a saloon setting is generally conceded to be uneven in inspiration and crude in technique, though its three individual numbers contain some good tunes (one of them shared with Gershwin's *Lullaby* for string quartet). It will nevertheless retain a permanent interest as Gershwin's first venture in operatic writing, complete with accompanied recitative. Originally presented as one segment of a revue, it was eliminated after the opening night. It has occasionally been staged (there was an abridged rendition in the ersatz Hollywood biography *Rhapsody in Blue*) and has been heard in concert since, with various orchestrations.

RECORDING Andrews, Mason, Richardson, Smith, Turnabout, 1977
MANUSCRIPT arranger's pf s. in New York Public Library at Lincoln Center

Primrose

Musical comedy in three acts
Libretto by George Grossmith and Guy Bolton; lyrics by Desmond Carter and Ira Gershwin (additional lyric by B. G. De Sylva)
PREMIERES 11 September 1924, Winter Garden, London; US: 15 May 1987, Library of Congress, Washington DC (concert)

Primrose was the first show for which Ira Gershwin dropped the pseudonym Arthur Francis. It was also the only Gershwin musical to be premiered in London and the first to be published in vocal score. The story deals with romantic misunderstandings among two pairs of easily confused young people, in a country estate on the Thames and in London. The music adapts itself to the English locale with surprising success; it has a gentler and less driving atmosphere than Gershwin's American shows.

EDITION v.s., Chappell & Co., 1924

Lady, Be Good!

Musical comedy in two acts
Libretto by Guy Bolton and Fred Thompson; lyrics by Ira
Gershwin
PREMIERES 1 December 1924, Liberty Theater, New York;
UK: 14 April 1926, Empire Theatre, London

Lady, Be Good! was the first successful full-length
collaboration for the Gershwin brothers. The show
provided roles for Fred and Adele Astaire as an
impoverished brother and sister whose schemes to
return to a life of wealth provide the plot. Also on
hand were the piano-duo team of Arden and
Ohman, and Cliff Edwards ('Ukelele Ike'). The score
includes the title song, 'The Half of It, Dearie, Blues',
and 'Fascinating Rhythm'. 'The Man I Love' was
dropped during the Philadelphia try-out.

RECORDING Morrison, Teeter, Maguire, Alexander, Stern,
Elektra/Nonesuch, 1992
EDITION Samuel French (on hire), 1924

Tip-Toes

Musical comedy in two acts
Libretto by Guy Bolton and Fred Thompson; lyrics by Ira
Gershwin
PREMIERES 28 December 1925, Liberty Theater, New
York; UK: 31 August 1926, Winter Garden, London

'Tip-Toes' Kaye (originally played by Queenie
Smith) finds herself and her vaudeville partners
penniless in Florida. She pretends to be a wealthy
lady in order to find a rich husband, and despite
amnesia and the uncovering of her ruse, she finds
true love as well. The score includes 'Looking for a
Boy', 'That Certain Feeling', and 'Sweet and Low-
Down'.

RECORDING Dickson, Kearns, Monmouth-Evergreen, 1926
EDITION 1947 orchestration: f.s., Tams Witmark (on hire);
Higgs (selected and arr.), Chappell, 1926

Oh, Kay!

Musical comedy in two acts
Libretto by Guy Bolton and P. G. Wodehouse; lyrics by Ira
Gershwin (additional lyrics by Howard Dietz)
PREMIERES 8 November 1926, Imperial Theater, New
York; UK: 21 September 1927, His Majesty's Theatre, London

The star of *Oh, Kay!* was Gertrude Lawrence, and
the plot devised for her involved liquor boot-legging,
a marriage that proves to be invalid, disguises, and
the obligatory misunderstandings. The songs include
'Maybe', 'Clap Yo' Hands', 'Do-Do-Do', and 'Someone to Watch over Me', as well as less-known gems
such as 'Dear Little Girl' and 'Fidgety Feet'.

RECORDING compilation of singles by Lawrence, Hulbert,
Gershwin *et al.*, Smithsonian, 1926–7
EDITION Musicscope (on hire), 1926; Higgs (selected and
arr.) Chappell, 1927

Strike Up the Band

Musical satire in two acts
Libretto by George S. Kaufman (1930 revision: Morrie
Ryskind); lyrics by Ira Gershwin

PREMIERES 29 August 1927, Reade's Broadway Theater,
Long Branch, New Jersey; rev. version: 14 January 1930,
Times Square Theater, New York

The original version, which was an out-of-town
failure, depicted a war between the US and
Switzerland over the quality and importation of
cheese. In the revised version of 1930, which reached
Broadway, the dispute was over chocolate, and the
war itself was a dream. This show marked Gershwin's
most striking turn towards an operetta style, with
extended finales and ensembles; the songs include
the ballad 'Soon', the cynical title song, some patter
numbers, 'The Man I Love' (one of many failed
attempts in the first version to find this song a home
in the theatre), and (in the second version) 'I've Got
a Crush on You'. Both Gershwin's versions of *Strike
Up the Band* are reconstructable; they display
striking differences. (The 1940 film has only the title
song in common with Gershwin's show, and two
revivals in recent years have used yet different
reconstructions.)

RECORDING Luker, Barrett, Graae, Chastain, unnamed Ch
and O, Mauceri, Elektra/Nonesuch, 1990: both the 1927 and
1930 versions were recorded and released separately
EDITION original version: Joseph Weinberger (on hire),
1927; rev. version (not available for performance): v.s., New
World, 1930

Funny Face

Musical comedy in two acts
Libretto by Fred Thompson and Paul Gerard Smith; lyrics by
Ira Gershwin
PREMIERES 22 November 1927, Alvin Theater, New York;
UK: 8 November 1928, Princes Theatre, London

A plot to steal back a young woman's diary (which
her guardian has taken) happens to coincide with a
professional jewel theft, and each gang takes the
wrong treasure. This pretext produced sufficient
complication to provide a framework for the singing
and dancing of Fred and Adele Astaire. The title
song, ''S Wonderful', 'He Loves and She Loves', and
'My One and Only' are highlights of the score,
and 'The Babbit and the Bromide' was a notable
showcase for the Astaires. Two subsequent entertainments took *Funny Face* as a primary source for
Gershwin songs (including in both cases 'How Long
Has This Been Going On?', which *Funny Face* had
discarded out of town) but included other songs as
well and told completely different stories: the 1957
film *Funny Face* with Fred Astaire and Audrey
Hepburn and the 1983 musical *My One and Only*.

RECORDING compilation of singles by F. and A. Astaire,
Gershwin, *et al.* Smithsonian, 1927–8

Girl Crazy

Musical comedy in two acts (1h)
Libretto by Guy Bolton and John McGowan; lyrics by Ira
Gershwin
PREMIERES 14 October 1930, Alvin Theater, New York;
UK: 12 July 1988, Guildhall School of Music and Drama,
London

During a period of experimentation in the form of musical comedy, *Girl Crazy* represented a partial return to the Broadway formula, with plenty of song hits. It included the hits 'I Got Rhythm', 'Bidin' My Time', 'But Not for Me', and 'Embraceable You', and used the comedian Willie Howard, several future big-band eminences in the orchestra pit, and two contrasted leading ladies in Ginger Rogers and Ethel Merman (the latter making her Broadway début). With such richness, the story about a New York playboy who takes a cab to Arizona and falls in love with the postmistress mattered little. A similar plot premiss, and some of the *Girl Crazy* songs, provided the basis for the 1992 musical *Crazy for You* (which otherwise raided the Gershwins' entire output for its score).

RECORDING Luft, Blazer, Carroll, Gorshin, Mauceri, Elektra/Nonesuch, 1990: the first of a series of recordings of works by the Gershwin brothers in carefully prepared complete versions
FILMS 1. Seiter (dir.), RKO, 1932; 2. Taurog (dir.), MGM, 1943
EDITION v.s., New World, 1954

Of Thee I Sing
Musical satire in two acts
Libretto by George S. Kaufman and Morrie Ryskind; lyrics by Ira Gershwin
PREMIERE 26 December 1931, Music Box, New York

This was the first musical to win the Pulitzer Prize for drama, but, in a decision that caused much consternation at the time, the restriction of the prize to writers of words meant that Gershwin's music was excluded from the honour. It satirizes the American political process by depicting a presidential election as a popularity contest won by promoting true love and corn muffins. Its extended finales combine solos, recitative, and ensembles in the Gilbert and Sullivan manner; its overture is noteworthy as a thoughtfully structured piece rather than a simple medley. The songs include 'Wintergreen for President', 'Love Is Sweeping the Country', 'Of Thee I Sing (Baby)', and 'Who Cares?'

RECORDING McGovern, Kert, O'Hara, Gilford, Thomas, CBS, 1986; with *Let 'Em Eat Cake*
EDITION v.s., New World Music, 1932

Pardon My English
Musical comedy in two acts
Libretto by Herbert Fields; lyrics by Ira Gershwin
PREMIERE 20 January 1933, Majestic Theater, New York

Gershwin's last two Broadway musicals were commercial failures, as was the opera that followed. *Pardon My English* takes place in Dresden and includes international jewel thieves and a police commissioner in its cast, and an interrupted wedding, a kidnapping, and a cure for kleptomania among its events. This was a troubled and much-revised production that involved several uncredited librettists and directors. But its score is one of Gershwin's richest, its contents including 'The Lorelei'

'My Cousin in Milwaukee', 'Isn't it a Pity?', and the two contrapuntally combined waltzes 'Tonight' (published for piano as Two Waltzes in C).

Let 'Em Eat Cake
Musical satire in two acts
Libretto by George S. Kaufman and Morrie Ryskind; lyrics by Ira Gershwin
PREMIERE 21 October 1933, Imperial Theater, New York

The reassembling of the *Of Thee I Sing* team for a sequel did not produce a critical or popular success equal to the original. The satire this time extended much further (the heroes form a blue-shirted army that overthrows the US government in favour of a dictatorship) but the resolution of the plot was less witty than in the previous show. The score however showed Gershwin extending his musical and theatrical skills wider than ever, with an emphasis on motivic development and transitional figuration that anticipates *Porgy and Bess*, and one lyric outpouring ('All the Mothers of the Nation') that might have come from that opera. Of the more songlike sections of the score, the most familiar is the contrapuntal ensemble 'Mine'.

RECORDING Kert, McGovern, Gilford, Garrison, Thomas, CBS, 1987; with *Of Thee I Sing*

Porgy and Bess
Opera in three acts (3h)
Libretto by DuBose Heyward, based on the play *Porgy* by Dorothy and DuBose Heyward; lyrics by DuBose Heyward and Ira Gershwin
Composed 1934–5
PREMIERES 10 October 1935, Alvin Theater, New York; UK: 9 October 1952, Stoll Theatre, London
CAST Porgy *b-bar*, Bess *s*, Crown *bar*, Serena *s*, Clara *s*, Maria *a*, Jake *bar*, Sporting Life *t*, Mingo *t*, Robbins *t*, Peter *t*, Frazier *bar*, Annie *ms*, Lily *ms*, Strawberry woman *ms*, Jim *bar*, Undertaker *bar*, Nelson *t*, Crab man *t*; *spoken roles*: Mr Archdale, Detective, Policeman, Coroner, Scipio (boy); Jasbo Brown *pianist*; *satb* chorus of residents of Catfish Row (including divisi and soli)
ORCHESTRATION 2 fl/picc, 2 ob/ca, 3 cl/2 alto sax, b cl/tenor sax, bsn, 3 hn, 3 tpt, 2 trbn, tuba, perc (2 players), pf, banjo, str; onstage: pf

Having wanted to base an opera on DuBose Heyward's novel *Porgy* since reading it in 1926, Gershwin had to wait while it enjoyed success as a play. In 1933 a contract was signed and the two men began their collaboration, mostly by correspondence, with Ira brought in later to help with some individual lyrics. During the composition of the score, Gershwin travelled to South Carolina to absorb the milieu at first hand; once back in New York, he tried out passages of the score with cast members as he selected them. The title roles were created by Todd Duncan, a baritone not previously associated with the popular idiom, and Anne Brown, a young Juilliard student; John W. Bubbles, a vaudeville star, played Sporting Life. A private concert performance in Carnegie Hall was followed by a try-out run in Boston during which cuts and alterations were made.

The New York production's run was 124 performances – short by Broadway standards, but quite extraordinary for an opera, old or new. Reviews from both music and drama critics expressed mostly condescension, and the general perceptiom was that *Porgy* failed as opera, however appealing its popular excerpts.

Todd Duncan and Anne Brown as Porgy and Bess (1935)

As the score had been printed before Gershwin's rehearsals began, it contains music that he cut before the New York opening (see the Hamm article cited below); but *Porgy*'s operatic identity remained unmistakable. Revivals after Gershwin's death established *Porgy* as a success – and also inaugurated a history of textual meddling. A 1941 production went far beyond any of the composer's cuts, reducing the cast and chorus, providing a new orchestration for a smaller orchestra, and replacing most of the connecting orchestral passages with spoken dialogue. A highly successful revival in the 1950s, which toured the world and included among its principals Leontyne Price and William Warfield (it was still touring in the 1960s), restored more music (often as underscoring) but still reshaped *Porgy* as a two-act operetta. Two recordings made in 1976, both complete according to the published score, marked an important new step, drawing attention again to the

work's operatic stature and establishing the merit of many of the passages that had seldom been heard. Productions at the Metropolitan, New York, and at Glyndebourne have espoused equally complete texts. Perhaps, now that these and similar presentations have proven the stature and quality of *Porgy and Bess*, it may become possible to consider whether some of Gershwin's own cuts might not be considered improvements after all.

SYNOPSIS
The action takes place in the early 20th century, in Charleston, South Carolina. The principal location is the waterfront courtyard called Catfish Row, formerly an elegant mansion, now a Negro tenement.

Act I Scene 1: The sounds of a honky-tonk piano ('Jasbo Brown Blues'), the young mother Clara's lullaby ('Summertime'), and a crap game permeate Saturday night in Catfish Row. Clara's husband Jake, a fisherman, jokingly quiets their baby ('A Woman is a Sometime Thing'), and all greet the crippled beggar Porgy as he arrives in his goat-cart. The mean-tempered stevedore Crown arrives with his woman Bess, and joins the game. It develops into a fight in which Crown kills Robbins and flees, leaving Bess to fend for herself. Porgy takes her in. Scene 2: All the Catfish Row residents (now including a subdued Bess) come to Robbins's room to mourn with his widow Serena ('Gone, gone, gone') and contribute money for the burial ('Overflow'). A policeman investigating Robbins's death takes Peter, a honey salesman, into custody for questioning. Serena mourns her loss ('My Man's Gone Now'), and Bess leads the group in a triumphant spiritual ('Leavin' for the Promised Land').

Act II Scene 1: Several weeks later, Jake and the other fishermen work on their nets ('It Take a Long Pull To Get There'). Bess's love has brought happiness to Porgy's life for the first time ('I Got Plenty o' Nuttin''). Events of the morning include Sporting Life's attempts to peddle 'happy dust' (frustrated by the shopkeeper Maria), the fraudulent lawyer Frazier's offer to divorce Bess from Crown ('Woman to Lady'), and the visit of a sympathetic white man, Mr Archdale, who promises to get Peter out of gaol ('Buzzard Song'). All are preparing for the church picnic, but Bess is content to stay behind with Porgy ('Bess, You Is My Woman'). As the picnic parade forms ('Oh, I Can't Sit Down'), Porgy and Maria persuade her to go and enjoy herself. Scene 2: At the picnic on Kittiwah Island ('I Ain't Got No Shame'), Sporting Life presents his cynical philosophy ('It Ain't Necessarily So'). Bess misses the boat back, detained by Crown. He has been hiding on the island and tries to persuade Bess to come back to him. She refuses ('What You Want wid Bess?'), but ultimately is helpless against his insistence. Scene 3: Jake and his men leave for an extended fishing trip. Bess is heard calling out in the delirium in which she has remained for the week since she was found on the island. Peter returns from gaol, and he, Serena, Lily (Peter's wife), and Porgy pray for Bess's recovery ('Oh, Doctor Jesus'). Time passes as the cries of strawberry, honey, and crab sellers are heard, and Bess awakes, restored to health. She tells Porgy she wants to stay with him, not Crown, and he assures her that she need fear Crown no longer ('I Loves You, Porgy'). A terrible storm rises. Scene 4: In Clara's room, all are gathered to pray for safety from the hurricane ('Oh, de Lawd Shake de Heavens'). Even Crown shows up, shocking everyone with his irreverence ('A Red-Headed Woman'). When Jake's empty boat is seen outside and Clara runs out to find him, Crown is the only one who will go after her. The others resume their prayers.

Act III Scene 1: Back in the courtyard, the prayers of everyone for Clara, Jake, and Crown are heard as night falls ('Clara, Clara'). Bess is now caring for Clara's baby. Crown crawls back to claim Bess, but in the ensuing fight Porgy manages to kill him. Scene 2: Policemen investigating Crown's death get no help from anyone, and finally take Porgy with them to identify the body. Sporting Life plays on Bess's fear that she is left alone, offering to take her with him to a new life up north ('There's a Boat Dat's Leavin' Soon for New York'). She resists, but finally takes the dope he offers and gives in. Scene 3: Porgy returns, triumphant after his release from gaol. When Bess fails to appear, he becomes desperate ('Oh Bess, Oh Where's My Bess'). The others finally tell him that she has gone to New York with Sporting Life; he resolves to follow her there and get her back. As the curtain falls, he starts on his journey ('Oh, Lawd, I'm on My Way').

With this score, Gershwin proved that the gifts he possessed – a gift for capturing emotion musically, theatrical skill, and the ability to accommodate and accentuate the skills of his chosen performers (in his first try at writing for classically trained voices, he succeeded masterfully) – count for far more in operatic composition than some of the academic techniques he lacked. His song-writing genius had not deserted him, of course; *Porgy* contains one hit after another. But each is precisely suited to its place in the drama, and hardly any observe the standard 32-bar form. If some of the connecting material sounds more dutiful than inspired, much of it fulfils its purpose effectively; different textures and rhythms are tellingly contrasted, and a few significant motifs recur effectively at key points (Porgy, Crown, Sporting Life, and the 'happy dust' are among the motivically defined elements). Larger musical recurrences play a role too: Porgy's solos in the first scene contain seeds of music to come in Act II (harmony for 'I Got Plenty o' Nuttin'', a melody for 'Bess, You Is My Woman'), and a jazzy strain associated with Catfish Row's social life is turned into a gentle barcarolle for the fishermen's fateful departure. As representative examples of resourcefulness in making the most of the libretto's potential, one might mention the powerful succession of recitative, arioso, and duet that comprises the scene between Bess and Crown (written by Heyward as a simple prose dialogue), the six simultaneous unmeasured prayers of the hurricane scene and the rhythmic and vocal contrasts that shape 'My Man's Gone Now'. Indeed, the entire scene containing this impassioned solo shows Gershwin's genius at achieving overall unity through variety: linked choral passages, expressive recitative, one section of spoken dialogue, and two arias (with chorus) combine to create a uniquely varied picture of grief. Even with its minor imperfections and infelicities acknowledged, *Porgy* stands as the most vital and completely successful of American operas. One of the great might-have-beens of 20th-century music is the thought of the scores Gershwin could have gone on to write if he had lived beyond the age of 38.

RECORDINGS 1. Dale, Lane, Shakesnider, Marshall, Albert, Smith. DeMain, RCA, 1976; 2. Mitchell, Hendricks, Quivar, Clemmons, White, Boatwright, Cleveland Ch and O, Maazel, Decca, 1976; 3. Hayman, Clarey, Blackwell, Evans, White, Baker, Glyndebourne Ch, LPO, Rattle, EMI, 1989: the Rattle recording has the excitement of a performance that originated in the opera house, but the older Maazel set, very well recorded, should not be ignored [A.B.]
FILM (adapted as a musical) Previn (cond.), Preminger (dir.), Goldwyn/Columbia, 1959
EDITION v.s., Gershwin/Chappell, 1935

Other musicals: *La-La-Lucille!*, 1919; *A Dangerous Maid*, 1921; *Our Nell* (coll. with William Daly), 1922; *Sweet Little Devil*, 1924; *Tell Me More*, 1925; *Song of the Flame* (coll. with Herbert Stothart), 1925; *Rosalie* (coll. with Sigmund Romberg), 1928; *Treasure Girl*, 1928; *Show Girl*, 1929
BIBLIOGRAPHY Charles Hamm, 'The Theatre Guild Production of *Porgy and Bess*', *JAMS*, vol. 40, no. 3 (fall 1987), pp. 495–532; Edward Jablonski, *Gershwin*, Doubleday, 1987; Robert Kimball and Alfred Simon, *The Gershwins*, Atheneum, 1973

J.A.C.

CHARLES-HUBERT GERVAIS
b 19 February 1671, Paris; *d* 15 January 1744, Paris

As well as holding important posts in the French Royal Chapel, Gervais had charge of the Duc d'Orléans's musical establishment. The duke (the future Regent) was a former pupil of Marc-Antoine Charpentier and, as such, developed a taste for Italian music. (He is said to have written some of the music of Gervais's *Penthée* (1705).) While Gervais's youthful *Méduse* (1697) shows little sign of Italian influence, his *tragédie Hypermnèstre* (1716) certainly does. Its action-packed plot unfolds in music that is both more diverse and more elaborate than that of most contemporary French opera and represents a successful fusion of native and foreign elements. Surprisingly in view of the considerable success of *Hypermnèstre* (it had three revivals, the last in 1765), Gervais reverted to a more traditional style in his final opera, the opéra-ballet *Les amours de Protée* (1720).

BIBLIOGRAPHY R. Fajon, *L'Opéra à Paris du Roi Soleil à Louis le Bien-Aimé*, Slatkine, 1984

G.S.

GIORGIO FEDERICO GHEDINI

b 11 July 1892, Cuneo, Piedmont, Italy; *d* 25 March 1965,
Nervi, nr Genoa, Italy

Ghedini was late in reaching artistic maturity. His
eclectic, relatively conservative early output attracted
little more than local attention in and around Turin,
where he worked as an assistant conductor and
teacher. Then suddenly, in the late 1930s and the
1940s, he found a bold, intensely personal idiom that
brought him into the forefront of modern Italian
music. The pieces with which he belatedly made his
name are mostly for the concert hall: three of the
most famous are *Architetture* (1940), the *Concerto
dell'albatro* (1945) and the *Concerto funebre per
Duccio Galimberti* (1948). But his major
compositions from this vintage period also include an
outstandingly impressive opera, *Le baccanti*, in which
the starkly sculpturesque manner of *Architetture* was
developed on a larger scale.

None of Ghedini's other stage works are on the
same level as *Le baccanti* (in all periods of his life he
remained an uneven, over-prolific composer). But his
first published opera, *Maria d'Alessandria* (1936),
though quite strongly influenced by Pizzetti, already
revealed its composer's own individual approach to
instrumental colour. *Re Hassan* (1937–8) marked a
further step towards maturity, and was successfully
revived in a new version at Naples in 1961. After the
culminating point represented by *Le baccanti*,
Ghedini wrote no more full-length operas. But the
two one-act pieces that rounded off his operatic
output both have at least curiosity value for the
English-speaking world. *Billy Budd* (1949) had the
misfortune to be overshadowed by Britten's larger
and more impressive version of the same subject,
which appeared just two years later; but Ghedini's
version of Max Beerbohm's *The Happy Hypocrite*
has proved more durable – at least in its original
form as the effectively characterized, deservedly
prize-winning radio opera *Lord Inferno* (1952),
which has often been broadcast in Italy.

Ghedini was much respected as a teacher: his many
distinguished pupils include Berio and Castiglioni.

Le baccanti

The Bacchae

Opera in a prologue and three acts (five scenes) (1h 45m)
Libretto by Tullio Pinelli, after the tragedy by Euripides
Composed 1941–4
PREMIERE   22 February 1948, La Scala, Milan

The opera retains the stylized, ritualistic quality of
ancient Greek tragedy, with much choral-writing and
an action featuring bold, simple movements and
gestures. The result is a kind of pagan stage oratorio
whose libretto, despite some liberties, remains
essentially true to Euripides. Pentheus, the young
King of Thebes, is trying to rid his city of the wild,
corrupting influence of the new religion of Dionysus.
Even his own mother Agave has become caught up
in the cult. After two face-to-face encounters with
the god – whose identity he does not at first know –

and whom he imprudently tries to imprison –
Pentheus agrees to let Dionysus accompany him to
Mount Cithaeron, so that he can observe and then
confront the maenads. But they tear him to pieces
and impale his head on a thyrsus staff, which is then
carried back to Thebes by Agave. Only with difficulty does her father, the old King Cadmus, bring
her to her senses and make her understand that the
head she is carrying is that of her own son. Dionysus
then condemns Cadmus to be turned into a dragon,
and Agave to wander the world mourning Pentheus
for the rest of her life.

Ghedini's powerful, starkly dissonant score owes
something to Stravinsky and especially to his
Oedipus Rex. However, the influence is well
integrated into a personal style whose characteristic
interval patterns – which often undermine the key
sense without wholly destroying it – may also
occasionally suggest a distant affinity with Frank
Martin. There is an extended stretch of gentler, more
sweetly lyrical music in Act II, Scene 2; but the
sustained, rugged fierceness of so much of the rest
may reflect the fact that the opera was composed
during the Second World War.

When *Le baccanti* was new, the Italian public was
not yet ready to appreciate it: only after the revival in
Milan in 1972 did it achieve wider recognition (at
least in Italy) as the major achievement that it is.

EDITION   v.s., Ricordi, 1948

Other operas: *Gringoire*, (1915); *L'intrusa*, (1921); *Maria
d'Alessandria*, 1937; *Re Hassan*, 1939, (rev.
1961); *La pulce d'oro*, 1940; *Billy Budd*, 1949, *Lord
Inferno* (radio opera), 1952, rev. as *L'ipocrita felice*, 1956
BIBLIOGRAPHY   Niccolò Castiglioni, 'Ghedini – a Many-
Sided Composer', *Ricordiana*, vol. 10, no. 2 (April 1965),
pp. 4–7

J.C.G.W.

CHRISTOPHER GIBBONS

baptized 22 August 1615, London; *d* 20 October 1676, London

Christopher was the eldest surviving son of Orlando
Gibbons. When he received an Oxford doctorate in
1664 he was said to have served at court 'from his
youth', but there are no records of appointments
there until after the Restoration. He lived in Exeter
with his uncle Edward Gibbons after his father's
death in 1625; in 1638 he became organist at
Winchester Cathedral. During the Commonwealth
(1649–60) he taught music in London, where he took
part in at least two dramatic productions: he played
in Davenant's operatic play *The Siege of Rhodes*
(1656) and some of his music is included in the score
Matthew Locke compiled for the 1659 production of
James Shirley's masque *Cupid and Death*; in its
original 1653 form it may have had music by Gibbons
alone. Christopher Gibbons was a colourful man – a
'grand debauchee' (Anthony Wood) – who wrote
colourful music, 'very bold, solid, and strong, but

desultory and not without a little of the barbaresque' (Roger North).

EDITION Edward J. Dent (ed.), *Musica Britannica*, vol. 2, Stainer and Bell, 1951
BIBLIOGRAPHY Edward J. Dent, *Foundations of English Opera*, CUP, 1928; *rp*, Da Capo, 1965; Ellen T. Harris, *Handel and the Pastoral Tradition*, OUP, 1980

P.H.

JEAN GILBERT

Max Winterfeld; *b* 11 February 1879, Hamburg; *d* 20 December 1942, Buenos Aires

Gilbert studied music in provincial Germany and then Berlin, becoming a theatre conductor first in his native Hamburg and then at the Apollo-Theater in Berlin. He quickly adapted the saucy, breezy, music-hall-tinged Berliner style and became one of its leading exponents, along with Lincke and Kollo. He contributed to numerous revues, farces, and operettas, having a substantial hit in 1907 in Magdeburg with *Die keusche Susanne – Modest Suzanne* in New York and *The Girl in the Taxi* in London (both 1912).

Autoliebchen and *Puppchen*, and *Die Kinokönigin* were Gilbert's greatest pre-First World War successes, while post-war hits included *Die Frau im Hermelin* and *Katja, die Tänzerin*, which were seen all over Europe. In 1933, Gilbert was forced to emigrate to South America, where his works, especially *La casta Suzanna* (*Die keusche Susanne*), are still heard occasionally. His son, Robert Gilbert, was the leading English-to-German translator of American musicals, including *My Fair Lady*, and also wrote numerous German-language songs for operettas and musical films.

Operettas: *Das Jungfernstift*, 1901; *Jou Jou*, 1902; *Der Prinzregent*, 1903; *Die keusche Susanne*, 1910; *Polnische Wirtschaft*, 1910; *Die moderne Eva*, 1911; *Die elfte Muse*, 1912; *Puppchen*, 1912; *Das Jungfernstift*, 1912; *Das Autoliebchen*, 1912; *Die Kinokönigin*, rev. of *Die elfte Muse*, 1913; *Fräulein Trallala*, 1913; *Die Tangoprinzessin*, 1913; *Die Reise um die Erde in vierzig Tagen*, 1913; *Die Sünden des Lulatsch*, 1914; *Wenn der Frühling kommt*, 1914; *Kamr'rad Männe*, 1914; *Woran wir denken*, 1914; *Jung muss man sein*, 1915; *Drei Paar Schuhe*, 1915; *Das Fräulein vom Amt*, 1915; *Arizonda*, 1916; *Blondinchen*, 1916; *Die Fahrt ins Glück*, 1916; *Die Dose Sr. Majestät*, 1917; *Der verliebte Herzog*, 1917; *Ehurlaub*, 1918; *Der ersten Liebe golden Zeit*, 1918; *Das Vagabundenmädel*, 1918; *Zur wilden Hummel*, 1918; *Die Schönste von allen*, 1919; *Die Frau im Hermelin*, 1919; *Onkel Muz*, 1920; *Prinzessin Olala*, 1921; *Die Braut des Lukullus*, 1921; *Katja die Tänzerin*, 1923; *Dorine und der Zufall*, 1923; *Die kleine Sünderin*, 1923; *Das Weib im Purpur*, 1923; *Die Geliebte Sr. Hoheit*, 1924; *Der Gauklerkönig*, 1924; *Zwei um Eine*, 1924; *Annemarie*, 1925; *Uschi*, 1925; *Der Lebenskünstler*, 1925; *Das Spiel um die Liebe*, 1925; *In der Johannisnacht*, 1926; *Lene, Lotte, Liese – Josefinens Töchter*, 1926; *Eine Nacht in Kairo*, 1928; *Hotel Stadt Lemberg*, 1929; *Das Mädel am Steuer*, n.d.; *Onkel Kasimir*, n.d.; *So bummeln wir*, n.d.; Die Dame mit dem Regenbogen, 1933

BIBLIOGRAPHY Otto Schneidereit, *Operette A–Z*, Henschelverlag, 1971

R.T.

ALBERTO GINASTERA

b 11 April 1916, Buenos Aires; *d* 25 June 1983, Geneva

Ginastera established his reputation as the leading Argentinian composer of his generation, and musical spokesman of the indigenous Indian and *gauchesco* traditions, with two ballets: *Panambí* (1940) and *Estancia* (1943). His work skilfully combines nationalistic traits with modern techniques, notably serialism (though rarely strict). He was fascinated by ritual, magic and man's solitude and cruelty; sexual violence and supercharged political intrigue are constant themes in his three operas. Ginastera was commissioned by the New York City Opera to write an opera on the story of Barabbas for the American Bicentennial in 1976, but it remained incomplete.

Don Rodrigo

Opera in three acts, Op. 31 (1h 30m)
Composed 1963–4
Libretto by Alejandro Casona
PREMIERES 24 July 1962, Teatro Colón, Buenos Aires; US: 22 February 1966, New York State Theater, Lincoln Center, New York

Set in 8th-century Toledo, the plot concerns Don Rodrigo, the last Visigoth king of Spain. Initially acclaimed a hero, Rodrigo is crowned king with splendid ceremony. But an ancient curse foretelling the Moorish rebellion, together with his rape of the governor of Ceuta's daughter, Florinda, lead to his eventual downfall and death.

The outstanding musical feature is Ginastera's use of serial technique, particularly to symbolize Rodrigo and Florinda. The nine scenes are organized with Bergian symmetry around a central event (Florinda's rape), with Rodrigo's heroic first appearance mirrored in his death, his coronation anticipating his defeat, and so forth. The dazzling orchestral palette includes 18 offstage horns sounding hunting calls from around the theatre, and 25 bells used at the end of the opera to ring a chord of hope for Spain after the Moorish rebellion. Heroically nationalistic and dramatically opulent, the work is Expressionistic in musical style.

EDITION v.s., Boosey & Hawkes, 1969

Bomarzo

Opera in two acts, Op. 34 (2h 15m)
Libretto by Manuel Mujico Láinez, after his novel (1962)
Composed 1966–7
PREMIERES 19 May 1967, Lisner Auditorium, Washington DC; UK: 3 November 1976, Coliseum, London (New Opera Company)

The opera recounts, scene by scene, episodes from the life of the evil Duke of Bomarzo in 16th-century

Pantasilea (Joanna Simon) and the Duke of Bomarzo (Salvador Novoa) in Ginastera's opera (Washington, 1967)

Beatrix Cenci

Opera in two acts, Op. 38
Libretto by William Shand and Alberto Girri
Composed 1971
PREMIERE 10 September 1971, Kennedy Center, Washington DC

Ginastera's preoccupation with violence and the downfall of nobility continues in this harrowing setting of the story of Francesco Cenci, who was murdered by his family in 1598 after imprisoning his wife and raping his daughter Beatrix. Renaissance musical forms are again employed, for example in the opera's one moment of light relief, the dances 'in the ancient style' for the masked ball. Greek dramatic forms also reappear, together with an eclectic musical vocabulary which expands still further that of the earlier operas: serialism, clusters, aleatoric sounds, indeterminacy and microtonality. Certain staging effects and the use of flashback are reminders that Ginastera was an experienced composer of film music.

EDITION f.s./v.s., Boosey & Hawkes (on hire), 1971

BIBLIOGRAPHY Alberto Ginastera, 'How and Why I Wrote *Bomarzo*', *Central Opera Service Bulletin*, no. 9 (May–June 1967), pp. 10–13; Irving Lowens, 'Ginastera's *Beatrix Cenci*', *Tempo*, no. 105 (1973), pp. 48–53; Pola Suarea Urtubey, 'Alberto Ginastera's *Don Rodrigo*', *Tempo*, no. 74 (1965), pp. 11–18

S.J.W.

Italy, from his childhood, through his marriage, the murder of his brother (with whom he suspects his wife, Julia Farnese, is unfaithful), and his own death at the hand of his nephew, avenging his father. Much of the opera is extremely violent and after the Washington premiere the mayor of Buenos Aires banned the scheduled South American premiere on grounds of immorality. This prompted Ginastera to prohibit performances of his music in Argentina until the work, dubbed by one critic 'Porno in Belcanto', was finally given at the Colón in 1972.

Bomarzo continues themes and techniques explored in *Don Rodrigo*; it begins on the chord cluster with which *Don Rodrigo* ends, and formal organization and symmetry are features of the work. Also like *Don Rodrigo*, it divides into structures reproducing the Greek dramatic forms of exposition, crisis, and *dénouement*, both in the entire opera and also in individual scenes. The opera contains an eclectic variety of music. Twelve-note techniques are explored more fully than in *Don Rodrigo*; aleatoric choral passages and Renaissance musical forms are also employed. Ideas from *Cantata Bomarzo* (1964) were expanded for the opera and Ginastera later extracted a concert suite (1967, rev. 1970).

RECORDING Penagos, Simon, Turner, Novoa, Ch and O of Opera Society of Washington, Rudel, American Columbia, 1967
EDITION v.s., Boosey & Hawkes (on hire), 1967

TOMMASO GIORDANI

b c. 1733, Naples; *d* late February 1806, Dublin

Tommaso Giordani's father Giuseppe ran a celebrated travelling opera company consisting almost exclusively of members of his own family. Tommaso probably played the harpsichord with them. They first came to London in 1753 and performed Cocchi's highly successful burletta *Gli amante gelosi* at Covent Garden. In 1756 the company visited Dublin and performed *Gli amanti gelosi* and an Italianate version of *The Beggar's Opera* at Smock Alley; for this visit 'the band was strengthened for the season and the clarinet introduced for the first time in Ireland'. Tommaso had a great success with his operetta *Love in Disguise*, in which the lead part was taken by the great castrato Tenducci.

In 1768 Giordani returned to London, and spent the next 14 years at the King's Theatre, where he turned out music for over 50 operas (including several collaborations, according to the custom of the time). He also composed many songs for Vauxhall Gardens and for numerous pasticcios as well as the original songs for Sheridan's *The Critic*. The best-known work attributed to him is the song 'Caro mio ben', familiar in collections of *Arie Antiche*.

His attempt to found an English opera house in Dublin after 1783 failed and he soon went bankrupt.

Giordani's numerous stage works are lost except for the following, published in whole or in part: *The Elopement*, 1767; *L'omaggio* (coll.), 1781; *Gibraltar*, 1783; *The Haunted Castle*, 1783; *The Island of Saints, or The Institution of the Shamrock*, 1785

BIBLIOGRAPHY Highfill, Burnim and Langhans, *A Biographical Dictionary of Actors, Actresses, Musicians . . . in London, 1660–1800*, South Illinois University Press, 1973; T. J. Walsh, *Opera in Dublin, 1705–1797*, Allen Figgis, 1973

T.T.C.

UMBERTO GIORDANO

b 28 August 1867, Fóggia, Italy; *d* 12 November 1948, Milan, Italy

Giordano studied at the Naples Conservatory and became caught up in the *verismo* movement after the sensational success of Mascagni's *Cavalleria rusticana* (1890). His first opera in this vein, *Mala vita* (1892), which tells of a labourer who vows to reform a prostitute if the Virgin will heal his tuberculosis, created a scandal for its sordidness. It was revised and performed five years later, retitled *Il voto*, but failed to improve Giordano's standing. In the meantime Giordano's next opera, *Regina Diaz* (1894), saw the composer retreat from *verismo* into the outworn world of romantic melodrama. However, this fared no better than *Mala vita* and it survived for only two performances. The same year Giordano left Naples for Milan with hopes of better fortune.

Success came at last with *Andrea Chénier* (1896). The French Revolutionary subject and Illica's literate libretto moved Giordano to write music of passionate conviction. It was followed by *Fedora* (1902), based on a play by Sardou; its ingenious and powerful second act has helped maintain the work on Italian stages. These works represent a plateau of accomplishment that Giordano never attained again. A few of Giordano's later operas have survived on gramophone records or in occasional revivals. *Marcella* is remembered for one aria ('O santa liberta!') for which Italian tenors have a weakness.

Giordano was not without talent, but he lacked the essential resourcefulness and inventiveness to develop beyond his own limitations. He had two veins: one, an emphatic, occasionally strident, emotionalism: and the other, a graceful and predictable nattering that rarely rises above the level of salon music. The shifting of gears between these is all too often crude.

Andrea Chénier

Dramma di ambiente storico in four acts (2h 15m)
Libretto by Luigi Illica
Composed 1894–6
PREMIERES 28 March 1896, La Scala, Milan; US: 13 November 1896, Academy of Music, New York; UK: 16 April 1903, Camden Town Hall, London
CAST Andrea Chénier *t*, Carlo Gérard *bar*, Maddalena di Coigny *s*, Contessa di Coigny *ms*, Bersi *ms*, Madelon *ms*, Roucher *b*, Pietro Fléville *bar*, Fouquier-Tinville *bar*,

Mathieu *bar*, the Abbé *t*, an 'Incroyable' *t*, Majordomo *b*, Schmidt *b*; *satb* chorus of courtiers, ladies, soldiers, servants, peasants, prisoners, merchants, etc.
LARGE ORCHESTRA including hp; onstage: bd, 8 small drums

A successful combination of naturalism and historical drama, *Andrea Chénier* has remained a popular repertoire piece since its premiere. Illica's libretto (which, he claimed in a note in the vocal score, did not draw on historical fact but was based on ideas suggested by the editors of the real-life Chénier's poetic works) had originally been written for Alberto Franchetti. Franchetti ceded it to Giordano, who made use of the French Revolutionary background, spicing the opera with quotations of period tunes. The characters are scarcely developed, but the opera is kept alive with effective solos for the three principals and a surging final duet.

SYNOPSIS

Act I The Contessa de Coigny is giving a *soirée*, at which her daughter Maddalena is struck by the ardent libertarianism of the poet Chénier, but the fête is interrupted by peasants in revolt, led by a servant, Gérard, who tears off his livery. The intruders are sent away, and the Countess's guests resume their gavotte.

Act II Five years later, Chénier is disillusioned by the excesses of the Terror, and his friend Roucher, who has procured him a passport, urges him to go abroad. He hesitates because an unknown woman has written to him, asking for an appointment that very evening. It is Maddalena who seeks out Chénier's protection. Gérard, now Robespierre's agent, appears and tries to abduct Maddalena, but Chénier wounds him, while Roucher spirits the girl away. When Gérard is asked to identify his assailant, he generously says he cannot.

Act III Chénier has been arrested, and Gérard denounces him as a counter-revolutionary. Maddalena comes to Gérard and begs him to save Chénier, even at the cost of giving herself to him. At his trial, in spite of Chénier's stirring self-defence, Gérard is unable to prevent the sentence of death.

Act IV Chénier awaits execution at the prison of St Lazare. With Gérard's help Maddalena comes, substituting herself for another prisoner, to die with Andrea.

Giordano's quest for veristic naturalism led to the inclusion of the Revolutionary songs 'Ça ira', the 'Carmagnole' and the 'Marseillaise', and contrasting (but historically equally accurate) 18th-century dances and pastoral music. Set against these are the beautiful lyrical melodies for which the opera is famous – Chénier's 'Improvviso', Gérard's 'Nemico della patria', Maddalena's 'La mamma morta', and the final duet 'Vicino a te'. The chorus, representing the 'people' in their many guises, plays a larger than usual part, the violence of some of their music (their part is marked *urlando* – 'yelling' – at one point) making a significant contribution to the *verismo* nature of the work.

Umberto Giordano with Rosetta Pampanini, Benjamino Gigli and other cast members of Andrea Chénier *(Milan, c. 1937)*

RECORDINGS   1. Caniglia, Gigli, Bechi, La Scala Ch and O, De Fabritiis, EMI, 1941: Gigli in his favourite role, but the rest a bit rough; 2. Milanov, Del Monaco, Warren, Metropolitan Ch and O, Cleva, Nuova Era, recorded 1954; 3. Scotto, Domingo, Milnes, John Alldis Ch, National PO, Levine, RCA, 1976: well cast, modern version [A.B.]
VIDEOS   1. Martin, Carreras, Cappuccilli, Ch and O of La Scala, Chailly, Castle, 1985; 2. Tomara Sintow, Domingo, Zancanero, Ch and O of Covent Garden, Castle, 1983: both videos of live recordings with strong casts
EDITIONS   f.s., Sonzogno, 1896; v.ss., Sonzogno, 1896, 1931

Fedora

Melodramma in three acts (1h 45m)
Libretto by Arturo Colautti, after the play by Victorien Sardou (1882)
Composed 1897–8
PREMIERES   17 November 1898, Teatro Lirico, Milan; UK: 5 November 1906, Covent Garden, London; US: 5 December 1906, Metropolitan, New York

Encouraged by the success of *Andrea Chénier*, Giordano soon produced another *verismo* opera which was again popular and secured more than a reputation for its composer: word at the time was that '*Fedora* fè d'oro' ('*Fedora* made money'). Like *Chénier* the opera has a revolution as its background, but the action is carried out principally in salons (with the exception of the short final act set in Switzerland) which excludes the 'people', prominent

in the earlier opera, and largely eliminates opportunities for choral writing.

In St Petersburg, Princess Fedora comes to visit her fiancé, Count Vladimiro. Shortly thereafter he is brought in, mortally wounded, and his assassin is alleged to be Count Loris Ipanov, who escaped. The suspected motive is a nihilist *coup*. When Vladimiro dies, Fedora vows to avenge him. Fedora and Loris go to Paris, where at a *soirée* she finds herself drawn to him, but she remembers her oath on Vladimiro's corpse and denounces Loris, along with his family, to a police agent. Fedora asks Loris why he killed Vladimiro. Loris frankly confesses it was a point of honour; he had caught him with his wife Wanda. Transported by love and pity, Fedora throws herself into his arms. Later, Fedora and Loris are living blissfully in the Swiss Oberland, when word comes from Moscow that Loris's brother has drowned in prison when the Neva overflowed into his cell; his mother has died of grief. Loris guesses that Fedora has been hounding his family and curses her. Fedora has recourse to poison that she carries in a Byzantine cross and, dying, begs Loris's forgiveness, which he grants with a final kiss.

The score of *Fedora* contains routine and trivial music, but Giordano's lyric gift sustains a number of agreeable arias, the most familiar of which is Loris's 'Amor ti vieta' (Act II). A novel effect is obtained when a pianist entertains the guests at the *soirée* with a Chopinesque nocturne, while Fedora and Loris converse tensely.

RECORDING 1. Olivero, Del Monaco, Gobbi, Ch and O of Monte Carlo Opera, Gardelli, Decca, 1969; 2. Marton, Carreras, Martin, Ch and O of Hungarian Radio and Television, Patanè, CBS, 1986
EDITIONS f.s., Sonzogno, 1898; v.ss., Sonzogno 1898, 1941

Siberia

Opera in three acts (1h 30m)
Libretto by Luigi Illica
Composed 1901–3, rev. 1927
PREMIERES 19 December 1903, La Scala, Milan; US: 13 January 1906, French Opera House, New Orleans; rev. version: 5 December 1927, La Scala, Milan; UK: 7 December 1972, Old Town Hall, Fulham, London

Giordano's music finds many opportunities for vehemence in this silly plot about the mistress of a St Petersburg prince who follows her lover, an army officer, to a Siberian prison camp and is shot trying to escape with him. The opera was quite widely performed when it was new, mainly on the strength of Giordano's reputation, but the score is basically a crude contrivance with local colour supplied by quotations from 'The Song of the Volga Boatmen'.

RECORDING Maragliano, Londi, Zambon, Monachesi, Milan Ch and O of Italian Radio, Belardinelli, MRF, 1974
EDITIONS f.s., Sonzogno, 1903; v.ss., Sonzogno, 1903; rev. version, 1927

Madame Sans-Gêne

Commedia in three acts (2h 15m)
Libretto by Renato Simoni, after the play by Victorien Sardou and Emile Moreau (1890)
Composed 1913–14
PREMIERES 25 January 1915, Metropolitan, New York; Italy: 28 February 1915, Teatro Regio, Turin

Derived from a successful play by Sardou (who also wrote *Tosca*, the play on which Puccini's opera was based) and Moreau, this comic opera tells the story of an ex-laundress promoted in the French Revolution to be Duchess of Danzig, but who refuses to abandon her rough and plebeian manner at court.

Giordano tries to endow his score with something approaching the pace of the original play. The laundress Caterina and her husband Lefebvre both have moments of lyric expansiveness (Caterina's 'Gli avrei detto: tenetevele' is the opera's best-known aria), but the score, for all its superficial attractiveness and Toscanini's conducting of the premiere, failed to prove memorable.

RECORDING Santunione, Fr. Tagliavini, Tagger, Zanasi, Capecchi, Ch and O of La Scala, Gavazzeni, MRF, 1967
EDITIONS f.s./v.s. Sonzogno, 1914

La cena delle beffe

The Feast of the Jesters
Poema drammatico in four acts (1h 45m)
Libretto by Sem Benelli, from his play (1917)
Composed 1923–4

PREMIERES 20 December 1924, La Scala, Milan; US: 2 January 1926, Metropolitan, New York; Ireland: 22 October 1987, Theatre Royal, Wexford

With some justification this work has been described as 'the most sadistic of *verismo* operas'. The action takes place in Florence at the time of Lorenzo il Magnifico. The grisly plot deals with the brutal and complicated revenge of poor Giannetto, who had been thrown in the Arno and stabbed by the Chiaramantesi brothers, Neri and Gabriello, angered by Gianetto's love for Neri's mistress Ginevra. In the end Neri is tricked into stabbing his own brother, whom he mistakes for Giannetto.

Giordano's choice of Sem Benelli as his librettist is an indication, echoed by the score, that he aimed to move away from strongly *veristic* opera. Although the plot is in the best *verismo* tradition, the characters' emotions and the structure of the text lean more towards an older convention; one example of this is the non-naturalistic scene in Act IV where Gabriello and Ginevra, having been viciously stabbed by Neri, find time to sing a farewell to life before they die. Giordano eschewed a chorus and concentrated instead on integrating ensembles among some of the 15 solo roles into a continuous texture. Despite the variety of elements in the score, however, much of the music is undistinguished and rarely takes wing. The most successful is a hymn to May in the vein of a Tuscan *stornello*, sung by an offstage voice (Act IV).

RECORDING Lantieri, Manci, Armiliato, Chingari, Piacenza SO, Sanzogno, Bongiovanni, 1989
EDITIONS f.s./v.s. Sonzogno, 1924

Il re

The King
Novella in three acts (1h 30m)
Libretto by Giovacchino Forzano
Composed 1927–8
PREMIERE 12 January 1929, La Scala, Milan

Colombello loves the miller's daughter, Rosalina, but she suddenly announces that she has fallen in love with the king, whom she saw passing one day. The king, hearing of this, arranges for Rosalina to spend the night with him, and when she sees him without his regalia, as an ugly old man with a cane, she calls for Colombello. The king pronounces her cured and insists that she and Colombello marry immediately and accept gifts from him.

Il re moves away from veristic subjects into a world of fantasy. Giordano's lighter vein exerts a certain charm in this unpretentious work. There are several graceful intermezzi, allowing the opera to be played without an interval, and a touching aria in Act I ('Colombello sposarti') for Rosalina, whose music is liberally laced with *fioriture* up to high E.

RECORDING Baggiore, Jankovich, Ferrara, Turtura, Ch and O of Foggia Opera, Biondi, MRF, 1971: live
EDITIONS f.s./v.s., Sonzogno, 1928

Other operas: *Marina*, (*c.* 1889); *Mala vita*, 1892; *Regina Diaz*, 1894; *Il voto* (rev. of *Mala vita*), 1897; *Marcella*, 1907; *Mese mariano*, 1910 (RECORDING Colosseum, 1952); *Giove a Pompeii* (coll. with Franchetti), (*c.* 1901), 1921; *La festa del Nilo* (inc.), (n.d.)
BIBLIOGRAPHY   D. Cellamare, *Umberto Giordano*, Palombi, 1967; H. Krehbiel, *A Second Book of Operas*, chapter 16, Garden City Press, 1916

W.A.

PEGGY GLANVILLE-HICKS
b 29 December 1912, Melbourne, Australia; *d* 25 June 1990, Sydney, Australia

Although for many years an expatriate, living in the US (1942–59) and then in Greece, Peggy Glanville-Hicks returned to her native Australia in 1975. She studied composition in Melbourne from the age of 15 then won a scholarship to the Royal College of Music in London, where her teacher was Vaughan Williams. A scholarship enabled her to study in Vienna with Egon Wellesz and in Paris with Nadia Boulanger. She won many more grants and scholarships which facilitated her studies of Indian music and demotic Greek music, interests reflected in the operas *The Transposed Heads* and *Nausicaa*. She was the first Australian composer to have a work played in an ISCM Festival concert (*Choral Suite*, 1938). She was also an important writer on music theory and criticism, and a colleague of Virgil Thomson as a critic on the *New York Herald Tribune* (1948–58). A leading participant in the formation of the International Music Fund, founded to assist musicians who had suffered as a result of the Second World War, she organized many avant-garde musical events in the US and championed young composers and new music. Her varied output includes several ballet scores for the American choreographer John Butler and an opera, *Sappho*, for Maria Callas.

The Transposed Heads
Opera in one act (six scenes) (1h 30m)
Libretto by the composer, based on the story by Thomas Mann
PREMIERES   4 April 1954, Louisville, Kentucky; 1970, Sydney

The Transposed Heads was commissioned and performed by the Louisville Opera Company and later performed in New York and Australia. The music combines 20th-century Western composition techniques and Eastern-style music, without being openly derivative.

RECORDING   Nossaman, Harlan, Pickett, Louisville Opera Company and O, Bombard, LOU, 1954
EDITION   v.s., Associated Music, 1958

Nausicaa
Opera in three acts (2h)
Libretto by the composer and Robert Graves, after Graves's novel *Homer's Daughter*

PREMIERE   19 August 1961, Theatre of Herod Atticus, Athens

The work, as described by the composer, 'followed a kind of artistic journey to the source of the river, both in musical idioms and in forms, that led to a study of antique and folk material on one hand, Greek theatre concepts on the other'.

RECORDING   excerpts: Stratas, Steffan, Ruhl, Modenos, Malas, Athens Symphony Ch and O, Surinach, CRI, 1961
EDITION   v.s., Franco Colombo, 1961

Other operas: *Cadmon*, 1933; *Rapunzel*, 1958; *The Glittering Gate*, 1959; *Sappho*, 1966
BIBLIOGRAPHY   Jane Weiner LePage, *Women Composers, Conductors, and Musicians of the Twentieth Century*, The Scarecrow Press, 1983

A.I.G.

PHILIP GLASS
b 31 January 1937, Baltimore, Maryland, US

Glass is the leading composer of so-called minimalist opera in the late 20th century. He is also one of the most widely performed composers in the world. During 1988, for instance, no fewer than eight of his full-length stage works with more or less continuous music (the simplest way of defining the 'operatic' in an output as varied as it is already alarmingly extensive) were performed. Several works have had more than one production, unusual these days for any composer under 60. Glass's operas are indisputably successful though their merits are hotly disputed.

Glass's compositions – like those of his fellow Americans La Monte Young, Terry Riley and Steve Reich, who were exploring repetition and often clearly audible structural processes even earlier than he was – have become known as 'minimalist'. Certain similarities to the art of such figures as the sculptor Richard Serra (for whom Glass had acted as an assistant) provide justification for the label, though ironically the term 'minimalism' was not regularly applied to such music until the early 1970s, by which time Glass and others had begun to move away from their early repetitive rigour.

In 1967 Glass returned to the US from lengthy trips to Europe, where he had studied with Nadia Boulanger, and India. Between then and 1978 he wrote most of his compositions for the small amplified ensemble of flutes, saxophones and electric keyboards that still plays his music today, even though much of his energy since has been devoted to writing for the conventional opera house. While the earlier works' high energy level and sheer volume derived in part from rock music, their driving force technically was a rhythmic notion of additive process that came from classical North Indian music.

Glass's reputation prior to the world tour of *Einstein on the Beach* in 1976 was achieved primarily via his contribution to the New York 'downtown' scene which flourished in the 1960s and 1970s, with its crossing of the usual boundaries: between, for instance, the 'cultivated' and 'vernacular' traditions and often between the different media of music, theatre, film and other kinds of performance art, even including the 'fine' arts of painting and sculpture, etc. In fact, much of Glass's early music was written to accompany stage performances. Part of the reason for this was the close involvement of his first wife, JoAnne Akalaitis, with the experimental theatre group Mabou Mines, active first in Paris (the couple's base before 1967) and later in New York. Non-Western theatrical traditions, including those of Indian Khatikali, also encouraged increasingly close collaboration between the writers, designers, directors, actors and musicians involved in the group's experimental productions.

The culmination of this activity came with *Einstein on the Beach*, the brainchild of the American Robert Wilson, who was responsible for the work's basic conception and visual realization (the description of Wilson as 'director–designer' scarcely does justice to his theatrical role). Though sometimes described as an opera, *Einstein* is perhaps more logically regarded as a manifestation of what Wilson himself referred to as the 'theatre of images'.

After *Einstein*, Glass's best-known stage works moved closer to conventional notions of opera. *Satyagraha*, *Akhnaten*, *The Making of the Representative for Planet 8* and *The Voyage*, together with the chamber opera *The Fall of the House of Usher*, all largely eschew the ambiguities of *Einstein*, and substitute aspects more familiar from 18th- and 19th-century operatic practice.

The 'theatre of images' still, however, plays an important part in Glass's work. *The Photographer*, the two contributions to Wilson's *CIVIL WarS* project, *1,000 Airplanes on the Roof* and *Hydrogen Jukebox* all avoid the forces normally found in the opera house; some were written for the composer's own ensemble. Perhaps more importantly, their approach to both dramatic and musical continuity brings them closer to the world of *Einstein* than to opera as conventionally defined. Yet the extent to which they remain disputed territory (even in the composer's own mind) is itself an important dimension of their vitality. Glass also continues to be particularly active as a composer for films and television, as well as for the concert hall.

Einstein on the Beach

Opera in four acts [and five 'kneeplays'] (4h 30m)
Spoken texts by Christopher Knowles, Samuel M. Johnson and Lucinda Childs
Composed 1974–5
PREMIERES 25 July 1976, Avignon Festival;
US: 21 November 1976, Metropolitan, New York
CAST s, t, Einstein *violinist*, actors, dancers; *satb* chorus (16 voices including second solo s and t) sometimes in the pit, sometimes part of the action
ORCHESTRATION 3 wind-players (doubling fl, saxes and b cl), 2 electric organs, vn (see above)

Behind the conception and realization of *Einstein on the Beach* lay Robert Wilson's approach to

performance art. Wilson's starting points are usually visual rather than textual: here a set of drawings to which Glass would respond by writing music, which in turn influenced a reworking of the drawings, which inspired further music and so on.

Einstein, according to its creators, concerns not only the German physicist Albert Einstein but also 'science, technology and ecology'. It eventually became the first part in a trilogy of operas by Glass, each taking a major historical figure and a major human issue for its theme. Since narrative and characterization in the usual sense are absent, it is impossible to give a conventional synopsis. Choreographed movement of various kinds, by no means confined to 'dance', is more important than the text. In addition, the close relationship between dramatic structure and *misé-en-scène* inherent in Wilson's approach presents any other director with unusual problems.

The work is 'about' Einstein, the discoverer of relativity, whose activity as a keen amateur violinist leads to his portrayal not as a singer but (in Wilson's original production at least) as an elderly man who punctuates the action with extended violin solos. A train – which forms the first of three recurring images: the others are a courtroom and a spaceship – also suggests that Einstein's theory of relativity is, however obliquely, being practised on the audience; so also do such things as the slow eclipse of a handless clock by a large black disc in the first trial scene. Yet at the time of its composition, Glass said that he and Wilson merely 'tried to find out where Einstein was in the piece'. Act I offers the train and a trial scene; Act II the spaceship, hovering above a field of dancers, and then the train again, this time at night. In Act III the courtroom also resembles a prison, and the spaceship moves closer to the dancers. In Act IV all three images are developed more drastically: the train, for example, turning into a building.

While all this can be taken as the main action, the five 'kneeplays', which form the prologue, interludes and epilogue to the four acts, seem of equal significance, even though the first kneeplay is already in progress as the audience enters the auditorium. Their subject matter is, however, related only tenuously to that of the main acts. In the original production, two women sat at tables downstage right; in the fourth kneeplay they lay on glass tables, and for the fifth they became two lovers sitting on a park bench. Other images counterpointed their action (or inaction); all somehow related to experiments in relativity or more directly to Einstein himself.

The recitation of numbers and *solfège* syllables accounts for a significant part of the 'text'. In Wilson's production, eleven other texts were included, the majority provided by Christopher Knowles, an autistic boy whom Wilson had encountered while working with handicapped children. None of their imagery relates in any obvious way to the stage picture; their respect for grammar is somewhat intermittent. The only text – the single one written by Lucinda Childs – even to mention either Einstein or the beach (only the latter, in fact)

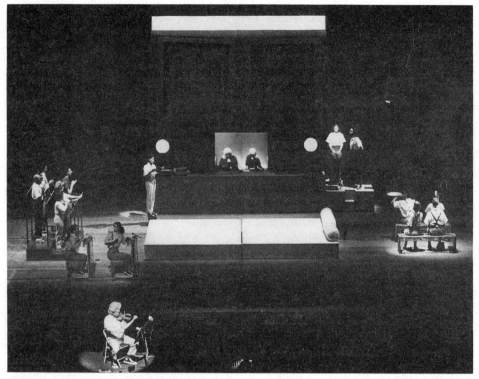

Einstein on the Beach *(New York, 1976)*

confines mention of the subject to avoiding the beach. Yet narrative, as well as grammatical, sense is by no means entirely forsaken in these texts, which are all spoken, never sung.

Musically, *Einstein* is crucially 'on the edge'. It retains not only a high degree of repetition but much of the non-developmental, 'non-narrative' approach of true minimalism. But while additive and cyclic rhythmic processes remain its driving forces, the more harmonically and melodically directed approach of Glass's later operas also begins to emerge. The impression that the grammar of a more familiar tonality is under reinvestigation is reinforced, in particular, by the use of chord sequences with clearly defined movement in the bass line.

RECORDING   LaBarbara, Zukovsky, Childs, Sutton, Johnson, Mann, Philip Glass Ensemble, Riesman, Tomato Records, 1979; *reissue*, CBS, 1985
EDITIONS   f.s./v.s. Dunvagen, 1984

Satyagraha: M. K. Gandhi in South Africa
Opera in three acts (2h 15m)
Libretto (in Sanskrit) by Constance DeJong and the composer, adapted by DeJong from the *Bhagavadgita*
PREMIERES   5 September 1980, Stadsschouwburg, Rotterdam; US: July 1981, Artpark, Lewiston, New York State
CAST   Miss Schlesen *s*, Mrs Naidoo *s*, Kasturbai *ms*, M. K. Gandhi *t*, Mr Kallenbach *bar*, Parsi Rustomji *b*, Mrs Alexander *a*, Arjuna *t*, Krishna *b*; *silent:* Count Leo Tolstoy,

Rabindranath Tagore, Martin Luther King; *satb* chorus of two hostile armies (Indians and Europeans), an Indian crowd, 8 European men; *silent:* 6 Indian workers, 6 Indian residents, 2 contemporary policemen
ORCHESTRATION   full ww, str, electric organ or synthesizer

Satyagraha became the second opera in Glass's trilogy. Based on Mahatma Gandhi's early years in South Africa, according to the composer it deals with 'politics: violence and non-violence'. *Satyagraha* literally means 'truth-force' but has come to stand for the concept of 'passive resistance'. The *Bhagavaadgita*, source of the libretto, is the Sanskrit religious text that was Gandhi's 'dictionary of daily reference'.

SYNOPSIS
Satyagraha covers the period from Gandhi's arrival in South Africa in 1893 to the New Castle March of 1913 (the event that brought the *Satyagraha* movement to an end in that country) as though it were a single day.

Act I introduces turn-of-the-century South Africa via a somewhat ambiguous invocation of the *Bhagavadgita*; Gandhi's workers build Tolstoy Farm and demonstrate against the imposition of identification cards.

Act II White resistance to Gandhi's arrival in Durban is thwarted by the wife of the superintendent of police; the newspaper *Indian Opinion* is set up and distributed; and identification cards are ceremonially burned in retaliation against the government's retraction of its promise to repeal the Black Act.

Act III The striking miners of New Castle and their families march with the *Satyagraha* army in peaceful protest against racial discrimination.

Satyagraha clarifies the crucial differences between Glass's early, minimalist music and his later, post-minimalist output. The opera is specifically concerned with the life of Gandhi who, while hardly subjected to conventional dramatic development, becomes a clearly delineated focus of attention. The structure of the opera is much more conventional than that of *Einstein*, with scenes and acts forming a sequence of tableaux. The use of Sanskrit encourages reflection on the moral lessons of each scene rather than engagement in the dynamic of narrative; the scenes of Gandhi's early life portrayed here do not, in any case, appear chronologically. In addition, the 'figurative counterpart' placed above the action of each of the opera's three acts – Count Leo Tolstoy, Rabindranath Tagore and Martin Luther King – suggest the historical continuity of what Gandhi's movement stood for.

Taken as a whole, however, the opera charts a readily comprehensible, conventionally motivated plot. Movement on stage plays a significant role, but the main thrust is conveyed through the conventions of solo aria, duets, trios, etc., and choral singing, in ways closely resembling those adopted by the traditional lyric stage. The more harmonically and melodically directed approach already noted in *Einstein* is here clarified by chaconne-like structures underpinning an often continuous flow of vocal melody.

RECORDING Cummings, Woods, Liss, Perry, Macfarland, Reeve, New York City Opera Ch and O, Keene, CBS, 1985
EDITIONS f.s./v.s. Dunvagen, 1979

Akhnaten

Opera in [a prologue,] three acts [and an epilogue] (2h 15m)
Libretto by the composer in association with Shalom Goldman, Robert Israel and Richard Riddell; drawn from Egyptian and Akkadian sources (some in English translation), Psalm 104 (in Hebrew), and sentences from Fodor's and Frommer's guides to Egypt
Composed 1980–83
PREMIERES 24 March 1984, Kleines Haus, Württembergischer Staatstheater, Stuttgart; US: 12 October 1984, Wortham Theater Center, Houston; UK: 17 June 1985, Coliseum, London
CAST Akhnaten *ct*, Nefertiti *a*, Queen Tye *s*, Horemhab *bar*, Aye *b*, High Priest of Amon *t*, Amenhotep *spoken role*, 6 daughters of Akhnaten and Nefertiti, 3 *s*, 3 *a*, funeral party, 4 *t*, 4 *b*; offstage: tourist guide (voice-over); *tb* chorus of mourners, priests of Amon, priests of Aten, soldiers, etc.; *satb* chorus of people of Thebes, Akhnaten's entourage, offstage chorus, people of Egypt, soldiers, outlawed priests of Amon; *silent*: funeral cortège, tourists; dancers; onstage musicians
FULL ORCHESTRA without vln, including 3 perc and synthesizer

Akhnaten, the final panel in the trilogy of operas beginning with *Einstein on the Beach*, has as its subject the Egyptian pharaoh of the 14th century BC

Akhnaten and his family; designs by Ilona and Achim Freyer for Glass's opera (Stuttgart, 1984)

and, more widely, 'religion: orthodoxy and reaction'. Sigmund Freud's *Moses and Monotheism* (1939) and Immanuel Velikovsky's *Oedipus and Akhnaton* (1960) were both crucial influences on the composer and his team of assistant librettists. Shalom Goldman compiled the text from original sources, and the opera is sung in ancient languages – Egyptian, Akkadian and Hebrew – as well as 'the language of the audience', which also serves for narration.

SYNOPSIS
The opera shows the rise and fall of Akhnaten in a series of tableaux. During an orchestral prelude, the narrator reads from ancient Pyramid texts to set the scene.

Act I The funeral of Amenhotep III, Akhnaten's father. Akhnaten's coronation is followed by a hymn announcing the revolution to come.

Act II Akhnaten launches an attack on the Amon temple, sings a love duet with his queen, Nefertiti, participates in a dance to mark the inauguration of the city of Akhetaten and sings his own 'Hymn to the Sun'.

Act III The progressive withdrawal of Akhnaten and his family from the world and the pharaoh's downfall are represented; the final scene moves to the present, as tourists visit what little remains of Akhnaten's former city.

The epilogue depicts the ghosts of Akhnaten and his entourage amid the ruins.

Akhnaten continues in the tradition of post-minimalist opera established by *Satyagraha*. Dramatically, it is concerned with a central character who – though somewhat distanced by voice type (David Freeman's Houston–London production also drew attention to Akhnaten's reputedly hermaphrodite aspect) – is sympathetically drawn and develops as a real human being. His pivotal 'Hymn to the Sun' in Act II is sung in 'the language of the audience', thus encouraging even greater identification. The sequence of scenes – here chronological, unlike in *Satyagraha* – may still be treated ritualistically (as in Achim Freyer's production); Freeman, however, attempted to demonstrate its propensity for dramatic development in tandem with the evolution of character.

Akhnaten has a wider musical range than its predecessor. The approach to harmony is often much darker and more chromatic. Careful consideration of overall key structure and the use of leitmotifs join the basic techniques already established in *Satyagraha*. Orchestration, too, is more subtle; the lack of violins provoked some original responses to the inevitably darker colouring, as well as an appropriate emphasis at times on somewhat militaristic wind and percussion; Akhnaten himself is frequently accompanied by a solo trumpet. The love duet for Akhnaten and his queen Nefertiti and Akhnaten's 'Hymn to the Sun' are powerfully lyrical utterances.

RECORDING   Esswood, Vargas, Liebermann, Hannula, Hauptmann, Holzapfel, Warrilow, Stuttgart State Opera Ch and O, Russell Davies, CBS, 1987
EDITIONS   f.s./v.s. Dunvagen, 1984

The Making of the Representative for Planet 8

Opera in three acts (17 scenes) (2h 15m)
Libretto by the composer and Doris Lessing, based on the novel by Lessing (1982)
Composed 1985–6
PREMIERES   8 July 1988, Wortham Theater Center, Houston; 9 November 1988, Coliseum, London

Doris Lessing's book is the fourth in a series of five with the overall title *Canopus in Argos: Archives*. Lessing says that *Planet 8* is concerned with 'loss of hope'. The story is of an innocent people meeting their physical end in the Ice Age that takes over their formerly temperate planet as a result of a shift in its axis; in the process, however, they come to a new understanding of their spiritual selves.

Though variously capable of interpretation as Christian, Sufist, or Third World allegory neatly encompassed within a single dramatic curve, the opera's 17 scenes retain a surprising amount of Lessing's prose. This results in a decision to alternate speech and sung text, which, though helping to deflect attention away from what is some of Glass's less memorable music, raises problems of dramaturgy. The composer's adoption of a vaguely leitmotivic as well as metrically very limited approach in conjunction with the new emphasis on text and narrative could in theory work well with better material, though the suspicion remains that Glass was unwise to set an entire opera to English words when also bringing narrative to the fore. The opera was jointly commissioned by four international houses in Houston, London, Amsterdam and Kiel.

EDITIONS   f.s./v.s. Dunvagen, 1988

The Fall of the House of Usher

Chamber opera in a prologue and two acts (1h 30m)
Libretto by Arthur Yorinks, based on the short story by Edgar Allan Poe (1837)
Composed 1987
PREMIERES   18 May 1988, American Repertory Theater, Cambridge, Massachusetts; UK: 9 August 1989, St Donat's Castle, Llantwit Major, Wales
CAST   William *t*, Roderick Usher *bar*, Madeline Usher *s*, Servant *b*, Physician *t*
CHAMBER ORCHESTRA   12 players

Poe's story of demented lust in a crumbling castle is well known; its air of Gothic horror and what Debussy (who never finished his *Usher* opera) called its 'sombre melancholy' are ideally suited to the more chromatic and doom-laden style Glass first developed in *Akhnaten*. Though first staged before *The Making of the Representative for Planet 8*, *The Fall of the House of Usher* was composed after it and exhibits a refinement lacking in *Planet 8*. The highly charged emotional content and structural compression of Poe's tale seem particularly well suited to the ambiguous ways in which Glass's exploration of familiar-sounding harmonic devices deals with tonal progression. Famously trounced by nearly all British critics, such an idiom perhaps works best when illustrating single emotional and dramatic states, as here, rather than attempting to match the cut and thrust of narrative, as in *Planet 8*.

Sunk in the weird introspection of Poe's text, which Glass sets with considerable rhythmic subtlety, *The Fall of the House of Usher* to some extent reclaims the more ambiguous territory between conventional opera and openly modernist notions of music-theatre, while doing full justice to a narrative of cumulative power and terrifying *dénouement*. As a result, it is one of Glass's best works since *Einstein*.

EDITIONS   f.s./v.s. Dunvagen, 1988

The Voyage

Opera in [a prologue,] three acts [and an epilogue] (3h)
Libretto by David Henry Hwang
PREMIERE   12 October 1992, Metropolitan, New York
CAST   The Scientist/1st Mate *t*, Commander *s*, Ship's Doctor/Space Twin 1 *s*, 2nd Mate/Space Twin 2 *lyric b*, Isabella *ms*, Columbus *b-bar*, Earth Twin 1 *ms*, Earth Twin 2 *b*; *satb* chorus of the Music of the Spheres, natives, the Spanish court

The Voyage was commissioned by the Metropolitan, New York, in commemoration of the 500th Anniversary of Columbus's arrival in America. It deals with the idea of voyage and exploration more as an activity of the mind and of the imagination than of geographical heroics.

SYNOPSIS
Prologue The Scientist (a character based on Stephen Hawking, the well-known physicist), though confined by illness to a wheelchair, encompasses the stars in his imagination.

Act I   A spaceship from outer space crashes on earth in prehistoric times. Each crew member takes one of the ship's directional crystals which will eventually link them again to their home planet. They are asked to imagine the time and place in

A scene from Act II of The Voyage *(New York, 1992)*

which they envisage existence on their new planet, and we see them journey towards these goals. The Commander in particular anticipates her sensual future among the 'natives', while they likewise await their new encounter with trepidation.

Act II   In 15th-century Spain Columbus is given a triumphant send-off at Isabella's court. But this turns out to be merely his vivid memory as he lies on his becalmed boat. He continues to fantasize that Isabella visits him on the boat; as his obsession with her reaches its climax, land is sighted.

Act III   The crystals from Act I have been found coincidentally by the Earth Twins. When these crystals are brought together the signals they emit lead the Space Twins to announce the discovery of a new planet. Another voyage sets off towards this new discovery.

Epilogue   Columbus is visited on his deathbed by the ghost of Isabella, unrepentant for her exploitation of his discoveries. He rejects her and his bed floats up to the stars.

The Voyage develops Glass's powerful choral writing, first shown in *Satyagraha*, to create a large-scale – even spectacular – work appropriate to the venue that commissioned it. In addition, Hwang's poetic and non-realistic text enables the music to remain at a distance from the narrative – as in *Einstein* and *Usher* – which is essential to its functioning in an operatic context.

EDITIONS   f.s./v.s. Dunvagen, 1992

Other operatic works: *Attacca – A Madrigal Opera*, 1980 (as *The Panther*, 1982; as *A Madrigal Opera*, 1985); *The Photographer*, 1982 (RECORDING CBS, 1983); *The CIVIL WarS* (Rome and Cologne Sections), 1984; *The Juniper Tree* (coll. with Robert Moran), 1985; *A Descent into the Maelstrom*, 1986; *1,000 Airplanes on the Roof*, 1988; *Hydrogen Jukebox*, 1990; *The White Raven*, 1993

BIBLIOGRAPHY   Constance DeJong and Philip Glass, *Satyagraha, M. K. Gandhi in South Africa, 1893–1914: The Historical Material and Libretto Comprising the Opera's Book*, Standard Editions, 1980; Philip Glass, edited and with supplementary material by Robert Jones, *Music by Philip Glass*, Dunvagen/Harper and Row, 1987; in UK as *Opera on the Beach: Philip Glass On His New World of Music Theatre*, Faber, 1988; John Rockwell, 'The Orient, the Visual Arts and the Evolution of Minimalism: Philip Glass', in *All American Music: Composition in the Late Twentieth Century*, Alfred A. Knopf, 1983; Vintage Books, 1984; Kahn and Averill, 1985, pp. 109–22

K.P.

REINHOLD GLIER

Reinhold Moritsevich Glier; *b* 11 January 1875, Kiev, Ukraine; *d* 23 June 1956, Moscow

Glier studied at the Moscow Conservatory with Arensky, Taneyev and Ippolitov-Ivanov, and became a legendary professor of composition there; he also gave private lessons to the young Prokofiev. He won numerous accolades and prizes throughout a long and successful career. He is considered the founder of Soviet ballet, his *The Red Poppy* (1927) being often performed. His operas have had wide currency within the Soviet Union, and several of them demonstrate his interest in ethnic music of the eastern republics. *Shakh-Senem*, premiered in Azerbaijan, uses Azerbaijani folk themes and is said to have established a tradition of professional opera and musical training in the republic. But Glier was a composer in the 19th-century Romantic tradition, his use of ethnic themes is Westernized and superficial, and he has been accused of 'Sovietizing' musical culture, thus suppressing more authentic Azerbaijani music. Other works include *Gyul'sara*, based on Tadzhik themes, and *Leyli and Mejnun* from Uzbekistan. Comparison of these works with Paliashvili's Georgian operas reveals how external the ethnic trappings are. Two non-operatic works hold the fringes of the repertoire: the 'Ilya Murometz' Symphony, revived by Stokowski, and a Concerto for coloratura soprano and orchestra, recorded by Joan Sutherland.

Operas: *Zemlya i nebo* (*Heaven and Earth*), 1900; *Shakh-Senem*, (1923), 1926, rev. 1934; *Gyul'sara*, 1937, rev. with Sadikov, 1949 (RECORDING Melodiya, 1960s); *Leyli and Mejnun*, 1940 (RECORDING Melodiya, 1970s); *Rachel*, 1942
BIBLIOGRAPHY   S. D. Krebs, *Soviet Composers*, George Allen and Unwin, 1970

J.G.

Glinka in 1854

MIKHAIL GLINKA

Mikhail Ivanovich Glinka; *b* 1 June 1804, Novospasskoye (now Glinka, Russia); *d* 15 February 1857, Berlin

Glinka was by no means the first Russian to compose opera, yet he is indisputably the founder of the Russian operatic tradition. Born into a minor landowning family, he was educated in St Petersburg, then settled into the role of a dilettante in the city's salons. Though he had had no proper musical education, he composed a good many undemanding songs and piano pieces, and shared in the current Russian taste for French opera, as well as for Rossini. But by the end of the 1820s Italian opera in general was becoming his central interest, and in 1830 he left for a three-year residence in Italy. He met Bellini, soaked himself in the Italian tradition, but by the end of his stay was turning against it; as he himself put it: 'I could not sincerely be Italian. A longing for my own country led me gradually to the idea of writing in a Russian manner.' On his return journey he delayed five months in Berlin for the only formal composition study of his whole life. The following year he began his first opera, *Ivan Susanin* (better known as *A Life for the Tsar*), and it was a sensation at its first performance in 1836.

Glinka promptly chose Pushkin's *Ruslan and Lyudmila* as the subject of his next opera, but the poet's death in a duel thwarted his hope that Pushkin himself would be the librettist. As it was, the totally unsystematic, even incompetent way in which the libretto was compiled, coupled with Glinka's equally unsystematic compositional process, could only result in a work hopelessly flawed, and it was a relative failure at its premiere in 1842.

Glinka's two operas are very different pieces. *A Life for the Tsar*, with its grand choruses and formal ballet, depended heavily on the French operatic tradition; but it treated a subject that was thoroughly Russian, and besides achieving an often remarkable synthesis of Italian and Russian melodic characteristics, Glinka devised a novel arioso-cum-recitative idiom for narrative and dialogue that was to become a fundamental element in many later Russian operas (*A Life for the Tsar* is the first Russian opera not to use spoken dialogue). The opera is very effective on the stage. By contrast, *Ruslan and Lyudmila* is dramatically a disaster. Nevertheless it represents a very remarkable achievement. Uneven the music may be, but there was abundant stimulus to the imagination in this fantastic tale of the supernatural set in a heroic past, and Glinka's music, at its imaginative best, was not only strikingly original and sometimes very beautiful, but also so new in a specially Russian way that later Russian composers could find in it a richness of stimuli and suggestion for their own creative ventures. *Ruslan and Lyudmila* could indeed claim to be the most seminal work in Russian music.

A Life for the Tsar

(*Ivan Susanin*)
Zhizn' za tsarya

Opera in four acts with an epilogue (3h)
Libretto by Georgy Fyodorovich Rosen; epilogue by Vasily Zhukovsky, rev. Glinka; scene at the monastery (Act IV) by Nestor Kukolnik
Composed 1834–6; scene at the monastery, 1837
PREMIERES 9 December 1836, Bolshoi Theatre, St Petersburg; UK: 12 July 1887, Covent Garden, London (in Italian); US: 4 February 1936, Schola Cantorum, New York (inc.; concert); 12 December 1936, War Memorial Theatre, San Francisco
CAST Ivan Susanin *b*, Antonida *s*, Vanya *a*, Bogdan Sobinin *t*, Polish commander *b*, Polish messenger *t*; *satb* chorus of Russian peasants, Poles
ORCHESTRATION 2 fl/picc, 2 ob/ca, 2 cl, 2 bsn, 4 hn, 2 tpt, 3 tb, ophicleide, timp, sd, hp, str; onstage: tpt, sd, glock

In 1613 the first of the Romanov Tsars was saved by a peasant, Ivan Susanin, who decoyed a detachment of pursuing Polish troops, perishing at their hands when his deception was uncovered. The subject was suggested to Glinka in 1834, and its Russianness immediately fired him. Having decided that certain incidents were bound to be part of the final work, he worked impulsively as these caught his imagination, sometimes running ahead of his amateur librettist, Georgy Rosen (secretary to the Tsarevich), who was thus forced to set words to existing music. Once rehearsals began, the Tsar himself showed much interest and, realizing its potential for stirring emotions of patriotic loyalty, approved the suggestion that *Ivan Susanin* should be renamed *A Life for the Tsar*.

The work's premiere was a sensational success, and within Russia it became the most performed of all native operas until the 1917 Revolution; indeed, it was then suggested that the melody of the final scene should become the new Soviet national anthem. In 1837 Glinka was persuaded to replace Sobinin's scene at the beginning of Act IV with a new one (Vanya at the gates of the monastery).

A Life for the Tsar had an enormous influence on later Russian music, setting the precedent for a succession of heroic works based on incidents from Russian history. Not surprisingly, it was slower to make its mark abroad; though in Russia it became customary to open the St Petersburg operatic season with it, it seems to have been 30 years before it crossed the frontier (to Prague in 1866).

In the USSR since 1939 Rosen's politically unacceptable libretto has been replaced by a grossly rewritten one by Sergey Gorodetsky. This version is used on Soviet recordings.

SYNOPSIS

Act I A chorus of male peasants enters the village of Domnino, to be greeted by their womenfolk; they give thanks that a new tsar has been found. Antonida sadly laments the absence of her betrothed, Sobinin, who has been fighting for the tsar – though today he is to return home. However, Susanin brings news: the Poles are threatening Moscow, and there can be no thought of a wedding. Sobinin arrives in a boat along the river (chorus of rowers). He too has news: Moscow is safe. But, Susanin begins the quartet, without a tsar Russia is still vulnerable. Sobinin is dismayed that his wedding will be delayed, and in the trio he and Antonida lament, while Susanin promises that Antonida shall finally be Sobinin's bride. However, when Susanin hears from Sobinin that 'their boyar' is to be crowned in Moscow, he agrees to the wedding and all rejoice.

Act II A ball in the fortress of a Polish commander. All are confident Russia will be vanquished But after the choral polonaise, *krakowiak*, waltz and mazurka, a messenger bursts in with news of defeat; Mikhail Romanov has been elected tsar, though he does not yet know, for he has retired to his estate at Kostroma. After recriminations, a detachment of soldiers leave to apprehend the new tsar. Those remaining resume dancing.

Act III In Susanin's cottage Vanya ('the orphan') reflects on how the peasant had adopted him after his mother had been killed. When Susanin enters, Vanya declares he will fight for the tsar when he is grown up. A chorus of men bids farewell to Susanin as they go off for the day's work, and he invites them to the eve-of-wedding celebration. Susanin and Vanya, now joined by Antonida and Sobinin, express in a quartet their happiness, and their hopes for Russia, now that a tsar has been chosen. Sobinin leaves to summon his friends. Suddenly Susanin hears horses, and the Polish detachment appears. Believing Susanin knows the Tsar's whereabouts, the Poles demand that he lead them to him. Susanin prevaricates and, as the intruders confer, whispers to Vanya to ride to Kostroma and warn the tsar. Susanin then pretends he will accept the bribe the Poles offer. Antonida enters and is distressed to see her father departing with Russia's enemies but, resisting her embrace, he tells her to celebrate her wedding without h/im, then leaves with the Poles. Vanya also slips out. A group of girls sings a bridal chorus, and Antonida voices her grief at her father's apparent abduction. Sobinin returns with his friends and they go off to collect others to help in rescuing Susanin. Sobinin lingers to comfort Antonida, then also leaves.

Act IV (1836 version) In a forest glade Sobinin rallies his followers in their search for Susanin, and thinks of Antonida.

Act IV (1837 version) At the gates of the Kostroma monastery Vanya wakens the inhabitants, and convinces them of the danger to the tsar. Susanin and the Poles enter the forest glade. While his captors rest, the peasant reflects on the coming dawn which will be his last, and recalls the wedding preparations and his family, then quietly sleeps. The Poles rouse him; finally he confesses his deception and is killed.

Epilogue On the square before the Kremlin in Moscow. An offstage chorus praises the new tsar and his warriors (Slavsya chorus). Sobinin, Antonida and Vanya enter and tell of Susanin's heroic death. All praise the new tsar and Susanin.

The fundamental problem for any 19th-century Russian composer was to reconcile indispensable forms and procedures that originated in the West with the kind of music that nature had decreed he should write. Glinka was the first composer to conquer this problem, and *A Life for the Tsar* marked his first victory. His strongest weapon was his outstanding gift for melodies basically Western, but often fused with characteristics stemming from folksong or church chant. And while the overall organization and structures of the opera remained Western, even these were occasionally shed to allow a passage that could never have occurred except in a Russian opera – the opening chorus of Act I, for instance, or the beautiful bridal chorus in 5/4 in Act III (the most Russian piece in the whole score).

Above all, *A Life for the Tsar* is good drama. True, the story is not very elegantly shaped, and the progress of the music is sometimes correspondingly fitful; the extended dances in the second act are simply the obligatory ballet, and the later use of extracts from these dances as leitmotifs for the Polish soldiers is dramatically disastrous. But when Glinka was faced with a situation of deep emotion or true drama, he could respond splendidly. Especially impressive are Susanin's great scena in Act IV, which is touchingly filled with recollections of earlier themes, and the corporate rejoicing at the opera's end, the first of those great tableau scenes which were to become one of the glories of the Russian tradition.

RECORDINGS 1. Stich-Randall, Bugarinovich, Gedda, Christoff, Belgrade Opera Ch, Lamoureux O, Markevich, HMV, 1958; 2. Pendachanska, Toczyska, Merritt, Martinovich, Sofia National Opera Ch, Sofia Festival O, Tchakarov, Sony, 1989
EDITIONS f.s., M. Balakirev, A. Lyadov and N. Rimsky-Korsakov (eds), St Petersburg, 1881; modern reprint f.s., *Polnoye sobrany sochineny*, 12 (3 parts), Moscow, 1965; v.s., St Petersburg, 1856/7

Ruslan and Lyudmila
Ruslan i Lyudmila

Opera in five acts (3h 10m)
Libretto by Konstantin Bakhturin (scenario); mostly Valerian Shirkov, but also Nestor Kukolnik, Nikolay Markevich, Mikhail Gedeonov; after the poem by Pushkin
Composed 1837–42
PREMIERES 9 December 1842, St Petersburg; UK: 4 June 1931, Lyceum, London; US: 26 December 1942, New York (concert); 5 March 1977, Boston
CAST Svetozar *b*, Lyudmila *s*, Ruslan *bar*, Ratmir *a*, Farlaf *b*, Gorislava *s*, Finn *t*, Naina *ms*, Bayan *t*, Chernomor *silent*; *satb* chorus of courtiers, the Gigantic Head, Naina's maidens, and Chernomor's followers
ORCHESTRATION picc, 2 fl, 2 ob/ca, 2 cl, 2 bsn, dbsn, 4 hn, 2 tpt, 3 tb, timp, perc (bd, sd, tambourine, cym, triangle, glock) glass harmonica, pf, hp, str; onstage: picc, 2 fl, 2 ob, picc cl, basset hn, b cl, 4 hn, 2 alto hn, 2 tenor hn, bass hn, 3 cornet, 4 tpt, 3 tb, 2 tuba, b tuba, perc (bd, sd, tambourine, cym, triangle)

Glinka began work on *Ruslan and Lyudmila* in 1837, and had completed several numbers before ever a scenario had been devised. His disorganized life-style ensured that the compositional process was even more disorderly and spasmodic than that of *A Life for the Tsar*, with the libretto provided by a succession of amateur writers (though incorporating some lines of Pushkin), and composition spread over five years. Interest in the work was fanned by public performances of separate numbers and Liszt was highly approving when Glinka showed him some of the score early in 1842. But despite radical changes during production, it was tepidly received. Appreciation of the opera seems, however, to have increased fairly steadily. Connoisseurs apparently appreciated its unusual qualities, and it retained an intermittent place in the repertoire. By 1893 it had been performed 300 times in St Petersburg, but there have been few productions outside Russia.

SYNOPSIS
Act I At the court of Svetozar, Prince of Kiev, celebrations are in progress before the marriage of his daughter, Lyudmila, to Ruslan, a warrior. The Bayan (a minstrel) sings of the trials in store for Ruslan, though he predicts the victory of true love. Nostalgically, Lyudmila bids farewell to her parents' home, and consoles her unsuccessful suitors, the eastern prince Ratmir and the Varangian warrior Farlaf. Suddenly all darkens; when light is restored, Lyudmila has vanished. Svetozar promises her hand and half his kingdom to the one who rescues her.

Act II In his cave Finn, a good magician, reveals to Ruslan that Lyudmila's abductor is the dwarf Chernomor (whose strength lies in his enormously long beard) and warns Ruslan against the evil enchantress Naina. The scene changes to a deserted place where Naina instructs a very frightened Farlaf to wait at home; she will help him defeat Ruslan and gain Lyudmila. Finally on a deserted battlefield Ruslan reaffirms his resolve, then defeats a gigantic head and draws from beneath it a sword; the head explains he is Chernomor's brother and one of his victims, and that the sword's magic can defeat the dwarf.

Act III In Naina's enchanted palace her maidens are directing their allure at a travel-weary Ratmir, to the distress of his slave, Gorislava, who loves him. Ruslan appears and is smitten with Gorislava, but Finn intervenes, breaks the seductive spell, unites Ratmir and Gorislava, and all set out to rescue Lyudmila.

Act IV Confined in Chernomor's enchanted garden, Lyudmila voices her despair and defiance, rejecting her captor's blandishments. On Ruslan's approach Chernomor casts a spell over her and goes out to fight with Ruslan. Chernomor's followers observe the offstage encounter, in which Ruslan catches hold of Chernomor's beard, then cuts it off. Triumphantly he returns onstage with it, but is in despair when he finds Lyudmila in an enchanted sleep. He decides to take her back to Kiev.

Act V Ratmir sings of his love for Gorislava. Farlaf steals Lyudmila and speeds to Kiev. Meanwhile Finn gives Ratmir the magic ring that will waken Lyudmila. In Kiev Farlaf cannot rouse her but when Ruslan arrives with Ratmir he breaks the spell with the aid of the ring. General rejoicing.

The fantasy and romance of Pushkin's *Ruslan and*

Ballet scene from Act IV of Ruslan and Lyudmila *(Moscow, 1846)*

Lyudmila had a natural appeal to Glinka; the problem was that the subject was totally unsuited to operatic treatment, and the work's fate was sealed when a friend, Konstantin Bakhturin, devised its scenario 'in a quarter of an hour while drunk'. For some four years Glinka worked intermittently on such individual incidents as caught his fancy; by the time he came to knit these together, far too much music of the wrong kind had been composed, and for all the drastic surgery during rehearsals, nothing could hide the unevenness or remedy the often misshapen structure. Dramatically, *Ruslan and Lyudmila* is an irreparable disaster, and some of the characterization is weak; Farlaf in particular is little more than a conventional opera-buffa figure.

Yet, at its musical best, *Ruslan and Lyudmila* contains some of the most strikingly original invention of 19th-century opera, some separate incidents are brilliantly treated, and some characters transcend the ludicrous situations in which they find themselves. The opera's Russianness is far deeper than that of *A Life for the Tsar*, springing not from the absorption of folk and chant idioms into what was still basically a Western idiom, but from the sometimes novel materials and free structures that Glinka's vivid and totally Russian imagination created. Hence the prodigious seminal importance of the opera. In addition, the clear and bright scoring, which contributes so much colour to the whole opera, established the fundamental style of Russian orchestration.

Though *Ruslan and Lyudmila* is mostly an opera of brilliant moments, Act I does have real consistency, establishing for Russian music its special heroic idiom, which is extended further in Ruslan's great Act II aria. (Act I also contains the famous passage where, to depict the disorientation caused by Chernomor's magic as he abducts Lyudmila, Glinka disrupts the music's tonal course with a descending whole-tone scale.) Earlier in Act II Naina's music introduces something of the special Russian 'magic' idiom, while the oriental idiom appears for the first time in Act III, notably in the voluptuous Persian chorus and the first part of Ratmir's aria. Between these is Gorislava's plangent cavatina, but there is a greater concentration of excellent music in Act IV: in Lyudmila's spirited scena and aria, for instance, and in the languorous delicacy of the choruses for Chernomor's houris – though most immediately arresting, perhaps, are Chernomor's splendidly grotesque march and the fierce oriental *lezhginka*. The most memorable movement in Act V is Ratmir's sultry romance.

RECORDINGS Rudenko, Sinyavskaya, Nesterenko, Morozov, Bolshoi Ch and O, Simonov, EMI/Melodiya, 1979
EDITIONS f.s., M. Balakirev, A. Lyadov and N. Rimsky-Korsakov (eds), St Petersburg, 1878; modern reprint f.s.,

Polnoye sobrany sochineny, 14 (3 parts), Moscow, 1966; v.s., Stellovsky, 1856

BIBLIOGRAPHY   David Brown, *Mikhail Glinka: A Biographical and Critical Study*, OUP, 1974; Richard B. Mudge (ed.), *M. Glinka: Memoirs*, University of Oklahoma, 1963; Alexandra Orlova, *Glinka's Life in Music: A Chronicle*, UMI Research Press, 1988

D.B.

Christoph Willibald Ritter von Gluck; contemporary aquatint by Edmé Quenedey

CHRISTOPH WILLIBALD GLUCK

Christoph Willibald Ritter von Gluck; *b* 2 July 1714, Erasbach, nr Berching; *d* 15 November 1787, Vienna

Gluck came from a family of foresters who worked for the minor nobility. His precocious musical talent led to studies in music (and law) in Prague, probably sponsored by Prince Lobkowitz (father of Beethoven's patron), and travel to Italy where he studied with G. B. Sammartini. His first operas were written for Milan and Venice; he then tried his luck in London, producing two operas in 1746. Years later he told Burney how he admired Handel and English musical taste (this may have been flattery as Gluck was to say much the same in France about Lully). His search for a permanent position took him to Saxony and Denmark. Recurring visits to Vienna, his wife's home, enabled him to ingratiate himself with the imperial family, some of whom became his pupils. The first of many operas commissioned by the Vienna court was *La Semiramide riconosciuta* (1748); Gluck settled there by about 1750.

His earliest output consisted of conventional opere serie, mainly to libretti by Metastasio. He wrote no opera buffa. Among his earliest surviving music are solidly composed *da capo* arias, not without anticipations of his later style; some pieces reappear in his greatest works. Recycling material was common enough at the time not to excite remark, and Gluck, never as fluent as his Italian contemporaries, was certainly justified in searching for better dramatic contexts for his most original conceptions. Some passages display a rugged boldness, as well as a grand melodic span, which were to continue to influence musicians as late as Berlioz.

From Vienna, Gluck made occasional journeys to fulfil commissions in Italy, and at last, most significantly, in Paris. His Viennese work quickly took him away from opera seria, although he continued to produce courtly entertainments. He owed the variety of his experience during the 1750s to the favour of the imperial theatre administrator, Count Durazzo, whose *L'innocenza giustificata* he set (1755), a gesture directed against the Caesarean poet, Metastasio. Durazzo fell in with the fashion for French culture, and gave Gluck the job of adapting and later composing a series of opéras comiques for the court theatre.

Such diverse experiences stood the composer in good stead in the 1760s when he was drawn towards reform movements in dramatic music. His first significant collaboration was in the ballet *Don Juan* by Angiolini (1761), after which came three operas to libretti by Calzabigi; *Orfeo ed Euridice*, *Alceste*, and *Paride ed Elena*. Besides his masterpiece of opéra comique, *Le rencontre imprévue* (1764), Gluck wrote other occasional works in the 1760s. He has sometimes been accused of backsliding from the radical position adopted in *Orfeo* and *Alceste*. There is, however, no reason to perceive *Orfeo*, an occasional work related to the courtly genres, as an irreversible step. Gluck composed no full-scale opera seria after 1756 (*Antigono*, which won him the Papal knighthood of the Golden Spur); even *Telemaco* (1765) can be associated with the spirit of reform.

With the publication of *Alceste*, however, Calzabigi penned a dedicatory preface which Gluck signed, and which is their manifesto of reform. The ideas they had assimilated from French opera and the Parmesan and Viennese reform operas of Traetta are justified as a return to the natural and poetic origins of opera, at the expense of mere musicianship, and especially of the virtuoso singer: 'I sought to restrict music to its true purpose of expressing the poetry and reinforcing the dramatic situation, without interrupting the action or hampering it with superfluous embellishments.' Later, in an open letter to the French press, Gluck said that in *Armide* he had striven to be 'more painter and poet than musician'. Consequences of the reform were the greater attention paid to orchestra, chorus, and dance; this, however, corresponded with French tragédie lyrique. In *Orfeo* and *Paride*, but not *Alceste* and *Telemaco*, Gluck orchestrated all the recitatives; and in *Alceste* he managed without a castrato. *Alceste* was followed by *Paride ed Elena*, which Gluck must have valued less, since he did not adapt it for Paris; instead he used parts of it (and *Telemaco*) in new operas.

If the architect of reform was Calzabigi, Gluck supported him wholeheartedly. In Paris he took control of his less experienced librettists; yet even when, like Mozart and Verdi, he demanded verses for music already composed, he kept in mind the needs of the drama rather than merely the music. Largely through the influence of his pupil Marie Antoinette (then Dauphine, later in 1774 Queen of France) he was contracted to present six French operas, including thorough recompositions of *Orfeo* and *Alceste* (he also adapted two opéras comiques). *Armide* completed his *rapprochement* with French tradition by using an old libretto. The threat from the partisans of Italian music, who brought Piccinni to Paris, was met by wholesale plunder of Gluck's own Italian music in his last and perhaps greatest masterpiece, *Iphigénie en Tauride*. He had not permanently affected the taste of Vienna, and Italy remained largely indifferent to his reforms. But, as Lully's partisans had feared, he killed off the old French opera; and he withstood the pressure of the Italians who displaced native talents at the Opéra. The failure of *Echo et Narcisse* (1779) sent him home in disgust, but his works continued to dominate the repertoire into the next century.

Gluck's last operatic undertaking was his only one in German, a version of *Iphigénie en Tauride*. He handed *Les Danaïdes* to his protégé Salieri, and abandoned a setting of Klopstock's *Hermann-schlacht*, but he wrote some songs and a *De profundis* before his death in 1787. He remained a talisman of dramatic art for several generations. Cherubini, Spontini, Weber and others paid him tribute; Berlioz (his most eloquent partisan), Wagner and Strauss supervised performances. A scholarly edition of his French operas was undertaken by musicians close to Berlioz. Major critical and historical studies have been undertaken this century, and a complete edition of his works is well advanced.

Note: *GW* = C. W. Gluck, *Sämtliche Werke* (*Collected Works*), published by Bärenreiter, Kassel; volumes published to date are listed as '*GW* series/ volume' – series 1: 'Reform' operas ('Musikdramen'); 2: ballets; 3: Italian opere serie and serenatas; 4: French opéra comique. The designation dramma per musica usually implies opera seria.

Demofoonte

Dramma per musica in three acts
Libretto by Pietro Metastasio (1733)
PREMIERE 6 January 1743, Regio Ducal, Milan

Gluck's third known opera and the first to survive as an entity, although the overture, one aria, and the recitatives are missing. Gluck's energetic style, which later won him both plaudits and enemies, is already

in evidence, as is a quite striking vein of pathos in the role of Dircea.

EDITION v.s. (inc.), J. Tiersot (ed.), Breitkopf und Härtel, 1914

Ipermestra

Dramma per musica in three acts
Libretto by Pietro Metastasio (1744)
PREMIERE 21 November 1744, San Giovanni Grisostomo, Venice

Gluck's sixth known opera; the first to survive complete. His lifelong habit of self-borrowing begins here (if not before), with reuse of an aria from *Demofoonte*. The subject was also proposed for what would have been Gluck's last opera. Instead Calzabigi's *Ipermestra* was set by Millico and converted into a French opera, Salieri's *Les Danaïdes* (1784).

MANUSCRIPT British Library, London

La caduta de'giganti

The Fall of the Giants
Dramma per musica in two acts
Libretto by Francesco Vanneschi
PREMIERE 7 January 1746, King's Theatre, Haymarket, London

Gluck's London operas were not outstandingly successful but they had sufficient following for inclusion in a collection of 'Favourite Songs' (including five arias and one duet from *La caduta*) published in full score by Walsh in 1746. Nothing else survives of the opera.

Le nozze d'Ercole e d'Ebe

The Wedding of Hercules and Hebe
Dramma per musica in two parts
Librettist unknown
PREMIERE 29 June 1747, Pillnitz, near Dresden

Le nozze d'Ercole e d'Ebe was Gluck's first commission after his visit to England, and his first work in the courtly genre, resulting from his association with the travelling impresario Pietro Mingotti. Despite the designation dramma per musica, it is not an opera seria but the first of many works in the courtly genres: it was later entitled serenata or festa teatrale.

The four characters are the ruling gods Jupiter (Giove) and Juno (Giunone), and the minor deities of the title. Hercules, like Apollo in equivalent pieces written for Vienna, was sung by a woman; the action takes place after his mortal death and his reception on Olympus. Juno and Jupiter conspire to have Hercules fall in love with Hebe under a false name; otherwise his mistrust of Juno would prevent him considering marriage to her daughter. This slender action – it is hardly a plot – is emblematic of the double dynastic marriage between the ruling Saxon and Bavarian families for which it was composed. The music represents Gluck's early style, which is closest to the Neapolitan school; Hebe's music is freshened by the spirit of opera buffa.

RECORDING Vulpius, Rönisch, Prenzlow, Schreier, Berlin Kammerorchester, Koch, Eterna, 1967
EDITION H. Abert (ed.), *DTB*, vol. 26, Breitkopf und Härtel, 1914

La Semiramide riconosciuta
Semiramide Revealed
Dramma per musica in three acts (3h 15m)
Libretto by Pietro Metastasio (1729)
PREMIERE 14 May 1748, Burgtheater, Vienna

Gluck's first commission for Vienna, composed, as the manuscript title page tells us, for 'the most glorious birthday of the reigning Empress Maria Theresia . . . sempre Augusta etc.', and also for the opening of the new court theatre. In one of his less attractive texts, Metastasio rejects the gruesome story of Semiramide (as in Rossini's opera and Gluck's ballet *Semiramis* of 1765) in favour of a complicated intrigue. Semiramide reigns in Assyria disguised as a man; her former lover Scitalce, who thinks he has killed her, is one of three suitors for the Bactrian princess Tamiri. Eventually Semiramide is revealed and marries Scitalce; her brother weds Tamiri.

This opera shows Gluck as a mature master of the Italian musical lingua franca while possessing considerable individuality. The arias show an impressive variety of moods and some variety of form. Coloratura is restrained, several arias being purely lyrical or, like Semiramide's 'Tradita, pressata', purely expressive, the abrasive tremolando strings a foretaste of the later Gluck. One aria reappeared in *Le feste d'Apollo* (1769).

EDITION f.s., facsimile, Garland, 1982

Ezio
Dramma per musica in three acts
Libretto by Pietro Metastasio
PREMIERE Carnival 1750, Prague

Ezio was revived in Vienna in December 1763, after *Orfeo*; yet much of the essence of Orpheus' 'Che puro ciel' is already evident in the aria 'Se povero il ruscello', the beauties of nature later serving as model for those of Elysium (an intermediate version is in *Antigono*). Other passages reappear as early as *La clemenza di Tito* (see below). 'Ecco alle mie catene' became Hercules' aria in the French *Alceste*, and another passage was used in *Echo et Narcisse*. Gluck recycled three arias from his previous opera, *La contesa de'numi*, in *Ezio*.

MANUSCRIPT Národní Muzeum, Hudební Oddělení, Prague

La clemenza di Tito
The Clemency of Titus
Dramma per musica in three acts (3h)
Libretto by Pietro Metastasio (1734)
PREMIERE 4 November 1752, Teatro San Carlo, Naples

Gluck reached a personal summit in this setting of Metastasio's popular royalist drama. Perhaps because Naples was remote from where his music was best known, he used an exceptional amount of earlier material (mainly from *Ezio*). A new aria, 'Se mai senti spirarti', later became 'O malheureuse Iphigénie' in *Iphigénie en Tauride*, its middle section forming the chorus 'Contemplez ces tristes apprêts'. Berlioz tells the story of its being shown by students, as an example of work by a German donkey ('asino tedesco'), to the old Neapolitan master Durante who replied that no rule existed to justify this harmony, but it needed a genius to think of it. Mozart set an adaptation of this libretto in 1791.

MANUSCRIPT Conservatoire National de Musique, Paris

Le Cinesi
The Chinese
Azione teatrale in one act (1h)
Libretto by Pietro Metastasio (1735)
PREMIERES 24 September 1754, Schlosstheater, Schlosshof, Vienna; UK: 28 June 1984, St Bartholomew's Hospital, London

When set by Caldara in 1735, this short entertainment was intended for performance by the Austrian archduchesses. Metastasio added a tenor part for the version set by Gluck, which was designed for professional performance; it is the nearest he came to Italian comedy. Three Chinese girls, illicitly joined by a young man newly returned from Europe, enact roles from fashionable operatic genres. According to Dittersdorf, 'exotic' percussion instruments were used. Otherwise the music has no local colour, but it sparkles with invention. Lisinga's aria (in an abbreviated form) treats of the sorrow of Andromache; the *da capo* arias of Silango (the man) and Sivene (one of Gluck's most original pieces) praise love and the pastoral life, and jealous Tangia pokes fun at Silango's European affectations. An elaborate danced ensemble forms the finale.

RECORDING Poulenard, Banditelli, von Otter, de Mey, O of the Schola Cantorum Basiliensis, Jacobs, EMI, 1985
EDITION G. Croll (ed.), *GW*, 3/17, 1958

La Danza
The Dance
Componimento drammatico pastorale in one act
Libretto by Pietro Metastasio (1744)
PREMIERE 5 May 1755, Laxenburg, Vienna

A slight work written as the introduction to a ballet, originally described as a cantata and consisting of an overture and five numbers, four of which Gluck drew on in *Echo et Narcisse*. It was designed for a minor celebration at court, and Gluck used an enlarged version of an old text. The two characters, Nice and Tirsi, engage in a lovers' dispute: she is flirtatious, he jealous of her joining the dance; the pastoral ballet follows naturally on their reconciliation.

RECORDING Ignatowicz, Myrlak, Warsaw Chamber O, Bugaj, Orfeo, 1988
EDITION G. Croll (ed.), *GW*, 3/18, 1969

L'innocenza giustificata

Innocence Justified
Festa teatrale in one act (2h)
Libretto by Giacomo Graf Durazzo (recitatives), using aria
texts by Pietro Metastasio
PREMIERE   8 December 1755, Burgtheater, Vienna

L'innocenza (revived in Vienna as *La vestale* as late as 1768) is a festa and therefore uses a classical subject with a supernatural element; for the first time in Gluck's operas the chorus plays a significant role. *L'innocenza* was identified by Einstein as an important stage in the development of Gluck's operatic reform. Certainly a criticism of convention is implied by the use of Metastasio's arias in a new dramatic context; yet Gluck was to set five more of his texts. Gluck used three of his own earlier arias; some material was used again in *Armide*. The most striking idea is at the *dénouement*, which interrupts an aria (Julia's 'Prayer', borrowed from *Issipile*: 'Ah rivolgi, o casta Diva' (1752)).

RECORDING   Ruffini, Lucarini, Benelli, Corale Amerina,
O Giovanile di Terni, Catalucci, Bongiovanni, 1991
EDITION   Alfred Einstein (ed.), *DTÖ*, Jg 44, vol. 82,
Artaria, 1937

Antigono

Antigono
Dramma per musica in three acts
Libretto by Pietro Metastasio
PREMIERE   9 February 1756, Torre Argentina, Rome

Antigono was Gluck's last full-scale opera seria. The music that was to become 'Che puro ciel' (*Orfeo*) makes its second appearance (see *Ezio*). The magnificent final aria 'Perchè se tanti siete', after reappearing in *Telemaco*, reached its final form as 'Je t'implore et je tremble' in *Iphigénie en Tauride*. Whether by conscious or unconscious imitation, or by coincidence, an important progression in this aria bears a close resemblance to the *Gigue* in J. S. Bach's Partita No. 1.

MANUSCRIPT   Conservatoire National de Musique, Paris

Il rè pastore

The Shepherd King
Dramma per musica in three acts
Libretto by Pietro Metastasio (1751), set by Giuseppe Bonno
PREMIERE   8 December 1756, Burgtheater, Vienna

Il rè pastore was composed for the birthday of the Emperor Franz I. It is an opera seria with strong overtones of pastoral (which colours the music of several numbers), based on a minor incident in the career of Alexander the Great.

Aminta, a shepherd, is about to marry Elisa, a shepherdess with royal blood. He is, however, heir to the throne of Sidon; the usurper, defeated by Alessandro, has committed suicide. Tamiri, daughter of the usurper, is hiding in the countryside, sheltered by Elisa; she is in love with Agenor, a Sidonian noble. Aminta tells Alexander, whom he does not recognize, that he is happy with his lot; his humility

and intelligence convince the conqueror that he will make an excellent king. Aminta receives the news of his destiny with mixed feelings, Elisa with simple joy. In Act II, they find that protocol prevents them from meeting; then Alexander, with the best of intentions, tells Agenor that Tamiri can reign as Aminta's wife. The four lovers give vent to their feelings in an extended quartet. In Act III, after an aria for each character, the four throw themselves in turn on Alexander's mercy, and Aminta, once more dressed as a shepherd, is ready to renounce his throne. Alexander is delighted to unite both couples, promising Aminta and Elisa the throne of Sidon, and another kingdom to Agenor and Tamiri.

Gluck linked the overture to the first scene; it ends on the dominant, resolved by the first aria. Following his experiment in *L'innocenza giustificata*, this aria is interrupted. In the quartet and the Act III arias Gluck achieved greater variety and intensity of feeling than in any previous opera seria. Otherwise the music is characteristic of his court operas; the roles of Elisa and Aminta demand the highest virtuosity. A characteristic vein of pathos is touched in Elisa's Act III aria 'Io rimaner divisa', her mood of questioning and defiance reflected in the sequence of tender *adagio* and forceful *andante*, both broken up with pauses. There are a few borrowings from *Ezio* and *Antigono*. Mozart set an adaptation of the libretto in 1775.

EDITION   L. Somfai (ed.), *GW*, 3/8, 1968

La fausse esclave

The Pretended Slave
Opéra comique in one act
Libretto by Louis Anseaume and P. A. L. de Marcouville
PREMIERE   8 January 1758, Vienna

The first in the series of Gluck's French opéras comiques, although he had already adapted music for similar texts. The structure of this type of opera required the composer to write the larger airs and the ensembles; much of the dialogue took the form of short verses set to familiar vaudeville melodies (*timbres*) indicated in the libretto.

MANUSCRIPT   Österreichische Nationalbibliothek,
Musiksammlung, Vienna

L'ile de Merlin, ou Le monde renversé

Merlin's Island, or The World Turned Upside Down
Opéra comique in one act (1h 30m)
Libretto by Louis Anseaume (1753), after Alain René Lesage's and 'd'Orneval's' libretto for Jean-Claude Gillier's vaudeville *Le monde renversé* (Paris, 1718)
PREMIERES   3 October 1758, Schönbrunn, Vienna;
US: 1 December 1927, Philadelphia

Pierrot and Scapin are shipwrecked on an island of plenty; they remember that Merlin has promised them this after three years of service. Drink, food, and susceptible girls appear in answer to their wishes; the girls (Argentine and Diamantine) are as rich as their names imply. By the island's law, they must marry poor men, a detail that particularly delights our heroes. They meet the people of the island and are astonished to find the philosopher amiable, the lawyer honest, the *galant* modest, and that fidelity obtains in marriage; this is indeed the 'world turned upside down'. They fear to lose the girls to a pair of rivals; fighting is forbidden, but the rivals win the substitute game of dice. However, Merlin appears to unite them with their lovers.

Gluck's second *opéra comique* begins with a 'descriptive overture' later developed (in reverse order) into the opening calm and storm of *Iphigénie en Tauride*. The libretto is in verse, with such frequent indication of *timbres* that it must have been sung throughout; most of the tunes are included in the *GW* edition. This opera is a satirical fantasy, and the music is nearly all light-hearted, Gluck displaying an unexpectedly light touch in a substantial score of 24 numbers. One aria is adapted from the finale of *Le cinesi*.

EDITION   G. Hausswald (ed.), *GW*, 4/1, 1956

La Cythère assiégée
Cythera Besieged
Opéra comique in one act
Libretto by Charles Simon Favart
Composed 1759; rev. as three-act opéra-ballet, 1775
PREMIERES   first version: spring 1759, Burgtheater, Vienna; second version: 1 August 1775, Opéra, Paris

The island of Cythera is dedicated to the cult of Venus. The maidens who live there are invaded by a male army; unable to defend themselves by force, they subdue the men by the charms of love, and peace prevails. The score is richer in varied forms and more developed musically than the previous opéras comiques by Gluck; but the plot is decidedly thin when spun out to three acts. The additional music for the 1775 version is almost entirely borrowed, some curiously enough from the recent *Iphigénie en Aulide* (1774).

MANUSCRIPT   first version: Österreichische Nationalbibliothek, Musiksammlung, Vienna
EDITION   second version: f.s., Deslauriers, 1775

L'ivrogne corrigé
The Drunkard Reformed
Opéra comique in two acts (1h 30m)
Libretto by Louis Anseaume and Lourdet de Sarterre (set by Jean-Louis Laruette, Paris, 1759), adapted by Charles Simon Favart
PREMIERES   April 1760, Burgtheater, Vienna; UK: 12 March 1931, Birkbeck College, London

Mathurin intends to marry his daughter Colette to his drinking companion, Lucas. His wife Mathurine is desperate to cure him of his habitual drunkenness, but her nagging only drives him out to drink at Lucas's house. Cléon, Colette's lover, has a plan which is executed in Act II with the aid of some actor friends. The drunken pair are conveyed to the cellar and are gently woken by a chorus mourning the death of Mathurin. A masquerade of devils terrifies both men out of their wits. Mathurin is persuaded

that his torment will be mitigated if he consents to his daughter's wedding to Cléon, who is acting the part of Pluto. Cléon reveals himself; Lucas goes off in disgust to get drunk, but Mathurin is truly reformed.

Amid the dialogue, *L'ivrogne corrigé* still includes airs to be sung to the indicated *timbres*; unfortunately these are not included in the *GW* edition. Gluck wrote an overture and 15 numbers, in which his relish for comedy is given full rein. The drinking music of Act I is contrasted with sentimental airs and, in Act II, mock heroics, Pluto and his retinue being more familiar in serious opera. Gluck also shows his developing skill in ensemble writing.

RECORDING   Collart, Betti, Benoit, Demigny, Paris PO, Leibowitz, Nixa, *c.* 1951
EDITIONS   F. Rühlmann (ed.), *GW*, 4/5, 1951; v.s., V. d'Indy (ed.), Legouix, 1925

Tetide
Thetis
Serenata in two parts
Libretto by Giovanni Ambrogio Migliavacca
PREMIERE   10 October 1760, Hofburg, Vienna

Tetide was written for the marriage of the future Emperor Joseph II. He and his wife are alluded to as Achilles and Deïdameia, but do not appear. The sea goddess Thetis (Tetide), mother of Achilles, is enthroned; the gods Mars (Marte, war) and Apollo (arts) dispute the honour of being Achilles' patron. Athene (Pallade) and Venus (Venere) have a similar dispute over Deïdameia. Hymen (Imeneo, marriage) reconciles them and all proceed to Skyros for the glorious wedding.

This is Gluck's last courtly work in the conventional idiom, performed by professionals and on a larger scale than most of these largely allegorical works (nine arias and ensembles, as well as a true chorus). The arias are still full-length pieces in *da capo* form, except one for Athene which is a vehement G minor piece in a single section. Formal variation is provided by a disputatious quartet.

EDITION   L. Somfai (ed.), *GW*, 3/22, 1978

Le cadi dupé
The Deception of the Calif
Opéra comique in one act (1h)
Libretto by Pierre René le Monnier, set by Pierre Alexandre Monsigny (14 September 1761, Paris)
PREMIERES   9 December 1761, Burgtheater, Vienna; US: 16 May 1932, Eastman School of Music, Rochester, NY

The last of Gluck's short opéras comiques and the only work intervening between the important reform ballet *Don Juan* and *Orfeo*. One aria contains an orchestral idea that Gluck used for the quarrel of Agamemnon and Achilles in *Iphigénie en Aulide*.

RECORDING   Rothenberger, Donath, Gedda, Berry, Vabavrian State Opera Ch and O, Suitner, Electrola, 1976
EDITION   v.ss., *Der betrogene Kadi*, J. N. Fuchs (ed.), Senff, *c.* 1884; Universal, 1881; *rp* (English words), 1966

Orfeo ed Euridice/Orphée et Euridice
Orpheus and Eurydice

Orfeo ed Euridice
First version
Azione teatrale per musica in three acts (1h 45m)
Libretto by Raniero de' Calzabigi
Composed 1762
PREMIERE 5 October 1762, Burgtheater, Vienna
CAST Orpheus *a castrato*, Euridice *s*, God of Love (Amore)
s; *satb* chorus of shepherds and nymphs, furies and infernal
spirits, heroes and heroines from Elysium, followers of Orfeo;
ballet of furies and blessed spirits
ORCHESTRATION 2 fl, 2 chalumeaux, 2 ob, 2 ca, 2 bsn,
2 cornetti, 2 hn, 2 tpt, 3 trbn, timp, hp, str

Orphée
Second version
Tragédie opéra (drame héroïque) in three acts (2h)
Libretto by Pierre Louis Moline, after Calzabigi
Composed 1774
PREMIERES 2 August 1774, Opéra (Académie Royale de
Musique), Salle des Tuileries, Paris; UK: 7 April 1770, King's
Theatre, Haymarket, London; US: 24 June 1794, Charleston
CAST Orpheus *high t* (*haute-contre*), Euridice *s*, God of
Love (Amore) *s*; *satb* chorus of shepherds and shepherdesses,
nymphs, demons and furies, blessed spirits, heroes and
heroines; ballet of furies and blessed spirits
ORCHESTRATION 2 fl, 2 ob, 2 cl, 2 bsn, 2 hn, 2 tpt, 3 trbn,
timp, hp, str

The performance of *Orfeo* on the Emperor Franz's
name day in 1762 involved a rare galaxy of talent and
must be accounted one of the major events in 18th-
century musical theatre. Calzabigi, with full support
from the administrator Durazzo, was the guiding
spirit (as Gluck admitted); he manipulated a familiar
subject and genre with the intention of restoring
naturalness and simplicity to dramatic music. Thus
Orfeo in no sense proposes the reform of Metastasian opera seria. The choreographer Angiolini,
for whom Gluck had composed a revolutionary
action ballet (*Don Juan*) the year before, was also
an innovator in his field; the sets were by the
ubiquitous Quaglio brothers, and the title role was
sung by Gaetano Guadagni, who ten years before
had worked with Handel in London and studied
acting with Garrick.

The festa or azione teatrale, like the serenata, an
Italian opera on a mythological subject with chorus
and dancing, was a feature of courtly celebrations
(Gluck had written several already and was to write
more). But its musical style was similar to opera
seria, particularly in the virtuoso writing for voices.
Calzabigi probably designed *Orfeo* to capitalize on
Gluck's particular musical strengths, and on his
recent dramatic experience. It was preceded by
Durazzo's reform gesture (*L'innocenza giustificata*),
and by Gluck's French comedies, which trained the
composer in directness of utterance. *Don Juan*
permitted Gluck to explore extremes of expression,
particularly in the final scenes. Calzabigi had been
inspired by traditional French opera, notably
Rameau; Gluck knew the reform operas of Traetta,
whose *Armida*, based on the French libretto Gluck
later used in Paris, was given in Vienna in 1761. From
this source came the richly developed tableaux in
which chorus, solo singing and dance are alternated
and combined. The subject had been used,
symbolically, at a critically early stage in the
development of opera and Gluck, unknowingly,
revived something of the spirit of those early 17th-
century operas by Peri, Caccini and Monteverdi,
particularly in the first two acts, by restoring to
recitative its original function as the most expressive
and articulate part of the protagonist's role. Yet
Orfeo feels like a new start rather than the climax of
a remarkable tradition. To posterity it has remained,
perhaps to an unfair degree, Gluck's masterpiece.

After performances in Italy and England, much
abused by additional music, a second authentic
version (*Orphée*, 1774) clinched Gluck's reputation
in Paris after the disputed success of *Iphigénie en
Aulide*. Gluck enlarged his work to occupy a whole
evening; he compromised the spirit of the original
by adding a bravura air for Orpheus to end the first
act, and introduced new ballets, most notably the
long *Dance of Furies* taken from *Don Juan* and
the famous *Dance of the Blessed Spirits* for flute
and strings, perhaps his most eloquent instrumental
solo.

SYNOPSIS (1762 version)
Act I Scene 1: Orpheus and the traditional pastoral
chorus of nymphs and shepherds are grouped round
Eurydice's tomb. The mournful C minor chorus, 'Ah,
se intorno a quest'urna funesta', is punctuated by
Orpheus' cries: he can only utter Eurydice's name. In
a grouping of movements characteristic of reform
works, the chorus is used to frame a recitative for
Orpheus and a dance-pantomime, during which the
tomb is strewn with flowers. Orpheus, alone, sings of
his grief, 'Chiamo il mio ben così'. The three verses
alternate with powerfully expressive recitatives. He
complains that only Echo hears him; her wordless
replies are confided to an echo orchestra with
chalumeaux. Orpheus shakes off his despair and
resolves to recover Eurydice from the dead. Scene 2:
Love appears to encourage him, for his music can
overcome any obstacle. After a short aria Love
disappears and Orpheus, in recitative, determines to
carry the adventure through. (In the 1774 version
Love has two songs; and Orpheus ends with the aria
'L'espoir renaît dans mon âme', a piece that aroused
controversy; its Italian style led to the accusation that
Gluck had stolen it from Bertoni. It actually comes
from *Il Parnaso confuso* and *Le feste d'Apollo* (see
below).)

Act II Scene 1: A hideous landscape near the
banks of the river Cocytus. After a fierce sinfonia,
Orpheus' lyre (represented by the harp) is heard
approaching. It arouses the Furies' wrath; they dance
frenziedly and sing of the hellish watchdog Cerberus
(whose barking is represented by orchestral
glissandi). When Orpheus explains his mission they
interrupt with cries of 'No!', but as his singing grows
in eloquence they display signs of compassion
and finally allow him passage. (The 1774 version at
this point somewhat incongruously inserts the
magnificent *Dance of Furies* which originally ended

Orpheus calms demons and furies at the entrance to Hades; from the autograph manuscript of Orphée, *Act II, Scene 1 (1774)*

the ballet *Don Juan*.) Scene 2: A delectable landscape in Elysium. Ballo. (This was expanded in the 1774 version to became the *Dance of the Blessed Spirits*.) The chorus and a soloist, sometimes taken to be Eurydice, sing of their bliss in such a place ('Cet asile aimable').) Orpheus, alone, sings of the beauty around him and its emptiness for him, because he cannot find Eurydice ('Che puro ciel'). Eurydice is brought to him, blindfold; the chorus ('Vieni a regni del riposo' repeated as 'Torna, o bella, al tuo consorte') exhorts her to return to Orpheus.

Act III Scene 1: A dark, twisted path in a repellent landscape, leading away from Hades. Eurydice is overjoyed at her release, but Orpheus, in fulfilment of conditions imposed by Love (in Act I, Scene 2), has to let go of her hand and must not look at her. She reproaches him for his apparent coldness and he suffers her unjust suspicions (the first long recitative dialogue of the opera is followed by the duet 'Vieni, appaga il tuo consorte'). Eventually she feels that death was preferable ('Che fiero momento'). Orpheus can bear it no longer; he turns to look at her, and she dies. His grief is embodied in the aria 'Che farò senza Euridice?' Scene 2: Love reappears in time to prevent his suicide; Eurydice is revived and the couple are united on earth to the happiness of their friends. Scene 3: All join in praise of Love. (In the 1774 version Orpheus joins in the central part of Eurydice's arias and a trio is added from *Paride ed Elena*; many changes were made in the dances, and the work is considerably longer as a result.)

For all the importance of Calzabigi in directing

Gluck towards a new type of opera, *Orfeo* owes its perennial freshness to Gluck's musical imagination. When Bertoni set the text, very beautifully but in a conventional idiom (Venice, 1776), the loss of Gluckian directness led to loss of magic and dramatic insight. The aim is truth to nature, in the 18th-century sense of 'imitation' – not only of natural phenomena but of human passions. The new directness of expression appears in the absence of *da capo* forms. Instead, Orpheus sings songs: strophic ('Chiamo il mio ben così') or rondo ('Che farò senza Euridice?') in form. 'Che puro ciel', potentially an aria text, is an obbligato recitative; and Orpheus overcomes the Furies by short, even fragmentary outpourings of lyrical intensity. These forms may derive from Renaissance or baroque traditions, particularly 18th-century French ones, but the directness is also from opéra comique, and the gestural exactness of the musical language, not only in the dances, derives from Angiolini's ballet d'action.

The experiment of building scenes out of blocks of interlocked ideas is taken further in *Alceste*, but is never more eloquent than in the dying away of the Furies' music. Gluck's other innovations include the abolition of simple recitative (the orchestra plays throughout), an experiment not resumed until *Paride*, and a richness of orchestral colouring unprecedented in his work and very unusual anywhere before the 1770s. Cornetti and chalumeaux, in their brief appearances, provide a haunting, antique colour; in 'Che puro ciel' a complex layered sonority includes solo flute, oboe, bassoon, horn and cello over a triplet continuum. The choral sonorities are remarkable, and the dances, in their appositeness to each scene, reveal an exceptional choreographic imagination.

Most prophetic, perhaps, is the continuity. Cadences are only occasionally omitted or elided, but many numbers are too short to be self-contained and in a good performance they flow into each other, forming single, extended complexes. But in addition to painting unforgettably Eurydice's tomb, Hades, and Elysium, Gluck discovered accents of grief, resignation, pleading, hope, and despair that make his conception of the mythological singer the equal of Monteverdi's and raised the possibilities of the musical language of his generation to a level otherwise attained only by his exact contemporary C. P. E. Bach (who wrote no operas).

Orpheus was produced in most European centres but the original version fell from favour. Berlioz, in 1859, restored the 1762 tessitura to the title role by assigning it to a woman, Pauline Viardot-García. Tenors still take the role occasionally, in the 1774 keys, but the majority of performances adopt Berlioz's sensible, albeit inauthentic, compromise solution, which involves restoring the 1762 key scheme, while retaining music added in 1774, transposed where necessary. The role has been taken by, among others, Giulia Ravogli, Clara Butt, Kathleen Ferrier and Janet Baker.

RECORDINGS 1. 1762 version, in Italian: Kowalski, Schellenberger-Ernst, Fliegner, Berlin Radio Ch, Carl

Philipp Emanuel Bach CO, Haenchen, Capriccio, 1990; 2. 1774 version, in French: Simoneau, Danco, Alarie, Ensemble Vocal Roger Blanchard, Concerts Lamoureaux O, Rosbaud, Philips, 1956; 3. 1859, Berlioz version, in Italian: Ferrier, Koeman, Duval, Netherlands Opera Ch & O, Bruck, EMI, recorded 1951; 4. 1859 version: Baker, Speiser, Gale, Glyndebourne Ch, LPO, Leppard, Erato, 1982 (also on video, Castle). All four performances stem from live productions, recorded either in the theatre (EMI) or committed to disc shortly after. The Capriccio set is the most moving to date of the 1762 version with counter-tenor Kowalski a superb Orpheus. Both sets of the 1859 version enshrine performances by much-loved interpreters of the title role – Kathleen Ferrier and Janet Baker – both of whom are heard to best effect. [A.B.]

EDITIONS first version (1762): Duchesne, 1764; H. Abert (ed.), *DTÖ*, Jg 21/2, vol. 44a, 1914; A. A. Abert and L. Finscher (eds), *GW* 1/1, Bärenreiter, 1963; v.s., Bärenreiter, 1962; second version (1774): Lemarchand, 1774; Pelletan, Saint-Saëns and Tiersot (eds), Durand, 1898; L. Finscher (ed.), *GW* 1/6, Bärenreiter, 1967; v.s., Bärenreiter, 1967; compromise version: A. Dorffel (ed.), Heinze, 1866; *rp*, Peters, 1873

Il trionfo di Clelia

The Triumph of Clelia
Dramma per musica in three acts
Libretto by Pietro Metastasio (1762)
PREMIERE 14 May 1763, Teatro Comunale, Bologna

The libretto was adjusted by Gluck to contain more orchestral recitative than usual; this puzzled the audience, which had not heard *Orfeo*. Gluck's visit to Italy is described in Dittersdorf's memoirs.

MANUSCRIPT Staatsbibliothek Preussischer Kulturbesitz, Berlin

La rencontre imprévue

The Unexpected Meeting
Comédie mêlée d'ariettes in three acts (2h)
Libretto by L. H. Dancourt, after Lesage's and d'Orneval's *Les pèlerins de la Mecque* (1726)
PREMIERES 7 January 1764, Burgtheater, Vienna; UK: 21 July 1939, Loughton, Essex
CAST Ali *t*, Rezia *s*, Dardane *s*, Amine *s*, Balkis *s*, Osmin *t*, Sultan of Egypt *t*, Vertigo *bar*, Calender *b*, a chief of the caravan *b*; 2 slaves (Banon and Morachin) *spoken roles*; Sultan's entourage and guard, Rezia's slave girl, porters, *silent*
ORCHESTRATION fl/picc, 2 ob/2 ca, 3 bsn, 2 hn, perc (cym, drum), str, hpd

Among oriental rescue operas, this is the most substantial precursor of Mozart's *Die Entführung*; it makes similar use of 'Turkish' percussion for 'local' colour. It is also Gluck's longest, finest and, in the 18th century, most popular opéra comique. As well as being widely performed in French it achieved great popularity in German (as *Die Pilgrimme von Mekka*), being played in most centres in the 1770s and 1780s, and it formed part of the repertoire of the German opera company in Vienna itself. In keeping with contemporary French development of the genre (it was performed five days after Philidor's *Le sorcier*), the dialogue is all spoken, in prose, without *timbres*.

SYNOPSIS

Act I The action takes place in Cairo. Osmin, servant of Ali, meets the Calender (leader of an order of mendicant Dervishes), who is singing a begging song in a traditional language which he professes not to understand himself. Osmin, being destitute, receives practical advice on begging ('Les hommes pieusement'/'Unser dummer Pöbel meint', well known from Mozart's piano variations, K. 455). He also meets the eccentric French painter Vertigo. Dressed like the Calender, Osmin acts the beggar before Ali, failing to grasp the ancient language ('Castagno' comes out as 'Castrato', etc.); but he is recognized, while the Calender recognizes Ali as Prince of Balsora. A serious note is struck by Ali's aria 'Je chérirai, jusqu'au trépas' (with solo violin and cor anglais, an instrument appearing quite frequently in Gluck's opéras comiques). Ali is seeking the Persian princess Rezia, whom he has secretly married, but who was kidnapped by pirates when trying to elope. Balkis, an attendant on the Sultan's favourite in the harem, tells them that her mistress has seen Ali and summons him secretly to the palace. Ali is reluctant but the promise of food decides Osmin and he drags his master inside.

Act II In the palace, Osmin enjoys the good life. Ali is approached in turn by Dardane, seductively, and Amine, provocatively, each pretending to be the mysterious beauty. He spurns their love graciously; nothing will make him unfaithful to Rezia. Amine laughs at him and bets that his constancy will not survive encounter with the real favourite. She is right; it is Rezia herself who has arranged this little test of his fidelity. Their ecstatic reunion is interrupted by Balkis: the Sultan is unexpectedly back from hunting. The act ends with a panic-stricken sextet; Osmin saves the day by rushing them off to the Calender.

Act III The Calender assures them of their safety in his house, and suggests they escape with a caravan on its way to Mecca. However, he seems dangerously interested when Osmin speaks of the huge reward the Sultan is offering for Rezia's return. There follows a long episode with Vertigo: after three trios with Balkis and Osmin, the painter sings of scenes of war (a 'rataplan' aria, 'Des combats j'ai peint l'horreur') and pastoral peace. Ali and Rezia have a loving duet; then disaster strikes, for the Calender has betrayed them. An octet is led by the angry Sultan in a brisk comic patter which foretells the happy end. When he learns the identity of the suppliants, who are quite prepared to die together, the Sultan unites them and offers to execute the Calender instead. The lovers plead for clemency.

Although replete with comedy *La rencontre imprévue* is a full-length opera with serious characters, on the pattern of the contemporary dramma giocoso (it is thus designated in Haydn's Italian version, *L'incontro improvviso*, 1775). There is even space for two ballets, near the ends of Acts II and III, but the music does not survive. The arias are longer, some being in a ternary form not unlike the Italian da capo; two are 'parodied' from *Il trionfo di*

Clelia, although the extreme virtuosity of Gluck's Italian style is eliminated except from Rezia's Act II *ariette*, 'Ah, qu'il est doux de se revoir'. The musical idiom is thus very close to that of Gluck's reform operas from *Alceste* on, and particularly his French operas.

RECORDING Dawson, Dubosc, de Mey, Viala, Cachemaille, Ch and O of Lyons Opera, Gardiner, Erato, 1990
EDITIONS *Die Pilger von Mekka*: M. Arend (ed.), Verlag der Gluck-Gesellschaft, 1910; H. Heckmann (ed.), *GW*, 4/7, 1964; v.s., J. B. Wekerlin (ed.), Legoux, 1891

Il Parnaso confuso
Parnassus in Turmoil
Azione teatrale in one act (1h)
Libretto by Pietro Metastasio
PREMIERE 24 January 1765, Schönbrunn, Vienna

Three new works by Gluck were performed for the celebrations of the second marriage of the Archduke Joseph (the others were *Telemaco* and the grim ballet *Semiramis*). *Il Parnaso confuso* was sung by members of the imperial family, which explains the distribution of difficulty within the four soprano roles, those of Erato and Euterpe being far shorter and simpler than those of Apollo and Melpomene; the future Emperor Leopold directed the orchestra.

Metastasio's poem belongs to the significant sub-genre of pieces about theatrical invention (cf. Casti and Salieri, *Prima la musica*; Bertati, *Capriccio drammatico*, preceding Gazzaniga's *Don Giovanni*). Apollo rouses the Muses to prepare an artistic offering for the royal wedding on the Danube, but they spend the day luxuriantly exchanging and rejecting ideas: when morning comes they have nothing ready. Apollo assures them that so vast and glorious a theme as this royal marriage is sure to inspire them, and they end with a confident chorus.

EDITION B. Baselt (ed.), *GW*, 3/2, 1970

Telemaco, o sia l'isola di Circe
Telemachus, or Circe's Island
Dramma per musica in two acts (2h 45m)
Libretto by Marco Coltellini, an adaptation of a text by Carlo Sigismondo Capeci, set by Alessandro Scarlatti in 1718
PREMIERE 30 January 1765, Burgtheater, Vienna

Ulysses and his men are imprisoned by Circe (changed into trees, not swine). She loves him; he pines for home. His son Telemachus appears, falling in love with Circe's attendant Asteria. An oracle in the Temple of Love forces Circe to free the Greeks, and the episodic plot is spun out by her attempts to win Ulysses by enchantment. In the kind of revelation typical of opera seria, Telemachus' friend Merione, son of Idomeneus, is reunited with his sister, Asteria, destined from childhood to be Telemachus' bride. The Greeks escape from the island and Circe turns her enchanted realm into a desert. *Telemaco* blends reform elements (chorus, dances of which the music, perhaps not Gluck's, is lost, short arias, expressive instrumentation) with a

residue of coloratura and a reversion to *recitativo semplice*.

Telemaco is something of a hybrid, and perhaps Gluck regarded it as an experiment. He left it unpublished; and he plundered it freely in later works. Several ideas reappeared in the new section of *Le feste d'Apollo*; the opening of *Iphigénie en Aulide* is expanded from Telemachus' invocation to his lost father; *Armide* was supplied with an overture and a wholesale reuse of material in Act III; and Circe's aria 'S'a estinguer', originally from *Antigono*, reappears in *Iphigénie en Tauride*. Yet Circe is a magnificent role, and with Ulysses' aria 'Fremer gonfio di torbide spume' and other attractive pieces not used again or only redeployed in occasional works, makes revival of *Telemaco* more than a curiosity.

EDITION K. Geiringer (ed.), *GW*, 1/2, 1972

La corona
The Crown
Azione teatrale in one act
Libretto by Pietro Metastasio

Composed (like *Orfeo*) for the Emperor Franz's name day (4 October 1765), *La corona* remained unperformed because of his sudden death. It was intended, like *Il Parnaso confuso*, for the four talented soprano archduchesses, the distribution of arias being identical.

The story represents a contest of magnanimity centred on the myth of the Kalydonian boar hunt; an offstage chorus, horn calls, and the unusual device of horns changing keys during an aria, contribute to the atmosphere. The Argive princess Atalanta determines to help hunt the giant boar menacing Klaydon, but reconsiders when her sister and friend insist they must join her; the prince of Etolia, Meleagro, does not want the women to endanger themselves. Eventually Atalanta enters the wood, and wounds the boar, which Meleagro kills while rescuing her. He credits her with dealing the mortal blow; she insists that the glory is his. Eventually the laurel crown of the title is dedicated to the goddess Diana.

RECORDING Slowakiewicz, Juranek, Gorzyńska, Nowicka, Bavarian Radio Ch, Warsaw CO, Bugaj, Orfeo, 1988
EDITION G. Croll (ed.), *GW*, 3/26, 1974

Alceste
Tragedia per musica in three acts (2h 15m)
First version
Libretto by Raniero Simone Francesco Maria da Calzabigi, after Euripides
Composed 1766–7
PREMIERE 26 December 1767, Burgtheater, Vienna
CAST Admeto *t*, Alceste *s*, Eumelo and Aspasia (children of Admeto and Alceste) 2 *s*, Evandro *t*, Ismene *s*, herald *b*, High Priest of Apollo *bar*, oracle *b*, infernal god *b*; *satb* chorus of courtiers and citizens, female attendants on Alceste, priests of Apollo, infernal deities

ORCHESTRATION 2 fl, 2 ob, 2 chalumeaux, 2 ca, 2 bsn, 2 tpt, 2 hn, 3 trbn, timp, str, hpd

Tragédie lyrique in three acts (2h 45m)
Second version
Libretto by Marie François Louis Gand Leblanc du Roullet, after Calzabigi
Composed 1775
PREMIERES 23 April 1776, Opéra, Paris; UK: 30 April 1795, London; US: 11 March 1938, Wellesley College, Massachusetts
CAST Admète *t*, Alceste *s*, High Priest of Apollo *b*, Evandre *t* (*haute-contre*), herald at arms *b*, Hercule *b*, 4 Coryphées *satb*, Apollon *bar*, Oracle *b*, infernal god *b*, 2 children of Admète and Alceste 2 *silent roles*; *satb* chorus of officers of the palace, female attendants on Alceste, Thessalians, infernal deities, priests and priestesses in the temple of Apollo
ORCHESTRATION 2 fl, 2 ob, 2 cl, 2 bsn, 4 hn, 2 tpt, 3 trbn, timp, str

Euripides' *Alkestis* is a tragi-comedy; but unlike Quinault and Lully, Calzabigi omitted the humour and concentrated on the loftiest sentiments whose unrelenting expression make the original (1767) version both the most radical reforming gesture of Gluck's career and the most persistently mournful opera ever written. Possibly the subject was intended to convey sympathy to the Empress Maria Theresia, widowed in 1765; the libretto is dedicated to her.

Alceste was performed by an opera-buffa troupe rather than singers used to the musical finery of opera seria; for the first time in a full-scale Italian opera, Gluck dispensed with a castrato. A buffo troupe would also be more amenable to being expected to act. Thus Sonnenfels said of Bernasconi, who sang Alceste, that 'her gestures followed only the movements of the heart'. The ballets were by Noverre, who sympathized less with Gluck and Calzabigi than had Angiolini; he presented a final 'grotesque ballet' which some, at least, enjoyed more than the opera. Nevertheless *Alceste* made a profound impression on the public, which included the 11-year-old Mozart and his father. It is the most challenging gesture of the Viennese reformers, but its severity is such that Gluck should not have been surprised, as he complained in the dedicatory preface to *Paride ed Elena*, that it had found no imitators. As an attempted reform of Italian opera seria, it must be accounted a failure; but in its French form, although preceded by *Iphigénie en Aulide*, it exerted considerable influence.

Alceste was the second Gluck opera revived with Pauline Viardot-García in the title role (Paris, 1861). Subsequent revivals have likewise usually used the French version, even if translated back into Italian: with Cigna under Gui (Florence, 1935) and Callas under Giulini (Milan, 1954). An exception was Flagstad's performance of the Italian original (see RECORDINGS). *Alceste* in the French version was the last new opera role undertaken by Janet Baker (Covent Garden, under Mackerras, 1981).

SYNOPSIS
Act I begins with the proclamation that Admetus, the young king of Thebes, is dying; his wife Alceste is drawn into scenes of communal mourning (1767: 'Io non chiedo, eterni dei'; 1776: 'Grands Dieux! Du destin qui m'accable'). After an imposing religious ceremony, Apollo's oracle pronounces: Admetus can live if someone dies in his place. The people flee (1767: 'Che annunzio funesto/Fuggiamo'; 1776: 'Quel oracle funestre/Fuyons'). Only his wife Alceste has the courage to take this step. 1776: her immense recitative is replaced by an incisive recitative and the new aria, which provides a resolution of her dilemma: to die for Admetus is not a sacrifice ('Non, ce n'est point un sacrifice'). She offers herself to the underworld gods ('Ombre, larve, compagne di morte'). 1767: a short scene for Evander and the chorus ends Act I. 1776: the aria (now 'Divinités du Styx'), provides a more fitting ending to the act.

Act II 1767: Alceste, dismissing Ismene, approaches the gods to beg respite so that she can see Admetus again (this scene is omitted in the French version, much of its music passing to Act III). In both versions, choral singing and dancing celebrate the recovery of Admetus, but nobody knows its price. When Alceste arrives her tears seem incomprehensible; in the French version she appears in the midst of the ballet, making explicit the irony behind this rejoicing which Rousseau found so incongruous. Gradually the truth is revealed. In a magnificent tableau she bids farewell to life; the act ends with the aria 'Ah per questo' ('Ah, malgré moi'), embedded in a splendid choral refrain in F minor ('O come rapida').

ALCESTE.

T.VI.P.305.

O ma mere! ma chère mere!

Illustration from an early French libretto for Alceste

Act III 1767: Admetus tries in vain to force Alceste to renounce her sacrifice and let him die ('Misero! E che farò!'). Alceste bids farewell and dies ('Piangi o Patria', a choral tableau of mourning with solos, reminiscent of the third act of Lully's *Alceste*). But Apollo comes to revoke his dreadful oracle: Alceste, as well as Admetus, can live after all. 1776: the revised version initially mounted in Paris was threatened with failure, so further revisions were undertaken and the final French version reverts more nearly to Euripides by bringing in Hercules, who owes Admetus a debt of hospitality. The act begins with the mourning tableau ('Pleure, o patrie'), abbreviated. Hercules arrives and learns the truth; he determines to rescue Alceste (Gluck refurbished an aria from *Ezio*). The scene changes to the underworld. Alceste, in music from the 1767 Act II, meets the infernal deities; Admetus appears to offer his own life ('Alceste, au nom des dieux'). The infernal deities call on Alceste; Hercules overpowers them and Alceste is returned to life with the blessing of Apollo.

Perhaps because *Orfeo* is concerned with a superhuman being, but *Alceste* with human society, the latter did more to set the pattern for tragic opera in years to come. Its elevated tone is reflected in Italian and French tragedies, notably Mozart's *Idomeneo* and Cherubini's *Médée*. The D minor overture and its link with Act I anticipate both *Idomeneo* and *Don Giovanni*. It has been argued that the arpeggio motif that begins the *Alceste* overture is a sort of leitmotif, anticipating the crucial preparation for the speech of the oracle. The thematic connection with the opera is less explicit than in some of Mozart's operas, or in *Iphigénie en Aulide*, but the oracle scene was certainly Mozart's model for the sacrifice scene in *Idomeneo*. One might go further and suggest that the presentation of the nobly suffering heroine is suggestive of the redeeming women of Romanticism, although the music and forms are neo-classical.

Gluck himself was the most constructive critic of the Italian version. Magnificent as it is, its high-flown sentiments and huge static tableaux of repeated choruses surrounding recitative, arias, and dance, demand absolute submission: if the tension is lost for a moment, it is bound to appear tedious. Tovey observed that Gluck had got rid of the abuses of opera seria by simplifying the drama almost out of existence. Rousseau made an extensive critique of the Italian score: much as he admired it, he deplored the multi-movement arias (which were to arouse opposition from the Piccinnists) and he criticized the cheerful divertissement which greets the king's recovery. For Paris, Gluck kept his style of aria, although he eliminated arias for minor characters and the touching intrusion of the children into one of Alceste's arias. But as well as introducing new dances (some taken from works written in the meantime, *Le feste d'Apollo* and *Paride ed Elena*) he changed the divertissement along lines suggested by Rousseau, omitted much repetition and added new material including a superb aria for Alceste in Act I. Like that

of *Iphigénie en Aulide*, which intervened between the two versions, the design is fluid; grandeur is lost but theatricality enhanced.

The Italian version follows *Telemaco* rather than *Orfeo* by returning to simple recitative. In proportion to the orchestral (obbligato) recitative it is, however, much reduced from the opera-seria norm. In the French version the recitatives are orchestrated throughout. Gluck's orchestration attains a new depth and richness in the tutti, particularly in the infernal scenes which are totally different from those in *Orfeo*. The Romantic orchestra, or at least its treatment of the darker colours, begins here, with Gluck's sonorous scoring for full woodwind and trombones, soon taken up in French opera by Piccinni. The orchestra, particularly in 'Ombre, larve, compagne di morte', is made to stand for the voices of the infernal deities, another foretaste of Romantic practice. Yet the orchestration continues the functional, symbolic use of instrumental timbre applied in *Orfeo*. The trombones are used to colour mourning and underworld scenes, while the cors anglais characterize only the former, and chalumeaux the latter. Low flutes colour the ritual march in Act I (which Mozart remembered in *Die Zauberflöte*). Standard orchestration, flutes, oboes, horns, bassoon, and strings, with occasional trumpets and timpani, represents normality.

RECORDINGS 1. 1767 version: Flagstad, Lowe, Jobin, Young, Hemsley, Geraint Jones Singers & O, Jones, 1956; 2. 1776 version: Norman, Gedda, Krause, Weikl, Nimsgern, Bavarian Radio Ch and SO, Baudo, Orfeo, 1982
EDITIONS 1767 version: (Vienna, 1769); G. Croll (ed.), *GW*, 1/3, 1988; 1776 version: Paris, 1776; F. Pelletan and B. Damke (eds), Richault, 1874; R. Gerber (ed.), *GW*, 1/7 (1957); v.s., Bärenreiter, 1987

Le feste d'Apollo

The Celebrations of Apollo
Festa teatrale in a prologue and three acts
Libretto by Carlo Innocenzio Frugoni and Raniero Simone Francesco Maria da Calzabigi
PREMIERE 24 August 1769, Teatrino della Corte, Parma

The marriage of the Austrian Archduchess Maria Amalia to the Infante Ferdinand of Parma was the occasion for this entertainment, its succession of dramatically self-contained acts generically related to French opéra-ballet. Gluck recycled much old music into a prologue (with the *Telemaco* overture), an act called *Philemon e Baucis*, and an act called *Aristeo*; the last act is a shortened version of *Orfeo*.

MANUSCRIPT Schweizerische Landesbibliothek, Berne

Paride ed Elena

Paris and Helen
Dramma per musica in five acts (1h 45m)
Libretto by Raniero Simone Francesco Maria da Calzabigi
PREMIERE 3 November 1770, Burgtheater, Vienna

Gluck's last reform opera written with Calzabigi, and the only one not adapted for France. Instead he reused dance movements in *Iphigénie en Aulide* and *Alceste*, a trio in *Orphée*, and an aria in *Echo et Narcisse*. This dismemberment of a score composed with as much care as either of the other Calzabigi operas is the more strange in that it had been published in 1770 with an important dedicatory preface (to the Duke of Braganza). Perhaps it has the fault of Calzabigi's *Alceste*, of too leisurely an argument; but the intention of the work is more clearly to entertain, and the extended choral and dance sequences, while they must stand in the way of modern revival except in a period style, are skilfully integrated into the action.

Arriving in Sparta with his Trojan followers, Paris comes to win Helen, the most beautiful woman in the world. The Trojans pay homage to Venus, whom Paris has declared the most beautiful of the goddesses, and request her help. Cupid, disguised as Helen's confidante Erasto, helps Paris. At first, Helen rejects Paris's advances. In Act III, having presented prizes at the games, Paris woos Helen in song, but his ardent desire succeeds only in frightening her. Finally, in Act V, 'Erasto' tells Helen that the Trojans are preparing to depart and succeeds in leading her to betray her true emotions. Cupid reveals himself and the lovers are united. Pallas Athene appears, uttering her terrible prophecy of the devastation Helen's abduction will bring on Troy. The work concludes with celebratory dancing in the Trojan camp.

The orchestration is simpler than in *Alceste*, although the harp is employed rather more freely than in *Orfeo*. The recitatives are orchestrated throughout, however, returning to the advanced position taken up by *Orfeo*, from which Gluck did not retreat again. Paris is a castrato role, the last Gluck wrote; as in many of his court works, there are no low voices.

Whatever Gluck's private opinion, *Paride* is a beautiful opera, some of his finest music clothing a psychological drama in which Helen gradually yields to her ardent lover. The idea that Gluck could not handle love music is given the lie by the title roles: Paris, the ardent wooer who enters with the direct and eloquent 'O del mio dolce ardor', and Helen, uncertain at first, then gradually overcoming her inhibitions before eloping in the final act. Paris's 'Le bell'imagine' and the trio 'Ah lo veggo!' are far more dramatic in their original context than their later incarnations in, respectively, *Echo* and *Orphée*. Gluck was proud of the contrasted national styles (rugged Spartans, effete Trojans) which are presented in the choral and ballet music. Paris is seconded throughout by Cupid in disguise. There are no other characters until Athene appears at the end to music from the overture.

RECORDINGS 1. Cotrubas, Greenberg, Fontana, Bonisolli, A. Schönberg Ch, Ch and O of Austrian Radio, Zagrosek, Orfeo, 1987; 2. Alexander, McFadden, Trey, La Stagione, Schneider, Capriccio, 1992
EDITIONS Trattner, 1770; R. Gerber (ed.), *GW*, 1/4, 1954; v.ss., Peters, 1863; Leduc, 1909; R. Gerber (ed.), Bärenreiter, 1957

Iphigénie en Aulide

Iphigenia in Aulis
Tragédie-opéra in three acts (2h 30m)
Libretto by Marie François Louis Gand Leblanc du Roullet after Jean Baptiste Racine's tragedy *Iphigénie* (1674)
Composed *c.* 1771–3
PREMIERES 19 April 1774, Opéra, Paris; UK: 20 November 1933, Oxford; US: 22 February 1935, Philadelphia
CAST Agamemnon *bar*, Clitemnestre *s*, Iphigénie *s*, Achille *t*, Patrocle *b*, Calchas *b*, Arcas *b*, Diane *s*, 3 Greek women 3 *s*, a slave from Lesbos *s*; *satb* chorus of Greek soldiers and people, Thessalian soldiers, guards, attendants on the princess, women from Aulis, slaves from Lesbos, priestesses of Diana; dancers
ORCHESTRATION 2 fl, 2 ob, 2 cl, 2 bsn, 2 hn, 2 tpt, b trbn (ad lib.), timp, str

Gluck's first French opera was written speculatively, in the hope of arousing interest in Paris. His campaign bore fruit only four years after the first performance of *Paride*. His objective was to found a new school in the cultural capital of Europe, in the interests of wider diffusion of his reform of serious opera. In so far as the old French operas rapidly dropped out of the repertoire after 1774, and his new works were widely performed in the original language or in translation, he succeeded. Gluck also created a revolution at the Paris Opéra by insisting that the principals (who included Sophie Arnould in the title role and the most distinguished French tenor and baritone of the time, Legros and Larrivée), and even the chorus, should act; according to

Sophie Arnould in the title role of Iphigénie en Aulide *(Paris, 1774)*

contemporary reports he had to behave like a sergeant-major to achieve this. He retained elements of French operatic tradition that had been taken over into the Calzabigian reform, notably the integration of choral and dance music, short and freely structured solo vocal numbers, and the serious use of orchestra, and could thus readily adapt *Orpheus* and *Alceste* for Paris; but in the *Iphigénies* and *Armide* he eschewed the monumentality of the latter, and the slowness of action in all three Calzabigi operas.

The subject of the sacrifice of Iphigenia had been treated in several Italian operas and by Algarotti in his *Saggio sopra l'opera in musica*. In essence, the story was intended to justify the murder of Agamemnon by his wife Clytemnestra on his return from Troy: Euripides invented the substitution of an animal for the human sacrifice by the offended goddess Artemis (Diana), and the translation of Iphigenia to Tauris. Du Roullet's libretto is adapted from Racine's *Iphigénie*, in which Iphigenia is married to Achilles; Eriphile, whose real name is also Iphigenia, turns out to be the intended sacrifice. Du Roullet's plot is less contrived, although the ending does not prepare for the Tauris drama.

Du Roullet's procedure became standard for the adaptation of neo-classical tragedy into opera. The plot is simplified (two major characters, Eriphile and Ulysses, are omitted); events only described in the play (notably the *dénouement*) are enacted to satisfy the requirement for choral involvement; danced divertissements are introduced. Other operas that treat plays in this manner included Grétry's *Andromaque* (1780), Salieri's *Les Horaces* (1786), Lemoyne's *Phèdre* (1786), and Gluck's (1779) and Piccinni's (1781) *Iphigénie en Tauride*.

Iphigénie en Aulide was never as successful as *Tauride*, but it retained a hold on the repertoire into the 19th century. Its most remarkable revival was organized by Wagner in Dresden (1847); in places this amounted to a recomposition in line with his own development (Mahler revived it in Vienna in 1904). Perhaps the most significant post-war revival was the one using 18th-century sets discovered in the theatre at Drottningholm (1965).

SYNOPSIS

Act I The Greeks are held up in Aulis by unfavourable winds on their way to attack Troy; a sacrifice is needed to propitiate Artemis. Agamemnon agonizes over his dilemma ('Diane impitoyable'); Iphigenia is sent for on the pretext of marrying her to Achilles, but in reality as the sacrifice. Calchas urges Agamemnon to do his duty; the Greek soldiers are heard fiercely demanding the sacrifice but he is defiant ('Peuvent-ils ordonner'). Agamemnon believes Arcas has forestalled his daughter's coming, but the chorus is heard greeting her and her mother. His next ruse is to tell Clytemnestra that Achilles has changed his mind. Iphigenia is devastated at the news, and greets her lover coldly; but his ardour overcomes her resistance.

Act II Preparations are made for the wedding but Arcas reveals the truth; Achilles promises to defend Iphigenia, but she is submissive. Achilles confronts Agamemnon (duet, 'De votre audace téméraire'). The infuriated king orders the sacrifice, but repents ('O toi, l'objet le plus aimable').

Act III The first part of the act is punctuated by the angry chorus of Greeks demanding blood. Iphigenia intends to submit to fate, despite Achilles' intention to fight and Clytemnestra's anguish. At the altar, after a solemn hymn, the sacrifice is prepared, but Achilles bursts in with his troops, threatening Calchas' life. The miraculous ignition of the pyre and a change of wind permits a happy ending.

For the Paris revival of 1775 minor changes were made in Act II, and at the end Artemis herself appears to bring about the happy ending and urge the Greeks on to the destruction of Troy (this was the version performed at the Paris Opéra into the 19th century, but not published until 1873). The ending, like that of *Tauride*, anticipates the 1790s vogue for operas ending in a rescue.

As the inception of the Gluckist era in France, *Iphigénie en Aulide* has a special place in operatic history. It is also, however, a logical development of his Viennese reform operas; in particular the overture is his finest, its contrasting thematic ideas, arranged in a free form, apparently representing the conflicting demands of authority and human affection that motivate the characters of the opera. In place of the sheer beauty of *Orfeo* and the grandeur of *Alceste*, Gluck concentrates on the variety and development of characterization, particularly of the title role and Agamemnon. To the almost saintly Iphigenia, who, however, is admirably severe when she believes herself jilted in Act I, and the noble, yet devious king are added a one-dimensional but vivid Achilles and a Clytemnestra whose anguish and fury in her arias (Act II, 'Par un père cruel'; Act III, 'Jupiter, lance la foudre') is worthy of the artistic, as well as actual, mother of Electra in Mozart's *Idomeneo*.

Gluck was criticized for surrendering beauty (particularly in the ballets, which are inferior to those in *Orphée*) to the portrayal of strong feeling; it was argued that opera is an art of illusion, and tragedy belonged in the spoken theatre. These qualities, which made *Iphigénie* only a qualified triumph, are precisely those which we value today. Both the orchestration and the recitative (albeit orchestrated throughout) are simpler than in the Calzabigi operas, perhaps because Gluck trusted the Paris orchestra less, and perhaps because he saw no place for trombones in an opera that in its original form had no true '*merveilleux*'. The forms are remarkably fluid, a personal adoption of a French model which was to influence the later revision of *Alceste*. In addition to arias, none long, some very short, there are fine ensembles, and complex scenes built out of arioso and recitative (especially those involving Agamemnon).

RECORDING Dawson, Von Otter, Aler, Van Dam, Monteverdi Ch, Lyons Opera O, Gardiner, Erato, 1990
EDITIONS earliest version: f.s., Le Marchand, [1774]; revised version: f.s., F. Pelletan and B. Damcke (eds),

Richault, 1873; M. Flothuis (ed.), *GW*, 1/5, 1987; v.s., Simrock, [1808–9]; numerous later v.ss, based on the 1774 score and therefore the first version; Wagner's version: v.s., Breitkopf und Härtel, [1859]; rev. version: Bärenreiter, 1991

Armide

Armida

Drame héroïque in five acts (3h)
Libretto by Philippe Quinault (1686), after an episode from Torquato Tasso's epic *La Gerusalemme liberata, ovvero Il Goffredo* (1575)
Composed 1776
PREMIERES 23 September 1777, Opéra, Paris; UK: 6 July 1906, Covent Garden, London; US: 14 November 1910, New York
CAST Armide *s*, Renaud *t*, 9 *s*, *a*, 2 *t*, 2 *bar*, *b*; *satb* chorus of *Coryphées*, people of Damascus, nymphs, shepherds and shepherdesses, followers of *la Haine*, demons, blessed spirits
ORCHESTRATION 2 fl, 2 ob, 2 cl, 2 bsn, 2 hn, 2 tpt, timp, str

In daring to use virtually unaltered the text of Lully's last completed opera, Gluck presented his strongest challenge both to the supporters of old French opera and to the newly ascendant partisans of Italian music. Usually, reset libretti were considerably altered (see Piccinni, *Atys*); Gluck merely omitted the Prologue and added a few telling lines for Armide at the end of Act III. In practice Armide goes only a little further than *Iphigénie en Aulide* in abandoning the Italian style and form in favour of a highly personal handling of French forms within a language forged for the purpose. It is, however, Gluck's one real success among the reform works that does not use the newly fashionable Greek mythology.

SYNOPSIS
Act I The pagan sorceress Armida has seduced many knights in the crusade led by Godfrey, but she cannot touch the pure Rinaldo whom she professes to hate. In fact her interest in him is disguised love (a comparison with the first act of Wagner's *Tristan* is not inapposite).
Act II Armida causes Rinaldo to be enticed into a place of beauty. He falls asleep but she cannot bring herself to kill him. She submits to love and carries him away to an enchanted place.
Act III After an aria that reveals her most intimate feelings, Armida summons Hate (*la Haine*) for conjurations against love, but then violently rejects them.
Act IV concerns the adventures of two knights coming to rescue the besotted Rinaldo.
Act V After the short love scene – the only time Armida and Rinaldo address one another – the knights shame Rinaldo into departure. Enraged, Armida, like Circe in *Telemaco*, destroys her magic works.

Gluck's setting matches Lully's in beauty and surpasses it in psychological insight. Gluck had the advantage, too, of the modern orchestra to paint Renaud's air 'Plus j'observe ces lieux' (Act II), underline sentiments (as in the wonderful end to Act III, with the composer's own text, a passage praised by Berlioz), and to end with a symphonic transfor-

mation scene, anticipating the orchestral end of Rossini's *Moses. Armide* is less likely to return to the repertoire than its contemporaries, however, because of the demands on staging, and because of its leisurely pace; it is surprising that Gluck included the whole of Act IV, in which the essential action is not advanced at all, and in it used less self-borrowing than in the dramatic parts of his work, notably Act III, which is based largely on older music including *Telemaco*, *Don Juan* and various opéra comiques.

RECORDING Palmer, Finnie, Rolfe Johnson, Roberts, Herincx, Richard Hickox Singers, City of London Sinfonia, Hickox, EMI, 1983
EDITIONS f.ss., Bureau du Journal du Musique, [1777]; F. Pelletan, C. Saint-Saëns and O. Thierry Poux (eds), Richault, [1889]; K. Hortschansky (ed.), *GW*, 1/8, 1987; v.ss., Rellstab, 1805–6; Bärenreiter, 1987

Iphigénie en Tauride

Iphigenia in Tauris

Tragédie lyrique in four acts (2h)
First version
Libretto by Nicholas-François Guillard, after Claude Guimond de la Touche's tragedy (1757) and Euripides
Composed 1778
PREMIERES 18 May 1779, Opéra, Paris; UK: 7 April 1796, London; US: 25 November 1916, Metropolitan, New York

Tragisches singspiel in four acts (2h)
Second version
Libretto by Johann Baptist von Alxinger, after Guillard
PREMIERE 23 October 1781, Burgtheater, Vienna

CAST Iphigenie *s*, Thoas *b*, Oreste *bar* (1781: *t*), Pylade *t* (*haute-contre*), 2 priestesses *s*, Diana *s*, a Scythian *b* (1781: *t*), a temple servant *b* (1781: *le ministre b*), 1779 only: a Greek woman *s*; *satb* chorus of priestesses, Scythians, Eumenides, Greeks, Thoas' guards
ORCHESTRATION 2 picc, 2 fl, 2 ob, 2 cl, 2 bsn, 2 hn, 2 tpt, 3 trbn, timp, perc (drum, cym, triangle), str

Gluck's last triumph at the Paris Opéra returns to Trojan War material. That Artemis (Diana) should save Iphigenia from sacrifice in Aulis and take her to Scythia (Crimea) as a priestess seems to negate the ending of the earlier opera; but the two themes were separately and incompatibly treated by Euripides, whose light-toned drama lies behind the more serious operas on the subject. The French pair (Piccinni's followed in 1781) were directly derived from Guymond de la Touche's play of 1757, still in repertoire at the Comédie Française in the 1770s. By coincidence Goethe's poetic drama on the subject was written at the same time as Gluck's opera. The second version, in German, is only a little altered. Its designation, tragisches singspiel, uses the latter word in its original sense, implying simply 'opera': there is no spoken dialogue.

Iphigénie en Tauride continues to be one of the most often revived of Gluck's operas. In the early 19th century the role was taken by Mme Branchu. The opera was a particular favourite of Berlioz; he wrote enthusiastically to Hallé (who gave a

Design by Pierre Adrien Paris for the prison in Iphigénie en Tauride *(Paris, c. 1785)*

performance in Manchester in 1860) about 'O malheureuse Iphigénie'; this aria was also singled out for praise by Tovey. Richard Strauss rearranged the operas, with additional orchestration and some musical 'modernization', in 1900 (repeated New York, 1916); but his version was considerably less radical than Wagner's of *Aulide*. Most of the major opera companies have put on the work since the Second World War. Callas took the title role under Giulini (Milan, 1957) and Gorr under Solti at the Edinburgh Festival in 1961, subsequently transferring to Covent Garden. The Paris Opéra revived it in 1965 with Régine Crespin.

SYNOPSIS

Act I Gluck prophetically began this opera without an overture. Instead the orchestra depicts calm at dawn, followed by the storm which (we learn later) brings Orestes to Tauris. Through this the voices of Iphigenia and her priestesses are heard imploring the gods' protection. The storm dies away; but Iphigenia declares that it is still raging in her heart. She has dreamed of the death of her father and mother, and then that she herself will raise the sacrificial knife to kill her brother. She turns to Artemis, who has brought her to Tauris, in prayer ('O toi, qui prolongeas mes jours'). The savage Thoas is afflicted

by foreboding ('De noirs pressentiments'); when two strangers appear, driven inland by the storm, he demands their immediate sacrifice in accordance with local custom.

Act II (Guillard originally wrote a five-act drama; it was on Gluck's insistence that two acts were conflated into Act II.) Orestes has been driven by the avenging Furies to seek absolution for killing his mother by recovering the statue of Artemis, profaned by human sacrifice in Tauris. The other captive is his close friend Pylades. They are separated by guards and Orestes, after a delusory moment of peace ('Le calme rentre dans mon coeur'), falls into a fit in which the Furies accuse him. At its climax his mother Clytemnestra's ghost appears and seems to merge into the real Iphigenia who comes to question him. Although unaware of Orestes' identity, Iphigenia feels drawn to him; she persuades him to tell her the history of her family, which he ends by announcing his own death. Lamenting his end ('O malheureuse Iphigénie') she turns for solace to ritual ('Contemplez ces tristes apprêts').

Act III Iphigenia resolves to free one captive, to take a message to her sister Electra. She hopes Orestes will be saved, but after a magnanimous dispute, in which Orestes cites his own madness as a reason for dying, Pylades agrees to go; he may find help and attempt a rescue ('Divinité des grandes âmes').

Act IV Iphigenia prays for release from her hated duty ('Je t'implore et je tremble'). At the sacrificial altar Iphigenia and Orestes recognize each other; Thoas enters in a rage, singing an air of invective which Gluck required his librettist to supply, and is about to slaughter the victim and priestess together when Pylades appears with the crew of the Greek ship, kills Thoas, and overcomes the superstitious barbarian guards. Artemis descends to confirm that her statue must no longer be profaned by human blood. (A ballet, *Les scythes enchaînés*, was added by Gossec, Gluck by this date (1779) apparently regarding such things as '*hors d'oeuvre*'.)

One remarkable aspect of this opera is the absence of sexual love. Gluck concentrates on his heroine, magnificently drawn in four contrasted arias, and on Orestes, whose frenzies, the result of the remorseless grip on his conscience of matricide (symbolized by the Furies) bring the trombones into play. The reminder, by the throbbing violas, that his peace ('Le calme rentre dans mon coeur') is illusory, is Gluck's most famous (though by no means unique) piece of psychological instrumentation. When it was criticized for the calm with which Orestes was speaking, Gluck replied: 'He is lying: he killed his mother.'

Iphigénie en Tauride may well be considered the most perfect of Gluck's serious operas. Yet he made even more use than usual of material salvaged from earlier works. The 1765 ballet *Semiramis* formed the basis for the Furies' music; Iphigenia's longer arias are from *La clemenza di Tito* and *Antigono* via *Telemaco*, which also supplied Orestes' Act II aria 'Dieux! qui me poursuivez' via *Le feste d'Apollo*; and the opening is derived from *L'île de Merlin*. The incorporation of Italian arias gives an expansiveness to the characterization which is markedly different from *Aulide* or *Armide*, though not unlike *Alceste*. None of these arias, however, retains its full *da capo* form, and they are balanced by shorter pieces. Iphigenia has an aria in each act; those in the first and third are considerably shorter, as are the arias for Thoas and Pylades. The small chorus of priestesses is handled with unprecedented freedom, intervening for single words as well as short choruses, and providing an additional dynamic and emotional resource at the climax of 'O malheureuse Iphigénie'. The divertissement is confined to the first act, a short abrasive set of choral and dance movements using 'Turkish' percussion instruments, following up the demonstration of national characteristic in *Paride*. Gluck continued to work in massive tableaux, notably in Act II; first Orestes' scene with the Furies, then Iphigenia's mourning, the central part of the original aria being converted into the chorus 'Contemplez ces tristes apprêts' (in the German version this is omitted, being replaced to considerably less effect by a sinfonia). The work also possesses a symphonic dimension unusual in Gluck, which, however, functions like a ritornello, connecting the opening storm music with the dénouement (the

intervention of Thoas to the arrival of Artemis), also in D major: the continuity of the music here exceeds even that of the climax of *Aulide*.

Gluck continued to cultivate flexibility of form, especially in recitatives, where the use of string texture, while prohibiting fast delivery, enabled him to exert an iron control over the tension even in the longest speeches. He makes more use than ever of sustained chordal accompaniment, which permits an immediate response from the orchestra to a crucial word or gesture. The principal formal achievement of this opera is the integration of arias derived from Italian works into a framework that seems entirely French. The revived *Alceste*, and earlier still Philidor in *Ernelinde*, provided precedents, but Gluck shortened his arias while retaining their expansiveness of gesture. This enabled him to move flexibly between recitative, aria and chorus.

RECORDING Montague, Aler, Allen, Massis, Monteverdi Ch, O of Lyon Opera, Gardiner, Philips, 1986
EDITIONS 1779 version: f.ss., Bureau du Journal de Musique, [1779]; F. Pelletan and B. Damcke (eds), Richault, 1874; A. Dorffel (ed.), Peters, [1884]; study s.: H. Abert (ed.), Eulenburg, [1927]; G. Croll (ed.), *GW*, 1/9, 1973; v.s., Rellstab, 1788–9; 1781 version: G. Croll (ed.), *GW*, 1/11, 1965; v.s., Bärenreiter, 1965; Strauss's version: Fürstner, 1891

Echo et Narcisse
Echo and Narcissus

Drame lyrique in a prologue and three acts (2h)
Libretto by Louis Theodore von Tschudi
PREMIERE 24 September 1779, Opéra, Paris

Gluck's last opera except for the German version of *Iphigénie en Tauride*. It belongs to the pastoral tradition, which seldom succeeded at the Paris Opéra in this period. Gluck lavished some of his loveliest instrumental invention on it, notably in the use of an echo orchestra, and was badly hurt by its failure, but he should not have been surprised. It was more successful when revived in a smaller theatre in 1780.

Echo loves Narcissus, but he is obsessed with a water nymph whom he cannot reach: she is, of course, his own reflection. This curse laid on him by Apollo is lifted by Love just in time to prevent Echo dying of grief. This slender material is spun out to three acts with great musical charm, but little dramatic impact, a version of 'Le bell'imagine' from *Paride* sounding incongruously powerful when coming from the drooping hero Narcisse.

RECORDING Boulin, Massell, Galliard, Streit, Hamburg Opera Ch, Concerto Köln, Jacobs, Harmonia Mundi, 1988
EDITIONS f.ss., Paris, 1780; Saint-Saëns and Tiersot (eds), Durand, 1902; R. Gerber (ed.), *GW*, 1/10, 1953; v.ss., Launer, [*c.* 1845]; Lemoine, 1908

Other operas: *Artaserse*, 1741 (2 arias survive); *Demetrio*, 1742 (8 arias survive); *Il Tigrane*, 1743 (11 arias and 1 duet survive); *La Sofonisba*, 1744 (11 arias and 1 duet survive); *Poro*, 1744 (overture, 4 arias and 1 duet survive); *Ippolito*, 1745 (11 arias and 1 duet survive); *Artamene*, 1746 (6 arias survive); *La contesa de'numi*, 1749; *Issipile*, 1752 (4 arias survive); *Le diable à quatre, ou La double métamorphose*, 1759; *L'arbre enchanté, ou Le tuteur dupé*, 1759, rev. 1775;

Il prologo, 1767 (overture and 3 numbers to precede Traetta's *Ifigenia in Aulide*)
BIBLIOGRAPHY Bruce Alan Brown, *Gluck and the French Theatre in Vienna*, OUP, 1991; Martin Cooper, *Gluck*, Chatto and Windus, 1935; Alfred Einstein, *Gluck*, Dent (Master Musicians Series), 1936; *rp*, 1964; L. Guichard (ed.), *Hector Berlioz, A travers chants*, Grund, 1971; C. Hopkinson, *A Bibliography of the Printed Works of C. W. von Gluck 1714–1787*, author, 1959; 2nd edn, 1967; P. Howard, *Gluck and the Birth of Modern Opera*, Barrie and Rockliff, 1963; P. Howard, *C. W. von Gluck: Orfeo*, CUP (Cambridge Opera Handbooks), 1981; P. Howard, *C. W. Gluck: A Guide to Research*, Garland, 1987; H. and E. H. Mueller von Asow (eds), trans. S. Thomson, *The Collected Correspondence and Papers of Christopher Willibald Gluck*, Barrie and Rockliff, 1962; Julian Rushton, 'The Musician Gluck', *MT*, vol. 128 (1987), p. 615; D. F. Tovey, 'Christoph Willibald Gluck and the Musical Revolution of the Eighteenth Century', *Essays and Lectures on Music*, OUP, 1949; A. Wotquenne, *Catalogue thématique des oeuvres de Chr. W. v. Gluck*, 1904; *rp* Georg Ohms, 1967

J.R.

FRANCESCO GNECCO
b c. 1769, Genoa; *d* 1810 or 1811, Milan

Little is known with certainty of Gnecco's life and career. He may have studied with Cimarosa, though his musical style gives no indication of his teacher's influence. Initially active as a church musician and composer – he was maestro di cappella at Savona Cathedral for a time – Gnecco enjoyed his greatest success as a composer of both comic and serious operas.

Gnecco often wrote his own libretti, including that to his best-known opera, *La prova di un opera seria*. This was the most successful – though not the first – of a genre of comic opera popular in the early 19th century based on backstage life at the theatre. Gnecco's libretto tells of a rehearsal for a non-existent opera seria, *Ettore in Trabisonda*, and parodies the musical styles of Paisiello and Cimarosa.

La prova di un opera seria held its popularity for over 50 years (it could still be seen in London in 1860), performed at Europe's principal theatres. Its success must be attributed at least in part to the flexibility of the score, which gave the prima donna and principal tenor opportunities to mould the work to their own taste and to show off their talents. Gnecco's 'fixed' elements are, in the manner of his remaining operatic output, unremarkable.

Operatic works: *Auretta e Masiello, ossia Il contrattempo*, 1792; *La contadina astuta*, 1792; *Il nuovo galateo*, 1792; *I filosofi burlati*, 1793; *L'indolente*, 1793; *Lo sposo di tre, marito di nessuno*, 1793; *Le nozze dei Sanniti*, 1797; *I due sordi*, 1798; *Vomina e Mitridate*, 1803; *La prima prova dell'opera 'Gli Orazi e Curiazi'*, 1803, rev. as *La prova d'un opera seria*, 1805; *Le nozze di Lauretta*, 1804; *Carolina e Filandro*, 1804; *Il geloso corretto*, 1804; *Arsace e Semiramide*, 1804; *L'amore in musica*, 1805; *Gli ultimi due giorni di Carnevale*, 1806; *I riti dei bramini*, 1806; *Il nuovo podestà*, 1807; *Argete*, 1808; *I falsi galantuomini*, 1809; *Gli amanti filarmonici*, 1810; *Amore scioglie i pregiudizi*, n.d.

BIBLIOGRAPHY Sabine Henze-Dohring, 'Francesco Gnecco', in *Pipers Enzyklopadie des Musik Theaters*, vol. 2, R. Piper, 1987, pp. 466–8

D.S.B.

ALEXANDER GOEHR
Peter Alexander Goehr; *b* 10 August 1932, Berlin

The son of the conductor Walter Goehr, Alexander Goehr went to England with his family in 1933 and has lived there ever since. He studied at the Royal Manchester College of Music (1952–5) with Richard Hall, and formed the so-called New Music Manchester group with, among others, Birtwistle and Maxwell Davies. He later spent a year in Paris studying with Messiaen and Yvonne Loriod. For a few years he was a BBC producer, and he directed the Music Theatre Ensemble (1967–72). Since 1971 he has been a university professor: first at Leeds (till 1976), then at Cambridge, where he has been a strong influence on the teaching, especially of composition, as well as reaching a wider audience through the medium of radio (he gave the BBC Reith Lectures in 1987).

Goehr's father had been a pupil of Schoenberg, and the son has always retained in his own music something of the intellectual rigour and system of that tradition. But he quickly outstripped its orthodoxy, and evolved a more personal and flexible harmonic grammar that also owes something to Messiaen. This harmonic 'feel' has given Goehr's mature work a distinctive flavour and in some ways made it more approachable, though the sort of music he writes is still intensely serious, with a consciousness of 'great traditions'. He has contributed to most of the standard instrumental forms (three symphonies, several concertos and three string quartets), and has written powerful oratorios. But his theatre music has had a chequered career. An early attempt at an opera on Euripides (*The Trojan Women*) was abandoned and its surviving fragments absorbed into the orchestral *Hecuba's Lament* (1959–61). His two subsequent full-length operas both had German premieres in which they fell foul of German theatrical politics, though at least Germany staged them – which, at the time of writing (1991), no established British company has done. As for the triptych of music-theatre pieces, they enjoyed a fashionable career in the early 1970s, when that genre was in vogue and when Goehr's ensemble existed to perform them, but have since fallen into relative neglect.

Arden Must Die
Arden muss sterben
Opera in two acts, Op. 21 (2h)
Libretto by Erich Fried (English version by Geoffrey Skelton), after the anonymous 16th-century play *Arden of Faversham*, and the Chronicle of Holinshed
Composed 1966
PREMIERES 5 March 1967, Staatsoper, Hamburg; UK: 17 April 1974, Sadler's Wells, London (New Opera Company)

CAST Arden *b*, Franklin *b*, Alice *ms*, Mosbie *t*, Susan *s*, Michael *t*, Greene *bar*, Reede *b*, Mrs Bradshaw *a*, Shakebag *t*, Black Will *b*, *s*, *bar*, *b*, *spoken role*; *satb* chorus of market people and (*tb*) constables
LARGE ORCHESTRA including amplified pf, organ, hpd, accordion

Goehr's first opera was commissioned by Hamburg State Opera, and played there to a noisy reception of the kind so often accorded by post-war German audiences to works with political content, however muted. Fried's adaptation enhances the play's 'morality' or (in Brecht's sense) 'epic' character: individual character is suppressed in favour of a semi-parodistic treatment of human frailty. Authority lines up with the most cynical individual self-interest (in fact is indistinguishable from it), while the majority, represented by the 'neighbour' Mrs Bradshaw (a character invented by Fried), stand by and pretend to be uninvolved.

A scene from Act I of Arden Must Die *(Hamburg, 1967)*

SYNOPSIS
Act I The characters plot Arden's murder: his wife, Alice, because she wants her lover, Mosbie; others because Arden is supposedly a hard landlord, etc. Arden, who in fact appears a decent man, is called to London to administer lands recently granted him. Alice feigns regret, but at once goes to bed with Mosbie. On the marshes in dense fog, Arden and Franklin cross the river by ferry, while the hired murderers Shakebag and Black Will blunder around and Shakebag falls into the river. A shepherd brings Alice and the others news of Arden's murder, but

soon afterwards Arden and Franklin themselves return. Arden makes to throw the would-be murderers out; Mosbie draws a dagger but then protests his innocence, and the act ends with a reconciliation.

Act II Shakebag and Will are in London (characterized by quotation from Gibbons's *Cries of London*) in pursuit of Arden, and observed by Mrs Bradshaw. But again they are thwarted, this time by a window shutter falling on Will's head at the crucial moment. Later they plot to enter Arden's London house at night, but the door is locked against them. Back at Faversham, Arden has dinner guests (the plotters) and this time, despite blunders, the murder is successful. But when the law arrives, in the person of the mayor and constables, the hired killers are appointed hangmen, and hope is offered to the others: 'For those who are contrite the law holds out no terrors. With true deeds they may strive to wipe out ancient errors.' In a spoken epilogue (done in Hamburg but later suppressed) the audience is ironically reassured of its own innocence.

Fried rhymed his text and included set pieces: 'Murderers' Songs', 'Ferryman's Song', etc., in the Brechtian manner. But Goehr's setting only partly respects this formula, and stylistically it owes little or nothing to Brecht–Weill. Like all Goehr's music it has a strong harmonic profile, materializing sometimes into tonal shapes. For a first opera, it is impressively considerate of the voices and as a score it is consistently intriguing. But as drama it perhaps lacks the speed and variety of pace called for by its black-comic subject matter, while the character portraiture is inevitably somewhat one-dimensional. Was Goehr, a self-declared man of the Left, interested in the political message as such? In the Hamburg programme he called Arden 'a political opera about the way we act in a crisis', but this remark is absent from the 1974 London programme, even though (in the broadest sense) it is no less than the truth.

EDITION f.s., Schott (on hire); v.s., Schott, 1967

Naboth's Vineyard
Dramatic madrigal, Op. 25 (20m)
Libretto by the composer, after I Kings 21
Composed 1968
PREMIERES 16 July 1968, Cripplegate Theatre, London; US: 11 December 1991, Manhattan School of Music, New York

After the founding of the Music Theatre Ensemble in 1967, it was inevitable that Goehr would write for it. This short piece, on the biblical story of King Ahab's ruthless acquisition of a coveted vineyard by false accusation and murder of its owner, was the first fruit. In its scoring (flute, clarinet, trombone, violin, double-bass, piano duet) *Naboth's Vineyard* reveals the fashionable influence of Schoenberg's *Pierrot lunaire*, which had moulded other music-theatre groups (such as the Pierrot Players, also in 1967), and, more distantly, of Monteverdi's hybrid *Il combattimento di Tancredi e Clorinda*. Britten's *Curlew River* (1964) is similarly suggested by the use of Noh theatre type masks, worn here by actors, who mime (as in Stravinsky's *Renard*) to a text in English and Latin sung by alto, tenor and bass soloists.

EDITION f.s., Schott, 1973

Shadowplay-2

Music-theatre, Op. 30 (20m)
Libretto by Kenneth Cavander, after Plato's *Republic*, Book 7
Composed 1970
PREMIERES 8 July 1970, Cripplegate Theatre, London; US: 11 December 1991, Manhattan School of Music, New York

Cavander and Goehr interwove three versions of the cave allegory that Plato used to illustrate his theory of Forms: 'an imaginative dramatization, a more explicit narrative version and finally a literal translation'. Men are chained in an underground chamber so that they experience only the shadows of the outside world, but then one of them is released and has to adjust to a new concept of reality. There is a singing narrator (tenor), an actor, and a small ensemble of alto flute, alto saxophone, horn, cello and piano.

EDITION f.s., Schott, 1976

Sonata about Jerusalem

Cantata – Music-theatre III, Op. 31 (20m)
Libretto by Recha Freier and the composer, after 12th-century Hebrew texts
Composed 1970
PREMIERES January 1971, Tel Aviv; UK: 7 May 1971, Palace Pier, Brighton Festival; US: 11 December 1991, Manhattan School of Music, New York

This completed Goehr's music-theatre triptych, often subsequently performed as such. Commissioned by Testimonium (Jerusalem), it tells how captive Jews in 12th-century Baghdad believed a rumour of a messiah. They climb to the roofs and as night falls, seeing a vision of Jerusalem, they pretend to fly there. But the next morning they have to descend once more, and face the mockery of the less credulous Jews. Goehr's somewhat ritualistic treatment, with a refrain in the form of a Latin chant about the Last Judgment, uses a small female chorus, soprano and bass soloists, and an ensemble of flute, clarinet, trumpet, trombone, piano, violin, cello and double-bass.

EDITION f.s., Schott, 1976

Behold the Sun

Opera in three acts, Op. 44 (3h)
Libretto by John McGrath and the composer
Composed 1981–4
PREMIERE 19 April 1985, Duisburg (as *Die Wiedertäufer*)
CAST Berninck *bar*, his Wife *ms*, Christian *coloratura s*, Matthys *bar*, Divara *s*, Bokelson *t*, Blacksmith *b*, Knipperdollinck *bar*, Prince-Bishop *bar*, *s*, 3 *t*, *bar*; *satb* chorus of townspeople; semichorus of Anabaptists
LARGE ORCHESTRA including alto sax, pf, vibraphone; onstage band, offstage band

Goehr's earlier study of religious delusion (in *Sonata about Jerusalem*) led him to this full-length treatment of the Anabaptist uprising in Münster in 1534–5. He had considered other more or less messianic subjects, and had sketched a libretto on Shelley's *Prometheus Unbound*. The eventual inspiration for *Behold the Sun* came from Norman Cohn's book *The Pursuit of the Millennium* and from Ernst Bloch's writings on the 'theology of Revolution'. The work uses the mass hysteria in the historical events as a basis for a choral opera with a flavour of the baroque Passion (the chorus is referred to as *turba*), while the big set-piece ensembles are offset by more intimate genre scenes. But the first production, by Deutsche Oper am Rhein, was both brutally cut and partly reorganized at the behest of the producer Bohumil Herlischka, wrecking Goehr's fine balance of the 'real' and the 'possible'.

SYNOPSIS

Act I The merchant Berninck comes home to find his wife reading the Bible and his son Christian unfed. In the Cathedral Square in (Lutheran) Münster the Anabaptists arrive from Leyden (Holland), led by Matthys, his wife Divara, and Bokelson. Their prophetic utterances and ecstatic manner infect the townspeople. They kiss, swooningly, to the dismay of the unaffected, including Berninck and the Burgomaster Knipperdollinck. Christian embarks on a visionary song with chorus, and the crowd becomes more and more abandoned.

Act II The Prince-Bishop determines to put down the rising. In Münster Matthys urges the people to be baptized anew and to give up their material wealth. Bokelson threatens a fishwife with a dagger for refusing, but is restrained by Matthys. Berninck, Knipperdollinck and the blacksmith stand up to Bokelson, who kills the blacksmith. Berninck tries to leave with his valuables but is prevented by the Anabaptists. Matthys walks out on to the town walls and is shot by the besiegers.

Act III Divara comforts the starving towns-people. A lame man utters prophecies. Bokelson, increasingly deranged, presents himself as king; he urges the men to polygamy and takes Divara as his wife. In the Bernincks' house Christian dies of starvation. In the square, the lame prophet works the people into a hysteria; there is an ecstatic dance and a play (*Dives and Lazarus*) is enacted, at the end of which Lazarus (Bokelson) orders the actual hanging of Dives. Divara intervenes. The Episcopal troops arrive, let in by Berninck, to be confronted by the ecstatic crowd led by Divara.

Goehr's score is closely related to a just earlier large-scale choral work, *Babylon the Great is Fallen*, and its choral scenes are the finest. The music uses refrain forms and recurrent harmonies brilliantly to suggest the gradual growth of mass hysteria. The genre scenes are more conventional and perhaps weaker, and the text, heavily dependent on prophetic utterances, sometimes lacks dramatic direction. But the vocal writing is excellent, and there is a magnificently extravagant soprano part for the visionary boy Christian, much of which was cut in Duisburg.

EDITION f.s., Schott (on hire); v.s., Schott, 1985

BIBLIOGRAPHY 'Naboth's Vineyard: Alexander Goehr talks to Stanley Sadie', *MT*, vol. 109 (1968), pp. 625–6; Bayan Northcott (ed.), *The Music of Alexander Goehr*, Schott, 1980; Bayan Northcott and Alexander Goehr, 'Working on *Die Wiedertäufer*', *Opera*, vol. 36 (1985), pp. 379–84; Nicholas Williams, '*Behold the Sun*: The Politics of Musical Production', in Christopher Norris (ed.), *Music and the Politics of Culture*, Lawrence and Wishart, 1989

S.W.

HERMANN GOETZ

Hermann Gustav Goetz; *b* 7 December 1840, Königsberg; *d* 3 December 1876, Hottingen, nr Zurich

Goetz studied music at the Stern Conservatory in Berlin, Hans von Bülow being among his teachers. In 1863 he moved to the Swiss town of Winterthur as a church organist, hoping not only to achieve musical success but also that the Swiss air would cure the tuberculosis he had contracted in childhood. Besides his duties in the organ loft he began teaching, performed as a concert pianist and started composing. His first stage work, a singspiel entitled *Die heiligen drei Königen* (1865), remains unpublished.

In spite of severe depression brought on by his illness, Goetz was able to produce joyful music. Of his published works, it is the chamber music, the Second Symphony and the two operas that reveal the best of this Romantic composer who stands in direct line from Weber, Marschner, Spohr and middle-period Wagner.

Der Widerspänstigen Zähmung

The Taming of the Shrew
Comic opera in four acts (2h 15m)
Libretto by Joseph Widmann and the composer, after the play by Shakespeare (1594)
Composed 1868–72
PREMIERES 11 October 1874, Mannheim; UK: 12 October 1878, Drury Lane, London; US: 4 January 1886, New York

Goetz began work on this opera only after rejecting Widmann's suggestion of *Parzifal*. It was a further six years before the premiere of the work, which, in the field of German comic opera, is a natural successor to Nicolai's *Die lustige Weiber von Windsor* and Cornelius's *Der Barbier von Bagdad*.

Set in Padua, the story relates the wooing of Baptista's daughter Katharine by Petruchio and, after fierce resistance by the shrewish and hot-blooded girl, her eventual submission to his domination. A sub-plot concerns the competition for the hand of Katharine's sister Bianca by two suitors, Hortensio and Lucentio.

The opera immediately spread its composer's name from Vienna to London and New York. Goetz had turned away from Wagner's concept of opera and drama (he denied that he had been influenced by *Die Meistersinger*, premiered in 1868) and remained loyal to the classicism of Mozart. He believed in preserving a 'unified, architectural musical form . . . in achieving the confluence of dramatic and musical development' (Kreuzhage). The opera has many ensembles, ranging from duets to the final septet, and is linked by arias and orchestrally accompanied recitative.

Der Widerspänstigen Zähmung elicited lavish praise from George Bernard Shaw in 1893: 'You have to go to Mozart's finest quartets and quintets . . . and *Die Meistersinger* . . . for work of the quality we find, not here and there, but continuously in the Symphony in F and *The Taming of the Shrew*, masterpieces which place Goetz securely above all other German composers of the last hundred years, save only Mozart and Beethoven, Weber and Wagner.'

RECORDING Teschemacher, Trotschel, Ahlersmeyer, Nilssen, Dresden State Opera Ch and O, Elmendorff, Urania, 1944
EDITIONS f.s./v.s., Kistner, [1875]

Francesca da Rimini

Romantic opera in three acts
Libretto by Joseph Widmann and the composer, after Canto V of Dante's *Inferno* (c. 1307–21)
Composed 1875–6; completed 1877 by Ernst Frank
PREMIERES 30 September 1877, Mannheim; UK: 3 December 1908, Royal College of Music, London

Goetz began work on his second opera, *Francesca da Rimini*, in 1875, but it was a race against time which he eventually lost. He completed only the first two acts, and it was left to his amanuensis, the conductor Ernst Frank, to flesh out the sketches of the overture and the last act. Joseph Widmann based his libretto on Silvio Pellico's 1812 adaptation of Dante's text, though Goetz himself was largely responsible for shaping and adapting the work.

The original story of Lanciotto Malatesta's jealousy of his wife Francesca, because of her love for his brother Paolo, provides the basis of the work. The second-act duet for the pair of ill-fated lovers may have drained the composer of his last strength, but it produced the best music in the opera. Brahms and Bruch were present at the first performance but even this eminent patronage, and a rescoring by Felix Mottl in 1893, failed to achieve for the opera anything like the success of its predecessor, largely because of its inherently weak and undramatic libretto.

EDITIONS f.s., Kistner, [1878]; v.s., Leipzig, [1878]

BIBLIOGRAPHY E. Kreuzhage, *Hermann Goetz, sein Leben und seine Werke*, Leipzig, 1916

C.F.

KARL GOLDMARK

Karl [Carl, Karoly] Goldmark; *b* 18 May 1830, Keszthely;
d 2 January 1915, Vienna

Goldmark was the second son in a very large Jewish family and his parents could not afford regular music tuition for him. Nevertheless he gained admission to the music school in Ödenburg in 1842 and showed such promise on the violin that he was sent to Vienna to study with Leopold Jansa. He later studied violin and rudimentary harmony at the Vienna Conservatory. During the next few years he earned a modest living as a theatre violinist and music teacher and continued to work at composition.

After several public performances of his works in the late 1850s, and a period in Budapest, during which he continued his composition studies, Goldmark suddenly gained recognition in 1860 with his String Quartet, Op. 8. He began to write music criticism and became a strong Wagner supporter. Grants from the Austrian and Hungarian governments enabled him to concentrate on composition. Having acqiired a reputation with his overture *Sakuntala*, Op. 13 (1865), he became a leading figure in Viennese musical life with the success of his opera *Die Königin von Saba*. Shortly afterwards he began a setting of Felix Dahm's libretto *Der Fremdling*, but abandoned it after composing the first act. With *Merlin*, composed in the early 1880s, Goldmark moved much closer to Wagner both in choice of subject and music. His next and only comic opera, *Das Heimchen am Herd* (1896), after a story by Charles Dickens, stands in sharp contrast to his previous operas, showing close affinities with the early 19th-century comic opera tradition. *Der Kriegsgefangene*, a grand heroic opera based on an episode from Homer's *Iliad*, followed only three years after *Das Heimchen am Herd* and reverted to something like the style of *Merlin*; it has impressive choral scenes, but the subject seems not to have been to the taste of the day and it was not widely performed. *Götz von Berlichingen*, premiered in Budapest in 1902, is the only one of Goldmark's operas to have a self-contained overture and, in other respects too, it is further removed from the Wagnerian conception of opera. However, it is perhaps the most uneven of Goldmark's operas and wavers uncomfortably between lyricism and Wagnerian gesture. In his final completed opera, *Ein Wintermärchen*, based on Shakespeare's *A Winter's Tale*, Goldmark seems to have shed Wagnerian influence almost entirely; it returns to a lighter, more melodious style. But though several of his later operas were enthusiastically greeted, none of them was as successful as *Die Königin von Saba*.

Die Königin von Saba

The Queen of Sheba
Opera in four acts, Op. 27 (3h 45m)
Libretto by Salomon Hermann Mosenthal
Composed 1866–75
PREMIERES   10 March 1875, Hofoper, Vienna;

US: 2 December 1885, Metropolitan, New York;
UK: 12 April 1910, Manchester

Goldmark spent almost ten years over the composition and revision of this opera. Its premiere, with a strong cast conducted by Gericke, was highly successful and it was soon being performed widely abroad. It remained in the repertoire until well into the 20th century.

Amalie Materna in the title role of Die Konigen von Saba *(Vienna, 1875)*

The Queen of Sheba is in love with Assad, a favourite of Solomon, who has been sent to invite her to Jerusalem. She secretly meets him incognito on several occasions, but publicly denies her liaison with him. When the queen appears at Assad's betrothal to Sulamith, he is so perturbed that he commits sacrilege in the temple; he is condemned to death. At the queen's intercession Assad's sentence is commuted to banishment in the wilderness. The queen meets Assad in the desert, but he rejects her. After a sandstorm he dies in the arms of Sulamith, who conveniently arrives on the scene just in time.

The opera is constructed on a large scale and richly orchestrated. A contemporary critic detected similarities between Goldmark's treatment of Solomon and Wagner's of Wotan in *Die Walküre*, but despite Goldmark's profound admiration for Wagner, his influence on the music of the opera is essentially superficial. Spohr, Mendelssohn, Schumann and Meyerbeer contributed more fundamentally to its style. The strength of *Die Königin von Saba* lies principally in Goldmark's effective use of oriental colour, his strong characterization of the main protagonists and his feeling for the powerful effect.

RECORDING Kalmár, Kincses, Takács, Jerusalem, Nagy, Miller, Hungarian State Opera Ch and O, Fischer, Hungaroton, 1980
EDITIONS f.s./v.s., Pohl, 1876

Merlin

Opera in a prelude and three acts
Libretto by Siegfried Lipiner
Composed 1882–4, rev. 1904
PREMIERES 19 November 1886, Hofoper, Vienna; rev. version: 14 February 1904, Frankfurt; US: 3 January 1887, New York

Merlin shows greater Wagnerian influence than *Die Königin von Saba*. A strong flavour of Wagner's *Ring* is already apparent in the prelude. Throughout the opera, chorus and orchestra are used powerfully and imaginatively. Although not as successful as its predecessor, it was performed on most of the major German stages during the years immediately following its premiere.

EDITIONS f.s./v.s., J. Schuberth & Co., 1886

Other operas: *Das Heimchen am Herd*, 1896; *Der Kriegsgefangene* (originally *Briseis*), 1899; *Götz von Berlichingen*, 1902; *Ein Wintermärchen*, 1908
BIBLIOGRAPHY Karl Goldmark, *Erinnerungen aus meinem Leben*, Vienna, 1922, trans. as *Notes from the Life of a Viennese Composer*, 1927; H. Truscott, 'Carl Goldmark', *MMR*, vol. 90 (1960), p. 62; R. von Perger, 'Karl Goldmark', *Die Musik*, vol. 7 (1907–8), pp. 131ff.

C.A.B.

BERTHOLD GOLDSCHMIDT

b 18 January 1903, Hamburg, Germany

Berthold Goldschmidt was one of the most promising young composers of Weimar Germany. A pupil of Schreker, he was a student companion of some of the most celebrated musicians of the age, including Krenek, Hába, and Horenstein. A répétiteur for the first performance of Berg's *Wozzeck*, at which he played the celesta, he made a growing reputation as a conductor while still young.

For his first opera he took the play *Le cocu magnifique* by Crommelynck, celebrated at the time in a touring production by the avant-garde Russian producer Meyerhold, and set it as *Der gewaltige Hahnrei*. It was produced in Mannheim in 1932, to wide acclaim, but a planned Berlin production by Carl Ebert was abandoned after the Nazi seizure of power. It was revived in a Berlin concert performance on 1 December 1992, and recorded by Decca.

Goldschmidt escaped to England in 1935 and made a precarious living until he was employed by the BBC European Service. He later made a career as a conductor, and was influential in the Mahler revival.

His second opera, *Beatrice Cenci*, to a libretto based on Shelley's tragedy *The Cenci*, by Martin Esslin, was written as an entry for the Arts Council's competition for operas to celebrate the Festival of Britain in 1951. Goldschmidt was one of the four winners but none was then produced. Extracts of *Beatrice Cenci* were broadcast in 1953; a full concert performance had to wait until 16 April 1988. The opera's post-Mahlerian Romantic idiom is reminiscent in turn of Busoni, Hindemith and Weill.

BIBLIOGRAPHY Nicholas Kenyon, 'New Deal' (interview with Goldschmidt about *Beatrice Cenci*), *Observer*, 10 April 1988, p. 39; David Matthews, 'Berthold Goldschmidt: A Biographical Sketch', *Tempo*, no. 144 (March 1983), pp. 2–6

L.F.

CARLOS GOMES

Antônio Carlos Gomes; *b* 11 July 1836, Campinas, Brazil; *d* 16 September 1896, Belém, Brazil

Gomes, one of 26 children, came from a typically provincial musical training to become Brazil's leading opera composer, revered equally at home and in Italy, where Verdi declared him a genius. During the period of fervid Brazilian political nationalism in the 1930s Gomes was posthumously proclaimed a national hero, the first composer to be so honoured, and his centenary in 1936 was celebrated throughout the country. His works are still revived in Brazil but receive few performances elsewhere, even in Italy, his adopted second home.

The success of Gomes's first two operas, *A Noite do Castelo* (1861) and *Joana de Flandres* (1863) brought his name to the attention of the Emperor Don Pedro II of Brazil, who granted him a studentship in Milan where he became an almost permanent resident. His subsequent operas and operettas, all in a thoroughly Italianate vein, won him acclaim as a worthy follower of Donizetti and Verdi. Although *Fosca* (1873) failed initially in Italy because of its Wagnerism, it had a more enthusiastic reception when it was revived five years later. Gomes's great success, however, both in Italy and Brazil, was *Il Guarani* which, like a later opera *Lo schiavo*, deals with a Brazilian subject. Towards the end of his life Gomes travelled frequently between Brazil and Italy, but died in his own country shortly after assuming a teaching post at the conservatory in Belém.

Il Guarany

The Guarani
Opera-ballo in four acts (3h 15m)
Libretto by Antonio Scalvini and Carlo d'Ormeville, after José de Alancar's novel *O Guarani* (1857)
Composed 1868–70

PREMIERES 19 March 1870, La Scala, Milan; UK: 13 July 1872, Covent Garden, London; US: 3 November 1884, New York

Il Guarany was Gomes's most important opera, in that it broke new ground in the treatment of nationalist subject matter. Himself a descendant of a Guarani Indian, Gomes was naturally drawn to José de Alancar's love story of 16th-century colonial Brazil. The opera tells of the love of Cecilia, daughter of a hidalgo, Antonio, and Pery, a Guarani Indian. Antonio disapproves of the match, wanting Cecilia to marry the Portuguese Don Alvaro; but after many complications – including Pery's capture and preparation for the pot by the cannibal Aimoré Indians – Pery and Cecilia are united.

Gomes's setting relies heavily on romantic stylization of tenuous 'folk' elements calculated to appeal to the 19th-century European ideal of the 'noble savage'. Native dances are tempered and choreographed for the stage, notably in the Act III 'Ballet of the Aimoré Indians', which culminates in an inevitable *Baccanale Indiano*. As there are no quotations from authentic Indian sources, local atmosphere is achieved entirely artificially; the opera is only as Brazilian as Verdi's *Aida* is Egyptian, with a traditional succession of choruses, arias and duets.

RECORDING A. Gomes, Maresca, Fortes, Ch and O of the Rio de Janeiro Municipal Theatre, Tavares, Voce, 1980
EDITION v.s., Ricordi, 1870

Lo Schiavo
The Slave
Dramma lirico in four acts (2h 30m)
Libretto by Alfredo Taunay and Rodolfo Paravicini
Composed 1883–7
PREMIERES 27 September 1889, Teatro Imperial Don Pedro II, Rio de Janeiro; UK: 31 January 1978, St John's, Smith Square, London (concert)

Although the action was transferred from the 18th to the 16th century and Indians replaced black slaves, *Lo Schiavo* clearly addressed the topical issue of slavery in Brazil. It was written at the height of the controversy surrounding the abolitionists and, like *Il Guarani*, is important for its social probing rather than for its musical content. Striking a claim for nationalism, the opera was premiered in Brazil two months before the collapse of the empire. The *Preludio Orquestrale* ('Dawn') in Act IV, with its realistic imitation of natural sounds, is a well-known concert piece, as is *The Dance of the Tamois*, in which Gomes creates a local flavour with a folklike melody and a habanera-type accompaniment.

RECORDING Martins, Godoy, Maresca, Teixeira, Feres, Ch and O of the São Paulo Municipal Opera, Machado, Voce, 1979
EDITIONS v.ss. Ricordi, 1889; *rp*, National Press (Rio), 1955

Other operatic works: *A Noite do Castelo*, 1861; *Joana de Flandres*, 1863; *Se sa minga*, 1867; *Nella Luna*, 1868; *Telegrafo Electrico*, 1871; *Fosca*, 1873, rev. 1878; *Salvator Rosa*, 1874 (RECORDING UORC, 1960s or 1970s); *Maria Tudor*, 1879

(RECORDING Voce, 1978); *Condor*, 1891 (RECORDING UORC, 1941); 10 inc. operas
BIBLIOGRAPHY Gerard Béhague, *Music in Latin America: An Introduction*, Prentice-Hall, 1979, pp. 113–16

S.J.W.

EUGENE GOOSSENS
(Sir) Aynsley Eugene Goossens; *b* 26 May 1893, London; *d* 13 June 1962, Hillingdon, England

Goossens began his career as a violinist after studying composition with Stanford at the Royal College of Music but soon followed in the family footsteps by conducting opera (both his father and grandfather, of Belgian origin, were principal conductors with the Carl Rosa Opera Company), and as assistant to Beecham (for whom he frequently deputized). His later conducting appointments in the US and Australia were not operatic, though he was a guiding force behind early plans for the Sydney Opera House.

Goossens's compositions are not well known and lack melodic character while echoing modernism. Nevertheless, his handling of voices and knowledge of the stage place his two operas, both to libretti by Arnold Bennett, among his major achievements. *Judith* (1929) is a melodramatic piece based on the violent Old Testament story (somewhat in the mould of Strauss's *Salome*). *Don Juan de Mañara* (1937) after the play by Dumas *père*, is notable for its attempt to promote opera in English through the extensive use of a *parlando* vocal style. Goossens himself conducted both works at their Covent Garden premieres.

BIBLIOGRAPHY Eugene Goossens, *Overture and Beginners*, Methuen, 1951

S.B.

FRANÇOIS-JOSEPH GOSSEC
originally Gossé; *b* 17 January 1734, Vergnies, Hainaut, France; *d* 16 February 1829, Passy, Paris

Gossec was one of France's most celebrated musicians during his lifetime, his career spanning over half a century. He is remembered principally for his symphonies, his religious and chamber music and his patriotic compositions during the Revolution and Empire periods, but he was also active in the field of serious and comic opera during the second half of the 18th century.

His early stage works were opéras comiques composed during the 1760s for the Comédie-Italienne. Of these, *Le tonnelier*, *Les pêcheurs* and *Toinon et Toinette* were his most successful. In their everyday subjects and simple characters they parallel the style of Duni, Monsigny and Philidor although Gossec developed certain musical aspects more fully than did his contemporaries. These include a richer harmonic language and more independent instrumental accompaniments particularly for woodwind and lower strings; both these features derive from his early symphonies.

With the advent of Grétry, Gossec ceased composing opéras comiques. After a break of several years, during which he wrote much instrumental music, he produced his first tragédie lyrique, *Sabinus*, performed after its court premiere at the Paris Opéra. Gossec had been employed by this establishment since 1757 as an orchestrator and arranger, rising to become maître de musique (1775) and eventually sous-directeur (1780). *Sabinus* was a failure but a succession of one-act pieces and a second tragédie lyrique, *Thésée*, proved more successful. Although overshadowed by Gluck in the field of serious opera, Gossec was one of his greatest admirers and wrote a highly successful ballet finale for his opera *Iphigénie en Tauride* (1779).

Operatic works: *Le tonnelier* (coll. with Alexandre, Ciapalanti, Kohaut, Philidor, Schobert and Trial), 1765; *Le faux lord*, 1765; *Les pêcheurs*, 1766; *Toinon et Toinette*, 1767; *Les agréments d'Hylas et Silvie*, 1768; *Sabinus*, 1773, rev. 1774; *Alexis et Daphné*, 1775; *Philémon et Baucis*, 1775; *La fête de village*, 1778; *Thésée*, 1782; *Nitocris*, (1783); *Rosine, ou L'épouse abandonnée*, 1786; *Le pied de boeuf* (including music by Grétry and Rameau), 1787, (n.d.): *Gustave Vasa* (inc.); *Perrin et Perrette* (overture survives)
BIBLIOGRAPHY L. Dufrane, *Gossec: sa vie, ses oeuvres*, Fischbacher, 1927

E.C.

CHARLES GOUNOD

Charles François Gounod; *b* 17 June 1818, Paris; *d* 18 October 1893, St-Cloud, nr Paris

Gounod, widely celebrated for a few years at the height of his career as France's leading composer, could count among his teachers two grand old men of French musical pedagogy in the 1830s, Antonin Reicha and Jean-François Lesueur. Thorough academic training fertilized his prodigious musical facility and led to the Prix de Rome at the early age of 20. Exposure to Italian cultural treasures on the prize-winner's trip left an indelible mark on Gounod, who was also a gifted painter. Unlike many of his contemporaries, he looked to Classical culture in a general way as a model of balance and control for his own work. And impregnated with Classical ideals about the higher role of art in society, he expressed alarm in letters home about the despoliation of music through commercialism. Not surprisingly, Gounod never became comfortable in business matters. His career was also unusual in that, on his return to Paris, he did not seek to achieve success in the world of opera, preferring to devote himself to sacred music and even seriously contemplating the priesthood.

It was entirely characteristic that Gounod was drawn to a Classical subject, the death of the poet Sappho, for his first opera. *Sapho* was composed for

the great mezzo Pauline Viardot, who championed the composer after he turned away from the seminary in 1848. Though it was a box-office failure during its first run at the Opéra in 1851, *Sapho* was enough of a *succès d'estime* to lead to another commission at the same house, *La nonne sanglante* (1854) to a libretto by Eugène Scribe. That work was no more enduring, mainly because of a poorly wrought libretto, but Gounod's continuing prominence was assured not only by favourable critical response to his music but also by his appointment in 1852 as director of an important choral society, the Orphéon de la ville de Paris. He began a number of operatic projects following the demise of *La nonne*, including an *Ivan le terrible* which he never completed; that libretto eventually passed into the hands of his young friend Bizet. The planning of *Faust* (1859), Gounod's first collaboration with Jules Barbier and Michel Carré, began in 1856 with encouragement from the newly appointed director of the Théâtre-Lyrique, Léon Carvalho. Before that work was staged, however, Gounod completed a very fine operatic adaptation of Molière's *Le médecin malgré lui* (1858). *Faust* itself was well received during its first run, though publishers were slow to take interest. A few weeks after the premiere, Gounod and his librettists struck an agreement with the Choudens firm. By arranging performances in other cities, that publisher set about effectively marketing *Faust*. Stagings at French provincial theatres were followed by productions in Germany, many of them under the title of *Margarete* to distance the work from Goethe and to reflect more accurately its substance.

Carvalho, eager to follow on the success of *Faust* with a new work by Gounod, persuaded him to reroute *Philémon et Baucis* (1860) from its intended destination, the summer theatre at Baden-Baden, to the Théâtre-Lyrique. Gounod rather artificially enlarged the scope of *Philémon* for the Parisian stage and it did not fare well until it was reduced to its original proportions many years later at the Opéra-Comique. In place of *Philémon et Baucis*, he supplied the Baden stage with *La colombe* (1860). Demonstrating remarkable productivity for a composer of his generation, Gounod soon completed the five-act *La Reine de Saba* (1862) after a story by Nerval, for the Opéra. For the first time in his career (and possibly that of any French composer) several reviewers described the music as *wagnérien*, a term that would be used with similar lack of discrimination in France until the end of the century. In part because of expectations roused by the success of *Faust*, the opera was Gounod's most resounding failure to date. His subsequent stage work, *Mireille* (1864), did little better at first; nevertheless, on revival and extensive modifications it eventually did entrench itself in French houses.

Another failure would almost certainly have led precipitously to the end of Gounod's operatic career. In *Roméo et Juliette* he scored a much needed critical triumph that was vigorously sustained at the Théâtre-Lyrique box office by an initial run during the Paris World Exhibition of 1867, when the city was well

Gounod in his study in 1893

populated by tourists. Personal turmoil brought about by a move to England after the war of 1870 and by a temporary estrangement from his wife produced a lengthy hiatus before his next operatic premiere. Because of a long-distance dispute with the management of the Opéra-Comique Gounod never completed the setting that he began of Molière's *Georges Dandin*, a most interesting project since he used Molière's prose text throughout instead of a more conventional verse reworking. Another project during these years was an adaptation of *Polyeucte*, Corneille's play about Christian martyrdom in Rome. A messy dispute over ownership of the complete autograph full score with Georgina Weldon, a singer of modest accomplishments with whom Gounod had become personally entangled while in England, caused a delay in a staging of that work.

After Gounod's return to France, Léon Carvalho, now hoping to replicate earlier Théâtre-Lyrique successes as director of the Opéra-Comique, commissioned *Cinq-Mars* (1877) from him. It disappointed, as did *Polyeucte* when it was finally unveiled on the stage of the Opéra in 1878. The latter failure was a bitter pill since Gounod himself valued the work highly, no doubt largely because of its fusion of Classical setting with Christian theme and the difficult personal circumstances surrounding its genesis. With scarcely better luck, he attempted radically different subject matter in his subsequent opera, *Le tribut de Zamora* (1881), a story set in Spain that prominently featured a madwoman's recovery of reason. By this time it was clear that Gounod's operatic career would not be resuscitated; he had not renewed himself musically and was left behind by younger composers such as Massenet. A

major overhaul of *Sapho* in 1884, with the addition of much new music, was Gounod's final operatic endeavour. That he could even undertake a recasting of his first opera late in his career is testimony to the short stylistic distance between his first opera and last.

Sapho

Opera in three acts (1h 30m)
Libretto by Emile Augier
Composed 1850–51
PREMIERES 16 April 1851, Opéra, Paris; UK: 9 August 1851, Covent Garden, London

Although the work did not last in the repertoire when first performed, nor at Opéra revivals in 1858 and 1884, parts of it were much admired by contemporaries. Berlioz savoured Gounod's evocation of Classical spirit, achieved both through purposeful archaicism, as in the Handelian introduction and march in Act I, and the sobriety of Sapho's numbers. One aria has achieved lasting fame, Sapho's final soliloquy 'O ma lyre immortelle', sung just before her suicidal leap into the sea because of the unfaithfulness of her lover, Phaon; it is a reworking of Gounod's earlier *mélodie* 'Chanson du pêcheur'.

RECORDING Cicsinski, Lublin, Vanzo, Vassar, Ch and PO of French Radio, Cambreling, Rodolfe, 1979
EDITION v.s., Choudens, 1860

Le médecin malgré lui

Opéra comique in three acts (2h 15m)
Libretto by Jules Barbier and Michel Carré, after Molière's play *Le médecin malgré lui* (1666)
Composed 1857–8
PREMIERES 15 January 1858, Théâtre-Lyrique, Paris; UK: 27 February 1865, Covent Garden, London; US: 10 May 1917, New York

Gounod and his librettists were given an opportunity to adapt Molière's play for the stage by Léon Carvalho when, early in 1857, he reneged (only temporarily, as it turned out) on his promise to produce *Faust* at the Théâtre-Lyrique. The spoken dialogue between the musical numbers is Molière's and the verse is closely fashioned after the model. Because of the work's proximity to a 17th-century masterpiece, the Comédie Française at first objected to the production of Gounod's opera, but with an appeal to the imperial household this obstacle was overcome.

The plot centres on the one hand around the attempt by Martine to inflict punishment on her husband, the woodcutter Sganarelle, by persuading others that he is a doctor in disguise and, on the other, around a romantic love interest between Léandre and Lucinde that is opposed by her father, Géronte. Lucinde feigns dumbness in order to resist Géronte's control and Sganarelle is brought in to effect a cure. Lucinde finds a ready recruit to his cause in Sganarelle and in the end the lovers are united.

Gounod exhibits a real talent for comedy in this work, in part through clever harmonic twists and pastiches of older musical styles. Among his less well-known operas, it alone deserves far more performances than it has received.

EDITIONS v.ss., Colombier, 1858; many rps, later by Tallandier

Faust

Opéra in five acts (3h 30m)
Libretto by Jules Barbier and Michel Carré, after Michel Carré's *Faust et Marguerite* (1850) and Johann Wolfgang von Goethe's *Faust*, Part I, in the French translation by Gérard de Nerval (1828)
Composed 1856–9; ballet 1868–9
PREMIERES 19 March 1859, Théâtre-Lyrique, Paris; UK: 11 June 1863, Her Majesty's Theatre, Haymarket, London; US: 25 November 1863, New York
CAST Faust *t*, Méphistophélès *b*, Wagner *bar*, Valentin *bar*, Siébel *s*, Marguerite *s*, Marthe *ms*; *satb* chorus of young girls, labourers, students, burghers, matrons, invisible demons, church choir, witches, queens and courtesans of antiquity, celestial voices
ORCHESTRATION 2 fl/picc, 2 ob/ca, 2 cl, 2 bsn, 4 hn, 2 tpt, 3 trbn (tenor), timp, perc, 2 hp, organ, str; onstage: 2 cornets à pistons, 3 saxhorn (soprano, bass, double-bass), 2 tpt, 3 trbn (2 alto, tenor)

Gounod's enthusiasm for Goethe's *Faust* was of long standing by the time he set about planning his opera with Barbier and Carré in 1856; he had even composed a setting of the church scene in the late 1840s (the present location of that autograph is unknown). Since Goethe's play offered little character interaction beyond the three principals (Faust, Gretchen, and Mephistopheles), Michel Carré allowed his own earlier adaptation of Goethe's *Faust* for the Théâtre du Gymnase-Dramatique, with its significantly expanded roles for Valentin and Siébel, to serve as the proximate source for the project. Gounod's opera follows Carré's light boulevard play quite closely, but reintroduces weightier elements from Goethe, such as Valentin's death, the *Walpurgisnacht* (rarely given outside France today), and Marguerite's imprisonment. The return to Goethean elements missing from Carré's play, however, seems to have been motivated in many instances as much, if not more, by purely musical and operatic considerations as by the principle of fidelity to the German playwright. Direct comparison of Gounod's opera with the Goethe play risks obscuring the opera's many qualities.

The work that Gounod originally composed was much longer than the one performed on the opening night. Many numbers, including an Act II duet for Valentin and Marguerite, a more extended *Nuit de Walpurgis* episode, and a mad scene for Marguerite alone in the last act – doubtless not well suited to the voice of Marie Miolan-Carvalho, creator of the role – were cut in the first rehearsal. At a late rehearsal stage, the 'Soldiers' Chorus' was lifted from Gounod's aborted *Ivan le terrible* to replace a set of couplets composed for Valentin in Act IV. Upheavals to *Faust* continued as its popularity spread. The original spoken dialogue between set pieces was soon replaced on most stages by recitatives supplied by the composer. In some productions, the church

scene appeared near the beginning of Act IV instead of in its original position after Valentin's death. For the second set of performances at Her Majesty's Theatre in 1864, the English baritone Charles Santley requested an arrangement of a melody from the orchestral prelude that became 'Avant de quitter ces lieux'; that piece has remained part of the work ever since, despite Gounod's reservations about it. Finally, Gounod composed the well-known ballet music when the work travelled from the Théâtre-Lyrique to the Opéra in 1869.

SYNOPSIS
Act I Faust, despondent and alone in his study, resolves to take poison but hesitates when he hears a pastoral chorus. An invocation to Satan conjures up a rather dapper buffo Méphistophélès. Faust yearns above all for sensual gratification and Méphistophélès readily promises to fulfil the philosopher's desires in return for service in the nether regions. When Faust hesitates, Méphistophélès conjures up a vision of Marguerite at her spinning wheel. Faust signs the document and is transformed into a young nobleman, singing of the pleasures that await him ('A moi les plaisirs').

Act II At the fair townspeople sing a virtuoso chorus ('Vin ou bière'). Valentin appears, clutching a medallion given him by his sister Marguerite; he is about to leave for battle and instructs his friends, including Wagner and Siébel, to look after her. Méphistophélès joins the group and provides blasphemous entertainment with a song about the golden calf ('Le veau d'or'). Valentin is incited to anger when Méphistophélès makes light of his sister, but his sword breaks in mid-air. Alarmed, the men brandish the crossed pommels of their weapons before him in a gesture of Christian exorcism. Temporarily emasculated, Méphistophélès is left alone on stage, but is soon joined by Faust and a group of waltzing villagers ('Ainsi que la brise légère'). When Marguerite appears among them, Faust offers her his arm; she modestly rejects his advance.

Act III Siébel leaves a bouquet for Marguerite in her garden. Faust, playing well the role of romantic idealist, apostrophizes her home and the protective embrace of nature ('Salut! demeure chaste et pure'). More worldly wise, Méphistophélès positions a jewel box near Siébel's flowers. Marguerite enters and sings a ballad tinged with modal inflexions about the King of Thule. She then discovers both the bouquet and jewel box and erupts in a buoyant *cabalette* (the 'Jewel Song' – 'Je ris de me voir') as she tries on earrings and a necklace. Her guardian Marthe is not immune to male attentions either and when Faust and Méphistophélès join the pair, she is attracted to the devil. Marguerite allows herself to be embraced by Faust in a duet ('Laisse-moi, laisse-moi contempler ton visage') but is suddenly overcome with shame. Encouraged by Méphistophélès, Faust completes the seduction.

Act IV Marguerite has given birth to Faust's child and is ostracized by girls in the street below. She sits down to spin ('Il ne revient pas') and Siébel,

A scene from Faust *(Paris, 1859)*

ever faithful, attempts to encourage her. The scene shifts to a public square for the return of Valentin, bombastic and self-assured ('Soldiers' Chorus'). While Valentin is inside the house, Méphistophélès trenchantly plays a lover delivering a serenade beneath Marguerite's window. Faust declares his responsibility for Marguerite's fall and successfully engages Valentin in a duel. As he dies, Valentin blames Marguerite and damns her for eternity. The next scene shows Marguerite attempting to pray in a church. She eventually succeeds, despite the musical efforts of a chorus of demons, but faints when Méphistophélès unleashes a final imprecation.

Act V It is the *Nuit de Walpurgis* in the Harz Mountains and Faust is first mesmerized by will-o'-the-wisps and witches and then titillated by legendary courtesans of antiquity. A vision of Marguerite redirects his thoughts to her. She has been imprisoned for infanticide. Through Méphistophélès, Faust obtains the keys to her cell. They sing a love duet about past bliss and he begs her to flee ('Oui c'est toi je t'aime'). With Méphistophélès impatiently goading the two to follow him, Marguerite resists and calls for divine protection ('Anges purs! anges radieux'). Faust looks on with despair and falls to his knees in prayer as her soul rises to heaven.

Faust was considered a difficult work by many during its first run of performances. In part this was due to a full-flowering of Gounod's mature melodic style, one that eschewed mechanistic spinning out of rhythmic

motifs and an abundance of coloratura in favour of a tapering of relatively simple surface rhythms around the expressive nuances of the text. Gounod also avoided certain conventions, for example the intro ductory chorus and concertato-type finale. It is easy to forget just how unusual the opening scene was in its day, with its long passages of arioso singing by Faust punctuated by offstage music. Marguerite's appearance late in the second act is a refreshingly understated first entry for the prima donna. The magnificent orchestral peroration at the curtain of Act III, a grand statement of a tune previously heard only at softer dynamic levels and fragmented, is another impressive moment, one that proved highly influential on later composers. To conclude with the threefold semitonal rise of 'Anges purs! anges radieux!' was an electrifying, and unprecedented, inspiration.

Marguerite is the most fully developed musical character in *Faust*. Her awakened sensuality is hinted at through recitative interruptions in 'The Ballade of the King of Thule' and later more fully exposed as she leans out of her window wishing for Faust's return. Her role displays a naturalism uncommon on the French stage at the time, as in her account of her sister's death in the Act III quartet where, with a brief turn to recitative in the prevailing arioso, she spontaneously recalls rushing to the side of the crib. Her spinning song compares favourably with other settings of this text and she achieves truly heroic musical stature in both the church scene and final trio. Méphistophélès is something of a demonic Leporello, light-hearted but dangerously cynical, a characteristic given effective musical form (particularly through orchestration) in the Act IV serenade.

RECORDINGS 1. Studer, Leech, Van Dam, French Army Ch, Toulouse Capitole Ch and O, Plasson, EMI, 1991; 2. de Los Angeles, Gedda, Christoff, Opéra de Paris, Cluytens, VSM, 1953: the young Gedda and de Los Angeles, Christoff in top vocal form; 3. Vezzani, Berthon, Journet, Opéra de Paris, Busser, HMV, 1930: 78s and poor sound, but brings the listener closer to earlier performing styles than later versions, but the 1991 Plasson, with an appendeix including discarded numbers, and offering a complete text, is highly recommendable [A.B.]
EDITIONS f.ss., Choudens, 1860; F. Oeser (ed.), modern critical edn, Alkor-Edition, 1972; v.s., Choudens, 1859

Philémon et Baucis

Opera in three acts (2h)
Libretto by Jules Barbier and Michel Carré, after
La Fontaine's story Philémon et Baucis
Composed 1859–60
PREMIERES 18 February 1860, Théâtre-Lyrique, Paris; UK: March 1888, Liverpool (amateur); 24 October 1891, Covent Garden, London; US: 16 November 1893, New York

Originally planned without chorus and in two acts for the summer theatre at Baden-Baden, it was expanded at Carvalho's request to include an additional act (the second) culminating in an impressive scenic coup, Jupiter's destruction of his own temple as a result of popular irreverence. Nevertheless, it was in a two-act version without the temple scene that the work was frequently performed at the Opéra-Comique in the first half of the 20th century.

Mythological comedy was in the air in Paris as Offenbach's Orphée aux enfers had recently completed its first run at the time Philémon et Baucis was conceived. The Offenbach and Gounod works both depict Jupiter in a dalliance with a mere mortal, but in spite of this similarity Philémon et Baucis is much more the moralizing, sentimental piece. In appreciation for the generosity that Philémon and Baucis extend to him in the first act, Gounod's Jupiter restores youth to the couple. By the third act he has fallen in love with Baucis, but in the end she outwits the god and willingly abandons youth out of devotion to her spouse. Coloratura in the role of Baucis effectively mirrors her rejuvenation and Gounod drew a Jupiter who is a paragon of musical bonhomie.

RECORDING Scotto, Misciano, Panerai, Montarsolo, Milan Ch and SO of RAI, Sanzogno, Myto, 1961
EDITIONS v.ss., Choudens, 1860; many later rps in two or three acts

La colombe

The Dove
Opéra comique in two acts (1h 15m)
Libretto by Jules Barbier and Michel Carré, after
La Fontaine's story Le faucon (1668)
Composed 1860

PREMIERES 3 August 1860, Theater der Stadt, Baden-Baden; UK: 20 September 1870, Crystal Palace, London

With four soloists, no chorus, and two acts La colombe has the dimensions originally intended for Philémon et Baucis. In the La Fontaine model a wealthy countess attempts to satisfy the demands of her capricious son by persuading an admirer to give her son his most prized possession, a pet falcon. By the conclusion of the story it appears on the dinner table. In Gounod's work the falcon becomes a dove and Sylvie desires to own it out of rivalry with another Florentine lady. Following the convention of happy endings in the genre of opéra comique the bird is eventually saved. Poulenc provided recitatives for a revival by Diaghilev in 1924.

EDITION v.s., Choudens, 1860

Mireille

Opera in five acts (3h)
Libretto by Michel Carré, after Frédéric Mistral's poem,
Mirèio (1859)
Composed 1862–4, rev. and reduced to three acts, 1864
PREMIERES 19 March 1864, Théâtre-Lyrique, Paris; rev. version (with recitative): UK: 11 July 1864, Her Majesty's Theatre, Haymarket, London; US: 17 November 1864, American Academy of Music, Philadelphia; 15 December 1864, Théâtre-Lyrique, Paris
CAST Mireille s, Vincent t, Ourrias bar, Maître Ramon b, Taven ms, Andreloun ms, Maître Ambroise b, Clémence s; satb chorus of mulberry gatherers, townspeople, spirits of the Rhône, farmhands, pilgrims to the Chapel of the Saintes-Maries
FULL ORCHESTRA

Mistral's epic Provençal poem was published in 1859 and soon afterwards Gounod was put into personal contact with him through their mutual friend the playwright Ernest Legouvé. Taking up the poet's invitation to visit Provence, he composed most of the score on location and actually visited the site of each tableau in the opera. Mireille was not successful in its original five-act form, despite frantic revisions and reorderings during the first run. Consequently, Gounod made important changes to the work within a few months of its premiere, including the addition of a light valse-ariette, 'O légère hirondelle', to the title role, a change in dénouement that had Mireille suddenly recover from sunstroke instead of expire, a reduction to three acts, and the conversion of the spoken dialogue into recitative for foreign stages. Mireille did not score a real success, however, until a three-act revival in 1889 at the Opéra-Comique, after which it became a staple of the repertoire of that house. Later productions at the Opéra-Comique, most prominently one in 1939 conducted by Henri Busser, sought to restore Gounod's original intentions, albeit with limited historical accuracy.

Though operas in pastoral settings were not uncommon at the Opéra-Comique in this period, Mireille struck a new note by depicting the unsuitability of an amorous relationship because of class entirely within a frame of Provençal peasant society. The choice of a classical five-act layout for such a setting was also unusual – a reflection of the epic nature of the Mistral model. That a farmer's daughter assumes real tragic stature in the opera was found objectionable in some critical circles after the premiere.

SYNOPSIS (original version)

Act I Mireille's friends gently tease her about having fallen in love with Vincent, the mere son of a basket-weaver, and the good witch Taven warns her that wealth and poverty are ill-matched. Vincent eloquently voices his love to Mireille and the two agree to meet at the chapel of the Saintes-Maries should danger befall either of them.

Act II The bull-tamer Ourrias tries to court Mireille but is rebuffed. She goes on to reveal her love for a boy from a lower class to her father, the wealthy farmer Maître Ramon. He vows that Mireille will never see Vincent again.

Act III In a fit of jealousy, Ourrias strikes the unarmed Vincent and for this ignoble act is drowned by a ghostly ferryman on the river Rhône. Taven, an old woman thought to be a witch, ministers to Vincent's wounds.

Act IV Despite asssurances given to her of Vincent's safety, Mireille decides to undertake a pilgrimage across the Crau desert to the Saintes-Maries. Exhausted by her journey, she sees a mirage of a city on the edge of a lake. She collapses, but shepherd's pipes in the distance revive her.

Act V At the chapel Vincent is the first to appear. Stumbling in on the point of death, Mireille is ecstatic at being reunited with him and has a vision of the sky opening to receive her. She dies, but her soul is summoned upward by a celestial voice.

As with Marguerite in *Faust*, Mireille herself is the best-drawn character. Her musical characterization spans the distance from the simple candour of her first appearance – a vocal line with narrow range and simple accompaniment – to music requiring real heroic projection, such as the aria she sings in the Crau desert ('En marche'). The best-known number is the 'Chanson de Magali' in Act II, not based on an actual Provençal folksong but now so popular as to have almost become one. Its strict alternation of two compound metres (6/8 and 9/8) is less interesting than the subtle musical ways in which Gounod paints the text of the metaphorical poem the lovers share. Less successful is the supernatural Rhône scene and the musical portrayal of Ourrias as antagonist.

RECORDING Freni, Rhodes, Vanzo, Van Dam, Bacquier, Ch ad O of Capitole de Toulouse, Plasson, EMI, 1979
EDITIONS five-act version: f.s., H. Busser (ed.), Choudens, 1947; v.s., Choudens, 1864; three-act version: v.s., Choudens, ?1888

Roméo et Juliette

Romeo and Juliet
Opera in a prologue and five acts (3h 15m)
Libretto by Jules Barbier and Michel Carré, after Shakespeare's *Romeo and Juliet* (1596)
Composed 1865–7

PREMIERES 27 April 1867, Théâtre-Lyrique, Paris; UK: 11 July 1867, Covent Garden, London (in Italian); US: 15 November 1867, New York
CAST Paris *bar*, Tybalt *t*, Capulet *b*, Juliette *s*, Roméo *t*, Mercutio *bar*, Benvolio *t*, Gertrude *ms*, Frère Laurent *b*, Stéphano *s*, The Duke *b*, Frère Jean *b*; *satb* chorus of servants, retainers and kinsfolk to the Capulet and Montaigu households; masquers
ORCHESTRATION 2 fl, picc, 2 ob, ca, 2 cl, 2 bsn, 4 hn, 2 cornets à pistons, 2 tpt, 3 trbn, timps, perc, 2 hp, str

In view of the widely recognized success of the love music in *Faust*, a setting of Shakespeare's *Romeo and Juliet* was a natural project for Gounod. Many episodes that do not centre directly on the relationship of the two protagonists in the play were cut by Gounod and his librettists, with the result that the encounters between the two main characters consume a far greater proportion of the opera than of the play. There is also a glaring discrepancy in the tomb scene: where in Shakespeare Juliet stirs only after Romeo has died, in Gounod (as well as other 19th-century versions, including Berlioz's dramatic symphony) she awakens in time to sing a final duet with him. In other respects Barbier and Carré followed Shakespeare closely, borrowing directly from existing French translations.

Sybil Sanderson as Gounod's Juliette in 1894

Like so many of Gounod's operas, *Roméo et Juliette* underwent much revision. The celebrated *valse-ariette*, 'Je veux vivre', was written at the request of Marie Miolan-Carvalho late in the rehearsal period. Because of her relatively light voice, the dramatic aria originally intended as the centrepiece for the role, 'Amour ranime mon courage' in Act IV, though printed in the first edition, was not performed at the first run, and is still rarely given today. The great confrontation between the Capulets and Montaigus at the end of Act III was repeatedly revised: in the first edition, for example, the entry and departure of the duke were accompanied by a pompous stage band that was soon cut. For the revival at the Opéra in 1888 Gounod composed a new musical phrase for Romeo and the chorus to bring down the curtain at the end of that episode, the imposing 'O jour de deuil', and also supplied a ballet for the next act.

SYNOPSIS (following the first edition)
The curtain opens to a declaimed choral prologue summarizing the tragedy about to be enacted.

Act I The assembled guests at a masked ball in the Capulet residence admire the beauty of Juliet when she is escorted into the hall by her father. Romeo Montaigu and his friends, Mercutio and Benvolio, emerge from hiding. Mercutio makes light of Romeo's dark premonitions with an account of the fantastic realm of the fairy queen Mab ('Mab, la reine des mensonges'). Juliet reappears accompanied by her nurse Gertrude and maintains that she is uninterested in marriage ('Je veux vivre') but after exchanging a few words with Romeo, she realizes that their destinies are intertwined. The guests return and Capulet restrains Tybalt from venting his anger at the trespassing Montaigus.

Act II Romeo has stealthily made his way into the Capulet garden and apostrophizes Juliet in the morning sun ('Ah! lève-toi soleil'). Shortly after she appears, he reveals his presence. Their tender words are interrupted by Capulet servants who run through the garden in search of the Montaigu page Stéphano, a comic foil to the elegiac tone of the act. The lovers agree to marry and reluctantly separate when Juliet is called in by Gertrude.

Act III Frère Laurent sings of nature's wonders and is soon joined by Romeo and Juliet. As the two kneel, he administers the sacrament of marriage. The scene changes to a street in front of the Capulet house where Stéphano is seen taunting the rival family ('Que fais-tu, blanche tourterelle'). The page's horseplay gives rise to serious consequences: Capulets come out; Montaigus appear and a succession of duels follows during which Romeo mortally wounds Tybalt. Romeo is exiled from Verona by the duke.

Act IV After spending the night with Juliet, Romeo suddenly breaks from her embrace on hearing the morning lark and Juliet sadly admits that they must separate again. Capulet gives his daughter the news that she is to marry Paris. Frère Laurent explains how she might escape with Romeo by means of a ruse enacted through a potion that will make her

appear dead. She summons her courage before drinking the liquid ('Amour ranime mon courage', a dramatic air often omitted). In the next scene Juliet is led into the family ballroom to the strains of a wedding march. She suddenly collapses.

Act V In the underground crypt of the Capulets, Frère Laurent learns from Frère Jean that Romeo has not received his letter explaining the ruse. After an instrumental interlude, Romeo appears. Believing Juliet to be dead he takes poison. At that moment, she awakens and the two sing of their love, largely through reminiscences of previous music, since a past is all that they now have. As he weakens, Juliet uncovers a sword hidden in her clothes and stabs herself.

The highlights of the score are the four duets for the two protagonists, certainly an unusual (and possibly unprecedented) number of tenor–soprano duets in a single opera: Massenet would follow suit in *Manon* and *Werther*. The passage for *divisi* cellos at the outset of the Act IV duet (surely a model for Verdi in the Act I duet of *Otello*) is a small tone poem about the wedding night; that entire duet exudes an air of sensuousness that was quite new to the French stage in its day. The concluding duet is one of Gounod's least conventional operatic numbers, at least in form: despite its length, it has few passages of ensemble singing or even of voice-dominated music constructed of phrases with regular lengths.

The opera also contains many other fine musical numbers. Romeo's ternary *cavatine* 'Ah! lève-toi, soleil' is justly renowned; its outer sections feature prominently a chromatic descent against a bass pedal note that illustrates the fading-star metaphor of the text without sacrificing lyric intensity. Mercutio's Queen Mab *ballade* is brilliantly orchestrated and in the Act III confrontation between the Montaigus and Capulets Gounod achieves a kind of momentum and excitement that is sometimes missing from his work.

RECORDINGS 1. Micheau, Jobin, A. Erede, Ch and O of Opéra de Paris, Decca, 1953; 2. Freni, Corelli, Ch and O of Paris Opéra, Lembard, EMI, 1968; 3. Malfitano, Kraus, van Dam, Ch and O of Capitole de Toulouse, Plasson, HMV, 1983: though vocally not outstanding, the 1953 recording exhibits a fine sense of the style; the others are fair rivals [A.B.]
EDITIONS f.ss., Choudens, 1870; *rp*, Kalmus, 1956; v.ss., Choudens, 1867; many subsequent 19th-century *rp*s reflecting later productions

Other operas: *La nonne sanglante*, 1854; *Ivan le terrible* (inc.), (1856–8); *La Reine de Saba*, 1862; *George Dandin* (inc.), (1873–4); *Cinq-Mars*, 1877; *Polyeucte*, 1878; *Maître Pierre* (inc.), (1877–8); *Le tribut de Zamora*, 1881
BIBLIOGRAPHY James Harding, *Gounod*, Allen and Unwin, 1973; Steven Huebner, *The Operas of Charles Gounod*, OUP, 1990; Camille Saint-Saëns, 'The Manuscript Libretto of *Faust*', *MT*, vol. 62 (1921), p. 553; T. J. Walsh, *Second Empire Opera: The Théâtre-Lyrique 1851–1870*, Calder, 1981

S.H.

LOUIS GRABU

Louis [Luis] Grabu [Grabue, Grabut, Grebus]; *b* ?Catalonia; *d c.* 1694, London

Unjustly maligned by both his contemporaries and modern historians, Grabu, who was born in Spain and trained at Paris, composed *Albion and Albanius* (1685), the first surviving full-length opera in English. Grabu came to England shortly after the Restoration and was appointed composer-in-ordinary to King Charles II in 1665, being promoted a year later to Master of the King's Musick in succession to Nicholas Lanier. Jealousy of the king's preferment of foreign (mostly French) musicians at court led to Grabu becoming the butt of much ridicule. In 1674 he directed and wrote additional music for Robert Cambert's opera *Ariane, ou Le mariage de Bacchus* (libretto by Pierre Perrin, a founder of the Académie Royale de Musique), the first all-sung opera, foreign or otherwise, to be professionally performed in London. Being a Roman Catholic, Grabu went into exile in 1679 following the Popish Plot. At the king's suggestion, he was recalled from Paris in 1684 to compose *Albion and Albanius*.

Like Purcell, Grabu also wrote music for plays, including Shadwell's version of *Timon of Athens* (1678), Dryden's *Oedipus* (1678, with the first setting of 'Music for a While') and an extraordinary ballet dream sequence for Lord Rochester's adaptation of *Valentinian* (1684), probably his finest music.

Albion and Albanius

'An Opera, or Representation in Musick' in a prologue and three acts
Libretto by John Dryden
PREMIERE   3 June 1685, Dorset Garden Theatre, London

A grand allegory of the Restoration, *Albion and Albanius* was originally designed as a prologue to *King Arthur*, which Dryden withdrew and later offered to Purcell. Unfortunately, Charles II did not live to see the premiere, for which the original opera had to be altered to conclude with a representation of the accession of James II. *Albion* is closely modelled on Lully's *tragédies en musique* and has been criticized for infelicitous setting of Dryden's poetry. In fact, much of the second act (which depicts the tribulations of Albion/Charles) is highly dramatic, and the instrumental music is of high quality throughout. The opera's failure owed more to Monmouth's Rebellion, which broke out the week of the premiere, than to any major artistic shortcoming. *Albion* clearly influenced Purcell in the composition of his first semi-opera, *Dioclesian*.

EDITION   f.s., London, 1687

BIBLIOGRAPHY   Edward J. Dent, *Foundations of English Opera*, CUP, 1928, *rp*, 1965; Curtis Price, *Henry Purcell and the London Stage*, CUP, 1984

C.A.P.

ENRIQUE GRANADOS

Enrique Granados y Campiña; *b* 27 July 1867, Lerida, Spain; *d* 24 March 1916, English Channel

Granados is remembered primarily for his songs and piano music, and his work is pervaded by the mood of the dark paintings of Goya, with whom he both became obsessed and has often been compared. This preoccupation is manifested in the piano cycle *Goyescas* (1911), each piece of which evokes the mood of a particular painting. The Paris Opéra persuaded Granados to rework the suite into an opera, a challenge accepted with relish, despite the fact that his previous stage works were all only moderately successful zarzuelas. The First World War prevented the opera's performance in Paris, but it was accepted by the New York Metropolitan.

It was a bitter irony that the only opera by a composer not remembered particularly for his stage works should have been the indirect cause of his death. While returning by sea from the world premiere of *Goyescas*, his ship was torpedoed by a German submarine, and the composer was drowned while trying to save his wife.

Goyescas

Opera in one act (three scenes) (1h)
Libretto by Fernando Periquet y Zuaznabar
Composed 1912–15
PREMIERES   28 January 1916, Metropolitan, New York; UK: 11 July 1951, Royal College of Music, London

Granados completed the musical arrangement of *Goyescas* before calling on Periquet to provide the text. The opera is set in the streets and gardens of Madrid, and is peopled by the characters and events of Goya's well-known cartoons and paintings. The plot tells of the fateful outcome of a flirtation between the bullfighter Paquiro and the beautiful Rosario. The music has the warmth and open-hearted passion of the piano pieces. Its most famous moment, the intermezzo, was added only to cover scene changes.

RECORDING   Rubio, Iriarte, Torrano, Ausensi, Madrid Cantores, Spanish National O, Argenta, Decca, 1956
EDITION   v.s., G. Schirmer, 1915

Zarzuelas: *Maria del Carmen*, 1898; *Petrarca*, 1900; *Picarol*, 1901; *Follet*, 1903; *Gaziel*, 1906; *Liliana*, 1911
BIBLIOGRAPHY   C. Wilson, 'The Two Versions of *Goyescas*', *MMR*, vol. 81 (1951), p. 203

S.J.W.

CARL HEINRICH GRAUN

b 1703/4, Wahrenbrück, Germany; *d* 8 August 1759, Berlin

Graun is frequently mentioned in the same breath as his older contemporary Hasse, and they had significant traits in common: both were important opera composers of Italian opera seria in 18th-century

Germany; both had trained and worked professionally as tenors; and both wrote opera for a court Though Graun's operas written for the court of Frederick the Great in Berlin were less crucial than Hasse's Dresden operas in the development of the genre, they are nevertheless significant in their combination of baroque and reform elements.

Graun studied at the Dresden Kreuzschule, singing in its choir, and from 1718 attended the University of Leipzig. He began his operatic career as a tenor at the Brunswick court. In 1731 he was appointed vice-kapellmeister there and wrote six operas, four to German texts, one in Italian, and one (*Pharao Tubaetes*) with German recitatives and Italian arias.

Frederick, Crown Prince of Prussia (later Frederick the Great) met Graun at the celebrations of his marriage to Princess Elisabeth Christine of Brunswick in 1733 for which Graun wrote *Lo specchio della fedeltà*. The prince subsequently took the composer under his patronage at Rheinsberg in 1735, and on Frederick's accession in 1740 Graun became kapellmeister to the Prussian court and was immediately charged with setting up an Italian opera company in Berlin. As a result he journeyed to Italy to engage singers, returning in 1741. That year his *Rodelinda* was given on a temporary stage in the royal palace, and in 1742 *Cesare e Cleopatra* opened the new court opera house (the famous Lindenoper). Thereafter Graun's work was closely supervised by his music-loving patron, who felt free to interfere in either composition or performance. Burney described an opera performance in which Frederick stood behind the conductor issuing instructions throughout.

For ten years Graun's operas dominated the repertoire in Berlin, though works by Hasse and Agricola were also performed. In 1756, however, the start of the Seven Years War brought with it the curtailment of court entertainments and Graun wrote no operas thereafter.

In his Berlin operas Graun furthered the development of the genre from the 18th-century baroque conventions of his earlier Brunswick works. In setting the great works of the French dramatists Corneille and Racine in Italian translation he paved the way for Mozart's Beaumarchais/Da Ponte operas. For the reform elements, some credit must go to Frederick, who eventually wearied of the relentless *da capo* arias of the high-baroque opera seria. Thus *Semiramide* (1754) contains *da capo* arias in the first half and less stylized cavatinas in the second. This trend reached its apogee the following year in *Montezuma*.

At his best Graun combined his lyrical gift with a flair for dramatic writing. The leading roles in his Berlin operas, written for a company dominated by Italian castrati, require virtuosity and a wide vocal range. In contrast to his Brunswick works, there are fewer major bass parts. The orchestra often plays a merely accompanying role, with bass line and strings filling out harmonies. Graun's operas often contain long tracts of recitative which are not always very carefully or dramatically set. Unlike Hasse, Graun had a limited command of Italian, and most of his operas were written under pressure. All 26 of the operas he composed in 15 years were fully staged.

Graun also wrote much other vocal and instrumental music, but only the *Te Deum* (1757) and the cantata *Der Tod Jesu* (1755) were still performed into the 19th century. With the growth of interest in baroque styles, perhaps his operas will receive the attention they deserve.

Artaserse

Dramma per musica in three acts (seven scenes) (2h)
Text by Pietro Metastasio, with additions from the version by 'Domenico Lalli' set by Hasse (1730)
PREMIERE 2 December 1743, Hoftheater, Berlin

This was Graun's third opera for Berlin, and only the second to be performed in the new Hoftheater. Metastasio's story, adapted by an anonymous hand, concerns Artabano's attempts to gain the Persian throne. Having murdered King Serse he incriminates his own son, Arbace, who is in love with Serse's daughter Mandane. Serse's son Artaserse is in turn in love with Semira, Artabano's daughter. Arbace is eventually returned to favour, his father exposed, and both pairs of lovers united.

Artaserse is typical of Graun's Berlin operas in the predominance of *da capo* arias and in the accompanying role of the orchestra. An unusual feature for an opera seria is the sextet in Act I, which replaces a series of three arias in Metastasio's original. The work was produced in Stuttgart in 1750 for the opening of the new Hoftheater.

EDITION facsimile of manuscript copy in Herzog-August-Bibliothek, Wolfenbüttel, Garland, 1978

Montezuma

Tragedia per musica in three acts (seven scenes) (2h 30m)
Libretto by Frederick the Great (in French), translated by Giampietro Tagliazucchi
Composed 1754
PREMIERE 6 January 1755, Hoftheater, Berlin

Frederick's libretto was unusual in being one of the first opere serie on a 'modern' (non-Classical) subject. In it Frederick deliberately attacked the Roman Catholic faith, in the shape of the treacherous Cortés, against whom stands the noble figure of Montezuma, representing the spirit of the Enlightenment. In form and style, too, the opera was the most experimental Graun set. As Frederick wrote to his sister Wilhelmine, 'Most of the arias are written to be sung without repetition [i.e. cavatinas] . . . one should employ repeats only when the singers know how to vary the music but it seems to me excessive anyway to repeat something four times.'

In Mexico in 1519–20, a messenger brings news that Cortés has landed. Despite the forebodings of his courtiers and his wife, Eupaforice, the Emperor Montezuma refuses to believe ill of the invaders. Cortés and his captain Narves arrive and are welcomed, but the Spaniards attack the Mexicans and Montezuma is taken prisoner. He breaks free but is recaptured. Cortés has designs on Eupaforice, who commits suicide rather than suffer dishonour.

As Montezuma is led away to execution a chorus of Mexicans revile Cortés's cruelty.

Graun's score combines lyricism (the Act III duet for Montezuma and Eupaforice is a good example) with a depth of characterization and drama not always evident in his other operas. Eupaforice's vengeance aria in Act II ('Barbaro, barbaro che mi sei') vividly portrays her conflicting emotions. *Montezuma* was revived in Berlin in 1771, but was then neglected until the 1980s, when there were productions in Berlin and Spoleto.

RECORDING excerpts: Sutherland, Elms, Harwood, Woodland, Sinclair, Ambrosian Singers, LPO, Bonynge, Decca, 1967
EDITION f.s., A. Mayer-Reinach (ed.), *DDT*, 1/15, Breitkopf und Härtel, 1904, *rp*, 1958

Other operatic works: *Sancio und Sinilde*, 1727; *Polydorus*, 1728; *Iphigenia in Aulis*, 1731; *Scipio Africanus*, 1732; *Lo specchio della fedeltà*, 1733; *Pharao Tubaetes*, 1735; *Rodelinda, regina de' Langobardi*, 1741; *Cesare e Cleopatra*, 1742; *Catone in Utica*, 1744; *Lucio Papirio*, 1745; *Adriano in Siria*, 1745; *Demofoonte, re di Tracia*, 1746; *Cajo Fabricio*, 1746; *Le feste galanti*, 1747; *Cinna*, 1748; *L'Europa galante*, 1748; *Ifigenia in Aulide*, 1748; *Angelica e Medoro*, 1749; *Coriolano*, 1749; *Fetonte*, 1750; *Mitridate*, 1750; *Armida*, 1751; *Britannico*, 1751; *Orfeo*, 1752; *Il guidizio di Paride*, 1752; *Silla*, 1753; *Semiramide*, 1754; *Ez io*, 1755; *I fratelli nemici*, 1756; *La Merope*, 1756
BIBLIOGRAPHY Charles Burney, *The Present State of Music in Germany*, London, 1773; Silke Leopold, 'Artaserse', and Hans-Joachim Bauer, 'Montezuma', in 'Carl Heinrich Graun', *Pipers Enzyklopädie des Musiktheaters*, R. Piper, 1986–

S.S.V.B.

CHRISTOPH GRAUPNER

Johann Christoph Graupner; *b* 13 January 1683, Kirchberg, Saxony; *d* 10 May 1760, Darmstadt

Graupner distinguished himself early in his career at the Hamburg Opera and later became a prolific composer of instrumental and sacred vocal music. He studied with Kuhnau at the Leipzig Thomasschule and became a friend of Telemann. In 1706 Graupner moved to Hamburg; he became the harpsichordist at the Opera, composed five successful operas (and possibly another three in collaboration with Keiser). In 1709 the Landgrave of Hessen-Darmstadt invited him to become his court vice-kapellmeister, and in 1712 he became kapellmeister, a position he retained for life. After 1719 he gave up opera and became an extraordinarily prolific composer of church cantatas and instrumental music. His fame was such that he was asked to compete for the position of kantor at St Thomas's in Leipzig. Though successful, he was forced to withdraw when the Landgrave refused to accept his resignation; J. S. Bach was later appointed.

Graupner's operas have not received the critical attention they deserve, and none has appeared in a modern edition. In form and style the Hamburg operas strongly resemble those of Keiser. Stylistically

they combine Italian, French, and more popular German elements. As with Keiser, Graupner's scores are often rich in instrumental colour (testimony to the excellence of the Opera orchestra) and many arias use Italian texts, though the recitatives and other arias use German. This peculiar practice seems to have been an idiosyncratic feature of the Hamburg Opera.

Surviving operas: *Dido, Königin von Carthago*, 1707; *L'amore ammalato: Die Krankende Liebe, oder Antiochus und Stratonica*, 1708; *La constanza vince l'inganno*, 1719; 6 lost operas
BIBLIOGRAPHY A. D. McCredie, 'Christoph Graupner as Opera Composer', *Miscellanea musicologica* vol. 1 (1966), pp. 74–116

G.J.B.

ALEKSANDR GRECHANINOV

Aleksandr Tikhonovich Grechaninov; *b* 25 October 1864, Moscow; *d* 3 January 1956, New York

A pupil of Arensky and Rimsky-Korsakov, Grechaninov achieved early success with orchestral works and songs. He worked as a piano teacher and for the Moscow University ethnographic society, arranging songs from all corners of the empire. His first opera, *Dobrinya Nikitich*, an opera-bylina modelled on Rimsky-Korsakov's *Sadko*, was a success with Chaliapin in the title role. Grechaninov was granted a pension in 1910 for his religious music, but later clashed with the Orthodox Church for attempting to use instruments in services, and for his Maeterlinck opera *Sister Beatrice*, withdrawn on religious grounds after three performances. His pension ceased after the Revolution and in 1925 he settled in Paris, earning a living as a pianist. In 1939 he emigrated to New York, taking US citizenship in 1946. His most significant works are religious or for children; the children's operas have a racy charm worth investigating.

Operatic works: *Dobrinya Nikitich*, 1901; *Sestra Beatrisa* (*Sister Beatrice*), 1910; *Elochkin son* (*The Fir Tree's Dream*), 1911; *Mishkin teremok* (*The Mouse's Tower*), 1921; *Kot, petukh i lisa* (*The Cat, the Cock and the Fox*), 1924; *Zhenit'ba* (*The Marriage*), 1946
BIBLIOGRAPHY A. Grechaninov, trans. R. Dwyer, *My Life in Music*, Knopf, 1951

J.G.

MAURICE GREENE

b 12 August 1696, London; *d* 1 December 1755, London

Greene, the youngest son of a prominent London clergyman who was a chaplain of the Chapel Royal, is believed to have been a chorister at St Paul's Cathedral. At the age of 17 he became organist of St Dunstan-in-the-West, and four years later of St Paul's. In 1727 he added to this the post of organist and composer to the Chapel Royal, and in 1735 the Mastership of the King's Musick. Not surprisingly the bulk of his compositions is anthems, but he also wrote three oratorios, numerous odes and three dramatic pieces. The latter were the fruits of his collaboration with the Reverend John Hoadly; their association is commemorated in a double portrait by Hayman. Hoadly, canon of Winchester and chaplain to the Prince of Wales, was also a devoted amateur of the stage with a knowledge of music. Of these pieces one, *The Judgment of Hercules*, has been lost. Despite the fact that they were never performed in the public theatres, the other two survive complete and reveal that Greene had a natural gift for opera and an almost Handelian ability to translate emotions into musical terms.

Maurice Greene and the Reverend John Hoadly by F. Hayman (1747)

Florimel, or Love's Revenge

Pastoral in two acts
Libretto by John Hoadly
PREMIERE   1734, Hall of the Bishop's Palace, Winchester

The orchestra for *Florimel* included flutes, oboes, bassoon, horns and strings. Myrtillo loves Florimel and hangs a song on a tree for her to find. Cupid, out of jealousy, changes her name. She quarrels with Florimel. In the second interlude Florimel is discovered asleep by a satyr (originally sung by Greene) who pricks her with a magical dart. She will love the first man she sees when she awakes. This proves to be Myrtillo, and the felicity of Arcadia is restored. Myrtillo was originally sung by a counter-tenor, but in revivals, such as that at the Three Choirs Festival in 1745, by a soprano. The title song, 'The Charms of Florimel', became a popular success.

MANUSCRIPT   f.s., British Library

Phoebe

Pastoral in three acts (2h)
Libretto by John Hoadly
PREMIERES   1737, London; UK modern revival:
28 September 1984, Holme Pierrepont Hall, Nottingham (Opera Restored)

Phoebe, disguised as Sylvio so as to be near Amyntas, who has rejected her, affects to be indifferent to love. Amyntas' sister, Celia, falls in love with Sylvio. The countryman, Linco, pursues Celia. In the second act Sylvio reveals her identity to Celia, but this is no help to Linco. In the last act Amyntas sees that Celia is wearing a bracelet he had given to Phoebe. Celia says it was given to her by Sylvio. Amyntas reveals that he has always been in love with Phoebe. Sylvio reveals that he is she. Of this excellent full-length opera Roger Fiske has justly observed: 'Its neglect in the composer's lifetime was as strange as is its neglect today.'

MANUSCRIPT   f.s., British Library

BIBLIOGRAPHY   H. Diack Johnstone, 'Greene's First Opera: *Florimel, or Love's Revenge*', *MT*, vol. 114 (1973), p. 1,112; Roger Fiske, *English Theatre Music in the Eighteenth Century*, OUP, 1973, 2nd edn, 1986

R.Lu.

ANDRÉ GRÉTRY

André-Ernest-Modeste Grétry; *baptized* 11 February 1741, Liège; *d* 24 September 1813, Montmorency, nr Paris

Grétry's operatic output extended over 30 years, bridging the span in Paris between the rococo age of the 1760s and the dawn of the Napoleonic era. He brought pre-Revolutionary opéra comique to its highest point of development. Grétry also successfully wrote larger-scale, light, recitative opera, and became one of the few composers of his century to publish not just his own memoirs (*Mémoires, ou Essais sur la musique*, 1797) but also philosophical speculation (*De la vérité*, 1801).

Grétry's first stage works were two intermezzi, *La vendemmiatrice* (1765), given in Rome, where he had studied since 1760, and an opéra comique, *Isabelle et Gertrude* (1766) for Geneva, where he was temporarily living and teaching. From then on he wrote exclusively for French singers in Paris. By dint of good luck and careful effort Grétry secured a libretto by the liberal intellectual Marmontel for *Le Huron* (1768), his first Parisian opera. Like all his opéras comiques, this was composed for the Comédie-Italienne company, later known as the Opéra-Comique. Success followed success. Marmontel's libretti were topical, yet bourgeois in moral sentiment; Grétry's music was melodious, Italian-influenced, closely fitted to French accentuation, and acutely responsive to the demands of the stage. Soon, Grétry's *Les deux avares* was honouring the royal wedding of the Dauphin and Marie-Antoinette, who later made the composer her personal director of music.

Through the 1770s Grétry expanded the dramatic range of his works, and was partnered by different librettists. Eventually he came to work with the greatest of them all, Michel-Jean Sedaine. In the 1780s Grétry's *Colinette à la cour*, *La caravane du Caire*, and *Panurge* successfully introduced the exotic spectacular as a genre to the Paris Opéra; *La caravane du Caire* in particular proved an enormous success over the following half-century.

Aside from triumphant visits to Liège in 1776 and 1782, Grétry left Paris only for Lyons, his wife's home city. He had three daughters, all of whom died young. The second of them, Lucile, composed two operas: *Le mariage d'Antonio* and *Toinette et Louis*, both performed at the Comédie-Italienne. In 1798 Grétry purchased Jean-Jacques Rousseau's former home, the Hermitage at Montmorency, and wrote his last works there.

Le Huron

Comédie in two acts, Oeuvre 1 (2h)
Libretto by Jean-François Marmontel, after Voltaire's novella *L'ingénu* (1767)
PREMIERES   20 August 1768, Comédie-Italienne, Paris;
UK: 2 August 1990, Opera House, Buxton

With this Grétry immediately caught the public eye. Voltaire's Huron is a 'noble savage' from Canada who lands on the Brittany coast; he captivates all with his handsomeness and heroism (fighting an English invasion) and, having discovered that he is in fact a Frenchman, marries Mlle de St Yves. Grétry's music contains richness and range, the Italianate sense of line, and the fidelity to verbal meaning that would in time make his work as a whole so influential.

EDITION   F. A. Gevaert, E. Fétis, A. Wotquenne *et al.* (eds), *Collection complète des oeuvres*, vol. 14, Breitkopf und Härtel, 1884–1936

Lucile

Comédie in one act, Oeuvre II (1h 30m)
Libretto by Jean-François Marmontel
PREMIERE   5 January 1769, Comédie-Italienne, Paris

Lucile is a good example of Marmontel's operatic style. Lucile, brought up as the daughter of a wealthy bourgeois, Timante, is about to be married to Dorval *fils* when it emerges that she is really the child of the poor Blaise, whose wife was Lucile's wet nurse: they substituted their own baby after Timante's daughter died. Timante accepts this fact, and obliges the father of Lucile's suitor to do likewise, since 'Thinking nobly creates all the worth of nobility.' Grétry's music is notable for the dramatic monologue expressing Blaise's struggle with his conscience ('Ah! ma femme!') and the equally dramatic ensemble portraying Lucile's anguish ('Ah! ma belle maîtresse'). The quartet 'Où peut-on être mieux qu'au sein de sa famille' became long famous: a musical picture of domestic happiness, sung round the table on Lucile's wedding morning.

RECORDING   François, Granger, Razador, Fontagnère, Mathieu, Opéra de Wallonie, Liège, Rossel, Monumenta Belgicae Musicae, 1975
EDITION   *Collection complète*, vol. 2

Zémire et Azor

Comédie-ballet in four acts, Oeuvre VII (2h)
Libretto by Jean-François Marmontel, after the story of Beauty and the Beast by J. M. Le Prince de Beaumont, and after the play *Amour pour amour* by P. C. Nivelle de la Chaussée (1742)
PREMIERES   9 November 1771, Fontainebleau;
UK: 5 December 1776, Drury Lane, London;
US: 1 June 1787, New York
CAST   Sander *bar*, Ali *t*, Zémire *s*, Azor *t*, Fatmé *s*, Lisbé *s*; *satb* chorus of genies and fairies
CLASSICAL ORCHESTRA; offstage: (Act III) 2 cl, 2 hn, 2 bsn; (Act IV) 2 fl, 2 hn

Zémire et Azor, like Grétry's *Les deux avares* and *L'amitié à l'épreuve*, was premiered at court as part of royal-wedding celebrations. But *Zémire* marks an expansion of scale in opéra comique. Only Duni's *La fée Urgèle* (1765) previously had four acts, and *Zémire* also contains a modest ballet sequence in Act III. The opera was a phenomenal success throughout the operatic world, and its libretto was adapted for later settings by Thomas Linley the Elder, Baumgarten, and Spohr. In France, Grétry's setting was revived in 1846–8 with orchestration by Adam.

SYNOPSIS

Act I   The Persian merchant Sander has just lost his fortune in a shipwreck, and is returning home to Ormuz with his servant Ali. The two shelter from a night storm outside a palace. Food and wine mysteriously appear. When Sander picks a rose for his daughter Zémire, the wrathful occupant of the palace appears: it is Azor, a prince who has been transformed by a vengeful fairy into a beastlike form. Only the surety of a genuine love can restore his handsomeness. Azor demands Sander's life, but allows him to visit his three daughters for a last time.

Act II   Sander meets his daughters, but conceals the news of his sacrifice. Zémire discovers the truth from Ali and determines to give her own life instead. She and Ali return to the palace.

Act III   Zémire discovers Azor's true and cultivated nature. A ballet of genies entertains her; he shows Zémire her family in a 'magic picture' or *tableau vivant*. Azor lets her visit them a last time.

Act IV   Zémire tries to explain matters to her family, then hurries back to where Azor languishes in a wild garden. Her confession of love breaks the spell, the fairy restores Azor's form, and the couple are married.

The artificiality of the tale is well reflected in the score, since the wide range of passions is contained within basically rococo idioms. But it is full of contrasts nevertheless: there are fear and despair, determination and jealousy, side by side with enchantment and childlike sensibility. The arias, which include Zémire's virtuoso 'La fauvette avec ses petits', vary greatly in style and subject; the three main duets, however, centre on conflict, displaying much rhythmic energy.

RECORDING Mesplé, Louis, Bufkens, Orliac, Van Gorp, Ch and O of Belgian Radio and Television, Doneux, Pathé Marconi EMI, 1975
EDITIONS *Collection complète*, vol. 13; v.ss., Launer, n.d.; Jobert, n.d.

Le jugement de Midas

The Judgment of Midas
Comédie in three acts, Oeuvre XIV (2h)
Libretto by d'Hèle (Thomas Hales) and Louis Anseaume (?versification), after Kane O'Hara's *Midas* (1760)
PREMIERES 28 March 1778, Palais-Royal, Paris (private); 27 June 1778, Comédie-Italienne, Paris; US: 11 June 1808, New Orleans

Thomas Hales is an enigma of Anglo-Irish literature: a fortune-hunter who, to pay his bills, created two of the best French comic libretti of the 18th century – *Midas* and *L'amant jaloux*. *Le jugement de Midas* burlesques both Classicism and tragédie lyrique in order to exalt the values of modern opéra comique. But the mixture of satire and more earthy humour is so finely controlled that the result defies categorization. In the impressive mimed overture, Apollo is seen falling from Olympus, where he had been spreading gossip about Jupiter. Employed as Palémon's farmhand, he loses no time in wooing the farmer's two daughters. Their current lovers are Pan (a woodcutter who sings common vaudeville tunes) and Marsias (a shepherd who sings in baroque-opera style). After intrigues in Act II there is a singing contest in Act III between Pan, Marsias and Apollo. Midas, the village bailiff, pronounces against Apollo and instantly grows ass's ears for his false taste. Apollo removes both daughters to Olympus, and all praise his (and Grétry's) music.

RECORDINGS excerpts only: 1. Degelin, Clini, Vandersteene, Devos, Schreurs, de Moor, CO of Belgian Radio and Television, Zollman, Musique en Wallonie, 1978; 2. Elwes, Van der Sluis, Vanhecke, Gari, Bastin, Verschaeve, La Petite Bande, Leonhardt, Ricercar, 1989
EDITIONS *Collection complète*, vol. 17; facsimile (extracts), Paul Culot (ed.), Bibliothèque Royale Albert 1er, Brussels, 1978

L'amant jaloux

The Jealous Lover
Comédie in three acts, Oeuvre XV (2h)
Libretto by d'Hèle (Thomas Hales) and F. Levasseur (versification), after Susannah Centlivre's *The Wonder: A Woman Keeps a Secret* (1714)
PREMIERES 20 November 1778, Versailles; UK: 17 November 1977, Sheffield University

L'amant jaloux is a masterpiece of ironic humour and of adaptation from its literary source. Beaumarchais and Da Ponte–Mozart borrowed from it. The Spanish merchant Lopez is trying to prevent his widowed daughter, Léonore, from remarrying. The reasons are financial. He tries to keep her closeted

from her jealous suitor, Don Alonze. In Act I Alonze accuses Léonore of harbouring a lover: but from the dressing room emerges Isabelle, who is her friend and Alonze's own sister. In Act II Isabelle's suitor, the French officer Florival, comes to the house to look for her. Later, his serenade under the windows causes another mighty explosion of jealousy from Don Alonze. Finally, in the garden at night, Florival and Alonze discover they are not rivals, and the couples are paired off. The music reflects the wit and irony of the plot, especially in the climactic ensembles of Acts I and II.

RECORDING Mesplé, Perriers, Burles, Brewer, Bastin, Ch and O of Belgian Radio and Television, Doneux, Pathé Marconi EMI, 1978
EDITION *Collection complète*, vol. 21

Richard Coeur-de-Lion

Richard the Lionheart
Comédie in three acts, Oeuvre XXIV (2h)
Libretto by Michel-Jean Sedaine, after the legend as retold in *Bibliothèque universelle des romans* (1776)
PREMIERES 21 October 1784, Comédie-Italienne, Paris; UK: 16 October 1786, Covent Garden, London (music adapted by Shield); US: 23 January 1797, Boston
CAST Richard *t*, Blondel *t*, Sir Williams *b*, Laurette *s*, Colette *s*, Florestan *b*, Marguerite d'Artois *s*, 3 *s*, 2 *t*, 3 *b*, silent; *satb* chorus of peasants, soldiers and militia
CLASSICAL ORCHESTRA

Richard Coeur-de-Lion is accepted as Grétry's masterpiece, and consequently as one of the greatest opéras comiques of its century. In it, the experience of composer and the genius of librettist combined to treat a subject that was unusually ambitious. It became a key work in the evolving genres of French neo-medieval 'Gothic' art, with its propensity for 'ancient' local colour. Additionally, the plot revolves round the music itself, i.e. in the romance sung by Blondel (which appears throughout) and his violin accompanying it, comparable to the flute in Mozart's *Die Zauberflöte*. (Blondel is supposed to play his violin onstage in Acts I and II.) Grétry's extensive use of chorus and the final siege angle the work towards serious opera.

SYNOPSIS
Act I The scene is 12th-century Austria. Blondel has been searching for his master King Richard I of England, who has been imprisoned by Leopold of Austria in the aftermath of the Third Crusade. Disguised as a blind troubadour, he arrives at Linz castle, where he meets Sir Williams (who lives near by), and his daughter Laurette. Blondel learns of the existence of an unknown prisoner, held in the castle. By chance, Richard's friend Marguerite of Artois arrives with a retinue: she has all but despaired of finding Richard alive.

Act II Richard is seen at dawn on the battlements. Below, Blondel sings the beginning of the romance that Richard had originally written for Marguerite. The king's sung reply identifies him as the unknown prisoner. Blondel contrives a plot.

Costume for M. Clairval as Blondel in Richard Coeur-de-Lion *(Paris, 1784)*

Act III Florestan, the castle governor, is arrested during festivities for Marguerite; the castle is attacked and breached, and Richard released.

The main romance, 'Une fièvre brûlante', is heard nine times, but always differently arranged, and sometimes only in the orchestra. This concept of a musico-dramatic thread was directly influential in France, and on C. M. von Weber. Other famous numbers are Blondel's 'O Richard! ô mon Roi', the king's 'Si l'univers entier m'oublie', the light duet 'Un bandeau couvre les yeux' and the couplets 'Et zig et zig' sung during the Act III festivities.

RECORDING Mesplé, Perriers, Burles, Van Gorp, Trempont, Ch and O of Belgian Radio and Television, Doneux, Pathé Marconi EMI, 1978
EDITIONS *Collection complète*, vol. 1; David Charlton (ed.), facsimile, *French Opera in the Seventeenth and Eighteenth Centuries*, Pendragon, in preparation; v.ss. Laurier, 1841; Heugel, 1874

Guillaume Tell

William Tell
Drame in three acts, Oeuvre XXXI (1h 30m)
Libretto by Michel-Jean Sedaine, after the play by A.-M. Lemierre (1766)
PREMIERES 9 April 1791, Comédie-Italienne, Paris; US: *c.* 1817, New Orleans; UK: 1 May 1984, John Lewis Partnership Music Society, Oxford Street, London

Guillaume Tell (together with *Pierre le Grand* composed the year before) is a direct response to the French Revolution. Sedaine had long preached the cause of justice for all, and Grétry was a natural liberal, not to say pragmatist. Musically, Grétry's style became tougher in the 1780s. In *Guillaume Tell* both solos and choruses have moments of considerable power and pathos.

SYNOPSIS
Act I portrays the Tell family and villagers (there is much use of Swiss local colour). Tell's daughter is to be married to Melktal *fils*. Suddenly news arrives that Melktal's father, having refused to salute Guesler's hat, has had his eyes put out by the Austrians.

Act II Tell has already refused to salute the hat, and been condemned to death. His wife and children plead vainly with Guesler. Guesler forces Tell to shoot the apple from his son's head; he succeeds, but when a second bolt, intended for Guesler, is discovered Tell is led away. The Swiss people express their revolutionary determination.

Act III sees Tell's escape from an Austrian boat, in a storm. He summons the cantons together; signal fires are lit. During final combats Guesler is shot by Tell; the last chorus tells future ages to fight for liberty, as they have done.

EDITION *Collection complète*, vol. 24

Denys le tyran, maître d'école à Corinthe

Dionysius the Tyrant, Schoolmaster at Corinth
Opera in one act (35m)
Libretto by Sylvain Maréchal, after Classical sources
PREMIERE 23 August 1794, Opéra, Paris

Denys is the historical Dionysius the Younger, former tyrannical king of Syracuse, now in exile in Corinth after being deposed by the republican leader Timoleon (in 343 BC). Denys runs a school, but his dictatorial methods cause suspicion, as do his politics. Eventually, while drunk, his identity is unmasked thanks to the old royal diadem he keeps about his person. He is driven out by Timoleon and the people.

Grétry kept the musical style and orchestration simple, matching the naïve treatment of the subject. There is humour in the children's music (their 'Alpha, beta, gamma' chorus anticipates *The Sound of Music*), and a heroic aria for Timoleon acts as the final focus.

RECORDING Donzelli, Franceschetto, Di Segni, De Simone, Coro Ars Pulcherrima Artium, O Internazionale d'Italia Opera, Vizioli, Nuova Era, 1989
EDITION *Collection complète*, vol. 28

Other operas: *Isabelle et Gertrude, ou Les sylphes supposés*, 1766; *Le tableau parlant*, 1769; *Silvain*, 1770; *Les deux avares*, 1770; *L'amitié à l'épreuve*, 1770, rev. 1786; *L'ami de la maison*, 1771; *Le magnifique*, 1773; *Céphale et Procris, ou L'amour conjugale*, 1773; *La rosière de Salency*, 1773, rev. 1774 (EDITION Pendragon, in preparation); *La fausse magie* (also known as *L'amant jaloux*), 1775 (RECORDING Pathé Marconi EMI, 1977); *Les mariages samnites*, 1776; *Matroco*, 1777; *Les trois âges de l'opéra*, 1778; *Les événements imprévus*, 1779; *Aucassin et Nicolette*, 1779; *Andromaque*, 1780; *Emilie, ou La belle esclave*, 1781; *Colinette à la cour, ou La double épreuve*, 1782; *L'embarras des richesses*, 1782; *La caravane du Caire*, 1783; *L'épreuve villageoise*, 1784; *Panurge dans l'île des lanternes*, 1785 (RECORDING excerpts: Musique en Wallonie, 1972); *Amphitryon*, 1786; *Les méprises par ressemblance*, 1786; *Le Comte d'Albert*, 1786; *Le prisonnier anglais*, 1787, rev. as *Clarice et Belton*, 1793; *Le rival confident*, 1788; *Raoul Barbe-bleue*, 1789; *Aspasie*, 1789; *Pierre le Grand*, 1790; *Cécile et Ermancé, ou Les deux couvents*, 1792; *Basile, ou A trompeur, trompeur et demi*, 1792; *Le congrès des rois* (coll. with 11 other composers), 1794; *Joseph Barra*, 1794; *La rosière républicaine, ou La fête de la vertu*, 1794; *Callias, ou Nature et patrie*, 1794; *Lisbeth*, 1797; *Anacréon chez Polycrate*, 1797; *Le barbier de village, ou Le revenant*, 1797; *Elisca, ou L'amour maternel*, 1799; *Le casque et les colombes*, 1801; *Delphis et Mopsa*, 1803; several unperformed, inc., and lost works

BIBLIOGRAPHY   David Charlton, *Grétry and the Growth of Opéra-Comique*, CUP, 1986; G. de Froidcourt (ed.), *La correspondance générale de Grétry*, Brepols, 1962

D.P.C.

EDVARD GRIEG

Edvard Hagerup Grieg; *b* 15 June 1843, Bergen, Norway; *d* 4 September 1907, Bergen

Grieg's genius was for the smaller forms. He possessed a highly developed feeling for vocal line and a subtle understanding of Norwegian poetry and folksong. He studied in Leipzig (1858–62) and later in Copenhagen with Gade (1863–6). He set many of the great Norwegian poets of the day, including Bjørnstjerne Bjørnson and, of course, Ibsen. In 1872 he composed music for a production of Bjørnson's play, *Sigurd Jorsalfar*, in Christiania (as Oslo was then known), and the following year Bjørnson sent him part of a libretto on the life of the national hero, Olav Trygvason. Trygvason was the Norwegian king (995–1000) who converted his countrymen to Christianity. Grieg had already drawn on an episode in his life as the basis of the cantata, *Landkjenning* (*Land-sighting*), to words of Bjørnson. But when, in January 1874, Ibsen asked Grieg to provide incidental music for a production of *Peer Gynt*, he put the opera on one side. Three scenes, scored in 1888, have been recorded (Unicorn, 1979), but this choral suite (Op. 50) has never succeeded in capturing the public imagination.

BIBLIOGRAPHY   Finn Benestad and Dag Schjelderup-Ebbe, William L. Halverson and Leland B. Sateren (trans.), *Edvard Grieg: The Man and the Artist*, Alan Sutton, 1988; John Horton, *Grieg*, Dent, 1974

R.La.

LOUIS GRUENBERG

b 3 August 1884, nr Brest-Litovsk, Belorussia; *d* 10 June 1964, Beverly Hills, California, US

Gruenberg was one of the earliest American composers to recognize the potential of jazz, which he called 'the musical expression of black, red and white people – the American race'. His choral piece *The Daniel Jazz* (1924) embodied his approach. Gruenberg's operas and operettas include one, *The Bride of the Gods*, with a text by Busoni, with whom he studied in Berlin. Two of them in particular made an impact in America: *Jack and the Beanstalk*, a fairy-tale for children (1931), and *The Emperor Jones*, based on the play by Eugene O'Neill (Metropolitan, 1933). The latter tells of Brutus Jones, an escaped convict who becomes the dictator of a Caribbean island. With its avoidance of arias and other set forms, *The Emperor Jones* has been described as a play with sound effects. However, the musical techniques Gruenberg uses to portray Jones's increasing terror – complex rhythmic patterns, discordant harmonies, a type of sprechstimme, all building up to a state of extreme tension – are precisely what make the work so dramatic. Perhaps surprisingly, given the central character and Gruenberg's interest in Negro spirituals and folk music (he had already edited four volumes of this music), there is just one episode in this style, 'Standin' in the Need of Prayer', which Jones sings near the end of the opera.

Operatic works: *Signor Formica*, 1910; *The Witch of Brocken*, 1912; *The Bride of the Gods*, 1913; *Piccadillymädel*, 1913; *Roly-boly Eyes*, 1919; *The Dumb Wife*, 1923; *Hallo! Tommy!*, *c.* 1924; *Lady X*, *c.* 1927; *Jack and the Beanstalk*, 1931; *The Emperor Jones*, 1933; *Green Mansions* (radio opera), 1937; *Helena's Husband*, (1938); *Volpone*, (1945); *One Night of Cleopatra* (television opera), 1954; *The Miracle of Flanders* (television opera), (1954); *The Delicate King*, (1955); *Antony and Cleopatra*, 1955, (rev. 1958), 1961

BIBLIOGRAPHY   David Ewen, *American Composers: A Biographical Dictionary*, Hale, 1983

P.D.

ADRIANO GUARNIERI

b 10 September 1947, Sustinente, nr Mantua, Italy

After completing his musical studies with Giacomo Manzoni at the Bologna conservatory, Guarnieri soon established himself as one of the most individual voices of his generation. The elaborate fluidity of his melodic writing allowed him to generate a magmatic counterpoint in which individual lines ebb and flow around each other. This idiom was put to telling use in his first opera.

Trionfo della notte

The Triumph of Night
Lyric action in four pictures (1h 30m)
Text extracted by L. Leonetti and the composer, from Pier Paolo Pasolini's *Religione del mio tempo*

Composed 1985–6
PREMIERE 3 February 1987, Teatro delle Celebrazioni, Bologna

Each of Guarnieri's four pictures sets fragments from a different poem by Pasolini – *Nostalgia della vita, Ad un ragazzo, Trionfo della notte*, and *Religione del mio tempo*. Divested of their more concrete context in the street life of Rome, these fragments create an open network of erotic imagery to which the producer can respond as he or she wishes (Guarnieri indicates only when singers perform on stage, and when off). Prompted by the example of Monteverdi, Guarnieri creates dense, ecstatic vocal counterpoints from two sopranos, a tenor, and an offstage 'madrigal chorus' of five women. The result is a non-narrative sequence of short groups of sounds, dramatically static and, as Guarnieri has stated, 'not a conventional opera'.

EDITION S. Camerini, 1987

Other Opera: *Medea*, 1991
BIBLIOGRAPHY Piero Moli, review of *Trionfo*, *Opera*, vol. 38 (1987), pp. 679–81

D.O.-S.

PIETRO ALESSANDRO GUGLIELMI

b 9 December 1728, Massa; *d* 19 November 1804, Rome

Guglielmi belonged to an old family of musicians and, having trained at home with his father and uncle (as well as with Giacomo Puccini the Elder), he was sent to study in Naples under Durante. His first known comic opera (1757) was followed by others that were staged in Naples and Rome and, thanks to the influence of patrons, he soon had the opportunity to tackle an opera seria (1763).

In 1767 he moved to London, as resident composer at the King's Theatre. He stayed until 1772, producing many operas, though, according to Burney, without great success. He returned to Italy, where his works were more appreciated, despite competition in Naples from Cimarosa and Paisiello. The three were recognized as the greatest living exponents of Neapolitan comic opera; indeed, according to Rossini (as quoted by Stendhal), after these three it would be unthinkable to write further opere buffe. Mozart himself, in Abert's opinion, owed a small debt to Guglielmi, being influenced by the Italian's way of 'fragmenting the melodic discourse in a rapid patter of syllables, scales, rests and fermatas' to achieve 'authentically comic effects'.

Throughout his career Guglielmi modified his style to reflect the latest developments in operatic fashion. Thus by the time he composed his last opere serie he had come a long way from the highly stylized Metastasian forms of his early works, and had adopted the more fluid structure and more dramatic approach of his contemporaries both in Italy and in France. His comic operas too increasingly moved away from rigid 'closed' forms, consequently allowing greater realism in the expression of emotion and in dramatic pacing. One of the most successful was *La pastorella nobile* (1788), a typical Neapolitan work, which was sufficiently popular to warrant an adaptation by Martín y Soler and Cherubini; it was staged at the Théâtre-Italien in Paris in 1807, and remained in the repertoire until 1822.

In May 1793 Guglielmi became maestro di cappella at St Peter's, Rome, and ended his days far from the vicissitudes of the operatic stage.

Surviving operas: *I cacciatori*, 1762, as *Gli uccellatori*, 1772; *Tito Manlio*, 1763; *L'Olimpiade*, 1763; *Siroe, re di Persia*, 1764; *Li rivali placati*, 1764; *Il Tamerlano*, 1765; *Il ratto della sposa*, 1765, as *Il vecchio deluso, o sia La bella aurora*, 1775; *Adriano in Siria*, 1765; *Lo spirito di contradizione*, 1766 (EDITION facsimile, Garland, 1983); *Sesostri*, 1766; *Il Demofoonte*, 1766; *La sposa fedele*, 1767; *Armida*, 1767, as *Rinaldo*, 1789; *Antigono*, 1767; *Il re pastore*, 1767; *Ifigenia in Aulide*, 1768; *I viaggiatori ridicoli tornati in Italia*, 1768; *Alceste*, 1768; *L'impresa d'opera*, 1769; *Ruggiero*, 1769; *Ezio*, 1770, rev. 1774; *Il disertore*, 1770; *Le pazzie d'Orlando*, 1771; *Il carnevale di Venezia, o sia La virtuosa*, 1772; *Mirandolina*, 1773; *La contadina superba, ovvero Il giocatore burlato*, 1774; *Tamas Kouli-Kan nell'India*, 1774; *Merope*, 1775; *Artaserse*, 1775; *Vologeso*, 1775; *Gli intrighi di Don Facilone*, 1775 or 1776; *L'impostore punito*, 1776; *La Semiramide riconosciuta*, 1776; *Il matrimonio in contrasto*, 1776; *Ricimero*, 1777; *Il raggiratore di poca fortuna*, 1779; *La villanella ingentilita*, 1779; *Narcisso*, 1779; *Le nozze in commedia*, 1781; *La semplice ad arte*, 1782; *La Quakera spiritosa*, 1783; *Le vicende d'amore*, 1784; *Le sventure fortunate*, 1785; *La finta zingara*, 1785, as *La finta zingara, ossia Il Solachianello*, 1791; *La virtuosa di Mergellina*, 1785; *Enea e Lavinia*, 1785; *L'inganno amoroso*, 1786; *Laconte*, 1787; *La pastorella nobile*, 1788; *Alessandro nell'Indie*, 1789; *La bella pescatrice*, 1789; *L'azzardo*, 1790; *La sposa contrastata*, 1791; *Il poeta di campagna*, 1792; *Amor tra le vendemmie*, 1792; *La lanterna di Diogene*, 1793; *Admeto*, 1794; *Il trionfo di Camilla*, 1795; *Tomiri*, 1795; *La morte di Cleopatra*, 1796; *Siface e Sofonisba*, 1802; Doubtful: *La pace tra gli amici*, 1766; *Il matrimonio*, 1770; *La virtuosa*, 1770; *La frascatana*, 1773; *Il vecchio deluso*, 1774; *La virtuosa alla moda*, 1780; *Didone*, 1785; *La clemenza di Tito*, 1785; *Li cinque pretendenti*, 1792; *Il ratto di Briseide*, 1794; *La scuola degli amanti*, 1794; *La schiava riconosciuta*, 1797; *La donna fanatica*, 1798; *Amore in caricatura*, n.d.; *Gli amanti teatrali*, n.d.; *Il regno delle Amazoni*, n.d.; *Il matrimonio villano*, n.d.; c. 37 lost operas
BIBLIOGRAPHY James L. Jackman, 'Pietro Alessandro Guglielmi (2)', in *Grove*, Macmillan, 1980

D.A.D'A.

MANFRED GURLITT

Manfred Hugo Ludwig Gurlitt; *b* 6 September 1890, Berlin; *d* 29 April 1973, Tokyo

An opera conductor as well as composer, Gurlitt studied composition in Berlin with Humperdinck. In 1908 he became a répétiteur at the Hofoper and, following posts in Bayreuth, Essen and Augsburg, kapellmeister and opera director in Bremen. In 1924 he was appointed generalmusikdirektor in Berlin, where he conducted at the Staatsoper. In 1939 he moved to Japan, where he helped popularize German opera.

Gurlitt's second opera, *Wozzeck* (Bremen, 1926) appeared just four months after Alban Berg's setting, and even at the time was known as 'the second *Wozzeck*'. Inevitably, despite critical success, it fell under the shadow of Berg's work and remained neglected until an Austrian Radio broadcast and a new production in Bremen (both 1987). *Soldaten* (1930, after Lenz) has prompted further comparisons with Berg's *Wozzeck*, with which Gurlitt had by then become familiar, but remains interesting in its own right for its exploration of polytonality and dissonances within a highly structured musico-dramatic context.

Operatic works: *Die Heilige*, 1920; *Wozzeck*, (1924), 1926; *Soldaten*, 1930; *Nana*, 1933; *Nächtlicher Spuk*, 1937; *Warum?*, 1940; *Nordische Ballade*, 1944; *Wir schreiten aus*, 1958

BIBLIOGRAPHY Rudolf Stephan, 'Wozzeck', and Michael Mackelmann 'Soldaten', in 'Manfred Gurlitt', in C. Dahlhaus (ed.), *Pipers Enzyklopädie des Musiktheaters*, R. Piper, 1986– , vol. 2, pp. 620–23

M.A.

H

ALOIS HÁBA
b 21 June 1893, Vizovice; d 18 November 1973, Prague

Like many Czech musicians, Hába worked first as a schoolteacher. He then joined Novák's composition masterclasses at the Prague Conservatory (1914–15), and studied at the Vienna Musikhochschule (1917–20) and under Schreker in Berlin (1920–22). In Vienna he came into contact with Schoenberg's atonal music, and in Berlin with Busoni. At the same time, however, he cultivated an interest in the folk music of his native Moravia. The instinctive use of micro-intervals he detected in it led to his own quarter-tone theories, which he tenaciously promoted in his own works and writings and in the quarter- and sixth-tone section of the Prague Conservatory, which he established in 1923.

Though Hába wrote some music in the semitonal system (for instance his second opera, *The New Land*), he is best known for his quarter-tone music. It gained notoriety at the time (*The Mother* was premiered in Munich under Scherchen), but the difficulties it poses have restricted performances. His two later operas have not been performed.

The Mother
Matka
Opera in the quarter-tone system in ten scenes, Op. 35
(1h 45m)
Libretto by the composer
Composed 1927–9
PREMIERES 17 May 1931, Munich (in German); 23 May 1947, Theatre of the Fifth of May, Prague (in Czech)

The Mother begins with a lament for a dead mother. Francek Křen's wife has died and he needs another to care for his six children. Maruša, the mother of the title, fills this need and bears four children of her own. Hába's opera, set in the same peasant world as Janáček's *Jenůfa*, charts the story of the new mother until just one child is left at home and the parents' lives are complete. The music is athematic, and uses quarter-tones both melodically (for emotional inflexion) and in the harmony, with the aid of specially constructed quarter-tone instruments: clarinets, trumpets, harmonium and piano.

RECORDING   Zikmundová, Urbanová, Jedenáctik, Spisar,

P. Kočí, Prague National Theatre Ch and O, Jirouš, Supraphon, 1956
EDITION   f.s., Dilia, 1963

Other operas: *The New Land* (*Nová země*), (1936); *Thy Kingdom Come* (*Prijd' království Tvé*), in the sixth-tone system, (1942)
BIBLIOGRAPHY   Jiří Vysloužil, *Alois Hába: život a díla* (*Alois Hába: Life and Works*), Panton, 1974

J.T.

PARASHKEV HADJIEV
b 27 April 1912, Sofia, Bulgaria

The son of Todor Hadjiev – conductor and early champion of Bulgarian opera – Parashkev Hadjiev is perhaps the most important post-war composer in Bulgaria. After early studies in Prague, he went to the Sofia State Academy and (from 1937 to 1940) studied composition in Vienna and Berlin. He joined the staff of the Sofia Academy in 1940. Though primarily known as a prolific composer of opera and especially operetta, he has written in a wide variety of other genres. His music is sparklingly melodious and untiringly inventive.

Hadjiev's first two operas were strongly in the folk tradition, both set in the years of the Ottoman oppression and consisting of a succession of contrasting lyrical and comic scenes. With *Albena* Hadjiev began to pare away the folk elements, at the same time replacing traditional numbers with a more recitative-based style. This was taken a stage further in the anti-fascist *July Night*. The next opera, *The Millionaire*, is a satire on bourgeois values, while another comedy, *The Knight*, set in the 14th century, mocks the following of foreign fashions, and its deliberately non-folkloric treatment makes clear the allegorical intent. The fairy-tale opera *The Golden Apple* heads a veritable stream of works written for children.

Operatic works: *Once Upon a Time* (*Imalo edno vreme*), 1957; *The Madcap* (*Lud gidiya*), 1959; *Albena*, 1962; *July Night* (*Julska nosht*), 1965 (RECORDING Balkanton, 1960s); *The Millionaire* (*Milionerat*), 1965; *The Masters* (*Maistori*), 1966; *The Knight* (*Rizaryat*), 1969; *The Golden Apple* (*Slatnata yabalka*), 1971; *Year 893* (*Leto 893*), 1973; *Cyrano de Bergerac*, 1973; *Midas the King has Donkey's Ears*, 1976;

Klvdii, 1982; *The Star* (*Zvezdata*), 1983; *Iniyat bolem*, 1988
Operettas: *Delyana*, 1952; *Aika*, 1955; *Madame Sans-Gêne*,
1958; *c.* 120 children's operettas for radio, 5 for stage
Musical: *The Conscript* (*Sluybogonzi*), 1972
BIBLIOGRAPHY   Venelin Krustev, trans. Jean Patterson-
Alexieva, *Bulgarian Music*, Sofia Press, 1978, pp. 228–35

E.A.

REYNALDO HAHN
b 9 August 1875, Caracas, Venezuela; *d* 28 January 1947, Paris

Hahn, the youngest of 12 children of a German-
Jewish father and a Spanish mother, came to Paris
when he was three and spent the rest of his life there.
At the Conservatoire he studied composition with
Massenet, and when he was only 15 he was noticed
by Alphonse Daudet (the author of *L'arlésienne*),
who commissioned him to write music for his play
L'obstacle (1890). This was the start of Hahn's
lifelong fascination and connection with the theatre.
He became a noted conductor of Mozart, especially
of the operas, and in 1906 (the 150th anniversary
of Mozart's birth) conducted *Don Giovanni* at
Salzburg. In the 1920s he conducted Mozart at the
Paris Opéra, where at the end of the Second World
War (during which, as a Jew, he suffered a ban on his
music) he finally became director. He was also a
noted music critic, including for the *Journal* (1909–
14), and for *Le Figaro* (1921–45).

Four years after the Daudet commission, Hahn
met the 22-year-old Marcel Proust, and they became
lovers, remaining close friends after their two-year
affair. There are no unmistakable individual Hahn
portraits in Proust. He does not figure in *A la*
recherche du temps perdu. But several characters in
the early, unfinished *Jean Santeuil* borrow traits from
him, including the musician Henri de Réveillon, and
the Marquis de Poitiers, with his habit of singing with
a cigarette dangling from the corner of his mouth.

Hahn is best remembered for his songs, of which
the popular 'Si mes vers avaient des ailes', written
when he was only 13, perhaps exaggerates the easy
salon elegance of his style. He was famous in his day
for his own performances of such pieces, in which he
would accompany himself at the piano. But his music
for the theatre is much more voluminous. As well as
several ballets and incidental scores, he wrote 17
operas, operettas, and musical plays, of which the
first, the 'Polynesian idyll' *L'île du rêve*, was staged
by the Opéra-Comique when he was only 23. Most of
these works are comedies, with singing and dialogue,
a genre in which Hahn, with his love of classical
lightness, wit and good taste, excelled. 'At all costs,'
he once said, 'heaviness and boredom are to be
avoided; the Muses do not wear glasses.' It could be
the motto for a whole strain in French art from
Offenbach (another German) to Cocteau.

Ciboulette
Operetta in three acts (2h)
Libretto by Robert de Flers and Francis de Croisset
Composed 1921–2
PREMIERE   7 April 1923, Théâtre des Variétés, Paris

Hahn's most successful operetta was composed at the
suggestion of Robert de Flers, the editor of *Le*
Figaro. Set in 1867 in the now vanished market of
Les Halles, it is about a pretty young market-
gardener and her quest for a husband. Dissatisfied
with her eight fiancés, she consults a clairvoyant, who
tells her that she must find her true lover in a pile of
cabbages, must win him from a woman who turns
white in a moment, and must receive his proposal in
a tambourine. Naturally these conditions are finally
satisfied, but not before Ciboulette has disguised
herself as a Spanish artiste, Conchita Ciboulero, to
entice her seemingly reluctant lover.

The absurd complexities of this plot are in the
Chabrier tradition, and Hahn's music – light, frothy
but inventive – is well worthy of Chabrier on, at any
rate, a moderate day. The music for 'Conchita', and
for the character of famous waltz-composer Olivier
Métra, reveals Hahn's gift for pastiche, a gift he used
to good purpose a year or two later in his music for
Sacha Guitry's play *Mozart*.

RECORDING   Mesplé, Alliot-Lugaz, Gedda, Van Dam,
O Philharmonique de Monte Carlo, Diederich, EMI, 1981
EDITION   v.s., Salabert, 1923

Operatic works and musical plays: *L'île du rêve*, 1898; *La*
Carmélite, 1902; *Pastorale de Noël*, 1908; *Fête triomphale*,
1919; *Nausicaa*, 1919; *La colombe de Bouddha*, 1921;
Ciboulette, 1923; *Mozart*, 1925 (RECORDING Musidisc, 1959);
La Reine de Sheba, 1926; *Une revue*, 1926; *Le temps d'aimer*,
1926; *Brummel*, 1931; *O mon bel inconnu!*, 1933
(RECORDING Musidisc, 1960s); *Malvina*, 1935; *Le marchand*
de Venise, 1935; *Beaucoup de bruit pour rien*, 1936; *Le oui des*
jeunes filles (orch. Henri Busser), 1949

Reynaldo Hahn

BIBLIOGRAPHY   R. Bebb, 'Reynaldo Hahn', *Listener*, 8 April 1971, pp. 458–9; B. Gavoty, *Reynaldo Hahn*, Editions Buchet/Chastel, Paris, 1976; G. Painter, *Marcel Proust: A Biography*, 2 vols, Chatto and Windus, 1959, 1965, *passim*

S.W.

FROMENTAL HALÉVY

Jacques-François-Fromental [Fromentin] -Elie [Elias] Halévy [Lévi]; *b* 27 May 1799, Paris; *d* 17 March 1862, Nice, France

The son of Jewish parents, Halévy entered the Paris Conservatoire at the age of nine. There he was a pupil of Cherubini, who was later to assist him considerably in his career. He also studied with Berton and Méhul. Before winning the Prix de Rome in 1819 he had already composed a comic opera, *Les bohémiennes*, which was never performed; in Italy he wrote part of an Italian opera, *Marco Curzio*. His first work to be staged was *L'artisan* at the Opéra-Comique in 1827 with a libretto by St-Georges; but his greatest successes were *La juive* and *L'éclair* (both 1835), the one grand opera, the other comic, written in collaboration with respectively Scribe and St-Georges. Four more grand operas were to follow: *Guido et Ginevra*, *La reine de Chypre*, *Charles VI*, and *Le juif errant*, all set in Renaissance or medieval Europe. There were at least a dozen more comic operas, a genre in which Halévy was equally at home.

Halévy was an intelligent composer and a good writer; he earned a fine reputation also as a choral director (at the Opéra) and as a teacher at the Conservatoire. His pupils included Gounod, Saint-Saëns and Bizet, the latter subsequently becoming his son-in-law. He was an accomplished administrator, indeed, one of the most prominent men of his time. Yet he felt overshadowed by Meyerbeer in the field of grand opera and by Auber and Adam in comic opera. His music is fluent and thoroughly professional; like Meyerbeer he was good at engineering impressive ensembles for a crowded stage, and he was adept at providing local colour and ballet music when required. He ably served the great singers in his vocal writing. His music was admired, though perhaps not whole-heartedly, by both Berlioz and Wagner.

La juive

The Jewess
Opera in five acts
Libretto by Eugène Scribe
PREMIERES   23 February 1835, Opéra, Paris; US: 13 February 1844, New Orleans; UK: 29 July 1846, Drury Lane, London
CAST   Eléazar *t*, Rachel *s*, La princesse Eudoxie *s*, Léopold *t*, Cardinal de Brogni *b*, Ruggiero *bar*, Albert *b*, Herald, Officer; *satb* chorus of the people
FULL ORCHESTRA with organ

The reopening of the Paris Opéra in 1847, with a performance of La juive

The most successful of Halévy's operas, *La juive* remained in the Opéra's repertoire throughout the 19th century and has occasionally been revived, especially as a vehicle for tenors in the role of Eléazar. It was Halévy's first grand opera, staged with unprecedented magnificence in its first production at a cost of 150,000 francs; such splendour in historical costumes, armour and equestrian equipage had never been seen before. The role of Eléazar was derived from Shylock, that of Rachel from Rebecca in Scott's *Ivanhoe*.

SYNOPSIS

Act I   The setting is Constance in 1414. Rachel, daughter of Eléazar, a Jewish goldsmith, is in love with 'Samuel', who is working in her father's workshop. The Jews are harassed by the people for working on a Christian holiday.

Act II   At the Passover meal Rachel notices that Samuel rejects the unleavened bread, and he confesses that he is a Christian, not a Jew at all. Rachel persuades her father not to kill him for the confession, so long as he marries her. He then admits, to their horror, that he is not free to marry her.

Act III   At a sumptuous fête Eléazar and his daughter deliver a gold chain which the Princess Eudoxie has ordered for her husband and find that the husband, Prince Léopold, is none other than Samuel. Rachel, in fury, denounces him for the seduction of a Jewess, namely herself, and the Cardinal Brogni pronounces an anathema on all three: Léopold, Eléazar, and Rachel.

Act IV   Léopold is saved from the scaffold by Rachel's declaration of his innocence, but although the Jews can be saved if they abjure their religion, they refuse.

Act V   Eléazar and Rachel are led to the scaffold. As she is thrown into the boiling cauldron Eléazar reveals his terrible secret to Brogni; Rachel is in fact Brogni's long-lost daughter, whom Eléazar saved from the sack of Rome many years before. She is not a Jewess at all.

This sensational dramaturgy with its 'spring-loaded' plot perfectly exemplifies Scribe's theatrical style; each successive revelation causes a horrified reaction, often expressed as a grand static ensemble. Halévy's models were Auber's *La muette de Portici* and Meyerbeer's *Robert le diable*, both of which he surpassed in many respects, earning the admiration of Wagner, Mahler and a faithful public for a whole century. He treated the Jewish scenes as local colour, not suggesting any particular identification as a Jew. The opera's orchestration is advanced for its time; Eléazar's air, 'Rachel! Quand du Seigneur', with its plaintive accompaniment by two cors anglais, is the best-known number in the opera.

RECORDING   Varady, Anderson, Carreras, González, Furlanetto, Ambrosian Opera Ch, Philharmonia O, de Almeida, Philips, 1989
EDITIONS   f.ss., Schlesinger, 1835; Garland (*Early Romantic Opera*, no. 36), 1980

L'éclair
The Lightning Flash
Drame lyrique in three acts
Libretto by Jules-Henri Vernoy de St-Georges and François-Antoine-Eugène de Planard
PREMIERES   16 December 1835, Opéra-Comique, Paris; US: 16 February 1837, New Orleans

A young naval officer, blinded by lightning on a seashore near Boston, is cared for by the shy young Henriette. But when her uncle has miraculously restored his sight, he mistakes her elder sister, a merry widow, for his benefactress. The misunderstanding is put straight in time for a happy ending. The opera is skilfully composed for two sopranos and two tenors and was greatly admired in its time.

EDITIONS   f.s., Schlesinger, 1836; v.s., Schlesinger, [1897]

La Reine de Chypre
The Queen of Cyprus
Opera in five acts
Libretto by Jules-Henri Vernoy de St-Georges
PREMIERES   22 December 1841, Opéra, Paris; US: 25 March 1845, New Orleans; UK: 7 July 1845, Drury Lane, London

The vocal score was arranged by Wagner during his first stay in Paris. He wrote admiringly of the opera, especially for its sense of period. Set in 1469 at the time of the Venetian annexation of Cyprus, the opera was regarded by some as superior even to *La juive*. It concerns Catarina Cornaro, designated by the Venetians as wife to Jacques de Lusignan, king of Cyprus. Her last-act duet with Gérard, to whom she had originally been betrothed, is one of Halévy's greatest scenes. Donizetti composed an opera, *Caterina Cornaro* (1843), based on an adaptation of this libretto.

EDITIONS   f.s./v.s., Schlesinger, 1842

Other operas: *Les bohémiennes*, 1819; *Marco Curzio*, 1822; *Les deux pavillons, ou Le jaloux et le méfiant*, 1824; *Pygmalion*, 1824; *Erostate*, 1825; *L'artisan*, 1827; *Le roi et le batelier*, 1827; *Clari*, 1828; *Le dilettante d'Avignon*, 1829; *Attendre et courir*, 1830; *La langue musicale*, 1830; *La tentation*, 1832; *Yella*, 1832; *Les souvenirs de Lafleur*, 1833; *Ludovic* (completion of inc. work by Hérold), 1833; *Guido et Ginevra*, 1838; *Les treize*, 1839; *Le shérif*, 1839; *Le drapier*, 1840; *Le Guitarrero*, 1841; *Charles VI*, 1843; *Le Lazzarone, ou Le bien vient en dormant*, 1844; *Les mousquetaires de la reine*, 1846; *Les premiers pas* (coll. with Adam, Auber and Carafa) 1847; *Le val d'Andorre*, 1848; *La fée aux roses*, 1849; *La tempestà*, 1850; *La dame de pique*, 1850; *Le juif errant*, 1852; *Le nabab*, 1853; *Jaguarita l'indienne*, 1855; *L'inconsolable*, 1855; *Valentine d'Aubigny*, 1856; *La magicienne*, 1858; *Noé* (completed by Bizet, renamed *Le déluge*), 1885; *Vanina d'Ornano* (inc.), (n.d.)
BIBLIOGRAPHY   'La juive', *L'avant-scène Opéra*, no. 100, 1987; Mina Curtiss, 'Fromental Halévy', *MQ*, vol. 39 (1953), p. 196; J. W. Klein, 'Jacques Fromental Halévy', *MR*, vol. 23 (1962), p. 13; Karin Pendle, *Eugène Scribe and French Opera of the 19th Century*, UMI, 1979

H.M.

IAIN HAMILTON

Iain Ellis Hamilton; *b* 6 June 1922, Glasgow, Scotland

Although a late starter in the genre, Hamilton is one of the most prolific British opera composers of the post-Britten era. After training as an engineer he entered the Royal Academy of Music at the age of 25, winning its highest distinction, the Dove Prize, in 1951. His early output, largely instrumental and choral, shows the expressive influence of Berg and, later, the serial techniques of Webern. After lecturing at Morley College in London he taught at Duke University, North Carolina, from 1961, moving back to London in 1981.

Hamilton's choice of epic or legendary subjects for his operas (for which he has written his own libretti) reflects a concern with the interaction and conflict between personal and public events. It also makes for imposing spectacle: for instance, *Lancelot* was mounted in the tilting yard of Arundel Castle. *Tamburlaine*, a BBC radio commission based on Marlowe, remains unstaged, as do *Agamemnon* and his treatment of the Dick Whittington legend.

The Royal Hunt of the Sun

Opera in two acts (24 scenes) (2h 15m)
Libretto by the composer, after the play by Peter Shaffer (1964)
Composed 1966–8; orch. completed 1975
PREMIERE 2 February 1977, Coliseum, London

The story deals with events in 1529–33 surrounding the Spanish conquest of Peru. The fatal clash of cultures is explored on a personal level in the relationship between the gold-hunting venturer, Pizarro, and the Inca king, Atahuallpa. Abandoning serial and atonal methods, the musical substance is generated by small musical units, including motivic use of chords. At the time of its production the work was criticized for being too declamatory, and Hamilton himself later described it as 'much more a music-theatre work than an opera'. Though it uses a large percussion section, no reference is made to Inca music.

EDITIONS v.s./lib., Theodore Presser Co., 1977

The Catiline Conspiracy

Opera in two acts (nine scenes) (2h)
Libretto by the composer, based on Ben Jonson's play *Catiline* (1611) and sources from Sallust and Cicero
Composed 1973
PREMIERE 16 March 1974, MacRobert Centre, Stirling (Scottish Opera)

Set in Rome in 64–63 BC, the opera deals with Catiline's conspiracy against the state in the final years of the Republic and its confounding by Cicero. When compared with his earlier works, Hamilton's music shows an increased lyricism and, as in *Royal Hunt*, the chorus plays an important role, particularly in the Act II Senate scene.

EDITIONS v.s./lib., Theodore Presser Co., 1974

Anna Karenina

Opera in three acts (15 scenes) (2h 30m)
Libretto by the composer, after the novel by Tolstoy (1877)
Composed 1978
PREMIERES 7 May 1981, Coliseum, London; US: 16 March 1983, Wilshire-Bell Theater, Los Angeles

Hamilton's version of Tolstoy's great tragedy further continued his move away from serialism and atonality towards a new exploration of tonality. Traditional set pieces and orchestral interludes assume an even greater importance. In other respects, it breaks with the pattern of earlier works: it was his first opera to take as its source not a play but a novel. It also focuses more on the personal aspect, though the conflict between Anna's and Vronsky's burgeoning affair and the moral judgement of society is felt. The figure of Levin is omitted.

EDITIONS v.s., Theodore Presser Co., 1979; lib., Theodore Presser Co., 1981

Other operatic works: *Agamemnon* (1960, rev. 1968, 1987); *Pharsalia*, 1969; *Tamburlaine*, 1977; *Dick Whittington* (1981); *Lancelot*, 1985; *Raleigh's Dream*, 1984
BIBLIOGRAPHY Noel Goodwin, 'Hamilton's 'Royal Hunt'', *Opera*, vol. 28 (1977), pp. 149–52, 169-70; Noel Goodwin, 'Hamilton's 'Anna Karenina'', *Opera*, vol. 32 (1981), pp. 457–62; Iain Hamilton, 'The Royal Hunt of the Sun', *MT*, vol. 118 (1977), pp. 23–5

M.A.

MARVIN HAMLISCH

Marvin Frederick Hamlisch; *b* 2 June 1944, New York

A prodigy who won a Juilliard scholarship at seven, Marvin Hamlisch was working on Broadway (making arrangements for *Funny Girl*) even before completing his university studies. Film composition occupied his attention for a number of years, until Joseph Papp and Michael Bennett lured him back to New York to provide the music (including almost continuous music under dialogue) for the Pulitzer prize-winning *A Chorus Line*. After that huge success, he has returned to the stage from time to time, creating scores in the same contemporary vein that informs his film song hits.

A Chorus Line

Musical in one act (2h 15m)
Libretto by James Kirkwood and Nicholas Dante; lyrics by Edward Kleban
PREMIERES 15 April 1975, Public Theater, New York; UK: 22 July 1976, Theatre Royal, London

A breakthrough in style and subject, *A Chorus Line* presents an audition for the dance chorus of a new musical. Each character is allowed to tell his or her life story in song, dance or speech, and the tension builds steadily to the final choice of only eight dancers. In its omission of customary plot elements,

The opening scene of A Chorus Line *(New York, 1975)*

A Chorus Line represents another step in the cross-breeding of dramatic and revue-type structure that was taking place in the 1970s. Hamlisch and his lyricist contributed an accomplished, probably underrated score; but undoubtedly it was the late Michael Bennett's shaping and staging that lifted this show into the realm of the classic.

RECORDING   McKechnie, Blair, Bishop, Lopez, Pippin, CBS, 1975
FILM (much rewritten)   Attenborough (dir.), Columbia, 1985
EDITION   v.s., Edwin H. Morris, 1975

They're Playing Our Song
Play with music in two acts (2h 30m)
Libretto by Neil Simon; lyrics by Carole Bayer Sager
PREMIERES   11 February 1979, Imperial Theater, New York; UK: 1 October 1980, Shaftesbury Theatre, London

The rocky romance of a composer and a lyricist is told with the characteristic Simon humour and Hamlisch zip. The only other characters are three 'inner voices' for each of the two main protagonists, to serve as miniature chorus. This is almost a play with music rather than a musical, as the songs either represent the actual products of the characters' collaboration or are incidental interruptions (sometimes as interior monologues) to the scenes.

RECORDING   L. Arnaz, Klein, Blank, Casablanca, 1979
EDITIONS   v.s., Samuel French (on hire); lib., Random House, 1980

Other musicals: *Jean Seberg*, 1983; *Smile*, 1986; *The Goodbye Girl*, 1993

BIBLIOGRAPHY   Ken Mandelbaum, *A Chorus Line and the Musicals of Michael Bennett*, St Martin's Press, 1989

J.A.C.

GEORGE FRIDERIC HANDEL
Georg Friedrich Handel; *b* 23 February 1685, Halle an der Saale; *d* 14 April 1759, London

Although Handel is best known in the English-speaking world for his oratorios and orchestral works, he was primarily an opera composer. Until he was in his mid-fifties, his career centred on the opera house: he took a leading role in the musical management of London's repertoire opera companies and between 1710 and 1740 he composed new operas at a rate averaging more than one major work per year. Working within the musical conventions of Italian opera seria, Handel mainly set libretti that had already been used by other composers in Italy, though he adapted them to the needs of his own performers and, to some extent, to the tastes of his audiences. The well-developed and mature genre of opera seria to which Handel attached himself in his early twenties was already being enriched by elements from French opera (Handel's operas normally begin with a 'French' *ouverture*) and influences from French drama. To this form Handel brought formidable composition skills, particularly in the control and extension of melody and harmony, that took the baroque operatic aria to a peak of its development: and, since opera seria relied on the exposition of character and of emotional states through arias, in both of which Handel was supremely skilled, his operas mark the highest point in the genre itself.

In the town of his birth Handel received a firm technical education in music at the hands of Friedrich Wilhelm Zachow, the organist of the Market Church. Just before his 17th birthday he registered as a student at Halle University, and soon after received his first musical appointment as organist of the Calvinist Domkirche. However, he apparently nursed musical ambitions that could not be fulfilled in Halle, and two years later left to join the opera house in Hamburg, initially as a violinist. He had already met one of the opera house's leading young musicians, Johann Mattheson, during a visit to Hamburg and Lübeck in 1703, and may have made preliminary contact with its leading composer, Reinhard Keiser, through his family connections in the area near Halle.

At Hamburg Handel advanced quickly from second violinist to keyboard accompanist. Early in 1704 he was involved in a duel with Mattheson over the occupancy of the harpsichord at the end of Mattheson's *Cleopatra*. The next year saw the production of Handel's own first operas, *Almira* and *Nero*: the first was a success but the second ran for only three performances. After this, Handel seems to have withdrawn somewhat from the opera company, though he composed one further opera, apparently so extensive that it was divided over two nights when it was first performed in 1708 (*Florindo* and *Dafne*) – but by then Handel had left Hamburg for Italy. Handel's Hamburg operas have not survived intact: *Almira* is the only one for which a sufficiently complete score survives for modern performance.

Handel's Italian visit lasted from the autumn of 1706 to the early months of 1710. Since he wanted to meet as many contemporary Italian musicians as possible, and to hear their music, he spent periods in a number of different centres. Considerable time was spent in Rome, where Handel enjoyed enlightened patronage and composed many chamber cantatas, developing in them the operatic forms of recitative and aria. But opera itself was absent from Rome owing to papal opposition. At Florence, on the other hand, opera flourished under the patronage of Ferdinando de' Medici. Handel probably heard works by Alessandro Scarlatti, Perti and Orlandini there, and became acquainted with the libretti of Antonio Salvi, a physician to the Florentine court: it was for Florence that he composed his first all-Italian opera, *Rodrigo*. Venice gave him the opportunity to hear operas by Gasparini, Lotti, Albinoni, Caldara and Alessandro Scarlatti, and to produce his own *Agrippina*.

During the Carnival season Venice was a resort for foreign diplomats as well as musicians. There Handel may have made contacts that brought him successively to Hanover and London, among them Agostino Steffani who had directed the court opera in Hanover during its heyday in the 1690s. When Handel accepted a post at Hanover in June 1710 he must have recognized that the court opera was in abeyance for the foreseeable future, and it was apparently agreed that he would enjoy generous leave of absence to pursue his operatic ambitions elsewhere. Before the year was out, Handel was in London and early the next year *Rinaldo* was produced at the Queen's Theatre, Haymarket. After a single dutiful return to Hanover, he settled permanently in London in 1712.

Handel's long operatic career in London falls into a number of phases. Although an overall musical continuity is apparent in the type of music presented, the administrations of successive opera companies lurched from one artistic or financial crisis to another. The decade preceding Handel's arrival had seen almost continuous chaos in the management of the London patent theatres: only recently had the idea of all-sung Italian opera become a reality, and the Haymarket Theatre its regular venue. Musical quality, some novel stage effects, and the presence of the leading castrato Nicolini brought success to Handel's first London opera, *Rinaldo*, and contributed to the permanent establishment of Italian opera in London. But managements came and went: sometimes, like Owen Swiney in 1713, they took the money with them. John Jacob Heidegger as manager brought some stability to the situation, but his efforts were temporarily beaten by a political division among the patrons in 1717, which came at the end of a period of gradual financial attrition.

The reunification of the sources of patronage, symbolized by the reconciliation between George I

The stage of the King's Theatre in the Haymarket, c. 1725

and the Prince of Wales in March 1720, coincided with the most determined attempt to establish Italian opera in London on a permanent footing. The Royal Academy of Music, established by Charter in 1719, named Handel as 'Master of the Orchestra', and he was given instructions to undertake a European tour to engage singers, including the castrato Senesino. The Academy presented repertoire seasons whose programmes included operas by several composers and pasticcios assembled from other works. In the first years of the Academy Handel had to share musical authority with other composers, most importantly Giovanni Bononcini, but gradually responsibility devolved to Handel alone. Unfortunately the Academy was eventually overcome by problems of artistic and financial management. By 1728 the commitment of its original patrons had probably run its course, and could not be revived even by the unedifying rivalry between the supporters of the opera company's two leading ladies, Cuzzoni and Faustina Bordoni. After a break during 1728–9, Handel and Heidegger resumed opera seasons under their own management, taking over the Academy's scenery and costume stock. Handel once again visited the Continent to collect singers, including the soprano Strada and the castrato Bernacchi; but within the year the latter had been replaced by the return of Senesino.

However, when a rival opera company (The Opera of the Nobility) was established in 1733 Senesino joined the opposition, taking most of the rest of the cast with him. After one season of rivalry, Handel had to cede the premier Haymarket opera house (known as the King's Theatre since the accession of George I in 1714) to the Nobility Opera, taking his own opera company to Covent Garden. The period of the two opera companies, which lasted until 1737, was an uncomfortable one for Handel, but it brought forth some fine operas. In Carestini and

Conti he found technically accomplished successors to Senesino, and his programmes were more diverse than those of the Nobility Opera. From 1732 onwards he mixed English oratorios, odes and serenatas with his Italian operas and in 1734–5 his operas were considerably enhanced by Madame Sallé's dance company.

On the collapse of the Nobility Opera, Handel reoccupied the King's Theatre for two seasons in 1738–9: the emphasis was on opera in the first season and oratorio in the second. Then Handel moved his performances to a less central venue, the theatre in Lincoln's Inn Fields, for two seasons: English works were given in the first season, but the second included new Italian operas, Imeneo and Deidamia. There Handel gave his last London opera performance in February 1741: the next year Imeneo saw a final revival at his hands as part of his concert season in Dublin. When Handel returned to London, his theatre career centred around English works. He looked back only once, when he inserted five of his Italian opera arias into a revival of Semele in December 1744, probably to accommodate Italian singers. It may be significant that this occurred in the one English work that, although performed 'after the manner of an oratorio', was composed to a libretto originally written c. 1706 for an English opera and intended for one of London's major theatres.

All of the original works that Handel brought to the public stage are covered in the following entries. None of his English works was given a staged performance in the theatre under the composer: Acis and Galatea and Esther were probably acted in their earlier versions, at private performances, but when they came to the public theatre Handel presented them as a serenata and an oratorio respectively, without stage action. The genre of theatre oratorio that Handel developed in his later years was differently paced, and differently constructed, from his operas: opinions are divided as to whether staged performances are successful.

Handel revived several of his operas, with consequent changes of cast and musical contents. The versions and voice types listed are those of the first performances; major changes on subsequent revivals are noted in the descriptions. Voices are described according to the clefs used by Handel for the original singer (soprano, alto, tenor, bass), and roles originally composed for castrati are noted as such. The operas generally end with a coro sung by all the soloists. The presence of other chorus movements (generally sung by the soloists alone until Handel's operas of the mid-1730s) is noted for the relevant operas. Handel composed his operas to a normal time-span of about three hours' music: the performances must have lasted about four hours with the intervals. Il pastor fido, Flavio, Atalanta and Imeneo are rather shorter; Giulio Cesare, Rodelinda and Alcina rather longer.

The Handel editions referred to below are as follows: F. W. Chrysander (ed.), G. F. Handels Werke: Ausgabe der Deutschen Handelgesellschaft, Leipzig/Bergedorf bei Hamburg, 1858–94, 1902; rp, 1965

(abbreviated to HG); M. Schneider, R. Steglich and others (eds), Hallische Handel-Ausgabe im Auftrage der Georg Friedrich Handel-Gesellschaft, Kassel, 1955– (abbreviated to HHA); HWV numbers refer to the thematic catalogue by Bernd Baselt, in W. and M. Eisen (eds), Händel-Handbuch, vols 1 and 2, Deutsche Verlag für Musik, Leipzig, 1978, 1984.

Almira

Der in Krohnen erlangte Glückswechsel, oder Almira, Königin von Castilien
In the Crown lies a change of fortune, or Almira, Queen of Castile
Opera in three acts, HWV 1 (3h 45m)

Libretto by Friedrich Christian Feustking, after L'Almira by Giulio Pancieri set by Boniventi (1691)
Composed 1704–5
PREMIERE 8 January 1705, Theater am Gänsemarkt, Hamburg

Almira is the only one of Handel's Hamburg operas to survive in a sufficiently complete form to permit modern performance, though the single surviving source does not give the opera complete as it was first performed: it is a copyist's score apparently derived from the version of Telemann's revival in 1732, which had various alterations and additions. Nevertheless, Handel's original can mainly be restored with the help of the original printed libretto, which incidentally describes the work as a 'Sing-Spiel' although there is no spoken dialogue.

The opera is episodic when compared with the well-rounded and monolithic opera seria dramas of Handel's maturity: the cosmopolitan and varied Hamburg audience wanted entertainment, incident and spectacle. The plot centres round the relationships of seven characters, three female and four male, with mistaken messages, jealousies and conflicting emotional intentions. Act I begins with a big coronation scene, Act III with a pageant of the Continents. A comic servant provides contrast to the main characters, commenting on the action. The recitatives are in rhymed German, and 15 of the 53 arias are in Italian (the rest in German). The choice of language seems to be related to whether or not the arias were taken from Pancieri's original libretto. Handel's music is lively but rather rough and ill-formed and reveals the extent to which his style had developed before he went to Italy. Although most of the arias are not lengthy, some of them make considerable technical demands on the singers.

EDITIONS HG, vol. 55; HHA, series 2, vol. 1 (forthcoming)

Rodrigo

Vincer se stesso è la maggior vittoria
Rodrigo; Conquest of one's self is the greatest victory
Drama per musica in three acts, HWV 5 (3h)
Composed 1707
Libretto adapted from Il duello d'Amore e di Vendetta by Francesco Silvani set by M. A. Ziani (1699)
PREMIERES autumn 1707, Teatro Cocomero, Florence; UK: 17 July 1985, Sadler's Wells, London

Handel's first Italian opera was composed for performance in Florence under Medici patronage. Rodrigo was the last king of the Vizigoths in Spain, but the plot is only loosely tied to historical events. In the opera Rodrigo is King of Castile, and his forces under Giuliano defeat those of Aragon: Evanco, heir to the Aragon title, is taken prisoner. Rodrigo alienates Florinda, Giuliano's sister, who has been seduced by Rodrigo and borne a son by him. Through Giuliano's treachery, Evanco's fortunes are reversed and he leads a successful rebellion. Rodrigo's wife Esilena prevents Florinda from executing the death sentence on Rodrigo by thrusting the infant son into his arms. Reconciliations follow: Evanco and Florinda are left to rule Aragon and the young boy is named as the heir to Castile.

Handel's score shows a great advance over *Almira* in musical and dramatic fluency: he has achieved an Italian manner in recitatives and arias, though not the expansiveness that came with maturity. The proportion of recitative to aria is unusually high: in later years Handel would no doubt have looked for a more effective balance in the libretto. The strongest music comes in Act II for Esilena, whose 'Empio fato' effectively strikes Handel's tragic tone for the first time. Sections of Handel's autograph score have been lost, as have the revisions that he made between composition and performance. Nevertheless viable modern performing versions have been produced, with reconstructed music for the lost scene at the beginning of Act I.

RECORDING Sharp, Hamblin, Ginzer, Kunz, Ragin, Olsen, Deutsche Handel-Solisten, Farncombe, Badisches Staatstheater, Karlsruhe, und Süddeutscher Rundfunk, Stuttgart, 1987
EDITION *HG*, vol. 56

A rehearsal; painting by Marco Ricci, c. 1709

Agrippina

Drama per musica in three acts, HWV 6 (3h)
Libretto by Vincenzo Grimani, based on events *c.* AD 40–50 as related by Tacitus and Suetonius
Composed 1709
PREMIERES ?January 1710, Teatro Grimani di San Giovanni Crisostomo, Venice; UK: 27 June 1963, Unicorn Theatre, Abingdon; US: 16 February 1972, Philadelphia (concert); 14 March 1985, Fort Worth (Opera Association)

CAST Agrippina *s*, Poppea *s*, Nerone *s* (castrato), Ottone *a*, Claudio *b*, Narciso *a* (castrato), Pallante *b*, Lesbo *b*, Giunone *a*
ORCHESTRATION 2 rec, 2 ob, 2 tpt, timp, str (including violetta), cont

Agrippina is arguably Handel's first operatic masterpiece. The plot is an anti-heroic satirical comedy. The characters (and their follies) are vividly portrayed with a light touch; yet the seriousness of the motivations and issues that produce the dramatic tensions are never undercut. The libretto is one of the best that Handel ever set and, unusually, was written specially for him. Handel probably composed the score in Venice late in 1709: the Carnival season began on 26 December, and *Agrippina* was apparently the second opera of the season.

SYNOPSIS
Act I Agrippina, wife of the Roman emperor Claudio, schemes that Nerone, her son by a previous marriage, should succeed to the throne. Hearing that Claudio has been drowned, she arranges to have Nerone proclaimed, but the ceremony is interrupted by news of the arrival of Claudio, who has been rescued by his lieutenant Ottone: in return Claudio has named Ottone as his successor. Ottone declares his love for Poppea. Agrippina, knowing that Claudio is also attracted to Poppea, suggests to Poppea that Ottone has agreed to yield her to Claudio in return for the succession.

Act II Poppea sets Claudio against Ottone, but subsequently discovers that she has been deceived by Agrippina. Meanwhile, Agrippina plays on Claudio's belief in Ottone's treachery and persuades him that he should name Nerone as his successor.

Act III Poppea receives three admirers, successively hiding Ottone and Nerone behind curtained doorways, and awaiting Claudio. To him she says that she was mistaken in her previous identification and that his traitorous rival is Nerone, not Ottone: to prove this, she reveals Nerone's presence in the room, and Claudio dismisses him in a fury. Agrippina realizes that Poppea has denounced Nerone, and that her own schemes are in danger of exposure. She responds to Claudio's accusations by saying that she acted for the safety of the city and the throne, and taxes him with being improperly influenced by Poppea. When she claims that Ottone loves Poppea, Claudio lays the blame for his actions on Nerone, and summons all three. He accuses Nerone of hiding in Poppea's room, and orders them to marry, meanwhile naming Ottone to the succession. Ottone renounces the throne in order to reclaim Poppea: Claudio approves the exchange of Ottone's and Nerone's ambitions, and invokes Juno to bless the marriage of Ottone and Poppea. (Giunone is not listed in the original printed libretto: the final scene, in which she appears, may have been cut before the first performance.)

Agrippina was a success: according to John Mainwaring, Handel's first biographer, 'The theatre, at almost every pause, resounded with shouts of *Viva il caro Sassone.* They were thunderstruck with the grandeur and sublimity of his style: for never had they known till then all the powers of harmony and modulation so closely arrayed, and forcibly combined.' The arias in *Agrippina* are shorter and more numerous than in Handel's later operas, but this is appropriate to the nature of the story, and the opera marks a great advance on *Rodrigo* in the balance and pacing of the scenes. The portrayal of Agrippina herself is particularly well managed in the second half of Act II, and Handel's music keeps pace with the succession of comic *dénouements* in Act III.

RECORDING Bradshaw, Saffer, Minter, Hill, Isherwood, Capella Savaria, McGegan, Harmonia Mundi, 1991
EDITION *HG*, vol. 57

Rinaldo

Opera in three acts, HWV 7 (3h)
Libretto by Giacomo Rossi, to a scenario by Aaron Hill, after *Gerusalemme liberata* by Torquato Tasso (1575)
Composed December 1710–January 1711; rev. 1731
PREMIERES 24 February 1711, Queen's Theatre, Haymarket, London; US: 16 October 1975, Jones Hall, Houston
CAST Rinaldo *a* (castrato), Goffredo *a*, Eustazio *a* (castrato), Almirena *s*, Armida *s*, Argante *b*, Magician *a* (castrato), Herald *t*, Woman *s*, Mermaids *s*
ORCHESTRATION flageolet, 2 rec, 2 ob, 2 bsn, 4 tpt, timp, str (including violetta), cont (one aria with hpd solo)

Handel first arrived in London towards the end of 1710. His music had preceded him: movements from the *Rodrigo* overture had provided incidental music to *The Alchemist* (by Ben Jonson) earlier that year, and an aria from *Agrippina* was introduced into a performance of Alessandro Scarlatti's *Pirro e Demetrio* in December, probably with Handel's co-operation. It can safely be presumed that Handel had received a firm invitation to compose for the Haymarket company before he set out for London. The composer obviously wished to make his mark on London; the opera management for its part welcomed the opportunity for an original work in their programme, which had hitherto been founded on second-hand Italian scores.

In the preface to the printed libretto of *Rinaldo*, Rossi claimed that Handel had composed the opera in a fortnight, and this is possible since he reworked many of his previous Italian arias into the score. No doubt it had been prudent for Handel to leave the composition until he arrived in London and could see him cast in action. The preface by Aaron Hill (manager of the Queen's Theatre) to the libretto indicated his attempt to remedy what he regarded as the defects in the Italian operas hitherto seen in London: 'First, That they had been compos'd for Tastes and Voices, different from those who were to sing and hear them on the English Stage; And Secondly, That wanting the Machines and Decorations, which bestow so great a Beauty on their Appearance, they have been heard and seen to very considerable Disadvantage.'

As the *Spectator* commented, with only slight exaggeration, on 6 March 1711, 'The opera of *Rinaldo* is filled with Thunder and Lightning, Illuminations, and Fireworks.' Hill exploited the full resources of the stage machinery at the Haymarket. His intention seems to have been to match the virtuosity of the Italian singers with extravagant scenic effects derived from the English masque tradition. In addition to the singers, *Rinaldo* required a full complement of spirits, fairies and armies.

SYNOPSIS
Act I The Christian camp outside the gates of Jerusalem. Rinaldo reminds Goffredo, the Captain General of the Crusade force, that he has been promised the hand of Almirena, Goffredo's daughter, if the city is conquered. Argante's mistress Armida (an 'Amazonian' enchantress, and Queen of Damascus) arrives from the air in a fiery chariot and tells him that success depends on detaching Rinaldo from the Christian army. In a delightful grove with singing birds, Almirena and Rinaldo affirm their love. Armida enters and leads Almirena away. When Rinaldo offers resistance, the two ladies are carried away in a black cloud, and Rinaldo is left disconsolate ('Cara sposa, amanta cara'). Goffredo and his brother Eustazio enter; Eustazio advises that they consult a hermit in order to defeat Armida. Rinaldo calls on winds and tempests to assist him ('Venti, turbini').

Act II On the seashore Goffredo and Rinaldo complain about the distance they must travel to find the hermit, but Eustazio assures them that they are close to their destination. A spirit in the shape of a lovely woman lures Rinaldo into a boat, telling him that she has been sent by Almirena. Rinaldo's companions try to prevent him from entering the boat, but he breaks free of them. The boat immediately sails away. In the garden in the enchanted palace of Armida, Almirena complains of her abduction. Argante makes advances, saying that he can prove his affection by breaking Armida's spell, even though this will provoke the enchantress's wrath, but Almirena pleads to be left alone ('Lascia ch'io pianga'). Armida rejoices at Rinaldo's capture but when he is led in, in defiant mood, Armida annoys him further by offering her own love. When this is refused, Armida changes her appearance to that of Almirena: Rinaldo is at first taken in, but when the deception is revealed Rinaldo leaves angrily. Armida is torn between her passion for Rinaldo and her anger that he will not respond to her ('Ah, crudel'). On Argante's arrival, she changes her appearance to that of Almirena again in order to disguise her own distress, only to expose Argante's designs on Almirena. Resuming her own appearance she upbraids Argante: the alliance between them is at an end and it is now Armida's turn to call for revenge ('Vò far guerra').

Act III A mountain prospect with the hermit's cave at the bottom and an enchanted palace at the top. The Magician–Hermit tells Goffredo and Eustazio that Rinaldo and Almirena are prisoners in the palace, but enormous force will be necessary to release them. The Christians' first attempt is repelled by 'ugly spirits', but they escape back to the cave, and the Magician gives them 'fatal Wands' that can conquer witchcraft. They climb the mountain and strike the gates of the palace, whereupon the palace, spirits and mountain vanish, and Goffredo and Eustazio are found hanging on to the sides of a vast rock in the middle of the sea. Armida, in her garden, makes to stab Almirena with a dagger; Rinaldo draws his sword to attack Armida, but is restrained by two spirits. Goffredo and Eustazio arrive and Armida invokes the furies, but with help of the Christians' wands the garden vanishes, transformed into the area near the city gate at Jerusalem. Rinaldo is united with his companions and, when Armida again attempts to stab Almirena, he attacks her again: Armida vanishes. Argante and Armida are reconciled. Eustazio announces the approach of the pagan army, and the Christian army gathers (Rinaldo: 'Or la tromba'). In the battle, Rinaldo swings the balance in favour of the Christians. Argante and Armida are captured, Rinaldo and Almirena are united. Armida, deciding that heaven may not intend her destruction, breaks her magic wand: she and Argante profess the Christian faith and are released by Goffredo.

With such an episodic scenario, the strength of *Rinaldo* lies in the power of individual events, their variety and contrast, rather than in dramatic continuity. Although his musical style had advanced enormously during the preceding six years, Handel was almost thrown back into the operatic world of *Almira*. He may have missed a few dramatic tricks, but he matched visual spectacle with its musical equivalent: tuneful hit numbers such as 'Lascia ch'io pianga', the song for the mermaids and the now famous march for the Christian army in Act III. It mattered not that the tunes were second-hand, for the audience had not heard Handel's previous works. Presumably the libretto was adapted, even in places distorted, to accommodate the texts for some of these arias, though from the musical point of view the old tunes were considerably improved. And, where the plot allowed, dramatic characterization was strong: one of the high points is Armida's scene near the end of Act II, beginning with the forceful accompanied recitative 'Dunque i lacci d'un volto' and ending in 'Vò far guerra', which was a showpiece for Handel too, at the harpsichord in the orchestra pit.

Rinaldo maintained its popularity through several seasons following 1711. Inevitably there were some changes to the score as casts varied: the part of Goffredo was taken over by successive sopranos and that of Argante by an alto castrato, and new arias were added. One of the factors contributing to the initial success of the opera had been the presence of the castrato Nicolini in the title role. When Handel revived *Rinaldo* in April 1731 this part fell to the equally famous Senesino and the rest of the cast was also differently balanced (Goffredo as a tenor, Armida a contralto and the Magician a bass); Handel rewrote virtually the whole score.

RECORDING Cotrubas, Scovotti, Watkinson, Esswood, Brett, Cold, La Grande Ecurie et La Chambre du Roy, Malgoire, CBS, 1977: 1711 version, but with bass Magician
EDITIONS *HG*, vol. 58 (the 2nd edn (1894) includes both 1711 and 1731 versions); *HHA*, series 2, vol. 4 (forthcoming)

Il pastor fido
The Faithful Shepherd
Opera in three acts, HWV 8 (2h 30m)
Libretto by Giacomo Rossi, after the play by Giovanni Battista Guarini (*c.* 1584)
Composed 1712; rev. 1734
PREMIERES 22 November 1712, Queen's Theatre, Haymarket, London; rev. version: 29 May 1734, King's Theatre, Haymarket, London; second rev. version: 9 November 1734, Covent Garden, London; US: August 1983, Castle Hill, Ipswich, Massachusetts
CAST Mirtillo *s* (castrato), Silvio *a* (castrato), Amarilli *s*, Eurilla *s*, Dorinda *a*, Tirenio *b*; in 1734 version: *satb* chorus of huntsmen, shepherds and shepherdesses, priests; dancers
ORCHESTRATION 1711 version: 2 fl, 2 ob, bsns, str, cont; 1734 version requires in addition 2 hn, also theorbo and organs in cont for *Terpsicore*

Il pastor fido is based on a play that was famous as an example of the pastoral literary mode: two versions had been performed in London in the early 1700s. While *Rinaldo* is mainly heroic and spectacular, *Il pastor fido* is intimate and charming. No doubt the artistic recipe of *Rinaldo* could not be repeated immediately, but there were also pressing practical reasons for the contrast: the Haymarket opera company began its 1712–13 season without its leading castrato (Nicolini), and was probably unable to finance another grand spectacle immediately. Rossi drastically pruned down the number of characters from Guarini's play for the opera: as in *Rinaldo*, Handel drew on his previous music for some of the arias.

SYNOPSIS
An oracle has told the people of Arcadia that their only escape from the annual sacrifice of a virgin to Diana is by the union of two people of 'Heavenly Race', and a match has been arranged between Silvio and Amarilli. But Mirtillo and Amarilli are attracted to each other, and Silvio is more interested in pursuing animal game than young ladies, though Dorinda would like his attentions. Eurilla, in love with Mirtillo and jealous of Amarilli, tricks Mirtillo and Amarilli into an assignation in a cave, in order to expose their relationship. Dorinda hides in a bush and is wounded by Silvio's spear, thrown in the belief that the bush harboured a wild animal. The accident at last produces an affectionate response from Silvio. Amarilli is sentenced to death for being unfaithful to the arranged match with Silvio, and Eurilla rejoices in the elimination of her rival: Mirtillo will now be free to receive her attentions. But Mirtillo offers to substitute himself for Amarilli as the sacrifice, and the lovers assert their fidelity. Tirenio, the high priest, announces that Diana is appeased and that the sacrifice is not to proceed: Mirtillo is of divine descent, and the terms of the oracle ('the exalted Passion of a Faithful Shepherd cancels the ancient

Crime of a perfidious Maid') have been fulfilled. The two pairs of lovers are united, and Eurilla is forgiven.

A contemporary diarist commented: 'The Scene represented only ye Country of Arcadia, ye Habits were old. – ye Opera Short.' Certainly *Il pastor fido* is lightweight when compared to *Rinaldo*, and was no doubt inexpensively staged, but the result was an amiable piece of intimate music drama, almost on a chamber scale. Eurilla is a strong character; the development of some of the others was partially controlled by Handel's reuse of previous music, but the audience probably came for good tunes as much as for anything else.

Handel's revivals of *Il pastor fido* in 1734 saw radical changes to the opera. Only eight of the original 32 numbers were retained. New music (much of it borrowed from other works) included some magnificent showy arias appropriate to the talents of the new Mirtillo (Giovanni Carestini), while the part of Eurilla (played by the ageing soprano Durstanti – Handel's Agrippina in Venice) was reduced. Choruses added some flesh to the structure. Further important changes were made for another revival in November the same year, this time at the Covent Garden theatre. To make good use of a French ballet company under Madame Sallé, dances were introduced into the closing scenes of each act, and the opera was preceded by a one-act opéra-ballet prologue, *Terpsicore*, composed by Handel following a model from Colin de Blamont. Some of the dances gained new popularity in the 20th century through their inclusion in Beecham's famous suite *The Faithful Shepherd*.

RECORDINGS   1. 1734 version, without *Terpsicore*: Farkas, Flohr, Lukin, Esswood, Kállay, Gregor, Savaria Vocal Ensemble, Capella Savaria, McGegan, Hungaroton, 1988; 2. 1712 version: Fusco, Bozzi Lucca, Gatta, Garazioti, Reynolds, Miville, I Commedianti in Musica della Cetra, Gerelli, Cetra, 1969; 3. Dance music from *Il pastor fido* plus *Terpsicore*: English Baroque Soloists, Gardiner, Erato, 1985
EDITIONS   1712 version: *HG*, vol. 59; *HHA*, series 2, vol. 5; 1734 versions: *HG*, vol. 34

Teseo

Dramma tragico in five acts, HWV 9 (3h)
Libretto by Nicola Francesco Haym, after Philippe Quinault's libretto set by Lully as *Thésée* (1675)
Completed 19 December 1712
PREMIERES   10 January 1713, Queen's Theatre, Haymarket, London; US: 30 May 1985, Boston College Theater Arts Center, Chestnut Hill, Boston

With *Teseo* the Haymarket operas returned to an emphasis on visual spectacle, particularly in the transformation scenes effected by Medea, an enchantress in the same musical mould as Armida.

Teseo, son of Egeo, the king of Athens, has fought incognito in his father's army. He is not recognized by his father until the end of the opera. His plans to marry Agilea, a princess under the guardianship of Egeo, are confused because Egeo expects to marry Agilea himself and has promised Teseo to Medea in return for her supernatural assistance to his military career. After making various mischief, Medea finally

fails to prevent the union between Teseo and Agilea. She leaves in thunder and lightning, which gives way to heavenly radiance as Minerva descends.

The libretto of *Teseo* was an attempt to convert a tragédie-lyrique directly into an Italian opera. The opera was Handel's first collaboration with the composer–performer Haym, who was in many ways his most talented librettist–adapter, thanks to his considerable experience in the opera house. Even so, in *Teseo* he had to work against the grain in converting the French form to the Italian one, with its different emphasis on the importance and function of solo arias. The result was rather sprawling, but there is some fine music, and some excellent theatre for Medea's scenes.

RECORDING   Gooding, Napoli, James, Dímes, Ragin, Gall, Musiciens du Louvre, Erato, 1992
EDITION   *HG*, vol. 60

Silla

(*Lucio Cornelio Silla*)
Drama per musica in three acts, HWV 10 (3h)
Libretto by Giacomo Rossi
PREMIERE   ?2 June 1713, Queen's Theatre, Haymarket, London

Silla was a Roman dictator from the second century BC. In this opera he is portrayed as violent and ruthless, with penchants for immediate and universal application of the death sentence, and for forcing his attentions on any ladies present. Some of his intended victims are saved by his wife Metella, who eventually stands by her husband when he is defeated by an insurrection: Silla retires and liberty is restored.

For some time it was believed that Silla might have been composed for private performance to the Earl of Burlington, but circumstantial evidence is strong that the opera was written for the Queen's Theatre, as it uses known scenic effects from the theatre's repertoire and voices that match the contemporary opera house cast. In spite of the repulsive story, Silla may have been given as a (?semi-private) performance in honour of the French ambassador, to whom the libretto is dedicated: it has also been suggested that the character of Silla may have borne contemporary identification with the Duke of Marlborough. But the opera may never have been performed. Rossi's libretto seems to be a drastically reduced version of an Italian original which still awaits identification. Handel's score also looks like a rushed job: in spite of some occasional flashes of good music, it is perhaps not surprising that *Silla* still awaits modern revival.

EDITION   *HG*, vol. 61

Amadigi

(*Amadigi di Gaula*)
Opera in three acts, HWV 11 (3h)
Libretto probably by Nicola Francesco Haym, after Antoine Houdar de la Motte's libretto *Amadis de Grèce*, set by Destouches (1699)

PREMIERE   25 May 1715, King's Theatre, Haymarket,
London; US: 17 February 1969, Princeton University (concert)

Amadigi combines the spectacle of *Rinaldo* with a second attempt to convert a tragédie-lyrique into an opera seria. The libretto is more successful than in *Teseo*, largely because the original five acts were converted into the three acts more appropriate to the Italian genre.

The plot bears many similarities to that of *Rinaldo*: once again an enchantress (Melissa) tries to break up the relationship between a pair of lovers, this time by detaining Oriana, the heroine, in an enchanted tower in order to separate her from Amadigi. The plot is further complicated when Amadigi shows a picture of Oriana to his ally Dardano, whereupon the latter realizes that they are rivals for the love of the same woman. Amadigi manages to release Oriana but he sees a false image (conjured up by Melissa) in the Fountain of True Love, depicting Oriana accepting Dardano's advances. Melissa alters Dardano's appearance to appear like that of Amadigi: in this guise, Dardano gains some acceptance from Oriana, but he is found by the 'real' Amadigi and slain in a duel by his rival. Having the lovers in her power, Melissa cannot bring herself to kill either Amadigi or Oriana: she calls on Dardano's ghost, which tells her that heaven approves the union of the lovers; Melissa kills herself.

The conversion from tragédie-lyrique to opera seria was not perfect, if viewed from the narrow perspective of stagecraft, but *Amadigi* is carried magnificently by Handel's music, which conveys the emotional forces at work in the drama more effectively than in any of his previous operas. Melissa's frustrated passion for Amadigi is entirely credible, and the jealousy between Amadigi and Dardano builds a powerful dramatic tension. The emotional concentration was greatly assisted by the reduction of the principal cast to only four main players (Orgando is a minor character, who only appears in the final scene). Vestiges of the ballet from the French source libretto were retained, including a 'Dance of Enchanted Knights and Ladies' near the end of Act I.

RECORDING   Smith, Harrhy, Fink, Stutzmann, Musiciens du Louvre, Minkowski, Erato, 1991
EDITIONS   *HG*, vol. 62; *HHA*, series 2, vol. 8

Radamisto

Opera in three acts, HWV 12 (3h)
Libretto by Nicola Francesco Haym, after 'Domenico Lalli's' *L'amor tirannico* set by Gasparini (1710, rev. 1712)
Composed early 1720, rev. autumn 1720, 1721 and 1728
PREMIERE   27 April 1720, King's Theatre, Haymarket, London; US: 16 February 1980, Washington (semi-staged; Handel Festival Orchestra); 10 January 1992, New York (Mannes College Opera Seminar)

In June 1717 the Haymarket Opera Company under Heidegger's management came to an end, partly through artistic and financial fatigue, but most immediately because of a political division in the patronage base of the audience, symbolized by the estrangement between George I and the Prince of Wales. In 1719 Handel was greatly involved with the construction of a new company, the Royal Academy of Music, on a broad patronage base with strong aristocratic support. *Radamisto* was his first opera for the new company, and may well have been intended for the Academy's first presentation: in the event the season opened on 2 April 1720 with Porta's *Numitore*. Handel's opera was probably delayed until the impending reconciliation between the king and the prince had been effected: they attended the first performance together, and the word-book for the first performance contains a dedicatory epistle to the king from Handel himself.

Handel's musical style matched the ambitious scale of the Academy's plans and the high social profile of its patrons. While human emotions and situations are dealt with, the tone is serious and (in the case of the leading characters) heroic. Handel showed just how much variety and power was available through the conventions of opera seria, working almost entirely within the formal *da capo* framework in the arias.

The story centres on the tribulations of Radamisto and his wife Zenobia at the hands of the tyrant Tiridate, in the internecine warfare that beset the ruling families of Asia Minor in the first century AD. Tiridate, married to Radamisto's sister Polissena, makes war on his father-in-law as an outlet for his 'unjust Amours' after falling in love with Zenobia. The plot is further complicated by the fact that Tiridate's wife Polissena attracts the attentions of Tigrane, one of Tiridate's allies. Both wives remain faithful to their husbands: Polissena becomes a political lever in the plot, while Zenobia is the model of self-sacrificing conjugal devotion. When Radamisto and Zenobia face defeat at Tiridate's hands, Zenobia asks her husband to kill her so that she would not fall a prey to the tyrant: Radamisto wounds her slightly, but she falls into the river and is rescued by Tiridate's soldiers. Radamisto believes her dead (his aria 'Ombra cara' is one of the most moving in the score) but, disguised, he gains entrance to Tiridate's court and is reunited with his wife. Tiridate is eventually defeated by a revolt led by Tigrane, and universal generosity and forgiveness ensues; the final *coro* is the longest in any Handel opera.

For revivals, Handel subjected *Radamisto* to unusually thorough-going revisions. The first was in December 1720, when he had a substantially different cast; in particular, he rewrote the title role for Senesino, who had recently arrived to take up his place as the Academy's leading castrato. (In the April performances Radamisto had been taken by the soprano Durastanti, who now took the role of Zenobia.) The December version is as fine as the original and contains some excellent new music. Handel's version for the 1728 revival was slightly less happy; the score was somewhat distorted to provide musically even-handed parts for the sopranos Cuzzoni and Faustina.

RECORDING   Kuhse, Kehl, Apreck, Leib, Kaphahn, Leipzig Radio Ch, Halle Handel Festival O, Margraf, Eterna, 1961

EDITIONS   HG, vol. 63 (includes material from the two 1720 and the 1728 versions of the opera); HHA, series 2, vol. 9 (forthcoming)

Muzio Scevola

Opera in three acts, Act III only by Handel, HWV 13 (3h)
Libretto by Paolo Antonio Rolli, after Nicolò Minato's *Il Miutio Scevola* set by Cavalli (1665)
Completed 23 March 1721
PREMIERES   15 April 1721, King's Theatre, Haymarket, London; US: 5 October 1992, Morkin Concert Hall, New York (concert)

The idea of mounting a three-act opera with one act composed by each of the resident composers (Filippo Amadei, Giovanni Bononcini, Handel) presumably came from the Academy management, and it was perhaps a diplomatic triumph that it ever came to tangible form on the stage (one of the striking features of the 1720–21 season was the success of Bononcini's operas). Connoisseurs commented on the superiority of Handel's music, but serious partisanship in the opera-going public was probably focused on singers rather than on composers. Handel's contribution included a substantial overture and some fine arias, but the conditions of the collaboration (and the quality of the libretto itself) militated against sustained character development. The story, based on Livy, has an episodic plot with heroic deeds (there is one set-piece 'valorous Action' in each act) and many conflicts between self-interest, sexual attraction and Roman honour. Rolli, the librettist, was Italian Secretary to the Academy.

RECORDING   Baird, Mills, Matthews, Fortunato, Lane, Urrey, Ostendorf, Brewer, Baroque CO, Palmer, Newport Classic, 1992
EDITION   HG, vol. 64

Floridante

(*Il Floridante*)
Opera in three acts, HWV 14 (2h 45m)
Libretto by Paolo Rolli, after Francesco Silvani's *La costanza in trionfo* (1696, rev. 1706)
Completed 28 November 1721, rev. 1722, 1727, 1733
PREMIERE   9 December 1721, King's Theatre, Haymarket, London

Radamisto set a tone that ran for nearly a decade in Handel's operas. In place of the spectacular attractions of she-devils and transformation scenes that were characteristic of Handel's first London operas, the Academy operas concentrated now on close relationships among characters at the centre of political and military power, matched by a dignified (though varied) cultivation of the conventions of opera seria. Since the operas were performed to a distinguished audience, the subject matter may have reflected contemporary interest in dramatic parables about the behaviour of public figures. Plots about the restoration of rightful heirs and about internecine strife at times moved close to contemporary concerns: Jacobites versus Hanoverians, or the King versus the Prince of Wales. Perhaps because of the danger of such an interpretation, Rolli moved the

scene of *Floridante* from the Norway of Silvani's original to Persia.

Oronte, the King of Persia, has gained the throne by military conquest and by killing King Nino, but he has taken Nino's only surviving infant relation into his household as his adopted daughter, Elmira, there joining his own daughter, Rossane. Apparently the two girls formed a bond of mutual loyalty. Floridante, Prince of Thrace, fell in love with Elmira, and Oronte promised her to him in marriage on the successful completion of a naval war against the King of Tyre. Rossane fell in love with Timante, Prince of Tyre, though without meeting him, but this liaison was blocked by the political/military situation.

When Floridante returns from his successful naval campaign he claims Elmira, whom he loves, as his reward. But Oronte has fallen in love with Elmira himself and refuses to yield her. Timante is brought to the Persian court as a prisoner, and Rossane's love for him is confirmed. Throughout the opera the two pairs of lovers remain faithful to their partners: the plot centres around Oronte's advances to Elmira and his threats against Floridante, whom Oronte imprisons and attempts to poison. In the end, Timante and the Persian satrap Coralbo lead a successful revolt against Oronte; Elmira is restored to the throne with Floridante as her consort, and Rossane and Timante are free to marry and reign in Tyre.

The human relationships are well sketched and Handel's music contrasts the lightweight pair of lovers (Timante and Rossane) with their more serious and powerful counterparts. This opera included the first of Handel's prison scenes for Senesino (as Floridante). Other highlights of the score are a scena for Elmira as she waits in the dark for Floridante ('Notte cara') and a duet for her and Floridante at the end of Act I. Handel subjected the score to many revisions to suit different casts in 1722, 1727 and 1733.

RECORDINGS   1. Farkas, Zádori, Markert, Minter, Gáti, Capella Savaria, McGegan, Hungaroton, 1990; 2. abridged: Argenta, Attrot, Robbin, McGuire, Braun, Tafelmusik Baroque O, Curtis, CBC Records, 1992: although the first is complete, the second is to be preferred: superior singing and conducting [A.B.]
EDITIONS   HG, vol. 65; HHA, series 2, vol. 11 (forthcoming)

Ottone

(*Ottone, Re di Germania*)
Otto, King of Germany
Opera in three acts, HWV 15 (3h)
Libretto by Nicola Francesco Haym, after Steffano Benedetto Pallavicino's *Teofane* set by Lotti (1719)
Completed 10 August 1722, rev. 1723, 1726, 1727, 1733
PREMIERE   12 January 1723, King's Theatre, Haymarket, London

The soprano Francesca Cuzzoni arrived in London towards the end of December 1722, and her incorporation into the cast led Handel to redraft *Ottone* considerably before the first performance. The cast was a strong one, with three accomplished ladies (Cuzzoni, Durastanti, Anastasia Robinson), Senesino, a good second castrato in Berenstadt, and the bass Boschi. Senesino, Durastanti and Boschi repeated the roles they had sung in the opera by Lotti which provided the 'parent' libretto. Handel had almost certainly heard it in Dresden in 1719 while he was abroad collecting singers for the Academy.

The story is set in Rome and based, though somewhat reordered and compressed, on historical events from the 10th century, when Otto I and Otto II were active in maintaining their Italian empire. The opera deals with Otto II, incorporating into his role some actions attributed to his father. Adalberto, son of the overthrown 'Italian tyrant' Berengario, has led Rome in a successful revolt against the empire, at the instigation of his mother Gismonda. Ottone been promised Teofane, the daughter of the emperor in Constantinople, as a bride. Ottone's cousin Matilda, who should have held Rome on his behalf, is now betrothed to Adalberto. Adalberto poses as Ottone when Teofane arrives in Rome, and the deception nearly leads to their marriage, but the ceremony is interrupted by news of Ottone's return to retake Rome. Adalberto carries off Teofane in a boat, accompanied by Teofane's brother Emireno, disguised as a pirate, but they are forced by a storm to land. Emireno discovers his sister's identity and the true situation, and places Adalberto under arrest: Adalberto and Gismonda concede defeat and swear loyalty to Ottone, leaving Ottone united with Teofane and Adalberto with Matilda.

Haym set himself a rather over-ambitious task when he tried to compress and adapt Pallavicino's libretto to London conditions: considerable effort in understanding the plot is required of an audience. Nevertheless, *Ottone* was very popular, partly on account of Cuzzoni's début and partly on account of the attractiveness of the arias, many of which were taken up separately as concert items: as Burney remarked, 'The number of songs in this opera that became national favourites is perhaps greater than in any other that was ever performed in England. Handel himself revived the opera four times, with many alterations: part of the Haymarket company also took the opera to Paris for a private performance in 1724.

RECORDING Saffer, Gondek, Spence Minter, Popken, Dean, Freiburg Baroque O, McGegan, Harmonia Mundi, 1992
EDITION *HG*, vol. 66, mixing items from several of Handel's versions

Flavio

(*Flavio, Re de' Longobardi*)
Flavius, King of Longobardi
Opera in three acts, HWV 16 (2h 30m)
Libretto by Nicola Francesco Haym, after Matteo Noris's *Flavio Cuniberto* (1696) set by Partenio (1682)
Completed 7 May 1723
PREMIERES 14 May 1723, King's Theatre, Haymarket, London; US: 25 April 1985, Westminster Choir College, Princeton

CAST Flavio *a* (castrato), Guido *a* (castrato), Emilia *s*, Vitige *s*, Teodata *a*, Ugone *t*, Lotario *b*
ORCHESTRATION fl, obs, bsns, str, cont

Although *Flavio*, like the other Academy operas, is set at a centre of political power and deals with motives of love, honour and duty, the tone is more domestic, with less emphasis on political or military changes of fortune. Furthermore, while circumstances threaten the destinies of the opera's intended lovers, sexual jealousy is not played up very forcefully. While it would be overstating the case to describe *Flavio* as a comedy, it does seem to move towards a more detached view of human interactions. The action is set in Lombardy during the dark ages: the stratagem of sending unwanted characters away to govern Britain, with mixed overtones of honour and punishment, was no doubt taken humorously by the London audiences.

SYNOPSIS
King Flavio has two elderly counsellors, Ugone and Lotario. Ugone has a son, Guido, and a daughter, Teodata; Lotario has a daughter, Emilia.

Act I Teodata invites her lover Vitige, a courtier, to attend her brother Guido's betrothal to Emilia, but Vitige's duty at court prevents this. After the betrothal, Ugone presents Teodata to the king, who is much taken with her, and Lotario invites him to the wedding of Guido and Emilia. The governorship of Britain is vacant: Flavio appoints Ugone, presumably so that he can pay attention to Teodata in her father's absence. The appointment inflames Lotario's jealousy: he strikes Ugone, who asks Guido to avenge the insult. When Emilia appears, Guido asks her for a pledge of her devotion – a request that leaves her puzzled. Meanwhile, Flavio has revealed to Vitige that he is attracted to Teodata.

Act II Teodata's interview with Flavio is interrupted by the arrival of her father, clearly upset: Teodata misinterprets the cause of Ugone's distraction as the discovery of her love for Vitige. Lotario forbids Emilia to marry Guido. Vitige is horrified when Flavio asks him to arrange an assignation with Teodata: he tells Teodata, and urges her to appear compliant lest Flavio's anger should be aroused. Guido meets Lotario and mortally wounds him in a fight, but Lotario identifies his murderer to Emilia before he dies.

Act III Emilia and Ugone appeal to Flavio concerning Lotario's murder, one demanding justice and the other defending the honourable action. Flavio dismisses them in order to fulfil his assignation with Teodata. He asks Vitige to plead his love to Teodata, but soon takes over on his own behalf: Teodata assents to becoming Flavio's 'queen'. Emilia denounces Guido and he gives her the sword that killed her father, asking her to turn it on himself: her resolve fails when she looks at him. Vitige and Teodata are discovered in an embrace by Flavio and confess their love. When Emilia arrives, Flavio taunts her that Guido has been beheaded for murdering her father: her reaction reveals her continuing attachment to Guido. Flavio commands the marriage

A scene believed to be from Flavio *(1723) with Gaetano Berenstadt (right), Senesino and Francesca Cuzzoni; engraving by John Vandenbank*

of the two pairs of lovers, and sends Ugone off to govern Britain.

Handel's music matches the scale of the drama, which demanded movement and variety rather than extended introspection, though the final aria for Guido (Senesino), 'Amor nel mio penar', is a fine piece in the 'pathetic' vein. Duets, one for each pair of lovers, frame the beginning and end of the opera. In Act III a new element is introduced, as one lover pleads the cause of his rival: there is an ambiguity of the situation whose treatment leaves motives uncertain and provides an ironical *frisson*. Handel revived *Flavio* once, in 1732: its modest success reflects the tastes of contemporary audiences rather than its musical or dramatic quality. This sort of opera introduced welcome variety into the programme, but was perhaps not appropriate as the basis of an opera-seria repertoire.

RECORDING Lootens, Högman, Fink, Gall, Ragin, Fagotto, Messthaler, Ensemble 415, Jacobs, Harmonia Mundi, 1989
EDITIONS *HG*, vol. 67 *HHA*, series 2, vol. 13

Giulio Cesare

(Giulio Cesare in Egitto)
Julius Caesar in Egypt
Opera in three acts, HWV 17 (3h 15m)
Libretto by Nicola Francesco Haym, after Giacomo Francesco Bussani's *Giulio Cesare in Egitto* set by Sartorio (1677) and a 1685 version of the same libretto
Composed 1723–4
PREMIERES 20 February 1724, King's Theatre, Haymarket, London; US: 14 May 1927, Smith College, Northampton, Massachusetts
CAST Giulio Cesare *a* (castrato), Cleopatra *s*, Cornelia *a*, Sesto Pompeo *s*, Tolomeo *a* (castrato), Achilla *b*, Nireno *a* (castrato), Curio *b*; *satb* chorus of Egyptians, conspirators
ORCHESTRATION fl, 2 rec, 2 ob, 2 bsn, 4 hn, str (vns *divisi à* 3), cont; onstage: ob, 2 vn, vla, hp, vg, theorbo, bsn, vc

Handel probably began the composition of *Giulio Cesare* in the summer of 1723, soon after the last performance of *Flavio* on 15 June. Compared to the compactness of *Flavio*, *Giulio Cesare* is on an enormous scale: it is one of the longest and most elaborate of Handel's operas. In *Flavio* Senesino

received four arias: as *Giulio Cesare* he had eight, as did Cuzzoni playing Cleopatra. During composition Handel subjected the music of Act I to a series of massive revisions, partly to accommodate cast changes but also apparently as a result of alterations to the libretto. Circumstantial evidence suggests that Haym, probably in collaboration with Handel, evolved and revised the libretto with careful thought, drawing ideas from more than one literary source and paying careful attention to dramatic coherence and characterization. The intricate plot and careful organization of the finished libretto make for an elaborate and delicately balanced opera: performances of a shortened version can be a rather bewildering experience.

Giulio Cesare and *Tamerlano* together form the climax of Handel's operas from the Royal Academy period, and indeed are among the greatest opera-seria creations by any composer, applying the formal conventions of the genre to superb and sustained dramatic effect. *Giulio Cesare* is also the opera of Handel's that has seen most modern revivals, perhaps because its title gives promise of recognizable historical subject matter.

SYNOPSIS
Cesare has defeated Pompeo at Pharsalia in Greece, and pursued him to Egypt: the events forming the historical basis for the action took place 18–17 BC.

Act I Cesare is welcomed by the Egyptians. He has agreed to an appeal by Pompeo's wife and son (Cornelia and Sesto) for a peaceful settlement. When gifts arrive, brought by Achilla on behalf of Tolomeo (who is joint ruler of Egypt with his sister Cleopatra), among them is the severed head of Pompeo. Cesare sends Achilla back with a message of contempt and disgust. Cornelia tries to kill herself, then faces an unwelcome proposal of marriage from Curio, the Roman tribune. Sesto swears to avenge his father's murder. Meanwhile Cleopatra, horrified to hear of Pompeo's murder, decides to seek an alliance with Cesare against her brother. On Tolomeo's arrival Achilla reports Cesare's reaction to the gifts and promises to kill Cesare, provided he can claim Cornelia as his reward. Cesare reflects on the transitoriness of human greatness. Cleopatra, in the guise of 'Lidia', a noble Egyptian maiden whose fortune has been stolen by Tolomeo, enters and appeals to Cesare for justice. He promises redress, captivated by her beauty. Cornelia pays her last respects to her husband's ashes and snatches his sword from the trophies, crying vengeance on Tolomeo; but Sesto seizes the sword and determines to take the task on himself. Tolomeo invites Cesare to occupy the royal apartments that have been prepared for him; Cesare recognizes that he must be cautious ('Va tacito e nascosto'). Sesto challenges Tolomeo to a duel: Tolomeo orders Sesto's arrest and consigns Cornelia to work in the garden of the seraglio. Achilla offers to secure the release of Cornelia and her son if she will consent to marry him, but she rejects the idea with contempt.

Act II Cleopatra has arranged an elaborate set piece for the seduction of Cesare ('V'adoro pupille').

Thomas Lediard's design for fireworks at the end of Giulio Cesare *(Hamburg, 1727); in the background, a magic lantern projection of London*

It works as planned, and Cesare is promised an assignation with 'Lidia', who will introduce him to Cleopatra. Cornelia, in the seraglio garden, repels advances from Achilla and Tolomeo; she threatens suicide but is restrained by Sesto. Cleopatra's eunuch, Nireno, brings Tolomeo's order that Cornelia be taken to the harem. Cleopatra waits for Cesare in another garden. After some flirtation, the pair are interrupted by Curio, who tells Cesare that he is betrayed and people are calling for his murder. Cleopatra reveals her true identity, and says that her royal presence will quell the tumult: but she fails, and urges Cesare to leave. He refuses, and goes to face his assailants. Cleopatra asks the gods to preserve him and to have pity on her ('Se pietà di me non senti'). In the seraglio, Tolomeo indicates that Cornelia is his choice. Sesto enters and snatches Tolomeo's sword from the table, but Achilla appears and takes it from him. Achilla tells Tolomeo to prepare for war: Cesare is believed drowned, and Cleopatra has fled to the Romans, who are mustering against Tolomeo. Tolomeo dismisses Achilla as a traitor when the latter reminds him that Cornelia had been promised as his reward for killing Cesare, and then departs expecting a quick victory over the Romans. Sesto attempts to stab himself, but is restrained by his mother: he renews his vengeance against Tolomeo.

Act III Achilla, exasperated by Tolomeo's broken promise, leads his soldiers to join Cleopatra. In the ensuing battle, Tolomeo's forces are victorious, and Cleopatra is taken prisoner. Alone, and mourning for Cesare, she bewails her fate ('Piangerò la sorte mia'): she is led away. But Cesare is not dead: he appears, having escaped drowning by swimming from the harbour. He has lost contact with his troops and prays for help ('Aure, deh, per pietà'). Achilla, mortally wounded, gives Sesto a seal that will guarantee the loyalty of his troops and tells him of a secret passageway to Tolomeo's palace. Cesare witnesses the scene, takes the seal from Sesto, and hurries off to assemble his forces. As Cleopatra bids her friends farewell Cesare appears with his soldiers to rescue her. Cesare and Cleopatra are reunited. In the 'Royal Hall', Cornelia once again has to repel Tolomeo's attentions: she draws a dagger, and is about to attack him when Sesto enters with drawn sword and claims the right of revenge. In the ensuing duel, Tolomeo is killed. At the port of Alexandria, Cesare and Cleopatra welcome Cornelia and Sesto as friends and proclaim their own undying love: everyone celebrates the return of peace.

In addition to a succession of fine arias, the score contains a remarkable novelty in the set-piece scene at the beginning of Act II. The nine Muses are represented on Mount Parnassus, and Handel provided an onstage band which may have had nine players to consort with Cleopatra/Lidia/Virtue. Another unusual feature was the use of four horns in the opening and closing scenes of the opera. The original (1724) run of *Giulio Cesare* had 13 performances, and it achieved double figures again in Handel's revivals of 1725 and 1730. For the revivals Handel subjected his score to the usual alterations necessitated by changing casts: but mostly these alterations weakened the original conception.

RECORDINGS 1. Masterson, Baker, Walker, Jones, Bowman, Tomlinson, Ch and O of English National Opera, Mackerras, HMV, 1974 (in English): English version with modern instruments, from the ENO production; 2. Schlick, Larmore, Rørholm, Ragin, Fink, Zanasi, Concerto Köln, Jacobs, Harmonia Mundi, 1991: in Italian with period instruments
VIDEO ENO production (as above)
EDITION *HG*, vol. 68

Tamerlano

Tamburlaine
Opera in three acts, HWV 18 (3h)
Libretto by Nicola Francesco Haym, after Agostino Piovene's *Il Tamerlano* (1711) and *Il Bajazet* (1719) both set by Gasparini; based on the play by Jacques Pradon, *Tamerlan, ou La mort de Bajazet* (1675)
Draft composition score dated 3–23 July 1724
PREMIERES 31 October 1724, King's Theatre, Haymarket, London; US: 26 January 1985, Indiana University Opera Theater, Bloomington
CAST Tamerlano *a* (castrato), Andronico *a* (castrato), Bajazet *t*, Leone *b*, Asteria *s*, Irene *a*
ORCHESTRATION 2 fl, 2 rec, 2 ob, 2 cl, bsns, str, cont

Tamerlano is significant not only as one of Handel's finest Academy operas, but also as one of the few opere serie with a leading role for the tenor voice. Opposite Senesino playing the part of Tamerlano, the self-made ruler of the Tartar empire, Handel cast the tenor Francesco Borosini as Bajazet, the Turkish sultan defeated by Tamburlaine in 1402 and who subsequently died while still in captivity to the Tartar. Borosini's contribution to the opera extended beyond that of a soloist. When Handel completed his draft composition score at the end of July 1724, he had been composing to a libretto adapted from Piovene's 1711 libretto for a Venice production with music by Gasparini. In 1719 a much revised version of Gasparini's opera was performed in Reggio, with a significantly changed title: *Il Tamerlano* became *Il Bajazet*, and the strengthened role of Bajazet played by Borosini. When Borosini arrived in London in September 1724 to take up his place in the opera company, he provided Handel and Haym with the libretto and score of the 1719 version: stimulated by this, Handel revised his own score, in particular incorporating new scenes at the beginning and end of the opera based on the 1719 libretto.

Plays on the subject of Tamburlaine already had a niche on the 18th-century London stage: the theatres regularly performed one (most often Nicholas Rowe's) around the beginning of November, to coincide with the triple anniversaries of the foiling of the Gunpowder Plot, the birthday of King William

III and his landing in Torbay in 1688. No doubt a political allegory was intended or imposed in these plays, but Handel's opera seems innocent of any such interpretation: nevertheless, the treatment of a familiar subject was no doubt intended as good box office.

SYNOPSIS
Bajazet has been defeated and captured by Tamerlano, who is betrothed to Irene, Princess of Trebizond. Tamerlano and Andronico (a Greek prince in alliance with Tamerlano) have both, unknown to each other, fallen in love with Asteria, Bajazet's daughter. The action takes place in Prusa, the first city that Tamerlano occupied after defeating the Turks.

Act I Bajazet despises his conqueror and attempts suicide, but desists when Andronico reminds him that this would leave Asteria an orphan ('Forte e lieto'). Rather than return to the throne of Byzantium, Andronico opts to remain with Tamerlano to learn more about warfare. Tamerlano hopes to use Andronico to break down Bajazet's resistance to his suit, in return for which Andronico will receive the hand of Irene. Andronico is appalled that his action in bringing Asteria to plead for her father's life should have this consequence. Tamerlano agrees to release Bajazet, on condition that he can marry Asteria. Bajazet rejects this proposal, and Asteria accuses Andronico (who has spoken for Tamerlano) of taking Tamerlano's part in order to gain Irene and a kingdom for himself. She tells Andronico that she no longer loves him. Irene, arriving at the palace, is surprised when Tamerlano does not come to greet his bride-to-be: she is yet more surprised to learn that Andronico is to be her husband instead. Alone, Andronico reflects that he can save Bajazet's life only by concealing his love for Asteria and bearing her anger ('Benchè mi sprezzi').

Act II Tamerlano claims that he now has Asteria's heart: he tells Andronico to look forward to the double wedding. Andronico and Asteria each accuse the other of sacrificing their love for a throne. Irene, disguised as a messenger at the suggestion of Andronico, reproaches Tamerlano for his betrayal, and refuses his offer of the alternative suit. Tamerlano responds that if Asteria does not prove a satisfactory consort, then he will embrace Irene. Andronico vows to kill both Tamerlano and himself if Asteria marries Tamerlano. Asteria herself approaches Tamerlano's throne, with murder in her heart. Bajazet enters to prevent the marriage of his daughter: Tamerlano orders Bajazet to prostrate himself – Asteria can mount the throne over his body. Asteria refuses to do so, nor will Bajazet rise when Tamerlano orders him to. Asteria asks her father's forgiveness, but he refuses and turns his back on the throne as she advances to it. Irene enters, still disguised, and says that Irene will not appear until she has a share in Tamerlano's throne: Tamerlano replies that she will have to force Asteria to leave the throne. Bajazet orders his daughter to descend, or he will renounce her and end his own life, but Asteria at first makes no move. She has to decide between marriage to Tamerlano and renewed imprisonment: she chooses the latter. Tamerlano orders the execution of both father and daughter.

Act III   Tamerlano says that he still loves Asteria, and orders Andronico to tell her that her place at the throne is still vacant. Andronico reveals his own love for Asteria, which she reciprocates ('Vivo in te'). When Tamerlano orders Bajazet's execution, Asteria pleads for her father's life. Father and daughter are sentenced to the indignity of being dragged forcibly to Tamerlano's table, where Tamerlano orders Asteria to kneel as a slave with his drinking cup. Asteria poisons the cup and offers it to Tamerlano, but Irene, who has seen her place the poison, restrains him from drinking and reveals both Asteria's plan and her own identity. Tamerlano tells Asteria that he will drink if Andronico and Bajazet will do so first: she decides instead to take the poison herself, but Andronico dashes the cup from her hands. Tamerlano orders her to be sent to the slaves' seraglio and now promises to marry Irene, who accepts him. Bajazet takes poison; he says farewell to Asteria, and dies breathing fury against Tamerlano. Andronico offers to kill himself, but Tamerlano restrains him: Bajazet's death has been sufficient bloodshed. He yields Asteria to Andronico, and will marry Irene himself.

The quality of Handel's music is no less high than in *Giulio Cesare*, but *Tamerlano* has not gained popularity on the strength of individual arias, though Andronico's 'Bella Asteria' had some circulation in the 18th century. This is perhaps rather surprising, since 'Se non mi vuol amar' (Asteria), 'Par che mi nasca' (Irene), 'A suoi piedi' (Bajazet) and 'Cor di padre' (Asteria) are among Handel's finest arias. The final scenes of Acts II and III are powerful musico-dramatic sequences. At the end of Act II, when Asteria appeals to Bajazet, Andronico and Irene in turn, they reply in short but pointed exit arias. The end of Act III is dominated by Bajazet's last scene: before the opera's first performance Handel cut out a substantial amount of music (including a fine aria, 'Padre amato', for Asteria) so that no concerted numbers remained between Bajazet's death scene and the final minor-key *coro* (sung by the soloists). The scoring of *Tamerlano* is fairly restrained, but there are some novelties. Recorders and flutes double in the duet 'Vivo in te'; the obbligato part in Irene's Act II aria 'Par che mi nasca in seno' was composed for clarinets, misnamed 'cornetti' in Handel's autograph. The unusual prominence of the tenor role limited the opera's appearance in Handel's opera repertoire: he revived *Tamerlano* only once, in 1731.

RECORDING   Argenta, Findlay, Ragin, Chance, N. Robson, Schirrer, English Baroque Soloists, Gardiner, Erato, 1985: a good performance, though including music in the final scene that Handel never performed and making some cuts elsewhere

EDITIONS   *HG*, vol. 69; *HHA*, series 2, vol. 15 (forthcoming); facsimile of autograph, Garland, 1979

Rodelinda

(*Rodelinda, Regina de' Longobardi*)
Rodelinda, Queen of Lombardy

Opera in three acts, HWV 19 (3h 15m)
Libretto by Nicola Francesco Haym, adapted from Antonio Salvi's *Rodelinda*, set by Perti (1710) after Pierre Corneille's *Pertharite* (1652)
Draft composition score completed 20 January 1725
PREMIERES   13 February 1725, King's Theatre, Haymarket, London; US: 9 May 1931, Smith College, Northampton, Massachusetts
CAST   Rodelinda s, Bertarido a (castrato), Grimoaldo t, Garibaldo b, Eudige a, Unolfo a (castrato)
ORCHESTRATION   fl, recs, 2 ob, bsns, 2 hn, str (vns *divisi à* 3) cont

Rodelinda was cast for the same singers as *Tamerlano*, with a major part for the tenor Borosini as well as leading roles for Senesino and Cuzzoni. For the subject, Haym returned to another libretto dealing with Lombard history: the infant Flavio appears here (as a non-singing role) in company with his mother Rodelinda. The action of the opera relies on a complex dynastic background. On the death of Ariberto of Lombardy (AD 681) his kingdom was divided between his sons Bertarido and Gundeberto. A war developed between the brothers; Gundeberto was mortally wounded, and called on the assistance of Grimoaldo, Duke of Benevento, promising him the hand of his sister Eudige. Faced with an attack from Grimoaldo, Bertarido fled to Hungary, leaving his family behind: he put out reports of his own death, planning to return disguised in order to rescue his wife, Rodelinda, and son. Grimoaldo is supported by Garibaldo, Duke of Turin, who had rebelled against Bertarido.

SYNOPSIS
Act I   Rodelinda mourns her supposedly dead husband. Grimoaldo proposes to Rodelinda that he will restore her to her husband's inheritance if she will marry him, but she rejects him. Garibaldo professes his love for Eudige, who has been rejected by Grimoaldo, but his real ambitions are set on her inheritance. Bertarido, in disguise, returns and sees Rodelinda receive a further proposal of marriage from Grimoaldo, accompanied by a threat that her non-compliance would lead to the young Flavio's death. Rodelinda agrees to Grimoaldo's terms, intending to ask for the traitor Garibaldo's death once she is in a position of influence. Bertarido is horrified by Rodelinda's acceptance of Grimoaldo.

Act II   Eudige is embittered by Grimoaldo's rejection. Rodelinda, saying that she cannot be mother of the lawful king and wife of a tyrant at the same time, tells Grimoaldo to murder Flavio before her eyes. In spite of encouragement from Garibaldo, Grimoaldo recoils from this. Eudige recognizes Bertarido and learns that his prime purpose is to regain his family, not his throne: after Bertarido's death, Eudige had a claim to Bertarido's kingdom. Unolfo tells his friend Bertarido that Rodelinda is faithful to him: the reunion between husband and wife ('Io t'abbraccio') is interrupted by the arrival of

Grimoaldo, who puts Bertarido under arrest and sentences him to death.

Act III Eudige and Unolfo plan Bertarido's escape. Grimoaldo is encouraged by Garibaldo to have Bertarido executed, but hesitates because this would alienate Rodelinda. Bertarido laments his fate ('Chi di voi'). Eudige throws a sword into the dungeon. Unolfo goes to release Bertarido, but in the darkness Bertarido wounds him, mistaking him for a potential executioner. Unolfo leads Bertarido to freedom by a secret passage. Rodelinda and Flavio, arriving at the dungeon, find blood (Unolfo's) and Bertarido's cloak: Rodelinda laments her husband's apparent fate ('Se'l mio duol'). Having bandaged Unolfo's wound, Bertarido then sets off to find Rodelinda. Grimoaldo approaches, tormented by jealousy, anger and love: eventually he falls asleep in the garden. Garibaldo takes the sleeping Grimoaldo's sword and goes to kill him, but Bertarido, who has been watching unobserved, intervenes and kills Garibaldo. On his return, Bertarido throws his sword at Grimoaldo's feet. Rodelinda, entering, is amazed to find her husband alive. Explanations ensue. Grimoaldo renounces his claim to Bertarido's inheritance and takes up Gundeberto's former kingdom, with Eudige as his queen.

Rodelinda, though less hot-headed as a heroine than Asteria in *Tamerlano*, is a strong and faithful wife. Borosini played Grimoaldo, a tyrant with a softer side that recoils from murdering the young Flavio: as in *Tamerlano*, he received a powerful 'distraction' scene in Act III. Senesino, as Bertarido, had a no less remarkable prison scene. Bertarido's aria, 'Dove sei', familiar as a concert aria to the sentimental text 'Art thou troubled?', remains as an example of the 'capital and pleasing airs' that Burney recognized as one of the strengths of the score. After the initial season, Handel revived *Rodelinda* twice, in 1725 and in 1731; as with *Tamerlano*, opportunities for revival may have been limited by the necessity for a good tenor.

RECORDINGS   1. Stich-Randall, Forrester, Rössel-Majdan, Watts, Young, Boyden, Vienna Radio O, Priestman, Westminster, 1964; 2. Sutherland, Buchanan, Nafé, Tourangeau, Rayam, Ramey, Welsh National Opera Ch and O, Bonynge, Decca, 1985; 3. Schlick, Schubert, Cordier, Wessel, Prégardien, Schwarz, La Stagione Frankfurt, Schneider, Deutsche Harmonia Mundi, 1990: a complete performance accompanied by authentic instruments, though the extensively cut Sutherland–Bonynge performance has some good scenes
EDITIONS   HG, vol. 70; HHA, series 2, vol. 16 (forthcoming)

Scipione

(Publio Cornelio Scipione)
Scipio (Publius Cornelius Scipio)
Opera in three acts, HWV 20 (3h)
Libretto by Paolo Rolli, after Antonio Salvi's *Publio Cornelio Scipione* (1704)
Draft composition score completed 2 March 1726
PREMIERE   12 March 1726, King's Theatre, Haymarket, London

This opera has been preserved in public consciousness through the popularity of the 'March from *Scipio*', which marks Scipione's arrival in New Carthage at the beginning of the opera. Although worthy enough, *Scipione* does not maintain the outstanding level set by its three brilliant predecessors. Some of the blame must lie with a rather pedestrian libretto: Rolli did not have Haym's flair for dramatic coherence and musico-dramatic pacing. But there is some fine music, particularly in Act II which culminates in one of Handel's most brilliant soprano arias for Cuzzoni.

Scipione the elder was the Roman proconsul in Spain who took New Carthage by siege in 210 BC. After the conquest, Scipione falls in love with one of his Spanish captives, Berenice, the daughter of Ernando, King of the Balearic Islands. But Berenice has already been promised in marriage to Lucejo, a prince of the Celtiberi, to whom she remains faithful. Lucejo, disguised as a Roman soldier, enters the palace: Berenice makes repeated attempts to send him away, partly for his own safety and partly so that he can collect troops of his own and her father's in order to rescue her. Lucejo returns later, is identified, and imprisoned by Scipione, though with a promise to Berenice that he will not be harmed. Scipione formally asks Ernando for Berenice's hand in return for her liberty, but Ernando says that he cannot set aside her promised union with Lucejo. Impressed by Ernando's emphasis on honour, Scipione decides to sacrifice his own feelings: he releases Lucejo and Berenice, and approves their union. Lucejo promises his allegiance to Rome, and all praise Scipione's magnanimity. The plot also involves a certain amount of interaction between the main characters and a secondary pair of lovers, Lelio, a Roman captain, and Armira, 'a captive Lady'.

In spite of the short time between commencement of composition and first performance (just over two months), Handel subjected the score to considerable last-minute revisions, including the removal of one minor character and a change in the division point between Acts II and III. It was also subjected to further major revision before Handel's only revival of the opera, in 1730.

RECORDING   Masterson, Watts, Esswood, Roden, Jeffes, Comboy, Ch and O of Handel Opera Society, Farncombe, FNAC Reppel, 1979: in English
EDITION   HG, vol. 71

Alessandro

Alexander
Opera in three acts, HWV 21 (3h 30m)
Libretto by Paolo Rolli, after Bartolomeo Ortensio Mauro's *La superbia d'Alessandro* (1690) set by Steffani
Draft composition score completed 11 April 1726
PREMIERES   5 May 1726, King's Theatre, Haymarket, London; US: 21 April 1985, New York (concert; Handel Opera Festival)
CAST   Alessandro *a* (castrato), Rossane *s*, Lisaura *s*, Tassile *a* (castrato), Clito *b*, Leonato *t*, Cleone *a*; *satb* chorus of soldiers

ORCHESTRATION 2 rec, 2 ob, bsns, 2 tpt, 2 hn, str (vns *divisi à* 3), cont

Alessandro had specific Hanoverian associations, for Mauro's original libretto had been written for performance at Hanover in 1690, in the heyday of the court opera there. As Electoral Prince, Georg Ludwig almost certainly saw the original production: as King George I he saw Handel's opera in London. Whether George was intended to be identified with the Alexander the Great of the opera is unknown, still less whether the ladies of the story were to be identified with his supposed mistresses. What is known is that the attention of the original audiences was not focused on the royal family but on the 'Rival Queens' on the stage, the sopranos Cuzzoni and Faustina Bordoni. Handel began the composition of *Alessandro* before that of *Scipione*, but laid it aside pending the arrival of Faustina, returning to finish the job after *Scipione* had gone into performance and Faustina had arrived.

Faustina Hasse-Bordoni (wife of the composer Johann Hasse); pastel by Rosalba Carriera

SYNOPSIS

Act I At the siege of the Indian city of Ossidraca, Alessandro scales the city walls and eventually triumphs, slaughtering his enemies. He receives the attentions of two ladies, Rossane (a slave) and Lisaura (a Scythian princess): he loves Rossane, but does not want to alienate Lisaura. Tassile, the Indian king, is in love with Lisaura but, since he owes his throne to Alessandro, is unable to intervene when she shows an interest in Alessandro. Cleone, one of the Macedonian captains, is also in love with Rossane, but fears the powerful Alessandro. Alessandro himself claimed descent from Jupiter: at a thanksgiving sacrifice in Jupiter's temple Clito, another Macedonian general, although a long-standing loyal supporter of Alessandro, refuses to take his claims of divine descent seriously.

Act II In a garden scene Lisaura, while still attracted to Alessandro, recognizes his attachment to Rossane. Rossane asks Alessandro to demonstrate his love by granting her freedom, which he does after some hesitation. Clito again refuses to acknowledge Alessandro's divine descent. The canopy over Alessandro's throne 'is by Conspiracy made to fall': he accuses Clito of treachery, and has him imprisoned, in spite of Clito's protestations of loyalty. Tassile leaves to assemble his army in case Alessandro should need support: fears for Alessandro's safety lead Rossane to reveal that she returns his love. Leonato, the Macedonian leader, loyal to Alessandro, reports that the Indians, believing Alessandro dead, are likely to join his enemies.

Act III Leonato, presumably feeling that the situation requires a loyal and experienced general, releases Clito from prison, substituting another general, the 'fawning Sycophant' Cleone. Cleone calls on his own soldiers, who break down the prison gates, and decides to challenge Alessandro. After an uneasy scene between Rossane and Lisaura, the latter asks Alessandro outright to return her love, but he replies that to do so would be robbing Tassile, and Lisaura is moved by his generosity. Supported by Tassile's troops, Alessandro conquers the rebels: Leonato and Clito prove their loyalty in action, and the conspirators are captured. Civil peace and the union of the two pairs of lovers are celebrated in Jupiter's temple.

Handel maintained a high level of invention in the arias, of which Rossane's Act I 'Lusinghe più care' has attained some popularity as a concert item. A nice touch of musical irony occurs in the garden scene of Act II, where the leading ladies in turn hear Alessandro in amorous conversation with the other: each lady then quotes back to him the music that he has been singing to her rival. However, the equal weighting of the two sopranos led Handel to a few *longueurs*: of all the late Academy operas, *Alessandro* is the one most inflated by this consideration. But that was what the audience wanted to hear, and it is not surprising that Handel revived the opera in the following season; he also revived a shortened version (with different sopranos) in 1732, and apparently co-operated with the 'Middlesex' opera company in the 1740s in allowing them to revive his opera under the title *Rossane*.

RECORDING Poulenard, Boulin, Nirouet, Bollen, Jacobs, de Mey, Varcoe, La Petite Bande, Kuijken, Harmonia Mundi, 1984: one of the best of all Handel opera recordings
EDITIONS *HG*, vol. 72; *HHA*, series 2, vol. 18 (forthcoming)

Admeto

(*Admeto, Re di Tessaglia*)
Admeto (Admeto, King of Thessaly)
Opera in three acts, HWV 22 (3h)
Libretto by ?Nicola Haym or ?Paulo Rolli, after Ortensio Mauro's *L'Alceste*, set by Trento (1679, rev. 1681), itself after Aurelio Aureli's *L'Antigona delusa d'Alceste*, set by P. A. Ziani (1660)

Draft composition score completed 10 November 1726
PREMIERE 31 January 1727, King's Theatre, Haymarket, London

The early Royal Academy operas had concentrated almost exclusively on personal, political and dynastic relationships, but *Alessandro* saw a slight swing back to the 'spectacle' operas of the previous decade with its lavish opening scene and the ceremonies in the Temple of Jupiter. *Admeto* took this trend one stage further with a plot whose substructure was rooted in Classical mythology: at the beginning of Act II Hercules visits hell, beating back the furies in order to rescue Alceste.

Admeto is dying. His wife Alceste prays to Apollo, and a voice from the god's statue says that Admeto must die unless someone else sacrifices their life in his place. Antigona, a Trojan princess, her companion Meraspe arrive disguised as shepherdesses: Antigona, who had been betrothed to Admeto, accuses him of unfaithfulness. Alceste kills herself to save her husband; Trasimede, Admeto's brother, identifies Antigona from a portrait. Ercole rescues Alceste from hell. Antigona's portrait is brought to Admeto, who is attracted to her but remembers his lost Alceste: he notes the portrait's resemblance to the 'shepherdess', but is told that Antigona died at Troy. Alceste returns disguised as a soldier, and finds Antigona admiring Admeto's portrait. Antigona's identity is revealed to Admeto and when Ercole tests him by saying that he had failed to rescue Alceste, Admeto appears unmoved. The betrothal of Admeto and Antigona is arranged, but Trasimede wants Antigona for himself and plans to kill his brother. As Admeto and Antigona enter, he hides, unaware that Alceste also has concealed herself in the room: he steps forward to stab Admeto, but is intercepted by Alceste. She reveals her identity and is reunited with her husband, yielded at last by Antigona.

Admeto has several fine scenes, and the major parts for the two leading ladies are nicely contrasted. Handel revived the opera in three subsequent seasons, and probably co-operated in supplying music for a revival by another opera company at the King's Theatre in 1754, a circumstance which, however, may have led to the loss of the autograph.

RECORDING Yakar, Gomez, Jacobs, Bowman, van Egmond, Cold, Il Complesso Barocco, Curtis, EMI, 1978
EDITIONS *HG*, vol. 73; *HHA*, series 2, vol. 19 (forthcoming)

Riccardo Primo

(*Riccardo I, Re d'Inghilterra*)
Richard I, King of England
Melo-Drama in three acts, HWV 23 (3h)
Libretto by Paolo Rolli, after Francesco Briani's *Isacio tiranno* set by Lotti (1710)
Draft composition score completed 16 May 1727; rev. autumn 1727
PREMIERE 11 November 1727, King's Theatre, Haymarket, London

Riccardo Primo received its first performance exactly a month after the coronation of King George II, at

which Handel's now famous coronation anthems had received their first performance. The choice of an 'English' topic (which Rolli adapted to current sensibilities by referring to 'Britanno' in the body of the libretto) may have been a loyal gesture: Handel had become a British citizen in February 1727, and the originally intended dedicatee may possibly have been George II while he was still Prince of Wales. However the opera is not set in Britain, and concerns a historical incident from the life of Richard Lionheart on the island of Cyprus during the time of the Third Crusade in 1191.

Costanza (historically, Berengaria of Navarre), travelling to meet and marry Riccardo, is shipwrecked on Cyprus, where she takes refuge under a false name at the court of the tyrant Isacio and is faced with approaches from Oronte, Prince of Syria, and Isacio. Riccardo approaches Cyprus with an armed force in order to free Costanza; he asks for her release, thus revealing the girl's true identity to Isacio. Isacio, knowing that Riccardo has never seen Costanza, sends Pulcheria, his daughter, to him. The deception is at first carried off successfully, but news of the plot reaches Oronte, who tells Riccardo and offers his own support against Isacio. Isacio rejects a peaceful exchange and determines on a war against Riccardo and Oronte. In the ensuing battle, Riccardo is victorious, Costanza is freed and Isacio captured. Costanza is given a sword with which to kill Isacio but she spares him on the entreaties of Pulcheria. Riccardo receives his true bride, and Pulcheria and Oronte, also united, are left to rule Cyprus in place of the deposed Isacio.

As did the previous two operas, *Riccardo Primo* provided carefully balanced soprano roles for the two leading ladies (as Costanza and Pulcheria) and opportunity for spectacular scenes with a shipwreck and a battle: the initial stormy sea is represented by a novel use of timpani with strings and oboes. The opera ran for 11 performances but was never further revived by Handel, probably partly because of its topical associations and partly because it was associated with the last struggling season of the Royal Academy.

EDITION *HG*, vol. 74

Siroe

(*Siroe, Re di Persia*)
Siroe, King of Persia
Opera in three acts, HWV 24 (3h)
Libretto by Nicola Haym, after Pietro Metastasio's libretto set by Vinci (1726) and Sarri (1727)
Draft composition score completed 5 February 1728
PREMIERES 17 February 1728, King's Theatre, Haymarket, London; US: 1 November 1990, New York (concert)

Siroe was Handel's first opera to a libretto by Metastasio, later to be regarded as the 'classic' poet–dramatist of 18th-century opera seria. Metastasio was still at the beginning of his career: he was not yet 30 when Handel completed his score. The original *Siroe*, with music by Leonardo Vinci, quickly became popular after the first performance in Venice in 1726, seeing five other different versions (by four different composers) in Italy during 1726–7. So here, unusually, Handel was dealing with a 'modern' text, based on the version performed in Naples in 1727. The libretto provided ready-made roles for Cuzzoni and Faustina, and Haym's intervention in adapting it seems to have been less extensive than usual.

Cosroe II, King of Persia, plans to settle the succession on Medarse, his younger son, at the expense of his older son, Siroe. Siroe himself falls in love with Emira, Princess of Cambaja, whose father has been slain by Cosroe, and has entered Cosroe's court disguised as a man (Idaspe). Siroe rejects Emira's demand that he should kill Cosroe, but he falls under suspicion of treachery. He narrowly avoids execution, and survives the plotting of Medarse and Laodice, Cosroe's lover. Rebels in support of Siroe are victorious over Cosroe's guards. Siroe prevents Emira from killing his father and Cosroe resigns the crown in favour of Siroe.

Siroe (with *Silla*) has had to wait longer than the rest of Handel's London operas for modern British revival. Perhaps its conventional (Metastasian) pattern, with unbroken *da capo* arias (many of them of the *simile* type), no duets and extensive passages of recitative, is unattractive to producers looking for novelty: but it is a straightforward opera seria, well executed by the composer, and Senesino (as Siroe) received a good prison scene. Under Handel the opera ran for 18 performances: that he did not revive it later may once again be attributed to the exceptional circumstances of the Academy's last season, which produced works difficult to adapt to subsequent conditions.

RECORDING Fortunato, Baird, Matthews, Ostendorf, Rickards, Brewer, Baroque Ch and O, Palmer, Newport Classic, 1989
EDITION *HG*, vol. 75

Tolomeo
(*Tolomeo, re di Egitto*)
Ptolemy, King of Egypt
Opera in three acts, HWV 25 (3h)
Libretto by Nicola Francesco Haym, after Carlo Sigismondo Capeci's *Tolomeo et Alessandro* set by Domenico Scarlatti (1711)
Draft composition score completed 19 April 1728
PREMIERES 30 April 1728, King's Theatre, Haymarket, London; US: 11 April 1987, Opera Theater, University of Maryland

Tolomeo was Handel's last opera for the Royal Academy of Music. Someone who had attended a dress rehearsal of *Riccardo Primo* described the operatic establishment as being 'at their last gasp' and doubted whether the operas would survive the winter: but they did, and with two fine new Handel operas as well. Although the scandals of the previous season involving the supporters of the two rival prima donnas had not been repeated, it must have been clear by mid-season that the fickle patronage base was not going to support the company in its present form much longer. *Tolomeo* is a less elaborate opera than its four immediate predeces-

sors, but there is no reason to regard it as a cut-price job for a dying company: rather, Handel returned to the type of opera that he (with Haym's collaboration) had brought off so successfully earlier in the Academy's history.

Like *Riccardo Primo*, *Tolomeo* is set on Cyprus, but this time the dynastic background is Egyptian. The plot refers to Cleopatra, Tolomeo and Alessandro, but none of these is historically identical to the characters of the same names in other Handel operas. Cleopatra has favoured her younger son Alessandro for the succession, forcing her elder son Tolomeo from Egypt and taking from him his wife Seleuce. Seleuce, shipwrecked on Cyprus, disguises herself as 'Delia', a shepherdess, and searches for her lost husband, who is also on Cyprus disguised as the shepherd 'Osmin'. Alessandro falls in love with Elisa, sister to Araspe, King of Cyprus, but Elisa pursues 'Osmin', while Araspe is attracted to 'Delia'. Tolomeo and Seleuce remain faithful to each other and, when their true identities are revealed, Araspe consigns Tolomeo to prison. Alessandro is unhappy with his mother's dynastic plans and, on hearing of her death, seeks to release Tolomeo and restore him to the title. Both Tolomeo and Seleuce narrowly escape death: Tolomeo is saved because Elisa substitutes a sleeping draught for the intended poison. Finally, Tolomeo is reunited with Seleuce and is greeted as King of Egypt by Alessandro.

The music of *Tolomeo* is nicely varied (with good use of *recitativo accompagnato*, and two duets for Tolomeo and Seleuce) and there are some good scenes: a particularly effective touch in the scene in the wood comes when Seleuce and Tolomeo, searching for each other, echo or answer each other's musical phrases ('Dite, che fa'). Senesino had a strong dramatic opening with the rescue scene, and one of his best-ever dramatic opportunities in the poisoning scene near the end: the heartbeats of his aria 'Stille amare' slow down and die away before he can complete his *da capo*. *Tolomeo* was rather simpler in scenic and musical demands than its immediate predecessors and the part of Elisa (Faustina) was not as dramatically heavy-weight as that of Seleuce (Cuzzoni). So it was a fairly practical proposition for Handel to revive the opera, as he did in 1730 and 1733. Alessandro's first aria, 'Non lo dirò col labro', gained popularity in the 19th century to a rather fatuous English text under the title 'Silent Worship'.

EDITION *HG*, vol. 76

Lotario
Opera in three acts, HWV 26 (3h)
Libretto by Giacomo Rossi, after Antonio Salvi's *Adelaide* set by Torri (1722)
Draft composition score completed 16 November 1729
PREMIERE 2 December 1729, King's Theatre, Haymarket, London

The Royal Academy of Music company broke up at the end of the 1727–8 season, but Handel and at least some of the former patrons wished to continue with

Italian opera in London. By the autumn of 1729 Handel had assembled a new company including good leading singers in Bernacchi (castrato), Strada (soprano) and Fabri (tenor). The artistic recipe remained much as before and with *Lotario*, his first opera for the new company, Handel even retraced his previous steps in subject matter. The opera deals with Italian history in the generation preceding that covered by *Ottone*, and indeed the events of *Lotario* partly provide the historical background to the earlier opera. Rather confusingly Berengario's wife appears here as Matilda but in *Ottone* under the name of Gismonda: in both operas, however, she is single-minded and ambitious. To add a little more confusion, the title role of the present opera is based on the historical Otto I.

The kingdom of Italy has been divided: the usurper Berengario rules one half from Milan and the widowed Adelaide the other from Pavia. Berengario, abetted by his forceful wife Matilda, has ambitions on the other half and is besieging Pavia: but his son Idelberto is in love with Adelaide. Lotario, King of Germany, approaches Pavia from the 'Alpine Hills' with a large force but Berengario takes the city before he arrives. Adelaide accepts Lotario's proposal of marriage: after her rejection of Idelberto she is consigned to prison by Berengario, where she is at Matilda's mercy. Lotario attacks and defeats Berengario's forces, capturing Berengario himself. Matilda's attempts to kill Adelaide are frustrated by Idelberto, but she then uses Adelaide as a hostage. In a second battle, Lotario gains the city: Berengario and Matilda ask the victor for clemency, which is granted because of the honourable devotion that their son showed to Adelaide, and Idelberto himself is rewarded with his father's throne.

As a whole, *Lotario* is a frustratingly uneven opera: some parts are outstandingly good, others rather routine. Matilda is a strong character, but the constant frustration of her plans by her son's actions borders on the comic. It is perhaps not surprising that Handel never revived *Lotario* after the initial season (where it ran for a respectable ten performances): but nor is it surprising that Handel later raided the score to use some of its best arias (such as 'Scherza in mar la navicella' and 'Se il mar promette clama') for use elsewhere.

EDITION   *HG*, vol. 77

Partenope

Opera in three acts, HWV 27 (3h)
Libretto, after Silvio Stampiglia's *La Partenope* set by Manzo, (1699) and (rev. 1707) by Caldara (1708)
Draft composition score completed 12 February 1730
PREMIERES   24 February 1730, King's Theatre, Haymarket, London; US: 15 September 1988, Opera Omaha, Omaha
CAST   Partenope *s*, Emilio *t*, Armindo *a*, Ormonte *b*, Rosmira *a*, Arsace *a* (castrato); *satb* chorus of soldiers
ORCHESTRATION   2 fl, 2 ob, bsns, tpt, 2 hn, str (vns *divisi à* 3) cont (including theorbo)

Partenope is a comedy: there is one battle, without any heroics, self-sacrifices or high policies at stake,

and this seems to have mainly a symbolic function. For a comparable previous work in Handel's output we have to return to *Agrippina*, and such comparison is appropriate because Handel probably saw a version of *La Partenope* (with music by Antonio Caldara) in Venice the year before he composed *Agrippina*. The libretto of *Partenope* had been considered and rejected by the Royal Academy of Music, so to some extent Handel was in 1730 reviving an old scheme. The result suggests that he found the exercise thoroughly congenial.

SYNOPSIS

Act I Partenope, queen of the city of that name (modern Naples), has three princely suitors: Arsace, Armindo and Emilio. (In Handel's original cast, Armindo was played by a contralto *en travesti*.) Rosmira, Princess of Cyprus, formerly betrothed to Arsace, has followed him to Partenope's court, disguised as a soldier, 'Eurimene'. She reveals her identity to Arsace, accusing him of infidelity and, still disguised as 'Eurimene', declares herself to be another suitor for Partenope. This provokes Partenope to assert her devotion to Arsace. Emilio states that he will order his troops to attack the city if Partenope will not promise him her hand. Partenope calls his bluff and after some complications decides to lead her forces herself. Armindo reproaches 'Eurimene' for setting up as his rival for Partenope, but is told that 'his' affections really lie elsewhere.

Act II The armies of Partenope and Emilio join battle: the former win and Emilio is captured. He acknowledges Arsace as his captor, but 'Eurimene' claims the credit for this and challenges Arsace to a duel. Partenope arrests 'Eurimene' and reasserts her love for Arsace. Puzzled by Arsace's defence of 'Eurimene' Partenope nevertheless agrees to his request to release him on condition that he leaves the city. Armindo declares his love to Partenope, who pities him but cannot respond further.

Act III 'Eurimene' explains to Partenope that he challenged Arsace on behalf of a Cypriot princess whom Arsace had betrayed. When Arsace admits the truth of the allegation, Partenope offers her hand to Armindo, rejecting Arsace. The duel between Arsace and 'Eurimene' is arranged. The contestants are allotted weapons and Arsace suddenly declares that he will fight bare-chested. Equity demands that his opponent should do the same. Faced with a choice about what to reveal, Rosmira chooses to declare her real identity, and that her motive had been to test Arsace's fidelity. The pairs of lovers are united and Emilio is consoled with an offer of friendship.

Partenope is a fast-moving story requiring a deft touch and, although there are some extended arias (mainly for the two leading ladies), Handel keeps pace with the drama in his score and there are a number of engaging ensembles: *coro* movements interspersed with sinfonie in the battle sequence, a lively trio for Arsace and his two ladies, and a rare musico-dramatic interaction in a 'quartet of perplexity' near the beginning of Act III. Handel revived the opera in the 1730–31 season and again in

1737, this time in a shortened form with some important voice changes. It must have been a refreshing contribution to the repertoire.

RECORDING Laki, Müller Molinari, Jacobs, York Skinner, Hill, Varcoe, La Petite Bande, Kuijken, Harmonia Mundi, 1979: a lively rendering of the original 1730 version
EDITION HG, vol. 78

Poro

(*Poro, Re dell'Indie*)
Porus, King of India
Opera in three acts (3h)
Libretto after Pietro Metastasio's *Alessandro dell'Indie*, set by Vinci (1729), possibly after the play *Alexandre le Grand* by Racine (1665)
Draft composition score completed 16 January 1731
PREMIERES 2 February 1731, King's Theatre, Haymarket, London; US: 8 January 1978, Washington (concert)

If variety was essential to the programmes of Handel's opera company, the craving would certainly have been satisfied by the contrast between the fast-moving *Partenope*, as light as it was possible to be within the opera-seria genre and based on an old Venetian libretto, and *Poro*, a heavy-weight drama on a libretto by Metastasio that was scarcely a year old. *Poro* was also an important landmark in the history of Handel's company, as it saw the return of Senesino to London as his 'primo uomo'.

The action takes place during Alexander the Great's conquest of India. Poro, a proud Indian prince, has suffered defeat: he assumes a false identity in order to gain access to Alessandro's court. His sister Erissena is brought as a prisoner to Alessandro, who is generous to her and severe with Timagene, the Greek captain who betrayed her. Cleofide, an Indian princess in love with Poro, tries to make peaceful overtures to Alessandro, but Poro misunderstands her motive and accuses her of infidelity. Poro attacks Alessandro as he is visiting Cleofide: he is defeated and imprisoned by Alessandro, but released by Timagene who hopes that Poro will raise opposition to Alessandro. Alessandro offers his hand in marriage to Cleofide, and Erissena brings a report of Poro's death. But later Erissena is surprised to discover her brother alive. Poro tells her not to reveal the secret to Cleofide, and enlists her in an unsuccessful attempt to assassinate Alessandro. At the temple where the marriage of Alessandro and Cleofide is being prepared, Poro hides behind a pillar, dagger in hand. When Alessandro moves to claim Cleofide, she reveals that her own funeral pyre has been prepared: she wishes to follow her true love, Poro, to death. Poro now comes forward, alive, and begs forgiveness of Cleofide for his doubts. They both face Alessandro, who recognizes their nobility and devotion and restores their kingdoms to each of them.

Although serious in tone and carefully organized, Handel's score is by no means stiff: the arias are well characterized and there are some particular high points, such as Cleofide's ground-bass lament 'Spirto amato' and Poro's 'Dov'è? s'affetti per me la morte',

an aria highly acclaimed by Burney. At the end of Act I, where Poro and Cleofide bitterly quote the vows, made earlier, Handel seizes on a hint in the libretto by giving Cleofide and Poro the music of each other's previous promises, but transposed to their own keys: their subsequent duet of discord ('Se mai turbo il tuo riposo') is complemented by another celebrating their reunion in Act II. Handel revived *Poro*, with considerable revisions, in two subsequent seasons.

RECORDING Fischer, Herzberg, Enders, Leib, Kaphahn, Stumpf, Halle Handel Festival O, Margraf, Eterna, 1958
EDITIONS HG, vol. 79; HHA, series 2, vol. 25 (forthcoming)

Ezio

Opera in three acts, HWV 29 (3h)
Libretto after Pietro Metastasio's *Ezio* set by Auletta (1728)
PREMIERES 15 January 1732, King's Theatre, Haymarket, London; US: 11 May 1959, Gate Theater, New York

Handel's next production after *Poro* was also based on a Metastasio libretto, though in the meantime he had attempted, and failed to complete, a 'Tito' opera after Racine. The end of the autograph of *Ezio* is missing, but it seems a fair assumption that it was written during the last couple of months of 1731. Handel had probably collected the word-book during his visit to Italy to gather a cast in 1729.

The action takes place in Rome in AD 451. The forces of the Roman Emperor Valentiniano, under their general Ezio, have defeated Attila the Hun. Ezio is betrothed to Fulvia, daughter of Massimo, a Roman patrician with a grudge against Valentiniano. Onoria, the emperor's sister, is in love with Ezio, while Valentiniano himself intends to marry Fulvia. Massimo plots Valentiniano's assassination: the attempt fails but suspicion falls on Ezio, whom Massimo has represented to the emperor as being over-ambitious. Though at first accepting Valentiniano's advances, Fulvia finally declares her devotion to Ezio, and Ezio himself remains faithful to her. Valentiniano's attacker is identified as Emilio, Massimo's follower. On the Capitol Massimo gathers the people against the emperor, and in the ensuing battle Ezio saves Valentiniano's life. Valentiniano in gratitude grants Fulvia to Ezio, and, on Ezio's pleading, spares Massimo.

Ezio ran for only five performances, and was never revived again by Handel, in spite of the fact that the production was lavish with new scenery and costumes. Though it does not attain the quality of the best scenes in *Poro*, *Ezio* perhaps deserved better. The arias are rather conventional, and mainly on a big scale. The new bass singer Montagnana (as Varo, a friend of Ezio) was given a magnificent aria in Act III ('Già risonar d'intorno') though unfortunately in a position where it held up the *dénouement*. As Ezio himself, Senesino was given an affecting prison aria ('Ecco alle mie catene') in Act II and a richly scored showpiece with recorders and horns ('Se la mia vita') in Act III when Valentiniano has granted him release. *Ezio* was Handel's last Metastasio libretto, though he continued to mount Metastasian operas (either with scores by other composers, or as pasticcios) in the course of his London seasons.

EDITION *HG*, vol. 80

Sosarme
(*Sosarme, re di Media*)
Sosarme, King of Media
Opera in three acts, HWV 30 (3h)
Libretto after Antonio Salvi's *Dionisio, Re di Portugallo* set by Perti (1707)
Draft composition score completed 4 February 1732
PREMIERE   15 February 1732, King's Theatre, Haymarket, London

Although *Sosarme* deals with tangible human relationships, it has something of a fairy-tale quality about it. The opera began as the reworking of a libretto set in Portugal, but halfway through composing the score Handel altered the title of the opera and all the character names, and moved the location to Sardis in the kingdom of Lidia. The change of location may have been made for political reasons, to avoid offending Britain's Portuguese allies, but the rather nebulous final location seems appropriate: 'far away and long ago'.

Argone is in rebellion against his father Haliate, Prince of Lidia, whom he suspects of a design to advance Melo (Haliate's natural son) to the throne. Argone has taken the city of Sardis. Haliate's army besieges the city, joined by the forces of Sosarme, King of Media, who has come to claim Elmira, Haliate's daughter, as his promised bride. Sosarme plans to try to reconcile the warring parties, but Haliate is bent on vengeance. Argone makes a sortie to gain supplies for the city, but returns with his sword covered in the blood of Sosarme, whom he has captured and injured. Haliate decides to offer peace and a pardon to Argone, and he sends his trusted counsellor Altomaro to parley. Altomaro's daughter was Melo's mother and in order to advance his grandson, he lies to Argone, claiming that Haliate will conclude peace only if Argone fights Haliate in single combat. Returning to Haliate, Altomaro tells him that Argone not only rejects his peace offer but challenges him to a single combat. Melo discovers the extent of Altomaro's duplicity. At the duel, Erenice and Melo interpose and are wounded. Haliate and Argone throw away their swords and Melo explains Altomaro's deception. (Altomaro himself has fled from the combat and committed suicide.) The generations are reconciled, and Sosarme and Elmira look forward to a bright future together.

Musically speaking, the crowning glories of the score are the two duets for Sosarme and Elmira (Senesino and Strada): 'Per le porte del tormento' even won instant acclaim as a separate item, being performed in the intervals of plays at the London theatres during 1733–4. But the arias are felicitous also, usually more than compensating for any deficiencies in the libretto. Handel revived the opera, in a much revised version, in 1734. Before the first

performance Handel, probably influenced by the flat reception that *Ezio* had received, drastically shortened the recitatives in an attempt to cut out all unnecessary Italian verbiage and to keep the opera on the move in the manner of *Partenope*; but it has to be admitted that some necessary recitative (from the point of view of character motivation) was removed in the process.

RECORDING   Ritchie, Evans, Watts, Deller, Herbert, Kentish, Wallace, St Anthony Singers and O, A. Lewis, Oiseau-Lyre, 1954–5: considerably cut, but some fine singing, and a landmark in the artistic revival of Handel's operatic music
EDITION *HG*, vol. 81

Orlando
Opera in three acts, HWV 31 (3h)
Libretto after Carlo Sigismondo Capeci's *L'Orlando, overo La gelosia pazzia* set by Domenico Scarlatti (1711) based on Lodovico Ariosto's epic *Orlando furioso* (1516)
Draft composition score completed 20 November 1732
PREMIERES   27 January 1733, King's Theatre, Haymarket, London; US: 16 December 1981, Cambridge, Massachusetts (American Repertory Theater)
CAST   Orlando *a* (castrato), Angelica *s*, Medoro *a*, Dorinda *s*, Zoroastro *b*
ORCHESTRATION   2 rec, 2 ob, bsns, 2 hn, str (including vns divisi à 3, and 2 'violette marine'), cont

Orlando returns to the sort of drama that Handel had developed 20 years before, involving a supernatural dimension and transformation scenes: this contrasts with the operas that had been his concern since the start of the Academy in which the characters, however much fired by jealousy or passion, generally behave rationally. A spectacular element had been creeping back into Handel's opera productions since *Alessandro*: for example, the opera house must have invested in a collapsible city wall, which featured in siege scenes in several operas. At all periods the London opera companies probably employed a fair number of non-singing 'supers', who represented servants or armies as required, and once (in *Admeto*) furies. In *Orlando* they made the significant transition to genii in the service of the magician Zoroastro, a substantial role written for the bass Montagnana, whose part was enhanced by a contrast in vocal ranges: his was the only low voice.

Unlike *Tolomeo*, *Orlando* had a libretto that had been developed considerably from Capeci's original: the identity of the adapter is not known (this is generally the case with Handel's new libretti after 1729), though it has been suggested that Handel worked from a version that Haym may have prepared before his death in 1729, or even that Handel himself had a hand in the adaptation. One factor in the shaping of the opera may have been the revival, if only temporarily, of English opera by a company in a theatre near to the opera house: perhaps opera was not, for the moment, such a 'foreign' medium. In December 1732 Aaron Hill, the artistic impresario who had promoted *Rinaldo*, wrote a letter to Handel encouraging him to take up opera in English: by then the score of *Orlando* had already been written and, like *Rinaldo*, it embodied spectacular scenes of the type that had been developed by the English masque.

SYNOPSIS

Act I   The magician Zoroastro surveys the stars at night and predicts from them that the knight errant Orlando will not always be a 'Foe to Glory'. Orlando, entering, promises that he will follow Glory rather than Love, but after the magician has gone he recants and dedicates himself to the service of Love. In a wood, the lovers Angelica, Queen of Catai, and Medoro, an African prince, are seen together; Angelica tells Medoro that he shall share her empire as well as her heart; Medoro has supplanted her former attachment to Orlando. After Angelica has gone, Medoro is detained by the shepherdess Dorinda, to whom he had previously paid court: Dorinda still loves him, but finds his reaction evasive. Zoroastro warns Angelica of Orlando's jealousy. Seeing Medoro approaching, she appeals for help. Zoroastro conjures up a fountain to conceal Medoro, and the scene is transformed, leaving Orlando alone in a garden ('Fammi combattere'). Angelica and Medoro embrace, and are seen by Dorinda: Angelica presents her with a jewel, which Dorinda thinks a poor substitute for Medoro himself.

Act II   In a wood, Dorinda laments her situation. Orlando accuses her of linking his name with Isabella, a princess he rescued, but Dorinda says that she believed him attached to Angelica, who is now betrothed to another man. Orlando is horrified by the last piece of news, and falls victim to anger and jealousy ('Cielo! se tu il consenti'). Zoroastro urges Angelica and Medoro to escape ('Tra caligni profonde'): as Medoro leaves, he carves their names on a tree. Orlando sees these names and follows in hot pursuit. He finds Angelica in the wood, and tries to catch her: but a large cloud descends and bears her away. Orlando now crosses the bounds of reason: he imagines himself following the lovers to the underworld, finding Medoro in the arms of Proserpina, who weeps for him. Zoroastro appears in his chariot, scoops up Orlando and rides off into the air.

Act III   Medoro takes refuge in Dorinda's cottage and rather shamefacedly confesses to her that he loves Angelica. Orlando meets Dorinda, but has clearly taken leave of his senses, entering into an imaginary battle with the murderer of Angelica's brother. Dorinda tells Angelica of Orlando's pitiful condition, and reflects on the pains brought about by love ('Amor è qual vento'). Zoroastro changes the scene to a 'horrid Cavern' ('Sorge infausta'). Dorinda, weeping, tells Angelica that Orlando has demolished her cottage, leaving Medoro in the wreckage. Orlando thirsts for revenge. He throws Angelica into the cave, which is transformed into the Temple of Mars, then sinks exhausted to sleep. Zoroastro announces that the time has arrived for Orlando to be released from the power of love. He waves his wand, and four genii descend with an eagle carrying a golden vessel in its beak. Zoroastro takes the vessel and sprinkles liquor from it over Orlando's

face. Orlando revives, restored to his senses, and is told by Dorinda that he has murdered Angelica and Medoro. Filled with remorse, Orlando determines to kill himself; but the lovers appear, having been saved by Zoroastro. Orlando announces that he has triumphed over 'himself and Love', and presents Angelica to Medoro. Dorinda, reconciled to her own situation, invites everyone to her cottage to celebrate the 'Festival of Love'.

The high point of *Orlando*'s score is the mad scene at the end of Act II, an extended scena in a recognized theatrical tradition, but which may also be related to English musical progenitors such as Purcell's 'Mad Bess' ('From Silent Shades'). The 5/8 passage as Orlando imagines himself reaching Pluto's throne is a novelty, but more telling overall are the obsessive recurrences of a simple gavotte melody ('Vaghe pupille') as Orlando fights for coherence. The opening scenes for Zoroastro and Orlando are hardly less remarkable: in them recitatives and set numbers flow naturally into each other. Although there are some conventional (though dramatically strong) set-piece *da capo* arias, the action often breaks anticipated moulds, and there are some particularly effective duets. Act I ends with a remarkable 'romantic triangle' trio ('Consolati, o bella') of great subtlety. All five soloists have strong roles, though Medoro receives fewer musical opportunities than the others. In *Orlando* Handel applied the fast-moving dramatic skills of *Partenope* and *Sosarme* to a richly symbolic libretto which showed off the powers of Senesino (Medoro), Strada (Angelica) and Montagnana (Zoroastro) to best advantage. It ran for 10 performances in 1733. That Handel never revived it is attributable to the confusion that overcame his opera company at the end of the season, when he lost Senesino and Montagnana to a rival operation.

RECORDINGS   1. Auger, Kirkby, Robbin, Bowman, Thomas, Academy of Ancient Music, Hogwood, Oiseau-Lyre, 1989–90; 2. Bogard, Sciutti, Steffan, Greevy, Rintzler, Vienna Volksoper O, Simon, RCA, 1971
EDITIONS   *HG*, vol. 82; *HHA*, series 2, vol. 28

Arianna

(Arianna in Creta)
Ariadne (Ariadne in Crete)
Opera in three acts, HWV 32 (2h 30m)
Libretto after Pietro Pariati's *Arianna e Teseo* (1714, rev. 1721 and 1729) set by Leo (1721, and 1729 (pasticcio))
Composition score completed 5 October 1733
PREMIERE   26 January 1734, King's Theatre, Haymarket, London

The formation of a rival opera company in London, a project that had probably been canvassed for some time and which was given a political incentive by the growing rift between George II and the Prince of Wales, came to fruition in 1734. The new Opera of the Nobility lured away most of Handel's cast, including Senesino and Montagnana, and opened at Lincoln's Inn Fields on 29 December 1733 with *Arianna in Nasso* (libretto by Rolli, music by

Porpora). Handel retained the premier opera house for the 1733–4 season, presumably because of the five-year agreement that had been made with the Academy in 1729, and he had in any case already composed his own 'Ariadne' opera. He gathered a new cast around his faithful soprano Strada, bringing in two excellent castrati, Carestini and Scalzi (Teseo and Alceste), and even renewing an old association by employing Durastanti, his soprano from *Agrippina* and *Radamisto*.

The action takes place on Crete, to which seven young men and seven maidens are sent from Athens every seven years as sacrifices in settlement of a dispute with King Minos: the arrangement can be ended only if an Athenian champion succeeds in killing the Minotaur, finding his way out of the labyrinth and beating Tauride, the Cretan general and son of Vulcan. Teseo, son of Aegeus, King of Athens, has accompanied one of the septennial expeditions intending to take on the role of champion and also to rescue Arianna (supposedly a Theban princess, but in reality Minos' daughter, believed lost in infancy) with whom he is in love. Carilda, one of the Athenian virgins, is named as the first virgin for sacrifice to the Minotaur. Tauride is confident that no one can overcome the monster, the labyrinth and the power of his own magic belt. Alceste, a friend of Teseo, persuades Carilda, whom he loves, to escape with him. But they are caught by Minos, who is furious and allocates Arianna to Carilda's place as the first sacrifice. In the darkness of the labyrinth Teseo slays the monster, and begins to make his way out following the thread he has unravelled on the way in. On his way he encounters Arianna, and he persuades her that she is the true object of his affections. Teseo then confronts Tauride, whom he brings to the ground and forces to hand over his magic girdle. Minos acknowledges Teseo as the successful champion and frees the hostages. Teseo asks for Arianna's hand in marriage, and reveals her identity: father and daughter greet each other and the pairs of lovers (Teseo and Arianna, Alceste and Carilda) are happily united.

The score of *Arianna* looks fairly conventional, though Teseo has two interesting scenas in his 'sleep' scene and at the battle with the Minotaur. But on the stage the arias are strong, well varied and effective, and the musical drama entirely coherent. Teseo's music is particularly striking, whether in the lyrical 'Sdegnata sei con me', the brilliant 'Nel pugnar' (both Act I) or the elegant 'Bella sorge la speranza' with which the opera ends – a 'hit' melody if there ever deserved to be one. The women did well also, with big arias for Strada at the end of Acts I and II and some lively arias for Durastanti (as Tauride), including one 'lion' *simile* aria ('Qual leon') in Act II with horn accompaniment. Not surprisingly, Handel revived *Arianna* in his next season.

EDITIONS   *HG*, vol. 83; *HHA*, series 2, vol. 29 (forthcoming)

Parnasso in Festa
Festival on Parnassus
Serenata in three parts, HWV 73 (3h)

PREMIERE   13 March 1734, King's Theatre, Haymarket, London

Parnasso in Festa is not strictly an opera, but a serenata or festa teatrale. Nevertheless it was a full evening's entertainment, produced at the same theatre in the midst of Handel's opera season, and with his opera company cast. The work formed part of London's celebrations for the marriage of Princess Anne, King George II's eldest daughter, to Prince William of Orange.

In Part One, Apollo calls on the Muses to sing in celebration of the marriage of Peleus and Thetis. Clio reminds Apollo of Dafne, whom he once loved but whom he lost when she was transformed into a laurel tree. Apollo drives away this memory by singing the praises of Bacchus and wine. Part Two is mainly devoted to Orfeo and begins by recounting the power of his music. Clori attempts to cheer Orfeo by leading a chorus in praise of hunting, but he remains inconsolable over the loss of Euridice: an example of wedded devotion. Apollo summons the Tritons from the sea to celebrate the wedding of Peleus and Thetis. In Part Three Marte (Mars) looks forward to the race of heroes that will result from the union. Nymphs, shepherds, fauns and the goddesses Iri (Iris) and Aurora are asked to bring tributes of fruit and flowers, and the whole company invokes blessings on the happy pair.

Handel's singers in 1733–4 were nearly all Italians, so it is not surprising that his theatre offering for the wedding season was an Italian work, and in a suitable Italianate tradition. Much of the score was reworked from *Athalia*, Handel's oratorio first performed in Oxford the previous year but not yet heard in London. Presumably the librettist, whose identity is unknown, had a brief to write texts to fit this music. However some of the *Athalia* music was reworked and about ten numbers were newly composed; above all, the design of the new work was original, seamlessly incorporating new and old material.

EDITION   *HG*, vol. 54

Ariodante
Opera in three acts, HWV 33 (3h)
Libretto after Antonio Salvi's *Ginevra, principessa di Scozia*, set by Perti (1708), itself after Ariosto's poem *Orlando furioso* (1516)
Draft composition score completed 24 October 1734
PREMIERES   8 January 1735, Covent Garden, London; US: 29 March 1971, Carnegie Hall, New York (concert); 14 September 1971, Washington (New York City Opera)
CAST   Ariodante *s* (castrato), Ginevra *s*, Polinesso *a*, Lurcanio *t*, Dalinda *s*, Il re *b*, Odoardo *t*; *satb* chorus of shepherds and shepherdesses; dancers
ORCHESTRATION   2 fl, 2 ob, bsns, 2 hn, 2 tpt, str (vns *divisi à* 3), cont

For his 1734–5 season Handel was driven from the Haymarket Theatre by the Opera of the Nobility and set up his company at John Rich's new theatre in Covent Garden, which had opened in December 1732. No doubt Handel had some misgivings about leaving London's premier opera house, which had been his musical home for a quarter of a century. But he took with him an excellent cast, including Carestini and Strada, and the first season was enlivened by the participation of a group of French dancers under the direction of Madame Sallé. Handel made good use of the dancers: ballets were written into Handel's new operas *Ariodante* and *Alcina*, and *Il pastor fido* was revived with a prologue (*Terpsicore*), in which dancing played the major part. At Covent Garden also Handel seems to have regularly employed an independent chorus, which gave a new sound to *coro* movements: these had formerly been rendered by the soloists alone.

Ariodante is set in Edinburgh, with the King of Scotland and Guinevere (Ginevra), his daughter, among the persons represented; but the basis of Salvi's story was from Ariosto's *Orlando furioso*. Handel may have seen Perti's opera on Salvi's libretto in Florence in 1708. The outlines of Ariosto's tale provided popular subject matter for dramatists, including Shakespeare in *Much Ado About Nothing*.

SYNOPSIS

Act I   In the Royal Palace Ginevra prepares to meet Ariodante, a vassal prince with whom she is in love. Polinesso, Duke of Albany, declares his love for Ginevra. She rejects him, but her lady-in-waiting Dalinda hints he would find a better response from her. Polinesso wonders whether he can use Dalinda's infatuation to take revenge on Ginevra. In the palace garden Ginevra and Ariodante pledge their love. The king interrupts them and, approving of Ariodante, tells Ginevra to prepare for her wedding the next day. Polinesso persuades Dalinda to dress as Ginevra that night and to admit him to the princess's apartments. Dalinda rebuffs Ariodante's brother Lurcanio, who is in love with her. Ariodante and Ginevra share their joy with shepherds and shepherdesses.

Act II   At night, Ariodante encounters Polinesso, who suggests that Ginevra is unfaithful to him, and offers to prove it. Ariodante vows to kill himself if the accusation proves true – if false, he will kill Polinesso. Polinesso tells Ariodante to hide and watch. Unknown to them both, Lurcanio is also concealed in the garden. Dalinda, dressed as Ginevra, is seen to admit Polinesso to Ginevra's apartments. Ariodante resolves to end his own life, but Lurcanio urges him to avenge his betrayal. In the palace the king is declaring Ariodante his heir when the courtier Odoardo brings the news that Ariodante has thrown himself into the sea and is dead. On hearing the news Ginevra faints. Lurcanio produces to the king a sworn statement of what he saw that night and accuses Ginevra of unfaithfulness: he offers a challenge to anyone prepared to defend Ginevra. Ginevra herself cannot understand why she is harshly disowned by the king. Furies torment her dreams.

Act III   Ariodante, wandering alone, hears cries for help and finds Dalinda, pursued by assassins sent by Polinesso. He drives them off and learns from her the story of Polinesso's deceit: Dalinda herself turns against Polinesso. At the palace, Polinesso offers himself as Ginevra's champion: the king accepts him

despite Ginevra's fierce opposition. In the combat Lurcanio mortally wounds Polinesso: it looks as if the heavens are signalling Ginevra's guilt. A stranger in a helmet with lowered visor comes to her defence. It is Ariodante, who says that he has knowledge of Ginevra's innocence, which he will reveal if the king will pardon Dalinda in advance. Odoardo reports that the dying Polinesso confessed his crime. Dalinda agrees to accept Lurcanio as her lover. The king brings Ariodante to Ginevra, releases her from her confinement, and celebrations begin for the two pairs of lovers, with dances for the 'Knights and Ladies'.

In *Ariodante* Handel managed to combine an intimate atmosphere, in which the cross-currents of personal attractions and conflicts flow strongly, with a platform for Carestini's skill, which reached its apogee in his arias 'Con l'ali di costanza', 'Scherza infida' (at the climax of one of Handel's most powerful scenes, in the garden at the beginning of Act II), 'Cieca notte' and 'Dopo notte'. The recitatives are short and the arias extended, reflecting exactly the balance between the simple actions and the great effects they have on the participants. At the other extremity of scale, there are few more effective scene-setting introductions in opera than the 'moonrise' sinfonia at the beginning of Act II – a mere ten bars. With ravishing arias, some splendid duets (including one in Act I ('Prendi, prendi') in which the king interrupts Ariodante and Ginevra as they are about to embark on their *da capo*), spectacular dancing integrated with the plot (particularly at the end of Act II) and, incidentally, a good libretto, *Ariodante* is one of the most rewarding of Handel's operas. But it relied to some extent on the individual skills of Carestini: Handel revived the opera only once, in 1736, in a revised form to accommodate another castrato, Conti.

RECORDING   Mathis, Burrowes, Baker, Bowman, Rendall, Oliver, Ramey, London Voices, ECO, Leppard, Philips, 1979: now rather old-fashioned in sound, but a sensitive performance with fine singing from Baker in the title role
EDITION   *HG*, vol. 85

Alcina

Opera in three acts, HWV 34 (3h 30m)
Libretto based on ?Antonio Fanzaglia's *L'isola d'Alcina* set by Broschi (1728) after Lodovico Ariosto's *Orlando furioso* (1516)
Draft composition score completed 8 April 1735
PREMIERES   16 April 1735, Covent Garden, London; US: 16 November 1960, Dallas Civic Opera, Dallas
CAST   Alcina *s*, Ruggiero *s* (castrato), Morgana *s*, Bradamante *a*, Oronte *t*, Melisso *b*, Oberto *s* (*boy treble*); *satb* chorus
ORCHESTRATION   picc, 2 rec, 2 ob, 2 hn, str (vns *divisi à* 3), cont

Alcina was the last of Handel's operas to be derived from Ariosto's *Orlando furioso*. Handel probably collected the libretto during his visit to the Continent in 1729: as usual, it was considerably rearranged to suit London conditions (recitatives were abbreviated and arias were tailored to the singers' abilities). Of the four Handel operas on libretti derived from Ariosto's epic poem, three (*Rinaldo*, *Orlando* and *Alcina*) include an enchantress and/or enchanter among the leading characters. The nature of the story, set here on Alcina's enchanted island, gave plenty of opportunities for spectacle and scene transformation. As in *Ariodante*, Marie Sallé's ballet troupe was integrated effectively into the opera. Names added by Handel to one of the *coro* movements show that the main cast singers were supplemented by at least one more soprano, an alto (or two), three tenors and two basses in the chorus movements.

Alcina seems to have done well for Handel in the period of rivalry between his company and the Opera of the Nobility: in the original run it had 18 performances. As Burney commented later, *Alcina* was 'an opera with which Handel seems to have vanquished his opponents, and to have kept the field near a month longer than his rival Porpora was able to make head against him'. Burney's further comments are also interesting: 'Upon the whole, if any one of Handel's dramatic works should be brought on the stage, entire, without a change or mixture of airs from his other operas, it seems as if this would well sustain such a revival.' *Alcina* was indeed one of the first operas to re-enter the repertoire and to sustain some place in modern productions of Handel's operas, though it is rarely revived 'entire'.

SYNOPSIS

Alcina has fallen in love with the knight Ruggiero and has detained him on her enchanted island.

Act I Bradamante, Ruggiero's betrothed, arrives at the island in an attempt to rescue him, accompanied by her guardian Melisso: she is disguised as her brother Ricciardo. Bradamante and Melisso are discovered by Morgana, Alcina's sister, who is attracted to 'Ricciardo'. The original scene (a mountain) breaks open to reveal Alcina adorning herself while Ruggiero holds her mirror. The new arrivals introduce themselves and are welcomed by Alcina. 'Ricciardo' asks Ruggiero if he remembers him, the brother of his betrothed: but, under Alcina's spell, Ruggiero has no recollection of any lover but Alcina ('Di te mi rido'). Oronte, Alcina's general, tells Ruggiero that, with the arrival of 'Ricciardo', he may suffer the same fate as the thousands of Alcina's previous lovers who have been turned into streams, beasts, trees and rocks. When challenged, Alcina tells Ruggiero that he still pleases her, for the moment. Ruggiero tries to encourage 'Ricciardo' to return home. Bradamante reveals her true identity, but Ruggiero thinks that this is just one of Alcina's tricks.

Act II In a hall of the palace Melisso, disguised as Ruggiero's tutor Atlante, gives Ruggiero a magic ring which returns him to his senses. He renews his devotion to Bradamante, but decides to conceal this from Alcina. Before the statue of Circe, Alcina is about to change 'Ricciardo' into a beast, when Morgana, who believes 'Ricciardo' is in love with her, and Ruggiero together persuade her to desist. Oberto, Bradamante's nephew, who has come to the

island in search of his lost father, Astolfo, asks Alcina for help, and is told that he shall see Astolfo soon. Bradamante tells Oberto that his father has been changed into a lion. Oronte tells Alcina that he is preparing to leave with the new guests; he taunts Morgana with the faithlessness of her new lover. At first inclined to disbelieve him, Morgana then finds Bradamante and Ruggiero together ('Verdi prati'). In a 'Subterraneous Appartment', Alcina tries to use her powers to detain Ruggiero, but to no avail – he is protected by the ring ('Ombre pallide').

Act III In a courtyard of the palace, Oronte and Morgana, previously lovers, are reconciled. Alcina tries unsuccessfully to dissuade Ruggiero from leaving ('Ma quando tornerai'). A ship awaits Ruggiero and Bradamante, but Bradamante declares that she will not leave until Alcina's enchantments are broken ('Mi restano le lagrime') and life has been restored to her victims. Outside Alcina's palace are the dens of the wild beasts and the urn that contains the 'whole power of the Inchantment'. Ruggiero goes to break the urn with his ring: Alcina and Morgana try to restrain him, but he throws the urn down, whereupon 'the Scene wholly disappears, changing to the Sea, which is seen thro' a vast subterraneous Cavaern where many Stones are chang'd into Men; among them is Astolfo, who embraces Oberto: They form the Chorus and the Dance'.

'Verdi prati' in Act II, which expresses perfectly Ruggiero's regret that the beautiful landscape of the island is about to decay, caught the public's imagination at an early stage: with its sarabande-like rhythm and measured phrases it is reminiscent of Handel's first 'hit' in London, 'Lascia ch'io pianga' from *Rinaldo*. Reputedly, Carestini dismissed the aria when it was first presented to him as being insufficiently brilliant. In the opera its effect is heightened because it is followed immediately by Alcina's attempt to hold Ruggiero by enchantment. Throughout the opera Handel's command of contrast and pacing is masterly, making the most of the interplay between rational and irrational elements in the plot. Remarkably, he makes no attempt to cover a potential weakness in the plot – the fact that Alcina is effectively beaten by the end of Act II – by hurrying over the *dénouement*. Her developing character, through to her final aria ('Mi restano le lagrime'), is among Handel's most subtly drawn creations. Act III begins with a chain of magnificent and luxuriant *da capo* arias, which serve to emphasize the change of pace in the final scenes, when a trio, recitatives, choruses and dances follow in quick succession to complete Alcina's downfall. Although Carestini (Ruggiero) and Strada (Alcina) naturally dominated the score and the stage, the other roles are also quite substantial: even the 15-year-old treble 'Young Mr Savage' as Oberto had a man-size part to sing. Handel revived *Alcina* at the beginning and end of his 1736–7 season, though without the dances at the later perfomances since the arrangement with Madame Sallé's troupe had ended. It may be that the scenic effects of *Alcina* were particularly geared to the facilities of Covent Garden

Theatre. Handel never revived the opera after he returned to the King's Theatre in 1738.

RECORDINGS 1. Auger, Kwella, Harrhy, Kuhlmann, Jones, Davies, Tomlinson, Kwella, Opera Stage Ch and City of London Sinfonia, Hickox, HMV, 1985; 2. Sutherland, Sciutti, Freni, Berganza, Sinclair, Alva, Flagello, LSO, Bonynge, Decca, 1962: the latter, though less authentic (and less complete) than the first, has some superb singing [A.B.] EDITION   HG, vol. 86 (originally issued as HG, vol. 27)

Atalanta

Opera in three acts, HWV 35 (2h 30m)
Libretto after Belisario Valeriani's *La caccia in Etolia*, set by Chelleri (1715)
Draft composition score completed 22 April 1736
PREMIERES   12 May 1736, Covent Garden, London; US: 28 June 1992, Connecticut Colleges, New London (concert)
CAST   Atalanta *s*, Meleagro *s* (castrato), Irene *a*, Aminta *t*, Nicandro *b*, Mercurio *b*; *satb* chorus
ORCHESTRATION   2 ob, [bsns], 2 hn, 3 tpt, timp, str, cont

By November 1735 Handel was probably feeling the effects of the competition from the Opera of the Nobility and – a critical factor – he had no leading castrato for his next cast. He consequently delayed the start of his forthcoming season until February 1736, and then chose to perform some of his English works – *Alexander's Feast* (ode), *Acis and Galatea* (serenata) and *Esther* (oratorio). Only in May did he put Italian operas into his programme, beginning with a revival of *Ariodante* and then completing the season with his new opera, *Atalanta*. The course of his programme was affected by the arrival of two people in London: the castrato Conti (who took over Carestini's former role in *Ariodante*) and Princess Augusta of Saxe-Coburg, who was rushed with considerable haste to her marriage with the Prince of Wales at St James's Palace on 27 April.

The general subject of the libretto of *Atalanta* was quite well known in Italy and Germany as an appropriate one for nuptial celebrations. As visits to the opera house were part of the normal social display of the royal family, Handel would have been foolish to miss a chance to contribute to the festive season. Two years earlier he had similarly produced the serenata *Parnasso in Festa* for the wedding of the George II's eldest daughter. On this occasion there was all the more reason to cultivate the mood of the moment because Frederick, Prince of Wales, had been to some extent identified with the Opera of the Nobility, and indeed *Atalanta* seems to have signalled the beginning of the prince's return to active support for Handel. Perhaps, without the incentive of the forthcoming royal wedding, Handel would not have bothered with Italian opera at all in 1736, but would have continued with his unstaged performances of English odes and oratorios.

SYNOPSIS

Meleagro, King of Etolia, has asked for Atalanta, daughter of the King of Arcadia, as his bride; but she has refused in order 'not to lose the Pleasure she took in hunting wild Beasts'. To follow her favourite pursuit, she assumes the name of Amarilli and joins the nymphs and shepherds in the woods. Meleagro follows her in the guise of the shepherd Tirsi, his identity known only to an old shepherd, Nicandro.

Act I   Meleagro meets Aminta, a shepherd in love with Nicandro's daughter Irene. Irene teases Aminta by flirting with Tirsi and joking that Aminta is more interested in her dowry than her person; Nicandro warns her not to press Aminta too far. Atalanta organizes a hunt, and she and the shepherds chase after a wild boar. Atalanta hints that, although she has gained a victory over the boar, she is less certain of her command over her heart.

Act II   After a celebratory hunting chorus, Atalanta reflects on her situation: she loves Tirsi, but must conceal this because he is only a shepherd and she is of royal blood. Meleagro overhears her and, overjoyed to learn that she loves him, tries to explain the true situation; unfortunately he does this by embarking on an elaborate allegorical tale that Atalanta cannot hear to the end. Meleagro asks Irene to act as a go-between and take a scarf to 'Amarilli'; but, when Aminta approaches, Irene pretends that the lover's favour was intended for herself, thus provoking Aminta's jealousy. Atalanta gives Aminta a 'well-wrought Dart' to convey (without revealing the sender) to 'Tirsi'. But when Meleagro tries to continue telling Atalanta his story, she dismisses him abruptly, afraid to reveal her true feelings.

Act III   The love tokens are delivered. Atalanta says that Aminta 'bears the secret of my heart' which Irene takes to mean that Aminta has transferred his affections to 'Amarilli'. Aminta uses this misunderstanding to make Irene jealous; worse still, when Irene tells 'Tirsi' of the supposed liaison between Aminta and 'Amarilli', he despairs at Atlanta's faithlessness. But, awaking Meleagro from troubled dreams, Atalanta denies any love for Aminta and reveals that only pride has kept her from embracing 'Tirsi', until now. Nicandro discovers the lovers together and reveals Meleagro's true identity; the reunion of 'Tirsi' and 'Amarilli' is complemented by that of Aminta and Irene. Mercury descends on a cloud as Jove's messenger to bless the nuptials. The chorus sings of the illustriousness of royal progeny and wishes long life to the bridal couple.

The last scene, Mercury's descent, was obviously designed to honour the newly-weds of 1736, and the masque-like ending is interesting in itself, with or without the fireworks that the stage directions specify. But the opera proper, although rather shorter than Handel's normal span, is also worthy of consideration in its own right. This was Handel's first serious venture into the mode of pastoral drama since *Il pastor fido*. It contains fine scenes and varied arias, some of which – as, for example, Meleagro's aria at the end of Act I ('Non sarà poco', in which the solo part rises to top C) – are far from insubstantial musically. Although the plot does not ask to be taken too seriously, there are moments of emotional weight, especially with Atalanta's 'Lassa! ch'io t'ho perduta' at the beginning of Act II: as with 'Verdi prati' in *Alcina*, the aria gains in effect by contrast with the surrounding material, in this case the preceding cheerful hunting chorus. The opera was strong enough to bear revival for two performances later in 1736, apart from the original run of eight during the wedding period.

RECORDING Farkas, Bártfai-Barta, Lax, Bándi, Gregor, Polgár, Savaria Vocal Ensemble, Capella Savaria, McGegan, Hungaroton, 1985: an engaging performance in many respects, though with some inauthentic flute parts added
EDITION HG, vol. 87

Arminio

Opera in three acts, HWV 36 (3h)
Libretto after Antonio Salvi's *Arminio* set by Alessandro Scarlatti (1703)
Draft composition score completed 14 October 1736
PREMIERE 12 January 1737, Covent Garden, London

In November 1736 Handel reverted to his normal theatre timetable, commencing a season at Covent Garden that was to run through to June of the next year. Although some English works were presented later in the season, Handel's emphasis lay mainly with Italian operas, and he composed three new operas for this season – *Arminio*, *Giustino* and *Berenice*. In *Arminio* he reverted to the type of dynastic/political opera with which he had found success the previous decade, in the early years of the Royal Academy. The libretto, which originated with a Florentine performance in 1703, enjoyed some popularity in Italy – rather surprisingly, perhaps, since the story concerns the defeat of Varo, a Roman general, by the German prince Arminio (Hermann).

The scene is set in the Rhineland, which has been successfully invaded by Varo. Arminio, though defeated, remains defiant: he is betrayed to the Romans by his father-in-law Segeste and put in chains. Tusnelda, Arminio's wife, remains faithful but attracts the attentions of Varo; her brother Sigismondo is in love with Arminio's sister Ramise. Segeste tries unsuccessfully to persuade Arminio to yield to Varo, and to persuade Sigismondo to leave Ramise. Knowing that the defiant Arminio is under a death sentence, Segeste hopes to marry off his widow to Varo: in prison, Arminio entrusts Tusnelda to Varo's care, but she will have none of it and Varo himself soon rejects the claims of love. Arminio's execution is interrupted by the news of a fresh attack from the Germans: Varo commands a counter-attack and Sigismondo engineers Arminio's escape. The enraged Segeste imprisons Sigismondo and Ramise in his palace. Arminio rallies his troops and defeats the Romans: Varo is killed in action, and Segeste contemplates suicide. But Arminio pardons him, and the two pairs of lovers are united.

The score of *Arminio* is rather uneven: some of the music, though appropriate, seems routine. Nevertheless there are some fine arias, particularly for Sigismondo and Arminio. The latter, who has to spend a large part of the opera in chains, has a good scene near the beginning of Act II. More significant, however, is the formal flexibility found in the construction of some scenes (e.g. Act III, where Tusnelda's contemplation of suicide is interrupted by

news that her husband is still alive). Moving away from the conventional recitative–exit aria structure, this flexibility (already tried on occasions such as the mad scene in *Orlando*) was to be further expanded in Handel's later operas. *Arminio* ran for six performances, and was not seen again in Britain until 1972.

EDITION HG, vol. 89

Giustino

Opera in three acts, HWV 37 (3h)
Libretto after that by Nicolò Beregan set by Legrenzi (1683) and adapted by Pietro Pariati for Vivaldi (1724)
Draft composition score completed 20 October 1736
PREMIERES 16 February 1737, Covent Garden, London; US: 27 June 1989, War Memorial Opera House, San Francisco

Although *Giustino* was performed after *Arminio*, its main composition took place during August–September 1736, before the companion opera. Handel made many revisions to the score before it came to performance: some of these were the natural consequence of adapting a Roman libretto to London conditions, but it also seems likely that, when he began the composition, the outlines of his forthcoming cast were not yet clear. Like *Arminio*, *Giustino* has seven leading singing roles, including parts for two castrati (Conti and Annibali), but has an additional minor character – the goddess Fortune, originally played by the treble William Savage. *Giustino* also contains three brief movements for independent chorus. Both scores reveal that Handel's orchestra for the season included a virtuoso oboe-player.

The opera opens as Arianna, widow of the Greek Emperor Xenon, crowns Anastasio with the imperial laurel (accompanied by a stage band). Polidarte, captain of the forces of Vitaliano, a noble 'tyrant of Asia Minor', enters and declares Vitaliano's plan to abduct Arianna. Anastasio sends Polidarte back with a defiant reply. In the fields, the ploughboy Giustino is visited in his sleep by the goddess Fortune, who promises him heroic deeds and a bright future. He subsequently rescues Leoncasta, the emperor's sister, from pursuit by a bear, and Arianna from a sea monster, to which she had been exposed by Vitaliano after she repelled his advances. Giustino captures Vitaliano, who is imprisoned by Anastasio but rescued by Polidarte. Arianna, in gratitude for her rescue, presents Giustino with a diamond girdle that had been given her by Anastasio. When discovered, this proves compromising for Giustino: Anastasio orders Giustino to prison, but Leoncasta arranges his escape. Wandering in the hills, Giustino is captured by Vitaliano, who is about to execute him when a voice from heaven interrupts, telling Vitaliano to stay his hand because Giustino is his brother; the relationship is confirmed by a birthmark. Giustino enlists the support of Vitaliano to rescue Anastasio, who has been captured (along with Arianna and Leoncasta) in an uprising led by an imperial general, Amanzio. Giustino successfully defeats Amanzio, who is dispatched to execution: the others are released, and Anastasio offers Giustino both a share of his throne and the hand of his sister.

Although there are some conventional extended arias in *Giustino*, the opera succeeds primarily through a fast-moving plot and a variety of scenic effects, more numerous than in any opera since *Rinaldo* (ten scene changes are called for), and Handel's score nicely matches the episodic nature of the drama. After the first respectable run of nine performances Handel never revived the opera, probably because many of the stage effects were specific to Covent Garden Theatre, which he left at the end of the season, and possibly also because there was a general decline in the popularity of Italian opera in London, encouraged by parodies such as Lampe's hugely successful *The Dragon of Wantley* (May 1737).

EDITION *HG*, vol. 88

Berenice

Opera in three acts, HWV 38 (3h)
Libretto after Antonio Salvi's *Berenice, Regina d'Egitto*, set by Perti (1709)
Draft composition score completed 27 January 1737
PREMIERE 18 May 1737, Covent Garden, London

For his third new opera of the season Handel turned to a libretto by Salvi, of much the same type as that for *Arminio*, though the setting this time was Egyptian. *Berenice* came late in the season, after a revival of *Esther*, and Handel may have been forced to leave the direction of the performance to a deputy. The newspapers for 14 May reported that the composer was indisposed 'with a Paraletic Disorder, he having at present no use of his Right Hand'; nevertheless, Handel continued his season through to late June, and four performances of *Berenice* were presented. His cast of seven leading soloists, including two castrati, remained in place from earlier in the season.

Queen Berenice of Egypt is in love with Demetrio, a Macedonian prince, but he loves Berenice's sister Selene. Fearing the prospective alliance with Egypt, the Roman Emperor Silla sends two suitors to pay court to Berenice: Fabio and Alessandro. Alessandro is attracted to her, but Berenice defends her right to choose her own husband. Arsace, a vassal prince, loves Selene, and Berenice persuades him to press his suit, so that Selene and Demetrio might be parted. Various intrigues and misunderstandings ensue, but Demetrio and Selene remain loyal to each other. Selene promises Arsace her hand if he will free Demetrio, whom Berenice has imprisoned. Berenice prepares to sacrifice Demetrio at the Temple of Isis, and Selene offers to die with him. Arsace announces that he has freed Demetrio. Berenice decides in favour of Alessandro and crowns him King of Egypt. Arsace generously yields Selene to Demetrio. Love and Politics are now in agreement.

The name of the opera has been kept alive through one movement, the 'Minuet from *Berenice*' that closes the overture, but *Berenice* has been one of the last Handel operas to see modern revival. Wrong conclusions must not be drawn from this: although *Berenice* does not rise to the heights of Handel's most exceptional operas, it has few weak movements, and has sufficient variety in duets, *recitativo accompagnato* and *sinfonia* movements to leaven the chains of recitative and aria. (The introductory sinfonia to Act III interestingly anticipates the *ouverture* to *The Music for the Royal Fireworks*.) And the arias themselves are far from perfunctory, even the conventional *simile* arias. Few movements demonstrate more vividly the gap between what is seen on the printed score and the effect of the music in performance than Fabio's 'bee' aria ('Vedi l'ape') or Selene's 'turtle dove' aria ('Tortorella') from this opera. It is almost as if Handel in *Berenice* is making a valedictory gesture by doing the conventional job well, foreseeing that in a year's time he will have moved on to a more ironic style of opera in which grand gestures lack conviction.

EDITIONS *HG*, vol. 90; *HHA*, series 2, vol. 37 (forthcoming)

Faramondo

Opera in three acts, HWV 39 (3h)
Libretto after Apostolo Zeno's *Faramondo* set by Pollarolo (1699) and rev. for Gasparini (1720)
Draft composition score completed 24 December 1737
PREMIERE 3 January 1738, King's Theatre, Haymarket, London

In June 1737 the Opera of the Nobility gave its last performance; for the next season, 1737–8, Handel moved back from Covent Garden to London's major opera house. This bald description probably oversimplifies the situation: it seems more likely that there was some sort of agreement between Handel on one hand and the management of the Nobility Opera on the other, for a season in which Handel and Heidegger had a leading role. The principal castrati of both companies – Conti, Annibali and Farinelli – had left London, and so had Porpora, the Nobility's principal composer. A new company was assembled, in which the only recognizable links with Handel's London past were the bass Montagnana and the treble William Savage. Handel had to deal with a new 'first man' (Caffarelli) and a new first soprano (Francesina). The first productions (in October) were revived from the old Nobility Opera repertoire. By mid-November Handel was at work on the score of a new opera, *Faramondo*, but both this and the opera season itself were interrupted by the death of the queen on 20 November. When the opera company reopened in January 1738, it was with *Faramondo*.

The opera begins with Gustavo, King of the Cimbri, taking an oath to avenge the death of his young son Sweno at the hand of Faramondo, King of the Franks. Rosimonda, Gustavo's daughter, is under attack from Faramondo's soldiers, but is saved by Faramondo himself; the two discover a mutual attraction which cuts across their political and family loyalties. Furthermore Faramondo finds himself an unwilling rival in love of his former ally, Gernando, King of the Suevi. It also transpires that both

Gustavo and his son Adolfo are in love with Faramondo's sister Clotilde, again crossing political loyalties. Two unsuccessful attempts are made on Faramondo's life: the second time he is protected by Rosimonda, who sends him to her apartment. Teobaldo, Gustavo's general, attempts to gain admittance and reveals that he is bent on vengeance on his own behalf, because Sweno was really his own son. Faramondo rescues Gustavo from defeat at the hands of Gernando and Teobaldo, and offers his life to end the old quarrel. Gustavo is impressed, but cannot go back on his own oath to avenge Sweno's death. Gustavo is about to execute Faramondo when the proceedings are interrupted by Childerico, Teobaldo's son, who reveals the truth. Teobaldo confesses that he exchanged the young sons so that his own issue (Sweno) should occupy the throne. The old enmities are ended, and Faramondo is united with Rosimonda.

Faramondo was the only Zeno libretto that Handel set, perhaps to placate the taste of the Nobility Opera patrons, but it was cut to such a degree that it must barely have been comprehensible to the audience. Faramondo himself acts with reckless generosity of spirit throughout the opera and it is difficult to know whether Handel took the work entirely seriously, though there are no direct hints of irony in the score, which contains some good arias and two duets, though few fluidly constructed scenes. It looks as if Handel was adjusting to the pretensions of the new company, but rather marking time.

EDITION *HG*, vol. 91

Serse

Xerxes

Opera in three acts, HWV 40 (3h)

Libretto after Silvio Stampiglia's *Xerse* set by Giovanni Bononcini (1694), itself based on Nicolò Minato's *Serse* set by Cavalli (1654)

Draft composition score completed 14 February 1738

PREMIERES 15 April 1738, King's Theatre, Haymarket, London; US: 12 May 1928, Northampton, Massachusetts

CAST Serse *s* (castrato), Arsamene *s*, Amastre *a*, Ariodate *b*, Romilda *s*, Atalanta *s*, Elviro *b*; *satb* chorus of soldiers, sailors, politicians, priests

ORCHESTRATION 2 rec, 2 ob, bsns, 2 hn, tpt, hn, str (vns *divisi à* 3) cont

To the 1737–8 opera season at the Haymarket Theatre Handel contributed two new operas, *Faramondo* and *Serse*, and a third work, *Alessandro Severo*, which was musically a 'self-pasticcio' using arias from Handel's previous operas. Otherwise, the programme consisted of revivals of operas by other composers, apparently to the taste of the former Nobility Opera patrons. The fact that Handel did not revive any of his own operas probably indicates that he was not in artistic control of the season as a whole. With *Serse* Handel returned to the librettist who had provided *Partenope*, with results in a similar spirit. If the tone of *Faramondo* is ambiguous, as the hero seems too innocently virtuous to be taken entirely seriously, there is no doubt about the ironic slant of *Serse*. The dialogue is quite light in tone; there are

no great causes or heroics. In addition to dealing in comic situations, the opera includes one unambiguously comic character, the servant Elviro, 'a facetious Fellow'. Even the paragraph 'To the Reader' that takes the place of the conventional 'Argument' in the printed word-book seems to be a parody of the normal historical and literary justification: 'The contexture of this Drama is so very easy, that it wou'd be troubling the reader to give him a long argument to explain it. Some imbecilities, and the temerity of Xerxes (such as his being deeply enamour'd with a plane tree, and the building a bridge over the Hellespont to unite Asia to Europe) are the basis of the story, the rest is fiction.'

SYNOPSIS

Act I Serse, King of Persia, enjoys the shade provided by the plane tree in a garden ('Ombra mai fu'). His brother Arsamene enters looking for Romilda, with whom he is in love, whose singing is heard coming from elsewhere in the garden: the sound impels Serse to love. Arsamene tries to deter his brother by saying that her social station (she is the daughter of a vassal, Ariodate) makes her unworthy of the king's attentions. Undeterred, Serse instructs his brother to convey his affectionate intentions to Romilda, much to Arsamene's consternation. Romilda's sister Atalanta, who has her own designs on Arsamene, is present when Arsamene carries out his duty. When Arsamene later interrupts Serse's attempt to command Romilda into matrimony, Serse banishes him from the court. Romilda rejects Serse's love. Amastre, Serse's betrothed, arrives disguised as a man and overhears Serse reflecting that his plans for a liaison with Romilda will entail deserting Amastre. Arsamene sends his servant Elviro with a love letter to Romilda, asking for a meeting. Atalanta tries to make Romilda doubt Arsamene's constancy. Romilda declares that she will not love Arsamene if he proves unfaithful ('Se l'idol mio'), but warns Atalanta against trying to steal Arsamene from her.

Act II In the city square Elviro, who is masquerading as a flower-seller ('Ah! chi voler fiora'), tells Amastre of the situation between Serse, Arsamene and Romilda. Atalanta intercepts Arsamene's letter to Romilda, and then persuades Serse that the letter was written to herself. Serse determines to force Arsamene to marry Atalanta, and shows the letter to Romilda as proof of Arsamene's infidelity. Romilda is overcome with jealousy, but will still not accept Serse as a husband. Serse seems convinced that Arsamene loves Atalanta, conveniently leaving Romilda available for himself. But Arsamene protests his continuing devotion to Romilda. Outside the town Serse meets Amastre, still dressed as a man. He tries to enlist her into his military service, but the conversation is interrupted by the arrival of Romilda. When Serse tries to force his claim on Romilda, Amastre intervenes and says that she will champion Romilda against Serse's pressure.

Act III Romilda taxes Arsamene with writing to Atalanta: the deception is revealed. Atalanta claims that Serse arrived so suddenly that she had to pretend to be the recipient in order to screen Romilda. Serse again makes an approach to Romilda, which she counters by saying that her father's permission is needed. Serse tells Ariodate that Romilda is to be given a 'consort of our royal blood': Ariodate gives his consent and agrees to receive the suitor in his apartment soon, assuming that Serse had been referring to Arsamene. Romilda claims that she is already committed to Arsamene. Serse is not sure whether to believe her, but orders Arsamene's arrest. Arsamene goes to the temple, where he meets Ariodate who, believing that he is following Serse's command, marries Arsamene to Romilda. When Ariodate goes to Serse, to thank him for the honour done to his family, Serse discovers what has taken place. As he accuses Ariodate of treachery, a page brings Serse a letter purporting to come from Romilda: it is from Amastre, who threatens suicide on account of Serse's infidelity. Serse commands Arsamene to kill his new wife, giving him a sword for the purpose. Amastre takes the sword and turns it on Serse himself, at the same time revealing her true identity. Serse is reconciled to her and, repenting the violence of his rage, approves the union of Arsamene and Romilda.

Like *Berenice*, the title of *Serse* has remained in public consciousness through one melody – Serse's first arietta, 'Ombra mai fu': few of those who recognize 'Handel's *Largo*' (though designated *larghetto* by the composer) are aware of its origin in Serse's paean to a plane tree. The score of *Serse* is indebted in some details to Giovanni Bononcini's setting of the same text, though considerably transformed by Handel. As a whole, *Serse* exhibits more variety in its arias than any other Handel opera: in complete contrast to 'Ombra mai fu' there are some full bravura *da capo* arias (e.g. Serse's 'Più che penso', 'Se bramate d'amar' and 'Crude furie'). But *da capo* arias account for only about half of the score: many arias are through-composed (e.g. Amastre's 'Anima infida' and Atalanta's 'Voi mi dite') and several are curtailed or modified in form by dramatic exigencies (e.g. Romilda's 'O voi che penate!'). Even the duets deviate from the conventional 'lovers' reunion' type: in 'Troppo oltraggi la mia fede' (Act III) Romilda and Arsamene are actually separating emotionally, while in 'Gran pena è gelosia' (Act II) Serse and Amastre sing their own separate (but related) thoughts, unaware that the other person is present. Elviro's first scene in Act II is amusingly punctuated by snatches of song as he interrupts his conversations with flower-seller's cries in local dialect.

Perhaps because the plot lacks substantial political overtones, the characters are clearly delineated both individually and in their relationships. The central characters are seriously motivated by love, though Serse's behaviour has a touch of exaggeration, which makes it impossible to take him entirely seriously. A lighter touch is provided not only by Elviro but also by Atalanta (who is clearly capricious and likely to get up to fraudulent tricks) and Ariodate. As in

Partenope, Handel achieved exactly the appropriate musical means to express both the characterization and the plot. That Handel never revived the opera is easily explained: he never again had seven evenly matched soloists for an opera season.

RECORDINGS 1. Popp, Tyler, Forrester, Lehane, Miller, Hemsley, Brannigan, Vienna Radio O, Priestman, Westminster, 1965; 2. Hendricks, Rodde, Watkinson, Wenkel, Esswood, Studer, Cold, La Grande Ecurie et la Chambre du Roy, Malgoire, CBS, 1979: neither set is ideal; the first is old-fashioned but worthy, the second capricious
EDITIONS *HG*, vol. 92; *HHA*, series 2, vol. 39

Imeneo

Opera in three acts, HWV 41 (2h 30m)
Libretto after Silvio Stampiglia's *Imeneo in Atene* set by Porpora (1723)
Draft composition score completed 10 October 1740
PREMIERES 22 November 1740, Theatre Royal, Lincoln's Inn Fields, London; US: 3 May 1965, Princeton University, Princeton
CAST Imeneo b, Tirinto s (castrato), Rosmene s, Clomiri s, Argenio b; satb chorus
ORCHESTRATION 2 ob, [bsns], str (vns *divisi à* 3), cont

Towards the end of May 1738 Heidegger invited subscriptions for the next opera season, but had to abandon his plans when the response proved to be insufficient. So it is rather surprising that Handel spent time in September drafting a new opera, *Imeneo*: perhaps he was involved with some other scheme that never came to fruition. Handel did give a season at the King's Theatre between January and April 1739, but it was mainly devoted to English works, in particular the new oratorios *Saul* and *Israel in Egypt*. Although this proved quite successful, Handel did not attempt another season of the same type. He changed venues in London, moving to the theatre in Lincoln's Inn Fields for two seasons, apparently at his own choice. His initial plan, which he followed in 1739–40, was to mount a programme of unstaged English oratorios, serenatas and odes, which did not need the resources of a high-profile opera theatre. In 1741, however, he added the castrato Andreoni to his basically 'English-speaking' cast, and decided to present operas as well as odes and oratorios. So he returned to his (as yet unperformed) score of *Imeneo*, revising it substantially to suit his present cast and to fill the gaps left by music that he had meanwhile used elsewhere (some in the pasticcio *Giove in Argo*). Thus the opera came to performance more than two years after it was composed – a unique occurrence in the career of a composer who usually wrote to fulfil immediate demand.

SYNOPSIS

Act I In ancient Athens Tirinto laments the absence of Rosmene, to whom he is betrothed, who has gone with other Athenian virgins to take part in the rites in honour of the goddess Ceres. Rumours are heard that the ship carrying the virgins has been captured by pirates. Tirinto determines to institute a search, but his plans are interrupted by the arrival of Imeneo: in order to be near his beloved Rosmene, he was with the virgins, disguised as a woman, and while the pirates were sleeping he killed them. As a reward he claims the hand of Rosmene: the Athenian senator Argenio (whose daughter Clomiri was also on board) agrees to support him, but Tirinto is horrified at the proposal. Clomiri is upset because she has fallen in love with Imeneo herself. Faced with the rival claims of Tirinto and her rescuer, Imeneo, Rosmene gives non-committal answers.

Act II Argenio tells Rosmene that she should favour Imeneo, even at the expense of breaking faith with Tirinto. Argenio announces that the Athenians support Imeneo, but are leaving the decision to Rosmene: both Imeneo and Tirinto urge her to make her choice.

Act III Rosmene again faces Imeneo and Tirinto, saying that her heart is torn between them. Imeneo's declaration that he will marry no one but Rosmene provokes Clomiri to reveal her ill-fated love. Rosmene resolves to announce her choice, but describes, feigning a trancelike state, her descent to Hades where she dreams she meets the great judge Radamanto carrying a sword in one hand and a balance in the other: he strikes her with the sword and her soul flies from her body. Momentarily overcome, Rosmene asks to be held up, and Tirinto and Imeneo rush to support her. She sends Tirinto away. Rosmene then reveals that she has chosen Imeneo and she urges Tirinto to accept the outcome calmly. The Athenians comment that the heart must yield to the dictates of reason.

Imeneo is clearly a 'domestic' drama: it needs no elaborate scenic effects (which indeed might not have been possible at Lincoln's Inn Theatre), nor are any wars or public issues at stake. Although Rosmene's choice is on one level a variant on the familiar love-versus-duty theme, there is little evidence that she feels any overwhelming attraction to either of her suitors. There are ironic aspects to the opera, especially when viewed against the background of Handel's long experience in opera seria. Tirinto, the part for the castrato, is clearly the leading man, signalled not only by his voice category but by magnificent arias such as 'Sorge nell'alma mia'. The pacing of the plot is extraordinary: instead of the multiplicity of incidents characteristic of opera seria, Rosmene's dilemma is set up quite early in Act I, and little now happens until Rosmene makes her choice in Act III. *Imeneo* works well as a chamber opera: Handel revived it as an unstaged serenata (with the title *Hymen*) at Dublin in 1742. In addition to a delicious mix of arias, it has a number of attractive short choruses: the Athenians cheer for Imeneo throughout, their weight counterbalancing the circumstance that Tirinto's music is more impassioned than Imeneo's.

RECORDING abridged: Baird, Hoch, Ostendorf, Fortunato, Opalach, Brewer Chamber Ch and O, Palmer, Vox Cum Laude, 1986

EDITIONS *HG*, vol. 93; *HHA*, series 2, vol. 40 (forthcoming)

Deidamia

Melodrama in three acts, HWV 42 (3h)
Libretto by Paolo Rolli possibly inspired by Metastasio's *Achille in Sciro* (1736) or Bentivoglio's (1663)
Draft composition score completed 20 November 1740
PREMIERES 10 January 1741, Theatre Royal, Lincoln's Inn Fields, London; modern revival: 3 June 1955, St Pancras Town Hall, London; US: 25 February 1959, Hartford, Connecticut

Deidamia was the first libretto for more than ten years with which the name of a definite London author–adapter can be associated. Rolli had adapted libretti for Handel in the Royal Academy period and, it may be assumed, had maintained some contact with the composer. While it is possible that Handel invited Rolli to contribute to his Lincoln's Inn Fields season, it seems at least as likely that Handel worked from a libretto prepared for him at an earlier period: the scenic settings, including a hunt, are more demanding than any in *Imeneo* and may have been conceived for the Covent Garden or Haymarket theatres. On the other hand the tone of the libretto, like that of *Imeneo*, is poised between a serious and a comic style, and so constructed as to call into question its superficial conclusion (that the demands of duty should triumph over those of love). Presumably Rolli followed some pre-existing Italian text when constructing his libretto: there were several on the same subject, though his precise model has not yet been identified.

The action takes place in 'The Royal seat of Scyro, an island kingdom in the Aegean'. Ambassadors from Greece – Fenice, Nestor and Ulisse (the last-named posing as Antiloco, Nestor's son) – come to King Lycomede to ask for assistance in the war against the Trojans: Greece needs naval forces, but also the help of Achille without whom, the gods have said, Troy cannot be beaten. Achille's father Peleus had sent his son to Scyro for safety: and Lycomede, because of another prophecy which has said that Achille will be killed if he goes to Troy, denies knowledge of his presence on the island. In fact Achille is at Lycomede's court disguised as a woman, Pirra: Deidamia, Lycomede's daughter, is in love with him. Deidamia and her friend, Princess Nerea, receive approaches from Ulisse and Fenice, respectively. Lycomede arranges a hunt for the entertainment of the ambassadors. In the forest, Ulisse remarks on the hunting prowess of one of the 'nymphs' who, he is certain, is Achille in disguise. When 'Pirra' appears, Ulisse declares that he is transferring his affections from Deidamia to her. Fenice also tests 'Pirra' by a declaration of love, and the response convinces him that Pirra is no woman. Later, Fenice and Ulisse bring presents for the ladies. Achille betrays himself by the way he puts on a helmet and takes a sword: he then responds enthusiastically to Ulisse's invitation to take a leading part in defending Greece's honour. Meanwhile, Deidamia charges Ulisse with ruining her life by taking Achille: Achille offers to ask Lycomede's permission for their marriage, but Deidamia spurns him for putting glory before love.

Fenice offers Nerea marriage and a share in the throne of Argos. Lycomede enters and asks Ulisse, who has revealed his true identity, to perform the marriage of Deidamia and Achille: Deidamia promises her constancy in respect for his valour. The final *coro*, however, is about the transience of love.

The atmosphere of ironic, even cynical, detachment with which *Deidamia* ends is perhaps strange: Handel concludes with neither a bang nor a whimper, but with a sidelong glance. As usual there are some good scenes (such as the initial arrival of the ambassadors, accompanied by an onstage band of trumpets, horns and timpani) and some attractive arias, but there is also some routine music. Handel's last operatic performance in London was of *Deidamia*, on 10 February 1741, within three months of the 21st anniversary of his first performance for the Royal Academy of Music.

EDITION *HG*, vol. 94

The Charming Brute, caricature of Handel by Joseph Goupy (1754)

Semele

(*The Story of Semele*)
Dramatic entertainment in three acts, HWV 58 (3h)
Libretto after William Congreve's (*c.* 1705–6) for John Eccles (unperformed; published 1710)
Draft composition score completed 4 July 1743
PREMIERES 10 February 1744, Covent Garden, London; US: January 1959, N.W. University, Evanston, Illinois
CAST Jupiter *t*, Cadmus *b*, Athamas *a*, Somnus *b*, Apollo *t*, Juno *a*, Iris *s*, Semele *s*, Ino *a*; *satb* chorus of priests and augurs, loves and zephyrs, nymphs and swains; (the score also includes one aria for Cupid (*s*), probably cut before the first performance)

ORCHESTRATION 2 ob, 2 bsn, 2 hn, 2 tpt, str (vns *divisi à* 3), hps, organ

Two secular-subject works that Handel performed 'after the manner of an Oratorio' have some claim to attention as near-operas – *Semele* and *Hercules*, and of the two *Semele* has more relevance here because its source libretto was actually written for an opera. (That for *Hercules* was written for a play.) The original text was published in 1710, as 'Semele, an Opera', in a sumptuous edition of Congreve's works. Handel's adapter followed most of Congreve's text fairly faithfully, but cut and adapted sections and added some new material (partly drawn from other works by Pope and Congreve himself), including a new scene at the end of Act II. Although Handel performed the work in 'oratorio' style, it is perhaps significant that he ended his first draft of the end of Act II with 'Fine dell' Atto 2do', but a second draft with 'Fine della parte 2da': the uncertainty between 'parts' and 'acts' seems to reveal an equivocation in Handel's view of the work.

SYNOPSIS

Act I The action begins in Boeotia, at the Temple of Juno where the marriage of Semele, daughter of Cadmus, King of Thebes, and Athamas, a prince of Boeotia, is about to be solemnized. Semele seems reluctant: she does not want to forgo her present liaison with Jove (Jupiter). Suddenly thunder is heard (a sign of Jove's activity), and the fire on the altar is extinguished: eventually the altar sinks from sight, and the wedding is abandoned in face of these omens. Ino, Semele's sister, reveals her love for Athamas, and Cadmus reports that, as his party was leaving Juno's temple, an eagle swooped down and carried Semele away; Jupiter now enjoys Semele's favours 'above' ('Endless pleasure, endless Love').

Act II Juno is incensed by Jupiter's affair with Semele, and she determines to destroy the woman who has displaced her. She invokes Saturnia to destroy Semele and also decides that she will need help from Somnus, the god of sleep. In her palace, Semele awakes ('O Sleep, why dost thou leave me?'); Jupiter enters and the two renew their affection. But Semele is not entirely happy: she is only a mortal, and feels frightened when Jupiter leaves her. In order to distract Semele from wishing for immortality, Jupiter brings Ino to Semele for company: he transforms the scene to Arcadia ('Where'er you walk') and leaves the sisters together to enjoy the harmony of the spheres.

Act III Juno and Iris visit Somnus' cave and (with some difficulty) awaken him. Among Juno's requests to Somnus is one that Ino should be immobilized by sleep so that Juno can impersonate her when she visits Semele: in return Juno guarantees to Somnus the lady he desires, Pasithea. Juno, disguised as Ino, goes to Semele; she asks whether Jupiter has consented to Semele's request to join the immortals. Semele replies that she is still mortal, and Juno gives her a mirror in order to admire her own features. Semele gains confidence from what she sees in the mirror and Juno suggests that Semele should use her attractions to make Jupiter approach her bed 'Not . . . In Likeness of a Mortal, but like himself, the mighty Thunderer': by that means, Juno says, Semele will 'partake of immortality' and be called from the mortal state. Juno leaves as she hears Jupiter approach. Jupiter allows himself to be lured into promising to grant whatever Semele requests. When Semele asks him to appear 'like Jove', Jupiter tries to dissuade her, but to no avail. Jupiter knows that if he appears as he really is, Semele will be consumed by his fire. And thus it turns out: Semele sees Jupiter afar in his true form, and dies. The chorus reflects on ambition that overreaches itself. Ino, returned to the world of mortals, relates that in a dream Hermes told Ino that it was Jove's wish that she should now marry Athamas. Athamas enters willingly into the union. A cloud descends on Mount Citheron, in which Apollo is discovered. He predicts that better times lie ahead, and specifically refers to the creation of Bacchus – 'From Semele's ashes a Phoenix shall rise'.

In terms of the dramatic and musical expectations familiar from Handel's operas, the libretto of *Semele* is entirely coherent. However, allowance must be made for the features that are more effective in unstaged performances and which inevitably affect the dramatic pacing. Semele's aria 'The morning lark', for example, is really a concert-room piece: here Handel effectively invites us to forget the onward pressure of the plot and just listen to the music. Similarly, although the choruses are so arranged that they are sung by participants in the drama (priests, zephyrs, and so on), the chorus movements inevitably delay the action: but no musician would want to be deprived of 'Nature to each allots his proper sphere' in any performance of *Semele*. Perhaps because *Semele* sat uneasily with the general tone of Handel's developing oratorio seasons, the composer revived it only briefly in December 1744 after its original run of four performances earlier that year. Modern circumstances provide more flexibility than Handel himself had for choice between staged or unstaged treatments.

RECORDINGS   1. Vyvyan, Watts, Whitworth, Herbert, Lewis, Oiseau-Lyre, 1954; 2. Burrowes, Kwella, Denley, Penrose, Jones, Rolfe Johnson, Davies, Thomas, Lloyd, Monteverdi Choir and English Baroque Soloists, Gardiner, Erato, 1981: the latter is the most complete modern recording with especially fine choruses; there are also some outstanding performances of individual movements on the older recording
EDITION   *HG*, vol. 7

Operas lost or surviving only in fragments: *Nero (Die durch Blut und Mord erlangte Liebe)* (music lost), 1705; *Florindo (Der beglückte Florindo)*, and *Daphne (Der verwandelte Dephne)*, (1706), music partially lost, performed as two operas, 1708; *Genserico (Olibrio)* (inc.), (1728); *Titus l'Empereur* (inc.), (1731)
London pasticcio operas constructed by Handel from his own music: *Oreste*, 1734; *Alessandro Severo*, 1738; *Giove in Argo*, 1739
London pasticcio operas with music by other composers, arr. (with some new composition of recitatives, etc.) Handel: *Elpidia*, 1725; *Ormisda*, 1730; *Venceslao*, 1731; *Lucio Papirio*,

1732; *Catone*, 1732; *Semiramide riconosciuta*, 1733; *Cajo Fabricio*, 1733; *Arbace*, 1734; *Didone abbandonata*, 1737
BIBLIOGRAPHY   Winton Dean, *Handel and the opera seria*, OUP, 1970; Winton Dean and A. Hicks, *The New Grove Handel*, Macmillan, 1982; Winton Dean and J. M. Knapp, *Handel's Operas, 1704–1726*, OUP, 1987; O. E. Deutsch, *Handel, A Documentary Biography*, Black, 1955; rev. with additions, S. Flesch (ed.) in *Händel-Handbuch*, vol. 4, Deutscher Verlag für Musik, 1985; E. T. Harris (ed.), *The Librettos of Handel's Operas*, 13 vols, Garland, 1988–9; Reinhard Strohm, *Essays on Handel and Italian Opera*, CUP, 1985

D.B.

HOWARD HANSON

b 28 October 1896, Wahoo, Nebraska, US; *d* 26 February 1981, Rochester, New York

The first American winner of a Prix de Rome to reside in Rome (1921), Hanson was celebrated as the Director of the Eastman School of Music (1924–64) and as the champion of American nationalism in music, performing and recording a huge repertoire of American music for over 40 years. He composed in a strongly neo-romantic idiom, and in an immediately recognizable personal style drawing (according to the composer) something from Sibelius, Grieg and Respighi. Others have cited Vaughan Williams, and Puritan hymnody as providing elements of his style. He is especially known for choral and orchestral works, including seven symphonies.

The aspiration to write the 'Great American Symphony' and the 'Great American Opera' was a characteristic preoccupation of many American composers in the 1930s. Indisputably it was Hanson who succeeded in the opera house with his New England opera *Merry Mount*.

Merry Mount

Opera in three acts, Op. 31 (2h)
Libretto by R. L. Stokes, after Nathaniel Hawthorne
Composed 1930–33
PREMIERES   20 May 1933, Ann Arbor (concert); 10 February 1934, Metropolitan, New York

Merry Mount portrays the conflict between Puritan and Cavalier colonists in the 17th century. With its sweeping choral writing, modal melodies, brilliant rhythmic Maypole Dances and vivid characteristic orchestration, it made a powerful impression at its first performance, but failed to hold the stage, perhaps partly for managerial reasons at the Met.

RECORDINGS   1. Ljungberg, Swarthout, Johnson, Tibbett, Metropolitan Opera Ch and O, Serafin (original cast), EJS, 1934; 2. excerpts: soloists, Eastman School of Music Ch, Eastman Rochester SO, Hanson, Mercury, n.d.
EDITIONS   f.s., Harms, 1938; v.s., Harms, 1933

BIBLIOGRAPHY   Isaac Goldberg, '*Merry Mount*', *Musical Record*, 1934, pp. 354–7

L.F.

JAN HANUŠ
b 2 May 1915, Prague

A composition pupil of Jeremiáš, Hanuš spent much of his working life in music publishing and administration. Among his stage works he has written three ballets of which the most successful, *Othello* (1956), has been given more than 120 times at the Prague National Theatre. For all his serious side, evident in his first opera, his later works have been based on comic texts such as Goldoni, *One Thousand and One Nights* and Aristophanes.

The Flames
Plameny
Operatic rhapsody in two parts, Op. 14
Libretto by Jaroslav Pokorný, after an idea by the composer
Composed 1944
PREMIERE 8 December 1956, Plzeň

Hanuš's first opera had to wait 12 years for production, but it is perhaps more remarkable that the work was produced at all in Czechoslovakia in the 1950s. Its chief protagonist is a priest experiencing (both in reality and in his imagination) the end of the war and examining the conflicting demands of conscience and patriotism.

RECORDING excerpts: Šeflová, Neaubarthová, Novotný, Hořický, O of the J. K. Tyl Opera in Plzeň, Liška, Supraphon, n.d.

A Servant of Two Masters
Sluha dvou pánů
Opera buffa in five scenes, Op. 42 (1h 45m)
Libretto by Jaroslav Pokorný, after the play by Goldoni
Composed 1958
PREMIERE 18 April 1959, Plzeň

Hanuš's good-natured and briskly paced conversational comedy has continued to make its way as his most popular work, with productions in several Czech opera houses, as well as in Germany and in Yugoslavia (the Slovene premiere was given in 1988).

The Torch of Prometheus
Pochodeň Prométheova
Opera in three acts, Op. 54
Libretto by Jaroslav Pokorný, after Aeschylus
Composed 1961–3
PREMIERE 30 April 1965, National Theatre, Prague

The Prometheus myth is expressed by orchestra and dancers; a modern commentary is added by soloists and chorus, whose different sphere of action is emphasized by the use of electronic music, film and other contemporary elements in the staging. Prometheus himself is an atomic scientist defying not the gods but the rulers of a modern state.

Other operatic works: *A Tale of One Night* (*Pohádka jedné noci*), 1971 (recorded concert); *Dispute about a Goddess* (*Spor o bohyni*), television opera, 1986

BIBLIOGRAPHY Ladislav Šíp, *Česká opera a jeho tvůrci* (*Czech Opera and Its Creators*), Supraphon, 1983

J.T.

JOHN HARBISON
John Harris Harbison; 20 December 1938, Orange, New Jersey, US

Harbison grew up at Princeton, where his father was a professor, and learned to play several instruments. After Harvard, where he won prizes for music and poetry, he studied with Blacher in Berlin and with Sessions and Kim when he returned. His early experience as a jazz pianist and later as a conductor of baroque choral works fused with serial influences characteristic of the Princeton context to create a personal response to texts and dramatic situations in his vocal works. After writing incidental music for *The Merchant of Venice* in 1971 Harbison turned again to Shakespeare for his first libretto, which he devised himself. *A Winter's Tale*, staged by the San Francisco Opera Company in 1979, requires ten singers and a chorus as well as a speaking part and employs mime. The one-act *Full Moon in March*, described by Harbison as an 'emblematic ritual opera', is scored for four singers, dancer, six instruments, percussion and prepared piano. It is based on the play by W. B. Yeats, again to the composer's libretto, and was given by the Boston Musica Viva in 1979. Both works were admired for their imagination and fluency and helped to establish their composer's reputation as one of the leading new romantics of his generation.

BIBLIOGRAPHY B. Morton and P. Collins, *Contemporary Composers*, St James' Press, 1992

P.D.

EDWARD HARPER
b 17 March 1941, Taunton, Somerset, England

Although born in the West Country and educated at Oxford, Harper has played a significant role in Scottish contemporary music, as senior lecturer at Edinburgh University and as founder and director of the New Music Group of Scotland. A pupil of Franco Donatoni, he has moved from a style using serial and aleatory techniques to a more lyrical, tonally based idiom employing the kind of cellular, motivic working implied in the title of his orchestral *Bartók Games* (1972). Other important works include the *Ricerari in Memoriam Luigi Dallapiccola* (1975) for ensemble, a symphony (1979), a clarinet concerto (1982) and a set of double variations for oboe, bassoon and wind ensemble (1989).

Harper's admiration of Thomas Hardy has been expressed in two of his three operas and in the orchestral song-cycle *Hommage to Thomas Hardy* (1990), in which traditional fiddle music is quoted.

Fanny Robin (1975), a one-act chamber opera, is derived from episodes from Hardy's *Far from the Madding Crowd* and *Wessex Tales*. Originally intended as a modern partner for Purcell's *Dido and Aeneas* performed by the Edinburgh University Opera Club, the opera evokes not only the emotional world of Dido's lament, but also the 19th-century landscape of Hardy's characters through its use of English folksong (taken from the Cecil Sharp collection) and the metrical psalms of Sternhold and Hopkins.

Harper's full-length opera *Hedda Gabler* (1985), commissioned by the BBC for Scottish Opera, requires seven soloists, two speaking parts and chorus. Harper retains Ibsen's original dramatic scheme, but adds a prologue to clarify from the beginning the tension between Hedda and her lover Loevborg, and engineers the loss of Loevborg's manuscript through an invented dance scene in Act II. The opera employs a variety of historical musical styles, among which the polka rhythm is used to symbolize Loevborg's dissolute former life.

The Mellstock Quire (1988) returns to Hardy, a story from *Under the Greenwood Tree* that cunningly links in a pastoral romance by means of an ironic flashback. The score calls for taped sounds and serpent.

RECORDING *Fanny Robin*, OUP, 1979
BIBLIOGRAPHY Edward Harper, 'An Ibsen Opera', *MT*, vol. 126 (1985), pp. 334–7

N.W.

TIBOR HARSÁNYI
b 27 June 1898, Magyarkanisza; *d* 19 September 1954, Paris

Hungarian by birth, Harsányi came to Western Europe in the early 1920s, living first in Holland and then, from 1924, in Paris, where he was associated with the loose grouping of composers known as the Ecole de Paris (it also included Martinů, Jean Wiéner, and Conrad Beck). Harsányi was pre-eminently an instrumental composer, and his music is not unlike Martinů's in its influences – jazz, neo-classicism, and the bravura orchestration of Ravel – with something of the more solid and exhuberant energy of Bartók, particularly in his piano-writing.

Harsányi wrote only one opera, *Les invités*, for the stage, though there is also a successful radio opera, *Illusion, ou L'histoire d'un miracle* (based on E. T. A. Hoffmann), which won the Italia Prize in 1948. *Les invités* (1927–8, premiered in 1930) is a period piece with resonances of Krenek's *Jonny spielt auf* and Schoenberg's *Von heute auf morgen*, in which a bored middle-aged couple console themselves by conjuring up more desirable partners (the 'guests' of the title). Harsányi makes sharp use of jazz idioms to satirize the modish futility of his main characters, and there is a clear hint of neo-classicism in the division of the score into separate musical numbers.

BIBLIOGRAPHY John S. Weissmann, 'Tibor Harsányi: A General Survey', *Chesterian*, no. 27 (July 1952), pp. 14–17

S.W.

J. P. E. HARTMANN
Johan Peter Emilius Hartmann; *b* 14 May 1805, Copenhagen; *d* 10 March 1900, Copenhagen

Hartmann pursued a dual career as lawyer (1828–70) and musician. He became assistant organist at Copenhagen Cathedral (1843–1900) and taught at the music academy from 1827 until 1867 when, together with his son-in-law, Niels Gade, he became co-director of the newly founded conservatory. His son Emil (1836–1898) was a notable composer and one of his descendants is Niels Viggo Bentzon (*b* 1919). Hartmann wrote in a variety of forms and tackled everything from symphonies and quartets to part-songs, as well as a ballet, *Valkyrien* (1861). Although not a major figure in his own right, Hartmann's music was much admired by figures as diverse as Spohr and Hans Christian Andersen. His opera *Liden Kirsten*, to a text by Andersen, represents a genuinely Danish voice in music. Aksel Schiøtz recorded *Sverkel's Romance* and the charming *Card Game Duet* in the 1940s.

Operas: *Ravnen, eller Broderprøven* (*The Raven, or The Brother Test*), 1832, rev. 1865; *Korsarerne* (*The Corsairs*), 1835; *Liden Kirsten* (*Little Christina*), 1846, rev. 1858

R.La.

JOHANN ERNST HARTMANN
b 24 December 1726, Gross Glogau (now Głogów, Poland); *d* 21 October 1793, Copenhagen

J. E. Hartmann, a Danish composer and violinist of German ancestry, was the father of a distinguished dynasty which dominated Danish music until the end of the 19th century. In 1754 he joined the orchestra of the Prince-Bishop of Breslau until its dispersal in 1757, and eventually settled in Copenhagen in 1766. As the Copenhagen court orchestra had neither regular concertmaster nor conductor, Hartmann filled both posts until his official appointment in 1768. He introduced Gluck's *Orpheus* and Salieri's *Armida* to Denmark.

Although Hartmann was a prolific composer, much of his music was lost in the Christiansborg Castle fire of 1794. His importance today lies in his singspiels, which survive. The poet Johannes Ewald provided him with libretti based on Norse mythology as well as simple country life. He was principally influenced by Italian opera, the reform works of Gluck and the opéras comiques of Monsigny and Grétry.

Operatic works: *The Death of Balder* (*Balders død*), ?1778/9; *The Fishermen* (*Fiskerne*), 1780; *The Shepherdesses of the*

Alps (*Hyrdinden paa Alpene*) 1783; *Gorm the Elder* (*Gorm den Gamle*), 1785; *The Blind Man of Palmyra* (*Den Blinde i Palmyra*), (unperformed)
BIBLIOGRAPHY   F. Weis, 'The Musical Inheritance of a Danish Family', *Chesterian*, vol. 30 (1956)

N.J.

KARL AMADEUS HARTMANN
b 2 August, 1905, Munich, Germany; *d* 5 December 1963, Munich

Hartmann was primarily a symphonist whose musical roots are to be found in Bruckner and Mahler. He belonged to no school and founded none, developing a unique, neo-classically orientated style. It is significant that the strongest influence on him was exerted by a conductor, Hermann Scherchen, and although he studied privately with Webern, 1941–2, there is little detectable influence of the Second Viennese School. His musical language is founded on a strong sense of form and powerfully expressive gesture.

Simplicius Simplicissimus
Originally *Des Simplicius Simplicissimus Jugend*
The Simplest Simpleton
Chamber opera in three scenes (1h 15m)
Libretto by Hermann Scherchen, Wolfgang Petzet and the composer, after the romance by Grimmelshausen (1668)
Composed 1934–5, rev. 1955
PREMIERES   2 April 1948, Munich (concert); 20 October 1949, Cologne

Grimmelshausen's romance narrates the adventures of Simplicius ('the simpleton') during the Thirty Years War. Hartmann found in this work an ideal vehicle to express his rejection of Nazi dogma and to justify the ten years of 'inner emigration' – a process of silent resistance and withdrawal – to which he subjected himself at a time when serious modern music was effectively outlawed in Germany. 'Our times are so confused, nobody can say whether he will survive them without losing his life,' says Simplicius. Hartmann wrote of his score: 'The music ranges from street ballad to chorale, interpolates songlike structures into a psalmodized recitative and frequently waxes to symphonic dimensions.' The score calls for a medium-sized orchestra with a large percussion section.

The first performance, scheduled for Brussels in 1935, had to be postponed until after the war. A striking piece of epic theatre, the work deserves to be performed more frequently.

EDITION   v.s., Schott, 1957

Other works: *Wachsfigurenkabinett* (five little operas; partly orch. by Bialas, Henze and Hiller), (1929–30), 1988
BIBLIOGRAPHY   Andrew D. McCredie, *Karl Amadeus Hartmann: sein Leben und Werk*, trans. Ken Bartlett, Heinrichshofen Verlag, 1980

A.C.W.B.

JONATHAN HARVEY
Jonathan Dean Harvey; *b* 3 May 1939, Sutton Coldfield, West Midlands, England

Harvey began composing at the age of six. As a student at Cambridge he found many of his contemporaries writing in an atonal style. At first he himself continued in a more traditional vein, but his phenomenal ear and grasp of the possibilities of electronic music have subsequently combined to make him one of the most adventurous figures in late 20th-century music. Between 1975 and 1987, alongside his large-scale avant-garde orchestral and electronic works, such as *Madonna of Winter and Spring* (1986), Harvey completed a number of less complex but innovative compositions for the Church and, in particular, ten works for Winchester Cathedral Choir, including the opera *Passion and Resurrection*. Harvey's second opera, *Inquest of Love* – an early one, *A Full Moon in March* (1966) was withdrawn – was premiered by English National Opera on 5 June 1993. The libretto, by the composer and David Rudkin, describes a couple's experiences of the afterlife after they are shot dead during their wedding service by the bride's elder sister. The complex music, scored for large orchestra including three synthesizers, shows such diverse influences as Wagner's *Parsifal* and Berg's *Wozzeck*.

Passion and Resurrection
Church opera/liturgical drama (1h 15m)
Text: Latin Benedictine church dramas, translated by Michael Wadsworth
Composed 1980
PREMIERE   21 March 1981, Winchester Cathedral

The libretto of this first classical (as opposed to rock) stage setting of the Passion story since the Middle Ages, comes from two monastic plays. The first, from the 12th century, tells the story of the Passion from the scene in Gethsemane to the death of Jesus, and the second (two centuries later) presents the Resurrection. The action grows out of the liturgy, with Jesus himself intoning the words 'Take, eat, this is my body' offstage, in a kind of expanded recitative derived from plainchant. This is the basis of the musical language for all the soloists in the first part. The accompaniment is ingeniously provided by violin harmonics, while each character has his own harmonic 'halo'. The plainsong element also comes out forcefully in two great Passiontide hymns, *Pange lingua* and *Vexilla Regis*, both of which are thrillingly introduced by vivid orchestral preludes (brass, organ, percussion and strings). The audience involvement is here as essential an ingredient as in the chorales in the Bach Passions. After the dark austerity of the Passion music, the mood changes with radiant, dancelike melodies for the three Marys after they have heard from two angels (sung by trebles) that Jesus is risen. The more exuberant music finally subsides after the Ascension, when the chorus picks up its themes aleatorically for the closing benediction. The cast and audience together sing the final 'Amen'.

EDITION   f.s., Faber (on hire), 1980

BIBLIOGRAPHY   Nicholas Soames, 'This Musical Majesty', *Radio Times*, 10–16 April 1982

M.N.

JOHANN ADOLF HASSE

Johann Adolf [Adolph] Hasse; *baptized* 25 March 1699, Bergedorf, nr Hamburg; *d* 16 December 1783, Venice

For more than three decades, from the 1730s, Hasse was a leading exponent of Italian opera throughout Europe. Immensely productive, he composed some 62 traditional opere serie and numerous shorter dramatic pieces. His earliest experience was gained as a tenor singer at Hamburg, and at Brunswick, where he took part in his own first major stage work, *Antioco*. Subsequently he settled in Naples, where he may well have received tuition from Alessandro Scarlatti. It was there, in 1725, that he produced his serenata *Antonio e Cleopatra*, with Carlo Broschi (Farinelli) and Vittoria Tesi in the title roles. Also written in Naples, for the San Bartolomeo theatre, were his first seven opere serie, the seventh of which, *Ezio* (autumn 1730), was his first setting of an unadapted Metastasio libretto. In June 1730, he married the Venetian mezzo-soprano Faustina Bordoni, one of the finest singers of her time, and in the same month became kapellmeister to the court of Friedrich August I at Dresden.

During the 1740s Hasse greatly deepened his appreciation of the classical grace of Metastasio's texts, and thereafter gradually set all of the poet's libretti (with the exception of *Temistocle*), and reset in 'pure' versions such earlier ones as he had previously treated only in altered form. Thus the relationship between the two men, first formed in Vienna in the 1730s, ripened into an artistic alliance comparable in importance to those between Lully and Quinault, or Gluck and Calzabigi.

Also during the 1740s, Hasse first encountered Frederick the Great, who became an ardent admirer of his work, and later invited him to Potsdam as an honoured guest. In June 1760, however, Frederick's bombardment of Dresden resulted in the destruction of the opera theatre, much of the court library, and Hasse's own house, together with many of his manuscripts. Inevitably, the Saxon court was left in straitened circumstances, with its musical activities severely curtailed, and Hasse was forced to leave without a pension. For the next eight years he lived mainly in Vienna, where, during 1773, he is said to have been cast unwillingly as the leader of a conservative faction among the opera public, in opposition to those who supported the reformists Gluck and Calzabigi. Whether or not this is wholly accurate, he must certainly have been deeply aware of the effect that new challenges were having on the traditions he had for so long represented; and late in 1773 he left Vienna for final retirement in Venice. His sole operatic composition during this last period was the aria 'Ah che manca' (added later to the score of *Adriano in Siria*), in which he expressed his sorrow at the death of his wife in November 1781. By the time of his own death, two years later, he was already largely forgotten, even in Italy where his popularity had formerly stood so high.

By comparison with his younger contemporaries, Galuppi and Jommelli, Hasse was stylistically unadventurous. But the Neapolitan type of opera he cultivated, with its precise formal structure and rigid conventions, provided him with an ideal vehicle for his principal objective, the exploitation of *bel canto* aria. The suppleness of his melodic lines, the simplicity of the harmony and the lightness of his orchestral writing all served to throw emphasis on the virtuoso role of the singer, allowing scope for liberal ornamentation. Unusual for the period is the detailed care with which he treated the recitatives; not only are the rhythms and pitch inflexions of speech precisely observed, but keys and cadences are subtly arranged so as to underline the expression of mood and character. For moments of high drama, such as the ghost scene in *Artaserse*, vivid use is made of *recitativo accompagnato*.

Cleofide

(*Alessandro nell'Indie*)
Cleofide (*Alexander in India*)
Opera in three acts (3h 45m)
Libretto by Michelangelo Boccardi, after Pietro Metastasio's *Alessandro nell'Indie* (1729)
PREMIERE   13 September 1731, Hoftheater, Dresden

The work, the first of Hasse's operas for the Dresden court, is a compilation typical of its period. Of its 29 arias only 16 have the original Metastasian texts, the remainder being provided from various sources by Boccardi, and the music for several of them was taken from earlier operas. Also an entirely new mad scene was incorporated by Boccardi, for which the composer provided accompanied recitative of vividly dramatic effect. At the time of the opera's production, Johann Sebastian Bach and his eldest son, Wilhelm Friedemann, were in Dresden, the former to give an organ recital in the Sophienkirche, and it is highly probable that they were present at the premiere.

The story of an Indian king, Poro, defeated by Alexander the Great, but eventually rescued by and united to an Indian queen, Cleofide, was a popular subject set by many composers. Boccardi's text focuses on the role of the queen, but when Hasse revised the work for Venice in 1736, the title was changed to *Alessandro* and, using the whole of Metastasio's text, the emphasis was slightly different.

RECORDING   Kirkby, Mellon, Ragin, Visse, Capella Coloniensis, Christie, Capriccio, 1986
MANUSCRIPT   Sächsische Landesbibliothek, Dresden

Arminio

Arminius
Opera seria in three acts
Libretto by Giovanni Claudio Pasquini
PREMIERE 7 October 1745, Hoftheater, Dresden

This is the second of Hasse's two versions of the Arminius story. The first, written for Milan in 1730, is a setting of a libretto by Antonio Salvi, which was also set by Handel seven years later. Pasquini, who was newly appointed as court poet at Dresden, prepared the later text specifically for Hasse's use. The plot recounts the heroic deeds of the German prince, Arminius (Hermann), as treated originally by Tacitus. The opera thus proved an appropriate choice for performance before Frederick the Great, in celebration of his military successes, the signing of the Treaty of Dresden, and the end of the Second Silesian War.

EDITION v.s., Rudolf Gerber (ed.), *EDM*, vols 27–8, Schott, 1957–66

Solimano

Soliman
Opera in three acts
Libretto by G. A. Migliavacca
PREMIERE 5 February 1753, Court Theatre, Dresden

Solimano, 'the prototype of all later *Türkenopern* by reason of its use of dramatic characterization in place of the purely sensuous charm of the exotic' (P. H. Lang), appears to have been conceived on particularly spectacular lines. Its production was intended to involve 800 persons, horses, camels, elephants, and other exotic livestock.

AUTOGRAPH MANUSCRIPT Conservatorio di Musica Giuseppe Verdi, Milan; copies in British Library, London (without recitatives) and Library of Congress, Washington DC

Piramo e Tisbe

Pyramus and Thisbe
Intermezzo tragico in two acts (1h 30m)
Libretto by Marco Coltellini
PREMIERE November 1768, Burgtheater, Vienna

This work represents Hasse's sole experimental departure from the standard operatic forms of the period, and gives evidence of the influence of Gluck. Certainly, with its tragic theme and well-developed plot, it ranges considerably beyond the limits of the normal intermezzi and serenatas of the period. The setting has only three characters (with both principals sopranos) and contains only one full *da capo* aria out of the nine included. In addition there are four duets and a liberal amount of accompanied recitative. Hasse intended it to be his last composition for the theatre, but at the Empress Maria Theresia's insistence he wrote one further opera, *Il Ruggiero* (1771).

Costume design by Francesco Ponte for Rusteno the Turk in Solimano *(Dresden, 1753)*

AUTOGRAPH MANUSCRIPT Conservatorio di Musica Giuseppe Verdi, Milan; copies in British Library, London (without recitatives) and Library of Congress, Washington DC

Il Ruggiero, ovvero L'eroica gratitudine

Ruggiero, or Heroic Gratitude
Opera seria in three acts (2h 30m)
Libretto by Pietro Metastasio, after the last three books of Ludovico Ariosto's *Orlando furioso* (1516)
PREMIERE 16 October 1771, Teatro Regio Ducale, Milan

Il Ruggiero, the last of Hasse's operas, was written at the request of the Empress Maria Theresia to mark the marriage of the Austrian Archduke Ferdinand and Princess Maria Beatrice d'Este.

Set near Paris in the reign of Charlemagne, the story recounts the fortunes of Bradamante, a warrior maiden of noble descent, and her lover Ruggiero, believed dead. Leone, son of the Emperor Constantine, attempts to win her hand, but she will yield only to the man who overcomes her in single combat. Leone persuades his friend Erminio (Ruggiero in disguise) to undertake the task for him. 'Erminio' wins but, his true identity revealed, renounces Bradamante's hand as promised in favour of Leone, who emulates his friend's 'heroic gratitude' by reuniting the two lovers.

Ruggiero's most forward-looking feature is the replacement, in several of the arias, of the customary *da capo* form by through-composed settings. Metastasio's libretto is unusual in being based on a medieval, rather than a Classical, legend, presumably to give the opera a distinctively 'modernist' image. However, though constructed with the poet's usual finesse, it lacks the scope for grand spectacle that the Milanese audiences of the time craved. Consequently, more widespread interest appears to have been aroused at the time of the opera's premiere by the serenata *Ascanio in Alba* (K. 111) – complete with dances and choruses – by the 15-year-old Mozart, which was premiered the following day. In a letter to his sister (of 2 November 1771) Mozart expressed warm admiration for Hasse's work. Referring to a performance he was compelled to miss, he wrote, 'I fortunately know nearly all the arias by heart and can therefore see and hear it in my head at home.' Hasse, on the other hand, is alleged to have remarked, ruefully and with undoubted prescience, 'This boy will put us all in the shade.'

EDITION f.s., K. Hortschansky (ed.), Concentus Musicus, vol. 1, Arno Volk Verlag, 1973

Other stage works: operas and serenatas: *Antioco*, 1721; *Antonio e Cleopatra*, 1725; *Il Sesostrate*, 1726; *La Semele, o sia La richiesta fatale*, 1726; *L'Astarto*, 1726; *Enea in Caonia*, 1727; *Gerone tiranno di Siracusa*, 1727; *Attalo re di Bittinia*, 1728; *L'Ulderica*, 1729; *La sorella amante*, 1729; *Tigrane*, 1729; *Artaserse*, 1730; *Dalisa*, 1730; *Arminio*, 1730; *Ezio*, 1730; *Catone in Utica*, 1731; *Cajo Fabricio*, 1732; *Demetrio*, 1732; *Euristeo*, 1732; *Issipile*, 1732; *Siroe re di Persia*, 1733 (EDITION facsimile, Garland, 1977); *Sei tu, Lidippe, o il sole*, 1734; *Tito Vespasiano [La clemenza di Tito]*, 1735; *Senocrita*, 1737; *Atalanta*, 1737; *Asteria*, 1737; *Irene*, 1738; *Alfonso*, 1738; *Viriate Siface*, 1739; *Numa Pompilio*, 1741; *Lucio Papiro*, 1742; *Asilio d'amore*, 1742; *Didone abbandonata*, 1742; *Endimione*, 1743; *Antigono*, 1744; *Ipermestra*, 1744; *Semiramide riconosciuta*, 1744; *La Spartana generosa, ovvero Archidamia*, 1747; *Leucippo*, 1747; *Demofoonte*, 1748; *Il natal di Giove*, 1749; *Attilio regolo*, 1750; *Ciro riconosciuto*, 1751; *Adriano in Siria*, 1752; *L'eroe cinese*, 1753; *Artemisia*, 1754; *Il re pastore*, 1755; *L'Olimpiade*, 1756; *Nitteti*, 1758; *Achille in Sciro*, 1759; *Alcide al bivio*, 1760 (EDITION facsimile, Garland, 1983); *Zenobia*, 1761; *Il trionfo di Clelia*, 1762 (EDITION facsimile, Garland, 1981); *Egeria*, 1764; *Romolo ed Ersilia*, 1765; *Partenope*, 1767; 2 lost operas Intermezzi: *Miride e Damari*, 1726; *Larinda e Vanesio*, 1726 (EDITION v.s., Gordana Lazarevich (ed.), *Recent Researches in the Music of the Classical Era*, vol. 9, A-R Editions, 1979); *Grilletta e Porsugnacco*, 1727; *Pantaleone e Carlotta*, 1728; *La finta tedesca*, 1728; *Scintilla e Don Tabarano*, 1728; *Merlina e Galoppo*, 1729; *Dorilla e Balanzone*, 1729; *Lucilla e Pandolfo*, 1730; *Pimpinella e Marcantonio*, 1741; *Rimario e Grilantea*, 1739 or 1741
BIBLIOGRAPHY   Daniel Heartz, 'Hasse, Galuppi and Metastasio', *Venezia e il melodramma nel settecento*, Venice, 1975; Fredrick L. Millner, *The Operas of Johann Adolf Hasse*, Studies in Musicology, vol. 2, UMI Research Press, 1979

B.S.

MATTHIAS HAUER

Josef Matthias Hauer; *b* 19 March 1883, Wiener Neustadt; *d* 22 September 1959, Vienna

An eccentric among 20th-century composers, Hauer sought a music that followed 'the law of the cosmos' and in 1919 devised a technique of composition with the 12 semitones. His system differed from Schoenberg's, which evolved somewhat later, and while the latter saw in his work an unbroken link with earlier generations, Hauer deprecated the music of the past and repudiated tonality. In 1938 his music was proscribed by the Nazis and he was obliged to retire from public life. In post-war Vienna he became a cult figure but remained a recluse whose library consisted only of the *I Ching*.

Hauer's first scenic work, *Wandlungen*, to a text by Hölderlin, is a chamber oratorio for concert or stage performance. It was premiered by Scherchen at the 1928 Baden-Baden Festival and taken up in 1930 by Klemperer, who also conducted the first performance of two scenes from his opera *Salambo*. In *Die schwarze Spinne*, which was not performed until 1966, a dramatically effective libretto (by H. Schlesinger based on a medieval horror story) is matched by a score almost bereft of rhythmic and harmonic variety.

Operatic works: *Wandlungen*, 1928; *Salambo*, (1930), 1983; *Die schwarze Spinne*, (1932), 1966
BIBLIOGRAPHY   W. Szmolyan, *J. M. Hauer*, Verlag Elisabeth Lafite, Österreichischer Bundesverlag, 1965

A.C.W.B.

JOSEPH HAYDN

Franz Joseph Haydn; *b* 31 March 1732, Rohrau; *d* 31 May 1809, Vienna

Although Haydn is best remembered as a composer of symphonies, quartets and oratorios, opera formed a substantial part of his output and from 1776 to 1790 it dominated his life. Haydn's first operatic music was written in the 1750s when he was living in Vienna and earning income from a variety of sources. For a singspiel company based at the Kärntnertortheater he wrote *Der krumme Teufel* and *Der neue krumme Teufel*; the music of both operas is lost. A miscellaneous collection of arias in the Austrian National Library suggests that he also composed individual numbers for the company as required. Haydn seems not to have had any contact with the Burgtheater, whose repertoire at the time was dominated by French opéra comique. His first full-time employment (1759–60) was as kapellmeister to Count Morzin, a position that required the composition of instrumental music only.

Haydn's first extant opera dates from the first years of his employment at the Esterházy court, the richest in the Austrian aristocracy; between 1761 and his death he was to serve four successive Esterházy

Joseph Haydn (c. 1770); engraving by Luigi Schiavonetti after a portrait by Ludwig Guttenbrunn

princes and all but one of Haydn's operas were written for the family. At first they were performed in a theatre in the hall (now Haydnsaal) of Eisenstadt Castle south-east of Vienna, the main residence, but from 1768 onwards the performances took place in Eszterháza, a new summer palace built in the countryside some 22 miles further south-east by the second and most extravagant of Haydn's masters, Prince Nicolaus. There were two theatres. The larger, for Italian opera and plays, held about 400 people with the prince's seats and retiring rooms on the first floor; the orchestra sat, as was the custom, in a double row in front of the stage; and the stage itself was capable of a deep perspective and was fully equipped with stage machinery. The second, smaller theatre, opened in 1773, was devoted mainly to marionette performances. Haydn, as Eszterháza kapellmeister, was responsible for supervising and directing the music at both these theatres. Until 1775 there were occasional performances, but from then on a full-time opera company was based at Eszterháza, their performances alternating with spoken plays given by visiting troupes of actors. Performances were given of works by most of the leading composers of Italian opera: Anfossi, Cimarosa, Gluck, Guglielmi, Paisiello, Piccinni, Sarti and others; the busiest year was 1786 when 125 performances of 17 different operas were given, eight of them for the first time at Eszterháza. In September 1790 Prince Nicolaus Esterházy died and the opera season came to an abrupt end just as performances of Mozart's *Le nozze di Figaro* were being prepared; none of Prince Nicolaus's successors was interested in opera and the theatres at Eszterháza, together with the main house, fell into disuse and later disrepair.

At its zenith, the Esterházy court opera employed some 25 people, singers, designers, administrators, copyists, painters, etc., plus the regular court orchestra of some 15 to 20 players. As a centre for Italian opera north of the Alps it could fairly be said to have vied in importance with London and St Petersburg. But there were certain characteristics that were peculiar to Eszterháza. The first was its isolation. The nearest large city, Vienna, was 40 miles away and it was on the way to nowhere; consequently, the company could not profit from the more aggressive operatic life of the large European cities. Secondly, the resident composer, Haydn, was unusual in that he was not an Italian, nor did he ever visit Italy and, moreover, had very little knowledge of Italian opera when he started. Lastly, the Esterházy court did not employ a resident poet so that Haydn did not have the benefit of working in partnership with a librettist in the way that Galuppi, Gluck and Mozart did. The libretti of Haydn's operas were sometimes 20 or more years old and had already proved popular in settings by other composers. It is not known who chose the operas that were to be performed at the court (no doubt the Prince had the final say) but the two persons who seem to have assisted Haydn in adapting libretti for use at Eszterháza were the tenor Carl Friberth, and the director Nunziato Porta.

Between 1762 and 1783 Haydn composed 16 Italian operas and five German operas. The composer was very proud of his achievement, singling out the operas for special mention in an autobiographical sketch that appeared in 1776 and, apropos *La fedeltà premiata*, writing as follows in a letter to his publisher, Artaria, in 1781: 'I assure you that no such work has been heard in Paris up to now, nor perhaps in Vienna; my misfortune is that I live in the country.' In assessing these two instances of genuine self-esteem it should be borne in mind that Italian opera was the most international of art forms and Haydn was clearly anxious to claim his rightful place as a figure of more than local significance. Gradually, however, Haydn came to realize that the European public was more interested in his instrumental music – symphonies, quartets, piano sonatas and piano trios – and in the 1780s his output became more and more directed towards meeting this demand, composing symphonies for Paris, quartets for various publishers in Vienna and abroad and the *Seven Last Words* (an orchestral work) for Cadiz. This courting of international recognition partly explains why Haydn did not compose any operas for the Esterházy court after 1783. In 1787 it was suggested that Haydn might like to compose a new opera for Prague; the composer refused, noting that 'scarcely any man can brook comparison with the great Mozart'.

Haydn's only extant opera for a theatre outside Eisenstadt and Eszterháza was also to be his last,

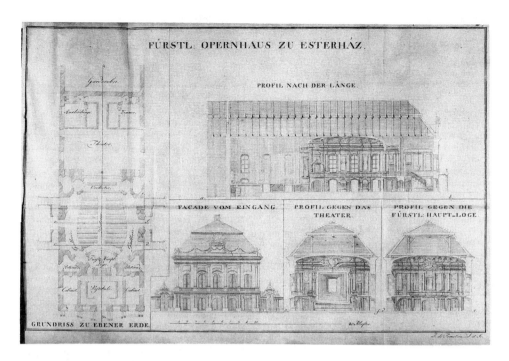

Ground plan and sections of the large theatre at Eszterháza

L'animo del filosofo, ossia Orfeo ed Euridice. Written for London in 1791, it was never performed in the composer's lifetime. During Haydn's last years in Vienna, when the composer's reputation was crowned by the oratorios *The Creation* and *The Seasons*, there was no hint of an operatic project.

Although opera played an insignificant part in his output in the last 25 years of his life, it should not be thought that Haydn's operas lay forgotten in Eszterháza. Some complete works and many extracts were known and distributed widely. For instance, *La fedeltà premiata* and *Orlando Paladino* were performed at several venues in Austria and Germany, usually in German translation; *La vera costanza* formed the basis of an opéra comique called *Laurette* given at the Théâtre Feydeau, Paris, in 1791; and *Armida* was performed in Turin in 1805. Some individual arias were published but the most substantial publication was that of 11 numbers from *L'anima del filosofo* issued, with the composer's co-operation, by Breitkopf und Härtel in 1806.

The modern revival of the composer's operas began with heavily edited performances in German of *La canterina*, *Lo speziale*, *L'infedeltà delusa*, *L'incontro improvviso*, *Il mondo della luna*, *L'isola disabitata* and *Orlando Paladino*, which took place in Austria and Germany between 1895 and 1939. With the development of Haydn scholarship after the Second World War, performances in the original language and in faithful editions began to be given and are now quite frequently encountered, though Haydn has not yet achieved an indisputable place in the centre of the operatic repertoire. Wider

appreciation of the operas has been encouraged by commercial recordings.

Modern evaluation of Haydn as a composer of opera has been conditioned by invidious comparisons with his contemporary Mozart. In general, Haydn's operas certainly lack the psychological insight into human behaviour and the sure-footed pacing of dramatic narrative that characterize Mozart's mature operas. On the other hand, comparison with popular Italian operas of the second half of the 18th century, many of which Haydn himself directed at Eszterháza, yields a more positive appreciation of the composer's talents. As might be expected from a composer whose wider reputation rested – then as now – on instrumental music, the arias frequently have a richness of orchestration, a security of structure and an individuality of melodic and, especially, harmonic content that are rare in operas by his Italian contemporaries. The influence of Gluck's reform operas is sometimes apparent, particularly in the two serious operas, *L'isola disabitata* and *Armida*, where extensive use of accompanied recitative coalescing into aria provides a continuity absent from number opera. Equally important for dramatic continuity is Haydn's interest in building his act finales into long sequences (up to ten consecutive sections) linked by their key structure, providing a powerful sense of mounting excitement.

Hob. numbers refer to A. von Hoboken, *Joseph Haydn: Thematisch-bibliographisches Werkverzeichnis*, vol. 2: *Vokalwerke*, Henle Verlag, 1957–71

La canterina
The Songstress
Intermezzo in musica in two acts, Hob. XXVIII:2 (1h)
Text from an intermezzo in Piccinni's *L'Orgille* (1760)
Composed 1766
PREMIERES   July 1766, Eisenstadt; US: 30 December 1940, Cleveland, Ohio (as *The Songstress*)

La canterina, Haydn's first extant comic opera for the Esterházy court, was probably performed in Eisenstadt Castle. Don Pelagio, a singing teacher, and Don Ettore vie for the attention of Gasparina. Confusion and intrigue lead to Gasparina and her mother being evicted from their house. Gasparina is eventually forgiven and everybody sings of their relief that this silly sequence of events is over. Of the six vocal pieces the accompanied recitative 'Che mai far deggio?' is an amusing take-off of a singing lesson and Gasparina's 'Non v'è chi mi aiuta' a stirring aria in C minor, an idiom more familiar from Haydn's symphonies in the minor key.

RECORDING   Brooks, Valente, Burgess, Humphrey, unnamed O, Schneider, MRF, 1967
EDITION   f.s., D. Bartha (ed.), *Joseph Haydn Werke* XXV/2, Henle, 1959

Lo speziale
The Apothecary
Dramma giocoso in three acts, Hob. XXVIII:3 (fragments: 2h 30m)
Libretto by Carlo Goldoni (1752), amended by Carl Friberth
PREMIERES   28 September 1768, Eszterháza; UK: 3 September 1925, King's Theatre, Hammersmith, London; US: 16 March 1926, Neighborhood Playhouse, New York

Haydn's first opera for the new theatre at Eszterháza. The composer's music for Act III Scenes 1–3 and the beginning of Scene 4 is missing. For modern performance the easiest option is to use the earlier setting (1754) of Goldoni's text by Domenico Fischietti.

RECORDING   Kalmár, Kincses, Fülöp, Rozsos, Ferenc Liszt CO, Lehel, Hungaroton, 1978
EDITION   f.s., H. Wirth (ed.), *Joseph Haydn Werke* XXV/3, Henle, 1959

Le pescatrici
The Fisherwomen
Dramma giocoso in three acts, Hob. XXVIII:4 (2h 30m)
Libretto by Carlo Goldoni (1751), ?amended by Carl Friberth
Composed 1769
PREMIERES   16 September 1770, Eszterháza; UK: 1965, Edinburgh

The first known performance was given as part of the celebrations accompanying the marriage of Countess Lamberg (Prince Nicolaus's niece) and Count Pocci. Several numbers in Act I and II are either entirely or partially lost.

EDITION   f.s., D. Bartha (ed.), *Joseph Haydn Werke* XXV/4, Henle, 1972

L'infedeltà delusa
Deceit Outwitted
Burletta per musica in two acts, Hob. XXVIII:5 (2h 15m)
Libretto by Marco Coltellini, amended by Carl Friberth
Composed 1773
PREMIERES   26 July 1773, Eszterháza; UK: 14 October 1960, Royal Festival Hall, London (concert; Haydn Opera Society); 18 March 1964, St Pancras Town Hall, London

The opera was written to be performed on the name day of Princess Maria Anna Louise Esterházy, widow of Prince Paul Anton, Haydn's first Esterházy patron. The performance in the Eszterháza theatre was followed by a masked ball and, on the following day, a firework display. A month later the Empress Maria Theresia made her first and only visit to the Esterházy court. *L'infedeltà delusa* was performed on the first night of the visit (31 August) and the marionette opera, *Philemon und Baucis*, on the second night. The success of the visit prompted Maria Theresa's later remark, 'If I want to hear good opera, I go to Eszterháza', an indication of the high standards in the Esterházy court in comparison with those in Viennese theatre at the time. After 1774, no further performances of *L'infedeltà delusa* are known in Haydn's lifetime.

Vespina wishes to marry Nencio, and Nanni wishes to marry Sandrina. But Sandrina's father (Filippo) thinks Nencio would make a better match for his daughter. To this end, he persuades Nencio to serenade his daughter. Sandrina spurns him and the spying Vespina strikes him. In Act II Vespina, in a series of disguises (a limping old woman, a German servant, the Marquis of Ripafratta and a notary), engineers the action so that Filippo is forced to accept the marriage of Sandrina and Nanni, and Vespina gets her man, Nencio.

The wily, yet sympathetic character of Vespina, a proto-Despina, is well caught in a series of arias in Act II. The innocent victim of the intrigue, Sandrina, is similarly well characterized, especially in the aria sung before the *dénouement*, 'È la pompa un grand'imbroglio'. The three ensembles, placed at the beginning and end of Act I and at the end of Act II, provide a broad framework for a charming narrative that unfolds through recitative (almost entirely *secco*) and aria.

RECORDINGS   1. Kalmár, Pászthy, Rozsos, Fülöp, Gregor, Ferenc Liszt CO, Sándor, Hungaroton, 1976: recorded in the Eszterháza Palace; 2. Mathis, Hendricks, Ahnsjö, Baldin, Devlin, Lausanne CO, Dorati, Philips, 1981; 3. Argenta, Lootens, Prégardien, Schäfer, Varcoe, La Petite Bande, Kuijken, Deutsche Harmonia Mundi/BMG, 1994
EDITIONS   f.s., D. Bartha and J. Vécsey, *Joseph Haydn Werke* XXV/5, Henle, 1964; v.s., H. C. Robbins Landon (ed.), Haydn Mozart Presse, 1961

Philemon und Baucis, oder Jupiters Reise auf die Erde
Philemon and Baucis, or Jupiter's Journey to Earth
Marionette opera in one act, Hob. XXIXa:1, rev. as singspiel in one act, Hob. XXVIXb:2 (1h)
Libretto after the play by Gottlieb Konrad Pfeffel (1763)
PREMIERES   2 September 1773, Eszterháza; second version:

1780, Regensburg; UK: 1950, King's Lynn; US: 3 October 1975, Baird Auditorium, Washington DC

The marionette opera (now lost) was preceded in the 1773 performance by *Der Götterrath* (Hob XXIXb:2) of which only the first number survives. *Philemon und Baucis* recounts the visit of Jupiter and Mercury to earth where they bring back to life Aret and Narcissa. The score of the singspiel version consists of 13 numbers; two are taken from Gluck's opera *Paride ed Elena* (1770) and one from Ordonez's marionette opera *Alceste* (1775).

RECORDING Naidic, Roon, Majkut, Kmentt, Vienna State Opera Ch, Vienna SO, Zallinger, Vox, 1951
EDITION f.s., J. Braun (ed.), *Joseph Haydn Werke* XXIV/1, Henle, 1971

L'incontro improvviso

The Unforeseen Encounter
Dramma giocoso in three acts, Hob. XXVIII:6 (2h 45m)
Libretto translated and adapted by Carl Friberth from L. H. Dancourt's libretto to Gluck's *La rencontre imprévue* (1764)
Composed 1775
PREMIERES 29 August 1775, Eszterháza; UK: 23 March 1966, St Pancras Town Hall, London (Handel Opera Society)

L'incontro improvviso was Haydn's largest and most ambitious opera to date. It was first performed as part of the lavish, four-day celebrations that marked the visit of Archduke Ferdinand and other members of the imperial court to Eszterháza in August 1775. (As well as Haydn's opera, two German plays and Ordonez's marionette opera, *Alceste*, were given.) There are 11 characters compared with, for example, the five found in *L'infedeltà delusa*, and the oriental setting encouraged appropriately lavish costumes and scenery.

Like many 'Turkish' operas of the 18th century the plot deals with imprisonment, rescue and clemency, all enlivened by broad comic interest – indeed, the plot has much in common with Mozart's *Die Entführung* (1782). Princess Rezia has been captured by the Sultan. Prince Ali, her lover, and a servant, Osmin, set out to rescue her. After many scrapes they gain the confidence of two ladies-in-waiting and some dervishes and plan their escape. The Sultan thwarts their plans and threatens vengeance but finally pardons everybody in an enlightened gesture of magnanimity.

The comic invention of the plot is enlivened by the customary 'Turkish' music with bass drum, cymbals and triangle and, in particular, by the attempts of the dervishes to teach Prince Ali's servant, Osmin, their strange music (Act I). Some numbers are very long, sometimes threatening the continuity of the drama. But Prince Ali's 'Il guerrier con armi avvolto' (Act II) is a splendid *aria di guerra* and the trio in Act I for Rezia and the two female slaves, Balkis and Dardane, 'Mi sembra un sogno, che diletta', is a lavish *andantino* featuring two cors anglais, one of Haydn's favourite alternative tone colours at this time.

RECORDING Zoghby, Marshall, Jones, Ahnsjö, Luxon, Trimarchi, Lausanne CO, Dorati, Philips, 1980
EDITION f.s., H. Wirth (ed.), *Joseph Haydn Werke* XXV/6, Henle, 1962

Die Feuersbrunst

The Conflagration
Singspiel in two acts, Hob. XXIXb:A (1h 15m)
Composed *c.* 1775–8
PREMIERE 18 July 1963, Bregenz Festival; US: 14 May 1963, Yale University, New Haven, Connecticut; UK: 1966, Collegiate Theatre, London

Haydn is known to have written a marionette opera entitled, in summary form in the composer's own catalogue, 'opera comique vom abgebrannten Haus' (Hob. XXIXa:4). This work is lost and it is a matter of scholarly dispute whether *Die Feuersbrunst* is a later singspiel version of this opera or an entirely different work by another, unknown composer.

EDITION f.s., Günther Thomas (ed.), *Joseph Haydn Werke* XXIV/3, Henle, 1990; v.s., H. C. Robbins Landon (ed.), Schott, 1963

Il mondo della luna

The World on the Moon
Dramma giocoso in three acts, Hob. XXVIII:7 (2h 45m)
Libretto by Carlo Goldoni
Composed 1777
PREMIERES 3 August 1777, Eszterháza; US: 7 June 1949, Greenwich Mews Playhouse, New York; UK: 8 November 1951, Scala Theatre, London (inc.; London Opera Club); authentic version: 22 March 1960, St Pancras Town Hall, London (Group Eight Productions)
CAST Ecclitico *t*, Ernesto *a*, Bonafede *b*, Clarice *s*, Flamina *s*, Lisetta *a*, Cecco *t*; 4 students of Ecclitico 4 *b*; scholars, knights, dancers, pages, servants, soldiers, followers of Ecclitico

Goldoni's text was one of his most popular, first set by Galuppi in 1750 and then by Avondano (1765), Paisiello (1774, as *Il credulo deluso*, and 1782) and Astarita (1775). The role of Ecclitico in the Astarita version was taken by Guglielmo Jermoli who from March to July 1777 was a member of the opera company at Eszterháza; he may well have suggested the libretto to Haydn. The opera was first performed as part of the celebrations accompanying the marriage of Count Nicolaus, second son of Prince Nicolaus I, and Countess Maria Anna Weissenwolf. The opera was evidently only a moderate success for it was not repeated in subsequent seasons at Eszterháza and no contemporary performances outside the court are known.

SYNOPSIS
The libretto is a delightful puncturing of the omniscience of the Age of Reason.

Act I Ecclitico and his students are observing the moon, eager to establish the presence of human life there. The ill-humoured Bonafede ('Good faith') is persuaded by them that a better life exists on the moon. Ernesto, a knight, and his servant Cecco enter, and it emerges that Ernesto and Ecclitico are in love with Bonafede's daughters, Flamina and Clarice, and

Cecco with Lisetta, the maid. Ecclitico convinces them that Bonafede can be tricked into allowing a triple marriage. Bonafede takes a potion which he is told will transport him to the moon. He bids everyone farewell: his daughters imagine that he is dying but are placated by the reading of a forged will leaving them a handsome dowry.

Act II In Ecclitico's garden, disguised as the moon, Bonafede wakes to the sound and sight of dancing and is prepared for his meeting with the emperor of the moon (Cecco in disguise). The old man, now rather a forlorn figure, woos Lisetta, who spurns him; she is about to be crowned the queen of the lunatics. Bonafede is duped into sanctioning the marriage of his two daughters. When he discovers the deceit everyone asks his forgiveness.

Act III In Ecclitico's house Bonafede agrees to forgive everyone and the triple marriage is sanctioned. Ecclitico announces that he is giving up astrology and everyone commends the good fortune that the world of the moon has brought.

The work is a typical dramma giocoso in that the characters are divided into three groups: the parti buffe are Bonafede, Lisetta and Cecco; the parti serie are Flamina and Ernesto; and the intermediate group, the parti di mezzo carattere, include Clarice and Ecclitico. Haydn's music resourcefully highlights these divisions, particularly in the three Act I arias for the female characters. Bonafede's aria in Act II ('Che mondo amabile') engages the sympathy of the listener as the old man describes his happiness (including whistling in imitation of birds) in the make-believe world of the moon.

Haydn reused many numbers from this opera in later works: the C major overture became the first movement of Symphony No. 63 ('La Roxelane'); Ernesto's aria ('Qualche volte non fa male') the Benedictus of the *Missa Cellensis* (1782), and other movements are included in the six trios for two violins (or flute and violin) and cello (Hob. IV:6–11, 1784).

RECORDING   Auger, Mathis, von Stade, Valentini Terrani, Alva, Rolfe Johnson, Trimarchi, Lausanne CO, Dorati, Philips, 1978
EDITION   f.s., G. Thomas (ed.), *Joseph Haydn Werke* XXV/7, Henle, 1979

La vera costanza

True Constancy
Dramma giocoso per musica in three acts, Hob. XXVIII:8 (2h)
Libretto by Francesco Puttini, written for Anfossi in 1775
Composed 1777–8, rev. 1785
PREMIERES   25 April 1779, Eszterháza; rev. version: April 1785, Eszterháza; US: 1980, Katonah, New York; UK: 5 March 1986, Royal College of Music, London

According to Dies, one of Haydn's first biographers, this opera was commissioned by Joseph II for performance in Vienna. Since there is no documentary evidence to support this statement many people have doubted its veracity. However, modern scholarship has also suggested that Haydn was indeed

commissioned to write an Italian opera by Joseph II, but that he composed only half of it because the Emperor became engrossed in the founding of the National Singspiel; Haydn then completed the work for performance in Eszterháza.

The true constancy of the title is that of the fishermaid, Rosina, who is secretly married to Count Errico, by whom she has a son. This fidelity is tested by Baroness Irene, Villoto and even Rosina's husband, all of whom plot at one stage to murder her. She and her son escape and it is only at the pathetic moment of her rescue from starvation that humanity's better nature triumphs and Rosina and the Count are reunited.

Rosina's music in Act II is strongly characterized, and the section in the finale when the boy (a spoken part) leads the rescuers to his mother is 18th-century sensibility at its most affecting. The 'chain' finales to Acts I and II are the most extensive to date in Haydn's operas, accounting for approximately a quarter and a third of their respective acts.

RECORDING   Norman, Donath, Lövaas, Ahnsjö, Rolfe Johnson, Trimarchi, Ganzarolli, Lausanne CO, Dorati, Philips, 1977
EDITION   f.s., H. Walter (ed.), *Joseph Haydn Werke* XXV/8, Henle, 1976

L'isola disabitata

The Deserted Island
Azione teatrale in two parts, Hob. XXVIII:9 (1h 30m)
Libretto by Pietro Metastasio for the azione teatrale (Vienna, 1753) by Giuseppe Giovanni Battista Bonno
Composed 1779
PREMIERES   6 December 1779, Eszterháza; US: 9 March 1936, Library of Congress, Washington; Ireland: 21 October 1982, Theatre Royal, Wexford

This was Haydn's first serious opera for almost seventeen years (since *Acide*) and his only complete setting of a Metastasio text. It was first performed on the name day of Prince Nicolaus, and because the Eszterháza opera house had been destroyed by fire the previous month the performance took place in the palace, possibly without scenery.

Two sisters, Costanza and Silvia, are shipwrecked on a desert island and after three years of solitude are rescued by their husband and lover, respectively. In Haydn's operatic output the work is notable for the fact that all the recitatives are accompanied by the orchestra, perhaps showing the influence of another azione teatrale, Gluck's *Orfeo*, which Haydn had directed in 1776. There is a good deal of music in slow tempo and Haydn, in later years, remarked that the work needed to be shortened.

RECORDING   Zoghby, Lerer, Alva, Bruson, Lausanne CO, Dorati, Philips, 1978
EDITION   f.s., H. C. Robbins Landon (ed.), Bärenreiter, 1976

La fedeltà premiata

Fidelity Rewarded
Dramma giocoso in three acts, Hob. XXVIII:10 (first version: 3h 15m; second version: 2h 45m)

Libretto adapted by Haydn and an unknown person from Giambattista Lorenzi's text for Cimarosa's *L'infedeltà fedele* (Naples, 1779)
Composed 1780; rev. 1782
PREMIERES 25 February 1781, Eszterháza; rev. version: September 1782, Eszterháza; UK: 27 April 1971, Collegiate Theatre, London
CAST Celia *s*, Fileno *t*, Amaranta *s*, Count Perrucchetto *b*, Nerina *s*, Lindoro *t*, Melibeo *b*, Diana *s*; *satb* chorus of nymphs and shepherds, hunters and huntresses, followers of Diana; dancers: shepherds, shepherdesses and satyrs

The opera was written for the reopening of the large opera house in Eszterháza, following its destruction by fire in November 1779, and revised for the 1782 season. It received 36 performances at Eszterháza in the 1780s and, translated into German, several in the Kärntnertortheater Vienna and in Pressburg.

In the 1782 libretto the genre title was modified to dramma pastorale giocoso, an indication of the setting of the opera: woodland, a grotto, rugged rocks and a distant lake, a scene populated by nymphs, shepherds and hunters. The story is of steadfastness eventually rewarded; fidelity (of Celia and Fileno) is contrasted with more fickle relationships (among Lindoro, Nerina, Amaranta, Melibeo and Perrucchetto).

SYNOPSIS

Act I A loving couple must be sacrificed to placate the sea monster. Amaranta and Melibeo connive to arrange the marriage of Lindoro and Celia, and Fileno is duped into assisting Nerina. Fileno and Celia meet, but realizing that they risk sacrifice they part. In the finale Amaranta, Lindoro and Melibeo persist in bullying Celia to marry Lindoro; Fileno's sadness turns to despair when he hears of these plans; suddenly, satyrs enter and save Celia.

Act II Fileno's despair leads him to contemplate suicide. Celia believes that Fileno is dead. Melibeo has now decided that the sacrificed couple should be Celia and Perrucchetto and the finale prepares for the fateful moment.

Act III Celia and Fileno are reunited but cannot see a just way of appeasing the sea god. At the moment of sacrifice, Fileno throws himself at the sea monster; it turns into a grotto revealing the goddess Diana. She resolves the action by sanctioning the marriage of Fileno and Celia, and of Perrucchetto and Amaranta. General rejoicing.

The overture was reused as the finale to Symphony No. 73. Celia's recitative and aria in Act II, 'Ah come il core/Ombra del caro bene', was published in Vienna and London as a cantata and was performed in Haydn's benefit concert on 16 May 1791 in the Hanover Square Rooms. This scena and others in Act II for Fileno and Amaranta are some of the highlights of the opera. Even more noteworthy are the 'chain' finales to Acts I and II, both propelled by a sequence of keys featuring a third relationship and forming a sustained drama that shows Haydn at his best in opera.

RECORDINGS 1. Cotrubas, Lövaas, von Stade, Valentini

Terrani, Alva, Landy, Titus, Mazzieri, Lausanne CO, Dorati, Philips, 1976; 2. Zempléni, Tokody, Kincses, Pászthy, Rozsos, Fülöp, Vághelyi, Gregor, Ferenc Liszt CO, Sándor, Hungaroton, 1977: recorded in Eszterháza Palace.
EDITIONS f.s., G. Thomas (ed.), *Joseph Haydn Werke* XXV/10, Henle, 1968; v.s., H. C. Robbins Landon (ed.), Haydn–Mozart Presse, 1970

Orlando Paladino
Knight Roland

Dramma eroicomico in three acts, Hob. XXVIII:11 (2h 45m)
Libretto by Nunziato Porta, after his own revision of Carlo Francesco Badini's *Le pazzie d'Orlando* written for Pietro Alessandro Guglielmi (London, 1771)
Composed 1782
PREMIERES 6 December 1782, Eszterháza; UK: 14 July 1988, St John's Smith Square, London (concert); 22 June 1990, Garsington Manor, Oxford

Pietro Travaglia's set design for Orlando Paladino *(Eszterháza, 1782)*

Porta was engaged from July 1781 as Director of the Opera at Eszterháza and he proposed the libretto for *Orlando Paladino*. The love of Angelica and Medoro is threatened by two errant knights, Orlando and Rodomonte, and protected by the timely interventions of the sorceress Alcina. Orlando is purged of all aggressive behaviour and the opera ends with the assembled cast declaiming the healing power of love.

As was typical of the dramma-giocoso genre (of which this is a subspecies) the serious-minded action of the higher ranks of society is contrasted with the more comic and human behaviour of Eurilla (a shepherdess) and Pasquale (Orlando's squire). In extravagant boasting the latter outdoes Mozart's Leporello, with two catalogue arias, the first recounting his endless travelling and the second his musical abilities; he also has a robust aria in C major of a type frequently encountered in Haydn's operas. The eponymous figure of Orlando is much talked about but appears too late in the first two acts to make any strong impact; his music, however, is unfailingly attractive, especially the Act III accompanied recitative and aria depicting the awakening of the knight from a long magic sleep. The opera ends with a vaudeville, a rondo-like structure in which the assembled cast declaims the moral for the main theme and the individual characters present their own viewpoint in the episodes. *Orlando Paladino*, Haydn's last comic opera, was the composer's most popular opera in his lifetime with documented performances in 20 towns in central Europe, usually in German translation.

RECORDING   Auger, Ameling, Killebrew, Shirley, Ahnsjö, Carelli, Luxon, Trimarchi, Mazzieri, Lausanne CO, Dorati, Philips, 1977
EDITION   f.s., K. Geiringer (ed.), *Joseph Haydn Werke* XXV/11, Henle, 1972

Armida

Dramma eroico in three acts, Hob. XXVIII:12 (2h 15m)
Libretto (after Torquato Tasso's *Gerusalemme liberata* (1575)) taken from Antonio Tozzi's opera *Rinaldo*; slightly amended by Nunziato Porta
Composed 1783
PREMIERES   26 February 1784, Eszterháza; UK: 21 July 1988, Opera House, Buxton

This was Haydn's last Eszterháza opera and it was the most frequently performed in the court theatre (there were 54 performances). It is part of a distinct trend towards featuring more opera seria in the Eszterháza repertoire in the 1780s.

The opera is set at the time of the Crusades and its theme is the superior call of duty on behalf of Christendom over the sweet voice of love. The person caught in this dilemma is Rinaldo (a former crusading knight) who is loved by Armida (a sorceress) and reminded of his calling by Ubaldo (a knight). Love seems to triumph but Armida's affection turns to hatred and the opera ends with the participants pondering their fate against the ironic background of martial music.

In Acts II and III several consecutive numbers run into one another providing dramatic continuity. The vocal writing is more virtuosic than in Haydn's previous operas and there are two splendid military arias in C major. In Act III, there is a vivid musical evocation of natural objects and phenomena – a notable foretelling of the composer's oratorios, *The Creation* and *The Seasons*.

RECORDING   Norman, Burrowes, Ahnsjö, Rolfe Johnson, Leggate, Ramey, Lausanne CO, Dorati, Philips, 1979
EDITION   f.s., W. Pfannkuch (ed.), *Joseph Haydn Werke* XXV/12, Henle, 1965

L'anima del filosofo, ossia Orfeo ed Euridice

The Spirit of Philosophy, or Orpheus and Euridice
Dramma per musica in four acts, Hob. XXVIII:13 (2h 15m)
Libretto by Carlo Francesco Badini after Ovid's *Metamorphoses*, Books IX and X
Composed 1791
PREMIERES   9 June 1951, Teatro della Pergola, Florence; UK: 25 May 1989, St John's, Smith Square, London (concert)

This opera was written in London. It was commissioned by John Gallini and was to have been performed at the newly opened King's Theatre in the Haymarket in 1791, but operatic and political intrigue conspired to deny Gallini the necessary licence and Haydn's opera was not performed. There

was possibly to have been a fifth act in which the lamenting Orfeo would have been taken to heaven and healed by the power of music, an appropriate sentiment for the newly opened theatre. The four completed acts make striking use of the chorus. The work received its premiere at the Florence Maggio Musicale in 1951 under the direction of Erich Kleiber, with a cast including Maria Callas and Boris Christoff.

RECORDINGS   1. Hellwig, Heusser, Handt, Poell, Berry, Vienna State Opera Ch and O, Swarowsky, Nixa, 1950; 2. Schmiege, Prégardien, McFadden, Schwarz, Netherlands Chamber Ch, La Stagione, Schneider, Deutsche Harmonia Mundi, 1992
EDITION   f.s., H. Wirth (ed.), *Joseph Haydn Werke* XXV/13, Henle, 1974

Other operas: *Acide* (inc.) 1763, rev. 1773; *La Marchesa Nespola*, 1763; *Die reisende Ceres* (doubtful), c. 1770; *Der Gütterrath*, 1773
Lost operas: *Der krumme Teufel*, 1751; *Der neue krumme Teufel*, c. 1758; *Il dottore*, c. 1761–5; *La vedova*, c. 1761–5; *Il scanarello*, c. 1761–5; *Hexenschabbas*, ?1773; *Dido*, 1776; *Genovevens vierter Theil*, 1777; *Die bestrafte Rachbegierde*, ?1779
BIBLIOGRAPHY   Dénes Bartha and László Somfai, *Haydn als Opernkapellmeister*, Verlag der Ungarischen Akademie der Wissenschaften, 1960; Mátyás Horányi, *The Magnificence of Eszterháza*, Hungarian Academy of Sciences/Barrie and Rockliff, 1962; H. C. Robbins Landon, *Haydn: Chronicle and Works*, 5 vols, Thames and Hudson, 1976–80; H. C. Robbins Landon and David Wyn Jones, *Haydn, His Life and Music*, Thames and Hudson, 1988

D.W.J.

MICHAEL HAYDN

Johann Michael Haydn; *b* ?10 September 1737, Rohrau; *d* 10 August 1806, Salzburg

Michael Haydn followed his now more famous elder brother, Joseph, to the cathedral school at St Stephen's, Vienna, where he was recognized as being the more talented singer of the two. In 1757, at the age of 20, he was appointed kapellmeister to the Bishop of Grosswardein in Hungary. In 1762 he entered the service of Archbishop Sigismund Schrattenbach in Salzburg, where he remained for the rest of his life. He was a close friend of both Leopold and Wolfgang Mozart and there are many complimentary references to Michael's abilities as a composer in the Mozart family correspondence. Michael Haydn's principal output consisted of church music, a genre in which he was more highly regarded than his brother, and over 40 symphonies. His many pupils included Diabelli and Weber.

His operas were all written in Salzburg and, with the exception of one opera seria, *Andromeda e Perseo*, and a serenata on a text by Metastasio, *L'Endimione*, are singspiels. For the university theatre Haydn wrote several short comic operas which were performed as intermezzi or afterpieces, to provide contrast with the main sacred work (usually a spoken drama). In the theatre at the

Residenz Haydn's oratorios were frequently given with costume and scenery. Even though a new public theatre featuring spoken drama and Italian opera was opened at the court in 1775, Haydn, like Mozart, composed little music for it.

Surviving operatic works: *Eliezer, oder Rebekka als Braut*, 1766; *Die Hochzeit auf der Alm*, 1768 and *c.* 1776; *Die Wahrheit der Natur*, 1769; *Hermann, ein Beyspiel der Liebe zum Vaterlande*, 1773; *Der Bassgeiger zu Wörgl*, *c.* 1773–5; *Endimione*, ?1775–6; *Abels Tod*, ?1778; *Der englische Patriot*, ?*c.* 1778–80; *Andromeda e Perseo*, 1787; *Die Ährenleserin von Weisse*, 1788

BIBLIOGRAPHY   Gerhard Croll and Kurt Vössing, *Johann Michael Haydn. Sein Leben – sein Schaffen – seine Zeit*, Paul Neff Verlag, 1987; Johanna Senigl, 'Johann Michael Haydn: Kompositionen für Salzburger Bühnen. Ein erster überblick', *Mozart-Jahrbuch* (1987/88), pp. 85–9

D.W.J.

JOHANN DAVID HEINICHEN

b 17 April 1683, Krössuln, nr Weissenfels; *d* 16 July 1729, Dresden

Heinichen wrote operas during his early years in Weissenfels and Leipzig, between 1710 and 1716 in Italy, primarily in Venice, and after 1717 one opera only for Dresden where he became kapellmeister to the court of August the Strong. He came into contact with several important composers: in Leipzig with Kuhnau, his teacher, and with Keiser, and in Italy with Gasparini, Pollaroli, Lotti, and Vivaldi. Two operas commissioned for the Sant' Angelo theatre in Venice, *Mario*, and *Le passioni per troppo amore*, brought Heinichen considerable fame during the Carnival season of 1713. *Mario* was brought to the Hamburg opera in 1716 under the title of *Calpurnia, oder Die römische Grossmut*.

Heinichen's musical style exhibits the prevailing tendency in the 18th century towards a confluence of German, French, and Italian elements, developed in a lighter texture with little contrapuntal complexity – frequently characterized as 'pre-classic'. His place in music history is the result of his thorough-bass treatise, *Der General-Bass in der Composition* (1728), which codifies methods of playing a continuo part according to contemporary practices, especially those found in 18th-century Italian opera houses. It includes instruction on accompanying operatic recitatives and also on how to compose music to less inspired operatic texts.

Surviving operas: *Le passioni per troppo amore*, 1713; *Mario*, 1713, trans. as *Calpurnia, oder Die römische Grossmut*, 1716; *Flavio Crispo* (inc.), (1720)
Arias survive for: *Der Karneval von Venedig, oder Der angenehme Betrug*, 1705; *Hercules*, *c.* 1709; *Olympia vendicata*, 1709; one opera and one collaboration lost
BIBLIOGRAPHY   G. J. Buelow, *Thorough-Bass Accompaniment According to Johann David Heinichen*, UMI Research Press, 3rd edn, 1992; G. Seibel, *Das Leben des*

königl. polnischen und kurfürstl. sächs. Hofkapellmeister Johann David Heinichen, Breitkopf und Härtel, 1913

G.J.B.

PETER HEISE

Peter Arnold Heise; *b* 11 February 1830, Copenhagen; *d* 12 September 1879, Stockkerup, Denmark

Peter Heise wrote no fewer than 200 songs in his relatively short life. He studied first with Niels Gade and then in Leipzig, before settling in Sorö as a teacher. Heise's music was conditioned by the school of Mendelssohn, Gade and Schumann, and he remained relatively indifferent to such modernists as Wagner and Tchaikovsky. He operated within the conservative Scandinavian tradition and yet there is something distinctly Danish, almost prophetic of Nielsen, who knew and indeed took part in performances of *Drot og Marsk*.

Drot og Marsk
King and Marshal
Opera in four acts (3h)
Libretto by Christian Richardt after Carsten Hauch
PREMIERE   25 September 1878, Royal Theatre, Copenhagen

Heise made many settings of A. E. Oehlenschläger, one of the Golden Age poets and dramatists, whose play *Erik Glipping* (1843) inspired *Drot og Marsk*. It deals with an incident in Danish history, the murder of King Erik V in 1286, which fascinated writers in much the same way as did the assassination of Gustav III in Sweden. The librettist made the king a Don Juan figure whose seduction of the marshal's wife becomes his downfall. The fresh diatonic flavour is outgoing with little of the introspective chromaticism encountered in the contemporary Weimar school.

RECORDING   I. Nielsen, Graener, Jensen, Landy, Hansen, Danish Radio SO, Frandsen, Unicorn, 1981
EDITION   v.s., C. C. Loses Bog-og Musikhandel, 1879

Singspiel: *Paschaens datter (The Pasha's Daughter)*, 1869
BIBLIOGRAPHY   G. Hetsch, *Peter Heise*, Copenhagen, 1926

R.La.

HANS WERNER HENZE

b 1 July 1926, Gütersloh, Westphalia

Henze has said of himself that all his music starts out from and returns to the theatre. One of his earliest musical memories was of listening enthralled to a performance on record of the overture to Mozart's *Le nozze di Figaro*. And though it would be an exaggeration to assert that it was this childhood experience that established the pattern of his creative life, he has been at pains to point out on more than one occasion that the theatre is his natural domain.

Even in his most seemingly abstract works the instruments often behave in an entirely theatrical way, like personages in a drama.

After a period of military service, during which he was for a short time a British prisoner-of-war, and while continuing his studies with the composer Wolfgang Fortner and the leading Schoenbergian theorist René Leibowitz, he also consolidated his more practical commitment to the theatre as a member of the staffs of the Bielefeld Stadttheater and the Deutsches Theater at Konstanz, and then as conductor and artistic director of the Wiesbaden ballet. Since then a substantial sequence of operas and music-theatre works has punctuated his prolific output like peaks in a mountain range, each with its own closely related series of orchestral, chamber and other vocal pieces. Sometimes, indeed, that relationship is particularly intimate, his Fourth Symphony being shaped directly out of part of Act II of the opera *König Hirsch* and an aria from the *Elegy for Young Lovers* providing the thematic basis of the finale of his Fifth Symphony.

Just when it seemed that he had achieved an impregnable position as one of the most prodigiously gifted and acclaimed of the new post-war generation of German composers Henze made a sudden, and wholly characteristic, decision in 1953 to break with his German roots and to settle permanently in Italy, first in the Bay of Naples and then in the country-side near Rome. As a composer who has always been responsive to the distinctive qualities of landscape and accent, the impact of his Mediterranean experience was first reflected in his music in its new vein of hedonistic lyricism and fantasy, and later by the slightly harsher inflexions typical of Roman speech.

Then, in the 1960s, the coincidence of his growing sense of disillusionment after the composition of *The Bassarids* and his personal identification with the aims of revolutionary socialism resulted in another radical change of direction, his music abandoning its passive attitude to contemporary reality in favour of a more active and astringently defined participation in its brutal struggles. Yet even at its most politically explicit that resolve can be diagnosed in hindsight as simply a further and logical step in the exploration of the clash between illusion and reality, authority and freedom, social constraints and individual liberty, that has been at the heart of Henze's artistic enterprise since his earliest years.

Das Wundertheater

The Magic Theatre
Opera for actors in one act (45m)
Libretto by the composer, after an intermezzo *El retablo de las maravillas* by Cervantes (c. 1605) in the German translation of Adolf Graf von Schack (1845)
Composed 1948, rev. for singers 1964
PREMIERES 7 May 1949, Heidelberg; rev. version: 30 November 1965, Kammerspiel, Frankfurt am Main (in triple-bill with *Ein Landarzt* and *Das Ende einer Welt*); UK: 8 March 1966, St Pancras Town Hall, London (triple-bill)

Arriving in a Spanish village whose pompous, self-satisfied inhabitants are obsessed by their sense of national honour, a group of strolling players puts on what is in reality a purely imaginary puppet play. Blinded by their racial pride and their fear of any taint of bastardy or Jewish blood, the villagers are easily persuaded that they are in fact witnessing invisible show. Only one sees through the sham, but he is rejected and viciously assaulted.

Just as the mature Cervantes used the traditional form of the rustic intermezzo to shed mocking light on the ridiculous posturing of ordinary people in a Spain in crisis, so the young Henze used Cervantes in turn to pour scorn on the myth of racial purity and to expose the dangerous rift between truth and falsehood. Written in a satirical cabaret style, and scored for an orchestra of wind, strings, percussion, harp and harpsichord, each of its tiny scenes has its own distinctive musical character, such as *Capriccio*, *Rondo*, *Ballade*, *March héroïque* and *Perpetuum mobile*. There is also a reduced orchestration for 11 players.

EDITION v.s. (rev. version), Schott, 1965

Boulevard Solitude

Lyric drama in seven tableaux (1h 15m)
Libretto by Grete Weil, after a play by Walter Jockisch based on the novel *Manon Lescaut* by the Abbé Prevost (1731)
Composed 1951
PREMIERES 17 February 1952, Landestheater, Hanover; UK: 25 June 1962, Sadler's Wells, London; US: 2 August 1967, Santa Fe

In the 25-year-old Henze's first full-length opera, the Abbé Prevost's famous 18th-century story of the doomed love of the passionate but weak-willed des Grieux for the morally unscrupulous Manon is

Hans Werner Henze in the 1970s

updated to Paris just after the Second World War. At their first meeting in the opening scene, set in the main railway station of some large French town and introduced and accompanied by an array of evocative percussion, the cigarette-smoking Manon is on her way to a finishing school in Lausanne, des Grieux to continue his lonely student life in Paris. Their burgeoning love in a Parisian attic is soon shattered, however, when the self-seeking Manon is forced by her rapacious brother Lescaut into a sexual liaison with a grotesque but rich old admirer, Lilaque, and then with Lilaque's young son. Des Grieux seeks oblivion in drugs, and when the elder Lilaque discovers the theft of a valuable modern painting from his son's apartment he is shot dead by Lescaut who cunningly transfers the gun to his unsuspecting sister's hand. She is arrested and imprisoned before the opera comes full circle with a final symbolic pantomime involving many of the incidental characters first encountered in the opening scene.

Drawing on influences as heterogeneous as Cocteau, the big-band jazz of Stan Kenton, Parisian music-hall and modern opera from Weill and Milhaud to Alban Berg, the score of *Boulevard Solitude* provides a striking early example of Henze's assimilative virtuosity. With its seven short scenes linked by orchestral intermezzi, and combining 19th-century operatic conventions with modern cinematic techniques, its music combines the tonal and atonal, jazz and a blues based on a chord progression borrowed from Puccini's *La bohème*, the atonal identified with the pains of love, the tonal with the bourgeois capitalist world.

RECORDING Vassilieva, Pruett, Falkman, Brewer, Ottevaere, O des Rencontres Musicales, Anghelov, Cascavelle, 1990
EDITIONS v.s./lib., Schott, 1952

Ein Landarzt
A Country Doctor
Radio opera in one act (35m)
Libretto by the composer, after a short story by Franz Kafka (1918)
Composed 1951, rev. for the stage 1964
PREMIERES 19 November 1951, Nordwestdeutscher Rundfunk, Hamburg (radio broadcast); rev. version: 30 November 1965, Kammerspiel, Frankfurt am Main (in triple-bill with *Das Wundertheater* and *Das Ende einer Welt*); UK: 8 March 1966, St Pancras Town Hall, London (triple-bill)

Henze's adaptation follows in meticulous detail every nuance and incident of Kafka's haunting tale of a dedicated country doctor's urgent journey through a fierce snow blizzard to a village ten miles away to attend a boy seriously ill with a gangrenous wound; and the ghostly betrayal of the doctor's good nature and professional concern by the superstitious villagers; and the eerie happenings in which he is engulfed. In its original radio version, which won the 1953 Prix Italia, the solo line encompasses straight recitation, speech in strictly notated pitches and rhythms, sprechgesang and singing, the effect produced by its dense, rigorously woven orchestral

counterpoint and predominantly dark instrumental hues, nightmarish and hallucinatory. In the stage version of 1964, the orchestra was reduced to more manageable proportions in keeping with the other two works. At about the same time Henze also made a concert version for solo voice and orchestra for the baritone Dietrich Fischer-Dieskau.

RECORDING Näslund, Langebo, Sannfrid, Grippe, Nilsson, Lundborg, Bäckelin, Swedish Radio O, Ehrling, Bis, [?1957]
EDITION f.s./v.s., Schott, 1965

Das Ende einer Welt
The End of a World
Radio opera in two acts with prologue and epilogue (50m)
Libretto by Wolfgang Hildesheimer, after a story in his collection *Lieblose Legenden* (1952)
Composed 1953, rev. for the stage 1964
PREMIERES 4 December 1953, Nordwestdeutscher Rundfunk, Hamburg (radio broadcast); rev. version: 30 November 1965, Kammerspiel, Frankfurt (in triple-bill with *Das Wundertheater* and *Ein Landarzt*); UK: 8 March 1966, St Pancras Town Hall, London (triple-bill)

The scenario devised by Wolfgang Hildesheimer for Henze's third radio opera has something of the quality of a sharply etched caricature. The action takes place on a man-made island in the Venetian lagoon where the guests of the rich American-born Marchesa Montetristo have gathered for a fashionable party. As a flautist plays a pastiche 18th-century sonata, the foundations shudder and the island begins to sink slowly into the sea. The guests, however, are either too stupid or too well mannered to notice, and scream delightedly for a repetition of the sonata as the island slips beneath the waves.

A number opera made up of strict forms like aria, rondo, barcarolle and *cabaletta*, Henze's score is dry, aggressive and coolly detached, its parodistic character underlined by the inclusion in the orchestra of such novel instruments as recorder, ocarina, an octet of jazz trumpets and trombones and electric guitar, as well as bizarre sound effects on three pre-recorded tapes. Most of these more unusual instruments, and the taped sounds, were discarded in the reduced orchestration of the revised 1964 stage version.

EDITION f.s., Schott, 1965

König Hirsch
King Stag
Opera in three acts (4h)
Libretto by Heinz von Cramer, after Carlo Gozzi's fable *Il re cervo* (1762)
Composed 1952–5; shortened and revised as *Il re cervo, oder Die Irrfahrten der Wahrheit*, 1962
PREMIERES 23 September 1956, Städtische Oper, Berlin (with extensive cuts); rev. version: 10 March 1963, Staatstheater, Kassel; UK: 20 January 1973, BBC Radio 3 (in English); rev. version: US: 4 August 1965, Santa Fe; complete original version: 5 May 1985, Staatsoper, Stuttgart
CAST *Il re Cervo*: The King (Leandro) *t*, The Girl (Costanza) *s*, The Governor (Tartaglia) *b-bar*, Scollatella I *s*, Scollatella II *s*, Scollatella III *ms*, Scollatella IV *a*, Checco *buffo t*, Coltellino *buffo t*, 2 statues 2 *s*, the Stag *silent*; *satb*

Scene from König Hirsch *with Sandor Konya as the King; set design by Jean-Pierre Ponnelle (Berlin, 1956)*

chorus of voices of forest, courtiers, animals, huntsmen, soldiers, city dwellers, etc.
LARGE ORCHESTRA including 6 timps, much percussion, pf, hpd, accordion, mand, gtr; onstage band including organ, mand, cel

Although the ideas for Henze's longest and most ambitious opera had begun to crystallize in the minds of its composer and librettist some time before Henze left Germany to settle permanently in Italy, the greater part of *König Hirsch* was written during many months of intense concentration, and in almost monastic seclusion at Forio d'Ischia in the Bay of Naples. Over a century ago the English translator of Carlo Gozzi's memoirs, John Aldington Symonds, had suggested that the theatrical fables of the 18th-century Venetian could well furnish excellent libretti for the composers of opera. And following in the footsteps of the young Wagner of *Die Feen*, of Busoni and Prokofiev, Henze was to discover in Gozzi's miraculous fairy-tale of the king who is metamorphosed into a stag, an ideal vehicle for all his most intimate dreams and aspirations, for his first revelatory encounters with Mediterranean culture and landscape and the haunting quality of Italian folksong.

SYNOPSIS
The place is somewhere between sea and forest near Venice, the period some time in antiquity.

Act I Preparations are underway for the coronation of the innocent King Leandro who has grown up among the forest animals. During a ferocious storm Scollatella and her doubles argue about who will become queen. The girl Costanza is brought in and is threatened by the malicious, scheming Tartaglia that to gain her freedom she must kill the new king. Instructed by Tartaglia that he must choose a queen, Leandro spurns the four quarrelsome Scollatellas and finds himself increasingly drawn to the gentle Costanza. When Tartaglis cunningly reveals the dagger hidden in Costanza's clothing, the broken-hearted Leandro's plea for her forgiveness is rejected and he decides to abdicate and return to the forest. Left alone, the victorious Tartaglia is joined by the hired assassin Coltellino whom he commands to follow Leandro and murder him.

Act II In the great living, breathing forest Leandro is pursued by Scollatella and her mirror images, and then by Tartaglia who tries to kill him but fails. A stag is wounded and dies. By means of a magic formula confided to him by the musician Checco, Leandro transforms himself into the stag.

But the evil Tartaglia, who has also learned the spell, assumes the appearance of the king and, as another storm breaks over the forest, orders a huge stag hunt that will rid him of Leandro for ever.

Act III The oppressed populace of the decaying city patiently awaits the King Stag which, according to legend, will free it from Tartaglia's tyrannical rule. Leandro in his form as the King Stag duly appears in the deserted streets and is greeted by Costanza. Tartaglia, still disguised as the king, is mistakenly shot and killed by Coltellino. Leandro, using the same transformation spell, is restored to human form and takes Costanza as his bride to general public rejoicing.

So bare an outline of the intricate scenario of *König Hirsch* can give little idea of the variety, richness and prodigality of a work whose music is saturated with the shimmering light, colour and enchanted atmosphere of the Italian landscape. Even before the scandal caused by its savagely cut Berlin premiere, Henze had recycled the evocative and already symphonically shaped music that accompanies the great stag hunt of Act II into his Fourth Symphony. And alerted by the enormous problems created by that first Berlin performance, he and his librettist also produced under the title *Il re cervo* their own official, much shortened and instrumentally reduced version. But as Henze has insisted, it is only when staged complete that it can be heard and understood correctly.

EDITIONS *König Hirsch*: v.s., Schott, 1959; lib., Schott, 1956; *Il re cervo*: v.s./lib., Schott, 1964

Der Prinz von Homburg

The Prince of Homburg

Opera in three acts (2h 15m)

Libretto by Ingeborg Bachmann, after the drama by Heinrich von Kleist (1811)

Composed 1958

PREMIERES 22 May 1960, Staatsoper, Hamburg; UK: 26 September 1962, Sadler's Wells, London

CAST Prince Friedrich *high bar*, Princess Natalie *s*, Elector Friedrich Wilhelm *t*, Electress *a*, Dörfling *bar*, Kottwitz *b*, Hohenzollern *t*; *satb* chorus of other officers, ladies-in-waiting, soldiers, servants, etc.

LARGE CHAMBER ORCHESTRA including 5 t-t, 3 tom-toms, vibraphone, marimbaphone; stage band: 11 players

The film director Luchino Visconti first suggested to Henze that the dramatic masterpiece of the late 18th-century German playwright Heinrich von Kleist would make ideal operatic material. What both drama and opera are about, in Henze's words, is the glorification of the dreamer, and what clearly appealed to him in Kleist's play was the tension it explores between the poetic individual as hero and the rigidity of its harsh, militaristic background. The libretto fashioned by the Austrian poet Ingeborg Bachmann falls naturally into recitative, aria and ensemble, and the composition of the opera came musically at a time when Henze was steeped, as he puts it, in early 19th-century Italian opera, in the serene melancholy of Bellini, the sparkling *brio* of Rossini and Donizetti's passionate intensity, all drawn together and condensed in Verdi's robust rhythms, hard orchestral colours and melodic lines that set the ears tingling.

SYNOPSIS

Act I As his fellow officers while away the time before the coming battle, Prince Friedrich Artur von Homburg sits musing in the moonlit garden of the castle of Fehrbellin. His reverie is interrupted by the arrival of Friedrich Wilhelm, Elector of Brandenburg, and his niece Princess Natalie whose hand the elector promises to the prince in marriage. After their departure, Friedrich remains dreamily fondling the glove left behind by the princess, the symbol of all his hopes and aspirations, of the coming victory and their glorious future together of love and happiness. In a conference room in the castle next morning Field Marshal Dörfling is giving his officers their orders of the day. The prince however, is still transfixed in his trancelike state. Later, on the battlefield, he checks the orders with his friend Hohenzollern, impetuously commands his cavalry to attack without waiting for the Field Marshal's signal and himself rushes into battle. The battle is won but, angered by the prince's reckless action, the elector orders him to be stripped of his honours and court-martialled.

Act II Prince Friedrich, who has been condemned to death, reflects in his prison cell on the gravity of his situation. In the electress's room he pleads with her to intervene on his behalf, but it is Natalie who goes to the elector to beg for clemency. Pardon will be granted, he tells her, only if Friedrich himself can argue convincingly in his own heart and soul that the sentence is unjust. When the prince rejects the offered compromise, preferring to die rather than betray his self-respect, Natalie decides that she will command her own dragoons to free him by force.

Act III Dörfling warns the elector of Natalie's intentions. What eventually moves him to tear up the death warrant is not, however, the pleading of Natalie or Friedrich's fellow officers, but the prince's adamant refusal to alter his decision that only an honourable death will cleanse his guilt. He is led into the garden prepared for execution, but as his blindfold is removed he realizes that instead of death all he had dreamed of in the opera's opening scene has now become reality.

With its orchestra used predominantly in the spirit of chamber music, each scene has its own specific instrumental grouping and colour, and each is based on a particular form such as fugue, rondo or passacaglia. As was noted at the time of the premiere, it is also in keeping with its themes of understanding and forgiveness, and with the aim of composer and librettist to lift its conflicts out of their strictly Prussian setting and to give them a more universal significance. Thus the elector's words in Kleist's play, 'He will teach you, be assured, what military discipline and obedience are', have been changed in the opera to '. . . what freedom and honour are'. The dedication is to Igor Stravinsky.

EDITIONS   v.s./lib. Schott, 1960

Elegy for Young Lovers

Opera in three acts (2h 30m)
Libretto by W. H. Auden and Chester Kallman
Composed 1959–61
PREMIERES   20 May 1961, Schlosstheater, Schwetzingen (in German); UK: 19 July 1961, Glyndebourne (in English); US: 29 April 1965, Juilliard School, New York
CAST   Mittenhofer *bar*, Reischmann *b*, Toni *t*, Elisabeth *s*, Carolina *a*, Hilda *s*, Mauer *spoken role*
CHAMBER ORCHESTRA with percussion (7 players), hp, cel, pf, gtr, mand

An inscription on the title page reads: 'To the memory of Hugo von Hofmannsthal, Austrian, European and Master Librettist, this work is gratefully dedicated by its three makers'. When Henze made his first tentative proposal to Auden and Kallman that they should write a libretto for him, what he had in mind was a chamber opera with a small, subtle orchestra and dominated by beautiful, tender noises. Set in an Alpine chalet in the year 1910, requiring a cast of just six solo voices and with its three acts made up of 34 short scenes each with its own individual title, the opera's true subject matter is the creation of a poem. At its centre is the poet Gregor Mittenhofer who ruthlessly exploits the personal obsessions of everyone around him to feed his monstrous creative appetites. Every year he returns to his Alpine retreat to write his spring poem, and to renew contact with the coloratura visions of the demented widow Hilda Mack who, still dressed in the style of the 1870s, has waited in lonely isolation at the inn for the return of her husband who disappeared on the mountain 40 years before.

SYNOPSIS
Act I   This year Mittenhofer has brought with him his wealthy patroness and unpaid secretary Carolina, his personal physician Dr Reischmann, and young companion Elisabeth, who are soon joined by Reischmann's son Toni. Morning life goes on with its everyday bustle as Mittenhofer calls impatiently for his breakfast egg and his daily injection, wheedles money out of Carolina, scolds her for her typing errors and makes notes of Hilda's hallucinatory visions. But the morning routine is suddenly interrupted when the guide Josef Mauer rushes in to tell them that a body has been found in the ice on the Hammerhorn and that it must be Frau Mack's husband. Elisabeth gently consoles the bewildered Hilda and the act ends with her ecstatic realization that her imprisoning crystal has at last been broken and Toni's ardent recognition of his love for Elisabeth.
Act II   Made aware by Carolina of the young couple's clearly expressed love for each other Mittenhofer first plays on Elisabeth's feelings of guilt but then, in a change of tack, asks Reischmann to bless them, and the lovers to bring him from the mountain a sprig of edelweiss that he needs to complete his poem. However, once they have departed his mood veers abruptly from apparent acceptance to furious rage.
Act III   The now completely cured Hilda says her farewells and Elisabeth and Toni leave for the mountain slope. But though a fine, warm day has been forecast a fierce snowstorm suddenly blows up and, in a switch of scene, the young couple are seen on the Hammerhorn, resigned to a loving death in one another's arms. Finally the scene shifts to an auditorium in Vienna where, after acknowledging the applause of his admirers, Mittenhofer silently mouths his newly finished poem, 'Elegy for Young Lovers', against the background of the offstage voices of Elisabeth, Toni, Hilda, Carolina, and the doctor.

With its predominance of silvery sounds and high tuned percussion the instrumental writing breathes an air of sharp, crystalline purity, depicting the sparkling atmosphere and the chill of the Alpine landscape in flashing, translucent colours. Each character is associated with a particular instrument or group of instruments; Mittenhofer, for instance, with horn, trumpet and trombone; Carolina with the plangent, submissive tone of a cor anglais, and Hilda with the flute, whose agile tracery, as it shadows the widely leaping intervals and brilliantly decorative figurations of her hallucinatory coloratura, is directly based on the mad scene from Donizetti's *Lucia di Lammermoor*.

RECORDING   excerpts: Gayer, Dubin, Mödl, Driscoll, Fischer-Dieskau, Hemsley, Members of the Berlin Radio SO and the Berlin Opera O, Henze, DG, 1964
EDITION   v.s./study s./lib., Schott, 1961

Der junge Lord

The Young Lord
Comic opera in two acts (2h 30m)
Libretto by Ingeborg Bachmann, after the parable *Der Scheik von Alessandria und seine Sklaven* by Wilhelm Hauff (1826)
Composed 1964
PREMIERES   7 April, 1965, Deutsche Oper, Berlin; UK: 14 October 1969, Sadler's Wells, London; US: 17 February 1967, Civic Theatre, San Diego
CAST   Sir Edgar *silent*, his secretary *bar*, Lord Barrat *t*, Begonia *ms*, Burgomaster *b-bar*, Councillor Hasentreffer *bar*, Councillor Scharf *bar*, Prof von Mucker *t*, Baroness Grunwiesel *ms*, Frau von Hufnagel *ms*, Frau Hasentreffer *s*, Luise *s*, Ida *s*, a maid *s*, Wilhelm *t*, Amintore La Rocca *t*, a lamplighter *b*, 3 *silent roles*; circus performers; *satb* chorus of townsfolk
MEDIUM-SIZED ORCHESTRA   onstage: military band, dance band

With his fifth full-length opera Henze fulfilled a long-held ambition that can be traced back through the clown scenes of *König Hirsch* and the satirical comedy *Das Ende einer Welt* – to write a fully-fledged opera buffa.

SYNOPSIS
Act I   In the German town of Hülsdorf-Gotha in 1830, the populace awaits the arrival of the rich English milord Sir Edgar. The grander citizens

rehearse their speeches of welcome while the children prepare a celebratory cantata. When Sir Edgar eventually arrives, their curiosity is further aroused by the black valet Jeremy, the Jamaican cook Begonia, the strange luggage and assorted animals that make up his bizarre retinue. As the confusion mounts, the town's wealthiest and most eligible girl, Luise, and the student Wilhelm take the opportunity to whisper their first secret words together. Later, in the salon of Luise's guardian Baroness Grunwiesel, the society ladies gossip excitedly about the mysterious newcomer whom they have invited to join them. The baroness does little to conceal her plans for a marriage between Luise and the English aristocrat, but when Jeremy comes in with a note from Sir Edgar declining their invitation she swears in barely contained fury that she will have her revenge for the supposed insult. Only a performance by a travelling circus in the town square can persuade Sir Edgar to leave his house. Incensed by what they believe to be another insult to their self-esteem, the members of the town council attempt to drive the circus away, but Sir Edgar invites the performers inside as his house guests.

Act II   As a lamplighter goes his rounds on a dark winter's night he hears blood-curdling screams coming from Sir Edgar's house. While Luise and Wilhelm confess their love, the mayor and his colleagues are called in to investigate, but Sir Edgar's secretary explains that what has been heard are no more than the exasperated cries of the milord's nephew Lord Barrat as he tries to learn German. They are put into an even better mood when invited to a grand reception at Sir Edgar's house at which the elegantly dressed Lord Barrat is introduced. Though he says nothing and behaves with unnerving eccentricity, Luise is irresistibly drawn to him and the dejected Wilhelm leaves in despair. At a party in the great ballroom of the casino, where it is confidently expected that the betrothal of Luise and Lord Barrat will be announced, everyone tries to imitate his bewildering eccentricities. As the dancing becomes increasingly frenzied and Lord Barrat's antics more wildly out of control, he suddenly tears off his clothes to reveal himself as a performing ape and Luise and Wilhelm are left clutching one another in horror amid the general panic.

It is perhaps no coincidence that the evening before he began work on the score Henze attended a performance in Berlin of Mozart's *Die Entführung*, a snatch of whose Turkish music is quoted early on in the first scene of Henze's opera. But for all the Mozartian economy of instrumentation, it is the *brio* of Rossini and the elegiac lyricism of Bellini, as filtered through Henze's 20th-century imagination, that cast the longest shadow over his comedy of early 19th-century bourgeois manners. It is a genuine ensemble opera, with a single aria and duet, its music is witty, elegant and briskly paced. But unlike the comedies of Rossini, Henze's comedy has an alarming sting in the tail, twisting into tragedy in Act II as music and libretto rip mercilessly away the bourgeois mask of small-town hypocrisy and self-delusion.

RECORDING   Mathis, Johnson, Little, Hesse, Driscoll, Grobe, McDaniel, Röhrl, Ch and O of the Berlin Opera, Dohnányi, DG, 1967
EDITIONS   v.s./lib., Schott, 1967

The Bassarids

Opera seria with intermezzo in one act (2h 30m)
Libretto by W. H. Auden and Chester Kallman, after the play *The Bacchae* by Euripides (407 BC)
Composed 1965
PREMIERES   6 August 1966, Grosses Festspielhaus, Salzburg (in German); UK: 22 September 1968, BBC Radio 3 (broadcast); 10 October 1974, Coliseum, London; US: 7 August 1968, Santa Fe
CAST   Pentheus *bar*, Dionysus *t*, Cadmus *b*, Tiresias *t*, Captain *bar*, Agave *ms*, Autonoe *s*, Beroe *ms*, 2 *silent*; intermezzo: Venus *ms*, Proserpina *s*, Kalliope *t*, Adonis *bar*; *satb* chorus of Bacchantes, Theban citizens, guards, servants
LARGE ORCHESTRA   onstage: 4 tpt, 2 mand, gtr (there is also an alternative version with reduced orchestration)

Before Henze started work on *The Bassarids*, his librettists demanded as a condition of their co-operation that he should go to a performance of *Götterdämmerung* and make his peace with Wagner. Already simmering in his imagination were ideas for a work that would no longer be influenced by the closed, Italianate forms that had mostly dominated his earlier operas, but which would instead be through-composed in a single, broadly designed span. From the great masterpiece of Euripides' old age, Auden and Kallman forged a scenario that falls naturally into four symphonic movements and whose language, Henze has written, is so richly expressive that it immediately suggested musical themes and textures.

SYNOPSIS

After the chorus has described the abdication of Cadmus as king of Thebes in favour of his grandson Pentheus a distant voice announces the arrival of Dionysus in Boeotia. Ignoring Pentheus' angry denunciation of the dangerous stranger, not only the Theban people, but the blind seer Tiresias, Pentheus' widowed mother Agave and her sister Autonoe are all gradually seduced into the service of the new, erotic god and the religion he embodies.

In the second movement the rash, severely rationalistic Pentheus orders the captain of the guard to round up Dionysus and his disciples. But his questioning of the prisoners produces no satisfactory answers.

Playing on the king's youthful voyeurism, Dionysus, in the pivotal third movement, reveals to Pentheus by means of a lascivious charade based on the Judgment of Calliope, and seen through a magic mirror, the true nature of his repressed sexual fantasies and desires. Pentheus is persuaded to dress in women's clothes and go to Mount Cytheron to observe for himself the Dionysian mysteries. The hunter thus becomes the hunted, and his dying screams can be heard in the darkness as the maenads, led by his own mother, tear him limb from limb. Slowly Agave is brought back to her senses, and as Henze's Dionysiac passion play reaches its tragic resolution Cadmus and his family are banished by the triumphant god from Thebes, and their palace ordered to be burnt to the ground.

The first section is a kind of large-scale sonata movement based on the interaction between the more harshly accented music associated with the rigid King Pentheus and the seductively sensuous music identified with the god Dionysus. The second is a scherzo made up of a suite of Bacchic dances, the third an extended *adagio* whose two parts are separated by a lighter intermezzo, the last a vast passacaglia. And woven into the musical texture at crucial moments are reminiscences of composers from Bach and Rameau to Mahler.

RECORDING   Lindsley, Armstrong, Wenkel, Riegel, Tear, Schmidt, Murray, Burt, South German Radio Ch and RIAS Chamber Ch, Berlin Radio SO, Albrecht, Schwann, 1991: recorded, presumably with the composer's agreement, without the third-movement intermezzo
EDITIONS   v.s./lib., Schott, 1966

We Come to the River

Actions for music in eleven scenes (2h 30m)
Libretto by Edward Bond
Composed 1974–6
PREMIERE   12 July 1976, Covent Garden, London

With its enormous cast of over a hundred individually named roles and its three orchestras, supplemented by a vast array of extra percussion, accordion, harp, portative organ and largish military band, Henze's first collaboration with the British playwright Edward Bond is the climactic work of his fiercest period of intense political engagement.

The action is set in an imaginary empire after the suppression of a bloody civil war. The victorious general who has been responsible for crushing the people's revolt is told that he is going blind. As his sight fails, his inner eye gradually awakens to the horrific suffering and carnage that the war has caused. Confined in a madhouse and with his eyes, in a *Lear*-like scene, put out on the orders of the emperor, he is transformed almost without knowing it into a popular symbol of resistance. But it is not so much the general's personal fate as the repressive nature of the cruelly authoritarian society in which such events can take place that is the work's principal concern.

Dispensing with the traditional pit orchestra, many scenes are performed simultaneously on three different stages each with its own individually constituted and clearly differentiated instrumental ensemble. In its dramatization of social conflict in the most harrowing and extreme of situations, the savage and the lyrical, the tragic and frivolously parodistic, action and reflection interpenetrate on every level in a score of a starkly realistic, hard-edged complexity. But it is the lyrical that ultimately wins through as the voices of the oppressed and the risen dead join together in a visionary song of hope, of liberation and the irrepressible march towards a better future. The reactions to the opera's first performance were nevertheless almost as complex as the work itself.

Though generally praised for its ambitious and stimulating theatrical daring, it was felt by many critics that the tripartite simultaneity of its orchestral writing and stage action, and the baldly expressed orthodoxy of its New Left anti-war, anti-bourgeois themes, created more problems of assimilation and audibility than they resolved.

EDITIONS   study s./lib., Schott, 1976

Don Chisciotte della Mancia

Don Quixote
Comic opera in two acts (1h 45m)
Adapted by Giuseppe Di Leva and Hans Werner Henze from the opera by Paisiello (1769)
Composed 1976
PREMIERES   1 August 1976, Montepulciano, Italy; UK: 28 March 1979, Round House, London (Phoenix Opera)

Designed for a mixed ensemble of professional and amateur performers, the adaptation by Henze and his librettist of Paisiello's opera *Don Chisciotte della Mancia* is much more than simply a colouristic, updated orchestration in the manner of Stravinsky's *Pulcinella*. Henze and Di Leva created an almost entirely new work out of Paisiello's original material. Arias and recitatives were added, the plot, dialogue and dramatic shape rearranged and newly invented. Exploiting the unresolved contrast between reality and pretence, Paisiello's opera becomes in their version a kind of play within a play, starting out as raw farce and ending in a mood of outrage. As the pretend Don Quixote and Sancho Panza act out some of their more ludicrously famous adventures, the real and now aged Quixote and Panza look on from the sidelines in growing distress at the indignities heaped on them. When they can bear the shame no longer, Quixote rushes on to the stage in despair and shatters the comic illusion. In a reversal of their original roles in Paisiello's opera, it is now Quixote and Panza who emerge as the victors and the rural aristocrats who are portrayed as foolish and degenerate.

In a note in the score Henze points out how the distinction in the orchestra betweeen its small ensemble of professional players and large wind band directly mirrors the dramatic action. The band music, he insists, must be played by amateurs, the imprecise roughness of their intonation underlining the work's quixotic dignity.

The English Cat

A story for singers and instruments in two acts (2h 45m)
Libretto by Edward Bond, after Honoré de Balzac's tale *Peines de coeur d'une chatte anglaise* (1840)
Composed 1980–83, rev. 1990
PREMIERES   2 June 1983, Schlosstheater, Schwetzingen; UK: 19 August 1987, Leith Theatre, Edinburgh (Frankfurt Alte Oper)

Henze's second operatic collaboration with playwright Edward Bond is also his fourth opera written to an original English text. The basic idea came initially from Henze himself after he had seen a dramatization in Paris of Balzac's feline parable. The cats in Balzac's brief satirical tales encompass all the familiar human types, from the amorous Tom, the demure, empty-headed Minette and her humble, but very pretty, sister Babette, to the aristocratic Lord Puff, his spendthrift nephew Arnold and moneylender Mr Jones. Bond's version updates the setting from the Directoire to London in the Edwardian period, and he provides a didactic framework for the interwoven stories of marriage and divorce, love and infidelity, vanity, deceit, loyalty and violent death, with the invention of the Royal Society for the Protection of Rats, whose members treat their fellow cats with an adamant, cruelly self-seeking conformity when it suits their own hypocritical ends, but who refrain from eating rats and are kindly to mice in a rather superior way.

In keeping with his aristocratic position, the RSPR's president elect, Lord Puff, is expected to breed and has chosen as his bride the simple country cat Minette. Determined to preserve his inheritance, Puff's insolvent nephew Arnold tries every trick in the book to prevent their marriage, but fails. The wedding goes ahead, but Minette cannot forget the seductive attractions of the basically decent but feckless Tom. When Puff and the entire RSPR burst in to find Tom at Minette's feet, divorce proceedings are instigated. Meanwhile Tom has been discovered to be the long-lost son and heir of the rich Lord Fairport, and when he learns that Puff's owner, Mrs Halifax, has arranged for the pathetic Minette to be drowned he quickly turns his attention to her pretty sister Babette. But just when he is about to claim his inheritance, which he has refused to hand over to the RSPR, Tom is himself murdered. The RSPR gets its money and the mouse Louise is left bemoaning its treachery.

The libretto is designed in the form of a ballad opera on the pattern established ˅by John Gay's *The Beggar's Opera*, by Brecht and by Auden in Stravinsky's *The Rake's Progress*. What Henze has called his 'sinister, oblique' music also pays its respects to Stravinsky while fleshing out the situations and characters by means of a continuously evolving variation technique modelled on the formal outlines of Beethoven's *Diabelli Variations*. The scoring is for large chamber orchestra with a lavish percussion section, in which various unusual instruments are subtly employed to underpin the distinctive traits of particular characters: Minette by a zither, Lord Puff by chamber organ and Arnold by a heckelphone or bass oboe.

RECORDING Berkeley-Steele, Coles, Watt, Platt, Pike, Parnassus Ensemble, Stenz, Wergo, 1991
EDITIONS v.s./lib., Schott, 1983

Das verratene Meer
The Sea Betrayed

Music drama in two acts (1h 45m)
Libretto by Hans-Ulrich Treichel, after the novella *Gogo No-Eiko* (*The Sailor who Fell from Grace with the Sea*) by Yukio Mishima (1963)
Composed 1986–9
PREMIERES 5 May 1990, Deutsche Oper, Berlin; US: 8 November 1991, War Memorial Opera House, San Francisco

In transferring Mishima's disturbing novella of repression, growing sexual awareness and adolescent dreams of glory to the public stage, Henze's opera meticulously preserves not only the story's tensely detailed incident but also its chilling atmosphere of latent violence and vibrant eroticism. As the widowed Fusako and her naval officer lover Ryuji consummate their physical relationship they are spied on through a hole in the bedroom wall, and in a state of almost incestuous love, by Fusako's precocious 13-year-old son Noboru. When he learns that Ryuji is apparently willing to sacrifice what he sees as a heroic naval destiny to assist Fusako in her fashionable dress shop, Noboru is outraged by so shameless a betrayal of his fervently idealistic sense of national honour, and he and his élite band of schoolboy friends plan a sinister revenge, culminating in Ryuji's ritual death.

Act I, subtitled 'Summer' like the first part of Mishima's book, is full of strong, explosive contrasts; the second, subtitled 'Winter', is much leaner, unfolding in ever longer lyrical lines. All four of the main participants in the drama are defined by a musical form and character specific to them alone and each is associated with a particular world of sound; Fusako with the strings, Ryuji with the wind, Noboru and his gang with piano and tuned percussion. The vocal writing for Fusako especially has an almost Bergian intensity, the opera reconciling Henze's earlier and more recent styles without a trace of merely decorative Japanesery.

EDITION lib., Schott, 1990

Other music-theatre works: *Moralities* (three scenic cantatas by W. H. Auden, after Aesop), 1967; *Der langwierige Weg in die Wohnung der Natascha Ungeheuer* (A Show for 17), 1971; *La Cubana* (vaudeville), 1973; *Pollicino* (children's opera, 1980); *Il ritorno d'Ulisse in patria* (free reconstruction of Monteverdi's opera), 1981
BIBLIOGRAPHY Robert Henderson, 'Henze's Progress from *Boulevard Solitude* to *The Bassarids*', *Opera*, vol. 25 (1974); Hans Werner Henze, *Music and Politics: Collected Writings 1953–1981*, Faber, 1981; Peter Heyworth, 'Henze and the Revolution', *Music and Musicians*, September 1970, pp. 36–40; Stephen Walsh (ed.), Programme of the BBC's 1991 Henze Festival (contains comprehensive Henze bibliography)

R.L.H.

VICTOR HERBERT
Victor August Herbert; *b* 1 February 1859, Dublin; *d* 26 May 1924, New York

As a young musician in Stuttgart, Victor Herbert earned his living as a cellist in a number of orchestras, moving to New York when he was engaged by the Metropolitan. He soon achieved fame as a soloist, conductor and orchestral composer. Though he maintained such activities throughout his life, it is through his stage works – 45 of them in 30 years – that he has achieved immortality.

These works, all but a handful ignored today, encompass a remarkable stylistic range from romantic operetta though children's fantasy, satire and grand opera, to musical comedy of the 1920s. Though most of these works are dated as stage pieces, Herbert's comprehensive skill entitles him to be considered a principal ancestor of American musical comedy, though he rarely seemed truly at ease in the more up-to-date styles he attempted later in life. His experience in the operatic pit served him well in his writing for orchestra (only when time pressed did he delegate this task to others). His operettas' combination of European grace with American vitality appealed to a wide public, and the best of his music remains appealing and stirring.

Babes in Toyland

Musical extravaganza in two acts (1h 45m)
Libretto by Glen MacDonough
PREMIERES 13 October 1903, Majestic Theater, New York

Intended to capitalize on the popularity of the musical play *The Wizard of Oz* (music by Paul Tieijens), *Babes in Toyland* follows the adventures of two shipwrecked children in a magical land. The song 'Toyland' and the instrumental 'March of the Toys' rank among Herbert's best-known compositions.

FILMS 1. Meins (dir.), Hal Roach, 1934 (1h 15m); 2. Donohue (dir.), Walt Disney, 1961 (1h 45m)
EDITIONS v.s., Witmark, 1903; rev. edn, Witmark, 1954

Naughty Marietta

Comic opera in two acts (film: 1h 45m)
Libretto by Rida Johnson Young
PREMIERES 7 November 1910, New York Theater, New York

In 18th-century New Orleans, Marietta vows to wed only the man who can complete a melody she heard in a dream. The tune, completed by faithful Captain Dick just before the play ends, is 'Ah, Sweet Mystery of Life'; other evergreen excerpts from this still-popular score include 'Tramp, Tramp, Tramp' and 'Italian Street Song'.

RECORDING Blazer, Green, Harrington, Turnage, Morris, Smithsonian, 1980: complete original score
FILM Van Dyke (dir.), MGM, 1935
EDITION v.s., Witmark, 1910

Eileen

Operetta in three acts
Libretto by Henry Blossom
PREMIERES 19 March 1917, Shubert Theater, New York

One of Herbert's most impressive creations and his own declared favourite among his scores, *Eileen* occupies an undeservedly obscure position. Originally titled (and first published as) *Hearts of Erin*, the story appealed to Herbert's Irish heritage. It is a romance set in 1798 on the west coast on Ireland, against a backdrop of the Irish conflict with England.

RECORDING Wrightson, Carroll, Greer, Goodman, RCA, 1946
EDITION v.s., Witmark, 1917

Other stage works: *Prince Ananias*, 1894; *The Wizard of the Nile*, 1895; *The Gold Bug*, 1896; *The Serenade*, 1897; *The Idol's Eye*, 1897; *The Fortune Teller*, 1898; *Cyrano de Bergerac*, 1899; *The Singing Girl*, 1899; *The Ameer*, 1899; *The Viceroy*, 1900; *Babette*, 1903; *It Happened in Nordland*, 1904; *Miss Dolly Dollars*, 1905; *Wonderland*, 1905; *Mlle Modiste*, 1905; *The Red Mill*, 1906; *Dream City* and *The Magic Knight* (double-bill), 1906; *The Tattooed Man*, 1907; *Algeria*, 1908, rev. as *The Rose of Algeria*, 1909; *Little Nemo*, 1908; *The Prima Donna*, 1908; *Old Dutch*, 1909; *Natoma* (opera), 1911; *When Sweet Sixteen*, 1911; *The Duchess*, 1911; *The Enchantress*, 1911; *The Lady of the Slipper*, 1912; *Sweethearts*, 1913; *The Madcap Duchess*, 1913; *Madeleine* (opera), 1914; *The Only Girl*, 1914; *The Debutante*, 1914; *The Princess 'Pat'*, 1915; *Her Regiment*, 1917; *The Velvet Lady*, 1919; *Angel Face*, 1919; *My Golden Girl*, 1920; *Oui Madame*, 1920; *The Girl in the Spotlight*, 1920; *Orange Blossoms*, 1922; *The Dream Girl*, 1924
BIBLIOGRAPHY Edward N. Waters, *Victor Herbert: A Life in Music*, Macmillan, 1955

J.A.C.

JERRY HERMAN
Gerald Herman; *b* 10 July 1933, New York

The most readily identifiable exponent of the traditional audience-pleasing musical in recent decades, Jerry Herman followed a drama degree from the University of Miami with song-writing for off-Broadway revues. He is most identified with the straightforward tunefulness of his two famous star vehicles, *Hello, Dolly!* and *Mame*, but later scores, such as *Mack and Mabel*, reveal a more subtle side to his talent, including some deftness as a lyricist.

Hello, Dolly!

Musical comedy in two acts (2h 15m)
Book by Michael Stewart, after the play *The Matchmaker* by Thornton Wilder (1954); lyrics by the composer
PREMIERES 16 January 1964, St James Theatre, New York; UK: 2 December 1965, Drury Lane, London

Dolly Levi matches up loving couples on a whirlwind day in old New York, and in the process secures a husband for herself. The musical, originally benefiting from the stylish staging of Gower Champion, has served as a vehicle for many eminent ladies of the musical stage, and its title song is the prototype of the endlessly repeated show-stopping refrain for which Herman is known.

RECORDING Channing, E. Brennan, Burns, Reilly, Coleman, RCA, 1964
FILM Kelly (dir.), Fox, 1969
EDITION v.s., Edwin H. Morris, 1964

Mame

Musical comedy in two acts (2h 30m)
Book by Jerome Lawrence and Robert E. Lee, based on their play and the novel *Auntie Mame* by Patrick Dennis; lyrics by the composer

PREMIERES   24 May 1966, Winter Garden, New York; UK: 20 February 1969, Drury Lane, London

Mame Dennis, inheriting a young orphaned nephew, brings him up with the same uninhibited enjoyment of life she has exemplified herself. *Mame* reinforced Herman's position, made a musical star of Angela Lansbury, and boasted another unstoppable title song.

RECORDING   Lansbury, Arthur, Connell, Pippin, CBS, 1966
FILM   Saks (dir.), Warner, 1974
EDITION   v.s., Edwin H. Morris, 1967

La Cage aux Folles
Musical in two acts (2h 30m)
Book by Harvey Fierstein, after the play by Jean Poiret; lyrics by the composer
PREMIERES   21 August 1983, Palace Theater, New York; UK: 7 May 1986, Palladium, London

A French homosexual couple (proprietor and star of a nightclub) are asked to disguise their relationship by the son they have raised, so that they will be acceptable to his fiancée's family. They attempt to oblige, but ultimately they disdain subterfuge and proclaim their pride in their identity. A timely subject, a lavish production, and several immediately popular songs gave Herman a hit on Broadway again, 17 years after *Mame*.

RECORDING   Hearn, Barry, Pippin, RCA, 1986
EDITION   v.s., Samuel French (on hire); lib., Samuel French, 1987

Other musicals:*Milk and Honey*, 1961; *Madame Aphrodite*, 1961; *Dear World*, 1969; *Mack and Mabel*, 1974; *The Grand Tour*, 1979
BIBLIOGRAPHY   Steven Suskin, *Show Tunes, 1905–1985*, Dodd Mead, 1986

J.A.C.

FERDINAND HÉROLD
Louis-Joseph-Ferdinand Hérold; *b* 28 January 1791, Paris; *d* 19 January 1833, Paris

In a short career Hérold composed much for both opera and ballet stages and achieved, at the end of his life in *Zampa* and *Le Pré aux Clercs*, two of the most successful of all French opéras comiques. A student at the Paris Conservatoire, he won the Prix de Rome in 1812 and travelled to Rome and Vienna. A collaboration with Boieldieu in 1816 led to an unbroken succession of works played at the Opéra-Comique, though none scored real success until *Le muletier* in 1823. Hérold belongs to the French tradition of Boieldieu and Isouard, although he was also much indebted to Weber.

Zampa, ou La fiancée de marbre
Zampa, or The Marble Bride
Opéra comique in three acts
Libretto by Anne-Honoré-Joseph Mélesville

Ferdinand Hérold

PREMIERES   3 May 1831, Opéra-Comique, Paris; UK: 19 April 1833, King's Theatre, Haymarket, London; US: 26 July 1833, Boston

Constantly in the repertoire in the 19th century, *Zampa* is still well known for its overture. The title role was written for Chollet, the leading light tenor of the day. The opera resembles a parody of *Don Giovanni*, for Zampa, a Sicilian pirate, is constantly threatened and finally consumed by a marble statue of Alice, whom he long ago abandoned. His attempts to snatch his brother's bride Camilla bring about his undoing.

EDITION   f.s./v.s., Meissonnier, 1831

Le Pré aux Clercs
Opéra comique in three acts (1h 30m)
Libretto by François-Antoine-Eugène de Planard, after Mérimée's *Les chroniques du temps de Charles IX*
PREMIERES   15 December 1832, Opéra-Comique, Paris; UK: 9 September 1833, Adelphi Theatre, London; US: 14 October 1833, Baltimore

Even more successful than *Zampa*, *Le Pré aux Clercs* offers a historical story of love and intrigue, set in 16th-century Paris (Le Pré aux Clercs was the area of the Left Bank opposite the Louvre), the kind of material more often set as grand opera than comic opera. It is a less weighty counterpart to Meyerbeer's *Les Huguenots*, but some imaginative orchestration and sharp characterization suggest that Hérold might have developed into a major opera composer if he had lived longer.

RECORDING   excerpts: Doria, le Bris, Louvay, Sénéchal, unnamed O, Etcheverry, Véga, 1960s
EDITION   f.s., Meissonier, 1835; v.s., Meissonnier, 1840

Other operatic works: *La gioventù di Enrico quinto*, 1815; *Charles de France* (coll. with Boieldieu), 1816; *Les rosières*, 1817; *La clochette, ou Le diable page*, 1817; *Le premier venu, ou Six lieux de chemin*, 1818; *Les troqueurs*, 1819; *L'amour platonique*, 1819; *L'auteur mort et vivant*, 1820; *Le muletier*, 1823; *Lasthénie*, 1823; *Vendôme en Espagne* (coll. with Auber), 1823; *Le Roi René, ou La Provence au XVe siècle*, 1824; *Le lapin blanc*, 1825; *Marie*, 1826; *L'illusion*, 1829; *Emmeline*, 1829; *L'auberge d'Auray* (coll. with Carafa), 1830; *La Marquise de Brinvilliers* (coll. with eight others), 1831; *La médecine sans médecin*, 1832; *Ludovic* (completed by Halévy), 1833

BIBLIOGRAPHY   Martin Cooper, *Opéra Comique*, Parrish, 1949

H.M.

recording eventually helped to secure its premiere by Portland Opera.

RECORDING   Beaton, Bainbridge, Bowden, Bell, Kitchiner, Elizabethan Singers, Pro Arte O, Herrmann, Pye, 1966
EDITION   v.s., Novello & Co, 1965

Other operatic works: *A Christmas Carol* (television), 1954; *A Child is Born* (television), 1955; *The King of Schnorrers* (musical comedy), 1968
BIBLIOGRAPHY   Steven S. Smith, *A Heart at Fire's Center, The Life and Music of Bernard Herrmann*, University of California Press, 1991

P.D.

BERNARD HERRMANN

b 29 June 1911, New York; *d* 24 December 1975, Los Angeles, US

Herrmann is remembered as one of the most accomplished film composers of the century. He studied at New York University with Percy Grainger and at the Juilliard School with Bernard Wagenaar. Herrmann worked as a conductor for films and television but he also directed major concert orchestras, often pioneering unusual repertoire such as the works of Charles Ives. The haunting qualities of Herrmann's film scores – *Citizen Kane* (1941), *Vertigo* (1958), *Psycho* (1960) and many more – are also evident in his magnum opus, the opera *Wuthering Heights*.

Wuthering Heights

Opera in four acts and a prologue (3h 15m)
Libretto by Lucille Fletcher, after the novel by Emily Brontë (1845–6)
Composed 1943–51
PREMIERE   6 November 1982, Portland Opera, Oregon

Herrmann and his then wife, Lucille Fletcher (the librettist of *Wuthering Heights*), visited Haworth and the Brontë home in 1945 (when Herrmann was conducting the Hallé Orchestra). This visit may have been the catalyst for his opera, although there are musical connections between it and his film score for Orson Welles's *Jane Eyre* (1943).

The opera follows the first half of Brontë's novel closely (differing only in the characterization of Heathcliff, here portrayed as a misunderstood tragic figure rather than Brontë's 'fierce, pitiless, wolfish man') but ends after Cathy's dream, thus reducing the narrative material to a manageable length. Herrmann and Fletcher took much of their text directly from the novel – both dialogue and description – adding apt extracts from Emily Brontë's poetry.

Herrmann's music, scored for a large orchestra and eight solo parts, avoids recitative, preferring a *parlando*-type style. The ostinati which are a Herrmann trademark appear frequently, helping to create atmospheric dramatic tension. The opera was never produced during Herrmann's lifetime, but his

HERVÉ

Florimond Ronger; *b* 30 June 1825, Houdain, France; *d* 3 November 1892, Paris

Hervé, together with Offenbach the founder of modern operetta, began his musical career as a church choirboy in Paris. At the Conservatoire he studied with Auber, and by the age of 15 was organist at the church of Bicêtre and was composing short vaudevilles for the inmates of the adjoining asylum. He began leading a double life, playing the organ and writing, conducting, acting and singing (tenor) at various theatres. His stage name was borrowed from a student, the Marquis d'Hervé.

A one-act tableau grotesque, *Don Quichotte et Sancho Pança* (1848), pointed the irreverent way to Hervé's burlesque future. The Palais-Royal theatre saw his five-act satire *Les folies dramatiques* in 1853 and by the following year Hervé was managing his own Folies-Concertantes (later the Folies-Nouvelles). Licensing restrictions prevented anything more ambitious than one-act diversions, which Hervé called 'lyric eccentricities' or one-act 'asphyxiations'. He also presented operettas by other composers, such as Delibes and Offenbach.

His witty short works were outmoded by the mid-1860s, by which time the full-length opéra-bouffe was licensed and in full flower. Hervé's contribution to this genre began in 1866 with the three-act *Les chevaliers de la table ronde*; the next year came a much greater success: *L'oeil crevé* (figuratively, 'Right in the Eye!'), which the critic on *Le Figaro* called 'distinguished, spiritual, joyous, really crazy, really Parisian . . . and wise!' *Chilpéric* (1868) was a world hit, a wacky travesty of 6th-century French history, with Hervé taking a leading part in the famous London presentation at the Lyceum. With *Le petit Faust* (1869) Hervé created perhaps his most interesting score.

Hervé had two more big international hits: the vaudeville-operettas *Lili* and *Mam'zelle Nitouche*. Because of his slapdash method of putting together so many instant parodies, Hervé's music lacks the sophistication of Offenbach's. His sometimes paltry tunes were not saved by elegant or lucid orchestration. But his comic invention and catchiness are evident, and his libretti are outlandish.

Le petit Faust
Little Faust

Opéra-bouffe in three acts (four tableaux) (2h)
Libretto by Hector Crémieux and Adolphe Jaime
PREMIERES 28 April 1869, Folies Dramatiques, Paris;
second version: 15 February 1882, Théâtre de la porte Saint-
Martin, Paris; UK: 18 April 1870, Lyceum, London; US: 26
September 1870, Grand Opera House, New York

This travesty of Gounod's 1859 opera appeared
barely two months after the premiere of a successful
production of the original at the Opéra. If it smacks
of speedy and raucous assembly, the operetta is
nevertheless one of his most happily madcap efforts.
The score not only features outright burlesque of
Gounod's music, but also hilariously inappropriate
tunes and similarly ridiculous lyrics. With its travesty
leads (Méphisto, Siebel), its considerable opportunity for spectacle, and its abundant high spirits,
Le petit Faust deserves more frequent revival.

RECORDING Disney, Dachary, Hamel, Rey, Ch and O of
French Radio, Clio, 1963
EDITIONS f.s., Heugel/Leduc (on hire); v.s., Heugel, [1869]

Mam'zelle Nitouche

Comédie-vaudeville in three acts (four tableaux) (2h)
Libretto by Henri Meilhac and Albert Millaud
PREMIERES 26 January 1883, Variétés, Paris; UK: 12 May
1884, Opéra Comique, London (as *Nitouche*); US: 1885,
Wallack's Theater, New York

This is one of the most celebrated and best-written
examples of the vaudeville-operetta, which took hold
in the 1880s and remained quite popular after
the turn of the century. The star was Anna Judic,
formerly of the *café-chantant* and Offenbach's
operettas. The plot shows off Hervé's own background – a
man who is a sober music master at a convent school
and a flashy operetta composer at the same time – to
tell the story of a demure convent girl Denise de
Flavigny (Miss Don't Touch), who enjoys a brief
escapade both on the stage and in the barracks
without too many finding out. Prominent among the
musical numbers are the song describing the music
man ('Pour le théâtre, Floridor, et pour le couvent
Celestin') and a military-accented drum song ('Le
long de la rue Lafayette').

The role of the organist–composer has attracted
top comedians, including Fernandel, assuring this
work's continued popularity – particularly in Central
Europe. However, the score is by no means as varied
and exhilarating as the ones Hervé supplied for his
1860s opéras-bouffes.

RECORDING Thibault, Fernandel, Ristori, Doniat,
unnamed O, Grassi, Decca, 1971
FILM Allégret, 1931
EDITIONS f.s., Heugel/Leduc (on hire); v.s., Heugel, [1883]

Other operettas: *L'ours et le pacha*, 1842; *Don Quichotte et
Sancho Pança*, 1848; *Les folies dramatiques*, 1853; *c.* 50 one-
act works, 1854–6; 9 revues and one-act operettas, 1858–62;
Les toréadors de Grenade, 1863, *Le joueur de flûte*, 1864; *La
liberté des théâtres*, 1864; *La revue pour rire, ou Roland à
Ronceveaux*, 1864; *La biche aux bois*, 1865; *Une fantasia,*

1865; *Les chevaliers de la table ronde*, 1866; *Les
métamorphoses de Tartempion*, 1866; *L'oeil crevé*, 1867;
Clodoche et Normande, 1867; *Trombolino*, 1868; *Chilpéric*,
1868; *Le Roi Amatibou*, 1868; *Les Turcs*, 1869; *Aladdin the
Second*, 1870; *Le trône d'Ecosse*, 1871; *La veuve du Malabar*,
1873; *Alice de Nevers*, 1875; *La belle poule*, 1875; *Estelle et
Némorin*, 1876; *La marquise des rues*, 1879; *Panurge*, 1879; *La
femme à papa*, 1879; *Le voyage en Amérique*, 1880; *La mère
des compagnons*, 1880; *La Roussotte* (completion of a Lecocq
work), 1881; *Lili*, 1882; *Le vertigo*, 1883; *Le Cosaque*, 1884;
La nuit aux soufflets, 1884; *Mam'zelle Gavroche*, 1885;
Frivoli, 1886; *Fla-Fla*, 1886; *Bacchanale*, 1892; *Le cabinet
Piperlin*, 1897
BIBLIOGRAPHY Louis Schneider, *Les maîtres de l'opérette
française: Hervé, Charles Lecocq*, Perrin, 1924

R.T.

RICHARD HEUBERGER

Richard Franz Joseph Heuberger; *b* 18 June 1850, Graz; *d* 28
October 1914, Vienna

Heuberger, now remembered solely as an operetta
composer, was in fact a highly respected member of
Vienna's classical music establishment, and held
several important posts including professor at the
Konservatorium and chorus master of the Vienna
Männergesangsverein. He was also an influential
critic, eventually becoming, in 1896, Hanslick's
successor on the *Neue Freie Presse* in Vienna. In
1902 he published one of the first truly perceptive
biographies of Schubert, and from 1904 to 1906 he
edited the *Musikbuch aus Österreich*. Although
readily performed, his operas did not achieve lasting
success; this was to come when he began writing
operettas with the avowed intention of restoring the
classical style and orchestral finesse of Johann
Strauss's *Die Fledermaus* to the genre.

Der Opernball
The Opera Ball

Operetta in three acts (1h 30m)
Libretto by Victor Leon and Heinrich von Waldberg, after
the farce *Les Dominos roses* by Alfred Delacour and Alfred
Hennequin
PREMIERES 5 January 1898, Theater an der Wien, Vienna;
US: 24 May 1909, New York

The story of *Der Opernball* is one of two wives
outwitting their supposedly philandering husbands at
an opera ball in Paris. The work, Heuberger's most
successful, is characterized by elegant and seductive
waltz motives (notably the duet 'Gehen wir ins
Chambre séparée'), one particularly vivacious gallop,
and consistently refined musicianship. Owing to
pressure of time, Zemlinsky was recruited to assist
with the orchestration of Act I. *Der Opernball* still
appears regularly in the repertoire of the Vienna
Volksoper.

FILM von Bolvary (prod.), 1939
EDITION f.s., V. Kratochwill, [?1898]; v.s., Bosworths,
[?1908]

Operas: *Die Abenteuer einer Neujahrsnacht*, 1886; *Manuel Venegas*, 1889, rev. as *Mirjam oder Das Maifest*, 1894 Other operettas: *Ihre Exzellenz*, 1899, rev. as *Eine entzückende Frau; Der Sechsuhrzug*, 1900; *Das Baby*, 1902; *Barfüssele*, 1905; *Der Fürst von Düsterstein*, 1909; *Don Quichotte*, 1910

BIBLIOGRAPHY A. Bauer, *Opern und Operetten in Wien*, Graz/Cologne, 1955

N.D.

JUAN HIDALGO

Juan Hidalgo [Ydalgo]; *b c.* 1612–16, Madrid; *d* ?May 1685, Madrid

Hidalgo was almost certainly the first Spanish opera composer and unquestionably the leading court composer in 17th-century Spain. He served, as harpist and keyboard-player, in the royal chapel in Madrid from about the age of 18 until his death. From 1658 or earlier he collaborated with the foremost Spanish playwrights, notably Calderón, in creating ten or more zarzuelas and operas for the Madrid court. The zarzuelas shared common musical, literary and scenic styles with his operas, both being modelled on Roman spectacle opera and the Venetian operas of Cavalli. They differed from his operas only in that spoken passages alternated with vocal passages. His two wholly sung operas, both performed in the Buen Retiro royal palace near Madrid in 1660, were – again like the zarzuelas – spectacularly staged, the aim being, in the words of Calderón, the political one of 'matching the splendours of other [European] nations'. The first, *La púrpura de la rosa*, was a one-act piece no doubt presented speculatively to the court because, again according to Calderón, the Spanish temperament preferred variety to the monotony of dramas sung throughout. It must have met with the court's general approval, nevertheless, since they received a second commission, this time for a three-act opera. Though this work, *Celos aun del aire matan*, was given a few more performances in Spain (and in Latin America even as late as 1728), Calderón's premonitions seem to have been well grounded for there is no record of any further such operas having been commissioned in Hidalgo's lifetime, whereas the demand for part-sung, part-spoken zarzuelas by him continued unabated.

Hidalgo's importance is attested also by the way later Spanish composers, responding to an 18th-century revival of interest in aristocratic opera from Durón in 1700 to Rodríguez de Hita with his popularizing zeal in the 1760s, followed in his footsteps with their adaptation of foreign operatic styles to Spanish traditions.

Celos aun del aire matan
Jealousy, even of air, is deadly
Comedia/fiesta cantada in three acts (1h 30m)
Libretto by Pedro Calderón de la Barca
Composed 1660

PREMIERES 5 December 1660, Buen Retiro Palace, near Madrid; US: March 1976, Trinity University, San Antonio (version by Pedro Sáenz); UK: 5 April 1983, London (BBC Radio 3)

Celos aun del aire matan is the earliest surviving Spanish opera. Together with other extant zarzuela music (especially *Los celos hacen estrellas*), it shows that Hidalgo did not lag behind other European composers in adopting the operatic practice of Italian masters such as Cavalli in his use of dramatic, affective recitative, fluid arias or ariosi and homorhythmic choruses, combining these techniques with traditionally Spanish rhythms (notably a swinging, syncopated style) and, arguably, the strophic form of the *villancico*. Calderón's intelligent libretto turns the well-worn story of the love of Cephalus for the nymph Procris into a symbolic conflict between Diana, the harsh goddess of chastity, and Venus, the compassionate goddess of love. The plot develops on two planes: on the visible, worldly level, Diana and most of the mortals behave egotistically and maliciously, while from the higher realm the unseen Venus prompts them to behave with more charitable understanding. The spectacular scenography of the 1660 performance served not only to amaze the courtly audience but to drive home the serious message Calderón aimed at them. Recent revivals suggest that the music, as well as the libretto, is of much more than mere historical interest.

EDITIONS Gerald R. Benjamin (ed.), performing edn, San Antonio, Trinity University, 1981; Ruth Landes Pitts, *Don Juan Hidalgo, Seventeenth-century Spanish Composer*, dissertation, George Peabody College for Teachers, Nashville, Tennessee, 1968; Pedro Sáenz, modern version, Buenos Aires, 1981

Other operatic works: *La estutua de Prometeo*, 1653; *Los celos hacen estrellas*, 1672; excerpts from other works; *c.* 6 lost works
BIBLIOGRAPHY Ruth Landes Pitts, *supra*; Jack Sage, 'La música de Juan Hidalgo', in Juan Vélez de Guevara, *Los celos hacen estrellas*, J. E. Varey and N. D. Shergold (eds), Tamesis, 1970; L. K. Stein, '*La plática de los dioses*: Music and the Calderonian Court Play', in M. R. Greer (ed.), Pedro Calderón de la Barca, *La estatua de Prometeo*, Kassel, 1986

J.W.S.

ALFRED HILL
Alfred Francis Hill; *b* 16 November 1870, Melbourne, Australia; *d* 30 October 1960, Sydney, Australia

Alfred Hill was one of the most significant of the first-generation Australian composers. His earliest musical experiences were as a player in theatre orchestras (violin and cornet) and, after studying in Leipzig (1887–91), as orchestra leader and conductor in New Zealand and Australia. He was one of the founding fathers of the New South Wales Conservatorium and its first Professor of Composition and Harmony (1916–34).

His works cover a wide range of genres, and include ten operettas or operas, all written in the early stages of his career. The music is basically late Romantic in idiom, with influences from Australian and New Zealand native music (*Hinemoa, Tawhaki, Tapu* and *Teora* use Maori music, of which he made a study) and Celtic folk music. The operas combine the opéra-comique style (with spoken dialogue), with through-composition, using leitmotifs. Some are comic operas, others are allegorical pageant-type works.

Operatic works: *The Whipping Boy*, (1891–3), fragments 1896; *Lady Dolly*, 1900; *Tapu, or A Tale of a Maori Pah*, 1903; *Don Quixote de la Mancha*, (1904); *A Moorish Maid, or Queen of the Riffs*, 1905; *Teora, or The Enchanted Flute*, (1913), 1929; *The Rajah of Shivapore*, (1914), 1917; *Giovanni the Sculptor*, 1914; *Auster*, (1919), 1922; *The Ship of Heaven*, 1923

BIBLIOGRAPHY John Mansfield Thomas, *A Distant Music – The Life and Times of Alfred Hill*, OUP, 1980

A.I.G.

FERDINAND HILLER

Ferdinand von Hiller; *b* 24 October 1811, Frankfurt am Main; *d* 11 May 1885, Cologne

Hiller was an influential figure in the musical life of mid-19th-century Germany, particularly through his friendships with many of the leading musicians of the day. From 1826 to 1828 he studied the piano with Hummel, then lived in Paris for seven years composing mainly chamber works. He went to Italy in 1837, and there his first opera, *Romilda*, was recommended to La Scala, Milan, by Rossini, but it did not survive its second performance. Returning to Germany in 1842, Hiller renewed his youthful friendship with Mendelssohn and was closely associated with the Schumanns and Wagner (1844–7). Greater success came with *Konradin der letzte Hohenstaufe*, to a text by Reinick (the librettist of Schumann's *Genoveva*), composed for Dresden. After several itinerant years, Hiller accepted the post of city kapellmeister in Cologne where he remained for the rest of his life. During this period he counted Brahms among his friends and Max Bruch among his pupils. Hiller's music is not strikingly original, and at its best is akin to that of Mendelssohn. His last three operas enjoyed no great success, but were respectfully received.

Operas: *Romilda*, 1839; *Der Traum in der Christnacht*, 1845; *Konradin, der letzte Hohenstaufe*, 1847; *Der Advokat*, 1854; *Die Katakomben*, 1862; *Der Deserteur*, 1865

BIBLIOGRAPHY R. Sietz (ed.), *Aus Ferdinand Hillers Briefwechsel*, Volk, 1958–70

C.Br.

JOHANN ADAM HILLER

b 25 December 1728, Wendisch-Ossig, nr Görlitz; *d* 16 June 1804, Leipzig

From his early studies at the Görlitz Gymnasium and at the Kreuzschule in Dresden, Hiller gained the sound general and musical education on which his remarkable career was based. In 1751, after matriculating at Leipzig University, he appears, while ostensibly reading law, to have devoted at least as much of his time to his varied musical activities. Subsequently, apart from three relatively short periods – as steward to Count Brühl in Dresden (1754–58), as kapellmeister to the Duke of Courland (1785) and as music director in Breslau (1787–89) – Leipzig was his home. His earliest compositions appeared there during the 1750s; and in 1754 his first considerable literary work was published, a treatise on the power of music to emulate nature (*Abhandlung über die Nachahmung der Natur in der Musik*). Thereafter he took an increasingly active role in the musical life of the city, as director of the Grosses Concert (1763–71), and from 1781 of the Gewandhaus concerts, as founder of an important song school, as music director at the Paulinerkirche in 1778 and additionally at the Neukirche in 1783, and as editor of, and major contributor to, the *Wöchentliche Nachrichten* (1766–70), the first modern-style periodical to specialize in music history, criticism and aesthetics. Ever idealistic in his aims, he sought constantly to serve the best interests of his fellow musicians and to raise public awareness of the significance of their work.

Hiller's reputation as a composer rests principally on the eleven singspiels he wrote between 1766 and 1773 in collaboration with the poet C. F. Weisse (1726–1804), mainly for the Rannstädter Thor theatre in Leipzig. Though not the earliest examples of the genre, they were the first to confirm its artistic significance, and served as a model for numerous later composers, including Johann André, Christian Neefe, Anton Schweitzer and Georg Benda. Initially, in 1766, he took Weisse's play *Die verwandelten Weiber, oder Der Teufel ist los* (a German version of the one-act ballad farce *The Devil to Pay* by Charles Coffey), and its sequel *Der lustige Schuster*, and added a number of new songs to the music already written previously by J. C. Standfuss. Also produced in 1766, but less successfully, was *Lisuart und Dariolette*, a fully-fledged 'romantic opera' in German, with *secco* recitatives and *da capo* arias, which reflects his admiration for the broad *cantabile* style of Hasse and Graun. In the works that followed Hiller adopted as his model the opéras comiques of the period, particularly those of Monsigny. By replacing the characteristic airs of the French genre with simple German lieder while retaining some Italianate expansiveness in various of the arias, and introducing short ensembles, he provided a significantly new stylistic compound, a kind of bourgeois antithesis to the aristocratic opera seria of the Italians and their German imitators.

After 1779 Hiller ceased writing for the stage and following his appointment in 1789 as kantor of St Thomas's (church and school), he further developed his long-standing interest in church composition. Greatly esteemed by his contemporaries, Hiller provided an example in artistic idealism of lasting benefit to German musical life. In 1832 a small monument was erected in Leipzig to his memory, close to the Bach memorial outside the kantor's residence at the Thomasschule.

A scene from Die Jagd: *engraving from a collection of libretti by Chr. F. Weisse (Leipzig, 1977)*

Die Jagd

The Hunt

Eine komische oper in three acts

Libretto by Christian Felix Weisse, after Charles Colle's *La partie de chasse de Henri IV* (1763)

PREMIERE 29 January 1770, Kleines Schlosstheater, Weimar

In *Die Jagd*, as also in *Die Liebe auf dem Lande* (1768), varied styles are skilfully deployed to match the social status of the characters portrayed – elevated arias for the upper classes and folk-style or comic songs for the more plebeian. The individual songs, which were written often for actors who

were not primarily singers, achieve directness of expression without descending to *naïveté* or banality and won widespread acclaim. *Die Jagd* appears to have inspired Goethe to write singspiel texts and its continuing popularity was attested by the regenerated and rescored version which Lortzing produced of it in 1830. It was highly regarded by Wagner.

EDITION f.s., facsimile, Garland, 1985; v.s., Breitkopf, 1770

Operatic works: *Die verwandelten Weiber, oder Der Teufel ist los, erster Teil* (12 numbers by Standfuss), 1766; *Der lustige Schuster, oder Der Teufel ist los, zweiter Teil* (7 numbers by Standfuss), 1766; *Lisuart und Dariolette, oder Die Frage und die Antwort*, 1766; *Lottchen am Hofe*, 1767; *Die Muse*, 1767; *Die Liebe auf dem Lande*, 1768; *Der Dorfbarbier* (some numbers by Neefe), 1771; *Der Aehrndtekranz*, 1771; *Der Krieg*, 1772; *Die Jubelhochzeit*, 1773; *Die kleine Aerenleserin* (children's operetta), 1778; *Das Grab des Mufti, oder Die beiden Geitzigen*, 1779; *Poltis, oder Das gerettete Troja*, ?1777

BIBLIOGRAPHY L. Hoffmann-Erbrecht and A. A. Abert, 'Johann Adam Hiller', in *MGG*; K. Kawada, *Studien zu den Singspielen von Johann Adam Hiller (1728–1804)*, dissertation, Marburg, 1969

B.S.

PAUL HINDEMITH

b 16 November 1895, Hanau, nr Frankfurt; *d* 28 December 1963, Frankfurt

Hindemith came to prominence in the rebuilding of German musical life after the First World War, by which time he had begun composing and was already working as a professional violinist, violist, clarinettist and pianist. As a violinist in the Frankfurt Opera orchestra he attracted the attention of the conductor Fritz Busch, who was on the look-out for new operas by young composers. In 1921 Busch conducted the Stuttgart premieres of Hindemith's one-act *Mörder, Hoffnung der Frauen* and *Das Nusch-Nuschi* as a double-bill.

Their provocative attitude to sexual matters in a continuing style of German Expressionism attracted public and critical attention. The next year they were supplemented by another one-act opera of a comparable nature, *Sancta Susanna*, first performed at Frankfurt in a triple-bill with the others. Taken in succession they reflect a progress in musical idiom from eclectic late Romanticism to a more disciplined control of structure and expressive character.

During the 1920s, while pursuing an active performing career, Hindemith embraced a style of severe contrapuntal neo-classicism in his music. His first three-act opera, *Cardillac*, premiered in 1926, is the major large-scale example of this (most of the others are chamber works). The following year Hindemith was appointed professor of composition at the Berlin Hochschule für Musik, where the practical application of his teaching was realized in what he termed *Gebrauchsmusik*: 'useful music' for amateurs as well as professionals.

At this time he also took an interest in popular music as exemplified in night-club jazz and the Berlin satirical cabarets, which led to the brief *Hin und zurück* (1927) followed by the three-act *Neues vom Tage* (1929), both with a libretto by Marcellus Schiffer, a leading cabaret writer/artist in Berlin. A concern with the position of the artist in society, partly suggested in *Cardillac* and renewed at a time when the darkening political scene in Germany brought the advent of the Nazi government, led to *Mathis der Maler* as a partly autobiographical allegory, for which he wrote his own libretto and adopted a more expressive musical style.

An outstandingly successful performance of the *Mathis der Maler Symphony*, extracted from the opera in advance of its production and conducted by Furtwängler, brought Hindemith into conflict with the Nazi authorities (Hitler having been offended by a bath scene in *Neues vom Tage*), and his Jewish connections led to a partial boycott of his music from 1934 and a full proscription in 1937. Hindemith left Germany for Switzerland, where *Mathis der Maler* was first staged in 1938, and in 1940 he went to the US, becoming a much admired professor at Yale University and taking US citizenship in 1946.

Mathis der Maler remained unperformed on the German stage until that year. After major revisions to *Cardillac* and *Neues vom Tage* in the early 1950s (published as separate editions), Hindemith turned to another historical subject for *Die Harmonie der Welt* – a commission for the 1957 Munich Opera Festival. By this time he had moved back to Europe and was living at Blonay, by Lake Lucerne. He gave up further teaching at Zurich University to concentrate on composition and conducting and, two years before he died, wrote his remaining opera on Thornton Wilder's *The Long Christmas Dinner* – his only setting of a libretto in English.

Mörder, Hoffnung der Frauen
Murder, Hope of Women
Schauspiel in one act, Op. 12 (25m)
Text by Oskar Kokoschka (1907)
Composed 1919
PREMIERE 4 June 1921, Württembergisches Landestheater, Stuttgart

A setting of a short, fragmented text evolved by Kokoschka from a series of his drawings of man and woman in violent combat, first presented in Vienna as a spoken play with improvised percussion. The text published in *Der Sturm*, an influential avant-garde magazine, attracted Hindemith's attention, and he set it for eight solo singers and mixed chorus with a large orchestra. Its Expressionist content involves a woman's carnal desire for a man who has abused her and whom she has physically wounded. Recovering his own strength from the satisfaction of her lust, the man abandons the woman and leaves her to die. Hindemith's musical idiom proved too indebted to the late Romanticism of Wagner and Strauss to be a satisfactory medium for the declamatory and sometimes gibberish text, though it interested Fritz

Busch sufficiently for him to conduct its premiere in a double-bill with *Das Nusch-Nuschi*.

RECORDING Schnaut, Peacock, Gahmlich, Grundheber, RIAS Ch, Berlin Radio SO, Albrecht, Wergo, 1988
EDITIONS f.s., *Samtliche Werke*, I/1, Schott, 1979; v.s., Schott, 1921

Das Nusch-Nuschi
Spiel for Burmese marionettes in one act (two scenes), Op. 20 (30m)
Text by Franz Blei (1904)
Composed 1920
PREMIERE 4 June 1921, Württembergisches Landestheater, Stuttgart

This is an operetta-style entertainment for 24 singers (including a counter-tenor and a coloratura soprano), one speaking role, one mime and small mixed chorus, and a medium-sized orchestra with celesta, mandoline, and percussion (four players). The Nusch-Nuschi is half alligator, half rat, and the irreverent parody of Expressionism includes an almost direct quotation from Wagner's King Mark for the King of Burma, whose drunken Field-Marshal is accused of enjoying the monarch's four wives and is sentenced to be castrated. A dance contest also takes place, and Hindemith uses musical *chinoiserie* similar to that previously ventured by Ravel and Stravinsky.

RECORDING Lindsley, Schreckenbach, Knutson, Stamm, von Halem, Berlin Radio SO, Albrecht, Wergo, 1988
EDITIONS f.s., *Samtliche Werke*, I/2, Schott, 1921; v.s., Schott, 1921

Sancta Susanna
Opera in one act, Op. 21 (35m)
Text by August Albert Bernhard Stramm (1913)
Composed 1921
PREMIERE 26 March 1922, Opernhaus, Frankfurt

As with *Mörder, Hoffnung der Frauen*, Hindemith's attention was drawn to a text first published in the magazine *Der Sturm*. He set it for three women soloists, two speaking roles and women's chorus, with a large orchestra including celesta and organ. It tells of Sister Susanna, a young nun inflamed by forces beyond her control, including the sight of a lovers' tryst and another nun's tale of sexual arousal, to remove her clothes and clutch at a crucified Christ on an altar. The music is more sympathetic to psychological expression, more tightly wrought and more personal than in the previous two one-act works, to which it was first added in a triple-bill of provocative scandal and corresponding public interest.

RECORDING Donath, Schnaut, Schreckenbach, RIAS Ch, Berlin Radio SO, Albrecht, Wergo, 1988
EDITIONS f.s., *Samtliche Werke*, I/3, Schott, 1975; v.s., Schott, 1921

Cardillac
Opera in three acts (four scenes), Op. 39 (1h 30m); rev. version in four acts (2h 15m)
Libretto by Ferdinand Lion, after E. T. A. Hoffmann's *Das*

Fraulein von Scuderi (1819); rev. version by the composer
after F. Lion
Composed 1926; rev. 1952
PREMIERES   9 November 1926, Staatsoper, Dresden; UK:
18 December 1936, BBC broadcast (in English); 11 March
1970, Sadler's Wells, London (New Opera Company); rev.
version: 20 June 1952, Stadttheater, Zurich; US: 26 July 1957,
Santa Fe
CAST   original version: Cardillac *bar*, His Daughter *s*, Lady
s, Officer *t*, Cavalier *t*, Gold Merchant *b*, Police Officer *high
b*, King *silent role*; chorus of knights, ladies, police, people,
satb; rev. version: Cardillac *bar*, His Daughter *s*, Her Friend *t*,
Opera Singer *s*, Officer *b*, Young Cavalier *t*, Singers in Lully's
Phaëton a, t, b, Rich Marquis *silent role*; *satb* chorus of
people, guards, chorus members, theatre staff, dancers
LARGE CHAMBER ORCHESTRA including tenor sax and
minimum 18 str; onstage band: 8 players (original version);
9 players (rev. version)

Hindemith was at the height of his concern with a
neo-classical baroque aesthetic, exemplified in
several works titled *Kammermusik* and in the
Concerto for Orchestra, when he composed *Cardillac*.
It also marked his first expression of a recurring
concern with the figure of a creative artist in society,
and applied his principles in a strictly musical
response to a psychopathic story which might earlier
have attracted the Expressionist approach of his one-
act operas. Avoiding psychological or illustrative
elements, it is laid out in the closed numbers of aria,
duet, fugato, passacaglia and the like, intended to
symbolize rather than express character and
situation, and to generate dramatic impetus by
contrast.

SYNOPSIS (original version)
Act I   Cardillac is a master goldsmith in late 17th-
century Paris, so obsessed by the beauty of his
artefacts that he cannot bear to be parted from them.
If persuaded to sell he regains the treasure by the
drastic expedient of murdering the purchaser.
Several such crimes have terrorized Paris. A Lady is
heard promising her favours to a Cavalier in return
for the finest example of Cardillac's art. When the
Cavalier brings a golden belt to her bedroom he is
attacked and killed by an intruder, who escapes with
the belt.

Act II   Cardillac's workshop is visited by a Gold
Merchant, who suspects the goldsmith. Cardillac's
Daughter and the Officer plan to elope. The King
and courtiers come to admire Cardillac's handiwork
but are rebuffed. He consents to his Daughter's
marriage; the Officer obtains a gold chain as a
wedding present but Cardillac follows after him.

Act III   He succeeds only in wounding the
Officer, who recognizes him. The Officer refuses to
betray Cardillac, who first tries to pin the guilt on the
Merchant before himself confessing, at which the
mob turn on him and put him to death.

By imposing set polyphonic forms on his text
Hindemith felt he was reasserting the music's pre-
eminence, but in performance it was found that the
two elements moved on separate planes of a
listener's perception. For instance, the murder at the
end of Act I is accompanied by a two-part flute

invention; the Daughter's aria is a concerto grosso
featuring violin, oboe and horn *concertante*; the
court's visit to the workshop is entirely in wordless
mime; the opera's finale is a passacaglia.

Hindemith's 1952 revision involved some rewriting
of the text which he undertook himself, adding an act
to incorporate parts of Lully's opera *Phaëton* (1683),
and altering the vocal line over a more richly scored
orchestral part. Hindemith put an embargo on
performing the first version, which was lifted at
Wuppertal and the Holland Festival in 1961. The few
productions since have preferred the stronger
original version.

RECORDINGS   original version: 1. Kirschstein, Söderström,
Katz, Grobe, Fischer-Dieskau, Kohn, Ch and O of Cologne
Radio, Keilberth, DG, 1966; 2. Schweizer, Schnaut,
Protschka, Schunk, Nimsgern, Stamm, Berlin Radio
Chamber Ch and SO, Albrecht, Wergo, 1989
EDITIONS   original version: f.s., *Samtliche Werke*, I/4, Schott
1979/80; v.s., Schott, 1926; rev. version: f.s., *Samtliche Werke*,
I/5, Schott, 1966; v.s., arr. composer, Schott, 1952

Hin und zurük
There and Back
Sketch with music in one act, Op. 45a (12m)
Libretto by Marcellus Schiffer
PREMIERES   15 July 1927, Stadthalle, Baden-Baden; US: 22
April 1928, Philadelphia; UK: 8 July 1958, Manchester,
Palace Theatre (Opera da Camera de Buenos Aires)

A brief skit on operatic Expressionism derived by
Schiffer from an English revue sketch, and set for
five singers and one spoken role, accompanied by
wind sextet, two pianos (three players) and backstage
harmonium. A young wife is killed by her husband in
a jealous moment, at which a Wise Man appears and
reverses time so that the same events (though not the
music) are then played backwards to the start.
Composed for a festival of chamber operas, it was
written in a light rhythmical and melodic style as
something of a preliminary study for *Neues vom Tage*
with the same librettist.

RECORDING   Miller, Bock, Schaible, Kuhnle, Berlin SO,
Gruber, FSM, *c.* 1982
EDITIONS   f.s., *Samtliche Werke*, I/6, Schott, 1982; v.s., arr.
composer, Schott, 1927; 2nd edn, 1955

Neues vom Tage
News of the Day
Lustige oper in three parts (eleven scenes) (2h)
Libretto by Marcellus Schiffer
Composed 1928–9; rev. 1953 (two acts and ten scenes)
PREMIERES   8 June 1929, Krolloper, Berlin; rev. version:
7 April 1954, Teatro San Carlo, Naples (in Italian); US: 12
August 1961, Santa Fe
CAST   original version: Laura *s*, Eduard *bar*, Hermann *t*,
Herr M. *t*, Frau M. *ms*; *s*, *t*, 3 *b*, sextet of Managers (2 *t*, 2 *bar*,
2 *b*); rev. version: Laura *s*, Eduard *bar*, Baron d'Houdoux *b*,
Frau Pick *a*, Herr Hermann *t*; 2 *s*, *a*, *t*, *bar*, 4 *b*, sextet of
Managers (2 *t*, 2 *bar*, 2 *b*); *satb* chorus of attendants, men,
secretaries, museum visitors, tourists, hotel staff, theatre-
goers, show girls; dancers
MEDIUM ORCHESTRA including alto sax, perc (2 players),
hp, mand, banjo, 2 pf (3 players), str

Hindemith's Neues vom Tage *(Darmstadt, 1929)*

Hindemith regarded the Berlin cabaret revues of the late 1920s as the most characteristic expression of urban life and 'it seemed logical that the features of this new form should be applied to an opera'. He asked Marcellus Schiffer, 'one of the most successful and sophisticated authors of such pieces', to collaborate with him. After an initial experiment with the short *Hin und züruck* they created the full-evening *Neues vom Tage* in which the revue technique was adapted for the operatic stage.

SYNOPSIS (original version)
Part I The domestic squabbles between two married couples, Herr and Frau M. and the newly wed Eduard and Laura, lead them to seek divorce through a co-respondent agency. The agency's chief, Herr Hermann, undertakes the work himself but usually falls in love with his female clients. This is much to the chagrin of his secretaries (accompanied by rhythmic typewriters, pianos and percussion). An assignation is arranged at a museum, but Eduard appears and is so infuriated that he shatters a valuable exhibit, is arrested and taken to gaol.

Part II Installed in a luxury hotel by the co-respondent, Laura is seen taking a bath, praising the joys of central heating and comparing the merits of gas and electricity. Violent argument is generated by the entry of Hermann from an adjoining room, followed by Frau M. and successive hotel staff, while Laura's bathwater is rapidly cooling. News of their

exploits appears in the tabloids and turns Laura and Eduard into celebrities.

Part III Receiving lucrative show-business contracts for their story, they become 'news of the day' with no private life. They enact their domestic rows at the top of a variety bill, watched by the newly remarried M.s among the audience. Though Laura and Eduard would rather return to peace together, public demand forces them continually to re-enact the cycle of disagreement and divorce.

The premiere conducted by Otto Klemperer enjoyed a partial success (thanks mainly to the jazz element in the music) though the composer disliked the staging. Certain operatic conventions were parodied, as in a 'hate duet' in foxtrot tempo instead of a love duet, and a blues waltz for the quartet of disaffected couples. The scene of Laura in her bath caused some scandal. The revision of 1953, first conducted by the composer, affected the story-line more than the music. Hindemith changed some characters and added others, and altered the ending to restore to Laura and Eduard their privacy.

RECORDING Werres, Nicolai, Pro Musica of Cologne Music Academy, NDR O, Latham-Koenig, Wergo, 1990
EDITIONS original version: f.s., *Samtliche Werke*, I/7, Schott, 1929; v.s., Schott, 1929; rev. version: f.s., *Samtliche Werke*, I/8, Schott, 1954; v.s., Schott, 1954

Mathis der Maler

Mathis the Painter
Opera in seven scenes (3h 15m)
Libretto by the composer
Composed 1934–5
PREMIERES   28 May 1938, Stadttheater, Zurich; UK: 15
March 1939, Queen's Hall, London (concert); 29 August
1952, King's Theatre, Edinburgh (Hamburg Staatsoper); US:
17 February 1956, Boston
CAST   Cardinal-Archbishop of Mainz *t*, Mathis *bar*, Lorenz
von Pommersfelden *b*, Wolfgang Capito *t*, Riedinger *b*, Hans
Schwalb *t*, Truchsess von Waldburg *b*, Sylvester von
Schaumberg *t*, Graf von Helfenstein *silent role*, Helfenstein's
piper *t*, Ursula *s*, Regina *s*, Grafin Helfenstein *a*; *satb* chorus
of monks, Catholics, Lutherans, women, students, citizens,
peasants, farm workers, demons
STANDARD ORCHESTRA   onstage: 3 tpt, bell

At a time when the Nazi regime in Germany was
beginning to tighten its grip, Hindemith based his
second treatment of the creative artist's position in
relation to social and political issues on Mathias
Grünewald (or Niethart), court painter in the early
16th century at Mainz, near where Hindemith was
born. Grünewald is remembered for the large linked
panels of the Isenheim altarpiece (now in the
Unterlinden Museum in Colmar), scenes from which

are regarded as a metaphor for the peasants' feelings
towards their overlords. They prompted ideas for
music and a libretto placing the artist at a crucial
point in the Peasants' Revolt of 1524.

SYNOPSIS

Prelude: *Engelkonzert*

Scene 1   In the courtyard of St Anthony's
monastery at Mainz, Mathis is painting a fresco; he
gives his horse to Schwalb, the peasant leader, to
help him and his daughter Regina to escape pursuing
troops, and promises his support.

Scene 2   Mathis pleads the peasants' cause to the
Cardinal-Archbishop, his patron, and is obliged to
leave his service.

Scene 3   Amid preparations for the burning of
Lutheran books, Mathis and Ursula pledge their love
though Riedinger, her father, plans she should marry
the Cardinal.

Scene 4   Mathis protests against the peasants'
brutality; Schwalb is killed and Mathis protects
Regina.

Scene 5   The Lutheran Ursula is introduced to the
Cardinal as a prospective bride to help solve his
financial problems; her faith wills her to submit to
marriage for the sake of her cause and the Cardinal,

Scene 7 from Mathis der Maler, *with Günther Reich (Mathis) and Sven-Olof Eliasson (Cardinal); (Düsseldorf, 1980)*

impressed, chooses to remain celibate while giving permission for Lutherans to declare themselves openly.

Scene 6 Mathis and Regina, in flight, rest in the Odenwald; Regina sleeps while Mathis endures visionary temptations as if he were St Anthony, finally redeemed by the Cardinal, in the guise of St Paul (a subject of the altarpiece).

Scene 7 In Mathis's studio, Regina is dying, tended by Ursula. The Cardinal takes a last leave of Mathis, who puts away the tools of his art in humble acceptance of his own impending death.

Into a musical style still predominantly contrapuntal, Hindemith incorporates folksongs such as the medieval 'Es sungen drei Engel' in the Prelude, subtitled *Concert of Angels* (another altarpiece subject), which also became the opening movement of the three-movement Symphony drawn from the opera in 1934. Use is made of Gregorian chant and of pentatonic melodies modelled on it, while the tonal structure of the opera moves chromatically from C♯ in Scene 1 to E in the central scene, then reverses the process. The opera is long when given uncut and slow-moving. If the more active scenes lack theatrically effective climaxes, the more reflective passages of exaltation and despair, and the final resignation to the will of God, remain both a metaphor for the circumstances of the composer's experience and a moving expression of artistic principles.

RECORDING Koszut, Wagemann, King, Fischer-Dieskau, Meven, Feldhoff, Bavarian Radio Ch and O, Kubelik, HMV, c. 1978
EDITIONS f.s., *Samtliche Werke*, I/9, Schott, 1938; v.s., Schott, 1935; study s., Schott, 1937

Die Harmonie der Welt

The Harmony of the World
Opera in five acts (fourteen scenes) (3h)
Libretto by the composer
Composed 1956–7
PREMIERE 11 August 1957, Prinzregententheater (Bavarian Staatsoper), Munich
CAST Johannes Kepler (Earth) *bar*, Susanna (Venus) *s*, Little Susanna *s*, Katharina (Moon) *a*, General Wallenstein (Jupiter) *t*, Christoph Kepler *t*, Ulrich Grüsser (Mars) *t*, Daniel Hizler/Regensburg priest (Mercury) *bar*, Tansur (Saturn) *bar*, Emperor Rudolf II/Emperor Ferdinand II (Sun) *b*, Baron Starhemberg *bar*; 2 *s*, 2 *a*, *t*, *bar*, 2 *b*; *satb* chorus of students, young men and women, maidens, witnesses, officers, Jesuits, nobles, electoral princes, executioners, bailiffs, servants, the Landstande (body of people's representatives), Bohemian nobles, voices from the moon, stars, constellations
LARGE ORCHESTRA onstage orchestra (10 players)

Another study of a creative mind in relation to politics and society, this time a scientist, the historical astronomer Johannes Kepler (1571–1630), whose theories of planetary laws culminated in a mathematical concept of 'harmony' in the solar system proposed in *De Harmonice Mundi* (1619). Hindemith began first ideas for such an opera in the 1930s; they came to fruition only under pressure to meet a commitment to launch the 1957 Munich

Opera Festival. He related Kepler's theories to his own ideas of an extended system of tonality (he compared the 'pull' of a tonic key directly to the force of gravity), and placed Kepler as an influential figure in the Thirty Years War – attacked by the Church, honoured by the state, troubled in family, and finding worldly disorder resolved in the harmony of the heavens only at his death.

SYNOPSIS
Act I 1608–11. The ambitious General Wallenstein hopes for support from Kepler's theories. Katarina, Kepler's mother, is suspected of witchcraft. Kepler and the Emperor Rudolf meet and discuss laws of the universe. When the emperor, Kepler's patron, is forced to abdicate, Kepler leaves Prague for Linz.

Act II 1613. The general, a Catholic convert, supports Archduke Ferdinand as emperor. Kepler's theories provoke conflict with religious dogma. He meets and falls in love with Susanna, who becomes his second wife.

Act III 1616–21. Katarina's unexpected arrival threatens Kepler's family stability. He gets her trial for witchcraft suspended but repulses her belief in alchemy.

Act IV 1628. General Wallenstein marches against the Swedes, and meets Kepler to enlist support from his theories.

Act V 1630. Susanna's religious faith is shaken, and she fears Kepler will soon die. He witnesses in hallucination the general's fall from power, and believes only death can bring the harmony of the universe. As he lies dying the figures in his life appear in the guise of heavenly bodies and become the music of the spheres.

Firm vocal lines and varied orchestral colour are handicapped by stodgy rhythms and a harmonic idiom largely deprived of sensuous appeal. At the premiere, conducted by the composer, the opera's musical strength was shown mostly to lie in the ensembles, of which there are several, though often concerned with philosophical or metaphysical discussion rather than the expression of character or feelings. The work's overall nature suggests more the category of masque. Hindemith preceded the opera in 1951 with a non-vocal symphony for concert performance with the same title.

RECORDING Koszut, Mathis, King, Cochran, Fischer-Dieskau, Ch and SO of Bavarian Radio, Kubelik, DG, 1970s
EDITIONS f.s., *Samtliche Werke*, I/10, Schott, 1959; v.s., arr. composer, Schott, 1957

The Long Christmas Dinner

Opera in one act (1h)
Libretto by Thornton Wilder, after his own play (1931); German version, *Das lange Weihnachtsmahl*, by the composer
Composed 1960
PREMIERES 17 December 1961, Mannheim Nationaltheater (in German); US: 13 March 1963, New York; UK: 20 November 1967, International Students' House, London

Hindemith's last opera, set to an English text, was a close collaboration between composer and librettist, who adapted his own short play to Hindemith's specifications. It encapsulates the 90 Christmas dinners over four generations in the Bayard household between 1840 and 1930, with new arrivals 'born' through a door at one side and making final exits through an opposite door, such as the soldier bound for Flanders in the First World War. There are 11 solo roles, and Hindemith's score is for chamber orchestra of modest size but including bass clarinet, double-bassoon and tuba, whose low registers help the voices to stand out clearly.

The writing is less concerned with musical dialectic than in previous operas and more with emotional expression, cast in strongly tonal terms whose highlight is an entirely triadic sextet which precedes the soldier's departure to war. Family chatter alternates with reflective interludes, mostly ensembles of quintet, quartet and trio, usually with canonic dialogue between the voices, and with a few short arias. The Christmas scene is set by an introduction based on the theme of 'God rest you merry gentlemen'. Hindemith conducted the premiere, and intended to compose a comedy to provide a double-bill, but his own death supervened.

EDITIONS f.s., *Samtliche Werke*, I/11, Schott, 1986; v.s., Schott, 1961

Other operatic work: *Tuttifanchen* (*Weihnachtsmarchen*), 1922
BIBLIOGRAPHY Paul Hindemith, *A Composer's World: Horizons and Limitations* (The Charles Eliot Norton Lectures 1949–50), Harvard University Press, 1952; *rp*, Peter Smith, 1969; Ian Kemp, *Hindemith*, OUP (Oxford Studies), 1970; Geoffrey Skelton, *Paul Hindemith: The Man Behind the Music*, Gollancz, 1975

N.G.

ALUN HODDINOTT
b 11 August 1929, Bargoed, Glamorgan, Wales

The Welsh composer Hoddinott showed an early talent for writing in abstract forms, which developed under the influence of Alan Rawsthorne and Bartók into an individual and chromatically inflected musical language of considerable rhetorical power. He came to opera comparatively late, having established his reputation with an impressive output of instrumental music. His first opera, *The Beach of Falesa*, to a libretto by Glyn Jones after Robert Louis Stevenson's short story, was premiered by Welsh National Opera in 1974.

A prodigious operatic output – five operas in six years – is not only characteristic of Hoddinott's ebullient creativity, but also suggests that his experience in instrumental music enabled him to tackle the dramatic challenges of opera successfully. Contemporary in sound without being avant-garde, his music possesses an unassailable melodic foundation, a highly polished surface making particular use of woodwind and tuned percussion, and an ability to modulate convincingly between contrasting

temperaments that has also ensured immediate accessibility for his stage works.

With the exception of *The Trumpet Major* (to a libretto by Myfanwy Piper after the novel by Thomas Hardy), his main baritone roles were written for the voice of Geraint Evans. Following the example of Britten's *Owen Wingrave*, two of his operas are for television: *The Magician* and *The Rajah's Diamond*, a 50th birthday commission from the BBC, also to a libretto by Piper.

Operas: *The Beach of Falesa*, 1974; *The Magician*, 1976; *What the Old Man Does is Always Right*, 1977; *The Rajah's Diamond*, 1979; *The Trumpet Major*, 1981
BIBLIOGRAPHY Basil Deane, *Alun Hoddinott*, University of Wales Press, 1978; Malcom Boyd, '*The Trumpet Major*', *MT*, vol. 122 (1981), pp. 237–8

N.W.

E. T. A. HOFFMANN
Ernst Theodor Amadeus (originally Ernst Theodor Wilhelm) Hoffmann; b 24 January 1776, Königsberg; d 25 June 1822, Berlin

Although he was also a conductor and a composer, Hoffmann's contribution to music was above all as a writer. He published a substantial number of valuable critical articles and reviews, especially of works by Beethoven, whose instrumental music he regarded as embodying the highest Romantic achievement. He also wrote a number of reviews advancing his views of Romantic opera. As with other German writers of the day, especially Weber, this involved taking a stand against Italian opera (he demolished Paer's *Sofonisba* for its dramatic triviality, and savaged Rossini as a frivolous composer not worthy of true art), and against the superficial stage devices of the day (in a sardonic article, 'Der vollkommene Maschinist'). It also involved advancing the cause of French opera. He upheld Boieldieu and especially praised Méhul for his orchestral mastery and for his ability to conceive a work as a totality. His greatest admiration went to Gluck, for the same qualities but also for depicting not details but states of mind, and to Mozart.

However, it is not possible to draw a line between criticism and fiction in Hoffmann's work. His story *Ritter Gluck* imagines an encounter between a young musician and the old composer, whom he sees as a mediator with the infinite. In *Don Juan*, the young musician is drawn into a mysterious relationship with Donna Anna, and hence with Mozart's ideals, during a performance of *Don Giovanni*: it was a pioneering story in associating love closely with death and in claiming the opera for Romanticism. In another story, *Der Dichter und der Komponist*, he argues in dialogue the problem of how to find good librettists and how to balance the requirements of drama and music in opera. These preoccupations absorbed him as a composer, and are most fully embodied in his *Undine*.

For much of his career, though, Hoffmann regarded himself as a musician rather than as a writer. As a young man, he taught music, and devoted himself to composition while working as a somewhat unpredictable government functionary. In Warsaw in 1804, he completed the first of his surviving operas, *Die lustigen Musikanten*; it was on the title page of this work that he signed himself for the first time with the middle name Amadeus, in token of an admiration for Mozart that is evident in the score. The nature of these early works is close to singspiel, though he is always careful to pay attention to the role of the chorus and the orchestra, and especially to the building up of a coherent dramatic structure from his separate numbers. It seems a paradox that the writer who was most associated with the extremes of the supernatural, the illogical and the mysterious in Romantic art should have attached himself to Mozartian values in his music. But his belief was that the language of Mozart should prove adaptable to new regions of feeling, as he declared Mozart himself had shown was possible with *Don Giovanni*.

From 1808 Hoffmann worked in Bamberg, though his post as theatre director was almost immediately removed from him and he was able to contribute to the theatre only as a composer. Thereafter, apart from a brief spell in Leipzig (1813–14), Hoffmann never succeeded in obtaining a permanent post as music director of a theatre. He was, however, able to pursue his musical interests, occasionally as scene designer but more intensively as composer and critic. He first wrote for the *Allgemeine musikalische Zeitung*, and was to be a regular and valued contributor, especially on opera. He also began publishing the tales in which opera and singing play a crucial role, which are to be variously found in the collections *Fantasiestücke in Callots Manier*, *Die Serapionsbrüder*, and *Kreisleriana*.

Even after the success of *Undine* in 1816, Hoffmann's career did not flourish any more vigorously. He worked in Berlin, including on the translation and preparation of Spontini's *Olympie*, which he admired as being capable of contributing to the establishment of German tragic opera. However, this brought him unwillingly into the rival party to Weber and *Der Freischütz* in 1821. His friendship with Weber was always equivocal, though he was probably not the author of some notorious anonymous articles attacking the new work: he did not live to fulfil his promise to Weber to review it. He may well also have felt himself overshadowed by a composer of greater gifts with a sensational success to his credit. Hoffmann himself was planning a new major opera at the time of his death: his ideas for it are not known. His loyalties to Gluck, to Beethoven (whose *Fidelio* he intended to, but did not, review) and to Mozart also inform his music. In the history of opera, he presents the case of an exceptionally gifted and intelligent critic whose compositional talent was of a different order from his literary imagination.

His character has haunted the imaginations of other artists, and his tales have provided the material for a number of other works. Among operas in which he appears, the most famous is Offenbach's *Les contes d'Hoffmann*, which uses three of his stories. Others on his stories include Busoni's *Die Brautwahl* and Hindemith's *Cardillac*. Wagner prepared a libretto on *Die Bergwerke zu Falun* for Dessauer, who did not use it.

Design by Carl Heinrich Schinkel for Kühleborn's water palace in Undine *(Berlin, 1816)*

Undine

Zauberoper in three acts, AV70 (2h 45m)
Composed February 1813 – 5 August 1814; rev. 1816
Libretto by Friedrich de la Motte Fouqué, after his own story
PREMIERES 3 August 1816, Königliches Schauspielhaus, Berlin; UK: 6 December 1991, Newman Rooms, Oxford

Undine is Hoffman's most important opera, hailed by Weber as representing the German ideal of opera, 'namely a self-sufficient work of art in which every feature and every contribution by the related arts are moulded together in a certain way and dissolve, to form a new world'. Weber was drawing attention to the unity of the work, which was in part achieved by some use of motif and also by its turning away from a series of isolated effects towards a more consistent whole. There is also an enterprising use of orchestration, as in the unaccompanied double-basses to usher in the Holy Man (Heilmann) at the start of the Act I terzetto. While keeping to a fairly conventional harmonic language, Hoffmann explores Romantic ideas that were novel at the time, among them the association of the hero and heroine in a transfigured death, described by Heilmann as a *Liebestod*. The music is in no way Wagnerian but it is possible that Wagner, a lifelong admirer of Hoffmann, remembered the term and its context.

SYNOPSIS

The plot concerns the love of the water spirit Undine, the adopted child of an old fisherman and his wife, for Huldbrand of Ringstetten: by marrying a mortal, she will gain a soul, but if betrayed by him will be destroyed. Fearing for her, the old water spirit Kühleborn opposes the relationship. Though she continues to be drawn to her native element, Undine is married to Huldbrand by the Holy Man. At Ringstetten, she is at first befriended by Berthalda, adopted child of the Count and Countess. When Berthalda discovers that her own true parents are the fisherfolk, she is enraged and storms out of the castle. Huldbrand follows with Undine. But he becomes increasingly uneasy at Undine's continued association with the other water spirits and rejects her. She sinks back into the waters. At the wedding of Huldbrand and Berthalda in Ringstetten Undine appears from a fountain, and she and Huldbrand are united in a loving death.

RECORDING Streich, Muszely, Grumbach, Kohn, Ch and SO of Bavarian Radio, Koetsier, Memories, c. 1970
EDITIONS f.ss., J. Kindermann (ed.) in E. T. A. Hoffmann, *Ausgewahlte musikalische Werke*, vols 1–3, Schott, 1971–2; v.ss., Hans Pfitzner (ed.), Peters, 1906; E. Hartzell (ed.), after Pfitzner, Doblinger, 1975

Singspiels: *Die Maske*, (1799); *Scherz, List und Rache*, ?1801–2 (lost); *Der Renegat*, (1804); *Faustina*, (1804); *Die lustigen Musikanten*, 1805 (RECORDING Schwann, 1983); *Die ungebetenen Gaste, oder Der Kanonikus von Mailand*, 1805 (lost); *Liebe und Eifersucht*, 1807
Melodramas: *Dirna*, 1809; *Sabinus* (inc.), (1810); *Saul, König in Israel*, 1811
Operas: *Der Trank der Unsterblichkeit*, 1808; *Aurora*, (1812), 1833; *Der Liebhaber nach dem Tode*, (1822) (inc., lost)

BIBLIOGRAPHY Gerald Abraham, 'Hoffmann as a Composer', in *MT*, vol. 83 (1942); *rp* in *Slavonic and Romantic Music*, London, 1968; David Charlton (ed.), *E. T. A. Hoffmann's Musical Writings*, CUP, 1989; R. M. Schafer, *E. T. A. Hoffmann and Music*, Toronto, 1975

J.W.

FRANZ ANTON HOFFMEISTER

b 12 May 1754, Rothenburg am Neckar; *d* 9 February 1812, Vienna

Hoffmeister is best remembered as one of the leading Viennese music publishers; by 1785 he was publishing music by all the leading Viennese composers, especially that of his close friend Mozart (including the 'Hoffmeister' Quartet, K. 499). Hoffmeister was also a prolific and talented composer in his own right and from 1806 he devoted himself to composition. Among his works the grand heroic–comic opera *Der Königssohn aus Ithaka*, to a libretto by Schikaneder, scored a great success and was performed all over central Europe.

Surviving operatic works: *Der Königssohn aus Ithaka*, 1795; *Rosalinde, oder Die Macht der Feen*, 1796; *Liebe macht kurzen Process, oder Die Heyrath auf gewisse Art*, 1801; 6 lost operas

T.T.C.

ROBIN HOLLOWAY

Robin Greville Holloway; *b* 19 October 1943, Leamington Spa, England

Holloway began composing while a chorister at St Paul's Cathedral. From 1960 he studied composition with Alexander Goehr, and established his reputation with a sequence of works culminating in the complex and violent First Concerto for Orchestra (1967). The musical paraphrases of *Scenes from Schumann* (1970) revealed an acute sensitivity of feeling leading to a rich new phase concentrating on the liberation of expressive resources hidden in apparently exhausted styles. Chiefly this involved Romanticism (Holloway's research on Debussy and Wagner has been highly praised), yet with a modernist stance most apparent in the cathartic Second Concerto for Orchestra (1979). In a number of other compositions, including the programmatic *Seascape and Harvest* (1984), the example of Richard Strauss – both early and late – seems relevant in Holloway's exploration of music's potential as a figurative medium, and as an art complete in itself. His second opera, provisionally entitled *Boys and Girls come out to play* to a libretto by Gavin Ewart after the composer's own scenario, was sketched in 1991. This is at the opposite pole from *Clarissa*, an operatic farce inspired by the life and work of Cynthia Payne, although not directly biographical. A lecturer in music at Cambridge University since 1974, Holloway is also a formidable literary stylist whose concern with the subtleties of language is reflected in a quantity of song-cycles, setting writers as diverse as John Ruskin and William Carlos Williams.

Clarissa

Opera in two acts, Op. 30 (2h 30m)
Libretto by the composer, after the novel by Samuel Richardson (1747/8)
Composed 1968–76
PREMIERE   18 May 1990, Coliseum, London

Holloway's intention to transform Richardson's vast epistolary novel into an opera dates from 1968, and the score was completed eight years later 'out of inner necessity' rather than for any prospect of performance. This period also produced a trio of key works in the composer's development: *Scenes from Schumann*, *Domination of Black* (1974) and the Wallace Stevens cantata *Sea Surface Full of Clouds* (1975). Stylistically, *Clarissa* can now be seen as the focus of all three in its rejection of modernism for a post-Stravinskian aesthetic filtered through an intense admiration for Wagner – evident in the music's quotations from *Die Walküre* – and an openness to the broad range of 20th-century opera from Berg's *Wozzeck* to the work of *Clarissa*'s twin dedicatees and 'masters of the native soil', Britten and Tippett.

As in Tippett's *Midsummer Marriage*, dance is used as an extension and symbol of the preoccupations of the central characters. The action revolves around the conflicting passions of Clarissa Harlowe and her pursuer, the libertine Lovelace. His sexual cravings, inflamed by her ambivalence towards him and her obvious desire to escape the clutches of her odious family, leads inexorably to her rape after she has been tricked into leaving home and has been installed in a brothel. The supporting cast – the family and Clarissa's confidante Anne Howe – plays a minor role. Essentially, like *Tristan*, this is a plot with two characters and one theme: the corruption of mutual physical and psychological attraction leading to the heroine's tragic downfall and enlightenment in death.

EDITIONS   f.s./v.s., Boosey & Hawkes (on hire), 1990

BIBLIOGRAPHY   Paul Griffiths, *New Sounds, New Personalities*, Faber, 1985; Peter Paul Nash, '*Clarissa* – Someone Who Needs to Sing', *Opera*, vol. 41 (1990)

N.W.

GUSTAV HOLST

Gustavus Theodore von Holst; *b* 21 September 1874, Cheltenham, England; *d* 25 May 1934, London

Holst's great-grandfather was a Swede who emigrated from Riga to London with his Russian wife in the early 1800s. But Holst himself seems to have been purely English in his preoccupations and intellectual tendencies. He went to Cheltenham Grammar School, then studied with Stanford at the Royal College of Music from 1893. Much of his working life was spent school-teaching (notably at St Paul's Girls' School, where he became Director of Music in 1905), or running evening classes (at Morley College from 1907); but he was also deeply involved with amateur music-making, to which he brought a quasi-political conviction of the worth of the common man. All this practical work restricted his time for composition and eventually undermined his health, but it had a significant effect on his own music, which is notably free of the conventional academic influences of the day. Like his friend Vaughan Williams, Holst was interested in folk music, as well as in Indian culture (though not specifically Indian music); he taught himself Sanskrit, set a number of Hindu texts in his own translations, and based two operas on Hindu subjects. He was also quick to pick up the sounds of the new Continental music of the years before the First World War. His most famous work, *The Planets* (1914–16), is full of echoes of Debussy, Stravinsky, Skryabin, even Mahler and Schoenberg, worked into a characteristic fusion that is completely radical and individual in its effect.

Despite the pressure on his time, Holst produced a large, if uneven, body of work, dominated by choral and other types of music that reflect his practical bent and his work with amateurs. But he also wrote about a dozen operas, at a time when British opera hardly existed as a serious commodity at all. Not surprisingly, they are a mixed bag, and several of them remain unperformed. *Lansdown Castle* was given an amateur production in Cheltenham in 1893, while the children's operettas *Ianthe* (1893) and *The Idea* (1894) were performed at Holst's aunt's school in Barnes, for which they were written. But *The Revoke*, a student one-act work about Beau Brummel (1894–5), has apparently never been performed. According to his biographer, Michael Short, all four works reveal the influence of Sullivan. But by this time Holst was an avid Wagnerite, and both his next two operas, *The Youth's Choice* (1900–1903) and *Sita* (1900–1906), reflect this enthusiasm. The former was submitted without success to the 1903 Sonzogno Competition for one-act operas. The three-act *Sita*, based by Holst on a story by the Hindu writer Valmiki (*c*. 500 BC), is a full-blown Wagnerian drama, with, however, a rambling and ill-organized libretto much of which, Holst confessed, had been written during orchestral performances in which he was taking part as a trombonist.

H. numbers refer to Imogen Holst, *A Thematic Catalogue of Gustav Holst's Music*, Faber, 1974.

Savitri

Chamber opera in one act, Op. 25, H. 96 (30m)
Libretto by the composer, after an episode from the *Mahabharata*
Composed 1908–9

PREMIERES 5 December 1916, Wellington Hall, London (amateur); 23 June 1921, Lyric Theatre, Hammersmith, London; US: 23 January 1934, Palmer House, Chicago
CAST Savitri *s*, Satyavan *t*, Death *b*; offstage *sa* chorus
ORCHESTRATION 2 fl, ca, 4 vn, 2 va, 2 vc, db

Holst's interest in Hindu literature seems to have begun while he was on tour with the Carl Rosa Opera Company in Scarborough in 1898, when a friend lent him a book on the subject. Back in London, he learned to decipher the Sanskrit, and began to make his own translations with the help of published cribs. On this basis he wrote the libretti of both *Sita* and *Savitri*, as well as the texts for the *Vedic Hymns* (1907–8) and the *Choral Hymns from the Rig Veda* (1903–12).

These works form a very loose grouping, since they spring from a common literary rather than musical impulse. *Savitri* is unimaginably different from *Sita* in musical conception, being drastically spare, compact, and with a tiny group of performers. It does away with almost all the normal operatic paraphernalia. It has no overture but opens with a long un-accompanied passage for Death and Savitri. In essence it is hardly a theatre piece at all. Holst wanted it played out of doors with 'a long avenue or path through a wood in the centre of the scene'. But his practical instincts warned him to allow 'a small building' as an alternative, and to suggest the 'Hymn of the Travellers' from the third group of *Choral Hymns from the Rig Veda* as an overture for anyone who could not bear to be without one.

SYNOPSIS
A wood at evening. Death announces to Savitri that he has come for her husband, the woodsman Satyavan. When Satyavan comes home from his day's work, he sings about the unreality (*Maya* – 'illusion') of the natural world. But Savitri tells him she now sees beyond *Maya* to 'the heart of every tree'. As Death approaches, Satyavan sinks to the ground lifeless. At first Savitri tries to protect her husband. But she then welcomes Death and invites him to stay. He offers her a wish for herself, and she asks for Life. When Death willingly grants her that which she has already, she points out that for her 'the life of woman, of wife, of mother' implies life for Satyavan too. Defeated, Death leaves at once, and Satyavan revives. As husband and wife go off, Death is heard singing of Savitri's freedom from illusion, 'for even Death is *Maya*'. At the very end Savitri's voice is heard singing alone.

The score has few exotic elements, and certainly none that are remotely Indian. Its modal character is partly English (from folksong), partly French, with a certain whole-tone colouring as in the recent piano works of Debussy. The music's main individuality lies in its spare but extremely delicate texture, its flexible metre, combining recitative with Holst's favourite seven-beat bars, and its use of a wordless female choir (originally a mixed choir, but changed at the suggestion of Herman Grunebaum, the work's first

conductor), a device that obviously anticipates *The Planets*.

RECORDINGS 1. Baker, Tear, Hemsley, Purcell Singers, English CO, I. Holst, Argo, 1965; 2. Palmer, Langridge, Varcoe, Hickox Singers, City of London Sinfonia, Hickox, Hyperion, 1983
EDITION f.s., Curwen, 1924; v.s., Goodwin, 1923; study s., Eulenburg, 1976

The Perfect Fool
Opera in one act, Op. 39, H.150 (1h)
Libretto by the composer
Composed 1918–22
PREMIERE 14 May 1923, Covent Garden, London

Towards the end of the First World War Holst penned an operatic revue under the title *Opera as She is Wrote*, full of heavy humour at the expense of 'composers' such as Verdizetti, Depussy, and Horridinsky-Kantakoff. *The Perfect Fool* might seem a follow-up. But Holst had been planning it at least since *Savitri*, and had simply had neither time nor incentive to write it. As a kind of spoof 'quest' opera, it reflects certain fashionable influences, including Rimsky-Korsakov's *Golden Cockerel*, as well as sharing common ground with Prokofiev's exactly contemporary *Love of Three Oranges*. But Holst was naturally unable to produce a text to match the rich fantasy of Pushkin or Gozzi, while his satire against Wagner, Italian opera, and Debussy tends to read, and sound, like amateurish Gilbert and Sullivan.

The Fool of the title is the sleepy centre of a sequence of events in which first a Wizard, then a Troubadour and finally a Traveller try in vain to woo the Princess. She of course falls for the Fool, who refuses her with the single word he utters, then yawns and falls asleep. The work pokes rather laboured fun at Wagner's *Parsifal* and *The Ring* (the Traveller sings in alliterative *Stabreim*, to Wanderer-type music), as well as, again, Verdi and Debussy. But the music is lame except when purely Holstian, as in the ballet music – effectively a mimed overture – much of which is drawn from Holst's incidental music to Clifford Bax's play *The Sneezing Charm* (1918).

EDITION v.s., Novello, 1923

At the Boar's Head
Musical interlude in one act, Op. 42, H.156 (1h)
Libretto by the composer, from Shakespeare's *Henry IV, Parts I and II*
Composed 1924
PREMIERES 3 April 1925, Manchester; US: 16 February 1935, MacDowell Club, New York

Some months before the premiere of *The Perfect Fool*, Holst fell while conducting and hit his head. Problems persisted, and he was ordered to spend 1924 resting in the country. His main activity during convalescence was to finish the First Choral Symphony, and to compose *At the Boar's Head*.

Leafing through a collection of folksongs, he noticed that one of the tunes fitted words he had been reading in Shakespeare's *Henry IV*, and this gave him the idea for a whole Falstaff opera set to folktunes. 'As the critics have decided that I can't write a libretto,' he told a friend, 'the words of my new opera have been written by Shakespeare.' He compiled the text mainly from the Falstaff scenes, including Hal's 'I know you all' monologue, together with two Sonnets ('Devouring Time' and 'When I do count the clock') and three traditional songs. The tunes, beautifully fused together by Holst's skilful hand, come mainly from published collections.

The 'plot' covers the incident in which Falstaff and his cronies, having committed a robbery, are themselves robbed by Prince Hal and Poins; Hal's determination eventually to break free of this criminal set; his and Falstaff's rehearsal for Hal's interview with the king; Falstaff's scene with Doll Tearsheet; Hal's recall to Westminster; and Falstaff's and Bardolph's departure for the war, touching at the end – and only by a tiny implication – on Falstaff's death in Act II of *Henry V*.

RECORDING Palmer, Langridge, Tomlinson, Wilson-Johnson, Royal Liverpool PO, Atherton, EMI, 1983
EDITION v.s., Novello, 1925

The Wandering Scholar

Chamber opera in one act, Op. 50, H.176 (30m)
Libretto by Clifford Bax, after Helen Waddell's book *The Wandering Scholars* (1927)
Composed 1929–30
PREMIERE 31 January 1934, David Lewis Theatre, Liverpool

The libretto of Holst's last opera was adapted from a brief account in Helen Waddell's book about the medieval *Vagantes* (or vagrant clerics), itself translated from a Boccacciesque French 13th-century tale called 'Le pauvre clerc'. A young scholar begs for food at a farm one spring day in medieval France, but unluckily arrives just as the farmer's wife is about to take advantage of her husband's absence at market to enjoy some hanky-panky with the local priest. There is pork, cake and wine to be seen, but the scholar is sent packing. Just as the wife and the priest are mounting the ladder to the bedroom, the farmer returns with the scholar, whom he has met on the road. The priest hides and the wife protests there is no food. But the scholar concocts an impromptu tale which leads to the revelation of the pork, the cake, the wine and, finally, the priest, who is kicked out as the scholar sits down to his meal and the farmer takes his wife aloft to administer a good thrashing.

The Wandering Scholar belongs firmly to Holst's austere final phase (the phase of *Egdon Heath* and the *Choral Fantasia*), and though hinting at the same folksong style as *At the Boar's Head*, its music is more obviously experimental and individual. In scale and density it harks back to *Savitri* (with which it forms an excellent short double-bill). But its style is that of the late 1920s, a time when Holst was extending his ideas of melody and harmony based on the perfect fourth – an idiom that lends a suitably dry piquancy to the medieval setting.

Holst was too ill to attend the first performance, or to carry out any post-premiere revision; the work remained unpublished for almost 40 years. For the Cheltenham Festival in 1951 Benjamin Britten produced a somewhat rescored version (with single wind, harp and percussion) to go with his own chamber operas. Holst's own scoring is for double woodwind and horns with strings.

RECORDING Burrowes, Tear, Rippon, Langdon, English CO, Bedford, Decca, 1975
EDITION f.s., Faber Music (on hire); v.s., Faber Music, 1968; study s., Faber Music, 1971, rev. edn, 1977

Other operatic works: *Lansdown Castle, or The Sorcerer of Tewkesbury*, 1893; *Ianthe*, (c. 1894); *The Revoke*, (1895); *The Magic Mirror* (inc.), (1896); *The Idea*, (c. 1896); *The Youth's Choice*, (1902); *Sita*, (1906); *Cinderella* (lost), (1902); *Opera as She is Wrote* (fragments only), (1918)
BIBLIOGRAPHY Imogen Holst, *The Music of Gustav Holst*, OUP, 3rd rev. edn, 1986; Michael Short, *Gustav Holst*, Clarendon Press, 1990

S.W.

IGNAZ HOLZBAUER

Ignaz Jakob Holzbauer; *b* 17 September 1711, Vienna; *d* 7 April 1783, Mannheim

After early study in Italy, during which he became committed to Metastasian ideals, Holzbauer settled in Mannheim in 1753 as kapellmeister to the electoral court, a post he was to occupy for the next 25 years. His large output for the stage during the first six years of this period included two important opere serie, *Nitteti* and *Alessandro nell'Indie*, both to Metastasio texts, which were premiered in Turin and Milan respectively. The latter, modelled on the style of Hasse, is probably his finest stage work. However, the achievement that gained him the most widespread recognition was his three-act German opera, *Günther von Schwarzburg*. Its success provided the climax to his career. In later life, though troubled by deafness, he continued to teach and compose, but produced little more for the theatre.

Günther von Schwarzburg

Singspiel in three acts
Libretto by Anton Klein
PREMIERE 5 January 1777, Schlosstheater, Mannheim

Unlike the typical singspiels of the day, this German historical opera included recitative for substantial portions of the text and elaborate arias with rich orchestral accompaniment. The break it represented with the all-pervading Italian traditions in German theatres of the time was later to have important repercussions. Mozart, who heard the work at Mannheim in November 1777, wrote to his father, 'Holzbauer's music is very beautiful. The poetry doesn't deserve such music. What surprises me most of all is that a man as old as Holzbauer [he was then 66] should still possess such spirit; for you can't imagine what fire there is in that music.'

EDITION   H. Kretzschmar (ed.), *DDT*, vols 8–9, Breitkopf und Härtel, *rp*, 1902

Other operatic works: *Il figlio delle selve*, 1753; *L'isola disabitata*, 1754; *L'issipile*, 1754; *Don Chisciotte*, 1755; *I cinesi*, 1756; *Le nozze d'Arianna*, 1756; *Il filosofo di campagna*, 1756; *La clemenza di Tito*, 1757; *Nitteti*, 1758; *Alessandro nell'Indie*, 1759; *Ippolito ed Aricia*, 1759; *Adriano in Siria*, 1768; *La morte di Didone*, 1779; *Tancredi*, 1783
BIBLIOGRAPHY   H. Kretzschmar, preface to *DDT*, vols 8–9, Breitkopf und Härtel, *rp*, 1902; J. Sittard, *Zur Geschichte der Musik und des Theaters am Württembergischen Hofe*, W. Kohlhammer, 1890–91, *rp* 1970

B.S.

ARTHUR HONEGGER

b 10 March 1892, Le Havre, France; *d* 27 November 1955, Paris

Honegger's Swiss origins, and his concomitant taste for the then unfashionable music of Germany singled him out from the rest of Les Six, the 1920s group of young composers to which he belonged. Honegger's preferred moderns were Richard Strauss and Max Reger rather than Satie and Stravinsky; his musical taste tended rather to structure and counterpoint than to the instant gratification of facile melody and 'chic' dissonance. The notion that the composer is merely an artisan doing an honest day's work is one that informed Honegger's whole creative life. He always strove to make his music logical, accessible and above all 'useful'.

Hence his many forays into the theatre and the new media of film and radio. Hence also his love of collaboration with other creative artists, even other composers, and his mastery of many compositional styles in his search for a music that was modern, muscular and immediate. The results of these collaborations were a series of dramatic works, many of which exist on the fringes of what can be strictly defined as opera. Some, such as *Judith* and *Antigone*, are quasi-operatic reworkings of theatrical incidental music, others, such as *Jeanne d'Arc au bûcher* and *Nicolas de Flue*, are described as 'dramatic oratorio' but are eminently stageable. In these works, as in his 'dramatic psalm' *Le roi David* and other cantatas and oratorios, Honegger enjoyed the use of spoken narration, of choral recitation, of soloists as protagonists then story-tellers – all devices intended to remove further the barriers between musical and theatrical genres.

Honegger's only opera (in the conventional sense), *L'aiglon* (1937), was written in collaboration with Ibert. He also wrote three operettas: the completely scandalous *Les aventures du roi Pausole* (the filthiest libretto in opera history), *La belle de Moudon* and his second collaboration with Ibert, *Les petites Cardinal*, based on Ludovic Halévy's novel (1880) about the girls of the Opera Ballet school in the 19th century.

Antigone

Opera in one act (1h)
Text by Jean Cocteau, after the play by Sophocles (*c.* 441 BC)
Composed 1924–7
PREMIERES   28 December 1927, Théâtre de la Monnaie, Brussels; US: 24 April 1930, American Laboratory Theater, New York

The story of the courage of Antigone in disobeying the edict of King Creon, her subsequent imprisonment, her death and the great suffering of all around her is told here with extraordinary celerity and power. Honegger's opera has much in common with Stravinsky's *Oedipus Rex* (also 1927), but Stravinsky's inexorable rhythms are replaced by grinding dissonance and headlong pace more reminiscent of Richard Strauss's *Salome*. In *Antigone* Honegger began his experiments with French prosody. He attempted to reclaim the importance of the sung word through eccentric, often very rhythmic stress, often on the first syllable (e.g. '*tou*-jours'). The result is frequently disconcerting, but always achieves the desired effect of making the listener sit up and take notice.

RECORDING   Serres, Verneuil, Collard, Giraudeau, Roux, Vessières, Ch and O of French National Radio, Le Roux, Bourg, 1960
EDITION   v.s., Senart/Salabert, 1928

Jeanne d'Arc au bûcher

Joan of Arc at the Stake
Dramatic oratorio in one act (prologue and eleven scenes) (1h 15m)
Text by Paul Claudel
Composed 1934–5
PREMIERES   12 May 1938, Basle (concert); UK: 20 October 1954, Stoll Theatre, London

In *Jeanne d'Arc* we see the Protestant oratorio burst its banks and aspire to the state of opera – The *St Matthew Passion* meets *Tristan und Isolde*. The spoken role of Jeanne places the work in the mainstream of melodrama at its most immoderate, but the pageant elements, the trial and the game of cards still have a very modern and precise cutting edge. The sheer scale of the rest is essentially decadent late Romantic, with a huge orchestra and choir and swooping ondes Martinot. But Honegger's greatest gift is the knowledge of when to cut away to reveal a simple shepherd's pipe, a voice from heaven, or a child's hymn. An interesting angle on the nature of collaboration is provided by Honegger's account (in his book, *I am a Composer*) of how Claudel would describe, in detail, the music he wished to hear, which the composer would then write.

RECORDING   Keller, Pollet, Command, Stutzmann, Ch and O of French National Radio, Ozawa, DG, 1989
EDITION   v.s., Salabert, 1938

L'aiglon

The Eaglet
Opera in five acts
Libretto by Henri Cain, after the play by Edmond Rostand (1900)

Fanny Heldry as the Duke of Reichstadt in Honegger's and Ibert's L'aiglon (Paris, 1937)

Composed 1936–7 in collaboration with Jacques Ibert
PREMIERE 11 March 1937, Salle Garnier, Monte Carlo

The eponymous role of the Duke of Reichstadt, the sickly son of the great Napoleon, was a famous triumph in the theatre for Sarah Bernhardt, and in the opera house for Fanny Heldy. This is a sad tale, of a son living in the shadow of his father's achievements and disasters. In the luxurious seclusion of the palace at Schönbrunn the young duke becomes a pawn in the various intrigues led by Metternich. His one deed of action, gathering troops on the windswept plain of Wagram, turns out to be a feverish delusion. The duke's death in Act V is touchingly accompanied by half-remembered folksongs of his beloved French homeland.

This is a conventional opera, designed as such. The plots, the masked balls, the pageantry and the pathos work as well as they always do. The only mystery is how such consistent, and consistently good, music came to be written by two composers. The received belief is that Ibert wrote Acts I and V, Honegger Act IV, and that the remaining music was somehow shared. But as the composers explained, 'The division of labour was very fair. One of us wrote the sharps, the other wrote the flats!'

RECORDING Boué, Berton, Bourdin, Peyron, Depraz, Lovano, Ch and O of French National Radio, Dervaux, Bourg, 1956
EDITION v.s. Heugel, 1937

Other operatic works: *Le roi David*, 1921 (RECORDINGS Decca, 1958; Supraphon, 1987; original version: Thorofon, 1991); *Judith*, 1926; *Les aventures du roi Pausole*, 1930; *Cris du monde* (stage oratorio), (1931); *La belle de Moudon*, 1933;

Les petites Cardinal (coll. with Ibert), 1938; *Nicolas de Flue*, 1941

BIBLIOGRAPHY Arthur Honegger, *Je suis compositeur*, Conquistador, 1951, W. O. Clough and A. A. Willman (trans.), *I am a Composer*, Faber, 1966; M. Landowski, *Honegger*, Paris, 1957

J.C.S.

JAMES HOOK
b ?3 June 1746, Norwich, England; *d* 1827, Boulogne, France

Despite a long association with the stage and a remarkable fluency in composition, Hook produced only a handful of works that can plausibly be classified as operas, and all of these have spoken dialogue, as well as frequent self-borrowings. The son of a cutler and born club-footed, he studied music with John Garland, organist of Norwich Cathedral; at the age of eight he composed a ballad opera (which does not survive). In about 1763 he established himself in London as a keyboard-player, teacher and composer. He became organist and composer at Marylebone Gardens, moving to Vauxhall Gardens in 1774. For Vauxhall he wrote 'musical entertainments' which were semi-staged; in the winter, when the gardens were closed, he turned his attention to the theatre.

The Lady of the Manor (Covent Garden, 1778) to a libretto by William Kendrick after *The Country Lasses* (1715) by Charles Johnson is a pasticcio derived from Hook's earlier compositions. The songs, as is usual with Hook, are tuneful and competent. Several of his later 'operas' (really plays with music) have libretti by his son Theodore Edward, the novelist and wit. He retired from performing in 1820, having given up composition a few years earlier.

Surviving operatic works: *The Country Courtship*, n.d. (RECORDING as *The Musical Courtship*, arr. F. Woodhouse, Decca, 1950); *The Lady of the Manor*, 1778; *The Peruvian*, 1786; *Jack of Newbury*, 1796; *Diamond Cut Diamond*, 1797
BIBLIOGRAPHY C. L. Cudworth, 'James Hook', *Norwich Journal*, 24 August 1946; Roger Fiske, *English Theatre Music in the Eighteenth Century*, OUP, 1973; 2nd edn, 1986

R.Lu.

KAREL HORKÝ
b 4 September 1909, Štěměchy u Třebíče; *d* 27 November 1988, Brno, Czechoslovakia

For many years Horký earned his living as a bassoonist. In 1937 he became a member of the Brno Theatre Orchestra, and began to study composition, first in Brno and then (1941–4) in Křička's masterclasses at the Prague Conservatory. After the war he taught in Brno at the Conservatory and at the Academy, and was Director of the Brno Conservatory from 1964 to 1971. Horký's experience as a theatre musician led at first to ballet and two of his three ballets have been performed in Brno (1945, 1951).

Horký's operas, all of which have received performances in Brno, range widely in their subject matter. Two are concerned with regional political–historical issues: a Moravian uprising in the 17th century (*Captain Šarovec*) and the dawning of political consciousness in Moravia in the 1870s (*Daybreak*). In *Atlantida* the last days of the doomed continent offer a warning to humanity about the destructive forces of science. *Poison from Elsinore* is a suggested reconstruction of events between the murder of Hamlet's father and Hamlet's return. Polonius discovers the murder, but decides to hush it up in the interests of the state.

Jan Hus

Oratorio-opera in six scenes
Libretto by Vladimír Kantor
Composed 1944–9, rev. 1956–7
PREMIERES 27 May 1950; rev. version: 5 December 1957, State Theatre, Brno

Horký's first complete opera is based on the life and work of the great Czech religious leader Jan Hus, whose martyrdom in 1415 is a key moment in Czech history. The work is cast in a series of large-scale historical frescoes along the lines of Pfitzner's *Palestrina*, with a large all-male cast of soloists, and scenes that include Hus's preaching at the Bethlehem Chapel in Prague and his denunciation as a heretic at the Council of Constance.

Other operas: *The Grave* (*Hrob*), (inc.); *Captain Šarovec* (*Hejtman Šarovec*) 1953; *Poison from Elsinore* (*Jed z Elsinoru*), 1969; *Daybreak* (*Svítání*) 1975; *Atlantida*, 1983
BIBLIOGRAPHY Pavel Eckstein, *The Czechoslovak Contemporary Opera*, Panton, 1967

J.T.

ALAN HOVHANESS

Alan Hovhaness [Hovaness]; originally Alan Vaness Chakmakjian; *b* 8 March 1911, Somerville, Massachusetts, US

Hovhaness is a prolific composer whose opus numbers exceed 400, not including the extensive early work he destroyed. His ancestry is Armenian and Scottish and the former particularly has provided him with a route to a neo-primitive modal style which has served him to a large extent since the later 1940s. He has said: 'Simplicity is difficult, not easy. Beauty is simple.' In that sense his quest for a world music is comparable to the work of other Americans such as Henry Cowell, but Hovhaness's stage works are virtually unknown. Most are designated as chamber operas and all use the composer's own texts. Of the most readily available works – *The Burning House, Spirit of the Avalanche* and *Travellers* – the longest lasts just over half an hour.

Operatic works: *Etchmiadz in*, 1946; *Blue Flame*, 1959; *The Burning House*, 1964; *Spirit of the Avalanche*, 1963; *Pilate*, (1963); *The Travellers*, (1965); *Pericles*, (1975); *Tale of the Sun Goddess Going into the Stone House*, 1979
BIBLIOGRAPHY David Ewen, *American Composers: A Biographical Dictionary*, Hall, 1983

P.D.

VOJTĚCH HŘÍMALÝ

b 30 July 1842, Plzeň, Bohemia; *d* 15 June 1908, Vienna

After studying at the Prague Conservatory as a violinist, Hřímalý worked in Rotterdam (1861) and Göteborg (from 1862) in his early years; from 1874 until retirement in 1902 he was music director in Czernowitz (now Chernovtsy, Ukraine). His professional years in Prague, and his career as a composer of Czech operas, occupy only a small part of his life. He joined the Prague Provisional Theatre in March 1868 as leader of the orchestra and occasional conductor. In 1873 he moved over to the rival German Theatre in Prague as second conductor, a move regarded as unpatriotic, and he soon left. He was known chiefly for *The Enchanted Prince*, a fairy-tale opera based on the complications arising from the exchange of roles between a prince and a poor tailor. The opera remained in the Prague repertoire for ten years, and was revived occasionally up to 1933–4. A second opera, based on the popular legend of Švanda the bagpiper, was given only in Hřímalý's native Plzeň.

Operas: *Zaklený princ* (*The Enchanted Prince*), 1872; *Švanda dudák* (*Švanda the Bagpiper*), (1885), 1896; *Strakonický dudák* (*The Bagpiper of Strakonice*), (n.d.)
BIBLIOGRAPHY John Tyrrell, *Czech Opera*, CUP, 1988

J.T.

JOHANN NEPOMUK HUMMEL

b 14 November 1778, Pressburg (now Bratislava, Slovakia); *d* 17 October 1837, Weimar

Although Hummel is remembered chiefly for his piano and chamber music he also wrote for the church and the theatre. His family moved to Vienna in 1786, where he studied with Mozart before touring Europe as a child prodigy. On his return to Vienna he became a composition pupil of Albrechtsberger and Salieri, and soon after began to try his hand at theatrical composition. From 1804 to 1811 he was konzertmeister to Prince Nicolaus Esterházy at Eisenstadt, acting as Haydn's deputy, after which came a period of intensive composition for Viennese theatres. After 1814 Hummel wrote little theatrical music, concentrating instead on smaller-scale compositions, concert tours, conducting and teaching. None of his operas was a great success, though some, notably *Die Eselshaut* and the revised version of *Mathilde von Guise* (the only one of his operas to be published) gained favourable recognition in their day. While his piano music shows hints of a more Romantic style, Hummel's operatic output remained firmly in the classical mould, using patterns set down by Mozart in a musical language that is pleasing if unadventurous.

Operas: *Il viaggiator ridicolo* (inc.), (1797); *Dankgefühl einer Geretteten*, 1799; *Don Anchise Campione* (inc.) (?*c.* 1800); *Le vicende d'amore*, 1804; *Die vereitelten Ränke* (rev. of *Le vicende d'amore*), 1806; *Die Messenier*, (?*c.* 1805–10); *Pimmalione*, (?*c.*1805–15); *Stadt und Land* (inc.), (*c.* 1810); *Mathilde von Guise*, 1810, rev. 1821; *Dies Haus ist zu verkaufen* (based on music from *Die vereitelten Ränke*), 1812; *Der Junker in der Mühle*, 1813; *Die Eselshaut, oder Die blaue Insel*, 1814; *Die Rückfahrt des Kaisers*, 1814; insertions to operas by other composers: duet, quartet for Isouard's *Jeannot et Colin*, 1815; march for Weigl's *Hadrian*, 1819; epilogue for Gluck's *Armide*, 1832; finale for Auber's *Gustave III*, 1836; 2 lost

BIBLIOGRAPHY K. Benyovsky, *J. N. Hummel: Der Mensch und Künstler*, Eos, 1934; J. Sachs, 'A Checklist of the Works of Johann Nepomuk Hummel', *Notes*, vol. 30 (1973–4), pp. 732–54

C.Br.

ENGELBERT HUMPERDINCK

b 1 September 1854, Siegburg; *d* 27 September 1921, Neustrelitz

Humperdinck's fame rests on his opera, *Hänsel und Gretel*, the success of which has been constant and extraordinary since its first performance. Of his six other operatic works only *Königskinder* is of similar scale and quality, and this enjoyed success in its early years.

Humperdinck studied architecture at the University of Cologne where he became friendly with the composer Ferdinand Hiller, who recognized his musical talent and persuaded him to become a student of composition, piano and cello. Considered brilliant by his professors, he won the Mozart Scholarship in 1876 which financed further study in Munich with Franz Lachner and Joseph Rheinberger. His first works were published at this time – the *Humoreske* for orchestra (1879) and choral ballade, *Die Wallfahrt nach Kevlaar* (1879). The latter won the Mendelssohn Prize. (Humperdinck was an inveterate prize-winner and in 1881, he also won the Meyerbeer Prize of 7,600 marks – a huge sum at the time.) This enabled him to visit France and Italy where, in Naples in 1880, he met Richard Wagner. Wagner invited him to Bayreuth as his assistant and, during 1881–2, he helped prepare the score of *Parsifal* for its premiere and publication. It is likely that he also composed a small fill-in passage, later discarded, for the Act III transition.

After Bayreuth, and short spells in Barcelona and Cologne, he joined the music publishers Schott in Mainz (1888) for whom in 1889 he published an arrangement of Auber's opera *Le cheval de bronze*. He later took three posts in Frankfurt: professor at Hoch's conservatory, teacher of repertoire at Stockhausen's music school and critic on the *Frankfurter Allgemeine Zeitung*.

In 1896 the Emperor William II bestowed on him the title of professor and, no doubt with massive royalties from *Hänsel und Gretel*, premiered with overwhelming success three years earlier, Humperdinck retired to Boppard on the Rhine in 1897 and devoted himself entirely to composition. He wrote spectacles, incidental music as well as orchestral works, songs, a string quartet and operas. In 1900 he was appointed (with only nominal duties) director of the Akademische Meisterschule in Berlin and a fellow of the Royal Academy of Arts there. With the premiere of the final operatic version of *Königskinder* at the Metropolitan in New York in 1910, his success grew abroad but at the same time he became somewhat pigeonholed at home. His last work to create any significant public impression was his spectacle, *The Miracle*, with a scenario by Max Reinhardt, premiered at Olympia in London on 23 December 1911. However, the large London crowds flocking to it appeared to have been drawn solely by the spectacular nature of the production and the work attracted little attention from musicians.

Hänsel und Gretel

Hansel and Gretel

Märchenoper in three acts (2h)
Libretto by Adelheid Wette, after the tale by the Brothers (Wilhelm and Jacob) Grimm (1812)
Composed 1890–93
PREMIERES 23 December 1893, Court Theatre, Weimar; UK: 26 December 1894, Daly's Theatre, London; US: 8 October 1895, Metropolitan, New York
CAST Hänsel *ms*, Gretel *s*, Gertrud *ms*, Peter *bar*, Sandman *s*, Dew Fairy *s*, Witch *ms* (sometimes *t*), 6 echoes 4 *s* 2 *a*; children's chorus, 14 angels *silent*
ORCHESTRATION 3 fl/picc, 2 ob/ca, 2 cl, b cl, 2 bsn, 4 hn, 2 tpt, 3 trbn, tuba, timp, perc (triangle, tambourine, blocks, castanets, xyl, glock, thunder machine, t-t, bd), hp, str

The early 1890s saw Germany reacting to the bombast of the lesser imitators of Wagner by developing a craze for Italian *verismo*. But German artists soon grew restive against the lurid plots and the brashness of composers such as Mascagni, and German audiences yearned for a work that was truly German in origin as well as popular. Humperdinck's very success with *Hänsel und Gretel* may have been the result of his avoidance of the mainstream German works of Weber, Marschner and Lortzing; his opera inhabits a very different world.

In 1890 Humperdinck's sister, Adelheid Wette, devised a dramatized version of the Grimm story of *Hänsel und Gretel* for her children to perform. In her version the parents are a much less alarming pair than they are in the fairy-tale where the mother (stepmother in the first version) is actually determined to leave the children out to die in the wood. Wette softened this, perhaps because she knew that her brother's music would supply some of the fear and drama. She also introduced the characters of the Father, the Sandman and the Dew Fairy, as well as the chorus of echoes and the angels, which provided Humperdinck with scope for a ballet.

At first Wette asked her brother to compose four songs for a dramatized family play (1890). Subsequently they decided to make it a full-scale opera. The premiere, conducted by Richard Strauss, was an instant success and within a year *Hänsel und Gretel* had been produced in over 50 theatres in Germany. It soon joined the repertoire of every lyric theatre in the German-speaking world, and within 20 years had been translated into about 20 languages. Richard Strauss, a constant supporter of Humperdinck (he also conducted the premiere of Humperdinck's *Die Heirat wider Willen* in 1905), described the work as 'a masterpiece of the highest quality . . . all of it original, new and so authentically German', despite his reservation that 'the orchestration is always a little thick'.

Hänsel und Gretel was the first complete opera to be broadcast on radio (from Covent Garden, London, 6 January 1923) and the first to be transmitted live from the Metropolitan, New York (25 December 1931).

Anna Jaeger and Hedwig Schacko as Hänsel und Gretel in the first Frankfurt production (1894)

SYNOPSIS

The self-contained overture is often performed as a concert piece.

Act I Hänsel and Gretel are at home waiting for their mother, Gertrude, to return. The interior displays the poverty of the family: Hänsel makes brooms for his broom-maker father, Peter, while Gretel knits. Both are bored, restless and hungry. To distract her brother, Gretel shows him a dance game ('Brüderchen, komm tanz' mit mir') but their playing is harshly interrupted by the arrival of their mother. She is cross at how little work the children have completed and in her anger she knocks over a jug of milk. She bursts into tears at losing the only food in the house, and sends the children out to pick strawberries in the nearby Ilsenstein forest. Depressed, she falls asleep but is wakened by the father singing on his way home. She is furious that he is obviously tipsy but her mood changes at the sight of the food he has bought as the result of a successful day selling brooms. After celebrating with his wife, he suddenly becomes aware that the children are not there and their mother admits that they have gone to the Ilsenstein for strawberries. Father is appalled; he knows this is the home of the Witch who entices children into her cottage and then turns them into gingerbread by baking them alive in her oven ('Eine Hex', steinalt'). Both parents rush out of the house to find their children. *Entr'acte: Hexenritt* - 'Witch's Ride'.

Act II Hänsel and Gretel are in the wood filling their baskets with strawberries ('Ein Männlein steht im Walde ganz still und stumm'). They eat them all, however, and soon Hänsel realizes that they are lost. They become frightened. A mist rises and a little Sandman appears and throws sand in the children's eyes ('Der kleine Sandmann bin ich'). They kneel down to say their evening prayers ('Abends wenn ich schlafen gehn'). Lying on a bank beneath the trees they fall asleep in each other's arms. The mist surrounds them and becomes a staircase of clouds as fourteen angels come down from heaven to guard the children through the night. This is accompanied by an extended orchestral postlude ('pantomime').

Act III opens with another orchestral prelude as dawn breaks and the Dew Fairy comes to shake dew drops over the children ('Der kleine Taumann heiss ich'). They cheerfully start to play. The mist clears to reveal a gingerbread cottage with a fence of gingerbread men ('O Himmel, welch Wunder ist hier geschehn'). Intrigued, the children eat little bits of the house but the Witch appears and throws a rope around Hänsel's neck. Hänsel tries to free himself but the Witch immobilizes both children with a spell ('Knusper, knusper knäuschen'). She puts Hänsel into a cage, intending to fatten him up. She frees Gretel with another spell and makes her help light the oven. Gretel uses the Witch's spell to free Hänsel from the cage. The Witch, unaware of this, tries to make Gretel look into the oven but Gretel pretends not to understand. When the Witch shows her what to do the children push her into the oven and slam the door ('Juchhei! Nun ist die Hexe tot'). The oven explodes and the fence of gingerbread men becomes a row of children; other children who have been baked in the oven rise up from the earth. As they thank Hänsel and Gretel for their deliverance Mother and Father appear. The Witch has been turned into gingerbread and everybody celebrates her downfall.

The influence of Wagner is evident in the use of leitmotifs (though Humperdinck uses them less strictly than Wagner), as well as in the orchestral and harmonic texture and in the symphonic character of the preludes and interludes. This does not, however, disguise the reliance on the style of traditional German children's songs, and two ('Ein Männlein steht im Walde' and 'Suse, liebe Suse') are taken from the well-known *Knaben Wunderhorn* collection. The work's originality derives from the synthesis of four opposite pairs of concepts – childhood/ adulthood, fairy-tale/reality, diatonic/chromatic and through-composition/episodic form. The subtle flexibility with which Humperdinck combined his resources gives the work its unique charm. As an heir to the Wagnerian tradition combined with folksong and realism – a strong influence on the composers of the time – *Hänsel und Gretel* occupies a startlingly individual place in musical history.

An arrangement of *Hänsel und Gretel* by Ludwig Andersen (1927) uses spoken dialogue and a much reduced orchestra. This less vocally demanding version is often used by schools and amateur groups.

RECORDINGS   1. Schwarzkopf, Grümmer, Felbermayer, von Ilosvay, Schürhoff, Metternich, Philharmonia O, Karajan, EMI, 1952; 2. Popp, Fassbaender, Gruberova, Burrowes, Hamari, Schlemm, Berry, Vienna PO, Solti, Decca, 1978; 3. Cotrubas, Te Kanawa, Welting, von Stade, Ludwig, Söderström, Nimsgern, Gürzenich O, Köln, Pritchard, CBS, 1982; 4. Bonney, Von Otter, Hendricks, Lind, Schwarz, Lipovšek, Schmidt, Bavarian Radio SO, Tate, EMI, 1990: the 1952 Karajan set is a classic but Schwarzkopf and Grümmer, though singing beautifully, might seem perversely mature at times; though the CBS benefits from Pritchard's benign conducting, the Decca, with the Vienna Philharmonic's ravishing playing captured in glorious sound, and the Tate set, excellent all-round, are the best modern recordings [A.B.]
VIDEO   Solti
EDITIONS   f.s., Schott, 1894; Eulenberg, c. 1955; v.s., Schott, 1894; 1972

Königskinder
Royal Children

Märchenoper in three acts, derived from an earlier melodrama (2h 30m)
Libretto by Ernst Rosmer (pseudonym for Elsa Bernstein-Porges)
Composed 1895–7 (melodrama), 1908–10 (opera)
PREMIERES   melodrama: 23 January 1897, Royal Court Theatre, Munich; UK: 13 October 1897, Court Theatre, London; US: 3 November 1902, New York; opera: US: 28 December 1910, Metropolitan, New York; Germany: 14 January 1911, Berlin; UK: 27 November 1911, Covent Garden, London
CAST   Goose-girl *s*, Witch *ms*, Prince *t*, Fiddler *bar*, Broom-maker *t*, Woodcutter *b*, 2 *ms*, 2 *t*, 2 *bar*, *b*; *satb* chorus of townspeople, children's chorus
FULL ORCHESTRA

Königskinder started out as a melodrama of a type that had no precedent at the time. In this first version the composer anticipated Schoenbergian sprechgesang by devising a speech-notation system that, although not as ambitious as sprechgesang, attempted to set the melodic line of speech without restricting the speaker. Humperdinck wrote, 'The notes for the spoken word generally indicate the relative, not the absolute pitch: the line of the risings and fallings of the voice.' His librettist was Elsa Bernstein-Porges, a distinguished playwright writing under the name of Ernst Rosmer. She knew Humperdinck from Bayreuth, where her father, Heinrich Porges, had been stage manager.

After the unsuccessful premiere of the melodrama Humperdinck abandoned the work until a summer holiday in 1908. He then took nearly three years to refashion it into a conventional opera, retaining nearly all the original music. The success of the New York premiere was undiminished by the fact that the same house had seen the first performance of Puccini's *La fanciulla del West* (with Caruso and Toscanini) 18 days earlier. There were 14 curtain calls after the first act and a 15-minute ovation at the end. American critics hailed *Königskinder* as the crowning work of post-Wagnerian opera but German critics, although complimentary, felt that Humperdinck had not matched the artistic heights of *Hänsel und Gretel*.

SYNOPSIS

Act I   The Goose-girl is kept in the forest by the Witch's spell. Together they bake a deadly magic loaf. A Prince finds her, and gives her his crown as a token of love, but when the spell prevents her leaving with him, he abandons her. The Fiddler guides the Broom-maker and the Woodcutter to the Witch's hut; the townspeople have sent them to ask her how they can find a king. The Witch prophesies that the new king of Hellabrun will be the first person to enter the town gates on the stroke of twelve. Meanwhile the Fiddler has spied the Goose-girl and he inspires in her the strength to break the Witch's spell. They leave together to find the Prince.

Act II   The townspeople, among them the Prince incognito, await the new king's arrival but it is the Goose-girl who enters the gates at noon wearing the crown, with her geese and the Fiddler. The people brand her as an impostor and when the Prince defends her they are both driven out.

Act III   Winter. The Fiddler now occupies the Witch's hut. The Woodcutter and Broom-maker implore him to return to Hellabrun where the town's children are in rebellion; they insist that he helps them search for the Prince and the Goose-girl. The Woodcutter and the Broom-maker take refuge in the hut. Frozen and starving the Prince and Goose-girl beg for shelter and finally barter the Prince's broken crown for a loaf, unaware of its deadly properties. The Fiddler returns to find them dead and he sings his last song as their requiem.

The elevated and romantic world of the fairy-tale appealed to *fin-de-siècle* German sensibilities, for whom the low life dramas of naturalism (or, operatically, *verismo*) were too coarse. Hence the vogue for Symbolist drama, of which Elsa Bernstein-Porges's invented fairy-tale is a typical example. Despite the apparatus of a fairy-tale the subject is serious, drawing heavily on Nietzsche for its concepts

Geraldine Farrar as the Goosegirl in Königskinder *(New York, 1910)*

of leadership and 'natural royalty'. There is therefore much less diatonic children's music than in *Hänsel und Gretel*, but instead a complex tonal carpet of Wagnerian development. Above all, Humperdinck found for this work a strain of exquisite elegiac melancholy, of which the Fiddler's final speech is a poignant example.

RECORDING opera: Donath, Schwarz, Unger, Dallapozza, Prey, Ridderbusch, Munich Radio O, Wallberg, EMI, 1970s: distinguished by Helen Donath's touching Goose-girl
EDITIONS melodrama: f.s./v.s. Brockhaus 1897; opera: v.s., Brockhaus, 1910

Other operas: *Die sieben Geislein*, 1895; *Dornröschen*, 1902; *Die Heirat wider Willen*, 1905 (RECORDING Melodram, 1940s); *Die Marketendrin*, 1914; *Gaudeamus*, 1919
BIBLIOGRAPHY Hans-Josef Irmen (ed.), *Engelbert Humperdinck, Letters and Diaries*, vol. 1: *1863–80*, A. Volk, 1975; vol. 2: *1881–3*, A. Volk, 1976; vol. 3: *1883–6*, Merseberger, 1983; E. F. Kravitt, 'The Joining of Words and Music in Late Romantic Melodrama', *MQ*, vol 62 (1976), pp. 571ff.; Robert Lawrence, *Hänsel und Gretel: The Story of Humperdinck's Opera*, Grosset and Dunlap, 1938

P.J.

ILJA HURNÍK
b 25 November 1922, Poruba, nr Ostrava

Hurník established a reputation first as a concert pianist, specializing in Janáček and Debussy, and came to opera comparatively late. However, he composed piano, chamber and vocal works from an early age (he published his first piano pieces at the age of 11), and completed his compositional training under Novák in Prague (1941–4). He is also a distinguished writer of tales and essays and was his own librettist for all his operas. Most have a comic or satirical character, some incorporate Hurník's own whimsical apocrypha to well-known stories, e.g. the one-act *Diogenes*, or *Salamo* (*King Solomon*), the first part of *Wise Men and Fools*. This opera and *Fishers in the Nets* contain three independent acts, each of which can be performed separately or as a whole.

The Lady and the Robbers
Dáma a lupiči
Tragicomic opera in four acts
Libretto by the composer, freely after William Rose's film scenario *The Ladykillers* (1955)
Composed 1966
PREMIERE 17 December 1966, Plzeň

Hurník's first opera is based on the famous Ealing black comedy *The Ladykillers*, about how a music-loving widow unknowingly provides a safe house for a gang of criminals (whom she takes for members of a string quartet – a quintet in the original film). The pretence is sustained by a gramophone record of Haydn string quartets and foiled by a faulty cello case, which reveals itself crammed with banknotes, though it is the widow rather than the robbers who survives to enjoy the loot. The result is an ironic comedy that pokes fun both at quaint English ways (observed from a central European vantage point) and operatic conventions: an aria about the magic of home is the song of a returning robber; a revenge aria is a complaint about a noisy cat; the police force provides a Gilbertian chorus.

Other operas: *Wise Men and Fools* (*Mudrci a bloudi*), 1971; *Diogenes*, 1975; *Fishers in the Nets* (*Rybáři v síti*), 1983; *Oldřich and Boženka* (*Oldřich a Boženka*), (1985)
BIBLIOGRAPHY Ladislav Šíp, *Česká opera a jeho tvůrci* (*Czech Opera and Its Creators*), Supraphon, 1983

J.T.

I

JACQUES IBERT

Jacques François Antoine Ibert; *b* 15 August 1890, Paris; *d* 5 February 1962, Paris

Although still known outside France mainly for his delightful *Divertissement* (1930), Ibert was one of the most versatile French composers of his generation, and less slave to the vogue for frivolity than some of his more notorious contemporaries. A Conservatoire pupil of Debussy's friend Paul Vidal, he won the Prix de Rome in 1919, and was later an influential administrator, himself director of the French Academy in Rome (1933–60).

As a composer, Ibert was prolific in all genres, but excelled in music for the theatre. The *Divertissement* itself derives from a theatre score (incidental music for Labiche's *Un chapeau de paille d'Italie*, 1929). This was only one of several incidental scores, to which should be added a quantity of film music (including, improbably, for Orson Welles's *Macbeth*, 1948) and several ballets. But Ibert's operas are by far his most substantial writing for the theatre. He wrote four for the stage, plus two more in collaboration with Honegger, and also, finally, a Bluebeard spoof for radio. They cover a surprising dramatic and expressive range, from the sparkling parody of the two one-act farces – *Angélique* (about a shrewish wife who drives her husband to offer her for sale) and *Gonzague* (about a piano-tuner who is invited to dinner to avoid thirteen at table) – to the rich fantasy of *Persée et Andromède*, based on a version of the myth by Jules Laforgue, and *Le Roi d'Yvetot*, a fairy-tale set in legendary Normandy and cast in the classic form of the opéra comique. The Honegger collaborations cover a similar range, *L'aiglon* being based on a romantic play by Edmond Rostand, while *Les Petites cardinal* is an operetta with dialogue. Ibert had the gift to turn a witty and tuneful comic song, but he could also write with profundity and a certain symphonic depth; his music invariably displays immaculate craftsmanship.

Operas: *Angélique*, 1927 (RECORDING Bourg, 1960s); *Persée et Andromède*, 1929 (RECORDING Bourg, 1963); *Le Roi d'Yvetot*, 1930 (RECORDING Bourg, 1958); *Gonzague*, 1931;

L'aiglon (with Honegger), 1937 (RECORDING Bourg, 1956); *Les petites Cardinal* (with Honegger), 1938; *Barbe-bleu* (radio opera), 1947

BIBLIOGRAPHY   Jacques Feschotte, *Jacques Ibert*, Ventadour, 1958

S.W.

VINCENT D'INDY

Paul Marie Théodore Vincent d'Indy; *b* 27 March 1851, Paris; *d* 2 December 1931, Paris

Teacher and theorist as well as composer, d'Indy studied music theory, composition and organ with César Franck at the Paris Conservatoire from 1872, becoming Franck's most ardent advocate, disciple and biographer. Beethoven and Wagner were also important influences on his style. He crystallized his thoughts in a four-volume treatise on composition (1903–5). D'Indy, a practical as well as a theoretical musician, was a prime mover in several organizations; he was one of the founders (1894) and director (1900) of the Paris Schola Cantorum.

An output of more than a hundred compositions includes several stage works. He wrote two light operas, *Attendez-moi sous l'orme* (1882) and *Le rêve de Cinyras* (1922), and music to three plays. More important are the légende dramatique, *Le chant de la cloche* (1883, a stage version of an earlier choral work, clearly influenced by *Parsifal*), and three operas to his own libretti. Two are described as actions musicales: the Wagnerian *Fervaal* (1889–95), and the musically leaner *L'étranger* (1898–1901), often considered to be d'Indy's most important opera. The third, described as histoire sacrée, is the large-scale *La légende de Saint-Christophe* (1908–15), in which the composer's patriotic, anti-Semitic sentiments emerge within a score which reflects his strong anti-modernist stance (he was a bitter opponent of Ravel).

BIBLIOGRAPHY   Norman Demuth, *Vincent d'Indy 1851–1931, Champion of Classicism*, Rockliff, 1951

F.A.

MIKHAIL IPPOLITOV-IVANOV

Mikhail Mikhailovich Ippolitov-Ivanov; *b* 19 November 1859, Gatchina; *d* 28 January 1935, Moscow

At the age of 23, Ippolitov-Ivanov graduated from the St Petersburg Conservatory and moved to Georgia, where he directed the Academy of Music and conducted the Opera at Tbilisi. In 1893 he was appointed professor at the Moscow Conservatory, where he remained until his death. A very active conductor, he worked at the Zimin, Mamontov and Bolshoi operas, and conducted the premieres of three of Rimsky-Korsakov's late operas. His conducting and teaching loom larger than his composition, which has charm, but little individuality. He was a lifelong conservative, even, in his book *Fifty Years of Russian Music*, considering some of Rimsky's late works a little decadent. His only work that is at all well known is *The Procession of the Sirdar* from his orchestral suite *Caucasian Sketches*, but he is also remembered for his completion of Musorgsky's *Zhenit'ba*. His operas *Ruth* and *Treachery* are in the nationalist oriental style, and *Asya*, subtitled 'Lyrical Scenes after Turgenev' is strongly influenced by Tchaikovsky's *Eugene Onegin*. His last opera, *The Last Barricade*, set in the time of the Paris Commune, remains unpublished and unperformed.

Operas: *Ruth*, 1887; *Azra* (destroyed), 1890; *Asya*, 1900; *Izmena* (*Treachery*), 1910; *Olye iz Nordlanda*, 1916; *Zhenit'ba* (*The Marriage*) (Acts II–IV, to follow Act I by Musorgsky), 1931 (RECORDING Melodiya, *c.* 1953); *Poslednyaya barrikada* (*The Last Barricade*), (1933)
BIBLIOGRAPHY S. D. Krebs, *Soviet Music*, George Allen and Unwin, 1970

J.G.

NICOLAS ISOUARD

Nicolas [Nicolo] Isouard; *b* 18 May 1773, Malta; *d* 23 March 1818, Paris

Isouard's career falls into two parts: the first spent in the south writing Italian opera, and the second spent in Paris composing mainly opéra comique. He was at first intended by his father for a non-musical career, but his musical gifts were so obvious that he was sent to study in Malta, Palermo, and Naples. Success came early with *L'avviso ai maritati*, which was premiered in Florence when Isouard was 19, and taken up in Madrid, Lisbon, Bologna and Dresden. Another eight works, predominantly opere buffe, followed rapidly.

Little has been written about the earlier works, but from the moment Isouard moved to Paris in 1799 his operas were destined for the widest exposure. Almost all were published in full score. His light yet rhythmic style of melody perfectly suited popular taste in the Napoleonic period. In gaiety and occasional use of exotic effect they more than rivalled the works of Dalayrac at the Opéra-Comique, and Isouard's successes were not supplanted until after his death, mainly by the ascendancy of Boieldieu's music.

His most successful works were *Les rendez-vous bourgeois*, *Cendrillon* and *Joconde*. *Joconde* was produced often in Germany and Austria, and reached London in 1876. *Cendrillon* was, in its turn, overtaken by Rossini's *La Cenerentola*, based on same libretto by C. G. Etienne.

Flaminius à Corinthe had been given at the Paris Opéra in 1801, but flopped. Isouard's posthumous *Aladin*, also for the Opéra, was very successful. This was in part because certain scenes used gas lighting for the first time in that theatre, creating the magic effects of Aladin's lamp. Isouard died after completing most of the first two acts. The last three acts were composed by A. M. Benincori, who himself died shortly before the premiere.

Operatic works: *L'avviso ai maritati*, 1794; *Artaserse, re di Persia*, 1794; *Rinaldo d'Asti*, 1796; *Il barbiere di Siviglia*, 1796; *L'improvvisata in campagna*, 1797; *Il tonneliere*, 1797; *I due avari*, 1797; *Ginevra di Scozia*, 1798; *Il Barone d'Alba Chiara*, 1798; *Le petit page, ou La prison d'état* (coll. with R. Kreutzer), 1800; *Flaminius à Corinthe* (coll. with R. Kreutzer), 1801; *Le tonnelier*, 1801; *L'impromptu de campagne*, 1801; *La statue, ou La femme avare*, 1802; *Michel-Ange*, 1802; *Les confidences*, 1803; *Le baiser et la quittance, ou Une aventure de garnison* (coll. with Méhul, Boieldieu, R. Kreutzer), 1803; *Le médecin turc*, 1803; *L'intrigue aux fenêtres*, 1805; *La ruse inutile, ou Les rivaux par convention*, 1805; *Léonce, ou Le fils adoptif*, 1805; *La prise de Passau*, 1806; *Le déjeuner de garçons*, 1806; *Idala, ou La sultane*, 1806; *Les rendez-vous bourgeois*, 1807; *Les créanciers, ou Le remède à la goutte*, 1807; *Un jour à Paris, ou La leçon singulière*, 1808; *Cimarosa*, 1808; *Zélomir, ou L'intrigue au sérail*, 1809; *Cendrillon*, 1810; *La victime des arts, ou La fête de famille* (coll. with H. M. Berton, Solié), 1811; *La fête du village, ou L'heureux militaire*, 1811; *Le billet de loterie*, 1811; *Le magicien sans magie*, 1811; *Lully et Quinault, ou Le déjeuner impossible*, 1812; *Le prince de Catane*, 1813; *Le Français à Venise*, 1813; *Bayard à Mézières, ou Le siège de Mézières* (coll. with Boieldieu, Catel, Cherubini), 1814; *Joconde, ou Les coureurs d'aventures*, 1814; *Jeannot et Colin*, 1814; *Les deux maris*, 1816; *L'une pour l'autre, ou L'enlèvement*, 1816; *Aladin, ou La lampe merveilleuse* (completed by Benincori), 1822; *Une nuit de Gustave Wasa* (completed by Gasse), 1825
BIBLIOGRAPHY E. Wahl, *Nicolo Isouard: sein Leben und sein Schaffen auf dem Gebiet der Opera Comique*, Munich, 1906

D.P.C.

J

WILLIAM JACKSON

b 29 May 1730, Exeter, Devon, England; d 5 July 1803, Exeter

Apart from two years in London as a pupil of John Travers, organist of the Chapel Royal, Jackson spent his whole life in Exeter, where his father was a grocer. As a boy he had lessons from the cathedral organist and his assistant; after his return from London (c. 1748) he established a reputation as a teacher, performer, and composer of keyboard and vocal music. In 1777 he became organist and master of the choristers at the cathedral. He was also an accomplished painter and writer; he exhibited at the Royal Academy and his essays on the aesthetics of music and the fine arts were controversial and influential. He composed an afterpiece, *Lycidas* (1767; lost) and two full-length stage works, *The Lord of the Manor* and *Metamorphosis* (1783), which failed. In the absence of both full score and dialogue the latter cannot be assessed today.

The Lord of the Manor

Comic opera in three acts (2h)
Libretto by General John Burgoyne ('Gentleman Johnny'), after Jean François Marmontel's one-act play *Sylvain*
PREMIERES 27 December 1780, Drury Lane, London; US: 2 February 1818, New York

The lord of the manor has disinherited his son and is unaware that, as 'Rashly', he is living on the estate with his two daughters (his wife has died). Contrast, Rashly's younger brother, forces his attentions on Sophia, the elder daughter (his niece), but she loves Truemore, who is in danger of conscription. Sophia's maid arranges that Contrast is conscripted instead. Contrast deserts and is brought before his father for judgement. Finally Rashly is forgiven and Sophia is united with Truemore.

The scoring is full and imaginative, but the chief virtue of the music is the amplitude of the melodies, typified by Rashly's lament for his wife, 'Encompass'd in an Angel's Frame'. *The Lord of the Manor* was a deserved success.

BIBLIOGRAPHY Roger Fiske, *English Theatre Music in the Eighteenth Century*, OUP, 1973; 2nd edn, 1986; Gertrude Jackson (ed.), *William Jackson of Exeter: A Short Sketch of My Life*, Verlag der Oesterreichischen Akademie der Wissenschaften, 1974

R.Lu.

VIKTOR JACOBI

b 22 October 1883, Budapest; d 12 December 1921, New York

Jacobi studied at the Budapest Musical Academy, along with Emmerich Kálmán and Albert Szirmai, and had his first operetta produced in 1904 while still a student. Further operettas exclusive to Hungary followed until he achieved an international breakthrough in 1911 with *Leányvásár* (*The Marriage Market*), a charming work set in the American West and aboard a ship. In 1914, an even more accomplished work, *Szibill* (*Sybil*) was widely popular; both works are still performed in Hungary. Jacobi went to New York (on the *Lusitania*) in 1915, and he worked on several American operettas, including *Apple Blossoms* with Fritz Kreisler, and an adaptation of Molnár's *The Wolf* entitled *The Love Letter*. His romantic music is enormously potent, particularly the slow waltz duets, and his bright comedy numbers are equally attractive, though less in the patently *csárdás* manner than those of Kálmán.

Operettas: *A rátartos királykisasszony* (*The Haughty Princess*), 1904; *A legvitézebb huszár* (*The Brave Hussar*), 1905; *A tengerszem tündére* (*The Nautical Fairy*), 1906; *Tüskerózsa* (*Rambler Rose*), 1907, rev. 1917; *Van, de nincs* (*There is, but there isn't*), 1908; *Jánoska*, 1909; *Leányvásár* (*The Marriage Market*), 1911; *Szibill* (*Sybil*), 1914 (RECORDING excerpts: Hungaroton, 1960s); *Apple Blossoms* (coll. with Fritz Kreisler), 1919; *The Half Moon*, 1920; *The Love Letter*, 1921
BIBLIOGRAPHY György Sándor Gál and Vilmos Somogyi, *Operettek Könyve*, Zenemükiadó, 1976

R.T.

EDITION J. Preston, 1781

Leoš Janáček with teachers and graduates of his Organ School (1914)

LEOŠ JANÁČEK

Leoš (Leo Eugen) Janáček; *b* 3 July 1854, Hukvaldy; *d* 12
August 1928, Moravská Ostrava (now Ostrava, Slovakia)

Janáček was almost 62 when his opera *Jenůfa* was
finally produced in Prague, bringing him unexpected
fame. By then he had written five operas, only two of
which had been previously produced (in his adopted
town of Brno) and the last had been abandoned in
sheer despair that it would ever be performed. The
success of *Jenůfa* in Prague in 1916, and its espousal
by the Viennese publishers, Universal Edition,
changed all this. He quickly completed his fifth opera
and in 1919, at the age of 65, embarked on an
astonishingly fertile last decade which saw the
composition of four major operas and a number of
substantial works in other genres such as the
Sinfonietta, the *Glagolitic Mass* and the two string
quartets. *Jenůfa* soon established his reputation in
Czechoslovakia and the German-speaking world, but
his later operas made less headway before the
Second World War. None of his operas was
produced in Britain, and the sole production in the
US (*Jenůfa*, in New York, 1924) was not a success.
Since the war, and especially from the 1960s and
1970s, Janáček has come to take his place as the best-
known Czech operatic composer and one of the
handful of the most important opera composers of
the 20th century.

Janáček was trained, like his father and grandfather before him, as a schoolteacher, leaving his
native Hukvaldy in northern Moravia in 1865 to
attend the Augustinian monastery school in Brno,
and thereafter a teacher-training course. The musical content in his schooling was substantial and
was supplemented by later training at the Prague
Organ School (1874–5), the Leipzig and Vienna
conservatories (1879–80), and above all by Janáček's
own particularly hard and systematic work. He read
widely in literature and philosophy. Other formative
influences were a fervent national pride that led to
his changing his name 'Leo' to the Czech 'Leoš', and
a fascination with the greater Slavonic world. He
made a crucial trip to Russia in 1896 and founded a
Russian Club in Brno which flourished up to the
First World War; two of his completed operas, *Kát'a
Kabanová* and *From the House of the Dead* were
based on works by Russian authors, Ostrovsky and
Dostoevsky respectively, but he also considered
settings of Tolstoy's *Anna Karenina* and his play
The Living Corpse. In 1880, his formal education
complete, Janáček returned to Brno, where he
married the young Zdenka Schulzová, and taught at
the Teacher Training College and elsewhere, notably
at the institution he founded, the Brno Organ School.
Apart from the Organ School, where he continued to
teach until 1919, he retired from all his teaching posts
by 1904 in order to devote himself to composition.

Until quite late in life Janáček's contact with opera
was minimal. As a young boy he had sung in a
performance of Meyerbeer's *Le prophète*. There was
no Czech opera in Brno at the time and no evidence
he attended (or could have afforded to attend) opera
in Prague during his year there as a student. So it is
likely that the first operas he saw were in Leipzig in

1880: Weber's *Der Freischütz* and, seven weeks later, Cherubini's *Les deux journées*. 'I wasn't taken by it at all, except for one single place,' he commented on the latter to his future wife. His orientation towards opera came only when, in his thirties, the tiny Brno Provisional Theatre was opened (1884), the first permanent institution in Brno to stage plays and operas in Czech. Janáček's response was characteristically positive. He founded a new musical periodical, *Hudební listy*, one of whose functions was to report on the activities of the Brno theatre. Janáček was the chief music critic, and his knowledge and opinions of the somewhat restricted repertoire (no Wagner, little Mozart, and much Smetana), can be charted in his reviews over the four years that the journal ran (1884–8). In the early 1900s, once he had retired from his schoolteaching, he had more time to travel to Prague, and pick up the novelties there. He was particularly enthusiastic about works such as Puccini's *Madama Butterfly* and Charpentier's *Louise*, and their influence can be detected respectively in his own operas *Fate* and *Kát'a Kabannová*. At a much later date he heard and championed Berg's *Wozzeck* at its controversial Prague premiere.

Although his last operas were written in the 1920s, Janáček was born in the middle of the 19th century and all he wrote was conditioned by a 19th-century training and attitude towards harmony and tonality. If his first opera, *Šárka*, had been a success at the time that he wrote it, Janáček might have been encouraged to remain with its musical idiom – essentially German-centred, though modified by the Czech romanticism of Dvořák and Smetana. But *Šárka* was not performed at the time and Janáček turned to other things. His preoccupation from the late 1880s with Moravian folk music, a particularly rich and distinctive resource in terms of mode and rhythm, had the long-term effect of enriching and fertilizing his musical language, though never obliterating its tonal roots. The result was a highly characteristic musical language, fresh and appealing, and one that a wide spectrum of 20th-century audiences have found accessible.

A second factor in Janáček's success arises from his gifts as a musical dramatist. While his mature operas have some of the oddest subject matter of any group of operas, all of them work, in their various ways, as effective stage pieces. They are astonishingly different from one another, inhabiting many distinctive worlds and atmospheres. These range from 19th-century Russian provincial life to Moravian peasant *verismo* and sophisticated Prague of the 1920s; from the life of animals in the Moravian woods to a Siberian prison camp. What binds them together is their succinctness, Janáček's uncanny ability to suggest and change mood with just a few notes, his terse but passionate lyricism, a compassionate humanity, and an emotional charge as powerful as any in the 20th century.

Šárka

Heroic opera in three acts (1h)
Libretto by Julius Zeyer (?1880), after Dalimil's Chronicle (14th century)

Composed 1887, 1888, rev. 1918, 1924–5
PREMIERE 11 November 1925, National Theatre, Brno
CAST Šárka *s*, Ctirad *t*, Přemysl *bar*, *t*; *satb* chorus of chieftains, women warriors, people, youths, girls
FULL ORCHESTRA

Janáček came across the text for his first opera in a periodical, set it over the summer of 1887, and sent it to his mentor and friend, Antonín Dvořák, for his comments. Only then did he approach Julius Zeyer for permission to use his text. This was refused. Zeyer, a distinguished poet and dramatist, had written his opera text specifically for Dvořák (who had toyed with it for years) and still hoped that he would eventually set it. Janáček nevertheless went on with the opera, composing a new version and orchestrating the first two acts (1888). Then he put it away, resurrecting it only thirty years later when the success of *Jenůfa* in Prague encouraged him to look at his other operas. Permission to use the text was now easily obtained from Zeyer's trustees. Janáček's pupil Osvald Chlubna orchestrated Act III while Janáček himself extensively revised the voice parts (1918). *Šárka* was staged in 1925 as a belated tribute to the composer's 70th birthday.

SYNOPSIS
The story of Šárka comes from the mythic history of Bohemia. After Libuše's death, the women of Bohemia, who had enjoyed special privileges during her lifetime, staged an armed revolt against the male rule of Libuše's consort, Přemysl. The rebellion is led by Vlasta (who does not appear in the opera); her chief captain is Šárka.

Act I Flagging male morale is restored by the young hero Ctirad, who, armed with magic weapons, vows to guard Libuše's tomb. Šárka and her women warriors invade the vault and are panicked into retreating by Ctirad's appearance. They vow revenge.

Act II Šárka plans to ambush Ctirad. She has herself tied to a tree, seemingly defenceless, while her warriors hide near at hand. Ctirad finds and takes pity on Šárka (who claims that she has been left there by the jealous Vlasta), and unties her. Ctirad falls in love with Šárka, as she does with him. Despite this, she summons her women with her horn-call. They kill Ctirad.

Act III Šárka is full of remorse and dramatically interrupts Ctirad's funeral rites by jumping on to his funeral pyre and dying in the flames.

Šárka continues the story of Smetana's *Libuše*, and was itself the basis for one of the symphonic poems in Smetana's *Má vlast*, and for Fibich's later opera. Musically *Šárka* shares the characteristics and conventions of Smetana's serious style, showing little hint of Janáček's future operas. The mostly iambic verse sets it apart from Janáček's later prose libretti, though his 1918 revision did much to disguise the basic regular periodic structure of the voice parts. There are full-blown choruses (a particularly attractive one for the women at the beginning of Act II) and ensembles (most of Act III is a slow-moving *tombeau* for soloists, chorus and orchestra). The music, however, catches fire only in the central Act II duet for Šárka and Ctirad where Janáček seems to have identified with the characters and their erotic involvement.

RECORDING Nováková, Jurečka, Kunc, Brno Radio O, Bakala, Multisonics (recorded 1958), 1993
MANUSCRIPT Universal Edition, Vienna; Ústav Dějin Hudby Moravského Zemského, Musea, Hudebněhistorické Oddělení, Brno

The Beginning of a Romance
Počátek románu
Romantic opera in one act (50m)
Libretto by Jaroslav Tichý (pseudonym of František Rypáček), after the short story by Gabriela Preissová (1886)
Composed 1891
PREMIERES 10 February 1894, Provisional Theatre, Brno; UK: 3 December 1974, Guildhall School of Music and Drama, London
CAST Poluška s, Tonek t, Baron Adolf t, Mudroch bar, Jurásek b, s, contralto, b; offstage satb chorus
FULL ORCHESTRA

Zeyer's refusal to sanction Janáček's setting of *Šárka* pushed the composer out into a new direction. Janáček, who had already shown interest in his native Moravian folk music, now became passionately involved in its collection and popularization. This sometimes took the form of arranging folkdances for orchestra and grouping them into larger performable units such as the *Lachian Dances* (1893), or the ballet *Rákos Rákoczy* (1891). *The Beginning of a Romance* represents a further stage along this path with, in many instances, Janáček simply adding lines from the libretto to his existing folkdance arrangements. Thus the duet for Poluška and Adolf is a version of the 'Starodávný' dance, familiar from the *Lachian Dances*. The result is a number opera, with clearly defined sections (it was originally composed as a singspiel, with spoken dialogue). Some folksongs, for instance Poluška's 'Žalo dívča, žalo trávu', were left with their original words and tunes; the offstage choruses, all folksong arrangements, provided sometimes ironic commentaries to the onstage action.

With almost two thirds of the opera consisting of previously written music, sensitive word-setting was consequently not a high priority, nor would one expect it to be from the poor level of the verse libretto. The original short story from which this was made has some charm, but most of its ironies were squeezed out in the adaptation. Its chief interest today is that it provided the first contacts between Janáček and Gabriela Preissová, the writer whose play *Her Stepdaughter* became the basis for Janáček's next opera.

SYNOPSIS
Poluška, a village beauty betrothed to Tonek, has attracted the attention of the young Baron Adolf. Their assignation (the beginning of their romance) is observed by Mudroch the gamekeeper, who runs off to report the news to Poluška's parents. Left alone, Poluška is joined by Tonek, who sadly observes the change in Poluška's attitude towards him without, however, guessing the reason. Meanwhile, Mudroch has found Poluška's parents and tells them of her new attachment. Confronted with this accusation, Poluška acknowledges its truth, arousing the anger of her father, Jurásek. Her mother, however, supports her. Thinking that Baron Adolf might perhaps marry Poluška, she and Mudroch encourage Jurásek to seek a meeting with Adolf's father, Count Halužanky. This turns out badly: the count completely misunderstands Jurásek's mission. The disappointed Poluška is comforted by Tonek and the young couple now swear fidelity to each other. Adolf meanwhile is seen happily paired with Countess Irma. In a cheerful concluding ensemble all express their delight at the outcome, believing that in marriage one should stick to one's class.

RECORDING Brno Radio, Jílek, Voce, 1982
EDITIONS v.s., Dilia/Alkor (on hire), 1978

Jenůfa
Její pastorkyňa
Her Stepdaughter
Opera in three acts (2h)
Libretto by the composer after Gabriela Preissová's play (1890)
Composed 1894–1903, rev. 1907 (rev. and reorch. 1916 by Karel Kovařovic)
PREMIERES 21 January 1904, National Theatre, Brno; Kovařovic version: 26 May 1916, National Theatre, Prague; US: 6 December 1924, Metropolitan, New York; UK: 10 December 1956, Covent Garden, London
CAST Grandmother Buryjovka contralto, Laca Klemeň t, Števa Buryja t, Kostelnička Buryjovka s, Jenůfa s, Mill Foreman bar, Mayor b, Mayor's Wife ms, Karolka ms, Maid ms, Barena s, Jano s, Aunt contralto; satb chorus of recruits, musicians, people from the mill, country folk, children
ORCHESTRATION picc, 2 fl, 2 ob, ca, 2 cl, b cl, 2 bsn, 4 hn, 2 tpt, 3 trbn, tuba, timp, perc (t-t, cym, tamburo piccolo, tamburo militaire, bd, glock, tubular bells, triangle), hp, str; onstage: hn, xyl, child's tpt, glock, 3 vn, va, vc, db

Janáček adapted his own libretto from Gabriela Preissová's controversial play, first produced in Prague 1890. The genesis of Janáček's opera is hard to document in view of his destruction of sketches and even his autograph score, but in 1894 he began work on the libretto and composed the prelude *Žárlivost* ('Jealousy'), originally planned as the work's overture though never performed as such during Janáček's lifetime. He probably completed Act I in about 1897 and then he seems to have let the project drop for a few years. He took it up again in 1901, and wrote the last two acts quite quickly.

The work was given in Brno, with some success (perhaps out of local patriotism) and was performed there and on local tours about 20 times up to 1913. Partly on the advice of the conductor of the premiere, Janáček's pupil Cyril Metoděj Hrazdira, Janáček revised the work and made several cuts, particularly in ensembles and other set numbers. The vocal score published by a local artistic society in 1908 incorporates these revisions and represents Janáček's definitive version of the piece.

Even before *Jenůfa* was accepted in Brno, Janáček had submitted the opera to the National Theatre in Prague, but the antagonism of its music director, Karel Kovařovic (allegedly hurt by Janáček's dismissive reviews of his opera *The Bridegrooms*) prevented its performance there until 1916. The Prague production under Kovařovic, however, proved a huge success. Two years later *Jenůfa* was given in Vienna in a German version by Max Brod, who subsequently translated most of Janáček's later opera texts. In the decade up to Janáček's death in 1928 *Jenůfa* became a repertoire piece in Czechoslovakia and in German-speaking countries. It remains the composer's most popular opera.

The version heard in Prague in 1916 was one that had been revised, and in particular reorchestrated, by Kovařovic (a condition of its acceptance). It was subsequently published by Universal Edition in this form and, until the 1980s, when Charles Mackerras conducted and subsequently recorded a version nearer to Janáček's original version, this was the only version that could be heard.

Maria Jeritza as Jenůfa (Vienna, 1918)

SYNOPSIS

Act I The Buryja mill in a remote village in Moravia. The mill-owner Števa Burjya and his older half-brother Laca are both in love with their cousin Jenůfa. But Jenůfa loves Števa, by whom she is pregnant. She anxiously awaits his return: if he is drafted into the army she will not be able to marry

him and her pregnancy will be discovered. Laca watches her jealously and learns from the mill foreman that Števa has not been conscripted.

The recruits can be heard approaching, singing a conscription song ('Všeci sa ženija') and accompanied by a small village band. At their head is Števa, who demands another song ('Daleko, široko') and then leads the reluctant Jenůfa in a wild dance. At the climax, a stern figure approaches and silences the company. This is Jenůfa's stepmother, known as the 'Kostelnička' (female sacristan). She forbids any marriage between Jenůfa and Števa for a year, during which time Števa must stop his drinking.

Grandmother Buryja dismisses the musicians and attempts to comfort Jenůfa, a cue for a slow ensemble ('Každý párek'). The company disperses, leaving a desperate Jenůfa confronting an unrepentant Števa. Laca has observed this scene, believes that Števa loves Jenůfa only for her beauty and, after her proud dismissal of him, Laca slashes her cheek in a fit of desperation. He is immediately remorseful, and in a short ensemble he pours out his anguish.

Act II The Kostelnička's cottage, five months later, winter. Jenůfa, kept in hiding by the Kostelnička, has given birth to a son. The Kostelnička sends her to bed with a sleeping draught. Having summoned Števa to the cottage, she shows him the baby and begs him to marry Jenůfa. But he offers money, not marriage, and hurries out. The next visitor is Laca. He is still anxious to marry Jenůfa, whom he believes, as does the rest of the village, to be in Vienna. The Kostelnička now tells him the truth. He is so dismayed to hear about the baby that the Kostelnička declares that the child died. She sends him away on an errand and, after a dramatic monologue in which she wrestles with her conscience ('Co chvíla'), runs from the cottage taking with her Jenůfa's baby, to drown it in the icy millstream.

Almost immediately, Jenůfa wakes up from her drugged sleep and discovers the baby is missing. Believing that the Kostelnička has taken it to show to the people at the mill, she offers up a prayer to the Virgin ('Zdrávas královno'). The Kostelnička returns frozen from her expedition, and tells Jenůfa that the child died while she was in a fever. Jenůfa accepts the news with tender resignation and when Laca returns soon after, she offers no resistance to his earnest proposal of marriage. As the Kostelnička blesses the union and then curses Števa, the window of the cottage blows open and the Kostelnička, filled with foreboding, cries out in terror.

Act III The Kostelnička's cottage, two months later. Preparations for Jenůfa's wedding to Laca are in progress, though the Kostelnička, broken by her deed, is a shadow of her former self. Guests arrive: the mayor and his wife, Števa and his betrothed (the mayor's daughter, Karolka). Jenůfa adroitly manages a reconcilation between the two half-brothers. Finally girls from the village come to sing a wedding song for Jenůfa ('Ej mamko, mamko'). Grandmother Buryja gives her blessing to the pair and just as the Kostelnička is about to add hers, a tumult is heard outside. Jano the herdboy runs on with the news that the frozen corpse of a little chld has been found in the mill-stream. Jenůfa thinks it is her child, and the gathering crowd accuses her of murder. Laca holds off the mob but it is the Kostelnička who silences the people with her own confession of guilt. At first appalled, Jenůfa begins to understand the motives that lie behind the Kostelnička's terrible action. She forgives her foster-mother, who is then led off to stand trial. Alone with Laca, Jenůfa thinks that he can no longer want her in these circumstances, but movingly, he pleads for and gains her love.

Superficially, there is much to link Janáček's second and third operas. Both were based on writings by Gabriela Preissová and both were set in the folklore-rich area of Slovakian Moravia. But whereas *The Beginning of a Romance* was tossed off in a few months, Janáček took almost a decade over his third opera, during which time he changed his whole attitude to the genre. The long pause before beginning Act II seems to have been particularly significant. Even in its final revision, the first act of *Jenůfa* shows traces of something like a number opera. It opens with what amounts to arias for Jenůfa and then Laca; towards the end there is a substantial *concertato* ensemble and a trio; and the chorus plays a large and fairly conventional part, especially in the folk scenes of Act I.

But even here Janáček had discarded his naïvely propagandist view of Moravian folksong. While *The Beginning of a Romance* consists mostly of folksongs, *Jenůfa* has a number of folksong texts in appropriate places (the recruits scene of Act I; the bridal chorus in Act III), but the tunes are by Janáček (who declared that the opera had not a single folksong in it). A further factor was Janáček's developing preoccupation with 'speech-melody' – his notations of fragments of everyday speech, often documented with details of their emotional context. Speech-melodies were not used to generate melodic material for his operas, but instead helped sharpen Janáček's awareness of the contours of natural speech. This led to a new style of writing whereby musical continuity was concentrated in the still regularly structured orchestra part, with the voice reciting increasingly freely over it. It was inevitable with such an approach that Janáček would set *Jenůfa* as a prose libretto, the first such in Czech opera.

RECORDINGS 1. Söderström, Randová, Dvorský, Ochman, Vienna Philharmonic, Mackerras, Decca, 1982: Janáček's original orchestration; 2. Beňačková, Kniplová, Přibyl, Krejčík, Brno Janáček Opera O, Jílek, Supraphon, 1978: two especially fine soloists (Beňačková, Přibyl) from a mainly Brno cast under the veteran Brno conductor; 3. Jelínková, Krásová, Blachut, Žídek, Prague National Theatre O, Vogel, Supraphon, recorded 1952: Janáček's biographer conducts some of the greatest Czech post-war singers, particularly Krásová and Blachut.
VIDEO Alexander, Silja, Langridge, Barker, Glyndebourne Festival Ch and O, Davis, Virgin, 1989
EDITIONS f.s., Universal, 1917, 1969 (Kovařovic version); v.ss., Klub přátel umění, 1908; Universal, 1917 (Kovařovic version), Vladimír Helfert (ed.), Hudební matice, 1934

Fate
(*Destiny*)
Osud

Three novelistic scenes (1h 15m)
Libretto by the composer and Fedora Bartošová
Composed 1903–5, rev. 1906, 1907
PREMIERES 13 March 1934 and 18 September 1934 (inc.; Brno Radio broadcast); 30 September 1934, Brno Stadion (concert); 25 October 1958, Brno State Theatre (Nosek 'flashback' arrangement); UK: 22 January 1972 (BBC broadcast); 14 August 1983, Queen Elizabeth Hall, London (concert); 8 September 1984, Coliseum, London
CAST Živný *t*, Míla Válková *s*, Doubek (at 5) *boy s*, Doubek (as student) *t*, Míla's Mother *contralto*, 6 *s*, 4 *contralto*, 5 *t*, 2 *bar*; *satb* chorus of schoolteachers, students and young girls, visitors at the spa, conservatory students
FULL ORCHESTRA including organ; onstage: pf

Even before *Jenůfa* had been produced, Janáček began a new opera. On holiday in the Moravian spa town of Luhačovice in August 1903 he met a Mrs Urválková, who told him how a malicious portrait of her had been drawn in an opera by Ludvík Čelanský, *Kamila* (1897). Janáček returned to Brno infatuated with Mrs Urválková and determined to write a new opera which would portray her in a different light. He took early retirement from his teaching post at the Teacher Training College and energetically began sketching a plot that included autobiographical scenes from Luhačovice and a music conservatory (similiar to the Brno Organ School which he had founded) and solicited the services of a young schoolteacher, Fedora Bartošová, to turn his scenario into 'Pushkinesque verse'. As his ardour for Mrs Urválková cooled (at the intervention of her husband), so the plot changed. It was further altered when Janáček began showing Bartošová's efforts to his friends, and by the time Janáček submitted his opera to the Brno National Theatre in October 1906 the work had been substantially revised. Negotiations with a producer and designer were started early in 1907 only to be scuppered by Janáček's wish to see the opera performed at the new Vinohrady Theatre in Prague, where it was immediately accepted by its musical director – ironically the same Ludvík Čelanský who had inspired it. But Janáček got cold feet over the libretto, which prompted another round of advice and further changes, which he completed in November 1907.

Čelanský took his time about the introduction of such an unusual work and a change of regime at the theatre produced even more delays. When in 1913 the work was eventually and reluctantly put into rehearsal, the singers rebelled, and the management seized on this as a pretext for abandoning the venture. Janáček took legal action, but was persuaded to drop the case on a vague promise of production by the now returned Čelanský. Meanwhile Brno showed further interest and Janáček withdrew the work altogether, submitting it to Brno in the spring of 1914. A production, however was shelved after the outbreak of the First World War.

After the success of *Jenůfa* in Prague, Janáček began to look at his earlier operas, including *Fate*, but the verdict on the libretto by Max Brod and others was so damning that he gave up all further thoughts about the work. Its first stage production, in Brno in 1958, was in an arrangement by Vaclav Nosek in which Act I and II were inserted in the middle of Act III as a flashback. Later productions at České Budějovice (1978) and London (1984) restored the original structure.

SYNOPSIS
Act I   A spa. The composer Živný meets up with a former mistress, Míla. Spa life is depicted in all its variety (various artists, fashionable society, women schoolteachers who rehearse a part-song, a noisy group of young people who leave for an 'excursion'). When left alone, the conversation between Živný and Míla reveals that a child had been born of their union, but submitting to pressure from her family Míla had married someone else. They decide to go off together, to the consternation of Míla's mother.

Act II   The study in Živný's house. Živný and Míla are living together with their five-year-old son, Doubek. Míla's mother, now insane and needing constant supervision, also lives with them and can be heard offstage mocking Živný as he plays through his opera to Míla. The opera has Míla's 'shame' depicted in it, and in a fit of remorse, Živný begins tearing pages from the score. Míla's mother breaks into the room, accusing Živný of stealing her daughter and her wealth. Míla tries to restrain her mother, and in the struggle both fall to their deaths.

Act III   The main hall of the conservatory (twelve years later). Students sing through a couple of the scenes in Živný's opera which is to be performed that evening in the theatre. Živný enters, and is persuaded to tell them something about the opera. As he does so a storm breaks out; he imagines that he can see his dead wife and hear her voice and collapses.

Fate is an important turning-point in Janáček's operatic career. His first three operas belong in different ways to the Czech operatic tradition: with *Fate* he began looking further afield for models, in particular to Gustave Charpentier's opera *Louise*, which had been hugely successful when given in Prague in February 1903, and which Janáček himself saw there in May of that year. He enthusiastically praised aspects of the opera such as its prose libretto, and its use of 'speech melodies', which he had already and independently employed in *Jenůfa*. Other features, not in *Jenůfa*, such as its contemporary subject matter, its more 'urban' style of music, its handling of a large individualized chorus, and its use of offstage 'symbolic' choruses he quietly purloined himself. These are all prominent aspects of *Fate* and some, for instance the offstage symbolic chorus, persist throughout his later operas.
In the wake of such a major stimulus, *Fate* is a surprisingly independent work. But its experimental character is none the less evident. The libretto was made up more or less as Janáček went along (the middle act in particular went through surprising metamorphoses), and is expressed in an art-nouveau floweriness of diction that makes it sometimes hard

to understand. The cinematic succession of scenes has caused problems for staging ever since, though it laid the foundation for Janáček's idiosyncratic dramatic pacing. The opera, however, was written with an overwhelming panache, right from the exuberant opening chorus (there is no overture). The solo sections, the long duet in Act I and Živný's monologue in Act III, are particularly fine.

RECORDING   1. Přibyl, Hajóssyová, Brno Janáček Opera O, Jílek, Supraphon, 1976; 2. in English: Field, Harries, Langridge, O and Ch of WNO, Mackerras, EMI, 1990
EDITION   v.s., Dilia/Alkor (on hire), 1978

The Excursions of Mr Brouček
Výlety páně Broučkovy
Opera in two parts (four acts) (2h 15m)
Libretto: Part I, the composer with František Gellner, Viktor Dyk, F. S. Procházka and others, after Svatopluk Čech's novel (1888); Part II, F. S. Procházka, after Svatopluk Čech's novel (1889)
Composed 1908–17
PREMIERES 23 April 1920, National Theatre, Prague; UK: 3 September 1970, King's Theatre, Edinburgh (Prague National Theatre); 28 December 1978, Coliseum, London: US: 23 January 1981, San Francisco Opera Ensemble (concert); 21 November 1981, Indiana University, Bloomington
CAST   Mr Brouček *t*, Mazal/Blankytný/Petřík *t*, Sacristan at St Vitus' Cathedral/Lunobor/Domšík od zvonu *b*, Málinka/Etherea/Kunka *s*, Würfl, landlord of the Víkarka/Čaroskvoucí/Town Councillor *bar*, Little Waiter/Child Prodigy/Student *ms*, *contralto*, 3 *t*, *bar*; *satb* chorus of artists, dancers, Etherea's companions, moon artists, armed men, Hussite people, Prague and Taborite soldiers, Taborite boys, Prague girls
FULL ORCHESTRA including organ and bagpipes

With *Fate* successfully accepted (as he thought) by the Vinohrady Theatre, Janáček began a new opera in March 1908. *The Excursion of Mr Brouček to the Moon* was designed as a one-act opera in four scenes based on Svatopluk Čech's satirical novel in which a philistine Prague landlord, Mr Brouček (Mr Beetle) is shown in comic confrontation with the aesthetes on the moon – a barb directed at the precious Art-for-Art's-sake movements of the period. Negotiations with a succession of librettists delayed work and resulted in Janáček's doing much of the adaptation himself (his first helpful librettist, František Gellner, who wrote most of the songs in what is now Act II, was brought in as late as 1912). By 1913, when any hope of staging *Fate* or *Jenůfa* in Prague had been abandoned, Janáček put away the three scenes he had written, but with Prague's change of mind over *Jenůfa*, he revised and completed his one-act opera (1916–17) with two more librettists (F. S. Procházka and Viktor Dyk). He finished the troublesome epilogue scene (depicting Brouček back at home), but later abandoned it, and added a second 'excursion' (1917), based on Čech's sequel, in which Mr Brouček is transported to the early 15th century, a heroic period in Czech history when the Czechs fought off armies of crusaders from the rest of Europe. Here Procházka provided the entire libretto, the last time Janáček was to employ a librettist. The complete 'bilogy' was given in Prague under Otakar Ostrčil in 1920, Janáček's only opera to be heard first outside Brno.

SYNOPSIS

The Excursion of Mr Brouček to the Moon
Výlet pana Broučka do měsíce

Act I Outside the Víkarka tavern, Prague. Mr Brouček, a Prague landlord, disgruntled by his troubles on earth, dreams of an idyllic life on the moon and, in a drunken stupor, is miraculously transported there. He meets the moon poet Blankytný (who resembles his difficult tenant on earth, Mazal), and Blankytný's betrothed Etherea (Málinka), accompanied by a chorus of singing maidens. Etherea promptly falls in love with Brouček and elopes with him on a winged horse, to the despair of Blankytný and her father Lunobor (Sacristan).

Act II The moon: the Temple of All Arts. Brouček and Etherea arrive at the court of the 'Maecenas', Čaroskvoucí (Würfl), pursued by Blankytný and Lunobor. Brouček gradually learns that the moon is inhabited by a breed of artistic beings who neither eat nor drink (they live by sniffing nectar) and are devoted entirely to artistic pursuits. He is horrified and manages to escape back to earth. He is found drunk in a beer barrel, while Mazal and Málinka make up their quarrel.

The Excursion of Mr Brouček to the 15th Century
Výlet pana Broučka do XV. století

Act I Jewel chamber of Wenceslas IV. Voices are heard (from the nearby Víkarka tavern) discussing the underground passages said to lead from there. Mr Brouček believes firmly in their existence. Soon after, he falls down a hole and finds himself in King Wenceslas's jewel chamber. He eventually makes his way out to the Prague Old Town Square which is mysteriously transformed to an earlier guise. Mr Brouček stumbles along the ill-lit streets (it is early dawn) and encounters a town councillor, who finds his 19th-century speech hard to understand and arrests him as a spy: Prague is on the eve of the great battle of 1420 where the Czechs, defending their Hussite faith, win a famous victory. Brouček's cause seems desperate until he is taken in by the kindly Domšík (Sacristan).

Act II Domšík's house. Brouček wakes up as an honoured guest and accustoms himself to his new surroundings. He is welcomed by Domšík's family and friends as a sturdy warrior who will fight with them in the coming battle. During a meal, Domšík's daughter Kunka enthuses over the sermon given that day and religious politics of the time are vigorously discussed. The alarm sounds, the men rush off to fight, Brouček reluctantly taking a pikestaff, against the background of prayers and Hussite war hymns. In the ensuing fight Domšík is killed, but the Czechs are victorious. Brouček manages to avoid fighting altogether, though he spins stories of his valour. However, his cowardice has been noticed and he is condemned to be burnt in a barrel. Just as the flames are at the highest, he wakes up in a barrel, and tells the indulgent Würfl about his latest escapade.

Brouček is Janáček's most overtly comic opera, the comedy essentially deriving from the confrontation of Mr Brouček with worlds beyond his limited imagination. The effect, however, is rather different in the two halves. In the first excursion Mr Brouček, in comparison with the rarefied moon-artists, offers the voice of sturdy common sense. In the second, Mr Brouček's 'reasonableness' makes a poor showing against the sacrifices of the patriotic Hussites: Janáček's motive for setting this second excursion was a moral appeal to the citizens of the future Czechoslovak Republic.

Despite this moral aim, the more coherent libretto, and often thrilling use of Hussite chorales (one traditional tune, the rest settings by Janáček of Hussite texts), the 15th-century excursion emerges as the weaker of the two. There are dry passages, especially in the doctrinal disputes among the Hussites, that suggest that Janáček did not completely engage with the material. However, the first excursion, for all its piecemeal production (a virtual scrapbook libretto) and seeming silliness, has music of great charm and liveliness and has proved surprisingly viable on the stage. *Fate* and *Brouček* can together be considered experimental transition pieces, uneven as artistic wholes but of great interest, and which considerably expanded Janáček's range through the impact of new influences (Charpentier, Puccini) and the exploration of new types of subject matter and structure.

RECORDING Přibyl, Švejda, Jonášová, Maršík, Novák, Czech Philharmonic Ch and O, Jílek, Supraphon 1980: a complete recording (Neumann's 1962 recording made cuts) with impressive choral and orchestral work
EDITION v.s., Universal, 1919

Katya Kabanova

Káťa Kabanová

Opera in three acts (1h 45m)
Libretto by the composer, after Ostrovsky's play *Groza* (*The Thunderstorm*, 1859) trans. Vincenc Červinka (1918)
Composed 1919–21
PREMIERES 23 November 1921, National Theatre, Brno; UK: 10 April 1951, Sadler's Wells, London; US: 26 November 1957, Karamu House, Cleveland, Ohio
CAST Savěl Prokofjevič Dikoj *b*, Boris Grigorjevič *t*, Marfa Ignatěvna Kabanová (Kabanicha) *a*, Tichon Ivanyč Kabanov *t*, Katěrina (Káťa) *s*, Váňa Kudrjáš *t*, Varvara *ms*, Kuligin *bar*, Glaša *ms*, Fekluša *ms*, Drunk Passer-by *silent*, Woman from crowd *contralto*, Passer-by *t*; *satb* chorus of townspeople, offstage chorus
ORCHESTRATION 4 fl/picc, 2 ob, ca, 3 cl/b cl, 3 bsn/dbsn, 4 hn, 3 tpt, 3 trbn, tuba, timp, perc (bass drum, sleigh bells), hp, cel, xyl, str (including viola d'amore)

With *Káťa Kabanová* Janáček entered his mature operatic period. His first five operas represent a painfully long operatic apprenticeship with only one clear-cut success (*Jenůfa*), for whose recognition he had to wait until he was almost 62. But what followed is without parallel. Janáček's amazing Indian summer – the last decade of his life – saw the composition of four major operas, on which, together with *Jenůfa*, his reputation rests today.

Kát'a Kabanová is Janáček's own adaptation of Ostrovsky's play *The Thunderstorm*, which he began considering late in 1919. The Russian material was congenial to him, but another strand in its inspiration was his identification of the principal character with a favourite operatic heroine of his, Madama Butterfly, and also with Kamila Stösslová. Janáček had met Mrs Stösslová on holiday in the Moravian spa town of Luhačovice in 1917. This marked the beginning of a passionate, though largely one-sided relationship which lasted until the end of Janáček's life, documented by the collection of over 700 letters which have only recently been published in full. According to these letters, Kamila Stösslová provided the inspiration for characters in all of Janáček's last four operas, and for the gypsy girl in *The Diary of One who Disappeared*. *Kát'a Kabanová* was dedicated to her.

Composition began early in 1920 and proceeded rapidly and unproblematically until the spring of 1921, though Janáček continued to tinker with the score up to its premiere. This took place in Brno in November 1921 under much grander circumstances than that of the Brno premiere of *Jenůfa*. Following the independence of Czechoslovakia the Czechs now had control of the excellent German opera house; *Kát'a Kabanová* was conducted by František Neumann, the new head of opera, who was to preside over all of Janáček's later premieres except for that of *From the House of the Dead*. *Kát'a Kabanová* also set a pattern for the later operas: all were given first in Brno, then in Prague, and published with Max Brod's German translation by Universal Edition. Despite the distinguished conductor of the first German production (Klemperer in Cologne, 1922), and a fine production in Berlin (1926) for which Janáček received the compliments of Schoenberg and Zemlinsky, the work made headway outside Czechoslovakia only after World War II. It was Janáček's first opera to be performed in the UK, and has been more frequently produced there than any other of his operas.

After difficulties in early productions with scene changes, Janáček wrote new interludes for Acts I and II which were first given in the Prague German Theatre production in 1928. Its conductor, Hans Wilhelm Steinberg, played the first two acts through without a break, a procedure Janáček enthusiastically endorsed.

SYNOPSIS

Act I Scene 1: Kalinov, Russia in the 1860s. In a public park on the bank of the Volga, Kudrjáš learns from Boris, his employer Dikoj's nephew, about his passion for a married woman, Kát'a Kabanová, and they watch the Kabanov family come back from church. The family is at loggerheads. Kát'a, a woman of great dignity and sweetness of nature, is married to the weak Tichon, a merchant under the thumb of his domineering mother, known as Kabanicha. He is unable to prevent Kabanicha from tyrannizing his wife, and he meekly complies when she orders him

off on a business trip. Scene 2: In a room in the Kabanov household, Kát'a tells Varvara, a foundling girl in the household, about herself. Her narration, at first joyful as she remembers her life at home and her church-going, clouds over as she tells Varvara of the dreams that trouble her, and of her guilty love for Boris. Tichon comes in, ready for his departure. Kát'a is anxious because of the temptations that might arise during his absence, and begs him not to go, or to take her with him. But he is helpless against his mother, who furthermore orders him to extract humiliating promises of good behaviour from Kát'a during his absence. Tichon departs.

Act II Scene 1: Towards evening on the same day, in another room in the Kabanov household, Kabanicha reprimands Kát'a for not showing enough grief at Tichon's departure. Varvara has already made plans for an assignation between Kát'a and Boris and gives her the key to the garden gate, which she has stolen from Kabanicha. Kabanicha is visited by Dikoj, Boris's unpleasant uncle, who derives pleasure from confessing his weaknesses to Kabanicha, and receiving her scolding. Scene 2: A hollow overlooked by the Kabanov garden, a summer evening. Kudrjáš sings a song as he waits for Varvara ('Po zahrádce děvucha'), and is surprised by the appearance of Boris, who tells him of the assignation arranged for him. Varvara joins them ('Za vodou za vodičkou') and runs off with Kudrjáš. Boris is soon joined by Kát'a, terrified by the 'sin' she is committing. Their courtship is interrupted by the other couple, whose more light-hearted relationship takes centre stage, with fragments from Boris and Kát'a's passionate love duet wafting in from offstage. Then it is time for the lovers to part and Kudrjáš calls Boris and Kát'a. The scene ends with another 'folksong' for Kudrjáš and Varvara ('Chod' si dívka do času').

Act III Scene 1: Two weeks later. People are taking refuge from the afternoon storm in the ruins of an abandoned church overlooking the Volga. Kudrjáš exchanges insults with his employer, Dikoj. The scientifically minded Kudrjáš advises the installation of lightning conductors; Dikoj pooh-poohs this since, as he asserts, storms are a punishment sent by God. Kudrjáš is sought out by Varvara, worried about Kát'a's distraught state at the imminent return of her husband. Kát'a runs on dishevelled and will not be calmed or comforted. Tichon and Kabanicha now enter, and Kát'a, overwrought by the thunderstorm which she sees as a punishment from God, confesses her adultery with Boris to the assembled company and rushes out into the storm. Scene 2: At twilight Tichon and Glaša, a servant, look in vain for Kát'a in a deserted place on the bank of the Volga. Kudrjáš and Varvara decide to leave for Moscow. Kát'a wanders on in a daze, wanting to see Boris once again and then die. Strange voices call her, but death does not come yet. Eventually Boris joins her. After a brief farewell he leaves (he is being sent off to Siberia by Dikoj), and Kát'a, now at peace with herself, finds death in the Volga. Her body is hauled out and presented to Kabanicha, who thanks the 'good people' for their kindness.

Kát'a Kabanová is Janáček's most lyrical opera. Central to the work is Janáček's conception of the heroine 'of such a soft nature that . . . if the sun shone fully on her she would melt'. Her first vocal utterance is gentle and regular, in sharp contrast to Kabanicha's noisy tirade. Similar 'Kát'a' music reappears in most scenes. Sometimes her music is confined to the orchestra, for instance her radiant appearance in Act I (modelled on the first appearance of Madama Butterfly) or the poignant music for the lovers' silent embrace in the final scene.

While Kát'a's presence is signalled by a type of music, two reminiscence themes are also important. Varvara's 'Za vodou' tune is heard in the opera even before it is given words in Act II, Scene 2. The eight strokes of the timpani represent a fate theme which is heard softly in the opening bars of the overture, and *fortissimo* at the end. Speeded up and heard on the oboe against a sleigh-bell accompaniment, it provides the music (first heard in the overture) for Tichon's departure, the event that precipitates the crisis.

Kát'a's gentle nature is contrasted not merely to the despotism of Kabanicha (Janáček's most evil female portrait), but to the light-hearted world of Varvara and Kudrjáš, characterized by their folksongs. The double love scene of Act II, Scene 2, with Kát'a's and Boris's love music heard in the distance against the more practical chatter of Varvara and Kudrjáš onstage, is one of the glories of the score. Equally fine are Kát'a's two monologues: the first (Act I, Scene 2), in which she travels imperceptibly from religious to sexual ecstasy in her vivid account of her inner life; the second (Act III, Scene 2) where her inner voices are made audible in an offstage chorus.

RECORDINGS 1. Söderström, Dvorský, Vienna PO, Mackerras, Decca, 1976: Mackerras's beautifully paced recording includes Janáček's additional interlude music; 2. Tikalová, Blachut, Prague National Theatre O, Krombholc, Supraphon, 1959: Talich's reorchestration; a fine Kát'a and Boris
EDITIONS f.s., Universal, 1921, 1971; study s., Universal, 1992; v.s., Universal, 1922

The Cunning Little Vixen

Příhody Lišky Bystroušky
(*The Adventures of the Vixen Bystrouška*)
Opera in three acts (1h 30m)
Libretto by the composer, after the novel *Liška Bystrouška* by Rudolf Těsnohlídek (1921)
Composed 1922–3
PREMIERES 6 November 1924, National Theatre, Brno; UK: 22 March 1961, Sadler's Wells, London; US: 7 May 1964, Mannes College of Music, New York
CAST Gamekeeper *bar*, Gamekeeper's Wife *contralto*, Schoolmaster *t*, Priest *b*, Harašta *b*, Pásek *t*, Mrs Pásková *s*, Bystrouška the Vixen *s*, Zlatohřbítek the Fox *s*, Young Bystrouška *child s*, Frantík *s*, Pepík *s*, Lapák the Dog *ms*, Cock *s*, Chocholka the Hen *s*, Cricket *child s*, Grasshopper *child s*, Frog *child s*, Midge *child s*, Woodpecker *contralto*, Mosquito *t*, Badger *b*, Owl *contralto*, Jay *s*; chorus of hens and creatures of the forest, children's chorus of fox cubs, offstage *satb* chorus; ballet (dragonfly, Vixen as a girl, midges, hedgehog, squirrels)

ORCHESTRATION 2 fl, 2 fl/picc, 2 ob, ca, 2 cl, b cl, 3 bsn/dbsn, 4 hn, 3 tpt, trbn, tuba, timp, perc (sd, triangle, cym, bd), hp, cel, xyl, tubular bells, glock, str

During the spring of 1920 the Brno newspaper *Lidové noviny* published in daily instalments a tale about a vixen who is captured by a gamekeeper and then escapes back to the woods to find a mate for herself and raise a litter. A particular feature of the serialization was the inclusion of a large number of illustrations. These had in fact come first. *Lidové noviny* acquired Stanislav Lolek's 200 line-drawings (which, in cartoon fashion, told their own story), and then instructed one of their reporters, Rudolf Těsnohlídek, to produce a text. The resulting 'novel', celebrating country life in the forests near Brno, was published in book form in 1921 and has remained popular to this day.

According to Janáček's housekeeper, Marie Stejskalová, it was she who drew the work to Janáček's attention as a possible opera text. But this could have come about through other means. Janáček took the paper and as a regular contributor himself had close contacts with its editors. In June 1921 he began dropping hints that *Liška Bystrouška* might be his next opera, but only the next year, with the premiere of *Kát'a Kabanová* out of the way, did he get down seriously to planning the libretto. He began the music in autumn 1922, and was essentially finished within a year, with the final act copied up by January 1924. The Brno premiere followed in November, a few months after Janáček's 70th birthday. The piece's foreign success dates from the celebrated Felsenstein production at the Komische Oper, Berlin in 1956.

Janáček wrote his own libretto. Invited to contribute, Těsnohlídek produced only the gamekeeper's song in Act II – other songs came from folk texts. The first two acts, with many omissions, follow Těsnohlídek closely. But since the Vixen's wedding at the end of Act II of the opera closes the novel, the structure of Act III is Janáček's invention, though drawing on various scenes and incidents earlier in the book. The Vixen's death, within a context of the cyclical renewal of life, is Janáček's own distinctive contribution.

SYNOPSIS

Act I The forest; summer, a sunny afternoon. The gamekeeper, interrupting the animal life of the forest, lies down and takes a nap. While he sleeps, a young frog tries to catch the mosquito, but lands instead on the gamekeeper's nose and wakes him up. The frog has attracted the attention of Bystrouška ('Sharp-ears'), the vixen cub. The gamekeeper catches her and takes her home. The farmyard: autumn, late afternoon sun. Installed at the gamekeeper's, Bystrouška exchanges stories with the dog and defends herself both against his sexual advances, and against the baiting by the two boys, Frantík and Pepík, for which she is tied up. When night falls she appears in her dreams as a young girl. Bystrouška's plan to entice the hens within her range begins with a harangue about their subservience to

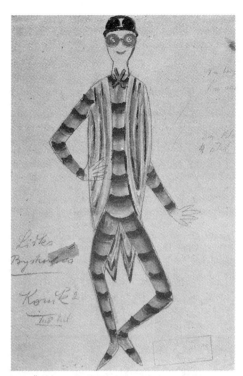

Josef Čapek's costume design for the caterpillar in The Cunning Little Vixen *(Brno, 1924)*

the cock; when this fails she threatens to bury herself alive in disgust at their conservatism. The cock is sent to investigate and is soon killed, as are all the hens in turn. Fearing retribution at the hands of the gamekeeper and his wife, Bystrouška bites through her leash and escapes into the forest.

Act II   The forest; late afternoon. Now at large in the forest, Bystrouška ruthlessly evicts the badger and takes over his comfortable home. The inn. The gamekeeper, the schoolmaster and the priest drink and play cards. The gamekeeper sings a song about the passing of time ('Bývalo, bývalo') and taunts the schoolmaster about his inactivity as a lover; in return the schoolmaster baits him about the escape of the vixen. The forest; moonlight. The schoolmaster, tipsy, has trouble finding his way home, and mistakes the vixen, hiding behind a sunflower, for his distant beloved, Terynka. The priest, separately wending his way home, lets his thoughts wander back to an incident in his youth when he was wrongly accused of seducing a girl. Both men are startled by the gamekeeper, who fires – in vain – at the vixen. The forest; summer, a moonlit night. The vixen meets a handsome fox, Zlatohřbítek ('Goldmane'); she tells him of how she was brought up by the gamekeeper and of her subsequent escapades. They fall in love, observed by gossiping birds, and she is soon obliged to marry. The animals of the forest join in the general merrymaking.

Act III   The forest; autumn, midday. Harašta, a poultry dealer, is heard approaching ('Déž sem vandroval'); he is accosted by the gamekeeper, who thinks he has been poaching. Harašta tells him he is about to marry Terynka. The gamekeeper leaves a trap for the vixen, but Bystrouška, her mate and litter make fun of the trap ('Beží liška k Táboru'). Bystrouška and her fox contemplate their growing family and possible additions. Harašta returns. Bystrouška, pretending to be lame, lures him into the forest, where he trips over. While he is nursing his injuries, Bystrouška and her family demolish the chickens. In his anger Harašta shoots and kills the vixen. The inn. The schoolmaster is tearful at the news of Terynka's marriage, and both he and the gamekeeper regret the absence of the priest. The gamekeeper, feeling his age, sets off home. The forest; as at the beginning. The gamekeeper contemplates the beauty of the scene around him, and remembers the day of his wedding. At peace with nature and with himself, he falls asleep. In his dream, the creatures seen at the opening reappear, including a little vixen, but when the gamekeeper tries to catch her he succeeds only in catching a frog – the 'grandson' of the one in the first scene. His gun falls to the ground.

As always, Janáček was an economical librettist. Where direct or indirect speech was available in the novel he used it, and where there was none, he simply wrote music. Thus, in comparison with his previous opera, *Kát'a Kabanová*, based on a play, there is a far greater proportion of purely instrumental music – essential for the short interludes between the many scenes. The music contains some of Janáček's most enchanting orchestral inspirations, for instance the dream sequence of the young vixen in Act I, or at the opening the evocation of the forest with its abundance of life. Janáček's score is articulated in half-act units held together by the recurrence of themes (e.g. the offstage chorus at the beginning of the second half of Act II transformed into the exuberant wedding chorus at the end), or by sets of variations.

Janáček had no inhibitions about the singing of animals. Size is more or less equated with pitch – ranging from the bass badger to the female voice hens and forest birds, and the inspired use of children's voices for the insects. Children's voices are also used delightfully for the vixen's cubs. Dance is another important element of the score in the evocation of animal life. Apart from the vixen herself, and memorably the little frog at the end of the opera, interactions between the human and animal worlds are sparing, though Janáček reduced his cast slightly by indicating suggestive doublings (e.g. priest/badger, schoolmaster/mosquito).

For such a curious libretto, the work has a surprisingly large emotional range, from the comic episodes with the hens in Act I, to the erotic courtship music in Act II, and the painfully nostalgic inn scene in Act III. Most memorable of all, however, is the gamekeeper's monologue which dominates the end of the opera, and which lifts the original text to an altogether different plane.

RECORDINGS   1. Böhmová, Domanínská, Asmus, Prague NT Ch and O, Neumann, Supraphon, 1957: Asmus's classic gamekeeper is unsurpassed; 2. Popp, Randová, Jedlička, Vienna PO, Mackerras, Decca, 1981: enchanting performances and digital sound; 3. Watson, Montague, Allen, Royal Opera House Ch and O, Rattle, EMI, 1991: in English VIDEO Gustafson, Palmer, McCauley, R. Davies, Adams, Glyndebourne Festival Ch and O, Davis, Virgin, 1988 EDITIONS   f.s., Universal (on hire), 1924; v.s., Universal, 1924

The Makropulos Affair

(*The Makropulos Case*)
Věc Makropulos
Opera in three acts (1h 30m)
Libretto by the composer, after Karel Čapek's comedy (1922)
Composed 1923–5
PREMIERES   18 December 1926, National Theatre, Brno; UK: 12 February 1964, Sadler's Wells, London; US: 19 November 1966, War Memorial Theatre, San Francisco
CAST   Emilia Marty (Elina Makropulos) *dramatic s*, Albert Gregor *t*, Vítek *t*, Kristina *s*, Jaroslav Prus *bar*, Janek *t*, Dr Kolenatý *b-bar*, Technician *b*, Cleaning Woman *contralto*, Hauk-Šendorf *operetta t*, Chamber Maid *contralto*; offstage: male chorus
ORCHESTRATION   4 fl/2 picc, 2 ob, ca, 3 cl/b cl, 2 bsn, dbsn, 4 hn, 4 tpt, 3 trbn, tuba, timp, perc (bd, castanets, cym, suspended cym, tamburo di bambini, tamburo militaire, tamburo picc, xyl, tubular bells), hp, cel, str (including viola d'amore); backstage: 2 hn, 2 tpt, timp

Janáček saw Karel Čapek's play *The Makropulos Affair* in Prague on 10 December 1922, three weeks after it opened, and was immediately attracted to it as a possible opera text, although he had only just started the composition of *The Cunning Little Vixen*. By February 1923 he was in correspondence with Čapek about it. Čapek himself was accommodating but there were legal problems to be overcome in securing the rights. On 10 September 1923 the composer heard from Čapek that these had been resolved and the next day set to work, even before the score of *The Cunning Little Vixen* was finalized. He worked quickly, with Act I drafted by February 1924 and the whole opera by December that year, though, as was his usual practice, he needed two more drafts before he was satisfied with his work, which he completed a year later on 3 December 1925. The Brno premiere followed under Neumann in December 1926, and the Prague premiere under Ostrčil in March 1928 – the last premiere Janáček attended. Though a German production followed under Josef Krips in Frankfurt in 1929, the work took time to establish itself internationally. However, outstanding productions by Sadler's Wells (1964) and Welsh National Opera (1978), both of which were later taken into the English National Opera repertoire, have ensured a regular following in the UK.

Janáček's libretto is a skilful compression keeping the original three-act framework of Čapek's play intact (though not the division of the final act into two scenes). But whereas Čapek wrote his play as a philosophical comedy, which dispassionately explored the merits and drawbacks of a life prolonged to over 300 years, Janáček impatiently cut out much of the speculative banter, and instead concentrated on the emotional state of the extraordinary central character, the 337-year-old Elina Makropulos.

SYNOPSIS
A young Cretan girl, Elina Makropulos, is given an elixir of life devised by her father, physician to Emperor Rudolf II at his court in Prague. She flees with the formula, 'Věc Makropulos' (the Makropulos thing, document), trains as a singer and with literally centuries to perfect her technique has become one of the greatest singers of all time. Moving from country to country to avert suspicion, she has undergone frequent changes of name, though always retaining the same initials. For the past few years (the date is 1922 – she is now 337), she has been known as Emilia Marty and returns to Prague where her extraordinary lease of life began. As it happens, a celebrated lawsuit, Gregor versus Prus, is reaching the end of its 100-year life. The present claimant, Albert Gregor, maintains that his ancestor Ferdinand Gregor should have inherited a large estate on the death in 1827 of its owner, Baron Josef Ferdinand Prus. The Prus family, however, have successfully contested the claim.

Josef Čapek's design for the lawyer's office in The Makropulos Case *(Brno, 1926)*

Act I Dr Kolenatý's chambers. Albert Gregor interrupts the historical ruminations of Kolenatý's clerk Vítek to find out the latest news of his case. Kristina, Vítek's daughter, returns from rehearsals at the theatre where Emilia Marty is currently appearing, infatuated by her artistry and beauty. She and Vítek leave just as Marty herself enters the office, accompanied by Dr Kolenatý. Marty wants to know about the Gregor–Prus case; her sharp questions and comments indicate an intimate knowledge of the people involved. She reveals that Ferdinand Gregor was Baron Josef Prus's illegitimate son, and that a will in his favour exists somewhere in the house of the present Baron Jaroslav Prus. Gregor makes the disbelieving Dr Kolenatý go and find it. Left alone with the mysterious Marty, Gregor hears more about Ferdinand Gregor's mother, the singer Ellian MacGregor. By then he is completely captivated. She repels his amorous advances and is distraught when he confesses ignorance of the 'Greek papers' she claims he must have. Kolenatý returns with Prus – and with a will. Prus, however, insists that some evidence is still missing. To Kolenatý's amazement, Marty undertakes to provide it.

Act II The empty stage of a large theatre. A cleaning woman and a technician discuss Marty's performance the night before. Prus comes to wait for Marty and, unobserved, witnesses the little scene between Kristina and her boyfriend, his son Janek – to the latter's embarrassment. Marty now appears, upsetting everyone who tries to congratulate her: the tongue-tied Janek, Gregor, and Vítek, who to her great annoyance compares her to a famous past singer. But she is strangely compassionate to her final visitor, the aged and demented Hauk-Šendorf, who sees in her a likeness of his 'gypsy girl', Eugenia Montez, long since dead. After giving Kristina her autograph, she dismisses everyone except Prus. Prus excites her interest by mentioning that together with the will there were letters and 'something else' in a sealed envelope. He adds that his investigations reveal that Ferdinand Gregor's mother is given on the birth register as Elina Makropulos, not Ellian MacGregor, as stated by the document Marty has provided. Consequently no MacGregor (or Gregor) can claim the Prus estates. Marty, however, is more interested in the sealed envelope and offers to buy it. Prus angrily stalks off. Gregor now finds her. She asks him to retrieve the document that she gave to Kolenatý – it needs another name. When he continues his advances to her, she brutally repulses him and then falls asleep. He tiptoes away, and Marty wakes up to find Janek with her. She urges him to steal the sealed envelope from his father. This scene, however, has been overheard, once again, by Prus who dismisses his son and who finally agrees to give Marty the envelope in exchange for an assignation that night.

Act III A hotel room. Prus and Marty have spent the night together. She gets her envelope, but Prus feels cheated and is broken by the news that Janek has committed suicide. Prus leaves, meeting Hauk-Šendorf on the way. Hauk-Šendorf proposes to Marty that they elope but they are forestalled by the arrival of Kolenatý and his party, who accuse her of forgery: the signature on the document she supplied has been written with modern ink. She goes to change while the others rifle her trunk, discovering a variety of historical documents relating to Ellian MacGregor, Eugenia Montez, Elina Makropulos and others. When she returns, dressed and a little tipsy. When cross-examined she insists that her name is Elina Makropulos and she is 337 years old. She tells them about her father and the elixir of life he devised and tried out on her. She had passed this on to the only man she loved, Josef Prus, but with the end of her

life approaching she wished to get back the formula. Eventually the company believes her. She collapses and is taken to the bedroom, attended by a doctor. She returns 'as a shadow', at last understanding that death will be a welcome relief – life has become quite meaningless for her. She offers the Makropulos formula to Kristina, who however sets fire to it, as Elina Makropulos dies.

Like the Vixen's, Elina's death at the end of the opera was Janáček's addition. This magnificent scene is the best illustration of how completely Janáček transformed Čapek's conversational comedy into a drama conceived on the grandest emotional scale. Here Janáček wrote one of his slow-waltz finales, a haunting, rocking tune played in the extremes of the orchestra with, in the middle, Elina's moving account of how meaningless life has become for her. Its otherworldliness is underlined by the slow pace and by the mysterious offstage male-voice choir repeating her words. This is the only substantial monologue in an opera that otherwise is characterized by its many memorable dialogues. Most striking of these is the verbal duel between Marty and Prus in Act II, complemented by their chilling, almost wordless encounter that brings down the curtain.

The success of the dialogues is due partly to the different atmospheres that Janáček creates in each of them, and partly to his virtuosity in handling the voice parts. Compared with those of The Vixen, or From the House of the Dead, this is a wordy libretto, an aspect that has often been criticized. And yet Čapek's elegant prose seems to have offered Janáček a wealth of phrases, whose memorable settings realized perhaps more than in any other work Janáček's speech-melody ideal of revealing a character's inner life. This is one reason why all the minor characters come alive in this more than in any other Janáček opera. The vocal writing is accompanied by some of Janáček's most sophisticated and imaginative orchestral developments which, for instance, help to bind the huge span of the long Marty–Gregor dialogue in Act I.

RECORDINGS 1. Söderström, Dvorský, Zítek, Švehla, Vienna PO, Mackerras, Decca, 1978: ideal casting in the title role, sumptuous playing, idiomatically conducted; 2. Prylová, Žídek, Kočí, Berman, Prague National Theatre O, Gregor, Supraphon, 1967
EDITION v.s., Universal, 1926

From the House of the Dead
Z mrtvého domu

Opera in three acts (1h 30m)
Libretto by the composer, after Dostoevsky's novel *Memoirs from the House of the Dead* (1862)
Composed 1927–8
PREMIERES 12 April 1930, National Theatre, Brno (Chlubna and Bakala arr.); UK: 28 August 1964, King's Theatre, Edinburgh (Prague National Theatre); 28 October 1965, Sadler's Wells, London (Janáček's original version); US: 3 December 1969 (NET Television); 24 March 1983, New York Philharmonic (concert)
CAST Alexandr Petrovič Gorjančikov *bar*, Aljeja *ms*, Luka Kuzmič (alias of Filka Morozov) *t*, Tall Prisoner *t*, Short Prisoner *bar*, Prison Governor *b*, Old Prisoner *t*, Prisoner

with Eagle *t*, Skuratov *t*, Čekunov *b*, Drunk Prisoner *t*, Cook *bar*, Smith *bar*, Priest *bar*, Young Prisoner *t*, Prostitute *ms*, Prisoner playing Don Juan and the Brahmin *b*, Kedril *t*, Šapkin *t*, Šiškov *bar*, Čerevin *t*, First Sentry *t*, Second Sentry *bar*, Voice offstage *t*, Knight, Elvira, Cobbler's Wife, Priest's Wife, Miller, Miller's Wife, Clerk, Devil *silent*; *tb* chorus of prisoners; guests and sentries *silent*

ORCHESTRATION   4 fl/3 picc, 2 ob, ca, 3 cl, 2 E♭ cl, b cl, 3 bsn, dbsn, 4 hn, 3 tpt, bass tpt, 3 trbn, tenor tuba, bass tuba, timp, perc (sd, cym, metal implements (hoe, shovel), chain, saw, tt, rattle, swords), hp, cel, xyl, bells, glock, str; onstage: 2 picc, tenor tuba, 3 trnb, tuba, sd, bd, triangle

After completing *The Makropulos Affair* in 1925, Janáček appeared to have no more operatic plans. The next year, 1926, he wrote the *Sinfonietta*, the piano *Capriccio* and the *Glagolitic Mass*, and made a brief visit to England. During this trip he mentioned to Mrs Rosa Newmarch his idea for a violin concerto called 'The Journeying of a Soul'. He made sketches, possibly in late 1926, and in 1927 these were revised to form the overture to his final opera, *From the House of the Dead*. Why he chose to set Dostoevsky's novel is not known, apart from his general sympathy towards Russian literature, but his total absorption with the appalling world depicted in the novel, and his feeling of urgency to set it, is vividly documented in his letters to Kamila Stösslová. By May 1928 the full score of his opera had been copied out, though he continued to revise the fair copy. Acts I and II of this copy contain many additions and corrections by Janáček; Act III was on his desk when he died in August 1928. If he had followed the pattern of previous works, Janáček would have submitted the score to the Brno Theatre that autumn for performance in 1929. In the event of his death, the premiere was delayed until 1930 and was complicated by the assumption that the work was incomplete, chiefly bcause of the sparsity of the verbal text and the thinness of the musical texture. Accordingly the first producer, Ota Zítek, filled out the words and stage directions, and Janáček's pupils Osvald Chlubna and Břetislav Bakala reorchestrated the work, throwing in for good measure an apotheosis-like 'optimistic' finale.

In this version the work was published and performed. In 1964 Universal Edition reissued the score with Janáček's original grim ending (the prisoners returning to their toils) added as an appendix, and thereafter productions began to respect this ending. Janáček's original orchestration has taken longer to establish itself despite the efforts of Rafael Kubelik (who revised the score on the basis of Janáček's autograph), Charles Mackerras and (in Brno) Václav Nosek. The final state of Janáček's opera was not, however, the autograph score, but the copyists' score that Janáček supervised, and to which he made many additions himself. This score provided the basis for Mackerras's Decca recording of 1980.

SYNOPSIS

Act I   The yard in a Siberian prison camp; winter, early morning. Prisoners come in from the barracks, wash and eat. An argument breaks out between two of them. Alexandr Petrovič, a new prisoner and a

'gentleman', arrives and is interrogated by the prison governor, who orders him to be flogged. The prisoners tease an eagle with a broken wing, but admire its defiance in captivity. The governor's sudden return puts an end to this; he orders them off to work. Half the prisoners go off to outdoor work, singing as they go ('Neuvidí oko již těch krajů'). Others remain, including Skuratov. His singing annoys Luka, who picks a quarrel with him. Skuratov recalls his life in Moscow, and his previous trade as a cobbler. He breaks into a wild dance, then collapses. As he sews, Luka recalls his previous imprisonment, for vagrancy. He tells how he incited the other prisoners to rebellion and how he killed the officer who came to quell the disturbance. He also describes how he was flogged for this. Petrovič, who has meanwhile been similarly punished, is brought back by the guards, half dead.

Act II   The bank of the river Irtysh. Summer, a year later. The prisoners are doing outdoor work. Petrovič asks the Tartar boy Aljeja about his family and offers to teach him to read and write. With the day's work over, guests appear, a priest gives his blessing on this feast day, and the prisoners sit down to eat. Skuratov tells his story – how he murdered the man that his sweetheart Lujza was forced to marry. The prisoners improvise a stage on which they perform two plays: 'Kedril and Don Juan', and 'The Miller's Beautiful Wife'. Darkness falls after the plays. The young prisoner goes off with a prostitute. Against a nostalgic background of offstage folksongs, Petrovič and Aljeja drink tea. The short prisoner, resenting this, picks a quarrel and attacks and wounds Aljeja. Guards rush on to restore order.

Act III   Scene 1: It is towards evening and Aljeja, who is recovering in the prison hospital, cries out in delirious fever. Čekunov waits on him and Petrovič, to the anger of the dying Luka. Šapkin describes how the police superintendant interrogated him and almost pulled his ears off. Night falls (short orchestral interlude). The silence is broken by the sighs of the old prisoner. Šiškov, encouraged by Čerevin, tells his story. He was made to marry Akulka (Akulina), a girl allegedly dishonoured by Filka Morozov, though in fact still a virgin. When Šiškov found out that she still loved Filka he killed her. Luka dies as the story ends; Šiškov recognizes him as Filka. His body is taken away by the guards. Petrovič is called for. Scene 2: the governor, drunk, apologizes to Petrovič before the other prisoners and tells him that he is to be released. Aljeja comes in from the hospital to say farewell. As Petrovič leaves, the prisoners release the eagle and celebrate its freedom as it flies away. The guards order them off to work.

This is Janáček's most extraordinary opera. The increasingly extreme musical style of Janáček's last years is here complemented by a dramaturgy in opera that was decades ahead of its time. Janáček's sound-vision of the work is perhaps best characterized by the initial sketches, which are often conceived in terms of voice parts, trombones and piccolos – and not very much else. For the first time

Design by František Hlavica for From the House of the Dead *(Brno, 1930)*

he adopted his practice, used in other genres, of ruling his own stave lines, and thereby encouraging great economy of texture. The harmonic style is similarly stark. As the curtain opens a motif is heard: a short rocking theme in which each chord is enriched with a dissonant semitone. This motif haunts and characterizes the entire first act (in a more purposeful way than in any other Janáček opera); its most searing version is as a ritornello between the lines of the prisoners going off to work, singing of their exile.

From the House of the Dead has almost no story and, except for one tiny part, its cast is exclusively male and made up of a collective, rather than of interacting soloists – a chorus opera from which individual speakers step out to tell their tales and then merge in with the others again. Janáček's libretto here is more his own work than in any other opera except *Fate*. He composed straight from the original Russian, translating as he went along, and made his own choice and ordering of events. While Dostoevsky's autobiographical account of his time in a Siberian prison is arranged chiefly by topic, Janáček, in order to give some idea of time passing, distributed some of the incidents (such as the account of the eagle or Petrovič's dealings with Aljeja) over the whole opera. He was particularly successful in producing emotional climaxes for the ends of the acts: for instance his juxtaposition of Petrovič's return from his flogging to end Act I just after Luka had described a similar event in horrifying detail, or the release and celebration of the eagle's freedom paired off with the release of Petrovič (whose arrival and departure provide the slender narrative frame of the piece). An important element in each act are the monologues in which a prisoner describes his crime (Luka in Act I; Skuratov in Act II; Šiškov in Act III) – all miniature dramas with the virtuosic depiction of a cast of characters, and all strongly contrasting in

tone and content with one another. Skuratov's lyrical account of his love for a German washerwoman is appropriately placed in the comparatively relaxed Act II, followed by the rough-and-tumble comedy of the two plays, given mostly in mime. The longest monologue of all, Šiškov's, told in the quietness of the prison hospital at night, is emblematic of the whole work: a harrowing tale held together by the recurrence of a transcendentally gentle theme in the same way that Janáček's warm compassion threads through and transforms his grimmest and yet most uplifting opera.

RECORDINGS   1. Zahradníček, Žídek, Zítek, Jedlička, Švorc, Janská, Vienna PO, Mackerras, Decca, 1980: a compelling, definitive performance in Janáček's final version; 2. Přibyl, Žídek, Souček, Novák, Jirglová, Prague PO, Neumann, Supraphon, 1979: some fine soloists; score mostly in Chlubna–Bakala arrangement, though with original ending
EDITIONS   f.s. (Chlubna–Bakala version), Universal, 1930; v.ss., Universal, 1930; with Janáček's ending, 1958
BIBLIOGRAPHY   Michael Ewans, *Janáček's Tragic Operas*, Faber, 1977; John Tyrrell, *Leoš Janáček: Káťa Kabanová*, CUP, 1982; John Tyrrell, *Czech Opera*, CUP, 1988; John Tyrrell, *Janáček's Operas: A Documentary Account*, Faber, 1992; Jaroslav Vogel, *Leoš Janáček*, Hamlyn, 1962; Orbis, rev. 2nd edn, 1981

J.T.

OTAKAR JEREMIÁŠ

b 17 October 1892, Písek, Bohemia; *d* 5 March 1962, Prague

The best-known member of a prominent Czech musical family, Otakar Jeremiáš made a career as a conductor, notably of the Prague Radio Orchestra (1929–45). Regarded as a potential successor to Ostrčil at the National Theatre in Prague, he was appointed there only after the Second World War. His tenure was short, interrupted by political infighting, and was terminated in 1949 by a stroke which left him partly paralysed. Jeremiáš was a private composition pupil of Novák; his two operas, *The Brothers Karamazov* and the one-act *Eulenspiegel* (*Enspigl*; composed 1940–44, premiered 1914), represent only a small part of his large output.

The Brothers Karamazov

Bratři Karamazovi
Opera in three acts (five scenes) (3h)
Libretto by Jaroslav Maria and the composer, after the novel by Dostoevsky (1880)
Composed 1922–7
PREMIERE 8 October 1928, National Theatre, Prague

The Brothers Karamazov is one of the finest of the inter-war Czech operas. A dramatic and forceful piece, it was written almost simultaneously with Janáček's Dostoevsky opera, *From the House of the Dead*. The emotional intensity is similar, as is some of the declamatory writing, though the important parts for women give Jeremiáš's opera a more conventional range of expression.

RECORDING excerpts: Tikalová, Pechová, Eremiáš, Jedenáctík, Kalaš, Prague National Theatre Ch and O, Košler, Supraphon, 1963
EDITION v.s., Hudební matice Umělecké besedy, 1930

BIBLIOGRAPHY Ladislav Šíp, *Česká opera a jeho tvůrci* (*Czech Opera and Its Creators*), Supraphon, 1983

J.T.

LEON JESSEL

b 22 January 1871, Szczecin; *d* 4 January 1942, Berlin

After musical training the Polish-Jewish composer Jessel accepted conducting posts in various German provincial theatres (including Bielefeld, Kiel and Lübeck); his first (one-act) operetta, *Die Brautwerbung*, was produced at Celle. There were fifteen more, of which only one, *Schwarzwaldmädel* (1917), remains popular. This is a well-constructed volksoperette, more like Zeller's *Der Vogelhändler* than the usual raucous Berliner operettas of its day by Gilbert, Kollo, and others. Jessel's works, including the popular piano piece, *Parade of the Tin Soldiers*, were banned in 1933, the year a film of *Schwarzwaldmädel* was released. He died after being tortured by the Gestapo for sending a letter to a friend complaining of his 'difficult circumstances'.

Operettas: *Die Brautwerbung*, 1894; *Kruschke am Nordpol*, 1896; *Die beiden Husaren*, 1913; *Schwarzwaldmädel*, 1917; *Die närrische Liebe*, 1919; *Verliebte Frauen*, 1920; *Schwalbenhochzeit*, 1921; *Die Postmeisterin*, 1921; *Das Detektivmädel*, 1921; *Schwalbenhochzeit*, 1921; *Des Königs Nachbarin*, 1923; *Der keusche Benjamin*, 1923; *Meine Tochter Otto*, 1927; *Prinzessin Husch*, 1925; *Die kleine Studentin*, 1926; *Mädels, die man liebt*, 1927; *Die Luxuskabine*, 1929; *Junger Wein*, 1933; *Die goldene Mühle*, 1936

BIBLIOGRAPHY Otto Schneidereit, *Operette A–Z*, Henschelverlag, 1971

R.T.

IVO JIRÁSEK

b 16 July 1920, Prague

Jirásek's studies included conducting and opera production in addition to composition with Hába at the Prague Conservatory. His career has been similarly broad: he was Kubelík's assistant at the Czech Philharmonic (1945–6), chief of opera in Opava (1953–6), and has held administrative posts in Prague. Opera is an important part of his output and ranges widely in its inspiration. The most successful has been a setting of *The Bear*, based on the same Chekhov vaudeville as Walton's opera. There are two more one-act operas, both slight and light-hearted tales of marital infidelity: *The Key* and, in a 16th-century monastic setting, *The Miracle*. Jirásek's first opera, *Mr Johannes*, is based on a patriotic fairy-story by an earlier writer, Alois Jirásek, and thus recalls Novák's best-known opera, *The Lantern*. *Dawn over the Waters*, on the other hand, is typical for its time in Czechoslovakia: an account of the conservative opposition (led by the local priest) to the construction of a dam that would bring prosperity to the area. His remaining two works share medieval subject matter, if little else: *Master Jeroným* is concerned with one of the followers of the religious reformer Jan Hus, while *Danse macabre* is an operatic reworking of Ingmar Bergman's celebrated film *The Seventh Seal*. His career has been one of the most prolific and versatile of contemporary Czech opera composers, and his style has moved in its technique from the line of Ostrčil and Jeremiáš to take in a sober use of atonal and aleatoric techniques.

Operas: *Mr Johannes* (*Pan Johannes*), (1952), 1956; *Daybreak over the Waters* (*Svítání nad vodami*), 1963; *The Bear* (*Medvěd*), 1965; *The Key* (*Klíč*), 1970; *Danse macabre* (*It was evening and was dawn*) (*Danse macabre* (*I byl večer a bylo jitro*)), 1972; *Master Jeroným* (*Mistr Jeroným*), (1980), 1984; *The Miracle* (*Zázrak*), 1981
BIBLIOGRAPHY Ladislav Šíp, *Česká opera a jeho tvůrci* (*Czech Opera and Its Creators*), Supraphon, 1983

J.T.

JAMES P. JOHNSON

James Price Johnson; *b* 1 February 1894, New Brunswick, New Jersey, US; *d* 17 November 1955, New York

Johnson was an outstanding figure in ragtime and early jazz piano. He also accompanied some of the great blues singers such as Ethel Waters and Bessie Smith. His family moved to New York in 1908 where he was able to absorb all types of music, including the classical tradition. Ten years later he had begun to make piano rolls; his songs were successful and his piano solos, like *Carolina Shout* (1921) were on their way to becoming classics.

Johnson's first Broadway show, *Runnin' Wild* (1923), contained the hit songs 'Old-fashioned Love' and 'The Charleston': it ran for 213 performances. Not all his shows achieved this level of success and at the same time he turned his attention to concert works where, along with William Grant Still, Johnson was part of the first generation of black composers to gain recognition. Unfortunately the scores of many of Johnson's musicals are lost; also lost, apart from a single number, 'Hungry Blues', is his one-act blues opera *De Organiser* (1940).

Operatic works: *Runnin' Wild*, 1923; *Mooching Along*, 1925; *Keep Shufflin'*, 1928; *Messin' Around*, 1929; *Shuffle Along of 1930*, 1930; *Sugar Hill*, 1931; *Harlem Hotcha*, 1932; *Policy Kings*, 1939; *Dreamy Kid*, (c. 1942); *Meet Miss Jones*, 1947; 4 lost musicals
BIBLIOGRAPHY Scott E. Brown, *J. P. Johnson: A Case of Mistaken Identity*, Scarecrow Press/Institute of Jazz Studies, Rutgers University, 1986

P.D.

ROBERT JOHNSON
b c. 1583, ?London; *d* 18 November 1633, London

Nothing is known about Johnson's origins except that he was indentured as a servant to the Lord Chamberlain, Sir George Carey, from 1596 to 1603; he was probably a relative of the Elizabethan lutenist John Johnson. He became a royal lutenist himself in 1604 and joined Prince Henry's household in 1610, a post later transferred to the household of Prince Charles. Johnson also became associated with one of London's commercial theatres, an unusual move for a court musician at the time. He wrote songs for many productions of the King's Men (Shakespeare's company), including *The Winter's Tale* (c. 1609–10), *Cymbeline* and *The Tempest* (both c. 1610–11); he was still writing for them as late as 1623. Johnson also wrote songs and dances for a number of Jacobean court masques, as well as a good deal of music for his own instrument. He mostly cultivated a cheerful, direct style, with clear tonality and memorable tunes.

Johnson wrote or arranged music for the following masques: *Oberon*, 1611; *Love Freed from Ignorance and Folly*, 1611; *The Lords' Masque*, 1613; *Masque of the Middle Temple and Lincoln's Inn*, 1613; and *Gypsies Metamorphosed*, 1621
EDITION A. J. Sabol (ed.), *Four Hundred Songs and Dances from the Stuart Masque*, Brown University Press, 1978
BIBLIOGRAPHY M. Chan, *Music in the Theatre of Ben Jonson*, OUP, 1980

P.H.

TOM JOHNSON
b 18 November 1939, Greeley, Colorado, US

Johnson is an idiosyncratic American composer who has also been an influential and prescient critic. Writing for the *Village Voice* in New York City from 1971 to 1982, he enthusiastically celebrated the avant-garde and minimalism. He attended Yale University, where his teachers included Elliott Carter, and then studied with Feldman. Johnson provides scintillating comedy in *Failing*, a very difficult piece for solo string bass (1975), where the player performs and tells a story simultaneously, and in *The Four Note Opera* (1972). By 1991 this one-act spoof had been produced over 60 times in nine different languages. The setting is 'any operatic room, the present' and Johnson calls the work 'a farce with the music built on four notes: A, B, D, E. It ends in mass suicide, as the singers become immobile, and the music slowly stops.'

Johnson became more committed to his conception of opera after moving to Paris in 1983. The half-hour *Réservé aux sopranes* was premiered there in 1984, conducted by the composer. The original text was in French and the six singers involved are named after solmization letters – Do, Re, Fa, Mi, Sol, La. There is no plot and the effect, as with *The Four Note Opera*, is further parody of the traditional apparatus of the genre.

Operatic works: *The Four Note Opera*, 1972; *The Masque of Clouds*, 1975; *Five Shaggy-Dog Operas*, 1978; *Réservé aux sopranes*, 1984; *Riemannoper*, 1988; *200 Ans*, 1989
BIBLIOGRAPHY Tom Johnson, *The Voice of New Music: New York City 1972–82*, Apollohuis, 1989

P.D.

NICCOLÒ JOMMELLI
b 10 September 1714, Aversa, nr Naples; *d* 25 August 1774, Naples

Jommelli was viewed by his contemporaries as one of the greatest opera composers of the mid-18th century. He is among the second generation of Italians who composed in the new Neapolitan style, and formed a link between Leo, Vinci, Hasse and Pergolesi, and Mozart, who heard Jommelli's *Armida abbandonata* at Naples in 1770, shortly before composing his first opera seria, *Mitridate* (1770).

Jommelli studied in Naples at the conservatories of San Onofrio and Pietà dei Turchini. Two comic operas for Naples in 1737–8 and an opera seria for Rome in 1740 earned him the patronage of Cardinal Henry Benedict, Duke of York, and initiated a succession of commissions from major opera houses throughout Italy. Jommelli also served as musical director of the Ospedale degli Incurabili in Venice (1743–7) and as maestro coadiutore to the papal chapel in Rome (1749–53).

For the 1749–50 season, he wrote two operas for Vienna, where he met the poet Metastasio. His opera sinfonias served as models for symphonic composers in both Mannheim and Vienna. Jommelli had offers from the courts of Lisbon and Mannheim but, in 1753, became maestro di cappella for the Duke of

Württemberg at Stuttgart. In this capacity he wrote numerous operas to celebrate special occasions, including no fewer than 11 for the duke's birthday, which fell on 11 February.

Jommelli was admired for his expressive accompanied recitatives and dramatic use of the orchestra, which, witnesses said, he caused to speak without words. Charles Burney describes the uncommon effect of Jommelli's accompanied recitative in Regolus' farewell to Rome from his *Attilio Regolo* (London, 1754), and Schubart found his programmatic orchestral effects in *Fetonte* (Ludwigsburg, 1768) overwhelming.

In Stuttgart, Jommelli built one of the finest operatic organizations in Europe, combining Italian singers with French dancers, choreographers, costumiers, and theatrical designers, and supported by an outstanding orchestra. The incursions of such French elements as chorus, ensemble, ballet and spectacle into Italian opera along with a gradual breaking down of formal opera-seria conventions, especially notable in his collaborations with the poet Mattia Verazi, predate many of Gluck's more highly publicized reforms. Furthermore, both the tonal planning in his operas and the open construction of his buffa finales predate Mozart.

Returning to Naples in 1769, Jommelli agreed to produce two operas a year for the Portuguese court. With debts still outstanding in Stuttgart and obligations as a Neapolitan subject, he found himself pressed to write new operas. A stroke in 1771 greatly reduced his productivity and a second ended his life.

L'uccellatrice

The Birdcatcher
Intermezzo in two parts
Libretto anonymous
Rev. as *Il paratajo* (*La pipée*), libretto by Charles François Clement, 1753
PREMIERES   6 May 1750, Teatro San Samuele, Venice; rev. version: 25 September 1753, Opéra, Paris

In 1753 *Il paratajo*, along with other works including Pergolesi's *La serva padrona*, indirectly provided fuel for the *querelle des bouffons*, which ultimately led to the incursion of Italianate elements into French opera. The Italian original involves only two singing characters and a mute role (Lesbino).

While hunting, Don Narciso comes upon Mergellina catching birds. Mistaking her for a woodland goddess, he falls in love with her. After she has teased him mercilessly, they are reconciled and rejoin the hunt. For the French version another pair of characters and several new arias were added.

EDITIONS   original version: v.s., Maffeo Zanon (ed.), Ricordi, 1954
MANUSCRIPTS   original version: copy in Conservatorio di Musica Nicolò Paganini, Genoa; rev. version: Conservatoire Royal de Musique, Brussels (also in Paris, Milan)

L'Olimpiade

The Olympiade
Dramma per musica in three acts (six scenes) (3h 30m)
Libretto by Pietro Metastasio (1733), adapted anonymously
PREMIERE   11 February 1761, Hoftheater, Stuttgart

L'Olimpiade, one of Metastasio's more frequently set libretti, takes place in Greece. The plot concerns conflicts between love and duty, is complicated by disguise, and is resolved by the discovery of a long-lost heir to the throne. The opera is notable for its generous use of accompanied recitative and independent writing for the wind instruments and is exceptional in including all of Metastasio's choruses and adding a trio in Act III. It provides an early example of the move away from the *aria da capo* to the *aria dal segno*, where the first setting of the first strophe of poetry is cut and only the second repeated to round the form and close the aria.

EDITION   *Recueil des opéra[s] composés par Nicolas Jomelli à la Cour du Sérénissime Duc de Wirtemberg*, Academie-Caroline, Stuttgart, 1783; facsimile, Garland, 1978: only this opera, the first in the series, was ever published; lacks simple recitatives

Didone abbandonata

Dido Abandoned
Dramma per musica in three acts
Libretto by Pietro Metastasio
PREMIERES   11 February 1763, Hoftheater, Stuttgart; other versions: 28 January 1747, Teatro Argentina, Rome; 8 December 1749, Burgtheater, Vienna

Jommelli's third version of *Didone*, one of Metastasio's most frequently set libretti, is typical of his Stuttgart operas in having acquired two new ensemble finales – a duet (Act I) and a trio (Act II). The plot treats the ill-starred love of Dido, Queen of Carthage, for the Trojan Aeneas, who eventually deserts her to pursue his destiny. Moors set fire to the vulnerable city, and Dido dies amid the ruins of her burning palace. Jommelli exploited the exceptional abilities of his excellent and well-trained orchestra with eloquent and dramatic expressive effects in both the obbligato recitatives and in the arias. His famed gift for vocal writing produced arias of ravishing beauty and stunning power.

EDITION   performing edn, Giovanni Carlo Ballola, Lugo, 1992
AUTOGRAPH MANUSCRIPT   Österreichische National-bibliothek, Vienna

Demofoonte

Dramma per musica in three acts (third version: 3h 30m)
Libretto by Pietro Metastasio (1733), adapted anonymously
PREMIERES   11 February 1764, Hoftheater, Stuttgart; rev. version: 11 February 1765, Hoftheater, Ludwigsburg; other versions: 13 June 1743, Teatro Obizzi, Padua; 1753, Teatro Regio Ducal, Milan; 4 November 1770, Teatro San Carlo, Naples

The plot, one of Metastasio's most appealing, concerns the deadly perils of a secretly married couple, Dircea and Timante, who have a child. Dircea has been chosen for human sacrifice, but because she is no longer a virgin, she is technically ineligible. When Timante is identified as the long sought after but unwitting usurper to the throne, a yearly sacrifice is no longer required.

The opera is notable for the trio that replaces the final scenes in Act I and the extensive scenes with accompanied recitative. It has demanding vocal parts and makes independent use of wind instruments with strong dynamic contrasts, chromatic harmony, and careful tonal planning.

EDITION facsimile, Garland, 1978
MANUSCRIPT Württembergische Landesbibliothek, Stuttgart (1764 version plus 1765 revisions)

Vologeso

Dramma per musica in three acts
Libretto by Mattia Verazi, after Apostolo Zeno's *Lucio Vero* (1700)
PREMIERE 11 February 1766, Hoftheater, Ludwigsburg

Verazi extensively reworked *Lucio Vero*, one of Zeno's most enduring libretti (which Jommelli had already set in 1754), in order to heighten its inherent drama. The theme is constancy of love in the face of unspeakable obstacles. The emperor, Lucio Vero, attempts to espouse Berenice, betrothed of Vologeso, who is presumed dead. The emperor finally admits defeat and agrees to mend his ways when the triumphant Vologeso appears leading an army.

This opera provided opportunities for lavish spectacle – an arena with wild animals in Act I and a sudden change of scene in Act III – and shows Jommelli's dramatic musical style at its height.

MANUSCRIPT copies: Gesellschaft der Musikfreunde, Vienna (also in Brussels, Berlin, Stuttgart, Paris)

Fetonte

Phaeton
Dramma per musica in three acts (ten scenes) (3h 30m)
Libretto by Mattia Verazi, after Philippe Quinault's libretto to Lully's *Phaeton* (1683), itself based on an episode from Book 2 of Ovid's *Metamorphoses*
PREMIERE 11 February 1768, Hoftheater, Ludwigsburg
CAST Fetonte *s*, Climene *s*, Libia *ms*, Teti/La Fortuna *s*, Orcane *t*, Sole/Proteo *s*, Epafo *a*; *satb* chorus of priests of Thetis, tritons, Ethiopian moors, river deities; ballet
CHAMBER ORCHESTRA

For Jommelli's last serious opera for the Duke of Württemberg, Verazi provided both an extravagant French spectacle of the kind for which the newly completed opera house at Ludwigsburg had been constructed, and an Italianate plot concerned with amorous and political intrigue. The libretto is distinguished by its many radical departures from Italian tradition: the overture doubles as the prologue; ensembles vary in size; ballet and chorus are incorporated into the drama, and the opera includes the first multi-section ensemble finale found in an opera seria.

According to Ovid, Phaeton (Fetonte), mortal son of Apollo, attempted to drive the chariot of the sun. In order to save both heaven and earth Jove struck him with a thunderbolt, causing him to fall from the sky. In Verazi's version, Fetonte undertakes the audacious enterprise to prove himself eligible to wed his beloved half-sister Libia. Her widowed mother Climene must ward off the advances of Orcane, King of the Congo, her suitor, and Epafo, King of Egypt, Libia's suitor – in order to see her two children happily united.

Jommelli himself admitted that the opera was principally intended to amaze the audience. The plot, like Quinault's libretto on which it is based, is little more than a vehicle for music and spectacle.

Jommelli's innovative tendencies reveal themselves in the almost total absence of *secco* recitative and the abandonment of traditional forms and conventional harmony, as in Libia's aria, 'Spargerò d'amare lagrime'. His ensembles move from trio, to solo, to duo in a manner uncommon even in opera buffa, and the finale moves freely from accompanied recitative, to chorus, to ensemble with a freedom unparalleled before Mozart's late operas.

EDITION f.s., Hermann Abert (ed.), *DDT*, vols 32–3, Breitkopf und Härtel, 1907; *rp*, 1958

La schiava liberata

The Liberated Slave
Dramma serio-buffo in three acts
Libretto by Gaetano Martinelli
PREMIERE 18 December 1768, Hoftheater, Ludwigsburg
CAST Selim *s* (or *ms*), Giulietta *s*, Dorimene *ms*, Elmira *s*, Solimano *t*, Pallottino *t*, Albumazar *b*, Don Garzia *a*; *satb* chorus of soldiers and people
CHAMBER ORCHESTRA

Jommelli's final Württemberg opera represents a unique blend of serious and comic which might have been impossible in an Italian theatre. Schuster set the libretto for Dresden in 1777, and Bretzner's reworked version, entitled *Belmont und Constanze*, was produced in Leipzig in 1781 with music by André. Bretzner's version subsequently became the basis of the libretto, by Stephanie, for Mozart's *Die Entführung aus dem Serail*.

SYNOPSIS

Act I Selim, son of the Bey of Algiers, Solimano, returns home from a sea raid having captured Dorimene, a Spanish noblewoman, and her betrothed servants Giulietta and Pallottino. In love with Dorimene, Selim defies his father's orders to remain faithful to his betrothed Elmira, daughter of the Circassian ruler, Albumazar. Selim engages Pallottino to disguise himself as an Armenian merchant and purchase Dorimene. The plan fails when Pallottino becomes more interested in protecting his Giulietta from the unwelcome attentions of Albumazar. Both men are discovered in the harem in female attire.

Act II Don Garzia offers Solimano a ransom to free Dorimene. Elmira attempts to kill the sleeping Selim, but Dorimene seizes the knife just as Selim awakens. Though shaken at her seeming treachery, Selim attempts yet again to attain Dorimene through Pallottino, this time posing as a French consul. When

Albumazar appears in the same disguise, both impostors are exposed.

Act III Elmira at last realizes that Dorimene will be no threat once she is safely on her way back to Spain and persuades Solimano to release the captives, thus paving the way for a happy ending.

Jommelli created the role of Selim for Giuseppe Aprile, primo soprano castrato of the Württemberg opera-seria troupe. For this supreme interpreter of his music Jommelli wrote arias of astonishing virtuosity ('Se il mio valor') and of ravishing beauty ('Dolce sonno, amor pietoso'). At the same time, Jommelli proves himself equally adept at the light accompaniments required for the buffa bluster of Albumazar or Pallottino's exaggerated strutting and preening.

Jommelli's use of tonality and careful construction of finales shows a close affinity with Mozart. He abandons the conventional finale comprised of closed forms, and responds freely to the dramatic situation with abrupt changes of tempo and tonality.

EDITION performing edn, Marita P. McClymonds and Alan Curtis (eds), Amsterdam, 1982
MANUSCRIPT copy in Conservatorio di Musica S Pietro a Majella, Naples

Armida abbandonata
Armida Abandoned
Dramma per musica in three acts (seven scenes) (3h)
Libretto by Francesco Saverio de Rogatis, after Tasso's poem *La Gerusalemme liberata ovvero Il Goffredo* (1575)
PREMIERE 30 May 1770, Teatro San Carlo, Naples

On 29 May 1770 Mozart wrote to his sister after a rehearsal of this opera, 'which is well composed and which I really like. [Jommelli] spoke to us and was very polite.' He modified his evaluation in a later report on 5 June, declaring it 'beautiful but too serious and old-fashioned for the theatre'. His change of heart may reflect the controversy that greeted this work, Jommelli's first for Naples after a 13-year absence. Even eye-witnesses do not agree. Leopold Mozart reported that the opera received 'no great acclaim', yet looking back, the poet and savant Saverio Mattei observed, 'What opera was ever so successful as *Armida*? . . . Who remembers such continuous applause throughout the entire work as for *Armida*, and universal applause of the old, the young, the ignorant and the connoisseur?' The unusual number of revivals – Naples, 1771 and 1780; Lisbon, 1773; and Florence, 1775 – and the numerous, widespread extant copies of both full scores and individual pieces, place this opera among Jommelli's most successful. Furthermore, the libretto served as model for a series of operas leading directly to Haydn's *Armida* (1784).

The text is the work of a Neapolitan literary amateur. Spectacular elements, unusual in a Neapolitan production, include two ballets (one with monsters), a ballet scene in Act I, a chorus scene in Act III and magical scene changes at the end of Acts II and III.

The plot centres around Tancredi's efforts to free Rinaldo from the enchantment of the Saracen witch Armida. Most previous texts end, as Act II does here, with Rinaldo's departure, to which Armida responds by vengefully destroying her palace and departing on a chariot drawn by winged dragons. Here the story is taken further. In Act III, Rinaldo braves Armida's wrath and monsters to break her powers, and the opera closes with a finale not entirely satisfactory from the 18th-century point of view because it lacks a repentant prima donna.

EDITION facsimile, Garland, 1983
MANUSCRIPT copy in Conservatorio di Musica S. Pietro a Majella, Naples

Ifigenia in Tauride
Iphigenia in Tauris
Dramma per musica in three acts
Libretto by Mattia Verazi
PREMIERE 30 May 1771, Teatro San Carlo, Naples

Verazi wrote this libretto in Mannheim, where it was set by Gian Francesco de Majo in 1764. This was a pioneering work, which featured a programmatic sinfonia that serves as a prologue to the opera (an idea subsequently borrowed in Gluck's version for Paris, 1779). During the initial *allegro* there is a storm at sea and a shipwreck. The survivors land during the *adagio*, and a battle with the natives takes place in the final *allegro*.

The exiled and tormented Oreste finds himself shipwrecked and a prisoner on the shores of Tauris, where his sister Iphigenia is high priestess. In many versions of the fable Iphigenia saves her brother from death by sacrificial knife when she assassinates the tyrant Thoas. Here Iphigenia departs with Oreste, and Thoas dies in the flames of his besieged temple, victim of the betrayed King Merodate's revenge.

The original version, typical of operas at Mannheim, had a number of ensembles and choruses all of which Jommelli asked Verazi to cut for the Naples production. The result was a more traditional aria opera retaining only the spectacular sinfonia and final conflagration.

Jommelli had just one month to compose his setting. It was so unsuccessful that it was almost immediately replaced with *Armida*. Nevertheless Mattei reports that 'that opera is now admired and appears, and will appear on every harpsichord as more beautiful than the two previous ones'. The work is the finest example of Jommelli's late style, concentrated, chromatic, complex and full of special effects. Typical of many arias in the last operas, Ifigenia's, 'Ombra cara', created for J. C. Bach's protégée, Anna de Amicis, is an astonishing combination of brilliant virtuosity and extreme contrasts of dramatic expression.

MANUSCRIPT copies: Conservatorio di Musica S. Pietro a Majella, Naples (also in Berlin, Munich, Florence, Milan)

Other operatic works (multiple dates indicate multiple versions): *L'errore amoroso*, 1737; *Odoardo*, 1738; *Ricimero*, *re de' Goti*, 1740; *Astianatte*, 1741; *Ezio*, 1741, 1748, 1758, 1771; *Merope*, 1741; *Semiramide riconosciuta*, 1742, 1753, 1762; *Eumene*, 1742, 1747; *Don Chichibio*, 1742; *Semiramide*, 1742; *Tito Manlio*, 1742, 1746, 1758; *Ciro riconosciuto*, 1743, 1749; *Alessandro nell'Indie*, 1744, 1760; *Antigono*, 1744, 1746; *Sofonisba*, 1746; *Cajo Mario*, 1746; *L'amore in maschera*, 1748; *La cantata e disfida di Don Trastullo*, 1749; *Artaserse*, 1749, 1756; *Demetrio*, 1749; *Achille in Sciro*, 1749, 1771; *La villana nobile*, 1751; *Ifigenia in Aulide*, 1751; *Ipermestra*, 1751; *Talestri*, 1751; *I rivali delusi*, 1752; *Attilio Regolo*, 1753; *La clemenza di Tito*, 1753, 1765; *Bajazette*, 1753; *Lucio Vero*, 1754; *Don Falcone*, 1754; *Catone in Utica*, 1754; *Pelope*, 1755; *Il giardino incanto*, 1755; *Enea nel Lazio*, 1755, 1766; *Creso*, 1757; *Temistocle*, 1757, 1765; *L'asilo d'amore*, 1758; *Nitteti*, 1759; *Endimione, ovvero Il trionfo d'amore*, 1759; *Cajo Fabrizio*, 1760; *L'isola disabitata*, 1761; *Il trionfo d'amore*, 1763; *La pastorella illustre*, 1763; *Il re pastore*, 1764; *Le cinesi*, 1765; *Imeneo in Atene*, 1765; *La critica*, 1766; *Il matrimonio per concorso*, 1766; *Il cacciatore deluso, ovvero La Semiramide in bernesco*, 1767; *L'unione coronata*, 1768; *L'amante cacciatore*, 1771; *Le avventure di Cleomede*, 1772; *Cerere placata*, 1772; *Il trionfo di Clelia*, 1774

BIBLIOGRAPHY   M. McClymonds, *Niccolò Jommelli: The Last Years, 1769–1774*, UMI Research Press, 1980; L. Tolkoff, *The Stuttgart Operas of Niccolò Jommelli*, dissertation, Yale University, 1974

M.P.M.

SCOTT JOPLIN

b 24 November 1868, nr Marshall, Texas, or Shreveport, Louisiana, US; *d* 1 April 1917, New York

Scott Joplin, 'The King of Ragtime Writers', perfected the classic piano rag as a polished miniature of great finesse, and although he attempted larger-scale works including operas, his finest achievements were his small-scale piano pieces. He grew up in Texarkana where his mother supported her seven children after her husband had left her. Joplin worked as a pianist locally and began to travel with his Texas Medley Quartette, which included one or two of his brothers. He moved to Sedalia around 1897 and there a friend persuaded him to write down his compositions. His partnership with the publisher John Stark paved the way for the phenomenal success of *The Maple Leaf Rag* (1899).

In spite of Joplin's enforced labours in the field of entertainment – the only scope available for black musicians at the time – he was deeply concerned to be regarded as a serious composer and longed to work in the theatre. *The Ragtime Dance* is a kind of folk ballet lasting about 20 minutes which was produced rather unsuccessfully at the composer's expense in 1902. In the following year the *St Louis Globe-Democrat* reported: '[Joplin] is assiduously toiling upon an opera.' This was *A Guest of Honor*, which was given in St Louis by Scott Joplin's Rag-Time Opera Company and advertised as 'the only genuine rag-time opera ever produced'. But, tantalizingly, there is no evidence of performances other than a try-out and the score has been lost.

Treemonisha, Joplin's second opera, brought him even greater frustration, although its revival in 1975 – long after his death – brought acclaim, a recording

and a posthumous Pulitzer Prize. Joplin published it at his own expense in 1911 and financed a single performance with piano in 1915 when his health was declining. He never recovered from *Treemonisha*'s failure. A rumoured musical comedy which followed has not survived.

Treemonisha

Opera in three acts (2h)
Libretto by the composer
Composed 1908–11
PREMIERES May 1915, Lincoln Theater, Harlem, New York City; 23 May 1975, Miller Outdoor Theater, Hermann Park, Houston (Houston Grand Opera; orch. Gunther Schuller); UK: 29 March 1990, Churchill Theatre, Bromley, Kent

Treemonisha is set on a plantation in Arkansas, reflecting the composer's own background. The Negroes are ignorant and superstitious. Before the opera starts, Ned and Monisha, who had not been able to have children, have come across a baby girl under a tree and adopted her. The white family for whom the couple worked have agreed to educate the girl, who was given the name of Treemonisha. Her intelligence brings her into conflict with pedlars of charms who make a living out of others' irrational fears. Treemonisha is abducted by them but she is rescued and finally chosen as the leader of her people.

Lost for over 50 years between its premiere and its discovery in 1970, *Treemonisha* has been nicknamed 'the sleeping beauty of American music'. Only parts of the opera are in ragtime style, but its climax is 'A Real Slow Drag' in which the whole company dances to lyrical syncopations in Joplin's best vein with choreographic instructions from the composer. His moral is that education can provide salvation and that harmony – 'Marching onwards, marching to the lovely tune' – can come from working together. In spite of effective numbers, the naïve libretto and static tableaux militate seriously against *Treemonisha*'s viability on stage.

Joplin's original orchestration is lost; recent performances have used an edition by Gunther Schuller scored for wind, reduced strings, piano, percussion and bongo drums, emulating the forces available to Joplin.

RECORDING Balthrop, Allen, Rayam, White, Houston Grand Opera Ch and O, Schuller, DG, 1976
EDITIONS v.ss., S. Joplin (New York), 1911; V. Brodsky Lawrence (ed.), facsimile *rp*, *The Collected Works of Scott Joplin*, New York Public Library, 1971; Dramatic Publishing (Chicago), 1972

BIBLIOGRAPHY   R. Blesh and H. Janis, *They All Played Ragtime*, Oak Publications, 1971; A. W. Reed, 'Scott Joplin: Pioneer', in J. E. Hasse (ed.), *Ragtime: Its History, Composers and Music*, Macmillan, 1985

P.D.

WILFRED JOSEPHS

b 24 July 1927, Newcastle upon Tyne, England

Although he qualified originally as a dentist, Josephs had early lessons in harmony and counterpoint from Arthur Milner. He studied at the Guildhall School of Music (1954–7) and in Paris with Max Deutsch, a pupil of Schoenberg (1958–9). One of the most prolific composers of his generation, he was influenced early on by the English pastoral tradition and later by the Second Viennese School, but he soon developed an individual gift for orchestration and melody which he combined with a reassimilation of tonal harmony. His output includes music for schools, and numerous film and television scores, and this wide experience has served him well as a composer of stage works. As well as *Rebecca* he has written a successful *Alice* diptych along with other works for children, and some effective music-theatre.

Rebecca

Opera in three acts, Op. 126 (2h)
Libretto by Edward Marsh, after the novel by Daphne du Maurier (1938)
PREMIERE 15 March 1983, Grand Theatre, Leeds

This highly effective adaptation of Du Maurier's melodramatic novel concerns a plain girl who marries into a household haunted by the memory of its previous mistress, the glamorous Rebecca. The expressive style of the music often recalls that of Britten. The most fully developed character is that of 'the girl', while the orchestra is used to suggest the pervasive atmosphere of the house itself, Manderley.

EDITION v.s., Novello, 1986

Other operatic works: *The Nottingham Captain* (music-theatre), 1962; *Pathelin* (opera-entertainment), 1963; *The King of the Coast* (children's musical), 1968; *The*

Appointment (television opera), 1968; *A Child of the Universe* (music-theatre), 1971; *Through the Looking Glass and What Alice Found There* (children's opera), 1978; *The Montgolfers' Famous Flying Glove* (operetta for schools), 1982; *Alice in Wonderland* (children's opera), 1990

BIBLIOGRAPHY Harold Rosenthal, review of *Rebecca*, *Opera*, vol. 34 (1983), pp. 1359–61

M.A.

JOHN JOUBERT

John Pierre Herman Joubert; b 20 March 1927, Cape Town, South Africa

Joubert came to England in 1946 to study at the Royal Academy of Music with Howard Ferguson and for a Durham University B. Mus. He later held university posts at Hull and Birmingham. He has written choral and orchestral music (including two symphonies), chamber music, and seven operas, including three for children.

Joubert's third opera, *Silas Marner*, based on George Eliot's novel, is very much in the tradition of Britten. It conveys character and atmosphere economically, particularly through florid vocal and instrumental writing. His best-known opera, however, is *Under Western Eyes*, after Conrad's novel. This is a vigorous traditional type of score with powerful orchestral interludes. Despite the problems posed by its unsympathetic main character, Razumov, it exhibits the same telling characterization as Joubert's earlier operas.

Operas: *Antigone*, 1954; *In the Drought*, 1956; *Silas Marner*, 1961; *The Quarry*, 1965; *Under Western Eyes*, 1969; *The Prisoner*, 1973; *The Wayfarers*, 1984
BIBLIOGRAPHY Ernest Bradbury, 'Joubert's *Under Western Eyes*', *Opera*, vol. 20 (1969), pp. 391–3

L.F.

DMITRI KABALEVSKY

Dmitri Borisovich Kabalevsky; *b* 30 December 1904, St Petersburg; *d* 14 February 1987, Moscow

Kabalevsky was one of the most politically conscious and astute of Soviet composers, weathering the composers' purge of 1948 lightly, and assimilating a large variety of political and musical directives within his copious output. He joined the Communist Party in 1940 and, as principal editor of the Soviet Music publishing house, acted as the main party spokesman on musical policy. His works for children, mainly books of piano pieces, are very well known in the West, as well as a triptych of 'Youth' concertos, for violin, cello, and piano, that have a Prokofiev-and-water tunefulness. Other works include many political oratorios, concertos, symphonies and much incidental music for the stage. His operas have been successful. His wartime works *Into the Fire* and particularly *The Taras Family*, patriotic anti-Nazi propaganda, are shameless in their sensationalism and sentimentality. He also wrote operettas and a children's opera.

Colas Breugnon

Opera in three acts, Op. 24 (2h 15m)
Libretto by V. Bragin, after the novel by Romain Rolland
Composed 1936–8, rev. 1953 and 1969
PREMIERE 22 February 1938, Maliy Opera Theatre, Leningrad

Rolland's tale of a 17th-century Burgundian artisan was used as an allegory for the Soviet present. Colas Breugnon is a Robin Hood figure who challenges the aristocracy, causes uprisings and comes to a sticky end. Kabalevsky makes extensive use of French folktunes, and derived an orchestral suite from the opera which became popular. The vivacious overture is sometimes performed in the West.

RECORDING Kayavchenko, Isakova, Mishchevsky, Boldin, Ch and O of Nemirovich-Danchenko Theatre of Moscow, Zhemchuzhin, Melodiya, 1970s
EDITION v.s., Moscow State Publishing House, 1973

Other operatic works: *V ogne* (*Into the Fire*), 1942; *Sem'ya Taras* (*The Taras Family*), 1947, rev. 1950, 1967; *Nikita Vershinin*, 1955 (RECORDING excerpts from *Sem'ya Taras* and *Nikita Vershinin*: Melodiya, *c.* 1953); *Vesna poyot* (*Spring Sings*), 1957; *V skazochnom lesu* (*In the Magic Forest*), 1958; *Sestry* (*The Sisters*), 1967

BIBLIOGRAPHY Nicholas Slonimsky, *Development of Soviet Music*, Coleman Ross, 1971

J.G.

MAURICIO KAGEL

Mauricio Raul Kagel; *b* 24 December 1931, Buenos Aires

Kagel was a leading figure of the 1950s avant-garde generation, who were committed to sweeping away traditional values and the search for a new musical language – in his case, one in which silence and gesture often seem to usurp the audible workings of music altogether. He was from the start an outsider. His first professional experience was in the theatre (including opera) and cinema; and from soon after his emigration to Germany in 1957, his own work incorporated film and radio, as well as a wide range of concert works that are nevertheless theatrical in conception, sometimes involving actors as well as or instead of musicians; sometimes almost excluding music as conventionally defined altogether.

Match, for two cellists and percussionists (1964, but better known in its 1966 film version), is typical of its composer's early 'instrumental theatre', questioning the virtuoso tradition through visual gestures welded to music in an entirely new, humorous yet rigorous, fashion. The theatrical aspects of works such as *Kantrimiusik* (i.e. 'Country Music') and *Mare Nostrum* (both 1973–5) are, on the other hand, more extensive, while similarly growing out of musical performance. *Kantrimiusik*, a 'pastorale for voices and instruments' (seven players and 'at least three singers'), draws obliquely on popular sources and can be staged with props including '1 mountain peak covered in snow', '1 incomplete horse' '1 'speaking' cow's head with full udder' and '1 compost heap'. *Mare Nostrum*, for two singers and six players, is subtitled 'discovery, pacification and conversion of the Mediterranean by an Amazonian tribe'.

All these works gain richness from their flexibility of genre. But the evening-length *Staatstheater* (1967–70) depends on the stage for what is essentially a critique of the modern opera house – its repertoire, social function, etc. Typical of this critique is *Scratching*, one of a hundred short scenes constituting *Repertoire*, one section of *Staatstheater*. An actor holds a gramophone record in front of his face, suddenly produces a nail and manically scratches the surface of the record with it.

Though Kagel has written mainly instrumental music since the late 1970s, there are also music-theatre works such as *Der mündliche Verrat* ('Oral Treason'), a 'Music-epic about the Devil' (1981–3) for three speakers and seven players, as well as two works which have been called operas: *Die Erschöpfung der Welt* (1976–8) and *Aus Deutschland* (1977–80). *Die Erschöpfung der Welt* ('The Exhaustion' – or perhaps collapse, or even uncreation – 'of the World') is a two-hour 'scenic illusion in one act' about the activities of a vengeful god who destroys the human race in a giant mincer. While far from conventionally operatic, it was conceived for, and first performed in, the opera house. *Auf Deutschland*, subtitled *Eine Liederoper* in 27 scenes, calls for a variety of vocal types in an extended parody of operatic conventions.

BIBLIOGRAPHY Mauricio Kagel, *Tam-Tam: Dialoge und Monologe zur Musik*, R. Piper, 1975; Richard Toop, 'Social Critic in Music', *Music and Musicians*, vol. 22 (1974), pp. 36–8

K.P.

EMMERICH KÁLMÁN

Imre Kálmán; *b* 24 October 1882, Siófok; *d* 30 October 1953, Paris

After Lehár, Kálmán remains the most popular Austro-Hungarian composer of the 20th century (or 'silver') period of operetta. The recent revival of his works outside Central Europe (where his operettas have always been firm favourites), particularly in the English-speaking world, harks back to the 1920s, when his works were seen everywhere.

Kálmán had a firm classical background and a middle-class Jewish upbringing. A hand injury interfered with the boy's desire to become a classical pianist, but he nevertheless continued his studies at Budapest's Royal Academy of Music. Fellow students in his composition class under Koessler included Bartók, Kodály and the future operetta composers Szirmai and Victor Jacobi. Kálmán's earliest compositions were tone poems and songs, but his cabaret songs were better received, and this encouraged him to write for the operetta stage. In 1908 at Budapest's Vígszínház (Comedy Theatre), Kálmán had his first operetta success, *Tatárjárás*. This quickly attracted attention in Vienna and was presented there several months later as *Ein Herbstmanöver*. As with the later *Autumn Manoeuvres* and *The Gay Hussars*, among other titles, this military operetta marched happily through Europe and the US.

Theatrical managers journeyed to Budapest to snap up the next Kálmán operettas. In the United States, Kálmán's popularity dated from the 1914 production of *Sari*, a version of *Der Zigeunerprimas* (1912), the success of which was due in part to one of Kálmán's most voluptuous waltzes, 'Du, du, du', or 'Love Has Wings', as it was christened in New York. Shuttling between Vienna and Budapest during the First World War, Kálmán witnessed the disintegration of the old empire, accompanied by the rise of pro-military comedies and revues and outright operetta escapism.

Berlin, Budapest and Hamburg were among many European cities charmed by *Die Csárdásfürstin* after the war. Kálmán scored several hits during the 1920s, particularly *Das Hollandweibchen* (1920), *Die Bajadere* (1921), *Gräfin Mariza* (1924) and *Die Zirkusprinzessin* (1926); the last two are still regularly performed today. Subsequent stage works were somewhat repetitive and not quite as popular. In the 1930s Kálmán and his family went into exile, first to Paris and then the US, despite the fascist offer of honorary Aryan citizenship.

Kálmán's works were banned by the Nazis, though not until after the great film success of the UFA version of *Die Csárdásfürstin* (1934). The composer returned to Paris after the Second World War, at which time his works instantly regained their popularity in Berlin, Vienna, and other cities. Following his death in 1953 he was given a state funeral and burial in Vienna's Zentralfriedhof.

Kálmán's blend of Viennese whipped cream and Hungarian paprika recalls Johann Strauss II's *Der Zigeunerbaron*, though Kálmán's inflexions and instrumentation seem more authentically, moodily Magyar. It was not a question of introducing cimbaloms and tambourines into stock operetta depictions of Hungary; songs such as 'Komm, Zigany' (from *Gräfin Mariza*) and the entrance song of *Die Csárdásfürstin* are virtual Hungarian folksongs. His waltzes are easily the equal of Lehár's, and in the supremely vital comedy duets he surpasses his rival in outright catchiness. The choral and ensemble writing is far ahead of most of his contemporaries, although, despite some excellent libretti, he did not often attempt to alter the standard routine of musical numbers.

Die Csárdásfürstin

The Csárdás Princess
Operetta in three acts (2h 30m)
Libretto by Leo Stein and Béla Jenbach
Composed 1913–15
PREMIERES 17 November 1915, Johann Strauss Theater, Vienna; US: 24 September 1917, New Amsterdam Theater, New York (as *The Riviera Girl*; libretto by Guy Bolton and P. G. Wodehouse, with several numbers by Jerome Kern); UK: 20 May 1921, Prince of Wales Theatre, London (as *The Gypsy Princess*; libretto by Arthur Miller and Arthur Stanley)

Certain critics found the plot of Kálmán's greatest operetta decidedly unpatriotic. The story was meant, however, as an exercise in nostalgia for an age when titled stage-door johnnies were rampant – the most famous being Kaiser Franz-Josef himself, who had a well-known liaison with an actress from the Burgtheater.

Prince Edwin Ronald is, much to the disapproval of his family, greatly attached to a cabaret singer, Sylva. Despite his parents' plan for him to marry Countess Anastasia, Edwin persuades Sylva to sign a marriage contract; she is henceforth known as the Csárdás Princess. After many confusions, and the discovery that Edwin's mother was originally a singer, the wedding takes place.

The work's orchestration was interrupted for a period by the death of Kálmán's brother, and a certain melancholy in the score is said to have resulted from the composer's grief. The first night was a sensation; the critical reaction to the music was very favourable – the *Neue Wiener Tageblatt* admired how the composer kept 'one foot in the Hungarian nightclub and the other in the Viennese dance hall that gave birth to the waltz'. Particularly notable are the cabaret turns, the soubrette–buffo duets, and the succession of pensive, and then ebullient waltzes.

RECORDINGS   1. Rothenberger, Miljaković, Gedda, Brokmeier, Anheisser, Bavarian State Opera Ch, Graunke SO, Mattes, EMI, 1970s; 2. Mottl, Kales, Wasserlof, Drahosch, F. Waechter, Ch and O of Vienna Volksoper, Bibl, Denon, 1985
FILMS   1. Jacoby (dir.), 1934; 2. Jacoby (dir.), 1951
EDITIONS   f.s., Weinberger, 1987; v.s., Weinberger, 1916, *rp*, 1944

Gräfin Mariza

Countess Maritza
Operetta in three acts (2h 30m)
Libretto by Julius Brammer and Alfred Grünwald
PREMIERES   28 February 1924, Theater an der Wien, Vienna; US: 18 September 1926, Shubert Theater, New York (as *Countess Maritza*; libretto by Harry B. Smith); UK: 6 July 1938, Palace Theatre, London (as *Maritza*; libretto by Robert Lager-Parker, Eddie Garr and Arthur Stanley)

This is another successful *mélange* of Vienna and Budapest, this time set in the present day in the Hungarian countryside. The titular countess, Mariza, falls in love with her estate manager, Tassilo, who is actually a Hungarian nobleman down on his luck. After misunderstandings involving Tassilo's sister and his financial interests, the lovers are united.

The supporting buffo characters have catchy numbers, particularly the duet 'Komm mit nach Varasdin', sung by Baron Zsupan and Mariza. Tassilo's two principal songs, 'Gruss' mir die süssen, die reizenden Frauen im schönen Wien' and 'Komm' Zigany!' both continue to stop the show, as they did at the premiere.

RECORDING   Rothenberger, Miljaković, Moser, Gedda, Boehme, Bavarian State Opera Ch, Graunke SO, Mattes, Electrola, 1970s
FILMS   1. Oswald (prod.), 1932; 2. Schündler (prod.), 1958
EDITIONS   v.ss., Karczag, 1924; Octava, 1936, *rp*, 1947

Die Zirkusprinzessin

The Circus Princess
Operetta in three acts (2h 30m)
Libretto by Julius Brammer and Alfred Grunwald
PREMIERES   26 March 1926, Theater an der Wien, Vienna; US: 25 April 1927, Winter Garden, New York (as *The Circus Princess*; libretto by Harry B. Smith)

The last Kálmán–Brammer–Grunwald international success of the 1920s has recently regained popularity in Europe, thanks to its catchy tunes and its circus background, set in St Petersburg and Vienna. The mysterious and romantic Mr X (originally Hubert Marischka) has an act involving a violin and a galloping horse; he woos and wins the Princess Fedora to the strains of 'Zwei Märchenaugen' and other moody or lilting numbers. The usual mix of song styles appears, moving in one instance ('My darling, my darling, muss so sein wie Du'), from Viennese waltz to contemporary foxtrot within the course of the number.

RECORDING   excerpts: Schramm, Katona, Fritz, Schock, Gruber, Ch of Deutsche Oper, Berlin, Berlin SO, Stolz, Eurodisc, 1960s
EDITION   v.s., Karczag, 1926

Other operettas: *Tatárjárás*, 1908, rev. as *Ein Herbstmanöver*, 1909; *Obsitos* (*The Veteran*), 1910, rev. as *Der gute Kamerad*, 1911, rev. as *Gold gab ich für Eisen*, 1914; *Der Zigeunerprimas*, 1912; *The Blue House*, 1914; *Kiskirály* (*Der kleine König; The Little King*), 1914; *Zsuzsi kisasszony* (*Miss Susie*), 1915; *Die Faschingsfee*, 1917; *Das Hollandweibchen*, 1920; *Die Bajadere*, 1921 (RECORDING excerpts: Németh, Zentay, Udvardy, Hungarian State O, Bródy, Hungaroton, 1960s); *Golden Dawn*, 1927; *Die Herzogin von Chicago*, 1928; *Das Veilchen von Montmartre*, 1930; *Ronny* (film), 1931; *Der Teufelsreiter*, 1932; *Kaiserin Josephine*, 1936; *Marinka*, 1945; *Arizona Lady*, 1954
BIBLIOGRAPHY   Vera Kálmán, *Emlékszel még . . . Kálmán Imre élete*, Zenemukiado, 1966; Rudolph Oesterreicher, *Emmerich Kálmán, der Weg eines Komponisten*, Amalthea Verlag, 1954

R.T.

MANÓLIS KALOMÍRIS

b 14 December 1883, Smyrna (now Izmir), Turkey; *d* 3 April 1962, Athens

Manólis Kalomíris was the founder of the modern Greek national school of music, and a highly influential figure in the development of Greek music into a European tradition. There were four main influences on his own musical style, the primary one, from his earliest days, being Greek folksong. After initial musical education in Greece, he continued his studies at the Vienna Conservatory 1901–6, where he developed a deep admiration for Wagner. Then followed four years as a piano teacher in Kharkov, in the Ukraine, where he gained a knowledge of the Russian national school. The fourth influence was his involvement, together with leading intellectuals and writers, in the movement for 'demotic' language – what is now the language of modern Greece, instead of the élitist pseudo-Classical language which was still officially insisted on at the time.

Kalomíris's five operas are all based on Wagnerian principles of the *unendliche Melodie* and the leitmotif; *The Mother's Ring* has always been the most popular.

The Masterbuilder

O Protomástoras

Musical tragedy in two parts and one interlude (2h 30m)
Libretto adapted by the composer, with Nikolaos Poriotis,
Giorgios Stefopoulos and Mirtiotissa (Theoni Drakopulu),
from the play by Níkos Kazantzákis (1910)
Composed 1913–15, rev. 1929, 1940
PREMIERE 11 March 1916, Athens

According to a Greek folk-tale, the bridge over the river at the city of Arta, which kept collapsing, would never stand unless a human sacrifice was made. Kazantzákis and Kalomíris developed this tale into a highly symbolic psychological drama. The masterbuilder's concentration on his work has been distracted by his passion for the daughter of the old master, and the bridge continually gives way. The master's wife foretells that the lover of the masterbuilder must be sacrificed and buried in the foundations of the bridge to ensure its safety, but neither she nor the master has realized that it is their own daughter who is thus condemned.

The music is written in an epic style, with strong characterization and dramatization of the main characters and their predicaments. The style of word-setting and declamation, and the way in which ethnic dance elements, played by a Wagnerian-scale orchestra, are incorporated into the score, are strongly reminiscent to a Western ear of the Russian school of Borodin and Rimsky-Korsakov, but are none the less convincing for the association.

RECORDING Pisarenko, Martinov, USSR Cinema Radio
Ch and O, Khachaturian, Greek Cultural Office, 1990
EDITIONS v.ss. Kalomíris, 1917; rev. version: Gaitanou, 1939/40

The Mother's Ring

To Dakhtylídi tis Mánas

Music drama in three acts (2h 15m)
Based on a play by Yánnis Kambýsis, with lyrics by Ágnis Orfikós
Completed 1917, rev. 1939
PREMIERE 8 December 1917, Athens

On Christmas Eve the village troubadour, Yannakis, lies at home dying. His mother decides to sell the family ring to help her son. In a dream Yannakis pursues a mountain nereid who has stolen the ring: he recaptures it, and then asks her to lead him to the highest mountain peak, where no man has trod. But he fails, and the nereid reveals herself as Erofili, his beloved. On Christmas morning, as his family prays by the village church, Yannakis suddenly appears, singing of his dream. But he dies, and in his hand is found the ring.

There are many layers of symbolism in the opera: an archetypal bond between mother and son, symbolized by the ring; the artist's drive to transcend his medium; the parallel with the Orpheus myth; the death of Yannakis coinciding with the feast of the birth of Christ. The music is written in a more gentle style than *The Masterbuilder*, generally underlaid with a folksong lilt, and also with elements from the music of the Eastern Orthodox Church, though clothed in a 19th-century harmonic tradition. The 'magic' element in the text is reflected in the more 'exotic' scoring, and the direct influence of Wagner is often apparent – to considerable expressive effect, when it does not saturate the genuine ethnic source.

RECORDING Karvelas, Terzakis, Koromantzou, Bulgarian National Chorus, Sofia PO, Daras, Concert Athens, 1983
EDITION v.s., Gaitanou, *c.* 1937

Other operatic works: *Anatolí* (*Sunrise*), 1945, rev. 1948; *Ta Xotiká Nerá* (*The Shadowy Waters*), 1950, rev. 1952; *Konstantínos Paleológos*, 1961
BIBLIOGRAPHY Fivos Anoyanákis, *Catalogue of Works of Manólis Kalomíris*, Rondas Publishing House, 1986

G.C.P.

MACIEJ KAMIEŃSKI

Maciej (Mathias) Kamieński; *b* 13 October 1734, Ödenburg
(now Sopron, Hungary); *d* 25 January 1821, Warsaw

After serving as a musician in Ödenburg Kamieński studied piano and composition in Vienna, and heard Mozart play at Schönbrunn in 1762. By 1778 he had settled in Warsaw where he taught, conducted and composed. In addition to the first operas in Polish, he wrote *A Short Outline of the Original Polish Opera*.

Misery Made Happy

Nędza uszczęśliwiona

Opera in two acts
Libretto by Wojciech Bogusławski
PREMIERE 11 July 1778, Palace Theatre, Warsaw

The earliest operatic setting of a Polish text, this was also the first Polish opera performed in a public theatre. Dedicated to King Stanisław Poniatowski, it was received with great enthusiasm. Bogusławski's libretto is based on a cantata text by Franciszek Bohomolec. Kamieński's music, as in his other operas, points to the emergence of a Polish national style, reinforced by folk-style settings.

EDITION f.s., *Opery Polskie*, vol 2, Cracow 1978

Other operatic works: *Tradycja dowcipem załatwiona* (*Tradition Settled by Ingenuity*), 1789; *Słowik, czyli Kasia z Hankana wydaniu* (*The Nightingale, or Kasia Persuaded by Hanusia*), 1790; 5 lost operas
BIBLIOGRAPHY Alina Nowak-Romanowicz, 'Maciej Kamieński', in *Grove*, Macmillan, 1980

G.A.

JOHN KANDER

John Harold Kander; *b* 18 March 1927, Kansas City, Missouri, US

A music student at Oberlin College and Columbia

University, John Kander acquired theatrical experience as rehearsal pianist and dance arranger (performing the latter function for Styne's *Gypsy*). After his first Broadway effort, *A Family Affair*, he established a long-term collaboration with Fred Ebb that has created a number of ambitious and offbeat projects over the years, often incorporating stylized, frankly theatrical presentation.

Cabaret

Musical in two acts (2h 30m)
Libretto by Joe Masteroff, based on the play *I Am a Camera* by John Van Druten (from stories by Christopher Isherwood); lyrics by Fred Ebb
PREMIERES 20 November 1966, Broadhurst Theatre, New York; UK: 28 February 1968, Palace Theatre, London

The story of Sally Bowles, a determinedly unconventional singer in Berlin in the 1920s, is framed by the show at the Kit Kat Klub, presented by a surreally decadent master of ceremonies. *Cabaret*, in addition to its quality as musical theatre, has a historical place as the first successful mixing of the formats of musical play and revue, an idea to be explored further by several writers in the following years.

Joel Grey as the Master of Ceremonies in Cabaret *(New York, 1966)*

RECORDING Haworth, Grey, Lenya, Gilford, Convy, Hastings, CBS, 1966
FILM (substantially rewritten) Fosse (dir.), Allied Artists, 1972
EDITION v.s., New York Times Music/Sunbeam, 1968

Chicago

Musical in two acts
Libretto by Fred Ebb and Bob Fosse, based on the play *Chicago* by Maurine Dallas Watkins; lyrics by Fred Ebb

PREMIERES 3 June 1975, 46th Street Theatre, New York; UK: 10 April 1979, Cambridge Theatre, London

The rise of Roxie Hart from condemned murderess to public favourite is retold in sardonic vaudeville terms, with almost every number simultaneously pertinent to its context and a parody of a recognizable 1920s musical style. This is Kander's and Ebb's own clearest development of the direction suggested by *Cabaret*, the use of revue format (addressing the audience directly), and typical vaudeville performance styles to tell a story in a heightened, deliberately unrealistic way. Original director (and co-librettist) Bob Fosse must rank as a primary creator of the show's shape and atmosphere.

RECORDING Verdon, Rivera, Orbach, Lebowsky, Arista, 1975
EDITIONS v.s., Samuel French (on hire); lib., Samuel French, 1976

Other musicals: *A Family Affair*, 1962; *Flora, The Red Menace*, 1965; *The Happy Time*, 1968; *Zorba*, 1968; *70, Girls, 70*, 1971; *The Act*, 1977; *Woman of the Year*, 1981; *The Rink*, 1984; *Kiss of the Spider Woman*, 1990
BIBLIOGRAPHY David Ewen, *American Songwriters*, H. W. Wilson, 1987

J.A.C.

RUDOLF KAREL

b 9 November 1880, Plzeň; *d* 6 March 1945, Terezín, Czechoslovakia

Karel was Dvořák's last pupil at the Prague Conservatory and he inherited a Romantic style that looked back unashamedly to his teacher. Later he himself became professor of composition and orchestration at the conservatory (1923–41). During the First World War Karel was interned in Russia, where he had been working; in 1943 he was interned again, this time by the Gestapo. His last opera was smuggled out of a concentration camp, where it was written, and completed by his pupil Zbynek Vostřák. His first opera, staged many years after its completion, had little success and he is remembered chiefly for *Godmother Death*.

Godmother Death

Smrt kmotřička
A merry tale of life and death in three acts, Op. 30
Libretto by Stanislav Lom after the folk-tale
Composed 1928–32
PREMIERE 3 February 1933, Brno

The fiddler cannot find a godparent for his thirteenth child. He tries to hang himself but Death prevents him and offers herself as a godparent. She predicts a career as a doctor for her godson who, thirty years later, seeks to cure the king's daughter. With help from his godmother and a little subterfuge, he accomplishes this and lives happily ever after with the princess. His father the fiddler, whose time has now come, goes off with Death.

The folk-tale is updated (the sick princess is tended in a modern sanatorium), but the central presence of the fiddler shows a traditional Czech preoccupation with musicians. With the dignified and sympathetic performance of Marta Krásová as Death in the Prague performances, the opera achieved special popularity before the war.

RECORDING   excerpts: Urbanová, Najmanová, Musilová, Krásová, Žídek, Zlesák, Mráz, Prague NT O, Vostřák, Supraphon, [c. 1955]
EDITION   v.s., Sadlo, 1936

Other operas: Ilsa's Heart (Ilseino srdce), (1909), 1924; The Taming of the Shrew (Zkrocení zlé ženy) (inc.), (1944); The Three [Golden] Hairs of Grandfather the Allknowing (Tři [zlaté] vlasy děda vševěda), 1948
BIBLIOGRAPHY   Ladislav Šíp, Česká opera a jeho tvůrci (Czech Opera and Its Creators), Supraphon, 1983

J.T.

LEO JUSTINUS KAUFFMANN

b 20 September 1901, Dannemarie [Dammerkirch], Alsace; d 25 September 1944, Strasbur, France

Kauffmann studied with Busoni's pupil Philipp Jarnach, Hermann Abendroth and Florent Schmitt. In 1926 he moved to Cologne, where, in 1929, he began to teach at the Rheinische Musikschule. In 1933 he was dismissed after the success of his Allemanische Suite at the ISCM Festival in Amsterdam, his music being deemed too modernistic. After 1937 he was supported by the conductor Hans Rosbaud, who gave the first performances of two of his operas. In 1940 he accepted a teaching post in Strasburg where he was killed in an air raid in 1944. Jarnach considered Das Perlenhemd to be 'a musical jewel and at the same time the very model of a new and valid style of chamber opera'.

Operatic works: Liebe um Gloria, 1924, rev. 1933; Das Ardwibele, 1928; Das Zauberflötchen, 1934; Gesang ins Glück, 1935; Die niegesehene Braut, 1937; Liebe im Park, 1937; Frühere Verhältnisse, 1939; Die Serenade, 1939; Elsässisches Tanzspiel, 1942; Die Geschichte vom schönen Annerl, 1942; Das Perlenhemd, 1944; Agnes Bernauer (inc.), (1944)
BIBLIOGRAPHY   H. von Radzibor, 'Leo Justinus Kauffmann', Rheinische Musiker, vol. 4, Cologne, 1966

A.C.

ULYSSES KAY

Ulysses Simpson Kay; b 7 January 1917, Tucson, Arizona, US

Kay comes from a rich musical background – the legendary jazz cornet-player Joe 'King' Oliver was his uncle – and learned to play the piano, violin and saxophone. At the Eastman School he was a student of Rogers and Hanson and at Tanglewood he went to Hindemith's classes before his progress was interrupted by war service in the US navy. After the war he attended Columbia University, where he was encouraged by William Grant Still, another pioneer Afro-American composer of a slightly older generation.

Between 1948 and 1964 Kay wrote 13 scores for films or television, but his first two operas, The Juggler of Our Lady and The Boor, based on Chekhov, both one-act, took some years to achieve production. Kay's music has been admired in some quarters for its generally melodic style and colourful orchestration. Jubilee, an American Bicentennial commission and Kay's first full-length opera, includes spiritual-like melodies and folk hymns amid more dissonant textures. Kay returned to an American setting in his next opera, which takes as its subject episodes from the life of the reformer Frederick Douglas.

Operas: The Boor (1955), 1968; The Juggler of Our Lady, (1956), 1962; The Capitoline Venus, 1971; Jubilee, 1976; Frederick Douglass, (1983), 1991
BIBLIOGRAPHY   D. Baker, L. Belt and H. Hudson, The Black Composer Speaks, Metuchen, 1978

P.D.

REINHARD KEISER

baptized 12 January 1674, Teuchern, nr Weissenfels; d 12 September 1739, Hamburg

Keiser was the most prolific composer of German baroque opera, and his catalogue of operas, serenades, and other types of dramatic vocal music numbers more than 100 works. This includes more than 60 complete operas, composed largely for Hamburg, of which 17 are extant. The German contemporary critic Johann Scheibe regarded him 'as perhaps the greatest original genius in music ever produced by Germany' (foreword to Über die musikalische Composition, erster Theil, 1773), while the contemporary composer Johann Mattheson described Keiser 'as the greatest opera composer of the world' and, with a play on the meaning of the composer's name, called him 'an emperor [Kaiser] of melody'.

Keiser was educated at the Leipzig Thomasschule, where he probably studied with Johann Schelle as well as the Thomaskirche organist and later kantor, Johann Kuhnau. From around 1692 Keiser lived in Brunswick where he was appointed 'Cammer-Componist' to the court, and wrote at least four operas. It was the attraction of Hamburg's flourishing commercial opera that led Keiser there around 1695, and during the next 45 years his career was firmly centred at the Hamburg Opera. In 1696 the opera director, Gerhard Schott, staged Keiser's Mahumeth II, and in 1697 Der geliebte Adonis, the first of numerous operas Keiser composed to libretti by Christian Heinrich Postel. Seven more operas

The stage of the Theater am Gänsemarkt in Hamburg, 1678–1738

followed in 1698 and 1699 and Keiser quickly confirmed his position as Hamburg's foremost opera composer.

In 1703 Keiser became director of the Theater am Gänsemarkt. For the next four years he led highly successful seasons for which he wrote ten of his best works; he also encouraged Mattheson and the young Handel to contribute their own operas. Handel, who had been employed by Keiser as *ripieno* violinist in the opera orchestra in 1704, gained his earliest foundation in opera composition here and later borrowed and adapted a number of Keiser's melodies in his operas. In 1707 Keiser gave up the management of the Theater am Gänsemarkt, but remained its most important composer until 1717, providing at least another 25 operas. He then sought permanent employment elsewhere, including an unsuccessful attempt to become kapellmeister at Stuttgart, but in 1721 returned to Hamburg where Telemann had taken on the directorship of the opera. With the exception of a brief spell in 1722 as kapellmeister at the Danish court in Copenhagen (where he wrote three operas), he remained in the city for the rest of his life, producing at least another ten works, as well as acting as cantor cathedralis at Hamburg Cathedral from 1728. Much of the last decade of his life was spent providing sacred compositions for the cathedral.

Keiser was a typical, 18th-century, eclectic composer, whose concepts of dramatic music were rooted in various operatic achievements by Italian (especially Venetian), French (the works of Lully), and German composers. His operas are usually in three acts constructed as a sequence of lengthy recitatives and arias derived from later 17th-century Italian opera. French elements include the insertion of various dances, the use of songs in dance rhythms and binary structure, and introductory instrumental pieces in French-overture style and form. From German opera Keiser received a considerable legacy which included various popular styles of music from north Germany, secular and sacred lieder, street cries and folksongs, as well as various German dances.

A number of Keiser's operas combined aria texts in Italian, which allowed for virtuosic vocal display, with recitative texts in German, which ensured that the audience could follow the action. In *Der Carneval von Venedig* (1707) Keiser caused consternation by including comic scenes (increasingly in demand in German opera) in Lower Saxon dialect (*Plattdeutsch*). The majority of Keiser's operas, however, are serious in tone, enabling him to put into practice his belief – later stated in the preface to a collection of his operatic arias – in the dramatic role of recitative. In response to the dramatic situation Keiser might write an affecting unaccompanied recitative passage or might score colourfully, also introducing effective, and sometimes sudden, shifts of harmony.

Keiser's use of instrumental timbres is, in fact, one

of the most individual features of his style. The resources at his disposal in Hamburg gave him the scope to produce a huge variety of aria accompaniments, ranging from fairly straightforward arias accompanied only by the continuo group to those demanding four or more solo instruments (a practice probably influenced by Graupner's example). Thus, for example, one aria in *Orpheus* (1709) calls for five flutes, one solo violin and double-bass, resulting in concerto-type contrasts and alternation between strings and wind as well as with the voice.

Der geliebte Adonis
The Beloved Adonis
Singspiel in three acts
Libretto by Christian Heinrich Postel
PREMIERE 1697, Theater am Gänsemarkt, Hamburg

This is the earliest preserved opera score by Keiser. The plot concerns the love of the goddess Venus for the mortal Adonis. Competing for each other's love are Mars for Venus and two shepherdesses, Dryante and Eumene, for Adonis. Mars takes revenge on Adonis by killing him while in the form of a boar. Venus, unable to follow her beloved to death, transforms her tears into anemones and Adonis' body into red roses, while all the roses in the field also turn red. Venus, clutching some roses to her breast, returns to her heavenly palace.

The title role is, in keeping with local practice in Hamburg, scored for an alto voice, and would have been sung by a falsettist (castrati were not introduced to the city until several years later). Since it predates Handel's arrival in Hamburg in 1703, the younger composer might have seen only selected arias from *Adonis*; however, a few fragments appear in his works, notably in 'O beauteous Queen' from *Esther*.

EDITION facsimile, John H. Roberts (ed.), *Handel Sources: Materials for the Study of Handel Borrowings*, vol. 1, Garland, 1986

Der bey dem allgemeinen Welt-Friede und dem grossen Augustus geschlossene Tempel des Janus
The Temple of Janus Closed by the Great Augustus Because of the General World Peace
Singspiel in three acts
Libretto by Christian Heinrich Postel
PREMIERE 1698, Theater am Gänsemarkt, Hamburg

Janus is one of Keiser's most important early operas, written to celebrate the end of the ten-year War of the League of Augsburg in 1697. The title refers to the Roman temple of Janus which remained open during war but was closed in peacetime. The story, based on Roman history, concerns the abandonment by Tiberius of his betrothed, Vipsania Agrippina, in order to marry Julia, the daughter of Emperor Augustus. This intrigue is inspired by Livia, wife of Augustus, who aspires to see Tiberius, her son, ascend to the throne as successor to Augustus.

Mattheson was particularly loud in his praise of this opera, commenting that 'The two authors [i.e. Keiser and Postel] . . . achieved many beautiful things.' Handel, too, was clearly impressed and borrowed, among other items, the opera's most popular aria, 'Holde Schatten'; this appears, reworked, in his opera *Il pastor fido* as well as in his oratorios *La Resurrezione* and *Esther*.

EDITION facsimile, John H. Roberts (ed.), *Handel Sources: Materials for the Study of Handel Borrowings*, vol. 1, Garland, 1986

La forza della virtù, oder Die Macht der Tugend
The Power of Virtue
Singspiel in three acts
Libretto by Domenico David, translated by Friedrich Christian Bressand
PREMIERE 1700, Theater am Gänsemarkt, Hamburg

The French princess Clotilde has arrived to take up her role as wife of Fernando, King of Castille. He, however, is in love with Anagilda, daughter of the noble Sancio, who covets the position of queen of Castille. Fernando attempts to dishonour Clotilde's reputation with false charges of infidelity, imprisons her and orders her to commit suicide. In an ensuing confrontation, however, she wins Fernando's sympathy with her virtuous conduct and also by saving him from an attempted assassination. Subsequently Anagilda attempts to kill her, but Clotilde responds with forgiveness, and the opera ends with Clotilde's coronation, Anagilda placing the crown on the new queen's head.

The contemporary success of *La forza della virtù* is confirmed by the fact that it was the first of Keiser's operas to have extracts published (in 1701). David's text had been set by Carlo Francesco Pollarolo in 1693, a setting Keiser must have heard since he adopts Pollarolo's highly unusual feature of leaving an aria for Anagilda, in which she combs her hair before a mirror, entirely without accompaniment. The libretto's Italian genesis also means that most of the arias are in *da capo* form, and the opera consequently has less formal variety than other Keiser works of this period. Among a number of Handel borrowings are passages from Clotilde's Act III aria 'Mit einem schönen Ende', reused in 'I know that my Redeemer liveth' in *Messiah*.

EDITION facsimile, John H. Roberts (ed.), *Handel Sources: Materials for the Study of Handel Borrowings*, vol. 2, Garland, 1986

Die römische Unruhe, oder Die edelmüthige Octavia
The Roman Unrest, or The Noble-minded Octavia
Singspiel in three acts (3h 45m)
Libretto by Barthold Feind
PREMIERE 5 August 1705, Theater am Gänsemarkt, Hamburg

The thrust of the plot is concerned with the Roman Emperor Nero's two-fold crisis: his infatuation with an Armenian Queen Ormoena, married to the King Tiridates, and the open rebellion within Rome as the result of Nero's failures as ruler. Nero's wife, Octavia, stands in the way of Nero's conquest of Ormoena, and he commands Octavia's suicide. The 'noble-minded' and dutiful Octavia would comply with her husband's order, but is saved by a compassionate Roman patrician, Piso, and the wisdom of Seneca, philosopher and adviser to the emperor. Finally Nero, realizing the extraordinary devotion and love of Octavia, asks for forgiveness, which she extends without enmity.

Despite a weak libretto, this opera includes some very attractive writing for voices and a richly varied use of the orchestra. *Octavia* was a particular favourite of Handel who borrowed 10 arias in original or modified form from it for use in his own works, most notably *Agrippina* (1709). This led the 19th-century Handel scholar, Friedrich Chrysander, to publish the first modern edition of a Keiser opera as a supplementary volume to the complete edition of Handel's works in order to facilitate comparisons of the original music by Keiser and Handel's various adaptations.

EDITION Friedrich Chrysander (ed.), *Supplemente, Enthaltend Quellen in Handels Werken*, vol. 6, Handel Gesellschaft, 1902

Masagniello furioso
Masagniello the Rebel
Drama musicale in three acts
Libretto by Barthold Feind
PREMIERES June 1706, Theater am Gänsemarkt, Hamburg; UK: 8 November 1973, University of Sheffield

The libretto is based on the historical acccount of the 1647 rebellion taking place in Naples against the Spanish rulers, led by a 27-year old fisherman Tommaso Aniello (Masagniello). The event was well known throughout Europe, and Feind's libretto may have purposefully reflected uncertain political times in Hamburg, as well as recalling the popular rebellion that shook the city in 1684–6. However, Feind seriously weakened the political thrust of the Masagniello rebellion by immersing it in an original plot involving the complications of love between Spanish noble couples: Aloysia, wife of General Don Velasco, and loved by Don Pedro, and Mariane, in love with Don Antonio, but loved also by the Duca D'Arcos.

Among the surviving operas by Keiser, this is one of the important examples of his operatic achievement both for its highly original scoring and its bountiful number of beautiful arias. *Masagniello furioso* retained its popularity in Hamburg through numerous repetitions. As late as 1722 Telemann directed a new version of the opera, making substantial changes in the original score and adding a number of new arias of his own.

EDITION Hans-Joachim Theill (ed.), *EDM*, vol. 89, Schott, 1986

Die grossmütige Tomyris
The Magnanimous Tomyris
Singspiel in three acts
Libretto by Domenico Lalli, translated and adapted by Johann Joachim Hoe
PREMIERE July 1717, Theater am Gänsemarkt, Hamburg

The libretto starts as a sequel to Herodotus' account of the death of the Persian King Cyrus at the hands of Tomyris, Queen of the Scythian Massagetae. The widowed Tomyris is courted by two rival kings, but is in love with her general Tigranes, who in turn loves Meroe, Cyrus' daughter. Meroe has come to court disguised as an Armenian magician with the purpose of avenging the death of her father. Tigranes, torn between two loyalties, accused of treachery, but protesting his innocence, is saved from execution in the last moment by the discovery that he is Tomyris' long-lost son.

Tomyris is one of only four operas extant from Keiser's second Hamburg period (1710–17). The score shows distinctive changes and a consolidation of style, and can be considered an important north German adaptation of Italian opera seria. Most of the arias, all *da capo*, are now placed at the ends of scenes. They are less varied in style than in earlier operas, but are frequently more virtuosic and cast in more extended forms. The style leans clearly in the direction of the *style galant*. Textures are thinner, seldom contrapuntal, and often *unisono* for the orchestra. Many arias omit the continuo bass, and harmonic colours are less varied than in previous operas.

RECORDING Fontana, Hirsti, Cemore, Dahlberg, Krohn, Prégardien, Linde-Consort, Pürgstaller, EMI, 1988
EDITION Klaus Zelm (ed.), *Die Oper: Kritische Ausgabe von Hauptwerken der Operngeschichte*, vol. 1, Henle, 1975

Der hochmütige, gestürtzte, und wieder erhabene Croesus
The Proud, Fallen, and Again Elevated Croesus
Singspiel in three acts (3h 30m)
Libretto by Lucas von Bostel, after Niccolo Minato's libretto *Creso* (1678)
PREMIERES 1711, Theater am Gänsemarkt, Hamburg; rev. version: 6 December 1730, Theater am Gänsemarkt

The libretto, based on Herodotus, recalls the life of Croesus, King of Lydia from 560 to 546 BC, who, as proud as he was rich, learned by his own bitter experience that he who rises highest is most likely to fall the farthest. Cyrus, King of the Assyrians, defeats Croesus' army. Croesus flees without his regal clothes, is captured, and is about to be killed. However, his mute son Atys suddenly recovers his voice and shouts, 'It is the king, stop, kill him not.' Cyrus condemns Croesus to death by fire. Tied to the stake, Croesus is temporarily saved by a cloudburst dousing the flames. As the fire is rekindled, Croesus realizes the folly of basing happiness on material wealth and willingly accepts his fate. Cyrus is so moved by Croesus' bravery that he frees him and restores him to power.

The burning of Croesus; engraving from the printed libretto of Der hochmütige gestürtzte, und wieder erhabene Croesus *(Hamburg, 1711)*

Of all Keiser's operas available in modern editions, *Croesus* has the greatest variety of music. The score is particularly rich in instrumental accompaniments to the arias, with interesting two- and three-part textures often based on motivic interplay. A few arias of the original version of this opera survive, but Keiser's 1730 revision made substantial changes. The ballets were omitted, along with the secondary character Olysius, and 37 arias were newly composed. These arias provide an interesting and specific example of the developments that had taken place in musical style between 1711 and 1730. This is also reflected in the strongly homophonic textures, with bass lines more often than not giving only harmonic support. Some of the arias are in a clearly focused buffo character; Italianate coloratura is prevalent, and at times there is a strong similarity to Telemann's operatic style.

RECORDING Klietman, Mizugushi, Grigorova, Van der Sluis, Martin, Tucker, Akerlund, Benet, Targler, Clemencic Consort, Ensemble Vocal La Cappella, Mildenhall, Nuova Era, 1990
EDITION Max Schneider (ed.), *DDT*, vols 37–8, Boosey & Hawkes, 1912, *rp* (with revs ed. by Hans Joachim Moser), 1958

Other operatic works: *Sieg der fruchtbaren Pomona*, 1702; *Die verdammte Staat-Sucht, oder Der verführte Claudius*, 1703 (EDITION facsimile, *Handel Sources*, vol. 3, Garland, 1986); *Der gestürzte und wieder erhöhte Nebucadnezar, König zu Babylon*, 1704 (EDITION facsimile, *Handel Sources*,

vol. 3, Garland, 1986); *La grandezza d'animo, oder Arsinoe*, 1710; *Fredegunda*, 1715; *Der die Festung Siebenbürgisch-Weissenburg erobernde und über Dacier triumphirende Kayser Trajanus*, 1717; *Ulysses*, 1722; *Der sich rächende Cupido*, 1724; *Der lächerliche Prinz Jodelet*, 1726; *Circe*, 1734; *c.* 48 lost operas (arias from several of these extant)

BIBLIOGRAPHY John D. Arnn, *Text, Music and Drama in Three Operas* [*La forza della virtù, Arsinoe, Croesus*] *by Reinhard Keiser*, dissertation, Rutgers University, 1987; Basil Deane, 'Reinhard Keiser: An Interim Assessment', *Soundings*, vol. 4 (1974), pp. 30–41; K. Zelm, *Die Opern Reinhard Keisers*, Emil Katzbichler, 1975

G.J.B.

RUDOLF KELTERBORN
b 3 September 1931, Basle, Switzerland

Kelterborn studied at the Basle Music Academy, and with Burkhard, Blacher, Fortner and Bialas. In the course of a distinguished professional career he has taught at Basle, Detmold, Zurich and Karlsruhe, edited the *Schweizerische Musikzeitung* (1969–74), and headed the music department of German and Rhaeto-Romanic Swiss Radio (1974–80). Since 1983 he has been Director of the Basle Music Academy. Whereas his early works owe something to Burkhard and Blacher, from 1954 to 1959 he was influenced by the avant-garde. He has since adopted an undogmatic approach to serialism and makes some use of aleatoric procedures. His first two operas were followed by three literaturopern, *Ein Engel kommt nach Babylon*, based on a play by Friedrich Dürrenmatt (who also wrote the libretto), *Der Kirschgarten*, based on Chekhov, and *Ophelia*, an operatic psychogram for which *Hamlet* is merely the starting point. His latest opera, *Julia*, is a conflation of Shakespeare's *Romeo and Juliet*, Gottfried Keller and an imaginary tragedy set in the context of the Palestinian *intifada*.

Operas: *Die Errettung Thebens*, 1963; *Kaiser Jovian*, 1967; *Ein Engel kommt nach Babylon*, 1977; *Der Kirschgarten*, 1984; *Ophelia*, 1985; *Julia*, 1991
BIBLIOGRAPHY   Rudolf Kelterborn, *Musik im Brennpunkt*, Bärenreiter, 1988

A.C.

JEROME KERN

Jerome David Kern; *b* 27 January 1885, New York; *d* 11 November 1945, New York

After musical studies in New York and Europe, Jerome Kern managed to establish himself as a writer of songs for interpolation in operettas by others – with such success that he was asked to write complete scores on his own. From 1915 onwards, he established the ground-breaking Princess Theater series of musicals, novel in their intimacy and their determination to relate all songs and comedy directly to the plot. He continued to write larger-scale shows as well, reaching a climax in the uniquely ambitious *Show Boat*.

After this landmark, Kern continued to experiment with new structures in musicals like *The Cat and the Fiddle* and *Music in the Air*, although the most popular of his later works, *Roberta* (remembered largely because of its film) was thoroughly conventional. From 1934 on, Kern lived and worked primarily in Hollywood. In his lifetime he encompassed, and indeed created, a complete change in attitude about what American musical theatre should be and could be; but however much it evolved with the years, Kern's music always remained recognizable by its deceptively simple melodiousness.

Show Boat

Musical play in two acts (2h 45m)
Libretto by Oscar Hammerstein II, based on the novel by Edna Ferber (1926); lyric for 'Bill' partly by P. G. Wodehouse
PREMIERES   27 December 1927, Ziegfeld Theater, New York; UK: 3 May 1928, Drury Lane, London; authors' rev. version: 5 January 1946, Ziegfeld Theater, New York
CAST   Magnolia Hawks/Kim Ravenal *s*, Gaylord Ravenal *t*, Julie Laverne *s*, Joe *b*, Queenie *a*, Ellie May Chipley *dancer/ms*, Frank Schultz *dancer/t*; speaking roles: Captain Andy Hawks, Parthy Ann Hawks, Steve Baker; other brief speaking and singing roles (mostly from chorus); *satb* chorus (white) of show-boat patrons, gamblers, World's Fair visitors, Trocadero patrons; *satb* chorus (black) of workers, show-boat patrons, Dahomey villagers
ORCHESTRATION (Robert Russell Bennett)   theatre orch., including gtr (doubling tuba) and banjo

The above voice ranges and orchestration apply to the original version; the authors began to make changes almost immediately after the premiere and created a major revised version for a 1946 revival. Alterations continue to this day, motivated by changes in vocal style (shifting Ravenal and Julie to lower vocal ranges), in propriety (elimination of offensive racial epithets), and theatrical habits (avoidance of 'front scenes' that exist only to cover scene changes). In all versions, the action remains deliberately episodic, encompassing nearly 40 years to emphasize that time passes, people grow and change, and only nature remains constant.

SYNOPSIS
Act I   The action begins in 1890. Captain Andy's show boat *Cotton Blossom* is docked in Natchez, Mississippi. His young daughter Magnolia falls in love with the gambler Gaylord Ravenal. When the boat's leading actors, Julie and Steve, are forced to leave because Julie is discovered to be part black, Magnolia and Ravenal take their places. Despite the objections of Magnolia's mother, the pair are married.
Act II   The Hawks family visit the 1893 Chicago World's Fair. By 1904, Ravenal's gambling is no longer successfully supporting Magnolia and their daughter Kim, and he leaves them in Chicago. Forced to find a job, Magnolia becomes a singer. In 1927, the newly modernized *Cotton Blossom* welcomes Magnolia and Kim, herself a Broadway star, and Ravenal finally returns.

The original score includes extended musical scenes encompassing solos, ensembles, and speaking over music. The songs themselves will always guarantee revivals, including 'Make Believe', 'Old Man River', 'Can't Help Lovin' Dat Man', 'You Are Love', 'Why Do I Love You?' and 'Bill'.

RECORDING   Von Stade, Stratas, Hadley, Hubbard, London Sinfonietta, McGlinn, EMI, 1988: a splendid complete performance of the 1927 score, followed by an appendix containing all numbers written for earlier and later versions, with full documentation
FILMS   1. Universal, 1929; 2. Whale (dir.), Universal, 1936; 3. MGM, 1951
EDITIONS   v.ss., Harms, 1927; London version, Chappell/Harms, 1928; the v.s. representing the (simplified) 1946 version also bears a 1927 date

Other musicals: *The Red Petticoat*, 1912; *Oh, I Say!*, 1913; *Ninety in the Shade*, 1915; *Nobody Home*, 1915; *Miss Information*, 1915; *Very Good Eddie*, 1915; *Have a Heart*, 1917; *Love o' Mike*, 1917; *Oh, Boy!*, 1917; *Leave It to Jane*, 1917; *Oh, Lady! Lady!*, 1918; *Toot-Toot*, 1918; *Rock-a-bye Baby*, 1918; *Head over Heels*, 1918; *She's a Good Fellow*, 1919; *Zip, Goes a Million*, 1919; *The Night Boat*, 1920; *Sally*, 1920; *The Cabaret Girl*, 1921; *Good Morning, Dearie*, 1921; *The Bunch and Judy*, 1922; *The Beauty Prize*, 1923; *Stepping Stones*, 1923; *Sitting Pretty*, 1924; *Dear Sir*, 1924; *Sunny*, 1925; *The City Chap*, 1925; *Criss-Cross*, 1926; *Blue Eyes*, 1928; *Sweet Adeline*, 1929; *The Cat and the Fiddle*, 1931; *Music in the Air*, 1932; *Roberta*, 1933; *Three Sisters*, 1934; *Gentlemen Unafraid*, 1938, *Very Warm for May*, 1939

BIBLIOGRAPHY Gerald Bordman, *Jerome Kern: His Life and Music*, OUP, 1980; Miles Krueger, *Show Boat: The Story of a Classic American Musical*, OUP, 1977

J.A.C.

TIKHON KHRENNIKOV

Tikhon Nikolayevich Khrennikov; *b* 10 June 1913, Elets

It is doubtful whether Khrennikov's international reputation, both musical and moral, can ever be salvaged after his unflattering portrayal in *Testimony*, Shostakovich's memoirs, where he is revealed as a toady and a henchman of Stalin. Throughout his career he showed immense skill as a politician, surviving many leadership purges as first secretary of the Soviet Composers' Union. His works show how closely he monitored current Party taste. *Into the Storm*, his first opera, composed in the wake of Stalin's denunciation of Shostakovich's *Lady Macbeth of Mtsensk*, is an optimistic patriotic piece, full of mass songs and simple folk melody and was praised by the Party for expressing a positive view of socialist culture. With Stalin's approval, it became a blueprint for future Soviet operas. Khrennikov was much to the fore in the 1948 denunciation that accused Prokofiev, Shostakovich, Myaskovsky, Shebalin (his old teacher) and Khachaturian of formalism, writing music incompatible with the needs of the people. From this time dates his leadership of the Union, a post he kept under various leaders, surviving to be made a Hero of Socialist Labour in 1973. His third opera, *Mother*, was a huge success, premiered simultaneously in three cities.

Operatic works: *V buryu* (*Into the Storm*), 1939, rev. 1952 (RECORDING Melodiya, 1960s); *Frol Skobeyev*, 1950, rev. as *Bezrodnyi zyat'*, 1966; *Mat'* (*Mother*) 1957 (RECORDING excerpts: Melodiya, 1950s); *100 chertei i odna devushka* (*One Hundred Devils and One Girl*), 1963; *Belaya noch'* (*White Night*), 1967; *Mal'chik-velikan* (*Boy Giant*), 1969
BIBLIOGRAPHY B. Schwarz, *Music and Musical Life in Soviet Russia, 1917–70*, Barrie and Jenkins, 1972

J.G.

WILHELM KIENZL

b 17 January 1857, Waizenkirchen; *d* 19 October 1941, Vienna

Kienzl studied in Graz with Wilhelm Mayer-Rémy (who also taught Reznicek, Heuberger, Weingartner and Busoni) and later in Prague he was a pupil of Krejci. In his youth he travelled extensively throughout Europe as pianist and conductor, attending the world premiere of Wagner's *Ring* at Bayreuth (1876), studying briefly with Liszt and for

one season (1883) conducting at the German opera in Amsterdam. He joined the inner circle of Bayreuth disciples, furthering the cause with lectures and essays before withdrawing after disagreement with other leading Wagnerians.

Not surprisingly his first opera, *Urvasi*, was stylistically indebted to Wagner. Its auspicious premiere in Dresden (1886) was followed by *Heilmar der Narr* (Munich, 1892). Plans for a third opera based on Immermann's *Münchhausen* were abandoned in favour of *Der Evangelimann*, which was an immediate success and enjoyed over 5000 performances in 40 years. *Don Quixote* (1898) was more ambitious in its dramatic form but met with little acclaim. For *Der Kuhreigen* (1911) Kienzl composed his own setting of a *Wunderhorn* poem, 'Zu Strasburg auf der Schanz', which became a popular hit. The opera was also performed in England and the US.

In 1917 Kienzl moved from Graz. He took a lively interest in contemporary developments, recording his opinions eloquently in essays and newspaper articles, but his compositional style never progressed far beyond the tonal chromaticism of his early years. During the 1930s the pendulum of musical fashion swung against him; yet *Der Evangelimann* later enjoyed several nostalgic revivals (particularly with excerpts on disc) and even *Der Kuhreigen* was staged (1954) and broadcast (1983) in Vienna.

Compared with other German post-Romantics, such as Pfitzner, Humperdinck, Thuille and Siegfried Wagner, Kienzl is characteristically Austrian. He succeeded in integrating elements of *verismo* and folk opera into his scores, unifying them with a natural if simplistic melodic gift.

Der Evangelimann

The Bible Preacher
Musical play in two acts (1h 30m)
Libretto by the composer, after Leopold Florian Meissner's story, *Papiere eines Polizeikommissars*
Composed 1894
PREMIERES 4 May 1895, Berlin; UK: 2 July 1897, Covent Garden, London; US: 1 January 1924, New York

The setting is the monastery of St Othmar; Act I takes place in 1820, Act II in 1850. The story tells of a schoolmaster, Johannes, and his brother Mathias. Johannes is jealous of his brother's love for Martha, whose uncle (Friedrich Engel) is the local magistrate. Engel is informed of the clandestine love affair and forbids any further contact. During a scene of rustic merry-making, including a graphically depicted game of skittles, Johannes overhears a fond exchange between the lovers. Beside himself with anger, he sets fire to a barn. Mathias is charged as chief suspect and arrested. In Act II Johannes, on his deathbed, is tormented by memories of the past. A roving preacher appears (the scene, *Selig sind, die Verfolgung leiden*, became well known as a separate item); it is Mathias. He tells Magdalena, a friend of Martha's, of his 20 years' imprisonment and subsequent life of penance. She urges him to visit his brother. After a lengthy scene of anguish and repentance, Mathias forgives Johannes, who dies to the sound of children's voices.

While substantial portions of the score are reminiscent of Wagner's *Die Meistersinger*, Kienzl contrived to establish a credible spirit of musical realism occasionally interspersed with moments of cloying sentimentality, as for instance in Magdalena's aria, 'O schöne Jugendtage'.

RECORDING Donath, Wenkel, Jerusalem, Hermann, Moll, Bavarian Radio Ch, Munich Radio O, Zagrosek, Electrola, 1981
EDITION v.s., Bote und Bock, 1894

Other operatic works: *Urvasi*, 1886, rev. 1909; *Heilmar der Narr*, 1892, rev. 1902; *Don Quixote*, 1898, rev. 1934; *In Knecht Ruprechts Werkstatt*, 1907; *Der Kuhreigen*, 1911; *Das Testament*, 1916; *Hassan der Schwarmer*, 1925; *Sanctissimum*, 1925; *Hans Kipfel*, 1926
BIBLIOGRAPHY H. Hagen (ed.), *Festschrift: Wilhelm Kienzl*, Graz, 1917; Wilhelm Kienzl, *Meine Lebenswanderung*, J. Engelhorns Nachfolger, 1926

A.C.W.B.

LEON KIRCHNER
b 24 January 1919, Brooklyn, New York

Kirchner has gradually achieved a distinguished reputation as a composer of complex, but never avant-garde, music. His teachers included Schoenberg, Bloch and Sessions but his allegiances, as composer, pianist and conductor, have been to the First Viennese School as well as to the Second. Aaron Copland found Kirchner's music 'charged with an emotional impact and explosive power that is almost frightening in intensity'.

The dramatic qualities of Kirchner's music pointed towards Expressionist opera. He himself wrote the libretto for *Lily* (1977), based on the first half of *Henderson, the Rain King* by Saul Bellow. The story follows the experiences and self-discovery of a wealthy American, Gene Henderson, amid a primitive African tribe. The orchestra includes electronic tape. Several concert works are related to the opera, which was originally entitled *Why Are We in Vietnam?*

BIBLIOGRAPHY D. Ewen, *American Composers: A Biographical Dictionary*, Hale 1983

P.D.

VOLKER DAVID KIRCHNER
b 5 June 1942, Mainz, Germany

Kirchner studied composition in Mainz and Cologne with Gunter Raphael and Bernd Alois Zimmermann.

For many years an orchestral viola-player, by 1974 he had composed incidental music for more than 20 plays. *Riten* (1971), a short work for music-theatre, preceded his first opera, *Die Trauung* (1975), based on the play by Witold Gombrowicz. Its concern with the nature of inhumanity remains a constant theme in Kirchner's work. *Die fünf Minuten des Isaak Babel* (1980), a staged requiem, was followed by *Das kalte Herz* (1980), based on the tale by Wilhelm Hauff. His latest operas, *Belshazar* (1986) and *Erinys* (1990), are both concerned to examine the nature of man's striving for power.

Belshazar
Music drama (1h 15m)
Libretto by Harald Weirich
Composed 1984–5
PREMIERE 25 January 1986, Bayerische Staatsoper, Munich

An apocalyptic vision, *Belshazar* is a critique of civilization's overweening pride. The central image is the progressive disintegration of the tower of Babel. Daniel – in the opera he is Belshazar's son – protests in vain against the inanity of luxury and is lynched. The musical stream of consciousness makes use of certain set forms such as passacaglia, rondo and canon.

EDITION f.s./v.s., Schott, 1986

Erinys
Threnody in two parts (1h 15m)
Libretto by the composer and Harald Weirich, after the *Oresteia* by Aeschylus (458 BC)
Composed 1986–9
PREMIERE 15 April 1990, Wuppertaler Bühnen, Wuppertal

The plot is the familiar story of the murder of Agamemnon after his return from the Trojan War, and the revenge exacted by Electra and Orestes. A particularly memorable moment is the frenzied 'insanity' aria assigned to Cassandra who sings in ancient Greek – thus no one can understand her. The opera also makes use of elements of ancient Greek music.

EDITION f.s./v.s., Schott, 1990

BIBLIOGRAPHY Wolf-Eberhard von Lewinski, 'Ein komponierender Individualist. Volker David Kirchner', *Mainz. Vierteljahresheft für Kultur, Politik, Wirtschaft, Geschichte*, vol. 1 (1981), no. 3; Lotte Thaler, 'Rufer in der Wüste. Ein Gespräch mit Volker David Kirchner', *Neue Zeitschrift für Musik*, 1990, no. 6, pp. 21–8

A.C.

JAN KITTL
Jan Bedřich Kittl/Johann Friedrich Kittl; *b* 8 May 1806, Orlík nad Vltavou, Bohemia; *d* 20 July 1868, Lissa (now Leszno, Poland)

A composition student of Tomášek, Kittl was a progressive and influential Director of the Prague Conservatory (1843–65). Through his links with composers such as Liszt, Berlioz and Wagner, he was one of the first Czech Romantics, encouraging the new generation of Czech nationalist composers. He taught composition to the young Šebor, and was on the committee that awarded Count Harrach's opera prize to Smetana for his first opera, *The Brandenburgers in Bohemia*. He is chiefly remembered in operatic history for setting a libretto by Wagner.

Bianca und Giuseppe, oder Die Franzosen vor Nizza

Bianca and Joseph, or The French at Nice
Opera in four acts, Op. 31
Libretto by Richard Wagner, after the novel by Heinrich König
Composed c. 1847
PREMIERE 19 February 1848, Estates Theatre, Prague

Wagner wrote the libretto originally for himself and later (1842) revised it for Reissiger, who did not set it either. It deals with revolutionary events in Savoy-ruled Nice in 1793 and its premiere shortly before Prague's own revolution has been seen as a contributory factor, especially the march in Act II (based on the French revolutionary song 'Ça ira'), which was taken up by the Prague National Guard. The opera continued to be revived in Germany into the 1880s.

EDITION v.s., Breitkopf und Härtel, [1848]

Other operas: *Daphnis' Grab* (lost), (1825); *Die Waldblume*, 1852; *Die Bildersturmer*, 1854
BIBLIOGRAPHY John Tyrrell, *Czech Opera*, CUP, 1988

J.T.

GISELHER KLEBE

b 28 June 1925, Mannheim, Germany

Klebe, a contemporary of Hans Werner Henze and Pierre Boulez, studied with Boris Blacher and Josef Rufer. After the Second World War he occupied a leading position in the avant-garde Darmstadt circle – indeed some contemporary commentators mention him in the same breath as Stockhausen. Yet the ideals of that school harmonized uncomfortably with Klebe's expressive instincts.

In 1958 W. E. von Lewinski wrote: 'Klebe has evidently chosen the path [of synthesis] . . . Whether he will come to terms with his inner intellectual conflicts and attain an equilibrium, we cannot yet tell.' Klebe's retreat from strict serialism to a more popular operatic language did little to resolve this dichotomy. Neither in literary operas, such as Schiller's *Die Räuber* or *Ein wahrer Held* (based on

Synge's *The Playboy of the Western World*) nor in the more popular genre (e.g. Ödon von Horváth's amusing contribution to the Almaviva saga, *Figaro lässt sich scheiden*) does his music entirely free itself of arid eclecticism.

Operatic works: *Die Räuber*, 1957 (rev. 1962); *Die tödlichen Wünsche*, 1959; *Die Ermordung Cäsars*, 1959; *Alkmene*, 1961; *Figaro lässt sich scheiden*, 1963; *Jacobowsky und der Oberst*, 1965; *Das Märchen von der schönen Lilie*, 1969; *Ein wahrer Held*, 1975; *Das Mädchen aus Domrémy*, 1976; *Das Rendezvous*, 1977; *Der jüngste Tag*, 1979; *Die Fastnachtsbeichte*, 1983
BIBLIOGRAPHY H. H. Stuckenschmidt, 'Giselher Klebe', in *Die grossen Komponisten unseres Jahrhunderts*, vol. 1, Piper, 1971

A.C.W.B.

OLIVER KNUSSEN

Stuart Oliver Knussen; *b* 12 June 1952, Glasgow, Scotland

The precocious son of a leading double-bass player, Knussen burst into prominence when at the age of 15 he conducted a performance of his First Symphony by the London Symphony Orchestra. He took some time to recover from this experience, yet his adult music has fulfilled a lot, if not all, of that early promise. Two further symphonies and several shorter chamber-orchestral works (including some with soprano solo) testify to a brilliant feel for movement and sonority, and a bold sense of the voice as a dramatic instrument, all of which is borne out, within their self-imposed limitations, by his two short operas. A pupil of John Lambert and the American composer–conductor Gunther Schuller, Knussen is a perfectionist who takes a long time to finish a piece. His increasing success in the 1980s as conductor and artistic guru, in the UK and in the US, may therefore be bad news for fans of his music.

Where the Wild Things Are

Fantasy opera in one act, Op. 20 (40m)
Libretto by Maurice Sendak and the composer, after the children's book by Sendak (1963)
Composed 1979–83
PREMIERES 28 November 1980, Théâtre de la Monnaie, Brussels (inc.); UK: 22 March 1982, Queen Elizabeth Hall, London (inc.; concert); 9 January 1984, Lyttelton Theatre, London (Glyndebourne Opera); US: 8 June 1984, New York (concert), 29 September 1985, St Paul, Minnesota

Knussen describes the work as 'an attempt to revive and develop the fantasy opera', and he acknowledges the influence of Ravel's *L'enfant et les sortilèges*, Musorgsky's *Nursery* (and *Boris*), and Debussy's *La boîte à joujoux* (they are quoted). Sendak's picture book supplied both an intense, child's-nightmare atmosphere, and strong scenic ideas, and for the Glyndebourne production Sendak himself made designs based on his original drawings.

Max, a naughty little boy in a white wolf suit, is sent to bed by his mother without any supper. He dreams of revenge. His room turns into a forest, and a boat appears, in which he sails away to an island inhabited by Wild Things (dream monsters of a rather sinister amiability). He quells them with a look. They perform a frenzied, galumphing dance (the 'Wild Rumpus'), after which Max sends the Wild Things to bed without any supper. But he is homesick and hungry, and decides to sail home. The monsters wake up and chase him, but he sets sail safely, the sea and forest dissolve, and he is back in his bedroom. A supper tray is waiting for him, still hot.

With only one main character (Max, a high soprano), assorted monsters (with amplification) and a large mixed chamber orchestra, the stage is set for aural fantasy rather than music drama. Knussen not only quotes his favourite children's composers, but also satirizes the funny-noise school of modern music. But his score is typically discriminating and brilliantly composed, if sometimes too loud for the clear audibility of words.

RECORDING Hardy, King, Hetherington, London Sinfonietta, Knussen, Unicorn, 1985
EDITIONS f.s., Faber Music (on hire); lib., Faber Music, 1985

Higglety Pigglety Pop!
or *There must be more to life*
Second fantasy opera in one act, Op. 21 (1h)
Libretto by Maurice Sendak and the composer, after the children's book by Sendak (1967)
Composed 1983–5, rev. 1990
PREMIERES 13 October 1984, Glyndebourne (inc.); 5 August 1985, Glyndebourne, Sussex; US: 7 June 1990, Los Angeles

The original story for this companion piece to *Where the Wild Things Are* is both more wordy and more sophisticated. Jennie, a discontented sealyham dog, decides to leave home and seek her fortune, first devouring a potted plant which tries to dissuade her. She meets a Pig in sandwich-boards advertising for a leading lady for the World Mother Goose (i.e. 'nursery rhyme') Theatre. But the successful candidate must have 'experience'. She sets out to acquire it. A Cat Milkman mistakes her for Baby's new nurse, explaining that Baby's previous nurses have all been fed to the Downstairs Lion for failing to get Baby to eat. Jennie, too, fails but resolves to save the situation by taking Baby to its parents at Castle Yonder. On the way she meets the Lion, who is about to eat Baby when Jennie saves it by accidentally saying its name (a spoof reference to Puccini's *Turandot*). The Lion goes off with Baby, and Jennie sadly goes to sleep under an ash tree. But it turns out that she has now acquired the experience she needed, and she joins the World Mother Goose Theatre (the Pig, the Cat, the Lion and the maid Rhoda) in enacting the nursery rhyme that gives the opera both its title and its *dramatis personae*.

Less sharp in narrative than its predecessor, the work is not without a certain wan sentimentality offset by Knussen's penetrating ear for kindly

musical satire. The influence of American neo-tonalists such as David del Tredici is palpable. As with the 'Wild Things', Sendak based his designs for the Glyndebourne production on the illustrations in his book.

EDITION f.s., Faber Music (on hire); lib., Faber Music, 1985

BIBLIOGRAPHY Max Loppert, review of *Where the Wild Things Are*, *Opera*, vol. 35 (1984), pp. 328–31

S.W.

ZOLTÁN KODÁLY
b 16 December 1882, Kecskemét; *d* 6 March 1967, Budapest

Kodály ranks second only to Bartók among Hungarian composers of the 20th century, and the two were close associates in a number of enterprises, including the collecting, cataloguing, arrangement and publication of Hungarian folksongs. Kodály believed that only through the absorption of folk models could modern music reach a wide audience; and folksong was also part of the basis of his Singing Youth movement, founded in the 1930s, and of the so-called Kodály Method of music teaching that grew out of it and which still holds sway in Hungary. After the Second World War, Kodály was a dominant figure in Hungarian musical life.

His own music is folk-influenced, like Bartók's but less complex and introspective. His orchestral suites (sets of dances, and the suite from *Háry János*) are among the genuinely popular 20th-century works. But his best music was choral. Large choral works such as the *Psalmus hungaricus* (1923) and the *Missa brevis* (1944) remain staple repertoire, while Kodály's shorter unaccompanied choruses are a major contribution to the genre. Of his theatre works, the one-act *Székely fonó* (*The Székely Spinning-Room*) (1924–32; recorded by Hungaroton in the 1970s) consists almost exclusively of solo and choral settings of folktunes outlining a slender love story set in a Transylvanian village. The work is scarcely an opera, since the music is not dramatically conceived. *Háry János* and *Czinka Panna* (1946–8) are classified as singspiels; but there is much less music in either of them than in, say, *Die Zauberflöte*. *Czinka Panna* is notable for having a libretto by Béla Balázs, the librettist of Bartók's *Duke Bluebeard's Castle*.

Háry János
[*János Háry's Adventures from Nagyabony to the Vienna Burg*]
[*Háry János kalandozásai Nagyabonytul a Burgváráig*]
Singspiel in four adventures, a prologue and an epilogue, Op. 15 (1h 15m)
Libretto by Béla Paulini and Zsolt Harsányi, after János Garay's comic epic poem *Az obsitos* (*The Veteran*)
Composed 1925–6, rev. 1927
PREMIERES 16 October 1926, Operház, Budapest; UK: 28 November 1966, Camden Town Hall, London (concert);

Playbill for the world premiere of Háry János *(Budapest, 1926)*

March 1972, Abingdon (amateur); 24 July 1982, Opera House, Buxton; US: 18 March 1960, Juilliard School, New York

The Baron Münchhausen-like hero actually lived. He fought in the Napoleonic wars, and seems to have recounted his adventures to the poet János Garay, who wrote them down in the form of a narrative poem. For Kodály, Háry is 'the personification of the Hungarian story-telling imagination. He does not tell lies; he imagines stories, he is a poet. What he tells us may never have happened, but he has experienced it in spirit, so it is more real than reality.'

Háry sits in the bar of the inn at Nagyabony, his native village in Transdanubia, spinning yarns about his daring but improbable exploits. In his first adventure he moves a frontier guardhouse across the Russian–Hungarian border in order to free the Austrian emperor's daughter Marie-Louise (Napoleon's wife), who is imprisoned inside. As a reward she invites him, and his girlfriend Ilka, to Vienna to live in the imperial palace. There he tames a wild horse and cures the emperor with a magic potion from Nagyabony. Later Háry, promoted to colonel, leads the imperial army against Napoleon at the Battle of Milan, defeats the French army single-handed and takes Napoleon prisoner. Marie-Louise offers to divorce Napoleon and marry him, with half the empire as dowry, but he prefers to return to Nagyabony with Ilka.

The work is best described as a play with music,

and again there is a lack of integration of the music into the drama. The story is entirely told in spoken dialogue, merely coloured and enlivened by songs, choruses and orchestral interludes (some of which Kodály made into a suite in 1927). The basis is Hungarian folksong, and there is a big part for the cimbalom, the Hungarian peasant dulcimer. It should be added that the title gives the character's name in reverse (as always in Hungarian), and he should be thought of in English as János Háry.

RECORDING 1. Szönyi, László, Komlóssy, Melis, Bende, Ustinov, LSO, Kertesz, Decca, 1969: Ustinov tells the story (complete with funny accents) in English, while the music keeps its Hungarian text – a compromise, but effective; 2. Meszóly, Takács, Poka, Nagy, Gregor, Hungarian State Opera Ch and O, Ferencsik, Hungaroton, 1981
EDITION f.s., Universal (1962 version; on hire); v.s.s., Universal, 1929; with English text and production notes: Universal, 1983

BIBLIOGRAPHY László Eösze, trans. István Farkas and Gyula Gyulás, *Zoltán Kodály: His Life and Work*, Collet's, 1962

S.W.

JOONAS KOKKONEN
b 13 November 1921, Iisalmi, Finland

Kokkonen, the grand old man of Finnish music, studied composition and the piano at the Sibelius Academy, and musicology at Helsinki University. He taught at the Academy from 1949 to 1963, for the last four years as professor of composition (Sallinen was among his pupils). Having dabbled with serialism as a young man, he settled down to a very Nordic tonality (Sibelius still casts a long shadow north of the Baltic). He has a substantial body of symphonic, chamber and sacred music to his credit, and his one opera, phenomenally popular in Finland and much toured abroad, was one of the cornerstones of the Finnish operatic renaissance in the 1970s. Since opera was the one form in which Sibelius did not excel, Finnish composers were out on their own, and Kokkonen's contribution as exemplar was crucial.

The Last Temptations
Viimeiset kiusaukset
Opera in two acts (14 scenes) (2h 15m)
Libretto by Lauri Kokkonen, the composer's cousin
PREMIERES 2 September 1975, Helsinki, Finnish National Opera; UK: 12 June 1979, Sadler's Wells, London; US: 26 April 1983, Metropolitan, New York

The protagonist of *The Last Temptations* is a historical figure, the itinerant revivalist preacher Paavo Ruotsalainen (1777–1852) whose stern fundamentalism brought him into conflict with the established Lutheran Church. The action of the opera, admirably fluid in its treatment of time, is seen in dream flashback from Paavo's deathbed: his meeting with his first wife, Riitta (the chorus reminds her of privations to come); her reproachful encounter with the blacksmith who set Paavo on his fundamentalist path; the young couple's battles with the implacable Finnish climate; a scene when Riitta attacks him with an axe as he tries to leave on a preaching mission with the last loaf of bread left between her and their son's starvation; the accidental killing of their son and – in the Act I finale – Riitta's own death of exhaustion and grief. In Act II, Paavo, sometimes the worse for drink and not unaware of the attractions of loose women, is humiliated at various official ceremonies in the big cities. The people from his past gather at his deathbed, and settle accounts before, to the sound of a rousing hymn, he goes confidently to meet his God.

The question of whether or not he really deserved to do so seldom arose in performance, which is tribute to the depth in which the character is portrayed through the music, and to the magnificent, superhuman performance of the bass Martti Talvela, for whom the opera was written. The score is studded with big, self-questioning monologues for Paavo in the face of the Temptations – or more properly reminders of the sins from which no human is immune, in his case especially the sin of pride. The musical language is defiantly tonal, yet organized in quasi-serial terms from the hymn sung briefly in the first scene and returning as apotheosis in the last. There are big, rolling tunes, and buoyant rhythms in the public and dance scenes; to British ears, Vaughan Willliams is never far away. The work struck a deep chord in the Finnish soul, achieving 150 performances within five years of the premiere.

RECORDING   Auvinen, Ruohonen, Lehtinen, Talvela, Finnish National Opera Ch and O, Söderblom, DG, 1978
EDITION   v.s., Fazer, 1975
BIBLIOGRAPHY   Erik Tawastsjerna (ed.), *Essays on 'The Last Temptations'*, Helsinki, 1976 (in Finnish)

R.M.

ERICH WOLFGANG KORNGOLD

b 29 May 1897, Brno, Moravia; *d* 29 November 1957, Hollywood, California, US

One of the last great Romantic composers, Korngold is today remembered principally for his opera *Die tote Stadt* and for his numerous Hollywood film scores.

At the age of ten (through the influence of his father Julius Korngold, Vienna's foremost music critic) Korngold was introduced to Mahler who, declaring the boy a genius, sent him to Zemlinsky for composition lessons. When the 13-year-old Korngold's ballet *Der Schneemann* (orchestrated by Zemlinsky) was given a successful premiere at the Hofoper in 1910, the young composer was hailed as a *Wunderkind*. And by the time his first two operas, *Der Ring des Polykrates* and *Violanta*, were premiered – as a double-bill – in 1916, he had amassed a distinguished band of supporters, among them Richard Strauss, Nikisch, Carl Flesch and Artur

Schnabel, all of whom championed the young composer's works.

Appointed musical director of his regiment, Korngold was able to keep composing throughout the First World War, producing much-acclaimed incidental music to Shakespeare's *Much Ado About Nothing* (1919), and working on what was to be his most successful opera, *Die tote Stadt*. In the 1920s, much to his own enjoyment but to his father's disapproval, Korngold undertook the arrangement of several operetta scores; these included Johann Strauss II's *Eine Nacht in Venedig*, which consequently became one of the composer's most popular works. In the same year (1923) he began work on *Das Wunder der Heliane*. Korngold always considered the opera his masterpiece, but the combination of hostility between Julius Korngold and supporters of Krenek's opera *Jonny spielt auf* and the disappointment of a public who expected a repeat of *Die tote Stadt* resulted in a less than enthusiastic response to the work.

Erich Wolfgang Korngold, c. 1926

Korngold was warned by his publisher in 1932 that the increase of anti-Semitism would make future productions of his operas inconceivable. He went to Hollywood in 1934 and the following year eagerly accepted an invitation from Warner Brothers to write an original score for the film *Captain Blood*, starring Errol Flynn. Over the next 12 years Korngold wrote 18 full-length film scores, which he referred to as 'opera without singing', winning Oscars for *Robin Hood* and *Anthony Adverse*.

Korngold returned to Vienna in 1949 but found that critical opinion no longer applauded his essentially lyrical, neo-romantic style, favouring instead the austere atonal idiom of Schoenberg and his followers. When his fifth opera *Die Kathrin* received its Viennese premiere in 1950 (its world premiere had taken place in Stockholm in 1939), the critics condemned it as old-fashioned, although it enjoyed considerable success with the public. During his last decade Korngold returned to concert music, making certain moves in the direction of a modern style, notably in his Symphony in F♯ (1949–50). Although he had plans for a sixth opera, based on a story by Grillparzer, he completed only one more stage work, a musical comedy, *Silent Serenade* (1946). His last works included the arrangement, in 1954, of music by Wagner for *Magic Fire*, a film biography of the composer.

Der Ring des Polykrates

The Ring of Polycrates
Heitere oper in one act (ten scenes), Op. 7 (1h)
Libretto by Julius Leopold Korngold and Leo Feld, after Heinrich Teweles's lustspiel (1888)
Composed 1913–14
PREMIERES 28 March 1916, Hoftheater, Munich; UK: 15 June 1972, BBC Radio 3 (South German Radio recording)

After the sensational success of earlier works, Korngold's first opera aroused great expectations. It was premiered in a double-bill with *Violanta* under Bruno Walter.

A happily married young couple are put 'on trial' by an old friend whose lack of success, financially and domestically, contrasts sharply with the couple's situation. The friend tells the husband about Polycrates, a successful man who, to avert the gods' envy, sacrificed his dearest possession – his ring. The husband discovers that his wife once loved the friend, though more out of pity than desire, and she still wears his ring. When she hurls it out of the window the friend catches it and returns it. The jewel is restored, so the couple's only sacrifice can be their friend. He leaves and the couple sit down to read together.

Concise and melodic, *Der Ring der Polykrates* confirmed Korngold's natural feeling for the theatre. The late-Romantic musical language has obvious debts to Wagner's chromaticism and to Richard Strauss's tone-colours, while the use of unifying motifs as an important part of the work's structure was surely an element Korngold learned from his teacher Zemlinsky. But there are also many individual passages, among the best of which is the aria 'Kann's nicht heute fassen' sung by the wife to the accompaniment of muted strings, celesta, harp and flute.

EDITIONS f.s./v.s. Schott, 1916

Violanta

Opera in one act, Op. 8 (1h 15m)
Libretto by Hans Müller
Composed 1914–15
PREMIERES 28 March 1916, Hoftheater, Munich; US: 6 November 1926, New York

Fearing that *Der Ring der Polykrates* might be paired with an unsuitable partner, Korngold decided to write an accompanying piece himself. German operas with Renaissance settings were much in vogue during the First World War: *Violanta* followed Schillings's *Mona Lisa* (1915) and preceded Zemlinsky's *Der*

florentinische Tragödie (1917) and Schreker's *Die Gezeichneten* (1918).

Carnival Night in 15th-century Venice. Violanta wants revenge on Alfonso, the Prince of Naples, since her sister committed suicide after he seduced her. Violanta has invited him to visit her, her plan being that her husband, Simone, will murder him. She will sing a blasphemous Carnival song as a signal. When Alfonso arrives she tells him why he is there. Alfonso replies that for him life is a sham, death a welcome release. When they acknowledge their mutual love Violanta cannot bring herself to sing the song. But Alfonso urges her to, and as she does she throws herself between him and her husband's dagger and dies.

Korngold had, at 18, already mastered all the elements of musical language and produced a highly charged emotional score – an effect resulting from his densely chromatic harmony. High tessituras in the vocal writing also contribute to the intense mood. Although the opera is built around melodic and chordal motifs rather than themes, there is one – a Venetian Carnival song – that runs through the work; sung initially by the chorus as an expression of ribald revelry, it later becomes the signal for Alfonso's murder and finally an expression of love fulfilled in death.

RECORDING Marton, Jerusalem, Berry, Bavarian Radio Ch, Munich Radio O, Janowski, CBS, 1980
EDITIONS f.s./v.s., Schott, 1916

Die tote Stadt

The Dead City
Opera in three scenes ('Bilder'), Op. 12 (2h 15m)
Libretto by Paul Schott (pseudonym for Julius and Erich Korngold), after Georges Rodenbuch's novel *Bruges-la-Morte* (1892)
Composed 1917–19
PREMIERES 4 December 1920, Stadttheater, Hamburg and Opernhaus, Cologne; US: 19 November 1921, Metropolitan, New York
CAST Paul *t*, Marie/Mariette *s*, Frank *bar*, Brigitta *a*, Juliette *s*, Lucienne *ms*, Victorin *t*, Count Albert *t*, Fritz (a pierrot) *bar*; Gaston *mime*; *satb* chorus of spirits
FULL ORCHESTRA several offstage instruments, including organ, perc, wind-machine, 7 low bells, 4 tpt, 2 cl, 2 trbn

With this work Korngold reached his operatic zenith. Its portrayal of the psychological damage of excessive mourning struck a chord in the aftermath of the First World War. At the same time its novel structure – much of it is a dream sequence – and memorable music heightened its impact. Korngold played a piano reduction of the score to Puccini, on a visit to Vienna in 1920, and he considered the work 'the strongest hope of new German music'. Productions were rapidly mounted throughout Europe and it was the first German opera to be performed at the Metropolitan after the war.

SYNOPSIS
Act I Although Paul is gloomily obsessed with the memory of his dead wife Marie (he preserves a room full of her memorabilia) he has met the vivacious

Mariette and impetuously asks her to visit him. But Mariette leaves when she sees a portrait of Marie and realizes how much she resembles her. Paul is torn by his devotion to Marie and his feelings for Mariette. In a vision Marie bids him 'see and understand'.

Act II takes place in Paul's imagination: a fantastic sequence of scenes portraying the loss of his friends, Mariette being serenaded, rising from a coffin, arguing with Paul, realizing her rival is a dead woman and deciding to exorcize her predecessor's ghost.

Act III The dream continues, with Mariette eventually desecrating Marie's possessions. Goaded beyond endurance Paul strangles her with a plait of Marie's hair. When he wakes the plait is intact and, though the memory remains, the mourning is over.

Korngold's Expressionistic opera, with its hallucinatory passages, was adventurous but proved to be a great success; it has remained his most popular opera. As with *Violanta*, the music throughout is intense, with Korngold making full use of the vast forces he had scored for. Rather than relying on full-blown melodies to propel the action, Korngold organizes his music around a number of short motifs representing various people, places or other aspects of the story. Many of these motifs include the interval of a perfect fourth (or its inversion, the perfect fifth), which consequently takes on a pivotal role in the musical structure of the entire opera. There are, nevertheless, identifiable arias – notably 'Gluck, das mir verblieb', sung first by the vision of Marie and later repeated by Paul, and the 'Pierrotlied', which is a serenade to Mariette performed by one of her admirers. Both numbers have enjoyed widespread performance independent of the opera.

RECORDING   Neblett, Kollo, Prey, Luxon, Bavarian Radio Ch, Munich Radio O, Leinsdorf, RCA, 1975
EDITIONS   f.s./v.s. Schott, 1920

Das Wunder der Heliane
The Miracle of Heliane
Opera in three acts, Op. 20 (2h 15m)
Libretto by Hans Müller, after the mysterium *Die Heilige* by Hans Kaltneker (1917)
Composed 1924–6
PREMIERE   10 October 1927, Staatsoper, Hamburg

In the seven years after the triumph of *Die tote Stadt*, Germany's operatic taste radically changed. Zeitoper ('opera of our time') arrived, with plots involving ordinary people and everyday events, and music incorporating jazz and popular dance forms. *Heliane*, with its mystical plot and Expressionist music, was eclipsed by Ernst Krenek's phenomenally successful *Jonny spielt auf*. It nevertheless rivalled Krenek's work sufficiently for a Viennese cigarette manufacturer to bring out two new brands – the working man's 'Jonny' and the more sophisticated 'Heliane'.

Heliane, a pure beauty with miraculous powers, is imprisoned by her husband, the prince of a kingdom of darkness, when he suspects her of infidelity with a

stranger. To save Heliane's honour, the stranger kills himself. But Heliane, having declared her love for him, uses her powers to restore the stranger to life. Overcome by jealousy, the prince stabs her. Now, however, the stranger is able, through the power of love, to restore Heliane to life. The people proclaim the miracle of indestructible love.

Scored for immense forces, *Heliane* contains some of Korngold's most modernistic music, using a complex harmonic language of constantly shifting tonal centres which occasionally hints at bitonality. The music seems at times closer to the world of cinema than to opera (e.g. the orchestral introduction to Act III), although Heliane's Act II aria, 'Ich ging zu ihm', the best-known number of the opera, is reminiscent of Richard Strauss.

RECORDINGS   1. excerpt: Heliane's Act II aria, Lehmann (recorded 1928): on several reissues; 2. Tomowa-Sintow, Runkel, Gedda, De Haan, Walker, Pape, Berliner Rundfunk Ch and SO, Mauceri, Decca, 1993
EDITIONS   f.s./v.s. Schott, 1927

Die Kathrin
Catherine
Opera in three acts (nine scenes), Op. 28 (2h 30m)
Libretto by Ernst Decsey, after H. E. Jakob's novella *Die Magd von Aachen*
Composed 1931–7
PREMIERE   7 October 1939, Royal Opera, Stockholm

Kathrin loves a soldier. When he is transferred to Africa, she is taken up by a night-club owner whose advances she resists. His mistress jealously shoots him. The soldier, now demobbed and searching for Kathrin, is present at the murder. They are both arrested; each pleads guilty in order to save the other. The soldier is gaoled but on release, six years later, he finds Kathrin waiting for him.

The music taps a lyrical, popular vein – it abounds in good tunes (such as Kathrin's 'letter' song to the soldier) and vivid orchestration.

EDITIONS   f.s./v.s. Weinberger, 1937

Musical comedy: *Silent Serenade* (1946); arrangements of works by Johann Strauss, Offenbach, Leo Fall and Rossini
BIBLIOGRAPHY   Brendan G. Carroll, *Erich Wolfgang Korngold, His Life and Works*, Wilfion Books (The Music Makers Series, vol. 1), 1984; *rp*, 1987; Luzi Korngold, 'Erich Walter Korngold', *Österreichische Komponisten des 20 Jahrhunderts*, vol. 10, Lafite-Verlag, 1967

C.B.

ARGHYRIS KOUNADIS
b 14 February 1924, Constantinople

The Greek composer Kounadis studied the piano at the Athens Conservatory and composition with Yannis Papaioannou at the Hellenic Conservatory, from which he graduated in 1956. From 1958 to 1961 he studied composition with Wolfgang Fortner at the Musikhochschule in Freiburg, where, in 1963, he was appointed assistant professor. From 1967 to 1974 he directed the Musica Viva concerts, and from 1973 to 1989 held the post of professor of theory and composition.

Kounadis, who has a penchant for surrealism, parody and satire, has made use of aleatory and serial procedures, of *objets trouvés*, quotation and collage. His works for the stage are mainly comedies (*Der Gummisarg*, based on a text by Basileios Zioghas, pokes fun at the bourgeois attitude to death). But there is a more recent chamber opera, based on E. T. A. Hoffmann's story *Der Sandmann*.

Operatic works: *Der Gummisarg*, 1968 (originally *Der liebe Nachbar*, 1967); *Die verhexten Notenständer*, 1971; *Der Ausbruch* (withdrawn), 1974; *Teiresias*, 1975; *Die Bassgeige*, 1979; *Lysistrate*, 1983; *Der Sandmann*, 1987; *Epilogos*, 1990; *Die Wiederkehr* (1961, rev. 1974), 1991
BIBLIOGRAPHY Alicia Padrós, 'Interview with Arghyris Kounadis', *Programmheft 9*, Freiburger Theater, 1990

A.C.

ANDOR KOVÁCH

András Kovach; *b* 21 April 1915, Szaszváros, Hungary (now Romania)

A pupil of Kodály and Bartók, Kovách left Hungary after the war and worked in Germany (he taught composition at the Musikhochschule in Saarbrucken, 1947–8), then Brazil – where he founded the Museo d'Arte Orchestra in São Paolo and took Brazilian citizenship – and Switzerland, where he taught at the Lausanne conservatory from 1962. Later he was composer in residence at the Massachusetts Institute of Technology.

Apart from concert works, Kovách is the composer of five operas, three of which, including a setting of T. S. Eliot's *Murder in the Cathedral*, were until recently still unperformed. His one-act *Médée*, based on the play by Anouilh, presents a powerful psychological portrait of its protagonist, and was praised after its premiere for its strong sense of theatre, matching a Puccinian richness of resource to a style owing something to Bartók. Kovách's only other performed opera, *Le Rendez-vous*, is quite different: a 40-minute comic chamber opera (on a story by Christine Arnothy), with music incorporating a strong element of pastiche and borrowed tunes. Like *Médée*, it was first staged at Saarbrucken and later (1974) at Divonne-les-Bains, in a double-bill with Weill's *Mahagonny Songspiel*.

Operas: *Meurtre dans la cathédrale* (1957); *Médée* (1960), 1967; *Le Rendez-vous* (1964), 1971; *Bal des voleurs* (1970); *L'Apollon de Bellac* (1972)
BIBLIOGRAPHY O. Trilling, 'Divonne-les-Bains . . .' (review), *Opera*, vol. 25 (1974; festival issue), pp. 60–61

S.W.

KAREL KOVAŘOVIC

b 9 December 1862, Prague, Bohemia; *d* 6 December 1920, Prague

When Kovařovic became head of opera at the Prague National Theatre in 1900 – a post he retained until his death – he was recognized as an excellent all-round theatre musician with experience as an orchestral player (harp), répétiteur and conductor. He was also a seasoned composer, one of the few Czech composers of the time to try his hand at ballet, and had a string of operas to his name. His first, *The Bridegrooms*, was famously rubbished by Janáček in the pages of *Hudební listy* after its showing in Brno in 1887 where Kovařovic was then conductor (with near-tragic consequences for Janáček's career: for 12 years Kovařovic refused to stage Janáček's *Jenůfa* in Prague). A decade later Kovařovic wrote the opera that made his name and that became one of the most popular Czech operas of the time, *The Dogheads* (1897). He completed only one more opera; his creative career was sacrificed to his post at the National Theatre during its heyday.

The Dogheads
Psohlavci
Opera in three acts (2h 45m)
Libretto by Karel Šípek, after the novel by Alois Jirásek
Composed 1895–7
PREMIERE 24 April 1898, National Theatre, Prague

The 'Dogheads' of the title are the Czechs of Chodsko, a border region whose emblem is a dog's head. The Habsburgs' attempt to deny their ancient privileges (received for defending the border) sparked off their rebellion in 1695. Though the folk hero Kozina, the leader of the rebellion, is executed, his dying threat to his Habsburg oppressor Laminger is fulfilled: Laminger dies exactly a year after Kozina. Kovařovic turned this melodramatic tale into a vigorous, somewhat old-fashioned historical opera, with numerous opportunities for sentimental nationalism including an offstage unaccompanied folksong to open the piece, and a folk sequence of general merrymaking, including a bagpiper.

RECORDING excerpts: Blachut, Tikalová, Veselá, Bednář, Kovář, Jedenáctík, Otava, Prague NT Ch and O, Folprecht, Supraphon, 1950
EDITION v.s., Hudební matice, 1898; 4th edn, 1950

Other operas: *Armida* (inc.), (1888–95); *The Bridegrooms* (*Ženichové*), 1884; *The Way through the Window* (*Cesta oknem*), 1886 (rev. 1914, 1920); *The Night of St Simon and St Jude* (*Noc Šimona a Judy*; originally *Frasquita*), 1892; *At the Old Bleachery* (*Na starém bělidle*), 1901
BIBLIOGRAPHY John Tyrrell, *Czech Opera*, CUP, 1988

J.T.

JOSEPH MARTIN KRAUS

b 20 June 1756, Miltenberg am Main; *d* 15 December 1792, Stockholm

Set design by Louis Jean Desprez for Aeneas i Carthago *(Stockholm, 1799)*

Kraus was the most gifted and influential composer at the court of Gustav III in Sweden, and the principal founder of the school of opera founded by Gustav with the intention of creating a national Swedish art form. Gustav's approach to opera was derived from Gluck's reforms, and his ideals were best realized in two operas by Kraus: *Proserpin* and *Aeneas i Carthago* (*Dido och Aeneas*). Kraus's musical idiom is individual and easily recognizable: it features a bold, richly textured harmonic structure, the abundant use of motivic material and a rhythmic drive influenced by Viennese *Sturm und Drang*.

In 1782 Kraus went on extended leave from court, travelling abroad. In Vienna he met Gluck and claimed friendship with him. Gluck confided to Salieri, 'This man has great style.' In 1784 Kraus joined Gustav in Paris and heard a number of performances of Piccinni's *Didon*, a work that had a profound effect on Kraus and caused him to revise much of his own opera on the subject.

VB numbers refer to Bertil H. van Boer jnr, *Die Werke von Joseph Martin Kraus: Systematisch-Thematisches Werkverzeichnis*, Kungliga Musikalista Akademien, 1988.

Proserpin

Opera in one act, VB19 (1h 15m)
Libretto by Johan Henrik Kellgren, after Gustav III's design
Composed June 1780–March 1781
PREMIERE 1 June 1781, Ulriksdal Castle, Stockholm

On 16 June 1780 Count Hans Axel de Fersen (remembered today chiefly for his assistance to the French royal family during the French Revolution) took over the management of the Royal Opera. Four days later he presented Kraus with the commission for *Proserpin* in Stockholm. Kraus's protector, the theatre director Zibet, foresaw possible difficulties in a collaboration with the poet Johan Henrik Kellgren. Kraus had attacked Kellgren in print for his infatuation with the elaborate yet decorative rococo style of the 1760s. Zibet diplomatically smoothed the ruffled feathers of both artists and, as a result, the dream of Gustavian opera became a reality.

The action takes place in Sicily and concerns Atis' love for Proserpin, his infidelity towards Cyane, and Proserpin's abduction by Pluto. Atis in desperation throws himself into the crater of Etna, and Cyane, guilt-ridden at betraying Proserpin, enters the underworld. Cyane and Atis rise from the volcano to reveal that Pluto has made Proserpin his queen. As the god and his new consort ascend from the underworld, Jupiter descends from heaven and all pay homage to him.

MANUSCRIPT Kungliga Musikaliska Akademiens Bibliotek, Stockholm

Aeneas i Carthago (Dido och Aeneas)

Aeneas in Carthage (Dido and Aeneas)
Lyric tragedy in a prologue and five acts, VB23 (4h 30m)
Libretto by Johan Henrik Kellgren, after a design by Gustav

III, after the tragedy *Didon* (1734) by Jean-Jacques Le Franc, Marquis de Pompignan
Composed 1781–2; rev. 1784–90
PREMIERES   18 November 1799, Royal Opera, Stockholm; US: 26 March 1980, Alice Tully Hall, New York (concert)

In 1781 Kraus was commissioned to compose *Aeneas i Carthago* for the opening of the new Royal Opera House, scheduled for the following year. The plot had been designed by the king, and Kellgren supplied the libretto. By January 1782 the overture, prologue and the first two acts were complete. When the prima donna fled Sweden (presumably because of debts), the projected production was replaced by *Cora och Alonzo* by Johann Gottlieb Naumann. Kraus did not live to see his opera; it was eventually presented seven years after his death, and then in a drastically cut version.

A storm blows up on the orders of Juno, driving the Trojan fleet under Aeneas off course to Carthage. Guided by his mother, Venus, Aeneas finds Queen Dido. He and Dido prepare to take vows of fidelity, but there are ill omens and Aeneas is ordered by the goddess Honor to continue on his journey. This he does, but not before defending Carthage against the forces of Jarbas, the jealous King of Numidia. Distraught, Dido throws herself on to a pyre built to celebrate the Trojan victory.

As well as telling the human story, the drama also involves the gods, including, at the end of Act II, a fiery jealousy duet in which Venus confronts Juno. In the revised ending, Jupiter welcomes Dido to Olympus, and there follows an enormous ballet, a chaconne.

MANUSCRIPT   Kungliga Musikaliska Akademiens Bibliotek, Stockholm

Other operatic works: *Azire* (ballet and final chorus extant), (1778); *Fintberg's Wedding* (*Fintbergs Brollop*), 1788; *Soliman II, or The Three Sultans* (*Soliman II, eller De tre Sultaninnorna*), 1789 (RECORDING Virgin, 1990s); *The Adventurers, or The Journey to the Island of the Moon* (*Afventyraren, eller Resan til Månans ö*), (singspiel; overture, two scenes and final chorus by Kraus), 1791; 2 lost operas
BIBLIOGRAPHY   Hans Åstrand and Gunnar Larsson (eds), *Kraus und das Gustavianische Stockholm*, Royal Swedish Academy of Music, 1984; F. W. Riedel (ed.), *Joseph Martin Kraus und Italien*, Katzbichler, 1987

N.J.

IŠA KREJČÍ

Iša (František) Krejčí, *b* 10 July 1904, Prague, Bohemia; *d* 6 March 1968, Prague

A composition pupil of J. B. Jirák and Novák, Krejčí held conducting posts in Bratislava (1928–32), Prague radio (1934–45), and Olomouc (head of opera, 1945–58), where he introduced many contemporary works. From 1958 to his death he was dramaturg at the National Theatre in Prague. A composer with strong neo-classical leanings, his *oeuvre* includes a one-act

opera–oratorio *Antigona* (1933–4, revised 1959–63, performed 1968) and the opera *Uproar in Ephesus*.

Uproar in Ephesus

Pozdvižení v Efesu
Comic opera in two acts
Libretto by Josef Bachtík after Shakespeare's play *The Comedy of Errors* (1593)
Composed 1939–43
PREMIERE   8 September 1946, National Theatre, Prague

Krejčí's witty and transparent style is ideally matched with its subject to make this one of the most successful Czech comic operas of the 20th century. Krejčí's practical experience in the theatre is evident from the work's sure pacing and its delightful ensembles – one of the many conventional operatic forms that are cleverly exploited in the work.

RECORDING   excerpts: Wysoczanská, Hlobilová, Kovář, Zlesák, Jindrák, Otava, Heriban, Vonásek, Berman, Haken, Prague NT Ch and Smetana Theatre O, Brock, Supraphon, [n.d.]
EDITION   v.s., Hudební matice Umělecké besedy, 1953

BIBLIOGRAPHY   Ladislav Šíp, *Česká opera a jeho tvůrci* (*Czech Opera and Its Creators*), Supraphon, 1983

J.T.

ERNST KRENEK

b 23 August 1900, Vienna; *d* 23 December 1991, Palm Springs, California, US

Krenek was one of the most prolific creative artists of the 20th century. He responded tirelessly to its major cultural transformations and succeeded in staying in tune with most of its significant musical developments. Fascinated by the potential of the genre through most of his long working life, Krenek completed 21 operas – 11 in Europe before the outbreak of the Second World War, and 10 later in America – his new homeland – as well as other music for the stage.

Krenek's compositional output is remarkable for its stylistic range. The operas make unique use of that colourful harmonic and textural palette established by 20th-century modernists – tonality, atonality, dodecaphony and serialism, jazz, dance music and electronic sounds. They also embody his changing attitudes to music itself: the aim of opera – its aesthetic function, role in society, the relationship of its music to extra-musical ideas – became a dominant concern in the critical and musicological work that Krenek pursued alongside composition.

Brought up by music-loving bourgeois parents in the vicinity of the Viennese Volksoper, Krenek was one of the youngest and most famous of the Imperial Academy composition class tutored by Schreker. Following his teacher to Berlin in 1920, he concentrated initially on instrumental works, rapidly developing an abstract and atonal style seemingly at odds with his training, but in line with the latest avant-garde tendencies influenced by Mahler, Bartók and Schoenberg. His interest in the written word, experience as Paul Bekker's assistant at the opera in Kassel and Wiesbaden (1925–7) and contact with recent artistic developments in Paris (which he visited in 1926) prompted him to write dramatic music relevant to contemporary taste. The tendencies of his first three stage works, in which he explored tragedy and comedy in Expressionist and lighter styles, came to fruition spectacularly in his fourth – the neo-classical jazz opera, *Jonny spielt auf* (1926). No other work by Krenek made such an impact on the public, and his instant fame brought sufficient financial security to enable him to compose full-time.

A trio of appealing one-act works in burlesque operetta and fairy-tale style followed in the afterglow of *Jonny*, and a comic work written in the spirit of Karl Kraus about contemporary Vienna, *Kehraus um St Stephan* (1930), deemed too satirical to be performed. But Krenek had already moved on to more serious subjects and the world of grand opera with *Leben des Orest* (1929), which reflected his childhood affection for the classics, as had his earlier setting of Kokoschka's Expressionist retelling of the myth *Orpheus und Eurydike* (1923). For Krenek himself the most important work of his European years, if not his entire career, was *Karl V* (1933), a philosophically complex and musically innovative work – the first full-length 12-note opera – which offended the authorities and led to enforced exile.

In America, after an initial period of obscurity, Krenek became increasingly sought after as a university teacher and wrote the chamber operas *Tarquin* (1940), *What Price Confidence?* (1945), *Dark Waters* (1950) and *The Belltower* (1956). Twenty years after *Karl V* he returned to large-scale opera. Prompted by renewed European interest in his music and the political conflicts caused by McCarthyism, Krenek revised *Karl V*, and completed two new works (for performance in Germany) inspired by Classical antiquity: *Pallas Athene weint* (1955) and *Der goldene Bock* (1963), the latter for the inauguration of Hamburg's new opera house. Krenek's later operas mark a return to his inimitable comic streak and predilection for special effects: *Ausgerechnet und verspielt* (1962), about gambling with computers which used serial techniques – one of two operas written for television – and the satirical parody *Sardakai* (1969). Thereafter Krenek continued to be fascinated by the possibilities of staged vocal music, working on chamber concert pieces (some using electronics) rather than opera.

Krenek explored the possibilities of opera to the full, experimenting with a variety of artistic intentions and expanding its expressive means. His earliest works were candidly zeitoper, but his subsequent stage works were also intended to have a contemporary application, even when set in the past. According to Krenek, all his operas reveal facets of his philosophical preoccupation with various conceptions of freedom. Most of his works are conspicuously absent from today's operatic repertoire.

Der Sprung über den Schatten

The Leap over the Shadow
Comic opera in three acts, Op. 17 (1h 30m)
Libretto by the composer
Composed 1922–3
PREMIERE 9 June 1924, Opernhaus, Frankfurt

Der Sprung was apparently the first opera to incorporate jazz. Its use is, however, more parodistic than authentic, in keeping with the satirical tone of the work, which makes fun of the fashion for psychoanalysis. The libretto concerns a poet, Goldhaar, and a married princess, Leonore, who are in unconfessed love with each other. Leonore's husband, Prince Kuno, hires a detective to spy on his wife. A hack psychoanalyst, Dr Berg, assumes the role because he also desires Leonore. At a masked ball where the dancers are trying to leap, to a mildly bluesy score, over their shadows in imitation of what they regard as the free-spirited hedonism of Negro foxtrotters, Goldhaar and Leonore meet. Goldhaar is mistaken for Dr Berg, arrested, accused of trying to seduce Leonore by means of hypnotism and spiritualism and tried to the accompaniment of a rather complicated fugue. Suddenly a revolution breaks out, the people overthrow Kuno's old regime and elect Dr Berg president of their newly formed republic. The lovers elope, and the popular voice wins the day.

The music caricatures atonal Expressionism, associating it with Dr Berg in scenes of absurdity and confusion. Various satirical allusions are also made to Mozart, Beethoven and Richard Strauss, using elaborate contrapuntal techniques. In spring 1928 *Der Sprung* became the first contemporary Western opera to be staged in the Soviet Union. It was then forgotten until its revival at Bielefeld in 1989.

RECORDING Kemeny, Dürmüller, Pflieger, Brüning, Bielefeld Stadttheater Ch and PO, de Villiers, CPO, 1989
EDITION v.s., Universal, 1923

Orpheus und Eurydike

Orpheus and Eurydice
Opera in three acts (11 scenes), Op. 21 (1h 45m)
Libretto: a reduction by the composer of the play by Oskar Kokoschka (1915, rev. 1917)
Composed 1923
PREMIERE 27 November 1926, Kassel

Kokoschka's version of the Orpheus myth is a modern psychological interpretation steeped in the artist's traumatic reactions to his First World War experiences and the ending of his relationship with Alma Mahler. The main twist in the traditional tale is that Orpheus' love turns to hatred when he learns of Eurydike's seduction by Hades in the underworld: a ring he had once given her is found in the jaws of a skull caught in the net of the ship taking them back to a new life. Mad with jealousy and with a storm raging, Orpheus murders her, thus condemning her to return to the underworld. Several years later a vision of his beloved appears to Orpheus as he is being hanged by a vicious mob; the ghost begs for release from its role in his torment. Orpheus, however, continues to deny Eurydike, choosing instead to triumph in his nihilism.

The music is completely atonal, powerfully traversing extremes of vocal and orchestral expression. Krenek's response to Kokoschka's hallucinatory style of writing was to underpin the poetic conception with music having its own expressionistic and symbolic autonomy. Intervallic motifs (notably fourth chords inspired by Debussy's *Pelléas*) structure and illuminate the chief psychological moments and events of the narrative. Initially acknowledged as one of Krenek's finest works, *Orpheus und Eurydike* was subsequently eclipsed by the enthusiasm for *Jonny*.

EDITION v.s., Universal, 1925

Jonny spielt auf
Jonny Strikes Up
Opera in two parts (11 scenes), Op. 45 (2h)
Libretto by the composer
Composed 1925–6
PREMIERES 10 February 1927, Stadttheater, Leipzig; US: 19 January 1929, Metropolitan, New York; UK: 14 November 1984, Grand Theatre, Leeds
CAST Max *t*, Anita *s*, Jonny *bar*, Daniello *bar*, Yvonne *s*, 4 *t*, *bar*, *b*; *satb* chorus of hotel guests, travellers and audience
FULL ORCHESTRA including t-t, flexaton, swannee whistle, cel, sax, loudspeaker, clock, radio, siren; onstage: jazz band

One of the greatest hits in 20th-century operatic history, this lively and thought-provoking work is a tribute to Krenek's diverse talents. Its capacity to entertain surprised both the musical establishment and the general public in Germany, where it achieved a record number of performances on more than 30 stages in its first season. Acclaimed for both its musico-dramatic dynamism and its kaleidoscopic impression of central European culture, which lent itself well to avant-garde staging, the opera also triumphed in more than 20 foreign cities over the next two years, although its New York and Parisian receptions were comparatively cool.

SYNOPSIS
Part I Max, a brooding intellectual composer (possibly a self-portrait), meets Anita, a sensual prima donna, on top of a glacier. Later at her house in a Central European city they begin an affair which results in the composition of a new opera. In Paris for its performance, Anita is unfaithful to Max with Daniello, a virtuoso violinist and womanizer. Meanwhile Jonny, a saxophonist performing at the hotel, steals Daniello's valuable violin. Blamed for the theft, Yvonne, a chambermaid, is sacked and returns with Anita to Germany as her maid. Jonny follows in pursuit having concealed the violin in Anita's banjo case.

Part II Max yearns for Anita's return, but on learning of her infidelity he seeks solace back in the Alps where he communes with a singing glacier. The sound of a loudspeaker transmitting a radio broadcast of Anita singing his aria, however, saves him and he decides to seek a new life with her just as Jonny's jazz band comes on the air. A police car-chase ends up in a railway station where Daniello is crushed by the locomotive arriving in the nick of time to take all the others, led by Jonny tuning up on the violin, to America.

Scene in the Alps, from Jonny spielt auf *(Leipzig, 1927)*

The music is striking in its juxtaposition of the dissonant chromaticism and traditional forms of the Second Viennese School with lyrically tonal Italianate romanticism and a Teutonic brand of jazz constructed from simple melodies, repetitive rhythms and seventh chords. The label 'jazz opera' is slightly misleading because Krenek's usage is textural rather than organic. The different styles successfully convey Krenek's idea that only an infusion of Jonny's uninhibited and 'primitive' American jazz can revitalize European music and thus its people, to whom such music appeals more than Max's.

Krenek expressed his commitment to bridging the divide between high art and popular culture in this opera's carnivalesque spirit and symbolic associations. More attention has, however, been paid to the opera's superficial aura of the exotic, and implicitly to Krenek's youthful desire for fame, than to any deeper meaning in the work. Yet *Jonny's* indulgence in the fashionably escapist fantasies of *Amerikanismus* was no less significant or influential than Kurt Weill's didactic brand of zeitoper, which promoted socio-political ideas more explicitly.

RECORDINGS 1. Popp, Lear, Blankenship, Feldhoff, Stewart, Vienna Academy Ch, Vienna Volksoper O, Hollreiser, Amadeo, 1960s; 2. Marc, Kruse, St Hill, Kraus, Scholz, Leipzig Opera Ch, Leipzig Gewandhaus, Zagrosek, Decca, 1993
EDITIONS f.s./v.s., Universal, 1926

Der Diktator

The Dictator
Tragic opera in one act (two scenes), Op. 49 (35m)
Libretto by the composer
Composed 1926
PREMIERE 6 May 1928, Staatstheater, Wiesbaden

Like the two other one-act operas – *Das geheime Königreich* and *Schwergewicht* – premiered with it, *Der Diktator* is true to the idiom and spirit of *Jonny*. These three zeitopers are usually presented as a set, but they are not strictly speaking a trilogy, even though they all explore facets of the nature of power.

The central figure of this first work is a caricature of Mussolini, but draws a psychological rather than political portrait. The plot focuses on the dictator as a womanizer, and the consequences of his lust for a blind officer's wife, Maria, who seeks him out intending to kill him, blaming him for her husband's disablement. Face to face with him, her emotional and physical state undergoes a rapid transformation as the dictator's hypnotic attractiveness overwhelms her and she offers him her body instead. The dictator's wife, Charlotte, arrives and, aiming at her husband, shoots Maria who throws herself into the bullet's path. The blind officer stumbles on to the scene screaming, and then mourning, for his dead wife.

True to the spirit of 'new objectivity' in the arts, Krenek's music is realistically evocative, using a clean, basically tonal neo-classical style akin to contemporary works by Hindemith or Prokofiev. The orchestral writing is full of humour and pathos, becoming both dramatically distorted and strikingly compressed in response to the anxiety and confusion inherent in the drama.

EDITIONS f.s./v.s., Universal, 1928

Das geheime Königreich

The Secret Kingdom
Marchenoper in one act (12 scenes), Op. 50 (55m)
Libretto by the composer
Composed 1926–7
PREMIERE 6 May 1928, Staatstheater, Wiesbaden

A king, under pressure from a rebellious people, abdicates, giving his crown to a fool. The fool had told him that he would suffer until he could find the right answer to the riddle: 'What contains the whole world in itself?' Ladies-in-waiting at the court try to seduce the fool. Then the ambitious queen wins the crown at cards, but is persuaded to give it to the strongest of the rebels. On discovering that the rebel only wants to kill her she flees into the forest after the king, pursued by her assailant. Undressing to try and ward off her attacker, the queen is magically transformed into a tree. Two drunken revolutionaries appear looking for the king, who, now dressed in the fool's clothes, wants to surrender. But the revolutionaries refuse to acknowledge him as king and, disillusioned, he prepares to hang himself from the tree. Suddenly the voice of his queen rings out telling him to take another look at the wonders of the world around him: the magic of nature is the answer to the fool's riddle.

Krenek makes effective use of contrasting musical idioms in response to the changing dramatic situation, e.g. the attempt to seduce the fool is accompanied by strains of a tango, steady in rhythm but veering harmonically between tonality and atonality. Although the opera is more consistently atonal than the others in the trilogy, its concluding scenes contain some of Krenek's most attractive tonal lyricism, such as the beautiful self-contained 'forest murmurs' chamber interlude which opens the second scene with notably luxuriant solo violin-writing and fluttering flutes articulating the secrets of the wood.

EDITIONS f.s./v.s., Universal, 1928

Schwergewicht, oder Die Ehre der Nation

Heavyweight, or The Pride of the Nation
Burlesque operetta in one act, Op. 55 (25m)
Libretto by the composer
Composed 1926–7
PREMIERE 6 May 1928, Staatstheater, Wiesbaden

Schwergewicht is a satire on the popularity of boxing and other sports in Germany and mocks the belief that sporting heroes were more capable of winning respect and acclaim for the nation than artists or intellectuals – a view that had been recently expressed by the German ambassador to the US. The choice of a prizefighter, Ochsenschwanz (Oxtail), as central character was inspired by the contemporary champion Max Schmeling. In his opera-buffa-style plot, Krenek shows the power of the heavyweight to be illusory outside his own sphere. Ochsenschwanz is duped by Gaston, a dancing master, who runs off with Evelyn, the champion's wife, leaving him strapped to an electric exercise machine at which he is shown being presented with various honours for his efforts on behalf of the nation. The colourful orchestration, incorporating banjo, flexatone, glockenspiel, tambourine and xylophone, enhances the light and witty character of the whole work.

EDITIONS f.s./v.s., Universal, 1928

Leben des Orest

The Life of Orestes
Grand opera in five acts (eight scenes), Op. 60 (2h)
Libretto by the composer, partly after Euripides
Composed 1928–9
PREMIERE 19 January 1930, Stadttheater, Leipzig

Leben des Orest is an ambitious, classically inspired work, which was intended to be musically and dramatically *aktuell*, that is, human, direct and relevant. Krenek's aim was to represent 'people of our own time who express their being and essence in the loosely depicted milieu of the timeless greatness of an eternal fable', and thus to comment on the fascist threat in Europe. The opera is concerned with the legendary liberation of Orestes from a brutal and animalistic way of life into one grounded in reason

Set design by Giorgio de Chirico for Orest's years of travel in the Krolloper production of Leben des Orest *(Berlin, 1930)*

and humanity. Based partly on Euripides, but augmented by two newly invented characters, the plot traces Orestes' journey through life from the savage murder of his mother and Aegisthus to his divine emancipation. In writing the work, Krenek recognized the need for music that was more emotional than the comic objectivity that had characterized his recent operas.

The music is neo-romantic and broadly tonal, signifying Krenek's continued desire to speak to his audience in an approachable lingua franca. There are some notable Schubertian touches, jazzy elements (which offset his portrait of Agamemnon), and dance music for the pleasure-loving Athenians.

EDITIONS f.s., Universal, 1930; v.s., Universal, 1929

Karl V

Charles V
Play with music in two parts, Op. 73 (3h)
Libretto (and English translation 1943) by the composer
Composed 1931–3; rev. 1954
PREMIERES 23 June 1938, Deutsches Theater, Prague; rev. version: 11 May 1958, Deutsche Oper am Rhein, Düsseldorf
CAST Karl V *character bar*, Juan de Regla *spoken role*, Juana *a*, Isabella *s*, Eleanore *s*, Luther *bar*, Sultan Soliman *bar*, Franz I *t*, Pope Clement VII *spoken role*, 4 *t*, 10 other *spoken roles*; offstage: God *t*; *satb* chorus of ghosts, monks, nuns, peasants and farmers
FULL ORCHESTRA onstage: tpts, bells, cym, thunder-machine

During the year Krenek spent researching the life of the 16th-century Holy Roman Emperor Charles V, his ideas about opera and its social role altered in response to the rapidly changing political and cultural situation of Europe in the early 1930s. As a result, Krenek built into this work his new-found belief that opera should have an intentionally spiritual function, and made *Karl V*, in his own words, 'explicitly anti-Nazi, pro-Austrian and Catholic'. The drama interpreted the meaning of the events of Karl's life in such a way as to encourage the audience to relate the nationalism which he thought

had destroyed Karl to that now also destroying Europe under the influence of Hitler. *Karl V* is perhaps Krenek's most ambitious work, but its conception as a kind of festspiel for national Austrian regeneration came too late to have the effect he had hoped, and his intentions were misunderstood in the climate of shifting Austrian political allegiances. The cancellation of the work in rehearsal at the Vienna Opera, which had commissioned it, was a bitter disappointment for Krenek and, his music already banned by the Nazis in Germany, he was forced into exile in the US in 1934. In 1984 the original version was produced at the Wiener Staatsoper, a tribute to the high esteem in which Krenek had come to be held in his native land.

The plot is presented as an on-going discussion between Karl V and his confessor. Flashbacks to significant moments take place in which events from Karl's life are selected and presented in a fluid and fragmented form rather than set numbers against the background of a divided stage. Philosophical and theological debate takes place in the foreground to suggest the broader political consequences of events resulting from Karl's decisions for the empire and its future development. Krenek's Karl is both a psychological subject and the object of a divine plan.

SYNOPSIS
Part I On his deathbed in the monastery of San Geronimo de Yuste in Spain, Karl is called by the voice of God to account for what he has achieved. Historical events are recalled such as the appearance of Luther at the Diet of Worms.

Part II Karl is afflicted by religious doubts and the question of his judgment is left to God rather than mankind. Finally, reminiscences of the past and present come together with Krenek's own vision for Austria made explicit.

The music uses 12-note technique exclusively, because at that point Krenek believed it to be intrinsically 'universal', and thus capable of achieving a mystical affinity with the dogmatic systematization of the Catholic Church. It also suggested a connection between the role of individual pitches within the chromatically based musical system and the relationship of the individual to political and religious institutions within society, both of which fit in with the overall theme of unity in the work. The constraints of the technique did not restrict Krenek's use of certain chords to create a network of symbolic relationships (C is important as a central note), nor his sense of rhythmic play and soaring lyricism.

RECORDING Jurinac, Schwarz, Schreier, Adam, Melchert, Hoffmann, Ch and O of ORF, Albrecht, Amadeo, 1980
EDITIONS f.s./v.s., Universal, 1933

What Price Confidence?

Vertrauenssache
Comic chamber opera in nine scenes, Op. 111 (40m)
Libretto by the composer
Composed 1944–5

PREMIERES 22 May 1962, Saarbrucken; US: 1970, Western Opera, San Francisco; UK: 27 April 1982, Clarendon College, Nottingham (East Midland Music Theatre)

A short, witty 12-tone work for four characters (two sets of lovers) and piano which, with its unorchestrated score and sharply well-knit script, is more of a play with music than an opera. For his first English language libretto Krenek set the action in London, with scenes including a suicide attempt from Waterloo Bridge and an assignation in the British Museum.

EDITION f.s., Bärenreiter, 1945

Pallas Athene weint
Pallas Athene Weeps
Opera in three acts, Op. 144 (2h 30m)
Libretto by the composer
Composed 1952–5
PREMIERE 17 October 1955, Staatsoper, Hamburg

This serious and important work marks a return to Krenek's humanistic philosophizing around live political issues, which he intended to have a universal application as well as an explicitly topical one. Inspired by what he considered to be the first real threat to democracy since the end of the Second World War, Krenek reinterpreted the life of Socrates in terms of his own reactions to McCarthyism (the figure of Melethos is inspired by the role of the senator) in the context of the downfall of democracy in Athens following the end of the Peloponnesian War. The profound message of the opera is enhanced by intense, passionate music: for example, the tragic tones of a solo voice in the introduction representing the Athenian goddess of wisdom mourning in Elysium over a muted bass drum roll. The orchestra has its own dramatic autonomy enabling it to represent emotions behind the actions on stage; it does not merely shadow the vocal lines, which have their own note rows and characteristic intervallic motifs. In 1954 Krenek created a symphony (Op. 137) from sections of the music.

EDITIONS f.s./v.s., Schott/Universal, 1955

Sardakai, oder Das kommt davon (Das kommt davon, oder Wen Sardakai auf Reisen)
Sardakai, or That Gets Away
Comic opera in one act (two parts), Op. 206
Libretto by the composer
Composed 1969
PREMIERE 27 June, 1970, Hamburg

One of Krenek's opera-buffa satirical works, *Sardakai* was commissioned by the Hamburg State Opera who requested a work using the same vocal forces as *Così fan tutte*. Krenek actually took a sub-plot from Mozart's opera, elaborating the bet made about women's fidelity into a complicated farce mocking on the one hand political radicalism and on the other Hollywood-style pornographic fantasy. The work's reputation has suffered from its controversial initial production, which emphasized the communist–capitalist conflict between Sardakai, virgin queen of a fictional South Seas island – Migo Mogo – and Urumuru, a revolutionary leader based in the European Romadra, thus seeming to focus attention on contemporary conflicts between the US, Cuba, Vietnam and Cambodia. Its outwardly frivolous Mozartian-style satire, involving sexual and military subterfuge manipulated by a psychiatrist and a poet, appeared absurd rather than entertaining. The music is composed in a complex serial style, but is employed more like incidental music illustrating a play text than as an integral part of the drama. It comes into its own only during scene changes, where it serves to create different moods, and at the end of the work where, as the ultimate joke, music by Mozart is played on the beach party's radio.

EDITION f.s., Bärenreiter, 1970

Other operatic works: *Die Zwingburg*, 1924; *Bluff*, (1925); *Kehraus um St Stephan*, (1930); *Cefalo e Procri*, 1934; *Tarquin*, (1940), 1950; *Dark Waters*, 1950; *The Belltower*, 1957; *Ausgerechnet und verspielt*, 1962; *Der goldene Bock*, 1964; *Der Zauberspiegel*, 1966

BIBLIOGRAPHY Garrett H. Bowles, *Ernst Krenek: A Bio-Bibliography*, Greenwood Press, 1989; Ernst Krenek, *Horizons Circled: Reflections on My Music*, University of California Press, 1974; John L. Stewart, *Ernst Krenek: The Man and His Music*, University of California Press, 1991

C.I.P.

CONRADIN KREUTZER
Conradin [Conrad] Kreutzer [Kreuzer]; *b* 22 November 1780, Messkirch, Baden; *d* 14 December 1849, Riga

Kreutzer was among the most prolific German theatre composers of his generation and a widely esteemed conductor. He wrote his one-act singspiel *Die lächerliche Werbung* while studying law at Freiburg University. In 1804 he went to Vienna and probably studied with Albrechtsberger. In Stuttgart, after the successful production of his operas *Konradin von Schwaben* and *Feodora*, he succeeded Danzi as hofkapellmeister in 1812. After a period as kapellmeister in Donaueschingen (1818–22) he was appointed kapellmeister at the Kärntnertortheater in Vienna, where his *Libussa* had been successfully produced in December 1822. Later engagements included a period in Paris (1827–9) and at the Theater in der Josephstadt (1833–5). His last years were spent largely accompanying his daughters Cäcilie and Marie on their singing engagements.

Influenced by Mozart, Beethoven, Schubert and contemporary French opera, Kreutzer's works are frequently described as typically 'Biedermeier' compositions – generally lightweight and undemanding. Most disappeared rapidly from the repertoire, probably due to their dramatic limitations. However, *Das Nachtlager in Granada* and the incidental music for Raimund's märchenspiel *Der Verschwender* (1834) proved more durable;

Raimund's play is still often performed in Austria with Kreutzer's music.

Libussa

Libuše
Romantic opera in three acts (2h 30m)
Libretto by Joseph Karl Bernard
PREMIERE 4 December 1822, Kärntnertortheater, Vienna

This was Kreutzer's first significant success and was widely produced in other cities during the few years after its premiere, securing the composer a national reputation. The libretto, by the author of the libretto of Spohr's *Faust* (1813), deals with an episode in Bohemian history (which was also to provide Smetana with an opera plot nearly 60 years later). Kreutzer rejects any nationalistic political overtones in favour of a simple tale of country love. Both libretto and music were highly praised at the time of the premiere.

EDITION v.s., Pennauer, 1822

Melusine

Romantic magic opera in three acts
Libretto by Franz Grillparzer
PREMIERE 27 February 1833, Königsstädtisches Theater, Berlin

Grillparzer's libretto was originally written for Beethoven who, however, disliking supernatural subjects, declined to set it. The text, which deals with the love of a mortal for a mermaid, was severely criticized at the premiere, although Kreutzer's music was praised. It makes extensive use of melodrama. The opera possibly prompted Mendelssohn to compose his *Fair Melusine* overture.

EDITION lib., J. B. Wallishauser, 1833

Das Nachtlager in Granada

The Night Camp in Granada
Romantic opera in two acts (2h 15m)
Libretto by Karl Johann Braun von Braunthal, after the play by Johann Friedrich Kind (1818)
PREMIERES 13 January 1834, Theater in der Josephstadt, Vienna; UK: 13 May 1840, Prince's Theatre, London; US: 15 December 1862, New York

By far Kreutzer's most popular opera, it was widely performed in Germany and abroad and has been occasionally revived in Germany this century. *Das Nachtlager in Granada* was admired for its attractive melodic qualities; the simple folklike songs (especially 'Ein Schütz bin ich' and the *a cappella* chorus 'Schon die Abendglocken klangen', which have remained popular as individual items) show Kreutzer at his best. The orchestration is elaborate and varied, with the Moorish setting allowed for some exotic colour. For a revival at the Kärntnertortheater in 1837, Kreutzer replaced the spoken dialogue with recitative.

RECORDING Ammersfeld, Fassler, Illavsky, Ruzicka, Arnold Schönberg Ch, Vienna Academy O, Etti, Preiser, [*c.* 1978]
EDITION v.s., Trentensky und Vieweg, [*c.* 1834]

Since many of Kreutzer's stage works were occasional pieces their dating and identification is difficult, and the borderline between opera and incidental music is not easy to draw. This list is undoubtedly imperfect: *Die lächerliche Werbung, c.* 1800; *Die zwei Worte, oder Die Nacht im Walde*, ?1803; *Aesop in Phrygien* [*Lydien*], ?1808; *Jery und Bätely*, 1810; *Panthea*, (1810); *Konradin von Schwaben*, 1812; *Feodora*, 1812; *Die Insulanerin*, 1813; *Der Taucher*, 1813, rev. 1823; *Alimon und Zaide, oder Der Prinz von Katanea*, 1814; *Die Nachtmütze* (*Die Schlafmutze* [*des Propheten Elias*]), 1814; *Die Alpenhütte*, 1815; *Der Herr und seiner Diener*, 1815; *Orestes*, 1818; *Cordelia*, ?1819; *Siguna*, 1823; *Erfüllte Hoffnung*, 1824; *Die lustige Werbung*, 1826; *Der Besuch auf dem Lande*, 1826; *Jadis et aujourd'hui*, 1826; *La folle de Glaris* (?a version of *Cordelia*), 1827; *L'eau de jouvenance*, 1827; *Die Insulanerinnen*, 1829 (rev. of *Die Insulanerin*); *Das Mädchen von Montfermeuil* (also as *Denise*, and *Das Milchmädchen*), 1829; *Baron Luft* (*Baron Lust*), 1830; *Die Jungfrau*, 1831; *Die Hochländerin*, (1831); *Der Lastträger an der Themse*, 1832; *Tom Rick, oder Der Pavian*, 1834; *Der Bräutigam in der Klemme*, 1835; *Die Höhle bei Waverley*, 1837; *Fridolin, oder Der Gang nach dem Eisenhammer*, 1837; *Die Verjüngerungsessenz* (rev. of *L'eau de jouvenance*), 1838; *Die beiden Figaro*, 1840; *Der Edelknecht*, 1842; *Des Sangers Fluch*, 1846; *Die Hochländerin am Kaukasus* (?rev. of *Die Hochländerin*), 1846; *Konradin der letzte Hohenstaufe* (rev. of *Konradin von Schwaben*), 1847; *Aurelia, Herzogin von Bulgarien* (*Die Prinzessin von Bulgarien*), 1849; *Zenobia*, (1849); *Der Apollosaal*, (n.d.); *Adela von Budoy* (?*Cordelia*); additional music for Auber's *Le serment, ou Les faux-Monnayeurs*, 1834, and for Hérold's *Ludovic*, 1834
BIBLIOGRAPHY K. P. Brecht, *Conradin Kreutzer: Biographie und Werkverzeichnis*, Messkirch, 1980

C.A.B.

RODOLPHE KREUTZER

b 16 November 1766, Versailles, France; *d* 6 January 1831, Geneva, Switzerland

Kreutzer's name is permanently linked with that of Beethoven, as the dedicatee of Beethoven's Violin Sonata, Op. 47. But in addition to his international importance as a violin virtuoso and composer of numerous concertos, Kreutzer built up a solid reputation as an opera composer.

In his earlier *opéras comiques* Kreutzer favoured dramatic and realistic subjects: in 1791 *Lodoïska* was premiered at the Théâtre Favart in direct competition with Cherubini's work of the same name (premiered two weeks earlier at the rival Théâtre Feydeau). From 1801 he began a significant series of works for the Paris Opéra. These included *Astyanax*, *Abel*, the opéra-ballets *Les dieux rivaux* and *Clari*, and the late opera *Ipsiboé*, which was recognized as a harbinger of Romantic opera in France, deriving from a recent novel by d'Arlincourt.

Berlioz waxed lyrical about a revival of Kreutzer's biblical opera *Abel*, which indeed contains magnificently epic pages; and *Paul et Virginie* was both adapted for balletic performance in 1806 and revived as an opera in 1830 and 1846.

Operatic works: *Jeanne d'Arc à Orléans*, 1790; *Paul et Virginie*, 1791; *Le franc breton* (coll. with Solié), 1792; *Lodoïska, ou Les tartares*, 1791; *Charlotte et Werther*, 1792; *Le siège de Lille*, 1792; *Le déserteur, ou La montagne de Ham*, 1793; *Le congrès des rois* (coll. with 11 other composers), 1794; *Le lendemain de la bataille de Fleurus*, 1794; *Encore une victoire, ou Les déserteurs liégeois*, 1794; *On respire*, 1795; *Le brigand*, 1795; *La journée du 10 août 1792*, 1795; *Imogène, ou La gageure indiscrète*, 1796; *Le petit page, ou La prison d'état* (coll. with Isouard), 1800; *Flaminius à Corinthe* (coll. with Isouard), 1801; *Astyanax*, 1801; *Le baiser et la quittance, ou Une aventure de garnison* (coll. with Boieldieu, Isouard, Méhul), 1803; *Les surprises, ou L'étourdi en voyage*, 1806; *François I, ou La fête mystérieuse*, 1807; *Aristippe*, 1808; *Jadis et aujourd'hui*, 1808; *Abel*, 1810; *Le triomphe du mois de Mars*, 1811; *L'homme sans façon, ou Les contrariétés*, 1812; *Le camp de Sobieski, ou Le triomphe des femmes*, 1813; *Constance et Théodore, ou La prisonnière*, 1813; *L'oriflamme* (coll. with Berton, Méhul, Paer), 1814; *Les béarnais, ou Henri IV en voyage* (coll. with Boieldieu), 1814; *La perruque et la redingote* (coll. with Kreubé), 1815; *La Princesse de Babylone*, 1815; *Les dieux rivaux* (coll. with Berton, Persuis, Spontini), 1816; *Le maître et le valet*, 1816; *Blanche de Provence, ou La cour des fées* (coll. with Berton, Boieldieu, Cherubini, Paer), 1821; *Le négociant de Hambourg*, 1821; *Le Paradis de Mahomet* (coll. with Kreubé), 1822; *Ipsiboé*, 1824; *Pharamond* (coll. with Berton, Boieldieu), 1825; *Matilde*, (1826–7)

BIBLIOGRAPHY Hector Berlioz, trans. David Cairns, *Memoirs*, Cardinal, 1990; Winton Dean, 'French Opera' in *The Age of Beethoven 1790–1830* (*New Oxford History of Music*, vol. 8), OUP, 1982, pp. 26–119

D.P.C.

JAROSLAV KŘIČKA
b 27 August 1882, Kelč; *d* 23 January 1969, Prague

Křička was one of the most prolific and versatile Czech opera composers of his generation. After studies at the Prague Conservatory and in Berlin, he worked as a music teacher in Russia (1906–9) before returning to Prague as choirmaster of the leading choral society, Hlahol (1909–20). In 1918 he was appointed professor of composition at the Prague Conservatory, serving as Director from 1942 to 1945.

Křička's first opera, *Hipolyta*, staged by Kovařovic in Prague in 1917, was taken up by all the main Czech theatres. Particularly remarkable were his pioneering attempts and skill in writing for amateur forces and children, beginning with the popular *Ogaři*, but he was also quick to make use of jazz elements, for instance in *The White Gentleman*, which had some success abroad. Křička's great local success, achieving 20 performances in the single year in which it was given in Prague (1949–50), was a simple evocation of the Christmas story, *The Czech Crib*, which incorporated traditional Czech carols and other folk elements. Křička also wrote a number of operettas, a generally neglected genre in Bohemia.

The White Gentleman, or It's hard for ghosts to haunt today; The Ghost goes West
Bílý pán, anebo Těžko se dnes duchům straší
Musical comedy in two parts with prologue and epilogue, Op. 50
Libretto by the composer and J. L. Budín, after Oscar Wilde's story *The Canterville Ghost* (1887)
Composed 1927–9, rev. 1930 in three acts in Max Brod's arrangement as *Spuk im Schlosse, oder Böse Zeiten für Gespenster*
PREMIERES 27 November 1929, Brno; rev. version: 14 November 1931, Breslau (Wrocław)

The Scottish setting of Wilde's tale was transposed to Czechoslovakia of the 1920s to provide a satirical reflection of 'modern times', wittily evoked with jazz and popular music elements.

EDITION v.s., Universal, 1931

Other operas: *Hypolyta*, 1917; *Ogaři*, children's opera, 1919; *It Turned Out Well, or The Stout Great-grandfather, the Thieves and the Detectives* (*Dobře to dopadlo, aneb Tlustý pradědeček, lupiči a detektivové*), children's opera, 1932; *The Czech Crib* (*České jesličky*), Christmas opera, (1937), 1949; *King Lávra* (*Král Lávra*), sung fairy-tale with dance, (1937, rev. 1939), 1940; *A Little Note from One's Travels* (*Psaníčko na cestách*), children's opera, (1941), 1944; *The Puppets of Matěj Kopecký Brought to Life* (*Oživlé loutky Matěje Kopeckého*), children's opera, 1943; *Joachim and Juliana* (*Jáchym a Juliána*), folk romance, 1951
Operettas: *The Czech Paganini, or Slavík and Chopin* (*Český Paganini, aneb Slavík a Chopin*), 1952; *The Zahořany Hunt* (*Zahořanský hon*), 1950, rev. as *Serenade, or Nocturne* (*Zastaveníčko, aneb Nokturno*), 1955; *Cradle Song* (*Kolébka*), 1951; *The Quiet House* (*Tichý dům*), 1952; *Victory Polka* (*Polka vítězí*), 1955; *Circus Humberto* (*Cirkus Humberto*), 1956
BIBLIOGRAPHY František Bartoš, 'Jaroslav Křička', *České umění dramatické*, vol. 2: *zpěvohra* (*Czech Stageworks*, vol. 2: *Opera*), Šolc a Šimáček, 1941; Pavel Eckstein, *The Czechoslovak Contemporary Opera*, Panton, 1967

J.T.

FRIEDRICH KUHLAU
Daniel Friedrich (Frederik) Rudolph Kuhlau: *b* 11 September 1786, Uelzen; *d* 12 March 1832, Copenhagen

Kuhlau left his native Germany when Hamburg was overrun by Napoleon's armies in 1810. He settled in Copenhagen where he made an important contribution to Danish musical life and in particular opera and singspiel. About half his output is for the piano and he contributed prolifically to the flute repertoire. In Denmark his songs are overshadowed by those of his contemporary Weyse, but his operatic music is full of delightful invention. His first singspiel, *Røverborgen*, scored a great success in Copenhagen in 1814, and was immediately published, though its successor, *Trylleharpen* (1817) was less well received. Next came *Lulu* and his best-known work, the incidental music for Heiberg's *Elverhøj* (*The Elves' Hill*) (1828).

Lulu

Opera in three acts, Op. 65 (2h)
Libretto by C. F. Guntelberg
PREMIERE 29 October 1824, Royal Theatre, Copenhagen

Great claims have been made for *Lulu* – 'not just Kuhlau's major dramatic work but one of the most significant operas in the history of Danish music' (Gorm Busk). The libretto is an adaptation of the same fairy-tale that inspired Schikaneder's *Die Zauberflöte*, though there is little likelihood of it being confused with Mozart, still less with Alban Berg. Its opening has overtones of the Wolf's Glen scene in Weber's *Der Freischütz* and the dance of the black elves in the moonlight is pure Mendelssohn. Much of it has charm (particularly the spinning song of the witches in Act II), though one cannot pretend that it has great depth. Unlike Mozart's Sarastro, the sorcerer Dilfeng has no redeeming features or nobility and Periferihme, unlike the Queen of the Night, is good.

RECORDING Kiberg, Frellesvig, Saarman, Harbo, Cold, Danish Radio Ch and SO, Schønwandt, Kontrapunkt/Harmonia Mundi, 1986
EDITION pf. arr., Johann August Bohme, 1825

Other operatic works: *Røverborgen* (*The Robbers' Castle*), 1814; *Trylleharpen* (*The Magic Harp*), 1817; *Elisa*, 1820; *Hugo og Adelheid*, 1827; *Trillingbrødrene fra Damask* (*The Triplet Brothers from Damascus*), 1830
BIBLIOGRAPHY Dan Fog (ed.), *Kompositionen von Fridr. Kuhlau: thematisch-bibliographischer Katalog*, Copenhagen, 1977

R.La.

RAINER KUNAD

b 24 October 1936, Chemnitz, Germany

Kunad studied composition in Leipzig and directed the stage music at the state theatre in Dresden (1960–74). Two one-act operas, *Bill Brook*, based on the story by Wolfgang Borchert, and *Old Fritz*, preceded *Maître Pathelin*, *Sabellicus*, a treatment of the Faust legend, and *Litauische Claviere*, an opera for actors. In 1978 he became professor of composition at the Dresden Conservatory. Before leaving the German Democratic Republic in 1984, Kunad completed *Vincent*, which is based on Van Gogh's final years at Arles, the comic opera *Amphitryon*, and *Der Meister und Margarita* (after Bulgakov). In his early- and middle-period works Kunad aimed at 'total theatre', his style progressing from free tonality to serialism. His latest works are eschatological and prophetic in character, and he now eschews serialism in favour of neo-tonal procedures. This is apparent in his mystery play *Die Menschen von Babel* and in the tetralogy *Der verborgene Name*.

Operatic works: *Bill Brook*, 1965; *Das Schloss*, (1962); *Old Fritz*, 1965; *Maître Pathelin*, 1969 (RECORDING Nova, 1979); *Sabellicus*, 1974; *Litauische Claviere*, 1976 (RECORDING excerpts: Nova, 1978/9); *Vincent*, 1979; *Der Eiertanz* (mini-opera), (1975); *Amphitryon*, 1984; *Der Meister und Margarita*, 1986; *Die Menschen von Babel*, 1986 (RECORDING Axel-Gerhard-Kühl-Verlag); *Der verborgene Name* (tetralogy), (1990); *Kosmischer Advent*, (1991)
BIBLIOGRAPHY Programme booklet, *Der Meister und Margarita*, Badisches Staatstheater, Karlsruhe, 1986; Ursula Stürzbecher, *Komponisten in der DDR*, Hildesheim, 1979

A.C.

EDUARD KÜNNEKE

b 27 January 1885, Emmerich; *d* 27 October 1953, Berlin

Künneke studied composition with Max Bruch in Berlin, and composed and conducted for Max Reinhardt at the Deutsches Theater. In 1919, after a number of attempts at opera, Künneke turned his attention to operetta, achieving a striking success with his second work in the genre, *Der Vetter aus Dingsda* (*The Cousin from Nowhere*, 1921). A chorus-less work that grafts an expansive Viennese style on to an intimate French *boulevard* plant (albeit written by two librettists from the Berlin revue world), it was very popular. Later in the 1920s, Künneke wrote works for Broadway and the West End, and in 1932 had another major hit in Berlin, *Glückliche Reise*. He remained in Germany during the Third Reich, when his works included the over-ambitious *Die grosse Sünderin* (1935).

Künneke's early works deserve re-examination as, on the evidence of *Der Vetter aus Dingsda* and other operetta songs that have been recorded, both his melodic and orchestral gifts were noteworthy.

Operas: *Robins Ende*, 1909; *Coeur As*, 1913; *Tobias Knopp*, (n.d.); *Nadja*, 1931; *Walther von der Vogelweide*, 1945
Operettas: *Das Dorf ohne Glocke*, 1919; *Der Vielgeliebte*, 1920; *Wenn Liebe erwacht*, 1920; *Der Vetter aus Dingsda*, 1921 (RECORDING RCA, 1982); *Die Ehe im Kreise*, 1921; *Verliebte Leute*, 1922; *Casinogirls*, 1924; *The Love Song* (with music by Offenbach), 1925; *Lover's Lane*, 1925; *Mayflowers*, 1925; *Die hellblauen Schwestern*, 1925; *Not so long ago*, *c.* 1925; *Riki Tiki*, 1925; *Lady Hamilton*, 1926; *Die blonde Liselott*, 1927 (rev. as *Liselott*, 1932); *Die singende Venus*, 1928; *Der Tenor der Herzogin*, 1929; *Glückliche Reise*, 1932; *Klein Dorrit*, 1933; *Die lockende Flamme*, 1933; *Die Fahrt in die Jugend*, 1933; *Herz über Bord*, 1935; *Die grosse Sünderin*, 1935; *Zauberin Lola*, 1937; *Der grosse Name*, 1938; *Traumland*, 1941; *Die Wunderbare*, 1941; *Hochzeit mit Erika*, 1949
BIBLIOGRAPHY Otto Schneidereit, *Eduard Künneke, der Komponist aus Dingsda*, Henschelverlag, 1978

R.T.

FRIEDRICH KUNZEN

Friedrich Ludwig Aemilius Kunzen; *b* 4 September 1761, Lübeck; *d* 28 January 1817, Copenhagen

Friedrich Kunzen belonged to the third generation of a distinguished musical family. He was influenced early in his life by the composer Johann Abraham Schulz, and through him established the Danish contacts that shaped much of his later career. The climax to a period in Copenhagen was provided by his opera *Holger Danske* (1789), which, though initially a failure, was eventually accepted in Denmark as an important national opera. Based on the Oberon story, with a libretto by Jens Baggesen, drawn from Wieland, it contains many attractive arias and choruses, but is marred by the weaknesses of its dramatic structure. In a striking but clearly coincidental anticipation of Weber, it begins with a 'magic' horn-call. After working in Berlin, Frankfurt-am-Main and Prague, as an opera director and musical journalist, Kunzen returned to Copenhagen in 1795, succeeding Schulz as royal kapellmeister; and there followed the most productive part of his career, during which he composed and directed numerous new operas and singspiels at the Kongelige Teater.

Operatic works: *Jokeyen*, 1797; *Ogier the Dane* (*Holger Danske*), 1789; *Das Fest der Winzer, oder Die Weinlese*, 1793; *Festival in Valhalla* (*Festen i Valhal*), 1796; *The Secret* (*Hemmeligheden*), 1796; *The Dragon Doll* (*Dragedukken*), 1797; *Erik Ejegod*, 1798; *The Cry of Nature* (*Naturens røst*), 1799; *My Grandmother* (*Min bedste moder*), 1800; *The Homecoming* (*Hjemkomsten*), 1802; *Eropolis*, 1803; *The Lodger* (*Den Logerende*), 1804; *The Hussites* (*Hussitterne*), 1806; *Ossians Harfe, c.* 1806; *Gyrithe*, 1807; *The Pirates* (*Kapertoget*), 1808; *Love in the Country* (*Kaerlighed paa landet*), 1810; *The Hussars Out Courting* (*Husarerne paa frieri*), 1813
BIBLIOGRAPHY   S. Lunn, 'Friedrich Ludwig Aemilius Kunzen', in *MGG*

B.S.

KAROL KURPIŃSKI
Karol Kazimierz Kurpiński; baptized 6 March 1785, Włoszakowice; *d* 18 September 1857, Warsaw

Kurpiński was one of the most important Polish opera composers before Moniuszko, and a leading figure in Warsaw musical life; conductor, teacher, founder–editor of the first Polish music periodical, and writer on music.

Apart from elementary lessons from his father and uncle, Kurpiński was self-taught. But he soon became a working musician: a church organist at the age of 12, and soon afterwards a violinist in the orchestra of a local aristocrat, where he first encountered operatic music. In 1810 he moved to Warsaw, and became an opera conductor, and most of his own operas were staged in the capital.

Kurpiński wrote orchestral, chamber and piano music, songs and ballets; but the bulk of his work is operatic, especially comic opera. Stylistically these works combine elements of Mozart, Cherubini and Rossini with Polish folktunes and dance rhythms. Many were popular in their day and, though now rarely performed, they have substantial historical importance as the first national Polish operas.

Operatic works: *Pygmalion* (lost), 1808; *Dwie chatki* (*Two Small Cottages*), 1811; *Pałac Lucypera* (*The Palace of Lucifer*), 1811; *Oblężenie Gdańska* (*The Siege of Gdansk*), 1811; *Ruiny Babilonu* (*The Ruins of Babylon*), 1811; *Marcinowa z Dunaju w Stambule w seraju* (*Martin's Wife from Dunaj in the Stamboul Harem*), 1812; *Szarlatan, czyli Wskrzeszenie umarłych* (*The Charlatan, or The Raising of the Dead*), 1814 (RECORDING excerpts: Veriton, ?1970s); *Łaska imperatora* (*The Emperor's Mercy*), 1814; *Agar na puszczy* (*Hagar in the Wilderness*), 1814; *Jadwiga, królowa polska* (*Jadwiga, Queen of Poland*), 1814; *Aleksander i Apelles* (*Alexander and Apelles*), 1815; *Nadgrodą, czyli wskrzeszenie Królestawa Polskiego* (*Rewards, or Resuscitation of the Polish Kingdom*), 1815; *Mała szkoła ojców* (*A Small School for Fathers*), 1816; *Zabobon, czyli Krakowiacy i górale* (*Superstition, or Cracovian Peasants and Mountaineers*), 1816; *Dziadek i wnuk* (*Grandfather and Grandson*), 1816; *Hero i Leander* (*Hero and Leander*), 1816; *Jan Kochanowski w Czarnym Lesie* (*Jan Kochanowski at Czarny Las*), 1817; *Bateria o jednym żołnierzu* (*Battery with One Soldier*), 1817; *Czaromyst, książę słowiański* (*Czaromyst, Slav Prince*), 1818; *Zamek na Czorsztynie, czyli Bojomir i Wanda* (*The Castle of Czorsztyn, or Bojomir and Wanda*), 1819; *Zbigniew*, 1819; *Kalmora, czyli Prawo ojcowskie Amerykanów* (*Kalmora, or The Paternal Right of the Americans*), 1820; *Leśniczy w Kozienickiej puszczy* (*The Forester of Kozienice*), 1822; *Cecylia Piaseczyńska*, 1829
BIBLIOGRAPHY   T. Przybylski, *Karol Kurpiński*, Państwowe Wydawnictwo Naukowe, 1980

Z.C.

L

FRANZ LACHNER

Franz Paul Lachner; *b* 2 April 1803, Rain am Lech, Upper
Bavaria; *d* 20 January 1890, Munich

Franz, the most renowned musician of the Lachner
family, went to Vienna in 1823 as organist at the
Lutheran Church, studying with Sechter and Stadler
and becoming acquainted with Beethoven and
Schubert. In 1827 he was appointed vice-
kapellmeister at the Kärntnertortheater, becoming
principal kapellmeister on Weigl's retirement two
years later. During this period he produced his first
opera, *Die Bürgschaft*. He became conductor of the
Mannheim opera in 1834 and hofkapellmeister in
Munich in 1836. His next three operas were all
written for the Munich Court Opera, including
Benvenuto Cellini (1849) to a German version of the
text set by Berlioz (1834–7). Lachner's last major
theatrical composition was the incidental music to a
German version of Sophocles' *Oedipus Rex* (1852),
and in the same year he was elevated to the position
of generalmusikdirektor. Though Lachner conducted
Tannhäuser in 1867, Wagner's influence in Munich
made his position increasingly difficult, and he
retired in 1868.

Caterina Cornaro

Opera in four acts
Libretto by Jules Henri Vernoy de Saint-Georges, in a
German version by Alois Joseph Büssel
PREMIERE   3 December 1841, Munich

This, Lachner's most successful opera, was widely
performed in Germany. It is grand historical opera in
the tradition of Auber's *La muette de Portici*. The
heroine is a 15th-century Venetian princess who
married the last Lusignan king of Cyprus. The same
libretto was set in French by Halévy (as *La reine de
Chypre*, premiered in 1842), in Italian by Donizetti
(as *Caterina Cornaro*, January 1844) and in English
by Balfe (as *The Daughter of St Mark*, November
1844).

Other operas: *Die Bürgschaft*, 1828; *Alidia*, 1839; *Benvenuto
Cellini*, 1849; additions to operas by Spohr, Auber, Cherubini
and Lindpaintner

BIBLIOGRAPHY   A. Würz, *Franz Lachner als dramatischer
Komponist*, dissertation, University of Munich, 1927

C.A.B.

IGNAZ LACHNER

b 11 September 1807, Rain am Lech, Upper Bavaria; *d* 24
February 1895, Hanover

Ignaz Lachner followed in the wake of his elder
brother Franz. After early musical instruction in
Augsburg and Munich he went to Vienna to study
with his brother in 1824, succeeding him as organist
of the Lutheran Church. He also became assistant
kapellmeister at the Kärntnertortheater. In 1831 he
went to Stuttgart as court musikdirektor, but after
five years joined Franz in Munich where he was
appointed assistant kapellmeister at the opera in
1842. Subsequently he held posts in Hamburg (1853),
Stockholm (1858) and Frankfurt am Main (1861). His
music is typical of German Romantic composers
influenced by Spohr and Weber.

Operatic works: *Der Geisterturm*, 1837; *Die Regenbrüder*,
1839; *Loreley*, 1846; *Alpenszenen* (comprising *'s letzti
Fensterln, Drei Jahrln nach'm letzten Fensterln, Die beiden
Freier, Der Freiherr als Wildschutz, Der Ju-Schroa*), c. 1850
BIBLIOGRAPHY   H. Müller, *Ignaz Lachner: Versuch einer
Würdigung, mit Verzeichnis*, Celle, 1974

C.A.B.

EDOUARD LALO

Edouard-Victor-Antoine Lalo; *b* 27 January 1823, Lille,
France; *d* 22 April 1892, Paris

Lalo's principal work was in the field of orchestral
and chamber music. He is now best known for his
Symphonie espagnole for violin and orchestra (1874),
but he always aspired to success in opera and would
probably have composed more if his work had been
staged earlier. Trained at the conservatories of Lille
and Paris, his career began as a violinist and violist.
He composed piano trios, a quartet and some
romances, but did not venture into opera until 1866
when, in response to an opera competition for the

Théâtre-Lyrique, he composed *Fiesque*, to a libretto by Charles Beauquier based on Schiller's *Fiesko*. Despite coming third and being published, it was never staged. Lalo abandoned this lively and melodious work in the 1880s when he reused its material in, for example, the G minor Symphony and the *Divertissement*. In the mid-1870s, at the height of his powers, he composed *Le Roi d'Ys*, although this had to wait until 1888 for production. By this time Lalo's invention had waned and he was unable to respond to its great success. In 1891 he began a third opera, *La Jacquerie*, concerning a 14th-century revolt, but finished only the first act, and that was almost entirely drawn from *Fiesque*. It was completed after the composer's death by Arthur Coquard and staged in Monte-Carlo in 1895.

Le Roi d'Ys

The King of Ys
Opera in three acts (1h 45m)
Libretto by Edouard Blau, after the legend of Ys
Composed 1875, rev. 1886
PREMIERES 7 May 1888, Opéra-Comique, Paris; US: 23 January 1890, New Orleans; UK: 17 July 1901, Covent Garden, London
CAST Margared *s*, Rozenn *s*, Mylio *t*, Karnac *bar*, Le Roi d'Ys *b*, St Corentin *b*, Jahel *bar*; *satb* chorus of citizens of Ys, warriors of Karnac
FULL ORCHESTRA offstage: organ

Despite its delayed premiere, *Le Roi d'Ys* was a long-lasting success, owing to its heroic Breton story and the vigour of its style; it has retained a place in the repertoire.

SYNOPSIS

Act I The people of Ys are celebrating the peace brought about by the betrothal of the king's daughter Margared with Karnac, their former enemy. Margared tells her sister Rozenn that she loves another man and repudiates Karnac who swears revenge on Ys. Rozenn is in love with Mylio, who promises to defend the city and its people.

Act II Margared is jealous of Rozenn; the stranger she loves is Mylio: the king tells Rozenn she may marry Mylio if he defeats Karnac. When Mylio is successful Margared plots with Karnac to destroy the city by opening the floodgates that protect it from the sea.

Act III Mylio and Rozenn are happily married. Mylio kills Karnac but it is too late; as the flood rises, Margared, full of remorse, hurls herself into the waves. The water subsides.

Planned for the Opéra rather than the Opéra-Comique, *Le Roi d'Ys* contains what Lalo claimed to be genuine Breton folksongs, reflecting the Wagner-inspired vogue for subjects drawing on a legendary Celtic past. Although essentially through-composed, fine individual arias and duets stand out. The best known of these is Mylio's aubade 'Vainement, ma bien aimée' in Act III. The opera requires grand staging and a strong chorus, whose function is to emphasize the emotions of the principal characters;

the orchestral and vocal style is impressively fresh and invigorating.

RECORDINGS 1. Micheau, Gorr, Legay, Borthayre, O of Radiodiffusion Française, Cluytens, EMI, 1957; 2. Hendricks, Ziegler, Villa, Courtis, O of Radiodiffusion Française, Jordan, Erato, 1990: the modern recording is more than adequate, but the earlier one (in mono) is a classic with Rita Gorr a superb Margared [A.B.]
EDITIONS f.s., Heugel, 1900; v.s., Hartmann, 1888

BIBLIOGRAPHY 'Lalo: *Le Roi d'Ys*', *L'Avant-Scène Opéra*, no. 65 (1984); Hugh Macdonald, 'A Fiasco Remembered: *Fiesque* Dismembered', in *Slavonic and Western Music: Essays for Gerald Abraham*, OUP, 1985

H.M.

JOHN FREDERICK LAMPE

John Frederick [Johann Friedrich] Lampe; *b* 1702 or early 1703, Saxony; *d* 25 July 1751, Edinburgh

Nothing is known about Lampe before he was admitted to the University of Helmstedt in May 1718, when he was described as 'Brunsvicensis' – from nearby Brunswick. Like his fellow Saxon Handel he studied law, graduating in 1720. Whether he practised as a lawyer is not known, though he may have come to England as a result of meeting the diplomat Thomas Lediard in Hamburg, who was later to write a libretto for him. An early associate in England was the poet and composer Henry Carey, who referred to him in a poem of 1726 as 'my Lamp obscure, because unknown' who 'shines in secret (now) to friends alone'. Carey foretold fame for him: 'Light him but up! let him in publick blaze,/He will delight not only but amaze', and indeed, fame was to come to him through his settings of Carey's comic opera libretti.

Lampe's first operas were serious. In 1732–3 he joined Carey, Thomas Arne and J. C. Smith in a project to put on English operas at the Little Theatre in the Haymarket. Three of his full-length works 'after the Italian manner' were performed there within the year: Carey's *Amelia* (13 March), Lediard's *Britannia* (16 November), and *Dione* (23 February), an anonymous adaptation of Gay's play. Only two airs survive from the first, but ten numbers from *Britannia* and eight from *Dione* exist in manuscript full score, perhaps copied in conjunction with the creation of later afterpiece versions. Lampe's first comic opera, *The Opera of Operas, or Tom Thumb the Great*, an adaptation of Fielding's play *The Tragedy of Tragedies*, was first performed at the Little Theatre in May 1733. Confusion surrounds the work: Arne's setting of the text was put on at Lincoln's Inn Fields in October, and Lampe revised his work as an afterpiece for Drury Lane, first performed on 7 November. However, there is little doubt that the anonymous publication *The Celebrated Aires in the Opera of Tom Thumb* (London, 1733) was taken largely from Lampe's original opera.

Engraving accompanying a published song by Lampe, showing a scene from The Dragon of Wantley

With *The Opera of Operas* Lampe discovered his true *métier*, the satire of Italian opera; he was familiar with the genre at first hand as a bassoonist in Handel's opera orchestra. His greatest success was the all-sung comic opera *The Dragon of Wantley* (1737). It came after a fallow period, perhaps spent teaching, writing a thorough-bass treatise (published in September 1737) or travelling abroad. *The Dragon* was a sensation. Carey's text was reprinted fourteen times in little more than a year, the work was quickly transferred to Covent Garden, and it held the stage until 1782.

After such a hit, Lampe's career could go only downhill. A sequel, *Margery, or A Worse Plague than the Dragon*, produced at Covent Garden in December 1738, was only mildly successful. In April 1741 his comic masque *The Sham Conjurer* failed after only three performances, and he took his company on tour in the provinces; the young Charles Burney saw them that summer in Chester. The early 1740s were not good years for music in the London theatres, for the attention of theatre-goers was engaged by the revolution in Shakespearean acting initiated by Charles Macklin and David Garrick. Lampe had only one more success in the London theatre, his opera *Pyramus and Thisbe*, but its success did not prolong his London career for long.

In September 1748 he went to Dublin for two years, and then on to Edinburgh; soon after his arrival he fell prey to a fever, and died there on 25 July 1751. He was buried in Canongate churchyard, and was commemorated by Charles Wesley in the hymn ''Tis done! the Sov'reign will's obey'd'.

The Dragon of Wantley

Burlesque opera in three acts (1h 45m)
Libretto by Henry Carey
PREMIERE   10 May 1737, Little Theatre, London

Carey's satire was similar to Gay's in *The Beggar's Opera* in that the artificial conventions and high-flown sentiments of Italian opera were transferred to a down-to-earth English setting – in this case, the legend of Moore of Moore Hall and the dragon of Wantley or Wharncliffe, set in his native Yorkshire. The story was also known nationally through the ballad printed by Thomas D'Urfey in *Pills to Purge Melancholy* (1699), and James Ralph suggested it as an opera libretto in *The Touchstone* (1728); Carey and Lampe worked on it together, and apparently offered it to Drury Lane as early as 1734–5. Lampe added to the comedy by setting the inane lines to deadpan Handelian music; it is his only opera to survive complete, with recitatives and choruses.

EDITIONS   f.s. (without recits), J. Wilcox, London, 1738; v.s., W. Smith, London, 1752
MANUSCRIPT   (with recits), Royal College of Music, London

Pyramus and Thisbe

Mock-opera in one act (1h)
Libretto anonymous: derived from the play-within-a-play in Act V of Shakespeare's *A Midsummer Night's Dream* (1596), by way of a text set by Richard Leveridge in 1716
PREMIERE   25 January 1745, Covent Garden, London; UK modern revivals: ?early 1970s (Opera da Camera); 20 September 1985, Holme Pierrepont Hall, Nottingham (Opera Restor'd)

The librettist (possibly the composer or Henry Carey) transferred the satire from plays and players to opera and opera singers, and Shakespeare's onstage audience, Duke Theseus and his court, became the impresario Mr Semibrief and his two guests, one of whom has experienced Italian opera at first hand on the grand tour. Lampe's music is largely deadpan, though it is now noticeably more *galant*, with folklike melodies featuring Scotch snaps in the manner of his brother-in-law Thomas Arne (Arne and Lampe married the singers Cecilia and Isabella Young in 1737 and 1738).

EDITIONS   f.s., J. Walsh, London, [c.1745]; facsimile, Roger Fiske (ed.), Music in London Entertainment, series C, vol. 3, Stainer and Bell, 1988

Other operatic works: *Amelia*, 1732; *Britannia*, 1732; *Dione*, 1733; *The Opera of Operas, or Tom Thumb the Great*, 1733; *Margery, or A Worse Plague than the Dragon*, 1738; *The Sham Conjurer*, 1741; 4 lost works
BIBLIOGRAPHY   B. Boydell, *A Dublin Musical Calendar 1700–1760*, Irish Academic Press, 1988; Roger Fiske, *English*

Theatre Music in the Eighteenth Century, OUP, 1973; 2nd edn, 1986; D. R. Martin, *The Operas and Operatic Style of John Frederick Lampe*, Detroit Monographs in Musicology, 1985

P.H.

GIOVANNI BATTISTA LAMPUGNANI

b 1708, ?Milan; *d* 12 June 1788, Milan

Nothing is known of Lampugnani's career before the early 1730s, when he wrote several heroic operas for Milan. His popularity can be judged from the commissions he received from other cities after 1737. From 1743 to 1746, he was resident composer at the King's Theatre in London; his first production there was *Rossane*, a pasticcio including music by Handel. After his return to Italy in 1746, several more of his operas were produced in Milan, Venice, Florence and elsewhere; *Vologeso* was performed in Barcelona in 1753, and *Siroe* in London two years later.

After 1758 Lampugnani settled in Milan as a singing teacher and harpsichordist at the opera house (he assisted at rehearsals and performances of Mozart's *Mitridate* in 1770); he developed an interest in comic opera and in 1760 produced what became his most successful work, *L'amor contadino*, to a libretto by Goldoni. The only one of Lampugnani's opere buffe to survive, the score has many features typical of mid-18th-century opera buffa. The arias, none of which is in strict *da capo* form, are varied according to the status and situation of the character who performs them, while the first two of the opera's three finales are constructed of sections of contrasting metres and tempi. Lampugnani ceased composing after 1769.

In his time Lampugnani was popular, but was less well received by the critics, who commented adversely on the elaborate and often vehement orchestral accompaniments in his arias, which also display his taste for vocal ornamentation as well as an attractive tunefulness; in his heroic operas this juxtaposition is somewhat jarring.

Surviving operas: *Didone abbandonata*, 1739; *Semiramide riconosciuta*, 1741; *Arsace*, 1741; *Alfonso*, 1744; *Alceste*, 1744; *Siroe Re di Persia*, 1755; *Il re pastore*, 1758; *L'amor contadino*, 1760 (EDITION facsimile, Garland, 1982); 21 lost operas
BIBLIOGRAPHY Michael F. Robinson, 'Giovanni Battista Lampugnani (ii)' in *Grove*, Macmillan, 1980

D.S.B.

STEFANO LANDI

Stefano Mattei; *baptized* 26 February 1587, Rome; *d* 28 October 1639, Rome

After his initial training and experience, working as an organist and singer in Rome, Landi was appointed maestro to Mauro Cornaro, Bishop of Padua, in 1618. The dedication of Landi's first opera, *La morte d'Orfeo*, was signed from Padua in 1619, but in the following year he returned to Rome. Landi held various ecclesiastical appointments, and continued to write church music, while developing his association with first the Borghese family, and then with the Barberini. His most important work, the opera *Il Sant'Alessio*, was written for the opening of the theatre in the Barberini palace in Rome in 1632. During his latter years he was most productive in the composition of secular arias for solo voice; he also wrote a volume of *prima prattica* masses (1639) which he modelled on the style of Palestrina.

La morte d'Orfeo

The Death of Orpheus
Tragicommedia pastorale in five acts (2h)
PREMIERE ?1619, Rome

This opera is unusual among those setting the Orpheus myth, since the narrative begins after the death of Euridice. Orpheus has renounced the pleasures of the world, but he still decides to celebrate his birthday without Bacchus and without women. Bacchus takes his revenge, and incites the maenads to kill Orpheus: the dead Orpheus arrives in the underworld; Euridice fails to recognize him; but he then drinks the waters of forgetfulness himself, and is conveyed to Olympus.

The opera is unusual too, in moving away from the Florentine tradition, with its heavy reliance on recitative, to a form incorporating more ensemble and choral passages anticipating the so-called 'Roman' opera that developed in the ensuing decades.

RECORDING Kozlowska, Chance, Cordier, Elwes, van der Kemp, Tragicomedia, Stubbs, Accent, 1988
EDITIONS Stampa del Gardano, Venice, 1619; extracts in Appendix F of Hugo Goldschmidt, *Studien zur Geschichte der italienischen Oper im 17. Jahrhundert*, Georg Olms Hildesheim, 1967 (*rp* of 1901 edn)

Il Sant'Alessio

Saint Alexis
Dramma musicale in three acts (4h)
Libretto by Giulio Rospigliosi
PREMIERES 21 or 23 February 1632, Palazzo Barberini, Rome; rev. version: Carnaval 1634, Teatro Barberini, Rome; US: 24 June 1988, Royce Hall, Los Angeles

Although this work conforms to the Roman tradition in presenting a moral story, it was the first to be based on a historical subject, the life of St Alexis (5th century). The Roman saint renounces the riches of his family to wander the world in poverty. Eventually he returns to Rome incognito where he becomes dependent on the charity of his father's household, and is forced to endure the mockery of the servants. Neither his family nor his wife recognizes him, and Alexis is sorely tempted to reveal his identity. But his own inner strength enables him to resist the thought of the joy his return would give to his relations. Only after his death does

Il Sant'Alessio, Act II; illustration by François Collignon (c. 1640) after sets ascribed to Bernini

his true identity become apparent to his family. The drama underlines the essential message of the work, as the Devil is engulfed in flames and Religion descends in triumph. The designer of the premiere was Bernini.

Most of the music is in a flowing recitative style, but each of the three acts closes with a ballo; there are also choruses of slaves and servants, demons and angels. The sinfonie are extended works, rather than being purely functional; they have been regarded as the first true overtures in operatic history. And the comic characters serve to highlight the moral seriousness of the main characters. The prologue of the printed version (1634) praises Prince Alexander Charles of Poland, for whom the work was revived (with a number of revisions) in that year.

EDITIONS rev. version: Masotti, 1634; facsimile, Forni, 1970
BIBLIOGRAPHY Silke Leopold, *Stefano Landi: Beiträge zur Biographie – Untersuchungen zur weltlichen und geistlichen Vokalmusik*, 2 vols, Hamburg, 1976; M. K. Murata, *Operas for the Papal Court (1631–1668)*, Ann Arbor, 1981

G.D.

BURTON LANE
Burton Levy; *b* 2 February 1912, New York

Burton Lane came late to the stage, having established himself first as a writer of isolated songs for other people's shows and, after 1933, of film scores. His only commercially successful stage musical was *Finian's Rainbow*, though his later scores, considered independently of their dramatic context, reveal consistently high quality and the same haunting melodic inspiration that characterizes all his work.

Finian's Rainbow
Musical in two acts (film: 2h 15m)
Libretto by E. Y. Harburg and Fred Saidy; lyrics by E. Y. Harburg
PREMIERES 10 January 1947, 46th Street Theatre, New York; UK: 21 October 1947, Palace Theatre, London

The combination of an imaginary state in the American South, an Irishman with a pot of gold, and the leprechaun from whom he has wrested it, give rise to magical transformation, romantic happy endings, and satire of racism and of the single-minded pursuit of wealth – a mixture of idealism and whimsy typical of lyricist Harburg. Lane's score provides its own riches, with songs like 'How Are Tings in Glocca Morra?', 'Look to the Rainbow', 'Something Sort of Grandish', and 'Old Devil Moon'.

RECORDING Logan, Richards, Wayne, Charles, CBS, 1947
FILM Coppola (dir.), Warner, 1968
EDITION v.s., Chappell, rev. edn, 1968

Other musicals: *Hold on to Your Hats*, 1940; *On a Clear Day You Can See Forever*, 1965; *Carmelina*, 1979

BIBLIOGRAPHY David Ewen, *American Songwriters*, H. W. Wilson, 1987

J.A.C.

NICHOLAS LANIER

baptized 10 September 1588, London; *buried* 24 February 1666, London

The Lanier family of wind-players arrived at the English court from Rouen in 1561; they were apparently Protestant refugees. Nicholas was the first to branch out into other activities: he was a singer, a lutenist, a composer, an artist and an art connoisseur. His court career began formally only in 1616 when he joined Prince Charles's household, though he had been a servant of the Cecil family since his teens and was composing for masques by 1613. In 1618 he was made master of Prince Charles's musicians and was given control over all the royal musicians when Charles became king in 1625. He made several trips to Italy in the late 1620s to buy pictures for the king, and spent the Commonwealth period on the Continent. As a result he was the most Italianate English court composer of his time and was largely responsible for the declamatory features in English song, taken in part from Italian monody.

Lovers Made Men, which Lanier contributed to, is often referred to as the first English opera on the strength of a reference to 'stilo recitativo' in Ben Jonson's text, a tenuous claim since the music is lost and Jonson also refers to stilo recitativo in the text of *The Vision of Delight*, performed a few weeks earlier. Despite numerous assertions to the contrary, there is no evidence that Lanier was involved in *The Vision of Delight*.

Court masques to which Lanier contributed: *The Masque of Squires*, 1613; *Lovers Made Men*, 1617; *The Gypsies Metamorphosed*, 1621; *The Masque of Augurs*, 1622
BIBLIOGRAPHY M. Chan, *Music in the Theatre of Ben Jonson*, OUP, 1980; I. Spink, *English Song: Dowland to Purcell*, Batsford, 1974

P.H.

GAETANO LATILLA

b 10 January 1711, Bari; *d* 15 January 1788, Naples

Latilla moved to Naples in 1726 to complete his musical studies at the Conservatorio di S. Maria di Loreto. He made his début as an opera composer in 1732 with a comedy, *Li marite a forza*, for the Teatro dei Fiorentini in Naples; his first serious opera, *Demofoonte*, was produced in Venice in 1738. The same year Latilla became assistant maestro at S. Maria Maggiore there but he resigned in 1741, possibly in order to concentrate on opera.

Latilla had a fluent gift for melody and might have become a composer of great originality, since he paid less overt homage than some other contemporaries

to Pergolesi. In 1752–3 Latilla found himself at the centre of the notorious *querelle des bouffons* in Paris alongside Pergolesi, Ciampi and Rinaldo di Capua. His set of intermezzi *Gli artigiani arricchiti* achieved fame all over Europe. Meanwhile, he had settled in Venice, where in December 1753 he was appointed maestro di coro at the Ospedale della Pietà.

He was dismissed from the Pietà in 1766, probably because of his outspoken criticism of the Republic's government and, though he at first remained as deputy to Galuppi at S. Marco, he was eventually exiled from the city. Charles Burney met him in 1770 and found him in a state of 'great indigence . . . which, considering his professional abilities, and former favour, excited indignation and melancholy reflections, at the caprice and ingratitude of the public'. From the mid-1760s onwards his reputation plummeted, suffering by comparison with Piccinni, Sacchini and other younger masters.

Surviving operas: *Angelica ed Orlando*, 1735; *Temistocle*, 1737; *Il Gismondo*, 1737 (later revs with various titles); *La finta cameriera*, 1738; *La giardiniera contessa*, n.d.; *Madame Ciana*, 1738 (later revs with various titles); *L'ambizione delusa*, 1749; *Ciana*, 1748 (as *Gli artigiani arricchiti*, 1753); *Romolo* (coll. with M. Terredellas), 1739; *Siroe*, 1740; *Zenobia*, 1742; *Don Calascione*, 1749; *Griselda*, 1751; *L'Olimpiade*, 1752; *Ezio*, 1758; *L'amore artigiano*, 1761; *Antigono*, 1775; 37 lost operas
BIBLIOGRAPHY M. Bellucci la Salandra, 'Vita e tempo di Gaetano Latilla', in *Archivo Storico Pugliese*, vol. 7 (1954), pp. 69–123

D.A.D'A.

HENRY LAWES

b 5 January 1596, Dinton, Wiltshire, England; *d* 21 October 1662, London

Henry and William Lawes, the sons of a choirman at Salisbury Cathedral, rose to become the two most prominent court composers during the reign of Charles I. After service with the Bridgewater family Henry was appointed as a Gentleman of the Chapel Royal (1626) and as a royal singer/lutenist (1631). During the Commonwealth he earned his living as a singing teacher in London, and at the Restoration he was one of the most senior surviving royal musicians; he then received a third post as a composer in the Private Music.

Lawes is remembered today mainly for his songs, though he also wrote a good deal of sacred music and a few dances. He excelled in the declamatory song idiom developed by Nicholas Lanier; in a famous sonnet, 'To my Friend Mr. *Henry Lawes*', John Milton praised the 'just note and accent' of his 'tunefull and well measur'd song'.

Henry Lawes wrote two acts of the lost music for *The Siege of Rhodes* (1656), one of the earliest all-sung English operas; Davenant's text states that it was 'sung in Recitative Musick', though performances after the Restoration were apparently spoken rather than sung.

Lawes contributed music to the following masques: *Arcades*, *c.* 1630; *Albion's Triumph*, 1632; *Comus*, 1634; *The Triumphs of the Prince d'Amour*, 1636; he also contributed to the masque-like *First Day's Entertainment*, 1656
BIBLIOGRAPHY   W. McC. Evans, *Henry Lawes, Musician and Friend of Poets*, Modern Language Association (New York), 1941; *rp*, Da Capo, 1966; Ian Spink, *English Song: Dowland to Purcell*, Batsford, 1974

P.H.

WILLIAM LAWES
baptized 1 May 1602, Salisbury, England; *d* 24 September 1645, Chester, England

The Lawes brothers William and Henry were the two leading court composers of Charles I's reign. After reputedly studying with John Coprario in the Earl of Hertford's household, William became a court viol-player in 1635. He joined the Royalist army at the beginning of the Civil War and was killed at the siege of Chester, quickly becoming a Royalist martyr commemorated by musicians and poets alike.

As a composer Lawes excelled in consort music, the best medium for his dissonant and angular style. However, he also wrote a great deal of vocal music, sacred and secular, including many songs and ensembles for plays and masques produced at court and in the London theatres. His masque music is novel in that songs, ensembles and instrumental passages are often brought together in sequences of continuous music, though the effect is usually more ceremonial than operatic.

The Triumph of Peace, to which Lawes contributed, is important because an unusual amount of its music survives and because, uniquely, the musical aspects of the production can be reconstructed in detail from documents in Bulstrode Whitelocke's papers at Longleat House.

Lawes contributed music to the following masques: *The Triumph of Peace*, 1634; *The Triumphs of the Prince d'Amour*, 1636; *Britannia Triumphans*, 1638; *The Triumph of Beauty*, 1645
BIBLIOGRAPHY   Edward J. Dent, *Foundations of English Opera*, CUP, 1928; Da Capo, 1965; Murray Lefkowitz, *William Lawes*, Routledge, 1960

P.H.

JEAN-MARIE LECLAIR
Jean-Marie Leclair *l'aîné*; *b* 10 May 1697, Lyons, France; *d* 22/23 October 1764, Paris

Though remembered mainly as a composer of instrumental music and a founder of the French violin school, Leclair was on several occasions extensively involved in music for the theatre. In his youth he trained not only as a violinist but as a dancer, and is listed in the ballet troupe at the Opéra

de Lyon in 1716. Among his first compositions, now lost, were ballet entrées added to various Italian operas performed at Turin in 1722 and 1727.

At the age of 50, having devoted the intervening years almost exclusively to a career playing and composing for the violin, Leclair completed his only extant full-length opera, *Scylla et Glaucus* (1746). It was given 18 times at the Paris Opéra with a star cast but was never judged particularly successful and was never revived there.

Around 1748 the Duc de Gramont, a former pupil, appointed Leclair to lead his private orchestra, a post the composer still held when he was mysteriously murdered 16 years later. The duke's house at Puteaux, near Paris, contained a well-equipped theatre, for which Leclair provided music for at least six productions. Apart from one ariette, none of this music can be identified; some probably survives, however, in his trios, Opp. 13 and 14, which contain other identifiable arrangements, including the overture to *Scylla et Glaucus*.

Scylla et Glaucus
Tragédie en musique in a prologue and five acts (2h)
Libretto by D'Albaret after Books X and XII–XIV of Ovid's *Metamorphoses* (first decade AD)
PREMIERES   4 October 1746, Paris Opéra (Académie Royale de Musique); modern revival: 14 June 1986, Opéra de Lyon, Göttingen Festival (concert)

Leclair's one surviving tragédie maintains a remarkably high level of invention. In style it most closely resembles the operas of Rameau: it has something of Rameau's forcefulness, harmonic richness and variety, without in any way being a pale imitation. Not surprisingly the violin-writing is often bold and elaborate, while the ballet music reveals a dancer's sensitivity to pace and gesture.

By the conventions of the day, D'Albaret's libretto works well, though its tragic ending was by then unusual. In an attempt to win the heart of the nymph Scylla, Glaucus enlists the help of the sorceress Circe. Infatuated with Glaucus herself, Circe tries unsuccessfully to win his love by supernatural means, and eventually takes revenge on Scylla by turning her into the huge rock that stands by the whirlpool Charybdis.

This *dénouement* is anticipated in the Prologue: the Propoetides, a cult of young Spartan women, deny the divinity of Venus, for which impiety the goddess turns them to stone. The ensuing divertissement is a thinly disguised glorification (unusual at the Opéra by that date) of Louis XV and the Dauphin.

RECORDING   Yakar, Brown, Crook, Monteverdi Ch, English Baroque Soloists, Gardiner, Erato, 1986: an exhilarating and stylish performance
EDITION   Paris, 1746; f.s., Neal Zaslaw (ed.), *French Opera in the 17th and 18th Centuries*, no. 46, Pendragon, forthcoming

G.S.

CHARLES LECOCQ
Alexandre Charles Lecocq; *b* 3 June 1832, Paris; *d* 24
October 1918, Paris

Lecocq compensated for being seriously crippled at
an early age by studying composition and music
theory assiduously. At the Paris Conservatoire from
1849, he was in Halévy's composition class with Bizet
and Saint-Saëns (one of his few friends). In 1856, he
shared with Bizet the first prize in Offenbach's
operetta competition at the Théâtre des Bouffes-
Parisiens: the one-act libretto they set was *Le
Docteur Miracle*, and the judges included Thomas,
Auber, Gounod, and Massé. Bizet's work, which was
performed second, is still occasionally heard today
while Lecocq's is forgotten.

There were further one-act works, including the
charming *Le Myosotis*, but his first substantial
success was *Fleur-de-thé*, which had French and
oriental characters and a score laden with enough
bouncy tunes to take it abroad. After the Parisian
disturbances of 1870, Lecocq took his new works to
Brussels for their premieres, and in 1872 came *Les
cent vierges*, which became another international hit
after its Paris production at the Variétés a few
months later. At the end of that year came *La fille de
Madame Angot*, a brilliantly sparkling and assured
score that has remained Lecocq's masterpiece.

When Offenbach consistently failed to recapture
the success of his glorious 1860s period, the immense
success of *Angot* saw Lecocq acclaimed as the new
king of French operetta. *Giroflé-Girofla*, an
enormous international success in its day, was
reminiscent of Italian opera buffa, with its French
twins entangled with Moors in Spanish Africa, and
the romantic nonsense of the plot encouraged
Lecocq to provide a suitably zany but tender score. It
remained quite popular until the 1920s, when it was
given a famous constructivist production in Moscow.

Two three-act works with diminutive leading
characters, *La petite mariée* (1875) (an Italian
equivalent of *Giroflé-Girofla*) and *Le petit duc* (1878)
(arguably Lecocq's second-best score) were conspicuously successful in France and abroad; two
other works of interest included a Japanese operetta
about the son of the Mikado, *Kosiki* (1876), and *La
Camargo* (1878) about the famous 18th-century
dancer and a celebrated bandit. *La petite mademoiselle* and *Janot* have libretti by Meilhac and Halévy,
but are not nearly as good as the works they wrote
with Offenbach.

Lecocq's formula was by now growing tedious, and
if the Parisian public still supported him, it was also
leaning towards Audran, Planquette, and the coarser
vaudeville-operettas of Hervé. Lecocq's exceptional
ensembles and finales, his brilliant orchestrations,
and his graceful pastiches were perhaps too refined
for the operetta audiences of the day.

La fille de Madame Angot
The Daughter of Madame Angot
Opéra-comique in three acts (2h 30m)
Libretto by Clairville, Paul Siraudin and Victor Koning

PREMIERES 4 December 1872, Théâtre des Fantaisies-
Parisiennes, Brussels; 21 February 1873, Folies-Dramatiques,
Paris; UK: 17 May 1873, St James's Theatre, London; US: 25
August 1873, Broadway Theater, New York

In Paris, during the corrupt Directoire period,
Clairette, the daughter of the late Madame Angot –
the famed, ribald fishwife – is to be married to the
bland wigmaker–hairdresser Pomponnet. She prefers
Ange Pitou, a singer of satirical songs who often
finds himself in gaol. To avoid a wedding, Clairette
sings one of his songs and is promptly arrested. Mlle
Lange, mistress of Directoire minister Barras,
arranges to have Clairette released through the
intercession of her hairdresser, Pomponnet. The
ladies find they were schoolmates, but Lange finds
herself attracted to Pitou. Conspirators plotting the
downfall of the regime meet at Lange's; to put off the
soldiers, she convinces them she is merely throwing a
ball. The rivalry for Pitou descends to quarrelling,
but Madame Angot's daughter goes back to the
faithful Pomponnet.

The combination of an intriguing plot set in a by
then romantic period, real characters (Pitou, Lange),
gorgeous sets and costumes – including the striking
conspirators' garb and the dresses of the Merveilleuses – plus a glittering and elegant score,
proved an irresistible mix for post-Franco-Prussian
War Parisians. Audiences wanted escape, preferring
romance to satire and, to some extent, silliness.
Lecocq's desire to avoid the Offenbach mould was
evident in his opéra-comique label for this work, and
there are numerous brilliant scenes, particularly in
Act II: the Lange–Clairette reminiscence duet ('Jours
fortunés de notre enfance') with its laughing refrain;
the enormously catchy, halting conspirators' chorus
('Quand on conspire'), and the magnificent finale-
waltz ('Tournez, tournez').

RECORDING Mesplé, Stutzmann, Burles, Sinclair, Roux,
Paris Opéra Ch, Paris Opéra-Comique O, Doussard, Pathé,
1976
FILM Derosne (dir.), 1935
EDITION v.s., Brandus, 1873

Other operatic works: *Le Docteur Miracle*, 1857; *Huis-clos*,
1859; *Le baiser à la porte*, 1864; *Liline et Valentin*, 1864; *Le
Myosotis*, 1866; *Ondines au champagne*, 1866; *Le cabaret de
Ramponneau*, 1867; *L'amour et son carquois*, 1868; *Fleur-de-
thé*, 1868; *Les jumeaux de Bergame*, 1868; *Gandolfo*, 1869;
Deux portiers pour un cordon, 1869; *Le Rajah de Mysore*,
1869; *Le beau Dunois*, 1870; *Le Testament de M. de Crac*,
1871; *Le barbier de Trouville*, 1871 (RECORDING Musidisc,
1973); *Sauvons la caisse*, 1871; *Les cent vierges*, 1872; *Giroflé-
Girofla*, 1874 (RECORDING Musidisc, 1963); *Les Prés Saint-
Gervais*, 1874; *Le pompon*, 1875; *La petite mariée*, 1875
(RECORDING Musidisc, ?1960s); *Kosiki*, 1876; *La marjolaine*,
1877; *Le petit duc*, 1878 (RECORDING Pathé, c. 1953); *La
Camargo*, 1878; *Le grand Casimir*, 1879; *La petite
mademoiselle*, 1879; *La jolie Persane*, 1879; *Janot*, 1881; *La
Rousotte* (completed by Hervé), 1881; *Le jour et la nuit*, 1881
(RECORDING Musidisc, ?1960s); *Le coeur et la main*, 1882;
La Princesse des Canaries, 1883; *L'oiseau bleu*, 1884; *La vie
mondaine*, 1885; *Plutus*, 1886; *Les Grenadiers de Mont-
Cornette*, 1887; *Ali-Baba*, 1887; *La volière*, 1888;
L'égyptienne, 1890; *Ninette*, 1896; *La Belle au bois dormant*,
1900; *Yetta*, 1903; *Rose Mousse*, 1904 (RECORDING Musidisc,

?1960s); *La salutiste*, 1905; *La trahison de Pan*, 1911; *Le Chevrier*, (c. 1888); *Renza*, (n.d.); *Ma cousine*, (n.d.)
BIBLIOGRAPHY   Louis Schneider, *Les maîtres de l'opérette française: Hervé, Charles Lecocq*, Perrin, 1924

R.T.

GIOVANNI LEGRENZI

baptized 12 August 1626, Clusone, nr Bergamo; *d* 27 May 1690, Venice

Most of Legrenzi's early career was spent in the service of religious institutions, S. Maria Maggiore in Bergamo and then the Accademia dello Spirito Santo in Ferrara. It was for Ferrara that he composed his first three operas, starting with *Nino il giusto* in 1662; he clearly found Ferrara a more stimulating musical environment after provincial Bergamo. Legrenzi applied his talents more diversely than many of his contemporaries, and he composed only 18 operas in total, five of which survive in their entirety. Indeed, Legrenzi does not seem to have sought a continuing operatic career: his church music and instrumental works appeared in print on a more regular basis than opera performances. His early operas must have enjoyed a certain amount of success, since they were revived in Venice and Vienna, as well as Bologna, Brescia and Macerata.

It is not clear where Legrenzi spent his time after leaving Ferrara in 1665: in that year he refused posts of maestro in Modena and in Bergamo, and asked Carlo II Gonzaga, Duke of Mantua, to assist him in obtaining a position at the Habsburg court in Vienna. Louis XIV seems to have invited him to Versailles at about the same time, but he was unable to accept due to ill-health. His next known appointment was as maestro at the church of S. Maria della Fava in Venice, where from 1677 he provided oratorios, until he succeeded to the posts of vice-maestro (1681) and maestro (1685) of St Mark's. He was also an influential teacher; his students included Gasparini, Caldara and Lotti. After 1685 he wrote no more operas, but his years as vice-maestro were some of his most productive in that field, writing for two Venetian theatres as well as the ducal palace in Mantua. *Giustino* (1683) was particularly successful, and was widely performed throughout Italy until the end of the century. As late as the 1720s his arias were still used to demonstrate the skills of singers; Bach and Handel borrowed themes from his works, which also had a discernible influence on Alessandro Scarlatti.

Despite the frequent presence of comic themes, Legrenzi was also capable of reflecting the drama of the plot in his music – for instance, in the battle songs that dominate his heroic works. But he also drew on the folksong heritage of the period, as well as the common dance rhythms; he introduces these into arias, which are increasingly differentiated into brisk diatonic and more languid chromatic ones. The simple accompaniments then give way to well-wrought instrumental ritornelli.

Moveable cloud scene from Legrenzi's Germanico sul Reno (1676)

La divisione del mondo (1675) was performed in an extremely expensive manner in Venice; the gods have come to earth, to the operatic stage, in order to satirize the Venetian nobility, whom they apparently represent. The kernel of the action is a dispute as to who shall win the goddess Venus. The small proportion of surviving music shows that the music benefited just as much from Legrenzi's imagination and craftsmanship as did the elaborate stage devices which he also designed. The composer also designed the stage machinery for *Germanico sul Reno* (1676). The drawings are still extant: pulleys and levers could make clouds descend and open, or give the effect of a mobile apotheosis. In the same opera, violin solos were apparently introduced to satisfy the public demand for the instrument.

Totila

Heroic–comic opera in three acts
Libretto by Matteo Noris
PREMIERE   February 1677, Teatro SS. Giovanni e Paulo, Venice

Totila is a historical opera, dealing with the history of Classical Rome, sacked by Totila, King of the Barbarians. It contains the confused love scenes common to many contemporary operas: the daughter of a Roman senator makes advances to and eventually marries Totila. A consul is sent mad by the supposed death of his wife and child, and is found singing love songs to his servant, whom he believes to be Narcissus. Mistaken identities, complex love affairs, unrealistically dramatic situations are all made more bizarre by the librettist: the stock-in-trade of Venetian late 17th-century opera is set against the depressing background of war and destruction, providing even more drama and giving the otherwise standard plot a curious twist.

EDITION facsimile, H. M. Brown (ed.), Garland, 1978

Il Giustino
Justin
Melodramma in three acts (3h 30m)
Libretto by Nicolo Beregan, based on the *Anekdota* (c. AD 553) of the Byzantine historian Prokop
PREMIERE 12 February 1683, Teatro San Salvatore, Venice

Like *Totila*, Legrenzi's last extant opera is a heroic work, designed as a protest against the frivolous works appearing on the Venetian stage at that period. The hero, Justin I, becomes emperor, despite his lowly birth; he saves the life of the Emperor Anastasius, and in doing so demonstrates remarkable loyalty and trustworthiness. Despite the intention to cultivate a more serious operatic genre, *Giustino* was so extravagant in its use of machines, that it was treated as a spectacle, rather than a serious medium: the second act calls for sea dragons, shipwrecked vessels on a stormy sea, two prisoners throwing travellers from a tower, and a carriage pulled by horses filled with warriors. The same libretto was the basis of later operas by Albinoni, Vivaldi and Handel.

EDITION L. Bettarini (ed.), Milan, 1980

Other operas: *Zenobia e Radamisto*, 1665; *Eteocle e Polinice*, 1675; *La divisione del mondo*, 1675; *Germanico sul Reno*, 1676; *Il Creso* (only arias survive), 1681; *Antioco il grande* (only arias survive), 1681; *Il Pausania* (only arias survive), 1682; *Lisimaco riamato* (only arias survive), 1682; *I due Cesari* (only arias survive), 1683; 8 lost operas
BIBLIOGRAPHY R. Bossard, *Giovanni Legrenzi: Il Giustino, Eine monographische Studie*, Koerner, 1988; P. Fogaccia, *Giovanni Legrenzi*, Orobiche, 1954

G.D.

FRANZ LEHÁR
b 30 April 1870, Komorn; *d* 24 October 1948, Bad Ischl, Austria

Lehár, the instigator and leading composer of 20th-century Viennese operetta, was of Czech and Hungarian descent. The son of a military band-master, he studied at the Prague Conservatory with Foerster, and briefly with Fibich and Dvořák, excelling at the violin. He played in his father's band (alongside Leo Fall) and later led his own ensembles for infantry regiments stationed in Trieste, Budapest and finally Vienna. During this period his grand 'Russian' opera *Kukuška* (1896) was unsuccessfully produced in Leipzig.

The popularity of his waltz *Gold und Silber* (1902) persuaded Lehár to leave the world of army bands

and once again to try the theatre. That same year, two of his operettas were performed at Vienna's two leading operetta theatres, *Wiener Frauen* (Theater an der Wien) and *Der Rastelbinder* (Carltheater), the latter making the more lasting impression with its provincial characters and a sensual, languorous love duet in Act II. After two less successful works, Lehár hit the jackpot in 1905 with one of the most popular operettas ever written, *Die lustige Witwe*.

Several undistinguished works followed *Die lustige Witwe*, until a series of Viennese and international triumphs began with *Der Graf von Luxemburg*, another Parisian romantic frolic (1909); *Zigeuner-liebe* (1910), and *Eva*, again set in Paris, but dealing with industrial relations (1911). Works written around the First World War period proved less durable as new rival composers were garnering many more performances.

In the mid-1920s, Lehár's fortunes began to rise again, thanks to his association with the Austrian tenor Richard Tauber. The singer had created a sensation taking over a leading part in *Frasquita* (1922) in Vienna, and later appeared in the Berlin premiere of *Paganini* (1925), the first of five new or refashioned romantic operettas written expressly for him. The contemporary charm and cohesive elegance of *Die lustige Witwe* gave way to quasi-historical exoticism. The romantic music instantly brought Puccini to mind, while the subsidiary comic numbers were written in a more vernacular style using modern dance rhythms that nevertheless sounded distinctively Lehárian. Though Tauber looked not remotely like Paganini or Goethe (in *Friederike*, 1928), the force of his voice and persona enraptured Europe. The climax of this partnership was reached with *Das Land des Lächelns* (1929).

The final original work was in fact an operetta transmogrified into an opera, *Giuditta* (1934). During the 1930s the composer wrote several film scores. With a Jewish wife, Lehár remained in retirement in Austria after 1938. His works were still performed (the non-Aryan librettists' names were omitted from the programmes); royalties continued to pour in, and the composer was occasionally feted by the Nazis – Hitler's favourite operetta was reputedly *Die lustige Witwe*.

Die lustige Witwe
The Merry Widow
Operetta in three acts (2h 30m)
Libretto by Viktor Léon and Leo Stein, adapted from the play *L'attaché d'ambassade* by Henri Meilhac (1861) in the German translation (*Der Gesandschafts Attaché*, 1862) by Alexander Bergen
PREMIERES 30 December 1905, Theater an der Wien, Vienna; UK: 8 June 1907, Daly's Theatre, London; US: 21 October 1907, New Amsterdam Theater, New York
CAST Baron Zeta *t*, Count Danilo Danilowitsch *t*, Camille de Rosillon *t*, Vicomte Cascada *t*, Raoul de St Brioche *t*, Bogdanowitsch *bar*, Kromow *t*, Pritschitsch *bar*, Njegus *bar*, Hanna Glawari *s*, Valencienne *soubrette*, Sylviane *s*, Olga *s*, Praskowia *ms*, 6 *s*; *satb* chorus of Parisians and Pontevedrians, *grisettes*, partygoers, dancers, etc.
FULL ORCHESTRA onstage: 3 tamburizzas, tambourine, gtr, str

No operetta conjures up Habsburg Vienna, turn-of-the-century Paris or the glittering Edwardian era of eternal waltzes quite like *The Merry Widow*. Lehár's rapturous score – which he was never to equal – was his ticket to immortality and enormous profits; it created an international furore the like of which had not been seen since Sullivan's *HMS Pinafore* or *The Mikado* 20 years before.

Lehár with Mizzi Guenther (Hanna) and Louis Treumann (Danilo) in Die lustige Witwe *(Vienna, 1905)*

SYNOPSIS

Act I   Baron Zeta, the Pontevedrian ambassador to Paris, anxiously awaits the fabulously wealthy Hanna Glawari, who has recently been widowed. To avoid her millions leaving Pontevedro, she must be prevented from marrying a foreigner. Hanna encounters the playboy Danilo; they once had an affair, but now that she is wealthy, he treats her coolly. Baron Zeta, oblivious of his own wife Valencienne's carrying on with Camille, informs Danilo that he must marry Hanna for the sake of his country. In the ballroom Hanna elects to dance with Danilo, despite his thoroughly obnoxious behaviour.

Act II   Hanna gives a party at her home with everyone in their national costumes. She tells her guests a story about a Vilja, a maid of the woods. Danilo and the men remark on the difficulties of handling women, but Danilo is falling in love again. Camille entices Valencienne into a pavilion in the garden. Zeta, looking through the keyhole, is surprised to see not his wife, but Hanna. She has taken Valencienne's place as much to save her friend as to tease Danilo, who angrily leaves.

Act III   Hanna explains the incident in the pavilion to Danilo, and they are drawn together by a sensuous waltz. Zeta's marital problems are settled, and when Hanna announces that she will lose her money on marriage, Danilo asks for her hand. She agrees, and then explains that the millions will pass to her husband.

Possibly the most frequently performed operetta of all time, the work offers a succession of brilliant scenes and superb finales, punctuated by operetta standards such as, in Act I, the entrance songs for both Hanna ('Bitte, meine Herr'n') and Danilo ('Da geh' ich zu Maxim'), in Act II, the 'Vilja' song, and the 'Weiber' march, and in the last act the famous waltz ('Lippen schweigen'). Just as glitteringly striking and memorable are the duets for Camille and Valencienne – including his passionate pavilion invitation in Act II, Hanna's description of life 'in the Parisian style' in the Act II finale, and the potent 'Ballsirenen' waltz in the Act I finale.

For the London production Lehár added two new numbers, and, later, a long, formal overture – the original short introduction is infinitely more satisfying in setting the scene. It is generally forgotten today that Lehár's score was considered quite bold and even *risqué* by some. The silver age of Viennese operetta is said to have begun with *Die lustige Witwe*. Love affairs could become comparatively more realistic, and the orchestra far more lush in support. Lehár had brought operetta into the 20th century.

RECORDINGS   1. Schwarzkopf, Loose, Gedda, Kunz, Philharmonia Ch and O, Ackermann, EMI, 1953; 2. Schwarzkopf, Steffek, Gedda, Waechter, Philharmonia Ch and O, Von Matačić, EMI, 1962; 3. Harwood, Stratas, Hollweg, Kollo, Ch of Deutsche Oper, Berlin, Berlin PO, Karajan, DG, 1972: the early EMI version is something of a classic, but it was rivalled by the stereo remake in 1962. Both these versions have a baritone Danilo. Karajan's super-glossy recording has a tenor in the role and Harwood challenging Scharzkopf's hegemony as Hanna. [A.B.]
FILMS   1. von Stroheim (dir.), MGM, 1925 (silent); 2. Lubitsch (dir.), MGM, 1934; 3. Bernhardt (dir.), MGM, 1952
EDITION   v.s., Doblinger, 1906

Der Graf von Luxemburg

The Count of Luxembourg
Operetta in three acts (2h 30m)
Libretto by Alfred Maria Willner and Robert Bodansky, after Willner's and Bernhard Buchbinder's libretto to Johann Strauss's *Die Göttin der Vernunft* (1897)
PREMIERES   12 November 1909, Theater an der Wien, Vienna; UK: 20 May 1911, Daly's Theatre, London; US: 16 September 1912, New Amsterdam Theater, New York; rev. version: 4 March 1937, Theater des Volkes, Berlin

Lehár's first success after *Die lustige Witwe* was based on a libretto previously set by Johann Strauss only under threat of a law suit. An impoverished count living in Paris marries a singer from the Opéra who needs a title in order later to remarry into the nobility. The count is handsomely recompensed, and the marriage takes place with the couple separated by a screen to avoid embarrassment. In due course the couple meet, oblivious of their relationship, and fall in love. Eventually the lovers are properly united. This unlikely story won widespread public acclaim. As in *Die lustige Witwe* a party scene in Act II provided the excuse for some memorable dance numbers, including the staircase waltz 'Mädel klein, Mädel fein'. Another favourite was the waltz song 'Bist du's, lachendes Glück', sung by the 'invisible' wedding couple. For the 1937 revision Lehár added an opening carnival scene in Montmartre, an entrance song for the count, and a ballet sequence.

RECORDING Popp, Gedda, EMI, 1970s
EDITIONS v.s., Karczag, [1909]; rev. version: Glocken Verlag, 1937

Zigeunerliebe
Gypsy Love
Romantic opera in three scenes (2h 45m)
Libretto by Alfred Maria Willner and Robert Bodansky
PREMIERES 8 January 1910, Carltheater, Vienna; 17 October 1911, Globe Theater, New York; UK: 1 June 1912, Daly's Theatre, London

Following hot on the heels of *Der Graf von Luxemburg*, *Zigeunerliebe* inhabited a more traditionally operatic world. Eschewing the Parisian gaiety of the previous work, it tells the story of a Hungarian girl who, at her engagement party, dreams that she has run off for a life among gypsies. Eventually, she comes to realize that such a life is not for her, and finds new love with her betrothed.

Once again, Lehár was able to indulge his gift for evoking the spirit of the Balkans though it was only later that he added the czárdás 'Hör' ich Cymbalklange' for Zorika, the heroine. Another highlight is the duet 'Es liegt in blauen fernen'. Lehár provided additional numbers for the London premiere and in 1943 he revised the work entirely as the Hungarian opera *Garabonciás diák*.

RECORDING excerpts: Schramm, Chryst, Schock, Katona, Günther Arndt Ch, Berlin SO, Stolz, Eurodisc, 1960s
EDITIONS f.s., Karczag and Wallner, 1909; v.s., Glocken Verlag, 1938

Paganini
Operetta in three acts (2h 30m)
Libretto by Paul Knepler and Béla Jenbach
PREMIERES 30 October 1925, Johann-Strauss-Theater, Vienna; UK: 20 May 1937, Lyceum, London
Knepler had originally intended to set his own libretto based on the rumours surrounding the relationship between the great violin virtuoso, Paganini, and Napoleon's sister, Anna Elisa, Princess of Lucca. However, a friend of the librettist gave the book to Lehár, and Knepler, on hearing some of the score, was happy to leave it in his hands.

The role of Paganini was designed for Richard Tauber, with plenty of opportunities for indulgent love songs, including the celebrated 'Gern hab' ich

die Frau'n geküsst'. Unfortunately, Tauber was unable to sing in the Vienna premiere, owing to a previously arranged concert tour, as was the intended Anna Elisa, Vera Schwarz. The result was a near disaster, but both singers were able to appear in the triumphant Berlin premiere on 20 January 1926, where Tauber's conspicuous lack of resemblance to the wiry Paganini failed to detract from the work's success.

RECORDING Rothenberger, Gedda, EMI, 1978
EDITIONS v.ss., Crescendo Verlag, 1925; Glocken Verlag, 1936

Das Land des Lächelns
The Land of Smiles
Romantic operetta in three acts (2h 15m)
Libretto by Ludwig Herzer and Fritz Beda-Löhner, after Viktor Léon's libretto to the earlier *Das gelbe Jacke* (1930)
PREMIERES 10 October 1929, Metropoltheater, Berlin; UK: 8 May 1931, Drury Lane, London; US: 5 September 1946, Shubert Theatre, New York (as *Yours is My Heart*)

With *Das Land des Lächelns* Tauber's fame and Lehár's commercial success reached their zenith. Herzer and Löhner greatly improved Léon's libretto, their most important changes being the replacement of the original happy ending with a tragic renunciation by the lovers, and the addition of the work's most famous number, 'Dein ist mein ganzes Herz'.

An aristocratic Viennese girl, Lisa, falls in love with the Chinese prince Sou-Chong, but is unable to adapt to the demands made on her in the prince's own country, where all passions are concealed behind enigmatic, disciplined smiles.

In Lehár's opulent score the worlds of Puccini and Richard Strauss meet that of operetta, with *chinoiserie* giving way to melancholy lyricism. Among the other numbers, Sou-Chong's 'Immer nur lächeln' and 'Von Apfelblüten einem Kranz' are particularly vocally demanding, while the duets include 'Bei einem Tee en deux' and the impassioned 'Wer hat die Liebe uns ins Herz gesenkt'. In 1930 alone – the year of the composer's 60th birthday – the work received some 200 productions.

RECORDING Schwarzkopf, Gedda, Kunz, Philharmonia Ch and O, Ackermann, EMI, 1953
FILMS 1. Reichmann (dir.), 1931; 2. Kiepura, Eggerth, 1952
EDITIONS v.ss., Glocken Verlag, 1929, 1957

Other operettas: *Fräulein Leutnant*, 1901; *Arabella, die Kubanerin* (inc.), (1901); *Das Club-Baby* (inc.), (1901); *Wiener Frauen*, 1902; *Das Rastelbinder*, 1902; *Der Göttergatte*, 1904; *Die Juxheirat*, 1904; *Der Schlüssel zum Paradies*, 1906; *Peter und Paul reisen im Schlaraffenland*, 1906; *Mitislaw der Moderne*, 1907; *Der Mann mit den drei Frauen*, 1908; *Das Fürstenkind* (1909); *Die Spieluhr*, 1911; *Eva*, 1911; *Rosenstock und Edelweiss*, 1912; *Die ideale Gattin* (rev. of *Der Göttergatte*), 1913; *Endlich allein*, 1914; *Der Sterngucker*, 1916; *A Pacsirta (Wo die Lerche singt)*, 1918; *Die blaue Mazur*, 1920; *Die Tangokönigin* (second rev. of *Der Göttergatte*), 1921; *Frühling*, 1922; *La danza della libellule*, 1922; *Frasquita*, 1922; *Die gelbe Jacke*, 1923; *Cloclo*, 1924; *Gigolette* (rev. of *Der Sterngucker* and *La danza delle libellule*), 1926; *Der Zarewitsch*, 1927; *Friederike*, 1928;

Frühlingsmädel (rev. of *Der Sterngucker* and *Frühling*), 1930; *Schön ist die Welt* (rev. of *Endlich allein*), 1930; *Der Fürst der Berge* (rev. of *Das Fürstenkind*), 1932; *Giuditta*, 1934
Operas: *Der Kürassier* (inc.), (1892); *Rodrigo* (inc.), (1893); *Kukuška*, 1896, rev. as *Tatjana*, 1905; *Garbonciás diák* (rev. of *Zigeunerliebe*), 1943

BIBLIOGRAPHY Stan Czech, *Franz Lehár, Sein Weg und sein Werk*, Franz Perneder, 1948; B. Grun, *Gold and Silver: The Life and Times of Franz Lehár*, David McKay, 1970; W. Macqueen-Pope and D. L. Murray, *Fortune's Favourite: The Life and Times of Franz Lehár*, Hutchinson, 1953

R.T.

JEAN-BAPTISTE LEMOYNE

[Lemoine, Le Moyne, Le Moine]; *b* 3 April 1751, Eymet, Dordogne, France; *d* 30 December 1796, Paris

Lemoyne was active in Paris during the late 18th century as a composer of serious opera and, towards the end of his career, of opéra comique. A contemporary of Gluck, Piccinni and Sacchini, his style was to a large extent imitative. Although his music contained some novel and innovative features, contemporary critics found it mediocre.

Lemoyne is remembered principally for three works, which were all performed at the Paris Opéra: *Electre* (1782), *Phèdre* (1786) and *Nephté* (1789). The first was dedicated to Gluck and ostensibly modelled on his style, but met with little success. The vocal writing lacks lyricism and the orchestration is somewhat cumbersome. However, much of the recitative is powerfully expressive and the unusual recurrence of selected musical motifs foreshadows later leitmotif practice.

Phèdre and *Nephté* subsequently attempted to emulate the style of Piccinni and Sacchini, *Nephté* proving particularly successful and enhancing Lemoyne's reputation. Its recitative, like that in *Electre*, is well styled and supported by interesting accompaniments, and the design of many arias is more carefully conceived. The colourful Egyptian setting also inspired a lavish staging. Lemoyne received a curtain call after the first performance – a then uncommon favour – which acknowledged his position as one of the most successful French stage composers during a period when competition from foreign musicians was great.

Operatic works: *Le bouquet de Colette*, 1775; *Electre*, 1782; *Phèdre*, 1786; *Nadir, ou Le dormeur éveillé*, (1787); *Les prétendus*, 1789; *Nephté*, 1789; *Les pommiers et le moulin*, 1790; *Louis IX en Egypte*, 1790; *Elfride*, 1792; *Silvius Nerva, ou La malediction paternelle*, (1792); *Miltiade à Marathon*, 1793; *Toute la Grèce, ou Ce que peut la liberté*, 1794; *Le compère Luc*, 1794; *Les vrais sans-culottes, ou Le batelier*, 1794; *Le mensonge officieux*, 1795; *L'île des femmes*, (1796)

BIBLIOGRAPHY Julian Rushton, 'An Early Essay in *Leitmotiv*: J. B. Lemoyne's *Electre*', *ML*, vol. 52 (1971)

E.C.

LEONARDO LEO

Leonardo Ortensio Salvatore de Leo; *b* 5 August 1694, San Vito degli Schiavi (now San Vito dei Normanni, Apulia, Italy); *d* 31 October 1744, Naples

A contemporary of Vinci and Hasse, Leo dominated musical life in Naples after 1730 until his death and contributed significantly to the development of comic opera. He was also an important composer of church music and the teacher of both Piccinni and Jommelli.

Trained under Nicola Fago at the Conservatory of Santa Maria della Pietà dei Turchini in Naples from 1709, Leo attracted early attention with a performance of his dramma sacro *Santa Chiara* at the same conservatory early in 1712. From 1713, before he was 20, Leo already held a number of positions: as supernumerary organist at the royal chapel, as maestro di cappella to the Marchese Stella and (perhaps) as maestro di cappella at the church of Santa Maria della Solitaria. In 1725, following the death of Alessandro Scarlatti, he was appointed first organist of the royal chapel. Later, following Leonardo Vinci's death in 1730, he became pro-vice-maestro there, then vice-maestro in 1737, after the death of Francesco Mancini. Finally, in 1744 just nine months before his death, he succeeded Domenico Sarro as maestro di cappella at the Neapolitan court. By this time he was more esteemed as a composer of oratorios and as primo maestro at two of the Neapolitan conservatories (Sant'Onofrio and Santa Maria della Pietà dei Turchini).

Leo's operatic career began at a precocious age with *Il Pisistrato*, performed at the Real Palazzo in 1714. It was only from 1720, however, that he began to fulfil a regular series of commissions for the court and the Teatro San Bartolomeo, writing both opere serie and comic operas in Neapolitan dialect. The first of the latter was *La 'mpeca scoperta* (1723). After 1725, with the advent of Vinci as a composer of serious opera and the arrival of Hasse in Naples, Leo's standing declined somewhat. As a composer of opera seria, his work was in some demand in Rome and Venice; in Naples itself he continued to be successful mainly with comic operas. Following the death of Vinci in 1730 and the departure of Hasse for Dresden, Leo's position in the forefront of Neapolitan music was reconfirmed. During the 1730s he consolidated his position with further court appointments. His relative standing is reflected in the number of occasions on which he was granted leave to produce his operas at other cities in Italy; he also received commissions from the Spanish court.

Less innovative in style than Vinci and somewhat tardy in setting the libretti of Metastasio (starting with *Catone in Utica* in a Carnival production in Venice in 1730), Leo also appears more old-fashioned in his use of richer textures and more contrapuntal detail than was the norm among his contemporaries; he was in other words more beholden to the ideals of Alessandro Scarlatti. Edward Dent compared his setting of *L'Olimpiade* (1737) somewhat unfavourably with that by Pergolesi (1735): while praising the solid construction of his melodies, Dent denied Leo the grace and dramatic sense of his younger contemporary. In his revival of the same opera in 1743, Leo reintroduced the chorus into Neapolitan opera.

One of Leo's most important contributions was in the field of orchestration where, despite restricting himself to simple, essentially background accompaniments to arias, he exhibited a sound awareness of the dramatic effects of instrumental colours. His introduction of notated dynamic contrasts in the orchestral parts was of significance in the development of independent orchestral writing later in the 18th century. Leo's vocal lines – like Vivaldi's – occasionally show an instrumental quality, including dramatic leaps amid the more usual conjunct vocal writing.

Among the most successful of Leo's 20 known comic operas was *Amor vuol sofferenza* (1739) which epitomizes many characteristics of Neapolitan opera: use of local dialect and folklike canzoni for the less socially elevated characters, combination of comic and heroic (or mock-heroic) arias, introduction of duets and trios to end acts, and the sentimental tone. As with a number of his operas, Leo later revised *Amor vuol sofferenza*, but he did not complete this revision; he was found dead at the harpsichord, the score in front of him.

Leo also composed much church music and wrote two important pedagogical works (*Istituzioni o regole del contrappunto* and *Lezioni di canto fermo*), reflecting his abiding interest in traditional skills.

Surviving operas: *Zenobia in Palmira*, 1725; *Il trionfo di Camilla, regina dei Volsci*, 1726; *Catone in Utica*, 1729 (EDITION facsimile, Howard Mayer Brown (ed.), Garland, 1983); *Demofoonte* (Act III of coll. with Sarro and Mancini), 1735; *Emira*, 1735; *Farnace*, 1736; *La simpatia del sangue*, 1737; *Olimpiade*, 1737 (EDITION facsimile, Garland, 1978); *Il Ciro riconosciuto*, 1739; *Amor vuol sofferenza*, 1739 (Società di storia patria per la Puglia, Bari, 1962); *Achille in Sciro*, 1740; *Demetrio*, 1741; *L'ambizione delusa*, 1742; *Andromaca*, 1742 (EDITION facsimile, Garland, 1979); 36 lost operas
BIBLIOGRAPHY Hellmuth Christian Wolff, 'Leonardo Leo' in *New Oxford History of Music*, vol. 5 (Opera and Church Music 1630–1750), OUP, 1975, pp. 108–16; Edward J. Dent, 'Leonardo Leo', *PRMA*, 32nd session (1905–6), p. 59; Michael F. Robinson, *Naples and Neapolitan Opera*, OUP, 1972

D.S.B.

RUGGERO LEONCAVALLO
b 8 March 1857, Naples; *d* 9 August 1919, Montecatini, Italy

Leoncavallo, the Italian composer and librettist, was admitted to the Naples Conservatory in 1866, where his principal teachers were Beniamino Cesi and Lauro Rossi. Graduating ten years later, he moved to Bologna, where he was much impressed by the poet Carducci's lectures. These had a strong influence on his literary interests, and prompted the completion of a libretto entitled *Chatterton*, which he had begun as a student and which he now also set to music. He also fell under the spell of Wagner and planned to write a

trilogy – both text and music – on the Italian Renaissance. Unable to interest a publisher in his proposals, he embarked on a journey to Egypt (1882) and later to Paris, supporting himself as an accompanist for *café-concerts*. In the French capital in 1888, he made friends with the baritone Maurel (the original Iago in Verdi's *Otello*), who persuaded the publisher Giulio Ricordi to take on the composer.

Ricordi was more impressed with Leoncavallo's abilities as a theatre poet than with his music, taking a dim view of *I Medici*, the only part of the proposed trilogy Leoncavallo had completed. In 1889 Leoncavallo worked with Puccini on the text for *Manon Lescaut*, but the collaboration lasted only briefly owing to differences of temperament. When Ricordi definitely refused *I Medici*, Leoncavallo, desperate to establish himself, quickly composed *I pagliacci*, modelling his work on Mascagni's *Cavalleria rusticana*, and exploiting the current trend for *verismo* opera. The successful premiere of *I pagliacci* in 1892, with Maurel as Tonio and with Toscanini conducting, made the composer famous overnight. *I pagliacci* became the almost inseparable companion of *Cavalleria* as a double-bill after the Metropolitan Opera House, New York, staged the combination in December 1893.

Fame, however, did not ensure a trouble-free future for the composer. Like *I pagliacci*, *I Medici* was taken up by Ricordi's rival publishing house, Sonzogno, who, hoping to capitalize on *Pagliacci*'s recent success, quickly arranged a performance. But the pretentious panorama of the Renaissance failed to measure up to expectations, despite the composer's unabashed promotion of it, and the opera was deemed a failure. Daunted by this setback, Leoncavallo wisely put aside the remainder of his projected *Crepusculum* trilogy (the title was a distant nod in the direction of *Götterdämmerung*). When Puccini began work on *La bohème*, Leoncavallo simultaneously embarked on the same subject, determined to better his rival with his memories of the Parisian atmosphere he had absorbed in his years of vagabondage. Leoncavallo's score, which was premiered some 15 months after Puccini's, never proved a serious threat, however, despite some beguiling local colour and vocally grateful moments.

Despite earlier failure *I Medici* was premiered in Berlin in 1894; Kaiser Wilhelm II was greatly impressed and commissioned an opera from Leoncavallo extolling the Hohenzollerns, placing the Court Opera at his disposal. Leoncavallo worked on the opera for ten years and – he wrote to Caruso – believed it to be his masterpiece. He was sadly mistaken: despite its illustrious patron *Der Roland von Berlin* (1904) utterly failed to hold its own.

In 1906 Leoncavallo toured the United States and Canada, imitating Mascagni's visit four years earlier, and here he first turned his hand to operetta, a genre that would periodically engage him for the rest of his life.

Leoncavallo's natural aptitude for lighter music, which had already been demonstrated in his song 'Mattinata' (one of the earliest compositions written for the gramophone, it was recorded by Caruso accompanied by Leoncavallo in 1904), was rather at odds with his intense desire to be taken seriously as a composer. Hoping to repeat the now distant success of *Pagliacci*, Leoncavallo set about the composition of *Tormenta*, based on a melodramatic play by Belvederi, set in Sardinia. The interruption of the First World War led to its abandonment and Leoncavallo completed no further operas. His final operatic project, a grand opera *Edipo Re* to a libretto by Forzano, was completed by Pennachio and premiered 17 months after Leoncavallo's death. It made only a temporary splash and that thanks to Titta Ruffo in the title role.

I pagliacci
The Clowns
Dramma in two acts and a prologue (1h)
Libretto by the composer
PREMIERES 21 May 1892, Teatro Dal Verme, Milan; UK: 19 May 1893, Covent Garden, London; US: 15 June 1893, Grand Opera House, New York
CAST Canio *t*, Nedda *s*, Tonio *bar*, Silvio *bar*, Beppe *t*; *satb* chorus of villagers
ORCHESTRATION 3 fl/picc, 2 ob, ca, 2 cl, b cl, 3 bsn, 4 hn, 3 tpt, 3 trbn, b trbn, timp, perc, 2 hp, str; onstage: ob, tpt, perc (drum, bells), vln

The only one of Leoncavallo's twelve operas and ten operettas to enter the permanent repertoire, *I pagliacci*, along with its almost inseparable sidekick, Mascagni's *Cavalleria rusticana*, best convey the

Self-caricature of Enrico Caruso as Canio in Pagliacci *(New York, 1913)*

ethos of *verismo*, the realistic representation of lower-class characters in the context of 'a bleeding slice of life', to quote Tonio in the prologue of *I pagliacci* – itself a manifesto of the naturalistic aesthetic. Drawing on his memories of a *crime passionel* adjudicated by his magistrate father, Leoncavallo combined the story of a jealous husband and his unfaithful wife with a performance by a *commedia dell'arte* troupe, attaining a climax when real-life emotion supplants the play-acting.

SYNOPSIS
Prologue Tonio alerts the audience that they are to see a drama taken from real life.

Act I On the feast day of the Assumption Calabrian villagers gather to greet a company of strolling players, and Canio, the troupe's leader, invites them to attend the performance. When one of the bystanders makes a teasing reference to the desirability of Nedda, Canio's wife, he brushes the taunt aside, but not without revealing his jealous nature ('Un tal gioco'). When the others go off, Nedda stays behind, half afraid that Canio is suspicious of her, but envying the birds their freedom to come and go as they please ('Stridono lassù'). The deformed Tonio, a member of the company, appears and plays clumsy court to Nedda, but she repulses him with a whip, leaving him vengeful. Her lover Silvio appears and they plan a rendezvous for later that evening ('Decidi il mio destin'). The latter part of their conversation is overheard by Tonio, who fetches Canio. Barely restrained by Beppe from assaulting his wife on the spot, Canio demands to know her lover's name, but Nedda will not tell him. Canio starts to paint his face and put on his clown's costume, although his heart is breaking ('Vesti la giubba').

Act II After a brief prelude (originally intended as an intermezzo), the audience gathers for the performance. First Harlequin (Beppe) serenades his beloved Colombine (Nedda). Next, with heavy irony Taddeo (Tonio) declares his love for the 'pure' Colombina, but Harlequin arrives and leads him off by the ear. He returns to enjoy a festive supper with Colombine, but soon they are interrupted by Taddeo's announcement that her husband Pagliaccio (Canio) is approaching. Harlequin leaves by the window, but Pagliaccio enters in time to hear Nedda repeating the same promise of an assignation that he heard her use in Act I. With difficulty Canio tries to sustain his comic role, but when Colombine refuses to divulge her lover's name, he can no longer control himself ('No, Pagliaccio non son!'). When Nedda continues to defy him, he stabs her in reality, and with her last breath she utters Silvio's name. Silvio, who has been in the audience, rushes to the stage, but, too late to save Nedda, he becomes Canio's second victim. Hoarsely, Canio announces 'La commedia è finita!' (Originally this line was intended for Tonio, but at least since the time of De Lucia and Caruso it has usually been spoken by the tenor.)

The score contains a wide variety of music, from Tonio's melodic prologue (which is in effect the midsection of the Act I prelude), to Nedda's languorous 'ballatella' 'Stridono lassù' (Act I) and her sensuous duet with Silvio, to Canio's two impassioned arias: 'Vesti la giubba' and 'No, Pagliaccio non son!' The dainty music of the harlequinade (the play within the play in Act II) adds a further fillip to the score, which also manifests traces of Leoncavallo's affection for Wagner in the form of a number of symbolic recurring themes. Although each act is cast as a continuous musical entity, the solos and duets usually end in full cadences, allowing for the applause that Leoncavallo knew was a vital ingredient to a success.

RECORDINGS 1. de Los Angeles, Björling, Warren, Merrill, Robert Shaw Ch, RCA Victor O, Cellini, RCA, 1954: rewardingly sung, vital but slightly dated account; 2. Carlyle, Bergonzi, Taddei, Panerai, La Scala Ch and O, Karajan, DG, 1965: sumptuous, slow, deep-throated reading; 3. Caballé, Domingo, Milnes, McDaniel, John Alldis Ch, LSO, Santi, RCA, 1972; 4. Stratas, Domingo, Pons, Rinaldi, La Scala Ch and O, Prêtre, Philips (also available on video and laserdisc), 1984: Zeffirelli directs the film version – *verismo* at its most realistic and histrionic, with singing to match [A.B.]
EDITIONS f.ss. Sonzogno, 1893; Broude, 1949; v.ss., Sonzogno, 1892; *rp*, 1977; Schirmer, 1934

La bohème

Commedia lirica in four acts (2h 15m)
Libretto by the composer, after Henri Murger's *Scènes de la vie de bohème* (1847–9) and his play (with Barrière) *La vie de bohème* (1849)
Composed 1895–6; rev. 1913
PREMIERES 6 May 1897, La Fenice, Venice; 14 April 1913, Teatro Massimo, Palermo (rev. version in three acts, as *Mimì Pinson, scene della vita di bohème*, later discarded); US: 31 January 1960, Columbia University, New York; UK: 12 May 1970, Camden Town Hall, London
CAST Mimì *s*, Musetta *ms*, Marcello *t*, Rodolfo *bar*, Schaunard *bar*, Colline *bar*, Barbemuche *b*, Gaudenzio *t*, Count Paolo *bar*, Durand *t*, Man on First Floor *t*, Lout *t*, Eufemia *ms*; *satb* chorus of students, neighbours, café patrons, waiters, salesmen
LARGE ORCHESTRA including hp

Although there are inevitable similarities with Puccini's better-known treatment of this subject, Leoncavallo's differs in some significant ways. Instead of, like Puccini, interweaving scenes of comedy and pathos, Leoncavallo restricts the comedy to his first two acts, while the last two are darkly tragic. Furthermore, he makes Marcello the leading tenor role, assigning Rodolfo to the baritone register and Musetta to the mezzo-soprano.

SYNOPSIS
Act I Christmas Eve. At the Café Momus, the proprietor Gaudenzio grumbles at the bohemians' habit of not paying their bills, but Schaunard assures him tonight will be different. The friends assemble; Mimì (already a friend of the group) and Eufemia bring along Musetta, who is attracted to Marcello. Their meal complete, they as usual find they cannot pay. Schaunard challenges Gaudenzio to a game of billiards, wins, and thereby wipes out their debt.
Act II The following April. Musetta has been evicted from her apartment, her wealthy lover unhappy with the attention she has been paying

Marcello. The friends gather and stage a party, replete with musical parodies. Tempted by the proposals of Count Paolo, Mimì decides to leave Rodolfo. The neighbours complain about the brouhaha below.
Act III October. In their garret, Marcello and Schaunard decide they must earn money. Musetta, tired of poverty, decides to leave Marcello and in his absence writes him a farewell note. Mimì returns to be reconciled with Rodolfo. He rejects her, and Marcello, convinced she has turned Musetta away from him, is furious with her.
Act IV Christmas Eve, the next year. As the friends are remembering the previous Christmas Eve, the consumptive Mimì, prematurely turned out of hospital, returns, her strength failing. When Musetta appears, she pawns her jewels to get help for Mimì, but it is too late and Mimì dies.

When Leoncavallo entered the contest with Puccini for *La bohème* (having once offered his text to him, which was refused), he had no idea how hugely successful his rival's opera would prove. Unfairly eclipsed, without being the equal of Puccini's score, Leoncavallo's can boast much attractive light music in the first two acts and several strong ariosi in the final two. In a pathetic attempt to compete with Puccini, Leoncavallo revised his score in 1913, making Rodolfo a tenor role, but this tinkering failed to give the work new life and the revision (which was renamed to distinguish it from its rival) was discarded.

RECORDINGS 1. Mazza Medici, Casei, Annaloro, Mazzini, Ch of Teatro Comunale, Bologna, San Remo PO, Zedda, Cetra, 1963; 2. Popp, Milcheva, Bonisolli, Weikl, Titus, Munich Radio, Wallberg, Orfeo, 1981; 3. Mazzaria-Scandiuzzi, Senn, Malagnini, Summers, Praticò, Ch and O of La Fenice, Latham-Koenig, Nuova Era, 1990
EDITIONS f.s./v.s., Sonzogno, 1897; *rp*, 1979; rev. version: v.s., Sonzogno, 1913

Zazà

Commedia lirica in four acts (1h 45m)
Libretto by the composer, after the play by Charles Simon and Pierre Berton (1898)
Composed 1899–1900
PREMIERES 10 November 1900, Teatro Lirico, Milan; US: 27 November 1903, Tivoli, San Francisco; UK: 30 April 1909, Coronet Theatre, London

Backstage at the music-hall where she is a star, Zazà awaits the arrival of her intended lover Milio Dufresne. She gives up her career for him. Cascart, her former music-hall partner, who loves Zazà himself, warns that Milio's unexplained absences are not a good sign. She learns that Milio is already married. With an effort, she calls at his house, using an assumed name, and is entertained by his young daughter. The child's innocent happiness forces Zazà to recall her own childhood, abandoned by her father and with a dypsomaniac mother. She resolves to break off the relationship with Milio, forgoing her own happiness.

Ruggero Leoncavallo (centre) with the cast of Zazà *(Milan, 1900)*

This opera, like Cilea's *Adriana Lecouvreur*, is a vehicle for a singer with a strong dramatic bent and an equally strong stomach for sentimentality. Zazà's Act III aria 'Mamma usciva da casa' and her Act IV arioso require skilful projecting of text and vocal colour to disguise their musical lameness. Leoncavallo's proclivity for light music finds expression in the Act I music-hall scene, where he was able to draw on his own experience as an entertainer in Paris. His congenial writing for the baritone voice is confirmed by Cascart's two effective arias.

RECORDINGS 1. Petrella, Campora, Turtura, Turin Ch and O of RAI, Silipigni, Cetra, 1970; 2. Favero, Dubbini, Prandelli, Tagliabue, Ch and O of RAI, Ghione, EJS, 1947
EDITIONS v.s., Sonzogno, 1900; rev. version by R. Bianchi: f.s,. Sonzogno, 1900; v.s., Sonzogno, 1947

Edipo Re
King Oedipus

Opera in one act (1h 15m)
Libretto by Giovacchino Forzano, after the play *Oedipus Tyrannus* by Sophocles (c. 435–25 BC)
Begun 1918–19; completed posthumously by G. Pennacchio
PREMIERES 13 December 1920, Auditorium, Chicago; Italy: 13 October 1939, RAI, Turin

Having arrived as a stranger from Corinth, Edipo has been made King of Thebes for ridding it of the murderous Sphinx, and he has married the widowed Queen Giocasta. He boasts that he will rid the city of the plague that infests it. By a series of disclosures, the truth is revealed that the unclean thing endangering the city is Edipo himself. He has both murdered his father (a stranger he encountered on the road) and married his own mother, crimes for which he accepts responsibility. Giocasta is unable to bear the shame and kills herself. Edipo blinds himself and goes into exile.

Even had Leoncavallo lived long enough to complete it, it is doubtful *Edipo* would have been a success. With the exception of some vigorous choruses, the composer's musical eloquence is stretched beyond its limits. The music is vocally grateful in an Italianate way (for instance with well-

prepared high notes), but it would take an exceptionally convincing baritone in the title role to arouse interest in *Edipo Re*.

RECORDING Malagrida, Infantino, Fioravanti, Malaspina, Dondi, Ch and O of the San Carlo, Naples, La Rosa Parodi, MRF, 1970
EDITION v.s., Baltramo (San Remo), c. 1959

Other operas: *Chatterton*, (1876), rev. 1896, 2nd rev. 1905; *Songe d'un nuit d'été*, 1889 (private performance); *I Medici* (inc.), (c. 1877–92), 1893; *Der Roland von Berlin*, 1904; *Maia*, (1908), 1910; *Gli zingari*, 1912 (RECORDING MRF, 1970); *Ave Maria* (abandoned 1915); *Tormenta* (inc.); *Prometeo*, (n.d.)
Operettas: *La jeunesse de Figaro*, 1906; *Malbrouck*, 1910; *La reginetta della rose*, 1912 (RECORDING excerpts: EJS, 1950s); *Are you there?*, 1913; *La candidata*, 1915; *Prestami tua moglie*, 1916; *Goffredo Mameli*, 1916; *A chi la giarrettiera?*, 1919; *Il primo bacio*, 1923; *La maschera nuda* (inc.; completed S. Allegra), 1925
BIBLIOGRAPHY J. W. Klein, 'Ruggero Leoncavallo (1857–1919)', *Opera*, vol. 9 (1958), pp. 158, 232; D. Rubboli, *Ridi, Pagliaccio*, Fazzi, 1985

W.A.

FRANCO LEONI
b 24 October 1864, Milan; *d* 8 February 1949, London

Leoni studied in Milan under Ponchielli, but when his first opera produced little impression (1890), he emigrated to London, where he made a modest place for himself. *L'oracolo*, the work by which he is remembered today, was preceded by two operas to English texts: *Rip Van Winkle* (1897) and *Ib and Little Christina* (1902).

Nothing in his subsequent career as an opera composer matched the success of *L'oracolo*. *Francesca da Rimini* (1913) survived at the Opéra-Comique for only seven performances, and three later stage works met no warmer welcome in his native Milan. Leoni's music is fluent but lacks a salient individuality.

L'oracolo
The Oracle

Opera in one act (1h)
Libretto by Camillo Zanoni, after Chester Bailey Fernald's story *The Cat and the Cherub* (1896)
PREMIERES 3 July 1905, Covent Garden, London; US: 4 February 1915, Metropolitan, New York

The lurid Grand-Guignol plot, set in San Francisco's Chinatown, provided the baritone Antonio Scotti with one of his most memorable characterizations as the sinister, opium-dealing Chim-Fen. For the seasons in which Leoni toured the States with his own Scotti Grand Opera Company, *L'oracolo* formed one of the linchpins of the repertoire. There have been few revivals since.

RECORDING Sutherland, Tourangeau, Davies, Gobbi, John Alldis Ch, National PO, Bonynge, Decca, 1975

EDITION f.s./v.s., Sonzogno, 1900

Other operas: *Reggio de Luna*, 1890; *Rip Van Winkle*, 1897; *Ib and Little Christina*, 1902; *Tzigana*, 1910; *Francesca da Rimini*, 1913; *Le baruffe chiozzotte*, 1920; *Falene*, 1920; *La terra del sogno*, 1920; *Massemarello*, (n.d.)

W.A.

XAVIER LEROUX

Xavier Henry Napoléon Leroux; *b* 11 October 1863, Velletri; *d* 2 February 1919, Paris

A pupil of Massenet at the Paris Conservatoire, Leroux won the Prix de Rome in 1885, and was thus in Rome (one of the requirements of the prize) at the same time as Debussy, who had won it the previous year. The two were close friends, and it was apparently Leroux who introduced Debussy to Shakespeare's works through a series of readings with another friend, Paul Vidal.

Leroux's first opera, *Evangeline*, dates from his Rome years, and most of his music thereafter was for the theatre, either as incidental music or as opera. His operatic work is broadly in the *verismo* tradition of Massenet and Charpentier, but that description is usually qualified in Leroux's case with praise for his poetic sensitivity and refined harmony and orchestration. His best-known opera, *Le chemineau*, adds vigour to its sentimental tale of a tramp who deserts his pregnant lover to follow the call of the road, through genre scenes of a vitality and freshness almost worthy of Bizet.

Operas: *Evangeline*, 1885; *Vénus et Adonis*, 1887; *Astarté*, 1901; *La Reine Fiammette*, 1903; *William Ratcliff*, 1906; *Théodora*, 1907; *Le chemineau*, 1907; *Le carillonneur*, 1913; *La fille de Figaro*, 1914; *Les cadeaux de Noël*, 1915; *1814*, 1918; *Nausithoé*, 1920; *La plus forte*, 1924; *L'ingénu*, 1931

S.W.

JEAN-FRANÇOIS LE SUEUR

b 15 February 1760, nr Abbeville, France; *d* 6 October 1837, Paris

Le Sueur's reputation was made before the Revolution as a church musician and composer of dramatic oratorios. He had studied with Sacchini before the latter's death in 1786. Thus, after the suppression of the churches, it was a short step to his first operas, produced in the thick of the Revolution. The first two, *Paul et Virginie* and *Télémaque*, performed at the Théâtre Feydeau, were – with *La caverne* – his biggest public successes. (*Télémaque* was actually the first to be written but was not performed until 1796.) In 1804 Le Sueur was fortunate to obtain the patronage of Napoleon, who placed him in musical charge of the Tuileries Chapel. In the same year the composer saw his most ambitious work to date, *Ossian*, given at the Opéra. This large-scale, unconventional treatment of its

source poem also covertly praised Napoleon's policy in restoring the Catholic church. Le Sueur's second grand opera, *La mort d'Adam*, inspired by Klopstock's drama, had already been partially composed. Winton Dean described the final result as 'the most spectacular opera ever conceived . . . The characters embrace not only the entire human race but the total population of heaven and hell.'

In 1818 Le Sueur began teaching at the Conservatoire where his pupils included Berlioz, Thomas and Gounod. His final opera, *Alexandre à Babylone*, was never staged, though it was privately engraved in full score. It had been ordered by Napoleon whose fall effectively sealed the opera's failure before it could even be seen. Le Sueur's final compositions were religious vocal works for the Chapel, where he worked until its closure in 1830.

La caverne
The Cavern
Drame lyrique in three acts (2h 30m)
Libretto by Palat, called Dercy, after Alain-René Lesage's novel, *Gil Blas de Santillane* (1735)
PREMIERE 16 February 1793, Théâtre Feydeau, Paris

The work is a representative example of a revolutionary 'tyrant' opera. The score specifies that the stage be divided horizontally: the cavern is below, a forest above. Séraphine, a noblewoman, and Gil Blas are held prisoner by a gang of robbers. Gil Blas hatches an escape plan. In Act II Alphonse, Séraphine's husband, who is searching for her in the forest, is captured and protects his wife. In the last act Rolando, the bandits' leader, in some danger from a *coup* by his own men, repents his ways, and discovers he is Séraphine's brother. Gil Blas appears with a group of rescuers who attack the cavern, free the prisoners, and shoot the robbers. The music is characterized by violent effects, sudden dynamic changes, unexpected harmonies, pounding rhythms and much use of the chorus.

EDITION f.s., facsimile, Jean Mongrédien (ed.), *French Opera in the 17th and 18th Centuries*, vol. 74, Pendragon, 1986

Ossian, ou Les bardes
Ossian, or The Bards
Opera in five acts (3h)
Libretto by Palat, called Dercy (rev. Jacques Marie Deschamps), after *Calthon and Colmal* by 'Ossian' (James Macpherson), trans. Felicien le Tourneur (1777)
PREMIERE 10 July 1804, Opéra, Paris

The setting is 3rd-century Scotland. A section of Caledonians, defeated by Scandinavians under Duntalmo, is threatened with imposition of Odin-worship. The senior Caledonian bard has a daughter, Rosmala, whom Duntalmo wants for his own son. Rosmala's lover, Ossian, arrives in Act II, but is captured by Duntalmo. The Caledonians deprecate the Scandinavian religion. In Act IV Ossian has a dream partially enacted behind backlit gauze (specified in the score); it features bards, heroes, young virgins, Rosmala, and a tomb. In the last act the Caledonians prepare for death, but Duntalmo's forces are defeated by another group of Ossian's confederates.

The score is replete with important curiosities: modal music for the Caledonians, 'songs of Selma', tam-tam strokes for the striking of ceremonial shields and 12 harps intended to suffuse the texture with Bardic glory. There are also several recurring motifs (a device Le Sueur was to develop further in *La mort d'Adam*), used with some subtlety. Berlioz was influenced both by the opera's techniques and by its visionary subjectivity. Moreover, its use of spectacle and religious themes alone places it directly in line with grand opera.

EDITIONS f.ss., Imbault, 1804–5; facsimile (with an introduction by Charles Rosen), *Early Romantic Opera*, no. 37, Garland, 1979; v.s., facsimile, Broude, 1970

Other operas: *Paul et Virginie*, 1794; *Télémaque dans l'isle de Calypso, ou Le triomphe de la sagesse*, (*c.* 1786); 1796; *L'inauguration du temple de la victoire* (coll. with L. L. de Persuis), 1807; *Le triomphe de Trajan* (coll. with L. L. de Persuis), 1807; *La mort d'Adam suivie de son apothéose*, (*c.* 1800), 1809; *Alexandre à Babylone*, (*c.* 1814)

BIBLIOGRAPHY Winton Dean, 'French Opera', in *New Oxford History of Music*, vol. 8, pp. 26–119, OUP, 1982

D.P.C.

RICHARD LEVERIDGE

b 1670 or 1671; *d* 22 March 1758, London

The singer Richard Leveridge was something of an institution in the 18th-century English theatre. In 1695 he came to prominence as Henry Purcell's leading bass after the break-up of the United Company. He created the role of the magician Ismeron in *The Indian Queen*. He went on to write for and sing in a number of post-Purcell plays and semi-operas, notably *The Island Princess* (his 'Enthusiastic Song' was famous for over 40 years) and *Macbeth* (his 1702 incidental music stayed in the repertoire for more than a century). With his comic masque, *Pyramus and Thisbe* (1716), Leveridge was the first composer to detach the mechanicals' play from Shakespeare's *A Midsummer Night's Dream*, switching the satire in the process from plays and players to opera and opera singers. Unfortunately, his setting is lost, though Lampe's 1745 version of essentially the same text is reconstructable. Leveridge also contributed to Peter Motteux's lost interlude, *Britain's Happiness* (1704).

As a composer Leveridge confined himself to vocal music and tended to hark back to Purcell, though he managed as a singer to adapt to the successive demands of Italian opera (including several by Handel) and pantomime. He continued to sing until 1751, though in later years he confined himself largely to undemanding ballads, typified by his most famous song, 'The Roast Beef of Old England'.

The Island Princess

Collaboration with Daniel Purcell, Jeremiah Clarke and others

Semi-opera

Text by John Fletcher, adapted by Nahum Tate and Peter Motteux

PREMIERE ?7 February 1699, Drury Lane, London

The Island Princess was the most successful and important post-Purcell semi-opera. Unusually for the period, it survives in its entirety. Set in the East Indies, it concerns the unjust imprisonment and threatened execution of the Portuguese hero, Armusia, and native heroine, Quisara. Leveridge contributed three songs.

EDITION facsimile, Curtis Price and Robert Hume (eds), *Music in London Entertainment*, series C, vol. 2, Macnutt, 1985

BIBLIOGRAPHY Roger Fiske, *English Theatre Music in the Eighteenth Century*, OUP, 1973; 2nd edn, 1986

P.H.

JOSÉ LIDÓN

José [Josef] Lidón; *b* ?1746, Béjar, nr Salamanca, Spain; *d* 11 February 1827, Madrid

Lidón was appointed as an organist to the Royal Chapel in Madrid in 1768, 'teacher of Italian-style singing' in the Real Colegio de Niños Cantorcicos in 1771 and finally chapel master of the Royal Chapel and rector of the Royal College in 1805. Though best known for his devotional and instrumental works, he wrote in 1791 a curious opera, *Glaura y Cariolán*, whose significance has often been misunderstood. The explicit aim of this *drama heroico* was to demonstrate that Spanish was an appropriate language for the expressive inflexions (*modulaciones*) and the tragic effects of Italian opera, as stated (probably by Lidón himself) in the prologue of the 1792 publication. However, the libretto is derived from an episode in Ercilla's New World epic of the Spanish conquest of the Araucanian Indians in Chile and Lidón explored more disturbing issues of non-Hispanic nobility and generosity in the face of despair, robbery, rape and incest. He was thus concerned to foster not just Italian operatic expressiveness but a supra-national perspective.

BIBLIOGRAPHY Antonio Martín Moreno, *Historia de la música española*, vol. 4: *Siglo XVIII*, Alianza, 1985; J. Subirá, *Historia de la música teatral en España*, Barcelona, 1945

J.W.S.

GYÖRGY LIGETI

György Sándor Ligeti; *b* 28 May 1923, Diciosânmartin [or Dicsöszentmárton], Transylvania (now Tirnaveni, Romania)

Ligeti came late not only to opera but also to the

music he really wanted to write. He began his musical life in Hungary where the political climate did not allow experiment. In 1956 he moved to Vienna and quickly became involved with Western Europe's most avant-garde circles, writing electronic music at the WDR studios in Cologne and producing in the 1960s a stream of works very different from the total serialism then in vogue. With the orchestral piece *Atmosphères* (1961) and the organ composition *Volumina* (1961–2, rev. 1966) Ligeti created huge swirling clouds of sound by writing an immensely complex web of closely packed polyphony. He went on to explore this further in his celebrated *Requiem* (1963–5, used in the soundtrack of the film *2001*), *Lontano* (1967, for orchestra), *Melodien* (1971, for chamber orchestra) and the Concerto for flute, oboe and orchestra (1972).

His operatic music belongs to a different line of thinking, a joking, perhaps cynical view of the world that produced the *Poème symphonique* (1962) for 100 metronomes set at different tempi, which lasts as long as it takes for them all to run down, *Continuum* for harpsichord (1968), where different metres are superimposed so that the music is in a perpetual rhythmic and colouristic flux determined by pitch changes, and *Clocks and Clouds* for female chorus and orchestra (1972–3), where the sound of metronomes becomes gradually less distinct.

The two dramatic entertainments from the early 1960s, *Aventures* and *Nouvelles aventures*, are like late manifestations of Dadaism, for though the texts are meaningless phonetics, when allied to the music they make a disconcerting blend of the playful and the menacing.

After their success Ligeti wanted to write a larger-scale 'imaginary opera' to a meaningless text but neither that idea nor his next operatic project, a version of the Oedipus myth, came to anything, though they amalgamated to some extent in the opera he did eventually write, *Le grand macabre*, a surrealist opera about death, conceived as a farce.

Aventures/Nouvelles aventures

Adventures/New Adventures
Originally concert works composed 1962 and 1962–5 (both 12m)
Rev. for the stage as musical-dramatic action in 14 scenes, 1966 (both 40m)
PREMIERES 19 October 1966, Württembergisches Staatstheater, Kammertheater, Stuttgart; UK: 3 August 1988, Queen Elizabeth Hall, London (Opera Factory)
CAST coloratura s, a, bar, mimes, dancers, extras
INSTRUMENTATION fl, hn, vc, (5-str) db, perc, hpd, pf/cel

Both works are scored for the same combination of three voices and seven players and explore, often humorously, the overlapping areas of vocally and instrumentally produced sounds. There are no intelligible words nor is there any conventional vocalizing; the works are undefined as to content but precisely defined as to the emotions expressed. They are like a stream of events that consist of different expressive character – mystical, idyllic, nostalgic, funereal, etc. In the stage version the original's bizarre and extravagant qualities are paralleled by

Ligeti's very precise staging requirements, surreal and apparently meaningless. Silence plays an important part and Ligeti requires that in these silences everyone, including the instrumentalists, freeze. Both works are subdivided into sections with individual titles, for example *Commerages* ('Gossip') – an exchange of fast repeated notes between the singers and some of the players – and *Communication*, where the singers use cardboard tubes to make them sound as if they are on long-distance telephone calls. The range of percussion noises includes bursting a paper bag, rubbing a suitcase with sandpaper and the scuffling of feet on the floor.

RECORDINGS 1. Charlent, Cahn, Pearson, International Kammerensemble Darmstadt, Maderna, Wergo, 1966: historically authentic; 2. Manning, Thomas, Pearson, Ensemble InterContemporain, Boulez, DG, 1983: more cautious
EDITIONS *Aventures*: study s., Litolff/Peters, 1964; *Nouvelles aventures*: study s., Litolff/Peters, 1966

Le grand macabre

Opera in two acts (four scenes) (2h)
Libretto by the composer and Michael K. J. A. Meschke freely adapted from the farce *La balade du grand macabre* (1934) by Michel de Ghelderode
Composed 1972–6
PREMIERES 2 April 1978, Royal Opera, Stockholm; UK: 2 December 1982, Coliseum, London
CAST Piet the Pot *high buffo t*, Miranda (originally Clitonia) s, Armando (originally Spermando) ms, Nekrotzar bar, Astradamors b, Mescalina *dramatic ms*, Venus *high s*, White Minister *spoken role*, Black Minister *spoken role*, Prince Go-Go ct, Chief of the Secret Police *coloratura s*, Ruffiak, Schobiak and Schabernak 3 bar; satb chorus of people of Breughelland; offstage: satb chorus of the spirits; echo of Venus sa chorus; boys' chorus; extras: men of the secret police, executioners, pages and servants at the court of Prince Go-Go, Nekrotzar's infernal entourage
ORCHESTRATION full (but only 3 vn, 2 va, 6 vc, 4 db), including 3 mouth organs, electronic and mental horns; onstage: picc, ob, ca, E♭cl, bsn, 2 tpt, 2 trbn, perc (1 player: Paradetrommel, siren, gong), retuned vn; bass tpt plays behind scenes or in auditorium throughout the opera

The opera was commissioned by the Stockholm Royal Opera in 1965 but took 13 years to be written and reach the stage. It was an immediate success and was quickly taken up by European opera houses. The plot is surreal though its essence is that the only certainty of life is that it will end in death and so one might as well eat, drink and be merry. The setting is also surreal, a place ruled over by anobese boy prince and populated by, among others, a transvestite visionary astronomer with a sadistic and sexually enterprising wife and a chief of police who is a manic coloratura soprano. It is called Breughelland, but it could perhaps be reality.

SYNOPSIS
Act I Scene 1: After a palindromic prelude for car horns, one of the citizens of Breughelland, the alcoholic Piet the Pot, sings the praises of his homeland while Miranda and Armando look for somewhere to make love; a mysterious figure, Nekrotzar, the figure of death (the *grand macabre*

Nils Johansson (Black Minister), Gunilla Slattegard (Prince Go-Go) and Dmitri Chermeteff (White Minister) in Le grand macabre *(Stockholm, 1978)*

himself), announces that the end of the world will occur at midnight. He forces Piet to help him in his task of world destruction. Scene 2: The astronomer Astradamors has to feign death to escape his appalling wife Mescalina's voracious and painfully unorthodox sexual appetites; she revives him by dropping a spider on him. Through his telescope he sees a fast approaching comet and other signs of Armageddon while his wife, in a drunken stupor, implores Venus to send her a man who will satisfy her desires. Nekrotzar is the man, and while Piet and her husband look on Mescalina dies in ecstasy. A satisfied Nekrotzar takes Piet off to destroy the palace, leaving a happy Astramadors.

Act II   Scene 3: The boy prince tries to chair a meeting between his two ministers but the absurdities of politics are beyond him so they play schoolboy games, understood by everyone, until the secret police burst in. They are all dressed as birds and their leader is a dazzling coloratura soprano. She tells the prince that the people are in revolt and are marching on the palace. He pacifies the people but they are all thrown into a panic when Nekrotzar threatens impending doom. Though drunk, before he passes out he utters the words that will bring the world to an end. Scene 4: No one is really sure whether the end of the world has actually happened.

Nekrotzar seems to think it has not, or if it has there are too many survivors. He tries to escape but is chased by the voracious Mescalina who remembers him well. He realizes his mission is a failure and dissolves. The two lovers emerge from their love nest, oblivious of the great events that have passed. Everyone realizes the moral: if death is coming for you, you cannot escape it, so do not fear it, ignore it.

The music is more in the quick-cutting comic style of *Aventures* than the almost static cloudlike sound of works such as *Lontano*. There are many direct references to other works as well as a feeling that the frequently tongue-in-cheek characterization is rooted in the past. The music of the two lovers, Miranda and Amando, has a Monteverdian richness as entwined as their bodies and the opera ends with a baroque conceit, a grand passacaglia. Nekrotzar's entrance in Act II is preceded by the opera's most obvious quotation and transformation, the 'Prometheus' theme from the finale of Beethoven's 'Eroica' Symphony.

RECORDING   Excerpts: Nielsen, Fredricks, Haage, Weller, Danish Radio Ch and O, Howarth, Wergo, 1970s
EDITIONS   v.s., Schott, 1978; lib. (trans Geoffrey Skelton), Schott, 1982

BIBLIOGRAPHY Paul Griffiths, *Gyorgy Ligeti*, Robson, 1983

C.B.

GIUSEPPE LILLO

b 26 February 1814, Galatina; *d* 4 February 1863, Naples

Lillo studied in Lecce and Naples, where he first appeared as a composer with a Mass for four voices with orchestra. But in 1834 the success of his first opera, *La moglie per 24 ore*, turned his attention to the theatre, and during the years that followed he achieved considerable fame as a good operatic composer in the Rossinian manner. He produced his best work, *L'osteria di Andujar*, in 1840. Its successors did not do so well, however, and he took up teaching in Naples, where he was appointed professor of composition at the conservatory in 1859. Not long after this he became insane and died aged 48.

Operas: *La moglie per 24 ore, ossia L'ammalato di buona salute*, 1834; *Il gioiello*, 1835; *Odda di Bernaver*, 1837; *Rosmunda in Ravenna*, 1837; *Alisia di Rieux*, 1838; *Il conte di Chalais*, 1839; *La modista*, 1839; *Le disgrazie d'un bel giovane, ossia Il zio ed il nipote*, 1840; *L'osteria di Andujar*, 1840; *Cristina di Svezia*, 1841; *Lara*, 1842; *Il cavaliere di S. Giorgio, ossia Il mulatto*, 1846; *Caterina Howard*, 1849; *La Delfina*, 1850; *La gioventù di Shakespeare, ossia Il sogno d'una notte estiva*, 1851; *Ser Babbeo*, 1853; *Il figlio della schiava*, 1853
BIBLIOGRAPHY Francesco Bussi, 'Giuseppe Lillo', *Grove*, Macmillan, 1980

M.R.

PAUL LINCKE

b 7 November 1866, Berlin; *d* 3 September 1946, Clausthal-Zellerfeld, Germany

Lincke, the founder of the Berlin operetta school, began as a bassoonist in theatre orchestras, later conducting and composing for music-halls. He wrote numerous popular songs, composed one-act operettas for the Apollo Theatre, Berlin, and conducted two seasons at the Folies-Bergère, Paris. *Frau Luna* (1899) established his fame, with its frankly Parisian basis and its bubbly, but more 'Prussian' numbers, of which the 'Berliner Luft' was the most celebrated. *Lysistrata* (1902) provided an even more famous extract, the 'Glühwürmchen-Idyll', played internationally by variety theatres, salon orchestras, and on parlour pianos. Many of the short operettas were later expanded, while the separate songs were ensured lasting popularity by the assiduous and lucrative activities of Lincke's own Apollo-Verlag publishing company.

One of the few operetta composers who could remain in Germany after 1933, Lincke presided over several revivals of his old works. He was honoured by the Nazi hierarchy, who capitalized on the public's nostalgia for the pre-Depression Berlin so cheerfully conjured up by Lincke's catchy tunes.

Operettas: *Ein Abenteuer im Harem*, 1897; *Eine lustige Spreewaldfahrt*, 1897, rev. 1908; *Venus auf Erden*, 1897; *Frau Luna*, 1899 (RECORDING excerpts: RCA, 1975); *Im Reiche des Indra*, 1899; *Fräulein Loreley*, 1900; *Lysistrata*, 1902; *Nakiris Hochzeit*, 1902; *Berliner Luft*, 1904; *Am Hochzeitabend*, 1904; *Prinzessin Rosine*, 1905; *Immer obenauf*, 1908; *Grigri*, 1911; *Casanova*, 1913; *Fräulein Kadett*, 1914; *Ein Liebestraum* (radio), (1940)
BIBLIOGRAPHY Otto Schneidereit, *Paul Lincke und die Entstehung der Berliner Operette*, Henschelverlag, 1974

R.T.

PETER LINDPAINTNER

Peter Joseph von Lindpaintner; *b* 9 December 1791, Koblenz; *d* 21 August 1856, Nonnehorn, Lake Constance

Lindpaintner was an important secondary figure in the history of German Romantic opera. He studied in Munich, where his first opera, *Demophoon*, was successfully performed in 1811, the year before he became music director at the city's Isartortheater. From 1819 he was kapellmeister in Stuttgart, establishing a reputation as one of Germany's leading conductors.

At Munich Lindpaintner turned out a stream of unambitious but tuneful stage works, but his Stuttgart operas are more enterprising, reflecting recent tendencies in the operas of Spohr and Weber. His greatest successes were *Der Bergkönig* (1825), based on the same folk-tale as Spohr's *Der Berggeist* (also 1825) and Weber's *Rübezahl/Der Beherrscher der Geister* (1804–5), and *Der Vampyr*.

Der Vampyr
The Vampire
Romantic opera in three acts
Composed 1828, rev. 1850 (original dialogue replaced with recitative)
Libretto by Caspar Max Heigel, after John William Polidori's story *The Vampyre* (1819), trans. L. Ritter (1822)
PREMIERES 21 September 1828, Stuttgart; rev. version: 26 April 1850, Stuttgart

Lindpaintner's most successful opera is based on the same sources as Marschner's better-known work, premiered just six months earlier. The influence of Spohr and Weber is apparent, particularly in the use of *polacca* rhythms and chromatic harmony.

EDITION v.s., Vienna, 1839

Other operas: *Demophoon*, 1811; *Der blinde Gärtner, oder die blühende Aloe*, c. 1812; *Die Pflegekinder*, c. 1812; *Die Prinzessin von Cacambo, c.* 1814; *Das Sternenmädchen/Die Sternkönigin*, 1815; *Das Christusbild, oder Kunstsinn und Liebe*, 1816; *Hans Alex Giesbrecht von der Humpenburg, oder Die neue Ritterzeit*, 1816; *Pervonte, oder Die Drei Wünsche*, 1816; *Das Rosenmädchen*, 1818; *Timantes*, 1819; *Sulmona* (rev. of *Demophoon*), 1823; *Der Bergkönig*, 1825; *Die Amazone, oder Der Frauen und der Liebe Sieg*, 1831; *Die Bürgschaft*, 1834; *Die Macht des Liedes*, 1836; *Die*

Genueserin, 1839; *Die Sicilianische Vesper*, 1843; *Lichtenstein*, 1846; *Giulia, oder Die Corsen*, 1853; *Libella*, (1855)

BIBLIOGRAPHY   R. Hänsler, *Peter Lindpaintner als Opernkomponist*, dissertation, University of Munich, 1928

C.A.B.

THOMAS LINLEY (Jnr)

b 5 May 1756, Bath, England; *d* 5 August 1778, Grimsthorpe, Lincolnshire, England

The most promising member of an exceptionally gifted musical family, Linley was drowned in the lake at Grimsthorpe Castle at the age of 22. His father, a West Country man, had been responsible for the concerts in the Bath Assembly Rooms from *c.* 1755 to *c.* 1774, thereafter becoming director of music (with John Stanley) at the Drury Lane Theatre. Thomas Jnr was an infant prodigy on the violin, and spent three years studying the instrument with Nardini in Florence, where he met and became close friends with Mozart. His significance in English operatic history is that he was the composer principally responsible for Sheridan's pasticcio opera *The Duenna*.

The Duenna

Comic opera with spoken dialogue in three acts (2h 30m)
Libretto by Richard Brinsley Sheridan
PREMIERES   21 November 1775, Covent Garden, London; US: 10 July 1786, New York

By far the most successful English ballad opera of the 18th century, *The Duenna* eclipsed even *The Beggar's Opera* in popular favour. Linley *père* seems to have had formal charge of the music, but there can be no question that his son did the bulk of the work of arrangement besides contributing the majority of the original airs, described by Hazlitt as having 'a joyous spirit of intoxication in them, and a strain of the most melting tenderness'. The result, according to Nigel Playfair, has often been damningly dismissed as 'Handel and water' but there is no justice in this. The songs and their harmonization come nearer to an authentic Mozartian idiom than anything else in the English repertoire. It is regrettable that when Playfair successfully revived the piece in 1924 he encouraged Alfred Reynolds to adapt the score to a point at which it is no longer recognizable as Linley's.

The scene is Seville. Don Jerome, a man of no patience and handy with a blunderbuss, attempts to compel his beautiful daughter, Louisa, to marry a rich Jew, Isaac. Louisa is in love with the impoverished Antonio and detests Isaac 'as a lover, and shall ten times more as a husband'. The duenna arranges assignations between Louisa and Antonio; Jerome sacks the duenna and incarcerates Louisa, who disguises herself as the duenna and flees, leaving Isaac to marry the duenna; in the ensuing imbroglio Antonio and Louisa are fortuitously and happily married. Isaac is sympathetically treated and by no means a stage villain. The anti-Semitic and anti-

feminist elements were noted at the time as being 'somewhat Irish'.

EDITION   v.s., C. and S. Thompson, 1775
MANUSCRIPTS   f.s., British Library, London; Guildhall Library, London

BIBLIIOGRAPHY   Roger Fiske, *English Theatre Music in the Eighteenth Century*, OUP, 1973; 2nd edn, 1986; Nigel Playfair (ed.), *The Duenna*, Constable, 1925; Cecil Price (ed.), *The Dramatic Works of Richard Brinsley Sheridan*, Clarendon Press, 1973

R.Lu.

VATROSLAV LISINSKI

Vatroslav Lisinski (Ignac [Ignacije] Fuchs); *baptized* 8 July 1819, Zagreb; *d* 31 May 1854, Zagreb

Lisinski was the founder of Croatian opera and a leading light in the nationalist 'Illyrian' movement of the 1830s and 1840s. Like many figures in Croatian music at the time he was essentially an amateur. Nevertheless in 1845 he composed the first Croatian opera, *Lyubav i zloba* (*Love and Malice*; orchestrated by his teacher, Wisner von Morgenstern). This played an important part in arousing nationalist sentiments; soon after its premiere in Zagreb in 1846 Croatian was made the official language in public affairs.

From 1847 to 1849 Lisinski studied in Prague, greatly improving his composing technique, though he was not eligible for a formal qualification. His second opera, *Porin* (1851), shows in its patriotic subject and use of folk idioms an increased awareness of Romantic nationalism, as well as of leitmotif technique. However, political events in the wake of 1848 forced Lisinski to abandon music and the opera had to wait until 1897 for its premiere.

BIBLIOGRAPHY   Josip Andreis, trans. Vladimir Ivin, *Music in Croatia*, Institute of Musicology/Academy of Music, Zagreb, 1973; 2nd edn, 1982

M.A.

FERENC LISZT

Ferenc (Franz) Liszt; *b* 22 October 1811, Raiding (now in Austria); *d* 31 July 1886, Bayreuth

Although Liszt completed only one opera – *Don Sanche* – and that at the age of 13, his preoccupation with the dissemination and performance of operas occupied him for much of his professional life, whether as a pioneering conductor–producer or as a pianist–composer.

Apart from his youthful work, Liszt made only sketches, during his most prolific period at Weimar, for various operatic projects which came to nothing – although the most significant attempt, *Sardanapole*, after Byron, runs to 111 pages. The only near-opera

Costume designs for Don Sanche *(Paris, 1825)*

that Liszt completed was his oratorio *The Legend of Saint Elizabeth*, which was successfully staged as an opera, against Liszt's wishes and without his attendance, at Weimar in 1881. It enjoyed a modest career in this form for half a century.

A word is due in praise of Liszt's achievement in elevating the piano work based on operatic themes to a height that has not been surpassed and seldom approached by other composers. The aims of these 50 or so piano works were many: the propagation of the deserving but unknown, the familiarization of an audience with the material, the challenge of a new form akin to but different from variation, the sedulous imitation of voices and orchestra at the keyboard and the encapsulation in a relatively small work of the dramatic ambit of a much larger one all play their part. In the largest and finest of the fantasies, such as *Don Giovanni* or *Norma*, Liszt reveals uncanny insight into the originals, and one can only regret that his interest in opera composition was stifled by his very enthusiasm for other men's work.

Don Sanche

(Le château d'amour)
(The Castle of Love)
Lyric opera in one act (with ballet) (1h 30m)
Libretto by Emmanuel Guillaume M. Théaulon de Lambert and de Rancé, after a story by Claris de Florian
Composed 1824–5

PREMIERES 17 October 1825 (five days before Liszt's 14th birthday), Théâtre de l'Académie Royale de Musique, Paris; UK: 20 October 1977, Collegiate Theatre, London; US: November 1986, Miami (semi-staged)

This opera was Liszt's first substantial composition of any sort, and almost the earliest surviving work from his pen. 'His pen' must, however, be taken cautiously, for it seems very likely that Paër, and perhaps Reicha and Kreutzer, had a hand, not just in the orchestration, but even in the general layout of the piece. That said, the opera is a remarkably professional work for any young composer, worthy of comparison with Mozart's *Lucia Silla*. The influences of Rossini and Gluck, among others, are plain, but exceedingly well digested.

The libretto afforded the young composer many opportunities to flex his musical muscles, but it is a shoddy piece of work, and the plot is quite preposterous.

SYNOPSIS
The magician Alidor presides over the castle of love. Don Sanche is suicidal because he may not enter since he loves but is not loved. Elzire, the object of his love, is affianced to the Prince of Navarre, whom she does not love. She arrives at the castle in search of shelter, thanks to some inclement weather organized by Alidor, but cannot meet the conditions of entry. A certain Romualde appears, with the

intention of kidnapping Elzire, who at least shows some sympathy for Don Sanche as he fights to save her. Don Sanche is fatally wounded. To save him, Elzire abandons the prospect of a royal wedding. Romualde then reveals himself to be Alidor, Don Sanche is miraculously cured, and everyone goes home happy.

The score is a straightforward number opera, with an independent overture, solo arias, ensembles, storm scene and a ballet, mostly in an agreeable and deftly constructed Italianate manner, with very occasional glimpses of the melodic style of the older Liszt.

RECORDING Hamari, Garino, Gáti, Hungarian Radio O, Pal, Hungaroton, 1986
EDITIONS f.s., Guy Woolfenden (ed.), Ariel Music, 1977; v.s., Chris de Souza (ed.), Ariel, 1977

BIBLIOGRAPHY Derek Watson, Liszt, Dent (Master Musicians Series), 1989; Chris de Souza, 'Teenage Opera', Listener, vol. 111, no. 2,859 (24 May 1984), p.34

L.H.

ANTONIO LITERES

Antonio Literes Carrión; b ?18 June 1673, Arta, Majorca; d 18 January 1747, Madrid

Literes received his musical education at the Real Colegio de Niños Cantorcicos in Madrid and from there was appointed viol-player in the royal chapel at the age of 20. It is very likely that, when Durón was exiled in 1700 with the fall of the Habsburgs, Literes effectively replaced him as music master in the Royal Chapel. In any case, his growing success as a composer of sacred works and especially of theatre music, linked to the lavish praise bestowed on him by the highly regarded Benedictine Feijoo, made him one of the most influential figures in the development of 18th-century Spanish music. Though Feijoo saw him as the champion of geniune Spanish tradition and an antidote to the corrupting Italianism allegedly purveyed by Durón, impartial studies of Literes's works have shown that in fact he, even more than Durón, carried on the process initiated by Hidalgo in the middle of the 17th century of marrying Italian operatic styles to the Spanish idiom.

Operatic works: Júpiter y Danae (zarzuela), ?1700; Con música y por Amor (drama with music), c. 1706; Acis y Galatea (zarzuela), 1708; Los elementos (ópera armónica al estilo italiano), ?1710; Hasta lo insensible adora (zarzuela), c. 1713; El estrago en la fineza: Júpiter y Semele (zarzuela), 1718
BIBLIOGRAPHY A. Martín Moreno, Historia de la música española, vol. 4: Siglo XVIII, Alianza, 1985

J.W.S.

GEORGE LLOYD

George W. S. Lloyd; b 28 June 1913, St Ives, Cornwall, England

Lloyd first came to notice with three early symphonies (1932–5) and with two operas, Iernin (1935) and The Serf (1938), both to libretti by his father. The Serf, premiered by the British Music Drama Opera Company at Covent Garden, is a story of feudal strife in Yorkshire during the reign of King Stephen. It is striking for its lyrical invention and most of all for its Verdian use of the chorus.

Lloyd's early success was cut short by the war; he suffered shell-shock, which resulted in a protracted physical collapse. His third opera, John Socman (1951), was commissioned for the Festival of Britain, but he subsequently had a breakdown and became a market gardener. Still composing, he was occasionally heard; John Ogdon performed his First Piano Concerto and recorded the piano piece An African Shrine.

Lloyd was relaunched in 1977 when Edward Downes performed his Eighth Symphony. He returned to full-time composition and moved to London, since when he has become an unintentional figurehead for those polemically opposed to modernist tendencies in music. The broadcast of John Socman in 1982 was felt by the composer not to be completely successful, but the BBC revival of Iernin in 1986 revealed a magical score, showing an intuitive grasp of the demands of the lyric stage.

BIBLIOGRAPHY Lewis Foreman, 'George Lloyd, Britten's Forgotten Contemporary', Records and Recordings, May 1980, pp. 26–9

L.F.

ANDREW LLOYD WEBBER

b 22 March 1948, London

Andrew Lloyd Webber was only 23 when Jesus Christ Superstar brought him worldwide acclaim, but his success was the natural consequence of his life to that date. Born into a family preoccupied with musical talent, his childhood grounding was in classical and church music, and his youth and maturity coincided with the golden age of pop. By investing the latter with the authority of the former, he and Tim Rice created three works, Joseph and the Amazing Technicolor Dreamcoat, Jesus Christ Superstar and Evita, that survived the era of popular music in which they were written.

Lloyd Webber's work since has generally been enormously successful in commercial terms but has escaped the full-blooded approbation of the critics. Of these later works, Cats (1981) suffers least from the imbalance of content and spectacle, while Starlight Express (1983) was privately considered extravagant by the composer. Aspects of Love marked a change of direction to the more traditional chamber opera.

At his worst, Lloyd Webber embodies the subjugation of dramatic and narrative content to marketing strategies aimed at the 'global' consumer. At his best, he is an accomplished tunesmith with a genuinely opportunist ear, and a talent for synthesis that is often unfairly ignored in assessments of his work.

Joseph and the Amazing Technicolor Dreamcoat

Cantata for children in two parts (original version: 15m; rev. version: 2h)
Libretto by Tim Rice, after the biblical story
Composed 1968; expanded and rev. 1972, 1973, 1991
PREMIERES 1 March 1968, Colet Court School, London (concert); 21 August 1972, Edinburgh (stage); US: 22 December 1976, Brooklyn Academy of Music, New York; 1991 version: 12 June 1991, Palladium, London

This cantata was originally commissioned for the choir of Colet Court School, London, to sing at an end-of-term concert. The Old Testament tale of Joseph and his envious brothers is given a fresh, witty telling and is conspicuous for its adroit parodies of popular music. Although it was subsequently expanded for the theatre, the main significance of the piece is as an established part of the school-music repertoire throughout the Christian world.

RECORDING original cast of the London Young Vic production, RSO, 1973
EDITIONS f.s., Chester (stage version; on hire); v.ss., The Really Useful Group, 1969 (choral version); 1975 (stage version)

Jesus Christ Superstar

Rock opera in two acts (1h 30m)
Libretto by Tim Rice
Composed 1969–70
PREMIERES 15 May 1971, Kansas City (concert); 12 October 1971, Mark Hellinger Theater, New York; UK: 9 August 1972, Palace Theatre, London

Jesus Christ Superstar was composed and recorded as an oratorio and its release in America catapulted the youthful composer and librettist to instant celebrity and considerable wealth. The application of the profane four-square rhythms of pop to the sacred subject of the Passion aroused great religious controversy to match the polarized critical responses to the work.

The early theatre productions of *Jesus Christ Superstar* ranged from the spectacularly vulgar to the chastely formal but, like *Joseph*, the piece has now become an established part of school and church repertoires. The composer's precocious facility for memorable light melodies and penchant for romantic orchestration stand out against the rather coarse and dated hard-rock elements of the piece.

RECORDINGS 1. original concept album, MCA, 1970; 2. London cast, MCA, 1972; 3. and VIDEO, Previn (cond.), Jewison (dir.), Universal/MCA, 1973

EDITION f.s., MCA Music (on hire), 1970

Evita

Opera in two parts (2h 15m)
Libretto by Tim Rice
Composed 1975–6
PREMIERES 21 June 1978, Prince Edward Theatre, London; US: 8 May 1979, Dorothy Chandler Pavilion, Los Angeles

Evita, like *Jesus Christ Superstar*, was advertised as an 'opera' but first released as a studio recording in the popular-music markets. This was followed by numerous successful stage productions.

Like *Jesus Christ Superstar*, *Evita* is a through-sung work with the movements of plot linked by the lyrics and the repetition of motifs by singer and orchestra. The story of Eva Perón and her ascent to power in Argentina again aroused polarized critical reactions (including comparison with Monteverdi's *The Coronation of Poppaea*). All responses start, however, with the acknowledgement that on its own terms *Evita* is probably the most successful example of the composer's eclectic talent at work.

RECORDINGS 1. original concept album, MCA, 1976; 2. London cast, MCA, 1978
EDITION v.s., Evita Music/MCA, 1977

Cats

Musical in two acts (2h 15m)
Libretto after T. S. Eliot, with additional material by Trevor Nunn and Richard Stilgoe

John Napier's design for the Rum Tum Tugger in Cats *(London, 1981)*

Composed 1980–81
PREMIERES 11 May 1981, New London Theatre, London;
US: 7 October 1982, Winter Garden Theatre, New York

Cats began as experimental musical settings of T. S. Eliot's *Old Possum's Book of Practical Cats* (1939) for a planned programme along the lines of the Walton–Sitwell *Façade*. The artfully variegated score none the less provoked one critic to recall Noël Coward's remark about the strange potency of cheap music, while the translation of the original idea into a full-length piece for singers and dancers made *Cats* the most commercially successful piece in the history of musical theatre.

RECORDING original cast, Polydor, 1981
EDITION songbook, Faber Music/The Really Useful Group, 1981

The Phantom of the Opera

Opera in two acts (2h 30m)
Libretto by Charles Hart, with additional lyrics by Richard Stilgoe
Composed 1985–6
PREMIERES 9 October 1986, Her Majesty's Theatre, London; US: 26 January 1988, Majestic Theater, New York

All versions of *The Phantom of the Opera*, including the three celebrated film versions, have their origins in Gaston Leroux's 1911 novel about the doomed affair between a young Swedish soprano and a disfigured composer who haunts the Paris Opéra. Lloyd Webber's version was written primarily as a vehicle for the coloratura soprano of his second wife, Sarah Brightman. The enormously successful productions in London and New York leaned heavily on spectacular staging, while two adept operatic pastiches did not distract either from the shallowness of the sung characters or the generally wooden nature of the composition.

RECORDING original cast, Polydor, 1987
EDITION songbook, The Really Useful Group, 1987

Aspects of Love

Opera in two acts (2h 30m)
Libretto by Don Black and Charles Hart, after the novella by David Garnett (1955)
Composed 1982–8
PREMIERES 17 April 1989, Prince of Wales Theatre, London; US: 8 April 1990, Broadhurst Theatre, New York

Aspects of Love is about the emotional entanglements of three generations of expatriates in the South of France. The subtleties of the story often suffer from overtly expository lyrics and an uneasy veering between the values of opera and musical theatre; but as an attempt at a through-sung chamber opera the piece was welcomed as a change from the dependence on spectacular production values that had characterized much of the composer's recent work.

RECORDING Really Useful Records/Polydor, 1989
EDITION songbook, The Really Useful Group, 1989

Other musicals: *The Likes of Us*, (1966); *Jeeves*, 1975; *Song and Dance*, 1982 (RECORDING Polydor, 1982); *Starlight Express*, 1984; *Sunset Boulevard*, 1993
BIBLIOGRAPHY Jonathan Mantle, *Fanfare: The Unauthorised Biography of Andrew Lloyd Webber*, Michael Joseph, 1989; Michael Walsh, *Andrew Lloyd Webber, His Life and Works*, Viking, 1989

I.J.M.

MATTHEW LOCKE

b 1622, ?Exeter, Devon, England; *d* August 1677, London

Locke must be reckoned the father of English opera. He was brought up at Exeter, where he was a chorister at the cathedral, and taught by Edward Gibbons, the eldest brother of Orlando. In 1648 he was in the Netherlands, possibly attached to the Royalist units from Devon which had retreated there. By 1651 he was back in England and composing consorts for viols; in 1653 he collaborated with Christopher Gibbons (the son of Orlando) in setting James Shirley's *Cupid and Death*, a privately staged masque in honour of the Portuguese ambassador. Though the Puritans of the Commonwealth abhorred stage plays they had no objections to masque, which was a moral and didactic form. Sir William Davenant, playwright, manager and former courtier, saw a loophole here and exploited it; the consequence was the first English opera, *The Siege of Rhodes*, staged at Rutland House in London in 1656.

Davenant appears to have conceived *The Siege of Rhodes* as a play in heroic couplets and then to have reworked it in such a way as to make its performance acceptable to the authorities, with acts described as 'entries' (a word borrowed from the masque), a

Matthew Locke, portrait (1662) attributed to Isaac Fuller

novel form of setting ('the art of Prospective in Scenes') and the whole 'sung in Recitative Musick'. This music was by various hands: Charles Coleman, George Hudson, Henry Lawes, Thomas Cooke and Matthew Locke; Locke acted the part of the Admiral. Locke also contributed to two later pre-Restoration operatic productions by Davenant.

No music for *The Siege of Rhodes* survives and Locke's two masques for Robert Stapleton's *The Step-mother* (1663) have also disappeared. So has the vocal music for Davenant's 1673 revival of *Macbeth*, a work that Downes, the prompter and historian of Davenant's and Thomas Betterton's company, described as 'being in the nature of an Opera'. By this he meant what would today be called a semi-opera, and later in the 17th century was referred to as a dramatic opera.

No great revenues can have been brought in by Locke's theatrical work. He earned his living as composer to the 24 Violins in the King's Musick and as organist to Charles II's queen, Catherine of Braganza, a task for which, as a Roman Catholic since at least 1654, he was well suited. His relations with his English colleagues were never easy: he failed to suffer fools gladly and made no attempt to disguise the fact. In his last years he turned almost exclusively to the theatre, composing the self-contained *Masque of Orpheus* for Settle's *The Empress of Morocco* in 1673, much of the music for the dramatic opera version of *The Tempest* in 1674 and (his most elaborate operatic enterprise) *Psyche* in 1675. Locke composed no complete opera, but he did resolve the problem of an operatic episode that could fuse an adequate English declamatory style with aria, chorus and dance. In so doing he laid the foundations for his pupil and devoted admirer Henry Purcell. He also established the principles of semi-opera, and, by publishing his music from *Psyche* and *The Tempest* as *The English Opera* (1675) with an eloquent preface, he put what he was doing into the public domain. Musically Locke never dwells on an idea for a moment longer than is necessary to establish it; his melodic lines can be unexpectedly angular and his harmony is frequently unorthodox. At its best, his music is as emotive as that of Henry Purcell.

The Tempest

Semi-opera in five acts
Libretto: an adaptation of the play by William Shakespeare (1611–12) by John Dryden and William Davenant, operatic version by Thomas Shadwell
PREMIERE 1674, London

The operatic *Tempest* was a collaborative effort. In 1667 Dryden and Davenant had adapted the play to the Restoration taste, cutting the exchanges between the courtiers, giving Miranda a sister (Dorinda) and introducing, to match these girls who 'never saw man', Hippolito, a man who had never seen a woman. They made the sailors comic and expanded the music in the play, adding songs and two musical 'dialogues'. In 1674 Shadwell continued this process in such a way as to exploit to the utmost the scenic and musical resources of the Dorset Garden theatre.

Locke wrote the incidental music, Giovanni Battista Draghi the dances, and Pelham Humfrey provided two masques. Songs by John Banister were taken over from the 1667 production. The orchestra was moved from its normal loft over the stage and doubled in size, so that 'the Band of 24 Violins, with the Harpsicals and Theorbo's which accompany the Voices, are plac'd between the Pit and the stage'. There were more than 30 singers. The curtain rose to reveal 'a thick Cloudy sky, a very Rocky Coast, and a Tempestuous Sea in perpetual agitation'; there was lightning, thunder and St Elmo's fire. Locke's accompanying music was equally innovative in its use of expressive dynamics: 'soft', 'lowder by degrees', 'violent', 'lowd', 'soft and slow by degrees'. This novel entertainment was immensely successful, the prompter recording that 'not any succeeding Opera got more money'.

EDITION   Michael Tilmouth (ed.), *Musica Britannica*, vol. 51

Psyche

Semi-opera in five acts
Libretto by Thomas Shadwell
PREMIERE   27 February 1675

Loosely derived from Lully's 1671 tragédie-ballet of the same name, *Psyche* was Betterton's attempt to follow up the success of his production of *The Tempest*, though in the event, as Locke reported, the experience did not answer the company's 'big expectation' and this in spite of, or perhaps because of, the fact that prices of admission were trebled. The story differs from the traditional version told by Apuleius in *The Golden Ass* in that Cupid is always visible to Psyche, and that rather than being forbidden to look at him she is forbidden to learn his name. In the event 'fatal curiosity' prompts her to force him to divulge it, and only after visiting the underworld is she able to be restored in the favour of Venus and marry him. All the music was provided by Locke except for the dances, which were set by Giovanni Battista Draghi, and choreographed by a Frenchman, St Andrée. According to Shadwell's stage directions, the instrumentation was elaborate and included trumpets, kettledrums, flageolets, recorders, oboes, strings and continuo. The scenery, painted by Stephenson, and the machines, devised by Betterton, occasioned much comment. Though *Psyche* did not match the success of *The Tempest* the mould of semi-opera was firmly established.

EDITION   Michael Tilmouth (ed.), *Musica Britannica*, vol. 51

BIBLIOGRAPHY   Edward J. Dent, *Foundations of English Opera*, CUP, 1928; Rosamond E. M. Harding, *A Thematic Catalogue of the Works of Matthew Locke*, OUP, 1971; Anthony C. Lewis, 'Matthew Locke, a Dynamic Figure in English Music', *PRMA*, vol. 74 (1948)

R.Lu.

EDWARD LODER

Edward James Loder; *b* 1813, Bath, England; *d* 5 April 1865, London

Loder's career as an operatic composer clearly illustrates the extent to which English composers were at the mercy of managerial success. Having studied with Ferdinand Ries in Frankfurt am Main (1826–8) Loder benefited from the reopening of the English Opera House, the Lyceum (1834), whose manager, Samuel Arnold, was influential in the development of English 19th-century opera. Though a small work, Loder's *Nourjahad* (1834) had the distinction of being the first new operatic piece to be performed at the theatre, predating John Barnett's *The Mountain Sylph*, a larger and historically more important opera, by two months. But whatever expectations the young Loder entertained were dashed by the financial collapse of Arnold's management. The composer contracted with the publishers Dalmaine & Co. to produce a new composition every week, and his theatrical work was limited to supplying small pieces, in particular songs. In 1838 some of the latter were cobbled together to form *Francis I*, Loder's only opera to be performed at Drury Lane, long the main venue for English opera. In 1846 Maddox, the manager of the smaller Princess's Theatre, appointed him musical director, thus providing the opportunity for Loder's first substantial opera, *The Night Dancers*, based on the story of *Giselle*. But in 1851 Maddox's management came to an end and, with no prospects in the capital, Loder moved to the Theatre Royal, Manchester.

In 1855 Loder's most expansive opera, *Raymond and Agnes*, was produced in Manchester, but serious illness now intervened: the composer contracted a cerebral disease. In due course he returned to London where, in June 1859, a revised version of *Raymond and Agnes* was given; it closed after a week. An operetta, *Never Judge by Appearances*, probably written while Loder was still in Manchester, appeared the following month, but his career was at an end. Much of the remainder of his life was spent in a coma.

Raymond and Agnes

Romantic opera in four acts (3h)
Libretto by Edward Fitzball, after Matthew Lewis's Gothic novel, *The Monk* (1795)
Composed 1855, rev. 1859
PREMIERE 14 August 1855, Theatre Royal, Manchester

Raymond and Agnes, strengthened by the supernatural assistance of the latter's namesake, St Agnes, overcome a villainous baron (Agnes's guardian) who is eventually killed by the very bullet he intended for Raymond. The final celebration is enhanced by a mute woman regaining the power of speech; hitherto a slave of the baron's henchman, she identifies herself as Raymond's long-lost mother.

Musically, Loder's basic affinity was with Weber. In *Raymond and Agnes* this emerges in the close relationship of the overture to the ensuing opera, the 'melodramatic' use of speech, thematic recurrence, various details in the arias, and the concern lavished on orchestral figuration. It also draws on Italian idioms, as in the Act II finale. However, the Act II duet for Raymond and Agnes is one of the most original and striking pieces in all English opera of this period and shows that Loder could write music of much power and originality.

EDITION v.s., Jeffreys, [*c.* 1859]

Other operatic works: *Nourjahad*, 1834; *The Covenanters*, 1835; *Francis I*, 1838; *The Night Dancers, or The Wilis*, 1846; *The Andulasian, or The Young Guard*, 1848; *Robin Goodfellow, or The Frolics of Puck*, 1848; *Never Judge by Appearances*, 1859; *Little Red Riding Hood*, (n.d.); *Pizarro*, (n.d.); *Sir Roger de Coverley*, (n.d.)

BIBLIOGRAPHY Nicholas Temperley, '*Raymond and Agnes*', *MT*, vol. 107 (1966), p. 307; Eric Walter White, *A History of English Opera*, Faber, 1983

G.B.

FRANK LOESSER

Frank Henry Loesser; *b* 29 June 1910, New York; *d* 28 July 1969, New York

Born into a German immigrant family, steeped in classical music, Frank Loesser taught himself popular-style pianism. His first song-writing efforts, for revues and films, were however as lyricist only. Beginning with the Second World War hit 'Praise the Lord and Pass the Ammunition', he always wrote both words and music.

Where's Charley?

Musical comedy in two acts (film: 1h 30m)
Libretto by George Abbott, based on the play *Charley's Aunt* by Brandon Thomas (1892); lyrics by the composer
PREMIERES 11 October 1948, St James Theatre, New York; UK: 20 February 1958, Palace Theatre, London

The venerable farce is given a musical treatment that allows a dancer–comedian (originally Ray Bolger) to disguise himself as Charley's Aunt and to charm the audience with songs including 'Once in Love with Amy'.

RECORDING Wisdom, Gale, Cooper, CBS, 1958
FILM Butler (dir.), Warner, 1952
EDITION v.s., Frank Music, 1964

Guys and Dolls

Musical fable in two acts (2h 30m)
Libretto by Abe Burrows and Jo Swerling, based on a story (1932) and characters by Damon Runyon; lyrics by the composer
PREMIERES 24 November 1950, 46th Street Theatre, New York; UK: 28 May 1953, Coliseum, London
CAST Sky Masterson *t*, Sarah Brown *s*, Nathan Detroit *bar*, Adelaide *ms*, Nicely-Nicely Johnson *t*, Benny Southstreet *bar*, Rusty Charlie *b*, Arvide *t*, Harry the Horse *bar*; smaller roles from *satb* chorus of gamblers, dolls, Cubans, frequenters of Times Square

ORCHESTRATION (George Bassman and Ted Royal) theatre orch, ww doubles, no vlas

Set in the colourful New York world of gamblers and night-clubs created in Damon Runyon's fiction, *Guys and Dolls* has proved consistently pleasing to audiences since its first performances. It is one of the rare traditional musicals whose interest is distributed equally among four main characters, among whom the male and female starring roles belong to different couples. It has an exceptional score, one equally strong in comedy ('Adelaide's Lament'), romance ('If I Were a Bell', 'I've Never Been in Love Before'), establishment of a milieu ('Fugue for Tinhorns', the title song), and response to a unique situation ('Luck Be a Lady', 'Sit Down, You're Rockin' the Boat').

SYNOPSIS
Act I Nathan Detroit is trying to find a safe home for the 'oldest established permanent floating crap game in New York'; to raise the fee for the only location he can find, he persuades newcomer Sky Masterson to make an unwinnable bet. Sky bets that he can persuade beautiful but icy Sister Sarah of the Salvation Army to go to dinner with him in Havana – and with a promise of an offering of twelve sinners to the Army, he succeeds. Nathan is also having bad luck with his girlfriend, nightclub chanteuse Adelaide, who is sure that her perpetual cold is caused by Nathan's failure to propose. On her return, Sarah finds the mission full of gamblers; assuming that was the purpose of her trip to Havana, she orders Sky away.

Act II The crap game takes place in the sewer. Sky wins, and orders the losers to the mission as his promised twelve sinners. Sarah and Adelaide confer and decide to marry their men, faults and all, and change them later. The final scene reveals that they have done exactly that.

RECORDINGS 1. Blaine, Bigley, Alda, Levene, Actman, US Decca, 1950; 2. McKenzie, Covington, Charleson, Hoskins, Britten, Chrysalis, 1982
FILM Mankiewicz (dir.), Goldwyn/MGM, 1955
EDITION v.s., Frank Music, 1953

The Most Happy Fella
Musical in three acts (2h 15m)
Libretto by the composer, based on the play *They Knew What They Wanted* by Sidney Howard; lyrics by the composer
PREMIERES 3 May 1956, Imperial Theater, New York; UK: 21 April 1960, Coliseum, London

The principal characters are Tony, a middle-aged Italian-American winemaker; Rosabella, a waitress whom he woos as a mail-order bride; and Joe, the young foreman whose picture Tony sends to Rosabella in place of his own. Rosabella, upset at the deception, at first finds comfort with Joe; but in time she and Tony both mature and learn each other's true worth. Loesser shaped *The Most Happy Fella* essentially as an opera (though he resisted the term) in the popular idiom. Its score includes pop tunes for

the secondary comic characters ('Standing on the Corner', 'Big D'), introspective character-revealing songs ('Joey, Joey, Joey'), appropriately Italian-flavoured choral and ensemble numbers, and a succession of musical scenes for the main characters depicting their growth. It stands as one of the most artistically successful examples of Broadway opera.

RECORDING Weede, Sullivan, Lund, Johnson, Greene, CBS, 1956: a recording of the complete show
EDITION v.s., Frank Music, 1957

How to Succeed in Business without Really Trying
Musical in two acts (film: 2h)
Libretto by Abe Burrows, Jack Weinstock, and Willie Gilbert, based on the book by Shepard Mead; lyrics by the composer
PREMIERES 14 October 1961, 46th Street Theatre, New York; UK: 28 March 1963, Shaftesbury Theatre, London

How to Succeed, an unusual example of a 'how-to' book (albeit a tongue-in-cheek one) transformed into a musical with a story, became the fourth musical to win the Pulitzer Prize. It tells the saga of a window-washer, Finch, who by deviousness and charm rises through the ranks at World Wide Wicket Corp. in record time, brushing aside all obstacles and winning the woman he loves as well. Its bright pop-style score enhanced the intentionally cartoonlike quality of the characters, and featured a most unusual love song, 'I Believe in You', sung by Finch – to himself.

RECORDING Morse, Vallee, Scott, Lawrence, RCA, 1961
FILM Swift (dir.), Mirisch/US, 1967
EDITION v.s., Frank Music, 1962

Other musicals: *Greenwillow*, 1960; *Pleasures and Palaces*, 1965
BIBLIOGRAPHY Martin Arthur Mann, *The Musicals of Frank Loesser*, dissertation, City University of New York, 1974

J.A.C.

FREDERICK LOEWE
b 10 June 1904, Vienna; *d* 14 February 1988, Palm Springs, Florida, US

The son of an operetta tenor, Frederick Loewe studied with Busoni, d'Albert, and Reznicek. In 1924, already successful as pianist and song-writer, he moved to New York but found his compositional skills ill-matched to the current tastes of his new country. A succession of jobs, musical and otherwise, supported him until he eventually found his compositional talents in demand; even after his first Broadway show he continued to play the piano in restaurants until his meeting with Alan Jay Lerner in 1942.

Lerner's lyrics and libretti proved the perfect complement for Loewe's romantically evocative music. Their first three collaborations revealed a steady growth in artistic assurance, without achieving popular success; but beginning with *Brigadoon* in 1947, the team established itself as one of the most reliable providers of artistically integrated musical entertainment. They maintained a level that Lerner failed to find with any of his subsequent collaborators (including Richard Rodgers, Burton Lane, André Previn, and Leonard Bernstein), Loewe having essentially retired from active work after *Camelot*.

Brigadoon

Musical play in two acts (2h 15m)
Libretto by Alan Jay Lerner
PREMIERES 13 March 1947, Ziegfeld Theater, New York; UK: 14 April 1949, His Majesty's Theatre, London
CAST Fiona MacLaren *s*, Tommy Albright *bar*, Meg Brockie *ms*, Charlie Dalrymple *t*, Jeff Douglas *spoken role*, Mr Lundie *spoken role*, Jean MacLaren *dancer*, Harry Beaton *dancer*; other solo roles from *satb* chorus of townsfolk; dancers
ORCHESTRATION (Ted Royal) theatre orchestra, including onstage bagpipes

With *Brigadoon*, Lerner and Loewe established themselves as worthy practitioners of the musical play as it had developed in the 1940s, with a combination of romance, picturesque fantasy, and humour that was to remain characteristic of the team. The score includes 'Almost Like Being in Love' and was one of several of its time that set aside substantial time for self-contained dance sequences (original choreography by Agnes De Mille).

SYNOPSIS

Act I Americans Tommy and Jeff, lost in the highlands of Scotland, discover Brigadoon, a village that magically appears for one day every hundred years. Tommy falls in love with Fiona, while Jeff amuses himself with Meg. At the wedding of Jean and Charlie, the future of Brigadoon is threatened when Harry, himself in love with Jean, announces that he is going to do what is forbidden to the villagers and flee to the outside world. He runs off with everyone else in pursuit.

Act II Before he passes the barrier, Harry falls and is killed. Tommy says goodbye to Fiona, but back in New York he finds that he made the wrong choice. Returning to Scotland, he finds that his and Fiona's love has created a new miracle: a return of Brigadoon long enough for him to enter it.

RECORDING Luker, Kaye, Barrett, Ainsley, Ambrosian Ch, London Sinfonietta, McGlinn, EMI, 1991
FILM Minnelli (dir.), MGM, 1954
EDITION v.s., Sam Fox, rev. edn, 1967

My Fair Lady

Musical play in two acts (2h 30m)
Libretto by Alan Jay Lerner, based on the play *Pygmalion* by George Bernard Shaw (1913)
Composed 1954–6
PREMIERES 15 March 1956, Mark Hellinger Theater, New York; UK: 30 April 1958, Drury Lane, London

CAST Henry Higgins *bar*, Eliza Doolittle *s*, Alfred P. Doolittle *bar*, Freddy Eynsford-Hill *t*, Colonel Pickering *bar*, Mrs Pearce *a*, Mrs Higgins *spoken role*; other solo roles from *satb* chorus of Londoners
ORCHESTRATION (Robert Russell Bennett and Philip J. Lang) theatre orchestra

Julie Andrews (Eliza Doolittle) and Rex Harrison (Henry Higgins) in My Fair Lady *(New York, 1956)*

This highly successful musical translation of Shaw's play had record-breaking runs in both New York and London – in both cases with the original stars, Rex Harrison, Julie Andrews and Stanley Holloway. Lerner's libretto followed the film version of *Pygmalion* in suggesting a romantic end for Higgins and Eliza, but otherwise generally maintained Shaw's tone and intent. Such songs as 'I Could Have Danced All Night', 'On the Street Where You Live', and 'I've Grown Accustomed to Her Face' are only the most familiar portions of a score highly attentive to character and situation.

SYNOPSIS

Act I London, 1912. Phonetics professor Henry Higgins, intrigued by the aspirations of Eliza, a young Cockney flower-seller, makes a bet with his friend Colonel Pickering that by changing her speech he can make her pass for a fine lady. She moves into the house where he, Pickering, and housekeeper Mrs Pearce live, and begins lessons. Her dustman father pays a visit, ostensibly to protest about the apparent immorality of the set-up but really to get some money out of it (Higgins, amused by his rhetoric, pays him and recommends him for a speaking engagement). The first attempt at showing Eliza off in society, at the Ascot races, ends in embarrassing failure – though it still wins her an ardent admirer,

Freddy Eynsford-Hill. But the final test, an embassy ball with a rival of Higgins looking on, is a success.

Act II After the ball, Eliza, furious with Higgins for his offhand dismissal of her share in the success of the experiment, leaves in the middle of the night and roams the city, followed by Freddy. She encounters her father, made miserably famous and wealthy by Higgins's advocacy, now forced to be respectable and to marry his mistress. Higgins, searching for Eliza the next day, finds her visiting his mother. They argue once more, and he storms out; on his way home he realizes that he misses her. She returns just as the curtain falls.

RECORDING Andrews, Harrison, Holloway, Allers, CBS, 1956: this is the original monaural recording; the London cast, with the same principals, conducted by Ornadel, made a stereo recording for CBS in 1958.
FILM Cukor (dir.), Warner, 1964
EDITION v.s., Chappell, rev. edn, 1959

Camelot

Musical play in two acts (2h 45m)
Libretto by Alan Jay Lerner, based on the tetralogy *The Once and Future King* by T. H. White (1938)
PREMIERES 3 December 1960, Majestic Theater, New York; UK: 19 August 1964, Drury Lane, London

This version of the story of King Arthur emphasizes his dream of a round table of knights fighting for right, and of its ruin by the romance between his wife Guenevere and his best friend Sir Lancelot. (Guenevere and Arthur – betrothed for state reasons – fall in love before being officially introduced, in an opening scene reminiscent of that of *Don Carlos*, even unto the forest setting.) Uneven in its dramaturgy, but the richest of all Loewe's scores, *Camelot* continues to exert a fascination for producers and performers because of its depiction of the conception, creation, and fall of an idealistic society, and also because of the musical opportunities its leading roles provide.

RECORDING Andrews, Burton, Goulet, Allers, CBS, 1960
FILM Logan (dir.), 7 Arts/Warner, 1967
EDITION v.s., Chappell, 1962; the British edition differs substantially, reflecting the first London production

Other musicals: *Salute to Spring*, 1937; *Great Lady*, 1938; *Life of the Party*, 1942; *What's Up?*, 1943; *The Day before Spring*, 1945; *Paint Your Wagon*, 1951; *Gigi* (originally film), 1973
BIBLIOGRAPHY Alan Jay Lerner, *The Street Where I Live*, Norton, 1978

J.A.C.

NICOLA LOGROSCINO

Nicola Bonifacio Logroscino; *baptized* 22 October 1698, Bitonto; *d* 1765–7, ?Palermo

Once credited with the 'creation' of comic opera, Logroscino was the most important composer of the genre in Naples for a decade (1744–54); but only two of his operas survive, making evaluation of his historical importance problematic.

He studied at the Conservatory of Santa Maria di Loreto in Naples and, after three years as organist to the Bishop of Conza in the province of Avellino, he returned to Naples in 1731. His first known work, the heroic opera *Il Quinto Fabio*, was not given until six years later in Rome: in the intervening period he had apparently been producing comic operas at small Neapolitan theatres. After 1738 he wrote numerous comic operas in Naples.

At some point, probably in the 1740s or 1750s, Logroscino took up a teaching post in Palermo, where he also wrote operas. There is no evidence of productions of his operas in Naples after 1756, and his last opera, *La gelosia*, was presented in Venice in 1765; nothing more is known of him after that.

Logroscino stands between Leo and Piccinni in the development of Neapolitan opera. Highly regarded in his day, he was described by a contemporary French writer as 'the god of the comic genre [who] has served as model for almost all composers of this type of work'. However, *Il governatore* – the only comic opera to survive complete – reveals few technical advances over Leo in terms of ensemble finales (with whose invention Logroscino has been credited in the past), and although he displays strong gifts of characterization and orchestration, the melodic invention is on the whole weak.

Surviving operatic works: *Il Leandro* (Act I finale), 1744; *Il governatore*, 1747 (EDITION facsimile, Garland, 1979); *Giunio Bruto*, 1748; 33 lost operas
BIBLIOGRAPHY Michael F. Robinson, *Naples and Neapolitan Opera*, OUP, 1972

D.S.B.

PAOLO LORENZANI

b 1640, Rome; *d* 28 November 1713, Rome

Arriving in France in 1678 as a refugee from Messina, Lorenzani was championed by those at court who wished to see Lully's musical monopoly and his antipathy towards Italian music challenged. In 1681 Lorenzani's pastorale *Nicandro e Fileno* was performed at Fontainebleau before Louis XIV, who had already expressed a liking for his style – a skilful amalgam of French and Italian elements. But Lully, fearful that the newcomer would replace him in the king's estimation, successfully schemed against his rival at court.

As one of the most talented composers in France, Lorenzani looked set to fill the void created by Lully's death in 1687, when his tragédie en musique, *Orontée* (the music of which is mostly lost), was given at Chantilly the following year. Inexplicably, that did not happen: after five years in obscurity, he departed for Rome where he remained until his death.

Lorenzani's one surviving opera, *Nicandro e Fileno*, is undeservedly little known. Although its libretto (by Filippo Mancini-Mazarini, Duc de Nevers) is undistinguished, the score is elegantly written in a somewhat old-fashioned style reminiscent of Cesti and Rossi but pleasingly diversified with elements derived from contemporary French music. For its time, the autograph is unusually explicit in matters of instrumentation and dynamics.

BIBLIOGRAPHY H. Prunières, 'Paolo Lorenzani à la cour de France (1678–1694)', *La revue musicale*, vol. 3 (1922), pp. 97–120 (includes edn of aria from *Nicandro e Fileno*)

G.S.

ALBERT LORTZING

Gustav Albert Lortzing; *b* 23 October 1801, Berlin; *d* 21 January 1851, Berlin

Lortzing was the leading German comic opera composer of the 19th century. Though he lacked the musical sophistication and ambition of such near-contemporaries as Weber and Spohr, his sure sense of theatre and his accomplished and inventive treatment of familiar forms have ensured the lasting popularity of his best works, particularly in Germany.

Lortzing's grasp – and willing acceptance – of the demands of the stage was the product of a lifetime's experience of provincial touring companies. His parents were amateur actors and musicians who turned professional after the failure of the family business. The composer's early experience as a child actor was followed by engagements as both actor and buffo tenor; he also worked as producer, conductor and orchestral cellist. His repertoire as an actor was not restricted to popular comedy but included plays by Schiller, Lessing and Raimund, as well as the Fool in *King Lear*. Several of his operas are based on plays in which he had appeared as an actor.

Lortzing was almost entirely self-taught as a musician, apart from some early theory lessons and piano studies. His earliest compositions included incidental music for several plays. His first opera was a one act singspiel, *Ali Pascha von Janina*, performed in 1828 by the Detmold Hoftheater company, of which he and his wife were then members. Other works of this period rely to a large extent on arrangements of music by other composers. *Szenen aus Mozarts Leben*, using material from various Mozartian sources, testifies to one of the most important influences on Lortzing's music. He may well have been drawn primarily to Mozart the successful theatrical professional, but the confident handling of ambitious ensembles in his best works suggests that deeper lessons were also learned.

Lortzing suffered acute financial difficulties throughout his career; in the absence of a rational system of royalty payments, the popularity his operas achieved was not enough to secure him an income on which to support his family. The success in 1837 of *Die beiden Schützen*, in which he began to move away from the limitations of singspiel and to develop a more personal operatic language, and the even greater enthusiasm which greeted the first full realization of that language in *Zar und Zimmermann* at its Berlin production two years later, encouraged him to concentrate on composition. But he still needed the financial security only a permanent engagement could provide. In the 1830s he worked in Leipzig at the Altes Theater, finally becoming kapellmeister there in 1844. The following year he was appointed to the same post at the Theater an der Wien, but he failed to find favour with Viennese audiences and was unhappy with his own work there. But he continued to compose, enjoying a repeat of his earlier triumphs with *Der Wildschütz* in 1842. He ventured outside comedy, with the musically ambitious Romantic magic operas *Undine* and *Rolands Knappen*, and, less successfully, with *Regina*, a work on a revolutionary subject, inspired by the events and ideals of 1848. Ultimately unsuccessful in his attempts to secure a contract at another major opera house following the termination of his Vienna engagement, Lortzing was obliged to return to acting. In 1850 he gladly accepted an appointment as kapellmeister at the Friedrich Wilhelm Stadttheater in Berlin, a third-rate house devoted mainly to vaudeville and farce. There he managed to compose a one-act comedy, *Die Opernprobe*, but was too ill to attend its premiere and died the following day.

Lortzing assimilated the influence of other composers as readily as he did popular forms, turning everything to his own theatrical ends. His works, nonetheless, display a sound grasp of musical structure, an accomplished – and sometimes original – approach to harmony, a sure sense of melody and orchestration, and, above all, an unfailing ability to match music to character and situation. The attention he devoted to writing and adapting his own libretti enabled him to achieve a successful fusion of music and text that eluded many of his contemporaries.

Die beiden Schützen

The Two Riflemen

Comic opera in three acts (2h 30m)

Libretto by the composer, after the comedy *Les deux grenadiers, ou Les quiproquos* (1796) by Joseph Patrat from his own libretto for Grétry's *Les méprises par ressemblance* (1786), via the German free adaptation by Gustav Cords, *Die beiden Grenadiere* (1811)

Composed 1835

PREMIERES 20 February 1837, Stadttheater Leipzig; US: 13 December 1859, New York; UK: 10 March 1898, St George's Hall, Langham Place, London

As with several of his later works, Lortzing chose a source with which he was already familiar; he had himself played one of the protagonists in Cords's German version of Patrat's comedy. In *Die beiden Schützen*, a comedy of mistaken identity like the best of Lortzing's mature operas, two soldiers return to their village after several years' absence.

Die beiden Schützen marks a decisive move away from singspiel and opéra comique and towards the more sophisticated spieloper Lortzing was to make his own. Here he still makes use of rhythmic patter and farce couplets, and the work does not attempt to conceal its debt to its French models; but the introduction of more lyrical, songlike melodies, the tendency to favour the ensemble (including here an impressive septet in Act II) over the solo number, and the strong concern for musical and dramatic organization establish an individual voice and point the stylistic way forward. At the premiere both the composer and his mother were in the cast. The opera was an enormous success and established Lortzing's reputation, but it was already beginning to lose its place in the repertoire by the time of his death.

RECORDING Nentwig, Lindermeier, Holm, Schmitt-Walter, Bavarian Radio Ch and SO, Koetsier, Melodram, 1950
EDITIONS v.ss. Wunder, 1838; Peters, 1882

Zar (originally Czaar) und Zimmermann, oder Die zwei Peter

Tsar and Carpenter, or The Two Peters
Comic opera in three acts (2h 45m)
Libretto by the composer (with Philip Düringer and Philip Reger), after Georg Christian Römer's German translation of *Le bourgmestre de Saardam, ou Les deux Pierres* by Mélesville (pseudonym for Jean Honoré Duveyrier), Merle and Boirie (1818)
Composed 1837
PREMIERES 22 December 1837, Theater der Stadt, Leipzig; US: 13 January 1857, New York; UK: 15 April 1871, Gaiety Theatre, London
CAST Peter the Great *bar*, Peter Ivanov *t*, Van Bett *b*, Marie *s*, Marquis de Chateauneuf *t*, Admiral Lefort *b*, Lord Syndham *b*, Widow Browe *a*; *satb* chorus of carpenters, citizens, soldiers, sailors, council officials
FULL ORCHESTRA

Like *Die beiden Schützen*, whose success it decisively consolidated, *Zar und Zimmermann* is a comedy of mistaken identity. Lortzing had acted the role of the French ambassador in Römer's translation of Mélesville's comic melodrama. His opera follows Römer closely until the third act, when the splendid comic set piece of the chorus rehearsal is introduced. At the Leipzig premiere the composer sang Peter Ivanov while his mother played Widow Browe. The popular enthusiasm that greeted the premiere was not matched by critical acclaim until the Berlin production of 1839.

SYNOPSIS
Act I The action takes place in Saardam in 1698. Peter the Great is working incognito as a shipyard carpenter (as he actually did) under the name of Peter Michaelov. A fellow Russian carpenter, an army deserter named Peter Ivanov, is in love with Marie, the niece of Burgomaster Van Bett. Informed by his ambassador, Lefort, of simmering rebellion in Moscow, the tsar resolves to return to Russia. Van Bett arrives, with instructions to locate a foreigner called Peter working in the shipyard. The interest of the English and French ambassadors, Syndham and Chateauneuf, convinces him of the foreign Peter's importance. His suspicions, and Syndham's, centre on Peter Ivanov. Chateauneuf, however, correctly identifies Peter Michaelov as the tsar.

Act II During a wedding celebration for the son of Widow Browe, owner of the shipyard, Chateauneuf (in disguise) concludes an alliance with the tsar, while Syndham (also in disguise) turns his attention on the bewildered Peter Ivanov. The arrival of a party of soldiers with instructions to detain all suspicious foreigners creates a general tumult in which the ambassadors throw off their disguises. Each identifies a different Peter as the tsar. Van Bett, after futile attempts to control the situation, looks on bewildered.

Act III While Van Bett prepares a musical homage to the wrong tsar, Peter Michaelov prepares to escape with the English passport Syndham has given to Ivanov. In return for their assistance in the temporary deception, the tsar gives Ivanov and Marie a letter that licenses their marriage and appoints Ivanov a general inspector of the imperial court. The tsar's ship leaves the harbour to general rejoicing. Van Bett remains confused.

In *Zar und Zimmermann* Lortzing's musical language reaches maturity. A powerful structural coherence underlies his virtuoso treatment of stock characters and situations. Familiar forms and set pieces are firmly integrated into the dramatic whole. The operatic lied is used in varying contexts to dramatic effect, made to carry psychological as well as atmospheric weight. The musical characterization of the pompous Van Bett, particularly in his buffo aria 'O sancta justitia', with its comic interplay of voice and bassoon and its mixture of nonsensical dog-Latin patter and grandiloquent vocal flourishes, can stand comparison with anything achieved in this vein by Donizetti (whose opera on the same subject, *Il Borgomastro di Saardam* was performed in Berlin in August 1837) or even Rossini. The accomplished construction of the Act II finale reveals a sophisticated – and Mozartian – understanding of comic ensemble, while the chaotic rehearsal of Van Bett's ponderous choral tribute is a masterpiece of self-conscious musical humour. As in several of the mature operas, a colourful and elegant ballet (here a clog dance) shows Lortzing at his most exuberant and unaffected.

RECORDING Köth, Burmeister, Gedda, Prey, Schreier, Frick, Leipzig Radio Ch, Dresden Staatskapelle, Heger, Electrola, 1966
EDITIONS f.s., Breitkopf und Härtel, 1985; v.ss., Breitkopf und Härtel, 1838; Kruse (ed.), Peters, [n.d.]

Hans Sachs

Comic opera in three acts (2h 15m)
Libretto by Philip Düringer and the composer, after the play by Johann Ludwig Deinhardstein (1827)
Composed 1840, rev. 1845
PREMIERE 23 June 1840, Leipzig; rev. version: 25 May 1845, Mannheim

Hans Sachs, shoemaker and poet, is defeated by Hesse, a member of the Augsburg town council, in a singing competition; the prize is the hand of Kunigunde, daughter of Steffen, the mayor of

Nürnberg, with whom Sachs is in love. Emperor Maximilian comes to Nürnberg to discover the author of a poem he admires. Hesse claims authorship but cannot recite the lines convincingly. The emperor recognizes Sachs as the true author and gives him Kunigunde as his bride.

Lortzing's opera, which enjoyed some success at its premiere but has since faded from the repertoire, is chiefly of interest as an earlier treatment of the subject Wagner was to use in *Die Meistersinger*. In *Die Meistersinger* Wagner adopted nearly all of the changes and additions made to Deinhardstein's original by Lortzing and Reger. There are parallels between characters too, and even some curious musical similarities. But the divergences are as significant; Lortzing's Steffen and Kunigunde, for instance, bear little relation to their Wagnerian counterparts, Pogner and Eva.

Scene from Act II of Der Wildschütz *(Leipzig, 1842)*

RECORDING   Sailer, Mikorey, Schmitt-Walter, Vogler, Kohl, Nürnberger Singgemeinschaft, Fränkisches Landesorchester, Loy, Melodram, 1950
EDITIONS   v.ss., Senff, Leipzig; Peters, 1911

Der Wildschütz, oder Die Stimme der Natur

The Poacher, or The Voice of Nature
Comic opera in three acts (3h)
Libretto by the composer, freely adapted from August von Kotzebue's comedy *Der Rehbock, oder Die schuldlosen Schuldbewussten* (1815)
Composed 1842
PREMIERES   31 December 1842, Altes Theater, Leipzig; US: 25 March 1859, New York; UK: 3 July 1895, Drury Lane, London
CAST   Count Eberbach *bar*, Countess *a*, Baron Kronthal *t*, Baroness Freimann *s*, Nanette *ms*, Baculus *b*, Gretchen *s*, Pancratius *b*; *satb* chorus of huntsmen, servants, villagers, schoolchildren
FULL ORCHESTRA

Lortzing's avowed preference was for literary sources of no great intrinsic merit, which allowed him freedom to create the musical and dramatic effects he required. Here he transforms the coarse impropriety of Kotzebue's original – in which he had acted in Detmold – into well-crafted and good-natured comedy. *Der Wildschütz* is Lortzing's comic masterpiece and proof that in the German spieloper he developed a native theatrical form that was in every way the equal of the French opéra comique or Italian opera buffa whose influences it assimilated.

SYNOPSIS

Act I   Celebration of the engagement of Baculus, a schoolmaster, and the much younger Gretchen is interrupted by a letter from Count Eberbach threatening Baculus with dismissal for poaching. Gretchen offers to intercede with the count, but Baculus, knowing his employer's reputation as a womanizer, refuses to let her go. Baroness Freimann, a young widow, sister of the count (whom she has not seen since childhood), arrives with her maid Nanette, both disguised as male students. The count has

proposed that his sister remarry; she intends first secretly to observe the suggested groom, Baron Kronthal, a young widower and brother of the count's own wife. The baroness offers to impersonate Gretchen. The count and the baron arrive with a hunting party. Immediately attracted to the supposed Gretchen, they invite her and Nanette (now also 'disguised' as a woman) to the castle.

Act II   In the castle Countess Eberbach is holding a reading of Sophocles. She attempts to engage the baron in a Greek love scene, unaware that he is the brother she has not seen since childhood, for he too is at the castle in disguise, as a stable lad, his true identity known only to the count. Baculus arrives and succeeds in impressing the countess with his apparent knowledge of the classics. The count, however, is not so easily mollified and Baculus summons 'Gretchen' to assist him. Both the count and the baron are carried away by their passion for her; they react with jealous astonishment to the knowledge that she is engaged to the elderly schoolmaster. A storm offers an excuse to invite the betrothed couple to stay the night. A game of billiards between the count and the baron degenerates into farcical chaos as they vie for the attentions of the disguised baroness, whom the countess finally rescues from beneath the billiard table. Alone with Baculus, the baron offers him 5000 thalers to relinquish his fiancée. Baculus, filled with thoughts of his own magnificent future, agrees.

Act III   The next morning Baculus presents the real Gretchen to the baron, explaining that the woman of the previous night was a male student in disguise. Gradually all involved reveal their true identities, protesting the innocence of their behaviour on the grounds that they had only been following the voice of nature. The tangle of relationships is unravelled and Baculus is pardoned, all the more readily when it emerges he had in fact shot his own donkey rather than one of the count's bucks.

The comic figures of Baculus and the steward Pancratius and the magnificent central billiards scene are among the many inventions and alterations with which Lortzing improved on his source material. The confidence of his musical characterization brings the familiar stock types vividly to life and lends timeless appeal even to his contemporary satire (of educational reformers and of the mania for all things Greek that swept Leipzig after the 1842 performance of *Antigone* with Mendelssohn's incidental music). Structurally the opera is a model of musical and dramatic refinement and coherence. In contrast to the reliance on operatic lieder in earlier works, *Der Wildschütz* has only four solo numbers but twelve ensembles. In the comically touching vanity of Baculus's 'Fünf Tausend Thaler' Lortzing demonstrates again his mastery of the buffo aria, while in the extended billiard table quintet ('Ich habe Num'ro eins'), which manages to integrate the cantus firmus of a chorale rehearsed by Baculus into the erotic warfare going on around the disguised baroness, he develops an increasingly complex comedy of musical and dramatic climaxes with Mozartian panache.

RECORDING Rothenburger, Schädle, Litz, Wunderlich, Prey, Ollendorf, Ehrengut, Bavarian State Opera Ch and O, Heger, Electrola, 1963
EDITIONS   f.s., Peters, 1928; v.s., Breitkopf und Härtel, 1842

Undine

Romantic magic opera in four acts (3h)
Libretto by the composer (with Philip Düringer) freely after the fairy-tale by Friedrich de la Motte-Fouqué (1811)
Composed 1844–5, rev. 1847
PREMIERES 21 April 1845, Magdeburg; US: 9 October 1856, New York; UK: 29 January 1980, University of Nottingham
CAST Berthalda *s*, Hugo von Ringstetten *t*, Kühleborn *bar*, Tobias *b*, Marthe *a*, Undine *s*, Pater Heilmann *b*, Veit *t*, Hans *b*; *satb* chorus of nobles, ambassadors, knights, ladies, heralds, pages, squires, hunt followers, peasants, fishermen; phantoms and water spirits
FULL ORCHESTRA

Undine represented a bold departure from Lortzing's previous work. Fouqué had already produced a libretto from his fairy-tale for E. T. A. Hoffmann in 1816. Fouqué's death in 1843 renewed interest in his work, and this may have influenced Lortzing's choice of subject. *Undine*, despite some obvious flaws, has retained a regular place in the German repertoire.

SYNOPSIS
Act I Hugo is about to marry Undine, the adopted daughter of a poor fisherman, Tobias. Undine's real father, the water prince Kühleborn, attends the wedding in disguise. Kühleborn knows that Hugo is already promised to Berthalda, the daughter of Duke Heinrich; Veit, Hugo's squire, confirms that his master is fickle. Kühleborn, anxious for his daughter, decides to follow the couple back to Hugo's homeland.
Act II Undine confesses to her husband that she is a water spirit. Berthalda greets the news of Hugo's marriage with assumed indifference; she treats Undine with sarcasm and announces her own engagement to the King of Naples. Kühleborn, still disguised, reveals in a song that Berthalda is in fact the lost daughter of the poor fisherman who had adopted Undine. He discloses his own identity.

Act III Undine takes pity on Berthalda and invites her to live in Hugo's family castle. Berthalda insinuates herself back into Hugo's affections. He resolves to leave his wife. The distraught Undine is taken back into the water by her father.
Act IV Preparations are underway for Hugo's marriage to Berthalda. On the stroke of midnight Undine appears at the celebrations in the great hall. Water floods the castle. Undine takes her faithless husband in her arms and carries him down into the depths. Kühleborn forgives Hugo and allows him to live on at Undine's side in the palace of the water spirits.

Lortzing did not feel entirely comfortable with the Romantic idiom and had to call on the assistance of his friend Philip Düringer for some of the verse writing in *Undine*. He also made extensive cuts and alterations after the first Vienna performance of 1847, removing and reworking passages he now found 'tedious and diffuse'. *Undine*'s Romanticism relies on essentially conventional effects, but it is not without sophistication, particularly in its structural use of the association, amounting effectively to leitmotif, of themes with particular characters. The first- and last-act finales are particularly ambitious in their incorporation of different musical elements into a larger dramatic and tonal structure. The most effective changes Lortzing made to Fouqué's original are those which allow an accommodation between Romantic magic and the earthier comic realism of which he was a master. But the decision to change the tragic ending undoubtedly weakens the work.

RECORDINGS 1. Rothenberger, Pütz, Gedda, Schreier, Prey, Frick, Berlin Radio Chamber Ch and SO, Heger, Electrola, 1966; 2. Krause, Hampe, Protschka, Janssen, Schmidt, Kruse, Cologne Radio Ch and O, Eichhorn, Capriccio, 1990
EDITIONS   f.s., Peters, 1925; v.ss., Breitkopf und Härtel, 1845; Peters (including Vienna revs), n.d.

Der Waffenschmied
The Armourer

Comic opera in three acts (2h 30m)
Libretto by the composer (with Philip Düringer), after Friedrich Wilhelm Ziegler's comedy *Liebhaber und Nebenbühler in einer Person* (1790)
Composed 1845–6
PREMIERES 30 May 1846, Theater an der Wien, Vienna; US: 4 February 1867, New York
CAST Hans Stadinger *b*, Marie *s*, Count Liebenau *bar*, Georg *t*, Adelhof *b*, Irmentraut *a*, Brenner *t*; *satb* chorus of apprentices, citizens, knights, squires, pages
FULL ORCHESTRA

Again Lortzing chose to adapt a play in which he had acted in Detmold. He took the newly completed work with him when he took up his appointment in Vienna and conducted the premiere there himself. *Der Waffenschmied*, a return to the popular German idiom the composer had briefly abandoned in *Undine*, was an immediate success and has retained its popularity.

SYNOPSIS

Act I The opera is set in Worms in the 16th century. Count Liebenau loves Marie, daughter of the famous armourer Hans Stadinger. Stadinger, who has disapproved of aristocrats since a knight stole his own wife, refuses to allow their marriage. The count assumes the guise of Konrad, an apprentice, and comes to work in Stadinger's forge. Marie is torn between the two lovers. Liebenau reappears in his own identity to test her love. She decides in favour of Konrad.

Act II Stadinger disapproves not only of the count, but of Konrad, who he thinks is a bad worker. He decides, after prompting from the Swabian knight Adelhof, that Georg, another apprentice, who is really Liebenau's squire in disguise, should marry Marie. At the celebrations of Stadinger's silver jubilee as a master armourer, Marie's governess, Irmtraut, rushes in to announce that she and Marie have been the victims of a kidnap attempt and were saved only by the intervention of Konrad. Stadinger still refuses to allow the match and threatens to send Marie to a convent.

Act III Adelhof has discovered, from the venal Brenner, who once worked for Liebenau, the real identities of Konrad and Georg. The count manages to prevent him from revealing this and uses Brenner (whom he has bribed back on to his side) to persuade Stadinger to act on a magistrate's letter ordering Marie's immediate marriage to Konrad, on the grounds that Liebenau is threatening to attack the city. Stadinger gives in. Furious to discover his daughter has married the count after all, he then relents and gives the couple his blessing. All ends happily.

Model of musical and dramatic coherence that it is, *Der Waffenschmied* none the less shows signs of a retreat from the complexity Lortzing could achieve even within the spieloper form. The use of ensemble is arguably less ambitious than in, say, *Der Wildschütz*, with a greater reliance on duets and simple, songlike, solo melodies. The opera's musical and dramatic crux, for instance, lies essentially in Stadinger's famous song in Act III (for which the composer provided extra stanzas in case a reprise was required).

RECORDING Schädle, Litz, Unger, Prey, Ollendorf, Böhme, Bavarian State Opera Ch and O, Lehan, Electrola, 1964
EDITIONS f.s., Peters, 1922; v.s., Breitkopf und Härtel, 1846

Die vornehmen Dilettanten, oder Die Opernprobe
The Elegant Dilettantes, or The Opera Rehearsal

Comic opera in one act (1h)
Libretto by the composer, after the comedy *L'impromptu de campagne* by Philippe Poisson (1733), via Johann Friedrich Junger's German translation *Die Komödie aus dem Stegreif* (1794)
PREMIERES 20 January 1851, Stadttheater, Frankfurt am Main; UK: 9 October 1934, London (concert); 26 March 1969, Sadler's Wells, London

Lortzing, his wife and his parents had appeared together in the German translation of Poisson's comedy in Cologne in 1825. Lortzing's last opera, with its engaging satirical exploration of the theatrical world he knew so well, enjoyed a popularity he did not live to see: it was regularly performed up to the Second World War. Its comparatively recent fall from favour is a mystery. Set in the castle of a count whose mania for opera is such that he addresses his staff in recitative and has made compulsory participation in opera performances a condition of employment, it is a delightful comedy of romantic confusion and mistaken identity. All is resolved in the course of a rehearsal conducted by the chambermaid, Hannchen. A charming distillation of Lortzing's lifelong experience and love of the theatre, *Die Opernprobe* can stand comparison with anything in the long tradition of operas about opera, from Cimarosa's *L'impresario in angustie* and Mozart's *Schauspieldirektor* to Strauss's *Ariadne*.

RECORDING Lövaas, Marheineke, Litz, Gedda, Berry, Ch and O of Bavarian State Opera, Suitner, Electrola, 1975
EDITIONS f.s., Senff, 1899; v.s., Senff, 1851

Other operatic works: *Ali Pascha von Janina, oder Die Franzosen in Albanien*, 1828 (RECORDING MD&G, 1989); *Der Pole und sein Kind, oder Der Feldwebel vom IV Regiment*, 1832; *Der Weinachtsabend*, 1832; *Andreas Hofer*, 1832; *Szenen aus Mozarts Leben*, 1832; *Die Schatzkammer des Ynka*, 1836; *Caramo, oder das Fischerstechen*, 1839; *Casanova*, 1841; *Zum Grossadmiral*, 1847; *Regina*, (1848), 1899 (arr. L'Arronge); *Rolands Knappen, oder Das ersehnte Glück*, 1849
BIBLIOGRAPHY M. Hoffmann, *Albert Lortzing, der Meister der Deutschen Volksoper*, Leipzig, 1956; E. Sanders, 'Oberon and Zar und Zimmermann', *MQ*, vol. 40 (1954), p. 521; R. R. Subotnik, 'Lortzing and the German Romantics: A Dialectical Assessment', *MQ*, vol. 62 (1976), p. 241

I.B.

MARK LOTHAR
b 23 May 1902, Berlin; *d* 6 April 1985, Munich, Germany

Lothar's composition teachers included Schreker and later Wolf-Ferrari, to whom he dedicated his 'magic opera', *Rappelkopf*. His early works, mainly lieder, were well received, while the success of his first opera, *Tyll*, led to his appointment as Max Reinhardt's musical director at the Deutsches Theater, Berlin, in 1933. He remained in Berlin throughout the war years. 'I am no nationalist,' he wrote, 'but I consider myself a German and sense a profound obligation to German culture and thought.'

Lothar was an all-round theatre musician. Apart from his eight operas, he composed incidental music for over 130 plays, 50 radio and television productions and 28 films. His best-known work is the score for Gustaf Gründgens's film production of Goethe's *Faust*. Gründgens, who also directed the premiere of the comic opera *Schneider Wibbel*, said

The auditorium of the Dresden Opera House during a performance of Lotti's Teofane *(1719)*

of Lothar's score, 'The opera is captivatingly light, attractive and warm-hearted, the music is entirely straightforward with no trace of "phonyness" – there are no problems.' Gründgens's remark can well be applied to all of Lothar's deftly written opera scores.

Operatic works: *Tyll*, 1928; *Lord Spleen*, 1930; *Münchhausen*, 1933; *Das kalte Herz* (radio opera), 1935; *Schneider Wibbel*, 1938; *Rappelkopf*, 1958; *Der Glücksfischer*, 1962; *Der widerspenstige Heiliger*, 1968
BIBLIOGRAPHY   Alfons Ott (ed.), *Mark Lothar, ein Musikerporträt*, Süddeutscher Verlag, 1968

A.C.W.B.

ANTONIO LOTTI
b c. 1667, Venice or Hanover; *d* 5 January 1740, Venice

A student of Legrenzi in Venice, Lotti held a number of posts at St Mark's, finally becoming maestro only four years before his death. Unfortunately, his name has become exclusively associated with a conservative style of church music, and it is nowadays difficult to imagine him as a successful composer of operas. Only a handful of his 30-odd operas survive in score, and they were written almost exclusively for performance in Venice. His operatic career began in

1692 with a performance of *Il trionfo dell'innocenza;* following his greatest period of operatic activity, the decade from 1706, Lotti was invited to compose for the court in Dresden, where there was a considerable vogue for Italian music. He stayed in the north from 1717 to 1719, composing for Dresden three operas and a festa teatrale on the occasion of the marriage of the Elector of Saxony to Maria Gioseffa of Austria. The remainder of his career seems to have been spent in Venice, and no further operas seem to have been composed in the final 20 years of his life, after his return from Dresden.

Lotti's style favoured the lightly accompanied voice in clear declamation with occasional flourishes to underline the text; the instruments come to the fore in ritornelli, introductions and interludes, which are well conceived and contrast with the vocal material. Some parallels have been drawn between this technique and that of the late-baroque concerto. Like his contemporary Gasparini, Lotti also composed independent comic intermezzi, such as *Le rovine di Troja* (1707).

Extant operatic works: *Tirsi* (coll. with Caldara and Ariosti), 1696; *Le rovine di Troja*, 1707; *Dragontana e Policrone*, 1707; *Porsenna*, 1712; *Irene augusta* (only arias survive), 1713; *Polidoro*, 1714; *Costantino* (coll. with Fux, Caldara and Matteis), 1716; *Foca superbo*, 1716; *Alessandro Severo*, 1716 (EDITION facsimile, H. M. Brown (ed.), Garland, 1977); *Giove in Argo*, 1717; *Ascanio, ovvero Gli odi delusi dal*

sangue, 1718; *Teofane*, 1719; *Griletta e Serpillo*, n.d.; 15 lost operas
BIBLIOGRAPHY C. Spitz, *Antonio Lotti in seiner Bedeutung als Opernkomponist*, dissertation, University of Munich, 1918

G.D.

JEAN-BAPTISTE LULLY
Giovanni Battista Lulli; *b* 28 November 1632, Florence; *d* 22 March 1687, Paris

Jean-Baptiste Lully

Lully's domination of late 17th-century French music was achieved by a combination of good fortune, musical and theatrical talent, skilful management of people and finance, and ruthless pursuit of power.

Lully came to France at the age of 13, to help perfect the Italian of Louis XIV's cousin, the 18-year-old Mlle de Montpensier. He soon became an accomplished violinist, guitarist and dancer, working closely with the composer and singer Michel Lambert. Lully was just 20 when he danced with the 14-year-old Louis XIV in the *Ballet royal de la nuit* (1653) and when he gained his first court post as Compositeur de la musique instrumentale de la Chambre. At 23, he was directing the smaller court string orchestra (Les Petits Violons or La Petite Bande) and composing for the ballets de cour, while also drawing on the vocal style of the airs de cour of Lambert. Within weeks of taking charge of the kingdom on the death of Cardinal Mazarin in 1661, Louis XIV appointed Lully as Surintendant and Maître de la musique de la Chambre, the two most powerful posts in the musical establishment. The composer was then 28, and was naturalized later the same year (as Jean-Baptiste Lully). The following year he became Maître de la Musique de la famille royale, and married Lambert's daughter, Madeleine.

The second decade of Lully's career at court centred on his successful collaborations with Molière; the first was the comédie-ballet *Le mariage forcé* (1664); the last the tragédie-ballet *Psyché* (1671, later in 1678 to be hurriedly transformed into a tragédie en musique). This experience, preceded by Lully's long apprenticeship with the ballet de cour, enabled him to refine the ingredients of the recipe he was to put together so successfully in his operas.

The first operas in 17th-century France were almost wholly imported Italian productions, between 1645 and 1662, concluding with Cavalli's *Ercole amante* with interludes by Lully. The first French-language operas resulted from initiatives by the poet Pierre Perrin, between 1659 and 1671. Ironically, Lully long opposed the notion, but, nettled by the spectacular success of Robert Cambert's *Pomone* to a text by Perrin, who had obtained Letters Patent for Académies d'Opéra, Lully seized the chance to acquire these rights when Perrin was imprisoned for debt in 1672. Establishing the Académie royale de Musique, Lully ensured his monopoly of staged music performance in France, with privileges obtained from Louis XIV. Until his death 15 years later, he produced a new opera almost every year. Thus, although not its inventor, Lully won acceptance for French-language opera. The form of tragédie en musique evolved by Lully and his librettist Philippe Quinault dominated French opera for the following century.

Lully's development of the 'French' overture widely adopted by Bach, Handel and contemporaries in England and Italy, his development of dance forms and of a fluid recitative have all long been acknowledged. Also widely admired was the legendary discipline Lully imposed on his performers, ensuring a perfection of ensemble remembered long after his death. Less recognized outside France has been the supremacy of the text itself; yet Lully's clear statement that 'my recitative is meant for speaking' unambiguously underlines the centrality of the dialogue, as important as it is in, say, the works of Gilbert and Sullivan. Contemporary writers emphasized the enormous appeal of the very human text, liberally sprinkled with witty aphorisms (usually emanating from lesser characters, rather than the main protagonists). These works were also unashamed propaganda on behalf of Louis XIV, the Sun King, and the plots, loosely based on mythology or fable, were mostly peopled by gods and mortals engaged in improbable confrontation, with the theme of love versus duty rarely absent. Yet, there are also many wry observations on the frailty of human nature, even when in godly form. To transmit both plot and commentary unambiguously, Lully uses flowing declamatory recitative (carefully notated in constantly varying time signatures), which frequently evolves from and returns to various forms of air, sometimes based on popular song, as well as comment from the static chorus, which functions much as does that of Classical drama. Monologue is a frequently used device at critical moments in the unfolding of the drama. Opera libretti (and candles) were sold to help the public follow the action, and audiences sometimes even sang along with the chorus, as they became familiar with each new work.

Of Lully's operas only *Atys, Phaëton* and *Armide* have an 'unhappy' ending. Nor is humour confined to a few early works as is sometimes suggested, even if it became more subtle later. The overture is heard twice: before and after the prologue, itself usually an allegory of the king's majesty. During the tragedy, audiences are rewarded with substantial divertissements of dances, solos and choruses, for which Lully required his librettists to fit their words to his musical design. Instrumental movements already heard are repeated as entr'actes. From *Bellérophon* (1679) onwards, the score of each opera was published the same year as its premiere (*Isis* had already appeared in separate parts in 1677); the earlier works appeared after Lully's death. Several of Quinault's libretti for Lully were used by later composers, such as Campra, Mondonville, F.-A.-D. Philidor, J. C. Bach, Piccinni, Gossec and, most notably, Gluck (*Armide*).

Lully's orchestra was organized as a small continuo group (the petit choeur), usually accompanying the solo singers and comprising solo violins and wind, bass viol(s), bass violin(s), theorbo(es) and harpsichord, and a larger one (the grand choeur) employed in instrumental movements and choruses, and based on a five-part string ensemble (violins, violas in three parts, bass violins), sometimes extended to seven parts. Flutes, recorders and oboes played in both groups; bassoons, trumpets (up to five parts) and timpani were frequently added to the grand choeur. Other instruments occasionally employed included guitar, musette, *taille* (tenor oboe), crumhorn and panpipes.

LWV numbers refer to Herbert Schneider, *Chronologisch-Thematisches Verzeichnis Samtlicher Werke von Jean-Baptiste Lully,* Hans Schneider, 1981.

Cadmus et Hermione

Tragédie in a prologue and five acts, LWV 49
Libretto by Philippe Quinault, after Book III of Ovid's *Metamorphoses*
PREMIERES   27 April 1673, Jeu de Paume du Bel-Air, Paris;
UK: 11 February 1686, Dorset Garden, London

Lully's first true opera contains elements soon modified in *Alceste* and subsequent works. The chorus, although contributing substantially to the prologue, are confined in the tragédie to Acts III and V. The prologue, unconnected with the tragedy

following, concerns the serpent Python overcome by the withering rays of the Sun – an allegory of the Sun King's power. In the tragédie, Lully's music carries the action forward with minimal distraction from the comic sub-plot. The dance and choral elements of the divertissements are integrated into the plot, serving to maximize the drama at critical moments.

The myth of Cadmus and Harmonia was considerably adapted by Quinault. Cadmus seeks to save his beloved from the giant keeping her captive, at the behest of her father Mars, and guarded by a dragon. After Cadmus slays the monster, Mars demands further trials of him. Cadmus sows the dragon's teeth in the ground, warned by Arbas that armed soldiers will spring up and do battle. Cupid provides him with a grenade to throw amidst the soldiers when they appear. In their panic, they fight one another until the few left surrender to Cadmus. Pallas turns the defiant giants to stone; she has prepared a palace for the lovers. But a cloud takes Hermione from Cadmus' sight: Juno has intervened because she still has scores to settle with her husband, Jupiter. When Pallas announces that Juno and Jupiter have settled their quarrel, Hermione returns from the heavens with Hymen. Jupiter, Juno and Venus all bless the lovers.

Much of the musical appeal of *Cadmus et Hermione* derives from the many instrumental movements. In the prologue, these include the entrée of Envy, depicting furious winds, and the pair of menuets that conclude it. The motif associated with Cadmus' slaying of the dragon returns for a later struggle when Hermione is taken to heaven by Juno; Lully also used this device in *Alceste* and later operas. The most eloquent air of the work is the monologue in rondo form which opens Act V, Cadmus' poignant lament for his 'Belle Hermione'.

RECORDING   excerpt: Souzay, ECO, Leppard, Philips, 1964; *reissue*, 1989
EDITIONS   f.ss., J.-B.-C. Ballard, 1719; Henry Prunières (ed.), *Oeuvres complètes,* vol. 1, Edition de la Revue Musicale, Paris, 1930; *rp,* Broude, 1966; v.ss., Lajarte (ed.), Michaelis, 1881; *rp,* Broude, 1971

Alceste, ou Le triomphe d'Alcide

Alceste, or The Triumph of Hercules
Tragédie in a prologue and five acts, LWV 50 (2h 30m)
Libretto by Philippe Quinault after the play *Alcestis* by Euripides (438 BC)
PREMIERES   19 January 1674, Jeu de Paume du Bel-Air, Paris; UK: 17 December 1975, London Opera Centre
CAST   *prologue:* Nymph of the Seine *s,* Glory *s,* Nymph of the Tuileries *s,* Nymph of the Marne *s; tragédie:* Alcestis *s,* Céphise *s,* Lycomedes *b,* Thetis *s,* Alcides *bar,* Admetis *t,* Pheres *t,* Charon *b,* Pluto *b,* Proserpine *s,* Apollo *haute-contre,* Alecto *haute-contre,* 5 *s,* 3 *haute-contre, t, bar,* 3 *b; satb* chorus of nymphs, naiads, people, soldiers, sea-sprites, spirits, etc.; ballet
ORCHESTRATION   2 tpts, timp, 3 fl/rec, 2 ob, musette, [bsns], str, continuo; onstage: wind band

Although described by Mme de Sévigné as a 'marvel of beauty', *Alceste* did not win immediate acceptance; nevertheless it held a particular place in Louis

XIV's affections, and remained in the repertoire for 83 years.

SYNOPSIS

The allegorical prologue is a colourful divertissement in praise of an unnamed hero.

Act I The rejoicings at the marriage of Alcestis and Admetis are shattered when the jealous Lycomedes abducts Alcestis to his island kingdom.

Act II Alcestis laments her fate, but Admetis and Alcides (who also secretly loves Alcestis) lead the expedition to free her. The rescuers are triumphant, but Admetis is mortally wounded. Apollo appears and announces that Admetis can be saved if someone will die in his place; such a person will be immortalized in a monument.

Act III Pheres, Admetis' father, and Céphise plead old age and youth respectively as excuses for not offering themselves for the sacrifice. When Admetis sees the image of Alcestis on the monument, he knows she has made the sacrifice. Alcides offers to rescue Alcestis from the underworld if Admetis will cede to him 'the beauty you have lost'. Admetis agrees, happy that Alcestis may return, even though denied to him. Diana, impressed with such selflessness, assists Alcides' expedition to Hades.

Act IV Pluto and Proserpine are entertaining Alcestis when Alcides arrives, having chained up the three-headed dog, Cerberus, guarding the entrance. Assured that Alcides' father, Jupiter, intends no other intervention in the underworld, Pluto agrees to Alcestis' release.

Act V Alcestis, although touched by Alcides' rescue and his love for her, confesses that it is Admetis she truly loves. Deeply moved by the heart-rending farewells between Alcestis and Admetis, Alcides accepts glory rather than love in renouncing his own passion for her. Apollo descends to join in the concluding divertissement of rejoicing.

The musical proportions of *Alceste* and subsequent operas gained much from Lully's experience with *Cadmus et Hermione*. Most notably, there is more for the chorus (which now sings in all five acts as well as the prologue) and less recitative. The musical portrayal of the storm evoked by Lycomedes' sister, Thetis, to prevent pursuit in Act I is matched in Act II by a colourful battle scene for double chorus, onstage wind band, and the full panoply of Lully's orchestra. The hauntingly evocative duo between the grief-stricken Alcestis and her dying husband includes the poignant refrain: 'Alceste, vous pleurez?' 'Admète, vous mourez?' In Act III, a ritournelle heard earlier when Alcestis declares that only love can save Admetis, heralds the news that he is healed. In an impressive rondeau, the heart-rending refrain 'Alceste est morte' is exchanged between Admetis and Céphise, the intervening recitatives expressing her remorse at failing to prevent Alcestis' death. In complete contrast are the comic rondeau that opens Act IV, 'Il faut passer tôt ou tard', in which Charon sings of his task ferrying the departed across the Styx, and the wordless 'barking' chorus to depict the dog, Cerberus.

RECORDING Palmer, Rodde, Nighogossian, Auphan, Brewer, Elwes, Le Maigat, Vento, Loup, Maîtrise National d'Enfants, Ensemble Vocal Raphaël Passaquet, La Grande Ecurie et La Chambre du Roy, Malgoire, CBS, 1975
EDITIONS f.s., Henry Prunières (ed.), *Oeuvres complètes*, operas, vol. 2, Edition de la Revue Musicale, 1932; *rp*, Broude, 1966; reduced s., Baussen, 1708; v.s., Lajarte (ed.), Michaelis, 1882

Thésée

Theseus

Tragédie en musique in a prologue and five acts, LWV 51 (2h 30m)
Libretto by Philippe Quinault
PREMIERE 11 January 1675, Saint-Germain-en-Laye
CAST *prologue*: Venus *s*, Mars *b*, Ceres *s*, Bacchus *haute-contre*; *tragédie*: Aeglé *s*, Arcas *b*, Priestess of Minerva *s*, Aegeus (Egée) *bar*, Medea *s*, Dorine *s*, Theseus *t*, Minerva *s*, 3 *s*, 4 *haute-contre*, 3 *t*, *bar*, 2 *b*; *satb* chorus of nymphs, shepherds, cupids, soldiers, spirits; ballet
ORCHESTRATION 4 tpt, 2 fl/rec, 2 ob, musettes, [bsns], str, cont

Thésée remained in the repertoire until 1779, the longest-running of all Lully's operas, its popularity sustained by the relentless pace of the plot and a colourful score.

SYNOPSIS

The prologue explains how, from the noise of war, 'a new Mars will make France triumphant' and 'the pleasures of peace' will follow. (Louis XIV's conquest of the Spanish Netherlands was in progress.)

Act I The young Aeglé prays to Minerva for the safety of her beloved, the warrior Theseus. The elderly king, Aegeus, also enamoured of Aeglé, determines to make her his queen, despite his betrothal to the sorceress Medea, herself in love with Theseus, whom she knows is the king's son. Theseus, secretly brought up abroad until old enough to bear his father's sword, wins renown as a warrior in Athens without his father realizing his identity. The battle over, Aegeus presses his suit with Aeglé. The Athenians offer a sacrifice of thanksgiving for their deliverance.

Act II Medea and Aegeus agree to forgo their betrothal in favour of their new infatuations. But when the people want Theseus named heir to the throne, the king's mood changes. Medea warns Theseus of Aegeus' annoyance. Confessing his love for Aeglé, Theseus learns that the king is his rival. Medea offers to intervene with both Aeglé and the king, but, alone, she passionately abandons herself to spite and jealousy.

Act III Medea tells Aeglé she, too, loves Theseus, and threatens vengeance if Aeglé doesn't renounce him. Medea evokes a bleak desert and calls up the spirits of hell to terrify Aeglé.

Act IV Medea warns Aeglé that to escape she must marry Aegeus. Theseus appears under a spell; Medea threatens to kill him. Aeglé agrees to her terms. When Theseus awakes, he cannot understand why Aeglé ignores him. He announces he is the king's son and Aeglé explains that she is promised to Aegeus. Medea, witnessing their pledges of love, appears to relent, renouncing her love for Theseus.

Act V Medea plans vengeance yet more appalling. She convinces the king that naming Theseus as heir will disinherit his missing son. Aegeus agrees to offer Theseus a poisoned chalice at the ceremonies in the hero's honour. As he is about to drink, the king recognizes Theseus' sword and, realizing his identity, dashes the cup from his grasp; Medea flees. All are reconciled – father to son, and son to his beloved, but Medea destroys the palace; confusion reigns until Minerva intervenes and the opera concludes with rejoicing.

The opera abounds with vigorous choruses and a rich variety of entrées and dances. Woodwind and trumpets are deployed in the prologue in impressive ensembles denoting Venus and Mars respectively; Act I includes further evocative 'military' scoring, with the offstage sounds of the Athenians battling for their city. Medea's powerful monologues concluding Act II and the stark 'Ah, faut-il me venger' of Act V are the most significant vocal expressions of the opera, showing Lully's dramatic talents at their best.

RECORDING excerpts: Ayer, Mattei, Cuenod, Vienna Volksoper O, Straight, RCA, 1973
EDITIONS f.s., C. Ballard, 1688; v.ss., Lajarte (ed.), Michaelis, 1878; *rp*, Broude, 1971

Atys

Tragédie en musique in a prologue and five acts, LWV 53 (2h 15m)
Libretto by Philippe Quinault, after Book IV of Ovid's *Fasti*
PREMIERE 10 January 1676, Saint-Germain-en-Laye; US: 17 May 1989, Brooklyn Academy of Music, New York (Les Arts Florissants)
CAST *prologue*: Time *bar*, Flora *s*, Melpomene *s*, Iris *s*, a zephyr *haute-contre*; *satb* chorus; *tragédie*: Atys *haute-contre*, Idas *b*, Sangaride *s*, Doris *s*, Cybèle *s*, Melisse *s*, Celenus *bar*, Le Sommeil *haute-contre*, Sangar *b*, 2 *haute-contre*, *t*, 2 *b*; *satb* chorus of nymphs, zephyrs, heroes, priestesses, spirits, pleasant and bad dreams; ballet
ORCHESTRATION 2 fl/rec, 3 ob, [bsns], str, cont

Costume design by Jean Bérain for Le Sommeil in Atys *(St Germain-en-Laye, 1676)*

SYNOPSIS

Prologue In a transparent allegory of the might of Louis XIV, Time promises the greatest of heroes eternal fame; Flora, goddess of spring, wishes to pay her tribute before the hero leaves for the wars. But Melpomene intervenes, distracting him with the story of Atys.

Act I At dawn, Atys awakens the Phrygians to prepare a welcome for the goddess Cybèle. Idas mocks his enthusiasm and asks if it is Love that keeps him awake? Sangaride enters and feigns delight at the prospect of her marriage to Celenus, king of Phrygia, especially as Cybèle will be present but, alone, she laments her fate and her unrequited love for Atys. Finding her distressed, Atys confesses his love to the astonished Sangaride.

Act II Both Atys and the king declare their wish to act as high priest for Cybèle. Cybèle, secretly loving Atys, chooses him, and admits it is for this love she has come, rather than for the nuptials of the king and Sangaride. Atys receives the accolades of his high office.

Act III Cybèle causes Atys to fall into a deep sleep. Pleasant dreams sing of love, but bad dreams warn him of the penalties of deceiving the gods. He wakens startled to find Cybèle only too ready to console him. Sangaride begs Cybèle to save her from marrying the king whom she does not love. Atys, confused, supports her pleas, and Cybèle guesses their mutual passion; she laments her fate.

Act IV Sangaride misinterprets Atys' confusion as hidden passion for Cybèle, and laments the ungrateful Atys. But he explains, and they swear eternal love. Atys, as high priest, goes to Sangaride's father, Sangarius, commanding him, in the name of Cybèle, to cancel the marriage arrangements between Sangaride and the king.

Act V Hearing of this, the king confronts Cybèle. Realizing Atys has deceived them, they decide to punish the lovers. Cybèle casts a spell on Atys, who, in his blindness, stabs Sangaride. When he sees what he has done, Atys attempts suicide, but Cybèle intervenes, transforming him into a tree. She is left to celebrate her hollow victory, and to lament him whom she has lost for ever.

Act I includes the chorus 'Nous devons nous animer d'une ardeur nouvelle', soon to become the source of a Purcell trumpet tune and thus of a score of further parodies. In the same act, in one of Lully's most eloquent recitatives, Atys confesses his love for Sangaride. Atys' dreams in Act III are depicted by a memorable orchestral *sommeil* with alternating strings and flutes, but the musical climax of the opera coincides with the tragic *dénouement*; the chorus attempts to warn Atys of his mistake as he stabs Sangaride: 'Arrête, arrête, malheureux!' they cry, but it is too late, and as Sangaride dies they wail, 'Atys lui-même fait périr ce qu'il aime'.

RECORDING Mellon, Laurens, Rime, de Mey, Ragon, Fouchécourt, Deletré, Bona, Les Arts Florissants, Christie, Harmonia Mundi, 1987
EDITIONS f.ss., C. Ballard, 1689; facsimile, *French Opera in*

the 17th and 18th Centuries, vol. 3, Pendragon, forthcoming; reduced s., Baussen, 1708, 1709; *rp*, Société de musicologie de Languedoc, 1987; v.ss., Lajarte (ed.), Michaelis, 1880; *rp*, Broude, 1971

Isis

Tragédie en musique in a prologue and five acts, LWV 54
Libretto by Philippe Quinault
PREMIERE   5 January 1677, Saint-Germain-en-Laye
CAST   *prologue*: La Renommée *s*, Neptune *b*, Apollo *haute-contre*, 2 Tritons *haute-contre, t*; *tragédie*: Hierax *bar*, Io *s*, Mercury *haute-contre*, Jupiter *b*, Juno *s*, Iris *s*, Hébé *s*, Argus *bar*, Pan *b*, 5 *s*, 8 *haute-contre*, 3 *t*, 5 *b*; *satb* chorus of nymphs, shepherds, satyrs, naiads, furies, frozen people, spirits; ballet
ORCHESTRATION   5 tpt, timp, 3 fl/rec, 2 ob, musettes, [bsns], str, cont

Quinault's critics cited Jupiter's pursuit of Io and Juno's jealousy as an allegory of Mme de Montespan's resentment of a younger rival for the king's affections. But performances continued and Quinault was soon rehabilitated, although at first 'ghosting' for others (in *Psyché* and *Bellérophon*).

SYNOPSIS
Prologue   Neptune acknowledges the hero who will 'fulfil the destiny of the French empire' (Louis XIV) and his powers over land and sea. Apollo, the Muses and the Arts announce new festivities to honour the hero.
Act I   Hierax doubts the fidelity of his beloved nymph, Io. But she asserts her constancy despite Jupiter's advances. Mercury tells Io that Jupiter has come to earth to see her, but she is already promised to another.
Act II   Jupiter hides Io and himself from the jealous Juno behind clouds. He sings of love and Io of duty until Mercury announces Juno has sent Iris to pursue them. Iris is unconvinced when Mercury tells her Jupiter has gone down to earth 'to do good', but she nevertheless tells Juno she cannot find Io. When the gods meet, Jupiter suggests Juno augment her court with a nymph; to his dismay, she chooses Io.
Act III   Near a lake, Hierax's brother, Argus of the hundred eyes, guards Io at Juno's behest. Jupiter sends Mercury to re-enact the story of Pan and Syrinx until all of Argus' eyes close, and Io can escape. The spurned Hierax awakens Argus, but Mercury's wand strikes them both dead. Juno revives Argus, sending a fury to pursue Io into the wilderness.
Act IV   There, Io is tormented – first, among the frozen people then surrounded by flames from the Chalybes' forges, driving her to such distraction that she dives into the sea, pursued by the Fury. The Fates threaten Io until she begs to die.
Act V   The Fury drags Io from the sea at the mouth of the Nile; she implores Jupiter to relieve the agony his love has caused her. He begs Juno to release the dying Io from her torments. Only when Jupiter admits he must learn to conquer himself does Juno relent; she abandons her vengeance in return for his love, and elevates Io to the ranks of the gods as Isis; the Egyptian people recognize her divinity.

Its variety of textures and forms bears witness to Le Cerf de la Viéville's description (1704) of Isis as the 'musicians' opera'. In the prologue, the chorus and five stage trumpets praise the hero, while Neptune is accompanied by flutes. In Act I, a beguiling echo chorus announces Jupiter's descent from heaven. In Act III, in one of Lully's most eloquent sequences, the sound of the reeds (flutes playing a three-note figure) intersperses Pan's lament when Syrinx dives into them to escape him and is transformed. Io's torments in Act IV are depicted in a chorus of shivering people (with repeated notes, an Italian device adopted in England as well as in France) contrasted with one portraying the relentless hammering of the forges of the Chalybes.

RECORDING   excerpts: Sautereau, Chamonin, Mallabrera, Soyer, Caillard Chorale, Paillard CO, Paillard, Erato, 1972
EDITIONS   f.s., J.-B.-C. Ballard, 1719; v.ss., Lajarte (ed.), Michaelis, 1882; *rp*, Broude, 1971

Bellérophon

Tragédie en musique in a prologue and five acts, LWV 57
Libretto by Thomas Corneille and Bernard le Bovier de Fontenelle after Philippe Quinault's tragédie (1665)
PREMIERE   31 January 1679, Palais Royal, Paris
CAST   *prologue*: Apollo *b*, Bacchus *haute-contre*, Pan *b*; *tragédie*: Stenobée *s*, Argie *s*, Philonoe *s*, Iobates *b*, Bellérophon *haute-contre*, Amisodar *b*, High Priest *b*, Pythia *haute-contre*, Apollo *b*, Pallas *s*, 6 *s*, *haute-contre, b*; *satb* chorus of followers of Bacchus and Pan, captives, magicians, people of Lycia; ballet
ORCHESTRATION   4 tpt, timp, 2 fl/rec, 2 ob, [bsns], str, cont

Quinault's temporary disgrace after the 1677 premiére of *Isis* obliged Lully to turn to other librettists for *Bellérophon*, but Quinault apparently 'ghosted' the final version of the libretto. The subject of a hero victorious in war and love aptly flattered Louis XIV, especially for his conquests in the Spanish Netherlands the previous year (1678).

SYNOPSIS
Prologue   Apollo, Bacchus and Pan sing of the joys of peace.
Act I   The warrior hero, Bellerophon, who believes his father is the sea god Glaucus, is loved by the widowed Stenobée, queen of Argos. Her late husband, Proetus, jealous of Bellérophon, had sent him to Iobates, king of Lycia, with secret letters praising his courage, but asking he be killed. Iobates disregards this request, rewarding Bellérophon's exploits with the hand of his daughter, Philonoe. Stenobée, outraged, challenges the magician, Amisodar, to invoke a monster to ravage Lycia.
Act II   Stenobée makes a final plea for Bellérophon's love, but he rejects her, believing her responsible for his banishment from Argos. Amisodar conjures up a monster, the Chimera.
Act III   Seeing the carnage left in the monster's wake, Stenobée is mortified, since she still loves Bellérophon, who decides to hunt the Chimera, while the High Priest offers a sacrifice. But Apollo appears and announces that a son of Neptune will save them,

providing he is rewarded with the hand of Philonoe. Bellérophon and Philonoe despair of their love, but agree to submit to the gods' will.

Act IV Amisodar is pleased with the devastation he has caused, but Argie, Stenobée's confidante, tries to persuade him to return the monster to the underworld, since the queen's motive for vengeance has evaporated now that Philonoe must marry Neptune's son. Bellérophon, sure that death can be his only reward, is about to attack the Chimera when Pallas, goddess of wisdom, provides him with the winged horse Pegasus, enabling him to defeat the monster.

Act V Neptune announces that he is Bellérophon's father, a fact he previously disguised to avoid the wrath of a jealous sea nymph. The lovers now rejoice, but Stenobée takes poison, and the opera concludes in praise of 'le plus grand des héros'.

Trumpets and drums announcing Bellérophon's triumphal entry to the court in Act I typify much of the scoring of this epic tale, contrasting with the scene of destruction in Act III, where the people's grief is poignantly depicted with chorus and strings alternating with flutes. The most eloquent of three monologues ('Heureuse mort') is sung by Bellérophon as he prepares to seek out the monster.

EDITIONS f.s., C. Ballard, 1679; v.s., Lajarte (ed.), Michaelis, 1880

Proserpine

Tragédie en musique in a prologue and five acts, LWV 58
Libretto by Philippe Quinault
PREMIERES 3 February 1680, Saint-Germain-en-Laye; UK: 18 March 1987, Hinde Street Church, Marylebone, London

The prologue depicts the victory of Peace over Discord. The tragédie recounts how Ceres grieved for Proserpine, her daughter by Jupiter, carried off to the underworld by Pluto. Jupiter would have effected her release if she had not eaten, but because she had consumed some pomegranate seeds, she had to marry Pluto, and spend half the year in Hades, but could return to her mother for the other half. Discord and War were then banned in favour of everlasting Peace. Lully's score includes a colourful scene in Act II (organized ABCDCDBA), where Proserpine and her companions are enjoying the beauties of Ceres' garden, and, in Act IV, flutes à 4 depicting the Elysian fields.

EDITIONS f.s., C. Ballard, 1680; v.ss., Lajarte (ed.), Michaelis, 1883; rp, Broude, 1971

Amadis

Tragédie en musique in a prologue and five acts, LWV 63
(2h 30m)
Libretto by Philippe Quinault, after Nicolas d'Herberay des Essart's translation of Garci Rodriguez de Montalvo's *Los quatros libros del virtuoso cavallero Amadis de Gaula* (c. 1492)
PREMIERES 15 January 1684, Palais Royal, Paris; UK: 14 June 1938, Twentieth Century Theatre, London

CAST *prologue*: Urgande *s*, Alquif *b*, follower of Alquif *s*; *satb* chorus; *tragédie*: Amadis *haute-contre*, Oriane *s*, Florestan *b*, Corisande *s*, Arcalaus *b*, Arcabonne *s*, Spirit of Ardan Canile *b*, Urgande *s*, 6 *s*, 2 *haute-contre*, 2 *t*, *b*; *satb* chorus of knights, nymphs, prisoners, gaolers, heroes, heroines; ballet
ORCHESTRATION 4 tpt, timp, 2 fl/rec, 2 ob, str, cont

Amadis marks Quinault's turn from Greek mythology to medieval chivalry. Unaware of the tale's British origins, he depicts the hero as a *gaulois*, while reducing the legend to manageable dimensions. Linking prologue and tragédie, he presents Amadis' heroism as an allegory of that of Louis XIV.

SYNOPSIS
Prologue The benevolent sorceress Urgande and her husband Alquif are roused by thunder from a spell, removed so that 'the world's destiny depends on an even more glorious hero' (than Amadis, whom they were mourning). They resolve to revive the Amadis story to 'bear witness to the glory of a king of kings'.

Act I Amadis, advised by his half-brother Florestan to console himself with the glory of his exploits, nevertheless pines with unrequited love for Oriane; she suspects he loves another, describing her rival as having 'the advantage on myself of being a new conquest' (a typical Quinault *bon mot*). A tournament in her honour provides a brilliant divertissement.

Act II The evil magicians Arcabonne and her brother Arcalaus determine to avenge the death of their brother Ardan Canile, killed by Amadis. Arcabonne, however, is in love with an unknown knight who rescued her from a monster. Arcalaus shadows Amadis in the forest, while the lovelorn hero encounters Corisande, searching for Florestan, kidnapped by Arcabonne. She too is then taken; Arcalaus challenges Amadis and although Arcalaus' demons fail to ensnare Amadis, a nymph succeeds.

Act III Arcabonne threatens death to all the prisoners and to Amadis. She passionately addresses the tomb of Ardan, foretelling the revenge she will take. The ghost of Ardan emerges, accusing Arcabonne of betrayal. Approaching Amadis, dagger in hand, she recognizes the knight who saved her, and her arm falls. She asks what reward he will accept; Amadis exacts freedom for the prisoners.

Act IV Arcalaus holds Oriane captive; when Arcabonne confesses love for Amadis, Arcalaus restores her hatred by conjuring the vision of Amadis and Oriane together. As he shows Oriane the apparently dead Amadis, Urgande returns, freezing the evil magicians with her wand.

Act V Saved by the love of Amadis, the lovers are reunited in the palace of Apollidon.

In *Amadis*, a new lyricism characterizes Lully's vocal writing, with fluid expressive settings eschewing previous adherence to caesura and rhyme, and memorable airs. The orchestra assumes an increasingly significant role in accompanied recitatives and airs, many of great dramatic power. In Act II, two successive monologues, accompanied by full orchestra, vividly contrast the threatening Arcalaus ('Dans un piège fatal son mauvais sort l'amène') and the unknowing Amadis ('Bois épais', one of the airs borrowed from traditional sources). In as dramatic a sequence as Quinault and Lully ever contrived, Arcabonne addresses the tomb of Ardan in Act III, with a 'shivering' bass line in the orchestra. The opera concludes with a chaconne surpassed in length and splendour only by that in *Roland*.

RECORDING excerpts: Tarr, Collegium Aureum, Peters, Harmonia Mundi, 1966
EDITIONS f.ss., C. Ballard, 1684; Henry Prunières (ed.), *Oeuvres complètes*, operas, vol. 3, Edition de la Revue Musicale Paris, 1939; *rp*, Broude, 1966

Roland

Tragédie en musique in a prologue and five acts, LWV 65
Libretto by Philippe Quinault
PREMIERES 8 January 1685, Versailles; UK: 14 January 1983, Wolfson Hall, London

The first opera by Quinault and Lully following the death of the Queen, Marie-Thérèse, and the king's marriage to the sober Madame de Maintenon, reflects a new seriousness in approach. Like *Amadis*, the story derives from medieval chivalry. The prologue debates the conflict between love and glory, and announces a re-enactment of the story of Roland, ending with a chorus in praise of Le Roi Soleil. In the tragédie, Roland (the only title role for bass in all Lully's operas) becomes enamoured of Angelica, Queen of Cathay, sent to entice the crusaders into a tournament to kill them. She responds to his advances, but, though torn by love and pride, cannot master her passion for a humble soldier, Medoro. She persuades her subjects to recognize Medoro as king, celebrated in a divertissement that includes Lully's most elaborate chaconne, and, after a hasty marriage, they flee to Cathay. Roland comes upon a village wedding, and hears the news of his betrayal when the story is unwittingly recited by the bridegroom. (Thus, Lully, with telling effect, turns a divertissement into a scene of dramatic action.) This revelation sends Roland mad, and his sanity is restored only when the fairy Logistille soothes him with music and convinces him to once again forgo love for glory.

EDITION f.s., C. Ballard, 1685

Armide

Tragédie en musique in a prologue and five acts, LWV 71 (2h 30m)
Libretto by Philippe Quinault, after the epic poem *Gerusalemme liberata* (1575), by Torquato Tasso
PREMIERES 15 February 1686, Palais Royal, Paris; UK: 14 May 1981, Barber Institute, Birmingham
CAST *prologue*: Glory *s*, Wisdom *s*; *satb* chorus; *tragédie*: Armida *s*, Phoenice *s*, Sidonia *s*, Hidraoth *b*, Arontes *b*, Rinaldo *haute-contre*, Artemidorus *t*, Hatred *t*, Ubalde *b*, Danish knight *haute-contre*, 4 *s*, *haute-contre*; *satb* chorus of heroes, nymphs, shepherds, demons, furies; ballet
ORCHESTRATION 2 fl/rec, 2 ob, [bsns], str, cont

Lully's and Quinault's last tragédie was their most highly developed, both musically and dramatically. A wealth of expressive melody and a spectacular, tragic *dénouement* helped to ensure its popularity in the Paris repertoire until 1764, being outlived among Lully's operas only by *Thésée* and *Amadis*.

SYNOPSIS
The prologue, eschewing mythology and spectacle, is a moral discourse between Wisdom and Glory, rivals yet both overcoming love, thus mirroring the newfound piety of the court in the era of Mme de Maintenon.

Act I The sorceress Armida's victory over the Christians besieging Jerusalem is incomplete while the most formidable knight, Rinaldo, remains resistant to her. Armida's uncle, Hidraoth, King of Damascus, urges her to turn from war to love but she will marry only Rinaldo's conqueror. The people's celebrations are interrupted by Arontes, Armida's general, dying after an encounter with Rinaldo. Hidraoth and Armida swear revenge.

Act II Rinaldo, in disgrace because of the defeat, is determined to rehabilitate himself. But Armida and Hidraoth find him and invoke spirits to enchant him. Rinaldo soliloquizes on the beauty of his surroundings. Armida demands to take her vengeance alone, but when she sees Rinaldo she cannot kill him, and commands her spirits to carry him to her enchanted palace.

Act III Armida and Rinaldo are happy together, but she knows that his love depends on her magic. She summons Hatred to exorcize her love for Rinaldo, but relents, and banishes the furies.

Act IV Artemidorus and Ubalde, knights sent to find Rinaldo, are armed with a diamond shield and a golden sceptre to penetrate the enchanted garden. Armida sends spirits to seduce them, but the spirits disappear when touched by the weapons of the knights, who enter the palace.

Act V Armida leaves Rinaldo with spirits to entertain him while she renews her spells. But the knights arrive and bring Rinaldo to his senses. Armida returns and desperately implores Rinaldo to stay, but the knights drag him away. She tries to summon Hate to rekindle her revenge, but she cannot bring herself to harm Rinaldo, and instead destroys the palace and all within it.

Much of Lully's music for *Armide* is on a higher plane than in any preceding work. In Act II, the enchantment of Rinaldo, to the muted-string accompaniment of the composer's most expressive *sommeil*, is followed by Armida's powerfully emotional soliloquy, 'Enfin il est en ma puissance', expressing the conflict within her between love and hate. This is Lully's most celebrated monologue, cited by his contemporaries, and later by Rameau, as the model for French recitative, achieving its effect by the skilful use of rests as much as by its melodic and rhythmic vitality.

RECORDING Yakar, Borst, de Reyghere, Poulenard, Vandersteene, de Mey, Egel, Cold, La Chapelle Royale,

Sketch by Jean Bérain for the destruction of Armide's palace at the end of Lully's opera (Paris, 1686)

Herreweghe, Erato, 1983: substantial cuts including the whole of Act IV

VIDEO Manning, Keys, Tunley (dir.), University of Western Australia, 1987 (prologue omitted)

EDITIONS f.s., C. Ballard, 1686; facsimile, *French Opera in the 17th and 18th Centuries*, vol. 6, Pendragon, 1992; v.ss., Lajarte (ed.), Michaelis, 1878; *rp*, Broude, 1981

Acis et Galathée

Acis and Galatea

Pastorale héroïque in a prologue and three acts, LWV 73 (2h)

Libretto by Jean-Galbert de Campistron, after Book XIII of Ovid's *Metamorphoses*

PREMIERES 6 September 1686, Anet; UK: 29 March 1937, BBC broadcast; US: 10 April 1980, New York

Lully's last complete stage work shows the composer at his most dexterous. The allegorical prologue, flattering the Dauphin, precedes the tragédie based on the Greek myth of the shepherd Acis lured by the nymph Galatea and killed with a rock by his rival, the cyclops, Polyphemus. Quinault being unavailable as librettist because of continuing illness (not for religious scruples as often alleged), Lully turned to Campistron, a member of the Duc de Vendôme's circle at Anet, where *Acis et Galathée* was staged in the Dauphin's honour. The pastoral elements are transformed by the same skilful development of plot and character so evident in *Armide*. The ridiculous figure of Polyphemus, his ungainly movement and pathetic infatuation with Galatea are all portrayed in mocking marches and a *gigue*. The giant's arrival in Act II also features panpipes in an air prescient of Papageno's in *Die Zauberflöte*. Act III is distinguished by the evocation of blessing on the lovers by the High Priest, scored for high strings and voices, Galatea's lament for Acis (Lully's most developed essay in monologue, its changes of mood heralded by brief instrumental preludes), and the noble bass air of Neptune, father of the cyclops, who responds to Galatea's plea for the return to life of Acis by making him immortal. The celebratory conclusion is a danced and sung *passacaille* equalling the splendour of the chaconne of *Amadis*.

EDITION f.s., C. Ballard, 1686

Other operatic works: *Les fêtes de l'Amour et de Bacchus*, 1672; *Psyché*, 1678; *Persée*, 1682; *Phaëton*, 1683; *Achille et Polixène* (overture and Act I by Lully; remainder by Colasse), 1687
BIBLIOGRAPHY J. R. Anthony, 'Jean-Baptiste Lully', *The New Grove French Baroque Masters*, Macmillan, 1986; J. H. Heyer (ed.), *Jean-Baptiste Lully and the Music of the French Baroque. Essays in Honour of James R. Anthony*, CUP, 1989; *Early Music*, vol. 15, no. 3 (August 1987), Lully 300th anniversary issue; Jérôme de La Gorce and Herbert Schneider (eds), *Jean-Baptiste Lully: Actes du Colloque* [1987], Laaber, 1991;

L.S.

ELISABETH LUTYENS

Elisabeth Agnes Lutyens; *b* 6 July 1906, London; *d* 14 April 1983, London

Elisabeth Lutyens, a daughter of the architect Sir Edwin Lutyens, studied in Paris in the 1920s and later at the Royal College of Music. Her operatic works reveal a fascinating paradox. While possessing a dramatic temperament and a wide literary knowledge, she was at her best writing vocal music that retained one mood throughout a piece. This is well illustrated in her short chamber opera, *Infidelio* – with its typically punning title – which focuses on an inner psychological drama rather than attempting real dramatic conflict. It is also partly autobiographical, as is *Time Off? Not a Ghost of a*

Chance!, a charade in four scenes (with three interruptions) which, unusually for Lutyens, resorts to collage techniques and a spoken role. It is significant that she did not call all her stage works operas. *Isis and Osiris* displays her interest in the very sources of our culture and is a lengthy, static and ritualistic piece containing some of the composer's finest lyrical music. It awaits a professional production, as does the Elias Canetti-based *The Numbered*, her most ambitious operatic project.
Operatic works: *The Pit* (dramatic scene), 1947; *Infidelio*, 1954; *The Numbered*, (1967); *Time Off? Not a Ghost of a Chance!* (charade), 1967; *Isis and Osiris* (lyric drama), 1970; *The Linnet from the Leaf* (music-theatre), 1972; *The Waiting Game*, 1973; *The Goldfish Bowl*, (1975)
BIBLIOGRAPHY Elisabeth Lutyens, *A Goldfish Bowl*, Cassell, 1972; Meirion and Susie Harries, *A Pilgrim Soul*, Michael Joseph, 1989

R.L.S.

NIKOLAI LYSENKO

Mykola Vital'yevich Lysenko; *b* 22 March 1842, Hrynky, nr Kremenchug, Poltava district, Ukraine; *d* 6 November 1912, Kiev, Ukraine

Lysenko is regarded as the founder of Ukrainian opera. A fervent patriot, his refusal to authorize Russian versions of his libretti lost him many opportunities of having his work more widely performed. As a child, he was deeply influenced by peasant songs, and his nationalism was fuelled by reading Shevchenko, the Ukrainian poet and nationalist, after whom the opera house in Kiev is named. Lysenko became involved with the anti-tsarist movement, and was an avid reader of the socialist philosophers Belinsky and Herzen. A hymn, 'The Great Revolution', supporting the events of 1905, earned him a spell in prison.

Throughout his life, Lysenko collected and published Ukrainian folksongs, and wrote essays analysing the differences between folk material from the Ukraine and from other Russian republics. He was an excellent pianist, and his improvisations on folk themes were legendary. From 1874 to 1876 he studied orchestration with Rimsky-Korsakov and was a friend of Tchaikovsky, who attempted to arrange performances of Lysenko's best opera, *Taras Bul'ba* in Moscow. His music tends to be short-winded and structurally flawed, but as a dramatist he portrays characters convincingly. His death was an occasion for national mourning, eloquently described by Gorky in *My Universities*.

Operatic works: *Harkusha* (fragment), 1864; *Andrashiada* (fragment), 1866; *Chernomortsy* (*Sailors of the Black Sea Fleet*), 1872; *Maryusa Boguslavka* (fragment), 1874; *Nich pid Rizdvo* (*Christmas Eve*), (1874, rev. 1877–82), 1883; *Ltopiennitsa* (*The Drowned Woman*), 1885; *Koza-Dereza*, (*The Goat*), children's opera, 1901; *Natalka-Poltavka*, 1889 (RECORDING Melodiya, 1960s); *Taras Bul'ba*, (1890), 1903

(RECORDING Melodiya, 1960s); *Pan Kotsky*, children's opera, 1891; *Zima i vesna, ili Snezhnaya krasavitsa (Winter and Spring, or The Snow Maiden)*, children's opera, 1892; *Volshebnyi son (The Magic Dream)*, 1894; *Sappho*, 1900; *Aeneid*, 1911; *Letney Nochu* (fragment), 1912; *Nocturne*, 1914

(EDITIONS   Complete, 20 vols, Ukrainian State Publishers)

BIBLIOGRAPHY   M. Skalya Staritisky, *Lysenko 1842–1912*, Kiev, 1962

J.G.

JOHN McCABE

b 21 April 1939, Huyton, Liverpool, England

One of the most fluent and prolific composers of his generation, McCabe is well known also as a concert pianist and as a writer on music. He studied in Manchester and at the Munich Hochschule für Musik (1964). He was resident pianist at University College, Cardiff (1965–8), and more recently Director of the London College of Music (1983).

A rapid and disciplined writer to commission, McCabe has had comparatively little occasion to work in the theatre. His orchestral music includes three symphonies, several concertos, and high-class *pièces d'occasion* such as *The Chagall Windows* (1974) and *The Shadow of Light* (1979), whose titles indicate his interest in colour and the idea of light as a property of sound. His most substantial theatre pieces are ballets but he has also written three operas: a successful work for children, *The Lion, the Witch and the Wardrobe* (1969), based on the book by C. S. Lewis; an entertainment, *This town's a corporation full of crooked streets*, with words by a group of Liverpool poets (1970); and a full-length chamber opera, *The Play of Mother Courage*, after Grimmelshausen (1974).

BIBLIOGRAPHY Gerald Larner, '*The Lion, the Witch and the Wardrobe*', *MT*, vol. 110 (1969), p. 372

S.W.

HAMISH MACCUNN

b 22 March 1868, Greenock, Scotland; *d* 2 August 1916, London

MacCunn's *Jeanie Deans*, commissioned by the Carl Rosa Opera Company and retained in their repertoire until the composer's death, was the first opera by a Scotsman to be premiered in Scotland. Nevertheless, MacCunn studied in England (at the Royal College of Music) and thereafter lived in London; teaching and conducting claimed his later energies, and despite his distinctive style his music failed to provide the foundations for a national Scottish style.

Jeanie Deans

Grand opera in four acts
Libretto by Joseph Bennett, after the novel *The Heart of Midlothian* by Walter Scott (1818)
PREMIERE 15 November 1894, Lyceum Theatre, Edinburgh

The musical freshness and dramatic simplicity of MacCunn's inevitably foreshortened account of Scott's great novel have not convinced all commentators, and periodic revivals (most recently in 1986 by Opera West) have not won the opera a place in the professional repertoire.

EDITION v.s., Mathias and Strickland, 1894

Diarmid

Grand opera in four acts, Op. 34
Libretto by the Marquis of Lorne (J. G. Campbell)
PREMIERE 23 October 1897, Covent Garden, London

MacCunn exchanged the 18th-century Scottish realism of *Jeanie Deans* for Celtic mythology in his setting of the story of Grania and Diarmid; again the music is impressive (and more assertive) but the stageworthiness questionable.

EDITION v.s., Boosey, 1897

Other operatic works: *Breast of Light* (inc.); *The Masque of War and Peace*, 1900; *The Golden Girl*, 1905 (lost); *Prue* (inc.); *The Pageant of Darkness and Light*, 1908
BIBLIOGRAPHY Jerome Mitchell, *The Walter Scott Operas: An Analysis of Operas Based on the Works of Walter Scott*, University of Alabama Press, 1977

S.B.

GALT MACDERMOT

Arthur Terence Galt MacDermot; *b* 18 December 1928, Montreal, Canada

MacDermot was a pioneer of the rock musical in the 1960s and 1970s, above all with the hugely successful *Hair*. This was followed by *Isabel's a Jezabel* (1970), the rock-Shakespeare *Two Gentlemen of Verona* (1971), *Dude* (1972), and *Via Galactica* (1972).

Hair

American tribal love-rock musical in two acts (2h 15m)
Lyrics and book by Gerome Ragni and James Rado
PREMIERES   29 October 1967, New York Shakespeare
Festival Public Theater, New York; rev. version: 29 April
1968, Biltmore Theater, Broadway, New York; UK: 27
September 1968, Shaftesbury Theatre, London

Hair, in which a group of young Americans search
for freedom from society's rules and celebrate their
own passions, caused a sensation at the time of its
premiere, but it was much more than an argument
for drug-taking and free sex. It challenged the US
establishment during the Vietnam War, and it proved
decisively that rock music was here to stay on the
musical stage. Other composers have since integrated
music and action more convincingly, but with songs
such as 'Frank Mills' and the anthem-like 'Aquarius',
Hair remains a milestone. The London production
had just failed to notch up 2000 performances when
the theatre roof fell in.

RECORDING   Broadway cast, RCA, 1968
FILM   Milos Forman (dir.), Panavision, 1979
EDITION   vocal selection: United Artists Music, 1968

BIBLIOGRAPHY   L. Davis, *Letting Down My Hair*, New
York, 1972

M.A.

GEORGE MACFARREN

(Sir) George Alexander Macfarren: *b* 2 March 1813, London;
d 31 October 1887, London

Macfarren learned much from his father, a theatre
manager, who wrote the libretti for some of his
operas. His formal training was received at the Royal
Academy of Music. In addition to operatic music he
composed works in most of the principal genres, and
wrote on a wide range of musical subjects. Despite
going blind in 1860, Macfarren reached an exalted
position in English 19th-century musical life,
becoming principal of the Royal Academy of Music
and professor at Cambridge University in 1875. He
was knighted in 1883.

Macfarren's early operas include echoes of Mozart
and Beethoven, whom, with Mendelssohn, he
revered throughout his life. He eschewed the more
recent operatic developments, particularly the Italian
style. Macfarren maintained a strong interest in
English folk music and in the study of harmony,
in 1847 resigning his teaching post at the Royal
Academy of Music rather than forswear his
theoretical beliefs. (He was reinstated in 1851.) Both
enthusiasms shaped his later works, in which he
strove to develop a distinctive national idiom marked
by plots set in Britain – for instance, *Robin Hood* –
folk-style material, and a restrained harmonic
vocabulary. The scale and pace of his 'opere di
camera' (*Jessy Lea* and *The Soldier's Legacy*)
probably influenced Sullivan's operettas.

Operatic works: *The Prince of Modena*, (1833); *Genevieve, or
The Maid of Switzerland, 1834; I and My Double*, 1835;
Innocent Sins, or Peccadilloes, 1836; *El Malhechor*, (1838);
The Devil's Opera, 1838; *Agnes Bernauer, the Maid of
Augsburg*, 1839; *Emblematic Tribute on the Queen's
Marriage*, 1840; *An Adventure of Don Quixote*, 1846; *King
Charles II*, 1849; *Allan of Aberfeldy*, (*c.* 1850); *Robin Hood*,
1860; *Freya's Gift*, 1863; *Jessy Lea*, 1863; *She Stoops to
Conquer*, 1864; *The Soldier's Legacy*, 1864; *Helvellyn*, 1864;
Kenilworth, 1880
BIBLIOGRAPHY   Henry Charles Banister, *George Alexander
Macfarren*, G. Bell & Sons, 1891

G.B.

OTMAR MÁCHA

b 2 October 1922, Ostrava

After studies in Ostrava and at the Prague
Conservatory, Mácha worked as a producer and
dramaturg at Prague radio (1947–62). Since 1962 he
has made a career as a freelance composer, chiefly of
orchestral and operatic works.

Infidelity Unmasked

Polapená nevěra
Operatic farce in five acts with prologue and epilogue (35m)
Libretto based on an anonymous old Czech text of 1608
Composed 1956–7
PREMIERE   21 November 1958, Theatre D34, Prague

The modest forces (four soloists) of Mácha's first
opera and his witty adaptation of earlier musical
styles has encouraged frequent performances in
Czechoslovakia and in Germany.

Lake Ukereve

Jezero Ukereve
Opera in five scenes (1h 30m)
Libretto by the composer, after the novel by Vladislav
Vančura
Composed 1960–63
PREMIERE   27 May 1966, National Theatre, Prague

The unusual setting of this much more ambitious
work (the Berlin Reichstag and the shores of Lake
Victoria in 1907) comes from a novel by a
distinguished Czech writer about the attempts by
the German biologist Robert Koch and the British
doctor Robert Forde to find a cure for sleeping
sickness. The opera centres on Forde's conflicts with
the colonial authorities over adequate resources for
combating the disease, and with the local white
settlers over his taking a black wife.

Other operas: *Roses for Johanka* (*Růže pro Johanku*), (1974,
rev. 1978), 1982; *Marriage for Show* (*Svatba na oko*), (1977);
A Cradle for Sinful Virgins (*Kolébka pro hříšné panny*),
(1976), 1982; *Proměny Prométheovy* (*The Metamorphoses of
Prometheus*), television opera, 1982
BIBLIOGRAPHY   Ladislav Šíp, *Česká opera a jeho tvůrci*
(*Czech Opera and Its Creators*), Supraphon, 1983

J.T.

ALEXANDER MACKENZIE

(Sir) Alexander Campbell Mackenzie; *b* 22 August 1847, Edinburgh; *d* 28 April 1935, London

Mackenzie studied in Germany and at the Royal Academy of Music in London, of which he was Principal from 1888 to 1924. His early operas, which reached the Continent, are grand in conception but suffer from old-fashioned libretti and belatedly cosmopolitan sympathies. His commercial operettas must be measured by different yardsticks. *His Majesty*, although light and tuneful, ran in London for only 61 performances. *The Knights of the Road* is short and trivial (Mackenzie saw it as 'an attempt . . . to stimulate an interest in operetta on the music-hall stage').

In his last works for the stage Mackenzie turned from both grand opera and operetta to something closer to the fairy-tale and the pastoral. *The Cricket on the Hearth* derives a certain refulgence from Dickens's story, while *The Eve of St John* explores a world of midsummer night's madness with a musical freshness that almost transforms conservatism into neo-classicism.

Operatic works: *Colomba*, 1883; *The Troubadour*, 1886; *Phoebe*, (1894); *His Majesty, or The Court of Vingolia*, 1897; *The Cricket on the Hearth*, (1901), 1914; *The Knights of the Road*, 1905; *The Eve of St John*, (1919), 1924
BIBLIOGRAPHY   Stan Meares (ed.), *British Opera in Retrospect*, British Music Society, 1986

S.B.

ELIZABETH MACONCHY

b 19 March 1907, Broxbourne, Hertfordshire, England

One of the outstanding women composers of her generation, Maconchy, a pupil of Charles Wood and Vaughan Williams at the Royal College of Music (1923–9), established her reputation with a Piano Concertino and an orchestral suite, *The Land* (both premiered in 1930). Tough and direct in its quality of utterance and deploying a contrapuntal idiom akin to Bartók's, her music was regularly heard in the 1930s and 1940s. Chamber music and vocal works accounted for much of her work over the next two decades and she continued to develop her idiom into the 1980s, retaining her essential interests in originality of structure and freedom of technique, together with a new-found concern for the character of individual instruments. The outstanding composition of this period was the dramatic monologue *Ariadne* for soprano and chamber orchestra (1970).

Maconchy has composed four one-act operas and two operas for children. The fourth of the one-act operas, *The Birds*, stands by itself, but the others, though spanning a period of ten years in their composition, have been performed as a triple-bill. *The Sofa* (1957) sets a verse libretto by Ursula Vaughan Williams based on the novel by Crebillon

fils. In this witty and improbable escapade, a young libertine can be released from his transmogrification into a sofa only when he becomes the rendezvous for a pair of lovers. In *The Departure* (1961), to a libretto by Anne Ridler, a woman reflects on her married life as she imagines her own funeral. *The Three Strangers* (1958–67) is based on one of Thomas Hardy's Wessex Tales, to a libretto by the composer. Andrew Porter described it as having 'the directness, the powerful simplicity, the honesty of Hardy's own work'. Maconchy's children's operas, *Johnny and the Mohawks* and *The King of the Golden River*, successfully overcome the problems of this difficult genre.

Operas: *The Sofa*, 1957; *The Departure*, 1961; *The Three Strangers*, 1967; *The Birds*, 1968; *Johnny and the Mohawks*, 1969; *The Jesse Tree* (church opera), 1970; *The King of the Golden River*, 1975
BIBLIOGRAPHY   Hugo Cole, *Elizabeth Maconchy*, Chester, 1986

N.W.

BRUNO MADERNA

b 21 April 1920, Venice, Italy; *d* 13 November 1973, Darmstadt, Germany

Maderna was one of the few 20th-century musicians to combine authoritative careers as conductor and composer. The hectic schedules that resulted may well have reinforced his fondness for constructing new works by reworking materials he had previously used elsewhere: a tendency apparent in his theatrical works.

His first skirmishes with musical drama were in the electronic studio at Milan radio. In 1960 he elaborated Cathy Berberian's varied readings of a phoneme text by Hans G. Helms into a tape piece, *Dimensioni II*. His radio version of Lorca's *Don Perlimplín* (1961–2) produced further experiments. The protagonist, an old man unwisely married to the beautiful Belisa, is impersonated not by a voice, but a flute, as is Belisa's caricature of a mother by a saxophone quartet. Belisa sings and speaks, other parts are spoken.

Hyperion/Hyperion en het Geweld/Hyperion-Orfeo dolente

Hyperion/Hyperion and Violence/Hyperion-Mourning Orpheus
Lirica in forma di spettacolo in one act (*Hyperion*: 55m; others variable)
Scenario by the composer and Virginio Puecher, with a text by Friedrich Hölderlin and phonemes by Hans G. Helms; additional text for *Hyperion en het Geweld* from *Morituri* by Hugo Claus
Composed 1964–8
PREMIERES   *Hyperion*: 6 October 1964, La Fenice, Venice; *Hyperion en het Geweld*: 17 May 1968, Théâtre Royale de la Monnaie, Brussels; *Hyperion-Orfeo dolente*: 18 July 1968, Courtyard of the Palazzo Bentivoglio, Bologna

The use of flautist and female vocalist as protagonists spilled over into Maderna's first theatrical project, *Hyperion*, whose first version was written for the Venice Biennale of 1964. Here the flautist represents the 'poet' struggling to assert himself against the instrumental forces in the pit and the forces of technology on stage (including a 'machine' – all moving parts and flashing lights – that exhibits itself to the wordless vocal acrobatics of *Dimensioni II*). Finally a woman appears in a great metal shell, and sings a setting of words from Hölderlin's *Hyperion*, to which the flautist responds. These and further materials composed in the interim were then combined with Hugo Claus's parable on violence and soldiering, *Morituri*, to produce a Flemish version, *Hyperion en het Geweld* (1968), and interleaved with an early 17th-century intermezzo by Belli to form *Hyperion-Orfeo dolente* (1968).

EDITION   Suvini Zerboni (on hire)

Satyricon

Opera in one act (1h 15m)
Libretto by the composer and Jan Strasfogel after the satire by Petronius (first century AD)
Composed 1971–2
PREMIERES   16 March 1973, Scheveningen, Holland; US: 6 August 1973, Tanglewood, Massachusetts; UK: 24 October 1990, Drill Hall Theatre, London

Satyricon belongs more straightforwardly within the operatic tradition in that it has a full range of singing characters. But this adaptation of the 'Dinner with Trimalchio' episode from the *Satyricon*, whose celebration of the anarchic pleasures of the flesh Maderna made no attempt to expurgate, is composed as a series of separate numbers. Since the events of Trimalchio's party follow no more logical pattern than most, Maderna felt free to permutate them in

Debria Browne (Fortunata) and Mihard Kraak (Eumolpus) in Satyricon *(Scheveningen, 1973)*

the few versions that he was able to supervise before his death.

EDITION   Salabert, [n.d.]

BIBLIOGRAPHY   Raymond Fearn, *Bruno Maderna*, Harwood Academic Publishers, 1990, pp. 128–60, 222–88

D.O.-S.

LEEVI MADETOJA
b 17 February 1887, Oulu, Finland; *d* 6 October 1947, Helsinki

Madetoja was considered one of the leaders of the so-called National Romantic School of Finnish composers, active before and after Finland's declaration of independence from Russia following the October Revolution of 1917. His opera *Pohjalaisia* bursts with nationalist patriotic sentiment. He studied with Sibelius in Helsinki, d'Indy in Paris, also in Vienna and Berlin. As well as a composer he was a conductor, an academic (teaching at the Helsinki Academy of Music and Helsinki University for most of his life) and for a time a critic. He was president of the Society of Finnish Composers.

Pohjalaisia
The Ostrobothnians
Opera in three acts, Op. 45 (2h)
Libretto by the composer, based on the play by Artturi Järviluoma (1914)
PREMIERE   25 October 1924, Helsinki

The Bothnians had the reputation of being the fiercest (and drunkest) of the various regional Finns, much given to brawling. In Madetoja's opera, set in the 1850s, the characters are united in their hatred of the high-handed Russian sheriff (Finland was then an autonomous Russian grand duchy). The burly hero Jussi befriends a prisoner on bail for a stabbing, and makes an enemy of the sheriff by breaking his whip. When the prisoner disappears, Jussi is arrested and, handcuffed and defenceless, beaten by the sheriff; he breaks the metal cuffs and is shot by his terrified tormentor, but heroically manages to stab him before dying. The music is tonal, tuneful – there is much rustic song and dance – and the general atmosphere is wholesomely patriotic.

RECORDING   Lokka, Luusoja, Erkkilä, Hynninen, Heikkilä, Ch and O of Finnish National Opera, Panula, Finnlevy, 1975
EDITION   v.s., Wilhelm Hansen, 1923

Other opera: *Juha*, 1935

R.M.

ALBÉRIC MAGNARD
Lucien Denis Gabriel Albéric Magnard; *b* 9 June 1865, Paris; *d* 3 September 1914, Baron, Oise, nr Paris

The son of a Parisian newspaper magnate (later

editor of *Le Figaro*), Magnard entered the Paris Conservatoire late, in 1886, having passed much of his youth in travel – including to Bayreuth. A pupil of Massenet, he eventually aligned himself with the 'enemy' camp of César Franck, and spent another four years studying with Franck's most distinguished pupil, d'Indy. A notoriously taciturn and austere character, Magnard made a musical virtue of this severity. His output of four symphonies and a handful of other orchestral and chamber works is characterized by an obsession with strict counterpoint and the structured working of themes, and often as a result by rather thick textures. Magnard's personal inflexibility was the direct cause of his death. He was killed in his house a few miles north-east of Paris by a platoon of German Uhlans, two of whom he had shot and killed from an upstairs window.

Magnard wrote three operas, which in specific gravity if not in style often reflect his enthusiasm for Wagner (and like Wagner, he wrote all his own libretti). The early one-act *Yolande*, which had one unsuccessful production in Brussels in December 1892 (probably, according to Martin Cooper, thanks to string-pulling by his father) was followed by two full-length works, of which *Guercoeur* was partly destroyed in Magnard's house in 1914 and only later reconstructed by his friend Guy Ropartz (it was eventually produced at the Opéra in 1931). The distantly Racinesque *Bérénice*, meanwhile, had been staged at the Opéra-Comique in December 1911. In true Gluckist fashion, the score carries a preface in which Magnard explains his severe ideas about music drama, admitting the Wagnerism of his style while in fact putting forward a rather coolly abstract theory of the role of music in the theatre. 'Perhaps my conception of dramatic music is wrong,' he wrote. 'I apologize in advance to our experts on aesthetics.'

Operas: *Yolande*, 1892; *Bérénice*, 1911; *Guercoeur*, (1914), 1931 (RECORDING EMI, 1986)
BIBLIOGRAPHY Laurence Davies, *César Franck and his Circle*, Barrie and Jenkins, 1970

S.W.

GIAN FRANCESCO DE MAJO
Gian Francesco [de Majo, Di Majo, di Maio; Ciccio De Majo]; *b* 27 March 1732, Naples; *d* 17 November 1770, Naples

De Majo was one of the Italian composers of opera who anticipated Gluck by including in their opere serie elements that would later become crystallized in the 'Gluckian reform'. At the age of 15 De Majo had already become an unpaid supernumerary organist in the royal chapel of the Bourbon monarchy, of which his father was primo maestro. In 1752 he made his professional début in the two musical genres that dominated his career: opera seria and sacred music. He achieved great success in both: his operas were commissioned for houses in Italy and

throughout Europe, while his sacred music was described as 'very beautiful' by the 14-year-old Mozart in a letter to his sister written from Naples in May 1770. De Majo's brilliant career ended when he died of tuberculosis at the age of 38. In 1795 the poet Wilhelm Heinse immortalized him in his novel *Hildegard von Hohental*.

A number of features that appear in De Majo's operas justify his inclusion, with Jommelli and Traetta, in the group of reform composers. A loosening of formal structures, permitting passages of expressive accompanied recitative and arioso, and a move away from the strict *da capo* aria form added to the dramatic impact of De Majo's operas, as did the expanded use of chorus and ensembles and greater independence for the orchestra, sometimes employing instrumental motifs that were varied according to mood and situation. These elements are most prominent in *Ifigenia in Tauride* (1764), written for Mannheim, when De Majo was probably aiming to show his flexibility in adapting his musical style to local taste. The later *Adriano in Siria* (Rome, 1769) adheres rather more closely to traditional *seria* conventions, though here too there are innovative features, notably the substitution of a duet for an aria at the end of Act II, and the rhythmic and chromatic nature of some of the melodic material – aspects that are said to have influenced Mozart in his composition of *Idomeneo*.

Surviving operas: *Ricimero re dei Goti*, 1758; *Astrea placata*, 1760; *Ifigenia in Tauride* (first version), 1760; *L'Almeria*, 1761; *Artaserse*, 1762; *Demofoonte*, 1763; *Alcide negli orti Esperidi*, 1764; *Ifigenia in Tauride* (second version), 1764; *Ipermestra*, 1768; *Adriano in Siria*, 1769 (EDITION facsimile, Garland, 1978); *Eumene* (inc.), 1771; 6 doubtful operas; 10 lost operas
BIBLIOGRAPHY David Di Chiera, *The Life and Operas of Gian Francesco de Majo*, dissertation, University of California, Los Angeles, 1962

D.A.D'A.

GIAN FRANCESCO MALIPIERO
b 18 March 1882, Venice; *d* 1 August 1973, Treviso

Like some other leading Italian composers of his generation, Malipiero rebelled openly against the established opera tradition. Unlike the young Casella, however, he did not avoid the opera house altogether: he preferred to seek new, less traditional solutions to the 'music-drama problem'. The results often anticipate aspects of post-war music-theatre. The searing, war-inspired *dramma sinfonico Pantea* (1917–19), for solo dancer, offstage voices and orchestra, has also been compared, in its hallucinatory turbulence, to *Erwartung*, although the musical language is not at all Schoenbergian. Together with *Sette canzoni*, *Pantea* marked the beginning of Malipiero's most drastically rebellious phase. His previous stage works had been much more conventional – although *Sogno d'un tramonto d'autunno* (1913) remains of considerable interest.

In *Sette canzoni* Malipiero's use of old Italian poetry in incongruous dramatic contexts gives parts of the work a distinctly surrealist character. Some of his theatre pieces of the 1920s are even more surreal in effect. The two outer 'panels' (1919–22) of the triptych *L'Orfeide* (in which *Sette canzoni* serves as centrepiece) are an extreme case: the last panel even mingles live singer–actors with marionettes. At the other end of the spectrum of Malipiero's personality stands *San Francesco d'Assisi* (1920–21), in which his interest in early music, from plainsong to Monteverdi, bore creative fruit. The resultant antique calm well suits a series of static, stylized tableaux depicting episodes in the saint's life. The *Tre commedie goldoniane* are different again: idiosyncratically concentrated adaptations of Goldoni, with a winsome Venetian charm. In the later 1920s Malipiero's use of symbolism, which had been relatively intelligible in *Pantea*, tended to become enigmatic and dreamlike. This is especially the case in *Filomela e l'Infatuato* (1925) and *Merlino mastro d'organi* (1926–7): the latter features a huge magic organ which kills all men who hear it, until a deaf mute kills the organist and then becomes articulate in the 'purifying fire' of the stake, revealing himself as his victim's reincarnation. *Filomela* and *Merlino* are best regarded as transitional – preparing the way for the remarkable *Torneo notturno*, which has been staged more often in Italy than any of Malipiero's other works apart from *Sette canzoni*.

During the 1930s Malipiero's musical style mellowed somewhat, and he became more conformist in his theatrical methods. In *La favola del figlio cambiato* he collaborated with Pirandello, with whose famous 'paradoxical' dramas he had a natural affinity. Though successful in Germany, *La favola* was banned by Mussolini after only one Italian performance, after which the composer could hardly be blamed for withdrawing into safe, traditional territory. *Giulio Cesare* (1934–5) is based on Shakespeare, and ends with a recognizable obeisance to the Duce. Further operas based on existing dramas followed; but Malipiero's more experimental side reasserted itself in *I capricci di Callot* (1941–2), freely based on a work by another of his natural 'soul mates' – *Prinzessin Brambilla* by E. T. A. Hoffmann.

The post-war operas show considerable stylistic changes after his basically diatonic idiom of the 1930s and 1940s. In the uneven but crucial *Mondi celesti e infernali* (1948–9) the first act ends with a 12-note chord; and in the best parts of *Venere prigioniera* (1955) Malipiero's new, more chromatic style achieves a fierce dramatic tension that had become rare in his music after the 1920s. The quality of these last-period works is variable, and too often they suffer from undistinguished vocal writing. Nevertheless *Il capitan Spavento* (1954–5) and *Il marescalco* (1960–68) recapture the comic zest of the *Tre commedie goldoniane* in more spikily chromatic terms; *Le metamorfosi di Bonaventura* (1963–5) recalls the more enigmatic and surreal aspects of pre-1930 Malipiero, and *Uno dei Dieci* (1970) presents a grotesque yet touching picture of intolerant old age, in which many have recognized a caricatured self-

portrait. A place apart is occupied by *Gli eroi di Bonaventura* (1968), which consists largely of scenes salvaged from previous Malipiero operas.

Malipiero's torrential productivity (not only in the field of theatre works) has bewildered the musical world: it was simply impossible to keep up with him. His obsessional creative urge often outstripped his self-criticism; yet the rich inventiveness of his best works has inspired reverence in many younger Italian musicians. Dallapiccola called him 'the most important [musical] personality that Italy has had since the death of Verdi'. Yet outside Italy unjustly he is more generally known as an editor of early music than as a composer.

Sette canzoni

Seven Songs

Sette espressioni drammatiche in one act (40m)
Libretto by the composer, using old Italian poems (some anonymous, some by Poliziano, one each by Jacopone da Todi and Luigi Alamanni)
Composed 1918–19
PREMIERES 10 July 1920, Opéra, Paris; 5 November 1925, Stadtsoper, Düsseldorf (as centre of *L'Orfeide*); US: 20 March 1925, League of Composers, New York (concert); UK: 17 March 1963, BBC Third Programme (radio broadcast); 5 September 1969, King's Theatre, Edinburgh

Unlike *Pantea* – which is almost entirely wordless – *Sette canzoni* includes several quasi-operatic singing characters, although there are also many mute parts. The work consists of seven miniature dramatic episodes, musically continuous but each with a separate cast and plot. Each has a song as its main musical focus, but is otherwise largely mimed to orchestral accompaniment. Recitative-like declamation is wholly excluded, but some use is made of a (mainly offstage) chorus.

1. A young ballad-singer tempts a girl to desert her blind companion. 2. A monk ejects a praying woman from a church because it is closing time. 3. A mother becomes demented because her son is away at the war – only to be driven completely over the edge when he seemingly returns. 4. A furtive assignation is ruined by the noisy singing of a drunkard. 5. A serenading lover is abruptly confronted with the fact that there has been a death in the house. 6. A bell-ringer shows by his inept choice of song that the raging fire which is the reason for his tocsin worries him not at all. 7. Symbols of Carnival and Lent are starkly contrasted when the latter takes over from the former in the small hours of Ash Wednesday.

Malipiero claimed to have based each of these miniature dramas on a personal experience. At a more abstract level, each depicts a collision between a positive and a negative principle. An especially eccentric feature is the use of old Italian poetry – usually quoted in dramatic situations that would have startled the original authors. Here it seems that Malipiero needed to find verbal counterparts to those conscious archaisms which were becoming increasingly prominent in his music. There are also strong 20th-century components in *Sette canzoni*'s style: Debussy and Stravinsky played important parts in shaping it, and echoes of Puccini can occasionally be heard, despite intentions to the contrary. Yet the total effect is profoundly personal, and can work remarkably well in the theatre.

EDITION v.s., J. & W. Chester, 1919

Tre commedie goldoniane
Three Goldoni Comedies
Triptych of one-act operas:
1. *La bottega da caffè* (*The coffee shop*) (18m)
2. *Sior Todero brontolon* (*Mr Todero, the grumbler*) (22m)
3. *Le baruffe chiozzotte* (*Quarrels in Chioggia*) (13m)
Libretto by the composer, after Carlo Goldoni (1707–1793)
Composed 1919–20 (3) and 1922 (1 and 2)
PREMIERES 24 March 1926, Hessisches Landestheater, Darmstadt; UK: 21 February 1936, BBC National Programme (concert suite only; radio broadcast)

Malipiero's reinterpretations of three of Goldoni's most famous comedies are characteristically high-handed and wilfully fragmentary: he said he was less interested in the plots than in the 18th-century Venice the plays evoke. In *La bottega da caffè* the shameless gossip Don Marzio is surrounded by suspicious wives, errant husbands and dishonest gambling. *Sior Todero brontolon* portrays a grumpy old miser who wants to avoid paying a dowry for his grand-daughter. Isidoro, the central figure of *Le baruffe chiozzotte*, is a long-suffering 'arm of the law' who has to cope with quarrelling women and violent men. All three operas are exceedingly brief, with unrealistically fast action and many details either invented by Malipiero or transferred from other Goldoni comedies. Many characters remain mute or almost mute, so that the effect comes considerably closer to that of *Sette canzoni* than one might expect.

Unlike *Sette canzoni*, however, the *Tre commedie* mingle lyrical utterances with rapid yet strongly characterized recitative. Musical references to the 18th century are nevertheless only of the freest kind; and the brightly glinting, pulsating orchestral textures suggest a quintessentially Venetian response to *Petrushka*.

EDITION v.s., Ricordi, 1924

Torneo notturno
Nocturnal Tournament
Sette notturni in one act (1h 15m)
Libretto by the composer, quoting texts by Poliziano and others
Composed 1929
PREMIERE 15 May 1931, Nationaltheater, Munich

The dreamlike symbolism of *Torneo notturno* casts a strange, unforgettable spell. Like *Sette canzoni*, the work consists of seven dramatic episodes linked by elaborate instrumental interludes. This time, however, there is a rudimentary plot which features two symbolic characters, defined as Il Disperato and Lo Spensierato ('The despairing one' and 'The carefree one'). They are brought together in an enigmatic series of nocturnal situations, in which the two are repeatedly in conflict over some lady or other. The brazen, unscrupulous Spensierato, unlike his rival, has at least some superficial successes; but in the last episode, when the two meet in prison, Il Disperato kills Lo Spensierato, steals his song, and regains what turns out to be an illusory freedom.

The writer Massimo Bontempelli once likened *Torneo notturno* to 'a lugubrious gyration of anguished faces within the walls of a bleak city', while the critic Piero Santi has called it 'a phantom drama, whose meaning is defined exclusively by the music'. Malipiero's growing interest in early music is reflected in some sombre neo-Monteverdian ariosi – interacting closely with 20th-century idioms of an almost Janáček-like poignancy. Running through it all is an obsessively recurring song (the one Il Disperato eventually steals): the *canzone del tempo*, with its insistent message about the inexorable destructiveness of time. *Torneo notturno* comes over particularly effectively as a radio opera.

EDITION v.s., Bote und Bock, 1930; *rp*, Ricordi, 1950

La favola del figlio cambiato
The Fable of the Changeling Son
Opera in three acts (five scenes) (1h 15m)
Libretto by Luigi Pirandello, taken partly from the fragmentary play-within-a-play in his *I giganti della montagna* (inc.)
Composed 1932–3
PREMIERES 13 January 1934, Landestheater, Brunswick; UK: 18 January 1984, BBC Radio 3 (radio broadcast)

In the 1930s Malipiero's music became more euphonious and expansive; he also reverted to more traditional ideals of dramatic continuity. Both tendencies are evident in *La favola del figlio cambiato*, yet the work is still unconventional in subject and expression.

A Sicilian mother is convinced that witches have substituted a misshapen idiot for her beautiful baby. Many doubt her story, but a clairvoyant assures her that her child is being well brought up in a distant royal palace, and that the best she can do for him now is to devote herself to the half-wit, since the fortunes of the two children are mysteriously interconnected. The handicapped boy grows up believing that he is 'the son of a king'. But a young prince arrives from a northern land, seeking to regain his health in the Mediterranean sun. He decides to play along with the mother's belief that he is her long-lost child, and refuses to go home when news arrives of the death of his father the king. Enchanted by the simple affection of his 'mother', he orders that the 'son of a king' should return to the court in his place.

The opera becomes more naturalistic as it proceeds. The moving yet stylized opening scene is remarkably akin to some in Malipiero's previous operas, whereas the relatively long last act is dominated by sustained dialogue of a kind he had previously avoided. The intermezzo-like second act is by any standards a vivid invention. After Mussolini's notorious ban on *La favola* in 1934, it remained for many years in the shadows, but attracted renewed interest when revived in the early 1980s.

EDITION v.s., Ricordi, 1933

Other operas and music-theatre works: *Elen e Fuldano*, (1909); *Canossa* (= *La notte dei penitenti*), 1914; *Schiavona* (lost), (?*c.* 1912); *Sogno d'un tramonto d'autunno*, (1913), 1963 (RAI broadcast), 1988; *Lancelotto del lago*, (1915); *Pantea*, (1919), 1932; *Orfeo, ovvero L'ottava canzone* (= Part 3 of *L'Orfeide*), (1920), 1925; *San Francesco d'Assisi* (mistero), 1922 (concert); 1949; *La morte delle maschere* (= Part 1 of *L'Orfeide*), (1972), 1925; *Filomela e l'Infatuato*, (1925), 1928; *Il finto Arlecchino* (= Part 2 of *Il mistero di Venezia*), (1925), 1928; *Merlino, mastro d'organi*, (1927), 1934 (radio), 1972; *Le aquile di Aquileia* (= Part 1 of *Il mistero di Venezia*), (1928), 1932; *I corvi di San Marco* (= Part 3 of *Il mistero di Venezia*), (1928), 1932; *I trionfi d'Amore* (triptych of one-act operas: only the second, *Il festino*, was not withdrawn by the composer), (1931), *Il festino*, 1937 (radio), 1954; *Giulio Cesare*, 1936; *Antonio e Cleopatra*, 1938; *Ecuba*, 1941; *La vita è sogno*, (1941), 1943; *I capricci di Callot*, 1942; *L'allegra brigata*, (1943), 1950; *Vergilii Aeneis* (secular oratorio), 1946 (RAI broadcast), 1958; *Mondi celesti e infernali*, 1950 (RAI broadcast), 1960; *Il figliuol prodigo*, 1953 (RAI broadcast), 1957; *Donna Urraca*, 1954; *Il capitan Spavento*, (1955), 1963; *Venere prigioniera*, 1957; *Rappresentazione e festa di Carnasciale e della Quaresima* ('opera with dance'), (1961), 1962 (concert); 1970; *Don Giovanni*, 1963 (RAI broadcast); *Le metamorfosi di Bonaventura*, 1966; *Don Tartufo bacchettone*, (1966), 1970; *Il marescalco*, 1969; *Gli eroi di Bonaventura* (largely excerpts from previous Malipiero operas), 1969; *Uno dei Dieci*, 1971; *L'Iscariota*, 1971
BIBLIOGRAPHY Luigi Dallapiccola, 'In memoriam Gian Francesco Malipiero' in Rudy Shackelford (trans. and ed.), *Dallapiccola on Opera*, Toccata Press, 1987, pp. 109–16; John C. G. Waterhouse, 'Between Opera and "Music-Theatre": Gian Francesco Malipiero's Rebellion against the Italian Operatic Establishment, 1917–29', *ATI Journal* (Journal of the Association of Teachers of Italian), no. 56 (summer 1989), pp. 27–38; John C. G. Waterhouse, *La musica di Gian Francesco Malipiero*, Nuova ERI, 1990

J.C.G.W.

LUIGI MANCINELLI
b 5 February 1848, Orvieto; *d* 2 February 1921, Rome

Luigi Mancinelli was at first a cellist but an impromptu début as an opera conductor (with Verdi's *Aida* at Perugia in 1874) launched him on a successful conducting career both in Italy and abroad. He has been referred to as a precursor of Toscanini, resembling the younger man in his musical thoroughness and insistence on discipline. Fragments of his conducting, including a tantalizing excerpt from his own *Ero e Leandro*, are preserved on the Mapleson cylinders, released on LP in 1985.

Mancinelli's first opera, *Isora di Provenza*, premiered at Bologna (1884), did not last though it was initially successful. His second and best-known opera, *Ero e Leandro*, to a libretto by Boito (previously set by Bottesini (1879)), was first performed (in English) at the Norwich Festival in 1896. It was first staged in Madrid the following year, and performances followed at both Covent Garden and the Metropolitan, always with Mancinelli conducting. The score has some atmospheric pages, but the dramatic temperature is tepid. After

Mancinelli's retirement it virtually disappeared from the stage.

Operas: *Isora di Provenza*, 1848; *Ero e Leandro*, 1896; *Paolo e Francesca*, 1907; *Sogno di una notte d'estate*, (*c.* 1916)
BIBLIOGRAPHY George Bernard Shaw, Dan H. Lawrence (ed.), *Shaw's Music*, 3 vols, The Bodley Head, 1981

W.A.

FRANCESCO MANCINI
b 16 January 1672, Naples; *d* 22 September 1737, Naples

Mancini studied the organ at the Conservatory of the Pietà dei Turchini in Naples and remained there as organist before gaining a reputation as an opera composer with *Ariovisto* (1702). Having become musical director at the Neapolitan court in 1707, he was demoted when Alessandro Scarlatti returned from leave in Rome in 1708. From then on Mancini was Scarlatti's greatest rival for the favour of the Neapolitan public. Mancini was Director of the Conservatory of Santa Maria di Loreto from 1720 to 1735 and after Scarlatti's death in 1725, regained the position of maestro di cappella to the court.

Between 1702 and 1723 Mancini wrote some 17 operas, mainly in the heroic mode. He is best known as the composer of *Idaspe fedele*, performed at the Haymarket Theatre in London in 1710, and one of the first operas to be performed wholly in Italian on the English stage.

Mancini's operas up to and including *Trajano* (1723) place him firmly in the tradition of late-baroque Neapolitan opera, with its Metastasian texts and heavy reliance on the alternation of recitative and *da capo* arias. Mancini's later operas show the more progressive influence of his younger contemporaries, e.g. Logroscino, Leo and Cafaro. His only known buffa work is *Don Aspremo*.

Operatic works: *Ariovisto*, 1702; *Lucio Silla*, 1703; *La costanza nell'honore*, 1704; *Gli amanti generosi*, 1705 (EDITION facsimile, Garland, 1978); *La serva favorita*, 1705; *Alessandro il Grande in Sidone*, 1706; *Turno Aricino*, 1708; *Engelberta, o sia La forza dell'innocenza* (coll. with A. Orefice and T. Albinoni), 1709; *Idaspe fedele* (rev. of *Gli amanti generosi*), 1710; *Mario fugitivo*, 1710; *Selim re d'Ormuz*, 1712; *Artaserse re di Persia*, 1713; *Il Gran Mogol*, 1713; *Il Vincislao*, 1714; *Alessandro Severo*, 1718; *La fortezza al cimento*, 1721; *Il Trajano*, 1723; *Orontea*, 1729; *Alessandro nelle Indie* (lost), 1732; *Don Aspremo*, 1733; *Il Demofoonte* (Act II of coll. with Sarro and Leo), 1735; 11 numbers for Handel's *Agrippina*, 1713
BIBLIOGRAPHY Winton Dean and John Merrill Knapp, *Handel's Operas 1704–1726*, Clarendon Press, 1987

D.S.B.

FRANCESCO MANELLI
Francesco Manelli [Mannelli, 'Il Fasolo']; *b* 1595–7, Tivoli; *d* before 27 September 1667, Parma

Francesco Manelli, with Benedetto Ferrari, inaugurated so-called public opera in Venice in 1637. Like Ferrari, too, Manelli developed a wide range of skills – as composer, singer, poet and impresario – to cater for new modes of operatic production.

Manelli was a singer at Tivoli Cathedral (c. 1605–24) and later its maestro di cappella (1627–9). His *L'Andromeda* (libretto by Ferrari, 1637) was the first opera staged at the Teatro San Cassiano, Venice, and composer and librettist collaborated again on *La maga fulminata* (1638). Manelli joined the choir of St Mark's in 1638, but continued to write operas, including *La Delia, o sia La sera sposa del sole* (1639), which inaugurated the Teatro SS. Giovanni e Paolo; *L'Adone* (1639–40), once thought to be by Monteverdi, and *L'Alcate* (1642). In 1640, Manelli and his family toured operas – including Monteverdi's *Il ritorno d'Ulisse in patria* – to Bologna. In 1645, they moved to Parma, where Manelli provided six stage works for the Farnese court. All his stage music is lost, but he published two books of agreeable chamber songs in 1629 and 1636.

BIBLIOGRAPHY P. Petrobelli, 'Francesco Manelli: documenti ed osservazioni', *Chigiana*, vol. 24 (1967), pp. 43–66

T.C.

GIACOMO MANZONI
b 26 September 1932, Milan

Manzoni is, along with Luigi Nono, the most forceful exponent of a challenging theatre of ideas in post-war Italian music. His education focused strongly on languages and literature, in which he took his degree in 1955. From 1959 to 1970 he published important translations of the writings of Adorno and Schoenberg. But during his teens he had begun to study music, soon immersing himself in the post-Schoenbergian tradition, which he explored in depth while pursuing studies at the Milan Conservatory alongside his university work.

In his final year at university, he tried his hand at a theatre piece (it was only his second fully-fledged composition). Entitled *La Legge* (*The Law*), it anticipated what was to come both in subject matter – a story of Sicilian peasants ground down by authority – and in its Expressionist musical idiom. It was not performed.

La sentenza
The Sentence
An act in two pictures (30m)
Libretto by Emilio Jona
Composed 1959–60
PREMIERE 13 October 1960, Teatro delle Novità, Bergamo

This Brechtian parable takes place during the Japanese occupation of China. A peasant woman, Sun-Te, protects a partisan on the run by pretending that he is her husband. When soldiers drag in her real husband, a decent but submissive man, she says she does not know him. He is taken away and shot. Later, with victory achieved, a revolutionary court debates Sun-Te's action, but neither condemns nor condones it. When she demands some resolution they respond, 'If there's going to be a sentence, it must come from you.' Manzoni fleshes out the parable with spare, vivid dodecaphonic writing.

EDITIONS f.s./v.s., Suvini Zerboni, [n.d.]

Atomtod
Atomic Death
Two acts (1h 15m)
Libretto by Emilio Jona
Composed 1963–4
PREMIERE 27 March 1965, Piccola Scala, Milan

With *Atomtod*, Manzoni and Jona moved into active confrontation, employing film and electronic music alongside conventional theatrical means. The work was the cause of lively displeasure among political and ecclesiastical authorities. *Atomtod* is set inside and outside private nuclear shelters. Inside, the proprietor and his chosen companions sit out a nuclear crisis in ever more empty observance of every-day social rituals. Outside, the mass of the human race is left to its fate. When the affluent men finally emerge to confront the devastation, they have lost the last traces of humanity: their blank hymn of joy demonstrates that they are as dead psychologically as are the mutilated remains around them.

EDITION Suvini Zerboni (hire material only)

Per Massimiliano Robespierre
For Maximilian Robespierre
Musical scene in two acts and a critical intermezzo (1h 15m)
Libretto assembled by the composer and Virginio Puecher from texts by Robespierre and others with the collaboration of Luigi Pestalozza
Composed 1974
PREMIERE 12 April 1975, Teatro Comunale, Bologna

If *Atomtod* stood at the boundaries of operatic narrative, *Per Massimiliano Robespierre* moved beyond them. Puecher (Manzoni's producer for both of the previous works) had proposed a scenography rich in incident and imagery, with many historical characters represented. Manzoni instead went further, scrutinizing our own ambivalences in the face of Robespierre's thought and achievement. Robespierre's texts are sung by a quartet of voices: some are also declaimed by speakers. The theatrical debate articulated by Manzoni's montage of quotations is historically anchored by scenes of flashback to their original context. Manzoni's score gives a sense of large-scale shape by cutting between strongly differentiated types of sound-mass. At one striking point Manzoni cuts Gossec's *Hymne à l'être suprême* into a complex assemblage of materials evoking the Festival of the Supreme Being. The work ends with an impassioned valediction from Charlotte, Robespierre's sister, accompanied by string quartet.

EDITIONS f.s., Ricordi, 1974

Doktor Faustus
Doctor Faust
Scenes from Thomas Mann's novel (1h 45m)
Libretto by the composer, after the novel by Thomas Mann
(1947)
Composed 1985–8
PREMIERE 16 May 1989, La Scala, Milan

The work has long roots in Manzoni's past career: he wrote his doctoral thesis on music in the work of Thomas Mann and immersed himself as translator and musician in the work of Adorno and Schoenberg, both of which were important influences on the writing of Mann's novel. Manzoni first wrote a symphonic work, *Scene sinfoniche per il Doktor Faust* (1984) out of which he then developed the music for the opera. Perforce, he was compelled to pare the libretto down to essentials: Mann's narrator, Serenus Zeitblom, speaks only at the very end; important subsidiary protagonists are removed.

Act I confronts us immediately with the composer Adrian Leverkühn's infection with syphilis. It ends as a diabolic Trinity spells out the price he must pay for the enjoyment of his genius: he must renounce love. Tertiary syphilis will in due course consume him. In Act II, Echo, Adrian's nephew, comes to stay. Adrian's love for him is punished by the boy's death. In Act III he makes his manic confession before an increasingly embarrassed assembly of friends and associates, and submits to his fate.

In this, his most personal statement, Manzoni moves beyond the texture-based idioms of previous works to reinstate melody as a central focus. Intensive thematic working thus takes on an important role. Much use is made of a five-note group rich in fourths, derived from the letters of the name 'Hetaera Esmeralda' (by which Leverkühn refers to the prostitute who infected him). The resultant harmony, like the intensive thematicism, reflects the musical concerns of Leverkühn's generation, notably the young Schoenberg; but Manzoni uses these resources to his own ends, rather than attempt a period piece.

EDITION f.s./v.s., Ricordi, 1988

D.O.-S.

MARIN MARAIS
b 31 May 1656, Paris; *d* 15 August 1728, Paris

Marais is best known today for his compositions for bass viol. He was, however, long associated with French opera. As a member of Louis XIV's *musique* he took part in the premieres of a number of Lully operas and, in 1705, became batteur de mesure (conductor) at the Paris Opéra. His four tragédies – *Alcide* (1693, written in collaboration with Lully's son Louis), *Ariane et Bacchus* (1696), *Alcyone* (1706) and *Semélé* (1709) – are cast, at least outwardly, in the Lullian mould. Their plots, however, and particularly those of the latter two, belong to the

lighter-weight *galant* type newly fashionable in the early 18th century. Marais is musically more adventurous than his model in his use of chromaticism and affective leaps. Moreover, his airs often have a lightness of touch rare in Lully. Above all, he did much to develop the descriptive element of French opera, notably the *tempête*: that of *Alcyone* was especially famous and contributed to the opera's longevity (it continued to be revived until 1771, though much revised by that date).

BIBLIOGRAPHY J. R. Anthony, *French Baroque Music from Beaujoyeulx to Rameau*, Batsford, rev. 2nd edn, 1978; Sylvette Milliot and Jérôme de La Gorce, *Marin Marais*, Fayard, 1991; Caroline Wood, 'Orchestra and Spectacle in the *tragédie en musique* 1673–1715: *oracle*, *sommeil* and *tempête*', *PRMA*, vol. 108 (1981–2), pp. 25–46

G.S.

MARCO MARAZZOLI
[Marco dell'Arpa]; *b c.* 1602–8, ?Parma; *d* 26 January 1662, Rome

Although Marazzoli's family came from Parma, he succeeded in winning the patronage of Cardinal Antonio Barberini by the early 1630s, and by the beginning of 1637 he was living in Rome. He stayed there for the rest of his life, apart from visits to northern Italy and Paris. Shortly after his arrival in Rome, Marazzoli was made a member of the papal chapel; he maintained his connection with the Barberini, and composed oratorios for the prestigious Oratorio del SS. Crocifisso.

In February 1637 his first opera for the Barberini family was performed, *Il falcone*, written in collaboration with Virgilio Mazzochi to a text by Giulio Rospigliosi; the work seems to have been revised for a further performance in 1639, under the title of *Chi soffre speri*. For the revival Marazzoli also (probably) provided an intermedio to the second act, *La fiera di Farfa*. In the early 1640s he travelled to Ferrara and Venice; in Ferrara his first serious opera, *L'Armida*, was performed, and in Venice he composed a festa teatrale for the Teatro SS. Giovanni e Paolo. In 1643 he developed connections with the French community in Rome, and the opera he composed for them, *Il capriccio*, was probably performed in Paris at the invitation of Cardinal Mazarin in 1645.

In 1653 he collaborated with Abbatini in producing a comic opera to celebrate the marriage of Maffeo Barberini with Olimpia Giustiniani, *Dal male il bene*. In 1656, shortly after she arrived in Rome, Queen Christina of Sweden described Marazzoli as her virtuoso da camera, and in that year he dedicated his final opera, *La vita humana*, to her. Marazzoli's operas mark an important development in the style of both recitatives and ensemble finales.

Operatic works: *Il falcone* (coll. with Virgilio Mazzochi), 1637, rev. as *Chi soffre speri*, 1639; *La fiera di Farfa*

(intermedio to Act II of the previous), 1639; *L'Armida*, or
L'amore trionfante dello sdegno, 1641; *Le pretensioni del
Tebro e del Po*, 1642; *Gli amori di Giasone e d'Issifile*, 1642; *Il
capriccio*, or *Il giudiz io della ragione fra la Beltà e l'Affetto*,
1643, rev. 1645; *Dal male il bene* (coll. with Antonio Maria
Abbatini), 1653; *Le armi e gli amori*, 1654, rev. 1656; *La vita
humana, overo Il trionfo della pietà*, 1656
BIBLIOGRAPHY M. K. Murata, *Operas for the Papal Court
(1631–1668)*, Ann Arbor, 1981

G.D.

FILIPPO MARCHETTI

b 26 February 1831, Bolognola, Macerata; *d* 18 January 1902,
Rome

Marchetti studied at the Naples Conservatory with
Lillo and Conti (1850–54). His first opera, *Gentile da
Varano*, was successfully premiered in Turin in 1856,
and this led to the performance the following year of
his second opera, *La demente*. However, unable to
secure performances of *Il paria*, he moved to Rome
where he taught singing and composition. From 1862
he lived in Milan, composing *Romeo e Giulietta* there
(first performed with moderate success in Trieste in
1865). Marchetti was a member of the committee
that awarded the first prize in the Sonzogno
competition of 1889 to Mascagni's *Cavalleria
rusticana*.

Ruy Blas

Dramma lirico in four acts (2h 30m)
Libretto by Carlo d'Ormeville, after the play by Victor Hugo
(1838)
PREMIERES 3 April 1869, La Scala, Milan; US: 14 October
1874, Academy of Music, New York; UK: 1875, London
(amateur), 24 November 1877, Her Majesty's Theatre, London

Ruy Blas was one of the first Italian operas to show
the influence of French grand opera, partly no doubt
in response to its French source. It enjoyed enormous
success and was widely performed well into the 20th
century.
  The story tells of the rise to power at the Spanish
court of Ruy Blas (disguised as 'Don Cesare'), a
youth of humble origins and the servant of Don
Sallustio. When Sallustio is disgraced, he threatens to
expose Ruy Blas's real identity to the queen. Ruy
Blas intervenes and kills first Sallustio and then
himself.
  Ruy Blas is notable for a certain refinement of
melody and good orchestration, but it is dramatically
weak and implausible.

EDITION v.s., Ricordi, [*c.* 1870]

Other operas: *Gentile da Varano*, 1856; *La demente*, 1856; *Il
paria*, (1859); *Romeo e Giulietta*, 1865; *Gustavo Wasa*, 1875;
Don Giovanni d'Austria, 1880
BIBLIOGRAPHY Jay Nicolaisen, *Italian Opera in Transition,
1871–1893*, UMI Research Press, 1980

C.T.

HEINRICH MARSCHNER

Heinrich August Marschner; *b* 16 August 1795, Zittau; *d* 14
December 1861, Hanover

The most important opera composer in Germany
between Weber and Wagner, Marschner made a
decisive and distinctive contribution to the development of German Romantic opera. Still
obviously rooted in the tradition of singspiel and
number opera, his best works nevertheless succeeded
in expanding the dramatic range of existing musical
forms and in integrating discrete elements into a
more ambitious theatrical whole. Adventurous in his
use of chromatic harmony and imaginative in the
deployment of instrumental effects, Marschner
attempted always to subordinate musical sophistication to the demands of the drama. Though he
excelled at the depiction of the supernatural and
the creation of an atmosphere of horror or suspense,
he was more interested in the portrayal of inner
conflicts and psychological turmoil than the evocation of setting and local colour.
  Marschner's parents were keen amateur musicians
and he showed early talent as a pianist and boy
soprano; he is reputed to have sung the role of Julia
in Spontini's *La vestale*. He composed his first
theatre work, the ballet *Die stolze Bauerin*, when still
at school and soon abandoned law studies in Leipzig
in favour of a musical career, taking up employment
in 1816 as domestic music teacher and kapellmeister
to noble families in Pressburg. His first attempt at
operatic composition, unperformed and apparently
intended mainly as a technical exercise, was a setting
of Metastasio's *Titus*, using the adaptation Mazzolà
made for Mozart. The breakthrough in Marschner's
career came when Weber accepted *Heinrich IV
und d'Aubigné* for production in Dresden in
1820. Marschner settled in Dresden the following
year, writing incidental music for plays, including
Kleist's *Prinz Friedrich von Homburg*. In 1824 he
became musikdirektor at the opera. Professional
responsibilities to both Italian and German resident
companies forced him to steer a diplomatic course
between the two national styles, but his personal
sympathies lay with the idea of a German national
opera, which he attempted to promote with his
singspiel *Der Holzdieb*, produced at the Hoftheater
in 1825 and published as the first in what was
intended to be a series of cheap, easy-to-play piano
scores of national operas.
  When Weber died in 1826, Marschner, who
combined zeal in self-promotion with an inability to
make himself agreeable, failed in his attempt to
succeed him as royal kapellmeister and left Dresden.
During the next year he travelled Germany with his
third wife, the singer Marianne Wohlbrück, spending
time in Berlin, Danzig, Breslau and Magdeburg
before settling in Leipzig in 1827. The premiere of
Der Vampyr, in Leipzig in March 1828, was his first
great success. His reputation was consolidated in
December 1829 by *Der Templer und die Jüdin*. In
1831 Marschner was appointed conductor at the
Hoftheater in Hanover. Two years later *Hans Heiling*

was produced in Berlin. It proved to be the highpoint of Marschner's career. He remained in Hanover for the rest of his life, though his opposition to the Italian tastes of the court made his position there uncomfortable. In the remaining years of his long career he attempted comic opera (*Der Babü*, premiered in Hanover, 1838), historical grand opera in the manner of Spontini (*König Adolf von Nassau*, staged in Dresden, largely thanks to Wagner, in 1845) and a quasi-Wagnerian exercise in through-composition (*Sangeskönig Hiarne*, performed posthumously, Frankfurt, 1863, after Rossini had tried unsuccessfully to secure a Paris production). Songs, male choruses, incidental music and pageants for royal occasions helped maintain his reputation, but changing public taste (and some undoubtedly weak libretti) denied him further major operatic successes. Despite Pfitzner's attempt at revival earlier this century, only the three operas most widely acclaimed during Marschner's lifetime survive on the fringes of today's repertoire.

Der Vampyr

The Vampire
Romantic opera in two acts (2h 45m)
Libretto by Wilhelm August Wohlbrück after the play *Der Vampir oder die Totenbraut* (1821) by Heinrich Ludwig Ritter, after John Polidori's story (published as *The Vampyre: a Tale by Lord Byron*, 1819)
Composed 1827–8
PREMIERES 29 March 1828, Sächsisches Hoftheater Leipzig; UK: 25 August 1829, Lyceum, London; US: 9 March 1980, Boston
CAST Malwina Davenaut *s*, Janthe Berkley *s*, Emmy Perth *s*, Edgar Aubry *t*, George Dibdin *t*, Sir Humphrey Davenaut *b*, Lord Ruthven, (the Vampire) *bar*, Sir John Berkley *b*, John Perth *spoken role*, The Vampire Master *spoken role*, *ms*, 2 *t*, 3 *b*; *satb* chorus of witches, goblins, ghosts, demons, servants, peasants, priests
FULL ORCHESTRA including serpent and extra perc. including thunder machine; onstage: 2 hn, 2 tpt

Marschner began work on *Der Vampyr* after leaving Dresden in 1826. The choice of subject undoubtedly exploited a contemporary vogue for such themes – Lindpainter's opera of the same title was premiered a few months after Marschner's – but the opera's success was not simply due to fashion. In *Lucretia*, begun in 1820 and staged in Leipzig in 1827, Marschner had attempted to treat a Classical subject in a manner that owed something to Spontini, dispensing with spoken dialogue. The work met with a lukewarm response. *Der Vampyr* offered a subject more obviously suited to Marschner's distinctive operatic voice.

SYNOPSIS

Act I The setting is the Scottish Highlands. At a midnight gathering of spirits, the vampire, Ruthven, is granted an extension of his stay on earth, on condition that he sacrifice three brides within the next 24 hours. His first victim is Janthe, whom he kills as Berkley, her father, arrives with a search party and stabs his daughter's assailant. The dying Ruthven asks Aubry, whose life he once saved, to

George shoots Ruthven; illustration (1831) of a scene from Act II of Der Vampyr

place his body where the moon's rays can revive it, and swears him to secrecy for 24 hours. Aubry flees in horror. His horror is compounded when he discovers his beloved Malwina is to be married to Ruthven before midnight.

Act II Ruthven's servants are celebrating the marriage of Emmy and George. Ruthven arrives to claim Emmy as his second victim, warning Aubry that he too will become a vampire if he tries to intervene. George is unable to save his bride, but manages to shoot Ruthven. In the moonlight the vampire revives again and hastens to Davenaut's castle for his own wedding to Malwina, his intended third victim. Aubry succeeds in delaying the marriage ceremony and, after wrestling with his conscience, resolves to break his oath. He denounces Ruthven. As the clock strikes one, the vampire is struck by lightning.

Der Vampyr represents a significant expansion of the dramatic possibilities of number opera. Sustaining tension with reminiscence motif and bold, shifting harmony, vividly underscoring changes of mood with choral and orchestral effects, Marschner combines and contrasts vocal forms of varying emotional range – melodrama, folksong, declamation, arioso, chorus – in a convincing dramatic whole. Pathos and terror are interwoven to create a powerful atmosphere of supernatural horror and suspense. The opera's central figure, victim as well as monster, is a creation of some psychological complexity.

RECORDING   Farley, Protschka, Nimsgern, Egel, Rome Ch and SO of Italian Radio, Neuhold, Fonit Cetra, 1980
EDITIONS   v.ss., Hofmeister, 1828; Pfitzner (ed.), Furstner, 1925

Der Templer und die Jüdin
The Templar and the Jewess
Romantic opera in three acts (3h 15m)
Libretto by Wilhelm August Wohlbrück, after the novel *Ivanhoe* by Sir Walter Scott (1819) and the play *Das Gericht der Templer* (1823) by Johann Reinhold Lenz
Composed 1828–9
PREMIERES   22 December 1829, Sächsisches Hoftheater, Leipzig; UK: 17 June 1840, Prince's Theatre, London; US: 29 January 1872, New York
CAST   Cedric *b*, Ivanhoe *t*, Rowena *s*, Lucas de Beaumanoir *b*, Brian de Bois-Guilbert *bar*, Maurice de Bracy *t*, Black Knight *b*, Locksley *bar*, Wamba *t*, Oswald *b*, Friar Tuck *b*, Rebecca *s*, Albert Malvoisan *bar*, Isaac of York *spoken role*; *satb* chorus of Saxons, Normans, Templars, knights, pages, squires, peasants, outlaws
FULL ORCHESTRA   onstage: fl, picc, ob, 2 cl, 2 bsn, 6 hn, 2 tpt, 3 trbn, b trbn, tambourine

Following the success of *Der Vampyr*, Marschner chose another subject that had captured the contemporary imagination. Scott's novel had already inspired a pasticcio by Rossini (1826) as well as a number of plays. It was to continue to fascinate composers throughout the 19th century. Despite its successful premiere, Marschner immediately began to revise the work, shortening it, rearranging the order of scenes and numbers, and cutting some of the spoken dialogue or replacing it with recitative. Pfitzner produced a more substantial revision, first performed in Berlin in 1904. During the composer's lifetime, and in the succeeding decades, *Der Templer und die Jüdin* was the most frequently performed of Marschner's operas.

SYNOPSIS
Act I   Rebecca and her father, Isaac, are nursing the wounded Ivanhoe when all three are kidnapped by Bois Guilbert, who hopes to force Rebecca to reciprocate his love for her. Bracy, similarly motivated, imprisons Rowena and her guardian, Cedric. Friar Tuck, the Black Knight and Locksley, an outlaw loyal to King Richard (and the original Robin Hood) resolve to free the captives. As the Saxons storm the castle Rebecca and Rowena continue to reject their captors' advances. The Black Knight saves Ivanhoe from the burning castle. Bois Guilbert saves Rebecca and flees. The castle falls to the Saxons. Bracy is killed. Cedric and Rowena are freed.
Act II   The Saxons recognize the Black Knight as their king, Richard the Lionheart. Rejoicing, they pledge their loyalty. The Knights Templar attribute Guilbert's love for Rebecca to her witchcraft. On Guilbert's advice she asks for her fate to be decided in trial by combat. If no champion appears on her

behalf, she will die. The Templars nominate the horrified Guilbert to fight on their behalf. Isaac, who has overheard, rushes to seek help.
Act III   Ivanhoe is betrothed to Rowena. Isaac begs him to fight on Rebecca's behalf. Guilbert continues to woo Rebecca. She rejects him. Ivanhoe defeats Guilbert in combat. Rebecca is declared innocent and ruefully relinquishes her champion to Rowena. King Richard asserts his authority over the Templars.

In turning Scott's novel into a feasible libretto, Wohlbrück was unable entirely to avoid structural weakness and had to rely extensively on spoken dialogue to provide necessary background information (hence the attempts at revision). Nevertheless, with the aid of Lenz's play he produced a remarkably vivid historical backcloth for the riveting psychological drama of Rebecca's conflict with Bois Guilbert, and Bois Guilbert's conflict with himself. Marschner responded with a score that exploits to the full his ability to combine and contrast musical forms and idioms. Local and historical colour is more prominent than in his other operas: simple strophic songs and rousing martial choruses bring the historical panorama to life, with the bluff, honest Saxons convincingly distinguished from the sophisticated Normans, and Rebecca's exotic and pure remoteness delicately suggested by vocal flourishes and more complex harmony. Tuck and Wamba the fool provide comic relief, and some of the opera's most immediately engaging music, while the principal conflict unfolds in boldly constructed scenes that move between set forms and gripping passages of dramatic declamation and free arioso. Bois Guilbert, vicious yet tragic, is the most compelling, and the most strikingly modern, of the tormented bass-baritones at the centre of Marschner's three best operas.

EDITIONS   v.ss., Hofmeister, [*c.* 1830]; Pfitzner (ed.), Brockhaus, 1912

Hans Heiling
Romantic opera in a prelude and three acts (2h 45m)
Libretto by Philipp Eduard Devrient, after a Bohemian legend
Composed 1831–2
PREMIERES   24 May 1833, Hofoper, Berlin; UK: 2 December 1953, Oxford
CAST   Queen of the Earth Spirits *s*, Hans Heiling *bar*, Anna *s*, Gertrude *ms*, Konrad *t*, Stephan *b*; *satb* chorus of spirits, peasants, wedding guests, guards
FULL ORCHESTRA including thunder-machine, 3 extra trbn beneath the stage

The libretto of *Hans Heiling* had been rejected by Mendelssohn, for whom it was written in 1827, on the grounds that it was too close in atmosphere to *Der Freischütz*. Devrient, a baritone who had a considerable reputation as an author and producer, sent the text anonymously to Marschner in July 1831 just before he sang Bois Guilbert in the Berlin production of *Der Templer und die Jüdin*. Marschner accepted it with enthusiasm. The success of the premiere, at which Devrient sang Heiling, turned to triumph with the Leipzig production two months later.

SYNOPSIS

Prelude Disregarding all warnings, Hans Heiling, son of the Queen of the Earth Spirits and a mortal man, leaves his mother's underworld realm to live on earth near his beloved Anna.

Act I Living among men, Heiling is troubled and uncomfortable. Only Anna's love can make him truly mortal. Anna is afraid of him and persuades him to burn the magic book he has brought with him. At a village celebration, she dances with Konrad, reducing Heiling to despair.

Act II Anna, lost in the forest, is confronted by the Queen of the Earth Spirits who demands that she give up Heiling. Anna faints and is found by Konrad. They declare their love for each other. Heiling appears and demands that she honour her promise to marry him. She cannot, she says, since she now knows he is not a mortal. In his rage Heiling stabs Konrad and flees.

Act III Heiling appeals to the earth spirits. Scornfully they inform him that Konrad has survived and will soon marry Anna. Determined on revenge, Heiling attends the wedding and calls on the spirits to help him. As he is about to attack Konrad, his mother appears and reminds him of his promise to return to her should his heart be broken. The mortals thank heaven for their salvation.

Devrient's drama of the conflict between two worlds, with its troubled protagonist at home in neither, drew from Marschner a score that blends the traditional with the radical. The rustic world of the mortal characters is depicted within the conventions of singspiel, where dialogue links songlike melodies and cheerful choruses. For the eerie spirit world, and Heiling's inner turmoil – especially in the long, through-composed prelude – a seamless flow of aria, recitative and ensemble that precedes the Romantic tone poem of the overture – Marschner calls on more elaborate resources of harmony and orchestral colour. Within and between the opera's two worlds, contrasting set forms are bridged, their emotional and theatrical range extended by expressive use of melodrama and of flexible, declamatory word-setting, while extensive motivic links and reminiscence ensure musical and dramatic coherence.

RECORDINGS   1. Kirschstein, Synek, Plümacher, Hering, Prey, West German Radio Ch and O, Keilberth, MRF, 1966; 2. Mohr, Hajóssyová, Seniglova, Eklöf, Markus, Neshyba, Slovak Philharmonic Ch and O, Korner, Marco Polo, 1991
EDITIONS   f.s., Peters, 1892; v.s., Hofmeister, 1833

Other operas: *Titus*, (1816); *Saidar und Zulima*, 1818; *Heinrich IV und d'Aubigné*, 1820; *Der Kyffhäuserberg*, 1822; *Der Holzdieb*, 1825; *Lukretia*, 1827; *Des Falkners Braut*, 1832; *Das Schloss am Ätna*, 1836; *Der Babü* (lost), 1838; *König Adolph von Nassau*, 1845; *Austin*, 1852; *Sangeskönig Hiarne*, 1863

BIBLIOGRAPHY   Georg Münzer, *Heinrich Marschner,*

Harmonie, 1901; A. Dean Palmer, *Heinrich Marschner, 1795–1861: His Life and Stage Works*, UMI Research Press, 1980

I.B.

FRANK MARTIN
b 15 September 1890, Geneva; *d* 21 November 1974, Naarden, Netherlands

Of French Huguenot descent, Martin was, at the time of his death, Switzerland's most important composer. Tenth and youngest child of a Calvinist pastor, he began to compose at eight, though his true gifts developed late. His only formal music teacher was Joseph Lauber in his native Geneva, but mathematics and physics were abandoned for a musical career when he was 20. He studied and later taught under Jacques Dalcroze, becoming active as pianist, harpsichordist and pedagogue. Martin's highly personal musical formation began with his lifelong devotion to Bach. Then, the revelation of Debussy, through his friend Ernest Ansermet's programmes with the Suisse Romande orchestra, had its influence. In his forties, Martin asked Ansermet for an exposé of Schoenbergian 12-note technique. It proved crucial, providing the key to his emancipation from a hitherto unremarkable tonal idiom into one that combined it with newly found chromaticism in a highly personal harmonic language.

Successful stagings of Martin's oratorio, *Le vin herbé*, the first fruit of this language, entitle it to be listed with Martin's two designated operas: *Der Sturm*, a grand opera, after Shakespeare's *The Tempest*, and *Monsieur de Pourceaugnac*. Between these two, Martin's *Mystère de la Nativité*, *Oratorio de Noël* (1959), first given in Geneva under Ansermet, was also intended to be staged, and first given thus in Salzburg under Heinz Wallberg (1960).

Le vin herbé
The Magic Potion
Dramatic oratorio in a prologue, three parts and an epilogue (1h 30m)
Libretto: excerpts from Joseph Bédier's French version (1900) of the Tristan legend (*Le roman de Tristan et Yseut*)
Composed 1938–41
PREMIERES   Part I: 16 April 1940, Tonhalle, Zurich; complete: 28 March 1942, Tonhalle, Zurich (concert); 15 August 1948, Landestheater, Salzburg; UK: 30 January 1948, Central Hall, Westminster (concert); 1 April 1982, Jeannetta Cochrane Theatre, London

Martin established his reputation with *Le vin herbé*. Its restrained scoring (for 12 solo voices, strings and piano) and harmonic freedom heightened the emotional impact of this concentrated version of a famous French conflation of five early versions of the Tristan legend that includes Isolde of the White Hands, the dark Isolde, among the characters. Martin was drawn to the legend after reading Charles Morgan's *Sparkenbroke*, a novel he recognized as 'impregnated' with the myth. In *Le vin herbé*, the voices supply not only the principal roles, but also, by doublings, the lesser characters, three narrators and the commenting chorus.

RECORDING Retchitzka, Tuescher, Tappy, Rehfuss, Vessières, Ensemble, Desarzens, Westminster, 1961
EDITION v.s., Universal, 1943

Der Sturm
The Tempest
Opera in three acts and an epilogue (2h 30m)
Libretto by the composer, from August Wilhelm von Schlegel's German translation of Shakespeare's *The Tempest* (1611)
Composed 1952–5
PREMIERES 17 June 1956, Staatsoper, Vienna; US: 11 October 1956, City Center Opera, New York

Der Sturm is a straight setting of most of Schlegel's text. The restrained scoring of *Le vin herbé* and the particular colouring of the *Petite symphonie concertante* (1945), informed the already very personal musical language and orchestral timbre of both *Der Sturm* and the later *Monsieur de Pourceaugnac*. In the original production, the part of Ariel was sung offstage and mimed by a dancer. Later it was spoken; the French version maintains the original text.

RECORDING 3 excerpts: Fischer-Dieskau, Berlin PO, Martin, DG, 1963
EDITION v.s., Universal, 1955

Monsieur de Pourceaugnac
Comédie mise en musique in three acts (1h 45m)
Libretto by the composer, from the comédie-ballet by Molière (1690)
Composed 1960–62
PREMIERE 23 April 1963, Grand Theatre, Geneva

In Molière's farcical divertissement, Pourceaugnac, an elderly provincial lawyer, is engaged to be married to Julie, daughter of his Parisian client, Orgon. Neither of them has yet set eyes on the lawyer, who is thwarted by Julie's young lover, Eraste, and is finally thankful to escape from Paris and the charges falsely laid against him. Martin's score, of Mozartean proportions, is an almost exact setting of Molière's text. The orchestral forces are appropriately reduced, but typical timbres recall those of previous works, as does Martin's personal harmonic idiom.

EDITION v.s., Universal, 1964

BIBLIOGRAPHY Frank Martin, *Un compositeur médite sur son art*, A la Baconniere, 1977; Frank Martin, *A propos de ... Commentaires de Frank Martin sur ses oeuvres*, A la Baconniere, 1984; Maria Martin, *Souvenirs de ma vie avec Frank Martin*, Lausanne, 1990

F.A.

JOHANN PAUL AEGIDIUS MARTINI
Jean-Paul-Egide Martin; Schwarzendorf; 'Il Tedesco'; *b* 31 August 1741, Freystadt, Bavaria; *d* 10 February 1816, Paris

After travelling in Europe, Martini settled in Paris in 1764 and established himself among the second generation of opéra-comique composers active during the closing decades of the 18th century. Although his works were few in number and composed sporadically over a 30-year period, Martini ranked in his lifetime alongside Grétry and Dalayrac, and produced works that were popular and highly acclaimed.

L'amoureux de quinze ans, Martini's first opéra comique, was one of his most successful. Light in character and charmingly expressive, it included many graceful tunes with simple accompaniments and earned Martini the title 'le doyen des vaudevillistes'. He developed his style in *Le droit du seigneur*, which included complex tonal structures and made greater use of the orchestra, the chorus and mixed ensembles. Certain works relied less on comic intrigues and favoured more serious scenarios. *Henri IV* – highly successful in Europe – used historical characters and furthered the style of the drame lyrique. Martini's one tragédie, *Sapho* – which retained spoken dialogue in the tradition of the opéra comique – enjoyed over a hundred performances.

Operatic works: *L'amoureux de quinze ans, ou La double fête*, 1771; *Le fermier cru sourd, ou Les méfiances*, 1772; *Le nouveau-né*, 1772; *Le rendezvous bien employé*, 1774; *Henri IV, ou La bataille d'Ivry*, 1774; *Le droit du seigneur*, 1783; *L'amant sylphe, ou La féerie de l'amour*, 1783; *Annette et Lubin*, 1789; *Sapho*, 1794; *Ziméo*, 1800; *Sophie, ou Le tremblement de terre de Messine*, (n.d.)
BIBLIOGRAPHY David Charlton, 'The Tragic Seascape: *Sapho* and its 12-note chord', in M. Arnold and M. Walter (eds), *Jahrbuch für Opernforschung*, 1984, pp. 46–72

E.C.

BOHUSLAV MARTINŮ
Bohuslav Jan Martinů; *b* 8 December 1890, Polička; *d* 28 August 1959, Liestal, Switzerland

After Janáček, Martinů is the major representative of Czech opera in the 20th century. Most of Martinů's creative life was spent away from his native Czechoslovakia, but – except during the Second World War – he maintained strong links with his homeland. Following three desultory years (1907–10) at the Prague Conservatory, from which he was expelled, Martinů made a career as a teacher and violinist with the Czech Philharmonic Orchestra, graduating in 1918 to frequent engagements after sporadic appearances beginning in 1913.

After a brief period of study with Josef Suk in 1922, Martinů was awarded a Czech government scholarship to study in Paris in 1923, where he remained for the next 17 years, marrying his French wife, Charlotte Quennehen, in 1931. In 1940, having been blacklisted by the occupying German authorities, Martinů left Paris for the south of France and, in 1941, travelled to the United States where he remained, apart from long summer holidays in Europe, until 1953. The last years of Martinů's life were spent in Europe, in Nice, Rome, and Schonenberg in Switzerland.

After the war Martinů had planned to return to Czechoslovakia, but timely warning of the communist takeover of 1948 deterred him. Although his musical output in these late years was deeply affected by his native land, Martinů's unmistakable musical style – with its springy, syncopated melodies, motor rhythms, warm and predominantly diatonic harmonies – crystallized from numerous influences. Early encounters with the English madrigal and the music of Debussy led to a fascination with counterpoint and French-tinted harmony. Jazz and Les Six were important to Martinů in the 1920s, but the signal influence on his music at the start of the 1930s was the baroque concerto grosso. By this stage Martinů's style was fully formed, although he was still to respond positively to musical influences as diverse as Notre Dame polyphony and Haydn.

Music for the theatre occupied Martinů at all stages of his career, some of his earliest works being ballets. Of his fourteen complete operas (*La semaine de bonté*, 1931, and *La plainte contre inconnu*, 1953, are substantial torsos), six, including his first, were full length (*The Soldier and the Dancer*, *The Three Wishes*, *The Plays of Mary*, *Julietta*, *Mirandolina* and *The Greek Passion*). Martinů's operas show that he set his face against Wagnerian music drama and the nationalist subject matter of many of his Czech predecessors, and reveal Martinů's variety of inspiration, based on wide reading, and his propensity for experiment. The latter encompasses contemporary incident and improvisation in *The Soldier and the Dancer*, jazz and surrealism in *Les larmes du couteau* (scored for jazz band), film in *The Three Wishes*, medieval mystery plays in *The Plays of Mary*, commedia dell'arte in *The Suburban Theatre* and *Mirandolina*, neo-classicism in *Alexandre bis* and *Ariadne*. Martinů was also a pioneer of opera for radio (*The Voice of the Forest* and *Comedy on a Bridge*) and television (*What Men Live By* and *The Wedding*). The more elusive background to the surreal *Julietta* and the political realism of *The Greek Passion* have not prevented these two works from becoming Martinů's most widely performed full-length operas.

H. numbers refer to H. Halbriech, *Martinů: Werkverzeichnis, Dokumentation und Biographie*.

The Plays of Mary
Hry o Marii
A cycle of four separate stories on Marian themes, H. 236 (2h 15m)
The Wise Maiden and the Foolish Maiden
(*Panny moudré a panny pošetilé*)

Libretto by Vítězslav Nezval, after a 12th-century French liturgical play
Mariken of Nimègue
(*Mariken z Nimègue*)
Libretto by Henri Ghéon and Vilem Zavada, after a 15th-century Flemish liturgical play
The Nativity
(*Narození Páně*)
Libretto by the composer, based on Moravian folk texts
Sister Pasqualina
(*Sestra Paskalina*)
Libretto by the composer, after a play by Julius Zeyer and folk texts collected by František Bartoš
Composed 1933–4
PREMIERE 23 February 1935, National Theatre, Brno

Based on medieval and folk sources, *The Plays of Mary* marks Martinů's return to a more identifiably Czech idiom in his operas. Typically, their inspiration derives from a number of sources, including the legend of St Dorothea, which Martinů had set in the ballet *Špaliček*, and the revival of mystery and Passion plays in Paris in the early 1930s. Martinů noted that the work was less to do with the pursuit of religious aims than a return to earlier forms of theatre.

RECORDING Mrázová, Marková, Kratochvílová, Děpoltová, Zítek, Kusnjer, Jedlička, Průša, Prague Radio Ch, Prague SO, Bělohlávek, Supraphon, 1984
EDITIONS f.s., Dilia, 1965; v.s., Panton, 1979

Comedy on a Bridge
Veselohra na mostě
Opera in one act, H. 247 (40m)
Libretto by the composer, after the play by Václav Kliment Klicpera
Composed 1935
PREMIERE 18 March 1937, Czech Radio

Comedy on a Bridge was the second of Martinů's pioneering radio operas and owing to its wit and irony remains a favourite for student performance. The vocal writing is largely brisk monody and the orchestral material based partly on a characteristically parodistic military march.

RECORDING Krátka, Barová, Krejčík, Tuček, Novák, Brno Janáček CO, Jílek, Supraphon, 1984
EDITION v.s., Boosey & Hawkes, 1951

Julietta: Snář
Julietta: The Book of Dreams
Lyric opera in three acts, H. 253 (2h 15m)
Libretto by the composer, after the play *Juliette, ou La clé des songes* (*Juliette, or The Key of Dreams*) by Georges Neveux (1930)
Composed 1936–7
PREMIERES 16 March 1938, National Theatre, Prague: UK: 5 April 1978, Coliseum, London (New Opera Company)
CAST Julietta *s*, Michel *t*, Man in helmet *bar*, Man at window *b*, Old Arab *b*, 19(9) other minor roles (maximum number given first, minimum in brackets), 2(1) *s*, 5(2) *ms*, 5(2) *t*, 2(1) *bar*, 5(3) *b*; 6 townsfolk/3 gentlemen, *women's voices*
FULL ORCHESTRA including pf, cel; offstage: hn, accordion

According to Šafránek, Martinů saw Neveux's surrealist play *Juliette* in 1932. Martinů wrote the libretto himself with the author's permission, deeply impressing Neveux with his understanding of the work's effect on stage. The subject was a radical departure from Martinů's previous operas and remained a favourite with the composer. In his introduction to the published vocal score Martinů said of *Julietta*, 'The libretto and play are not a philosophical dissertation, but an extraordinarily beautiful and poetic fantasy in the form of a dream.' Martinů responded well to the sharply observed wit and fantasy of his own libretto in what may be described as his operatic masterpiece. The plot, which Martinů himself found difficult to relate, is built up of many apparently disjointed episodes.

Set design by Frantisek Muzika for Julietta *(Prague, 1938)*

SYNOPSIS

Act I Michel, a travelling bookseller from Paris, has returned to a small harbour town to find a girl, Julietta, whose voice has haunted his memory since a previous visit. The strange behaviour of the inhabitants of the town is explained by their lack of memory: they live in a continuous present seeking to acquire the reminiscences of others for themselves. Michel, with his memory, is understandably, if inevitably somewhat sporadically, an object of fascination. Eventually he finds Julietta. Although it is not clear that she remembers him he is greeted as a lost lover and the act ends with her asking him to meet her in a wood.

Act II A series of surreal incidents forms a prelude to the meeting of Julietta and Michel. Michel's memories, feeding Julietta's fantasies, form the basis of the exchange. When she eventually runs away from him he shoots at her, but it is not clear whether the shot has hit her. The act concludes when Michel, uncertain why he came to the town, is preparing to leave by boat when he hears Julietta's voice again.

Act III In the Central Office of Dreams many come to experience dreams. Michel, wanting to

return to his, hears Julietta calling. As the office closes, Michel rushes back into his dream to find himself once again in the harbour town as at the start of the opera.

Julietta is characterized by subtle orchestral colouring and an acute command of situation. In an opera where large numbers of brief stage appearances form the substance of the action, the composer provides highly effective character studies. Julietta herself, by emerging forcefully as a heroine, does not threaten the dreamlike qualities of the whole. Her exchanges with Michel in Act II are a virtuoso mixture of aspiring lyricism and ironic bathos. Throughout, Martinů preserves the fantasy atmosphere of Neveux's original although, as he was to recognize in a production at Wiesbaden in 1959, the opera maintains dramatic tension and explores disturbing psychological depths.

RECORDING Tauberová, Žídek, Otava, Kalaš, Prague NT Ch and O, Krombholc, Supraphon, 1964
EDITIONS f.s., Dilia, 1959; v.s., Karel Šolc (ed.), with an introduction by the composer, Melantrich, 1947

The Greek Passion
Řecké pašije
Opera in four acts, H. 372 (1h 45m)
Libretto by the composer and Nikos Kazantzakis, after Kazantzakis's novel *Christ Recrucified* (1948), translated into English by Jonathan Griffin
Composed 1956–7, rev. 1958 and 1959; invariably it is the 1959 revision that is performed
PREMIERES 9 June 1961, Opernhaus, Zurich; UK: 29 April 1981, New Theatre, Cardiff
CAST Manolios *t*, Katerina *s*, Grigoris *b-bar*, Fotis *b-bar*, Kostandis *bar*, Yannakos *t*, Lenio *s*, Panait *t*, 8 minor roles (3 *s*, *a*, 2 *t*, *bar*, *b*), Ladas *spoken role*; *satb* chorus of villagers and refugees; children's chorus
ORCHESTRATION 3 fl/picc, 3 ob/ca, 3 cl, 3 bsn, 4 hn, 3 tpt, 3 trbn, tuba, timp, perc, hp, pf, accordion, str; offstage: rec, cl, harmonica, vn, accordion, bells

By 1954 Martinů was looking for a libretto with a Czech subject. He was diverted, however, by his discovery of Nikos Kazantzakis's novel *Zorba the Greek*. Since *Zorba* was unsuitable as an opera, Martinů began to write a libretto on another Kazantzakis novel, *Christ Recrucified*, retitling it *The Greek Passion*. Though the basic musical text was complete by early in 1957 Martinů cut and revised it over the next two years. Despite the Greek setting, the musical language is close to the Czech cantatas of the composer's late years. The adaptation of the novel skilfully reduces the Turkish element of the original in order to focus on the drama of the village set against a band of refugees.

SYNOPSIS

Act I A Greek village, Lykovrissi, in the early 20th century. On Easter morning the priest, Grigoris, distributes parts for next year's Passion play. Katerina, a young widow, is chosen as Mary Magdalene, Manolios, a shepherd, as Christ, and Panait, Katerina's lover, as Judas. As the characters dwell on the significance of their roles night falls and a band of refugees, driven from their homes by Turks, arrives exhausted in the village. Grigoris, suspecting conflict and impoverishment for Lykovrissi orders them to leave. The act ends with Katerina offering help and Manolios suggesting that the refugees settle near by.

Act II   It becomes clear that Katerina is obsessed with Manolios. The miser Ladas persuades the pedlar Yannakos, who is to play the apostle Peter, to offer money for the valuables of the needy refugees. Witnessing the simple dignity and hope of the refugees, Yannokos is ashamed of his attempt to cheat them, and presents them instead with Ladas's money.

Act III   Manolios's and Katerina's relationship comes to a head when he persuades her that their love can be only spiritual. She learns to accept the fulfilment of the love of Mary Magdalene for Christ. Manolios, becoming still more Christ-like, persuades the villagers to help the refugees as the village elders plot to prevent him.

Act IV   As the villagers celebrate a wedding, Grigorios excommunicates Manolios and denounces him. After explaining his actions as the substitute of Christ, Manolios is killed by Panait as the refugees approach. Both parties mourn the death of Manolios and the refugees prepare to leave the village.

Although built as a series of tableaux, *The Greek Passion* has a powerful sense of dramatic continuity. The characters grow at the same pace as the Passion tragedy, leading to a *dénouement* of extraordinary power. Much of the force of the work in Acts I and IV is generated through the use of antiphonal choruses. The musical language is warmly diatonic, coloured both by the extensive use of Greek Orthodox chant and the gentle lyricism associated with many of the works of Martinů's last decade.

RECORDING   Field, Mitchinson, Davies, Tomlinson, Czech Philharmonic Ch, Kuhn Children's Ch, Brno State PO, Mackerras, Supraphon, 1981
EDITIONS   f.s., Universal, 1960; v.s., Universal, 1961

Ariadne

Ariane/Ariadna
Opera in one act, H. 370 (45m)
Libretto by the composer, after Georges Neveux's play, *Le voyage de Thésée* (1943)
Composed 1958
PREMIERE   2 March 1961, Stadtische Buhnen, Gelsenkirchen

In contrast to the neo-romantic warmth of *The Greek Passion* Martinů employed a neo-baroque formula of sinfonias and arias as the structural basis of this work. The large-scale coloratura aria for Ariadne in the third scene was inspired by the art of Maria Callas.

EDITIONS   f.s./v.s., Bärenreiter, 1960

Other operas: *Voják a tanečnice* (*The Soldier and the Dancer*), (1927), 1928; *Les larmes du couteau* (*Slzy nože*),

(1928), 1968; *Trois souhaits, ou Les vicissitudes de la vie* (*Trojí přání, aneb vrtkavosti života*), film opera, (1929), 1971; *La semaine de bonté* (inc.), 1931; *Hlas lesa* (*The Voice of the Forest*), radio opera, 1935; *Divadlo za branou* (*The Suburban Theatre*), 1936; *Dvakrát Alexandr* (*Alexander bis*), (1937), 1964; *What Men Live By* (*Čím lidé žijí*), television opera, (1952), 1953 (premiered in English); *The Marriage* (*Ženitba*), television opera, (1952), 1953 (premiered in English); *La plainte contre inconnu* (inc.), (1953); *Mirandolina*, (1954), 1959
BIBLIOGRAPHY   Brian Large, *Martinů*, Duckworth, 1975; Miloš Šafránek, trans. Roberta Finlayson-Samsour, *Bohuslav Martinů: His Life and Works*, Allan Wingate, 1962

J.A.S.

VICENTE MARTÍN Y SOLER

Vicente Martín y Soler [also known as 'il Valenziano', 'Martini lo Spagnuolo' (misleadingly), Vicente Martínez (wrongly)]; *b* 2 May 1754, Valencia, Spain; *d* 11 February 1806, St Petersburg

Remembered nowadays chiefly for Mozart's quotation in *Don Giovanni* of a tune from his opera *Una cosa rara* and allegedly for having invented the Viennese waltz, Martín quite outshone Mozart in popularity for several years as a composer of opera buffa in Vienna.

Early in his career, he gave up native forms of the zarzuela and turned to opera in the Italian manner, composing ten such works, mostly opere serie, between 1779 and 1785 with apparent success in Naples, Turin, Lucca, Venice and probably Florence and Parma. By 1786, the Emperor Joseph II brought Martín to Vienna in his quest to install distinguished foreign as well as national composers in his court. Lorenzo da Ponte, the librettist of the three opere buffe Martín wrote here, perceptively noted his knack for composing 'the sweetest melodies that go straight to the heart but which very few can match'.

By 1788, he had moved to St Petersburg, following Sarti and a long line of Italian composers, where he was rewarded in 1790 with a four-year commission in the court of Catherine II as composer–conductor of Italian and Russian operas and with other appointments such as that of singing teacher in the Imperial Theatre School. Though he fell somewhat out of favour later as the fashion for Italian opera began to wane, the esteem with which he was held may be gauged by his appointment in 1798 as Imperial Russian Privy Counsellor.

In 1794–5, he visited London, probably by invitation, given the popularity excerpts from *Una cosa rara* and his two other Viennese opere buffe had come to enjoy there, producing three new works again with libretti by Da Ponte. By 1796, he was back in St Petersburg and, apart from an appointment as inspector of the Italian court theatre in 1800, he spent most of the later years of his life there, apparently as much from choice as from necessity.

Martín's decision to abandon Spain at the age of 25, like that of Terradellas before him, may be seen as an eloquent comment on the trivializing within Spain of a general debate about nationalism in European countries throughout the 18th century (and beyond) and the consequent discouragement – on both artistic and financial grounds – felt by its most talented opera composers. No other Spanish opera composer achieved greater fame than Martín did in his day: his success in Italy, Vienna, Russia and England is unquestionable, while even in Spain itself performance of his works in the Teatro de los Caños del Peral, Madrid, in the 1780s alongside those of revered foreigners such as Corradini, shows how highly this expatriate came to be regarded.

Da Ponte's praise of Martín's knack for catchy tunes was surely well founded; the variety and aptness with which he matched text and character types to music has been justifiably defended by Roy Jesson; and the accusation that he was over-fond of dance rhythms ignores the underlying folklike quality – supra-national rather than just Spanish – that adds spice to his modish style. No doubt this concern to incorporate the rhythms of popular music explains also both his interest in fostering the Viennese waltz and his success in doing so.

Various interpretations have been put forward to explain Mozart's quotations from Martín, Sarti and finally himself at the end of Act II of *Don Giovanni*: was Mozart expressing envy, disdain, sarcasm, a subtle, threefold juxtaposition of Don Juans . . . ? The pertinent facts about the Martín quotation are these: the tune ('O quanto un si bel giubilo') is sung (first) by the queen in *Un cosa rara* to celebrate a double village wedding, a scene in which rejoicing takes precedence over donjuanism. Sarti's is 'Come un agnello' from *Fra i due litiganti* and Mozart's own is the march 'Non più andrai' from *Figaro*. All three were well known in Vienna at the time, a fact that Leporello's comments make quite clear. There seems to be no need to suppose that Mozart was concerned to do more than create an enjoyable background of modish, light music in comic vein (not least as regards his own) as an ironic prelude to the tragically serious turn of events about to unfold.

Una cosa rara, o sia bellezza ed onestá

A Rare Thing, or Beautiful and Virtuous
Opera buffa in two acts (2h 30m)
Libretto by Lorenzo da Ponte, after the play *La luna de la sierra* by Luis Vélez de Guevara (1652)
Composed 1785 or 1786
PREMIERES 17 November 1786, Burgtheater, Vienna; UK: 10 January 1789, London; US: 1987, Vineyard Opera, New York

Da Ponte's libretto neatly simplifies Guevara's original plot, bringing out the staunch yet down-to-earth virtue of the village girl Lilla, vindicated by the Queen in the face of the lustful attentions of the village mayor, Podesta, as well as the Infante of Spain and his retinue. Martín responded with nicely characterized and discreetly contrasting music for the lovers, Lilla and Lubino, the villagers, the courtiers and huntsmen. Apart from the famous waltz tune, catchy dance rhythms and tunes that linger in the memory abound. It is easy to see why, for instance, the Act II duet, 'Pace mio caro sposo', was

The cover of the German piano score, published in 1790, of Una cosa rara

apparently encored at the Vienna premiere against the encoring ban of the Emperor. For all the music's charm, there is an underlying seriousness, even earthiness, not least in the way the folklike affiliations are set against the waywardness of the nobles and the sophisticated good sense of the queen.

Martín's most famous opera will presumably never again be as triumphantly successful as it was all over Europe up to the 1830s but it certainly deserves more than the mere notoriety it had won from Mozart's passing quotation from it.

RECORDING   Peters, Figueras, Palacio, Belaza-Leoz, La Capella Reial de Catalunya, Le Concert des Nations, Savall, Atrée, 1991
EDITIONS   f.s., G. Allroggen (ed.), Henle, 1990; Roy Jesson (ed.), performing edn (in English), Opera 61 (London), 1968

L'arbore di Diana

Diana's Arbour
Opera buffa in two acts
Libretto by Lorenzo da Ponte
PREMIERES 1 October 1787, Burgtheater, Vienna; UK: 1797, London

Martín's second Viennese opera is commonly supposed to have been proposed by Da Ponte as a sly parallel between the subversion of Diana's temple by Endymion in the opera and the dissolution of the convents by the emperor but this is probably a simplistic view of Da Ponte's cultured treatment of the post-Renaissance theme of the humbling of Diana as a symbol of inhuman, unloving chastity. The plot is initiated by Amore, in transvestic disguise as an attractive girl, who bribes Doristo, the buffo guardian of Diana's temple of chastity, in order to get Endymion and Silvius into the temple and the company of Diana and her band of nymphs. The nymphs' vows of chastity are exposed as fragile, as is Diana herself when Amore, now in the role of a guiding spirit, reveals Endymion, sleeping nude, to her. Diana's capitulation to true love is symbolized by Amore's transforming her life of abnegation and hunting into a kingdom of love.

Roy Jesson has convincingly analysed Martín's score and the effective way he differentiates the characters with consistent musical styles as well as the expressive way he characterizes Diana's changing outlook as she develops in the opera. Her aria at the end of Act I has been compared with 'Come scoglio' in Mozart's *Così fan tutte*, a comparison that gains strength from the possibility that the Diana in the 1788 Vienna performance was Adriana Ferraresi del Bene (known as La Ferrarese and reputedly Da Ponte's mistress) who was also the first Fiordiligi.

EDITION   Roy Jesson (ed.), performing edn in English (unpublished), Opera 61 (London), 1972

Other operatic works: *La madrileña o Tutor burlado* (zarzuela), ?1776; *Ifigenia in Aulide*, 1779; *Ipermestra*, 1780; *Andromaca*, 1780; *Astartea*, ?1781; *Partenope*, 1782; *L'amor geloso*, 1782; *In amor ci vuol destrezza, o sia L'accorta cameriera, c.* 1782; *Vologeso*, 1783; *Le burle per amore*, 1784; *La vedova spiritosa*, 1785; *Il burbero di buon cuore*, 1786; *Gli sposi in contrasto*, or *La capricciosa corretta*, or *La scuola dei maritati*, ?1788; *Gore-bogatyr Kosometovich* (*Hapless, Herculean Kosometovich*), 1789; *Melomania ovvero L'amore per il canto*, 1790; *Il castello d'Atlante*, 1791; *L'isola del piacere*, 1795; *Le nozze dei contadini spagnuoli*, 1795; *La festa del villaggio*, 1798
BIBLIOGRAPHY   Roy Jesson, 'Una cosa rara', *MT*, vol. 109 (1968), p. 619; Roy Jesson, 'Martín y Soler's *L'arbore di Diana*', *MT*, vol. 113 (1972), p. 551; Antonio Martín Moreno, *Historia de la música española*, vol. 4: *Siglo XVIII*, Alianza, 1985

J.W.S.

PIETRO MASCAGNI

b 7 December 1863, Livorno, Italy; *d* 2 August 1945, Rome

Although younger than his contemporaries Puccini and Leoncavallo, Mascagni was the first to taste triumph, and fame came to him in an unlikely way. Against family opposition (his father wanted him to continue the family bakery business), he was determined to follow a musical career, and at the age of 19 was admitted to the Milan Conservatory to study composition, where his teachers included Ponchielli. Dismissed during his second year for failure to complete assignments, he supported himself by playing the double-bass at the Teatro Dal Verme in Milan (where he played in the premiere of Puccini's *Le villi*) and conducting opera at Cremona. Unable to interest a publisher in his attempts at writing for the stage, he settled down in Cerignola (Puglia) to give music lessons. In 1889 he saw an advertisement for Sonzogno's second competition for one-act operas. He was fired with enthusiasm and quickly wrote *Cavalleria rusticana*. Once it was completed, however, he was besieged with doubts and had all but decided to submit Act IV of his *Guglielmo Ratcliff* instead. But unbeknown to him, his wife dispatched the score of *Cavalleria rusticana* and it was awarded the first prize.

Together with the other two winning works,

Cavalleria rusticana was performed at the Teatro Costanzi in Rome in May 1890. Mascagni was fortunate to have in the cast two of the most popular singers in Italy: the tenor Stagno and his fiery wife Gemma Bellincioni. *Cavalleria* scored an immediate success, and amazingly soon it was heard in theatres all over the world.

Cartoon of Mascagni conducting Cavalleria rusticana *(Vanity Fair, 1893)*

Mascagni was instantly famous and was soon acknowledged the harbinger of the group that came to be known as the *veristi* or 'The Young Italian School' (among its leaders would be Leoncavallo, Puccini, Giordano and Cilea). Predictably, anticipation was great for his next work, but instead of trying to emulate *Cavalleria*, he brought out a naïve idyll set in Alsace, *L'amico Fritz* (1891). In no way an outright failure, this work puzzled and disappointed those who expected Mascagni to exploit the vein of *Cavalleria*.

A string of operas followed over the next decade, ranging in subject from a maritime drama (*Silvano*) to the Japanese *Iris*. But a repeat of the success of *Cavalleria* eluded him and, restlessly seeking to prove himself as something more than a one-opera composer and to avoid the generally unfavourable attitude of Italian critics, Mascagni decided to give the premieres of his next two operas outside his native country. *Amica*, to a French text by de Choudens, was premiered at Monte Carlo in 1905, but failed to sustain itself. Better fortune greeted *Isabeau* (Buenos Aires, 1911), a sensational variant of the Godiva story, although its success, too, was short-lived. With *Parisina* (1913) Mascagni attempted another premiere in Italy but, yet again, neither this long-winded score nor that of the sentimental *Lodoletta* (1917) exerted much appeal. The closest Mascagni came to a major success in the later part of his career was *Il piccolo Marat*, based on a French Revolutionary subject, though the opera still failed to enter the repertoire.

In 1929, however, Mascagni's opportunistic nature was confirmed when he succeeded Toscanini as musical director of La Scala, as he had no scruples against beginning performances with the fascist hymn. In 1932 he reworked the score of an early cantata and brought out *Pinotta* in the unlikely precincts of the San Remo Casino. His last opera, *Nerone*, was introduced at La Scala in 1935 with much preliminary hullabaloo. After the obligatory first round of productions on Italian stages, it started to gather dust which has scarcely been disturbed since. At Venice, Rome and Milan in 1940, on the occasion of the 50th anniversary of *Cavalleria*, Mascagni conducted his chief claim to fame, filling out the evening with excerpts from its less fortunate sisters. Mascagni did not long survive the collapse of fascism, dying in an obscure Roman hotel.

It is all too easy to dismiss Mascagni as a self-promoting opportunist and a composer of limited achievements. But there is not a score of his that is without some arresting moments, although his creative impetus was short-breathed and lacked continuity. He too readily mistook emotion for the expression of deep feeling. Yet his experiments in setting text and his choice of subjects reveal his responsiveness to the temper of his times. *Cavalleria* will remain his monument, a symbol of his accomplishment as well as his limitations.

Cavalleria rusticana

Rustic Chivalry

Melodrama in one act (1h 15m)
Libretto by Giovanni Targioni-Tozzetti and Guido Menasci, after the play by Giovanni Verga (1883)
Composed 1889
PREMIERES 17 May 1890, Teatro Costanzi, Rome; US: 9 September 1891, Grand Opera House, Philadelphia; UK: 19 October 1891, Shaftesbury Theatre, London
CAST Santuzza *s* or *ms*, Lola *ms*, Mamma Lucia *a*, Turiddu *t*, Alfio *bar*; *satb* chorus of villagers
ORCHESTRATION 2 picc, 2 fl, 2 ob, 2 cl, 2 bsn, 4 hn, 2 tpt, 3 trbn, b trbn, timp, perc, organ, hp, str; offstage: bells, organ, hp

The rapidity with which *Cavalleria rusticana* spread throughout the world has been unmatched by any other opera. Within the space of little more than a year it had promulgated operatic *verismo* and soon spawned a host of imitations, of which only Leoncavallo's *I pagliacci* firmly established itself in the repertoire, supplying the other member of the most performed double-bill of modern times. The idea of writing an opera on Verga's dramatization of his novella was Mascagni's, and he persuaded two of his friends to provide him with the libretto. In terms of influence, the opera's chief significance lies in the fact that it presents ordinary people in credible situations and thus seems to tell a story sufficiently realistic and simple to be true to life.

SYNOPSIS
Some time before Turiddu went off to serve in the army, he had had an affair with Lola. While he was away, Lola married the carter Alfio. On his return Turiddu seduced Santuzza, who is now pregnant by him and has been excommunicated because of her condition. She loves him sincerely, but to her chagrin Lola could not endure seeing him with another and has resumed her affair with the inconstant Turiddu.

Easter morning in a village in Sicily. Before the curtain rises, Turiddu is heard singing a siciliana ('O, Lola') to his mistress (this forms the final part of the opera's prelude). The villagers comment on the season ('Gli aranci alezzano'). Alfio enters ('Il cavallo scalpita') and soon asks Turiddu's mother Lucia about her son's whereabouts. Lucia says he has gone to Francofonte to fetch some wine for the family inn. When Alfio says he has seen Turiddu near his house, Santuzza hurriedly tells Lucia to keep silent. Further conversation is halted by the Easter Hymn ('Inneggiamo il Signore; non è morto'). When all but Santuzza and Lucia have entered the church, the young woman pours out her heart to Lucia, telling her how Lola has stolen Turiddu and left her desperate. Lucia goes into the church, leaving Santuzza to wait for Turiddu. He soon appears and she implores him to come back to her, informing him that he has been seen at dawn near Lola's house ('Tu qui, Santuzza?'). Turiddu accuses her of jealousy, but then they are interrupted by Lola on her way to church ('Fior di giaggiolo'). After an exchange of barbed remarks between the women, Lola goes to attend the service. Ever more desperately, Santuzza begs him to return her love, but he rejects her forcibly, throwing her down and running into the church. Now blinded by jealous fury, she sees Alfio and pours out her story of Lola's infidelity ('Oh! Il Signor vi manda, compar Alfio'), while Alfio vows vengeance. After the intermezzo, the congregation throngs out and Turiddu urges them to have a post-ecclesiastical tipple ('Viva il vino spumeggiante'). When Alfio appears, Turiddu offers him a glass of wine, but Alfio refuses, saying it would turn to poison inside him. The villagers draw Lola away. Alfio, in the way of the traditional challenge, bites Turiddu's earlobe. Before they go off to duel behind the church, Turiddu takes leave of his mother, asking that she look out for Santuzza ('Mamma, quel vino è generoso'). The women gather in the piazza, and suddenly a female voice is heard screaming that Turiddu has been killed. Santuzza and Lucia faint.

A contemporary illustration of the last scene of Cavalleria rusticana *(Rome, 1890)*

This concise, passionate tale of Sicilian peasants, ironically occurring on Easter Sunday, elicited from Mascagni crude but effective music that seemed the inevitable mode of expression for his characters. The score, except for Turridu's serenade in the prologue, begins conventionally enough with an opening chorus and a 'characteristic' song for Alfio, soon followed by the Gounod-esque Easter Hymn. It is only with Santuzza's arioso, 'Voi lo sapete, o mamma', that the dramatic temperature begins to rise, reaching a climax with the Santuzza–Alfio duet. The tragic outcome is assured at this point, but then comes the contrast of the serene intermezzo played to an empty stage. This calm before the inevitable storm serves, oddly enough, only to increase the tension.

RECORDINGS 1. Rasa, Gigli, Bechi, La Scala Ch and O, Mascagni, HMV, 1940: authoritative, but one wonders whether the slow tempi represent a choice or indicate the composer's advanced age; 2. Callas, Di Stefano, Panerai, La Scala Ch and O, Serafin, EMI, 1953: still the most earthy, exciting performance, but a dated recording; 3. Tebaldi, Björling, Bastianini, Ch and O of Maggio Musicale Fiorentino, Erede, Decca, 1958; 4. Scotto, Domingo, Elvira, Ambrosian Opera Ch, National PO, Levine, RCA, 1978: strongly sung, vivid performance; 5. Varady, Pavarotti,

Cappuccilli, London Voices, National PO, Gavazzeni, Decca, 1978: most convincingly recorded and eloquently sung [A.B.]
VIDEO Obraztsova, Domingo, Bruson, Ch and O of La Scala, Prêtre, Philips, 1986
EDITIONS f.s., Sonzogno, 1890; v.ss., Sonzogno, 1891; Broude, 1950

L'amico Fritz
Friend Fritz
Commedia lirica in three acts (1h 30m)
Libretto by Nicola Diaspuro, based on the novel *L'ami Fritz* by Emile Erckmann and Alexandre Chatrian (1864)
Composed 1890–91
PREMIERES 31 October 1891, Teatro Costanzi, Rome; UK: 23 May 1892, Covent Garden, London; US: 8 June 1892, Grand Opera House, Philadelphia

Mascagni's publisher Sonzogno was, understandably, keen that Mascagni should present another opera while the success of *Cavalleria* was still at its height. Aware that some critics were attributing its success solely to its libretto, Mascagni stated that he wanted 'a simple libretto, with almost a flimsy plot, so the opera could be judged on the music alone'. Sonzogno suggested Erckmann's and Chatrian's play (adapted from the same authors' novel).

Set in Alsace, the plot concerns a wealthy

landowner, Fritz Kobus, a bachelor. His friend Rabbi David ignores his protests against marriage, assuring him he will soon wed. When David offers to wager, Fritz offers his vineyard at Clairfontaine. The young daughter of one of his tenants, Suzel, brings him a bouquet. Later, she comes to gather cherries, and Fritz is charmed by her unspoiled innocence. Fritz is unable to come to terms with his new emotions and decides to move to town. Later he returns, realizing that he is in love. In his absence, Suzel's father wants her to marry another, but she must get Fritz's permission to do so. Fritz gradually acknowledges his attachment to her, feelings she readily reciprocates. Rabbi David wins his bet and gives the vineyard to Suzel as a wedding gift.

Although Mascagni was happy with his text, others were less impressed: Verdi considered it 'the worst libretto I've ever seen'. However, the opera's public reception, though nowhere near the level of *Cavalleria*'s, was not unenthusiastic. As in *Cavalleria* the opera's strength lies in Mascagni's skill as a melodist, most famously demonstrated here in the so-called 'cherry duet' ('Suzel, buon dì') for Fritz and Suzel. Progressing from *parlando* to arioso before arriving at the duet 'proper', the scene also displays a flexibility of formal structures and a continuity which advance considerably on that of *Cavalleria* and which were to influence other composers.

RECORDINGS   1. Tassinari, Pini, Tagliavini, Meletti, Ch and O of RAI, Mascagni, Cetra, 1942; 2. Freni, Didier Gambardella, Pavarotti, Sardinero, Ch and O of Royal Opera, Covent Garden, Gavazzeni, HMV, 1967
EDITIONS   f.s., Sonzogno, 1891; v.ss., Sonzogno, 1891; Schirmer, 1891

Guglielmo Ratcliff
William Ratcliff
Tragedia in four acts (2h 15m)
Libretto by Andrea Maffei, his translation of Heinrich Heine's *William Ratcliff* (1822)
Composed 1882–94
PREMIERE   16 February 1895, La Scala, Milan

This dark tragedy was the second opera Mascagni composed, but the fourth to be performed. All his life he claimed it as his favourite among his scores. He had seen Heine's play, in Maffei's translation, in Milan in 1882 and was immediately struck by it. Instead of commissioning a libretto, he used Maffei's text, cutting only a hundred lines from it. This direct setting of a play, rather than a libretto, came to be known as literaturoper, and *Guglielmo Ratcliff* is the earliest known Italian example.

Maria, the daughter of the MacGregor clan, is about to marry Douglas. He arrives telling of a hairbreadth escape from highwaymen. The student Ratcliff is suspected: he was rejected by Maria and since then, two of her other suitors have been murdered at Black Rock. At an inn, Ratcliff relates his story: his mad love for Maria and his hatred for any other man who might have her. He confesses he is haunted by a pair of ghosts and, imagining he sees them, he becomes delirious. At Black Rock, Ratcliff

and Douglas fight a duel; Ratcliff loses but Douglas spares his life. At MacGregor's castle, preparations are underway for the wedding. The wounded Ratcliff suddenly appears and, maddened by his ghosts, stabs Maria, her father, and lastly himself. When Douglas arrives Maria's nurse shows him the three corpses.

Musically, *Guglielmo Ratcliff* is interesting as pre-*Cavalleria* Mascagni. The score contains few of those restless modulations and surprising harmonic shifts that the post-*Cavalleria* Mascagni employed to add interest. There is a vein of straightforward lyricism, at its most intense in the final duet for Maria and Guglielmo, but also numerous stretches where the composer lacked the resources to cope interestingly with Maffei's stream of 11-syllable lines.

RECORDING   Mattioli, Truccato Pace, Ferraro, Ciminelli, Mazzoli, Rome Ch and SO of RAI, La Rosa Parodi, RAI, Nuova Era (live), 1963
EDITION   v.s., Sonzogno, 1895

Iris
Melodrama in three acts (2h 45m)
Libretto by Luigi Illica
Composed 1897–8
PREMIERES   22 November 1898, Costanzi, Rome; US: 14 October 1902, Academy of Music, Philadelphia; UK: 8 July 1919, Covent Garden, London

Osaka, a rich young libertine, abducts the poor Iris, a laundry-girl, and sets her up in a bordello. But he fails to make her yield to his advances. The bordello owner, meanwhile, advertises her publicly on a balcony, where her father sees her and throws muck at her, whereupon Iris throws herself into a sewer.

Illica's libretto, an uneasy mixture of exoticism and crude *verismo* suggestiveness, contains elaborate directions to stress the symbolism of his plot. Mascagni's resourceful score contains effective moments such as Osaka's Act I serenade and Iris's various solos, but the opera attains true eloquence only in the resonant 'Hymn to the Sun' that begins and ends it. An unusual feature for an Italian opera of 1898 is the prelude to the last act written on a whole-tone scale.

RECORDING   Tokody, Domingo, Pons, Giaiotti, Bavarian Radio Ch, Munich Radio O, Patané, CBS, 1988
EDITIONS   f.s., Ricordi, 1911; *rp*, 1925; v.s., Ricordi, 1898

Le maschere
The Maskers
Commedia lirica e giocosa in prologue and three acts (3h)
Libretto by Luigi Illica
Composed 1899–1900, rev. 1905 and 1931
PREMIERES   17 January 1901 (six simultaneous): La Scala, Milan; Teatro Costanzi, Rome; La Fenice, Venice; Teatro Regio, Turin; Carlo Felice, Genoa; Filarmonico, Verona; a seventh, at the San Carlo, Naples, was delayed two days; first rev. version: 28 November 1905, Adriano, Rome; second rev. version: 8 March 1931, La Scala, Milan

Wanting to write a 'quintessentially Italian opera', Mascagni and Illica turned to the traditional figures of the *commedia dell'arte* maskers. Rosaura, the daughter of Pantalone, loves Florindo, but her father is determined to make her marry the braggart Captain Spaventa. The course of true love is aided by Rosaura's maid Colombina, her love, the vendor Brighella, and the stuttering servant Tartaglia. Various tricks are played before Rosaura and Florindo finally receive Pantalone's blessing.

Illica's use of chorus as commentary, even including political satire, fails to give the work freshness and spontaneity. Mascagni's score is deliberately old-fashioned, dubiously eclectic and heavy-footed. The revision of 1905 involved cutting the prologue and changing the Act III finale. In 1931 these were restored but other cuts from 1905 retained. (In 1916 the work was given as an operetta with spoken dialogue, but Mascagni had no part in this.)

RECORDING Broggini, Rizzieri, Ferrari, Poli, Cassinelli, Ch and O of Trieste Opera, Bartoletti, MRF, 1961
EDITION v.s., Sonzogno, 1901

Isabeau

Leggenda drammatica in three acts (2h)
Libretto by Luigi Illica
Composed 1908–10
PREMIERES 2 June 1911, Teatro Colón, Buenos Aires; Italy: 20 January 1912, La Scala, Milan, and La Fenice, Venice; US: 12 November 1917, Auditorium, Chicago

Looking back to a different tradition from that of *Le maschere*, Mascagni's aim in *Isabeau* was to 'attempt to return to that romanticism which inspired so much Italian opera'. This evocation of medieval courtly chivalry was, the composer acknowledged in his autobiography, a far cry from the tone of *Cavalleria* which had brought him such success: 'I began with *verismo*. But *verismo* kills music. It is in poetry, in romanticism, that inspiration may spread its wings.'

Isabeau, only daughter of King Raimondo, is offered in marriage to the victor of a tournament, but she refuses the winner, Faidit (actually Raimond's banished nephew). For this disobedience, Raimondo orders her to ride naked through the town. Folco, a falconer, unaware of the king's decree, alone observes her with rapture; for this he is condemned to death. Isabeau is moved through pity to love, and as Folco is led away to his fate, she stabs herself.

Illica's libretto, inspired by the legend of Lady Godiva, is full of high-flown rhetoric, and Mascagni responds to it with trite bombast. The opera was popular until the 1940s, thanks largely to Bernardo De Muro who performed the high tenor part of Folco regularly until his farewell performance in 1938. It is now seldom revived.

RECORDING Pobbe, Ferraro, Carroli, Ch and O of San Carlo, Rapalo, MRF, 1972
EDITION v.s., Sonzogno, 1910

Parisina

Tragedia lirica in four acts (3h 30m)
Libretto by Gabriele D'Annunzio, (to some extent) after Byron's epic (1816)
Composed 1912–13; reduced to three acts after the premiere

PREMIERES 15 December 1913, La Scala, Milan

D'Annunzio's text (the only specifically designated opera libretto he wrote) was offered first to Puccini and then to Franchetti before Mascagni agreed to set it. He, too, had doubts about accepting the project, fearing that the libretto's literary quality and the reputation of the author would subsume his own contribution.

The plot differs from Romani's text for Donizetti's *Parisina*, for here the emphasis is more on the lovers, Parisina and Ugo, than on the jealousy of the Ferrarese duke. After rescuing his stepmother, Parisina, from the hands of pirates, Ugo (the son of Niccolò d'Este from a previous affair) declares his love for her. Eventually Niccolò learns of their relationship and sentences his unfaithful wife and son to death.

The work is long because D'Annunzio opposed cuts in his elaborate verse text, although Mascagni shortened the original 1400 lines by some 330. The final act, performed at the premiere but then discarded, consisted of a posthumous encounter between the spirits of Parisina and Ugo, which only the poet regarded as indispensable. Mascagni's score is innocent of motivic ideas that might lend it coherence; instead it is for the most part little more than highly charged musical declamation.

RECORDING Renzi, Parutto, Molese, Di Bella, Mazzoli, Milan Ch and O of RAI, Urbini, MRF, 1976
EDITION v.s., Sonzogno, 1914

Lodoletta

Dramma lirico in three acts (2h)
Libretto by Giovacchino Forzano, after Ouida's tale *Two Little Wooden Shoes* (1874)
Composed 1916–17
PREMIERES 30 April 1917, Teatro Costanzi, Rome; US: 12 January 1918, Metropolitan, New York

Lodoletta ('little lark') is a flower-seller living in a small Dutch village. A stranger arrives, Flammen, a Parisian painter who has been exiled for insulting the emperor. He falls in love with Lodoletta and, when he is allowed to return to Paris, decides to leave before he corrupts the girl. But she follows him on foot, only to die of cold on arrival.

This sentimental subject, another rejected by Puccini, evoked a trivial response in Mascagni. The children's choruses and the waltzes (Act III) have a vulgar predictability. Two arias, Lodoletta's 'Flammen, perdonami' (Act III) and Flammen's 'Ah, ritrovarla' (Act III), are touchstones of late-Mascagni sentimentality.

RECORDING Tavolaccini, Campora, Fioravanti, Milan Ch and O of RAI, Paoletti, GAO, 1957
EDITION v.s., Sonzogno, 1917

Il piccolo Marat

Little Marat
Dramma lirico in three acts (2h)
Libretto by Giovacchino Forzano and Giovanni Targioni-Tozzetti, after Victor Martin's novel *Sous le Terreur* (1906)

Composed 1919
PREMIERE   2 May 1921, Teatro Costanzi, Rome

After the avowed melodiousness of *Lodoletta*, *Il piccolo Marat* marked another shift in Mascagni's operatic intentions: 'Do not look for melody or learning . . . there is only blood.' The result is, not surprisingly, a *verismo* work set – like Giordano's *Andrea Chenier* – against the background of the French Revolution. A sentimental relationship is juxtaposed with the dangers of the Reign of Terror. The Prince de Fleury disguises himself as a revolutionary ('the little Marat') in order to rescue his imprisoned mother from the guillotine. He finds a kindred spirit in Mariella, the niece of the ruthless President of the Committee, and falls in love with her. Together they save his mother and escape.

At first this opera was the greatest success of Mascagni's post-*Cavalleria* period, but it has failed to sustain its original promise. The tenor role of *Il piccolo Marat* has a daunting tessitura. A large-scale work, with vigorous choruses and an attractive love duet in Act II, it contains a discouraging number of pages of mingled rhetoric and sentimentality.

RECORDING   Zeani, Gismondo, Poli, Rossi-Lemeni, Ch and O of San Remo, Ziino, Cetra, *c.* 1960
EDITIONS   f.s., Sonzogno, 1921; v.s., Sonzogno, 1921; *rp*, 1963

Other operas: *Pinotta* (adapted from the cantata *In filanda*), (*c.* 1880), 1932 (RECORDING UORCI Rantzau, 1892; *Silvano*, 1895 (RECORDING Nuova Era, 1973); *Zanetto*, 1896 (RECORDINGS MRF, 1970; Bongiovanni, 1986); *Amica*, 1905; *Nerone*, 1935 (RECORDING Bongiovanni, 1986) Operetta: *Sì*, 1919 (RECORDING Bongiovanni, 1987)
BIBLIOGRAPHY   J. Maehder, 'The Origins of Italian *Literaturoper*', in Arthur Groos and Roger Parker (eds), *Reading Opera*, Princeton University Press, 1988; David Stivender (ed. and trans.), *The Autobiography of Pietro Mascagni*, Kahn and Averill, 1975

W.A.

VICTOR MASSÉ

Felix Marie Massé; *b* 7 March 1822, Lorient, Morbihan, France; *d* 5 July 1884, Paris

A pupil of Halévy at the Paris Conservatoire, and winner of the Prix de Rome in 1844, Massé is remembered chiefly today for a single work, the likeable if somewhat pallid one-act operetta *Les noces de Jeannette*. Students of Wagner also come across him as the chorus master at the Opéra at the time of the Paris production of *Tannhäuser* in 1861.

Massé composed a string of comic operas characterized by a vein of facile melody in the manner (though without the brilliance) of Auber, whose chair he inherited at the Institut de France in 1872. Most of these works enjoyed temporary success followed by oblivion. But there is something peculiarly French about the fact that this fluent composer of what amounted to commercial stage works was also (from 1866) professor of composition

at the Conservatoire. Massé's later works are more in keeping with the dignity of that post. *Paul et Virginie* is an opéra comique in the serious tradition of *Carmen*. But Massé seems not to have been at his best in melodrama, and the consensus of opinion about this work and its successor, *Une nuit de Cléopâtre*, is that they aimed beyond their composer's modest talents.

Operatic works: *La favorita e la schiava*, (*c.* 1845), 1855; *La chambre gothique*, 1849; *La chanteuse voilée*, 1850; *Galathée*, 1852; *Les noces de Jeannette*, 1853 (RECORDINGS Pathé, 1950s; RCA, 1960s); *La fiancée du diable*, 1854; *Miss Fauvette*, 1855; *Les saisons*, 1855; *Le prix de famille*, (1855); *La Reine Topaze*, 1856; *Le cousin de Marivaux*, 1857; *Les chaises à porteurs*, 1858; *La fée Carabosse*, 1859; *Mariette la promise*, 1862; *La mule de Pedro*, 1863; *Fior d'Aliza*, 1866; *Le fils du brigadier*, 1867; *Les enfants de Perrette*, (1872); *La petite soeur d'Achille*, (1873); *La trouvaille*, (?1873); *Paul et Virginie*, 1876; *Une loi somptuaire*, (1879); *Une nuit de Cléopâtre*, 1885
BIBLIOGRAPHY   Guy Ropartz, *Victor Massé*, Sagot, 1887

S.W.

JULES MASSENET

Jules-Emile-Frédéric Massenet; *b* 12 May 1842, Montaud, nr St Etienne, France; *d* 13 August 1912, Paris

Massenet was one of the most successful of all French opera composers, for although his work never equalled the grandeur of Berlioz's *Les troyens*, the genius of Bizet's *Carmen*, or the profundity of Debussy's *Pelléas et Mélisande*, he provided the French operatic stage between 1867 and his death in 1912 with a series of remarkable works of great variety and invention. Two of them, *Manon* and *Werther*, are masterpieces that will always grace the repertoire, and a considerable number of others offer rewarding operatic experience in terms of vocal and orchestral technique, scenic invention, comedy, pathos, sentiment, local colour, and so on. He was a thoroughly professional composer who perfected his craft at an early age and enjoyed the fruits of success. His works fell victim, for the most part, to the very different tastes of the post-1918 generation and some have not been revived. But he embodies many enduring aspects of the *belle époque*, one of the richest cultural eras of history.

Massenet was trained at the Paris Conservatoire and he won the Prix de Rome in 1863. He was influenced by Meyerbeer, Berlioz, Gounod, and his teacher, Thomas. He was a timpanist at the Opéra for a spell, learning the craft of orchestration from the experience. His grounding in opera came less from his first two operas (both opéras comiques), *La grand' tante* (1867) and *Don César de Bazan* (1872), than from the 'sacred dramas' *Marie-Magdeleine* (1873) and *Eve* (1875), in which human passion is set against a background of religious fervour, a dramatic contrast that was to inform some of his most successful operas, notably *Hérodiade*, *Thaïs* and *Le jongleur de Notre-Dame*. In the field of grand opera with epic scenic effects and abundant local colour, he maintained a long French tradition, although none of the operas of that type (*Le roi de Lahore*, *Hérodiade*, *Le Cid*, *Le mage*, *Ariane*) was able to equal his intimate tragedies (*Manon*, *Werther*), his veristic dramas (*La navarraise*, *Thérèse*), or his comedies (*Cendrillon*, *Don Quichotte*). The variety of his work is indeed astonishing since there is no ready category for a magical opera such as *Esclarmonde*, nor for the unusual blend of sex and religion found in *Thaïs*, nor for the monastic mystery *Le jongleur de Notre-Dame*.

Massenet was strictly regular in his working habits, a characteristic of many highly fertile composers, and he usually composed with great speed, keeping revision to a minimum. He would sometimes have a vocal score printed before a work went into rehearsal. His full scores are mostly annotated with great precision concerning dates and locations. He worked with a variety of librettists, although the obliging Henri Cain was a regular partner. He liked to find unusual settings for his operas, ranging from Classical mythology to the contemporary, and his fondness for the 18th century is manifest. He relished providing special music, such as ballets or set-piece songs within the drama, or 'symphonies' to suggest dramatic action. He had a rare understanding of the human voice and worked enthusiastically for certain singers, usually sopranos with whom gossip was wont to link his name. For Sybil Sanderson, for instance, he felt a particular tenderness and wrote some remarkable roles, notably Esclarmonde and Thaïs; for Georgette Wallace (whose stage name was Lucy Arbell) he similarly composed with great sympathy; her chief roles were Ariane, Thérèse, and Dulcinée. He always notated vocal parts with extreme precision, a practice he may have learned from studying Verdi's scores.

His affection for his leading ladies has led many to suppose that Massenet depicted only his female characters with real understanding, but this notion is easily refuted. The role of Athanaël in *Thaïs* is hard to project convincingly, but there is no mistaking the depth of Des Grieux's agony in *Manon*, or of Werther's, or of Jean's in *Sapho*. *Le jongleur de Notre-Dame* offers a rich variety of male types, and both Don Quichotte and Sancho Panza evoke the audience's sympathy with a few deft strokes.

Massenet's fondness for religious scenes was derived not from faith but simply from an acute sense of the dramatic in religious ritual and devotions, a striking feature of Catholicism. He loved the 18th-century style, using Handelian mannerisms freely, often for minor characters of the buffo type. He could equally call on medieval pastiche when required. He liked to evoke the world of magic in the manner of Rimsky-Korsakov, or the world of children, as he does in both *Werther* and *Cendrillon*. He could slip easily from tragedy to sentiment to high comedy. His sense of theatrical timing is hard to fault, an operatic instinct he shared with Verdi and Puccini. His structural skill is best observed in the way single scenes are constructed, using tonality and motifs – both vocal and orchestral – to build movements of rounded musical shape and appropriate dramatic pace.

While he aroused the envy of other composers who lacked his success (Saint-Saëns) or his fertility (Debussy), Massenet enjoyed popular acclaim in France and abroad. As a teacher he had a considerable influence on the younger generation, especially on Bruneau, Charpentier and Schmitt, all of them sharply individual in their approach to opera. His best work was written in the last two decades of the 19th century, and although some of his later operas maintained this high level, the lack of any modernity began to disappoint audiences seduced by the shock of Richard Strauss, Dukas and Florent Schmitt, or by the mysterious murmurings of Debussy. His main works survived in the repertoire, though, and will always continue to do so as long as great singing and high operatic craft are held in esteem.

Don César de Bazan

Opéra comique in three acts (four tableaux)
Libretto by Adolphe Philippe d'Ennery and Jules Chantepie, after the play by d'Ennery and Philippe Françoise Pinel Dumanoir (1844)
Composed 1872
PREMIERE 30 November 1872, Opéra-Comique, Paris

The subject, the same as that of Vincent Wallace's *Maritana*, is derived from characters in Victor Hugo's play *Ruy Blas* (1838). Though not a lasting success, *Don César de Bazan* established Massenet's reputation as a composer for the theatre and gave him opportunities for comic action which find echoes in his later work. The opera was composed in six weeks and reorchestrated many years later; the original full score was lost.

Don César is to be hanged for duelling in Holy Week. In his last hours he agrees to marry Maritana, a street singer whom the king wished to take as his mistress but could not until she was a member of the nobility. But Don César escapes with the aid of a boy, Lazarille, and tells the king that he has killed the prime minister, who was paying attentions to the queen. In gratitude, the king declares Don César governor of Granada.

There are some effective and popular Spanish numbers, including Maritana's *Ballade aragonnaise* and the *Entr'acte sevillana* at the beginning of Act III. In the roles of Charles VI and the boy Lazarille the opera brought together Lhérie and Galli-Marié, who were to sing the leading roles in Bizet's *Carmen* just over two years later.

EDITION v.s., Hartmann, 1873

Le roi de Lahore

The King of Lahore
Opera in five acts (3h 15m)
Libretto by Louis Gallet, after the Comte de Beauvoir's *Voyage autour du monde*, based on a story from the *Mahabharata*
Composed 1875–6

PREMIERES   27 April 1877, Opéra, Paris; UK: 28 June 1879, Covent Garden, London; US: December 1883, French Opera House, New Orleans
CAST   Alim *t*, Scindia *bar*, Timour *b*, Indra *b*, Un chef *bar*, Sita *s*, Kaled *ms*; *satb* chorus of priests, priestesses, chiefs, soldiers, people, spirits; ballet
FULL ORCHESTRA including 2 cornet, 3 sax, 4 hp; offstage band (5 players)

This was the first new work to be staged at the Palais Garnier, and its production was appropriately magnificent. The Indian setting allowed for all kinds of exotic sets and costumes, with dances and processions to reinforce the sense of locale. Act III, in addition, is set in the Garden of the Blessed in the Hindu paradise on Mount Mehru with a series of celestial ballets. Massenet's gifts were well suited to such colourful material, and he was able too to characterize his protagonists with considerable force, his first opportunity on a big stage. The three leading roles of Sita, Alim and Scindia, though conventionally distributed as heroic lovers and villainous rival, are strongly depicted. Massenet's natural gift for vocal declamation was here in evidence for the first time. The Indian setting and the story of a lover breaking through the temple sanctuary to reach his beloved follow in the tradition of Bizet's *Les pêcheurs de perles* (1863).

SYNOPSIS
Act I   For the sin of paying court to Sita, a priestess of the temple, Alim, King of Lahore, is ordered by Timour, the high priest, to raise an army against the invading Muslims. Scindia, Alim's chief minister, is also in love with Sita.
Act II   Alim is defeated and slain. Scindia seizes the throne.
Act III   In the Hindu paradise Alim's soul longs for Sita's love: the god Indra takes pity on him and permits him to return to earth not as a king but as a beggar.
Act IV   Lying destitute in the streets, he watches as Scindia, his jealous rival, prepares to mount the throne of Lahore in great pomp and take Sita as his queen. Alim intervenes; Scindia would have the beggar put to death, but the priests and people insist that beggars have divine illumination, so he is saved.
Act V   Alim and Sita take refuge in the temple sanctuary. In the face of Scindia's threats Sita kills herself, thereby ending Alim's dispensation on earth. The lovers are received into the bosom of heaven.

In *Le roi de Lahore* the essential elements of Massenet's style are evident for the first time: a strong vocal line, the pre-eminence of melody, an abundance of scenic colour, and clear control of scene structure. The libretto is full of conventional postures, but it well serves the demands of both stage and pit.

RECORDING   Sutherland, Tourangeau, Lima, Milnes, Morris, Ghiaurov, Tomlinson, National PO, Bonynge, Decca, 1980
EDITION   v.s., Hartmann, 1877

Hérodiade

Opera in four acts (3h)
Libretto by Paul Milliet, 'Henri Grémont' (Georges Hartmann) and Angelo Zanardini, after Flaubert's *Hérodias* (in the *Trois contes*, 1877) (Though Grémont and Zanardini, Ricordi's agent, are credited as co-librettists, their contribution was more impresarial than literary.)
Composed 1878–81; rev. 1883
PREMIERES   three-act version: 19 December 1881, Théâtre de la Monnaie, Brussels; final version: 1 February 1884, Théâtre-Italien, Paris; US: 13 February 1892, French Opera House, New Orleans; UK: 6 July 1904, Covent Garden, London (as *Salome*)
CAST   Jean *t*, Hérode *bar*, Phanuel *b*, Vitellius *bar*, Le Grand Prêtre *bar*, une voix *t*, Salomé *s*, Hérodiade *ms*, a young Babylonian *s*; *satb* chorus of merchants, soldiers, Jews, Roman soldiers, priests, Levites, temple attendants, sailors, Pharisees, Scribes, Galileans, Samaritans, Ethiopians, Nubians, Arabians, Romans; dancers
FULL ORCHESTRA including 3 sax, 2 hp; on- and offstage bands

Four years, an unusually wide gap, separate *Le roi de Lahore* from Massenet's next opera, *Hérodiade*. Massenet had suggested to Paul Milliet that he write a love poem which mingled Christian mysticism and sensual passion, as if 'a woman's hair became a man's hair-shirt'. The poem was set aside, but it influenced their collaboration on an adaptation of Flaubert's *Hérodias*, encouraged by Massenet's publisher, Georges Hartmann. When the opera was completed, Vaucourbeil, director of the Paris Opéra, judged the work to be *incendiaire*, owing to its biblical-amorous subject (the same objection that kept Saint-Saëns's *Samson et Dalila* from that stage for many years), so Massenet gladly accepted an offer from the Théâtre de la Monnaie, a much more enterprising stage for young French composers in those years. For the Paris premiere of 1884, Massenet revised his original version, rearranging a number of passages, expanding the opera to four acts and adding the slaves' chorus and dance (Act II, Scene 1).

SYNOPSIS
To Flaubert's colourful retelling of the biblical Salome story Milliet added the supposition that Salome is in love with John the Baptist.
Act I   Herod the Tetrarch is indifferent to the Jews' resentment of the Romans. Salome confesses to Phanuel, an astrologer, that she loves John (the Baptist) who has been prophesying the coming of the Messiah. Herodias, Herod's wife, hates John for his preaching.
Act II   Herod is obsessed with the image of Salome, who, unknown to Herodias, is her long-lost daughter; she sees Salome only as her rival.
Act III   Furious, because Salome refuses to yield to him, Herod orders both her and John to be beheaded.
Act IV   They await their execution and hope that their love may continue in heaven. Salome wants to kill Herodias as the person responsible for John's death sentence, but when she discovers that Herodias is her mother, she kills herself instead.

Hérodiade was very successful, at least until the

advent of Strauss's *Salome* based on Wilde's much more sensational version of the story. It has occasionally been revived in recent years, although the comparison with Strauss is inevitably unfavourable.

In *Hérodiade*, Massenet is master of his technique, but the work is exuberantly overlong, especially in the last act when a chorus of Roman soldiers and a set of ballets precede the *dénouement*. The vocal style, full of boldly shaped phrases, is fully characteristic, and the variety of colour considerable. Massenet uses a number of recurrent motifs. The opera can succeed only when staged in a grandly sumptuous manner. Salome does not dance.

RECORDINGS 1. De Channes, Denize, Brazzi, Blanc, Thau, French Radio Lyric Ch and O, Lloyd-Jones, Rodolphe, 1974; 2. excerpts: Crespin, Gorr, Lance, Dens, Mars, Paris Opéra O, Prêtre, EMI, 1960s
EDITIONS f.s., Heugel, [1900]; v.s., Hartmann, 1881

Manon

Opéra comique in five acts (six tableaux) (2h 30m)
Libretto by Henri Meilhac and Philippe Gille, after the Abbé Prévost's novel *Manon Lescaut* (1731)
Composed May–October 1882, orch. March–August 1883; last scene rev., gavotte inserted in Cours-la-Reine scene, 1884; *fabliau* replaced Act III gavotte (this rev. not generally used), 1898
PREMIERES 19 January 1884, Opéra-Comique, Paris; UK: 17 January 1885, Liverpool; US: 23 December 1885, Academy of Music, New York
CAST Manon Lescaut *s*, Le Chevalier Des Grieux *t*, Lescaut *bar*, Le Comte Des Grieux *b*, Guillot de Morfontaine *t*, De Brétigny *bar*, Poussette *s*, Javotte *s*, Rosette *ms*, innkeeper *b bouffe*, two guards *t*; spoken roles: maid, seminary porter, sergeant, constable, gambler; *satb* chorus of elegant society, citizens of Amiens and Paris, travellers, porters, postilions, merchants, churchgoers, gamblers, cardsharpers, croupiers
ORCHESTRATION 2 fl/picc, 2 ob/ca, 2 cl, 2 bsn, 4 hn, 2 tpt, 3 trbn, perc, hp, str; onstage: cl, bsn, str quintet, organ

Manon is Massenet's most successful opera and, with *Faust* and *Carmen*, one of the mainstays of the French repertoire to this day. The Abbé Prévost's novel had been set as an opéra comique by Auber in 1856, but had soon faded from the repertoire. The idea for *Manon* came to Massenet in a conversation with Henri Meilhac who had written numerous libretti for Offenbach and others in collaboration with Ludovic Halévy, but who now collaborated with Philippe Gille, a journalist and dramatist. Despite the claim of Massenet's autobiography that the opera was begun in 1881, his correspondence shows that it was not composed until after *Hérodiade* had been performed. *Manon* was conceived as a quite different opera from his two preceding grandiose works. It was to be an opéra comique with some speech over music and a more continuous and integrated structure than usual. It called for some 18th-century pastiche and a more intimate manner.

It was completed in October 1882, some of it composed in The Hague, where Massenet occupied the Abbé Prévost's own rooms, at that time a hotel. Part of the gambling scene used music originally intended for *Hérodiade*. In February 1883 a contract was signed with the publisher Hartmann, and the orchestration of the work followed. At the premiere in January 1884 Talazac was Des Grieux and Marie Heilbronn was Manon, although Massenet had hoped to engage the very young Marguerite Vaillant-Couturier for the role. The conductor was Danbé. *Manon* remained a regular item of the Opéra-Comique's repertoire almost without interruption until 1959. It quickly conquered the world's stages. Ten years later Massenet followed up the story of Manon with *Le portrait de Manon* (see below), by which time Puccini had set his version of the novel as *Manon Lescaut* (1893).

SYNOPSIS
Act I The courtyard of a hostelry at Amiens, *c.* 1720. De Brétigny, a *fermier-général*, and Guillot de Morfontaine, a financier, are calling noisily for food and drink. They are accompanied by three young ladies of doubtful virtue, Poussette, Javotte and Rosette. A bell rings, announcing the forthcoming arrival of the stagecoach from Arras. People crowd into the courtyard to inspect the new arrivals, among them Lescaut, awaiting his young cousin Manon who is on her way to a convent. Lescaut's interest, it is clear, is in drinking and gambling. Travellers arrive in some confusion and Manon is greeted by Lescaut. She chatters eagerly about her first experience of travel ('Je suis encor tout étourdie'), then Lescaut goes in search of her luggage. Guillot appears, catches sight of Manon and makes immediate advances. Lescaut, returning, is offended. He sends Guillot away and gives Manon, who is fascinated by the sophisticated world she sees around her, a few timely words of warning about unwelcome strangers ('Regardez-moi bien dans les yeux'). Des Grieux appears. He has missed the coach which was to take him to his father ('J'ai manqué l'heure du départ'). Entranced by Manon, he introduces himself. She is captivated too. After only a little hesitation she agrees to leave with Des Grieux, taking the coach which Guillot had arranged to abduct her in. Both Lescaut and Guillot are furious when they learn what has happened. Everyone else is amused.

Act II In the apartment in the rue Vivienne, Paris, where he and Manon are now living, Des Grieux is writing to his father to explain their relationship and to sing Manon's praises ('On l'appelle Manon'). After a noisy disturbance offstage Lescaut comes in with De Brétigny, disguised as a guardsman. Des Grieux calms Lescaut by assuring him that he plans to marry Manon and shows him the letter to his father. Meanwhile De Brétigny is tempting Manon to abandon Des Grieux for a life of pleasure and riches, a temptation she cannot easily resist. While Des Grieux goes out to post the letter, she sings a farewell to their humble life together ('Adieu, notre petite table'). When he returns he tells her of a daydream he had in which all is paradise, except Manon is not there with him ('En fermant les yeux'). Suddenly a knock is heard. Manon, who knows that Des Grieux is to be abducted, fails to stop him answering the door, yet she is overcome by grief as he is taken away.

OPÉRA-COMIQUE : *MANON*, OPÉRA EN 5 ACTES ET 6 TABLEAUX. — PAROLES DE MM. MEILHAC ET GILLE, MUSIQUE DE M. J. MASSENET

Scenes from Manon, *published in* L'Illustration *(Paris, 1884)*

Act III Scene 1: The Cours-la-Reine by the Seine. There is much merry-making with merchants selling their wares and a crowd enjoying a public holiday. Lescaut is spending freely. Manon is arm in arm with De Brétigny, enjoying his attention and wealth. A gavotte is danced ('Profitons bien de la jeunesse'). Des Grieux's father, the count, tells De Brétigny that his son plans to take holy orders and is to preach that evening at St-Sulpice. Manon sends De Brétigny away on an errand and then questions the count about Des Grieux's feelings. Guillot lays on a divertissement, danced by a troupe from the Opéra, but Manon's thoughts are now elsewhere.

Scene 2: The seminary at St-Sulpice. The service is over at which Des Grieux was preaching. His father congratulates him ('Epouse quelque brave fille'), but he is still full of bitterness. He is determined to take his vows. After the count has left, Des Grieux confesses the image of Manon still haunts him ('Ah! fuyez, douce image'). He goes into the church. When he comes back he finds Manon waiting for him. The reunion overcomes all their doubts and they run off together again.

Act IV An illicit gaming room in the Hôtel de Transylvanie. Lescaut, Guillot and their friends are at the tables when Manon and Des Grieux enter.

With Lescaut's support Manon urges an unwilling Des Grieux to try his luck. She is again dazzled by the glitter of money and the lure of laughter. Guillot loses to Des Grieux, exchanges some sharp words and goes off to fetch the count and the police. Lescaut escapes but Guillot has his revenge: Des Grieux and Manon are arrested, accused of cheating.

Act V The road to Le Havre. Des Grieux has been freed but Manon is to be deported as a prostitute. Lescaut's plan to rescue her has failed. When the guards appear, Lescaut bribes the sergeant to let Manon stay behind for a while, under guard. He then bribes the guard too and leads him away. Des Grieux and Manon are now alone, but she is too weak to flee. She dies in Des Grieux's arms.

Manon brought out the best of Massenet's operatic genius. The score shows his great feeling for human passion and also his incomparable skill in scenic management. The principle of dramatic contrast is abundantly used: in the depiction of Manon's character, torn between her devotion to Des Grieux and her fatal weakness for a glittering social milieu; in the contrast between adjacent scenes (the solitude of their room in the rue Vivienne followed by the bustle of the Cours-la-Reine, the devotional atmosphere of St-Sulpice followed by the gaming tables of the Hôtel de Transylvanie); and in the contrast of musical styles between the elegant 18th-century pastiche in the Cours-la-Reine scene and the sweeping romantic phrases with which real passion is expressed. The use of speech over music is purposeful (although in a New York performance Massenet allowed these passages to be sung) and the choral scenes are invariably handled with great skill. The opera contains a well-developed set of leitmotifs, two for Lescaut, one each for De Brétigny and Guillot, for example. Manon's earlier motifs pass out of sight as she grows up with great rapidity. Massenet also uses orchestral motifs to identify a scene, for example the gambling motif in Act IV and the soldiers' motif in Act V.

Des Grieux's complex characterization explodes the belief that Massenet could portray only female characters with true feeling, and once Manon has been lured into the social world it is difficult ever quite to believe in her attachment to him as wholly as in his for her. Yet because Manon is the only female character (apart from the puppet-like trio of Poussette, Javotte and Rosette) against five males with various claims on her, she cannot fail to hold our attention when she is on stage. Her plight is no less touching because she appears at times both fickle and shallow. Massenet's sense of her impudence and gaiety makes this image of the eternal feminine perfectly sympathetic.

RECORDINGS 1. de Los Angeles, Legay, Dens, Borthayre, Ch and O of Paris Opéra-Comique, Monteux, EMI, 1955; 2. Feraldy, Rogatchewsky, Villier, Guénot, Ch and O of Paris Opéra-Comique, Cohen, EMI, 1932: two classic, authentically performed, sets both still sound well [A.B.]
EDITIONS f.ss., Heugel, [c. 1884]; *rp*, Editio Musicus, [c. 1947]; v.ss., Hartmann, 1884; rev. edn, Heugel, 1895; Schirmer, 1963

Le Cid

Opera in four acts (ten tableaux) (2h 15m)
Libretto by Adolphe d'Ennery, Louis Gallet and Edouard Blau, after Corneille's drama *Le Cid* (1637) and Guillen da Castro y Bellvis's play *Las mocedades del Cid* (1618)
Composed 1884–5
PREMIERES 30 November 1885, Opéra, Paris; US: 23 February 1890, French Opera House, New Orleans
CAST Chimène *s*, L'Infante *s*, Rodrigue *t*, Don Diègue *b*, Le Roi *bar*, Le Comte de Gormas *b*, St Jacques *bar*, L'Envoyé Maure *b*, Don Arias *t*, Don Alonzo *b*; *satb* chorus of lords, ladies, bishops, priests, monks, captains, soldiers, people; dancers
FULL ORCHESTRA including 2 hp, organ

Corneille's *Le Cid* had served many earlier composers when Massenet accepted Gallet's libretto, previously offered to Bizet in 1873. Part of the libretto came from a project by d'Ennery, part directly from Corneille, and the vision scene in Act III was taken from Castro's *Cid* and from Flaubert's *S. Julien Hospitalier*. For the music Massenet reused some fanfares written in Venice in 1865 and an unused draft for *Hérodiade*. He collected one motif on a visit to Spain.

SYNOPSIS
Act I The Comte de Gormas and his friends talk about Rodrigue, who is to be knighted by the king. Chimène, the comte's daughter, is planning to marry Rodrigue and has her father's approval. At the ceremony in Burgos Cathedral a quarrel breaks out between Gormas and Don Diègue (Rodrigue's father) over the latter's appointment as preceptor for the infanta.

Act II Rodrigue challenges Gormas on his father's behalf and kills him; Chimène learns that Rodrigue has killed her father, and asks the king to serve justice on him. When war with the Moors is announced, the king appoints Rodrigue at the head of the army in place of Gormas.

Act III There is first a love scene for Chimène (despite her loyalties) and Rodrigue, then a vision for Rodrigue in which St Jacques de Compostella promises him victory. The Moors are defeated.

Act IV Rodrigue is reported dead. Chimène at last confesses her love for him. When after all he returns alive, Chimène overcomes her sense of duty and allows herself to be united with him.

Le Cid reverted to the spectacular style of *Le roi de Lahore* and *Hérodiade*, still the prevalent taste at the Paris Opéra, with plenty of Spanish and Moorish colour and many opportunities for lavish settings: the cathedral square at Burgos, for example. The first performance featured the two de Reszke brothers – Jean and Edouard – who had also sung in the first Paris production of *Hérodiade*. The ballets from Act II are still popular in the concert hall, but the popularity of the opera itself scarcely lasted beyond Massenet's lifetime. It has some fine scenes, notably those for Rodrigue and Don Diègue at the end of Act I, Chimène's solo scene at the opening of Act III ('Pleurez, pleurez, mes yeux'), and the duet with Rodrigue that follows.

RECORDING Bumbry, Domingo, Plishka, Byrne Camp Ch,
Opera O of New York, Queler, CBS/Sony, 1976
EDITIONS v.s., Hartmann, 1885

Werther

Drame lyrique in four acts (five tableaux) (2h 30m)
Libretto by Edouard Blau, Paul Milliet and Georges
Hartmann, after Goethe's *Die Leiden des jungen Werthers*
(1774)
Composed 1885–7, orch. March–July 1887
PREMIERES 16 February 1892, Hofoper, Vienna; France: 16
January 1893, Opéra-Comique, Paris; US: 29 February 1894,
Chicago; UK: 11 June 1894, Covent Garden, London
CAST Werther *t*, Albert *bar*, Le Bailli *b*, Schmidt *t*, Johann
bar, Charlotte *ms*, Sophie *s*, Bruhlmann *t*, Katchen *s*,
6 children 6 *s*
ORCHESTRATION 2 fl/picc, 2 ob/ca, 2 cl, 2 bsn, 4 hn, 2 tpt,
3 trbn, alto sax, timp, perc, hp, str; onstage: t-t, wind-machine;
offstage: organ, glock

Werther may claim to be Massenet's masterpiece and,
next to *Manon*, his best-known opera. In a letter of
September 1880 Massenet spoke of his intention to
follow *Hérodiade*, then just completed, with *Werther*.
The idea had emerged from a conversation in Milan
in 1879 with Hartmann, Massenet's publisher, and
Milliet, librettist of *Hérodiade*. The plan was shelved
in favour of *Manon* and then *Le Cid*, and Milliet's
role as librettist was taken over by Edouard Blau
(one of *Le Cid*'s librettists). *Werther* was eventually
started in 1885, but evidently it did not go well.
Hartmann, knowing Massenet's need for appropriate
stimuli, acquired an 18th-century apartment in
Versailles for him to work in, and then, on a trip to
Bayreuth in August 1886, suggested that they visit
Wetzlar, north of Frankfurt, where Goethe had
conceived his *Werther*; a similar absorption of the
Abbé Prévost's rooms in The Hague had assisted the
composition of *Manon* three years earlier.

This visit, though not the original inspiration
for *Werther*, as Massenet's autobiography claims,
provided a tremendous spur to the completion of
the opera. But it was turned down by the Opéra-
Comique as too depressing. After that theatre's
destruction by fire, its new management preferred
the more glamorous *Esclarmonde*. Thus *Werther* did
not appear in Paris until 1893; its premiere took place
in Vienna in February 1892, following the great
success there of *Manon* two years before.

It soon conquered every stage and has been a
repertoire work ever since. Great interpreters have
included, in the role of Werther, van Dijck (the role's
creator), Beyle, de Reszke, Thill, Schipa, Tagliavini,
Gedda, Vanzo, Kraus, Carreras and Domingo, and
in the role of Charlotte, Farrar, Lehmann, Lubin,
Crespin and von Stade.

SYNOPSIS

The action takes place near Frankfurt between July
and December 178...

Act I 'The Bailli's House', July. On the terrace of
his house the Bailli, a magistrate, is rehearsing his six
small children in a Christmas carol. A widower, he is
cared for by his elder daughters, Charlotte (20) and
Sophie (15). Johann and Schmidt, two of his friends,

Ernest van Dijck, the first Werther (Vienna, 1892)

come in and discuss a ball to be given that evening
in Wetzlar, the possibility that Werther (a melancholy young man of 23) may be sent away as an
ambassador, and the imminent arrival of Charlotte's
fiancé, Albert. They leave, and soon Werther
appears, entranced by the beauty of nature and by
the children's singing within the house ('O nature,
pleine de grâce'). He watches as Charlotte comes out
of the house and busies herself with the children. The
Bailli greets Werther and introduces Charlotte. All,
including a number of other guests, go off to the ball,
leaving Sophie to care for the children. Albert then
arrives, anxious to have news of Charlotte ('Quelle
prière de reconnaissance'), and goes into the house.
As darkness falls, Charlotte and Werther return, arm
in arm. Werther becomes increasingly amorous until
the Bailli's voice is heard telling Charlotte that
Albert is back. When she tells Werther she is to
marry Albert since her mother made her promise to,
Werther, in despair, tells her to fulfil her promise.

Act II 'The Lime Trees'. September. The church square at Wetzlar. Johann and Schmidt are drinking outside a tavern. Charlotte and Albert, now married, arrive for church, blessing their happiness. Werther appears, cursing the happiness he has missed ('Un autre son époux!'). When Albert comes out of the church, he offers Werther consolation for any regrets he may feel at their marriage and suggests Sophie as an alternative bride. Left alone, Werther realizes he has to leave, and when Charlotte emerges from the church she begs him to go, conceding that they may meet again at Christmas. After she has gone Werther thinks at once of suicide ('Lorsque l'enfant revient d'un voyage') and leaves, telling Sophie that he will not be back. Charlotte, hearing this from Sophie, is so clearly distraught that Albert realizes that Werther is in love with her.

Act III 'Charlotte and Werther'. Christmas Eve, 5 o'clock. Albert's house. Charlotte confesses that her thoughts are all with Werther and that his letters stir her deeply ('Werther . . . Werther . . .'). Sophie attempts to cheer her up. Charlotte breaks into a passionate prayer for spiritual aid ('Va, laisse couler mes larmes'), then Werther appears at the door. Before long she finds herself in his arms. Overcome with guilt and remorse, she rushes from the room. Werther leaves. Albert enters, calling for Charlotte. She appears, obviously distraught. A servant brings a message for Albert from Werther: since he is leaving for a distant country, would Albert lend him his pistols? Albert orders Charlotte to fetch the pistols. As soon as Albert has gone, she rushes out, praying that she is not too late.

Act IV The same evening. Scene 1: 'Christmas Night', an orchestral tableau leading directly into Scene 2: 'The Death of Werther', in Werther's study. Werther lies mortally wounded, the pistols at his side. Charlotte rushes in, finds him, and attempts to revive him. She confesses she loves him and they kiss for the first time. As Werther dies, he hears the children singing 'Noël' and imagines he hears angels promising forgiveness.

Goethe's novel was based on the story of a young lawyer, Karl Wilhelm Jerusalem, who shot himself in October 1772 because of his unhappy love for the wife of a diplomat. Jerusalem had borrowed pistols from a friend of Goethe's who gave a full account of Jerusalem's death, quoting the text of the note asking for the loan of the pistols. This note was copied by Goethe in his novel and by Massenet in his opera.

The libretto is necessarily a free adaptation of the novel, which consists simply of Werther's letters. Some of Werther's complex pantheistic personality is lost, whereas Charlotte is a more immediate and real figure. Sophie's role is almost entirely the invention of the librettists, and the final act, bringing Charlotte and Werther together for a final death scene, is their creation too; in the novel Werther dies alone. In Goethe, Werther's malaise may be seen as the hopeless dissatisfaction of a searching, Romantic melancholic, whereas Massenet's Werther is more narrowly the victim of an amorous passion that cannot be satisfied.

Charlotte in the opera presents a wonderfully touching portrait of a girl gradually moved to pull against her mother's wishes and the constraints of her marriage (in Goethe, Charlotte never returns Werther's love with the same ardour). Her solo scene at the beginning of Act III represents one of the greatest moments of self-discovery and self-revelation in opera, and at the same time the reading of the letter in that scene pays tribute to Goethe's epistolary mode. By the end of the opera her diffidence is thrown aside and she can confess, too late, that she returns Werther's love.

As in *Manon*, Massenet finds the intimate style very much to his taste. There are no chorus and no large orchestral effects. He relies particularly on the cor anglais and there is an unforgettable solo for the saxophone to accompany Charlotte's 'Les larmes qu'on ne pleure pas' in Act III. In contrast to *Manon*, he does not attempt any pastiche musical touches except in the rather exaggerated counterpoint that supports Johann and Schmidt. His melodic invention in creating striking motifs was at its peak, and although there are some deliberately facile melodies that seem too plain to convey their message, the match of feeling and melody is masterly. Albert's correct *bon ton* is perfectly conveyed, for example, by inner octaves in the texture. Most striking, too, is the wider harmonic palette Massenet draws on in this opera, perhaps a reflection of Wagner's influence (although that never extended to his dramaturgy), and we may detect some darker string textures possibly derived from *Parsifal*. The very opening of the *prélude*, with its strong melodic dissonances, captures the tone of the opera, followed by a plain diatonic melody that suggests the beauty of nature. Using the children's 'Noël' as contrast and also as ironic accompaniment to Werther's death might have risked banality, but Werther's vision of angels, the idea of rebirth at Christmas, and the straightforward musical coherence of recalling the opera's beginning at its end, plus Massenet's incomparable skill in musical manipulation of such materials, all ensure a deeply tragic, satisfying close.

RECORDINGS 1. Vallin, Feraldy, Thill, Roque, Ch and O of Paris Opéra-Comique, Cohen, EMI, 1931; 2. von Stade, Buchanan, Carreras, Allen, O of Covent Garden, Davis, Philips, 1981; 3. Troyanos, Barbaux, Kraus, Manuguerra, LPO, Plasson, EMI, 1979; 4. Obraztsova, Auger, Domingo, Grundheber, Cologne Radio O, Chailly, DG, 1979: the most idiomatic performance is the first, now sounding excellent on CD – Vallin and Thill are unsurpassed; of the others the second is just preferable, but Domingo is a fine Werther in the fourth [A.B.]
EDITIONS f.ss., Heugel, 1892; 2nd edn, 1909; v.ss., Heugel, 1892; 4th edn, 1946

Esclarmonde

Opéra romanesque in a prologue, four acts (eight tableaux) and an epilogue (2h 45m)
Libretto by Alfred Blau and Louis de Gramont, after the French romance *Partenopoeus de Blois* (before 1188)
Composed 1888
PREMIERES 15 May 1889, Opéra-Comique, Paris; US: 10 February 1893, French Opera House, New Orleans; UK: 28 November 1983, Covent Garden, London

CAST Esclarmonde *s*, Parséis *ms*, Roland *t*, Phorcas *b*,
L'Evêque de Blois *b*, Enéas *t*, Cléomer *b*, un envoyé sarrazin
b, un héraut byzantin *t*; *satb* chorus of dignitaries, knights,
warriors, guards, monks, priests, penitents, children, spirits,
people; dancers
FULL ORCHESTRA including dbsn, hp, organ; onstage band:
4 tpt, 3 trbn, 3 tuba, perc

Massenet met the American soprano Sybil
Sanderson in 1887. She was 22, strikingly beautiful,
and endowed with a voice of remarkable range
and quality. Captivated, Massenet arranged for her
to sing the role of Manon in Holland in January
1888 and at the same time began a new opera,
Esclarmonde, whose principal role was for her. The
libretto was procured by Hartmann, Massenet's
publisher, who planned the first performance to
coincide with the Universal Exhibition in 1889.

SYNOPSIS
Prologue At an assembly of the Byzantine court,
Phorcas, the emperor, decrees that power shall pass
to his daughter Esclarmonde, on condition that she
remain veiled until she reaches the age of 20.

Act I Esclarmonde is in love with Roland, a
young knight, but may not show her feelings. Her
sister Parséis counsels Esclarmonde to use her magic
powers to win Roland.

Act II Roland has been mysteriously transported
to a magic isle, where he falls asleep amid the
flowers. Esclarmonde arrives and wakes him with a
kiss. Roland falls in love with her and promises never
to seek to know who she is. She gives him the sacred
sword of St George with which to fight the Saracens:
if he is not true to her, the sword will break.

Poster for the world premiere of Esclarmonde *(Paris, 1889)*

Act III Near Blois, King Cléomer and his people
are at the mercy of the invading Saracens. Roland
challenges the Saracen chief in single combat and
wins, but he is unable to explain why he then refuses
the hand of Cléomer's daughter as a reward. The
bishop of Blois, keen to penetrate the mystery, tricks
Roland into confessing his love for Esclarmonde.
The bishop denounces him. Esclarmonde arrives and
is saved from the bishop's threats by her spirits, but
Roland's sword has broken trying to defend her.

Act IV Phorcas announces that a tournament
will be held with Esclarmonde's hand as prize. He
has ordered Esclarmonde to renounce her love for
Roland and has spirited her away from him. Roland
is distraught.

Epilogue Esclarmonde is given to the knight with
the lowered visor who won the tournament; it is
Roland, and the lovers are finally united.

First played in the Opéra-Comique's temporary
home in the old Théâtre-Lyrique building,
Esclarmonde is far from that company's traditional
repertoire. It is a 'magic' opera, full of enchantment
and spectacular effects (the first production used a
series of projections to suggest rapid scene changes);
it also evokes medieval chivalry, and Massenet
relished the task of providing music for such scenic
riches, not to mention Sybil Sanderson's voice. It was
thus, as he often repeated, his favourite opera, and its
quality and invention are much finer than its patchy
stage history would suggest. The harmonic language
shows the benefit of advances he had made in
Werther and his orchestral imagination is wonderfully
rich. Like *Le Cid*, it was successful in Masssnet's
lifetime but not much played thereafter, although it
has featured in Joan Sutherland's stage repertoire.

RECORDING Sutherland, Tourangeau, Aragall, Quilico,
Lloyd, John Alldis Ch, National PO, Bonynge, Decca, 1976
EDITIONS f.s./v.s., Hartmann, *c.* 1890

Le mage
The Magus
Opera in five acts (six tableaux)
Libretto by Jean Richepin
Composed 1889–90
PREMIERE 16 March 1891, Opéra, Paris

Although one of Massenet's least successful operas
(it was given only in Paris and in Holland in 1896),
Le mage has some fine scenes. A grand opera, with
crowd scenes, ballet, etc., it has some resemblance to
Aida in the plot since Zarâstra, the Persian general, is
secretly in love with Anahita, a Turanian captive,
who, unknown to him, is queen of Turan. Varedha, a
Persian priestess, is in love with Zarâstra, supported
by her father, the high priest. By denouncing
Zarâstra, Varedha forces him to flee to the
mountains, and arranges that Anahita shall marry the
king. An attack by the Turanians foils the plan.
Zarâstra and Anahita are reunited while Varedha
dies as the temple collapses. The best music is found
in the big ensemble at the end of Act II. As in

Hérodiade, the final scenes fuse religious and amorous fervour.

EDITION v.s., Hartmann, 1891

Thaïs

Comédie lyrique in three acts (seven tableaux) (2h 15m)
Libretto by Louis Gallet, after Anatole France's novel *Thaïs* (1890)
Composed 1892–3, rev. 1897
PREMIERES 16 March 1894, Opéra, Paris; rev. version: 13 April 1898, Opéra, Paris; US: 25 November 1907, Manhattan Opera Company, New York; UK: 18 July 1911, Covent Garden, London
CAST Athanaël *bar*, Nicias *t*, Palémon *b*, un serviteur *bar*, Thaïs *s*, Crobyle *s*, Myrtale *ms*, Albine *ms*, 12 Cenobites 6 *t*, 6 *b*, la Charmeuse *dancer*; *satb* chorus of actors, actresses, comedians, philosophers, Nicias' friends, people
FULL ORCHESTRA including dbsn, hp; onstage band including t-t, crotales, wind-machine, thunder-sheet, hp, cel, harmonium, pf, organ

Like *Esclarmonde*, *Thaïs* was written for Sybil Sanderson, Massenet's favourite soprano at that time. Anatole France's novel had caused a sensation in 1890, with its remarkable description of the Thebaid and its story of Paphnutius the desert monk (Athanaël in the opera), who converts the Egyptian harlot Thaïs to the faith but falls himself a victim to the very carnality he professes to reject. The libretto was written in prose, breaking with a long tradition in French opera; the idea may have come from Charpentier. The antique setting – Egypt in the early years of the Christian era – appealed greatly to Massenet, and the interlocking claims of religion and love were now established as his special dramatic domain.

SYNOPSIS

Act I Athanaël returns to the Thebaid from Alexandria to report to his brother Cenobites that Thaïs, whom he once knew as a good child, is the leading courtesan in that sinful city. He goes to Alexandria to save her and contrives to meet her at the house of Nicias. Intrigued by the strange visitor, Thaïs puts on her most lascivious act. Athanaël flees in disgust.

Act II Athanaël visits Thaïs and attempts to draw her away from the cult of Venus. Her conscience is troubled. Nicias and his friends find her modestly dressed when they expect her to be decked for more conviviality. They threaten Athanaël when they learn that she is destroying her house and her wealth at Athanaël's bidding, but Nicias holds them back.

Act III Athanaël leads Thaïs to a desert retreat where she is to offer her repentance. But he imposes such duress on her that her strength is failing. Back in the Thebaid, Athanaël is troubled by impure thoughts and visions of Thaïs as she first appeared to him; he also hears voices that tell him she is dying. He hurries to her side, drawn by her beauty and confessing his carnal passion for her while she expires, full of dreams of divine felicity.

Sybil Sanderson as Thaïs (Paris, 1894)

The wide success of *Thaïs* added to Massenet's great celebrity, and the famous 'Meditation' (between Acts II and III), symbolizing Thaïs's awakening conscience, is one of the most famous of all violin solos. Although written for the Opéra, the work lacks large-scale scenes of pageantry and crowd conflict, and concentrates more on the personal predicaments of its two central characters, as in *Werther*. But their simultaneous conversions – Athanaël from self-denial to lust and Thaïs from sin to saintliness – are inherently improbable, for all the passionate intensity of the music, which displays some of the most flexible and lyrical qualities in all Massenet's work. Thaïs's 'Miroir, dis-moi que je suis belle' has enjoyed great celebrity as an operatic extract.

RECORDINGS 1. Doria, Collard, Sénéchal, Massard, unnamed Ch and O, Etcheverry, Decca, 1962; 2. Esposito, Michel, Mollien, Massard, French Radio Lyric Ch and O, Wolff, Chant du monde, 1959: neither set is ideal, but both have affecting interpreters of the two main roles [A.B.]
EDITIONS f.ss., Heugel, 1894, 1898; v.ss., Heugel, [1894], 1900

Le portrait de Manon

The Portrait of Manon
Opéra comique in one act (1h)
Libretto by Georges Boyer
Composed 1893
PREMIERES 8 May 1894, Opéra-Comique, Paris; US: 13 December 1897, New York

The plot imagines Des Grieux treasuring a portrait of his beloved Manon and given over to a life of sorrow. He has taken charge of his nephew, the young Vicomte de Montcerf, who tells his uncle of the young girl, Aurore, with whom he has fallen in love. Des Grieux warms to this reminder of his own former passion but objects that Aurore is not worthy of the family name. The lovers find the portrait of Manon and dress Aurore (who happens to be Manon's niece) to look like Manon in the portrait. Des Grieux is so deeply touched by the lovers' devotion that he consents to their marriage. The score recalls a number of appropriate motifs from *Manon*. Although only occasionally revived, this little 'niece' to the well-known *Manon* can give nothing but pleasure to Massenet's admirers.

EDITIONS   f.s./v.s., Heugel, 1894

La navarraise

The Girl from Navarre
Episode lyrique in two acts (1h 15m)
Libretto by Jules Claretie and Henri Cain, after Claretie's story *La cigarette* (1890)
Composed 1893
PREMIERES   20 June 1894, Covent Garden, London; France: 27 March 1895, Bordeaux; US: 11 December 1895, Metropolitan, New York
CAST   Anita *s*, Araquil *t*, Garrido *bar*, Remigio *bar*, Ramon *t*, Bustamente *b*; *satb* chorus of Basque women, officers, wounded soldiers, surgeon, chaplain, peasants
FULL ORCHESTRA   offstage: 6 tpt, 3 sd, cannon, 2 deep bells

Mascagni's *Cavalleria rusticana* arrived in Paris in January 1892 and its enormous success prompted Massenet to try his hand at the violent immediacy of *verismo*. *La navarraise* is set in the thick of the Spanish Carlist War in 1874 near Bilbao. The blood and heartbreak of civil war is counterpointed by the tragic passion of Anita, the girl from Navarre, for Araquil, a sergeant in the defeated royalist army. Desperate to win a dowry with which to marry him, she crosses enemy lines and assassinates the Carlist leader. She earns the reward but loses Araquil, who out of jealousy has pursued her into dangerous and, for him, fatal territory.

The score is full of strong effects of local and scenic colour: deep bells, the calls of battle trumpets, the click of castanets, the clapping of hands. Anita's line is sometimes wildly disjunct, sometimes marvellously melodic in Massenet's familiar manner. The opening of each short act is an orchestral symphony depicting, in turn, the clamour of battle and the tranquillity of night.

RECORDINGS   1. Popp, Vanzo, LSO, Almeida, CBS, 1975; 2. Horne, Domingo, LSO, Lewis, RCA, 1975; the first is slightly preferable, being more histrionic [A.B.]
EDITION   v.s., Heugel, 1894

Grisélidis

Conte lyrique in three acts with a prologue (2h)
Libretto by Armand Silvestre and Eugène Morand, after their play *Grisélidis* (1891) based on a story in Boccaccio's *Decameron* (1349–51)
Composed 1894, rev. 1898

PREMIERES   20 November 1901, Opéra-Comique, Paris; US: 19 January 1910, Manhattan Opera Company, New York; Ireland: 22 October 1982, Theatre Royal, Wexford
CAST   Grisélidis *s*, Fiamina *s*, Bertrade *s*, Loys *treble*, Le Diable *bar* or *b*, Alain *t*, Le Marquis *bar*, Le Prieur *bar*, Gondebaud *bar*; *satb* chorus of men at arms, spirits, night voices, celestial voices, women in the château, etc.
STANDARD ORCHESTRA   offstage: 4 tpt, bells, harmonium, cel

Grisélidis was commissioned by the Opéra-Comique some years before it was performed there. It was based on a play that had been successful at the Théâtre-Français.

SYNOPSIS
In a Prologue, Alain, a young shepherd, hopes he may win Grisélidis, but she is wooed and won instead by the marquis.

Act I   The marquis is called away to fight in the Holy Land. He is sure of his wife's fidelity, but the Devil, watching, has other ideas.

Act II   In various disguises the Devil tempts Grisélidis. He brings the adoring Alain to meet her, and she is on the point of yielding when the sight of her son Loys reminds her of her duty.

Act III   The Devil abducts the little boy. When the marquis returns from the Crusades he and his wife pray to St Agnes to bring him back. The Devil is confounded, and seraphic voices sing the Magnificat.

Like the later *Le jongleur de Notre-Dame*, *Grisélidis* evokes a medieval setting, with the Devil presented as a comic role. There are touching sections for Grisélidis herself and her ardent suitor Alain, and the evocation of nature draws some fine orchestral pages from the composer.

RECORDING   Moizan, Betti. Mallabrera, Depraz, Ch and O of French Radio, Alpress, EJS, 1963
EDITIONS   f.s./v.s., Heugel, 1901

Cendrillon

Cinderella
Fairy-tale in four acts (six tableaux)
Libretto by Henri Cain, after Charles Perrault's story *Cendrillon*, in *Contes de ma mère l'oye* (1697)
Composed 1895
PREMIERES   24 May 1899, Opéra-Comique, Paris; US: 23 December 1902, French Opera House, New Orleans; UK: 24 December 1928, Little Theatre, London (by puppets)
CAST   Cendrillon *s*, Madame de la Haltière *ms*, Le Prince Charmant *s*, La Fée *s*, Noémie *s*, Dorothée *ms*, Pandolfe *b* or *bar*, Le Doyen de la Faculté *t*, Le Surintendant des Plaisirs *bar*, Le Premier Ministre *b* or *bar*, Le Roi *bar*, 6 spirits 4 *s*, 2 *a*; *satb* chorus of spirits, servants, courtiers, doctors, ministers, lords, ladies; dancers
FULL ORCHESTRA   onstage band including viola d'amore, cel, harmonium, hp

While composing *Cendrillon* Massenet again found inspiration by immersing himself in the appropriate surroundings, in this case a 17th-century house on the Seine in Normandy that had belonged to the celebrated Duchesse de Longueville; he even bought a large antique table on which to spread the pages of his manuscript.

SYNOPSIS

Act I   Mme de la Haltière and her two daughters are making ready for the royal ball. Her husband, Pandolfe, groaning at his unhappy lot, is sorry to be leaving his daughter Cinderella behind. Cinderella, alone, falls asleep. A fairy appears, provides her with a magnificent dress, and gives her a glass slipper to make her unrecognizable. She must promise to leave the ball at midnight.

Act II   Prince Charming is inconsolable, not even touched by the ballets in his honour. When Cinderella arrives, everyone is captivated by her. She and Prince Charming fall in love. Midnight strikes.

Act III   Scene 1: In her flight Cinderella has lost her slipper. The trio of women upbraid Pandolfe for his bad behaviour at the ball and tell Cinderella that the prince took only a passing interest in the unknown stranger. Scene 2: Cinderella takes refuge in the fairy domain where the spirits conjure up a meeting with Prince Charming. They join in a fervent embrace.

Act IV   The prince is said to be searching for the owner of the mysterious slipper. Before the whole court Cinderella claims it as hers, and 'all ends happily', in Pandolfe's words.

Cendrillon is one of Massenet's most attractive operas. The characterization of Cinderella's long-suffering father and of her bossy stepmother is deft, and the composer relished the opportunity to write fairy music. There is some pseudo-baroque pastiche (including the use of a viola d'amore) and much witty music in the manner of *Falstaff*. There seem to be parodies of Meyerbeer and Wagner's *Parsifal*, too, and occasional hints of Debussy's style. The love music is some of the finest he ever wrote. Cinderella's 'Vous êtes mon Prince Charmant' is one of the opera's best-known extracts. Considering its abundant opportunities for spectacular staging, it has been surprisingly neglected. It should truly be acknowledged as on a par with Humperdinck's *Hänsel und Gretel*. The role of Prince Charming is written for a voice designated *falcon* or *soprano de sentiment*.

RECORDING   von Stade, Welting, Berbié, Gedda, Bastin, Ambrosian Opera Ch, Philharmonia O, Rudel, CBS, 1979
EDITIONS   f.s./v.s., Heugel, 1899

Sapho

Pièce lyrique in five acts
Libretto by Henri Cain and Arthur Bernède, after the novel by Alphonse Daudet (1884)
Composed 1896, rev. 1909
PREMIERES   27 November 1897, Opéra-Comique, Paris; US: 17 November 1909, Manhattan Opera Company, New York; UK: 14 March 1967, St Pancras Town Hall, London
CAST   Fanny Legrand *s*, Divonne *s*, Irène *s*, Jean Gaussin *t*, Caoudal *bar*, Césaire *b*, La Borderie *t*, Le Patron du Restaurant *b*; *satb* chorus of maskers, guests, artists, gypsies, strolling musicians, etc.
FULL ORCHESTRA   offstage: 2 vn, vcl, db, fl, harmonium, pf, tuba, cornet

This opera was written, like *La navarraise*, for Emma Calvé. It gave Massenet great satisfaction, especially since he knew Daudet and won the author's warm praise for his work. It was successful in Massenet's lifetime, but has not often been revived since. The unusually strong second scene in Act III was added in 1909.

SYNOPSIS

Act I   A young man from Provence, Jean Gaussin, arrives in Paris and attends a party given by the sculptor Caoudal. Fanny Legrand, an artist's model known as 'Sapho' and the centre of attraction at the party, notices Jean. They get acquainted and soon leave the party together.

Act II   Despite the concern of Jean's family, who have come to Paris to visit him, he is still obsessed with Fanny and she with him. She wins his heart by singing Provençal songs to him.

Act III   Jean and Fanny have been living for a year at Ville d'Avray. Caoudal and his friends arrive while Fanny is out and express surprise that she has been so faithful for so long. Fanny's promiscuous past begins to haunt Jean and he repudiates her when she returns. In the next scene Jean finds a box of letters, one of which reveals that Fanny has a child by a former lover. After a bitter exchange of insults he leaves.

Act IV   Jean has returned alone to his family in Provence. Fanny arrives, but fails to persuade him to rejoin her. His family have persuaded him to stay.

Act V   Fanny is alone in Ville d'Avray when Jean arrives; he cannot live without her. But an incautious reminder of her past shatters the dream. Without melodrama or fuss she leaves.

The impossible passion of a naïve young man from the country and the worldly-wise Parisienne makes for an opera of nuance and feeling, not a violent drama. *Sapho* is a love story in a modern setting based, like *Thaïs*, on a successful novel. Dramatically it perhaps recalls *La traviata*. The Provençal setting of Act IV provides some local colour, including the 'Magali' melody used by Gounod in *Mireille*. There are kinships too with Bizet's *L'arlésienne*. Massenet delights in the vicissitudes of love as he had in *Manon*; *Sapho* is thus one of his most lyrical works. The Act V solo scene for Fanny may be compared in dramatic force to Charlotte's solo in Act III of *Werther*; both use the device of reading a letter.

RECORDING   Doria, Sirera, Gamboa, Chorale Stéphanie Caillat, O Symphonique de Garde Républicaine, Boutry, Peters, 1978
EDITIONS   v.ss. Heugel, 1898; rev. version: Heugel, 1909

Le jongleur de Notre-Dame

The Juggler of Notre-Dame
Miracle in three acts (1h 30m)
Libretto by Maurice Léna, after the short story *L'étui de nacre* by Anatole France (1892), based in turn on the tale *Le tombeur de Notre-Dame* by Gaston Paris (1870s)
Composed 1900
PREMIERES   18 February 1902, Salle Garnier, Monte Carlo; UK: 15 June 1906, Covent Garden, London; US: 27 November 1908, Manhattan Opera Company, New York

CAST   Jean *t*, Boniface *bar*, Le Prieur *b*, un moine poète *t*, un moine peintre *bar*, un moine musicien *bar*, un moine sculpteur *b*, deux anges *trebles* (*s*, *ms*), La Vierge *silent*; *satb* chorus of monks, invisible angels, knights, townspeople, peasants, merchants, clerks, vagabonds
FULL ORCHESTRA including viola d'amore; offstage: cel, pf, harmonium, organ

Le jongleur de Notre-Dame took Massenet into a medieval setting, that of the Benedictine abbey at Cluny in the 14th century. Although there is a mixed chorus with female voices for peasants and angels, all the singing roles are for men. Yet the figure of the Virgin dominates the action and at the end her statue is seen to glow and offer a blessing. It makes an interesting comparison with Puccini's *Suor Angelica* with its single-sex cast in a religious setting.

SYNOPSIS
Act I   Cluny in the 14th century. Jean is a juggler, acrobat and minstrel who relies on his wits to earn a living. After leading the crowd in a drinking song he is rebuked by the prior but forgiven on the condition that he joins the Benedictine order. Jean is worried that monastic life may be too austere, but Boniface, the corpulent cook, assures him that it is not.
Act II   Jean is teased by the more artistic monks of the order, but he realizes with emotion that shepherd and minstrel are equal to a king in the Virgin's eyes. He falls into a trance of pious ecstasy.
Act III   Jean steals into the sanctuary and, addressing the Virgin, begins to play his tricks, sing, and dance; it is the only way he knows to honour her. The prior is summoned, but before Jean can be seized invisible angels are heard singing and the Virgin is seen enthroned in glory. As Jean dies in ecstasy, all acknowledge a miracle.

This libretto offered Massenet many features he responded to warmly: a chance for musical pastiche (in an imagined medieval style), religious fervour, a town-square scene with all walks of life going about their business, a disputation between a musician, a sculptor, a poet and a painter, and a choir rehearsal. There is also a comic character, Boniface, the abbey's cook. Even without any love interest, this is an unusual and inventive score which gave Massenet much pleasure. The orchestral textures are kept thin, and opulence and complexity are avoided. He told Pierre Lalo in 1900 that he was sure this would be his masterpiece. At the New York premiere the tenor role of Jean was sung by the soprano Mary Garden, by which Massenet confessed he was 'somewhat bewildered'.

RECORDING   Vanzo, Bastin, Vento, Monte Carlo Opera Ch and O, Boutry, EMI, 1979
EDITIONS   f.s./v.s., Heugel, 1902

Chérubin
Cherubino
Comédie chantée in three acts (1h 45m)
Libretto by Francis de Croisset and Henri Cain
Composed 1902–3
PREMIERE   14 February 1905, Salle Garnier, Monte Carlo

Just as *Le portrait de Manon* had imagined the character Des Grieux in later life, *Chérubin* follows Cherubino, from *Le nozze di Figaro* (or, to be accurate, from Beaumarchais's *Le mariage de Figaro*) to the advanced age of 17. He is now commissioned as an officer and he is still hopelessly vulnerable to female charm. The Count and Countess reappear from Beaumarchais, and there are new characters, such as L'Ensoleillad, a singer from Madrid, and the Philosopher, Cherubino's tutor. His final choice falls on Nina, the Count's ward, and the opera ends with an appropriate reference to the serenade from *Don Giovanni*. The opera allowed some music in 18th-century style, as in *Manon*, but its large cast and inconsequential dramatic structure kept it from wide success. Chérubin, a *travesti* role as in Mozart, was first played by Mary Garden.

RECORDING   Anderson, Upshaw, Von Stade, Sénéchal, Ramey, Ch of Bavarian State Opera, Munich Radio O, Steinberg, RCA, 1992
EDITIONS   f.s./v.s., Heugel, 1905

Ariane
Opera in five acts
Libretto by Catulle Mendès, after the Greek myth
Composed 1904–5
PREMIERE   31 October 1906, Opéra, Paris

Massenet's first new production at the Opéra for 12 years (since *Thaïs*), *Ariane* was designed on a grand scale and grandly staged. Mendès's libretto recounts Ariadne's flight from Crete with Theseus; he has invited her to Athens as his queen in gratitude for her saving him from the Minotaur. Her sister Phaedra, also in love with Theseus, manages to win his attentions while they are stranded on the island of Naxos. When Ariadne discovers this, Phaedra pleads with a statue of Adonis which falls on her, killing her. Ariadne descends to the Underworld to implore Persephone to restore Phaedra to life. She succeeds in her mission, but finds that Theseus still prefers Phaedra's passion to Ariadne's devotion. Theseus leaves with Phaedra, while Ariadne, in despair, is consumed by the waves.

There are three fine female roles in *Ariane*. Persephone, who dominates Act IV and has the famous 'Rose Scene', was sung by Lucy Arbell, the leading lady in most of Massenet's late works. The best act is the third: the scene where Ariadne pleads with Phaedra to intercede with Theseus on her behalf is very touching and superbly crafted. This is followed by a strong duet for Phaedra and Theseus, and then by Ariadne's plaintive solo scene 'Ah! le cruel! Ah! la cruelle!', among the best of such pieces in Massenet's work. *Ariane* was performed 60 times in its first production and revived at the Opéra in 1937.

EDITIONS   f.s./v.s., Heugel, 1906

Thérèse
Drame musical in two acts (1h 15m)
Libretto by Jules Claretie
Composed 1905–6

PREMIERES 7 February 1907, Salle Garnier, Monte Carlo; UK: 22 May 1919, Covent Garden, London

The setting of *Thérèse* is the French Revolution, Act I taking place in October 1792 and Act II in June 1793. It is a compact and compelling drama with some of the force of *La navarraise*, and the same librettist – Jules Claretie. At the same time Massenet was anxious to convey a sense of autumnal nature in Act I and the scents of summer at the start of Act II. Part of the love music is a minuet, rendered by an offstage harpsichord.

The Girondin Thorel is protecting the residence of his old friend the Marquis de Clerval, now an émigré. The marquis returns not only to see his house but also to declare his love for Thorel's wife, Thérèse. Her feelings are responsive, but in Act II when the Girondins are overthrown and her husband is led off to the scaffold she knows her duty lies in following him. By shouting 'Vive le roi!' she draws a violent fate down on herself, while the marquis escapes.

The contrast of nature's placidity with human menace is a forceful element of this very successful score. Massenet's judgement of stage effect is as precise as ever and his invention still strong. The atmosphere of Revolutionary Paris is well evoked. The title role was written for Lucy Arbell and the setting of Act I (Clagny, near Versailles) was to be based on a house in the Bois de Boulogne built by the Comte d'Artois.

RECORDING Tourangeau, Davies, Quilico, Linden Singers, New Philharmonia O, Bonynge, Decca, 1974
EDITIONS f.s./v.s., Heugel, 1907

Bacchus

Opera in four acts (seven tableaux) with a prologue
Libretto by Catulle Mendès, after the Sanskrit epic
Râmayana by Palmiki
Composed 1907–8
PREMIERE 5 May 1909, Opéra, Paris

Bacchus is a sequel to *Ariane*, intended to capitalize on the latter's success. The same characters, Ariadne, Theseus and Persephone, appear, sung in the first production by the same singers as in *Ariane* in 1906. But Massenet and Mendès did not work well together, and the latter died shortly before the opening. The opera was a resounding failure and received only six performances.

The opera imagines that Bacchus, who according to the myth rescued Ariadne from the island of Naxos, is the reincarnation of Theseus in a Buddhist afterlife in Nepal. He proclaims the Bacchic delights of life and love, but is opposed by the queen Amahelli and her army of monkeys. Amahelli in fact falls in love with Bacchus and persuades Ariadne to offer her life on Bacchus' behalf. It is a highly fanciful story, 'too literary' as many thought, but it offered Massenet the opportunity for effective music for the Bacchic scenes and especially for the battle with the monkeys in the forest, for which he sought inspiration in the Jardin des Plantes.

EDITION v.s., Heugel, 1909

Don Quichotte
Don Quixote

Comédie héroïque in five acts (2h 15m)
Libretto by Henri Cain, after Jacques Le Lorrain's play *Le chevalier de la longue figure* (1906), based on Cervantes's *Don Quixote* (1605, 1615)
Composed 1908–9
PREMIERES 19 February 1910, Salle Garnier, Monte Carlo; US: 27 January 1912, New Orleans; UK: 18 May 1912, London Opera House, London
CAST Dulcinée a, Don Quichotte b, Sancho Panza *bar*, Pedro s, Garcias s, Rodriguez t, Juan t, Le chef des bandits *spoken role*, 2 valets 2 *bar*, 4 bandits 2 *t*, 2 *bar*; *satb* chorus of lords, Dulcinée's friends, bandits, crowd
FULL ORCHESTRA including 2 hp, gtr; offstage: 2 fl, ob/ca, perc, hp, pf, organ, str; onstage: 20 pairs of castanets

It was appropriate that Massenet's last operatic success should make gentle fun of an elderly man with a fondness for beautiful women. The mockery of Cervantes's masterpiece makes excellent operatic material and it offered Massenet yet another opportunity for mingling sentiment and comedy, pastiche and contemporary styles. The title role was written for Chaliapin, the role of Dulcinée for Lucy Arbell.

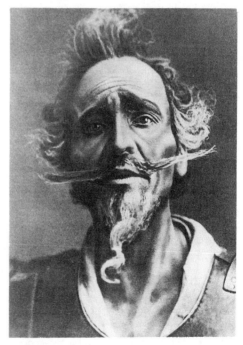

Fyodor Chaliapin as Massenet's Don Quichotte (Monte Carlo, 1910)

SYNOPSIS

Act I In a crowded square in full fiesta Dulcinée is courted by four suitors. When Don Quichotte and his faithful servant Sancho Panza arrive, one of the suitors, Juan, mocks Don Quichotte's eccentric ways, while another, Rodriguez, reminds us of the knight's noble ambitions. When all have departed Don Quichotte serenades Dulcinée, but the jealous Juan interrupts and a duel inevitably follows. Dulcinée intervenes, sends Juan on an errand, and upbraids Quichotte for his hot blood. She asks him to retrieve a necklace stolen from her by the bandit Ténébrun. The Don instantly undertakes the heroic task.

Act II   The Don and his servant have set out in the morning mist. Sancho sings a fierce tirade against women. As the mist clears Quichotte mistakes some windmills for giants and, attacking them, is borne aloft on one of the sails.

Act III   Don Quichotte is close in pursuit of the bandits. While he takes his rest (standing up, like all good knights) he and Sancho are overpowered by the bandits, but their wicked hearts are quickly won by Quichotte's evocation of his mission as knight errant, and they hand over the stolen necklace.

Act IV   Dulcinée is singing of the caprice of love. Don Quichotte returns with the necklace to everyone's amazement, but his proposal of marriage is turned down on the grounds that since she must be generous in her love she could not bear to deceive him. The old knight is disconsolate, but Sancho protects him from the crowd's mockery.

Act V   Death is near as the Don promises Sancho an 'island of dreams'. He dies, fondly imagining that the planet in the heavens is a fleeting image of Dulcinée.

Don Quichotte is a highly crafted comedy full of affection and charm. There is some traditional Spanish colour and some folk pastiche, in this case a romanesca antica in Act IV. The scene of Don Quichotte's death mostly presents a quiet pastoral simplicity but with a touch of harmonic tension as he dies. The boisterous music of Act I recalls both *Cendrillon* and *Falstaff*, with mocking counterpoint for the suitors, a manner used later also for the windmills. The Don himself is characterized with much subtlety and sympathy, an achievement that reflects Massenet's enormous experience and skill. The opera enjoyed considerable popularity and has been revived several times in recent years.

RECORDING   Crespin, Ghiaurov, Bacquier, Suisse Romande Ch and O, Kord, Decca, 1978
EDITIONS   f.s./v.s., Heugel, 1909

Roma

Opéra-tragique in five acts
Libretto by Henri Cain, after the play *Rome vaincue* by Alexandre Parodi
Composed 1902, 1909
PREMIERE   17 February 1912, Salle Garnier, Monte Carlo

The play on which Cain's libretto is based was one of Sarah Bernhardt's great successes, played in 1876 when Massenet first considered it for an opera. The opera was finally staged in 1912, his last premiere before his death. Set in Rome in 216 BC, it concerns a vestal virgin, Fausta, who is condemned to be immured for transgressing her vows. Her blind patrician grandmother, Posthumia, manages to bring

her a dagger to save her from a drawn-out death, but has to strike the blow herself since Fausta's hands are bound. The gods, appeased, bring Rome success in battle.

Massenet evokes the ancient world with a dignified and restrained musical style that was far from fashionable in 1912. The noble choral dirge at the opening, 'O tristes jours!', might be compared to the similar scene in *Samson et Dalila*. The chorus plays a prominent part throughout and the third act contains a solemn ceremonial scene. The dream recounted in Act II by another vestal, Junia, 'Le soleil se couchait', is a fine solo scene. The role of Posthumia was played by Lucy Arbell. The opera was briefly successful, but soon disappeared from the stage.

EDITIONS   f.s./v.s., Heugel, 1912

Panurge

Haulte farce musicale in three acts
Libretto by Georges Spitzmuller and Maurice Boukay, after the novel *Pantagruel* by Rabelais (1532–3)
Composed 1911
PREMIERE   25 April 1913, Théâtre Lyrique de la Gaîté, Paris

Panurge was not heard until after Massenet's death. Massenet had hoped to set a libretto in old French but settled instead simply for a musical style that evokes Renaissance mannerisms, as he had in *Le jongleur de Notre-Dame*. The tone is farcical and often gross, as befitted an operatic setting of Rabelais. Bruneau described the score as 'lively, witty, light and seductive', but its stage life was short. The libretto gives Panurge a wife, Colombe (another strong role for Lucy Arbell), and their adventures and misunderstandings amid a colourful and large supporting cast make excellent operatic comedy.

EDITIONS   f.s., Heugel, 1913; v.s., Heugel, 1912

Amadis

Opéra légendaire in four acts (1h 45m)
Libretto by Jules Claretie, after the romance *Los quatros libros del virtuoso cavallero Amadis de Gaule* by Garci Rodriguez de Montalvo (*c.* 1492)
Composed 1889–90, 1910–11
PREMIERE   1 April 1922, Salle Garnier, Monte Carlo

Amadis has the most prolonged compositional history of any of Massenet's operas and was the last to receive a performance. It was started in 1889 but set aside when Hartmann's publishing house was taken over by Heugel. Massenet resumed work on the score in 1901–2 and finally completed it in 1911, though it had to wait until ten years after his death to be staged. Based on the epic *Amadis de Gaule* (the source of operas by Lully, J. C. Bach and others), it tells of twin brothers separated at birth who later find themselves both in love with the same woman, Floriane, daughter of the king of Brittany. Only when the brother Amadis, whom Floriane prefers, has killed his rival Galaor does he recognize him, from a magic jewel he wears, to be his brother. Notable moments in the score include Floriane's ballad in Act II, 'Le chevalier de la mer', and

Amadis's solo that follows, 'Si je tenais un pied en paradis'.

RECORDING Perraguin, Streiff, Henry, Ch and O of Paris Opéra, Fournillier, Forlane, 1988
EDITIONS f.s., Heugel, 1921; v.ss., Heugel, 1913, 1922

Cléopâtre
Opéra in four acts
Libretto by Louis Payen
Composed 1911–12
PREMIERES 23 February 1914, Salle Garnier, Monte Carlo; US: 10 January 1916, Chicago

The last fruit of Massenet's productive last years, *Cléopâtre* was not performed until after his death. Its large canvas embraces Rome, Egypt, and the eastern Mediterranean, and concerns the famous story of Antony and Cleopatra, with Octavian's eventual victory at Actium and the deaths of both Antony and Cleopatra. It is a traditional grand opera with scenes of celebration, carousal and high passion. There are ballet movements and strong roles for the principal characters. Lucy Arbell's claim to the title role was overturned in the courts, although she sang it in Nantes and Bordeaux. Massenet's style is dignified and restrained, as in *Roma*, and the opera has been successfully revived in recent years.

RECORDINGS Harries, Streiff, Maurette, Henry, Massenet Festival Ch, Nouvel O de Saint-Etienne, Fournillier, Koch-Schwann, 1990
EDITIONS f.s., Heugel, 1915; v.s., Heugel, 1914

Other operas: *Esmeralda* (lost or destroyed) (c. 1865); *La coupe du roi de Thule*, 1866; *La grand'tante*, 1867; *Manfred* (inc.), (c. 1869); *Méduse* (inc.), (c. 1869); *L'adorable Bel'-Boul'* (destroyed), 1874; *Les templiers* (inc.; lost); *Bérangère et Anatole*, 1876; *Robert de France* (lost or destroyed), (c. 1880); *Les Girondins* (lost or destroyed), (1881); *L'écureuil du deshonneur* (early, lost or destroyed); *Montalte* (lost or destroyed), 1882–3
Sacred and profane dramas: *Les erinnyes*, 1873, rev. 1876; *Marie-Magdaleine* (originally performed as oratorio, 1873), 1906 (RECORDING BJR, 1976); *Eve*, 1875; *Narcisse*, 1877; *La Vierge*, 1880 Orchestration of Delibes's last opera, *Kassya*, 1893
BIBLIOGRAPHY *Don Quichotte*, *L'Avant-Scène Opéra*, no. 93 (December 1986); *L'Esclarmonde*, *Grisélidis*, *L'Avant-Scène Opéra*, no. 148 (September 1992); *Manon*, Calder (ENO Opera Guide), 1984; *Manon*, *L'Avant-Scène Opéra*, no. 123 (September 1989); *Thaïs*, *L'Avant-Scène Opéra*, no. 109 (May 1988); *Werther*, *L'Avant-Scène Opéra*, no. 61 (March 1984); James Harding, *Massenet*, Dent, 1970; Jules Massenet, *Mes souvenirs*, Pierre Lafitte, 1912, translated as *My Recollections*, Boston, 1919; *rp*, 1970; Condé (ed.), Paris, 1992; Louis Schneider, *Massenet: l'homme, le musicien*, Carteret, 1908; 2nd edn, Charpentier, 1926

H.M.

FILIPPO MATTEI
[Filippo Amadei; Sigr Pippo; Pippo Amadio]; *fl* 1690–1730

The first record of Mattei is as an instrumentalist in concerts and services organized under the patronage of Cardinal Pietro Ottoboni in Rome in the early 1690s. He also composed cantatas and oratorios for the cardinal. In 1719 he was in London, where he gave concerts and joined the orchestra of the new Royal Academy of Music under Handel's direction. He added a number of arias to Orlandini's opera *Amore e maestà*, given by the Academy under the title *Arsace* in 1721. In the same year he collaborated with Handel and Bononcini by composing the first act of the opera *Muzio Scevola*. It has been suggested that he returned to the service of Ottoboni in Rome in 1729.

BIBLIOGRAPHY H. J. Marx, 'Die Musik am Hofe Pietro Kardinal Ottobonis unter Arcangelo Corelli', *Analecta Musicologica*, vol. 5 (1968), pp. 104–77

G.D.

JOHANN MATTHESON
b 28 September 1681, Hamburg; *d* 17 April 1764, Hamburg

Mattheson was the most important contemporary writer on the music of the German Baroque. At the age of nine he sang in J. W. Franck's opera, *Aeneas*, and he continued to sing with the Hamburg opera (as treble and later tenor) for some 15 years. Mattheson's own operas are lost, except for *Cleopatra* (1704), which gained some notoriety after a performance that Handel conducted from the harpsichord while Mattheson sang the role of Antonius. After the death of Antonius in Act III, Mattheson went to the orchestra to assume his role as composer–conductor at the keyboard. When Handel refused to yield his place, an argument ensued which led, according to Mattheson in his *Grundlage einer Ehrenpforte*, to a duel in which Handel's life was spared only because Mattheson's sword struck a large button on Handel's jacket.

Mattheson also composed numerous oratorios and other vocal and instrumental music. In 1706 he became secretary to the English ambassador, a position he retained for the rest of his life. He also recorded his views on almost every aspect of music of his day. He viewed opera as a cultural necessity for the educated citizen. Indeed, in Mattheson's view: 'A good opera theatre is nothing less than an academy of many of the fine arts – architecture, perspective, painting, mechanics, dancing, acting, ethics, history, poetry, and especially music . . . The downfall of opera causes the downfall of the very essence of music.' (*Der neueste Untersuchung der Singspiele*)

Surviving operas: *Die unglückselige Cleopatra*, 1704 (EDITION G. J. Buelow (ed.), *EDM*, vol. 69, Schott, 1975); *Die geheimen Begebenheiten Henrico IV, Königs von Castilien und Leon, oder Die getheilte Liebe* (arias only), 1711; 5 lost operas
BIBLIOGRAPHY G. J. Buelow, 'Johann Mattheson, the Composer, an Evaluation of his Opera *Cleopatra*', in H. C.

Robbins Landon (ed.), *Studies in Eighteenth Century Music, a Tribute to Karl Geiringer*, Allen and Unwin, 1970, pp. 92–107

G.J.B.

SIEGFRIED MATTHUS

b 13 April 1934, Mallenuppen, East Prussia

A pupil of Wagner-Régeny and Eisler, Matthus was appointed composer-in-residence at the Komische Oper in Berlin in 1964. Here he worked with Walter Felsenstein, who exerted a profound influence on his operatic thinking. In 1966, with Götz Friedrich, he prepared a performance of Monteverdi's *Il ritorno d'Ulisse*. He also wrote incidental music for plays. His first opera, *Lazarillo von Tormes*, is still largely tonal, though in his second opera, *Der letzte Schuss* (based on the novella by Laurenyov), which established him as a leading East German composer, he had progressed to dodecaphonic and serial procedures. His third opera, *Noch ein Löffel Gift, Liebling?*, was a combination of comedy and detective story based on Saul O'Hara's *Risky Marriage*. In *Omphale*, Matthus made use of ancient Greek modes and *Klangfarben*.

The orchestral work *Responso* (1977) marked a turning point in his stylistic development. He now favours a kind of Expressionist free atonality, and, from the second act of *Judith* onwards, has derived his melodic and harmonic material from an unusual 8-note scale. His approach to vocal writing owes something to the baroque doctrine of the affections. In his three most recent operas the theme is the perennial conflict between the individual and society in times of political crisis. Significantly, *Graf Mirabeau*, written to celebrate the anniversary of the French Revolution, was first performed in 1989 – the year in which his fellow countrymen shook off the shackles of dictatorship.

Die Weise von Liebe und Tod des Cornets Christoph Rilke

The Lay of Cornet Christoph Rilke's Love and Death
Operatic vision
Libretto by the composer, after the poem by Rainer Maria Rilke (1899)
Composed 1983
PREMIERES   16 February 1985, Semperoper, Dresden; US: 5 December 1990, Manhattan School of Music, New York

Written for the reopening of the Semperoper in Dresden, this protest against war depicts the tragedy of a young man who experiences an overwhelming love affair and then rushes headlong to his death on the battlefield. Twinned voices are assigned to the principal characters. The work is framed by a choral *Dies irae*, and a setting of a line by Rilke, 'In such nights there was a fire in the opera', an appropriate reference to the catastrophic bombing of Dresden during the Second World War.

EDITION   v.s., Deutscher Verlag für Musik, 1986

Judith

Opera in two acts
Libretto by the composer, after Friedrich Hebbel and the Old Testament
Composed 1980–84
PREMIERES   28 September 1985, Komische Oper, East Berlin; US: 28 July 1990, Santa Fe

The plot is based on the familiar story of the Jewish widow who, in the besieged city of Bethulia, saves her people by ensnaring and then decapitating the brutal Assyrian general Holofernes. It is a strident and Expressionist portrait of a tormented and impassioned heroine who at the end commits suicide.

RECORDING   Bundschuh, Hasclau, Hellmich, Rundfunkchor Berlin, Komische Oper Berlin, Reuter, Eterna, [n.d.]
EDITION   v.s., Deutscher Verlag für Musik, 1985

Other operatic works: *Lazarillo von Tormes*, 1964; *Der letzte Schuss*, 1967 (RECORDING excerpts: Eterna/Nova, *c.* 1978); *Noch ein Löffel Gift, Liebling?*, 1972; *Omphale*, 1976; *Graf Mirabeau*, 1989; *Desdemona und ihre Schwestern*, 1992
BIBLIOGRAPHY   Andrew Porter, 'Moral Tales Retold', *New Yorker*, 24 December 1990, pp. 16–17; Ursula Stürzbecher, *Komponisten in der DDR*, Gerstenberg Verlag, 1979

A.C.

NICHOLAS MAW

John Nicholas Maw; *b* 5 November 1935, Grantham, Lincolnshire, England

Maw worked in a bicycle factory before being accepted to study at the Royal Academy of Music with Lennox Berkeley. Later he studied in Paris with Max Deutsch, himself a pupil of Schoenberg. But though serialism affected Maw briefly and superficially, his music has generally avoided system or codifiable method. His first great success, the 1962 BBC Prom commission *Scenes and Arias*, already established the sumptuous idiom, based on expressive line and much extended tonal harmony, which has served him ever since. Its lyric–dramatic treatment of the female voice also looked forward directly to his two operas (especially the second), a genre he cultivated briefly but with considerable success in the 1960s.

One Man Show

Comic opera in two acts (2h)
Libretto by Arthur Jacobs, after an idea from the short story *The Background* by Saki (1911)
Composed 1964, rev. 1966
PREMIERES   12 November 1964, Jeannetta Cochrane Theatre, London; US: 7 March 1975, Pittsburgh

The satirical story about a young man with a tattoo who is elevated into a national exhibit by pretentious art critics (with, ironically, a libretto by a well-known music critic) presented problems of pace and timing to the inexperienced composer. Nevertheless *One Man Show* revealed seeds of musical wit and theatrical invention that were to bear fruit in Maw's next opera. Its first performance marked the opening of the Jeannetta Cochrane Theatre.

EDITIONS f.s., Boosey & Hawkes (on hire); v.s., Boosey & Hawkes, 1968

The Rising of the Moon

Opera in three acts (2h 30m)
Libretto by Beverley Cross
Composed 1967–70
PREMIERE 19 July 1970, Glyndebourne, Sussex
CAST Brother Timothy *high t*, Donal O'Dowd *bar*,
Cathleen Sweeney *ms*, Colonel Lord Jowler *b-bar*, Major von Zastrow *high bar*, Captain Lillywhite *t*, Lady Eugenie Jowler *s*, Frau von Zastrow *ms*, Atalanta Lillywhite *s*, Corporal Haywood *bar*, Cornet Beaumont *t*, Widow Sweeney *a*, Lynch *b*; *tb* chorus of Lancers
LARGE ORCHESTRA including stage band

The Rising of the Moon is a bitter-sweet romantic comedy. While the Irish peasants and the English soldiers are to some extent caricatured, the intended core of the work is a strain of sentiment not unduly disturbed by psychological probability. The genuinely funny if occasionally gauche libretto is based on an original idea, set in Ireland in 1875, the time the Fenians, and the year in which Parnell entered Parliament (the title is a phrase of one Fenian song, sung in Act II by Lynch to the tune of another, 'The Wearing of the Green').

SYNOPSIS
Act I The 31st Royal Lancers arrive in the Mayo town of Ballinvourney 'to show the flag . . . and to stop young men from talking revolution'. They include a monocled Prussian 'observer' (Zastrow) and, among their retinue, three ladies (the CO's and Zastrow's wives, and the captain's daughter Atalanta). When a candidly unmilitary but handsome and self-assured young officer (Beaumont) arrives to join the regiment, Zastrow suggests an initiation test involving the conquest of three women in one night. The locals plan to lead him by a roundabout route to the ladies' hotel.

Act II Beaumont easily breaks down Lady Eugenie's 'defences', and conquers Frau von Zastrow by reading poetry to her. But his third victory is interrupted by the arrival of Zastrow, with the beautiful Irish girl, Cathleen, in his sights. He is, however, tricked into Atalanta's room, leaving Cathleen to woo Beaumont for herself.

Act III The next morning, the fuddled Lancers are rudely awoken by Beaumont's return. His trophies reveal the identity of his conquests, but to save the regiment's honour he offers to resign his commission. As the Lancers leave Ballinvourney in

A scene from Act II of The Rising of the Moon *(Glyndebourne, 1970)*

disarray Beaumont also gently detaches himself from Cathleen and departs.

Full of charm and sharp musical observation, and much cleverer in comic pacing than its predecessor, the work follows purely traditional models, including Britten and perhaps Strauss. In style it inhabits a middle ground between the atonal and the extendedly tonal, with occasional passages of simple melody, tonally set. There are several big, effective ensembles and the orchestration is rather full for a comic opera, but individual characterization is precise; for instance, Maw manages to distinguish his four leading female characters without ever lapsing into stereotype.

EDITION v.s., Boosey & Hawkes, 1971

BIBLIOGRAPHY Anthony Payne, 'Nicholas Maw's *One Man Show*', *Tempo*, no. 71 (winter 1964–5), pp. 2–14; Stephen Walsh, 'Nicholas Maw's New Opera [*The Rising of the Moon*]', *Tempo*, no. 92 (spring 1970), pp. 2–15

S.W.

SIMON MAYR

Johannes [Johann] Simon [Giovanni Simone] Mayr [Mayer]; *b* 14 June 1763, Mendorf, nr Ingolstadt, Bavaria; *d* 2 December 1845, Bergamo

Mayr was the leading composer of Italian opera in the first decade of the 19th century, filling an important position between Paisiello and Rossini. Little is known of his early life and education other than that he gained a place at the Jesuit seminary at Ingolstadt on the strength of his skill as a boy chorister and later studied law at Ingolstadt University. In 1786 a Swiss patron took him to Italy where Mayr was to remain, bar a few excursions, for the rest of his life. He studied first with Carlo Lenzo, maestro di cappella at Bergamo, and then with Ferdinando Bertoni in Venice. It was under the latter that he embarked in earnest on his career as a composer, concentrating initially on sacred music.

Mayr's first opera, *Saffo*, an opera seria, was performed at the Teatro La Fenice (where Mayr played the viola in the orchestra) in 1794. Despite its success, it was two years before he wrote his next stage work, *La Lodoiska* (which, like the later *Due Giornate*, borrowed its subject from a work by Cherubini). From then on a stream of operas followed. The early works were principally comic operas and one-act farsas but – after 1801 – Mayr's output also included a significant number of works described as eroico or eroicomico. Combining elements of both opera seria and opera buffa, these contributed to a tradition of opera semi-seria popular in Italy at the time, of which Paer was the greatest exponent.

By 1813 Mayr's reputation was well established (his *Adelasia e Alemaro* had been the work chosen by Ricordi in 1808 to publish as its first (more-or-less) complete opera), and he consolidated his position as one of Italy's leading opera composers with two works that were to prove his greatest successes – *La rosa bianca e la rosa rossa* and *Medea in Corinto*. In the succeeding years, however, due at least in part to the growing popularity of Rossini, Mayr's interest in opera waned and he turned his attention increasingly to cantatas. Several of Mayr's later operas, including his last, *Demetrio*, return to the Metastasian type of texts he set early in his career, a regressive move in the face of a fast-developing Italian operatic scene. After 1824 blindness prevented the composition of any further operas and Mayr concentrated on liturgical music and on the work of the music school he had founded in 1802.

Towards the end of his life Mayr recorded his memoirs and his thoughts about music. Among his comments is one regarding his own position in the development of Italian opera, which history has confirmed: 'The operas of Mayr and Paer, introducing into Italian music German harmony and instrumentation, modified the physiognomy and prepared a revolution.' Certainly Mayr's deliberate and original use of specific instrumental colours (he regularly scored for harp, guitar and cor anglais, wrote solo violin or woodwind obbligati and passages for unaccompanied woodwind 'banda') influenced later Italian composers. And, perhaps less conspicuously, several other features of Mayr's operas continued in those of the next generation, most notably in the works of Donizetti – a pupil at Mayr's school from 1806 to 1814. Among shared elements are the choice of dramatic scenes: pagan rituals, storms, and battles, and historical British subjects. Donizetti may also have been influenced by formal devices of his teacher's works – the stringing together of short melodic fragments to create a dramatic scene, the use of the chorus, the avoidance of vocal embellishments, etc. A relative lack of melodic ingenuity on Mayr's part weakens the effects of his more innovative elements and few of his works are seen today.

Medea in Corinto

Medea in Corinth
Melodramma tragico in two acts (2h 45m)
Libretto by Felice Romani
Composed ?1812–13, rev. 1823
PREMIERES 28 November 1813, Teatro San Carlo, Naples; UK: 1 June 1826, King's Theatre, Haymarket, London; US: 14 February 1961, Alice Tully Hall, New York (semi-staged)

Probably Mayr's most successful opera, *Medea* was no doubt inspired by Cherubini's opera on the same subject (1797) and by Spontini's *La vestale*, which had been a huge success in Naples (1811). The opera's popularity was such that, for a while, it eclipsed the works of Rossini (and is said to have inspired Turner to paint *The Vision of Medea*); but it was a triumph Mayr failed to repeat.

Medea, abandoned by her husband Giasone, interrupts his new marriage to Creusa. Imprisoned, she calls on the gods of the Underworld to help her wreak vengeance. At a resumption of the wedding

Contemporary illustration of Giuditta Pasta as Medea and her children in Medea in Corinto *(Naples, 1813)*

della lettera, 1797; Il segreto, 1797; Avviso ai maritati, 1798; Lauso e Lidia, 1798; Adriano in Siria, 1798; Che originali, 1798; Amor ingegnoso, 1798; L'ubbidienza per astuzia, 1798; Adelaide di Guesclino, 1799; L'accademia di musica, 1799; Labino e Carlotta, 1799; L'avaro, 1799; La locandiera, 1800; Il caretto del venditore d'aceto, 1800; L'inconvenienze teatrali (2 numbers survive), 1800; L'equivoco, ovvero Le bizzarie dell'amore, 1800; Gli sciti, 1800; Ginevra di Scozia, 1801; Le due giornate, 1801; I virtuosi, 1801; Argene, 1801; I misteri eleusini, 1802; Ercole in Lidia, 1803; Le finte rivali, 1803; Alonso e Cora, 1803; Amor non ha ritegno, 1804; Elisa, ossia Il monte San Bernardo, 1804; Zamori, ossia L'eroe dell'Indie, 1804; Eraldo ed Emma, 1805; Di locanda in locanda e sempre in sala, 1805; L'amor coniugale, 1805; La roccia di Frauenstein, 1805; Gli americani, 1805; Palmira, ossia Il trionfo della virtù e dell'amore, 1806; Il piccolo compositore di musica, 1806; Adelasia e Aleramo, 1806 (EDITION facsimile, Garland, 1991); Nè l'un, nè l'altro, 1807; Belle ciarle e tristi fatti, 1807; I cherusci, 1808; Il vero originale, 1808; Il matrimonio per concorso, ?1809; Il ritorno di Ulisse, 1809; Amore non soffre opposizione, 1810; Raùl di Créqui, 1810; Il sacrifizio d'Ifigenia, 1811 (?rev. of Ifigenia in Aulide (lost), 1806); L'amor filiale, 1811; Tamerlano, 1812; La rosa bianca e la rosa rossa, 1813; Elena, 1814; Atar, ossia Il serraglio d'Ormus, 1814; Le due duchesse, o sia La caccia dei lupi, 1814; Cora, 1815 (reworking of Alonso e Cora); Mennone e Zemira, 1817; Amor avvocato, 1817; Alfredo il grande, re degli Anglo Sassoni, 1819; Le danaide, 1819; Fedra, 1820; Demetrio, 1824; 5 lost operas

BIBLIOGRAPHY   John Stewart Allitt, J. S. Mayr: Father of 19th-century Italian Music, Element Books, 1989; Arrigo Gazzaniga (ed.), Giovanni Simone Mayr: Zibaldone preceduto dalle Pagine autobiographiche, Biblioteca Civica A. Mai, Bergamo, 1977

G.H.

ceremony, Creusa wears a poisoned robe given to her by Medea and dies. As the people approach Medea seeking retribution, she stabs her own children. The heavens darken and a chariot drawn by a dragon carries her away across the skies.

Mayr's technique of constructing scenes from short musical fragments is extremely effective in dramatic scenes, of which Medea offers many. The gripping effect of, in particular, the heroine's invocation of the powers of hell ('Antica notte', Act II) is achieved through constantly changing tempi, melodic motifs, and orchestral accompaniments. Like Mozart in *Don Giovanni*, Mayr makes dramatic use of trombones in conjuring up his image of hell, and the instrument's regular inclusion in Italian opera orchestras after this date was probably due at least in part to his example. For *Medea*'s 1823 revival at La Scala, Mayr was persuaded to modify his melodic style to include longer lyrical periods (à la Rossini) and to introduce more modern *cabalettas*. The result is weaker and modern revivals have reverted to the original score.

RECORDING   Galvany, Patenaude, Cathcart, Clarion Concerts Ch and O, Jenkins, Vanguard, 1970
EDITIONS   f.s., Opera Rara, 1972; v.s., Carli, Paris, ?1823; facsimile, Garland, 1986

Other surviving operas: Saffo, ossia I riti d'Apollo Leucadio, 1794; La Lodoiska, 1796 (rev. twice, 1799); Un pazzo ne fa cento, 1796; Telemaco nell'isola di Calipso, 1797; L'intrigo

DOMENICO MAZZOCCHI

baptized 8 November 1592, Civita Castellana; *d* 21 January 1665, Rome

After studying for the priesthood in his home town, Mazzocchi settled in Rome where he entered the service of Cardinal Ippolito Aldobrandini as a musician. The cardinal's brother, Giovanni Giorgio, commissioned the opera *La catena d'Adone* (1626) from Mazzocchi. Rather unusually, it contains four duets and ten trios. Mazzocchi was fortunate in attracting the support of many influential patrons, including members of the Farnese, Barberini and Pamphili families. After the performance of his sacred opera based on the life of Roman saints, *Il martirio de'Sant Abundio prete, Abundantio diacono, Marciano, e Giovanni suo figliuolo, cavalieri romani* (1641, music lost), Mazzocchi devoted little time to music.

BIBLIOGRAPHY   W. Witzenmann, 'Domenico Mazzocchi, 1592–1665', Analecta musicologica, vol. 8, Cologne–Vienna, 1970

G.D.

VIRGILIO MAZZOCCHI

baptized 22 July 1597, Civita Castellana; *d* 3 October 1646, Civita Castellana

Like his brother Domenico, Virgilio Mazzocchi was intended for the priesthood, and although he was never ordained his career was spent in the service of major Roman churches including the Cappella Giulia of St Peter's, where he was a respected teacher of the choirboys. Most of his output consists of sacred music, though he wrote two operas to texts by Giulio Rospigliosi. The first, *L'Egisto* or *Che soffre speri*, was performed at the Palazzo Barberini in 1637, and Mazzocchi set the convoluted story of love and mistaken identity in collaboration with Marco Marazzoli. Although it included none of the divertissements, chorus passages and spectacular stage effects that were often to be found in works of this period, and lasted over five hours, the opera was a success. A similar style prevails in the second opera, *L'innocenza difesa*, or *San Bonifatio* (1641). This is a spiritual opera which tells the story of Bonifacio, who, encouraged by his love to fight for the Christian cause, dies a martyr.

BIBLIOGRAPHY   Margaret Murata, *Operas for the Papal Court 1631–1668*, UMI Research Press, 1981

G.D.

ALBERTO MAZZUCATO

b 28 July 1813, Udine; *d* 31 December 1877, Milan

Mazzucato's first opera, *La fidanzata di Lammermoor*, preceded Donizetti's setting of the same subject by 18 months. A mathematician by education, Mazzucato was regarded as something of a modernist even in his early works, and a visit to Paris, where he became acquainted with the music of Beethoven and Meyerbeer, confirmed this impression: *Esmeralda*, the first opera he produced on his return, was widely performed but had a mixed reception from the more traditional sections of the establishment. Mazzucato was, in any case, one of several composers who abandoned their operatic careers with the arrival of Verdi on the operatic scene. From 1839 until his death he was a teacher at the Milan Conservatory, first of singing, later of composition, and finally as director. In this capacity he counted Boito and Gomes among his pupils.

Operas: *La fidanzata di Lammermoor*, 1834; *Don Chisciotte*, 1836; *Esmeralda*, 1838; *Fede*, 1838; *I corsari*, 1840; *I due sergenti*, 1841; *Luigi V, re di Francia*, 1843; *Hernani*, 1843; *Alberico da Romano*, 1847
BIBLIOGRAPHY   Andrea Lanza, 'Alberto Mazzucato', in *Grove*, Macmillan, 1980

M.R.

RICHARD MEALE

Richard Graham Meale; *b* 24 August 1932, Sydney, Australia

Meale, a dominating force in Australian music, studied piano, harp and clarinet at the New South Wales Conservatorium, but never formally studied composition. In 1960, on a Ford Foundation grant, he studied non-Western music at the University of California. As a member of the music department of the Australian Broadcasting Commission for seven years, he was responsible for the broadcasting of much new music. His instrumental and orchestral works include commissions from Paul Sacher for the Collegium Musicum Zurich and from the Fires of London. Early works were uncompromisingly avant garde, but more recent compositions show a more melodic idiom. Meale is reader in composition at the University of Adelaide.

Voss

Opera in two acts (2h)
Libretto by David Malouf, based on the novel by Patrick White (1957)
Composed 1979–86
PREMIERE   1 March 1986, Adelaide Festival

The libretto is a skilful reduction of White's complex novel to a manageable shape. It is not a naturalistic story of exploration, but concentrates on the strange spiritual union between Voss and Laura Trevelyan, who remains in Sydney. The device of having two characters sing simultaneously is put to brilliant use, uniting their thoughts although they are widely separated geographically. Act I employs quotations from collections of 19th-century Australian salon music to emphasize the normality of the society from which Voss sets out. Distorted reference to these occurs when the expedition and its leader are disintegrating. The music is more lyrical than most of Meale's earlier compositions.

RECORDING   Richardson, Grant, Begg, Gard, Eddie, Chard, Pringle, Tomlinson, Australian Opera Ch, Sydney SO, Challender, Philips, 1987
EDITION   manuscript, Boosey & Hawkes (Australia) (on hire), 1986

Mer de glace

Sea of Ice
Opera in a prologue and seven scenes (2h 30m)
Libretto by David Malouf
Composed 1986–91
PREMIERE   7 October 1991, Sydney Opera House

Set against the background of the *Mer de glace* in Switzerland, the opera describes Mary Shelley's invention of her Frankenstein monster. In a bizarre and confusing turn to the story, the monster is created out of Byron, who is visiting, while Percy Bysshe Shelley (Mary's husband) becomes Frankenstein. The entire action takes place as a memory relived by the dying Claire Clairmont, half-sister of Mary and mother of Byron's child.

As in *Voss* Meale refers to pre-existent music whose style helps establish the atmosphere of the drama. Here this evolves into a post-Romantic style with snatches reminiscent of composers ranging from Ravel to Richard Strauss, a language that is then deliberately broken down as the terror caused by the monster takes control.

EDITION   v.s., Boosey & Hawkes, 1991

BIBLIOGRAPHY   Essay by Roger Covell accompanying recording of *Voss*; Australian Music Centre brochure

A.I.G.

ETIENNE MÉHUL

Etienne-Nicolas Méhul; *b* 22 June 1763, Givet, France; *d* 18 October 1817, Paris

Méhul was the leading French-born composer in the age of Beethoven. His output included four symphonies and many opéras comiques, and he was an important contributor to the development of the latter, furthering its progress towards Romantic opera in several significant areas.

Méhul went to Paris in 1778/9 and studied with J. F. Edelmann. The 1780s was a decade of high achievement in French opera, so when Méhul burst on the scene in 1790 with *Euphrosine* (in its original form the first-ever five-act opéra comique), its success was significant. His earlier tragédie-lyrique *Cora* was soon produced at the Opéra, for which he also wrote *Adrien* (derived from Metastasio's *Adriano in Siria*). Its imperial subject caused opposition and postponement. But Méhul's next projects were opéras comiques of startling variety, culminating in *Mélidore et Phrosine*, which was ahead of its time in several respects.

Like most composers in Paris, Méhul wrote works engaging in some way with the political revolution (*Horatius Coclès, Doria*); but he wrote far more occasional music for the Empire of Napoleon. After the relative failures of *La caverne* and *Ariodant*, Méhul switched to comedy: *L'Irato* was actually premiered under an Italian pseudonym (Fiorelli) to emphasize the concomitant change of style. The score was dedicated to Napoleon Bonaparte. In the two most original works of his final period, *Uthal* and *Joseph*, Méhul took local colour to radical degrees of expression. *Joseph*'s simplicity, counterpoint, and 'antique' chants anticipate traits in Halévy's *La juive* and Meyerbeer's *Les Huguenots*. The work had an especially strong following in 19th-century Germany, where Méhul's integrity of style was favourably contrasted with the lightweight idiom of many of his compatriots. He remained, though, an essentially Parisian figure, finally defeated by illness and the unhappy reception accorded to *Les amazones* in 1811. However, certain of his opera overtures, which were generally designed to paint the scene for the opera, had independent success, such as that to *Le*

Etienne Méhul

jeune Henri, known as *La chasse du jeune Henri*, with its descriptive horn-calls.

Euphrosine, ou Le tyran corrigé

Euphrosine, or The Tyrant Reformed

Comédie in three acts (2h)

Libretto by François-Benoît Hoffman

PREMIERES   five-act version: 4 September 1790, Théâtre Favart, Paris; three-act version with rev. Act III: 13 August 1795

Alibour, Coradin's doctor, welcomes three orphaned sisters to his master's castle: Euphrosine, Louise and Léonore. Coradin, who has agreed to house the sisters, is a tyrannical, feudal lord. They plot to reform him. Euphrosine learns of the existence of prisoners, including a knight. The Countess of Arles arrives and is angered by Euphrosine's assertion that she will marry Coradin since she has been rejected by him already. In Act II Coradin is falling in love with Euphrosine. Reassured that the knight is not her lover (as the malicious countess had tried to persuade him), Coradin kneels to Euphrosine and places her in charge of the castle during the impending battle with the knight's forces. In Act III, encouraged by the countess, Coradin orders that Euphrosine be poisoned; however his remorse when he believes her dead earns him forgiveness, and the countess's schemes are exposed.

Méhul's score is distinguished by variety, force, and passion. The fateful role of jealousy is underlined by thematic cross-references, and the Act II duet 'Gardez-vous de la jalousie' established a new standard of psychological realism for the post-Gluckian age.

EDITION f.s. (3-act version), Cousineau, [n.d.]; facsimile, with an introduction by Charles Rosen, *Early Romantic Opera*, vol. 38, Garland, 1980

Stratonice

Comédie héroïque in one act (1h)
Libretto by François-Benoît Hoffman, after the Classical story concerning Antiochus I Soter, of Syria
PREMIERE 3 May, 1792, Théâtre Favart, Paris

Seleucus, king of ancient Syria, and his court pray for the recovery of his son, Antiochus. A doctor arrives and suspects a love malady. The son is on the point of confessing it, when sight of his father causes him to be silent. When Stratonice, Seleucus' betrothed, appears the doctor finds his silent patient's pulse rate has accelerated, confirming his diagnosis. He suggests an interview between Antiochus and Stratonice, persuades the couple that he knows they are in love, then uses an expedient to inform the king of it. Seleucus tests the motives of each young person in turn, and finally relinquishes the princess to his son.

Whereas *Euphrosine* was famous for the violent 'jealousy' duet, *Stratonice* breathes an antique calm and reason. Seleucus' solo, 'Versez tous vos chagrins dans le sein paternel', was a favourite for many years.

EDITION facsimile, Elizabeth Bartlet (ed.), *French Opera in the 17th and 18th Centuries*, Pendragon, 1993

Mélidore et Phrosine

Drame lyrique in three acts (2h 15m)
Libretto by Antoine-Victor Arnault
PREMIERE 6 May 1794, Théâtre Favart, Paris

Phrosine and her lover Mélidore plan to elope, since their intended marriage is opposed by Phrosine's brothers, Aimar and Jule. They are overheard and, in a fight in the darkness, Aimar is fatally wounded. He dies naming the innocent Mélidore as the assassin. Mélidore's friends drag him away to safety. Act II takes place across the straits of Messina on an island. Mélidore assumes the identity of a local hermit, who has recently died. When Jule comes to consult the 'hermit' about finding his brother's supposed killer he is told that the latter has drowned. Mélidore manages to explain the truth to Phrosine; they swear fidelity. In Act III Mélidore lights a beacon to guide Phrosine's boat to the island. But a storm rises, and the boat yields only Jule; he has thwarted his sister and, seeing her trying to swim across, pushed her away from his boat. Mélidore saves her. Jule finally renounces his incestuous love and agrees to Phrosine's wedding to Mélidore.

The experimental nature of this extraordinary libretto was matched in the score by many forward-looking techniques: large-scale tonal wanderings; Berlioz-like use of stopped horn notes; thematic cross-references; and a pervading sense of the wild elements, formed in the orchestral writing.

EDITION facsimile, Elizabeth Bartlet (ed.), *French Opera in the 17th and 18th Centuries*, vol. 73, Pendragon, 1990

Ariodant

Opéra in three acts (2h 15m)
Libretto by François-Benoît Hoffman, after Cantos V and VI of the poem, *Orlando Furioso* by Ariosto (1516)
PREMIERE 11 October 1799, Théâtre Favart, Paris

Hoffman's plot is based on the same original source as Handel's *Ariodante* (1735). Othon has failed in his suit for the hand of Ina, Princess of Scotland, and is violent and resigned by turns. On hearing of a rival, Ariodant, he becomes uncontrollably jealous. Ina's father, King Edgard, refuses to influence her. Othon plans a *coup* and persuades Dalinde to help. Ariodant confronts Othon's insults, and is challenged by him to a duel. In Act II celebrations are in train. Othon is still furious; Ariodant's brother, Lurcain, arrives with friends to witness the duel. Othon announces instead he will prove Ina unchaste, and so cause her judicial punishment by death. Dalinde, disguised as Ina, admits Othon to her rooms and Ariodant believes Ina has betrayed him; the princess's protestations of innocence are disbelieved. In Act III Othon tempts Ina to pretend she and Othon were married already; but Ina will not save herself by perjury. Othon is informed of Dalinde's murder (which he ordered), but in fact Ariodant has rescued her and now arranges for her to impersonate Ina at the latter's trial. At the crucial moment Othon rushes in to claim that they are already married. But Dalinde unveils and exposes his crimes publicly.

Once again Méhul memorably depicts the demonic power of jealousy, now tempered by a spacious sense of medieval chivalry. Edgard's anguish is also portrayed; only the limited participation of the chorus restricts the full expansion of the subject. Among technical novelties are the bridge passages that link set pieces to spoken dialogue.

EDITION f.s., Imbault, [n.d.]; facsimile, with an introduction by Charles Rosen, *Early Romantic Opera*, vol. 39, Garland, 1978

Uthal

Opera in one act (50m)
Libretto by Jacques Benjamin Saint-Victor, after the poem *Berrathon* by 'Ossian' (pseudonym for James Macpherson)
PREMIERE 17 May 1806, Opéra-Comique, Paris

Larmor, aged chief of Dunthalmon, has been dispossessed and is sheltering at night in the storm-ridden countryside. The voice of his daughter Malvina is heard in the overture, searching for him. Larmor tells Malvina that an envoy – the bard Ullin – has gone to get help from Fingal, chief of Morven. War is inevitable, and Malvina is caught between loyalty to her father and her husband Uthal, who has occupied Larmor's palace. Fingal's warrior bards approach, ready to attack at dawn. Uthal appears, seeking Malvina. She approaches, and when she eventually recognizes him (he is armed), Uthal's excessive pride prevents him from seeing reason. It is now daybreak and Uthal, Larmor and the warrior bards prepare for action. Uthal is defeated. His pride is further subdued by the ultimate sacrifice of

Malvina, who offers to follow him into exile. The opera ends in reconciliation.

The Ossianic subject was as far removed from typical Empire-period comedy as can be imagined. As if to alienate popularity further, Méhul removed violins from the orchestra altogether, asking their players to play violas instead. To this attempt at northern tone-painting is added harp-writing for the bards, and the whole work, especially taking account of the spoken episodes, attains a unique sort of nobility.

EDITION f.s., Magasin de Musique, [n.d.]; facsimile, with an introduction by Charles Rosen, *Early Romantic Opera*, vol. 40, Garland, 1978

Joseph

Opera in three acts
Libretto by Alexandre Duval after Genesis, Chapters 37 and 41–5
PREMIERES 17 February 1807, Opéra-Comique, Paris; US: 15 October 1828, Philadelphia; UK: 7 April 1841, Drury Lane, London (concert); 3 February 1914, Covent Garden, London

The opera has no female solo characters; however, the role of Benjamin is a *travesti* role, and there are female voices in the chorus. The action takes place in Memphis, in the palace of Joseph. He is seen telling his confidant Utobal how his brothers sold him into slavery, and of his subsequent rise to power under the pharaoh. Famine is in the land, and Jacob's sons arrive to seek asylum for the Israelites. Unrecognized by his family, Joseph (now named Cléophas) admits the starving people. After an entr'acte Joseph goes to the Hebrew encampment, at night. A hymn is heard. Benjamin appears and describes the effect of Joseph's presumed death on their father, Jacob. Jacob, now blind, converses with 'Cléophas'; the latter is summoned to a triumphant ceremony, and insists on sharing the experience with Jacob's family. Siméon appears and confesses his 15-year-old crime against Joseph. Jacob curses his sons, except for Benjamin. But Joseph can now reveal his identity. All praise the God of goodness and mercy.

Méhul's music is pervaded by a sober antiquity of mood, yet is true to his melodic style. The various hymns and entr'actes (not to mention the overture with its chant-like motifs) establish the setting, while the characters are distinguished by a range of strong statements: Joseph's celebrated romance, 'A peine au sortir de l'enfance', Siméon's 'Non! non! l'Eternel que j'offense' and the 'curse' ensemble. A harp is prominent, and also a 'tuba' (presumably the antique 'tuba curva' invented under the Revolution for use in open-air festivals) is heard.

RECORDING Lafon, Dale, Massis, Vassar, Intermezzo Choral Ensemble, O Regionale de Picardie, Bardon, Chant du Monde, 1989: the most famous number, Joseph's aria ('Champs paternels'), has been recorded separately by McCormack, Tauber and Simoneau among others
EDITIONS f.s., Magasin de Musique, [n.d.]; facsimile, Philip Gossett and Charles Rosen (eds), *Early Romantic Opera*, vol. 41, Garland, 1979; v.ss., Leduc, [c. 1860]; Breitkopf, [c. 1913]

Other operas: *Cora*, 1791; *Le jeune sage et le vieux fou*, 1793; *Horatius Coclès*, 1794; *Le congrès des rois* (coll. with 11 others), 1794; *Doria, ou La tyrannie détruite*, 1795; *La caverne*, 1795; *Le jeune Henri*, 1797; *La prise du pont de Lodi*, 1797; *Adrien*, 1799; *Epicure* (coll. with Cherubini), 1800; *Bion*, 1800; *L'Irato, ou L'emporté*, 1801; *Une folie*, 1802; *Le trésor supposé, ou Le danger d'écouter aux portes*, 1802; *Joanna*, 1802; *Héléna*, 1803; *Le baiser et la quittance* (coll. with Boieldieu, Kreutzer and Isouard), 1803; *L'heureux malgré lui*, 1803; *Les deux aveugles de Tolède*, 1806; *Gabrielle d'Estrées, ou Les amours d'Henri IV*, 1806; *Les amazones, ou La fondation de Thèbes*, 1811; *Le prince troubadour*, 1813; *L'Oriflamme* (coll. with Berton, Kreutzer and Paer), 1814; *La journée aux aventures*, 1816; *Valentine de Milan* (inc.), (1817), completed by Daussoigne-Méhul, 1822; *La taupe et les papillons*, (c. 1797); *Sésostris*, (c. 1810); 9 other lost operas
BIBLIOGRAPHY David Charlton, 'Motive and Motif: Méhul before 1797', *ML*, vol. 57 (1976), p. 362; Winton Dean, 'French Opera' in *The New Oxford History of Music*, vol. 8, OUP, 1982; Winton Dean, 'Opera under the French Revolution', *PRMA*, vol. 94 (1967–8), pp. 77–96

D.P.C.

JACOPO MELANI

baptized 6 July 1623, Pistoia; *d* 18 August 1676, Pistoia

Jacopo Melani pursued a somewhat provincial career in his native Pistoia and nearby Florence. Nevertheless, he remains a major composer of mid-17th-century opera. He was organist (1645) and then choirmaster (1657) of Pistoia Cathedral, and may also have spent some time in Venice and Rome. Most of his stage works, however, were written for Florentine academies and the Medici court. In 1655, he supplied a set of intermedi for the Accademia dei Sorgenti and, from 1657 to 1662, he wrote four operas for the Accademia degli Immobili for their Teatro della Pergola, plus a splendid festa teatrale, *Ercole in Tebe*, for the wedding of Cosimo III de' Medici and Marguérite Louise d'Orléans in 1661. His *Il Girello*, a comic opera written for Rome (1668) and with a prologue by Alessandro Stradella, is an important example of its genre and provides a link between the styles of the 17th- and 18th-century comic opera. It became one of the most frequently performed operas of the century.

Stage works surviving in manuscript: *Il potestà di Colognole, ovvero La Tancia*, 1657; *Ercole in Tebe*, 1661; *Il Girello*, 1668; *Enea in Italia*, 1670; 10 lost works
BIBLIOGRAPHY R. L. and N. W. Weaver, *A Chronology of Music in the Florentine Theater, 1590–1750*, Detroit Studies in Music Bibliography, Information Coordinators, 1978

T.C.

FELIX MENDELSSOHN

Jakob Ludwig Felix Mendelssohn-Bartholdy; *b* 3 February 1809, Hamburg; *d* 4 November 1847, Leipzig

In 1831 Mendelssohn remarked to the singer Eduard Devrient: 'Put a real libretto in my hands and in a few moments it will be composed, for every day I long anew to write an opera . . . I will not set a text that does not suit me. If you know a man who is able to write a libretto, for heaven's sake tell me about him: I look for nothing else.' When he said this, at the age of 22, he had already completed six operas but, though he was to live for another 16 years and to consider many operatic projects, he never finished another. His reputation rests firmly on his instrumental compositions and oratorios, and it was these works that established him as one of the greatest composers of the day. Nevertheless, his early operatic efforts are a remarkable testimony to the precocity of his genius.

His earliest dramatic work dates from 1820, the year of his first extant compositions. For his father's 44th birthday he began words and music of a little domestic piece, a three-scene Lustspiel, Ich, J. Mendelssohn, but seems only to have completed the first scene and part of a second. Later that year, however, he completed a one-act comic opera to a text by a family friend, Dr Johann Ludwig Casper, entitled Die Soldatenliebschaft; like the three subsequent libretti provided by Casper it was probably based on a French original. The 11-year-old composer's overture and 11 numbers show that he was familiar with the conventional treatment of stock operatic characters, that he knew Mozart's operas and that he was benefiting from his training in counterpoint with Carl Friedrich Zelter (begun the previous year).

The second Mendelssohn–Casper opera, Die beiden Pädagogen, written in 1821, while still firmly grounded in the most conventional singspiel idiom, shows remarkable advances on its predecessor. The third, a one-act singspiel, Die wandernden Komödianten, composed the following year, is dramatically less convincing (largely as a result of its libretto, recently rediscovered in the Bodleian Library, Oxford) but nevertheless testifies to the remarkably rapid musical advances Mendelssohn was making at that time. Characterization is stronger than in his previous works, created in longer, more varied vocal numbers (mostly ensembles) and sustained in a deftly constructed finale. The last product of Mendelssohn's collaboration with Casper was the three-act comic opera Der Onkel aus Boston, oder Die beiden Neffen (1823). A fair appraisal of the work is hindered by the loss of the dialogue to Act III (the dialogue to Acts I and II has recently come to light in the Bodleian Library, Oxford); but it seems clear that, despite the advances of technique and conception shown in much of the music, it is, like its predecessor, dramatically feeble.

Far more impressive is Die Hochzeit des Camacho, Mendelssohn's only full-scale opera, and the only one of his stage works to be publicly performed and published during his lifetime. He wrote his final opera, the modest liederspiel Die Heimkehr aus der Fremde, in 1829. And although his search for suitable operatic subjects continued for many years, he was never able to complete another such work. Several projects were begun with enthusiasm – notably settings of Shakespeare's The Tempest (1831) and of

Wieland's Pervonte (1834), and a Loreley opera, of which he completed only the Act I finale and a chorus. In later years Mendelssohn's dramatic interests found outlets only in the oratorios St Paul (1836) and Elijah (1846) and in incidental music to a number of plays.

Like his contemporary Schubert, Mendelssohn strove for success on the operatic stage, his continuing interest belied by the fact that he wrote his last completed stage work at the age of 20. With the exception of Die Hochzeit des Camacho and Die Heimkehr aus der Fremde, Mendelssohn's stage works are neglected, belonging to the category of ordinary works of their time which now seem of little interest.

Die beiden Pädagogen
The Two Pedagogues
Singspiel in one act (2h 30m)
Libretto by J. L. Casper, after Eugène Scribe's comedy Les deux précepteurs, ou Asinus asinam fricat (1817)
Composed 1821
PREMIERES 1822, Mendelssohn's home, Berlin (private); 27 May, 1962, Komische Oper, Berlin

A wealthy landowner, Herr von Robert, arranges for a Viennese professor to come as private tutor to his more-or-less grown-up son, Carl. Instead of the professor, however, his assistant, Lustig, arrives impersonating him. Unfortunately for him he is recognized by a former lover, Hännchen, niece of the village schoolmaster, Kinderschreck (literally 'Scarechild'). Eventually Lustig is exposed, but the piece ends happily with the betrothals of Lustig to Hännchen and Carl to his sweetheart, Elise, while Herr von Robert admits the unrealistic nature of his plans.

Mendelssohn was barely 12 years old when he set Casper's skilful adaptation of Scribe's comedy. The music follows the standard singspiel patterns but shows a definite understanding and competent handling of stereotyped situations resulting in some effective characterization, most notably of the buffo pedant Kinderschreck. The trio for Carl, Elise and Hännchen and the quartet in which the two pedagogues dispute the merits of Pestalozzi's and Basedow's educational theories to the astonishment of Carl and his father are particularly strong.

RECORDING Laki, Fuchs, Dallapozza, Fischer-Dieskau, Hirte, Wewel, Bavarian Radio Ch and O, Wallberg, EMI, 1979
EDITION f.s., Leipziger Ausgabe der Werke Felix Mendelssohn-Bartholdys, vol. 5, no. 1, Deutscher Verlag für Musik, 1966

Die Hochzeit des Camacho
Camacho's Wedding
Opera in two acts, Op. 10
Libretto possibly by Friedrich Voigt, after an episode in Cervantes's Don Quixote (1605, 1615)
Composed 1824–5
PREMIERES 29 April 1827, Schauspielhaus, Berlin; US: 1 May 1875, Chicago (concert); UK: 24 February 1987, Playhouse, Oxford

CAST Quiteria *s*, Basilio *t*, Carrasco *bar*, Lucinda *ms*, Vivaldo *t*, Camacho *t*, Sancho Panza *b*, Don Quixote *b*, Alcade *b*; *satb* chorus of villagers
FULL ORCHESTRA

Completed in August 1825, a few weeks before the famous Octet, Mendelssohn carried out a thorough revision of the score before its first performance. The original version vividly illustrates the rapidity with which the 16-year-old composer's gifts were developing; by the time he came to write Act II he himself seems to have recognized that he was already a far more mature composer and he made particularly extensive changes to Act I, deleting several numbers. The Act II finale, too, was largely rewritten. However, his revised version was not used intact for the 1827 production; the composer seems to have been persuaded to make cuts and alterations which, on the evidence of the 1829 vocal score, he later regretted.

SYNOPSIS
Act I Quiteria and Basilio are in love, but Quiteria's father, Carrasco, wants her to marry the rich Camacho. The lovers' friends, Lucinda and Vivaldo, determine to help them. Camacho announces a lavish wedding feast, to which he invites Sancho Panza and his master, Don Quixote, who are said to be searching for the haunted cave of Montesinos. Basilio goes into hiding in the woods while Vivaldo tries to persuade Carrasco that Basilio has come into a fortune. Meanwhile Quiteria has gone to join Basilio; on the way she meets Don Quixote who unwittingly terrifies her. When the angry Carrasco and Camacho go in search of the lovers, they are confronted by Basilio disguised as the ghost of Montesinos and the act ends in general confusion.

Act II Preparations for the wedding are under way. Vivaldo's entertainment (a barbed allegory about love and wealth) is abruptly ended by the crazy intervention of Don Quixote. Just as Quiteria, in despair, is about to sign the marriage contract, Basilio arrives. He pretends to stab himself and is allowed to marry Quiteria so that he can die happy. He then confounds everyone by miraculously returning to full health.

The harmonic and melodic language of *Camacho* seem to indicate Mendelssohn's definite decision to try to move away from the small scale of his previous dramatic works to a style closer to that emerging in the works of Weber and Spohr – he was undoubtedly familiar with his contemporaries' operas and aware of the developments taking place. Despite the continuing use of spoken dialogue, there are long sections of uninterrupted music, building up multipartite scenes; the score also contains significant use of reminiscence motif and resourceful ensemble and chorus-writing. The imaginative instrumentation, showing Mendelssohn at his best, is another more modern aspect. While characterization is quite strong, the opera nevertheless lacks dramatic momentum – a fault attributable to the composer's inexperience. A particular weakness is the decision to present the work's dramatic climax, Basilio's feigned death, in spoken dialogue.

EDITIONS f.s., F. Mendelssohn-Bartholdy, *Werke*, vol. 15, no. 7, Breitkopf und Härtel, 1874–7; v.s., Breitkopf und Härtel, 1829

Die Heimkehr aus der Fremde
The Return from Abroad
Liederspiel in one act, Op. 89 (1h)
Libretto by Karl Klingemann
Composed 1829
PREMIERES 26 December 1829, Mendelssohn's home, Berlin (private); 10 April 1851, Leipzig; UK: 7 July 1851, Little Haymarket Theatre, London

Written in celebration of Mendelssohn's parents' silver-wedding anniversary, this slight liederspiel was first staged at the family home, with Mendelssohn's sisters and brother-in-law (who, by all accounts, could not sing a note) taking part. It was written during the composer's first visit to Britain and orchestrated on his return.

Kauz, a travelling pedlar, arrives in a small town and decides to pass himself off as the son of a local magistrate, returning home after six years. Unfortunately for him, the genuine son – Hermann – has also arrived; both pursue the same girl, but Kauz is eventually found out and driven away.

Heimkehr is a step back in the direction of homely, conventional singspiel, presenting a sequence of finely crafted individual numbers with scarcely any attempt to link these into a dramatic whole. Intended, as it was, for private use, this was entirely apt. However, *Heimkehr* was, ironically, to become the most frequently performed of Mendelssohn's stage works. After its public premiere it was seen regularly on German stages and – as *Son and Stranger* – enjoyed some popularity in England. The drama is inconsequential and the music uncomplicated, but Mendelssohn managed to characterize situations and people attractively.

RECORDING Donath, Schwarz, Schreier, Fischer-Dieskau, Kusche, Bavarian Radio Ch and O, Wallberg, EMI, 1979
EDITION f.ss., F. Mendelssohn-Bartholdy, *Werke*, vol. 15, no. 8, Breitkopf und Härtel, 1874–7; facsimile, Gregg, 1967; v.s., Breitkopf und Härtel, [c. 1850]; study s., Belwin Mills, 1975

Other operatic works: *Ich, J. Mendelssohn* (inc.), (1820); *Die Soldatenliebschaft*, 1821; *Die wandernden Komödianten*, (1822); *Der Onkel aus Boston, oder Die beiden Neffen*, 1824; *Die Loreley* (inc.), (1847)
BIBLIOGRAPHY G. Schünemann, 'Mendelssohns Jugendopern', *ZMw*, vol. 5 (1922–3), pp. 506–45; John Warrack, 'Mendelssohn's Operas' in Nigel Fortune (ed.), *Essays in Honour of Winton Dean*, CUP, 1987

C.A.B.

GIAN CARLO MENOTTI

b 7 July 1911, Cadegliano, Italy

For at least a generation, in the years following the Second World War, Menotti was the most acclaimed American composer of opera. He has a natural sense of theatre, which stems from his Italian background, and has always shown an intuitive grasp of character and situation.

By the time he was 11, Menotti had written his first opera, *The Death of Pierrot*, and regularly attended theatre and opera in Milan where the family lived. On Toscanini's advice he went to the Curtis Institute in Philadelphia where, in 1928, Menotti met Samuel Barber, who became his close companion: they both studied composition with Rosario Scalero, who gave a solid grounding based on Brahms rather than on opera.

Menotti and Barber travelled in Italy and Austria, and in Vienna Menotti began composing the one-act opera buffa *Amelia al ballo* (later known as *Amelia goes to the Ball*). The Curtis Institute and New York performances were so successful that the Metropolitan Opera placed it in a double-bill with Richard Strauss's *Elektra* in 1938. The *New York Times* recognized '*something that has not materialized so far from an American-born composer*' and admired Menotti's tuneful flexibility and spontaneity. This success brought the composer an NBC radio commission for *The Old Maid and the Thief*, which *became a favourite among students and amateurs*, and a production at the Metropolitan of an opera seria, *The Island God*, which flopped.

The highly original double-bill of *The Medium* and *The Telephone*, both, as usual, to Menotti's own ingenious texts, was a huge success. These were premiered separately and then united on Broadway. When the backers were losing money Toscanini again intervened in Menotti's destiny – his three visits to the operas provided enough publicity to boost a long run.

The Consul as a gripping topical tragedy maintained Menotti's high profile as, in a completely different way, did the charm of *Amahl and the Night Visitors*, which gained special fame through being the first opera written expressly for television. After *The Saint of Bleecker Street*, and in the changing climate of the 1960s, Menotti's work began to be received with less enthusiasm and often downright hostility in the press. He changed his focus slightly, writing *Labyrinth* for television, a church opera, *Martin's Lie*, and *Help, Help, the Globolinks!*, a children's opera, for Hamburg. He also wrote the libretti for two of Samuel Barber's operas. Seven more operas, three for children, were premiered during the 1970s; since then he has written four more operas of which *The Boy Who Grew Too Fast* has been the most successful.

In 1958 Menotti inaugurated the Festival of Two Worlds at Spoleto and in 1977 expanded it to Charleston, South Carolina. He enjoyed the entrepreneurial activity involved, although some connected it with a decline in his own work. The power of his earlier operas has never been in question, but in an interview for his 60th birthday in 1971, Menotti tried to disguise his bitterness about the impact of changing fashions on his reputation.

The Medium

Tragedy in two acts (55m)
Libretto by the composer
Composed 1945
PREMIERES 8 May 1946, Brander Matthews Theater, Columbia University; UK: 29 April 1948, Aldwych Theatre, London

Menotti had the idea for *The Medium* as early as 1936 when he attended a seance in Austria. In his libretto he created what he called 'a play of ideas [which] describes the tragedy of a woman caught between two worlds, a world of reality which she cannot wholly comprehend and a supernatural world in which she cannot believe'. Along with *The Telephone*, *The Medium* had a run of 211 performances at the Ethel Barrymore Theater on Broadway during 1947–8.

Madame Flora, her daughter Monica and Toby, the mute servant boy, prepare their shabby parlour with tricks to be used during the evening's seance. Mr and Mrs Gobineau arrive, regular clients, and Mrs Nolan, a widow coming for the first time. During the seance Mrs Nolan recognizes her dead daughter but Madame Flora becomes hysterical when a cold hand seems to touch her throat: she suspects Toby but he cannot answer her accusations. In the end, Madame Flora, after drinking heavily, shoots Toby in the dark.

Menotti's The Medium *(New York, 1947)*

The mainstay of the score is a powerfully dramatic recitative-like music, influenced by Puccini. The only aria is Monica's wistful, naïve 'Black Swan' – a gypsy-type tune she sings to calm her mother – which stands in stark contrast to the increasingly dissonant music that reflects Madame Flora's growing alarm. Menotti scored the work for an orchestra of 14 players, including a piano duet, though the original string quintet can be expanded for larger venues.

RECORDING   Keller, Mastice, Dame, Powers, Rogier, unnamed O, Balaban, CBS, 1948
EDITIONS   f.s., Schirmer, 1947; v.s., Schirmer, 1947; *rp*, 1967

The Telephone, or L'amour à trois
Comedy in one act (22m)
Libretto by the composer
Composed 1946
PREMIERES   18 February 1947, Heckschner Theater, New York; UK: 29 April 1948, Aldwych Theatre, London

The Telephone, subtitled *L'amour à trois*, is a light comedy designed as a curtain-raiser for *The Medium*. Ben wishes to propose to Lucy but is unable to gain her attention for long because of her obsession with her telephone. In desperation he goes out and telephones with his proposal.

A short typically opera-buffa overture is followed by a light-hearted score which employs a number of recognizable musical styles in a partly satirical fashion. Lucy's telephone conversations (of which we hear only one side) are miniature arias, the first of which, 'Oh Margaret, it's you', is sometimes performed independently.

RECORDING   Cotlow, Rogier, unnamed O, Balaban, CBS, 1947
VIDEO   Farey, Saltir CO, Serchrier, Decca, 1992
EDITION   v.s., Schirmer, 1947

The Consul
Musical drama in three acts (1h 45m)
Libretto by the composer
Composed 1949
PREMIERES   1 March 1950, Philadelphia; UK: 7 February 1951, Cambridge Theatre, London

The New York premiere of *The Consul* on 15 March 1950 established the opera as a classic of its period and it ran for some 8 months. It was awarded the Pulitzer Prize and the Drama Critics' Circle Award and was translated into at least a dozen languages and seen in more than 20 countries.

Somewhere in Europe after the Second World War the secret police are after John Sorel who has had to leave his wife and baby and go abroad. His wife, Magda, is obstructed by bureaucracy in her efforts to get a visa to follow him. Meanwhile she too is hounded by the secret police and the baby dies. Hearing of this, John braves danger and returns to fetch his wife. But it is too late – he is arrested and Magda commits suicide.

The subject of Menotti's first full-scale, full-length opera – obtaining a passport to leave a police state – has obvious parallels with Puccini's *Tosca*. The music, too, has Puccinian touches, especially the sentimental 'Now lips, say goodbye' in Scene 1. These echoes are as important to the opera's overall dramatic effect as Menotti's use of a pedantic 5/4 march to represent the secret police and the hallucinatory, naïve 6/8 waltz of the final suicide scene.

RECORDING   Neway, Powers, Lane, McKinley, MacNeil, Lishner, Jongeyans, unnamed O, Engel, American Decca/New World, 1950
EDITION   v.s., Schirmer, 1950

Amahl and the Night Visitors
Opera in one act (45m)
Libretto by the composer
Composed 1951
PREMIERES   24 December 1951, NBC Studios, New York (television); 21 February 1952, Bloomington University, Indiana; UK: 6 December 1963, Royal College of Music, London

In this perennial Christmas favourite, Amahl, a boy cripple, sits outside his hut watching the brilliant new star. The Three Kings, looking for hospitality, arrive with presents for the Holy Child they are seeking. During the night Amahl's mother tries to steal part of the treasure and there is a struggle. Eventually Amahl offers his crutch as a gift, is miraculously healed, and joins the Kings in search of the Christ Child.

Hieronymous Bosch's painting *The Adoration of the Magi* gave Menotti the idea for this opera, which, since its television premiere, has been broadcast annually at Christmas in the US. The opera's appeal to young audiences has made it a popular choice with amateur operatic groups. Menotti composed melodious, short numbers and scored the opera for a small orchestra; he insists that the part of Amahl should always be sung by a boy and not taken by a soprano.

RECORDING   Haywood, Rainbird, Dobson, Maxwell, Watson, Covent Garden Ch and O, Syrus, That's Entertainment, 1978
EDITION   v.s., Schirmer, 1952

The Saint of Bleecker Street
Musical drama in three acts (2h)
Libretto by the composer
Composed 1953–4
PREMIERES   27 December 1954, Broadway Theater, New York; UK: 4 October 1956, BBC Television, London; 27 July 1962, Orpington Civic Hall, Kent (Kentish Opera Group)

Menotti's tragedy gained the Drama Critics' Circle Award as well as the New York Music Critics' Circle Award and brought the composer his second Pulitzer Prize.

The story is set in Little Italy in New York City. Annina is a deeply religious girl who has been having visions and performing miracles. Her brother, Michele, wants to protect her from public exploitation but is overpowered. Desideria, Michele's mistress, objects to his obsession with his saintly sister and when she accuses him of being in love with Annina, Michele stabs her. Finally Annina dies at the moment of becoming a nun.

Menotti considered *The Saint of Bleecker Street* 'melodically . . . an improvement over *The Consul*'. Certainly the melodic style of the opera – and many of its other features – is more large-scale. Significant use of the chorus (not present in *The Consul*) and a large orchestra give the feeling of 'grand' opera. Critics were loud in their praise, hailing the opera as a technical and dramatic masterpiece. Broadway audiences, however, perhaps put off by its religious subject matter and rather ambiguous message, were not as enthusiastic.

RECORDING Ruggiero, Di Gerlando, Lane, Poleri, Cassilly, Reardon, Lishner, unnamed Ch and O, Schippers, RCA, 1955
EDITION v.s., Schirmer, 1955

Other operas: *Amelia al ballo*, 1937 (RECORDING Columbia, 1953); *The Old Maid and the Thief*, 1939 (RECORDING Turnabout, 1979); *The Island God*, 1942; *Maria Golovin*, 1958 (RECORDING RCA, 1958); *Labyrinth*, 1963; *Le dernier sauvage*, 1963; *Martin's Lie*, 1964; *Help, Help, the Globolinks!*, 1968; *The Most Important Man*, 1971; *Tamu-Tamu*, 1973; *The Egg*, 1976; *The Hero*, 1976; *The Trial of the Gypsy*, 1978; *Chip and his Dog*, 1979; *La Loca*, 1979; *A Bride from Pluto*, 1982; *The Boy Who Grew Too Fast*, 1982; *Goya*, 1986 (RECORDING Nuova Era, 1991); *Giorno da Nozze*, 1988
BIBLIOGRAPHY J. Ardoin, *The Stages of Menotti*, Garden City, 1985; J. Gruen, *Menotti: A Biography*, Macmillan, 1978

P.D.

SAVERIO MERCADANTE

Giuseppe Saverio Raffaele Mercadante; *baptized* 17 September 1795, Altamura, nr Bari; *d* 17 December 1870, Naples

After the death of Bellini, and in the absence abroad of Rossini and Donizetti, Mercadante was the most important composer in Italy in the period immediately before Verdi. He studied at the Naples Conservatory, where his first interest seems to have been instrumental composition. At the age of 24, encouraged by Rossini, he produced an opera, *L'apoteosi d'Ercole*, and four more the next year. The brilliantly successful comic opera *Elisa e Claudio*, given at La Scala, Milan, in 1821, rapidly established his reputation in Italy, and subsequently all over Europe. But the 30-odd operas that succeeded it during the next 14 years were mainly serious in character. These included three in Vienna, and seven during extended visits to Spain and Portugal; the highlights of this period were *Donna Caritea* in 1826 and *I Normanni a Parigi* in 1832.

For all these works Rossini is clearly the model, with a tendency, from *Donna Caritea* onwards, towards the lyric style soon to be associated with Bellini. But in 1836 Mercadante was invited to write an opera for Paris and, though the piece itself was a failure, exposure to Parisian musical life and in particular to the operas of Meyerbeer (*Les Huguenots* had its first performance during

Mercadante's visit) provided a new and valuable stimulus. With *Il giuramento* at La Scala in 1837 Mercadante broke away from his earlier manner and created a genuine music drama that has a voice of its own and has remained his best-known work. In this and the succeeding operas he worked consciously at a series of dramatic reforms that are of the greatest importance in the development of Italian 19th-century melodrama. This is the period of Mercadante's best operas: *Le due illustri rivali*, *Elena da Feltre*, *Il bravo*, *La vestale* and *Il reggente*.

From 1840 Mercadante was Director of the Naples Conservatory. In his later operas the zeal for reform tends to get forgotten, though his last great triumph, *Orazie Curiazi* in 1846, must count among his finest achievements. In 1862 he became totally blind but continued to compose by dictation, leaving a 59th opera unfinished when he died.

Mercadante's work is uneven and sometimes laboured – painstaking in both good and bad senses – but from *Il giuramento* onwards his best operas show a seriousness of purpose, a richness of harmony and orchestration and a concern for dramatic continuity without equal among his contemporaries. He has always been recognized as a precursor of Verdi, whom he certainly influenced and by whom he was decisively overshadowed; nevertheless revivals of his operas at the centenary of his death, and at occasional festivals since, suggest that Mercadante also merits consideration for his own sake.

Elisa e Claudio, ossia L'amore protetto dall'amicizia

Elisa and Claudio, or Love Protected by Friendship
Melodramma semiserio in two acts
Libretto by Luigi Romanelli, after F. Casari's play *Rosella*
Composed 1821
PREMIERES 30 October 1821, La Scala, Milan; UK: 12 April 1823, His Majesty's Theatre, London; US: 18 October 1832, New York

Mercadante's first great success and his only comedy to have been revived in recent years. The plot turns on the secret marriage of Elisa and Claudio, son of Conte Arnoldo, and Arnoldo's alternative plans for a union between his son and Silvia, daughter of Marchese Tricotazio. Unfortunately Silvia is herself in love – with a former fellow student of Claudio's, conveniently to hand in the guise of valet to the marchese. The intrigues that follow end happily, and provide the young Mercadante with scope for a more spontaneous vein of melody than he was able to command in his later and more serious operas.

RECORDING Zeani, Fioroni, Lazzari, Trimarchi, Trama, Ch and O of Teatro San Carlo, Naples, Rapalo, MRF, 1971
EDITION v.s., Ricordi, [1821/2]

Il giuramento

The Oath
Melodramma in three acts
Libretto by Gaetano Rossi, after the melodrama *Angelo, tyran de Padoue* by Victor Hugo (1835)
Composed 1836–7

PREMIERES   11 March 1837, La Scala, Milan; UK: 27 June 1840, London; US: 14 February 1848, New York

Mercadante's best-known opera and the one that was most highly regarded by his contemporaries. The libretto is taken from the same darkly melodramatic source as Ponchielli's *La gioconda*, though Rossi's treatment of it is less flamboyant than Boito's 40 years later. The action is set in Sicily (not Venice), and the rich and beautiful society hostess Elaisa takes the place of *la gioconda*. Her love for Viscardo, her generosity to her rival Bianca, the treachery of Brunoro and her ultimate death at Viscardo's hand (not her own) add up to an implausible but well enough constructed libretto from which Mercadante was able to create a music drama of considerable originality and power.

RECORDING   Zylis-Gara, Tremblay, Pecchioli, Molese, Miller, Plantey, French Radio Ch and O, Arena, Rodolphe, 1984
EDITION   v.s., Ricordi, 1837; 2nd edn, 1860

Il bravo, ossia La Veneziana
The Bravo [Assassin], or the Venetian Girl
Melodramma in three acts
Libretto by Gaetano Rossi and Marco Marcelliano Marcello, after Bourgeois's *La vénitienne*, from J. Fennimore Cooper's *The Bravo* (1813)
Composed 1838–9
PREMIERE   9 March 1839, La Scala, Milan

One of the most interesting of Mercadante's reform operas. The story, set in 16th-century Venice, is a complex tissue of passion, violence and dark deeds, spiced with mistaken identity and ultimate generosity; it revolves around the enigmatic figure of the Bravo, an unwilling desperado who has been blackmailed by the Council of Ten and forced to act as their official assassin – 'Rigoletto and Sparafucile rolled into one', as Frank Walker observed. The comparison is apt: Act I in particular shows a real attempt to weld the disparate elements of early 19th-century Italian melodrama into a continuous dramatic whole, and anticipations of Verdi are evident.

RECORDINGS   1. Parazzini, Matsumoto, Johns, Savastano, Washington, Rome Opera Ch and O, Ferro, Italia, 1977; 2. Di Domenico, Tabiadon, Perry, Bertocchi, Antonucci, Bratisalava Ch and Italian International O, Aprea, Nuova Era, 1991
EDITION   v.s., Ricordi, 1839; 2nd edn, 1860

La vestale
The Vestal Virgin
Tragedia lirica in three acts
Libretto by Salvatore Cammarano
Composed 1839–40
PREMIERES   10 March 1840, Teatro San Carlo, Naples; as *Emilia*: 1842, Rome; as *San Camillo* (azione sacra): 1851, Rome

Regarded by some as Mercadante's masterpiece and certainly one of his most consistent works. The story is the same as Spontini's opera, though differently handled in detail: instead of the happy ending required by French convention, Cammarano's version follows the priests' condemnation of the vestal virgin (here Emilia) with her burial alive and the suicide of her lover on her tomb. All this inevitably suggests *Aida*, as do other passages in the opera (including a full-blown triumph scene in Act I and at least one almost literal anticipation to the words 'Decio ritorna, dei Galli vincitor!'); though plagiarism is obviously not in question, subconscious memory is another matter and it is an interesting fact that Verdi was present when *La vestale* was first performed at Genoa in 1841, and was living and working in Milan when it had a long and successful run at La Scala later in the same year.

RECORDING   Vejzovic, Romano, Cecchele, Sioli, Croatian NT Ch and O, Sutej, Bongiovanni, 1987
EDITION   v.s., Ricordi, 1840

Il reggente
The Regent
Tragedia lirica in three acts
Libretto by Salvatore Cammarano, after the drama *Gustave III* by Eugène Scribe (1833)
Composed 1842–3, rev. 1843
PREMIERES   2 February 1843, Teatro Regio, Turin; rev. version: 1843, Trieste

The subject is the same as Verdi's in *Un ballo in maschera*, based on the same drama by Scribe and with much the same succession of scenes and disposition of characters, though Cammarano has transferred the action to Scotland in 1570 – a distinct improvement on 17th-century Boston. Among Mercadante's operas *Il reggente* stands out for its more personal, human atmosphere, with a score of greater refinement and richness of invention backed by a well-balanced dramatic structure.

RECORDING   Chiara, Vajna, Merighi, Montefusco, Ch of the Maggio Musicale Fiorentino, Angelicum O of Milan, Martinotti, MRF, 1970
EDITION   v.s., F. Lucca, 1843

Orazi e Curiazi
The Horaces and Curaces
Tragedia lirica in three acts
Libretto by Salvatore Cammarano
Composed 1845–6
PREMIERE   10 November 1846, Teatro San Carlo, Naples; UK: 23 April 1975, Colston Hall, Bristol (Opera Rara)

Regarded by contemporaries as the culmination of Mercadante's career, *Orazi e Curiazi* is an effective, powerful and competent summing-up of early 19th-century Italian melodrama. There is perhaps less of the reformer here than in the operas that immediately preceded it, but the heroic subject, based on the story of the three Orazi and three Curiazi chosen by lot to defend Rome and Alba in battle, is well served by the strong scoring, robust vocal writing and fine ensembles of this energetic score.

EDITION   v.s. Ricordi, 1846

Set design by Baldassare Cavalotti and Domenico Menozzi for Mercadante's La vestale *at La Scala in 1842*

Other operas: *L'apoteosi d'Ercole*, 1819; *Violenza e costanza, ossia I falsi monetari*, 1820 (as *Il castello dei spiriti*, 1825); *Anacreonte in Samo*, 1820; *Il geloso ravveduto*, 1820; *Scipione in Cartagine*, 1820; *Maria Stuarda, regina di Scozia (Maria Stuart)*, 1821; *Andronico*, 1821; *Il posto abbandonato, ossia Adele ed Emerico*, 1822, rev. 1828; *Amleto*, 1822; *Alfonso ed Elisa*, 1822 (as *Aminto ed Argira*, 1823); *Didone abbandonata*, 1823; *Gli sciti*, 1823; *Costanzo ed Almeriska*, 1823; *Gli amici di Siracusa*, 1824; *Doralice*, 1824; *Le nozze di Telemaco ed Antiope* (with others), 1824; *Il podestà di Burgos, ossia Il signore del villaggio*, 1824; *Nitocri*, 1824; *Ipermestra*, 1824, ?rev. 1832; *Erode, ossia Marianna*, 1825; *Les noces de Gamache* (doubtful), 1825; *Caritea, regina di Spagna (Donna Caritea), ossia La morte di Don Alfonso re di Portogallo*, 1826; *Ezio*, 1827; *Il montanaro*, 1827; *La testa di bronzo, ossia La capanna solitaria*, 1827; *Adriano in Siria*, 1828; *Gabriella di Vergy*, 1828, rev. 1832; *La rappresaglia*, 1829; *Don Chisciotte [alle nozze di Gamaccio]*, ?1829; *Francesca da Rimini*, ?1830; *Zaïra*, 1831; *I normanni a Parigi*, 1832; *Ismalia, ossia Amore e morte*, 1832; *Il conte di Essex*, 1833; *Emma d'Antiochia*, 1834; *Uggero il danese*, 1834; *La gioventù di Enrico V*, 1834; *I due Figaro*, 1835; *Francesca Donato, ossia Corinto distrutta*, 1835, rev. 1845; *I briganti*, 1836, rev. 1853; *Le due illustri rivali*, 1838, rev. 1839 (RECORDING MRF, 1970); *Elena da Feltre*, 1838; *La solitaria delle Asturie, ossia La Spagna ricuperata*, 1840; *Il proscritto*, 1842; *Leonora*, 1844; *Il Vascello de Gama*, 1845; *La schiava saracena, ovvero Il campo di Gerosolima* (originally *Il campo de' crociati*), 1848, rev. ?1850; *Medea*, 1851; *Statira*, 1853; *Violetta*, 1853; *Pelagio*, 1857; *Virginia*, 1866; *L'orfano di Brono, ossia Caterina dei Medici* (inc.), (c. 1869)

BIBLIOGRAPHY Santo Palermo, *Saverio Mercadante*, Schena Editore, 1985; Michael Rose, 'Saverio Mercadante', in *Grove*, Macmillan, 1980

M.R.

AARE MERIKANTO

b 29 June 1893, Helsinki; *d* 29 September 1958, Helsinki

Aare Merikanto's father Oskar was one of Finland's leading musicians, composer of the first opera set to a Finnish text and founder in 1911 of what was to become the Finnish National Opera. Aare wrote his first opera, the one-act *Helena*, in 1912 (he subsequently destroyed it). His father then sent him to Leipzig to study with Reger, and later to Moscow. On his return, his music proved too avant garde for conservative local audiences. He wrote *Juha* in 1920–22, to a libretto by the soprano Aino Ackté, but it was rejected by the Helsinki Opera; later Ackté recalled her text, and gave it to Madetoja, whose more acceptable setting was premiered in 1935. Merikanto's *Juha* was not staged until after his death. Embittered, depressive and alcoholic, he earned his living as a teacher; his pupils included Sallinen and Rautavaara.

His *Juha*, now recognized as the first operatic masterpiece by a Finnish composer, is a mainstay of the repertoire in Finland; Madetoja's has sunk into oblivion.

Juha

Opera in three acts (1h 45m)

Libretto by Aino Ackté, based on the novel by Juhani Aho (1911)
PREMIERES 1958, Finnish Radio (broadcast); 28 October 1963, Lahti Concert Hall, Lahti; UK: 28 August 1987, King's Theatre, Edinburgh (Finnish National Opera)

The opera presents a clash of cultures at the turn of the century between a static farming community in north-eastern Finland (Lutheran) and the more nomadic, worldly people of Karelia (Russian Orthodox). The smallholder Juha is middle-aged and lame; his young wife Marja is tempted by the attentions of a dashing Karelian merchant, and after a row with her mother-in-law runs away with him. Juha believes she was taken by force. In Act II Marja discovers the truth: each year the merchant picks up a 'summer girl', and when he has done with her she joins his household as a servant. Juha passes by searching for Marja but, pregnant, she hides in shame. The merchant returns with his new 'summer girl'. In Act III Marja returns to Juha, who welcomes her without question, and even suggests that they should go to collect her child from the merchant. When the latter tries to persuade Marja to stay, Juha attacks him with an axe, and to save her lover's life Marja blurts out the truth, that she left willingly. Juha drowns himself in the rapids.

The word-setting and use of speech-rhythm melodic fragments recall Janáček; the lush harmonies and orchestration remind one that Merikanto fell under Skryabin's spell in Moscow. The characterization through music is faultlessly achieved. The tragedy is that after *Juha's* rejection Merikanto wrote no more for the stage. He was without doubt a born opera composer.

RECORDING Kostia, Valjakka, Krumm, Lehtinen, Finnish National Opera O, Söderblom, Finlandia, 1972
EDITION v.s., Foundation for the Promotion of Finnish Music, 1973

BIBLIOGRAPHY Rodney Milnes, 'A Finnish Janáček', *Opera*, vol. 38 (1987), pp. 868–71

R.M.

ANDRÉ MESSAGER

André Charles Prosper Messager; *b* 30 December 1853, Montlucon, France; *d* 24 February 1929, Paris

Messager, the last true master of classical French operetta, was trained as an organist at the Ecole Niedermeyer under Saint-Saëns and Fauré (both of whom remained lifelong friends). He became organist at St Sulpice in 1874, and four years later had a symphony performed at the Concerts Colonne. At the same time he was writing ballets for the Folies-Bergère, where he also conducted. In 1883 came his first attempt at operetta, when he was commissioned to complete Firmin Bernicat's *François les Bas-Bleus*, which had a respectable run at the Folies-Dramatiques.

In 1885, two operettas appeared that showed further promise; the second, *La béarnaise*, exhibited the delicacy and period flavour for which Messager later became celebrated. In 1886, Saint-Saëns recommended Messager's graceful ballet *Les deux pigeons* to the Opéra; it is still performed. But little else found much favour in the 1880s, not even the *Souvenirs de Bayreuth* (*c.* 1886), a quadrille-fantasy for four hands on 'favourite themes from Wagner's Ring', written in collaboration with Fauré.

In 1890, Messager's fortunes changed with the successful premiere at the Opéra-Comique of *La Basoche*. The 1891 London production followed Sullivan's *Ivanhoe* as the second and last attraction at D'Oyly Carte's ill-fated Royal English Opera House. The through-composed *Madame Chrysanthème* (with an oriental/occidental theme that predated both Sidney Jones's *The Geisha* and Puccini's *Madama Butterfly*) was followed by several operettas and finally, a sensational hit, *Les p'tites Michu* (1897), which recalled the tuneful frivolity of Lecocq's *Giroflé-Girofla* and *La fille de Madame Angot*, but which was perhaps more charmingly florid and more tastefully constructed. The succeeding work, *Véronique*, was even more successful.

In 1898, Messager became Musical Director of the Opéra-Comique, and there conducted the premieres of several new works, notably Debussy's *Pelléas et Mélisande*, and significant revivals, including Beethoven's *Fidelio*. In 1901, he became manager of the Grand Opera Syndicate in London until he was appointed to direct the Paris Opéra in 1907, where he remained until 1914. One operetta from this period, *Les dragons de l'impératrice* (1905), deserves re-

Esa Ruutunen (Juha), Eeva-Liisa Saarinen (Marja) and Jukka Salminen (Shemeikka) in Juha *(Finnish National Opera, 1967)*

examination. *Monsieur Beaucaire* (1919), a 'romantic opera' composed to an English libretto, looks back through the ragtime craze to the more genteel time of Edward German. Its centrepiece, a pastoral episode that includes the Arcadian soprano aria 'Philomel', was famously sung by Maggie Teyte.

Messager moved with the times, lightened his style, and by 1921, was writing for the 'comédie-musicale' stage. Two years later, he collaborated with the actor–playwright Sacha Guitry on *L'amour masqué*, which fortuitously starred the author's brilliant wife, Yvonne Printemps. The ageing composer had succumbed to the 1920s taste for tangos and foxtrots, but gave them a refined touch.

Messager has not enjoyed the revival of interest shown towards Offenbach, but raucousness was not his style; elegance, neatness, tripping melodiousness, orchestral refinement, and a decidedly French grace were the composer's hallmarks.

Véronique

Opéra comique in three acts (2h 30m)
Libretto by Albert Vanloo and Georges Duval
PREMIERES 10 December 1898, Bouffes-Parisiens, Paris;
UK: 5 May 1903, Coronet Theatre, London; US: 30 October
1905, Broadway Theater, New York

At a Parisian florist's in the 1840s, Hélène de Solanges, a noblewoman, pretends to be a shop-girl to check up on her prospective bridegroom, the rakish Vicomte Florestan de Valaincourt. Florestan gives a picnic for the employees of the flower shop (purchased with non-existent funds), and, predic-

Poster design for Véronique *(Paris, 1898)*

tably, falls for the disguised Hélène (who calls herself Véronique). Instead of reporting to a ball at the Tuileries that evening to be presented to his so-far unknown bride, he risks debtor's prison and remains at the picnic grounds. At the ball, complications are sorted out between the lovers and, in the presence of the king, the marriage contract is signed.

Messager's grace and refinement are apparent throughout this radiant score; even entrance songs are imbued with a lilting glitter, and more elaborate ensembles (such as the quartet in Act I with the refrain 'Charmant, charmant') are unexpectedly moving. The finales to Acts I and II are dazzling, the latter with its 'marié ou coffré' tag line. The score's two most popular numbers are the two duets for the lovers in Act II: the 'donkey' ('De ci, de là') and 'swing' ('Poussez, poussez, l'escarpolette') songs, which became Edwardian favourites.

RECORDING Mesplé, Guiot, Dens, Benoît, René Duclos
Ch, Lamoureux O, Hartemann, Pathé, 1970
EDITION v.s., Choudens, 1898

Other operatic works: *François les Bas-Bleus* (completion of operetta by F. Bernicat), 1883 (RECORDING Musidisc, ?1960s); *La fauvette du temple*, 1885; *La béarnaise*, 1885; *Le bourgeois de Calais*, 1887; *Isoline*, 1888 (RECORDING Musidisc, ?1960s); *Le mari de la reine*, 1889; *La Basoche*, 1890 (RECORDING Musidisc, ?1960s); *Miss Dollar*, 1893; *Madame Chrysanthème*, 1893; *Mirette*, 1894; *La fiancée en loterie* (coll. with P. Lacome), 1896; *Le Chevalier d'Harmental*, 1896; *Les p'tites Michu*, 1897 (RECORDING excerpts: Pathé, 1970); *Les dragons de l'impératrice*, 1905; *Fortunio*, 1907 (RECORDING Erato, 1987); *Béatrice*, 1914; *Cyprien, ôte ta main d'là*, 1916; *Monsieur Beaucaire*, 1919 (RECORDING excerpts: Pathé, c. 1951); *La petite fonctionnaire*, 1921; *L'amour masqué*, 1923 (RECORDING excerpts: Decca, 1970); *Passionément*, 1926 (RECORDING Musidisc, 1964); *Coups de roulis*, 1928 (RECORDING Musidisc, ?1960s)
BIBLIOGRAPHY M. Auge-Laribe, *André Messager: Musicien de théâtre*, La Colombe, 1951; H. Février, *André Messager: Mon maître, mon ami*, Amiot-Dumont, 1948; John Wagstaff, *André Messager: A Bio-Biography*, Greenwood, 1991

R.T.

OLIVIER MESSIAEN

b 10 December 1908, Avignon, France; *d* 28 April 1992, Paris

Despite a conventional musical training (he was a pupil of Dukas and Dupré at the Paris Conservatoire) Messiaen was a radical from the first. He rejected German symphonic thought and post-Wagnerian opulence as well as the mechanical or synthetic neo-classicism of Les Six. In the 1930s, saying he wanted to return mystery to music, he began to write a series of works in which the mysteries of the Roman Catholic Church play a central inspirational role. It was natural, since he was organist at La Trinité in Paris, that his deeply held religious beliefs should find expression in composition for his own instrument (*La nativité du Seigneur, Les corps glorieux*) but they also feature in his instrumental and orchestral music (*L'ascension, Visions de l'amen*) and in his vocal music. Birdsong was a major influence: he went on field trips, wrote down hundreds of individual songs and integrated these brief snatches of nature into his music.

From quite early on, these aspects of Messiaen's spiritual and physical environment found a response in certain technical procedures. In the search for contemplative depth and richness, he interested himself in elaborate symmetries: in what he called 'non-retrogradable' rhythms (palindromes), and in 'modes of limited transposition', where the traditional major and minor scales are replaced by specially constructed scales with symmetrical interval divisions (the whole-tone scale, much used by Musorgsky and Debussy – both profound influences on Messiaen – is his Mode 1). The audible effect of all this on the harmony, melody and rhythm is of a kind of suspension in musical space, or, if the music is quick, of some mystical orbital dance of the spirit. But for a time after the war Messiaen brought these various elements under strict control and laid the foundations for a school of composition led by his pupils and followers (such as Boulez and Stockhausen) which extended the serial organization of pitch formulated by Schoenberg into all the elements of composition.

But the organizational principles were always the means of expressing emotions for Messiaen. His *Turangalîla Symphony* (1946–8), with its sumptuous orchestration, and the extraordinarily erotic sound of that purest of instruments, the electronic ondes Martinot, is a vast love song related to the myth of Tristan and Isolde, while *Et exspecto resurrectionem mortuorum* (1964) is an immensely personal affirmation of the composer's faith.

After 1964 Messiaen's music became, if not simpler, certainly more accessible. The intricacies of its construction became less apparent and have been replaced by a static, hieratic vision where clock time is less important than the space needed for a musical expression of spiritual contemplation.

It was natural that his only opera, commissioned by Rolf Liebermann for the Paris Opéra in 1975, should fuse these features in portraying the spiritual development of St Francis of Assisi. It is an opera of ritual, not of action, requiring the involvement of the audience's spiritual being rather than its earthy theatrical responses. It has been suggested that it would be better staged in a vast Gothic cathedral than in the decadent interior of our opera houses. It requires enormous forces – a huge orchestra and a chorus of at least 150. The practical problems of rehearsing so long and difficult a work probably mean it will never become a repertoire piece.

Saint François d'Assise

(*Scènes Franciscaines*)
St Francis of Assisi
Opera in three acts (eight tableaux) (4h)
Libretto by the composer, after 14th-century Franciscan writings: the *Fioretti* and *Reflections of the Stigmata*, and St Francis's own *Cantico delle creature*
Composed 1975–83

PREMIERES 28 November 1983, Opéra, Paris; UK: 26 March 1986, Royal Festival Hall, London/BBC Radio 3 (concert performance of tableaux 3, 7 and 8); US: 10 April 1986, Boston (concert performance of tableaux 3, 7 and 8); UK: 10 December 1988, Royal Festival Hall, London (semi-staged, complete)
CAST St Francis *bar*, the Angel *s*, the Leper *t*, Frère Léon *bar*, Frère Massée *t*, Frère Elie *t*, Frère Bernard *b*, Frère Sylvestre *b*, Frère Rufin *b*; *satb* chorus (invisible)
ORCHESTRATION 3 picc, 3 fl, alto fl, 3 ob, ca, 2 E♭ cl, 3 cl, b cl, contrabass cl, 3 bsn, dbsn, 6 hn, tpt in D, 3 tpt, 3 trbn, 2 tuba, db tuba, 3 ondes Martenot, perc (including xylophone, xylorimba, marimba, glock, vibraphone, wind-machine, géophone, 5 more players), str

The opera depicts the path of St Francis of Assisi towards a state of spiritual grace.

SYNOPSIS

Act I Tableau 1: *The Cross*. St Francis explains to one of his fellow monks, Frère Léon, that all life's contradictions and sufferings must be endured for the sake of Christ's love, for only through these sufferings will man reach perfect joy. The invisible chorus sings Christ's words 'He who wishes to follow in my footsteps must take up his cross and follow me.' Tableau 2: *Lauds*. After the service in a small dark chapel has ended and the brothers have left, St Francis pours out his heart. The God who has created so many simple but wonderful things – time, light, space, the taste of clear water, the song of the wind that changes its note in every tree – has also created ugliness – the poisonous mushroom, the rotting pustulation of leprosy. Francis feels revulsion at the physical presence of the disease and begs that God will help him overcome his nausea and be able to love a sufferer. Tableau 3: *Le baiser au lepreux*. In a colony a Leper rejects God and Francis's homilies; he has done nothing to deserve his disfiguring, revolting, painful, ostracizing disease, so why should he listen to the platitudes of monks who can scarcely conceal their disgust for his fetid appearance? An Angel, visible only to the audience, sings of God's love and convinces the Leper that his own self-disgust is as strong as the disgust others feel for him. Francis is deeply moved and overcoming his repugnance embraces the Leper, effecting a miraculous cure and, at that moment, becoming a saint. The Leper dances ecstatically and the chorus sings that, to those who have truly loved, all is forgiven.

Act II Tableau 4: *L'ange voyageur*. The Angel is assumed to be another traveller who has come to the monastery to seek advice from Francis; his knock on the door is a terrifying sound that symbolizes the inrush of grace. The vicar, Elias, will not answer the Angel's questions about predestination but he receives an answer of great wisdom from Bernardo, one of the brothers. It is only after the Angel equivocates about where he has come from and has left in search of Francis that the brothers wonder if their visitor was indeed an Angel. Tableau 5: *L'ange musicien*. In a grotto Francis recognizes the Angel as a messenger from God and is literally entranced by the wonderful music he plays. When the brothers revive him he is ecstatic – had he not fainted the

A scene from Saint François d'Assise *(Paris, 1983)*

exquisite pain of the heavenly music would have torn his soul from his body. Tableau 6: *Le prêche aux oiseaux*. At the hermitage at the Carceri in Assisi Francis preaches to and blesses the birds, who answer with a massive chorus – the orchestra alone – divided, as Francis tells one of the brothers, into four groups representing the points of the Cross. He reminds the brother of Christ's words about the birds being looked after by their heavenly father: 'Search for the Kingdom and you will find it through faith.'

Act III Tableau 7: *The stigmata*. Francis prays that before he dies he should be allowed to experience the pain Christ endured on the Cross and feel in his heart the love for mankind which allowed Jesus to die for its salvation. The chorus, symbolizing the voice of Christ, grants him his wish and inflicts the stigmata upon him. Tableau 8: *La mort et la nouvelle vie*. Francis, near to death, says goodbye to the brothers and the partly visible chorus. While they sing Psalm 114, the Angel and the Leper he cured come to comfort his last moments. Francis's final words are, 'Music and poetry have led me to you, by image, by symbol and in default of Truth . . . deliver me, enrapture me, dazzle me for ever by your excess of Truth!' One of the brothers observes that his death is like a golden butterfly which flies from the Cross to go beyond the stars. The chorus praises the mystery of the Resurrection.

Messiaen was adamant that, for all its static drama, his opera is more than a symphonic spectacle. It is an opera in the tradition of the theatre of the fantastic, of the imagination, of the operas which he analysed with his students while he was professor at the Paris Conservatoire – Monteverdi's *Orfeo*, the opéra-ballets of Rameau, Mozart's *Don Giovanni*, Berlioz's *Damnation of Faust*, *Carmen*, *The Ring*, *Boris Godunov*, *Wozzeck* and *Pelléas et Mélisande*.

The music too gives an impression of stasis, for each of the characters has his own theme, orchestrated with individual and instantly recognizable timbres, and an associated bird song; the major characters, Francis and the Angel, have several. Because Messiaen uses his vast orchestra more as a complex of chamber colours than as an endless stream of loud noise – though the climaxes are overwhelming – only those themes associated with characters who develop emotionally or spiritually are developed equivalently. He also uses two more abstract leitmotifs, one associated with the symbolism of the Cross (a sequence of two highly characteristic chords), the other, a little fanfare associated with the concept of 'joy'.

The two purely orchestral episodes are unusual. In the first, the Leper's dance in Act I, the music is based on a transformation and expansion of the theme with which he reviled God and Francis before his cure. In the second, the birds' response to Francis's sermon, Messiaen allows the players complete freedom to choose their own tempi, so that the aural and emotional effect is more naturalistic than in his earlier birdsong pieces such as *Réveil des oiseaux* and *Catalogue d'oiseaux*.

RECORDING   Eda-Pierre, Sénéchal, Riegel, Van Dam, Courtis, Paris Opéra Ch and O, Ozawa, Cybelia, 1988

EDITIONS f.s., Leduc/UMP, Act I: Tableau 1, 1991; Tableau 2, 1991; Tableau 3, 1988; Act II: Tableau 4, 1992; Tableau 5, 1992; Tableau 6, 1989; Act III: Tableau 7, 1990; Tableau 8, 1991; lib., Leduc/UMP, 1983

BIBLIOGRAPHY Paul Griffiths, *Olivier Messiaen and the Music of Time*, Faber, 1985; Robert Sherlaw Johnson, *Messiaen*, Dent, 2nd edn, 1989; Roger Nicholls, *Messiaen*, OUP (Oxford Studies of Composers), 2nd edn, 1986

C.B.

GIACOMO MEYERBEER

Jakob Liebmann Meyer Beer; *b* 5 September 1791, Vogelsdorf, nr Berlin; *d* 2 May 1864, Paris

The name of Meyerbeer is synonymous with French grand opera, which flourished in Paris in the mid-19th century. With his librettist, Eugène Scribe, he was responsible for the creation of operas more flamboyant than anything seen previously, writing spectacular dramatic works which enjoyed huge public success. Changing fashions and a lack of suitable voices have combined to make performances today a rarity, but Meyerbeer nevertheless retains an important place in operatic history.

Brought up in one of Berlin's wealthiest families, Meyerbeer received the best possible education, including piano lessons from Muzio Clementi. He had a natural aptitude for the instrument, giving public concerts from the age of 11, and for a number of years his performing career took precedence over his composing. Nevertheless, he received training in composition first from Carl Zelter, the *Lieder* composer, and then from Abbé Vogler in Darmstadt from 1810. It was during his two years of study with Vogler that the young Meyerbeer (he had just adopted the one-word form of his name) wrote his first operatic works.

In 1816 Meyerbeer visited Italy for the first time. What started as a short study tour turned into a nine-year sojourn, and was decisive in shaping the composer's subsequent career. At this time Rossini was beginning to dominate the Italian stage and Meyerbeer no doubt became familiar with his work, while pursuing his own interests in collecting traditional folksongs. His first Italian opera, *Romelda e Costanza*, was staged with some success in 1817. Five more operas followed, received with increasing enthusiasm, and Meyerbeer was seen by many as the great new hope of Italian opera. The premiere of *Il crociato in Egitto* in 1824 was his greatest triumph yet. Years later, the poet Heine recalled, 'Never have I seen such frenzy as during the performance of *Il crociato.*' The work was a watershed in more than one respect – not only was it one of the last works written for a castrato, but it also established Meyerbeer as a composer of international standing.

Performances of *Il crociato* in London and in Paris were equally successful and Meyerbeer, fulfilling a long-held ambition, was invited to produce a work for the Opéra. The result was *Robert le diable*, Meyerbeer's first collaboration with Scribe. Paris was to remain the centre of Meyerbeer's operatic activity for the rest of his life, though he never set up home in the city and maintained ties with his native Berlin, composing his only mature German opera, *Ein Feldlager in Schlesien*, for the Prussian court in 1844.

Robert le diable, with its notorious nuns' ballet, was an even greater success than *Il crociato*. Such was its triumph that it was responsible at least in part for Rossini's decision to write no further works for the Opéra (his last, *Guillaume Tell*, had been premiered in 1829). Over four years elapsed between *Robert le diable* and the premiere of Meyerbeer's next opera, *Les Huguenots*. Work had begun and been abandoned on several projects, including an opéra comique entitled *Les brigands*, which was to have been a collaboration with the author Alexandre Dumas *père*. After overcoming a number of censorship problems *Les Huguenots* was premiered in 1836 to great acclaim. Meyerbeer's reputation went from strength to strength.

Throughout his career Meyerbeer tailored the roles in his operas to particular singers – a fact that sometimes caused delays or necessitated rewriting when the singer had to drop out. This happened with *L'africaine*, which Meyerbeer began in 1837, soon after *Les Huguenots*, but which he did not live to see premiered. In this case work was halted when the soprano who was to have sung the title role withdrew, and Meyerbeer turned his attention instead to *Le prophète*. But this, too, ran into difficulties when the principal tenor withdrew and the opera, completed in 1840, remained unperformed for nine years until, despairing of ever finding a

Meyerbeer; lithograph by Antoine Maurin

suitable tenor, the composer rewrote the opera giving greater prominence to the alto role Fidès.

In the meantime the man described by Fétis as 'the leader of the German School' had in 1842 been appointed Prussian generalmusikdirektor, with responsibilities for composing occasional music for the Prussian court in Berlin. It was in this guise that Meyerbeer composed *Ein Feldlager in Schlesien*, a patriotic Prussian work which was later successfully adapted for Vienna (as *Vielka*). Meyerbeer never attempted to stage the work in Paris but later reused substantial parts of it in his opéra comique *L'étoile du nord*.

Commitments in Berlin were too heavy and in 1848 Meyerbeer returned to Paris where he was able to renew work on *Le prophète*. It was ten years since Meyerbeer's last Paris premiere, but any fears the composer may have had about his popularity proved completely unfounded: *Le prophète* was an unprecedented success. It received over 100 performances at the Opéra in little over two years, and Paris was swept by a craze for 'Prophet Skates', the roller skates used in the opera to simulate a ballet 'on ice'. Two opéras comiques followed before *L'africaine* eventually went into rehearsal in September 1863. Eugène Scribe, Meyerbeer's collaborator on all but one of his French works, had died in 1861 and Meyerbeer was anxious about who would be able to make the necessary changes to the text during rehearsals. This worry no doubt contributed to the stress of the rehearsals. On the morning of 2 May 1864, Meyerbeer died, unexpectedly, in his sleep. After an interruption, rehearsals for *L'africaine* continued, the critic Fétis having agreed to sort out a final performing version of the score. (It was Meyerbeer's habit constantly to make revisions as rehearsals progressed.) The work's posthumous premiere in April 1865 was another triumph.

Not everyone was enthusiastic, however. German musicians in particular felt Meyerbeer's success had been achieved by pandering too much to public taste, and they accused him of compromising his artistic integrity. Schumann wrote scathingly of *Les Huguenots*, and Wagner, who early in his career had benefited from Meyerbeer's personal support, did not exclude him from the vitriolic attack in his essay 'Das Judentum in der Musik'.

Although his output was fairly small, Meyerbeer's influence on the development of opera was far-reaching. He retained the spectacle of operas such as Auber's *La muette di Portici*, which had been so popular with the public, and added more exciting – sometimes, as in the case of the dancing nuns in *Robert le diable*, even shocking – elements to the plot. The works made unprecedented demands on the singers, were longer, and increasingly blurred the formal distinctions of recitative, aria and ensemble. And even if the composers who followed did not adopt the dramatic excesses and grand stagings, they made use of the ranges of orchestral colour Meyerbeer had introduced (Adolphe Sax was a friend and the instruments he invented appear in a number of Meyerbeer's works) and shared his concern that opera be a whole art form – an equal combination of words, music, movement and visual elements.

Il crociato in Egitto
The Crusader in Egypt
Melodramma eroico in two acts (3h 30m)
Libretto by Gaetano Rossi
Composed 1823–4
PREMIERES 7 March 1824, La Fenice, Venice; UK: 3 June 1825, Haymarket Theatre, London
CAST Armando *s* (castrato), Palmide *s*, Alma *ms*, Aladino *b*, Osmino *t*, Felicia *s*, Adriano *t*, Mirva *silent*; *satb* chorus of prisoners, Egyptians, knights, slaves, etc.; ballet
LARGE ORCHESTRA including hp; onstage: banda (picc, 2 fl, 2 ob, F cl, 5 cl, 2 bsn, 4 hn, 2 key tpt, 6 tpt, 3 trbn, serpent, sd, bd)

This was the last of Meyerbeer's Italian operas. It was composed in close collaboration with Rossi, as the surviving correspondence shows. Armando was the last major operatic castrato role, written for the celebrated Velluti. Within two years of *Il crociato*'s successful premiere in Venice it was staged in Florence, Trieste, Padua, London and Paris. For each of these productions Meyerbeer revised the work and composed new music for parts of it.

SYNOPSIS
Act I Armando, a knight of Rhodes, is the sole surviver of an attack on Egypt during the Sixth Crusade. He assumes an Egyptian identity, becomes the confidant of the Pasha Aladino and secretly marries the Pasha's daughter Palmide. A peace mission arrives from Rhodes, among its members Armando's erstwhile betrothed Felicia and his uncle Adriano. Felicia agrees to give up Armando after meeting Palmide and the couple's five-year-old son, Mirva. Adriano discloses Armando's true identity and he and his fellow Christians are all imprisoned by Aladino.

Act II Aladino learns of Mirva's existence and orders the boy's death, but Palmide mollifies him and he agrees to release Armando. When he discovers Palmide has converted to Christianity, however, he reimprisons the Christians. Osmino, the Pasha's vizier, schemes to overthrow Aladino and releases and arms the knights; but instead of helping Osmino they defend Aladino who, in gratitude, allows Armando and Palmide to depart in peace.

Il crociato contains many of the elements that are associated with Meyerbeer's later French grand operas. It is written on a grand scale and has a larger orchestra than any of Rossini's Italian operas; for instance, in the introduction Meyerbeer demands six trumpets on stage in addition to two in the orchestra. The first finale, where Christians and Egyptians confront one another, includes two large stage bands of contrasting instruments, the usual brass instruments for the Christians and high-pitched instruments such as the piccolo clarinet for the Egyptians. The style of the music shows an amalgam of German and Italian influence, but the Italian predominates, particularly in the vocal lines, which are often highly ornamented. Perhaps surprisingly, the original version contains a great deal of *secco* recitative (with figured bass) though this was changed in later versions.

RECORDINGS 1. Kenny, Palmer, Blake, Diaz, Sacred Music Society Ch and O, Masini, Voce, 1979; 2. Kenny, Montague, D. Jones, Ford, Geoffrey Mitchell Ch, RPO, Parry, Opera Rara, 1991
EDITIONS f.s., *Early Romantic Opera*, vol. 18, Garland, 1980; v.ss., Ricordi, 1824; Schlesinger, 1826

Robert le diable
Robert the Devil

Grand opera in five acts (4h)
Libretto by Eugène Scribe, after a sketch by Germain Delavigne
Composed 1828–31
PREMIERES 21 November 1831, Opéra, Paris; UK: 20 February 1832, Drury Lane, London (as *The Fiend-Father*, version by Rophino Lacy); 11 June 1832, London (original version); US: 7 April 1834, Park Theater, New York (Lacy's version)
CAST Alice *s*, Isabelle *s*, Robert, Duke of Normandy *t*, Bertram *b*, Raimbault *t*, Priest *b*, Master of Ceremonies *t*, Alberti *b*, 10 *t*, 8 *b*, Abbess *dancer*; *satb* chorus of nobles, courtiers, populace, evil spirits, ghostly nuns; dancers
ORCHESTRATION picc, 2 fl, 2 ob/ca, 2 cl, 2 bsn, 4 hn, 2 tpt, 2 trbn, ophicleide, timps, perc, t-t, 2 hp, str; onstage: picc, 4 hn, 4 tpt, 3 trbn, ophecleide, timps, perc, 2 hp, organ, thunder-machine

After the success of *Il crociato*, Meyerbeer, taking his cue from Rossini, spent some time revising his Italian operas for the French stage. However, the success of Auber's *La muette de Portici* (1828) and Rossini's *Guillaume Tell* (1829) convinced him that the future lay with grand opera. Meyerbeer persuaded Scribe to change *Robert le diable* from a three-act opéra comique to a five-act grand opera and completed the music in 1831. Its extraordinarily successful premiere transformed Meyerbeer overnight into the most celebrated opera composer of the day. Chopin, who was present, observed: 'If ever magnificence was seen in the theatre, I doubt it reached the level of splendour shown in *Robert le diable* . . . It is a masterpiece . . . Meyerbeer has made himself immortal.' And Fétis wrote: 'It is not only M. Meyerbeer's masterpiece; it is a work remarkable in the history of art.'

SYNOPSIS

Act I The action takes place in the 13th century. Robert, the Duke of Normandy, in exile because of his evil doings, has come to Sicily, where he has fallen in love with the Sicilian princess Isabella. His father, the devil, follows him under the guise of Bertram. Raimbault, a minstrel betrothed to Robert's virtuous half-sister Alice, sings of Robert's misdeeds and is saved from Robert's wrath only by the intercession of Alice. She urges Robert, in vain, to reform and to avoid Bertram. At Bertram's instigation Robert gambles away all his possessions, including his armour, without which he cannot attend the forthcoming tournament where he hopes to win the hand of Isabella.

Act II Isabella and Robert meet in the palace during court celebrations; they pledge their love and

The Paris Opéra during a performance of Robert le diable *in the 1840s*

Isabella gives him new armour. However, Bertram prevents him attending the tournament. Robert's honour is compromised, and the Prince of Granada wins Isabella's hand in his stead.

Act III After a bantering encounter with Raimbault, Bertram attends an orgy of evil spirits, where he pledges that Robert will soon join their number. Alice, terrified, observes some of Bertram's sinister activities. In a ruined convent Bertram summons from their graves nuns who have broken their vows; they entice Robert to take a magic cypress bough from above the grave of St Rosalie, by means of which his wishes will be granted.

Act IV Now under Bertram's power, Robert uses the bough to gain access to Isabella's rooms. He threatens to carry her off, but she calms him and persuades him to break the bough, thus ending its power.

Act V Bertram attempts to inveigle Robert into making a contract with him, for which his soul is the price; but Alice intervenes, delaying him signing it until eventually, on the stroke of twelve, Bertram disappears. Robert is finally freed from his power. The great doors of the cathedral then open revealing Isabella in her wedding robe.

Robert le diable was the first collaboration between Meyerbeer, Scribe and the designers Duponchel and Cicéri, whose spectacular atmospheric sets were an integral part of the opera. The work of this team came to represent the most typical features of grand opera: a plot that wavers between history and the supernatural, an amalgam of musical styles and tableaux that (as in the Act III finale) used technical resources to achieve the maximum expressive effect.

Meyerbeer's use of extensive orchestral resources achieves bold and powerful effects throughout the opera. However, its success depended to a considerable extent on the effectiveness of the solo vocal parts. Meyerbeer was pre-eminent in giving his singers the opportunity to shine. Robert's *sicilienne* in the first finale, 'Au tournois, Chevaliers', Isabella's solos in Act II and much else are vocally brilliant. Bertram's solo in the Act II finale, 'Nonnes, qui reposez', where he calls the dead nuns from their graves, is splendidly atmospheric with its use of the tam-tam, while the unaccompanied trio, 'Fatal moment' for Alice, Robert and Bertram, interrupted after an elaborate three-part cadenza by tremolando strings, is highly effective. One of the finest things in the opera is the extended dramatic trio 'Que faut-il faire?' for the same three characters, at the end of which Bertram disappears.

RECORDING Anderson, Lagrange, Vanzo, Ramey, Paris Opéra Ch and O, Fulton, HRE, 1985
EDITIONS f.ss., Schlesinger, 1832; facsimile, *Early Romantic Opera*, vol. 19, Garland, 1980; v.s., Schlesinger, 1831

Les Huguenots

Grand opera in five acts (4h)
Libretto by Eugène Scribe and Emile Deschamps; additions by Gaetano Rossi

Composed 1832–6; original title, *La Barthélemy*, then *Léonore*, then *Valentine*
PREMIERES 29 February 1836, Opéra, Paris; US: 29 April 1839, Théâtre d'Orléans, New Orleans; UK: 20 June 1842, Covent Garden, London
CAST Marguérite de Valois *s*, Le Comte de St Bris *b*, Valentine *s*, Le Comte de Nevers *bar*, Cosse *t*, Thore *b*, Tavannes *t*, Meru *b*, Retz *b*, Raoul de Nangis *t*, Marcel *b*, Urbain *s*, Queen's maid of honour *s*, Maurevert *b*, Bois-Rose *t*, 3 monks *t*, 2 *b*, 2 witches 2 *s*, 2 girls *s*, *a*, student *t*, 2 *silent*; *satb* chorus of Huguenots, Catholics, soldiers, pages, citizens, populace, night watch, students, monks, etc.; ballet
ORCHESTRATION picc, 2 fl, 2 ob/a, 2 cl, b cl, 2 bsn, 4 hn, 3 trbn, ophicleide, 2 tpt *à piston*, 2 tpt, timps, perc (including bd, t-t), 2 hp, str (including oboe d'amore); large stage band

After the completion of *Robert le diable*, but before its premiere, Meyerbeer and Scribe began working on an opéra comique, *Le portefaix*. Following the tremendous success of *Robert le diable*, Meyerbeer decided to transform the three-act *Le portefaix* into a five-act grand opera, but when Scribe refused, he abandoned it. In October 1832 they signed an agreement for *La St Barthélemy* (later *Les Huguenots*). Meyerbeer promised to complete the music by December 1833 but failed to do so. He could not persuade Scribe to alter Act IV to include more opportunity for female voices, and instead had additions made by his old librettist Rossi. Other changes to the work were made shortly before the premiere to placate the censors, while for Adolphe Nourrit Meyerbeer added the duet 'O ciel! où courrez vous'. In later performances the last act was often omitted.

SYNOPSIS
Act I France, 1572. The Catholic Comte de Nevers is holding a banquet in Touraine ('Des beaux jours de la jeunesse'). Because of the king's desire for peace, he has invited a Huguenot nobleman, Raoul. The guests tell tales of amorous adventure: Raoul's story concerns an unknown lady, whom he rescued from a band of riotous students, and with whom he has fallen in love ('Plus blanche que la blanche hermine'). Raoul's servant, Marcel, is horrified to see his master consorting with Catholics and protests ('Seigneur, rempart', 'Piff, paff, piff, paff'). Nevers is summoned to meet a lady in the garden; the guests observe through a window ('L'aventure est singulière'). Raoul recognizes her as the unknown lady. She is Valentine, Nevers's fiancée, and has come to request that she be released from her engagement. Raoul receives a note summoning him to a secret rendezvous.

Act II At the château of Chenonceaux, Marguérite de Valois, sister of the king and fiancée of the Huguenot Henri de Navarre, awaits Raoul's arrival ('O beau pays de la Touraine'). For the sake of peace she plans to promote his marriage to Valentine, daughter of the Catholic leader St Bris. Raoul is brought in blindfold and, once his eyes are uncovered, swears devotion to her ('Beauté divine'). She proposes he marry the daughter of St Bris and he agrees. She explains her plan to a delegation of Catholic and Huguenot nobles and all swear eternal friendship ('Par l'honneur'). But when Valentine arrives Raoul, who does not know of her engagement, mistakenly presumes she is Nevers's mistress and repudiates his promise. Valentine does not understand his reaction; the antagonism between Catholics and Huguenots is renewed.

Act III In Paris a crowd is enjoying the day of rest ('C'est le jour du dimanche'). Huguenot soldiers sing a battle song while a Catholic service is heard from a nearby chapel ('Rataplan'). Nevers is about to be married to Valentine. Marcel delivers a message from Raoul to St Bris challenging St Bris to a duel. Nevers, St Bris and Maurevert plot to ambush Raoul ('Rentrez habitants de Paris'). Valentine, praying in the chapel, has overheard the conversation and, still in love with Raoul, warns Marcel ('Dans la nuit'). The duellers arrive and a fight between their followers ('Nous voilà') is averted only by the arrival of Marguérite. Valentine emerges from the church and St Bris is shocked to discover that it is his daughter who had warned Marcel ('Ma fille'). Marguérite clarifies Raoul's misunderstandings about Valentine and Nevers.

Act IV Raoul visits Valentine, now married to Nevers, and resolves to die after seeing her for a last time. She hides him when St Bris and his companions enter, and he overhears their plan for a massacre of Huguenots that night, St Bartholomew's Eve ('Des troubles renaissants'). Nevers refuses to join in. Raoul takes leave of Valentine ('O ciel! où courez vous') and rushes off to warn the Huguenots.

Act V The Huguenot leaders are celebrating the marriage of Marguérite and Henri de Navarre (entr'acte et ballet) when Raoul bursts in summoning them to arms ('A la lueur'). Later, sheltering in a churchyard, Raoul and Marcel are joined by Valentine: Nevers has been killed and she wishes to marry Raoul; she renounces her faith. Catholic soldiers challenge them, but they escape to the street with the dying Raoul ('Par le fer'). St Bris orders his men to fire on them, fatally wounding Valentine; he recognizes her too late. Marguérite arrives and helplessly witnesses the continuing savagery of the soldiers.

Les Huguenots is widely regarded as the finest of Meyerbeer's operas; it was the work chosen to open the current opera house at Covent Garden, London, in 1842. It puts immense strains on the resources of an opera house, for seven of its principal roles require singers of the very highest calibre; this has hindered its production during the 20th century, especially since the types of voice and vocal technique that Meyerbeer required are scarcely to be found today. The modern singer's pitch vibrato, so different from the vibrato of intensity in the *bel canto* tradition, is not suited to this kind of writing. Marguérite's air, 'O beau pays de la Touraine', and her duet with Raoul, 'Beauté divine', are outstanding examples of this style.

The musical style of Les Huguenots is, if anything, even more eclectic than that of *Robert le diable*, Meyerbeer's choice of style depending on the particular dramatic function of each section. For instance, while choral numbers that progress the action often seek to use local colour to reflect the emotions of specific characters (sometimes through instrumental timbres), solo numbers are frequently written in popular, more conventional forms. Many numbers show Meyerbeer's keen ear for instrumental effect; for example, Raoul's romance, 'Plus blanche que la blanche hermine', with its solo viola accompaniment shows great artistry in the creation of a feeling of simplicity. An incoherent effect is avoided by grouping contrasting numbers into larger units.

One example of this skilful combination of contrasting styles comes at the opening of Act III where the interweaving of the Huguenot soldiers' 'Rataplan' alternates with the song of the Catholic maidens accompanying Valentine's bridal procession and the protests of the Catholic populace against the Huguenot song (perhaps inspired by a similar scene in Spohr's *Pietro von Abano*, which Meyerbeer greatly admired). Another highlight of the score is the finale of Act III where a military band is on stage – an excellent example of Meyerbeer's skill in creating an arresting effect with large forces. The septet 'En mon bon droit j'ai confiance' immediately preceding the duel scene in Act III is highly effective on a smaller scale. And Act IV, as a whole, is perhaps Meyerbeer's greatest dramatic achievement. The scene of the 'benediction of the daggers' and the passionate duet for Valentine and Raoul, 'O ciel! où courez vous', are magnificent theatre.

RECORDINGS 1. Sutherland, Arroyo, Tourangeau, Vrenios, Bacquier, Cossa, Ghiuselev, Ambrosian Singers, New Philharmonia O, Bonynge, Decca, 1969; 2. Raphanel, Pollet, Borst, Leech, Cachemaille, Ghiuselev, Martinovich, Montpelier Opera Ch, Montpelier PO, Diederich, Erato, 1990: the live Montpelier recording, with a predominantly French cast, is to be preferred for all except Sutherland enthusiasts [A.B.]
EDITIONS f.ss., Schlesinger, 1836; facsimile, *Early Romantic Opera*, vol. 20, Garland, 1980; v.s., Schlesinger, 1836

Le prophète
The Prophet
Grand opera in five acts (4h)
Libretto by Eugène Scribe
Composed 1836–49
PREMIERES 16 April 1849, Opéra, Paris; UK: 24 July 1849, Covent Garden, London; US: 2 April 1850, Théâtre d'Orléans, New Orleans
CAST Jean de Leyde *t*, Fidès *ms*, Berthe *s*, Le Comte d'Oberthal *b*, Zacharie *b*, Jonas *t*, Mathisen *b*, 2 treble, 2 ms, 6 *t*, 7 *b*; *satb* chorus of peasants, anabaptists, soldiers, nobles, children; ballet
ORCHESTRATION picc, 2 fl, 2 ob, ca, 2 cl, b cl, 4 bsn, 4 hn, 4 tpt, 3 trbn, ophicleide, timp, perc, 2 hp, str; stage band: saxhorns of various sizes, 2 cornets *à cylindres*, 2 trompettes *à cylindres*

Within a few weeks of the premiere of Les Huguenots, Meyerbeer and Scribe began consideration of a new grand-opera text. Both Le prophète and L'africaine were discussed. Initially L'africaine was chosen to be Meyerbeer's next opera; he contracted to complete it in 1840, but in 1838 the completion date was extended by two years. Meyerbeer also signed a contract for *Le prophète*. Two years later *Le prophète* was substantially finished, but Meyerbeer's appointment as generalmusikdirektor in Berlin in 1842 delayed further progress. When he finally returned to *Le prophète* it needed thorough revision: the tenor part, originally intended for Gilbert Duprez, who had a remarkable chest-voice range, had to be rewritten for Gustave Roger; the part of Fidès was also rewritten and expanded for Pauline Viardot-García.

The premiere was again triumphant: leading critics, including Berlioz, regarded it as even surpassing the previous operas. Meyerbeer was promoted to Commandeur du Légion d'honneur; the publishing rights were hotly competed for, and the opera was taken up by almost every major theatre in Europe. It held its place in the repertoire throughout the 19th century and it continued to be performed, though with decreasing frequency, in the 20th. As with Meyerbeer's other grand operas, the difficulty of casting the operas satisfactorily, as well as changing taste, has militated against its production.

SYNOPSIS

Act I The countryside near Dordrecht, Holland. On the eve of the anabaptist uprising of 1,532 people are gathered outside Count Oberthal's castle ('La brise est muette'). Berthe aproaches the castle to obtain permission for her marriage to the innkeeper Jean (John of Leyden). Jean's mother, Fidès, accompanies her ('Fidès, ma bonne mère'). Three anabaptists, Zacharie, Jonas and Mathisen, also arrive to incite the people against their rulers but are driven away by Oberthal's men ('Ad nos ad salutarem undam'). Berthe makes her plea to the count ('Un jour, dans les flots') but he, struck by her beauty, refuses. He has her seized and taken into the castle. The onlooking populace is dismayed and, when the anabaptists return, is roused to the verge of revolt.

Act II In Jean's inn in Leyden the three anabaptists, struck by Jean's likeness to a picture of King David in the cathedral, try to persuade him to assume the role of prophet. He, however, is absorbed in his love for Berthe ('Pour Berthe'). Then Berthe rushes in begging to be hidden; she is hotly pursued by Oberthal, who orders Jean to hand her over ('Ils partent'). When Jean refuses, Oberthal threatens to execute Fidès. At this Jean gives way. After Oberthal's departure, Jean agrees to lead the anabaptists. They leave secretly; Fidès is deceived into thinking that Jean has been murdered by the prophet and his followers.

Act III The anabaptists, camped in a forest outside Münster, are making merry. Oberthal is brought into Zacharie's tent as a prisoner. Jean learns that Berthe has escaped and is in Münster. The three anabaptists wish to execute Oberthal, but Jean decrees that Berthe must decide his fate. When a group of the anabaptists led by Mathisen is defeated in an attack on the city, Jean, who has been

proclaimed a prophet of God, exerts his authority to prevent chaos in the camp. He rallies the people and leads a successful assault.

Act IV In a square in the city, people discuss the situation. Fidès is begging; she meets Berthe and tells her that Jean is dead, murdered by the prophet. Berthe vows revenge ('Un pauvre pèlerin'). In the cathedral Jean is to be crowned king (*Marche du sacre*). When he speaks Fidès recognizes his voice and cries out to him. Jean is then in danger from the people, since they thought him divine, but he escapes the crisis by denying that she is his mother, reasserting his divine parentage.

Act V In the palace at Münster the three anabaptists plot against Jean; the emperor, who is advancing on the city, has promised them pardon if they will betray the prophet ('Ainsi, vous l'attestez'). Jean and Fides meet secretly. He implores her pardon for denying her, but she refuses it until he agrees to renounce his position and return to Leyden ('Ma mère! ma mère!'). Berthe bursts in with a flaming torch, intending to ignite the building near to the powder magazine, to kill the prophet, his followers and herself. When she recognizes Jean she is happy, but when a soldier enters to report that the emperor is at the gates she realizes that Jean is also the prophet, curses him and stabs herself to death ('Voici le souterrain'). Jean determines to revenge himself on the anabaptists. He and Fidès go to the banquet knowing that the powder magazine is about to explode; they, along with the anabaptists, Oberthal and imperial troops, are all killed in a great explosion.

The music of *Le prophète* contains all the characteristic features of Meyerbeer's earlier grand operas, but the degree of fusion among these is even greater than before. The strongest characterization is that of Fidès, a role written specifically for Pauline Viardot. Her aria-cabaletta 'O prêtres de Baal' in Act V is an excellent example of the skills employed by Meyerbeer to achieve his dramatic ends. Interesting instrumentation – here, the use of harp and bass clarinet in particular – adds excitement to an otherwise conventional structure, infusing the music with additional emotional depth.

Variety is provided by the grotesque music allotted to the three anabaptists: for instance, their trio in Act III with its rhythmical striking of a flint to light a lantern. Meyerbeer's remarkable ability to create an effect by bizarre juxtaposition is nowhere better revealed than in the final scene where a boisterous drinking song ('O versez que tout respire l'îvresse et le délire') is the prelude to the explosion in which everyone perishes. For sheer grandiose magnificence the coronation scene, with its 22-piece stage band, is scarcely to be rivalled; it provided a model for many later opera composers.

Meyerbeer's calculation of effect extended to details of the staging. *Le prophète* was the first work to be staged at the Opéra with electric lighting. This was put to particularly fine use in the final scene of Act III where, as Jean leads his men to victory, the sun breaks through the mist which had shrouded the earlier part of the scene. Another *coup de théâtre* in the first production was the use of roller-skates to create the effect of ice-skating on the frozen lake at the beginning of Act III.

RECORDING Scotto, Horne, McCracken, Dupouy, Hines, Bastin, Ambrosian Opera Ch, RPO, Lewis, CBS, 1976
EDITIONS f.ss., Brandus, 1851; facsimile, *Early Romantic Opera*, vol. 21, Garland, 1978; v.s., Brandus, 1851

L'étoile du nord
The Star of the North
Opéra comique in three acts (3h)
Libretto by Eugène Scribe (partly after his ballet *La cantinière*)
Composed 1849–54
PREMIERES 16 February 1854, Opéra-Comique, Paris; US: 1 April 1855, Théâtre d'Orléans, New Orleans; UK: 19 July 1855, Covent Garden, London

Meyerbeer had briefly considered revising his Prussian opera *Ein Feldlager in Schlesien* for Paris, but he soon dropped this idea and worked with Scribe on a completely new text. However, since he still intended to use some of the music from *Ein Feldlager* in the new opera, he provided Scribe with appropriate metrical patterns to which he could fit some of his words. The premiere, attended by Napoleon III, was a brilliant occasion and the opera enjoyed considerable popularity in succeeding years.

Peter the Great of Russia is in love with a peasant girl, Katherine. She disguises herself as a man and takes the place of her brother, who has been drafted into the Russian army. Having learned of a conspiracy against the tsar, she warns him of it and, consequently, the conspiracy is soon suppressed. The tsar then disguises himself as a carpenter in order to woo Katherine. He wins her heart and makes her his tsarina.

The overture is for 'two orchestras', the concluding section containing a separate band of instruments designed by Adolphe Sax. Since spoken dialogue is used, unlike in the grand operas, Meyerbeer included several sections of melodrama in which he notated the speech rhythm: for instance, 'Et dans ce moment même' in Act I. As usual there are some charming effects; in the Act I finale he imitates the tuning of violins, while in the 'Chanson d'infantri' the chorus mimics the effect of side drums. The finale to the last act is unusual, containing a string of extended reminiscences of earlier numbers. A particularly delightful section in this finale is a piece for Katherine accompanied only by two solo flutes (supposedly played by characters on stage) which imitate her elaborate vocal coloratura.

EDITIONS f.ss., Brandus, 1854; facsimile, *Early Romantic Opera*, vol. 22, Garland, 1980; v.ss., Brandus, 1854

Le pardon de Ploërmel
(Also performed as *Le chercheur du trésor* and *Dinorah, oder Die Wallfahrt nach Ploërmel*)
Dinorah
Opéra comique in three acts (2h 30m)

Libretto by Jules Barbier and Michel Carré
Composed 1854–9
PREMIERES 4 April 1859, Opéra-Comique, Paris; UK: 26 July 1859, Covent Garden, London (in Italian, as *Dinorah*); US: 4 March 1861, French Opera House, New Orleans
CAST Dinorah *s*, Hoël *bar*, Corentin *t*, Huntsman *b*, Reaper *t*, 2 goatherds *s*, *a*; *satb* chorus of peasants, villagers, etc.
LARGE ORCHESTRA including thunder-sheet and wind-machine

Shortly after the premiere of *L'étoile du nord*, Jules Barbier sent Meyerbeer the synopsis of a one-act comic opera entitled *Le chercheur du trésor*. Meyerbeer was attracted to the story and requested Barbier and Carré to make a three-act opera of it. In fact the story was scarcely substantial enough to fill three acts since the essential action of the opera is over by the end of Act II; but Meyerbeer made a virtue of necessity and used the opportunity to produce some charming scenic tableaux with plenty of local colour in the final act.

SYNOPSIS
Act I Because of a catastrophe in which all Dinorah's father's property is destroyed, Hoël deserts her on their wedding day (the day of the religious procession known as the *pardon de Ploërmel*) to seek a cache of treasure he has been told about. She, unaware of his motive for leaving, loses her reason and wanders aimlessly with her pet goat. A year later, Coretin, a wandering minstrel, encounters Dinorah who, believing him to be Hoël, makes him dance with her. Hearing someone approach, she flees. Hoël enters; he tells Coretin of the treasure and offers to share it: he knows that the first to touch it will die. They hear the tinkling of Dinorah's goat-bell and decide to follow it.

Act II Dinorah broods sadly. At midnight in the Cursed Valley, Coretin and Hoël prepare to secure the treasure. A storm is brewing. Dinorah appears; she is swept away in a flood. Hoël, recognizing her, jumps in to save her.

Act III As hunters and reapers begin the day's work, Hoël carries in the unconscious Dinorah. At last he realizes he wants her, not riches. She wakes, her sanity restored. It is the day of the *pardon* and they go off to be married.

During the overture, snatches of a distant choir, singing a processional hymn, are heard from behind the curtain; as the music proceeds they appear to come closer. Throughout the opera Meyerbeer sustains interest by similar imaginative and ingenious touches. For example, in the Act III finale, as Dinorah slowly regains consciousness, Meyerbeer requires half of each section of the strings to be muted while the other half remains unmuted; the muted strings accompany Dinorah while the unmuted accompany Hoël.

The part for Dinorah gives the opera its special charm. Her Act II scene serves as the central axis of the work and is, typically, made up of three contrasting sections – a melancholy romance, in which she imitates the phrases of a solo clarinet (Coretin's 'cornemuse'), then a virtuoso rondo,

'Ombre légère' (the so-called 'shadow aria'), and finally a melodrama that recalls musical motifs from earlier parts of the opera.

RECORDING Cook, Hill Smith, Jones, Oliver, du Plessis, Geoffrey Mitchell Ch, Philharmonia O, Judd, Opera Rara, 1979
EDITIONS f.ss., Brandus et Dufour, 1859; facsimile, *Early Romantic Opera*, vol. 23, Garland, 1981; v.s., Brandus et Dufour, 1859

L'africaine
The African Girl
Grand opera in five acts (4h)
Libretto by Eugène Scribe, completed by François-Joseph Fétis
Composed 1837–64
PREMIERES 28 April 1865, Opéra, Paris; UK: 22 July 1865, Covent Garden, London; US: 1 December 1865, Academy of Music, New York
CAST Vasco da Gama *t*, Don Pedro *b*, Don Alvar *t*, Don Diego *b*, Inès *s*, Anna *ms*, Sélica *s*, Nelusko *b*, Grand Inquisitor *b*, High Priest of Brahma *b*, Anna *s*, 14 other solo parts 4 *t*, 10 *b*; *satb* chorus of priests, inquisitors, councillors, sailors, Indians, attendants, ladies, soldiers; ballet
LARGE ORCHESTRA including 4 hp; stage band of 26 Sax instruments

L'africaine had the longest gestation period of any of Meyerbeer's operas. The idea was first conceived in 1837, shortly after the premiere of *Les Huguenots*. When Meyerbeer died it was not fully complete, despite being put into rehearsal a few weeks earlier (his practice was to make substantial modification to both music and words of his operas during the

extensive rehearsal periods he insisted on). After the composer's death it was left to François-Joseph Fétis to supervise the final alteration to the work. The title is curious, for Sélica is actually an Indian queen.

The production of *L'africaine* was one of the most magnificent spectacles in the history of the Opéra. However, despite the fact that Meyerbeer himself thought it his best opera, it was not as successful as his three other grand operas. Though it contains some of Meyerbeer's finest music, its looser structure and somewhat unconvincing characterization undoubtedly make it dramatically weak. These defects might have been minimized to some extent had Meyerbeer lived to make thorough revisions in rehearsal.

SYNOPSIS
Act I In the Admiralty in Lisbon, Inès longs for news of her beloved Vasco da Gama, who has been away for two years. Her father, Don Diego, assuming Vasco to be dead, urges her to marry Don Pedro. During a council meeting Vasco and two captives, the only survivors of the expedition, unexpectedly arrive. When the council refuses to furnish a new expedition Vasco protests and is imprisoned together with his two captives, Sélica and Nelusko.

Act II Sélica loves Vasco; Nelusko loves Sélica and wants to kill the sleeping Vasco, but Sélica watching over Vasco forbids him. She wakes Vasco and explains that she can guide him to India. Inès enters just as Vasco embraces Sélica in gratitude (she had married Pedro in order to secure Vasco's release). Vasco gives her Sélica as a slave, but is doubly shattered when he learns that Pedro is Inès's

The storm scene in Act III of L'africaine *(L'Illustration, 1865)*

husband and is mounting an expedition to the Indies; the jealous Nelusko offers to act as Pedro's guide.

Act III On board ship a storm is brewing. Nelusko plans to guide it on to a reef. Vasco, having mounted his own expedition, comes alongside and boards; he warns them of the reefs. Pedro tries to kill Vasco, but is prevented by Sélica; he orders Nelusko to kill her, but Nelusko refuses. The storm breaks and the ship is wrecked. Indians board and begin to massacre the crew. Recognizing their queen, Sélica, they pay homage to her.

Act IV Sélica is triumphantly enthroned. Inès has been taken to the mancanilla grove to die by inhaling the poisonous fragrance of the trees. Sélica saves Vasco's life by claiming he is her husband and they declare their love. Inès has not died, however, and when she and Vasco meet, their passion is overwhelming. Sélica nobly renounces Vasco and sends the lovers home.

Act V From a promontary Sélica watches the departure of Vasco's ship. She inhales the perfume of a mancanilla tree and dies in Nelusko's arms. As the curtain falls he, too, inhales the perfume.

The opera shows Meyerbeer's continuing development towards a more through-composed style, which had been increasingly apparent in his previous operas, and is mostly constructed in a fluid mixture of recitative, arioso and aria; there are fewer self-contained numbers. Throughout Meyerbeer uses solo wind instruments resourcefully to accompany the solo voices. The scene of Sélica's enthronement at the beginning of Act IV gives him the opportunity to use a large stage band, as in the coronation scene of *Le prophète*, but here he makes the most of the chance to create exotic musical colouring. The final scene is extraordinary and can fairly be described as Meyerbeer's *Liebestod* (he had carefully studied the vocal score of Wagner's *Tristan und Isolde* in 1860): Sélica dies ecstatically to the accompaniment of an offstage chorus.

RECORDING Mandac, Verrett, Domingo, Mittelmann, San Francisco Opera Ch and O, Perisson, MRF, 1972
VIDEO Verrett, Domingo, Diaz, San Francisco Opera Ch and O, Arena, Virgin, 1980s
EDITIONS f.ss. (completed Fétis), Brandus et Dufour, 1875; facsimile, *Early Romantic Opera*, vol. 24, Garland, 1980; v.s., Brandus et Dufour, 1865

Other operas: *Abu Hassan* (inc.), (1810); *Der Admiral, oder Der verlorene Prozess* (inc.), (1811); *Jepthas Gelübde*, 1812; *Wirth und Gast, oder Aus Scherz Ernst*, 1813; *Das Brandenburger Tor*, (1814); *Romilda e Costanza*, 1817; *Semiramide riconosciuta*, 1819; *Emma di Resburgo*, 1819; *Margherita d'Anjou*, 1820; *L'Almanzore*, (1821); *L'esule di Granata*, 1821; *Ein Feldlager in Schlesien*, 1844, rev. as *Vielka*, 1847
BIBLIOGRAPHY Heinz and Gudrun Becker, trans. Mark Violette, *Giacomo Meyerbeer: A Life in Letters*, Christopher Helm, 1989; J. W. Klein 'Giacomo Meyerbeer (1791–1864)', *MR*, vol. 25 (1964), p. 142; Karin Pendle, *Eugène Scribe and French Grand Opera of the 19th Century*, UMI Research Press, 1979

C.A.B.

MINORU MIKI
b 16 March 1930, Tokushima, Shikoku, Japan

Like most Japanese composers since the war, Miki was trained in Western styles, even though he came from a musical family in which traditional Japanese instruments were played. He studied at the Tokyo National University of Fine Arts and Music, and was already a successful composer for the European orchestra, as well as for choir, when in the early 1960s he began to interest himself in Japanese instruments. In 1964 he founded the Ensemble Nipponia, a group that played on these instruments, and in the following years Miki wrote a number of works for the group, as well as other works combining Japanese and Western instruments.

In his theatre music too, Miki has sought to fuse Western elements with the traditional styles and stories of Japanese theatre. His first full-length opera, *Shunkin-Sho*, a love story set in 19th-century Osaka (just before the opening up of Japan), beautifully combines the slow pace and delicate texture of Japanese drama with the sound-world of the Western orchestra treated, however, in a highly personal way. Its immediate successor, *An Actor's Revenge* (commissioned by English Music Theatre, and first staged in London in 1979) is an even more vigorous fusion of Western music-theatre elements (themselves admittedly Eastern-influenced) with the stark, statuesque idioms of Kabuki theatre, applied to the Otokichi Mikami story on which Ichikawa based his film of the same name. Since then, Miki has added a second Kabuki-based opera, *Joruri*, inspired by the 17th-century puppet plays of Chikamatsu Monzaemon, and commissioned by the Opera Theatre of St Louis, two further large-scale ('grand') operas, as well as several so-called 'folk operas', or musical plays in Japanese dialect, for whose performance Miki founded the performing group Uta-za (named after his first folk opera, *Utayomizaru, or The Monkey Poet*) in 1985.

Stage works: *Husband the Hen*, 1963; *Kikimimi* (for children), 1967; *Shunkin-Sho*, 1975; *Urakagura Seikai-no-Hokoku*, 1976; *An Actor's Revenge*, 1979; *Toge no muko ni naniga aruka* (choral opera), 1983; *Utayomizaru* (folk opera), 1983; *Joruri*, 1985; *At the Flower Garden* (mini-opera), 1985; *Wakahime*, 1992; *Vomigaeru* (folk opera), 1992; *Orochi-Den* (folk opera), 1992; *Shizuka and Yoshitsune*, 1993

S.W.

DARIUS MILHAUD
b 4 September 1892, Aix-en-Provence, France; *d* 22 June 1974, Geneva, Switzerland

Milhaud's operatic output spans his creative life. His love of literature, encouraged by his childhood literary friends Léo Latil and Armand Lunel, developed from an interest in poets such as Maeterlinck, Jammes and Claudel whom he admired for their departure from the Symbolist aesthetic. At this early stage he found in them his own musical alternative to Impressionism. In 1911 he began work on a setting of Jammes's *La brebis égarée* and in 1913 embarked on an *Oresteia* trilogy with Claudel.

After arriving in Paris to study at the Conservatoire in 1909, Milhaud discovered the music of Stravinsky, Koechlin and Satie. From 1917 to 1919 he accompanied Claudel to Rio de Janeiro as his secretary, and there began *Les Euménides*, the third and most substantial part of the *Oresteia*, also collaborating with Claudel on the ballet *L'homme et son désir* (1918). These works show increasing rhythmic polytonal and contrapuntal experimentation.

Returning to France in 1919, Milhaud was caught up in the Parisian artistic scene and soon found himself a member of Les Six, the clique of subversive young composers promoted by Cocteau under the wing of Erik Satie. He gained considerable notoriety with his pantomime ballet *Le boeuf sur le toit* (1919) and his involvement with novel projects such as Satie's apparently frivolous *musique d'ameublement* (1920); the popular tunes and unconventional subject matter of these works gave him a reputation for being whimsical and interested in novelty at all costs, but he always regarded himself as a serious composer. Milhaud heard jazz in London (1920) and New York (1922), and in the ballet *La création du monde* (1923) endeavoured to assimilate it into his musical language. His exposure to new and varied influences at this time helped formulate his aesthetic principles, which changed remarkably little thereafter (these are presented in several contemporary articles on music). The six operas he wrote between 1924 and 1927 are in striking contrast with the mammoth scale of *Oresteia*, being short, frequently satirical and more contemporary in setting.

Christophe Colomb (1928) marked a return to large-scale operatic writing and forms the apex of Milhaud's experimental years. During the 1930s he became more of an Establishment composer; the performance of *Maximilien* at the Paris Opéra in 1932 and the state commission for *Médée* (1938) are indications of his respectability. As a Jew, he was forced to flee to America in 1939. He taught at Mills College in California, and after the war in 1947 became professor of composition at the Paris Conservatoire, holding both posts simultaneously. He completed his last opera, *Saint-Louis, Roi de France*, in 1971.

Variety and versatility are the keys to Milhaud's operatic success. They can be seen in his choice of collaborators (from Hoppenot and Cocteau, to his wife Madeleine), the length of the works (9m to 3h 15m), choice of subject matter, and stylistic range. Milhaud's versatility arose from his belief that a composer should be capable of writing in whatever style a project demanded and that each task demanded an individual solution. He has frequently been charged with hastiness and lack of self-criticism. Yet apart from occasional insensitivity to textural balance his craftsmanship was superb and his musical and dramatic achievements were immense.

L'Orestie
The Oresteia

Trilogy:
Agamemnon, play with only one scene set to music, Op. 14 (10m)
Les Choéphores (*The Libation Bearers*), theatre music in seven scenes, Op. 24 (30m)
Les Eumenides, opera in three acts, Op. 41 (1h 30m)
Libretti by Paul Claudel, after the trilogy by Aeschylus (458 BC)
Composed 1913–24
PREMIERES *Agamemnon*: 14 April 1927, Paris (concert); *Les Choéphores*, 15 June 1919, Paris (concert; extracts), 8 March 1927, Paris (concert; complete), 27 March 1935, Brussels; *Les Eumenides*: 18 November 1949, Brussels Radio (concert); *L'Orestie*: 5 May 1963, Berlin

As *Agamemnon* opens, Argos awaits the king's return from the Trojan War. During Agamemnon's absence his wife Clytemnestra has taken Aegisthus as her lover and on Agamemnon's homecoming she kills her husband. In *Les Choéphores*, Orestes returns and avenges his father's death by killing his mother and her lover. In *Les Eumenides*, Orestes is pursued by the Furies, although forgiven by Apollo for his crime. A trial is held in Athene's temple, but the vote is split. Athene casts the deciding vote and acquits Orestes, pacifying the Furies by promising them a respected position within the new world order.

The composition of *L'Orestie* spans a formative period of Milhaud's creative life. The first two parts of the trilogy are not operas as such, but contain nascent techniques that become prominent in *Les Eumenides*. In *Agamemnon* there is no music until Clytemnestra comes out of the palace to face the elders. In *Les Choéphores* Claudel felt that the violence of two of the scenes demanded something between speech and song and Milhaud's solution was to employ solo declamation accompanied by choral recitation and unpitched percussion. Detailed harmonic organization is prominent in all three works. Milhaud subtitled *Les Choéphores* 'harmonic variations' and the second scene marks his first use of chordal polytonality. But the finale of *Les Eumenides* has a complex polytonal plan, and Milhaud shows how he was also beginning to view polytonality melodically.

RECORDINGS   *Les Choéphores* and Processional of *Les Eumenides*: Jordan, Bobikian, Boatwright, Zorina, Schola Cantorum, New York PO, Bernstein, CBS, 1960s
EDITIONS   *Agamemnon*: v.s., Heugel, 1927; *Les Choéphores*: v.s., Heugel, 1926; *rp*, 1947; *Les Eumenides*: v.s., Heugel 1927

Les malheurs d'Orphée
The Sorrows of Orpheus

Chamber opera in three acts, Op. 85 (35m)
Libretto by Armand Lunel
Composed 1924
PREMIERES   7 May 1926, Théâtre de la Monnaie, Brussels; US: 29 January 1927, Town Hall, New York (concert); 22 May 1958, Hunter College, New York; UK: 8 March 1960, St Pancras Town Hall, London

In sharp contrast to *L'Orestie*, *Les malheurs d'Orphée* is the first of a series of chamber operas.

Milhaud wanted to transport the Orpheus myth to a modern setting and, with the help of Lunel, Orphée became a healer of people and animals from the Camargue. He falls in love with a visiting gypsy, Eurydice, and the two escape to the mountains where Eurydice becomes ill despite Orphée's medical skills. When she dies Orphée returns to his village, where he is pursued and killed by Eurydice's sisters, who realize too late that he was innocent of their sister's death.

A series of miniature dramatic and musical pictures are presented, pared down to the essentials, giving momentary glimpses of the drama unfolding. Again in contrast to *L'Orestie*, Milhaud uses a limited amount of musical material. The vocal parts are simple, although the angularity of Eurydice's lines contributes to a sense of exoticism in keeping with her gypsy nature. The reflective solo and duet passages overshadow and contrast with more fleeting fast-paced ensemble numbers, and the music is fashioned with a delicacy that is moving and direct.

RECORDINGS 1. Brumaire, Collart, Collard, Demigny, soloists of the Paris Opéra, Milhaud, Vega, 1957; 2. Steiger, Bickley, Bardon, Walker, Matrix Ensemble, Ziegler, ASV, 1990
EDITION v.s., Heugel, 1926

Le pauvre matelot
The Poor Sailor

Complainte (chamber opera) in three acts, Op. 92 (30m)
Libretto by Jean Cocteau
Composed 1926, rev. (with reduced scoring) 1934
PREMIERES 16 December 1927, Opéra-Comique, Paris (with reduced scoring); rev. version: 15 November 1934, Grande Théâtre, Geneva; US: 1 April 1937, Academy of Music, Philadelphia; UK: 9 October 1950, Fortune Theatre, London
CAST Wife *s*, Sailor *t*, Friend *bar*, Sailor's Father *b*
CHAMBER ORCHESTRA (rev. version)

Le pauvre matelot has the same dramatic and musical precision as *Les malheurs d'Orphée*. In this opera Milhaud set a subject rooted in folk-tale and everyday life. Cocteau's libretto was inspired by a newspaper article, to which he added a seafaring setting, and Milhaud, while working on the opera, visited the harbour at Marseilles in order to absorb the musical atmosphere of the bars and streets. This slight but dramatically potent work remains his most frequently performed opera.

SYNOPSIS
Act I A sailor's wife has waited faithfully for 15 years for her husband's return, refusing to remarry despite her father-in-law's urgings and her poverty. She believes that her husband will return rich from his travels. The sailor does indeed return a wealthy man; he decides to visit his wife without revealing his identity, in order to view her constancy for himself.

Act II He finds his wife hungry for news of her husband and tells her that her man is alive but very poor. She expresses concern because she herself is penniless, but her joy breaks through at the knowledge that her husband is alive. The sailor

boasts of his own wealth and of the pearls he carries with him, to which she responds, 'And what about my husband?' When he asks for accommodation for the night, she consents.

Act III The wife picks up a hammer and kills the sailor because, as she explains to her father-in-law, the wealth of this stranger will help to pay the debts of her loved one.

The music is imbued with the simplicity and repetitiveness of folksong. The opening 'java' melody is strikingly modal and cleverly depicts the shabby bar where the sailor's wife works. Act III is dominated by the well-known folksong 'Blow the man down'. On its first appearance its exaggerated slowness, combined with a jazz-inspired rhythmic figure on the bassoon, double-bass and percussion, skilfully encapsulates the tragic events.

The wife's music is simple and tuneful. Her unsuitably triumphant song, when she has killed the sailor, makes her appear ridiculous, and the excessive pride and confidence of her husband are matched with a high, fast-paced vocal line. The story is related with a dispassionate musical voice that heightens its dramatic power.

RECORDING Brumaire, Giraudeau, Depraz, Vessières, soloists of the Paris Opéra, Milhaud, Vega, 1957
EDITIONS v.ss., original version, Heugel, 1927; rev. version, Heugel, c. 1960

Les Opéras-minutes
Three-Minute Operas

L'enlèvement d'Europe (*The Abduction of Europa*), eight scenes, Op. 94 (9m)
L'abandon d'Ariane (*Ariadne Abandoned*), five scenes, Op. 98 (10m)
La délivrance de Thésée (*The Deliverance of Theseus*), six scenes, Op. 99 (8m)
Libretti by Henri Hoppenot
Composed 1927
PREMIERES *L'enlèvement d'Europe*: 17 July 1927, Town Hall, Baden-Baden; *L'abandon d'Ariane* and *La délivrance de Thésée*: 20 April 1928, Wiesbaden Opera

In 1927 Hindemith commissioned Milhaud to write an opera of the smallest proportions for the festival at Baden-Baden. Milhaud took him at his word and responded with a nine-minute opera, *L'enlèvement d'Europe*. His publisher, Hertzka, then proposed that he should transform this fleeting work into a trilogy.

In these works Milhaud went a step further than the chamber operas in terms of concise dramatic statement. Complete with arias, ensembles and choruses, the notion of time is so accelerated as to give a sense of unreality. The reactions and asides of the chorus add a satirical touch to the bare outlines of the Greek legends.

RECORDING Ensemble Ars Nova and Ensemble Vocal Jean Laforge, Sirnossian, Arion, 1983
EDITIONS f.s., Universal, 1928; *rp*, [c. 1970]; v.ss., Universal, 1927, 1928; *rp*, 1953

Set design by Panos Aravantinos for the sailors' revolt in Christophe Colomb *(Berlin, 1930)*

Christophe Colomb
Christopher Columbus

Opera in two parts (27 tableaux), Op. 102 (2h 30m)
Libretto by Paul Claudel, after his play *Le livre de Christophe Colombe* (1927)
Composed 1928, rev. (the order of the two parts reversed) *c.* 1955
PREMIERES 5 May 1930, Theater unter den Linden, Berlin; France: 6 December 1936, Salle Pleyel, Paris (concert); UK: 16 January 1937, Queen's Hall, London (concert); US: 6 November 1952, Carnegie Hall, New York (concert); revised version: 31 May 1956, Théâtre des Champs-Elysées, Paris (concert); 27 June 1968, Opernhaus, Graz
CAST Christophe Colomb *bar*, Isabella *s*, Narrator *spoken role*, 41 other solo parts from *satb* chorus
LARGE ORCHESTRA offstage band including harmonium; onstage band

The composition of *Christophe Colomb* marks a return to large-scale opera, after the chamber operas and the 'minute' operas directly preceding it, and to Milhaud's collaboration with Claudel. In the trilogy Claudel and Milhaud had been preoccupied with the balance between music and words in drama. In *Christophe Colomb* they attempted to focus on all aspects of drama: words, music, gesture, scenery and even film, in order to achieve Claudel's ideal of 'total theatre', an ideal not far removed from Wagner's *Gesamtkunstwerk*.

The opera is a symbolic and religious presentation of the life of Christopher Columbus. The story is presented as a book from which the narrator draws at will in order that posterity (the chorus), with Christophe Colomb among them, may judge his life. The opera does not progress chronologically and indeed Part II mirrors Part I rather than following on from it. Columbus's worldly and spiritual journeys are examined from various perspectives: his calling as a child, his help from Isabella the Catholic, his adventures in quest of the New World, his conflicts with the sailors, with the Spanish court and, finally, his miserable death at the Inn of Valladolid.

Many of the experiments of *L'Orestie* are here combined with the experience of the shorter operas. Declamation is exploited in the spoken role of the narrator. Polytonality, both harmonic and melodic, is prominent and the texture in the scene *Irruption des Colombes* is a well-wrought combination of melodically, tonally and rhythmically independent layers. his is achieved partly through skilful orchestration, each line maintaining autonomy of timbre while the texture remains light.

Contrast is essential to the dramatic impact: the often short scenes are self-contained units fluctuating between harsh dissonance and simple melody, declamation and the combined forces of orchestra and chorus: chaotic action-packed scenes alternate with those of calm reflection. This musical and dramatic balance and contrast make the work one of Milhaud's finest, and arguably his best opera.

RECORDING Micheau, Giraudeau, Massard, Depraz,

Lovano, French Radio Ch and Lyric O, Rosenthal, Disques
Montaigne, 1956
EDITION   v.s., 2 vols, Univeral, 1939

La mère coupable
The Guilty Mother
Opera in three acts, Op. 412 (1h 45m)
Libretto by Madeleine Milhaud and the composer, adapted
from the play by Beaumarchais (1792)
Composed 1964–5
PREMIERE   13 June 1966, Grand Theatre, Geneva

The idea of setting the third play of Beaumarchais's
Figaro trilogy was the result of the director of
Ricordi's request for an opera from Milhaud. The
characters are those familiar from *The Barber of
Seville* and *The Marriage of Figaro*, but later in their
lives, when Rosine (the guilty mother) has had a
child by Cherubin. The monotonous and complicated
series of intrigues is scarcely alleviated by Milhaud's
setting; there is negligible musical contrast between
characters and only a few lyrical moments. Frequent
changes of mode create a tonal fluidity typical of
Milhaud's late style.

EDITION   v.s., Ricordi, 1966

Other operatic works: *La brebis égarée*, (1914), 1923; *Esther
de Carpentras*, (1927), 1937; *Maximilien*, 1932; *Médée*, 1939;
Bolivar, (1943), 1950; *David*, 1954; *Fiesta*, 1958; *Saint-Louis,
Roi de France* (opera-oratorio), 1972
BIBLIOGRAPHY   Paul Collaer, trans. and ed. Jane Hohfeld
Galante (with a catalogue of works by J. H. G. and
Madeleine Milhaud), *Darius Milhaud*, San Francisco Press,
1988; Jeremy Drake, *The Operas of Darius Milhaud*,
Garland, 1989; Darius Milhaud, trans. Donald Evans, *Notes
without Music*, Dobson, 1952

B.L.K.

KARL MILLÖCKER
b 29 April 1842, Vienna; *d* 31 December 1899, Baden, nr
Vienna

The son of a Viennese goldsmith, Millöcker studied
the flute at the Vienna Conservatory. He played in
the orchestra at the Theater in der Josefstadt, then
led by Franz von Suppé, and later conducted at the
Thalia-Theater, Graz. His initial one-act operettas
were produced there in 1865, among them *Der tote
Gast*. Another, *Diana*, was produced in Vienna two
years later, and a three-act work, *Die Fraueninsel*, in
Budapest in 1868.

The following year he became second conductor at
the Theater an der Wien, where he scored a distinct
success in 1871 with the songs for a farce, *Drei Paar
Schuhe*, which starred Alexander Girardi, a former
locksmith from Graz who would become one of the
theatre's greatest stars. There were several other
farces and musical comedies throughout the 1870s,
until *Das verwunschene Schloss* (1878), his first
substantial operetta success. In 1879 appeared *Gräfin*

Dubarry, which achieved international fame in a
heavily revised version by Theo Mackeben in 1931.

Millöcker was meanwhile conducting the first runs
of such operettas as Johann Strauss's *Die Fledermaus*
(1874). But in 1882, he produced a masterpiece that
challenged Strauss's stage works: *Der Bettelstudent*,
which made its merry way across Europe and to
America and made its composer wealthy. Its
successor, *Gasparone*, was a bandit caper in the *Fra
Diavolo* mould that remains quite popular in
Germany and Austria.

Subsequent operettas – usually starring Girardi –
were eagerly sought by German-speaking theatres
and American managers as well, the most notable
being *Der Feldprediger* (1884), *Der Vize-Admiral*
(1866), and *Der arme Jonathan* (1890), while works
written before *Der Bettelstudent* were performed to
capitalize on Millöcker's reputation. His last three
operettas were set, respectively, in Scotland, the
Black Forest, and Russia, and various pasticcios were
concocted after the composer's death.

Der Bettelstudent
The Beggar Student
Operetta in three acts (1h 30m)
Libretto by F. Zell and Richard Genée, after the plays
Fernande by Victorien Sardou (1870) and *The Lady of Lyons*
by Edward Bulwer-Lytton (1838)
PREMIERES   6 December 1882, Theater an der Wien,
Vienna; US: 19 October 1883, Thalia Theater, New York;
UK: 12 April 1884, Alhambra Theatre, London

This historical romantic comedy is set in Saxon-
occupied Poland in 1704 and combines themes of
honour, revenge, masquerade, political plotting and
romance. Millöcker's score rises to the lively action
and is full of incisive musical characterization.
It is studded with eminently hummable polkas,
krakowiaks, polonaises, marches, and waltzes, and
brilliantly constructed and scored. It was one of the
most successful Viennese operettas – between 1896
and 1921 there were almost 5000 performances in
German; it has been filmed many times in Germany.

RECORDINGS   1. Gueden, Schädle, Konetzni, Schock,
Ollendorf, Ch of Deutsche Oper, Berlin, Berlin SO, Stolz,
Eurodisc, 1960s; 2. Streich, Holm, Litz, Gedda, Prey,
Bavarian Radio Symphony Ch and O, Graunke, EMI
Electrola, 1970s
FILMS   1. Janson (dir.), 1931; 2. Jacoby (dir.), 1936; 3.
Carlton (dir.), 1956; 4. Houwer (dir.), 1970
EDITION   v.s., Cranz, 1883

Other operettas: *Der tote Gast*, 1865; *Die lustigen Binder*,
1865; *Diana*, 1867; *Die Fraueninsel*, 1868; *Der
Regimentstambour*, 1869; *Abenteuer in Wien*, 1873; *Das
verwunschene Schloss*, 1878; *Gräfin Dubarry*, 1879; *Apajune
der Wassermann*, 1880; *Die Jungfrau von Belleville*, 1881;
Gasparone, 1884; *Der Feldprediger*, 1884; *Der Dieb*, 1886;
Der Vize-Admiral, 1886; *Die sieben Schwaben*, 1887; *Der
arme Jonathan*, 1890; *Das Sonntagskind*, 1892; *Der
Probekuss*, 1894; *Das Nordlicht, oder Der rote Graf*, 1896
BIBLIOGRAPHY   Otto Schneidereit, *Operette A–Z*,
Henschelverlag, 1971; Richard Traubner, *Operetta: A
Theatrical History*, Gollancz, 1983

R.T.

FRANCISZEK MIRECKI

Franciszek Wincenty Mirecki; *baptized* 31 March 1791,
Cracow; *d* 29 May 1862, Cracow

Mirecki came from a family of musicians, studying
first with his father, who was an organist, then in
Vienna with Hummel and in Paris with Cherubini.
He was conductor of an Italian opera company in
Lisbon (1825–6) and with it visited England and
France. Later he taught singing in Genoa and
Cracow, where he was the director of a music school;
he conducted opera in both cities.

Thanks to these conducting activities, operas form
the major part of his work; some of them were
written specially for staging in Lisbon and Genoa and
were published by Ricordi, either in vocal score or as
excerpts. They enjoyed a certain fame and popularity
in Mirecki's day, being very much in the fashionable
Italian, Rossinian style. He also composed a
symphony, chamber music, piano music (including
sonatas), arranged a set of psalms by Benedetto
Marcello for orchestra, and published a treatise on
instrumentation in Italian (Milan, 1825).

Operas: *Cyganie* (*The Gypsies*), 1822; *Evandro in Pergamo*,
1824; *I due forzati* (*The Two Convicts*), 1826; *Adriano in Siria*
(inc.), (*c.* 1826); *Cornelio Bentivoglio*, 1844; *Nocleg w
Apeninach* (*A Night in the Apennines*), 1845; *Rajmund mnich*
(*Raymond the Friar*), (n.d.); 2 lost operas
BIBLIOGRAPHY   W. Sandelewski, 'Francesco Mirecki,
campione polacco del melodramma italiano', *RMI*, vol. 55
(1953), p. 426

Z.C.

HENRY MOLLICONE

b 20 March 1946, Providence, Rhode Island, US

Mollicone is a composer, conductor and pianist. His
composition teachers included Gunther Schuller and
his conducting appointments have largely been with
opera companies. As a composer Mollicone has
specialized in opera. His best-known example is *The
Face on the Bar Room Floor* (1978), written for
Central City Opera in Colorado and performed in
the bar where a face is painted on the floor, which
was given on the fringe of the Edinburgh Festival by
Opera Theater of St Louis in 1983 and was enjoyed
as a successful entertainment for three singers and
piano. Mollicone's subsequent operatic works include *Emperor Norton*, *The Starbird*, *The Mask of
Evil* and *Hotel Eden*.

RECORDING   *The Face on the Bar Room Floor*, Foss, CRI,
[*c.* 1980]

P.D.

LIONEL MONCKTON

John Lionel Alexander Monckton; *b* 18 December 1861,
London; *d* 15 February 1924, London

Monckton was a leading composer of late Victorian
and Edwardian musical comedy. His contributions
to several popular shows generally stand out
from adjacent songs by fellow composers thanks to
a joyous, often haunting infectiousness that
foreshadows such musicians as Kern, Novello and
Ellis. Monckton was involved with amateur
theatricals at Oxford University but trained for the
bar. He then became a music critic at the *Daily
Telegraph*. After contributing effective numbers to
Gaiety burlesques and to *The Geisha* (1896),
Monckton most frequently collaborated with Ivan
Caryll. Some of his best works were, however, shared
with Howard Talbot, including the best of all
Edwardian operettas, *The Arcadians*.

The Arcadians

A fantastic musical play in three acts (2h 30m)
Libretto by Martin Ambient and Alexander Mattock
Thompson; lyrics by Arthur Harold Wimperis
PREMIERE   28 April 1909, Shaftesbury Theatre, London;
US: 17 January 1910, Liberty Theater, New York

James Smith, an ageing aviator from London, bales
out over Arcady where he is introduced to the ideas
of Truth and Beauty and, after immersing himself in
the Well of Truth, becomes the young Simplicitas.
With other Arcadians, he returns to London to 'set
up truth in England for ever more', with adventures
at a racecourse and the Arcadian Restaurant, before
returning to his former self.

One of the best examples of British musical
comedy, *The Arcadians* clearly inherits the mantle of
Gilbert and Sullivan's *Iolanthe*, but was a huge
success in its own right. Among the numbers
supplied by Monckton, 'Arcady is ever young', 'The
pipes of Pan', 'The girl with a brogue' and 'All down
Piccadilly' (added after the first performances) retain
much of their appeal, while the 'Askwood' racecourse scene in Act II looks forward to Lerner's and
Loewe's *My Fair Lady*.

RECORDING   excerpts: Bronhill, Howard, Tausky, EMI, 1968
FILM   Saville (dir.), 1927
EDITION   Chappell

Other musicals: *The Circus Girl* (coll. with Caryll), 1896; *A
Runaway Girl* (coll. with Caryll), 1898; *The Messenger Boy*
(coll. with Caryll), 1900; *The Toreador* (coll. with Caryll),
1901; *A Country Girl* (coll. with Caryll), 1902; *The Orchid*
(coll. with Caryll), 1903; *The Cingalee*, 1904; *The Spring
Chicken* (coll. with Caryll), 1905; *The Girls of Gottenberg*
(coll. with Caryll), 1907; *Our Miss Gibbs* (coll. with Caryll),
1909; *The Quaker Girl*, 1910; *The Mousmé* (coll. with Talbot),
1911; *The Dancing Mistress*, 1912; *The Boy* (coll. with
Talbot), 1917
BIBLIOGRAPHY   Kurt Gänzl, *The British Musical Theatre*,
vol. 1, Macmillan, 1985

R.T.

JEAN-JOSEPH CASSANÉA DE MONDONVILLE

baptized 25 December 1711, Narbonne, France; *d* 8 October 1772, Belleville, France

Settling in Paris in 1733, Mondonville soon established a reputation as a composer and violinist. Helped by powerful allies including Madame de Pompadour, he secured a succession of important posts in the Royal Chapel and eventually became director of the Concert spirituel. His operatic career began badly with the failure of *Isbé* (1742). By contrast, *Le carnaval du Parnasse* (1749) was spectacularly successful, with a first run of over 60 performances. During the *querelle des bouffons* he became a natural champion of the French cause: *Titon et l'Aurore* (1753) scored an important psychological victory for devotees of native opera opposed to Italian infiltration. For *Daphnis et Alcimadure* (1754) he wrote both music and libretto, the latter entirely in Languedoc dialect.

In 1765 Mondonville took the unprecedented step of resetting a Quinault libretto immortalized by Lully in the previous century: his version of *Thésée* was given first before the court at Fontainebleau. While the recitative was regarded as a poor substitute for Lully's, some of the new music was admired. But when the work appeared two years later at the Paris Opéra, it was savaged: after only four performances it was replaced, by popular demand, with Lully's original.

Thésée apart, Mondonville eschewed the lofty tragédie in favour of the lighter-weight pastorale and opéra-ballet. His style seems designed to appeal to the widest audience; it ranges from simple vaudeville-like melodies to brilliant Italianate coloratura arias and from old-fashioned French-style dances to orchestral writing reminiscent of the latest German symphonies. His operas are not lacking in scenes of pathos and passion, which benefit from an expressive harmonic vocabulary and imaginative orchestration; such scenes are seldom prolonged, however, and are often quickly contrasted with others of a lighter character.

Surviving operatic works: *Isbé*, 1742; *Bacchus et Erigone*, 1747; *Le carnaval du Parnasse*, 1749; *Vénus et Adonis*, 1752; *Titon et l'Aurore*, 1753 (RECORDING Erato, 1991); *Daphnis et Alcimadure*, 1754; *Les fêtes de Paphos*, 1758; *Thésée*, 1765; *Les projets de l'Amour*, 1771

BIBLIOGRAPHY R. Machard, *Jean-Joseph Cassanéa de Mondonville, virtuose, compositeur et chef-d'orchestre*, Centre international de documentation occitane, Société de musicologie du Languedoc (Béziers), 1980

G.S.

STANISŁAW MONIUSZKO

b 5 May 1819, Ubiel, nr Minsk; *d* 4 June 1872, Warsaw

Moniuszko is generally regarded as the creator of Polish national opera and the most important Polish composer of the 19th century after Chopin. He composed operas throughout his working life and, along with other works for voices and orchestra, they form the most important part of his output.

Moniuszko first studied music in Minsk, and then from 1837 to 1840 was a composition student in Berlin with Carl Friedrich Rungenhagen, whose conservatism influenced his own language: it remained deeply rooted in early Romanticism. Moniuszko encountered the European operatic repertoire in Berlin, and gained experience in preparing opera for performance through his work as a chorus master. His first opera dates from this time.

In 1840 he moved to Vilnius, where he soon became the leading figure in local musical life. He was church organist and choir conductor, and conductor of the theatre orchestra. Here he composed *Halka*, and after its highly successful Warsaw premiere Moniuszko was appointed first conductor at the Warsaw Opera (1858). From then on he wrote mainly for the stage, and all his new operas were premiered in Warsaw. In addition to opera, he wrote ballets, and incidental music to Shakespeare's *Hamlet* and *The Merchant of Venice*, Schiller's *Die Räuber*, Racine's *Phèdre*, Słowacki's *Lilla Wenda*, and many others. But there are also instrumental pieces, religious music, cantatas, and many songs of the domestic variety, rather simple and unvirtuosic – a style that is also characteristic of some of his operatic arias.

His work was directly addressed to Polish audiences of the day, and reflected its expectations and needs, and this in turn influenced his choice of genre and his musical language, which stayed within the grasp of the general public. He wrote operetta and comic opera, as well as grand opera. His early operas are on the border between opera and operetta, influenced by French vaudeville and German singspiel. His more important later operas are influenced, in both structure and musical language, by Auber and by early 19th-century Italian opera. Nevertheless, most of them have a national character which comes from their specifically Polish subject matter, and from the use of rhythms and musical phrases typical of Polish national and folkdances (dance rhythms figure not only in the ballet music, but also in the arias and choruses).

Moniuszko's operatic output is artistically uneven. His operettas, early operas, and also later ones such as *Paria*, had few performances in his lifetime and are not performed today. *The Raftsman*, *The Countess* and *Verbum Nobile* were popular in the 19th century, but his best operas, *Halka* and *The Haunted Manor*, are still in the repertoire of Polish opera houses.

Halka

Opera in four acts (2h 30m)
Libretto by Włodzimierz Wolski, after a story by K. W. Wójcicki
Composed 1846–7 (in two acts); rev. 1857 (four acts)
PREMIERES 1 January 1848, Vilnius (concert); 16 February 1854, Vilnius; rev. version: 1 January 1858, Wielki Theatre, Warsaw; US: June 1903, Manhattan Opera House, New York

(Russian Opera Company); UK: 8 February 1961, Collegiate Theatre, London
CAST Halka *a*, Janusz *bar*, Jontek *t*, *s*, 2 *t*, 2 *b*; *satb* chorus; ballet
FULL ORCHESTRA

Halka was Moniuszko's first grand opera of a nationalistic character, reflecting the social conflicts and injustices of the time in music of recognizably ethnic cut.

SYNOPSIS
The opera is set in the countryside near the Tatra Mountains in the first half of the 19th century. Halka is a village girl in love with Janusz, an impoverished nobleman. Previously, she loved Jontek, a boy from the same village, until she was seduced by Janusz and had a child by him.

Act I The opera opens with Janusz's engagement to Zofia, the daughter of a rich nobleman. Halka is unaware of the engagement, and when she hears about it refuses to believe it.

Act II In order to see Janusz, she goes to the manor house, where the engagement is being celebrated. Jontek follows her. When she realizes what is happening, she goes mad. She and Jontek are thrown out by a servant.

Act III In Halka's and Jontek's village everyone is rejoicing, but Halka paces around, crazy and unaware that Janusz's wedding is imminent.

Act IV In the hope of curing Halka of her hopeless love, Jontek takes her to the wedding. At first she tries to set fire to the church to avenge herself and her dead child. But she changes her mind, decides to leave Janusz with his happiness and, jumping into the river, commits suicide.

Halka reverts to an early 19th-century operatic form consisting of arias, ensembles and choruses. The influence of Donizetti and Auber is particularly evident in the duets, while ensemble scenes such as the celebration of Janusz's engagement allow the introduction of Polish dances, which are the most colourful parts of the score. Specific dances are used for specific social circles: for example, the polonaise and mazurka, the typical dances of the Polish gentry, are danced by the noblemen, while the peasants dance local mountain dances. Hence the music follows the needs of the drama and the types of character involved, and in fact folk tunes are the sole model for Moniuszko's melody in the episodes involving country people.

Halka is superior to all previous Polish operas in artistic quality and in its control of large form, and its popularity has continued to grow ever since the Warsaw premiere of the four-act version.

RECORDINGS 1. Woytowicz, Ochman, Hiolski, Polish Radio S Ch and O, Semkow, Polskie Nagrania/Le Chant du Monde, 1972; 2. Kawecka, Domienizcki, Wocznieko, Ch and O of Poznań Opera House, Bierdiajew, Polskie Nagrania/Colosseum, 1955; 3. Sokolova, Nelepp, Lisitsian, Bolshoi Ch and O, Kondrashin, Melodiya, 1952: the Melodiya set is abridged
EDITIONS f.s./v.s., PWM, 1952

The Haunted Manor

Straszny Dwór
Opera in four acts (2h 30m)
Libretto by Jan Chęciński
Composed 1861–4
PREMIERE 28 September 1865, Wielki Theatre, Warsaw
CAST Stefan *t*, Zbigniew *b*, Czesnikowa *ms*, Hanna *s*, Jadwiga *ms*, Miecznik *bar*, Damazy *t*, 2 *s*, 1 *t*, *bar*; *satb* chorus of country folk, Miecznik's guests, hunters; ballet
FULL ORCHESTRA

After the collapse of the uprising against Russia in 1864, Poles lost hope of their national independence, and writers and artists turned back for their subject matter to an idealized view of Polish history. *The Haunted Manor* sprang from this tendency; the opera presents an idyllic view of life in a Polish manor in the second half of the 17th century, and the simple courage of an ordinary Pole. After the third performance it was removed from the Wielki Theatre's repertoire by the tsar's censor.

SYNOPSIS
Act I Two brothers, Stefan and Zbigniew, return home from a victorious campaign. In parting from their comrades, they swear not to marry, so as always to be ready to fight for their country. When they get home, they decide to visit their old friend Miecznik, although they know his house is haunted.

Act II At a New Year's Eve celebration at Miecznik's manor the brothers meet his two beautiful daughters, Hanna and Jadwiga, and fall in love with them. But the brothers' aunt, Czesnikowa, wants them to marry other girls and Damazy, who himself wants to marry Hanna, is angry with the brothers. Miecznik describes the virtues needed by his daughters' husbands: they should be brave and devoted to their country. Czesnikowa and Damazy decide to prove that the brothers are not brave.

Act III Stefan and Zbigniew spend the night in a room with an old clock, where strange things happen every night. As soon as they are alone, the pictures on the wall start to move and the clock starts to chime. But the brothers are not afraid, especially when they find the girls hidden behind the pictures and Damazy hidden in the clock.

Act IV Miecznik tells the story of the manor, the brothers propose to the girls and are accepted, and all ends happily.

The Haunted Manor is Moniuszko's best opera, as well as being the most original – harmonically more advanced than *Halka*. Its musical features include finely constructed ensembles, colourful instrumentation and melodic inventiveness. Some of the arias, such as Stefan's so-called 'aria with chimes', are comparable to the best-known Italian tenor arias, while the colourful and vivacious mazurka is often played as a separate orchestral piece.

RECORDINGS 1. Betley-Sieradzka, Baniewicz, Hiolski, Ochman, Mróz, Saciuk, Polish Radio S Ch and O, Krenz, Polskie Nagrania, 1981; 2. Kostrzewska, Kurowiak,

A scene from The Haunted Manor *(Warsaw, 1875)*

Woźniczko, Paprocki, Kossowski, Poznań Opera House Ch and O, Bierdiajew, Polskie Nagrania, 1981
EDITIONS   f.s./v.s., Towarzystwo Wydawnicze Muzyki Polskiej, 1937

Other operas: *Biuraliści* (*The Bureaucrats*), (*c.* 1835); *Nocleg w Apeninach* (*A Night in the Apennines*), 1839; *Ideał, czyli Nowe Precjoza* (*Ideał, or The New Preciosa*), 1841; *Karmaniol, czyli Francuz i lubią żartować* (*Carmagnole, or The French Like Joking*), 1842; *Nowy Don Kichot, czyl Sto szaleństw* (*The New Don Quixote, or 100 Follies*), 1842; *Żółta szlafmyca* (*The Yellow Nightcap*) (lost), 1841; *Loteria* (*The Lottery*), 1843; *Sielanka* (*Idyll*), 1852; *Woda cudowna* (*The Miraculous Water*), (*c.* 1843); *Cyganie* (*The Gypsies*), 1852, rev. as *Jawnuta*, 1860; *Bettly*, 1852; *Flis* (*The Raftsman*), 1858 (RECORDING Polskie Nagrania, 1960s); *Hrabina* (*The Countess*), 1860 (RECORDING excerpts: Polskie Nagrania, 1960s); *Rokiczana* (inc.), (1859); *Verbum nobile*, 1861; *Paria*, 1869; *Beata*, 1872; *Trea* (inc.), (1872)
Undated: *Sen wieszcza* (*The Seer's Dream*) (inc); *Pobór rekrutów* (*Conscription*) (lost); *Walka muzyków* (*The Musicians' Struggle*) (lost); *Nowy dziedzic* (*The New Landlord*)
BIBLIOGRAPHY   Z. Jachimecki, 'S. Moniuszko and Polish Music', *Slavonic Review*, vol. 2 (1924), p. 533; Z. Jachimecki, 'Stanislaus Moniuszko', *MQ*, vol. 14 (1928), p. 54; Tadeusz Kaczyński, *Dzieje sceniczne 'Halki' Stanisława Moniuszki* (*Performance History of Moniuszko's 'Halka'*), PWM, 1969;

W. Rudziński, *Stanisław Moniuszko. Studia i materiały*, 2 vols, PWM, 1955, 1961

Z.C.

MEREDITH MONK
b 20 November 1943, Lima, Peru

Monk exhibits talents in a variety of media: her importance as a choreographer and film-maker rivals her significance as a composer, and she is also well known as a singer, pianist, dancer and mime artist, and to some degree as a theatre director (all chiefly these days in her own work).

Monk's early work in a theatrical context is typical of its time: her first 'theater cantata', *Juice* (1969), is scored for 85 solo voices, 85 jew's harps and two violins and was premiered in New York's Guggenheim Museum. Yet she was soon happy to use the term 'opera' – as her experimental colleagues in New York and elsewhere were also doing – for works that no traditionalist opera-goer would regard as more than remotely operatic: *Education of the*

Girlchild (1972–3), for instance (one of Monk's best-known works), is described as an 'opera' for six solo voices, electric organ and piano. Recent works reveal an interest in narrative and character development on a larger scale, as well as the use of more tradional forces. *Atlas* (1991), for instance – an 'opera in three acts' scored for chamber orchestra and voices – concerns an explorer, Alexandra Daniels, whose journey through life is told in terms of spiritual as well as geographical discovery. Monk's emphasis on wordless vocals rather than text remains, however, an important feature.

BIBLIOGRAPHY Gregory Sandow, 'Invisible Theater: The Music of Meredith Monk', in J. L. Zaimont (ed.), *The Musical Woman: An International Perspective*, Greenwood Press, 1984

K.P.

PIERRE-ALEXANDRE MONSIGNY

b 17 October 1729, Fauquembergues, nr St Omer, France; *d* 14 January 1817, Paris

Monsigny ranks as one of the creators of the opéra comique. He was one of a generation of composers active during the 1760s and 1770s, a period of rapid expansion in which the genre was transformed from the comédie en vaudevilles – reliant on popular melodies – to the comédie mêlée d'ariettes (opéra comique) – which used original music throughout. Performances in Paris of *La serva padrona* and other Italian comic works by the famous Bouffon troupe between 1752 and 1754 had encouraged this development. They had introduced French composers to the idea that libretti be designed to serve and enhance the music; in the comédie en vaudevilles the composer had played only a subservient role. The musical content of the Bouffons' repertoire also proved influential since many ariettes were firstly transferred literally to new works (parodied) and then used as models for original compositions.

Monsigny developed both the subject matter and the musical style of the opéra comique. His early works (1759–61), composed for the fair theatres of Saint Germain and Saint Laurent, were all comic intrigues revolving around disguises, deceptions, misunderstandings and reconciliations. *On ne s'avise jamais de tout* was the most popular of these, and was the first of many successful collaborations with the librettist Michel Sedaine. In 1762 Monsigny departed significantly from an overtly comic style with *Le roi et le fermier*, whose literary source was Robert Dodsley's play *The King and the Miller of Mansfield*. This work juxtaposed royalty and members of the nobility with rural characters – the class most usually portrayed in the opéra comique – and painted the picture of an enlightened monarch dealing humanely with his subjects. The emphasis in Sedaine's libretto on the virtues of common folk, on personal freedom and equality were themes then popularized by

philosphers of the Enlightenment. Seven years later Monsigny and Sedaine extended the scope of the genre further with *Le déserteur*.

The musical content of Monsigny's works became increasingly complex. He rapidly dispensed with vaudevilles, wrote original ariettes in their place, and composed a great many vocal ensembles. Although his lack of technique has been emphasized, his concerted writing often belies such criticism. The vocal textures of many ensembles are complex – noteworthy examples including the trio for three sopranos opening Act III of *Le roi et le fermier*, and an extensive fugal trio in *Rose et Colas* – and some incorporate dramatic action. The first example of a septet in an opéra comique is found in *Le roi et le fermier*, predating Philidor's use of the same device (in *Le bûcheron*) by a year.

However, Monsigny's rather limited creative imagination and technical prowess – compared to his contemporaries Grétry and Philidor – are evident from his somewhat repetitive musical style, his unadventurous harmonic language and occasional weaknesses in instrumentation. However, his skills as a melodist, the comic spirit of his lighter works, and the immediacy of the dramatic expression in his more serious compositions leave Monsigny with few rivals among his contemporaries.

Le déserteur

The Deserter
Opéra comique in three acts
Libretto by Michel Jean Sedaine
PREMIERES 6 March 1769, Comédie-Italienne, Paris; UK: 2 November 1773, Drury Lane, London; US: 8 June 1787, New York

Le déserteur, Monsigny's most successful opéra comique, is unprecedented in its juxtaposition of comic and serious elements, which established a more passionate and dramatic style of opéra comique, the drame larmoyante. It tells a melodramatic tale of a soldier condemned to death for desertion. While on leave, Alexis, the hero, is deliberately led to believe that Louise, his fiancée, has wed her cousin Bertrand. In despair, he announces his intention to flee in the then unusual form (for an opéra comique) of *recitative accompagnato*; his capture, by a quartet of guards, concludes Act I with a rousing ensemble. Act II is set in the prison cell Alexis shares with the drunken Montauciel, a fellow soldier. Alexis is visited by Louise and her father who explain the misunderstanding. Emotional scenes between the three are punctuated with outbursts from Montauciel – among these the celebrated air 'Je ne deserterai jamais' – and the act concludes with a comic duet between Bertrand and Montauciel juxtaposing two solo *chansons*. Act III is an admirable blend of pathos and suspense: Alexis prepares to face his death, Louise undertakes a desperate offstage Journey in search of a royal pardon and, having obtained this, returns in time secure the traditional happy conclusion.

EDITION f.s., Chez Des-Lauriers, 1769; v.s., Mme Ve. Launer, *c.* 1845

Other operas: *Les aveux indiscrets*, 1759; *Le maître en droit*, 1760; *Le cadi dupé*, 1761; *On ne s'avise jamais de tout*, 1761; *Le roi et le fermier*, 1762; *Rose et Colas*, 1764; *Aline, reine de Golconde*, 1766; *L'isle sonnante*, 1767; *La rosière de Salency*, (coll. with Philidor, ?Duni, Blaise, Swieten), 1769; *Pagamin de Monègue*, (c. 1770); *Le faucon*, 1771; *La belle Arsène*, 1773, (rev. 1775); *Félix, ou L'enfant trouvé*, 1777; *Robin et Marion*, (n.d.); 3 lost operas

BIBLIOGRAPHY   P. Druilhe, *Monsigny*, La Colombe, 1955

E.C.

MICHEL PIGNOLET DE MONTÉCLAIR

baptized 4 December 1667, Andelot, Haute-Marne, France; *d* 22 September 1737, Aumont, France

From 1699 until the year of his death Montéclair served as basse de violon-player at the Paris Opéra; it was he who introduced the double-bass to the Opéra orchestra around 1701, having doubtless encountered the instrument during an early visit to Italy in the service of the Prince de Vaudrémont. He enjoyed a considerable reputation as composer and theorist, though his output in both spheres is small: for the Opéra he wrote only two works, both of them successful – the opéra-ballet *Les festes de l'été* and the tragédie *Jephté*.

Though marred by occasional short-windedness and banality, Montéclair's music often anticipates Rameau's in its forcefulness, harmonic richness and complexity. Rameau admired the chorus 'Tout tremble devant le Seigneur' from *Jephté*, a work that probably sowed the seed for his own biblical opera, *Samson*. *Les festes de l'été* (whose last entrée foreshadows the plot of *Così fan tutte*) helped establish the hunting scene, much imitated in later French opera. Its use of offstage *cors de chasse* is characteristic of Montéclair's inventive scoring, which includes antiphonal contrasts between bass instruments and pieces for up to five sizes of recorder, as well as double and *a cappella* choruses.

Operatic works: *Les festes de l'été*, 1716; *Jephté*, 1732
(RECORDING Harmonia Mundi, 1991)
BIBLIOGRAPHY   J. R. Anthony, *French Baroque Music from Beaujoyeulx to Rameau*, Batsford, rev. 2nd edn, 1978; Caroline Wood, 'Orchestra and Spectacle in the tragédie en musique 1673–1715: oracle, sommeil and tempête', *PRMA*, vol. 108 (1981–2), pp. 25–46

G.S.

ITALO MONTEMEZZI

Antonio Italo Montemezzi; *b* 4 August 1875, Vigasio, nr Verona, Italy; *d* 15 May 1952, Vigasio

Montemezzi was a relatively minor, conservative composer whose fame now rests on one opera, *L'amore dei tre re*. None of his other works made so lasting an impact, although *Giovanni Gallurese* (1905) had considerable initial success and reached New York in the mid-1920s. The subject here is a grim, barbarous tale set in Sardinia during the Spanish domination, with touches of local colour that may suggest an affinity with *Cavalleria rusticana* (which the composer is said to have had in mind as a precedent). However, unlike *Cavalleria*, the work is in three acts, and it introduces touches of Wagnerian harmony and orchestration within its traditional Italian framework. Wagner's influence became more pervasive in *Hellera* (1909), which seems not to have received a stage revival since its first run. There is also a strong Wagnerian component in *L'amore dei tre re*.

After that opera's big international success – which proved more durable in the US than in Italy – Montemezzi's subsequent output was disappointing. His most ambitious opera, *La nave* (1918), based on D'Annunzio's controversial, sumptuously decadent play of the same name, contains some fine passages, but is laboured and uneven as a whole. Although Montemezzi here showed occasional mild signs of Strauss's influence, he was not greatly disposed to move with the times. His unassuming, unadventurous last two operas aroused no more than passing interest when they appeared. In addition to his operas, Montemezzi wrote a small handful of works for the concert hall.

L'amore dei tre re

The Love of Three Kings
Opera in three acts (recording: 1h 35m)
Libretto by Sem Benelli, adapted from his own play
Composed *c.* 1911–13
PREMIERES   10 April 1913, La Scala, Milan; US: 2 January 1914, Metropolitan, New York; UK: 27 May 1914, Royal Opera House, Covent Garden, London

When Sem Benelli, one of D'Annunzio's best-known disciples, wrote his drama *L'amore dei tre re* in 1910, he had already agreed to convert it into a libretto for Montemezzi. As things turned out, the opera's success far outshone that of the play – perhaps because the characters (recalling Maeterlinck's) have a symbolic dimension that needs music in order to become wholly convincing in the theatre.

The time is the 10th century, when a part of Italy was dominated by barbarian invaders from the north. They include Archibaldo who, 40 years earlier, established himself as king of Altura. Now he is old and blind, but he remains extremely strong-willed and acutely aware of his surroundings. The story centres on the continuing love between Fiora – who has been married against her will to Archibaldo's son, Manfredo – and one of her own countrymen, Prince Avito, to whom she had previously been betrothed. The drama reaches its climax in Act II, when Archibaldo surprises the lovers together. Avito escapes; but the old king strangles Fiora when she refuses to reveal her lover's name. In order to catch his son's unknown rival, Archibaldo spreads poison on the dead Fiora's lips, as she lies in the crypt of the castle chapel. This results in the death not only (as intended) of Avito, but also of the gentle, altruistic Manfredo, who has forgiven Fiora for her infidelity, knowing that it was the result of a great love.

Montemezzi's musical depiction of Archibaldo – with his characteristic halting yet menacing motif, epitomizing both his infirmity and his determination – is one of the opera's most memorable features. The love music, especially in Act II, is also fine, though obviously indebted to *Tristan und Isolde*. At other times one is more aware of Montemezzi's Italian heritage, from Verdi and perhaps from Catalani; and there is some unexpectedly Slavonic-sounding choral writing in Act III.

RECORDING   Moffo, Domingo, Elvira, Siepi, LSO, Santi, RCA, 1977: observes the Act II cuts sanctioned in the 1913 v.s., but includes an Act III prelude not in that score
EDITION   v.s., Ricordi, 1913

Other operas: *Bianca*, (c. 1901); *Giovanni Gallurese*, 1905; *Hellera*, 1909; *La nave*, 1918; *La notte di Zoraima*, 1931; *L'incantesimo*, 1943 (NBC broadcast), 1952
BIBLIOGRAPHY   Lawrence Gilman, 'A Note on Montemezzi' in *Nature in Music and Other Studies in the Tone-poetry of Today*, John Lane, 1915, pp. 155–66

J.C.G.W.

CLAUDIO MONTEVERDI

Claudio Giovanni Antonio Monteverdi; *b* 15 May 1567, Cremona; *d* 29 November 1643, Venice

Monteverdi was undoubtedly the most significant composer of opera as it emerged in the first decade of the 17th century. He studied in Cremona with Marc'Antonio Ingegneri, choirmaster of the cathedral, whose solid teaching in the traditional polyphonic style was apparent in Monteverdi's earliest publications.

In 1590 or 1591, Monteverdi moved to Mantua to join the court musicians of Duke Vincenzo Gonzaga. Although employed as a string-player, he continued to publish madrigals and must have become involved in court entertainments. Mantua, then one of the most exciting musical centres in northern Italy, was host to some of the best composers of the period, including, as head of the ducal chapel, Giaches de Wert (1535–1596). Wert, perhaps the leading madrigalist of his generation, significantly influenced Monteverdi's maturing style. Moreover, the Gonzaga dukes (Vincenzo and later his two sons, Francesco and Ferdinando) were keen patrons of music as more than just an essential adjunct of court life. They provided a climate in which all the arts flourished in their city.

Monteverdi participated in the grand performance of Battista Guarini's *Il pastor fido* in Mantua in late 1598. He also accompanied Duke Vincenzo on several trips outside his kingdom, including to Hungary and Flanders, and perhaps to Florence for the wedding celebrations of Maria de' Medici and Henri IV of France in October 1600: the festivities included the first opera to survive complete, *Euridice* by Jacopo Peri. In 1601 Monteverdi finally received a long-sought-for appointment as the head of the duke's musical establishment.

Monteverdi's first opera was *Orfeo*, to a libretto by the court secretary Alessandro Striggio. Although Monteverdi built on the example of the Florentines, by his cautious approach to their revolutionary stance and his own flexibility he removed the element of dilettante experimentation from the new genre of dramma per musica, and established it as a more powerful force in its own right. *Orfeo* was presumably intended to emphasize Mantua's cultural rivalry with Florence. Exchanges between the two cities were hardly surprising: Duke Vincenzo's wife, Eleonora, was a Medici princess, and Prince Ferdinando spent a good deal of his early life in Florentine circles and was closely involved with musicians there, especially Marco da Gagliano.

For the wedding festivities of Prince Francesco Gonzaga and Margherita of Savoy, celebrated in May–June 1608, Monteverdi contributed an opera, *Arianna*, to a libretto by Ottavio Rinuccini (who had collaborated with Peri), plus a dance entertainment, *Il ballo delle ingrate*. But Monteverdi resented what he felt was the shabby treatment accorded him by the Mantuan court, and he disliked the unhealthy climate there. Events were further marred by personal tragedy; after the death first of his wife and then of his favourite pupil, Caterina Martinelli (who was to have sung the title role in *Arianna*), Monteverdi began to look elsewhere for work. His *Sanctissimae Virgini missa . . . ac vespere* (the 'Vespers' of 1610) clearly advertises his availability, and on 19 August 1613 he was appointed director of music at the Basilica of St Mark in Venice.

Monteverdi now enjoyed the fame, responsibility and security of what was possibly the leading musical position in Italy. He was also working for a republic rather than a court. His former employers continued to press him for music for operas, ballets and tournaments, but many of these requests remained unanswered. Monteverdi blamed the pressures of time and his duties at St Mark's, but in fact he now disliked catering for court tastes, where entertainments had to be peopled with mythological, allegorical and (super)natural characters. As he wrote to Striggio in 1616 about one such entertainment, *Le nozze di Tetide*, 'I have noticed that the interlocutors are Winds, Cupids, little Zephyrs and Sirens . . . [but] how can I, by such means, move the passions? Ariadne moved us because she was a woman, and similarly Orpheus because he was a man, and not a wind.' Monteverdi did in fact provide some more entertainment music for Mantua, but in his heart he had left the court behind.

Inevitably, Monteverdi's duties in Venice led him to concentrate on church music. However, as he grew older and relied more on his assistants to provide liturgical music, his thoughts returned to the stage. In the Carnival of 1624 he presented *Il combattimento di Tancredi et Clorinda*, adapting a poet who had been one of his favourite sources for madrigal texts, Torquato Tasso. He was also involved in the entertainments for the wedding of Duke Odoardo Farnese of Parma and Margherita de' Medici, which was celebrated in Parma in 1628, with a prologue, four intermedi and a licenza for the performance of Tasso's *Aminta* as well as music for a tournament. Monteverdi also wrote music for other entertainments in Venice and Vienna.

However, Monteverdi's most striking achievements for the stage came in the last years of his life. In 1637, the first public opera house opened at the Teatro S. Cassiano in Venice, encouraging a new type of opera catering not for a court but for a paying public. This led to inevitable changes both in subject matter and in musical content. Subjects, whether mythological or historical, had to be more accessible and appealing; musical resources, particularly in terms of the chorus and orchestra, had to be pared down to ensure maximum profitability; tuneful arias had to dominate over recitative; and the success or failure of an opera depended ever more on the virtuoso qualities of its lead singers. The resulting changes were striking and far-reaching.

Title page of Fiori Poetici *with a portrait of Monteverdi, published in 1644, after the composer's death*

Monteverdi first revised his *Arianna* for the Teatro S. Moisè in Carnival 1640: his choice of a work always close to his heart is significant, but *Arianna* was a court opera and cannot have been entirely appropriate for the new audience. It was far better to begin anew, as he did with *Il ritorno d'Ulisse in patria*, performed in the same season. Here Monteverdi stayed with the mythological world of the court, but now the cast are real-life characters experiencing and conveying immediate, human emotions.

For his second Venetian opera, Monteverdi turned from Homer to Virgil: his *Nozze d'Enea in Lavinia* (now lost) was staged at the Teatro SS. Giovanni e Paolo in Carnival 1641. However, the gradual move towards more concretely historical subject matter was completed only with his last work, *L'incoronazione di Poppea*. With *Orfeo*, Monteverdi had participated in the very birth of opera, marking the genre's first maturity. With *Poppea*, he celebrated a revolution of no less significance that inaugurated a new age in operatic history.

Orfeo

Favola in musica in a prologue and five acts (1h 45m)
Libretto by Alessandro Striggio jnr, after Rinuccini's *Euridice* (1600)
PREMIERES 24 February 1607, Palazzo Ducale, Mantua; UK: 8 March 1924, Institut Français, London (concert); 7 December 1925, Oxford; US: 14 April 1912, Metropolitan, New York (concert); 11 May 1929, Smith College, Northampton, Massachusetts
CAST La Musica *s*, Orfeo *t*, Euridice *s*, Silvia *s*, Speranza *s*, Charon *b*, Pluto *b*, Proserpina *s*, Apollo *t*; *satb* chorus of nymphs and shepherds, infernal spirits
INSTRUMENTALISTS 5-part str ensemble (2 to a part); brass ensemble (2 cornetts, 4 trbn); 2 rec, 2 small vln 'alla francese', and muted tpts for the opening 'toccata'; continuo: 2 hpd, 3 chitarroni, 2 'organi da legno', regal, double hp, 3 vg, 2 db viols

Orfeo was first performed under the auspices of Prince Francesco Gonzaga and the Accademia degli Invaghiti. The title role was taken by Francesco Rasi, a famous virtuoso from Arezzo who had also sung in Peri's *Euridice* (1600). There was a second performance a week later and a third was planned, though this seems not to have taken place. Unlike the early Florentine operas, the work is clearly divided into acts, although these were probably played without a break. The libretto published for the first performance contains an ending different from the score and closer to the myth: after Orpheus has vowed to renounce women, a crowd of Bacchantes enter, berating him for his decision and singing in praise of Bacchus. The two endings may reflect different conditions at different performances, although it is not clear which was used when.

SYNOPSIS

Prologue After three statements of the opening fanfare-like 'toccata' (which reappears in the 1610 'Vespers'), Music enters to a ritornello for strings. This ritornello returns at key points in the opera where music and its power come into play. The prologue consists of five short stanzas sung over the same bass line, each separated by a shortened version of the ritornello. The theme of the opera is the power of music, which can 'soothe each troubled heart and . . . inflame the coldest minds now with noble anger, now with love'.

Act I In the fields of Thrace, Orpheus is to be married to Eurydice. He sings a hymn to his beloved ('Rosa del Ciel') and nymphs and shepherds rejoice in song and dance.

Act II Eurydice has left with her companions. Orpheus sings to the woods, which once heard his laments but now ring to his joy ('Ecco pur ch'a voi ritorno . . . Vi ricordi, o boschi ombrosi'). But the mood of celebration, so carefully built up over this first part of the opera, is shattered by the sudden entrance of Sylvia, the messenger ('Ahi caso acerbo!'). Her tale slowly emerges ('In un fiorito prato'): Eurydice has died from a snakebite. Orpheus, at first scarcely believing the shattering news, laments his bride ('Tu sei morta') and then resolves to recover her from Hades. The chorus repeats 'Ahi caso acerbo', Sylvia decides to enter solitary exile and the act ends in lamentation.

Act III A sinfonia of sombre brass instruments marks the change of scene to the Inferno. Orpheus is led by Hope (Speranza) to the gates of Hades, where she must leave him ('Lasciate ogni speranza, voi ch'entrate', 'Abandon all hope, you who enter', quoting Dante). Orpheus reaches the river Styx and the boatman Charon, who, singing to the rough sound of the regal, refuses to let him pass. The shepherd summons up all his musical powers to meet his greatest task, and the ensuing aria, 'Possente spirto', is the literal centrepiece and the climax of the opera. The text is in *terza rima* stanzas (as used by Dante), and each is set as a variation over the same bass, with florid vocal ornamentation reinforcing Orpheus' magical powers. Various instruments (two violins, two cornetts, a double harp) provide ritornelli and echo-like interjections. As Charon remains unmoved, Orpheus changes tack, adopting a much simpler style accompanied by strings. Eventually, the boatman is lulled to sleep by a sinfonia for strings, and Orpheus takes the oars. The chorus comments on the power of man to triumph over all obstacles.

Act IV Pluto, king of the underworld, and his wife Proserpina have heard Orpheus' lament. She pleads on Orpheus' behalf, and Pluto grants that Eurydice return to earth, with the condition that Orpheus leads her from the underworld without looking back. The chorus comments on the mercy to be found even in Hades. Orpheus takes up a joyful song in praise of his lyre ('Qual onor di te sia degno') over a walking bass and two-violin accompaniment. But as he moves earthwards, he has doubts; is Eurydice really behind him? He turns to look, only to see her disappearing before his eyes. Orpheus returns to earth alone, and the final chorus comments on the paradox of a man who can conquer Hades, but not his own emotions.

Act V In the fields of Thrace, Orpheus laments his second loss of Eurydice; only an echo responds, and he decides to renounce women. Suddenly the heavens open and Apollo, Orpheus' father, appears in a chariot. He consoles his son, and in a duet ('Saliam cantando al cielo') they both return to heaven, where Orpheus will see Eurydice in the stars. The chorus rejoices in Orpheus' apotheosis and dances a final *moresca*.

Both composer and librettist clearly knew Peri's *Euridice*. Alessandro Striggio was certainly in Florence when it was first performed, and so, probably, was Monteverdi. Striggio's libretto contains many echoes of Rinuccini in both structure and content, although significantly he avoids much of Rinuccini's self-indulgent artistry in favour of a more concise dramatic presentation, as seen in their different narrations of Euridice's death. Monteverdi's recitative, too, owes much to Peri.

However, *Orfeo* also has much broader roots. There are many references to the tradition of the Florentine intermedi: the spectacular stage effects, the mythological subject matter, the allegorical figures, the number and scoring of the instruments, and the extended choruses. The opera also harks back to Classical tragedy in the five-part division, the use of a messenger, and the commenting choruses at the ends of acts, and to the pastoral tragi-comedies of Tasso and Guarini. Similarly, Monteverdi's music is redolent of 16th-century techniques: the choruses are madrigalian in style, the technique of variation over a repeated bass was typical of earlier improvisatory procedures, and even in his new recitative, Monteverdi exploits expressive devices first explored in his polyphonic madrigals, including carefully crafted vocal lines, dissonances and chromaticism.

These backward-looking, Renaissance aspects of the opera are reinforced by its various humanist messages about the power of man and music. But *Orfeo* also looks forward to the Baroque. Monteverdi demonstrates his openness to the new styles developed by his Florentine contemporaries, and also to other techniques then being developed, particularly in the duple- and triple-time arias and in the duet textures for voices and/or instruments (as in Monteverdi's *Scherzi musicali* of 1607). Another novel aspect of his score is the detail with which Monteverdi notes his precise intentions in matters of instrumentation and ornamentation (e.g. the ornaments in 'Possente spirto' are written out): here he asserts his control over elements previously left to the performer. As a result, *Orfeo* contains an intriguing mixture of old and new elements. Rather than rejecting previously perfected techniques in an iconoclastic search for novelty, Monteverdi reinterprets the old in the light of the new (and vice versa) to produce a powerful synthesis of undeniable dramatic force. Moreover, and unlike the Florentines, Monteverdi is unquestionably a masterful composer. His attention to the drama, to large-scale structure (witness his symmetrical patterning and tonal planning) and to expressive detail demonstrate his skills to the full; and they produced what is arguably the first great opera.

RECORDINGS 1. Petrescu, Reynolds, Bowman, Rogers, Hamburg Monteverdi Ch, Hamburg Camerata Accademica, Jürgens, Archiv, 1974: a reliable performance with a large-scale sound, an outstanding Orpheus from Rogers; 2. Kwella, Kirkby, Denley, Rogers, Chiaroscuro, London Cornett and Sackbut Ensemble, London Baroque, Medlam, EMI, 1984: a small-scale reading reflecting the performing practice of the 1980s; 3. Michael, Watkinson, Quilico, Ensemble vocale de la chapelle royale, Lyons Opera Ch, Corboz, Erato, 1986: highly dramatic performance taken from stage performances and film; 4. Gooding, Ainsley, George, New London Consort,

Pickett, L'Oiseau-Lyre, 1992: a new, authentic recording with spare orchestration [A.B.]
EDITIONS *L'Orfeo: favola in musica*, Venice, 1609, 2nd edn, 1615; facsimile of 1615, Farnborough, 1972; G. F. Malipiero (ed.), *Tutte le opere di Claudio Monteverdi*, Asolo, 1926–42, vol. 11; D. Stevens (ed.), Novello, 1967

Arianna

Libretto by Ottavio Rinuccini
PREMIERE 28 May 1608, Mantua

Arianna, Monteverdi's first 'opera', was performed (like his dance entertainment, *Il ballo delle ingrate*) as part of the wedding celebrations of Prince Francesco Gonzaga and Margherita of Savoy. It was a great success. *Arianna* remains one of the great enigmas of Monteverdi's output as all its music is lost, except for the lament, one of the most famous works of its time, which was arranged as a madrigal and published in that form as well as a solo. The libretto was also published, and the opera was revived in Venice, in the 1639–40 season.

EDITION 'Lament', included in *Il sesto libro di madrigali*, Venice, 1614; solo version published 1623; see G. F. Malipiero, *Tutte le opere di Claudio Monteverdi*, Arolo, 1926–42, vols 6, 11

Il ballo delle ingrate

Ballo in one act (40m)
Libretto by Ottavio Rinuccini
PREMIERE 4 June 1608, Mantua

This ballo in genere rappresentativo combines dramatic action and dancing. Cupid and Venus visit Hades to discuss with Pluto the harsh fate of those ungrateful women who scorn love. The simple message was entirely appropriate for the occasion of the first performance, the wedding festivities for Prince Francesco Gonzaga and Margherita of Savoy (although the score that survives reflects revisions for a performance at the imperial court in Vienna perhaps in 1636). It also gave Monteverdi the opportunity to create his first large-scale bass role, Pluto (compare Neptune in *Il ritorno d'Ulisse in patria* and Seneca in *L'incoronazione di Poppea*).

RECORDINGS 1. Harper, Watson, Howells, Dean, Ambrosian Singers, ECO, Leppard, Philips, 1971; 2. Mellon, Laurens, Reinhart, Les Arts florissants, Christie, Harmonia Mundi, 1983; 3. Tubb, Nichols, A. Ewing, Rooley, Consort of Musicke, Virgin, 1990
EDITIONS included in *Madrigali guerrieri et amorosi . . . libro ottavo*, Venice, 1638; G. F. Malipiero (ed.), *Tutte le opere di Claudio Monteverdi*, Asolo, 1926–42, vol. 8

Il combattimento di Tancredi et Clorinda

The Battle between Tancredi and Clorinda
Dramatic cantata in one scene (25m)
Libretto after Torquato Tasso's *Gerusalemme liberata*, Canto XII, and *Gerusalemme conquistata*, Canto XV
PREMIERE 1624, Venice

Like *Il ballo delle ingrate*, *Il combattimento* is one of those curious mixed genres, part opera, part ballet, part cantata, which was characteristic of early opera. However, Monteverdi is precise about the fact that it was (or at least could be) acted by characters in costume. The Narrator conveys the bulk of this short drama, although Tancredi and Clorinda have their own dialogue. Tancredi calls to battle an anonymous opponent; they fight bravely, and Tancredi defeats his enemy, only to discover that the soldier is in fact his beloved Clorinda.

Here Monteverdi returned to problems that had always occupied him in his secular vocal music, the imitation and effective presentation of strong emotions. Now, however, he adopts a more directly mimetic approach, exploiting new sonorities to re-create the sounds of battle (*tremolando* effects, triadic fanfares, etc., for strings; quick-fire declamation in the voices). This produced the so-called *stile concitato* that appears in a number of Monteverdi's late works.

RECORDINGS 1. Harper, Alva, Wakefield, ECO, Leppard, Philips, 1971; 2. Lerer, Eliasson, Concentus Musicus Wien, Harnoncourt, Telefunken, 1971; 3. Rogers, Kwella, Thomas, Musica Antiqua Köln, Goebel, Archiv, 1981; 4. Schmidt, Hollweg, Monteverdi-Ensemble Opernhaus Zurich, Harnoncourt, Telefunken, 1981: the sound-track from the broadcast of the Ponnelle production; 5. Kirkby, Tubb, Nichols, Rooley, Consort of Musicke, Virgin, 1990
EDITIONS included in Monteverdi's *Madrigali guerrieri, et amorosi . . . libro ottavo*, Venice, 1638; G. F. Malipiero, *Tutte le opere di Claudio Monteverdi*, Asolo, 1926–42, vol. 8, pp. 132–56; Malipiero (ed.), English trans. by Peter Pears, Chester, 1931

Il ritorno d'Ulisse in patria

The Return of Ulysses
Opera in a prologue and three acts (3h)
Libretto by Giacomo Badoaro (1602–1654) after Homer's *Odyssey* XIII–XXIII
PREMIERES Carnival, February 1640, Teatro S. Cassiano, Venice; UK: 16 January 1928, London (broadcast); 16 March 1965, St Pancras Town Hall, London; US: 18 January 1974, Washington, DC
CAST L'Humana fragilità (Human Frailty) *s*, Tempo (Time) *b*, Fortuna (Fortune) *s*, Amore (Cupid) *s*, Ulisse (Ulysses) *t*, Penelope *s*, Telemaco (Telemachus) *t*, Antinoo (Antinous) *b*, Pisandro (Peisander) *t*, Anfinomo (Amphinomus) *a*, Eurimaco (Eurymachus) *t*, Melanto (Melantho) *s*, Eumete (Eumaeus) *t*, Iro (Irus) *t*, Ericlea (Eurycleia) *ms*, Giove (Jupiter) *t*, Nettuno (Neptune) *b*, Minerva *s*, Giunone (Juno) *s*; *satb* chorus of Phaeacians, celestial spirits, maritime spirits
ORCHESTRATION 5-part str ensemble; continuo group

Ulisse was Monteverdi's first new opera for Venice, and it reveals him coming to terms both with the demands of the new public theatres and with the stylistic developments of his younger contemporaries. Its authenticity, once doubted, now seems clear. The score survives in manuscript in Vienna but there are significant differences between this score and the surviving manuscript copies of the libretto. The text is a straightforward adaptation of Homer, and Badoaro exploited all the devices now becoming standard in Venetian opera: the moralizing prologue, comic characters (Iro and Ericlea, Melanto and Eurimaco (cf. Damigella and Valletto in *Poppea*)) and spectacular scenic effects. However, the subject matter of the opera also has a somewhat archaic, courtly feel: witness the prominence of the gods and an almost 'super-human' hero in the manner of *Orfeo*. The opera seems to have been a success: it was also staged in Bologna in 1640 and again in Venice in 1641.

SYNOPSIS

Prologue Human Frailty acknowledges its submission to Time, Fortune and Cupid, as the following drama will reveal.

Act I In her palace in Ithaca, Penelope awaits the return of her husband Ulysses from the Trojan Wars. She cannot be consoled by her nurse, Eurycleia. Melantho, a maid, and Eurymachus, a shepherd, comment on the pains yet pleasures of their own love ('De' nostri amor concordi'). Neptune, supported by Jupiter, condemns the rescue of Ulysses by the Phaeacians. They have brought him back to Ithaca, leaving him sleeping on the beach. As a punishment, Neptune turns their ship into a rock. Ulysses awakes ('Dormo ancora') and believes himself to have been abandoned. Minerva enters disguised as a shepherd ('Cara e lieta gioventù') and tells Ulysses that the island is his home. She reveals herself to his amazement ('O fortunato Ulisse') and tells him to bathe in a sacred fountain (a chorus of naiads is missing in the score). Here Ulysses will change into an old man so as to enter his palace unrecognized and outwit Antinous, Peisander and Amphinomus, the suitors who have insinuated themselves into the offices of state and are seeking his wife's hand. Meanwhile, Minerva will bring back Ulysses' son Telemachus from Sparta. Ulysses again rejoices ('O fortunato Ulisse'). Melantho urges Penelope to forget Ulysses and love another ('Ama dunque'). Eumaeus, a shepherd faithful to Ulysses, tends his flocks and argues with the social parasite Irus. Ulysses, now disguised, enters and warns Eumaeus of the imminent return of his sovereign ('Ulisse, Ulisse è vivo').

Act II Minerva brings Telemachus on her chariot. Eumaeus welcomes the prince ('O gran figlio d'Ulisse') and presents the old man, who, he says, has news of his father's return. A ray of light descends from heaven to reveal Ulysses in his true form. Father and son are joyfully reunited in a duet ('O padre sospirato/O figlio desiato'), and they plan their return to the palace. Melantho and Eurymachus discuss Penelope's continued devotion to Ulysses. The suitors enter to pursue their advances ('Ama dunque') but Penelope staunchly resists ('Non voglio amar'). Eumaeus announces the imminent return of Telemachus and Ulysses, and the suitors are disconcerted. They plot to kill Telemachus, but the sight of Jupiter's eagle flying overhead warns them against the plan. They decide instead to redouble their wooing of Penelope ('Amor è un'armonia'). Minerva outlines to Ulysses a plan to remove the suitors, and Eumaeus recounts to Ulysses Penelope's lasting fidelity. Ulysses rejoices ('Godo anch'io') and they plan to go to the palace. Meanwhile,

Telemachus discusses his recent travels with Penelope. Antinous and Irus meet Eumaeus and Ulysses, now disguised as a beggar. Antinous treats them badly and Ulysses is provoked to fight Irus, thrashing his fat adversary. Penelope orders that the beggar be made welcome. The suitors redouble their efforts to gain her favours with rich gifts. She proclaims that she will marry whoever manages to string Ulysses' great bow. The suitors agree willingly ('Lieta, soave gloria') but all three fail the test. The beggar asks to enter the competition, while renouncing the prize, and succeeds in stringing the bow. Invoking Minerva's protection, Ulysses looses arrows at the suitors and kills them all.

Act III Irus grieves for his colleagues in a splendid take-off of the typical lament scene (a following scene for Mercury and the ghosts of the suitors is missing). Penelope refuses to believe Eumaeus' claim that the beggar who bent the bow was indeed Ulysses ('Ulisse, Ulisse è vivo'), and even Telemachus cannot convince her. Minerva and Juno decide to plead with Jupiter on Ulysses' behalf ('Ulisse troppo errò'). Neptune is pacified, and choruses of celestial and maritime spirits praise the new accord ('Giove amoroso'). Eurycleia ponders how best to act with Penelope, who still refuses the assurances of Eumaeus and Telemachus ('Troppo incredula'). Even when Ulysses enters in his true form, she fears a trick. Eurycleia claims that it is indeed he ('È questo, è questo Ulisse'): she has seen him in his bath and recognized a scar. But Penelope is finally convinced only when Ulysses correctly describes the embroidered quilt on their nuptial bed ('Hor sì ti riconosco . . . Illustratevi, o cieli'). Husband and wife are rejoined in a blissful love duet ('Sospirato mio sole').

There are clear parallels between *Ulisse* and the styles found in Monteverdi's other later works (e.g. the *stile concitato* first seen extensively in *Il combattimento*). The opera also contains several echoes of *Orfeo*; the recitative laments (e.g. Penelope at the opening of Act I), the virtuosic ornamental writing for Minerva and Juno, the five-part sinfonias, and even the care for large-scale symmetrical structures. But whereas in *Orfeo* it was the recitative that carried the bulk of the action, with arias and duets, etc., interposed only where they could be used realistically (rather as songs in a play), now the style is one of a flexible shifting between recitative, arioso and aria. The duple- and triple-time arias, whether just short phrases or more developed structures, are points of intensification prompted by the drama, by the need to emphasize particular words and by the emotional effect. They also reflect changes in the verse structure of the text. The sensuous triple-time melodies, so much more developed than the simple hemiola patterns of *Orfeo*, are a truly modern characteristic. Indeed, at the age of 73 Monteverdi shows himself to be remarkably *au fait* with the most up-to-date Venetian idioms.

RECORDINGS 1. Lehane, English, Santini CO, Ewerhart, Turnabout, 1964: rather dated; 2. Lerer, Eliasson, Concentus

Musicus Wien, Harnoncourt, Telefunken, 1971; 3. Schmidt, Hollweg, Monteverdi-Ensemble Opernhaus Zurich, Harnoncourt, Telefunken, 1981: taken from the broadcast of the Ponnelle production; 4. von Stade, Stilwell, Glyndebourne Ch, LPO, Leppard, CBS, 1979 (also VIDEO, Virgin); 5. Fink, Prégardien, Concerto Vocale, Jacobs, Harmonia Mundi, 1992

EDITION G. F. Malipiero (ed.), *Tutte le opere di Claudio Monteverdi*, Asolo, 1926–42, vol. 12; f.s., Paul Daniel (ed.), unpublished, 1989

L'incoronazione di Poppea

The Coronation of Poppea
Opera in a prologue and three acts (3h 30m)
Libretto by Giovanni Francesco Busenello (1598–1659), after Tacitus, Suetonius and perhaps Seneca
PREMIERES Carnival 1643, Teatro SS. Giovanni e Paolo, Venice; UK: 6 December 1927, Oxford; US: 27 April 1926, Smith College, Northampton, Massachusetts
CAST Fortuna (Fortune) *s*, Virtù (Virtue) *s*, Amore (Cupid) *s*, Poppea *s*, Nerone (Nero) *s*, Ottavia (Octavia) *ms*, Seneca *b*, Ottone (Otho) *a*, Drusilla *s*, Arnalta *a*, Nutrice (Nurse) *a*, Lucano (Lucan) *t*, Valletto *s*, Damigella *s*, Liberto *t*, Littore (a Lictor) *b*, maidservant *s*, 2 soldiers 2 *t*, Pallade (Pallas Athene) *s*, Mercurio (Mercury) *b*, Venere (Venus) *s*; *atb* chorus of consuls and tribunes, Seneca's companions
ORCHESTRATION str ensemble (2 vn, vn/va, bass vn); continuo group (probably at least 2 hpd, chitarrone, 1 bass instrument); 2 cornetts (for the Act III consul scene)

Poppea is the first known opera to adopt a factual historical subject: it is set in Rome in AD 64. The earthy, sensuous plot, tempered by Busenello's trenchant view of the world, is typical of new Venetian trends. Certainly there are no high-minded allegories here, and important precedents are established by the oft-remarked 'immorality' of the plot, by the comic interludes and by the emphasis on virtuoso singers (Ottavia was sung by the young Anna Renzi, who later had an outstanding operatic career in Venice).

The surviving sources are complex. We have a scenario associated with the first performances, some manuscript libretti of uncertain date, and Busenello's edition of the libretto in his *Delle hore ociose* (Venice, 1656). The music survives in two manuscripts: one in Naples, perhaps associated with a performance by the travelling Febiarmonici in 1651 (a libretto printed for this performance also survives); the other in Venice, largely copied in the early 1650s by Francesco Cavalli's wife, with performance alterations and annotations by Cavalli himself. These various sources differ, sometimes considerably. The music was first definitely assigned to Monteverdi in 1681 (although the Venice manuscript also bears an attribution of uncertain date) and the extent of his authorship is not entirely clear. Certainly there seems little doubt that *Poppea* as it survives mixes the work of various composers. The text of the final duet between Nero and Poppea was used in a revival of Benedetto Ferrari's *Il pastor reggio* (Bologna, 1641; now lost), and in an entertainment (1647) by Filiberto Laurenzi. There is also music almost certainly by Cavalli (the opening sinfonia is reworked from his *Doriclea* of 1645) and by Francesco Sacrati (the sinfonias in the consul scene in

Act III appear in his *La finta pazza* of 1641). These and other problems pose obvious difficulties for modern productions. The leading exponent of mid-17th-century Venetian opera in the 1960s, Raymond Leppard, viewed these manuscripts as essentially skeletons that were then, and should be now, fleshed out in various ways. He added lavish string accompaniments and made extensive cuts and alterations. One can sympathize with the intent (such pragmatism was clearly characteristic of 17th-century operatic performances) but Leppard's overly romantic 'realizations' have now gone out of favour. More recent productions have followed the surviving scores and contemporary resources more closely, with the result that the dramatic and musical effect, although considerably less opulent, is more stringent and arguably more effective.

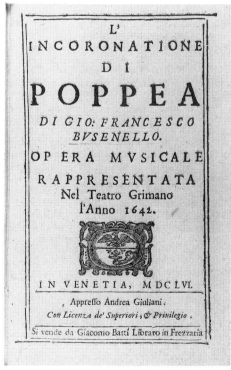

L'incoronazione di Poppea; *title page of the printed libretto (Venice, 1656)*

SYNOPSIS (Venice manuscript)
Prologue Fortune, Virtue and Cupid dispute their respective powers. Cupid claims to be master of the world, as the story of Nero and Poppea will prove.

Act I Otho arrives at his house and sees Nero's soldiers outside, asleep. He realizes that his betrothed, Poppea, is together with Nero and curses her faithlessness. The soldiers are aroused and complain about their job and the decline of Rome. Nero and Poppea enter: they take a sensuous farewell as Poppea emphasizes her love for him

('Signor, sempre mi vedi') and seeks to guarantee their marriage. She is left alone with her nurse, Arnalta, to discuss tactics and ignores Arnalta's common-sense warnings, for Cupid is on her side ('Per me guerreggia Amor e la Fortuna'). Arnalta is left to grumble at her mistress's folly ('Ben sei pazza'). In the emperor's palace Octavia, Nero's wife, acknowledges her humiliation ('Disprezzata regina') while her nurse suggests that she should take a lover. Seneca, shown in by Octavia's secretary, Valletto, urges restraint and appeals to her dignity: Valletto responds by cursing Seneca's pedantry. As Seneca reflects on Octavia's power and the transitory nature of life ('Le porpore regali e le grandezze'), Pallas Athene appears to warn him of his impending death. Seneca welcomes the news. Nero debates his plans about Octavia and Poppea with Seneca ('Son risoluto al fine'). The philosopher urges reason, but Nero is inflamed to anger. Poppea enters to calm him down ('Come dolci signor, come soavi'), suggesting that Seneca must be killed. Otho confronts Poppea over her infidelity, but she dismisses him ('Chi nasce sfortunato di se stesso si dolga e non d'altrui'). He tries to come to his senses ('Otton, torna in te stesso') and vows revenge. Then he turns to Drusilla, who has always loved him, and swears that he will favour her over Poppea.

Act II Seneca praises Stoic solitude. Mercury appears, warning him again of death, which the philosopher accepts happily ('O me felice'). Liberto, a freedman, enters with Nero's command: Seneca must die by the end of the day. He welcomes his fate, despite the urgings of his companions ('Non morir, Seneca') and they leave to prepare the bath in which he will open his veins. The tension is broken by a flirtatious scene between Valletto and Damigella. Nero and Lucan celebrate the news of Seneca's death with wine and song ('Son rubini amorosi'). Otho rededicates himself to Poppea, whom he still loves ('Sprezzami quanto sai') but Octavia orders him to assume female garb and kill her. He cannot refuse. Drusilla delights in her love for Otho ('Felice cor mio'), and Octavia's nurse wishes she were in her place. Otho enters and explains his plan for Poppea: Drusilla gives him her clothes. Meanwhile Poppea rejoices in Seneca's death ('Hor che Seneca è morto') and prays for Cupid to support her. Arnalta lulls her to sleep ('Oblivion soave') as Cupid watches overhead. Otho, dressed as Drusilla, enters and tries to kill Poppea, but he is prevented by Cupid. She wakes and gives the alarm as Otho escapes. Cupid proclaims his success ('Ho difeso Poppea').

Act III Drusilla joyfully anticipates Poppea's death, but she finds herself arrested for the attempted murder (Otho was wearing her clothes) and Nero sentences her to death. Otho in turn confesses his guilt, despite Drusilla's persistent attempts to protect her beloved, and Nero banishes them. Nero and Poppea rejoice now that the way is clear for their marriage ('Non più s'interporrà noia a dimora'). Octavia enters and, in a lament, bids a halting farewell ('Addio Roma'). Arnalta revels in the exaltation of her mistress as empress of Rome (these two scenes are reversed in some sources).

Nero crowns Poppea ('Ascendi, o mia diletta') and the consuls and tribunes pay homage. Cupid proclaims his triumph to his approving mother, Venus ('Io mi compiaccio, o figlio'). Nero and Poppea have a final ecstatic duet ('Pur ti miro, pur ti godo').

The uncertain status of Poppea, upsetting though it may be for devotees of the single-composer masterpiece, is itself revealing. First, the fact that Monteverdi can be so easily conflated with his contemporaries and successors suggests the similarity of styles exploited in Venetian opera around the middle of the century. Second, it emphasizes the priorities of contemporary opera production, where the librettist and stage designer held sway over such lesser functionaries as musicians. In contrast with Ulisse, Poppea has a drastically pared-down orchestration and places much more emphasis on the tuneful melodies given to the lead singers. Again the style is one of a flexible shifting between recitative, arioso and aria, although here the arias become more extensive and structurally self-contained. To be sure, Monteverdi, if it is he, can still provide some splendid recitative, such as Octavia's great Act III lament, harking back to Orfeo and Arianna. But the splendidly lyrical arias now carry the emotional and musical weight of the drama and point the way forward to the prime concerns of later baroque opera.

RECORDINGS 1. Laszlo, Lewis, Glyndebourne Festival Ch, RPO, Pritchard, EMI, 1964: an abridged recording of Leppard's realization which is now something of a historical curiosity; 2. Donath, Söderström, Concentus Musicus Wien, Harnoncourt, Telefunken, 1974: too fussy to be a classic; 3. Balthrop, Watkinson, Il Complesso Barocco Curtis, Fonit Cetra, 1981: a thoughtful, 'authentic' reading marred by the noises of a live recording (at the Fenice Theatre, Venice, 5 September 1980); 4. Auger, Jones, City of London Baroque Sinfonia, Hickox, Virgin, 1989: a wholly theatrical recording [A.B.]

VIDEOS 1. Yakar, Tappy, Salminen, Zurich Monteverdi Ensemble, Harnoncourt, Decca, 1980s: Ponnelle's arresting production; 2. Ewing, Bailey, Glyndebourne Ch, LPO, Leppard, RM Arts, 1984: from Glyndebourne, Leppard's realization

EDITIONS H. Goldschmidt (ed.), Studien zur Geschichte der italienischen Oper im 17. Jahrhundert, vol. 2, Leipzig, 1904; G. F. Malipiero (ed.), Tutte le opere di Claudio Monteverdi, Asolo, 1926–42, vol. 13; R. Leppard (ed.), Faber Music, 1966; C. Bartlett (ed.), Huntingdon, 1988; A. Curtis (ed.), Novello, 1988

MANUSCRIPTS AND EDITIONS Biblioteca del Conservatorio di Musica S. Pietro a Maiella, Naples (facsimile, T. Walker (ed.), 'Drammaturgia musicale veneta', forthcoming); Biblioteca Nazionale Marciana, Venice (facsimile, Bologna, 1969)

Other stage works surviving in whole or part: De la bellezza le dovute lodi, 1607; Tirsi e Clori, 1616 (RECORDING Quintana, 1991); 'Su le penne de' venti il ciel varcando' (prologue for G. B. Andreini's La Maddalena), 1617; Volgendo il ciel per l'immortal sentiero, 1638
Lost: Gli amori di Diana ed Endimione, 1605; 'Ha cento lustri con etereo giro' (prologue for B. Guarini's L'idropica), 1608; Le nozze di Tetide (inc.), (1617); Andromeda, 1620; Apollo, 1620; La contesa di Amore e Cupido, etc. (intermedi for E. Marigliani's Li tre costanti), 1622; Armida abbandonata,

(1626); *La finta pazza Licori* (?inc.), (?1627); *Gli Argonauti*, 1628; *Teti e Flora*, etc. (intermedi for T. Tasso's *Aminta*), 1628; *Mercurio e Marte*, 1628; *Proserpina rapita*, 1630 (one canzonetta survives in Monteverdi's *Madrigali e canzonette*, Venice, 1651); *La vittoria d'Amore*, 1641; *Le nozze d'Enea in Lavinia*, 1641
BIBLIOGRAPHY   Denis Arnold and Nigel Fortune (eds), *The New Monteverdi Companion*, OUP, 1985; A. Curtis, 'La Poppea imposticciata or, Who Wrote the Music to *L'incoronazione* (1643)?', *JAMS*, vol. 43 (1989), pp. 23–54; Paolo Fabbri, *Monteverdi*, CUP, forthcoming; Silke Leopold, *Claudio Monteverdi, Music in Transition*, Clarendon Press, 1991; D. Stevens (ed.), *The Letters of Claudio Monteverdi*, Faber, 1980; G. Tomlinson, *Monteverdi and the End of the Renaissance*, OUP, 1987; John Whenham (ed.), *Claudio Monteverdi: Orfeo*, CUP, 1986

T.C.

DOUGLAS S. MOORE

Douglas Stuart Moore; *b* 10 August 1893, Cutchogue, New York; *d* 25 July 1969, Greenport, Long Island, US

Moore studied at Yale University with Horatio Parker. After service in the US navy, he studied composition in Paris with d'Indy and Nadia Boulanger and, on returning to the US, with Ernest Bloch. His operas, most of which are based on American subjects, are considered his best works, particularly *The Devil and Daniel Webster* and *The Ballad of Baby Doe* which are still regularly performed. *Giants in the Earth*, concerned with the troubled life of a pioneer family in the Dakota Territory, won a Pulitzer Prize in 1951 but has never enjoyed the same success. Like Virgil Thomson in his operas, but less idiosyncratically, Moore deals with traditional, simple materials. His musical language echoes the patterns of American folksongs, hymns and popular songs, though he rarely quotes from these directly. His operas, especially *The Ballad of Baby Doe*, the story of the loyalty of a silver prospector's widow, have an appealing style in which straightforward music matches well-sustained narrative. His final work, *Carry Nation*, is based on the life of the eponymous campaigner for women's suffrage.

Operas: *Jesse James* (inc.), (1928); *White Wings*, (1935), 1949; *The Headless Horseman*, 1937; *The Devil and Daniel Webster*, 1939 (RECORDING Westminster, 1958); *The Emperor's New Clothes*, 1949, rev. 1956; *Puss in Boots*, 1950; *Giants in the Earth*, 1951, rev. 1963; *The Ballad of Baby Doe*, 1956 (RECORDING DG, 1959); *Gallantry*, 1958; *The Wings of the Dove*, 1961; *Carry Nation*, 1966 (RECORDING Desto, 1968)
BIBLIOGRAPHY   David Ewen, *American Composers: A Biographical Dictionary*, Hale, 1983

P.D.

FRANCESCO MORLACCHI

Francesco Giuseppe Baldassare Morlacchi; *b* 14 June 1784, Perugia; *d* 28 October 1841, Innsbruck

Morlacchi studied with Zingarelli and later with Mattei at Bologna. His earliest works were mainly sacred and choral, but in 1807 he produced his first two operas, launching a reputation that grew rapidly with the next seven and was confirmed, in 1809, by the success of *La principessa per ripiego* in Rome and, particularly, by *Le Danaidi* the next year. In 1810 Morlacchi was invited to Dresden as director of the Italian Opera, and after the performance there of *Raoul di Créqui* in 1811 the appointment was confirmed for life. This opera was remarkable for its musical continuity, without recitatives, cadenzas or instrumental introductions, but in general Morlacchi's continuing success in Dresden was based on the fluent Italian style of the day, as well as on his undoubted talents as a practical musician. He was jealous of his position, however, and when Weber was appointed director of the German Opera in 1817 Morlacchi did his utmost to undermine his colleague's activities; he made frequent long visits to Italy on the plea of ill-health, delegating his duties to the overworked Weber, whose own health suffered in consequence. As a composer, Morlacchi perhaps succeeded best in his comic operas: of his *Nuovo barbiere di Siviglia* (rather cheekily produced only a few months after Rossini's *Barber*), Weber commented, 'The man has little musical knowledge, but talent, a lot of ideas, and above all a fund of good comedy.'

Operas: *Il poeta in campagna, ossia Il poeta spiantato*, 1807; *Il ritratto, ossia La forza dell'astrazione*, 1807; *Il Corradino*, 1808; *Enone e Paride*, 1808; *Oreste*, 1808; *Rinaldo d'Asti*, 1809; *Il tutore deluso*, 1809; *Il Simoncino*, 1809; *La principessa per ripiego*, 1809; *Le avventure di una giornata*, 1809; *Le Danaidi*, 1810; *Raoul di Créqui*, 1811; *La capricciosa pentita*, 1812; *Il nuovo barbiere di Siviglia*, 1816 (RECORDING Bongiovanni, 1989); *La simplicetta di Pirna*, 1817; *Laodicea*, 1818; *Gianni di Parigi*, 1818; *Donna Aurora, ossia Il romanzo all'improvviso*, 1819; *Tebaldo e Isolina*, 1820; *La gioventù di Enrico V*, 1823; *Ilda d'Avenello*, 1824; *I saraceni in Sicilia, ossia Eufemia da Messina*, 1828 (also as *Il rinnegato*, 1832); *Il Colombo*, 1828; *Don Desiderio, ovvero Il disperato per eccesso di buon cuore*, 1829; *Francesca da Rimini* (inc.), (1836)
BIBLIOGRAPHY   Dieter Härtwig, 'Francesco Morlacchi', in *Grove*, Macmillan, 1980

M.R.

JEROME MOROSS

b 1 August 1913, Brooklyn, New York; *d* 25 July 1983, Miami, Florida, US

Jerome Moross followed his Juilliard and New York University training with ballet, concert, and theatre composition, and created some classic film scores. His sung-theatre works all qualify as genuine operas, usually from an offbeat perspective. His musical style occupies a place between the serious and popular, able to inhabit either world convincingly.

The Golden Apple

Musical play in two acts (2h)
Libretto by John Latouche, suggested by Homer's *Iliad* and *Odyssey* (late 8th century BC)

Composed 1948–50
PREMIERE　11 March 1954, Phoenix Theatre, New York

A through-composed comic opera combining the musical idioms of the popular musical and of Moross's concert and film works (somewhat reminiscent of Copland), *The Golden Apple* alludes to the two Homeric epics in a tale set right after the American Civil War (and waggishly set near Mount Olympia, Washington). The Judgment of Paris is a pie-baking contest, General Ulysses's wanderings a visit to the temptations of the big city. This musical, worthy of more frequent production, contains one song that achieved classic status, 'Lazy Afternoon'.

RECORDING　P. Gillette, Douglass, Ballard, Whiting, Ross, RCA, 1954
EDITIONS　v.s., Chappell (on hire), 1954; lib., Random House, 1954

Other operatic works: *Ballet Ballads* (four one-act ballet operas): *Susanna and the Elders*, 1940; *Willie the Weeper*, 1945; *The Eccentricities of Davy Crockett*, 1946, and *Riding Hood Revisited*, 1948; *Gentlemen, Be Seated!*, 1963; *Sorry, Wrong Number*, (1977), 1982
BIBLIOGRAPHY　David Ewen, *American Composers: A Biographical Dictionary*, Hale, 1983

J.A.C.

JEAN-JOSEPH MOURET
b 11 April 1682, Avignon, France; *d* 22 December 1738, Charenton, France

Arriving in Paris from his native Provence, Mouret became surintendant de la musique to the Duchesse de Maine in 1709, providing much of the music for the duchess's spectacular *Grandes Nuits de Sceaux* (1714–15). At the Paris Opéra his opéra-ballet *Les fêtes, ou le triomphe de Thalie* (1714) proved enormously popular, thanks to its lifelike characters, naturalistic dialogue and attractive, light-hearted music. *Le mariage de Ragonde*, first given at Sceaux that year, enjoyed similar success when eventually staged at the Opéra in 1742 in a revised version (*Les amours de Ragonde*). In three further opéra-ballets – *Les amours des Dieux* (1727), *Le triomphe de sens* (1732) and *Les grâces* (1735) – Mouret followed the trend away from flesh-and-blood situations in favour of a return to mythological characters. Mouret had a flair for elegant, simple and, at times, folklike melody (he eventually became known as *le musicien des grâces*); it is best seen in such lighter genres of French opera and in his many divertissements for the Théâtre-Italien. By contrast, his two tragédies, *Ariane* (1717) and *Pirithoüs* (1723), are disappointingly trite, and only the second proved at all successful.

BIBLIOGRAPHY　J. R. Anthony, *French Baroque Music from Beaujoyeulx to Rameau*, Batsford, rev. 2nd edn, 1978

G.S.

WOLFGANG AMADEUS MOZART
Joannes Chrysostomus Wolfgangus Theophilus Mozart; *b* 27 January 1756, Salzburg; *d* 5 December 1791, Vienna

Mozart is the most famous of all infant prodigies, the little boy who charmed kings and princes as his music continues to charm us today. But far more remarkable than his precocity was his development by the time he was 30 into the composer of works of the greatest beauty, depth and humanity.

After three operas composed by the time he was 12, Mozart had the extraordinary honour of being commissioned to compose the opera seria *Mitridate* for the royal ducal theatre of Milan in 1770 when he was 14, with two more operas for 1771 and 1772. His own personality gradually gained the upper hand over the Italian models he had assimiliated. The next years were frustratingly short of opera commissions. Salzburg had no regular theatre or opera, only occasional touring companies and formal gala occasions, for one of which he wrote the totally undramatic *Il re pastore*. Fortunately the court of the Bavarian Elector in Munich gave him the chance of composing *La finta giardiniera* in 1775 and *Idomeneo* – his first truly great opera – in 1781. Soon after, he left the service of the Prince Archbishop of Salzburg in a stormy scene and settled in Vienna, where his first major task was the composition of *Die Entführung aus dem Serail* (1782), a resounding success. Yet, neither the beautiful music of this singspiel, nor the Italian operas begun but soon abandoned because of their hopeless libretti, prepare us for his next major opera, *Le nozze di Figaro* (1786). There is no accounting for perfection, but the genius of the librettist Lorenzo da Ponte (to be confirmed in the next two operas which lacked the benefit of Beaumarchais's brilliant play as a basis), played its part, along with Mozart's greater maturity, deeper experience of life, and the intense application of a unique intelligence. After *Don Giovanni* (1787) and *Così fan tutte* (1790) to da Ponte's libretti, Mozart wrote two totally different operas, both produced within three months of his death in 1791. In *Die Zauberflöte* he miraculously combines a new simplicity with great seriousness and comedy; *La clemenza di Tito* is at the same time a backward glance at opera seria and a work of neo-classical nobility ushering in the new century.

The creation of *Le nozze di Figaro* coincided with two comparable achievements, the series of great piano concertos and the six quartets dedicated to Haydn, but he had a special love for opera: its influence is audible throughout his instrumental music in many a 'vocal' phrase and in the dramatic juxtapositions of mood. The influence of Mozart the instrumental composer on the operas is equally important. Whereas his highly successful contemporary, Paisiello, regarded modulation as an unsatisfactory substitute for melody, patterns of tonality form the architecture of Mozart's mature operas, both in the total plan and within the individual sections. Could Mozart expect a listener lacking absolute pitch (as most of us do) to take in

Mozart; unfinished portrait (c.1789) by his brother-in-law Joseph Lange

then the reconciliation of the return to the tonic key. The key relationship between the movements is also significant in this finale: from Figaro's entrance in the fourth section it moves to the subdominant every time (G–C–F–B♭–E♭) each move therefore expressing a lowering of tension, but this always proves to be momentary since a new problem soon appears.

Although Mozart rigorously adheres to the harmonic structure (of sonata, rondo or ternary form), his operas become ever freer about the recapitulation of the melodies. From the time of *Figaro*, Mozart is less liable to repeat words and music for the sake of musical form. New events and emotions arise, requiring new music. By the time of *Die Zauberflöte* the recapitulation of melodies may be vestigial, just a hint to give the listener his bearings.

Not only do keys have a special significance, but melodic phrases or intervals reappear throughout Mozart's vocal music to express similar moods: in *Die Zauberflöte* the exultant rising major sixth that opens Tamino's aria 'Dies Bildnis' is echoed by the equally rapturous 'Tamino mein' sung by Pamina in the Act II finale. These are in different keys, but there is a link of melody and key in the vengeance sworn by Donna Anna's 'Fuggi crudele' in *Don Giovanni* and the Queen of the Night's 'Der Hölle Rache' in *Die Zauberflöte*. Attempts to codify a distinct musical language as used by Mozart go too far, since his thinking was deep and instinctive, but nearly everything in his great opera scores, melody, harmony and orchestration, has a dramatic purpose as well as a purely musical one.

K. numbers refer to L. von Köchel (ed.), *Chronologisch-Thematisches Verzeichnis sämtlicher Tonwerke Wolfgang Amade Mozarts*, Breitkopf und Härtel, 1862; 6th edn, F. Giegling, A. Weinmann and G. Sivers (eds), 1964. Editions referred to are: L. von Köchel *et al.* (eds), *Mozarts Werke*, Breitkopf und Härtel, 1877–83 supplements, 1877–1910, abbreviated to *MW*; and E. F. Schmid, W. Plath and W. Rehm (eds), *Neue Ausgabe sämtlicher Werke*, Internationale Stiftung Mozarteum Salzburg, Bärenreiter, 1955– , abbreviated to *NMA*.

Apollo et Hyacinthus

Apollo and Hyacinth
Latin intermezzo in three acts, K. 38 (1h 30m)
Libretto by P. Rufinus Widl, after Palaiphatos (300 BC) or Lucian (2nd century AD)
Composed March–April 1767
PREMIERES 13 May 1767, Great Aula, Salzburg University; UK: 24 January 1955, Fortune Theatre, London; US: April 1956, Alice Tully Hall, New York
CAST Melia *s*, Hyacinthus *s*, Apollo *a*, Zephyrus *a*, Oebalus *t*, [2 priests of Apollo *b*; *satb* chorus of Lacedaemonians]
CHAMBER ORCHESTRA

his schemes of tonality, even when an 18th-century opera-goer was lucky to see a work more than once in a lifetime? The answer must be yes, perhaps subconsciously, since the whole use of sonata form is based on that assumption.

Apart from the formal consideration that operas and finales ended in the key they started with and apart from the traditional keys, C and D for martial occasions, E♭ for solemn ones and so on, Mozart had his own instinct. The most sensual key for him was A major, for most seductions were performed or attempted in it. In *Die Zauberflöte*, C minor always refers to death, while A♭, not the relative major (E♭) but its subdominant, usually brings relief, as in the opening scene. The same key relationship, a tone higher, takes on a structural role in *Don Giovanni*, where D minor, the key of the Commendatore and his vengeance opposes and finally overcomes B♭ major and D major – the Don's principal keys.

The supreme example of Mozart's architecture is perhaps the Act II finale of *Figaro*, which presents a chain of crises appearing and being resolved in turn, each depicted in a 'movement' in sonata form with its rise of tension at the modulation to the dominant and

Latin plays interspersed with musical intermezzi were an old tradition of the Benedictine school in Salzburg. The soprano and alto parts were performed by boys from the school, the tenor part by a student; the opening chorus was probably sung by the soloists.

Unlike Mozart's first dramatic work, the cantata *Die Schuldigkeit des ersten Verbotes*, K. 35, two months earlier, *Apollo et Hyacinthus* was fully staged with scenery and many stage effects. The original legend of Hyacinth, killed by the discus of his lover Apollo, which was blown off course by the jealous south wind Zephyr, was made respectable: Apollo loves Hyacinth's sister (invented for the occasion) and intends to marry her.

SYNOPSIS
Act I The Lacedaemonian king Oebalus and his son Hyacinthus prepare a sacrifice to Apollo. When lightning destroys the altar they fear his wrath, but the god himself arrives and promises Hyacinthus his friendship and his sister Melia his love.

Act II Melia's joy at the prospect of marrying a god is cut short by Zephyrus, who reports that Apollo has killed Hyacinthus with his discus. Apollo arrives in angry pursuit. Zephyrus is transformed into a wind and carried off. Melia refuses to hear Apollo's protestations and orders him to leave.

Act III With his dying breath Hyacinthus tells his father that it was the jealous Zephyrus who killed him. The king and Melia lament his death and their treatment of the god. But Apollo returns because of his love for Melia: he covers the boy's grave with flowers which shall bear his name.

In the music of the *intrada* and nine vocal numbers we soon take the 11-year-old Mozart's skill in harmony, form and counterpoint for granted. His individual ear for sound and the use of full, rich harmonization is already evident. The beautiful duet 'Natus cadit' is scored for first violins playing a long melody, in which they are joined first by the tenor, then by the soprano, finally by both together, the whole accompanied by horns, *pizzicato* second violins, continuo and divided violas (the latter, modelled on the work of the Salzburg composer J. E. Eberlin, would become a lifelong addiction for Mozart). The accompanied recitative for the dying Hyacinthus is short but moving. There are also good examples of characterization, as when Hyacinthus sings, in 'Saepe terrent Numina', of the gods threatening mankind and then laughing.

RECORDING Auger, Mathis, Wulkopf, Schwarz, Rolfe Johnson, Mozarteum O, Hager, Philips, 1982
EDITIONS f.ss., *MW*, V, no. 2; *NMA*, II:5/i, 1959

La finta semplice
The Pretended Simpleton

Opera buffa in three acts, K. 51/46a (2h 30m)
Libretto by Carlo Goldoni, rev. Marco Coltellini, after the comedy *La fausse Agnès, ou le poète campagnard* by Philippe Néricault Destouches (1734)
Composed April–July 1768
PREMIERES ?May 1769, Archbishop's Palace, Salzburg; UK: 12 March 1956, Palace Theatre, London; US: 27 January 1961, Boston (as *The Clever Flirt*)
CAST Rosina *s*, Don Cassandro *b*, Don Polidoro *t*, Giacinta *s*, Ninetta *s*, Fracasso *t*, Simone *b*
FULL ORCHESTRA including 2 ca, 2 hn

In September 1767 Leopold Mozart brought his 11-year-old son to Vienna in the hope of obtaining a commission for an opera. The Emperor Joseph II expressed his interest and in due course Giuseppe Afflisio, director of the two principal theatres, gave Wolfgang the libretto, 100 ducats and the best singers in Vienna. The opera was composed, but envy and intrigue prevented its performance despite Leopold's furious protests.

SYNOPSIS
Act I The Hungarian captain, Fracasso, and his sergeant, Simone, are billeted on Don Cassandro, a vain and miserly gentleman of Cremona, who does not intend to let his sister, Giacinta, marry the captain nor her maid, Ninetta, go off with Simone. Fracasso summons his sister, Rosina: she pretends to be a simpleton who would like to marry not only Cassandro but his silly young brother Polidoro as well. She succeeds in wheedling a precious ring from the miser.

Act II Rosina has to put up with the boorishness of Polidoro and the drunkenness of Cassandro, who narrowly escapes fighting a duel with the captain. Persuaded that Giacinta has run off with the family treasure, Cassandro promises her hand to whoever can find her and bring her back.

Act III Rosina would naturally rather marry Cassandro than his penniless brother. The two other couples are found, forgiven and betrothed.

'I can more or less assimilate and imitate every sort and style of composition, as you know,' the 22-year-old Mozart was to write to his father. One must consider his earlier operas in relation to the Italian operas from which he learned his craft, from Pergolesi to the 'new Neapolitans' such as Traetta, Jommelli and J. C. Bach. Ensembles had achieved increasing importance in opera buffa and the 1750s saw the arrival of the chain finale, a succession of ensembles in different keys and tempi, each handling one link of the plot. First used by Mozart in *La finta semplice*, it became crucial to his masterpieces.

Like all opere buffe this libretto is about the war of the sexes. Unfortunately half the arias are old clichés about the pros and cons of marriage, not calculated to bring out the best in a 12-year-old composer. Mozart provides charming tunes and deft orchestrations, but the contemporary fashion for the aria in two tempi for the sake of variety misses its aim when there are no fewer than eight of them, as well as three minuets and four pert *allegretti* in 2/4 time. The two gems of the opera are Rosina's garden aria, 'Senti l'eco ove t'agiri', with its solo oboe and two cors anglais and, above all, 'Amoretti, che ascosi qui siete', an exquisite E major *andante* with pairs of bassoons and violas under an expressive violin line. Mozart uses every opportunity for descriptive music, partly following the conventions of opera buffa and partly with an individual touch of his own – a dog barking, a drunk, a serenade with *pizzicato* accompaniment and Rosina tiptoeing to steal the ring in the pantomime that follows, a duel scene with Cassandro trembling. The lively finales leave little room for vocal characterization of person or situation, yet there are anticipations of the magic to come – Simone's arrival in the Act I finale, like Figaro's in the Act II finale, and a beautiful G major plea for forgiveness (here by the women) near the end as in the Act IV finale of *Figaro*.

RECORDING Hendricks, Murray, Lind, Johnson, Blochwitz, Lorenz, Schmidt, Kammerorchester CPE Bach, Schreier, Philips, 1991
EDITIONS f.ss., *MW*, V, no. 4; *NMA*, II:5/ii, 1983; v.s., Ricordi, 1955

Bastien und Bastienne
Bastien and Bastienne

Singspiel in one act, K. 50/46b (45m)
Libretto translated from the French parody of Jean Jacques Rousseau's *Le devin du village* (1752), *Les amours de Bastien et Bastienne* by Harny de Guerville, Charles Simon Favart and Marie Justine Benoite Favart (1753), trans. by Friedrich Wilhelm Weiskern and Johann Heinrich Müller, rev. Johann Andreas Schachtner
Composed ?1767–8
PREMIERES October 1768, the garden of Dr Anton Mesmer's house in Vienna; UK: 26 December 1894, Daly's Theatre, London; US: early 1905, Habelmann's Opera School, New York
CAST Bastienne *s*, Bastien *t*, Colas *b*; shepherds and shepherdesses *silent*
CHAMBER ORCHESTRA

The success of Rousseau's naïve little pastoral opera *Le devin du village* soon gave birth to a parody, in which the Arcadian shepherds were turned into French peasants, while the music consisted of popular melodies. This was performed in Vienna in French and Mozart set its translation. Nissen's biography of Mozart states that his 'operetta' was performed in the suburban garden of Dr Mesmer (who gave 'mesmerized' to the language and who was mocked in *Così fan tutte* by Despina with her magnet). For a later performance Mozart wrote some recitatives with the part of Colas in the alto clef.

SYNOPSIS
The shepherdess Bastienne, regretting the infidelity of her beloved Bastien, consults the magician Colas. He promises that all will be well but urges her to show some fickleness too. He then warns Bastien that Bastienne no longer loves him but confirms that they can be reunited with the help of his magic. And so they are, after a while. They praise Colas and he cheerfully joins in.

Mozart's first singspiel finds the right style long before the emergence of Joseph II's National Singspiel: homely texts in a mild Viennese dialect to simple melodies. The bagpipe imitation for the entry of Colas has a rustic colour and the *intrada*'s single theme (with its oft remarked anticipation of Beethoven's 'Eroica' Symphony) is of the same family. There are several expressive airs in minuet rhythm, but half the pieces are in the two-tempo form learned from opéra comique. Colas has a splendid hocus-pocus aria 'Diggi, daggi, schurry,

murry' in C minor, but Mozart is so far from characterizing the young people that he gives them a duet with the same music but sung to different words. Perhaps the fact that they have such similar names and aims made it seem an amusing idea. Their big duet 'Geh! geh! geh, Herz von Flandern' begins with the two at first obstinately refusing a reconciliation, but then, with a hint of the minor, holding out olive branches and, in a short free *adagio*, turning to happiness, ending with a delicious 3/8 finale. The very simplicity of the 13-year-old's composition is appropriate to this little work.

RECORDINGS 1. Ilse Hollweg, Kmentt, Berry, Wiener Symphoniker, Pritchard, Philips, 1956; 2. Gruberova, Cole, Polgár, F. Liszt CO, Leppard, Sony, 1991; 3. with boy sopranos and alto: Nigl, Oriesching, Busch, Wiener Symphoniker, Harrer, Philips, 1987
EDITIONS f.ss., *MW* V, no. 3; *NMA* II:5/iii, 1974; v.ss., Universal, [1926]; Schott, 1948

Mitridate, re di Ponto
Mithridates, King of Pontus

Opera seria in three acts, K. 87/74a (3h 30m)
Libretto by Vittorio Amedeo Cigna-Santi, originally set by Quirino Gasparini (1767), after Racine's tragedy (1673) trans. into Italian by Giuseppe Parini (*c.* 1765)
Composed September–December 1770
PREMIERES 26 December 1770, Teatro Regio Ducal, Milan; UK: 17 March 1979, Logan Hall, London (concert); US: 15 August 1985, Avery Fisher Hall, New York (concert); Ireland: 27 October 1989, Theatre Royal, Wexford; US: 30 June 1991, Loretto-Hilton Centre, St Louis
CAST Mitridate *t*, Aspasia *s*, Sifare *s*, Farnace *a*, Ismene *s*, Marzio *t*, Arbate *s*, guards and Roman soldiers *silent*
FULL ORCHESTRA

In March 1770 the 14-year-old Mozart presented three magnificent arias at a soirée of Count Firmian's in Milan: this led to his first commission, for an opera seria for one of Italy's three principal theatres. It had a powerful orchestra including 28 violins, as opposed to the 12 he would find at the Vienna Burgtheater and the six at the premiere of *Die Zauberflöte*. Mozart duly handed in the recitatives by the end of October, but the arias had to be tailored to the singers. The primo uomo (principal castrato) in the role of Sifare did not arrive until the end of November. The tenor Guglielmo d'Ettore (Mitridate) was the most troublesome – Mozart had to rewrite his opening aria three times. The premiere, which lasted six hours (including ballets by another hand), was a great success. The opera was given 22 times and the composer was re-engaged for the following year.

Mithridates VI Eupator (132–63 BC), King of Pontus (on the Black Sea), was finally defeated by the Romans after a reign of 50 years and many conquests. Like *Figaro* this libretto has the advantage of being based on a great play. The tension of the drama is maintained throughout in a way that was impossible for tragedies of 18th-century origin with their genteel, rather bloodless behaviour. Unusually for Racine, nobody dies except the fierce old king; it thus conforms to the Age of Enlightenment's wish for a happy ending.

The Teatro Regio Ducale in Milan, where Mitridate *was premiered in 1770; the theatre was destroyed by fire in 1776*

SYNOPSIS

Act I King Mitridate has left his empire in the care of his sons Sifare and Farnace while he is away at the wars. Deceived by a rumour of his father's death, Farnace declares his love to the king's betrothed, Aspasia. She seeks the protection of Sifare. Mitridate returns with Ismene as a bride for Farnace. When he hears of Farnace's guilt, he determines to kill him.

Act II Aspasia and Sifare declare their love for each other and mourn that she must marry the king.

Act III When Farnace's treacherous plotting with the Romans is discovered, he reveals in his despair that Sifare is his father's real rival. Mitridate traps Aspasia into confessing her love for Sifare and condemns them both to death. Ismene holds off the king's wrath for long enough to let both sons beat off the Roman attack. Mitridate, mortally wounded, rejoices at their loyalty and their coming betrothals.

An Italian composer would have avoided some of Mozart's mistakes, such as setting Aspasia's pleading in the first aria to fierce coloratura or giving the angry king staccatos in the manner of opera buffa. Gasparini's setting of the same libretto is less attractive, but his version of Mitridate's last aria, 'Vado incontro al fato', with its six top Cs was used in place of Mozart's frankly weaker one. One can always admire Mozart's craftsmanship, for example

in Sifare's first aria, 'Soffre il mio cor', the organization of short phrases of the orchestral ritornello, some of which return at the end of the exposition while others are reserved for the end of the aria, or the coloratura subtly varied at its return. He also does his best to characterize – Mitridate's ferocity with great leaps and dynamic contrasts, the gentleness of Sifare opposed to the far more angular music of his impulsive brother. But when in doubt he turns out a well-made all-purpose piece with a busy orchestra over a drumming bass and a good deal of coloratura, his general stand-by until after *Il re pastore* (1775).

The formal patterns of the day demanded long arias, even with the shortened *da capo* form. Another type, a succession of slow and fast sections, is used tellingly by Mozart when Mitridate speaks gently to Sifare, then fiercely to Aspasia in 'Tu, che fedel mi sei', but formal convention weakened the drama by demanding a complete repeat (in appropriate keys). The Italian composers generally kept their arias shorter than Mozart at this stage.

There is, however, more and more music of great beauty as the opera proceeds. There are two *agitato* pieces in minor keys with no contrasting section to destroy the mood and some delicious lyrical music, especially in Sifare's 'Lungi da te' with horn obbligato (inspired by contact with the orchestra, for there is an earlier version without the horn) and in the one duet, 'Se viver non degg'io', in which Aspasia and Sifare declare their doomed love. The original version, presumably rejected by the singers, is even more beautiful. The greatest piece is 'Pallid' ombre' with its accompanied recitatives, sung by Aspasia when she receives the king's poisoned cup. Her long incantation has the earnestness of Gluck's *Alceste*. When she sings at the lowest range of the voice, it is as a means of intense expression and not to show what the singer could do.

RECORDING Auger, Gruberova, Cotrubas, Baltsa, Hollweg, Mozarteum-Orchester, Hager, Philips, 1977
VIDEO Kenny, Rodgers, Murray, Gjevang, Winbergh, Vienna Concentus Musikus, Harnoncourt, Decca, 1992: a somewhat cut but highly dramatic performance given in the arena at Vicenza [A.B.]
EDITIONS f.ss., *MW*, V, no. 5; *NMA*, II:5/iv, 1966; (March, no. 7, also *NMA*, VII:17/2)

Il sogno di Scipione

Scipio's Dream
Azione teatrale in one act, K. 126 (1h 30m)
Libretto by Pietro Metastasio (1735), after Cicero's (106–43 BC) *Somnium Scipionis ex lib. de Republica VI*
Composed April–August 1771, rev. April 1772
PREMIERES ?May 1772, Archbishop's Palace, Salzburg; UK: 7 March 1968, Camden Town Hall, London (Handel Opera Society Chorus)
CAST Scipione *t*, Costanza *s*, Fortuna *s*, Publio *t*, Emilio *t*, Aria della Licenza *s*; *satb* chorus of heroes
FULL ORCHESTRA

Mozart composed *Il sogno di Scipione* for the jubilee of Prince Archbishop Schrattenbach due to take place in January 1772, but as he had to be in Milan for *Ascanio in Alba* from late August, he prepared *Il sogno* well in advance. After Schrattenbach's death in December the Mozarts hoped to have it performed for the installation of the new Archbishop Colloredo in March 1772. Both the handwriting of the score and the change of names from the old to the new Archbishop in the *Licenza*, the recitative addressed directly to him, confirm this account. The well-known parsimony of Colloredo and the lack of any mention of a performance make it unlikely that it took place.

The subject of the opera is the historical Publius Cornelius Scipio Aemilianus (185–129 BC)

SYNOPSIS
Scipio dreams that he is visited by the goddesses Fortune and Constancy, who demand that he choose between them. They take him to Elysium, where his father and adoptive grandfather tell him about the immortality of the soul and urge him to live virtuously. When Scipio finally chooses Constancy, Fortune in her fury overwhelms him with a cataclysm, at which he wakes up to find Constancy still with him. In an epilogue the Prince Archbishop is addressed directly, for 'the heart exalts him though the tongue may speak of Scipio'.

Despite the use of chorus, trumpets and high horns, Mozart is unable to convey much personality to the music. There is little to distinguish between the music of the three tenor Scipios or the two soprano goddesses. He does occasionally illustrate the words, as in the Metastasian cliché of the rock assailed by high seas, 'Biancheggia in mar lo scoglio', with coloratura and busy strings, but surviving to enjoy a calm *andante*. He passes by the opportunity of setting Constancy's description of the Harmony of the Spheres to an *accompagnato*. The only *accompagnato* – for the cataclysm – is an academic collection of random modulations. As with *Ascanio*, the main pleasure is in the neat workmanship, in the way the violins weave a decorative line around the sung melody, above all in the sheer energy of some of the music, for example Publio's 6/8 'Quercia annosa'. But there is a very revealing contrast between the epilogue addressed to the Archbishop, frivolous but charming enough, and another setting of the same text, apparently composed in March or April 1772 to conclude or replace *Il sogno di Scipione* at Colloredo's installation ceremony. In it the melodies are more memorable, and the harmonies and the chains of coloratura have a sense of direction.

RECORDING Popp, Gruberova, Mathis, Schreier, Ahnsjö, Moser, Mozarteum-Orchester, Hager, Philips, 1977
EDITIONS f.ss., *MW*, V, no. 7; *NMA*, II:5/vi, 1977

Ascanio in Alba

Ascanius in Alba
Festa teatrale in two acts, K. 111 (2h 45m)
Libretto by Giuseppe Parini, after Virgil's *Aeneid* (c. 19 BC)
Composed September 1771
PREMIERES 17 October 1771, Teatro Regio Ducal, Milan
CAST Venere *s*, Ascanio *ms*, Silvia *s*, Aceste *t*, Fauno *s*; *satb* chorus of spirits, shepherds and shepherdesses, nymphs; ballet
FULL ORCHESTRA including 2 serpenti (ca)

After the success of *Mitridate* Mozart was commissioned to compose a festa teatrale for the celebrations following the wedding of the 17-year-old Archduke Ferdinand with Princess Maria Beatrice d'Este of Modena. The libretto, by one of Italy's most distinguished poets, is an allegory on the Empress Maria Theresa, the bridegroom's mother, as Venus and on the young couple, represented by Ascanio and Silvia. Ascanius, the son of Aeneas, meets Silvia, daughter of the Latin king. Legend has it that he went on to marry her and found Alba, cradle of Rome. The incongruity of the empress as the queen of love and of the young people impersonated by a 50-year-old castrato and a prima donna at the end of her career did not hinder the success of the opera. The great Hasse, who had said of Mozart 'this boy will cause the rest of us to be forgotten', composed an opera seria for the occasion. 'Unfortunately,' Leopold wrote home, 'Wolfgang's serenata has beaten Hasse's opera by so much that I cannot describe it.' The young archduke actually asked his mother if he could take Mozart into his service, to which the bountiful mother of her people (as seen in this work) replied, 'I cannot see how you can have any use for a composer or useless people of that sort, but if it nevertheless gives you pleasure I do not wish to stop you.'

SYNOPSIS

Venus descends to tell her grandson Ascanio that he is to marry the nymph Silvia. As a test of Silvia's virtue and fortitude, the identity of the handsome stranger, whom she has already loved in her dreams through Cupid's arts, is concealed from her until it is time for the happy ending. A priest and a Faun add their flattery.

One of countless similar elegant effusions to flatter sovereigns, this libretto received on the whole the uninteresting music it deserved. The success of the evening was due mainly to the beautiful scenery and the stage effects, as well as to the use of chorus and ballet. The arias, as in *Mitridate*, mostly have the full or shortened *da capo* form or the two-tempo form. The main quality of the work lies in the well-made accompaniments and in Mozart's already infallible ear for the sonorities to be derived from wind instruments, and divided violas. There is also a real exuberance in the wild coloratura flights for Silvia and Fauno, the second castrato, who rises to a top E♭. Mozart reserves his more tender moments for the poor tormented female used as a pawn in dynastic games (like Pamina in *Die Zauberflöte*): Silvia's 'Sì, ma d'un altro Amore' and 'Infelici affetti miei' (especially its *recitativo accompagnato*) are clearly based on emotion rather than on pure technique.

RECORDING Mathis, Auger, Sukis, Baltsa, Schreier, Mozarteum-Orchester, Hager, Philips, 1976
EDITIONS f.ss., *MW*, V, no. 6; *NMA*, II:5/v, 1956

Lucio Silla

Lucius Sulla

Opera seria in three acts, K. 135 (3h 30m)
Libretto by Giovanni de Gamerra
Composed November–December 1772
PREMIERES 26 December 1772, Teatro Regio Ducal, Milan; UK: 7 March 1967, Camden Town Hall, London; US: 19 January 1968, Peabody Concert Hall, Baltimore
CAST Lucio Silla *t*, Giunia *s*, Cecilio *s*, Lucio Cinna *s*, Celia *s*, Aufidio *t*; *satb* chorus of noble Romans, senators, people; guards *silent*
FULL ORCHESTRA

Mozart had to compose *Lucio Silla* more rapidly than *Mitridate*. He could not begin on the arias until the singers were present: the primo uomo, the famous castrato Venanzio Rauzzini (Cecilio), arrived on 21 November, the no-less-famous prima donna, Anna de Amicis (Giunia) on 5 December, but a totally inadequate tenor in the title role, 'a church singer from Lodi' and a late substitute, turned up only eight days before the first performance! So he was given just two vocally very unambitious arias, which may account for the total lack of motivation for Silla's change of heart at the end. The premiere had only a moderate success but there were 20 performances. Although the Mozarts stayed on and on, no further commissions were forthcoming and early in March 1773 Wolfgang left Italy, never to return.

The Roman Lucius Cornelius Sulla (138–78 BC)

did indeed retire unexpectedly from his tyrannical dictatorship.

SYNOPSIS

Act I Cecilio, a senator banished by the dictator Silla, returns secretly to Rome to hear from his friend Cinna that his bride Giunia has been taken into Silla's household. There we see her wooed by the dictator, who is urged to use gentle ways by his sister Celia but force by Aufidio. Giunia spurns his advances and goes to pray at her father's tomb, together with other noble Romans who hope to free their country from Silla's yoke. She meets her beloved Cecilio.

Act II Giunia turns down Cinna's suggestion to marry Silla in order to murder him. Silla confronts her publicly on the Capitol with a demand for her hand as a way to end the civil strife. Cecilio appears with drawn sword and is seized.

Act III Cecilio is visited in prison by Cinna who begs his own bride Celia to mollify her brother. Giunia is ready to die with Cecilio, but on the Capitol Silla forgives everybody and abdicates.

Nothing in the recent Salzburg works, mostly instrumental, prepares us for the great leap forward Mozart made with *Lucio Silla*. The much stronger emotional engagement must be a sign of the adolescent taking over from the child. The use of the chorus and the dark moods with their *ombra* (shadow) scenes are partly the consequence of the young librettist's leanings towards the reforms of Gluck and the neo-Neapolitans. But Mozart's *recitativi accompagnati* are marvellous compositions, some of which would not be out of place in his later operas. He gives the orchestra a bigger role in them than the Italians did: the harmonic movement is sometimes surprising but always purposeful. At the end of Act I two short orchestral links (added during rehearsals) produce a long stream of continuous, music including the powerful chorus 'Fuor di queste urne' with Giunia's interpolated aria and the happy duet that concludes the act. All these are big steps towards *Idomeneo*, his next opera seria, still eight years away.

Many of the 18 arias still suffer from a rather generalized busy manner, from excessive length and from long stretches of coloratura. The most awe-inspiring of these are in Giunia's 'Ah se il crudel periglio', of which Leopold wrote, 'Wolfgang has put passages in it which are new and quite especially and astonishingly difficult: she sings them to amaze you and we are on the best of terms with her.' But de Amicis also had the vivid breathless 'Parto, m'affretto' and the solemn 'Fra i pensier più funesti' with its excited middle section. On the other hand, Rauzzini preferred showing his skill in enormous leaps, as from bottom A to the A♭ nearly two octaves higher in 'Ah se a morir mi chiama', rather than in coloratura – surprisingly in view of the motet 'Exsultate, jubilate' with its brilliant and famous concluding 'Alleluia', which Mozart wrote for him soon after. His little minuet in rondo form, 'Pupille amate', is one of those infinitely touching melodies in which the young Mozart excelled his master J. C. Bach. The trio 'Quell'orgoglioso sdegno' predicts the quartet in *Idomeneo* in some ways, such as the imitative entries: Giunia and Cecilio naturally sing in thirds for much of it, but it is touching to find Silla, moved by the intrepid love of the two, finally joining them. The grand finale is a *ciaconna* with three verses for the chorus alternating with the soloists. Performances usually ended with a danced chaconne, as *Idomeneo* was to do: perhaps there were dancers for this sung chaconne.

Mozart later wrote out Cecilio's 'Ah se a morir mi chiama' with decorations in nearly every bar, both in the first section and then differently in the *da capo*, as an example to singers, who were always expected to improvise their own version.

RECORDING Auger, Varady, Mathis, Donath, Schreier, Mozarteum-Orchester, Hager, Philips, 1977
EDITIONS f.ss., *MW*, V, no. 8; *NMA* II:5/vii, 1986

La finta giardiniera
The Pretended Gardener

Dramma giocoso in three acts, K. 196 (3h 30m)
Libretto by ?Giuseppe Petrosellini, originally for Anfossi (1774)
Composed December 1774; accompanied recitatives rev. by Mozart for German singspiel version, *Die verstellte Gärtnerin* (*Die Gärtnerin aus Liebe*), 1779–80, libretto trans. ?Johann Franz Joseph Stierle the elder
PREMIERES 13 January 1775, Salvatortheater, Munich; 7 January 1930, Scala Theatre, London; US: 18 January 1927, Mayfair Theater, New York; singspiel version: ?1 May 1780, Komödienstadl, Augsburg
CAST Don Anchise (the Podestà) *t*, La Marchesa Violante/'Sandrina' *s*, Belfiore *t*, Arminda *s*, Ramiro *s* or *ms*, Serpetta *s*, Roberto/'Nardo' *b*
FULL ORCHESTRA

Commissioned for the Munich Carnival, Mozart's opera was twice postponed and then had only three performances amidst problems with an ailing prima donna and a 'large but rather untidy orchestra'. It was not done again in his lifetime except in the German translation, nor could the Italian version be performed in our own day until the missing recitatives of Act I were found in a copy in Moravia in the 1970s. Piccinni's *Buona figliuola* (1760) had started the fashion for opera buffa with a sentimental story, the operatic daughter of Richardson's virtuous maltreated Pamela and, like *La finta giardiniera*, an aristocratic girl working as a gardener's assistant (they all clung to this pastoral activity rather than descend to housework). Petrosellini, the probable author, had written several libretti in this vein – *L'incognita perseguita* and *La Metilde ritrovata*. Mad scenes were also popular: Haydn was to write them for *La vera costanza* (1778) with a similar plot and *Orlando paladino* (1782), but the afflicted heroes were the tenor heroes (in the tradition of Ariosto's *Orlando furioso*) until Paisiello's *Nina, o sia La pazza per amore* (1789) changed all that. Belfiore and Sandrina proclaim their madness by believing themselves to be all sorts of mythological figures. Auden took up the same idea for the chilling Bedlam finale in Stravinsky's *The Rake's Progress* (1951).

SYNOPSIS

Act I Don Anchise, the Podestà (mayor) of Lagonero, has fallen in love with the new gardener's assistant, Sandrina, to the annoyance of the jealous maid, Serpetta. Sandrina is really the disguised Marchesa Violante, who has fled from her violent lover, the Count Belfiore. She is accompanied by her servant Roberto under the name of Nardo. The Podestà's haughty niece, Arminda, arrives to receive her bridegroom, none other than Count Belfiore. Arminda is recognized by her moping cavalier, Ramiro. Reproaches all round.

Act II Sandrina, meaning to test Belfiore, denies that she is Violante, but when the Podestà appears with a warrant for the arrest of Belfiore on the charge of having murdered Violante, she saves him by admitting that she is Violante. Left alone with him, she denies it again. At this point Belfiore, who has always acted a little strangely, goes completely mad. The jealous Arminda and Serpetta contrive to abandon Sandrina in a wild forest, but Nardo, who has been wooing the maid, discovers the plot and goes to the rescue, followed by the entire cast. Unfortunately Sandrina now seems to have gone mad as well.

Act III Sandrina and Belfiore awaken to refound sanity and love. Arminda makes do with Ramiro and Serpetta accepts Nardo. The Podestà decides to wait until another Sandrina turns up.

Serpetta and Nardo are the traditional buffo soubrette and valet; the Podestà is a buffo tenor (not bass) with the hoary old cliché of an aria imitating various musical instruments; Arminda and Ramiro are the opera seria characters; but the heroine wavers between the Marchesa Violante she is and the Sandrina she pretends to be; Belfiore is mainly cast in a buffo light, for his first entry reminds us of Ferrando and Guglielmo taking their mock tender leave in *Così fan tutte*, and the aria 'Da Scirocco a Tramontana', boasting of his good breeding, is certainly comic. Perhaps his mad scenes were meant to be comic too. The idea that the count needs a process of trial and purification to make him worthy of Violante is in the tradition of great comedies. While the librettist hops awkwardly in and out of the comic and serious implications, the score shows the beginning of Mozart's ability to combine these two elements of life – to become the cornerstone of his operatic masterpieces.

Musically, Mozart had taken another gigantic step in the two years since *Lucio Silla*. 'Most of the pieces show the imprint of Mozart's style so clearly,' wrote Abert, 'that it would be impossible to think of any other composer.' The arias are mostly in sonata form and mostly of suitable length; there are no *da capos*. Where there is a change of tempo it is for the sake of the text or to heighten the tension towards the end of an aria. Some of Serpetta's arias would not be out of place among Despina's in *Così fan tutte*. The most striking novelty is in the Act I and II finales with their rich palette of harmony, instrumentation and rhythm, far beyond anything achieved or indeed even considered by his Italian contemporaries. For the two *allegro* sections in the Act I finale Mozart employs a loose rondo form, in which the characters impart their own flavour to the main tune by singing it in the minor, or by continuing it in a different way. The excitement mounts as all the voices join in. The finale to Act II, linked by orchestral sections or accompanied recitatives to the three previous arias, provides 26 minutes of continuous music – compared to the great *Figaro* Act II finale of under 20 minutes! It opens in darkness (like the Act IV finale in *Figaro*), though here with an *andante sostenuto* in E♭, the traditional key for an *ombra* scene, as in *Lucio Silla*. The nocturnal sounds of the forest, expressed by the orchestra, are broken by single voices here and there, until Ramiro enters followed by servants with torches. They are accompanied by a busy violin figure until the scene is lit up to the sound of flutes and horns and everybody's identity is revealed. There are so many touches of Mozart's real genius that one cannot help regretting the weaknesses of the libretto.

RECORDINGS   1. Conwell, Sukis, Ihloff, Fassbaender, Moser, di Cesare, McDaniel, Mozarteum-Orchester, Hager, Philips, 1981; 2. singspiel version: Donath, Norman, Cotrubas, Troyanos, Hollweg, Prey, NDR Ch and O, Schmidt-Isserstedt, Philips, 1972
VIDEO   Aruhn, Biel, Piat, Kale, Croft, Striglund, Salonica. Drottningholm Court Theatre Ch and O, Ostman, Virgin, 1980s
EDITIONS   f.ss., *MW*, V, no. 9; *NMA*, II:5/viii, 1978; v.s., Bärenreiter, 1985

Il re pastore
The Shepherd King
Serenata in two acts, K. 208 (2h)
Libretto by Pietro Metastasio (1751)
Composed March–April 1775
PREMIERES 23 April 1775, Archbishop's Palace, Salzburg; 8 November 1954, St Pancras Town Hall, London; US: 7 July 1971, Norfolk, Virginia
CAST   Alessandro *t*, Aminta *s*, Elisa *s*, Tamiri *s*, Agenore *t*
FULL ORCHESTRA including 2 ca

Two operas on libretti by Metastasio were commissioned by Archbishop Colloredo for the visit of the youngest archduke, Maximilian Franz. The text chosen by (or for) Mozart had been set a dozen times, chiefly for occasions honouring Habsburg princes. (The well-meaning bungler Alexander, as depicted here, predicts the career of the archduke's elder brother, the Emperor Joseph II.) The opera, or serenata, was virtually performed as a cantata with a minimum of scenery and movement. After this, Mozart was not to see a new opera performed for five years. He began to loathe Salzburg, where musicians were held in no regard and where there was no opera or theatre.

Metastasio cites the ancient historians Cursius and Justinian as his sources for the story that Alexander the Great placed an obscure gardener named Abdolonymus on the throne of Sidon. But this name 'made him sound like a hypochondriac with a stomach ache', so Metastasio changed him into the shepherd Aminta.

SYNOPSIS
Act I   Having freed Sidon from the usurper Strato, Alexander determines to put the rightful heir on the throne. With the help of Agenore, he discovers him in Aminta, who was unaware of his origins. Agenore recognizes his own beloved Tamiri, Strato's daughter, disguised as a shepherdess. Aminta, only concerned with his beloved Elisa, is dismayed by Alexander's news. He and Elisa reaffirm their love.

Act II   Agenore refuses to admit Elisa to the new king but Aminta has no desire for the crown. Alexander tells the devastated Agenore that he will arrange for Aminta to marry Tamiri, thus making everybody happy. In the end Tamiri and Elisa pluck up courage to tell him that he is actually making everybody miserable. Aminta hands in his royal robes: let Tamiri reign with another, he says, for he himself prefers Elisa's love to a crown. Alexander appoints Tamiri and Agenore to rule over Sidon, promising Aminta and Elisa the next kingdom he comes upon (another unconsciously ironic reflection on the Habsburgs).

The nature of the occasion and of the libretto precluded anything dramatic in the music, but the melodies are more truly Mozartian than in his earlier opera-seria music. Since his main preoccupation at this time was with instrumental music, it is not surprising to find Mozart using instrumental form for some of the arias, sharing the theme of Aminta's first aria with the G major Violin Concerto (September 1775) and providing extremely enjoyable scoring, including the virtuoso flutes of Alexander's 'Se vincendo vi rendo felice'. The duet exactly follows the pattern of all his previous opera-seria duets and the finale is strictly formal in its writing for the 'chorus' of soloists. The most moving music is in Aminta's protestation of love, the famous *rondeaux* 'L'amerò, sarò costante' with solo violin and an accompaniment of flutes, cors anglais, bassoons, horns and muted strings. Almost as touching is Tamiri's simple rondo 'Se tu di me fai dono' that follows it.

RECORDING   Blasi, McNair, Vermillion, Hadley, Ahnsjö, Academy of St Martin, Marriner, Philips, 1991 (also on Philips Laserdisc)
EDITIONS   f.ss., *MW*, V, no. 10; *NMA*, II:5/ix, 1985; v.s., Breitkopf und Härtel, [1855]

Thamos, König in Egypten
Thamos, King of Egypt
Choruses and interludes to the heroic drama in five acts, K. 345/336a (45m)
Text by Tobias Philipp, Freiherr von Gebler
Composed 1773 (original version of choruses nos 1 and 6), Salzburg; 1776–7 (interludes), Salzburg; 1779–80 (final version of choruses), Salzburg; possibly not performed in Mozart's lifetime
PREMIERES ?4 April 1774, Kärntnertortheater, Vienna (inc.); ?3 January 1776, Salzburg (rev. with additions); ?1779-80, Salzburg (with further new material)
CAST   Sethos, high priest *bar*, 4 soloists *s, a, t, b*; *satb* chorus of priests and priestesses
FULL ORCHESTRA including 3 trbn

The fictitious ancient Egyptian setting of Gebler's play has some of the same roots as *Die Zauberflöte*. Everybody speaks in the solemn language of Sarastro and the characters are as clearly divided into very good and very bad. As late as 1783 Mozart regretted that the play had fallen out of favour in Vienna so that there was no chance of using his music.

SYNOPSIS

King Thamos, son of the usurper Rameses, loves Sais, a priestess of the Sun. Without knowing it, she is really the daughter of the rightful king Menes, and it is Menes, temporarily disguised as the high priest Sethos, who brings about the happy end. The treacherous general Pheron is struck by lightning (an 18th-century compromise for divine retribution, as used by Goldoni for his *Don Giovanni*) and his wicked aunt, the head priestess Mirza, kills herself.

The orchestral interludes are examples, rare in Mozart, of *Sturm und Drang* vehemence, displayed by German dramatists in the 1770s and adopted by many composers including Haydn. Mozart kept it for theatrical effects as here. These movements, in sonata form except for the short fifth movement, are filled with syncopated accents, tremolos and diminished sevenths. They were an interesting exercise in expressing events and emotions in purely instrumental terms. Leopold's annotations tell us what is being expressed: 2. 'The resolution of the conspirators'; 3. (the only gentle piece) 'Pheron's duplicity' with *fp* contrasts, 'Thamos's honesty' in an oboe solo, then both together; 4. 'The treacherous plan of Pheron and Mirza' in an angry G minor (generally the key for vehemence, not for pathos, in Mozart), which leads to the melodram of the virtuous Sais; 5. 'The fourth Act ends in general confusion', but there is a noble theme contrasting with the wild music, depicting the goodness of Thamos and triumphing in the coda; 7a A short wild piece about 'Pheron's despair, sacrilege and death' (later replaced by a chorus, see below).

The two original choral pieces already show an interesting independence in the scoring of trombones to alternate with the chorus, rather than merely double it as in the church music, and the wind to alternate with the strings. The revision of 1778–9, following his radical experience with the Mannheim orchestra and the Paris opera with its important choral parts, shows Mozart on his way to the mastery he was soon to use in *Idomeneo*. Yet these two choruses are still somewhat wooden compared to the entirely new chorus that opens with the amazingly grand address by the high priest, 'Ihr Kinder des Staubes, erzittert und bebet', and continues with the jolliest of prayers, accompanied by the guitar-like *pizzicati* of violas and bass. The melodic and harmonic wealth of this chorus make it the masterpiece of *Thamos*.

RECORDING Adam, Berlin Radio Ch, Staatskapelle Berlin, Klee, Philips, 1974
EDITIONS f.ss., *MW*, V, no. 12; *NMA*, II:6/i, 1956; v.s., Peters, [?1866]

Zaide

(*Title first used in first edition, 1838*)
Fragment of a singspiel in two acts, K. 344/336b (1h 15m)
Libretto by Johann Andreas Schachtner, after Franz Josef Sebastiani's *Das Serail* (c. 1778)
Composed 1779–80
PREMIERES 27 January 1866, Opernhaus, Frankfurt; UK: 10 January 1953, Toynbee Hall, London; US: 8 August 1955, Tanglewood
CAST Zaide *s*, Gomatz *t*, Allazim *bar*, Sultan Soliman *t*, Osmin *b*, 4 Slaves 4 *t*, Zaram *spoken role*, guards *silent*
FULL ORCHESTRA

Mozart wrote the 15 pieces of this singspiel (Leopold described it as 'not quite completed') in the hope of a performance by a touring company in Salzburg or by Joseph II's new National Singspiel.

SYNOPSIS

Act I A group of working slaves tries to remain cheerful, but the new captive, Gomatz, bemoans his fate. As he sleeps, the sultan's favourite, Zaide, falls in love with him and leaves her portrait and a jewel for him to find on awakening. When she reappears they plan to escape with the help of the overseer Allazim, who has decided to join them.

Act II The sultan is furious at the news. After Osmin's cynical laughing song he sings a grand aria of revenge. Zaide in prison laments her plight but defies Soliman. Allazim begs him to spare the captives and a final quartet encompasses all the conflicting emotions.

Zaide contains some striking advances and much music of great beauty. A fascinating innovation is the melodram or melologo, as Mozart called it. In *Thamos* Mozart has Sais speaking over continuous music, but in *Zaide* he interrupts the music for speech. By the time of *Die Entführung* he had forgotten about melodram and wrote sung accompanied recitatives as in Italian opera.

The first aria, Zaide's 'Ruhe sanft', has a melody with an exultant octave leap, which is startlingly beautiful: the muted violins and divided *pizzicato* violas for Gomatz's slumbers and the oboe for the newly awakened love help to make this one of Mozart's unforgettable pieces. The tiny duet expresses the heart leaping for joy in five-bar phrases. The trio is one of the ravishing E major 'nature' pieces that recur in the operas. Allazim has strong, virtuoso writing for the baritone voice (Mozart's first), especially in 'Ihr Mächtigen' the best text in the libretto, a noble appeal to the mighty of this world to consider their lower brethren. Soliman's arias are in danger of making him a comic figure: in one he compares himself to a roaring lion (complete with sound effects). Zaide confuses the picture by calling him a tiger in a vehement G minor aria. Mozart made the best of a poor text in 'Ich bin so bös' als gut', Soliman's revenge aria, by loading it with a rich instrumentation. The quartet is the greatest piece in *Zaide*: as in the *Lucio Silla* trio the lovers bravely facing death are joined by the angry tyrant; Allazim adds his sorrow.

RECORDING Mathis, Schreier, Hollweg, Wixell, Staatskapelle Berlin, Klee, Philips, 1975
EDITIONS f.ss., *MW*, V, no. 11; *NMA*, II:5/x, 1957; v.s., Breitkopf und Härtel, [1917]

Idomeneo

Dramma per musica in three acts, K. 366 (3h 30m) and ballet (30m)
Libretto by Giambattista Varesco, after Antoine Danchet's five-act tragédie lyrique *Idomenée* set by André Campra (1712)
Composed October 1780–January 1781
PREMIERES 29 January 1781, Cuvilliés Theater, Munich; UK: 12 March 1934, Glasgow (amateur); 20 June 1951, Glyndebourne, Sussex; US: 4 August 1947, Tanglewood
CAST Idomeneo *t*, Idamante *s* (or *t*), Ilia *s*, Elettra *s*, Arbace *t*, High Priest *t*, Oracle *b*; *satb* chorus of Trojan captives, Cretan sailors, Cretan people, priests; ballet
ORCHESTRATION picc, 2 fl, 2 ob, 2 cl, 2 bsn, 4 hn, 2 tr, 3 trbn, timp, str, cont; offstage fanfare: 2 tr, timp

The artistic Karl Theodor had succeeded to the Bavarian Electorate in 1778 and brought his famous orchestra and opera company with him from Mannheim. Mozart's letters home from his arrival in Munich (on 8 November 1780) until his father joined him (on 25 January 1781) give a fascinating detailed account of the creation of his first operatic masterpiece. His problems with the 67-year-old tenor Raaff and the untalented 'amato castrato del Prato', his Idomeneo and Idamante ('the two worst actors any stage has ever borne'), were not without

Watercolour of Anton Raaff, Mozart's first Idomeneo, in a heroic role

influence on the music he wrote for them. Mozart's dramatic instinct and common sense are in evidence when he remarks that 'the thunder is presumably not going to cease for Mr Raaff's aria' or 'it seems naïve to think that everybody hurries off (after the Oracle has spoken) just to leave Mme Elettra alone'. The music for the Oracle was written at least four times, for he believed that it must be short to be credible, adding that the Ghost in *Hamlet* would have benefited from greater brevity. In the interests of dramatic tightness he cut three arias from Act III at a late stage (among many smaller cuts). The opera was given only three performances, but Mozart continued to believe in it: nothing came of his hope of making a German opera of it with a bass Idomeneo in Vienna in 1781, but there was one revival by aristocratic amateurs in the Palais Auersperg, Vienna in March 1786 (when he was completing the score of *Figaro*). For this Mozart made some important changes: Idamante was now apparently a tenor (though the music is mysteriously written in the soprano, not the tenor, clef) and has a new aria with violin obbligato ('Non temer, amato bene', K. 490). The Act III duet was almost wholly rewritten to its great advantage ('Spiegarti non poss'io', K. 489) and small adjustments were made to the trio and quartet.

Gluck's and Piccinni's operas on *Iphigenia in Aulis* and Gluck's *Alceste* were the most famous of the sacrifice operas, but the genre continued into the 19th century. Melchior von Grimm, who had been Mozart's patron in Paris in 1778–9, remarked that sacrifice operas were 'a very interesting spectacle to behold and offered many situations at once strong and pathetic and suitable for music'. There was certainly more pathos than drama to be got out of them, for all humans can do is submit to the gods. The too pliant and generous Idamante plays the Metastasian role of dying cheerfully for a father he has only just met. Yet the story does contain, at least potentially, the perennial tragedy of the young generation condemned to death by the vows or treaties of their elders.

SYNOPSIS

Act I The action takes place in Crete after the Trojan War. In the royal palace the captive Trojan princess Ilia laments her fate ('Padre, germani, addio!'), but the Cretan prince Idamante loves her ('Non ho colpa') and sets all the Trojan captives free to prove it. Arbace brings the news that Idomeneo has been drowned at sea. The fierce Greek princess Elettra is jealous of Ilia's power over Idamante ('Tutte nel cor vi sento'). On a stormswept shore the pitiful cries of the sailors ('Pietà! Numi, pietà!') finally give way to the appearance of Neptune himself (in a pantomima) calming the storm in answer to Idomeneo's prayer. As the king comes ashore he is profoundly unhappy at the vow he has just taken, to sacrifice the first being he meets ('Vedrommi intorno'). His victim, the friendly young man who comes to his aid, turns out to be his son Idamante, saddened that his father seems to reject him ('Il padre adorato ritrovo'). The Cretan people celebrate Idomeneo's safe return.

Act II In the palace alone with Arbace, Idomeneo resolves to send Idamante to safety in Argos with Elettra. Ilia involuntarily reveals her love for his son ('Se il padre perdei'), which increases his despair at the storm in his soul ('Fuor del mar'). Only Elettra rejoices at her coming departure with the prince, hurrying down to the harbour to join the chorus ('Placido è il mar') and the leave-taking of the king and his son ('Pria di partir'). But suddenly Neptune, infuriated by Idomeneo's attempts to break the vow, sends a monster in a storm ('Qual nuovo terrore!'). Idomeneo begs Neptune to punish him alone, but the tempest continues and the people flee in terror ('Corriamo, fuggiamo').

Act III In the royal garden Ilia sings to the breeze of her love for Idamante ('Zeffiretti lusinghieri') and when he promises to kill the monster or die in the attempt, she at last confesses her love. The momentary happiness of their duet ('S'io non moro a questi accenti') is followed by the bleak tragedy of the quartet ('Andrò ramingo e solo'), when Idomeneo once more urges his son's departure. Arbace now warns him that the people demand action and threaten revolt. Idomeneo goes to meet them in a large square before the palace. Urged by the High Priest, he at last reveals that the victim is his own son, to the sorrow of the people ('Oh voto tremendo!'). The scene of the sacrifice is the temple of Neptune near the shore. After Idomeneo's prayer ('Accogli, oh re del mar') there is a momentary ray of hope at the news that Idamante has killed the monster. But he is brought on as the willing sacrificial victim. Idomeneo's sword is already raised when Ilia rushes in to implore him to kill her, an enemy of Greece, instead. Now the nobility of Ilia and Idamante melts Neptune's anger and the Oracle announces that they shall henceforth reign in Crete. This is followed by universal rejoicing with the notable exception of Elettra, a prey to the furies who had tormented her brother, Orestes ('D'Oreste, d'Aiace ho in seno i tormenti').

Seen as a whole, *Idomeneo* is a flawed masterpiece without the tension of a great tragedy, but Mozart's score contains some of the greatest operatic music ever written. Traditional elements of opera seria struggle with innovations based on Gluck and the tragédie lyrique, especially in the great dramatic choruses. Infinitely expressive *recitativi accompagnati* link the arias and ensembles to form long stretches of continuous music, leaving few opportunities for the old applauded exit aria: they also bind the music by quoting themes from arias just heard or yet to come and achieve great tension by merging into rhythmic arioso at the approach of an aria or of some important revelation. Ilia has the most beautiful of the arias; her 'Se il padre perdei' early in Act II is one of Mozart's very greatest, accompanied by a *concertante* wind quartet, not as a virtuoso or merely colourful element but to express every hidden emotion. Mozart avoided giving del Prato coloratura or other problems and made up for this with his orchestration, for example the string runs and chromatic wind to express Idamante's perplexity in 'Non ho colpa'. Idomeneo has the noble prayer 'Accogli, oh re del mar' with the unison chant of the priests and a unique accompaniment of *pizzicato* strings with a web of interlinking woodwind, but also the return to an earlier style in the coloratura of 'Fuor del mar', ineptly triumphant even if it is meant to represent the storm in his heart. The two other characters have virtually no impact on the story at all. The confidant Arbace sings two very conventional arias, which were heavily cut by Mozart and can easily be omitted. But Elettra has the most varied and difficult role in Mozart (along with the equally fierce Vitellia in *La clemenza di Tito*): she can sing of the joys of love as sweetly as any Zaide ('Idol mio') or in her solo in 'Placido è il mar', but her first and last arias express fury beyond the limits of sanity, especially in the manic laugh that concludes the latter. No wonder conductors are reluctant to follow Mozart in cutting 'D'Oreste' at the end of the opera. Unfortunately nobody ever takes the slightest bit of notice of Elettra. Perhaps that is why she goes mad.

The duet is little more than a charming pastoral piece: Mozart's 1786 version is the most pertinent criticism of it. The trio ('Pria di partir'), a beautiful piece of conflicting emotions, is, however, overshadowed by the quartet ('Andrò ramingo e solo'), one of Mozart's great tragic utterances – he himself later burst into tears while singing it with friends. The dramatic choruses at the appearance of the monster in Act II and at the revelation of Idamante's fate in Act III are of incomparable eloquence. And there is also the sheer happy lilt of the barcarolle 'Placido è il mar'.

If Mozart tailored each aria to his singer, how much more he must have fitted the score to his admired Mannheim orchestra. Mozart never created such a rich orchestral part in any other opera. His father wondered how the musicians could survive three hours of it (four hours would be closer if the ballet was done complete) – 'I know your style. Every musician needs astonishing continuous concentration.' Mozart is suddenly freed from the old conventions, the woodwind are wholly independent; he lovingly uses the clarinet for the first time in an opera, as well as the virtuoso oboe of his friend Ramm and all the power of four horns, two trumpets and timpani. One must also imagine all the effects of thunder, lightning, crowd movements, swift scene changes and a monster and a god out of the machine, as produced by the experts of the Munich theatre.

For the first time Mozart uses little phrases, not quite leitmotifs, but expressions of a particular emotion, such as the anxious trill-like trembling we hear in Elettra's first aria and in Idamante's first two arias and throughout the chorus 'Qual nuovo terror', or the falling phrase associated with Idamante's fate and first heard towards the end of the overture. Lacking Gluck's bold simplicity, Mozart hints at subtler shades of emotion with an orchestral, melodic and harmonic richness far beyond his contemporaries. The premiere took place two days after his 25th birthday.

RECORDINGS 1. McNair, Martinpelto, von Otter, Rolfe Johnson, N. Robson, Monteverdi Ch, English Baroque Soloists, Gardiner, Archiv, 1990; 2. Yakar, Palmer, Schmidt, Hollweg, Equiluz, Zurich Opera Ch and O, Harnoncourt, Teldec, 1986; 3. Rinaldi, Tinsley, Shirley, Davies, Tear, BBC Ch and SO, Davis, Philips, 1969; 4. Mathis, Varady, Ochman, Schreier, Winkler, Leipzig Radio Ch, Dresden Staatskapelle, Böhm, DG, 1977: the Gardiner performance, using period instruments, offers the tautest, leanest, most dramatic performance to date, and one notably well sung; it includes the alternative arias, etc. Harnoncourt's reading is predictably idiosyncratic – and thought-provoking. The two older, more 'traditional' readings are also worthy of consideration, directed by two acknowledged Mozartians with loving care. The first two sets use a female singer for Idamante; the last two employ a tenor. [A.B.]
VIDEO Kenny, Vaness, Hadley, Langridge, Glyndebourne Festival Ch, LPO, Haitink, Castle, 1983
EDITIONS MW, V, no. 13; NMA, II:5/xi, 1972; v.s. (2 vols), Bärenreiter, 1983

Die Entführung aus dem Serail

The Abduction from the Harem

Singspiel in three acts, K. 384 (2h 15m)
Libretto by Gottlieb Stephanie the Younger, after *Bellmont und Constanze, oder Die Entführung aus dem Serail* by Christoph Friedrich Bretzner set by Johann André (1781)
Composed July 1781–May 1782
PREMIERES 16 July 1782, Burgtheater, Vienna; UK: 24 November 1827, Covent Garden, London; US: 16 February 1860, Brooklyn Athenaeum, New York
CAST Bassa Selim *spoken role*, Konstanze *s*, Blonde *s*, Belmonte *t*, Pedrillo *t*, Osmin *b*, Klaas, a sailor *spoken role*, guards *silent*; *satb* chorus of jannisaries and attendants
ORCHESTRATION flauto piccolo, 2 fl, 2 ob, 2 cl/2 basset hn, 2 bsn, 2 hn, 2 tpt, timp, sd, bd, cym, triangle, str, cont

The composition of *Die Entführung aus dem Serail*, commissioned for Joseph II's singspiel company under Stephanie's direction, took an unusually long time to complete, although Mozart composed three major numbers for it in one day. It had been intended for a visit by the Russian Grand Duke at the end of 1781, which kept being postponed. The opera was Mozart's main preoccupation between May 1781, when he broke with the Archbishop of Salzburg and settled in Vienna, and his marriage in August 1782. He wrote three long letters to his father in the autumn of 1781 that give a vivid insight into his creative thinking. He describes how he expressed the emotions, the very heartbeats of Belmonte in 'O wie ängstlich, o wie feurig' and the unbridled fury of Osmin: at the end of 'Solche hergelauf'ne Laffen' he is 'beside himself, so the music must be too, but because passion, however strong, must never be expressed to the extent of disgusting the hearer and music must remain music, I have chosen a key [for 'Erst geköpft, dann gehangen'] that is not a stranger to F [the key of the aria], but a friend, not the closest one D minor, but A minor'. The actual words of Stephanie's undistinguished text did not really worry him, for Osmin's aria 'was already walking around' in his head before he saw the libretto. He thought that a good composer who understood the stage, helped by the right poet, could steer the drama in the right direction, that words should be the obedient daughters of the music and that rhyming texts were a

waste of time. But there has probably never been a really satisfactory production of *Die Entführung* and Mozart must bear the main responsibility for this. Stephanie added little to Bretzner's text. They even copied the idea of a speaking Selim: a tenor had been planned for the role, but Mozart must have turned against the thought of three tenors and remembered his failure in *Zaide* to give Soliman a serious profile. This means that the only musical opposition comes from the comic Osmin. In the opera that was their model Bretzner and his composer Johann André had produced a lively ensemble for the elopement scene in Act III: Mozart began a finale for Act II presumably to contain the elopement, with an unfinished duet for Belmonte and Pedrillo ('Welch ängstliches Beben' K. 389/384A), but eventually the elopement and recapture of the lovers was allowed to take place in silence. Thus, both the main action of the opera and its main character, Selim, in the sense that the plot hangs on his moods and their changes, remain without music. In spite of this the opera was an instant success and was played in 40 cities during Mozart's lifetime. Goethe, who had himself written libretti for singspiels, said, '*Die Entführung* knocked everything else sideways.' Weber saw that Mozart's artistic experience had reached maturity in *Die Entführung*. The Emperor apparently remarked: 'An awful lot of notes, my dear Mozart.'

SYNOPSIS

Act I The Spanish nobleman Belmonte has arrived on the Barbary or Turkish coast to search for his betrothed Konstanze, who was captured by pirates, together with her maid Blonde and his servant Pedrillo ('Hier soll ich dich denn sehen'). With great difficulty he learns from the grumpy overseer Osmin that he is standing before the palace of Bassa Selim ('Wer ein Liebchen hat gefunden'). When Pedrillo appears, Osmin expresses his lethal loathing for him ('Solche hergelauf'ne Laffen'). When he has gone, Belmonte learns that Konstanze is alive and well: his emotion is boundless ('Konstanze! . . . O wie ängstlich'). The Bassa arrives with his retinue ('Singt dem grossen Bassa Lieder') and begins to woo Konstanze once more, but her heart belongs to another from whom she was cruelly parted ('Ach, ich liebte'). Selim gives her one more day to change her mind. She leaves and Pedrillo introduces Belmonte to the Bassa as a talented architect. Selim takes him on, but Belmonte and Pedrillo have the greatest difficulty in getting past Osmin to enter the palace ('Marsch, marsch, marsch!')

Act II Outside Osmin's house in the palace garden. Blonde has been assigned to Osmin but soon shows that she has the upper hand. 'I am a free-born Englishwoman,' she tells him and proceeds to tease him into submission ('Ich gehe, doch rate ich dir'). Konstanze still has nothing to say to the Bassa except to express her sorrow ('Welcher Wechsel herrscht in meiner Seele . . . Traurigkeit ward mir zum Lose'), but when he threatens her with torture, she replies defiantly ('Martern aller Arten'). Blonde is delighted to hear from Pedrillo that they are to escape that very night ('Welche Wonne, welche Lust'). Pedrillo summons up as much courage as he can ('Frisch zum Kampfe!'), then proceeds to get Osmin drunk to be out of the way ('Vivat Bacchus!'). Belmonte meets his beloved at last ('Wenn der Freude Tränen fliessen'). The women assure their lovers that they have always been faithful to them despite all the hazards of life in a harem ('Ach Belmonte, ach mein Leben!').

Act III   Outside the palace Pedrillo sings an old ballad as a signal ('Im Mohrenland gefangen war') and the two men succeed in abducting the women, but a guard discovers the ladder and they are soon brought before Osmin, who is seething with vengeful fury ('O, wie will ich triumphieren'). Condemned to die by the Bassa, Belmonte reveals that his father is Lostados, governor of Oran. 'He is my greatest enemy,' Selim answers, 'who has robbed me of my beloved, my wealth, my fatherland.' Belmonte and Konstanze await their death, each longing to die for the other ('Welch ein Geschick . . . Meinetwegen sollst du sterben'). But the Bassa has no wish to emulate the despised Lostados, so he pardons them and sends all four home. The opera ends in the gratitude and rejoicing of everybody except Osmin.

The wonderful freshness of the musical invention more than makes up for the dramatic weakness. Mozart gave the magnificent buffo bass Ludwig Fischer, in the part of Osmin, music of great brilliance and range with frequent descents to evil thoughts and bottom D. The Konstanze, Caterina Cavalieri, was famous for her coloratura and her two-octave leaps: Mozart admitted that he had to sacrifice something to her 'fluent throat' and that he had to express the mood within the limitations of an Italian bravura aria. Her second aria ('Traurigkeit') with its recitative is one of his most moving creations, but when he came to the great showpiece of the opera, 'Martern aller Arten', Mozart abandoned dramatic

relevance by adding a virtuoso *concertante* quartet of flute, oboe, violin and cello. Belmonte opens with a lied, taken from the middle section of the overture, and then Mozart gives him 'O wie ängstlich' – 'everybody's favourite, including mine'. The famous tenor Johann Valentin Adamberger demanded four arias, so he sings one on meeting Konstanze, when a duet would have been far more appropriate, and another in Act III, which is generally omitted. The duet in Act III avoids tragic tones except in the opening recitative, for the lovers are quietly exulting in thoughts of self-sacrifice. Pedrillo's arias are both full of character: in the first a not very courageous little man is trying to wind himself up to the necessary courage for the daring rescue. The romance, *sotto voce*, with only *pizzicato* strings, is one of Mozart's strangest compositions: the first three lines pass though the keys of D, A, C, G, F♯ minor and F♯ major. The soubrette Blonde is lyrical and vixenish as the occasion demands.

The quartet, though it does not fit the customary picture of an Act II finale as a crescendo of noise and confusion, is one of Mozart's most enchanting creations. The beginning and end express generalized joy, but the middle part contains its own little drama: the two tenors ask the sopranos, not without due hesitation and embarrassment, if in spite of all the temptations and threats they have remained faithful to them. The women's reactions reassure them. This is not so much a quartet as two simultaneous duets – the two noble lovers with their *legato* lines, the servants in *staccato* phrases, the culmination being in Blonde's triplet fireworks (she is still smarting at the insult) against the blissful reconciliation of the others. At the very heart of the quartet there is a serene siciliana in A major of only 15 bars, in which Mozart celebrates the profound happiness of love. He was about to marry his Constanze despite a father rather less forgiving than the Bassa.

One should mention the vivid Turkish music, with its C major, its repeated little phrases and, of course, percussion, which fills the overture and the choruses. The characters take their leave in a charming vaudeville, the form borrowed from opéra comique.

RECORDINGS   1. Dawson, Hirsti, Heilmann, Gahmlich, von Kannen, Academy of Ancient Music Ch and O, Hogwood, L'Oiseau Lyre, 1991; 2. Kenny, Watson, Schreier, Gahmlich, Salminen, Zurich Opera House Ch and O, Harnoncourt, Teldec, 1988; 3. Auger, Grist, Schreier, Neukirch, Moll, Leipzig Radio Ch, Dresden Staatskapelle, Böhm, DG, 1974: the Hogwood performance, using period instruments, sheds a new and revealing light on the work; it is also remarkably well sung by an appropriately youthful cast. Harnoncourt's account is arrestingly immediate and vital. The Böhm is more orthodox, beautifully sung and played. [A.B.]
VIDEO   Winska, Hellstrom, Croft, Morgan, Szule, Schaffe, Drottningholm Theatre Ch and O, Ostman, Virgin, 1980s
EDITIONS   f.ss., *MW*, V, no. 15; *NMA*, II:5/xii, 1982; v.ss., Bärenreiter, 1982; Peters, 1926

L'oca del Cairo

The Goose of Cairo
Fragment of an opera buffa, K. 422 (45m)
Libretto by Giambattista Varesco

Catarina Cavalieri, the first Konstanze; silhouette by Hieronymous Löschenkohl (1785)

Composed November–December 1783
PREMIERES 1860, Frankfurt (concert); 6 June 1867, Paris (arr. Victor Wilder including numbers from *Lo sposo deluso* and inserts Mozart wrote for Bianchi's *La villanella rapita*); UK: 12 May 1940, Sadler's Wells, London (in one act, orch. Hans Redlich); US: 1 June 1953, Greenwich Playhouse, New York (as *Don Pedro's Heimkehr*, arr. Hans Erismann, containing numbers from *L'oca del Cairo* and *Lo sposo deluso*); 27 July 1991, Battignano, Italy (with additions by Stephen Oliver)
CAST Don Pippo *b*, Celidora *s*, Biondello *t*, Calandrino *t*, Lavina *s*, Chichibio *b*, Auretta *s*; *tb* chorus of guards
FULL ORCHESTRA

Following the success of *Die Entführung* Mozart was thrilled to be asked for an Italian opera by Count Orsini-Rosenberg, director of the court theatre. In May 1783 he reported that he had looked through at least a hundred libretti without finding one that would do without a great many changes 'and then you might as well have an entirely new one. A certain Abbate da Ponte has promised me one but who knows if he can or will keep his word. If he is in league with Salieri I'll never in my life get one – and I would so love to show what I can do in an Italian opera . . .' In despair he asked for a libretto from Varesco, the Salzburg chaplain with whom he had struggled so hard over the text for *Idomeneo*. He began composing during a stay in Salzburg, but on his return to Vienna he protested at Varesco's amateurish efforts and the ridiculous idea of the goose: after December nothing more was heard about *L'oca del Cairo*.

SYNOPSIS
The Marchese Don Pippo intends to wed the unwilling Lavina and marry off his daughter, Celidora, to an unattractive suitor of his choice. The women's lovers, Biondello and Calandrino, form various plans to rescue them with the help of the majordomo Chichibio and the maid Auretta. In the Act I finale (which is as far as Mozart got with the composition), the marchese interrupts the escape from a tower. In Act II Biondello was to enter the house inside a huge mechanical goose provided by Don Pippo's lost wife, Donna Pantea.

A short score has survived, consisting of the voice parts with texts, the instrumental bass part and indications of instrumental melodies at the beginning of each piece (Mozart drafted all his operas in this way). There are three arias, two duets, a quartet and a 13-minute finale, as well as Pippo's aria plus trio recently found in complete score in an early copy. The music has its good moments, but the libretto offers few situations for Mozart's talent. What could he do with a scene about building a bridge to reach the captive ladies in their tower? At least he learned to avoid hopeless libretti.

RECORDING realization by Erik Smith: Wiens, Nielsen, Coburn, Schreier, Johnson, Fischer-Dieskau, Scharinger, Kammerorchester CPE Bach, Schreier, Philips, 1990
EDITIONS f.ss., *MW*, XXIV, no. 37; *NMA*, II:5/xiii, 1960

Lo sposo deluso, ossia La rivalità di tre donne per un solo amante

The Deceived Bridegroom, or The Rivalry between Three Ladies for One Lover
Fragment of an opera buffa, K. 430/424a (20m)
Anonymous libretto, after *Le donne rivali* set by Cimarosa (1780)
Composed 1783 or early 1784
PREMIERES US: 1 June 1953, Greenwich Playhouse, New York (see *L'oca del Cairo*, above); UK: 11 February 1956, City Opera Club, London (arr. John Coombs as *The Deluded Bridegroom*, using much the same music as Paris 1867, see *L'oca del Cairo*)
CAST Bocconio *b*, Eugenia *s*, Don Asdrubale *t*, Pulcherio *t*, Bettina *s*
FULL ORCHESTRA

Bocconio Papparelli, a rich old fool, intends to marry the beautiful but proud Eugenia, formerly loved by the quarrelsome officer Don Asdrubale, who is also loved by Bocconio's niece Bettina who, however, finally marries the misogynist Pulcherio.

Only an overture leading to a quartet (incompletely scored), two arias in short score (voice part with text and orchestral bass only) and a complete trio were written. There is no reference to it in Mozart's letters nor any evidence that da Ponte wrote the libretto, as is sometimes maintained. Against the characters Mozart noted the names of the singers in the new Italian company for which he was to write *Figaro*.

RECORDING realization by Erik Smith: Cotrubas, Palmer, Rolfe Johnson, Tear, Grant, LSO, C. Davis, Philips, 1975
EDITIONS f.ss., *MW*, XXIV, no. 38; *NMA*, II:5/xiv, 1988; v.ss., Johann André, [1855]; English version by John Coombs, *The Deluded Bridegroom*, Chappell, [1960]

Der Schauspieldirektor

The Impresario
Comedy with music in one act, K. 486 (music only: 30m)
Text by Gottlieb Stephanie the Younger
Composed January–February 1786
PREMIERES 7 February 1786, Orangerie, Schloss Schönbrunn, Vienna; UK: 30 May 1857, St James's Theatre, London; US: 9 November 1870, Stadttheater, New York
CAST Buff *b*, Monsieur Vogelsang *t*, Mme Herz *s*, Mlle Silberklang *s*; *spoken roles*: Frank, Eiler, Mme Pfeil, Mme Krone, Mme Vogelsang
FULL ORCHESTRA

In the midst of one of the most astonishing creative periods of Mozart's life, which included the composition of *Figaro*, the piano concertos K. 482, K. 488 and K. 491 and a dozen other major works, came the imperial command for a few songs for a comedy to be presented at a court festivity in honour of the governor-general of the Austrian Netherlands, the Archduchess Christine and her husband. The 80 guests were given lunch in the centre of the hall, then this German comedy on a stage at one end followed by an opera buffa, *Prima la musica poi le parole* by Casti, with music by Salieri, at the other end. Mozart wrote an overture and four vocal numbers. Stephanie, director of the National Singspiel, obviously saw himself in the role of the good-natured impresario Frank (though Mozart was one of the few who spoke well of him). The two prima donnas, Caterina Cavalieri (Salieri's mistress and the first Konstanze in *Die Entführung*) as Mlle Silberklang and Aloysia Lange (née Weber, Mozart's sister-in-law and first love) as Mme Herz, must have had a sense of humour to take part in this parody on the vanity of singers.

SYNOPSIS
The impresario Frank, assisted by the buffo singer Buff, is forming a theatrical company to play in Salzburg. Two actresses perform for him and are engaged. Then Mme Herz sings a pathetic arietta ('Da schlägt die Abschiedsstunde') and Mlle Silberklang a rondo ('Bester Jüngling!') to exhibit their strongest points. Each then gives brilliant vocal backing to her claim for the higher fee, but Monsieur Vogelsang manages to effect a truce ('Ich bin die erste Sängerin'). When Frank threatens to abandon the whole plan of forming a company, all unreasonable demands are instantly withdrawn. In a vaudeville ('Jeder Künstler strebt nach Ehre'), everybody, including Buff, recognizes the need for the ambition of artists, provided that it is not at the expense of their colleagues.

Mozart would have preferred to compose the opera buffa (if his work on *Figaro* had permitted it), but he made the very best of his trivial task. The overture is a brilliant, symphonic work with rich orchestration. The pathos of the first aria anticipates the parodies of *Così*: the horn imitating the tolling bell is an especially good touch. A sketch of the vocal line, of which only the first five bars remain in the final version, is a rare surviving example to show us how much Mozart sometimes departed from his initial ideas. Mlle Silberklang has a delicious wind-band accompaniment and the same coloratura figure that is the undoing of many a Donna Anna in 'Non mi dir' in *Don Giovanni*. The trio is a very funny scene in which each lady sings about the nobility of her art while trying to defeat her rival with ever higher notes. The closing song is a simple rondo in gavotte time.

RECORDING Te Kanawa, Gruberova, Heilmann, Jungwirth, Vienna PO, Pritchard, Decca, 1990
EDITIONS f.ss., *MW*, V, no. 16; *NMA*, II:5/xv, 1958; v.s., Bärenreiter, 1958

Le nozze di Figaro
Figaro's Wedding

Opera buffa in four acts, K. 492 (3h)
Libretto by Lorenzo da Ponte, after the comedy *La folle journée, ou Le mariage de Figaro* by Pierre-Augustin Caron de Beaumarchais (1784)
Composed October 1785–April 1786
PREMIERES 1 May 1786, Burgtheater, Vienna; UK: 2 May 1812, Pantheon, London; US: 10 May 1824, Park Theater, New York
CAST Il Conte di Almaviva *bar*, La Contessa di Almaviva *s*, Susanna *s*, Figaro *b*, Cherubino *s* (or *ms*), Marcellina *s*, Bartolo *b*, Basilio *t*, Don Curzio *t*, Barbarina *s*, Antonio *b*; *satb* chorus of peasants and the Count's tenants

ORCHESTRATION 2 fl, 2 ob, 2 cl, 2 bsn, 2 hn, 2 tpt, 2 timp, str, cont

We know very little about the process of composition of *Figaro*, for none of Mozart's letters survives from the months that preceded the first performance on 1 May 1786. When da Ponte came to relate his tale many years later in his autobiography, he was himself the hero of the story: it was he who hurried to the emperor and persuaded him to permit the musical version of a play that had been banned as subversive and he who later foiled the typical Viennese plots. But even da Ponte admitted that the idea of setting *Figaro* came from Mozart. The play had everything to commend it, not least the thrill of having been banned. It used most of the old ingredients of comedy, but in a new way: there was a pair of lovers but they were a valet and a lady's maid; the comic servant has become his master's successful rival; in the concluding scene of clemency, common to nearly all of Mozart's operas, it is the Count, the representative of emperor, bassa or god, who has to beg for it. We are in the new topsy-turvy world of the French Revolution. Cherubino is a new invention, 'drunk with love' (according to Kierkegaard), the first of the many *travesti* roles which succeeded the youths impersonated by castrati. Beaumarchais, who recognized the potential *frisson*, specified that 'he could be played only by a young and very pretty woman'. The play is brilliantly theatrical, for each act has its *coup de théâtre*: the discovery of the page in Act I, Susanna emerging from the closet in Act II, the revelation of Figaro's parentage in Act III and the Countess as *dea ex machina* in Act IV – and how quietly, almost casually, Mozart brings each one about. The actual plotting does not bear too much scrutiny. How many people in the audience realize that there are actually three mysterious pieces of paper at different points? Unlike *Così fan tutte* with its schematic plot, *Figaro* teems with plots, as life does: all the characters are involved with intrigues of their own, sometimes even against their allies, as when Susanna and Figaro set out to teach each other a lesson in Act IV. But the main plot is clear: although the Count is doing everything to cancel or postpone the wedding because of his feelings for Susanna, Figaro and Co. defeat him and bring him back to his wife.

Da Ponte apologized in his preface to the libretto for having had to reduce the number of acts, characters and *bons mots* in the interests of the music. He also had to omit Figaro's more politically subversive remarks, though the tone of 'Se vuol ballare' is defiant enough. The essential difference between the play and the opera was perceptively described by Stendhal in his *Lettre sur Mozart* (1814): 'Mozart, with his overwhelmingly sensitive nature, has transformed into real passions the superficial inclinations which amuse the easy-going inhabitants of Aguas Frescas in Beaumarchais . . . In this sense then it might be said that Mozart could not have distorted the play more. I do not really know if music is capable of depicting French flirtation and frivolity for the course of four acts and in all the

Etching by Daniel Chodowiecki for Beaumarchais's
Le mariage de Figaro, published in 1785

characters: I should say it was difficult, for music needs strong emotions, whether of joy or unhappiness . . . the wit remains only in the situations: all the characters have been filled with feeling and passion . . . Mozart's opera is a sublime mixture of wit and melancholy, which has no equal . . .'

The cast included the great actor Francesco Benucci as Figaro (later the first Vienna Leporello and the first Guglielmo), Francesco Bussani as Bartolo and Antonio (later the first Vienna Commendatore and Masetto and the first Don Alfonso), his wife, Dorotea as Cherubino (later the first Vienna Zerlina and the first Despina), the 12-year-old Anna Gottlieb as Barbarina (later the first Pamina) as well as the English Nancy Storace as Susanna and the Irish Michael Kelly as Basilio and Don Curzio.

On 29 August 1789 began a series of performances of a revival in Vienna with a new cast for which Mozart made a number of revisions, including changes in the Count's aria and in the Countess's second aria. The new Susanna, Caterina Cavalieri, made him replace her two arias with 'Un moto di gioia' (K. 579) and 'Al desio' (K. 577).

SYNOPSIS

Act I   A half-furnished room in Count Almaviva's Castle of Aguas Frescas near Seville. The Count's valet, Figaro, and Susanna, the Countess's maid, are preparing for their wedding ('Cinque, dieci, venti'). How convenient, thinks Figaro, for us to be between the Count and the Countess; and how convenient, Susanna adds, for the Count who has started making advances to her – not that Figaro should doubt

her for a moment ('Se a caso madama la notte ti chiama'). Left alone, Figaro is distraught but vengeful ('Se vuol ballare signor Contino'). When he has gone out, Dr Bartolo and his housekeeper, Marcellina, enter: though old enough to be his mother, she is trying to force Figaro into marriage in acquittal of a loan he cannot repay. Bartolo is eager to help her in order to avenge himself on Figaro, who had planned the abduction of his ward Rosina, now the Countess ('La vendetta'). Susanna returns and she and Marcellina soon abandon ironic politeness ('Via resti servita, madama brillante') until Marcellina storms out. Cherubino darts in. He is in love with all women ('Non so più cosa son, cosa faccio') but most of all with his godmother, the Countess. Hearing the Count approach, he hides behind the armchair. The Count at once begins to flirt with Susanna but, hearing the music master Don Basilio outside, he too hides behind the armchair – though not before Cherubino has had time to jump into the armchair and be covered up by Susanna with a dress. Basilio taunts Susanna about Cherubino's passion for the Countess. At this the Count springs up in a rage ('Cosa sento!'); Basilio enjoys the mischief and Susanna nearly swoons. The Count complacently relates how he has recently discovered Cherubino in the room of the gardener's young daughter, Barbarina, hiding under the tablecloth. Acting out the story, he lifts the dress from the armchair and is stunned to see the page again. There is to be no pardon this time and Figaro had better know about his bride's relations with the page, thunders the Count, a little uneasy that Cherubino had witnessed his scene with Susanna. Figaro leads in the peasants to praise the Count for abolishing the wicked old feudal rights over his female tenants. The Count, with great presence of mind, postpones the wedding and sends Cherubino off with a commission to his regiment. Figaro warns Cherubino in a rousing finale ('Non più andrai') that a soldier's life is very different from that of an 'amorous great butterfly'.

Act II   The grand bedroom of the Countess. She is alone, regretting the loss of her husband's love ('Porgi amor'). Figaro unfolds his plan to bring him back to fidelity: he will send the Count an anonymous letter claiming that the Countess has made a secret assignation with a lover; at the same time Susanna is to make an assignation with him, but they will send Cherubino dressed as a girl in place of her. All this will at least distract the Count from averting their marriage. When he has left, Cherubino arrives to perform his latest love song ('Voi che sapete') and to be fitted with his disguise by Susanna ('Venite inginocchiatevi'). The Countess is touched to find that he has wrapped a ribbon of hers round his arm. Suddenly the Count is heard knocking on the door and demanding entry. Susanna happens to be out in the dressing room, so the Countess quickly shuts Cherubino into a closet and opens the door to the Count. She cannot allay his suspicions when a noise is heard from the closet. 'It is only Susanna,' she claims. In a trio ('Susanna, or via sortite') the Count orders Susanna to come out, the Countess is affronted by his behaviour and Susanna, who has come into the room unseen by both of them, observes the situation. As soon as the Count has gone off with the Countess to fetch a hammer to break the closet door down, Susanna releases the page. After a moment of panic ('Aprite presto aprite'), he jumps out of the window. The Count returns and the Countess confesses that he will not find Susanna in the closet but Cherubino. The finale opens with the Count ordering Cherubino out and threatening to kill him. When Susanna emerges, all innocence, the Count and Countess are equally surprised but he asks to be forgiven for his suspicions. Figaro now arrives to remind him that it is time for the wedding ceremony. The Count confronts him with the anonymous letter but Figaro denies any knowledge of it. A new threat appears: Antonio, the drunken gardener, complains that somebody had jumped out of the Countess's window on to his geraniums. To allay suspicion Figaro admits that it was he. 'In that case,' says Antonio, 'you will want these papers you dropped.' The Count challenges Figaro to tell him what they are. Prompted by the Countess and Susanna, Figaro gradually reveals that they are the page's commission which needed the official seal. Just as the Count fears he has lost the campaign, Marcellina storms in with Bartolo and Basilio to urge her legal claim over Figaro. The Count declares that he will hear it at a proper trial in due course, to the noisy despair of Figaro's party.

Act III A grand hall prepared for the wedding feast. The Count is puzzled by events but delighted with a surprisingly compliant Susanna, sent in to him by the Countess in pursuit of Figaro's plot ('Crudel! perchè finora'). Unfortunately he overhears Susanna whisper to Figaro of her success and bursts out in jealous fury ('Hai gia vinta la causa! . . . Vedrò mentr'io sospiro'). The trial has gone against Figaro, who, confronted by all his enemies, reveals that his parents are unknown: it gradually emerges that he is the bastard son of Bartolo and Marcellina. The rejoicing over this reunion ('Riconosci in questo amplesso'), not shared by the baffled Count, is interrupted by Susanna with the money to pay off Marcellina. Seeing him in the embrace of her rival, she slaps his face, but the necessary explanations soon bring general contentment. The Countess comes in alone to sing of her hope of regaining her husband's love ('E Susanna non vien! . . . Dove sono . . .') and then to dictate to Susanna a letter of assignation to the Count ('Che soave zeffiretto'). The village girls bring her flowers. Cherubino, who has joined them in disguise, is unmasked by Antonio and the Count. Nevertheless the wedding celebrations commence. Figaro is amused to see the Count pricking himself on a pin which had sealed a letter of assignation.

Act IV The garden that night, with various arbours and pavilions. Barbarina is desperately looking for the pin the Count had given her to return to Susanna in acknowledgement of their rendezvous. Figaro wheedles this out of the innocent creature and gives way to his despair at being cuckolded on his wedding night. After Marcellina and Basilio each sing a superfluous aria (normally cut), Figaro has his diatribe about women ('Tutto è disposto . . . Aprite un po' quegl'occhi'), then hides to spy on Susanna. She sings of the coming joy of love ('Giunse alfin il momento . . . Deh vieni non tardar') but poor Figaro does not realize that she is thinking of him, not of the Count. The moment of the Count's assignation is at hand: the plot has been modified in that the Countess will herself take Susanna's place, disguised as Susanna, while Susanna is disguised as her mistress. The amorous Cherubino opens the finale, pleased to find Susanna, as he thinks, in the dark: he tries to kiss her, but in the confusion it is the Count who gets the kiss and Figaro who receives the Count's answering slap. When the Count's seduction of the supposed Susanna is getting too close for comfort, Figaro chases them off. He eventually recognizes Susanna's voice beneath her disguise and the injustice of his suspicions. He teases her for a while by pretending to declare his love to the 'Countess' and receives another slap for his pains. They make peace and prepare to tease the Count, as Figaro flings himself down before Susanna to declare his love for 'Milady'. The Count calls the whole establishment to witness this outrageous betrayal by his wife and his servant. He is deaf to universal pleas for mercy, until at last the Countess appears, in her disguise as Susanna, and he realizes that it is he who must ask forgiveness. She grants it. There is serene happiness, which explodes into great rejoicing.

Though seven years older than the composer, Lorenzo da Ponte had written only three libretti compared to Mozart's 12 operas. Mozart doubtless played a leading role in their collaboration, but da Ponte was able to understand and satisfy his requirements to a very high degree. The fluidity and freedom of his metres and line lengths, which could blur the transition from recitative to aria, fitted in with Mozart's preference for arias of action rather than contemplation – Susanna's Act II aria ('Venite . . . inginocchiatevi') is sung while dressing Cherubino, her Act IV aria ('Deh vieni non tardar') is designed to tease the eavesdropping Figaro and Mozart's music follows the words and their meanings, not merely the metre of the verse.

Time and time again Mozart's music humanizes the farce of the libretto. *Figaro* stands out, even in Mozart's work, for having the greatest human warmth and the most natural characters, especially in the central figures. Instead of operatic conventions and vain repetitions we get something like a stream of consciousness. In 'Deh vieni non tardar', for example, the melody winds on rhapsodically, while just enough feeling of formal unity is given by the siciliana rhythm and the recapitulation of the wood-wind phrases. Susanna's opening phrase, a sort of quote from 'Che Susanna ella stessa si fè' in the opening duet, is recapitulated, but in disguise – a third higher. When she changes from teasing the jealous, eavesdropping Figaro to real emotion, the serenade-like *pizzicato* of the violins changes magic-ally to *con arco* sighs, the same accompanying figure Mozart used for the beginning of the *Lacrymosa* in the *Requiem* six years later, the last note he ever wrote down. The letter duet, an exquisite piece in which the woodwind illustrate the breezes of the nocturnal tryst, treats the dictating of the letter absolutely realistically with suitable pauses for Susanna to write, then follows this with the two women reading the letter together and overlapping in their eagerness. Da Ponte once wrote that a finale should be a complete little opera in itself. The sextet in Act III, reputedly a great favourite of Mozart's, could stand alone as the epitome of Mozartean opera buffa. The action is, of course, a parody of the sentimental pieces of the time, in which long-lost parents and children discover each other (and still a subject for parody in Oscar Wilde's *The Importance of Being Earnest*). There is a long calm opening over a pedal for the quiet joy of the reunited family. Susanna arrives with the ransom money, not at all overjoyed at what she sees – the music has moved to the dominant and agitated violins accompany her. She relieves her feelings by slapping Figaro, but she and the Count, whose plans have been spoiled by the discovery, continue to sing in angry dotted rhythms against the serenity of the others. When we arrive at the recapitulation, back in F major, Marcellina has an entirely new text to explain things to Susanna and therefore new music – which Mozart elegantly combines with the original opening melody now played by the woodwind. The next section, in which the incredulous Susanna is introduced over and over again to Figaro's new parents, is the most delicious passage in all comic opera. But the miracle is still to come when the laughter dissolves in tears of happiness, as Susanna's voice lightly runs over the *sotto voce* accompaniment of the others (Mozart crossed out his original idea of doubling her line with flute and bassoon). In the end the Count and his henchman, Don Curzio, provide a mildly threatening movement, in case we should lapse into sheer blissful sentimentality.

These are just three examples, briefly described, but every piece in *Figaro* deserves more, from the magic of the overture (with no musical quotation from the opera, but instead an embodiment of its feeling of excitement and tenderness) to the finale of Act IV. Earlier operas had placed the *dénouement* in an extra act after the second big finale. Mozart and da Ponte accomplish everything within the great Act IV finale – the mounting excitement and gathering of all the characters as well as both reconciliations, Figaro's with Susanna in a playful tone, the Count's with the Countess in a still moment of the utmost beauty.

RECORDINGS 1. Bonney, Auger, Nafé, Hagegård, Salomaa, Drottningholm Court Opera Ch and O, Östman, L'Oiseau Lyre, 1987; 2. Moffo, Schwarzkopf, Cossotto, Waechter, Taddei, Philharmonia Ch and O, Giulini, EMI, 1959; 3. Gueden, Della Casa, Danco, Poell, Siepi, Vienna State Opera Ch and Vienna PO, E. Kleiber, Decca, 1955: these three performances are among the best in recordings of Mozart opera. The period-instrument Östman suggests the intimate intrigues and machinations of a small household in a quicksilver, seemingly spontaneous reading, intimately recorded. The Giulini, sumptuously cast, is fiercely Italianate in character (it omits the arias for Marcellina and Basilio).

The Kleiber represents the tradition of Viennese ensemble at its best under a superb conductor. [A.B.]

EDITIONS f.ss., *MW*, V, no. 17; *NMA*, II:5/xvi; v.ss., Bärenreiter, 1976; Ricordi, *rp*, 1980

Il dissoluto punito, o sia Il Don Giovanni

The Rake Punished, or Don Giovanni

Dramma giocoso in two acts, K. 527 (2h 45m)
Libretto by Lorenzo da Ponte, after Giovanni Bertati's opera *Don Giovanni Tenorio, o sia Il convitato di pietra* (1787)
Composed April–October 1787
PREMIERES 29 October 1787, Gräflich Nostitzsches Nationaltheater, Prague; 7 May 1788, Burgtheater, Vienna; UK: 12 April 1817, His Majesty's Theatre, Haymarket, London; US: 7 November 1817, Park Theater, New York
CAST Don Giovanni *b* or *bar*, Il Commendatore *b*, Donna Anna *s*, Don Ottavio *t*, Donna Elvira *s*, Leporello *b*, Zerlina *s*, Masetto *b*; *satb* chorus of peasants, *tb* chorus of servants; peasants, servants, musicians and ministers of justice *silent*; offstage: *b* chorus of demons
ORCHESTRATION 2 fl, 2 ob, 2 cl, 2 bsn, 2 hn, 2 tpt, 3 trbn, timp, mandolin, str, cont; onstage: 3 bands (Act I): (1) 2 ob, 2 hn, str; (2) vn, db; (3) vn, db (wind-band music in Act II played by members of the orchestra; originally they remained in the pit)

The extraordinary amount of works of one sort or another about Don Juan must surely exceed the alleged number of his conquests. Faust and Don Juan were created by the Counter-Reformation as warnings against exceeding the bounds set for man – Faust in seeking metaphysical knowledge and power, Juan for living in unbounded sensuality without any spiritual belief. Both are finally overtaken by divine retribution. Juan first appears in *El burlador de Sevilla*, a play written in 1630 by a monk, Tirso de Molina. But the play is much more than a pious text. The story was rewritten many times before (and after) Mozart's opera, most notably as a play by Molière and as a ballet by Gluck. By the late 18th century it had become little more than an effective puppet show: the two elements that were common to all versions make for good entertainment – a libertine who seduces innumerable ladies and a statue that gets up and comes to dinner. There were at least two new operas on the subject in 1787 before Mozart's: one was seen in Rome by Goethe, who noticed the universal delight in the farcical representation of the story; the other, by Gazzaniga, performed in Venice in January 1787, became the direct model for da Ponte and, to some extent, for Mozart. There are some striking similarities in the text and sometimes even in the music, such as the use of 'Tafelmusik' for the supper scene.

The death of the Commendatore and his revenge are the essential parts of the opera. 'The rest is a parenthesis, the most beautiful and delightful parenthesis in the history of opera but still a parenthesis' (Luigi Dallapiccola). Gazzaniga's opera was based on these essentials but it was only in one act: da Ponte and Mozart had to fill out the time between the Commendatore's death and his reappearance in the form of the avenging statue. Apart from a call to repentance and a supernatural warning, which already occur in Tirso's play, no events have any real bearing on the dénouement,

*Alabaster relief (1789) of Don Giovanni and the
Commendatore's statue in the graveyard*

since Don Juan is not defeated by any human revenge or pursuit. The rest of the opera is therefore filled with the opera-buffa game of disguises.

Da Ponte later claimed that Mozart had wanted to write a serious opera and had to be persuaded to add the comedy. Mozart probably never considered if he was writing about crime and punishment or divine vengeance. After all, most of his operas had concluded in the theatrical convention of divine or imperial clemency; this time the divine intervention was simply of the opposite sort. But he must have seen this as his first opportunity since *Idomeneo* to write serious, heroic, tragic operatic music. Mozart is inevitably compared to Shakespeare, not least for the mingling of laughter and tears, but while Shakespeare used the powerful close juxtaposition of tragedy and comedy, he surely has no parallel to *Don Giovanni*'s last scene in which the great heroic duet with the Commendatore is not merely followed, as Duncan's murder is, but actually accompanied by the patter of the buffoon.

Mozart had enjoyed witnessing the triumph of *Figaro* during his first visit to Prague in January 1787. Only the Bohemian audience seems to have understood what Mozart was, as we believe we do today. Bondini, the manager of the Italian company, commissioned *Don Giovanni* and may have even proposed the subject. *Don Giovanni* proved to be a triumph and Mozart was cheered on entering and leaving the pit. Vienna saw it the following May with a number of changes demanded by the new cast. The ever exigent Caterina Cavalieri as Elvira got an extra *scena ed aria* ('Mi tradì'); Benucci as Leporello lost his aria but got a farcical duet with Zerlina ('Per queste tue manine'), which is now seldom performed; Ottavio had his aria changed for one with less coloratura ('Dalla sua pace'). Mozart made some other changes including cutting the Anna–Ottavio duet in the final scene, but there is no conclusive evidence that he authorized the cut of the entire final scene, which became the rule from the 1790s until the 1920s.

SYNOPSIS

Act I A garden by night. Leporello is complaining that he has to keep watch in all weathers while his master is enjoying himself indoors ('Notte e giorno faticar'), when Don Giovanni rushes out, trying to escape and hide his face from a furious Donna Anna. Her father, the Commendatore, enters with a sword: Don Giovanni kills him in a duel and escapes with Leporello. Anna returns with her betrothed, Don Ottavio; distraught at finding her father dead, she swears vengeance ('Fuggi, crudele, fuggi!'). A street scene as dawn breaks. An unknown beauty accosted by Don Giovanni ('Ah chi mi dice mai') turns out to be Donna Elvira, whom he had cozened into a pretended marriage and abandoned. Leporello tells her of his master's 2065 conquests and of his technique ('Madamina, il catalogo è questo'). Don Giovanni spies a new prey in the peasant Zerlina, who appears with her bridegroom, Masetto. Masetto is removed by Leporello and Don Giovanni has just persuaded Zerlina to follow him to his pavilion ('Là ci darem la mano') when Elvira returns to warn her off ('Ah fuggi il traditor'). She warns Anna and Ottavio too ('Non ti fidar, o misera'), but Giovanni brushes off her accusations as a sign of madness. As he leaves, Donna Anna recognizes Don Giovanni as her nocturnal assailant: she describes the attempted rape to the horrified Ottavio and implores him to join in her vengeance ('Or sai chi l'onore'). (Ottavio then usually sings 'Dalla sua pace', added for the Vienna revival.) Don Giovanni gives Leporello instructions about his party for the peasants ('Fin ch'han dal vino'). In a garden on Don Giovanni's estate, Zerlina, reproached for her flirtation with the noble stranger, mollifies Masetto ('Batti, batti, o bel Masetto'), but as soon as Giovanni appears, she grows weak again (finale, Act I), only being saved by Masetto's presence. Donna Anna, Donna Elvira and Don Ottavio, arriving masked to pursue their vengeance, are invited to join the ball. In Don Giovanni's brightly lit ballroom with servants and peasants, the masked strangers are welcomed and the three orchestras strike up: Anna and Ottavio dance the stately minuet, Zerlina and Giovanni the middle-class contredanse, and Leporello whisks Masetto off in a rustic German dance. All is confusion when Zerlina's scream is heard offstage. She rushes in distraught and Giovanni tries to pin the blame on Leporello. The guests now unmask to tell Don Giovanni that he has been found out and that vengeance is nigh.

Act II A street. Leporello cannot stand his job any longer and tells his master he is leaving him ('Eh via buffone'). Giovanni persuades him with money but vehemently rejects the notion of giving up his mission to make all women happy. At the moment he is thinking of Elvira's maid, but it is Elvira herself who appears on the balcony. He plans to put on Leporello's clothes and seduce the maid, while Leporello in his master's clothes is to keep Elvira out of the way. When he speaks to Elvira of his love, she all too soon falls for his honeyed words again ('Ah taci ingiusto core'), while Leporello is half amused, half pitying. Don Giovanni's plan works, but he has hardly sung his serenade ('Deh vieni alla finestra') when Masetto enters with a band of peasants intending to kill Don Giovanni. The Don, disguised as Leporello, gives Masetto directions on how to find the evil-doer ('Metà di voi qua vadano') and then, getting him on his own, beats him up mercilessly. Zerlina finds Masetto and comforts him ('Vedrai, carino'). In a dark courtyard before Donna Anna's house, Leporello is tired of the amorous Elvira ('Sola, sola in buio loco'), but just as he tries to escape, Donna Anna and Don Ottavio enter with servants bearing torches and Zerlina and Masetto come in through another door. They think they have cornered Don Giovanni at last. Ottavio is quite ready to kill him. Elvira pleads for the life of 'her husband', but the others agree that he must die. At this point Leporello reveals himself and whines for mercy. When he escapes, Don Ottavio decides that it is time to call the police ('Il mio tesoro'). (At this point Elvira's scene and aria ('Mi tradì'), composed for the Vienna revival, is usually inserted.) Meanwhile Don Giovanni has been enjoying himself seducing Leporello's wife. When he laughingly boasts of this to Leporello, whom he meets in the cemetery, it is not only Leporello who is shocked: a mysterious voice tells him that his laughter will be silenced before morning. They find the statue of the Commendatore with the inscription that he waits to be avenged. Don Giovanni orders the terrified Leporello to invite the statue to supper ('O statua gentilissima'). Donna Anna tells Don Ottavio that she loves him but cannot think of marriage during her sorrow. The finale to Act II takes place in Don Giovanni's dining room. He is eating alone, waited on by Leporello and enjoying a wind band playing an opera pot-pourri, when Elvira bursts in to make one more attempt to reclaim him from his wicked life. He answers her scornfully; she runs out and is immediately heard sceaming frantically. Leporello goes to investigate and screams too; he returns to report breathlessly that the statue is arriving. Don Giovanni himself opens the door to his stone guest, who bids him amend his life and repent. He refuses but in spite of Leporello's terrified entreaties, he accepts the statue's return invitation. As he takes its hand, his strength drains from him. The Commendatore leaves, but an invisible chorus of demons warns Don Giovanni of his coming perdition. With a terrible scream he is swallowed up amidst flames. Leporello describes these events to the others. They resolve to get on with their own lives: Don Ottavio to woo Donna Anna once again, Elvira to enter a convent, Leporello to seek a new master, Zerlina and Masetto to have a jolly dinner. The opera ends with the moral that sinners meet with their just reward.

The opening *andante* of the overture is taken almost entirely from the scene in which the statue confronts Don Giovanni: thus Mozart daringly anticipates the crucial event of the opera, though without the trombones and without the chord of the diminished seventh. Mozart used more ensembles than his contemporaries: *Don Giovanni* in its original form has over 80 minutes of ensemble against less than 40 of arias, and even the arias are ensembles in that each one is sung to somebody or overheard.

Within the vast dramatic range of *Don Giovanni* Mozart still adheres to a semblance of the opera-buffa types. Leporello and the peasants are clearly in the buffa category; Donna Anna and Don Ottavio in the seria, hence her rondo 'Non mi dir' before the Act II finale, suitable to an opera-seria heroine. Donna Elvira has to be *mezzo carattere* (in between): for all her true pathos, she is always being made fun of by Giovanni or Leporello (except in the Vienna addition 'Mi tradì', preceded by the most beautiful of all Mozart's *recitativi accompagnati*, but clearly alien to the original concept).

What of the Don himself? He is everything and nothing. He dominates every moment of the opera, even when not on stage, but he subordinates his own character to that of the others – he adopts Anna's music at their first appearance, then the Commendatore's when the challenges are exchanged, he falls into peasant 2/4 and 6/8 rhythms to seduce Zerlina and into Leporello's buffo terseness when persuading him to stay in his service. Apart from the brief 'Fin ch'han dal vino', the epitome of his energy (he only once draws breath in it), he does not have a real aria of his own. The 21-year-old Luigi Bassi, who created the role, is said to have complained about it. What a *Credo* he might have sung after Leporello's well-meant suggestion that he should 'lasciar le donne'! But why should he waste time (that could be much better spent) on revealing himself, when his servant can do it for him, as in 'Madamina'? In his last scene he turns into a hero, dramatically and musically, defying heaven and hell as no other operatic hero ever did.

RECORDINGS 1. Auger, D. Jones, Bonney, van der Meel, Hagegård, Cachemaille, Terfel, Sigmundsson, Drottningholm Court Theatre Ch and O, Östman, L'Oiseau-Lyre, 1989; 2. Sutherland, Schwarzkopf, Sciutti, Alva, Waechter, Taddei, Cappuccilli, Frick, Philharmonia Ch and O, Giulini, EMI, 1959; 3. Arroyo, Te Kanawa, Freni, Burrows, Wixell, Ganzarolli, van Allan, Roni, Royal Opera House Ch and O, Davis, Philips, 1973; 4. Bampton, Novotná, Sayão, Kullmann, Pinza, Kipnis, Harrell, Cordon, Metropolitan Ch and O, Walter, Music and Arts, 1942; 5. Souez, Helletsgruber, Mildmay, von Pataky, Brownlee, Baccaloni, Henderson, Franklin, Glyndebourne Opera Ch and O, Busch, EMI, 1936: there is a veritable cornucopia of interpretations here. For a period-style account, the Östman will do well, though it isn't the most convincingly cast. The Giulini is dynamically conducted and generously cast. Colin Davis's is a vital, middle-of-the-road reading. The two historic, live performances enshrine classic interpretations, forward-moving and highly dramatic, even daemonic in character. The Met discs are also a reminder of Ezio Pinza's famous Giovanni. [A.B.]
VIDEO Gruberova, Murray, Mentzer, Araiza, Allen, Desderi, De Carolis, Kopcák, Ch and O of La Scala, Milan, Muti, Castle, 1989
EDITIONS f.ss., *MW*, V, no. 18; *NMA*, II:5/xvii, 1968; v.ss., Bärenreiter, 1975; Ricordi, 1959

Così fan tutte, ossia La scuola degli amanti

Thus Do All Women, or The School for Lovers
Dramma giocoso in two acts, K. 588 (3h)
Libretto by Lorenzo da Ponte

Composed September–December 1789
PREMIERES 26 January 1790, Burgtheater, Vienna; UK:
9 May 1811, His Majesty's Theatre, London; US: 24 March
1922, Metropolitan, New York
CAST Fiordiligi *s*, Dorabella *s* or *ms*, Ferrando *t*, Guglielmo
b, Despina *s*, Alfonso *b*; *satb* chorus of soldiers, serenaders;
silent: servants, musicians
ORCHESTRATION 2 fl, 2 ob, 2 cl/basset cl, 2 bsn, 2 hn, 2 tpt,
timp, str, cont; onstage: sd

Nothing is known about the creation of *Così* except
that the commission is supposed to have followed the
successful revival of *Figaro* in Vienna beginning on
29 August 1789. The performances of *Così* were
interrupted by the death of the Emperor Joseph II
on 20 February 1790, but there was a second run
from June to August. Mozart entered the Guglielmo
aria 'Rivolgete a lui lo sguardo' (K. 584), composed
for Benucci, into his thematic index in advance of the
rest, but then replaced it in the opera with the
shorter and more apt 'Non siate ritrosi'.

Through most of the 19th century and a good part
of the 20th *Così fan tutte* was regarded as being
immoral and frivolous, utterly unworthy of Mozart's
genius. Even George Bernard Shaw, one of the few
people a hundred years ago to have admired Mozart
much as we do today, wrote of its libretto: 'The
despised book after all has some fun in it, though
quite as good plays have often been improvised in
ten minutes in a drawing room at charades or dumb
crambo.' The story of a lover testing the fidelity of
his wife or bride by approaching her in a disguise or
magical transformation goes back through Ariosto to
Ovid. In our own time it has become as popular as
Mozart's other greatest operas, because we believe
that the psychological truths beneath the play are
revealed by Mozart's music. It just steers clear of the
rocky side of 18th-century tales of wagers such as *Les
liaisons dangereuses* with its sensual cruelty, but it
certainly does not leave the audience with a happy
glow. One asks, will any of the four ever feel so
deeply again? Mozart, who was responsible for
deriving the title from the text (da Ponte referred to
the opera as the 'school for lovers'), might equally
well have called it *Così fan tutti*, but, though he can
enter fully into female emotions, his obsessive
insistence on repeating the multiplicity of women's
deceptions in Guglielmo's 'Donne mie, la fate a tanti,
a tanti, a tanti', etc., looks like personal participation.

SYNOPSIS

Act I In a coffee-house two young officers are
boasting about the fidelity of their betrothed. Their
sceptical friend, Don Alfonso, wagers 100 zecchini
that Dorabella and Fiordiligi would be no more
faithful than any other woman, if put to the test.
Ferrando and Guglielmo indignantly accept the bet
and the condition to obey Alfonso's orders all day. In
a garden by the seashore the daydreams of Dorabella
and Fiordiligi ('Ah guarda, sorella') are interrupted
by Alfonso's desperate report that Ferrando and
Guglielmo have been ordered to depart at once to
the wars. They come to take a tender leave ('Sento,
oddio, che questo piede'): everybody is overcome by
emotion ('Di, scrivermi ogni giorno'). The women

and Alfonso wave to the departing ship ('Soave sia
il vento'). A room in the house of the sisters.
Dorabella's vehement sorrow ('Smanie implacabili')
is brushed aside by the maid, Despina: do as soldiers
do, she advises them, and find yourselves new lovers
('In uomini, in soldati'). Alfonso bribes her to help
him to introduce his two Albanian friends to the
sisters. Despina does not recognize them ('Alla bella
Despinetta'), but they are, of course, Ferrando and
Guglielmo in disguise and under oath to Alfonso to
woo the sisters but with new partners – Ferrando,
engaged to Dorabella, is to pursue Fiordiligi and
Guglielmo Dorabella. They are reassured by the
women's indignant reaction to the strangers,
especially by Fiordiligi's 'Come scoglio', but their
satisfaction in these proofs of constancy is beginning
to be mingled with the delights of play-acting and the
chase. Ferrando, especially, is intoxicated by love
('Un'aura amorosa'). A more dangerous attack is
made in the Act I finale: distraught at the coldness
of the strong-hearted maidens, the Albanians gulp
poison and drop lifeless at their feet. Despina begs
the women to revive them with affection, and then
reappears disguised as a doctor to restore the
patients to life with an enormous magnet according
to the latest principles of Dr Mesmer. They rise
dazedly and beg for a kiss to complete the cure, but
the sisters still just manage to resist.

Act II The women hardly need Despina's
encouragement ('Una donna a quindici anni') for
they have already decided that there cannot be
much harm in a mild flirtation ('Prenderò quel
brunettino'). In the garden by the shore the
Albanians woo them with a serenade ('Secondate,
aurette amiche'). Now that Fiordiligi and Dorabella
are at last in a romantic mood, the men are overcome
by bashfulness. But Alfonso and Despina persuade
the two pairs to link hands and to stroll off
in different directions ('La mano a me date').
Guglielmo, outrageously overacting the part of the
forlorn lover, finds Dorabella succumbing ('Il core vi
dono'), and they exchange their lockets as tokens
of love. Ferrando, seeing Fiordiligi's agitation,
expresses hope of success in an aria ('Ah, lo veggio'),
which is normally omitted. When he has left,
Fiordiligi admits to herself the tremors of her heart
('Per pietà'). The men compare notes: Guglielmo
confesses smugly that he has found Dorabella less
pure than the driven snow and adds some cynical
observations about women ('Donne mie, la fate a
tanti'). Alfonso takes advantage of Ferrando's
despair ('Tradito, schernito') to taunt him into
making one more supreme attempt on Fiordiligi's
honour. Dorabella is altogether happier now that she
has given in and tries to persuade Fiordiligi to follow
her example ('E amore un ladroncello'), but her
sister is planning to escape temptation by seeking her
Guglielmo on the battlefield disguised in one of his
own uniforms. There she will be safe in his arms. But
Ferrando enters at that moment and it is into his
arms that she falls ('Fra gli amplessi'). Alfonso's bet
is won: the two officers have to agree that women are
all the same, but the finale is needed for the written
proof. A grand room brightly lit, with dinner laid,

Playbill for the premiere of Così fan tutte *(Vienna, 1790)*

etc. The wedding celebrations include a chorus and a toast sung in canon. The versatile Despina impersonates a notary to perform the mock marriage. The ink is not dry on the contract before the sound of a familiar military march freezes the ladies' blood. The Albanians flee in terror and soon Ferrando and Guglielmo return from what was clearly a very short war. But what is a notary doing here and whose is this contract of marriage? They rush off in pursuit of the Albanians and return to confront the terrified women in the costumes of the Albanians and with the whole truth. Guglielmo taunts Dorabella with the melody that had so idyllically united them. The officers pull Despina's ears to the trill of the magnetic doctor and pay Alfonso's wager. Fiordiligi and Dorabella beg to be forgiven and are soon reunited with their original lovers.

As so often in Mozart, the whole opera expresses a comic–serious duality. The division is not always clear, for the sheer beauty of the music hits the listener at a deeper emotional level than the libretto would warrant. The overture provides just the right introduction: after the shortest of *andantes* (with the five chords to which the men later sing the words 'Così fan tutte') there is a *presto*, entirely constructed of single-bar phrases of the type that usually links more important themes, music of intrigue and laughter behind one's back with nothing lyrical or sweet about it. Da Ponte's originality was in taking the old plot of the disguised husband or lover testing the fidelity of his own wife or sweetheart and doubling it, providing, as it were, two diagonal seductions. The music of Act I underlines the farcical element of the schematic nature of the plot, for the men and the women tend to move in pairs like puppets – a reminiscence of the popular Casti–Salieri *Grotta di Trofonio* of 1785. The ensemble writing postulated by the double action demanded a taut style based less on melody than on short motifs – for which the overture has prepared us. In 'Alla bella Despinetta', the first piece to bring all six characters on stage, the men and the women move in pairs (singing in thirds); Despina is generally linked to Alfonso though she sometimes supports the men's pleas. Musically, the whole piece is a pattern of short clichés. The effect is strangely electrifying and exactly what the situation calls for.

The despair of Dorabella and Fiordiligi explodes in two arias parodying opera seria. Despina predictably propounds the conventional cynicism of the soubrette, though with many a tender musical thought. Mozart cannot resist striking at us with moments of piercing beauty – in the burlesque leave-taking quintet 'Di scrivermi', accompanied by a laughing Don Alfonso, or in the trio 'Soave sia il vento', one of his irresistible E major 'nature' pieces. In the Act I finale the C minor 'death' scene of the poisoned lovers, with a comic bassoon to allay any fears, is followed, after the opera-buffa business of Despina disguised as the doctor, by a reawakening of the men which would be blissful enough to serve for Adam and Eve waking in Paradise.

Abert for once missed the point when he regretted that Mozart had not continued in Act II with another delicious ensemble to complete both seductions instead of giving us a string of arias and duets. Mozart and da Ponte realized that the game became serious only in a one-to-one confrontation. So do Ferrando and Guglielmo when first left alone with their victims. Moreover, it is time to see each one as an individual. Guglielmo uses a Don Giovanni touch to get Dorabella at his mercy and still to have time for the aside, 'Poor old Ferrando!' In his total confusion the less cynical Ferrando first gives vent to the rather artificial rondo 'Ah lo veggio' on his hopes about Fiordiligi, then to the more heartfelt 'Tradito, schernito' on his despair about Dorabella. The deepest feelings are expressed by the (relatively) constant Fiordiligi in her rondo 'Per pietà', a wonderful piece with obbligato horns and woodwind, the most moving aria in the opera. The horn, usually the mocker of cuckolds, speaks of fidelity. The duet 'Fra gli amplessi', in which the music convinces us that Fiordiligi's sincerity wins Ferrando from his play-acting to true love, is the climax of the serious side of the opera. But there is one more astonishing moment during the wedding celebration in the Act II finale – 'E nel tuo, nel mio bicchiero', the toast to forgetfulness of the past. The melody is very similar to the moving 'Volgi a me' in which Ferrando had found his true voice in the duet just before, but now (a semitone lower) sung as a canon, the only one in Mozart's operas, to intensify the beauty. When it is Guglielmo's turn to join in he cannot hide his disgust at his recent betrayal by Fiordiligi's capitulation (nor can he manage the higher reaches of the melody), so he merely mutters that he wishes the drink was poison while Fiordiligi sings his line. An enharmonic change abruptly returns us to the world of farce with the appearance of Despina in the guise of the notary, then of the returning warriors humiliating the women and finally pardoning them. It is a shock to go back to stylized symmetry after all those deeper emotions have been invoked.

RECORDINGS 1. Yakar, Nafé, Resick, Winbergh, Krause, Feller, Drottningholm Court Opera Ch and O, Östman, L'Oiseau-Lyre, 1984; 2. Schwarzkopf, Ludwig Steffek, Kraus, Taddei, Berry, Philharmonia Ch and O, Böhm, EMI, 1962; 3. Souez, Helletsgruber, Eisinger, Nash, Domgraf-Fassbaender, Brownlee, Glyndebourne Opera Ch and O, Busch, EMI, 1935; 4. Mattila, von Otter, Szmytka, Araiza, Allen, van Dam, Ambrosian Ch, Academy of St Martin, Marriner, Philips, 1991: the Böhm performance, expertly recorded by Walter Legge, has been the yardstick by which other performances have long been judged. It remains a lovable, warm-hearted reading, sensuously sung, firmly conducted. The earlier Busch version pioneered the revival of the opera and it is a reminder of what Busch and his pre-war Glyndebourne ensemble achieved in Mozart. But neither of these performances is complete. For a modern, wholly integral recording the Marriner is securely paced and full of life, while the Östman, swift and intimate, is a welcome alternative for those wanting period-instrument authenticity [A.B.]
VIDEO Dessi, Ziegler, Scarabeli, Kundák, Corbelli, Desderi, Ch and O of La Scala, Milan, Muti, Castle, 1990: Michael Hampe's intelligent, 'straight' staging, splendidly sung and conducted [A.B.]
EDITIONS f.ss., MW, V, no. 19; NMA, II:5/xviii, 1991; v.s., Ricordi, 1961

Die Zauberflöte

The Magic Flute
Eine Deutsche Oper in two acts, K. 620 (2h 30m)
Libretto by Emanuel Schikaneder
Composed April–July and September 1791
PREMIERES 30 September 1791, Freihaustheater auf der Wieden, Vienna; UK: 6 June 1811, His Majesty's Theatre, Haymarket, London; US: 17 April 1833, Park Theater, New York
CAST Sarastro *b*, Tamino *t*, Speaker *b*, First Priest *b*, Second Priest *t*, Third Priest *spoken role*, Queen of the Night *s*, Pamina *s*, First Lady *s*, Second Lady *s*, Third Lady *s* or *a*, 3 Boys *3 s*, Old Woman (Papagena *s*), Papageno *b* or *bar*, Monostatos *t*, First Man in Armour *t*, Second Man in Armour *b*, 3 slaves *spoken roles*; *satb* chorus of priests, slaves, Sarastro's subjects
ORCHESTRATION 2 fl/picc, 2 ob, 2 cl/2 basset hn, 2 bsn, 2 hn, 2 tpt, 3 trbn, timp, str, 'istromento d'acciaio' (glock)

The premiere of *Die Zauberflöte*, after which Mozart only had another 10 weeks to live, was followed by the most successful run of any of his operas, 197 performances in two years. In his first opera for a popular rather than a court theatre, all the 18th-century irony about the war of the sexes was replaced by an exotic fairy-tale with mystical elements, features of the new German Romanticism. The chivalric quest of the outset turns into a philosophical search for love and virtue. Considering the commonly held view that it is no more than a bungled children's story, the sources of the libretto are surprisingly wide and complex. The opening scene, with the rescue by the three ladies and the appearance of a strange semi-human being, is derived from the 12th-century *Yvain, ou Le chevalier au Lion* by Chrétien de Troyes, then recently translated into German; magic instruments had appeared in Wranitzky's singspiel *Oberon* (1789); the three boys and a model for Monostatos came into *Lulu, oder Die Zauberflöte*, one of the stories in Wieland's collection *Dschinnistan* (1786); another singspiel *Der Fagottist, oder Die Zauberzither* (1791) by Wenzel Müller is also based on one of these stories but with comic additions; Jean Terrasson's recently translated novel *Sethos* (1731), with its ancient Egyptian setting, provided the basis for the trials; the essay on the *Mysteries of the Freemasons* (1784) by one of Austria's most eminent Masons, Ignaz von Born, suggested the words of Sarastro.

Emanuel Schikaneder, since playing Hamlet at 25, had also been singer, playwright, composer, producer and manager. He had first met Mozart in Salzburg in 1780 and they seem to have had a friendly relationship. He wrote later that he and Mozart had thought *Die Zauberflöte* through very busily together. In spite of the naïve versification and some poor jokes the whole libretto has a natural strength in its very illogicality and a mysterious quality that

Emanuel Schikaneder as Papageno, from the original libretto for Die Zauberflöte, *published in 1791*

was perceived by Goethe. Its great superiority over Schikaneder's other works is evidence for Mozart's contribution. Like Mozart, he had been a Freemason. In fact, Mozart continued to be one despite Joseph II's stringent restriction of the order in 1786, and seems to have had a devout belief in the principles of the order as well as obviously enjoying the possibility it offered of mixing with the aristocracy and the intelligentsia on equal terms. The opera made no secret of the fact that the Temple's brotherhood represented the Freemasons, as the libretto had a frontispiece full of Masonic symbols. This glorification of Masonry could not have won the opera any popularity, least of all in official circles. The general public enjoyed the stage tricks, the comedy and the music, but Mozart must have had a purpose in courageously bringing in Freemasonry:

it was surely to defend it through allegory. The audience shares Tamino's bewilderment in finding Sarastro no ogre at all but wise and virtuous, while the Queen changes from apparently good to clearly evil. It has even been suggested that the plot must have been altered when Schikaneder and Mozart arrived at the Act I finale. The moral he intended is surely: do not believe what the detractors of the order say, for it is they that turn out to be evil when you look for yourself. Every element in the music of *Die Zauberflöte* and, indeed, in Mozart's late instrumental music, has been described in terms of Freemasonic symbolism – especially the three chords, the key of E♭ with its three flat signs, bound pairs of notes, counterpoint, clarinets and basset horns – but as all these are present in a great deal of non-Masonic music, it is impossible to assess the precise influence of Freemasonry on his music.

It is notable in the masculine world of the time in general and of the Freemasons in particular, that Pamina increasingly takes on the central role, both in her suffering and when she leads Tamino through the fire and water. The three boys are a puzzle, since they were recommended as guides by the three ladies and then turn out to be ministers of goodness. They are not servants of the Temple, but rather forces of nature, the constellations that guide our paths, the voice of conscience which keeps us from suicide, the quiet reminder of what we really know. At the start of the finale to Act II they look forward to the end of superstition and the triumph of human wisdom.

Schikaneder gave Papageno – played by himself – the lion's share. The Tamino was another versatile man of the theatre, Benedikt Schack, a composer and a good musician, who could have played the flute on stage (if Mozart had allowed him the tiniest of breaths between singing and playing). The Queen was Mozart's sister-in-law, Josepha Hofer.

SYNOPSIS

Act I A rocky region. Prince Tamino is fleeing a huge serpent ('Zu Hilfe! Zu Hilfe!'). As he faints in terror three ladies appear and kill it. They reluctantly leave the handsome stranger to bring their Queen the news. As Tamino comes to, Papageno, a birdcatcher dressed up as a bird, appears ('Der Vogelfänger bin ich ja'). He claims to have throttled the serpent himself, but soon regrets his lie when the three ladies appear and padlock his mouth as punishment. They give Tamino a portrait of the Queen's daughter, Pamina, with which he instantly falls in love ('Dies Bildnis ist bezaubernd schön'). The scene changes, for the next aria only, to reveal the Queen of the Night enthroned among transparent stars. She promises Tamino her daughter's hand if he will rescue her from the demon who has kidnapped her ('O zittre nicht, mein lieber Sohn'). The ladies free Papageno but order him to accompany the prince on his dangerous quest. Tamino is given a magic flute and Papageno a magic set of bells. Three mysterious boys are to show them the way. In a splendid Egyptian room Pamina is being bullied by the lustful Moor, Monostatos. At that moment Papageno wanders in: the feathered man and the black man put the fear of the devil into each other, but Papageno remains to tell Pamina about Tamino's mission and his love for her, whereupon she falls in love with the prince without as much as seeing his picture. She and Papageno sing about love ('Bei Männern, welche Liebe fühlen'). Meanwhile Tamino, guided by the three boys, has come to a grove with three temples (finale Act I). An old Priest emerges from the central temple of wisdom to dissipate Tamino's hatred for Sarastro, the ruler who has imprisoned Pamina. A distant chorus reveals that she is still alive. Tamino plays his magic flute and wild beasts come out to enjoy the music. Hearing Papageno's pipes, he rushes out. A moment later Pamina and Papageno run through in their attempt to escape, but Monostatos gleefully captures them. Now it is Papageno's turn to try his magic instrument: Monostatos and all the slaves are bewitched by the music and march off singing happily. Sarastro arrives in his chariot drawn by lions. Pamina confesses that she fled because of Monostatos's importunities. Sarastro, too, loves her more than he should, but he recognizes that she loves another. At that moment Monostatos drags in his latest capture and thus Tamino and Pamina ecstatically behold each other for the first time. Sarastro orders the two strangers to be led to the Temple of Examination. The chorus praises his wisdom.

Act II A palm grove with pyramids. Sarastro and the assembled priests resolve to let Tamino undergo the trials for admission to the brotherhood. The gods have decided that Pamina is to be his wife. All join in a hymn ('O Isis und Osiris'). Amid thunder the scene changes to a temple court filled with broken pillars. Two priests lead in the candidates: Tamino, resolved to undergo all the trials, the first of which is to keep silent, and Papageno, caring only about food and drink and his hope of finding Papagena, the woman of his dreams. The three ladies try in vain to rally them back to the Queen ('Wie? Wie? Wie?'). In a garden where Pamina is asleep, the lustful Monostatos flees at the approach of the Queen, who orders her daughter to murder Sarastro ('Der Hölle Rache kocht in meinem Herzen'). Left alone in despair, Pamina is once more subjected to Monostatos's lewd propositions, but Sarastro drives him off and reassures her ('In diesen heil'gen Hallen'). In another hall Papageno breaks all the rules and chats to an old crone who tells him she is eighteen years and two minutes old and has a sweetheart named . . . Papageno. Before she can reveal her identity, she disappears at a thunderclap. The three boys remind him and Tamino to be steadfast ('Seid uns zum zweitenmal willkommen'). Pamina is heartbroken when Tamino will not speak to her ('Ach ich fühl's'). In the vault of the pyramids. After another hymn, Sarastro tells Pamina and Tamino that they must part but that they will meet again ('Soll ich dich, Teurer, nicht mehr sehn?'). A glass of wine is all that Papageno really asks of life: it instantly appears, but having drunk it, he is filled by thoughts of love ('Ein Mädchen oder Weibchen'). The old woman promptly reappears. Only after she

reveals that the alternative is eternal incarceration does Papageno promise her his hand. She immediately turns into Papagena, only to be whisked away. The finale to Act II opens in a garden with the three boys who save Pamina from her attempted suicide. The final trial is set between two large mountains, one a volcano, the other with a waterfall. Two men in black armour lead Tamino in and tell him that whoever walks this difficult path will be purified by fire, water, air and earth and that if he overcomes the fear of death, he will be worthy to be consecrated to the mysteries of Isis. He agrees to undergo the tests and is reunited with Pamina, who guides him through fire and water, protected by the magic flute. They are welcomed by the chorus in a brightly lit temple. Back in the garden it is now Papageno who is suicidal for lack of his Papagena. Just in time the three boys remind him of his magic bells, which bring Papagena to him with the prospect of domestic bliss. The Queen and her ladies, abetted by Monostatos, make a secret onslaught on the temple, but they are routed by storms, thunder and lightning. The stage is transformed into a sun. Sarastro receives Tamino and Pamina. Night has been dispersed. The chorus gives praise and thanks.

The overture's only direct quote is in the three chords before the development, which in the opera precede the trials of Act II, but the entire sublime amalgamation of sonata form and fugue is a metaphor for the opera's mingling of narrative with philosophy.

There are traditional ingredients in *Die Zauberflöte* – five strophic numbers (three of them for Papageno), derived from the singspiel, and opera-seria arias for the Queen, but now Mozart completed the revolutionary process begun in *Figaro*. Away with the vain repetition of words for the sake of the music! The musical form had to fit the text. In 'Dies Bildnis' Tamino is led, through admiration of Pamina's portrait (first subject) and the awakening of love (second subject in the dominant), to the thought of finding her (development ending on a chord of the dominant seventh). The thought is almost too much for him (a whole bar's rest). What would he do then? Well (although he is back in the tonic key), certainly not go back to mere admiration of a portrait, as sonata form would demand. The violins lead him on with a tender phrase, while he expresses with gradually increasing confidence his hopes of embracing Pamina. There is only a vestigial recapitulation of five bars of melody to suggest the musical form. Apart from formal considerations, there is an emotional effect in hearing a melody for the second time, never more so than in those quintessentially Mozartean moments when a melody first heard in the major returns in the minor. In 'Ach, ich fühl's' neither words nor music are recapitulated except Pamina's magical rising phrase 'meinem Herzen' which returns to the words 'so wird Ruhe', but now with the poignant sweetness of the B♭ major phrase turned to the heartbreaking sorrow of G minor. The orchestral coda of this aria seems to echo her cry of 'Sieh, Tamino', with the music fractured as though she was looking at him dazzled by tears. Mozart always maintains the harmonic pattern of sonata form or other forms: the Act I quintet is in rondo form harmonically, but the music is always new for the new events that occur, except for a few short returning phrases that give the hearer at least a suggestion of thematic form. This freedom, which is hinted at in *Figaro*, has now become universal.

A new freedom is apparent too in the finale to Act I. In this opera the finales are not scenes of mounting numbers of participants and excitement but a free expression of the words and the emotions hidden behind the words. Tamino's dialogue with the old priest goes freely from recitative to arioso, then to the distant chorus: in spite of the stern tone of their conversation, a gentle recurring phrase in the strings indicates that Tamino is drawn to the wisdom of the order. Later in the same finale the duet between Pamina and Sarastro offers another way in which the emotions are painted by the orchestra, which indicates heartbeats of different speed and intensity – Pamina's when she thinks of her mother, Sarastro's when he recognizes that she is not for him, as he had hoped, since she now loves another. The passage from recitative, to melody, and later in the next scene, to a chorus interjection, is performed with absolute freedom.

The finale to Act II contains the essence of the opera, four pieces so separate that they have even been performed in a different order. Between the scene in which Pamina is held back from suicide by the three boys and the one in which they perform the same service for Papageno is the heart of the opera – in which Tamino and Pamina undergo the ultimate tests. Mozart opens it with six solemn bars in C minor, then an old chorale melody sung by the two men in armour doubled by woodwind and trombones, all in octaves and accompanied by a four-part fugato on the strings, done with the mastery of Bach but with late 18th-century sensibility in the frequent appoggiaturas. It is one of the most overwhelming pieces in any opera, but there is more to come. After a delightfully perky *allegretto*, in which the two men in armour turn out to be good fellows after all and assure Tamino that Pamina is near and all will be well, comes the final, simple, exultant reunification – 'Tamino mine! What happiness!'/'Pamina mine! What happiness!' There is a very hesitant beginning by sustained horns and strings before the lovers speak again. This is the greatest of many moments which make *Die Zauberflöte* the most moving of all Mozart's operas.

The scoring is extremely simple, compared with the richness of *Idomeneo* or *Figaro*, but each piece has exactly the right orchestration – for example, no double-basses for the airborne three boys. There were various reasons for this simplicity, an orchestra less brilliant than that of the court theatre, the singspiel tradition and a less sophisticated audience, but it is a tendency shared with *La clemenza di Tito* and the instrumental works of 1791 – the concentration on essentials. The music of *Die Zauberflöte* becomes increasingly concentrated as the opera proceeds: from being quite indulgent about the not very relevant, though absolutely delightful palaver of the three ladies at the start, Mozart allows Tamino and Pamina a final duet after the completion of the trials of only two bars!

RECORDINGS   1. Jo, Ziesak, Heilmann, M. Kraus, Moll, Vienna State Opera Ch, Vienna PO, Solti, Decca, 1991; 2. Serra, Price, Schreier, Melbye, Moll, Leipzig Radio Ch, Dresden Staatskapelle, C. Davis, Philips, 1984 (also VIDEO Philips); 3. Hoch, Upshaw, Rolfe Johnson, Schmidt, Hauptmann, Schütz Ch of London, London Classical Players, Norrington, EMI, 1991; 4. Anderson, Hendricks, Hadley, Allen, Lloyd, Scottish Chamber Ch and O, Mackerras, Telarc, 1991: ideal performances have proved oddly elusive. The Davis is highly recommendable apart from the fact that the dialogue is spoken by a separate team of actors. As the Solti avoids that solecism and has a delightfully youthful aspect, it is probably just preferable though the cast is not as convincing all round as Davis's. Norrington's period-instrument reading hardly fulfilled expectations, being unevenly cast. The Mackerras, also unevenly cast, has some of the most convincing conducting ever recorded in this piece. Both the venerable Beecham version of 1938 and the fine 1964 Klemperer reading suffer from an absence of all dialogue. [A.B.]
VIDEO   Gruberova, Popp, Araiza, Brendel, Moll, Bavarian State Opera Ch and O, Sawallisch, Philips, 1983
EDITIONS   f.ss., *MW*, V, no. 20; *NMA*, II:5/xix, 1970; v.ss., Bärenreiter, 1970; Ricordi, 1959

La clemenza di Tito

The Clemency of Titus
Opera seria in two acts, K. 621 (2h 15m)
Libretto by Caterino Tommaso Mazzolà, after Pietro Metastasio (1734)
Composed July–September 1791
PREMIERES   6 September 1791, Gräflich Nostitzsches Nationaltheater, Prague; UK: 27 March 1806, His Majesty's Theatre, London; US: 4 August 1952, Tanglewood
CAST   Tito *t*, Vitellia *s*, Servilia *s*, Sesto *s* or *ms*, Annio *s* or *ms*, Publio *b*; *satb* chorus of Roman people; guards
ORCHESTRATION   2 fl, 2 ob, 2 cl/basset cl/basset hn, 2 bsn, 2 hn, 2 tpt, timp, str, cont

La clemenza di Tito was commissioned as part of the celebrations in Prague for the coronation of the new Emperor Leopold II as King of Bohemia. Though the Prague public loved Mozart, he was approached only when it became clear that the court composer, Salieri, was not available. He received the definite commission from Domenico Guardasoni, director of the Italian company, in July 1791 while he was working on *Die Zauberflöte*, but he may have written at least the *allegro* section of Vitellia's 'Non più di fiori' by April 1791, when it perhaps was performed by Josephine Duschek, and his sketches for a tenor Sesto must have preceded the July contract with the Bohemian Estates which stipulated a castrato Sesto. When Mozart arrived in Prague on 28 August, together with his wife and his pupil Süssmayr, the score was nearly complete.

The Roman emperor Titus Vespasianus, famous for the noble qualities he had shown in his short reign (AD 79–81), was an ideal subject for a coronation opera: Leopold had been likened to a latterday Titus during his reign as Grand Duke of

The burning of the Capitol in La clemenza di Tito; *engraving on the title page of the Breitkopf und Härtel piano score by Johann August Rosmässler (Leipzig, 1795)*

Tuscany. If Mozart went back to an opera-seria libretto to please the Italian taste of the new emperor, he had it converted into a 'true opera' (as he noted in his thematic index) to please himself. One third of Metastasio's text was cut; the rest was turned into three duets, three trios, three choruses and two finales for soloists and chorus, leaving just 11 arias. Metastasio's libretto had often been modified in the 40 settings it had inspired but never so radically as this. That may have been the cause of 'a certain prejudice at court against Mozart's opera', of which Guardasoni complained to the Estates. In spite of all the changes, the libretto for each ensemble concerned a single static situation without any real action or interaction of the characters. For example, in the beautiful trio 'Quello di Tito è il volto' when the guilty Sesto appears before his betrayed emperor and friend only inner feelings are expressed.

Metastasio's elegant plots and verses are on the whole more suited to the tangled love stories of his famous *L'Olimpiade* and *Demofoonte* than to political subjects. Titus is the only historical character in the drama. The ferocious Vitellia is derived from

Hermione in Racine's *Andromaque*, who also sends her doting lover to kill the king who spurned her: she is therefore in marked contrast to the virtuous 18th-century Romans around her, until in her final great scena she turns her back on Racinian passion and becomes another self-sacrificing Metastasian heroine.

When the court left, the public took the opera to their hearts. Mozart was delighted to hear of the applause that every number received at the last performance on the day of the equally triumphant first performance of *Die Zauberflöte* in Vienna. For 30 years it remained among Mozart's most popular operas (it was the first to be performed in England), before going underground for the next 150.

SYNOPSIS

Act I Vitellia's apartments. Vitellia, daughter of the deposed Emperor Vitellius, had hoped to marry the Emperor Titus, but he is paying court to the Jewish princess, Berenice. The opera opens as she persuades Sesto, who is in love with her, to join the conspiracy to assassinate Titus ('Come ti piace imponi'). In the forum Titus is praised by the crowd and organizes help for the victims of the eruption of Vesuvius. He tells Sesto that he has decided to send away the foreigner, Berenice, and marry Servilia, Sesto's sister. Sesto's friend, Annio, who is himself in love with Servilia, nobly keeps silent, but when he breaks the news to her, they declare their mutual love ('Ah perdona al primo affetto'). Servilia reveals this to Titus and he praises her candour. Vitellia, hearing that she has been passed over again, promises her hand in marriage to Sesto if he will instantly murder Titus. He departs reluctantly to murder his beloved emperor and friend ('Parto, parto'). No sooner has he left than Annio and the prefect Publio come to pay homage to her as the newly chosen empress. She hysterically tries to call Sesto back, while the others attribute her emotion to excessive joy ('Vengo . . . aspettate . . .'). Below the Capitol. Sesto is torn by conflicting emotions ('Oh Dei, che smania è questa') but, just as he resolves to save Titus from the conspiracy, he sees the flames leap up (finale Act I, 'Deh conservate, oh Dei'). The soloists run around in confusion, but Vitellia keeps her head enough to warn Sesto not to blurt out the truth. The Roman people are heard mourning Titus offstage.

Act II In a garden on the Palatine hill. Annio tells Sesto that Titus has survived and advises him to seek his mercy. As the identity of the conspirators still seems to be unknown, Vitellia begs Sesto to flee. But Publio approaches to arrest him. Sesto takes a tender leave of her ('Se al volto mai ti senti'). In a great throne room. Thanks are given for Titus' survival ('Ah grazie si rendano'). He cannot believe that his friend is guilty but Publio warns him not to judge others by his own heart. Annio can only recommend mercy. Titus is torn by inner conflict ('Che orror! che tradimento!'): he envies the happy lot of a simple peasant. Sesto is led in but refuses to reveal Vitellia's complicity ('Quello di Tito è il volto!') and takes his leave of Titus ('Deh per questo istante solo'). Titus eventually tears up the death sentence, for he wishes to be seen by posterity as a clement ruler ('Se all'impero'). Servilia begs Vitellia, the empress elect, to save Sesto ('S'altro che lacrime'). Vitellia resolves to sacrifice her own happiness and life for the noble Sesto who had not betrayed her. ('Ecco il punto, oh Vitellia . . . Non più di fiori'). A crowd has collected by the entrance to the arena, where the wild beasts await the condemned. As Titus is about to pass sentence on the conspirators, Vitellia flings herself at his feet and confesses that she is guiltier than anyone – mistaking his goodness for love, she had hated him for seeming to spurn her. Titus forgives them all. Amidst their praise he resolves to devote himself only to the well-being of Rome ('Tu, è ver, m'assolvi Augusto').

Vitellia is the driving force in the opera: her role contains an amazing range of emotions, from wheedling to hectoring, from feigned love to real despair and hysterical terror, together with a no less amazing vocal range from bottom A to top D. The most famous piece in the opera, is her rondo 'Non più di fiori' with basset horn obbligato. The rondo, always reserved for principal singers, had an important place in Italian opera in the 1780s, especially in the works of Cimarosa and Sarti. It was always in two parts, a slow and a faster, usually a sentimental gavotte. Apart from allowing himself some wild modulations at the start of the *allegros*, Mozart is true to the Italian model, both in this aria and in Sesto's 'Deh per questo istante'. But Sesto also has his coloratura aria with clarinet obbligato 'Parto, parto'. (Both obbligati were performed by Mozart's friend Anton Stadler, for whom he also composed the Concerto (K. 622), the Quintet (K. 581) and the Kegelstatt Trio (K. 498).) Titus is too predictably merciful ('What will posterity say of us?') and becomes ridiculously obliging when he contemplates marriage to three different women in the course of one day. Antonio Baglioni (also the first Don Ottavio) inspired a gentle lyrical style with long coloraturas. His set-piece aria, 'Se all'impero', might have been found in *Lucio Silla*, but the other arias are in the 1791 pattern of simplicity and brevity, the most beautiful being in the heart of the chorus 'Ah grazie si rendano'. Servilia's tiny gem of an aria and Annio's two affecting pictures of loyalty are surpassed by their delicate duet, 'Ah perdona al primo affetto', as irresistible as it is sentimental.

The opera lacks the rich scoring of the previous operas, whether in deference to Italian style, or to the 1791 concentration on essentials found in *Die Zauberflöte*. The *recitativo semplice* is most probably by Süssmayr; however, Mozart provided highly dramatic *recitativi accompagnati* at all the decisive moments. The most striking piece is the finale to Act I, in which the people of Rome are heard far away lamenting the assassination of their beloved emperor, at first with exclamations on diminished seventh chords and then antiphonally with the quintet of soloists on stage, in poignant harmonies prophetic of the 19th century. This coronation opera opens with a brilliant overture, its first subject like cheering crowds and pealing bells, and closes with the emperor's almost ecstatic devotion to his people, an exuberant finale which must have inspired the end of Beethoven's *Fidelio*.

RECORDINGS 1. McNair, Varady, von Otter, Robbin, Rolfe Johnson, Hauptmann, Monteverdi Ch and English Baroque Soloists, Gardiner, Archiv Production, 1990; 2. Popp, Baker, Minton, von Stade, Burrows, Lloyd, Royal Opera Ch and O, C. Davis, Philips, 1976; 3. Mathis, Varady, Berganza, Schiml, Schreier, Adam, Leipzig Radio Ch, Dresden Staatskapelle, Böhm, DG, 1977: the urgency of the period-instrument performance under Gardiner is hard to deny, and it is excellently sung. But both the Davis and the Böhm are splendidly vital readings. The Davis contains the greatest amount of the recitative. [A.B.]

VIDEO Sildh, Poulson, Nilsson, Höglind, Dahlberg, Arvidson, Drottningholm Court Ch and O, Ostman, Virgin, 1987: Järvefelt's highly charged, highly erotic staging, superbly executed [A.B.]

EDITIONS f.ss., *MW*, V, no. 21; *NMA*, II:5/xx, 1970; v.s., Bärenreiter, 1984

Concert and Insertion Arias

From his ninth till his last year Mozart wrote arias with orchestral accompaniment, half a dozen for bass, a few more for tenor and two dozen for soprano, not including first drafts and new arias for revivals of his own operas. Each was written with a particular singer in mind. The arias for use in concerts were usually to famous Metastasio verses. They often served a special purpose: 'Misero me . . . Misero pargoletto' (K. 77) was performed at Count Firmian's soirée in Milan in March 1770 and resulted in the commission for *Mitridate*. Singers had to be satisfied with all their arias in a new opera; in the case of a revival they could ask to have any aria replaced by a composer of their choice. Thus, in June 1783, Mozart wrote two arias for Aloysia Lange in Anfossi's *Il curioso indiscreto* (K. 418 and K. 419) and reported that 'nobody liked anything about Anfossi's opera except my two arias of which the second, a bravura aria, had to be repeated' (he was certainly not doing Anfossi a favour). He wrote three arias for Louise Villeneuve as practice for composing her role of Dorabella in *Così fan tutte*. Some arias had a personal touch, like Nancy Storace's wonderful 'Ch'io mi scordi di te' (K. 505; 1786) with a text from *Idomeneo* and a keyboard obbligato for the composer himself on the occasion of her farewell concert in Vienna. He even wrote a trio and quartet (K. 480 and K. 479) for insertion into Bianchi's *La villanella rapita* during his work on *Figaro*.

RECORDING Complete Mozart Edition, vol. 23, Philips, 1991
EDITIONS f.s., *NMA*, II:7/i–iv, 1967, 1968, 1971, 1972

BIBLIOGRAPHY Hermann Abert, *W. A. Mozart: neu bearbeitete und erweitere Ausgabe von Otto Jahn's 'Mozart'*, Breitkopf und Härtel, 1919–21; 3rd edn, 1955–66; Emily Anderson (trans. and ed.), *The Letters of Mozart and his Family*, 3 vols, Macmillan, 1938; 3rd edn, 1985; Daniel Heartz, *Mozart's Operas*, University of California Press, 1990; Giorgio Pestelli, *The Age of Mozart and Beethoven*, Cambridge University Press, 1984; Andrew Steptoe, *The Mozart–Da Ponte Operas*, Clarendon Press, 1988; Alan Tyson, *Mozart: Studies of the Autograph Scores*, Harvard University Press, 1987; Cambridge Opera Handbooks (all published by Cambridge University Press): Thomas Bauman, *Die Entführung aus dem Serail*, 1987; Peter Branscombe, *Die Zauberflöte*, 1991; Tim Carter, *Le nozze di Figaro*, 1987; John A. Rice, *La clemenza di Tito*, 1991; Julian Rushton, *Don Giovanni*, 1981; ENO Opera Guides (all published by John Calder): *Così fan tutte*, 1983; *Don Giovanni*, 1983; *The Magic Flute*, 1980; *The Marriage of Figaro*, 1983

E.S.

WENZEL MÜLLER

b 26 September 1767, Tyrnau (now Trnava); *d* 3 August 1835, Baden, nr Vienna

Müller studied with Dittersdorf and was first employed as violinist at the theatre in Brunn (1782). There he began writing singspiels, which quickly won him recognition and, in 1786, employment as kapellmeister at the Leopoldstadttheater in Vienna. He remained there until 1830 except for a spell at the German Opera in Prague (1807–13). Müller composed altogether some 250 singspiels, pantomimes, ballets, melodramas and plays with, music. Some of his works from the 1790s were particularly successful: [*Kaspar*] *Der Fagottist* (1791) received 125 performances before 1819, yet Mozart describe it as 'shoddy stuff' in a letter to his wife (12 June 1791). Beethoven used the song 'Ich bin der Schneider Kakadu' from *Die Schwestern von Prag* for his Variations for Piano Trio, Op. 121. Other melodies have entered the German folksong repertoire, and are still performed today.

Das Sonnenfest der Braminen
The Sun Festival of the Brahmins

Heroisch-komisches original singspiel in two acts (2h)
Libretto by Karl Friedrich Hensler
PREMIERE 9 September 1790, Leopoldstadttheater, Vienna

Das Sonnenfest der Braminen continues the popular exotic theme demonstrated in Mozart's *Die Entführung aus dem Serail* and the plots have several similarities. Eduard, a young Englishman, has arrived on an island off the Indian coast to rescue his beloved Laura from kidnappers. Learning that Bella, a girl who saved him from a shipwreck, is due to be sacrificed to Brahma, he manages to substitute his servant in her place. The god suddenly decrees that the victim shall be spared and it finally emerges that Bella is in fact Eduard's long-lost sister, kidnapped years ago by the ship's captain.

Sonnenfest includes the customary mix of German folk-type songs and ornate Italian arias (though fewer of the latter than usual since the artists at the Leopoldstadttheater were actors rather than singers). Despite the fact that Mozart's *Die Zauberflöte* was premiered in the city a year later, *Sonnenfest* retained its tremendous popularity and was seen frequently in Vienna well into the next century.

EDITION f.s., facsimile, *German Opera 1770–1800*, vol. 16, Garland, 1986

Other operatic works (inc. list): [*Kaspar*] *Der Fagottist, oder Die Zauberzither*, 1791; *Das Neusonntagskind*, 1793; *Die Schwestern von Prag*, 1794; *Der alte Überall und Nirgends*, 1795; *Das lustige Beilager*, 1797; *Die zwölf schlafenden Jungfrauen*, 1797; *Der Sturm, oder Die bezauberte Insel*, 1798; *Die Teufelsmühle am Wienerberg*, 1799; *Die Belagerung von Ypsilon*, 1804; *Die neue Alceste*, 1806; *Der Schlossgärtner und der Windmüller*, 1813; *Der Fiaker als Marquis*, 1816; *Tankredi*, 1817; *Doktor Fausts Mantel*, 1817; *Der verwunschene Prinz*, 1818; *Die travestirte Zauberflöte*, 1818; *Die Fee aus Frankreich, oder Liebesqualen eines Hagestolzen*, 1821; *Aline, oder Wien in einem anderen Weltteil*, 1822; *Der Barometermacher auf der Zauberinsel*, 1823; *Herr Josef und Frau Baberl*, 1826; *Die gefesselte Phantasie*, 1828; *Der Alpenkönig und der Menschenfeind*, 1828; *Der Sieg des guten Humors, oder Die Lebenslampen*, 1831; *c.* 225 other stage works

BIBLIOGRAPHY Robert Haas, 'Wenzel Müller', in *Mozart-Jahrbuch*, 1953, p. 81

M.F.

VANO MURADELI

Vano Ilyich Muradeli; *b* 6 April 1908, Gori, Georgia; *d* 14 August 1970, Tomsk, Russia

Muradeli graduated from the Tbilisi Conservatory in 1931, and studied with Myaskovsky in Moscow. During the Second World War, his mass song 'The Buchenwald Alarm' gained international fame. He was a praesidium member of the Composers Union from 1939 until he was denounced in the 1948 purge. This was prompted by his opera *The Great Friendship*, which unfortunately muddled the history of the Georgians and Ossetians and thus displeased Stalin, himself an Ossetian. However, *October*, complete with a singing Lenin, was a great success. There is nothing subtle about Muradeli's musical style: forged to appeal to the Stalinist ideal of art for the masses, it favours elementary march rhythms, simple strophic songs and thickly effective orchestration. Galina Vishnevskaya refers to him in her autobiography as 'having the musical abilities of a child'.

Operatic works: *Velikaya druzhba* (*The Great Friendship*), 1947 (RECORDING excerpts: Melodiya, 1960s); *Oktyabr'* (*October*), 1961 (RECORDING excerpts: Melodiya, 1967); *Moskva–Parizh–Moskva* (*Moscow–Paris–Moscow*), 1969
BIBLIOGRAPHY B. Schwarz, *Music and Musical Life in Soviet Russia, 1917–70*, Barrie and Jenkins, 1972

J.G.

THEA MUSGRAVE

b 27 May 1928, Barnton, nr Edinburgh

Musgrave studied music at Edinburgh University (and composition privately with Hans Gal), then spent four years at the Paris Conservatoire, studying privately with Nadia Boulanger. Returning to the UK, she established a reputation in the early 1960s as the composer of well-wrought, rather subdued instrumental works in an eclectic modernist idiom with its roots in free serialism. But she was also, from early on, much involved with music for the theatre. She wrote a ballet, *The Tale of Thieves* (1953), based on Chaucer's *Pardoner's Tale*, and a one-act comic opera, *The Abbot of Drimock*, based on one of John Mackay Wilson's *Tales of the Border*. Later, theatrical motifs began to enter her concert works (as they did the works of leading figures such as Berio, Stockhausen and, in Britain, Maxwell Davies in the early and mid-1960s). She wrote a series of orchestral and chamber concertos in which the inherent drama of the concerto is turned into stylized action, with the soloists as *dramatis personae*. She also continued to write for the theatre, and – to date – five full-length operas, all but the first commissioned, are solid witness to her aptitude in this field.

In 1970 Musgrave held the post of guest professor at the Santa Barbara campus of the University of California, and since 1972 has lived in the US. She teaches at Queen's University, New York. An opera about Simon Bolivar, with a lead tenor role for Placido Domingo, is to be premiered in Los Angeles in September 1993.

The Decision

Opera in three acts (2h)
Libretto by Maurice Lindsay, after the television play *The Devil and John Brown* by Ken Taylor (1963)
Composed 1964–5
PREMIERE 30 November 1967, Sadler's Wells, London (New Opera Company)

The play, for which Musgrave had written incidental music, was based on a real incident at a mine in Ayrshire in 1835. A trapped miner was rescued after 23 days underground but died soon afterwards. The opera enriches the story with a network of personal relationships, whose history is narrated partly in flashback; the trapped miner has been having an affair with the foreman's wife, and it is the foreman's decision – how hard to try to rescue him – that gives the opera its title. Though somewhat overwritten and at times overscored, *The Decision* is a remarkably effective, if technically conventional, opera, rich in strongly characterized music, and its stage complexities (involving vigorous crowd scenes) handled with great aplomb.

EDITIONS f.s./v.s., Chester (on hire), 1965

The Voice of Ariadne

Opera in three acts (2h 15m)
Libretto by Amalia Elguera, after the short story *The Last of the Valerii* by Henry James (1874)
Composed 1972–3
PREMIERES 11 June 1974, Aldeburgh Festival (English Opera Group); US: 30 September 1977, Lincoln Center, New York

Musgrave's second substantial opera coincided with her best concerto-writing (for horn, 1971, and viola, 1973) and was closely followed by a fine ensemble work called *Space Play* (1974); it belongs very much with them. The orchestra is a chamber ensemble of 13 players, plus an operator for the tape which projects the voice of the title 'from nowhere' – a spatial idea itself reminiscent of the composer's contemporary instrumental preoccupations.

James's story is expanded, with some new characters and a changed emphasis. A statue is unearthed in the grounds of the Roman villa of the Valerii, the ancestral home of Count Marco Valerio, apparently confirming an old family legend. In James the statue is of Juno; in the opera it is Ariadne. But only the pedestal is found, while Ariadne herself begins to haunt the count with her disembodied voice, drawing him away from his young American wife. Gradually the countess herself assumes the identity of the missing goddess, merging vocally with her taped voice, and finally stepping on to the vacant pedestal (like Hermione in *The Winter's Tale*), at which point the voice of Ariadne fades away for the last time.

The opera is notable musically for its impressionistic tone poetry, with the 'tangled shrubs and twisted trees' of James's garden depicted in dense free polyphony, and for its sure handling of the tense emotions implied by its central allegory. The vocal writing, especially for the count and countess, is splendid, whether lyrical or dramatic, and shows the increase in Musgrave's range since *The Decision*. Less effective are the quasi-comic sub-plot (involving an elderly English woman, Mrs Tracy, and her Italian escort Baldovino), and the jealousy motive supplied by the Marchesa Bianca Biancchi, who loves the count and so foments his marital problems – these characters are all invented for the opera. However, the score – already leaning back towards a clear tonal/ harmonic style – is good enough for its neglect since the early performances to be a matter of serious regret.

EDITIONS   f.s., Novello (on hire); v.s., Novello, 1977

Mary, Queen of Scots

Opera in three acts (2h 15m)
Libretto by the composer, after the play *Moray* by Amalia Elguera
Composed 1976–7
PREMIERES   6 September 1977, King's Theatre, Edinburgh Festival (Scottish Opera); US: 29 March 1978, Norfolk, Virginia
CAST   Mary *s*, Moray *bar*, Darnley *t*, Bothwell *t*, Riccio *b-bar*, Gordon *b*, Cardinal Beaton *bar*, Earl of Ruthven *t*, Earl of Morton *bar*, the four Marys 2 *s*, 2 *ms*; *satb* chorus of soldiers, courtiers, Lords of the Congregation, monks, people of Edinburgh
STANDARD ORCHESTRA including chamber organ, hp

Ashley Putnam as Mary Queen of Scots (Norfolk, Virginia, 1978)

A much more direct and conventional opera than its predecessor, *Mary, Queen of Scots* shows Musgrave's expertise at handling the raw materials of the genre in an effective and approachable way. The Elguera play offered strong dramatic situation and character conflict, with the accent on Mary's bastard half-brother, James Stewart, the Earl of Moray. Musgrave accepts the play's flexible view of history, further reduces its burden of marginal characters, but retains its main emphases. It still manages to cover much – perhaps too much – of the essential incident in the period from 1561, when Mary returned to Scotland as queen, and 1568, when she was imprisoned by Queen Elizabeth, appending the murder of Moray (which actually happened 19 months later).

SYNOPSIS

Act I   On the eve of Mary's return, the ambitious Moray seizes and imprisons Bothwell's supporter Cardinal Beaton. Mary arrives and is met by Bothwell and Moray, who quarrel. Mary succeeds in holding the balance, but later Gordon tries unsuccessfully to rouse the people against Moray. At a ball in honour of Darnley, Moray reproves Mary for dancing with her young English cousin. Bothwell, also jealous, disrupts the French dancing with a wild Scottish reel which Mary joins in. Bothwell physically attacks Darnley and is banished with his men; Moray also leaves.

Act II   Despite his unsuitability, Mary has married Darnley and appointed his friend Riccio as secretary. But the lords refuse to accept Darnley as king. Mary summons Moray to appease them, while Moray's agents incite Darnley to demand the crown. Moray expects power, but Mary rejects him. In revenge Moray incites Darnley to murder Riccio in Mary's presence. Mary flees, pursued by Moray's accusations of complicity in the murder. But as James seems about to seize power, she returns, accuses him publicly, and banishes him.

Act III   Weak from the birth of her son, Mary nevertheless refuses Gordon's suggestion that she take refuge from Moray in Stirling Castle. To Gordon's horror, she puts her trust in Bothwell. Bothwell seduces her, but they are discovered by Moray. In the ensuing fight, Bothwell is wounded but escapes. At Moray's urging, the people demand Mary's abdication. She flees to England, but as she leaves Gordon kills Moray, leaving her baby son to be proclaimed King James VI.

The score makes fluent and effective use of traditional means, as refracted (perhaps most obviously) through the operas of Britten. As in Britten, drama and text are kept scrupulously clear, and action and reflection are very skilfully balanced. More tonal than before, Musgrave's own music nevertheless retains a muscularity and a technical economy which fit the turbulent subject well. And her use of borrowed material (plainsong, contemporary dances, Scottish pipe music and reels, etc.) is never merely picturesque, but always works to dramatic ends.

RECORDING Putnam, Busse, Garrison, Gardner, Virginia Opera Association, Mark, MMG, 1979: live performance from Norfolk, Virginia, 1978
EDITIONS f.s., Novello (on hire); v.s., Novello, 1978

A Christmas Carol

Opera in two acts (1h 45m)
Libretto by the composer, after the story by Charles Dickens (1843)
Composed 1978–9
PREMIERES 7 December 1979, Norfolk, Virginia; UK: 16 December 1981, Sadler's Wells, London

The work simplifies Dickens effectively, with a series of cast doublings (the three embodiments of the Spirit of Christmas are played by one singer). Musically, it draws on Musgrave's now established technique of absorbing traditional material into her own post-tonal idiom, notably the carol, 'God rest you merry, gentlemen', which runs through the two acts.

EDITIONS f.s., Novello (on hire); v.s., Novello, 1981

Harriet, the Woman called Moses

Opera in two acts (2h 15m)
Libretto by the composer
Composed 1984, rev. 1985
PREMIERES 1 March 1985, Norfolk, Virginia; UK: 3 March 1985, BBC Radio 3 (broadcast of the Norfolk production)

Musgrave's libretto is based on the true story of Harriet Tubman, an escaped Maryland slave who, in the 1850s, helped some 300 other slaves to escape to Canada by way of the so-called 'Underground Railroad'. As before, Musgrave weaves traditional material (Negro spirituals and other types of American folk music) into her own post-tonal style, and it is typical of her that she does not see the politically fashionable aspects of the subject (feminism, human rights) as an excuse for fudging the dramatic issues. *Harriet* is by any standards strong musical theatre.

The opera was commissioned jointly by the Virginia Opera Association and the Royal Opera, Covent Garden, but still awaits its UK stage premiere. After the Norfolk production, Musgrave made a reduced version called *The Story of Harriet Tubman*, designed to make the work accessible to companies with more limited resources. Described as a 'narrated music-drama in one act', it has a smaller cast, a narrator and an orchestra of eight players.

EDITIONS *Harriet, the Woman called Moses*: f.s., Novello (on hire); *The Story of Harriet Tubman*: f.s., Novello (on hire)

Other operas: *The Abbot of Drimock*, 1959; *An Occurrence at Owl Creek* (radio opera), 1981
BIBLIOGRAPHY Charles Haws and Thea Musgrave, '*Mary, Queen of Scots*: Fact or Fiction', *Opera*, vol. 28 (1977), pp. 730–34; Thea Musgrave, '*Mary, Queen of Scots*', *MT*, vol. 118

(1977), pp. 625–7; Stephen Walsh, 'Musgrave's *The Voice of Ariadne*', *MT*, vol. 115 (1974), pp. 465–7

S.W.

MODEST MUSORGSKY

Modest Petrovich Musorgsky; *b* 21 March 1839, Karevo, Pskov District; *d* 28 March 1881, St Petersburg

Musorgsky and Tchaikovsky (one year his junior) are universally acknowledged as the outstanding masters of 19th-century Russian music. There are, however, two notable factors that distinguish them. Tchaikovsky was the first of a new conservatory-trained generation of professional composers, whereas Musorgsky remained a largely self-taught amateur, albeit one of genius. The scope of their achievement also differs markedly. In contrast to Tchaikovsky's voluminous and masterly output in every genre, Musorgsky's reputation rests essentially on his 65 songs, *Pictures at an Exhibition* for piano (1874, later orchestrated by Ravel), the orchestral *St John's Night on Bare Mountain* (1867, reworked by Rimsky-Korsakov 1886), and three operas, two of them still unfinished at his early death aged 42. Of these *Boris Godunov* is in the repertoire of every major opera company and revered as a music drama of astonishing theatrical power, integrity and trailblazing originality.

Musorgsky's musical ability was first displayed in his prowess as a gifted pianist and improviser. While still an army cadet in St Petersburg he met Balakirev and from him received vital encouragement and the only form of compositional guidance he ever had. Operatic projects were among his very first attempts at composition (*Oedipus in Athens*, 1858–60; *Salammbô*, 1863–6); but it was as a song-writer – often to his own texts – that he first found his highly individual voice as a composer. For these he chose diverse subjects that were often humorous, satirical or taken from low life. With an astonishing directness of utterance he displayed an ability to sympathize with and depict in the most uncompromisingly vivid way those whom Dostoevsky classed as 'the humiliated and the injured'. Closely allied to this desire for musical realism was Musorgsky's determination to fashion a vocal line that reflected, with as little recourse as possible to conventional melody, the contours and intonations of human speech. As a result the songs, especially those written between 1864 and 1870, and the three great cycles, *The Nursery* (1870–72), *Sunless* (1874), and *The Songs and Dances of Death* (1875–7), are unique in their dramatic and realistic power of expression. It is significant that Musorgsky is possibly the only one of the world's supreme song-writers to achieve comparable success in opera.

Musorgsky's artistic credo, then, as displayed in his greatest songs, *Boris Godunov* and, to a lesser extent, *Khovanshchina* (for which broad canvases they served as preliminary sketches), resided in his belief in the intimate relationship between the inflexions of the spoken Russian language, the idea and emotion expressed by it and the intonation of voice and accompaniment with which it is communicated. This could create a new, fresh form of music that was part of everybody's experience and would serve as an unprecedentedly direct means of communication. At the same time he repudiated the cult of art for art's sake as displayed by the German school of conservatory-trained composers whose works in sonata form he castigated as 'musical mathematics'.

Having resigned his commission in the Guards to devote himself fully to music, Musorgsky found that the sharp drop in his private income caused by the emancipation of the serfs obliged him to undertake part-time work in the Civil Service. The great turning point of his career came in 1868 when a friend proposed Pushkin's *Boris Godunov* as a subject that was perfectly suited to his rapidly developing gifts. In order to put his ideas into practice in his first full-length opera, Musorgsky perfected a novel and idiosyncratic musical style which, thanks to his lack of formal training and contempt for conventional musical disciplines, is largely free from formative influences. The voices of Glinka, Serov, Liszt and Berlioz – all highly individual composers in their own right – can be detected at times. For the most part, however, Musorgsky's predominantly chordal language, often presupposing a vocal line and incorporating audacious harmonic procedures, must have been discovered almost empirically at the piano.

The long-delayed production of *Boris* sadly proved to be the watershed of his short life. Though

Musorgsky in 1876, drawing by Alexandrovsky

acclaimed by the public and fellow artists, it met with critical incomprehension and hostility, and this, together with the drudgery of his job and more personal, emotional problems, made Musorgsky increasingly introspective and dependent on alcohol. His St Petersburg musical friends tried to help him, but he became disillusioned and listless, and failed to complete, let alone orchestrate, the even larger historical canvas of *Khovanshchina* and his comic Gogol opera *Sorochintsy Fair* which he had unwisely undertaken at the same time. The well-intentioned but excessively distorting editorial work of his friend Rimsky-Korsakov to which most of his output, unfinished or finished, was subjected after his death is now increasingly rejected in favour of a return to the originality of his own texts whenever possible.

Salammbô

Opera in four acts (inc.) (recording: 1h 30m)
Libretto by the composer, after the novel by Flaubert (1862)
Composed 1863–6

Musorgsky's first serious attempt at a full-scale opera. In choosing Flaubert's exotic oriental story he was clearly influenced by the example of Serov's grand opera *Judith* (1863).

Six scenes from all four acts survive, of which three were scored. These fragments, fascinating in their own right, have the additional interest of acting as the original source material for certain passages in *Boris*. The Hungarian conductor Zoltán Peskó has orchestrated all six scenes. These were given a concert performance (later recorded) on 10 November 1980 in Milan, and the torso has since been staged in various European cities.

RECORDING Shemchuk, Seleznyev, Stone, Surian, Italian Radio Ch and O, Peskó, CBS, 1980
EDITION v.s., P. Lamm (ed.), Russian State Music Publishers, 1939

The Marriage

Zhenit'ba
Comic opera (inc.)
Libretto from the (four-act) play by Gogol (1842)
Composed 1868
PREMIERES 4 January 1909, Moscow, (concert, with pf);
28 October 1917, Theatre of Music Drama, Petrograd (orch. A. V. Gauk); UK: 1981, Bloomsbury Theatre, London (Nexus Opera; orch. Colin Matthews and Oliver Knussen, 35m)

Written under the direct influence of Dargomyzhsky's *The Stone Guest* (1872), this word-forword setting of Act I of Gogol's comedy (entitled 'an experiment in dramatic music in prose') represents Musorgsky's most extreme attempt to portray in music the precise inflexions of Russian speech.

In his bachelor apartments the lawyer Podkolesin finally decides to get married. Fyokla Ivanovna, the marriage broker, has been trying to persuade him to do this for over two months. She arrives to give him a vivid description of his future wife and her dowry, and urges him to make up his mind. His friend

Kochkarov is amazed to learn that he is contemplating matrimony and, after trying to dissuade him, decides to take over the role of matchmaker himself.

The first act was orchestrated and the missing three acts newly composed by Ippolitov-Ivanov. More recently the fragment has been orchestrated for smaller forces by Gennadi Rozhdestvensky and others.

RECORDINGS both of Ippolitov-Ivanov completion: 1. Act I only: Matiushina, Pontryagin, Demyanov, USSR State Radio O, Kovalev, Melodiya, c. 1954; 2. Desmazures, Mollien, Agroff, Paris PO, Leibowitz, Olympic, c. 1952
EDITIONS v.ss., Rimsky-Korsakov (ed.), Bessel, 1908; authentic text, P. Lamm (ed.), Muzgiz, 1933; completed Ippolitov-Ivanov, Muzgiz, 1934; completed A. Tcherepnin, Universal, 1938 (as Die Heirat)

Mlada

Opera-ballet (inc.)
Libretto by Viktor Krylov
Composed 1872, with Cui, Rimsky-Korsakov and Borodin

Not to be confused with Rimsky's full-length opera-ballet of the same name (1890), this hare-brained collective project soon collapsed, though not before each composer had written a considerable amount of music for it. Two Musorgsky numbers survive. The market scene (later to be used as the opening chorus of Sorochintsy Fair) is a reworking of the 'Chorus of the People' from an earlier projected opera (1858–61) based on Ozerov's play Oedipus in Athens. The 'March of the Princes and Priests' reappeared with a new trio as an orchestral piece, The Capture of Kars, in 1880.

EDITION v.s. (arr. 4 hands), Market Scene and 'March of the Princes and Priests', Muzgiz, 1931

Boris Godunov

Opera in four acts with a prologue (3h 15m)
Libretto by the composer, based on Pushkin's historical drama and Karamzin's History of the Russian State (1824)
Composed 1868–9; rev. 1871–2
PREMIERES Definitive version: 8 February 1874, Mariinsky Theatre, St Petersburg; UK: 30 September 1935, Sadler's Wells, London; Rimsky-Korsakov version: 17 October 1908, Bolshoi Theatre, Moscow; US: 19 March 1913, Metropolitan, New York; UK: 24 June 1913, Drury Lane, London; Shostakovich version: 4 November 1959, Leningrad
CAST Boris Godunov b, Ksenia s, Fyodor ms, Nurse a, Prince Vasily Ivanovich Shuisky t, Andrei Shchelkalov bar, Pimen b, Grigori (later the Pretender Dimitri) t, Marina Mnishek ms, Rangoni bar, Varlaam b, Missail t, Hostess of the Inn ms, Simpleton t, Nikitich b-bar, Mitukha bar, Boyar in attendance t, Khrushchov silent, Lavitzky b-bar, Chernikovsky b-bar (voice categories not designated by Musorgsky himself); satb chorus of boyars and their children, Streltsy (guards), soldiers, police officers, Polish noblemen and ladies, Sandomir girls, blind mendicants, people of Moscow, urchins, vagabonds
ORCHESTRATION Musorgsky: 3 fl/picc, 2 ob/ca, 2 cl, 2 bsn, 4 hn, 2 tpt, 3 trbn, tuba, timp, perc, hp, pf (4 hands), str; offstage: tpt in F; onstage: bells; Rimsky-Korsakov: 3 fl/picc, 2 ob/ca, 3 cl/b cl, 2 bsn, 4 hn, 2 tpt, 3 trbn, tuba, timp, perc, bells, hp, pf, str; offstage: alto tpt in F; Shostakovich: 3 fl/picc, 3 ob/ca, 3 cl/E♭ cl, b cl, 3 bsn/dbsn, 4 hn, 3 tpt, 3 trbn, tuba, timp, perc, bells, cel, 2–4 hp; stage band: 2–4 cornet, 4 tpt, 3–6 hn, 2–4 baritones (euphoniums), 2–4 tuba, balalaikas and domras

Musorgsky broke off work on his experimental setting of Gogol's comedy The Marriage when he became fired by the idea of making an operatic version of Pushkin's Boris Godunov. Having condensed the Shakespeare-like 25-scene drama down to a mere seven, adding material and rewriting considerably in the process, he began the composition in October 1868, finished it in July 1869 and completed the orchestration in December – an astonishing achievement considering his lack of experience. When the opera in this compact seven-scene initial version was rejected for performance by the Mariinsky Theatre for a complex variety of reasons (novelty, fear of imperial and ecclesiastic censorship, lack of a leading female role, personal intrigues, etc.), Musorgsky set about revising it.

The two most notable features of this revision are the addition of an entirely new act (Act III) set in Poland, thereby providing the leading female role of Princess Marina, and the removal of the scene outside St Basil's Cathedral in order to accommodate a new scene depicting the advance of the Pretender's anti-Boris forces and the defection of the Russian people. Musorgsky boldly decided that this wonderful new choral scene should follow and not precede the highly impressive death of Boris scene, and thus end the opera with the simpleton singing his solitary lament over the fate of Russia. Act II, in which the character of Boris is most fully revealed, was also substantially revised. Here, in addition to writing new songs for the nurse and Fyodor, Musorgsky largely recast the tsar's great monologue, added a touchingly domestic scene between Boris and his son and recomposed the Boris–Shuisky confrontation and final hallucination scene, making the whole act incomparably richer in the process. He also rewrote parts of the Pimen cell scene (Act I, Scene 1) and added the hostess's song at the beginning of the following inn scene.

This 'definitive' version was eventually accepted for production largely thanks to the tenacity of the singer Julia Platonova who demanded that the opera be staged as her benefit performance. At the highly successful premiere, with Melnikov as Boris, Platonova as Marina and Nápravník conducting, the scene in Chudov monastery (Pimen's cell) was omitted for censorship reasons; it was never staged during the composer's lifetime. It may be safely asserted that no other first opera which has subsequently been acknowledged as a masterpiece has ever been created with such meagre compositional experience and against such a negative cultural and political background.

SYNOPSIS

(The sequence of scenes in the initial version is shown in square brackets.)

Ivan the Terrible died in 1584 leaving two sons: Fyodor, who became tsar, and Dimitri, the tsarevich. Soon the boyar Boris Godunov was appointed regent

Ivan Melnikov in the title role of Boris Godunov
(St Petersburg, 1874)

to the weak-minded Fyodor. In 1591 Dimitri was found dying from a knife wound and it was rumoured that Boris was responsible.

Prologue   Scene 1 [i]: The year 1598. Boris is in retreat in the Novodevichy monastery following the death of Tsar Fyodor. The apathetic people are exhorted to beg him to assume the throne by the police and the boyar Shchelkalov. A procession of pilgrims enters the monastery. The people comment cynically on developments. Scene 2 [ii]: A square in the Kremlin. To the famous orchestral evocation of bells, supplemented by real peals on stage, the chorus greets Boris as he emerges from his coronation. In a contemplative monologue Boris acknowledges the people's acclamation, but his soul is filled with foreboding.

Act I   Scene 1 [iii]: Six years later. In his cell the old monk Pimen is completing his chronicle of Russian history ('Yeshcho odno' – 'Still one more tale'). His novice Grigori is tormented with dreams of greatness. Pimen vividly recalls how the child Dimitri was discovered murdered. Grigori realizes that had he lived the tsarevich would have been his own age. Scene 2 [iv]: Grigori has fled from the monastery and is making for Poland to raise an army against Boris. He arrives at an inn on the Lithuanian border with two vagabond monks, Varlaam and Missail. Varlaam sings a racy ballad describing Ivan the Terrible's victory at Kazan. Police arrive with a warrant for Grigori's arrest but he manages to escape.

Act II [vi] The tsar's apartments in the Kremlin. Ksenia mourns the death of her betrothed while Fyodor and the nurse try to comfort and amuse her.

Boris enters and speaks affectionately to his children. In his great monologue ('Dostig ya vysshei vlasti' – 'I stand supreme in power') he meditates on his crime and the sufferings of Russia. Prince Shuisky, a rival boyar, brings news that a pretender has appeared calling himself Dimitri, the resurrected tsarevich. Shuisky gives an unbearably graphic account of the murdered child's features and, aghast, Boris dismisses him. As a mechanical clock with figures begins to chime, the guilt-racked Boris breaks down, haunted by a vision of the murdered child.

Act III   Scene 1: A castle in Poland. Princess Marina has fallen in love with the pretender and her Jesuit confessor Rangoni commands her to ensnare him in order to convert Russia to Catholicism. Scene 2: Grigori/Dimitri awaits a rendezvous with Marina in the garden. After a courtly choral polonaise the guests return indoors and Marina taunts Dimitri over his infatuation with her. When she realizes that he is determined to seize the Russian throne she pours out her love for him in a short but richly melodic love duet that is one of the opera's few concessions to tradition.

[vi, omitted in the definitive version] Outside St Basil's Cathedral, Moscow. The starving and disaffected people beg Boris to give them bread as he emerges from the cathedral. There is an astonishing confrontation between him and a simpleton, who publicly accuses him of murder. Left alone, the simpleton foretells Russia's troubled future. (Musorgsky himself orchestrated the St Basil scene, although Ippolitov-Ivanov reorchestrated it in 1926 so that it could be used as an additional scene to the Rimsky version if required.)

Act IV   Scene 1 [vii]: An emergency meeting of the Council of Boyars is in progress in the Kremlin. Shuisky's description of the overwrought state in which he had recently found the tsar is interrupted by the sudden arrival of the deranged Boris. Pimen enters and describes a miraculous cure performed at the tomb of the Tsarevich Dimitri. Boris collapses and then, left alone with Fyodor, begins his simple and intensely moving prayer and death scene ('Proshchai, moi syn, umirayu' – 'Farewell, my son, I am dying') in which he advises his son on the government of Russia and prays for God's protection for his children. Scene 2: In a forest near Kromy an unruly mob taunts a half-lynched boyar. After short scenes between a simpleton and some urchins (transferred from the discarded St Basil scene), Varlaam and Missail and two Jesuit monks, the crowd greets the arrival of the false Dimitri and follows him to Moscow. The simpleton is left alone singing a haunting lament foretelling the troubled times that lie in store for Russia.

The most immediately striking feature of the music of *Boris* is the simplicity and economy of means by which Musorgsky achieves the maximum dramatic and expressive effect. Just as in the first movement of Beethoven's Fifth Symphony, short phrases, harmonized either simply or with audacious originality, etch themselves indelibly on the memory and create an impression of human emotion in the raw. Counterpoint is largely absent as are colouristic orchestral effects. Instead attention is directed with unprecedented clarity to the vocal line which graphically communicates the rapidly changing moods of the text. When a character pauses for thought, so, more often than not, does the orchestra; no opera contains more telling silences. In the same way the scenes are all made to fade out at the end, as if in anticipation of cinema technique. The only exception to this is the brilliant coronation scene in which Musorgsky makes impressive use of the folksong 'Slava' that Beethoven had earlier used in his second 'Razumovsky' Quartet.

Musorgsky understood the expressive possibilities of the human voice to the full. A more than capable singer and accompanist himself, he extracted the maximum from his singers, and his vocal line is provided with an unusually comprehensive and detailed set of dynamics, expression marks and verbal indications as to how the voice is to be used. Furthermore, in the still modern-sounding Act II 'hallucination' scene his frequent use of the term *glukho* – a word that implies a combination of muffled, toneless and dull – anticipates the technique that Schoenberg and his pupils were to term sprechgesang.

Perhaps Musorgsky's greatest innovation is his promotion of the chorus from its normal subordinate role to that of one of the most important characters in the drama; many would say the chief one. From the very opening pages the people are shown to have unusually lifelike character, and much use is made of individual groups voicing their own thoughts. Given the opera's episodic construction, the treatment of the chorus lends cohesion to the whole more than anything else.

Mention must be made of the notorious editorial problem that besets *Boris*. Although Musorgsky completed and orchestrated two different versions, the second of which was successfully performed during his lifetime, the opera was for many years exclusively performed in the reorchestrated revision of Rimsky-Korsakov. Rimsky believed that the opera's disappearance from the repertoire after Musorgsky's death was largely due to its lacklustre orchestration and 'faulty' compositional technique. It is unfortunate that the appearance of his edition coincided with Chaliapin's magisterial assumption of the title role, for the two became synonymous and established a norm. Since 1945 the tendency to return to Musorgsky's own versions has greatly accelerated worldwide, although the Bolshoi Theatre in Moscow still clings to the more sumptuous Rimsky version. Quite frequently the two authentic versions are conflated in performance, for instance by incorporating the St Basil scene from the initial version into the text of the definitive version. Shostakovich made a reorchestration in 1940 which, unlike Rimsky's, at least remained faithful to the text of Musorgsky's vocal score.

RECORDINGS 1. Rimsky orchestration: Zareska, Bielicki, Gedda, Christoff (3 roles), Russian Ch of Paris, ORTF O, Dobrowen, EMI, 1952: classic recording of this version;

2. Rimsky orchestration: Arkhipova, Shulpin, Ivanovsky, Kibkalo, Petrov, Reshetin, Guleva, Bolshoi Theatre Ch and O, Melik-Pashayev, Melodiya/Chant du Monde, 1962: splendidly cast, authoritatively conducted, somewhat venerable Bolshoi set; 3. Vedernikov, Arkhipova, Koroleva, Shkolnikova, Sokolov, USSR Television and Radio Ch and O, Fedoseyev, Philips, 1984: uncut definitive version performed by Russian forces; 4. original scoring: Vishnevskaya, Riegel, Polozov, Storozhev, Raimondi, Plishka, The Choral Arts Society of Washington, the Oratorio Arts Society of Washington, National SO, Rostropovich, Erato, 1990: reasonable modern set of Musorgsky's uncut definitive version, plus the St Basil scene. Chaliapin's famous 78rpm discs (both studio and live) are worth investigating on reissues [A.B.]
VIDEO Sinyavskaya, Piavko, Nesternko, Bolshoi Theatre Ch and O, Lazarev, Castle, 1987
EDITIONS f.s., David Lloyd-Jones (ed.), OUP, 1975: a critical edition of both the 'initial' and 'definitive' versions; v.s. (English only), OUP, 1968

Khovanshchina
The Khovansky Affair/Plot
National music drama in five acts (3h)
Libretto by the composer
Composed 1872–80 (inc.)
PREMIERES 21 February 1886, St Petersburg; UK: 1 July 1913, Drury Lane, London; US: 18 April 1928, Philadelphia
CAST Prince Ivan Khovansky *b*, Prince Andrei Khovansky *t*, Prince Vasily Golitsyn *t*, Shaklovity *b-bar*, Dosifei *b*, Marfa *ms*, Susanna *s*, Scribe *t*, Emma *s*, Lutheran Pastor *bar*, Varsonofev *bar*, Kuzka *t*, Streshnev *t*, 3 Streltsy 3 *b* (voice categories not designated by Musorgsky himself); *satb* chorus of Streltsy, Old Believers, serving girls and Persian slaves, Peter the Great's bodyguards, the people
ORCHESTRATION Rimsky-Korsakov: 3 fl/picc, 2 ob/ca, 2 cl, 2 bsn, 4 hn, 2 tpt, 3 trbn, tuba, timp, perc, hp, pf, str; Shostakovich: 3 fl/picc, 3 ob/ca, 3 cl/b cl, 3 bsn/dbsn, 4 hn, 3 tpt, 3 trbn, tuba, timp, perc, 2–4 hp, pf, cel, str; banda of hns, tpts and tbns

Musorgsky began work on *Khovanshchina* as soon as he finished revising *Boris*. He avidly collected a vast amount of historical and social detail about the

Fyodor Chaliapin as Prince Ivan Khovansky in Khovanshchina *(St Petersburg, 1886)*

turbulent period of change from 'old' to 'new' Russia in the years following Peter the Great's accession (1682–98), conflating a number of incidents in the interests of concision. Also involved are the religious sect known as Old Believers who were violently opposed to the new reforms introduced into the ritual of the Orthodox Church. Instead of putting his libretto into a finished state before beginning composition, Musorgsky tried to work on text and music simultaneously and soon after began a similar process with *Sorochintsy Fair*. As a result the ends of Act II and V (final chorus) had not been composed by the time of his death; neither had he managed to subject the mass of disparate episodes that he had composed to rigorous revision. Nevertheless *Khovanshchina*, though at times opaque and slow-moving, contains some very fine music and the roles of Marfa, Dosifei, Ivan Khovansky and Golitsyn are particularly rewarding. The haunting prelude to Act I, subtitled 'Dawn over the Moscow River', and the 'Dance of the Persian Slaves' from Act IV are regularly performed in the concert hall.

SYNOPSIS
The complex story of the opera largely concerns the interaction of the chief characters against the political and religious background at the time of the accession of the young Peter the Great. Ivan Khovansky and his son Andrei, in charge of the unruly Streltsy guards, are custodians of old, feudal Russia. Prince Golitsyn, wily lover of the Regent Sophia, is the representative of the new, Westernized ideas that are being introduced by Tsar Peter. The reactionary Old Believers are represented by the monk Dosifei and Marfa.

Act I The boyar Shaklovity dictates a letter to a scribe warning the rulers and nobility that Prince Ivan Khovansky and his son Andrei are plotting against the state. Khovansky arrives amid general rejoicing and announces his determination to crush the enemies of the throne. Andrei pursues a young German girl, Emma, but Marfa, a former lover of Andrei, intervenes. A quarrel between father and son over Emma is interrupted by the arrival of Dosifei, who restores peace but foretells times of trouble ahead.

Act II Prince Golitsyn reads a letter from Sophia and decides to be wary of her. In a divination scene Marfa foretells his disgrace and ruin. After he has dismissed her a meeting takes place between him, Khovansky and Dosifei. They are interrupted by Shaklovity who announces that the Khovanskys have been proclaimed traitors.

Act III Marfa sings of her past love for Andrei. She is scolded by Susanna but comforted by Dosifei. The unruly Streltsy appear singing a drinking song and quarrelling with their wives. The scribe warns them that Tsar Peter's troops are advancing on them. Khovansky advises them to disperse quietly; Tsar Peter has clearly gathered the reins of power.

Act IV Scene 1: Khovansky is entertained by his serving girls and Persian slaves. Shaklovity arrives, ostensibly to summon him to a council of state, but assassinates him as he prepares to leave. Scene 2:

Golitsyn leaves Moscow for exile and Dosifei reflects on his fall and that of Khovansky. Andrei and Marfa have an altercation and Marfa defies him to summon his Streltsy. They arrive, but carrying blocks for their own execution. An emissary from Tsar Peter pardons them.

Act V The Old Believers' cause is lost and they prepare for death rather than compromise their faith and yield to the tsar's soldiers. They are joined by Dosifei, Marfa and Andrei who prepare to immolate themselves in a chapel in a forest clearing. The tsar's soldiers arrive in time to see everyone consumed in flames.

Although very much the work of Musorgsky throughout, *Khovanshchina* can, in a good performance, create an almost Wagnerian cumulative impact which some find more satisfying than the more kaleidoscopic and tersely constructed *Boris*. However, even they would be obliged to concede that here the composer's genius declares itself more fitfully, and that the grandiose concept is handled with less imagination and originality than in *Boris*.

At his death Musorgsky had orchestrated only two short scenes (Marfa's short folklike aria at the start of Act III and the Streltsy scene in Act IV, Scene 1). In order for the work to be performed, Rimsky-Korsakov undertook the heavy assignment of completing and orchestrating it. In trying to give the material a more manageable shape, he cut some 800 bars while also compressing, transposing and recomposing much else. His most substantial cuts (all restored in the Shostakovich version) can be summarized as follows: in Act I the extended scene (over 200 bars) between the people and the scribe immediately preceding Khovansky's arrival; in Act II Golitsyn's reading of his ex-lover's letter, his scene with a German pastor, and nearly half of the scene between Golitsyn, Khovansky and Dosifei; in Act III, Shaklovity's aria is shortened and the Strelets Kuzka's song with chorus is lost entirely. Rimsky's version held the stage until 1958 when Shostakovich made his own orchestration, faithfully keeping to Musorgsky's vocal score as reconstructed and published by P. Lamm and B. Asafyev in 1931. Diaghilev commissioned Stravinsky and Ravel to orchestrate additional material for the Paris premiere in 1913. Of this, only Stravinsky's reworking of the final chorus exists in published vocal score (1914).

RECORDING Shostakovich's edition but with the two sections orchestrated by Musorgsky and Stravinsky's new ending: Poschner-Klebel, Lipovšek, Atlantov, Popov, Kocherga, Haugland, Burchuladze, Vienna State Opera Ch and O, Abbado, DG, 1990
EDITIONS f.ss., Shostakovich (ed.), Russian State Music Publishers, 1963; Marfa's song, orch. Musorgsky, Russian State Music Publishers, 1931; v.s. (the 1931 edn with some added material), A. Dmitriev and A. Wuffsohn (eds), Leningrad, 1976

Sorochintsy Fair
Sorochinskaya Yarmaka
Comic opera in three acts (1h 45m)

Libretto by the composer, after the story *The Fair at Sorochintsy* by Gogol (1831–2)
Composed 1876–81 (inc.)
PREMIERES   13 October 1917, Petrograd (in Cui's edition); US: 29 November 1930, Metropolitan, New York; UK: 17 February 1934, Fortune Theatre, London

Musorgsky originally decided to start work on this in order to avoid composing two 'heavyweights' one after another, and to provide a good comic role for his friend, the bass Osip Petrov. The opera is set in the Ukraine. Parasya, the daughter of Cherevik, falls in love at the fair with the young peasant (*parabok*) Gritsko. There are many humorous and fantastic complications to the plot which involve the popular legend of a 'devil in a red jacket' and Gritsko's rather improbable 'dream' (an excuse to recycle the *Bare Mountain* witches' sabbath music). In the end true love is able to triumph thanks to a crafty gypsy who exposes a love affair between Cherevik's wife Khivrya and the priest's son. All express their joy at this outcome in a gopak.

In keeping with the light-hearted Ukrainian atmosphere as depicted in Gogol, the music is simple, folky and largely devoid of the originality that characterizes the two previous operas. At the time of Musorgsky's death, despite some desperate last-minute borrowing from earlier pieces such as the *Bare Mountain* music, there was much that remained unwritten; even important stretches of the libretto had not been finalized, only two numbers had been orchestrated: the prelude ('A hot day in little Russia') and Parasya's song (completed by Rimsky-Korsakov); neither has been published. A number of attempts to put the material into performable shape have been made by Lyadov (orchestrations of the prelude, Khivra's song, Gritsko's dumka and final gopak), Karatygin, Sakhnovsky, Cui and Nikolay Cherepnin (Monte Carlo, 1923). Pavel Lamm's 1933 edition in the complete works gave all the Musorgsky material in its original form and included Vissarion Shebalin's completion of the unfinished scenes and orchestration of the whole (1934). This version is probably as authentic as is possible and the one used almost invariably since then.

RECORDING   Shebalin version: Belobragina, Kleshcheva, Usmanov, Troitsky, Moscow Radio Ch and O, Ahronovich, Melodiya, 1960s
EDITIONS   Lyadov's excerpts: f.s., Bessel, 1904, 1914; Cui (ed.), f.s./v.s., 1916; Cherepnin (ed.), v.s., Bessel, 1923; Lamm and Shebalin (eds), f.s., Russian State Music Publishers, 1934; v.s., Russian State Music Publishers, 1933

BIBLIOGRAPHY   M. H. Brown (ed.), *Musorgsky: In Memoriam 1881–1981*, UMI Press (Ann Arbor), 1982; M. D. Calvocoressi (with additions by Gerald Abraham), *Musorgsky*, Dent, 1946; rev. edn, 1974; J. Leyda and S. Bertensson (eds), *The Musorgsky Reader: A Life of M. P. Musorgsky in Letters and Documents*, W. W. Norton, 1947; rev. edn, 1970; Richard Taruskin, *Mussorgsky: Eight Essays and an Epilogue*, Princeton University Press, 1993; booklet with DG recording of *Khovanshchina*, for a rp of Musorgsky's edited libretto, first revealed in 1972

D.L.-J.

JOSEF MYSLIVEČEK

Josef Mysliveček [Mysliweczek, Mislliveček]; *b* 9 March 1737, Horní Šárka, nr Prague; *d* 4 February 1781, Rome

Mysliveček was apprenticed to his father's trade as a miller but he also received an excellent and musically rich schooling under the Dominicans and Jesuits in Prague. After working briefly as a church violinist he left in 1763 for Venice where he studied with Giovanni Pescetti.

The success of his first opera ('opera–cantata'), *Il parnasso confuso*, in Parma in 1765 led to further commissions, notably for the San Carlo Theatre in Naples. (*Medea*, frequently given as his first opera, does not survive apart from the text; there is no evidence that Mysliveček set it.) In January 1767 *Bellerofonte* was given in Naples with a distinguished cast, including Raaff, Mozart's first Idomeneo, and Caterina Gabrielli, with whom Mysliveček formed a long-standing attachment. Over the next decade Mysliveček wrote nearly 20 more operas, four of them for the San Carlo, the others for Turin, Venice, Milan and elsewhere.

Mysliveček's operas were taken up outside Italy, for instance in Munich which Mysliveček visited in 1777 to oversee a revival of *Ezio* and a new version of his oratorio *Isacco, figura del Redentore* (Florence, 1776) as *Abramao ed Isacco*. The year 1777 was the first since 1767 to see no new Mysliveček opera, chiefly owing to his treatment for venereal disease. Mozart, an old friend from Bologna in 1770, visited him in hospital and wrote to his father (in October 1777) about the visit. Mysliveček returned to Italy the next year and wrote six more operas, mostly failures, the last given in Rome at the end of 1780, six weeks before his death.

Mysliveček's great popularity, which earned him the nickname of 'Il boemo' ('divino' was a later inauthentic accretion), was not founded on any particularly individual voice. He wrote operas in the standard Neapolitan style of the time, basically involving strings of *da capo* arias and recitatives. Texts were in the Metastasian mould (more than half of Mysliveček's operas were composed directly on Metastasio texts). Where he departed from it, for instance in the late Quinault-based magic opera *Armida*, he failed to achieve popular success. Although he knew Gluck's *Orfeo* (he conducted a version in Naples in about 1774), he had no reformist tendencies and condoned the performance of ballets between the acts of his operas. More significant is Mysliveček's link with Mozart, and his possible influence on the younger composer.

Most of Mysliveček's operas survive in contemporary copies (which attest their great popularity at the time), and from the 1930s Czech scholars began to investigate these sources. Excerpts from *Motezuma* and *Ezio* were performed in Prague in 1931 and 1937. Since 1960 a modest Mysliveček renaissance has taken place in Czechoslovakia, with productions of *Medonte* (whose manuscript turned up in Leningrad in 1955) in Opava (1961) and of *Tamerlano* in Brno (1967) (also given in Prague

(1977) and in Italy). Concert performances have been given in Brno of *L'Ipermestra* (1970, 1987) and *Demofoonte* (1973) and in Prague of *Bellerofonte* (1987).

Operas: *Il parnasso confuso* (opera–cantata), 1765; *Bellerofonte*, 1767 (RECORDING Supraphon, 1987); *Il Farnace*, 1767; *Il trionfo di Clelia*, 1767; *Demofoonte*, 1769; *L'Ipermestra*, 1769; *La Nitteti*, 1770; *Motezuma*, 1771; *Il gran* *Tamerlano*, 1771; *Demetrio*, 1772; *Romolo ed Ersilia*, 1773; *La clemenza di Tito*, 1773; *Antigona*, 1774; *Atide*, 1774; *Artaserse*, 1774; *Ezio*, 1775; *Adriano in Siria*, 1776; *La Calliroe*, 1778; *Armida*, 1778; *Olimpiade*, 1778; *La Circe*, 1779; *Antigono*, 1780; *Medonte, re di Epiro*, 1780

BIBLIOGRAPHY   Josef Pečman, *Josef Mysliveček*, Supraphon, 1981

J.T.

NICOLAS NABOKOV

b 17 April 1903, Novogrudok, Belorussia; *d* 6 April 1978, New York

Nicolas Nabokov, a cousin of the writer Vladimir Nabokov, was a composer of cosmopolitan background and varied interests. His composition teachers included Rebikov and Busoni. After studying literature at the Sorbonne and working in France and Germany, Nabokov emigrated to the US in 1933. In Paris he had met Diaghilev, who commissioned his ballet-cantata, *Ode*, successfully produced by the Ballets Russes in 1928, and Stravinsky, a strong influence on his work, with whom he remained friendly.

Nabokov's operas came relatively late in his career, when he was active in promoting international festivals and engaged in university teaching. His first, *The Holy Devil*, to a libretto by Stephen Spender (1958), later revised as *Der Tod des Grigorij Rasputin* (1959), shows the influence of Nabokov's compatriots, Tchaikovsky and Musorgsky, but also includes elements of French popular music, ragtime and serial technique. For his second opera, *Love's Labour's Lost* (after Shakespeare), Nabokov turned to W. H. Auden and Chester Kallman for the libretto. Plans for the premiere in Edinburgh and then Berlin were abandoned and it was eventually performed in Brussels in 1973. The most effective passages are those which recall the neo-classical style of Stravinsky's *The Rake's Progress*.

BIBLIOGRAPHY Nicolas Nabokov, *Old Friends and New Music*, Hamish Hamilton, 1951; Nicolas Nabokov, *Bagázh: Memoirs of a Russian Cosmopolitan*, Athaneum, 1975

P.D.

EDUARD NÁPRAVNÍK

Eduard (Frantsevich) Nápravník; *b* 24 August 1839, Býšt', nr Hradec Králové, Bohemia; *d* 23 November 1916, Petrograd (St Petersburg)

Nápravník studied at the Prague Organ School (1853–4) and privately with Kittl. In 1861 Prince Yusupov engaged him as conductor of his private orchestra in St Petersburg, and in 1863 he joined the staff of the Mariinsky Theatre, where he was appointed chief conductor in 1869. In his 50 years at the Imperial Theatre he introduced over 80 operas – including most of the Russian nationalist repertoire. His importance as a conductor overshadowed his compositional career, most of which took place in Russia. All his four completed operas were written in Russian, two on Russian topics.

Dubrovskiy

Opera in four acts, Op. 58
Libretto by Modest I. Tchaikovsky, after the tale by Pushkin
PREMIERES 15 January 1895, St Petersburg; US: 14 January 1922, San Francisco

Nápravník's most successful opera is nearest to the type of lyrical realism of Tchaikovsky's *Eugene Onegin*. It continues to be played occasionally in Russia.

RECORDING Chubenko, Pokrovskaya, Kozlovsky, Ivanov, Bolshoi Theatre Ch and O, Nebolsin, Melodiya, *c.* 1949
EDITION v.s., Muzika, 1972

Other operas: *Nizhegorodtsï*, 1869; *Garol'd* (*Harold*), 1886; *Francesca da Rimini*, 1902
BIBLIOGRAPHY E. Gordeyeva, *'Dubrovsky' Napravnika*, Moscow, 1949; 2nd edn, 1960

J.T.

JOHANN GOTTLIEB NAUMANN

b 17 April 1741, Blasewitz, nr Dresden; *d* 23 October 1801, Dresden

Naumann was one of the most prolific German opera composers of the late 18th century. He studied initially at the Kreuzschule in Dresden, and at the age of 16 he began an extended visit to Italy, during which he aroused the interest of Tartini, Padre Martini and Hasse. In 1762 he produced his first operatic work, the intermezzo *Il tesoro insidiato*. Two years later, with Hasse's aid, he was appointed as church composer to the Dresden court, and in 1776 became kapellmeister. During two later visits to Italy his operatic successes included settings of such well-known Metastasio texts as *L'Achille in Sciro*, *La clemenza di Tito* and *L'isola disabitata*. Particularly important are the stage works that he composed in Sweden during a visit there, from 1778 to 1782, to advise on the development of the nation's opera. Of these *Cora och Alonso*, performed at the inauguration of the New Opera House in Stockholm in 1782, became his most popular work, though the composer himself rated his lyric tragedy *Gustav Wasa* even more highly. His earliest works reflect seria and buffo elements drawn from Hasse and Piccinni; but later, under the influence of Gluck, he also embraced features of the French style, including extended choruses and ballets.

Operatic works: *Il tesoro insidiato*, 1762; *Li creduti spiriti* (coll.), 1764; *L'Achille in Sciro*, 1767; *Alessandro nelle Indie* (inc.), (1768); *La clemenza di Tito*, 1769; *Il villano geloso*, 1770; *Solimano*, 1773; *L'isola disabitata*, 1773; *Armida*, 1773; *Ipermestra*, 1774; *La villanella incostante*, 1773, as *Le nozze disturbate*, 1774; *L'ipocondriaco*, 1776; *Amphion*, 1778; *Elisa*, 1781; *Cora och Alonso*, 1782; *Osiride*, 1781; *Tutto per amore*, 1785; *Gustav Wasa*, 1786; *Orpheus og Eurydice*, 1786; *La reggia d'Imeneo*, 1787; *Medea in Colchide*, 1788; *Protesilao*, 1789; *La dama soldato*, 1791; *Amore giustificato*, 1792; *Andromeda*, 1792; *Aci e Galatea, ossia I ciclopi amanti*, 1801
BIBLIOGRAPHY   R. Engländer, *Johann Gottlieb Naumann als Opernkomponist (1741–1801)*, E. Haberland, 1922; *rp*, Gregg International, 1970

B.S.

JOSÉ DE NEBRA

José Melchor Gaspar y Baltasar Nebra y Blasco [Joseph (de) Enebra]; *baptized* 6 January 1702, Catalayud, nr Saragossa, Spain; *d* 11 July 1768, Madrid

The most influential of an extraordinary family of musicians spanning 1672 to 1782, José de Nebra progressed precociously from the post of organist at the convent of the Descalzas Reales (where earlier Cristóbal Galán had reluctantly spent most of his career) in 1719, to that of second organist in 1724 and vice chapel master in 1751 of the Royal Chapel in Madrid under the Italian Francesco Courcelle (Corselli). Here he made his mark in a number of ways: he worked tirelessly at reforming the Royal Chapel, played a leading part in rewriting and restoring scores lost in the archives after a disastrous fire at the Alcázar Real in 1734, and wrote, as well as nearly 100 devotional works, some 20 operas and zarzuelas commissioned more often by the public theatres than by court impresarios. These operatic works show that, contrary to the received view of him as a staunch upholder of Spanish traditions in the face of foreign musical fashion, Nebra was as zealous an innovator as were Hidalgo, Durón and Literes before him in grafting Italianate melismatic styles and *da capo* forms on to Spanish roots.

Surviving operatic works: *Amor aumenta el valor* (dramma

armónico; coll.), 1728; *Viento es la dicha de amor* (zarzuela), 1743
BIBLIOGRAPHY   William M. Bussey, *French and Italian Influence on the Zarzuela, 1700–1770*, UMI Research Press, 1980; Nicolás A. Solar-Quintes, 'El compositor español José de Nebra . . . ', *Anuario musical*, vol. 9 (1950)

J.W.S.

OSKAR NEDBAL
b 26 March 1874, Tabor, Bohemia; *d* 24 December 1930, Zagreb

Nedbal studied the violin with Bennewitz and composition with Dvořák at the Prague Conservatory; he was a noted violinist and leader of the Bohemian String Quartet (with Suk as second violinist). He conducted widely, with the Czech Philharmonic (1896–1902) and later with the Vienna Tonkünstler Orchestra; he was subsequently prominent in the musical life of Slovakia. He committed suicide before a performance at the National Theatre, Zagreb.

Nedbal is remembered chiefly for his operettas, premiered mainly in Vienna, of which *Polenblut* (1913) is the best known. This is set in Russian-occupied Warsaw, and is peppered with mazurkas and krakowiaks, filtered through a recognizably Czech-nationalist dance-music sensibility, reminiscent of Smetana or even Nedbal's mentor, Dvořák. There are also the obligatory waltzes, so relished by the Viennese public.

Nedbal's one grand opera is forgotten, but his ballets and pantomimes, with their Czechoslovak themes, are still occasionally recorded.

Operettas: *Die keusche Barbara*, 1910; as *Cudná Barbora* (*Chaste Barbara*), 1911; *Polenblut*, 1913 (rev. as *Die Erntebraut*, 1942); *Die Winzerbraut*, 1916; *Die schöne Saskia*, 1917; *Eriwan*, 1918; *Mamsell' Napoleon*, 1920; *Donna Gloria*, 1925; *Das Dorf ohne Männer*, (n.d.)
Opera: *Sedlák Jakub* (*Peasant Jacob*), 1922

R.T.

CHRISTIAN NEEFE
Christian Gottlob Neefe; *b* 5 February 1748, Chemnitz; *d* 26 January 1798, Dessau

Although remembered chiefly as the most important of Beethoven's earliest teachers, Neefe is also noted as a composer, particularly of lieder and singspiels. His earliest theatrical experience was gained with Hiller who commissioned him to compose songs for inclusion in his *Der Dorfbarbier* (1771) and then, in 1776, relinquished to him the music directorship of the Seyler theatre troupe. Three years later Neefe moved with the Grossman-Helmut company to Bonn and there he first met the young Beethoven.

Neefe's stage works are distinguished by their melodic charm and effective sense of theatre; one that achieved particular popularity is his *Adelheit von Veltheim*, notable for its use of 'Turkish' effects akin to those in Mozart's *Die Entführung aus dem Serail*. Attracted to melodrama, on Benda's model, he not infrequently used the technique to enhance moments of dramatic intensity and produced an extended work of the type, a monodrama entitled *Sophonisbe*.

Operatic works: *Die Apotheke*, 1771; *Amors Guckkasten*, 1772; *Die Einsprüche*, 1772; *Heinrich und Lyda*, 1776; *Die Zigeuner*, 1777; *Sophonisbe*, 1778; *Adelheit von Veltheim*, 1780; *Der neue Gutsherr* (?1783–4); one lost opera
BIBLIOGRAPHY L. Hoffmann-Erbrecht: 'Christian Gottlob Neefe', in *Grove*, Macmillan, 1980

B.S.

ALBERTO NEPOMUCENO

b 6 July 1864, Fortaleza, Brazil; *d* 16 October 1920, Rio de Janeiro, Brazil

Working principally in Rio de Janeiro, Nepomuceno, concert adminstrator, pianist, teacher, conductor and composer, became the leading champion of the nationalist cause in Brazilian music during the early years of the Republic. His compositions employ traditional melodies and instruments; his songs set Portuguese as opposed to Italian texts; and he included contemporary Brazilian music in his popular concert series. Controversially he sponsored a folk guitarist to appear at the Instituto Nacional de Música, and he provoked the wrath of conservative critic Oscar Guanabarino by steering the works of the young Villa-Lobos into print.

Nepomuceno wrote a large body of music in all genres, including four operas. Unlike his well-known piano piece *Galhofeira* and the string quartet *Brasileiro*, none of these displays any more than superficially Brazilian characteristics, remaining firmly rooted in Italianate romanticism. The unfinished lyrical comedy *O Garatuja*, based on a novel by José de Alencar, tells of a colonial Brazilian Till Eulenspiegel. Possibly this persuaded Richard Strauss to conduct the opera's fine *prelúdio* in 1920, while on tour in Rio de Janeiro.

Operas: *Porangaba*, 1887; *Artemis*, 1898; *Abul*, (1905), 1913; *O Garatuja* (inc.), (1904); *A cigarra*, 1911
BIBLIOGRAPHY David Appleby, *The Music of Brazil*, University of Texas Press, 1983

S.J.W.

OTTO NICOLAI

Carl Otto Ehrenfried Nicolai; *b* 9 June 1810, Königsberg; *d* 11 May 1849, Berlin

Nicolai is considered a significant figure in early German Romantic opera on the strength of a single

work – *Die lustigen Weiber von Windsor* – which is still regularly performed in German opera houses. It comes as something of a surprise, then, to learn that this was Nicolai's only German opera and that his remaining four operas, now never performed, were all Italian works.

Early studies in Berlin with the lieder composer Carl Friedrich Zelter obviously influenced Nicolai's early works: his first published compositions, which appeared in 1830, were solo songs and part-songs. In 1833 he went to Rome as organist at the Prussian embassy and undertook a study of Italian music, paying particular attention to the works of Palestrina. However, Nicolai, like Meyerbeer before him, soon developed a strong interest in traditional Italian folksong and, again like Meyerbeer, soon felt the pull of the theatre. The final impetus in Nicolai's case came as a result of his composing a funeral cantata for the mezzo-soprano Maria Malibran: 'Even if it's not an opera,' he wrote, 'at least it's a beginning.' His longed-for first commission came in 1838, though Nicolai had already begun work on *Rosamunda d'Inghilterra* two years earlier. The opera was performed, as *Enrico II*, in Trieste in 1839.

Enrico II and the three other Italian operas that followed – *Il templario* (based on Sir Walter Scott's *Ivanhoe*), *Gildippe ed Odoardo*, and *Il proscritto* (to a text rejected by Verdi) – are all firmly cast in the *bel canto* style, with graceful flowing melodies in the manner of Bellini, and following conventional Italian forms and structures. The success of *Enrico II* and *Il templario* led to Nicolai being hailed as a great Italian composer. In 1841 he was invited to conduct *Il templario* at the Hofoper in Vienna; its success led to his appointment as kapellmeister there, a post he held for six years. During this time Nicolai reworked *Il templario* as *Der Tempelritter* and *Il proscritto* as *Die Heimkehr des Verbannten* and eventually found in Shakespeare's *The Merry Wives of Windsor* the new operatic subject he had long been seeking. The intendant at the Opera turned it down and this probably prompted Nicolai to leave Vienna, having secured a post as kapellmeister at the court opera in Berlin. *Die lustigen Weiber von Windsor* received its premiere there in March 1849, only two months before Nicolai's untimely death after a stroke.

Die lustigen Weiber von Windsor

The Merry Wives of Windsor
Comic-fantastic opera in three acts (2h 30m)
Libretto by Hermann Salomon Mosenthal, after Shakespeare's *The Merry Wives of Windsor* (1600–1601)
Composed 1845–8
PREMIERES 9 March 1849, Hofoper, Berlin; UK: 3 May 1864, Her Majesty's Theatre, Haymarket, London; US: 16 March 1863, Philadelphia
CAST Sir John Falstaff *b*, Herr Fluth *bar*, Herr Reich *b*, Fenton *t*, Junker Spärlich *t*, Dr Caius *b*, Frau Fluth *s*, Frau Reich *ms*, Jungfer Anna Reich *s*, Citizen *t*, 3 other Citizens *spoken roles*, Innkeeper *spoken role*; *satb* chorus of men and women of Windsor, children, masks of elves and spirits; ballet

FULL ORCHESTRA onstage: hp, bell in G

Before arriving at Shakespeare's *The Merry Wives of Windsor*, Nicolai had considered and rejected texts by Goldoni, Gozzi and Calderón. He had even, in his desperation, advertised a prize competition to find a suitable subject, but none of the 30 entries he received pleased him. *The Merry Wives of Windsor* was suggested by Siegfried Kapper, who had helped Nicolai make German versions of two of his Italian works. It proved to be a felicitous choice: the opera has remained in the repertoire in Germany ever since.

SYNOPSIS

Act I   Frau Fluth and Frau Reich discover they have received identical love letters from Sir John Falstaff and vow to get their revenge. Frau Fluth invites him to a rendezvous, having made sure that her husband – whom she considers to be over-possessive – learns of the arrangement. In mid-assignation, Frau Reich enters, as planned, to warn of Fluth's imminent arrival. Falstaff is bundled into a laundry basket to be thrown into the river.

Act II   At the Garter Inn, Falstaff receives a second invitation from Frau Fluth. Her husband arrives, in disguise, to try to discover his wife's supposed lover. Meanwhile Frau Reich's daughter Anna is receiving the attentions of two unwanted suitors, Dr Caius and Spärlich, and one wanted one – Fenton. The young couple pledge their love. Falstaff visits Frau Fluth again, and is again interrupted by the arrival of her husband; this time he escapes dressed in women's clothes.

Act III   The women have explained everything to their husbands and they discuss how to punish Falstaff further. Anna's father arranges that she shall marry Spärlich while her mother arranges that she shall marry Caius. In Windsor Park, Fluth, Reich and their neighbours torment the terrified Falstaff. Meanwhile Spärlich and Caius have gone off together, disguised as elves, each thinking the other is Anna, while Anna and Fenton have hurried off to be married. Finally Anna's parents give their blessing, and Falstaff asks forgiveness for his foolish behaviour.

The form of the opera is that of the singspiel. But the Italian influence on much of the music is obvious and the result is a deep-rooted fusion of the two national styles. Among the most easily identifiable examples of Italian traits are Nicolai's *parlando*-type handling of the voices in the Act II comic duet between Falstaff and Fluth ('Ja, Sir Bach'), and the melodic construction of Fenton's romance ('Horch, die Lerche'). Colourful handling of the orchestra – evidence here of the influence of German composers, notably Weber – adds a further dimension to this ebullient score.

RECORDING Pütz, Mathis, Litz, Wunderlich, Gutstein, Engen, Frick, Bavarian State Opera Ch and O, Heger, EMI, 1963
EDITIONS f.s., Bote und Bock, 1850; v.s., Peters, 1933; *rp*, 1961

Other operas: *Enrico II (Rosmonda d'Inghilterra)*, 1839; *Il templario*, 1840 (rev. as *Der Tempelritter*, 1845); *Gildippe ed Odoaro* (only a cavatina survives), 1840; *Il proscritto*, 1841 (rev. as *Die Heimkehr des Verbannten*, 1846)
BIBLIOGRAPHY J. W. Klein, 'Verdi and Nicolai: A Strange Rivalry', *MR*, vol. 32 (1971), p. 63

G.H.

GIUSEPPE NICOLINI

b 29 January 1762, Piacenza; *d* 18 December 1842, Piacenza

Nicolini left his birthplace to travel, with the help of Duke G. Girolamo Sforza Fogliani, to Naples, where he finished his training at the Conservatory of San Onofrio, but tradition has it that, between 1778 and 1784, Nicolini took lessons from Cimarosa. If this is so, the tuition must have been private, since Cimarosa never held a post at a conservatory.

During the 40-odd years of his career Nicolini composed about 50 operas. Beginning with comedy, he made his début in Parma with *La famiglia stravagante* (1793), and later broadened his field to include serious and semi-serious genres. Basing his style on the late works of Cimarosa and Paisiello, and blessed with a gift for comic writing, Nicolini reached the apex of his career between 1811 and 1820, the period when Rossini achieved maturity. By nature a traditionalist and averse to the new stirrings of the time, Nicolini made little effort to keep up with new trends in opera composition, led by Rossini, and was content to remain a musician of the late 18th century – antiquated, but also sensitive and balanced, with a full command of the requisite professional skills.

Surviving operas: *I molinari*, 1794, as *L'amor mugnaio, ossia I mulinari*, 1795; *Le nozze campestri*, 1794; *La clemenza di Tito*, 1797; *Gli Sciti*, 1799; *Il trionfo del bel sesso*, 1799; *Quinto Fabio*, 1801; *I baccanali di Roma*, 1801; *I Manlii*, 1801; *Il geloso sincerato*, 1804; *Peribea e Telamone*, 1804; *Le nozze inaspettate*, 1805; *Abenamet e Zoraide*, 1805; *Traiano in Dacia*, 1807; *Le due gemelle*, 1808; *Coriolano o L'assedio di Roma*, 1808; *Angelica e Medoro*, 1810; *Abradate e Dircea*, 1810; *Le nozze dei Morlacchi*, 1811; *L'ira d'Achille*, 1814; *Annibale in Bitinia*, 1821; 34 lost operas
BIBLIOGRAPHY A. Rapetti and C. Censi, 'Un Maestro di musica piacentino: Giuseppe Nicolini', *Biblioteca storica piacentina*, vol. 24 (1944)

D.A.D'A.

CARL NIELSEN

Carl August Nielsen; *b* 9 June 1865, Sortelung, nr Nørre Lyndelse on Funen, Denmark; *d* 3 October 1931, Copenhagen

Although Nielsen wrote two successful operas, he is today chiefly considered as a symphonist. He also wrote chamber music, including four fine string quartets, incidental music for more than a dozen plays, many songs and choral works.

Carl Nielsen

Nielsen came from a poor family and was brought up in rural surroundings. Together with his father, he played the violin at local weddings, dances and other celebrations. At the age of 14 he left school and for five years was employed in a military band at Odense, playing the signal horn and trombone. For recreation he played Haydn and Mozart string quartets with his friends. Helped by money supplied by benefactors in Odense, he studied for two years at the Royal Conservatory in Copenhagen. From 1889 until 1905 he played second violin in the orchestra of the Royal Theatre, Copenhagen.

A grant from the Ancker Bequest enabled him to visit Germany in the autumn of 1890. He went to Dresden, where he heard *Der Ring des Nibelungen*, then to Berlin, where he attended a performance of *Die Meistersinger*. But though overwhelmed by the music of Wagner's operas, he did not succumb to their dramatic theory. In 1894 he went abroad again, to Germany and to Vienna, where he heard *Tristan und Isolde*. He also visited Brahms, who had a greater influence on Nielsen's own compositions than Wagner. Another influence was Johan Svendsen, whom Nielsen succeeded in 1908 as conductor of the Royal Opera, Copenhagen, a post he held until 1914.

The operas date from the period of his early maturity, when he had evolved a personal style of his own. Nielsen had strong views on the nature of opera. In the diary he kept while travelling in 1894 he wrote: 'The plot must be the pole that goes through a dramatic work; the plot is the trunk, words and sentences are fruit and leaves, but if the trunk is not strong and healthy, it is no use that the fruits look beautiful.'

For his two operas, Nielsen chose strong poles or trunks: the Books of Samuel in the Old Testament for the first, *Saul og David*, and a comedy by Ludvig Holberg, the 18th-century dramatist, for the second, *Maskarade*. Given their success and the composer's interest in the genre, the question must be asked, why did Nielsen stop writing operas at the age of 41? Vilhelm Andersen, the librettist of *Maskarade*, offered him an adaptation of another Holberg comedy, but he thought the subject too similar. Then in 1930, on the 125th aniversary of Hans Andersen's birth, he considered setting the dramatization of one of Andersen's fairy-tales, but instead contributed incidental music and a few songs to a play, *Amor og Digteren* (*Cupid and the Poet*), about Andersen and his love for Jenny Lind.

Nielsen began work on his Second Symphony, 'The Four Temperaments', while still composing *Saul og David*; he began the third, *Sinfonia espansiva*, four years after finishing *Maskarade*, which is called to mind in the scherzo of the symphony. The Fourth Symphony, 'The Inextinguishable', would follow in another four years. There, perhaps, lies the answer to the question raised above: the symphonist had finally found his true *métier*, and opera, like the string quartet, was abandoned.

Saul og David
Saul and David

Opera in four acts, Op. 25 (2h 15m)
Libretto by Einar Christiansen, based on the Books of Samuel
Composed 1898–1901
PREMIERES 28 November 1902, Royal Theatre, Copenhagen; UK: 23 February 1977, Collegiate Theatre, London
CAST Saul *b-bar*, Jonathan *t*, Mikal *s*, David *t*, Samuel *b*, Abner *b*, The Witch of Endor *ms*, Abisay *t*; *satb* chorus of maidservants, priests, soldiers and people
FULL ORCHESTRA

Throughout the composition period of *Saul og David*, Nielsen was a member of the Royal Theatre orchestra. Obsessed by the subject of his opera, he wrote that 'for long periods I could not free myself from it, no matter where I was – even when I was sitting in the orchestra with my second violin, busy with ballets and vaudevilles'. This obsession, apparent in Nielsen's score, lends the opera its particular dramatic strength.

SYNOPSIS

Act I Samuel prophesies that Saul's reign as King of Israel will be over shortly. To comfort his father, Jonathan asks his friend David to sing to the king. David declares his love to Saul's daughter, Mikal.

Act II David defeats the Philistines by slaying the giant Goliath, but Saul is jealous at the people's praise of David and banishes him.

Act III David returns and proves his loyalty by sparing the sleeping king's life. Samuel anoints David as king of Israel and then dies.

Act IV Saul visits the Witch of Endor to consult the spirit of Samuel, who prophesies the deaths of

Saul and Jonathan at the hands of the Philistines. The prophecy comes true as Jonathan is mortally wounded and Saul kills himself rather than fall into the hands of the enemy. David is proclaimed king by the Israelites.

Musically and dramatically, the dominant figure of the opera is Saul, who has a fine monologue in the first act as well as an impressive death scene in the fourth. David's music is less original, but the choral music is splendid throughout, while the orchestral preludes and interludes are also highly evocative, in particular those depicting battle scenes.

RECORDING Söderström, Christoff, Hartmann, Young, Langdon, John Alldis Ch, Danish Radio Symphony Ch and O, Horenstein, Unicorn-Kanchana, 1975
EDITIONS v.ss., Wilhelm Hansen, 1904; 2nd edn, 1931

Maskarade
Masquerade
Opera in three acts, Op. 39 (2h 15m)
Libretto by Vilhelm Andersen, after the play by Ludvig Holberg
Composed 1904–6
PREMIERES 11 November 1906, Royal Theatre, Copenhagen; US: 23 June 1972, St Paul, Minnesota; UK: 9 May 1986, Morley College, London
CAST Jeronimus *b*, Magdelone *ms*, Leander *t*, Henrik *b-bar*, Leonard *t-bar*, Leonora *s*, Pernille *s*, *s*, *t*, 3 *bar*, *b-bar*, *b*; *satb* chorus of masqueraders – officers, students, girls; dancers
FULL ORCHESTRA

By the time he had completed composition of two-thirds of *Maskarade*, Nielsen was free, after 16 years, from the nightly grind of playing in the Royal Theatre orchestra and had not yet taken up his post as conductor of the Royal Opera. This unaccustomed freedom is reflected in the exhilaration, high spirits and even frivolity of much of the music.

SYNOPSIS
Act I Copenhagen, early 1723. Jeronimus has arranged a marriage between his son, Leander, and Leonora, daughter of his friend Leonard. Leander, however, has fallen in love with a girl he met the night before at a masquerade and refuses the match. According to Leonard, his daughter is also unwilling – she too has fallen in love with an unknown young man.

Act II In the street outside, Leander and Leonora meet on their way to the masquerade and sing ecstatically of their love, still unaware of each other's identity. Their respective servants, Henrik and Pernille, are also taken with each other.

Act III At the masquerade Magdelone (wife of Jeronimus) flirts and dances with Leonard, while the two pairs of young lovers express their feelings. At midnight, when everyone unmasks, Leander and Leonora discover that the marriage arranged for them is much to their taste.

Maskarade inevitably invites comparison with Mozart's *Le nozze di Figaro*, especially as regards the characters of Henrik and Mozart's Figaro. But the revolutionary side of Beaumarchais's valet is entirely missing from Holberg's, while the atmosphere of *Maskarade* is light-hearted. Nielsen's music, in particular the dance music of the third act, is sparkling and joyous. The passionate love duet for Leander and Leonora, parodied in the scene between Henrik and Pernille, reveals genuine feeling, while the ensemble pieces are as impressive as those in *Saul og David*, though very different in style. The opera has become a classic in Denmark.

RECORDING Brødersen, Hydgaard, Plesner, Landy, Schmidt-Johansen, Hansen, Sørensen, Bastian, Klint, Haugland, Danish Radio Ch and SO, Frandsen, Unicorn, 1977
EDITIONS f.s., facsimile, Wilhelm Hansen, 1948; v.ss., Wilhelm Hansen, 1906; *rp*, 1946

BIBLIOGRAPHY Johannes Fabricius, *Carl Nielsen 1865–1931: A Pictorial Biography*, Copenhagen, 1965; Carl Nielsen, *Min fynske barndom*, Martins Forlag, 1927 (English trans. by Reginald Spink, *My childhood on Fyn*, Hutchinson, 1953); Robert Simpson, *Carl Nielsen: Symphonist 1865–1931*, J. M. Dent, 1952; rev. edn, 1979

E.F.

LUIGI NONO
b 29 January 1924, Venice; *d* 8 May 1990, Venice

Nono's use of sound as a medium for social and personal challenge gave his work a distinctive edge. He was born into a family that pursued a wide range of cultural interests, and his own concern for music became dominant only in his teens. He thereafter threw himself into a study of musical technique, guided first by Malipiero, a friend of the family, and subsequently by his near-contemporary Maderna. From the start, he rooted himself in the more radical traditions of 20th-century modernism.

For Nono, technical and ideological radicalism were natural allies, and music's role as a shaper of collective enthusiasms was self-evident. Words and, from the early 1960s on, recorded sound therefore had a decisive role to play in his work. To this, his theatre added a further, visual layer. It was not a narrative form, but a 'theatre of ideas' grasped through the scrutiny of given situations. In its willingness to embrace discontinuity it looked back to some of Malipiero's theatrical work; but its prime source of inspiration was the experimental theatre of revolutionary Russia, on which Nono's first theatrical collaborator, A. M. Ripellino, was a noted authority.

Although Nono nurtured a number of theatrical projects, he completed only two of them: *Intolleranza 1960*, and *Al gran sole carico d'amore* (1972–5). The latter is in effect a *summa* of his aggressively confrontational work to date. Thereafter, critics registered a substantial volte-face: Nono's music became increasingly spare and contemplative, and intensively involved with the real-time electronic manipulation of sound in space. At the same time, as a result of a long collaboration with the philosopher Massimo Cacciari, the texts to which Nono turned also showed a change of direction with a new emphasis on the achievement of inner focus and clarity. Their major work together, *Prometeo* (1981–5), started life as a theatrical project, but mutated into a tragedia dell'ascolto – a tragedy of and for listening alone. In retrospect, this vast post-theatrical hymn to inwardness seems not so much a rejection of the politicized work of previous decades as a complement to it; for commitment to keeping alive the 'infinite possibilities' of human sensibility was also the motive force behind Nono's earlier denunciations of political oppression, and his often naïve exaltation of alternative political systems.

Intolleranza 1960

Intolerance 1960
Azione scenica in two parts (1h 15m)
Text by the composer, after *Materiali per un' opera* by Angelo Maria Ripellino and drawing on texts by Henri Alleg, Bertolt Brecht, Aimé Césaire, Paul Eluard, Vladimir Mayakovsky, Julius Fucík and Jean-Paul Sartre
Composed 1960–61, rev. 1970
PREMIERES 13 April 1961, La Fenice, Venice; US: 21 February 1965, Boston

Although Nono chose to frame the various source texts employed in *Intolleranza 1960* within a rudimentary narration, the story served only to link emblematic situations – of which a number at the time had immediate political resonances. In brief, an emigrant worker longs to escape from a mining town and return home, albeit turning his back on a woman who has cared for him. He gets caught up in a demonstration, arrested, interrogated and tortured. Thrown into a concentration camp, he escapes with 'an Algerian'. In Part II, montages demonstrating the 'absurdities of contemporary life' and the abiding presence of fanaticism alternate with episodes in the progress of the emigrant. He meets a female companion; together, they confront society's intolerance; finally they find themselves on the banks of a swollen river used to drive turbines: the river breaks through the dam, sweeping all before it.

Within this frame, different materials invite different treatment. The poems of Brecht, Eluard, Mayakovsky, etc., are set in a more direct version of the choral idiom that Nono had richly developed in *Il canto sospeso* (1955–6) and *Cori di Didone* (1958). Syllables are thrown from voice to voice throughout the full vocal gamut. By direct contrast the prose materials of Alleg or Sartre, or the extracts from Nazi interrogations of Julius Fucík, are presented in documentary fashion. Only the emigrant and his companion are permitted moments of vehemently expressive lyricism. The same violent contrasts inform the orchestration: at one moment pointillist, at the next a massive, almost undifferentiated wall of sound. A revised version, *Intolleranza 1970*, made for a performance in Nuremberg, modifies the text and

reworks the opera into one part; the music remains unchanged.

EDITION f.s. (with German text only), Ars Viva Verlag, 1962

Al gran sole carico d'amore

In the great sun, heavy with love
Azione scenica in two acts (1h 30m)
Texts assembled by the composer and Yuri Liubimov, from Bertolt Brecht, Tania Bunke, Fidel Castro, Ernesto Che Guevara, Giorgi Dimitrov, Maxim Gorky, Antonio Gramsci, Vladimir Lenin, Karl Marx, Louise Michel, Cesare Pavese, Arthur Rimbaud, Celia Sanchez, Haydée Santamaria and popular sources
Composed 1972–5
PREMIERES first version: 4 April 1975, Teatro Lirico, Milan; definitive version: 11 February 1978, Teatro Lirico, Milan; UK: 8 September 1978, King's Theatre, Edinburgh (concert; Frankfurt Opera)

Initiated by Nono, *Al gran sole* was the fruit of intensive collaboration involving the producer, Yuri Liubimov, of the Taganka Theatre, Moscow, his scenographer David Borovsky, and in due course the conductor Claudio Abbado. Moving entirely beyond traditions of narrative developed round individual protagonists, this choral opera, as Nono defined it, celebrates two great moments of social revolt: the Paris Commune, and the Russian Revolution of 1905. Both were bloodily suppressed and yet served to inspire others that came after. In each half, the role played by women in revolution is repeatedly underlined with individual characters such as Louise Michel, one of the heroines of the Commune, the poetess/guerrilla Tania Bunke and the street-walker Deola (a character of Pavese's and the remnant of an unrealized operatic project from the 1960s), represented by a quartet of sopranos – that nexus of female voices to which Nono was to return time and again.

The resources at Nono's disposal were wide: soloists, small chorus, large chorus, orchestra, tape. So the work's sectional nature could be underlined by constant changes of texture. Liubimov's production (his first in the West) matched this with a virtuoso manipulation of the elements of stagecraft: lights, moving platforms, and above all large numbers of performers, insistently present, as befits this eminently 'collective' work. The combined network of resources was pushed to its logical extremes: action without music, and orchestral 'reflexions' without stage action.

Looking back on *Al gran sole*, Nono described the work, somewhat unkindly, as 'an elephant'. But at the same time, this ambitious and vivid collective work marked a high point in the history of Italian political music theatre, and also in some measure a swan song. The challenging path that it marked out is one that younger composers have not chosen to follow.

EDITIONS rev. version: f.s./v.s., Ricordi (on hire), 1978

A scene from Nono's Al gran sole carico d'amore *(Milan, 1978)*

BIBLIOGRAPHY Enzo Restagno (ed.), *Nono*, Edizione de Torino, 1987; Jurg Stenzl (ed.), 'Azione scenica und Literatur oper' in *Luigi Nono: Musik-Konzepte 20*, edition text + kritik, 1981

D.O.S.

PER NØRGARD
b 13 July, 1932, Gentofte, Denmark

Nørgard studied at the Copenhagen Conservatory and in Paris with Lili Boulanger. After three years in Odense, he taught at the Copenhagen Conservatory from 1960 to 1965, then, after a difference of opinion with the authorities, moved to Aarhus. His early compositions were influenced by Sibelius; then, during the 1950s, he adopted various avant-garde techniques and evolved an infinite serial process that is used in his first opera, *Labyrinten*. By the time he came to write *Det Guddommelige Tivoli*, based on the writings of Adolf Wölfli, who spent the last 35 years of his life in a mental hospital, Nørgard's style had become complex in the extreme, but it remains sufficiently lyrical to attract the listener.

Operatic works: *Labyrinten*, 1967; *Gilgamesh*, 1973; *Det Guddommelige Tivoli* (*The Divine Circus*) 1983; *Siddharta*, 1983

E.F.

FREDERICK NORTON
George Frederic(k) Norton; *b* 11 October 1869, Salford, Lancashire, England; *d* 15 December 1946, Holford, Somerset, England

Norton trained as a baritone and after singing with the Carl Rosa Opera Company appeared on the variety stage; he played Ali Baba several times during the run of *Chu Chin Chow*.

Chu Chin Chow
Musical tale of the East in three acts (film: 1h 45m)
Book and lyrics by Oscar Asche, based on 'Ali Baba and the Forty Thieves' from *The Arabian Nights*
PREMIERES 31 August 1916, His Majesty's Theatre, Haymarket, London; US: 22 October 1917, Manhattan Opera House, New York

A mixture of pantomime, bloodthirsty melodrama and romantic operetta, this ran for five years in London and set a theatrical record. Its exotic escapism appealed to soldiers on leave, and the production was lavish. The music, picturesque rather than memorable, is full of minor-mode fingerprints (for example, in 'The Cobbler's Song') that relate more to the parlour ballad than to contemporary trends in musical theatre.

RECORDING excerpts: Bryan, Te Wiata, The Williams Singers, Michael Collins O, Collins, HMV, 1959
FILM Forde (dir.), Gaumont British/Gainsborough Films, 1934
EDITION v.s., Keith Prowse and Co., 1916

Musical comedies: *Pamela*, 1917; *The Willow Pattern Plate* (n.d.); *The Stone of Destiny* (n.d.)

BIBLIOGRAPHY Kurt Gänzl, *The British Musical Theatre*, vol. 2: *1915–1984*, Macmillan, 1986

S.B.

VÍTĚZSLAV NOVÁK

b 5 December 1870, Kamenice nad Lipou; *d* 18 July 1949, Skuteč, Czechoslovakia

A Dvořák pupil, Novák was himself the most influential Czech composition teacher of his day. He lived long, but peaked early, with the high point usually regarded as his cantata *The Storm* (1910), composed a few years before he embarked on his operatic career. His operas were thus written at a disappointing time in his life, when he had been overtaken by Suk in the orchestral field and in opera by Janáček, whose surprising later career was virtually contemporary. Novák wrote four operas, all of which show great musical craftsmanship but little flair for the stage. The first three are based on plays by major figures in the flowering of Czech drama between 1880 and 1914. Two are somewhat wordy comedies, both set in 'medieval' Bohemia, the second, *Karlštejn*, based on an incident in the life of the greatest Czech king, Emperor Charles IV. The most successful is his third opera, *The Lantern*. In his final opera, *The Grandfather's Legacy*, Novák abandoned many of the naturalistic conventions of the preceding operas by including substantial choruses, dances and long symphonic interludes.

The Lantern

Lucerna
Musical fairy-tale in four acts, Op. 56 (2h)
Libretto by Hanuš Jelínek, after Alois Jirásek's play
Composed 1919–22, rev. 1930
PREMIERE 13 May 1923, National Theatre, Prague; rev. version: 28 September 1930, National Theatre, Prague

The lantern of the title is a symbol of serfdom: the lantern with which the young miller must light the way of the lady of the manor should she step on to his property. This is an opera of reconciliation and at the end the lantern is no longer needed. The charm of the work lies chiefly in its affectionate depiction of local colour: village musicians, minor gentry and two most articulate water goblins.

RECORDING Děpoltová, Jonášová, Tuček, Berman, Zítek, Prague Radio Ch and O, Vajnar, Supraphon, 1986
EDITION v.s., Hudební matice, 1923

Other operas: *The Imp of Zvíkov* (*Zvíkovský rarášek*), 1915; *Karlštejn*, 1916 (rev. 1925, 1930); *The Grandfather's Legacy* (*Dědův odkaz*), 1926 (rev. 1942)
BIBLIOGRAPHY John Tyrrell, *Czech Opera*, CUP, 1988

J.T.

IVOR NOVELLO

David Ivor Davies; *b* 15 January 1893, Cardiff; *d* 6 March, 1951, London

Novello (he took his mother's name) was a silent-film matinee idol in the 1920s before he composed his most successful works for the musical theatre. He not only wrote his own plays and sometimes lyrics (which came after the melodies) but also acted the, often multiple, male leads; however, these were not singing parts and most of the songs in his operettas were sung on dramatic pretext (*The Times* astutely recognized in *Perchance to Dream* that 'all the songs gain much from the rapture with which Mr Novello listens to them'). Hence he could indulge the utmost romance with the alibi of a framework. As he was a superb melodist excelling in vocal waltzes, even the critics could hardly bring themselves to begrudge him this formula.

Glamorous Night

Romantic musical play in three acts (film: 1h 15m)
Book by the composer, lyrics by Christopher Hassall
PREMIERE 2 May 1935, Drury Lane, London

Amid wide-ranging and spectacular settings, a fascist revolution provides the Ruritanian element, television the reminder that we are in the contemporary world. The title song, one of Novello's finest melodies, epitomizes the smoothness of the late romantic vocal waltz.

RECORDING original cast, HMV, re-release, 1955
FILM Hurst (dir.), ABPC, 1937
EDITION v.s., Chappell, 1938

The Dancing Years

Romantic musical play in two acts (film: 1h 30m)
Book by the composer, lyrics by Christopher Hassall
PREMIERE 23 March 1939, Drury Lane, London

The setting is Hitler's invasion of Austria, the romantic operetta a flashback to the early work of the composer Rudi Kleber (played originally by Novello). The work's highlights include 'Waltz of My Heart', 'My Dearest Dear' and 'I Can Give You the Starlight'.

RECORDING original cast, HMV, re-release, 1954
FILM French (dir.), ABPC, 1949
EDITION v.s., Chappell, 1938

Perchance to Dream

Musical romance in two acts
Book and lyrics by the composer
PREMIERE 21 April 1945, Hippodrome, London

Here the pretext is history (the play is set in an English house in three different eras), but the romantic number 'We'll Gather Lilacs', portrayed as a Victorian ballad sung by two women, became hugely popular.

RECORDING   original cast, Decca, re-release, 1958
EDITION   v.s., Chappell, 1945

King's Rhapsody

Musical romance in three acts (film: 1h 30m)
Book by the composer, lyrics by Christopher Hassall
PREMIERE   24 August 1949, Palace Theatre, Manchester

Novello starred as Nikki, the playboy King of Murania, who has to be taught by his spirited wife Christiane that love and duty can flourish together in their politically arranged marriage. Ironically, romantic pathos eventually flourishes too, in the form of their separation when Nikki has to return to exile because of his democratic policies. Romantic hit songs include 'Some Day My Heart Will Awake', 'Fly Home, Little Heart' and 'If This Were Love'.

RECORDING   original (1949) cast, HMV, re-release (World Record Club)
FILM   Wilcox (dir.), Everest, 1955

Other musical comedies/plays: *Theodore & Co.* (coll. Kern), 1916; *The Golden Moth*, 1921; *Careless Rapture*, 1936; *Crest of the Wave*, 1937; *Arc de triomphe*, 1943; *Gay's the Word*, 1950
BIBLIOGRAPHY   James Harding, *Ivor Novello*, Allen, 1987

S.B.

MICHAEL NYMAN

b 23 March 1944, London

Nyman was well known as a critic (and author of a standard book on *Experimental Music* (1974)) before he established himself as a composer in the late 1970s. In 1976 he formed the Michael Nyman Band, with which he gave concerts of mainly minimalist music, including his own. It specialized in minimalism of the more aggressive and assertive type, with much amplification; and it is also to this genre that most of Nyman's own music belongs.

Nyman is best known as the composer for the films of Peter Greenaway (including *The Draughtsman's Contract* and *Prospero's Books*). He has also, however, composed several operas, including two for television: *The Kiss* (1985) and *Letters, Riddles and Writs* (1991, for the Mozart bicentenary); and three for the stage: *Vital Statistics* (partially performed in 1987, completed 1992), *Orpheus's Daughter* (1988, but then withdrawn), and, most successfully, *The Man Who Mistook his Wife for a Hat* (1986). In addition an opera-ballet, *La Princesse de Milan* (based, like *Prospero's Books*, on Shakespeare's *Tempest*), was staged at Avignon in 1991.

The Man Who Mistook his Wife for a Hat

Chamber opera in one act (50m)
Libretto by Christopher Rawlence, after the case study by Oliver Sacks (1985)
Composed 1985–6
PREMIERE   27 October 1986, ICA, London

Sacks's case study concerns a singer suffering from visual agnosia (mental blindness), for whom musical ability acts as 'a substitute for his loss of visual cognition'. The plot simply tracks the neurologist in his investigation of this strange and disturbing condition.

Nyman's score, obsessive and repetitive in style, is ideally suited to the subject, even if its unvarying amplified forte does become wearisome. It is built round a succession of Schumann songs – a kind of musical correlative of the patient's own fulfilment in the world of music – and its centrepiece is a performance of 'Ich grolle nicht', from Schumann's *Dichterliebe*. The tiny orchestra consists of string quintet (with two cellos) plus harp and piano. The opera was filmed for television and shown, episodically, in 1987 as part of a Channel 4 documentary on the Sacks case study.

RECORDING   Leonard, Belcourt, Westcott, Ensemble Instrumental, Nyman, CBS, 1987

S.W.

JACQUES OFFENBACH

Jacob Offenbach; *b* 20 June, 1819, Cologne; *d* 5 October 1880, Paris

Offenbach, the creator of French operetta, was the second son of a German cantor who had replaced his original surname, Eberst, with that of Offenbach, the town outside Frankfurt where he had once lived. All the Offenbach children were musical, but Jacob was enough of a cello prodigy for his father to have him enrolled at the Paris Conservatoire in 1833. He soaked up Paris's rich musical-theatre attractions; his disposition for the Opéra-Comique and the works of Adam, Auber, Hérold and others was rewarded by a spell as a cellist in the theatre's orchestra.

His experience playing at private salons led to his first compositions, sentimental waltzes such as *Fleurs d'hiver*, or *Rebecca* (using synagogue motifs), and also to public cello-recitals. His cello-playing was acclaimed, even by the young Queen Victoria. Offenbach's first stage music was for an 1839 Palais-Royal vaudeville, *Pascal et Chambord*, which was unsuccessful. During the political crisis of 1848, after composing further minor stage works, Offenbach returned to Germany. But, in 1850, he was back in Paris as chef d'orchestre at the Comédie-Française, a job that entailed conducting a great deal of incidental music and songs, much of which he composed himself. His first notable song, 'La chanson de Fortunio', with its haunting refrain, was written for Alfred de Musset's *Le chandelier*.

Dissatisfied with the Opéra-Comique's reluctance to mount truly comic operas, Offenbach set out to write his own, short operettas much in the style being popularized by Hervé – one-act buffooneries with a few songs sung by two or three characters. The licensing restrictions that deprived Offenbach and his early librettists of more than two or three characters, let alone a chorus, did not seem to dull the success of the first bill at the Bouffes-Parisiens in 1855. Here, at a tiny, rickety magic theatre off the Champs-Elysées, a four-part programme was riotously ended with *Les deux aveugles*, the raffish story of two sham blind beggars. Other one-act works followed, notably *Le violoneux*, and the theatre shifted its operations to winter quarters in the Passage Choiseul.

The permanent theatre opened merrily with a bill that included *Ba-ta-clan*, a musical *chinoiserie* of considerable cleverness and silliness by Offenbach and Ludovic Halévy (a civil servant and a nephew of Fromental Halévy, the composer of *La juive*). It indulged in musical satire (on Meyerbeer and grand Italian opera), put its contemporary Parisian characters in a fantastic (Chinese) setting, and had them sing and dance an entrancing waltz. Thus, the pattern for many of Offenbach's works was already set. Within a year, the Bouffes was offering not only new Offenbach works, but reprises of short comic works by Mozart and Rossini, as well as two winning operettas in a competition for new composers – one by Lecocq and the other by Bizet (both to the same libretto, *Le docteur Miracle*).

The opéras-bouffes were popular not only in Paris, but on tours of the Bouffes company to the French provinces, London, and Vienna. In Britain, as in Austria–Hungary, the frivolity of Offenbach's one-act operettas led to local translations and, later, frank imitations. Suppé's *Das Pensionat* (1860) and Sullivan's *Cox and Box* (1868) were both influenced by Offenbach's style and were instrumental in establishing the national operetta styles of both countries.

By 1858, several characters and a full chorus were permitted at the Bouffes, and on 21 October the first great, full-length, classical French operetta was produced: *Orphée aux enfers*. Its enormous success led to worldwide productions, and the composition of the full-length *Geneviève de Brabant* (1859). Several accomplished short works followed, including *M. Choufleuri restera chez lui le . . .*, *Les bavards*, *Lieschen et Fritzchen*, as well as a ballet, *Le papillon*, and a work for the Opéra-Comique, the three-act *Barkouf*. Neither *Le Pont des Soupirs* (1863) nor *Les Géorgiennes* (1864) was particularly memorable at the Bouffes, nor was Offenbach's romantic opera for the Court Opera in Vienna: *Die Rheinnixen* (1864), although one of its numbers was transformed much later into the barcarolle in *Les contes d'Hoffmann*. But with a new star, Hortense Schneider, a new theatre (the Variétés), and a new team of librettists, there was another triumph, *La belle Hélène*. The fortuitous partnership of librettists Henri Meilhac and Ludovic Halévy ensured almost perfect texts for the great works that followed: *Barbe Bleue*, *La vie parisienne* and *La Grande Duchesse de Gérolstein*.

La Princesse de Trébizonde (1869), although coming at the very height of Offenbach's powers, also marked the beginning of the end of the public's enchantment with the old opéra-bouffe style. It was tired of the old burlesque methods and operatic parodies, the puns, the travesty, and was beginning to seek a more romantic, heavier weight to its stories, though it did not tire of clever plots and jokes if well written. It also craved spectacle. *Les brigands* (1870) was a compromise between silliness, satire, and romanticism of operas such as Auber's *Fra Diavolo*. The Franco-Prussian War brought to an end the frivolity of the Second Empire with its saucy operettas; Offenbach (still ashamed of his Germanic origins) fled France.

But Lecocq's prediction that operetta would be killed by Prussian shells was wrong; post-war Paris craved either an excess of spectacle or a surfeit of sentimentality. Offenbach, who returned to take over the management of the Théâtre de la Gaîté in 1873, failed, however, to find the perfect recipe for new works. *Le Roi Carotte*, although lavish, was too satirical; *Fantasio* was bland and *Les braconniers* was a weak rehash of *Les brigands*. (Lecocq's *La fille de Madame Angot*, an immense success in Paris in 1873, was exactly what Parisians wanted: a costume romance with reduced silliness and satire.) Offenbach could still write effective short works (*La leçon de chant*, *La permission de 10 heures*) and risqué longer ones with modern settings (*La jolie parfumeuse*), but he increasingly channelled his enormous energies into massive, spectacular versions of older works, and new extravaganzas, at the Théâtre de la Gaîté, which after a profitable start he mismanaged into debt. An aggrandized *Orphée aux enfers* in 1874 was followed much less profitably by an amplified *Geneviève de Brabant*.

In an attempt to recapture his imperial crown, Offenbach worked again with Meilhac and Halévy (*La boulangère a des écus*, *La créole*) and then with Lecocq's writers Chivot and Duru on *Madame Favart*, and, most successfully, *La fille du tambour-major*, a work that harked back to Donizetti and even Méhul, but which displayed Offenbach's late-period charms at their most delightful. But by the end of the 1870s, the triumphs of Planquette and Audran were foremost in the minds and throats of the Paris operetta public and Offenbach's works fell out of favour. *Les contes d'Hoffmann* was unfinished at the time of the composer's death and was completed at the request of his family by Ernest Guiraud. Standing outside the operetta tradition, it has become, rather ironically, the most frequently performed of Offenbach's works.

Orphée aux enfers
Orpheus in the Underworld

Opéra-bouffon in two acts (1h 45m; rev. version: 2h 45m)
Libretto by Hector Crémieux and Ludovic Halévy
Composed 1858, rev. in four acts 1874
PREMIERES 21 October 1858, Bouffes-Parisiens, Paris; US: March 1861, Stadt Theater, New York; UK: 26 December 1865, Her Majesty's Theatre, Haymarket, London (as *Orpheus in the Haymarket*); rev. version: 7 February 1874, Théâtre de la Gaîté, Paris
CAST Aristée/Pluton *t*, Jupiter *bar*, Orphée *t*, John Styx *t*, Mercure *t*, Bacchus *silent*, Mars *b*, Eurydice *s*, Diane *s*, L'Opinion Publique *ms*, Vénus *s*, Cupidon *s*, Junon *s*, Minerve *s*, Cybèle *s*, Hebé *s*; *satb* chorus of gods, goddesses; ballet
STANDARD ORCHESTRA (rev. version has larger orchestra)

Orphée aux envers was the first classical (in both senses of the term) full-length operetta, although it was supported by other pieces at its original presentation. What began as a burlesque sketch on the Orpheus legend became something far more substantial, its foolery striking the right, impudent note. The original targets were the posturing excesses of classical performances at the Comédie-Française, still considered sacrosanct during the Second Empire, and the attack was handled by contemporary party-goers in Gustave Doré-style togas. An orgiastic climax was reached during the Act II bacchanal, with a stately minuet of the gods holidaying in hell followed immediately by the *galop infernal* (the can-can).

SYNOPSIS

Act I Orpheus and Eurydice are bored with each other; the wife particularly loathes her husband's dreadful violin-playing. The shepherd/beekeeper

M. Marchand, the original Orphée; an illustration from the first vocal score

Aristaeus has attracted Eurydice's attentions – in fact he is Pluto, disguised – and he sets a poisonous snake in the fields, which conveniently bites Eurydice. She dies euphorically and is happily transported to hell. Orpheus is delighted at the news, but Public Opinion requires him to journey to Jupiter to demand the return of his wife. On Mount Olympus, the gods are seditious, demanding more excitement and better food. To quell their revolt, Jupiter decides to allow them to accompany him down to the Underworld to investigate Orpheus' predicament.

Act II Once there, Jupiter – disguised as a fly – falls for Eurydice himself. At a rowdy farewell party for the Olympians, Jupiter consents to let the less-than-enthusiastic Orpheus retrieve his wife, providing he does not turn around on his way out. Jupiter then throws a thunderbolt, causing Orpheus to turn. Eurydice is forced to remain down under as a bacchante, to everyone's joy save Public Opinion's.

Because of its irreverent merriment (snatches of Gluck's 'Che faro senza Euridice?' appear), its catchy score, and most of all its can-can – Offenbach's most famous composition (often rather dubiously interpolated into many of his other works) – Orphée – is constantly performed. Generally, the original two-act version is used, but since the EMI recording of the four-act 1874 aggrandisement, parts of that overblown score have been heard in recent revivals.

RECORDINGS Mesplé, Rhodes, Sénéchal, Burles, Trempont, Ch and O of the Capitole de Toulouse, Plasson, EMI, 1979
EDITIONS original version: v.s., Heugel, 1858; rev. version: v.s., Heugel, 1874

La belle Hélène

Beautiful Helen
Opéra-bouffe in three acts (3h)
Libretto by Henri Meilhac and Ludovic Halévy
Composed 1864
PREMIERES 17 December 1864, Théâtre des Variétés, Paris; UK: 30 June 1866, Adelphi, London (as *Helen, or Taken from the Greek*); US: 14 September 1867, Chicago
CAST Paris *t*, Ménélaus *t*, Agamemnon *bar*, Calchas *b*, Achille *t*, Ajax I *t*, Ajax II *bar*, Hélène *s*, Oreste *s* or *t*, Leøna *s*, Parthenis *s*, Bacchis *ms*; *satb* chorus of guards, slaves, people, princes, princesses, mourners for Adonis, Helen's entourage
STANDARD ORCHESTRA

La belle Hélène marked a return to Classical antiquity for its creators, who aimed to repeat the triumph of *Orphée aux enfers* – and succeeded. The libretto and characters are far more developed, and its musical pattern subsequently became the basic mould for the classical three-act operetta. There was also a romantic or sentimental streak that Offenbach and his librettists, their followers, and the Viennese, later developed. Meilhac and Halévy turned the events of the rape of Helen of Sparta into a boulevard farce, but a musical farce, and it is the delirious activity of the chorus and principals in their various ensembles that makes *La belle Hélène* so deliciously immortal.

SYNOPSIS

Act I Queen Helen of Sparta is troubled by her marriage to the weak King Menelaus, and feels she is being hounded by the Fates. The shady soothsayer Calchas tells her that he too has heard the rumours of a divine beauty contest involving a golden apple and a handsome shepherd. The shepherd appears and tells Calchas that Venus has promised him the heart of the most beautiful woman in the world. The shepherd wins a wordplay contest and reveals himself as Paris, Prince of Troy. Calchas makes sure that Paris and Helen will be alone by manufacturing a divine message that forces Menelaus to journey to Crete.

Act II Paris steals into Helen's boudoir, disguised as a slave. Helen thinks she is dreaming, until Menelaus barges in, discovering the two in bed. She reproaches her husband for having returned without warning. Paris tactfully withdraws, vowing to return.

Act III The royals have gone to the beach at Nauplia for their holidays. A priest arrives on a barge, to proclaim that Helen must now take a trip to Chytherea, to atone for the gods' displeasure. As soon as she sails away, the priest reveals himself as Paris, and the Trojan War is set in motion.

While the subject matter of *La belle Hélène* and its disrespectful treatment echoed that of *Orphée*, Offenbach adopted a different musical style, moving away from 18th-century pastiche towards a more modern idiom that involved a greater degree of chromaticism (often in the melodies, for example in Helen's 'Amours divins', where the stepwise falling motion perfectly captures her sadness and longing). There is even an oblique quip at Wagner's *Tannhäuser* during the competition scene, a raucous fanfare which Menelaus passes off as 'German music I commissioned for the ceremony'.

RECORDINGS Norman, Alliot-Lugaz, Aler, Burles, Lafont, Bacquier, Ch and O of the Capitole de Toulouse, Plasson, EMI, 1984
EDITIONS f.s., Bote und Bock, 1865; v.s., Bote und Bock; rp, c. 1945

Barbe-Bleue

Bluebeard
Opéra-bouffe in three acts (four scenes) (2h)
Libretto by Henri Meilhac and Ludovic Halévy
Composed 1866
PREMIERES 5 February 1866, Théâtre des Variétés, Paris; UK: 2 June 1866, Olympic Theatre, London (as *Bluebeard Re-Paired*); US: 13 July 1868, Niblo's Garden, New York

Barbe-Bleue took the same group of Variétés comedians that had made *La belle Hélène* such a hit and set them loose in the farcical medieval-legend territory that had previously been evoked in *Geneviève de Brabant* (1859).

Bluebeard, having murdered no fewer than five wives, is determined to find a sixth. He sends his ministers to the village to crown a Rose Queen, to be chosen by lottery. The winner is the buxom, 'Rubensesque' but uncouth Boulotte, and Bluebeard is delighted. They go off to be married at the castle. When Bluebeard later fancies Fleurette, daughter of King Bobèche, he must rid himself of Boulotte. The alchemist Popolani is instructed to carry out the execution. But he has a good heart, and offers Boulotte the choice between a vial of poison and one of sugared water. She chooses the latter, and is drugged to sleep. When she awakes, she discovers her five predecessors are also alive, kept by Popolani in his cellar. They seek revenge. Boulotte, dressed as a gypsy palmist, interrupts the nuptials of Bluebeard and Hermia (as Fleurette is now known), and reveals that the gypsy band with her are Bluebeard's five other wives and male victims who similarly avoided the monarch's death sentences. Boulotte rejoins Bluebeard, who not too convincingly pledges to reform himself.

There are moments of horror and suspense, particularly in Act III, where an extended scene of great drama foreshadows *Les contes d'Hoffmann*. The Act II court shenanigans, in which Offenbach satirizes the obsequiousness of courtiers, have little to do with the murderous goings-on of the title character, and have not worn as well. Because of this and other dull libretto patches *Barbe-Bleue* is not played as often today as its delightful score warrants.

RECORDING Dachary, Stiot, Legay, Lenoty, Doniat, Ch and O of French Radio, Doussard, Bourg, 1967
EDITIONS f.s., Bote und Bock, c. 1867; v.s., Gérard, 1866; rp, Belwin Mills, 1985

La vie parisienne

Parisian Life

Opéra-bouffe in four (originally five) acts (3h)
Libretto by Henri Meilhac and Ludovic Halévy
Composed 1866, rev. 1873
PREMIERES original version: 31 October 1866, Théâtre du Palais-Royal, Paris; US: 29 March 1869, Théâtre Français, New York; UK: 30 March 1872, Holborn Theatre, London; rev. version: 25 September 1873, Théâtre des Variétés, Paris

With *La vie parisienne*, Meilhac, Halévy and Offenbach turned to the troupe of the Théâtre du Palais-Royal and its dizzy farceurs for an unusual contemporary opéra-bouffe planned to capitalize on the forthcoming 1867 World Exhibition. The work was in fact suggested by a one-act farce the authors had written for the same playhouse two years earlier, which was now craftily embroidered.

A Swedish baron and baroness come to Paris to see the Great Exhibition. At the railway station, a boulevardier, Raoul de Gardefeu, spies the attractive baroness and passes himself off as a tour guide. Raoul has taken the couple to his house, which he passes off as an annexe of the Grand Hotel. While Raoul attempts to seduce the baroness, the baron insists that he be introduced to a courtesan, Métella, who was recently Gardefeu's lover. Stalling the baron for a while, Raoul invites him to dine with his glove-maker, his cobbler, and their friends, passing themselves off as higher-class hotel guests. At another party at a vacant townhouse – arranged so that Raoul can spend some time alone with the baroness – a group of dressed-up servants carouse

drunkenly with the baron. At the Café Anglais, a duel beween the baron and Gardefeu is prevented when Métella and the baroness reveal that nothing at all happened the previous evening.

Though a thoroughly 'integrated' modern operetta, with gorgeous ensembles and finales, *La vie parisienne* harks back endearingly to the old vaudeville pattern of couplets so familiar to the Palais-Royal audiences. Offenbach was prevented from incorporating many of his usual vocal cadenzas by the fact that the company of the Palais-Royal were essentially actors rather than singers, but he made up with a wealth of memorable dance tunes. The two brilliant party scenes also influenced *Die Fledermaus* (1874), itself based on a Palais-Royal farce by Meilhac and Halévy.

RECORDING Crespin, Mesplé, Sénéchal, Masson, Trempont, Benoit, Ch and O of the Capitole de Toulouse, Plasson, EMI, 1976
EDITIONS f.s., F. Treumann, 1867; v.s., V. Boullard, 1866

La Grande-Duchesse de Gérolstein

The Grand Duchess of Gerolstein

Opéra-bouffe in three acts (2h 45m)
Libretto by Henri Meilhac and Ludovic Halévy
Composed 1866–7
PREMIERES 12 April 1867, Théâtre des Variétés, Paris; US: 24 September 1867, Théâtre Français, New York; UK: 18 November 1867, Covent Garden, London

La Grande-Duchesse de Gérolstein, which was the Variétés's contribution to the 1867 Exhibition, was one of the great smash hits of 19th-century operetta. Effectively planned and marketed to coincide with a barrage of royal visitors to Paris, its satire at the expense of militaristic petty states and court intrigue – especially amorous – was directly on target.

Private Fritz of the Gerolstein army is in love with a peasant girl, Wanda. The Grand-Duchess, reviewing her troops, falls for the private. When he explains his military strategy to her, she is so impressed that she makes him a general. In due time, he returns victorious from battle. All of this does not sit well with the displaced General Boum, who with his confederates plots to bring down Fritz. They are eventually joined by the Grand-Duchess herself, exasperated by Fritz's coldness towards her. Fritz's honeymoon with Wanda is disrupted, and he becomes a private once more.

The score is less full of consistently great invention than its predecessors, despite a marvellous first act that is a model of bombastic silliness. More so than la belle Hélène, the Grand-Duchess was a star part for Hortense Schneider, whose offstage reputation remained as loose as possible, perhaps partially for publicity purposes. The operetta was rapturously received around the world, no doubt preceded by whiffs of scandal. The craze for French opéra-bouffe in Britain and the US dates from the *Grande-Duchesse*'s initial performances in those countries.

RECORDING Crespin, Mesplé, Vanzo, Burles, Massard, Ch and O of the Capitole de Toulouse, Plasson, CBS, 1977

EDITIONS f.s., Bois, 1983; v.ss., Brandus et Dufour, 1867; Bote und Bock, *c.* 1870; F.-H. Heddenhausen (ed.), Bote und Bock, 1967

La Périchole

Perichole
Opéra-bouffe in two (later three) acts (2h 30m)
Libretto by Henri Meilhac and Ludovic Halévy, after the play *Le Carrosse du Saint-Sacrement* (1830) by Prosper Mérimée
Composed 1868, rev. 1874
PREMIERES two-act version: 6 October 1868, Théâtre des Variétés, Paris; US: 4 January 1869, Pike's Opera House, New York; UK: 27 June 1870, Princess's Theatre, London; three-act version: 25 April 1874, Théâtre des Variétés, Paris

La Périchole is set in 18th-century Peru. The usual Meilhac–Halévy silliness is all there, but there is also a more sentimental vein in the leading character, which Offenbach exploited in several numbers, most famously the Act I letter song. The heroine's romantic predicament was still considered quite *risqué* to British audiences in 1875, when the operetta shared the bill with the first run of Gilbert and Sullivan's *Trial by Jury*.

The street singers La Périchole and Piquillo, much in love, are too poor even for a marriage licence. The viceroy, Don Andrès, is taken by La Périchole's beauty and wants her to move in to his palace as a lady-in-waiting. To do this officially, she must be a married woman, so the viceroy arranges for the lovesick Piquillo – who has just received a despairing farewell letter from his beloved – to marry La Périchole, without knowing her identity. The two are so tipsy by the time of their wedding that they do not recognize one another. Piquillo eventually recognizes her as his wife, and as the viceroy's favourite, and publicly humiliates her. For this, the viceroy has Piquillo dragged down to the dungeon reserved for recalcitrant husbands. Eventually the viceroy pardons them.

Offenbach's score is rich in Spanish (if not Peruvian) suggestions – boleros, seguidillas and fandangos abut galops, waltzes and marches – and is one of his most magical creations; the finales in particular are superb. *La Périchole* was restaged at the Variétés in 1874, in three (rather than two) acts. Since then, the operetta has had a chequered career, but certain productions have been very successful.

RECORDINGS 1. Crespin, Vanzo, Trigeau, Friedmann, Bastin, Ch of the Opéra du Rhin, Strasbourg PO, Lombard, Erato, 1977; 2. Berganza, Carreras, Sénéchal, Trempont, Bacquier, Ch and O of the Capitole de Toulouse, Plasson, EMI, 1981: both recordings are recommended for authenticity of style [A.B.]
EDITION v.ss., Brandus et Dufour, 1868

Les contes d'Hoffmann

The Tales of Hoffmann
Fantastic opera in five acts (4h)
Libretto by Jules Barbier, based on the play by Jules Barbier and Michel Carré (1851), in turn based on several tales by E. T. A. Hoffmann, in particular *Der Sandman* (1816), *Rat Krespel* (1818) and *Die Abendteuer der Silvester-Nacht* (1815)
Composed 1877–80

PREMIERES 10 February 1881, Opéra-Comique, Paris (orchestrated, re-arranged and with recitatives by Guiraud); US: 16 October 1882, Fifth Avenue Theater, New York; UK: 17 April 1907, Adelphi Theatre, London
CAST Hoffmann *t*, Nicklausse *ms*, Olympia *s* (sometimes also sings Antonia *s*, Giulietta *s*, Stella *s*), Lindorf *b* (also sings Coppélius *bar*, Dr Miracle *bar*, Dappertutto *b* or *bar*), Andrès *t* (also sings Cochenille *t*, Pittichinaccio *t*, Frantz *t*), Spalanzani *t*, Nathanael *t*, Crespel *b* or *bar*, Luther *b*, Hermann *b* or *bar*, Schlemil *b* or *bar*, Wolfram *t*, Wilhelm *b*, voice of Antonia's mother *ms*; *satb* chorus of students, party-goers, Venetians, servants
ORCHESTRATION 2 fl/picc, 2 ob, 2 cl, 2 bsn, 4 hn, 2 tpt, 3 trbn, timp, perc, 2 hp, str

One of the repertoire favourites, *Les contes d'Hoffmann* has been subjected to many well-intentioned alterations and, more recently, expansions seeking to provide either a satisfying evening at the opera or the format Offenbach perhaps would have wanted had he been alive at the premiere. The celebrated tales of fantasy by E. T. A. Hoffmann inspired many other composers for the stage, including Tchaikovsky, Adam, Audran, Hindemith, and previously Offenbach himself (*Le Roi Carotte*, 1872).

The composition of *Les contes d'Hoffmann* (announced for the Gaîté-Lyrique season of 1877–8) taxed Offenbach's powers, especially as he was continually turning out operettas for other theatres to support his family. When bankruptcy hit the Gaîté-Lyrique, Offenbach continued composing. In May 1879, two years after he had begun the work, a *musicale* at his house featuring songs from the opera attracted the attention of Carvalho, manager of the Opéra-Comique. Many of the recitatives were replaced by spoken dialogue, traditionally used at the Opéra-Comique, and vocal assignments were altered. When he died Offenbach had not completed much of Act IV or the end of Act V, nor begun the orchestration.

Shortly after Offenbach's death, Ernest Guiraud was asked to finish the work for production in early 1881. The original Venetian act was dropped entirely, except for the barcarolle, and the role of Nicklausse was shortened because of the star's vocal short-comings. Since it was Offenbach's habit to revise his works in the light of the public reaction to the premiere, we can never know what finished form *Les contes d'Hoffmann* might have taken. The closest we can come to the composer's original intentions is to follow the critical edition made by Fritz Oeser in 1977, which revokes alterations made in other performing versions and, drawing on original vocal parts and on sketches by Offenbach, restores missing passages and probably most nearly approaches the composer's conception.

SYNOPSIS
Act I In a German tavern, adjoining an opera house, the Muse of the poet Hoffmann calls on spirits to separate him from his adored Stella, a diva. The Muse becomes Nicklausse, Hoffmann's friend. The councillor Lindorf, rival for Stella's affections, plots to undo Hoffmann. During the interval for *Don*

Hoffmann and the Muse; from a series of illustrations by Pierre Auguste Lamy and Antonin-Marie Chatinière (Paris, 1881)

Giovanni, the tavern becomes filled with students, who prevail on Hoffmann to sing them a song about the deformed dwarf Kleinzach ('Il était une fois à la cour d'Eisenbach'). In the middle of the song, Hoffmann unexpectedly starts indulging in a reverie about Stella. Brought back to his senses, Hoffmann sees Lindorf, and tells his friends that the councillor has previously thwarted his love affairs. Mellowed by punch, he begins to describe them.

Act II Hoffmann is in love with a woman he thinks is the daughter of an inventor, Spalanzani. The inventor is afraid that Coppélius, who also specializes in gadgets – particularly eyes – will want a share of the profits from his latest invention, and offers to buy him out. The inventor introduces Olympia, the singing doll, to the public; Hoffmann sings of his love for her ('Ah, vivre deux'). While Olympia sings ('Les oiseaux dans la charmille'), Spalanzani winds her clockwork mechanism up whenever it runs down. Despite Nicklausse's warnings, Hoffmann is more and more enchanted by her, though somewhat surprised at her strange behaviour. When Coppélius returns, having been given a bad cheque, he destroys Olympia and Hoffmann finally realizes his error, to the public's delight.

Act III In Munich, Hoffmann has fallen in love with Antonia, seriously ill and hidden away by her father, Crespel, to prevent her from exerting herself. Although forbidden to, she sings ('Elle a fui, la tourterelle!'). Hoffmann finds her and the two declare their love ('C'est un chanson d'amour'). The evil Dr Miracle, who attended the death of Crespel's late wife, enters and proceeds to 'examine' Antonia by hypnosis, making her sing. Crespel forces Miracle out, but he returns, takes a violin, and urges Antonia to sing with the voice emanating from her mother's portrait. Antonia collapses as Hoffmann re-enters; the doctor declares her dead.

Act IV In Venice, Hoffmann listens to Nicklausse and the courtesan Giulietta sing a languorous barcarolle ('Belle nuit, o nuit d'amour'). Hoffmann has given up amorous adventures for the pleasures of wine. The shadowy Dappertutto tempts Giulietta with a diamond into obtaining Hoffmann's soul ('Scintille diamant'). Hoffmann falls in love with

Giulietta ('O Dieu de quelle ivresse'), and they sing an ecstatic duet ('Si ta presence m'est ravie') during which Giulietta succeeds in obtaining the reflection of Hoffmann Dappertutto demanded. Hoffmann is drawn into a duel with Schlemil, a rival for Giulietta's hand. Hoffmann kills Schlemil, and obtains the key with which Giulietta is locked up at night, only to see his beloved disappearing in a gondola with Pittichinaccio.

Act V Back in the tavern, Nicklausse admits that Hoffmann's loves were different personifications of the same woman – Stella. She appears, but leaves the tavern on Lindorf's arm. Nicklausse reassumes the character of the Muse and tells Hoffmann that his poetry will be enriched by his sorrow.

Although, shortly before his death, Offenbach sanctioned the replacement of his planned recitatives with spoken dialogue, *Les contes d'Hoffmann* is far removed from his much essayed operetta tradition. Serious in tone, it eschews the parodistic element of many previous works, instead following closely the combination of reality and fantasy, of the romantic and the grotesque, found in Hoffmann's writings. The removal of the need to ape Meyerbeer or Bellini, for example, allowed Offenbach the opportunity to formulate his own musical style – a style that was not, melodically or harmonically, hugely innovative, but could adapt more readily to a new type of dramatic pacing. Where simple strophic songs were previously presented in the most straightforward manner, here they are often the vehicles of some dramatic development, e.g. Antonia's aria 'Elle a fui, la tourterelle' (Act IV) or in Hoffmann's telling of the legend of Kleinzach (Act II). Nevertheless, when appropriate, Offenbach was happy to echo earlier stylistic mannerisms, for instance Olympia's doll song, 'Les oiseaux dans la charmille', which, with its vocal virtuosity, conjures up an effective portrait of a mechanical toy. The famous barcarolle, 'Belle nuit, o nuit d'amour', had originally been composed for *Die Rheinnixen*, Offenbach's ill-fated German Romantic opera, but transferred happily to its Venetian setting; the drinking song that follows was also from that source.

RECORDING 1. Doria, Bovy, Boué, Revoil, Jobin, Pernet, Soix, Bourdin, Opéra-Comique Ch and O, Cluytens, EMI, 1948: represents the now lost Opéra-Comique style at its authentic best; 2. D'Angelo, Schwarzkopf, de Los Angeles, Benoit, Gedda, London, Blanc, Ghiuselev, René Duclos Ch, Paris Conservatoire O, Cluytens, EMI, 1964: a strong reading of the traditional Choudens version; 3. Sutherland (all three female leads), Tourangeau, Domingo, Bacquier (all four villains), Lausanne and Swiss Radio Ch, Suisse Romande O, Bonynge, Decca, 1972: a conflation prepared by Bonynge restoring some of the usually omitted music and preferring dialogue to recitative [A.B.]
FILM *The Tales of Hoffmann*, Powell (dir.), Beecham (cond.), British Lion, 1951
VIDEO Serra, Cotrubas, Baltsa, Domingo, Nimsgerra, Ghiuschev, Lloyd, Royal Opera House Ch and O, Prêtre, Castle, 1981: John Schlesinger's imaginative Covent Garden production
EDITIONS f.ss., Choudens, 1907; *rp*, 1930 (four acts with recitatives); F. Oeser (ed.), Alkor, 1977 (five acts); Kalmus,

1980; v.ss., Choudens, 1881 (four acts); W. Felsenstein (ed.), Weinberger, 1959; F. Oeser (ed.), Alkor, 1977 (five acts)

Other operatic works: *L'alcôve*, 1847; *Le trésor à Mathurin*, 1853, rev. as *Le mariage aux lanternes*, 1857; *Pépito*, 1853; *Luc et Lucette*, 1854; *Oyayaie, ou La reine des îles*, 1855; *Entrez messieurs, mesdames*, 1855; *Les deux aveugles*, 1855 (RECORDING Bourg, ?1960s); *Une nuit blanche*, 1855; *Le rêve d'une nuit d'été*, 1855; *Le violoneux*, 1855 (RECORDING Bourg, ?1960s); *Madame Papillon*, 1855; *Paimpol et Périnette*, 1855; *Ba-ta-clan*, 1855 (RECORDING Erato, 1960s); *Elodie, ou Le forfait nocturne*, 1856; *Le postillon en gage*, 1856; *Trombalcazar, ou Les criminels dramatiques*, 1856; *La rose de Saint-Flour*, 1856; *Les dragées du baptême*, 1856; *Le '66'*, 1856; *Le savetier et le financier*, 1856; *La bonne d'enfants*, 1856; *Les trois baisers du diable*, 1857; *Croquefer, ou Le dernier des paladins*, 1857 (RECORDING Bourg, ?1960s); *Dragonette*, 1857; *Vent du soir, ou L'horrible festin*, 1857; *Une demoiselle en lôterie*, 1857; *Les deux pêcheurs*, 1857; *Mesdames de la Halle*, 1858 (RECORDING EMI, 1982); *Le chatte métamorphosée en femme*, 1858; *Un mari à la porte*, 1859; *Les vivandières de la grande armée*, 1859; *Geneviève de Brabant*, 1859, rev. 1867 and 1875 (RECORDING Bourg, 1960s); *Le carnaval des revues*, 1860; *Daphnis et Chloé*, 1860; *Barkouf*, 1860 (rev. as *Boule de neige*, 1871); *La chanson de Fortunio*, 1861 (RECORDING Musidisc Gaieté Lyrique, 1963); *Le Pont des Soupirs*, 1861, rev. 1868 (RECORDING Bourg, 1960s); *M. Choufleuri restera chez lui le . . .* (?coll. with Duc de Morny), 1861 (RECORDING EMI, 1982); *Apothicaire et perruquier*, 1861; *Le roman comique*, 1861; *Monsieur et Madame Denis*, 1862; *Le voyage de MM. Dunanan père et fils*, 1862; *Les bavards*, 1862; *Jacqueline*, 1862; *Il Signor Fagotto*, 1864; *Lischen et Fritzchen*, 1864 (RECORDING Bourg, 1960s); *L'amour chanteur*, 1864; *Die Rheinnixen*, 1864; *Les Géorgiennes*, 1864; *Jeanne qui pleure et Jean qui rit*, 1864; *Le fifré enchanté, ou Le soldat magicien*, 1864; *Coscoletto, ou Le Lazzarone*, 1865; *Les refrains des bouffes*, 1865; *Les bergers*, 1865; *La permission de dix heures*, 1867; *Robinson Crusoe*, 1867 (RECORDING Opera Rara, 1981); *Le château à Toto*, 1868; *l'île de Tulipatan*, 1868; *Vert-vert*, 1869; *La diva*, 1869; *La Princesse de Trébizonde*, 1869; *Les brigands*, 1869 (RECORDING EMI, 1988); *La romance de la rose*, 1869; *Mam'zelle Moucheron*, (c. 1870), rev. Delibes, 1881; *Le Roi Carotte*, 1872; *Fantasio*, 1872; *Fleurette, oder Naherin und Trompeter*, 1872; *Der schwarze Korsar*, 1872; *La leçon de chant*, 1873; *Les braconniers*, 1873; *Pomme d'api*, 1873 (RECORDING EMI, 1982); *La jolie parfumeuse*, 1873; *Bagatelle*, 1874; *Madame l'archiduc*, 1874 (RECORDING Musidisc Gaieté Lyrique, 1963); *Whittington*, 1874; *Les Hannetons*, 1875; *La boulangère a des écus*, 1875; *La créole*, 1875; *Le voyage dans la lune*, 1875; *Tarte à la crème*, 1875; *Pierrette et Jacquot*, 1876; *La boîte au lait*, 1876; *Le docteur Ox*, 1877; *La foire Saint-Laurent*, 1877; *Maître Péronilla*, 1878; *Madame Favart*, 1878; *La marocaine*, 1879; *La fille du tambour-major*, 1879 (RECORDING EMI, 1966/7); *Belle Lurette* (completed Delibes), 1880

BIBLIOGRAPHY Antonio de Almeida, *Thematic Catalogue* (in preparation); Alexander Faris, *Jacques Offenbach*, Faber, 1980; James Harding, *Jacques Offenbach: A Biography*, John Calder, 1980

R.T.

STEPHEN OLIVER

Stephen Michael Harding Oliver; *b* 10 March 1950, Liverpool, England; *d* 29 April 1992, London

Oliver wrote his first opera when he was 12, inspired more by his singing of 'the most profound utterances of the human spirit' as a chorister at St Paul's Cathedral than by any conventional example. His desire to render into song any striking line of verse led him to write some 44 operas before his untimely death. Three of them were performed while he was still an undergraduate at Worcester College, Oxford, where he studied with Leighton and Sherlaw-Johnson. In 1971 *The Duchess of Malfi* attracted wider attention, leading among other things to the robust comedy *Tom Jones* (1976) and a series of works for the Batignano Festival: *Il Giardino* (1977), *Euridice* (1981) (using Peri's vocal lines), *Beauty and the Beast* (1984), *Mario and the Magician* (1988) and *L'oca del Cairo* (1991) written around existing numbers by Mozart.

Inventive in theatrical devices (he generally wrote his own libretti), and with an ear for unusual instrumental combinations, he based his technique on a naturalistic delivery of the text, the voice never dominated by the often complex expressionistic instrumental writing.

An exceptionally versatile composer, Oliver balanced his operatic output with scores for over 80 plays and films, and a musical, *Blondel* (he also translated several libreti). If his 'popular' work was often exuberant and optimistic, in the operas he explored darker feelings, especially in the works of the 1980s, where qualities of nervous melancholy and despair were heightened by the use of a strict modal system. The secular cantata *Prometheus* (1988) proved a turning point, opening up new possibilities of warmth and rhythmic vigour.

A Man of Feeling

'Sketch' for soprano, baritone and piano (20m)
Libretto by the composer, after the short story *Der Empfindsame* by Arthur Schnitzler (1895)
Composed 1980
PREMIERE 17 November 1980, King's Head Theatre Club, London

The opera begins with a *coup de théâtre*: while an opera singer rehearses with her pianist, a young man comes on stage, puts a revolver to his head and shoots himself. The ensuing action explains this moment: after losing her voice, the singer has consulted a series of doctors, to no avail until the twenty-fourth doctor tells her to take a lover. This seems to do the trick. But when the lover discovers the use to which he has been put, it proves too much for him.

Part of the charm of this piece is the ingenuity of the adaptation, in which the baritone in turn plays the young man, Fritz; Fritz's friend; the opera singer; and seven of the twenty-four doctors. At first the soprano's rehearsal forms a musical 'backdrop' to the baritone's narration; she comes into the foreground for scenes with Fritz and the doctors. While practical and entertaining, the work is given an effect beyond its scale by a nostalgic waltz that permeates the score.

EDITION f.s., Novello, 1983

La Bella e la Bestia

Beauty and the Beast
Opera in two acts (1h 15m)
Libretto by the composer taken from Carlo Collodi's Italian
translation of the story by Mme Le Prince de Beaumont
Composed 1984
PREMIERES 26 July 1984, Batignano Festival; UK: 21 June
1985, St John's, Smith Square, London

Conceived for a promenade performance to
celebrate the tenth anniversary of Musica nel
Chiostro, with instrumental interludes to lead the
audience to the next scene, the piece makes
resourceful use of a small band with a large
percussion section. A curious effect of fable is
achieved by the device of having characters narrate
their own actions, with relatively little direct speech.
This potentially alienating device has magical properties: the vocal writing reveals the scenes that are
going on beneath the simple text. Although there
is plenty of wonder in the scoring, with some
exquisitely sensuous ensemble-writing, there is more
than enchantment: as in his setting of *The Dong with
the Luminous Nose*, Oliver charges a childhood story
with adult longing and distress. The musical
characterization of the Beast's self-loathing and
despair gives a great intensity to this parable of
'generous love'.

EDITIONS   f.s., Novello (on hire), 1984; v.s., Novello, 1987

Mario ed il Mago

Mario and the Magician
Opera in one act (1h)
Libretto by the composer, based on the story by Thomas
Mann (1930)
Composed 1988, rev. 1989
PREMIERES   5 August 1988, Batignano Festival; UK: 2 July
1992, Almeida Theatre, London

It is 1929. Cipolla, a conjuror with a gift for hypnosis,
comes to the Italian seaside resort of Torre di Venere
to give a show. He conquers the minds of all the
townspeople except for Mario: in his attempts to win
the youth over, Cipolla goes too far and Mario shoots
him. This allegory of the rise of fascism, with its play
on the ambiguities of the language of seduction
and conquest, exploits Oliver's gift for suggesting
dark subterranean forces at work in an apparently
innocent setting. A mood of unease and foreboding
pervades the score from the start, the town's
instability suggested by shifting textures and fleeting
images. The nine-piece ensemble sometimes suggests
a sour circus band, with snatches of what could be
popular music, but corrupt and infected.

EDITION   f.s., Novello (on hire), 1989

Timon of Athens

Opera in two acts (1h 30m)
Libretto by the composer, after the play by Shakespeare
Composed 1990–91
PREMIERE   17 May 1991, Coliseum, London

Although not his last opera, *Timon* has the character
of a summation. In writing it, Oliver drew widely
from his own previous work, notably from two
cantatas, *Prometheus* (1988) and *The Vessel* (1990).
The new sound of *Prometheus*, robust, pagan and
harmonically generous, is fused with the nervously
melancholic lyricism of his earlier operas, giving
Timon a mellow depth of tone. There is longer-
breathed melody, too, for the majestic lines of blank
verse.

Written in the shadow of the composer's
knowledge of his own mortality, *Timon* is a dramatic
meditation on what lies beyond man's dealings with
man. The action is simple. Timon, known for his
extreme generosity, finds he has given away all his
wealth. When his friends fail to help him, he invites
them to a banquet of stones and water. Act II depicts
his self-imposed exile in the wilderness. Here Oliver
extends Shakespeare's scenes of vituperation into a
spiritual journey: Timon hears a 'summoning music'
(of trumpets and glittering metal percussion). At first
he resists; later, at the moment he yields to this force,
he finds himself confronting human goodness in the
shape of his faithful steward. Finally, with the help of
his friend Alcibiades, Timon kills himself in front of
the senators of Athens.

Although the vocal palette is restricted to an all-
male darkness, the orchestral colour is often brilliant;
the story may be pessimistic, but Oliver achieves
beauty in anger and splendour in despair. Striking
musical images abound, among them the excitement
of being in Timon's company, suggested by a texture
of upward-rushing scales; the calm before the storm
of the second banquet, expressed in deceptively
serene 'white-note' music; the disquiet of Sempron-
ius and Philotus conjured in a haunting duet;
Apemantus' oblique views characterized by a wry,
primitive pipe music. Perhaps most powerful of all is
the threatening drumbeat that Alcibiades brings with
him, lit with flashes of lightning, which underscores
the final purging hymn of the assembled Athenians.

EDITIONS   f.s., Novello (on hire), 1991; v.s., Novello, 1991

Other operatic works: *Elymas*, (1962); *The Warden of the
Tower*, (1964); *Thespis*, (1966); *Dr Faustus*, (1967); *Comus*,
(1968); *All the Tea in China*, 1969; *Slippery Soules*, 1969, rev.
1988; *A Phoenix too Frequent*, 1970; *The Enchanted Shirt*,
(1970); *The Duchess of Malfi*, 1971, rev. 1978; *The Dissolute
Punished*, 1972; *The Three Wise Monkeys*, 1972; *The Donkey*,
1973; *Three Instant Operas*, 1973; *A Furcoat for Summer*,
(1973); *Sufficient Beauty*, (1973); *Perseverance*, (1974); *Past
Tense*, 1974; *Bad Times*, 1975; *Tom Jones*, 1976; *The Great
McPorridge Disaster*, 1976; *The Waiter's Revenge*, 1976; *Il
Giardino (The Garden)*, 1977; *A Stable Home*, 1977; *The Girl
and the Unicorn*, 1978; *Jacko's Play*, 1979; *The Dreaming of
the Bones*, (1979); *Euridice*, 1981; *Sasha*, 1983; *Britannia
Preserv'd*, 1984; *The Ring*, 1984; *Exposition of a Picture*, 1986;
Commuting, (1986); *Waiting*, 1987; *The Ring II*, 1989; *Tables
Meet*, 1990; *L'oca del Cairo*, 1991; *Cinderella* (television
opera), (1991)

BIBLIOGRAPHY   Paul Griffiths, *New Sounds, New
Personalilties: British Composers of the 1980s*, Faber, 1985,
pp. 140–47

J.D.

ANTONIO OREFICE

Antonio Orefice [Arefece, Orefici]; *b c.* 1685, Naples; *d c.*
1727, Naples

Few biographical details survive about Orefice,
composer of the first comic opera in Neapolitan
dialect performed on stage (*Patrò Calienno de la
Costa*, 1709). Apparently educated as a lawyer, the
success he enjoyed as a composer probably indicates
that he had a professional musical training. His first
opera, *Il Maurizio*, produced in Naples in 1708, was
heroic, but with *Patrò Calienno* he helped establish
the Neapolitan comic genre and contributed several
others of the same type.

Little of Orefice's music survives; his largest extant
work, *Engelberta*, shows the influence of Alessandro
Scarlatti, the leading Neapolitan opera composer of
the day. The other main sources of Orefice's music
are seven arias from his *Le finte zingare*, which form
the earliest surviving music from a Neapolitan comic
opera, and a comic intermezzo – precursor of the
Neapolitan comic opera – *Melissa e Serpillo* (1708),
written in collaboration with Francesco Mancini.

Extant operatic works: *Il Maurizio*, 1708; *Melissa e Serpillo*
(coll. with Francesco Mancini), 1708; *Engelberta, ossia La
forza dell'innocenza*, 1709 (coll. with F. Mancini, T.
Albinoni); *Le finte zingare* (arias), 1717; 15 lost operas
BIBLIOGRAPHY   Michael F. Robinson, *Naples and
Neapolitan Opera*, OUP, 1972

D.S.B.

CARL ORFF

b 10 July 1895, Munich; *d* 29 March 1982, Munich

Carl Orff was one of the most influential German
composers of his generation. At a time when the
majority of composers were concerned with an ever-
increasing degree of thematic and structural complexity, he succeeded in evolving a distinctive style
in which deliberate simplification was coupled with
the ability to design large paragraphs and textures
which at their best, as in *Carmina burana*, are both
compelling and memorable.

Orff, who came from an old Bavarian military
family, studied at the academy of music in Munich.
From 1915, apart from a brief spell of military service
in the First World War, he worked as a conductor
at various theatres in Munich, Mannheim and
Darmstadt. Returning to Munich in 1919, he
embarked on a study of early music; at the instigation
of Curt Sachs he developed an interest in Monteverdi, and, with the writer Dorothee Günther, prepared a stage version of *Orfeo* (1923–5). He
also made arrangements of Monteverdi's *Ballo
dell'ingrate* and *Lamento d'Arianna*. These works
helped him to find and define his own style and thus
represented more than a mere revival of neglected
masterpieces. Orff also admired the dancer Mary
Wigman, a pupil of Emile Jacques-Dalcroze, and the
'elemental' quality of her art. In 1924, with Dorothee
Günther, he opened a school in Munich, embarking
on a 'regeneration of music' from movement and

Stage design by Ludwig Sievert for Carmina Burana *(Frankfurt am Main, 1937)*

dance, and laying the foundations for his famous educational music, the *Schulwerk*. It adumbrated many of the stylistic features that now strike the listener as characteristic, especially the combining of music with movement, dance and speech, a large variety of percussion instruments, ostinati, prominent rhythm, and pentatonic modes. Orff first made his mark as a composer with *Carmina burana* in 1937. Thereafter, although he continued to be involved in educational activities, his career is essentially defined by a succession of works, most of which were not operas in the accepted sense of the word. *Carmina burana*, *Catulli Carmina* (1943), *Trionfo di Afrodite* (1953) are in fact combinations of cantata and ballet. *Der Mond* (1939), *Die Kluge* (1943), *Die Bernauerin* (1947) and *Astutuli* (1953) are to all intents and purposes folk plays with music, whereas *Antigonae* (1949), *Oedipus* (1959) and *Prometheus* (1968) are an attempt to recapture the spirit of ancient Greek tragedy. Orff's last work for the stage, *De temporum fine comoedia* (1973), has a mystical dimension that is prefigured in these tragedies.

Carmina burana
Songs from Beuren
Staged cantata in three parts (50m)
Libretto by the composer, after the Benediktbeuren manuscript
Composed 1934–6
PREMIERES   8 June 1937, Frankfurt am Main; US: 3 October 1958, San Francisco; UK: 26 January 1960, Royal Festival Hall, London (concert)

Orff's most famous work is based on a manuscript collection of medieval Latin and Middle High German verse that once belonged to the Bavarian monastery of Benediktbeuren and was first published in 1847 under the title of *Carmina burana*. A staged cantata rather than an opera, *Carmina burana* consists of a succession of tableaux illustrating how fortune governs the affairs of man. Although Orff uses the traditional symphony orchestra, the large percussion section and much of the music clearly derives from the *Schulwerk*, while the melodic material alludes to Gregorian chant and other medieval models.

Although Orff was of the opinion that *Carmina burana* marked 'the start of his collected works', none of the pieces that followed proved so enduringly successful.

RECORDINGS   1. Janowitz, Stolze, Fischer-Dieskau, Schönberg Boys' Ch, Berlin Deutsche Oper Ch and O, Jochum, DG, 1970s; 2. Armstrong, English, Allen, St Clement Danes Grammar School Ch, London Symphony Ch and O, Previn (HMV, 1975): both versions are vital and dramatic [A.B.]
VIDEO   Battle, Lopardo, Allen, various Chs, Berlin PO, Ozawa, Philips, 1980s
EDITIONS   f.s., Schott, 1953; v.s., Schott, 1937

Der Mond
The Moon
Ein kleines Welttheater (1h 30m)
Libretto by the composer, after the story by the Brothers (Jacob and Wilhelm) Grimm (1812–15)

Composed 1936–8, rev. 1957
PREMIERES   5 February 1939, Munich; US: 16 October 1956, City Center Theater, New York

From an imaginary place without moon or stars, four young men journey to the neighbouring country, where the nights are pleasantly illuminated by moonlight. They steal the moon and take it home with them. Before they die, they each arrange to be buried with a quarter of the purloined moon, which thus reaches the underworld. Here its light awakens the dead from their slumbers. The ensuing commotion – the dead leave their coffins and begin to carouse and quarrel – is heard by St Peter, who descends to join the revellers, and at length sends them back to their coffins. He then takes the moon back to its rightful place in the heavens.

As befits a fairy-tale, *Der Mond* begins and ends with a (singing) narrator. Some of the musical material clearly derives from the *Schulwerk*, and some from the tavern music of *Carmina burana*.

RECORDING   Christ, Kuén, Schmitt-Walter, Hotter, Philharmonia Ch and O, Sawallisch, EMI, 1957
EDITIONS   f.s., Schott, *c.* 1975; v.s., Schott, 1939

Die Kluge
The Wise Maiden
Märchenoper (1h 30m)
Libretto by the composer, after the story *Die Geschichte von dem König und der klugen Frau* (1812–15)
Composed 1940–42

A scene from Die Kluge *(Frankfurt am Main, 1943)*

PREMIERES   20 February 1943, Frankfurt; US: 7 December 1949, Karamu House, Cleveland; UK: 27 July 1959, Sadler's Wells, London

The plot tells the story of a wise maiden. Not having heeded her advice, her father, a peasant, is in prison. When the king hears of the daughter's wisdom, he commands her to appear. She does so, and correctly answers three riddles, whereupon the king offers to marry her. Next we see three ruffians and a muleteer conspiring to make a fool of the king. They easily outwit him, for he mistakenly believes that a mule can produce offspring, and thus assigns the donkeyman's animal to the muleteer – obviously a travesty of justice. In her wisdom his wife does not at once object to his error, though in disguise she comforts the disconsolate donkeyman. When the king realizes what she has done, he is enraged and orders her to leave the castle, allowing her to take a trunk and 'that which she loves most'. She first serves up his dinner, administers a sleeping draught and sings a lullaby. In the final scene the king awakens in the trunk some distance from the castle to realize that his wife is in fact the wisest person imaginable.

In compiling the libretto Orff made use of an old collection of German proverbs. This, the combination of sung and spoken scenes characteristic of the singspiel tradition, and a deliberate stylistic simplicity, contributed to making *Die Kluge*, which has been translated into more than 20 languages, one of Orff's most successful works for the stage.

RECORDINGS   1. Schwarzkopf, Kuén, Cordes, Frick, Philharmonia O, Sawallisch, EMI, 1957; 2. Popp, Gruber, Stewart, Frick, Munich Radio O, Eichhorn, Eurodisc, 1970s
EDITIONS   f.s., Schott, 1957; v.s., Schott, 1942

Catulli Carmina
Songs of Catullus
Ludi scaenici (45m)
Libretto by the composer, after Catullus
Composed 1941–3
PREMIERES   6 November 1943, Leipzig; UK: 4 March 1958, Arts Theatre, Cambridge

The poet Gaius Valerius Catullus (84–55 BC) was enamoured of a patrician lady named Clodia Pulcher whose capricious inconstancy drove him to despair. In 1930 Orff set seven poems by Catullus for unaccompanied chorus, and in 1941 arranged six of them for stage performance. A framing prologue and epilogue are assigned to singers placed on the proscenium. The exuberance of youth is first contrasted with the disillusionment of old age, and this is followed by a play within the play designed to show the true nature of love. Here the action is presented by dancers, and the music sung by an unaccompanied choir in the orchestra pit.

RECORDINGS   1. Blegen, Kness, Temple University Chs, Philadelphia O, Ormandy, CBS, [n.d.]; Auger, Ochman, Berlin Opera Ch, 4 pf and perc, Jochum, DG, 1971; Stoyanova, Kaludov, Bulgarian Radio and Television SO and Ch, Milkov, Forlane, 1988
EDITION   f.s., Schott, 1955

Die Bernauerin
Agnes Bernauer
A Bavarian drama in two acts
Libretto by the composer
Composed 1942–6, rev. 1954
PREMIERES   15 June 1947, Staatstheater, Stuttgart; US: 21 March 1968, Kansas City

A combination of singspiel and mystery play, *Die Bernauerin* is based on a lurid episode in Bavarian history. In 1432 Albrecht, Duke of Bavaria, the only son of the reigning duke, Ernst, fell in love with Agnes, the daughter of Kaspar Bernauer, who kept a bathing establishment in Augsburg. Against the wishes of his father and the Church, Albrecht married Agnes. Three years later, accused of witchcraft, Agnes was imprisoned by Albrecht's father and sentenced to death. On 12 October 1435 she was drowned in the Danube. Albrecht, bent on revenge, planned to make a funeral bonfire of Munich, but was dissuaded from doing so by his father's death and his own succession to the ducal throne. The work concludes with a vision of Agnes in heaven.

In stark contrast to Friedrich Hebbel's sentimental drama *Agnes Bernauer*, Orff was concerned to emphasize the plot's Bavarian origins. He made use of the *Liederbuch der Clara Hätzlein* of 1471, and of Johann Andreas Schmeller's four-volume Bavarian dictionary (1827–37), which prompted him to exploit the rough musicality of the Bavarian dialect.

RECORDING   Popp, Laubenthal, Bavarian Radio Ch, Munich Radio O, Eichhorn, RCA, 1981
EDITIONS   f.s., Schott, 1974; v.s., Schott, 1946

Antigonae
Antigone
Tragedy (2h 30m)
Libretto by the composer, after Hölderlin's translation of the play by Sophocles (*c.* 441 BC)
Composed 1940–49
PREMIERES   9 August 1949, Salzburg; US: 21 April 1968, Brooklyn Academy of Music, New York

After Oedipus has been banished from Thebes, his sons, Eteocles and Polyneices, kill each other in combat. The king, Creon, denies burial to Polyneices, who led the Seven against Thebes. By burying her brother's body, Antigone transgresses the royal command, is condemned to death, and immured alive. Warned by the seer Tiresias, Creon attempts to liberate Antigone. However, she has committed suicide, and, piling horror on horror, so has Creon's son Haemon and Euridice, his wife.

Antigonae was the first of Orff's trilogy of Greek tragedies. Enthralled by the power of Hölderlin's translation, he made no changes to the text. The music follows the formal patterns of Greek drama, such as alternating lines of dialogue (*stichomythia*), speeches and choruses. Over long stretches the dialogue is intoned on the same held note. The chief weight rests on the main speeches, which take the place of arias. They are marked by rhythmic displacements, interval leaps and coloratura melismas.

A striking feature is the ubiquitous use of ostinati to form a sombre musical background. *Antigonae* requires an unusual orchestra: 6 pianos (also used as percussion instruments), 4 harps, 9 double-basses, 6 flutes, 6 oboes, 6 trumpets, 7–8 timpani, and a large percussion section (10–15 players) that includes xylophones specially constructed at the composer's behest.

RECORDING Borkh, Plümacher, Haefliger, Uhl, Alexander, Borg, Bavarian Radio Ch and SO, Leitner, DG, 1961
EDITIOND f.s., Schott, 1959; v.s., Schott, 1949

Trionfo di Afrodite
The Triumph of Aphrodite
Concerto scenico (45m)
Libretto by the composer, after Catullus, Sappho and Euripides
Composed 1947–51
PREMIERE 13 February 1953, Milan

The Triumph of Aphrodite concludes Orff's triptych of staged cantatas: the other two works are *Carmina burana* and *Catulli Carmina*. Based on poetry by Catullus (in Latin) and Sappho and Euripides (in Greek), this work describes in seven sections the ceremony of an antique wedding. Orff also called the complete triptych *Trionfi*, referring to the allegorical masked processions of Renaissance courts in which virtue was presented as triumphing over the forces of darkness.

RECORDING Nawe, Büchner, Stryczek, Ch and O of Leipzig Radio, Kegel, Philips, [n.d.]; Tattermuschová, Žídek, Berman, Czech Radio Ch, Prague SO, Smetáček, Supraphon, 1970s
EDITIONS f.s., Schott, 1952; v.s., Schott, 1951

Astutuli
A Bavarian Comedy (50m)
Libretto by the composer
Composed 1949
PREMIERE 20 October 1953, Munich

The plot is based on a colourful medieval farce that Orff himself recast in Bavarian dialect. *Astutuli* is a work for actors, and with two brief exceptions relies entirely on the spoken word, though rhythms are carefully notated on a single line. Orff restricts his orchestra to a large battery of percussion.

EDITION f.s., Schott, 1953

Oedipus der Tyrann
King Oedipus
Tragedy
Libretto by the composer, after Hölderlin's translation of the play by Sophocles
Composed 1951–8
PREMIERE 11 December 1959, Staatstheater, Stuttgart

The plot is based on the familiar story of how Oedipus gradually learns that he has murdered his father and married his mother. The truth emerges in the three scenes with, respectively, Tiresias, who recognizes that Oedipus is the source of the gods' displeasure; the messenger from Corinth, who reveals that he is not the son of the king and queen of Corinth; and the servant, who admits to not having killed the son of Laius as he had been ordered to do. The tragedy concludes with Oedipus putting out his own eyes. The music centres on the note C, and the vocal style ranges from the spoken word to an insistent *parlando* on a single note, though there are moments of lyricism and the occasional telling melisma. *Oedipus der Tyrann* requires an unusual orchestra that follows the pattern established in *Antigonae*: a very large percussion section (12–18 players), 6 grand pianos, 4 harps, mandoline, celesta, glass harp, 9 double-basses, 6 flutes, 6 oboes, 6 trombones, electric organ, 5–6 timpani; and, offstage, 8 trumpets and several large Javanese gongs.

RECORDING Varnay, Stolze, Harper, Engen, Bavarian Radio Ch and SO, Kubelik, DG, 1967
EDITIONS f.s., Schott, 1965; v.s., Schott, 1959

Prometheus
Tragedy
Libretto after the play *Prometheus Bound* by Aeschylus (5th century BC)
Composed 1963–7
PREMIERE 24 March 1968, Staatstheater, Stuttgart

This drama of suffering and defiance depicts the Titan Prometheus, overpowered by Zeus and nailed to a lonely crag in distant Scythia, where an eagle feeds on his liver. He is pitied by Oceanus and the ocean nymphs, who try to persuade him to yield to Zeus' demands. Prometheus eloquently describes his plight, what he has done for mankind, and the sorry nature of his reward. A further element is the appearance of the tortured and delirious Io. Prometheus remains defiant, and with the nymphs is engulfed by a tempest.

Prometheus, which completes Orff's trilogy of Greek tragedies, retains the original Greek text, which he considered to be superior to the German translation. (He was in any case primarily concerned with the symbolic images on the stage.) For long stretches the music is reduced to the notated rhythm of the words. Long passages of intoned declamation are interspersed, at crucial points, with expressive melodic phrases. As in the preceding tragedies, the orchestra is unusual, comprising 4 pianos, 6 flutes, 6 oboes, 6 trumpets, 6 trombones, 4 tenor banjos, 4 harps, organ and electronic organ, 9 double-basses, and a large percussion section (for 15–18 players) including wind- and thunder-machines.

RECORDING Greindl, Cramer, Hermann, Engen, Moser, Sante, Kostia, Lorand, Uhl, West German Radio Ch and O, Leitner, Acanta, 1972
EDITION f.s./v.s., Schott, 1967

De temporum fine comoedia
A Drama of the End of Time
Opera-oratorio
Libretto by the composer

Composed 1969–71
PREMIERE   20 August 1973, Salzburg Festival

A final summing up of Orff's musical and mystical preoccupations, *De temporum fine comoedia* is a kind of eschatological endgame in three sections, with a text in Greek, Latin and German. The first section, *The Sybils*, based on the *Sibylline Prophecies*, is a lament for mankind, damned without hope of redemption. *The Anchorites*, the second section, offers an opposing view based on the ideas of Origen (AD 185–254), who believed that even the devil will be saved at last (a teaching later condemned as a heresy). The third section, *Dies illa*, depicts the last of mankind, the masses who have lost their bearings after the catastrophe that marks the end of time. An unanswered prayer is followed by an evocation of evil. Lucifer appears, and, having acknowledged his sins, is transformed back into the bright being he was before the fall, thereby illustrating Origen's idea that 'the end of all things will be the abolition of sin'.

RECORDING   Ludwig, Schreier, Greindl, Cologne Radio Ch and SO, Karajan, DG, 1973
EDITIONS   f.s., Schott, 1974; v.s., Schott, 1972

Other operatic works: *Gisei* (withdrawn), (before 1914); *Ein Sommernachtstraum*, 1939; *Comoedia de Christi resurrectione*, 1956 (television), 1957; *Ludus de nato infante mirificus*, 1960
BIBLIOGRAPHY   Lilo Gersdorf, *Carl Orff*, Rowohlt, 1981; Andreas Liess, *Carl Orff, His Life and His Music*, Calder and Boyars, 1966; *Carl Orff und sein Werk, Dokumentation*, vol. 1: *Carl Orff, Erinnerung*, Schneider, 1975; vol. 2: *Carl Orff, Lehrjahre bei den alten Meistern*, Schneider, 1975; vol. 3: *Carl Orff, Schulwerk. Elementare Musik*, Schneider, 1976; vol. 4: *Carl Orff, Trionfi. Carmina burana. Catulli Carmina. Trionfo di Afrodite*, Schneider, 1979; vol. 5: *Carl Orff, Märchenstücke*, Schneider, 1979; vol. 6: *Carl Orff, Bairisches Welttheater*, Schneider, 1980; vol. 7: *Carl Orff, Abendländisches Musiktheater*, Schneider, 1981; vol. 8: *Carl Orff, Theatrum mundi*, Schneider, 1983; Werner Thomas, *Das Rad der Fortuna*, Schott, 1990

A.C.

NIGEL OSBORNE

b 23 June 1948, Manchester, England

Osborne studied at Oxford under Kenneth Leighton and Egon Wellesz (1966–71), then in Warsaw with Rudziński. Despite Rudziński's influence, his work in the 1970s was largely for the concert hall, though he worked on a number of projects with Ballet Rambert, including *Wildlife* (1984). An operatic setting of Bulgakov's *The Master and Margarita* was abandoned for copyright reasons, and instead *Hell's Angels*, to a text by David Freeman, was produced by Opera Factory (1986). Based partly on Oskar Panizza's play *Das Liebeskonzil* (1893), the work dealt controversially with the subject of AIDS sent as divine judgment on Vatican politicking. Its musical

achievements were overshadowed as a result. In 1988 Osborne wrote music for a major production of Goethe's *Faust*, including songs and music for untuned percussion. Since 1990 he has been Reid Professor of Music at Edinburgh University.

The Electrification of the Soviet Union
Opera in two acts and epilogue (29 scenes) (2h 15m)
Libretto by Craig Raine, after Boris Pasternak's novella *The Last Summer* (1929) and poem 'Spectorsky' (1930)
PREMIERE   5 October 1987, Glyndebourne, Sussex

Based on two quasi-autobiographical works by Pasternak and cast in the form of a flashback, the opera is set at the time of the Russian Revolution. It explores the feelings and experiences of the young Serezha Spectorsky, particularly his relationship with the women in his life – an idealistic sister, an intense governess and the prostitute he visits – as well as his ambivalent attitude to the Revolution.

The work was the result of a close collaboration between Osborne, Raine and the director, Peter Sellars. As the number of scenes suggests, the treatment of time involves much cinematic intercutting. Musically, it demonstrates Osborne's eclecticism and intellectual rigour, making extensive use of song form in a stylized but integrated fashion. It includes music for electronic tape.

EDITIONS   f.s./v.s., Universal, 1987; lib., Faber, 1986

Terrible Mouth
Opera in six scenes (1h 15m)
Libretto by Howard Barker
PREMIERE   10 July 1992, Almeida Theatre, London

Barker's libretto is a portrait of the Spanish painter Francisco Goya y Lucientes (1746–1828). Set amid the horrors of the Peninsular War, it looks at Goya's objectification of events around him – including his relationship with the Duchess of Alba – and his place within them. This is a Grand Guignol full of anguished cries, dismembered limbs and dead babies thrown on to the stage by the mysterious Hooded Figure.

Despite its modest dimensions, this is Osborne's most substantial operatic work to date. The part of the deaf Goya is divided between an actor and a singer, the latter representing the Voice of Goya – his inner self. In the composer's words: 'Goya the actor heightens speech to the point where it meets the speechlike singing of Goya the singer.' The cast includes a six-part Chorus of the Maimed which explores similar vocal possibilities, while the instrumental ensemble, in addition to wind, percussion and harp, contains six cellos which extend and fill out the vocal sonorities.

EDITIONS   f.s./v.s./lib., Universal, 1992

BIBLIOGRAPHY   Paul Driver, 'Osborne's *Electrification of the Soviet Union*', *MT*, vol. 128 (1987), pp. 560–62; Paul

Griffiths, *New Sounds, New Personalities: British Composers of the 1980s*, Faber, 1985, pp. 125–32

M.A.

OTAKAR OSTRČIL

b 25 February 1879, Smíchov, nr Prague; *d* 20 August 1935, Prague

Although impressively educated in music (notably under Fibich, whose amanuensis he became), Ostrčil continued to earn his living as a language teacher until he was 40. In 1914 he also became chief conductor at the Vinohrady Theatre in Prague, which had opened in 1907 as the first permanent Czech-language opera house and theatre to be built in Prague after the National Theatre. In 1919 he moved to the National Theatre as dramaturg and after Kovařovic's death in 1920 took over as chief of opera until his own death in 1935, continuing one of the most fruitful periods of opera at the National Theatre.

Ostrčil showed an interest in opera from an early age, writing his first opera while still a student, and despite his onerous duties continued to compose until his death. His first adult opera, *The Death of Vlasta*, continues the tradition of Czech mythological operas (such as *Libuše* and *Šárka*), but his following works take a more personal path, notably an increasing preoccupation with moral values, climaxing in *Johnny's Kingdom*, which proclaimed a pacifist message to a Europe busily rearming itself.

The Bud
Poupě

Comic opera in one act, Op. 12
Libretto by the composer, after the comedy by F. X. Svoboda
Composed 1909–10
PREMIERE   25 January 1911, National Theatre, Prague

Like Smetana's later operas, *The Bud* explores the theme of personal growth: the title is a metaphor for a young girl's awakening into womanhood. It was the first Czech prose opera after Janáček's *Jenůfa* (a direction Ostrčil did not pursue) and carefully avoided simultaneous singing, with musical continuity provided by the orchestra. Ostrčil's first opera to be published, it continued to be revived up to the 1960s.

EDITION   v.s., Hudební matice, 1911, 2nd edn, 1950

Johnny's Kingdom
Honzovo království

Musical play in seven scenes, Op. 25 (2h)
Libretto by Jiří Mařánek, after Tolstoy's story *The Tale of Ivan the Fool and his Two Brothers*
Composed 1928–33
PREMIERE   26 May 1934, National Theatre, Brno

Ostrčil's harmonic language, formed at the height of the late-Romantic period with Richard Strauss as model, became much simplified in his final opera, perhaps to accommodate an important folksong element. Also jettisoned were the rather nebulous symbolisms of *The Legend of Erin* and *Kunála's Eyes*, and the stern avoidance of set numbers and simultaneous singing in *The Bud*. Instead, Ostrčil and his librettist adapted a Russian tale, a celebration of a simple-minded but pure-hearted hero whose goodness of heart wins out against terrible adversities, and placed this in a convention that allowed large-scale choruses and a much greater reliance on the voice at emotional climaxes, including a *concertato* ending to Act I.

RECORDING   excerpts: Jonášová, Průša, Ježil, Tuček, Horáček, Czechoslovak Radio Ch and O, Jílek, Supraphon, 1980
EDITION   v.s., Hudební matice, 1950

Other operas: *Jan Zhořelecký*, (1898), 1939 (excerpts); *The Death of Vlasta* (*Vlasty skon*), 1904; *Kunála's Eyes* (*Kunálovy oči*), 1908; *The Legend of Erin* (*Legenda z Erinu*), 1921
BIBLIOGRAPHY   John Tyrrell, *Czech Opera*, CUP, 1988

J.T.

P

LUIS DE PABLO

Luis Alfonso de Pablo Costales; b 28 January 1930, Bilbao, Spain

Pablo was at first self-taught as a composer, having embarked on a legal career. But after attending the conservatory in Madrid, he went to Paris where he was taught by Boulez and Messiaen. He led the summer seminars at Darmstadt in 1958, and organized modern performing groups in Spain, particularly Tiempo y Musica in 1958, and Alea (which succeeded it) in 1965. In his early compositions Pablo followed the fashionable dictates of Falla's nationalist school but he soon devised a peculiarly personal approach to serialism, flexible enough to cross-fertilize with many different styles and compositional techniques. The influence of Bartók, for example, may be discerned in his work. His theatrical style has favoured lighting and plastic objects as well as dance and acting in the musical discourse. His *Protocolo* (1968), with a text by the composer, is variously described as music theatre, pièce scènique Buñuelesque, and pantomime. In *Kiu* (1983) Pablo sought to create a modern tradition for Spanish opera independent of the conventions of the zarzuela and free of the self-conscious 'Spanish' voice adopted by (usually foreign) composers. The opera, based on Alfonso Vallejo's expressionistic play *El cero transparente*, is deliberately less experimental than much of Pablo's output. In 1991 Pablo said that several of his works had been temporarily withdrawn, for further revision.

BIBLIOGRAPHY 'De Passage à Paris: Entretien avec Luis de Pablo', *Salabert-Actuel*, no. 4, Editions Salabert, 1989; T. Marco, *Luis de Pablo* (Artistas espanoles contemporaneos, serie musicos VI), Madrid, 1971

S.J.W.

GIOVANNI PACINI

b 17 February 1796, Catania, Sicily; d 6 December 1867, Pescia, Italy

Pacini seems to have been of Tuscan origin though he is often claimed a Sicilian because of his birthplace. He studied in Venice and wrote his first two operas when he was 17 years old. The second of these, *Annetta e Lucindo*, was given in Milan (1813) and a dozen comedies in similar vein led to his first real successes (also in Milan), *Adelaide e Comingio* in 1817, and *Il barone di Dolsheim*, which ran for 47 nights at La Scala in the following year. Further successes in Rome and Naples brought him the position of director at the Teatro San Carlo, and he rapidly became one of the most sought-after opera composers in Italy.

Pacini's fluent but rather superficial style, as he candidly admits in his *Memoirs*, was based entirely on Rossini and cleverly tailored to meet the demands of singers and public alike. He bothered little about harmony and instrumentation: 'God help us if he knew music,' said Rossini. 'No one could resist him.' By 1833, however, Pacini began to realize that he had been 'surpassed' by Bellini and Donizetti and retired to Viareggio where he founded a school of music (later transferred to Lucca).

After an absence of five years, during which he had time to reassess the Italian operatic scene, he returned to the stage and in 1840 achieved a triumph with his masterpiece, *Saffo*. This is a more solidly written work, and the operas that follow it generally maintain the new level of quality; this declines, however, towards the end of the composer's life, when the developing genius of Verdi began to make Pacini's style seem old-fashioned. The best of the later works is perhaps *Niccolò de' Lapi*, written for Rio de Janeiro but produced posthumously at Florence. Pacini's music never did particularly well outside Italy: it was very much a product of its period and place, and the nickname 'il maestro della cabaletta' aptly suggests the abundant if not always very distinguished melodic energy that was the main source of its appeal. His energy was prodigious: in half a century he produced nearly 90 operas as well as a quantity of other music; he married three times, had nine children and counted among his mistresses the redoubtable Countess Samoyloff and Napoleon's sister Pauline.

Saffo

Tragedia lirica in three acts (1h 45m)
Libretto by Salvatore Cammarano
Composed 1840
PREMIERES 29 November 1840, Teatro San Carlo, Naples; UK: 1 April 1843, Drury Lane, London; US: 1847, New York

The plot is based on the story of Sappho's love for the ferryman Phaon and ends with her death as she leaps from the Leucadian rock. The score is Pacini's best: harmonically, instrumentally and even dramatically it is a great advance on its predecessors, and the influence of Bellini is entirely beneficial (for example the fine ensemble in the Act II finale). It certainly deserves the attention that, almost alone among Pacini's works, it has received sporadically since the composer's death.

EDITION v.s., Ricordi, 1841
RECORDING Gencer, Mattiucci, Del Bianco, L. Quilico, Ch and O of San Carlo, Naples, Capuana, MRF, 1967

Maria, regina d'Inghilterra

(*Maria Tudor*)
Mary Tudor
Tragedia lirica in three acts (2h 15m)
Libretto by Leopoldo Tarantini after the play by Victor Hugo (1832)
PREMIERE 11 February 1843, Real Teatro Carolino, Palermo; UK: 23 March 1983, Bloomsbury Theatre, London (Opera Rara)

This is a good example of Pacini's best work. The libretto, based very remotely indeed on English history, concerns the queen's love for Riccardo Fenimore, an upstart Irishman (or Scotsman: the score is indecisive) whom she raises to high rank and considers marrying. Discovering his liaison with Clotilde Talbot she consigns him to the Tower, along with Clotilde's unfortunate fiancé, who is innocent of any crime but very nearly (though not quite) dies in Riccardo's place.

EDITION v.s., Ricordi, 1843
RECORDING Hill Smith, Walker, Lewis, Vassilev, Opera Rara Ch, English SO, Parry, MRF, 1983

Other operas: *Don Pomponio*, (1813); *Annetta e Lucindo*, 1813; *L'escavazione del tesoro*, 1814; *Gli sponsali de' silfi*, 1814; *Bettina vedova* (*Il seguito di Ser Mercantonio*), 1815; *La Rosina*, 1815; *La Chiarina* (doubtful), 1815; *L'ingenua*, 1816; *Il matrimonio per procura*, 1817; *Dalla beffa il disinganno, ossia La poetessa*, 1817, rev. as *Il carnevale di Milano*, 1817; *Piglia il mondo come viene*, 1817; *I virtuosi di teatro* (doubtful), 1817; *La bottega di caffè* (doubtful), 1817; *Adelaide e Comingio*, 1818 (also as *Isabella e Florange*); *Atala*, 1818; *Gl'illinesi*, (1818); *Il barone di Dolsheim*, 1818 (also as *Federico II, re di Prussia* and *La colpa emendata dal valore*); *La sposa fedele*, 1819; *Il falegname di Livonia*, 1819; *Vallace, o L'eroe scozzese*, 1820 (also as *Odoardo I re d'Inghilterra*); *La sacerdotessa d'Irminsul*, 1820; *La schiava in Bagdad, ossia Il papucciajo*, 1820; *La gioventù di Enrico V*, 1820 (also as *La bella tavernara, ossia Le avventure d'una notte*); *Cesare in Egitto*, 1821; *La vestale*, 1823; *Temistocle*, 1823; *Isabella ed Enrico*, 1824; *Alessandro nelle Indie*, 1824; *Amazilia*, 1825, rev. 1827; *L'ultimo giorno di Pompei*, 1825; *La gelosia corretta*, 1826; *Niobe*, 1826; *Gli arabi nelle Gallie, ossia Il trionfo della fede*, 1827, rev. as *L'ultimo dei clodovei*,

Alessandro Sanquirico's design for the eruption of Vesuvius in Pacini's L'ultimo giorno di Pompei *(Milan, 1825)*

1855; *Margherita, regina d'Inghilterra*, 1827 (also as *Margherita d'Anjou*); *I cavalieri di Valenza*, 1828; *I crociati a Tolemaide, ossia Malek-Adel*, 1828; *Il talismano, ovvero La terza crociata in Palestina*, 1829; *I fidanzati, ossia Il contestabile di Chester*, 1829; *Giovanna d'Arco*, 1830; *Il corsaro*, 1831; *Il rinnegato portoghese (Gusmano d'Almeida)*, (1831); *Ivanhoe*, 1832; *Don Giovanni Tenorio, o Il convitato di pietra*, 1832; *Gli elvezi, ovvero Corrado di Tochemburgo*, 1833; *Fernando duca di Valenza*, 1833; *Irene, o L'assedio di Messina*, 1833; *Carlo di Borgogna*, 1835; *Bellezza e cuor di ferro*, 1835; *La foresta d'Hermanstadt*, 1839; *Furio Camillo*, 1839; *L'uomo del mistero*, 1841; *Il duca d'Alba*, 1842 (also as *Adolfo di Werbel*); *La fidanzata corsa*, 1842; *Medea*, 1843; *Luisella, ossia La cantatrice del molo*, 1843; *L'ebrea*, 1844; *Lorenzino de' Medici*, 1845, rev. as *Rolandino di Torresmondo*, 1858 (also as *Elisa Valasco*); *Bondelmonte*, 1845; *Stella di Napoli*, 1845; *La regina di Cipro*, 1846; *Merope*, 1847; *Ester d'Engaddi*, 1848; *Allan Cameron*, 1848; *L'orfana svizzera*, 1848; *Zaffira, o La riconciliazione*, 1851; *Malvina di Scozia*, 1851; *L'assedio di Leida (Elnava)*, (?1852); *Rodrigo di Valenza*, (1852); *Il Cid*, 1853; *Lidia di Brabante*, 1853 (probably the original version of *Lidia di Bruxelles*, 1858); *Romilda di Provenza*, 1853; *La donna delle isole*, (1853); *La punizione*, 1854; *Margherita Pusterla*, 1856; *I portoghesi nel Brasile*, 1856; *Niccolò de' Lapi*, (1857), 1873; *Il saltimbanco*, 1858; *Lidia di Bruxelles*, 1858; *Gianni di Nisida*, 1860; *Il mulattiere di Toledo*, 1861; *Belfagor*, 1861; *Carmelita*, (1863); *Don Diego di Mendoza*, 1867; *Berta di Varnol*, 1867

BIBLIOGRAPHY Giovanni Pacini, *Le mie memorie artistiche*, Florence, 2nd edn, 1875; Michael Rose, 'Giovanni Pacini', in *Grove*, Macmillan, 1980

M.R.

IGNACY PADEREWSKI

Ignacy Jan Paderewski; *b* 6 November 1860, Kuryłówka, Podolia; *d* 29 June 1941, New York

Although best known as a pianist, Paderewski was also a composer and a politician (after the First World War he was Prime Minister of Poland and signed the Treaty of Versailles as his country's representative). As a musician, he studied at the Music Institute in Warsaw, and was later (1886) a pupil of Leschetizky in Vienna. His own compositions, written mainly before he was 50, include piano pieces, a symphony, a piano concerto, a violin sonata, songs and one opera.

Manru

Lyric drama in three acts, Op. 20
Libretto (in German) by Alfred Nossig, after Józef Ignacy Kraszewski's novel *Chata za wsią* (*A Cottage Outside the Village*)
Composed 1892–1901
PREMIERES 29 May 1901, Dresden; 8 June 1901, Lwów (now Lviv) (in Polish); US: 14 February 1902, Metropolitan, New York

A village girl has married a gypsy, but their life-styles conflict. When the other gypsies persuade him to leave his wife and return to them, the girl drowns. To avenge her death, a villager pushes the gypsy over a precipice.

Manru is a typical late-Romantic melodrama with

leitmotifs and a dominant part for orchestra. It was briefly popular in several countries.

EDITION v.s., Bote und Bock, 1901

BIBLIOGRAPHY Adam Zamoyski, *Paderewski*, Atheneum, 1988

Z.C.

FERDINANDO PAER

b 1 June 1771, Parma; *d* 3 May 1839, Paris

Together with Mayr, Paer was the dominating figure in Italian opera during the first decade of the 19th century. Having studied music locally, he gained a reputation in Parma with his earliest opera, *Orphée et Euridice* (1791), and then with *Circe*, produced in Venice the following year. Appointed honorary maestro di cappella at the court of Parma in 1792, Paer also wrote several operas to commission for Padua, Florence and Naples, as well as for his home town. The most important of these was *Griselda* (1798), written in the semiserio style for which he is chiefly remembered.

In 1797 Paer moved to Vienna to take up the musical direction of the Kärntnertortheater. Here he made the acquaintance of Beethoven and produced some of his best work, including *Camilla* (1799) and *Achille* (1801). In 1801 he moved to Prague and then to Dresden.

Greatly admired by Napoleon, Paer joined the emperor's train and, after sojourns in Posen (Poznań) and Warsaw, followed him to Paris in 1807 as his maître de chapelle. Paris was to be Paer's home for the rest of his life, even after Napoleon's defeat, when the composer had to relinquish many of the positions and benefices he had held. He maintained his standing during the 1820s as director of the Théâtre-Italien and as a singing master; the young Liszt studied composition with him. The arrival of Rossini as director of the Théâtre-Italien in 1824 resulted in a period of controversy, until Paer was dismissed in 1827: opinion was that he had intrigued against the younger man. Paer himself was given further honours, including the cross of the Légion d'honneur; in 1832 he was appointed as director of the private chapel of King Louis Philippe.

Beyond a certain indebtedness to Gluck (in his opere serie) and Mozart (in his rhythmic drive and instrumental richness), Paer was gifted with a sure technique and Italianate gifts of melodic facility; he can stand as a representative of those Italian musicians who occupied prime positions in the European musical scene in the 18th and early 19th centuries. At the same time, he was conservative by nature. The most significant portion of his output was of opere semiserie, the Italian equivalent of the kind of opéras comiques cultivated during and after the French Revolution, which combined serious and comic elements, fully developed airs and homespun ditties, and in which the chorus retained an important role. This very variety gave rise in turn to new formal practices, where the tendency was to go beyond single numbers or scenes towards the creation of a kind of dramatic continuity. One particularly effective example of this episodic structure is the Act II trio ('Che l'eterna provvidenza') in *Leonora*. According to Julian Budden, the best of Paer is in his lighter numbers, which are full of wit and melodic grace, instrumental skill and writing of great vocal dexterity.

Leonora, ossia L'amour coniugale

Leonora, or Conjugal Love
Dramma semiserio in two acts (2h 30m)
Libretto by Giovanni Schmidt or ?Giacomo Cinti, after Bouilly's libretto *Léonore, ou L'amour conjugal* (1794)
PREMIERE 3 October 1804, Kleines Kurfürstliches Theater, Dresden

Like Beethoven's version, Paer's opera is set in Spain and sticks closely to Bouilly's original text (though here it is Marcellina who secures Florestano's release). The changes that do occur are principally side-effects of transferring a French opera to an Italian framework and include the lengthening of the finales into multi-section scenes. The role of Pizzaro, which is a spoken part in Beethoven's opera, is here scored for tenor; but the part of Rocco is reduced and he is not allocated any solo arias. Paer's opera does not include a chorus – probably because none was available to him in Dresden.

The overture presents, and repeats, a motif representing Leonora's devotion and reappears during one of her recitative passages and in the Act II trio when she tends to Florestano in his cell. Although rescue operas were much in vogue, *Leonora* enjoyed only moderate success and was eclipsed by Beethoven's 1814 revision of his opera (by then called *Fidelio*). However, there have been a number of modern revivals.

RECORDING Koszut, Gruberova, Jerusalem, Bavarian Symphony O, Maag, Decca, 1979
EDITION v.s., Breitkopf und Härtel, [c. 1805]

Other surviving operas: *Circe*, 1792; *Le astuzie amorose, o Il tempo fa giustizia a tutti*, 1792; *Laodicea*, 1793; *I pretendenti burlati*, 1793; *L'oro fa tutto*, 1793; *I molinari*, 1794; *L'Idomeneo*, 1794; *Ero e Leandro*, 1794; *Una in bene e una in male*, 1794; *La Rossana*, 1795; *Il Cinna*, 1795; *L'intrigo amoroso*, 1795; *L'orfana riconosciuta*, 1796; *L'amante servitore*, 1796; *Il principe de Taranto*, 1797; *Griselda, ossia La virtù al cimento*, 1798; *Camilla, ossia Il sotteraneo*, 1799; *Il morto vivo*, 1799; *La testa riscaldata*, 1800; *La sonnambula*, 1800; *Poche ma buone, ossia Le donne cambiate*, 1800; *Achille*, 1801; *Ginevra degli Almieri*, 1802; *I fuorusciti di Firenze*, 1802; *Sargino, ossia L'allievo dell'amore*, 1803; *Sofonisba*, 1805; *Il maniscalco*, 1805; *Numa Pompilio*, 1808; *Diana e Endimione, ossia Il ritardo*, 1809; *Agnese di Fitzhenry*, 1809; *La Didone*, 1810; *I Baccanti*, 1813; *L'oriflamme* (coll. with Méhul, Berton, Kreutzer), 1814; *L'eroismo in amore*, 1815; *La primavera felice*, 1816; *Le maître de chapelle, ou Le souper imprévu*, 1821 (RECORDING Concert Hall, ?1960s); *Blanche de Provence, ou La cour des fées* (coll. with Berton, Boieldieu, Cherubini, Kreutzer), 1821; *La marquise de Brinvilliers* (coll.

with Auber, Berton, Boieldieu, Cherubini *et al.*) 1831; *Olinde et Sophronie* (inc.); 14 lost operas

BIBLIOGRAPHY Julian Budden, 'Ferdinando Paer', in *Grove*, Macmillan, 1980; Winton Dean, in *The New Oxford History of Music*, vol. 8: *The Age of Beethoven 1790–1830*, OUP, 1982, chapter 9: 'Italian Opera', pp. 387–9

D.B.

GIOVANNI PAISIELLO

Giovanni Gregorio Cataldo Paisiello; *b* 9 May 1740, Roccaforzata, nr Taranto; *d* 5 June 1816, Naples

Paisiello was one of the most prolific and successful opera composers of his generation; his success was matched only by that of Cimarosa. The exact number of his operas is unknown but probably reaches 90. His reputation throughout Europe was at its highest during the last two decades of the 18th century. After about 1800 the popularity of his music declined due to changes of taste which have never swung back in his favour.

He received his musical education between 1754 and 1763 at the Conservatorio San Onofrio in Naples and then in 1764 began a successful career as a freelance composer of opera. He became a court musician for the first time in 1776, when he was appointed music director at the court of the Empress Catherine II in St Petersburg. For the rest of his life he was always in the employ of a European ruler: the Empress Catherine II of Russia whom he served from 1776 to 1784; King Ferdinand IV of Naples (most of the period 1784–1806); Napoleon I (1802–4); King Joseph of Naples (1806–8); King Joachim Murat of Naples (1808–15); and finally King Ferdinand again (1815–16). He did not want to go to Paris in 1802 to become Napoleon's maître de chapelle, but was forced to as part of a diplomatic agreement between King Ferdinand and Napoleon. He was not happy in Paris and returned to Naples two years later. Napoleon's friendship was, however, invaluable to him between 1806 and 1815, the years of the French occupation of Naples. Napoleon's brother, Joseph, and Napoleon's brother-in-law, Joachim Murat, occupied the throne of Naples in

Giovanni Paisiello with Giacomo Tritto, Giuseppe Sarti and Niccolò Zingarelli

turn and both retained Paisiello's services as court composer.

Paisiello produced a constant flow of new operas for the theatres of Naples and elsewhere until the mid-1790s. Thereafter his interest in opera gradually declined as his interest in religious music increased. His late sacred compositions for the chapels of his royal employers have never, however, acquired the fame of his earlier works for the secular theatre. He himself believed that some of his serious operas showed his art at its best. Nowadays his reputation is based primarily on his comic operas, for which his brand of effervescent, melodious music is eminently suitable.

La serva padrona
The Servant as Mistress
Intermezzo in two parts (1h)
Libretto by Gennaro A. Federico
PREMIERES 10 September 1781, Palace of Tsarskoie Selo, nr St Petersburg; UK: 21 June 1858, Her Majesty's Theatre, Haymarket, London (concert); US: 13 November 1858, New York

Paisiello was ordered to compose this intermezzo for the nameday of the Grand Duke Alexander, the Empress Catherine's grandson, who was then not quite four years old. The libretto tells of how a servant girl, Serpina, traps her master, Uberto, into offering her marriage. Being short and humorous, it was as suitable as any that could be found for the Grand Duke's amusement. Paisiello rightly feared that his score would be unfavourably compared with the famous earlier setting of the same text by Pergolesi. His version had some initial success but did not dent the reputation of Pergolesi's score which has always been regarded as the superior of the two.

RECORDING 1. Donat, Artysz, Warsaw CO, Dobrzanski, Muza, 1971; 2. Banks, Ricci, O da Camera di Milano, Vaglieri, Nuova Era, 1991
EDITION Artaria, [c. 1780]; f.s., Choizeau, 1803

Il barbiere di Siviglia, ovvero La precauzione inutile
The Barber of Seville, or The Useless Precaution
Dramma giocoso per musica in four acts (2h)
Libretto by an unknown author, based on the play *Le barbier de Seville* (1775) by Pierre Augustin Caron de Beaumarchais
PREMIERES 26 September 1782, Imperial Court, St Petersburg; UK: 11 June 1789, Her Majesty's Theatre, Haymarket, London; US: 10 December 1805, Théâtre Français, New Orleans
CAST Rosina *s*, Il Conte D'Almaviva *t*, Figaro *bar*, Bartolo *b*, Don Basilio *b*, Svegliato *b*, Giovinetto *t*, Lawyer *b*, Spanish Sheriff *t*
CHAMBER ORCHESTRA including mandoline

Il barbiere di Siviglia is the best and most original opera Paisiello composed during his period in Russia. The subject was selected in the knowledge that the Empress Catherine was an admirer of Beaumarchais and the librettist was careful to retain all the general features of the play (merely reducing the number of words and translating what was left into Italian verse). The rather uneven distribution of the arias and ensembles is another noticeable feature of this work – Figaro's solos, for instance, all come near the beginning. This seems the result of a conscious decision by Paisiello and his librettist to make the music fit the action rather than vice versa.

The success of this opera when it reached Vienna in 1783 spurred Mozart and Da Ponte to create a new opera on Beaumarchais's *Le mariage de Figaro* (the sequel to *Le barbier*). Many of the musical details of Mozart's *Le nozze di Figaro* show Paisiello's influence.

For performances in Naples in 1787, Paisiello and Giovanni Battista Lorenzi revised the opera in a three-act form, modifying the work to suit local taste. The original version remained, however, more widely performed.

Il barbiere was one of the few Paisiello works still popular with the general public in 1816, when Rossini composed his own *Il barbiere di Siviglia*. The audience at the Rome premiere that year of the Rossini work criticized him for having dared to compose an opera on the same subject as Paisiello. However, opinion changed once it was perceived that Rossini's was the stronger setting.

SYNOPSIS
Act I Figaro, an itinerant barber, meets Count Almaviva who is courting Rosina, Bartolo's ward, disguised as a student. Bartolo wishes to marry her himself and jealously guards her. Rosina drops the 'student' a message from her balcony. He sings her a serenade, declaring his name is 'Lindoro'.

Act II Figaro tells Rosina of Lindoro's love and obtains from her a letter to give him. The Count arrives, now disguised as a soldier billeted on Bartolo. His attempt to hand a written reply to Rosina miscarries, for Bartolo catches him. Rosina saves the situation by exchanging his letter for another.

Act III The Count, dressed as 'Alonso', a supposed pupil of Don Basilio, the music master, meets Rosina (who still believes he is Lindoro) and gives her a music lesson. Don Basilio, knowing nothing of the Count's stratagem, appears and is bribed to leave at once. Figaro shaves Bartolo while the lovers plan their escape. Bartolo breaks up their tête-à-tête.

Act IV At midnight Bartolo, informed by Don Basilio, tells Rosina that Alonso is an impostor believed to be an agent of Count Almaviva. Disillusioned, she reveals the escape plans. Bartolo goes off triumphantly to find the guard. The Count and Figaro climb in at the window and meet Don Basilio and a notary ready with the marriage contract. Once Rosina is told of the Count's identity and his love, she signs the contract. Bartolo returns too late and the captain refuses to arrest the supposed housebreaker, recognizing the Count.

RECORDINGS 1. Laki, Gulyás, Gáti, Gregor, Sólyom-Nagy, Hungarian State O, Fischer, Hungaroton, 1985; 2. Cuberli, Visconti, Corbelli, Dara, Menicucci, Romanian PO, Campanella, Frequenz, 1982: live recording from Valle d'Itria Festival

EDITIONS f.s., Firenze Stabilimento Musicale, 1869; v.s.,
Ricordi, 1961

L'amor contrastato

Commedia per musica in three (originally two) acts (2h)
Libretto by Giuseppe Palomba
PREMIERES autumn 1788, Teatro Fiorentini, Naples; UK:
21 May 1791, Pantheon, London

There is confusion about the title of this work. The
original title was the one retained for most revivals of
the opera in southern Italy in Paisiello's lifetime. But
elsewhere the title *La molinara* (or one of its
variants, *La molinarella* or *La mulinara*) was often
used instead. The *molinara* is Rachelina, the maid of
the mill, who is wooed by three suitors. These are
two members of the gentry, Don Calloandro and
Don Rospolone, and a comical advocate, Notar
Pistofolo. The first two employ Pistofolo to present
their suits to her, but the lady prefers him and the
wrath of the other two descends on the couple. The
lovers flee when Calloandro becomes insane, but
when he regains his sanity the opera ends amid
general reconciliation.

L'amor contrasto was one of Paisiello's most
successful works. Several songs and duets became
popular favourites, notably 'Nel cor più non mi
sento' whose tune was a major hit of the 1790s, and
became in turn the basis of instrumental fantasias
and sets of variations by many other composers,
including Beethoven.

RECORDING *La Molinara*: Sciutti, Lazzari, Misciano,
Bruscantini, Calabrese, Alessandro Scarlatti O of Naples,
Caracciolo, Fonit Cetra, 1959
EDITION f.s., Aldo Rocchi (ed.), Otos, 1962

Nina, o sia La pazza per amore

Nina, or The Girl Driven Mad by Love
Commedia in un atto in prosa ed in verso per musica (1h 30m)
Libretto by Giuseppe Carpani and Giambattista Lorenzi,
after Benoît Joseph Marsollier
PREMIERES original version in one act: 25 June 1789,
Belvedere, S. Leucio (nr Caserta); rev. version in two acts:
autumn 1790, Teatro Fiorentini, Naples; UK: 27 April 1797,
London

Nina has one of the most sentimental plots of any
18th-century opera – although officially 'comic' its
brand of pathos puts it almost in the 'tragic' class.
Denied marriage to her lover Lindoro and hearing
that he has been killed by another suitor for her
hand, Nina becomes mentally deranged. Throughout
most of the opera she mopes for her lover's return
while her father and friends try unsuccessfully to
cheer her up. Only the real return of Lindoro
towards the end restores her sanity.

The model for *Nina* was a French opéra comique
called *Nina, ou La folle par amour*, with words by
Marsollier and music by Dalayrac, first seen in Paris
in 1786. Most unusually for an Italian opera but in
line with the practices of opéra comique, Paisiello's
work has spoken dialogue between the arias rather
than sung recitative. Several productions of the opera
during the composer's lifetime were staged with

recitative; this change, though, never had his
personal sanction.

RECORDING Orciani, Lojarro, Bolognesi, Verducci, Ch
Franceso Cilea, Piacenza SO, Panni, Bongiovanni, 1987
EDITIONS v.ss., Carisch, 1940; Ricordi, 1987

Other operas: *Il Ciarlone (La pupilla)*, 1764; *I Francesci
brillanti*, 1764; *Madama l'umorista*, 1765; *L'amore in ballo*,
1765; *Le virtuose ridicole*, 1765; *Le nozze disturbate*, 1766; *Le
finte contesse*, 1766; *La vedova di bel genio*, 1766; *Le
imbroglie de le bajasse*, 1767 (rev. as *La serva fatta padrona*,
1769); *L'idolo cinese*, 1767; *Lucio Papirio Dittatore*, 1767; *Il
furbo malaccorto*, 1767; *Olimpia*, 1768; *La luna abitata*, 1768;
La finta maga per vendetta, 1768; *L'osteria di Marechiaro*,
?1769; *La Claudia vendicata*, ?1769; *Don Chisciotte della
Mancia*, 1769; *L'arabo cortese*, 1769; *La Zelmira*, 1770; *Le
trame per amore*, 1770; *Il Demetrio*, 1771; *Annibale in Torino*,
1771; *La somiglianza de' nomi*, 1771; *I scherzi di amore e di
fortuna*, 1771; *Artaserse*, 1771; *La Semiramide in villa*, 1772
(RECORDING excerpts: Cetra, 1967); *Montezuma*, 1772; *La
Dardané*, 1772; *Gli amanti comici*, 1772; *L'innocente
fortunata*, 1773 (rev. as *La semplice fortunata*, 1773); *Sismano
nel Mogol*, 1773; *Il tamburo*, 1773 (rev. as *Il tamburo
notturno*, 1773); *Alessandro nell'Indie*, 1773; *Andromeda*,
1774; *Il duello*, 1774 (rev. as *Il duello comico*, 1774),
(RECORDING Haydn Society, 1953); *Il credulo deluso*, 1774;
La Frascatana, 1774; *Il divertimento de' numi*, 1774; *Il
Demofoonte*, 1775; *La discordia fortunata*, 1775; *Le astuzie
amorose*, 1775; *Socrate immaginario*, 1775; *Il gran Cid*, 1775;
Le due contesse, 1776; *La disfatta di Dario*, 1776; *Dal finto il
vero*, 1776; *Nitteti*, 1777; *Lucinda ed Armidoro*, 1777; *Achille
in Sciro*, 1778; *Lo sposo burlato*, 1778; *I filosofi immaginari*,
1779; *Il Demetrio*, 1779 (new setting); *Il matrimonio
inaspettato*, 1779; *La finta amante*, 1780; *Alcide al bivio*, 1780;
Il mondo della luna, 1783; *Il re Teodoro in Venezia*, 1784;
Antigono, 1785; *L'amore ingegnoso*, 1785; *La grotta di
Trofonio*, 1785; *Olimpiade*, 1786; *Le gare generose* (later as
Gli schiavi per amore), 1786; *Pirro*, 1787; *Giunone Lucina*,
1787; *La modista raggiratrice*, 1787; *Fedra*, 1788
(RECORDING Nuova Era, 1958); *Catone in Utica*, 1789; *I
zingari in fiera*, 1789; *Le vane gelosie*, 1790; *Zenobia in
Palmira*, 1790; *Ipermestra*, 1791; *La locanda*, 1791 (rev. as *Il
fanatico in Berlina*, 1792); *I giuochi d'Agrigento*, 1792;
Elfrida, 1792; *Elvira*, 1794; *Didone abbandonata*, 1794; *La
pace*, 1795; *La Daunia felice*, 1797; *Andromaca*, 1797;
L'inganno felice, 1798; *Proserpine*, 1803; Epilogue to Simone
Mayr's *Elisa*, 1807; *I Pittagorici*, 1808
BIBLIOGRAPHY Andrea della Corte, *Settecento italiano
Paisiello, con una tavola tematica*, Fratelli Bocca, 1922; Alfred
Loewenberg, 'Paisiello's and Rossini's *Barbiere di Siviglia*',
ML, vol. 20 (1939), pp. 157–67; Michael F. Robinson,
'Giovanni Paisiello', in *Grove*, Macmillan, 1980

M.F.R.

ZAKHARY PALIASHVILI

Zakhary Petrovich Paliashvili; *b* 16 August 1871, Kutaisi,
Georgia; *d* 6 October 1933, Tbilisi, Georgia

Paliashvili is considered one of the founders of
Georgian nationalist music, though unlike his
contemporaries Arakashvili and Dolidze, he studied
in Moscow with Serge Taneyev (1900–1903), who
introduced him to Western musical trends. In 1906 he
founded the Fraternity of the Creation of Georgian
Opera, and throughout his life was a rigorous

A scene from Act IV of Abesalom and Eteri, *the 1947 production at Tbilisi*

folklorist, publishing two volumes of Georgian folksongs that set new standards of research. His first opera, *Abesalom and Eteri* (1919), is regarded as a Georgian national monument. His later operas, *Daisi* (1923) and *Latavra* (1928), were also highly successful, the former being Stalin's favourite opera (there is a 1950s Melodiya recording conducted by V. Paliashvili). Other works include a *Georgian Suite* for orchestra, a number of choral works based on Georgian melodies, and some songs.

In Georgia Paliashvili is regarded as a Westernized composer, and indeed his musical language is a hybrid of Eastern and Western elements. The folk-derived melodic lines are very distinctive; usually modal with exotic chromatic intervals, they tend to centre obsessively around a note or small phrase. These simple shapes are then decorated with florid melismas that always circle around the note and fall. The melodic phrases are often of irregular length, highlighted by Paliashvili's very simple harmonic settings which feature bare fifths and a distinctive ambiguity between major and minor modes. His choral writing favours massive block-chordal effects and is notable for its fervour. The Western elements sometimes mingle uncomfortably and his occasional forays into chromatic harmony can be clumsy. For the early 20th century such ideas seem very old-fashioned, further exaggerated by stock features from Western operas; for example, Abesalom's death is accompanied by strings of diminished-seventh chords that sound as if they have strayed in from early Verdi. Structurally, the operas are discursive and the characterization not always well defined. Recurring themes are used, but with no great consistency. His orchestration is simple, though very effective, and he employs traditional percussion instruments such as the *daira*, *doli*, and *dimplipito*. The later operas are lusher in tone than *Abesalom and Eteri*, but lack its exuberance of invention. Ironically, they are better constructed as operas, but contain larger proportions of second-hand Westernisms, with some deeply banal martial music that anticipates the Soviet propaganda operas of the 1930s and 1940s.

Abesalom and Eteri

Abesalom da Eteri

Opera in four acts (2h 15m)
Libretto by P. Mirianashvili, after *Eteriani*, an ancient Georgian legend
Composed 1909–18
PREMIERE 21 February 1919, Tbilisi

Eteriani exists in a number of tribal variants, the first written versions dating from the early 19th century. The story concerns a shepherdess, Eteri, who is wooed by the king's son, Abesalom. However, a court official, Murman, who has reputedly sold his mother's soul to the devil, loves her too, and casts a disfiguring and diseasing spell on her. She is presumed dead, but Murman restores her to health, abducts her, and forces her to live in his castle as his wife. Abesalom pines away and is finally restored to Eteri on his deathbed.

A great deal of the action takes place offstage and the opera is a chain of static set pieces, in which events are narrated and commented on. There are few linking recitatives, so the opera is very formalized, more a ritual than a Western drama. However, much of the music is spellbinding, its simplicity and sincerity at times very moving, especially the love music of Abesalom and Eteri, the joyful music of Abesalom's young sister, Marich, and the extended choral numbers. Murman is not a convincing villain, despite Paliashvili's attempts to portray him with music that is unstable in tonality; his scenes are the weakest in the opera. Act II – Abesalom and Eteri's betrothal – is the most consistent: here, significantly, no action occurs and Paliashvili can indulge his lyric gifts to the hilt. The jewel of the opera is a quintet, in which Abesalom, Eteri and the royal family sing of love and fidelity, interrupted by the wedding guests' call for *tamada* (Georgian toasts). Starting as a simple ensemble, the solo toasts become ever more elaborate and florid, with Paliashvili winding the tonality up step by step. The melismas tumble over each other and collide, building to a thrilling climax of vocal display redolent of a convention of champion muezzins. For this number alone, the opera deserves revival. It was successfully revived in Germany in the 1970s.

RECORDING Z. Tatishvili, Chkonya, L. Tatishvili, Sotkilava, Kiknadze, Shushanya, USSR Radio Ch and O, Mirtschulava, DG, 1978
EDITION f.s., Moscow State, 1949; v.s., Muzfond Gruzii (Tbilisi), 1925

BIBLIOGRAPHY K. Franke, *Orientalism with a Western Finish*, DG booklet, 1978

J.G.

CARLO PALLAVICINO
b ?1640, Salo, Lake Garda; *d* 29 January 1688, Dresden

While working as an organist at San Antonio in Padua, Pallavicino produced his first two operas at the Teatro San Moisè in Venice: *Demetrio* (1666) and *Aurelimo* (1666). In the following year he was employed alongside distinguished foreigners and Schütz at the Dresden court. In 1673 he returned to Padua for a brief period, becoming maestro di coro at the Ospedale degli Incurabili in Venice in the following year. His residence in Venice led to his second group of operatic works. In 1685, he was persuaded back to Dresden, though he seems to have reserved the right to return to Venice to supervise productions of his operas. His operas, many of which are now lost, seem to have been revived frequently, both in Venice and elsewhere, particularly *Vespasiano* (1678), commissioned for the opening of the Venetian Teatro San Giovanni Crisostomo. Much of his music is based on simple melodies and rhythms, and with the increasing vogue for the aria he seems to have set the trend towards the regular use of *da capo* form. Much of his writing is quite sparse, and often the orchestra is introduced merely for the dramatic effect required in magic or sleep scenes or in the frequent and various sinfonias.

Surviving operas: *Demetrio*, 1666; *Diocletiano*, 1674; *Enea in Italia*, 1675; *Galieno*, 1675; *Vespasiano*, 1678; *Il Nerone* (one aria survives), 1679; *Le Amazoni nell'isole fortunate*, 1679; *Messalina*, 1679; *Bassiano, overo Il maggior impossibile*, 1682; *Carlo, re d'Italia*, 1682; *Il re infante* (only arias survive), 1683; *L'Amazone corsara, overo L'Alvilda, regina de'Goti*, 1686 (EDITION facsimile, H. M. Brown (ed.), Garland, 1978); *Elmiro re di Corinto* (only arias survive), 1686; *La Gierusalemme liberata*, 1687 (EDITION H. Abert (ed.), *DDT* 60, Leipzig, 1916); 10 lost operas
BIBLIOGRAPHY J. Smith, 'Carlo Pallavicino', *PRMA*, vol. 96 (1969–70), p. 57

G.D.

DOMENICO PARADIES
Pietro Domenico Paradies [Paradisi]; *b* 1707, Naples; *d* 25 August 1791, Venice

Probably a former pupil of the great teacher Nicolo Porpora, Paradies came to London in 1746 or 1747; between 1753 and 1756 he held the licence for the King's Theatre with Francesco Vaneshi – the librettist for his opera *Alessandro in Persia*. The orchestral concerts that were regularly given there frequently opened with one of his 'overtures' – what we would now describe as symphonies. Although he composed much for the stage, including *Fetonte*, which is unusual for the amount of ballet music for the chorus, and many arias for pasticcios, he had a greater success as singing teacher and harpsichordist. His most famous composition is the second movement of his Harpsichord Sonata in A (1754), familiarly known as 'Toccata by Paradies'.

Stage works surviving in manuscript: *Alessandro in Persia*, 1738; *Il decreto del fato*, 1740; *Le muse in gara*, 1740; *Fetonte*, 1747; *La forza d'amore*, 1751; *Antioco*, (n.d.); *Nerina*, (n.d.); *The Judgement of Paris*, (n.d.)
BIBLIOGRAPHY Highfill, Burnim and Langhans, *A Biographical Dictionary of Actors, Actresses, Musicians . . . in London, 1660–1800*, South Illinois University Press, 1973

T.T.C.

HORATIO PARKER
Horatio William Parker; *b* 15 September 1863, Auburndale, Massachusetts, US; *d* 18 December 1919, Cedarhurst, Long Island, US

In his lifetime Parker was one of America's most celebrated composers. He studied with Rheinberger in Munich (1882–5) and after his return to New York his reputation as a choral composer grew, largely due to the success of his oratorio *Hora novissima* (1893). It was much admired by Elgar, who heard it at the Three Choirs Festival in 1899.

By this time Parker was Battell Professor at Yale, a position he held until his death. His pupils included Ives – who admired him but did not agree with him – and Sessions. In 1902 Parker wrote that opera was 'a form with such manifest limitations that one may also regard it as outside the sphere of reasonable activity among Anglo-Saxons'.

But he soon became involved in operatic activity and seven years later Parker found opera 'just now the largest figure on our musical horizon'. One incentive seems to have been the cash prize of $10,000 and production at the Metropolitan (1912), both of which his first opera, *Mona*, achieved. Set in England under Roman occupation during the first century, *Mona*, steeped in Wagner and early Strauss, is a predominantly chromatic and highly expressive work. After its premiere it was not revived; critics felt this neglect was unjust.

His only other opera, *Fairyland*, won another prize and a premiere in Los Angeles (1915) as well as a contest designed to celebrate the inauguration of the Panama Canal. Its style is simpler and more tuneful than that of *Mona*, with emphasis on the chorus and mellifluous solo arias.

BIBLIOGRAPHY   W. K. Kearns, *Horatio Parker 1863–1919: His Life, Music and Ideas*, Scarecrow Press, 1990

P.D.

HUBERT PARRY

(Sir) Charles Hubert Hastings Parry; *b* 27 February 1848, Bournemouth, Hampshire, England; *d* 7 October 1918, Rustington, Sussex, England

Parry was one of the architects of the English musical renaissance as composer, teacher, administrator and writer. He became a musician against the wishes of his family, who forced him into a job in the City of London for seven years. He came into prominence at the 1880 Gloucester Festival with his setting of scenes from Shelley's *Prometheus Unbound*. His best-known choral work is a Milton setting, *Blest Pair of Sirens*, but he also wrote symphonies, chamber music, incidental music, songs and oratorios. He was Director of the Royal College of Music (1894–1918) and Professor of Music at Oxford University (1900–1908). His only opera, *Guinevere* (1885–6), to a libretto by U. Taylor, remains unpublished and unperformed.

BIBLIOGRAPHY   Jeremy Dibble, *C. Hubert Parry, His Life and Music*, Clarendon Press, 1992

M.K.

JOSEPH PARRY

b 21 May 1841, Merthyr Tydfil, Wales; *d* 17 February 1903, Penarth, Wales

After studying at the Royal Academy of Music, London, Parry returned for a time to Pennsylvania (where he had lived since he was 13) before becoming Professor of Music at Aberystwyth in 1874. With little practical experience of the stage, he completed the first Welsh opera, *Blodwen*, four years later. Although it is no masterpiece, it was more successful than all his subsequent operas.

Blodwen

Opera in three acts
Libretto by Richard Davies
PREMIERE   1878, Aberystwyth (concert); 1878, Swansea

Set in Wales in 1413, *Blodwen* is a chivalric tale of the love between Sir Hywel Ddu and his adopted daughter Blodwen. Sir Hywel is imprisoned at Chester by King Henry's invading soldiers, but is eventually pardoned on the death of the king, and Blodwen is reunited with her true father, long believed to be dead. Traditional Welsh tunes add

local colour to a score rooted in the style of early Verdi.

RECORDING   Bowen, Lloyd-Davies, Roberts, Barker, Rees, unnamed O, Hywel, Sain, 1978
EDITION   v.s., private publication, Aberystwyth, 1878

Published operas: *Arianwen*, 1890; *Sylvia*, 1895; *Ceridwen*, 1900
Operas in manuscript at the National Library of Wales, Aberystwyth: *Cap and Gown*, (1898); *King Arthur*, (1899); *His Worship the Mayor*, (1900); *Y ferch o'r scer*, (1902); *The Maid of Cefn Ydfa*, (1902)
Lost opera: *Virginia*, (1883)
BIBLIOGRAPHY   O. T. Edwards, *Joseph Parry, 1841–1903*, University of Wales Press, 1970

M.B.

THOMAS PASATIERI

b 20 October 1945, New York

A prolific American composer, Pasatieri has specialized in opera, adhering to the established *bel canto* traditions represented by Puccini and Menotti. In his teens Pasatieri arranged for Nadia Boulanger to comment on his scores sent by post, and at the Juilliard School he worked with Giannini and Persichetti and at the Aspen summer school with Milhaud. While Pasatieri's music has usually lacked critical approval owing to its derivative nature, its grateful and idiomatic vocal writing is much appreciated by singers. His operas have been commissioned by Houston Grand Opera, Baltimore Opera, Michigan Opera Theatre and for television.

Operatic works: *The Trysting Place*, (1964); *The Flowers of Ice*, (1965); *The Women*, 1965; *La Divina*, 1966; *Padrevia*, 1967; *Calvary*, 1971; *The Trial of Mary Lincoln*, 1972; *Black Widow*, 1972; *The Seagull*, 1974; *Signor Deluso*, 1974; *The Penitentes*, 1974; *Ines de Castro*, 1976; *Washington Square*, 1976; *Three Sisters*, (1979) 1986; *Before Breakfast*, 1980; *The Goose Girl*, 1981; *Maria Elena*, 1983
BIBLIOGRAPHY   R. H. Kornick, *Recent American Opera: A Production Guide*, 1991, pp. 222–32

P.D.

BERNARDO PASQUINI

b 7 December 1637, Massa da Valdinievole, nr Lucca; *d* 21 November 1710, Rome

The details of Pasquini's early musical training are unclear, but by 1650 he was in Rome where he remained until his death. He was employed by various churches as organist, and in 1664 he was appointed at Santa Maria in Aracoeli; though he held this position for the rest of his life, he seems also to have been involved with the Oratorio del SS. Crocifisso too. Pasquini made his name as a keyboard-player, and it was as a harpsichordist that he developed contacts with members of the leading Roman families, as well as with Queen Christina of

Sweden. In about 1670 he became musical director to Prince Giambattista Borghese but he also composed and performed secular music in the palaces and theatres of Rome. He was closely connected with Corelli and Alessandro Scarlatti, and many musicians came to study with him.

Pasquini's first known opera is *La sincerità con la sincerità, overo Il Tirinto*, which was performed at the Palazzo Borghese in 1672; the plot is a typical collection of false identities, falling in love with someone in disguise, and amorous intrigues, which eventually come to a happy resolution. His next opera, *L'Alcasta* (1673), is a more substantial work, and it was dedicated to Queen Christina of Sweden when it opened the Carnival season at the Tordinona theatre. Three years later he fulfilled his first commission for the Colonna with *La donna ancora è fedele*, a comedy in miniature. Papal directives against theatres and entertainment in general from 1680 onwards caused the wane of the Roman operatic tradition: but during one of the few years of respite, operas were allowed during Carnival. In 1692 his final opera, *L'Eudossia*, was performed at the Seminario Romano; the music has not survived. In 1693 Innocent XII issued another ban, initiating a period of intense activity in the field of the oratorio, and before the end of the century the leading opera theatre had disappeared.

Pasquini's operas, like those of his contemporary Stradella, mark a stage in the development of opera when it was gradually moving away from expressive recitative towards greater emphasis on arias. The forms had not, however, yet acquired the rigidity of later opera seria and the result is a fluid structure that moves easily between recitative, arioso, aria and, especially in *L'Idalma*, duets and ensembles. As arias took on an increasingly important role, so the function of the orchestra that accompanied them, was also expanded. A device particularly favoured by Pasquini was the ostinato aria, numerous examples of which occur in his later operas.

Surviving operas: *La sincerità con la sincerità, overo Il Tirinto*, 1672; *La forza d'amore*, 1672, rev. 1679 (RECORDING Bongiovanni, 1987); *L'amor per vendetta, overo L'Alcasta*, 1673; *Trespolo tutore*, ?1675; *La donna ancora è fedele*, 1676; *La caduta del regno dell'Amazzoni*, 1678, rev. 1690; *Dov'è amore è pietà* (one aria survives), 1679; *L'Idalma, overo Chi la dura la vince*, 1680 (EDITION facsimile, H. M. Brown (ed.), Garland, 1977); *Il Lisimaco*, 1681; *La Tessalonica*, 1683; *L'Arianna*, 1685; 2 lost operas
BIBLIOGRAPHY Carolyn Gianturco, 'Evidence for a Late Roman School of Opera', *ML*, vol. 56 (1975), pp. 4–17

G.D.

JIŘÍ PAUER
b 22 February 1919, Libušín, nr Kladno

Pauer has had the most successful career of any postwar Czech opera composer, much of it due to his deft theatrical instinct and his clear, melodic and generally undemanding musical style.

He qualified as a schoolteacher and while working as a teacher took private composition lessons. Later (1943–50) he attended the Prague Conservatory and Academy (under Hába and Bořkovec). Of his many administrative posts the most significant were those of artistic director of the Czech Philharmonic (1958–80) and at the National Theatre as head of opera (1953–5; 1965–7) and artistic director (1979–89). His first opera, and one of his most popular, *The Garrulous Snail*, was a graduation work. Its witty and light-hearted approach characterizes all of Pauer's later operas except for the historical *Zuzana Vojířová*. Other stage works include a ballet, *Ferdie the Ant* (*Ferda mravenec*, 1976), and a monodrama for male voice and orchestra, *Swan Lake* (*Labutí píseň*, 1976).

The Garrulous Snail
Žvanivý Slimejš
Opera in one act (50m)
Libretto by Míla Mellanová, after the tale by Joe Hloucha
Composed 1949–50
PREMIERE 5 April 1958, Academy of Music, Prague

The snail of the title is in search of fresh monkey liver to cure the illness of the beautiful daughter of the sea king. The hunt is successful: the snail (a pompous diplomat) flatters a monkey into coming with him, only to be betrayed by his talkativeness into revealing to the monkey what is in store for him.

RECORDING Tattermuschová, Soukupová, Votava, Berman, Czech PO, Liška, Supraphon, (n.d.)
EDITION v.s., Státní Hudební nakladatelství, 1963

A scene from The Garrulous Snail *(Prague, 1984)*

Zuzana Vojířová
Opera in five scenes (2h 15m)
Libretto by the composer, after the play by Jan Bor
Composed 1954–7
PREMIERE 30 December 1958, National Theatre, Prague

The play that Pauer adapted received its premiere during the Occupation and its audience read a coded message of hope and regeneration into its action concerning the last of the Voks of Rožmberk, one of the greatest aristocratic families of the Bohemian kingdom (Smetana's *The Devil's Wall* concerns an earlier member).

Petr Vok is childless, but fathers an illegitimate child from his loving union with Zuzana. Years after Vok's death (in 1611) Zuzana, now destitute and near death, has a chance meeting with her long-lost son. She dies happy in the knowledge that the line has been preserved.

RECORDING Beňačková, Márová, Soukupová, Havlák, Zítek, Švorc, Czech Radio Ch, Prague NT O, Vajnar, Supraphon, 1981
EDITION v.s., Panton, 1965

Little Red Riding Hood
Červená Karkulka
Opera in one act (45m)
Libretto by Míla Mellanová
Composed 1958–9
PREMIERE 1960, Prague

This was written as a companion piece for *The Garrulous Snail*. The two operas were performed together with great success at the Prague National Theatre in 1966.

RECORDING Šormová, Tattermuschová, Mrázová, Jedličková, Jindrák, Prague NT O, Chaloupka, Supraphon, [n.d.]
EDITION v.s., Dilia, [n.d.]

Marital Counterpoints
Manželské kontrapunkty
Five (originally three) operatic grotesqueries (50m)
Libretto by the composer, after the tales by Stefanie Grodzieńská
Composed 1961–2 (1–3); 1965 (4–5)
PREMIERES 1–3: 17 March 1962, Ostrava; complete: 1966, Liberec

These are musical settings of five independent and very cynical vignettes about family life: choosing a meal at a restaurant; a photographic session with an unruly child; preparations for a visit (a divided stage depicting hosts and guests simultaneously, neither showing much enthusiasm for the coming event). After the popular success of these first three, Pauer added two more, the first about a family holiday, the second about a writer constantly interrupted by wife and mother.

RECORDING 1 and 3: Soukupová, Blachut, Tattermuschová, Berman, Prague NT O, Gregor, Supraphon, 1965
EDITION v.s., Supraphon, 1977

The Hypochondriac
Zdravý nemocný
Opera in three acts
Libretto by the composer, after the play *Le malade imaginaire* by Molière (1673)
Composed 1965–8
PREMIERE 22 May 1970, Tyl Theatre, Prague

Molière's familiar play lends itself well to Pauer's talents, particularly in the depiction of well-contrasted comic characterizations, though there are

lyrical and moving moments associated with the invalid's daughter, Angelica.

RECORDING excerpts: Fidlerová, Márová, Frydlewicz, Jedenáctík, Blachut, Berman, Czech PO, Liška, Panton, 1973

Other opera: *The Haunted House* (*Strašidelný dům*), (1986)
BIBLIOGRAPHY Ladislav Šíp, *Česká opera a jeho tvůrci* (*Czech Opera and Its Creators*), Supraphon, 1983

J.T.

STEPHEN PAULUS
Stephen Harrison Paulus; *b* 24 August 1949, Summit, New Jersey, US

Paulus is a successful composer of opera in the American vernacular tradition, although his work is by no means limited to the stage. At the University of Minnesota he worked with Argento when he was creating an important centre for opera at St Paul and Minneapolis.

The Village Singer
Opera in one act
Libretto by Michael Dennis Browne, based on the short story by Mary Wilkins Freeman (1891)
PREMIERE 9 June 1979, Opera Theatre of St Louis

The story charts the musical warfare that follows the enforced retirement of a village-choir soprano in favour of a younger replacement, and provides opportunity to cite hymns and parlour songs which Paulus welds into a tonal (and occasionally bitonal) idiom that is conservative but individual. The opera was praised for its dramatic timing and character-ization, especially of the central character, Candace Whitcomb, written for – and first performed by – Pauline Tinsley.

EDITION v.s., European American, 1985

The Postman Always Rings Twice
Opera in two acts (2h)
Libretto by Colin Graham, after the novel by James Cain (1934)
PREMIERES 17 June 1982, Opera Theatre of St Louis; UK: 6 September 1983, King's Theatre, Edinburgh (Opera Theatre of St Louis)

As a result of *The Village Singer*'s success, Opera Theatre of St Louis commissioned a second opera. *The Postman Always Rings Twice* is a more sinister piece, with a libretto by Colin Graham based on James Cain's first novel. Graham, who was both librettist and producer, described it as 'a tragedy of two people who have no knowledge of good or evil, and only become aware of their true natures when they are on the way down'. The story, which is real *verismo*-Americano, is told in a series of flashbacks. It concerns the murder of a restaurant owner by two lovers; they escape but the woman dies in a car crash and the man is executed for her murder. *When The Postman Always Rings Twice* was performed at the

Edinburgh Festival in 1983, Max Loppert found it disappointing with 'little consistent interest, let alone dramatic excitement – or originality'.

EDITION   v.s., European American, 1988

The Woodlanders

Opera in three acts
Libretto by Colin Graham, based on the novel by Thomas Hardy (1887)
PREMIERE   13 June 1985, Opera Theatre of St Louis

The Woodlanders shows a rather tighter, more assured handling of operatic structure than its predecessor. Paulus sustains the drama more effectively, moving easily from vocal recitative to arioso and aria against a discreet chamber-orchestra accompaniment that relies heavily, but not monotonously, on characteristic repeated figures.

Other opera: *Harmoonia*, 1991
BIBLIOGRAPHY   B. Morton and P. Collins, *Contemporary Composers*, St James Press, 1992

P.D.

STEFANO PAVESI

b 22 January 1779, Casaletto Vaprio, nr Crema; *d* 28 July 1850, Crema

Pavesi began his studies with Piccinni in Naples, but in 1799 he was expelled from the conservatory for republican views and escaped to Marseilles; in Dijon he enlisted as a military bandsman in Napoleon's army and in this capacity returned to Italy. Leaving the army at Crema, he completed his studies with Gazzaniga; in 1803 he produced his first (or possibly his second) opera, *Un avvertimento ai gelosi*, in Venice, and from then on continued to turn out operas at the rate of four and sometimes even six a year – mostly buffe or semiserie in the accepted style of the period. His greatest success came with *Ser Marcantonio* which ran for 54 nights at La Scala in 1810 and became a popular favourite all over Italy. In 1818 he succeeded Gazzaniga as maestro di cappella at Crema, and from 1826 to 1830 spent half of each year as director of the Court Opera in Vienna, following Salieri. He produced his last opera, *Fenella, ovvero La muta di Portici* (to a libretto by Rossi based on Scribe's for Auber's opera, 1828), another major success, in 1831.

Pavesi was one of the most individual and richly gifted of the composers between Paisiello and Rossini, but his talent could not long survive once Rossini, Donizetti and Bellini had cornered the market – and in fact he wrote no operas at all during the last 19 years of his life.

Operas: ?*La pace*, 1801; *Un avvertimento ai gelosi*, 1803; *L'amante anonimo*, 1803; *I castelli in aria*, 1803; *La forza dei simpatici, ovvero Lo stratagemma per amore*, 1803; *Andromaca*, 1804; *La fiera*, 1804; *L'accortezza materna*, 1804; *L'amore prodotto dall'odio*, 1804; *La vendetta di Medea*,

(1804); *Fingallo e Camala*, 1805; *Il trionfo d'Emilia*, 1805; *Amare e non voler essere amante*, 1805 (also as *L'incognito, o L'abitatore del bosco*, 1805); *Il giuocatore*, 1806; *Le donne fuggitive*, 1806; *I baccanali di Roma*, 1806; *La sorpresa, ovvero Il deputato di grosso latino*, 1806; *Ines de Castro* (with G. Farinelli and N. Zingarelli), 1806; *Amore vince l'inganno*, 1806; *I Cherusci*, 1807; *Sapersi scegliere un vero sposo, ovvero Amor vero e amor interessato*, 1807; *Aristodemo*, 1807; *Il maldicente, ovvero La bottega del caffè*, 1807/?1808; *L'amore perfetto, ovvero Il servo padrone*, 1808; *La festa della rosa*, 1808; *Il trionfo della bella, ovvero Corradino Cuor di Ferro*, 1809; *Ippolita regina delle Amazzoni*, 1809; *Arminia*, 1810; *I gaurî*, 1810; *Elisabetta regina d'Inghilterra*, 1810; *Il tributo di Gedeone* (sacred drama), 1810; *Ser Marcantonio*, 1810; *Odoardo e Cristina*, 1810; *La giardiniera abruzzese, ovvero Il signorino e l'ajo*, 1811; *Il monastero*, 1811; *Il trionfo dell' amore, ovvero Irene e Filandro*, 1811; *Nitteti*, 1811; *Tancredi*, 1812; *Amore e generosità*, 1812; *L'ostregaro*, 1812; *Aspasia e Cleomene*, 1812; *Teodoro*, 1812; *Una giornata pericolosa*, 1813; *Agatina, ovvero La virtù premiata*, 1814; *Celanira*, 1815; *La villanella fortunata*, 1816; *Le Danaidi romane*, 1816; *La gioventù di Cesare*, 1817; *I Pitocchi fortunati*, 1819; *Gli esiliati da Firenze* (doubtful); *Don Gusmano*, 1819; *Il gran naso*, 1820; *Eugenia degli Astolfi*, 1820; *Arminio, ovvero L'eroe germano*, 1821; *Sandrina*, 1822; *Antigona e Lauso*, 1822; *Anco Marzio*, 1822; *Ines d'Almeida*, 1822; *I cavalieri del Nodo*, 1823; *Egilda di Provenza*, 1823; *Ardano e Dartula*, 1825; *Il solitario ed Elodia*, 1826; *Gli arabi nelle Gallie*, 1827; *La donna bianca d'Avenello*, 1830; *Fenella, ovvero La muta di Portici*, 1831; *La testa riscaldata*, (n.d.)

BIBLIOGRAPHY   Mario Morini, 'Stefano Pavesi', in *Enciclopedia dello Spettacolo*, G. C. Sansoni, 1960

M.R.

CARLO PEDROTTI

b 12 November 1817, Verona; *d* 16 October 1893, Verona

Pedrotti is significant as a representative figure of a largely forgotten generation. Pedrotti was four years younger than Verdi, and his career as an opera composer was launched in 1840, one year after the premiere of Verdi's first opera, *Oberto*. Although he made a favourable impression with his first two works, Pedrotti was unable to make a living as an opera composer. For want of anything better, he embarked on a path as an opera conductor, first in Amsterdam, and later and more valuably in Turin (1868–82).

Never in a position to devote himself entirely to composition, he nevertheless wrote 17 operas between 1840 and 1872. Of these, only the opera buffa *Tutti in maschere*, with a plot after Goldoni, proved to have staying power. It shows Pedrotti's facility and grace, even his contagious high spirits, but he lacked the capacity for creative growth and the ability to find new and more complex solutions to the question of revitalizing operatic tragedy as did Verdi. Pedrotti was in a sense a prisoner of a largely moribund tradition and he came to realize it himself. Aware of his limitations, and of his deteriorating health, he committed suicide.

Operas: *Antigone*, (n.d.); *La sposa del villagio*, (n.d.); *Lina*, 1840; *Clara di Mailand*, 1840; *Matilde*, 1841; *La figlia dell'arciere*, 1844; *Romeo di Montfort*, 1846; *Fiorina, o La fanciulla di Glaris*, 1852; *Il parrucchiere della reggenza*, 1852; *Gelmina, o Col fuoco non si scherza*, 1853; *Genoveffa di Brabant*, 1854; *Tutti in maschere*, 1856; *Isabella d'Aragona*, 1859; *Guerra in quattro*, 1861; *Mazeppa*, 1861; *Marion de Lorme*, 1865; *La Vergine di Kermo* (coll.), 1870; *Il favorito*, 1870; *Olema la schiava*, 1872

BIBLIOGRAPHY   Carlo Schmidl, *Dizionario universale dei musicisti*, vol. 2, Casa Editrice Sonsozgno, 1938

W.A.

VICTOR PELISSIER

[Pelisier, Pelesier, Pellesier]; *b c.* 1740–50, ?Paris; *d c.* 1820, ?New Jersey, US

Pelissier was one of the earliest French composers active in America, arriving initially in Philadelphia in 1792 and settling a year later in New York. He was employed by the Old American Company from 1793 as principal horn-player and thereafter became one of its resident composers and arrangers. He adapted operas, ballets and pantomimes – many of which were imported English works by Storace, Dibdin and Arnold – and provided incidental music to spoken plays.

Pelissier's original stage works were important achievements in their time. He wrote one of the earlist American operas, *Edwin and Angelina* (1796), whose 'outlaw' setting was highly romantic in tone. *Ariadne Abandoned* (1797) was one of the first American melodramas and greatly influenced the development of this genre during the 19th century. Other original compositions included the opera *Sterne's Maria* (1799) and a pantomime extravaganza, *The Fourth of July* (1799). Much of Pelissier's stage music is lost.

BIBLIOGRAPHY   J. Mates, *The American Musical Stage Before 1800*, Rutgers University Press, 1962

E.C.

KRZYSZTOF PENDERECKI

b 23 November 1933, Dębica, Poland

Penderecki completed his composition studies at Cracow Music Academy in 1958, and thereafter quickly came to prominence. In 1959 he won the first and two second prizes in the composers' competition of the Polish Composers' Union. Soon afterwards, he received his first overseas commission (Donaueschingen Festival); since then his international fame has grown rapidly. His early, mainly instrumental, works are short, modern in musical language, and have a richness of expression which informs all his music. In some vocal works the sound of the words is actually more important than their meaning, and this feature persists in many more recent compositions. Devices such as the cluster and the glissando were also typical from the start.

In about 1964 a change came over Penderecki's music, connected with his growing interest in ritual and archaism. Elements of traditional musical styles from earlier periods (chords based on thirds, quasitonal harmony) are combined with modern techniques. He began to write large-scale choral, often religious, works (such as the *St Luke Passion* and *Utrenia*), as well as operas, using Gregorian or Orthodox chant and chorales. This is demonstrated in his operas, particularly the first two. Penderecki has written orchestral and chamber music, vocal works including oratorios, operas and more than 50 incidental and film scores. He has consistently espoused such universal subjects as evil and expiation, intolerance, fanaticism and death. His international success is due to the fact that his music appeals to a broader audience than most avant-garde music, which in its turn has led to Penderecki being criticized on the grounds that his music is superficial and intended purely for show.

The Devils of Loudun

Diably z Loudun
Opera in three acts (30 scenes) (2h 15m)
Libretto by the composer, based on John Whiting's dramatization (1961) of the novel by Aldous Huxley (1952), in the German translation by Erich Fried
Composed 1968–9, rev. 1972
PREMIERES   20 June 1969, Staatsoper, Hamburg; US: 14 August 1969, Santa Fe; UK: 1 November 1973, Coliseum, London (Sadler's Wells Opera)
CAST   Grandier *bar*, Jeanne *dramatic s*, Father Barre *b*, Philippe *high lyric s*, de Laubardemont *t*, Father Mignon *t*, Adam *t*, Mannoury *bar*, Prince Henri de Conde *bar*, d'Armagnac *spoken role, s, ms*, 2 *a, b-bar, b, basso profondo*, 2 *spoken roles*; *satb* chorus of Ursuline nuns, Carmelites, people, children, guards, soldiers (often offstage)
VERY LARGE ORCHESTRA including 2 alto sax, 2 baritone sax, pf, organ, harmonium, electric bass gtr, 4 perc players and *nastro magnetico con scampanata* (tape)

The story of Father Grandier, who was burned at the stake in Loudun, near Poitiers, in 1634, has exerted a strong fascination for artists and writers. But Penderecki was more interested in the contemporary and universal symbolism of the subject than in its historical aspect. The number of characters and sub-plots in the play is reduced and the dialogues shortened, the psychological change in Grandier is made less clear, and instead the accent is placed on his fight against fanaticism and evil.

SYNOPSIS
Act I   The nuns of the Ursuline convent and their mother superior, Jeanne, have been seized with erotic obsession. Jeanne has had frequent sexual visions of Father Grandier, a handsome parish priest and ladies' man. She tells Father Mignon about them, and her confession is subsequently used against Grandier, as well as influencing the political battle between the town's governor and Cardinal Richelieu over the threatened dismantling of the town's fortifications.

Act II   Exorcisms are performed on Jeanne. She tells how she and other nuns have been forced by

Tatiana Troyanos as Jeanne in The Devils of Loudun *(Hamburg, 1969)*

Grandier to take part in a sexual orgy in the chapel. Further exorcisms (in effect torture) produce nothing of use to Grandier's enemies, but despite this he is arrested by de Laubardemont, the king's special commissioner.

Act III The innocent Grandier refuses to sign a confession. He is tortured and burned at the stake.

The opera's many-layered structure and division into short scenes brings it closer to the form of film, while demanding rapid and frequent change in the music itself, which is characterized by dramatic contrast and great expressive tensions. The characters sing, speak, laugh and scream; the chorus sings in the manner of Gregorian chant, but also shouts and screams. Such devices appeared in earlier works such as the *St Luke Passion*. There is no purely orchestral music; the instruments are mostly used in small groups to produce rapid changes in colour, or for solos.

RECORDING Troyanos, Ahlin, Boese, Steiner, Hiolski, Ładysz, Sotin, Marschner, Blankenburg, Melchert, van Mill, Hamburg Staatsoper Ch and O, Janowski, Philips, 1972
EDITIONS f.s., PWM-Edition/Schott, 1969; v.s., Schott, 1970

Paradise Lost

Sacra rappresentazione in two acts (2h)
Libretto by Christopher Fry, after the poem by John Milton (1665)
Composed 1975–8
PREMIERE 29 November 1978, Lyric Opera, Chicago
CAST Milton *spoken role*, Adam *lyric bar*, Eve *lyric s*, Satan *dramatic bar*, Archangel Michael *heroic t, coloratura s, ms*, 3 ct, 3 t, 2 bar, basso profondo, 5 *dancers*; boys' chorus, satb chorus
VERY LARGE ORCHESTRA including triple ww and brass, 3 Wagner tubas, harmonium, cel, organ and vast perc section

Milton's poem about sin and the fall of Man provides further material for Penderecki's moral preoccupations: here again the subject is the fight against evil and the method of expiation.

SYNOPSIS
The scene is set in Hell and the Garden of Eden.

Act I The expulsion of Adam and Eve from Paradise is followed by a sequence of retrospective tableaux such as the Fallen Angels being thrown into the pit in the struggle against God, the creation of Man (who is intended by Satan as an instrument in this struggle) and Satan tempting Eve to eat the forbidden fruit.

Act II Before leaving the Garden, Adam and Eve observe the consequences of their sin, and Adam is shown images of disasters which will afflict his progeny: war, flood, plague. He is shaken, but the Archangel Michael instils in him faith in God's justice, and Adam and Eve leave Paradise calmly.

The work derives certain features from the baroque sacra rappresentazione: the narrator (Milton himself), allegorical characters and elements of pantomime, extensive use of chorus in the role of commentator, and the generally static character of the treatment. It marks a turn towards a more traditional musical language, particularly that of Wagner. This is mainly evident in the quasi-tonal harmony, and in the actual sonority of the orchestral writing.

EDITIONS f.s., Schott (on hire), 1978; v.s., Schott, 1978

Die schwarze Maske

The Black Mask
Opera in one act (1h 45m)
Libretto by Harry Kupfer and the composer, after the play by Gerhard Hauptmann (1928)
Composed 1984–6
PREMIERES 15 August 1986, Kleines Festspielhaus, Salzburg (Vienna Staatsoper); UK: 15 May 1990, Dome Theatre, Brighton (State Opera Company of Poznań)
CAST Silvanus Schuller *t*, Benigna *s*, Johnson *spoken role*, Arabella *s leggiero*, Daga, Jedidja Potter *buffo t*, François Tortebat *b*, Lowel Perl *bar*, Dedp *b bar*, Wendt *b*, Hadank *lyric t*, Ebbo Huttenwachter *buffo b*, Laura Huttenwachter *a*, Schedel *t*, Knoblochzer *b*, masked dancer *silent, a*; satb chorus offstage
LARGE ORCHESTRA including organ; onstage: 2 picc, 3 rec (soprano, alto, tenor,), 2 E♭ cl, 3 tpt, 3 trbn, perc, cimb, vc

Hauptmann's play is condensed and modified for the libretto, using closed forms with clear-cut endings. The work is a vision of the world at a time of impending catastrophe, and suggests the image of a dance of death. The masked man (Johnson) is the most ambiguous and symbolic of the characters; all the evil is focused on him, and he is both the herald and the cause of imminent disaster.

SYNOPSIS
In the small Silesian town of Bolkenhain in the winter of 1662 guests are arriving at the house of Schuller, the mayor. Each professes a different religion and, in spite of apparent harmony, there is some tension, which gradually increases as the action proceeds. Everyone is horrified when an unknown man in a black mask jumps into the garden. In the eerie situation that results, the guests' secret conflicts, desires and hatreds begin to come to the surface. Relations between certain characters prove complicated. Benigna, Schuller's wife, tells the secret

story of her life. She was seduced by a Negro, Johnson, an escaped slave, who afterwards forced her to marry a rich, elderly merchant. The merchant died soon afterwards, and Johnson was suspected of his murder. He escaped, but Benigna has been blackmailed by him ever since. She married Schuller, and they moved to Belkenhain to get away from Johnson, but she has just received a letter from him making new demands. She begins to suspect that the masked man is Johnson. Suddenly, seeing the dead body of her servant, she is now sure of her suspicions. She goes mad and dies, and her husband, in despair, commits suicide.

The scenes of Benigna's confession and madness are the climactic points of the opera. The tension is resolved in a concluding dance of death which uses motifs from the introduction; thus the opera is enclosed in a musical frame. The musical language harks back to Penderecki's early works, without completely resembling them. Though the harmony is now more dissonant there are quotations from chorales and 17th-century dance music (which create an appropriate period atmosphere) and from the composer's own early religious works. Rhythm plays a vital role in portraying individual characters along leitmotivic lines.

EDITION   lib., Schott, 1986

Ubu Rex

Opera buffa in two acts
Libretto by Jerzy Jarocki and the composer, after the play *Ubu roi* by Albert Jarry (1896)
PREMIERE   6 July 1991, Bayerische Staatsoper, Munich

Penderecki's operatic version of Jarry's schoolboy satire of despotism had a long gestation. In 1963 he had provided incidental music for a marionette production of the play, and work with Jarocki on the libretto also dated back to the 1960s. The original plan for a wind-only orchestra was abandoned in favour of a large orchestra (including stage music) and cast.

Ubu is the archetypal tyrant – Nero, Hitler, Stalin, Amin and Hussein rolled into one – drawn in comic-book fashion. Jarry's play relentlessly pokes fun at theatrical and social conventions. Penderecki's opera buffa is an amalgam of a wide variety of styles – Mozart, Rossini (Ma Ubu is a coloratura mezzo-soprano), Wagner, Richard Strauss – incorporating traditional ensembles and arias. However, this eclecticism frequently robs the music of any individuality. Combined with the persistent attempts to sustain the comic element (with use of *parlando*, *staccato*, continuous musical action), this highlights the problem of writing contemporary opera buffa.

EDITIONS   f.s./v.s. (on hire), Schott, 1991

BIBLIOGRAPHY   L. Erhardt, *Spotkania z Krzysztofem Penderekim* (*A Meeting with Penderecki*), PWM-Edition,

1975; W. Schwinger, *Penderecki: Begegnungen, Lebensdaten, Werkkommentare*, Deutsche Verlags-Anstalt, 1979; trans. by William Mann as *Krzysztof Penderecki, His Life and Work*, Schott, 1989

Z.C.

JOHANN CHRISTOPH PEPUSCH

b 1667, Berlin; *d* 20 July 1752, London

Composer, harpsichordist, violinist, theorist and antiquarian, Pepusch was one of the most important musicians resident in London during the time of Handel. Their paths frequently crossed. Though overshadowed by Handel (whose music he supposedly disliked) in every endeavour except scholarship, Pepusch was closely involved in three important phases of opera in London: the introduction and establishment of opera seria; the creation of an English-language alternative, and the invention of ballad opera, which nearly annihilated the other two species.

Pepusch came to England shortly after 1700, having been previously employed at the Prussian court from the age of 14. He may have been introduced into London musical circles through the Clerkenwell concerts of the small-coal man Thomas Britton (one of Pepusch's early trio sonatas bears the title 'Smalcoal'). Advertisements for his compositions first appear in London newspapers in 1704, and in 1706 he was employed by the Drury Lane Theatre as harpsichordist. Later that season Pepusch directed the production of *Thomyris*, a pasticcio in the Italian style which was the second opera produced in London to feature a castrato, Valentino Urbani. He sang in Italian, the rest of the cast in English. Pepusch wrote the recitatives (to a libretto by P. A. Motteux) and arranged various arias by Alessandro Scarlatti, Dieupart, Gasparini, Albinoni and (the majority) G. Bononcini. The title role was sung by Margarita de l'Epine, for whom Pepusch was acting as agent and whom he later married. *Thomyris* was successful enough to be revived in 1708, but Pepusch had been replaced as director. About this time he joined the Haymarket opera orchestra as a first violinist and probably played in the 1711 premiere of *Rinaldo*, Handel's first London opera.

Pepusch received the Oxford D. Mus. in 1713, and in 1715 his theatre career once again changed direction when, in direct competition with the Italian opera at the Haymarket, he composed a series of all-sung English masques for Drury Lane. These charming and generally successful works included *Venus and Adonis* (1715, libretto by Colley Cibber), *Apollo and Daphne* (1716) and *The Death of Dido* (1716). The last is simple, tuneful and, although it is invidious to compare it with Purcell's masterpiece, it is nevertheless dramatic and, like *Dido and Aeneas*, a true opera in miniature. After 1716 Pepusch seems to have withdrawn from the theatre to become music

Satirical engraving after The Beggar's Opera, *1728*

director to James Brydges (later Duke of Chandos) at Cannons, where Handel was composer-in-residence.

Pepusch's final flourish on the London stage gained him immortality. He composed the overture to John Gay's enormously successful *The Beggar's Opera* (28 January 1728). Whether he also helped Gay select the tunes is unknown, but Pepusch provided rough-and-ready accompaniments for this and two other ballad operas, including Gay's *Polly*, which was banned and never performed during his lifetime. In later years Pepusch retreated into music history and theory.

Dramatic works: *Thomyris, Queen of Scythia* (pasticcio; recitatives, arrangements), 1707; four masques: *Venus and Adonis*, 1715; *Myrtillo*, 1715; *Apollo and Daphne*, 1716, and *The Death of Dido*, 1716; ?*The Prophetess, or The History of Dioclesian* (lost), 1724; *The Beggar's Opera* (overture, accompaniments), 1728; *The Wedding* (?overture), (1729); *Polly* (accompaniments), (1729), 1777

BIBLIOGRAPHY   D. F. Cook, *John Christopher Pepusch in London: His Vocal Music for the Theatre*, dissertation, University of London, 1983; Roger Fiske, *English Theatre Music in the Eighteenth Century*, OUP, 2nd edn, 1983; J. Milhous and R. D. Hume (eds), *Vice Chamberlain Coke's Theatrical Papers, 1706–1715*, Carbondale, 1982

C.A.P.

MARIO PERAGALLO
b 25 March 1910, Rome

Peragallo's creative development has been guided by his own changing preferences rather than by loyalty to a single school or trend. He first made his name with *Ginevra degli Almieri* (1937) and *Lo stendardo di San Giorgio* (1941), *verismo* operas showing affinities with Zandonai. After the Second World War he drastically modernized his style, under the influence of serial technique.

La gita in campagna
The Trip in the Country
Opera in one act (three scenes) (35m)
Libretto adapted by the composer, from Alberto Moravia's short story *Andare verso il popolo*
PREMIERE   24 March 1954, La Scala, Milan

This brilliantly effective little work is perhaps the most striking operatic manifestation of the Italian 'neo-realist' movement, centred on writers such as Moravia and film directors such as De Sica. The story unflinchingly takes the lid off the chaos left by the departing Germans in 1945. When their car breaks down Ornella and Mario, a bourgeois couple, are brought face to face with peasants who have lost nearly everything. The peasant woman Leonia willingly offers to help them, while revealing that the members of her family now live as thieves. Mario's academic interest in the problems of the peasantry is put through a severe test, and when he and Ornella eventually drive away, they have been robbed of their money and even most of their clothes.

Peragallo's score combines suitably barbed dodecaphonic textures with singable vocal lines, not unlike Menotti's. An accordion, a saxophone and jazz drums help to contribute a (wryly distorted) undertone of popular music. Stormily received in Milan when new, *La gita* then quickly won success in Germany and the US, and later in Italy too.

EDITION v.s., Universal, 1955

Other operatic works: *Ginevra degli Almieri*, 1937; *Lo stendardo di San Giorgio*, 1941; *La collina* (madrigale scenico), 1947; *La parucca dell' imperatore* (rondò scenico), 1959
BIBLIOGRAPHY Massimo Mila, 'La contadina e il trasvolatore', in his *Cronache musicali 1955–1959*, Einaudi, 1959, pp. 217–18

J.C.G.W.

DAVIDE PEREZ
b 1710–11, Naples; *d* 30 October 1778, Lisbon

Born in Naples to parents of Spanish descent, Perez studied at the Conservatory of S. Maria di Loreto (1723–33). In 1735 he made his début as an opera composer at the court opera house, earning the description 'outstanding virtuoso' from the impresario Angelo Carasale. Three years later he obtained a post in the Cappella Palatina at Palermo, which gave him, until 1748, the economic security to undertake the risky business of opera.

Preceded by the fame resulting from performances of his opere serie in Palermo, Perez produced his works in the major Italian centres and in Vienna. In 1752 Don José I, King of Portugal, invited him to Lisbon to take charge of the capital's musical activities. The ample resources of the court were put at his disposal and in 1755 Perez's production of a second version of his *Alessandro nell'Indie* employed a complete cavalry corps and an imitation of a Macedonian phalanx.

Perez brought dramatic conviction and originality to opera seria by relaxing some of the conventional rigid forms and borrowing techniques from comic opera. He had the technique and sensibility to express melancholy, a quality evident in his two masterpieces of the Portuguese period, *Solimano* (1757) and *Demetrio* (1766).

Surviving operatic works: *Il trionfo di Venere*, 1738; *L'Atlanta*, 1739; *L'amor pittore*, 1740; *I travestimenti amorosi*, 1740; *Siroe re di Persia*, 1740, rev. 1752; *Demetrio*, 1741, rev. 1765–6; *Il natale di Giunone*, 1742; *Merope*, 1744; *Alessandro nell'Indie*, 1744, rev. 1755; *Artaserse*, 1748, rev. 1754; *La Semiramide riconosciuta*, 1749; *Farnace*, 1750; *L'amor prigioniero*, 1751; *Didone abbandonata*, 1751, rev. 1753; *La Zenobia*, 1751; *Demofoonte*, 1752; *L'Adriano in Siria*, 1752 or

?1754; *L'eroe cinese*, 1753; *L'Olimpiade*, 1753; *L'Ipermestra*, 1754; *Lucio Vero*, 1754; *L'eroe coronato*, 1775; *Solimano*, 1757, rev. 1768; *L'isola disabitata*, 1767; *Creusa in Delfo*, 1774; *La pace fra la virtù e la bellezza*, 1777; 22 lost operas
BIBLIOGRAPHY P. J. Jackson, *The Operas of Davide Perez*, dissertation, Stanford University, 1967

D.A.D'A.

GIOVANNI BATTISTA PERGOLESI
b 4 January 1710, Jesi, nr Ancona; *d* 16 March 1736, Pozzuoli, nr Naples

Pergolesi's stage works include four serious operas, two comic operas, two intermezzi, and a sacred drama. These were written during a period of less than six years in Pergolesi's short lifetime and were all first produced in Naples with the exception of his last opera seria, *L'Olimpiade*.

In any discussion of works attributed to Pergolesi, the question of authenticity is an overriding concern. This is particularly true of the many sacred works, instrumental pieces, and independent arias fraudulently inscribed with the celebrated name. This wholesale production of false Pergolesiana by unscrupulous publishers and copyists was a result of the resounding posthumous success of his intermezzo *La serva padrona* in Paris in 1752 and the ensuing battle of words – the so-called *querelle des bouffons* – between the partisans of French and Italian opera.

Nevertheless, with few exceptions, the authenticity of the Pergolesi *oeuvre* for the stage remains not only secure but well documented, even including a partial autograph of his last opera, *Il Flaminio*. Pergolesi also wrote an oratorio, *La morte di San Giuseppe*, a complete autograph of which has recently been authenticated. Among the relatively few Pergolesi misattributions for the stage are the intermezzo *Il maestro di musica* (a pasticcio based on Pietro Auletta's *Orazio*) and the comic opera *Il geloso schernito* (a 1746 work by the Venetian composer Pietro Chiarini, with an overture by Baldassare Galuppi).

Pergolesi was sent at an early age to study at the Conservatorio dei Poveri di Gesù Cristo in Naples. There he had the advantage of studying with such masters as Greco, Vinci, and Durante. His sacred drama, *La conversione e morte di San Guglielmo*, was presented, probably as a conservatory exercise, at the monastery of Sant' Agnello in the summer of 1731. Later the same year, Pergolesi was commissioned to write his first opera seria, *La Salustia*, which was received with indifference when it was produced in January 1732. In sharp contrast, his first comic opera, *Lo frate 'nnamorato*, presented later in the same year, was an unqualified success.

Pergolesi's second opera seria, *Il prigionier superbo*, is best known as the conduit for the intermezzo placed between its acts, the immortal *La serva padrona* (1733). The following year saw another intermezzo, *Livietta e Tracollo*, sandwiched

Caricature portrait of Pergolesi by Pier Leone Ghezzi

between the acts of Pergolesi's third, and perhaps most powerful, opera seria, *Adriano in Siria*. Pergolesi's two final works for the stage were produced in 1735: the opera seria *L'Olimpiade*, in Rome, and the commedia musicale *Il Flaminio*, in Naples.

The diversity of style among these works is remarkable: from the buffo scenes of *La conversione e morte di San Guglielmo* to the virtuosic and extended arias of *Adriano in Siria*; from the folklike canzonas of *Lo frate 'nnamorato* to the delicate and expressive arias of *L'Olimpiade*. They reflect in microcosm the vast stylistic range of much of Pergolesi's non-dramatic work: from the simple textures of his Violin Sonata to the multitudinous sonorities of his Mass in F; from the sensitivity of his *Stabat Mater* to the virtuosity of his Violin Concerto.

Aside from *La serva padrona* and the *Stabat Mater* – which have been performed almost continually since their creation – Pergolesi performances were uncommon until relatively recently. Sparked by a renewal of scholarly interest in the composer in the 1970s, there were revivals of *Il Flaminio* in 1983, *Adriano in Siria* and *Livietta e Tracollo* in 1986, and *Lo frate 'nnamorato* in 1989.

La conversione e morte di San Guglielmo

The Conversion and Death of St William
Dramma sacro in three parts
Libretto by Ignazio Mancini
PREMIERE summer 1731, Monastery of Sant' Agnello Maggiore, Naples

The two chief characters in Pergolesi's first stage work are St William, the tenth Duke of Aquitaine, who ruled from 1127 to 1137, and St Bernard of Clairvaux, the Cistercian monk who was the motivating force behind the Second Crusade. Other characters include an Angel, the Devil, and a boastful personage, Captain Cuosemo, who provides comic relief with his buffo numbers in Neapolitan dialect. The first and third movements of the sinfonia to this work are almost identical with the parallel movements of Pergolesi's sinfonias for *Adriano in Siria* and *L'Olimpiade*. Besides the usual recitatives and arias, there are several duets as well as a closing quartet to Part I, 'Cieco che non vid'io', for St William, St Bernard, the Angel, and the Devil.

RECORDING Lucarini, Caldini, Gamberucci, Gatti, Herron; Province of Terni CO, Maestri, Bongiovanni, 1986
EDITION f.s., R. Nielsen (ed.), Ricordi, 1965

La Salustia

Salustia
Opera seria in three acts
Libretto adapted by ?S. Merelli, from Apostolo Zeno's *Alessandro Severo* (1716)
PREMIERE January 1732, Teatro San Bartolomeo, Naples

La Salustia is based on Roman history: specifically, the Censor Alexander Severius, who ruled from AD 222 to 235. Alexander's mother, Giulia Mammea, slanders his wife, Salustia, thus provoking her father to seek revenge. Characters include Marziano, a general of Caesar's troops, and two Roman patricians: Claudio, a friend of Marziano's, and Albina, the beloved of Claudio. The singer Nicolini (Nicolo Grimaldi) was scheduled to play the leading role, but his death on 1 January 1732 necessitated some last-minute changes in the opera to accommodate his replacement, Gioacchino Conti. Despite this effort, the opera met with little success.

EDITION v.s., F. Caffarelli (ed.), *Opera omnia di Giovanni Battista Pergolesi*, vol. 9, Gli amici della musica da camera, 1941

Lo frate 'nnamorato

(Neapolitan)
Il fratello innamorato (Italian)
The Enamoured Brother
Commedia musicale in three acts (2h 45m)
Libretto by Gennarantonio Federico
PREMIERE 27 September 1732, Teatro dei Fiorentini, Naples

Pergolesi's first comic opera was an immediate success and was often performed in Naples in the years following its premiere. The plot takes place in contemporary Naples, specifically the district of Capodimonte around 1730, and many of the characters sing in Neapolitan dialect. *Lo frate 'nnamorato* is a comedy of manners involving two sisters, Nina and Nena, who are both secretly in love with a youth named Ascanio. He in turn is loved by another woman, Lucrezia. Since all three of these young ladies are slated to marry other men, nobody is happy until Ascanio reveals by a birthmark that he is in reality a brother of Nina and Nena. Thus, unencumbered by the adoration of his two sisters, he is free to marry Lucrezia.

The music of this delightful opera contains folklike and buffo elements side by side with parodies of opera seria.

RECORDING Focile, Felle, Manca di Nissa, D'Intino, Corbelli, Di Cesare, O of La Scala, Milan, Muti, Ricordi, 1989
EDITION E. Gerelli (ed.), Zerboni, [1961]

Il prigionier superbo
The Proud Prisoner

Opera seria in three acts
Librettist unknown; libretto adapted from Francesco Silvani's *La fede tradita e vendicata* set by Gasparini (1704)
PREMIERE 28 August 1733, Teatro San Bartolomeo, Naples

The action of Pergolesi's second opera seria takes place in Norway at the time of the birth of that country's national identity. The plot revolves around six characters: Sostrate, usurper to the throne of Norway; Rosmene, his daughter, who is in love with Viridate; Metalce, King of the Goths; Ericlea, heiress to the throne of Norway; Viridate, Prince of Denmark, who loves Rosmene; and Micisda, Prince of Bohemia, who loves Ericlea. The plot is essentially the same as Silvani's and many of the lines are identical, but the setting as well as the characters' names are entirely different in the two libretti. Although *Il prigionier superbo* is best known for its association with *La serva padrona*, it is able to stand on its own; much of its music is dramatically expressive and deeply moving, as, for example, Sostrate's aria in Act II, 'Vado a morte'. The opera begins and ends with a short choral number and also includes a duet and a trio, both in Act III.

EDITION v.s., F. Caffarelli (ed.), *Opera Omnia di Giovanni Battista Pergolesi*, vol. 20, Gli amici della musica da camera, 1942

La serva padrona
The Maid Turned Mistress

Intermezzo in two parts (50m)
Libretto by Gennarantonio Federico
PREMIERES 28 August 1733, Teatro San Bartolomeo, Naples; UK: 27 March 1750, His Majesty's Theatre, Haymarket, London; US: 13 June 1790, Baltimore
CAST Uberto *b*, Serpina *s*, Vespone *silent*
INSTRUMENTATION str, cont

La serva padrona is one of the most universally popular works in the operatic repertoire. Also one of the most influential of stage works, it served as a model for Jean Jacques Rousseau in his polemic war and long served as a prototype of the opera-buffa

style. The sparkling and witty score is comprised of a brief instrumental introduction and two separate parts, each of which contains both spoken and sung passages and includes an aria for each principal as well as a duet.

SYNOPSIS
Part I Uberto, a bachelor, complains about the incompetence and wilfulness of his maidservant, Serpina, who rules the household with an iron hand and keeps him waiting for his chocolate. He instructs his servant, Vespone, to find him a wife, no matter how ugly, who will bow to his wishes. Overhearing this, Serpina asks her master to take her as his wife, but Uberto refuses.

Part II Serpina conspires with Vespone to trick her master into marrying her. She tells Uberto that she intends to marry a certain Captain Tempest. When her master asks to meet this soldier suitor, she produces Vespone in disguise. Then she informs him that the silent captain requires a dowry or else he will insist that Uberto marry Serpina in his place. Uberto, choosing what he considers to be the lesser of two evils, agrees to marry his servant. When Vespone pulls off his false moustache and reveals his true identity, Uberto realizes that he loves Serpina. Her future as mistress of the house is secured.

Among the outstanding arias in the first part are Uberto's frivolous 'Sempre in contrasti' and Serpina's peevish 'Stizzoso, mio stizzoso'. A highlight of the second intermezzo is Serpina's reflective aria, 'A Serpina penserete', in which she at first appears to have a softer side. However, later in the same aria, her true nature is revealed. The music of Uberto's aria, 'Son imbrogliato io già', is capricious, with alternating buffo and serious elements, thus reflecting his uncertain feelings towards Serpina.

RECORDING Scotto, Bruscantini, Virtuosi di Roma, Fasano, Ricordi, c. 1965
EDITIONS f.s./v.s., Karl Geiringer (ed.), Wiener Philharmonischer, 1925

Adriano in Siria
Hadrian in Syria

Opera seria in three acts (3h 30m)
Libretto by Pietro Metastasio (1732), rev. anon.
PREMIERE 25 October 1734, Teatro San Bartolomeo, Naples

Adriano in Siria was given to celebrate the birthday of the Queen of Spain, mother of the Infante Don Carlos, King of Sicily, and was conceived as a vehicle for the celebrated castrato Caffarelli (Gaetano Majorano), who played the part of Farnaspe. The text was extensively revised to accommodate Caffarelli.

Hadrian, the Roman emperor, is in love with Emirena, the recently captured daughter of the Parthian king, Osroa. Farnaspe, a Parthian warrior, is also in love with Emirena. To compound matters further, Hadrian is betrothed to Sabina, with whom the emperor's confidant, Aquilio, is secretly in love.

By the opera's end, all is sorted out in typically Metastasian fashion: Osroa is restored to his kingdom, Emirena is bestowed on Farnaspe, Aquilio is forgiven, and Sabina is promised to the emperor.

The opera's highlights occur at the end of each act. Act I ends with Farnaspe's *da capo* aria, 'Lieto così tal volta', a remarkable showcase for Caffarelli's talents replete with all kinds of ornamentation and a cadenza for oboe and voice. Act II closes with another *tour de force* for Farnaspe, the striking *da capo* aria 'Torbido in volto e nero', characterized by strong dynamic contrast and an ominous accompaniment suggestive of the sea. A short joyful choral number in praise of the magnanimous Hadrian ends the opera.

RECORDING Jankovic, Dessy, Di Cesare, Devia, Browne, Rossi, O del Maggio Musicale Fiorentino, Panni, Bongiovanni, 1985
EDITION Dale Monson (ed.), *Giovanni Battista Pergolesi: Opere Complete*, vol. 3, Pendragon Press/Ricordi, 1986

Livietta e Tracollo, ossia La contadina astuta

Livietta and Tracollo, or The Wise Peasant Girl
Intermezzo in two parts (30m)
Libretto by Tomasso Mariani
PREMIERES 25 October 1734, Teatro San Bartolomeo, Naples

This charming intermezzo has been given a variety of other titles besides *Livietta e Tracollo* and *La contadina astuta*, among them *La finta Polacca*, *Il ladro finto pazzo*, and *Il Tracollo*. One of the most popular intermezzi of the 18th century, it appeared throughout Europe in many variations. The plot involves a number of tricks and disguises. Livietta, dressed as a Frenchman, seeks revenge against Tracollo – a petty thief who poses as a pregnant woman – and his wily companion, Faccenda. Livietta and her friend Fulvia catch the rascals in the act of thievery. To placate Livietta, Tracollo promises to marry her. This she refuses to do, and pretends to be dying. In the second intermezzo, Tracollo disguises himself as a crazed astrologer. Finally the two are reconciled after Tracollo promises to reform. The sprightly music is a paragon of Pergolesi's opera-buffa style.

A highlight of the first intermezzo is Tracollo's *da capo* aria, 'Ecco il povero Tracollo', written in a capricious style featuring repeated notes, broken chords, and a two-octave range. Each intermezzo ends with a joyful duet.

RECORDINGS 1. Baiano, Pagliuca, Villani, Marcelli, O del Maggio Musicale Fiorentino, Panni, Bongiovanni, 1985; 2. Sciutti, Cortis, O della Scuola di Arzignano, Gallini, Barclay Fonit, 1950s
EDITION Gordana Lazarevich (ed.), *Giovanni Battista Pergolesi: Opere Complete*, vol. 6, Pendragon Press/Ricordi, 1991

L'Olimpiade

The Olympiad
Opera seria in three acts (3h 30m)
Libretto by Pietro Metastasio (1733), rev. anon.
PREMIERES Carnival, 1735, Teatro Tordinona, Rome; UK: 20 April 1742, His Majesty's Theatre, London

Pergolesi's last opera seria was based on one of Metastasio's most popular libretti, set by many other composers, including Leo, Caldara, Vivaldi and Cimarosa. The plot takes place in ancient Greece, and revolves about Clistene, the King of Sicyon, and his daughter Aristea, who has been promised in marriage to the winner of the Olympic Games. Licida, who loves Aristea, wants the prize but has no hope of winning it. Therefore, he asks Megacle to compete in his place. Thus Megacle, who also loves Aristea, must choose between love and friendship; he decides for the latter. When Argene, a Cretan who loves Licida, tells the king about the deception, Clistene banishes Licida from the kingdom. Licida, in turn, attempts to assassinate the king and is condemned to death. But Argene produces a necklace that proves that Licida is Clistene's son. Finally all is resolved: Megacle marries Aristea and Licida marries Argene.

Four arias from *Adriano in Siria* were revised and given new texts for *L'Olimpiade*; another aria from *Adriano*, Caffarelli's 'Torbido in volto e nero', was retained with the original text. The sinfonias of the two operas (as well as that of *La conversione e morte di San Guglielmo*) are also essentially the same. Musical highlights include Megacle's and Aristea's duet closing Act I, 'Ne giorni tuoi felici', and Megacle's plaintive aria in Act II, 'Se cerca, se dice', one of Pergolesi's most famous numbers, noted for its effective chromaticism.

EDITIONS facsimile of copy in Conservatoire Royale de Musique, Brussels, Garland, 1979; v.s., F. Caffarelli (ed.), *Opera Omnia di Giovanni Battista Pergolesi*, vol. 24, Gli amici della musica da camera, 1942

Il Flaminio

Commedia musicale in three acts (4h)
Libretto by Gennarantonio Federico
PREMIERES autumn 1735, Teatro Nuovo, Naples; US: 4 June 1983, Spoleto Festival

Pergolesi's last theatrical work is the only one to exist in autograph; a holograph of Act III is held in the library of the Naples Conservatory. As with *Lo frate 'nnammorato*, the action takes place in 18th-century Naples. The plot centres on a young widow named Giustina who is engaged to marry an eccentric Neapolitan named Polidoro. Giustina lives just outside Naples with her maidservant Checca. Polidoro, along with his sister Agata, moves into Signora Giustina's villa in order to arrange a marriage between Agata and Ferdinando. Accompanying Polidoro is his servant, Bastiano, as well as his secretary, who goes by the name of Giulio. Giustina soon realizes that the so-called Giulio is in reality her ex-lover Flaminio. But Giulio/Flaminio, whom she previously had rejected, pretends not to recognize her. To further complicate matters, Agata is also in love with Flaminio, who she knows as Giulio. By the end of the comedy, everything falls into place, with pairings between Flaminio and Giustina, Agata and Ferdinando, and Bastiano and Checca.

The work opens with a Neapolitan canzona in the style of a siciliana, 'Mentre l'erbetta pasce l'agnella', accompanied by solo guitar. Flaminio's aria in Act I, 'Scuote e fa guerra', is full of octave leaps and virtuosic melismas. There are also three duets, a trio and an ensemble finale.

EDITION   v.s., F. Caffarelli (ed.), *Opera Omnia di Giovanni Battista Pergolesi*, vol. 22, Gli amici della musica da camera, 1941

BIBLIOGRAPHY   Francesco Degrada (ed.), *Studi Pergolesiana*, vols 1 and 2, La Nuova Italia Editrice, 1986, 1988; Marvin E. Paymer and Hermine W. Williams, *Giovanni Battista Pergolesi: A Guide to Research*, Garland, 1989

M.E.P.

JACOPO PERI

b 20 August 1561, ?Rome; *d* on or before 12 August 1633, Florence

Peri is often known as the 'inventor' of opera. He studied in Florence with Cristofano Malvezzi and began his career in various musical positions in churches in the city. In the 1580s he was enrolled among the musicians at the Medici court as a tenor and keyboard-player. He made his début as a composer for court entertainments with music for the first intermedio (entr'acte) of Giovanni Fedini's *Le due Persilie* (16 February 1583). In 1589 Peri participated in the magnificent festivities for the wedding of Grand Duke Ferdinando I de' Medici and Christine of Lorraine, most prominently in the spectacular intermedi that accompanied the performance of Girolamo Bargagli's comedy *La pellegrina* (Peri composed and performed an echo madrigal for the fifth intermedio). The 1589 wedding, and indeed the reign of Grand Duke Ferdinando I (*reg.* 1587–1609), marked a glorious 'Indian summer' in Florence's chequered history. It also initiated a decade of exciting experiment in dramatic entertainments, in part because of the presence of Emilio de' Cavalieri, a Roman now in charge of the court music.

In the 1590s, Peri became associated with the leading patron of music in Florence, Jacopo Corsi. Corsi and the artists under his protection took their lead from the so-called Florentine *camerata* headed by Giovanni de' Bardi and active in the 1580s. Both groups speculated on the modern arts and their aesthetic position – some felt inadequacy – compared with Classical Greece and Rome. Corsi, perhaps in competition with Cavalieri, encouraged Peri and the poet Ottavio Rinuccini to experiment on a new theatrical genre that would merge drama with music in the manner that many assumed was typical of Classical tragedy. Their first colloboration, *Dafne*, was begun in 1594; it was staged semi-privately in

early 1598, 1599 and 1600, and before the court (and the Duke of Parma) on 26 December 1604.

Rinuccini's and Peri's next collaboration, *Euridice*, was performed during the festivities celebrating the marriage of Maria de' Medici and Henri IV of France in October 1600. It is the first opera to have survived complete (the score was published in early 1601). The 1600 wedding was a decisive political event for Florence, and clearly the idea was to match the occasion with novel entertainments. As well as Peri's new opera (again sponsored by Corsi) there was a musico-dramatic spectacle by the poet Gabriello Chiabrera, *Il rapimento di Cefalo*, with music by Giulio Caccini and others. The performance of *Euridice* was marred by Caccini's insisting that his singers should sing his and not Peri's music, and the work was not a success. Indeed, the Medici seem to have been unenthusiastic about opera, perhaps because it was less suited to providing the blatant propaganda they required of court entertainments. By the time Peri next contributed to Medici wedding festivities, for the marriage of Prince Cosimo de' Medici and Maria Magdalena of Austria in 1608, the court had reverted to the tried-and-tested formula of a comedy with spectacular intermedi that had proved so successful in 1589. Opera took roots elsewhere, notably in Mantua in the hands of Claudio Monteverdi.

During the reign of Grand Duke Cosimo II (*reg.* 1609–1621) Peri continued to write music for court tournaments, ballets, intermedi and other entertainments, particularly as Caccini's star waned. He generally collaborated with other Florentine musicians, especially Marco da Gagliano. Most of this music is lost, apart from a few items scattered in Florentine prints and manuscripts. Peri's chamber songs, published as *Le varie musiche* in 1609 (reprinted in 1619), also reflect music-making in a courtly environment, while his reputation was emphasized first by a performance of *Euridice* in Bologna on 27 April 1616 and then by commissions for theatrical performances in Mantua in 1620.

In the 1620s Peri collaborated with Giovanni Battista da Gagliano (Marco's brother) on several sacre rappresentazioni (sacred dramas) performed in the leading confraternity in the city, the Compagnia dell'Arcangelo Raffaello. They matched the new religious climate in Counter-Reformation Florence. However, although Peri continued to provide entertainment and other music for the court, he increasingly retired from official duties, whether because of age and other business interests, or just because of the distaste of a nobleman (as he claimed he was) for practical activity. His last known involvement in court entertainments was for the wedding of Margherita de' Medici and Duke Odoardo Farnese of Parma in 1628. Peri collaborated with the poet Andrea Salvadori (1591–1635) on a new opera, *Iole ed Ercole*, which was eventually abandoned through the machinations of Francesca Caccini. He then contributed to Marco da Gagliano's opera, *La Flora*, which was performed at the wedding and later published. Peri provided the recitatives for the part of Clori in a style that was becoming rather old-fashioned in the face of newer developments in opera.

Dafne

Favola in musica
Libretto by Ottavio Rinuccini, after Ovid
PREMIERE Carnival 1598, ?Palazzo Corsi, Florence

Dafne was the first collaboration between Jacopo Peri and Ottavio Rinuccini and ostensibly the first opera. The plot elaborates an episode from the third of the 1589 intermedi and deals with the myth of Apollo and his unrequited passion for the nymph Daphne. Only fragments of the work now survive (some by Jacopo Corsi), and Rinuccini's libretto is better known from its setting by Marco da Gagliano of 1608. However, these fragments reveal the first experiments in the new recitative and aria styles that were to come to fruition in *Euridice*.

MANUSCRIPTS fragments in Biblioteca Nazionale Centrale, Florence, and Conservatoire Royal de Musique, Brussels

First edition of Ottavio Rinuccini's libretto for Dafne, *published in 1600*

Euridice

Favola in musica in a prologue and one act
Libretto by Ottavio Rinuccini, after Ovid
PREMIERE 6 October 1600, Palazzo Pitti, Florence
CAST La Tragedia *s*, Orfeo *t*, Euridice *s*, Plutone *b*,
Proserpina *s*, Venere *s*, Aminta *t*, Arcetro *ct*; *satb* choruses of nymphs and shepherds, infernal deities

Euridice, like *Dafne*, is based on Classical myth and again concerns a demi-god with famed musical powers. The representation of Orpheus' musical magic, an important self-justification for early opera, was to challenge many later composers. Peri himself sang the title role, and another virtuoso tenor, Francesco Rasi, the role of Aminta (Rasi later sang the title role in Monteverdi's *Orfeo*). At the first performance, the continuo group included a harpsichord (played by Jacopo Corsi), a chitarrone, a lirone and a 'liuto grosso'.

There are no scene divisions in the libretto or the score, although the work is in three sections reckoning by setting (earth–Hades–earth), and in five according to the strophic choruses (on Classical precedent). Orpheus' bride, Eurydice, dies of a snakebite. He descends to Hades, guided by Venus, to plead with Pluto, king of the underworld, for her return. Now Rinuccini deviates from the myth, as was perhaps inevitable in a wedding entertainment. Pluto, charmed by Orpheus' singing, releases Eurydice, and the couple return to earth and universal celebration.

Rinuccini and Peri were anxious to connect *Euridice* with Classical tragedy ('Tragedy' sings the prologue). Thus they linked the opera to humanist inquiry in what was perhaps the last flowering of the Florentine Renaissance. But the humanist resonances were intended largely for the sake of academic respectability as a way of justifying the apparently unrealistic use of music on stage, and Peri eventually admitted (in the preface to his score) that the parallels with Greek and Roman practice were at best tenuous. In fact, the opera is entirely typical of its time: it takes over many characteristics of the intermedi, including the mythological subject and particular scenic effects (especially the inferno scene), and belongs generically to the modern pastoral drama recently established by Torquato Tasso's *Aminta* and Battista Guarini's *Il pastor fido*.

Euridice contains strophic arias, choruses and instrumental items. But its most distinctive feature, emphasized as such in Peri's preface, is the recitative, a declamatory musical style midway between speech and song. Here Peri developed a free style of writing for the new combination of solo voice and basso continuo that closely followed the form and content of Rinuccini's fine text, matching its emotional and dramatic peaks by intense vocal lines and often exploiting chromaticism and dissonance in a manner reminiscent of contemporary polyphonic madrigals. The reaction of observers was mixed – some felt that the result was too much 'like the chanting of the Passion' – and clearly the opera was on too intimate a scale to impress a court accustomed to spectacular scenic extravaganzas. However, for the first time a musical style for solo voice flexible enough to respond to dramatic effect appeared on stage. The lessons offered by Peri were taken to heart by many early opera composers, not least Monteverdi.

RECORDING Santini, Farolfi, Coro Polifonico di Milano, I Solisti di Milano, Ephrikian, Telefunken, 1966: the added instrumental parts produce something of a travesty

EDITIONS *Le musiche sopra l'Euridice*, Florence, 1601; facsimile, Bologna 1969; H. M. Brown (ed.), *Recent Researches in the Music of the Baroque Era*, vols. 26–7, Madison, 1983

Other stage works: 'Dunque fra torbid'onde' (part of Intermedio 5 for G. Bargagli's *La pellegrina*, 1589; in *Intermedio et concerti . . .*, 1591); 'Poichè la notte con l'oscure piume' (final chorus Act III, of Buonarroti's *Il giudizio di Paride*), 1608, music with new text in Peri's *Le varie musiche*, 1609; *Mascherata di ninfe di Senna* (coll. with M. da Gagliano, F. Caccini *et al.*), 1611; one song in P. Benedetti, *Musiche*, 1611; ?untitled tournament (coll. with M. da Gagliano, L. Allegri), 1613; *La Flora* (coll. with M. da Gagliano), 1628; *Iole ed Ercole* (one lament survives in manuscript), (1628); *c.* 18 lost works

BIBLIOGRAPHY Howard Mayer Brown, 'How Opera Began: An Introduction to Jacopo Peri's *Euridice* (1600)', in E. Cochrane (ed.), *The Late Italian Renaissance, 1525–1630*, Macmillan, 1970, pp. 401–43; Tim Carter, 'Jacopo Peri', *ML*, vol. 61 (1980), pp. 121–35; Tim Carter, 'Jacopo Peri's *Euridice* (1600): A Contextual Study', *MR*, vol. 43 (1982), pp. 83–103; B. R. Hanning, *Of Poetry and Music's Power: Humanism and the Creation of Opera*, UMI Research Press, 1981

T.C.

GIACOMO ANTONIO PERTI
b 6 June 1661, Bologna; *d* 10 April 1756, Bologna

Perti, first taught by his uncle, Lorenzo Perti, maestro di cappella at the Cathedral of San Pietro in Bologna, studied in Parma in the early 1680s; his first complete opera, *Marzio Coriolano*, was written in 1683. He was closely associated with the Church throughout his career, holding a succession of maestro di cappella posts in Bologna, and his sacred music forms a major part of his output. Perti was also an influential teacher, his pupils including Torelli and G. B. Martini.

Perti wrote his operas mainly for theatres in Bologna, but he was also patronized by Ferdinando III de' Medici, who commissioned several operas for the Tuscan court. Most fall into the earlier part of his composing career: although Perti continued to hold his post at the cathedral of S. Pietro until his death at the age of 94, his last known opera was written in 1709. The scores of the seven operas that survive are rich in melodic inventiveness and, while adhering largely to conventional *da capo* form, show Perti's ability to create apt dramatic effects. A characteristic feature – found in many Bolognese operas of the time – is the inclusion of virtuoso obbligato parts for various solo instruments in aria accompaniments.

Surviving operas: *Oreste in Argo*, 1685; *La Flavia*, 1686; *La Rosaura*, 1689 (EDITION facsimile, Garland, 1982); *L'inganno scoperto per vendetta*, 1691; *Furio Camillo*, 1692; *Nerone fatto Cesare*, 1693; *Rosinde ed Emireno*, (n.d.); 20 lost operas
BIBLIOGRAPHY M. Fabbri, 'Giacomo Antonio Perti', *Musicisti lombardi e emiliani*, Chigiana, vol. 15 (1958)

D.S.B.

GIOVANNI BATTISTA PESCETTI
b c. 1704, Venice; *d* 20 March 1766, Venice

A pupil of Antonio Lotti, and a fellow student of Galuppi, Pescetti was a prolific composer of operas from 1725. In 1736 he resided in London, where he worked at Covent Garden and the King's Theatre, Haymarket, as well as succeeding Porpora in directing the Opera of the Nobility, a rival company to that of Handel. Nine of his Italian operas were intended for the London stage. He probably left England due to the political instability of the 1745 rebellion. On his return to Venice he devoted himself once more to composing operas, receiving commissions from throughout northern Italy. Burney regarded him – in comparison with Handel – as a composer of simple, uninventive music, which relied on the greatest of singers to achieve any effect. But he had a certain melodic gift, as well as an ability to write good counterpoint.

Extant operas: *Nerone detronato* (only arias survive), 1725; *Artaserse*, 1751: 25 lost operas

G.D.

WILHELM PETERSON-BERGER
Wilhelm Olof Peterson-Berger: *b* 27 February 1867, Ullånger, Ångermanland, Sweden; *d* 3 December 1942, Ostersund, Sweden

Peterson-Berger grew up in the north of Sweden and studied the piano and composition in Stockholm and Dresden, where he taught at the Musikschule (1892–4). He was active as a critic for Stockholm's *Dagens Nyheter* (1896–1930), his musical outlook being highly conservative. His music belongs to the national Romantic tradition and includes five symphonies, a violin concerto and about 100 songs and piano pieces. His operas enjoyed some popularity in their day and were influenced by Wagner.

Arnljot
Opera in three acts
ibretto by the composer, based on Snorre Sturlasson's *The Saga of St Olav* and Bjornstjerne Bjornson's *Arnljot Gelline*
Composed 1907–9
PREMIERE 13 April 1910, Royal Swedish Opera, Stockholm

The opera tells of the vicissitudes of Arnljot, a member of a declining clan in Jamtland. He eventually becomes its chief and declares Jamtland's independence. Long thought of as the Swedish national opera, *Arnljot* was performed some 80 times at the Royal Opera, Stockholm, and successfully revived in 1960. It is the only Peterson-Berger opera to have retained a foothold on the repertoire.

RECORDING Prytz, Ericsson, Svedenbrant, S. Björling, Björker, Ch and O of Royal Opera, Stockholm, Ehrling, Caprice, 1960
EDITION v.s., A. Lundquist, 1911

Other operas: *Ran*, 1903; *Lyckan (Happiness)*, 1903; *Domedagsprofeterna (Prophets of Doomsday)*, 1919; *Adils och Elisiv*, 1927

BIBLIOGRAPHY Birger Carlberg, *Peterson-Berger*, Bonniers Fürlag, 1950

R.La.

GOFFREDO PETRASSI

b 16 July 1904, Zagarolo, nr Palestrina, Italy

Although Petrassi was subsequently to establish himself as the most authoritative Italian instrumental composer of his generation, for a single decade he devoted himself predominantly to musical theatre. This development came in the wake of his choral work *Coro di morti* (1940–41), in which he achieved a distinctive amalgam of hard-edged Stravinskian textures and a brooding chromaticism.

There was already a hint of the operatic in his *Lamento d'Arianna* (1936) for voice and piano, recast for chamber ensemble in 1938: an experience developed further in his first ballet, *La follia d'Orlando* (1942–3) which incorporated narrative recitatives for baritone after Ariosto. (A further ballet, *Ritratto di Don Chisciotte*, followed in 1945.)

Il cordovano

The Cordovan Mat
Opera in one act (50m)
Libretto: Eugenio Montale's translation of Cervantes's *Entremes del Viejo Geloso* (1615)
Composed 1944–8, rev. 1958
PREMIERE 12 May 1949, La Scala, Milan

A sardonic rendering of the old joke: a crotchety, jealous old man, Cannizares, married to a charming young wife, Donna Lorenza, to whose laments her neighbour, Donna Hortigosa, promises a speedy cure. Hortigosa smuggles a pretty boy into the house concealed in a Cordovan leather mat which she claims to wish to sell to Cannizares. With the boy in her bedroom, Donna Lorenza gives all too lyrical an account of his charms from behind closed doors. Cannizares, unsure whether this is teasing or truth, tries to get in but has a bowl of water thrown in his face while the boy escapes. Much in the manner of a buffo finale, Donna Lorenza raises a hubbub at her husband's unworthy suspicions; neighbours rush in, and Cannizares is compelled to reassure them that nothing is wrong. Petrassi's crisp setting faithfully paces Cervantes's intermezzo, but takes musical wing above all at the erotic climax, and the *dénouement* that follows.

RECORDING Paoletti, Rigacci, Condò, Barbacini, Luccardi, Orecchia, Rome Ch and SO of Italian Radio, Panni, Dischi Ricordi, 1987
EDITIONS f.s./v.s., Suvini Zerboni, [n.d.]

Morte dell'aria

Death in the Air
Tragedy in one act (30m)
Libretto by Toti Scialoja

Composed 1949–50
PREMIERE 24 October 1950, Teatro Eliseo, Rome

Scialoja developed the libretto from an early documentary film showing a man with a flying apparatus throwing himself off the Eiffel Tower. In the opera, the Inventor has summoned journalists, a Scientific Observer and the Chief of Police to witness his attempt at flight. It is plain to all, and becomes increasingly so to the Inventor, that his attempt is doomed to failure. Twice he draws back, but the third time, knowing that he faces certain destruction, he keeps dogged faith with his project and jumps to his death. In the wake of this all-male endgame, a hidden female chorus enters to affirm the value of human faith within this nihilistic context. This provides the musical climax to a score that makes telling use of dark instrumental colours through an unusually constituted chamber orchestra.

EDITION v.s. and hire material, Suvini Zerboni, 1951

BIBLIOGRAPHY John S. Weissman, *Goffredo Petrassi*, Suvini Zerboni, 1957; rev. edn, 1980

D.O.-S.

ERRICO PETRELLA

b 10 December 1813, Palermo; *d* 7 April 1877, Genoa, Italy

Petrella studied at the Naples Conservatory. While still only 15 he was invited to write an opera for the local Teatro della Fenice. Although he had apparently never even seen an opera performed, he accepted, wrote and produced *Il diavolo di color rosa* in 1829 with considerable success, and found himself expelled from the conservatory as a result. He continued his studies privately and produced four more comedies during the next ten years, but in 1839 his career was interrupted (characteristically) by a quarrel over fees and for 12 years he composed very little.

In 1851 he re-entered the opera world with *Le precauzioni* which was widely admired as a late example of the Neapolitan buffo tradition. His first serious opera, *Marco Visconti*, carried his name all over Italy and was followed by his best-known work, *Jone*, at La Scala in 1858. During this period he was taken up by the Milanese publisher Lucca (Ricordi's chief rival) who hoped to use him as a counterblast to Verdi. But Petrella never looked like matching up to his great competitor, who regarded him with scant respect and refused to join the chorus in praise of *Le precauzioni*: 'Let's have the honest truth . . .' he wrote, 'Petrella doesn't know music.' In fact, Petrella was a vigorous, instinctive composer, but unequal and often commonplace – particularly in serious opera where melodic exuberance and what Verdi called 'a few brilliant violin figures' were no substitute for the deeper involvement his subjects demanded. His later works show more refinement, particularly *I promessi sposi* to a text by Antonio

Ghislanzoni, the librettist of *Aida*, from the novel by Manzoni (who was generally believed to have been present at the much publicized first performance).

Operas: *Il diavolo color di rosa*, 1829; *Il giorno delle nozze, ovvero Pulcinella marito e non marito*, 1829; *Lo scroccone*, 1834; *La Cimodocea*, (1835); *I pirati spagnuoli*, 1838, rev. 1856; *Le miniere di Freinbergh*, 1839, rev. 1843; *Galeotto Manfredi* (doubtful), 1843; [*Le precauzioni, ossia*] *Il carnevale di Venezia*, 1851, rev. 1858; *Elena di Tolosa*, 1852; *Marco Visconti*, 1854; [*Elnava, o*] *L'assedio di Leida*, 1856; *Jone, o L'ultimo giorno di Pompei*, 1858 (RECORDING Bongiovanni, 1981); *Il duca di Scilla*, 1859; *Morosina, ovvero L'ultimo de' Falieri*, 1860; *Il folletto di Gresy*, 1860; *Virginia*, 1861; *La contessa d'Amalfi*, 1864; *Celinda*, 1865; *Caterina Howard*, 1866; *Giovanna* [*II*] *di Napoli*, 1869; *I promessi sposi*, 1869 (RECORDING excerpts: Tiberi, 1973); *Manfredo*, 1872; *Bianca Orsini*, 1874; *Diana, o La fata di Pozzuoli*, (1876); *Salammbò* (opera-ballo; inc.); *Solima*, (n.d.)
BIBLIOGRAPHY G. Cosenza, *Vita e opere di Errico Petrella*, Rome, 1909; Michael Rose, 'Errico Petrella', in *Grove*, Macmillan, 1980

M.R.

EMIL PETROVICS

b 9 February 1930, Nagybecskerek [now Zrenjanin]

The Hungarian composer Emil Petrovics was brought up in Belgrade, but moved to Budapest in 1941, where he was a pupil of Ferenc Szabó and Ferenc Farkas at the Academy of Music. He was director of the Petőfi Theatre (1960–64), professor at the Academy of Dramatic and Film Arts (from 1964) and director of the Budapest Opera House (1986–90). He has also been a member of the Hungarian parliament.

Petrovics made his name with two one-act operas, *C'est la guerre* (1961) and the comic 'concert opera' *Lysistrate* (1962). But since his third opera, *Crime and Punishment* (1969), his only theatre score has been a ballet about *Salome* (1978).

C'est la guerre
That's War
Opera in one act (1h)
Libretto by Miklós Hubay
Composed 1960–61
PREMIERES 1961, Hungarian Radio (broadcast); 1962, Operaház, Budapest; UK: 19 February 1967, BBC Radio 3 (broadcast)

At the end of the Second World War, a Budapest couple hide a deserter in their flat, spied on by an ex-army officer with binoculars and by the janitor's wife, a police informer. While the husband is at work, there is a brief entanglement between the wife and the deserter. Later the deserter and the husband are arrested and the wife throws herself from the balcony.

The taut treatment reveals an instinctive theatre composer who knows Berg's *Wozzeck*, as well as Puccini and, of course, Bartók. Cheap gramophone music played by the ex-army officer provides the action with a sinisterly inconsequential backcloth. Yet Petrovics's own style is well integrated, and he paces the drama with natural flair.

RECORDING Dunst, Ilosfalvy, Réti, Radnai, Hungarian State Opera Ch and O, Blum, Hungaroton, 1964
EDITION Artisjus (on hire)

Crime and Punishment
Bün és bünhödés
Opera in three acts
Libretto by Gyula Maár, after the novel by Dostoevsky (1866)
Composed 1969
PREMIERE 26 October 1969, Operaház, Budapest

Maár's adaptation concentrates, even more than Dostoevsky's, on the hero Raskolnikov and his psychological development. Other characters retreat into the background as stereotypes, and the score is dominated by monologue. The novel's outline remains, however, from the decision to murder the old woman, through Raskolnikov's unwitting self-betrayal in the police station, to his final public confession. Petrovics's style is basically atonal (free 12-note), with a more banal music for ironic contrast; but much of Raskolnikov's part is sprechgesang, and there is also a pre-recorded tape with which he carries on an internal dialogue.

RECORDING Polga, unnamed O, Koniz, Hungaroton, 1980
EDITION Artisjus (on hire)

Other operatic work: *Lysistrata*, 1962 (concert), 1971, (RECORDING Hungaroton, 1970s)
BIBLIOGRAPHY Imre Fabian, 'Two Opera Composers', *Tempo*, no. 88 (spring 1969), pp. 10–15; Imre Fabian, 'Petrovics's *Crime and Punishment*', *Tempo*, no. 91 (winter 1969–70), pp. 25–7

S.W.

HANS PFITZNER
Hans Erich Pfitzner; *b* 5 May 1869, Moscow; *d* 22 May 1949, Salzburg

Pfitzner was born in Moscow because his father, a Saxon choirmaster, happened to be working there as a violinist. The family soon returned to Germany. Once the young Pfitzner had completed his musical education, he became a teacher and then kapellmeister at the Theater des Westens in Berlin; later he was appointed director of the Strasburg Conservatory and conductor of the symphony orchestra. From 1910 he was director of the opera there, joined in 1914 by Otto Klemperer as his deputy. His first two operas (exactly contemporary with Richard Strauss's *Guntram* and *Feuersnot*) had impressed Humperdinck and Mahler favourably, and for a few years they were performed on many German stages. As with all his stage works, their subjects were consciously Teutonic and Christian.

Pfitzner's interest turned to symphonic music. He had begun as a gentle post-Wagnerian modernist (with a lifelong devotion to the pessimistic philosopher Schopenhauer), but he felt growing dismay at the radicalism of Schoenberg and Busoni, and published angry polemics against their malign influence. His *Palestrina* is plainly a declaration of loyalty to conservative tradition – about which his writings found nothing very articulate to say, beyond reiterating his faith in lyrical spontaneity. Two comparably ambitious imposing works followed later, the huge cantata *Von deutscher Seele* (1921) and the 'choral fantasy' *Das dunkle Reich* (1929).

Notoriously, the first of these came to be venerated within the Nazi movement – which had certainly not inspired it; but until 1936 Pfitzner's career certainly throve with the Nazis. There are conflicting accounts of what his real political sentiments were (as also of his character: sour and waspish; contrariwise, humane and witty). In any case, the end of the Second World War found him bombed out of his Munich house and soon to face a denazification court, his public credit severely devalued. His miserable last years were spent in a Munich old people's home. Shortly before he died, the Vienna Philharmonic Society found him a house in Salzburg, and his 80th birthday was decently celebrated in the Austro-German musical world.

The international musical world has been gingerly about reviving Pfitzner. Among German works from between the wars, Hindemith's are neglected, and only Richard Strauss's have been steadily honoured: one effect of the radical revelations from the Schoenberg–Berg–Webern axis has been the dismissal of lesser conservative composers from hearing. Since Pfitzner counts (by stern recent standards) as unrigorous and sentimentally eclectic, he must survive – or not – by his individual lyrical stamp, and his knack for broad, intuitive construction. As the winds of fashion veer this way and that, his music will doubtless enjoy intensive short-term rediscoveries.

Der arme Heinrich

Poor Heinrich
Musikdrama in two (originally three) acts (2h 15m)
Libretto by James Grun, after the medieval legend
Composed 1891–3
PREMIERE 2 April 1895, Mainz (two-act version)

The opera is set around the year 1100. The cast is small: besides the knight Heinrich, there are only his wife, his 14-year-old daughter – hopelessly ill, but of exemplary piety – her monk–physician from Salerno, and Dietrich, one of Heinrich's menservants, with a chorus of monks whose solemn *Dies irae* underpins much of the long redemption scene at the end. As in later Pfitzner stage pieces, the elevated theme is salvation; almost any modern audience, however, would find the terms in which *Der arme Heinrich* presents it fairly queasy. Though like his next opera, the score has been described as Wagnerian, closer attention to either of them will reveal great differences in musical procedure. The prelude to *Der arme Heinrich* begins on four muted violas – an early and striking example of Pfitzner's attachment to the inner voice, troubled but quietly exalted.

EDITIONS v.ss., in three acts, text by the composer, Brockhaus, 1900; two-act version, B. Firnberg, 1896; f.s., two-act version, Brockhaus, 1901

Die Rose vom Liebesgarten

The Rose from the Garden of Love
Romantische oper in two acts, with vorspiel and nachspiel (2h)
Libretto by James Grun
Composed 1897–1900
PREMIERE 9 November 1901, Elberfeld

The inspiration for this fantasy opera, again medieval and elaborately symbolic, came from a painting by Hans Thoma, a friend of the composer. The names of the first conductors indicate the early prestige that Pfitzner enjoyed: Felix Mottl for the premiere (as for *Das Christ-Elflein*) and Fritz Reiner for the second production. *Die Rose* has none the less faded from view.

RECORDING Eipperle, Aldenhoff, Proebstl, Ch and O (?Munich Radio), Heger, Rococo, 1950s
EDITION v.s., J. Feuchtinger, 1901

Das Christ-Elflein

The Little Elf of Christ
Spieloper in two acts, Op. 20/Op. 54 (1h 30m)
Libretto by Ilse von Stach and the composer
Composed 1906, rev. 1917
PREMIERES 11 December 1906, Munich; rev. version: 11 December 1917, Dresden

Before it was revised as a spieloper, *Das Christ-Elflein* was a domestic-sized liederspiel – a series of sung numbers interspersed in a quaint Christmas pantomime. Amid the spoken dialogue, that first version boasted not only a singing Christchild, a Knight Rupert (the seasonal reckoner-up of children's demerits) and the eponymous elfin soprano who learns about the Christian miracle, but a singing St Peter. In the 1917 revision St Peter became mute, and the original three acts were reduced to two, some minor characters excised and new numbers added. The piece remains mawkish.

EDITION first version: v.s., Ries und Erler, 1906; second version: f.s./v.s., Fürstner/Boosey and Hawkes, 1918

Palestrina

Musikalische legende in three acts (3h 30m)
Libretto by the composer, after historical sources
Composed 1912–15
PREMIERES 12 June 1917, Prinzregententheater, Munich; UK: 10 June 1981, Collegiate Theatre, London; US: 14 May 1982, Berkeley (concert)
CAST Pope Pius IV *b*, 2 Cardinal Papal Legates: Giovanni Morone *bar*, Bernardo Novagerio *t*, Cardinal Christoph Madruscht, Prince Bishop of Trent *b*, Carlo Borromeo, Cardinal from Rome *bar*, Cardinal of Lothringen [Lorraine] *b*, Abdisu, Patriarch of Assyria *t*, Anton Brus von Muglitz, Archbishop of Prague *b*, Count Luna, Orator to the King of Spain *bar*, Bishop of Budoja *t*, Theophilus, Bishop of Imola *t*, Avosmediano, Bishop of Cadiz *b-bar*, Giovanni Perluigi Palestrina *t*, Ighino *s*, Silla *ms*, Bishop Ercole Severolus, Master-of-Ceremonies at the Council of Trent *b-bar*, Singers of the Chapel of Santa Maria Maggiore 2 *t*, 3 *b*; 9 great dead

A scene from Palestrina *(Munich, 1917)*

composers 3 *t*, 3 *bar*, 3 *b*; angelic voices 3 *s*, Lucrezia's spirit *s*; 2 Papal nuncios; Lainez and Salmeron, Jesuits; Massarelli, Bishop of Thelesia, Secretary of the Council; Giuseppe, Palestrina's aged servant, *silent*; *satb* chorus of singers from the Papal Chapel, archbishops, bishops, abbots, heads of religious orders, envoys, ambassadors (procurators) of princes spiritual and temporal, theologians, scholars from all Christendom, servants, soldiers, crowd
ORCHESTRATION   4 fl/2 picc, alto fl, 3 ob/ca, 3 cl/2 E♭ cl, 2 b cl in B♭ and A, 3 bsn, dbsn, 6 hn, 4 tpt, 4 trbn, tuba, timp, perc (sd, cym, t-t, triangle, bells, antique cym), organ, cel, 2 hp, 2 mand, str (including viola d'amore)

Many a work has been designed as a *magnum opus* without attaining any such status, but in its crochety way *Palestrina* succeeds. Though it deploys awkwardly many performers for a very long time, it justifies its overweening proportions as creditably as it represents Pfitzner's best strengths. The proportions are wilfully odd, with two quite disparate 90-minute acts – visibly linked only by the figure of Cardinal Borromeo – followed by a third which takes a mere half-hour. Preparing his libretto, Pfitzner had immersed himself in the history of the Council of Trent for two years. The 'historical' gist of his operatic conclusions is this: in 1563 the aged Palestrina composed his *Missa Papae Marcelli*, thereby reaffirming the eternal spirit of pure music, and triumphantly persuading the Roman Church not to relinquish it. It is irrelevant that every clause of that proposition is now thought dubious (Palestrina was under 40 in 1563). There is no romantic interest, nor any real note of tragedy – only Palestrina's private despair, and his wry acquiescence to fame. A seasoned opera company is presupposed: the central

Council act depends on a ripe team of singing actors who know how to play to one another. The premiere was conducted by Bruno Walter.

SYNOPSIS
Act I Rome, November 1563. Palestrina's pupil Silla has written a new song in the avant-garde Florentine style. His master's son Ighino joins him and they worry over the ageing composer's gloomy lethargy since the death of his wife Lucrezia. He enters with an old friend, Cardinal Borromeo, who warns him that the Council of Trent – nearing its conclusion after 18 years – may resolve to ban polyphonic church music in favour of plainchant, recoiling from fashionably over-ornamented, verbally opaque settings. Borromeo wants Palestrina to compose a Mass that will persuade Pius IV that polyphony can be properly devout. The weary composer declines: nothing has any meaning for him now. Borromeo departs angrily; but while Palestrina drowses, his great musical ancestors – Josquin, Isaac *et al.* – appear to urge him on. Angels in glory prompt his *Missa Papae Marcelli* as he begins to write, and his wife's spirit comforts him. After dawn, the boys find him asleep before the completed Mass.

Act II At Trent, the Council is lengthily embroiled in national and personal rivalries. Merely *en passant*, the topic of sacred music is raised; Borromeo reports that he has commanded a Mass from Palestrina, who after steadfastly refusing has been imprisoned. The act ends with a punitive slaughter of embattled hangers-on and rabble.

Act III Back home two weeks later, the dazed composer learns that his secret Mass is being sung in

St Peter's: to save him from punishment, his Santa Maria Maggiore choristers have handed over the parts to the authorities. The papal singers arrive, full of praise, and then the delighted Pope himself comes with Borromeo and an entourage to demand Palestrina's lifelong services. Borromeo exults (but Silla has decamped to Florence); the composer resigns himself to his destiny, and begins to muse at the organ.

To the static outer acts, Pfitzner's idiosyncratic art lends subtle musical lines as well as pungent character, and Borromeo's long dramatic monologue in Act I is a *tour de force*. In our 'authenticity'-conscious time the grand close of Act I sounds touchingly dated, with its 'Palestrina' fragments drenched in celestial harps. But Pfitzner never lapses here into plaintive sentiment; and his sardonic sketch of committee futility in Act II is brilliantly calculated for variety and pace. (None of the debate is theological, but any performance must either be sung in the audience's language or enlist surtitles.) A vision is transmitted with considerable power, and it is not a simple one. At the end, Palestrina's tight-lipped reaction to his 'triumph' and the significant absence of young Silla – whose defection to the trendy Florentines is not rebuked – leave an astringent aftertaste. To the extent that *Palestrina* is a grandiose exercise in self-exposure, it eschews self-justification: it is sadder, wiser and more far-sighted than that. The wealth of invention in Pfitzner's score speaks for itself.

RECORDINGS 1. Nentwig, Sabo, Patzak, Klarwein, Hotter, Frantz, Bavarian State Opera Ch and O, Heger, Melodram, 1952: historic 'live' performance with Patzak (Palestrina) and Hotter (Borromeo); 2. Donath, Fassbaender, Gedda, Steinbach, Fischer-Dieskau, Weikl, Ridderbusch, Prey, Bavarian Radio Symphony Ch and O, Kubelik, DG, 1973: rewarding but less intense performance than the former [A.B.]
EDITIONS f.s./v.s., Fürstner/Schott, 1916; study s., Schott, 1963

Das Herz
The Heart

Drama für musik in three acts, Op. 39 (2h 45m)
Libretto by Hans Mahner-Mons
Composed 1930–31
PREMIERES 12 November 1931, simultaneously in Munich and Berlin

Again, the names of the first conductors of Pfitzner's final opera testify to the respect he commanded: Fürtwangler for Berlin, Knappertsbusch for Munich. (His Piano Concerto had been introduced by Gieseking and Fritz Busch.) The story concerns occult 17th-century diabolism in south Germany. Engaged to resuscitate a prince, Dr Athanasius enlists the services of the demon Asmodeus; the price of the deal is a human heart, to be plucked from the Realm of Dreams where every sleeper's heart temporarily resides. Unfortunately, the heart Dr Athanasius picks is that of his own wife. The 'spiritual' aspects of the story have much in common

with Pfitzner's first two operas, which may explain why he accepted the foolish text; but it inspired him to nothing more than thumping triadic harmony and predictable chromatic swirls for the devilry. Nothing in the opera is as shocking as the sad decline it marks in the composer's work.

EDITIONS f.s./v.s., Fürstner, 1931

BIBLIOGRAPHY W. Abendroth (ed.), *Hans Pfitzner: ein Bild in Widmungen anlässlich seines 75. Geburtstages*, Helling, 1944; Carl Dahlhaus, trans. J. B. Robinson, *Nineteenth-century Music*, University of California Press, 1989, pp. 339–42; H. Rectanus, 'Leitmotivik und Form in den musikdramatischen Werken Hans Pfitzners', *Literarhistorisch-musikwissenschaftliche Abhandlungen*, vol. 18, Triltsch, 1967; John Williamson, *The Music of Hans Pfitzner*, Clarendon Press, 1992

D.M.

FRANÇOIS-ANDRÉ DANICAN PHILIDOR
b 7 September 1726, Dreux, France; *d* 31 August 1795, London

Philidor was the first composer to achieve distinction in the newly refined genre of the opéra comique in the mid-18th century. His musical pedigree was impeccable, the Philidor family having been in royal service as wind-players since the 1650s. However, he had another passion, chess, by which he earned a living for at least part of his life, dividing his time between France and England, where he was particularly admired. His *L'analyse des échecs* (1748), later revised as *Analyse du jeu des échecs*), much translated and reprinted, means that even today his name is well known to chess enthusiasts who may have no idea of his musical activities.

After early musical training under André Campra as a choirboy at Versailles, he began to compose chiefly motets. From 1745 Philidor spent a period of nearly ten years in England, where he established his reputation as a chess-player, continued some musical studies and probably heard Italian music. Unsuccessful in his bid to become maître de chapelle at Versailles in 1754 and to gain entry to the Opéra (both institutions found his composition 'too Italian'), he turned to opéra comique and produced a steady stream of works in that genre, which, up to about 1765, were mostly well received.

Philidor also essayed tragédie lyrique: his *Ernelinde* (1767) enjoyed success in a later (revised) version. Two later serious operas were comparative failures, however, and the comic operas of this period did not enjoy the success of the earlier ones. He was also giving more time to chess again. Stranded in London when war broke out with France, he died there.

Philidor made a major contribution to the emergence of the opéra comique as a respectable musical genre, with realistic characters and situations. He handled his limited orchestral resources cleverly, making a particular feature of descriptive effects. He also showed originality and skill in writing for vocal ensembles of up to seven voices (*Le bûcheron*, 1763, includes the first known comic septet). The only shadow on his reputation was a series of accusations of plagiarism: there were suggestions (by Berlioz and others) that he had plundered the work of Gluck, Galuppi, Pergolesi and Jommelli. Certainly, the resemblance of numbers in *Le sorcier* and *Ernelinde* to others in Gluck's *Orfeo* (which Philidor saw through the press in 1764) laid him wide open to such a charge. The degree of intent remains unproven, however, and suspicion should not be allowed to cloud recognition of Philidor's considerable achievements.

Blaise le savetier

Blaise the Cobbler
Opéra comique in one act
Libretto by Michel-Jean Sedaine, after La Fontaine's *Conte d'une chose arrivée à Château-Thierry*
PREMIERES 9 March 1759, Opéra-Comique, Paris; UK: 23 June 1783, Sadler's Wells, London (as *The Landlord Outwitted, or The Cobbler's Wife*); modern revival: 25 February 1976, French Institute, London

This was Philidor's first solo venture in the operatic field, and was a notable success. The theme of the plot is the contrast between bourgeois greed and moral corruption on the one hand and peasant virtue and quick-wittedness on the other. The cobbler's wife secures release from a debt by apparently allowing the creditor to seduce her. At the critical moment, she alerts her concealed husband by coughing. Philidor's originality in the handling of ensembles is already apparent in an amusing pseudo-duet in which Blaise fakes his wife's voice in falsetto.

EDITION f.s., facsimile, *French Opera in the 17th and 18th Centuries*, vol. 54, Pendragon, forthcoming

Le jardinier et son seigneur

The Gardener and His Master
Opéra comique in one act
Libretto by Michel-Jean Sedaine, after the fable by La Fontaine
PREMIERES 18 February 1761, Opéra-Comique, Paris; UK: 23 May 1977, French Institute, London

This little fable may seem an unlikely choice for an opera libretto. It concerns a gardener whose lettuces are being eaten by a hare. He appeals for help to the lord of the manor, whose 'help' wreaks havoc and who attempts to seduce the gardener's daughter. The vein of social criticism is expressed frankly by the girl's mother: 'Ces seigneurs-là n'ont qu'un doigt pour faire du bien; ils en ont neuf pour faire du mal' ('These seigneurs do good with only one of their fingers; with the other nine, they do evil'). The librettist's boldness and his attempts to make his peasants speak like peasants were criticized, but the music was well received.

EDITION v.s., Chez M. de la Chevardière, Paris, 1761

Le maréchal ferrant

The Farrier
Opéra comique in two acts
Libretto by François-Antoine Quétant, after Boccaccio
PREMIERES 22 August 1761, Opéra-Comique, Paris; US: 25 March 1793, Boston; UK: December 1978, French Institute, London

This opera was a major success, enjoying many revivals. The plot is a lightweight tangle of would-be lovers. Marcel, the farrier, wants to marry off his daughter Jeanette to his friend, La Bride. Both have other ideas: Jeanette prefers the farmer, Colin, with whom she is united in the end.

The illustrative effects for which Philidor was noted are here displayed with particular resourcefulness: the clang of hammer on anvil, the crack of a coachman's whip, a braying donkey and the village carillon are all depicted.

EDITION v.s., Chez M. de la Chevardière, Paris, *c.* 1765

Le sorcier

The Sorcerer
Opéra comique in two acts
Libretto by Antoine A. H. Poinsenet
PREMIERES 2 January 1764, Comédie-Italienne, Paris; modern revival: 6 May 1980, Maison de la Culture, Rennes

In this lightweight opera Julien disguises himself as a sorcerer to frighten off Blaise, a peasant, who is to marry Julien's sweetheart, Agathe. Blaise marries Agathe's mother instead, and everyone pairs off happily.

The opera contains its share of descriptive effects, notably the evocation of a storm at sea in the accompaniment to one of Julien's arias. A mock incantation parodies similar scenes in serious operas.

RECORDING Bouveret, Orliac, Reinemann, Rennes O, Soustrot, Arion, 1980
EDITION f.s., facsimile, *French Opera in the 17th and 18th Centuries*, vol. 54, Pendragon, forthcoming

Tom Jones

Opéra comique in three acts
Libretto by Antoine A. H. Poisenet, rev. Michel-Jean Sedaine, after the novel *The History of Tom Jones, a Foundling* by Henry Fielding (1748)
PREMIERES 27 February 1765, Comédie-Italienne, Paris; rev. version: 30 January 1766; UK: March 1978, French Institute, London

In its revised version, *Tom Jones* was Philidor's most successful opera. The plot concerns the escapades of Tom Jones, a foundling, and the obstacles that have to be overcome before Tom and his sweetheart Sophia Western can be united; the *dénouement* is brought about by the revelation of Tom's parentage. The opera follows the novel quite closely, although the hero is a somewhat tame version of Fielding's original.

Particularly noteworthy are a lively hunting air for Squire Western, 'D'un cerf dix cors' (Act I), full of tally-ho, the duet 'A ton père', in which Sophia's

M. Caillot, the first Squire Western in Tom Jones *(Paris, 1765)*

pleadings are set against her father's anger (Act II), and an extended scena for Sophia at the inn, 'Respirons un moment' (Act III). There is an unusual unaccompanied quartet of drunken servants and an effective septet, which closes Act III, in which Philidor manages to distinguish each character's reaction to the situation.

EDITIONS f.s., facsimile, *French Opera in the 17th and 18th Centuries*, vol. 55, Pendragon, forthcoming; v.s., Nicholas McGegan and Adrian Salter (eds), Boosey & Hawkes, 1978

Ernelinde, princesse de Norvège
Ernelinde, Princess of Norway
Tragédie lyrique in three acts (five acts in 2nd rev.)
Libretto by Antoine A. H. Poisenet, after Matteo Noris's libretto *Ricimero, re di Vandali* (1684), rev. Michel-Jean Sedaine
PREMIERES 24 November 1767, Opéra, Paris; 24 January 1769, Opéra, Paris (as *Sandomir, prince de Danemarck*); 11 December 1773, Versailles (five-act version)

An alliance between Denmark and Sweden brings victory over Rodoald, King of Norway. Ricimer, King of Sweden, wants to marry Rodoald's daughter Ernelinde, but she loves Sandomir, the Prince of Denmark. Ricimer tells Ernelinde that he will spare the life of either Rodoald or Sandomir: she must decide which. She chooses her father; Sandomir remains in prison. Rodoald rallies his army and, together with the Danes, overcomes Ricimer's forces. Sandomir extends clemency to Ricimer, who eventually gives his blessing to the marriage of Ernelinde and Sandomir.

Generally more Italianate than Philidor's previous operas, there are many remarkable passages in this score, especially Ernelinde's scene at the end of Act II in which, having chosen to spare her father's life, she sees a vision of the spectre of her reproachful lover.

EDITIONS f.s., facsimile, *French Opera in the 17th and 18th Centuries*, vol. 56, Pendragon, forthcoming; v.s., *Chefs d'oeuvre*, vol. 27, [1883]; *rp*, Broude Bros, 1971

Les femmes vengées, ou Les feintes infidélités
The Women Revenged, or Pretended Infidelities
Opéra comique in one act
Libretto by Michel-Jean Sedaine, after the tale *Les remois* by La Fontaine
PREMIERES 20 March 1775, Comédie-Italienne, Paris; modern revival: 27 July 1978, Albi

Courted by two judges, a painter's wife confides in their wives, and the three conspire to outwit the philanderers. Surprised by the pre-arranged return of the husband, the judges hide and are forced to watch helplessly as their wives apparently respond enthusiastically to the painter's advances. The plot revealed, they can only beg their wives to forgive them.

In the choice of librettist, the source of the subject and musical style, this opera is reminiscent of Philidor's earlier works. Well-known tunes appear alongside newly composed material. Philidor's gift for ingenious ensembles is here given ample scope, particularly in a quartet between the painter, one of the wives and the two concealed judges.

EDITION Chez le Duc, Paris, 1775

Other operatic works: *Le diable à quatre, ou Le double métamorphose* (coll. with J. L. Laruette), 1756; *Le soldat magicien*, 1760; *Sancho Pança dans son isle*, 1762; *Le bûcheron, ou Les trois souhaits*, 1763; *Les fêtes de la paix*, 1763; *La bagarre* (coll. with Van Maldere), 1763; *Le jardinier de Sidon*, 1768; *L'amant déguisé, ou Le jardinier supposé*, 1769; *La rosière de Salency* (coll. with Monsigny, von Swieten, ?Duni), 1769; *La nouvelle école des femmes*, 1770; *Le bon fils*, 1773; *Mélide, ou Le navigateur/Zémire et Mélide*, 1773; *Berthe* (coll. with Gossec, Botson), 1775; *Persée*, 1780; *Thémistocle*, 1785; *L'amitié au village*, 1785; *La belle esclave, ou Valcour et Zélia*, 1787; 4 lost operas
BIBLIOGRAPHY C. M. Carroll, 'François-André Danican Philidor', *Recherches sur la musique française classique*, vol. 2 (1961–2), p. 159; David Charlton, *Grétry and the Growth of Opéra-comique*, CUP, 1986; Martin Cooper, *Opéra Comique*, Max Parish, 1949

C.W.

NICCOLÒ PICCINNI

Vito Niccolò [Nicola] Marcello Antonio Giacomo Piccinni
[Piccini]; *b* 16 January 1728, Bari; *d* 7 May 1800, Passy, Paris

Piccinni, remembered mainly as Gluck's rival in Paris, is equally significant as a composer of Italian opera. He studied in Naples, probably under Leo and Durante and spent much of his career there, holding church posts and teaching as well as writing an astonishing number of operas. According to Burney, Sacchini claimed that Piccinni had composed nearly 300. The actual total, which is *c.* 110, is remarkable enough.

Piccinni's first successes were in opera buffa in the minor theatres of Naples, where he introduced the multi-movement finale, created by Galuppi in Venice. His style anticipates the 'high classical' idiom, and he had no need to develop it over 30 years; the fundamental patterns of phrasing, motifs and harmony in his music, as well as his fertility, inventiveness and charm, epitomize the late Neapolitan school.

Prestigious opera-seria commmissions came from the San Carlo in Naples (*Zenobia*, 1756) and Rome (*Alessandro nelle Indie*, 1758). After *La Cecchina* (1760) Piccinni dominated the stage in both cities until his former student Anfossi supplanted him in Rome around 1773, while in Naples he had to share the honours from 1766 with Paisiello. He had attracted attention in France in the early 1770s, and in 1776 he agreed terms with the Opéra. At first, knowing no French, he was in need of constant supervision by his librettist Marmontel, both for his accentuation of the language and for the use of such French forms as short arias, choruses, and ballets, which were rarely present in Italian opera. He nevertheless established himself with *Roland* (1778). Gluck's triumph with *Iphigénie en Tauride* (1779) caused postponement of Piccinni's version, but it attained a creditable number of performances, as did *Atys*; *Didon* was a notable success.

In Paris Piccinni directed an Italian buffo troupe, and took charge of singing at the Ecole Royale de Musique et de Déclamation (1783). But fashion moved on, and his last French opera, *Clytemnestre*, was not performed. With the Revolution he returned to a warm welcome in Naples. He wrote a few more Italian operas, but fell foul of the authorities in Venice because his son-in-law was a Jacobin. After four years under house arrest, during which he composed some religious music, he returned to Paris in 1798. He was appointed to the staff of the Conservatoire and his pension was restored, but he died soon afterwards.

La Cecchina, ossia La buona figliuola

Cecchina, or The Good-Natured Girl
Opera buffa in three acts (2h 30m)
Libretto by Carlo Goldini, after the novel *Pamela, or Virtue Rewarded* by Samuel Richardson (1740)
PREMIERES 6 February 1760, Teatro delle Dame, Rome;
UK: 25 November 1766, King's Theatre, Haymarket, London; US: 6 January 1967, Madison, Wisconsin

CAST   The Marquis *t*, Lucinda *s*, Armidoro *s castrato*, Paoluccia *s*, Cecchina *s*, Sandrina *s*, Mengotto *b comico*, Tagliaferro *b-bar*
ORCHESTRATION   2 fl/picc, 2 ob, 2 hn, 2 tpt, str, bc

The libretto had previously been set by Duni (1756) and Perillo (*c.* 1760). Piccinni's setting (supposedly composed in 18 days) became a trendsetter and was performed in all the main European houses, reaching Paris in 1771; by 1779 it was known from Ireland to Russia and was rumoured to have been performed in Peking. Piccinni hoped to repeat his success with a sequel, *La buona figliola maritata* (1761), which was widely performed but did not achieve the same popularity. Numerous other sequels and pasticcios were also composed – a sure sign of the opera's reputation.

SYNOPSIS

Act I The Marquis loves his servant Cecchina and is determined to marry her despite the opposition of his sister and the entire household. Only Mengotto, a peasant, who loves Cecchina, defends her. Cecchina herself cannot believe in her master's love, but nevertheless returns it. The plotters persuade the Marquis that Cecchina loves Mengotto and she is driven out of the house.

Act II Cecchina, under arrest thanks to the schemings of Armindoro, the Marquis's potential brother-in-law, who wants to keep her out of the way, is rescued by Mengotto, and carried off by the Marquis. Mengotto is comforted by a German stranger, Tagliaferro, who then presents himself to the Marquis. His mission is to trace Mariandel, daughter of his noble colonel; it is, of course, Cecchina (the main point of Richardson's novel, a gentleman's marriage to a girl of humble birth, is thus lost).

Act III The overjoyed Marquis persuades Cecchina of the truth. All objections to the marriage are now removed and love takes it course.

This perfect example of operatic lingua franca is inventive in comic scenes, adroitly delineating the characters, while also touching on more serious feelings; Cecchina's sleep scene with flutes, *pizzicato* bass and muted strings represents an effective transfusion from opera seria.

RECORDING   Rinaldi, Aliberti, Ravaglia, Zilio, Benelli, Corbelli, Dara, Ch and O of Rome Opera, Gelmetti, Fonit Cetra, 1981
EDITIONS   facsimile (manuscript; the inclusion of arias by Duni and Galuppi is typical of the time), Garland, 1983; v.s., G. Benvenuti (ed.), *I classici musicali italiani*, Milan, 1942

La pescatrice, ovvero L'erede riconosciuta

The Fishermaid, or The Heiress Revealed
Opera buffa (intermezzo) in two acts; expanded to three acts (1771), probably by Perillo (1h 45m)
Librettist unknown
PREMIERE   9 January 1766, Teatro Capranica, Rome

La pescatrice is a lengthy intermezzo, a simple drama for four characters to be performed between the three acts of an opera seria. The existence of several manuscripts indicates its success in Germany as well as Italy. Silvia, heiress to a usurped estate, is believed dead, but has been brought up in ignorance of her parentage by Licone, a fisherman. A storm forces them to land on an island, where they are succoured by Dorilla; the castle where they are entertained proves to be rightly Silvia's. The reigning count, son of the usurper, is easily overthrown, and all ends happily with his marriage to Silvia and Licone's to Dorilla. Among the conventional arias are two cavatinas. There are also three duets and two short finales.

RECORDING Pennicchi, Garbato, Comencini, Gatti, Sassari SO, Rizzi, Bongiovanni, 1988
EDITION v.s., D. Boschan (ed.), Edito Musica Budapest, 1982

Roland

Tragédie lyrique in three acts (2h 30m)
Libretto by Jean-François Marmontel, after Phillipe Quinault (1685)
PREMIERE 27 January 1778, Académie Royale, Paris

In this, his first French opera, Piccinni successfully combined both the French and Italian styles. The arias are predominantly Italianate but, no doubt advised by Marmontel, the composer took care to include the traditional French divertissements, and was obviously concerned with adhering to French speech rhythms. Gluck was reported to have been setting the same story but to have abandoned his opera on hearing of Piccinni's.

Roland suffers through unrequited love for Angélique, and tries to destroy her lover Médor. Roland's music is effective, especially the aria 'Je me reconnais' in which the hero believes he has recovered his martial pride, and the subsequent mad scene, which uses typically French short musical units.

EDITIONS f.s., Dezauche, 1778; v.s., Chefs d'oeuvre de l'opéra français, Michaelis, 1883; rp, Broude, 1971

Atys

Tragédie lyrique in three acts (3h)
Libretto by Jean-François Marmontel, after Quinault's Atys (1676)
Composed 1779, rev. 1783
PREMIERE 22 February 1780, Académie Royale, Paris
CAST Atys t, Sangaride s, Cybèle s, Céloenus bar, 5 small solo parts; satb chorus of worshippers of Cybèle, good and bad dreams
STANDARD ORCHESTRA including 3 trbn

Atys was Piccinni's third French opera seria, but was performed before the delayed Iphigénie en Tauride. The tragic end was coolly received, but a slightly shortened and revised version was successful in 1783 and revivals continued into the 1790s. Its fine arias and ensembles, and the richness of its instrumentation, make this perhaps Piccinni's finest French opera. Marmontel adapted Roland and Atys from libretti by Quinault set originally by Lully, eliminating the prologues, compressing the plot into three acts, pruning the cast, and reducing recitative and dances to create space for arias and ensembles and give free rein to the more expansive Italian musical style (the action of Atys climaxes in a quartet of over 200 bars). The main dramatic alteration to Quinault's Atys is the removal of the final metamorphosis of the hero into a pine tree.

SYNOPSIS
Act I Atys is sworn to indifference in love, and Sangaride is to marry the king, Céloenus; but they cannot conceal their mutual affection. The goddess Cybèle descends and proclaims Atys her high priest.

Act II Cybèle reveals her love for Atys in a dream sequence of solo, chorus, and dance. Atys pretends to misunderstand; Cybèle is jealous.

Act III Atys and Sangaride are compromised and condemned. Atys is driven mad by the goddess and, taking Sangaride for a monster, kills her. When he recovers his senses, he commits suicide, cursing Cybèle.

The 1783 revision substituted a perfunctory happy ending. The pastoral atmosphere and dream scenes aroused in Piccinni a new picturesque vein, and the emphatic arias of despair in minor keys have a pathos totally unlike Gluck's, deriving directly from opera seria.

EDITIONS f.ss., Paris, 1780; 2nd edn, Paris, 1783; facsimile of 1783 edn, J. Rushton (ed.), Pendragon, vol. 65, 1991

Iphigénie en Tauride

Iphigenia in Tauride
Tragédie lyrique in four acts (2h 30m)
Libretto by Alphonse de Congé Dubreuil, after G. de la Touche and Euripides (414–12 BC)
PREMIERE 23 January 1781, Académie Royale, Paris

The librettist's source was the same as for Gluck's Tauride, and it has long been thought that Devismes, then director of the Opéra, set both composers the same task to perpetuate the rivalry between the opposing factions, promising Piccinni that his version would be staged first. More probably, he gave Piccinni the libretto as the first that came to hand when he wanted to offer an alternative should Marmontel have trouble preparing the libretto of Atys in time.

In Piccinni's version the Scythian king Thoas is in love with Iphigenia. The libretto was immediately recognized as inferior, but although worsted by Gluck's in a box-office battle, Piccinni's opera won many supporters and was revived in 1785 and 1790.

RECORDING Baleani, Bertolo, Noli, Massis, Ch and O of the Teatro Petruzzelli, Bari, Renzetti, Fonit Cetra, 1986
EDITIONS f.ss., Des Lauriers, 1781; facsimile, Gregg International, 1972

Didon

Dido
Tragédie lyrique in three acts (2h 30m)
Libretto by Jean-François Marmontel

PREMIERE 16 October 1783, Fontainebleau
CAST Didon *s*, Elise *s*, Enée *t*, Iarbé *bar*; *satb* chorus of
Carthaginians and Trojans
STANDARD ORCHESTRA including 3 trbn

Didon was Piccinni's most successful French opera. Confidently expected to be another failure after that of *Adèle de Ponthieu*, it overcame opposition thanks to the exceptional singing actress Mme de St Huberty, who made Dido her greatest role. It remained in the repertoire of the Paris Opéra for 40 years and was widely performed abroad. Critics suggested that Piccinni was now a Gluckist, but in fact, by enhancing the flow between musical numbers while including more short ones, he built on his own previous achievements and preserved his own style. An original libretto by Marmontel, *Didon* owes surprisingly little to Metastasio's *Didone abbandonata* (1724).

SYNOPSIS
Act I Dido is torn between loyalty to her dead husband, who has reproached her in a dream, and love for Aeneas. The powerful African king Iarbas asks for Dido's hand and can be rejected only with tact.
Act II Destiny bids Aeneas depart for Italy; love bids him stay. War with Iarbas is inevitable.

Mme de St Huberty as Dido (Paris, 1783)

Act III Aeneas returns truimphant from battle but departs after a warning from his father's ghost. With a subdued apology to her husband ('O toi qui me condamnes'), Dido kills herself; the Carthaginians, anticipating Berlioz's *Les troyens*, swear eternal hatred for Aeneas and his race.

Dido's opening aria (a Gluckian sequence of three sections) contrasts several moods, ending with preparations for the hunt. Her confrontation with Iarbas in Act I shows her regal grandeur, and Piccinni allows glimpses of her innermost feelings by the use of short, almost fragmentary, arias – a technique he shared with Sacchini – as well as violent agitation in her Act III aria 'Hélas, pour nous il s'expose'. Aeneas's dilemma is exposed in the pathetic C minor aria which opens Act II and the powerful 'Au noir chagrin qui me dévore'. The trombone accompaniment for the ghost of his father effectively underlines the supernatural background to the tragedy.

EDITIONS f.s., Paris, 1783; facsimile, Forni, 1970; v.s., *Chefs d'oeuvre de l'opéra français*, Michaelis, 1881; *rp*, Broude Bros, 1971

La Griselda
Griselda

Opera eroicomico in two acts (2h)
Libretto by Angelo Anelli, after Boccaccio's *Decameron*, and probably influenced by Zeno's libretto
PREMIERE 8 October 1793, Teatro San Samuele, Venice

The Griselda story was also set by many other composers, including Alessandro Scarlatti and Vivaldi. Griselda is of lowly birth and has married above her station. She is rejected, but her virtues win her husband back. The genre is close to the French comédie larmoyante, as represented by Dalayrac's *Nina*, but here the heroine triumphs not through luck but entirely as the result of her own efforts. The opera therefore has a didactic angle, which culminates in a moralistic final chorus. The subject is serious, but of the everyday world, so the forms are those of opera buffa. This blend perfectly suits Piccinni's mature style and results in the finest work of his last years.

MANUSCRIPT Conservatorio di Musica Luigi Cherubini, Florence

Other surviving operas: *Le gelosie*, 1755; *Il curioso del suo proprio danno*, 1756; *Zenobia*, 1756; *L'amante ridicolo*, 1757; *La schiava Siria*, 1757; *Caio Mario*, 1757; *Alessandro nelle Indie* (first setting), 1758; *Madama Arrighetta*, 1758; *La scaltra letterata*, 1758; *Ciro riconosciuto*, 1759; *L'Origille*, 1760; *Il rè pastore*, 1760; *La furba burlata*, 1760; *Le vicende della sorte*, 1761; *Olimpiade* (first setting), 1761; *Tigrane*, 1761; *Demofoonte*, 1761; *La buona figliuola maritata*, 1761; *L'astuto balordo*, 1761; *L'astrologa*, 1761; *Artaserse*, 1762; *Le avventure di Ridolfo*, 1762; *La bella verità*, 1762; *Antigono*, 1762; *Il cavaliere per amore*, 1762 or 1763; *Le donne vendicate*, 1763; *Le contadine bizzarre*, 1763; *Gli stravaganti*, 1764; *Il perrucchiere*, 1764; *L'incognita perseguitata*, 1764; *La donna vana*, 1764; *Il barone di Torreforete*, 1765; *L'incostante*, 1766; *La molinarella*, 1766; *Il gran Cid*, 1766; *La notte critica*,

1767; *La finta baronessa*, 1767; *Olimpiade* (second setting), 1768; *Li napoletani in America*, 1768; *La locandiera di spirito*, 1768; *Lo sposo burlato*, 1769; *Demetrio*, 1769; *Gli sposi perseguitati*, 1769; *Cesare in Egitto*, 1770; *Didone abbandonata*, 1770; *Il regno della luna*, 1770; *Gelosia per gelosia*, 1770; *Catone in Utica*, 1770 (EDITION facsimile, Garland, 1978); *Le finte gemelle*, 1771; *La donna di bell'umore*, 1771; *La Corsala*, 1771; *L'americano*, 1772; *L'astratto*, 1772; *Le trame zingaresche*, 1772; *Ipermestra*, 1772; *La sposa collerica*, 1773; *Gli amanti mascherati*, 1774; *Alessandro nelle Indie* (second setting), 1774; *Il sordo*, 1775; *L'ignorante astuto*, 1775; *I viaggiatori*, 1775; *Enea in Cuma*, 1775; *La contessina*, 1775; *Vittorina*, 1777; *Phaon*, 1778; *Il vago disprezzato*, 1779; *Adèle de Ponthieu*, 1781; *Le dormeur éveillé*, 1783; *Le faux lord*, 1783; *Diane et Endymion*, 1784; *Lucette*, 1784; *Pénélope*, 1785; *Clytemnestre*, (1787); *Ercole al Termedonte*, 1793; *Il servo padrone*, 1794; *Il Decemviri*, (n.d.); *Il finto turco*, (n.d.); *La pie voleuse*, (n.d.); 20 lost operas; collaborations include: *Farnace* (with Perez), 1757; *Nitteti* (with Cocchi), 1757; *L'orfana insidiata* (with Astarita), 1765
BIBLIOGRAPHY Julian Rushton, 'The Theory and Practice of *Piccinnisme*', *PRMA*, vol. 98 (1971–2), p. 31; Julian Rushton, '*Iphigénie en Tauride*: The Operas of Gluck and Piccinni', *ML*, vol. 53 (1972), p. 411; M. Hunter, 'The Fusion and Juxtaposition of Genres in Opera Buffa 1770–1800: Anelli's and Piccinni's *Griselda*', *ML*, vol. 67 (1986), p. 363; E. Schmierer, 'Piccinni's *Iphigénie en Tauride*: 'chant périodique' and dramatic structure', *Cambridge Opera Journal*, vol. 4 (1992), p. 91

J.R.

GABRIEL PIERNÉ

Henri Constant Gabriel Pierné; *b* 16 August 1863, Metz, France; *d* 17 July 1937, Ploujean, Finistère, France

Pierné was one of the most versatile and prolific of all French composers. A pupil of Massenet and César Franck, he succeeded Franck as organist at St Clothilde in Paris (1890), but was later more widely known as a conductor. He was principal conductor of the Concerts Colonne (1910–34), where, in his first year, he directed the first performance of Debussy's *Ibéria*, four months before conducting, for Diaghilev, the epoch-making premiere of Stravinsky's *Firebird*.

Like Mahler, Pierné composed mainly when on vacation from conducting. But this hardly seems to have restricted him. He wrote about 25 theatre scores (operas, ballets, incidental music), as well as many orchestral and chamber works, some of which survive on the fringes of the repertoire. Though facile, in the French Romantic manner, much of this music is highly attractive and approachable. Most of his nine operas are comédies, and it was in the slightly frothy and gay that Pierné excelled. The exception is the drame lyrique *Vendée*, about the revolutionary turmoil in western France in 1793. But most revivable is perhaps his last opera, *Fragonard*, a sumptuously light-hearted romance on the life and loves of the painter.

Operas: *Le chemin d'amour*, (1883); *Don Luis*, (1886); *Lizarda*, (1894); *La coupe enchantée*, 1895; *Vendée*, 1897; *La fille de Tabarin*, 1901; *On ne badine pas avec l'amour*, 1910; *Sophie Arnould*, 1927; *Fragonard*, 1934

BIBLIOGRAPHY Laurence Davies, *César Franck and his Circle*, Barrie and Jenkins, 1970

S.W.

WILLEM PIJPER

b 8 September 1894, Zeist, Netherlands; *d* 18 March 1947, Leidschendam, Netherlands

Pijper was the leading Dutch composer of his generation, as well as a highly influential teacher. He studied with Johann Wagenaar in Utrecht (1911–16), and taught at the Amsterdam Conservatory from 1918 to 1930, when he was appointed director of the Rotterdam Conservatory, a post he held until his death. Early influences included Mahler and Debussy. His output embraces many choral and instrumental works, as well as incidental music to three Greek dramas and to Shakespeare's *The Tempest*.

Pijper's only completed opera was the 'symphonic drama' *Halewijn* (1933). This had its roots in the earlier *a cappella* choral work *Heer Halewijn* (1929), itself based on a medieval ballad. Both employ the composer's 'germ cell' technique, whereby an entire composition is generated by a chord or series of notes. Although it is the music rather than the dramatic action that carries the main interest, the work gave new impetus to Dutch opera. A second opera, *Merlijn*, remained incomplete, but was posthumously performed in 1952.

BIBLIOGRAPHY Wouter Pap, 'Composer', Eduard Reeser (ed.), trans. Ian F. Finlay, *Music in Holland*, J. M. Meulenhoff, [n.d.], pp. 19–24

M.A.

LYUBOMIR PIPKOV

b 19 September 1904, Lovech, Bulgaria; *d* 9 May 1974, Sofia

The son of the composer Panayot Pipkov (1871–1942), Lyubomir studied at the Sofia Music School, financing himself by working as a restaurant pianist. In 1926 he went on a French scholarship to Paris where his teachers included Nadia Boulanger. Returning to Bulgaria in 1932, he joined the Sofia National Opera as répétiteur and chorus master, a post previously held by his father. He subsequently became director of the Opera (1944–7), president of the Union of Bulgarian Composers and editor of *Music* magazine.

Pipkov was the leading Bulgarian opera composer of the generation after Athanassov: *Momchil* was the only new Bulgarian opera to appear between 1944 and 1957. In his first two operas, both on historical subjects, Pipkov turned his back on Romantic opera and, particularly in the second, *Momchil*, based on the life of the eponymous Bulgarian folk hero, achieved a depth of characterization coupled with an imaginative handling of crowd scenes that recall his model, Musorgsky. *Antigone 43* – the first Bulgarian opera on a contemporary theme – is a psychological drama based on Sophocles.

Operas: *Yaninite devet bratya* (*Yana's Nine Brothers*), 1937; *Momchil*, 1948; *Antigone 43*, 1963
BIBLIOGRAPHY   Venelin Krustev, trans. Jean Patterson-Alexieva, *Bulgarian Music*, Sofia Press, 1978

E.A.

ILDEBRANDO PIZZETTI

b 20 September 1880, Parma, Italy; *d* 14 February 1968, Rome

Among the Italian composers of his generation, Pizzetti occupied a distinctive intermediate position between the conservatives and the modernists. Unlike Casella and G. F. Malipiero, he was never much interested in the radical innovations of, say, Stravinsky. Yet he was not content simply to accept the Italian operatic tradition with minor modifications: already in his first published opera, *Fedra*, he made a firm stand against the methods of Puccini and his contemporaries. Pizzetti's operatic approach was conditioned by a musico-dramatic theory which outlawed self-sufficient lyricism (except in special circumstances) and replaced it by a continuous, usually rather rapid declamation, highly sensitive to the nuances of the text. The result has a personal, often modally inflected physiognomy that can be profoundly expressive, despite a serious danger of monotony in the less inspired scenes.

Fedra was composed in close collaboration with the flamboyantly decadent poet Gabriele D'Annunzio, who for a time seems to have regarded Pizzetti as his musical alter ego. However, the young composer's second D'Annunzio opera, *Gigliola* (1914), remained unfinished, and he used no further libretto derived directly from D'Annunzio until long after the poet's death. Meanwhile he usually wrote his own libretti – although the strong influence of D'Annunzio can still be detected in their general style, interacting strangely with a high-minded if sometimes rather confused tendency to moralize.

Pizzetti's next completed opera, *Dèbora e Jaéle*, is commonly regarded as his masterpiece, and gave some credibility to G. M. Gatti's description of him (in 1921 when Puccini was still alive) as 'doubtless the greatest musician in Italy today'. However, his subsequent operas failed – some of them dismally – to live up to the huge expectations *Fedra* and *Dèbora* had aroused. The unpretentious *La sacra rappresentazione di Abram e d'Isaac* is a special case, originating in incidental music composed before the completion of *Dèbora*. But Pizzetti already showed dangerous signs of repeating himself in *Lo straniero* (1923–5), which resembles *Dèbora* in style while being more static dramatically and musically less compelling. *Fra Gherardo* (1926–7) is theatrically more effective than *Lo straniero*, revealing a certain

rapprochement with Verdi: here the choral writing, as usual in Pizzetti, is a strong feature; but the opera is long-winded, and lacks the visionary evocativeness that made *Fedra* and *Dèbora* so memorable. It was in his next three operas, however, that Pizzetti entered his most disappointing phase: his arrogant refusal to open his ears to virtually any music more 'advanced' than his own too often led, during this middle period, to a stultifying reliance on self-imitation.

The post-war years saw a partial recovery of his creative vitality, already evident in the concise radio opera *Ifigenia* (1950). *La figlia di Iorio* (1954), again based on a D'Annunzio play, is more uneven, though it was initially well received. But the climax of creative renewal came with *Assassinio nella cattedrale*, undoubtedly his best opera since *Fedra* and *Dèbora*. By comparison, his last two operas are of very small account.

Fedra

Phaedra
Opera in three acts (2h 30m)
Libretto by Gabriele d'Annunzio, adapted from his own play (1909)
Composed 1909–12
PREMIERE   20 March 1915, La Scala, Milan

Although indebted to Euripides and Seneca, D'Annunzio added many significant details to the Classical legend, clothing it in characteristically ornate, archaically coloured verse. Phaedra's compulsive passion for Hippolytus – son of her husband, King Theseus, by a previous marriage – leads her to rejoice in the king's supposed death in battle, and then to murder the beautiful slave girl whom he brings with him (as a present for Hippolytus) when he comes home safely after all. When, in desperation, she kisses her stepson as he sleeps, he wakes up and fiercely rejects her. Incensed, she tells Theseus that Hippolytus tried to rape her, whereupon the king invokes the revenge of the sea god, causing the young man to fall from his horse and be trampled to death. Phaedra belatedly confesses her guilt to the crowd that has gathered round the corpse. She has taken poison but remains defiant, believing that her love will triumph in the hereafter.

Pizzetti's score, though usually rather sober in its orchestral colouring, clothes D'Annunzio's text in an evocative, finely woven fabric in which linear chromaticism and modality are subtly balanced. The heroine, and her effect on the other characters, are forcefully presented in the solo writing, despite occasional *longueurs*; while the chorus, though more static than in some later Pizzetti operas, contributes some of the work's most expressive music – above all in the unaccompanied, sublimely neo-madrigalian 'Threnody for the Dead Hippolytus' at the beginning of Act III, which (like the opera's prelude) has often been performed in the concert hall. The opera was frequently revived in Italy until the late 1960s.

EDITIONS   v.ss., Lorenzo Sonzogno, 1913; 3rd edn (with minor modifications dating back to 1915), Casa Musicale Sonzogno, 1959

Design by Rovescalli for Act II of Dèbora e Jaéle *(Milan, 1922)*

Dèbora e Jaéle

Deborah and Jael

Opera in three acts (2h 45m)

Libretto by the composer, very freely based on Chapters 4 and 5 of the Book of Judges

Composed 1917–21 (libretto begun 1915)

PREMIERE   16 December 1922, La Scala, Milan

While preserving the broad outline of the well-known biblical story, Pizzetti drastically transformed its underlying motivation and almost reversed its apportionment of 'good and evil'. Sisera (himself the king of Canaan in this version) is a far more complex and sympathetic character than Deborah: whereas she represents the inflexibly established Jewish law, he has been to Greece and has begun to develop a new vision of life that sets him apart from his own people. On a more purely intuitive level, Jael too senses that the old law is outdated: consequently when Deborah sends her to persuade Sisera to lead his army into an ambush, she finds a bond of sympathy with the king which creates a conflict between love and duty. In due course, when the defeated Sisera seeks refuge in Jael's tent, the two renew their doomed love, after which the king falls deeply asleep. As the victorious Israelites close in on them, Jael drives a tent peg into Sisera's skull; but her motive, in Pizzetti's version, is simply to save him from a worse death at the hands of her compatriots.

The logic of this plot may at times seem questionable; but the effect in the theatre remains deeply moving, thanks above all to some remarkably intense music. Methods already established in *Fedra*

are enriched by new elements: the chorus is now given a far more dramatic role, which sometimes calls to mind *Boris Godunov*. Bloch, too, is an important new influence. As in *Fedra*, there is an undeniable risk of prolixity, especially in scenes featuring lengthy ethical discourses. Yet the opera's best parts are more than enough to justify its exceptionally high standing with the Italian critics during Pizzetti's lifetime. Its total neglect since his death thus seems all the more outrageous.

EDITIONS   f.s., Ricordi, 1924; v.s. Ricordi, 1922

La sacra rappresentazione di Abram e d'Isaac

The Miracle Play of Abraham and Isaac

Opera in one act, expanded from incidental music (1h)

Libretto adapted by Onorato Castellino from the sacra rappresentazione by Feo Belcari (15th century)

Composed in three stages: original incidental music, 1917; further incidental music, 1926; remainder of text set, 1928

PREMIERES   original incidental music: 9 June 1917, Politeama Fiorentina, Florence; full operatic version: 2 October 1937, Teatro Morlacchi, Perugia; second incidental-music version: US: 4 December 1927, Town Hall, New York

Feo Belcari's presentation of the Genesis story is simple yet telling, giving a touching prominence to Sarah as she wonders why Abraham and Isaac have been away so long. (Her scenes are intercut with others depicting the journey to the place of sacrifice.) An angel announces and rounds off the drama; another plays a key role. Both of them sang already in the 1917 incidental music, which also contained choruses, whereas the other characters' vocal lines date from 1928. The work's structure, which reflects its gradual transformation from a play with music into an opera, differs markedly from Pizzetti's usual practice: the frankly self-contained numbers (some of them for orchestra alone) and the winsome charm and simplicity of much of the musical material make this perhaps his most instantly appealing stage piece. Yet the spirit of the Old Testament is evoked by means that are recognizably akin to those used in *Dèbora e Jaéle*: the powerful climax, when an angel's voice and a chorus from heaven prevent the sacrifice of Isaac in the nick of time, is worthy of comparison with some of that opera's finest moments.

EDITION   v.s. (final, fully operatic version), Ricordi, 1929

Assassinio nella cattedrale

Murder in the Cathedral

Opera in two acts and an intermezzo (1h 45m)
Libretto shortened and adapted by the composer, from Alberto Castelli's translation of the play by T. S. Eliot (1935)
Composed 1956–7
PREMIERES   1 March 1958, La Scala, Milan; US: 17 September 1958, Carnegie Hall, New York; UK: 12 June 1962, Coventry Theatre, Coventry

Pizzetti's partial recovery, in the 1950s, after the creative decline that had afflicted his middle years, was undoubtedly helped by well-chosen subjects for his libretti. This was especially the case in *Assassinio nella cattedrale*; for T. S. Eliot's skilful mix of plentiful choruses, eloquent ethical pronouncements, a pervasive religious atmosphere and a central character racked by moral conflicts could hardly have been better attuned to the composer's natural preferences.

After a long exile in France following his disagreement with King Henry II, Thomas Becket returns to Canterbury where he is archbishop, and is welcomed (though with some misgivings) by local women and priests. He is then visited by four tempters: his struggle to resist their well-aimed enticements brings Act I to its climax in a powerful concluding monologue. Act II is preceded by an intermezzo, which evokes Thomas's Christmas sermon in mainly orchestral terms, with token fragments of sung text at the beginning and end. Likewise controversially reduced is the famous address to the audience with which the four knights, towards the end of Eliot's play, seek to justify their murder of the archbishop for his refusal to submit to the king. Pizzetti's depiction of the knights is generally disappointing, and his orchestration, too, is less effective in this opera than in *Dèbora e Jaéle*. However, there is much to admire in the intense and varied choral writing, and in the vivid portrayal of Thomas himself.

Given the subject, it is understandable that this should be the only Pizzetti opera that has yet been staged in the UK and repeatedly performed in North America. The cool reception that greeted it in England in 1962 (after notable successes elsewhere)

did the work less than justice, and might well be reversed in the different critical climate of today.

RECORDING   Zeani, Rota, Ortica, Borriello, Cormanni, Rossi-Lemeni, Turin Ch and SO of Italian Radio, Pizzetti, Stradivarius, 1958
EDITION   v.s., Ricordi, 1958

Other operas: *Sabina* (destroyed), (1897); *Romeo e Giulietta* (virtually destroyed), (1900); *Il Cid* (destroyed), (1903); several fragments, 1904–8, including a *Fedra* based directly on Euripides, (1908); *Gigliola* (inc.), (1914); *Lo straniero*, (1925), 1930; *Fra Gherardo*, 1928; *Orsèolo*, 1935; *L'oro*, (1942), 1947; *Vanna Lupa*, 1949; *Ifigenia*, 1950 (RAI broadcast), 1951; *Cagliostro*, 1952 (RAI broadcast), 1953; *La figlia di Iorio*, 1954; *Povera gente* (inc.), (1956); *Il calzare d'argento*, 1961; *Clitennestra*, 1965

BIBLIOGRAPHY   Guido M. Gatti, *Ildebrando Pizzetti*, Dennis Dobson, 1951; Bruno Pizzetti, *Ildebrando Pizzetti, cronologica e bibiografia*, La Pilotta, 1980; reviewed and summarized in *ML*, vol. 63 (1982), pp. 141–6; Andrew Porter, 'Coventry and London: *Murder in the Cathedral*', *MT*, vol. 103 (1962), pp. 544–5

J.C.G.W.

ROBERT PLANQUETTE

Jean Robert Planquette; *b* 31 July 1848, Paris; *d* 28 January 1903, Paris

Planquette studied at the Paris Conservatoire; his earliest published music included several operatic reductions and military songs, including the march of the Sambre and Meuse regiment (1867), which became very popular. In 1877, the Folies-Dramatiques offered Planquette an operetta libretto, *Les cloches de Corneville*, turned down by Hervé because it contained too few puns; it became perhaps the most successful French operetta ever written with over 400 consecutive performances originally, and hundreds more in Paris revivals and tours, not to mention countless foreign productions. This set a style which Planquette himself exploited for *Rip Van Winkle*, composed for London (1882, after Washington Irving's novel, seen as *Rip* in 1884 in Paris), which remained quite popular until the 1930s. None of Planquette's later works rivalled the success of *Les cloches*, which enabled him to retire to his villa on the coast of Normandy.

Les cloches de Corneville

The Bells of Corneville

Opéra comique in three acts
Libretto by 'Clairville' (Louis François Nicolaie) and Charles Gabet
PREMIERES   19 April 1877, Folies-Dramatiques, Paris; UK: 23 February 1878, Folly Theatre, London (as *The Chimes of Normandy*); US: 22 October 1977, 5th Avenue Theater, New York

Set in Normandy during the reign of Louis XIV, the story concerns an abandoned castle and the search for its rightful heir. He eventually emerges in the shape of Henri, but not before the castle is wrongly given to the foundling Serpolette and Henri has met Germaine, whose life he once saved.

With its haunted castle, errant marquis, and picturesquely dressed village maidens, *Les cloches* harks back to older works such as Boieldieu's *La dame blanche*, and the music, correspondingly, has a more romantic–sentimental opéra comique feel to it, unlike the Offenbach buffooneries Paris had become used to. Among its most popular numbers are Henri's *valse-rondeau* 'J'ai fait trois fois le tour du monde' and the charming barcarolle 'Va, petite mousse'.

RECORDING Mesplé, Stutzman, Burles, Sinclair, Giraudeau, Paris Opéra Ch, Paris Opéra-Comique O, Doussard, EMI, 1974
EDITION, v.s., Editions Joubert, 1877

Other operettas: *Méfie-toi de Pharaon*, 1872; *Le serment de Mme Grégoire*, 1874; *Paille d'avoine*, 1874; *La confession de Rosette*, 1876; *Le chevalier Gaston*, 1879; *La péage*, 1879; *Les voltigeurs de la 32ème*, 1880 (rev. as *The Old Guard*, 1887); *La fiancée de Margot*, 1880; *La cantinière*, 1880; *Les cheveau-légers*, 1881; *Rip van Winkle*, 1882 (RECORDING excerpts: Pathé, 1950s); *Nell Gwynne*, 1884 (as *La Princesse Colombine*, 1886); *La crémaillère*, 1885; *Surcouf*, 1887 (as *Paul Jones*, 1889); *Le capitaine Thérèse*, 1890; *Le cocarde tricolore*, 1892; *Le talisman*, 1893; *Panurge*, 1895; *Mam'zelle Quat' Sous*, 1897; *Le paradis de Mahomet*, 1906 (completed by Louis Ganne)
BIBLIOGRAPHY F. Bruyas, *Histoire de l'opérette en France*, Vitte, 1974

R.T.

JOHANN NEPOMUK POISSL
Johann Nepomuk (Freiherr von) Poissl; *b* 15 February 1783, Haukenzell; *d* 17 August 1865, Munich

The aristocratic Poissl, after receiving a good education and a basic grounding in music, settled in Munich in his early twenties and studied composition with Danzi and Abbé Vogler. Danzi encouraged him, and in 1806 his first stage work, the singspiel *Die Opernprobe*, was staged at the Munich Court Opera, but without conspicuous success. Poissl then turned his attention to grand opera with continuous music, probably influenced by Danzi's through-composed German grand opera, *Iphigenia in Aulis* of 1807, and his next two operas, *Antigonus* (in German) and *Ottaviano in Sicilia* (in Italian), both to libretti adapted by the composer himself from Metastasio, enjoyed considerable local success. The singspiel *Aucassin und Nicolette* was coolly received but the tragic opera *Athalia* was widely acclaimed, and in the wake of this success Poissl quickly produced *Der Wettkampf zu Olympia*. These two operas established him as a major figure in the attempt to create a quality of German opera that could challenge the supremacy of foreign works on the German stage.

Poissl was an important link between the Mannheim–Munich German grand-opera tradition, which stemmed from Holzbauer, and the Romantic grand operas of Weber and Spohr. However, despite his two considerable successes, Poissl's rather outmoded approach, relying on Classical or mytho- logical texts in the manner of Gluck, proved less appealing than Weber's and Spohr's more Romantic conception of German opera. His efforts to handle Romantic themes in his last three operas, composed after the appearance of Weber's *Der Freischütz* and *Euryanthe* and Spohr's *Jessonda*, were not particularly successful.

Of his later operas, *Nittetis*, *La rappresaglia* and *Die Prinzessin von Provence* were quite well received, but the poor reception of *Der Untersberg* in 1829 probably deterred him from further efforts for more than a decade. His last opera, *Zaide*, roused little interest. When Poissl died at the age of 82, after a life intermittently troubled by financial difficulties, his works had long been relegated to obscurity.

Athalia
Grand tragic opera in three acts
Libretto by Johann Gottfried Wohlbrück, after the play *Athalie* by Jean Racine (1691)
PREMIERE 3 June 1814, Residenztheater (Cuvilliés), Munich

Athalia was performed in most of the major German theatres during the decade following its premiere. The *Münchner Theaterjournal* hailed its appearance as marking the start of 'the longed-for era of a national art, the creation of a national artistic model which we have so far lacked', while a critic said in the *Allgemeine musikalische Zeitung* that Poissl, in this work, had discovered the style of a truly national opera.

MANUSCRIPT Bayerische Staatsbibliothek, Munich

Der Wettkampf zu Olympia, oder Die Freunde
The Contest at Olympia, or The Friends
Grand opera in three acts
Libretto by the composer, after *L'Olimpiade* by Metastasio (1733)
PREMIERE 21 April 1815, Residenztheater (Cuvilliés), Munich

Like *Athalia*, *Der Wettkampf zu Olympia* was widely performed for some years after its premiere. In an introduction to the Dresden production of 1820, Weber described Poissl's style as follows: 'In addition to scrupulous attention to prosody, a rich harmonic palette and apt and varied instrumentation, Baron Poissl's music is remarkable for its fluent and clearly defined melodies, which have the virtue of being extremely singable as well as tender in character.'

MANUSCRIPT Bayerische Staatsbibliothek, Munich

Other operas: *Die Opernprobe* (singspiel), 1806; *Antigonus*, 1808; *Ottaviano in Sicilia*, 1812; *Aucassin und Nicolette*, 1813; *Dir wie mir, oder Alle betrügen*, 1816; *Nittetis*, 1817; *Issipile*, (1818); *La rappresaglia*, 1820; *Die Prinzessin von Provence*,

1825; *Der Untersberg*, 1829; *Zaide*, 1843; overture and 9 numbers in Nasolini's *Merope*, 1812; additional numbers to operas by Dittersdorf, Pilotti and Rossini
BIBLIOGRAPHY E. Reipschläger, *Schubaur, Danzi und Poissl als Opernkomponisten*, Berlin, 1911

C.A.B.

CARLO FRANCESCO POLLAROLO

b c. 1653; *d* 7 February 1723, Venice

Pollarolo was brought up in Brescia, where his father worked as an organist. His earliest musical activity was in the field of church music, and he became organist of the cathedral in Brescia in 1680. From the mid-1680s he increasingly devoted himself to the composition of operas, which were performed not only in the major centre of Venice, but also in many other cities of northern Italy, as well as in Vienna. In 1690 Pollarolo was appointed second organist at St Mark's, Venice, and two years later vicemaestro. Much of his time must however have been devoted to the stage since he wrote some 85 operas. Not only was he the leading composer for the Teatro San Giovanni Crisostomo in Venice, but he also supplied works for other houses. Curiously, the great popularity he enjoyed during his lifetime ceased almost immediately on his death.

His operas are mainly cited for the greater flexibility he brought to the orchestra: unusual combinations of instruments, with and without continuo; adoption of the orchestral aria in preference to the continuo aria; offstage use of obbligato instruments and small instrumental groups; echo effects. He seems to have been aware of developments in French stage writing under Lully: on one occasion he included a vaudeville in French, and one act of *Onorio in Roma* includes a final chaconne. Pollarolo clearly had an original mind, and was prepared to take risks for the cause of dramatic expression. His operas do not deserve the oblivion into which they have fallen.

Surviving operas: *Il Roderico*, 1686; *Onorio in Roma*, 1692; *La forza della virtù*, 1693; *Alfonso primo*, 1694; *Ottone*, 1694; *La Santa Genuinda* (coll. with Lulier and Alessandro Scarlatti), 1694; *Irene* (coll. with Alessandro Scarlatti), 1695; *Il pastore di Anfriso*, 1695; *Gl'inganni felici*, 1696 (EDITION facsimile, H. M. Brown (ed.), Garland, 1977); *Almansore in Alimena* (only arias survive), 1696; *Tito Manlio* (only arias survive), 1696; *La Rosimonda*, 1696; *La clemenza d'Augusto* (coll. with S. de Lucca and Bononcini), 1696; *Il Faramondo*, 1699; *Il repudio d'Ottavia* (only arias survive), 1699; *Il colore fa' la regina*, 1700; *Le pazzie degli amanti*, 1701; *Semiramide* (only arias survive), 1713; *Marsia deluso* (only arias survive), 1714; *Ariodante*, 1716; *Astinome* (only arias survive), 1719; *Giulio Cesare nell'Egitto*, n.d.; *c.* 63 lost operas
BIBLIOGRAPHY H. C. Wolff, *Die venezianische Oper in der zweiten Hälfte des 17 Jahrhunderts*, Berlin, 1937

G.D.

AMILCARE PONCHIELLI

b 31 August 1834, Paderno Fasolaro (now Paderno Ponchielli), nr Cremona; *d* 17 January 1886, Milan

Ponchielli, of humble origins, received his first musical instruction at home. His talents were recognized early, however, and he was admitted to the Milan Conservatory on a scholarship at the age of nine. He remained there for 11 years (the last three studying composition with Alberto Mazzucato), and graduated in 1854.

He returned to Cremona as a church organist, and for the next 18 years from there and nearby Piacenza he attempted to establish himself as an opera composer. *I promessi sposi* (1856), to a libretto the composer himself probably hacked from Manzoni's epic novel, had some local success, but failed to interest directors of important theatres. An extensive revision of this score, to a new text by Emilio Praga, premiered in Milan at the Teatro dal Verme in 1872, would prove his means of escape from the provinces. Before that lucky event, he composed three more operas, none of which produced the desired impression. The first of them was rejected after being rehearsed in Turin, the second was a turning back to the outworn semiseria genre, and the third received only one performance.

The revised *I promessi sposi* was the pivotal event in Ponchielli's career. It brought him an invitation to compose a ballet for La Scala, *Le due gemelle* (1873), which won him a contract with the publishing house of Ricordi. The prima donna of the refashioned *I promessi sposi*, Teresina Brambilla, married Ponchielli in 1874 (and her relatives harried him for the rest of his life). His reputation, improving with his next work, *I lituani* (1874), was solidified by *La gioconda* (1876). This work entered the international repertoire. His last two operas were respectfully received but have failed to find a place in repertoire.

In 1880, Ponchielli became professor of composition at the Milan Conservatory, where he taught Puccini and, briefly, Mascagni. Two years later he assumed the additional duties of maestro di cappella at Santa Maria Maggiore in Bergamo. He held both these positions until his death.

As an opera composer, Ponchielli has frequently been dismissed as crude and vulgar, but such snap judgements do not really describe his capacities. Afflicted by torturing self-doubt, he frequently arrived at his ideas by a painful process of trial and error, as the compositional sketches for La Cieca's 'Voce di donna' in Act I of *La gioconda* and the progressive transmogrifications that four of his operas underwent demonstrate. None the less, he is said to have composed 'The Dance of the Hours' (*La gioconda*, Act III) at a single sitting. He possessed a gift both for creating atmosphere, as in the prisoner's chorus of *I lituani*, and for powerful dramatic confrontations, witness the final duet for Gioconda and Barnaba. His works show considerable skill in laying out large-scale structures coherently, and many passages are impressive for their adroit orchestration. His influence on Puccini is evident in the *concertato* in *Edgar* and in des Grieux's impassioned outburst in the embarkation scene of *Manon Lescaut*, which inevitably reminds one of Gioconda's 'Suicidio!' And the intermezzo from *Il figliuol prodigo* set an example that was not lost on Mascagni and the other *veristi*. As an Italian opera composer attempting to launch himself in the mid-1850s, Ponchielli, unlike Verdi, had no firm underpinning in the flourishing tradition of the 1830s, and as a result he laboured and forged a personal idiom, which would later serve Mascagni, Puccini, and other members of the 'Young Italian School' as a point of departure.

I lituani

The Lithuanians
Dramma lirico in a prologue and three acts
Libretto by Antonio Ghislanzoni, after Adam Mickiewicz's narrative poem, *Konrad Wallenrod* (1828)
Composed 1872–4; rev. 1875 and, as *Aldona*, 1884
PREMIERES 7 March 1874, La Scala, Milan; first rev. version: 6 March 1875, La Scala, Milan; second rev. version, as *Aldona*: 20 November 1884, St Petersburg

The action takes place in the Middle Ages when Teutonic knights overran Lithuania, a subject full of resonance for those seeking liberty anywhere in the 19th century. Walter (Mickiewicz's Konrad) leaves his wife Aldona to wreak vengeance on the Teutons for the invasion of his homeland. In disguise as Corrado he becomes chief of the Teutonic knights and uses his authority to spare Lithuanian prisoners. Aldona arrives, seeking news of her husband. Eventually 'Corrado's' cover is blown; he takes poison minutes before the victorious Lithuanians burst in.

Having been taken on by the publishing house Ricordi (as a result of the success of his ballet *Le due gemelle*), Ponchielli was commissioned to set Ghislanzoni's libretto for La Scala. The bombastic libretto is no model of clarity, but Ponchielli's score is filled with grandiose scenes, characteristic choruses and dances, and vocal lines of wide-ranging cantilena which foreshadow *La gioconda*. Enthusiastic critics drew parallels between it and *Aida* (also with a libretto by Ghislanzoni and seen in Milan two years earlier), reminding readers how audiences had at first failed to find melody in Verdi's opera and implying that the greatness of *I lituani* would be seen as its equal. Yet in spite of felicities of orchestration and a certain local colour, the work lacks true coherence and has now fallen into neglect.

RECORDING Hayashi, Garaventa, Cassis, De Bortoli, Turin Ch and O of Italian Radio, Gavazzeni, MRF, 1979
EDITION v.s., Ricordi, 1876

La gioconda

The Ballad Singer (literally, *The Joyful Girl*)
Dramma lirico in four acts (2h 30m)
Libretto by 'Tobia Gorrio' (Arrigo Boito), loosely based on the play, *Angelo, tyran de Padoue* by Victor Hugo (1835)
Composed 1874–5; rev. 1876, 1877, 1880
PREMIERES 8 April 1876, La Scala, Milan; first rev. version:

18 October 1876, Teatro Rossini, Venice; second rev. version: January 1877, Rome; definitive version: 12 February 1880, La Scala, Milan; UK: 31 May 1883, Covent Garden, London; US: 20 December 1883, Metropolitan, New York
CAST La Gioconda *s*, La Cieca *contralto*, Alvise Badoero *b*, Laura *ms*, Enzo Grimaldo *t*, Barnaba *bar*, Zuane *bar*, singer *b*, Isepo *t*, pilot *b*; *satb* chorus of monks, senators, sailors, shipwrights, ladies, gentlemen, populace, masquers, guards; ballet
ORCHESTRATION picc, 2 fl, 2 ob/ca, 2 cl, 2 bsn, 4 hn, 4 tpt, 2 trbn, bombardone, timp, perc, str, 2 hp, organ; Act I finale: banda; onstage: cl, 2 hn, 2 bsn, hp, bells

Boito's libretto bears but a slight resemblance to Hugo's play. He transferred the action from Padua to Venice, as the latter afforded more opportunities for spectacle and local colour. He changed the names of the characters and reduced the role of Alvise (Hugo's Angelo) to a subordinate one. During the series of revisions, he telescoped motivation to the point of occasional obscurity, sacrificing credibility for harsh contrasts, laden with irony.

SYNOPSIS
Act I ('The Lion's Mouth') The greedy Barnaba wants to possess the street-singer Gioconda, but she rejects him. In revenge, he stirs up the crowd to believe that her blind mother, La Cieca, is a witch. They are about to drag the pious old woman away, when Enzo, a Genoese noble in exile in Venice disguised as a fisherman, attempts to save her. Alvise and his wife Laura appear, and the Venetian leader quells the riot. In gratitude, La Cieca gives a rosary to Laura ('Voce di donna'). Enzo recognizes Laura, whom he had loved before her marriage, and Gioconda is filled with passionate gratitude toward Enzo. Barnaba, however, knows Enzo's true identity and offers to arrange for him a rendezvous with Laura on Enzo's brigantine ('Enzo Grimaldo, principe di Santafior'). Alone, Barnaba concocts a letter, denouncing Enzo to the Council of Ten.

Act II ('The Rosary') Fishermen gather on the wharf and Barnaba is on hand to watch developments ('Pescator'). Enzo comes on deck to await Laura ('Cielo e mar!'). Laura is rapturously greeted ('Deh, non turbare'), but when Enzo leaves to attend to their departure, Gioconda appears and faces her rival ('L'amo come il fulgor del creato!'). Suddenly Alvise's ship is seen approaching; Laura prays to the Virgin for help and, recognizing her rosary, Gioconda determines to rescue her mother's saviour. Enzo returns to find not Laura but Gioconda, who alerts him to his danger, whereupon Enzo sets fire to his ship and they escape.

Act III ('The House of Gold') Alvise plans revenge on his unfaithful wife. He commands her to drink poison ('Morir! è troppo orribile!') but Gioconda emerges from hiding and substitutes a sleeping potion for the poison. At Alvise's mansion, the Ca d'Oro, guests are entertained by 'The Dance of the Hours'. Enzo is shocked that these festivities are going on while Laura lies 'dead' in the next room and tries to stab Alvise. Alvise orders Enzo's arrest, but Gioconda tells Barnaba she will submit to him to save Enzo.

Design by Carlo Ferrario for La gioconda *(Milan, 1876)*

Act IV ('The Orfano Canal') Gioconda contemplates suicide ('Suicidio!'). Enzo is furious when he learns she has brought Laura's body to her house. Soon Laura returns to consciousness, and Gioconda sends the lovers away to safety ('Quest' ultimo bacio'). Awaiting Barnaba, Gioconda tries to pray. He appears but, as he moves to embrace her, she stabs herself ('Ebbrezza! Delirio!'). Frustrated, Barnaba tells her corpse that he has thrown La Cieca into a canal.

La gioconda can produce a powerful effect, especially when well sung, though oddly enough its best-known moment, the ballet divertissement 'The Dance of the Hours', is a non-vocal one. There are a number of unconventional arias: La Cieca's 'Voce di donna'; the spy Barnaba's soliloquy, 'O monumento' (Act I); Enzo's tenor *romanza* 'Cielo e mar!', and Gioconda's monologue in Act IV. There are also three dramatic duets: for the rivals, Gioconda and Laura, in Act II; Alvise and Laura in Act III; and at the end between the desperate Gioconda feigning gaiety and Barnaba as he gloats at the prospect of possessing her. The chorus is treated prominently in *La gioconda*, and the *concertato* at the end of Act III develops momentum on a truly grandiose scale. A particular feature of Ponchielli's style is a *fortissimo* peroration of a prominent tune, as at the close of the *concertato* or at the end of the trio in Act IV, a practice not lost on the composers of the next generation.

La gioconda, along with *Aida*, is representative of the absorption during the 1870s of the spectacular effects of French grand opera, including the insertion of ballet into the plot, coupled with overtly emotional Italian vocalism, to produce an amalgamated 'international' style. Apart from its occasional disjointedness, both musically and dramatically, *La gioconda* exemplifies both the strengths and weaknesses of a particular aspect of Italian operatic history.

RECORDINGS 1. Milanov, Elias, Di Stefano, Warren, Clabassi, Accademia di Santa Cecilia Ch and O, Previtali, Decca, 1958: Milanov in one of her best roles, well supported; 2. Callas, Cossotto, Ferraro, Cappuccilli, Vinco, La Scala Ch and O, Votto: Callas at her most vivid and commanding; 3. Caballé, Baltsa, Pavarotti, Milnes, Ghiaurov, London Opera Ch, National PO, Bartoletti, Decca, 1980: evenly cast, modern set [A.B.]
VIDEO Martin, Semtschuk, Lilowa, Domingo, Manuguerra, Rydl, Vienna State Opera Ch and O, A. Fischer, Virgin, 1986
EDITIONS f.s., Ricordi, 1916; v.s., Ricordi, 1881; *rp*, 1980

Il figluol prodigo
The Prodigal Son
Melodramma in four acts (2h 45m)
Libretto by Angelo Zanardini
Composed 1878–80
PREMIERE   26 December 1880, La Scala, Milan

The Assyrian Amenofi and the adventuress Nefte lure Azaele away from the tent of his father Ruben and from his intended bride, Jeftele, to roister in the fleshpots of Nineveh. There Amenofi plans to trap Azaele into committing sacrilege so that he can be sacrificed to the local goddess by being cast into the river Tigris. Jeftele and Ruben come to Nineveh to find Azaele, but Jeftele succeeds only in inflaming Amenofi's desire, while the fate of his son turns Ruben mad. Azaele stumbles home to Gessen, saved from the river by Jehovah. He is about to wander into the desert to die, when he is recognized by Jeftele. The sight of the prodigal returned restores his father's reason.

Operas with exotic settings or subjects were popular in Italy in the second half of the 19th century (e.g. Verdi's *Aida*). Ponchielli had already composed music with a slavic flavour for *I lituani* and the biblical setting of *Il figluol prodigo* provided further opportunity for elements of local colour to invade the music. The dominating feature of the score, however, is its scale: it is replete with massive ensembles, varied choruses and exotic dances, as well as a number of expressive arias. The work as a whole, despite the obvious pains Ponchielli expended on it, is largely static, saddled with Zanardini's self-consciously biblical text.

EDITION   v.s., Ricordi, 1881

Other operas: *I promessi sposi*, 1856, rev. 1872; *Bertrando dal Bormio*, (1858); *La savoiarda*, 1861, rev. 1870, rev. as *Lina*, 1877; *Roderico, re dei Goti*, 1863; *Il parlatore eterno*, 1873; *I mori di Valenza*, (inc.), (1874; completed by Cadore, 1911), 1914; *Marion Delorme*, 1885
BIBLIOGRAPHY   Julian Budden, *The Operas of Verdi*, Cassell, 1981, vol. 3, pp. 281–5; J. Nicolaisen, *Italian Opera in Transition: 1871–1893*, UMI (*Studies in Musicology*, no. 31), 1980, pp. 71–122

W.A.

JÓZEF PONIATOWSKI
Józef Michał Ksawery Franciszek Jan Poniatowski; *b* 20 February 1816, Rome; *d* 3 July 1873, Chislehurst, England

A nephew of Prince Józef Poniatowski (Marshal of France) and of the last Polish king, Stanisław August, Poniatowski was a singer, conductor and composer. He studied with Ceccherini in Florence, where he conducted the local premieres of some of Beethoven's symphonies. He also sang (tenor) in opera at the Teatro Pergola in Florence, and from 1860 to 1870 was conductor of the Italian Opera in Paris. Poniatowski's musical activities were to some extent conditioned by his career as a politician. He was Tuscany's ambassador in Brussels (1849),

London (1850–53) and Paris. In France he was made a Senator of the French Empire. After 1870 he followed his friend Napoleon III into exile in England.

Poniatowski's operas are typical of early 19th-century Italian opera, in which solo arias and *cantabile* melodies predominate. They were much performed in Italy and France and his last opera, *Gelmina*, written for Adelina Patti, was premiered in London at Covent Garden. He also wrote two masses, oratorios and songs as well as chamber and piano music. His ballad 'The Yeoman's Wedding Song' was popular in England and went through many editions and arrangements.

Operas: *Giovanni da Procida*, 1838; *Don Desiderio, ossia Il disperato per eccesso di buon cuore*, 1840; *Ruy Blas*, 1843; *Bonifazio de' Geremei*, 1843, rev. as *I Lambertazzi*, 1845; *La sposa d'Abido*, 1845; *Malek-Adel*, 1846; *Esmeralda*, 1847; *Pierre de Médicis*, 1860; *Au travers du mur*, 1861; *L'aventurier*, 1865; *La Contessina*, 1868; *Gelmina*, 1872

Z.C.

NICOLA PORPORA
Nicola Antonio Porpora; *b* 17 August 1686, Naples; *d* 3 March 1768, Naples

Porpora was one of the foremost Neapolitan composers of the first half of the 18th century. He spent ten years as a pupil at the Neapolitan Conservatorio dei Poveri di Gesù Cristo (between 1696 and 1706) and then another 12 establishing his name as an opera composer in Italy and Austria. His operas were most in demand during the period 1718–42. One of the chief reasons he wrote few operas thereafter was that contemporary audiences started to consider his music old-fashioned and lost interest in it.

During his lifetime Porpora was as well known for his teaching as for his compositions. Among his private singing pupils were the castratos Farinelli (who made his début in a performance of Porpora's cantata *Angelica* in 1720) and Caffarelli. Porpora taught composition and singing at music schools in both Naples and Venice. His school duties, however, sometimes came into conflict with his desire to write operas and other music, which explains why he changed jobs frequently. In 1747 he accepted the invitation of the Princess Maria Antonia to become her singing instructor at the Saxon court in Dresden. The pension he acquired on retiring from this post in 1752 allowed him to settle in Vienna. Here he came into contact with, among others, the young Joseph Haydn, who acted as his valet, pupil and keyboard accompanist. Haydn later acknowledged the debt he owed to Porpora's composition lessons. Porpora lost his pension around 1759 as a result of the Seven Years War and returned to Naples to eke out his last years in rather straitened circumstances.

The musical structures of Porpora's operas follow the normal early 18th-century conventions: apart from a very few accompanied recitatives, short songs and ensembles, each score consists of a series of simple recitatives and *da capo* arias. The overriding sense of uniformity created by these recurrent structures is not compensated for, on paper at least, by Porpora's too common liking for a particular style characterized by a florid top line and simple repetitive rhythms underneath. We should bear in mind however that the composer wrote as he did knowing that his skilled singers would enhance the musical expression by adding improvised embellishments to their parts.

Exceptional in Porpora's output are the operas he wrote during his stay in London between 1733 and 1736. In 1733 a group of English noblemen hired him to become chief composer of a new Italian company they were forming to compete with Handel's company in London. Because his task was to outclass Handel (who had an uncommon flair for making opera theatrically effective) and beat him at his own game, Porpora tried to enliven his London operas by composing them more in the Handelian manner and by introducing into them a greater variety of musical forms and styles than he had been accustomed to. His efforts, however, were not good enough to prove him the superior composer. He left England in 1736 having made up his mind that the competition was not working to his long-term advantage. None the less his London operas contain some good music and some effective dramatic moments. If the question ever arises of a revival of any of his works, these are the first that should be considered.

Operas: *Agrippina*, 1708; *Flavio Anicio Olibrio*, 1711; *Basilio re d'oriente*, 1713; *Arianna e Teseo*, 1714; *Berenice, regina d'Egitto* (coll. D. Scarlatti), 1718; *Temistocle*, 1718; *Faramondo*, 1719; *Eumene*, 1721; *Adelaide*, 1723; *Amare per regnare*, 1723; *Damiro e Pitia*, 1724; *Semiramide, regina dell'Assiria*, 1724; *Didone abbandonata*, 1725; *Siface*, 1725; *La verità nell'inganno*, 1726; *Meride e Selinunte*, 1726; *Imeneo in Atene*, 1726; *Siroe, re di Persia*, 1727; *Arianna e Teseo* (2nd version), 1727; *Ez io*, 1728; *Semiramide riconosciuta*, 1729; *Mitridate*, 1730; *Tamerlano*, 1730; *Poro*, 1731; *Annibale*, 1731; *Germanico in Germania*, 1732; *Issipile*, 1733; *Arianna in Nasso*, 1733; *Enea nel Laz io*, 1734; *Polifemo*, 1735; *Ifigenia in Aulide*, 1735; *Mitridate*, 1736; *Lucio Papirio*, 1737; *Rosbale*, 1737; *Carlo il calvo*, 1738; *Il barone di Zampano*, 1739; *L'amico fedele*, 1739; Intermezzo for the marriage of the Infante D. Filippo, 1739; *Il trionfo di Camilla*, 1740, rev. 1760; *Tiridate*, 1740; *Statira*, 1742; *La Rosmene*, 1742; *Temistocle*, 1743; *Le nozze d'Ercole e d'Ebe*, 1744; *Filandro*, 1747
BIBLIOGRAPHY Michael F. Robinson, 'Porpora's Operas for London, 1733–1736', *Soundings*, vol. 2 (1971–2), pp. 57ff.; Frank Walker, 'A Chronology of the Life and Works of Nicola Porpora', *Italian Studies*, vol. 6 (1951); pp. 29ff.

M.F.R.

GIUSEPPE PORSILE

Giuseppe Porsile [Porcile, Porsille]; *b* 5 May 1680, Naples; *d* 29 May 1750, Vienna

The son of a musician, Porsile was trained at the Conservatorio dei Poveri di Gesù Cristo in Naples.

He spent several years in Barcelona at the court of Charles III before moving with the royal family (after Charles became Holy Roman Emperor) to Vienna in 1713. He remained there for the rest of his life, playing a central role in the musical life of the Habsburg court, which employed poets such as Zeno and Metastasio, musicians such as Antonio Draghi, Giovanni Bononcini and Fux, as well as Galli Bibiena, the most highly regarded theatre designer of his time.

Porsile wrote 21 stage works for the imperial court. Among the most popular of his opere serie was *Spartaco*, which, if a little old-fashioned by contemporary Italian standards, suited Vienna's rather conservative taste. Porsile clung to the long phrases and fast-moving bass accompaniments espoused by his predecessors Fux and Caldara, and his writing also shows a predilection for fugal and imitative passages. In combination with the more natural melodic style inherited from his Neapolitan training, these elements – and the use of the French overture, introduced to satisfy Viennese taste – Porsile evolved a dramatic style that served his patrons well.

Operas: *Il ritorno di Ulisse alla patria*, 1707; *Il giorno nataliz io dell'imperatrice Amalia Wilhelmina*, 1717; *La virtù festeggiata*, 1717; *Alceste*, 1718; *Meride e Selinunte*, 1721; *Spartaco*, 1726 (EDITION facsimile, Garland, 1979); *Telesilla*, 1729; *Sesostri, re d'Egitto, ovvero Le feste d'Iside*, 1737; *Psiche*, n.d.
BIBLIOGRAPHY Otto Ernst Deutsch, 'Das Repertoire der höfischen Oper, der Hof- und der Staatsoper', *Österreichische Musikzeitung*, vol. 24 (1969), pp. 369–421; Michael F. Robinson, *Naples and Neapolitan Opera*, OUP, 1972

D.S.B.

COLE PORTER

Cole Albert Porter; *b* 9 June 1891, Peru, Indiana, US; *d* 15 October 1964, Santa Monica, California, US

Unlike most of the Broadway song-writers of his time, Cole Porter was born into affluence and avoided the Tin-Pan-Alley, rehearsal-accompanist, and amateur-show routes to theatre composition. His interest in music, though it diverted him from the law career his family had planned for him, did not bring him to Broadway on a regular basis until he agreed to write the score for *Paris* in 1928. Thereafter he became a regular contributor to the Broadway scene.

His earlier work tended to feature Parisian locales and naughty lyrics that sometimes provoked trouble with radio censors. His subsequent efforts from the 1930s, with the exception of *Anything Goes*, are never revived, due to libretti deemed hopelessly dated; as with Gershwin and Rodgers and Hart, such a harsh verdict may be undeserved in certain cases. In particular, *Jubilee*, with a libretto by Moss Hart and a workable comic premiss of a royal family taking time off from its duties, might merit investigation; its score would be no problem, boasting as it does 'Why Shouldn't I?', 'A Picture of Me without You', 'Begin the Beguine', and 'Just One of Those Things'. Other shows from this period with well-remembered Porter songs include *Gay Divorce* ('Night and Day'), *Red, Hot and Blue!* ('Ridin' High', 'It's De-Lovely'), *Leave It to Me* ('My Heart Belongs to Daddy', sung and stripteased by Mary Martin in her Broadway début), and *DuBarry Was a Lady* ('Friendship').

Porter's string of successes, only temporarily interrupted in 1937 when a riding accident permanently damaged his legs and left him in pain for the rest of his life, reached a climax with the classic *Kiss Me, Kate*. Though too often stereotyped as a purveyor of either throbbing ballads with a Latin beat or ultra-chic 'list' songs, Porter commanded a wide stylistic range, and adapted himself to changing tastes over the years. His music is especially notable for its balance between passion and a chaste coolness, while his lyrics are acknowledged as gems of wit and romance.

Anything Goes

Musical comedy in two acts (1h 45m)
Libretto by Guy Bolton and P. G. Wodehouse, revised by
Howard Lindsay and Russell Crouse; lyrics by the composer
PREMIERES 21 November 1934, Alvin Theater, New York;
UK: 14 June 1935, Palace Theatre, London

Taking place mostly on board an ocean liner, this farce of flirtation and disguise (originally starring Ethel Merman) remains one of the more revived 1930s musicals because of its wonderful score: 'I Get a Kick out of You', 'All through the Night', 'You're the Top', 'Blow, Gabriel, Blow', and the title song. The New York revivals of 1962 and 1987 (the latter especially well executed) have been recorded; each involved libretto changes, deletion of songs, and interpolation of other Porter songs.

RECORDING Criswell, Von Stade, Groenendaal, McGlinn, EMI, 1988: the original version, to the extent that it can be reconstructed
FILMS 1. Merman, Crosby, Bradley, Ruggles, Milestone (dir.), Paramount, 1936; 2. Crosby, O'Connor, Jeanmaire, Gaynor, Lewis (dir.), Paramount, 1956
EDITION v.s., Harms, 1936

Kiss Me, Kate

Musical play in two acts (1h 45m)
Libretto by Sam and Bella Spewack, based on the play *The Taming of the Shrew* by William Shakespeare (1593–4); lyrics by the composer
PREMIERES 30 December 1948, New Century Theater, New York; UK: 8 March 1951, Coliseum, London
CAST Fred Graham (Petruchio) *bar*, Lilli Vanessi (Kate) *s*, Lois Lane (Bianca) *ms*, Bill Calhoun (Lucentio) *t/dancer*, 2 men *bar*, Hattie *a*, Paul *bar*; other roles from *satb* chorus of actors
ORCHESTRATION (Robert Russell Bennett) theatre orchestra, including double ww, gtr/mandoline

The combination of a musicalized *Taming of the Shrew* with the troupe enacting it provided Porter

with the context for his richest and most consistently inspired score. It is the only one that has maintained a constant performance history, and was the proof that Porter could provide an integrated score in the new Rodgers and Hammerstein mould. 'Another Op'nin', Another Show', 'Wunderbar', 'So in Love', and 'Brush Up Your Shakespeare' are especially well known, but nearly every song is familiar to lovers of musicals.

Cole Porter with Kathleen Grayson (Kate) and Ann Miller (Bianca) on the film set of Kiss Me, Kate *(1953)*

SYNOPSIS

Act I The action takes place in and around a theatre. Actor–manager Fred Graham's floral gift to *ingénue* Lois is delivered by mistake to his leading lady (and ex-wife) Lilli Vanessi, to her pleasure and his embarrassment. Meanwhile Lois's boyfriend Bill has signed Fred's name to a gambling debt to avoid his creditors; Fred cannot understand the threats of the two men who show up to collect the money. The performance of *The Taming of the Shrew* is complicated by the presence of the men (in costume) to prevent Fred's escape, and by Lilli's discovery that the flowers were not meant for her. Fred keeps her from walking out by persuading the men that her departure will close the show, leaving him unable to repay 'his' debt.

Act II The intrigue proceeds offstage and on, with the men finally giving up when they hear that their boss has been bumped off and they now report to a new boss. Lilli is now free to leave the theatre and does so. Fred/Petruchio puts on a brave front onstage, but is sure he has lost Lilli/Kate – until she returns to him at the last moment.

RECORDINGS 1. Morison, Kirk, Drake, Lang, Davenport, CBS, 1949; 2. Barstow, Criswell, Hampson, Dvorsky, Ambrosian Ch, London Sinfonietta, McGlinn, EMI, 1989: the only recording of the complete score
FILM Keel, Grayson, Miller, Rall, Van, Fosse, Sidney (dir.), MGM, 1953
EDITION v.s., Chappell, 1951

Can-Can

Musical in two acts (film: 2h 15m)
Libretto by Abe Burrows; lyrics by the composer
PREMIERES 7 May 1953, Shubert Theater, New York; UK:
14 October 1954, Coliseum, London

A lightweight story about the supposed origin of the scandalous titular dance allowed Porter once again to exploit the Parisian flavour that had permeated much of his early work. *Can-Can*'s fertile score ('I Love Paris', 'C'est Magnifique', 'It's All Right with Me'), Porter's most consistent from the time following *Kiss Me, Kate*, earns its occasional revival.

RECORDING Lilo, Cookson, Conried, Verdon, Rosenstock, Capitol, 1953
FILM Sinatra, MacLaine, Chevalier, Jourdan, Prowse, Lang (dir.), Suffolk-Cummings/Fox, 1960
EDITION v.s., Chappell, 1954

Other musicals: *See America First*, 1916; *Kitchy-Koo*, 1919; *Paris*, 1928; *Wake Up and Dream*, 1929; *Fifty Million Frenchmen*, 1929; *The New Yorkers*, 1930; *Gay Divorce*, 1932; *Nymph Errant*, 1933; *Jubilee*, 1935; *Red, Hot and Blue!*, 1936; *You Never Know* (coll.), 1938; *Leave It to Me*, 1938; *DuBarry Was a Lady*, 1939; *Panama Hattie*, 1940; *Let's Face It*, 1941; *Something for the Boys*, 1943; *Mexican Hayride*, 1944; *Around the World in Eighty Days*, 1946; *Out of This World*, 1950; *Silk Stockings*, 1955
BIBLIOGRAPHY Stanley Green, *Ring Bells! Sing Songs! Broadway Musicals of the 1930s*, Arlington House, 1971; Tommy Krasker and Robert Kimball, *Catalog of the American Musical: Musicals of Irving Berlin, George and Ira Gershwin, Cole Porter, Richard Rodgers and Lorenz Hart*, National Institute for Opera and Musical Theater, 1988; Charles Schwartz, *Cole Porter: A Biography*, Dial Press, 1977

J.A.C.

MARCOS PORTUGAL

Marcos António da Fonseca Portugal [Portogallo]; *b* 24 March 1762, Lisbon; *d* 7 February 1830, Rio de Janeiro, Brazil

Portugal studied with João de Sousa Carvalho at the Seminário da Patriarcal in Lisbon, where all the main Portuguese composers of the late 18th century were trained. In 1785 he became music director of the Teatro do Salitre, where several Portuguese farces and burlettas with music by him were performed.
In 1792, under royal patronage, he went to Naples to complete his studies but soon became active as an opera composer, obtaining instant success in Florence with *La confusione della somiglianza* (1793); it was performed during the next few years at Dresden, Milan, Vienna, Berlin, Hamburg and London. Over 20 operas followed, produced with great success in the major Italian theatres during the next seven years. In 1799 he wrote an opera on the theme of Figaro's marriage, *La pazza giornata*.
Portugal returned to Lisbon in 1800 and was appointed mestre de capela of the royal chapel and director of the Teatro de S. Carlos. During this period he wrote or revised twelve opere serie and composed one opera buffa, *L'oro non compra amore*

(1804). His opere buffe won him greatest popularity in Italy and elsewhere, the spread of the opere serie being due mainly to performances by Angelica Catalani, the prima donna at the S. Carlos, in France, England and Ireland.
Although the French invasion in 1807 forced the court to transfer to Rio de Janeiro, Portugal remained in Lisbon until 1811 when he joined the court in Rio. Here he was immediately reappointed mestre of the royal chapel, and director of the new Teatro de São João which opened in 1813. In 1811 he suffered an apoplectic fit and in 1817 another; he remained in Rio when the court returned to Lisbon in 1821.
Although Marcos Portugal wrote much church music, his fame rests on his comic works, as well as on the virtuoso arias he wrote for Madame Catalani. Stylistically his music relates to the late 18th-century Neapolitan tradition of Cimarosa. For Brazil's independence he composed the *Hino da independência* (1822).

Surviving operas: *La confusione della somiglianza, o siano I due gobbi*, 1793; *Il Cinna*, 1793; *Lo spazzacamino principe*, 1794; *Rinaldo d'Aste*, 1794; *Demofoonte*, 1794; *La vedova raggiratrice, o siano I due sciocchi delusi*, 1794; *L'inganno poco dura*, 1796; *Zulima*, 1796; *La donna di genio volubile*, 1796; *Il ritorno di Serse*, 1797, rev. as *L'Argenide*, 1804; *Le donne cambiate*, 1797; *Fernando nel Messico*, 1798; *La maschera fortunata*, 1798; *Alceste*, 1798; *Non irritar le donne, ossia Il chiamantesi filosofo*, 1798; *La pazza giornata, ovvero Il matrimonio di Figaro*, 1799; *Idante, ovvero I sacrifici d'Eccate*, 1800; *La morte di Semiramide*, 1802; *La Zaira*, 1802; *L'oro non compra amore*, 1804; *La Merope*, 1804; *Il duca di Foix*, 1805; *La morte di Mitridate*, 1806; at least 15 lost operas; 10 lost Portuguese comic operas
BIBLIOGRAPHY E. Vieira, *Diccionario biographico de musicos portugeses*, Lisbon, 1900, vol. 2, pp. 191–230

M.C.B.

FRANCIS POULENC

Francis Jean Marcel Poulenc; *b* 7 January 1899, Paris; *d* 30 January 1963, Paris

Poulenc came to opera comparatively late in his composing career; late, that is, for one who started so early. Various historical accidents pushed the young Poulenc into the musical vanguard. His family was rich and well connected and he soon met all the fashionable composers and artists, who discovered that Poulenc's slender gifts – an infallible ear for melody, an ironic sense of humour – were just what was required by Jean Cocteau, Erik Satie and a whole band of anti-Establishment propagandists. Even his compositional shortcomings, a complete ignorance of structure, orchestration or musical orthography, seemed to suit the post-war fashion for *naïveté* and primitivism.
Fashion was Poulenc's making, and his undoing. It led him to Diaghilev and the Ballets Russes, to worldwide success for his earliest piano pieces and songs. But occasionally it led him to complicate and

over-embellish his natural style, which was at its most authentic when at its simplest. By the early 1930s Poulenc the *enfant terrible* was beginning to look a little long in the tooth. His muse faltered and then deserted him completely. The missing ingredient – his rediscovery of his Catholic faith (1935) – unlocked his soul, his psyche and his music. He also rediscovered, via the baritone Pierre Bernac, his love of song, and via Paul Eluard – the most spiritual of the Surrealist poets – a new sensual and lyrical strain.

This can be further heard in the music of the war years. The brittle influence of Stravinsky gives way to that of Ravel and Chabrier: warmer, more French. *Les mamelles de Tirésias* (1944), for all its high jinks, is shot through with this new nostalgia. The final ingredient in the making of an opera composer is to be found in Poulenc's post-war compositions, which can best be described as an acknowledgement of human frailty in music. Poulenc suffered much from depression and hopelessly doomed love affairs (often with younger men). His last two operas, *Les dialogues des Carmélites* and *La voix humaine*, have the courage to depict the blacker moments of human life in terrifying detail. Poulenc ended his career completely out of step with fashion – shamelessly tonal, unembarrassed about emotion, pain, even sentimentality. He had come a long way from the cynical stylist of the early 1920s.

Les mamelles de Tirésias

The Breasts of Tiresias
Opera bouffe in a prologue and two acts (1h)
Libretto prepared by the composer, from the play by Guillaume Apollinaire (1903, rev. 1917)
Composed 1944
PREMIERES 3 June 1947, Opéra-Comique, Paris; US: 13 June 1953, Brandeis University, Massachusetts; UK: 16 June 1958, Jubilee Hall, Aldeburgh
CAST Theatre Director *bar*, Thérèse *s*, the Husband *high bar* (later rev. for *t*), the Policeman *bar*, Presto *bar*, Lacouf *t*, Journalist *t*, the Son *b*, newspaper vendor *ms*, members of the audience 2 *ms*, *b*; *satb* chorus of the people of Zanzibar

The word 'Surrealist' was coined by Apollinaire in his introduction to the revisions to his play in 1917. The drama's high-spirited topsy-turvydom seems to define the term, but in reality it conceals a deeper and sadder theme – the need to repopulate and rediscover a France ravaged by war. This message, however absurdly stated, must have been at the forefront of Poulenc's mind in 1940, soon after the fall of France, when he began his sketches for the libretto and the prosody of *Les mamelles* – one of many specifically and quintessentially French works written during the dark days of the Occupation.

SYNOPSIS

Prologue Over a long pedal point the Theatre Director appears before the curtain, exhorting the audience to 'make children'. He disappears and the curtain rises on the town/city of Zanzibar.

Act I Thérèse is bored with being a woman and decides to change sex; her breasts (two balloons) float away to the sound of a *valse chantée*. Her

husband arrives, assumes she has been abducted, and assumes her clothing.

Act II The husband has become a paterfamilias on a grand scale – he has given birth, single-handed, to over 40,000 children in one day. We can hear them yowling in the orchestra pit. He has to find them ration cards which are supplied by the Cartomancer, Thérèse – alias Tirésias – in disguise. They are reunited. Around this touching domestic tale mad people pop up and do mad things – always with the conviction that what they are saying and doing makes some semblance of sense. It doesn't.

Design by Erté for the title page of the vocal score of Les mamelles de Tirésias *(Paris, 1947)*

To set this irresistible nonsense Poulenc deploys the most familiar, almost mundane, of forms – the French operetta from opéra comique to café-concert. Thus the music veers from the giddy prestos and polkas of Offenbach and Lecocq to the sentimental waltzes of Messager, even Maurice Chevalier. The harmonies are freely borrowed from Ravel and Stravinsky, the melodies from Chabrier. In other words, it is typical Poulenc. He considered it to be one of his most 'authentic' works and added much private feeling to it. For example, the setting was, in Poulenc's mind at least, relocated to Monte Carlo in the 1920s, the scene of his earliest triumphs. But the predicament of fallen France is sensible throughout. Whenever Paris is mentioned the music swoons and weeps for a moment before the madness starts up again.

RECORDING Duval, Giraudeau, Jeantet, Thirache, O of Opéra-Comique, Cluytens, EMI, 1953
EDITION v.s., Heugel, 1947

Les dialogues des Carmélites

Dialogues of the Carmelites

Opera in three acts (12 scenes) (2h 45m)
Libretto prepared by the composer, from the drama by
Georges Bernanos (1948)
Composed 1953
PREMIERES 26 January 1957, La Scala, Milan; US: 14 July
1957, San Francisco; UK: 16 January 1958, Covent Garden,
London
CAST The Marquis de la Force *bar*, Blanche *lyric s*, The
Chevalier de la Force *t*, Madame de Croissy *a*, Madame
Lidoine *s*, Mother Marie of the Incarnation *ms*, Sister
Constance *light s*, Mother Jeanne *a*, Sister Mathilde *ms*,
Mother Gerald/Sister Claire/Sister Antoine and 5 others
choristers, Father Confessor *t*, First Officer *t*, Second Officer
bar, Gaoler *bar*, Thierry *bar*; M. Javelinot *bar*; *satb* chorus of
nuns, officials of the municipality, officers, police, prisoners,
guards, townspeople
ORCHESTRATION 2 fl, ob, 3 cl, 4 bsn, 4 hn, 3 tpt, 3 trbn,
tuba, timp, perc, pf, 2 hp, str

Les dialogues des Carmélites has a provenance
complicated even by operatic standards. The tale of
the martyrdom of the sisters of Compiègne was first
told by one of their number, Mother Marie, who
survived the French Revolutionary Terror and
published her memoirs. The subsequent canonization
of the nuns inspired a young German Catholic,
Gertrude von le Fort, to tell their story in a novel,
Die letzte am Schafott (1931), which describes, with
grim prescience, the fate of religion under
totalitarianism. Le Fort gave life, and indeed her own
name, to the heroine Blanche de la Force. There
followed various attempts to turn the book into a
play, then a film, to which end it arrived in the hands
of Georges Bernanos, who was living, or more
precisely dying, in South America. He invented
further characters and added further personal details,
even giving the dying Prioress his own age, 59, 'a
good age to die'.

By a bizarre coincidence Poulenc's lover at the
time was dying as the composer was writing the
music for the same Prioress. Indeed, as Poulenc
noted in a letter, he breathed his last just as the work
was finished. The opera had been commissioned by
Ricordi for La Scala, Milan, but the length of time
between conception and birth indicates the
complications both legal, financial (the rights were a
nightmare as one can see on the title page of the
score), and indeed emotional, that the opera brought
with it. All this took its toll on Poulenc's health and
happiness, both of which, as we can see and hear in
the opera, were fragile at the best of times. It is an
opera about terror. Personal terror played against
state terror. It opens as it means to go on, in fear.

SYNOPSIS

Act I Blanche's father and brother, the Marquis
and Chevalier de la Force – French aristocrats – are
frightened that Blanche might be frightened. She is
not home yet and the streets are unsettled. She is
indeed frightened when she arrives, but maintains a
great, albeit spurious, calm as she announces her
intention to join the Carmelite order. We then meet
the ageing Prioress who explains to Blanche that the

Order can protect nobody. She is touched by
Blanche's devotion, however, and gives her her
blessing. Blanche joins the convent where she meets
Constance, a happy-go-lucky peasant girl who voices
one of the opera's themes, that, when we die,
perhaps we die in someone else's stead, perhaps we
die their deaths. Certainly the Prioress is dying a
death which she does not deserve: slow, agonizing,
undignified and depicted in unflinching detail in both
music and words. Mother Marie is in attendance,
loyal and solid, keen to avoid involuntary blasphemy.
Blanche arrives to watch her new spiritual mother
die in torment.

Act II Blanche's solitary fears begin to be
matched by real dangers from the outside world. The
first scene opens with the first of the sung prayers
that punctuate this act. It is a Requiem for the
Prioress. Blanche, left alone with the body, panics;
she is calmed by Mother Marie, ever watchful. The
new Prioress arrives and preaches to the nuns.
Blanche's brother is admitted and, in a scene that
could almost be described as a love duet, attempts to
take Blanche away to safety. The finale is of Verdian
proportions. The sisters are led in prayer, then the
Prioress warns them against the temptation of
martyrdom. The noise of the Terror grows; officers
arrive and the mob threatens to attack the convent.
In the uproar Blanche drops the statue of the infant
Jesus.

Act III The convent is desecrated, the Order
declared illegal. Blanche runs away to her late
father's house, where she lives disguised as a servant.
She hears that the Carmelites have been arrested.
They have been imprisoned in the *conciergerie* where
we see the new Prioress inspiring her sisters with
strength and courage to face the ordeal ahead. This
is depicted with extraordinary realism in the great
final scene consisting of one long prayer, the Salve
Regina, sung by the nuns as they go, one by one, to
their death by guillotine. The crowd looks on amazed
as Blanche steps forward, transfigured and joyful, to
join her sisters in martyrdom.

'You must forgive my Carmelites,' wrote Poulenc.
'They can sing only tonal music.' And, indeed,
compared to most operas written in the 1950s
Poulenc's is astonishingly old-fashioned. His models,
indeed the work's dedicatees, were Verdi, Monteverdi, Debussy and Musorgsky. The structure,
the alternation of recitative and arioso, is Verdian;
the recitative itself owes a huge amount to Monteverdi's *Poppea* and to Debussy's *Pelléas*. From
Musorgsky Poulenc learned the sense of menace and
nightmare that suffuses the whole work.

The tessituras are meticulously planned, and
borrowed from grand opera. Poulenc's models were
Verdi's Amneris (Mother Marie) and Desdemona
(new Prioress), Wagner's Kundry (Prioress),
Massenet's Thaïs (Blanche) and Mozart's Zerlina
(Constance). Each of these characters has leitmotifs
that stand not only for them but also for the
emotions they embody, even in other characters.
Thus Mother Marie's music (strong, in C major)
indicates loyalty and steadfastness not only in Marie

Poulenc with two of the Carmelites during rehearsals for the UK premiere of his opera at Covent Garden (1958)

but also in Blanche. This is an apt device in an opera in which the sharing of suffering and the universality of grace loom so large. Underpinning everything are two sorts of music: first the prayers, the pulse and counterpoint of Renaissance religious music, which in a cloistered life is at once miraculous and mundane; then the music of fear (typified by a rising minor third which we hear throughout), which always threatens to destroy the age-old structures of the religious world. The Terror versus the Order. It is in the extraordinary final scene that the two are combined; the nuns sing over repeated minor thirds, drowning the mob, conquering fear, moving into posterity.

RECORDINGS 1. Duval, Crespin, Berton, Gorr, Scharley, Ch and O of Opéra de Paris, Dervaux, EMI, 1958; 2. Dubosc, Yakar, Fournier, Dupuy, Van Dam, Gorr, Sénéchal, Lyons Opera Ch and O, Nagano, Virgin, 1992: the 1958 set enshrines the premiere cast and remains a classic, but the 1992 version is as well sung and conducted; it is also an uncut version [A.B.]
EDITION v.s., Ricordi, 1957

La voix humaine
The Human Voice
Tragédie lyrique in one act (40m)
Text by Jean Cocteau, after his play (1928)
Composed 1958
PREMIERES 6 February 1959, Opéra-Comique, Paris; US: 23 February 1959, Carnegie Hall, New York; UK: 30 August 1960, King's Theatre, Edinburgh
CAST 'Elle' s

The joke at the time was that Poulenc was writing a solo opera for Maria Callas – then notorious for her reluctance to share the stage with anybody. In fact the piece was devised as a showcase for Denise Duval, the leading lady of all of Poulenc's operas and his preferred mouthpiece when trying to describe and depict the nature of fear, depression, nervous exhaustion, which he himself knew so well.

SYNOPSIS
The heroine spends the whole opera on the telephone talking mostly to her lover, but also to various crossed lines and wrong numbers. It becomes evident that her relationship has also been, as it were, 'cut off' – she can no longer get through to him. As she talks, variously, love, lies and self-pitying nonsense, it becomes quite clear that he no longer cares – indeed is probably not even at his home – and she is at the end of her tether, certainly suicidal. In the end she wraps the telephone cord round her neck and takes the receiver to bed with her, murmuring 'Je t'aime' to an unhearing earpiece.

Poulenc's opera is scored for a large sensual orchestra which is then used with extraordinary economy. There is almost more silence than 'music' as the heroine chatters away, listens, responds, chatters again. The overall mood is one of blind panic, punctuated by febrile moments of calm. The only melody is a nostalgic theme, cloying and sickly – purely sentimental and therefore doubly desperate.

This neurotic atmosphere is drawn from life: Poulenc himself was no stranger to obsession and rejection. Indeed *La voix humaine* was written at a time of enforced separation from his then lover, Lucien. The composer described it as 'a sort of musical confession' – 'the protagonist is more or less myself'.

RECORDING Duval, O of Opéra-Comique, Prêtre, EMI, 1958: the definitive recording by the original 'Elle'
VIDEO Farey, Sultin CO, Serebriev, Decca, 1992
EDITION v.s., Ricordi, 1958

BIBLIOGRAPHY Sidney Buckland (trans. and ed.), *Francis Poulenc, 'Echo and Source', Selected Correspondence 1915–1963*, Gollancz, 1991; Keith W. Daniel, *Francis Poulenc, His Artistic Development and Musical Style*, UMI Research Press, 1982; Henri Hell, trans. and with an introduction by Edward Lockspeiser, *Francis Poulenc*, Grove Press, 1959; George R. Keck (comp.), *Francis Poulenc, A Bio-Bibliography*, Greenwood Press, 1990

J.C.S.

EZRA POUND
Ezra Loomis Pound; *b* 30 October 1885, Hailey, Idaho, US; *d* 1 November 1972, Venice

The poet Ezra Pound occupies an eccentric corner of operatic history. Although one of Pound's biographers asserted that he had no ear for music, the subject held continuous fascination for him and he began work on several operas. Like Bernard Shaw, he also worked as a music critic and promoted concerts. Pound was particularly interested in the music of the medieval troubadours of Provence, and was encouraged by his friend Arnold Dolmetsch (the pioneering performer of early music).

With his first opera, *The Testament of François Villon*, Pound acknowledged the help of George Antheil, the American composer he had championed in his unorthodox *Treatise on Harmony*. In the opera, the near-monodic style and overall restraint of the amateur composer strangely anticipate the gestures of the later minimalists, but also relate to a distant past. Two songs from the opera were performed in a Paris concert in 1924 and a fuller (though still incomplete) version in 1926 at the Salle Pleyel. The complete *Villon* has been broadcast by the BBC (1931), performed as a ballet at the Spoleto Festival (1965) and staged by Western Opera Theater in Berkeley, California (1971).

Operas: *The Testament of François Villon*, 1931 (RECORDING Fantasy, 1972); *Cavalcanti*, (1932), 1983
BIBLIOGRAPHY R. Murray Schafer (ed.), *Ezra Pound and Music: The Complete Criticism*, Faber, 1978

P.D.

HENRI POUSSEUR

Henri Léon Marie Thérèse Pousseur; *b* 23 June 1929, Malmédy, Belgium

Pousseur was one of the central members of the 1950s avant-garde associated with the Darmstadt summer school, and there are parallels in Boulez and Berio in his movement from a deep attachment to Webern, through a quick response to the possibilities of mobile form, to, in the 1960s, an inquisitive search for ways to embrace tonal harmonies and style references within a serially ordered world. All these concerns are alive in his opera, which characteristically has given rise to a number of dependent works and commentaries: *Miroir de Votre Faust* for piano, *Jeu de miroirs de Votre Faust* on tape, etc. Other later works in his multiform output include partly improvisatory, partly theatrical pieces, but no more operas.

Votre Faust

Fantaisie variable genre opéra, in two parts
Libretto by Michel Butor, after numerous Faust sources
Composed 1960–67, rev. ?1981
PREMIERES 15 January 1969, Piccola Scala, Milan; rev. version: 1981, Gelsenkirchen
CAST main roles taken by 5 actors; also participating are 4 singers (*s, a, t, b,*), tape-recordings, the audience
INSTRUMENTATION fl/picc, E♭ cl/B♭ cl, a sax, bsn, hn, tpt, pf, hp, perc, vn, vc, db: all also playing perc

In the first part Henri, a young composer, is commissioned to write a Faust opera: the theatre director offers him all the time, money and resources he needs. But Maggy, a waitress, tries to rescue him from this diabolical opportunity, and during the interval the audience has to decide whether he follows the impresario or the waitress. There are also, particularly in the second part, other variabilities in the score. For instance, the central portion of the second part is a puppet play which can be performed in any of four national versions (with different backgrounds): French (Gluck's *Orphée*), German (the evolution of tonal music during the

19th century), Italian (*Don Giovanni*) and English (church music). The dramatic atmosphere is appropriately that of a fairground, with the musicians stationed at rostra on the stage, the narrative fluid and circuitous, the text obsessive with repetitions and lists.

RECORDING *Jeu de miroirs de Votre Faust*: Retchitzka, Berberian, Bastin, Mercenier (pf), Wergo, 1970
EDITION f.s., Universal (on hire)

BIBLIOGRAPHY Henri Pousseur, *Fragments théoriques I sur la musique expérimentale*, Institute de Sociologie de l'Université Libre de Bruxelles, 1970

P.G.

PETER PRELLEUR

baptized 16 December 1705, London; *buried* 27 June 1741, London

A writing master, keyboard-player and composer from an immigrant Huguenot family, Prelleur is best known today for his educational publications, particularly *The Modern Musick-master, or The Universal Musician* (1731), a popular compendium containing instruction in singing and playing various instruments. Prelleur also wrote a good deal of music for London's parish churches and the theatre, his two spheres of employment. He was organist of St Alban's, Wood Street, from around 1728 to 1736, when he moved to Christ Church, Spitalfields. From around 1728 he also worked at the Goodman's Fields Theatre (after 1737 at the New Wells Theatre), writing songs for plays, ballad operas and pantomimes as well as orchestral music. Prelleur was an accomplished exponent of an attractive, light-weight idiom.

All-sung masques with pantomime interludes: *Jupiter and Io* (lost), 1735; *Baucis and Philemon*, 1740
BIBLIOGRAPHY Roger Fiske, *English Theatre Music in the Eighteenth Century*, OUP, 1973, 2nd edn, 1986

P.H.

SERGEY PROKOFIEV

Sergey Sergeyevich Prokofiev; *b* 23 April 1891, Sontsovka, Ukraine; *d* 5 March 1953, Moscow

Prokofiev considered himself essentially a man of the theatre. Before graduating from the St Petersburg Conservatory in June 1914 he had already worked on five operas; he completed six more over the next 40 years and left three unfinished. He also wrote nine ballets, including two of this century's most successful (*Romeo and Juliet* and *Cinderella*), incidental music to several dramatic works, and the scores for seven films.

Only one of the operas – the first to be performed, *The Love for Three Oranges* – was a success in his lifetime. All the others had to wait until after his death before their worth could be realistically assessed, divorced from the political considerations that had affected Prokofiev throughout his life.

His first four operas were schoolboy efforts and have not been published or professionally performed. His first mature opera, *Maddalena* (1911), was written when he was still a student at the St Petersburg Conservatory. He orchestrated the first scene but left the other three in piano score when the institution's proposed performance was abandoned because the singers found the music too difficult. A similar fate befell his second opera, *The Gambler*, in 1917, though this time the music was fully orchestrated. The following year, feeling the current state of political turmoil in Russia offered him few opportunities, Prokofiev left for a tour of the US (he had also developed a fearsome reputation as a pianist), and after a successful concert in Chicago the opera house there commissioned an opera from him based on a Russian version of Gozzi's *fiaba The Love for Three Oranges*.

The premiere was beset by delays and, uncommissioned, Prokofiev began work on his next opera, *The Fiery Angel*. With the exception of *War and Peace* this was to occupy him for longer than any other composition (1919–27), and although it was never staged during his lifetime, Prokofiev never abandoned his belief that it contained some of his best music.

In 1920 Prokofiev, still unwilling to return to Russia, had moved to Paris where his ballet *The Tale of the Buffoon* was well received at its premiere the following spring. Over the next few years he built up a successful career in Europe but, from the mid-1930s, commissions for compositions came increasingly from the USSR rather than from the West. Unlike Stravinsky and Rakhmaninov, Prokofiev had stayed away for practical rather than political reasons and so, with an apparent change in Russia's musical climate, he moved to Moscow in 1936.

He soon made his name with *Peter and the Wolf* and the patriotic film score *Alexander Nevsky*. The latter, written in collaboration with the celebrated film director S. M. Eisenstein, transformed Prokofiev's way of thinking about constructing a dramatic musical work: instead of writing long, musically developing scenes, he chose a format of many short scenes, cut together cinematically. With his imagination fired, he quickly found a suitable story for an opera, heroic and uplifting as the Soviet authorities required, full of incident but easy to follow. This was *Semyon Kotko*, the tale of a young soldier returning from the Great War to the newly founded Soviet Ukraine. Despite all Prokofiev's hopes and efforts the authorities condemned both its musical style and its dramatic content and the work was not a success.

For his next two operas Prokofiev returned to the individual kind of neo-classicism he had earlier demonstrated in the *Classical Symphony* (1916–17) and the film score *Lieutenant Kijé* (1933). In *Betrothal in a Monastery* (1940) and *War and Peace* (1941–52) the music re-creates the period atmosphere through use of musical forms such as minuet and gavotte, using classical period phrasing and melodic contours familiar in Mozart and Haydn, and simple, but never simplistic harmonies. In these works Prokofiev adopted rhymed verse and musical set pieces – elements he had eschewed during his early, radical period. He emphasized the romantic elements in the stories, writing lyrical tunes which are a far cry from the brittle style of the early days.

But once again, Prokofiev was unlucky with performances. Russia's entry into the Second World War made opera production difficult; and after the war, despite numerous revisions carried out at the suggestion of the authorities, a satisfactory format was never arrived at and *War and Peace* was never staged in Prokofiev's lifetime in anything like a form that represented his original concept. Meanwhile the notorious 1948 Moscow Congress of Composers condemned Prokofiev, along with virtually every Soviet composer of any distinction, for writing 'formalist' music (Zhdanov's catch-all opposite to socialist realism; Prokofiev himself defined formalism as 'music people don't understand at first hearing'). He sought official rehabilitation with his last opera, *The Story of a Real Man*, based on a patriotic true story of a wartime fighter pilot. The music includes folksongs from the hero's north Russian homeland linked by uncomplicated and bland arioso passages. As in *Semyon Kotko*, Prokofiev wrote almost cinematically, but added nothing of his own personality to the folksongs and the opera has little dramatic thrust. It was proscribed as 'modernistic, anti-melodic' and was denied a public performance until many years later.

After Prokofiev's death there was a relaxation of the official Russian position and only *The Fiery Angel* remained unknown to Soviet audiences. In the West there has been a different reaction: of the Soviet operas, only *War and Peace* is at all well known but the early operas are increasingly being performed.

Maddalena

Opera in one act (four scenes), Op. 13 (50m)
Libretto by the composer, after Magda Gustavovna Liven's play
Composed 1911 (in pf score); rev. and Scene 1 orch. 1913; remainder orch. Edward Downes
PREMIERES 25 March 1979, BBC Radio 3 (studio recording); 28 November 1981, Opernhaus, Graz, Austria; US: 9 June 1982, Loretto-Hilton Center, St Louis

Prokofiev's first mature opera reflects the influence of his teacher at the St Petersburg Conservatory, Nikolay Tcherepnin. Its musical language owes much to the extravagantly chromatic music of Skryabin and the charged late-Romanticism of Richard Strauss – a style that contrasts greatly with that of Prokofiev's later operas. Its construction is symphonic in that themes associated with the different characters or their emotions are fragmented and then developed for essentially musical rather than dramatic reasons. Consequently the opera is more a symphonic poem about the action than a musical reflection or parallel of it.

In 15th-century Venice Maddelena admires the sunset. When her artist husband Genaro returns home, they embrace in loving ecstasy. She hides when his old friend, Stenio, an ugly recluse, arrives with a secret he can no longer keep. For three months he has been having a torrid affair with a beautiful woman who made him promise never to try to discover her identity; now his curiosity has got the better of him and they have quarrelled. During his narrative a storm has been brewing and as it breaks he realizes that his secret has been overheard by Genaro's wife. He recognizes her as the woman he loves and Genaro realizes that his wife has been unfaithful to him. Both men decide that she should die but she persuades Genaro that he should kill her lover first. In the struggle both men are mortally wounded. Maddelena looks at the corpses and wonders which, if either, she really loved. She calls from the window for help – her husband has been murdered by an intruder.

RECORDING Ivanova, Martynov, Yakovenko, Russian State Chamber Ch, Ministry of Culture SO, Rozhdestvensky, Olympia, [c. 1988]
EDITION f.s. (orch. and trans. Edward Downes), Boosey & Hawkes, 1990; v.s., Boosey & Hawkes, 1990

The Gambler
Igrok

Opera in four acts (six scenes), Op. 24 (2h)
Libretto by the composer, after the novella by Dostoevsky (1866)
Composed 1915–17 (1st version withdrawn); rev. 1927–8
PREMIERES 29 April 1929, Théâtre de la Monnaie, Brussels; US: 4 April 1957, 85th Street Playhouse, New York; USSR: March 1963 (concert; radio broadcast); 7 April 1974, Bolshoi Theatre, Moscow; UK: 28 August 1962, King's Theatre, Edinburgh (Belgrade Opera Company); 28 April 1983, Coliseum, London
CAST The General *b*, Pauline *s*, Alexei *t*, The Marquis *t*, Mr Astley *bar*, Blanche *a*, Babulenka (Grandmother) *ms*, Prince Nilsky *t*, Potapitsch *bar*, 21 gamblers and croupiers 2 *s*, 2 *ms*, 1 *a*, 7 *t*, 3 *bar*, 6 *b*; *satb* chorus of gamblers, hotel guests, domestics, porters
STANDARD ORCHESTRA including 2 hp

This was the first significant opera to be based on a Dostoevsky text. Prokofiev himself adapted it and kept his own additions to a minimum. His aim was to write a new, conversational kind of opera, free of the influence of acknowledged giants such as Wagner, Tchaikovsky and Rimsky-Korsakov, with their reliance on set pieces. There are virtually no themes but a succession of short, highly characterful and varied motifs, which either exaggerate the natural inflexions of the Russian text or, in the orchestra, serve to amplify the action. The opera had been promised a performance at St Petersburg's Mariinsky Theatre by Albert Coates, the theatre's conductor. But by February 1917 political upheaval added to the problem of a cast and orchestra who would not or could not master the music and rehearsals stopped. The work's premiere did not take place until 1929 in Brussels, by which time Prokofiev had revised it to include more repetition and development, less motivic complication.

After its premiere the opera was not heard until shortly after Prokofiev's death, when Hermann Scherchen conducted it in Naples in 1953.

SYNOPSIS
Act I In 1865 in Roulettenburg (a mythical German spa) Alexei, tutor of the General's children, obsessively in love with the General's step-daughter Pauline, has lost the money she asked him to gamble with. He is contemptuous of his social superiors, particularly his employer, the General, who is deeply in love with an impoverished opportunist, Blanche, and, because of his gambling, deeply in debt to the Marquis. However, all the General's problems will be solved when he inherits his elderly relation's fortune.

Act II The General threatens to dismiss Alexei because of his rudeness to Baroness Wurmerhelm (the tutor was carrying out Pauline's orders) but rescinds at the threat of scandal. Alexei realizes that the Marquis is a former lover of Pauline's. Babulenka arrives in person, confounding deathbed rumours, and proceeds to gamble away her fortune.

Act III His inheritance gone, the General is abandoned by Blanche. Babulenka returns home.

Act IV The Marquis too returns to his homeland and releases Pauline from her debt to him (it transpires that this debt was why she asked Alexei to gamble her money in the opening scene). Alexei becomes convinced that with her money he will win and thus win her too. To the astonishment of the other gamblers, Alexei breaks the bank twice and runs to Pauline with the money. She throws it back in his face. He has lost her but fallen for a far more capricious mistress.

RECORDINGS 1. Polyakova, Makhov, Ch and O of USSR Radio, Rozhdestvensky, Melodiya, 1963; 2: Kasrashvili, Maslennikov, Bolshoi Theatre Ch and O, Lazarev, Olympia, 1982
EDITIONS f.ss., Boosey & Hawkes, 1919; rev. version, 1928; v.s., Edition Russe, 1930

A scene from the US premiere of The Gambler *(New York, 1957)*

The Love for Three Oranges

Lyubov k tryom apel'sinam
Opera in a prologue and four acts, Op. 33 (1h 45m)
Libretto by the composer, after Gozzi's *Fiaba dell'amore
delle tre melarancie* (1761)
Composed 1919
PREMIERES 30 December 1921, Auditorium, Chicago;
USSR: 18 February 1926, Mariinsky Theatre, Leningrad (St
Petersburg); UK: 24 August 1962, King's Theatre, Edinburgh
(Belgrade Opera Company); 17 September 1988, Grand
Theatre, Leeds
CAST King of Clubs *b*, The Prince *t*, Princess Clarice *a*,
Leandro *bar*, Truffaldino *t*, Pantaloon *bar*, Chelio *b*, Fata
Morgana *s*, Princess Linetta *a*, Princess Nicoletta *ms*, Princess
Ninetta *s*, a Gigantic Cook *b*, Farfarello *b*, Smeraldina *ms*,
Master of Ceremonies *t*, Herald *b*, 10 Ridiculous People 5 *t*,
5 *b*, advocates of Tragedy *b* chorus, advocates of Comedy *t*
chorus, advocates of Lyric Drama *st* chorus, advocates of
Farce *ab* chorus, little devils *b* chorus; *satb* chorus of
courtiers; *silent*: monsters, drunkards, gluttons, guards,
servants, 4 soldiers
ORCHESTRATION picc, 2 fl, 2 ob, ca, 3 cl/E♭ cl/b cl, 3
bsn/dbsn, 6 hn, 3 tpt, 3 trbn, tuba, 2 hp, timp, perc (sd, bd,
cym, suspended cym, triangle, t-t, tubular bells), str; offstage:
3 tpt, 2 trbn, cym, triangle, sd, hp

At the time of this opera's composition, Prokofiev's
eclectic style ranged from the aggressiveness of the
Scythian Suite (which sought to outdo Stravinsky's
The Rite of Spring in its portrayal of primitive
Russian life) to the quasi-18th-century elegance of
the *Classical Symphony*. In Gozzi's story Prokofiev
saw the chance to synthesize these elements, its
fantasy world providing scope for glittering orchestration, brilliant effects and strongly differentiated
characterization. Also, he thought his American
audience would appreciate a mercurial setting of the
type of brittle fairy-story then in operatic vogue;
Busoni (and soon Puccini) also selected a Gozzi
fiaba, *Turandot*, for operatic treatment. Prokofiev
wrote his own libretto, in Russian, from a translation by Meyerhold, Vogak and Solovyov of the
play, and created a whimsical opera buffa full of
the fantastic and grotesque, the comic and the sad,
set within a framework of utmost unreality and maximum theatricality.

The commission, from the Chicago Opera, was
signed in January 1919 for production that autumn
but the work was not staged until 1921 when the
soprano Mary Garden had become the theatre
director. Since its European premiere, on 14 March
1925 in Cologne, it has been the most frequently
performed of Prokofiev's operas.

SYNOPSIS

The King believes his son and heir will die unless he
can be cured of his melancholia. His enemies, his
niece Princess Clarice and the Prime Minister,
Leandro, are determined to prevent a cure, for
Leandro plans to marry Clarice and succeed to the
throne. The King's magic protector is Chelio, his
enemies' is the evil Fata Morgana. The action is
played out before the Ridiculous People who, like a
Greek Chorus, comment on the events. At crucial
moments they intervene to ensure that Good prevails.

*Costume design by I. Rabinovich for the Blackamoor in an
early production of* The Love for Three Oranges *(1927)*

In an allegorical prologue champions of different
kinds of theatre (Tragedy, Comedy, Lyric Drama
and Farce) demand to see their favourite entertainment. The Ridiculous People chase them away and a
herald proclaims the beginning.

Act I Doctors tell the King that his son's
melancholia is fatal. They say that laughter is the
only cure, so the King commands lavish and comic
entertainments. Leandro tries unsuccessfully to
dissuade him. Chelio loses a symbolic card game to
Fata Morgana; Good is endangered. Leandro tells
Princess Clarice he has fed the Prince a diet of Tragic
Verses to hasten his demise; she wants swifter action.
Both are worried that the clown Truffaldino might
make the Prince laugh. Smeraldina announces that
her mistress, Fata Morgana, will be at the entertainment to stop Chelio from intervening.

Act II The Prince, in his bedroom, does not
laugh at Truffaldino's antics but vomits the Tragic
Verses into a bucket. The Prince refuses to attend
the King's festivities but, to the strains of the
celebrated March, Truffaldino forces him out. The
first two divertissements fail to amuse the Prince. But
when Fata Morgana, disguised as an old woman, slips
and falls, legs kicking in the air, the Prince laughs
hysterically. So does everyone else except Clarice,
Leandro and Fata Morgana, who pronounces a spell
on the Prince: he will fall in love with three oranges
and will scour the earth in search of them. It takes
effect immediately and the Prince leaves on his quest,
accompanied by Truffaldino, blown on their way by
the mighty bellows of the devil Farfarello. The King
is in despair.

Act III In a desert Chelio persuades Farfarello to disclose the Prince's destination – the castle of Creonte, where the oranges are kept. Chelio's magical powers are too weak to break Fata Morgana's spell, but he warns the Prince and Truffaldino to open the oranges only near water and arms them with a magic ribbon, to distract Creonte's Gigantic Cook. They are blown into the courtyard and head for the kitchen. While the dreaded cook is distracted by the magic ribbon the Prince steals the oranges and escapes back to the desert, followed by Truffaldino. The oranges have grown very large and their return is slow. The Prince falls asleep exhausted as Truffaldino, forgetting Chelio's warning, cuts into one hoping for a drink. Out steps a beautiful princess who tells him she must have water otherwise she will die. Truffaldino thinks the second orange might contain some liquid, but when he cuts it out steps another thirsty princess. Both collapse and Truffaldino flees in panic. When the Prince awakes he is angry at Truffaldino's disappearance and puzzled by the two corpses. Realizing that his future is with the remaining orange and heedless of Chelio's warning, he splits it open and the beautiful Princess Ninetta steps out. They fall in love and the Ridiculous People intervene with a reviving bucket of water. The Prince leaves to arrange for the Princess's reception at the palace. Smeraldina appears, changes the Princess into a rat and usurps her place as the entire court arrives. Smeraldina insists that she is the one the Prince promised to marry and the King believes her. The court returns to the city.

Act IV Fata Morgana accuses Chelio of cheating; though he lost the card game he continues to help his protégés. The Ridiculous People lock Fata Morgana up so that Chelio can return to the palace. The King, the Prince and Smeraldina arrive with the rest of the court. But the throne is occupied by a giant rat. As the soldiers begin to shoot at it Chelio, to the Prince's joy and the King's confusion, turns it back into Princess Ninetta. The King finally realizes that Smeraldina, Leandro and Clarice are traitors and orders their exccution, but they escape along with Fata Morgana. In the shortest final chorus in all opera, the Ridiculous People drink a toast to the happy couple.

In its subject and its anti-realism *The Love for Three Oranges* is quite different from Prokofiev's previous operas. However, its musical construction bears similarities with his earlier works. As in *The Gambler*, Prokofiev works with short motifs and their repetition contributes to the ostinato sound of the score. In *The Love for Three Oranges* these function more by association with specific qualities of the *commedia dell'arte*-type characters than with their feelings. Those who are essentially good have music that is essentially diatonic, with smooth, undisturbed rhythms. The music for the evil characters is more chromatic and rhythmically unstable, with brittle orchestration. Prokofiev usually constructed even his symphonic works in this 'patchwork' way, but its success in *The Love for Three Oranges*

is to a large extent due to the flamboyance of the motifs themselves and the exuberant manner in which Prokofiev combines them.

The opera's anti-realism was in tune with prevailing post-war artistic attitudes, but it is the strength of the invention and the skill of Prokofiev's handling of his material that have kept the opera in the repertoire. In 1919 Prokofiev composed an orchestral suite on *The Love for Three Oranges*, which enjoyed instant success; this was revised in 1924. It consists of six sections from the opera, including the famous March.

RECORDING Dubosc, Gautier, Viala, Bacquier, Bastin, Opéra de Lyon, Nagano, Virgin, 1990 (also on video, Virgin)
EDITIONS f.s., Boosey & Hawkes, [c. 1949]; v.s., Gutheil, [c. 1922]

The Fiery Angel
Ognennyi Angel
Opera in five acts, Op. 37 (2h)
Libretto by the composer, after the historical novel by Valery Bryusov (1908)
Composed 1919–23, rev. 1926–7
PREMIERES 25 November 1954, Théâtre des Champs-Elysées, Paris (concert); 15 September 1955, La Fenice, Venice; UK: 27 July 1965, Sadler's Wells, London (New Opera Company); US: 22 September 1965, City Opera, New York; Russia: 28 December 1991, Mariinsky Theatre, St Petersburg
CAST Ruprecht *bar*, Renata *s*, Count Heinrich *silent*, Jacob Glock *t*, Agrippa of Nettesheim *t*, Mephistopheles *t*, Faust *b-bar*, 10 solo parts 2 *s*, 2 *ms*, *a*, *t*, 3 *bar*, *b*, 3 skeletons *s*, *t*, *b*, 3 neighbours *bar*, 2 *b*; *sa* chorus of nuns; *tb* chorus of Inquisitor's retinue, *satb* offstage chorus
ORCHESTRATION picc, 2 fl, 2 ob, ca, 2 cl, b cl, 2 bsn, dbsn, 4 hn, 3 tpt, 3 trbn, tuba, timp, perc, 2 hp, str

This study of neurotic female sexuality set in Reformation Germany is far removed from the pantomime world of Gozzi, and the music of *The Fiery Angel* has an Expressionist intensity quite unlike the dispassionate music Prokofiev had previously been writing. He spent some four years composing the short score, but with no performance in view he did not start orchestrating it in detail. In 1926, when Bruno Walter, head of the Berlin State Opera, accepted it for performance the following season, Prokofiev revised it, reorganizing Act II and much of Acts I, III and V and orchestrating the whole opera. The Berlin performance did not materialize but Prokofiev transferred some of the music into his Symphony No. 3. In the early 1930s there was talk of the opera being staged by the Metropolitan Opera in New York and Prokofiev began preliminary work on another major revision. This was never finished, the American performance did not take place and the opera was not staged in Prokofiev's lifetime. Even though it has been widely praised as his strongest and most dramatically intense score, productions (which always use the version prepared for Berlin) have not been frequent.

SYNOPSIS
Act I Since childhood Renata has been obsessed with her protective angel, Madiel, at first spiritually,

Act I, Scene 1 of The Fiery Angel *(Venice, 1955)*

then, after puberty, physically. For a year she lived with Count Heinrich, the man she imagined to be Madiel, but he left her. Since then she has been searching for him. She tells all this to Ruprecht after he has found her having hysterical visions and although everyone else agrees that she is a witch, Ruprecht, who has fallen in love with her, agrees to help.

Act II Renata and Ruprecht turn to magic in the quest for Heinrich, acquiring forbidden books and conjuring up dark spirits, though the leading proponent of black philosophy, Agrippa, refuses to assist them.

Act III Renata has seen Heinrich but he has again rejected her. She demands that Ruprecht avenge her honour. As Ruprecht challenges him to a duel Renata, seeing Heinrich bathed in light, is again convinced that he is her Fiery Angel; she commands Ruprecht not to harm him but when Ruprecht is badly wounded in the duel she is full of remorse. She vows to love him and nurse him back to health. Unseen voices mock her.

Act IV Ruprecht has recovered and Renata leaves him again, determined to punish her own sinfulness by entering a convent. Ruprecht encounters Faust and Mephistopheles; Mephistopheles takes Ruprecht under his wing.

Act V Renata has corrupted the nuns with her visions and obsessions with her Angel. The Inquisition tries to exorcize the evil to no avail. While Ruprecht looks on, with a triumphant Mephistopheles beside him, Renata is condemned to torture and death.

Prokofiev began *The Fiery Angel* at the only time in his life when religion featured in his intellectual considerations, and it is unique among his theatre works in being written with neither a commission nor a production in view. Its theme of obsession looks back to his pre-Revolution operas *The Gambler* and *Maddelena*. Its form – a set of more or less free-standing tableaux – looks back even further, to Musorgsky. But its musical and dramatic portrayal of ambiguity (the story comes from one of Russia's greatest Symbolist poets) was totally new for him.

Individuals, atmospheres and emotional responses are all given specific themes of characterization – most of them chromatic to some degree. There is only one unambiguously tonal (and therefore stable) character motif in the opera, and this is associated, quite improbably, with the forces of evil. The opera is seen largely through Renata's eyes and consequently, although the text is ambivalent about whether her visions are hallucinatory, the music makes it apparent that for her they are real and terrifying. During the narrative of her life the orchestra abounds in motifs which return when she later experiences similar feelings. Among the most memorable of these are the soaring theme of her love for Madiel, and the theme – first heard in the orchestra during Ruprecht's attempted rape – which recurs whenever Renata's responses to physical masculinity are displayed.

RECORDINGS 1. Rhodes, Kolassi, Depraz, Giraudeau, Paris Opera O, Bruck, Véga, 1957: a historic event now showing its age; 2. Secunde, Engert-Ely, Lorenz, Zednik, Moll, Gothenburg Symphony Ch and O, Järvi, DG, 1991: obviously better in sound than the earlier recording but not so electrifying in effect [A.B.]
EDITIONS f.s., Boosey & Hawkes, [c. 1960]; v.ss., Gutheil, 1927; Musyka, 1981; Boosey & Hawkes, [c. 1960]

Semyon Kotko

Opera in five acts, Op. 81 (3h 45m)
Libretto by the composer and Valentin Katayev, after the
novella *I, Son of the Working People* by Katayev
Composed 1939
PREMIERES 23 June 1940, Stanislavsky Theatre, Moscow;
Germany: May 1961, Karl-Marx-Stadt (Chemnitz)
CAST Semyon Kotko *t*, his Mother *a*, Frosa *s*, Sofia *s*,
Tkachenko *b*, Khivra *a*, Mikola *t*, 4 *s*, *a*, 4 *t*, 3 *bar*, 7 *b*; *satb*
chorus of peasants, Red Army soldiers, Germans
LARGE ORCHESTRA including offstage: accordion, gtr,
military band

Semyon Kotko, written 15 years after *The Fiery
Angel*, marked a major change in Prokofiev's
thinking. The composer felt that, for such a contemporary, patriotic opera, 'many forms applicable
to classical opera might prove unsuitable'. He chose
a cinematically inspired structure of almost 50 very
short scenes, which, despite his wish to portray 'live
flesh-and-blood human beings', resulted in characters
that are often one-dimensional. Prokofiev's attempt
to create a 'Soviet' opera acceptable to the authorities
failed. Its planned premiere was delayed following
the arrest of the theatre director Meyerhold,
who was to have staged the work. When it was
eventually performed, in 1940, the authorities were
less than enthusiastic and it was dropped from the
repertoire.

SYNOPSIS
Act I Returning to his Ukrainian village after
fighting in the First World War, Semyon Kotko is
given a hero's welcome. Anxious to marry his
girlfriend Sofia, he sends a matchmaker to plead his
cause with her wealthy landowner father, Tkachenko.
   Act II Although he would prefer a richer
husband for his daughter, Tkachenko agrees to the
match. Betrothal celebrations are interrupted by a
German detachment.
   Act III Tkachenko co-operates by naming
Bolshevik sympathizers, including Semyon, whose
house is consequently burned down.
   Act IV Semyon has escaped and has established
a resistance movement. News arrives at their camp of
the German's continuing oppression; Semyon also
learns that Sofia, at her father's wish, is to marry
Klembovski.
   Act V Storming the village, Semyon lobs a hand-
grenade at the church, wounding Klembovski. The
Germans are defeated and the village reclaimed for
the Bolshevik cause.

Both dramatically and musically *Semyon Kotko* was
new. Set-piece arias are included as integral parts
of the drama or when the event of the aria is in
itself dramatic. For the first time Prokofiev gave
the chorus a major role as representatives of
the collective consciousness. In place of recitative
he wrote arioso and unpitched rhythmic speech
depending on whether the moment was emotional
or mundane. His melodies had what he called a
new simplicity, so that the music was more readily
approachable. That all this came close to Stalin's

ideal of a 'song opera', in which the tunes were light
and the situations uplifting, was probably not
coincidental.

RECORDING Antipova, Gres, Gelovani, Timchenko, USSR
Radio SO, Zhukov, Melodiya, 1960
EDITIONS f.s., Musyka, 1967; v.ss., Musgis, 1960;
Henschelverlag, 1961

Betrothal in a Monastery (The Duenna)

Obrucheniye v Monastire
Lyric-comic opera in four acts, Op. 86 (2h 30m)
Libretto by the composer and Mira Mendelson, after the play
The Duenna by Richard Brinsley Sheridan (1775)
Composed 1940–41
PREMIERES 5 May 1946, Narodni Divadlo Theatre, Prague;
USSR: 3 November 1946, Kirov Opera, Leningrad (St
Petersburg); US: 1 June 1948, Greenwich Mews Playhouse,
New York; UK: 12 May 1963 (BBC broadcast of
performance at Stanislavsky Theatre, Moscow); 15 February
1980, Collegiate Theatre, London
CAST Don Jerome *t*, Ferdinand *bar*, Louisa *s*, her Duenna
a, Antonio *t*, Clara *ms*, Mendoza *b*, Don Carlos *bar*, 9 other
solo parts *s*, *a*, 4 *t*, 2 *bar*, *b*; *satb* chorus of servants, maskers,
tradespeople, monks, nuns, guests
LARGE ORCHESTRA including several on- and offstage
players

Prokofiev's first collaboration with the young literary
student Mira Mendelson (for whom he was soon to
leave his wife) put more emphasis on the romance in
Sheridan's sparkling and successful play than on its
farce or cynicism. Described by Shostakovich as 'one
of Prokofiev's most radiant and buoyant works', it
remains – after *Oranges* – his most popular opera.

SYNOPSIS
Act I In 18th-century Seville Don Jerome arranges
to marry his daughter Louisa to Mendoza, an ugly
but very rich old fish merchant who has not seen
the girl but is enthusiastic. He hears the penniless
Antonio serenading Louisa and vows that the
wedding must take place soon.
   Act II Louisa's duenna hatches a plan that will
allow Louisa to marry Antonio and herself to snare
Mendoza and his money: Don Jerome must believe
that the duenna is acting as a go-between for the
lovers; he will then dismiss her but Louisa will put on
the duenna's clothes, escape and elope with Antonio.
The duenna, disguised as Louisa, will marry
Mendoza instead. Having escaped, Louisa comes
across her friend Clara who, feigning distress at her
lover's over-ardent behaviour (her lover is Louisa's
brother Ferdinand), has decided to take refuge in a
monastery. Disguised, this time as Clara, Louisa
enlists Mendoza's help in finding Antonio – the
merchant is only too pleased to divert his rival's
attentions away from Louisa (as he thinks). At Don
Jerome's house, Mendoza meets 'Louisa' (the
duenna); he is won over by her flattery and the
couple plan to elope.
   Act III Antonio meets the real Louisa and
Mendoza, still ignorant of her identity, smiles on
young love. Don Jerome, interrupted in his amateur
music-making, unwittingly blesses the separate
marriages of Louisa and Mendoza. At the convent
Clara pines for Ferdinand.

Act IV A visit from Mendoza and Antonio interrupts the alcoholic revelry of the monks at the monastery. Ferdinand also arrives and, believing that Antonio is about to marry Clara, starts a fight. Confusions are resolved and the monks bless all three marriages. At the wedding ball planned for Louisa, Don Jerome learns of the turn of events and is eventually reconciled to them: his daughter has married a pauper, but Ferdinand has married an heiress.

In *Betrothal*, with its farcical plot, its disguises, mistaken identities and outwitted father, Prokofiev re-created the opera-buffa world of Rossini. The music is diatonic, lucidly harmonized, limpidly orchestrated (with some unexpected tone colours, such as the glass harmonica played by Jerome at the end), and distinctively varied according to the characters on stage. Prokofiev still uses his system of motifs to introduce characters, but they are now the raw material of arias.

RECORDING Kayevchenko, Isakova, Mishchevsky, Korshunov Stanislavsky Musical Theatre Ch and O, Abdullayev, Melodiya, c. 1964
EDITIONS f.ss., Musyka, 1967; Henschelverlag, 1975; v.ss., Leeds Music Corp., 1948; Chant du Mond, 1964; Henschelverlag, 1975

War and Peace

Voina i mir
Lyric dramatic scenes – opera in five acts (two parts) – an epigraph and 13 scenes, Op. 91 (4h)
Libretto by the composer and Mira Mendelson, after the novel by Tolstoy (1863–9)
Composed 1941–3, rev. 1946–52
PREMIERES 16 October 1944, Moscow (eight scenes, concert with pf); 7 June 1945, Conservatory, Moscow (nine scenes, concert with orch.); two-evening version: 12 June 1946, Maly Theatre, Leningrad (St Petersburg) (Part I); July 1947, Maly Theatre, Leningrad (Part II, private performance); new one-evening version: 26 May 1953, Teatro Comunale, Florence; USSR: June 1953, Moscow, (concert; All-Russian Theatrical Association); 1 April 1955, Maly Theatre, Leningrad (11 scenes of 13); 8 November 1957, Stanislavsky Theatre, Moscow (13 scenes, with cuts); another 13-scene version (with epigraph): US: 13 January 1957, NBC TV, New York (broadcast); USSR: 15 December 1959, Bolshoi Theatre, Moscow; UK: 19 April 1967, Town Hall, Leeds (concert); 11 October 1972, Coliseum, London (Sadler's Wells Opera); US: 8 May 1974, Boston
CAST principal characters: Prince Andrei Bolkonsky *bar*, Countess Natasha Rostova *s*, Sonya *ms*, Maria Dmitrievna Akhrosimova *a*, Count Ilya Rostov *b*, Count Pyotr Bezukhov (Pierre) *t*, Helene Bezukhova *ms*, Prince Anatol Kuragin *t*, Lt Fedya Dolokhov *bar*, Vasska Denisov *bar*, Field-Marshal Prince Kutuzov *b*, Napoleon Bonaparte *bar*, Platon Karataev *bar*; other characters: the host *t*, Major Domo *t*, Madame Peronskaya *s*, Countess Rostova, Natasha's mother *ms*, Tsar Alexander I *silent*, Maria Antonovna *silent*, Prince Bolkonsky's Major-Domo *b*, an old valet *bar*, a housemaid *s*, Maria Bolkonskaya *ms*, Prince Bolkonsky *b-bar*, Balaga *b*, Matriosha *ms*, Josef *silent*, Dunyasha *s*, Gavrilla *b*, Metivier *bar*, French abbé *t*, Tikhon *bar*, Fyodor *t*, 2 Prussian Generals *spoken roles*, Andrei's orderly *t*, 2 Russian Generals *t, bar*, Kaizarov *t*, Adjutant to General Compans *t*, Adjutant to Murat, King of Naples *treble*, Prince Berthier, Marshal of France *bar*, Marquis de Caulaincourt, French Ambassador to Russia *silent*, General Belliard *bar*, Adjutant to Prince

Eugene *t*, Baron Gourgaud, aide-de-camp to Napoleon *b*, Monsieur de Bausset-Roquefort *t*, General Count Bennigsen *b*, Prince Mikhail Barclay de Tolly *t*, General Yermolov *bar*, General Konovnitsin *t*, General Rayevsky *bar*, the Peasant's daughter *silent*, Captain Ramballe *b*, Lt Bonnet *t*, Mavra *a*, Ivanov *t*, Marshal Davout *b*, a French Officer *bar*, 3 madmen *t, bar, silent*, 2 French actresses *s, ms*; *satb* chorus of guests, citizens of Moscow, Russian soldiers, French people, partisans
ORCHESTRATION picc, 2 fl, 2 ob, ca, 2 cl, b cl, 2 bsn, dbsn, 4 hn, 3 tpt, 3 trbn, tuba, timp, perc (including campanelli and xylophone), hp, str; offstage: str orchestra (Scene 4), military band (Scene 8)

In choosing to make an opera from selected scenes of one of Russian literature's most revered masterpieces (and also one that was hailed as a cornerstone of socialist realism) Prokofiev was laying himself open to attack. He felt he could infuse the heroic story with his own very popular and characteristic kind of neo-classicism. The work immediately ran into difficulties. In May 1942, with Russia and Germany at war, he was asked to strengthen the patriotic element of the 11-scene piano score he had submitted, so he added heroic marches, arias and choruses to the 'war' sections. This shifted the balance away from the affairs of the individuals to the affairs of the state; it monumentalized the opera's substance. For the first proposed staged performances in 1946 Prokofiev added two more scenes, the glittering ball in Part I and the epic war council at Fili (Scene 10). This 13-scene version was designed to be performed over two evenings but in fact only the first eight scenes were heard in public. After that the political climate made further performances of any of the music impossible and although Prokofiev continued revising the work until the end of his life, he never heard the complete opera and was never able to give his approval to a final version. The first Russian performances in the late 1950s were all cut.

SYNOPSIS
Part I: Peace
Epigraph The Russian people affirm their invincibility and the sanctity of their country against all invaders. Scene 1: The young, recently widowed Prince Andrei loses his melancholia when he hears Natasha singing of her happiness at the coming of spring. Scene 2: New Year's Eve 1810. Natasha, at her first society ball, dances with Andrei and the two fall in love. But she has been noticed by the predatory Prince Anatol. Scene 3: February 1812. Natasha and Andrei are engaged but his father refuses to accept her and insults her. She fears that the year's absence imposed on Andrei will weaken their love. Scene 4: May 1812. At a party Natasha is swept off her feet by the charming Prince Anatol, even though she realizes that an affair will sully her love for Andrei. Scene 5: 12 June 1812. Dolokhov, Anatol's friend, tries to persuade him not to elope with Natasha; neither her fiancé nor his wife would acquiesce. Anatol is adamant, summons his troika driver and after a few more drinks leaves. Scene 6: The same night. The elopement is foiled by Natasha's hostess's servants but Anatol escapes. Her

Prokofiev and the conductor Samuil Samosud during a rehearsal of War and Peace *in the Large Hall of the Moscow Conservatory (June 1945)*

aunt rails at her and makes an old family friend, Count Pierre, tell her that Anatol is already married. Pierre also tells her that he has fallen in love with her himself, which confuses her further. Scene 7: The same night. Pierre goes home and finds his wife entertaining friends, including Anatol. He demands that Anatol give up Natasha and leave Moscow immediately. News arrives that Napoleon and his army have crossed the Russian border.

Part II: War. Scene 8: 25 August 1812, before the Battle of Borodino. The Russian volunteer army is assembling, convinced of its invincibility. Andrei joins up hoping to forget Natasha, whom he still loves, and expecting to die. He rejects Field-Marshal Kutuzov's offer of a post at a staff headquarters and as he leaves with his men the first shots of battle are heard. Scene 9: Later that day, behind the French lines, Napoleon cannot believe the extent of the Russian resistance. He feels destiny is turning against him. When a cannonball lands at his feet he calmly pushes it away before it can explode. Scene 10: Field-Marshal Kutuzov, having lost the Battle of Borodino and retreated to Fili, holds a war council to discuss whether or not to defend the ancient and sacred city of Moscow and risk defeat or retreat further so as to regroup and fight again. Against all advice he decides to abandon Moscow. Alone, Kutuzov meditates on his momentous decision but is confident that the Muscovites will win in the end. Scene 11: French-occupied Moscow is virtually deserted; Count Pierre hears that Natasha's family has fled, taking with them some wounded soldiers, including Andrei (though Natasha has not recognized him). To Napoleon's

anger the Muscovites fire their city. Scene 12: Behind the Russian lines. Andrei, wounded and delirious, recalls his love for Natasha. She begs his forgiveness; he longs to live only for her. But it is too late. He dies. Scene 13: November 1812. In the terrible Russian winter the French army, with its prisoners, is in chaotic retreat on the Smolensk road. Those prisoners who cannot keep up are shot. Partisans attack an escort party and free the Russians, among them Pierre. He learns that Andrei is dead and that Natasha is sick, but he dreams that his love for her might now flower. Field Marshal Kutuzov congratulates everyone on a great victory, the people cheer him and reassert their belief in themselves and their country.

In the form and style of *War and Peace* Prokofiev harks back to the historical-tableaux operas of 19th-century Russia, such as Musorgsky's *Khovanshchina* and *Boris Godunov*. The opera's structure is traditional with set-piece arias and Tchaikovskyan dances. Within each scene there are many short episodes involving different characters, a cinematic technique already encountered in Prokofiev's earlier Soviet operas but here developed more effectively. The composer brought the characters alive by relaxing his insistence that the music needed to reflect every inflexion of the original words. In fact some of the words were made to fit pre-existing music, for Prokofiev, ever a prolific inventor of ideas and an inveterate hoarder of those not used, pillaged sketchbooks and unperformed scores for *War and Peace*; one of the most pervasive themes, associated with the love of Andrei and Natasha first heard in Scene 1, was taken over from the incidental music of an unstaged dramatization of Pushkin's *Eugene Onegin* written in 1936, where it also portrayed innocent love destined to be thwarted.

The opera is fundamentally a lyrical work, with expansive melodies, infectious dances and stirring choruses. The good characters (Natasha, Andrei, Pierre) are provided with opulent orchestration; the bad ones (Anatol and his sister Helene, who together bring about Natasha's fall) have music that matches Tolstoy's description of them as 'false and unnatural' with a spare sound. Napoleon has no melodies, only broken phrases more or less unaccompanied, perhaps symbolizing his distance from the people over whom he rules; the Russian commander, Kutuzov, on the other hand, has finely proportioned themes, strong, slow-moving and full of gravitas. The parallels of these two characters with the contemporary leaders, Hitler (Napoleon) and Stalin (Kutuzov) was played up by Prokofiev on the advice of the authorities.

RECORDINGS   Vishnevskaya, Miller, French National Radio Ch and O, Rozhdestvensky, Erato, 1988: the first absolutely uncut performance, including both overture and epigraph (transferred to before Scene 8); 2. Bareva, Vidonev, Sofia National Opera Ch and O, Raichev, Fidelio, 1986: overture (but no epigraph) and 13 scenes: a good modern recording but slightly cut
EDITIONS   f.s., Musgis, vols 6A, B and C, 1958; v.ss. (Bolshoi version), Boosey & Hawkes, [c. 1943]; Musgis, vols 7A and B, 1958

The Story of a Real Man

Porest' o Nastoyashchem Cheloveke
Opera in four acts, Op. 117 (cut version: 1h 45m)
Libretto by the composer and Mira Mendelson, after the novel by B. Polevoy
Composed 1947–8
PREMIERES   3 December 1948, Kirov Theatre, Leningrad (St Petersburg) (a closed concert performance for Soviet cultural officials and musicians); 7 October 1960, Bolshoi Theatre, Moscow (edn by M. Mendelson, in three acts with scenes rearranged and many cuts)

Prokofiev was confident that his opera's new style – folk melodies, simple tunes, short scenes and a fervently uplifting and patriotic story – would rehabilitate him after his public humiliation at the now notorious 1948 Composers' Union Conference where, along with other notable Soviet composers, he was accused of formalism. He was particularly anxious that *War and Peace*, shelved since its condemnation by the authorities in July 1947, should be restored to favour. Sadly the single closed performance of *The Story of a Real Man* was feeble ('As I was listening I couldn't even recognize my own music,' he said later); the opera was proscribed and not revived until after the composer's death.

The plot comes from a prize-winning wartime novel about a heroic Soviet fighter pilot shot down over central Russia. Despite terrible injuries, and drawing strength from a photograph of his girlfriend, he manages to crawl through the snow to the next

village and is transferred to hospital in Moscow where both his legs are amputated. Inspired by the determination of his fellow patients, he vows to return to flying so that he will be a real man again and can face his girl. He forces himself to walk and achieves his ambition.

RECORDING   Deomidova, Kibkalo, Pankov, Eizen, Bolshoi Ch and O, Ermler, Melodiya, 1961: well sung and recorded but of the inauthentic version made by Mira Mendelson
EDITIONS   v.ss., Musfond, 1960; Henschelverlag, 1962

Early operas: *The Giant (Velikan)*, 1900; *Desert Islands (Na pustinnikh ostrovakh)* (inc.), (1900–2); *A Feast in Time of Plague (Pir vo vremya chumi)*, (1903; one scene rev. 1908–9); *Undina*, (1904–7)
BIBLIOGRAPHY   David Gutman, *Prokofiev*, Alderman Press, 1988; Sergei Prokofiev, *Materials, Documents, Reminiscences*, Moscow Progress, 1978; Harlow Robinson, *Sergei Prokofiev*, Robert Hale, 1987

C.B.

FRANCESCO PROVENZALE

b ?1626/7, Naples; *d* 6 September 1704, Naples

Next to nothing is known about Provenzale's early life. His marriage banns, dated 5 January 1660, state that he was then 'about 33 years old'. He was among the first Neapolitan composers to take an interest in opera, a theatrical genre unknown in Naples before 1640, and also taught at two of the four Neapolitan conservatories. Provenzale was among the first to train students to become professional opera composers and performers. This practice bore significant fruit later in the 18th century, when the conservatories educated many composers who later acquired fame and fortune in European opera houses.

Provenzale composed four operas between 1653 and 1658. Of these *Il Ciro* (1653) is the only one to have been preserved, albeit in a form with musical additions and alterations by other composers. The high reputation he has gained in recent times rests on two later operas of his that still exist: *Il schiavo di sua moglie* (1671) and *La Stellidaura vendicata* (1674). His two sacred operas (both 1672) are lost.

BIBLIOGRAPHY   Romain Rolland, *Les origines du théâtre lyrique moderne: L'histoire de l'opéra en Europe avant Lully et Scarlatti*, Bibliothèque des Ecoles françaises d'Athènes et de Rome, 1895, 4th edn, 1936

M.F.R.

GIACOMO PUCCINI

Giacomo Antonio Domenico Michele Secondo Maria Puccini; *b* 22 December 1858, Lucca, Italy; *d* 29 November 1924, Brussels

Puccini is generally regarded as the greatest Italian composer of the post-Verdi generation. All but the first two of his operas remain a firm part of the

Puccini – who owned a motor boat called Cio -Cio -San, *after Madam Butterfly – with his son Antonio*

unfortunately, Fontana's melodramatic style was ill-suited to Puccini's expressive powers and, in spite of years of work, *Edgar* (1889) was never a success. The failure nearly cost Puccini Ricordi's support, but the young composer was given a second chance.

With his next work, *Manon Lescaut* (1893), Puccini found a personal voice, and with this and the next three operas, *La bohème* (1896), *Tosca* (1900) and *Madama Butterfly* (1904), all of them written to libretti by Luigi Illica and Giuseppe Giacosa, established himself as the leading Italian composer of his generation. His sense of dramatic pacing was acute, in particular his ability to juxtapose action sections with ones of lyrical repose; and he had a masterly control over balancing the various systems – words, music and staging – that make up an opera, only rarely allowing indulgence of one aspect over the others. On the purely musical level, he managed to assimilate into his personal style such weighty foreign influences as those of Massenet and Wagner; his treatment of recurring motifs, for example, is cavalier on the semantic level precisely because it takes into account the intense dramatic presence of his operatic language.

The relatively long gaps between operas were due to a number of factors. Puccini was eager to taste the fruits of his success, and spent much time indulging his passions for hunting and for the newly invented motor car. On the professional level, work in progress was interrupted by the series of promotional tours that Ricordi arranged in order to launch Puccini's works on the national and international stage. Perhaps most seriously, however, each new creation underwent a tortured genesis. As if in vivid illustration of the fragmented condition of the Italian operatic tradition, the structure of each opera had to be achieved through a painful process of discovery, Puccini's obsession with details of dramatic pacing causing him frequently to change his mind in mid-composition, driving his long-suffering librettists almost to despair.

The three works that secured his international reputation all succeed in part by characterizing a particularly evocative ambience: Bohemian Paris in the 1830s; Rome in 1800, seething with revolutionary and religious tension; modern-day Japan. Indeed, one senses that the choice of dramatic setting always had a critical effect on stimulating his desire and ability to find fresh ideas. After *Madama Butterfly*, however, Puccini found it increasingly difficult to locate subjects that were both novel enough to kindle his imagination, and at the same time firmly enough structured to sustain dramatic treatment. Finally, three years after the premiere of *Butterfly*, Puccini discovered a subject set in the California gold rush of 1849. *La fanciulla del West* (1910) had the usual protracted genesis, and was further interrupted by a crisis in his – frequently stormy – relationship with his wife Elvira. There was an even longer gap before his next work, *La rondine* (1917), which started life as a Viennese operetta and remains (outside a few popular excerpts) the least well known of Puccini's mature operas.

Puccini's next project took up a different dramatic

operatic repertoire, and several are among the most popular ever written. During a period in which the Italian operatic tradition was finally coming to an end, he alone among his contemporaries managed to renew himself creatively, to fashion a convincing series of works, repeatedly forging a successful compromise between his native inheritance and the French and German influences that increasingly gained sway in his country.

Puccini was born into a family whose musical tradition extended back five generations. From an early age he received training in Lucca as a church musician, but a performance of Verdi's *Aida* in Pisa in 1876 apparently turned his thoughts to operatic music. In 1880 he went to Milan to study composition at the conservatory with Ponchielli. While still studying there, he achieved some critical acclaim for his final composition exercise, an orchestral *Capriccio sinfonico* (1883); Puccini later borrowed music from this early piece for his operas *Edgar* and *La bohème*. His first opera, the one-act *Le villi*, was written immediately after leaving the conservatory for a competition sponsored by the publishing house of Sonzogno. Puccini's submission failed to receive even an honourable mention but, undeterred by the lack of success, some influential friends arranged a performance of *Le villi* in a revised, two-act version (1884). This provided the impetus for Puccini's career, as soon afterwards the publisher Ricordi offered him a contract for a new opera. Part of his contract stipulated that the librettist of *Le villi*, Ferdinando Fontana, would write the new libretto;

challenge. *Il trittico* (1918) is a group of three sharply contrasting one-act operas that together make up a complete evening: a sinister melodrama (*Il tabarro*); a sentimental religious tragedy, written entirely for women's voices (*Suor Angelica*); and a comic opera (*Gianni Schicchi*). It is clear from the relative speed with which *Il trittico* was produced that the reduced scope of these works allowed Puccini to experiment more freely with dramatic types, to immerse himself in a particular ambience without the necessity of developing a protracted narrative structure. For his final opera, *Turandot*, he returned to exoticism, but this time employed a bold mixture of dramatic types within one work, showing that his creative imagination and dramatic insights remained intact in spite of the increasing self-doubt and pessimism of his later years. Puccini died of throat cancer in 1924, leaving the final scene of *Turandot* unfinished. It was completed by Franco Alfano, a member of the younger Italian generation, and first performed in 1926.

Although Puccini has been cast as a conservative figure in early 20th-century music, he continued to respond to contemporary music when it suited his dramatic purpose. One can, for example, trace through his mature operas a gradual development in complexity of harmonic idiom, and an increasingly sophisticated use of the orchestra. However, Puccini's central innovation lay in his continual attempts to fashion new types of musical drama, to invent for each new work a particular structure, a particular dynamic relationship between its various narrative strands. In spite of these efforts, and in spite of an unprecedented success with the public, Puccini has never been fully accepted by the critical establishment. His operas respond only faintly to the Wagner-influenced analytical and critical techniques that have been in vogue for so long, and this has encouraged some to accuse him of lacking complete artistic seriousness of purpose, of cynically manipulating an easily moved mass audience. But there are signs of a general change in critical attitude. As time passes, and as we gain an increasingly broad perspective on the progress of 20th-century music, Puccini's reputation as a musical dramatist of the highest quality, and as a significant representative of his age, seems bound to grow.

Le villi

The Willis
Opera-ballet in one act (first version entitled *Le willis*); final version in two acts (1h)
Libretto by Ferdinando Fontana, based on the story *Les wilis* by Alphonse Karr (1852)
Composed August–December 1883; expanded into two acts 1884; rev. for La Scala, Milan, performance (24 January 1885); further revs 1888, 1892
PREMIERES 31 May 1884, Teatro Dal Verme, Milan (in one act); 26 December 1884, Teatro Regio, Turin (in two acts; final version); UK: 24 September 1897, Carl Rosa Company, Manchester; US: 17 December 1908, Metropolitan, New York

The success of the premiere of *Le villi* gave Puccini his *entrée* into the world of Italian opera, but the work soon faded from the repertoire and is today only occasionally revived.

In the heart of the Black Forest: Roberto inherits a fortune from a distant relative and must go to Mainz to claim it. Anna, Roberto's betrothed, is forlorn at the prospect of separation. Although Roberto assures her of his undying love, he soon forgets his promises and she eventually dies of a broken heart. Roberto later returns to the forest, unaware of her death and hoping for forgiveness. But he is met by the Willis, the spirits of maidens forsaken by their lovers. The Willis force their faithless lovers to dance until they fall dead from exhaustion; Anna's avenging spirit pulls Roberto, overcome with terror, into the dance of death.

Fontana's libretto was heavily influenced by the *scapigliatura* (a 'Bohemian' literary society in Milan, whose members had included Arrigo Boito and the poet Emilio Praga), in its evocation of the bizarre and its wide range of genres – opera, dance, spoken narrative and orchestral interlude. Puccini's treatment is interesting for the glimpses of his mature melodic style that it affords, especially in Anna's 'Romanza', in parts of the love duet, and in Roberto's 'Scena Drammatica-Romanzo'.

RECORDING Scotto, Domingo, Nucci, Gobbi, Ambrosian Opera Ch, National PO, Maazel, CBS, 1980
EDITION v.s. (two-act version), Ricordi, 1892

Edgar

Lyric drama in four – subsequently three – acts (1h 30m)
Libretto by Ferdinando Fontana, based on the verse play *La coupe et les lèvres* by Alfred de Musset (1832)
Composed 1885–8, rev. 1889; reduced to three acts 1891–2; further revs 1901, 1905
PREMIERES in four acts: 21 April 1889, La Scala, Milan; in three acts: 28 February 1892, Teatro Comunale, Ferrara; final version: 8 July 1905, Teatro de la Opera, Buenos Aires; UK: 6 April 1967, Hammersmith Town Hall, London; US: 13 April 1977, Carnegie Hall, New York (concert)

The opera is set in medieval Flanders. Edgar is caught between two women: the wild gypsy Tigrana, his former mistress, and Fidelia, an innocent young maiden. Edgar loves Fidelia and will not listen to Tigrana's enticements. But Tigrana manages to win him by stirring up the villagers against Fidelia and enlisting Edgar to defend her. Edgar burns down his house and duels with Fidelia's brother Frank (who is infatuated with Tigrana), wounding him before fleeing with Tigrana. Edgar soon tires of Tigrana, however, and escapes her clutches by enlisting in the army. Later a military funeral is held for Edgar, who is presumed to have died in battle; but he arrives disguised as a Friar, reveals his true identity, and enjoys a brief reunion with Fidelia. Tigrana, in a vicious act of revenge, stabs Fidelia, mortally wounding her.

Fontana's libretto was outdated even as it was written and the resulting disjunction between musical style and dramatic ambience is one reason for *Edgar*'s lack of success. The opera is, however, interesting in that it shows that the major Italian influence on the young Puccini was Ponchielli rather than Verdi. Youthful imitations notwithstanding, the score contains many foreshadowings of the mature Puccini: harmonic progressions, melodic and orchestral details, and a distinctive vocal declamation. Puccini later used some of the music from Act IV, which was cut in the second version, for the love duet in Act III of *Tosca*.

RECORDING Scotto, Killebrew, Bergonzi, Sardinero, NY Schola Cantorum and Opera O, Queler, CBS, 1977
EDITION v.s., Ricordi, 1905

Manon Lescaut

Lyric drama in four acts (2h)
Libretto by Ruggero Leoncavallo, Marco Praga, Domenico Oliva, Luigi Illica and Giuseppe Giacosa (with contributions by Giulio Ricordi and the composer), based on the novel *L'histoire du Chevalier des Grieux et de Manon Lescaut* by Abbé Prévost (1731)
Composed 1889–October 1892, rev. 1893, 1922
PREMIERES 1 February 1893, Teatro Regio, Turin; UK: 14 May 1894, Covent Garden, London; US: 29 August 1894, Grand Opera House, Philadelphia (Hinrich's company)
CAST Manon Lescaut *s*, Il Cavaliere Renato des Grieux *t*, Lescaut *bar*, Geronte di Ravoir *b*, Edmondo *t*, a musician *ms*, Dancing Master *t*, Lamplighter *t*, Landlord *b*, Sergeant of the archers *b*, Naval Captain *b*, Hairdresser *silent*; *satb* chorus of girls, townspeople, men and women, students, musicians, old men and abbés, courtesans, guards, naval officers, sailors
ORCHESTRATION 3 fl/picc, 2 ob, ca, 2 cl, b cl, 2 bsn, 4 hn, 3 tpt, 3 trbn, tuba, timp, perc (triangle, sd, t-t, bd, cym, carillon), cel, hp, str; onstage: fl, cornet, bells, sd, sleigh bells

Puccini began searching for a new opera libretto soon after *Edgar* was first performed. Ruggero Leoncavallo – then better known as a librettist than a composer – was the first to sketch a text, but he soon dropped out of the project and was succeeded by an alarming succession of further librettists, each striving to accommodate a composer who was increasingly difficult to please in matters of dramatic structure and fine verbal detail. An added problem was the existence of Massenet's opera on the same subject: Puccini felt constrained to make his work sufficiently different from Massenet's, in order to avoid the charge of plagiarism. The text was eventually completed by Luigi Illica and Giuseppe Giacosa, who were destined to become the composer's most faithful – and long-suffering – collaborators. The opera underwent many subsequent revisions and even today several competing versions exist, of Act IV in particular (at one point Puccini cut the famous aria 'Sola, perduta, abbandonata . . .'). The composer probably never reached a 'definitive' form for this opera, his first international success.

SYNOPSIS

Act I A square in 18th-century Amiens, outside an inn. A student, Edmondo, and his companions are interrupted by Des Grieux, who mocks love before joining the others in praise of carefree pleasure. A coach arrives and Geronte (a rich, elderly adventurer), Lescaut and his sister Manon alight. Des Grieux is captivated by Manon, and soon contrives a personal encounter in which he discovers that she

Poster design for Manon Lescaut *(Turin, 1893)*

must go to join a convent the following day. As Lescaut calls Manon into the inn, Des Grieux persuades her to meet him again later. Left alone, the young man muses over Manon's beauty and his awakening love for her ('Donna non vidi mai'). Geronte admits to Lescaut that he too is interested in Manon, and plans to take her off to Paris – with Lescaut's blessing. Edmondo overhears the plot to abduct Manon and warns Des Grieux, who convinces Manon of his love and persuades her to run off with him to Paris, taking advantage of Geronte's waiting carriage. Geronte is furious that his plan has been foiled, but Lescaut calms him, assuring him that when Des Grieux's money runs out, Manon will again be available.

Act II opens on to a luxurious boudoir in Geronte's Parisian house. Manon has left Des Grieux, tempted away by Geronte's money. Although she relishes her new-found wealth, she nostalgically recounts to Lescaut the simple joys of her humble life with Des Grieux ('In quelle trine morbide'). After a dancing lesson, Manon is left alone. Des Grieux appears – having at last discovered Manon's whereabouts – and angrily reproaches her for her desertion. In an extended love duet, she gradually reawakens his love for her, but they are discovered by Geronte. When Manon taunts the old man, he retires with a vague threat. Des Grieux urges her to run away with him, but she lingers reluctantly over her jewels, causing him to despair over her foolishness ('Ah Manon, mi tradisce il tuo folle pensier'). As they at last prepare to depart, Lescaut appears, warning them that Geronte has denounced Manon and the police are on their way to arrest her. Manon again delays, attempting to gather up some of her treasures, and in a hectic climax Geronte bursts in and triumphantly sends her off in the hands of the police.

Act III, which is preceded by an orchestral intermezzo, takes place at the port of Le Havre, where Manon is about to be deported. Lescaut and Des Grieux are waiting for dawn in order to attempt her rescue. Des Grieux locates the room where Manon is imprisoned, and tells her through the window of their plan. But the attempt quickly fails. The convicted women are brought out one by one and the crowd comments on each of them; Manon and Des Grieux sing a bitter farewell. At the last moment, as the women are led to the convict ship bound for North America, Des Grieux attempts a last desperate rescue, and then flings himself at the feet of the captain, pleading to be allowed to accompany his beloved ('Guardate, pazzo son'). The captain takes pity on him, lets him come aboard, and gives orders for the departure.

Act IV takes place in the Louisiana desert, as night is falling. Manon and Des Grieux are again on the run. Manon, in the last stages of exhaustion, faints, and Des Grieux tries desperately to revive her ('Manon, senti, amor mio'). He goes off in search of water, and Manon bemoans her fate ('Sola, perduta, abbandonata . . .'). Soon after Des Grieux returns empty-handed, she falls dead at his feet, singing to the end that her love will never die.

As befits a youthful work, *Manon Lescaut* still betrays the influences that formed Puccini's mature style. Passages in the Act II love duet, for example, recall Wagner's harmonic language (particularly that of *Tristan*), while the close of that act is strongly reminiscent of middle-period Verdi. On the other hand, in Des Grieux's Act III aria, 'Guardate, pazzo son', and elsewhere, Puccini showed himself adept at the more 'modern' style of Ponchielli. Whatever the influences, almost all the music bears the stamp of Puccini's emerging mature style. We can also see the composer's growing awareness of large-scale structure, of the careful shaping of individual acts. Act I skilfully alternates hectic action sequences with moments of lyrical repose (a type of rapid juxtaposition that was much used in the opening acts of subsequent operas). Act II, on the other hand, is made up of two sharply contrasting musical ambiences: first a nostalgic re-creation of 18th-century musical manners; then a sudden plunge into the torridly expressive world of Manon and her

rejected lover. Act III is perhaps the most perfectly achieved large structure, the action sequences framing a magnificently controlled and highly original ensemble movement in which Manon and her fellow prisoners are paraded before the public. Act IV is something of a disappointment, its lack of outward action encouraging Puccini to attempt a 'symphonic' style that interferes with his usually impeccable sense of dramatic pacing. But this final uncertainty does little to shake a general feeling that with this opera Puccini found his authentic voice as a musical dramatist.

RECORDINGS 1. Albanese, Björling, Merrill, Calabrese, Rome Opera Ch and O, Perlea, RCA, 1954: mainly valuable for Björling's unsurpassed Des Grieux; 2. Callas, Di Stefano, Fioravanti, Calabrese, La Scala Ch and O, Serafin, EMI, 1957: most vivid and authentic interpretation; 3. Freni, Domingo, Bruson, Rydl, Royal Opera Ch, Philharmonia O, Sinopoli, DG, 1984: splendidly sung, eccentrically conducted; best stereo set [A.B.]
VIDEO Te Kanawa, Domingo, Allen, Royal Opera House Ch and O, Sinopoli, Castle, 1983: filmed live at Covent Garden
EDITIONS f.s., Ricordi, 1958; v.s., Ricordi, 1960

La bohème

Bohemian Life

Opera in four quadri (scenes) (1h 45m)
Libretto by Giuseppe Giacosa and Luigi Illica, based on Henry Mürger's *Scènes de la vie de bohème* (1845) and Mürger's and Théodore Barrière's play *La vie de bohème* (1849)
Composed 1893–5, rev. 1896
PREMIERES 1 February 1896, Teatro Regio, Turin; UK: 22 April 1897, Comedy Theatre, Manchester; US: 14 October 1897, Los Angeles Theater, Los Angeles (Royal Italian Grand Opera)
CAST Mimì *s*, Musetta *s*, Rodolfo *t*, Marcello *bar*, Schaunard *bar*, Colline *b*, Parpignol *t*, Benoit *b*, Alcindoro *b*; Act II: *satb* chorus of students, working girls, bourgeois, shopkeepers, street vendors, soldiers, waiters, children; Act III: Customs officer *b*, tavern drinkers 6 *s*, 3 *a*, scavengers 8 *b*, carters, milkmaids 6 *s*, peasant women 6 *s*
ORCHESTRATION picc, 2 fl, 2 ob, ca, 2 cl, b cl, 2 bsn, 4 hn, 3 tpt, 3 trbn, b trbn, timp, perc (sd, musical glasses, triangle, cym, bd, xyl, carillon, bells), hp, str; onstage: 4 pifferi (piccs in C), 6 tpt, 6 sd (tamburi in B♭)

La bohème was, it seems, born in litigation: the first we hear of Puccini's interest in the subject is in March 1893, when he engaged in a public quarrel with Ruggero Leoncavallo over the rights to Mürger's source. Around this time, the team of Luigi Illica and Giuseppe Giacosa (who had safely completed Puccini's previous opera, *Manon Lescaut*) were engaged, and work started in earnest. However, and in spite of the continuing 'race' with Leoncavallo (who insisted on continuing work on his own *Bohème*, which was eventually performed in 1897), the opera progressed slowly, in part because the success of *Manon Lescaut* obliged Puccini to undertake a number of extensive promotional tours. The composer overcame a characteristic loss of confidence in the subject (during which he toyed with an opera entitled *La lupa*, based on a short story by Giovanni Verga), and eventually completed the score in late 1895. As would become a regular feature of

Puccinian creation, the protracted period of composition saw numerous changes of direction and modification: at one point an entire act (to take place in the courtyard outside Musetta's flat) was discarded; at another the decision was made to divide the original first act into two separate acts. The first performance, given in Turin to delay the inevitable trial by fire at La Scala, Milan, was conducted by the 29-year-old Arturo Toscanini. The Turin audience, fresh from the first Italian performances of *Götterdämmerung*, gave *Bohème* a lukewarm reception, but the opera very soon found its way on to the international circuit, and is today one of the three or four most often performed works in the repertoire. Some time soon after the first performance, Puccini made various adjustments to the score, notably adding the 'bonnet' episode in Act II.

SYNOPSIS

Act I On Christmas Eve (1830) in Paris two Bohemian artists, Rodolfo (a poet) and Marcello (a painter), are working in their scantily furnished and unheated garret. They are joined by two friends,

Costume design by Adolfo Hohenstein for the first Mimì *(Turin, 1896)*

Colline (a philosopher) and Schaunard (a musician), and the group decides to visit the Café Momus. Benoit, their landlord, enters to ask for the rent, but they skilfully evade him. As the others leave, Rodolfo stays behind to finish an article, promising to join them soon. A young seamstress, Mimì, shyly knocks at the door to ask for a light for her candle. Rodolfo is charmed and prolongs the encounter; he tells her about himself, and shares with her his dreams of love ('Che gelida manina'). Mimì in turn introduces herself, describing her loneliness and her attic lodgings ('Mi chiamano Mimì'). The shouts of Rodolfo's friends from the courtyard below call him to the window; the moonlight, flooding the room, shines directly on Mimì's face, and Rodolfo is overcome with emotion ('O soave fanciulla'). He and Mimì declare their love, and together go off to join Rodolfo's friends at the Café Momus.

Act II begins in a bustling, brightly lit street in the Latin quarter where Rodolfo and Mimì meet the other Bohemians outside the Café Momus. The entrance of Marcello's erstwhile mistress, Musetta, causes a sensation: she is on the arm of a rich admirer, Alcindoro. She places herself at a neighbouring table and tries to attract Marcello's attention by singing of the amorous attention her looks inspire ('Quando me'n vo''). Marcello, after initial irritation, capitulates; Musetta creates a scene to get rid of Alcindoro, and throws herself into her former lover's arms. But then, disaster: the bill is presented. Who can pay? As a military band approaches, the Bohemians disappear into the crowd. Alcindoro returns to find Musetta gone and collapses in amazement at the huge bill she has left on his table.

Act III opens outside a tavern on the fringes of Paris. It is a bleak and snowy dawn in February; street-sweepers and peasants pass by on their way to the city. Mimì, weak and afflicted by a terrible cough, enters looking for Marcello who, at that moment, comes out of the tavern. She pours out her troubles, telling him how Rodolfo torments her with his constant jealousy. When Rodolfo himself appears Mimì retreats in confusion, hoping to avoid a confrontation. Rodolfo tells Marcello a different tale: his jealous fits hide despair over Mimì's increasingly serious illness. Mimì's coughing and sobs reveal her presence just as Marcello, hearing Musetta's laugh, rushes back inside. Rodolfo and Mimì agree that they must part, but sing poignantly of their love. Marcello and Musetta come out of the tavern, quarrelling heatedly. In the ensuing quartet, Marcello and Musetta exchange insults while Rodolfo and Mimì agree to stay together until the coming of spring.

Act IV returns us to the Bohemians' garret. Several months have passed. Rodolfo and Marcello are discussing Mimì and Musetta. They feign indifference, but reveal their true feelings in a duet ('O Mimì, tu più non torni'). Colline and Schaunard come in, and the four friends enact a series of charades culminating in a furious mock duel. Musetta's sudden appearance shatters the mood with news that Mimì is outside, very ill. Mimì is brought in and her condition spurs the Bohemians to scrape money together for a doctor. Colline decides to pawn his old coat, singing it an aria of mournful farewell ('Vecchia zimarra'). Left alone, Rodolfo and Mimì reminisce about their first meeting. The others return, and Mimì gently drifts into unconsciousness. As Rodolfo busies himself with her comfort, Schaunard discovers that her sleep will be permanent. The curtain falls to anguished cries from Rodolfo as he discovers the truth.

One of the greatest strengths of *La bohème* is the clarity of its overall structure. Although there are connecting musical links across the score (notably certain recurring themes), each of the four acts projects a characteristic musical atmosphere, and each is placed in telling contrast to its surroundings. Act I (as so often with Puccini, the longest and most musically dense) introduces the hectic energy of the Bohemians but closes with a prolonged period of stasis: the two autobiographical arias and the love duet of Rodolfo and Mimì. Acts II and III might be seen as complementary, the former showing the gaudy exterior of Parisian life, the latter its more sombre side; and each contrasts this evocation of ambience with a central lyrical moment (in Act II the ensemble 'Quando me'n vo'', and in Act III the famous quartet). Act IV returns us to the mood of Act I, but in subtly changed colours: the opening scene for the Bohemians is even more hectic than in Act I, while the conclusion casts a veil of nostalgia over the lovers' first meeting. As mentioned above, certain musical connections heighten this sense of pattern and reprise. The raucous descending triads that open Act II are converted to the fragile descending fifths of Act III; the characteristic, bumpy rhythm associated throughout with the Bohemians predominates in both the opening scenes of Act I and IV, and fragments of the famous Act I arias form the basis of the close of the drama. In the eyes of many perceptive commentators, *La bohème* is the composer's most perfectly achieved score: the one in which subject matter and musical style are most suited, and in which the overall dramatic effect is most consistently controlled.

RECORDINGS 1. De Los Angeles, Amara, Björling, Merrill, Reardon, Tozzi, RCA Victor Ch and O, Beecham, HMV, 1956: this remains the classic, atmospheric interpretation; 2. Callas, Moffo, Di Stefano, Panerai, Spatafora, Zaccaria, La Scala Ch and O, Votto, EMI, 1956: deeply moving performance from Callas as Mimì, well supported; 3. Tebaldi, D'Angelo, Bergonzi, Bastianini, Cesari, Siepi, Santa Cecilia Academy Ch and O, Serafin, Decca, 1958: regally cast, thoroughly Italianate reading; 4. Freni, Harwood, Pavarotti, Panerai, Maffeo, Ghiaurov, Deutsche Oper Ch and Berlin PO, Karajan, Decca, 1973: sensuous, slow-moving, gorgeously sung performance in modern sound [A.B.]
VIDEOS 1. Freni, Martino, Raimondi, Panerai, Maffeo, Vinco, Ch and O of La Scala, Karajan, DG Laserdisc, 1988; VHS, 1990: famous La Scala–Zeffirelli production of the 1960s, with a fine cast, led by Freni's touching, young Mimì; 2. Cotrubas, Zschau, Shicoff, Rawnsley, Allen, Hawdl, Ch and O of Covent Garden, Gardelli, Castle, 1970s: film of John Copley's long-lasting production with excellent cast; 3. Freni, Paceth, Pavarotti, G. Quilico, Dickson, Ghiaurov, San Francisco Opera Ch and O, Siverini, Virgin, 1992: Francesca Zambello's stage production [A.B.]
EDITIONS f.ss., Ricordi (folio), 1898; Ricordi (quarto), 1920; v.ss., Ricordi, 1896; 1944

Tosca

Opera in three acts (2h)
Libretto by Giuseppe Giacosa and Luigi Illica, based on Victorien Sardou's play *La Tosca* (1887)
Composed 1896–9
PREMIERES 14 January 1900, Teatro Costanzi, Rome; UK: 12 July 1900, Covent Garden, London; US: 4 February 1901, Metropolitan, New York
CAST Floria Tosca *s*, Mario Cavaradossi *t*, Baron Scarpia *bar*, Cesare Angelotti *b*, Sacristan *bar*, Spoletta *t*, Sciarrone *b*, Gaoler *b*, Shepherd Boy *treble*; *silent*: a Cardinal, a Judge, Roberti the executioner, a Scribe, an Officer, a Sergeant; *satb* chorus of priests, pupils, choir singers, soldiers, police agents, ladies, nobles, bourgeois, populace
ORCHESTRATION 3 fl/2 picc, 2 ob, ca, 2 cl, b cl, 2 bsn, dbsn, 4 hn, 3 tpt, 3 trbn, b trbn, timp, perc (sd, triangle, cym, t-t, bd), carillon (chimes), cel, glock (campanelli), str; onstage: fl, vla, hp, 4 hn, 3 trbn, church bells, organ, 2 sd, guns, cannon

The first reference to *Tosca* in Puccini's correspondence dates from more than ten years before its premiere. The subject had been suggested by Ferdinando Fontana (librettist of *Le villi* and *Edgar*), but the subject was given by Ricordi to the by now trusted team of Illica and (later) Giacosa. For Puccini, work on *Manon* and *La bohème* intervened, and the subject passed to another composer,

Poster for the premiere of Tosca *(Rome, 1900)*

Alberto Franchetti. But during 1895, with work on *Bohème* coming to a close, Puccini's interest in *Tosca* revived and, with Ricordi's help, Franchetti was persuaded to give up his interest in the opera. In spite of continuing reservations on the part of Giacosa about the subject's suitability, work on the opera progressed steadily. As with *Bohème*, the main interruptions were caused by Puccini's increasingly far-flung visits to supervise revivals of his previous successes. In the later stages of composition, the composer went to considerable trouble to establish a precise sense of local colour: he made a trip to Rome in 1897 to listen to the sound of church bells from the heights of the Castello Sant'Angelo, and he enlisted the help of a priest, Don Pietro Panichelli, to check certain religious details. As the opera neared completion, Ricordi attempted to persuade Puccini to revise part of Act III, in particular a passage in the love duet which Puccini had taken from a discarded passage in *Edgar*. But the composer managed to defend himself and the opera moved into rehearsal with few further changes. Puccini had great faith in the premiere cast, which included Ericlea Darclée (Tosca), Emilio De Marchi (Cavaradossi) and Eugenio Giraldoni (Scarpia), but the first performance (conducted by Leopoldo Mugnone) was greeted by a mixed reception. In spite of this, the composer made few alterations to his score, and *Tosca* fairly soon established itself as a staple of the operatic repertoire.

SYNOPSIS

Act I opens in the church of Sant'Andrea della Valle, Rome, in June 1800. Angelotti, an escaped prisoner, takes refuge in a side chapel. A Sacristan enters, followed shortly afterwards by Cavaradossi, an artist working on a painting of the Madonna. As Cavaradossi prepares to start work, he muses over his painting; although this Madonna is blonde she reminds him of his dark mistress, the singer Tosca ('Recondita armonia'). The sound of the Sacristan leaving brings Angelotti from his hiding-place. Angelotti and the painter recognize each other, and Cavaradossi promises to help his friend to escape from Rome. They hear Tosca's voice outside; Angelotti hides again before she enters. The sound of conversation has aroused Tosca's jealousy, but Cavaradossi's assurances calm her, and they join in a passionate duet. When Tosca leaves, Angelotti reappears and he and Cavaradossi plan his flight, but a distant cannon warns them that the prison escape has been discovered; they exit hurriedly together. As a crowd gathers for a celebratory *Te Deum*, Scarpia, the chief of police, enters with his henchman Spoletta and orders a search for the escaped prisoner. Tosca returns and Scarpia, suspicious of Cavaradossi and enamoured of Tosca, tries to trick her into revealing information by inciting her jealousy. When she leaves to seek out her lover, Scarpia has her followed, and, as the crowd intones the *Te Deum*, Scarpia vows to bring Cavaradossi to the gallows and Tosca into his arms ('Va, Tosca! Nel tuo cuor s'annida Scarpia').

Act II takes place in Scarpia's room in the Farnese Palace. Scarpia muses over his violent desire for Tosca ('Ha più forte sapore'). Spoletta enters to report that Angelotti has not been found, but that he has arrested Cavaradossi for suspicious behaviour. Cavaradossi is brought in and questioned, but he denies all knowledge of Angelotti's escape. Scarpia has sent for Tosca, and she comes in as Cavaradossi is led to the next room to be tortured. Tosca is left alone with Scarpia, and Cavaradossi's cries of pain eventually drive her to reveal Angelotti's hiding-place. Cavaradossi is dragged back onstage just as Napoleon's victory at Marengo is announced. The news elicits a stirring response from Cavaradossi, and the outraged Scarpia has him taken off to prison. Scarpia and Tosca are once again left alone, and Scarpia offers Tosca a hideous choice: she must submit to his lust or cause Cavaradossi's execution. She sings a despairing aria ('Vissi d'arte'), but finally agrees to submit. Scarpia summons Spoletta and pretends to order a faked execution. Scarpia writes a safe-conduct from Rome for her and Cavaradossi, Tosca surreptitiously takes a knife from the dinner table and, when Scarpia comes forward to claim his prize, plunges it into his chest. She taunts him in his death throes and, when he expires, takes the safe-conduct from his clenched hand and starts to leave. At the last moment she returns to place candles around Scarpia's body and a crucifix on his chest.

Act III opens a few hours later, just before dawn on a platform of the Castello Sant'Angelo. Church bells ring and a shepherd boy sings in the distance. Cavaradossi awaits his final hour, overcome by memories of Tosca and thoughts of his approaching death ('E lucevan le stelle'). Tosca appears and triumphantly displays their safe-conduct. She instructs him on his role in the mock execution and they sing of their love and hopes for the future. As four o'clock strikes, the firing squad arrives and Cavaradossi is prepared for execution. Tosca watches, hardly managing to restrain herself as the shots ring out and Cavaradossi falls. In an agony of suspense, she waits for the soldiers to depart. At last she tells Cavaradossi to rise, but he does not respond: Scarpia has betrayed her even in death and her lover lies dead before her. Soldiers rush on to arrest Tosca for Scarpia's murder but, with a final defiant gesture, she flings herself over the parapet.

The famous opening chords of *Tosca* (associated with Scarpia's evil), which recur during the first two acts of the opera, have been said to herald a new dramatic and musical potential in Puccini's work. In these chords and elsewhere the composer uses 'modernistic' harmonic devices to thrilling dramatic effect. Indeed, the opera as a whole attempts a dramatic level far more grandiose and impressive than *La bohème*, and in some senses it achieves its expanded goals. Act I in particular is a *tour de force*; in spite of a weight of stage action that made his librettists dubious of its operatic viability, Puccini managed to characterize musically all the essential elements of the drama, and even to allow time for the lyrical pauses so necessary to the development of his dramatic intentions. Act II, scarcely less dense in its activity, though necessarily more sparse in its musical invention, is again magnificently paced, with passages such as the final, orchestrally accompanied mime showing that Puccini was capable of finely calculated dramatic effect even without the stimulus of the voice. As his publisher and friend Giulio Ricordi so acutely observed, Act III is, in spite of many fine moments, hardly on a level with the other two, and tends to flag in its central love duet. However, taken as a whole and with the help of first-class singing actors, *Tosca* can reach an intensity of dramatic effect rarely equalled in Puccini's theatre.

RECORDINGS 1. Caniglia, Gigli, A. Borgioli, Rome Opera Ch and O, De Fabritiis, EMI, 1938: memorable for Gigli's Cavaradossi, an unsurpassed interpretation, and for Caniglia's impetuous Tosca; sounds amazingly well on CD; 2. Callas, Di Stefano, Gobbi, La Scala Ch and O, De Sabata, EMI, 1953: the classic set with Callas and Gobbi unsurpassed; 3. L. Price, Di Stefano, Taddei, Vienna Staatsoper Ch, Vienna PO, Karajan, Decca, 1963: another classic set; 4. Caballé, Carreras, Wixell, Royal Opera House Ch and O, C. Davis, Philips, 1977: most successful modern version [A.B]
VIDEOS 1. Kabaivanska, Domingo, Milnes, Ambrosian Singers, New Philharmonia O, Bartoletti, Decca Laserdisc, 1988; VHS, 1990: colourful 1976 film made on location in Rome; 2. Behrens, Domingo, McNeil, Ch and O of Metropolitan, New York, Sinopoli, DG, 1992: film of Ponnelle's exciting production [A.B.]
EDITIONS f.ss., Ricordi (folio), 1899; Ricordi (quarto), 1924; 1954; v.ss., Ricordi, 1899; 1960

Madama Butterfly
Madam Butterfly

A Japanese tragedy in three acts (2h); second and third versions in two acts/Act II in two parts; fourth version in three acts
Libretto by Giuseppe Giacosa and Luigi Illica, based on David Belasco's play *Madame Butterfly*, itself based on a short story by John Luther Long (1898)
Composed 1901–3 (in two acts); rev. (second version) 1904; further revs 1905; cuts, alterations for Paris, 1906
PREMIERES 17 February 1904, La Scala, Milan; second version: 28 May 1904, Teatro Grande, Brescia; third version: UK: 10 July 1905, Covent Garden, London; US: 15 October 1906, Savage Opera Company, Washington DC; definitive version (with minor exceptions): 28 December 1906, Opéra-Comique, Paris
CAST Madama Butterfly (Cio-Cio-San) *s*, Suzuki *ms*, Kate Pinkerton *ms*, B. F. Pinkerton *t*, Sharpless *bar*, Goro *t*, Prince Yamadori *t*, Bonze *b*, Yakuside *b*, Imperial Commissioner *b*, Official Registrar *b*, Butterfly's mother *ms*, aunt *s*, cousin *s*, Sorrow *silent*; *satb* chorus of Butterfly's relatives and friends, servants
ORCHESTRATION 3 fl/picc, 2 ob, ca, 2 cl, b cl, 2 bsn, 4 hn, 3 tpt, 3 trbn, b trbn, timp, perc (sd, triangle, cym, t-t, bd, keyed glock (campanelli a tastiera), Japanese campanelli, bells, Japanese t-t), str; onstage: campanella, tubular bells, viola d'amore, bird-calls, t-t, b t-t

Puccini's first exposure to *Madama Butterfly* (in June 1900) was at a performance of David Belasco's play in London. It is clear that what initially caught the composer's interest – he knew little English – was a drama intimately tied to a striking new ambience (Japan); and we can guess that this immediately awakened musical possibilities. Very soon after-

wards, Puccini expanded his vision. With the help of material from John Luther Long's novella (the source for Belasco's play), he planned to make a two-act opera: the first set in North America, the second in Japan, thus establishing a dramatic juxtaposition between two distinctive musical ambiences. Once the rights to *Butterfly* had been cleared, Illica set to work on a scenario, and in March 1901 came up with a different plan: Act I would be a kind of prologue, depicting the meeting and marriage of Butterfly and Pinkerton in Japan. Act II was to be in three scenes, with episodes in Butterfly's house framing a scene at the American Consulate. Thus, in both parts, the contrast between 'European' and 'Oriental' values could be explored. This plan (elaborated by Illica and Giacosa) held good for over a year, but then, in November 1902, the composer insisted that the Consulate scene be discarded. This decision had considerable repercussions. Act II now concentrated single-mindedly on Butterfly: the other principal characters, Pinkerton and Sharpless, were now embarrassingly peripheral, so much so that it later became clear that Pinkerton's part would have to be 'artificially' filled out in the new Act II. The opera's premiere at La Scala, Milan, was a resounding failure, and in the coming years Puccini continued to revise the score, including taking out some of the detailed Japanese local colour in Act I, and adding new material for Pinkerton, notably his aria 'Addio fiorito asil', in Act II/Part II.

SYNOPSIS
The opera takes place near Nagasaki in the early 1900s.

Act I opens outside a little house on which Pinkerton, an American naval officer, has taken out a 999-year lease and is making the final arrangements with the Japanese marriage-broker, Goro, for a Japanese wedding. From a discussion with the American consul, Sharpless, we gather that according to Japanese law the marriage will not be binding. Pinkerton revels in his carefree attitude as a 'Yankee vagabondo' who takes his pleasure where he finds it ('Dovunque al mondo'); Sharpless tries in vain to warn him that his 15-year-old bride, Butterfly, is serious about the marriage. Butterfly enters amid a bustle of friends and relatives, singing happily of the love that awaits her. After shyly greeting Pinkerton, she shows him her few belongings – including the ceremonial dagger with which her father killed himself – and the commissioner performs the wedding ceremony. But the festivities are short-lived; her uncle (the Bonze) arrives and curses her for converting to Christianity, and her relatives and friends immediately join him in rejecting her. Butterfly is left alone with Pinkerton, who tries to comfort her. Her servant Suzuki prepares her for the wedding night, and she joins Pinkerton in the garden for an extended love duet ('Viene la sera'). He is enchanted with his plaything-wife and, while she speaks tenderly of her love, ardently claims his fluttering, captured butterfly.

Act II (Part I) is in the same house, several years later. Butterfly and Suzuki are alone. Pinkerton sailed for America three years ago, but Butterfly remains fiercely loyal and describes to Suzuki her dream of his return ('Un bel dì'). Sharpless, knowing that Pinkerton has taken an American wife and will soon be arriving in Nagasaki with her, attempts to prepare Butterfly for the shock. But Butterfly will not listen and remains stubbornly faithful; she shows Sharpless the child she has borne Pinkerton without his knowledge, convinced that this revelation will ensure her husband's return. Sharpless leaves, unable to face Butterfly with the truth. A cannon shot is heard and Butterfly and Suzuki see Pinkerton's ship coming into harbour. Butterfly jubilantly prepares for his return, filling the room with flowers and again donning her bridal costume. With preparations complete, the two women and the child sit down to wait for Pinkerton's arrival. Night falls; as Suzuki and the child sleep and Butterfly waits motionless, a humming chorus is heard in the distance.

Act II (Part II) It is dawn and Butterfly has fallen asleep at her post. Suzuki rouses her and she carries the sleeping child into the next room, singing a sad lullaby. Pinkerton and Sharpless arrive and ask Suzuki to talk to Pinkerton's new wife, Kate, who is waiting outside. Suzuki agrees, but the sight of her distress, together with memories of the past, overcome Pinkerton. He is filled with remorse ('Addio fiorito asil'), and he leaves rather than face the woman he deserted. Butterfly rushes in, searching desperately for Pinkerton, but she sees only the strange woman waiting in the garden. Suzuki and Sharpless manage to break the news that this is Pinkerton's wife, and that her husband will never return to her. Butterfly seems to accept the blow, and agrees to give up her son, asking only that Pinkerton come in person to fetch him. Kate and Sharpless leave; Suzuki tries to comfort Butterfly, but she asks to be left alone. She takes her father's dagger from the wall and prepares to kill herself. Suzuki pushes the child into the room, and Butterfly drops the dagger, momentarily deterred. After an impassioned farewell ('O a me, sceso dal trono'), she blindfolds the child and, going behind a screen, stabs herself just as Pinkerton rushes in calling her name.

The play of varied 'local colours', always an important feature of Puccini's writing, takes on particular importance in Act I of *Madama Butterfly*, which was structurally conceived along lines very similar to those of *La bohème*. As in the earlier opera, though on a much larger scale, an opening section established a musical and dramatic atmosphere of hectic activity, which is then juxtaposed with a lyrical and comparatively static close. However, in *Butterfly* there is a central shift in musical ambience marked by the entrance of the heroine. The final duet in Act I breaks new musical ground and although, as Illica pointed out early on, it superficially resembles that of Rodolfo and Mimì in *La bohème*, it is actually a far more complex musical and dramatic structure. By mediating between contrasting musical ambiences and then gradually blending them, the duet ends with the lovers subsumed in a new musical medium, one that

somehow arises from their two quite separately established styles. As mentioned earlier, Act II focuses on the heroine with (for Puccini) unprecedented concentration, and leads inexorably to the tragic *dénouement*. Whether the music of this final scene is capable of sustaining its weight of dramatic expectation is a matter of debate, but few will deny that *Butterfly* makes an important and brave attempt to break away from established dramatic patterns.

RECORDINGS 1. Callas, Danieli, Gedda, Borriello, La Scala Ch and O, Karajan, EMI, 1955: Callas in one of her most affecting performances, admirably supported, with Karajan a highly charged conductor; 2. de Los Angeles, Pirazzini, Björling, Sereni, Rome Opera Ch and O, Santini, EMI, 1960: Victoria de Los Angeles in one of her most famous roles, Björling in one of his final recordings; 3. Scotto, Di Stasio, Bergonzi, Panerai, Rome Opera Ch and O, Barbirolli, EMI, 1967: probably the most successfully cast and conducted recording of all; 4. Freni, Ludwig, Pavarotti, Kerns, Vienna Staatsoper Ch, Vienna PO, Karajan, Decca, 1974: sumptuous singing, playing and recording [A.B.]
VIDEO Freni, Ludwig, Domingo, Kerns, Vienna Staatsoper Ch, Vienna PO, Karajan, Decca VHS, 1990: over-imaginative Ponnelle production, well sung and conducted [A.B.]
EDITIONS f.ss., Ricordi (folio), 1907; Ricordi (quarto), 1923; 1955; v.ss., Ricordi: 1904 in two acts, 1904; in three acts, 1904; third version, 1906; fourth version (in French), 1906

La fanciulla del West

The Girl of the Golden West
Opera in three acts (2h)
Libretto by Guelfo Civinini and Carlo Zangarini, based on the play *The Girl of the Golden West* by David Belasco (1905)
Composed 1908–10
PREMIERES 10 December 1910, Metropolitan, New York; UK: 29 May 1911, Covent Garden, London; Italy: 12 June 1911, Teatro Costanzi, Rome
CAST Minnie *s*, Jack Rance *bar*, Dick Johnson (Ramerrez) *t*, Nick *t*, Ashby *b*, Sonora *b*, Trim *t*, Sid *bar*, Bello (Handsome) *bar*, Harry *t*, Joe *t*, Happy *bar*, Larkens *b*, Billy Jackrabbit *b*, Wowkle *ms*, Jake Wallace *bar*, José Castro *b*, postilion *t*; *tb* chorus of men of the camp
ORCHESTRATION picc, 3 fl, 3 ob, ca, 3 cl, b cl, 3 bsn, dbsn, 4 hn, 3 tpt, 3 trbn, b trbn, timp, perc (bells, glock) 2 hp (second also offstage), cel, str: offstage: hp, harmonica, wind-machine, t-t, tubular bells

After considering a variety of subjects – including Victor Hugo's *The Hunchback of Notre-Dame* – and being constantly distracted by foreign and domestic travels, Puccini finally settled on another 'exotic' subject for his next opera. The composer saw Belasco's *The Girl of the Golden West* in New York in early 1907 (he was there to see the Metropolitan premieres of both *Manon Lescaut* and *Madama Butterfly*), and decided to set it to music after reading an Italian translation. His librettists Zangarini and Civinini were on occasion slow to produce, and a personal tragedy – in which a servant girl of Puccini's was driven to suicide by his wife's unfounded jealousy – forced him to put the work aside for some time. Appropriately enough, the opera received its first performance in America, where it was conducted by Toscanini and greeted with great

Caricatures by Enrico Caruso, of Emmy Destinn as Minnie and of himself as Johnson, drawn during a rehearsal for La fanciulla del West *(New York, 1910)*

enthusiasm. The star cast was headed by Emmy Destinn, Enrico Caruso and Pasquale Amato.

SYNOPSIS
At the foot of the Cloudy Mountains (Nubi) in California. A miners' camp at the time of the 1849–50 gold rush.

Act I takes place in the Polka Bar. The bandit Ramerrez is at large and a $5000 reward has been set for him. Sheriff Jack Rance declares his love for Minnie, the chaste darling of the miners ('Minnie, dalla mia casa'), but she rejects him, reminiscing about her parents' love for each other and hoping that she will find true love ('Laggiù nel Soledad'). A man announcing himself as Dick Johnson arrives. He has met Minnie before, and their friendly relationship angers Rance. All the men go out in search of Ramerrez, leaving Minnie alone with Johnson. In their ensuing conversation, Johnson becomes increasingly enamoured, and they agree to meet later in her cabin.

Act II begins one hour later in Minnie's cabin, where Minnie is excitedly preparing for her visitor. Johnson arrives, and as they have supper Minnie tells him how much she loves her life in the mountains ('Oh, se sapeste'). Completely enchanted, Johnson embraces her; she succumbs ecstatically to her 'first kiss'. As he prepares to leave, he discovers that snow is falling heavily outside, and Minnie agrees to let him stay the night. As he goes off to bed, Rance arrives to tell Minnie that 'Johnson' is none other than the bandit Ramerrez. When Rance has left, Minnie angrily confronts Johnson, who pleads for her understanding, telling her how he was fated from birth for the bandit's life ('Una parola sola'), but she orders him to leave. As soon as he has gone, shots ring out and Johnson's body slumps against the door. Minnie drags him in and succeeds in hiding him in

her loft. Rance again enters, searching for the bandit, and drops of blood falling on his hand eventually reveal Johnson. In a desperate ploy, Minnie plays Rance at poker: if she wins, Johnson will go free; if she loses, she will agree to marry Rance. She wins by cheating on the last hand, Rance leaves and she collapses, laughing hysterically.

Act III takes place in a nearby forest. Rance and friends sit by a fire. News arrives that Johnson has been caught, and the miners prepare to string him up. Johnson is brought in and, after speaking tenderly of Minnie and begging the miners not to tell her how he died ('Ch'ella mi creda libero'), is led to the makeshift gallows. But Minnie arrives just in time and pleads with the miners to spare him. They eventually agree, unable to refuse her after all she has done for them, and Minnie and Johnson depart for a new life together.

Parts of *Fanciulla* present a musical–dramatic problem even more severe than that in Act I of *Tosca*: the sheer complexity of stage action allows very little time to 'place' events musically, and crowds out the opportunity for those lyrical pauses and developments so necessary to Puccini's art. Clearly the composer willingly embraced this type of drama, but it is at least arguable that by the time of *Fanciulla* his powers of musical invention were less able to sustain such extreme concentration. Like *Tosca* – and perhaps even more so – the opera needs singing actors of the first quality in order to succeed on stage. What is undeniable is that *Fanciulla* is harmonically and orchestrally one of Puccini's most innovative scores, and in these two areas represents a high point in experimentation and musical daring. For this, and for many other reasons, it deserves a better relative placing in the Puccinian canon than it today enjoys.

RECORDING Neblett, Domingo, Milnes, Royal Opera House Ch and O, Mehta, DG, 1978
VIDEO Neblett, Domingo, Carroli, Royal Opera House Ch and O, Santi, Castle, 1978: recorded live at Covent Garden
EDITIONS f.ss., Ricordi (folio), 1910; Ricordi (quarto), 1925; v.ss., Ricordi 1910; 1963

La rondine
The Swallow
Lyric comedy in three acts (1h 45m)
Libretto by Giuseppe Adami, based on the German libretto by Alfred Maria Willner and Heinz Reichert
Composed 1914–16; rev. 1919; further revs 1920
PREMIERES 27 March 1917, Salle Garnier, Monte Carlo; Italy: 5 June 1917, Bologna; UK: 24 June 1929 (broadcast), 9 December 1965, Fulham Town Hall, London; US: 10 March 1928, Metropolitan, New York
CAST Magda de Civry *s*, Ruggero Lastouc *t*, Rambaldo Fernandez *bar*, Lisette *s*, Prunier *t*, 4 *s*, 2 *ms*, *t*, *bar*, 3 *b*; *satb* chorus of citizens, students, artists, dancers
FULL ORCHESTRA

After *La fanciulla del West* Puccini spent some fruitless years searching for a suitable libretto for his next work. The plan for *La rondine* emerged from a proposal made in 1913 for Puccini to write a Viennese operetta for the Karltheater. Eventually

Puccini agreed, though he insisted on writing a comic opera (with no spoken dialogue) and on setting the text in Italian. In due course a German text arrived and was translated by Giuseppe Adami. Puccini finished the score in October 1915, but the outbreak of the First World War had put the whole project in jeopardy, and it was some time before he could secure the rights to arrange a first performance and Italian publication. *La rondine* was finally premiered in 1917 in Monte Carlo.

SYNOPSIS

Paris and Nice during the Second Empire.

Act I takes place in a Parisian salon. Magda (the mistress of Rambaldo, a rich banker) and her maid Lisette playfully discuss the joys of love with Prunier. Ruggero, the son of one of Rambaldo's friends, joins the party and all decide that, for his first night in Paris, he should go to the popular night spot Bullier. When the guests leave, Prunier and Lisette decide to go out together. Magda, who is feeling wistful and has had adventures there in the past, dons a disguise and decides she too will go to Bullier.

Act II takes place in Bullier. Magda and Ruggero meet and dance, becoming strongly attracted to each other. Even though Rambaldo appears and confronts Magda, she will not break off, and eventually she and Ruggero admit their love and leave together.

Act III occurs some months later. Magda and Ruggero are living together blissfully in Nice. Ruggero tells Magda that he has written to his mother for consent to marry her, but Magda realizes that she will never receive his family's approval. Lisette and Prunier are together again, although Prunier's attempt to put Lisette on the stage in Nice has proved a disaster. Ruggero bursts in with his mother's letter, which blesses his marriage; but Magda tells him she can never become his wife and sadly decides that she must leave him for ever.

La rondine has always been the least performed of Puccini's mature operas, and this in spite of certain well-known extracts such as Magda's Act I aria 'Che il bel sogno' and the Act II *concertato* 'Bevo al tuo fresco sorriso'. Various reasons for its comparative lack of success have been suggested, among which the weaknesses of Ruggero's characterization and the shaky motivation of Magda's *Traviata*-like renunciation are clearly well founded. But perhaps the central problem is with the extensive sub-plot between Lisette and Prunier, which vies with the Magda–Ruggero plot in length and development, but in which Puccini found little to stimulate his lyrical fantasy. However, for those who know the opera well, *La rondine* cannot be easily dismissed; its restraint and lightness of touch suggest a surprising new range in Puccini's musical language, one that many regret he did not explore further.

RECORDING   Te Kanawa, Watson, Domingo, Rendall, Nucci, Ambrosian Opera Ch, LSO, Maazel, CBS, 1983
EDITIONS   f.s., Sonzogno (folio), [1917]; v.ss., first version, Sonzogno, 1917; second version, Eibenschütz und Berté, 1920; third version, Sonzogno, 1921–2

Il trittico

Triptych of one-act operas
PREMIERES   14 December 1918, Metropolitan, New York; Italy: 11 January 1919, Teatro Costanzi, Rome; UK: 18 June 1920, Covent Garden, London

The idea of combining a collection of one-act operas into a single evening had been on Puccini's mind through most of his career, but had consistently been opposed by his publisher, Ricordi. Puccini first saw Didier Gold's play *La houppelande* in Paris in 1912, and by 1913 he was in negotiations with Illica about the subject. Eventually, though, a libretto was fashioned by Giuseppe Adami, and work on *Il tabarro* began in October 1915, immediately after Puccini had completed *La rondine*. He finished this first panel of the 'triptych' in 1916, with no idea of what the companion pieces were going to be. After considering a host of topics, the answer eventually came from Giovacchino Forzano, who in early 1917 offered Puccini the libretto for a one-act opera set in a convent, *Suor Angelica*, and (soon afterwards) a second, comic subject entitled *Gianni Schicchi*. Puccini accepted both gladly, and finished the remaining two operas by early 1918 – for him, something like record time. The Metropolitan in New York paid a considerable sum for the rights to the world premiere, which was given that same year conducted by Roberto Moranzoni. Though *Il trittico* has occasionally been revived in its complete form, today it is more usual to find two of the three operas performed as a double-bill.

Il tabarro

The Cloak
Opera in one act (55m)
Libretto by Giuseppe Adami, based on the play *La houppelande* by Didier Gold (1910)
Composed 1915–16
PREMIERES   see *Il trittico* above
CAST   Giorgetta (25) s, Luigi (20) t, Michele (50) bar, La Frugola (50) ms, Tinca (35) t, Talpa (55) b, a song-vendor t, 2 lovers s, t, an organ-grinder *silent*; *satb* chorus of stevedores and seamstresses
ORCHESTRATION   picc, 2 fl, 2 ob, ca, 2 cl, b cl, 2 bsn, 4 hn, 3 tpt, 3 trbn, b trbn, timp, perc (sd, triangle, cym, bd), str; onstage: cornet in B♭, car horn (both in the distance), hp, siren, low bell

SYNOPSIS

The opera takes place in contemporary Paris. A barge is tied to a quay beside the Seine, and its owner, Michele, watches the sun set as the stevedores finish the day's work. Michele's wife Giorgetta goes about her chores, and as workers come and go and street musicians pass she steals a few moments with her lover Luigi, who is one of the stevedores. They are interrupted by Michele, who looks at them suspiciously but leaves them alone long enough for them to arrange a rendezvous for later that night. After Luigi has gone, Michele returns and speaks of the past, begging Giorgetta to return to their former love and happiness. But Giorgetta evades his caresses and Michele grimly watches her go inside,

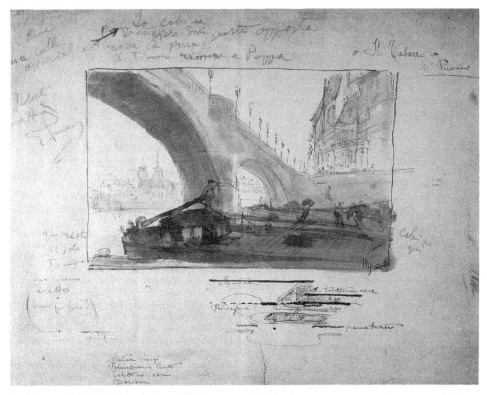

Study for a set design for Il tabarro *by Santoni, 1918*

convinced of her infidelity. He remains alone in the dark, tormenting himself with thoughts of her betrayal ('Nulla, silenzio'). In silence he lights his pipe and Luigi, who mistakes the light for Giorgetta's pre-arranged signal, runs aboard the barge. Michele catches Luigi and, after forcing him to confess his love for Giorgetta, chokes him to death. When Giorgetta reappears, Michele conceals the corpse under his cloak; as she approaches, he removes the cloak and triumphantly reveals Luigi's lifeless body.

Il tabarro has many admirers, some even considering it the composer's finest work. The orchestration is highly innovative (as is demonstrated, for example, by the orchestral introduction, in which a texture of Debussy-like clarity and subtlety sets forth the governing ambience of the score); the musical characterization is surprisingly well defined considering the duration of the action, with even minor figures such as Il Tinca (a stevedore) and La Frugola (wife of another stevedore, Talpa) sharply focused. Perhaps most importantly, the timing of the musical drama is impeccable, with lyrical scenes always balancing the action sequences. Realistic touches such as the motor horn in the opening, or the music-seller who offers his clients a snatch of *La bohème*, are subtly integrated into the generally sombre atmosphere and, as the major characters all

grow out of this ambience, the effect of the drama is all the more compelling.

RECORDINGS   1. Mas, Prandelli, Gobbi, Rome Opera Ch and O, Bellezza, EMI, 1955: torrid, melodramatic performance with Gobbi's unbeatable Michele; 2. Tokody, Lamberti, Nimsgern, Bavarian Radio Ch, Munich Radio O, Patané, Eurodisc, 1988: good modern version (the Eurodisc *Trittico* is available as a CD box) [A.B.]
VIDEO   Sass, Gasdia, Plowright, Vejzovic, Martinucci, Cappuccilli, Ch and O of La Scala, Milan, Castle, 1983 (*Trittico* complete)
EDITIONS   f.ss., Ricordi (folio), 1918; Ricordi (quarto), 1927; 1956; v.ss., Ricordi, 1918; 1960

Suor Angelica
Sister Angelica
Opera in one act (1h)
Libretto by Giovacchino Forzano
Composed 1917
PREMIERES   see *Il trittico* above
CAST   Suor Angelica *s*, La Zia Principessa *a*, Suor Genoveva *s*, Suor Osmina *s*, Suor Dolcina *s*, La Badessa (the Abbess) *ms*, La Suora Zelatrice (the monitor) *ms*, La Maestra delle novizie (the mistress of the novices) *ms*, La Suora Infermiera (the nursing sister) *ms*; *sa* chorus of alms-collectors, novices, lay sisters
ORCHESTRATION   picc, 2 fl, 2 ob, ca, 2 cl, b cl, 2 bsn, 4 hn, 3 tpt, 3 trbn, b trbn, timp, perc (triangle, cym, bd, glock), cel, hp, str; onstage: bronze bell; offstage: picc, 2 pf, organ, 3 tpt, bells, cym, tavolette

SYNOPSIS

A convent in late 17th-century Italy. As the curtain opens, the nuns are finishing their prayers and joyfully go about their business, while Sister Angelica tries unsuccessfully to hide her unhappiness; in the seven years she has spent in the convent, she has heard no news of her family. But soon the Abbess announces that her aunt, a princess, has come to visit. When the aunt is ushered in, Angelica is checked by the coldness of her aunt's greeting. From their conversation we learn that Angelica has been put in the convent by her family as punishment for having an illegitimate child. As Angelica begs for compassion, her aunt coldly informs her that the child is now dead. The princess leaves Angelica alone to weep despairingly, desiring only to end her sorrows and join her child in heaven ('Senza Mamma'). The other nuns join her in ecstatic praise of the Holy Virgin; when she is again left alone, she drinks poison, singing a joyful farewell to life. Suddenly her calm is shattered: by killing herself she is damned to eternal separation from the child she loves. She prays desperately to the Madonna; angels' voices join in her prayer as the Madonna herself appears, bringing the child to lead his mother into heaven.

As the plot summary indicates, this is an unashamedly sentimental drama, and perhaps gains its full effect only in its original context, framed by the more vivid and immediate *Tabarro* and *Gianni Schicchi*. The religious setting allowed Puccini to indulge in some pastiche of the world of his musical ancestors, and if the resulting pseudo-ecclesiastical vein works well in the less elevated context of the opening section of the opera, it seems strained at the more demanding, miraculous close. But there are moments of considerable effect, in particular the tension-laden meeting between Sister Angelica and her glacial aunt – the latter certainly the most extraordinary of Puccini's female creations; and Angelica's 'Senza Mamma', which follows the princess's exit, remains one of Puccini's greatest soprano arias.

RECORDINGS 1. de Los Angeles, Barbieri, Rome Opera Ch and O, Serafin, EMI, 1957: touching performance of title role from de Los Angeles; 2. Scotto, Horne, Desborough School Ch, National PO, Maazel, CBS, 1977: most notable for Horne as the Old Princess; 3. Popp, Lipovšek, Bavarian Radio Ch, Munich Radio O, Patané, Eurodisc, 1988: well-recorded modern version, with Popp an appealing Angelica (the Eurodisc *Trittico* is available as a CD box) [A.B.]
EDITIONS f.ss., Ricordi (folio), 1918; Ricordi (quarto), 1927; 1958; v.ss., Ricordi, 1918; 1943

Gianni Schicchi

Opera in one act (55m)
Libretto by Giovacchino Forzano, based on an episode (Canto XXX, l. 32) in Dante's *Inferno* (c. 1307–21)
Composed 1917–18
PREMIERES see *Il trittico* above
CAST Gianni Schicchi (50) *bar*, Lauretta (21) *s*, Rinuccio (24) *t*, Nella (34) *s*, La Ciesca (38) *ms*, Zita (60) *a*, Gheraldino (7) *a*, Gheraldo (40) *t*, Marco (45) *bar*, Ser Amantio di

Nicolao *bar*, Betto di Signa (indefinable age) *b*, Simone *b*, Maestro Spinelloccio *b*, Pinellino *b*, Guccio *b*
ORCHESTRATION picc, 2 fl, 2 ob, ca, 2 cl, b cl, 2 bsn, 4 hn, 3 tpt, 3 trbn, b trbn, timp, perc (sd, triangle, cym, bd, campana grave (interna)), cel, hp, str

SYNOPSIS

Late 13th-century Florence. The curtain opens on the bedroom of Buoso Donati, a rich old gentleman who has just died. His relatives are gathered round the deathbed, feigning grief to impress each other, until a rumour that Buoso has left all his money to a monastery sends them into a feverish search for his will. The young Rinuccio finds it first but withholds it from the others until he has extracted a promise from them: when they receive Buoso's money, he will be allowed to marry Lauretta, the daughter of Gianni Schicchi. The relatives hurriedly agree, but are sorely disappointed when they find out that all Buoso's money is indeed left to the Church. Rinuccio suggests turning the problem over to Gianni Schicchi, who is famed for his cunning, even though the relatives scoff at Schicchi's low birth ('Avete torto'). Schicchi himself arrives in answer to a secret summons from Rinuccio, bringing Lauretta with him. The relatives condescend to ask for Schicchi's help, but he refuses; finally Lauretta intercedes, begging her father to make her marriage to Rinuccio possible ('O mio babbino caro'). Schicchi comes up with a plan: they are to hide Buoso's death long enough for him, disguised as Buoso, to make a new will. Delighted, the relatives send for the notary, individually bribing Schicchi to give them the most favourable portion of the inheritance. Schicchi agrees to everything, reminding them that to reveal the trick will mean severe punishment according to Florentine law. When the notary arrives, Schicchi awards the lion's share of Buoso's property to his 'devoted friend, Gianni Schicchi' and the relatives are helpless to intervene. Once the notary has gone, Schicchi drives the relatives from his new home. Rinuccio and Lauretta remain on the terrace, singing of their love for each other. Schicchi returns and, seeing the young lovers, announces to the audience his satisfaction with the way Buoso's money has been used.

It is unfortunate that *Gianni Schicchi* was the only outright comic opera that Puccini wrote. Throughout his career he periodically toyed with comic subjects, but in the end refused to commit himself to anything that strayed so far from the paths in which he had achieved his greatest successes. Again, it is probably thanks to the one-act format, whose more discrete, short-term goals released the composer from his usual doubts, that we have this masterly vignette of medieval Florence. As with *Il tabarro*, the musical characterization is on a very high level, in particular the portraits of Gianni Schicchi and his daughter Lauretta; and the sheer musical invention of the opera, as well as many of its most characteristic idioms, places in the clearest possible context the debt Puccini owed to his great predecessor, Giuseppe Verdi, whose final opera, *Falstaff*, paved the way for Puccini's comic masterpiece.

RECORDINGS   1. de Los Angeles, Del Monte, Gobbi, Rome Opera Ch and O, Santini, EMI, 1958: Gobbi's classic portrait of Schicchi; 2. Donath, Seiffert, Panerai, Bavarian Radio Ch, Munich Radio O, Patané, Eurodisc, 1988: Panerai rivals Gobbi in attractive modern version (the Eurodisc *Trittico* is available as a CD box) [A.B.]
EDITIONS   f.ss., Ricordi (folio), 1918; Ricordi (quarto), 1927; 1957; v.ss., Ricordi, 1918; 1962

Turandot

Opera in three acts (1h 45m)
Libretto by Giuseppe Adami and Renato Simoni, after the play by Carlo Gozzi (1762)
Composed 1920–24; completed by Franco Alfano 1925–6
PREMIERES   25 April 1926, La Scala, Milan; US: 16 November 1926, Metropolitan, New York; UK: 7 June 1927, Covent Garden, London
CAST   Princess Turandot *s*, the Unknown Prince (Calaf) *t*, Liù *s*, Timur *b*, Emperor Altoum *t*, Ping *bar*, Pang *t*, Pong *t*, a Mandarin *bar*, Prince of Persia *t*, executioner *silent*; *satb* chorus of imperial guards, the executioner's servants, children, priests, mandarins, dignitaries, the eight wise men, Turandot's handmaidens, soldiers, flag-carriers, musicians, ghosts of the dead, the crowd
ORCHESTRATION   3 fl/picc, 2 ob, ca, 2 cl, b cl, 2 bsn, dbsn, 4 hn, 3 tpt, 3 trbn, b trbn, timp, perc (triangle, sd, bd, cym, t-t, chinese gongs, glock, xyl, bass xyl, tubular bells), cel, 2 hp, organ, str; onstage: 2 alto sax, 6 tpt, 3 trbn, b trbn, wooden sd, b gong or t-t

The idea of setting Gozzi's *Turandot*, and thus of returning to the Far Eastern ambience of *Madama Butterfly*, was first mooted by Giuseppe Adami and Renato Simoni in March 1920, nearly three years after the premiere of Busoni's short opera on the same story. Puccini was enthusiastic, but the opera went through the kind of agonizing genesis that had become the norm in Puccinian creation. Endless prose and verse scenarios were proffered and rejected; and there was a crisis during which Puccini, having completed about half the work, became convinced that its shape should be radically altered: until a fairly late stage, Act I was planned – and, what is more important, musically sketched – to encompass a good deal more of the action than the version we know today, ending where the present Act II now ends, with Calaf's solving of the riddles. When the decision came to split this sequence in two, both halves had to be enlarged: Act I with the finale after Calaf's and Liù's arias, and the new Act II with the addition of an opening scene for Ping, Pang and Pong, and a grand aria for Turandot, 'In questa reggia'.

Everything up to the final scene was finished by the end of March 1924, but the closing duet between Calaf and Turandot was still to be written when the composer died in November. The opera was completed (in part by following sketches left by Puccini) by the young composer Franco Alfano. The first performance (which did not include Alfano's ending) was conducted by Arturo Toscanini.

SYNOPSIS
The action takes place in ancient Peking. Princess Turandot has decreed that she will marry any prince who can solve three riddles, but that if he fails in the attempt he must die. Many have tried; all have failed.

Act I   The curtain opens on a crowded scene at sunset amid preparations for the execution of the latest contestant, the Prince of Persia. The young Prince Calaf recognizes his father, Timur, who is accompanied by Liù, a slave girl. (Timur's throne has been usurped, and he has escaped penniless from his kingdom.) The execution proceeds; Turandot appears on the palace balcony, luminous in the light of the newly risen moon, to give the signal of death. Calaf is dazzled by her beauty and, as the Prince of Persia's death cry rings out, Calaf determines to win Turandot for himself. The Emperor of China's three ministers, Ping, Pang and Pong, attempt to dissuade Calaf, and are joined in this by Timur and Liù. Calaf tries to comfort his father, asking Liù to continue to care for Timur ('Non piangere, Liù!'). But his purpose cannot be deflected and, crying out 'Turandot', he strikes three blows on a gong to signal the arrival of a new suitor.

Act II   Scene 1 opens in a pavilion of the palace as Ping, Pang and Pong review the endless cycle of executions they have witnessed since Turandot first issued her decree. They dream of a princess transformed by love and restoring peace to China, but a fanfare recalls them to the reality of another trial. Scene 2 takes place in the square of the royal palace. The Emperor Altoum, weary of the needless deaths, pleads with Calaf to give up the challenge but Calaf insists on proceeding. Turandot places herself in front of the emperor's throne. She explains that, inspired by an ancient princess who was cruelly betrayed by a man, she has vowed to keep herself pure ('In questa reggia'). The trial begins. One by one, Turandot announces her riddles. To the crowd's gathering excitement, Calaf answers each one correctly. As he solves the third riddle, Turandot collapses in despair, begging her father to release her from her own decree. The emperor is unyielding, but Calaf offers her a chance of release. He gives her a riddle of his own: if she can discover his name by daybreak, he will pay the forfeit and die; if not, she will be his.

Act III   Scene 1: Calaf is lying on the steps of a pavilion in the palace garden that same night lyrically contemplating his coming victory over the princess ('Nessun dorma'). Ping, Pang and Pong arrive, desperate over Turandot's new decree by which all their lives are forfeit if the prince's name is not discovered by dawn. They tempt Calaf with a variety of delights. Calaf remains unmoved until the guards drag in Timur and Liù, who had been seen earlier in the company of Calaf. Turandot herself enters to question Timur, but Liù courageously steps forward, saying that she alone knows the secret of the prince's name. When the soldiers try to force the name from her, her love for Calaf gives her the strength to resist. Finally Liù turns to Turandot and, crying that through her sacrifice, Turandot will learn love ('Tu che di gel sei cinta'), she grabs a soldier's dagger and stabs herself, dying at Calaf's feet. Timur, heartbroken at her death, follows as her body is carried off in mournful procession. Calaf and

Eva Turner as Turandot (Brescia, 1926)

Act I, and thus discretely dominate sections of the drama. These 'colours' are not restricted to individual characters: there are several distinct sides to the exotic ambience, for example, not merely a blanket characterization of all things 'Eastern'. There is also an unusually large system of recurring motifs and melodies: one thinks immediately of the motif that regularly accompanies Turandot's entrances, or the choruses that welcome the emperor. These are hardly ever used in a developmental way, and almost invariably return in exact repetition and within the same broad musical context. They thus serve to articulate the various contrasting blocks of colour rather than to create connections between them. And all this musical variety is wrapped in an orchestral texture whose richness and invention Puccini had not previously equalled.

RECORDINGS   1. Nilsson, Tebaldi, Björling, Tozzi, Rome Opera Ch and O, Leinsdorf, RCA, 1960: Nilsson's unrivalled Turandot, Björling's heroic Calaf; 2. Sutherland, Caballé, Pavarotti, Ghiaurov, John Alldis Ch, Wandsworth School Boys' Ch, LPO, Mehta, Decca, 1973: no-expenses-spared cast, living up to reputations, though Sutherland not ideally suited to the role [A.B.]
VIDEO   Marton, Ricciarelli, Carreras, Vienna State Opera Ch and O, Maazel, ORF Productions, 1983: Marton is leading exponent of title role [A.B.]
EDITIONS   f.s., Ricordi, 1926; v.ss., Ricordi, 1926 (first and second versions); 1929 (from second version)

BIBLIOGRAPHY   G. Adami (ed.), *Giacomo Puccini: Epistolario*, A. Mondadori, 1928; second edn, 1982; trans. by E. Makin as *Letters of Giacomo Puccini*, London, 1931; AMS Press, 1971; William Ashbrook, *The Operas of Puccini*, Cassell, 1968; 2nd edn, Cornell University Press, 1985; Mosco Carner, *Puccini: A Critical Biography*, Knopf, 1st US edn, 1959; 2nd edn, Duckworth, 1974; E. Gara, *Carteggi pucciniani*, Ricordi, 1958; C. Hopkinson, *Bibliography of the Works of Giacomo Puccini 1858–1924*, Broude Bros, 1968

E.H./R.P.

Turandot are left alone. Their extended duet comes to a first climax as Calaf kisses Turandot passionately. Overcome with a mixture of passion and shame, she begs him to leave for ever, but instead he gives her the answer to his riddle, telling her his name and so placing his life in her hands. Trumpets announce the coming of dawn. Scene 2: In the palace square Turandot announces triumphantly to the emperor and the crowd that she knows the stranger's name. But then to everyone's surprise she cries out: 'His name is love!' and, to a reprise of 'Nessun dorma', all join in rejoicing.

Turandot has many of the qualities of Puccini's earlier operas – superb dramatic pacing in particular – but what distinguishes it from its predecessors, and is perhaps its most remarkable quality, is its extraordinary richness of musical invention; something all the more surprising from a composer who constantly complained that advancing age was sapping his creative powers. As in many of the best *fin-de-siècle* operas, there is in *Turandot* a riot of competing musical colours, each primarily associated with an element of the drama: the heroic prince, the proud princess, the pathetic slave girl, the bizarre ministers, even the hapless Persian suitor; all create their own musical atmosphere during the course of

DANIEL PURCELL
b ?1663, London; *buried* 26 November 1717, London

Daniel Purcell came to prominence only after his elder brother Henry's death, though by then he had been organist of Magdalen College, Oxford, for seven years and had already begun to compose. In 1695 he came to London, started a career as a theatre composer and soon became organist of St Dunstan in the East; he retained the post until his death and also became organist of St Andrew's, Holborn, c. 1713. Purcell was most active as a composer from 1696 to 1707, when he wrote music for over 40 plays, published several collections of instrumental music and wrote a number of court odes. After 1707 the advent of Italian opera brought an end to his theatre career and he seems to have concentrated largely on church music, though he published a set of Italianate cantatas in 1713, the earliest by an Englishman. As a composer he is uneven: he was too inclined to lift ideas from his brother and he never really escaped his influence.

The Indian Queen
Collaboration with Henry Purcell
Semi-opera
Text by John Dryden and Sir Robert Howard
PREMIERE   ?late 1695, Dorset Garden Theatre, London

The Indian Queen was Henry Purcell's last semi-opera; Daniel completed it around the time of his brother's final illness and death in November 1695. The play, in whose setting the Incas and Aztecs live adjacent to and at war with each other, deals with the rivalry of the Peruvian Montezuma and his prisoner, the Mexican Acacis, for the hand of the Inca's daughter Orazia. The title character is Zempoalla, the usurping Aztec queen. Daniel Purcell's Act V wedding masque, celebrating the union of Monte-zuma and Orazia, Peru and Mexico, is inevit-ably on a lower level than the rest of the work, though, as Price points out, it completes his brother's tonal scheme and would probably be effective on stage.

EDITION   facsimile: Curtis Price and Robert Hume (eds), *Music in London Entertainment*, series C, Stainer and Bell, forthcoming; *The Works of Henry Purcell*, vol 19, no. 1, The Purcell Society, 2nd edn, 1961–9

The Island Princess
Collaboration with Jeremiah Clarke, Richard Leveridge and others
Semi-opera
Text by John Fletcher, adapted by Nahum Tate and Peter Motteux
PREMIERE   (?)7 February 1699, Drury Lane, London

The Island Princess was the most successful and important post-Purcell semi-opera. Unusually for the period, it survives in its entirety. Set in the East Indies, it concerns the unjust imprisonment and threatened execution of the Portuguese hero, Armusia, and the native heroine, Quisara. Daniel Purcell composed about half the music, inluding the whole of the masque at the end of Act II.

EDITION   facsimile: Curtis Price and Robert Hume (eds), *Music in London Entertainment*, series C, vol. 2, Macnutt, 1985

The Judgement of Paris
All-sung masque
Text by William Congreve
PREMIERE   1 April 1701, Dorset Garden Theatre, London

Congreve wrote *The Judgement of Paris* for the Musick Prize, the famous operatic competition unexpectedly won by John Weldon in 1701. He called *The Judgement of Paris* a masque because it is based on Classical myth and has elements of allegory: the shepherd Paris has to choose whether to award the golden apple of beauty (symbolic of the 'Musick Prize') to Juno, Pallas Athene or Venus; Venus wins. Purcell's setting came third in the competition, after those by Weldon and Eccles; it is

less modern than the former and less accomplished than the latter. It is Purcell's only surviving all-sung dramatic work.

EDITION   facsimile: Curtis Price and Robert Hume (eds), *Music in London Entertainment*, series C, Stainer and Bell, forthcoming

Daniel Purcell also wrote music for the following semi-operas: *Brutus of Alba*, 1696; *Cinthia and Endymion*, 1696; *The World in the Moon*, 1697; *The Grove*, 1700; *The Rival Queens*, 1701; he also set John Dryden's all-sung *Secular Masque*, 1700 (coll. with Finger)
BIBLIOGRAPHY   Roger Fiske, *English Theatre Music in the Eighteenth Century*, OUP, 1973, 2nd edn, 1986; Curtis Price, *Henry Purcell and the London Stage*, CUP, 1984

P.H.

HENRY PURCELL
b 1658 or 1659, London; *d* 21 November 1695, London

Purcell is generally regarded as the greatest English opera composer before the 20th century, yet he wrote only one true opera, *Dido and Aeneas*. A pupil of Matthew Locke and John Blow, he also endeavoured to emulate the new French and Italian styles, though his music remained conservative and distinctively English in its predilection for dissonant counterpoint. Purcell is particularly admired for his genius at setting the English language.

Purcell was appointed composer-in-ordinary (that is, with salary) for the King's Violins in 1677 and co-organist of the Chapel Royal in 1682, having already succeeded Blow as organist of Westminster Abbey in 1678, and his early career was naturally centred on the court. He served four monarchs – Charles II (to 1685), James II (1685–88) and William and Mary (1689–95) – during the turbulent years of the Exclusion Crisis and the Glorious Revolution. His earliest public works are anthems for the Chapel Royal and royal welcome songs. During these formative years he also composed much instrumental music, including the fantasias for viol consort – contrapuntal *tours de force* and the last of their kind – and trio sonatas, supposedly in imitation of the new Italian style but in reality continuing to explore the same English vein as the fantasias.

Purcell's first contribution to the professional stage was the incidental music for Nathaniel Lee's tragedy *Theodosius* of 1680. The songs and choruses are modelled on the music of his teacher Locke, who had dominated the London musical theatre until his death in 1677. The *Theodosius* pieces are rather stiff and awkward in comparison to the highly sophis-ticated instrumental music Purcell was com-posing at the same time, and give little indication of his later achievement in dramatic song. The political upheavals and management crises of the London theatres during the 1680s afforded him few other opportunities to write for the stage, his output being restricted to anthems, coronation music and festive odes, most notably those associated with the

Henry Purcell; portrait after the life-drawing attributed to Godfrey Kneller

recently established London St Cecilia's Day celebrations.

In the last five years of his life, Purcell's career turned decisively towards the theatre, largely in consequence of William's and Mary's drastic curtailment of the Royal Musick, which forced Purcell and many of his colleagues to seek employment outside the court. In 1690 he composed the music for *The Prophetess, or The History of Dioclesian*, adapted by the actor Thomas Betterton from a Jacobean tragi-comedy. *Dioclesian* (as it became known) is a semi-opera, that is, a play with substantial musical episodes or masques which are sung and danced by minor characters – spirits, soldiers, priests, fairies and the like; the main characters do not sing. The choice of Purcell as composer of *Dioclesian*, which proved a great financial and artistic success, was probably influenced by the amateur performance in 1689 of *Dido and Aeneas* at a girls' boarding school in Chelsea. The libretto was written by Nahum Tate, soon to become Poet Laureate, and the school was run by Josias Priest, a choreographer at the Theatre Royal; both were men of considerable influence in the London theatrical world.

Dioclesian attracted the attention of John Dryden, who offered Purcell the libretto of his semi-opera *King Arthur*, which was produced in 1691, another great success for the Theatre Royal. Because it was conceived as a semi-opera rather than being adapted from an old play, *King Arthur* is much more cohesive than *Dioclesian*, and here Purcell came close to matching the quality of *Dido*; two numbers, the so-

called frost scene and the nostalgic song 'Fairest Isle', have achieved immortality.

Purcell's next semi-opera, *The Fairy Queen* of 1692, was to be the grandest and most lavish of all such works. Adapted anonymously from Shakespeare's *A Midsummer Night's Dream*, it includes Purcell's finest and most sophisticated dramatic music, all of which is collected into four self-contained masques; a fifth was added to a revival in 1693. But *The Fairy Queen*, which proved as popular as Purcell's previous works, nearly bankrupted the Theatre Royal because of the expense of the scenes, music and dances. No new semi-opera was planned for 1694, and Purcell concentrated instead on writing orchestral incidental music (collected in the posthumous *Ayres for the Theatre* of 1697) and songs for plays. In the latter genre he was eclipsed in popularity by his younger contemporary John Eccles, whose simple and highly dramatic songs were better suited to the actor–singers (such as the celebrated Anne Bracegirdle) than were Purcell's more difficult, highly decorated vocal music.

In early 1695 Purcell's theatrical career suffered another setback when Betterton was given permission to set up a rival theatre in a converted tennis court in Lincoln's Inn Fields. Not only did the old actor persuade most of his colleagues to follow him, but Eccles and virtually all of the professional stage singers also joined the renegades, leaving Purcell with a handful of young and inexperienced singers. He nevertheless composed a great deal of theatre music during the last year of his life, including masques and entertainments for *Timon of Athens*, *The Libertine*, *Bonduca*, a song or two for *The Tempest* and his last semi-opera, *The Indian Queen*. He did not live to complete this score, and his younger brother Daniel was called down from Oxford to compose the final masque.

Purcell's only opera thus came at the beginning of his brief theatre career. Because *Dido and Aeneas* is through-composed and seems to conform to the 19th-century ideal of musical tragedy, it has assumed a central position in Purcell's *oeuvre*. Yet there is no evidence that he was dissatisfied with semi-opera as a genre or frustrated at not having the opportunity to write another all-sung opera. One needs to understand the conventions of semi-opera to appreciate how much better a composer Purcell became after *Dido and Aeneas*.

Dido and Aeneas

Tragic opera in three acts (1h)
Libretto by Nahum Tate, after his tragedy *Brutus of Alba* (1678) and the fourth book of Virgil's *Aeneid*
PREMIERES spring 1689, Josias Priest's boarding school for girls, Chelsea; US: 13 January 1924, New York, Town Hall (concert); 18 February 1932, Juilliard School, New York
CAST Dido *s*, Belinda *s*, Second Woman *s*, Sorceress *ms* or *b-bar*, First Witch *s*, Second Witch *s*, Spirit *ms*, Aeneas *t*, Sailor *s*; *satb* chorus of courtiers, witches, sailors and cupids
INSTRUMENTATION 4-pt str orch, bc; gtrs

The circumstances behind the composition and performance of *Dido and Aeneas* are unknown. According to the sole surviving copy of the libretto of the Chelsea production, the opera was performed 'by young gentlewomen', presumably the girls of Priest's boarding school. It was modelled very closely on John Blow's opera *Venus and Adonis*, which had also been performed by an all-female cast at Priest's school in April 1684. That *Dido* was also a spring production is suggested by a couplet of Thomas Durfey's spoken epilogue: 'Like nimble fawns, and birds that bless the spring/Unscarr'd by turning times we dance and sing.' The opera originally included a prologue (music lost) which alludes to William and Mary and welcomes the arrival of spring; so *Dido* may have formed part of the celebrations of their joint coronation on 11 April 1689. Like *Venus and Adonis*, *Dido* is highly unusual for baroque opera in having a tragic ending. Tate based the plot on Virgil's account of Aeneas at Carthage, the main difference being that in the opera the Trojan prince, rather than being prompted by the gods to sail on to Italy, is tricked into leaving Dido by an evil Sorceress, Tate's invention.

SYNOPSIS
Act I After escaping from the sack of Troy, Prince Aeneas sets sail for Italy where he is destined to found Rome. Blown off course to Carthage, he is welcomed by Queen Dido who, being burdened by affairs of state and unspoken grief ('Ah! Belinda'), is reluctant to reveal a growing love for her guest. Urged on by her confidante Belinda and her attendants ('Fear no danger'), Dido tacitly succumbs to Aeneas and the court rejoices ('To the hills and the vales').

Act II Scene 1: With the playing of a sombre prelude, the scene changes to a cave, where a Sorceress and her witches plot Queen Dido's downfall ('Wayward sisters'). Hoping to trick Aeneas into leaving Dido by reminding him of his destiny in Italy, they prepare the charm in an echo chorus ('In our deep vaulted cell'). Scene 2 is set in a grove where Dido and Aeneas, having consummated their love during the previous night, are entertained by Belinda and an attendant ('Thanks to these lonesome vales'/'Oft she visits this lone mountain'). The Sorceress (unseen) conjures up a thunderstorm which sends the courtiers running for shelter ('Haste, haste to town'), while Aeneas lags behind to hear an elf disguised as Mercury order him to leave Carthage ('Stay, Prince'). He agonizes over his decision to comply with the command.

Act III On the quayside Aeneas' men are preparing to weigh anchor ('Come away, fellow sailors'). The Sorceress and witches reappear to gloat over the impending tragedy ('Destruction's our delight'). The scene shifts back to court where Dido, having got wind of Aeneas' decision to leave, seeks Belinda's advice ('Your counsel all is urg'd in vain') before bitterly confronting the cowardly Aeneas, who offers to stay but then ignominiously departs. Dido realizes that she cannot live without him. Inconsolable ('Thy hand, Belinda'), she sings her great lament ('When I am laid in earth'), dies and is mourned by a chorus of cupids ('With drooping wings').

Dido is remarkable for the swift concision of action, its widely contrasting moods (including the comic relief of the sailors' scene) and a deeply tragic ending. For most of these features and a carefully controlled key scheme Purcell was indebted to Blow's *Venus and Adonis*. But *Dido* is much more structured; each scene is built up of units of recitative (or declamatory song), arioso, aria, chorus and dance. Purcell was thus following the formal model offered by Lully's *tragédies en musique*, but his chief innovation, inspired by contemporary Venetian opera, was to concentrate the greatest musical interest in the arias. Dido's are placed at the beginning and end of the opera and both are constructed over ostinato basses: 'Ah! Belinda!' in Act I also displays a *da capo* structure, while the famous lament is built over a repeated chromatically descending five-bar bass, also common in Italian opera of the time.

Purcell's recitatives, which have been called the finest in the English language, are regularly measured but with great flexibility of rhythm to reflect the slightest nuance of speech; important words are often decorated with elaborate melismas. The Sorceress's part, which Purcell may have conceived for bass-baritone rather than mezzo-soprano as usually heard today, is notable for being set almost entirely in recitative accompanied by four-part strings.

Perhaps because of the involvement of Josias Priest, a professional choreographer, dance dominates the score; key pieces are the triumphing dance (another ground) at the end of Act I, the witches' echo dance (in the style of a French furies' dance) in Act II, Scene 2, and the sailors' dance in Act III, each being radically different in character one from the other. And in its brief, sharply contrasting sections, the final witches' dance, which included Jack o' Lantern, resembles a Jacobean antimasque. The opera was even supposed to end with a cupids' dance, which has not survived.

The earliest score of *Dido and Aeneas* dates from nearly a century after the Chelsea performance and differs from Tate's original libretto in several significant ways. Besides the missing prologue mentioned above, the score lacks a dance and chorus of witches at the end of Act II. Many modern producers have therefore felt the need to add music between Aeneas' soliloquy and the beginning of Act III, perhaps the most successful being that arranged by Benjamin Britten from other Purcell works. The original music for this scene, along with the prologue and final cupids' dance, may have been cut from the first public production of *Dido* at Lincoln's Inn Fields Theatre, London, in 1700, when the opera was reordered and inserted into an adaptation of Shakespeare's *Measure for Measure*.

RECORDINGS 1. Baker, Clark, Sinclair, Herincx, St Anthony Singers, ECO, Lewis, Oiseau-Lyre, 1962: the most notable of 'traditional' recordings; 2. Kirkby, Nelson, Norman, Thomas, Taverner Ch and Players, Parrott, Chandos, 1981: small-scale, intimate, at times bizarre; a memorable Dido from Kirkby; 3. von Otter, Rogers, Varcoe,

Dawson, The English Concert, Pinnock, Archiv, 1989: expansive and highly dramatic; first recording in which the Sorceress is sung by a man (Rogers) at the lower octave
EDITIONS   Margaret Laurie (ed.), *The Works of Henry Purcell*, vol. 3, Novello, 1979; Ellen Harris (ed.), OUP, 1988

Dioclesian (The Prophetess, or The History of Dioclesian)

Semi-opera in five acts (3h 30m)
Libretto by Thomas Betterton, 1690, an adaptation of P. Massinger's and J. Fletcher's tragi-comedy *The Prophetess* (1622)
PREMIERES   spring 1690, Dorset Garden Theatre, London

Dioclesian, Purcell's first semi-opera and indeed his first major work for the professional stage, was designed and produced by Betterton with choreography by Josias Priest, with whom Purcell had worked the year before on *Dido and Aeneas*. While conceived on a grand scale and published by the composer himself, the music does not mesh with the lively and cynical plot as well as in the other semi-operas. Delphia, a prophetess, predicts that Diocles, a common soldier, will become emperor of Rome after slaying a mighty boar. Eventually he kills the regicide Volutius Aper ('the boar'), is proclaimed emperor, renames himself Dioclesian, discards his betrothed Drusilla (Delphia's ugly niece) and courts instead Princess Aurelia ('What shall I do to show how much I love her?'). Pressured by Delphia, Diocles abdicates in favour of his nephew Maximinian. Purcell provided music for Diocles' coronation in Act II and for the celebration of the defeat of the Persian army in Act IV; most important, however, is the long masque in Act V that welcomes Diocles and Drusilla into retirement. The masque was revived as a separate work well into the 18th century.

RECORDING   Dawson, Fisher, Covey-Crump, Elliott, Varcoe, George, Monteverdi Ch, English Baroque Soloists, Gardiner, Erato, 1988
EDITION   f.s., Bridge and Pointer (eds), rev. by Margaret Laurie, *The Works of Henry Purcell*, vol. 9, Novello, 1961

King Arthur, or The British Worthy

Semi-opera in five acts (3h 30m)
Libretto by John Dryden, 1684, rev. 1690–91
PREMIERES   May or June 1691, Dorset Garden Theatre, London; US: 24 April 1800, New York
CAST   Philadel *s*, Grimbald *b-bar*, Shepherd *t*, Cupid *s*, Cold Genius *b*, Aeolus *b-bar*, Venus *s*
ORCHESTRATION   2 rec, 2 ob, bsn, 2 tpt, 4-pt str, bc

King Arthur was Purcell's second semi-opera (or 'dramatick opera', as Dryden preferred to call it), that is, essentially a tragi-comedy with four or five long musical episodes. As is typical of the genre, the protagonists (King Arthur, Merlin, Oswald, Emmeline *et al.*) only speak, while most of the music is performed by minor characters; exceptionally, the spirits Philadel and Grimbald both speak and sing. Unlike all of Purcell's other semi-operas, *King Arthur* is not based on an earlier play, and therefore

the music is much more closely integrated with the main action. Dryden, who had the year before acknowledged Purcell as an English composer 'equal with the best abroad', conceded that in writing *King Arthur* 'my Art, on this occasion, ought to be subservient to his'. With its spectacular staging, dances and fine music, it was an outstanding success, being frequently revived well into the 18th century.

SYNOPSIS
In a series of set battles with the Saxons, King Arthur and the Britons have regained all the kingdom except Kent. After a heathen sacrifice, Oswald and the Saxons launch a final assault but are defeated. Urged on by the evil spirit Grimbald, the Saxons resort to treachery, first by trying to lead the Britons on to quicksand and then by kidnapping King Arthur's betrothed, Emmeline, the blind daughter of the Duke of Cornwall. Aided by Merlin and Philadel, a good spirit, Arthur attempts to rescue Emmeline from the snares and illusions of an enchanted forest. Meanwhile, the heroine is nearly raped by her gaoler, the Saxon magician Osmond. After breaking the magic spell, Arthur defeats Oswald in a single combat, is reunited with Emmeline (now restored to sight) and magnanimously forgives the Saxons. The opera concludes with a masque in praise of Britain – its people, natural resources and institutions.

Apart from the final masque, which lies quite outside the main action, Purcell's music is tightly bound to the drama. The sacrifice scene in Act I ('Woden first to thee') draws somewhat incongruously on the style of the verse anthem, while the scene in Act II in which the Britons pursue the Saxons ('Hither this way') is highly original in the way it advances the plot by rapid alteration between opposing groups of singers. The so-called frost scene in Act III ('What power art thou'), though inspired by a similar episode in Lully's opera *Isis* (1677), is memorable for its quivering string effects and chromatic harmony. Probably the most impressive piece of the score is the long passacaglia in Act IV ('How happy the lover'), a rich tapestry of solos, choruses and dances spun out over a continuously varied four-bar ground bass. The masque in Act V is loosely structured, at times purposefully chaotic, but includes what has been described as Purcell's most perfect song, 'Fairest Isle'.

RECORDINGS   1. Smith, Fisher, Priday, Ross, Elliott, Varcoe, Monteverdi Ch, English Baroque Soloists, Gardiner, Erato, 1983; 2. Argenta, Perillo, Gooding, MacDougall, Bannatyne-Scott, Finley, English Concert, Pinnock, Archiv, 1992
EDITION   Denis Arundell (ed.), rev. by Margaret Laurie, *The Works of Henry Purcell*, vol. 26, Novello, 1971

The Fairy Queen

Semi-opera in a prologue and five acts (4h)
Libretto, anon., 1692, after the play *A Midsummer Night's Dream* by William Shakespeare (1596)
Composed ?1692, rev. 1693

PREMIERES   first version: May 1692, Dorset Garden Theatre, London; second version: February 1693, Dorset Garden Theatre, London; US: 30 April 1932, San Francisco CAST   Drunken Poet *b-bar*, First and Second Fairies 2 *s*, Night *s*, Mystery *s*, Secresy *ct*, Sleep *b*, Coridon *b-bar*, Mopsa *s* or *a*, Phoebus *t*, Spring *s*, Summer *a*, Autumn *t*, Winter *b-bar*, Juno *s*, Chinese Man *a*, Chinese Woman (Daphne) *s*, Hymen *b*
ORCHESTRATION   2 rec, 2 ob, 2 tpt, timp, 4-pt str, bc

The Fairy Queen, Purcell's third semi-opera, was the most lavish and expensive of all such works. Collaborating again with Thomas Betterton as producer (and perhaps the adapter of Shakespeare's play) and Josias Priest as choreographer, Purcell was able for the first time to write exclusively for professional singers, as opposed to actor–singers; the vocal music is correspondingly more elaborate and challenging than any he had written before. The operatic version generally follows the original plot, except that two minor characters are omitted, much of the lyric poetry is modernized or reduced and the masque of Pyramus and Thisbe, which in Shakespeare is rehearsed by the mechanicals in Act III and performed in Act V, is ingeniously compressed into a single scene in the adaptation. All four masques (a fifth was added to the second version) are self-contained and textually unrelated to *A Midsummer Night's Dream*, but each captures and enhances the atmosphere of the original fairy scenes.

A page from the manuscript of The Fairy Queen

SYNOPSIS
Act I In accordance with Athenian law, Duke Theseus requires Demetrius to marry Hermia, as her father wishes. But Hermia is beloved of Lysander, while Demetrius is betrothed to Helena. To avoid being mismatched, the pairs of lovers flee the town. In a nearby wood some tradesmen are preparing a play to celebrate the expected weddings. Titania, the fairy queen, has also come into the wood to escape the rage of her jealous husband, Oberon. The queen's attendants (in the 1693 version) torment a drunken poet (possibly a satire on Thomas Durfey or Thomas Shadwell or both) who has wandered into the wood.

Act II Puck helps Oberon prepare the love potion while Titania is sung to sleep. The philtre is administered with the familiar confusion.

Act III Bottom the weaver (with ass's head) entertains the besotted queen with rustic and highly erotic music.

Act IV Oberon tries to bring the rightful pairs of lovers back together and releases Titania from the spell. The fairy monarchs' reconciliation is celebrated with a masque of the seasons.

Act V Oberon presents the disbelieving duke and the other mortals with a Chinese masque (symbolizing enlightenment) in celebration of the state of matrimony.

The music of *The Fairy Queen* is of the highest quality. The scene added to Act I in 1693 ('Fi– fi– fill up the bowl') is a purposefully disjointed series of ariettas and choruses in which drunkenness and tomfoolery are acutely depicted. In stark contrast the masque of sleep in Act II is an elegant sequence of pieces which grow ever more complex and mysterious. Bottom's masque in Act III juxtaposes the highly dissonant air and chorus 'If love's a sweet passion' and the rollicking dialogue for Coridon and Mopsa 'Now the maids and the men', two of Purcell's best-known vocal pieces. The Act IV masque, framed by a grand chorus in praise of Phoebus ('Hail, great parent'), is rather muted in its differentiation between the seasons. The final masque, which is more loosely organized, includes the counter-tenor air 'Thus, the gloomy world', one of Purcell's finest trumpet songs. *The Fairy Queen* is remarkable for the way in which all the music, however diverse, complements rather than detracts from the play.

RECORDINGS   1. Harrhy, Smith, Nelson, Priday, Penrose, Stafford, Evans, Hill, Varcoe, Thomas, Monteverdi Ch, English Baroque Soloists, Gardiner, Archiv, 1981; 2. Vyvyan, Morison, Whitworth, Boggis, Pears, Hemsley, Anthony, St Anthony Singers, Boyd Neel O, Lewis, Oiseau-Lyre, 1958; 3. Argenta, Dawson, Fouchécourt, Loonen, Randle, Corréas, Deletré, Les Arts Florisants, Christie, Harmonia Mundi, 1989; 4. Fisher, Anderson, Murray, Chance, Ainsley, Partridge, George, The Sixteen, Christophers, Collins, 1990: the Lewis version, using modern instruments, is tried and tested; the three period-instrument versions are recommendable, the Christie is most vital, based on a live performance [A.B.]
EDITION   J. S. Shedlock (ed.), rev. Anthony Lewis, *The Works of Henry Purcell*, vol. 12, 1968

The Indian Queen

Semi-opera in five acts (3h)
Libretto of 1694–5 adapted from the tragedy by John Dryden
and Sir Robert Howard (1664)
PREMIERES spring or autumn 1695, Drury Lane, London

Purcell's last major dramatic work (probably unfinished at the time of his death), *The Indian Queen*, was meant to be another Betterton show, but the actor left the Theatre Royal before production began. Because of financial constraints and a lack of good singers, it had to be on a much smaller scale than Purcell's other semi-operas and includes hardly any scenic spectacle or dancing; the music is none the less excellent. Closely following Dryden's and Howard's original play (and hence with scant regard for history or geography), the plot turns round the military conflict between the Mexicans and the Peruvians, each side being helped in turn by the great mercenary Montezuma – of 'unknown race' but actually the long-lost son of the rightful queen of Mexico. Most of the music is focused on Zempoalla, the usurping queen, who faces a series of heroic dilemmas. In the central musical episode she consults her magician Ismeron, a role created by the famous bass Richard Leveridge, then at the beginning of his long career; Ismeron refuses to reveal the future but agrees to conjure up the God of Dreams ('You twice ten hundred deities'). The force of the tragedy is unfortunately blunted by the hymeneal masque added to Act V and set by Purcell's younger brother Daniel; but at least the imposed happy ending is quite outside the drama.

RECORDINGS 1. Cantelo, Brown, Tear, Partridge, Keyte, St Anthony Singers, ECO, Mackerras, Oiseau-Lyre, 1966; 2. Smith, Hardy, Fisher, Harris, Hill, Elwes, Varcoe, Thomas, Monteverdi Ch, English Baroque Soloists, Gardiner, Erato, 1980: two lively sets, the first using modern instruments, the second period ones [A.B.]
EDITION f.s., Edward J. Dent (ed.), *The Works of Henry Purcell*, vol. 19, Novello, 1912

BIBLIOGRAPHY Curtis Price, *Henry Purcell and the London Stage*, CUP, 1984; Curtis Price (ed.), *Henry Purcell: Dido and Aeneas* (includes edn of score by Margaret Laurie and Thurston Dart, which formed the basis of the complete works edn), W. W. Norton, 1986; Ellen Harris, *Purcell's Dido and Aeneas*, OUP, 1988; Robert E. Moore, *Henry Purcell and the Restoration Theatre*, Heinemann, 1961; *rp*, Greenwood Press, 1974; Jack Westrup, *Purcell*, Dent (Master Musicians Series), 1937; rev. edn by N. Fortune, 1980; Franklin B. Zimmerman, *Henry Purcell*, Macmillan/St Martin's Press, 1967; 2nd edn, University of Pennsylvania Press, 1983

C.A.P.

R

HENRI RABAUD

b 10 November 1873, Paris; *d* 11 September 1949, Paris

Parisian born and bred, a pupil of Massenet at the Conservatoire, Rabaud won the Premier Grand Prix de Rome in 1894. In 1899, after two orchestral symphonies, he composed *La procession nocturne*, a symphonic poem by which he became best known outside his native France. Illustrating an episode from Lenau's *Faust*, its musical language, which draws on Franck as well as on Wagner, but more akin to Saint-Saëns than to Strauss, reveals a skilled orchestrator. Rabaud worked as opera conductor from 1908, in Rome and Vienna, then at the Paris Opéra and in Boston, before becoming director of the Paris Conservatoire 1920–41, and a highly respected administrative and French Establishment figure. Of Rabaud's operas, *Marouf* has proved the only survivor.

Marouf, savetier du Caire

Opera in five acts (2h 15m)
Libretto by L. Nepoty, after J. C. Mardrus's *Arabian Nights*
Composed 1914
PREMIERE 15 May 1914, Opéra-Comique, Paris

Marouf, instantly successful with its appropriate musical orientalisms, was widely performed. Based on a story from *The Arabian Nights*, it traces the emancipation of the cobbler Marouf from a state of conjugal misery, with a harridan of a wife, to the bliss of acquiring a beautiful princess as her successor.

RECORDING Blanzat, Barraud, Lecocq, Petri, Loup, Nantes Opera Ch, Pays de la Loire PO, Etcheverry, IPG, 1976
EDITION v.s., Choudens, 1914

Other operas: *La fille de Roland*, 1904; *Le premier glaire*, 1908; *Antoine et Cléopâtre*, 1917; *L'appel de la mer*, 1924; *Rolande et le mauvais garçon*, 1934; *Martine*, 1947; *Le jeu de l'amour et du hasard*, 1948
BIBLIOGRAPHY Max d'Ollone, *Henri Rabaud: sa vie et son oeuvre*, Paris, 1958

F.A.

SERGEY RAKHMANINOV

Sergey Vasil'yevich Rakhmaninov; *b* 1 April 1873, Semyonovo, Russia; *d* 28 March 1943, Beverly Hills, California, US

Rakhmaninov's operas have never enjoyed a good press, and productions of them are rare. But while it is easy to detect the flaws in the libretti of the three completed works (each in a single act), the scores contain some of his finest music. As one might expect from a great song-composer, the writing for the voice is always grateful, and the instinctive flair for arioso writing only makes one regret that a suitable libretto for a full-length opera eluded him. The vocal scores of all three operas are by Rakhmaninov himself, and are excellently laid out for the piano.

Sergey Rakhmaninov (right) with Fyodor Chaliapin in 1916

Rakhmaninov's earliest attempts at opera remain unfinished: at the age of 15 he sketched parts of *Esmeralda*, based on Hugo's *Notre Dame de Paris*, and various other early operatic fragments may only be exercises from his days at the Moscow Conservatory. His last attempts at opera were merely a scenario for *Salammbô*, after Flaubert (a subject earlier chosen by Musorgsky), from 1906, and the first act in piano score of *Monna Vanna*, after

Maeterlinck, from 1907. *Monna Vanna* has recently been scored by Igor Buketoff, and given in concert performance in America (Buketoff has also prepared and published an orchestral suite), but the piece remains a tantalizing torso whose completion was prevented by a contractual problem. Rakhmaninov achieved great distinction as an opera conductor in Russia around the turn of the century, working first with Mamontov's company (where he met Fyodor Chaliapin, whom he influenced greatly, and who, in turn, inspired some of his finest vocal writing) and later at the Bolshoi. Pressure of other compositions and his piano-playing fought with conducting, and Rakhmaninov's operatic connections petered out in 1908.

Aleko

Opera in one act (1h)
Libretto by Vladimir Nemirovich-Danchenko, after the poem *Tsygany* by Aleksandr Pushkin (1824)
Composed 1892
PREMIERES 9 May 1893, Bolshoi Theatre, Moscow; US: 1926, New York; UK: 15 July 1915, London Opera House, London
CAST Aleko *bar*, Young Gypsy *t*, Old Gypsy *b*, Zemfira *s*, Old Gypsy Woman *a*; *satb* chorus of gypsies
FULL ORCHESTRA

Although the composition was primarily an examination requirement for the Moscow Conservatory (which explains why Rakhmaninov was not in a position to alter the libretto), *Aleko* was certainly a successful piece in its day, praised by Tchaikovsky, and often compared with *Cavalleria rusticana*, with which there are some structural similarities. Rakhmaninov won the Great Gold Medal of the Moscow Conservatory for the work, which he completed and scored in just 17 days, and it has since enjoyed many more productions than its musically superior successors.

SYNOPSIS

Aleko has renounced society to take up with a band of gypsies, and his former loneliness has been alleviated by the love of Zemfira. Zemfira, however, has grown tired of Aleko and has taken a young gypsy lover. The Old Gypsy (Zemfira's father) sings of his own past tragedy: his mistress deserted him for a younger man. Aleko impatiently suggests that if he had been in that position he would not have hesitated to kill both mistress and lover. Zemfira rocks her child's cradle, singing an old song about 'my old and terrible husband', deliberately goading Aleko, who storms off. He sings of his misery while the camp sleeps. The Young Gypsy is heard singing of free love. Aleko finds Zemfira with the Young Gypsy and stabs them to death – Zemfira defiantly affirming her new love as she dies. The shocked but peaceable gypsies gather, and punish Aleko with that which he fears most: exile.

The enthusiasm of the young Rakhmaninov for his subject crowds the pages of this work, and almost disguises the rather patchwork nature of the libretto,

which calls for separate numbers, includes dances and an intermezzo, and allows very little drama to develop without interruption. The influence of many of the great Russian opera composers is clear, but, especially in Aleko's famous cavatina (recorded three times by Chaliapin), more than a hint of the grand sweep of Rakhmaninov's mature melodic style is evident. There are several recurring motifs, which help to hold the numbers together, and the piece is splendidly orchestrated and gratefully composed for soloists and chorus, the character of Aleko drawn with much sympathy. A real burgeoning understanding of musical drama is apparent in the two scenes where the libretto allows for it: the quarrel between Aleko and Zemfira, and the discovery *in flagrante delicto* of the lovers.

RECORDINGS 1. Pokrovskaya, Zlatogorova, Orfenov, Petrov, Ognivtsev, Ch and O of USSR Radio, Golovanov, Melodiya, [c. 1950]; 2. Karnobatlova, Christova, Kurshumov, Ghiuselev, Petkov, Bulgarian Radio Ch, Plovdiv PO, Raichev, Balkanton, [c. 1970]; 3. Volkova, Kotova, Fedin, Nesterenko, Matorin, USSR Television and Radio Large Ch. Moscow Philharmonic SO, Kitaenko, Melodiya, 1987
EDITIONS f.ss., Moscow, 1953; Muzyka, 1965; v.ss., Gutheil, 1892; Muzyka, 1966

The Miserly Knight

Skupoi Rytsar'
Opera in three scenes, Op. 24 (1h)
Libretto by the composer, an almost word-for-word setting of the 'little tragedy' by Aleksandr Pushkin (1830)
Composed 1903–5
PREMIERES 24 January 1906, Bolshoi Theatre, Moscow; US: 2 December 1910, Boston
CAST the Baron *bar*, Albert *t*, the Duke *bar*, Jewish Moneylender *t*, Servant *b*
FULL ORCHESTRA

Written as a vehicle for Chaliapin, and as the first half of a double-bill with *Francesca da Rimini*, this opera remains a connoisseur's piece whose very storyline precludes much in the way of dramatic opportunity (Pushkin never intended his original playlet to be acted on stage), but allows none the less for very strong musical characterization. The want of female principals or chorus has been unfairly stressed by critics; the drama could not have been treated otherwise, and the second opera provided all possible contrast. Rakhmaninov himself conducted the premiere of both works.

SYNOPSIS

Scene 1 Albert, an impoverished apprentice knight with a miserly father (the Baron), has resorted to a moneylender. Asked for collateral, Albert offers his word and his father's reputation. The moneylender refuses, but offers a supply of poison to ensure a speedy inheritance. Albert, appalled, threatens to hang the fellow for his notion, and is immediately offered a loan. But Albert resolves to ask for the Duke's help to extract some support from the Baron.

Scene 2   The Baron gloats over the power his wealth brings, and reflects, unmoved, on the human misery he has caused. He is then seized by fear and mistrust of his son. His desire is to rise from the grave to protect his treasure from inheritance.

Scene 3   The Duke agrees to assist Albert. The Baron arrives. Albert retires into the next room and overhears the conversation in which the Baron accuses his son of robbery and intended patricide. Albert bursts in, calls his father a liar, is challenged to a duel, and accepts the glove as 'the first gift from my father'. The Duke takes the glove and turns to calm the apoplectic Baron, who collapses and dies.

To a large extent, the shape of the poem determines that of the music: each scene is through-composed and there are leitmotifs for the principals as well as for the various states of mind of the Baron. The Baron's motifs are outlined in the sombre prelude, which moves straight into the first scene, where a forced levity is an important component in the irony of the conversation between Albert, his servant and the moneylender, showing a side of Rakhmaninov unfamiliar from his orchestral works. More familiar is the unrelieved misery of the Baron's monologue, in which Rakhmaninov artfully reflects his judgement on a character intent on self-justification. The short final scene again has more interaction of character and the *dénouement* is skilfully done. Although the amount of stage action in this piece is relatively small, it is compensated for by the depth of the psychological drama.

RECORDING   Kuznetsov, Yakovenko, Usmanov, Dobrin, Budrin, Moscow Radio SO, Rozhdestvensky, HMV/Melodiya, 1973: entitled *The Covetous Knight*
EDITIONS   f.ss., Gutheil/Breitkopf (now Boosey), 1905; Muzyka, 1972; v.ss., Gutheil (now Boosey), 1904; Muzyka, 1968

Francesca da Rimini

Franceska da Rimini
Opera in two tableaux with prologue and epilogue, Op. 25 (1h 15m)
Libretto by Modest Tchaikovsky, after Canto V of Dante's *Inferno* (c. 1307–21)
Composed 1904–5 (second tableau duet 1900)
PREMIERES   24 January 1906, Bolshoi Theatre, Moscow (cond. Rakhmaninov); UK: 28 June 1973, Chester Festival
CAST   Ghost of Virgil *bar*, Dante *t*, Lanciotto Malatesta *bar*, Francesca *s*, Paolo *t*, Cardinal *silent*; *satb* chorus of spectres of hell, retinues of Cardinal and Malatesta
FULL ORCHESTRA   onstage 2 hn, 2 tpt

Critics have unanimously attacked the many faults in the libretto by Pyotr Tchaikovsky's younger brother, and it is a pity that Rakhmaninov was apparently not in a position to alter it or even to reject it outright, but it came to him in 1898 during his period of great depression after the failure at the premiere of the First Symphony, and the composition of the love duet in 1900 marks the real return of his creative ability. Later conflict with Modest Tchaikovsky produced an unsatisfactory solution of a new revised

libretto being printed as an adjunct to the published score with the earlier libretto. Despite the faults of balance – the prologue is larger than either tableau and the epilogue is very short – the music is full of originality, and the 'infernal' side of Rakhmaninov's musical character was never better expressed.

SYNOPSIS
Prologue   The Ghost of Virgil reassures a frightened Dante on the steps from the First Circle of Hell Hell to the abyss. The sounds of tormented spirits are heard, and the ghosts of Paolo and Francesca tell Dante that 'the greatest sadness is the recollection of past happiness amidst present sorrow'.

Tableau 1   At the Malatesta Palace in Rimini, Lanciotto receives the Cardinal's blessing before setting off to defend the Pope against the Ghibellines. Lanciotto's monologue laments the deceit whereby his brother Paolo wooed Francesca, ostensibly to have her marry Lanciotto. Francesca had then married the lame Lanciotto while loving the handsome Paolo. Lanciotto tells Francesca that he is going away leaving his brother to look after her. He seeks some expression of love from her; she replies only that she will remain dutiful and obedient.

Tableau 2   Paolo reads to Francesca from the story of Lancelot and Guinevere and they recognize similarities to their own story. Eventually they can suppress their feelings no longer. They are surprised by the planned return of Lanciotto, who stabs them both.

Epilogue   Virgil's Ghost observes the doomed lovers, who cry Dante's great line: 'That day we read no more', and the chorus repeats the lament of 'The greatest sadness . . .'

The dramatic problems are several: the time the music requires to depict hell – including a doleful fugue which would have delighted Max Reger with its chromatic ingenuity – allows for very little stage action, and Lanciotto's monologue occupies much of the first tableau. The scene where the lovers read ogether cannot help but be dull although the love duet is a mighty compensation. The return of Lanciotto and the *crime passionnel* is practically unstageable as it stands – here, as elsewhere, there are simply too few lines of text. The most interesting feature of the work is the use of the chorus, who sing no words at all until the very end of the opera, but act as part of the orchestra, either humming or intoning over a range of sounds that culminates in screaming terror. The demonic power of Rakhmaninov in his 'D minor' mood – comparable with the First Symphony, the First Piano Sonata, the Third Piano Concerto and the *Corelli Variations* (which quotes a passage from the opera) – is sufficient to excuse the faults of the libretto, and this opera, especially with the other half of the double-bill, remains an area of shameful neglect.

RECORDING   Kasrashvili, Laptyev, Atlantov, Maslov, Nesterenko, Bolshoi Ch and O, Ermler, HMV/Melodiya, 1976

EDITIONS f.ss., Gutheil/Breitkopf (now Boosey), 1905; Muzyka, 1974; v.ss., Gutheil (now Boosey), 1904; Muzyka, 1964

BIBLIOGRAPHY S. Bertensson and J. Leyda, *Sergei Rachmaninoff*, George Allen and Unwin, 1965; Geoffrey Norris, *Rakhmaninov*, Dent (Master Musicians series), 1976; R. Threlfall and Geoffrey Norris, *A Catalogue of the Compositions of Sergey Rakhmaninov*, Scolar Press, 1982

L.H.

JEAN-PHILIPPE RAMEAU

baptized 25 September 1683, Dijon, France; *d* 12 September 1764, Paris

With excusable exaggeration, the *Mercure de France* (1765) concluded its epitaph to Rameau with the words: 'Here lies the God of Harmony.' It was a fitting tribute to the man who, then as now, was seen not only as the outstanding European musical theorist of his era but as France's leading 18th-century composer. To many music-lovers he may nowadays be best known for his keyboard and chamber works. Yet his finest and most ambitious compositions are in the field of dramatic music and include some of the most powerful operas of the period between Monteverdi and Mozart.

Rameau came late to opera. Although his music covers the best part of six decades (1706–*c.* 1763), all his dramatic works belong to the last three. As he

Jean-Philippe Rameau, portrait after Chardin

later admitted: 'I have attended the theatre since I was 12, yet I first worked for the [Paris] Opéra only at 50, and even then I did not think myself capable.'

Much of Rameau's early life was spent in comparative obscurity of the provinces. When he eventually settled in Paris at the age of 39, it was as a music theorist that he first came to public attention: the epoch-making *Traité de l'harmonie* appeared in 1722, and was followed by some three dozen books and pamphlets on music theory. During his first decade in the capital he published his two best-known keyboard collections, the *Pièces de clavessin* in 1724 and the *Nouvelles suites de pièces de clavecin* and a volume of cantatas in 1729 or 1730; he also tried his hand at incidental music (now lost) for some knockabout comedies at the fair theatres.

For all its undoubted imagination, skill and refinement, there was little in Rameau's previous output to prepare contemporary audiences for the power and complexity of *Hippolyte et Aricie*, his first opera. Never had the French been confronted with a musical style so intensely dramatic. There were those who immediately hailed Rameau as 'the Orpheus of our century'. Others, however, found the music over-complex, unnatural, misshapen – in a word, baroque. (*Hippolyte* has the dubious distinction of being the first musical work to which that epithet, still pejorative in those days, is known to have been applied.) At the Paris Opéra (the Académie Royale de Musique) two factions soon formed – the *Ramistes*, as his supporters became known, and the *Lullistes*, devotees of the traditional repertoire, who compared the new music unfavourably with that of their revered Lully. The dispute raged around all Rameau's operas of the 1730s; although it gradually subsided during the following decade, echoes could still be heard in the 1750s and beyond.

Increasingly, though, Rameau began to win the acclaim of the French musical public. In 1745 he was adopted as a court composer, with a royal pension and the title Compositeur de la chambre du roy. From that time too, he enjoyed the esteem of the intelligentsia, and his works were received at the Opéra and elsewhere with growing enthusiasm. Yet controversy was never far away; during the *querelle des bouffons* (1752–4) – a notorious pamphlet war between supporters of opera buffa and those of serious French opera – this former threat to the musical Establishment was himself attacked as an Establishment figure. And although he was increasingly regarded as the Grand Old Man of French music, criticism that his style seemed outmoded could more often be heard. While a number of Rameau's works remained in the Opéra's repertoire after his death, few survived the radical change in taste brought about by the arrival of Gluck's operas in the mid-1770s.

To his contemporaries, Rameau's operas at first seemed revolutionary. With hindsight, however, they appear securely rooted in French operatic tradition both in their subject matter and overall dramatic structure and in many musical details. Rameau's achievement was to rejuvenate that tradition by bringing to it an astonishingly fertile musical imagination, a harmonic idiom richer and more varied than that of any French predecessor, and a boldness of expression that can still seem almost overpowering. Throughout his operatic career Rameau remained receptive to new musical fashions; consequently the lofty and dignified idiom of his first operas became noticeably influenced during the 1740s and 1750s by the lighter German and Italian styles and softened by a proliferation of ornamental detail.

Even in his late seventies the composer's creative powers remained largely unimpaired, as the amazing quality of his last work, *Les Boréades*, demonstrates. But few would deny that, with the exception of that work and of *Platée* and *Pigmalion*, his most enduring operas almost all belong to the period 1733–44. It is especially sad that in his later years he found few libretti with the dramatic potential of *Hippolyte*, *Castor* or the 1744 version of *Dardanus*.

OC: C. Saint-Saëns, C. Malherbe *et al.*, *Jean-Philippe Rameau: Oeuvres complètes*, Paris, 1895–1924; *rp*, New York, 1968.

Hippolyte et Aricie

Hippolytus and Aricia
Tragédie en musique in five acts with prologue (2h 45m)
Libretto by Simon-Joseph Pellegrin
PREMIERES 1 October 1733, Opéra (Académie Royale de Musique), Paris; 11 September 1742 (with changes); modern revivals: 28 March 1903, Geneva; UK: 13 May 1965, Birmingham University (in English); US: 11 April 1954, New York (concert); 4 April 1966, Boston
CAST Thésée *b*, Phèdre *ms*, Hippolyte *t* (*haute-contre*), Aricie *s*, Diane *s*, Pluton *b*, Tisiphone *t* (*taille*), 7 *s*, 4 *t*
(2 *hautes-contre*; 2 *tailles*), 3 *b*; *satb* chorus of nymphs, forest-dwellers, priestesses of Diana, citizens of Troezen, gods of the underworld, sailors, hunters and huntresses, shepherds and shepherdesses; *ballet*: priestesses of Diana, gods of the underworld, furies, sailors and citizens of Troezen, hunters and huntresses, shepherds and shepherdesses, zephyrs, people of the forest of Aricia
ORCHESTRATION standard Académie Royale de Musique orchestra: 2 fl, 2 ob, 2 bsn, 2 musettes, (all ww parts doubled), 2 hn, 2 tpt, timp, perc (tambourin), str (with divided vas), hpd

In reworking the story of Phaedra's incestuous love for her stepson Hippolytus, Pellegrin borrowed elements (including a number of lines) from Racine's *Phèdre* (1677); he also returned to features of Racine's models, Euripides' *Hippolytos* and Seneca's *Phaedra*. His setting, however, alters the balance between the main characters, not so much in its treatment of the young lovers Hippolytus and Aricia as of Theseus, whose role becomes both more extensive and more powerful than that of Phaedra, his queen.

SYNOPSIS

Prologue Diana is forced to concede that, one day a year, her normally chaste forest dwellers should be permitted to serve Cupid. She promises to protect Hippolytus and Aricia.

Act I As the last descendant of Theseus' enemy Pallas, Aricia is compelled to take vows of chastity in the Temple of Diana. Before the ceremony, she and Hippolytus discover their mutual love. When Phaedra arrives to ensure that Aricia 'takes the veil', she learns with rage of Diana's pledge to protect the lovers.

Act II Theseus, who is presumed dead, has descended to Hades to rescue a comrade. Eventually realizing his mission is hopeless, he invokes the help of his father, Neptune. Before he can escape the Fates make their all-important prediction: Theseus may be leaving Hades, but he will find hell in his own home.

Act III Phaedra, believing herself a widow, reveals her love to Hippolytus but is rebuffed even when she offers him the crown. In despair, she tries to kill herself with the prince's sword. As Hippolytus seizes it back, Theseus appears. Recalling the Fates' prediction and misled by various insinuations (which his son is too honourable to counter), Theseus jumps to the conclusion that Hippolytus has attempted rape. Concealing his anguish from the loyal subjects who celebrate his return, he calls on Neptune to punish Hippolytus.

Act IV Hippolytus has escaped with Aricia to Diana's grove. During celebrations in the goddess's honour, a sea monster carries him off. As the horrified onlookers react to his apparent death, Phaedra confesses her guilt.

Act V Theseus eventually learns the truth from the dying Phaedra and is himself about to commit suicide when Neptune reveals that Hippolytus is alive. For accepting his son's guilt too readily, Theseus is condemned never to see him again. The scene shifts to the forest of Aricia, where Diana causes Hippolytus to be reunited with his beloved.

Despite some obvious flaws, Pellegrin's libretto comes nearer to real tragedy than any other that Rameau set (Voltaire's still-born *Samson* excepted; see below). It provides the composer with the outlines of two of his most monumental creations. The magnanimous but fatally gullible Theseus is given music of consistently elevated tone, its broad contours and rich harmonies conveying the king's noble and generous bearing. It reaches its high points in Theseus' two invocations to Neptune and in his final dignified acceptance of his punishment, all of which have a Bach-like harmonic intensity and (unusual for France) consistently patterned accompaniments. Phaedra, though less subtle or rounded than her Racinian counterpart, is still a powerful embodiment of passionate jealousy and remorse. Though initially an unsympathetic character, she gains our compassion in her anxious prayer to Venus and, above all, in her final confession of guilt; this last, with its involvement of the grief-stricken bystanders, is one of the most powerful moments of pure tragedy in the entire pre-Romantic operatic repertoire. By comparison, the eponymous young lovers seem pale, though they project a touching innocence.

The second *Trio des Parques* (Fates) in Act II has become justly famous for its bold use of enharmonic progressions – too bold, indeed, for contemporary

HIPPOLYTE
ET
ARICIE,
TRAGEDIE,
REPRÉSENTÉE

POUR LA PREMIERE FOIS

PAR L'ACADÉMIE ROYALE
DE MUSIQUE,

Le Jeudi premier Octobre 1733.

Reprife le Mardi 11 Septembre 174

Et remife au Théâtre, le Vendredi 25 *Février* 1757.

PRIX XXX SOLS.

AUX DÉPENS DE L'ACADÉMIE,

A PARIS, Chez la V. Delormel & Fils, Imprimeur de ladite Académie, rue du Foin, à l'Image Ste. Geneviéve.

On trouvera des Livres de Paroles à la Salle de l'Opéra.

M. DCC. LVII.

AVEC APPROBATION ET PRIVILEGE DU ROI.

Title page of the libretto of Hippolyte et Aricie, *published in 1757*

performers, so that it had to be cut by about two-thirds. Scarcely less remarkable are the orchestral representation of thunder (Act I) and of the boiling sea (Act III), the latter with the orchestra of strings and bassoons divided into eight parts. Performance difficulties and criticism of the work's dramatic structure led to a series of damaging cuts, both before and during the first run and at successive revivals, so that in Rameau's day the work was seldom valued as highly as his other tragedies. It is, however, the most human of them all and the most consistently moving.

RECORDINGS 1. Hickey, Baker, Tear, Shirley-Quirk, St Anthony Singers, ECO, Lewis, L'Oiseau-Lyre, 1966: despite its inclusion of d'Indy's rescorings (see EDITIONS below) and

its dated approach to stylistic matters, this is the most genuinely dramatic of all Rameau recordings; 2. Auger, Watkinson, Caley, Cold, English Bach Festival Ch, La Grande Ecurie et la Chambre du Roy, Malgoire, CBS, 1978: uses the dramatically weaker 1742 version; stylish singing and playing, but little sense of involvement in the drama
EDITIONS f.s., *OC*, vi (includes extensive rescoring by Vincent d'Indy); reduced s., Paris, *c.* 1733

Samson

Tragédie en musique in five acts with prologue
Libretto by Voltaire
Music lost, unperformed

This collaboration between Voltaire and Rameau, the first of three, was begun in December 1733, soon after the premiere of *Hippolytus et Aricie*. Although a substantial amount of music was complete (Acts III and V and some of the ballet music were rehearsed in 1734), the opera was abandoned in 1735 or soon after. By then Rameau appears to have lost interest in a project that, given its mixture of sacred and profane and its librettist's political notoriety, was bound to be controversial.

That is especially unfortunate, for the libretto is one of the finest he set. Its theme is a powerful one – the liberation of the oppressed Israelites from evil tyranny: Samson, though tragically flawed in succumbing to Dalila's charms, defiantly causes the destruction of the Philistines' temple and, in the process, his own death. (Voltaire's text was known to Saint-Saëns and inspired his first sketch for the libretto of his *Samson et Dalila*.) Rameau evidently employed the discarded music in several subsequent operas, though little can be positively identified.

EDITION lib., L. Morland (ed.), *Voltaire: Oeuvres complètes*, vol. 3, Paris, 1877–85

Les Indes galantes

The Amorous Indies
Opéra-ballet, with prologue and four entrées (2h 30m)
Libretto by Louis Fuzelier
PREMIERES 23 August 1735, Opéra, Paris (prologue and first two entrées only); third entrée added 28 August 1735; fourth entrée added 10 March 1736; modern revival: 18 June 1952, Opéra, Paris (complete); US: 1 March 1961, New York (concert); UK: 22 May 1974, Banqueting House, London (concert); 1977, Edinburgh
CAST prologue: Hébé *s*, L'Amour *s*, Bellone *b*; first entrée: Osman *b*, Emilie *s*, Valère *t* (*haute-contre*); second entrée: Huascar *b*, Phani *s*, Don Carlos *t* (*haute-contre*); third entrée: Tacmas *t* (*haute-contre*), Fatime *s*, Ali *b* (replaced in rev. by Roxane *s*), Zaïre *s* (replaced in rev. by Atalide *s*); fourth entrée: Damon *t* (*haute-contre*), Don Alvar *b*, Zima *s*, Adario *t* (*taille*); *satb* chorus (in prologue and all entrées) of French, Italian, Spanish and Polish allies, warriors, sailors, Provençale men and women, Incas, sacrificers, Peruvians, Persian musicians and slaves, Indian savages; *ballet*: French, Italian, Spanish and Polish young people, warriors, Hebe's retinue, cupids, sports and pleasures, Osman's African slaves, sailors and sailor girls, Pallas, Incas and Peruvians, Persians, Bostangis, flowers, male and female savages, French women dressed as Amazons, French and Indian soldiers, Indian women, colonial shepherds and shepherdesses
ORCHESTRATION 2 picc, 2 fl, 2 ob, 2 bsn, 2 musettes (all ww parts doubled), 2 tpt, timp, perc (tambourin), str (with divided vas), hpd

Ignoring the contemporary preference for opéra-ballets based on mythological themes, Fuzelier's libretto reverted to an older type involving believable modern characters, initiated by Campra's *L'Europe galante* (1697) and briefly in vogue during the first two decades of the 18th century. The prologue retains its allegorical character in order to introduce the work's theme – aspects of love in far-flung lands: the young men of four allied nations (France, Spain, Italy and Poland) forsake the goddess Hebe and, despite Cupid's exhortations, are led off to war by Bellona. The Cupids, realizing that Europe was forsaking them, decide to emigrate to the various 'Indies' (then a generic term for any exotic land). These colourful locations become the settings for the ensuing entrées.

The third entrée, added shortly after the premiere, was criticized for what the French regarded as the absurdity of disguising the hero as a woman. Two weeks later, its plot was entirely changed and all but the final divertissement replaced with new music. The final entrée, added the following year, eventually became one of Rameau's best-loved works of the type.

SYNOPSIS
First entrée: *Le turc généreux* (*The Generous Turk*) On a Turkish island in the Indian Ocean,

Costume design by N. Bocquet for a revival of Les Indes galantes *(Paris, 1761)*

Emilie, a young Provençal girl, has been captured and sold as a slave to the pasha Osman. Although the pasha has fallen in love with her, Emilie cannot forget her lover Valère, a French marine officer. During a sudden storm, Valère is shipwrecked on the island and captured. Osman recognizes him as the one who freed him from slavery. After first feigning anger at seeing the couple embracing, Osman shows his gratitude to Valère by releasing them both.

Second entrée: *Les Incas du Pérou* (*The Incas of Peru*) In the Peruvian desert, the Incas prepare to celebrate the Festival of Sun in the shadows of a nearby volcano, while Don Carlos, a Spanish officer, and Phani, a young Peruvian princess, declare their love for each other. Phani spurns Huascar, the Inca in charge of the ceremonial. As the sun worship begins, Huascar artificially provokes the eruption of the volcano to convince her that the sun god disapproves of her love for an alien. But Carlos foils his attempt to abduct her, and the jealous Inca, now mad with rage, provokes a further eruption of the volcano and is crushed by molten rocks.

Third entrée: *Les fleurs, fête persane* (*A Persian Flower Festival*) (a) Original version: the young Persian prince Tacmas and his confidant, Ali, are each in love with one of the other's slaves: Tacmas loves Zaïre, spurning his own slave Fatima whom Ali loves. On the day of the flower festival, the four meet in a confusing encounter in Ali's garden, where Tacmas is disguised as a woman and Fatime as a Polish slave; but when it emerges that Zaïre and Fatime each love the other's master, the men exchange slaves and the two satisfied couples take part in the festival. (b) Revised version: Fatime (here the sultana rather than a slave) suspects her husband Tacmas of infidelity with Atalide. Disguised as a Polish slave, she gains Atalide's confidence and thus learns, to her astonishment, of Tacmas's utter fidelity. The happy couple takes part in the flower festival.

Fourth [new] entrée: *Les sauvages* (*The Savages*) In a North American forest near the French and Spanish colonies, a tribe of Indian savages prepares to celebrate peace with its European vanquishers. Two officers – Don Alvar, a jealous Spaniard, and Damon, a fickle Frenchman – are rivals for the hand of Zima, the chief's daughter. But she, declaring that the Spaniard loves too much and the Frenchman too little, follows the instincts of a true child of nature and chooses the honourable Indian brave, Adario. Somewhat shamefacedly the Europeans join with the Indians in the ceremony of the Great Pipe of Peace.

With *Les Indes galantes*, the lightweight genre of opéra-ballet was raised to a new level. Fuzelier's libretto, though widely condemned in Rameau's day, can now be seen to have considerable merits. Each entrée has its own distinct character; each tiny plot holds rather more dramatic interest than is usual in works of this sort. Moreover, apart from the prologue, there are no supernatural interventions. Instead, Fuzelier generates much of the necessary visual and dramatic interest from his cleverly chosen

exotic locations and the indigenous ceremonial they provide. (Some of the ethnic detail was culled from published reports of recent events or from first-hand experience.) In the process he manages to portray the interaction of and contrast between European and other cultures – not always to the former's advantage, as the final entrée with its lighthearted but moving tribute to the 'noble savage' demonstrates.

Rameau's response to this unusual material is superb, and the opera is surely among his very finest. He brings to *Les Incas* a dramatic intensity no less than that of the tragedies. The passage from the start of the earthquake to the end of the entrée is an almost unbroken sequence of some 350 bars, during which voices and orchestra interact with extraordinary vehemence. The entrée is dominated by Huascar, whose harsh and fanatical but wholly credible character is established with a sureness of touch not found outside *Hippolyte et Aricie*. In the other entrées and the prologue it is the grace and variety of the vocal airs and ballet music that impress most. Appropriately, the entrée *Les sauvages* includes a reworking of Rameau's harpsichord piece *Les sauvages*, itself inspired by the dancing of two American Indians in Paris in 1725, which had involved a peace-pipe dance. The movement, as indeed the whole entrée, was to become one of Rameau's most popular in the 18th century.

RECORDINGS 1. Poulenard, McFadden, Fouchécourt, Crook, Deletré, Les Arts Florissants, Christie, Harmonia Mundi, 1992; 2. Hartmann, Smith, Devos, Elwes, Huttenlocher, Coeur Joie, Jean-François Paillard CO, Paillard, Erato, 1974
EDITIONS f.s., *OC*, vii (includes some rescoring by Paul Dukas); abridged reduced score, Paris, *c*. 1736

Castor et Pollux

Tragédie en musique in five acts with prologue (2h 45m)
Libretto by Pierre-Joseph Justin Bernard
PREMIERES 24 October 1737, Opéra, Paris; ?8/?11 June 1754 (rev. version: no prologue, new Act I and other changes), Opéra, Paris; modern revivals: 29 January 1903, Schola Cantorum, Paris (concert); 23 January 1908, Montpellier; UK: 27 April 1929, Glasgow (amateur production in English); 1754 version: US: 6 March 1937, Vassar College, New York (concert); UK: 11 October 1981, Covent Garden, London (English Bach Festival)
CAST Télaïre *s*, Phébé *s*, Castor *t* (*haute-contre*), Pollux *b*, Jupiter *b*, High Priest of Jupiter *t* (*taille*), 3 *s*, 2 *t* (*haute-contre*), 2 *b*; (additional soloists, *s*, *t* (*haute-contre*) and *b*, added in 1754); *satb* chorus of arts and pleasures, Spartans, athletes, priests, people, celestial pleasures, Hebe's retinue, demons, blessed spirits, stars; *ballet*: graces, arts, pleasures, cupids, athletes, warriors, Spartan women, Hebe's retinue, celestial pleasures, monsters, demons, blessed spirits, stars, planets and constellations
ORCHESTRATION 2 picc, 2 fl, 2 ob, 2 bsn (all ww parts doubled), 2 tpt, timp, perc (tambourin), str (with divided vas), hpd

In its choice of subject matter – the brotherly love of the twins Castor and Pollux, the one mortal and the other immortal – this work is unusual, since contemporary French opera normally gave the central place to romantic love. After an initially reception, *Castor* was eventually regarded as Rameau's crowning achievement, especially after the triumphant revivals of 1754 and 1764.

SYNOPSIS

The prologue relates to the Peace of Vienna (1736) which ended the Polish War of Succession: Venus and Cupid, at Minerva's bidding, succeed in subduing Mars with the power of love.

Act I   Castor has been killed in battle. As the Spartans mourn, Pollux is persuaded by Telaira to ask his father Jupiter to restore Castor to life. Pollux agrees for love of Telaira, though he knows that she loves only Castor.

Act II   At first Jupiter tries to dissuade Pollux from his mission. He eventually consents to let Castor return from Hades, but on one condition – that Pollux gives up his immortality and take his brother's place there. Pollux selflessly agrees.

Act III   At the mouth of Hades, the spurned Phoebe tries to prevent him from entering. Urged on by Telaira, and with Mercury's help, he braves the demons who bar his way and descends to the Underworld.

Act IV   In Elysium, Castor has found no happiness, for he still longs for Telaira. He is naturally overjoyed when Pollux arrives. Yet, despite the prospect of seeing Telaira again, he cannot bring himself to accept Pollux's sacrifices. He finally agrees to return to earth, but for one day only.

Act V   Reunited with Telaire, Castor holds to his promise despite her pleas and taunts. Eventually relenting, Jupiter restores Pollux to life. For their selflessness he grants both brothers immortality and a place in the firmament.

At the 1754 revival, the dramatically irrelevant prologue was omitted, and a new expository first act inserted before the original Act I. To compensate for this, the original Acts III and IV were telescoped into one; at the same time, the libretto was pruned by well over a quarter, the compression achieved largely by reducing the amount of recitative. The resulting libretto, tauter and better paced, is arguably the best Rameau ever set. Apart from the loss of the prologue (some of it, in any case, incorporated into the revised Act IV divertissement), almost all the most memorable music remains – the mourning chorus 'Que tout gémisse'; Telaira's aria 'Tristes apprêts' grudgingly admired by Berlioz; Castor's ethereal but nostalgic soliloquy 'Séjour de l'éternelle paix' to name only a few. In general too, the substituted music is scarcely inferior to the original: Pollux's monologue 'Nature, Amour' is replaced by an almost equally moving hymn to friendship, 'Présent des dieux'; moreover, we should scarcely suspect from the liveliness, grace and variety of the new ariettas and dance movements that their composer was by now over 70.

RECORDINGS   1. 1754 version: Smith, Buchan, Jeffes, Huttenlocher, English Bach Festival Singers and O, Farncombe, Erato, 1982: a generally stylish and persuasive performance; 2. 1737 version: Scovotti, Lerer, Vandersteene, Souzay, Villisech, Stockholm Chamber Ch, Concentus Musicus Wien, Harnoncourt, Telefunken, 1972: incorporates Chapuis's rescorings, on period instruments (see EDITIONS below), but otherwise sounds remarkably fresh despite its age.
EDITIONS   f.s., *OC*, viii (includes extensive rescoring by Auguste Chapuis); reduced study s., Paris, *c.* 1737 and *c.* 1754

Les fêtes d'Hébé, ou Les talents lyriques

Hebe's Festivities, or The Lyric Talents
Opéra-ballet, with prologue and three entrées
Libretto by Antoine Gautier de Montdorge (with additions by Pierre-Joseph Justin Bernard, Simon-Joseph Pellegrin, Alexandre le Riche de la Pouplinière and possibly others)
PREMIERES   21 May 1739, Opéra, Paris; modern revival: 21 March 1910 (first entrée only), Brussels; 24 January 1914, Monte Carlo (complete); UK: 29 March 1974, Queen Elizabeth Hall, London (concert); US: 1986, Los Angeles
CAST   prologue: L'Amour *s*, Hébé *s*, Momus *t* (*taille*); first entrée: Sappho *s*, Alcée *b*, Hymas *b*, Thélème *t* (*haute-contre*), 1 *s*, 1 *t* (*haute-contre*), 1 *b*; second entrée: Iphise *s*, Tirtée *b*, Lycurgue *t* (*haute-contre*); third entrée: Eglé *s* (and dancer), Mercure *t* (*haute-contre*), Eurilas *b*, Palémon *silent* (required to play the oboe); *satb* chorus of Thessalians, water-dwellers, Lacedemonians, shepherds and shepherdesses; *ballet*: graces, Thessalians, water-dwellers, warriors, Lacedemonians, Terpsichore's nymphs, fauns, sylvans, shepherds
ORCHESTRATION   2 picc, 2 fl, 2 ob, 2 bsn, 2 musettes (all ww parts doubled), 2 hn, 2 tpt, timp, perc (tambourin), str (with divided vas), hpd

In Rameau's day this work was generally known by its subtitle, *Les talents lyriques*, which gives a better idea of the content.

SYNOPSIS

The prologue establishes the theme: the gods' cup-bearer Hebe, dissatisfied with Olympus, persuades her attendant divinities to journey to the banks of the Seine to celebrate those gifts most cherished on the lyric stage – poetry, music and dance. These lyric talents form the subject matter of the ensuing entrées.

First entrée: *La poésie*   On the island of Lesbos, the poet Alcaeus and poetess Sappho are in love. As a result of Thelemus' jealous scheming, Alcaeus

Costume designs for M. Tribou (Castor) and Mlle Pelissier (Télaïre) in Castor et Pollux *(Paris, 1737)*

has been banished by the Lesbian king, Hymas. But Hymas is greatly touched by an allegorical entertainment mounted by Sappho in his honour, which enables her to reveal Thelemus' treachery. The king rescinds the banishment order and the lovers are reunited.

Second entrée: *La musique* The Spartan Princess Iphise is betrothed to Tyrtaeus (Tirtée), famed for the ethical effects of his singing. However, an oracle unexpectedly reveals that she must marry the warrior who vanquishes the Messenians threatening the city. In order to marry Iphise, Tyrtaeus uses the powers of his vocal art to inspire the Spartan army to defeat their attackers.

Third entrée: *La danse* The shepherdess Eglé, a favourite of Terpsichore, Muse of dancing, must choose a husband. Her choice falls on an unknown stranger, who later reveals himself to be the god Mercury. At his request, Terpsichore receives Eglé into her court as Nymph of the Dance.

Rameau's first opéra-ballet, *Les Indes galantes*, had involved believable modern characters. In returning to stock Classical Greek subject matter, its successor may seem retrogressive but was actually in line with current trends. Montdorge's libretto was initially much criticized and the second entrée in particular had to be radically revised, probably by the Abbé Pellegrin: the character of Lycurgus was eliminated (it was anachronistic by some two centuries) and scenes involving Tyrtaeus' exhortations of his soldiers and the women's vigil during the battle were substantially reworked; the revision was extensive enough to be described in one libretto as a 'nouvelle entrée', and involved much new music.

For all its lack of distinction, the libretto serves Rameau quite well. Each embryo plot provides just enough dramatic momentum to maintain our interest up to the all-important divertissement. Rameau, by now at the height of his powers, contributes a score of astonishing inventiveness. 'C'est une musique enchantée,' wrote one contemporary with little exaggeration. This is specially true of the third entrée, wonderfully rich in that languorous and often deeply nostalgic pastoral music that is one of Rameau's hallmarks. The *loure grave* and two sumptuously scored musettes (the second borrowed from the *Pièces de clavessin* of 1724 along with the dionysiac tambourin and 'L'entretien des muses') must surely be among the century's finest ballet music, yet are only marginally finer than many other movements. Among numerous gems in the earlier entrées, Sappho's water-pastoral entertainment includes an exhilarating mariners' chorus, 'Ciel, O ciel! le fleuve agite son onde', notable for an accompaniment consisting entirely of rapid unison scales.

RECORDING Third entrée, *La danse*: Gomez, Rodde, Orliac, Monteverdi Ch and O, Gardiner, Erato, 1979
EDITIONS f.s., *OC*, ix; and in M. Cyr, *Rameau's 'Les fêtes d'Hébé'*, dissertation, University of California, Berkeley, 1975; reduced ss, Paris, *c.* 1739 and *c.* 1756

Dardanus

Tragédie en musique in five acts with prologue (2h)
Libretto by Charles-Antoine Le Clerc de La Bruère
PREMIERES 19 November 1739, Opéra, Paris; 23 April 1744 (as 'nouvelle tragédie' with three acts rewritten); 15 April 1760 (with new alterations); modern revival: 26 April 1907, Schola Cantorum, Paris (concert); December 1907, Dijon; UK: February 1973, Queen Elizabeth Hall, London (concert)
CAST Dardanus *t* (*haute-contre*), Iphise *s*, Anténor *b*, Teucer *b*, Isménor *b*, Venus *s*, L'Amour *s*, Arcas *t* (*haute-contre*) added in 1744; 3 *s*, 1 *t* (*haute-contre*), 2 *b*; *satb* chorus of retinue of Venus and Cupid, retinue of Jealousy, warriors, people, magicians, Phrygians, dreams, cupids; *ballet*: pleasures, Jealousy and her retinue, troubles, suspicions, mortals, warriors, Phrygians, dreams
ORCHESTRATION 2 picc, 2 fl, 2 ob, 2 bsn (all ww parts doubled), 2 tpt, timp, perc (tambourin), str (with divided vas), hpd

Despite its initial run of some 26 performances, *Dardanus* was harshly criticized for its absurd plot and abuse of the supernatural (the latter more or less admitted in the libretto). Rameau and La Bruère subsequently revised the work to the extent of giving Acts III, IV and V an entirely new plot. This version, staged in 1744, at first excited little comment; but when revived in 1760 with further, though less extensive, changes, it was rightly acclaimed as one of Rameau's finest achievements.

SYNOPSIS
In Greek legend, Jupiter's son Dardanus was founder of the royal house of Troy. He was assisted in this by the Phrygian king Teucer, whose daughter he then married. La Bruère's libretto invents a stormy pre-history to these events.

Act I Dardanus is at war with Teucer; at the same time, he has fallen in love with Teucer's daughter Iphise and she with him, though neither knows the other's feelings. Meanwhile Teucer has promised Iphise to a neighbouring prince, Anténor, in return for a military alliance.

Act II Dardanus obtains from the magician Isménor a magic ring that disguises him as the magician himself. Iphise comes to beg this pseudo-Isménor to exorcize her love for her father's enemy; in so doing, she unwittingly reveals to Dardanus the state of her emotions. Overjoyed at the revelation, Dardanus appears in his own form and declares his own love, to Iphise's consternation and dismay.

Act III Up to this point the 1739 and 1744 versions have virtually identical plots. The former continues with Dardanus' capture. His enemies' celebrations, however, are interrupted by news that Neptune has sent a sea monster to avenge this imprisonment of a son of Jupiter. Anténor resolves to combat the monster.

Act IV By now, Dardanus has escaped. In his sleep he is visited by Venus and her attendant Dreams, who exhort him to slay the monster. When he eventually does so, Dardanus rescues Anténor and takes advantage of the latter's gratitude to extract a promise that Iphise be allowed to refuse Anténor's hand.

Act V After Teucer reveals Neptune's decree

Design for the prison scene from Dardanus *(Paris, 1739), based on a drawing by Piranesi*

times almost frightening in its intensity. The dream sequence, Iphise's two tortured monologues, her consultation with the pseudo-Isménor, the scene where Dardanus slays the monster, all are among Rameau's very best. The main problem with this version is that the momentum generated by such passages is continually sapped by the plot's ill-motivated twists and turns and by what come to seem increasingly puerile supernatural happenings.

In simplifying the plot and eliminating the supernatural excesses, La Bruère brings to the drama much greater human interest. The action now focuses far more on the conflicting emotions of the principal characters. Musically, it is true, the revision entails the removal of many beauties, among them the dream sequence, the monster scenes and Iphise's second monologue. (Her first monologue is drastically curtailed, too.) But the prologue and Acts I and II, with their two great ceremonies, remain largely intact, while the considerable quantity of new music generally maintains the high quality of the original. Especially notable is Dardanus' F minor prison monologue, with its amazingly bold bassoon obbligato, wonderfully contrasted with the luminous music for Isménor that immediately follows.

For all its dramatic superiority, the 1744 version has never been revived in modern times, largely because no modern edition exists. (Only the passages where it differs from the original appear in *OC*, consigned to an appendix volume.) Yet it is easily the equal of *Castor* and *Les Boréades* if not of *Hippolyte et Aricie*.

RECORDING Von Stade, Eda-Pierre, Gautier, Van Dam, Ch and O of the Théâtre National de l'Opéra de Paris, Leppard, Erato, 1981: an unsatisfactory and drastically abbreviated conflation of the 1739 and 1744 versions. Some impressive vocal moments, but wooden and unstylish playing
EDITIONS f.s., *OC*, x; reduced ss, Paris, *c.* 1739 and *c.* 1744

that Iphise should marry whoever vanquishes the monster, Anténor is eventually forced to concede to Dardanus. Venus descends to celebrate the marriage.

The last three acts of the 1744 and later versions involve fewer supernatural interventions.

Act III The jealous Anténor devises a plan to murder the now-captive Dardanus without appearing to be the perpetrator.

Act IV Isménor visits Dardanus' cell and foretells his rescue but warns that his liberator will instead become the victim. Consequently, when Iphise gives Dardanus the chance to escape, he refuses. It is Anténor, remorseful and now mortally wounded, who eventually makes possible Dardanus' escape. In the ensuing battle (represented as an entr'acte between Acts IV and V) Dardanus defeats Teucer.

Act V The king defiantly refuses to give him Iphise's hand. It is only when the despairing hero asks to be struck down with his own sword that Teucer relents. As in the original, Venus descends to celebrate the union.

In purely musical terms, the first version of *Dardanus* is without doubt one of Rameau's most inspired creations. The two superb ceremonies in Acts I and II – the first where Teucer and Anténor pledge allegiance and prepare for battle, the second where Isménor displays his occult powers by changing day into night – contain music of astonishing power, at

La princesse de Navarre

The Princess of Navarre
Comédie-ballet in three acts
Libretto by Voltaire
PREMIERES 23 February 1745, La Grande Ecurie, Versailles; 26 November 1763, Bordeaux (with new prologue by Voltaire); UK: 24 April 1977, Covent Garden, London (English Bach Festival)

This was the first of Rameau's operas commissioned by Louis XV's court: with *Platée*, it marked the wedding of the Dauphin with the Infanta Maria Teresa of Spain. Like the comédies-ballets of Molière, the work consists of a spoken play with musical intermèdes.

SYNOPSIS
The plot concerns the vicissitudes of Constance, Princess of Navarre, who has escaped from the King of Castille and seeks refuge with the ludicrous Don Morillo. Constance does her best to evade the amorous advances of the Duc de Foix, who is

Engraving after a scene from La princesse de Navarre *(Versailles, 1745)*

disguised as one of Morillo's officers; meanwhile, the naïve young Sanchette has become infatuated with the duke and believes she is the true object of his affections.

Rameau's three divertissements, one in each act, are only tenuously linked to this plot. The first is a pretext to divert Constance from leaving the château, while the second celebrates her reunion with the court of Navarre. The final divertissement alludes directly to the wedding festivities: at Cupid's command the Pyrenees collapse and are replaced by a magnificent Temple of Love.

Rameau's contribution is characteristically lively and well varied, and was to provide an extensive fund of material for use in later operas.

RECORDING Hill Smith, Harrhy, Goldthorpe, Caddy, English Bach Festival Ch and Baroque O, McGegan, Erato, 1980
EDITIONS f.s., *OC*, xi

Platée
Plataea
Comédie lyrique in three acts with prologue (2h 15m)
Libretto by Adrien-Joseph Le Valois d'Orville, after the play *Platée, ou Junon jalouse* by Jacques Autreau
PREMIERES 31 March 1745, La Grande Ecurie, Versailles; 4 February 1749, Opéra, Paris (text altered by Bellot du Sovot); modern revivals: 26 January 1901 (in German), Kaim-Saal, Munich; 5 April 1917, Monte Carlo (in French); UK:

4 October 1983, Sadler's Wells, London (English Bach Festival); US: 24 May 1987, Dock Street Theater, Charleston (Spoleto Festival)
CAST Thespis *t (haute-contre)*, Thalie *s*, L'Amour *s*, Platée *t (haute-contre)*, Cithéron *b*, La Folie *s*, Momus *t (taille)*, Clarine *s*, Jupiter *b*, Junon *s*, 3 *s*, 1 *t (haute-contre)*, 2 *b*; *satb* chorus of satyrs, maenads, frogs, nymphs, retinue of Momus, Mercury and Cithéron; *ballet*: satyrs, maenads, harvesting peasants with their wives and children, nymphs, aquilons of the North Wind, retinue of Momus, Mercury and Cithéron, Folly's retinue, dryads, graces, country-dwellers
ORCHESTRATION flageolet, 2 picc, 2 fl, 2 ob, 2 bsn (all ww parts doubled), 2 tpt, timp, perc (tambourin), str (with divided vas), hpd

Comedy had traditionally played little part in French opera. Lully soon eliminated comic episodes from his tragedies; from then until the appearance of the present work, only a handful of operas had comic themes. That for *Platée* is the mock marriage between the god Jupiter and an ugly marsh nymph. As such, it seems grotesquely ill-suited to the occasion for which it was commissioned – the wedding of the Dauphin and the evidently unattractive Spanish princess Maria Teresa – though it was well enough received at the time. Once transferred in modified form to the Paris Opéra in 1749, it became one of Rameau's best-loved works and was ultimately regarded by many (including D'Alembert) as his masterpiece.

In Le Valois d'Orville's libretto little more than the outline of Autreau's original play remains.

SYNOPSIS

The prologue, entirely the librettist's invention, is subtitled *La naissance de la Comédie* (*The Birth of Comedy*). Thespis, represented here – unusually – as the inventor of comedy, plans with Momus, god of ridicule, Thalie, Muse of comedy, and L'Amour to teach mortals and gods a moral lesson: they decide to re-enact the episode in which Jupiter cures his wife Juno of jealousy. The comedy itself, the story of which can be traced back to the ancient Greek writer Pausanius, is set throughout in a marsh at the foot of Mount Cithaeron. (It is thus the only multi-act work by Rameau without elaborate scene changes.) Here, with her attendant frogs and cuckoos, lives the marsh nymph Platée who, though incredibly ugly, is convinced of her own charms.

Act I   In consultation with King Cithaeron, Mercury conceives a plan to cure Juno's tiresome jealousy: Jupiter is to court the ludicrous nymph and go through with a mock marriage. Juno, when she is led to uncover the plan, will be made to look foolishly jealous as the object of her husband's 'affections' is revealed.

Act II   In courting Platée, Jupiter undergoes various metamorphoses – as a cloud, a donkey, an owl – to the nymph's consternation and delight. At last he appears in his own form amid a shower of fire. After making amorous advances, he arranges a divertissement in her honour, led by Momus and La Folie, whose followers are dressed respectively as babies and as Greek philosophers.

Act III   By now Juno has been alerted and arrives incognito at the mock wedding. Heavily disguised, Platée is led in on a chariot drawn by two frogs. After an interminable chaconne, danced in *le genre le plus noble*, Momus appears disguised as L'Amour with a ridiculously large bow and quiver. Just as Jupiter is about to pronounce his marriage vows, Juno snatches away Platée's veil . . . and starts to laugh. Mocked by the entire assembly, Platée retreats to her marsh.

Such a description may well give the impression that the humour of *Platée* is rather sick. On the stage, however, that is not how it seems. While we may laugh at Platée's plight, our sympathies are with the nymph throughout. Moreover, the cruelty of laughing at an ugly but hopelessly vain woman is kept at a distance by the role of Platée being sung by a tenor. (This *travesti* role, one of the very few in French operas of the period, was created by the famous *haute-contre* Pierre Jelyotte.) The work's humour comes not just from the extravagant situations but also from wicked parodies of the conventions of serious opera, its descents and transformations, its musical and poetic language. For example, the chaconne that precedes the impatient Platée's marriage is comic not just because of its absurd length or because it is danced in mock-serious style, but because it is misplaced: chaconnes belong at the culmination of the final divertissement. Musical parody takes many forms – exaggerated vocalises, misaccentuations, vocal acrobatics; imitations of frogs, cuckoos, frightened birds, donkey-

Jupiter; elaborate *pizzicati* for La Folie's lyre, double-stoppings for her hurdy-gurdy; even glissandos when Momus presents Platée with L'Amour's gifts (tears, sorrow, cries, languor). The burlesque use of language is seen in Platée's frequent recourse to a frog-like 'Quoi!', her comic alliterations and her colloquial expressions, including the decidedly unoperatic expletive 'Ouffe!'

Yet there is more to *Platée* than a series of comic effects, genuinely funny though many of them are. Whether mock serious, quirkily descriptive or uninhibitedly gay, Rameau's music is a constant delight. He seems to have relished particularly the chance for elaborate ensembles; those in the Prologue and at the ends of Acts II and III have a breadth almost without parallel in his output.

RECORDINGS   1. Micheau, Sénéchal, Gedda, Huc-Santana, O de la Société du Conservatoire, Rosbaud, EMI, 1956; 2. Smith, Ragon, de Mey, le Texier, Françoise Herr Vocal Ensemble, Musiciens du Louvre, Minkowski, Erato, 1989: the first is a recording of a famous Paris staging and has a dated charm; the second is an authentic performance with period instruments [A.B.]
EDITIONS   f.s., *OC*, xi; reduced s., Paris, *c*.1749

Les fêtes de Polymnie

Polyhymnia's Festivities
Opéra-ballet, with prologue and three entrées
Libretto by Louis de Cahusac
PREMIERES   12 October 1745, Opéra, Paris; UK: prologue and first entrée: 5 October 1983, Sadler's Wells, London (English Bach Festival)

Cahusac was among the very few librettists to work with Rameau more than twice: *Les fêtes de Polymnie* was the first of at least seven collaborations (though see *Io* below). It was one of two Rameau operas commissioned to celebrate the Maréchal de Saxe's famous victory at Fontenoy – this one for Louis XV's court, *Le temple de la Gloire* for the Paris Opéra.

SYNOPSIS

The prologue, *Le temple de Mémoire* (*The Temple of Memory*), alludes to this victory: the Arts erect a statue of the king and the Muses extol his glory – a rare return to the kind of panegyric addressed to his predecessor Louis XIV in Lully's prologues. The Muse of lyric poetry, Polyhymnia (Polymnie), then introduces the work's main theme in preparing to refresh the victors with her *fêtes*.

First entrée: *La fable* (*Legend*)   The legend is the marriage of Alcide (Hercules) and Hebe, drawn from Greek mythology.

Second entrée: *L'histoire* (*History*)   The true story is told of how the Syrian King Seleucus and his son Antiochus both discover they love Stratonice and how the king, finding that she loves his son, generously renounces his own love and unites the couple.

Third entrée: *La féerie* (*Fairy-Tale*)   Set in the world of Middle Eastern fairy-tale, this concerns the love of Argélie for Zimès, son of her guardian fairy,

Oriade. But Zimès has been turned by the wicked fairy, Alcine, into a bloodthirsty brute and can be released from this state only when he feels true love.

While this opera contains a quantity of agreeable airs, dances and choruses, it seems at times to be straining for effect and occasionally routine or even clumsy. (The pressure of having to complete four commissioned operas in one year seems to have taken its toll.) Most remarkable, perhaps, is the overture, the first of Rameau's not even to pay lip-service to the Lullian model; the piled-up dissonances of the first section (which recurs later in the prologue when the statue is raised) have the character of magnificent organ improvisation, while the music of the second would not seem out of place in a contemporary German symphony.

EDITIONS f.s., C. Debussy (ed.), *OC*, xiii; reduced s., Paris, c. 1753

Le temple de la Gloire
The Temple of Glory
Opéra-ballet, with five acts (1h 15m)
Libretto by Voltaire
PREMIERES 27 November 1745, La Grande Ecurie, Versailles; 7 December 1745, Opéra, Paris; 19 April 1746, Paris Opéra, rev. as prologue (*La caverne de l'Envie*) and three entrées (*Belus*, *Bacchus* and *Trajan*)

Voltaire believed that opera should be edifying as well as entertaining and that the conventional love element, generally thought essential to French opera, could be minimized. Characteristically, his libretto to celebrate the Battle of Fontenoy is concerned not with romance but with the nature of kingship.

SYNOPSIS
Three kings of markedly different character come in turn to the Temple of Glory. Belus, the power-hungry Assyrian, is judged unworthy to enter because of his bloodthirsty and unjust nature. The self-indulgent Bacchus, having subjugated the Indies with the weapon of drunkenness, is refused because of his unbridled debauchery. Only the Roman Emperor Trajan proves himself worthy: after quelling a revolt led by five kings, he shows magnanimity and duly receives a crown of laurels.

In its original form, the work devoted one act to each king; these were framed by a prologue-like Act I and an epilogue-like Act V, where the Temple of Glory was transformed at Trajan's request into the Temple of Happiness. In 1746 the work was made to conform with the conventional opéra-ballet format: Act I became the prologue, while Acts IV and V were condensed into one and the entrée *Belus* almost entirely rewritten. It is this later version that virtually all musical sources preserve. The score, which contains an abundance of later borrowings, is full of interest, notably the pastoral music of Act I and

Rameau's elaborate reworking of his harpsichord piece *La Cupis* (*Pièces de clavecin en concerts*, 1741) in the prologue.

RECORDING Bellamy, Reinhardt, Elwes, Poulenard, La Grande Ecurie et La Chambre du Roy, Malgoire, CBS, 1982: 1746 version, abridged
EDITION *OC*, xiv

Les fêtes de Ramire
Ramiro's Festivities
Acte de ballet
Libretto by Voltaire (with additions by Jean-Jacques Rousseau)
PREMIERE 22 December 1745, Versailles

When Voltaire and Rameau were busy on *Le temple de la Gloire*, Rousseau was asked to complete *Les fêtes de Ramire*, the libretto of which had been devised by Voltaire to combine in a single act Rameau's divertissements for *La princesse de Navarre*. Rousseau claimed to have composed the overture and linking recitatives as well as some of the text; yet the only music that can be more than tentatively identified as his is the undistinguished monologue, 'O mort, viens terminer les douleurs de ma vie'.

EDITION *OC*, xi

Les fêtes de l'Hymen et de l'Amour, ou Les dieux d'Egypte
The Festivities of Hymen and Cupid, or The Egyptian Gods
Opéra-ballet, with prologue and three entrées
Libretto by Louis de Cahusac
PREMIERE 15 March 1747, La Grande Ecurie, Versailles; 9 July 1754 (without prologue), Opéra, Paris

To celebrate the Dauphin's second marriage, to Maria-Josepha of Saxony, Rameau and Cahusac adapted an opéra-ballet nearing completion. Its theme was well suited to the occasion: the three entrées, *Osiris*, *Canope* and *Aruéris, ou Les Isies*, each culminate in the marriage of one of the Egyptian gods.

SYNOPSIS
First entrée Osiris pacifies a tribe of Amazons and successfully woos their warlike queen Orthésie.
Second entrée The water god Canopus is in love with a young virgin, Memphis, whom the Egyptians are preparing to sacrifice to him. At the height of the ceremony, the offended god causes the Nile to overflow and appears on a chariot drawn by crocodiles. He reveals to Memphis that he is the young mortal, Nilée, whom she loves, and claims her as his spouse.
Third entrée Aruéris (Horus, god of the arts), presides over 'les Isies', a competitive festival in honour of his mother Isis, which awards prizes for singing, playing and dancing. Though diffident of her abilities, Aruéris' beloved Orie enters and wins the vocal competition, for which the prize is union with the object of her love – Aruéris himself.

Les fêtes de l'Hymen is one of the most unjustly neglected of all Rameau's operas. The plots of the three colourful entrées are simple but effective, while the music is consistently interesting and sometimes quite outstanding, as in the sacrificial scene in *Canope* with its ten-part chorus as the Nile overflows. Equally fine is the pastoral music in *Osiris* and the competition music in *Aruéris*.

EDITIONS   f.s., *OC*, xv; reduced score, Paris, *c.* 1748

Zaïs

Pastorale héroïque in four acts with prologue
Libretto by Louis de Cahusac
PREMIERES   29 February 1748, Opéra, Paris; 19 May 1761
(without prologue), Opéra, Paris

Rebel's and Francoeur's *Zélindor, roi des sylphes* and the entrée *La féerie* in Rameau's *Les fêtes de Polymnie* (both 1745) rapidly established a vogue for operas set in the enchanted world of Middle Eastern myth. While elements of this may be found in *Zoroastre*, *La guirlande* and *Les Paladins*, the clearest examples of *la féerie*, as it was known, are the present work and *Acante et Céphise*.

Zaïs is a *génie de l'air*, an elemental being, who has fallen in love with the mortal shepherdess Zélide. Having gained her love disguised as a shepherd, he is commanded by Love to prove her constancy. Zélide emerges unsullied from the various tests she is forced to undergo, but is distressed to learn of Zaïs's royal lineage. The genie decides to sacrifice all for his love, and breaks the magic ring that is the token of his power. Zaïs's palace collapses, and the lovers find themselves alone in a frightful desert. Touched by this sacrifice, Oromases, the benevolent king of the genies, restores to Zaïs his power and grants immortality to Zélide.

Insubstantial though it is for a four-act work, the plot provides Rameau with wonderful opportunities for music that is thoroughly diverting and often unexpectedly moving, as in Zélide's fine monologue 'Coulez mes pleurs'. The composer makes some interesting use of symbolic thematic cross-reference, a technique only hinted at in his earlier scores. The prologue (including the astonishingly bold overture depicting the distillation of the elements from primordial chaos) represents the formation of the universe and the awakening of the elemental spirits.

RECORDING   Elwes, Kweksilber, Van Egmond, Thomas, Collegium Vocale Gent, La Petite Bande, Leonhardt, Stil, 1979
EDITIONS   f.s., *OC*, xvi (includes extensive rescoring by Vincent d'Indy); reduced s., Paris, *c.* 1748

Pigmalion

Acte de ballet
Libretto by Ballot de Sovot, after Antoine Houdar de La Motte
PREMIERES   27 August 1748, Opéra, Paris; modern revivals: 1913, Théâtre des Arts, Paris; UK: 23 May 1985, Hinde Street Church, London

CAST   Pigmalion *t* (*haute-contre*), La Statue *s* (also required to dance); Céphise *s*, L'Amour *s*; *satb* chorus of people, Cupid's retinue; *ballet*: graces, sports, smiles
ORCHESTRATION   2 picc, 2 fl, 2 ob, 2 bsn (all ww parts doubled), timp, str (with divided vas), hpd

According to the *Mercure de France*, Rameau wrote *Pigmalion* in less than eight days in an attempt to help the new Opéra management out of financial difficulties. While it never achieved that wellnigh impossible aim, the work proved immensely popular: from its premiere in 1748 until its final 18th-century revival in 1781 it was given more than 200 times at the Opéra and the French court.

SYNOPSIS
The action is simple but effective: the sculptor Pygmalion has fallen passionately in love with one of his statues and rejected the love of Céphise. In desperation, he implores Venus' aid. Suddenly, at a signal from Cupid, the Statue comes to life and reveals her love to the ecstatic Pygmalion.

The work borrows its subject matter and some 30 lines from La Motte's libretto for the entrée *La sculpture* in *Le triomphe des arts*, first set by La Barre in 1700. While such resettings were commonplace elsewhere in Europe, it was not until *Pigmalion* that the practice was adopted in France, 76 years after the emergence of French opera. Even then it was initially criticized, though the work deservedly became one of Rameau's most popular. Prefaced by a vivacious overture said to depict the sculptor's chisel, the slender but well-paced plot offers a wide variety of moods: the deeply felt yearning of Pygmalion's opening monologues, his bewilderment and elation as the statue comes to life, the uninhibited joy of the final divertissement. It also provides an ingenious pretext for the obligatory ballet, as the Statue, once she has come to life, needs to be shown how to move. Cupid duly leads in the Graces and others, who teach her the characteristics of each dance type, each more animated than the last.

RECORDINGS   1. Crook, Piau, Mellon, Michel-Dansac, Les Arts Florissants, Christie, Harmonia Mundi, 1992: outstandingly good; 2. Goldthorpe, Hill Smith, Rodde, English Bach Festival Singers and Baroque O, McGegan, Erato, 1984; 3. Elwes, Van der Sluis, Yakar, La Petite Bande, Leonhardt, Deutsche Harmonia Mundi, 1981
EDITIONS   f.s., *OC*, xvii/1; reduced s., Paris, *c.* 1748

Les surprises de l'Amour

Cupid's Surprises
Opéra-ballet, originally with prologue and two entrées
Libretto by Pierre-Joseph Justin Bernard
PREMIERES   27 November 1748, Théâtre des Petits Cabinets, Versailles; rev. version: 31 May 1757, Opéra, Paris

Although Louis XV's mistress Madame de Pompadour was evidently no great lover of Rameau or his music, she commissioned this work for her private theatre and created two of the roles. In its original form the opera comprised two entrées, *La lyre enchantée* and *Adonis*. These were preceded by a prologue (*Le retour d'Astrée*) which, like that of *Naïs*, celebrated the Treaty of Aix-la-Chapelle. When the work first appeared at the Paris Opéra in 1757, this prologue was omitted and the original two entrées appeared in a drastically revised form along with a new one, *Anacréon* (not the same as the *Anacréon* with libretto by Cahusac listed below). A few weeks later a further entrée, *Les sibarites* replaced *La lyre enchantée*, the various component entrées being further reshuffled from time to time. By far the best music in an otherwise rather routine score is found in the entrée *Anacréon* (see separate entry, *Anacréon (ii)*, below).

EDITIONS f.s., *OC*, xvii/1; reduced s., Paris, *c.* 1757

Naïs
Neis

Pastorale héroïque in three acts with prologue (2h)
Libretto by Louis de Cahusac
PREMIERES 22 April 1749, Opéra, Paris; 7 August 1764 (with additions by Pierre-Monton Berton); modern revival: June 1980, Opéra Royal, Versailles; UK: July 1980, Old Vic, London
CAST Naïs *s*, Neptune *t* (*haute-contre*), Jupiter *b*, Pluton *b*, Astérion *t* (*haute-contre*), Télénus *b*, Tirésie *b*, 3 *s*, 1 *b*; *satb* chorus of Titans and giants, gods and goddesses, Corinthians, sea divinities, shepherds and shepherdesses, Tiresias' retinue; *ballet*: Titans and giants, retinue of Neptune and Pluto, gods and earth-dwellers, zephyrs, nymphs, Corinthians, athletes, sea divinities, shepherds and shepherdesses, herdsmen
ORCHESTRATION 2 picc, 2 fl, 2 ob, 2 bsn, 2 musettes (all ww parts doubled), 2 tpt, timp, perc (tambourin, tambour voilé), str (with divided vas), hpd

Rameau's *Opéra pour la Paix*, as it was known, celebrated the Treaty of Aix-la-Chapelle which concluded the War of the Austrian Succession (1740–48). Topicality is confined to the prologue, *L'accord des dieux* (*The Gods' Agreement*), an allegory in which the war is represented as the attempt of the Titans to storm the heavens. Magnanimous in victory, Jupiter (Louis XV) shares jurisdiction over the universe with Pluto and Neptune, the latter popularly seen as an inept portrayal of France's former enemy, the English King George II. (No one seems to have noticed the incongruity of making Neptune the hero of the ensuing drama.)

The opera itself is set on the Isthmus of Corinth and concerns Neptune's wooing of the water nymph Naïs. Since classical sources mention only her beauty and her entrancing voice, Cahusac supposes Naïs to have been daughter of the blind soothsayer Tiresias, who could predict the future by interpreting birdsong.

SYNOPSIS

Act I After fending off two suitors, Télénus and Astérion, Naïs presides over the Isthmian Games; but as she crowns the *victor ludorum*, her emotions are troubled by the arrival of a handsome stranger – Neptune in disguise.

Act II In front of Tiresias' grotto, where the shepherds consult the soothsayer, Astérion asks whether the cold-hearted Naïs will ever respond to love. From the awakening birds Tiresias divines that a stranger will conquer her heart and that Astérion and Télénus should beware the god of the seas.

Act III At daybreak over the Corinthian coast, Naïs warns the still-disguised Neptune that his rivals are taking up arms against him. But when their ships attack, Neptune causes them to be engulfed. Only then does he reveal his true identity. The lovers find themselves in the god's magnificent underwater palace surrounded by welcoming sea divinities.

As befits a work in one of the lighter genres, *Naïs* contains little of the serious emotional conflict of the tragédie and little attempt at characterization. It is, however, rich in the spectacle and local colour for which Cahusac was renowned. Moreover, these elements are well integrated, the action continuing to some extent during the colourful divertissements. The disguised Neptune, for example, first pays court to Naïs as she presides over the Isthmian Games, involving onstage wrestling, boxing and athletics; a certain dramatic tension arises from the nymph's attempts to conceal her aroused emotions from the other participants. Similarly, Tiresias' interpretation of birdsong (the Act II divertissement) furthers the action in motivating Neptune's rivals to take up arms against him.

The boldest music appears in the prologue. The violent syncopations and pungent dissonances of the overture (representing the Titans' storming of the heavens) continue into the first two choruses to create a long and astoundingly strong opening sequence – and a further anticipation of Gluck. Thereafter the score provides rich contrasts and consistently imaginative music. The pastoral music and birdsong of Act II are particularly fine, as is the music representing the games (a huge chaconne full of gestures suggesting athletic movement), the jaunty arrival of the sea divinities and the final sequence in Neptune's underwater palace.

RECORDING Russell, Caley, Caddy, Tomlinson, English Bach Festival Singers and Baroque O, McGegan, Erato, 1982
EDITION f.s., *OC*, xviii

Zoroastre
Zarathustra

Tragédie en musique in five acts (2h 30m)
Libretto by Louis de Cahusac
PREMIERES 5 December 1749, Opéra, Paris; 19 January 1756 (three acts largely rewritten); modern revival: 26 November 1903, Schola Cantorum, Paris (concert); 7 June 1964, Opéra, Paris; UK: 1 May 1979, Queen Elizabeth Hall, London (concert; 1756 version, abridged); US: 24 May 1983, Sanders Theater, Harvard University (1756 version)
CAST Zoroastre *t* (*haute-contre*), Abramane *b*, Amélite *s*, Erinice *s*, Céphie *s*, Zopire *b*, La vengeance *b*, Oromasès *b* (1756 version only), Narbanor *b* (1756 version only), 5 *s* (2 in 1756), 2 *t* (*haute-contre*) (1 in 1756), *b*; *satb* chorus of Bactrian men and women, Indian savages, magi, elemental beings, idolatrous priests, demons, retinue of Vengeance, shepherds and shepherdesses; *ballet*: Bactrian men and

women, Indian savages, elemental beings, priests of Ahriman, cruel spirits of darkness, shepherds and shepherdesses
ORCHESTRATION   2 picc, 3 fl, 2 ob, 2 bsn (all ww parts doubled), 2 hn, timp, str (with divided vas), hpd

The subject matter of *Zoroastre* represents a deliberate break with the Classical legend and medieval romance of the conventional French tragédie en musique. Inspired by ancient Persian sources, it concerns the conflict between the great religious reformer Zoroastre (Zarathustra) and an ambitious sorcerer Abramane, 'inventor of the cult of idols' (and himself the librettist's invention). The one is portrayed as representative of the Supreme Being, the other as servant of Ahriman, spirit of evil.

SYNOPSIS
Zoroastre, who has been exiled after the death of the King of Bactria, is summoned by a divine voice to deliver the Bactrian people from Abramane's cruel domination. This he does after a series of confrontations with the magician and with much supernatural assistance. In emphasizing the central struggle between the forces of good and evil the opera pays far less attention than usual to the amorous entanglements of the characters. Indeed, the two main female characters, both Bactrian princesses with claims to the throne, play fairly minor roles: Amélite, Zoroastre's beloved, functions mainly as a pawn in the power struggle; Erinice, whose spurned love for the hero has turned to hate and who has thus joined forces with Abramane, exists largely to provide the sorcerer with a claim to the Bactrian throne.

In its original form, *Zoroastre* was only a qualified success. Revising it for the 1756 revival, Cahusac and Rameau largely recast Acts II, III and V, giving them an entirely different plot and much new music. Zoroastre is now sent on his mission not by an impersonal divine voice but by Oromasès, King of Genii, whose high priest he has become. The hero is portrayed less as a messianic figure and is motivated at least as much by his love for Amélite as by his sacred mission. Aware that this conventional element diminishes Zoroastre's religious stature, Cahusac elevates the mission itself from the simple liberation of Bactria to the more momentous one of freeing the world from the powers of evil. Greater stress is laid on Zoroastre's preparation for the task, which now includes an impressive initiation scene. In this way the libretto's Masonic symbolism is greatly enhanced (Cahusac was secretary to the Comte de Clermont, Grand Master of the French Grand Lodge). Despite its high ideals, however, the work, even in revised form, involves too many arbitrary reversals of fortune brought about by supernatural agents. While the characters – Abramane in particular – are by no means without interest, the dualistic Persian religion comes to seem a struggle not so much between good and evil as between goodies and baddies.

That said, *Zoroastre*'s most impressive passages involve religious ceremonial. The huge occult sac-rifice that occupies virtually the whole of Act IV is superbly handled, working itself gradually into a frenzy and culminating in a series of colossal ensembles and choruses. This is balanced by the hero's devotions to the Supreme Being, represented by the rising sun. Cahusac believed Zoroastre to have initiated a sun cult, and the inclusion of this ritual helps invest him with a mystical quality that effectively counterbalances the love scenes with Amélite. In 1756 a serene 'Hymne au Soleil' was added (a further Masonic element) and the whole ceremony moved from Act II to Act III where it forms a better contrast with the occult ceremonial that follows. Impressive, too, are the scenes involving Zoroastre and his religious mentor Oromasès, whose words (like Christ's in Bach's *St Matthew Passion*) are characterized by a halo of sustained double-stopped strings. The passage in which he initiates the hero has something of the same ecstatic character as the sun-worship scenes, the two passages containing some of the most spiritually elevated music in all Rameau.

Zoroastre set an important precedent in abandoning the traditional French prologue. The overture, deliberately intended to replace it, is the first in which Rameau anticipated Gluck by prefiguring not just the opening scene but the entire drama: its three movements depict in turn Abramane's barbarous rule, the renewal of hope, and the rejoicing of the liberated people.

RECORDING   Elwes, Reinhart, de Reyghere, Van der Sluis, Mellon, Bona, Collegium Vocale Gent, La Petite Bande, Kuijken, Deutsche Harmonia Mundi, 1983: fine singing and playing, but little sense of drama
EDITIONS   1749 version: reduced s., Paris, *c.* 1749; v.s., T. Lajarte (ed.), Michaelis, 1881; 1756 version: f.s., F. Gervais (ed.), ORTF, 1964, transposed down a tone and with all the ornaments editorially realized

La guirlande, ou Les fleurs enchantées
The Garland, or The Magic Flowers
Acte de ballet
Libretto by Jean-François Marmontel
PREMIERES   21 September 1751, Opéra, Paris; modern revival: 22 June 1903, Schola Cantorum, Paris (concert)

It was the 1903 revival that prompted Debussy's patriotic if rather intemperate cry of 'Long live Rameau, down with Gluck!' Debussy's enthusiasm for this work was well founded, for *La guirlande* is a modest but near-perfect creation, little inferior to that better-known miniature masterpiece, *Pigmalion*.

The slender plot indulges in a thinly veiled but ingenious symbolism: the shepherd Myrtil and shepherdess Zélide have exchanged garlands that will stay fresh as long as the lovers remain faithful. But after a flirtation the unfortunate Myrtil's garland wilts embarrassingly. When Zélide discovers it on Cupid's altar, she generously substitutes her own. Myrtil, believing a miracle to have happened, tries to maintain that he has remained faithful. He becomes suspicious when Zélide cannot produce her garland, and they quarrel. But Cupid, touched by Zélide's loyalty, brings about a reconciliation.

The various conflicts of sentiment are made to seem sincere enough and give rise to some touching exchanges. Throughout, the music is characterized by extreme delicacy of decorative detail (Girdlestone described the work as 'a flawless piece of Dresden-china Rameau'), and there are some wonderfully languorous pastoral movements, several borrowed from *Le temple de la Gloire*.

RECORDING Saneva, Lesueur, Versailles CO, Wahl, Nonesuch, 1960s
EDITIONS f.s., G. Beck (ed.), Le Pupitre, Heugel, 1981; reduced s., Paris, *c.* 1751

Allegorical representation of Rameau and Gluck

Acante et Céphise, ou La sympathie
Acanthus and Cephisa, or Telepathy
Pastorale héroïque in three acts (2h 15m)
Libretto by Jean-François Marmontel
PREMIERES 19 November 1751, Opéra, Paris; UK: 21 November 1983, BBC radio

The plot of this occasional work, written to celebrate the birth of the Duke of Burgundy, has the dubious distinction of being the most puerile of any that Rameau set.

The lovers Acante and Céphise have the protection of the good fairy Zirphile. To safeguard them from the menacing genie Oroès, who is in love with Céphise, Zirphile gives the lovers a talisman: this provides them with a kind of telepathic power (*la sympathie* of the work's subtitle) whereby they can experience each other's feelings even when they are separated. After a series of spectacular confrontations with the genie and his evil spirits, in the course of which Oroès tortures Acante and tries to seduce Céphise with his magic, the lovers are rescued from certain death by Zirphile: destiny has decreed that on this day – that of the Duke of Burgundy's birth – the fairy will at last have some power over the evil genie.

Ludicrous though it is, this plot evokes from Rameau a score of remarkable imagination. While some of the vocal music suffers, perhaps, from the haste with which the work was put together, the lovers' reactions to their various tribulations are often unexpectedly moving, while Oroès has much the same menacing character as Abramane in *Zoroastre*. The opera is rich in attractive instrumental items – some, like the entr'acte between Acts II and III, remarkably forward-looking in adopting a quasi-classical musical style. The overture, which celebrates the royal birth with a *feux d'artifice* (Fireworks) complete with cannon fire, is one of Rameau's most ambitiously scored pieces. Like a number of other movements, it includes parts for two clarinets – the earliest surviving examples of their use in French opera (although these instruments are known to have been used two years earlier in *Zoroastre*, their parts have not survived).

EDITIONS manuscript f.s., G. Vaubourgoin (ed.), Paris, 1969; reduced s., Paris, *c.* 1751

Linus
Tragédie en musique in five acts
Libretto by Charles-Antoine Le Clerc de La Bruère

All that survives of *Linus* is the manuscript libretto and two copies of the violin part (all in the Bibliothèque Nationale, Paris). Rameau's son Claude-François told the collector J. J. M. Decroix that the work was in rehearsal at the home of the Marquise de Villeroy when she was suddenly taken seriously ill. In the resulting confusion, the score and all the other parts were lost or stolen. Other evidence suggests that this rehearsal must have taken place by 1752. The diarist Charles Collé claimed that Rameau had never quite completed the music after La Bruère had made changes to his libretto.

Daphnis et Eglé
Pastorale héroïque in one act
Libretto by Charles Collé
PREMIERE 30 October 1753, Fontainebleau

Collé's pastoral acte de ballet contrasts love and friendship. Thinking they are merely friends, Daphnis and Eglé are alarmed to find themselves debarred from the Temple of Friendship. But Cupid shows them the true nature of their feelings, and the temple becomes the Temple of Love, into which they are joyfully received. The work, which includes a fine ariette ('Oiseaux, chantez') and a wealth of attractive instrumental items, has never been published.

MANUSCRIPTS   Paris: Bibliothèque Nationale, Bibliothèque-Musée de l'Opéra

Lysis et Délie
Pastorale in one act
Libretto by Jean-François Marmontel

Although the printed libretto (Paris, 1753) declares that this pastoral was performed in the court theatre at Fontainebleau on 6 November 1753, the *Mercure de France* makes clear that the performance never took place: its subject matter – love disguised as friendship – was thought too similar to that of *Daphnis et Eglé*, performed in the same theatre the week before. The music has not survived.

Les sibarites
The Sybarites
Acte de ballet
Libretto by Jean-François Marmontel
PREMIERE   13 November 1753, Fontainebleau

Though it began life as an independent acte de ballet, this work was eventually incorporated in *Les surprises de l'Amour* at its 1757 revival. The action concerns the peaceful Sybarites, whose life of pleasure is shattered by the invasion of the harsh Crotoniates. On the orders of their queen, Hersilide, the Sybarites put up no resistance but present their conquerors with flowers. The Crotoniate king, Astole, gradually succumbs to Hersilide's charms, and the Sybarites' flower power finally causes the Crotoniates to renounce war. Rameau effectively characterizes the contrast between the voluptuous Sybarites and their warlike opponents, and although his score is somewhat uneven it contains some particularly appealing ballet music.

EDITIONS   f.s., *OC*, xvii/2; reduced s., Paris, *c.* 1757

La naissance d'Osiris, ou La fête Pamilie
The Birth of Osiris, or The Pamylia Festival
Acte de ballet
Libretto by Louis de Cahusac
PREMIERES   12 October 1754, Fontainebleau; US: 1972, Berkeley

This simple ballet allégorique, as it was subtitled, marked the birth of the Duc de Berry (the future Louis XVI), who is represented as the god Osiris. The plot, set in ancient Egypt, is even sketchier than usual: Jupiter descends to his temple at Thebes and announces to Pamilie (Pamyles) and the waiting shepherds the god's birth, which they duly celebrate as the Pamylia Festival. The music, much of it

appropriately pastoral in character, is consistently attractive and does not deserve the indignity of never having appeared in a modern edition.

MANUSCRIPTS   Paris: Conservatoire National de Musique, Bibliothèque Nationale, Bibliothèque-Musée de l'Opéra

Anacréon (i)
Acte de ballet
Libretto by Louis de Cahusac
PREMIERE   23 October 1754, Fontainebleau

One of the two actes de ballet by Rameau that confusingly have the same title. Both concern the ageing poet Anacreon, but are otherwise wholly independent. In this one, Anacreon prepares a betrothal celebration for his two protégés, Cloé and Bathylle, but teasingly leads them to think that it is for his own betrothal to Cloé. The celebration evokes from Rameau music of great charm, while the lovers' desolation that precedes it is touchingly conveyed. The work has never been published.

MANUSCRIPTS   Paris: Conservatoire National de Musique, Bibliothèque Nationale, Bibliothèque-Musée de l'Opéra

Anacréon (ii)
Acte de ballet
Libretto by Pierre-Joseph Justin Bernard
PREMIERES   31 May 1757, Opéra, Paris; UK: 19 August 1985, Lyceum Theatre, Edinburgh (Les Arts Florissants)

The theme of this entrée, added to *Les surprises de l'Amour* at its 1757 revival, is a debate as to whether love and wine are compatible. No, according to the Maenads (priestesses of Bacchus); yes, according to the poet Anacreon. Naturally the latter view prevails, a view shared by a librettist whose life had been largely given over to practical experiment in both spheres. The music may not be the best vintage but is full of good things – a gorgeous *sommeil*, some lovely airs for Anacreon and Cupid and a string of intoxicating ballet movements of which the final *contre-danse* is the most striking.

RECORDING   Schirrer, Feldman, Mellon, Visse, Les Arts Florissants, Christie, Harmonia Mundi, 1982
EDITIONS   f.s., *OC*, xvii/2; reduced s., Paris, *c.* 1757

Les Paladins
The Knights Errant
Comédie lyrique in three acts
Libretto attributed to Duplat de Monticourt and (less reliably) to Pierre-Joseph Bernard, the Abbé Claude-Henri de Voisenon and the Comte de Tressan
PREMIERES   12 February 1760, Opéra, Paris; modern revival: June 1967, Lyons Festival

The libretto is an undistinguished adaptation of La Fontaine's conte *Le petit chien qui secoue de l'argent et des pierreries*, which in turn is based on Canto XVIII of Ariosto's *Orlando furioso* (1516).

Set in medieval Venetia, the plot concerns the love between Atis, a young knight errant, and Argie, a young Italian girl. Argie is kept in a fortress under the surveillance of a cowardly gaoler, Orcan, on the orders of her absent guardian, the aged senator Anselme, who wishes to marry her. By various means, including several disguises and some help from the fairy Manto, Atis attempts to outwit the jealous Anselme to win Argie's hand.

In making Anselme guardian rather than husband of Argie, the librettist changes the theme from one of cuckoldry (unsuitable for opera in mid-18th-century France) to one of rivalry between an old and a young suitor. The opera includes elements of farce and knockabout comedy, but is by no means wholly comic and was criticized for its inclusion of serious elements. The only character to emerge as more than a stereotype is Orcan, a genuinely comic creation who engages our sympathy despite his craven behaviour.

While scarcely Rameau's *Falstaff*, as a reviewer of the Lyons revival deemed it, the score is astoundingly lively for a composer well into his seventies (it was possibly begun in 1756). The instrumental items include some of his most adventurous orchestration. The deployment of several fully developed *da capo* arias in the main action rather than solely in the divertissements is one symptom of a new wave of Italian influence, probably sparked off by the notorious *querelle des bouffons*.

MANUSCRIPTS   Paris: Conservatoire National de Musique, Bibliothèque Nationale, Bibliothèque-Musée de l'Opéra
RECORDING   extracts: Rodde, Farge, Benoit, La Grande Ecurie et La Chambre du Roy, Malgoire, CBS, 1973
EDITIONS   f.s., in R. P. Wolf, *Jean-Philippe Rameau's comédie lyrique 'Les Paladins' (1760): A Critical Edition and Study*, dissertation, Yale University Press, 1977; facsimile f.s., R. P. Wolf (ed.), Pendragon, 1986

Les Boréades

The Sons of Boreas
Tragédie en musique in five acts (2h 45m)
Libretto attributed to Louis de Cahusac
PREMIERES   unperformed in Rameau's lifetime; modern performance: 16 September 1964, Maison de la Radio, Paris (extracts; concert); 21 July 1982, Théâtre de l'Archevêche, Aix-en-Provence; UK: 14 April 1975, Queen Elizabeth Hall, London (concert); 21 November 1985, Royal Academy of Music, London (abridged); 21 April 1993, Mayfair Suite, Bullring Shopping Centre, Birmingham
CAST   Alphise *s*, Abaris *t* (*haute-contre*), Sémire *s*, Borilée *bar*, Calisis *t* (*haute-contre*), Adamas *b*, Borée *b*, 4 *s*, 1 *b*; *satb* chorus of pleasures and graces, Alphise's retinue, Bactrian people, muses, arts, subterranean winds, Boreas' retinue; *ballet*: pleasures and graces, priests, Alphise's retinue, Oritheia and her companions, Boreas' disciples, Bactrian people, north winds, hours, seasons, zephyrs, talents
ORCHESTRATION   2 picc, 2 fl, 2 ob, 2 cl (optional), 2 bsn (all ww parts doubled), 2 hn, str (with divided vas), hpd

Until recently, *Les Boréades* was widely believed to have been in rehearsal at the Paris Opéra at the time of Rameau's death but then abandoned for reasons unknown. Archival evidence now reveals that the work was rehearsed more than a year earlier, in April 1763, and that it was probably intended for performance not at the Opéra but before the court at Choisy. Why this remarkable opera should have been put aside can only be guessed at, though it must have to do with changing musical tastes in the 1760s, with the opposition of Madame de Pompadour and others at court, with the fact that the music presents formidable problems, perhaps even with the burning down of the Académie Royale's theatre in the very month of the rehearsals. It has been suggested, too, that since the libretto includes elements that could be construed as Masonic (an initiatory voyage, a magic talisman and various Apollonian symbols) the opera might have been considered politically subversive.

SYNOPSIS

The action, set in the ancient kingdom of Bactria, concerns the love between the Queen Alphise and a noble foreigner, Abaris, who has been brought up by Adamas, high priest of Apollo, in ignorance of his origin. The obstacle to their love is a tradition that the queen must marry a descendant of Boreas, god of the north wind. Rather than lose Abaris by marrying one of the 'Boréades', Alphise abdicates, much to her subjects' surprise and regret and the god's displeasure. During a violent tempest, she is carried off to his domain among the subterranean winds. The efforts of Abaris to rescue her are assisted by the interventions of the muse Polyhymnia and the god Apollo; Abaris also has the magic arrow which Cupid had given to Alphise. Eventually Apollo reveals that Abaris is his child by a nymph daughter of Boreas, and may therefore marry Alphise with impunity.

While the libretto is ascribed to Cahusac by two independent 18th-century writers, there are problems in accepting the attribution unreservedly. The work takes considerable (and uncharacteristic) liberties with its Classical source material, while compared with *Zoroastre* it makes little of the Masonic elements. Moreover, the hymns and ballets figurés, which are such a feature of Cahusac's work, are each represented by a single, undeveloped example; at the same time, the presence of three *simile* arias and other anomalies have no parallel in his other works, though such arias may be found, for example, in Marmontel's libretti. It is, however, always possible that the text was among Cahusac's papers at the time of his death (1759) and that the perceived anomalies result from subsequent tinkerings by others.

That said, the libretto is among the more serviceable of those that Rameau set. Despite its overuse of the supernatural and reduction of hero and heroine to the status of mere agents in a battle between superior forces, it is paced in such a way that successive stages of the plot generate increasing dramatic momentum; this is especially so from the moment of the queen's unexpected abdication in Act III, through the tempest that dominates the rest of that act and most of the next, to the torture scenes in Act V. Rameau takes full advantage of this to produce a work with greater forward drive than any of his others, exemplified by the way his fearsome tempest continues straight through from the middle of Act III well into Act IV (and, less innovatory, his overture into the first scene). Among musical highlights in a particularly inventive score are the *simile* arias 'Un horizon serein' (Act I), Abaris' despairing monologue 'Lieux désolez', and the descent of Polyhymnia and the Muses (Act IV), this last one of the most ravishing single movements in the whole of his output.

RECORDING Smith, Rodde, Langridge, Aler, Lafont, Cachemaille, Le Roux, Monteverdi Ch, English Baroque Soloists, Gardiner, Erato, 1982
EDITIONS f.s., in M. Terey-Smith, *Jean-Philippe Rameau: 'Abaris ou Les Boréades': A Critical Edition*, dissertation, University of Rochester, Eastman School of Music, 1971; facsimile f.s., Stil (Paris), 1982

Io

Acte de ballet
Incomplete
Librettist unknown

There is no evidence that *Io* was performed in Rameau's lifetime. It was once suspected of being the composer's last work, on the grounds that all sources lack the final divertissement. But the work includes a duet found in a more polished form in *Les fêtes de Polymnie*, suggesting that *Io* may have been written by 1745. Since the duet's text is much the same in both operas, and since French librettists did not generally borrow from each other, Cahusac seems the most likely author of *Io*, in which case this would precede his first documented collaboration with Rameau. In its surviving form the work is of little musical or dramatic interest.

MANUSCRIPTS Paris: Conservatoire National de Musique, Bibliothèque Nationale

Zéphyre

Zephirus
Acte de ballet
Librettist unknown
PREMIERES apparently unperformed in Rameau's lifetime; modern revivals: UK: 15 June 1967, Jubilee Hall, Aldeburgh (concert); 1976, Albi

Although we know neither the date of *Zéphyre* nor the occasion for which it was written, the work was possibly composed or at least revised in the early 1750s. Of all the actes de ballet of that decade it is one of the most delightful. Its anonymous libretto, which presents the wooing of one of Diana's nymphs by Zephirus, god of the west wind, may allow little scope for drama. But it gives Rameau a chance to write some of his most charmingly evocative and descriptive music – whether in depicting the flowers that sprout under the nymph's feet or the various effects of Zephirus' breezes. The score contains several references to a musical figure clearly derived from Rameau's harpsichord piece *Les niais de Sologne* (*Pièces de clavessin*, 1724).

RECORDING Langridge, Pena, Garcisanz, Ensemble Instrumental de France, Wallez, IPG, 1976
EDITION f.s., *OC*, xi

Nélée et Myrthis

Acte de ballet
Librettist unknown
PREMIERES apparently unperformed in Rameau's lifetime; modern revival: 22 November 1974, Victoria State Opera, Melbourne

The history of this work is as obscure as those of *Io* and *Zéphyre*. It was evidently to have been included in an opéra-ballet entitled *Les beaux jours de l'Amour*, of which nothing further is known. The skeletal plot takes place during the Argive Games. The athlete Nélée, rebuffed by the feigned indifference of the poetess Myrthis, manages to arouse her jealousy by courting Corinne. But Myrthis' true feelings for Nélée are revealed as she crowns him *victor ludorum*, to the onlookers' delight. As in *Naïs*, the athletics take place during an impressive chaconne. The remaining music is generally attractive if not outstanding.

RECORDING Mellon, Corréas, Semellaz, Les Arts Florissants, Christie, Harmonia Mundi, 1992
EDITION f.s., *OC*, xi

BIBLIOGRAPHY *Early Music*, special Rameau issue, October 1983; D. Foster, *Jean-Philippe Rameau: A Guide to Research*, Garland, 1989; Cuthbert Girdlestone, *Jean-Philippe Rameau: His Life and Works*, Dover, rev. and enlarged 2nd edn, 1969; Graham Sadler, 'Jean-Philippe Rameau', in J. R. Anthony *et al.*, *The New Grove French Baroque Masters*, Macmillan, 1986

G.S.

EINOJUHANI RAUTAVAARA

b 9 October 1928, Helsinki

Rautavaara, one of the most prolific and respected of contemporary Finnish composers, studied in Helsinki with Merikanto, and later at Tanglewood with Copland and Sessions. Definable neo-classical and serial periods of compositional style gave way in the 1960s to the free tonality of what became known in Finland as the 'new Romantic' movement. He has a substantial list of symphonic, chamber and choral works to his credit.

The style of Rautavaara's first opera, *Kaivos* (*The Mine*), written in 1957 and inspired by events in the Hungarian uprising of the previous year, was much influenced by Alban Berg; it was first performed on Finnish television in 1963. His comedy *Apollon contra Marsyas* (1970) used elements of jazz as part of its treatment of the mythological aesthetic confrontation; *Marjatta matala neiti* (*Marjatta the Lowly Maiden*, 1975), drawn from the *Kalevala*, is a one-act Christmas mystery play.

His most substantial work for the stage is *Thomas*, commissioned by the Joensuu Song Festival as part of the 100th anniversary celebrations of the first publication of the *Kalevala*, and premiered on 21 June 1985 (and recorded by Ondine the following year). Thomas was the English bishop and missionary who attempted to set up a papal state in Finland in the mid-13th century; he was thwarted after an over-ambitious invasion of pagan Russia, and his defeat by Alexander Nevsky in the famous battle on the ice is also celebrated in Eisenstein's film and the cantata Prokofiev drew from his incidental music. In Rautavaara's opera, written for the baritone Jorma Hynninen, Thomas's Christianity is also in conflict with the shamanistic pantheist culture of Finland's national epic.

BIBLIOGRAPHY Mikko Heinio, 'Einojuhani Rautavaara at 60', *Finnish Musical Quarterly*, February 1988, pp. 3–14; Einojuhani Rautavaara, 'Thomas – Analysis of the Tone Material', *Finnish Musical Quarterly*, January–February 1985, pp. 47–53

R.M.

VENANZIO RAUZZINI

b 18 December 1746, Rome; *d* 8 April 1810, Bath, England

Rauzzini, a male soprano and composer, studied in Rome, but may also have spent some time at Naples with the great teacher Nicolo Porpora. He made his début at Rome in 1765 in Piccinni's *Il finto astrologo*. There followed performances in Munich, Venice and Vienna, where Mozart heard him in Hasse's *Partenope*. His first operas, *Piramo e Tisbe* and *L'eroe cinese*, were performed in Munich, where Burney admired his voice but preferred his compositions. Mozart's virtuosic solo motet 'Exsultate, jubilate' was composed for him.

Rauzzini occasionally appeared at London's King's Theatre between 1774 and 1777, settling in England in 1779. From autumn 1779 he was often in Bath, where he successfully managed concerts. Meanwhile he continued to compose operas and ballets for the King's Theatre. His operas were usually well received. After a revival of *La vestale* in 1787 flopped he settled in Bath, where his frequent musical guests included Haydn whose visit prompted his well-known canon about Rauzzini's recently deceased and much-loved dog: 'Turk was a faithful dog, and not a man'.

Operatic works surviving in whole or in part: *Piramo e Tisbe*, 1769, rev. 1775; *L'ali d'amore*, 1770, rev. 1776; *L'eroe cinese*, 1770, rev. 1782; *Astarto* (dubious), 1772; *Pompejo* (dubious), 1773; *Armida*, 1774; *Creusa in Delfo*, 1783; *L'omaggio* (coll. with Bianchi and Giordano), 1781; *Alina, o sia La regina di Golconda*, 1784; *La vestale, o sia L'amore protetto dal cielo*, 1777

BIBLIOGRAPHY W. van Lennep *et al.* (eds), *The London Stage*, South Illinois University Press, 1960–68

T.T.C.

MAURICE RAVEL

Joseph Maurice Ravel; *b* 7 March 1875, Ciboure, France; *d* 28 December 1937, Paris

Ciboure is by the Pyrenees, and though Ravel's family moved to Paris when he was three months old he kept a lifelong affection for things Basque (and Spanish) through his mother. His father was a Swiss civil engineer. It is hard not to see familial traces in the composer's love of polished, ingenious mechanisms, and the frequent Spanish irruptions in his music. They are highly characteristic features of his scores – most obviously, of *L'heure espagnole*; and yet they are marginal. Ravel's basic musical language developed from his revered teacher Fauré, with vital influences from Chabrier, Debussy (up to *Pelléas*), early Satie and the New Russian School: Rimsky-Korsakov, Borodin, Balakirev. The oft-told story of his repeated failures to win the Prix de Rome at the Paris Conservatoire (at the fifth and last attempt, in 1905, he was rejected at the preliminary round, and a great scandal ensued) is misleading. Ravel was no revolutionary young Turk challenging the Establishment, but an inquiring, fastidiously original composer who was neither interested in the kind of academic exercise prescribed for that competition, nor particularly good at it. The piquant 'injustice' of the final rebuff lay in the fact that his *Jeux d'eau*, his String Quartet and the *Shéhérezade* songs were already widely admired; the terms of the Prix de Rome, however, excluded independent works from consideration.

That failure cannot have wounded him gravely, since his most prolific period followed at once. (Of all petits-maîtres Ravel was among the least prolific: rigorously self-critical throughout his 40-odd years of composing, he published only a few hours' worth of music.) Between 1905 and 1911 came the *Introduction and Allegro* for harp and ensemble, the *Sonatine*, *Miroirs*, *Gaspard de la nuit* and the *Valses nobles et sentimentales* for piano, the suite *Ma mère l'oye* for piano duet, the *Rapsodie espagnole*, the first sketches for *Daphnis et Chloé*, many songs, and *L'heure espagnole*. Ravel's name is not popularly associated with opera, no doubt because the two he completed are brief and therefore awkward to programme, and they afford no spectacular vocal or dramatic opportunities to their leading singers. In fact his thoughts turned early to the medium. In the late 1890s he had planned an opera on Maeterlinck's *Intérieur*, as well as a Hoffmann operetta *Olympia* (the robot doll of Offenbach's celebrated piece), and later – like several other composers of the day – a fairy opera after Hauptmann's *Die versunkene Glocke* (*La cloche engloutie*, or *The Sunken Bell*). His sketches were not wasted, for it seems that Dr Coppelius' entry music from *Olympia* was recycled as the prelude to *L'heure espagnole*, and much later some musical ideas for *La cloche engloutie* were transferred to *L'enfant et les sortilèges*.

After the successful premieres of *L'heure espagnole* (though one critic did call it 'a mildly pornographic vaudeville') and *Daphnis* (with

Nijinsky), Diaghilev asked Ravel to collaborate with Stravinsky in an unexpected operatic task. They were to produce a reorchestrated version of *Khovanshchina*, which Musorgsky had left unfinished and Rimsky-Korsakov had adapted according to his own lights. The new version was completed and performed by the Ballets Russes in 1913; unfortunately, the score has never been retrieved. Then came the First World War, in which Ravel did non-combatant military service. During that time the novelist Colette agreed to write a libretto for the Paris Opéra, and hit upon Ravel as a suitable composer for the divertissement she conceived. It took him some time to agree; he was profoundly depressed by the war, and by the death of his mother in 1917, and his glum response to Colette's original title, *Ballet pour ma fille*, was that he *had* no daughter. Eventually he warmed to the project, but his *Tombeau de Couperin* and *La valse* were completed long before *L'enfant et les sortilèges* was finally staged, with de Sabata conducting and Balanchine as maître de ballet.

Ravel's health was declining. After *L'enfant* he composed, slowly, the newly austere *Chansons madécasses* and his Violin Sonata, then the *Boléro* for the dancer Ida Rubinstein and the two concertos for piano. Between the premieres of the latter, he was involved in the taxi-cab accident that may have triggered his final collapse. He accepted a film commission to write three songs for Chaliapin as Don Quixote (he had actually begun contemplating an opera after Cervantes's novel), but was late in fulfilling it. Those songs were Ravel's last music; in summer 1933 his muscular co-ordination began to fail, and aphasia set in. He became unable to compose, and in the sad four years left to him could manage only some bare sketches for *Morgiane*, another ballet meant for Ida Rubinstein.

L'heure espagnole
Spanish Time

Comédie musicale in one act (introduction and 21 scenes) (50m)
Libretto by Franc-Nohain (Maurice-Etienne Legrand), after his own comedy
Composed 1907-9
PREMIERES 19 May 1911, Opéra-Comique, Paris; UK: 24 July 1919, Covent Garden, London; US: 5 January 1920, Chicago
CAST Concepción *s*, Gonzalve *t*, Torquemada *t* (*Trial*), Ramiro *bar* (*baryton-Martin*), Don Inigo Gomez *b*
ORCHESTRATION picc, 2 fl, 2 ob, ca, 2 cl, b cl, 2 bsn, sarrusophone (dbsn), 4 hn, 2 tpt, 3 trbn, tuba, 2 hp, cel, timp, perc (sd, cym, triangle, glock, bells, castanets, tambourine, whip, xyl, 3 metronomes), str

Franc-Nohain was surprised when Ravel asked permission to set his highly improper, cod-poetical vaudeville to music, and when at last Ravel came to play and sing him the result, the playwright's cautious reaction was that it went on rather long. In fact the composer set his own Spanish time with expert precision and crisp habanera rhythms; there are no longueurs, except in performances that seek to

humanize the characters by letting them moon over their recitatives. Ravel's score expanded Franc-Nohain's comic analogy between wound-up automata and erotically driven people much further than the text could do alone, and yet kept the sung lines natural and colloquial enough to incur some disapproving sniffs in 1911 (as with his Jules Renard songs four years earlier, the *Histoires naturelles*). The vocal writing permits the ripe double meanings to be lucid, but they are never crudely underlined. Nor are the characters guyed: besides its poise and verve, the score often glows with the famous Ravel *tendresse*.

SYNOPSIS
Eighteenth-century Toledo. A muscular mule-driver, Ramiro, takes his broken watch to the shop of the clockmaker Torquemada. But it is Thursday, the day when Torquemada regulates all the town clocks; he must leave Ramiro to wait, and his wife Concepción to entertain him. Both are embarrassed: Ramiro because he is shy ('Les muletiers n'ont pas de conversation'), Concepción because she is expecting her poet lover imminently. Her husband has promised her either of two large grandfather clocks, and it occurs to her to beg the muleteer to carry one up to her bedroom. Delighted to have a task, he goes off with it just as Gonzalve drifts in, warbling poetically.

To Concepción's frustration, he is still warbling when Ramiro comes back. She declares a sudden preference for the other clock, and dispatches the muleteer to retrieve the first one; meanwhile she conceals her poet in the second, whereupon the stout banker Don Inigo Gomez arrives unannounced to court her. Ramiro, back again with the first clock, duly carries off the second clock with negligent ease and Concepción as anxious escort. Don Inigo, abandoned, decides that flirtatious whimsy is the card to play, and squeezes himself into the first clock – but prudently shuts the door when Ramiro returns alone, musing on the mysteriousness of woman. Suddenly Concepción reappears in a temper, demanding the instant removal of the second clock. While the muleteer obeys, Don Inigo pursues his lascivious strategy with the lady; the upshot is that Ramiro, all unawares, is soon hefting the first clock upstairs once more with Concepción on his heels.

The dismissed poet sings an effusive farewell to his clock dungeon, but hides again as Ramiro comes back, still musing romantically. Concepción descends in a fury – the first clock must go. While Ramiro fetches it, she voices her bitter disappointment ('Oh! la pitoyable aventure!'): Gonzalve would do nothing but rhapsodize, and now Don Inigo is inextricably stuck in his clock. Ramiro returns bearing that clock, ready and eager for the next job. She looks at him with new eyes, and proposes going upstairs again 'sans horloge . . .'. Torquemada comes home to find two gentlemen occupying his clocks and explaining brightly that they are interested customers. By the time his wife reappears, much happier, their reluctant purchases are settled. It takes Ramiro to heave Don Inigo out of his expensive prison, and he also promises to tell Concepción the time each morning when he comes by with his mules. In a final quintet, everybody agrees on a Boccaccian moral: through plain efficiency, the muleteer eventually gets his turn.

The glittering surface of Ravel's score, all Spanish snap with horological icing (continual chimes high and low, a mechanical cuckoo and clock, even three metronomes ticking throughout the prelude), disguises its pure musical invention. Ravel expressly intended to write something more like Italian buffo than French opérette, but what he devised was *sui generis* – an elegantly comic piece for orchestra and singers, through-composed in patterns as intricately and ingeniously connected as those of any watch. The music is aptly laden with displacement jokes: just as the rigorously ticking metronomes in the prelude are all at odds, so the brisk Hispanic dance-rhythms are prone to fractures, the 'popular' harmonies derailed by post-Fauré sophistication, Gonzalve's exquisite little effusions rudely interrupted, and an impossibly low note demanded from Don Inigo by the finale is supplied by a helpful double bassoon. Ravel's Spanishry here surely owes far less to his maternal memories than to Albéniz, whose music he adored (and who died in the year Ravel completed the opera).

Costume design by A. Maré for Torquemada in L'heure espagnole *(Paris, 1921)*

Recent French operas had embraced the Wagnerian leitmotif method to a fault, and Ravel extends it here to absurdity. Don Inigo is identified by a pompous fanfare of short brays, Gonzalve purely by his constant mimicking of effete *fin-de-siècle* art song, Ramiro by a lusty rhythm on timpani – but in his two dreamy fantasies, he is also allotted the most richly developed music.

No tag is attached to Concepción, the only character who is both clever and sensible. The music for the gentle Torquemada, to whom perhaps the situation is perfectly clear and the outcome perfectly satisfactory, is of a piece with the tintinnabulating serenity of his shop. That, in turn, is not so very far removed from the magical garden of *L'enfant et les sortilèges.*

RECORDINGS 1. Duval, Hérent, Giraudeau, Vieuille, Clavensy, Paris Opéra-Comique O, Cluytens, Columbia, 1953: a treasurable performance, its well-seasoned manners unlikely to be recaptured; 2. Berbié, Giraudeau, Sénéchal, Bacquier, Van Dam, O National de Paris, Maazel, DG, 1965: the unusually strong, characterful cast compensates for Maazel's heavier touch; 3. E. Laurence, Sénéchal, Raffalli, G. Quilico, Loup, Nouvel O Philharmonique, Jordan, Erato, 1985: lighter, admirably stylish, full of verve [A.B.]
EDITIONS f.s., Durand, 1911; v.s., Durand, 1908

L'enfant et les sortilèges
The Child and the Sorceries
Fantaisie lyrique in two parts (45m)
Libretto by Colette (Sidonie-Gabrielle Colette)
Composed 1920–25
PREMIERES 21 March 1925, Monte Carlo Opera; 1 February 1926, Opéra-Comique, Paris; US: 19 September 1930, San Francisco; UK: 3 December 1958, Oxford University Opera Club
CAST (The multiple roles marked * are prescribed by the composer) The Child *ms*, Maman *a*, Louis XV chair *s*, Chinese Cup *a*, Fire/Princess/Nightingale* *light s*, Little Old Man (Arithmetic)/Tree Frog* *t*, Cat *ms*, Dragonfly *ms*, Bat *s*, Little Owl *s*, Squirrel *ms*, Shepherdess *s*, Shepherd *a*, Armchair *b chantante*, Grandfather Clock *bar*, Teapot *t*, Tom Cat *bar*, Tree *b*; children's chorus of Settle, Sofa, Ottoman, Wicker Chair and Numbers; *satb* chorus of shepherds, frogs, animals and trees
ORCHESTRATION picc, 2 fl, 2 ob, ca, 2 cl, E♭ cl, b cl, 2 bsn, dbsn, 4 hn, 3 tpt, 3 trbn, tuba, pf, hp, cel, timp, perc (sd, bd, cym, t-t, triangle, crotales, wb, whip, rattle, cheese-grater, wind-machine, slide fl, xyl), str

Both Colette and Ravel were cat-lovers, and the feline duet at the centre of *L'enfant et les sortilèges* was conceived *con amore*. Ravel was undoubtedly pleased to have inanimate objects to animate, too, including a much noisier clock than the ones in *L'heure espagnole*, and he must have imagined the garden of the opera on the model of his own at his recently acquired villa, *Le Belvédère*, in Montfort L'Amaury. It was the composer who tilted Colette's divertissement towards the style of a revue, with her approval: his interest in American popular music had been growing, and would surface again in the 'Blues' of the Violin Sonata and in both the piano concertos. (There is a curious likeness between the cup-and-teapot duet in *L'enfant* and Gershwin's 'Our love is here to stay'.) The challenges the opera presents to a producer's imagination are severe; whimsy would be ruinous in the garden scene, and it would be a rare mezzo-soprano indeed who could make a plausible child of 'six or seven years' as prescribed by the text. After seeing a Disney animated film, Ravel's brother exclaimed that *that* must be the way to do *L'enfant et les sortilèges*.

SYNOPSIS
A naughty child, dawdling over his homework, is reproved by his mother. Left alone, he flies into a tantrum and assaults everything in the room, including the family cat. Then, one after another, all the things he has maltreated come to plaintive life: the long-suffering furniture, the broken clock and the tea service, the offended fire in the grate, the printed shepherds from the slashed wallpaper, the princess from his torn story book. He regrets bitterly the lost ending of the tale ('Toi, le coeur de la rose'), but suddenly his neglected arithmetic pops up to challenge him with impossible exercises. By now quite unstrung, he expects even the cat to speak. Instead, it miaows a mock-Wagnerian erotic duet with its mate in the garden: meanwhile the scene revolves from indoors to outdoors.

At first the garden twitters and murmurs with innocent animal voices; but the trees break in to lament their cruel wounds from the child's pocket knife and a dragonfly cries after the mate whom he pinned dead to a wall. A bat grieves for a lost mate too and a squirrel – reliving its cruel captivity – tries to warn a dim frog of omnipresent danger. A Utopian wildlife ballet ensues, but at the climax the squirrel addresses a poignant rebuke to the child: 'You caged me for the sake of my beautiful blue eyes, but did you know what they reflected? – The free sky and the wind, and my free brothers!' Chastened, the child feels himself rejected from this harmonious animal realm, and he whimpers for his Maman. At once some unforgiving trees and beasts close in upon him; in the commotion, a small squirrel who has been wounded limps towards the child, who binds the squirrel's paw with a ribbon. The other animals reflect on his instinctive kindness and decide to practise calling 'Maman!' on his behalf. Eventually they manage it in chorus, and a light goes on in the house. As Maman comes to the call, they sing, 'Il est bon, l'enfant, il est sage . . .' The child holds out his arms to her, then the opera is suddenly over.

Ravel's score is far more intricately constructed than it pretends to be, with disguised connections between seemingly disparate numbers. There are interesting echoes, too: obviously from the *jardin féerique* of *Ma mère l'oye* in the benedictory final chorus, more subtly from the Violin and Cello Sonata in the princess's opening monologue – and the winding oboe duet that starts the opera and returns reassuringly at the end suggests a delicate shadow of Musorgsky's 'Promenade' in his *Pictures at an Exhibition*. Maman first enters on the same sighing cadence that closes the opera. Two matching

Ravel with a feline friend at his home in Montfort L'Amaury in 1929

modulations, among the most poignantly beautiful in all Ravel's music, adorn the squirrel's plaint (after 'Sais-tu ce qu'ils reflétaient, mes beaux yeux?') and the climax of the farewell chorus.

There are extraordinary and bewitching sounds from the orchestra pit throughout, as well as a prominent piano, which ranges from furious arpeggios to plonking revue-style accompaniments. Ravel wanted it equipped with a *luthéal*, apparently a device for altering and distorting the timbre of the instrument in various ways (he wanted it for his gypsy rhapsody *Tzigane* as well); as far as anyone knows, it is now extinct.

RECORDINGS 1. Sautereau, Angelici, Turba-Rabier, Scharley, Michel, Vessières, Ch of the RTF and O National, Bour, French EMI/American CBS, 1948: uniquely magical and close to the heart of the score, despite fallible execution and dated recording; 2. Ogéas, Gilma, Collard, Berbié, Sénéchal, Rehfuss, Ch of the RTF, O National, Maazel, DG, 1960: uncommonly straight, faithful account (especially in respect of Ravel's proposed role doublings), a bit cool; 3. Wyner, Auger, Taillon, Berbié, Langridge, Bastin, Ambrosian Singers, LSO, Previn, EMI, 1981: more wayward, sometimes more directly appealing [A.B.]
VIDEO Netherlands Dance Theatre, Paris Opéra O, Maazel, Pioneer, 1990s
EDITIONS f.s./v.s., Durand et Cie, 1925

BIBLIOGRAPHY Vladimir Jankelevitch (trans. Margaret Crosland), *Ravel*, Grove Press/John Calder, 1959; Roger Nichols, *Ravel*, Dent (Master Musicians series), 1977; Arbie Orenstein, *Ravel: Man and Musician*, Columbia UP, 1968

D.M.

FRANÇOIS REBEL

b 19 June 1701, Paris; *d* 7 November 1775, Paris

and François Francoeur

b 21 September 1698, Paris; *d* 5 August 1787, Paris

For well over 40 years Rebel and Francoeur enjoyed such a close association as composers (and, indeed, as players and administrators) that they can scarcely be treated separately. Both came from musical families; both were child prodigies, joining the Paris Opéra orchestra as violinists at the ages of 13 and 15 respectively. In 1723 they travelled to Vienna and Prague in the retinue of General Bonneval. Three years later the Opéra produced their tragédie *Pyrame et Thisbé*, the first of some 20 joint creations. Together they held a succession of important administrative posts at the Opéra, including those of inspector general (1743–53) and director (1757–67).

Surviving sources of the operas give no indication as to which of the two was responsible for each piece; according to Laborde, however, Rebel wrote the more forceful movements and Francoeur the more expressive. Their style evolved considerably. The original version of *Scanderberg* (1735), for instance, seems distinctly old-fashioned alongside Rameau's first operas, though its composers were almost a generation younger than Rameau. By the time it was revived in 1763, thoroughly reworked, Rebel and Francoeur had incorporated into their idiom many Ramellian stylistic traits and much of his orchestral practice. This later version, like *Pyrame et Thisbé*, contains some powerful moments and generates considerable pathos. The remaining operas are mostly in the lighter genres and contain less of interest.

Operatic works: *Pyrame et Thisbé*, 1726; *Tarsis et Zélie*, 1728; *Scanderberg*, 1735; *Le ballet de la Paix*, 1738; *Le retour du roi à Paris*, 1744; *Les Augustales*, 1744; *Zélindor, roi des Sylphes*, 1745; *Le trophée*, 1745; *Ismène*, 1747; *Le Prince de Noisi*, 1749
BIBLIOGRAPHY J.-B. de La Borde, *Essai sur la musique ancienne et moderne*, Paris, 1780; *rp*, 1972

G.S.

VLADIMIR REBIKOV

Vladimir Ivanovich Rebikov; *b* 31 May 1866, Krasnoyarsk, Siberia; *d* 4 August 1920, Yalta

Known as the father of modernism in Russia, Rebikov studied in Moscow and Berlin, later founding a branch of the Russian Musical Society in Odessa. He had a career as a concert pianist and later lived in Vienna, Berlin and Moscow before ending his days in Odessa. His early works are in Tchaikovskian vein, but at the turn of the century he became more experimental, using extensive whole-tone harmony and chords of superimposed fourths that prefigure Skryabin. His most iconoclastic works are his 'musico-psycholographic dramas' which probe characters, and even inanimate objects, in an expressionistic vein; these range from ten-minute dramas for one voice and piano to full-scale works.

Operatic works: *V grozu* (*In the Storm*), 1894; *Yolka* (*The Christmas Tree*), 1904; *Bezdna* (*The Abyss*), 1907; *Thea*, 1907; *Snow-White*, 1909; *Zhenishchina s kinzhalom* (*The Woman with the Dagger*), (1911); *Alpha and Omega*, 1911; *Narcissus*, 1913; *Prince Charming and Princess Beautiful*, (n.d.); *The Gentry's Nest*, 1918
BIBLIOGRAPHY M. Montagu-Nathan, 'Rebikov', in *Contemporary Russian Composers*, Frederick A. Stokes, 1916

J.G.

JOHANN FRIEDRICH REICHARDT

b 25 November 1752, Königsberg; *d* 27 June 1814, Giebichenstein, nr Halle

Not surprisingly, in view of his parallel literary and musical interests, Reichardt's most successful works are his numerous lieder (which point significantly forward to Schubert), and his many stage works. Widely travelled in his youth, he made early contact with prominent composers and authors, including Franz Benda, J. A. Hiller, C. P. E. Bach, Lessing and Klopstock, who exercised a continuing influence on his career. As a *littérateur* he published writings on many aspects of contemporary music and, anticipating Schumann, did much to shape public taste through his editorship of the influential *Musikalisches Kunstmagazin* (Berlin, 1782–91).

In 1775, after boldly recommending himself, he was appointed kapellmeister to Frederick the Great's royal opera in Berlin. At first his plans to convert the court to new operatic styles were frustrated by conservative attitudes, and it was during periods of leave abroad, in the course of which he met Goethe and Herder, as well as Galuppi in Venice and Gluck in Vienna, that he was chiefly able to widen his experience. However, following the king's death in 1786 he successfully liberalized the operatic policies of Berlin, overcoming in particular a long-standing bias towards old-fashioned opera seria. In 1787 his three-act *Andromeda*, in which his study of Gluckian techniques is reflected, was successfully produced; and two years later he achieved a powerful response, both from the court and the general public, with his spectacular opera *Brenno*, written in a grand heroic manner that points towards Spontini and Meyerbeer. Also in 1789 he won the Prussian court's support for German stage works with his setting of Goethe's

Claudine von Villa Bella (a play later partly set by Schubert), and thereafter concentrated most successfully on singspiels. Particularly characteristic of his German works is the simple, folksong-like nature of their arias. But a capacity for elaborate theatrical writing is also to be found, especially in his incidental music. The witches' scenes he wrote in 1787 for G. A. Burger's version of *Macbeth*, which contain Gothic effects, particularly in their orchestration, foreshadow Weber's *Der Freischütz*.

Operatic works: *Hänschen und Gretschen*, ?1772; *Amors Guckkasten*, ?1773; *Le feste galanti*, 1775; *Der Holzhauer, oder Die drei Wünsche*, 1775; *Cephalus und Prokris*, 1777; *Ino*, 1779; *Der Hufschmied*, 1779; *Liebe nur beglückt*, 1780; *Tamerlan*, (1786), 1800; *Panthée*, 1786; *Andromeda*, 1788; *Orfeo*, 1788; *Protesilao* (coll.), 1789; *Claudine von Villa Bella*, 1789; *Brenno*, 1789; *Jery und Bätely*, (1789), 1801; *L'Olympiade*, 1791; *Erwin und Elmire*, 1793; *Macbeth*, 1795; *Die Geisterinsel*, 1798; *Lieb' und Treue*, 1800; *Der Jubel, oder Juchei*, 1800; *Rosmonda*, 1801; *Das Zauberschloss*, 1802; *Hercules Tod*, 1802; *Kunst und Liebe*, 1807; *L'heureux naufrage*, 1808; *Bradamante*, 1809; *Der Taucher*, 1811
BIBLIOGRAPHY   Eugene Helm, 'Johann Friedrich Reichardt', in *Grove*, Macmillan, 1980; R. Pröpper, *Die Bühnenwerke Johann Friedrich Reichardts*, Bonn, 1965

B.S.

ARIBERT REIMANN
b 4 March 1936, Berlin

Reimann's parents were musicians; his father was an organist and Bach specialist, and his mother, a concert singer and voice teacher. As a child he experienced the Blitz in Berlin at first hand; a brother was killed in a bombing raid and the family home was subsequently destroyed. In 1945 he fled with his parents before the advancing Russian troops. Later he experienced the desolation of the first post-war years, alleviated only in 1949 by a period spent in Stockholm. By the age of ten he had composed some first songs and piano pieces; after completing his schooling he studied composition with Boris Blacher and Ernst Pepping in Berlin from 1955 to 1960. There followed periods of study in Vienna and at the Villa Massimo in Rome. An extremely fine pianist, Reimann is in great demand as soloist and lieder accompanist.

A song-cycle with chorus and orchestra, *Lieder auf der Flucht*, and a piano sonata, both dating from 1957, were Reimann's first published works. An extensive list of subsequent compositions includes a cello concerto, two piano concertos, *Variations* for orchestra and a substantial string trio. However, Reimann's output is predominantly vocal and displays a catholic taste in poets (Celan, Byron, Shelley, Joyce, Rilke, Louize Labé, e. e. cummings). His choral works include a cantata, *Verrà la morte* (1966), and a *Requiem* (1982). He has also composed two ballets, *Die Vogelscheuchen* (1970, scenario by Günter Grass) for large orchestra (a revision of *Stoffreste*, 1957), and *Chacun sa chimère* for tenor

and chamber orchestra (1981). In Germany he has received several major prizes, while the opera *Lear* has brought him worldwide recognition.

Having spent many hours accompanying his mother's voice lessons, Reimann acquired a unique understanding of singing technique. Like earlier opera composers, he rarely creates new roles until the premiere has been cast, tailoring his vocal writing to the specific qualities of the singers chosen. His operatic music is distinguished above all by its intense and brooding qualities, a tendency to sustained hysterical outbursts, complex textures and dark colours. Reimann's childhood experiences have influenced him in his frequent choice of pessimistic or apocalyptic texts. Yet since completing his fifth opera, *Troades*, his touch has lightened appreciably and he has reached a turning-point in his creative development.

Ein Traumspiel
A dream-play, in a prelude and 13 scenes (2h 45m)
Libretto after the play *A Dream Play* by August Strindberg (1901), translated by Peter Weiss, adapted by Carla Henius
Composed 1963–4
PREMIERE   20 June 1965, Stadttheater, Kiel

Reimann's two Strindberg libretti bear witness to his profound respect for the great Swedish author. *A Dream Play* is 'an attempt to imitate the unconnected yet apparently logical shape of a dream' and itself calls for a considerable amount of music. Carla Henius's libretto is comprehensive yet remarkably terse, allowing space for expansive orchestral interludes.

In a brief prelude the god Indra (sung by offstage chorus) commands his daughter to descend to earth and discover the cause of mankind's grief. Indra's daughter adopts the name Agnes (Lamb of God) and attempts initially to comfort those she encounters and free them from their spiritual incarceration. Later she becomes an actress, but her marriage to a tormented advocate (a self-portrait of the author) ends in disaster. The loosely constructed plot also includes scenes in Fingal's Cave, the 'ear of Indra', where God hears the groans of the oppressed, on the 'beach of shame', and at a mysterious seaside resort, the 'beautiful bay'. Agnes gradually comes to realize the hopelessness of the human condition and, in a final act of self-immolation, returns to her father.

Orchestra and offstage chorus are almost continuously dominant in Reimann's intricate score, but are interrupted by a Bach fugue, played on the piano, and remain entirely silent when the poet, in Fingal's Cave, sings verses of bitter supplication.

EDITION   v.s., Ars Viva (Schott), 1965

Melusine
Opera in four acts (2h 30m)
Libretto by Claus H. Henneberg, after the play by Yvan Goll (1922)
Composed 1970

PREMIERES   29 April 1971, Schwetzingen; UK:
2 September 1971, King's Theatre, Edinburgh (Deutsche
Oper); US: 21 August 1972, Santa Fe

Reimann's interest in Goll's little-known tragi-comedy, as with *Ein Traumspiel*, was principally motivated by the climax of the story – in this case death in a burning house, which reflects the tragic death of his own brother.

Melusine, whose marriage to Oleander has never been consummated, spends her days in an enchanted park. The land has been sold, but Melusine employs her charms to protect and ensnare: the surveyor dies in an on-site accident; the bricklayer loses his sanity; even the architect falls hopelessly in love with the enigmatic heroine. She appeals to the nature spirits, Pythia and Oger, to safeguard her park, but in vain. The castle is built and in it Melusine surrenders her virginity to Lusignan, the owner. Pythia sets the castle on fire: Melusine and Oger are both consumed in the blaze.

The orchestra, which played a relatively dominant role in *Ein Traumspiel*, functions in Melusine as discreet colouristic background, with high-pitched clusters to illustrate the realm of Melusine and percussive string effects for the nature spirits. The vocal writing is acrobatic; indeed the title role is a brilliant show piece for coloratura soprano.

EDITIONS   f.s./v.s., Schott, 1971

Lear

Opera in two parts (2h 15m)
Libretto by Claus H. Henneberg, after *King Lear* by William Shakespeare (1605)
Composed 1976–8
PREMIERES   9 July 1978, Nationaltheater, Munich; US: 12 June 1981, War Memorial Opera House, San Francisco; UK: 24 January 1989, Coliseum, London
CAST   King Lear *bar*, King of France *b-bar*, Duke of Albany *bar*, Duke of Cornwall *t*, Kent *t*, Gloucester *b-bar*, Edgar *ct*, Edmund *t*, Goneril *s*, Regan *s*, Cordelia *s*, Fool *spoken role*, servant *t*, knight *spoken role*; *tb* chorus of followers of Lear and Gloucester, soldiers, servants
LARGE ORCHESTRA including quadruple ww, 6 hns, 2 hp

Hearing a performance of his Celan cycle (1971) – 'the dark colour, massive brass agglomerations, concentrated areas in the lower strings' – Reimann became convinced of the possibility of a third opera. 'From then on all the pieces I wrote . . . were paths towards Lear,' he wrote. It was bold indeed to approach an operatic subject that Berlioz, Debussy and, above all, Verdi had contemplated and abandoned, yet the task was made possible by Claus Henneberg's skilful reduction of Shakespeare's drama to its textual bare bones, making full use of ensembles and scenic simultaneity. The German version, based on a translation by Eschenburg, also makes some use of the anonymous *Ballad of King Lear and His Three Daughters*, which served Shakespeare himself as source material.

SYNOPSIS
Part I   Lear abdicates the throne and divides his kingdom between his daughters, Regan and Goneril. Cordelia, who remains silent out of love for her father, is disinherited and married off to the King of France. Edgar, son of Gloucester, is banished on a false charge of plotting to kill his father. Kent attaches himself to Lear as faithful servant, but Goneril and Regan drive their father away. In a ferocious storm on the heath Lear becomes demented; Kent and the Fool bring him to a hovel where Edgar, feigning madness, has also taken refuge. Gloucester rescues the king and takes him to Dover.

Dietrich Fischer-Dieskau in the title role of Lear *(Munich, 1978)*

Part II   Cornwall (Regan's husband) takes Gloucester captive, blinds him and is himself stabbed to death. Edgar leads Gloucester to Dover, where he is reunited with Lear. The king is led to Cordelia in the French camp; both are captured by Edmund and Cordelia is strangled. Goneril poisons Regan but, when Edmund is killed by Edgar in single combat, she commits suicide. Lamenting over the corpse of Cordelia, Lear dies of grief.

The strength of *Lear* lies primarily in Reimann's delineation of character. He exploits every musical resource of the voice but strictly avoids extraneous vocal effects, hence his roles are approachable by classically trained opera singers. In the interests of clarity, the vocal lines are set in orchestral frames (a 'window' technique derived from Mozart's operatic scoring), while the Fool, a spoken role, is accompanied by string quartet. The complex and frequently aggressive orchestral textures come close to those of Penderecki. There is, however, a considerable difference in the means employed, for in *Lear* every parameter of the sound picture is notated in minutest detail: the strings are divided into 48 separate parts, rhythmic structures are strictly specified (except, on occasion, in the voice parts), clusters are exactly notated, while quarter-tones are employed to compress the harmony still further.

Dietrich Fischer-Dieskau was the moving force behind *Lear* and the eloquent first interpreter of the title role. Since its highly successful premiere the work has been widely accepted as a masterpiece of the post-war German operatic repertoire.

RECORDING Varady, Dernesch, Lorand, Knutson, Götz, Fischer-Dieskau, Nöcker, Boysen, Bavarian State Opera Ch and O, Albrecht, DG, 1978

EDITIONS f.s./v.s., Schott, 1978

Die Gespenstersonate
The Ghost Sonata
Chamber opera in three scenes (1h 30m)
Libretto by the composer and Schendel, after the play by August Strindberg (1907)
Composed 1983
PREMIERES 25 September 1984, Hebbel-Theater, Berlin; UK: 20 February 1989, Queen Elizabeth Hall, London
CAST Director Hummel *b-bar*, Arkenholz *ct*, Colonel *t*, the Mummy *a*, the Young Lady *s*, Johansson *t*, Bengtsson *b*, the Dark Lady *ms*, the Cook *a*, 5 *silent roles*
CHAMBER ORCHESTRA 12 players including hp, prepared pf/harmonium

Reimann's German libretto closely follows the text and dramatic structure of the original play, incorporating a Strindberg poem for Scene 2, where the Mummy sings a dirge accompanied by solo viola. The three scenes of the opera, which correspond exactly to the original three acts, run without a break and are linked by orchestral interludes.

The ghosts to whom the title refers are living dead, the exploiters and the exploited, the murderers and the murdered. The one outsider in this macabre society is the student Arkenholz. He possesses special qualities, for he is a Sunday's child who, as Director Hummel enviously acknowledges, 'can see things that others cannot see'. The old man introduces him into his house. At the 'ghost supper' Arkenholz witnesses Hummel's unmasking. The old man's guilt, once revealed, demands atonement: he withdraws and hangs himself. In a room filled with hyacinths, a lengthy dialogue ensues between Arkenholz and Hummel's daughter. Sympathy, even love, appears to unite the two, but the Cook, a brutal, avaricious figure, disturbs the intimacy of the moment, and Arkenholz comes to realize that his fiancée, like all the others, is diseased to the depths of her soul. As she collapses and dies, he despairingly

intones the Icelandic hymn to the sun with which the scene began.

The thematic material is developed almost exclusively from two figures superimposed in the opening bars, an oscillating chordal expostulation for wind instruments and an extended chorale-melisma for string trio, in which the cello plays harmonics. Reimann's use of quarter-tone harmony is here expanded to a new system of mathematical chord division. In the opening two scenes these harmonies are associated with an enigmatic milkmaid; in the final scene, a passacaglia, quarter-tone harmony is sustained throughout. In the richly characterized vocal writing little use is made of microtones but, as in *Lear*, much is made of the 'window' principle, here often refined to rhythmic micro-structures. Using an ensemble of 12 players, Reimann succeeds in condensing the bleak, brutal sound-world of *Lear* to the dimensions of chamber music.

EDITIONS f.s./v.s., Schott, 1984; study s., Schott, 1992

Troades
The Trojan Women
[Opera in one act] (2h 15m)
Libretto by Gerd Albrecht and the composer, after Franz Werfel's translation of the play by Euripides
Composed 1984–5
PREMIERE 7 July 1986, Nationaltheater, Munich

In his fifth opera, Reimann evokes once again the traumatic experiences of his childhood. Euripides wrote *The Trojan Women* as a warning to his fellow Athenians (of which they took no heed) not to embark on the disastrous Sicilian expedition. Werfel's free translation, written in 1914, is a bitter indictment of war.

At the close of the Trojan War, in a long dialogue structurally comparable to a baroque prologue, Poseidon and Athene agree to unite in hindering the homecoming of the triumphant Greeks. Hecuba bewails the fate of her country. Talthybios announces the fate of the Trojan women: Cassandra is to become Agamemnon's concubine and Andromache is to be married off to the son of Achilles, while Hecuba herself is allotted to Odysseus. Cassandra, half demented, prophesies the death of Agamemnon. Menelaus comes to take Helen, who blames Hecuba for letting Paris live. Talthybios returns with the body of Astyanax, Andromache's young son. The signal to depart is sounded and Troy set ablaze.

Werfel's polished phraseology strikes a false note in Reimann's world, and it seems regrettable that he did not find a version better suited to his musical language. The libretto is uneven, with little attempt to alleviate the static quality of the play, while the score, which runs for over two hours without a break and inhabits much the same sound-world as *Lear*, does not always succeed in holding the listener's attention.

RECORDING Reppel, Dernesch, Soffel, Koper, Brinkman, Bavarian State Opera Ch and O, Albrecht, EMI, 1986

EDITIONS f.s./v.s., Schott, 1986

Das Schloss
The Castle

Opera in two parts (2h 30m)
Libretto by the composer, after the unfinished novel by Franz
Kafka (1921–2), adapted for the stage by Max Brod
Composed 1989–91
PREMIERE 2 September 1992, Deutsche Oper, Berlin

Kafka's unfinished novel is a horrendous vision of humanity stifled by its own bureaucracy; Brod's stage adaptation uncovers a metaphysical interpretation, symbolically spreading the action over seven days. While faithfully following Brod's structure, Reimann shifts the emphasis towards present-day German traumas of xenophobia and racism.

A land-surveyor called K. arrives in a village dominated by a nearby castle. From the outset he is greeted with hostility. Artur and Jeremias, two buffoons who have ostensibly been assigned to him as his assistants by Klamm, an official from the castle, are in fact spies. Messages from Klamm are sporadically brought by an outcast named Barnabas, but K. is unable to establish contact with his employers and is subjected to intrigue and humiliation. In search of living quarters, he falls in love with Frieda, Klamm's mistress. Eventually they are forced to part. In a nocturnal meeting with an official named Bürgel, K. comes to realize the utter hopelessness of his situation. He dies of exhaustion. During the burial service Barnabas brings news that K. has been granted a residence permit.

In many respects Reimann's score is the logical outcome of those vocal, instrumental and dramatic techniques developed in his previous works. Yet in *Das Schloss* the relationship between voices and orchestra is radically altered. The almost hieratical alternation of vocal line and instrumental interpolation, which determined much of the structure of *Lear* and *Die Gespenstersonate*, is abandoned. In its place Reimann unfolds static orchestral landscapes, moving almost imperceptibly from bleak monody to dense polyphony and serving as the background for vocal lines that often burst into wild melismatic cries.

EDITION v.s., Schott, 1992

BIBLIOGRAPHY Horst Koegler, 'Reimann: Musical Vision', *Opera*, vol. 40 (1989), pp. 39–43; Klaus Schulz (ed.), *Aribert Reimann 'Lear'*, Deutscher Taschenbuchverlag, 1984

A.C.W.B.

CARL GOTTLIEB REISSIGER
b 31 January 1798, Belzig; *d* 7 November 1859, Dresden

Although Reissiger's operas have long disappeared from the stage, he was an important figure in German opera in the second quarter of the 19th century. In the early 1820s he studied with Salieri in Vienna and Winter in Munich. He was strongly influenced by Spohr and Weber. His opera *Didone abbandonata* was successfully staged by Weber in Dresden in 1824, and on Weber's death in 1826 Reissiger took over the direction of the Dresden Opera. In 1842 he conducted the premiere of Wagner's *Rienzi*. After Wagner became second Kapellmeister in Dresden the following year, he invited Reissiger to set his libretto *Die hohe Braut*; Reissiger's refusal soured their relationship. Reissiger's most successful opera was *Die Felsenmühle zu Etalières*, though his melodrama *Yelva* was also widely popular for a time.

Operas: *Das Rockenweibchen*, (1821); *Didone abbandonata*, 1824; *Der Ahnenschatz* (inc.), (1825); *Libella*, 1829; *Die Felsenmühle zu Etalières*, 1831; *Turandot*, 1835; *Adèle de Foix*, 1841; *Der Schiffbruch der Medusa*, 1846

BIBLIOGRAPHY W. Neumann, *K. G. Reissiger*, Kassel, 1854

C.A.B.

OTTORINO RESPIGHI
b 9 July 1879, Bologna, Italy; *d* 18 April 1936, Rome

Although not the most deeply original of the Italian composers born around 1880, Respighi alone among them has won a big international popular following, thanks especially to the huge success of his brilliantly orchestrated tone poems and his free, decorative arrangements of early music. His operas have remained little known. This neglect is scarcely justified, although his achievements in this field are variable in quality and eclectic in approach.

His involvement with opera was, moreover, intermittent, being concentrated principally in the opening and closing phases of his relatively short career, in which he excelled also as a teacher of composition (notably at the Conservatorio di Santa Cecilia, Rome, 1913–26).

Of Respighi's first three completed operas *Semirama* (1910), the only one to be published and professionally staged, is more interesting for what it foreshadowed than for what it achieved. Hailed when new as the first Straussian opera written by an Italian, it in fact combines rather crude attempts at *Salome*-like turbulence with a colourful exoticism evoking the ancient Babylonian setting. The 'Danza dell'aurora' from *Semirama* was to resurface many years later in the composer's garishly exotic ballet score *Belkis, regina di Saba* (1930–31).

During the war and immediately afterwards, when he was reaching maturity in the orchestral field, Respighi largely ignored opera composition: the one exception, the unpretentious and wholly delightful *La bella dormente nel bosco*, was originally written for Vittorio Podrecca's world-famous puppet theatre. Then, in 1923, Respighi returned to the opera house with the relatively unsuccessful *Belfagor*. His last two full-length operas, *La campana sommersa* and *La fiamma*, won considerably greater success; while the smaller and more stylized *Maria egiziaca* has become, over the years, his most frequently performed opera in Italy.

La bella dormente nel bosco

(Originally *La bella addormentata nel bosco*)
The Sleeping Beauty
Fiaba musicale in three acts (1h)
Libretto by Gian Bistolfi, after the fairy-tale by Perrault
Composed 1916–21 (for puppets, with singers in the orchestra); rev. 1933 (for child mimes with singers in the orchestra); rev. by Gian Luca Tocchi, 1966
PREMIERES original version: 13 April 1922, Teatro dei Piccoli di Podrecca (in Sala Verdi, Palazzo Odescalchi, Rome); UK: July 1923, Coliseum, London (Podrecca's company); 1933 version: 9 April 1934, Teatro di Torino, Turin; 1966 version: 13 June 1967, RAI (broadcast); UK: 17 July 1969, BBC Radio 3 (broadcast)

While retaining the broad outline of Perrault's tale, Bistolfi added many disarmingly whimsical details. For example, the princess finally awakes in the 20th century, roused by a prince who has just taken part in a paper chase with a rich American whose Italian is absurdly limited. Dancing plays an important part, well suited to the child performers for whom the opera's second version was intended. The final dance was updated in each version: in 1966 Respighi's 1933 foxtrot was replaced, regrettably, by a banal 'twist' by Gian Luca Tocchi.

Respighi's own concise, elegantly colourful music perfectly serves its simple purposes. There are many touches of parody, evoking styles that range from late-baroque pomp to Debussy, from Wagner to 20th-century popular music. Yet the overall effect seems surprisingly unified, thanks to the score's unfailing appropriateness to the details of the story.

Podrecca's puppets performed the first version of *La bella* throughout the world for over two decades. Yet that version remained unpublished, as did its successor until 1958; and even today the lack of a readily available printed score prevents this undemanding little opera from winning the popularity that it deserves.

EDITIONS Ricordi (on hire), 1958; 1966 version: f.s./v.s., Ricordi (on hire), 1966

Belfagor

Comic opera in a prologue, two acts and an epilogue (2h 15m)
Libretto by Claudio Guastalla, freely based on the play by Ercole Luigi Morselli (*c.* 1919), itself tenuously related to Machiavelli's story (*c.* 1520)
Composed *c.* 1921–2
PREMIERE 26 April 1923, La Scala, Milan

The protagonist is a devil, whose task is to test whether wives really are the source of all evil, as damned souls often claim. Belfagor chooses as his 'experimental bride' the high-minded Candida, who is determined to remain faithful to her lover Baldo. The wedding nevertheless takes place when Baldo is temporarily absent, since the girl's father has been bribed to overrule her. But the marriage remains unconsummated, to Belfagor's great chagrin since he has genuinely fallen in love; and when Baldo returns, Candida's mother helps her to escape with him. In a last effort to divide the young lovers, Belfagor disguises himself as a tramp and manages to persuade Baldo that Candida may not have remained true to him. But a miracle intervenes to prove her fidelity: the church bells – which have remained obstinately mute since her wedding – suddenly start ringing by themselves.

While lacking the sharply characterized wit of Machiavelli's very different story, the opera contains some effective scenes and some radiant love music. Moreover Respighi shows enterprise not only in his picturesque orchestration but also in the harmonic boldness of some of the 'devil' music; the score actually begins with a build-up of superimposed perfect fourths. Badly received when new, *Belfagor* has only occasionally been revived, although the concert overture based on material from the opera is comparatively well known.

RECORDING Sass, Lamberti, Miller, Polgár, Hungarian Radio and TV Ch, Hungarian State O, Gardelli, Hungaroton, 1989
EDITIONS f.s., Ricordi, 1924; v.ss., Ricordi, 1923; rev. edn, 1924

La campana sommersa

The Sunken Bell
Opera in four acts (with authorized cuts: 2h 15m)
Libretto by Claudio Guastalla, based on Gerhart Hauptmann's Symbolist drama *Die versunkene Glocke* (1896)
Composed *c.* 1924–7
PREMIERES 18 November 1927, Stadttheater, Hamburg; US: 24 November 1928, Metropolitan, New York

Hauptmann's play, depicting the incompatibility of the fairy realm with the world of mortals, is also a metaphor for the conflict between creative inspiration and domesticity. The skilled bell-maker Enrico (Heinrich in the play) strays by chance into fairy territory, where his finest bell is caused by magic to tumble into a lake. He is brought home wounded; but the elf Rautendelein, who has fallen in love with him, follows him home. When she kisses his eyes, Enrico has a vision that abruptly eclipses his home life: deserting his wife Magda, he withdraws into a magic workshop on the mountain, where his work rises to supremely inspired heights. But the lost bell tolls as news reaches him that Magda has killed herself. Filled with remorse, he rejects Rautendelein, who returns to her own kind and marries the King of the Frogs. But Enrico cannot live without her, and she is allowed to comfort him as he dies.

Respighi's score, though uneven, is outstandingly vivid in the more fantastic scenes: in Act I, set in the fairy realm, its multicoloured brilliance can match that of his best tone poems. The various tolling, chiming effects that reverberate through the opera are another memorable feature, whereas the music evoking human passions tends to lapse into an anonymous, sub-Puccinian lingua franca.

RECORDING Taskova Paoletti, Tucci, Millauro, Tagger, Saccomani, Ferrin, Rome Ch and SO of Italian Radio, Bartoletti, MRF, 1976
EDITIONS f.s./v.s., Bote und Bock (now Ricordi), 1927

Maria egiziaca
St Mary of Egypt
Trittico da concerto in three episodes (1h)
Libretto by Claudio Guastalla, after Domenico Cavalca's *Le vite dei santi padri* (14th century)
Composed *c.* 1929–31
PREMIERES 16 March 1932, Carnegie Hall, New York (semi-staged); Italy: 10 August 1932, Teatro Goldoni, Venice; UK: 11 April 1937, Hyde Park Hotel, London (concert)

Commissioned as a so-called 'concert opera', *Maria egiziaca* was later transferred to the stage. Guastalla aimed to create a modern counterpart to a medieval mystery play. St Mary, a young Alexandrian prostitute, feels a sudden need to sail to the Holy Land and pays for her passage with her body. In Jerusalem she finds herself excluded from the temple until she has repented: an angel then tells her to become a hermit in the desert. She does so, and remains there into old age, when a lion digs a grave in readiness for her death.

Guastalla's verbal archaisms are matched, in the music, by Gregorian, Renaissance and Monteverdian influences; there is even a harpsichord in the small orchestra. As usual with Respighi, such archaic features mingle eclectically with others of more recent origin: there is a touch of Richard Strauss in the first orchestral interlude. At its best, however, the music speaks with its own dignifiedly authoritative voice, as in Mary's superb, calmly spiritual aria 'O bianco astore', addressed to the angel in the temple.

RECORDING Kincses, Nagy, Miller, Hungarian Radio and TV Ch, Hungarian State O, Gardelli, Hungaroton, 1990
EDITIONS f.s./v.s., Ricordi, 1931

La fiamma
The Flame
Melodramma in three acts (2h)
Libretto by Claudio Guastalla, freely based on Hans Wiers-Jenssen's play *Anne Pedersdotter* (1908)
Composed 1931–3
PREMIERES 23 January 1934, Teatro Reale dell'Opera, Rome; US: 2 December 1935, Chicago; UK: 22 May 1956, BBC Third Programme (broadcast)

Respighi persuaded Guastalla to transfer Wiers-Jenssen's turbulent drama from 16th-century Norway to Byzantine Ravenna. Silvana, the young second wife of the exarch Basilio, falls in love (Phaedra-like) with her stepson Donello. Meanwhile the old witch Agnese, just before being burned at the stake, reveals that Silvana's dead mother used magic powers to bring about her daughter's marriage. Realizing that she too may have inherited such powers (the 'flame' of the title), Silvana bewitches Donello into returning her love. When the couple are found together, she confesses that she needs this liaison as an escape from a stifling marriage; whereupon Basilio dies of shock, and Silvana, having

been tried for murder and witchcraft, is condemned to death.

In this opera Respighi reverted in some ways to 19th-century methods, with the orchestra playing a more subsidiary role than in *Belfagor* or *La campana sommersa*. The solo lines contain frequent neo-Verdian inflexions. But the Byzantine setting also brought out the exotic and archaic sides of the composer's vocabulary – notably in the choral climax at the end of Act I and in parts of the last scene, set in San Vitale's basilica. Though less personal than *La campana sommersa* at its best, *La fiamma* became Respighi's most widely performed larger opera.

RECORDING Tokody, Klára Takács, Tamara Takács, Kelen, Sólyom-Nagy, Hungarian Radio and TV Ch, Hungarian State O, Gardelli, Hungaroton, 1985
EDITION v.s., Ricordi, 1933

Lucrezia
Opera in one act (three scenes) (1h)
Libretto by Claudio Guastalla after the poem *The Rape of Lucrece* by William Shakespeare (1594)
Composed 1935, orch. completed by Elsa Respighi, 1936
PREMIERES 24 February 1937, La Scala, Milan; UK: 13 September 1979, BBC Radio 3 (broadcast)

Respighi's last opera must be regarded as a work of decline. Here his eclecticism degenerates into mere stylistic indecisiveness, with echoes ranging from Monteverdi to Puccini. But the work was not quite finished; it was completed after the composer's death by his widow, who had been his pupil. Had Respighi lived longer, he might well have revised what he had written.

RECORDING Byrne, Jori, Jäggi, Morino, Washington, Junge Philharmonie der A.M.O.R., Gracis, Bongiovanni, 1981
EDITIONS f.s./v.s., Ricordi, 1936

Other operas: *Re Enzo*, 1905; *Al mulino* (inc.), (1908); *Semirama*, 1910 (RECORDING Hungaroton, 1990); *Marie Victoire*, (1914)
BIBLIOGRAPHY Elsa Respighi, *Ottorino Respighi*, Ricordi, 1954; drastically abridged English trans., Ricordi, 1962; Giancarlo Rostirolla (ed.), *Ottorino Respighi*, ERI Edizioni RAI, 1985

J.C.G.W.

HERMANN REUTTER
b 17 June 1900, Stuttgart, Germany; *d* 1 January 1985, Heidenheim, Germany

Reutter was a distinguished pianist, a highly respected teacher and a prolific composer. In the 1920s and 1930s he was near the forefront of German contemporary music: his chamber opera *Saul* was first performed at the influential 1928 Baden-Baden Festival, *Der neuer Hiob*, a lehrstück, was commissioned by Hindemith in 1930 and *Doktor Johannes Faust* (1936), an opera on the grandest scale, was premiered to great acclaim in Frankfurt.

Like Busoni's *Doktor Faust*, the opera is based on the 16th-century puppet play. But where Busoni uses Faust to expound the composer's personal aesthetic and philosophical views, Reutter, composing under fascist rule, leaves the legend unchanged. His apparent fidelity to an old German *Urtext* paid lip service to contemporary nationalist ideals, but the foolishness with which Faust rushes to his damnation can be taken as a shrewder comment on the Nazis, from whom Reutter kept a discreet distance.

The brief radio opera *Lübecker Totentanz* and the touching *Weg nach Freudenstadt*, both dating from 1948, are objective comments on the horrors of war. Reutter's post-war style subsequently tended towards conservatism, and later operas such as *Die Brücke von San Luis Rey*, based on a novel by Thornton Wilder, lack the incisive clarity of earlier scores. Common to all Reutter's theatrical works is a frieze-like presentation of the characters, which recalls Orff or the Stravinsky of *Oedipus Rex*.

Operatic works: *Saul*, 1928, rev. 1947; *Der verlorene Sohn*, 1929, rev. 1952; *Der neuer Hiob*, 1930; *Doktor Johannes Faust*, 1936, rev. 1955; *Die Prinzessin und der Schweinehirt*, 1938; *Odysseus*, 1942; *Der Lübecker Totentanz*, 1948; *Der Weg nach Freudenstadt*, 1948; *Don Juan und Faust*, 1950; *Die Witwe von Ephesus*, 1953, rev. 1966; *Die Brücke von San Luis Rey*, 1954; *Der Tod des Empedokles*, 1965; *Hamlet*, 1980
BIBLIOGRAPHY H. Lindlar (ed.), *Festschrift, Hermann Reutter: Werk und Wirken*, Schott, 1965

A.C.W.B.

ERNEST REYER
Louis-Etienne-Ernest Reyer [Rey]; *b* 1 December 1823, Marseilles, France; *d* 15 January 1909, Le Lavandou, Var, France

Early evidence of musical talent was opposed by Reyer's father, who sent him to a maternal uncle in Algiers to work in a ministry; but the youth's passion for composing survived. He was then moved to Paris to another uncle whose wife, a competent musician, gave him instruction. In the capital Reyer made literary friends including Gautier and Flaubert, and won praise from Berlioz for his 'oriental symphony' *Le Sélam* (1850). Two comic operas, *Maître Wolfram* and *La statue*, were produced at the Théâtre Lyrique; the latter was one of this enterprise's greatest successes. *Erostrate* was given at Baden-Baden in 1862. About this time Reyer started work on *Sigurd*, which was not finished until 1884. In 1866 he began a 30-year association with the *Journal des débats* where, at one remove, he followed Berlioz as critic. For this newspaper he reviewed the Cairo premiere of *Aida* in 1871. Journalism (he contributed to many publications) and the recurrent failure to arouse interest in *Sigurd* slowed down his rate of composition. Reyer's only remaining opera was the five-act *Salammbô*, based with the author's cooperation on Flaubert's novel. Like *Sigurd*, *Salammbô* was

given at the Monnaie in Brussels before beginning a half-century's career at the Paris Opéra. As well as Berlioz, Reyer's idols were Gluck and Weber. Wagner he admired greatly while remaining level-headed about him. For patriotic rather than musical reasons he stayed away from Bayreuth.

Sigurd
Opera in four acts (nine tableaux)
Libretto by Camille du Locle and Alfred Blau
Composed 1860s–1883
PREMIERES 7 January 1884, Théâtre de la Monnaie, Brussels; UK: 15 July 1884, Covent Garden, London; US: 24 December 1891, French Opera Company, New Orleans

Sigurd is a mythological-fantastic grand opera stuffed with romantic spectacle. The action covers roughly similar events to the last scene of Wagner's *Siegfried* and to *Götterdämmerung*. The final act (the opera was begun many years before) was written shortly before the premiere. Meanwhile the incomplete score had been unsuccessfully offered round, the Paris Opéra being notably unwelcoming. *Sigurd* was conceived independently of Wagner, before the *Ring* poem was published in Germany.

Brunehild, Odin's disobedient daughter, is woken from magic sleep by the hero Sigurd, disguised as Gunther, King of the Burgundians. Gunther plans to wed Brunehild but she and Sigurd fall in love. When Gunther has Sigurd slain, Brunehild dies of grief. Gunther's sister Hilda, a more fully developed equivalent of Wagner's Gutrune, who secretly loves Sigurd, sends for a distant suitor Attila to claim her and take possession of Gunther's kingdom.

There are predictable reminders of early Wagner (and brief hints of his mature works) but the overriding presence is the Berlioz of *La damnation de Faust* and *Les Troyens*. In the orchestral writing Weber and Meyerbeer share the honours with Berlioz. Middle-period Verdi is also an influence, yet *Sigurd* stands on its own feet, with an innocent, storybook quality which explains its long popularity with the public and with singers.

RECORDING Guiot, Esposito, Chauvet, Massard, Blanc, Bastin, French Radio Ch and PO, Rosenthal, Chant du Monde/INA, 1989
EDITIONS f.s., Heugel, [*c.* 1900]; v.s., G. Hartmann, [1884]

Other operas: *Maître Wolfram*, 1854; *La statue*, 1861; *Erostrate*, 1862; *Salammbô*, 1890
BIBLIOGRAPHY A. Julien, *Ernest Reyer*, Laurens (Les musiciens célèbres), [n.d.]

R.H.C.

E. N. VON REZNIČEK
Emil Nikolaus von Reznicek; *b* 4 May 1860, Vienna; *d* 2 August 1945, Berlin

The son of a high-ranking Austrian army officer, Rezniček enjoyed thorough training in harmony and counterpoint with Mayer-Rémy in Graz. His subsequent theatre career included conducting posts in Zurich, Jena, Mainz, Weimar and Warsaw, interrupted by a spell as military bandmaster in Prague.

All Rezniček's stage works after the famous *Donna Diana* are characterized by fast-moving action underlined by frequent tempo changes, effective vocal writing with a particular fondness for comtopplex ensembles, and brilliant orchestration. *Till Eulenspiegel* was Rezniček's contribution to the genre of popular German folk opera inspired by Wagner's *Die Meistersinger*, while *Ritter Blaubart* reflects post-war taste in the morbidity of its libretto. A further serious opera, *Holofernes*, gave Rezniček an opportunity to exploit the public's taste for exoticism. This 1920s post-*verismo* predilection for traditional plots set in unusual surroundings was taken to extreme lengths in a further tragic opera, *Satuala*: it is set in Hawaii and the score includes a hula-hula dance.

In the comic opera *Benzin* the basic situation of *Donna Diana* is moved to an 'unnamed island' which boasts a gigantic well of self-refining oil. The score includes a polka and a foxtrot, Boston and Viennese waltzes, while the orchestra is supplemented by sirens, hammers, anvils and propellers. *Spiel oder Ernst?* plays behind the scenes during a rehearsal of Rossini's *Otello* and is an amusing tale of rivalry between the tenor, the bass and Peulemann, the répétiteur. *Das Opfer* comes close to Brecht and Weill with its story of Martha, a Salvation Army girl who falls in love with a drinker, and music that ranges from classical counterpoint to imitation jazz.

Donna Diana

Opera in three acts
Libretto by the composer after the play *El desdén con el desdén* by Moreto y Cavana (1654)
Composed 1894, rev. 1908 and 1933
PREMIERE   16 December 1894, Deutsches Theater, Prague

Rezniček read Moreto's play in 1894, reworked it into a libretto and hastily wrote the music. Within the year *Donna Diana* had been accepted by Angelo Neumann for the Deutsches Theater, Prague, where it enjoyed an instant success. In 1933 Rezniček revised the libretto, transferring the plot from 17th-century Spain to the present day and tightening the action by making cuts.

The plot is an operatic archetype: a haughty heroine is surrounded by suitors whom she rejects; the hero, by stealth or by force, humbles her into loving him. Although including dashing ensembles and some fine arias, the opera is best remembered today for its brilliant overture.

EDITIONS   f.s., Universal, [*c.* 1950]; v.s., Schubert, [*c.* 1895]

Other operatic works: *Emmerich Fortunat* (partly lost), 1889; *Till Eulenspiegel*, 1902, rev. 1937; *Die verlorene Braut*, 1910; *Die Angst vor der Ehe*, 1914; *Eros und Psyche*, 1916; *Ritter Blaubart*, 1920; *Holofernes*, 1923; *Satuala*, 1927; *Benzin*, 1929;

Spiel oder Ernst?, 1930; *Der Gondoliere des Dogen*, 1931; *Das Opfer*, 1932; *Tenor und Bass*, 1934
BIBLIOGRAPHY   F. von Rezniček, *Gegen den Strom*, Amalthea, 1960

A.C.W.B.

FEDERICO RICCI

b 22 October 1809, Naples; *d* 10 December 1877, Conegliano, nr Treviso, Italy

Like his elder brother Luigi, Federico studied at Naples, and first appeared as an opera composer in collaboration with his brother in 1835. Later the same year he brought out an opera of his own, and in 1838 scored a big success with *La prigione di Edimburgo*, one of his best works in the more serious vein. Serious subjects continued to occupy him for the next few years, *Corrado d'Altamura* being particularly successful in this field. But in 1850 his last collaboration with his brother, *Crispino e la comare* (see Luigi Ricci), was greeted as the masterpiece of both composers and from then on he devoted himself entirely to comedy. However, after another success followed in quick succession by a total failure in Vienna, he accepted an official teaching appointment in St Petersburg and for 16 years wrote no operas. In 1869 he transferred to Paris, where *Une folie à Rome* ran for 77 nights, and other French comedies – mainly revisions of his own and his brother's earlier works – had some success.

Though lacking the gusto of his more prolific brother, Federico's scores are the more skilfully written of the two: his share of *Crispino e la comare* displays the greater elegance of style, and a work such as *La prigione di Edimburgo* shows a sensitivity towards its subject (from Scott's *The Heart of Midlothian*) that is rare among Italian operas of this period.

Operas: *Il colonello* (coll. with L. Ricci), 1835 (also as *La donna colonello*); *Monsieur de Chalumeaux*, 1835; *Il disertore per amore* (coll. with L. Ricci), 1836; *La prigione di Edimburgo*, 1838; *Un duello sotto Richelieu*, 1839; *Luigi Rolla e Michelangelo*, 1841; *Corrado d'Altamura*, 1841, rev. 1844; *Vallombra*, 1842; *Isabella de' Medici*, 1845; *Estella di Murcia*, 1846; *L'amante di richiamo* (coll. with L. Ricci), 1846; *Griselda*, 1847; *Crispino e la comare, ossia Il medico e la morte* (coll. with L. Ricci), 1850, rev. as *Le docteur Crispin*, 1869; *I due ritratti*, 1850; *Il marito e l'amante*, 1852, rev. as *Une fête à Venise*, 1872; *Il paniere d'amore*, 1853; *Une folie à Rome*, 1869; *Le docteur Rose, ou La dogaresse*, 1872; *Don Quichotte* (inc.), (1876)
BIBLIOGRAPHY   Julian Budden, 'Federico Ricci', in *Grove*, Macmillan, 1980

M.R.

LUIGI RICCI

b 8 July 1805, Naples; *d* 31 December 1859, Prague

Luigi Ricci studied at Naples, producing his first

opera at the conservatory in 1823. A triumph at Milan with *Chiara di Rosembergh* in 1831 and another three years later with *Un'avventura di Scaramuccia* carried his name all over Europe, and in 1835 he collaborated with his younger brother Federico in the first of the four operas they were to write together. In 1837 financial insecurity (due mainly to his uninhibited life-style) forced him to accept an appointment at Trieste, and for seven years he composed no operas. But, falling in love simultaneously with the 17-year-old twin sisters of the singer Teresa Stolz, he produced at Odessa in 1845 an opera for them both to sing in. Back in Trieste he married one (without, however, relinquishing the other) and produced three more operas of his own which were favourably received. But the greatest success of these years was the last collaboration with his brother, *Crispino e la comare*, of which he wrote the greater part. Luigi's strength, in fact, lay mainly in comedy and *Crispino*, though not quite reaching the level of Donizetti (whom he himself so much admired), is unquestionably one of the best Italian comic operas of this period. In 1859, shortly after the production of his last opera, he became insane and ended his life in a mental hospital in Prague.

La serva e l'ussero
The Cook and the Hussar
Farsa in one act
Librettist unknown
PREMIERE spring 1835, Pavia; Ireland: 21 October 1977, Theatre Royal, Wexford

This short farce, set in a kitchen, involves a young couple who want to marry, a stepmother who is against it, and a rather wet alternative suitor. The plot is complicated by the disguises to which the hero and heroine resort (as *serva* and *ussero* respectively), as a result of which they fail to recognize one another. The heroine's father makes a pass at the hero, and the alternative suitor gets challenged to a duel by the cook. Stylish and tuneful in the characteristic idiom of the period, the piece had a notable success as the centrepiece of a triple bill in Wexford in 1977.

EDITION v.s., Ricordi, 1841

Crispino e la comare
Collaboration with Federico Ricci
Crispin and the Fairy Godmother
Melodramma fantastico-giocoso in four acts (2h)
Libretto by Francesco Maria Piave, after a comedy by Salvatore Fabbrichesi
PREMIERES 28 February 1850, Teatro San Benedetto, Venice; UK: 17 November 1857, St James's Theatre, London; US: 24 October 1865, New York; Ireland: 26 October 1979, Theatre Royal, Wexford

One of the most successful comic operas in Italy in the 19th century, and one of the last popular examples of the Neapolitan buffo tradition. The plot, set in Venice, is a satire on the medical profession. A

poor cobbler, about to put an end to his wretched existence, is saved in the nick of time by his fairy godmother who turns him into a fashionable doctor; his remarkable success in this capacity makes him rich, conceited, and so insufferable that, after giving him a glimpse of what Hell has in store for such behaviour, she turns him back into a cobbler and restores him to his family in a more reasonable frame of mind.

RECORDING Ravaglia, Ciaffi-Ricagno, Pastine, Corbelli, Chiappi, Turin Ch and SO of Italian Radio, Della Chiesa, MRF, 1977
EDITION v.s., Ricordi, 1850

Other operas: *L'impresario in angustie*, 1823; *La cena frastornata*, 1824; *L'abbate Taccarella, ovvero Aladino*, 1825 (also as *La gabbia de' matti, Poeta Taccarella*, etc.); *Il sogno avverato* (with D. Pogliani-Gagliardi and ?N. Zingarelli), 1825; *Il diavolo condannato nel mondo a prender moglie*, also as *Il diavolo mal sposato*, 1826; *La lucerna di Epitteto*, 1827; *Ulisse in Itaca*, 1828; *Il Colombo*, 1829; *Amina, ovvero L'orfanella di Ginevra*, 1829; *Il sonnambulo*, 1829; *Fernando Cortez, ovvero L'eroina del Messico*, 1830; *Annibale in Torino*, 1830; *La neve*, 1831; *Chiara di Rosembergh*, 1831, also as *Chiara di Montalbano in Francia*, 1835; *Il nuovo Figaro*, 1832; *I due sergenti*, 1833; *Un'avventura di Scaramuccia*, 1834; *Gli esposti, ovvero Eran due or son tre*, 1834; *Chi dura vince, ovvero La luna di miele*, 1834 (rev. by F. Ricci as *La petite comtesse*, 1876); *Il colonello* (with F. Ricci), 1835, also as *La donna colonello*; *Il disertore per amore* (with F. Ricci), 1836; *Le nozze di Figaro*, 1838; *La solitaria delle Asturie*, 1845; *L'amante di richiamo* (with F. Ricci), 1846; *Il birraio di Preston*, 1847; *La festa di Piedigrotta*, 1852 (RECORDING Voce, 1967); *Il diavolo a quattro*, 1859
BIBLIOGRAPHY Julian Budden, 'Luigi Ricci', in *Grove*, Macmillan, 1980

M.R.

VINCENZO RIGHINI
b 22 January 1756, Bologna; *d* 19 August 1812, Bologna

In his day, Righini was renowned both as a singing teacher and as a composer. (One of his songs, 'Venni amore', is the theme of a set of Beethoven variations.) His first opera, *Il convitato di pietra, ossia Il dissoluto punito*, a version of the Don Giovanni story (1776), scored some success in Austria and Germany. He was appointed director of the Italian Opera in Vienna in 1780; after seven productive years Righini moved to Mainz, where he continued to compose operas. In 1793 he was appointed kapellmeister and director of the Italian Opera in Berlin, and composed *Il trionfo d'Arianna* for the wedding of the Crown Prince Frederick William. War caused the disbandment of the Italian Opera in 1806, but Righini was retained at court and appointed kapellmeister in 1811.

The craftsmanship of Righini's music was praised, but also its expressive powers and beauty, and above all the superb writing for the voice. This quality is evident in the operas, which have been criticized as lacking dramatic power, often as a result of the mediocre libretti Righini was obliged to accept from the court poet Filistri. Righini's posthumous reputation, like those of others of his generation, has always suffered by comparison with his contemporary Mozart, but his operas were highly praised in his time and deserve to be heard again.

Operatic works: *Il convitato di pietra*, 1776; *La bottega del cafè*, 1778; *La vedova scaltra*, 1778; *Armida*, 1782; *L'incontro inaspettato*, 1785; *Il Demogorgone*, 1786; *Antigono*, 1788; *Alcide al bivio*, 1790; *Vasco di Gama*, 1792; *Enea nel Lazio*, 1793; *Il trionfo d'Arianna*, 1793; *Atalante e Meleagro*, 1797; *La Gerusalemme liberata*, 1799; *Tigrane*, 1800; *La selva incantata*, 1803

BIBLIOGRAPHY   Hellmut Federhofer, 'Vincenzo Righinis Opera *Alcide al Bivio*', in Jack Westrup (ed.), *Essays Presented to Egon Wellesz*, Clarendon Press, 1966, pp. 130–44

T.T.C.

WOLFGANG RIHM
b 13 March 1952, Karlsruhe

Rihm studied composition with Eugen Werner Velte, Stockhausen, Huber, Fortner and Searle. A former participant, then tutor, at the Darmstadt summer school, he was appointed to a professorship at the Musikhochschule in Karlsruhe in 1985. One of modern Germany's most prolific composers, he has written numerous orchestral and chamber works, including three symphonies and eight string quartets. Of particular importance in his development were the five *Abgesangsszenen* (1979–81), the *Chiffre* cycle (1982–8) and *Klangbeschreibung I–III* (1982–7). In the mid-1970s Rihm was one of a group of young German composers (they included von Bose, von Schweinitz and Trojahn) who were occasionally termed neo-romantics. This was a misnomer, for Rihm was primarily concerned to break away from the aridity of doctrinaire post-serialism. His aesthetic position became apparent in *Sub-Kontur* (1974–5), an orchestral work that attempted to plumb the depths of the subconscious. The unfavourable response to the piece at the time of its premiere in Donaueschingen in 1976 did not deter Rihm from pursuing his chosen path. In 1976 he also composed his first work for the stage, the chamber opera *Faust und Yorick*, which revealed a penchant for the theatre of the absurd. A second chamber opera, *Jakob Lenz*, followed a year later. This clearly demonstrated that Rihm's rejection of serialism was linked with an interest in suffering artists on the verge of madness. Psychology tended to be eschewed by the avant garde in the 1960s, and thus the plight of the schizophrenic historical Lenz, a representative of the *Sturm und Drang* aesthetic who rejected classicism, could be construed in symbolical terms.

Jakob Lenz was followed by *Tutuguri* (Berlin, 1982), a poème dansé based on Antonin Artaud's description of the black rites of the Tarahumara Indians. Artaud's Theatre of Cruelty, which was 'created in order to restore to the theatre a passionate and convulsive conception of life', left its mark on Rihm's next work for the stage, *Die Hamletmaschine*. Based on the play by Heiner Müller, the work dwells on images of horror and despair. This vein is further explored in *Oedipus*. Rihm's latest stage work was first performed in Hamburg on 9 February 1992. Based on Artaud's *Die Eroberung von Mexico* (1989), it is a threnody for the victims of the discovery of America.

Faust und Yorick
Faust and Yorick
Chamber Opera No. 1 (40m)
Libretto by Frithjof Haas, after the sketch by Jean Tardieu
Composed 1976
PREMIERE   29 April 1977, Nationaltheater, Mannheim

Tardieu was a contemporary of Samuel Beckett and Ionesco. Faust, having come to the conclusion that the solution to all that remains unsolved resides in Yorick's skull, is seen measuring skulls. His scholarly obsession makes him neglect his family and all else. After his death his pupils find the proof of his theories in Faust's own skull. In *Faust und Yorick* Rihm strove to attain the kind of technical perfection propounded by Busoni, and thus appended to the score the words '. . . thinking of Busoni'.

EDITION   v.s., Universal (on hire), 1976

Jakob Lenz
Chamber Opera No. 2 (1h 15m)
Libretto by Michael Fröhling, after the novella *Lenz* by Georg Büchner (1836)
Composed 1977–8
PREMIERES   8 March 1979, Staatsoper, Hamburg; UK: 3 June 1987, Almeida Theatre, London

Büchner's incomplete novella describes with almost clinical accuracy the fate of the schizophrenic 18th-century poet Jakob Lenz. In the opera this psychogram of a personality drifting inexorably to destruction and madness is cast in the form of a kind of multi-layered rondo comprising 15 scenes and five instrumental interludes.

Lenz is seen wandering through the Vosges, pursued by voices. He jumps into the water and is found by Oberlin, a Protestant minister and philanthropist, who takes him home to console him. Unable to sleep, Lenz thinks of Goethe's beloved Friederike Brion. Plagued by voices, he once more jumps into the water. He is permitted to preach to Oberlin's congregation.

His friend Kaufmann incorrectly considers his illness to be eccentricity. The events that follow show that this is not the case. Lenz becomes obsessed with the idea that Friederike will die and bursts into Oberlin's room at night to ask after her. Later he comes across a dead girl, whom he tries in vain to bring back to life. His condition continues to deteriorate, and Oberlin and Kaufmann are finally forced to put him into a straitjacket. Totally oblivious of his surroundings, he is reduced to uttering the word 'Konsequent!'

One of the opera's principal ideas is a basic chord, B–F–G♭, that, significantly, is a transposed version of Schoenberg's seminal D minor plus G sharp chord. The contrast between the world of normality and Lenz's inner torments is brought out by the evocative use of sarabande, motet, madrigal and chorale on the one hand, and the vocal resources of Expressionist music-theatre on the other. A small and unusual orchestra provides predominantly chamber-music textures.

RECORDING Deutsche Harmonia Mundi, 1983
EDITIONS v.s., Universal, 1986; study s., Universal, 1984

Die Hamletmaschine
The Hamlet Machine
Music-theatre in five acts
Libretto by the composer, after the play by Heiner Müller (1977)
Composed 1983–6
PREMIERE 30 March 1987, Nationaltheater, Mannheim

Müller's play owes much to the example of Samuel Beckett and T. S. Eliot. It is a kind of German *Endgame*, and reflects the frustrations that beset German intellectuals in the 1980s. Significantly, the programme of the premiere reprinted a poem by the 19th-century German poet Ferdinand Freiligrath which begins with the words 'Germany is Hamlet'.

Shakespeare's *Hamlet* is merely the starting-point. Although the play revels in nauseating imagery, gratuitous cruelty and bloodcurdling insanity, it is also intended as a kind of black comedy. In keeping with the tenets of the Theatre of Cruelty, Rihm in turn discards continuity and discursive logic, in favour of a spontaneous response to dramatic occurrence. However, there are certain allusions, including a parody of a Handel aria, and chorales reminiscent of Kagel.

In the first section, *Family Album*, the actor who once played Hamlet passes his role in review. It is never quite clear whether he is the actor or the role, an ambiguity the composer renders by having three Hamlets (two actors and a singer). Müller's heap of sordid and broken images are grouped around the assertion that 'something is rotten in this age of hope'.

The second act, *The Europe of Woman*, makes significant use of chiaroscuro lighting effects. Set in an enormous room, it depicts Ophelia as the archetypal woman, oppressed and driven to suicide and insanity. However, she protests volubly and hysterically, tearing up the photographs of the men she has loved.

The third act is a grotesque and surrealistic scherzo (though Rihm notes in the score: 'This is not a scherzo.'). Hamlet is pelted with books by dead philosophers. Dead women tear his clothes from his body. Ophelia performs a striptease, and then Hamlet dresses in her clothes. The act concludes with a particularly revolting image, the Virgin with breast cancer.

In the fourth act, *Pest in Buda Battle for Greenland*, Hamlet (the actor) admits that he is not Hamlet (the character). The drama is no longer played because no one is interested in it. He has a vision that if it were played, it would be in a time of revolution. However, in keeping with his indecisive character, he would be impartial, taking part on both sides of the barricades. In reality he goes home to watch television. In a *danse macabre* the three Hamlets enter three oversized television sets to express their disgust at the inanity of consumer society. Three naked women representing Marx, Lenin and Mao appear. At the end of the act Hamlet splits open their heads with an axe, thereby symbolizing the end of one particular Utopian vision.

In the final act, *Wildly waiting/In dreadful armour/Millennia*, Ophelia is seen sitting in a wheelchair in the depths of the ocean. Dead bodies and parts of corpses float past. Two men dressed as doctors wrap bandages around her. Nevertheless, she continues in the defiant vein of Act II. Her concluding words are: 'Long live hatred, contempt, rebellion, death. When it goes through your bedrooms with butchers' knives, you will know the truth.'

EDITION f.s., Universal, 1987

Oedipus
Music-theatre in one act (1h 15m)
Libretto by the composer, after Hölderlin's translation of Sophocles' *Oedipus der Tyrann*; Nietzsche's *Oedipus, Reden des letzten Philosophen mit sich selbst*, and Heiner Müller's *Oedipuskommentar*
Composed 1986–7
PREMIERE 4 October 1987, Deutsche Oper, Berlin

After *Die Hamletmaschine* Rihm turned his attention to Oedipus. The plot, which unfolds in 21 continuous sections, gradually reveals that Oedipus has killed his father and married his mother. He himself brings the unbearable truth to light, and then blinds himself in order to expiate his sins. There are three tableaux: Oedipus and the Sphinx; A child limping through a dreary rocky desert; Oedipus at the crossroads; four internal monologues: Nietzsche; five commentaries: Müller; and six scenes. The violence, pain and despair at the heart of the work are rendered with the help of an unusual orchestra: quadruple woodwind, quadruple brass, two harps, a piano, and six percussionists. A large drum and a pendant metal plate onstage are played by Oedipus and Jocasta, and taped passages introduce unseen voices.

EDITION f.s., Universal, 1987

BIBLIOGRAPHY Dieter Rexroth (ed.), *Der Komponist Wolfgang Rihm*, Schott, 1985; Programme booklet, *Die Hamletmaschine*, Nationaltheater, Mannheim, 1987

A.C.

Rimsky-Korsakov (second from left) at his home with Igor Stravinsky, Maximilian Steinberg with his wife (Rimsky-Korsakov's daughter) and Stravinsky's first wife, Catherine

NIKOLAY RIMSKY-KORSAKOV

Nikolay Andreyevich Rimsky-Korsakov; *b* 18 March 1844, Tikhvin, nr Novgorod, Russia; *d* 21 June 1908, Lyubensk, nr St Petersburg, Russia

By the time Anton Rubinstein founded the St Petersburg Conservatory in 1862, four young men had joined a circle dominated by the pianist–composer Mily Balakirev: César Cui, Musorgsky, Borodin and, the youngest of the group, Nikolay Rimsky-Korsakov. All had originally been destined for careers other than music, but were persuaded to compose by the force of their mentor's magnetic personality. Balakirev's circle was nicknamed *moguchaya kuchka* or Mighty Handful by their ardent supporter, the connoisseur and critic Vladimir Stasov.

In the early 1860s, Balakirev started the 17-year-old naval cadet Rimsky on a full-scale symphony, but before it was completed the latter had to interrupt his studies, sailing on a lengthy cruise to the New World. It was not until after his return to St Petersburg in 1865 and the completion of a second symphony based on the legend of Antar, that he attempted his first opera, *The Maid of Pskov*.

After a change to a more sympathetic conservatory director, Rimsky joined the staff as a professor of practical composition and instrumentation in 1871. (He resigned his naval commission

in 1873, and was instead appointed to the part-time civil post of inspector of naval bands.) He studied Tchaikovsky's harmony treatise avidly and immersed himself in academic music, writing a number of fugues and chamber works (of which Balakirev thoroughly disapproved), and getting to know pre-19th-century music. Balakirev's insistence, in 1876, that Rimsky should assist him with the preparation of Glinka's operas for publication helped turn his own thoughts back to opera, though the academic experience he had gained could not be forgotten. His own most lyrical operas, *May Night* and *The Snow Maiden*, soon followed.

After Musorgsky's death in 1881, Rimsky set about arranging and completing the unfinished music for performance and publication. By the time he wrote the three great orchestral pieces of the late 1880s (*Capriccio espagnol, Scheherazade* and the *Russian Easter Festival* overture), Rimsky's already assured orchestral technique was matched by his compositional virtuosity. After hearing Wagner's *Ring* in 1889 he determined to concentrate on writing opera. Relations with Balakirev (known for his intransigence) became increasingly strained and he would have nothing to do with any of Rimsky's later operas; the two men broke off relations in the early 1890s.

Rimsky's influence as a composition teacher was enormous. The most important of his pupils was Stravinsky. More significant than actual technical derivations, however, was the model of the calculating, sensual, pattern-creating world of the later operas. Most of his operas are based on Russian topics and contain folk material or folk intonations. He found fantastic or mythological subjects particularly congenial, but was less successful in treating full-blooded human emotions, achieving this satisfactorily only in *The Maid of Pskov*. The middle-period operas, *May Night* and *The Snow Maiden*, reveal a genuine lyrical gift combined with an ability to depict supernatural and fantastic elements with suitable harmonic piquancy clothed in imaginative and original orchestral colours. But the characterization lacks conviction.

All the operas published in the Soviet edition of the complete works of Rimsky were reissued, with English translations of the introductory articles, by Belwin Mills, Melville, New York, 1981–4 (hereafter referred to as *RKBM*).

The Maid of Pskov (or Ivan the Terrible)

Pskovityanka
Opera in four acts (first version); prologue and three acts (second version); three acts (third version; 2h 30m); see also *Boyaryna Vera Sheloga* (1898)
Libretto by the composer, after the play by Lev Alexandrovich Mey (1860)
Composed 1868–72; second version 1876–7; third version 1891–2
PREMIERES   13 January 1873, Mariinsky Theatre, St Petersburg; second version: not performed; third version: 18 April 1895, Panayevsky Theatre, St Petersburg; UK: 8 July 1913, Drury Lane, London
CAST   Tsar Ivan the Terrible *b*, Prince Yury Tokmakov *b*, Boyar Nikita Matuta *t*, Prince Afanasiy Vyazemskiy *b*, Mikhail Tucha *t*, Princess Olga Tokmakova *s*, Stefanida Matuta *s*, 2 *ms*, *t*, 2 *b*; *satb* chorus of officers, judges, boyars, burghers' sons, *oprichniki*, pages, Muscovite archers, serving maids, boys, people, huntsmen
FULL ORCHESTRA

Although the text is loosely based on Mey's drama, Rimsky wrote most of it himself, and it is in the best tradition of the Mighty Handful. Their realist music dramas, in which the chorus actively participates in the drama and the principal characters are often revealed with psychological intensity, include Cui's *William Ratcliff*, Musorgsky's *Boris Godunov* and Borodin's *Prince Igor*. Tchaikovsky's *Oprichnik* is of the same type and all these works, except Cui's, were the result of the social and artistic conditions that also inspired Tolstoy's *War and Peace*.

SYNOPSIS (third version)
Act I   The action takes place in 1570. Olga loves the young Mikhail Tucha but has been promised to the much older Boyar Matuta by her supposed father Prince Tokmakov, the vice-regent of Tsar Ivan the Terrible in Pskov (her real father is unknown). The lovers meet secretly. In the marketplace, news is brought of the destruction of Novgorod by Ivan, who is marching on the similarly semi-autonomous Pskov. Tokmakov persuades the people to receive him

peacefully, but Tucha and his followers resolve to resist.

Act II   Ivan's initial wrath disappears when Olga is presented to him and he decides to forgive Pskov.

Act III   During a royal hunt, the young lovers again meet clandestinely, but are discovered by Matuta; he, however, is dismissed angrily by Ivan, who has revealed in a soliloquy that Olga is his daughter. Olga's faith in him, despite his reputation, moves him deeply, but when Tucha appears to rescue her she is killed by a shot intended for him.

This is Rimsky's only opera in which the human characterization is wholly satisfactory. Tsar Ivan's character is very well drawn, both at his most bloodthirsty and, for example, when his heart melts at Olga's trusting and loving nature. Tokmakov is depicted as a kindly, understanding prince, and the young lovers, so often mere ciphers with Rimsky, are exceptionally well portrayed. Tucha is convincing both as a lover and as a young rebel leader. At the close of Act I, Tucha induces a number of men (divided tenors and basses of the chorus) to defend themselves against the tyrannical Tsar to the strains of a folksong. Here the chorus propels the action forward in one of the finest scenes in Russian opera, singled out for praise by contemporary critics.

RECORDING   Shumilova, Nelepp, Shchegolkov, Pirogov, Bolshoi Ch and O, Sakharov, Melodiya, 1947
EDITIONS   f.s., *RKBM*, vols 1a–d; v.s., *RKBM*, vols 29a–b

Mlada

(Collaboration with Borodin, Cui, Musorgsky and Minkus; unfinished; existing music: 2h 15m)
Libretto by Viktor Alexandrovich Krilov
Composed 1872

The collective *Mlada* was commissioned by A. Gedonov, director of the Imperial Theatres. It was to have been a spectacular opera-ballet. For reasons of expense the project was aborted, but not before Cui's Act I and Borodin's Act IV had been substantially completed. Musorgsky and Rimsky were to share Acts II and III between them, an arrangement that proved difficult even though they were sharing lodgings at the time. Rimsky's eventual contribution to the opera was small, and what little he did write was later either subsumed in his own opera of the same name, or used elsewhere; for example, the final *khorovod* (choral dance) of Act II, celebrating the festival of Kupala, was used (for the *khorovod* of the *rusalki*) in the last act of *May Night*.

May Night

Maiskaya noch'
Opera in three acts (2h 30m)
Libretto by the composer, after the comic short story in the volume *Evenings on a Farm near Dikanka* by Nikolay Gogol (1831–2)
Composed 1878–9
PREMIERES   21 January 1880, Mariinsky Theatre, St Petersburg; UK: 26 June 1914, Drury Lane, London

Fyodor Stravinsky (Igor's father) as the Mayor in May Night *(St Petersburg, c. 1880)*

CAST The Mayor *b*, Levko *t*, Hanna *ms*, Pannochka *s*, Mayor's sister-in-law *ms*, Kalenik *bar*, Distiller *t*, 3 water sprites 2 *s*, *ms*; *satb* chorus of villagers
FULL ORCHESTRA including t-t, bells, 2 hp, pf

In basing his next opera on Gogol's story, Rimsky abandoned the dramatic realism of *Pskovityanka*. With Balakirev, he had been editing the operas of Glinka, and the score is indebted to that composer in many ways, especially to his *Ruslan and Lyudmila*.

SYNOPSIS
Act I The village Mayor disapproves of his son Levko's love for Hanna, since he wants her himself. Horrified to learn that his father is his rival, Levko gathers together a band of village lads who sing a mocking song outside the Mayor's house.

Act II In the confusion that follows this performance, the Mayor's sister-in-law is captured in error and bundled into prison. She chides the Mayor, saying his philanderings are common knowledge in the village. He eventually calms her and restores order.

Act III Levko sits on the shores of a nearby lake singing of his love for Hanna. Suddenly *rusalki* (water sprites) appear. Their leader, Pannochka, asks Levko to identify a witch from among them (this was Pannochka's cruel stepmother in a former mortal life, who drove Pannochka to drown herself). He succeeds and, in gratitude for being released from the evil spell, Pannochka gives Levko a document. The Mayor, when he sees it, believes this to be a decree from the Commissar sanctioning Levko's marriage to Hanna and reluctantly agrees to the wedding.

There are some excellent comic episodes, including the Mayor's ridiculous wooing of Hanna and, later on, his interruption of the reading of the 'Commissar's' letter and the bitchy chatter of his sister-in-law depicted by bustling semiquavers. Excellent folk choruses include the finale of Act I, in which Levko eggs on the villagers to play practical jokes on his father, to a driving orchestral accompaniment (piano and harp) which imitates his vigorous strumming on the bandora. The stylized musical patterns employed for the fantastic episodes are more highly organized than the rest of the material. The opera's head motif, which occurs in its most characteristic form at the opening of Act III, is strikingly similar to the opening of Weber's *Oberon*.

RECORDING Sapegina, Matyushina, Lisovsky, Krivchenya, Moscow Radio Ch and O, Fedoseyev, DG/Melodiya, 1971
EDITIONS f.s., *RKBM*, vols 2a–b; v.s., *RKBM*, vol. 30

The Snow Maiden
Snegurochka
Opera (spring fairy-tale) in four acts with a prologue (3h 15m)
Libretto by the composer, after the play by Aleksandr Nikolayevich Ostrovsky (1873) in turn based on a folk-tale
Composed 1880–81; second version, *c.* 1895
PREMIERES 10 February 1882, Mariinsky Theatre, St Petersburg; US: 5 January 1922, Seattle; UK: 12 April 1933, Sadler's Wells, London
CAST Snegurochka *s*, Lel' *a*, Kupava *s*, Mizgir *bar*, Tsar Berendey *t*, Bobyl' *t*, Bobylikha *ms*, Red Spring *ms*, Father Frost *b*, Woodsprite *t*, *ms*, *t*, 2 *b*; *satb* chorus of peasants, followers of Spring, followers of the Tsar, boyars; dancers
FULL ORCHESTRA including pf

SYNOPSIS
Prologue Snegurochka is the daughter of Father Frost and Red (i.e., beautiful) Spring. She seems beautiful and warm but her heart is ice; she will die if it melts. Fearful for her safety from Yarilo the sun god, her father entrusts her to the care of the Woodsprite and she is adopted by a peasant couple, Bobyl' and Bobylikha. The true nature of love, controlled by Yarilo, must remain hidden from her.

Act I Snegurochka takes a platonic interest in the warm-hearted shepherd boy Lel', but he prefers Kupava, who is betrothed to Mizgir, who in turn falls in love with Snegurochka.

Act II At a royal feast held to celebrate the end of winter, Snegurochka tells Tsar Berendey that she is incapable of love. He promises a reward to the man who can disprove this.

Act III When Lel' overlooks Snegurochka and kisses Kupava, Snegurochka is distraught. Mizgir tries to comfort her but she flees from him. Mizgir is prevented from catching her by the Woodsprite.

Act IV Snegurochka prevails on her mother, Spring, to warm her heart and soon consents to marry Mizgir, but she is struck by a ray of sun just before the wedding, and melts. Heartbroken, Mizgir throws himself into the lake.

Viktor Vasnetsov's costume design for peasants in The Snow Maiden *(St Petersburg, 1882)*

The Snow Maiden was written at one of the happiest times in Rimsky's life and it contains some of his most spontaneously lyrical music. According to his autobiography, there are six authentic folk melodies, some of them treated modally, as well as many folk intonations. Birds are imitated: for example, the cock in the prologue and the bullfinch in the prologue and in Act IV. Though he knew little of Wagner at the time, Rimsky makes use of leitmotifs, such as the delicate motif for Snegurochka, the rough one for the peasant Bobyl', and the tsar's motif (first heard in the splendid little march to which he enters in Act II, derived from Chernomor's march in Glinka's *Ruslan and Lyudmila*). Rimsky draws particular attention to his invention of a chord of six whole-tone notes of the scale used when the Woodsprite embraces Mizgir. The opera abounds in instrumental solos for violin, cello, flute, oboe and, above all, clarinet. Yet the work is ultimately unconvincing, for some of the finest music is thrown away on unimportant scenes, while those which should be dramatically the strongest, such as the final duet of the now warm-hearted Snegurochka and Mizgir, are insipid and ineffective. Nevertheless, because of the fine quality of much of the music, it deserves to be better known.

RECORDING Sokolik, Arkhipova, Grigoriev, Moksyakov, Vedernikov, Moscow Radio Ch and O, Fedoseyev, EMI/Melodiya, 1977
EDITIONS second version: f.s., *RKBM*, vols 3a–b; v.s., *RKBM*, vols 31a–b

Mlada

Magic opera-ballet in four acts (2h 30m)
Libretto by the composer, based on Viktor Alexandrovich Krilov's libretto for the collective *Mlada*
Composed 1889–90
PREMIERES 1 November 1892, Mariinsky Theatre, St Petersburg; UK: 7 May 1989, Barbican Hall, London (semi-staged); 3 August 1990, Scottish Exhibition and Conference Centre, Glasgow (Bolshoi Company)
CAST Prince Mstivoy *b*, Princess Voyslava *s*, Yaromir *t*, Veglasniy *bar*, Lumir *a*, Morena *ms*, *s*, 2 *ms*, *a*, 3 *t*, *bar*, 2 *b*; the ghost of Mlada, the ghost of Cleopatra, dancers; *satb* chorus of witches, ghosts, serving girls, weapon carriers, worshippers, peasants, priests and priestesses, werewolves, slaves; ballet
LARGE ORCHESTRA including alto fl, E♭ cl, D cl, 6 hn, B♭ tpt, F tpt, chromatic timp, large perc, 3 hp; offstage: organ; onstage: 12 natural hns, 2 panpipes, 8 lyres, perc

Mlada was Rimsky's first composition after he heard Wagner's *Ring* cycle in St Petersburg in 1889; from then on, he composed almost exclusively for the theatre. The work calls not only for huge forces but also for spectacular scenery and stage effects. Despite its many derivations from the works of other composers and his own previous compositions, it is an extraordinarily original and unusual work; it is therefore hardly surprising that it puzzled contemporary audiences and was unsuccessful, soon being edged out of the repertoire by more popular works, such as the one-act operas *Iolanta* (Tchaikovsky) and *Cavalleria rusticana* (Mascagni). Rimsky arranged Act III for a smaller orchestra, as well as assembling an orchestral suite from the opera.

SYNOPSIS

Act I In ancient, pre-Christian Retra (modern-day Pomerania) on the Baltic coast, Prince Mstivoy and his daughter Voyslava have murdered Mlada, the fiancée of Prince Yaromir, with a poisoned ring so that Yaromir will be free to marry Voyslava and unite their princedoms. Voyslava appeals to Morena, the goddess of darkness, to make Yaromir forget Mlada and love her instead. But in a dream Mlada reveals the murder to Yaromir.

Act II The Kupala games are celebrated in a festival which includes a song by the Czech Lumir, the procession of the nobles (the best-known number in the opera), the interpretation of auguries, Lithuanian and Indian dances, and a final *khorovod* in which, each time Voyslava attempts to lead Yaromir into the dance, the spirit of Mlada appears, finally leading him away to Mount Triglav.

Act III At a witches' sabbath on the mountain, after the appearance of Chernobog, the god of darkness, and the skeletal Kashchei, who can manifest himself in any form at will, the ghost of Cleopatra is conjured up to ensnare Yaromir, but Mlada prevents this.

Act IV In the temple of the sun god Radegast, Yaromir consults Veglasniy, the high priest, and the shades of the ancestors appear and proclaim that Voyslava is guilty and must be avenged; she confesses and appeals for forgiveness, but Yaromir kills her. After claiming her soul, Morena unleashes the forces of nature and the temple and city are destroyed. Mlada and Yaromir are united in death.

Mlada was a turning point in Rimsky's career. The influences on it are legion. Foremost is that of Wagner, evident in the orchestration and in the leisurely opening of Act III, as well as in the use of leimotifs. The witches' sabbath in Act III contains echoes of Berlioz and Weber, as well as Musorgsky's *Night on the Bare Mountain* (1867, then subsequently intended for the same scene in the collective *Mlada*) and references to Glinka's *Ruslan and Lyudmila* (1842) and Balakirev's symphonic poem *Tamara* (1882). Paradoxically the work emerges with an original flavour that Rimsky never managed again. Though the work failed to achieve lasting success in the theatre, its influence was considerable, not least on Stravinsky.

In *Mlada* Rimsky tried to do for the Russian psyche what Wagner did for the German. The drama is to be found not in the conventional development of characters on stage, but rather in the underlying psychological disturbance that is created. The result is of exceptional interest.

RECORDING Kulagina, Klepatskaya, Tugarinova, Bolshakov, Korolev, Makhov, Moscow Radio Ch and O, Svetlanov, Melodiya, *c.* 1966
EDITIONS f.s., *RKBM*, vols 4a–b; v.s., *RKBM*, vol. 32

Christmas Eve
Noch' pered Rozhdestvom
Opera in four acts (2h 15m)
Libretto by the composer, after the story by Gogol (1831)
Composed 1894–5
PREMIERES 10 December 1895, Mariinsky Theatre, St Petersburg; US: 15 December 1977, Indiana University Opera Theatre, Bloomington; UK: 24 December 1987, BBC Radio 3 (studio recording); 14 December 1988, Coliseum, London

Gogol's Ukrainian story tells of the young black-smith Vakula, son of the witch Solokha, and his endeavours to woo the coquettish Oxana, whose father is a drunken Cossack with a roving eye. Oxana sets Vakula the seemingly impossible task of bringing her the empress's slippers (literally high-heeled leather boots) from St Petersburg. Returning home, Vakula finds four heavy sacks in the kitchen: the sociable Solokha has been receiving visitors – the devil, the mayor, the priest, and Oxana's father – each of whom has hidden when the next arrived. Ignorant of their contents, Vakula drags them to the smithy where, after his departure, the villagers open three of them with great relish. The remaining sack Vakula takes with him and, once he realizes its contents, forces the devil to fly with him to St Petersburg, where he succeeds in obtaining the slippers. On his return he finds his efforts have been unnecessary – Oxana loves him anyway.

Tchaikovsky's opera *Vakula the Smith*, revised as *Cherevichki*, was based on the same story,

and Rimsky's version, in spite of the effective use of Ukrainian folk intonations, is inferior in characterization and lyricism. In his autobiography Rimsky himself pointed out one of the basic weaknesses: 'In *Christmas Eve* the fantastic and mythological elements are so well developed as to seem to have been foisted upon the light humour and comedy of Gogol's subject to a much greater extent than in *May Night*.' As this implies, the fantastic episodes, which he himself has interpolated into the story, are the most successful in the opera.

RECORDING Shpiller, Kulagina, Tarkhov, Migai, Krasovsky, USSR Radio Ch and O, Golovanov, Melodiya, [*c.*1950]
EDITIONS f.s., *RKBM*, vols 5a–b; v.s., *RKBM*, vol. 33

Sadko
Opera-bylina in seven scenes (three or five acts) (3h 45m)
Libretto by the composer and Vladimir Ivanovich Bel'sky, based on a bylina (epic poem) from the 11th-century 'Novgorod cycle'
Composed 1894–6
PREMIERES 7 January 1898, Solodovnikov Theatre, Moscow; US: 25 January 1930, Metropolitan, New York; UK: 9 June 1931, Lyceum, London

According to Rimsky's autobiography, both *Mlada* and *Christmas Eve* were large-scale studies for *Sadko*, an opera of which he was especially proud. The story is essentially the same as that behind Rimsky's early orchestral 'musical picture' *Sadko* (1867, rev. 1869 and 1892).

Princess Volkhova, daughter of the King of the Sea, helps the poor minstrel Sadko to catch golden fish. Flushed with this success he sets sail, but on his return journey his ship is becalmed; his companions set him adrift as a propitiation to the Sea King and he sinks to the bottom of the sea. There he wins Volkhova's hand by the beauty of his singing, but the dancing to his *gusli* (a strummed folk instrument) becomes so frenzied that it causes a terrible storm. Sadko is compelled to return to land and Princess Volkhova is turned into a river.

The opera's finest moments include the complex folk scene at the quayside (Scene 4), with its songs of the Viking, Venetian and Indian merchants, as well as Sadko's own bardic-style melodies, as adumbrated by Glinka in *Ruslan and Lyudmila* but considerably developed by Rimsky. In the end, however, the earlier, succinct orchestral piece succeeds where the opera fails.

RECORDING Shumskaya, Antonova, Davydova, Nelepp, Kozlovsky, Lisitsian, Reizen, Krasovsky, Ch and O of Bolshoi Theatre, Moscow, Golovanov, Melodiya, [*c.* 1950]
EDITIONS f.s., *RKBM*, vols 6a–c; v.s., *RKBM*, vol. 34

Mozart and Salieri
Mozart i Sal'yeri
Opera (Dramatic Scenes from Pushkin) in one act (two scenes), Op. 48 (40m)
Composed 1897

Libretto: the 'little drama' by Aleksandr Pushkin (1830)
PREMIERES   7 December 1898, Solodovnikov Theatre,
Moscow; UK: 11 October 1927, Albert Hall, London; US: 6
August 1933, Unity House, Forest Park, Pennsylvania

This chamber opera is dedicated to the memory of
Dargomyzhsky. As with that composer's *The Stone
Guest*, Rimsky set Pushkin's lines without alteration. The result is a continuous 'recitativo-arioso' style
which Rimsky, according to his autobiography,
considered to be 'purely vocal'. The two scenes were
originally to have been connected by an intermezzo,
but the composer rejected this, though his assertion
that it had been destroyed is untrue.

The plot concerns the envy of talent (Salieri,
baritone) for genius (Mozart, tenor) the former
eventually poisoning the latter. The only other
character is a blind violinist who comes on the stage
to play, badly, part of an aria from *Don Giovanni*,
much to Mozart's merriment. Towards the end, after
Mozart has unwittingly drunk the poison but before
it has taken effect, he 'extemporizes' part of his
Requiem on the piano (here an optional chorus sings
offstage). Three (optional) trombones and timpani
accompany the effective final soliloquy of Salieri.

While the 'Mozartian' music and the melodic
recitative can be dry, this experimental piece is, on
the whole, curiously telling. Tchaikovsky included
'neo-classical' numbers in some of his operas, but
never before had a complete stage work, albeit a
short one, been based on such material.

RECORDINGS   1. Fedin, Nesterenko, USSR Bolshoi
Theatre O, Ermler, Olympia, 1989; 2. Kozlovsky, Reizen, Ch
and SO of USSR Radio, Samosud, Melodiya, [1950s]
EDITIONS   f.s., *RKBM*, vol. 7; v.s., *RKBM*, vol. 35

Boyaryna Vera Sheloga

Opera in one act, Op. 54 (50m)
Composed 1877, partly rewritten 1898
Libretto by the composer, after the play *The Maid of Pskov*
by Lev Alexandrovich Mey (1860)
PREMIERES   27 December 1898, Solodovnikov Theatre,
Moscow (as prologue to *Pskovityanka*); US: 9 May 1922, New
Amsterdam Theatre, New York (as one-act opera)

Originally the prologue to the second version of
Pskovityanka: as this had been discarded in the third,
definitive, version, Rimsky rewrote the scene with
the intention that it should be performed either as a
prologue to that version, or as a one-act opera in its
own right.

Vera Scheloga confesses to her sister Nadesha that
her daughter Olga is the result of an affair Vera has
had with Tsar Ivan IV during her husband's absence
fighting in the Tsar's army. She consequently fears
her husband's return. Nadesha saves the situation by
pretending that Olga is her own child.

Rimsky stated that the new material he added
when adapting the prologue as a separate work was
written 'in my new vocal style'. Certainly Nadesha's
recitative passages strive to steer a course between
melodic stylization and imitation of actual speech
patterns. Also notable are the motifs representing

the Tsar and Olga which add to the orchestra's
dramatic function.

RECORDINGS   1. Panova, Gribova, Gavriushov, O of
Bolshoi Theatre, Sakharov, Melodiya, 1947; 2. Evstatieva,
Milcheva, Bakardzhiev, Bulgarian National Radio O,
Angelov, Harmonia Mundi, 1980
EDITIONS   f.s., *RKBM*, vol. 8; v.s., *RKBM*, vol. 36

The Tsar's Bride

Tsarskaya nevesta
Opera in four acts (2h 45m)
Libretto from the drama by Lev Alexandrovich Mey (1849),
with an additional scene by I. F. Tyumenev
Composed 1898–9
PREMIERES   3 November 1899, Solodovnikov Theatre,
Moscow; US: 6 January 1922, Seattle; UK: 19 May 1931,
Lyceum, London

The idea for this conventional four-act opera may
have been inspired by Rimsky's work on *Boyaryna
Vera Sheloga*, also based on a play about Ivan the
Terrible by Mey. He was particularly pleased with
the ensembles, and his intention was that the voices
should 'invariably be to the fore' with special
attention to the vocal cantilena.

Marfa is loved by both Lykov, whom she loves,
and the oprichnik Gryaznoy; without Gryaznoy's
knowledge, his mistress Lyubasha substitutes poison
for the love potion he gives Marfa. In addition,
Marfa is chosen as the bride of Ivan the Terrible,
who has Lykov beheaded for the poisoning. On
learning of Lyubasha's treachery, Gryaznoy kills her
and is led away while Marfa, who has gone mad on
hearing of Lykov's death, lies dying.

Rimsky endeavoured to avoid a narrowly Russian
opera, but besides the folksong 'Slava' (also
employed by Musorgsky in the coronation scene of
Boris Godunov), other traditionally based material
includes the excellent 'hop' chorus and Lyubasha's
unaccompanied aria in Act I, as well as the chorus
during the ceremony of the betrothal of Marfa to
Lykov near the end of Act III. Marfa's aria in Act II
is one of Rimsky's most beautiful creations. Much of
the rest of the opera is commonplace; the theatrical
scene near the end where Lyubasha confesses to
Gryaznoy is far from successful.

RECORDING   Vishnevskaya, Arkhipova, Atlantov, Valaitis,
Nesterenko, Bolshoi Ch and O, Mansurov, EMI/Melodiya,
1974
EDITIONS   f.s., *RKBM*, vols 9a–b; v.s., *RKBM*, vol. 37

The Tale of Tsar Saltan, of his son the famous and mighty hero Prince Gvidon Saltanovich and of the beautiful Swan Princess

*Skazka o Tsare Saltane, o syne evo slavnom i moguchem
bogatyre knyaze Gvidone Saltanovich i o prekrasnoi tsarevne
lebedi*
Opera in a prologue and four acts (3h 15m)
Libretto by Vladimir Ivanovich Bel'sky after the poem by
Aleksandr Pushkin (1832)
Composed 1899–1900

PREMIERES 3 November 1900, Solodovnikov Theatre,
Moscow; UK: 11 October 1933, Sadler's Wells, London; US:
27 December 1937, St James Theatre, New York (as *The
Bumble-Bee Prince*)
CAST Tsar Saltan *b*, Princess Militrissa *s*, Prince Gvidon *t*,
Swan Princess *s*, Povarikha *s*, Tkachikha *ms*, 2 *t*, 2 *bar*, 2 *b*;
satb chorus of nobles, courtiers, nurses, guards, soldiers,
sailors, astrologers, squirrel, bumble-bee, 33 sea-knights, etc.
FULL ORCHESTRA including cel; onstage: B♭ tpt, bd, bells

The recurrent formulaic material employed by
Pushkin in his poem was well suited to Rimsky's
creative gifts. The opera opens with a fanfare in
which are juxtaposed two unrelated harmonies
pivoting on a common note. As the composer wrote,
it 'has the significance of an invitation to see and
hear what will presently be enacted, a novel device
eminently suitable for a fantastic tale'.

SYNOPSIS
Act I Two evil sisters send a false message to Tsar
Saltan, who has marched away to the wars, that his
wife, their beautiful younger sister Militrissa, has
given birth to a monster. He orders that she and her
son, Prince Gvidon, be cast into the sea in a barrel.

Act II They are washed up on an island. Gvidon,
now miraculously full-grown, rescues a swan from a
pursuing kite. The swan, having turned out to be a
maiden, causes a marvellous city with onion-domed
churches, gardens and palaces, to rise from the
ground. Gvidon rules over it.

Act III Gvidon is anxious to learn of his father,
so the swan changes him into a bee and he flies to
tsar Saltan's court (the well-known *Flight of the
Bumble-Bee*). The tsar has heard of the magical
island, though does not know that his wife and son
are there. When Militrissa's sisters try to dissuade the
tsar from visiting the island, the bee stings them.

Act IV The tsar, nevertheless, crosses to the
island, where he sees its three wonders: a squirrel
that cracks golden nuts containing emerald kernels
while whistling a folktune, 33 handsome young warriors cast up on the shore and the swan maiden.
She reveals herself to be a princess. Gvidon, whom
the tsar has now realized is his son, falls in love with
her, and the tsar and his wife are reunited.

Though it bears some resemblance to a folksong,
the swan princess's motif is based, probably
subconsciously, on a beautiful melody from Tchaikovsky's opera *Vakula the Smith*; the opening is
identical though changed to the major mode. Instead
of Tchaikovsky's deeply felt lyricism we have a
sharply etched illusion of beauty created by
accompanying washes of sound. Like other material
in the opera, it gives an impression of sound for its
own sake. It is the logical consistency of Pushkin's
fairy-tale world together with its absence of obvious
human significance that, as the Russian literary
historian D. S. Mirsky has written, makes *Tsar Saltan*
paradoxically 'the most universally human of
Pushkin's works'. Rimsky's opera, too, has elements
of sophisticated beauty and a naïve directness that
contribute enormously to its charm. In this context

Nadezhda Zabela-Vrubel as the Swan Princess in The Tale
of Tsar Saltan, *painted by the set designer Mikhail Vrubel,
who was also her husband (Moscow, 1900)*

the lack of full-blooded human emotions in the
conventional operatic sense does not detract from
Rimsky's achievement.

RECORDING Smolenskaya, Oleinichenko, Ivanovsky,
Petrov, Bolshoi Theatre Ch and O, Nebolsin, Chant du
Monde, 1950s
EDITIONS f.s., *RKBM*, vols 10a–b; v.s., *RKBM*, vol. 38

Serviliya

Opera in five acts
Composed 1900–1901
Libretto by the composer, after the play by Lev
Alexandrovich Mey
PREMIERE 14 October 1902, Mariinsky Theatre, St
Petersburg

Rimsky again turned to a play by Mey for *Serviliya*
but this one was not based on a Russian subject, but
on the life of ancient Rome. This gave him, Rimsky
wrote, 'free rein with regard to style. Here anything
was appropriate except for what was clearly
contradictory, like the obviously German, the
evidently French, the undoubtedly Russian.' Yet the
best number is 'the closing multi-voiced Credo'
which he 'borrowed from the closing Amen of the

second version of *The Maid of Pskov*, where it was out of place'. Elsewhere, in spite of the widespread use of leitmotifs, the music is pallid and stilted. The opera was a failure both in St Petersburg, where it received only seven performances, and at the Solodovnikov Theatre in Moscow two years later, where it received only six performances.

EDITIONS   f.s., *RKBM*, vols 11a–b; v.s., *RKBM*, vol. 39

Kashchei the Immortal
Kashchei bessmertnyi
Opera (autumn fairy-tale) in one act (three scenes) (1h 15m)
Libretto by the composer, after an idea by E. M. Petrovsky
Composed 1901–2; conclusion rewritten, 1906
PREMIERE   25 December 1902, Solodovnikov Theatre, Moscow

At its premiere in Moscow, *Kashchei the Immortal* was given in a double-bill with Tchaikovsky's one-act *Iolanta*, which, ironically enough, Rimsky had earlier called 'one of Tchaikovsky's feeblest compositions'. The two go particularly well together, both being concerned with the emergence from darkness into light.

The Princess of Supreme Beauty, betrothed to Ivan Korolevich, is a prisoner of the wicked old Kashchei. Korolevich comes to the magic garden of Kashchei's daughter Kashcheyevna, who plans to poison him while he is in a state of enchantment. Hesitating because of his good looks, she fails to strike the fatal blow before the arrival of the Storm Knight, who creates a wind which disperses the spell and carries them all to Kashchei's domain. Though Kashchei has been put to sleep by the Princess's lullaby, Korolevich is prevented from rescuing the Princess by Kashcheyevna. But the Princess sympathetically kisses Kashcheyevna who is turned into a weeping willow and Kashchei dies with the flowing of her tears. The Storm Knight opens the gates and the lovers emerge into the warm spring sunshine.

This is Rimsky's most chromatic opera. The depiction of Kashchei and his domain is extra-ordinarily original. There is evidence here, too, of influence on Stravinsky's *Firebird*. Rimsky told a friend that his very elaborate harmonies would be suitable for every possible 'table of harmonies'.

RECORDINGS   1. Gradova, Kleshchova, Pontryagin, Lisitsian, Polyayev, Moscow Radio Ch and O, Samosud, Melodiya, 1948; 2. Zhurina, Terentieva, Arkhipov, Verestnikov, Matorin, Yurlov Academic Ch, Bolshoi Theatre O, Chistyakov, Chant du Monde, [c. 1990]: two authentic performances, the former better sung, the latter better recorded [A.B.]
EDITIONS   f.s., *RKBM*, vol. 12; v.s., *RKBM*, vol. 40

Pan Voyevoda
The Commander
Opera in four acts
Composed 1902–3
Libretto by I. F. Tyumenev
PREMIERE   16 October 1904, St Petersburg Conservatory

This opera, on a Polish subject, is dedicated to the memory of Chopin. Perhaps trying to emulate Glinka's Polish scenes and dances in *A Life for the Tsar*, and thinking that he was 'capable of writing something Polish', Rimsky was of the opinion that Tyumenev 'had cleverly hit upon the [Polish] folk element' in his specially written libretto, providing opportunities for dances such as a mazurka and a *krakowiak*, as well as for an orchestral nocturne.

The plot deals with the unrequited love of Yaduriga for the powerful Pan Voyevoda. He, however, plans to marry Maria. Yaduriga persuades Olesruki, a young admirer, to poison Maria on her behalf; but the youth errs and Voyevoda dies instead. Yaduriga loses her mind but Maria is now free to marry her beloved Tchaplinsky.

There were only seven performances at the St Petersburg Conservatory, five in Warsaw in the summer of 1905 and six at the Bolshoi Theatre in Moscow later that year, conducted by 'the talented Rakhmaninov'. This excursion into the realm of Polish nationalism is unsuccessful and subsequent performances have been rare.

RECORDING   Rozhdestvenskaya, Legostaeva, Orfenov, Polyaev, Korolev, All-Union Radio Ch and O, Samosud, Melodiya, 1951
EDITIONS   f.s., *RKBM*, vols 13a–b; v.s., *RKBM*, vol. 41

The Legend of the Invisible City of Kitezh and the Maiden Fevroniya
Skazaniye o nevidimom grade Kitezhe i deve Fevronii
Opera in four acts (six scenes) (3h 15m)
Libretto by Vladimir Ivanovich Bel'sky, after a Russian legend
Composed 1903–5
PREMIERES   20 February 1907, Mariinsky Theatre, St Petersburg; UK: 30 March 1926, Covent Garden, London (concert); US: 21 May 1932, Ann Arbor (concert); 4 February 1936, Philadelphia
CAST   Prince Yury *b*, Prince Vsevolod Yur'evich *t*, Fevroniya *s*, Grishka Kuterma *t*, *s*, *ms*, *a*, 2 *t*, 4 *b*; *satb* chorus of *streltsy*, people, domra-players, Tartars
LARGE ORCHESTRA including muted obs, ca, bsns, cel; onstage: F tpt, tenor and bass tubas, 8 large bells, domras, balalaikas

The story is based on a legend that blends Christianity with nature worship and pantheism, and it may have been this religious element, together with Wagnerian orchestration, that led some con-temporary critics to call it a Russian *Parsifal* – rather a fanciful notion. In the decades after its first production it was one of Rimsky's most popular operas but, since the Second World War, it has been heard less frequently outside the Soviet Union.

SYNOPSIS
Act I   The maiden Fevroniya lives in the forest and reveres God and Mother Earth. She promises to marry a young man whom she meets when he is injured while hunting. She afterwards learns that he is Prince Vsevolod, son of Prince Yury and joint ruler of the Sacred City of Great Kitezh and its domains.

Act II The bridal procession in Little Kitezh is derided and cursed by the drunken ne'er-do-well Grishka; a horde of Tartars sacks the village and carries off Fevroniya, together with Grishka who is forced to act as the Tartars' guide to Great Kitezh.

Act III Vsevolod leads the army against the enemy while his father prays; in answer to his prayer, the city is enveloped in a golden mist and disappears into Paradise. Meanwhile Vsevolod and his companions have been slain. The Tartars view with astonishment a flaming cross, all that is left of Kitezh. Grishka and Fevroniya manage to escape but get lost in the forest.

Act IV The terrified Grishka imagines that he sees the Devil wildly dancing, and sings and whistles to appease him. Soon the birds and flowers spring up around Fevroniya and the spirit of Vsevolod leads her to Kitezh in Paradise where they are united beyond death.

Kitezh contains some of Rimsky's most beautiful music; the symphonic interlude between Scenes 1 and 2 of Act IV (which forms the finale of the orchestral suite from the opera) is a marvellous instance of the composer's ability to build a fresco of instrumental sounds, including the orchestral sound of churchbells, touched on in his *Russian Easter Festival* overture but here taken to unprecedented lengths. Fevroniya's religious, nature-worshipping *naïveté* comes over with great charm – her principal leitmotif is similar to the Snow Maiden's. Grishka's scene with the Devil in Act IV is masterly, and almost bears comparison with Musorgsky's essays in the same vein, while Prince Yury, in his pious stateliness, is not unlike Pimen in *Boris Godunov*. But other characterization is less satisfactory and the opera as a whole lacks that crucial dimension of creative inspiration and judgement which would have transformed it into a masterpiece.

RECORDINGS 1. Rozhdestvenskaya, Tarkhov, Ivanovsky, Petrov, USSR Radio Ch and O, Nebolsin, Melodiya, [*c.* 1950]; 2. Kalinina, Piavko, Raikov, Vedernikov, Bolshoi Theatre Ch and O, Svetlanov, Melodiya, 1983: the first of these sets is slightly the better performance; the second has a superior recording [A.B.]
EDITIONS f.s., *RKBM*, vols 14a–b; v.s., *RKBM*, vol. 42

The Golden Cockerel

Zolotoi petushok
Opera (dramatized fairy-tale) in three acts with prologue and epilogue (2h 15m)
Libretto by Vladimir Ivanovich Bel'sky, after a poem by Aleksandr Pushkin (1834)
Composed 1906–7
PREMIERES 7 October 1909, Solodovnikov Theatre, Moscow; UK: 15 June 1914, Drury Lane, London; US: 6 March 1918, Metropolitan, New York
CAST Tsar Dodon *b*, Prince Gvidon *t*, Prince Afron *bar*, General Polkan *b*, Amelfa *a*, Astrologer *t altino*, Queen of Shemakha *s*, Golden Cockerel *s*; *satb* chorus of people, boyars, guards, soldiers, cannoniers, female slaves
ORCHESTRATION picc, 2 fl/picc, 2 ob, 2 cl, b cl, 2 bsn, dbsn, 4 hn, 2 C tpt, F tpt, 3 trbn, tuba, timp, perc (sd, bd, switches, cym, tambourine, triangle, xyl, glock), cel, 2 hp, str

The designer of the first production of *The Golden Cockerel* was the Russian fairy-tale illustrator I. Ya. Bilibin, whose cartoon of Tsar Dodon, 'sovereign of the entire earth' contemplating the notion of annexing the moon – a skit on the Tsarist expansionism – may well have given Rimsky the idea of using Pushkin's poem as the basis of an opera. Whereas *Tsar Saltan* is Pushkin's longest *skazka*, the ironic *Golden Cockerel*, written three years later, is one of his shortest. This was no disadvantage, since the composer and his librettist Bel'sky (who had also written the libretto for *Tsar Saltan*) were able to expand the original to suit their purpose, adding elements of irony and political satire; for example, the passage in which the astonished tsar asks what the word 'law' means does not occur in Pushkin; new also was the close of Act II in which the Queen's slaves sing of Dodon, a tsar by rank and dress, but a slave in body and soul.

Russia had just lost the Russo-Japanese war, and the resultant unrest caused the temporary closure of the St Petersburg Conservatory and the suspension of Rimsky for his support of the students. As *The Golden Cockerel* is a satire on incompetence in war, it is not surprising that, after completion of the opera on 11 September 1907, there was trouble with the censor. This may have contributed to the recurrence of the composer's angina of which he died, never having heard what many consider to be his greatest work. Perhaps in order to veil the more obvious examples of satire there was obfuscation of the 'meaning' of the tale, but to look for deeper symbolism would be fruitless.

Significantly, the premiere was in Moscow, away from the seat of government, and certain changes were made by the censor. Because some of the parts entail dancing as well as singing, in the Western premiere, on 25 May 1914 in Paris, and in subsequent London performances, Diaghilev's ballet dancers mimed the actions while the singers sat in the theatre boxes, a version originally devised by Fokine for St Petersburg. However, later interpreters of the roles of the Queen and Dodon have been able to cope with the stage business in Act II, and the opera's frequent modern performances are always in Rimsky's authentic version.

SYNOPSIS
Prologue The Astrologer informs the audience that the fantastic tale it is about to witness has a moral.

Act I The curtain rises on the palace of the aged Tsar Dodon, with a view of the town in the distance which includes people walking about and armed guards soundly asleep. With Dodon are his two sons, Gvidon and Afron, General Polkan and assembled boyars. Dodon asks advice on how to counter threatened attack. Each prince in turn makes a futile proposal which is greeted with rapturous approval by all but the crusty old general. Not knowing how to solve the problem, they suggest the possibility of consulting an augury, and as they quarrel the Astrologer appears. He gives Dodon a golden cockerel which will crow to predict peace, or as an alarm, point in the direction of the enemy. The

Set design by Ivan Bilibin for Act I of The Golden Cockerel *(Moscow, 1909)*

delighted Dodon promises the Astrologer he may have anything he wishes as a reward. When the Astrologer asks that Dodon should put this in writing, according to the law, the astonished tsar exclaims, 'According to the law? What does that word mean? I have never heard of it. In all cases my caprice, my command – that is the law.' The Astrologer withdraws and Dodon dismisses the boyars, climbs into bed, plays with a parrot and, with the cockerel proclaiming that all is safe, is sung to sleep by his housekeeper Amelfa. Dodon's dreams of a lovely maiden are twice interrupted by the cockerel crowing to raise the alarm. The first time his none too willing sons are sent off at the head of an army, but the second time he dons his rusty armour and, to the cheers of his subjects, himself sets off to war.

Act II A narrow rocky pass on a misty night. The army has been defeated and among the bodies are those of Gvidon and Afron who have slain each other in the battle. Dodon and Polkan, with their force, lament but cannot avenge the dead, since they do not know where the enemy is. With the dawn, the mists rise to reveal a magnificent tent. Assuming it to belong to the enemy general, they bombard it with singular lack of success. A beautiful maiden emerges and sings an aria in praise of the sun. She tells Dodon that she is the Queen of Shemakha who can conquer all by her beauty. Polkan, who is getting in the way, is dismissed, and she seduces Dodon, eventually prevailing on him to sing and dance, and laughing at his grotesque endeavours. She accepts his hand in marriage and they start for home.

Act III Back in Dodon's capital the procession enters – one of the most spectacular processional marches in the whole of Russian opera. But the rejoicing is interrupted by the appearance of the Astrologer who now claims his reward – the Queen of Shemakha herself. Dodon tries to excuse himself and offers alternatives; but the aged eunuch insists, stating that he wishes to take a wife. Dodon, enraged, strikes him fiercely with his sceptre and is disconcerted when he dies as a result, but the Queen of Shemakha laughs; when Dodon tries to embrace her she repulses him. Amid dark clouds and thunder, the cockerel suddenly gives a loud crow, flies down from its perch and pecks Dodon on the head. He falls down dead and when the clouds clear the Queen and the cockerel have vanished. The people lament, singing of the virtues of their dead tsar.

Epilogue The Astrologer asks the audience not to be alarmed by the tragic outcome, for 'the Queen and I were the only living persons in it, the rest – a pale illusion, emptiness . . .'

The many leitmotifs are used as vivid, descriptive recurrent patterns which are treated to various metamorphoses, resulting in an elaborate fresco of sound. Three of the four most important motifs occur in the prologue. First, that of the golden cockerel, a trumpet call initially juxtaposing the triads of D flat and E major. But this is no mere 'invitation to . . . hear what will presently be enacted' as in *Tsar Saltan*, for it is interwoven into the music in many different places; the second phrase becomes the soothing accompaniment to Dodon's slumbers in Act I, and is sung by the frightened chorus after the alarm has been raised. Secondly, the chromatic motif of the Queen of Shemakha, redolent of the Orient and depicting her insidious beauty, which accompanies not only the Queen herself but also Dodon's dreams in Act I. More importantly, the Queen's motif occurs during the Astrologer's music in Act I, thus cleverly revealing that there is a subtle connection between him and the Queen. And thirdly, the Astrologer's own motif of unrelated arpeggiated chords tinkled out by the glockenspiel and the harps in their highest register. Together with the very high tenor register of his voice, this depicts the brittleness of his old age. Finally, the most important of Tsar Dodon's prosaic motifs occurs at the very beginning of Act I and is adroitly incorporated, in inverted form, in the march at the end of that act. There is no important new material in Act III; Rimsky skilfully employs existing material in endless permutations.

RECORDING   Kadinskaya, Pishchayev, Yelnikov, Polyakov, Korolev, Moscow Radio Ch and SO, Kovalyov and Akulov, Melodiya/ Chant du monde, [c. 1960]
EDITIONS   f.s., *RKBM*, vols 15a–c; v.s., *RKBM*, vol. 43

Other operas (sketches only): *Bagdadskii borodobrei* (*The Barber of Baghdad*), (1895); *Sten'ka Razin*, (1906); *Zemlya i nebo* (*Heaven and Earth*), (1906)
BIBLIOGRAPHY   Gerald Abraham, *Studies in Russian Music*, Reeves, 1935; Gerald Abraham, *On Russian Music*, Reeves, 1939; Steven Griffiths, *A Critical Study of the Music of Rimsky-Korsakov, 1844–1890*, Garland, 1989; Nikolay Rimsky-Korsakov, trans. by Judah A. Joffe, *Autobiography: My Musical Life*, Knopf, 1942; 2nd edn, Eulenburg, 1974; 3rd edn, Faber, 1989

E.G.

RINALDO DI [DA] CAPUA
b c. 1705, Capua or Naples; *d c.* 1780, ?Rome

The surviving details about Rinaldo's life are contradictory and confusing. Nothing is known about his musical training, but the style of his works firmly places him within the Neapolitan school, a fact supported by Burney's description of him in 1770 as 'an old and excellent Neapolitan composer'. Most of his life, however, was spent working in Rome, where his first comic opera – title unknown – was performed at the Teatro della Valle in 1737. In the following year his satirical opera, *La commedia in commedia*, was performed there too; it was so well received that it was repeated in Florence, London, Venice, Munich and other major centres. In 1739 his opera seria, *Vologeso re de' Parti*, was performed in Rome, and his increasing reputation in the seria field led to an invitation to Lisbon, where he composed a number of operas for the Rua dos Condes theatre. By 1742 he had returned to Rome, and it was here that almost all his remaining works were produced. After 1758 he devoted himself exclusively to comic opera.

Although many of Rinaldo's operas are lost, it seems clear that he was an influential composer in the development of opera buffa; some of his works entered into the stylistic controversy in Paris known as the *guerre des bouffons*, and their impact on contemporary opéra comique is certain. Among his most characteristic and influential elements are his

careful text-setting and his experimentation with extended and contrasting aria forms. Burney also credited Rinaldo with being 'among the first who introduced long ritornellos . . . into the recitatives of passion and distress [of opera seria]'.

Surviving operatic works: *Vologeso re de' Parti*, 1739 (EDITION facsimile, Garland, 1977); *Il bravo burlato* or *Il capitan Fracasso*, 1745; *Gli impostori*, 1751; *La zingara*, 1753 (RECORDING Turnabout, [c. 1963]), rev. as *La bohémienne*, 1755; *I finti pazzi per amore*, 1770; *La donna vendicativa e l'erudito spropositato*, 1771; 25 lost operas
BIBLIOGRAPHY   Claudio Gallico, 'Rinaldo da Capua: Zingara o Bohémienne', in M. T. Muraro (ed.), *Venezia e il Melodramma nel settecento*, vol. 1, pp. 425–36, Leo S. Olschki Editore, 1978

G.D.

GIOVANNI ALBERTO RISTORI
b 1692, ?Bologna; *d* 7 February 1753, Dresden

By the time he was appointed as composer to the Italian comic theatre in Dresden in 1717, Ristori, the son of an actor and musician, had had two operas performed successfully in Padua and Venice (both in 1713). He also held a position as director of the cappella polacca at Warsaw, and may have returned to Italy in the 1720s, since his opera *Cleonice* was performed in Verona in 1723. Although only chamber organist in Dresden from 1733, Ristori contributed notably to the court's music with occasional compositions, including a coronation opera, *Le fate* (1736). He probably accompanied the Saxon princess Maria Amalia to Naples in 1738: two of his operas, *Temistocle* and *Adriano in Siria*, were performed there, in 1738 and 1739 respectively. In 1750 he was named as vice-kapellmeister at Dresden in recognition of long years of service.

Although Ristori set three Metastasian texts, he was more at home in pastoral or comic works, which make up the major part of his operatic output. *Calandro* is frequently cited as one of the earliest Italian comic operas staged in Germany. A good feeling for characterization emerges, while effective simile arias also display a sure handling of orchestral colours.

Surviving operas: *Pallide trionfante in Arcadia*, 1713; *Orlando furioso*, 1713; *Euristeo*, 1714; *Pigmalione*, 1714; *Cleonice*, 1718; *Calandro*, 1726; *Un pazzo ne fà cento, ovvero Don Chisciotte*, 1727; *Le fate*, 1736; *Didone abbandonata*, 1737; *Temistocle*, 1738; *Adriano in Sirio*, 1739; 2 lost operas
BIBLIOGRAPHY   C. R. Mengelberg, *Giovanni Alberto Ristori*, Leipzig, 1916

D.S.B.

LODOVICO ROCCA
b 29 November 1895, Turin, Italy; *d* 25 June 1986, Turin

Rocca won fame principally with *Il Dibuk*, which was

so successful at its premiere that some hailed it as the most exciting new Italian opera since Puccini's *Turandot*. During the next few years it was performed in several other countries, including the US, and it continued to be revived in Italy – even as recently as 1982 in the composer's native Turin. The most successful of Rocca's other operas was *Monte Ivnor*. He also wrote non-operatic works, which often reuse devices found in *Il Dibuk*.

Il Dibuk

The Dybbuk

Opera in a prologue and three acts (2h 15m)
Libretto by Renato Simone, based on the play by Shalom Anski
Composed 1928–30
PREMIERES 24 March 1934, La Scala, Milan; US: 6 May 1936, Masonic Temple, Detroit

Il Dibuk owes much to its very striking libretto. The story centres on the old Jewish belief that a despairing lover can return after death in the form of a *dybbuk* and enter the body of his former beloved. In this case Hanan, prevented from marrying Leah by the girl's father, dies and then enters her invisibly in the midst of her wedding to another man. As a result Leah behaves as if possessed by a demon, and only with difficulty is Hanan persuaded to leave her. But he reappears, now as a visible ghost; Leah dies too, and the lovers are united beyond the grave.

Musically, *Il Dibuk* is a strange mixture. Sombre Musorgskian modal writing, orientalisms reminiscent of Bloch and abrupt outcrops of harsh dissonance rub shoulders with a more traditional, even sentimental Italian style. The orchestration is resourceful and often suitably macabre, the choral writing sometimes genuinely powerful. The crudity of some of the musical gestures is usually offset by their undeniable appropriateness to the drama.

EDITION v.s., Ricordi, 1934

Other operas: *La morte di Frine* (1920), 1936 (radio), 1937; *In terra di leggenda* (1923), 1933 (concert), 1936; *Monte Ivnor*, 1939; *L'uragano*, 1952
BIBLIOGRAPHY Gastone Rossi-Doria, 'La stagione lirica a Roma: *Il Dibuk* di L. Rocca', *Nuova antologia*, vol. 383 (January–February 1936), pp. 351–2

J.C.G.W.

RICHARD RODGERS

Richard Charles Rodgers; *b* 28 June 1902, New York; *d* 30 December 1979, New York

Richard Rodgers began writing songs for the stage when aged 14, contributing to summer-camp and club shows. He attended Columbia University where he wrote for the Varsity Show in collaboration with fellow student Lorenz Hart and, in one song, Oscar Hammerstein II. After a period of intense frustration

a lucky break came with the revue *The Garrick Gaieties* in 1925. The team of Rodgers and Hart thereupon embarked on a remarkable series of collaborations that lasted until 1943, when they revised their *A Connecticut Yankee* for revival. Their work together was characterized by the vivacity and sophistication of Hart's lyrics, for which Rodgers's music provided sometimes a lively support, sometimes a lyrical contrast.

The partnership with Hammerstein that began with *Oklahoma!* in 1943 formed a second career for Rodgers, as illustrious as the one with Hart but today the more familiar of the two; to perform one of their major plays hardly constitutes a revival, for they have remained popular in performance since their premieres. The team's determination that songs should pertain directly to character and situation (reflected in their tendency to write lyrics before music – Hart had worked the other way) justified itself in such popular success that the approach inaugurated a new era and was emulated by most other Broadway writers into the 1960s. The repertoire thus created, by Rodgers and Hammerstein and by others, continues to form the backbone of American musical theatre.

Hammerstein's death in 1960 left Rodgers without a long-term collaborator for the first time in his professional career. He composed one stage score to his own lyrics (*No Strings*), one with Hammerstein's protégé Stephen Sondheim (*Do I Hear a Waltz?*), one with Sheldon Harnick (*Rex*), and two with Martin Charnin. At his death he left behind one of the richest legacies of any Broadway composer: half-a-dozen musicals that stand up as well as any ever written, and one unforgettable song after another from his other ventures.

On Your Toes

Musical comedy in two acts (film: 1h 30m)
Libretto by Richard Rodgers, Lorenz Hart and George Abbott; lyrics by Lorenz Hart
PREMIERES 11 April 1936, Imperial Theater, New York; UK: 5 February 1937, Palace Theatre, London

In a version of the 'tap versus ballet' conflict so popular in the 1930s, a music professor whose heart is in tap dancing becomes the protégé of a Russian ballerina and joins her in the ballet *Slaughter on Tenth Avenue* (originally choreographed by George Balanchine). The score contains such standards as 'There's a Small Hotel' and 'Glad to be Unhappy'.

RECORDING Andreas, Merrill, Teeter, Irving, Mauceri, Polydor, 1983: the revival from which this recording comes marked a turning-point in recapturing the sounds (including original orchestrations) and style of pre-1940 musicals
FILM Enright (dir.), Warner, 1939: most of score omitted
EDITION v.s., Chappell, 1985

Babes in Arms

Musical comedy in two acts (film: 1h 30m)
Libretto by Richard Rodgers and Lorenz Hart; lyrics by Lorenz Hart
PREMIERE 14 April 1937, Shubert Theater, New York

This standard story of young people putting on a show is still occasionally performed. Its remarkable score contains 'Where or When', 'My Funny Valentine', 'Johnny One Note', and 'The Lady is a Tramp'.

RECORDING Blazer, Kaye, Kane, Edelman, Graae, Haile, New World, 1989
FILM Berkeley (dir.), MGM, 1939: most of score omitted
EDITION v.s., Chappell; rev. edn, 1959

The Boys from Syracuse

Musical comedy in two acts (film: 1h 15m)
Libretto by George Abbott, based on the play *The Comedy of Errors* by William Shakespeare (1592–3); lyrics by Lorenz Hart
PREMIERES 23 November 1938, Alvin Theater, New York; UK: 7 November 1963, Drury Lane, London

Shakespeare's tale of two sets of identical twins, separated at birth and reunited after a day of misunderstanding, is retained intact in this lively adaptation. Its songs include 'Falling in Love with Love', 'This Can't Be Love', and 'Sing for Your Supper'.

RECORDING Nelson, Osterwald, Cassidy, Engel, CBS, 1953
FILM Sutherland (dir.), Universal, 1940: much of score omitted
EDITION v.s., Chappell; rev. edn, 1965

Pal Joey

Musical comedy in two acts (1h 45m)
Libretto by John O'Hara, based on his short stories in the *New Yorker* (1940); lyrics by Lorenz Hart
PREMIERES 25 December 1940, Ethel Barrymore Theater, New York; UK: 31 March 1954, Princes Theatre, London

The cynical saga (considered excessively distasteful when it was new) of Joey, a sleazy night-club performer who comes under the protection of a bored, wealthy socialite (her troubled feelings expressed in 'Bewitched, Bothered, and Bewildered').

RECORDING Segal, Lang, Engel, CBS, 1950
FILM Sidney (dir.), Columbia, 1957: with additional Rodgers and Hart songs
EDITION v.s., Chappell, 1962

Oklahoma!

Musical play in two acts (2h 45m)
Libretto by Oscar Hammerstein II, based on the play *Green Grow the Lilacs* by Lynn Riggs
PREMIERE 31 March 1943, St James Theater, New York; UK: 29 April 1947, Drury Lane, London
CAST Laurey *s*, Ado Annie *ms*, Aunt Eller *a*, Curly *bar*, Will Parker *bar*, Jud Fry *bar*, Ali Hakim *t*, Ike Skidmore *bar*, Andrew Carnes *spoken role*; *satb* chorus of farmers and ranchers; dancers
ORCHESTRATION (Robert Russell Bennett) small theatre orch, including gtr

Rodgers's first collaboration with Hammerstein was not necessarily intended to be groundbreaking; nevertheless the tastes of the two writers in adapting

Howard de Silva (Jud) and Alfred Drake (Curly) in Oklahoma! *(New York, 1943)*

this piece of Americana produced the first musical to survive intact as written through several decades. At this distance its old-fashioned aspects are at least equally apparent (strict plot–subplot demarcation, conventional handling of the chorus), but its overall rightness, each song suited to the story and the specific situation, remains convincing and satisfying. Besides the title song, the score includes 'Oh, What a Beautiful Morning', 'The Surrey with the Fringe on Top', 'I Cain't Say No', and 'People Will Say We're in Love'.

SYNOPSIS
Indian Territory (present-day Oklahoma), in the early 1900s.

Act I Laurey and Curly have been carrying on a teasing courtship; she declines to accompany him to a party and finds that the sinister hired hand Jud wants her to go with him. Laurey decides that less harm will ensue if she goes with Jud.

Act II At the party, Curly saves Laurey from Jud. On the day of his wedding to Laurey, Curly kills Jud in self-defence. At his immediate trial by the assembled community he is declared innocent.

RECORDING Andreas, Guittard, Ebersole, Vidnovic, Groener, Blackton, RCA, 1979
FILM Zinneman (dir.), Magna/Fox, 1955
EDITION v.s., Williamson, 1943

Carousel

Musical play in two acts (2h 45m)
Libretto by Oscar Hammerstein II, based on an adaptation by Benjamin F. Glazer of the play *Liliom* by Ferenc Molnar (1909)
PREMIERES 19 April 1945, Majestic Theater, New York; UK: 7 June 1950, Drury Lane, London
CAST Julie Jordan *s*, Billy Bigelow *bar*, Carrie Pipperidge *s*, Enoch Snow *t*, Nettie Fowler *a*, Jigger Craigin *b*, Starkeeper *spoken role*, Louise *dancer*, other roles from *satb* chorus of New Englanders, dancers, children
ORCHESTRATION (Don Walker) large theatre orch, needs relatively large str section (originally 8.6.4.4.2) for proper balance

For the successor to *Oklahoma!*, Rodgers and Hammerstein chose similarly to adapt an existing play, but with a more serious outlook and with additional importance given to the music. All the leading roles were written with trained voices in mind, and the 40-piece orchestra was one of the largest ever seen in a Broadway pit.

SYNOPSIS
The coast of New England, 1873.

Act I Julie, a young millworker, meets Billy, a tough carnival worker who gives Julie a ride on the carousel; the two fall in love and get married. When Billy learns he is going to be a father, he decides to join his old crony Jigger in a robbery.

Act II Billy is killed attempting the robbery, and in heaven is ordered to do a good deed for his unhappy daughter Louise, now 15 years old. After some unsuccessful attempts, Billy does bring comfort to her, and to Julie as well.

Several songs (including 'Mister Snow', 'If I Loved You', 'June is Bustin' Out All Over', and 'When the Children are Asleep') emerge as the final portions of through-composed musical scenes. With Billy's 'Soliloquy' as an extended piece of character development through song, the 'Carousel Waltz' as the accompaniment for the entirely instrumental first scene, and such additional gems as 'What's the Use of Wondrin'' and 'This Was a Real Nice Clambake', the score may be seen as an exceptionally bountiful one. The final song, 'You'll Never Walk Alone', was adopted as an unofficial anthem by Liverpool Football Club after Gerry Marsden recorded it in the 1960s. *Carousel* was reportedly Rodgers's own favourite among his works.

RECORDINGS 1. Clayton, Darling, Johnson, Raitt, Littau, US Decca, 1945; 2. Cook, Brightman, Forrester, Ramey, Gemignani, MCA Classics, 1987; though reorchestrated and unevenly cast, the MCA recording contains more music than any other and thus gives the best idea of the work's scope
FILM King (dir.), Fox, 1956
EDITION v.s., Williamson, 1945

South Pacific

Musical play in two acts (2h 45m)
Libretto by Oscar Hammerstein II and Joshua Logan, based on *Tales of the South Pacific* by James A. Michener; lyrics by Oscar Hammerstein II
PREMIERES 7 April 1949, Majestic Theater, New York; UK: 1 November 1951, Drury Lane, London
CAST Nellie Forbush *ms*, Emile De Becque *b*, Bloody Mary *a*, Joe Cable *t*, Luther Billis *comedy bar*, Liat *spoken role*, other roles from mostly unison chorus of islanders, sailors, marines, officers
ORCHESTRATION (Robert Russell Bennett) theatre orch.

After the artistically ambitious, commercially unsuccessful personal statement of *Allegro* (1947), Rodgers and Hammerstein again adapted an existing source for their next work. Concentrating on two of Michener's stories, for the first time they fashioned a musical for established stars – Ezio Pinza and Mary Martin, appropriately cast as people from different worlds. Nearly every song became a hit; among them 'Dîtes-moi', 'Some Enchanted Evening', 'Nothing Like a Dame', 'Bali Ha'i', 'A Wonderful Guy', 'Younger than Springtime', and 'Happy Talk'.

SYNOPSIS
An island in the South Pacific during the Second World War.

Act I Nellie, a naïve navy nurse from Arkansas, meets the French *émigré* planter Emile De Becque. Despite the dissimilarity of their backgrounds, they seem perfect for each other – until she discovers he has two young Eurasian children. Meanwhile Lt Joe Cable, on temporary duty for a secret assignment, is introduced by the trinket-seller Bloody Mary to her daughter Liat.

Act II Liat wants to marry Cable, who despite his feelings for her cannot imagine bringing her home as his wife. Leaving for his mission behind enemy lines, he is joined by De Becque as an expert on local terrain; Cable is killed, but De Becque returns to find Nellie caring for his children and waiting for him.

RECORDING Martin, Pinza, Hall, Tabbert, Dell'Isola, CBS, 1949
FILM Logan (dir.), Fox, 1958
EDITION v.s., Williamson, 1949

The King and I

Musical play in two acts (2h 15m)
Libretto by Oscar Hammerstein II, based on the novel *Anna and the King of Siam* by Margaret Landon
PREMIERES 29 March 1951, St James Theater, New York; UK: 8 October 1953, Drury Lane, London
CAST Anna *ms*, King *bar*, Tuptim *s*, Lun Tha *t*, Lady Thiang *s*, Louis *boy s*, Prince Chulalongkorn *boy s*, Kralahome *spoken role*, Sir Edward Ramsay *spoken role*, mostly unison chorus of wives, amazons, priests, slaves; children's chorus of royal princes and princesses; royal dancers
ORCHESTRATION (Robert Russell Bennett) theatre orch.; onstage: perc. for ballet

Conceived as a vehicle for Gertrude Lawrence (who died during its initial run), *The King and I* served

Gertrude Lawrence (Anna) showing Yul Brynner (the King) how to polka in The King and I *(New York, 1951)*

Yul Brynner equally well, giving him the role with which he remained most associated all his life. The production also provided a showcase for Jerome Robbins's choreography, particularly the ballet based on Harriet Beecher Stowe, *The Small House of Uncle Thomas*. In this score Rodgers stood by his principle of allowing period and locale to affect his musical language in only minor colouristic ways. His score always sounds recognizably Rodgers, and as with the previous three Hammerstein collaborations described, nearly every number achieved familiarity outside the theatre. They include 'I Whistle a Happy Tune', 'Hello, Young Lovers', the instrumental 'March of the Siamese Children', 'Getting to Know You', and 'Shall We Dance'.

SYNOPSIS

Siam in the early 1860s.

Act I Anna, with her son Louis, comes to Bangkok to serve as governess to the royal children. Though not friendly at first, she and the King agree on a plan to receive a visiting English dignitary in a way that will reflect well on Siam.

Act II Despite minor mishaps, all goes well at the reception and Sir Edward, the visitor, is impressed by what he has seen. Anna and the King congratulate each other afterwards, but their closeness is shattered when the slave Tuptim (captured while trying to escape) is brought in and the King discovers that he cannot beat her with Anna looking on. On the point of leaving Siam, Anna answers a call to the King's sickbed. He passes his authority to his young son

Chulalongkorn (who announces policies reflecting Anna's teaching) and dies.

RECORDINGS 1. Stevens, Venora, Neway, McGavin, Allers, RCA, 1963; 2. Towers, Angela, Choi, Brynner, RCA, 1977: together, these two recordings contain virtually every note of the score
FILM Lang (dir.), Fox, 1956
EDITION v.s., Williamson, 1954

The Sound of Music

Musical play in two acts
Libretto by Howard Lindsay and Russel Crouse, based on *The Trapp Family Singers* by Maria Augusta Trapp; lyrics by Oscar Hammerstein II
PREMIERES 16 November 1959, Lunt–Fontanne Theater, New York; UK: 18 May 1961, Palace Theatre, London
CAST Maria *ms*, Captain von Trapp *bar*, Abbess *s*, Liesl *ms*, Rolf *t*, Max *bar*, Elsa *s*, 3 nuns *s*, *ms*, *a*, 6 children *s* and *a*, other roles from chorus; *sa* (men in unison) chorus of nuns, novices, postulants, friends of Captain von Trapp, concert contestants
ORCHESTRATION (Robert Russell Bennett) theatre orch., including gtr

For what turned out to be their final collaboration, Rodgers and Hammerstein turned to a true story, with a libretto supplied by others. Though they did not abandon their determination to make songs spring from dramatic necessity, the result resembled older operettas to a greater extent than had their previous musicals. This did not stop *The Sound of Music* from being one of their most popular efforts (even more so in its film version). Rodgers again exhibited considerable versatility within his personal style, successfully evoking church music and folksong in a score that includes the title song, 'My Favourite Things', 'Do-Re-Mi', 'Climb Every Mountain', and 'Edelweiss'.

SYNOPSIS
Austria in 1938.

Act I The novice Maria is told by her abbess that she is not suited for convent life and is given a job as governess to the seven children of the widowed Baron von Trapp. She succeeds in brightening the life of the children and (despite his involvement with his more sophisticated friends Max and Elsa) with the baron too, as they all find a common love for music. Maria realizes she is falling in love with him.

Act II Maria and the baron are married; their honeymoon interrupted by the *Anschluss*, they find their life threatened by the constant Nazi presence. They finally manage to flee while performing in a concert; as they reach the Swiss border, the curtain falls.

RECORDING Von Stade, Farrell, Hagegård, Kunzel, Telarc, 1988
FILM Wise (dir.), Fox, 1965
EDITION v.s., Williamson, 1960

Other musicals: *Poor Little Ritz Girl* (coll. with Sigmund Romberg), 1920; *Dearest Enemy*, 1925; *The Girl Friend*, 1926; *Lido Lady*, 1926; *Peggy-Ann*, 1926; *Betsy*, 1926; *A Connecticut Yankee*, 1927, rev. 1943; *She's My Baby*, 1928; *Present Arms*, 1928; *Chee-Chee*, 1928; *Spring Is Here*, 1929; *Heads Up!*, 1929; *Simple Simon*, 1930; *Ever Green*, 1930; *America's Sweetheart*, 1931; *Jumbo*, 1935; *I'd Rather Be Right*, 1937; *I Married an Angel*, 1938; *Too Many Girls*, 1939; *Higher and Higher*, 1940; *By Jupiter*, 1942; *Allegro*, 1947; *Me and Juliet*, 1953; *Pipe Dream*, 1955; *Cinderella* (from television musical), 1957; *Flower Drum Song*, 1958; *No Strings*, 1962; *Do I Hear a Waltz?*, 1965; *Two by Two*, 1970; *Rex*, 1976; *I Remember Mama*, 1979
BIBLIOGRAPHY Stanley Green (ed.), *Rodgers and Hammerstein Fact Book*, Lynn Farnol Group, 1980; Frederick Nolan, *The Sound of Their Music*, Walker, 1978; Richard Rodgers, *Musical Stages*, Random House, 1975

J.A.C.

JOAQUÍN RODRIGO
Joaquín Rodrigo Vidre; *b* 22 November 1901, Sagunto, Spain

While Rodrigo's voice does not have the vital originality of that of his friend Falla, it is Spanish enough, despite its somewhat synthetic use of national idioms, to identify him in the minds of many as Spain's leading modern composer. Though blind from the age of three, he studied composition in Valencia and later in Paris under Dukas at the Ecole Normale de Musique.

Essentially a miniaturist, Rodrigo is at his best in songs and short instrumental pieces evoking Spain's musical and literary heritage (the famous *Concierto de Aranjuez* is something of an exception, never successfully repeated). Although experienced as a composer of incidental music for stage and screen he has written only one zarzuela, *El hijo fingido* (1964). Although the work is not important in the composer's output the lyrical beauty of the main protagonist's three main arias is outstanding.

BIBLIOGRAPHY Vicente Vayá Pla, *Joaquín Rodrigo: su vida y su obra*, Real Musical, 1977

S.J.W.

ANTONIO RODRÍGUEZ DE HITA
Antonio Rodríguez de Hita [Yta]; *b* ?1724–5, Valverde, Madrid; *d* 21 February 1787, Madrid

A precociously gifted musician, Rodríguez de Hita appears to have been appointed second organist at the Colegio de Alcalá at the age of 13 or 14, maestro de capilla at Palencia Cathedral when about 20 and finally maestro de capilla at the Convento de la Encarnación in Madrid when about 40 (in 1765). In the protracted 18th-century debate in Spain between the patriotic traditionalists and the European-oriented progressives, Rodríguez de Hita sided discreetly but authoritatively with the latter, emphasizing the need for a composer to be intuitively creative. A prolific composer of devotional music and the author of a treatise on music teaching (*Diapasón instructivo*, 1757), his most significant achievement was probably the fostering of a more racy and down-to-earth brand of zarzuela in collaboration with the popular dramatist Ramón de la Cruz. Though neither composer nor librettist turned their backs entirely on the more heroic and aristocratic kind of music drama created by Hidalgo and Calderón, it was their plebeianized zarzuelas that were to stand as models for the 19th and 20th centuries. Of the former kind, the two surviving are *La Briseida* (1768) and *Scipión en Cartagena* (1770); of the latter, *Las segadoras de Vallecas* (1768) and *Las labradoras de Murcia* (1769).

BIBLIOGRAPHY Francisco Bonastre, 'Estudio de la obra teórica y práctica del compositor Antonio Rodríguez de Hita', *Revista de musicología*, vol. 2 (1979); William M. Bussey, *French and Italian Influence on the Zarzuela, 1700–1770*, UMI Research Press, 1980

J.W.S.

JEAN ROGER-DUCASSE
Jean Jules Aimable Roger-Ducasse; *b* 18 April 1873, Bordeaux, France; *d* 19 July 1954, Taillan-Médoc, Gironde, France

A Paris Conservatoire pupil of Fauré, Roger-Ducasse was typical of that fusion of administrative and creative talent so common in French musical life. He was inspector of the teaching of singing in Paris schools, and later professor of composition at the Conservatoire. But he was also a versatile and prolific composer, who combined a streak of intellectual intensity (particularly apparent in his piano music) with a feeling for large-scale effect, which comes out in choral–orchestral works such as his symphonic poem *Ulysse et les sirènes*.

He wrote two works for the stage, both substantial. *Orphée* (1913) is strictly pantomime, dominated by dance but also incorporating singing by a chorus, while *Cantegril* (1931) is a conventional comic opera in four acts with a libretto by Raymond Escholier, set in the Pyrenees in the 1880s.

BIBLIOGRAPHY P. Landormy, *La musique française après Debussy*, Gallimard, 1943, pp. 234–7

S.W.

SIGMUND ROMBERG

b 29 July 1887, Nagykanizsa, Hungary; *d* 9 November 1951, New York

Romberg studied in Vienna with Heuberger, though he also studied to be an engineer. In 1909 he moved to the US, where he earned his living as a pianist and later conductor with restaurant orchestras. In 1914 he contributed songs to the revue *The Whirl of the World*, and became a house composer for the Shubert brothers, contributing to the *Passing Show* series from 1914, and the (Franz) Schubert concoction *Das Dreimäderlhaus* (*Blossom Time*, 1916), among several other adaptations and interpolations.

Not until well into the 1920s did Romberg decide to stop interpolating and write his own works. The result was his greatest hit, *The Student Prince* (1924). Two years later came the more enduringly popular *The Desert Song* and in 1928 Romberg collaborated with Gershwin on *Rosalie*. Later that year came his third great success, *The New Moon*, which, despite an attractive score, was let down by its weak comic elements.

Romberg had a very lean period in the 1930s and early 1940s. He moved to Hollywood, where he wrote some works for the screen, and from 1942 he toured the country with his own orchestra.

A late success was the picture-book musical comedy set in old New York, *Up in Central Park* (1945), which war-weary Broadway audiences supported for over 500 performances.

The Student Prince

Musical play in two acts (1h 45m)
Libretto by Dorothy Donnelly, based on *Old Heidelberg* by Rudolf Bleichmann (1903), a dramatization of the romantic novella *Alt Heidelberg* by Wilhelm Meyer-Forster (1899)
PREMIERES 2 December 1924, Jolsons Theater, New York; UK: 3 February 1926, His Majesty's Theatre, London.

Orchestrated by Emil Gerstenberger, this was the first operetta that Romberg could nevertheless justi-

fiably call his own. Donnelly had already worked with Romberg on *Blossom Time*. *The Student Prince* is thoroughly European in character but recalls in its verve and sentiment the Broadway works of Victor Herbert. The tale – of a young crown prince who falls for a barmaid but has to renounce her for the sake of his royal duty – has a bittersweet flavour and an emotional power that can still move audiences. Romberg's score is correspondingly dashing and sincere, and takes full advantage of the student setting with rousing marching and drinking choruses, including a version of 'Gaudeamus igitur'. More realistic than many turn-of-the-century Ruritanian operettas, its characters are better developed. It enjoyed the longest run of any of Romberg's operettas – 608 performances.

RECORDINGS 1. Kirsten, Rounseville, Engel, CBS, 1952; 2. MacRae, Kirsten, unnamed O, Roger Wagner Ch, Alexander, EMI, [*c.* 1960]
FILM Thorpe (dir.), MGM, 1954
EDITION v.s., Warner, 1932

The Desert Song

Musical play in two acts (1h 45m)
Libretto by Otto Harbach, Oscar Hammerstein II and Frank Mandel
PREMIERES 21 October 1926, Wilmington, Delaware (as *Lady Fair*); 30 November 1926, Casino Theater, New York (as *The Desert Song*); UK: 7 April 1927, Drury Lane, London

The publication of T. E. Lawrence's desert exploits and the 1925–6 uprisings against French rule in Morocco lay behind the choice of subject for Romberg's second independent operetta. The year 1926 also saw the box-office hit *Son of the Sheik*, and the death of its star, the matinee idol Rudolph Valentino. With the fashion for Arabiana at its peak, *The Desert Song* was inevitably a success, with a run of 471 performances on Broadway, though first reviews were muted.

The son of the governor of French Morocco feigns foolishness when not leading the Arab rebellion as the masked Red Shadow. At the same time he has a rival in love – a French captain bent on defeating the 'Shadow'. After some improbably speedy changes of costume the hero wins his girl.

Romberg's first collaboration with Hammerstein resulted in his lushest and most romantic score. With its deathless title love duet, its 'Riff' and 'Sabre' songs, and a spectacular ensemble contrasting 'Eastern and Western Love', *The Desert Song* has remained effective and popular to this day.

RECORDINGS 1. Hockridge, Bronhill, Williams Singers, Collins, 1959; 2. MacRae, Kirsten, unnamed O, Roger Wagner Ch, Alexander, EMI, [*c.* 1960]
FILMS 1. Florey (dir.), Warner, 1943; 2. Humberstone (dir.), Warner, 1953
EDITION v.s. Chappell, 1927

Other operettas: *The Blue Paradise* (coll. with L. Edwards), 1915; *Her Soldier Boy*, 1916; *My Lady's Glove*, 1917; *Maytime*, 1917; *The Magic Melody*, 1919; *Love Birds*, 1921; *Blossom Time*, 1921; *The Rose of Stamboul*, 1922; *Springtime of Youth*, 1922; *Caroline*, 1923; *Princess Flavia*, 1925; *Cherry Blossoms*, 1927; *My Maryland*, 1927; *My Princess*, 1927; *The Love Call*, 1927; *The New Moon*, 1928; *Nina Rosa*, 1930; *East Wind*, 1931; *Melody*, 1933; *May Wine*, 1935; *Forbidden Melody*, 1936; *Sunny River*, 1941; *Up in Central Park*, 1945; *My Romance*, 1948; *The Girl in Pink Tights*, 1954

BIBLIOGRAPHY Elliott Arnold, *Deep in my Heart*, Duell, Sloan and Pearce, 1949; Richard Traubner, *Operetta: A Theatrical History*, Gollancz, 1983

R.T.

GUY ROPARTZ

Joseph Guy Marie Ropartz; *b* 15 June 1864, Guingamp, Côtes-du-Nord, France; *d* 22 November 1955, Lanloup, Côtes-du-Nord

Like several of his French contemporaries, Ropartz started his musical studies as a pupil of Massenet at the Paris Conservatoire and ended them as a private pupil of César Franck. A law graduate, the son of a local Breton historian in the Côtes-du-Nord, he became director of the conservatory in Nancy (1894), and was later (1919) put in charge of rebuilding musical life in Strasburg after almost 50 years in which Alsace had been part of Germany. In 1929 Ropartz returned to Brittany, and died there at the age of 91.

Ropartz wrote a vast quantity of music, little of which is now played, though his use of Breton folksong in orchestral works such as *La cloche des morts* gives it an individuality that eluded some of his fellow Franckians. His single opera, *Le pays* (1910, first staged in Nancy in February 1912 and at the Opéra-Comique in Paris the following year), also has a strong Breton atmosphere. Based on *L'islandaise*, a novel by the Breton writer Charles Le Goffic, it tells of a shipwrecked fisherman who settles and marries on a remote island but abandons his pregnant wife to return to his native Brittany, only to meet his death by drowning. Ropartz also wrote a sacred drama, *Le mystère de Saint Nicolas*.

BIBLIOGRAPHY Laurence Davies, *César Franck and His Circle*, Barrie and Jenkins, 1970

S.W.

NED ROREM

b 23 October 1923, Richmond, Indiana, US

Rorem is the leading American composer of solo songs – he has written hundreds – and is also a compulsive, incautious, and therefore entertaining, diarist (several volumes are published). He spent his youth in Chicago, where his enthusiasms ranged from Stravinsky to Billie Holiday, and then studied with Menotti at the Curtis Institute and Bernard Wagenaar at the Juilliard School. Rorem encountered Copland at Tanglewood, and in New York Virgil

Thomson became a major influence when Rorem worked as his copyist.

In 1949 Rorem went to France, where he studied with Honegger and also got to know Poulenc and Milhaud. He spent considerable periods in Morocco before returning to New York in 1958. His compositional sources have always been varied and his style, within its limits, personal. The orchestral piece *Lions* (1963) is neatly woven around a jazz combo and his major song-cycle, *Poems of Love and the Rain* (1963), ingeniously contains two different settings of the same poems laid out palindromically. In terms of his musical philosophy Rorem is a conservative: 'Music comes from tonality the way babies come from sperm.'

Rorem's two-act opera, *Miss Julie*, based on Strindberg's play, was commissioned by the New York City Opera and premiered at the City Center (1965). The work was admired for its lyrical arias, choral ensembles and dramatic power. Rorem revised it, shortening it considerably, in 1979.

Operatic works: *Cain and Abel*, (1946); *A Childhood Miracle* (1952); *The Robbers*, 1958; *The Anniversary* (inc.), (1961); *Miss Julie*, 1965 (RECORDING excerpts, Painted Smile, 1979); *Last Day*, (1959), 1967; *Three Sisters who are not Sisters*, 1971; *Bertha*, 1973; *Fables* (five short operas), 1971; *Hearing* (song-cycle arr. for stage), 1976

BIBLIOGRAPHY David Ewen, *American Composers: A Biographical Dictionary*, Hale, 1983; Arlys L. McDonald, *Ned Rorem – A Bio-Bibliography*, Greenwood, 1989

P.D.

HILDING ROSENBERG

Hilding Constantin Rosenberg; *b* 21 June 1892, Bosjökloster Skåne, Sweden; *d* 19 May 1985, Stockholm

Rosenberg was the leading Swedish composer of his generation. After studies in Stockholm with Richard Andersson, a pupil of Clara Schumann, and Wilhelm Stenhammar, he studied piano and conducting on the Continent. His music reflects neo-classical influences including Sibelius, Hindemith and Schoenberg. He is best known for his powerful symphonies and for his string quartets.

In the early 1930s he was on the staff of the Royal Opera and first attracted attention with his opera *Resan till Amerika*, to a libretto by the poet–historian Alf Henriksen. The two orchestral interludes, including the *Jarnvägsfuga* ('Railway Fugue'), are periodically heard. *Marionetter* (1939), after Benavente's *Los intereses creados*, is best known for its rather Hindemithian overture. This inventive and vivacious opera has been revived in Stockholm (1981/2) and televised. *Lycksalighetens ö*, from a Swedish classic by Per Daniel Amadeus Atterbom (1790–1855), includes music of considerable lyrical strength. The immediate post-war years saw the composition of a four-part opera–oratorio, *Josef och hans bröder*, based on Thomas Mann's novel. Rosenberg possessed enormous facility, which at times outstripped his inventive resources, but his best music has nobility and breadth.

Operatic works: *Resan till Amerika* (*Journey to America*), 1932 (RECORDING excerpts: RCA); *Marionetter* (*Marionettes*), 1939 (RECORDINGS Caprice; EMI); *De två Konungadöttrarna* (*The Two Daughters of the King*), 1940; *Lycksalighetens ö* (*The Isle of Felicity*), 1945 (RECORDING closing scene Act IV: Caprice); *Josef och hans bröder* (*Joseph and His Brethren*), Parts 1 and 2, 1946; Part 3, 1947; Part 4, 1948; *Kaspers fettisdag* (*Punch's Shrove Tuesday*), 1954; *Porträttet* (*The Portrait*), (radio opera), 1956; *Hus med dubbel ingång* (*The House with Two Doors*), 1970
BIBLIOGRAPHY   Peter Lyne (ed.), *Hilding Rosenberg: Catalogue of Works*, Royal Academy of Music, Stockholm, 1970; Hilding Rosenberg, *Toner från min örtagård* (*Autobiographical Essays*), Natur och Kultur, 1978

R.La.

JERRY ROSS
See Adler, Richard

LAURO ROSSI
b 19 February 1812, Macerata; *d* 5 May 1885, Cremona, Italy

Rossi, who studied in Naples, produced his first opera there in 1829. But his greatest success came five years later with the comic opera *La casa disabitata* – subsequently revised as *I falsi monetari*, in which form it held the stage for many years. In 1835, after a fiasco at Naples, he left for Mexico where he set up an opera company of his own and married its prima donna, Isabella Obermayer. Returning to Italy in 1843, he produced another 16 operas, but in later life he was famous mainly as an academic figure – from 1850 to 1870 as director of the Milan Conservatory, and from 1870 to 1878 in the equivalent post at Naples.

Operas: *Le contesse villane*, 1829, rev. as *La villana contessa* (also as *Le principesse villane*), 1830; *Costanza e Oringaldo* (coll. with P. Raimondi), 1830; *La sposa al lotto*, 1831; *La casa in vendita*, *ovvero Il casino di campagna*, 1831; *La scommessa di matrimonio*, 1831; *Baldovino, tiranno di Spoleto*, 1832; *Il maestro di scuola*, 1832; *Il disertore svizzero, ovvero La nostalgia*, 1832; *Le fucine di Bergen*, 1833; *La casa disabitata, ovvero Don Eustachio di campagna*, 1834, rev. as *I falsi monetari*, 1844 (?also as *Don Eutichio e Sinforosa*); *Amelia, ovvero Otto anni di costanza*, 1834; *Leocadia*, 1835; *Giovanna Shore*, 1836; *Il borgomastro di Schiedam*, 1844; *Dottor Bobolo, ovvero La fiera*, 1845; *Cellini a Parigi*, 1845; *Azema di Granata, ovvero Gli Abencerragi ed i Zegrini*, 1846; *La figlia di Figaro*, 1846; *Bianca Contarini*, 1847; *Il domino nero*, 1849; *Le Sabine*, 1852; *L'alchimista*, 1853; *La sirena*, 1855; *Lo zingaro rivale*, 1867; *Il maestro e la cantante*, 1867; *Gli artisti alla fiera*, 1868; *La contessa di Mons*, 1874; *Cleopatra*, 1876; *Biorn*, 1877
BIBLIOGRAPHY   Julian Budden, 'Lauro Rossi', in *Grove*, Macmillan, 1980

M.R.

LUIGI ROSSI
b c. 1597, Torremaggiore; *d* 20 February 1653, Rome

Rossi's earliest years were spent at the Neapolitan court, where he learned organ, lute, singing and composition. In about 1621, he moved to Rome, where he entered the service of the Borghese family. In 1633 he was appointed organist of the French church, S. Luigi dei Francesi, a post he held until his death. In 1635 he spent some time at the Medici court in Florence, at the invitation of Ferdinando II. In 1641 he left the service of the Borghese in favour of Cardinal Antonio Barberini, and it was Barberini who commissioned Rossi's first opera, *Il palazzo incantato* (1642). Many leading singers were involved in the production, including members of the papal choir, and the expense of the machines and costumes was enormous.

Title page of a manuscript score of Luigi Rossi's Il palazzo incantato *(Rome, 1642)*

In the mid-1640s Rossi was one of the leading musicians in Rome, and his house was a meeting place for other virtuosi. His first opera was generally reckoned a great success, and in 1646 Cardinal Mazarin invited him to France to compose another opera, *Orfeo*. While in Paris, Rossi participated in the court chamber music, and the opera – a six-hour performance – was eventually heard on 2 March 1647. Feeling against such lavish entertainment was running high among the common people, and when Rossi returned to France in 1648 with the intention of producing another opera, no production was possible because the court had sought refuge outside Paris. By 1650 Rossi was back in Rome, where he died three years later, leaving only two operas, a number of oratorios, and about 300 cantatas in a large variety of forms. Although Rossi's work marked the end of an era in early Roman baroque opera, it had a significant influence on Lully in France.

Orfeo
Opera in three acts (3h 15m)
Libretto by Francesco Buti

PREMIERES 2 March 1647, Palais Royal, Paris; US: 2 April 1988, Indiana University Opera Theater, Bloomington; UK: 27 November 1990, Queen Elizabeth Hall, London

Orpheus takes Euridice as his wife; Aristeo, son of Bacchus, is also in love with Euridice and calls Venus to help him. Eventually she causes a snakebite to kill Euridice. Orpheus goes with his lyre to the underworld to seek her; he is successful, but soon he loses her again. He wishes to die, and Venus makes him fall at the hands of the *baccanti*.

The story is more complex and elaborate than that based on Monteverdi's courtly version of *Orfeo*, but it is splendidly worked out, and Rossi's music is extrovertly characterized, with flashes of humour and pathos. Buti's libretto is very fine, and at the end has a remarkable passage suggesting that the 'marvellous tale' of the opera must now give way to reality. Detailed descriptions of the original production survive, and they indicate that no expense was spared in making it as lavish as possible: 200 men were employed to work on the scenery alone, and musicians from Rome, including Marc'Antonio Pasqualini, travelled to France to take part. Two of the performances were given in honour of the English Queen Catherine of Braganza (consort of Charles II) then in exile in Paris. Though the score contains no suggestions, contemporary accounts indicate that a large number of instruments participated. The style of writing for the solo voice has moved from dry declamation to well-shaped melodies (this is possibly the earliest opera in which arias outnumber recitatives): particularly memorable is the lament of Orpheus, 'Lasciate averno'.

Statuette of Rossini by the caricaturist J. R. Dantan (Milan, 1830s)

RECORDING Zanetti, Pelon, Boyer, Mellon, Les Arts Florissants, Christie, Harmonia Mundi, 1991

Other opera: *Il palazzo incantato, overo La guerriera amante*, 1642 (EDITION facsimile, H. M. Brown (ed.), Garland, 1977)
BIBLIOGRAPHY A. Ghislanzoni, *Luigi Rossi: biografia e analisi delle composizioni*, Milan, 1954; M. K. Murata, *Operas for the Papal Court (1631–68)*, Ann Arbor, 1981

G.D.

GIOACHINO ROSSINI

Gioachino Antonio Rossini; *b* 29 February 1792, Pesaro; *d* 13 November 1868, Paris

Rossini's theatrical works dominated the repertoire for three decades, from the 1810s through the 1830s. His comic operas were considered supreme examples of the buffo style that had flourished in 18th-century Italy; his Italian serious operas were models for generations of composers; his French operas were fêted and reviled by opposing camps in the contentious Parisian musical world. Although he ceased writing new operas before 1830 and although his serious operas had all but disappeared from public view well before his death in 1868, every operatic composer working in Italy or France during his lifetime had to come to grips with this legacy.

Both Rossini's parents were professional musicians (his mother a singer, his father a horn-player). Even before he entered the Bologna Conservatory in 1806, he had learned to play the piano and cello, performed as a singer, and composed chamber works, overtures, and sacred music. In Bologna he regularly served as maestro al cembalo in the theatre. Early commissions for operas came through the good offices of performers who were family friends and knew the boy's talents. By the end of his 21st year, Rossini had written ten operas for northern Italian theatres. Among them were: a series of five one-act operas (called *farse*) for the Venetian Teatro San Moisè, which specialized in this genre; an important comic opera, *La pietra del paragone* (1812), for the Teatro alla Scala of Milan, and his first major serious opera, *Tancredi* (February 1813), for the Teatro La Fenice of Venice.

Tancredi and Rossini's next opera, the madcap *L'italiana in Algeri* (May 1813), had an explosive effect: here was a new voice characterized by energy and wit, overflowing with melodic ideas, and sensitive to the most delicate shades of orchestral colour. What is more, Rossini brought to his work a structural clarity that transformed Italian opera: his characteristic forms, which gradually evolved over a period of ten years, were later developed into a system of formal rules as basic for 19th-century Italian composers as the sonata principle was for German ones.

Over the next four years, Rossini composed operas for a wide variety of Italian theatres. During this period, he prepared his major comic and semi-serious operas: *Il turco in Italia* (Milan, 1814), *Il barbiere di Siviglia* (Rome, 1816), *La Cenerentola* (Rome, 1817), and *La gazza ladra* (Milan, 1817), all of which were performed extensively throughout Europe. Working quickly, Rossini sometimes employed collaborators to prepare recitative or even musical numbers (arias for minor characters), but he frequently returned to these works and substituted new pieces of his own composition for those of the collaborators. He also borrowed from himself, usually turning to works unlikely to circulate further and making extensive revisions to suit the new dramatic and musical context.

Naples, where he had made his début in 1815 with *Elisabetta, regina d'Inghilterra*, was the composer's centre of activity from 1817 until 1822. Many modern critics consider Rossini's nine serious operas for Naples, together with his last opera for Italy, *Semiramide* (Venice, 1823), to be his most impressive achievement. Complex works, formally inventive, orchestrally lavish, vocally extravagant, the Neapolitan operas and *Semiramide* defy easy categorization: despite their external similarities, each has its individual character. The range of their sources (from Italian Renaissance verse epic through Shakespearean tragedy, French classical drama, and English Romantic poetry) is noteworthy. Some of these works (*Otello, La donna del lago, Semiramide*) were widely known; others, particularly the more experimental operas (*Armida, Ermione, Maometto II*), did not circulate. Their highly florid vocal style, written to measure for some of the finest singers of Rossini's day (including his future wife, the soprano Isabella Colbran), made them difficult to mount even in Rossini's time and almost impossible after the mid-19th century, when vocal techniques changed radically.

After *Semiramide*, Rossini took up residence in Paris, and became musical director of the Théâtre-Italien, where his operas were already the backbone of the repertoire. His reputation as the composer of the political 'Restoration' was enhanced by *Il viaggio a Reims* (1825), written for the coronation of Charles X. Between 1826 and 1829 he prepared four works for the Opéra. Two were revisions of Neapolitan operas; the third (*Le Comte Ory*, 1828) borrowed extensively from *Viaggio*. Only with *Guillaume Tell* (1829) did Rossini compose an entirely new opera in French, a work of monumental proportions, mediating between the worlds of Italian melodramma and French tragédie-lyrique. The artistic growth Rossini achieved in the period of 20 years between his earliest operas and this final masterpiece is extraordinary.

Guillaume Tell was Rossini's last opera. Many have speculated about the motive behind this retirement, but no single answer is sufficient. The factors were political (the change of government in France), emotional (the death of Rossini's mother, to whom he was deeply attached), economic (a wealthy man, he had no need to continue composing), physical and psychological (his bodily and mental health was deteriorating), and his favoured position at the Opéra was threatened after the 1830 Revolution and the 1831 premiere of Meyerbeer's *Robert le diable*; new styles of singing were becoming common, requiring modifications in his compositional technique.

From 1830 to 1836 the composer remained in Paris, overseeing the fortunes of the Théâtre-Italien and lending support to his younger Italian colleagues (Bellini, Donizetti and Mercadante). He then returned to Italy, where despite ill-health he served a term as director of the Bologna Conservatory. Only in 1855 did he return to Paris, where he regained his health, resumed active composition (though not in the field of opera), and lived out his final years, an esteemed presence from another era. The musical soirées in Rossini's apartment at the Chaussée d'Antin were attended by *tout Paris*.

Rossini's reputation for more than a hundred years, that of a composer of comic opera, has changed considerably in the past few decades. Thanks to the efforts of the Fondazione Rossini of Pesaro, many of his operas, particularly the serious ones, have been edited anew. The Rossini Opera Festival of Pesaro has provided models for intelligent stagings of these works; singers have successfully mastered their vocal style, and major theatres around the world have incorporated the operas into their repertoires. Thus, the depth and breadth of Rossini's achievement can be experienced anew by modern audiences.

Demetrio e Polibio

Dramma serio per musica in two acts
Libretto by Vincenzina Vigano-Mombelli
Composed before 1809
PREMIERE   18 May 1812, Teatro Valle, Rome

Even before the young Rossini completed his studies at the Bologna Conservatory, he composed his first opera. It was commissioned by the tenor Domenico Mombelli, whose wife prepared the libretto. Rossini did not participate in the premiere of *Demetrio e Polibio*, performed by Domenico and his two daughters. Mombelli may well have added music of his own composition.

This post-Metastasian story of rival dynasties, betrayals, and disguises is set at the Persian court. A young man ('Siveno'), raised by King Polibio and ignorant of his true lineage, falls in love with Polibio's daughter, Lisinga. Siveno's real father, Demetrio (King of Syria and long believed dead), comes in search of his son. After many conflicts, true identities are revealed, families reconciled, and the royal children joined in marriage.

Rossini's first opera is notable for the musical quality of its finest numbers. The lyrical love duet ('Questo cor ti giura amore'), which Rossini reused in several other operas, became highly popular. Stendhal called the quartet ('Donami omai Siveno') 'one of Rossini's masterpieces'. Its impressive integration of dramaturgical organization and musical form became increasingly characteristic of the mature Rossini.

RECORDING Bisi, Valdenassi, Pecchioli, Bramante, Coro 'Guido Monaco' Prato, Youth O of Opera Barga, Rigacci, Bongiovanni, 1979
EDITION v.s., Ricordi, 1825/6

La cambiale di matrimonio
Marriage by Promissory Note
Farsa comica da rappresentarsi in musica in one act (1h 15m)
Libretto by Gaetano Rossi, after the play *La cambiale di matrimonio* by Camillo Federici (1791) and the libretto *Il matrimonio per lettera di cambio* (first set to music by Carlo Coccia) by Giuseppe Checcherini (1807)
PREMIERES 3 November 1810, Teatro San Moisè, Venice; US: 8 November 1937, 44th Street Theater, New York
CAST Tobia Mill *b*, Fanni *s*, Edoardo *t*, Slook *b*, 2 servants *ms*, *b*
CHAMBER ORCHESTRA with cont

Of Rossini's first nine operas, five were written for the San Moisè of Venice, which specialized in farse, operas in a single act, often comic (as are 4 of Rossini's) but sometimes serious or 'semi-serious'. The commission for *La cambiale di matrimonio* probably came through the good offices of Rosa Morandi, a singer and family friend, who played Fanni at the premiere. Composing for the relatively small San Moisè, Rossini could hone his musical and theatrical skills without the pressures associated with major theatres such as La Scala or La Fenice. What is astonishing is how much of Rossini's mature comic style is anticipated in these early efforts.

SYNOPSIS
Mill, an English merchant, has received an unusual request from a Canadian businessman, Slook. Not finding an appropriate wife in Canada, Slook has ordered one from Mill by means of a promissory note in which he agrees to marry whoever presents the note to him. Encouraged by the Canadian's indifference to a dowry, Mill decides to offer his own daughter. Fanni has quite different plans: she is in love with the poor but honest Edoardo Milfort. Slook arrives, having decided to 'examine the merchandise' in person. Naïve but sincere, ingenuous but noble, he is delighted with his prize. But delight soon turns to distress, as Edoardo and Fanni threaten to pluck out his eyes and ship him back to Canada. The horrified Slook tries to escape from his pact, but Mill insists that it be maintained, then challenges him to a duel. After Fanni and Edoardo admit their love for one another to Slook, the generous colonial agrees to turn his 'merchandise' over to Edoardo and offers to make them his heirs. Mill's objections soon evaporate, and the lovers are united.

In *La cambiale di matrimonio*, Rossini already demonstrates remarkable fluency and an unfailing sense of proportion in constructing individual numbers. Inexperience manifests itself chiefly in the generic quality and brevity of many musical ideas. His treatment of comic characters is particularly successful. Slook's cavatina, 'Grazie . . . grazie', is a model buffo aria (Rossini reused ideas from it for the Poet's entrance in *Il turco in Italia*). The duets for Slook and Mill splendidly contrast the precipitous Englishman and the phlegmatic Canadian. Nor are the lyrical moments slighted: in fact, Rossini liked the *cabaletta* of Fanni's aria so much that he recycled it, almost unchanged, in *Il barbiere di Siviglia*.

RECORDINGS 1. Scotto, Fioroni, Monti, Panerai, Capecchi, Petri, I Virtuosi di Roma, Fasano, Delysé, c. 1965; 2. Rossi, Baiano, Comencini, Praticò, De Simone, Facini, ECO, Viotti, Claves/Albany, 1990: the older set is superior in virtually every respect [J.H.]
EDITION v.s., Ricordi, 1847; *rp*, 1960

L'equivoco stravagante
The Absurd Misunderstanding
Dramma giocoso per musica in two acts (1h 45m)
Libretto by Gaetano Gasbarri
PREMIERE 26 October 1811, Teatro del Corso, Bologna

Returning to Bologna, where he was 'maestro al cembalo and director of the chorus', Rossini wrote his first full-length comic opera. A young woman (Ernestina), defying her father (Gamberotto), avoids an unwanted marriage with a rich but stupid suitor (Buralicchio) by spreading the rumour that she is a castrato in disguise, a deserter from the army. When the credulous Buralicchio reports 'the deserter', Ernestina is bundled off to prison, from which (disguised as a soldier) she escapes. Once the stratagem is explained, Ernestina is permitted to marry her beloved Ermanno.

The story is badly served by the libretto's language, loaded down with double meanings and puns (the original reviewer cites the public's 'nausea at the indecent libretto'), and its poor arrangement of the action and musical numbers. None the less, Rossini found several situations congenial: the heroic aria for Ernestina as a soldier ('Se per te lieta ritorno'), for example, became the prototype for a series of analogous pieces, such as Isabella's 'Pensa alla patria' in *L'italiana in Algeri*. After the fiasco of *L'equivoco stravagante*, Rossini rescued several numbers by placing them in later operas.

RECORDING Rinaldi, Bottazzo, Pedani, Badioli, O of Angelicum, Milan, Zedda, EJS, 1965
EDITION v.s., Ricordi, 1851

L'inganno felice
The Fortunate Deception
Farsa per musica in one act (1h 15m)
Libretto by Giuseppe Foppa, after G. Palomba's libretto for Paisiello (1798)
PREMIERES 8 January 1812, Teatro San Moisè, Venice; UK: 1 July 1819, King's Theatre, Haymarket, London; US: 11 May 1833, New York

CAST Bertrando *t*, Isabella *s*, Ormondo *b*, Batone *b*,
Tarabotto *b*
CHAMBER ORCHESTRA with cont

Second of Rossini's farse for the Teatro San Moisè, *L'inganno felice* was much loved by the contemporary public. It was frequently revived in Italy for over half a century, and also performed throughout Europe and even in America. This farsa belongs to to the genre of opera semiseria, mixing comic and serious elements. Typically these operas feature an innocent heroine, persecuted and in danger of losing her life, and an obligatory happy ending. The genre is related both to Italian late-18th-century models (e.g. Piccinni's *La buona figliola*) and to French Revolutionary rescue opera (e.g. Cherubini's *Les deux journées*). After the success of *L'inganno felice*, the impresario of the Teatro San Moisè immediately contracted Rossini to write three more farse for his theatre.

SYNOPSIS
Ten years before the opera begins, the treacherous Ormondo, close friend of Duke Bertrando, having failed to seduce the duke's wife Isabella, convinced her husband that she was guilty of adultery. Ormondo turned her over to his henchman Batone, who abandoned her in a small boat to the fury of the sea. Her boat was washed ashore in a remote area of the duke's realm, where she was rescued by Tarabotto, chief of the iron miners, with whom she has lived ever since. Believing Isabella dead, Bertrando remarried but his second wife subsequently died.

When Isabella hears that the duke is coming to inspect the mines, she lays plans to win back his love. Tarabotto, to whom she now explains her history, offers to assist her. Bertrando arrives with his followers, among them Ormondo and Batone. The duke cannot forget Isabella, whom he still loves. Seeing the 'niece' of Tarabotto ('Nisa'), Batone and Bertrando are astonished at her resemblance to Isabella. Ormondo's suspicions are aroused, and he orders Batone to abduct and kill the woman. Under cover of night Batone and his followers approach, but the planned abduction is foiled, Ormondo's treachery is revealed, Isabella (dressed in the finery with which Tarabotto found her ten years earlier) is identified, and reunited with Bertrando.

In *L'inganno felice* Rossini melds the comic and serious registers into a splendid equilibrium. Comic elements are entrusted to Batone and Tarabotto, particularly in their duet, 'Va taluno mormorando' – here and elsewhere Rossini is notably successful at writing comic duets for two basses. But Batone is more than a basso buffo: his aria 'Una voce m'ha colpito' demands a rich vocal presence. The arias of Bertrando and Isabella are solemn and virtuosic. Bertrando's 'Qual tenero diletto' features an obbligato part for flute. The opera's most impressive music is found in the trio (in which Bertrando first encounters Isabella, while Tarabotto functions musically as a Leporello figure) and the finale, where

Rossini beautifully captures the mysterious nocturnal atmosphere that precedes the joyous conclusion.

RECORDINGS 1. Cundari, Jacopucci, Pezzetti, Montarsolo, Tadeo, Alessandro Scarlatti CO of RAI (Naples), Franci, Fonit Cetra, 1963; 2. Gonzales, Amato, Buoso, Desderi, Fissore, Alessandro Scarlatti CO of RAI (Naples), De Masi, ANNA, 1972
EDITIONS f.s., Ratti, Cencetti, 1826; v.ss., Breitkopf und Härtel, 1819; OTOS, 1976

Ciro in Babilonia, ossia La caduta di Baldassare

Cyrus in Babylon, or The Downfall of Belshazzar
Dramma con cori per musica in two acts
Libretto by Francesco Aventi
PREMIERES Lent (?14 March) 1812, Teatro Comunale, Ferrara; UK: 30 January 1823, Drury Lane, London (concert)

During Lent many Italian theatres were closed; others performed works with biblical settings. The central event of *Ciro in Babilonia*, the first of Rossini's two Lenten operas (*Mosè in Egitto* being the other), is the feast of Belshazzar, King of Babylon, at which a mysterious hand traces the words 'Mane, Thecel, Phares'. The prophet Daniel (poorly realized in the music) interprets the words as announcing the fall of Babylon. Earlier, Belshazzar abducts Amira (the wife of Cyrus, the Persian king), falls in love with her, and offers her his throne. Although Cyrus, disguised as an ambassador, gains access to Amira, he is unmasked and imprisoned. The prison scene inspired an impressive trio (Amira, Cyrus and Belshazzar). After an extended solo aria in many parts (a so-called gran scena and the highlight of the score), in which the condemned Cyrus bids farewell to his wife and child, the victorious Persians free their king and queen.

Ciro suffers from an excess of *secco* recitative and arias (some of ample proportions, such as Belshazzar's 'Qual crudel, qual trista sorte' and Amira's 'Deh! per me non v'affliggete', with an elaborate violin solo). Amira's 'Vorrei veder lo sposo' resurfaces in the 1818 version of *Mosè in Egitto*.

RECORDING Dessì, Calvi, Palacio, Ferraris, Antonucci, Cossutta, Serraiocco, Francesco Cilea Ch of Reggio Calabria, San Remo SO, Rizzi, Hunt, 1988
EDITION v.s., Ricordi, 1852

La scala di seta

The Silken Ladder
Farsa comica in one act (1h 30m)
Libretto by Giuseppe Foppa, after François-Antoine-Eugène de Planard's libretto (first set to music by Pierre Gaveaux), *L'échelle de soie* (1808)
PREMIERES 9 May 1812, Teatro San Moisè, Venice; UK: 26 April 1954, Sadler's Wells, London (Teatro dell'Opera Comica, Rome); US: 18 February 1966, War Memorial Opera House, San Francisco
CAST Dormont *t*, Giulia *s*, Lucilla *s*, Dorvil *t*, Blansac *b*, Germano *b*
CHAMBER ORCHESTRA including ca, cont

With *La scala di seta*, third of his farse for the Teatro San Moisè, Rossini produced an operatic jewel. Although its basic situation recalls Cimarosa's *Il matrimonio segreto* (1792), other aspects of the story – its silken ladder to facilitate nocturnal rendezvous, its profusion of characters in various hiding places, etc. – invoke French comedy, particularly the plays of Beaumarchais. *La scala di seta*, in fact, is the first of many Rossini operas with a libretto derived from the French theatre. The most original character, in both literary and musical terms, is the servant Germano. Little performed in the 19th century, *La scala di seta* has now begun to circulate widely.

SYNOPSIS

Giulia, against her tutor Dormont's wishes but with the approval of an aunt, has secretly married Dorvil. Every night her husband visits by means of a silken ladder, which she lowers from her balcony. Learning that Dormont intends her to marry the vain Blansac, Dorvil's friend, Giulia vows to turn Blansac's affection towards her cousin Lucilla. She enlists Germano's help, without explaining what she wants. The servant imagines himself the object of Giulia's love, but this mistake is soon cleared up. Blansac arrives, bringing along Dorvil (found near the house, from whence he had just departed) as a witness to his triumph. Although Giulia's plan advances, Germano overhears her musing about a nocturnal rendezvous. Thinking Blansac to be the object of Giulia's love, he congratulates the suitor on his good fortune. Blansac is delighted at the prospect of a rendezvous with Giulia. Meanwhile, Germano also informs Lucilla, and each of them decides to hide in Giulia's apartment to learn the ways of love. As midnight strikes, Germano and Lucilla are already present. Dorvil arrives, then hides as Blansac appears, who in turn conceals himself when Dormont, who has heard the racket, climbs up the ladder. After Dormont discovers the concealed characters in their various hiding places, Giulia reveals the secret of her marriage. Blansac gallantly agrees to marry Lucilla, and the tutor accepts the *fait accompli*.

Long known exclusively for its superb overture, the earliest in the Rossini canon to have survived as a concert piece, *La scala di seta* fulfils the promise of its opening pages. The key characters are Giulia and Germano. Her aria, 'Il mio ben sospiro e chiamo', is notable for its rich orchestration and cor anglais solo. Rossini lavished his most fascinating music on Germano. Like that of Batone in *L'inganno felice*, the role incorporates comic and serious elements, but Germano's ability to pass from lyricism to pure buffoonery is unique. The length, diversity, and complexity of 'Amore dolcemente' justifies comparison with a gran scena. It begins with a splendid melody and coloratura spanning almost two octaves, but concludes with extreme caricature (ingeniously supported by the raucous use of bassoon and horn). All major ensembles involve Germano (a duet with Giulia, a quartet, and the extended finale), and all represent the young Rossini at his finest.

RECORDING   Serra, Bartoli, Matteuzzi, Di Credico, Coviello, De Carolis, O of Teatro Comunale Bologna, Ferro, Ricordi–Fonit Cetra/Rossini Opera Festival Pesaro, 1988: complete recording based on the critical edition
VIDEO   Serra, Kuebler, Rinaldi, Corbelli, Stuttgart Radio SO, Gelmetti, Teldec, 1980s
EDITIONS   f.s., Fondazione Rossini, 1991; v.ss., Ricordi, 1852; Fondazione Rossini/Ricordi (on hire), 1988

La pietra del paragone
The Touchstone
Melodramma giocoso in two acts (2h)
Libretto by Luigi Romanelli
PREMIERES   26 September 1812, La Scala, Milan; US: 4 May 1955, Hart College of Music, Hartford; UK: 19 March 1963, St Pancras Town Hall, London
CAST   Clarice *a*, Aspasia *s*, Fulvia *ms*, Asdrubale *b*, Giocondo *t*, Macrobio *b*, Pacuvio *b*, Fabrizio *b*; *tb* chorus of gardeners, guests, hunters, soldiers of the count
FULL ORCHESTRA   with cont

Through the influence of two singers (Maria Marcolini and Filippo Galli) who already knew his extraordinary gifts, Rossini obtained his first major commission, from the Teatro alla Scala. Romanelli, poet in residence, provided a libretto rich in incident and character. Around the misogynistic Count Asdrubale and the three claimants to his hand, he wove a tapestry of absurd poets, venal journalists, and hangers-on. The poet Pacuvio's ballad, 'Ombretta sdegnosa del Missipipi' ('Haughty little ghost of the Mississippi'), became so popular that Rossini's authorship was forgotten and the novelist Antonio Fogazzaro, in *Piccolo mondo antico* (1895), considered it a folksong.

SYNOPSIS

A 'touchstone' determines the purity of gold and silver; Romanelli's 'touchstone' tests the sincerity of emotions.

Act I Marquise Clarice (a widow), Baroness Aspasia, and Lady Fulvia all wish to marry the rich Count Asdrubale. Taken with Clarice but dubious about the faithfulness of all women, Asdrubale disguises himself as a Turk. Claiming that the count is indebted to him, the 'Turk' begins to repossess Asdrubale's goods and those of his guests. 'Sequestrara . . . Sigillara' ('Take possession . . . seal them'), he says in pidgin-Italian. False friends (Aspasia, Fulvia, Macrobio, Pacuvio) abandon him; true ones (Clarice and Giocondo) rally to his defence. When Asdrubale's servant, Fabrizio, announces that the debt was previously paid, everyone is thrown into confusion.

Act II The offended Aspasia and Fulvia order Macrobio and Pacuvio to challenge the count and Giocondo to a duel. The action culminates in a reverse masquerade, with 'Lucindo' (Clarice disguised as her soldier brother) seeking to take his unhappy 'sister' home. The thought of losing Clarice is the 'touchstone' that reveals to the count his own feelings. When he admits his love, 'Lucindo' is transformed into Clarice, and the opera concludes with general rejoicing.

The prolix libretto offered Rossini many challenges, and provided situations rich in musical possibilities. From the easy melodiousness of Pacuvio's 'Ombretta sdegnosa' to the extreme caricature of Macrobio's narrative aria, 'Chi è colei che avanza', built largely over orchestral themes, Rossini explores diverse aspects of his comic language. But it is the Act I finale, particularly its absurd 'Turkish' scene, that fully reveals his genius. Turks, both comic and serious, appear in several Rossini operas. (Curiously, Filippo Galli, the original Asdrubale, was the protagonist of three of them: *L'italiana in Algeri*, *Il turco in Italia* and *Maometto II*.)

Alongside comic scenes and ensembles, *La pietra del paragone* features music of quite a different cast for Asdrubale and Clarice. Clarice's cavatina, 'Quel dirmi oh Dio! non t'amo', to which the count (unseen) provides an echo, is particularly appealing. (Its *cabaletta* anticipates Tancredi's 'Di tanti palpiti'.) In his final aria, 'Ah! se destarti in seno', Asdrubale's music gains dignity and depth of feeling.

RECORDINGS 1. Elgar, Wolff, Bonazzi, Carreras, Reardon, Foldi, Díaz, Murcell, Clarion Concerts Ch and O, Jenkins, Vanguard, 1971; 2. Trovorelli, Nocentini, Molinari, Barbacini, Scaltriti, Rumetz, Di Matteo, Ch of Teatro Comunale, Modena, O Camerata Musicale, Desderi, Nuova Era, 1992
EDITIONS v.ss., Ricordi, 1846; Ricordi (on hire), [n.d.]

L'occasione fa il ladro
Opportunity Makes the Thief

Burletta per musica in one act (1h 15m)
Libretto by Luigi Prividali, partly after the play *Le prétendu par hazard, ou L'occasion fait le larron* by Eugène Scribe (1810)
PREMIERES 24 November 1812, Teatro San Moisè, Venice; UK: 14 January 1929, Little Theatre, London (marionette performance, in English)
CAST Don Eusebio *t*, Berenice *s*, Count Alberto *t*, Don Parmenione *bar*, Ernestina *ms*, Martino *b*
CHAMBER ORCHESTRA with cont

With the successful *La pietra del paragone* behind him, Rossini returned to Venice to write his final two farse for the Teatro San Moisè. *L'occasione fa il ladro*, the first of them, was the fifth new work by Rossini to be staged in that year; thus we should not be surprised that a contemporary review claims it was written in 11 days. Although it was not warmly received at first (there were only five performances during the season), recent revivals have revealed the opera's superb construction, lyrical melodic language, and careful differentiation of characters.

SYNOPSIS
Surprised by a storm, two travellers take refuge at a country inn. Don Parmenione is charged with finding and returning to her family a runaway girl; Count Alberto is going to meet for the first time Berenice, his fiancée. Alberto's servant accidentally switches their valises, and after the count leaves, Parmenione opens the count's valise and finds Alberto's passport together with a picture of a beautiful girl whom he assumes to be the fiancée (it is actually Alberto's

sister, who is sending it as a gift to Berenice). Parmenione decides to pose as the count and marry her himself. He presents himself at the house of Don Eusebio, uncle and guardian of Berenice. The lady, to discover the character of her betrothed, pretends to be a servant, while her guest, Ernestina, assumes the role of the fiancée. Alberto soon arrives, and each of the men claims to be the count. In the meanwhile, Alberto falls in love with the 'servant' while Parmenione falls in love with the 'mistress' (even though she bears no resemblance to the woman in the portrait). After various humorous and sentimental episodes, everyone's identity is revealed. The count is united with Berenice, while Parmenione gives his hand to Ernestina, the very girl he was sent to trace.

L'occasione fa il ladro is notable for the precise way in which Rossini differentiates the two pairs of lovers. For Alberto and Berenice, he reserves a simple, sentimental melodic style (as in the duet within the finale, 'Oh quanto son grate le pene d'amore'); for Parmenione and Ernestina, one filled with movement and energy (Parmenione's aria, 'Che sorte, che accidente'). The opera is constructed around three anchoring ensembles: the sinfonia (actually a brief prelude and storm, the latter taken from *La pietra del paragone* and reappearing in *Il barbiere di Siviglia*) and introduction; the central quintet ('Quel gentil, quel vago oggetto'); and the finale. Although the design of the opera is compact, most numbers are expansive, and some have quite complex structures. The orchestration is unusually rich in this farsa. Particularly charming among the four arias are Berenice's cavatina ('Vicino è il momento') and Martino's Leporello-like assessment of his master ('Il mio padrone è un uomo').

RECORDING Serra, D'Intino, Giménez, Gavazzi, Raftery, Desderi, O Giovanile Italiana, Accardo, Ricordi–Fonit Cetra/Rossini Opera Festival Pesaro, 1987: complete recording based on the critical edition
EDITIONS f.s., Fondazione Rossini/Ricordi (on hire), 1987; v.ss., Ricordi, 1853; Fondazione Rossini/Ricordi (on hire), 1987

Il Signor Bruschino, ossia Il figlio per azzardo
Signor Bruschino, or The Son by Chance

Farsa giocosa per musica in one act (1h 15m)
Libretto by Giuseppe Foppa, after the play *Le fils par hazard* by Alissan de Chazet and E. T. Maurice Ourry (1809)
PREMIERES 27 January 1813, Teatro San Moisè, Venice; US: 9 December 1932, Metropolitan, New York; UK: 14 July 1960, Orpington (Kent Opera Group)
CAST Gaudenzio *b*, Sofia *s*, Bruschino padre *b*, Bruschino figlio *t*, Florville *t*, Police Commissioner *t*, Filiberto *b*, Marianna *s*, servants *silent*
CHAMBER ORCHESTRA including ca, cont

This last of Rossini's farse marked his third collaboration with Foppa in slightly over a year. Its poor reception by the Venetian public and its highly inventive comedy style gave rise to a host of anecdotes purportedly demonstrating that Rossini wrote *Il Signor Bruschino* to humiliate the impresario of the San Moisè, Antonio Cera. Rossini's biographer Alexis Azevedo spoke of uproarious laughter from those who understood the supposed plot and outraged whistles from those who did not. But these anecdotes are baseless. In *Il Signor Bruschino*, Rossini reveals a fully developed and outrageous opera-buffa style; a few months later it would lead to *L'italiana in Algeri*.

SYNOPSIS

Florville loves Sofia, but she is promised by her guardian, Gaudenzio, to the son of one Bruschino, known to them only through letters. Learning that Bruschino junior is being held prisoner at a local inn until he pays his bill, Florville pretends to be Bruschino junior so he can marry Sofia. When Bruschino senior unexpectedly arrives at Gaudenzio's house and refuses to recognize Florville as his wayward 'son', he is made to appear as if he is both disowning the poor lad and trying to break the marriage contract. Bruschino senior even sends for the police, but they fail to unravel the mystery. Only when the innkeeper Filiberto arrives does Bruschino begin to understand. Discovering, furthermore, that Florville is the son of Gaudenzio's worst enemy, he revenges himself by accepting the impostor as his son and persuading Gaudenzio to bless the couple. When the repentant Bruschino junior arrives and the plot is uncovered, Gaudenzio is furious, but it is too late. He bows to the inevitable, while the lovers rejoice.

Although it is hard for modern audiences to comprehend the initial failure of *Il Signor Bruschino*, for the work is a masterpiece of comic verve and invention, one must not underestimate the novelty of Rossini's music. This is already revealed in the overture, where the composer has the second violins tap their bows on the metal candle holders attached to their music stands in a rhythmic gesture that pervades the melodic fabric of the entire piece. The sense of heightened burlesque is well represented throughout the opera: the flustered Bruschino senior incessantly exclaims 'Uh che caldo' ('Oh I'm so hot!'), while Bruschino junior begs forgiveness in a mournful march, babbling 'Padre mio! . . . mio mio, mio mio! . . . son pentito! –tito, –tito . . . –tito, –tito . . .'

One of the highlights of the score is the preposterous trio ('Per un figlio già pentito'), in which Florville (as Bruschino junior) begs his 'father' for forgiveness, while Gaudenzio upbraids Bruschino senior for not yielding to paternal feelings. (Bruschino senior will turn Gaudenzio's words against him at the end of the opera, and Rossini underlines the verbal reference by quoting the music of the trio.) Even apparently sentimental pieces, such as Sofia's aria with cor anglais ('Ah donate il caro sposo'), are permeated with a spirit of irony. Indeed, the only character for whom we develop sympathy is Bruschino senior: his comic aria 'Ho la testa o è andata via? . . .' ends up being both hilarious and touching.

RECORDING Devia, Gonzalez, Rinaldi, Dara, Favano, Farruggia, Antoniozzi, SO of the RAI (Turin), Curiel, Ricordi–Fonit Cetra/Rossini Opera Festival Pesaro, 1988: complete recording based on the critical edition
VIDEO Hall, Kuebler, Rinaldi, Feller, Stuttgart Radio SO, Gelmetti, Teldec, 1989
EDITIONS f.s., Fondazione Rossini, 1986; v.ss., Ricordi, 1854; Fondazione Rossini/Ricordi, 1993

Tancredi

Melodramma eroico in two acts (2h 45m)
Libretto by Gaetano Rossi, with additions by Luigi Lechi, after Voltaire's play *Tancrède* (1760)
PREMIERES 6 February 1813, La Fenice, Venice; rev. with tragic finale, March 1813, Teatro Comunale, Ferrara; UK: 4 May 1820, King's Theatre, Haymarket, London; US: 31 December 1825, Park Theater, New York
CAST Argirio *t*, Tancredi *a*, Orbazzano *b*, Amenaide *s*, Isaura *a*, Roggiero *s* or *t*; *tb* chorus of nobles, knights, squires, populace, Saracens (the latter in the original version only); *silent*: warriors, pages, guards, populace, ladies, Saracens
ORCHESTRATION 2 fl/picc, 2 ob, ca, 2 cl, 2 bsn, 2 hn, 2 tpt, timp, banda turca, str, cont

With *Tancredi*, Rossini both achieved his first maturity as a composer of opera seria and established himself in Italy and abroad as the leading contemporary composer of Italian opera. Although working simultaneously on the two preceding farse, his attention was focused principally on *Tancredi*, for which he composed the *secco* recitatives himself. At the first two performances the indisposition of the Tancredi (Adelaide Malanotte) and the Amenaide (Elisabetta Manfredini) caused the curtain to be brought down during Act II. None the less, enough was heard to enable the reviewer to comment on 'the melodious song, the animated action of the first; the most sweet voice, the ardent and agile coloratura dared by the second'.

After the Venetian season Rossini, Malanotte, and Todran took a revised version of the opera to Ferrara. Important changes made for this production were partially due to the suggestions of Luigi Lechi, a Brescian nobleman and the lover of Malanotte, who provided the revised text. The most significant alteration was the introduction of a tragic finale, which brought the plot closer to Voltaire.

The public, however, preferred the happy ending. A production for the Teatro Re of Milan in December 1813, most likely under Rossini's direction, included some of the Ferrarese revisions but restored the Venetian finale. In this production the role of Roggiero was assigned to a tenor, rather than to the original soprano, and both of Argirio's arias were replaced, and the new ones ('Se ostinata ancor non cedi' and 'Al campo mi chiama') were widely performed, even outside Italy. In this form, *Tancredi* continued to be given until the mid-19th century, when it disappeared from the repertoire, although Tancredi's cavatina, 'Di tanti palpiti' (actually the text of the *cabaletta*), remained popular as a concert number. *Tancredi* was revived successfully in 1952 at the Florentine Maggio Musicale. Since the 1974 rediscovery of the tragic finale, which has become the standard ending, the opera has regained a firm place in the repertoire.

Set design for an early performance of Tancredi

SYNOPSIS (original, Venetian version)
Rossini borrowed the overture from *La pietra del paragone*.

Act I The action takes place in Syracuse, Sicily, in 1005. Faced with an impending attack by the Saracens (led by Solamir), the Syracusans celebrate the newly forged alliance between their ruler, Argirio, and his family's hereditary enemy, Orbazzano. To cement the pact, Argirio promises Orbazzano the hand of his daughter, Amenaide. She joyfully greets her father ('Come dolce all'alma mia') and in an aside expresses her longing for the return of the exiled and outlawed Tancredi, whom she knows to be in Sicily and to whom she has secretly written. (The son of a noble Norman family, Tancredi was forced by factional strife to leave Syracuse with his family when he was a child. He grew up in the court of Byzantium, where he and Amenaide met and fell in love.) Informed of her betrothal to Orbazzano, Amenaide begs Argirio to delay the wedding. In the next scene Tancredi, disguised and accompanied by his squire Roggiero, arrives in Syracuse. He expresses his love for Amenaide in a cavatina ('Tu che accendi'/'Di tanti palpiti'). Because of the Saracen threat, Argirio presses the wedding and informs Amenaide that all enemies of Syracuse, even Tancredi, will be condemned to death by the Senate. In his aria ('Pensa che sei mia figlia'), Argirio demands again that she marry Orbazzano. When Amenaide is left

alone, Tancredi re-enters. In a duet ('L'aura che intorno spiri') she warns him to flee a country where he is in danger of death, while he asks in vain for assurance that she loves him. In anticipation of the wedding, a chorus of nobles and people, joined by Orbazzano's knights, throngs the square in front of the church. Tancredi, incognito, offers to join them in battle against the Saracens. At that moment, Orbazzano arrives bearing Amenaide's letter, which he believes to have been addressed to Solamir. (At the court of Byzantium, Amenaide was also courted by Solamir, but rejected his advances.) In the first finale Amenaide, accused of treachery, is disowned by her father, rejected by Tancredi, and taken prisoner.

Act II Orbazzano urges Argirio to sign the order for Amenaide's death, while her confidante, Isaura, seeks to stir his paternal pity. Although struggling with the decision ('Ah! segnar invano io tento'), Argirio signs the order. Isaura sorrowfully prays that Amenaide may find consolation ('Tu che i miseri conforti'). Amenaide, in prison, meditates on her fate and resolves to die faithful to Tancredi ('No, che il morir non è'). Since no champion has come forward to defend Amenaide, Orbazzano and a reluctant Argirio arrive with guards to escort her to the execution. Still unidentified, Tancredi appears and challenges Orbazzano. Argirio and Tancredi share their differing sorrows in a duet ('Ah se de' mali miei'), of which the *cabaletta* is a martial call to battle

('Ecco le trombe'). Amenaide's prayer for Tancredi's victory ('Giusto Dio che umile adoro') is interrupted by joyful music: the chorus proclaims her vindication. Tancredi's triumphal appearance (chorus 'Plaudite, o popoli') is suspended as the unhappy Tancredi, still believing Amenaide unfaithful, prepares to leave Syracuse. Amenaide stops him. In their duet ('Lasciami: non t'ascolto') Tancredi refuses to accept Amenaide's protestation of fidelity, while Amenaide cannot reveal the truth in front of other characters, since to do so would endanger Tancredi's life. Tancredi leaves alone, while Roggiero hopes in a brief *aria di sorbetto* that love and joy will return ('Torni alfin ridente').

In the gran scena ('Dove son io?'), a distracted Tancredi has wandered close to the camp of the Saracens; they appear, vaunting their imminent triumph ('Regna il terror nella Città'). Argirio, Amenaide, and the Syracusan forces arrive in search of Tancredi, who accuses the maiden of having come to meet Solamir. The Saracens offer peace in return for Amenaide's marriage to Solamir; Tancredi upbraids Amenaide and defies the Saracens ('Va! palese è troppo omai'). The warriors take the field, while Amenaide and Isaura listen to sounds of battle. Argirio and Tancredi re-enter. Tancredi has killed Solamir who, dying, has reassured Tancredi of Amenaide's innocence. In the second finale the principal characters express their happiness.

The most important changes in the Ferrara revision occur at the end of the opera. In the new version of the gran scena the Saracens are replaced by Syracusans who already know Tancredi's identity and want him to lead them against the enemy. When Argirio and Amenaide enter, Tancredi orders her to leave for Solamir's camp. Amenaide vainly tries to explain. In his new rondo ('Perché turbar la calma?') Tancredi asks himself why a traitress has come to disturb him. Though moved against his will by Amenaide's tears, he leaves with the soldiers for the battlefield. The new finale opens with recitative: Argirio returns alone. The Syracusans are victorious, but Tancredi is mortally wounded. The chorus accompanies the entrance of the hero, who invokes Amenaide's name. Argirio informs him that Amenaide's fated letter was directed to Tancredi himself, not to Solamir, and that she has always loved him. As death approaches, the lovers join hands. Their union is blessed by Argirio. After bidding a final farewell to his wife, Tancredi dies to the fading sound of *tremolo* strings.

Tancredi is Rossini's first great opera seria. Stendhal held it high among the composer's masterworks, referring to its blend of youthful lyricism and rhythmic vitality as 'virginal candour'. The formal procedures Rossini employed in later operas, which so influenced the development of Italian opera, are crystallized in *Tancredi*. Although the division of the opera into closed numbers separated by *secco* recitatives remains, a flexibility of style makes possible extensive dramatic activity within numbers. Lyrical moments, incorporated into larger musical

units, are motivated by dramatic events. Rossini's approach is well exemplified in Amenaide's 'Giusto Dio che umile adoro'. Her lyrical prayer is followed by a passage in contrasting tempo and tonality, the chorus describing Tancredi's victory over Orbazzano. The concluding section, or *cabaletta*, returns to the opening tonality, and Amenaide first expresses her joy lyrically, then exuberantly in florid style.

In the duets Rossini also employs a sectional form. The opening section allows dramatic confrontation between the characters, who express their often differing emotions in parallel stanzas. A more lyrical second section is followed by further dramatic interaction, concluding with a *cabaletta* in which the changed dramatic configuration is rendered in a new moment of conflict or accord. Although *Tancredi* lacks the larger ensembles which become integral to Rossini's later style, his technique is shown in the first act finale: it is similar in structure to the duets, balancing musical and dramatic forces. In *Tancredi*, these forms are given life through clear melodies, energetic rhythms, and simple but interesting harmonies. The orchestra is used carefully, with numerous wind solos enhancing the idyllic and heroic moods.

RECORDING Cuberli, Schuman, Horne, Manca di Nissa, Palacio, Zaccaria, O and Ch of La Fenice, Venice, Weikert, CBS, 1985: complete recording of the Venetian version, with the concluding rondo and tragic finale from Ferrara, based on the critical edition
EDITIONS f.s., Fondazione Rossini, 1984; v.ss., Breitkopf und Härtel, *c.* 1817; Fondazione Rossini/Ricordi, 1991

L'italiana in Algeri
The Italian Girl in Algiers
Dramma giocoso per musica in two acts (2h 15m)
Libretto by Angelo Anelli (1808) for Luigi Mosca
PREMIERES 22 May 1813, Teatro San Benedetto, Venice; UK: 26 January 1819, His Majesty's Theatre, London; US: 5 November 1832, New York
CAST Mustafà *b*, Elvira *s*, Zulma *ms*, Haly *b*, Lindoro *t*, Isabella *a*, Taddeo *b*; *tb* chorus of eunuchs, corsairs, slaves, Pappataci; *silent*: women, European slaves, sailors
ORCHESTRATION fl/2 picc, 2 ob, 2 cl, bsn, 2 hn, 2 tpt, bd, cym, banda turca, catuba, str, cont

Following *Tancredi* by only a few months, *L'italiana in Algeri* was an equal success for the 21-year-old composer. The subject – the liberation, through a deception and an encounter with a lost lover, of a woman abducted by a tyrant – has roots in Greek and Roman theatre.

Because Rossini was called on to prepare the opera only at the last minute, after another composer failed to respect his contract, it was decided to employ an earlier libretto, by Angelo Anelli, first set by Luigi Mosca for the Teatro alla Scala of Milan in 1808. The few modifications show the dramaturgical hand of Rossini: Anelli's entrance aria for Taddeo (preceding Isabella's appearance) and a duet for Isabella and Lindoro were eliminated, the latter with the effect that the two lovers, like Rosina and the Count in *Il barbiere di Siviglia*, never have an intimate scene. The second-act aria for Isabella was added, as were the zany sections of the large ensembles: 'Nella testa ho un campanello' in the first finale and 'Sento un fremito' in the quintet. Perhaps because of the pressing schedule, *secco* recitatives and probably two short arias (Haly's 'Le femmine d'Italia' and Lindoro's 'Oh come il cor di giubilo') were composed by a collaborator. For a Milanese revival in 1814 Rossini replaced the Lindoro piece with a new aria of his own composition, 'Concedi, amor pietoso'.

The first Isabella was Maria Marcolini, the popular alto who had participated in the premieres of three previous Rossini operas (*L'equivoco stravagante*, *Ciro in Babilonia*, and *La pietra del paragone*). Mustafà was Filippo Galli, perhaps the finest bass of the day. Lindoro was sung by Serafino Gentili and Taddeo by Paolo Rosich. Rossini participated in and composed music for three later revivals: in Vicenza during the summer of 1813; at Milan's Teatro Re in April 1814, and at the Teatro dei Fiorentini in Naples in the autumn of 1815.

SYNOPSIS
The action takes place in Algiers. The overture, while not melodically related to the opera, captures its spirit delightfully. Rossini never reused it elsewhere.

Act I Elvira, the wife of Mustafà, the Bey, grieves that her husband no longer loves her. Her confidante Zulma and a chorus of eunuchs (tenors and basses) advise her to accept this common lot of women. Mustafà enters in a temper; he wants an Italian woman, and gives his captain, Haly, six days in which to produce one. In another part of the palace Lindoro, an Italian recently enslaved by Mustafà's corsairs, languishes for his distant love ('Languir per una bella'). Mustafà informs Lindoro that he must marry Elvira so that Mustafà can be rid of her; Lindoro describes the woman he wants to marry and Mustafà assures him Elvira is perfect ('Se inclinassi a prender moglie'). Offshore a ship has been wrecked and its passengers taken prisoner. Among them Haly and his men discover an Italian woman, Isabella, and her companion and would-be suitor, Taddeo. Isabella has been seeking her lover, Lindoro, and laments her cruel destiny ('Cruda sorte!'). She determines to conquer the Algerians through womanly wiles. Isabella and Taddeo argue about their relationship ('Ai capricci della sorte'), but they agree to pose as niece and uncle. Back at the palace Mustafà offers to allow Lindoro to leave immediately for Venice if he takes Elvira along. Seeing his opportunity to escape, Lindoro accepts. Haly brings news of the Italian woman, and Mustafà orders his court to assemble. He anticipates his new pleasure ('Già d'insolito ardore'). As the first finale begins, Mustafà is hailed by the eunuchs. Isabella is brought in and Mustafà and the chorus marvel at her beauty; she flirts with the Bey to entrap him. When Taddeo forces his way into the hall, Mustafà threatens to impale him, but then accepts Isabella's 'uncle'. Elvira, Zulma, and Lindoro come to say farewell; Isabella and Lindoro recognize each other and all express stupefaction in a grand ensemble of

Costume design for Isabella in L'italiana in Algeri *(1823)*

onomatopoeic nonsense during which Isabella acquires Lindoro as her slave.

Act II Mustafà has fallen in love with Isabella. Haly counsels Elvira to be patient while Isabella's wiles make a fool of the Bey. Isabella and Lindoro plan their escape; the latter rejoices at being reunited with Isabella ('Oh come il cor di giubilo'). In order to impress Isabella, Mustafà makes Taddeo his 'Kaimakan' and has him dressed in Turkish costume. Taddeo, not wishing to be a go-between, first declines the title ('Ho un gran peso sulla testa') but accepts with much obsequiousness on seeing Mustafà's anger. Isabella prepares to receive the Bey. She orders Lindoro to bring coffee for at least three and tells Elvira to observe from another room how to handle a man. Mustafà, Taddeo, and Lindoro watch from within while Isabella, completing her dressing, invokes Venus to make her more lovely ('Per lui che adoro'). Mustafà arranges to signal by sneezing the moment that the others should leave him alone with Isabella; the subsequent quintet ('Ti presento di mia man') is punctuated by numerous 'atchoos' which are conspicuously ignored. The ensemble is complete when Isabella invites Elvira to take coffee with them, and Mustafà understands that he has been tricked. Haly declares that Italian women excel at making men love them ('Le femmine d'Italia'). Lindoro tells Mustafà that Isabella loves the Bey and wants to make him her 'Pappataci', an honourable title given to men who sleep and eat while allowing their women to do just as they please. Isabella has arranged a ceremony involving the other Italian captives and has given the eunuchs and guards much wine. She encourages the Italians with patriotic passion ('Pensa alla patria'). In the second finale the chorus of Pappataci dresses the Bey in wig and costume, and Isabella confers the oath in which he swears to be deaf and blind to all her enterprises. Mustafà eats and drinks as the Italians slip away to the waiting ship. Taddeo, realizing that Isabella loves Lindoro, tries to alert the Bey but the latter fulfils his duty as Pappataci; rather than face Mustafà's wrath, Taddeo joins the Italians. Elvira, Zulma, and Haly reveal the deceit to Mustafà; he begs Elvira's forgiveness and renounces Italian women. The entire ensemble proclaims that a woman cannot be kept from having her way.

Within Rossini's bubbling score the scenes range from the sentimental and the patriotic to the farcical and the lunatic. Rossini's treatment of the two genres of opera seria and opera buffa permits considerable overlap and exchange of elements, so we find noble sentiments present within the comic framework. The formal designs seen in *Tancredi* re-appear in *L'italiana*, although with greater internal finesse.

Rossini characterizes well each of Isabella's three lovers. Mustafà's aria 'Già d'insolito ardore' combines buffoonery, elegance, and virtuosity. Lindero is a sweet, sentimental tenor who describes his sadness in the beautiful cavatina 'Languir per una bella'. Rossini emphasizes its poignancy with solo horn. Taddeo is the stock buffo of the opera and as such can hardly hope to end up with Isabella. His character is displayed in rapid patter and exaggerated leaps, a musical language that mocks its own pretensions.

The Italian girl must assume multiple personalities to triumph over cruel fate. She expresses erotic tenderness in 'Per lui che adoro'. (Rossini in 1814 rewrote the original solo cello obbligato as a flute solo.) Isabella tricks Mustafà and Taddeo time and again, from her initial meeting with the Bey in the first finale, to the pretended *tête-à-tête* which turns into a quintet, to the investiture of Mustafà as a Pappataci in the Act II finale. Yet she is also a woman of strength, who encourages her countrymen to escape with profound patriotic sentiments ('Pensa alla patria'). This rondo was considered subversive in an Italy with awakening hopes of nationhood – the words were often changed or the piece omitted.

Despite the censors, Rossini made his point musically: in the chorus preceding 'Pensa alla patria' he embedded a quotation from the 'Marseillaise'.

RECORDINGS All recordings are complete and based on the critical edition: 1. Battle, Horne, Foti, Palacio, Trimarchi, Ramey, Zaccaria, Prague Philharmonic Ch, I Solisti Veneti, Scimone, Erato, 1980: includes replacement arias as an appendix (omitted on CD version); 2. Bima, Valentini Terrani, Rizzi, Araiza, Dara, Ganzarolli, Corbelli, West German Radio Male Ch, Capella Coloniensis, Ferro, CBS–Sony, 1984: Ferro conducts the most lively, well-cast performance; 3. Pace, Baltsa, Gonda, Lopardo, Dara, Raimondi, Corbelli, Vienna State Opera Ch and O, Abbado, DG, 1989: rather straight-faced version in spite of deriving from stage performances [A.B.]

EDITIONS f.s., Fondazione Rossini, 1981; v.ss., Schott, *c.* 1819; Fondazione Rossini/Ricordi, 1982

Aureliano in Palmira

Dramma serio per musica in two acts
Libretto by Felice Romani, probably based on a libretto by Gaetano Sertor, *Zenobia in Palmira*, originally set by Anfossi (1789)
PREMIERES 26 December 1813, La Scala, Milan; UK: 22 June 1826, London

After the successes of *Tancredi* and *L'italiana in Algeri* Rossini spent several months in Milan, revising those operas for the Teatro Re and writing two new ones for La Scala: *Aureliano in Palmira* and *Il turco in Italia*. *Aureliano* is the only Rossini opera with a leading part for a castrato, Giambattista Velluti, the last great example of that vocal type. Velluti created the role of Arsace, prince of Persia. The opera was not well received in Milan, but was widely performed in Italy for 20 years.

In the centre of the action is Zenobia, Queen of Palmyra (Syria), heroine of tales and dramas since ancient times. Romani and Rossini present the story as an operatic love triangle surrounded by the exotic grandeur of Classical Rome and the Middle East. Zenobia (soprano) and Arsace (soprano castrato) love each other. The enemy Aureliano (tenor), who has imprisoned both of them, desires Zenobia. Faced with her heroic resistance, Aureliano magnanimously gives them both their freedom in return for fealty to Rome.

While effectively mixing heroic and pathetic elements, the subject did not fire Rossini's imagination. Despite some fine individual numbers, especially Arsace's pastoral gran scena ('Perché mai le luci aprimmo'), *Aureliano in Palmira* does not live up to the promise of *Tancredi*. Several numbers were reused in later operas, including the overture, which Rossini inserted into *Il barbiere di Siviglia*.

RECORDING Serra, Müller Molinari, Barbacini, Trotta, Cava, Gregorio Magno Ch, O of the Teatro dell'Opera Giocosa, Genoa, Zani, Ars Nova, 1981
EDITION v.s., Ricordi, 1855

Il turco in Italia

The Turk in Italy
Dramma buffo per musica in two acts (2h)

Libretto by Felice Romani, after the libretto by Caterino Mazzola, first set to music by Joseph Seydelman (1788)
PREMIERES 14 August 1814, La Scala, Milan; UK: 19 May 1821, His Majesty's Theatre, London; US: 14 March 1826, Park Theater, New York
CAST Selim *b*, Fiorilla *s*, Geronio *b*, Narciso *t*, Prosdocimo *b*, Zaida *s*, Albazar *t*; *satb* chorus of gypsies, Turks, masqueraders; *silent*: friends of Fiorilla, gypsies, Turks, masqueraders
ORCHESTRATION 2 fl/2 picc, 2 ob, 2 cl, 2 bsn, 2 hn, 2 tpt, trbn, timp, bd, cym, str, cont

The Milanese audience, believing *Il turco in Italia* to be a mere inversion of *L'italiana in Algeri*, with numerous self-borrowings, felt cheated by Rossini and did not receive the opera warmly. Except for a few short motifs, however, the work was newly composed, and it is one of Rossini's most carefully constructed comic operas. It is also his most Mozartian work and shows particularly the influence of *Così fan tutte*, which was being produced at the Teatro alla Scala immediately before the premiere of *Il turco*.

Il turco in Italia suffered much from severe alterations during its early career, such as the ravages perpetrated at the Théâtre-Italien in Paris for an 1820 revival, in which a dismembered torso of Rossini's score was refitted with numbers lifted from *La Cenerentola*, *L'italiana in Algeri* and *Ciro in Babilonia*, as well as an aria not by Rossini. The composer shared some blame, for he apparently had prepared a one-act reduction for the Théâtre-Italien, but no trace of this version survives. The Parisian pastiche was published, thereby confusing critics for a century and a half. After the mid-19th century, *Il turco in Italia* virtually disappeared from the repertoire, returning to the stage in a production with Maria Callas in 1950. The critical edition of the Fondazione Rossini has now made Rossini's original version available.

Several items in the original version are not by Rossini: the *secco* recitatives, the cavatina for Geronio ('Vado in traccia d'una zingara'), the aria for Albazar ('Ah! sarebbe troppo dolce'), and the entire Act II finale. After the premiere Rossini made several changes to this version. Narciso's Act II aria, 'Tu seconda il mio disegno', was added some time during the first season. An alternative cavatina for Fiorilla, 'Presto amiche', and additional pieces for Narciso and Geronio were prepared in the autumn of 1815 for a revival at Rome, where Rossini also omitted the two arias (for Geronio and Albazar) by his original collaborator.

SYNOPSIS

Act I In their camp on a solitary shore near Naples, gypsies sing about their happy life ('Nostra patria è il mondo intero'), while Zaida, former slave and fiancée of the Turk Selim, mourns her lost love. Prosdocimo the poet thinks gypsies would provide a fine introduction for the *dramma buffo* he must write. Geronio is searching for a fortune-teller to advise him how to cure his wife, Fiorilla, of her passion for men ('Vado in traccia d'una zingara'). When Zaida and the gypsy girls tell him he was born

under the fatal constellation of the ram, he flees. The poet learns that Zaida's rivals for Selim deceived him into condemning her to death, but the Turk's confidant, Albazar, saved her. Coincidentally, the poet reports, a Turkish prince is about to visit Italy to observe European customs; perhaps Zaida will find a mediator in him. Fiorilla muses on the folly of loving only a single object ('Non si dà follia maggiore'). Selim's boat appears, and he disembarks, greeting the wonderful country he has so longed to see ('Bella Italia, alfin ti miro'). He is further delighted by the appearance of the Italian ladies, especially Fiorilla. Geronio reveals to the poet and to Narciso (who also loves Fiorilla) that the Turk is taking coffee with Fiorilla. Geronio and Narciso are both distressed at Fiorilla's inconstancy. The quartet 'Siete Turchi' develops with protestations of anger and love. Fiorilla wants Geronio to allow her complete freedom, but he will have neither Turkish nor Italian men in his house ('Per piacere alla signora'). She threatens to punish him for his cruelty by having a thousand lovers. Selim has prepared his ship to flee with Fiorilla; while the Turk waits on the shore by the gypsy camp, Zaida reveals herself to him and they are reconciled. Narciso enters, complaining of his unrequited love ('Perché mai se son tradito'). Fiorilla and her friends arrive, then Geronio. The interaction of all six characters ('Ah! che il cor non m'ingannava'), particularly the two rival women, concludes the act in what the poet describes as a *finalone*.

Act II Geronio and the poet are drinking at an inn. Selim arrives, and the poet withdraws to observe. The Turk offers to buy Fiorilla from Geronio, according to Turkish custom; Geronio describes the better Italian custom of breaking the would-be buyer's nose ('D'un bell'uso di Turchia'), and the business conversation turns to threats of violence. As the men leave, Fiorilla and her friends arrive ('Non v'è piacer perfetto'). She has come at Selim's invitation and expects to triumph over Zaida, who arrives followed by Selim. The women ask him to choose between them, but he cannot decide. Zaida leaves him to Fiorilla; they muse on the fickleness of the opposite sex, then avow their mutual love ('Credete alle femmine'). The poet tells Geronio and Narciso that Selim plans to abduct Fiorilla from the masked ball that evening. To thwart him, Zaida will attend, dressed exactly as Fiorilla with Narciso disguised as Selim. At the ball the masked lovers pair off – Fiorilla with Narciso, Selim with Zaida. Geronio in confusion sees the two couples, and a comic quintet ensues in which Geronio demands his wife, whichever she may be ('Oh! guardate che accidente'). Even the chorus joins in calling Geronio crazy as the lovers leave him breathless and desperate. The poet suggests that the unhappy husband send Fiorilla away and pretend to sue for divorce. Albazar assures Geronio that Selim is departing with Zaida. Outside Geronio's house the poet relays this news to Fiorilla and gives her Geronio's letter of dismissal. Chastened, she divests herself of her finery and prepares to return to her parents' home ('Squallida veste, e bruna'). The poet advises Geronio to follow and pardon her. In the Act II finale they are reconciled ('Son la vite'). Selim and Zaida – taking leave of Italy – and Narciso receive Geronio's forgiveness, and the poet hopes his public will enjoy the happy ending.

Il turco in Italia shows Rossini at his comic best. He responds to the buffoonery of the plot with an inspired and constantly amusing score. *Il turco in Italia* is largely an ensemble opera; only in Fiorilla's role do solo arias play an important part. There is abundant madcap motion, but time and again the composer steps back and, whether for specifically dramatic or more purely musical reasons, creates moments of extraordinary beauty and sensitivity. The Act I finale begins with all the noisy bumptiousness one expects of a Rossini finale. The scene is in turmoil, motivated by the jealous battle of Fiorilla and Zaida, but suddenly the noise stops and the orchestra disappears. The solo voices sing a remarkable unaccompanied phrase, 'Quando sono rivali, rivali in amor'. The effect of the entire *stretta* depends on Rossini's explicit wide-ranging indications of dynamics with phrases developing in unexpected ways.

The quintet in which Geronio tries to find Fiorilla, while the four disguised lovers dance around him, is extraordinarily funny; but underneath a passage of unaccompanied singing, Geronio declaims his perplexity on a single note, emerging as a genuinely touching character. The little canonic *allegro* that follows, 'Questo vecchio maledetto', is Rossini's best piece in this genre. Its counterpoints are perfectly placed to set off the tune and help the modulations along.

The trio for Narciso, Geronio, and the poet ('Un marito scimunito!'), in which the latter expresses his glee at the developing plot while the other two plan their own revenge on him, is most unusual in design. The ensemble is largely built around a four-bar orchestral phrase in semibreves which appears both as a melody and as an accompanimental figure. Equally delightful is the duet for Fiorilla and Geronio ('Per piacere alla signora'). With wonderful mock realism Rossini follows husband and wife through their confrontation, showing them in scenes of anger and sentimentality.

RECORDINGS 1. Callas, Gedda, Stabile, Calabrese, Rossi-Lemeni, La Scala Ch and O, Gavazzeni, EMI Odeon, 1972; 2. Caballé, Berbie, Palacio, Barbacini, Nucci, Dara, Ramey, Ambrosian Opera Ch, National PO, Chailly, CBS–Sony, 1981; 3. Jo, Giménez, Fisson, Corbelli, Alaimo, Academy of St Martin in the fields, Marriner, Philips, 1992: the earliest set, memento of performances at La Scala with Callas, has historic significance in restoring the piece to the repertoire, but is incomplete; the 1981 set is uncut and heard in the critical edition of the Fondazione Rossini, as is the 1992 version, a vital, well-sung reading [A.B.]
EDITIONS f.s., Fondazione Rossini, 1988; v.ss., Breitkopf und Härtel, 1821; Fondazione Rossini/Ricordi (on hire), 1978

Sigismondo

Dramma per musica in two acts
Libretto by Giuseppe Foppa

PREMIERE 26 December 1814, La Fenice, Venice

After his two Milanese operas, *Aureliano in Palmira* and *Il turco in Italia*, Rossini returned to Venice with another opera seria for the theatre that had welcomed *Tancredi*. Although the orchestra applauded *Sigismondo* in rehearsals, the opera was criticized by a Venetian reviewer for having a libretto made of a 'confused mass of indigestible words' that 'pretended to be poetry'.

Ladislao, lieutenant of King Sigismondo of Poland, falsely accused the queen, Aldimira, of infidelity, and the king condemned her to death. Sigismondo now faces the avenging armies of her father, Ulderico. But Aldimira has been secretly saved by Zenovito, who plans to present her to Sigismondo as his daughter, Egelinda. Because of 'Egelinda's' remarkable resemblance to the supposedly dead Aldimira, Ulderico will believe Aldimira is safe. Sigismondo accepts the plan; Ladislao, suspicious of 'Egelinda', reveals the plot to Ulderico. When Aldimira appears, Ulderico cannot decide whether she is his daughter or not. A letter from Ladislao to Aldimira proving her identity is produced, Ladislao is sentenced to life imprisonment, and Ulderico, Aldimira and Sigismondo are all reconciled.

While the reviewer admitted that Rossini must have had difficulty making sense of the text, the music, however beautiful certain passages, was not up to expectations and seemed to lack originality: indeed, Rossini was correctly accused of having borrowed melodies from earlier operas. *Sigismondo* received few revivals in Italy, and apparently none outside it; by 1827 it had left the repertoire, but parts of it live on in later operas, such as *Elisabetta, regina d'Inghilterra Il barbiere di Siviglia* and *Adina*.

EDITION v.s., Ricordi, 1826

Elisabetta, regina d'Inghilterra

Elizabeth, Queen of England
Dramma per musica in two acts (2h 15m)
Libretto by Giovanni Schmidt, after the play by Carlo Federici (1814) based on the novel *The Recess* by Sophie Lee (1783–5)
PREMIERES 4 October 1815, Teatro San Carlo, Naples; UK: 30 April 1818, King's Theatre, Haymarket, London
CAST Elisabetta *s*, Leicester *t*, Matilde *s*, Enrico *a*, Norfolk *t*, Guglielmo *t*; *satb* chorus of knights, courtiers, Scottish nobles, royal guards, populace
FULL ORCHESTRA including 2 ca

Elisabetta, regina d'Inghilterra opens Rossini's Neapolitan period. Between 1815 and 1822 he was to write ten operas for Naples (eight for the Teatro San Carlo). In Naples the impresario Domenico Barbaja had assembled a superb orchestra, a large and excellent mixed chorus (only a male chorus had been available for most of Rossini's earlier operas), and some of the greatest singers of the epoch, among them Isabella Colbran, who created the role of Elisabetta and later became Rossini's first wife. Unusually, the Neapolitan company regularly included two first tenors: one of high tessitura and very florid style, usually Giovanni David (but in

Elisabetta Emanuele Garcia), and one more heroic with a baritonal extension, Andrea Nozzari.

Elisabetta borrows many musical phrases, sections, and entire numbers from earlier works. For the most part, however, these were extensively reworked and fully integrated into the new context. It is as if Rossini wished to present himself to the Neapolitan public by offering a selection of the best music from operas unlikely to be revived in Naples.

SYNOPSIS

Rossini thoroughly reorchestrated the overture from *Aureliano in Palmira* for *Elisabetta* (he later used it a final time in *Il barbiere di Siviglia*).

Act I At the royal palace, the Earl of Leicester is to be honoured by Queen Elizabeth for his victories against the Scots. Elizabeth enters, overjoyed at the prospect of seeing Leicester again, but Leicester is shocked to find among the Scottish hostages his secret wife, Matilda, and her brother, Henry. Torn between love for Matilda and loyalty to Elizabeth, Leicester confides in his friend Norfolk, unaware of the latter's jealousy. Norfolk promptly informs Elizabeth that Leicester has betrayed her. The queen resolves that Leicester and Matilda will pay and announces to the court that Leicester will become her consort; when Leicester hesitates, she imprisons the traitors.

Act II Elizabeth offers to spare Leicester, Henry and Matilda if the latter will renounce her marriage. Although Matilda (to save her husband) agrees, Leicester proclaims that they prefer to die. Elizabeth, disgusted with Norfolk's betrayal of his friend, exiles the duke, who plays on the people's sympathy for Leicester to raise a revolt. When Norfolk informs the imprisoned Leicester of his plan, Leicester refuses to act dishonourably. Elizabeth comes to the prison (where Norfolk, Matilda, and Henry variously hide themselves) to offer to help Leicester escape; Leicester again refuses dishonour. When Elizabeth implicates Norfolk, the latter, fearing further exposure, attempts to kill the queen, but he is disarmed by Matilda and Henry and arrested. Elizabeth gratefully pardons the three, sanctions the marriage of Leicester and Matilda, and renounces love in her own life.

In his Neapolitan operas Rossini explored the dramatic possibilities of opera seria. His experiments were not always understood or accepted by his audiences. In *Elisabetta* he wrote a conservative bridge between the earlier periods and the mature Neapolitan operas, adapting much of the music from prior works rather than composing a fully original opera, but he invested the older ideas with the rich Neapolitan orchestral palette and surrounded them with new music to suit the context. Notable are the two male solo scenes in Act II: the interaction between chorus and soloist in Norfolk's aria ('Qui sosteniamo'/'Che intesi') anticipates the scene for Assur and chorus in *Semiramide* and Leicester's prison scene ('Della cieca fortuna') is remarkable for the flexibility of its first sections and its orchestration, with solo writing for two cors anglais.

RECORDING Caballé, Masterson, Creffield, Carreras, Benelli, Jenkins, Ambrosian Singers, LSO, Masini, Philips, 1976
EDITIONS f.s., facsimile of the autograph manuscript, Garland, 1979; v.s., Breitkopf und Härtel, 1819–20

Torvaldo e Dorliska

Dramma semiserio in two acts (2h 15m)
Libretto by Cesare Sterbini, based on the novel *Vie et amours du chevalier de Faubles* by J.-B. de Coudry's (1790)
PREMIERE 26 December 1815, Teatro Valle, Rome

In the autumn of 1815 Rossini not only began his important relationship with the theatres of Naples but also worked for the first time in Rome. He presented a revised version of *Il turco in Italia* at the Teatro Valle, and later composed a new rescue opera in the semiseria genre for the same theatre.

The evil Duke of Ordow has vanquished Torvaldo, his rival for the hand of Dorliska. Dorliska seeks refuge at a nearby castle that turns out to be Ordow's. Her persecutor threatens to kill her if she continues to reject him. Torvaldo, whom the duke had thought dead, comes in disguise to the castle in search of Dorliska, who unwittingly reveals his identity. The duke threatens to kill the imprisoned Torvaldo if Dorliska will not yield, but she remains resolute. The governor's troops, summoned by Giorgio, the castle's keeper, are admitted to the castle by the servants. In a confrontation in the dungeon, Torvaldo disarms the duke, who is led away by the soldiers amidst general rejoicing.

This nicely constructed opera makes much use of the basso-buffo character of Giorgio to enliven the ensembles, contrasting with the duke's florid bass and Torvaldo's lyrical tenor. The semiseria genre encourages Rossini to write in a simpler melodic style, alongside more fully developed compositions. Particularly touching is the duettino for the lovers, 'Quest'ultimo addio'.

RECORDING Cuberli, Valentini Terrani, Bottazzo, Nimsgern, Dara, Socci, Milan Ch and SO of RAI, Zedda, Voce, 1975
EDITION v.s., Ricordi, 1855

Il barbiere di Siviglia

(Originally *Almaviva, ossia L'inutile precauzione*)
The Barber of Seville (originally *Almaviva, or The Useless Precaution*)
Commedia in two acts (2h 45m)
Libretto by Cesare Sterbini, after the play by Beaumarchais (1775) and G. Petrosellini's libretto for Paisiello (1782)
PREMIERES 20 February 1816, Teatro Argentina, Rome; UK: 10 March 1818, King's Theatre, Haymarket, London; US: 3 May 1819, Park Theater, New York
CAST Count of Almaviva *t*, Bartolo *b*, Rosina *ms*, Figaro *bar*, Basilio *b*, Berta *s*, Fiorello *bar*, Ambrogio *b*, official *b*, notary *silent*; *tb* chorus of police, soldiers, musicians
ORCHESTRATION 2 fl/2 picc, 2 ob, 2 cl, 2 bsn, 2 hn, 2 tpt, bd, cym, sistrum, gtr, str, cont

During the years of his association with Naples, Rossini wrote several important operas for other Italian cities, including *Il barbiere di Siviglia*, the oldest opera by an Italian composer never to have disappeared from the repertoire and perhaps the greatest of all comic operas. Set to a beautifully constructed libretto and drawing effectively on an important literary source, Rossini's opera achieves melodic elegance, rhythmic exhilaration, superb ensemble writing, original and delightful orchestration. In it Rossini, with cleverness and irony, adapted the formal models of his art to specific dramatic situations.

In Rome for the premiere of *Torvaldo e Dorliska* in December of 1815, Rossini signed a contract with the Teatro Argentina to compose an opera for the conclusion of the imminent carnival season. After a subject offered by Jacopo Ferretti had been rejected, Cesare Sterbini, author of *Torvaldo*, was selected to prepare the text. The resulting libretto was *Almaviva, or The Useless Precaution*, a title chosen to distinguish it from Paisiello's well-known *Barber of Seville*. In no more than two weeks, Rossini had prepared the score; probably from lack of time he adapted the overture of *Aureliano in Palmira*, which also had formed the basis for the overture to *Elisabetta, regina d'Inghilterra*. The opening-night audience reacted unfavourably to this new and hastily mounted *Barbiere*, but on the second night its brilliance won them over. For the Bologna revival of 1816 there was no necessity to maintain the original title; Rossini's *Barbiere di Siviglia* had come into its own.

The opera was known in corrupt versions from the end of the 19th century until the 1960s. Furthermore, its modern performance tradition stressed slapstick gags rather than elegant comedy. The critical edition of the score, edited by Alberto Zedda (1968), and the performances based on it, have allowed the public to hear the work afresh.

SYNOPSIS

Act I At dawn in Seville Count Almaviva serenades the beautiful Rosina ('Ecco ridente il cielo'). When Rosina fails to appear at her window, he pays off the musicians who, delighted by his generosity, make an enormous racket before departing. Figaro, the barber, approaches; he loves his profession, which opens every door in the city to him ('Largo al factotum'). He recognizes the count, but the latter wants his identity hidden, for he has secretly followed Rosina. Figaro says she is the ward of old Dr Bartolo, who wishes to marry her himself. Bartolo appears, locks Rosina in, and hurries off to organize the wedding. The count, not wanting Rosina to marry him for his title, pretends to be Lindoro, a poor student ('Se il mio nome'). As Rosina starts to respond, the shutters are firmly closed. Promised gold for his assistance, Figaro concocts a plan: the count will enter Bartolo's house disguised as a drunken soldier and claim lodgings ('All'idea di quel metallo'). Inside the house Rosina has written a letter to Lindoro ('Una voce poco fa'). Figaro appears, promptly followed by Bartolo. Don Basilio, music master and friend of Bartolo, brings word that Count Almaviva, attracted by Rosina's beauty, has arrived in Seville. He suggests they spread malicious rumours about the count ('La calunnia'). Bartolo

prefers to marry that day, and they go off to draft the contract. Having overheard the conversation, Figaro warns Rosina. Assuring him she can handle the situation, Rosina inquires about the handsome youth she has just seen with Figaro. He tells her it was his impoverished cousin, madly in love with Rosina. Though feigning surprise when Figaro suggests she write to Lindoro, Rosina produces her finished letter ('Dunque io son') and Figaro goes to deliver it. The suspicious Bartolo accuses Rosina of having written to her lover and threatens to lock her up ('A un dottor'). The disguised count arrives noisily ('Ehi, di casa'). He tells Bartolo he seeks lodging. When Rosina appears, the count manages to reveal that he is Lindoro. Bartolo produces an exemption from billeting, but the count dismisses it. In the uproar, he slips Rosina a letter, which she promptly exchanges with a laundry list as the servant Berta and Don Basilio enter. Figaro soon reappears, reporting that their noise can be heard throughout the city. Soldiers knock at the door. All the characters try to explain the situation, creating even more chaos. The officer arre 's the count, who shows a document and is prom tly set free. Bartolo explodes in anger and everyone expresses total confusion.

Act II Another knock at the door announces the count, disguised as a music master, 'Don Alonso' ('Pace e gioia'). He claims to be a student of Don Basilio, sent because his master is ill. To gain Bartolo's confidence, he tells him he has stolen from Almaviva a note written by Rosina. With this evidence, he will try to convince Rosina that the count merely plays with her affections. Tricked, Bartolo goes to fetch his ward for her lesson. Rosina performs a 'Rondo' from a new opera, *The Useless Precaution*, and as Bartolo dozes, she and Lindoro express their mutual affection ('Contro un cor'). Bartolo awakens, bored by this 'contemporary music', and sings some 'music of my time' ('Quando mi sei vicina'). Figaro comes to shave Bartolo, who sends the barber to get shaving materials. Figaro grabs the opportunity to obtain the balcony key, then drops crockery, forcing Bartolo to come after him. Rosina and Lindoro again swear their love. As Figaro begins to shave Bartolo, Don Basilio arrives for Rosina's lesson. The lovers and Figaro provide Basilio with an ample purse, claim he has scarlet fever, and make him withdraw ('Don Basilio! Cosa veggo!'). Figaro continues to shave Bartolo while Lindoro plans with Rosina to elope at midnight. Bartolo overhears the count speak of his disguise and breaks into a rage. Alone, Berta, Dr Bartolo's housekeeper, comments on the foolishness of old men who would marry young women ('Il vecchiotto cerca moglie'). Basilio admits to Bartolo he does not know 'Don Alonso' – perhaps it was the count himself. Bartolo instructs Basilio to fetch the notary immediately. Producing Rosina's letter to Lindoro, Bartolo tells her he obtained it from Count Almaviva and persuades her to agree to marry him. A storm rages outside. As Figaro and the count enter through the balcony, Rosina accuses 'Lindoro' of intending to sell her to that vile Count Almaviva. The count throws himself at her feet and admits his true

Luigi Salvi (Almaviva), Fanny Persiani (Rosina), Giorgio Ronconi (Figaro) and Agostino Rovere (Bartolo) in the first Covent Garden performance of Il barbiere di Siviglia *(1847)*

identity. The lovers express their joy, while Figaro urges them to escape ('Ah! qual colpo inaspettato'). By the time they are ready, their ladder has disappeared. Basilio enters with the notary. Figaro has him marry the count and Rosina. Offered the choice between a valuable ring and two bullets in the head, Basilio agrees to be a witness. Bartolo, too late, arrives with soldiers. Count Almaviva reveals his identity and announces that Rosina is his wife ('Cessa di più resistere'). With no choice remaining, Bartolo blesses the marriage. All wish the happy couple love and eternal fidelity ('Di sì felice innesto').

In *Il barbiere di Siviglia* Rossini most successfully uses his musical style to provide a metaphoric interpretation of, or an ironic commentary on, the unfolding drama. The basic techniques and forms of his musical vocabulary embody in a precise and often delightful way the dramatic situations and characters. For example, the 'Rossini crescendo' (a technique for building musical tension by repeating a short phrase with added instrumental forces, expansions of register, alterations in articulation, and gradual increases in dynamics), though rarely inappropriate for its context, frequently lacks specific links to the drama. In Figaro's cavatina, as the orchestral crescendo gathers force, the barber describes how the demands of his clients become ever more insistent; his words come faster and faster until the momentum reaches its climax and he is left to sing unaccompanied: 'Figaro, Figaro, Figaro, Figaro . . .'

In Don Basilio's 'calumny' aria the crescendo becomes the central musical force of the number. As Basilio describes how the soft voice of rumour gradually spreads until it explodes like a cannon shot, the orchestral crescendo builds to the *colpo di cannone* of the bass drum.

In the trio near the end of Act II Rossini uses another standard musical technique to comment ironically on the action rather than describe the dramatic situation. While the lovers react with ecstasy to their new-found happiness, Figaro urges them to leave. It is standard for Rossini to echo a lyrical vocal melody in the orchestra, giving the singer a chance to breathe at the end of a phrase while maintaining melodic interest. In this trio the echo is both played by the first violins and sung by Figaro, who tries to shake Rosina and the count out of their happy delirium. Although he imitates their very words, the lovers simply do not hear him; it is as if Figaro served as nothing more than the traditional instrumental echo. Furthermore, when the lovers finally realize they must hurry, the three sing 'Presto andiamo via di qua'; as the characters wait for the music to work itself out with standard repeats of the *cabaletta* theme and cadential phrases, their ladder disappears from under them.

In one number after another, Rossini both captures the essence of the characters and comments ironically, even maliciously, on them. This is an opera that combines the elegance of its literary source with the buffoonery of the Italian *commedia dell'arte* tradition. Even with the recovery of so many of the composer's significant operas over the past 20 years, it remains Rossini's masterpiece.

RECORDINGS 1. Berganza, Malagu, Alva, Prey, Dara, Montarsolo, Cesari, Ambrosian Opera Ch, LSO, Abbado, DG, 1972: first important recording of the Rossini revival; 2. Baltsa, Burgess, Araiza, Allen, Trimarchi, Lloyd, Best, Ambrosian Opera Ch, Academy of St Martin in the Fields, Marriner, Philips, 1983: rounded, characterful account; 3. Horne, Pierotti, Barbacini, Nucci, Dara, Ramey, Alaimo, Ch and O of La Scala, Chailly, CBS–Sony, 1988; 4. Bartoli, Banditelli, Matteuzzi, Nucci, Fissore, Burchuladze, Pertusi, O and Ch of Teatro Comunale, Bologna, Patané, Decca, 1989: the last two are both good modern performances, one with the veteran Horne as an experienced Rosina, the other with the young, succulent-voiced Bartoli in the role [A.B., P.G.] VIDEOS 1. Berganza, Alva, Prey, Dara, Montarsolo, Ch and O of La Scala, Milan, DG, 1970s: Ponnelle's noted staging of the 1970s, finely conducted; 2. Ewing, Cosotti, Rawnsley, Desderi, Furlanetto, Glyndebourne Festival Ch, LPO, Cambreling, Castle, 1982. EDITIONS f.s., Ricordi, 1969; v.ss., Breitkopf und Härtel, 1820; Ricordi, 1969

La gazzetta
The Gazette
Dramma per musica in two acts (1h 45m)
Libretto by Giuseppe Palomba, rev. by Andrea Leone Tottola, after the play *Il matrimonio per concorso* by Goldoni (1763)
PREMIERE 26 September 1816, Teatro dei Fiorentini, Naples

La gazzetta, the second opera Rossini wrote for Naples (and the only comic one), is even more derivative than *Elisabetta*. Various numbers are lifted whole from *Il turco in Italia*, a trio comes unchanged from *La pietra del paragone*, and several pieces are largely derived from *Torvaldo e Dorliska*, all of which were unknown in Naples. The opera was favourably received, although the libretto was criticized. Noteworthy is the use of Neapolitan dialect for the buffo roles, a characteristic of the comic-opera tradition in Naples.

The plot involves the intrigues of two pairs of lovers: Alberto, who has travelled the world in search of a wife, and Doralice, daughter of the peevish Anselmo; Filippo, the keeper of the inn where the action occurs, and Lisetta, crafty daughter of the *nouveau-riche* Don Pomponio. The latter has placed an advertisement for a good husband for Lisetta in the daily paper, *La gazzetta*. Anselmo decides to marry Doralice to Monsù Traversen. After various ridiculous situations, Filippo devises a Turkish masquerade at which Don Pomponio is mocked by Doralice, Lisetta, Alberto, and Filippo, who are all dressed alike. (The number is taken from *Il turco in Italia*.) In the end, Monsù Traversen renounces the hand of Doralice and the two pairs of lovers receive the consent of their fathers to their marriages.

RECORDING Galli, Tuccari, Casoni, Lazzari, Borriello, Tajo, Ch of San Carlo, Naples, Alessandro Scarlatti CO of RAI, Caracciolo, Fonit Cetra, 1960
EDITION v.s., Ricordi, 1854

Otello, ossia Il moro di Venezia
Othello, or The Moor of Venice
Dramma per musica in three acts (2h 15m)
Libretto by Francesco Maria Berio di Salsa, after the play *Othello* by William Shakespeare (1604–5)
PREMIERES 4 December 1816, Teatro del Fondo, Naples; UK: 16 May 1822, King's Theatre, Haymarket, London; US: 7 February 1826, Park Theater, New York
CAST Otello *t*, Desdemona *s*, Elmiro *b*, Rodrigo *t*, Iago *t*, Emilia *ms*, Lucio *t*, the Doge *t*, a Gondolier *t*; *satb* chorus of senators, followers of Otello, ladies-in-waiting to Desdemona, people
FULL ORCHESTRA including hp, sistrum, thunder-machine

Otello, written for Naples between the Roman operas *Il barbiere di Siviglia* and *La Cenerentola*, was staged at the Teatro del Fondo because the principal theatre, the San Carlo, had been destroyed by fire. Although the title suggests the Shakespearean drama, the libretto actually explores archetypical situations of Italian opera: a secret marriage, a disapproving father, a duel between rivals. Only in Act III, with the scene for Desdemona and Emilia and final confrontation and tragedy, is the literary source apparent.

SYNOPSIS
The overture, a reworking of that of *Sigismondo*, is distinctly old-fashioned in the context of the opera: it is the last traditional overture Rossini wrote in Naples.

Act I Otello returns victorious to Venice while the jealous Iago and Rodrigo plot his downfall. Desdemona's father, Elmiro, has intercepted a letter she sent to Otello and believes it was intended for Rodrigo. Desdemona fears that Otello will doubt her love. Elmiro, who has offered his daughter's hand to Rodrigo, tells her only that he has found her a husband. As friends gather for the wedding, Desdemona realizes she is to marry Rodrigo, not Otello, and is torn between filial duty and love. Otello enters and reveals that Desdemona has pledged herself to him.

Act II Rodrigo pleads his case with Desdemona. Iago gives Desdemona's letter to Otello; not realizing it was meant for him, Otello is consumed by a desire for revenge. Despite Desdemona's efforts to separate them Rodrigo and Otello fight. Elmiro, furious, curses his daughter.

Act III Otello has been exiled by the Senate; the grief-stricken Desdemona, hearing a gondolier singing verses of Dante outside her window, intones a doleful song of her own, ending with a prayer for Otello's return. When she is asleep, Otello stealthily enters. Although Desdemona, awakening, protests her innocence, he stabs her. The Doge, Elmiro, and Rodrigo arrive. Iago, attempting to murder Rodrigo, has been killed, but before his death he confessed his plotting. The Senate has therefore pardoned Otello; Rodrigo withdraws his claim to Desdemona, and Elmiro is prepared to grant her hand to Otello. Overcome with grief, the Moor stabs himself.

The opera lies at a significant juncture in Rossini's compositional development. Although the first two

Giovanni Battista Rubini as Rossini's Otello, a role in which he caused a sensation in Paris in 1825

acts are musically and dramatically effective, even inspired, it is the third that elicited Rossini's most original and profound music. Conceived as a whole, the act ranges from the richly scored prelude through Desdemona's magnificent 'Willow Song' to the powerful *dénouement*. The 'Willow Song' is a masterful demonstration of music's power to enrich a strophic framework with emotional depth. As Desdemona becomes more agitated the vocal line grows more florid; when she attempts to sing the final strophe, the vocal line is stripped of ornament, and she abandons the song without bringing it to completion; finally, she offers her beautiful prayer to the accompaniment of winds alone. Although the first section of the Otello–Desdemona 'duet' is conventional, its ending, which builds in intensity until Otello kills her, is not. Rossini offers no *cabaletta*, although the text had been fashioned to suggest the typical structure. Throughout this act, the drama is the controlling element; Rossini had come of age as a musical dramatist.

RECORDING von Stade, Condò, Carreras, Fisichella, Pastine, Ramey, Ambrosian Opera Ch, Philharmonia O, López-Cobos, Philips, 1979
EDITIONS f.ss., facsimile of the autograph manuscript, Garland, 1979; Fondazione Rossini/Ricordi (on hire), 1988; v.ss., Breitkopf und Härtel, 1819–20; Fondazione Rossini/Ricordi (on hire), 1988

La Cenerentola, ossia La bontà in trionfo

Cinderella, or Goodness Triumphant
Dramma giocoso in two acts (2h 30m)
Libretto by Giacomo (Jacopo) Ferretti, after Charles

Perrault's tale *Cendrillon* (1697), G.-G. Etienne's libretto *Cendrillon* (1810), and F. Fiorini's libretto *Agatina* for Stefano Pavesi (1814)
PREMIERES 25 January 1817, Teatro Valle, Rome; UK: 8 January 1820, King's Theatre, Haymarket, London; US: 27 June 1826, Park Theater, New York
CAST Don Ramiro *t*, Dandini *b*, Don Magnifico *b*, Clorinda *s*, Tisbe *ms*, Angelina (known as Cinderella) *ms*, Alidoro *b*; *tb* chorus of courtiers; *silent*: ladies
ORCHESTRATION 2 fl/2 picc, 2 ob, 2 cl, 2 bsn, 2 hn, 2 tpt, trbn, str, cont

Rossini was originally commissioned by the Teatro Valle to set a different libretto, based on a French comedy, but the ecclesiastical censors demanded so many changes that Rossini ultimately rejected it, requesting a new libretto from his friend Ferretti. Because of the shortness of time – Ferretti and Rossini chose the subject on 23 December 1816 – Ferretti did not write a new poem based on the fairy-tale, but rather turned to two earlier libretti, written for Paris and Milan, respectively. Practically none of the elements familiar from Perrault's fairy-tale figures in Ferretti's libretto. His transformation of the glass slipper into a bracelet was probably to placate the Roman censors, who would not wish to see an unshod feminine foot on stage.

The opera was staged a month later. Rossini borrowed the overture from the Neapolitan *La gazzetta* and employed a Roman musician, Luca Agolini, to assist him in his preparations. Agolini composed all the *secco* recitative and three pieces: an aria for Alidoro ('Vasto teatro è il mondo') in Act I, a chorus ('Ah della bella incognita') to open Act II, and an aria for Clorinda ('Sventurata! me credea') near the end of the opera. For a Roman revival in 1821 Rossini replaced Alidoro's aria with a new composition, 'Là del ciel nell'arcano profondo'.

The nature of the libretto makes *La Cenerentola* significantly different from Rossini's previous comic operas. Although Don Magnifico and Dandini are comic characters in the great Italian tradition, the principal characters, Cinderella herself and Ramiro, are sentimental, not comic. They are heirs of Richardson's Pamela, the virtuous servant girl loved and finally married by a noble patron. From Piccinni's setting of Goldoni's *La buona figliola* (1760) on through the century, Italian opera buffa more and more frequently had sentimental and pathetic heroines, expressing their emotions in a musically simple and popular style.

SYNOPSIS
Act I In a hall of Don Magnifico's castle, his vain daughters Clorinda and Tisbe are primping. Their stepsister, Cinderella, consoles herself with a song about a king who chose a kind-hearted bride ('Una volta c'era un re'). A beggar (actually Prince Ramiro's tutor Alidoro) comes in; Cinderella gives him some breakfast, angering the stepsisters. The prince's knights enter, announcing the imminent arrival of the prince himself, who at a ball will choose the most beautiful woman as his wife. The ensuing excitement generates great confusion. The knights leave; so does the 'beggar', foretelling that Cinderella

will be happy by the next day. Quarrelling for the privilege of telling their father the good news, Clorinda and Tisbe awaken him. Don Magnifico interprets a dream he was just having as a prediction of his fortune: the impoverished baron's vision of himself as grandfather of kings is apparently confirmed by his daughters' announcement ('Miei rampolli femminini'). Ramiro, having decided to explore the situation, has exchanged clothing with his attendant, Dandini. When the disguised prince enters the house, he and Cinderella fall in love immediately ('Un soave non so che'). Dandini arrives, awkwardly playing the prince ('Come un'ape ne' giorni d'aprile'). Clorinda and Tisbe are introduced to him. Cinderella begs her stepfather to take her to the ball ('Signor, una parola'), but Magnifico orders her to stay at home. Alidoro, with a list of the unmarried women of the region, asks Don Magnifico about a third daughter; he says she died. Everyone is confused. Later Alidoro reveals his identity to Cinderella and invites her to the ball, alluding to a change in her fortunes ('Là del ciel'). At the palace Dandini, still disguised as the prince, appoints Magnifico his wine steward; Magnifico proclaims new drinking laws. Clorinda and Tisbe scornfully mistreat Ramiro, believing him to be the squire. All are enchanted by the arrival of a mysterious lady. When she unveils herself they are struck by her uncanny resemblance to Cinderella.

Act II The courtiers laugh at the sisters' distress. Magnifico imagines himself the prince's father-in-law, making money in exchange for his favours ('Sia qualunque delle figlie'). Ramiro overhears Cinderella refusing Dandini's attentions because she loves his 'squire'. Ramiro asks her to be his, but she gives him a bracelet, saying he will find her wearing its twin. If he still likes her, she will marry him. Ramiro reassumes his princely role and determines to look for Cinderella ('Sì, ritrovarla, io giuro'). Dandini encourages Magnifico's fantasies, then reveals his real identity ('Un segreto d'importanza'). Returning home, the sisters find Cinderella by the fire and berate her because she looks like the lady at the ball. Alidoro arranges an accident for the prince's carriage, which overturns in front of the house. Cinderella and Ramiro recognize each other ('Siete voi'), and everyone expresses amazement ('Questo è un nodo avviluppato'). Ramiro whisks Cinderella away, while Alidoro convinces the sisters to ask forgiveness so as to avoid ruin. At the wedding banquet Cinderella intercedes with the prince for Magnifico and her stepsisters. She reflects on how her fate has changed ('Nacqui all'affanno, al pianto').

La Cenerentola is far from a simple comic opera. Rossini adapts for his purposes not only the popular semiseria genre but even the exalted vocal style of opera seria. When we first meet Cinderella she is a naïve girl singing a little ditty: 'Once upon a time there was a king . . .' The disguised prince begins their duet ('Un soave non so che') with a simple melody that is a transformation of her tune. In the sextet Rossini gives Cinderella a coloratura style that none the less remains attached to simple melodic

patterns ('Ah signor, s'è ver che in petto'). But in her first appearance at the ball ('Sprezzo quei don') and at the beginning of her rondo ('Nacqui all'affanno, al pianto') she emerges a queen, her florid flights approaching those we normally associate with Rossini's serious operas. Ramiro's Act II aria ('Sì, ritrovarla, io giuro') is a thoroughly elegant piece with spectacular vocal fireworks and a range that ascends repeatedly to exposed and sustained high Cs.

The opening comic aria for Don Magnifico is rather standard, with almost continuous comic patter. Dandini, however, is a more subtle comic character. When he first appears disguised as the prince, Rossini gives him a princely *coro e cavatina* in mock-heroic style, in which extravagant coloratura alternates with patently buffo declamation. The witty duet with Magnifico ('Un segreto d'importanza') is superbly set. Once the secret is out, the tentative opening phrase is transformed into a spirited *allegro* in which Dandini's buffo style emerges gloriously, with Magnifico babbling in confusion. More revelations lead to the sextet of confusion ('Questo è un nodo avviluppato'), one of the most inspired moments in all Rossini's operas. By using a remarkable palette of musical styles throughout the opera, Rossini leads us through each stage. In the end, Cinderella's transformation is brought about not by supernatural arts, but by the magic of music.

RECORDINGS 1. Gabarain, Oncina, Bruscantini, Wallace, Alan, Glyndebourne Festival Ch and O, Gui, EMI, 1953: cut and ageing set redeemed by Gui's supreme gifts as a Rossinian; 2. Berganza, Guglielmi, Zannini, Alva, Capecchi, Montarsolo, Trama, Scottish Opera Ch, LSO, Abbado, DG, 1972: excellent set using the critical edition; 3. Baltsa, Malone, Palmer, Araiza, Alaimo, Raimondi, Del Carlo, Ambrosian Opera Ch, Academy of St Martin in the Fields, Marriner, Philips, 1988: reasonably lively modern version [A.B.]
VIDEO Denning, Evangelatos, Murray, Araiza, G. Quilico, Berry, Schöne, Vienna State Opera Ch, Vienna PO, Chailly, Virgin (video)/Pioneer (laserdisc): a conventional staging, by Michael Hampe; very well sung [A.B.]
EDITIONS f.s., facsimile of the autograph manuscript, Forni, 1969; v.ss., Carli, 1822–3; critical edn, Ricordi (on hire)

La gazza ladra
The Thieving Magpie
Melodramma in two acts (3h 15m)
Libretto by Giovanni Gherardini, after the play *La pie voleuse* by J.-M.-T. d'Aubigny and L.-C. Caigniez (1815)
PREMIERES 31 May 1817, La Scala, Milan; UK: 10 March 1821, King's Theatre, Haymarket, London; US: October 1827, Philadelphia
CAST Fabrizio Vingradito *b*, Lucia *ms*, Giannetto *t*, Ninetta *s*, Fernando Villabella *b*, the Mayor *b*, Pippo *ms*, Isacco *t*, Antonio *t*, Giorgio *b*, Ernesto *b*, magistrate *b*, gaoler *silent*, usher *silent*; *satb* chorus of men at arms, peasants, servants; a magpie
ORCHESTRATION 2 fl/2 picc, 2 ob, 2 cl, 2 bsn, 4 hn, 2 tpt, 3 trbn, timp, bd, cym, triangle, 2 sd, bell, str, cont

From the second half of 1817 until 1822, Rossini's creative activity was dominated by his artistic ties with Naples, where he concentrated his attention primarily on the production of serious operas. The winter and spring seasons of 1816–17, however, proved to be one of the composer's most intensely prolific periods. Working in a variety of theatres and across a number of genres, Rossini had already affirmed his genius in opera seria (with *Otello* for Naples) and opera buffa (with *La Cenerentola* for Rome). Now he returned to Milan, the scene of his earliest important success, and a city where a large number of works by German and Austrian composers (Mozart, Weigl and Winter) had been produced since his last visit. Mindful of the lack of enthusiasm generated by his two previous works for La Scala, Rossini devoted considerable attention to his new opera semiseria.

Gherardini, a leading personality in Milanese cultural life, had offered the libretto the preceding year to Paër, but it was not used. The plot is based on a true story: a French servant girl, accused of theft, was tried and executed. When her townspeople later discovered that the thief was a magpie, they instituted an annual mass in her memory, called the 'mass of the magpie'. In a letter to his mother, Rossini proclaimed 'the subject is wonderful'.

La gazza ladra belongs to the 'mixed' genre, born in the mid-18th century. During the revolutionary period, semiseria operas were frequently rescue operas (the most famous example being Beethoven's *Fidelio*). *La gazza ladra* is a classic example of opera semiseria, but its fusion of comic and dramatic elements is clearly weighted towards the latter.

The opera was an immediate and enormous success. It quickly circulated outside Italy, being heard throughout Europe in the following decade, and remained in the repertoire for over 50 years. Rossini himself directed revivals in Pesaro and Naples, writing some remarkable new arias for the character of Fernando.

SYNOPSIS
The opera begins with one of Rossini's finest overtures, whose opening snare drums and military tone infiltrate much of the drama. Many themes are derived directly from the opera and anticipate its emotional content.

Act I Fabrizio Vingradito, a well-to-do tenant farmer, would like to see his son Giannetto, who is returning from military service, marry Ninetta, their serving girl and the daughter of an honourable soldier, Fernando Villabella: the young couple are in love ('Oh che giorno fortunato!'). Lucia, Fabrizio's wife, complains that the girl is irresponsible and has recently mislaid a silver fork. Ninetta enters ('Di piacer mi balza il cor'); Fabrizio and Lucia go to meet Giannetto. Isacco the pedlar arrives selling his wares ('Stringhe e ferri da calzette'), but is sent on his way by Pippo, a friend of Ninetta in Fabrizio's service. Everyone returns with Giannetto, who embraces Ninetta ('Vieni fra queste braccia'); Pippo sings a drinking song ('Tocchiamo, beviamo'). Alone in the household, Ninetta is joined by a ragged man: it is her father. Having been refused permission to visit his daughter, Fernando fought with his commander, was imprisoned and condemned to death, and now has escaped. He gives Ninetta a silver

fork and spoon to sell so that he will have some money ('Come frenar il pianto!'). The mayor, coming to renew his unwelcome amorous overtures to Ninetta ('Il mio piano è preparato'), receives an urgent message; not having his eye-glasses, he asks Ninetta to read it aloud. It is an order to arrest her father, which she falsifies by changing the description of the fugitive ('M'affretto di mandarvi'). Fernando reproaches the mayor for his unwanted attentions to Ninetta ('Respiro. Mia cara!'). Meanwhile, the pet magpie, unobserved, steals a silver spoon. Lucia accuses Ninetta of stealing the missing silver fork and spoon. Pippo inadvertently reveals to the mayor that Ninetta has sold some trinkets to Isacco. The pedlar is summoned and a deposition is taken ('In casa di Messere'); Isacco has already resold the fork and spoon, but he testifies that they had the initials F.V. – those of both Fabrizio and Fernando. Ninetta, unwilling to betray her father, is arrested.

Act II Ninetta, in prison, is visited in turn by Giannetto, to whom she declares her innocence but not the truth about her father ('Forse un dì conoscerete'); by the mayor, whose offer of freedom in return for his love she rejects ('Sì, per voi, pupille amate'); and by Pippo, to whom she gives the money to hide for her father ('E ben, per mia memoria'). Lucia reveals Ninetta's plight to Fernando, who determines to save her at the cost of his own life ('Accusata di furto'). Lucia repents of her accusations ('A questo seno'). At the trial Ninetta is sentenced to death; all react in pity and horror ('Tremate o popoli'). Fernando bursts in; too late to help his daughter, he is himself arrested. While Pippo is counting his money in the village square, the magpie steals a coin. The mournful procession to the execution enters the square as the townspeople console Ninetta ('Infelice, sventurata'); it pauses in front of the church while Ninetta prays for her father ('Deh tu reggi'), then leaves the square. Pippo and Antonio climb to the magpie's nest in the belltower, where they discover the stolen fork and spoon. However, it seems to be too late; gunfire is heard in the distance. Then a joyful chorus announces it is a signal that Ninetta is safe. A royal pardon arrives for Fernando. All rejoice, except the mayor.

Despite the great wealth of beautiful music in *La gazza ladra*, a modern audience may find its semi-serious tone difficult to grasp. The music moves from a light-hearted, pastoral tone to one of deep tragedy, only to wrest itself back at the last moment. The two most ambiguous characters are Pippo and the mayor. The youthful Pippo announces the return of Giannetto, plays with the magpie, and sings a drinking song; then, in the prison scene, he and Ninetta perform a duet whose beauty and tenderness create a powerful dramatic tension. In the mayor's cavatina there are elements of opera buffa (in the orchestra, in the comic declamation), but in the following trio he is much more threatening. Showing his 'official' side during the Act I finale, he reveals his fury against Ninetta in a musical language that leaves no doubt about the evil of which he is capable. During the highly charged quintet, he finally

Design by Alessandro Sanquirico for Act II of La gazza ladra *(Milan, 1817)*

expresses remorse but is unable to find a way out. In the finale, when it seems that Ninetta has been executed, it is to the mayor that Rossini gives the weightiest part, while in the face of communal joy, he feels intense shame.

The funeral march of the Act II finale is laden with such grief as to set aside the lighter elements. The procession approaches, the orchestra *sotto voce*; it draws nearer, adding chorus (always with the accompanying drums that opened the overture and called the court to session). The prayer, with its introduction for two bassoons and two horns leading to a simple melody, does not end the scene but leads to a reprise of the march, swelling to *fortissimo*, then dwindling until only bassoon, horn, trombone, and drum remain, fading to nothing. And then the sudden change from clouds to sunlight: Ninetta and Fernando return in triumph, and one of the principal dramaturgical requirements of opera semiseria, a happy ending, is fulfilled, with each character (except the mayor) expressing joy.

RECORDING Ricciarelli, Manca di Nissa, D'Intino, Matteuzzi, Coviello, Furlanetto, Ramey, Philharmonic Ch of Prague, Symphonic O of RAI (Turin), Gelmetti, Sony, 1990; complete recording, live from the Rossini Opera Festival of 1989, based on the critical edition

VIDEO Cotrubas, Kuebler, Rinaldi, Ellis, Feller, Cologne Opera Ch, Gürzenich O, Bartoletti, Virgin, 1980s
EDITIONS f.s., Fondazione Rossini, 1979; v.ss., Simrock, 1819–20; Fondazione Rossini/Ricordi, 1989

Armida

Dramma per musica in three acts (2h 30m)
Libretto by Giovanni Schmidt, after scenes from the epic *Gerusalemme liberata* by Torquato Tasso (1575)
PREMIERES 11 November 1817, Teatro San Carlo, Naples; UK: 30 January 1922, Covent Garden, London (concert); US: 29 February 1992, Tulsa Opera, Tulsa
CAST Goffredo *t*, Rinaldo *t*, Idraote *b*, Armida *s*, Gernando *t*, Eustazio *t*, Ubaldo *t*, Carlo *t*, Astarotte *b*; *satb* chorus of paladins, warriors, demons, spirits
FULL ORCHESTRA including serpentone, hp, banda turca, sistrum, t-t

With *Armida* Rossini returned to the medieval setting of *Tancredi*, but the opera is far from the pastoral idyll of that youthful work. Rather it indulges the Romantic passion for the exotic and supernatural, while at the same time deeply probing human passion. In Naples Rossini became the lover of the star soprano Isabella Colbran, who created the title role of *Armida*; perhaps the emotion he felt for her poured out in the magnificent love duets of the opera.

SYNOPSIS

Act I Armida, princess of Damascus and a sorceress, comes to the French crusaders' camp outside Jerusalem, ostensibly to ask their aid against a usurper in Damascus but actually to weaken the Christian forces. She finds there Rinaldo, whom she loves. Gernando boastfully taunts Rinaldo concerning which of them will succeed their recently dead leader, Dudone. Rinaldo angrily kills Gernando and is spirited to safety by Armida.

Act II On Armida's enchanted island the chief spirit Astarotte and a chorus of demons proclaim her magic powers and true intentions. Armida and Rinaldo, arriving in a dragon-borne chariot, declare their love. Nymphs and spirits sing and dance, exalting love's reign.

Act III Carlo and Ubaldo, sent to announce Goffredo's pardon and retrieve Rinaldo, wander in Armida's enchanted garden, where a chorus of nymphs attempts to seduce them. Rinaldo enters with Armida; the knights recall him to his duty. He vacillates; she beseeches; ultimately he goes with them. The desolate Armida, torn between love for Rinaldo and a desire for revenge, calls on her demons to destroy the island. The dragon chariot carries her off amid flame and smoke.

Armida is one of Rossini's most individual operas. In it Rossini presents the differing worlds of manly duty and erotic love through musical contrasts. Act I, set in the 'real world', displays the leadership of Goffredo ('Ardite all'ire') and the bravado of Gernando ('Non soffrirò l'offesa'). Rossini brings us from this into Armida's magical domain of Acts II and III where the solo violin, solo cello, and colourful combinations of winds predominate. Perhaps the clearest example of Rossini's deliberate 'distortion of reality' is the form the duets for Armida and Rinaldo take in these acts. In Act I they have a standard duet ('Amor, possente nome') with *primo* tempo, *tempo di mezzo*, and *cabaletta*. In Act II Rinaldo awakens in Armida's arms and begins a 'duettino' ('Dove son io?') of only 56 bars (nearly half of which is an introduction featuring a cello solo), in which their voices echo at close intervals and entwine with alternating coloratura phrases. In the equally short Act III duet ('Soave catene'), with an introduction for solo violin, the two voices never separate but declaim together.

RECORDINGS 1. Callas, Ziliani, Albanese, Filippeschi, Raimondi, Salvarezza, Frosini, Stefanoni, Ch and O of Maggio Musicale Fiorentino, Serafin, various labels, 1952: although the Callas recording has poor sound and a portion missing, it is historically important; 2. Gasdia, Matteuzzi, Merritt, Furlanetto, Ford, Workman, Ambrosian Opera Ch, I Solisti Veneti, Scimone, Europa, 1991
EDITIONS f.s., Fondazione Rossini/Ricordi (on hire), 1991; v.ss., Pacini, 1823–4; Fondazione Rossini/Ricordi (on hire), 1991

Adelaide di Borgogna

Dramma per musica in two acts
Libretto by Giovanni Schmidt

PREMIERES 27 December 1817, Teatro Argentina, Rome; UK: 19 November 1978, Queen Elizabeth Hall, London (concert)

Berengario has poisoned Lotario, first king of Italy, and usurped the throne. To assure his authority he tries to marry his son, Adelberto, to Lotario's widow, Adelaide of Burgundy. Instead, the German emperor Ottone invades Lombardy, defeats Berengario, and marries Adelaide himself. Captures and deliverances precede the final *dénouement*.

Although the other operas Rossini wrote for Rome during his Neapolitan tenure (*Il barbiere di Siviglia* and *La Cenerentola*) are comic, contrasting with the serious works produced for Naples, *Adelaide di Borgogna* is very different. Critics have called it trivial, even (in the absence of an autograph score) doubting its authenticity. The latter is unlikely, for Rossini used several numbers from it in later operas, especially his pastiche *Eduardo e Cristina* (1819). The numbers are unusually short and undeveloped for this period of Rossini's career. Indeed, Schmidt's libretto is remarkable for the place accorded *secco* recitative and the brevity of the musical set pieces, which exalt a kind of Metastasian poetry. At the same time there are fine numbers: Adelaide's eloquent aria in Act II ('Cingi la benda candida'), Ottone's cavatina ('Soffri la tua avventura'), and the Act II quartet. Perhaps Rossini set aside the newest aspects of his art for this Roman commission, or maybe he was experimenting with a more classical approach to opera seria.

RECORDING Devia, Dupuy, Bertolo, Caforio, Tandura, Farruggia, Fallisi, New Cambridge Ch, O of Martina Franca Festival, Zedda, Fonit Cetra, 1986: derived from a live performance at the Festival della Valle d'Istria (1984)
EDITION v.s., Ricordi, 1858

Mosè in Egitto

Moses in Egypt
Azione tragico-sacra in three acts (1h 30m)
Libretto by Andrea Leone Tottola, after the play *L'Osiride* by Francesco Ringhieri (1760)
PREMIERES 5 March 1818, Teatro San Carlo, Naples; UK: 30 January 1822, Covent Garden, London (concert); 23 April 1822, King's Theatre, Haymarket, London (as *Pietro l'Eremita*); US: 2 March 1835, New York
CAST Pharaoh *b*, Amaltea *s*, Osiride *t*, Elcia *s*, Mambre *t*, Moses *b*, Aaron *t*, Amenophis *ms*
FULL ORCHESTRA including serpentone, hp, banda turca; onstage: band

Rossini's azione tragica is an opera in sacred garb, a way to circumvent official sanctions against performing secular works during Lent. The plight of Elcia, the Israelite girl secretly married to the Egyptian crown prince, has little to differentiate it from other depictions of the conflict between love and duty pervading Italian melodramma of the time, and Rossini provides the lovers with music similar to that of his frankly secular opere serie.

At its premiere *Mosè in Egitto* was well received except for the short final act, the crossing of the Red Sea, the staging of which elicited howls of derision.

On 7 March 1819 Rossini presented the opera with a revised third act (the version known today), including the prayer, 'Dal tuo stellato soglio', one of Rossini's most popular compositions. In 1827 he presented *Mosè in Egitto* in a revised form, *Moïse*, at the Paris Opéra (see below).

SYNOPSIS

Act I Afflicted by the plague of darkness, Pharaoh agrees to let the Israelites depart from Egypt. In response to the prayers of Moses, the light returns. Osiride, the crown prince, and Elcia lament their resulting separation. Pharaoh, induced by Osiride to revoke his permission, confronts Moses, who brings a new plague of hailstones and fiery rain.

Act II Again Pharaoh agrees to let the Israelites go, after which he will marry his son to the princess of Armenia. Osiride and Elcia hide but are caught by Aaron and Queen Amaltea, who has protected the Israelites during their bondage in Egypt. Pharaoh once more revokes his permission and Moses threatens the death of Osiride and the other Egyptian first-born at God's hand. Amaltea vainly tries to tell Pharaoh about Osiride and Elcia. Moses and Elcia are brought before Pharaoh and Osiride; revealing that she is Osiride's wife, Elcia offers her life for that of Moses and the Israelites' freedom. When Osiride raises his sword to kill Moses, he is struck dead by a bolt of lightning.

Act III On the shores of the Red Sea, Moses and the Israelites pray for God's help. The waters part. The Egyptian army pursues the Israelites and is overwhelmed by the sea.

What gives the work its particular profile is its treatment of the biblical story. Rossini employs massive ensembles, choral movements, and declamatory solos to relate the story of the exodus from Egypt. The music associated with Moses is in large part declamatory, noble recitative that gives the character weight and dignity. Innovative is the orchestral introduction (the opera has no overture), with a threefold unison C for the entire orchestra, after which the curtain rises on a dark stage, the chorus bewailing in C minor the plague of darkness. Only after the Egyptians vow to free the Israelites does Moses invoke the Lord; the return of light is marked by a radiant change to C major. The interaction of C minor and C major dominates the opera.

RECORDING Anderson, Gal, Browne, Fisichella, Palacio, Lewis, Nimsgern, Raimondi, Ambrosian Opera Ch, Philharmonia O, Scimone, Philips, 1982
EDITIONS f.ss., Ratti, Cencetti, 1825–6; facsimile of the autograph manuscript, Garland, 1979; v.s., Boieldieu, 1822

Adina, o Il califfo di Bagdad

Adina, or The Caliph of Baghdad
Farsa in one act (1h 15m)
Libretto by the Marchese Gherardo Bevilacqua-Aldobrandini, related to Felice Romani's libretto for Francesco Basili, *Il califfo e la schiava* (1819)
Commissioned 1818

PREMIERES 22 June 1826, Teatro São Carlo, Lisbon; UK: 27 June 1968, Holywell Music Room, Oxford (English Bach Festival)

Rossini was commissioned to write his last one-act farsa by Diego Ignazio de Pina Manique, police superintendent of Lisbon and inspector of the Portuguese theatres. Rossini apparently had little enthusiasm for the project and refused to write an overture, saying it was not in his contract. In fact, the only pieces newly composed for the opera are the introduction, a quartet, and the final aria for Adina; Rossini also prepared Adina's cavatina, although partially basing it on previous music. Most other numbers are taken without change from earlier operas, especially *Sigismondo*. *Adina* shares its plot and a number of verses with a libretto Romani wrote in 1819; that leaves some uncertainties concerning the date of composition of the opera.

The story belongs to the tradition of abductions from various Middle-Eastern seraglios. The Caliph of Baghdad is in love with a slave girl, Adina. She is torn between affection for him and for her former beloved, Selimo, who has reappeared. With the help of Mustafa, his servant, Selimo convinces Adina to elope, but they are discovered and arrested. When Selimo is condemned to death, Adina faints. At that moment, the Caliph discovers she is wearing a medallion that reveals her to be his long-lost daughter.

Despite its compositional history and conventional libretto, *Adina* functions reasonably well as a musical drama. The ensembles Rossini composed for the opera, and Adina's final aria, are fully developed compositions with an attractive melancholy tone.

RECORDING Adani, Spina, Andreolli, Pedani, Tadeo, Cantori Pisani, O of Angelicum, Milan, Rigacci, Voce, 1963
EDITIONS v.ss., Ricordi, 1859; OTOS, 1977

Ricciardo e Zoraide

Dramma in two acts
Libretto by Francesco Berio di Salsa, after Niccolò Forteguerri's *Ricciardetto* (1716–25)
PREMIERES 3 December 1818, Teatro San Carlo, Naples; UK: 1823, King's Theatre, Haymarket, London

Rossini exploited the abundance of lyrical and dramatic situations in *Ricciardo e Zoraide* through a profusion of exquisite numbers. That these were highly appreciated by his contemporaries is evidenced by the opera's thoroughly respectable career in European theatres for over 20 years.

Agorante, King of Nubia, has conquered the Asian prince Ircano and kidnapped his daughter Zoraide; Agorante intends to repudiate his wife, Zomira, and marry Zoraide. Zoraide's beloved, the Christian knight Ricciardo, comes to rescue her, disguised as an African. Agorante proposes a duel between a crusader and an African champion; he appoints the disguised Ricciardo champion, and a mysterious knight appears to fight him – Ircano. Zomira plots revenge. Pretending to abet the lovers' escape, she prepares a trap. With Ircano, wounded in the duel, they are condemned to death. Agorante agrees to spare Ircano's life in return for Zoraide's love, to which she reluctantly agrees. At that moment the knight Ernesto arrives with his troops and defeats the Africans. Ricciardo spares the lives of Agorante and Zomira, while Ircano consents to the union of Ricciardo and Zoraide.

Ensembles dominate the work: indeed, the major characters have only a single solo number each. There are three major duets, a trio, a quartet, several choral movements, and an impressive first-act finale. *Ricciardo e Zoraide* is the first opera in which Rossini employed a stage band.

EDITIONS   f.ss., Fondazione Rossini/Ricordi (on hire), 1990; facsimile of the early printed edition, Garland, 1980; v.s., Fondazione Rossini/Ricordi (on hire), 1990

Ermione
Hermione

Azione tragica in two acts (2h)
Libretto by Andrea Leone Tottola, after the play
Andromaque by Jean Racine (1667)
PREMIERES   27 March 1819, Teatro San Carlo, Naples; UK: 10 April 1992, Queen Elizabeth Hall, London (concert); US: 26 June 1992, San Francisco Opera (concert)
CAST   Ermione *s*, Andromaca *a*, Pirro *t*, Oreste *t*, Cleone *ms*, Pilade *t*, Fenicio *b*, Cefisa *a*, Attalo *t*; *satb* chorus of lords of Epirus, Phrygian prisoners, followers of Oreste, Spartan maidens
FULL ORCHESTRA   onstage: band

Of all Rossini's mature operas, *Ermione* made the least impression on his contemporaries; despite a superb cast for its premiere (Colbran, Pesaroni, Nozzari and David), it was soon forgotten and never revived during Rossini's lifetime. Yet Rossini treasured it and spoke of it in later years as his 'little *William Tell*'. In its protagonist he created one of the most fully developed characters in 19th-century Italian opera.

SYNOPSIS
Act I   Orestes, already pursued by the Furies for having murdered his mother Clytemnestra and her husband Aegisthus, arrives at the court of Pyrrhus, son of Achilles, leading a Greek delegation. They seek the death of Astyanax, to prevent this child of Hector from ever trying to avenge his father. Using the boy as a pawn, Pyrrhus wrests from his captive mother, Andromache, a promise to marry him.

Act II   Pyrrhus' legitimate wife Hermione (daughter of Menelaus and Helen) plays on Orestes' passion for her to persuade him to kill Pyrrhus. Orestes, returning with the bloody dagger, describes the murder of Pyrrhus at the wedding ceremony. Hermione turns on Orestes in fury, berating him for not having understood that she still loves Pyrrhus. Together they acknowledge the Furies that have driven Orestes to this fate. Hermione swoons and Orestes is dragged off by the fleeing Greeks.

Rossini treats this powerful tale of passion and murder with the utmost artistic integrity. This is focused primarily on the musical realization of the four major characters, as he constantly presses against convention to realize dramatic ends. Each character has a major aria, and there are four intensely dramatic duets: Pyrrhus encounters each woman once, and there are two especially impressive encounters for Orestes and Hermione (one of which opens the first-act finale). Yet the chorus and minor characters participate in most of these numbers, giving them greater dramatic weight.

Rossini's willingness to mix elements from different musical genres is apparent already in the overture, during which a men's chorus of Trojan prisoners sings from behind the curtain. The gran scena for Hermione in Act II is Rossini's finest achievement in a genre that goes back to *Ciro in Babilonia* and recurs in several serious operas. The quality of the recitative is noteworthy. Hermione passes through three lyrical sections of intensely contrasting emotions: grief, love and anger. After Orestes and the chorus enter, the crescendo, already heard in the overture, is transformed to a *pianissimo* accompaniment. In her *cabaletta* Hermione thinks only of revenge. Her melodic line, extremely irregular, flies chromatically from one measure to another and soars in coloratura to its cadence. The final duet for Orestes and Hermione, with its preceding scene of dramatic declamation for Hermione alone, has its roots in French tragédie-lyrique. Rossini is sensitive to each nuance of the text. Modern revivals of the opera have confirmed that *Ermione* holds a special place among Rossini's works.

RECORDINGS   1. Gasdia, Zimmerman, Palacio, Merritt, Matteuzzi, Alaimo, Ch of Radio Budapest, Monte Carlo PO, Scimone, Erato, 1986; 2. Caballé, Horne, Merritt, Blake, Surian, Philharmonic Ch of Prague, O Giovanile Italiana, Kuhn, Legato, 1987; the latter is a live recording of the critical edition from the Rossini Opera Festival, Pesaro
EDITIONS   f.s., Fondazione Rossini/Ricordi (on hire), 1987; v.ss., Ricordi, 1858; Fondazione Rossini/Ricordi (on hire), 1987

Eduardo e Cristina
Edward and Christina

Dramma per musica in two acts
Libretto by Giovanni Schmidt for Stefano Pavesi (1810), with revisions by Gherardo Bevilacqua-Aldobrandini and Andrea Leone Tottola (1819)
PREMIERES   24 April 1819, Teatro San Benedetto, Venice; US: 25 November 1834, New York

Eduardo e Cristina is a pastiche for which Rossini, not having had time to write a new work in the month following the premiere of *Ermione*, largely borrowed numbers from *Adelaide di Borgogna*, *Ermione*, and *Ricciardo e Zoraide*, supplementing them with new choruses, a duettino, and a 'battle and skirmish'. A bass aria, 'Questa man la toglie a morte', is actually taken over from Pavesi's original setting of Schmidt's libretto in 1810. Following the tradition of northern theatres in these years, Rossini reverted to *secco* recitative instead of the accompanied recitative of the Neapolitan serious operas.

King Carlo of Sweden wants to marry his daughter Cristina to Prince Giacomo of Scotland, but discovers that the princess is already married to Eduardo, a loyal officer of the Swedish army, and has borne his child. Carlo condemns to death Cristina, Eduardo, and the child. Giacomo is willing to marry Cristina even though she is a mother, but Cristina prefers to die with her husband and son. When Russian forces suddenly attack Sweden, however, Eduardo is called upon to lead the country's defence. He returns victorious, and the grateful king forgives him and embraces Cristina and his grandson.

Despite its origins as a pastiche, *Eduardo e Cristina* was enthusiastically received by Venetian audiences. The local newspaper reported that the performance took six hours because the public demanded repetitions of almost every piece. It is significant, however, that the history of the opera demonstrates it was heavily altered from revival to revival. In this, *Eduardo e Cristina* was different from most of Rossini's Neapolitan operas, whose performance traditions show relatively stable texts.

EDITION v.s., Carli, 1826–7

La donna del lago
The Lady of the Lake
Melodramma in two acts (2h 15m)
Libretto by Andrea Leone Tottola, after the poem *The Lady of the Lake* by Sir Walter Scott (1810)
PREMIERES 24 October 1819, Teatro San Carlo, Naples; UK: 18 February 1823, King's Theatre, Haymarket, London; US: 26 August 1829, New York
CAST Giacomo (James) V (Uberto of Snowdon) *t*, Douglas of Angus *b*, Rodrigo of Dhu *t*, Elena *s*, Malcolm Groeme *a*, Albina *s*, Serano *t*, Bertram *t*; *satb* chorus of Scottish shepherds and shepherdesses, bards, Scottish lords and ladies, Clan Alpine warriors, huntsmen, royal guards
ORCHESTRATION 2 fl/2 picc, 2 ob, 2 cl, 2 bsn, 4 hn, 2 tpt, 3 trbn, timp, bd, cym, triangle, hp, str; onstage: 6 hn, band

La donna del lago is the most Romantic of Rossini's Italian operas. The source of its libretto is a good clue to its character, being drawn not from the general stock of 17th- or 18th-century French tragedy but rather from a narrative by Sir Walter Scott. Interest in things Scottish was fashionable throughout Europe in this period, and the 'Ossianic' poems of James Macpherson captured a large following, but *La donna del lago* was the first operatic setting in Italy of a libretto based on Scott. The poem was apparently brought to Rossini's attention by a young French composer, Désiré-Alexandre Batton, who was studying in Italy. The spirit and essential story of Scott's poem are respected, and Tottola supplied Rossini with a framework that excited the composer's musical imagination. What makes the opera so unusual in the context of Rossini's works is its local colour, derived largely from Scott. In this, *La donna del lago* clearly anticipates *Guillaume Tell*. Although Rossini does not seem to have quoted Scottish tunes, elements such as the so-called Scotch snap rhythm and the use of hunting horns (six solo horns onstage in the introduction) and bardic harps pervade the score.

The atmospheric writing is particularly apparent in the large ensembles opening and closing Act I.

To favour the tenor Giacomo Rubini, Rossini inserted an aria from *Ermione* into the opera at a later revival in Naples; for a Parisian revival he also inserted two numbers from *Bianca e Falliero* into Act II, replacing the difficult trio. Under normal circumstances, however, there can be little doubt that the original version of *La donna del lago* is preferable.

SYNOPSIS
In 16th-century Scotland, King Giacomo V is trying to subdue the Alpine Clan of the Highlands. Among the Highlanders are the chieftain Rodrigo (Roderick) of Dhu, Malcolm Groeme and Douglas of Angus.

Act I At dawn, around Lake Katrine, the shepherds return to work ('Del dì la messaggiera'). Elena crosses the lake on a small boat, singing of her love for Malcolm ('Oh mattutini albori!'). She comes across Uberto (King Giacomo in disguise), who claims to have lost his fellow huntsmen. He is struck by her beauty. She offers him hospitality, and they sail to the island in the middle of the lake, the site of her father's cottage. Huntsmen appear, vainly looking for Uberto ('Uberto! ah! dove t'ascondi?'). In the cottage, Uberto learns that Elena's father is Douglas, once a trusted follower of the king – now a rebel against his rule. Douglas, sheltered by the warrior Rodrigo, has agreed to reward him with Elena's hand. Elena's friends sing of her imminent wedding with Rodrigo ('D'Inibaca donzella'). She alludes to her love for another, and the infatuated Uberto mistakenly imagines himself to be the fortunate one ('Le mie barbare vicende'). Everyone leaves, and Uberto is escorted back to shore. Malcolm, returning to the island after a long absence, enters the deserted room and sings of his love for Elena ('Elena! oh tu, che chiamo!'). Serano informs him that Rodrigo's troops are gathering in a valley nearby. Hearing Elena and Douglas enter the room, Malcolm hides. Elena angers her father by resisting the wedding ('Taci, lo voglio'). When Douglas leaves, Elena and Malcolm swear they will die rather than renounce their mutual love ('Vivere io non potrò'). In the valley, Rodrigo is joyously received by his warriors (chorus 'Qual rapido torrente' and cavatina 'Eccomi a voi, miei prodi'). Douglas leads in Elena, and Rodrigo is struck by her lack of enthusiasm (chorus 'Vieni, o stella' and first finale 'Quanto a quest'alma amante'). Malcolm joins them; his reaction on hearing of Elena's engagement leads Rodrigo to suspect Elena's secret love. But the royal troops are approaching, and everyone joins the bards in a warlike chorus ('Già un raggio forier').

Act II Uberto desires to see Elena again, in order to declare his love ('Oh fiamma soave'). Disguised as a shepherd, he reaches the cavern where Elena is taking shelter during the battle. She reveals her love for Malcolm. Respecting her feelings, he gives her a ring that he claims to be a gift from the king: should she or her family ever be in danger, she must show the ring to the king in person, and he will protect her. When Rodrigo arrives, Uberto declares himself to be on the king's side ('Alla ragion deh rieda'). The two challenge each other to a duel and leave together. Malcolm is lamenting his loss of Elena ('Ah si pera: ormai la morte') when he hears that the Alpine Clan has been defeated by the royal troops and that Rodrigo is dead. Douglas goes to the royal castle of Stirling and offers his life to the king in exchange for his people's safety. Elena also goes to the castle, to beg mercy for her father by showing the ring. In the final scene in the throne hall, Elena hears Uberto singing ('Aurora! ah sorgerai'); when she sees him before the assembled court, she realizes that Uberto is actually the king. Giacomo forgives Douglas and Malcolm and joins the latter in marriage with Elena, who rejoices in her happiness ('Tanti affetti in tal momento').

Nearing the end of his Neapolitan career, Rossini was fully in control of his expanded musical style, using more and longer ensembles, with a corresponding decrease in the prominence of solo arias, a more dramatic accompanied recitative, and a chorus that has become a participant in the action. The forms of *Tancredi* seem rudimentary in comparison with the complexity and originality of *La donna del lago*. The introduction, for example, encompasses: a chorus of shepherds and hunters; a solo for Elena ('Oh mattutini albori!'), one of the most beautiful melodies Rossini ever wrote; a scene between Elena and the incognito king; their duet based on Elena's solo; and a final chorus of huntsmen that draws on melodic ideas from the opening chorus. In the final tableau of the act, the Scottish warriors sing a martial piece to the accompaniment of trumpets and stage band. Then the Scottish bards sing a hymn to the warriors, to the accompaniment of harp, violas and celli *pizzicato*, and a single double-bass – a fine orchestral effect. Finally, in the *stretta*, Rossini brings all the tunes together contrapuntally, with full orchestra, three separate choruses, soloists, band, trumpets and harp. Throughout the opera Rossini makes unusual use of counterpoint. When Elena and Uberto sing together in the introduction, Elena's original solo tune is treated to imitative counterpoint. In the final return of the *cabaletta* theme of the long Act I duet, the theme is imitated between the voices.

This tunefulness is an important aspect of *La donna del lago*. There are moments of tender pathos. The 'duettino' for Elena and Malcolm in Act I, 'Vivere io non potrò', is an intimate composition: the orchestra is restricted to strings, clarinets and bassoons. Subtle harmonic effects show Rossini's mastery of detail. When Rodrigo's bluster turns to thoughts of Elena, the music of 'Ma dov'è colei che accende' is of extraordinary sweetness and delicacy, again seconded by an almost chamber orchestration. In contrast are the vocal fireworks of the two arias for Malcolm and the final rondo for Elena: *bel canto* at its finest.

RECORDING Ricciarelli, Valdenassi, Valentini Terrani, Gonzáles, Ramey, Raffanti, Di Credico, D'Uva, Philharmonic Ch of Prague, CO of Europe, Pollini, CBS, 1983: complete recording, live from the Rossini Opera Festival, based on the critical edition
EDITIONS f.s., Fondazione Rossini, 1990; v.ss., Carli, 1822–3; Fondazione Rossini/Ricordi (on hire), 1981

Bianca e Falliero, o sia Il consiglio dei Tre

Bianca and Falliero, or The Council of Three

Melodramma in two acts (3h)
Libretto by Felice Romani, after the play *Blanche et Montcassin* by Antoine-Vincent Arnault (1798)
PREMIERES 26 December 1819, La Scala, Milan; US: 7 December 1987, Greater Miami Opera, Miami
CAST Priuli *b*, Contareno *t*, Capellio *b*, Loredano *spoken role*, Falliero *a*, Bianca *s*, Costanza *ms*, Pisani *t*, officer *t*, bailiff *t*; *satb* chorus of senators, noblemen and women, bailiffs, soldiers, servants
FULL ORCHESTRA with cont

Although structurally conservative by comparison with the Neapolitan operas of the same period, *Bianca e Falliero* is an opera of such musical riches in harmonic style, melodic character, and orchestral subtlety that one still recognizes the fully mature Rossini. It also provides a host of vocal opportunities for fine singers. Felice Romani, the most accomplished librettist of the period, provided Rossini with four distinct personalities to depict musically, although he was also responsible for changing the original tragic ending of the source to an unlikely happy one. The cast was excellent, including many who had sung other Rossinian roles. A fine orchestra and an accomplished set designer, Alessandro Sanquirico, completed the recipe for success. The opera had 39 performances, the longest initial run ever enjoyed by a Rossini opera at La Scala.

SYNOPSIS

Act I Capellio and Contareno, two senators of Venice, look forward to the resolution of a dispute through Capellio's marriage to Contareno's daughter Bianca. She loves the victorious general Falliero and is stunned when Contareno names Capellio as her future husband; she submits when her father threatens to disown her and ruin Falliero's career. Bianca tells Falliero of her father's opposition.

Act II In a final meeting, Falliero begs Bianca to elope with him. To avoid the approach of Contareno, Falliero climbs over a wall bordering the Spanish embassy. Capellio comes to sign the marriage contract; Bianca refuses and Capellio leaves in anger. The chancellor Pisani reports that Falliero has been caught in the Spanish embassy and will be tried as a traitor by the Council of Three: Loredano, Capellio and Contareno. Believing Bianca unfaithful to him and destined for Contareno, Falliero refuses to defend himself before the Council and agrees to sign a confession. He is prevented from doing so by the appearance of an unknown witness: Bianca. When she explains what has happened, Capellio refuses to condemn Falliero; the case is remanded to the Senate, which absolves Falliero. Capellio does not press his suit on Bianca and Contareno resigns himself to her marriage with Falliero.

The external framework of *Bianca e Falliero* might suggest a conservative opera: 11 large-scale numbers, with five arias, joined by *secco* recitative, and with accompanied recitative reserved for points of emphasis; and a traditional overture of the kind Rossini was avoiding in his Neapolitan works. But the score reveals a complexity of musical style and beauty of line that gives the opera a well-defined character. With few exceptions, the music is newly composed and Rossini's autograph manuscript shows an unusual sensitivity to detail. (The most important borrowing is Bianca's final rondo, adapted – with many changes – from the rondo for Elena that concludes *La donna del lago*.) Among the particular beauties of *Bianca e Falliero* must be numbered the chorus 'Negli orti di Flora' sung by Bianca's ladies-in-waiting and her cavatina 'Della rosa il bel vermiglio' with its lilting *cabaletta*; the brilliant duet for Bianca and Falliero, 'Sappi che un dio crudele' (in which the sections are thematically related); the prison scene for Falliero, and the quartet of Act II, 'Cielo, il mio labbro ispira'.

RECORDINGS 1. Ricciarelli, Horne, Orciani, Merritt, Gavazzi, Riva, Surian, Philharmonic Ch of Prague, London Sinfonietta Opera O, Renzetti, Legato Classics, 1986: live recording using the critical edition from the 1986 Rossini Opera Festival, Pesaro
EDITIONS f.s., Fondazione Rossini/Ricordi (on hire), 1986; v.ss., Ricordi, 1828; Fondazione Rossini/Ricordi (on hire), 1986

Maometto II

Dramma per musica in two acts (3h)
Libretto by Cesare della Valle, after his own play *Anna Erizo* (1820)
PREMIERES 3 December 1820, Teatro San Carlo, Naples; US: 17 September 1988, War Memorial Opera House, San Francisco
CAST Paolo Erisso *t*, Anna *s*, Calbo *a*, Condulmiero *t*, Maometto II *b*, Selimo *t*; *satb* chorus of Muslim ladies, Venetian soldiers, Muslim soldiers
ORCHESTRATION 2 fl/2 picc, 2 ob, 2 cl, 2 bsn, 4 hn, 2 tpt, 3 trbn, serpentone, hp, timp, bd, cym, triangle, bells, sd, str; onstage: band

Rossini wrote *Maometto II* at the height of his Neapolitan career. Although it was not a popular success, he must have felt great confidence in what was to prove his next-to-last opera for Naples, for he chose this work to open the Venetian Carnival season of 1823 and to revise it for his début at the Paris Opéra in 1826, where it became *Le siège de Corinthe* (see below).

Maometto II sets a love story against the background of historical events, the wars between the Turks and the Venetians, culminating in the fall of Negroponte in 1476. (For Paris the locale was shifted to Corinth, since wars between Greeks and Turks were topical in the 1820s.) In the Naples and Paris versions, the Turks destroy Negroponte/Corinthe; in Venice, the Venetians are victorious, and Rossini instructed his copyist to close the resulting happy ending with the final rondo, 'Tanti affetti in tal momento', from *La donna del lago*.

In some ways *Maometto II* is Rossini's most ambitious opera. Here he avoids altogether many 'standard' formal conventions of Italian opera, which he had codified almost single-handedly during the preceding decade, while expanding other forms internally. One can trace stages of the development from *Otello* onwards. But in *Maometto II* Rossini carried his art beyond the capabilities of his Neapolitan audience. That he knew this all too well is seen in the gradual retrenchment after *Maometto II*; in *Semiramide* (1823) Rossini regains a more classical pose, though one that shows the influence of the Neapolitan experiments. To help ensure the success of the opera in Venice and Paris, he smoothed out the more audacious elements of the score. Yet in *Maometto II*, we find a work that brings together Rossini's pre-eminent gift for music of immediate appeal and vocal splendour with a considered and profound understanding of musical and dramatic structure. An opera of greater unity than the revised *Siège de Corinthe*, it is a key work in the history of Italian opera during the early 19th century and gives a clear vision of the directions Rossini might have pursued further had his career as a composer of Italian opera not ended a few years later.

SYNOPSIS (Naples version)
Act I The local governor, Paolo Erisso, is holding a council: Negroponte is besieged by the Turks, led by Maometto; Constantinople has fallen. General Condulmiero proposes surrender, but the young general Calbo urges them to resist. Meanwhile Erisso's daughter Anna laments her father's peril ('Ah che invan su questo ciglio'). Erisso arrives with Calbo, and proposes that Anna marry him. She cannot conceal her secret affection for a young man called Uberto, whom she met in Corinth during her father's absence. But the real Uberto had been with Erisso at the time, and Anna is abashed to find she has been duped by an impostor ('Ohimè qual fulmine'). Gunfire interrupts them. As the men leave, Anna hurries to the church, where the women tell her a traitor has opened the gates to the Turks. They join in a prayer ('Giusto Cielo'). Erisso and Calbo appear with the news that the Turks will not venture farther until daylight. Erisso sends forces to the citadel; Anna, together with other women, offers to join the defenders of the city ('Figlia, mi lascia'). Refusing, Erisso gives her a dagger with which to kill herself should she be captured. Anna and the women seek refuge in the church. At daylight Turkish soldiers appear, threatening fire and slaughter ('Dal ferro, dal foco'). Maometto acknowledges the obeisance of his followers ('Sorgete!'). With his vizier Selimo he plans the assault on the citadel. Maometto reveals that he knows the city, having once travelled in Greece as a spy. Warriors bring news that the Venetian leaders have been seized ('Signor, di liete nuove'). Calbo and Erisso are brought forward in chains. When Erisso discloses his identity Maometto is momentarily confused. He asks if Erisso was governor of Corinth and if he is a father. Learning this is so, he offers to spare him and the prisoners if Erisso will persuade his men to open the gates of the

citadel. Erisso turns to Calbo in his dilemma ('Giusto Cielo') but remains steadfast. Maometto orders them tortured ('Guardie, olà'). Anna rushes from the church. Maometto recognizes her, and she him as the impostor Uberto. She threatens to kill herself if he does not release her father and Calbo, whom she calls her brother. Maometto yields, promising Anna a life of luxury if she will be his. Calbo is moved by Anna's concern, but her father spurns her in shame.

Act II Anna grieves in Maometto's tent. The Muslim girls tell her to enjoy love ('E' follia sul fior degli anni'). Anna is protesting indignantly when Maometto enters. He professes love and repeats his wish to make her queen. Spurning him, Anna begins to weep; Maometto is moved by her distress ('Anna tu piangi'). He orders his troops to mount another assault on the citadel. Anna, fearing for her safety in his absence, asks for a token of security and receives the ultimate proof of his love – the imperial seal of authority. Maometto exhorts his forces to new efforts and takes the standard himself ('All'invito generoso'). Anna is inspired to what she calls 'a task of honour'. Erisso and Calbo have hidden in the crypt of the church. Erisso laments Anna's treachery; Calbo defends her, but to no avail ('Non temer'). When Anna appears Erisso repulses her until she swears fidelity. She gives him Maometto's seal, which will give them free passage through the city. At her request, Erisso marries her to Calbo before the tomb of her mother; the three express their anguish as father and husband prepare for battle, leaving her to almost certain death ('In questi estremi'). Anna hears the women praying in the church ('Nume, cui 'l sole'). They inform her that the Venetians have put the sultan's army to flight; intent on revenge, the Turks are now seeking her ('Sventurata! fuggir sol ti resta'). Anna prepares to meet her fate. The Turks enter the crypt and rush upon her, but her calm demeanour in offering herself to their swords stops them. Maometto enters and demands his seal. Anna reveals that she gave it to her father and Calbo, whom she now names openly as her husband. She stabs herself and falls dying on her mother's tomb.

There are many striking aspects of the music of *Maometto II*. The richness of the orchestration is immediately apparent. Although Rossini uses a full complement of orchestral resources, in each piece he uses only those instruments he truly needs, and many fine effects are achieved with a reduced palette. Rossini also effectively employs thematic transformation and a series of thematic references across the entire work. The introduction, for example, is bracketed by choral movements for the Venetian warriors. Though the two choruses are separated by a lengthy ensemble, Rossini transforms the opening, hesitant, triple-time movement into a strong final section in 4/4, giving the entire number dramatic and musical unity.

Of the five independent arias in the opera, only two – Maometto's cavatina (a show-stopper, timed to unleash a torrent of applause) and Calbo's aria – conclude with regular *cabalettas*. Anna's cavatina is a single slow section; the concluding quick section of Maometto's aria in Act II never develops into a regular *cabaletta*. The final aria for Anna, a multi-sectional piece, also ends without a *cabaletta*; Rossini gives the *dénouement* appropriate musical expression without forcing it into a predetermined mould. Thus *Maometto II* concludes with dialogue for Maometto and Anna over an orchestral crescendo, her suicide, and the horrified reaction of the chorus and Maometto.

But it is in the Act I 'terzettone' (Rossini's own term) that the flexibility of structure is most apparent. In this ensemble Rossini forces us to perceive musical and dramatic events – passing over even a major change of scene – as a single, coherent composition. He does this by assuming and playing on our knowledge of the way ensembles in Italian opera are conventionally constructed. As a result the entire first act of *Maometto II* reduces to only five separate numbers – this in one of Rossini's longest operas.

RECORDING   Anderson, Zimmermann, Palacio, Dale, Ramey, Ambrosian Opera Ch, Philharmonia O, Scimone, Philips, 1983
EDITIONS   f.ss., Fondazione Rossini/Ricordi (on hire), 1985; facsimile of a contemporary manuscript, Garland, 1981; v.ss., Artaria, 1823; Fondazione Rossini/Ricordi (on hire), 1985

Matilde (di) Shabran, o sia Bellezza, e cuor di ferro

Mathilde (di) Shabran, or Beauty and Heart of Stone

Melodramma giocoso in two acts

Libretto by Jacopo Ferretti after François Benoît Hoffmann's libretto for Méhul, *Euphrosine* (1790), and J. M. Boutet de Monvel's play *Mathilde* (1799)

PREMIERES 24 February 1821, Teatro Apollo, Rome; UK: 3 July 1823, King's Theatre, Haymarket, London; US: 10 February 1834, New York

CAST Corradino *t*, Matilde (di) Shabran *s*, Raimondo Lopez *b*, Edoardo *a*, Aliprando *bar*, Isidoro *buffo*, Contessa d'Arco *ms*, Ginardo *b*, Egoldo *t*, Rodrigo *t*; *tb* chorus of guards and peasants; *silent*: peasant women

FULL ORCHESTRA with cont

After the premiere of *Maometto II*, Rossini proceeded to Rome in mid-December 1820, to fulfil what was to be his last commission for that city. The subject was also his last foray into the semiseriagenre. The resulting score is complex and demanding. The composer adapted a few pieces from earlier works: the overture from *Eduardo e Cristina*, a duet and chorus from *Ricciardo e Zoraide*. He also asked the composer Pacini to supply three numbers: the introduction of Act II, a trio ('Padre . . . Figlio . . .'), and part of the duet for Matilde and Edoardo ('No, Matilde, non morrai'). Pacini probably also composed the *secco* recitative.

After some delay, the production was staged. On the opening night Rossini's admirers and opponents engaged in a battle of applause and boos; the victory seemed to go to the Rossinians, but international critics reported a fiasco. None the less, the music pleased, and the opera was widely performed in Italy and abroad. For a revival in Naples later that year,

Rossini replaced the Pacini compositions and the most important borrowed ones with new pieces of his own.

SYNOPSIS

Act I Corradino, a feudal tyrant and woman-hater, lives shut up in his castle and threatens with death those who bother him. A poor poetaster, Isidoro, happens by and is imprisoned for annoying Corradino. Matilde, a spirited and clever young woman, proposes to tame the beast. Corradino refuses to see her, but Aliprando, the castle's physician, is on her side. A rival appears in the person of the proud Countess Arco, but Matilde succeeds in winning over Corradino. Don Raimondo arrives, searching for his son, Prince Edoardo, whom Corradino has imprisoned. The tyrant comes out of the castle to battle with his old enemy, and the countess helps Edoardo escape.

Act II The countess induces Edoardo to write a thank-you note to Matilde, which falls into Corradino's hands. The latter orders Isidoro to push Matilde over a cliff into the sea, but the poet abandons her in the woods instead. When Corradino hears of this, he repents his anger and, fearing she may be dead, goes to find her. She forgives him and they are united.

Rossini's final semiseria opera is written on a grand scale, with many sub-plots, a host of characters and incidents, and a sense of spaciousness that anticipates (in another vein) the style of *Semiramide*. In the introduction Ginardo, the keeper of the tower, describes the dreadful Corradino in great detail, with a back-hand reference to the 'catalogue' aria of *Don Giovanni*: 'He hates the female sex. Beautiful or ugly, if they are women, he hates them all.' In the many ensembles, the individual styles of the comic, serious, and sentimental characters come together as part of a complex whole. There are frequent reminiscences, dramatically and musically, of earlier operas, and the character of Matilde herself has roots in Clarice (*La pietra del paragone*) and Isabella (*L'italiana in Algeri*). None the less, the opera has many beauties of its own.

RECORDING Valdenassi, Casula, Rochow-Costa, Bottazzo, Ercolani, Polotto, Panerai, Trimarchi, Ferrin, Zardo, Ch and O of Teatro Comunale, Genoa, Martinotti, MRF, 1974
EDITIONS f.s., Ratti, Cencetti, 183?; v.s., Artaria, 1822

Zelmira

Dramma in two acts (2h 30m)
Libretto by Andrea Leone Tottola, after the play *Zelmire* by Dormont de Belloy (1762)
PREMIERES 16 February 1822, Teatro San Carlo, Naples; UK: 24 January 1824, King's Theatre, Haymarket, London
CAST Polidoro *b*, Zelmira *s*, Ilo *t*, Antenore *t*, Emma *a*, Leucippo *b*, Eacide *t*, High Priest of Jupiter *b*, Zelmira's child *silent*; *satb* chorus of priests of Jupiter, people of Lesbos, warriors of Mitilene, followers of Ilo
FULL ORCHESTRA including hp; onstage: band

Zelmira was composed with an eye to the proposed Viennese tour of impresario Barbaja's Neapolitan company and opened that season on 13 April 1822. The major roles were written for Naples's fine company: Isabella Colbran (who, between the Neapolitan and Viennese premieres, became the composer's wife), Andrea Nozzari (Antenore), with his unusual extension at the top and bottom registers and a heroic vocal quality, and Giovanni David (Ilo), with a stratospheric range and unsurpassed ability in florid music.

SYNOPSIS

Act I Zelmira, daughter of Polidoro, elderly king of Lesbos, is married to Ilo, a prince of Troy. In Ilo's absence, Lesbos was conquered by Azorre, ruler of Mitilene. Zelmira has hidden Polidoro in the royal mausoleum; pretending to side with Azorre, she announced that her father was in the temple, which Azorre then burned. Antenore, aspiring to rule Mitilene, has secretly had Leucippo assassinate Azorre, accusing Zelmira of the deed. Ilo returns; when Zelmira greets him, they are surrounded by others, so that she has to conceal what has happened. Antenore and Leucippo, plotting to kill Ilo and his son, persuade Ilo that Zelmira has murdered Polidoro and now plans to kill him. The high priest crowns Antenore king. Ilo searches desperately for his son, whom Zelmira has consigned to the care of her friend Emma. Ilo collapses with grief, and Leucippo tries to stab him. Zelmira disarms Leucippo, who promptly accuses her of trying to kill her husband. She is arrested.

Act II Leucippo and Antenore suspect that Polidoro is not dead and free Zelmira in order to discover her father's whereabouts. Polidoro tells Ilo of Zelmira's self-sacrifice, and Ilo takes up arms against Antenore. Leucippo tricks Zelmira into revealing her father's refuge, and Polidoro is captured. In the prison, Antenore and Leucippo are about to kill Polidoro when Ilo and his troops arrive and Antenore and Leucippo are carried off in chains. To general rejoicing Zelmira restores Polidoro to the throne.

In *Zelmira* the experimentation of the preceding years reaches a culmination. Forgoing an overture, the opera begins directly with the introduction, establishing a dark, dramatic tone that dominates much of the work. The harmonic language features intense chromaticism, and the minor mode is much in evidence. Antenore's joy when he is named king is expressed in a theme so rich with syncopations as to leave him (and the listeners) breathless. In almost every piece in *Zelmira* Rossini tries to interpret afresh the conventions of his style. Particularly striking is the quality of the recitatives. The path traversed by Rossini in this area within the space of some six years, from *Otello* to *Ermione* and then to *Zelmira*, gives a measure of the composer's artistic growth.

The opera has public moments of solemnity, lamentation, or terror that reproduce the initial tone of dark drama, but the chromaticism also strikes more intimate chords of pathos. The duettino 'Perché me guardi, e piangi', in which Zelmira entrusts her child to Emma, is one of the most pathetic moments in Rossini's work. The melodic chromaticism has a Bellinian aura; the accompaniment is reduced to harp and cor anglais. In the first recitative of the second finale, when Zelmira and her son are reunited, the use of these two instruments recalls the atmosphere of the duettino and thus the touching moment of separation. Especially in the ensembles one finds pages of a refined, classical style, a celebration of the abstract power of music: the slow section of the first finale (for quintet and chorus) or the *andante* of the quintet perfectly exemplify this ideal of beauty.

RECORDING Gasdia, Fink, Matteuzzi, Merritt, García, Ambrosian Singers, I Solisti Veneti, Scimone, Erato, 1989
EDITIONS f.ss., Ricordi (on hire), 1989; facsimile of the autograph manuscript, Garland, 1979; v.ss., Artaria, 1822; Ricordi (on hire), 1989

Semiramide

Semiramis

Melodramma tragico in two acts (3h 45m)
Libretto by Gaetano Rossi after the play *Sémiramis* by Voltaire (1748)
PREMIERES 3 February 1823, La Fenice, Venice; UK: 15 July 1824, King's Theatre, Haymarket, London; US: 19 May 1937, St Charles Theatre, New Orleans
CAST Semiramide *s*, Arsace *a*, Assur *b*, Idreno *t*, Azema *s*, Oroe *b*, Mitrane *t*, Ghost of Nino *b*, Arbate *silent*; *satb* chorus of Magi, Babylonians, foreigners, ladies-in-waiting; *silent*: satraps, wizards, Babylonians, bards, foreign ladies, royal guards, ministers of the temple, Indians, Scythians, Egyptians, slaves
ORCHESTRATION 2 fl/2 picc, 2 ob, 2 cl, 2 bsn, 4 hn, 2 tpt, 3 trbn, timp, bd, cym, triangle, t-t, str; onstage: band

After his definitive departure from Naples in 1822, Rossini composed only one more opera for Italy, *Semiramide*, which had its premiere at the Teatro La Fenice of Venice almost exactly ten years after the premiere of *Tancredi* at the same theatre. Both were written to libretti by Gaetano Rossi, and both were based on dramas by Voltaire, parallels that are not accidental. After the more tormented and experimental Neapolitan works, Rossini sought to recapture a more classical spirit, one that would gain the favour of a wider public. *Semiramide* occupies a unique place in the Rossini canon: a consolidation of past triumphs and a step towards his future French operas. The work captivated the Venetian public, was performed everywhere in Europe, and remained in the repertoire throughout the 19th century.

SYNOPSIS

Act I In the Babylonian Temple of Baal a throng waits for Queen Semiramide to name the successor to the throne of her husband, Nino, dead for 15 years. Idreno, King of Indus, pays homage ('Là dal Gange'), and Prince Assur, Semiramide's former lover and her accomplice in the murder of Nino, brings offerings ('Sì, sperate'); both aspire to the throne and to the hand of Princess Azema. Semiramide, awaiting the return of the young commander Arsace, whom she loves, reluctantly begins to name the successor; lightning, thunder, and wind

extinguish the sacred altar fire, frightening everyone. Arsace, summoned by Semiramide, arrives in Babylon hoping to marry Azema, who loves him ('Ah! quel giorno'). He brings to the high priest, Oroe, tokens of the dead Nino and a letter that reveals the truth about Nino's murder. Assur reminds Arsace that Azema was betrothed to missing Prince Ninia, but Arsace's love knows no obstacle ('Bella imago degli dei'). In a separate aria, Idreno professes his love to Azema ('Ah dov'è, dov'è il cimento'). In the Hanging Gardens Semiramide anticipates Arsace's arrival ('Bel raggio lusinghier'). When Arsace enters he diffidently tries to tell of his love for Azema, but Semiramide believes he loves her ('Serbami ognor'). The queen demands of her subjects an oath of loyalty to the future king, and then names Arsace as king and consort. The ghost of Nino appears and says Arsace must avenge his death with the blood of the murderers ('Qual mesto gemito'). The crowd wonders who is the guilty one ('Ah! Sconvolto nell'ordine eterno').

Act II Assur tries to force Semiramide to make him king; they each threaten to reveal the other's crime ('Se la vita ancor t'è cara'). Oroe reveals to Arsace that Nino was his father and that his mother, Semiramide, conspired with Assur. Arsace accepts the duty of avenging his father ('In sì barbara sciagura'). Idreno entreats Azema to accept him ('La speranza piu soave'). Arsace tells Semiramide the marriage cannot take place and shows her the accusing scroll; she offers herself as the sacrificial victim. Arsace pities her, but he will follow his father's instructions and descend into his tomb ('Ebben . . . a te: ferisci'). Assur learns that Oroe has turned the people against him. Shaken by a vision of Nino, he vows to kill Arsace ('Deh . . . ti ferma . . .'). He searches for Arsace in the tomb of Nino; Semiramide follows to protect Arsace; Oroe and the Magi are close behind. Groping in the darkness, the three principals are fearful ('L'usato ardir'). When Oroe tells Arsace to strike at Assur, Semiramide steps between them and is killed. Assur is arrested. The horrified Arsace, prevented by Oroe from killing himself, accepts the throne at the behest of the populace.

Continuing Neapolitan developments, *Semiramide* provides attractive vocal opportunities for accomplished singers, and without such singers it makes no sense to perform the work, for Rossini uses this vocalism to project the drama. *Semiramide* is the first of Rossini's non-Neapolitan operas to abandon *secco* recitative: indeed, the accompanied recitative of *Semiramide* is a model of passionate and expressive declamation.

Important differences from its Neapolitan predecessors are the presence of a conventionally constructed overture and a preponderance of arias and duets rather than ensembles. None the less, most of the striking dramatic events in *Semiramide* occur in the three great ensembles, each centred on a supernatural intervention: the expansive introduction, the monumental Act I finale, and the Act II finale.

The arias and duets of *Semiramide* are all constructed according to standard Rossinian design, but in many cases each section is enormously expanded (see, for example, the entries for *Tancredi*, *Armida* and *Maometto II*, where this is already discussed). In duets, the formal confrontation between characters takes place in an opening section, leading to a meditative *cantabile*. Some of the most stunning music in *Semiramide* is found here, including the famous 'Giorno d'orror! . . . e di contento' in the Act II duet for Semiramide and Arsace, after the queen learns he is her son. A short *tempo di mezzo* leads the characters to a new dramatic stance, expressed in the *cabaletta*. Rossini often wrote his most memorable melodies in these duet *cabalettas*: 'Va, superbo, in quella reggia' for Arsace and Assur, or 'Alle più care immagini' in Act I for Semiramide and Arsace. These pieces breathe a majesty and expansiveness that give the opera its sense of monumentality. Even within these numbers, however, there are remarkably original musical and dramatic effects. Most notable is Assur's mad scene preceding the Act II finale, where his tormented mind reels from one emotion to another. Rossini's music leads him graphically through these shifts.

The *andantino* of the Act I finale, in which all swear to obey Semiramide's command, is particularly beautiful: it uses the theme for four horns that Rossini also employs in the overture. But the centrepiece of the finale is the canonic ensemble in which all the characters react to the appearance of the ghost ('Qual mesto gemito'), a passage accompanied by an ostinato rhythmic figure in the orchestra. One of the musical ideas in this ensemble recurs several times during Act II, recalling the ghost of Nino. In the Act II finale the trio 'L'usato ardir' seems suspended in time.

Semiramide represents the apotheosis of musical neo-classicism in Italy. It is the opera to which the next generation of Italian composers returned almost compulsively, both to imitate and to abjure. Its forms provided models. Its sounds resonated in their hearts. But they rejected its classicism, its unabashed glorification of the power of music.

RECORDING Sutherland, Clark, Horne, Serge, Rouleau, Malas, Fyson, Langdon, Ambrosian Opera Ch, LSO, Bonynge, Decca, 1966
EDITIONS f.ss., Fondazione Rossini/Ricordi (on hire), 1990; facsimile of the autograph manuscript, Garland, 1978; v.ss., Artaria, 1823; Fondazione Rossini/Ricordi (on hire) 1990

Il viaggio a Reims, ossia L'albergo del giglio d'oro

The Voyage to Rheims, or The Inn of the Golden Lily
Dramma giocoso in one act (3h)
Libretto by Luigi Balocchi, after the novel *Corinne, ou l'Italie* by Mme de Staël (1807)
PREMIERES 19 June 1825, Théâtre-Italien, Paris; 18 August 1984, Auditorium Pedrotti, Pesaro; US: 12 June 1986, Loretto-Hilton Center, St Louis; UK: 8 June 1987, Guildhall School of Music, London
CAST Corinna *s*, Marquise Melibea *a*, Countess of Folleville *s*, Madame Cortese *s*, Chevalier Belfiore *t*, Count Libenskof *t*,

Lord Sidney *b*, Don Profondo *b*, Baron Trombonok *b*, Don Alvaro *b*, Don Prudenzio *b*, Don Luigino *t*, Maddalena *s*, Delia *ms*, Modestina *ms*, Zefirino *t*, Antonio *b*, Gelsomino *t*; *satb* chorus of musicians, peasants, gardeners, dancers, servants, travellers
ORCHESTRATION picc obbligato, 2 fl, 2 ob, 2 cl, 2 bsn, 4 hn, 2 tpt, 3 trbn, hp, timp, banda turca, str

Rossini's last Italian opera and the first he wrote in France had its premiere as part of the festivities honouring the coronation of Charles X. Although an occasional piece *Viaggio* was calculated to establish Rossini's reputation. Conceived for the greatest voices of the time, including Giuditta Pasta as Corinna, the work requires an exceptional cast: three prima donna sopranos, an alto, two tenors, and four baritones and basses have leading roles. Lavish costumes, magnificent sets, and a ballet for 40 dancers enhanced the splendour. Contemporary reviews were uniformly ecstatic, but Rossini was jealous of this opera. Aware that a work so tied to a particular historical occasion could not hope to circulate widely, he reused about half the music for *Le Comte Ory* in 1828. He was pressed to permit three further performances of *Viaggio*, the proceeds of the last going to charity.

The libretto is inextricably bound to the specific event for which it was written. Hope for a strong Europe at peace, under the leadership of monarchies newly restored after the decisive defeat of Napoleon in 1815, gives symbolic meaning to the international clientele at the inn, and each character during the finale brings his own country's music to the festivities.

The manuscript sources of *Viaggio* were presumed lost until, in the mid-1970s, part of Rossini's autograph was recovered at the Library of the Conservatory Santa Cecilia in Rome. Other sources were located in Paris and Vienna, permitting a reconstruction of the entire work. (The so-called overture to *Il viaggio a Reims*, a 20th-century invention, is derived from a ballet movement written for one of Rossini's French operas: *Viaggio* never had an overture.)

SYNOPSIS

Travellers on their way to the coronation in Rheims are staying overnight at the Inn of the Golden Lily. The inn-keeper, Madame Cortese, and her staff assist them in preparing for the last leg of their journey ('Presto, presto . . . su, coraggio!'). The Parisian Countess of Folleville, learning that the carriage bringing her wardrobe has overturned, laments her loss ('Partir, oh ciel! desio'). Baron Trombonok, keeper of the travellers' purse and a lover of music, is responsible for making final arrangements ('Sì, di matti una gran gabbia'). Other travellers arrive: Don Profondo, an antiquarian; the Spanish admiral Alvaro, who escorts the Marquise Melibea, a Polish widow; a jealous Russian general, Count Libenskof, in love with Melibea. When Madame Cortese enters to explain that their departure has been delayed, Alvaro and Libenskof are already about to duel. From behind the scenes, the Roman poetess Corinna improvises an ode to fraternal love ('Arpa gentil'), and momentary peace returns. An English officer in love with Corinna, Lord Sidney, places flowers at her door ('Invan strappar dal core'). The French chevalier Belfiore tries to woo Corinna, but she wants nothing to do with him ('Nel suo divin sembiante'). Don Profondo lists the possessions the travellers are bringing with them ('Medaglie incomparabili'). The baron and Zefirino inform the travellers that they cannot go to Rheims after all, because no horses remain to take them there ('Ah! A tal colpo inaspettato'). Madame Cortese suggests an alternative: her husband has written to describe the festivities being prepared for the king's return to the capital, and the travellers decide to proceed directly to Paris the next morning. In the meantime, they will give a public banquet that evening. Melibea and the count quarrel; he tries once again to win her hand ('D'alma celeste, oh Dio!') and she finally yields. In the garden the banquet is under way. Musicians and dancers provide entertainment. The baron proposes a series of musical tributes to the royal family, with each singing in his or her own national style. Corinna offers an improvisation in honour of the new king, and the assembled guests (representing all the nations of Europe) proclaim the glory of Charles X and France.

Because the orchestra of the Théâtre-Italien was strengthened with soloists from the Opéra for the first performance of *Viaggio*, instrumental lines could be made particularly demanding (see, for example, the flute solo in the aria of Lord Sidney, 'Invan strappar dal core'). And because each of his singers was a master of Italian vocal style, Rossini could allow his vocal writing to luxuriate in their strengths. Moreover, the musical numbers of *Viaggio* perfectly realize the dramatic situations. The Countess of Folleville's aria of misery over the loss of her finery is delectable, precisely because of the contrast between the grandeur of the musical expression and the triviality of the dramatic cause. In Don Profondo's aria ('Medaglie incomparabili'), he is preparing a list of the effects of each traveller so that luggage can be prepared for the journey. He invokes each traveller and writes down what each will be bringing; each strophe characterizes a single person.

The 'Gran Pezzo Concertato a 14 Voci' ('Ah! A tal colpo inaspettato') is one of the glories of *Viaggio*. A slow opening section of astonishment, largely unaccompanied, is motivated by the news that no horses are available. In the second, quick section, the letter from Madame Cortese's husband in Paris alters the dramatic situation. The final section is constructed as a formal *cabaletta*, in which the characters react to the altered circumstances. The overwhelming effect of the audacious scoring for fourteen solo voices may be seen most clearly in the Rossini crescendo that serves as the concluding section of the *cabaletta* theme. The first phrase is sung by two voices, the second by nine, and the third by all fourteen.

The national toasts of the finale are either taken from patriotic hymns or based on national musical

styles. Among the melodies that flow past are Haydn's 'Gott erhalte Franz den Kaiser', 'God Save the King' and the French 'Charmante Gabrielle'. They are joined by a polonaise, a Russian hymn, a Spanish song, and a tyrolese complete with yodels. The entire company joins in an apotheosis of Charles X to the well-known French song 'Vive Henri Quatre'.

RECORDING Gasdia, Cuberli, Ricciarelli, Valentini Terrani, Giménez, Araiza, Nucci, Dara, Raimondi, Ramey, Surian, Prague Philharmonic Ch, CO of Europe, Abbado, DG, 1985: complete recording, live from the Rossini Opera Festival of 1984, based on the critical edition
EDITIONS f.s./v.s., Fondazione Rossini/Ricordi (on hire), 1984

Le siège de Corinthe

The Siege of Corinth
Tragédie-lyrique in three acts (2h 30m)
Libretto by Luigi Balocchi and Alexandre Soumet, after della Valle's libretto (1820) for Rossini's *Maometto II*
PREMIERES 9 October 1826, Théâtre de l'Académie Royale de Musique, Paris; US: 6 February 1833, New York; UK: 5 June 1834, King's Theatre, Haymarket, London
CAST Mahomet II *b*, Cléomène *t*, Pamira *s*, Néoclès *t*, Hiéros *b*, Adraste *t*, Omar *t*, Ismène *s*; *satb* chorus of Turks, Greeks, Muslims
FULL ORCHESTRA including ophicleide

For his first encounter with the audience of the Théâtre de l'Académie Royale de Musique, home of French opera, Rossini faced the task of developing an original synthesis, firmly based in the Italian manner yet appropriate for the French stage, to rouse the ailing Opéra from its torpor. Having to learn French and master the intricacies of its declamation, Rossini approached this task circumspectly. He reserved two Neapolitan works for adaptation to the French stage, withholding them from production at the Théâtre-Italien during his tenure as director. Thus *Maometto II* became *Le siège de Corinthe* and *Mosè in Egitto* became *Moïse*.

SYNOPSIS
Following the plan of *Maometto II* with the place, time, names of characters, and some plot details changed, the opera relates the victory of the Turks over the Greeks at Corinth in 1459.

Act I Cléomène, governor of Corinth, has promised the hand of his daughter, Pamira, to the young officer Néoclès, but Pamira is in love with a man named Almanzor whom she knew in Athens. When the Turks enter the city, Mahomet confides to his friend, Omar, that his thoughts still dwell on the Greek girl he met while travelling under the name of Almanzor. The remainder of the first act follows the events of Act I of *Maometto II*.

Act II Pamira, in Mahomet's tent awaiting her wedding, prays to her dead mother for guidance. Ismène, her confidante, arrives with women who joyfully anticipate the wedding, dancing and singing a marriage hymn. Néoclès tries to prevent the wedding;

the Greek battle call interrupts and Pamira, leaving with Néoclès, swears she will die with her own people.

Act III Néoclès brings Pamira to her father in the catacombs, where the Greeks have prepared their last defence. When the victorious Turks burst in, Pamira stabs herself. Flames engulf the stage, for the Greeks have set fire to their city, leaving only ruins to the conquerors.

In *Maometto II* extremely florid vocal lines co-exist with experiments in musical structure. In *Le siège de Corinthe* both extremes are planed down, resulting in a more consistent, if less audacious, dramatic continuum and a reduced gulf between declamatory lines and florid passages. In some reworked passages much of the original vocal splendour is lost. Similarly modifying the bolder structural experiments, Rossini eliminated internal sections from the 'terzettone' of *Maometto II*, leaving a truncated and conventional residue. In the solo arias for Mahomet, Pamira and Néoclès he adapted essentially Italian material.

In the newly composed music Rossini continued to explore larger units combining solo voices and chorus more dramatically. The scene in which Hiéros blesses the soon-to-be-martyred Greek warriors is particularly impressive. *Le siège de Corinthe* also features much ceremonial music in the Parisian style: dances, hymns, choruses, and a brilliantly scored overture.

RECORDING Sills, Verrett, Wallis, Theyard, Scano, Díaz, Howell, Lloyd, Ambrosian Opera Ch, LSO, Schippers, EMI, 1975: this recording, in Italian, is based on an edition that distorts Rossini's opera through cuts, manipulations, and insertions (including music by other composers); it is not recommended [P.G.]
EDITIONS f.ss., Troupenas, 1827; *rp*, Garland, 1980; v.ss., Troupenas, 1826; (in Italian) Ricordi, [n.d.]

Moïse et Pharaon, ou Le passage de la Mer Rouge
Moses and Pharaoh, or The Passage through the Red Sea
Opera in four acts (2h 30m)
Libretto by Luigi Balocchi and Etienne de Jouy, after Tottola's libretto (1818 and 1819) for *Mosè in Egitto*
PREMIERES 26 March 1827, Théâtre de l'Académie Royale de Musique, Paris; UK: 20 April 1850, Covent Garden, London (as *Zora*); US: 7 May 1860, Academy of Music, New York
CAST Moïse *b*, Pharaoh *b*, Aménophis *t*, Eliézer *t*, Osiride *b*, Aufide *t*, Sinaïde *s*, Anaï *s*, Marie *s*, a mysterious voice *b*; satb chorus of Egyptians and Israelites
FULL ORCHESTRA including ophicleide and hp

Mosè in Egitto was already known in Paris in its revised version. The original three-act libretto by Tottola, in its 1819 adaptation, was extended to four acts by the French revisers, who expanded the original action, placed the Italian pieces (supplied with French texts) within this grander context, and provided both appropriate dramatic situations for new musical numbers and connecting recitative. Rossini supervised their work, suppressing the more old-fashioned numbers of *Mosè in Egitto*, while carrying over unchanged the finest music.

SYNOPSIS
The plot of *Moïse* is similar to that of *Mosè in Egitto* (see above), but the names of the characters differ and additional episodes have been inserted.

Act I Moses and the Israelites await the return of his brother, Eliézer, who has gone to Pharaoh to plead the Israelite cause. Pharaoh's son, Aménophis, is in love with Anaï, daughter of the sister of Moses.

Act II This begins with the opening scene of *Mosè in Egitto*. Pharaoh agrees to permit the Israelite departure, and Queen Sinaïde persuades Aménophis to marry the princess of Assyria.

Act III An extended ballet divertissement occurs in the Temple of Isis, where Osiride, the high priest, demands that the Israelites pay homage to the goddess. Pharaoh orders the Israelites bound and expelled from Egypt.

Act IV In the desert near the Red Sea, Aménophis tells Anaï he will give up the throne if she will marry him. Anaï chooses to follow her people; Aménophis warns that Pharaoh will attack them and goes to join his father. On the shores of the sea Moses leads the anxious people in prayer. The sea divides and the Israelites cross over. When the pursuing Egyptians attempt to follow, they are drowned.

Moïse has a more consistent score than its model, but the addition of so much spectacle for Paris weakens the dramatic effect of the work. However strong the new choral opening, transposing the scene of 'darkness' to the beginning of Act II was a strategic error. But Anaï's aria ('Quelle horrible destinée') is a superb addition to the score. One of the most interesting revisions affects Elcia's aria from *Mosè in Egitto*, which is placed in a profoundly different dramatic context in *Moïse*. In *Mosè in Egitto* Elcia pleads with Osiride to marry the Armenian princess and to let her depart with her people. When Osiride threatens to kill Moses, a bolt of lightning strikes him down; Elcia's *cabaletta* expresses her despair. In *Moïse* the piece is sung by Sinaïde, the Egyptian queen and mother of Aménophis (Osiride). She makes the same plea as did Elcia, but now the prince acquiesces, so that the final *cabaletta*, whose music is essentially unchanged, expresses Sinaïde's joy. That it functions well in both contexts is a measure of Rossini's belief that music is 'ideal' in its expression, not imitative of particular emotions.

RECORDINGS 1. (in Italian) Mancini, Rizzoli, Danieli, Filippeschi, Lazzari, De Palma, Taddei, Rossi-Lemeni, Mazzoli, Clabassi, Ch and O of Teatro San Carlo, Naples, Serafin, Philips, 1957; 2. (in French) Le Bris, Saneva, Capderou, Sénéchal, Finel, de Peyer, Massard, Rouleau, Serkoyan, Ch and Symphonic O of French Radio, Matheson, Voce, 1974
EDITIONS f.ss., Troupenas, 1827; *rp*, Garland, 1980; v.ss., Troupenas, 1827; (in Italian) Ricordi, [n.d.]

Le Comte Ory
Count Ory
Opéra [comique] in two acts (2h 15m)
Libretto by Eugène Scribe and Charles Gaspard Delestre-

Poirson, after their own play (1816), based on a medieval ballad
PREMIERES 20 August 1828, Théâtre de l'Académie Royale de Musique, Paris; UK: 28 February 1829, King's Theatre, Haymarket, London; US: 22 August 1831, New York
CAST Count Ory *t*, the Tutor *bar*, Isolier *ms*, Raimbaud *bar*, Countess of Formoutiers *s*, Ragonde, Alice *s*, two knights *t*, *bar*; *satb* chorus of Ory's men, ladies, Crusaders, peasants
ORCHESTRATION picc obbligato, 2 fl, 2 ob, 2 cl, 2 bsn, 4 hn, 2 tpt, 3 trbn, timp, bd, cym, triangle, str

About half of Rossini's music for *Il viaggio a Reims* resurfaced in *Le Comte Ory*. How should one think about an opera in which such a large proportion of the music derives, essentially without change, from a work whose substance is entirely different? How should one think about an opera in which the confusion of identity extends so far as to present a tenor disguised as a woman who thinks he is making love to a soprano, when in fact he is making love to an alto in the role of a man who takes the place of the soprano?

If gender is a problem in the libretto, genre is problematic concerning the opera as a whole. Superficially *Le Comte Ory* might seem to be an opéra comique. That it was conceived not for the Théâtre de l'Opéra-Comique but for the Opéra, however, transforms it. Whereas a typical opéra comique consists of relatively short lyrical numbers separated by spoken dialogue, *Le Comte Ory* is made up of highly developed, even massive musical forms, linked by accompanied recitative. Whereas the orchestration of a contemporary typical opéra comique is relatively light, Rossini's forces are large. Despite the Italianate forms of many of its lyrical numbers, the use of accompanied recitative was at odds with the Italian practice of *secco* recitative for comic operas. Furthermore, there is no hint of buffoonish characters, no exaggeratedly rapid declamation. Instead, *Le Comte Ory* sparkles with Gallic wit, grace and charm.

In the medieval ballad Count Ory and his men give siege to nuns in a convent; their notable success became evident nine months later. Scribe and Delestre-Poirson created a one-act vaudeville first performed in Paris in 1816, changing the nuns to ladies whose husbands are away on a Crusade; the Crusaders return before Count Ory and his men achieve their goal. This becomes essentially Act II of the opera. Act I presents events that are described in an air at the beginning of the vaudeville. The librettists grafted a first act to the vaudeville, arranging the action and poetry so that Rossini's music from *Il viaggio a Reims* could be reused. They were also compelled by the enormous differences between the two genres to rewrite the text of their vaudeville, accommodating another two numbers from *Il viaggio a Reims*. Little wonder they originally declined to have their names on the printed libretto! Yet despite its difficult birth, *Le Comte Ory* works splendidly.

SYNOPSIS
The opera takes place *c.* 1200 in and around the castle of the counts of Formoutiers.

Act I The men are on a Crusade, and their wives have taken a vow of chastity and locked themselves in the castle. In order to court the beautiful Countess Adèle, Count Ory disguises himself as a hermit said to specialize in affairs of the heart, and his friend Raimbaud stirs up interest among the local people. Ragonde, stewardess of the castle, announces that her mistress wishes to consult him ('Jouvencelles, venez vite'). The count's tutor, together with his page Isolier, arrive in search of him. Hearing about the hermit, the tutor becomes suspicious ('Veiller sans cesse'). Isolier, not recognizing his master, seeks advice from the 'hermit' about gaining Adèle's love. When he reveals his plan to penetrate the castle disguised as a female pilgrim, Ory decides to adopt the plan himself ('Une dame de haut parage'). Adèle comes to consult the hermit, who advises her to distrust the page of the notorious Count Ory (Isolier), with whom she confesses to be half in love ('En proie à la tristesse'). The tutor recognizes the count and unmasks him ('Ciel! Ô terreur, ô peine extrême'). A letter arrives announcing the successful conclusion of the Crusade: Adèle's brother and the knights will be home the next day. The ladies invite Ory to celebrate with them, but he resolves to use the time remaining to devise another plan to conquer Adèle.

Act II Within the walls of the castle, the women await their men's return, thankful at having escaped Ory's wiles ('Dans ce séjour calme et tranquille'). Outside a storm is raging and cries of distress are heard. Pilgrim women say they are being threatened by Ory. 'Soeur Colette', who turns out to be the count in disguise, thanks Adèle profusely ('Ah! quel respect, Madame'). Left alone, the 'pilgrim women' revel ('Ah! la bonne folie!'); having discovered the wine cellar, Raimbaud provides wine for all ('Dans ce lieu solitaire'), and they sing a lively drinking song ('Buvons, buvons'). Isolier arrives and reveals the hoax to Adèle. Taking advantage of the darkness of her bedroom, Adèle hides behind Isolier; 'Soeur Colette', deceived by his voice, makes advances to the page, whom he mistakes for the countess ('A la faveur de cette nuit obscure'). When trumpets announce the return of the Crusaders, Count Ory and his men are forced to flee ('Ecoutez ces chants de victoire').

From *Il viaggio a Reims* Rossini salvaged numbers that could be transferred most easily to other dramatic situations. The introduction is from *Viaggio*, though the short overture is new; part of the *air* of the tutor is derived from Lord Sidney's aria; the countess's air from the contessa's aria; the first finale from the 'Gran Pezzo Concertato'; the duet between the count and the countess from that between Corinna and Belfiore; Raimbaud's air from Don Profondo's. Only a single piece in Act I of *Le Comte Ory* is entirely new: the duet for Ory and Isolier. In Act II, however, Rossini reused only two compositions from *Viaggio*.

Although the borrowed numbers are artfully adapted to their new surroundings, there are losses. The carefully wrought structure of Don Profondo's aria, where parallel strophes describe different characters, seems arbitrary as the musical setting for Raimbaud's narrative of his discovery of the castle's wine cellar. But most situations, while different in detail, are structurally and emotionally similar. When the drama or characters are markedly different, Rossini intervened: for the tutor, he altered the first section of Lord Sidney's aria, whose sentimentality was ill-suited to the new laments, and made changes in the *cabaletta* (adding, for example, the canonic obbligato for flute and clarinet in the repetition of the theme).

The jewels of the score are the pieces Rossini prepared directly for *Le Comte Ory*. The choral songs for the count and his followers, as pilgrims, are spirited in tone and subtle in their musical realization. The original ballad tune, heard twice before in the opera, becomes the central episode of the drinking chorus. The Act II trio is magical in the nocturnal and insinuating quality of the opening section, its delicate orchestral shading, its erotic chromaticism, the shifting pairings of the voices. Rossini has centred the drama in the sexual and musical shadows, disguises, and illusions of his score.

RECORDINGS 1. Barabas, Canne-Meier, Sinclair, Oncina, Roux, Wallace, Glyndebourne Festival Ch and O, Gui, EMI, 1956: stylish (though cut) version conducted by a born Rossinian; 2. Jo, Montague, Pierotti, Aler, G. Quilico, Cachemaille, Lyons Opera Ch and O, Gardiner, Philips, 1990: more straight-faced than Gui, Gardiner none the less conducts a superb version (complete) with a cast worthy of the piece [A.B.]

EDITIONS f.ss., Troupenas, 1828; *rp*, Garland, 1978; v.ss., Troupenas, 1828; (in Italian) Ricordi, [1883]

Guillaume Tell
William Tell

Opera in four acts (3h 45m)
Libretto by Etienne de Jouy and Hippolyte Louis-Florent Bis, with additions by Armand Marrast and Adolph Crémieux, after the play *Wilhelm Tell* by Johann Christoph Friedrich von Schiller (1804)
PREMIERES 3 August 1829, Théâtre de l'Académie Royale de Musique, Paris; UK: 1 May 1830, Drury Lane, London (as *Hofer, or The Tell of the Tyrol*); US: 19 September 1831, New York
CAST Guillaume Tell *bar*, Arnold *t*, Walter *b*, Melchthal *b*, Jemmy *s*, Gesler *b*, Rodolphe *t*, Ruodi *t*, Leuthold *b*, Mathilde *s*, Hedwige *a*, Huntsman *b*; *satb* chorus of Swiss, huntsmen, soldiers
ORCHESTRATION picc, 2 fl, 2 ob, ca, 2 cl, 2 bsn, 4 hn, 2 tpt, 3 trbn, timp, bd, cym, triangle, bell, t-t, 2 hp, str; onstage: 4 hn

With *Guillaume Tell* Rossini finally offered Parisian audiences an original opera in French. It was intended to initiate his true career as a French composer, after his years at the Théâtre-Italien and his earlier arrangements at the Opéra. During the months preceding the premiere he struggled to obtain two long-term commitments from the French government: a lifetime annuity and a ten-year contract.

Rossini wove into the historical panorama of *Guillaume Tell* pastoral elements, patriotic deeds

A sketch made in Switzerland by Pierre-Luc-Charles Cicéri before he designed the sets for Guillaume Tell

(much in vogue on the eve of the revolutionary wave soon to sweep Europe), and superbly drawn characters. Yet the development of the libretto, freely derived from Schiller's play, was tormented. The original draft by Etienne de Jouy underwent considerable alteration at various hands. Finally, changes were made during the long rehearsal period and even after the premiere. Some were incorporated into printed editions of the opera (in preparation before the first performance). Others survived in manuscripts of the opera; they have been reconstructed for the critical edition.

What is most fascinating about *Guillaume Tell*, however, is the imaginative way in which its composer responded to the challenge of creating a work for the French Opéra without abandoning his Italian roots. Though certain elements are more 'Italian', others more 'French', it is the combination of these elements that is extraordinary. More than in any other work, Rossini integrates the *bel canto* lyricism and formal refinement of Italian opera with the declamatory immediacy and scenic splendour (the latter expressed in extensive choruses and ballet) characteristic of French opera. The grandiose structure, finally, is tied together with a system of musical motifs derived from popular Swiss melodies known as *ranz des vaches*.

SYNOPSIS

Act I The action takes place in medieval Switzerland. The villagers at Bürglen, in the canton of Uri, anticipate a triple wedding, the culmination of their traditional festival ('Quel jour serein le ciel présage!'). A fisherman serenades his beloved, while Guillaume Tell laments the tyrannical rule of the Austrians and their governor, Gesler. Melchthal, patriarch of the village, urges his son Arnold to think of marriage, but Arnold, who serves in the Austrian garrison, loves the Habsburg princess Mathilde. Distant horns announce the governor's hunt. As Arnold seeks to rush off to join Mathilde, Tell reappears. He tries to gain Arnold's support against the increasingly oppressive Austrian rule ('Où vas-tu?'). Arnold swears to join Tell when the moment to strike arrives. Melchthal blesses the couples. The festivities proceed with songs, dances, and an archery contest, which Jemmy (Tell's son) wins. His triumph is interrupted by Leuthold, an old herdsman. He has killed an Austrian soldier who was trying to rape his daughter. While Tell ferries Leuthold across the dangerous rapids, Austrian soldiers arrive ('Dieu de bonté'). The Swiss refuse to identify the ferryman; Rodolphe drags Melchthal away as a hostage and orders the soldiers to loot the village.

Act II In the dusk, huntsmen pass ('Quelle sauvage harmonie'), while villagers return to their homes. Mathilde muses on her feelings for Arnold ('Sombre forêt'). When he approaches, they declare their love ('Oui, vous l'arrachez à mon âme'). As Tell and Walter appear, Mathilde hurries off, having agreed to meet Arnold the next day. The men reveal that Gesler has murdered Melchthal; Arnold swears to avenge his father ('Quand l'Helvétie est un champ de supplices'). Representatives of the three cantons arrive. The patriots vow to throw off the Austrian yoke and gain their liberty ('Des profondeurs du bois immense').

Act III Meeting in a ruined chapel near Gesler's palace, Mathilde and Arnold bid each other farewell ('Pour notre amour, plus d'espérance'). In the main square at Altdorf, the townspeople celebrate Gesler's power ('Gloire au pouvoir suprême'), while the soldiers force the Swiss to sing and dance (*pas de trois*, 'Toi qui l'oiseau', and *pas des soldats*) and to bow before a symbol of Gesler's authority. When Tell refuses to bow, Rodolphe recognizes him as the man who saved Leuthold ('C'est là cet archer redoutable'). Having heard of Tell's skill as an archer, Gesler announces that he can save his life only by shooting an apple from Jemmy's head: otherwise, father and son will die together. Sustained by his son's courage, Tell shoots his arrow through the apple ('Sois immobile'). In the general relief that follows, Tell drops a second arrow, held in reserve for the governor, should his first arrow have killed his son. Tell is thrown into chains, but Mathilde takes Jemmy under her own protection. When Gesler orders that Tell be transported across Lake Lucerne and thrown to the reptiles living in the waters of Küssnacht Castle, the riotous reaction of the Swiss is barely contained by the soldiers.

Act IV Arnold visits his birthplace ('Asile héréditaire'). His companions announce that Tell is a prisoner. Arnold shows them where his father and Tell concealed arms for the day of insurrection. Hedwige is about to beg mercy from Gesler, when Mathilde arrives with Jemmy. The princess offers herself as a hostage in return for Tell. The storm breaks. Leuthold reports that Tell's captors have freed his hands, since he alone can control the boat in the storm. Jemmy gives the signal for the revolt. Tell reaches the shore and, with the bow handed to him by Jemmy, kills Gesler. Arnold and his forces capture the castle of Altdorf. As the storm subsides, the Swiss join in a prayer of thanksgiving for the liberation of their country ('Tout change et grandit en ces lieux').

Carefully written, harmonically daring, melodically purged of ornamentation, orchestrally opulent, *Guillaume Tell* represents a final purification of Rossini's style. Ensembles dominate and the interests of the drama are well served. The great overture is unabashedly programmatic, and Rossini's orchestral palette is fuller than ever before. The extensive spectacular elements, ballets, and processions, which derive from French operatic tradition, are effectively integrated into the opera.

Many parts of *Guillaume Tell* adhere to Italian structures, most obviously the duet for Mathilde and Arnold in Act II, Mathilde's aria at the opening of Act III, and Arnold's aria in Act IV – all three part of the dramatically ancillary sub-plot. Also frankly Italianate in design is the Act I finale, whose action comes into focus in two major ensemble movements. Within these structures, however, the music remains highly responsive to details of the drama.

Already during his Neapolitan years Rossini began integrating French elements into his style: concern with declamation, spectacle, chorus and dance. In *Tell* the recitative is extremely powerful, blending into passionate, yet lyrical declamation, enhanced by a consistently rich orchestral texture. This happens especially in complex scenes, such as the Act III finale (including Tell's admonishment to his son) and the concluding scene of the opera. The chorus is central both musically and dramatically, and much of the opera revolves about magnificent choral ensembles such as 'Vierge que les chrétiens adorent' in the Act I finale, or the final ensemble. Some of these choruses are part of large-scale divertissements with ballet.

Act II was particularly appreciated by Rossini's contemporaries, even by hostile critics such as Berlioz. He found 'sublime' the finale, in which the three Swiss cantons, each characterized musically, are called together to plan the revolt. The chorus is the central protagonist of *Guillaume Tell*: the fate of the Swiss people is the subject of the drama. Rossini's quotation and transformation of popular Swiss tunes throughout the melodic fabric of the entire work gives it a strong, unified colour. The whole opera is a rich tapestry of Rossini's most inspired music.

RECORDINGS 1. (in French) Caballé, Mesplé, Taillon, Gedda, Burles, Cassinelli, Bacquier, Fyson, Howell, Hendrickx, Kovács, Christou, Ambrosian Opera Ch, RPO, Gardelli, EMI, 1973; 2. (in Italian) Freni, D. Jones, E. Connell, Pavarotti, Milnes, Ghiaurov, Tomlinson, Ambrosian Opera Ch, National PO, Chailly, Decca, 1979; 3. (in Italian) Studer, Felle, D'Intino, Merritt, Terranova, Gavazzi, Zancanaro, Panariello, De Grandis, Roni, Surian, Noli, Ch and O of La Scala, Milan, Muti, Philips, 1988: live recording based on the critical edition
VIDEO Studer, Merritt, Zancanaro, Ch and O of La Scala, Milan, Muti, Castle, 1989: same, controversial performance as CD version [A.B.]
EDITIONS f.ss., Troupenas, 1829; *rp*, Garland, 1980; Fondazione Rossini, 1992; v.ss., Troupenas, 1829; Fondazione Rossini/Ricordi (on hire), 1988

BIBLIOGRAPHY Philip Gossett (ed.), *Ediz ione critica delle opere di Gioachino Rossini*, Fondazione Rossini, 1979–; Richard Osborne, *Rossini*, Weidenfeld and Nicholson, 1986;

G. Radiciotti, *Gioacchino Rossini: Vita documentata, opere ed influenza su l'arte*, Arti grafiche majella di Aldo Chicca, 1927–9; Stendhal, trans. Richard Coe, *Life of Rossini*, Calder and Boyars, 1970; F. Toye, *Rossini: A Study in Tragi-Comedy*, Norton, 1963; H. Weinstock, *Rossini: A Biography*, OUP, 1968

P.G. and P.B.B.

NINO ROTA

Nino Rota Rinaldi; *b* 3 December 1911, Milan; *d* 10 April 1979, Rome

Although best known outside Italy for his resourceful scores for Fellini's films, Rota also composed fluent, unproblematical music in a wide variety of other genres, including opera. His *Il cappello di paglia di Firenze* is the most frequently performed relatively traditional opera to have appeared in Italy since 1945. His shorter operatic works range from the children's 'musical fable' *Lo scoiattolo in gamba* (*The Clever Squirrel*, 1959) to the radio operas *I due timidi* (1950, staged in London 1952) and *La notte d'un nevrastenico* (1959). The latter in particular is a classic of its kind, often revived in Italy.

Il cappello di paglia di Firenze

The Italian Straw Hat (literally, *The Florentine Straw Hat*)
Musical farce in four acts (five scenes) (1h 45m)
Libretto by Nino and Ernesta Rota, based on the comedy *Le chapeau de paille d'Italie* by Eugène Lebiche and Marc Michel
Composed 1945–6, rev. 1955
PREMIERES 21 April 1955, Teatro Massimo, Palermo; US: 6 July 1977, Santa Fe; UK: 19 March 1980, Collegiate Theatre, London

Rota's decision to convert one of the best loved of all French farces into a latter-day opera buffa was a happy inspiration; and the music, though slight and unpretentious, is unfailingly apt. The complex and hilariously hectic action is set in motion when the bridegroom Fadinard's horse calmly eats a straw hat belonging to Anaide, the young, unfaithful wife of the aged Beaupertuis. Since the result of this little mishap may seriously arouse Beaupertuis's jealousy, Anaide insists that before doing anything else (he is about to get married) Fadinard must find an identical replacement for the lost headgear. This proves more easily said than done. But eventually all is resolved when it is found that the deaf Uncle Vezinet has all along been about to give an identical hat to Fadinard's fiancée Elena, as a wedding present.

Rota's free 20th-century re-creation of Rossinian opera buffa broadly recalls Wolf-Ferrari, while the friskily unpredictable twists and turns of harmony and tonality sometimes show affinities with the Prokofiev of, say, the *Classical Symphony*. Although certain non-Italian critics have taken a condescending view of this opera, its lasting success in Italy has even won the respect of some avant-garde

musicians, whose outlook seems worlds away from Rota's.

RECORDING Mazzuccato Meneghini, Cortez, Martelli, Benelli, Basiola, Mariotti, Rome Ch and SO, Rota, RCA, 1975
EDITION v.s., Ricordi, 1956

Other operas: *Il principe porcaro*, (1926); *Ariodante*, 1942; *Torquemada*, (1943) 1976; *I due timidi*, 1950 (RAI broadcast), 1952; *Lo scoiattolo in gamba*, 1959 (RAI broadcast), 1973; *La notte d'un nevrastenico*, 1959 (RAI broadcast), 1960; *Aladino e la lampada magica*, 1968; *La visita meravigliosa*, 1970; *Napoli milionaria*, 1977
BIBLIOGRAPHY Pier Marco De Santi, *La musica di Nino Rota*, Laterza, 1983

J.C.G.W.

JEAN-JACQUES ROUSSEAU

b 28 June 1712, Geneva, Switzerland; *d* 2 July 1778, Ermenonville, France

Opinions have always been divided about the merit of Jean-Jacques Rousseau as a composer. His own estimation put him alongside Rameau, with whom he had a series of increasingly bitter disagreements on musical topics. Others have concluded that, had he not also been a great philosopher with powerful supporters, his intermède *Le devin du village* would quickly have sunk into oblivion instead of holding the stage for more than half a century.

The extraordinary fact is that Rousseau thought of himself primarily as a composer, even though he had little musical training; music copying also brought him an income at various times in his life. In 1743–4 Rousseau lived in Venice and for the first time saw Italian opera on stage. He became a passionate enthusiast, and progressively more critical of French music thereafter.

The successful second production of Pergolesi's *La serva padrona* in Paris in 1752 unleashed a whole new round of the French *v.* Italian quarrels which had beset French musical life for the best part of a century; this episode became known as the *querelle des bouffons*. Later the same year Rousseau wrote *Le devin du village* in which he sought to exemplify his views on the superiority of the Italian style. The work was a huge success.

Rousseau contributed several articles on music theory to the *Encyclopédie*; these later formed part of his *Dictionnaire de musique* (1768). His disputes with Rameau were a feature of Rousseau's life; the two first tangled over a theoretical system that the latter had proposed. Rameau uttered disparaging views on Rousseau as both composer and theoretician. Rousseau's most extreme views on French opera were propounded in the *Lettre sur la musique française*, 1753, in which he declared (notwithstanding his own contribution to the genre) that opera in the French language was impossible, since the language was inherently unmusical. He later experimented with *Pygmalion*, a spoken drama with instrumental interludes, and left another

Cross-section of the Théâtre de la Belle Cheminée in Fontainebleau during a performance, c. 1778

pastorale, *Daphnis et Chloé*, unfinished at the time of his death.

Rousseau's philosophy of music, like that of the Encyclopedists, was of art imitating nature: music was capable of expressing nothing if not depicting or imitating nature. Melody, or melodic declamation, was the basis of all music; Rousseau said that he believed that Greek tragedies were the true operas. Nevertheless, he expressed his profound admiration for Gluck. The Romantics laid claim to Rousseau, though it was his ideals and the spirit of his music rather than his compositional style that was truly influential.

Les muses galantes
The Muses of Love
Opéra-ballet in three acts
Libretto by the composer
PREMIERE   ?1745, Residence of La Pouplinière, Paris

Although the music of the original version of *Les muses galantes* is lost, a new entrée, *Hésiode*, composed soon after the first performance to replace the original first entrée, *Le Tasse*, survives in manuscript. According to the composer, *Hésiode* was written at the suggestion of the Duc de Richelieu to make the work suitable for court performance. Although in his preface to the libretto Rousseau repudiated the work as a mediocre specimen of a

mediocre genre, he had a high opinion of the music of *Hésiode*; Rameau, however, who was reluctantly persuaded to attend the first performance, was not impressed, and later declared that Rousseau could not have been the composer responsible for such merits as the work possessed.

EDITION   *Hésiode*: v.s., Henri Chapuis, [c. 1960]

Le devin du village
The Village Soothsayer
Intermède in one act (1h)
Libretto by the composer
PREMIERES   18 October 1752, Fontainebleau; UK: 21 November 1766, Drury Lane, London; US: 21 October 1790, New York

The long-lasting success of this little work was an extraordinary phenomenon. Following its public Paris premiere on 1 March 1753, it was played all over France and in several European countries: both Marie-Antoinette and Madame de Pompadour took part in early private performances. In its representation of Rousseau's 'back to nature' philosophy *Le devin* had an important influence on the style and content of many opéras comiques and singspiels. Its popularity also ensured it several parodies, one of which served as a basis for the libretto of Mozart's *Bastien und Bastienne*.

The story is far from the world of serious opera, but is not without its artificialities. A shepherdess, Colette, goes to consult a soothsayer about her sweetheart, Colin, who is attracted by a higher-born lady. The soothsayer advises her to appear cool towards Colin, then goes to suggest to Colin that Colette is interested in another man. After a 'magic spell', Colin comes to his senses. The couple offer gifts to the soothsayer, who says that their happiness is his reward (but he takes the presents anyway). The young men and women of the village join in the celebrations with dancing, pantomime and a vaudeville.

The style of the music is – following Rousseau's avowed philosophy – for the most part simple, and many of the airs are accompanied only by continuo. Critics have pointed out numerous faults in Rousseau's compositional technique and drawn attention to the contradictions in the work's style and *raison d'être*. Nevertheless, it remains one of those works which was precisely right for its time.

RECORDING Kirchner, Choy, Müller de Vries, Gottardo Tomat Ch of Spilimberg, Alpe Adria Ensemble, Clemencic, Nuova Era, 1991
EDITION facsimile, *French Opera in the 17th and 18th Centuries*, vol. 50, Pendragon, forthcoming

Pygmalion

Scène lyrique in one act
Libretto by the composer after Book X of the *Metamorphoses* by Ovid
PREMIERES May 1770, Hôtel de Ville, Lyons; US: 9 or 10 November 1790

With this work, Rousseau claimed to initiate a new approach to musical drama, one in which the music depicted each action or thought before the (spoken) text revealed it. The music, however, is mostly not Rousseau's: he sent the monodrama to Horace Coignet in Lyons in 1770, some eight years after it was written. Early publications of the text (apparently printed without the author's permission) were prefaced by a letter from Coignet stating that he had written the music (with the exception of two sections). *Pygmalion* was given in Paris in March 1772, with a reprise in 1775 which Rousseau disowned. In his *Consolations des misères de ma vie* (1781) Rousseau stated that the only composer who could have done justice to his conception was Gluck. Nevertheless, the new genre was very influential, particularly on German opera.

EDITION v.s. (in Russian), Glumov, 1955

Other operatic work: *Daphnis et Chloé* (inc.), (1779); 3 lost operas
BIBLIOGRAPHY J. F. Strauss, 'Jean-Jacques Rousseau: Musician', *MQ*, vol. 64 (1978), pp. 474–82; Arnold Whittall, 'Rousseau and the Scope of Opera', *ML*, vol. 45 (1964), p. 369

C.W.

ALBERT ROUSSEL

Albert Charles Paul Marie Roussel; *b* 5 April 1869, Tourcoing, France; *d* 23 August 1937, Royan, France

When Roussel decided to take up music as a profession he was 25, a naval officer with service at home and in the Far East. After leaving the navy he studied with Gigout in Paris before joining the Schola Cantorum for a long period of tuition under d'Indy, during which he himself became a teacher of counterpoint. In 1909 Roussel and his wife made a private journey to India and Indo-China. During the war, prevented by ill-health from rejoining the navy, he served in the Red Cross and in the army until he was invalided out in 1918. From 1922 Roussel lived at Varengeville in Normandy, writing a steady stream of music, active as a public figure with 'a strong sense of social responsibility' (Basil Deane). He was president of the music section of the 1937 Paris International Exhibition. His 60th birthday in 1929 was marked by a festival in Paris.

Roussel occupies an independent position between the Schola Cantorum and the Impressionists – the respective worlds of Franck and d'Indy, Debussy and Ravel. While in his later works the search for clarity and concision led to a form of neo-classicism, he did not lose the hyper-sensitive gift for atmosphere conspicuous in the earlier orchestral works. Prominent features in his music are astringent, sometimes harsh, harmony and a fondness for motoric rhythms. Sensitivity is balanced by a robust strain possibly deriving from his Franco-Flemish background.

The stage works reveal a strong attraction to mixed genres with a desire to tackle new problems rather than to repeat himself. Of the two hybrids, *Padmâvatî*, though described as an opera-ballet, is

Albert Roussel at Varengeville

less close to Lully and Rameau than the conte lyrique *La naissance de la lyre*. When he died, Roussel was planning a large-scale multi-media spectacle for actors, singers and dancers on the subject of Charles the Bold, Duke of Burgundy. The most conventional of his operas is the third, *Le testament de la tante Caroline*, designated opéra bouffe. Roussel wrote three ballets: *Le festin de l'araignée* (*The Spider's Banquet*) (1913), *Bacchus et Ariane* (1931) and the choral *Aenéas* (1935). Non-theatrical music includes four symphonies, several other orchestral works, *Psalm 80* (choral), chamber music and songs.

Padmâvatî

Opera-ballet in two acts, Op. 18 (1h 30m)
Libretto by Louis Laloy
Composed 1914–18
PREMIERES 1 June 1923, Opéra, Paris; UK: 6 July 1969, Coliseum, London (concert)
CAST Padmâvatî *a*, Nakamti *ms*, Ratan-Sen *t*, Alaouddin *bar*, the Brahmin *t*, Gora *bar*, Badal *t*, 3 *s*, 1 *a*, 3 *t*, 1 *bar*, 1 *b*; *satb* chorus of warriors, priests, women of the palace, populace
LARGE ORCHESTRA with quadruple ww

The origins of *Padmâvatî* lie in a visit to the ruins of Chitor in Rajasthan during Roussel's eastern journey of 1909. A few years later the critic and orientalist Laloy devised a libretto out of local legends concerning Chitor. The short score was ready before the outbreak of war; the orchestration was finished after Roussel's demobilization. The work, intended to inaugurate Jacques Rouché's directorship of the Opéra, was not given until 1923. The exotic tradition in French music, present at least from the time of Rameau, erupted towards the end of the 19th century under the stimulus of the Universal Exhibition of 1889. Unlike Debussy and others, Roussel had the advantage of first-hand experience. In *Padmâvatî* his use of Hindu scales suits his harmony, more complex and acrid here than in previous scores.

SYNOPSIS
Act I The 13th-century siege of the Hindu city of Chitor by the Mogul Sultan Alaouddin has reached stalemate. Alaouddin comes in person to discuss peace with Chitor's ruler, Ratan-Sen. Their meeting is polite but inconclusive. Alaouddin asks to be shown the city's splendours, adding that he prefers flesh and blood to the marvels of stone. Ratan-Sen shows off his warriors, then his dancing girls. Aware that these are foreign slaves, Alaouddin demands to see the palace women. While he praises their charms, he inquires slyly after Ratan-Sen's queen, Padmâvatî, famed equally for her beauty and her virtue. Unwillingly Ratan-Sen allows the queen to appear on a balcony and, at Alaouddin's insistence, permits her to unveil. Alaouddin departs without concluding a pact. His Brahmin counsellor remains behind. The crowd, recognizing him as a malefactor who had fled the city, kills him. Padmâvatî comes down to the deserted square, sees the body and is filled with foreboding.

Act II Negotiations have broken down. The Moguls are attacking the city. Padmâvatî and her companions have taken refuge in the temple of Siva. Ratan-Sen appears, wounded. There is a truce until dawn. Padmâvatî assures him she will die with him. Ratan-Sen has vowed to Siva to save his people: if Padmâvatî will not consent to give herself to the conqueror, the people will be massacred. She indignantly refuses. When Ratan-Sen tries to compel her to obedience she stabs him, preferring the widow's death by burning dictated by their religion to eternal shame. A long ceremony follows during which spirit deities emanating from Siva threaten and coax Padmâvatî. Finally she is allowed to descend to the funeral pyre. When the temple doors are broken down and Alaouddin appears all he finds is smoke rising from the crypt.

The big dance scenes (the parading of the warriors, dancers and palace women in Act I, and the funeral rites in Act II) arise directly out of the action. The mood is dark, urgent and sinister, relieved only by the lyrical descriptions of Padmâvatî's beauty by the Brahmin and by a girl in the crowd, Nakamti. By French standards of the time the orchestral writing had unusual density. In spite of its high reputation among musicians, *Padmâvatî*, which needs a large company and considerable outlay, has had few stagings. Concert performances, sometimes of Act II only, have been more frequent. The score must be classed among the major achievements of French opera in the present century.

RECORDING Horne, Berbié, Gedda, Van Dam, Ch Orfeón Donostiarra, O Capitole Toulouse, Plasson, EMI, 1983
EDITIONS f.s., Durand, 1924; v.s., Durand, 1919

La naissance de la lyre

The Origin of the Lyre
Conte lyrique in one act (three tableaux), Op. 24
Libretto by Théodore Reinach, based on the *Ichneutae* of Sophocles and on a Homeric hymn
Composed 1923–4
PREMIERE 1 July 1925, Opéra, Paris

The precocious infant Hermes has stolen his brother Apollo's cattle. Silenus and the satyrs track him down; the nymph Kyllene shields him. Out of the remains of one of the cattle Hermes, using horns, skin and entrails, has fashioned a musical instrument. Enchanted by the sounds Apollo forgives Hermes and adopts the lyre. Nymphs and satyrs dance in celebration as the two gods regain Olympus. The work employs soloists, dancers, chorus and orchestra, with some spoken lines. The original choreographer was Bronislava Nijinska. There are some resemblances to Stravinsky's melodrama *Persephone*.

EDITIONS f.s., Durand, 1927; v.s., Durand, 1924

Le testament de la tante Caroline

Aunt Caroline's Will
Opéra bouffe in three acts, rev. as opérette in one act
Libretto by Nino (pseudonym for Michel Veber)

Composed 1932–3; rev. as opérette by Marcel Mihalovici
PREMIERES original version: 14 November 1936, Olomouc,
Czechoslovakia; 11 March 1937, Opéra-Comique, Paris; UK
(rev. version): 29 November 1968, The Playhouse, Oxford
(Oxford University Opera Club; one-act version)

Aunt Caroline, shunned by her family for her way of
life, leaves her fortune to the first of her three nieces
to produce a male child within one year of her death.
The two elder nieces, although they employ the
services of a midwife and of a doctor who runs a
crèche, are unable to comply. The third niece, a
charitable spinster, unexpectedly rediscovers a lost
love-child in the person of the doctor's chauffeur.
The original three-act version, produced shortly
before the composer's death, was coolly received.
A one-act reduction approved by the librettist was
prepared by Marcel Mihalovici. This is quite frequently performed, yet since the lively music feels
too weighty for the narrow framework, a return to
the original is surely desirable.

EDITIONS original version: f.s./v.s., Editeur (Paris/Brussels),
1936; rev. version: v.s., Heugel, 1966

BIBLIOGRAPHY Basil Deane, *Albert Roussel*, Barrie and
Rockliff, 1961; N. Demuth, *Albert Roussel, A Study*, UMP,
1947

R.H.C.

GIOVANNI ROVETTA
b 1596 or 1597, Venice; *d* 23 October 1668, Venice

Rovetta devoted his entire career to St Mark's,
Venice, first as a singer and finally succeeding
Monteverdi as maestro di cappella in 1644. Not
surprisingly, his musical style owes a great deal to his
Venetian colleagues, especially Monteverdi and
Alessandro Grandi. He published nine volumes of
sacred music (1626–62) and three books of *concertato* madrigals (1629, 1640, 1645). His opera
Ercole in Lidia (1645) is lost, although John Evelyn's
account of a performance splendidly captures the
flavour of new operatic trends in Venice: 'This night
. . . we went to the Opera, which are Comedies &
other plays represented in Recitative Music by the
most excellent Musitians vocal & Instrumental,
together with variety of Seeanes painted & contrived
with no lesse art of Perspective, and Machines, for
flying in the aire, & other wonderfull motions. So
taken together it is doubtlesse one of the most
magnificent & expensfull diversions the Wit of Men
can invent.'

BIBLIOGRAPHY E. S. de Beer (ed.), *The Diary of John
Evelyn*, OUP, 1955, vol. 2, pp. 449–50

T.C.

JOSEPH-NICOLAS-PANCRACE ROYER
b c. 1705, Turin; *d* 11 January 1755, Paris

Among Rameau's younger contemporaries, Royer
was one of the brighter spirits. Of aristocratic
descent, he took up music as an amateur, but turned
professional when his father left him destitute, and
soon gained a reputation as a keyboard-player. By
1725 Royer was in Paris, where he contributed music
to two of Alexis Piron's opéras comiques, *Le fâcheux
veuvage* (1725) and *Crédit est mort* (1726). In 1730 his
first opera, the tragédie *Pyrrhus*, was unsuccessfully
staged at the Paris Opéra; in that same year he began
a four-year period as maître de musique at the
Opéra, a post he resumed in 1753.

Much the most successful of Royer's operas was
Zaïde, reine de Grenade (1739), a ballet héroïque in
three acts, revived in a revised form in 1745 for the
Dauphin's wedding festivities and further revived in
1756 and 1770. In this work Royer demonstrates
a talent for adventurous orchestration and for
capturing vividly a wide range of mood, even if
by comparison with Rameau's his music seems
somewhat shallow. None of his subsequent operas,
which include *Le pouvoir de l'Amour* (1743) and
Almasis (1748), enjoyed much success. Royer
recycled some of the dances from *Zaïde* and *Le
pouvoir de l'Amour* in his *Pièces de clavecin* (1746).
His setting of Voltaire's *Pandore*, rehearsed privately
in 1752, is now lost.

G.S.

JOSEF ROZKOŠNÝ
Josef Richard Rozkošný; *b* 21 September 1833, Prague;
d 3 June 1913, Prague

Though well trained as a musician (under Tomášek,
Proksch and Kittl among others), Rozkošný worked
all his life as a bank clerk. This did not prevent his
becoming one of the most prolific Czech opera
composers of his generation and, after Smetana, one
of the most performed. *The St John's Rapids* was
played 35 times in Prague; *Cinderella*, an astonishing
68 times. Furthermore Rozkošný continued composing to an advanced age, writing his last opera at 71.
He lacked the distinctive musical personality of
Dvořák or Smetana, but had a solid technique and an
instinct for effective dramatic writing. His operas
range over a number of different genres: the early
Mikuláš is a village comedy in the *Bartered Bride*
vein, *Záviš z Falkenštejna* is a historical drama,
Cinderella is a fairy-tale opera based on the familiar
story, and *Stoja* is the first Czech *verist* opera.

The St John's Rapids
Svatojanské proudy
Romantic opera in four acts
Libretto by Eduard Ruffer (in German), translated by
František Adolf Šubert

Composed 1869
PREMIERE 3 October 1871, Provisional Theatre, Prague

The St John's Rapids was one of the most popular Czech operas of the 1870s and Rozkošný's only opera to be published. Its subject matter was drawn from the world of early German opera, with hunters' choruses, bridesmaids' choruses and a central focus on the supernatural. With its character of the Vltava sprite who charms the hero and when later rejected takes her revenge, it anticipates Dvořák's water-sprite opera, *Rusalka* (both derive from the German Undine legend). Its overture, an evocation of the Czech river Vltava, similarly looks forward to the more famous Vltava tone poem by Smetana, who conducted the premiere.

EDITION v.s., Hudební matice, 1882

Other operas: *Ave Maria* (dubious), 1855; *Mikuláš*, 1870; *Záviš z Falkenštejna* (*Záviš of Falkenštejn*), 1877; *Pytláci* (*The Poachers*) (dubious), 1878; *Popelka* (*Cinderella*), 1885; *Krakonoš*, 1889; *Stoja*, 1894; *Satanela*, 1898; *Černé jezero* (*The Black Lake*), originally *Šumavská víla* (*The Šumava Fairy*), 1906; 2 lost operas
BIBLIOGRAPHY John Tyrrell, *Czech Opera*, CUP, 1988

J.T.

LUDOMIR RÓŻYCKI

b 6 November 1884, Warsaw; *d* 1 January 1953, Katowice, Poland

Różycki is the outstanding Polish opera composer of the early 20th century. He studied in the Warsaw Conservatory and then at the Berlin Academy with Humperdinck. Together with Szymanowski, Grzegorz Fitelberg and Apolinary Szeluto he founded the Publishing Company of Young Polish Composers. From 1907 Różycki was director of the opera in Lvov where he wrote his first operas. After 1912 he travelled to Italy, Switzerland, France and Germany. From 1918 to 1939 he taught piano and composition at the conservatory in Warsaw and composed operas, ballets, symphonies, chamber music, piano works and songs. After the war Różycki was a professor in the State Higher Music School in Katowice. Many of his works were lost during the war and he reconstructed and altered them later.

His music is stylistically within the conventions of German neo-Romanticism, and was modelled in harmony and instrumentation on the music dramas of Wagner and Strauss, using leitmotifs and a large orchestra (*Boleslaw the Bold, Eros and Psyche*). Later Różycki was influenced by Italian *bel canto*, and paid more attention to vocal *cantabile* (*Beatrix Cenci*), with a corresponding simplification of harmonic language (*Casanova*).

Operatic works: *Bolesław Śmiały* (*Boleslaw the Bold*), 1909; *Meduza* (*Medusa*), 1912; *Eros i Psyche* (*Eros and Psyche*), 1917; *Casanova*, 1923, rev. 1948; *Beatrix Cenci*, 1927; *Młyn diabelski* (*The Devil's Mill*), 1931; *Lili chce śpiewać* (*Lily*

Wants to Sing), 1932; *Pani Walewska* (inc.), (1935)
BIBLIOGRAPHY J. Kański, *Ludomir Różycki*, PWM, 1955

J.M.

PAUL RUBENS

Paul Alfred Rubens; *b* 29 April 1875, London; *d* 5 February 1917, Falmouth, Cornwall, England

Rubens, along with Lionel Monckton, was the best of the Edwardian tunesmiths. In the immemorial tradition of training himself for the comedy theatre while he should have been studying law at Oxford, he subsequently wrote interpolations for George Edwardes's shows before providing complete scores of his own. His ill-health and early death prevented him from realizing his full potential. The violin song from *Tina* is still heard.

Miss Hook of Holland

A Dutch musical incident in two acts
Book by Paul Rubens and Austen Hurgon; lyrics by Paul Rubens
PREMIERES 31 January 1907, Prince of Wales Theatre, London; US: 31 December 1907, Criterion Theater, New York

Spirited tunes (such as 'Little Miss Wooden Shoes') are only to be expected when the second-act setting of an operetta is a liqueur distillery. The plot concerns the wealthy proprietor's daughter, Sally Hook, who has invented a famous recipe (echoes of Leslie Stuart's *Florodora*, 1899), and van Vuyt, the composer she wishes to marry.

RECORDING excerpts: studio cast, HMV, 1930
EDITION v.s., Chappell, 1907

Other musical comedies (selective list; some are collaborations): *Three Little Maids*, 1902; *Lady Madcap*, 1904; *Mr Popple (of Ippleton)*, 1905; *My Mimosa Maid*, 1908; *Dear Little Denmark*, 1909; *The Balkan Princess*, 1910; *The Sunshine Girl*, 1912; *The Girl from Utah*, 1913; *After the Girl*, 1914; *To-Night's the Night*, 1915; *Betty*, 1915; *Tina*, 1915
BIBLIOGRAPHY Kurt Gänzl, *The British Musical Theatre*, Macmillan, 1986

S.B.

ANTON RUBINSTEIN

Anton Grigoryevich Rubinstein; *b* 28 November 1829, Vikhvatinets, Podolsk district, Russia; *d* 20 November 1894, Peterhof, nr St Petersburg

Rubinstein, one of the greatest piano virtuosi of the 19th century, was also an exceptional teacher (who directed the St Petersburg Conservatory from 1862 to 1867 and from 1887 until his death) and a prolific composer. However, of his 19 operas, five symphonies, five piano concertos, numerous piano pieces, chamber works and songs, only the 'Melody in F' for piano is still regularly heard. Paderewski remarked that Rubinstein 'had not the necessary concentration of patience for a composer', and his works are generally uneven, insufficiently developed or contain evidence of note-spinning. From a German-Jewish family, he studied in Berlin with Siegfried Dehn, who had previously taught Glinka, and there met Meyerbeer and Mendelssohn, who were to remain major influences on his work. Rubinstein regarded the Russian nationalists as hopeless dilettantes, and often crossed swords with their leader, Balakirev, who remarked of Rubinstein, 'He is not a Russian composer, but a Russian who composes.' Eleven of Rubinstein's operas are set to German texts, many of them with biblical subjects, and musically they are indebted to Handel, Mendelssohn and Gounod. In the 1860s he attempted to adopt a nationalist approach, though this tended towards the superficial, usually involving dance rhythms rather than inflected harmonic and melodic material. His two Lermontov operas, *The Demon*, and *The Merchant Kalashnikov*, contain some of his best music.

The Demon

Fantastic opera in three acts (3h)
Libretto by P. A. Viskovatov, after the poem by Lermontov
Composed 1871
PREMIERES 13 January 1875, Mariinsky Theatre, St Petersburg; UK: 21 June 1881, Covent Garden, London; US: 17 January 1922, San Francisco

The Demon, a gloomy Byronic figure, falls in love with Tamara and pursues her to a convent where he hopes she can redeem him – a mixture of *The Flying Dutchman* and *Faust*. An uneven work, ranging from palely Victorian choruses of angels, to some

P. A. Khokhlov, the first interpreter of The Demon *at the Bolshoi Theatre, Moscow, 1880–90*

attractive oriental pastiche, its best music is reserved for the two principals. Tamara's music has some striking pre-echoes of Tatyana in *Eugene Onegin* (Tchaikovsky was Rubinstein's pupil), and there is a sumptuous final duet for her and the Demon. *The Demon* was a huge success, despite objections from the censor, who insisted on changing the Demon to a 'Good Genius' and removing all the ikons from Tamara's cell.

RECORDING Talakhadze, Kozlovsky, Al. Ivanov, Krasovsky, Bolshoi Theatre Ch and O, Melik-Pashayev, Melodiya, 1950
EDITION v.s., A. Gutheil, 1875

Other operas: *Dmitry Donskoi*, 1852; *Sibirskiye okhotniki* (*The Siberian Huntsmen*), 1854; *Stenka Raz in* (fragment), (1852); *Hadji-Abrek*, 1858; *Fomka-durachok* (*Tom the Fool*), 1853; *Das verlorene Paradies*, 1875; *Die Kinder der Heide*, 1860; *Feramors*, 1863; *Der Thurm zu Babel*, 1870; *Die Makkabäer*, 1875; *Nero*, 1879; *Kupets Kalashnikov* (*The Merchant Kalashnikov*), 1880; *Sulamith*, 1883; *Unter Räubern*, 1883; *Der Papagei*, 1884; *Goryusha*, 1889; *Moses*, 1892; *Christus*, 1894
BIBLIOGRAPHY Gerald Abraham, *Anton Rubinstein, Russian Composer*, Faber, 1968

J.G.

WITOLD RUDZIŃSKI

b 14 March 1913, Siebież, Poland (now Russia)

Rudziński studied composition in Vilnius (until 1937) and in Paris (1938–9) with Nadia Boulanger and Koechlin and at the Gregorian Institute. He was a member of the Association of Young Polish Composers in Paris. From 1942 he taught at the conservatory in Vilnius, in 1946–7 in Łódź, and from 1948 to 1949 he was artistic director of the State Philharmonic Orchestra and Opera in Warsaw. Since 1957 he has taught at the Warsaw Music Academy and has been widely active as composer, writer and administrator. Rudziński's operas are late Romantic in style while leaning towards a more modern musical language. Folk music informs his works on rural themes, especially the chorus and ballet scenes. Many of his libretti are based on classical literary works (Kochanowski, Thackeray, Sienkiewicz, Reymont).

Operas: *Janko Muzykant* (*Janko the Fiddler*), 1953; *Komendant Paryża* (*The Commandant of Paris*), 1960; *Odprawa posłów greckich* (*The Dismissal of the Greek Envoys*), (1962). 1966 (RECORDING Muza, 1960s); *Sulamita* (*The Shulamite*), 1964; *Żółta szlafmyca* (*The Yellow Nightcap*), 1970; *Chłopi* (*The Peasants*), 1974; *Pierścień i róża* (*The Rose and the Ring*), radio opera, 1982
BIBLIOGRAPHY *Kto jest kim w Polsce* (*Who's Who in Poland*), Wydawnictwo Interpress, 1984; 2nd edn, 1989

J.M.

JÓZSEF RUZITSKA

b c. 1775, ?Pápa, Western Hungary; *d* after 1823

Ruzitska is remembered today as the composer of the two earliest surviving Hungarian operas, *Béla futása* (*Béla's Flight*) and *Simon Kemény*, both of which were staged in Kolozsvár (Clausenburg, now Cluj) in 1822. Like their predecessors (notably the lost operas of József Chudy) they are singspiels in the popular German tradition to which Mozart's *Seraglio* and *Die Zauberflöte* belong (as well as Weber's *Der Freischütz*, first performed in Pest in 1822). As with so much embryonic national music, from Glinka downwards, there is a sometimes uncomfortable fusion of styles. Elements of Rossini and Mozart rub shoulders with the specifically Hungarian *verbunkos* music.

Ruzitska vanished after 1823, when he left Kolozsvár for Italy, but his music did not. Loewenberg mentions a performance of *Béla futása* as late as 1862 (but attributes the work to the wrong Ruzitska). But by then Ruzitska's music had largely been driven out by the more solidly operatic works of Erkel.

BIBLIOGRAPHY　Bence Szabolcsi, trans. Sára Karig, *A Concise History of Hungarian Music* (includes one song from *Béla futása*, pp. 171–2), Corvina, 1964

S.W.

ANTONIO SACCHINI

Antonio Maria Gasparo Gioacchino Sacchini; *b* 14 June 1730, Florence; *d* 6 October 1786, Paris

Sacchini was one of the most significant composers of opera seria in the late 18th century. His career, which spanned 30 years and extended beyond the major Italian cities to Stuttgart and Munich, London and finally Paris, brought him great acclaim, a considerable fortune and its share of controversy.

Taken by his father to Naples when he was four, Sacchini began his musical education there in 1740, when he entered the Loreto Conservatory, studying violin, singing, harpsichord, organ and composition (the last with Durante). He established a reputation with his intermezzo *Fra Donato* in 1756; a similar success the following year brought him commissions for comic works from two Neapolitan theatres. His first opera seria, performed at the Teatro San Carlo in 1762, was *Andromaca*. By this time he was secondo maestro at the conservatory. The same year he travelled to Venice to fulfil two more commissions, *Alessandro Severo* and *Alessandro nell'Indie*. Their success, coupled with the much greater one of *Olimpiade* in Padua in 1763 and a series of further triumphs in Rome, Florence and Naples, led Sacchini to give up his position at the conservatory in Naples.

From 1762 to 1772 he worked mainly in Venice and Rome, both as composer and singing teacher (his pupils included Nancy Storace – the first Susanna in Mozart's *Figaro*). A series of comic operas written for the Teatro Valle in Rome were widely performed and established his European reputation. In 1768 he was appointed director of the Conservatorio dell'Ospedaletto in Venice, for which he composed several oratorios. In 1770 he travelled to Germany where he wrote three operas for Stuttgart and Munich; these were followed by several more operas for Italian cities.

Sacchini spent nearly a decade in London from 1772; Burney described him as 'the most promising composer in the serious [style]'. He wrote ten theatrical works for the King's Theatre, seven opere serie, two comic operas and a contribution to a pasticcio. Despite great popular success, he left London in 1781, when he was under threat of imprisonment for debt. He spent the final six years of his career in Paris, where his reputation was already well established. Patronized by Marie Antoinette, Sacchini was able to command high fees from the directors of the Opéra but was drawn into the controversy between the supporters of Gluck and those of Piccinni in the so-called *guerre des bouffons*. Because of intrigue against him and his works, his success in Paris was less assured: *Renaud* and *Chimène* (both 1783) were criticized severely, and *Dardanus* (1784) was at first a failure. He completed his penultimate opera, *Oedipe à Colone*, in 1785, but it was first performed in 1787, after his death. It proved to be a great success, however, becoming part of the standard repertoire at the Opéra for 43 years, and is generally regarded as his masterpiece.

Costume design for M. Chardini as Thesée in Sacchini's Oedipe à Colone *(Versailles, 1786)*

Sacchini's music bears all the hallmarks of the classical style, making use of relatively simple textures and balanced phrasing. His melodic style, especially that of his serious operas, was much praised by his contemporaries. Although not always particularly original, it does possess an immediate appeal and is capable of depicting a wide range of emotion. This is less the case with the comic operas, where a lack of differentiation in melodic style tends to limit their power of characterization. His harmony ranges beyond the norm of classical music and is consistently enlivened and enriched by the introduction of diminished sevenths and augmented sixths. In both his melody and harmony there are prefigurations of 19th-century practice. His instrumental writing is also adept, especially that for the violin, and is always carefully gauged according to the requirements of the vocal part.

Operas: *Olimpia tradita*, 1758; *Il copista burlato*, 1759; *Il testaccio*, 1760; *I due fratelli beffati*, 1760; *Andromaca*, 1761; *La finta contessa*, 1761; *Li due bari*, 1762; *L'amore in campo*, 1762; *Alessandro Severo*, 1763; *Alessandro nell'Indie*, 1763; *Olimpiade*, 1763; *Semiramide riconosciuta*, 1764; *Eumene*, 1764; *Il gran Cidde*, 1764; *Lucio Vero*, 1764; *Il Creso*, 1765; *L'isola d'amore*, 1766; *Le contadine bizzarre*, 1766; *Artaserse*, 1768; *Nicoraste*, 1769; *Scipione in Cartagena*, 1770; *Calliroe*, 1770; *L'eroe cinese*, 1770 (EDITION facsimile, Garland, 1982); *Adriano in Siria*, 1771; *Ezio*, 1771; *Armida*, 1772; *Vologeso*, 1772; *Tamerlano*, 1773; *Perseo*, 1774; *Nitteti*, 1774;

Montezuma, 1775; *Didone abbandonata*, 1775; *Erifile*, 1778; *L'amore soldato*, 1778; *L'avaro deluso, o Don Calandrino*, 1778; *Enea e Lavinia*, 1779; *Mitridate*, 1781; *Dardanus*, 1784; *Oedipe à Colone*, 1786 (RECORDING MRF, 1971); *Arvire et Evelina* (inc.; completed by J.-B. Rey), 1788

BIBLIOGRAPHY David DiChiera, 'Antonio Sacchini', in *Grove*, Macmillan, 1980

D.S.B.

FRANCESCO SACRATI

baptized 17 September 1605, Parma; *d* 20 May 1650, ?Modena

Sacrati participated in the first flowering of 'public' opera in Venice in the 1640s, working regularly with the Italian stage designer Giacomo Torelli: he was particularly associated with the short-lived Teatro Novissimo, which established its reputation on the basis of spectacular sets and machines. He also toured operas, with performances perhaps in Bologna, and certainly in Reggio Emilia (1648). Like his colleagues Benedetto Ferrari and Francesco Manelli, however, he eventually exchanged the uncertainties of a freelance career in the Republic of Venice for more stable, if less exciting, prospects in a duchy: he was appointed maestro di cappella of Modena Cathedral on 3 June 1649.

Garden in the king's palace; engraving by Giacomo Torelli from his own design for La finta pazza *(Paris, 1645)*

Sacrati's operas were among the most popular of his time: not for nothing did Giacomo Badoaro, the librettist of *L'Ulisse errante* (a sister piece to Monteverdi's *Il ritorno d'Ulisse in patria*), describe him as the moon to Monteverdi's sun.

La finta pazza

Drama in a prologue and three acts (3h)
The Fake Madwoman
Libretto by Giulio Strozzi
PREMIERE 1641, Teatro Novissimo, Venice; modern revival: July 1987, Venice

La finta pazza was perhaps the most travelled opera of the 1640s, thanks not least to the support of the touring company or companies known as the *Febiarmonici*. It was also one of the first Italian operas to be staged in France (Paris, 1645).

The plot centres on Achilles in female disguise on the isle of Scyros, and the numerous editions of the libretto issued between 1641 and 1662, some with splendid engravings, and other descriptions of performances all bear witness to its popularity. A score was rediscovered in 1984 (his other six stage works remain lost) and contains music already known from Monteverdi's *L'incoronazione di Poppea* (1643) – the overture combines the two sinfonias from the coronation scene in *Poppea*, Act III – and other triple-time passages in *Poppea* are very close in style to *La finta pazza*. It now seems likely that Sacrati played a significant part in bringing Monteverdi's last opera to the stage; in turn, the *Poppea* that survives probably contains music by the younger composer.

EDITION facsimile, in *Drammaturgia musicale veneta*, forthcoming
BIBLIOGRAPHY A. Curtis, '*La Poppea impasticciata* or, Who Wrote the Music to *L'incoronazione* (1643)?', *JAMS*, vol. 42 (1989), pp. 23–54

T.C.

CAMILLE SAINT-SAËNS

Charles Camille Saint-Saëns; *b* 9 October 1835, Paris; *d* 16 December 1921, Algiers

The career of Saint-Saëns, one of the most gifted and versatile musicians of the 19th century, whose accomplishments were solid as well as brilliant, covered a momentous span of musical history. Born the year before the premiere of Meyerbeer's *Les Huguenots*, he died when Berg had nearly completed *Wozzeck* and Britten was a schoolboy. At the age of ten Saint-Saëns made his début as pianist in Paris playing concertos by Mozart and Beethoven. His last public appearance took place in Dieppe 75 years later. His first numbered symphony was written when he was 18. His last works, the three woodwind sonatas, were written in the final year of his life.

In between, Saint-Saëns was unremittingly active as composer and executant. In the latter capacity

he was a much travelled concert pianist, organist (notably at the Madeleine church in Paris), author, teacher (not at the Conservatoire where he had studied but at the Ecole Niedermeyer in Paris) and scholar, who did much to make Mozart's music known in France and was general editor of the complete edition of Rameau. As composer he produced over the years five symphonies, sacred and secular choral works, numerous concertos and concerted works, four orchestral tone poems, and a quantity of chamber music and songs. To his regret his operas, with the exception of *Samson et Dalila*, failed to win the success he achieved in other, by Parisian standards less important, fields. Including his part (with Dukas) in the completion of Guiraud's unfinished *Frédégonde*, Saint-Saëns wrote 13 operas, two of them opéras comique. There were in addition a ballet, *Javotte*, incidental music for several plays and a film score. As a widely cultivated man he understood what was wanted, yet with all his competence and experience he lacked the 'nose', the instinct of the theatre animal granted, for example, to Massenet, who in other forms of music was his inferior. His choice of libretti showed more education than flair, yet he skilfully adapted the procedures of grand opera to the needs of the period between the death of Meyerbeer and the conquest of France by Wagner. The operatic music of Saint-Saëns by and large has the same strengths and weaknesses as the rest – lucidity, Mozartian transparency, greater care for form than content. His facility, a quality misprized by those who lack it, tempted him to accept ideas good or bad, often memorable if rarely profound, as they came to him. There is a certain emotional dryness; invention is sometimes thin but the workmanship is impeccable.

Samson et Dalila

Samson and Delilah
Opera in three acts (four tableaux) (2h)
Libretto by Ferdinand Lemaire, based on the Book of Judges
Composed 1868–77
PREMIERES 2 December 1877, Grand Ducal Theatre, Weimar; US: 25 March 1892, New York (concert); 4 January 1893, New Orleans; UK: 25 September 1893, Covent Garden, London (concert); 26 April 1909, Covent Garden
CAST Dalila *ms*, Samson *t*, High Priest of Dagon *bar*, Abimélech *b*, an Old Hebrew *b*, a Philistine Messenger *t*, First Philistine *t*, Second Philistine *b*; *satb* chorus of Hebrews and Philistines
ORCHESTRATION 3 fl, 3 ob, 3 cl, 3 bsn, 4 hn, 4 tpt, 3 trbn, tuba, 2 ophicleides, timp, perc (including glock), str

Saint-Saëns, who had experience of the English oratorio tradition and shared the national admiration for Mendelssohn's *Elijah*, intended to use the biblical story of Samson's betrayal and death for an oratorio. His librettist, Ferdinand Lemaire, sensing theatrical possibilities, suggested an opera. Musical friends showed little enthusiasm for the first passages the composer tried out on them. On a visit early in 1870 to Liszt in Weimar, Saint-Saëns spoke of his discouragement. Liszt, the champion of the new and unfamiliar, offered, if Saint-Saëns finished *Samson*, to produce it in Weimar. Owing to the outbreak of

Caricature portrait of Saint-Saëns by Gabriel Fauré

the Franco-Prussian War and local difficulties, Liszt could not keep that promise until 1877. Meanwhile there had been no takers in France. The singer Pauline Viardot organized a private performance in Paris of Act II at which she sang Dalila and the composer played the orchestral part on the piano, but the audience, including the director of the Opéra, remained unconvinced: the biblical subject would not do. Rameau and Voltaire had had similar difficulties 150 years earlier with a projected *Samson*. There was a public concert performance of the first act at the Châtelet theatre in 1875, but the opera was not performed on the French stage until 3 March 1890, at the Théâtre des Arts at Rouen. That production was brought to Paris, not to the Opéra but to the nearby Théâtre Eden, in October the same year. The Opéra was at last emboldened to accept *Samson* and it was first seen there on 23 November 1892 with Deschamps-Jehin, Vergnet and Lassalle, conductor Colonne. (Viardot, for whom the role of Dalila was designed, and to whom the opera is dedicated, was now over 70.) Success with the general public in Paris was great and prolonged, but was overshadowed for progressives by the vogue for Wagner. Audiences outside Paris, however, were enthralled: *Samson* became one of the most widely popular of operas.

SYNOPSIS

Act I A public place at Gaza, before the temple of Dagon. The Hebrews lament their subjugation by the Philistines. They fear their God has forsaken them. Samson, claiming that God speaks through his mouth ('Arrêtez, ô mes frères!'), attempts to raise their spirits. The satrap Abimélech rebukes the Hebrews for praying to the wrong deity – Dagon would help

them. His words incite Samson and the Hebrews to a fervent outburst ('Israël! Romps ta chaîne!'). Abimélech attacks Samson, who slays him. The Hebrews melt away as the temple gates open, revealing the high priest of Dagon, heavily guarded. As he scolds his followers for showing fear, a messenger brings news of an uprising among the Hebrews. The high priest curses Israel. Ready to celebrate the turn of events, Dalila and a group of priestesses advance, ostensibly to crown the victor Samson. Vowing that he reigns in her heart, she beseeches him to visit her again in her lonely dwelling. An old Hebrew warns Samson against the wiles of Dalila. As she dances among her priestesses the troubled Samson is compelled against his will to follow her voluptuous movements. She sings provocatively ('Printemps qui commence') of her nocturnal vigil, waiting for the hero.

Act II Outside Dalila's house in the valley of Sorek. Night is falling and a storm is brewing. Dalila, sensing Samson's perplexity, calls on Love to help her ('Amour! Viens aider ma faiblesse!'). Her first visitor is the high priest, to inform her that since the Israelites have recaptured the city, the downfall of Samson is essential. He reminds Dalila that her previous encounter with the hero had not brought his total submission. She admits that her attempts to prise from him the secret of his strength were unsuccessful. She is their only hope, the high priest assures her; through her Samson must be enslaved and die. When the coast is clear, Samson steals in, the more shamefully because God has smiled on the Hebrews. This must be the lovers' farewell. Dalila dismisses thoughts of Israel's fate and invokes a more powerful god – Love. Samson dares the lightning to strike him down as he confesses his love. Dalila demands total surrender ('Mon coeur s'ouvre à ta voix') adding that he must entrust her with his secret. Assuming that the thunder is the voice of God, Samson refuses, but finally follows her indoors. Philistine soldiers approach silently. Dalila signals to them to enter the house.

Act III Tableau 1: The prison in Gaza. Blinded, his hair shorn, Samson turns the treadmill ('Vois ma misère, hélas') while Hebrew voices are heard bemoaning his apparent betrayal of them and their God for a woman's charms. Tableau 2: Interior of the temple of Dagon with two marble columns in the centre. A celebration is in progress. The high priest, Dalila and their followers watch a bacchanal. Samson is led in by a small boy. The high priest mocks the hero's weakness. Dalila reminds him of her successful extraction of his secret (the nature of this secret is never revealed in words). At the sacrificial table they invoke their god ('Gloire à Dagon vainqueur!'). A flame appears, signifying the god's presence. The high priest commands Samson to kneel and worship. Samson asks the boy to lead him to the two columns, prays to God to give him back his old strength and, pushing them outwards, brings the temple roof crashing down.

Lemaire's libretto is an intelligent compression of the established five-act formula of Meyerbeerian grand

The character of Dalila is carefully drawn. Each of her three arias adds something. The first is the most purely feminine. The second is an appeal for help and reassurance. In the third, Dalila, who has Samson in her power but still has not discovered his secret, gives him the full works. One may doubt her professions of love. Any tender feelings she may harbour disappear once he is helpless. Her gloating over him at this point and her earlier refusal of the high priest's offer of money imply that patriotism is a motive but, although as an expert she may appreciate Samson's physique, deeper feelings than endangered *amour propre* seem unlikely.

RECORDINGS 1. Bouvier, Luccioni, Cabanel, Paris Opéra Ch and O, Fourestier, EMI, 1946: the most authentically French performance; 2. Obraztsova, Domingo, Bruson, Ch and O de Paris, Barenboim, DG, 1978: high-quality orchestral playing and conducting; a weak Delilah, but Domingo a splendid Samson; 3. Meier, Domingo, Fondary, Bastille Ch and O, Chung, EMI, 1992: probably the best modern performance; finely sung, conducted and recorded [A.B.]
EDITIONS f.s./v.s., Durand, 1877

Henry VIII

Opera in four acts (3h)
Libretto by Léonce Détroyat and Armand Silvestre
Composed 1883; rev. as three-act version, 1889; full version restored, 1909
PREMIERES 5 March 1883, Opéra, Paris; UK: 14 July 1889, Covent Garden, London; US: 1983, New York

A slimmed-down grand historical opera about Henry's defiance of the Pope, the annulment of his marriage to Catherine of Aragon and his subsequent marriage to Anne Boleyn. Catherine, to save her rival Anne from the king's wrath, burns an incriminating love letter to her from the Spanish ambassador, Gomez. The music is of superior quality, the mood predominantly sombre. The portrait of Henry differs from the conventional view of 'bluff King Hal'. The opera can now be seen as a bridge between Meyerbeer and the serious French operas of the early 1890s. *Henry VIII* remained in the Opéra repertoire until 1919. The revival of interest in French opera has recently extended to this work in the US and elsewhere.

RECORDING Command, Vignon, Rouillon, Rouen Théâtre des Arts Ch, French Lyrique O, Guingal, Chant du Monde, 1992

Other operas: *La princesse jaune*, 1872 (RECORDING MRF 1957); *Le timbre d'argent*, 1877; *Etienne Marcel*, 1879; *Proserpine*, 1887; *Ascanio*, 1890; *Phryné*, 1893 (RECORDING MRF, 1960); *Frédégonde* (completion, with Dukas, of opera by Guiraud), 1895; *Les barbares*, 1901; *Hélène*, (1903), 1904; *L'ancêtre*, 1906; *Déjanire*, 1911
BIBLIOGRAPHY Martin Cooper, *French Music from the Death of Berlioz to the Death of Fauré*, OUP, 1951; J. Harding, *Saint-Saëns and His Circle*, Chapman and Hall, 1965

R.H.C.

The destruction of the palace in Act III of Samson et Dalila
(L'Illustration, *1890*)

opera. The customary spectacle and ballets form a logical part of the action. The clash between the austere Hebrews and the pleasure-loving Philistines is kept well in the foreground. In Act I the entry of Dalila and her maidens brings refreshment after the Hebrews' lament and Samson's killing of the satrap. In Act III the pathetic scene of Samson at the treadmill is followed by the appropriately superficial tinklings of Philistine rejoicing. Saint-Saëns made use of his knowledge of the classics: Bach (experienced perhaps through Mendelssohn) goes mainly to the Hebrews, Handel (his light, pagan side) to the Philistines, for instance in the canonic duet for the high priest and Dalila. In Act II the conflict is left to the protagonists. In the interview between Dalila and her master, Saint-Saëns works short, jagged instrumental phrases in a manner that makes one understand how theatre people in the 1870s were put off by the 'symphonic' nature of the writing in addition to the, to them, unacceptable subject matter. The symphonic aspect blinded them to the attraction of the set numbers. The eventual popularity of these numbers, ground out by café orchestras and pulled out of context, diverted serious musicians from the score's finer qualities. The orchestration is masterly throughout, especially in the second act where the dramatic tension is heightened by the sultry atmosphere – a summer storm circling round and breaking at the climax, the cooing of doves transformed into rushing storm scales.

ANTONIO SALIERI

b 18 August 1750, Legnago; *d* 7 May 1825, Vienna

At a time when it was the greatest wish of every young musician to be trained in Italy, Salieri crossed the Alps in the opposite direction. Orphaned at 15, he was already receiving financial help from a wealthy Venetian nobleman when he met Florian Gassmann, who invited the young composer to travel with him to Vienna. Under Gassmann's tutelage he received an excellent education and was introduced to three people who were to have a decisive influence on his subsequent career: Emperor Joseph II, who employed him as a chamber musician; the poet Metastasio, who taught him the art of declamation; and the composer Gluck, who was to become his friend and patron.

Salieri, therefore, is not a typical representative of the Italian opera tradition but a composer steeped in a mixture of styles who received a decisive stimulus from Gluck (though he never became his pupil) and who, in his best works, sought to end the distinction between opera seria and opera buffa by creating a *stile misto*. He first attracted attention in 1771 with *Armida*, described in the autograph score as an 'opera di stile magico-eroico-amorosa toccante il tragico'. Gluckian in its dramaturgy (but with its own identifiable musical language), it is a psychologically impressive work. In 1774 Salieri was appointed conductor of the Italian opera in Vienna (a post he retained until 1790), taking leave of absence when the 'German singspiel' was established at the Nationaltheater in 1778. When Gluck was prevented from writing *L'Europa riconosciuta* for the opening of La Scala, Milan, he passed on the commission to Salieri, who followed up this success with *La scuola de' gelosi*, written for Venice and soon taken up all over Europe. When the National Singspiel Theatre closed in Vienna in 1783, Salieri returned to the city and resumed control of the Italian opera, where he encouraged Da Ponte to work as librettist. He was soon invited to write *Les danaïdes* for Paris (again at Gluck's instigation), the great success of the work leading to other commissions from that city. When Mozart was composing *Le nozze di Figaro* to Da Ponte's adaptation of Beaumarchais's comedy, Salieri (now back in Vienna) was writing another Beaumarchais opera, this time to an original libretto, *Tarare*. It was a sensational success in pre-Revolutionary Paris. Salieri fully subscribed to Beaumarchais's belief that the music should be strictly subordinated to the words, an extreme development which turned Gluck's tragédie lyrique into a fully fledged music drama with what almost amounted to sprechgesang. Two further operas with political overtones and satirical exaggeration, *Cublai, gran kan de Tartari* (1788) and *Catilina* (1792), remain unperformed.

In 1788 Salieri was appointed hofkapellmeister and president of the Tonkünstler-Sozietät and thus became the most influential musician in Vienna. Posterity has accused him of hostility towards Mozart on account of his jealousy of the latter's genius

(a view propounded by Peter Shaffer in his play *Amadeus*). Certainly, Mozart's letters contain occasional references to Salieri's 'cabals', but these appear to relate to institutional disputes at the Nationaltheater involving, for example, questions of casting and scheduling. During this period Salieri was by far the more successful of the two composers and the later legend that Salieri poisoned Mozart is altogether without foundation. Both men clearly valued each other highly.

Salieri's operas are uneven in quality. Often the problem lies with an inferior libretto, but equally to blame was his loyalty to the Nationaltheater, which obliged him to fill gaps in the repertoire with hastily written works. After 1802 he wrote no more operas but transferred his energies to teaching both composition (to Beethoven, Czerny, Hummel, Liszt, Moscheles and Schubert, among others) and singing, his pupils including many famous names. He was also one of the leading figures in the musical life of Vienna. In addition to his operas, Salieri also wrote a handful of instrumental works, a great deal of church music and some shorter secular songs. Many of his operas were extraordinarily popular but after his death Salieri was quickly forgotten and is only now being rediscovered.

Les danaïdes

The Danaïdes

Tragédie lyrique in five acts (1h 45m)

Libretto by François Bailly du Roullet and Louis Théodore Baron de Tschudy, after Raniero de Calzabigi

PREMIERE 26 April 1784, Opéra, Paris

Raniero de Calzabigi's adaptation of the Hypermnestra legend was intended originally for Gluck and the Paris Opéra, but, finding himself unable to meet the terms of the commission, the latter invited Salieri to write the opera instead. The names of the two composers appeared together on the libretto, but Gluck wrote on the day of the first performance to Bailly du Roullet, instructing that a notice be inserted in the press saying that 'The music of *Les danaïdes* is completely by Salieri, my only part in it having been to make suggestions which he willingly accepted.' Salieri, in reply, acknowledged that he wrote 'completely under [Gluck's] supervision, guided by his light and genius'.

Believing himself betrayed, Danaus orders his 50 daughters to murder their husbands. Only Hypermnestra refuses, torn, as she is, between loyalty to her father and love of her husband Lynceus. The opera is planned entirely around its final scene in which the danaïdes are shown in hell, atoning for their crime. The work is in the grand operatic style, with its successful integration of choruses and ballets, and is notable, not least, for its great solo scene for Hypermnestra, which anticipates Cherubini's *Médée* (1797). It remained a great box-office success at the Paris Opéra until 1820.

RECORDING Marshall, Bartha, Giménez, Kavrakos, Stuttgart Radio Ch and O, Gelmetti, EMI, 1990
EDITIONS f.s., Des Lauriers, 1784; v.s., Paris, [c. 1880]

La grotta di Trofonio

Trofonio's Cave
Opera comica in two acts (2h)
Libretto by Giambattista Casti
PREMIERE 12 October 1785, Burgtheater, Vienna

Michael Kelly claimed that this opera was intended to rival Mozart's *Le nozze di Figaro*. But Mozart had barely started work on his own opera when Salieri's received its first performance (with Nancy Storace, Mozart's first Susanna, as Ophelia). The witty story tells of Trofonio's magic cave, which can turn people's characters into their complete opposites, and deals with two contrasted couples who are thrown into confusion as a result of the spell that is cast on them. Salieri's inventive music succeeds in distracting attention away from the weakness of the drama and produces an effective pastorale by mixing the most disparate stylistic elements. Trofonio and his infernal spirits recall the world of Gluck. The opera was one of Salieri's greatest successes.

EDITION f.s., Artaria, 1786

Prima la musica e poi le parole

First the Music and then the Words
Operetta in one act (1h)
Libretto by Giambattista Casti
PREMIERE 7 February 1786, Orangery, Schönbrunn Palace, Vienna

Written for an official function held for Emperor Joseph II, Salieri's operetta was first performed in a double-bill with Mozart's *Der Schauspieldirektor*. Both works deal with the problems of theatrical life; Salieri's is concerned with the difficulties of writing and rehearsing an opera, in the course of which librettist and composer, prima donna and soubrette come close to blows. One particularly amusing episode is the scene in which the female singers introduce themselves and the castrato Luigi Marchesi is parodied in the role of Giulio Sabino in Sarti's opera of the same name. The scene also includes a 'mad' aria. Although modest in scale, the work reveals Salieri's consummate skill as a buffo composer with an inclination towards satire.

RECORDINGS 1. Gamberucci, Casula, Polidori, Gatti, CO of the North Bohemian Philharmonia, Sanfilippo, Bongiovanni, 1989; 2. excerpts: Alexander, Hamari, Hampson, Holl, Concertgebouw O, Harnoncourt, Teldec, 1987
EDITIONS f.s./v.s., J. Heinzelmann and F. K. Wanek (eds), Schott, 1972

Tarare

Opera in five acts with a prologue (2h 45m)
Libretto by Pierre-Augustin Caron de Beaumarchais, after a Persian story
PREMIERES 8 June 1787, Opéra, Paris; UK: 15 August 1825, Lyceum, London

Beaumarchais was determined to create a sensation with this opera and so he included every possible trick in an attempt to excite attention. Pre-

Revolutionary Paris was a suitable backdrop for such an undertaking. An extended prologue depicts the state of primordial chaos in which Nature intervenes by creating humankind. It is human behaviour that the opera itself examines, with its tale of a cruel and cynical despot for whom no crime is too horrible to perpetrate. He is so jealous of the good fortune enjoyed by Tarare, one of his officers, that he determines to see him suffer in every possible way. He begins by setting fire to Tarare's home and follows this up by having his wife Astasie carried off to the royal seraglio. He suborns his priests into making false prophecies and finally condemns Tarare and Astasie to be burned at the stake. But Tarare is so popular with the people that their anger is finally stirred: the despot is overthrown (he stabs himself) and replaced by a new king chosen by the people – none other than Tarare himself, who accepts the challenge only with reluctance. To end the work, the gods of the prologue return and draw the moral: 'Man! Your greatness on this earth derives not from your social standing but solely from your character.'

The opera is highly unusual in form, using all kinds of recitative (which was praised as 'expressive and rapid') and including brief arioso passages, but never extending to traditional aria forms. As a music drama, it shows a radical treatment which develops the approach of Gluck and which was not to be repeated until Wagner embarked on his programme of operatic reform. *Tarare* represents an extreme experiment in operatic style, in which the music

Mlle Maillard as Astasie in Tarare *(Paris, 1786)*

reflects the outspoken text in its outright rejection of traditional forms.

EDITIONS f.ss., Imbault, 1787; Rudolph Angermüller (ed.), 2 vols, Henle, 1978; v.s., Paris, [c. 1880]

Axur, rè d'Ormus

Axus, King of Ormus

Dramma tragicomico in five acts (2h)
Libretto by Lorenzo Da Ponte adapted from Beaumarchais's libretto for *Tarare*
PREMIERE 8 January 1788, Burgtheater, Vienna

This revised version of *Tarare* was commissioned by Emperor Joseph II to celebrate the wedding of Archduke Franz (the future emperor of Austria) and was intended as a graphic demonstration of the rules of kingship. Originally only an Italian translation was planned, but Da Ponte and Salieri soon realized that there was a difference between 'music for French singing actors and music for Italian acting singers'. The result was a new version which changed the names of the characters, dispensed with the prologue and epilogue and tightened up some of the scenes to make them more dramatic, but which left unchanged the picture of the cruel tyrant. Da Ponte's adaptation could be compared with the changes he made to *La folle journée* when he turned it into *Le nozze di Figaro* and removed allusions to contemporary France, while retaining the original's political focus. Salieri adapted the musical material of *Tarare* to produce a melodically richer, largely through-composed opera with arias and ensembles, so that, of all his operas, *Axur* comes closest in its musical language to Mozart. The work was heard all over Europe in this Italian version, and during the Napoleonic Wars was used by both sides for propaganda purposes.

RECORDING Mei, Vespasiani, Rayam, Martin, Nova, Coro 'Guido d'Arezzo', Soviet PO, Clemencic, Nuova Era, 1989
EDITION v.s., Simrock, 1796

Falstaff, ossia Le tre burle

Falstaff, or The Three Pranks

Opera comica in two acts (2h)
Libretto by Carlo Prospero Defranceschi after *The Merry Wives of Windsor* by Shakespeare (1602)
PREMIERE 3 January 1799, Kärntnertortheater, Vienna

One of the earliest operas to be based on Shakespeare, Salieri's comedy – one of his last operas – is based on a skilful adaptation of *The Merry Wives of Windsor*, successfully reducing Shakespeare's large cast of characters to more manageable proportions by dispensing with various confusing sub-plots such as the one involving Anne's three suitors, concentrating instead on Falstaff himself and the two couples, the Fords and the Pages (here renamed Slender). The dialogue is extremely witty, and inspired Salieri to write some particularly light and sparkling music, highly effectively orchestrated. Unostentatious and full of subtle nuances,

the music breathes a mellow wisdom, while remaining wholly within the 18th-century tradition.

RECORDING Zempléni, Pánczél, Vámossy, Gulyás, Gáti, Csurja, Gregor, Salieri Chamber Ch and O, Pál, Hungaroton, 1985
EDITIONS f.s., Eva Riccioli (ed.), Edizioni musicali Otos, 1969; v.s., Vienna, 1799

Other operas: *Le donne letterate*, 1770; *L'amore innocente*, 1770; *Don Chisciotte alle nozze di Gamace*, 1770; *La moda*, 1771; *Armida*, 1771; *La fiera di Venezia*, 1772; *Il barone di Rocca antica*, 1772; *La secchia rapita*, 1772; *La locandiera*, 1773 (RECORDING Nuova Era, 1989); *La calamità de'cuori*, 1774; *La finta scema*, 1775; *Daliso e Delmita*, 1776; *L'Europa riconosciuta*, 1778; *La scuola de' gelosi*, 1778; *La partenza inaspettata*, 1779; *Der Rauchfangkehrer*, 1781; *Semiramide*, 1782; *Il ricco d'un giorno*, 1784; *Les Horaces*, 1786; *Cublai, gran kan de Tartari*, (1788); *Il talismano*, 1788; *Il pastor fido*, 1789; *La cifra*, 1789; *Catilina*, (1792); *Il mondo alla rovescia*, 1795; *Eraclito e Democrito*, 1795; *Palmira, Regina di Persia*, 1795; *Il moro*, 1796; *Cesare in Farmacusa*, 1800; *L'Angiolina*, 1800; *Annibale in Capua*, 1801; *La bella selvaggia*, (1802); *Die Hussiten vor Naumburg*, 1803; *Die Neger*, 1804
BIBLIOGRAPHY Rudolph Angermüller, *A. Salieri: Leben und weltliche Werke*, 3 vols, Munich, 1971–4; Volkmar Braunbehrens, *Salieri, ein Musiker im Schatten Mozarts*, Munich, 1989; E. E. Swenson, *A. Salieri: A Documentary Biography*, dissertation, Cornell University, UMF Ann Arbor, 1974

V.B.

AULIS SALLINEN

b 9 April 1935, Salmi, Finland

With four operas under his belt, Sallinen is firmly established as Finland's most successful composer for the stage. He was a leading figure in the national operatic renaissance of the 1970s, when 14 new works were staged in what is a small country with little operatic tradition; to a certain extent this was something of which Finnish composers took advantage, since the absence of tradition presupposed audiences without prejudice.

Sallinen studied in Helsinki with Merikanto and Kokkonen. Early preoccupation with atonality and orthodox serialism – in the 1950s still seen as the only true path – gradually gave way to a more personal, lyrical and tonal style. He has composed prolifically in all forms, chamber and symphonic music, oratorio as well as opera, and his music is melodious, colourfully yet fastidiously orchestrated, and notable for a certain sardonic wit that leavens his whole-hearted commitment to the subjects he chooses for his operas. His compositional ancestors include Shostakovich and Bartók, as well as the inescapable Sibelius, but their influence is subsumed into a highly personal style. His use of melody is especially individual; his tunes are like coiled springs, full of tension based on small intervals whose latent energy is eventually released, or, as a Finnish commentator has put it, a current bubbling through the winter ice gradually increasing in force (climate and landscape have always been crucial to Finnish composers). He writes extremely rewardingly for the voice.

Sallinen's music does not always find favour with the sterner critics in his homeland, who see him as conservative if not reactionary, but his operas have all been heard abroad and he is one of his country's most persuasive cultural ambassadors.

The Horseman

Ratsumies
Opera in three acts (2h 15m)
Libretto by Paavo Haavikko
PREMIERE   17 July 1975, Savonlinna Festival

The Horseman won the competition for a new opera to celebrate the 500th anniversary of the water fortress of Olavinlinna, built by the Swedes in 1475 at a strategic point in the lake system of eastern Finland to counter threats from Russia. The courtyard of Olavinlinna is the site of the annual Savonlinna opera festival.

Haavikko, one of Finland's leading poets, fashioned a dreamlike, symbolic action for Sallinen to set, a meditation on the historical fate of Finland. 'A dark forest set between two robber states', Finland was for 500 years part of the Swedish empire, and from the early 19th century until 1917 an autonomous Russian grand duchy.

In Act I Antti the Horseman and his wife Anna are serfs in the home of a rich Merchant in Novgorod, Russia. The Merchant takes Anna to his bed, as if by right. The Merchant's wife plays sadomasochistic games with the resentful Antti. Antti sets fire to the house, and before the doomed Merchant dies he has a vision of the Horseman's death. Haunted by the crime, Antti and Anna escape to Finland. Act II is set in Olavinlinna castle itself, at a Swedish assize. Anna appeals to be declared a widow, and an old man backs her claim, but the disguised Antti is recognized and imprisoned. In Act III Antti, having escaped, leads an assault by dissident Finns on a Swedish manor house. The plot is betrayed, and Antti is shot. Anna mourns him, and the final tableau – the pile of corpses illuminated by rat-chewed candles – is as foretold by the Russian Merchant.

The Horseman is very much a first opera, big, bold, broad in gesture, epic in treatment. The dreamlike scenario is weirdly compulsive, the music brooding and darksome, with flashes of melodic and orchestral energy. The writing for chorus in the trial scene is especially compelling.

RECORDING   Valjakka, Välkki, Erkkilä, Wallén, Salminen, Ch and O of the Savonlinna Festival, Söderblom, Finlandia, 1975
EDITIONS   f.s., Foundation for the Promotion of Finnish Music (on hire), 1975; v.s., Foundation for the Promotion of Finnish Music, 1977

The Red Line

Punainen viiva
Opera in two acts (1h 45m)

Libretto by the composer, based on the novel by Ilmari Kianto (1911)
PREMIERES   30 November 1978, Finnish National Opera, Helsinki; UK: 14 June 1979, Sadler's Wells, London; US: 27 April 1983, Metropolitan, New York
CAST   Topi *bar*, Riika *s*, Puntarpää *t*, Simana Arhippaini *b*, young priest *bar*, vicar *t*; *satb* chorus of country people
FULL ORCHESTRA including perc (4 players), hp, cel; onstage: brass band

Sallinen's second opera, commissioned by the Finnish National Opera, was perhaps wisely very unlike his first: tauter, neo-realist rather than Symbolist, painfully direct in its dramaturgy and musical treatment, yet still deeply embedded in the Finnish national experience. It is set at the time of the election of 1907; following the reverses of the Russo-Japanese War, Russification of Finland was relaxed and direct parliamentary elections allowed, the first in Europe in which women were allowed the vote.

SYNOPSIS
Act I   The action centres on a peasant family living at starvation level in a remote northern province. The husband Topi finds the remains of a sheep eaten by a marauding bear, and swears to kill it when it awakes from hibernation. The tensions between Topi and his wife Riika caused by their struggle to feed themselves and their three children are painfully explored. Topi dreams of his application to the vicar for poor relief being turned down; the latter offers cheap burial for the children, since the three little corpses can be accommodated in a single coffin. Simana Arhippaini, a pedlar from Russia, passes by, bringing rumours of unrest; Topi returns from the village with news of something called social democracy – words he cannot even pronounce – which will solve all their problems. Husband and wife attend a political meeting, at which Puntarpää, a professional agitator, exhorts the barely literate villagers to draw a red line on their voting slips to usher in the golden age.

Act II   Topi and his neighbours ponder how to register their votes: he has never held a pen in his life. They hear dogs barking at what they themselves cannot hear: the bear stirring in its sleep. On election day all proudly go to vote, brushing aside the protests of a young priest, who warns of social strife. While Topi is away earning money at a logging camp, Riika waits in vain for the changes promised by the agitator and looks on helplessly as her children die of malnutrition. Topi returns in time to bury them. News arrives that the election has been won. But the barking of the dogs and the lowing of Topi's one remaining cow indicate that the bear has awoken. Topi rushes out to do battle with it. Riika finds his corpse with his throat slit in a red line.

The greatest single strength of *The Red Line* lies in Sallinen's ability to write about inarticulate and underprivileged human beings without a hint of condescension, indeed with a compassion that suggests burning and furious identification. Despite the doom-laden narrative, this is not a depressing opera: Sallinen has Janáček's secret of using music to turn death and disaster into a celebration of the indomitability of the human spirit. The musical ideas have intense theatricality, from the use of stage brass and chorus to denote the ever-present bear, the catchy quasi-folktune of the Russian pedlar, or the searing funeral march to which Topi displays the corpses of his children to the audience, one by one. The political meeting is a virtuoso piece of operatic composition: the slithery clarinet tune to which the professional agitator insinuates his panaceas into the minds of his victims is gradually transformed into a march of undeniably stirring revolutionary fervour –this is operatic manipulation of audience emotion at its most insidious. *The Red Line* is one of the most immediately theatrical of all post-war operas, silencing through its sheer anger any critical reservations about its generally conservative musical idiom.

Heikki Siukola (Guide) in The King Goes Forth to France *(Savonlinna, 1984)*

RECORDING Valjakka, Viitanen, Hynninen, Hietikko, Ch and O of Finnish National Opera, Kamu, Finlandia, 1980
EDITION v.s., Novello, 1982

The King Goes Forth to France
Kuningas lahtee Ranskaan
Opera in three acts (2h 15m)
Libretto by Paavo Haavikko, based on his own play for radio
PREMIERES 7 July 1984, Savonlinna Opera Festival; US: 26 July 1986, Santa Fe; UK: 1 April 1987, Covent Garden, London

After the success of *The Red Line*, news of a remarkable new opera composer at work in Finland spread quickly, and resulted in a joint commission for Sallinen's third opera from the Savonlinna Opera Festival, the Royal Opera House, London, and the BBC. The result may have surprised the commissioners: Haavikko's radio play is a contemporary fantasy on themes from Froissart's account of the Hundred Years War. At a first encounter the surreal action seems teasingly inconsequential: precisely what, listeners ask themselves nervously, are Sallinen and Haavikko trying to tell us?

England is threatened by a new ice age. The Prime Minister presents the Prince with four possible fiancées, one of whom, Caroline, starts to show signs of mental instability. Instead of concerning himself with marriage, the Prince assumes power and leads his army, his people and his fiancées across the frozen channel to France, leaving England to its icy fate. In Act II the unstable Caroline becomes more so, imagining her royal wedding; the King has in fact married a German princess, and pawned both her and the crown jewels to raise money for the campaign. A new Battle of Crécy is fought and won through a combination of French incompetence (they slaughter their own Genoese allies) and England's secret weapon – an outsize cannon called Parliament. The Prime Minister advises a march on Paris; the King decides instead to besiege Calais. Outside the walls of Calais in Act III an English Archer asks for his discharge. The King orders him to be flayed; he teams up with the increasingly mad Caroline. The Six Burghers of Calais are spared, having warned the King against the treacherous peasantry; the King promotes them to membership of his War Tribunal. He announces his plans: a march on Paris, the flaying of the French King for war crimes (the English Archer enthusiastically applauds this wise move) and a march to the south – to sun, warmth and wine. The army sets off.

The oblique, cynical humour of *The King* should not disguise its essential seriousness: if it is about anything concrete, it is – in the words of the critic and Sallinen enthusiast Max Loppert – about 'mankind's cynical urge to debase and destroy itself through irrational violence'. The protagonist starts out as an innocent idealist and ends up a drunken, power-crazed tyrant. Sallinen's sardonic sense of humour is well to the fore (the Genoese bowmen march to Crécy to a raucous version of Schubert's D major *Marche militaire*), as is his compassion for the underdog: the flayed English Archer and the mad Caroline share the score's most lyrical passages, and the former's sudden conversion to cynical time-serving in the last scene seems almost an act of betrayal by the composer. In general, good sense and beautiful music are shared by the four fiancées – a politically correct *aperçu avant la lettre* – and the use of orchestral colour to suggest the iron entering the protagonist's soul is extremely cunning.

EDITION v.s., Novello, 1986

Kullervo
Opera in two acts (2h 30m)
Libretto by the composer, based on Runos 31–6 of the *Kalevala* and the play by Aleksis Kivi (1864)
Composed 1988
PREMIERE 25 February 1992, Dorothy Chandler Pavilion, Los Angeles (Finnish National Opera)
CAST Kullervo *bar*, Kimmo *t*, Kullervo's mother *s*, Kalervo *b-bar*, Kullervo's sister *s*, Unto *bar*, Unto's wife *ms*, Blind Ballad Singer *bar*, Smith's wife *ms*; *satb* chorus of observers

FULL ORCHESTRA including perc (4 players), hp, synthesizer, 15 voices on pre-recorded tape

Sallinen's fourth opera was commissioned by the Finnish National Opera to open their new opera house in Helsinki; as the completion of the building was further and further delayed, the company instead gave the premiere as part of celebrations of the 75th anniversary of Finnish independence on tour in Los Angeles.

SYNOPSIS
The choral prologue describes wars between the tribes in which Kullervo's parents are slaughtered by his uncle, Unto.

Act I Kullervo and his friend Kimmo are slaves in his uncle Unto's household and, on discovering the identity of his parents' murderer, Kullervo swears vengeance. Unto resists his wife's urgings to kill the troublesome youth, and instead sells him to the blacksmith Ilmarinen. The Smith's wife tries to seduce the inexperienced youth, taunts him for his lack of response, and bakes a stone in his bread on which he breaks the knife he inherited from his father. Kullervo murders her. Kimmo discovers that Kullervo's parents are not dead after all, and reunites the family. This is not a success: when his father Kalervo learns that his son is a murderer, he disowns and rejects him, but his mother cannot bear to lose her son a second time and begs him to stay.

Act II The Blind Ballad Singer describes in his 'Ballad of the Sister's Ravishing', how Kullervo met a beautiful girl and seduced her. When their relationship became known, she committed suicide. This makes it doubly impossible for Kullervo to stay in his parents' house; although his mother is pre-pared to forgive even this latest crime, he leaves, determined to take revenge on his uncle's tribe. His mother dies of grief, and his father commits suicide. Kullervo teams up with a gang of outlaws, and the slaughter of Unto's tribe is duly accomplished. Kullervo seeks out Kimmo, his last hope of human companionship, only to find that he has gone mad. Kullervo immolates himself.

All myths are interconnected: there are elements of Orestes and Siegmund in the character of Kullervo, a man raised to be alienated from society against a background of unrelenting violence and emotional trauma. 'Am I afraid of death?' he asks before immolating himself. 'It could not be worse than life. This is what the world has made of me.'

To tell this grisly tale Sallinen fined down his musical language to its essentials; it is a score at once sardonic, horror-struck and profoundly compassion-ate. The deliberately cheap yet insistently catchy pop-song setting of the 'Ballad of the Sister's Ravishing' is alienating in a peculiarly unsettling way, while the mother's song of love for her errant child is one of the the most heartfelt passages in all Sallinen's operas. There is a prominent role for chorus, describing and commenting on the continuous acts of violence, at times recoiling in horror, at others – as in *Turandot* – conniving in them. In telling audiences how

society creates monsters in its midst, Sallinen can-not possibly have known that within weeks of the premiere the Los Angeles riots would break out; that particular audience could not say that it hadn't been warned.

RECORDING Saarinen, Jakobsson, Silvasti, Hynninen, Salminen, Finnish National Ch and O, Söderblom, Ondine, 1992
EDITION v.s., Novello, 1989

BIBLIOGRAPHY Erkki Arni, *The Horseman, the Line and the King*, Savonlinnan kirjapaino Oy, 1984, in Finnish; Mikko Heinio, 'Aulis Sallinen – Seeking the Truth in Performance', *Finnish Music Quarterly*, vol. 1 (1991), in English

R.M.

JOHANN PETER SALOMON
baptized 2 February 1745, Bonn; *d* 28 November 1815, London

The son of a Bonn oboist, Salomon became music director to Prince Heinrich of Prussia. When the prince's orchestra was disbanded in 1780 he travelled to Paris and to London, joining the Covent Garden orchestra as a violinist in 1781. He soon began to act as an impresario, starting his famous series of subscription concerts in 1783. It was for these concerts that Salomon brought Haydn to London in 1791–2 and again in 1794–5.

Salomon composed operas throughout his career, and his most important stage work was the medieval extravaganza *Windsor Castle*, composed to com-memorate the wedding of the Prince of Wales to the musically gifted Princess Caroline of Brunswick in April 1795. Salomon's librettist, William Pearce, originally intended that the second act should consist of a tournament, in tune with his chivalric theme, but at the insistence of the choreographer, Noverre, it was turned into a 'masque' (actually a ballet). Although the printed score contains Salomon's extended overture, he asked Haydn to provide the one used in the performances (the *Overture to an English Opera* published in 1951).

Stage works: *Titus*, 1774; *La reine de Golconde*, 1776; *Windsor Castle, or The Fair Maid of Kent*, 1795; 2 others lost
BIBLIOGRAPHY Roger Fiske, *English Theatre Music in the Eighteenth Century*, OUP, 1973, pp. 554–5

T.T.C.

SPYRIDON SAMARAS
Spyridon Filískos Samaras; *b* 29 November 1861 or 22 November 1863, Corfu; *d* 7 April 1917, Athens

The first Greek composer to achieve an international reputation, Samaras was an established member of the Italian *verismo* school of opera, though his operas are now totally neglected. He is remembered only as the composer of the official *Hymn of the*

Olympic Games; this was commissioned for the first modern Olympics, held in Athens in 1896, and was later adopted as a permanent anthem.

Born to a Greek father and English mother, Samaras studied with Spyros Xyndas (the first opera composer to set a Greek libretto) and at Athens University under Stancampiano, a pupil of Mercadante, who collaborated with Samaras on the latter's first opera, *Olas*. After further study in Paris with Delibes, Samaras wrote *Flora mirabilis*, which anticipates many features of *verismo* opera (it predates Mascagni's *Cavalleria rusticana* by four years) and was premiered in Milan (1896) to great acclaim. Further successes in Italy followed including *La martyre*, which has a libretto by Puccini's librettist Illica. Such was Samaras's popularity that he threatened at one time to overshadow Mascagni. His musical style was essentially Italian, though it also includes some distinctively French elements and his last opera, *Rhea* (performed as far afield as Cairo), introduces Greek folksongs and Byzantine melodies.

Samaras returned to Greece in 1911 and turned his attention to lighter stage works, composing three operettas in his native language. An opera, *Hi Tigris*, was unfinished at the time of his death.

Operatic works: *Olas*, 1882; *Flora mirabilis*, 1886; *Medgè*, 1888; *Lionella*, 1891; *La martyre*, 1894; *La furia domata*, 1895; *Storia d'amore*, 1903; *Mademoiselle de Belle Isle*, 1905; *La biondinetta*, (1906); *Rhea*, 1908; *Polemos en polemo* (*War in War*), 1914; *Pringipissa tis Sasson* (*The Princess of Sasson*), 1915; *Criticopoula* (*The Cretan Girl*), 1916; *Hi Tigris* (*The Tiger*), (inc.)

BIBLIOGRAPHY   Th. N. Synadines, *History of Modern Greek Music 1824–1919*, Athens, 1919

G.C.P.

GIOVANNI BATTISTA SAMMARTINI

Giovanni Battista Sammartini [St Martini, San Martini, San Martino]; *b* 1700 or 1701, ?Milan; *d* 15 January 1775, Milan

Sammartini, the son of a French oboist and brother of Giuseppe Sammartini, another oboist and composer, was Milan's greatest composer in the 18th century and an important figure in the development of the classical style; his reputation stretched far beyond his native city, to Paris, Vienna and London. He is remembered chiefly for his contribution to the symphony and to chamber music.

His three operas, which show a mixture of baroque and classical elements, belong to a decade in the early part of his career, when he had established a firm reputation in Milan as maestro di cappella in several churches, including Sant'Ambrogio. They follow the conventions of opera seria, with mostly *da capo* arias. Sammartini used movements from two of his symphonies, the earliest known dated examples of the genre, as introductions to Acts II and III of his opera *Memet* in 1732. His influence on Gluck, who borrowed movements from Sammartini's sym-

phonies in his operas *Le nozze d'Ercole* (1747) and *La contesa dei numi* (1749), is well known. There are also similarities between Gluck's *Demofoonte* (Milan, 1742) and Sammartini's *L'Agrippina* (1743), suggesting that the influence was not entirely one way.

Operas: *Memet*, 1732; *L'ambizione superata dalla virtù*, 1734; *L'Agrippina*, 1743

BIBLIOGRAPHY   Newell Jenkins and Bathia Churgin, *Thematic Catalogue of the Works of Giovanni Battista Sammartini: Orchestral and Vocal Music*, Harvard University Press, 1976

D.S.B.

GIUSEPPE SAMMARTINI

Giuseppe Francesco Gaspare Melchiore Baldassare Sammartini [St Martini and other variants]; *b* 6 January 1695, Milan; *buried* 22 November 1750, London

Sammartini was an oboist and recorder-player from a French family of professional musicians in Milan; he was the son of the oboist Alexis Saint-Martin and the elder brother of the composer Giovanni Battista Sammartini. Giuseppe arrived in London probably in 1729 and quickly established himself as an eminent performer (he was Handel's first oboist) and as a composer of instrumental music. In 1736 he became a member of the household of the Prince and Princess of Wales; he directed Prince Frederick's chamber ensemble and taught Princess Augusta music. His only major vocal work, a setting of Congreve's masque *The Judgement of Paris*, was written for an outdoor entertainment given for the third birthday of Frederick's daughter, Lady Augusta. He was an accomplished composer, though more conservative than his brother; he followed Handel and Geminiani in contributing to the English genre of the post-Corelli concerto grosso.

The Judgement of Paris

All-sung masque
Text by William Congreve
PREMIERE   1 August 1740, Cliveden House, nr Maidenhead

Congreve wrote *The Judgement of Paris* for the Musick Prize, the famous operatic competition unexpectedly won in 1701 by John Weldon in the face of competition from John Eccles, Daniel Purcell and Gottfried Finger. Though the settings are all-sung it was called a masque because it is based on Classical myth and has elements of allegory: the shepherd Paris has to choose whether to award the golden apple of beauty (a symbol of the 'Musick Prize') to Juno, Pallas Athene or Venus; Venus wins. Sammartini's fine setting came at a moment when English theatre composers were turning to old libretti; it was the first since 1701 and clearly inspired the later one by Thomas Arne (1742).

MANUSCRIPT   The British Library, London

BIBLIOGRAPHY   Roger Fiske, *English Theatre Music in the Eighteenth Century*, OUP, 1973; 2nd edn, 1986

P.H.

DOMENICO SARRO

Domenico Natale Sarro [Sarri, Sarra]; *b* 24 December 1679, Trani, Apulia; *d* 25 January 1744, Naples

Trained at the music conservatory of Sant'Onofrio, Sarro was employed at the court in Naples from 1704 to 1707, and again from 1720 onwards. His period of greatest activity and fame as an opera composer was during the 1720s, but his role in the development of opera has been consistently underrated: he has been viewed as a transitional figure and imitator of his famous contemporaries, such as Vinci. Rather, he was one of the most significant Neapolitan composers of his generation, among the earliest and most important products of the city's conservatory system in the 18th century with its unique process of theatrical training.

His early musical style is modelled on that of Alessandro Scarlatti, but by the mid-1720s he had abandoned his older contemporary's more contrapuntal manner for one in which the musical texture was generally clearer and pronouncedly melodic, with the top part prominent and the other voices functioning simply as accompaniment. Within his own lifetime he was already regarded as somewhat old-fashioned, and his later works (few of which survive) show little of the technical innovation apparent earlier.

Surviving operas: *Le gare generose tra Cesare e Pompeo*, ?1706; *Il Vespasiano*, 1707; *I gemelli rivali*, 1713; *Armida al campo*, 1718; *Arsace*, 1718 (EDITION facsimile, Garland, 1978); *Ginevra Principessa di Scozia*, 1720; *Lucio Vero*, 1722; *La Partenope*, 1722; *Didone abbandonata*, 1724; *Tito Sempronio Gracco*, 1725; *Il Valdemaro*, 1726; *Siroe, re di Persia*, 1727; *Artemisia*, 1731; *Berenice*, 1732; *Achille in Sciro*, 1737; 14 lost operas
BIBLIOGRAPHY   Michael F. Robinson, *Naples and Neapolitan Opera*, OUP, 1972

D.S.B.

GIUSEPPE SARTI

baptized 1 December 1729, Faenza; *d* 28 July 1802, Berlin

Sarti, an important opera composer of the late 18th century, won an early success with *Pompeo in Armenia*, written for the local theatre in Faenza in 1752; this was followed by further acclaim for *Il re pastore*, performed in Venice in 1753. From 1755, except between 1765 and 1768, he served for 20 years as kapellmeister and director of Italian opera at the Danish court in Copenhagen. There he wrote many Metastasian settings and a few Danish singspiels. Returning to Italy, he gained a European reputation

with a series of operas produced in Milan, while serving as maestro di cappella at the cathedral. His many pupils included Cherubini.

Giulio Sabina, first performed in Venice in 1781, was one of the most popular and widely performed opere serie of the last quarter of the 18th century. Metastasian in structure, it anticipates later operas in its celebration of conjugal love, though its flavour remains neo-classical. It was staged throughout Europe, and was the first opera seria performed at Eszterháza (1783), where its success probably influenced Haydn's composition of *Armida*, his first opera seria, the following year. *Giulio Sabina*'s popularity, and Sarti's subsequent fame, was no doubt instrumental in prompting Grand Duke Paul of Russia to invite Sarti to succeed Paisiello as director of the imperial chapel in St Petersburg in 1784. On his way there, he stopped in Vienna, where he was honoured by the Emperor Joseph II and where he met Mozart, who later parodied one of the arias ('Come un agnello') from *Fra i due litiganti* in the dinner scene in *Don Giovanni*. Under him, the Italian Opera at St Petersburg reached its artistic zenith; Sarti also composed a Russian opera, *The Early Reign of Oleg* (1790). After the death of the emperor in 1801, he decided to return to Italy, but died in Berlin while visiting one of his daughters.

Popular in their time, Sarti's works have not stood up to modern-day examination, betraying a conventionality of melody and harmony and a lack of dramatic sense, despite considerable technical accomplishment. His formal practices are more interesting, however: he made little use of the *da capo* aria, *preferring a two-part, slow–fast structure or else* a through-composed form, particularly noticeable in his comic operas. According to DiChiera, his accompanied recitative shows him at his best, with its rich harmonies and expressive instrumentation. Ensembles and choruses are insignificant in his serious operas but frequent and extremely varied in his comic works.

Surviving operas: *Vologeso*, 1754; *Antigono*, 1754; *Ciro riconosciuto*, 1754; *Gram og signe eller Kiaerligheds*, 1756; *Anagilda*, 1758; *Nitteti*, 1760; *Alessandro nell'Indie*, 1761; *Semiramide*, 1762, rev. 1768; *Didone abbandonata*, 1762; *Cesare in Egitto*, 1763; *Ipermestra*, 1766; *La giardiniera brillante*, 1768; *Soliman den Anden*, 1770; *Demofoonte*, 1771; *Tronfælgen i Sidon* (*The Succession to the Throne in Sidonia*), 1771; *Le gelose villane*, 1776; *Ifigenia*, 1777; *Medonte, re di Epiro*, 1777; *Il militare bizzarro*, 1777; *Olimpiade*, 1778; *Scipione*, 1778; *I contratempi*, 1778; *Adriano in Siria*, 1778; *Mitridate a Sinope*, 1779; *Achille in Sciro*, 1779; *Siroe*, 1779; *Didone abbandonata*, 1782 (EDITION facsimile, Garland 1982); *Alessandro e Timoteo*, 1782; *Fra i due litiganti il terzo gode*, 1782; *Idalide*, 1783; *Erifile*, 1783; *Olimpiade*, 1783; *Gli amanti consolati*, 1784; *I finti eredi*, 1785; *Armida e Rinaldo*, 1786; *Castore e Polluce*, 1786; *Andromeda*, 1798; *Enea nel Lazio*, 1799; *La famille indienne en Angleterre*, 1799; 33 lost operas
BIBLIOGRAPHY   Mario Baroni and Marra Gioia Tavoni (eds), *Giuseppe Sarti, Musicista faentino*, Atti del convegno internazionale (Faenza), 1983; David Di Chiera and Denis Libby, 'Giuseppe Sarti', in *Grove*, Macmillan, 1980

D.S.B.

ANTONIO SARTORIO

b 1630, Venice; *d* 30 December 1680, Venice

Sartorio was one of the foremost Venetian opera composers of the mid-17th century. He first emerged in the early 1660s and in 1666 formed an association with the Teatro S. Salvatore. But his career was not confined to Venice; in the mid-1660s he became Kapellmeister to the Catholic convert and Italophile Duke Johann Friedrich of Brunswick-Luneburg in Hanover, and he remained there for almost a decade, while frequently returning to Venice to produce operas for Carnival. In Hanover his energies were directed more towards the stage than the composition of church music.

In 1673 Sartorio was called in to salvage Cavalli's *Massenzio*. Taste was changing fast and the older composer's work, lacking in arias, was considered to be of little interest. The impresario of the Teatro S. Salvatore asked Sartorio to inject some spectacle and excitement into the drama, effectively to rewrite it, in less than two weeks. Like many of Sartorio's operas, *Massenzio* is based on one of the heroes of Classical Rome, but the seriousness of the music is frequently punctuated by comic scenes.

Sartorio was fond of introducing chromatic, augmented and diminished intervals for expressive ends. *L'Orfeo*, among other operas, contains word-painting that is expressive of the language rather than directly pictorial.

Extant operas: *Gl'amori infruttuosi di Pirro* (only arias survive), 1661; *Seleuco*, 1666; *La prosperità d'Elio Seiano*, 1667; *La caduta d'Elio Seiano*, 1667; *L'Adelaide*, 1672 (EDITION facsimile, H. M. Brown (ed.), Garland, 1978); *L'Orfeo*, 1672; *Massenzio*, 1673; *Giulio Cesare in Egitto* (only arias survive), 1676; *Antonino e Pompeiano*, 1677; *L'Anacreonte tiranno*, 1677; *Ercole su'l Termodonte* (only arias survive), 1678; *La Flora* (inc.; completed M. A. Ziani), 1680; 3 lost operas

G.D.

ERIK SATIE

Erik (Eric) Alfred Leslie Satie; *b* 17 May 1866, Honfleur, France; *d* 1 July 1925, Paris

A composer of rarefied and sometimes deliberately gauche miniatures, Satie occupies the pole opposite the gargantuan Wagnerian music drama that dominated the late 19th century. He was a gifted dilettante, not a highly trained or even competent composer. But the austere charm and originality of his early music, especially piano pieces such as the *Gymnopédies* (1888), influenced his talented colleagues, including Debussy and Ravel, and, later, the minimalist thinking of John Cage.

Satie's music was scarcely known outside a tiny professional circle until Ravel and Debussy gave performances in 1911. The subsequent interest of publishers liberated his imagination and in the next 10 years he created his most lasting works, the

ballets *Parade* and *Relâche*, which drew on his early experiences as a composer of café music, and the symphonic drama *Socrate*. In his later years, although he was idolized by a group of young composers, he became a reclusive alcoholic.

Geneviève de Brabant

Genevieve of Brabant

Miniature opera for marionettes in a prelude and three acts (15m)
Libretto by J. P. Contamine de Latour
Composed 1899; orch. Roger Desormière, 1926
PREMIERES 17 May 1926, Théâtre des Champs-Elysées, Paris; UK: 30 May 1989, Queen Elizabeth Hall, London (orch. Dominic Muldowney)

SYNOPSIS
Act I A narrator tells how Genevieve's husband Sifroy has gone off to war leaving his pregnant wife in the care of his chamberlain Golo, who attempts, unsuccessfully, to seduce her. Golo accuses her of adultery and she is sent to prison, where she gives birth to a son.

Act II On his return, Sifroy regretfully orders the death of his wife and son. Soldiers cannot bear to carry out his command, however, and allow the two to escape into the forest. While out hunting, Sifroy is led by a doe to a grotto where he is reunited with his wife and child.

Act III The wicked Golo is flayed alive. Genevieve, committed entirely to God, dies. A heavenly light illuminates her funeral procession.

This tiny opera is, in the manner of the *Gymnopédies*, calm and simple and, because it is for marionettes, unreal and distant. The puppet characters sing in simple, clichéd words to simple, syllabic tunes and the harmony is gently soporific.

RECORDING Mesplé, Benoit, Ch of the National Theatre Opera, O de Paris, Dervaux, Arabesque, 1970s
EDITIONS f.s., Universal, 1930; new edn with original lib., Universal, 1986

Socrate

Socrates

Drame symphonique avec voix (35m)
Libretto by the composer, drawn from V. Cousin's translation of Plato's *Dialogues*
Composed 1918
PREMIERE 1918, Princess de Polignac's theatre, Paris (private); 14 February 1920, Société Nationale de Musique, Paris

Often considered Satie's masterpiece, this austere, disciplined work was described by the composer as 'white and pure as antiquity'. Its deceptively simple surface focuses attention on the smallest changes in the sound itself. Although it has four characters, it can be performed by a single singer (probably originally intended to be a soprano) with chamber ensemble or piano. Alcibiades praises Socrates' charm; the philosopher deflects such praise and, charmingly, begins complementing another in the group. Phaedrus and Socrates then discuss philosophy, myth and legend. Finally Phaedrus describes Socrates' imprisonment and suicide.

RECORDINGS 1. Millet, Guiot, Esposito, Mesplé, O de Paris, Dervaux, EMI, 1972; 2. Cuenod, Parsons (pf), Nimbus, 1977
EDITIONS f.s., Eschig, 1950; v.s., Eschig, 1919; arr. for 2 pf by John Cage, Eschig, 1984

Other operatic work: *Pousse l'amour* (operetta; inc.), *c.* 1905
BIBLIOGRAPHY Alan M. Gillmor, *Erik Satie*, Macmillan, 1988; Nigel Wilkins, *The Writings of Erik Satie*, Eulenburg, 1980

C.B.

HENRI SAUGUET
Henri-Pierre Poupard; *b* 18 May 1901, Bordeaux, France; *d* 22 June 1989, Paris

Born Henri Poupard, Sauguet bore his mother's name from 1920, when, after a concert in Bordeaux that included works by such modernist composers as Falla, Stravinsky, Schoenberg, Milhaud, Auric, Poulenc, Bartók and Satie, he was enjoined by his father not to compromise the family honour by playing at such scandalous events except under a pseudonym. Sauguet came under the spell of Debussy's music as a boy, writing a letter to his idol on 26 March 1918 – the day Debussy died and the day Sauguet resolved to become a composer. Invited to Paris by Milhaud in 1921, Sauguet studied there with Charles Koechlin. He met Satie in 1922, and became one of the four young composers who, as l'école d'Arceuil, grouped themselves around that composer. Sauguet's first success, with his opéra bouffe *Le Plumet du colonel* (1924), was followed by 27 ballets, among them *La Chatte* (1927) and *Les forains* (1945). Of his succeeding stage works, the most important is *La Chartreuse de Parme*.

La Chartreuse de Parme
The Charterhouse of Parma
Opera in four acts (ten tableaux)
Libretto by Armand Lunel, after the novel by Stendhal (1839)
Composed 1927–36, rev. 1968
PREMIERE 20 March 1939, Opéra, Paris

For ten years Sauguet dreamed of deriving an opera from Stendhal's lengthy story of the life, loves, relations and intrigues surrounding a minor Italian court in the Napoleonic period. Lunel's text reduces the narrative to depict the inter-relationships of the principal characters: the youthful Fabrice del Dongo, compromised as a Napoleonic volunteer; his doting aunt, the Countess Gina, mistress of Count Mosca; the General Conti, and his daughter Clélia. Sauguet matches the complexity of the plot with music that is unashamedly tonal (though modern), direct in its appeal and transparently scored.

EDITION v.s., private publication by the composer

Other operatic works: *Le Plumet du colonel*, 1924; *Un amour du Titien* (inc.), (1928); *La contrebasse*, 1930; *La gageure imprévue*, 1944; *Les caprices de Marianne*, 1954; *Soledad, ou Peau d'Espagne* (inc.), (1963); *Le pain des autres*, (1974); *Boule de suif*, 1978; *Tistou-les-pouces-verts*, 1981
BIBLIOGRAPHY Marcel Schneider, *Henri Sauguet*, Vantadour, 1959

F.A.

ROBERT SAXTON
Robert Louis Alfred Saxton; *b* 8 October 1953, London

Saxton started young as a composer, but came to opera comparatively late, having made his name through a succession of brilliant orchestral works such as *The Ring of Eternity* (1983) and *The Circles of Light* (1986). He was composing by the age of six and when he was nine began corresponding with Britten (who remains a strong spiritual influence); later he took private composition lessons with Lutyens, then studied at Cambridge with Holloway. He has also worked with Berio.

Saxton's concert music soaked up many of the fashionable influences of the 1960s and early 1970s, without ever sacrificing its individuality for long. An obsession with intricate textural workings gradually gave way to a more architectural kind of thinking, with planned (atonal) harmony and a more symphonic, propulsive style. For a time he wrote little for the voice, though much inspired by poetry. But in the 1980s a succession of choral works led naturally to his first opera since a schoolboy effort (*Cinderella*).

Caritas
Opera in two acts without interval (1h 15m)
Libretto by Arnold Wesker, from his play *Caritas* (1980)
Composed 1988–91
PREMIERE 21 November 1991, Opera House, Wakefield

Wesker's drama, set in Norfolk in 1377–81 at the time of the Peasants' Revolt, is based on the true story of a young woman, Christine Carpenter, who became an anchoress (actually in 1329 at Shere) but had to be re-enclosed after persistently leaving her cell. In the opera, Christine prays with increasing intensity for a divine 'showing', but finally despairs and pleads in vain to be released.

Saxton's Christine (a taxing part for a dramatic soprano) is portrayed in music of strong line and considerable emotional depth. But the punctuating short scenes, depicting the reactions of her family and fiancée together with events in the Peasants' Revolt, are more problematical and seem to parry the work's main psychological thrust. The idea of (religious) authority versus individual consciousness is familiar from other contemporary operas (Maxwell Davies's *Taverner*, Goehr's *Behold the Sun*). What distinguishes *Caritas* especially is the fascinating craftsmanship of its instrumental writing for chamber orchestra.

RECORDING   Davies, Best, Ventris, Hibberd, Bryson, Chamber O of Opera North, Masson, Collins Classics, 1991
EDITIONS   f.s., Chester Music (on hire), 1991; v.s., Chester Music, forthcoming

BIBLIOGRAPHY   Andrew Clements, 'Getting It Right' (interview with Saxton and Wesker), *Opera*, vol. 42 (1991), pp. 1273–6

S.W.

ALESSANDRO SCARLATTI

Pietro Alessandro Gaspare Scarlatti; *b* 2 May 1660, Palermo; *d* 22 October 1725, Naples

Alessandro Scarlatti was the most important opera composer of his generation in Italy, but such titles as 'Founder of the Neapolitan School', often attached to him, cannot be accepted without qualification. Scarlatti spent much of his working life in Rome, and also wrote operas for Florence and Venice; moreover he seems to have had little direct influence on the next generation of opera composers at Naples, although Hasse was his pupil for a short time. Finally, the extent to which the operatic style of these composers (who include Leo, Vinci and Porpora as well as Hasse) can be said to represent a school, as distinct from a pan-Italian tradition, is a matter of dispute.

Scarlatti left Sicily with other members of his family in 1672 and settled in Rome. His first operas were written for private patrons there and were immediately admired for their tunefulness, attracting the attention of Queen Christina of Sweden, who made Scarlatti her maestro di cappella in 1680. Some were heard also in Naples, and Scarlatti was already well known as an opera composer when he was appointed maestro di cappella to the Spanish viceroy there in 1684. The staple operatic diet of Naples consisted of Venetian imports, and the operas that Scarlatti composed up to about 1700 reflect this. They consist mainly of simple recitatives and numerous short arias: *La caduta de' Decemviri* (1697), for example, has no fewer than 51 arias and 11 duets. This opera nevertheless exemplifies some new features associated with the last four or five years of Scarlatti's first period at Naples: the so-called 'Italian' overture (fast–slow–fast) replaces the earlier Venetian type; arias with more than one strophe, or which use a ground-bass structure, are no longer found; and the string band is more actively employed. In Scarlatti's later operas the number of arias gradually decreases as their proportions become more ample, and their accompaniments become richer and more diversified; also, accompanied recitative plays a gradually increasing role in lending emotional depth or dramatic impact to the music.

In 1702 Scarlatti left Naples with his family and went to Florence, where he hoped for employment with Prince Ferdinando de' Medici. The attempt failed, though it did result in a series of operas (1702–6) for the prince's private theatre at Pratolino.

Engraving after Filippo Juvarra's set for Alessandro Scarlatti's Il Ciro (Rome, 1712)

The scores of these have unfortunately not survived. Scarlatti's attempt to establish himself as an opera composer in Venice, with two five-act tragedies to libretti by Frigimelica Roberti, also met with no success, partly because the operas were considered too serious, but also, it seems, because of Scarlatti's arrogant behaviour towards the Venetians and their own xenophobic attitude towards him. Scarlatti meanwhile had found employment as a church musician in Rome. He resumed his former post in Naples in 1709, but he remained in close touch with Rome (where his son Domenico was still active) and some of his finest late operas, including the last one to survive, *La Griselda* (1721), were composed for the city in which he had made his operatic début some 40 years earlier.

Gli equivoci nel sembiante
Mistaken identities

Dramma per musica in three acts (1h 45m)
Libretto by Domenico Filippo Contini
PREMIERE   February 1679, private theatre of D. F. Contini, Rome

This was the earliest of Scarlatti's operas to be staged. It is an Arcadian pastoral on an intimate scale, with a single set and four characters. Twin shepherds become the victims of mistaken identity, leading to jealousies and misunderstandings between them and their lovers. The opera was an immediate success, and was soon repeated in other major Italian cities and as far afield as Vienna (1681).

EDITION Frank A. D'Accone (ed.), *The Operas of Alessandro Scarlatti*, vol. 7, Harvard University Press, 1982

Il Pompeo
Pompey
Dramma per musica in three acts
Libretto by Nicolò Minato
PREMIERE 25 January 1683, private theatre of Cardinal Colonna, Rome

Il Pompeo, the first of Scarlatti's many operas based on events in Roman history (though with a liberal admixture of spurious events and characters), is not one of the best of his early works; among its arias only 'O cessate di piagarmi' from Act II is remembered today. The opera was, however, very successful in the 1680s, and Handel used some material from it in oratorios and other works he composed between 1732 and 1744.

EDITION facsimile, John H. Roberts (ed.), *Handel Sources: Material for the Study of Handel Borrowings*, vol. 6, Garland, 1986

La Statira
Statira
Dramma per musica in three acts
Libretto by Pietro Ottoboni
PREMIERES 5 January 1690, Teatro Tordinona, Rome; UK: 8 May 1970, Jeanetta Cochrane Theatre, London

The plot combines incidents from Plutarch's *Lives* and Pliny's *Natural History*, and tells of Alexander the Great's love for Statira, daughter of Darius, the Persian king, and of the painter Apelles' love for Alexander's mistress, Campaspe. After the usual intrigues, as well as renunciations on the part of Alexander and the Persian prince, Orontes, the two pairs of lovers are united. The opera was composed for the reopening of the Teatro Tordinona after its long closure during the pontificate of Innocent XI, and the choice of subject was perhaps intended as a tribute to the magnanimity of the new pope, Alexander VIII (great-uncle of the librettist), in allowing the Roman theatres to reopen their doors to the public.

EDITION William C. Holmes (ed.), *The Operas of Alessandro Scarlatti*, vol. 9, Harvard University Press, 1985

La caduta de' Decemviri
The Fall of the Decemvirate
Dramma per musica in three acts
Libretto by Silvio Stampiglia after incidents in Livy, Book III
PREMIERE 15 December 1697, Teatro San Bartolomeo, Naples

In Rome, where Alexander VIII had been succeeded by Innocent XII, papal opposition again made conditions difficult for opera, and in 1697 the Pope ordered the demolition of the Teatro Tordinona. In the same year in Naples the first of Scarlatti's several collaborations with Stampiglia, one of the most gifted

of the Arcadian dramatists, was staged. This was *La caduta de' Decemviri*, the action of which takes place at the time of the Roman Decemvirate (451–449 BC). Stampiglia cleverly manipulates his four male and four female characters so that, after the customary intrigues and deceptions, they are paired off in the mandatory happy ending. As was customary in Naples, the cast includes two comic servants, whose machinations are skilfully combined with the events of the main plot. Their love scene in Act I is notable for the inclusion of a *colascione*, a folk instrument of the lute family, which helps to convey the rustic simplicity of the servant Flacco.

EDITION Hermine Weigel Williams (ed.), *The Operas of Alessandro Scarlatti*, vol. 6, Harvard University Press, 1980

Il Mitridate Eupatore
Mitridate Eupatore
Tragedia per musica in five acts
Libretto by Girolamo Frigimelica Roberti
PREMIERES Carnival 1707, Teatro San Giovanni Grisostomo, Venice; UK: 6 December 1961, Town Hall, Oxford; US: March 1975, New York

This is among Scarlatti's most admired works; E. J. Dent spoke of it as 'a masterpiece worthy of the glorious traditions of Venetian opera' and called it 'perhaps the finest [opera] that Scarlatti ever wrote'. It is certainly his most classical and dignified in tone, in five acts and without either love scenes or comic characters. The plot draws on three Greek dramas, notably the *Electra*s of Euripedes and Sophocles, and is based on the same events as those depicted in Richard Strauss's *Elektra*. Despite the high quality of its music, *Mitridate* was revived only once during Scarlatti's lifetime (at Milan in 1717), but it has received several modern productions.

RECORDING Sutherland, Sinclair, Cameron, Boyce, MRF, 1957
EDITION v.s., Giuseppe Piccioli (ed.), Curci, 1953: unreliable

Il Tigrane, o vero L'egual impegno d'amore e di fede
Tigrane, or The Equal Ties of Love and Faith
Dramma per musica in three acts
Libretto by Domenico Lalli
PREMIERE 16 February 1715, Teatro San Bartolomeo, Naples

Donald J. Grout's evaluation of this work echoes Dent's of *Mitridate*: 'one of the greatest, if not the very greatest, of Scarlatti's operas'. Like *Mitridate*, it has enjoyed more than one modern revival, but unlike that work it was also very successful with Scarlatti's first audiences. The plot is a gloss on Herodotus' account of the defeat of the Persians and the slaying of their emperor, Cyrus (*d* 529 BC), by Thomyris, queen of the Massagetae, in revenge for the defeat and death in captivity of her son. In the opera Thomyris has another son, Tigrane, who (like many another hero of 18th-century opera) was kidnapped by pirates as a young boy, and whose true identity is revealed only at the end of the opera to untangle the net that has by then enmeshed the other characters. The comic scenes are here completely unrelated to the events of the main drama.

EDITION   Michael Collins (ed.), *The Operas of Alessandro Scarlatti*, vol. 8, Harvard University Press, 1983

Il trionfo dell'onore

The Triumph of Honour
Commedia in musica in three acts (2h 30m)
Libretto by Francesco Antonio Tullio
PREMIERES   26 November 1718, Teatro dei Fiorentini, Naples; UK: 23 July 1937, Loughton, Essex

The Teatro dei Fiorentini specialized in comic opera, a genre to which this is Scarlatti's only known contribution. Cynics might argue that the plot, which revolves around the amatory intrigues, misunderstandings and deceptions of its eight characters. is not so very different from those of Scarlatti's serious operas. But the action moves more quickly (hence the particularly long stretches of recitative and the opera is peopled not by historical, mythological or Arcadian personages, but by characters that the first audiences might easily have recognized among their contemporaries.

RECORDING   Zerbini, Zareska, Pini, Berdini, Borriello, Poli, Milan Ch and SO of Italian Radio, Giulini, Cetra, 1950
EDITION   v.s., Virgilio Mortari (ed.), Carisch, 1941: unreliable

Marco Attilio Regolo

Marcus Attilius Regulus
Dramma per musica in three acts
Librettist unknown
PREMIERE   Carnival 1719, Teatro Capranica, Rome

The libretto has often been attributed, erroneously, to Matteo Noris. It deals with an episode from Roman history during the period of the First Punic Wars. The consul Marcus Attilius Regulus, held captive at Carthage, was allowed to return to Rome to negotiate a peace and an exchange of prisoners with the senate. In fact, he urged exactly the opposite and then, as he had promised, returned to Carthage to face death. In the opera the plot is filled with other characters and a happy ending is contrived. Included in the original production were the intermezzi *Leonzio e Eurilla*.

EDITION   Joscelyn Godwin (ed.), *The Operas of Alessandro Scarlatti*, vol. 2, Harvard University Press, 1975

La Griselda

Griselda
Dramma per musica in three acts (3h 15m)
Librettist unknown, after Zeno
PREMIERE   January 1721, Teatro Capranica, Rome

The anonymous arranger of the libretto (possibly Scarlatti's patron, Prince Ruspoli) based it on the *Griselda* that Apostolo Zeno wrote for Pollarolo in 1701, eliminating one of the lesser characters and shifting the dramatic emphasis in places, but retaining much of Zeno's original text. The

nauseating story of the submissive peasant girl whose constancy and obedience are cruelly tested by a tyrannical husband–king is familiar from the versions in Boccaccio's *Decameron* (which Zeno drew on) and Chaucer's *Canterbury Tales*. It is here decked out with additional characters as well as with the intrigues and volte-faces customary in baroque opera. This is the last of Scarlatti's operas to survive complete and, musically at least, one of the most richly satisfying.

RECORDING   Freni, Alva, Luchetti, Panerai, Bruscantini, Naples Ch and SO of Italian Radio, Sanzogno, Nuova Era, 1970
EDITION   D. J. Grout (ed.), *The Operas of Alessandro Scarlatti*, vol. iii, Harvard University Press, 1975

Scarlatti reckoned he had composed over 100 operas (70 are now attributed to him). This total probably included *rifacimenti* of other composers' operas and collaborative works.

Operas surviving complete: [title unknown], (1678); *L'honestà negli amori*, 1680; *Tutto il mal non vien per nuocere*, 1681; *La guerriera costante*, 1683; *Olimpia vendicata*, 1685; *La Rosmene, o vero L'infedeltà fedele*, 1686; *Clearco in Negroponte*, 1686; *L'Amazzone corsara, o vero L'Alvilda*, 1689; *Gli equivoci in amore, o vero La Rosaura*, 1690; *La Teodora augusta*, 1692; *Gerone, tiranno di Siracusa*, 1692; *Il Pirro e Demetrio*, 1694; *Le nozze con l'inimico, o vero L'Analinda*, 1695; *Massimo Puppieno*, 1695; *L'Emireno, o vero Il consiglio dell'ombra*, 1697; *La donna ancora è fedele*, 1698; *Il prigioniero fortunato*, 1698; *Dafni*, 1700; *Laodicea e Berenice*, 1701; *Il pastor di Corinto*, 1701; *Il Flavio Cuniberto*, 1702 (or earlier); *L'amor volubile e tiranno*, 1709; *La fede riconosciuta*, 1710; *Il Ciro*, 1712; *Scipione nelle Spagne*, 1714; *L'amor generoso*, 1714; *Carlo, re d'Allemagna*, 1716; *Telemaco*, 1718; *Il Cambise*, 1719
Incomplete operas: *L'Aldimiro, o vero Favor per favore*, 1683; *La Psiche, o vero Amore innamorato*, 1683; *L'Etio*, 1686; *Il Flavio*, 1688; *La Dori* (doubtful), 1689; *L'Anacreonte tiranno*, 1689; *Il nemico di se stesso*, 1693; *Nerone fatto Cesare*, 1695; *Penelope la casta*, ?1696, or ?1694; *La Didone delirante*, 1696; *Comodo Antonino*, 1696; *Gli'inganni felici*, 1699; *L'Ereclea*, 1700; *Odoardo*, 1700; *Tito Sempronio Gracco*, 1702; *Tiberio, imperatore d'Oriente*, 1702; *Turno Aricino*, 1704; *Il trionfo della libertà*, 1707; *La principessa fedele*, 1710
Collaborations: *La santa Dinna* (Act I by A. Melani; Act II by B. Pasquini; Act III by Scarlatti), 1687; *La santa Genuinda* (Act I by G. L. Lulier; Act II by Scarlatti; Act III by C. F. Cesarini), 1694; *Giunio Bruto, o vero La caduta dei Tarquini* (Act I by F. Cesarini; Act II by A. Caldara; Act III by Scarlatti), 1711; the music to 8 other operas is lost
BIBLIOGRAPHY   E. J. Dent, *Alessandro Scarlatti: His Life and Works*, Arnold, 1905; rev. edn by Frank Walker, 1960; D. J. Grout, *Alessandro Scarlatti: An Introduction to His Operas*, University of California Press, 1979; C. R. Morey, *The Late Operas of Alessandro Scarlatti*, dissertation, University of Indiana, 1965

M.B.

DOMENICO SCARLATTI

Giuseppe Domenico Scarlatti; *b* 26 October 1685, Naples; *d* 23 July 1757, Madrid

Domenico Scarlatti has always been remembered for his remarkable series of harpsichord sonatas, numbering over 550, which he composed mainly for his most important patron, Queen Maria Barbara of Spain. His vocal music, which includes Masses, motets and secular cantatas as well as operas, has been undervalued and largely ignored.

When Scarlatti was born in 1685 – the same year as J. S. Bach and Handel – his father Alessandro was working as maestro di cappella to the Spanish viceroy in Naples and was already making a name for himself as one of the leading opera composers of his generation. At the age of 16 Domenico, too, received a court appointment at Naples and his first opportunity to try his hand at opera came two years later. His father had by then left for Rome, and the younger Scarlatti took his place as composer and adapter of three operas for the 1703–4 season. After a year or two in Venice, Domenico also moved to Rome, in 1708, and remained there for 11 years. He was employed during most of this time as a church musician and in December 1713 was made maestro of the prestigious Cappella Giulia at St Peter's, but from 1710 he also collaborated with the librettist C. S. Capece and the stage designer Filippo Juvarra in producing operas, at the rate of one or two a year, for the dowager queen of Poland, Maria Casimira, who had installed a small theatre in her residence in the Piazza della Trinità de' Monti. The last of these works, *Amor d'un ombra e gelosia d'un aura*, was composed in 1714, and the queen's departure for her native France shortly afterwards brought the collaboration to an end. Scarlatti subsequently composed only two more operas (one of them with intermezzi, the other in collaboration with Nicola Porpora), for the carnival seasons at the Teatro Capranica in Rome in 1715 and 1718. There is no record of any operatic involvement during the remaining 40 years of his life, which were spent mainly in Lisbon in the service of the Portuguese King João V, and (from 1728) in Spain, as music master to the king's daughter, Maria Barbara de Bragança.

Scarlatti's operas were by no means failures in their time, and those he wrote for Queen Maria Casimira were, in fact, often praised as the best in Rome. Later historians have mostly dismissed them as pale imitations of his father Alessandro's, but this view has too often reflected an inadequate first-hand knowledge of the scores and no experience at all of how they work in the theatre. When Ralph Kirkpatrick published his definitive monograph on the composer in 1953 not one of Domenico's operas was known to have survived complete. Now, with four complete operas and substantial extracts from three others to judge from, it can be seen that Scarlatti possessed a well-developed sense of the theatre and showed an often original approach to even the most conventional of late-baroque operatic structures, the *da capo* aria.

Tetide in Sciro

Thetis on Scyros
Dramma per musica in three acts
Libretto by Carlo Sigismondo Capece

PREMIERE ?10 or 16 January 1712, private theatre of Queen Maria Casimira in the Palazzo Zuccari, Rome

Achilles has been detained on the island of Scyros and dressed as a girl by his mother so that he may evade the death she knows awaits him in Troy. Ulysses arrives on Scyros to seek the hand of Deidameia for his son Orestes, and Antiope also comes there, disguised as a man, to avenge her father (Theseus), whom she believes was murdered by Deidameia's father, Lycomedes. The plot involves a mesh of misunderstandings and disguises which is resolved only in the final scene when Lycomedes is proved guiltless and Achilles is united with Deidameia. Some of Scarlatti's liveliest music is in the first-act ensembles, in which the *da capo* convention makes way for adroit characterization.

RECORDING Martino, Pio-Fumagalli, Madonna, Franzini, Meucci, Ferrein, O dell'Angelicum di Milano, Janes, Angelum, 1958
EDITION f.s. (inc.), Ochlewski (ed.), Polskie Wydawnictwo Muzyczne, 1963–6

Narciso

Narcissus
Dramma boscherrecio in three acts (1h 45m)
Libretto by Carlo Sigismondo Capece, rev. Paolo Rolli
PREMIERE 30 May 1720, King's Theatre, London

The plot, based on incidents in Ovid's *Metamorphoses*, tells of the rivalry between Aristeus, Cephalus and Narcissus to rid Athens of a dangerous wild beast and so win the hand of the Princess Procris. It is Cephalus who does the deed and wins the prize, while Narcissus, at first disdainful of female beauty, falls in love with the nymph Echo. The opera is a revision of *Amor d'un ombra e gelosia d'un aura*, composed originally for Queen Casimira in Rome and first performed there, with much success, in 1714.

EDITION songs: *The New Opera call'd Narcissus*, Walsh and Hare, 1720

La Dirindina

Farsetta per musica in two parts (30m)
Libretto by Girolamo Gigli
Composed c. 1715
PREMIERES 1725, Teatro San Samuele, Venice; modern revival: 18 May 1985, Teatro Sannazzaro, Naples

The two scenes that make up this short comic opera were originally intended as intermezzi for Scarlatti's serious opera *Ambleto*, performed at the Teatro Capranica, Rome, during Carnival 1715. As it turned out, the cast found the intermezzo's subject so repugnant that they schemed to have it banned, and it was replaced by an innocuous pastoral piece (probably not by Scarlatti). Dirindina is a young and inexperienced soprano who arouses the jealousy of her lustful teacher, Don Carissimo, by her liaison with the castrato Liscione. Carissimo overhears Liscione rehearsing Dirindina in the part of Dido and, thinking the girl to have been made pregnant somehow by the castrato, intervenes to prevent what he takes to be her suicide.

Gigli's spicy satire on the ways of opera singers, teachers and impresarios is not quite matched by Scarlatti's music, which is nevertheless witty and amusing. It is not absolutely certain that the Venetian performance in 1725 used Scarlatti's music, but it was in Venice that the only surviving manuscript score came to light in 1965.

RECORDING   Gamberucci, Gatti, Mari, Complesso da camera dell'Associazione Filarmonica Umbra, Maestri, Bongiovanni, 1985
EDITION   f.s., Francesco Degrada (ed.), Ricordi, 1985

Other surviving operas: *Tolomeo et Alessandro*, 1711; *Amor d'un ombra e gelosia d'un aura*, 1714; known from libretti and extensive aria collections: *L'Ottavia ristituita al trono*, 1703; *Il Giustino*, 1703; *L'Irene* (rev. of C. F. Pollarolo's opera, 1694), 1704; 6 other operas known from libretti and a few arias
BIBLIOGRAPHY   Malcolm Boyd, *Domenico Scarlatti, Master of Music*, Weidenfeld and Nicolson, 1986; Ralph Kirkpatrick, *Domenico Scarlatti*, Princeton University Press, 1953, *rp*, 1991; O. Termini, '*L'Irene* in Venice and Naples: Tyrant and Victim, or the Rifacimento Process Examined', in B. W. Pritchard (ed.), *Antonio Caldara: Essays on his Life and Times*, Scolar Press, 1987, pp. 365–407

M.B.

PETER SCHAT
b 5 June 1935, Utrecht, Netherlands

Schat is one of the leading Dutch composers of the post-war generation, and has consistently made important contributions to the world of music-theatre. He studied at the Utrecht Conservatory (1952–8), then with Mátyás Seiber in London, and Pierre Boulez in Basle (1960–62). Other influences include Stockhausen. Schat's early works employed strict serialism, which he came to use in all parameters. This led to an interest in the 'conquest of space' and resulted in 1962 in the complex multi-media opera *Labyrinth*. By the time it was premiered in 1966, a series of related concert works had appeared.

In 1969 Schat combined forces with four fellow composers in the anti-imperialist 'morality' opera *Reconstructie*. The 'circus opera' *Houdini* (to a libretto by Adrian Mitchell) combines entertainment with an underlying seriousness of purpose, and includes parts for three Houdinis: singer, escapologist and dancer. A more recent success was the smaller-scale *Monkey Subdues the White-bone Demon*, based on a 16th-century Chinese tale.

Operatic works: *Labyrinth*, (1962), 1966; *Reconstructie* (coll. with Louis Andriessen, Reinbert De Leeuw, Misha Mengelberg and Jan Van Vlijmen), 1969 (RECORDING Gaudeamus, 1969); *Het vijde seizoen* (*The Fifth Season*); *Houdini*, 1977 (RECORDING Composers Voice, 1977); *Aap verslaat de knekelgeest* (*Monkey Subdues the White-bone Demon*), 1980; *Symposion*, 1992

BIBLIOGRAPHY   Peter Schat, '*Labyrinth*: A Kind of Opera', in Charles Osborne (ed.), *Opera 66*, Alan Ross, 1966, pp. 250–60

M.A.

JOHANN BAPTIST SCHENK
b 30 November 1753, Wiener Neustadt, Austria; *d* 29 December 1836, Vienna

Schenk belongs to the Viennese classical school though he is now solely remembered as a composer of singspiels. As a boy he became a versatile musician and in 1773 began studying composition with Wagenseil in Vienna. Between 1780 and 1802 he wrote a number of singspiels, at a time when the Emperor Joseph II was trying to establish a theatre for this genre. In the last 30 years of his life Schenk worked primarily as a piano teacher (Beethoven studied with him, 1793–4).

Schenk's most successful work was *Der Dorfbarbier*, an energetic character comedy with a striking variety of melodies in the lyrical, sentimental, witty and ironic styles mingling arias, ensembles (including a septet) and choruses. It was performed all over Europe and remained extremely popular for at least 25 years.

Singspiels: *Der Schatzgräber*, 1780; *Die Weinlese*, 1785; *Die Weihnacht auf dem Lande*, 1786; *Im Finstern ist nicht gut tappen*, 1787; *Das unvermutete (unterbrochene) Seefest*, 1789; *Das Singspiel ohne Titel*, 1790; *Der Erntekranz, oder Das Schnitterfest*, 1791; *Achmet und Almanzine*, 1795; *Der Bettelstudent, oder Das Donnerwetter*, 1796; *Der Dorfbarbier*, 1796 (EDITION f.s., Robert Haas (ed.), *DTÖ*, vol. 66 (1927), *rp*, 1960); *Die Jagd*, 1799; *Der Fassbinder*, 1802; 6 lost singspiels
BIBLIOGRAPHY   F. Hadamowsky, *Die Wiener Hoftheater (1776–1966)*, 1966

M.F.

MAX VON SCHILLINGS
b 19 April 1868, Düren; *d* 24 July 1933, Berlin

Schillings became a member of Richard Strauss's circle in Munich in his twenties. Strauss championed both him and his music and he became a professor there, his pupils including Wilhelm Furtwängler. His first three operas were all considered needlessly and erivatively Wagnerian both in language and plot. In 1908, after refusing offers of employment in a number of important provincial German opera houses, he moved to the Royal Opera House, Stuttgart, as assistant to the intendant and three years later became general music director. He made Stuttgart a centre of novelty: there were more than 45 world premieres there in ten years, including Strauss's *Ariadne auf Naxos* and Schillings's own most successful stage work, *Mona Lisa*. In 1919 he became intendant of the Berlin State Opera but although he introduced Berliners to new works too, his administrative skills proved inadequate and his right-wing politics and prickly personality led to many clashes, though he did not resign until 1925. For the next six years he developed his career as a conductor, but always holding a grudge against those who had crossed him earlier. He was able to exact his revenge when his administrative career resumed as Nazi influence grew. In 1932 he was appointed president of the Prussian Academy of the Arts and, in 1933, intendant of Berlin's City Opera. In both posts he lost no time in dismissing, or demanding the resignations of, artists not favoured by the Nazi authorities. In many cases these were the same people with whom he had quarrelled previously.

Moloch

Musical tragedy in three acts (2h)
Libretto by Emil Gerhäuser, freely based on Friedrich Hebbel's *Moloch Fragment*
PREMIERE 8 December 1906, Sächsisches Staatstheater, Dresden

Set in the years after the destruction of Carthage, the opera illustrates the gradual civilizing of a primitive people through religion. The music's high-flown rhetoric and search for spiritually uplifting sounds draw strongly on the language of Wagner's *Parsifal*. It was used, in later years with Schillings's approval, as an anti-Semitic tract.

RECORDING Act III (78s) with Barbara Kemp, the composer's wife
EDITIONS f.s./v.s., Bote und Bock, [1906]

Mona Lisa

Opera in two acts with a prologue and epilogue, Op. 31 (1h 30m)
Libretto by Beatrice Dovsky
Composed 1915
PREMIERES 26 September 1915, Kleines Haus, Stuttgart; US: 1 March 1923, Metropolitan, New York; UK: 21 April 1986, BBC Radio 3 (1983 Karlsruhe production; broadcast)

Schillings's last and most successful opera, written at white heat in only a month, sets lurid imaginary events during the 1492 Florence carnival within a frame of contemporary action.

The central two acts describe the infidelity of Mona Lisa (Leonardo's model), her husband's murder of her lover by suffocation, and her similar murder of him after he has raped her on the trap door of the vaults where her lover is imprisoned. This is framed by a prologue and epilogue in which a modern tourist and his young wife are shown Mona Lisa's house and told her story.

After the Wagnerism of Schillings's previous operas this essay in *fin-de-siècle verismo* brought out a more obviously dramatic style. The three characters from modern times double as the protagonists in the opera proper, creating an uneasy ambivalence. Schillings's orchestration is Straussian, his melodies Puccinian. *Mona Lisa* held the German stage well into the Nazi period but after 1945 went into limbo. Its first modern revival (Karlsruhe, 1983)

showed that it sustained its dramatic drive. There have been a few productions in Germany since then.

RECORDING Anderson, Götz, Munkittrick, Kiemer, Baden State Opera Ch and O, Perick, MRF, 1983
EDITIONS f.s., Drei-Masken-Verlag, 1915; v.s., Universal, 1921

Other operas: *Ingewelde*, 1894; *Der Pfeifertag*, 1899, rev. 1931
BIBLIOGRAPHY Peter Heyworth, *Otto Klemperer, His Life and Times*, vol. 1: *1885–1933*, CUP, 1983

C.B.

FRANZ SCHMIDT

b 22 December 1874, Pozsony (now Bratislava);
d 11 February 1939, Perchtoldsdorf, nr Vienna

Born in the same year as Arnold Schoenberg, whose revolutionary *Pierrot lunaire* he greatly admired, Schmidt was a composer of precocious mastery whose own idiom remained tonally conservative all his life. He has never enjoyed an international reputation, despite the reverence long accorded in Austria to his apocalypse oratorio *Das Buch mit sieben Siegeln* (1938); but in recent years his four symphonies and his chamber music (two string quartets and three late piano quintets) – poignantly lyrical, with a mature, melancholy sweetness of character – have begun to attract many devotees. His operas came before the high-water mark of his best work.

Three-quarters Magyar by parentage, the young Schmidt made a great local impression in Pozsony before moving to Vienna for piano studies with Leschetizky, who recognized his talent but was

Franz Schmidt

annoyed by him ('Someone with a name like Schmidt shouldn't become an artist!'). His other instrument – besides the organ – was the cello, and in 1896 he joined the orchestra of the Vienna Court Opera and the Vienna Philharmonic; Gustav Mahler, who became director of the Opera the next year, regularly insisted on using him as first cellist (though he was not commensurately paid). In 1902 Schmidt conducted the premiere of his own First Symphony with the Konzertvereinsorchester, and began to compose the music for *Notre Dame* – which Mahler eventually rejected for performance at the Opera, as did Weingartner after him. By 1913, the year of a notable success with his Second Symphony, Schmidt gained a better teaching post in the Vienna Academy and resigned from the Philharmonic.

Notre Dame was performed at last in 1914 with some success, and his second opera, *Fredigundis* – fairly disastrously – in 1922, six years before his Third Symphony won the Austrian regional prize in a competition (sponsored by the Columbia record company) for a symphony 'in the spirit of Schubert'. He wrote no more operas.

Notre Dame

Romantische oper in two acts (2h)
Libretto by Leopold Wilk and the composer, after *Notre-Dame de Paris* by Victor Hugo (1831)
Composed '1902–4'/1904–6 (see below)
PREMIERE 1 April 1914, Hofoper, Vienna

Hugo's *Hunchback of Notre Dame* might seem to offer ripe opportunities for operatic treatment. The weaknesses of Schmidt's opera are directly connected with the doubt about its composition dates, given above as in Schmidt's own 'Autobiographical Sketch'. In fact the manuscript of the opera is dated 1904–6; but the basic orchestral music probably was composed during the preceding two years – and not all of it expressly for Hugo's tale. When the composer and his colleague, a chemist cum amateur poet, concocted their naïve libretto from Hugo, much of the sumptuous score was already done. (Its sole familiar excerpt, the Hungarian romantic *Intermezzo* on 'Esmeralda's theme', was premiered in 1903.)

The tale is baldly recounted. Every man loves the fey gypsy Esmeralda – the young officer ardently, the ruined poet Gringoire (who long ago rescued her by marrying her) chastely, the hunchbacked bell-ringer Quasimodo selflessly, the Archdeacon of Notre Dame guiltily – and it all ends in comprehensive disaster, rather tamely represented in the music. A few numbers offer some rewards to the voices – Esmeralda's carnival song and her duet with her dashing lover, poor Gringoire's reminiscent visions, the fallen Archdeacon's anguished soliloquy – and there are solid choruses, but too often the vocal lines are merely tacked on to the expansive 'symphonic' music. The young Schmidt lacked Wagner's gift for inspired compromise in this line, and the leisurely unfolding precludes anything much like theatrical pace. Pending some unforeseeably clever production, the virtues of the score are best appreciated away

from the stage. The opera is revived occasionally in Vienna.

RECORDING G. Jones, Berry, Laubenthal, King, Welker, Moll, Choirs of St Hedwig's Cathedral and RIAS, Berlin Radio SO, Perick, Capriccio, 1988
EDITION v.s., Drei-Masken-Verlag, 1913

Fredigundis

Opera in three acts (2h 15m)
Libretto by Bruno Warden and I. M. Welleminsky, after a tale from Felix Dahn's *Kleine Romane aus der Völkerwanderung*
Composed 1916–21
PREMIERE 19 December 1922, Staatstheater, Berlin
CAST King Chilperich *bar*, Drakolen *b*, Landerich *t*, Fredigundis *s*, Rulla *s*, Galswintha *silent*; *satb* chorus of the royal household, armed men, the people, etc.
LARGE ORCHESTRA including organ

Rich and strange, *Fredigundis* is a true *opéra maudit*. It was brusquely misjudged at its unhappy first performances; never again staged, it awaits a happy rediscovery. Though the plot, which the Berlin audience found repellently unedifying as well as silly, is all Gothic horror (a close parallel would be a bloodthirsty Jacobean tragedy), Schmidt's feral, amoral heroine is a *fin-de-siècle* archetype – the dangerous New Woman, infinitely seductive but a ruthless mistress of her own fate: she might have been painted by Gustav Klimt or Odilon Redon.

SYNOPSIS
Act I Late 6th century; sunset. As Chilperich, King of the Franks, brings his silent bride Galswintha home by wedding ship along the Seine, he is lured by flame-haired Fredigundis, a maid in his household, who is watching from a high bluff. Already young Landerich has come to court her – but she has had a vision of a royal destiny. His father, Duke Drakolen, enraged at finding him with the temptress, orders him to a monastery. A storm breaks; though Fredigundis excitedly invokes the Wild Huntsman, it is Chilperich who appears from the forest. They embrace passionately, and depart in his boat. Landerich resigns himself to holy orders.

Act II Some months later, as the king escorts Galswintha to her bedchamber, Drakolen warns him privately to give up Fredigundis; Chilperich rebuffs him. The veiled Fredigundis emerges from hiding, assassinates the queen and flees – though Drakolen seizes a lock of her hair, which Landerich (now Bishop of Rouen, but still devoted to her) recognizes and hastily burns. An orchestral interlude leads to the wedding of Chilperich and Fredigundis. While the bishop agonizes over whether he can crown a murderess, Drakolen bursts in to denounce her publicly. The king has him savagely blinded, and himself crowns his new queen.

Act III Years later, the child of the royal pair lies gravely ill. Fredigundis fears that this is a judgement on her; while faithful Chilperich tries to reassure her, the ruined Drakolen is heard lamenting outside. She pleads with Landerich to pray for her child, but he will do so only if she renounces the crown and confesses. Pretending to accept, she prepares a poisoned draught for him. By misfortune it is the king who drinks it; he dies, and so does the child. A funereal interlude follows. Before dawn, Fredigundis enters Rouen Cathedral, where Drakolen mourns the dead king, lying in state. She appeals to her pagan gods to revive him, and dances wildly. The sarcophagus lid crashes down and traps her long hair. By morning light, it has turned snow white; with Drakolen and Landerich as awestruck witnesses she repents, has a consoling vision of her lost husband and child, and expires in peace.

It seems more than coincidence that throughout the long composing of *Fredigundis*, Schmidt's mentally unstable first wife was becoming ever more unpredictable and violent. (She ended in an asylum, and Schmidt remarried within a year of the premiere.) Biographical speculation aside, the most striking aspects of *Fredigundis* are its confident operatic art, however lurid the tale, and its wealth of remarkable musical ideas. *Fredigundis* marks an enormous advance over the creaky *Notre Dame*; evidently Schmidt had learned much from his further years of playing the operatic repertoire under Mahler. It represents five years' worth of the creative energy of a composer approaching his prime. Strauss declared that this score contained the material for four symphonies; certainly the Third Symphony can already be heard in it and even *Das Buch mit sieben Siegeln*. The voices lead strongly this time, with music that invites mature nuances (firm tone and histrionics were enough for *Notre Dame*), and the drama is set out in high profile.

From its unhurried opening – the long duologue between Landerich and the temptress – *Fredigundis* steadily acquires momentum. No doubt the text was designed for Expressionist shock effects in the wake of Strauss's *Salome* and *Elektra*; instead, Schmidt dressed it in music of cogent breadth and dispassionate sympathy. The characters sing out their feelings without any moralizing authorial nudges. There are no melodramatic or 'evil' passages, though there are deep, astonishing orchestral colours – never gimmicky or *outré*, but real symphonic inventions that make for visionary scene-setting. Perhaps, indeed, what the Berlin audience found most unpalatable was the combination of the gruesome plot with such calmly balanced, glowing, peculiarly tender music. But an imaginative producer with insight might make it cohere memorably.

RECORDING   Vejzovic, Edel, Hollweg, Bunger, Sandu, ÖRF Ch and O, Märzendorfer, Voce, 1979
EDITIONS   f.s./v.s., Weinberger, 1922

BIBLIOGRAPHY   Harold Truscott, *The Music of Franz Schmidt*, vol. 1: *The Orchestral Music*, includes the 'Autobiographical Sketch' as an appendix, Toccata Press, 1984; vol. 3 (forthcoming) will deal with the operas and vocal music; Norbert Tschulik, *Franz Schmidt: A Critical Biography*, Österreichischer Bundesverlag Für Unterricht, 1972; trans. Angela Tolstohev, Glover and Blair, 1980

D.M.

HARVEY SCHMIDT
Harvey Lester Schmidt; *b* 12 September 1929, Dallas, Texas, US

Harvey Schmidt, a self-taught pianist, met Tom Jones while studying at the University of Texas. The two collaborated on college shows, and, after military service, resumed their writing in New York. They had an unprecedented success with their first musical for New York: *The Fantasticks* was still running in its tiny off-Broadway theatre in 1991. It established their preferred pattern of intimate musical stories told with stylized simplicity. They have since written both for the Broadway stage and for special situations such as their own workshop studio and regional production.

The Fantasticks
Musical in two acts (1h 15m)
Libretto, based on *Les romantiques* by Edmond Rostand, and lyrics by Tom Jones
PREMIERES   3 May 1960, Sullivan Street Playhouse, New York; UK: 7 September 1961, Apollo Theatre, London

A simple tale of a boy and girl falling in love because of the separations and trials contrived by their fathers is given additional meaning by a second act in which romantic fantasy does not survive the light of day, but real love does. The small cast and spare staging give *The Fantasticks* much of its appeal, aided by a score with such memorable ballads as 'Try to remember' and 'Soon it's gonna rain'.

RECORDING   Gardner, Nelson, Orbach, Stein, MGM, 1960
EDITION   v.s., Chappell, 1963

110 in the Shade
Musical play in two acts
Libretto by N. Richard Nash, based on his play *The Rainmaker*; lyrics by Tom Jones
PREMIERES   24 October 1963, Broadhurst Theatre, New York; UK: 8 February 1967, Palace Theatre, London

A drought-parched western town and a young woman who considers herself unattractive both blossom under the attention of a travelling rainmaker. The score is one of Schmidt's most evocative.

RECORDING   Swenson, Horton, Douglass, Pippin, RCA, 1963
EDITION   v.s., Chappell, 1964

I Do! I Do!
Musical in two acts (2h)
Libretto by Tom Jones, based on *The Fourposter* by Jan de Hartog; lyrics by Tom Jones
PREMIERES   5 December 1966, 46th Street Theatre, New York; UK: 16 May 1968, Lyric Theatre, London

This two-character, one-setting *tour de force* about 50 years of a marriage provided a vehicle irresistible to mature musical stars, and to sentimentally minded audiences as well.

RECORDING Martin, Preston, Lesko, RCA, 1966
VIDEO Linden, Remick, RKO, 1984
EDITION v.s., Portfolio Music, 1968

Other musicals: *Celebration*, 1969; *Philemon*, 1975; *Colette*, 1982; *Grover's Corners*, 1987
BIBLIOGRAPHY Donald C. Farber and Robert Viagas, *The Amazing Story of the Fantasticks: America's Longest-running Play*, Carol Publishing Group, 1991

J.A.C.

GEORG ABRAHAM SCHNEIDER

b 19 April 1770, Darmstadt; *d* 19 January 1839, Berlin

Schneider began his musical career in the Darmstadt court orchestra. As a member of Prince Heinrich of Prussia's orchestra at Rheinsberg between 1795 and 1803 he published orchestral and chamber works. In 1803 he joined the Berlin Hofkapelle as a horn-player. He wrote his first opera after he became conductor at the theatre in Reval (now Tallinn) in 1813. An appointment at the Berlin Königliche Theater followed in 1820. This period saw his major operatic works, which include the four-act Romantic opera *Aucassin und Nicolette* and the singspiel *Die Verschworenen*. The latter was produced shortly after Schubert completed his setting of the same libretto; Schneider's version is referred to in one of Schubert's letters, where he bewails the fact that in consequence of its success no one would now stage his. Schneider also wrote eight ballets and incidental music for 17 plays.

Operatic works: *Der Orakelspruch*, 1813; *Die Alpenhütte*, (*c.* 1814); *Das entschlossene Mädchen*, (*c.* 1815); *Der Onkel*, 1817; *Hero*, 1817; *Die ungebetenen Gäste*, (*c.* 1820); *Aucassin und Nicolette, oder Die Liebe aus der guten alten Zeit*, 1822; *Die Verschworenen, oder Der häusliche Krieg*, 1824; *Der Traum*, (*c.* 1825); *Der Wärwolf*, (*c.* 1830)

BIBLIOGRAPHY *Berliner Studien zur Musikwissenschaft*, vol. 7: A. Meyer-Hanno, *Georg Abraham Schneider, 1770–1839, und seine Stellung im Musikleben Berlins*, Berlin, 1965

C.A.B.

ALFRED SCHNITTKE

b 24 November 1934, Engels, German Volga Republic

Officially Russian, though of partly German and Jewish descent, Schnittke has, against considerable personal odds, recently become one of the best-known living composers. His relatively late move into opera is a cause of especial interest. Resident in Germany, since 1990, he has over the last 30 years evolved a highly original style through a re-evaluation of musical modernism and extensive use of musical quotation. Though he has now seemingly abandoned direct quotation of music of the past, the invocation of popular forms – in particular the tango, which Schnittke usually manages to transform into an emblematic and forcefully personal state-ment – is crucial to the current work of a composer who represents post-modernism (the composer's own term is 'polystylism') at its most eloquent and serious, as well as often delightfully entertaining. That Schnittke should feel the lure of opera appears due in part to his long experience of writing music for films, his chief living during the socialist-realist years. Schnittke's musical breakthrough is, happily, mirrored by political and other developments around him, so that what his fellow Russian composer Dimitri Silvestrov has called 'the genetic well of culture' can now be drawn on openly, and yet with increasing subtlety. An operatic collaboration with the director Yuri Lyubimov on the theme of Faust was apparently first planned more than ten years ago; the so-called *Faust Cantata* (1982–3) was a kind of pilot project for it.

Life with an Idiot

Zhizn' s idiotom
Opera in two acts (2h 30m)
Libretto by Viktor Yerofeyev, based on his own short story (1980)
Composed 1990–92
PREMIERE 13 April 1992, Het Muziektheater, Amsterdam

Life with an Idiot tells of a married couple forced, through some unspecified misdemeanour, to share their flat with an idiot who can say only one word, 'Ech', but who, unlike the others, has a name, Vova. Initially, all goes reasonably well in the circumstances. But soon the Idiot starts to create havoc around him, and eventually he even has sexual encounters with each of the couple in turn, leading, for the wife (whose increasing derangement is compounded by visions of Marcel Proust), first to an abortion and finally to her murder at Vova's hands, possibly with the approval of her husband, who at the close commits himself to the asylum from which the Idiot came.

The premiere production, directed by the 80-year-old Boris Pokrovsky, interpreted this as an allegory of life in the former Soviet Union, with the Idiot not merely the dupe but the architect of a situation that renders normal life impossible. The opera is notable for bringing the full panoply of Schnittke's 'polystylism' to the stage for the first time. The ubiquitous tango was performed in the original production by a small pit band led by the conductor, Mstislav Rostropovich, who played the honky-tonk piano.

EDITION v.s., Sikorski, 1992
BIBLIOGRAPHY Michael Davidson, review in *Opera*, vol. 43 (1992), pp. 965–7

K.P.

OTHMAR SCHOECK

b 1 September 1886, Brunnen, Schwyz, Switzerland; *d* 8 March 1957, Zurich, Switzerland

Schoeck spent most of his life in Switzerland, conducting, composing and accompanying singers. His reputation has never spread very far outside German-speaking territories primarily because most of his compositions set German texts in a style that makes performance in translation not very effective. His music is also traditionally romantic, owing much to Richard Strauss but without that composer's melodic imagination. Even devotees of Schoeck's music admit that at first glance it can appear dull; with repeated hearing, however, the best of it can show a fastidious craftsmanship which intermittently bursts into something more subtle and memorable.

He came from an artistic family; his father, a painter, hoped he would follow in his footsteps but the boy's natural inclination was to music. After a period at the Zurich Conservatory he went to Leipzig to study, briefly, with Reger (1907–8) but there was little exchange of ideas. Studies with Busoni, who had moved to Zurich during the First World War, proved more fruitful; at his suggestion Schoeck wrote a comic opera, *Don Ranudo*, and the music for Busoni's own 'scene and pantomime' *Das Wandbild*, but ultimately Schoeck decided that Busoni's neo-classicism was also infertile ground.

After 1918 Schoeck's music became more radical. In *Venus* there is a freer approach to tonality, while *Penthesilea* contains some of his most dissonant music. But it was a modernity that already seemed old-fashioned to the German avant-garde. Schoeck was out of sympathy with the industrialization of Art that dominated the work of the most progressive figures during the Weimar Republic, and *Penthesilea* looks back to the musical world of Strauss's *Elektra*

Schoeck in the early 1920s

and Schreker's *Der ferne Klang*, the most advanced music of the pre-war years.

Small wonder then that, though he was critical of the Nazi regime, he had no objection to his music being championed by it since it was the only bastion of the artistic tradition in which he believed. His next opera, *Massimilla Doni*, with its theatrical opera-within-an-opera format, recalls the world of Strauss's *Ariadne*. Its premiere, conducted by Karl Böhm in Dresden in 1937, was one of that season's great successes. After Goering's criticism of *Das Schloss Durande*, Schoeck wrote no further operas.

After 1945 his music became increasingly unfashionable and performances of the operas were few and far between. Latterly more interest has been shown in them.

Penthesilea

Opera in one act, Op. 39 (1h 30m)
Libretto by the composer, after the tragedy by Heinrich von Kleist
Composed 1923–5
PREMIERE 8 January 1927, Staatsoper, Dresden
CAST Penthesilea *ms*, Prothoe *s*, Meroe *s*, High Priestess of Diana *a*, Achilles *bar*, Diomedes *t*, *s*, *bar*, 4 spoken roles (3 female, 1 male); *sa* chorus of Amazons, *tb* chorus of Greeks
FULL ORCHESTRA including ob, 8 cl, 2 pf, 2 solo vn, low str; offstage: 3 tpt

Kleist's tragedy struck a sympathetic chord in Schoeck who, in the years after the First World War, felt culturally isolated and personally lonely. But the music shows no sign of depression. Its taut libretto and whirlwind setting – 'The piece must rush by like a tempest,' Schoeck said – lend a dissonant, expressionistic fervour that well matches the horrific story. Schoeck believed that Kleist's poetry constituted the real melody and his music was only a counterpoint to it. Consequently the musical argument is in the voice parts and the orchestra has essentially an accompanying role although the resources Schoeck draws on in this, his largest orchestral score, allow him plenty of vivid colours as well as overpowering volume.

SYNOPSIS

After Achilles has defeated the Amazons during the Trojan War he claims Penthesilea, their queen, as his prize. To preserve her self-respect he agrees to pretend that he is Penthesilea's captive; they fall in love. The tide of battle turns and the Amazons overrun the Greeks. Achilles is saved by Penthesilea but her followers condemn her for betraying her vows and falling in love with a man. She accepts Achilles' challenge to another battle and calls on the gods to bring her victory. One of her arrows fells the unarmed Achilles and her dogs close in for the kill. The victory deranges and elates Penthesilea. Only when she sees the corpse's face does she realize whom she has killed. She stabs herself.

RECORDING Smith, Janku, Hermann, Cologne Radio SO, Macal, Harmonia Mundi, 1975
EDITIONS f.s., Huni, 1927; v.s., Huni (later Bärenreiter), 1927

Massimilla Doni

Opera in four acts (six scenes), Op. 50 (2h 30m)
Libretto by Armin Rueger, after the novel by Balzac
Composed 1934–5
PREMIERES 2 March 1937, Staatsoper, Dresden; UK:
8 March 1986, BBC Radio 3 (studio recording)

Schoeck's penultimate opera, premiered under Nazi aegis, turns its back on socially significant matters and instead reflects on aesthetics. It is set in and around the Venice opera house, La Fenice, in 1830. Massimilla Doni is a virtuous wife, but finds herself falling in love with the young Emilio. She tries to resist his advances. Her husband, Duke Cattaneo, does not notice, preferring intellectual debate on the merits of artistic naturalism (exemplified by Tinti, a coloratura soprano) against those of refinement (Genovese, an operatic tenor). But Genovese loves Tinti (who prefers Cattaneo but seduces Emilio) and when, in an opera within the opera, his passion transcends good taste, Massimilla reflects that strong emotions require rational responses. Nevertheless, she gives in to Emilio as a distant children's chorus seems to proclaim the triumph of natural emotions over rationalism.

The music is more classically structured than that of *Penthesilea*. Closed forms (set-piece arias, duets, ensembles, etc.) and more regular phrase lengths are combined with suitably Bellinian melodies, with hints of Puccini in the love music.

RECORDING Mathis, Lindsley, Protschka, van der Walt, Cologne Radio SO, Albrecht, Schwann, 1986: the only commercial recording, containing a number of small but disfiguring and significant cuts
EDITIONS f.s., Universal (on hire); v.s., Universal, 1936

Das Schloss Durande

Count Durande's Castle

Opera in four acts, Op. 53 (2h 30m)
Libretto by Hermann Burte, after the novel by Eichendorff (1837)
Composed 1937–41
PREMIERE 1 April 1943, Staatsoper, Berlin

Schoeck completed the sketch of his last opera the week the Second World War broke out. Although he sent postcards to his friends inscribed with a line from Claudius, 'And I wish to have no guilty part in it', inevitably he was caught up in the attendant destruction and the Nazi propaganda machine. He had arranged the premiere of his previous opera in Dresden, one of the jewels of the Nazi cultural crown, but managed to ensure that *Das Schloss Durande* opened at the even more prestigious Berlin Staatsoper.

The story of a young huntsman at the time of the French Revolution, searching for his sister, who has been abducted by the Count of Durande, provided scope for many traditional operatic set pieces: the celebration of Mass, country scenes of peasants, hunting choruses, and numerous conspiratorial and confrontational civil-war scenes. After the premiere Goering anathematized the plot, effectively sealing the opera's fate in Germany. The Zurich premiere

in June 1943 was also scathingly criticized and the autumn revival survived for only three performances.

EDITIONS f.s., Universal (on hire); v.s. (pf. reduction by Webern), Universal, 1942

Other operas: *Der Schatz am Silbersee*, (c. 1901); *Don Ranudo de Colibrades*, 1919; *Das Wandbild*, 1921; *Venus*, 1922, rev. 1933; *Vom Fischer und syner Fru* (dramatic cantata), 1930
BIBLIOGRAPHY H. Corrodi, *Othmar Schoeck*, Huber, 1956

C.B.

ARNOLD SCHOENBERG

Arnold Franz Walter Schoenberg [Schönberg]; *b* 13 September 1874, Vienna; *d* 13 July 1951, Los Angeles, US

The son of a Hungarian-born father and a Czech-born mother (both Jews), Schoenberg was brought up in straitened circumstances and had little academic musical training. He learned the violin and taught himself the cello, and for a time in the mid-1890s he had composition lessons from Zemlinsky, but he was otherwise self-taught. He played in a string quartet, and his earliest surviving works are mainly for string groups, including the sextet *Verklärte Nacht* (Op. 4, 1899). Their style is late Romantic and complicatedly tonal, like contemporary works by Richard Strauss, Reger or Zemlinsky. But they also have an extreme melodic and motivic density, and it was in developing this idea to its limits that Schoenberg found himself, within ten years, consciously abandoning tonality. In the D minor String Quartet (1905) and Chamber Symphony No. 1 (1906) the relentless working of melodic motifs tends to pull the harmony out of focus. So it was logical of Schoenberg, if characteristically intransigent, to ditch tonal harmony altogether and instead, in works such as the song-cycle *Das Buch der hängenden Gärten* and the *Three Piano Pieces*, Op. 11, to allow the chords as well as the melodies to emerge from the motivic process.

In 1906 Schoenberg sketched a first opera, based on Gerhard Hauptmann's play *Und Pippa tanzt*, but abandoned it when Hauptmann held out for a stiff percentage (Alban Berg had a similar experience with this play in 1928). Two unconventional one-act works date from the early atonal period: the so-called 'monodrama' *Erwartung* (1909) and the 'drama with music' *Die glückliche Hand* (1910–13). These are characteristic products of Expressionism, inhabiting a world of neurotic hyper-sensibility. They belong to a group of vocal works, including *Pierrot lunaire* (1912) and the *Four Orchestral Songs*, Op. 22 (1913–16), in which Schoenberg attempted to resolve certain problems of form, syntax and harmony arising from his rejection of tonality. In the course of writing his next work, the oratorio *Jacob's Ladder* (never completed), he began to evolve the more systematic processes which led, in a series of instrumental works of the early and mid-1920s to the 12-note, or serial, method that was to have such

Portrait drawing of Schoenberg by Egon Schiele

profound consequences for subsequent 20th-century music.

By this time, Schoenberg was already an established *enfant terrible*, surrounded by a small but fervent group of admiring disciples (including Berg and Anton Webern, who had become his pupils in 1904, and remained attached to him as apostles and assistants until 1933). In Vienna before the First World War performances of his music were greeted with incomprehension and sometimes disruption, and he was the victim of open anti-Semitism. In Berlin, where he settled in 1911, he fared better, and *Pierrot lunaire* had a successful run there in the autumn of 1912. But the outbreak of war curtailed such activities, and in 1915 Schoenberg returned to Vienna and volunteered for military service (within ten months he was invalided out). There in 1919 he founded his Society for Private Musical Performance, which for three seasons gave concerts of new works to member audiences, with the notoriously factious Viennese press specifically excluded. Schoenberg, Berg and Webern themselves did much of the organizing and took part in performances. But the worsening inflation put paid to the venture after 1921. In 1926 Schoenberg returned to Berlin as professor of composition at the Prussian Academy of Arts, and he remained there until driven out by the Nazis in 1933. Among several substantial works composed during these Berlin years were two further operas: the one-act *Von Heute auf Morgen* (1928–9), and his single attempt at a full-length opera, *Moses und Aron* (1930–32; but incomplete). In October 1933 he and his family took ship for the US, where he taught briefly at the Malkin Conservatory in Boston before preferring the more benign climate of the West Coast. He spent the last 17 years of his life in Hollywood and Los Angeles.

While there may still be debate about Schoenberg's artistic stature, there is none about his in-

fluence, which has been vast. This is partly because of the innate strength of his best music, but it is also because he took procedural decisions that later composers saw as axiomatic, and because he managed to invest these decisions with a sense of moral and historical necessity which has gone on impressing lesser composers faced with similar decisions in their own work. Schoenberg saw the rejection of tonality and the reliance on dense motivic workings as a logical and inevitable consequence of the music of Wagner and Brahms. His serial method was worked out directly from his existing atonal music: the idea of giving equal status to the 12 semitones; the idea of avoiding letting any one note take precedence (as a 'keynote'); the idea of deriving melody and harmony from the same material; the idea of free dissonance; even the idea of a fixed note order, which follows from the concept of an all-pervading motif – all this was already implicit, if unsystematic, in the works he wrote between 1908 and 1915.

This earnest and doctrinaire thinking might not encourage confidence in Schoenberg's potential as a theatre composer. But in fact his theatre music is some of his most brilliant and innovative. This is especially true of *Erwartung* – with its mercurial psychic scenario and spectacular orchestration – and *Pierrot lunaire*, with its witty adaptation of the idea of a cabaret sequence to a cycle of gruesome Symbolist poems accompanied by a small mixed band. During these years, Schoenberg also painted. He exhibited with the Blaue Reiter group and corresponded energetically with its co-founder, Vassily Kandinsky. Though apparently worked out quite independently, Schoenberg's *Die glückliche Hand* is close in concept to Kandinsky's so-called 'stage composition' *Der gelbe Klang*. There is valuable information on both works in their published correspondence, one of the most fascinating exchanges on any aspect of modern music. The later operas perhaps suffer from the streak of academicism in Schoenberg's serial writing, with its tendency towards stereotyping. Even so, *Moses und Aron* has remained his most staged opera, thanks to its vivid crowd scenes, which admirably (and relevantly) offset the somewhat abstract discussions of the issues of language and artistic integrity that form its basic subject matter.

Erwartung
Expectation
Monodrama in one act (30m)
Libretto by Marie Pappenheim
Composed 1909
PREMIERES 6 June 1924, Prague; UK: 9 January 1931 (BBC broadcast conducted by the composer); 25 April 1960, Sadler's Wells, London; US: 28 December 1960, Washington DC (Opera Society of Washington)
CAST A Woman *s*
ORCHESTRATION picc, 3 fl/picc, 4 ob/ca, D cl, B♭ cl, 2 A cl, b cl, 3 bsn, dbsn, 4 hn, 3 tpt, 4 trbn, tuba, hp, cel, glock, xyl, timp, perc, str (at least 16.14.10.10.8)

Schoenberg met Marie Pappenheim, a young medical student and poet, in the summer of 1909 and asked her to write an opera text for him. It seems that the choice of subject, and also possibly the idea of limiting the drama to a single character, were hers, though at that time Schoenberg had already sketched *Die glückliche Hand*, which, in its final form, also has only one solo singer. He had recently been setting Expressionist poems by Stefan George (the last two movements of the String Quartet No. 2 and the cycle *Das Buch der hängenden Gärten*). Perhaps Fräulein Pappenheim also knew that the previous year Schoenberg's wife Mathilde (the sister of Zemlinsky) had run off with his and her painting teacher, Richard Gerstl. Mathilde had been persuaded to return, and Gerstl had committed suicide.

Such events may find oblique echoes in the nightmarish dramaturgy of *Erwartung*, with its unfaithful lover slain (possibly) by the 'expectant' protagonist. But the literary apparatus and symbolic imagery (forest, moon, blood) are in fact conventional for the time, as is the Freudian dramatization of guilt. The most striking thing about *Erwartung*, apart from its sheer musical brilliance, is the sense of helpless striving for clarity: for self-knowledge followed by self-communication, in the face of an overwhelmingly alien yet terrifyingly familiar environment. The idea that profound experience is a dream inaccessible to logical explanation or description crops up regularly in the work of the Symbolists and Expressionists of the 1910s (in opera it is the theme of Debussy's *Pelléas*, a subject Schoenberg had used for an early symphonic poem, as well as Dukas's *Ariadne* and Bartók's *Bluebeard*). It would be hard to imagine a better musical analogy than Schoenberg's free-association atonality – all haunted atmosphere and elusive substance.

According to the draft short score, Schoenberg composed this complex work between 27 August and 12 September (the orchestral score took a further three weeks). But it had to wait 15 years for its first performance, at the 1924 ISCM Festival in Prague, conducted by Zemlinsky (with Marie Gutheil-Schoder). Since then stage productions have been rare.

SYNOPSIS
Scene 1 In moonlight, the woman approaches the edge of a dark forest. She is looking for her lover, and knows this means entering the forest, but fears to do so. She plucks up courage and enters.

Scene 2 Groping in the darkness, she feels something crawling, and hears someone weeping. She thinks longingly of the peaceful garden where she had vainly awaited her lover. She hears a rustling and the screech of a night-bird and starts to run, but trips over what she at first thinks is a body but then recognizes as a tree trunk.

Scene 3 She approaches a moonlit clearing. She is startled by her own shadow and imagines it crawling towards her with goggling yellow eyes on stalks. She cries out for help.

Scene 4 On the edge of a forest, by a broad, moonlit road. The woman is exhausted and dishevelled; there is blood on her face and hands. She has not found him, and cannot return home for fear

of 'the stranger woman'. Then she touches something; it is her lover's bloodstained corpse. She tries to convince herself that it is a figment of the moonlight. Then she tries to rouse him, remembering that they were to have spent the night together. She imagines it is day, and that the moonlight is sunlight. She lies down beside him and kisses him. But in his staring eyes she finds a memory of his suspected infidelity. She tries to banish the memory. Why was he killed? Where is the other woman? She becomes hysterically angry and kicks the body; then again self-pitying, grieving for her love. What is she to do now, since her existence was defined by him? And as she awaits the 'eternal day of waiting', she feels again the darkness, his presence and his kiss.

Erwartung is rare among Schoenberg's early atonal works in being one long continuous movement. There is little doubt that he saw the text as a crucial element in the musical syntax, and that Pappenheim's long-drawn interior monologue was exactly what he needed. Much of the setting is slow, but with rapid instrumental figuration within the texture. But the music moves swiftly from idea to idea, often with little obvious pattern. Linking motifs are hard to detect, though certain harmonies recur. The woman's consciousness – flickering between dream and reality – is reflected in the endlessly varied melodic and rhythmic figures, while her lurking derangement finds a potent metaphor in the tonal instability, incessant tempo changes and general lack of repose of the musical language.

All the same, much of the musical vocabulary is that of late-Romantic German music. The interval of a third is fundamental, just as it is to classical and Romantic harmony, though some chords are based on the fourth, in a way remote from textbooks such as Schoenberg's own *Harmonielehre*, published, curiously enough, a mere two years after he wrote *Erwartung*. Locally, continuity is sometimes achieved by repeated melodic/rhythmic patterns (ostinati). But the main thread is always the voice, with the orchestra providing sympathetic commentary. The vocal writing itself is strenuous but Schoenberg generally avoids the huge leaps of some of his other Expressionist works for soprano, and there is no sprechgesang. The orchestra is huge, but much of the scoring is of chamber dimensions, with a kaleidoscopic variety of colouring and sudden explosions of full orchestra.

RECORDINGS 1. Pilarczyk, Washington Opera O, Craft, CBS, 1962; 2. Martin, BBC SO, Boulez, CBS, 1977; 3. Silja, Vienna PO, Dohnányi, Decca, 1980: Boulez's version is most diaphanous, Dohnányi's the most sensuous, Craft's the most authentic in spirit [A.B.]
EDITIONS f.s., Universal, 1916; v.s., Universal, 1922

Die glückliche Hand
The Fateful Hand (or *The Knack*)
Drama with music in one act (20m)
Libretto by the composer
Composed 1910–13
PREMIERES 14 October 1924, Vienna; UK: 17 October

1962, Royal Festival Hall, London (concert); US: 22 April 1930, Metropolitan, New York
CAST A Man *bar*, a Woman *silent*, a Gentleman *silent*; chorus: 3 *s*, 3 *a*, 3 *t*, 3 *b*
LARGE ORCHESTRA including quadruple ww, hp, cel, glock, xyl; offstage: band

At the time of his first atonal works, Schoenberg was also intrigued by the possibilities of (as he later expressed it) 'music-making with stage media': that is, of using a stage scenario, with its movement and lighting, to act directly on the audience's responses, without the mediation of realistic narrative or characterization in the usual sense. The painter Kandinsky was also fascinated by this possibility, and the published Schoenberg–Kandinsky correspondence is a mine of information on this subject, and reproduces stage designs by Schoenberg for *Die glückliche Hand*, as well as his comments on a proposal (never carried out) to film it.

The text is largely stage directions, with detailed instructions about coloured lighting and a complicated scheme for cueing specific actions and lighting changes to the music. The action itself is rather woodenly symbolic (the Man is either the artist torn between following his inner voice and succumbing to the lures of success, or he is the genius who cannot relate to the ordinary world, an interpretation which anticipates *Moses und Aron*).

SYNOPSIS
Scene 1 The Man is face down on a darkened stage, with a hyena-like monster crouching on his back. The chorus (mixing sprechgesang with normal singing) urge him not to compromise his inner vision. There is a burst of jollity offstage, and the Man leaps to his feet, showing his ragged clothes and bleeding body.

Scene 2 A glaring yellow light suggests the man's visionary longing. A beautiful young Woman enters carrying a goblet which (without seeming to move) the Man takes and drains. As he does so her sympathy turns to disdain. An elegantly dressed Gentleman appears and she goes to him and they embrace. As the Man shows his dejection, she returns to him; but as he moves his hand towards hers she again rejects him, this time without his noticing: 'Now', he sings, still gazing at his hand, 'I possess you for ever.'

Scene 3 Rocky landscape: the Man in a ravine with a bloody sword. Goldsmiths are working at an anvil. Ignoring their hostility, he shows them how to make a diadem out of the gold with a single stroke of the hammer. There is a storm. The Woman re-enters, with part of her dress missing. The Gentleman holds the missing fragment, but the Man cannot reach him. The Gentleman throws him the scrap, but the Woman recovers it, and as the Man pleads with her, she pushes a large boulder down on to him.

Scene 4 As in Scene 1, there is a burst of jollity, and the man is again face down with the monster on his back. The chorus resumes its expostulations.

Work on *Die glückliche Hand*, begun in 1910, was interrupted by other work, including *Pierrot lunaire*,

Sketch for The Man in Die glückliche Hand

and the pedagogical *Harmonielehre*. The music, nevertheless, is closest in style to *Erwartung*, with which it shares its kaleidoscopic orchestra and bewildering montage of melodic and rhythmic figures. Being more compact, and with a clear reprise of Scene 1 music in the final scene, it perhaps gives a more structured sense as a whole. Moreover in a stage performance the score gains an extra dimension from the lighting scheme. The work remains intriguing but elusive and, in the concert performances most often encountered, problematical.

RECORDING Nimsgern, BBC Singers and SO, Boulez, CBS, 1977

EDITIONS f.s., Universal, 1916; v.s., Universal, 1923

Von Heute auf Morgen

From One Day to the Next
Opera in one act (50m)
Libretto by Max Blonda (pseudonym of Gertrud Schoenberg)
Composed October 1928–January 1929
PREMIERES 1 February 1930, Frankfurt; UK: 12 November 1963, Royal Festival Hall, London (concert)
CAST Husband *bar*, Wife *s*, Singer *t*, Friend *s*, Child *spoken role*
STANDARD ORCHESTRA plus 3 sax, pf, mand, gtr

This slice-of-life comedy was the first opera composed with the 12-note method (it was followed by Schoenberg's own *Moses*, Berg's *Lulu* (1929–35), and Krenek's *Karl V* (1930–33)). Schoenberg had devised the method as a purely personal solution to the difficulty he had found with large-scale structure after abandoning tonality in about 1908. The idea was that by treating the 12 notes to a process of serial ordering, unity and continuity would become semi-automatic, and the composer would once again be free to compose as he liked. But Schoenberg's earliest serial works (1920–28) do nevertheless suggest some residual anxiety on this score; they are instrumental works leaning heavily on classical formal stereotypes. Why Schoenberg turned from such things to a comic opera about marital infidelity is not known. Perhaps he wanted to prove that serial music did not have to be earnest and intellectual. Perhaps he was prompted by some incident in his own marriage or that of a friend (Franz Schreker has been suggested). Or perhaps, above all, he saw in the subject an allegory about the superficiality of modern aesthetic fashion, of which he felt he was himself a victim. 'The merely modern', he told the director Hans Wilhelm Steinberg, 'lives only "from one day to the next" . . . in marriage, but at least as much in art, politics and people's outlooks.'

SYNOPSIS

A Husband and Wife come home late from a party at which, it transpires, he has flirted with an old friend of hers and she with a well-known tenor. With growing irritation they bicker about their life together, until they both announce their intention of henceforth abandoning propriety and pursuing only their own pleasure. At this point the Wife suddenly appears in altered guise, elegantly dressed and freshly made up. Abruptly the Husband redirects his passionate attentions to her, but she rejects him with scorn. She is teaching him a lesson. Their little boy comes in sleepily, but the Wife ostentatiously ignores him. There is (oddly) a ring at the door: the gasman demanding payment. But rather than worry about the gas being turned off, she insists they move into an hotel. The tenor now telephones, and elaborately invites them to join him and the Wife's old friend in a nearby bar. Husband and Wife continue bickering, then suddenly she is back in a drab housecoat and they are reconciled. The tenor and the friend arrive, and express their disappointment at this sweet accord. They leave, as the reunited family settles down to breakfast.

Von Heute auf Morgen has obvious elements of the 1920s zeitoper, but without the diversity of idiom. Fleeting allusions to modern dance styles, and to Wagner, as quoted by the tenor, are swiftly dispersed by the intensive working of serial motifs. Those who have seen the work staged complain of Schoenberg's lack of real humour, and there certainly are problems of comic pacing (the device of the gasman is an absurdity with no apparently surreal intention; the Wife's reversion to type is too abrupt, etc.). The score is nevertheless consistently intriguing, even if its contrapuntal intensity seems ill-suited to a 1920s conversation piece.

RECORDING Schmidt, Harper, Schachtschneider, RPO, Craft, CBS, 1964
EDITION v.s., Schott, 1961

Moses und Aron

Moses and Aaron
Opera in three acts (Acts I and II: 1h 45m)
Libretto by the composer
Composed 1930–32
PREMIERES 12 March 1954, Hamburg (concert); 6 June 1957, Zurich; UK: 28 June 1965, Covent Garden, London (in English); US: 2 November 1966, Boston
CAST Moses *spoken role*, Aaron *t*, Young Girl *s*, Invalid Woman *a*, Young Man *t*, Naked Youth *t*, Another Man *bar*, Ephraimite *bar*, Priest *b*, 4 Naked Virgins 2 *s*, 2 *a*; *satb* chorus of voice(s) from the Burning Bush, beggars, elderly persons, elders, tribal leaders, bricklayers, priests, tribeswomen, butchers, guardsmen, herdsmen
ORCHESTRATION 3 fl/picc, 3 ob/ca, E♭ cl, 2 cl, b cl, 2 bsn, dbsn, 4 hn, 3 tpt, 3 trbn, tuba, timp, perc (sd, bd, large tenor d, tambourine, cym, t-t, gong, triangle, glock, xyl, flexatone, high and low bells, unpitched high bell, rattle), hp, pf, cel, mand, str; onstage: picc, fl, ca, cl, hn, 2 tpt, 3 trbn, timp, perc (muffled bd, tambourine, high and low gongs, cym, xyl), pf, 2 mand, 2 gtr

The first drafts of the libretto were made in October 1928, just as Schoenberg was also starting work on *Von Heute auf Morgen*. He then composed the *Accompaniment to a Film Scene* and the *Six Pieces* for male chorus, before starting serious composition on *Moses und Aron* (so spelt because he was superstitious about a title with 13 letters) in the summer of 1930. We have his own account, in a letter to Berg of 8 August 1931, of progress on the work. With chorus parts to write out and the libretto to revise as he went along, he was finding composition more laborious than usual. Nevertheless Acts I and II were complete by March 1932. Work on Act III did not proceed beyond a few sketches; Schoenberg was suffering from severe asthma, and instead of returning to Berlin he spent the winter of 1931–2 in Barcelona. By the spring of 1933, with the Prussian Academy being purged of Jewish elements, Schoenberg's position in Berlin had become untenable. He left Germany and in October sailed for the US, where he again (in 1934) revised the text of Act III but could not find time to compose the music. In 1944, he applied to the Guggenheim Foundation for a grant to enable him to complete the work, but his application was turned down.

There may also, however, have been internal, creative reasons why the music for Act III eluded him. In a letter to Walter Eidlitz (15 March 1933) he complained of contradictions in the biblical account of Moses's smiting of the rock, and mentioned that he was engaged on his (at least) fourth revision of the text for Act III. Because this final act consists almost entirely of an extended diatribe by Moses against Aaron's love of graven images, details of the argument were obviously crucial. And yet in sung drama such things cut little ice. If the only meaning of Act III was one the audience would be unlikely to grasp in performance, then it is not surprising that Schoenberg found it hard to compose. Nor would it have escaped him that his difficulty was precisely Moses's: how to put a lofty, abstract vision into words and images without distorting and ultimately destroying it.

SYNOPSIS
Act I Scene 1: Moses hears the Voice in the burning bush, instructing him to free the Israelites and lead them to the Promised Land. Moses objects that he lacks eloquence, but God tells him that three miracles will serve as a sign, aided by Aaron's eloquence. (Moses 'speaks' throughout in sprechgesang, which stands for his lack of articulacy: the Voice of God is given to six singers, backed here by a sprechgesang group, standing for the two aspects of God: the word, and the hidden meaning). Scene 2: Moses and Aaron meet in the wilderness. Aware of his role, Aaron (a fluid, lyric tenor) consistently interprets Moses's words in a superficial, concrete sense, while Moses insists on God's unknowability. Scene 3: The Israelites discuss the meeting of Moses and Aaron, expressing various attitudes to the new god: a young girl sees him as the embodiment of love, a young man of spiritual aspiration, and an older man of political hope. A priest reminds them that Moses is a murderer. Two chorus groups sum up the different reactions, for and against. Moses and Aaron are seen approaching, and the chorus describe their contrasting ways of moving. Scene 4: Aaron interprets Moses's idea of the only, infinite, invisible God, but the people are hostile to an invisible god, even one who, Aaron says, is visible to the righteous. Moses expresses his helplessness in the face of Aaron's simplifications and the people's ridicule. But Aaron wins them over by changing Moses's staff ('the Law') into a writhing snake. Can the power of Moses and the new god force Pharaoh's hand? Aaron now turns Moses's hand leprous, then cures it, as a sign that the sickly, spiritless Israelites must make themselves whole in order to challenge Pharaoh. The people are now on the point of breaking their bonds. But what will they live on in the desert? Pure contemplation, says Moses. But Aaron promises that God will provide for his children by turning 'sand into fruit, fruit into gold, gold into ecstasy, and ecstasy into spirit'; he shows how God has changed the water in his pitcher to blood. God will lead them to a land flowing with milk and honey. The chorus takes up the ideas of the Chosen People and the Promised Land.

Interlude: In the darkness, the people ask after Moses (who has been absent on the Mount of Revelation for 40 days).

Act II Scene 1: The people are restive, and the rule of law beginning to break down. The Elders tell Aaron that they will not wait for Moses's return from the mountain with the new Law. Scene 2: The people demand their old gods back. Aaron tries to calm them but lets slip that God might have killed Moses. As the people threaten to slaughter their priests, Aaron gives way and promises to build them a visible image of gold. Scene 3: Aaron calls on the people to worship the Golden Calf. First, animals are brought in for slaughter, and the people devour hunks of raw meat. Then a crippled woman is healed; beggars dedicate their last scraps of food to the calf; old men sacrifice their last moments of life; the Ephraimite and Tribal Chieftains ride in and bow down to the image. The spiritual young man of Act I Scene 3 remonstrates with them and is slaughtered. Next comes an orgy of drunkenness, characterized by mutual generosity. Finally four naked virgins are embraced by priests and stabbed at the moment of ecstasy. This leads to an orgy of self-destruction and sexual excess. At the end, lassitude takes over. Scene 4: Moses is seen descending the mountain. He dismisses the calf with a gesture. The people flee. Scene 5: Aaron defends himself against Moses's reproof. Even Moses, he claims, needs images, like the tablets of the Commandments which he holds in his hands. In response, Moses smashes the tablets. Aaron reproaches him for his frailty. The Vision, he says, is not so easily falsified. In the background the Israelites are seen following the fiery and cloudy pillars. Aaron follows them, leaving Moses in an agony of frustration at his inarticulacy.

[Act III (uncomposed; late in his life, Schoenberg suggested it might be spoken) Aaron is brought in in chains. Once more, Moses reproves him for preferring the Image to the Idea. The guards ask if they should kill Aaron, but Moses orders his release, whereupon Aaron instantly falls dead.]

The obvious predecessor of *Moses und Aron* in Schoenberg's work is the unfinished oratorio *Jacob's Ladder*, and *Moses* itself has attributes of oratorio. The chorus is consistently treated like the *turba* in Bach's Passion settings. Individual characters emerge from it, but in essence it is a symbolic group, reacting collectively to the central dilemma. Much of the choral writing is fugal, as in Bach or Handel. But even in the freer sections, the serial method constantly throws up melodic similarities which suggest the imitative vocal styles of earlier times. This 'strictness' of technique is offset by the perhaps surprising vitality of the choral dramaturgy (considering that Schoenberg had never written for a stage chorus before). The final scene of Act I, in particular, is a brilliantly co-ordinated piece of extended ensemble writing. The notorious *Dance round the Golden Calf* is also skilfully paced, though it contains relatively little vocal writing, while as an orchestral piece it has the vividness of detail and colour, but not the melodic or rhythmic thrust, of the greatest stage dance tableaux, such as the *Danse sacrale* in Stravinsky's *Rite of Spring*.

Like all Schoenberg's other serial works, *Moses* is entirely based on a single 12-note row.

Since the 1950s, *Moses* has had several stage productions, without ever quite establishing itself as a repertoire piece. Its dramatic complexities make it difficult to put on, but it also lacks the ingredients for even highbrow popularity. This would not have worried Schoenberg (he expected it) but it is worrying to his admirers. They look, without much hope, for any previous example of great music drama that has not, in the long run, achieved a wide audience. The irony of this is that Schoenberg always saw history as his main justification and support as an artist, yet in his determined unapproachability it gives him no support at all.

RECORDINGS 1. Palmer, Cassilly, Winfield, Angas, Reich, BBC Singers and SO, Boulez, CBS, 1974; 2. Bonney, Langridge, Mazura, Haugland, Chicago Symphony Ch and O, Solti, Decca, 1985
EDITIONS f.s., Schott, 1958; also in collected edition; v.s., Schott, 1957

BIBLIOGRAPHY Jelena Hahl-Koch (ed.), trans. by John C. Crawford, *Arnold Schoenberg–Wassily Kandinsky: Letters, Pictures and Documents*, Faber, 1984; Malcolm MacDonald, *Schoenberg*, Dent (Master Musicians series), 1976; Charles Rosen, *Schoenberg*, Fontana, 1976; Erwin Stein (ed.), trans. by Eithne Wilkins and Ernst Kaiser, *Arnold Schoenberg Letters*, Faber, 1964; Leonard Stein (ed.), *Style and Idea: Selected Writings of Arnold Schoenberg*, Faber, 1975

S.W.

CLAUDE-MICHEL SCHÖNBERG
b 6 July 1944, Vannes, France

In partnership with Alain Boublil, Schönberg created one of the great hits of 1980s musical theatre in *Les Misérables*. It was hoped this would breathe fresh life into the French popular musical, but it began to look like a one-off until the appearance of the equally successful *Miss Saigon*, the story of a Vietnamese girl who falls in love with an American soldier in Saigon in 1975. Inevitably it invited comparisons (not all of them unfavourable) with Puccini's *Madama Butterfly*.

Les Misérables
Musical tragedy in two acts (3h)
Original text by Alain Boublil and Jean-Marc Natel, based on the novel by Victor Hugo (1862); rev. version by Herbert Kretzmer (1985)
PREMIERES 17 September 1980, Palais des Sports, Paris; UK: 30 September 1985, Barbican Theatre, London (rev. version); US: 12 March 1987, Broadway Theater, New York

The cult status achieved by *Les Misérables* is all the more remarkable given that its French premiere was something of a flop. However, the London production by the Royal Shakespeare Company of Hugo's epic tale set in the turmoil of post-Revolutionary Paris more than redressed the balance. The combination of individual emotional entanglements, thrilling spectacle and Schönberg's through-composed, tuneful score brought together all the trappings of opera with a popular accessibility.

RECORDING London cast, First Night Records, 1985
EDITION vocal selection: Editions Musicales Alain Boublil/Faber Music, 1985

BIBLIOGRAPHY Edward Behr, *Les Misérables: History in the Making*, Jonathan Cape, 1989

M.A.

FRANZ SCHREKER
b 23 March 1878, Monaco; *d* 21 March 1934, Berlin

From 1912 to 1924, Schreker rivalled Richard Strauss as Germany's leading opera composer. He provided musical and dramatic novelty through complicated and advanced harmonies which skilfully delineate characters and illustrate the emotionally charged atmosphere of the text. The brilliantly orchestrated scores, akin to French Impressionism, require grandiose resources to match their spectacularly theatrical music. Schreker largely discarded the traditional German notion of harmony defining structure or musical argument.

Schreker drew his plots more from his own imagination than from pre-existing myths or literature. Their mystical, erotic, post-Freudian themes combine fairy-tales and realism; the fairy-tales usually required a specific musical illustration or dominating concept (*Der ferne Klang* is about the mystical 'distant sound' sought by the hero) while realism provided the framework for the drama.

Schreker studied in Vienna and continued living in the city after leaving the conservatory. There, in 1908, he had his first success with the ballet *Der Geburtstag der Infantin* (after Oscar Wilde's tale for children). The following year the performance of an interlude from an opera he had put aside in 1903 inspired him to complete the score, and this work, *Der ferne Klang* (1912), established his reputation. The music's exhilarating opulence and hedonistic chromaticism, and the fanciful and erotic plot, matched the spirit of the times. Schreker became a sought-after teacher and accepted a post at Vienna's music academy. But his next opera failed, his orchestral music made little impact, and with the First World War intervening Schreker's greatest triumphs, *Die Gezeichneten* (1918) and *Der Schatzgräber* (1920), had to wait. In these works the harmonies are more conventional, post-Debussy, post-Strauss. But in *Irrelohe* (1924) Schreker again assumed the experimental mantle, writing highly chromatic and strongly contrapuntal music which explores the furthest reaches of tonality and polytonality.

In 1920 he had become head of the Berlin Hochschule für Musik and thus a figure of considerable influence, but by 1924 his pupils and the new generation of critics were turning against the luxuriance of his style and his mystical plots. *Irrelohe* was not a critical success. Schreker changed style again and embraced the 'New Objectivity', but none of his later operas found favour. He faced violent anti-Semitic demonstrations at performances in 1932, and never recovered from being swiftly and brutally dismissed from his post after Hitler came to power.

Der ferne Klang
The Distant Sound
Opera in three acts (2h)
Libretto by the composer
Composed *c.* 1901–3 (Acts I and II); completed 1910
PREMIERES 18 August 1912, Frankfurt am Main;
UK: 3 February 1957, BBC Third Programme (Hamburg Radio recording); 14 January 1992, Grand Theatre, Leeds
CAST Grete *s*, Fritz *t*, 2 *s*, 4 *ms*, *a*, 3 *t*, 3 *bar*, 7 *b*, *spoken role*;
satb chorus of guest-house clients, waiters and waitresses, guest-house servants, girls, female dancers, men and women, theatre staff, theatre-goers, *Wagenausrufer* (literally: 'coach criers')
VERY LARGE ORCHESTRA with several on- and offstage ensembles

Schreker's first operatic success brought him a reputation as a leading modernist along with Schoenberg and Richard Strauss. But Schreker's music, unlike Schoenberg's, found a ready and eager public, charming and exciting them in its novel use of chromaticism and its iridescent colours. Schreker dedicated the work to Bruno Walter, at the time Kapellmeister at the Vienna Hofoper alongside Mahler.

Karl Gentner (Fritz) and Lisbeth Sellin (Grete) in Der ferne Klang *(Frankfurt, 1912)*

Act I A 'distant sound' plays in the imagination of Fritz, a young musician; it sounds like the wind playing with ghostly fingers over a harp. His quest is to find its source, for then he will be famous and return to claim his beloved Grete as his bride. But Grete's family does not share his mysticism. Her father is a drunkard and has gambled Grete away to an innkeeper in a bet. Rather than marry, Grete runs away. She collapses in a wood where she is overcome by the magical beauty of the light on a lake. A mysterious old woman offers her untold happiness and wealth; Grete accepts.

Act II After ten years as a successful high-class prostitute Grete is working a sophisticated Venetian nightclub. She recalls the pure beauty of the wood and compares it with her beauty and the lecherousness it provokes in her customers. She suggests a song contest and offers her love as the prize. The winner is Fritz, led to her after many tribulations by the 'distant sound'. When he learns of her past he angrily rejects her.

Act III Five years later the negative ending of Fritz's new autobiographical play has given great offence. Grete, now a low-class prostitute, hears that Fritz is seriously ill and begs to be taken to him. Their meeting is ecstatic; Fritz realizes the significance of the 'distant sound' – it is enduring love – and now, too late, he has found his Grete again. He realizes that his play's despairing last act is misconceived.

Schreker's score, though suffused with leitmotifs, contains several set pieces, notably Fritz's narration and declaration of love in Act II and the duet at the climax of Act III. There are also significant passages of melodrama, orchestral preludes and entr'actes of transcendental beauty. The first scene of Act II requires, in addition to the orchestra in the pit, a number of different ensembles playing on different parts of the stage. Alban Berg made the piano reduction of the full score; several commentators have found elements derived from this work's technical and structural innovations in *Wozzeck*.

RECORDINGS 1. Grigorescu, Harper, Hagen Opera Ch, Hagen PO, Halasz, Marco Polo, 1989; 2. Schnaut, Moser, RIAS Chamber Ch, Ch and SO of Berlin Radio, Albrecht, Capriccio, 1990
EDITIONS f.s./v.s., Universal, 1911

Das Spielwerk und die Prinzessin
The Glockenspiel and the Princess
Opera in a prologue and two acts (1h 30m)
Libretto by the composer
Composed 1909–12
PREMIERES 15 March 1913, Frankfurt am Main and Hofoper, Vienna
EDITION v.s., Universal, 1912

Revised as:

Das Spielwerk
The Glockenspiel
Mysterium in one act (1h 30m)
Libretto by the composer
Revised 1916

PREMIERES 30 October 1920, Nationaltheater, Munich; UK: 3 December 1984, BBC Radio 3 (Austrian Radio recording)

In his third opera Schreker pushed chromaticism still further. The public did not like it; even his shortened and dramatically altered revision (he excised the prologue and softened the tragic climax) failed to rehabilitate it.

SYNOPSIS

(*Das Spielwerk*)

In medieval times the wife and son of a master-craftsman, Florian, have been corrupted by a wicked and licentious Princess. Despite the son's popularity as the village violinist, Florian has banished them both and since then the magic glockenspiel he made has been silent, its pure music defiled by their sinfulness. A simple itinerant musician brings the glockenspiel back to life and the Princess orders a celebration. But she has a mysterious illness and proposes to expiate her guilt by death. The simple musician believes his music will cure her. He plays his flute, the glockenspiel joins in, as does a violin – played by the corpse of Florian's recently deceased son. Music and love triumph and, with the Princess and the musician united, the corpse sinks back.

EDITIONS f.s., Universal, 1921; v.s., Universal, 1919

Die Gezeichneten

The Stigmatized Ones
Opera in three acts (2h 45m)
Libretto by the composer
Composed 1913–15
PREMIERES 25 April 1918, Frankfurt am Main; UK: 31 January 1965, BBC Third Programme (North German Radio recording)
CAST Alviano *t*, Count Tamare *bar*, Carlotta *s*, Duke Antoniotto Adorno *b-bar*, 2 *s*, 2 *a*, 7[5] *t*, 5[4] *bar*, 11[7] *b*; *satb* chorus of nobles, citizens, soldiers, maids, servants, women, maidens, people; *silent*: children, fauns, naiads, bacchants
FULL ORCHESTRA

After the success of Schreker's ballet *Der Geburtstag der Infantin* (1908), Alexander Zemlinsky commissioned Schreker to write him an opera libretto on the same story. Schreker became so absorbed in the idea of external ugliness making the expression of physical love impossible that Zemlinsky went elsewhere for his libretto and Schreker wrote *Die Gezeichneten* instead. It re-established him as Germany's leading progressive opera composer. There are three 'stigmatized ones': Alviano, a mis-shapen cripple who after years of repressing his need for love finds a beautiful woman who truly needs him; Carlotta who is that woman, but who for years has so repressed her deepest physical responses that she mistakes pity for true love; and Tamare, the embodiment of handsome masculinity who cannot tolerate rejection.

SYNOPSIS

Act I In 16th-century Genoa Alviano has created Elysium, an island of beauty which houses a grotto where noble young profligates (including Tamare) have orgies with abducted women. Alviano does not participate, wanting to end these debaucheries. Tamare desires Carlotta but she, a painter, prefers to capture Alviano's soul by painting his portrait.

Act II Tamare vows to win Carlotta, by force if necessary, and conspires with the local duke to prevent the orgy–grotto's closure. Carlotta, while painting Alviano, confesses she loves him; he is emotionally overwhelmed but restrains himself.

Act III Carlotta, though betrothed to Alviano, is now appalled by his ugliness and feels drawn towards Tamare. She goes with Tamare into the grotto. Alviano finds them and murders his rival. Carlotta expires with Tamare's name on her lips; Alviano goes insane.

The violence and eroticism of the plot elicit music more yearning than Schreker had written before. Its chromaticism is lyrical and the textures, even at their densest, are transparent, more like Debussy and Skryabin than Schoenberg. There are soaring tunes (the prelude's opening is an important leitmotif) and arresting character pieces, such as the bacchanal that opens Act III.

RECORDING Schmiege, Cochran, Cowan, Van Tassel, Netherlands Radio Philharmonic Ch and O, De Waart, Marco Polo, 1991
EDITIONS f.s./v.s., Universal, 1916

Der Schatzgräber

The Treasure Seeker
Opera in four acts with prologue and epilogue (2h 30m)
Libretto by the composer
Composed 1915–18
PREMIERES 21 January 1920, Frankfurt am Main; UK: 9 August 1971, BBC Radio 3 (Austrian Radio recording)
CAST Els *s*, Elis *t*, Jester *t*, King *b*, Innkeeper *b*, Albi *lyric t*, 2 *ms*, *a*, 3 *t*, 4 *bar*, 4 *b*, *silent role*; *satb* chorus of dukes, counts, knights, nobles and their wives, soldiers, monks, people
FULL ORCHESTRA

Schreker's last operatic success synthesizes the main elements of his previous operas: a medieval setting, a fairy-tale plot dominated by the mystic power of a musical instrument (here a lute that seeks out both hidden sorrows and treasure – symbolic of Art and the Artists) and the destructive power of sexual repression. Musically it is even more approachable than his previous operas and it was instantly a huge success.

SYNOPSIS

Prologue The court jester offers to recover the queen's magic jewels with the help of Elis, a wandering minstrel with a magic lute. The wearer of the jewels wins eternal youth; since their theft the queen has visibly aged. The jester's reward will be the woman of his choice.

Act I Els, an innkeeper's daughter, orders her servant to murder her third fiancé and steal his

Act II of Der Schatzgräber *(Frankfurt, 1920)*

wedding present, a necklace, the last of the queen's jewels. She has acquired the remainder already and feels herself growing daily more beautiful; she longs to escape her menial existence. She sees in the mysterious minstrel Elis the man of her dreams; he has found the necklace. When the villagers arrest Elis for the murder of her fiancé, Els realizes she can save him by confessing her guilt.

Act II In the village square Els tells the jester that the minstrel is about to be hanged. The jester saves him but demands that he help find the queen's jewels. Els orders her servant to steal the lute; without it Elis will be helpless.

Act III In her bedroom, Els offers Elis the queen's jewels provided he never asks her about them. She puts them on and looks ravishing in the moonlight. They sing a love duet.

Act IV At a palatial banquet, Elis, still entranced, claims that the jewels are rightfully Els's. Only the news that Els's servant has confessed both to the murders of her fiancés and to the theft of the jewels saves him from arrest. The king orders Els's execution but the jester claims her as his reward. Els tells Elis she sinned only for love but he rejects her.

Epilogue A year later, Els is near to death. The jester has sent for Elis. All he can offer is consolation; in the afterlife their love, untrammelled by moral constraints, will flourish.

The long melodic lines of the love music soar lyrically and ardently. The musical characterization of the main roles and their integration into the crowd scenes in the village square (Act II) and at the

banquet (Act IV) make this Schreker's most consistently successful opera.

RECORDING Schnaut, Protschka, Haage, Stamm, Hamburg State Opera Ch and O, Albrecht, Capriccio, 1989
EDITIONS f.s/v.s., Universal, 1918

Irrelohe
Opera in three acts (four scenes) (2h 15m)
Libretto by the composer
Composed 1919–23
PREMIERE 27 March 1924, Cologne

Schreker's concern with medievalism and purification, as shown in *Das Spielwerk*, returns here. The music moves away from the opulence of his previous opera to a grittier sound; the big tunes, waltzes, love music and other Romantic gestures are still in evidence, but so is dissonant counterpoint and polytonality. The orchestral interludes to the outer acts are consummate examples of Schreker's mastery. Conducted at its premiere by Klemperer, *Irrelohe* was not well received: the plot was found derivative, the music too modern-sounding for the conservatives and too opulent for Germany's postwar progressive faction.

SYNOPSIS
Act I is largely narrative. Although the present Count Henry of Irrelohe is free of his family's terrible curse, his father raped Lola, an innkeeper, in front of Christobald, her bridegroom, on her

wedding night. Peter, the innkeeper's son, realizes he is the offspring of the rape; meanwhile Eva, his girlfriend, becomes infatuated with Count Henry.

In Act II Christobald swears vengeance on the world and vows to purge it by burning Irrelohe castle. Eva visits Count Henry and offers herself to him.

In Act III, sensing diabolic intervention, Eva implores Peter not to dance at her wedding to the count. At the height of the celebrations Peter tries to rape Eva but Henry kills him – not realizing Peter is his brother – as the castle bursts into flame. Henry's incipient madness is cured by Eva's love; light triumphs over darkness.

EDITIONS   f.s./v.s., Universal, 1923

Christophorus, oder Die Vision einer Oper
St Christopher, or The Vision of an Opera
Opera in a prologue, two acts and an epilogue (1h 45m)
Libretto by the composer
Composed 1924–5, 1928
PREMIERES   1 October 1978, Freiburg; UK: 1 March 1979, BBC Radio 3 (recording of the 1978 premiere)

After the critical failure of *Irrelohe*, Schreker embraced zeitoper – opera brought up to date by the inclusion of jazz and modernisms such as the telephone. Schreker wrote the libretto in 1924 but abandoned the work in 1925, completing it after writing his next opera. Universal Edition was reluctant to accept it and in the face of Germany's growing anti-Semitism Schreker failed to find a publisher sufficiently influential to persuade an important house to stage it. The projected Freiburg premiere, in 1931, was cancelled.

A music teacher tells his composition class to compose a string quartet on the life of St Christopher. One of the students, Anselm, prefers to write an opera on the subject, casting the girl he is infatuated with, Lisa, as the incarnation of evil. The opera, dedicated to Schoenberg, is obliquely critical of much of Germany's contemporary musical and aesthetic thinking.

EDITIONS   f.s./v.s., Adler (now Bärenreiter), 1931

Der singende Teufel
The Singing Devil
Opera in four acts (2h 15m)
Libretto by the composer
Composed 1924–8
PREMIERE   10 December 1928, Staatsoper, Berlin

The failure of *Irrelohe* caused Schreker much heartache. *Christophorus* and *Der singende Teufel* show him moving, in his choice of plots, towards the aesthetic of the 'New Objectivity', but not towards the new realism of Weill or Krenek.

The Singing Devil is the church organ; the characters are medieval monks and devils; the subject the deep hate and merciless war between good and evil in which the organ, begun by a builder burnt for witchcraft and completed by his son, is the

means both of raising men to war fever and of calming passions. The pagans are mesmerized by its sound when they enter the cathedral bent on killing the monks; as they fall to their knees the monks slaughter them instead.

The opulence of the earlier works is here replaced by hard, aggressive music with modal melodies, driving rhythms and contrapuntal textures. The massacre scene includes on- and offstage ensembles in cacophonously different metres. The premiere was conducted by Erich Kleiber.

EDITIONS   f.s./v.s., Universal, 1928

Der Schmied von Gent
The Blacksmith of Ghent
Grosse Zauberoper in three acts (nine scenes) (2h 30m)
Libretto by the composer, after Charles de Costa's 'Smetse Smee' from *Vlämischen Mären*
Composed 1929–32
PREMIERE   29 October 1932, Deutsches Opernhaus, Berlin

In his last opera, Schreker turned his back on philosophy and set a folk opera not dissimilar to Weinberger's popular *Schwanda the Bagpiper* (1928). It was a complete failure. The plot, set in earth, hell and heaven, concerns a cunning blacksmith who makes a pact with the devil but escapes his fiery destiny through the help of St Joseph. Eventually, after opening a tavern outside the pearly gates, he is allowed into heaven. The libretto allows for more closed forms than in Schreker's previous works; he responded with simple folklike songs, marches, a waltz and a passacaglia, but was unable to shake off his naturally complex and often violent musical language.

EDITION   v.s., Universal, 1932

Other operas: *Flammen*, 1902; *Memnon* (inc.), (1933)
BIBLIOGRAPHY   Christopher Hailey, *Franz Schreker: Life and Works*, CUP, 1992; Haidy Schreker-Bures, H. H. Stuckenschmidt and Werner Oehlmann, *Franz Schreker*, (*Österreichische Komponisten des XX. Jahrhunderts*, 17), Verlag Elisabeth Lafite/Österreichischer Bundesverlag für Unterricht, 1970

C.B.

FRANZ SCHUBERT
Franz Peter Schubert; *b* 31 January 1797, Vienna; *d* 19 November 1828, Vienna

Though Schubert's songs and instrumental music place him among the greatest composers, none of his operas has joined the standard repertoire. Musically they contain fine moments, but fail because of their dramatic weaknesses. Whether this is due to an innate inability to construct large-scale dramatic works or to lack of stage experience is impossible to say. Schubert evidently felt constrained by theatrical demands and conventions which hampered the boundless creativity that found a natural and sublime expression in his songs. But there are elements in his last operas which suggest that, had he lived longer, he might have arrived at a highly original conception of opera.

Schubert's exceptional musical talents were already apparent when he became a pupil at the K. K. Stadtkonvikt in 1808 and his composition studies under Salieri were continued after he left the school in 1813. Salieri impressed on him that a composer should prove himself primarily through his dramatic works: it was certainly expected that composers should write operas. At the Stadtkonvikt Schubert had already made an abortive attempt at a singspiel, *Der Spiegelritter*, but his first substantial operatic work, *Des Teufels Lustschloss*, was composed during the 12 months immediately after he left. In 1815, when he was working as an assistant master in his father's school, he wrote no fewer than four stage works which, following the current popular trend, were all singspiels. The influences of Mozart and of Beethoven's *Fidelio* on these are clear; Schubert was also evidently familiar with the work of contemporary French composers such as Le Sueur, Dalayrac and Méhul as well as the popular Viennese singspiels of the day by such composers as Wenzel Müller, Weigl and Hummel.

From 1816, when he gave up teaching, to 1818 Schubert made only abortive operatic efforts, but in 1819, as a result of the influence of the singer Johann Michael Vogl, he was commissioned to write *Die Zwillingsbrüder*. The 1820 productions of this and

the melodrama *Die Zauberharfe*, with its spectacular magic effects, though by no means resounding successes, brought his stage works to public notice.

Schubert wrote four further complete stage works – his last – between 1821 and 1823. Only the incidental music to Helmina von Chezy's *Rosamunde* was performed during his lifetime. His last opera, *Fierrabras*, and sketches for an unfinished work, *Der Graf von Gleichen*, show clearly how far Schubert had progressed since his apprentice days. An individual theatrical style was beginning to emerge which in more than one respect (e.g. stage settings, instrumental accompaniments) anticipates later developments in German Romantic opera.

EDITIONS W. Dürr, A. Feil, C. Landon *et al.*, *Neue Ausgabe sämtlicher Werke*, Kassel, 1964–, abbreviated to *NSA*, series/volume. D. numbers refer to O. E. Deutsch with D. R. Wakeling, *Schubert: A Thematic Catalogue* of his Works, London, 1951; rev edn, Kassel, 1978.

Der Spiegelritter

The Looking-glass Knight
Singspiel in three acts (inc.), D. 11
Libretto by August von Kotzebue
Composed 1811–12
PREMIERES 11 December 1949, Swiss Radio (broadcast); 1 March 1975, Stadttheater Weilheim, nr Munich

Towards the end of his time at the Stadtkonvikt, Schubert worked on a setting of this light-hearted libretto (previously set by at least five other composers) which Kotzebue himself described as 'droll, romantic and silly'. Schubert completed only the overture and seven numbers of Act I; the plot, as far as it goes, sees the young prince Almador setting off for adventure with his squire and armed with a magic mirror given to him by the sorcerer Burrudusussusu. Obviously an experimental work, the influence of Mozart – especially of *Die Zauberflöte*, which Schubert saw in 1812 – is clear. Ideas for orchestral accompaniments (often heavy and elaborate) are his own, but the overall style is distinctly Mozartian.

RECORDING Mathis, Büchner, T. Moser, Austrian Radio Ch and SO, Guschlbauer, DG, 1978
EDITION f.s., *NSA*, ii/11

Des Teufels Lustschloss

The Devil's Pleasure House
Opera in three acts, D. 84 (1h 45m)
Libretto by August von Kotzebue
Composed [30 October] 1813–[15 May] 1814, rev. 1814–15
PREMIERES 12 December 1879, Musikvereinssaal, Vienna; US: 15 June 1988, Cambridge, Massachusetts

The 16-year-old Schubert began work on this opera two days after completing his First Symphony. He is reputed to have absented himself from his lessons with Salieri while working on it and to have presented the completed opera to his surprised teacher. Probably at Salieri's prompting, he then undertook a full revision.

Schubert (at the piano) with the singer Johann Michael Vogl (standing) and Josephine Fröhlich; pencil drawing by F. G. Waldmüller (1827)

The plot bears similarities to Mozart's *Die Zauberflöte*. The noble knight Oswald, his wife, Luitgarde, and his humble squire, Robert, are put through a series of absurd ordeals in a reputedly haunted castle. The perpetrator of these ordeals turns out to be Luitgarde's uncle who wanted to test Oswald's worthiness of his niece. The opera ends with a chorus in praise of the true love which gave the couple their strength to endure their trials.

While *Des Teufels Lustschloss* shows decided technical advances on Schubert's earlier singspiel, it is still very much a student work. His recitatives are clearly modelled on those of Gluck and of his teacher Salieri while hints of Mozart and Beethoven appear in the ensembles. The revised version of Luitgarde's and Oswald's reunion duet in Act II shows the influence of the reunion duet in Beethoven's *Fidelio*: Schubert had heard the opera in May 1814.

EDITION   f.s., *NSA*, ii/1

Der vierjährige Posten
The Four-year Posting
Singspiel in one act, D. 190 (35m)
Libretto by Theodor Körner
Composed [8–19 May] 1815
PREMIERES   23 September 1896, Hoftheater, Dresden; UK: 12 June 1928, Court Theatre, London

Körner's slight play concerns a French soldier whose superiors had forgotten that he was on sentry duty when the army moved on. He has fallen in love with a village girl and decides to stay. But four years later the army returns and he is in danger of being shot as a deserter, so he dons his uniform and returns to his post claiming that he has never been relieved of duty. His captain is unwilling to accept his excuse, but the general gives him an honourable discharge and the situation is happily resolved.

Composed within 12 days, Schubert's lively music consists of an overture and eight numbers. His arias and ensembles are more assured and successful than those of the earlier stage works. However, obviously constrained by the dramatic structures, the composer's solo vocal writing never approaches the standard of his contemporary lieder such as the first version of 'An den Mond', written on 17 May, or 'Erlkönig'.

RECORDING   Donath, Schreier, Brokmeier, Fischer-Dieskau, Bavarian Radio Ch and O, Wallberg, Electrola, 1977
EDITIONS   f.s., *NSA*, ii/2; v.s., Schott, 1922

Fernando
Singspiel in one act, D. 220 (25m)
Libretto by Albert Stadler
Composed [27 June–9 July] 1815
PREMIERES   13 April 1907, Vienna (concert); 18 August 1918, Viktoriatheater, Magdeburg; US: 13 October 1975, Alice Tully Hall, New York (concert); UK: 15 May 1960, Arts Council, St James's Square, London (Park Lane Opera Group)

Stadler, a fellow pupil at the Stadtkonvikt, produced a libretto which, with its Spanish setting and tale of a wife going in search of her long-lost husband, was obviously modelled on *Fidelio*.

Fernando killed his brother-in-law in a fit of rage and, fearing for his life, took refuge as a hermit. When he is granted a pardon his wife Eleonore and son Philipp go in search of him. Amidst wolves and thunderstorms the family is reunited.

This 'sensational' type of opera was popular in Vienna at the time, but Schubert seemed not to feel at home with this type of plot, nor was he helped by Stadler's clumsy libretto which does not bring the characters to life.

RECORDING   Mathis, Sima, Hopfner, Holl, Austrian Radio Ch and O, Zagrosek, Orfeo, 1982
EDITION   f.s., *NSA*, ii/2

Die Freunde von Salamanka
The Friends from Salamanca
Singspiel in two acts, D. 326 (1h 15m)
Libretto by Johann Mayrhofer
Composed [18 November–31 December] 1815
PREMIERE   6 May 1928, Theater des Friedens, Halle

Now best remembered as the author of 47 poems which Schubert set as lieder, this was Mayrhofer's first collaboration with the composer. The dialogue, now lost, was probably destroyed by Mayrhofer who was unhappy with it.

Don Alonso loves Countess Olivia. With the help of Fidelio and Don Diego (the other two eponymous friends), he wins her affection and her hand, thwarting the designs of Count Tormes; his friends become happily paired with Eusebia and Laura. While it still remains within the rather limited singspiel tradition of Schubert's predecessors, *Die Freunde von Salamanka* has some striking musical features, notably the coherence of the finales and range of styles (if not always total originality) of the ensembles. Schubert reused the theme of Laura's and Diego's duet in Act II, in the *Andante con variazioni* of the Octet.

RECORDING   Mathis, Büchner, T. Moser, Orth, Prey, Austrian Radio Ch and SO, Guschlbauer, DG, 1978
EDITION   f.s., *NSA*, ii/3

Die Zwillingsbrüder
The Twin Brothers
Singspiel in one act, D. 647
Libretto by Georg Ernst von Hofmann, possibly from the vaudeville *Les deux Valentins* (presumably by several authors) or the play *Les ménechmes*, or *Les jumeaux* (1705) by Jean-François Regnard
Composed 1818–January 1819
PREMIERES   14 June 1820, Kärntnertortheater, Vienna; modern revival: 26 June 1938, Collegium Musicum, Leipzig University

The first of Schubert's stage works to be produced, it was also the only one performed during his lifetime. It was written at the instigation of the well-known baritone Johann Michael Vogl, whose advocacy of Schubert's lieder was an important factor in spreading their popularity. Vogl, a member of Süssmayr's German opera company, secured Schubert the commission for *Die Zwillingsbrüder* from the Kärntnertortheater where, after several postponements, it was premiered (with Vogl in both the title roles!). There were only six performances and most of the contemporary reviewers found it too serious and complicated. Nevertheless, its performance was an important factor in gaining wider recognition of Schubert's talent in Vienna.

The opera begins with preparations for Lieschen's betrothal to Anton. Franz Speiss, however, returns after 18 years to claim Lieschen as his bride; she had been promised to him at her birth by her father, just before Franz went away to search for his missing twin brother, Friedrich. Unknown to Franz, Friedrich, whom everyone believes dead, returns on the very same day. The rest of the plot develops out of this potentially confusing situation. Eventually everything is clarified and Anton is united with Lieschen.

Obviously anxious to make his mark in this, his first professional commission, Schubert exaggerated the depth of his characters' emotions and wrote arias when naïve, simple songs might have been more apt. He also modelled some of his vocal ensembles on the style of Rossini, who was enjoying increasing popularity in Vienna at the time.

RECORDING Donath, Gedda, Fischer-Dieskau, Moll, Bavarian State Opera Ch and O, Sawallisch, EMI, 1978
EDITIONS f.s., *NSA*, ii/5; v.s., Peters, 1872

Alfonso und Estrella

Romantic opera in three acts, D. 732 (3h)
Libretto by Franz von Schober
Composed 1821–2
PREMIERES 24 June 1854, Hoftheater, Weimar (shortened version); 1946, Swiss Radio Beromunster (complete; broadcast); UK: 7 September 1968, Usher Hall, Edinburgh (concert); 22 February 1977, Reading University; US: 11 November 1978, Ford Auditorium, Detroit (concert)
CAST Froila *bar*, Alfonso *t*, Mauregato *bar*, Estrella *s*, Adolfo *b*; *satb* chorus of hunters, soldiers, people
FULL ORCHESTRA including hp

Much of the opera was composed in the castle of Ochsenburg near St Pölten, where Schubert and Schober were on holiday. Guided by enthusiasm rather than skill, they produced an opera which is rich in variety (Schober happily provided a wide range of situations and settings) but dramatically weak. It is likely that a premiere at the Kärntnertor was offered but later withdrawn after the two intended principal singers expressed unhappiness about the work. Schubert tried in vain to have it staged in Dresden, Berlin and Graz. Its posthumous premiere was conducted by Liszt.

SYNOPSIS

Act I Froila, the deposed king of Leon, has lived peacefully for 20 years in a mountain retreat, with his son Alfonso (who is unaware of his identity) and a few faithful retainers. Meanwhile, in Leon, Estrella, daughter of the usurper Mauregato, spurns the love of the general, Adolfo. When Adolfo asks Mauregato for her hand as a reward for a successful campaign, the king – knowing Estrella's feelings – temporizes, saying that only he who returns the Chain of Eurich to the royal treasury (it is in Froila's possession) can marry his daughter.

Act II Estrella, who has lost her way during a hunt, is discovered by Alfonso. They fall in love and Alfonso gives her the Chain of Eurich as a token. She returns to Leon, much to the joy of Mauregato, who recognizes the chain. Suddenly a guard brings news of a revolt led by Adolfo: he wants to usurp the throne and win Estrella's hand. The court flees.

Act III The battle between Adolfo's and Mauregato's forces has separated Estrella from her father. Alone with Estrella, Adolfo is trying to force her to submit to him when Alfonso and hunters arrive. Adolfo is captured and Alfonso defeats the rebels. Mauregato willingly surrenders the throne to the rightful king, and Froila, in turn, abdicates in favour of Alfonso. The opera ends with general rejoicing.

That Schubert considered this his best stage work demonstrates his lack of dramatic understanding. There is an attempt to build up dramatic tension, but all too often the momentum that has been achieved is dissipated by the insertion of a languorous duet. Taken individually, however, these duets are some of the score's strongest numbers. Schubert had heard Rossini's *Otello* and *Tancredi*, and his aim was probably to write something less frivolous than the average singspiel. The Italian composer's influence can be seen directly in some of the larger ensembles and may have inspired Schubert's decision to abandon spoken dialogue.

RECORDING Mathis, Schreier, Prey, Fischer-Dieskau, Adam, Berlin Radio Ch, Berlin Staatskapelle, Suitner, EMI, 1978
EDITIONS f.s., *NSA*, ii/6; v.s., Berlin, 1882

Die Verschworenen

(*Der häusliche Krieg*)
The Conspirators
(*Domestic Warfare*)
Singspiel in one act, D. 787
Libretto by Ignaz Franz Castelli, based on his play *Die Verschworenen* (1820) after the play *Lysistrata* by Aristophanes (c. 406 BC)
Composed [February–April] 1823
PREMIERES 1 March 1861, Musikverein, Vienna (concert); 29 August 1861, Städtisches Comödienhaus, Frankfurt; UK: 2 March 1872, London (concert); US: 16 June 1877, New York

In the preface to his play, Ignaz Castelli challenged contemporary German composers, who frequently complained about the lack of suitable material, to set it as an opera. His libretto (he also wrote the text for Weigl's phenomenally popular *Die Schweizerfamilie*) was certainly superior to anything Schubert had previously set and he produced a comic singspiel perfectly in tune with the popular style of the day. That the work was not premiered until nearly 30 years later was probably due partly to the censors (in deference to whom the original 'potentially political' title was changed); however, when performed, it was successful.

The familiar story of women who try to prevent their husbands from waging war by refusing to sleep with them is transferred to a medieval castle at the time of the Crusades.

Part of the overture is now lost but what remains shows that Schubert uses themes from the main body of the opera – a device new to him and one he repeated (though with only one theme) in *Fierrabras*. The remainder of the opera shows none of the desire for 'seriousness' which had beset some of his earlier works. Instead, Schubert was content to reflect the rather obvious humour of Castelli's text, introducing elements of comedy alongside uncomplicated melodious arias. The opera's ensembles are less effective, tending to repetitiveness, but the work enjoyed great popularity for several decades.

RECORDING Moser, Fuchs, Schary, Moll, Dallapozza, Finke, Bavarian Radio Ch and Munich Radio O, Wallberg, EMI, 1977
EDITIONS f.s., *NSA*, ii/7; v.ss., Spina, 1862; Peters, *c.* 1870

Fierrabras

Opera in three acts, D. 796 (2h 30m)
Libretto by Joseph Kupelwieser, after the play *La Puente de Mantible* by Pedro Calderón de la Barca and an old German legend, *Eginhard und Emma*
Composed [May–October] 1823
PREMIERES 7 May 1835, Josefstadt Theatre, Vienna (three numbers; concert); 9 February 1897, Hoftheater, Karlsruhe (shortened version); US: 9 May 1980, Walnut Street Theater, Philadelphia; UK: 6 November 1938, London (excerpts; concert); 10 April 1971, BBC Radio (studio recording); 19 February 1986, Playhouse, Oxford (Oxford University Opera Club)
CAST King Karl *b*, Emma *s*, Eginhard *t*, Roland *bar*, Ogier *t*, Boland *b*, Fierrabras *t*, Florinda *s*, Maragond *ms*, Brutamonte *b*; *satb* chorus of ladies, knights, soldiers
FULL ORCHESTRA

Late in 1821 Domenico Barbaja, director of the Kärntnertortheater, asked Schubert for a German opera for the 1822–3 season. The composer offered both *Alfonso und Estrella* and *Die Verschworenen* (neither of which had yet been performed), but they were rejected and Schubert, anxious to see his stage works performed, set to work on a new full-length opera. Although it was completed in time, *Fierrabras* too was rejected and its 26-year-old composer did not live to see his last – and most individual – opera performed. *Fierrabras* disappeared until its publication in 1886. It has enjoyed a few revivals since the 1970s (including a significant production at the 1988 Vienna Festival).

SYNOPSIS
Act I Emma, daughter of King Karl, and Eginhard, a young knight, are secretly in love. After a victory against the Moors, Karl sends a mission of peace led by his general, Roland, and including Eginhard. He declares an amnesty for the Moorish prisoners. Among these is Fierrabras, son of the Moorish leader Boland, whose valour has won Roland's admiration. It transpires that Fierrabras has loved Emma since

Watercolour costume design for Fierrabras by the opera's librettist Joseph Kupelweiser

seeing her during a visit to Rome and that Roland had simultaneously fallen in love with Fierrabras's sister Florinda. That night Fierrabras observes a secret meeting between Eginhard and Emma. Despite his jealousy he does not give them away, even when he is wrongly blamed for trying to abduct Emma and imprisoned.

Act II Eginhard and the rest of the peace mission are incarcerated by Boland. Florinda, recognizing Roland, determines to save them. She unlocks their prison and provides weapons, but only Eginhard escapes, while the rest of the knights remain barricaded in the tower.

Act III Karl, having discovered the truth about Emma and Eginhard, orders Fierrabras's release. Eginhard, arriving with news of the knights' plight, begs to lead a rescue party. Fierrabras accompanies him. The rescue party arrives just in time to prevent the executions of the knights and Florinda. The opera ends with the couples united and Fierrabras accepted into the chivalric brotherhood of the Frankish knights.

While Schubert employed many of the stock-in-trade devices of contemporary German opera (e.g. the women's spinning chorus, the men's unaccompanied patriotic hymn), *Fierrabras*, undeniably Schubert's strongest stage work, rises above the commonplace and presents a tantalizing example of the composer's fully formed theatrical style. Elements familiar from other composers are here not so much borrowed or copied as assimilated into Schubert's own musical language. Much of the most effective writing is for Florinda (the best-drawn female character in Schubert's theatrical music), whose numbers include an aria accompanied by male-voice chorus ('Des Jammers herbe Qualen') and a highly dramatic melodrama, as she watches her beloved Roland in battle. Particularly haunting too is the serenade between Eginhard and Emma, 'Der Abend sinkt aus stiller Flor', which begins the Act I finale.

RECORDING   Mattila, Studer, Protschka, Gambill, Hampson, Holl, Polgár, Arnold Schoenberg Ch, CO of Europe, Abbado, DG, 1990
EDITIONS   f.s., *NSA*, ii/8; v.s., Austrian Music Confection, 1987

Other operatic works (all inc.): *Claudine von Villa Bella*, (1815), 1913; *Die Bürgschaft*, (1816), 1908; *Adrast*, (1820), 1985; *Die Zauberharfe*, 1820; *Sakuntala*, (1820), 1971; *Rudiger*, (1823), 1868; *Der Graf von Gleichen*, (1827)
BIBLIOGRAPHY   Peter Branscombe, 'Schubert and his Librettists', *MT*, vol. 119 (1978), p. 943; M. J. E. Brown, 'Schubert's Two Major Operas', *MR*, vol. 20 (1959), p. 104; Elizabeth Norman Mckay, *Schubert's Music for the Theatre*, Schneider, 1991

C.A.B

GUNTHER SCHULLER
Gunther Alexander Schuller; *b* 22 November 1925, New York, US

Schuller is one of the most versatile figures in American music. A prolific composer, he has also been a horn-player, a jazz musician, a conductor, the inventor of 'third-stream' music (1957), an author and an influential teacher. His two books on jazz – *Early Jazz: Its Roots and Development* (1968) and *The Swing Era* (1989) – are landmarks in the field. Schuller was central to the revival, after 50 years, of Joplin's *Treemonisha*, reorchestrating the opera and conducting its complete premiere in 1975.

Schuller was commissioned to write an opera for Hamburg and eventually decided to adapt Kafka's *The Trial* as *The Visitation* in terms of racial problems in the US. In 'third-stream' tradition, the opera's musical language combines elements of contemporary classical music with aspects of jazz. The score is basically serial and atonal, but opens with a recording of a blues song, 'Nobody knows you when you're down and out', and calls for a seven-piece jazz band in addition to the conventional orchestra. At its premiere in 1966 *The Visitation* gave every appearance of being a smash hit with 'thunderous applause and 50 curtain calls'. But the American premiere, at the Metropolitan in 1967, received a mixed response: some felt *The Visitation* was simply a play set to music of no great character in spite of strong effects.

Operas: *The Visitation*, 1966; *The Fisherman and His Wife*, 1970
BIBLIOGRAPHY   Gunther Schuller, *Musings: The Musical Worlds of Gunther Schuller*, OUP, 1986

P.D.

WILLIAM SCHUMAN
William Howard Schuman; *b* 4 August 1910, New York; *d* 15 February 1992, New York

Schuman was one of the major American symphonists of the later 20th century and a distinguished teacher and administrator. In his youth he wrote many songs with Frank Loesser. He began business studies, but after a Toscanini concert in 1930 he decided to become a musician. Roy Harris, who taught him at the Juilliard School (1936–8), was a profound influence. Schuman had written three ballets before he composed his only opera, *The Mighty Casey* (1953). Casey was a baseball star, one of Schuman's youthful idols. The composer explained: 'It was not a matter of my being interested in baseball as a youth. It was my youth.' In 1976 Schuman arranged parts of the opera as a cantata, *Casey at the Bat*.

BIBLIOGRAPHY   C. Rouse, *William Schuman Documentary*, Schirmer, 1980

P.D.

ROBERT SCHUMANN
Robert Alexander Schumann; *b* 8 June 1810, Zwickau, Saxony; *d* 29 July 1856, Enderich, nr Bonn

The son of a bookseller–publisher, Schumann was brought up surrounded by books, and was all his life drawn almost as much to words as to music. He was one of the most literate of composers, and his songs reflect both the breadth of his reading and the subtlety of his response to poetry. For many years he was the editor of the *Neue Zeitschrift für Musik* in Leipzig and one of Germany's most trenchant and effective writers on music.

Despite this, and though strongly attracted to opera from quite an early stage, he composed nothing for this pre-eminently literary medium until his late thirties. His first published works are all for piano, after which he occupied himself obsessively with songs, then symphonies and chamber music, coming to music for the theatre only in 1844. Around 1830 he had considered an opera on Shakespeare's *Hamlet*, but committed only eight bars to paper. Ten years later he seriously entertained the idea of an opera, *Doge und Dogaressa* (on material from E. T. A. Hoffmann's *Seraphions-Brüder*), as a wedding present for Clara. In 1842 he wrote to Carl Kossmaly: 'Do you know what I pray about morning and evening? It's German opera. There's something to be done there.' The formidable list of Schumann's

Robert Schumann

known operatic plans includes: *Abelard und Heloise*, *Till Eulenspiegel*, *Hermann und Dorothea*, *Die Nibelungen*, *Faust*, *Columbus*, *Der Corsar*, *König Arthur*, *Romeo und Juliet* and *Tristan und Isolde*.

Few of Schumann's numerous ideas led directly to the composition of any music. *Hermann und Dorothea* resulted in the Overture, Op. 136. *Der Corsar*, based on Byron's *The Corsair*, which occupied Schumann during June and July 1844, was pursued as far as an opening chorus and the beginning of an aria. Work on this was interrupted by growing interest in *Faust*, which eventually led not to an opera but to the *Szenen aus Goethe's Faust*, completed in 1853.

The disappointing reception in 1850 of *Genoveva*, his only completed opera, was a great blow to Schumann, who perhaps set greater store by success on the operatic stage than in any other genre. From 1852 encroaching mental illness prevented any further attempts. *Genoveva* has never enjoyed the popularity of the overture and incidental music to Suckow's translation of Byron's *Manfred* (1849), Schumann's most enduring theatre work.

Genoveva

Genovieve
Opera in four acts, Op. 81 (2h 30m)
Libretto by Robert Reinick and the composer, after the plays
Das Leben und Tod der heiligen Genoveva (1799) by C. F.
Hebbel and *Genoveva* (1843) by L. Tieck

Composed 1847–8
PREMIERES   25 June 1850, Stadt Theater, Leipzig; UK:
6 December 1893, Drury Lane, London
CAST   Genoveva *s*, Siegfried *bar*, Golo *t*, Drago *b*,
Margaretha *s*, Hidulfus *bar*, Balthasar *b*, Caspar *bar*, Angelo
silent, Conrad *silent*; *satb* chorus of knights, squires, priests,
servants, people, spirits
FULL ORCHESTRA

The two plays Schumann chose as the basis for *Genoveva*, though founded on the same story, were contrasting: Hebbel's was morbid while Tieck's was a fairy-tale version of the story. Unhappy with Reinick's libretto, Schumann reworked most of it himself. The result was a text that lacks coherence – a problem the composer was unable to surmount with his relative lack of operatic experience. *Genoveva* was given three performances under Schumann's inexpert baton before being withdrawn. It was seen only once more in the composer's lifetime – conducted by Liszt at Weimar in 1855 – but although it was performed in several German cities and in Paris and St Petersburg, by the turn of the century it was confined to a limbo from which it seldom emerges. Historical perspective has, however, shown *Genoveva* to form a significant link between the Romantic operas of Weber and the mature works of Wagner.

SYNOPSIS
Act I Siegfried goes to fight the Saracens, leaving his wife Genoveva in the care of his servant Golo, who harbours a secret passion for her. The sorceress, Margaretha, promises to help Golo.

Act II Genoveva scornfully rejects Golo's advances. Planning revenge, he arranges for Margaretha to spread rumours of Genoveva's unfaithfulness; he persuades Drago, Siegfried's steward, to hide in her room to observe her. Margaretha incites the other members of the household to search Genoveva's chamber. They find Drago, and before he can protest his innocence, a servant, Balthasar, kills him. Genoveva is imprisoned for adultery.

Act III Siegfried is about to return home when Golo brings news of Genoveva's unfaithfulness. Siegfried orders her execution. Margaretha shows Siegfried a magic mirror in which Genoveva's guilt appears to be confirmed. Smashing it in fury he hurries away; the ghost of Drago then appears and commands Margaretha to confess the plot.

Act IV Genoveva is brought out for execution. Golo promises to spare her if she will be his, but she again scorns him. Genoveva, praying fervently, is about to be killed when Siegfried, guided by Margaretha, arrives, and everything is happily resolved.

As his choice of subject indicates, Schumann was intent on composing a truly 'German' opera. Although his aim was to do this by introducing traditional chorale melodies and folktunes rather than by writing singspiel-type songs, the lied is the main type of vocal solo found in the opera. This despite the work's continuous musical texture (anticipating Wagner), which eschews recitative in favour of a more seamless arioso type of writing. The use of a folksong – 'Wenn ich ein Vöglein wär', sung as a duet between Genoveva and Golo in Act II – emerges as one of the opera's highlights: presented at first in a straightforward setting, its increasingly expressive harmonization reflects the gradual perturbation in Golo's mind. In spite of this and the constantly modified leitmotifs, characterization is weak. Orchestration, too, is generally unimaginative, though tuba, piccolo and gong are introduced for the appearance of Drago's ghost.

It is not surprising that *Genoveva*, premiered two months before Wagner's *Lohengrin*, shows some Wagnerian traits. While working on the score, Schumann regularly showed his work to Wagner (they had known each other since being students together in Leipzig), eventually occasioning a rift when Wagner's criticism became too severe.

RECORDING E. Moser, Schroeter, Schreier, Fischer-Dieskau, Lorenz, Vogel, Berlin Radio Ch, Leipzig Gewandhaus O, Masur, Electrola, 1977
EDITIONS f.ss., Breitkopf und Härtel, 1886 (vol. 9 of complete edn); *rp*, Gregg International, 1967; Peters, [*c.* 1890]; v.ss., Peters, 1851; Novello, [n.d.]; study s., Kalmuss (no. 478), [n.d.]

BIBLIOGRAPHY Gerald Abraham, 'The Dramatic Music' in G. Abraham (ed.), *Schumann: A Symposium*, OUP, 1952, pp. 260ff.; Frank Cooper, 'Operatic and Dramatic Music', in Alan Walker (ed.), *Robert Schumann: The Man and His Music*, Barrie and Jenkins, 1972; rev. edn, 1976, pp. 324ff.; Linda Siegel, 'A Second Look at Schumann's *Genoveva*', *MR*, vol. 36 (1975), pp. 17–41

C.A.B.

JOHANN GEORG SCHÜRER
b c. 1720, ?Raudnitz (now Roudnice), Bohemia; *d* 16 February 1786, Dresden

Schürer was one of a celebrated line of musicians, including Hasse, Naumann and Schuster, who served the Dresden court during the 18th century. He first made his mark there in October 1746 with a performance of his opera *Astrea placata* to a libretto by Campagnari. Further theatrical works appeared in quick succession, including a singspiel entitled *Doris*, and a comic opera, *Calandro*. After 1748 he appears to have abandoned opera and to have devoted himself to writing a large quantity of sacred works, many of which are now lost.

His operatic idiom reflects the age of transition in which he worked, combining elements of the late Baroque with the elegant rococo style, later associated with Florian Gassmann and the young Mozart. Although widely acknowledged in his lifetime as a skilled craftsman, and particularly as a fine contrapuntist, his continuing reputation was limited by a lack of notable melodic writing.

Operatic works: *Astrea placata, ovvero La felicità della terra*, 1746; *La Galatea*, 1746; *L'Ercole sul Termodonte*, 1747; *Doris*, 1747; *Calandro*, 1748
BIBLIOGRAPHY R. Haas, *J. G. Schürer (1720–1786): Ein Beitrag zur Geschichte der Musik in Dresden*, Dresden, 1915

B.S.

GEORG CASPAR SCHÜRMANN
George Caspar Schürmann [Schurmann, Scheuermann]; *b* ?1672/3, Idensen, nr Hanover; *d* 25 February 1751, Wolfenbüttel

Schürmann, a major composer in the history of German baroque opera, began his career in Hamburg as a male alto, performing music by Keiser, Steffani and others. In 1697 he was appointed as solo alto and court conductor by Duke Anton Ulrich of Brunswick-Lüneburg. Except for two periods of absence, Schürmann remained at the Brunswick–Wolfenbüttel court until his death. The ducal family supported a major opera activity, often in direct competition with Hamburg, and an impressive theatre was constructed there for which Schürmann composed more than 40 operas. Only three survive complete and excerpts of others remain in manuscripts. The existing music shows an amalgamation of the Hamburg opera style, as exemplified by the works of Keiser, with Venetian characteristics. The operas are aria-orientated and, perhaps because of the composer's long singing career, impressively lyrical. They are also reminiscent of the later works of Handel, being less in the baroque mould than those of many Hamburg composers and with traits pointing towards the classical style.

Surviving operatic works: *Salomon*, 1701; *Giasone, overo Il conquisto del vello d'oro*, 1707; *Der getreue Alceste*, 1719
Operatic works surviving in part: *Leonilde, oder der siegende Beständigkeit*, 1705; *Das verstöhrte Troja*, 1706; *Porsenna*, 1718; *Ixion*, 1722; *Ludovicus Pius, oder Ludewig der Fromme* (some music by Graun), 1726; several lost operas
BIBLIOGRAPHY G. F. Schmidt, *Die frühdeutsche Oper und die musikdramatische Kunst Georg Caspar Schürmanns*, Gustav Bosse, 1933–4

G.J.B.

JOSEPH SCHUSTER
b 11 August 1748, Dresden; *d* 24 July 1812, Dresden

Like many other German composers of his time, Schuster learned his basic operatic skills in Italy, where he studied with Girolamo Pera in Venice and Padre Martini in Bologna. His earliest operas were performed in Italy, notably *Didone abbandonata* (Naples, 1776), to a Metastasio text. In Germany, where he gave lifelong service to the electoral court at Dresden as kapellmeister from 1787, it was mainly as a composer of opera buffa and singspiel that he gained renown, achieving a popularity that extended well beyond his immediate locality. He is, however, remembered particularly for his divertimenti for violin and keyboard, six of which Mozart sent to his sister on 6 October 1777 saying, 'They are not bad . . . I shall write six myself in the same style as they are very popular here.'

Der Alchymist, oder Der Liebesteufel

The Alchemist, or The Devil of Love
Singspiel in one act
Libretto by A. G. Meissner
PREMIERE   2 October 1778, Kleiner Kurfürstliches Theater, Dresden

An attractive example of Schuster's graceful style, this work retained a place in the repertoire of German theatres until well into the 19th century. Consciously Viennese in manner, it achieves a fine theatrical effect by means of its warm melodiousness and colourful instrumentation.

EDITION   R. Engländer (ed.), Bärenreiter, 1958

Other operatic works: *La fedeltà in amore*, 1773; *L'idolo cinese*, 1776; *L'amore artigiano*, 1776; *La Didone abbandonata*, 1776; *Demofoonte*, 1776; *La schiava liberata*, 1777; *Die wüste Insel*, 1779; *Creso in Media*, 1779; *Amor e Psyche*, 1780; *Il marito indolente*, 1782; *Il pazzo per forza*, 1784; *Lo spirito di contradiz ione*, 1785; *Gli avari in trappola*, 1787; *Rübezahl, ossia Il vero amore*, 1789; *Il servo padrone, ossia L'amore perfetto*, 1793; *Osmano dey d'Algeri*, 1800; *Il giorno natalizio*, 1802; *Der Schauspieldirector* (doubtful); one lost opera
BIBLIOGRAPHY   R. Engländer, 'Die Opern Joseph Schusters (1748–1812)', *ZMw*, vol. 10 (1927–8), pp. 257–91

B.S.

HEINRICH SCHÜTZ

baptized 9 October 1585, Köstritz (now Bad Köstritz), nr Gera; d 6 November 1672, Dresden

The greatest German composer of the 17th century, Schütz composed largely sacred vocal music for the Protestant Church. He is a significant figure in the history of opera because he composed the first German opera, *Dafne* (1627), based on a libretto by Opitz (a translation of Rinuccini's libretto for Peri's *Dafne*, 1597). The libretto has survived but the music is lost.

Schütz was brought to court by the Landgrave Moritz of Hessen-Kassel to serve as a choirboy. In 1610 Moritz funded Schütz's further musical education in Venice; he studied composition there with Giovanni Gabrieli. He thus returned to Germany with a complete command of the various Italian compositional practices and undoubtedly the earliest experiences of any German musician of the new Italian operatic practice. By 1617 Schütz had become a member of the music staff of the Dresden court of Elector Johann Georg I where he remained as kapellmeister until his death. No secular music is preserved although Schütz is known to have composed ballets and dramatic vocal music. *Dafne*

Title page of the libretto for Schütz's Dafne *by Martin Opitz, published in 1627*

was written for the celebrations for the wedding of the elector's daughter Sophia Eleonora to Landgrave Georg II of Hessen-Darmstadt during spring 1627. Another dramatic work, of which the music is also lost, was an opera-ballet in five acts, *Orpheus und Euridice* (1638) for the wedding of Prince Johann Georg of Saxony and the Princess Magdalena Sybilla of Brandenburg.

BIBLIOGRAPHY   Hans Joachim Moser, *Heinrich Schütz, His Life and Work*, Concordia, 1959

G.J.B.

STEPHEN SCHWARTZ

Stephen Lawrence Schwartz; b 6 March 1948, New York

Schwartz studied at the Juilliard School (1960–64). In 1971 he collaborated with Leonard Bernstein on the text of the latter's *Mass*, which opened the John F. Kennedy Center in Washington DC. But it is for his work as a composer and lyricist in the musical theatre that he is best known. *Pippin* (1972), set at the court of Charlemagne, and *The Magic Show* (1974), though both successes, failed to match that of *Godspell*.

Godspell

Musical in two acts (1h 30m)
Book by Michael Tebelak; lyrics by the composer; based on the Gospel according to St Matthew
PREMIERES   17 May 1971, Cherry Lane Theater, Greenwich, New York; UK: 17 November 1971, The Roundhouse, London

Godspell and Lloyd Webber's *Jesus Christ Superstar* (which appeared some five months later) were the definitive 1970s 'Jesus Rock' musicals. In *Godspell* a group of high-school students in clowns' costumes retell various gospel stories before acting out the last days of Jesus's life.

Despite a loosely constructed and now rather dated narrative, *Godspell* contains some memorable songs which have been absorbed into the evangelical repertoire, including 'Prepare ye the way of the Lord', 'Day by day' and a version of a harvest hymn 'All good gifts'. The cast of the UK premiere included David Essex and Jeremy Irons. A film version appeared in 1973.

RECORDING   Schwartz *et al.*, Arista, 1974
EDITION   v.s., Hal Leonard, 1971

BIBLIOGRAPHY   Kurt Gänzl and Andrew Lamb, *Gänzl's Book of the Musical Theatre*, Bodley Head, 1988, pp. 835–7

M.A.

ANTON SCHWEITZER
baptized 6 June 1735, Coburg; *d* 23 November 1787, Gotha

After initial experience at the court of the Duke of Hildburghausen, Schweitzer served in Weimar and Gotha with the Seyler theatrical company for whom he composed the majority of his dramatic works. His importance lies in the contribution he made to the development of German-language opera during the late 18th century, particularly with his *Alkeste* (1773). Based on a libretto by Wieland, drawn from Euripides, this large-scale work adopts the musico-poetic schemes of opera seria and reshapes them to accord with reform principles founded on Gluck and Calzabigi. Unhappily, Schweitzer's creative ability seems rarely to have matched the loftiness of his aims. Mozart, (in a letter of 18 December 1778) admired the dramatic scene 'O Jugendzeit' from Act IV of *Alkeste* but attributed the opera's success more to its novelty than its intrinsic merits. Many of Schweitzer's stage works are lost, including the music he wrote in 1772 for a German version of Rousseau's *Pygmalion*. Predating Benda's *Ariadne* by three years this was probably the first German melodrama.

Operatic works: *Die Dorfgala*, 1772; *Aurora*, 1772; *Ariadne auf Naxos* (inc.), (1772); *Alkeste*, 1773; *Die Wahl des Herkules*, 1773; *Polyxena*, 1775; *Rosamunde*, 1780; 7 lost operas
BIBLIOGRAPHY   J. Maurer, *Anton Schweitzer als dramatischer Komponist*, Breitkopf und Härtel, 1912: contains excerpts from *Die Dorfgala*, *Alkeste*, *Die Wahl des Herkules* and *Rosamunde*; F. Peters-Marquardt and W. Pfannkuch, 'Anton Schweitzer', in *MGG*

B.S.

KURT SCHWERTSIK
b 25 June 1935, Vienna

From 1955 Schwertsik pursued a career as an orchestral horn-player. In 1958, with Friedrich Cerha, he founded the ensemble die Reihe, and studied in Darmstadt and Cologne (1959–62) with Stockhausen, Kagel and Cage. Schwertsik began to experiment with tonality in 1961, feeling that serial and aleatoric methods yielded only simple musical results, and that simpler musical material would lead to greater and more meaningful complexity. He senses an affinity to the music of Cornelius Cardew, the American minimalist school, Hanns Eisler and Erik Satie. *Das Märchen von Fanferlieschen Schönefusschen*, a parable of 'Imagination and Piety versus Enlightenment and Revolution', was a great success at its Stuttgart premiere in 1983.

Operatic works: *Der lange Weg zur Grossen Mauer*, 1975; *Das Märchen von Fanferlieschen Schönefusschen*, 1983; *Die verlorene Wut*, 1989; *Das Friedensbankett*, (1990)
BIBLIOGRAPHY   Kurt Schwertsik, 'Looking into the Mirror', *Tempo*, nos 161–2 (1987); Friedrich Spangemacher (ed.), *Kurt Schwertsik*, Boosey & Hawkes, 1990

A.C.

SALVATORE SCIARRINO
b 4 April 1947, Palermo, Italy

Sciarrino is a precocious autodidact, whose initial fascination with the visual arts ceded to even stronger musical compulsions. At 22 he moved to Rome where he rapidly attracted notice. At 30 he became artistic director of the Teatro Comunale in Bologna for three years, since when he has taught extensively: principally in Milan, Florence, and in Città di Castello where he now lives.

His musical language quickly evolved into one of the most distinctive of his generation, obsessive in its use of marginalized sounds: string and wind harmonics, ancillary performance noises, the full, and sometimes disconcerting gamut of vocal sound. His theatre has proved equally idiosyncratic. Rooted in the surreal, re-examining with an oblique, wistfully sardonic eye myths ancient and modern, it anatomizes the precariousness of human attempts at relationships through protagonists whose infantilism mixes neurotic immediacy and invincible solipsism in a disturbing, but frequently hilarious, fusion.

Amore e Psiche
Love and Psyche
Opera in one act (45m)
Libretto by A. Pes, based on Apuleius
Composed 1972
PREMIERE   2 March 1973, Piccola Scala, Milan

Unlike Sciarrino's later operas, *Amore e Psiche* sets an elaborate, and emphatically poetic libretto – but in a manner so idiosyncratic as to have made an instant impression when the work was first performed. Sciarrino employs only high voices: a coloratura mezzo-soprano for Psyche, sopranos for her two attendant sisters, and a counter-tenor for Amore. Actors play four fantastic creatures who comment on proceedings: a salamander-man, a bull-man, a tree-man and a sprouting potato.

A dense play of symbols and images is articulated around skeletal action: Psyche, a luminous figure, conjures with magic ingredients, and unknowingly summons up another luminous figure, Love. Unperceived by her, he collapses behind her and his light fades. When finally she recognizes his presence, she bends over and reanimates him: he becomes a source of blinding light and departs.

EDITION f.s./v.s., Ricordi (on hire)

Cailles en sarcophage

Entombed Quails
Acts for a museum of obsessions (opera in three parts) (1h 30m)
Libretto by Giorgio Marini
Composed 1979
PREMIERES 26 September 1979, Teatro Malibran, Venice; definitive version: 17 October 1980, La Fenice, Venice

'A self-evidently surreal opera', as Sciarrino defined it, this 'museum of obsessions' rotates around a series of modern myths: Dietrich, Garbo, etc. The text is an extraordinary montage of quotations, from Genet and Cocteau to Lacan and Foucault. The music draws on Sciarrino's wide knowledge of classic American songs of the 1930s and 1940s, brief fragments of which are transformed as they are drawn into Sciarrino's sound-world. Three singers take a long series of parallel roles as they move from one fragment to the next: otherwise the text is given to nine actors.

EDITION f.s., Ricordi (on hire)

Lohengrin

Invisible Action
Text by the composer, after *Lohengrin fils de Parsifal* from *Moralités légendaires* by Jules Laforgue (1887)
Composed 1982–4
PREMIERE 15 January 1983, Piccola Scala, Milan

Laforgue's ironic rethinking of the Lohengrin story is in two parts. On a moonlit seashore, the chorus accuses Elsa, a vestal virgin, of impurity. Lohengrin arrives on a swan to defend her. The scene changes to the gardens and rooms of the nuptial villa made available to them by the Ministry of Cults. The gauche Elsa tries every gambit appropriate to a wedding night, but Lohengrin seems less than interested. His cushion mutates into a swan; mounting on it Lohengrin flies out of the window and back to the moon.

Sciarrino increases the sense of ironic uncertainty by reversing the two halves. Furthermore both Elsa and Lohengrin are interpreted by a single female protagonist whose part encompasses an extra-ordinary range of vocal nuance. At the end all is made plain: Elsa is a patient in a mental hospital.

RECORDING Dischi Ricordi
EDITION Ricordi, 1983

Perseo e Andromeda

Perseus and Andromeda
Opera in one act (1h 15m)
Text by the composer after *Moralités légendaires* by Jules Laforgue (1887)
Composed 1990–91
PREMIERE 27 January 1991, Staatstheater, Stuttgart

A bored Andromeda, marooned on her island, is indulged by an avuncular Dragon. Perseus flies in on Pegasus and duly slays the Dragon. But he proves a self-satisfied oaf: mortified, Andromeda retorts that he has got the wrong island. Perseus flies off, and Andromeda is left to mourn her Dragon.

For the first time, Sciarrino uses voices and live electronics – particularly the complex analogues to wind and sea that he obtains by subtractive synthesis from white noise.

EDITION f.s., Ricordi, 1991

Other operatic works: *Aspern*, 1978; *Vanitas*, 1981
BIBLIOGRAPHY Horst Koegler, review of *Perseo e Andromeda*, *Opera*, vol. 42 (1991), pp. 565–6

D.O.-S.

CYRIL SCOTT

Cyril Meir Scott; *b* 27 September 1879, Oxton, Cheshire, England; *d* 31 December 1970, Eastbourne, Sussex, England

Scott was one of the 'Frankfurt Gang' of British composers which included Percy Grainger, Balfour Gardiner, Norman O'Neill and Roger Quilter. He studied from the age of 12 at the Hoch Konservatorium in Frankfurt am Main where his teachers included Iwan Knorr. His early works were widely performed, particularly in Germany where he was known as the 'English Debussy'. His First Symphony, performed at Darmstadt when he was 20, was given in five European capitals. Later, in spite of a lasting reputation for piano miniatures and songs, he was unable to capitalize on this enviable beginning, and yesterday's modernism began to look increasingly dated. During the First World War he produced several works, including the First Piano Concerto (1915) and the opera *The Alchemist* (1917), the only one of his four operas to be produced (in Essen) and published (Schott, 1924). Vivid and colourful, it tells of a sorcerer's apprentice who invokes the assistance of 'The Elemental' who will provide him with all he wants, but who is liable to run out of control.

Operas: *The Alchemist*, 1917; *The Saint of the Mountain*, (1925); *Maureen O'Mara*, (1946); *The Shrine*, (1946)

BIBLIOGRAPHY   Jonathan Frank, 'Cyril Scott in the Opera House', *Musical Opinion*, July 1964, p. 597

L.F.

PETER SCULTHORPE

Peter Joshua Sculthorpe; *b* 29 April 1929, Launceston, Tasmania

Sculthorpe is Australia's most successful contemporary composer, both at home and abroad. He studied at the University of Melbourne Conservatorium (1945–50) and Oxford (1958–60). He has been composer-in-residence at Yale University (1966–7) and visiting Professor of Music at the University of Sussex (1972–3). His work has a distinctive Australian quality, which he has been the first to achieve, based partly on an exclusion of what he considers to be specifically European elements, and partly on a notion of Michael Hannan's that 'Australians, unlike Europeans, have a visual rather than an aural culture and awareness' – the music is said to reflect the harshness and open spaces of the Australian landscape; it also shows the influence of Asian music. *Rites of Passage* was his first major choral work and was followed by a music-theatre piece, *Eliza Fraser Sings*, a monodrama for soprano and small ensemble (1978), and a television opera, *Quiros*,

commissioned by the Australian Broadcasting Commission in 1982. He is Reader in Music at the University of Sydney.

Rites of Passage

Opera in one movement (1h 45m)
Libretto by the composer, based on the anthropological work *Les rites de passage* by Arnold van Gennep
Composed 1971–3
PREMIERE   27 September 1974, Opera House, Sydney

Although *Rites of Passage* has no soloists, being written for chorus, orchestra and dancers, the composer classifies it as an opera, stressing that it is at the same time 'a return to the idea of drama as ritual'. In structure the work alternates between chorales (for chorus and orchestra – consisting only of cellos, double-basses, tubas and percussion) with reference to Aboriginal and other tribal chants, and the 'rites enacted by movers, accompanied by singers and music-makers', reflecting the composer's wish to convey simultaneously the concepts of change and permanence.

EDITION   f.s., Faber Music (on hire), 1972

BIBLIOGRAPHY   Michael Hannan, *Peter Sculthorpe – His Music and Ideas 1929–79*, University of Queensland Press, 1982

A.I.G.

Peter Sculthorpe's Rites of Passage *(Sydney, 1974)*

HUMPHREY SEARLE

b 26 August 1915, Oxford, England; *d* 12 May 1982, London

Searle received a conventional middle-class English education (Winchester, Oxford, the Royal College of Music with Gordon Jacob and John Ireland), then went to the Vienna Conservatory (1937–8), and studied privately with Webern. He was a pioneer of the techniques of the Second Viennese School and an active worker for contemporary music. With the asceticism of Webern and the complexity of Schoenberg came a passionate regard for the music of Liszt, on whom he wrote a monograph. These influences resulted in an idiosyncratic personal style which informs his operas.

Between 1949 and 1951 Searle wrote three extended works for speaker and orchestra – *Gold Coast Customs* and *The Shadow of Cain* to words by Edith Sitwell, and *The Riverrun* after Joyce. These were the precursors of his first opera, *The Diary of a Madman*, after Gogol. Presented at the 1958 Berlin Festival and subsequently at Sadler's Wells in 1960, it was noted for its effective vocal writing combining arioso and sprechgesang. Although mainly serial in technique, it also uses *musique concrète* in a comic way to underscore a bizarre conversation between two dogs. In his second opera, a three-act setting of Ionesco's play *The Photo of the Colonel* (1964), Searle responded vividly to the symbolic world of the play with expressive use of serial technique. The climax of his operatic ambitions came with *Hamlet*, but his earlier achievements are more likely to be remembered.

Hamlet

Opera in three acts, Op. 48 (2h 30m)
Libretto by the composer, after the play by William Shakespeare (1600–1601)
Composed 1965–8
PREMIERES 5 March 1968, Hamburg Staatsoper; UK: 18 April 1969, Covent Garden, London; Canada: 12 February 1969, Toronto

Hamlet was commissioned by the Hamburg State Opera. Its subsequent London production was not a success. Searle's more or less verbatim setting of Shakespeare proved a barrier to the opera's musical effectiveness. This was underlined by the positive audience reception of the 'play within a play' in which he adopted a parody romantic idiom, in contrast to the *moderato* pace of most of the work, without ensembles. All the opera's themes are based on the same 12-note series.

EDITIONS f.s., Faber Music, 1968; rev. version: v.s., Faber Music, 1971

BIBLIOGRAPHY R. Murray Schafer, *British Composers in Interview*, Faber, 1963, pp. 125ff.

L.F.

KAREL ŠEBOR

Karel Richard Šebor [Carl Schebor]; *b* 13 August 1843, Brandýs nad Labem; *d* 17 May 1903, Prague

Šebor's first opera, *The Templars in Moravia*, was performed when he was 22 and was so successful that he was taken on at the Prague Provisional Theatre as second conductor, with a contract obliging him to deliver an opera annually, a requirement he almost managed to satisfy with four premieres in four years. At first his popularity with the public grew. His third opera, *The Hussite Bride*, remained in the Czech repertoire until the 1880s, but with the comparative failure of his next opera, *Blanka*, Šebor abruptly left Prague and settled for an itinerant life as a military bandmaster in the Austro-Hungarian army. His final opera, *The Frustrated Wedding*, written from the exile of Slovakia, also failed, partly because its would-be folk style was not his *métier*. He excelled, as is testified by his early works, in full-blooded historico-romantic opera. An inventive orchestrator and a distinctive melodist with the ability to handle long spans, Šebor had genuine theatrical gifts. But his instincts for, or luck in, finding adequate librettos, were less evident, and his promising career was soon overshadowed by that of his contemporary, Smetana.

The Templars in Moravia

Templáři na Moravě
Romantic opera in three acts (2h 30m)
Libretto by Karel Sabina
Composed 1865
PREMIERE 19 October 1865, Provisional Theatre, Prague

The Templars in Moravia occupies an important historical position as the first newly written Czech opera to be staged at the Prague Provisional Theatre, narrowly preceding Smetana's first opera, *The Brandenburgers in Bohemia* (which was, however, written two years earlier). With its Italianate arias and voice types, it is typical of Šebor's early output. Like all of Šebor's operas, it was not published, and after its first successful run of performances was unheard until a concert performance in 1980 demonstrated that Šebor's neglect was unjustified.

Other operas: *Drahomíra*, 1867; *Nevěsta Husitská* (*The Hussite Bride*), 1868; *Blanka*, 1870; *Zmařená svatba* (*The Frustrated Wedding*), 1879
BIBLIOGRAPHY John Tyrrell, *Czech Opera*, CUP, 1988

J.T.

ALEKSANDR SEROV

Aleksandr Nikolayevich Serov; *b* 23 January 1820, St Petersburg; *d* 1 February 1871, St Petersburg

Dubbed the Russian Meyerbeer, Serov was similarly despised, imitated and successful. Originally a civil servant, he resigned in 1851, living off his musical criticism while studying informally and composing salon pieces of little promise. An opera based on Gogol's *May Night* dates from this period, but Serov destroyed it after his friend Vladimir Stasov, historian and later mentor to the Mighty Handful, condemned it. They later became implacable enemies after Serov wrote an article criticizing the revered Glinka's *Ruslan and Lyudmila*. Serov also made an enemy of Rubinstein, thus managing to alienate both Westernizers and nationalists, the two main opposing factions in Russian musical life. Serov's connections with the Grand Duchess Helena Pavlovna paved the way for the staging of *Judith* (1863), and Serov confounded his many enemies, and even his friends, who had never seen evidence of much composing talent, by producing a work of genuine inspiration – and a success to boot. The financial success of *Judith* enabled him to marry Valentina Bergman, who later became an opera composer in her own right. *Rogneda* (1865), based on a Russian subject, was an even greater triumph, scoring 70 performances at the Mariinsky in its first five years: as a result, the tsar granted Serov a pension. His last opera, *The Power of Evil*, was almost complete at his death, and was finished by his widow and a pupil, Solovyev.

In his last years, Serov's critical polemics softened somewhat, and he gave some in-depth lectures to the Russian Musical Society on Glinka and Dargomizhsky, and was even sympathetic to the early works of Tchaikovsky and Rimsky-Korsakov. Ironically, his posthumous reputation suffered from vicious attacks by Stasov; and this judgement has been parroted by commentators in the absence of knowledge of his works. Act IV of *Judith* was staged in Paris in 1909, as part of Diaghilev's opera–ballet season, and this is the only performance of Serov's music traced outside Russia. There, by contrast, his operas were mainstays of the repertoire until the Revolution, when they quickly dropped from favour. That he was an ardent Wagnerian is evident only from his writings (though he also arranged the first Russian performance of *Lohengrin* in 1868). Musically, the operas are indebted to Meyerbeer, Verdi, Gounod and Glinka, with occasional lapses into Mendelssohn's Victorian oratorio style. *Judith* and *Rogneda* are both number operas with few recurring themes, and their structure is that of the five-act French grand opera; but, within this format, there is considerable musical invention, as well as a great deal of padding. His scores show him to be as great an influence on the next generation of Russian composers as Glinka and Dargomizhsky, with surprising harmonic and rhythmic experiment and a real talent for garish, piquant orchestration.

Judith

Yudif'
Opera in five acts (2h 30m)
Libretto by the composer, Apollon Nikolaevich Maykov, Dmitry I. Lobanov and Konstantin Zvantsev, after the drama *Giuditta* by Paolo Giacometti (1857)
Composed 1861–3
PREMIERE 28 May 1863, Mariinsky Theatre, St Petersburg

A simple retelling of the Old Testament tale of Judith and Holofernes in French grand-opera style. Wagner would have been horrified at Serov's working methods, which often consisted of his roughing out music and getting one of a stream of librettists to fit words and situations to it. Acts I, II and V are epic in tone, set in the besieged Jewish city of Bethulia. Acts III and IV are Assyrian, with Serov providing music in an oriental vein. This structure foreshadows that of *Prince Igor*, though Serov's oriental music is decidedly diluted compared to Borodin's and Glinka's in *Ruslan*. Serov was no melodist, though the standard is higher in *Judith* than in his later operas. There are some striking similarities between Judith's prayer in Act II and Musorgsky's death of Boris. Musorgsky sat with Stasov at the premiere and was obviously intimidated by the latter's criticisms. Musorgsky's true reaction to *Judith* was that it inspired him to start a spectacular opera of his own, *Salammbô*. The ballet music of *Judith* has a lightness of touch and brilliance of scoring that anticipate Tchaikovsky, who was a lifelong enthusiast of this opera.

RECORDING Udalova, Zaremba, Kudriachev, Krutikov, USSR Academy Ch, Bolshoi Theatre O, Chistyakov, Chant du Monde, 1991
EDITIONS f.s., Röder, 1903; v.s., A. Gutheil, 1885

Rogneda

Opera in five acts (2h 45m)
Libretto by Dmitry Vasileyvich Averkiev and the composer
Composed 1863–5
PREMIERE 8 November 1865, Mariinsky Theatre, St Petersburg

Vladimir the Great has abducted Olava (who never appears), bride of Ruald, a Christian warrior. Ruald has shown magnanimity in rescuing Vladimir from a bear, so when Vladimir awakes to find his wife, Rogneda, trying to murder him, he is persuaded by Christian monks to pardon her; he then forces his subjects to embrace Christianity. The libretto is an utter hotch-potch of theatrical and spectacular events with no motivation or relevance to the plot. A witch, idol-worshippers, dancing bears and mummers who turn into geese, dwarf the story and render it inconsequential. The music is much more uneven than that of *Judith*, but at its best is thoroughly soaked in folk idioms; some pages sound as if they could be by Borodin or Rimsky-Korsakov. Rimsky, in his memoirs, acknowledges his fascination with this work and how the scene with the witch influenced the opening of *Sadko* and a chorus in 7/4 time encouraged his own metric experiments in *The Snow Maiden* and *Mlada*. The hunt scene features the same two oscillating dominant seventh chords, a tritone apart, that open the coronation scene in Musorgsky's *Boris Godunov* – and Serov's handling of the chorus anticipates *Boris* in its division into many solo character parts.

RECORDING excerpts: Rayevskaya, Koroliev, Russian Radio Ch and O, Samosud, Melodiya, 1949

EDITIONS f.s., Stellowski Petersburg, [n.d.]; v.s., A. Gutheil, 1904

The Power of Evil
Vrazh'ya sila

Opera in five acts (2h 15m)
Libretto by Aleksandr Nikolaevich Ostrovsky, Piotr Kalashnikov and the composer, after the play *Ne tak zhivi, kak khochetsya, a tak zhivi, kak Bog velit* (*Don't live as you'd like to, but as God commands*) by Ostrovsky (1855)
Composed 1867–71 (Act V completed by N. F. Solovyov and V. S. Serova)
PREMIERE 1 May 1871, Mariinsky Theatre, St Petersburg

As a reaction to the inflated Meyerbeerian *Rogneda*, Serov settled on a realistic Russian subject. The story concerns the machinations of an evil smith and a merchant bored with his wife. Unfortunately Serov and Ostrovsky quarrelled over the last two acts, so the original ending of the story is sensationalized with a murder, and a new librettist was brought in. A feature of the original play is the incorporation of Russian folktunes as an integral part of the drama, and these Serov carried over into the opera. Some of these melodies are exceptionally beautiful, a bonus here as Serov's melodic invention is usually weak. He treats these melodies very simply, so ironically it is this work, rather than anything by Cui or Dargomizhsky, that most closely approaches the theoretical operatic ideals of the emergent nationalists. Serov's characterization of the evil smith, Eremka, is vivid and worthy of comparison with Musgorgsky (and was a favourite role of Chaliapin's). There are further musical experiments, brash whole-tone harmony accompanying the murder and a Shrovetide fair scene, where fragments of folk melodies collide in separate keys in a manner astonishingly prophetic of Stravinsky's *Petrushka*. The opera was only a moderate success, but was the last of Serov's operas to be revived, in 1948.

RECORDING excerpts: Antonova, Sokolova, Borisenko, Al. Ivanov, Shchegolkov, Bolshoi Theatre O, various conductors, Melodiya, various dates
EDITION v.s., A. Gutheil, 1904

Other operas: *The Miller's Wife in Marli* (*Mel'nichka v Marli*) (inc.), (1846); *May Night* (*Maiskayr noch'*) (destroyed), (1853); *Christmas Eve* (*Noch' pod rozhdestvo*) (inc.), (1866)
BIBLIOGRAPHY Gerald Abraham, *The Operas of Serov*, Clarendon, 1985; Richard Taruskin, 'Opera and Drama in Russia: The Case of Serov's *Judith*', *JAMS*, xxxii (1979), pp. 74–117.

J.G.

ROGER SESSIONS

Roger Huntingdon Sessions; *b* 28 December 1896, Brooklyn, New York; *d* 16 March 1985, Princeton, US

Sessions was a major figure in American musical life as composer and teacher, but his operas are more esteemed than regularly performed. The son of a lawyer, he gained a Harvard degree at 18 and went on to study with Horatio Parker at Yale. The influence of Bloch was profound, both in private lessons and when Sessions was his assistant at the Cleveland Institute. Sessions spent seven years in Italy and Germany in the late 1920s and early 1930s; his reaction against the rise of fascism later affected some of his works, including the operas.

On returning to the US Sessions established himself primarily at Princeton University where he taught several distinguished pupils (including Milton Babbitt and Edward T. Cone) built up a substantial *oeuvre* and expressed his ideas in regular critical writings. Sessions's earlier work was influenced by Stravinsky, but has a personal vein of complexity. By the 1950s he had moved towards Schoenberg's 12-note technique. His uncompromising stance was recognized by Virgil Thomson: 'The monumental music of Roger Sessions seems to yearn toward all of Europe . . . If in its pursuit of excellence it occasionally stumbles over its own coils, it is nevertheless work of a high viscosity, a stubborn obscurity, and some grandeur.'

Sessions wrote an early (unpublished) opera, *Lancelot and Elaine*, based on Tennyson, and another incomplete opera on Poe's *The Fall of the House of Usher* (1925); otherwise the only vocal works to precede his first staged opera, *The Trial of Lucullus*, are two songs (one with orchestra) and a choral piece.

The Trial of Lucullus

Opera in one act
Libretto: the radio play *Das Verhor des Lukullus* by Bertolt Brecht (1939), translated by H. R. Hays
Composed 1947
PREMIERE 18 April 1947, University of California, Berkeley

Written at great speed, this opera was designed to partner Stravinsky's *The Soldier's Tale* in a double-bill performed by students at the University of California. Sessions's long wait, until 1966, for the New York premiere was rewarded by enthusiastic reviews. Particular praise was given to the expressive declamatory style of the word-setting. This was guided, the composer wrote, 'by my strong convictions . . . that opera can become once more . . . a vital dramatic medium; that music and drama . . . must be welded into an ensemble in which neither is subservient to the other'.

Brecht's text, also set by Dessau (1949), is a diatribe against war and tyranny. Lucullus, the great Roman general, has died and is brought before a jury of ordinary people who will decide his fate in the realm of the dead. Lucullus summons witnesses – characters from a frieze brought to life – to cite his great conquests of ruined cities and looted treasure. The jury is unimpressed, but looks upon him more kindly for his respect for learning and good food, and for having introduced the cherry tree to Italy.

EDITION Marks Music (on hire)

Montezuma

Opera in three acts
Libretto by Antonio Borgese and the composer
Composed 1941–63
PREMIERES 19 April 1964, Deutsche Oper, West Berlin;
US: 30 March 1976, Boston Opera Company

Sessions met the Sicilian poet Borgese in 1934 but the libretto was not completed until 1941. Unhappy with its length and style, Sessions reworked it after Borgese's death in 1952. However, he could do nothing to mitigate the flowery language and the use of Spanish, Aztec and Latin as well as English.

The plot of *Montezuma*, like that of *Lucullus*, concerns the futility of conquest – here the 16th-century Spanish conquest of Mexico. Cortés claims Mexico for Charles V and, because of his fair skin, the Aztecs confuse him with their god Quetzalcoatl. Montezuma, the Mexican leader, is taken prisoner and eventually stoned by his own people.

Montezuma, Sessions's largest work, reflects the changes in his musical style, in particular his adoption of 12-note technique, that occurred during the opera's long gestation period. It is consequently seen as a pivotal work in his output. The immensely dense and complex score, which relies heavily on melodic and rhythmic ostinati for dramatic effect and to achieve unity, was described as 'a sea of grey monotony'; but Andrew Porter found *Montezuma* 'a stunning achievement' and went on to provide Sessions with a libretto for a comic opera, *The Emperor's New Clothes*, which the composer did not live to complete.

EDITION v.s., Edward B. Marks, 1967

BIBLIOGRAPHY E. T. Cone (ed.), *Roger Sessions on Music: Collected Essays*, Princeton University Press, 1979; Andrea Olmstead, *Roger Sessions and His Music*, UMI Research Press, 1985; Andrea Olmstead, 'The Plumed Serpent: Antonio Borgese's and Roger Sessions's *Montezuma*', *Tempo*, no. 72 (1986), pp. 13–22; Andrea Olmstead (ed.), *The Correspondence of Roger Sessions*, Northeastern University Press, 1992

P.D.

DÉODAT DE SÉVERAC

Marie-Joseph-Alexandre Déodat de Séverac; *b* 20 July 1872, St Félix de Caraman en Lauragais, Haute-Garonne, France; *d* 24 March 1921, Céret, Pyrénées-Orientales, France

The son of a well-known Languedoc painter (Gilbert de Séverac) and a descendant of the royal house of Aragon, Déodat de Séverac spent most of his life in the south-west, and is today remembered chiefly for a substantial body of piano music, much of it inspired by the scenery and atmosphere of that part of France. He studied in Paris at the Schola Cantorum with d'Indy and Magnard. But he disliked the centralizing tendencies in Parisian artistic life, and his graduation thesis at the Schola was an amiable attack on the institutions which perpetuated those tendencies.

Severac wrote a quantity of music for the stage, though his leanings towards improvisation and mood music equipped him better for incidental music than for formal opera. His most successful independent stage work, *Héliogabale*, is a hybrid of opera, ballet and pantomime, written in 1910 for performance in the outdoor arena at Béziers (where Fauré's *Prométhée* had been premiered ten years earlier), and including parts for Catalan oboes, trumpets and drums. It was revived at Béziers in 1972 on the centenary of Séverac's birth. The more conventional *Le coeur du moulin* is notable for its attractive use of folk material including dances, but is dramatically wooden. A fifth opera, *Les Antibels* (begun in 1907 but unfinished), is apparently lost.

Operas: *Le coeur du moulin*, 1909; *Héliogabale*, 1910; *La fille de la terre*, 1913; *Le roi pinard*, (1919)
BIBLIOGRAPHY Elaine Brody, 'Déodat de Séverac: A Mediterranean Musician', *MR*, vol. 29 (1968), pp. 172–83

S.W.

YURI SHAPORIN

Yuri Alexandrovich Shaporin; *b* 8 November 1887, Glukhov, Ukraine; *d* 9 December 1966, Moscow

Encouraged by Lysenko, Shaporin moved from the Ukraine to the more stimulating atmosphere of St Petersburg. There his studies with Glazunov, Steinberg and Nikolay Tcherepnin formed his style within the 19th-century nationalist tradition. With Gorky, Lunacharsky and Blok, he founded the Grand Drama Theatre in 1919, working as musical director until 1928, when he became associated with the Academic Drama Theatre until 1934. During this period he wrote incidental music for about 80 plays, comprising some of his most experimental work. With the advent of Stalin, such work ceased and he diverted his attention to film scores and oratorios. Apart from his theatre work, he was a painstaking and slow composer, leaving behind only a handful of works, including one opera.

The Decembrists

Dekabristy
Opera in four acts (2h 45m)
Libretto by V. Rozhdestvensky, after Alexei Tolstoy's and P. E. Shchegolev's libretto for *Paulina Goebbel*
Composed 1920–53
PREMIERE 3 June 1953, Moscow

The Decembrists originated in a two-scene opera, *Paulina Goebbel* (1925), which was later incorporated into the larger work. It concerns the Decembrist uprising in 1825, a revolt of the young élite protesting the lack of reform by Tsar Alexander I, which was ruthlessly suppressed by the newly crowned Nicholas I. It is a well-made opera, showing no signs of its monstrous gestation, far superior to the plentiful propaganda works of this period, though it remains wholly within the 19th-century Russian tradition. The original production was of legendary opulence, and for a long while it was the only Soviet opera to be regularly performed at the Bolshoi.

RECORDING Pokrovskaya, Verbitskaya, Nelepp, Ivanov, Pirogov, Petrov, Ch and O of Bolshoi Theatre, Melik-Pashayev, Melodiya/Parlophone, c. 1954
EDITIONS f.s., State Music Publishers, 1955; v.s., State Music Publishers, 1953

BIBLIOGRAPHY S. D. Krebs, *Soviet Composers*, George Allen and Unwin, 1970

J.G.

RODION SHCHEDRIN
Rodion Konstantinovich Shchedrin; *b* 16 December 1932, Moscow

Shchedrin trained at the Moscow Conservatory with Shaporin and soon became prominent with the success of his ballet *The Hunchbacked Horse* (1955). He is a prolific composer in most disciplines, and his early work derives from the tradition of Prokofiev and Shostakovich, though his later compositions assimilate avant-garde techniques and show an increased colouristic awareness. His best-known work is *Carmen Ballet*, a quirky version of Bizet, scored for strings and percussion.

Not Love Alone
Ne tol'ko lyubov'
Opera in three acts and an epilogue (1h 30m)
Libretto by V. Katanyan
Composed 1961
PREMIERES 25 December 1961, Moscow; new chamber version: 20 January 1972, Moscow

A much performed work in the Soviet provinces about a love triangle on a collective farm, *Not Love Alone* contains spoken dialogue and veers in tone from operetta to music drama. There is no overture, and in some productions this function is filled by recordings of tractors.

RECORDING Ambrazaitite, Noreika, Kupris, Lithuanian State Opera and Ballet Theatre Ch and O, Geniusas, Melodiya, 1976
EDITIONS f.s., Sovetsky Kompozitor Moscow, 1976; v.s., Sovetsky Kompozitor Moscow, 1965

Dead Souls
Myortvye Dushi
Opera in three acts (2h)
Libretto by the composer, after the novel by Gogol (inc.; 1842)
Composed 1966–76
PREMIERE 7 June 1977, Bolshoi Theatre, Moscow; US: 12 March 1988, Opera House, Boston

The central character of Gogol's great unfinished novel is a traveller, Chichikov, who journeys through Russia buying up the dead souls of serfs whose names are still registered with their masters, and who are therefore, in bureaucratic eyes, still alive. On his picaresque odyssey, Chichikov amasses imaginary wealth, though his motives for doing so are unclear.

The opera culls scenes from the novel, and is an episodic and sometimes rambling work with moments of great theatrical effectiveness. The scoring is unusual, with violins replaced by a female semi-chorus, huge amounts of percussion and harpsichord, electric guitar and balalaika. It was a great success when artists from the Bolshoi and the Kirov toured it to the US in 1988.

RECORDING Avdeyeva, Borisova, Piavko, Maslennikov, Voroshilo, Morozov, Bolshoi Theatre Ch and O, Temirkanov, Melodiya, 1982
EDITION f.s., Muzika, 1980

BIBLIOGRAPHY S. D. Krebs, *Soviet Composers*, George Allen and Unwin, 1970

J.G.

VISSARION SHEBALIN
Vissarion Yakovlevich Shebalin; *b* 11 June 1902, Omsk; *d* 28 May 1963, Moscow

A pupil of the symphonist Myaskovsky, Shebalin belonged to the first generation of composers to be educated totally under the Soviet system. Thus, early predilections for Skryabin and French Impressionism were soon replaced by mass songs, patriotic cantatas and a prodigious amount of cinema, theatre and radio scores. He was director of the Moscow Conservatory from 1942 to 1948, and during this time won two Stalin prizes and became a 'People's Artist'. He was a victim of the famous purge of 1948 that also denounced Prokofiev and Shostakovich, and was demoted. During this same period he suffered a stroke and was in bad health for the rest of his life. Popular success came with his opera *The Taming of the Shrew*. His only other opera, *Sun over the Steppe*, is a propaganda work that was never performed in full and was left in conflicting versions at the time of the composer's death. He was an inspired teacher and editor, and produced the best performing version of Musorgsky's *Sorochintsy Fair*.

The Taming of the Shrew
Ukroshcheniye stroptivoi
Opera in four acts, Op. 46 (2h 15m)
Libretto by A. Gozenpud, after the play by Shakespeare (1594)
Composed 1946–56
PREMIERE 3 May 1957, Moscow

Reactionary in style, recalling Rossini, Tchaikovsky and Borodin, this is nevertheless a well-characterized opera with memorable lyrical ideas, aided by a libretto that is taut and skilful. The music matches this with a light touch and robust humour.

RECORDING Vishnevskaya, Deomidova, Timchenko, Pankov, Kibkalo, Eizen, Bolshoi Theatre Ch and O, Chalabala, Melodiya, c. 1956

EDITION v.s., Moscow State Publishing House, 1957

Other operatic works: *Sun over the Steppe* (*Solntse nad step'yu*), (1939–59); *The Embassy Bridegroom* (*Zhenikh iz posol'stva*), 1942
BIBLIOGRAPHY Winton Dean, *Shakespeare and Opera*, St Martin's Press, 1966; S. D. Krebs, *Soviet Composers*, George Allen and Unwin, 1970

J.G.

WILLIAM SHIELD

b 5 March 1748, Swalwell, Co. Durham, England;
d 25 January 1829, London

Shield, the son of a music master, was orphaned at nine years old and served an apprenticeship as a boat builder. He moved to London in 1773 and in 1778 his first opera, *The Flitch of Bacon*, was produced as an afterpiece at the Little Theatre. Like the rest of his stage compositions this was in part derived from other composers, though Shield was unusual in drawing extensively on folksong; here he was well served by his friendship with Joseph Ritson, the radical Jacobite ballad collector. Shield was himself a notable musical antiquary, and the climax of his professional career was the Mastership of the King's Music. In all he wrote 43 works for the stage, full-length operas, afterpieces and pantomimes of which only *Rosina* survives in full score. He was not a natural musical dramatist; his arias are static, but his output is consistently workmanlike, and during his 15 years as resident composer at Covent Garden he kept the standard of music at a minimally acceptable level by his extensive borrowings from Continental composers, sometimes acknowledged, more often not. As soon as he was financially independent he abandoned the stage and concentrated on theory and history. His home at Taplow was a happy resort for many musicians, including Haydn on his London visits.

Rosina

Afterpiece with spoken dialogue in two acts
Libretto by Frances Brooke, after Charles Simon Favart's *Les moissoneurs* (1768)
PREMIERES 31 December 1782, Covent Garden, London; US: 19 April 1786, New York

Two brothers from the gentry, good Mr Belville and wicked Captain Belville, see Rosina harvesting and both fall in love with her. The Captain attempts to abduct her but is foiled by Irish labourers. In the meantime the good Belville has discovered that she is of noble birth. Finally the Captain sees the error of his ways and his brother wins her hand. The overture contains a version of 'Auld Lang Syne' and the majority of the songs have ballad-like characteristics; six of them are in fact traditional. The tunes are consistently charming and the orchestration deft and light-hearted. *Rosina* continued to be played as late as the 1870s.

RECORDING Harwood, Elkins, Sinclair, Tear, Macdonald, Ambrosian Singers, LSO, Bonynge, Decca, 1966
EDITION v.s., Napier, 1785
MANUSCRIPT The British Library, London

Other surviving operatic works: *The Flitch of Bacon*, 1778; *The Siege of Gibraltar*, 1780; *The Poor Soldier*, 1783; *Robin Hood*, 1784; *The Noble Peasant*, 1784; *Fontainbleau*, 1784; *The Choleric Fathers*, 1785; *Love in a Camp*, 1786; *The Farmer*, 1787; *Marian*, 1788; *The Highland Reel*, 1788; *The Woodman*, 1791; *Hartford Bridge*, 1792; *The Midnight Wanderers*, 1793; *The Travellers in Switzerland*, 1794; *Netley Abbey*, 1794; *The Mysteries of the Castle*, 1795; *Lock and Key*, 1796; *The Lord of the Hills*, 1796; *Abroad and at Home*, 1796; *Two Faces under one Hood*, 1807
BIBLIOGRAPHY Roger Fiske, *English Theatre Music in the Eighteenth Century*, OUP, 1973; 2nd edn, 1986; J. Robinson, *Life of William Shield*, Newcastle, 1891

R.Lu.

DMITRY SHOSTAKOVICH

Dmitry Dmitriyevich Shostakovich; *b* 25 September 1906, St Petersburg; *d* 9 August 1975, Moscow

Shostakovich's mother was a professional pianist, and he entered the Petrograd (St Petersburg) Conservatory as a pianist at the age of 13. But he also developed rapidly as a composer, under Maximilian Steinberg, the Rimsky-Korsakov pupil. He was still only 19 when his First Symphony was premiered in the again renamed Leningrad in May 1926 (he had already destroyed a student opera based on Pushkin's *The Gypsies*); within two years this brilliant, if derivative, symphony had made him world-famous. A Second and Third Symphony followed – both quite experimental in style – and several theatre works, including the sparkling Gogol opera *The Nose*, two or three ballets, and incidental music to Mayakovsky's play *The Bedbug*. By the early 1930s, Shostakovich was already moderating his style (as many west European progressives of the 1920s were also doing), and his second opera, *The Lady Macbeth of the Mtsensk District*, mixes modernism and biting satire with revived Romantic-cum-Expressionist elements.

Shostakovich was not yet 30 when this work was violently attacked in *Pravda* in January 1936, and its composer left shattered and fearful – at a time when even artists were beginning to pay with their lives for deviating from the new ideal of Socialist Realism. Thereafter, he seldom risked serious theatre work. An operetta, *The Silly Little Mouse*, composed early in 1939, is lost, as is the film material of a miniature Pushkin comic opera, *The Tale of a Priest and His Servant Balda*, composed in 1941 but destroyed in the Leningrad bombing that year (a concert suite survives). His setting of Gogol's *The Gamblers* was left unfinished, he tells us in *Testimony*, because he suddenly realized it was morally unacceptable in wartime Russia (and it would certainly have been so in post-war Russia, when in 1948 Shostakovich was carpeted, along with most of his gifted compatriots, for 'formalism and anti-democratic tendencies').

Shostakovich at a rehearsal

worshippers, poor matrons, travellers, passers-by, onlookers, eunuchs, policemen (also spoken roles) – numbers depend on various possibilities of role-doubling
SMALL ORCHESTRA   single wind, but with large perc section (10 players)

Shostakovich wrote his first opera at the height of the 'anything-goes' period of early Soviet art. For a few years after the end of the civil war the Soviet Union was in a ferment of artistic experiment, as seemed to befit an emerging revolutionary state. In music, the influence of Western avant-gardists such as Schoenberg, Hindemith and Stravinsky was strong. Berg's *Wozzeck* was staged in Leningrad while Shostakovich was writing *The Nose*, and its influence is apparent, as is that of Prokofiev's *Love of Three Oranges* (Leningrad, 1926). At the same time the work's absurdism and unremitting grotesquerie suggest a knowledge of Cocteau and Les Six, though its satire against civil servants is purely Russian. In tone and outline it follows Gogol's short story closely, while incorporating material from other books by Gogol, as well as a song from Dostoevsky's *Brothers Karamazov*.

The Nose enjoyed some success in Leningrad, but was not taken up elsewhere. The political climate was already turning against such things, and in any case the piece is forbiddingly hard to stage, with its spiky and difficult orchestral writing and its cast of 70 characters. It returned to favour in the Soviet Union in the 1970s, but has had only occasional productions abroad.

He seems to have made little progress with an opera based on Tolstoy's *Resurrection* (1940). Later he composed only the operetta *Moskva, Cheryo-mushki*, though at the time of his death he was planning an opera on Chekhov's *The Black Monk*. The core of his work post-1936 is symphonic, with a parallel stream of chamber works dominated by 15 string quartets. But even while seeking safety in 'abstract' forms, or in film music or cantatas on officially acceptable topics, Shostakovich found it hard to deny his theatrical talent. Both his symphonies and his chamber works are full of essentially graphic writing and barely concealed psychological drama. Though he never wrote an unmistakable operatic masterpiece, it seems quite possible that he would have been one of the great modern opera composers – a worthy successor to Musorgsky and Tchaikovsky – if circumstances had allowed.

The Nose

Nos

Opera in three acts and an epilogue (1h 45m)
Libretto by the composer, after the short story by Gogol (1835)
Composed 1927–8
PREMIERES   16 June 1929, Leningrad (concert); 18 January 1930, Leningrad; UK: 21 October 1972 (broadcast; in English); 4 April 1973, Sadler's Wells, London (in English; New Opera Company); US: 11 August 1965, Santa Fe
CAST   Kovalyov *bar*, Yakovlevich *b-bar*, Police Inspector *very high t*, Ivan *t*, Nose *t*, Madame Podtochina *ms*, her daughter *s*, old countess *a*, Praskovya Ossipovna *s*, advertising employee *b-bar, s*, 7 *t*, 9 *b*; *satb* chorus of

SYNOPSIS

Act I After a brief prologue (Kovalyov being shaved by the barber Yakovlevich), we see Yakovlevich at breakfast. To his (moderate) surprise he finds a nose in his roll, but manages – not without difficulty – to dispose of it in the river Neva. Meanwhile Kovalyov discovers his loss. He tracks the Nose down to Kazan Cathedral, where it appears dressed as a state councillor.

Act II Kovalyov tries to report the loss to the police, and to place a newspaper advertisement.

Act III Eventually the Nose is apprehended trying to board the Riga coach, and the Police Inspector returns it to Kovalyov. But the Doctor is unable to reattach it. Kovalyov writes to Madame Podtochina, accusing her of masterminding the theft to blackmail him into marrying her daughter. Everyone discusses the rumours about Kovalyov's nose walking the streets.

Epilogue The Nose suddenly reappears in its rightful place. The delighted Kovalyov is again able to hold his head up in St Petersburg.

Shostakovich maintained that his music for *The Nose* was not comical. But this may have been to pre-empt the criticism of unseriousness. The work is in fact rich in satire and grotesquerie, and the music is generally graphic rather than symphonic. Its structure is a montage of short scenes with orchestral interludes (cf. *Wozzeck*, whose Captain may also have inspired Shostakovich's Police Inspector, with his ludicrously high-tenor squeak), and there is little sustained dramatic growth or psychological development.

Although he never again wrote music so dependent on parody, many typical Shostakovich-isms appear in *The Nose* for the first time. The spiky scherzo ostinati were to become standard in his symphonies, and the jogging minimalism of episodes such as Ivan's balalaika-playing scene (with flexatone), or the final scene on the Nevsky Prospect, was to serve Shostakovich much later in serious or ironic contexts. In general the ability to absorb naïve musical styles into a sophisticated idiom was to prove one of his most individual traits and greatest strengths. *The Nose* may not be a masterpiece, but it is remarkably rich in musical possibilities.

RECORDING   Lomonosov, Akimov, Moscow Chamber Ch and O, Rozhdestvensky, Chant du Monde, 1980s
EDITIONS   v.ss., Universal, 1962 (German text only); Muzika, 1975

The Lady Macbeth of the Mtsensk District

Ledi Makbet Mtsenskovo uyezda
Opera in four acts (2h 30m)
Libretto by Alexander Preis and the composer, after the short story by Nikolay Leskov (1865)
Composed 1930–32; rev. 1935, and (as *Katerina Ismailova*) 1956–63
PREMIERES   *Lady Macbeth*: 22 January 1934, Maly Opera House, Leningrad; UK: 18 March 1936, Queen's Hall, London (concert); 22 May 1987, Coliseum, London; US: 31 January 1935, Cleveland, Ohio (semi-staged); *Katerina Ismailova*: 26 December 1962, Stanislavsky–Nemirovich-Danchenko Music Theatre, Moscow; UK: 2 December 1963, Covent Garden, London; US: 23 October 1964, War Memorial Opera House, San Francisco
CAST   Katerina Ismailova *s*, Boris Ismailov *high b*, Zinovy Ismailov *t*, Sergei *t*, Mill-hand *bar*, Coachman *t*, Aksinya *s*, Shabby Peasant *t*, Porter *b*, Steward *b*, 3 Foremen 3 *t*, Priest *b*, Chief of Police *bar*, Policeman *b*, Teacher *t*, Drunken Guest *t*, Old Convict *b*, Sentry *b*, Sonyetka *a*, Woman Convict *s*, Sergeant *b*; *satb* chorus of workers, policemen, guests, convicts
ORCHESTRATION   *Lady Macbeth*: picc, 2 fl, 2 ob, ca, E♭ cl, 2 cl, b cl, 2 bsn, dbsn, 4 hn, 3 tpt, 3 trbn, tuba, timp, perc (triangle, wb, tambourine, td, sd, whip, flexatone, cym, bd, t- t, bells, xyl), 2 hp, cel, str; onstage (ad lib): 5 cornets, 2 tpt, 8 saxhorns; *Katerina Ismailova*: as above, except fl 2 = picc 2/bass fl; no sd; onstage: 4 cornets only

Shostakovich first encountered Leskov's brutal tale (published a few years after the emancipation of the serfs) through his artist friend Boris Kustodiev, who illustrated an edition of 1930. But from the start he reacted very differently from Leskov to the tragic heroine. The original Katerina is irredeemably cruel and self-seeking, and is treated by Leskov ironically, whereas Shostakovich saw her as a sympathetic figure driven to crime by intolerable boredom and despair. The social and psychological implications of her predicament struck him as important; it clearly never occurred to him that his graphic treatment of her actions would be taken as signifying approval.

'As a Soviet composer,' he wrote in 1934, 'I determined to preserve the strength of Leskov's

novel, and yet, approaching it critically, to interpret its events from our modern point of view.' 'So little was socialist realism understood at first,' Gerald Abraham wrote in *Eight Soviet Composers*, 'that *The Lady Macbeth of Mtsensk* was accepted as an embodiment of it.' In 1934–5 the work was a considerable popular success and was widely performed in and out of the Soviet Union, attracting generally appreciative notices. But on 28 January 1936 there appeared in *Pravda* a lengthy editorial denouncing the opera as 'Muddle instead of Music', attacking its 'deliberately discordant, confused stream of sounds . . . [its] din, grinding and screaming', and its sexual naturalism, in which '"love" is smeared all over the opera in the most vulgar manner'. 'Is its success abroad not explained', *Pravda* demanded smugly, 'by the fact that it tickles the perverted bourgeois taste with its fidgety, screaming, neurotic music?'

The editorial apparently reflected the opinion of Stalin himself, who had attended a performance in December 1935. In any case, the denunciation was official, and the opera was instantly withdrawn, followed in December by the composer's Fourth Symphony, which had just gone into rehearsal. His Fifth Symphony, which followed in 1937, was subtitled 'the practical reply of a Soviet artist to justified criticism', and is certainly more direct and transparent than either of the withdrawn works, though less of a reaction against their style than is often said. *Lady Macbeth* vanished from the Soviet scene (there was a post-war production in Düsseldorf) until, in the more tolerant early 1960s, Shostakovich produced a major revision under the title *Katerina Ismailova*. This revision is a compromise. It purges textual and scenic details that would still have offended Soviet primness in 1962, but it also makes purely musical changes, especially to vocal lines, as well as somewhat lightening the orchestral texture. However, some of these changes already appear in the published edition of 1935. In particular, the orchestral depiction of Katerina's love-making with Sergei in Act I Scene 3 is toned down (it completely disappears in 1962). Moreover the

Scene from Eisenstein's production of Lady Macbeth of the Mtsensk District *(Moscow, 1934)*

passacaglia interlude after the murder of Boris is reduced for solo organ, and the stage band is cut (both these changes were cancelled in 1962). Since the composer's death, the original (1932) version has returned to favour, both on record and on the stage, and today there seems little reason to prefer the expurgated score.

SYNOPSIS (original version)

Act I   Scene 1: Katerina is lying on her bed, bored and frustrated. Boris, her father-in-law, nags her for not giving his son Zinovy a child. Zinovy meanwhile leaves to attend to a burst mill-dam, but before going he presents a new labourer, Sergei, to his father. Boris forces Katerina to swear fidelity in her husband's absence. Aksinya, a cook, tells Katerina that Sergei lost his previous job for carrying on with his master's wife. Boris berates her for not weeping at Zinovy's departure. Scene 2: Sergei and the men are brutally molesting Aksinya when Katerina appears and threatens Sergei with a thrashing. He in turn challenges her to a wrestling match, whose thinly veiled sexual intention takes them both to the ground as Boris comes in. He promises to report her behaviour to Zinovy. Scene 3: Boris orders Katerina to bed and goes out. She undresses, but as she lies down Sergei knocks on the door and asks to borrow a book. He complains of boredom, and she too admits she is bored and would like a child. He makes a pass at her and they make love. Boris is heard calling Katerina, but Sergei refuses to leave.

Act II   Scene 4: A week later Boris is walking about outside, musing on his sexual prowess when young. Seeing a light in Katerina's window, he decides to pay her a visit, and catches Sergei leaving her room. He at once calls in the workers, and personally whips Sergei, watched by Katerina, who slides down the drainpipe and tries to stop him. Sergei is taken away to the store room, while Boris orders Katerina to prepare him some mushrooms and sends the porter for Zinovy. Katerina slips rat poison into the mushrooms, and as Boris collapses, she takes the store-room keys from his pocket. A gang of workers arrives, and one of their foremen brings a priest. Boris manages to get out a garbled accusation against Katerina before dying. The priest pronounces a (somewhat light-hearted) requiem. Scene 5: Katerina and Sergei are in bed, but Sergei warns her that when Zinovy returns their love will end. She promises that all will be well. But as he sleeps, Boris's ghost appears to her and curses her. Suddenly Katerina senses Zinovy's return. Sergei hides and she admits Zinovy, who remonstrates with her for her philandering. Seeing Sergei's belt, he whips her with it, but Katerina and Sergei batter him to death with a candlestick and shove his body into the cellar.

Act III   Scene 6: Katerina and Sergei are about to get married, though Zinovy's body is still in the cellar. The Shabby Peasant sings a drunken song and breaks into the cellar in search of wine. Finding Zinovy's putrid corpse, he rushes off to the police station. Scene 7: At the station, the police sing a jolly hymn to bribery and corruption. They are incensed

at not being invited to Katerina's wedding. A 'socialist' teacher is brought in and questioned. When the Shabby Peasant arrives with news of the corpse, the police see it as 'a gift from God'. Scene 8: At the wedding, the guests are drunk and the Priest makes lascivious advances to Katerina. Suddenly Katerina notices that the store-room lock is broken, but as she suggests to Sergei that they steal the money and run away, the police arrive and the two give themselves up.

Act IV   Scene 9: In the convict line by a river on the road to Siberia, Katerina bribes the sentry to let her through to Sergei. But Sergei rejects her, and goes instead to Sonyetka, a convict who demands that he bring her Katerina's stockings. He tricks Katerina, and takes the stockings to Sonyetka, while the other women convicts, and then Sonyetka herself, taunt Katerina. As the convicts begin to move off, Katerina pushes Sonyetka into the river and jumps in after her. The remaining convicts trudge off.

Technically *Lady Macbeth* is a major advance on *The Nose*. Shostakovich himself drew attention to its symphonic character. The crucial orchestral interludes link the scenes into an unbroken musico-dramatic thread, as well as adding psychological depth and tragic foreboding to the superficially crude narrative. The same expansiveness is apparent in the Fourth Symphony, but it might well be argued that the opera is the more successful work. Its few satirical episodes – the two appearances of the Priest, and the scene in the police station – only mildly disrupt the melodramatic texture; indeed, they lighten it usefully. Overall, the pacing is astonishingly assured for a first serious opera.

At the same time, the musical invention is consistently brilliant. Among several superb interludes, the passacaglia (Scenes 4/5) is equal to anything in the symphonies; but so is much else, particularly the bedroom scenes, where Shostakovich shows a rare and astonishing ability to use sustained orchestral counterpoint dramatically. This skill he combines with a strong sense of harmonic architecture and a mastery of ostinato (in *The Nose* an amusing mannerism) as a device for generating tension. Even more unexpectedly, the vocal writing is grateful and effective, notwithstanding a few passages where screaming takes over. Like Britten, Shostakovich devised a vocal style that adheres to traditional principles without limiting the musical idiom. One of the work's most memorable vocal melodies served him again (in the String Quartet No. 8: Katerina's 'Seryozha, khoroshi moy' in the last scene of the opera). But there are others as good. It is easy to understand why *Lady Macbeth* was popular until Stalin took against it.

Shostakovich had planned a tetralogy of operas about women. That the other three were never written must be accounted one of the major losses of 20th-century opera, even if his choice of heroines (the fourth was to be a Stakhanovite worker at the Dnieper Hydroelectric Works) might seem less than ideally promising. After completing *Lady Macbeth*, late in 1932, he worked instead on a comic opera, *The Big Lightning*, but soon laid it aside (the fragments were glued together by Gennadi Rozhdestvensky, and performed in Leningrad in 1981).

RECORDINGS *Lady Macbeth* (original 1932 version): Vishnevskaya, Valjakka, Gedda, Krenn, Petkov, Ambrosian Opera Ch, LSO, Rostropovich, EMI, 1979; *Katerina Ismailova*: Andreyeva, Yefimov, Bulavin, Ch and O of Moscow Musical Theatre, Provatorov, EMI/Melodiya, 1964
EDITIONS *Lady Macbeth*: original 1932 version: f.s., Kalmus (on hire); v.s., Sikorski, 1979; rev. version: v.s., Universal/Muzgiz (Moscow), 1935; *Katerina Ismailova*: f.s., Collected Edition, vols 20–21, Muzika, l985; v.s., Collected Edition, vol. 22, Muzika, 1985

The Gamblers

Igroki
Opera in one act (inc.; 45m)
Libretto: the play by Gogol (1842)
Composed 1941–2
PREMIERES 18 September 1978, Leningrad (concert); 12 June 1983, Wuppertal (completion by Krzysztof Meyer)

According to his Soviet biographer, Rabinovich, Shostakovich began this straight setting of Gogol's comic play the day after completing the epic Seventh Symphony, in December 1941 (during the Siege of Leningrad). He composed 8 scenes (out of 25) then gave up, he tells us himself, when he realized there was no chance of such a work being acceptable in wartime Russia.

The gambler Ikharyov arrives at a provincial hotel and inquires whether any of his fellow guests play cards. Before long Ikharyov, who is a systematic card-sharp, has set up a crooked game, bribing the hotel servant and his own valet to provide specially 'fixed' packs as required. The other players soon see through this, but, impressed by Ikharyov's thoroughness, they pretend to join forces with him. In the uncomposed part of the play, the supposed cartel gang up on a rich merchant's son; but the original guests go off with his money, leaving Ikharyov with an IOU that turns out to be worthless when it emerges that the son was in the pay of the other players.

Setting the play, as he did, straight through without alteration, Shostakovich admitted that the opera began to be unmanageable. The existing scenes are wordy, and musically sometimes mechanical, though with many fine and characteristic touches (including an episode of spoof 18th-century recitative). One problem, musically, would have been that the cast is entirely male. Nevertheless, the score is complete as far as it goes, and was performed (under Gennadi Rozhdestvensky) with an added three-page conclusion to tidy up the musical loose end. Shostakovich himself later used some of the music in his his Viola Sonata, Op. 147.

RECORDING Tarkhov, Kurpe, Rybasenko, Byelykh, Leningrad PO, Rozhdestvensky, EMI/Melodiya, 1979
EDITIONS f.s., Muzika (on hire); v.ss., Muzika, 1979; Collected Edition, Muzika, 1986

Moscow, Cheryomushki

Moskva, Cheryomushki
Operetta in three acts
Libretto by V. Mass and M. Chervinsky
Composed 1958
PREMIERE 27 November 1958, Moscow; US: 21 November 1964, Cameo Theater, New York (as *Song over Moscow*)

Shostakovich was one of several Soviet composers commissioned by the Mayakovsky Operetta Theatre in Moscow in the 1950s. His comedy about the suburban lives of Moscow incomers is no more than a skilful *pièce d'occasion*, reminding us that through all his troubles he remained outwardly a good socialist artist, providing what was required of him. The work was made into a film in 1962, directed by Herbert Rappoport.

EDITIONS f.s., Collected Edition, vol. 24, Musicka, 1986; v.ss., Sovietsky Kompozitor, 1959; Collected Edition, vol. 25, Muzika, 1986
BIBLIOGRAPHY I. MacDonald, *The New Shostakovich*, Fourth Estate, 1990; B. Schwarz, *Music and Musical Life in Soviet Russia, 1917–1981*, Indiana University Press, 2nd edn, 1983; S. Volkov (ed.), *Testimony: The Memoirs of Shostakovich*, Hamish Hamilton, 1979

S.W.

JEAN SIBELIUS

Johan Julius Christian Sibelius; *b* 8 December 1865, Hämeenlinna, Finland; *d* 20 September 1957, Järvenpää, Finland

Although known to modern audiences almost exclusively as the composer of seven orchestral symphonies and a number of symphonic poems, Sibelius also wrote much excellent vocal music, including songs, cantatas with orchestra, and the large-scale choral symphony *Kullervo* (1891), on texts from the Finnish national epic poem, *Kalevala*, as well as incidental music for many plays. But he composed only one opera. In 1893 he began writing a Wagnerian music drama, *The Building of the Boat*, based on an episode from the *Kalevala*, but abandoned it after writing the prelude (which became *The Swan of Tuonela*).

The Maiden in the Tower

Jungfrun i tornet
Opera in one act (eight scenes) (40m)
Libretto by Rafael Hertzberg
Composed 1896
PREMIERES 9 November 1896, Helsinki (concert); 5 December 1990, Joensuu, Finland; UK: 19 April 1982, BBC Radio 3 (broadcast)

The Maiden in the Tower, Sibelius's only completed opera, was written to raise money for the Helsinki Philharmonic Society. It is far from the post-Wagnerian drama Sibelius had previously intended. Hertzberg's libretto (in Swedish) is a lifeless concoction based on a medieval Finnish tale about a maiden imprisoned in a castle by a wicked bailiff but eventually freed to marry her lover in the final scene. The score includes conventional folksy elements, but also some authentic early Sibelius, including a beautiful choral scene and some refined writing for a smallish theatre orchestra. In spite of this, Sibelius withdrew the work after its initial performances, and it was not heard in public again until it was broadcast by Finnish Radio in the early 1980s.

RECORDING Häggander, Kruse, Hagegård, Hynninen, Gothenburg Concert Hall Ch, Gothenburg SO, Järvi, Bis, 1985
EDITIONS f.s./v.s., facsimile, Wilhelm Hansen, 1984

BIBLIOGRAPHY Erik Tawaststjerna, trans. Robert Layton, *Sibelius*, vol. 1, Faber, 1976

S.W.

LARRY SITSKY
b 10 September 1934, Tientsin, North China

Arriving in Australia at the age of 17 with his Russian-Jewish parents, Sitsky studied piano and composition (with Raymond Hanson) at the New South Wales Conservatorium. From 1958 to 1961 he studied in San Francisco with Egon Petri. On his return to Australia he joined the staff of the Queensland Conservatorium and in 1966 was appointed head of keyboard studies at the Canberra School of Music, subsequently taking over both the composition and musicology departments.

The Fall of the House of Usher
Opera in one act
Libretto by Gwen Harwood, after the story *La chute de la maison Usher* by Edgar Allan Poe (1839)
PREMIERE 18 August 1965, Hobart

One of the most frequently performed Australian operas, *The Fall of the House of Usher*, Sitsky's first vocal work, was the first opera presented in the Sydney Opera House, in a try-out of the Opera Theatre two months before the official opening in October 1973.

The narrative follows Poe's story closely and proceeds through a series of distinct, named sections ('Narrator's Aria', 'Madeleine's Arietta', etc.). This surrealistic piece is most expressive in its orchestral writing; a prepared tape is included. Vocal techniques include sprechstimme and shrieks.

RECORDING excerpt: Hansford, West Australian SO, Schönzeler, Festival Disc, 1971
EDITION Ricordi, 1974

Other operas: *Lenz*, 1974; *Fiery Tales*, 1975; *Voices in Limbo* (radio opera), 1977; *The Golem*, 1980; *De Profundis*, 1982 (RECORDING MOVE, 1984)
BIBLIOGRAPHY Essay by Donald Thornton in Frank Callaway and David Tunley (eds), *Australian Composition in the 20th Century*, OUP, 1978

A.I.G.

FRANTIŠEK ŠKROUP
František Jan Škroup; *b* 3 June 1801, Osice, nr Pardubice, Bohemia; *d* 7 February 1862, Rotterdam, Netherlands

Škroup studied law, but soon became involved with amateur theatricals in Prague, helping to organize a Czech group that put on operas in Czech at the Estates Theatre. In their first production, a Czech version of Weigl's *Die Schweizerfamilie* (1823), Škroup sang tenor and also distinguished himself as répétiteur and conductor. In 1827 he was engaged as assistant conductor of the (German) opera company at the theatre, and in 1837 became chief conductor. He remained there until 1857, making a fine contribution to German operatic life in Prague with his introduction of many new works, notably the first performance of Wagner's operas up to *Lohengrin*. As a Czech patriot, he was also able to introduce a limited number of operas in Czech until the clampdown on such activities in the early 1850s.

His own operatic career began early with *The Tinker* (1826), sometimes described as the first Czech opera, though this description ignores an amateur tradition of Czech singspiels from about the 1740s until the end of the 18th century and several plays with music given professionally at the Patriotic Theatre (1786–1807) in which the musical content was such that they might well be described as singspiels.

The Tinker was successful, and continued to be performed even up to the opening of the Provisional Theatre in 1862. Also popular was his music to Tyl's play *Fidlovačka* (1834). But Škroup's later operatic career was disappointing. Two more Czech operas, *Oldřich and Božena* and *Libuše's Marriage*, had little success (the latter was not performed in full until 1850). Both were through-composed and thus much more ambitious than the earlier works. Czech audiences, however, failed to find in them the naïve folklike elements that had made the earlier singspiels popular. This is despite familiar patriotic subject matter: Oldřich is an early Czech king who took as his wife a humble subject, while Libuše is the Libuše of Smetana's opera, though curiously devoid of the patriotic charge that the topic was to acquire 40 years later. Škroup also wrote a number of German operas and singspiels, but they were no more successful.

The Tinker
Dráteník
Singspiel in two acts
Libretto by Josef Krasoslav Chmelenský
Composed 1825
PREMIERE 2 February 1826, Estates Theatre, Prague

Almost a century before the creation of Czechoslovakia, *The Tinker* pointed to Bohemia's future political links by building a work round a Slovak, the tinker of the title, who speaks and sings in dialect. His main function is to help the hero (disguised as a tinker) gain access to his sweetheart. Despite an extensive sonata-form overture, the work is modest in scale, with no chorus. Half of the 15 numbers are solos and most of these are simple strophic or ternary songs. Much of the action takes place through spoken dialogue, though the end of Act II has a series of cumulative ensembles in which the successive *dénouements* are presented.

EDITION v.s., Hudební matice, 1913; 2nd edn, 1926

Fidlovačka, or No Anger and No Brawl
Fidlovačka, aneb Žádný hněv a žádná rvačka
Play in four acts by Josef Kajetan Tyl
PREMIERE 21 December 1834, Estates Theatre, Prague

With its overture and 21 musical numbers, this play is hardly different in genre from *The Tinker*. Most of the numbers are choruses and strophic songs, but there are two extensive duets (one in German, and one in Czech and German) and a couple of multi-tempo finales. 'Fidlovačka' is the name of a traditional spring fair, and one of the chief functions in these 'scenes from Prague life' is to introduce a number of genre figures seen at the fair. In particular they include a blind violinist, Old Mareš, whose Act IV song, 'Kde domov můj?' ('Where is my homeland?'), became popular as a patriotic song and in 1918 was adopted as the first (Czech) half of the Czechoslovak national anthem.

EDITION v.s., Orbis, 1952

Other operas: *Der Nachtschatten*, 1827; *Oldřich a Božena* (*Oldřich a Božena*), 1828; *Der Prinz und die Schlange*, 1829; *Bratovrah* (*The Brother-killer*), 1831; *Die Drachenhöhle bei Rothstein, oder Der Hammer um Mitternacht*, 1832; *Udalřich und Božena* (German reworking of *Oldřich a Božena*), 1833 (rev. in Czech, 1847); *Libušin sňatek* (*Libuše's Marriage*), (1835, rev. 1849), 1850; *Die Geisterbraut*, 1836; *Drahomíra*, (?1840), 1848; *Der Meergeuse*, 1851; *Columbus* (1855), 1942 (RECORDING excerpts: Multisonic, 1962 (issued 1992))
BIBLIOGRAPHY John Tyrrell, *Czech Opera*, CUP, 1988

J.T.

FRANTIŠEK SKUHERSKÝ
František Zdeněk Xavier Alois Skuherský, *b* 31 July 1830, Opočno, Bohemia; *d* 19 August 1892, Budweis (now České Budějovice)

Like many 19th-century Czech musicians, Skuherský made his career abroad, chiefly in Innsbruck (1854–66) as conductor at the theatre and the university church. In 1866 he returned to Bohemia as director of the Prague Organ School (1866–89), where he himself had been a pupil. During his long tenure there (he was the last director before the Organ School was amalgamated with the Prague Conservatory), many distinguished pupils passed through his hands, notably Foerster and Janáček. He adapted his three German operas, written in Innsbruck, for performance in Prague. The historical *Vladimír*, based on Bulgarian history from the 9th century was given as the first new 'Czech' opera at the Provisional Theatre in 1863. Neither it nor its

successors, the romantic *Lóra* and the comic opera *Rector and General*, achieved more than a handful of performances, and they were overshadowed by the operas of Smetana, Šebor and Bendl.

Operas: *Samo* (?inc.), excerpts, 1854; *Der Apostat* (1860), Czech version as *Vladimír, bohův zvolenec* (*Vladimír, God's Chosen One*), 1863; *Der Liebesring*, 1861, Czech version as *Lóra*, 1868; *Der Rekrut*, (before 1866), Czech version as *Rektor a generál* (*Rector and General*), 1873; *Smrt krále Václava* (*The Death of King Wenceslas*) (inc.), (?1868); *Jaroslav ze Šternberka* (inc.), (?1869/73)
BIBLIOGRAPHY John Tyrrell, *Czech Opera*, CUP, 1988

J.T.

JULIAN SLADE
Julian Penkivil Slade; *b* 28 May 1930, London

Slade became musical director at the Bristol Old Vic in 1951, and *Salad Days* was devised as a light summer filler for the company, with piano, bass and drum-kit accompaniment. Its success and transfer to London inaugurated a period in which provincial experimentation or revivals gave a lead to the capital.

Salad Days
Musical entertainment in two parts
Book and lyrics by Dorothy Reynolds and the composer
PREMIERE 1 June 1954, Theatre Royal, Bristol

The simple plot concerns two university graduates, Timothy and Jane, resisting parental pressures to find work and the personal pressure to indulge in nostalgia ('We said we wouldn't look back'). A magic piano proves catalytic and holds the action, cast as a series of light-hearted revue sketches, together.

RECORDING original London cast, Oriole, 1954
EDITION v.s., Francis, Day and Hunter, 1957

Other musical comedies: *Free as Air*, 1957; *Follow That Girl*, 1960; *Vanity Fair*, 1962; *Nutmeg and Ginger*, 1963; *The Pursuit of Love*, 1967; *Trelawny*, 1972
BIBLIOGRAPHY Kurt Gänzl, *The British Musical Theatre*, vol. 2: *1915–1984*, Macmillan, 1986

S.B.

ANTONIO SMAREGLIA
b 5 May 1854, Pola, Istria; *d* 15 April 1929, Grado, Istria

Smareglia's composing career was beset by misfortunes which limited his success and later greatly reduced his productivity. Though blessed with a rich imagination and a resourceful technique, he failed (for personal rather than musical reasons) to win the support of either Ricordi or Sonzogno – the two great Milanese publishing houses that dominated Italian operatic life. His problems were aggravated further when his increasing blindness became virtually total from 1900 onwards (his amanuenses included the young Gian Francesco Malipiero).

Smareglia was brought up in an environment where Italian, Germanic and Slavonic traditions mingled. Although his native language was Italian and his higher musical studies were pursued in Milan, his mixed background is apparent in his operas: as time went on, he gravitated towards a personal variant of Wagnerian principles, and he had fervent admirers in the German-speaking world, notably Brahms and Hans Richter. Two of his operas (*Il vassallo di Szigeth* and *Cornill Schut*) actually had their premieres north of the Alps. But he won his most durable success, with *Nozze istriane*, in Trieste – the one place where his works are still regularly revived.

Nozze istriane
Istrian Wedding

Opera in three acts (1h 45m)
Libretto by Luigi Illica
Composed 1893–4
PREMIERES 28 March 1895, Teatro Comunale, Trieste; UK: 27 October 1966, BBC Third Programme (broadcast)

Illica's libretto was intended as an evocation of an Istrian village community: the action takes place in Dignano, a few miles north of Smareglia's native Pola. Marussa rebels against her father, Bara Menico, who wants her to marry the rich young farmer Nicola, although she is in love with Lorenzo. Menico tricks his daughter into believing that Lorenzo no longer loves her. She sadly agrees to marry Nicola, but then learns the truth: the lovers are reconciled, but Nicola stabs Lorenzo to death in a jealous rage.

The *Cavalleria*-like brutality of this ending is matched by traces of Mascagni's melodic influence. However, the harmony and orchestration are more subtle – with signs of the Wagnerian tendencies that were to become still stronger in Smareglia's subsequent operas. Meanwhile, the Slavonic aspects of the community portrayed are backed up by musical images that at times recall Smetana.

EDITION v.s., Friedrich Hofmeister (later Carlo Schmidl), 1906

Oceàna

Opera in three acts (2h 15m)
Libretto by Silvio Benco
Composed c. 1900–1902, later rev.
PREMIERES 20 January 1903, La Scala, Milan; UK: 4 April 1974, BBC Radio 3 (excerpts)

Benco is said to have cited Shakespeare's fantastic comedies and Böcklin's visionary paintings as his main models, though the libretto's language is extravagantly indebted to D'Annunzio. The setting is Syria in patriarchal times. Nersa, a servant of the tribal chief Vadar (who loves her), yearns for escape into a fantasy world, and is indeed abducted as bride of the sea god Init. Restored to Vadar, she still longs for Init, who reappears to marry her, leaving Vadar insane.

Despite Wagnerian influence, *Oceàna* has an atmosphere all its own, with Italian qualities in the vocal writing and a spaciously evocative orchestral fabric, which reaches sublime inspirational heights at the end of Act II (pervaded by the sirens' haunting song and the inexorable swell of the sea). However, the music is more atmospheric than dramatic, and the concert suite has been much more often performed than the opera.

EDITION composer's copyright; original version: v.s., Giudici e Strada (Milan), 1902; rev. version: L. Smolars e Nipote (Trieste), 1929

Other operas: *Preziosa*, 1879; *Bianca di Cervia*, 1882; *Re Nala* (destroyed by composer), 1887; *Il vassallo di Szigeth*, 1889; *Cornill Schut* (originally *Cornelius Schut*), 1893, rev. as *Pittori fiamminghi*, 1928; *La falena*, 1897; *Abisso*, (1911); 1914; one lost opera
BIBLIOGRAPHY Ariberto Smareglia, *Vita ed arte di Antonio Smareglia*, Cesare Mazzuconi, 1932

J.C.G.W.

BEDŘICH SMETANA
b 2 March 1824, Litomyšl, Bohemia; d 12 May 1884, Prague

Smetana is the outstanding figure in Czech opera of the 19th century. Before him there were only spasmodic and inconsistent attempts to write operas in Czech and together they form no continuous tradition. Smetana bequeathed to the Czech nation a work taken to be the very embodiment of 'Czechness' in opera (*The Bartered Bride*), and explored a variety of contrasting operatic genres as a basis for the future course of Czech opera. These range from large-scale historical and legendary operas to village operas, though his most personal contribution may well be the bitter-sweet questing dramas of his last years. Smetana's legacy was zealously defended after his death and turned into a cult that was used to stifle the works of his contemporaries and successors, Dvořák and Janáček in particular.

Smetana's musical education, at the Proksch Institute in Prague (1844–7), allied him to the Liszt–Wagner school and his earliest mature orchestral works were a series of Lisztian tone poems, striking in their harmonic freedom and their use of thematic transformation. After working abroad in Sweden (1856–61), Smetana returned to Prague at a crucial stage in the city's operatic history: the opening of the Provisional Theatre in 1862, the first theatre built exclusively for Czech use. In 1866, after his first opera, *The Brandenburgers in Bohemia*, was given at the Provisional Theatre and won first prize in the Harrach Competition for new Czech operas, he was quickly taken on at the theatre as chief conductor, ousting Jan Nepomuk Maýr, who had built up the company from scratch. Smetana remained at the Provisional Theatre for eight years (1866–74) in an increasingly embittered tenure, during which

The Provisional Theatre in Prague

his musicianship was unchallenged, but conservative factions, unhappy with his Wagnerian orientation, sought to question his ability as a conductor and as music director of an opera company. This period saw more Smetana premieres, though only his second opera, *The Bartered Bride*, in its final redaction of 1870, achieved real popularity.

What Smetana's critics sought to achieve, however, came about through the sudden onslaught of deafness in 1874. He had to resign his post as conductor and courageously set about a career exclusively as a composer. This period saw the composition of his First String Quartet (which depicts the tragic interruption of his working life by the high-pitched tinnitus which was now all he heard), the completion of his cycle of six tone poems, *Má vlast*, and the composition of three new operas. The first of these, *The Kiss*, became his most popular opera after *The Bartered Bride*. But his later years were increasingly unhappy as his illness took its toll, slowing down the rate of composition until he was able to compose only for short stretches at a time. At his death he left incomplete an earlier opera, *Viola* (after *Twelfth Night*), which he had returned to in his final years.

For all Smetana's Wagnerian affiliation and inclination, his operas derive from the French and Italian tradition of opera cultivated in the Provisional Theatre. (The German repertoire was the mainstay of the rival German Opera in Prague.) There is evidence of *cabaletta* technique and *concertato* in his

first opera and such elements can be found even in his later operas. He never abandoned resources such as the chorus or ensemble singing. With its ability for genre painting, the chorus was one of the mainstays of Czech national opera and was far too popular to sacrifice; even a serious historical opera such as *Dalibor* has a popular drinking chorus for the soldiers. The use of solo ensemble is a feature of Smetana's later operas and derives in part from the fervent belief of his last librettist, Eliška Krásnohorská, in this resource. Such ensembles are not found in *Dalibor*, which has a more austere libretto, though there are important duets even in this work.

Smetana's operas are Italianate also in their use of voice types. He employed tessituras more in keeping with Verdian voices, relying on lighter, brighter voices, rather than the lower, helden- or dramatic voice types of Wagner. In this, he was guided by the voices available in the small pool of solo singers at the Prague Provisional Theatre. No dramatic soprano or heldentenor was a regular or long-lived member of the ensemble. Similarly the absence of low bass parts is related to the early departure of the finest (and lowest) Czech bass, Josef Paleček. Smetana's inactive baritone roles, in contrast to Verdi's villainous baritones or German demonic baritones, are connected with the long-term presence in the company of Josef Lev, a poor actor, but the possessor of a baritone voice of great beauty, heard at its best in slow lyrical music.

Smetana in 1880

The character of Smetana's operas varies noticeably with the different strengths and concerns of his four librettists. The historical operas *Dalibor* and *Libuše*, with much emphasis on patriotic sentiments, had librettos from a conservative patriot Josef Wenzig. Eliška Krásnohorská, the librettist of *The Kiss*, *The Secret* and *The Devil's Wall*, preferred small-scale exploration of character psychology and the evocation of typical Czech milieus. Smetana seemed happy to take over the subjects offered him. He never suggested a libretto topic himself, and seldom went against the conventions implicit in each libretto.

Smetana was emphatically against the direct use of folksong in his operas as a means of conveying 'Czechness' and there are only a handful of documented borrowings in his operas. He had less hesitation in writing imitation folksongs, from Ludiše's 'Byl to krásný sen' in his first opera to Blaženka's 'Což ta voda' in *The Secret*. Mostly, however, the national character that most Czechs find in his works derives from Czech dance patterns such as the polka (not just in actual dances, but as the basis for other numbers) and from an identification of 'national style' with that of Smetana himself.

The Brandenburgers in Bohemia

Braniboři v Čechách

Opera in three acts (2h 15m)
Libretto by Karel Sabina
Composed February 1862–April 1863
PREMIERES 5 January 1866, Provisional Theatre, Prague; UK: 6 April 1978, Hurlingham School, London (Hammersmith Municipal Opera)
CAST Junoš *t*, Tausendmark *bar*, Varneman *t*, Jíra *t*, Ludiše *s*, Elder *b*, *s*, *a*, *bar*, 2 *b*; *satb* chorus of knights and armour-bearers, Volfram's retainers, countryfolk, the Brandenburg army, deserters, Prague beggars, judges
FULL ORCHESTRA stage band: tpt and sd

Smetana's first opera was submitted for an opera competition sponsored by the Czech patriot Count Jan Harrach. From September 1863, when an extended deadline for entries closed, the judges deliberated on the four entries for two and a half years. By the time they finally awarded the prize to Smetana in March 1866, their decision had been pre-empted by the opera's successful production at the Provisional Theatre, not quite the first newly written Czech opera to be performed there, as it had been shortly preceded by Šebor's *The Templars in Moravia*.

Following the requirements of the competition, Sabina's libretto was based 'on the history of the Czech crownlands' set in 1279 at a time of turmoil in the Czech state, when the Czech King Přemysl Otakar II had died, leaving a seven-year-old successor. His guardian was Otto of Brandenburg, who held the young king hostage while his troops ransacked Bohemia. None of these characters appears in the opera; instead the effect of the interregnum is vividly portrayed in other sectors of society. The opening of the opera is a debate on the political situation between two well-to-do Prague burghers. Later we witness the excesses of the Prague mob and, in Act II, the devastation of the countryside, with a village elder leading his people in a solemn choral prayer. Against this historical canvas is depicted the plight of Ludiše, threatened and abducted (together with her two sisters) by a Prague burgher, Tausendmark, taking advantage of the turbulent situation. When Jíra, the leader of the Prague mob, intervenes, Tausendmark accuses him of his own crime and has him arrested. The situation is resolved only with the departure of the Brandenburgers.

The Brandenburgers in Bohemia shows assured knowledge of Italianate and French conventions of the time in its *cabaletta* duet for heroine and villain and slow *concertato-stretta* finale in Act I, and a well-placed choral *preghiera* in Act II. The expected double chorus, in which Bohemians might confront Brandenburgers, is, however, unforthcoming, perhaps for fear of the censor: the only singing Brandenburger is the captain Varneman, who is portrayed as a straightforward military man. The villain of the piece is instead Tausendmark, one of Smetana's few real villains, though even he is compromised by the lyrical aria ('Tvůj obraz') added at the beginning of Act III. A more folk-orientated style is evident in Ludiše's would-be folksong in Act II ('Byl to krásný sen') and the spirited chorus and dance for the Prague mob in Act I.

RECORDING Šubrtova, Zídek, Vích, Otava, Haken, Prague NT Ch and O, Tichý, Supraphon, 1963
EDITIONS f.s., Studijní vydání děl Bedřicha Smetany, 9, 1952; v.ss., Družstvo ctitelů Smetanových/Umělecká beseda, 1899; Hudební matice Umělecké besedy, 1946

The Bartered Bride

Prodaná nevěsta
(*The Sold Bride*)
Comic opera in three acts (2h 15m)

Playbill for the premiere of The Bartered Bride *(Prague, 1866)*

Libretto by Karel Sabina
Composed July 1863–spring 1865; orch. by 15 March 1866; rev. 1869–70
PREMIERES two-act version with spoken dialogue: 30 May 1866, Provisional Theatre, Prague; definitive three-act version, sung throughout: 25 September 1870, Provisional Theatre, Prague; US: 20 August 1893, Haymarket, Chicago; UK: 26 June 1895, Drury Lane, London
CAST Krušina *bar*, Ludmila *s*, Mařenka *s*, Mícha *b*, Háta *ms*, Vašek *t*, Jeník *t*, Kecal *b*, Circus-master *t*, Esmeralda *s*, Red Indian *b*, circus artistes, *silent*; *satb* chorus of villagers
ORCHESTRATION picc, 2 fl, 2 ob, 2 cl, 2 bsn, 4 hn, 2 tpt, 3 trbn, timp, perc (triangle, bd, cym, sd), str; onstage: picc, tpt, sd, bd, cym

The Bartered Bride was not especially popular when it was first given, seeming not to achieve the success of its predecessor, *The Brandenburgers in Bohemia*. But while the latter opera dropped out of the repertoire after 1870, *The Bartered Bride* maintained its place with a steadily increasing number of performances each year. By 1927 it had been performed 1000 times in Prague. From the 1870s it was recognized as the quintessential Czech national opera, setting a standard by which other operas, including those by Smetana himself, were judged.

Especially in its original version, with spoken dialogue and without the dances, it made only modest demands. Unlike the ambitious *Branden-burgers in Bohemia* (with three tenor parts) or the later *Dalibor* (which called for a dramatic soprano and a heldentenor), voice parts were written around the fledgling Czech company, which then included an operetta component. The first Esmeralda was a well-known soubrette; the first circus-master was a Czech actor, Jindřich Mošna, who got through his undemanding part in a sort of *parlando*, playing it altogether 446 times over 30 years.

Smetana tinkered with the opera from the third performance onwards. The first change was the omission of an ironic couplet for the circus-master and Esmeralda (thought to be too risky to be played before Emperor Franz Josef), and its replacement by the ballet from Act I of *The Brandenburgers in Bohemia*, an unnecessary precaution since the emperor left after the first act. A more drastic revision followed on 29 January 1869, when the first act was divided into two scenes, the first ending with the duet for Mařenka and Vašek, and the second beginning with the newly written drinking chorus. Act II began with a newly composed polka, and Mařenka acquired a new aria ('Ten lásky sen'). The Esmeralda–circus-master couplet was omitted for good.

After four performances, Smetana produced another version (1 June 1869) in which the opera was split into the present three acts, Act I ending with a newly written *furiant*. The circus scene in Act III was expanded with a march and a *skočná*, a fast dance in duple time of a light or comic nature. It was not until the final version of 25 September 1870, however, that the spoken dialogue was replaced by sung recitatives (written for a performance in St Petersburg) and the *furiant* received its final position in Act II, after the drinking chorus.

SYNOPSIS

Act I The action takes place at a village fair in Bohemia. During a lull in the opening chorus ('Proč bychom se netěšili'), Mařenka confesses her fears to her lover Jeník. She cannot love anyone but Jeník, but her father is obliged to Mícha, and so she may be forced to marry Mícha's son. Jeník seems strangely unconcerned. Mařenka is also puzzled by Jeník's mysterious past. Why did he leave his home, she asks in the following aria ('Kdybych se co takového')? Jeník explains that after the death of his mother, his father married again and his stepmother soon sent him packing: he went off into the world and worked among foreign people. In a duet they swear eternal love ('věrné milování'). The next scene introduces Mařenka's parents, Krušina and Ludmila, and the ebullient marriage-broker Kecal ('Jak vám pravím, pane kmotře'), who gives them a glowing picture of Vašek, the bridegroom proposed for their daughter. Mařenka, who now returns, is less enthusiastic, and to the strains of 'věrné milování' in the orchestra she declares she loves another. Kecal resolves to seek out Jeník, whom he regards as the chief obstacle. The act ends in a polka with a choral conclusion.

Act II After the opening drinking chorus and *furiant*, Mařenka's would-be suitor makes his appearance on an empty stage. Vašek is dressed up for the occasion, but is nervous and stammers: his mother has told him that if he does not marry, the whole village will laugh at him ('Má ma-ma-matička'). Mařenka accosts him and, having established that he is her proposed bridegroom (he has no idea who she is), informs him that everyone is sorry for him. Mařenka, she tells him, loves another and will make sure that Vašek meets an early death. She coquettishly woos him in a duet ('Známt' já jednu dívčinu'), in which she makes the infatuated Vašek swear that he will not marry 'Mařenka'. Meanwhile Kecal has found Jeník, and in an extended duet attempts to bribe him into renouncing Mařenka. Jeník agrees to a final figure of 300 gulden on condition that Mařenka marry no one but Mícha's son, and that Krušina's debt to Mícha will be cleared. Afterwards Jeník wonders how Kecal could believe that he would have sold his Mařenka ('Jak možná věřit'). Kecal, however, brings back Krušina and the chorus to witness his negotiating triumph. The chorus is angry about the 'sale' of Jeník's bride.

Act III Vašek's confusion ('To to mi v hlavě leží') is brushed away by the arrival of the circus people, who give a preview of their skill in a lively *skočná*. Disaster has struck, however. The man appearing as the star attraction ('the big American bear') is too drunk to perform. Esmeralda the dancer and the circus-master persuade Vašek to take his place ('Milostné zvířátko'). Vašek's parents are astonished to hear that he does not want to marry Mařenka, but as soon as Vašek discovers that the girl who charmed him earlier is actually the feared Mařenka, he gladly agrees to marry her. Mařenka, now downcast at Jeník's supposed perfidy, also agrees to think things over. The pathos of her predicament is underlined in a slow sextet ('Rozmysli si, Mařenko') and in the moving aria she sings after it

('Ten lásky sen'). When Jeník joins her to explain, she will not listen ('Tak tvrdošijná divko, jsi'). Kecal calls the company to announce his final success. But Vašek's parents, Háta and Mícha, are amazed to see Jeník, now insisting on his rights as 'Mícha's son' to marry Mařenka. Mařenka realizes how Jeník has outwitted the others and gladly forgives him. Kecal is humiliated, but it is only when Vašek makes his appearance as the 'bear', that Mícha finally concedes that he is too young to marry and gives his blessing to the union of Jeník and Mařenka.

The Bartered Bride is so full of spontaneous charm that it is hard to credit how long it took to reach its final form. The fact that the dances were a late addition is particularly surprising since dance rhythms underline much of the basic substance of the opera. Many of the numbers are based on polka-type rhythms (fast two-in-a-bar) or *sousedská* rhythms (slow three-in-a-bar). Very few have complex forms, with introductions or changes of tempo and metre: isolated by the spoken dialogue, they must have seemed especially dancelike in the original version. Surprisingly in a 'folk opera', the chorus is given comparatively little to do (the male drinking chorus was another late addition), and instead the heart of the opera is the dazzling succession of duets: a loving duet for hero and heroine at the beginning and an angry one at the end; an immensely skilful one for Mařenka and the stuttering Vašek and, in another contrast of opposites, the brilliant duet for the high-spirited Jeník and the ponderous Kecal. Smetana's character drawing was especially sharp in this opera, and the self-important Kecal, established in just a few notes of limited range in his opening solo, spawned a whole generation of Czech comic successors. The overture, in Smetana's most brilliant fugal scherzando style, is a frequently performed concert piece in its own right. The opera's successful production by the Prague National Theatre at the Vienna Music and Theatre Exhibition in June 1892 initiated its popularity abroad, the only Czech opera to achieve this before the advent of Janáček.

RECORDINGS   1. Beňačková, Dvorský, Novák, Kopp, Czech PO, Košler, Supraphon, 1980–81: excellently cast and recorded; 2. Tikalová, Žídek, Haken, Kovář, Prague NT O and Ch, Chalabala, Supraphon, 1959: particularly idiomatic orchestral playing under Chalabala; 3. Nordenová, Tomš, Pollert, Gleich, Prague NT O and Ch, Ostrčil, HMV, 1933; reissued Supraphon, 1980: a classic performance from a golden period at the Prague National Theatre
EDITIONS   f.s., Studijní vydání děl Bedřicha Smetany, i, 1940; 2nd edn, 1953; v.ss., Hudební matice, 1872; Státní nakladatelství krásné literatury, hudby a umění, 1982

Dalibor

Opera in three acts (2h 15m)
Libretto by Josef Wenzig (in German); trans. Ervin Spindler
Composed April 1865–December 1867
PREMIERES   16 May 1868, New Town Theatre, Prague; 2 December 1870, Provisional Theatre, Prague (rev. with cuts and a new ending); US: 13 April 1924, Sokol Hall, Chicago (Prague National Theatre Company); UK: 17 August 1964,

King's Theatre, Edinburgh (Prague National Theatre Company)
CAST Vladislav *bar*, Dalibor *t*, Budivoj *bar*, Beneš *b*, Milada *s*, *s*, *t*; *satb* chorus of judges, royal household, vassals of the king, messengers, servants, people
FULL ORCHESTRA onstage band: 4 (8) tpt, 3 trbn, tuba, bells

SYNOPSIS
The action takes place in 15th-century Prague, where the people await the trial of Dalibor, a Czech knight whose crime has been to avenge the death of his friend the musician Zdeněk. Dalibor killed the Burgrave of Ploškovice; Milada, the burgrave's sister, demands of King Vladislav that Dalibor forfeit his life. Dalibor's appearance and his brave and defiant defence of his action, however, have an unexpected effect on Milada, who now begs the king to spare Dalibor. But the king declares that the law must take its course and Milada vows to free him herself.

By disguising herself as a boy musician Milada enters the service of Beneš, Dalibor's gaoler. Beneš is charmed by his young assistant and allows him down to the cell with a violin that Dalibor has asked for to while away the time. She reveals her identity to Dalibor, who greets her as his liberator. Milada's attempt to buy off Beneš, however, does not succeed. When the king hears about the plot to rescue Dalibor he takes the advice of his council, and gives instructions for Dalibor to be executed. Milada waits outside with her followers, but instead of Dalibor's signal she hears the death knell. She charges into the prison and, though mortally wounded, she rescues Dalibor before dying in his arms. Dalibor is recaptured and led away to execution.

After the success of Smetana's first two operas, *Dalibor* was received at first politely, then with increasing hostility. It was thought that Smetana had deserted the path of 'Czechness' in search of foreign gods, Wagner in particular. There is some truth in the first part of this accusation. Apart from the soldiers' chorus at the beginning of Act II, *Dalibor* has none of Smetana's usual folk-sounding lighter numbers. The orchestra was used not as a purveyor of Czech dances, but as a powerful scene-setter, for example in the processional music for King Vladislav, a sort of Czech 'pomp and circumstance'. Instead of a succession of dancelike numbers, audiences were confronted with long, declamatory sections ingeniously spun out of relatively little material so that the opera is often claimed to be monothematic. The story, for all its claims as a Czech historical opera, bears a striking resemblance to that of *Fidelio* (though with a typically Czech insistence on the musicianly accomplishments of its main characters). The text was not merely a translation of a German libretto, but one that aped the metrical scheme of the original. It is hardly surprising that the resulting voice parts are frequently mis-stressed and seldom display typical Czech speech rhythms. It was only in 1886, two years after Smetana's death, that true dramatic voices could be found for the two main parts and a new attempt to stage it was made at the new National Theatre. The result was a triumph that revealed some

of Smetana's finest dramatic music and established the work's lasting place in the Czech repertoire.

RECORDINGS 1. Podvalová, Blachut, Prague NT O and Ch, Krombholc, Supraphon, 1950: a particularly distinguished team, with Blachut in his prime; 2. Děpoltová, Přibyl, Brno State PO, Smetáček, Supraphon, 1979: more modern sound, with Přibyl in his finest role, though a disappointing Milada
EDITIONS f.s., Studijní vydání děl Bedřicha Smetany, v. 1945, 2nd edn, 1960; v.ss., Družstvo ctitelů Bedřicha Smetany, 1884; Hudební matice Umělecké besedy, 1950

Libuše
Ceremonial opera in three acts (2h 45m)
Libretto by Josef Wenzig (in German); trans. Ervin Spindler
Composed 1869–November 1872
PREMIERE 11 June 1881, National Theatre, Prague
CAST Libuše *s*, Přemysl ze Stadic *bar*, Chrudoš od Otavy *b*, Šťáhlav na Radbuze *t*, Krasava *s*, *a*, *bar*, *b*, 4 offstage voices: 2 *s*, *a*, *t*; *satb* chorus of elders, knights, chieftains, women and girls from Libuše's court, Přemysl's retainers, people
FULL ORCHESTRA onstage band: 4 tpt, 2 bass tpt

Smetana's fourth opera was first performed out of sequence, a decade after it was written. This upset the regular pattern of Smetana premieres and resulted in a six-year gap between *Dalibor* and *The Two Widows*. The opera was originally destined to celebrate the belated coronation of Franz Josef as King of Bohemia. Franz Josef changed his mind and the opera was then held in readiness to open the long-planned Czech National Theatre. This it did, but only after a decade of waiting. Ever since, the opera has been treated as a special pageant of a somewhat official kind, thanks to its consciously grand and ceremonial character.

SYNOPSIS
The plot is based on a Czech legend about the mythical founder of Prague, Libuše, and her union with Přemysl, the founder of the first Czech dynasty. After the death of her father, Libuše has become ruler of the Czechs. Her authority is challenged in a land dispute between two brothers, Šťáhlav and Chrudoš. Chrudoš, the unsuccessful claimant, proclaims that he will not obey a woman. Libuše offers to marry to give the nation a male ruler and instructs her messengers where to find her future husband. He is a simple countryman, Přemysl, ploughing with his oxen in the village of Stadice. Přemysl accepts Libuše's delegation and agrees to the marriage. This simple framework is expanded with the story of Krasava, who had pretended to favour Šťáhlav, to encourage her real love, Chrudoš. When Krasava confesses the truth, Chrudoš accepts Libuše's judgement, and the two brothers are reconciled. The climax of the opera is Libuše's prophetic vision: a *tableau vivant* of future kings and heroes culminating in the promise of a glorious future.

The libretto for *Libuše* came from the same team as its predecessor and was similarly a metrically exact translation of a German libretto, but there was an enormous difference in the way Smetana set the text. During the composition of *Libuše* his attention was drawn to the faulty word-setting that had marred his three previous operas. Smetana carefully revised his score and from then on set a standard of immaculate Czech prosody that has served as a model ever since. A prominent feature of the score is the enhancement of the 'pomp and circumstance' style of *Dalibor* (for instance in the festive overture). Only seldom, for instance in the scene where Krasava confesses her love, does full-blooded emotion break the ceremonial surface of the work. The most memorable part of the opera, and one of the most tangible expressions of Czech nationalism in music, is Libuše's prophecy at the end.

RECORDINGS 1. Beňačková, Vodička, Zítek, Švorc, Prague NT O and Ch, Košler, Supraphon, 1983: a live recording of the performance that reopened the National Theatre on 17 November 1983; Beňačková shows extraordinary stamina in the unstrained beauty of her voice in the final prophecy at the end of one of the most taxing parts in Czech opera; 2. Kniplová, Žídek, Bednář, Kroupa, Prague NT O and Ch, Krombholc, Supraphon, 1965
EDITIONS f.s., Studijní vydání děl Bedřicha Smetany, vi, 1949; v.ss., Hudební matice, 1881; Státní nakladatelství krásné literatury, hudby a umění, rev. 9th edn, 1955

The Two Widows

Dvě vdovy
Comic opera in two acts (1h 45m)
Libretto by Emanuel Züngel, after the play *Les deux veuves* by Felicien Mallefille
Composed July 1873–January 1874; rev. 10 June–July 1877, 1882
PREMIERES 27 March 1874, Provisional Theatre, Prague (with spoken dialogue); 15 March 1878, Provisional Theatre, Prague (with recitatives and extra numbers); US: 23 October 1949, Sokol Hall, New York; UK: 17 June 1963, Guildhall School of Music and Drama, London
CAST Karolina *s*, Anežka *ms*, Ladislav Podhajský *t*, Mumlal *b*; added in 1877: *s*, *t*; *satb* chorus of young countryfolk

The Two Widows is Smetana's only completed opera based on a non-Czech subject, a light French bourgeois comedy.

SYNOPSIS
The two widows of the title, Karolina and Anežka, are quite different in temperament. Karolina has energetically taken over the running of her estate, where the action is set; her cousin Anežka is mourning guiltily for her unloved husband and is consequently deaf to the pleas of her suitor Ladislav. Ladislav contrives to be arrested as a poacher by Karolina's slow-witted and self-congratulatory gamekeeper, Mumlal. The culprit is duly sentenced and imprisoned within the house. It takes not only Ladislav's protestations of love, but also a little jealousy of an artful Karolina for Anežka to yield. A subsidiary love affair was added in the 1877 revision between Mumlal's daughter Lidka and his assistant Toník which, at first resisted by Mumlal, is also happily resolved.

Richard Strauss is said to have demanded per-

formances of *The Two Widows* on his visits to Prague. One can see why: the appeal of the work, both in the origin of the text and the sophisticated charm of the music, is superficially cosmopolitan and easily accessible. But of all Smetana's operas this is the one most permeated by the rhythm of the polka, which, with its down-beat rhythms, reflects the natural down-beat patterns of Czech speech. Trochaic (i.e. polka-like) verse was provided by the highly experienced librettist and translator Emanuel Züngel, though this is set by Smetana with a virtuosity that avoids monotony. Furthermore, the nub of the plot – the overcoming of internal obstacles that hinder a marriage – foreshadows the concerns of Smetana's later operas set to Krásnohorská libretti. Despite this, the opera was not popular in its original version. As in *The Bartered Bride*, Smetana later replaced original spoken dialogue with through-composed recitatives. At the same time there was an attempt to establish a more identifiably 'Czech' milieu, introducing a comic country couple and a convincing imitation of a folksong for Ladislav at the beginning of Act II. Much later, for a German production in Hamburg in 1882, Smetana reluctantly added a trio in Act I and an alternative ending to Anežka's Act II aria, and consented to a redivision of the opera into three acts.

RECORDINGS 1. Tauberová, Tikalová, Žídek, Haken, Prague NT O and Ch, Krombholc, Supraphon, 1956: a distinguished team; 2. Šormová, Machotková, Horáček, Zahradníček, Prague NT O and Ch, Jílek, Supraphon, 1975
EDITIONS f.s. (critical edn of 1877 edn with 1882 appendix of additions), Studijní vydání děl Bedřicha Smetany, 7, 1950; v.ss. (in German, in three acts with extra Hamburg numbers), Bote und Bock, 1893; Hudební matice Umělecké besedy, 1914; 7th edn (1877 version, in Czech), 1949

Viola

Comic opera in three acts (inc.; 15m)
Libretto by Eliška Krásnohorská, after the play *Twelfth Night* by William Shakespeare
Composed ?1874, 1883–4
PREMIERES 15 March 1900, Prague (concert); 11 May 1924, National Theatre, Prague

Smetana completed a total of 365 bars (276 in full score) comprising a storm scene, the respective rescuing of Sebastian and Viola (played by the same mezzo-soprano) and the beginning of a fourth scene at Orsino's court. Most of the music, though not its orchestration, dates from the early 1870s, at the beginning of Smetana's collaboration with Krásnohorská.

RECORDING Štěpánová, Kalaš, Kočí, Prague NT O and Ch, Krombholc, Supraphon, 1953
EDITIONS v.ss. (with *The Devil's Wall*), Hudební matice, 1902; 3rd edn (alone), 1946

The Kiss

Hubička
Folk (*prostonárodní*) opera in two acts (1h 45m)
Libretto by Eliška Krásnohorská, after the tale by Karolina Světlá
Composed November 1875–31 August 1876

PREMIERES   7 November 1876, Provisional Theatre, Prague; UK: 8 December 1938, Liverpool (amateur); US: 17 April 1921, Blackstone Theater, Chicago; 18 October 1948, King's Theatre, Hammersmith, London (Carl Rosa Company)
CAST   Father Paloucký *b*, Vendulka *s*, Lukáš *t*, Tomeš *bar*, Martinka *a, s, t, b*; *satb* chorus of neighbours, girls, musicians, smugglers
FULL ORCHESTRA

Smetana's contacts with Eliška Krásnohorská, the librettist of his final years, began in 1869 with the proposed *Lumír* and were taken further in 1871 with *Viola*, but even this work was soon set aside. *The Kiss* was their first completed collaboration. For all their apparent *naïveté*, Krásnohorská's libretti had the virtue of inspiring the composer – he said he found 'music' in them. He could have found this in her carefully crafted verse, with different metres employed according to character or mood or to differentiate stages in multi-sectioned arias. But equally the subject matter seems to have been congenial for the ageing composer, locked in a loveless marriage. All the Krásnohorská heroes are middle-aged and have difficulty getting together with a suitable partner. It is only through personal learning that success is achieved.

The Kiss, set in a Czech border village, deals with the relationship of Lukáš, now a widower, and his former sweetheart, Vendulka, who has remained unmarried. Lukáš is anxious to return to his real love and to give his young baby a mother. The engagement party, however, runs into trouble: out of respect for Lukáš's dead wife, Vendulka refuses to seal the engagement with a kiss. Both stubbornly refuse to budge from their positions, despite a touching scene where they are left together to resolve their differences, but where their strong

Marie Sittova (Vendulka) singing to her baby in The Kiss *(Prague, 1876)*

characters increasingly clash. The engagement party is spoilt; Lukáš storms off and gets drunk; Vendulka sings lullabies to the infant. The quarrel is solved only after both have fled into the borderland forest; Vendulka with her spirited aunt Martinka on a smuggling expedition, Lukáš in a fit of remorse poured out to his best man, Tomeš. The reconciliation is finally sealed with a kiss.

The Kiss was the first opera Smetana wrote after going deaf. If this left any trace in the work it is in the depth of feeling he brought to the chief characters. Father Paloucký, conceived by the librettist as a comic bore, emerges as a figure of real and touching concern for his daughter. The positions of both Lukáš and Vendulka are made believable, transforming a naïve plot into a work of real depth and tenderness. It was a success from the start, and has remained popular with Czech audiences. Contemporary audiences were particularly taken with what appeared to be the work's 'Czechness'. This was advertised by the work's genre designation and by a rare borrowing by Smetana of a well-known traditional *pastorella* song ('Hajej mů andílku') for Vendulka's first lullaby. But her second lullaby ('Letěla bělounká holubička'), though Smetana's invention, is regarded as no less Czech. As in *The Two Widows*, certain numbers are based on polka rhythms, most prominently in Lukáš's drunken song at the end of Act I.

RECORDINGS   1. Červinková, Krásová, Blachut, Prague NT O and Ch, Chalabala, Supraphon, 1952, reissued Rediffusion Heritage, 1977: well worth putting up with the elderly sound for a cast such as this; 2. Děpoltová, Márová, Vodička, Haken, Brno Opera Ch and O, Vajnar, Supraphon, 1980
EDITIONS   f.s., Studijní vydání děl Bedřicha Smetany, 3, 1942; v.ss., Fr. A. Urbánek, 1880; Státní nakladatelství krásné literatury, hudby a umění, 1959

The Secret

Tajemství
Comic opera in three acts (1h 45m)
Libretto by Eliška Krásnohorská
Composed July 1877–July 1878
PREMIERES   18 September 1878, New Czech Theatre, Prague; UK: 7 December 1956, Oxford University Opera Club; US: 7 January 1989, New York (Bronx Opera Company)
CAST   Malina *b*, Kalina *bar*, Panna Roza (Miss Roza) *a*, Blaženka *s*, Vít *t*, Bonifác *b*, Skřivánek *t, s, t, bar, b*; *satb* chorus of aldermen, neighbours, boys and girls, threshers, apprentice bricklayers, spirits and apparitions in Kalina's dreams, bagpiper
FULL ORCHESTRA

SYNOPSIS

The setting is a small town beneath the Bezděz mountain in northern Bohemia towards the end of the 18th century. The plot initially concerns itself with the rivalry of two aldermen, Malina and Kalina. Behind this is the story of bitter love which has left its mark on the main characters. Years ago Kalina had loved Roza, the daughter of Malina, but had been refused by her father, on grounds of his poverty. Kalina and Roza each misinterpreted this as unfaithfulness on the other's part: he married in a fit of pique, and she has remained a spinster. Roza is particularly embittered as Friar Barnabáš told her before his death that he has left a 'secret' with Kalina that would enable him to marry her.

This 'secret' comes to light during a fracas between the followers of the two rivals, and knowledge of it is soon passed around the inhabitants of the small town. The 'secret', which gives hint of buried treasure, inspires Kalina to go out digging along a secret tunnel, but what he finds at the end of it is human rather than monetary treasure: the secret tunnel leads to Malina's house, and thus to Roza, who accepts her former sweetheart.

The Secret is a development of several aspects of the previous Krásnohorská–Smetana collaboration. Again at its centre is an older couple who missed their chance of happiness earlier on. And again after a symbolic gesture of searching – the dramatic, almost Freudian journey down the tunnel – the internal obstacle is removed. The location of a small town rather than a village provides a different type of genre painting. There is a particularly rich variety of town 'types' – small cameo parts that include a cantankerous foreman, a ballad singer (accompanying himself on the guitar and attempting to sing a song to flatter both rivals simultaneously), a retired soldier (Bonifác), who tries to woo Roza with his bragging, and a bagpiper, who provides one of the many bagpipe episodes in Czech opera. Most of the cast is assembled for one of Smetana's most appealing late *concertatos* in Act II which reverses the usual scheme: a gossamer-textured scherzo, followed by a slow ensemble of perplexity ('Ó klamné domnění'). This, rather than the over-used portentous 'secret' motif ('Ted' slavně, těžce slibte mi'), provides one of the chief musical delights of the piece, though there are also some of Smetana's finest arias, such as the multi-sectioned 'gold' aria for Kalina at the beginning of Act II and the delightful songs for Blaženka ('Což ta voda') and Skřivánek ('Aj k čemu') in Act III.

RECORDINGS 1. Soukupová, Horáček, Zítek, Prague NT O and Ch, Košler, Supraphon, 1982; 2. Štěpánová, Kočí, Kalaš, Prague NT O and Ch, Krombholc, Supraphon, 1953
EDITIONS f.s., Studijní vydání děl Bedřicha Smetany, 10, 1953; v.ss., Hudební matice, 1892; Státní nakladatelství krásné literatury, hudby a umění, 1958

The Devil's Wall

Čertova stěna

Comic-romantic opera in three acts (2h 15m)
Libretto by Eliška Krásnohorská
Composed September 1879–June 1882
PREMIERES 29 October 1882, New Czech Theatre, Prague; UK: 17 February 1987, Bloomsbury Theatre, London
CAST Vok Vítkovic *b*, Záviš *ms*, Jarek *t*, Hedvíka *s*, Michálek *t*, Katuška *s*, Beneš *b*, Rarach *b*; *satb* chorus of peasants, inhabitants of the castle, messengers, knights, ladies, attendants, villagers, devilish apparitions
FULL ORCHESTRA onstage: 2 tpt

The title of the opera refers to a bizarre group of rocks in the river Vltava, the source of several legends and the setting of the final scene. The devil (Rarach) also makes an appearance (usually, and confusingly, as a double of the hermit Beneš), though like all Czech devils he is essentially a comic character. Despite these elements and the medieval setting (mid-13th century), Smetana's last completed opera shared concerns similar to the previous Krásnohorská operas: in this case the older man seeking a wife is the head of one of the most famous Czech aristocratic families, the Rosenbergs. The fact that he is a wealthy man accounts for most of the comic complications of the plot, the attempts to find him a wife or to acquire his wealth.

SYNOPSIS
Vok Vítkovic is still a bachelor, his sweetheart having married elsewhere. All efforts to find him a wife are a failure, to the despair of Vok's friend, the knight Jarek, who vows he will not marry before Vok does. Others are less selfless. Michálek, Vok's castellan, hopes to marry him to his daughter Katuška (Jarek's sweetheart). Beneš, Vok's rascally adviser, plans to keep the status quo in order to endow the monastery where he hopes to become abbot. The problem appears to be solved by the appearance of Hedvíka, the daughter of Vok's old sweetheart, now dead, who has entrusted her daughter to Vok's care. Hedvíka is the image of her mother, but Vok is too cautious to woo her. It is only Vok's apparent decision to become a monk that makes Hedvíka realize her own love for him. Beneš sees the error of his ways; Rarach takes his revenge by getting his minions to dam the Vltava (creating 'the devil's wall') and flood the monastery. Hedvíka sets off over the wall to rouse the inhabitants, but she also rouses Vok's love for her, and Beneš, now in the moral ascendancy, vanquishes the devil and his wall.

Krásnohorská tried hard to carry out Smetana's instructions for a comic opera, but there are too many complications for the piece to work properly. Besides, Krásnohorská's gifts were for the lyrical and the tender rather than the comic, and Smetana's own sad state of mind and health meant that he was chiefly inspired by the predicament of the lonely Vok. It is into this lyrical baritone part (written expressly for Josef Lev) that he poured out his feelings, and it is Vok's 'Jen jediná mě ženy krásná tvář' that is a high point and not the comic elements such as Vok's tediously fussy castellan Michálek, or the pantomime-devil conception of Rarach. Ensembles and duets, the glories of the two previous Krásnohorská operas, were almost beyond Smetana by this stage (he was able to concentrate only for short periods) and are brief. For all this, the work's best moments have all the tenderness and poignancy of Smetana's other late operas.

RECORDING Šubrtová, Domanínská, Mixová, Žídek, Votava, Bednář, Mráz, Berman, Prague NT O and Ch, Chalabala, Supraphon, 1960
EDITIONS f.s., Studijní vydání děl Bedřicha Smetany, 12, 1959; v.ss., Družstvo ctitelů Smetanových/Umělecká beseda,

1902 (with *Viola*); Hudební matice Umělecké besedy, Prague, 6th edn, 1949

BIBLIOGRAPHY John Clapham, *Smetana*, Dent (Master Musicians series), 1972; Jaroslav Jíranek, *Smetanova operní tvorba* (*Smetana's Operatic Works*), Supraphon, 1984–8; Brian Large, *Smetana*, Duckworth, 1970; John Tyrrell, *Czech Opera*, CUP, 1988

J.T.

DMITRI SMIRNOV
b 2 November 1948, Minsk, Byelorussia

Smirnov is one of the younger generation of Soviet composers who have recently become prominent in the West. His musical language could be labelled neo-romantic, paying homage to Strauss and Mahler, and the unforced lyricism of his writing can recall Britten. A major artistic preoccupation is with the poetry, painting and thought of William Blake; his two operas, a symphony, two song-cycles and various chamber works have all been inspired by Blake. *Tiriel*, which attracted international attention at its premiere in 1989 in Freiburg, is a full-scale piece, and *The Lamentations of Thel* (also premiered in 1989) is a chamber-sized pendant to it, a lyric meditation on an episode from Blake's *Tiriel*.

BIBLIOGRAPHY G. McBurney, *Introduction to Smirnov*, Boosey & Hawkes, 1990

J.G.

JOHN CHRISTOPHER SMITH
Johann Christoph Schmidt, jnr; *b* 1712, Ansbach; *d* 3 October 1795, Bath, England

Smith's father, also Johann Christoph, came to England in 1716 as manager and amanuensis to Handel. The son took lessons from Pepusch and Thomas Roseingrave, acquiring the basis of a considerable keyboard technique and composing two sets of six sonatas (1732 and 1735) which show a clear debt to Handel. In 1732 an opera, *Teraminta*, to words by Henry Carey, was produced at Lincoln's Inn Fields; the music may have been by Smith, but a case has been made out for John Stanley as composer. However, there can be no question that *Ulysses* (1733), also performed at Lincoln's Inn Fields, to a libretto by Samuel Humphries, is by Smith; it is musically much more advanced and has been revived despite its imperfect state. The subject is that of the final eight books of the *Odyssey*, Ulysses' return to Ithaca and the slaying of the suitors. *Teraminta* ran for three nights; *Ulysses* only one.

Smith's later life took an unexpected course. He married into the aristocracy, wrote two Shakespearean operas for Garrick and took on

Handel's oratorio practice. His later operatic works were published only in part and he abandoned the unsuccessful composition of opera for the moderately successful composition of oratorio. He left Handel's manuscripts, bequeathed to him through his father, to the king; they constitute his real legacy.

Surviving operatic works: *Teraminta*, 1732; *Ulysses*, 1733; *Issipile*, 1743; *Il Ciro riconosciuto*, 1745; *The Fairies*, 1755; *The Tempest*, 1756; *The Enchanter, or Love and Magic*, 1760
BIBLIOGRAPHY Roger Fiske, *English Theatre Music in the Eighteenth Century*, OUP, 1973; 2nd edn, 1986; Alfred Mann, 'Handel's Successor, J. C. Smith the Younger', in Christopher Hogwood and Richard Luckett (eds), *Music in Eighteenth-Century England*, CUP, 1983, p. 135

R.Lu.

ETHEL SMYTH
(Dame) Ethel Mary Smyth; *b* 22 April 1858, Marylebone, London; *d* 9 May 1944, Woking, Surrey

The daughter of a general, Smyth became a composer against every convention of Victorian life. Not surprisingly, she had little early success in Britain. She studied in Leipzig, and was for a long time better known in Germany than at home. Her first three operas, *Fantasio* (1898), *Der Wald* (1901) and *The Wreckers* (1906), were all premiered there, while her later fame in Britain was more like notoriety, because of her activities as a suffragette (she was imprisoned in 1911 for throwing a brick through the Home Secretary's window), as a campaigner for women's rights in music, and as an all-round social, sartorial and sexual eccentric, whose association with Bloomsbury included a lesbian affair with Virginia Woolf.

Outside opera, Smyth's most ambitious works (the Mass in D and a late vocal–orchestral piece called *The Prison*) are eclectic in style and uneven in execution. Of her six operas, only *The Wreckers* has been revived since the war, though *The Boatswain's Mate* was popular during her lifetime. She was a prolific and entertaining *mémoiriste*, and a vigorous lobbier of newspaper editors; she never allowed the cause to smother her essential humanity and good humour.

The Wreckers
Opera in three acts
Libretto by Henry Brewster; an adaptation of a Cornish drama, *Les naufrageurs*
Composed 1903–4
PREMIERES 11 November 1906, Neues Theater, Leipzig (as *Standrecht*); UK: 30 May 1908, Queen's Hall, London (concert); 22 June 1909, His Majesty's Theatre, London

Long famous as a step towards a national British opera (its London stage premiere was conducted by Beecham), *The Wreckers* looks forward in its subject to another tide-mark of British opera, Britten's *Peter Grimes*. *The Wreckers* are almost the entire population of a Cornish fishing village, who, in times of famine, supplement their livelihood by luring storm-bound shipping on to the rocky coast. Even the local Wesleyan preacher, Pascoe, abets them; but his wife, Thirza, helps her lover, Mark, to warn the ships off, and for their pains the two are walled up in a tidal cave and left to drown.

For obvious reasons, Smyth's models are mainly German. Though no Wagnerite, she makes some use of his motivic technique, while the texture, orchestration, and even some of the music's dramatic density, show knowledge of the works of Richard Strauss. At its best (for instance in the love music of Act II) *The Wreckers* has genuine music-theatrical power. But it also slips too readily into operatic convention, and, as a whole (like other works by Smyth), lacks a strong musical personality of its own.

RECORDING Molteno, Clements, Short, Bradford Opera Group, Dawson, RRE, 1982
EDITIONS v.ss., Breitkopf und Härtel, 1906; Forsyth and Universal, 1916

Other operas: *Fantasio*, 1898; *Der Wald*, 1901; *The Boatswain's Mate*, 1916; *Fête galante*, 1923; *Entente cordiale*, 1925
BIBLIOGRAPHY C. St John, *Ethel Smyth*, Longman, 1959

S.W.

TEMISTOCLE SOLERA

b 25 December 1815, Ferrara; *d* 21 April 1878, Milan

Solera is best remembered as Verdi's first librettist, who provided the texts for *Oberto, Conte di S. Bonifacio*, *Nabucco*, *I lombardi alla prima crociata*, *Giovanna d'Arco* and *Attila*. But he was also a composer in his own right, producing four operas to his own libretti between 1840 and 1845. None of them had any great success, however, and after working as an impresario in Spain, while being confidential adviser (and probably lover) to Queen Isabella, he became a religious correspondent in Milan and secret courier between Napoleon III and Cavour (1859). He was superintendent of police in the Basilicata region (1860) and elsewhere and later to the Khedive of Egypt, and lastly an antique dealer in Paris. He died penniless in Milan.

Operas: *Ildegonda*, 1840; *Il contadino d'Agliate*, 1841, rev. as *La fanciulla di Castelguelfo*, 1842; *Genio e sventura*, 1843; *La hermana de Pelayo*, 1845
BIBLIOGRAPHY Antonio Cassi Ramelli, 'Temistocle Solera', in *Libretti e librettisti*, Casa Editrice Ceschina, 1973

M.R.

STEPHEN SONDHEIM

Stephen Joshua Sondheim; *b* 22 March 1930, New York

Having studied the writing of musicals in his youth with Oscar Hammerstein II – a neighbour – and

composition with Milton Babbitt, Stephen Sondheim earned his living for a time writing television scripts. As early as 1954 he was given the opportunity to write a Broadway score, *Saturday Night*, a project ended by the death of its prospective producer. This exposure secured Sondheim the chance to write lyrics for prestigious shows composed by Leonard Bernstein (*West Side Story*) and Jule Styne (*Gypsy*). Thereafter, with rare exceptions, he has written both lyrics and music for all his projects, and done so on an exceptionally high level.

His recognition as a significant contributor to musical theatre began with *Company* and has grown ever since; each of his new projects is eagerly awaited well in advance of its appearance. His lyrics can exhibit, as the case demands, either a memorable simplicity or a dazzling complexity unmatched even by Hart or W. S. Gilbert. His music, supported by reworking of recurring motifs and by textural and rhythmic invention that set new standards for the Broadway score, can encompass extended ensembles and through-composed musical scenes, fragmentary recitative-like passages, or catchy 32-bar show tunes. Though he does not make much use of the classically defined operatic voice categories, his biggest scores are indeed operatic in their scope and integrity.

A Funny Thing Happened on the Way to the Forum

Musical in two acts (film: 1h 45m)
Libretto by Burt Shevelove and Larry Gelbart, based on the works of Plautus; lyrics by the composer
PREMIERES 8 May 1962, Alvin Theater, New York; UK: 3 October 1963, Strand Theatre, London

This fast-paced farce depicts, in broad vaudeville style, the convoluted efforts of the slave Pseudolous (who acts as narrator) to gain his freedom. Though seemingly old-fashioned in subject, *Forum* was innovative stylistically: its songs (including 'Comedy Tonight' and 'Lovely'), rather than being integrated into the story in the then-approved manner, serve as moments of calm among the frantic goings-on, and are often addressed openly to the audience.

RECORDING Mostel, Gilford, Hastings, Capitol, 1962
FILM Lester (dir.), UA, 1966: much of score omitted
EDITION v.s., Burthen Music, 1964

Company

Musical comedy in two acts
Libretto by George Furth; lyrics by the composer
PREMIERES 26 April 1970, Alvin Theater, New York; UK: 18 January 1972, Her Majesty's Theatre, London

Company was a ground-breaking experiment in form, combining the continuing characters of a musical with elements of a revue: alternating sketch–song structure (with songs usually delivered by those not involved in the scene) and unity through a central theme – the difficulty of committed relationships in contemporary urban society – rather than a plot. Despite some difficulty in bringing the action to a satisfying close, the attempt was successful enough to suggest exciting new directions for Sondheim and others to follow.

RECORDING   Jones, Barrie, Stritch, Hastings, CBS, 1970
EDITION   v.s., Valando and Beautiful Music, 1971

Follies

Musical in one act (two acts in 1987 version)
Libretto by James Goldman; lyrics by the composer
Composed (intermittently) 1965–71
PREMIERES   4 April 1971, Winter Garden, New York; UK: 26 April 1985, Library Theatre, Manchester; rev. version: 21 July 1987, Shaftesbury Theatre, London

Follies represented a remarkable expansion of the possibilities suggested by *Company*. It presents a reunion of the Follies girls who used to perform in an annual revue in years gone by. Two of the women in particular, along with the men they married, find themselves dealing with their lifelong problems through reminiscence and a final dreamlike show in which each exposes his or her own 'folly' in song and dance. The show is thus structured as a book musical interspersed with revue songs (the individual reminiscences of Follies veterans) and culminating in a full-scale surrealistic Follies re-creation. In its original form, *Follies* was probably the most affecting of the shows Sondheim has written, and its score may well rank as his richest work.

RECORDINGS   1. Collins, Smith, De Carlo, Nelson, McMartin, Hastings, Capitol, 1971; 2. Cook, Remick, Burnett, Patinkin, Hearn, Gemignani, NYP, RCA, 1985; 3. McKenzie, Rigg, Gray, Healy, Massey, Koch, First Night, 1987: in the absence of a truly complete recording of the long score from the original cast, one must combine all three sets to get an adequate idea of *Follies*
VIDEO   Remick, Cook, Patinkin, Hearn, Burnett, Fries, 1985: concert excerpts plus documentary
EDITION   v.s., Charles Hansen, n.d.

A Little Night Music

Musical in two acts (film: 2h)
Libretto by Hugh Wheeler, based on the film *Smiles of a Summer Night* by Ingmar Bergman (1955); lyrics by the composer
PREMIERES   25 February 1973, Shubert Theater, New York; UK: 15 April 1975, Adelphi Theatre, London
CAST   Desirée Arnfeldt *a*, Fredrik Egerman *bar*, Mme Arnfeldt *a*, Charlotte *ms*, Carl-Magnus *bar*, Anne *s*, Henrik *t*, Petra *a*, Fredrika *child s*, Liebeslieder Quintet *s*, *ms*, *a*, *t*, *bar*, 4 servants *silent*
ORCHESTRATION (Jonathan Tunick)   theatre orch., including ww doubles, pf/cel

Those who had imagined that they understood the direction of Sondheim's work in the 1970s found *A Little Night Music* a surprise: a conventional period story albeit theatrically stylized. It deals with the contemporary themes of suppressed longings, missed connections and sensual fulfilment: it also contains an effervescent waltzing score and Sondheim's best-known song ('Send in the Clowns').

SYNOPSIS
Sweden at the turn of the century.
   Act I   After an overture by the Quintet, the lawyer Fredrik Egerman, frustrated with the unwillingness of his young wife Anne to consummate their marriage, turns to his old flame Desirée, an actress. Desirée herself is currently involved with the Count, whose wife is a friend of Anne's. Fredrik's son from his first marriage, Henrik, is unhappy with his dedication to religious purity, finding himself attracted to the maid Petra and to his new stepmother. Desirée, in collusion with her mother and daughter, decides to invite everyone to her mother's villa for the weekend.
   Act II   After confrontations, seductions, duels, and disappointments, the pairs are recombined. Anne runs off with Henrik, the Count and Countess reunite, and Fredrik returns to Desirée.

RECORDING   Johns, Cariou, Gingold, Elliott, Guittard, Hastings, CBS, 1973
FILM   Prince (dir.), New World, 1978
EDITION   v.s., Revelation and Beautiful Music, 1974

Pacific Overtures

Musical in two acts (2h)
Libretto by John Weidman, with additional material by Hugh Wheeler; lyrics by the composer
PREMIERES   11 January 1976, Winter Garden, New York; UK: 26 April 1985, Library Theatre, Manchester

The opening up of Japan to Western influence is presented in Kabuki-influenced style by an all-male (originally all-Asian) cast. The story, presented by a formal Reciter, shows the reactions of various Japanese to the arrival of Commodore Perry's fleet, and the attempts to deal with the US and other foreign powers. Only a few continuing characters unite the stylized vignettes that embody this conflict; at the end, a large jump in time and deliberate breach of style bring the action to the present day.

RECORDINGS   1. Shimono, Sato, Mako, Gemignani, RCA, 1976; 2. Angas, Booth-Jones, Rivers, English National Opera O, Holmes, TER, 1987: the latter, though less convincingly performed, is noteworthy as an absolutely complete recording including dialogue
EDITION   v.s., Revelation and Rilting, 1977

Sweeney Todd, the Demon Barber of Fleet Street

Musical thriller in two acts (2h 15m)
Libretto by Hugh Wheeler, based on a version of *Sweeney Todd* by Christopher Bond; lyrics by the composer
PREMIERES   1 March 1979, Uris Theater, New York; UK: 3 July 1980, Drury Lane, London
CAST   Sweeney Todd *b-bar*, Mrs Lovett *ms*, Anthony Hope *t*, Johanna *s*, Judge Turpin *b*, beggar woman *ms*, beadle *high t*, Tobias Ragg *t*, Pirelli *t*, Jonas Fogg *spoken role*; *satb* chorus of Londoners
ORCHESTRATION (Jonathan Tunick)   theatre orch., including ww doubles, organ

The score for this brutal melodrama is Sondheim's most ambitious: rarely interrupted for dialogue, tightly interwoven motivically (several of the motifs derive from the *Dies irae*), with intricate ensembles and a central role for the chorus, which frames the action with 'The Ballad of Sweeney Todd'.

SYNOPSIS

Act I A deported criminal returns to 19th-century London to take revenge on the judge who destroyed his family. With the help of a neighbour, the baker Mrs Lovett, he resumes his trade as a barber under the name Sweeney Todd. He misses his opportunity to cut the judge's throat, and resolves to expand his murderous activities.

Act II A multiple murderer now, with his victims baked into Mrs Lovett's pies, Todd finds his daughter Johanna and uses her as bait to draw the judge back to the barber shop. He finally kills the judge – and also a beggar woman who turns out to be his own wife, whom he had supposed dead. By the time the story ends, he and Mrs Lovett are dead too.

RECORDING Lansbury, Rice, Cariou, Garber, Gemignani, RCA, 1979
VIDEO Lansbury, Cariou, Joslyn, Groenendaal, RKO, 1982
EDITION v.s., Revelation and Rilting, 1981

Merrily We Roll Along

Musical in two acts (2h 30m)
Libretto by George Furth, based on the play by George S. Kaufman and Moss Hart; lyrics by the composer
Composed 1980–81; rev. 1985, 1989–90
PREMIERES 16 November 1981, Alvin Theater, New York; UK: 28 March 1983, Guildhall School of Music and Drama, London

The lives of three friends who mostly failed to fulfil their early promise are given poignancy by being shown (as in the source play) in reverse time order, so that their first meeting forms the last scene. The brief New York run has been followed by many amateur productions; the authors have also made some revisions.

RECORDING Walton, Price, Morrison, Gemignani, RCA, 1981
EDITION v.s., Revelation and Rilting, 1984

Sunday in the Park with George

Musical in two acts (2h 30m)
Libretto by James Lapine; lyrics by the composer
PREMIERES 2 May 1984, Booth Theater, New York; UK: 15 March 1990, National Theatre, London

SYNOPSIS

Act I follows the life and obsessions of Georges Seurat as he neglects his personal life in favour of gathering characters for his Parisian painting *A Sunday Afternoon on the Island of La Grande Jatte* – which is created as a tableau at the close of the act.

Act II shifts to New York and George, the painter's great-grandson, and contrasts his present-day struggles for artistic expression with those of his ancestor.

This show marked a change in collaborators for Sondheim, and to some extent a stylistic reorientation too, with many songs merging into each other in through-composed recitative-like passages. Despite its seemingly esoteric subject and manner, it had enough popular appeal to run on Broadway for a year and a half, and won a Pulitzer Prize for drama (the sixth to go to a musical).

RECORDING Patinkin, Peters, Gemignani, RCA, 1984
VIDEO Patinkin, Peters, Lorimar, 1985
EDITION v.s., Revelation and Rilting, 1987

The Act I finale of Sunday in the Park with George *(New York, 1984)*

Into the Woods

Musical in two acts (2h 30m)
Libretto by James Lapine; lyrics by the composer
PREMIERES   5 November 1987, Martin Beck Theater, New
York; UK: 25 September 1990, Phoenix Theatre, London

Four familiar fairy-tales interact with a newly
invented one: a baker and his wife, in order to
remove the curse of barrenness placed by a witch on
his family, must obtain Jack's cow, Little Red Riding
Hood's cape, Rapunzel's hair, and Cinderella's
slipper. All five stories are happily resolved at the
end of the first act, after which the second act explores the destructive consequences of their actions.
Into the Woods continued the trend of *Sunday*
in the Park towards stretches of near-continuous
music combining underscoring, songs (sometimes
very short), and gradual transitions. It proved accessible enough to enjoy the second-longest Broadway
run of any of Sondheim's shows (after *Forum*).

RECORDING   Peters, Gleason, Zien, Westenberg,
Gemignani, RCA, 1987
VIDEO   Peters, Gleason, Zien, Westenberg, Image
Entertainment, 1991
EDITION   v.s., Rilting, 1989

Assassins

Musical in one act (1h 45m)
Libretto by John Weidman
PREMIERES   27 January 1991, Playwrights Horizons, New
York; UK: 29 October 1992, Donmar Warehouse, London

Seen by fewer theatre-goers during its initial run than
any other Sondheim musical (at a limited subscription engagement at a very small off-Broadway
theatre), *Assassins* is also the most controversial of
Sondheim's shows. Its main characters are the
historical figures who have assassinated presidents
of the US (or tried to), and its format suggests a
revue while utilizing such typical styles of traditional
popular music as march, cakewalk, barbershop quartet, guitar ballad and hymn. The score departs from
the near-continuous musical texture of Sondheim's
previous two creations, instead alternating songs
and spoken scenes, sometimes with a framework
provided by a folksinging narrator. Some scenes are
re-creations of historical events; others allow figures
from different eras, such as John Wilkes Booth
and Lee Harvey Oswald, to interact. The resultant
merging of fantasy and jumbled chronology has an
appropriate resemblance to a nightmare.

RECORDING   Garber, Mann, Hadary, P. Cassidy,
Gemignani, RCA, 1991
EDITIONS   v.s., Music Theatre International (on hire); lib.,
Theatre Communications Group, 1991

Other musicals: *Anyone Can Whistle*, 1964; *The Frogs*, 1974
BIBLIOGRAPHY   Ethan Mordden, *Broadway Babies: The
People Who Made the American Musical*, OUP, 1983; Craig
Zadan, *Sondheim & Co.*, Harper and Row, 1974; 2nd edn,
1986

J.A.C.

FERNANDO SORS

Joseph Fernando Macari Sors [Sor]; *b* 13 February 1778,
Barcelona, Spain; *d* 10 July 1839, Paris

Acclaimed throughout Europe and Russia in his
day as a virtuoso guitarist, author of two standard
treatises on guitar-playing and composer for various
instruments and for orchestra, Sors achieved early
fame in his native Catalonia as an opera composer.
Telemaco nell'isola di Calipso, written when the
composer was aged 18 or 19, was staged 15 times in
Barcelona soon after its first performance there in
1797. In 1801 or 1802, he was commissioned by the
Duchess of Alba, while in her service in Madrid as
organist and music teacher, to write an opera, *Don
Trastulio*, completion of which was frustrated by the
duchess's death in 1802. Soon after, while in the
service of the Duke and Duchess of Medinaceli,
he also composed an operatic drama, *Elvira la
portuguesa*.

BIBLIOGRAPHY   Brian Jeffery, *Fernando Sor: Composer
and Guitarist*, Tecla Editions, 1977

J.W.S.

JOHN PHILIP SOUSA

b 6 November 1854, Washington DC, US; *d* 6 March 1932,
Reading, Pennsylvania, US

The American 'March King' was in fact of
Portuguese and Bavarian descent. Band practice
started early; his father was a member of the US
Marine Band and Sousa began there as an enlisted
apprentice. He also played the violin in and
conducted several touring operetta orchestras – one
of which included performances of an early,
unauthorized production of Sullivan's *HMS Pinafore*
– and was first violinist in Offenbach's orchestra in
Philadelphia for the 1876 centennial celebrations.
The influence of these two masters on Sousa is
unmistakable; his operettas even include a rehash of
Sullivan's *The Contrabandista*, *The Smugglers*. *El
Capitan* (1895) was a resounding success, thanks to
the performance of De Wolf Hopper and a very
snappy title march. If Sousa's operettas were written
as star vehicles, as most US operettas then were, the
stars were effective, and the vehicles were agreeably
European in styling. What makes them interesting
musically (and the reason for their occasional
revival) are their stirring martial sections.

Sousa's most successful period of operetta
composition was the 1890s, when his finest marches
were also composed – several were derived from his
theatre songs. In 1880, he was named conductor of
the US Marine Band, but real success came 12 years
later with the formation of his own band, which he
conducted for nearly 40 years and which frequently
played medleys based on his operettas.

Operettas: *Katherine*, 1879; *The Smugglers* (after Sullivan's
The Contrabandista), 1882; *Desirée*, 1884; *The Queen of*

Hearts, 1885; *The Wolf*, 1888; *The Devil's Deputy* (inc.), (1893); *El Capitan*, 1896; *The Bride Elect*, 1897; *The Charlatan*, 1898; *Chris and the Wonderful Lamp*, 1899; *The Free Lance*, 1906; *The American Maid*, 1909; *The Irish Dragoon*, 1915

BIBLIOGRAPHY   Paul E. Bierley, *John Philip Sousa: American Phenomenon*, Appleton-Century-Crofts, 1973

R.T.

NICOLA SPINELLI
b 29 July 1865, Turin, Italy; *d* 17 October 1909, Rome

Spinelli, composer, conductor and pianist, entered the Naples Conservatory in 1881 where his first opera, *I guanti gialli*, was his graduation exercise. His second opera, *Labilia*, finished second to Mascagni's *Cavalleria rusticana* in Sonzogno's first competition for one-act operas in 1889. Though *Labilia* was well received, it never won anything approaching the acclaim of Mascagni's work. However, Spinelli's third opera, *A basso porta* (1894), earned him an international reputation. A *verismo*-style work, it was one of the most successful of the many direct imitations of *Cavalleria rusticana* that proliferated in the 1890s, but it lacks the kind of melodic force and dramatic energy that has kept Mascagni's work on the stage. Spinelli began one further operatic project, *Trilogia di Dorina*, but it was left unfinished when he died.

BIBLIOGRAPHY   A. Colombani, *L'opera italiana nel secolo XIX*, Tipografia del Corriere della Sera, 1900

C.T.

LOUIS SPOHR
Ludewig [Ludwig] Spohr; *b* 5 April 1784, Brunswick; *d* 22 October 1859, Kassel

Spohr's importance in the development of German Romantic opera is far greater than the current neglect of his operas would suggest. Several were in the standard German repertoire during the 19th century and *Jessonda* held the stage until it was banned (because its plot centred on the liaison between a European and an Indian) by the Nazis. Spohr's reputation declined after his death, but his works – particularly his chamber music – are now being increasingly performed and recorded, though stagings of his operas remain rare.

Spohr showed an early interest in dramatic composition. As a child he attempted an opera on Weisse's *Kinderfreunde*, which he based on the pattern of Hiller's singspiels *Die Jagd* and *Lottchen am Hofe*. His musical education included several years as a violinist in the Brunswick theatre orchestra, where he became thoroughly familiar with the dramatic techniques of Cherubini and Mozart (who was to remain a strong influence throughout his life) as well as a host of other German and French opera composers. These influences are evident in his one-act singspiel *Die Prüfung* (1806), a sentimental piece in which the conflict between the ideas of the Enlightenment and of Romanticism are personified. Spohr was dissatisfied with it, however, and withdrew it after a single concert performance. Though his second opera, *Alruna* (1808), shows a considerable advance in technique and conception, the text had weaknesses, which Goethe insisted should be altered and, again unhappy with his music, Spohr withdrew the opera before the planned premiere.

Already established as a virtuoso violinist and conductor, during the next few years Spohr's reputation as a composer grew rapidly, and in 1810 he was commissioned to write *Der Zweikampf mit der Geliebten* for Hamburg. It enjoyed moderate success, but Spohr was convinced that he was capable of better things. Three years later, having moved to Vienna as orchesterdirektor at the Theater an der Wien, he composed *Faust*, in which, for the first time, his own distinctive characteristics as a dramatic composer were fully developed. Its innovative and forward-looking use of leitmotif was not lost on Weber, who conducted its premiere in 1816, and its expressive use of chromatic harmony foreshadows later developments in German opera.

Zemire und Azor (1818–19), written while he was director of the opera in Frankfurt, and especially *Jessonda* (1822–3), composed after he had taken up his position as kapellmeister at Kassel, established Spohr as one of the leading composers of German Romantic opera; many regarded him as seriously rivalling Weber. But his later operas, despite their fine musical qualities, did not play a significant part in furthering his reputation and, discouraged, Spohr turned his attention to other musical forms for over a decade. Then in 1843, perhaps prompted by Wagner's *Der fliegende Holländer*, which he had just conducted, he began work on his last opera, *Die Kreuzfahrer*. But, though it had a considerable success in Kassel, Berlin and elsewhere, the opera showed little progress since *Jessonda*, written over 20 years earlier, and Spohr found himself overtaken by the tide of developments which he himself had helped to initiate.

Faust
Originally Romantic opera in two acts
Rev. as grand opera in three acts (2h 30m)
Libretto by Joseph Carl Bernard
Composed 1813, rev. 1852
PREMIERES   1 September 1816, Prague; UK: 21 May 1840, Prince's Theatre, London; rev. version: 15 July 1852, Covent Garden, London
CAST   Faust *bar*, Mephistofeles *b*, Röschen *ms*, Franz *t*, Kunigunde *s*, Sir Gulf *b*, Count Hugo *t*, Wohlhaldt *t*, Wagner *t*, Kaylinger *bar*, Moor *b*, Sycorax *s*; *satb* chorus of townspeople, soldiers, demons, imprisoned women, witches, wedding guests
FULL ORCHESTRA

The libretto is based on various versions of the Faust legend, but was not influenced by the recently published first part of Goethe's *Faust*. The opera was premiered under Weber in Prague, while Spohr was in Italy, and by the 1820s *Faust* was being widely performed in other major theatres.

In 1851 Spohr agreed to turn *Faust* into a grand opera for performance in London. He retained the original music, but set the dialogue to music, divided the opera into three acts and composed a prelude to the third act; he also included 'Ich bin allein' from *Der Zweikampf* as an extra aria for Kunigunde. The new version was performed in many German theatres during the 1850s. Individual arias and duets were, on account of their melodic and harmonic richness, popular in the concert hall during the 19th century.

SYNOPSIS (revised version)

Act I Faust has made a compact with Mephistofeles, but believes that he can use his powers for good and outwit him. In reality he is the victim of his own passions; he wavers between his love for the pure Röschen and his lust for Countess Kunigunde, whom, with the aid of Mephistofeles, he has rescued from the clutches of a robber knight, Sir Gulf.

Act II From the witches on the Blocksberg Faust obtains a magic potion with which he plans to seduce Kunigunde. At the feast after her marriage to Count Hugo, Kunigunde consequently finds herself irresistibly attracted to Faust. When Hugo intervenes Faust kills him in a duel.

Act III Mephistofeles exults over Faust's impending damnation. Röschen, distressed by Faust's infidelity with Kunigunde, drowns herself and Faust himself is dragged off to hell by Mephistofeles's demons.

Faust is a significant landmark in the development of German Romantic opera. Spohr's concern to create scene complexes, rather than merely writing a string of individual numbers, points the way towards the continuity of his later operas. His striking use of chromatic harmony was a powerful influence on his contemporaries. The overture, which was described by Spohr as portraying Faust's inner conflict, introduces an important feature of the opera: the use of short musical motifs which, in Weber's words, 'hold it together artistically'. The principal motifs appear, together with other instances of thematic reminiscence, at various key points in the opera.

RECORDING Dean, Bryson, Winter, Hetherington, Ritchie, Winslade, Ch and O of University College, London, Fifield, 1986
EDITIONS f.s., Garland, 1990; v.ss., Peters, 1822; rev. version: Peters, 1854

Zemire und Azor

Romantic opera in two acts
Libretto by Johann Jakob Ihlee after Jean François Marmontel's comédie-ballet *Zémire et Azore* (1771)
Composed 1818–19
PREMIERES 4 April 1819, Frankfurt am Main; UK: 5 April 1831, Covent Garden, London

After moving to Frankfurt in 1817 Spohr considered several opera subjects. He started to compose a version of Apel's tale *Der schwarze Jäger* but abandoned it when he heard that Weber was writing an opera on the same story (*Der Freischütz*). *Zemire und Azor* is essentially the story of Beauty and the Beast.

The opera was well received and held a minor place in the 19th-century German repertoire. Individual numbers were frequently performed in the concert hall. The popularity of Zemire's *Romanze*, 'Rose wie bist du reizend und mild', continued into the 20th century and has been recorded by Joan Sutherland. As in *Faust* musical motif is used, but not so pervasively. It was revived in Kassel for the composer's bicentenary in 1984.

EDITION v.s., Cranz, [1823]

Jessonda

Grand opera in three acts, Op. 63 (2h 30m)
Libretto by Eduard Gehe, after the drama *La veuve de Malabar* by Antoine Lemierre (1770)
Composed 1822–3
PREMIERES 28 July 1823, Hoftheater, Kassel; UK: 18 June 1840, Prince's Theatre, London; US: 15 February 1864, Philadelphia
CAST Dandau *b*, Nadori *t*, Jessonda *s*, Amazili *s*, Pedro Lopes *t*, Tristan d'Achuna *bar*; *satb* chorus of Brahmins, Bayaderes, Portuguese and Indian soldiers, Indian people
FULL ORCHESTRA

During a visit to Paris in the winter of 1820–21 Spohr read Lemierre's drama. The following summer he drew up a rough scenario which he passed on to Gehe. He began work on the music shortly after taking up his post in Kassel. The premiere was successful and its Leipzig production in November 1823 was a triumph on a similar scale to that of *Der Freischütz*. By the end of the 1820s *Jessonda*, though never as universally popular as *Der Freischütz*, was a standard repertoire piece in Germany. It was staged in many other European countries and remained in the repertoire until the early 20th century.

SYNOPSIS

Act I The raja of Goa has just died and his young widow, Jessonda, is to be a suttee (sacrificed by burning). Dandau, the ruthless high priest, sends Nadori, a young Brahmin who abhors the priesthood, to take the message of death to Jessonda. Meanwhile a Portuguese army is advancing on the city. Delivering the message, Nadori is overcome by the beauty of Jessonda's sister, Amazili, and vows to help save Jessonda.

Act II The Portuguese general, Tristan, still grieves for his true love who mysteriously disappeared some years ago. When the Bayaderes bring Jessonda to the sacred stream for purification, Tristan recognizes her as his lost love; but having given his oath not to intervene with the religious ceremonies, he is forced to allow her to be taken away.

The Portuguese camp; design by Carlo Broschi for Jessonda *(Vienna, 1856)*

Act III Nadori informs Tristan that the Indians have broken the truce by attacking the Portuguese ships. A tempest is raging, and a colossal image of Brahma is struck by lightning. Believing that the god is angry, Dandau decides to expedite the sacrifice. But, guided by Nadori, the Portuguese storm the city in time to prevent it and the opera ends with the joyful union of Tristan with Jessonda and Nadori with Amazili.

Jessonda contains some of Spohr's most appealing music. After its London premiere, one critic declared, 'It is a tissue of the most lovely melodies and delicious combinations of harmony we ever heard', while another asserted, '*Jessonda* is not surpassed by any opera that we know, and it is equalled by very few.' It differs from Spohr's earlier operas in its extensive use of chorus and ballet and its replacement of spoken dialogue with recitative, making the music continuous throughout. Musical motif and reminiscence play a significant part in strengthening the opera's dramatic coherence. Its success was far greater than that of Weber's *Euryanthe*, and it remained the standard bearer of German grand opera until the advent of Wagner.

RECORDING Varady, T. Moser, Fischer-Dieskau, Moll, Hamburg State Opera Ch, Hamburg PO, Albrecht, Orfeo, 1990
EDITIONS f.s., Peters, 1881; *rp*, Garland, 1989; v.s., Peters, 1824

Other operatic works: *Die Prüfung*, 1806; *Alruna, die Eulenkönigin*, (1808); *Der Zweikampf mit der Geliebten*,

1811; *Der Berggeist*, 1825; *Pietro von Albano*, 1827; *Der Alchymist*, 1830; *Die Kreuzfahrer*, 1845
BIBLIOGRAPHY Clive Brown, *Louis Spohr: A Critical Biography*, CUP, 1984

C.A.B.

LUIGI SPONTINI

Gaspare Luigi Pacifico Spontini; *b* 14 November 1774, Maiolati; *d* 24 January 1851, Maiolati

Spontini played a vital part in the formation of early Romantic opera. He enjoyed his greatest success under Napoleon. Like many Italians he found France a propitious place to work, for although he had composed a dozen operas in Italy, mostly comedies, he made little impression as a composer until he won the patronage of the Empress Josephine in Paris. His career there began with three opéras comiques and then blossomed overnight with the appearance of *La vestale* in 1807. This was his masterpiece, and it caught the imagination of the times. Its simple plot and its strongly expressive musical language give it an important place in the development of French opera leading from the tradition of Gluck and Piccinni towards the styles of Berlioz and Meyerbeer.

Two years later he produced *Fernand Cortez*, in which a tendency towards spectacular staging is evident, perhaps reflecting the grandeur of Napoleonic ambition; and the same emphasis on scenic effect is found in the last of his Parisian operas, *Olimpie* of 1819. His centre of activity then moved to Berlin, as generalmusikdirektor to the King of Prussia, where his work never equalled the standard of his Parisian operas and he found himself embroiled in controversy. Politically conservative and inclined to touchiness, he was a difficult colleague. Yet Berlioz, to whom he was always generous in his support, declared that he loved Spontini; he was a widely respected figure, especially in France. Berlioz's early music owes much to Spontini, and Wagner too drew ideas freely from Spontini's scores.

He was advanced as an orchestrator, often trying new groupings, new effects, especially with mutes, and managing offstage bands with considerable care to create the illusion of distance. He was one of the first to use the metronome. He had an Italian's gift of melody but a Frenchman's care for the expressive projection of words. His operas contributed much to the increasing power required of leading singers, since they not only had to compete with a louder, larger orchestra, they were also expected to maintain a high level of intensity. His heroic tenors already belong to the modern type. Spontini exercised a powerful influence over the following generation, but his work did not survive beyond the end of the 19th century; revivals and recordings in modern times have been rare.

Milton

Opéra comique in one act
Libretto by Etienne de Jouy and A. M. Dieulafoy, a fait historique
PREMIERE 27 November 1804, Théâtre Feydeau, Paris

Milton was the most enduring of the three opéras comiques that opened Spontini's career in Paris. It concerns the poet Milton in his old age, now blind, and the efforts of William Davenant to restore Milton to Charles II's favour and to win the hand of Milton's daughter Emma for his son. Milton dictates *Paradise Lost* while his daughter accompanies herself on the harp. There is an unusual number of ensembles – a duet, a trio, a quartet, and a quintet with some adventurous scoring. Milton's 'Hymn to the Sun' foreshadows *La vestale*. Spontini converted the dialogue into recitatives for an Italian version.

RECORDING Devia, Savastano, Ciminelli, Micalucci, Milan Ch and SO of RAI, Paoletti, Voce, 1974

La vestale

The Vestal Virgin
Tragédie lyrique in three acts (2h 15m)
Libretto by Etienne de Jouy
Composed 1805
PREMIERES 15 December 1807, Opéra, Paris; US: 17 February 1828, Théâtre d'Orléans, New Orleans; UK: 9 June 1842, Covent Garden, London
CAST Licinius *t*, Cinna *t*, Julia *s*, High Priestess *ms*, Supreme Pontiff *b*, Chief Soothsayer *b*, *satb* chorus of vestal virgins, priests, matrons, young women, senators, consuls, lictors, warriors, gladiators, children, prisoners
FULL ORCHESTRA

La vestale was Spontini's first work for the Paris Opéra and his greatest success. It was accepted only through the intervention of the Empress Josephine. He had composed no opera in Italy or France that gave any foretaste of this modern brand of Gluckian serious opera, and it set a standard that was to be incorporated into French grand opera after the Napoleonic period. It remained in the repertoire during the first half of the 19th century and profoundly influenced both Berlioz and Wagner. The drama presents the classic conflict of love and duty in the person of Julia, the vestal virgin whose vows forbid her to yield to Licinius' passion.

Alexandrine Caroline Branchu (Julia) in La vestale *(Paris, 1807)*

SYNOPSIS

Act I Licinius, the victorious Roman general, confides to his friend Cinna that he cannot enjoy acclamation and honour since Julia, whose hand he has long sought to win, has been forced by her father to become a priestess of Vesta, sworn to chastity. Julia still loves Licinius, despite her vows, and it falls to her to place the crown of victory on Licinius' head. During the ceremony Licinius learns that Julia has to guard the sacred flame at night.

Act II Licinius visits the temple where Julia is on watch. In the excitement of passion they allow the flame to go out. With Cinna's help Licinius escapes, but Julia is stripped of her insignia and condemned to death, refusing to name the man who was with her.

Act III Licinius attempts to persuade the Supreme Pontiff to exercise his mercy, even admitting his part in Julia's guilt, but is rebuffed. Julia prepares to be entombed alive, when suddenly a storm breaks and a thunderbolt strikes the altar, relighting the sacred flame and proving Vesta's forgiveness. The lovers are reunited.

The tragédie has a happy ending but the emotional intensity of the opera, especially in Act II, is on a high dramatic level, worthy of a genuine tragedy. The scenes of solemnity and celebration are inherited from a long tradition in French opera, including Gluck, but the expressive intensity of Julia's music belongs truly to the new century. Its orchestration was considered noisy in its time, but it simply reflects the grandiose tastes of the Empire. In *La vestale* Spontini first revealed his striking gift for dramatic recitative, absorbing elements found in Gluck and Cherubini. The role of Julia, first sung by Madame Branchu, is particularly taxing in its high tessitura.

RECORDINGS 1. Callas, Stignani, Corelli, Ch and O of La Scala, Votto, Cetra, 1954; 2. Gencer, Mattiucci, Merolla, Bruson, Ch and O of Teatro Massimo di Palermo, Previtali, Nuova Era, 1969; 3. Plowright, Pasino, Araiza, Bavarian Radio Ch, Munich Radio O, Kuhn, Orfeo, 1992: an opera depending on its protagonist to succeed – as do Callas, Gencer and Plowright in their various ways [A.B.]
EDITION f.s., Philip Gossett and Charles Rosen (eds), facsimile of printed orchestral score, Garland, 1979

Fernand Cortez, ou La conquête du Méxique

Fernand Cortez, or The Conquest of Mexico
Tragédie lyrique in three acts
Libretto by Etienne de Jouy and J.-A. d'Esmenard, after the play by Alexis Piron (1744)
Composed 1808–9, rev. 1817 and 1832
PREMIERES 28 November 1809, Opéra, Paris; US: 6 January 1888, Metropolitan, New York
CAST Fernand Cortez *t*, Montézuma *b*, Telasco *t*, Amazily *s*, Alvar *a*, Mexican Officer *t*, High Priest *b*; *satb* chorus of prisoners, officers, Spanish soldiers
FULL ORCHESTRA

The subject of Cortez's conquest of Mexico is said to have been selected by Napoleon himself in order to symbolize his own planned conquest of Spain, and the success of *La vestale* made Spontini the obvious choice as composer. The plan backfired since the opera's message only emphasized the valour of the Spaniards as conquerors, and the performances were soon curtailed. A revised version was staged in 1817, and it remained in the repertoire until 1840. The staging of 1809 was particularly lavish, notorious for the introduction of horses on stage. These were supposed to amaze the audience just as they had astonished the Mexicans themselves.

SYNOPSIS
The Aztecs are portrayed as barbarous and fanatical, the Spaniards as Christian and noble.

Act I Montezuma, the Aztec king, interrupts the sacrifice of some Spanish prisoners and his nephew Telasco argues that they may serve as hostages with which to reclaim Amazily, his sister, now in Cortez's hands. Amazily, though, has fallen in love with Cortez and adopted his faith. When Cortez's approach is announced, she agrees to intercede on behalf of the Mexicans and seek peace.

Act II Cortez's soldiers are disgruntled, and despite elaborate overtures by the Aztecs Cortez refuses to be bought off with gold. Telasco is taken hostage. Cortez has the Spanish fleet set on fire to assert his determination never to abandon the conquest of Mexico.

Act III Cortez prepares for battle while Amazily secretly plans to avert the slaughter by surrendering herself to the Aztec priests. Just as Montezuma and Telasco prepare for Cortez's onslaught Amazily arrives and proclaims a general peace.

This gives an outline of the opera after its 1817 revision; in the original version there is no Montezuma and Amazily is not in love with Cortez. Despite the changes the libretto is still seriously flawed and personal motivation is never clear. The opera was designed as a spectacle, and its success rested on the scuttling of the ships, the scenes of battle and celebration, the entry of the horses, the marches and the colourful Aztec ceremonies as much as on its opportunities for fine singing. The music rises occasionally to the heights of *La vestale*, but it has a certain inertia and scenic effects often distract. In the first version there was a stronger epic dimension and less personal conflict. Cortez is heroic and magnanimous, and Montezuma is the perfect noble savage. The role of Amazily, like Julia in *La vestale*, was sung by Madame Branchu, but is a rather less taxing role than that of Julia.

RECORDING Gulin, Prevedi, Bottion, Blancas, Turin Ch and SO of RAI, von Matačić, MRF, 1974
EDITION f.s., Philip Gossett and Charles Rosen (eds), facsimile, Garland, 1980

Olimpie

Olimpia
Tragédie lyrique in three acts (2h 45m)
Libretto by A.-M. Dieulafoy and C. Brifaut, after the tragedy by Voltaire (1762)
Composed 1815–19, rev. 1820 and 1826
PREMIERE 22 December 1819, Opéra, Paris
CAST Cassandre *t*, Antigone *b*, Statira *s*, Olimpie *s*, L'Hiérophante *b*, Hermas *silent*; *satb* chorus of priests, priestesses, warriors, soldiers
FULL ORCHESTRA onstage band

Like *Fernand Cortez*, *Olimpie* was intended as a spectacular opera, although it was not a success in Paris in 1819. Spontini then moved to Berlin and put it on there (with E. T. A. Hoffmann's help). Of all Spontini's operas it contains the most formal pageantry. The play on which it is based had an old-fashioned ring in 1819, since the librettists had not strayed far from Voltaire's text and had preserved many of his alexandrines intact.

SYNOPSIS
Act I After the death of Alexander the Great his empire is disputed by Cassandre, King of Macedonia, and Antigone, King of Asia. Efforts at making peace are hindered by the two kings' love of Amenais, a young priestess. Amenais is in fact Olimpie, Alexander's lost daughter, and the priestess who is to

marry her to Cassandre is in fact Statira, Alexander's widow, both in disguise. The wedding is disrupted when Statira denounces Cassandre as Alexander's murderer.

Act II Olimpie and Statira recognize each other, and Olimpie says that Cassandre saved her life many years ago. Statira is still bent on revenge, however.

Act III Olimpie is torn between her love of Cassandre and her duty to her mother. Cassandre's and Antigone's forces do battle and Antigone is mortally wounded. He confesses that he, not Cassandre, killed Alexander. Thus Cassandre is vindicated and he and Olimpie are united.

The predominance of festive, noisy music in *Olimpie* obscures the high quality of much of the score, with its expressive recitative and excellent ensembles. The orchestration is inventive, with special muting effects and much percussion. There is a touching duet in Act II for mother and daughter, and the role of Cassandre is the type of heroic tenor now established as the principal male lead in romantic opera. The constant use of disguise and the world of high priests and sacred vows smacked too strongly of 18th-century opera, and *Olimpie* was never the same success as its two brothers, even though Berlioz described it as 'a sublime work, in every way worthy of the composer of *La vestale*'. The closing ceremonial scene is of extraordinary length and splendour; Cassandre is directed to enter on an elephant, and in the Berlin production in 1821 he did so.

RECORDING Varady, Toczyska, Tagliavini, Fischer-Dieskau, Ch of the Deutsche Oper, Berlin SO, Albrecht, Orfeo, 1987
EDITION f.s., Philip Gossett and Charles Rosen (eds), facsimile, Garland, 1980

Nurmahal, oder Das Rosenfest von Caschmir

Nurmahal, or The Rose Festival of Cashmir
Lyrisches drama in two acts
Libretto by Carl Alexander Herklotz, after Thomas Moore's *Lalla Rookh* (1817)
PREMIERE 27 May 1822, Königliches Opernhaus, Berlin

Nurmahal has the character of a fairy opera-ballet and it used material written the year before for a ballet on *Lalla Rookh*, as well as music composed for a revival of Salieri's *Les danaïdes* in 1817. The atmosphere is comparable to that of Weber's *Oberon*, but the music is not of that order, nor does it claim comparison with Spontini's three great Paris works.

EDITION v.s., Schlesinger, 1823

Alcidor

Zauberoper in three acts
Libretto by Emmanuel Guillaume Marguérite Théaulon de Lambert, after Rochon de Chabannes's *Alcindor* (1787), translated into German by Carl Alexander Herklotz
PREMIERE 23 May 1825, Berlin

Composed for the marriage of Louise, the King of Prussia's third daughter, and Prince Frederick of the Netherlands, *Alcidor* allowed some attractive staging and costumes but its music was never much admired. There are some good choruses and a canon trio, and it begins with a chorus of gnomes accompanied by tuned anvils.

AUTOGRAPH MANUSCRIPT Bibliothèque, Musée de l'Opéra, Paris

Agnes von Hohenstaufen

Historisch-romantisch oper in three acts (2h 15m)
Libretto by S. B. E. Raupach
PREMIERE 12 June 1829, Königliches Opernhaus, Berlin

Although originally planned as a 'lyrical drama' in two acts, *Agnes von Hohenstaufen* became a grand historical opera in three acts, and it was revised again in 1837. It has a medieval subject and belongs to the German tradition that runs from *Euryanthe* to *Rienzi* and *Tannhäuser*. Spontini's invention is much richer than in his previous two, lighter operas, with large ensembles and continuous action. There is some kinship with the Scribe type of French grand opera, and the work was much admired by Wagner.

RECORDING Caballé, Stella, Prevedi, Guelfi, Bruscantini, Rome Ch and SO of RAI, Muti, Myto, 1970

Other operas: *I puntigli delle donne*, 1796; *Adelina Senese, o sia L'amore secreto*, 1797; *L'eroismo ridicolo*, 1798; *Il Teseo riconosciuto*, 1798; *La finta filosofa*, 1799; *La fuga in maschera*, 1800; *Gli Elisi delusi*, 1800; *La petite maison*, 1804; *Julie, ou Le pot de fleurs*, 1805; *Pélage, ou Le roi et la paix*, 1814; *Les dieux rivaux, ou Les fêtes de Cythère*, 1816; 4 lost operas
BIBLIOGRAPHY Gerald Abraham, 'The Best of Spontini', *ML*, vol. 23 (1942), p. 163; Charles Bouvet, *Spontini*, Rieder, 1930; Gerald Abraham (ed.), *New Oxford History of Music*, vol. 8: *The Age of Beethoven*, OUP, 1982
AUTOGRAPH MANUSCRIPT Bibliothèque, Musée de l'Opéra, Paris

H.M.

SIGMUND STADEN

Sigmund Theophil Staden; *baptized* 6 November 1607, Kulmbach; *buried* 30 July 1655, Nuremberg

Staden is remembered today for *Seelewig*, his only complete stage work and the oldest surviving German opera. He received his musical grounding from his father, a composer of sacred vocal works, and after mastering several instruments was employed by the Nuremberg authorities as a city instrumentalist. He remained in the city throughout his life, organizing civic musical events and composing. His output consists largely of secular vocal music, although he is known to have written one oratorio and also contributed incidental music for religious plays.

Seelewig

Full title: *Die geistliche Waldgedicht, oder Freudenspiel, genant Seelewig, Gesangsweis auf Italienische Art gesetzet* The Soul (*The Sacred Forest Poem, or Play of Gladness, called The Soul, set vocally in the Italian manner*)
Spiritual pastorale in a prologue and three acts
Libretto by Georg Philipp Harsdorffer
PREMIERE 1644, Nuremberg

Harsdorffer, the librettist of *Seelewig*, founded an academy known as the Shepherds of the Pegnitz. This society advocated the purification of the German language and, in attempting to arrive at their own aesthetic concerning opera, vigorously debated varying views of dramatic genres from antiquity to contemporary theatre. Harsdorffer sought to synthesize the different arts in *Seelewig*, whose text and music he published interspersed with extensive didactic commentary in his *Frauenzimmer Gesprechspiele*, a popular periodical of the day.

In his attempt to win over the nymph Seelewig (Soul), Trugewald enlists another nymph, Sinnigunda (Sensuousness), and three shepherds, Kunsteling (Artifice), Reichmut (Wealth) and Ehrelob (Power). However, Gwissulda (Conscience) and Herzigilde (Wisdom) help the virtuous Seelewig to triumph in the end.

Staden's setting is remarkable in its use of both poetry and music to advance the drama. The composer drew upon rhyme scheme, metre, rhythm, tempo, melodic patterns, the use of choruses and independent instrumental pieces, and scoring to portray the allegorical characters in this 'spiritual pastoral'. The most striking association between character and its instrumental counterpart is that of the villain, a devious satyr named Trugewald, with the 'grosses Horn'. Modelled on the school dramas of the 16th and 17th centuries, *Seelewig* contains numerous strophic songs with typically German syllabic text setting. A symphony introduces each act, and Acts II and III both conclude with a chorus.

EDITION originally printed in Harsdorffer's *Frauenzimmer Gesprechspiele*, vol. 4 (1644); *rp* as v.s. in vol. 13 of *Monatshefte für Musik-Geschichte* (1881)

An engraving of a scene from Seelewig *(Nuremberg, 1644)*

BIBLIOGRAPHY Ellen T. Harris, *Handel and the Pastoral Tradition*, OUP, 1980, 'The Pastoral in Germany' (chapter 3), pp. 58–70

J.D.A.

NICHOLAS STAGGINS

d 13 June 1700, Windsor, Berkshire, England

The son of Isaac Staggins, a London wait and a court musician, Nicholas obtained his own place in the Restoration Twenty-four Violins in 1671. In 1673 or 1674 he unexpectedly became the Master of the King's Musick in place of the Catholic Louis Grabu, a victim of the recent Test Act. His first major task, in the spring of 1675, was to compose and direct the music for the lavish court production of *Calisto*. In 1676–7 Staggins was sent to study abroad, probably as part of Charles II's continuing attempts to bring opera to England; in 1683 he collaborated with John Blow in a project to establish an opera house in London, though it came to nothing. Staggins apparently owed his position as Master of the Musick under successive monarchs to his abilities as an administrator and musical director; his music seems trivial, though too much of it is lost for a proper assessment to be made.

Calisto

Play with operatic episodes
Text by John Crowne
PREMIERE 15 February 1675, Hall Theatre, Whitehall

Although called an opera at the time, *Calisto* is a lively play based on Ovid's tale of Jupiter's attempt to seduce the virtuous nymph by disguising himself as Diana, goddess of chastity. Staggins's music is confined mainly to episodes at the end of each act; about half of it survives, scattered in manuscripts in England, Eire and the US. Detailed information on the production is contained in court documents; much of it throws light on more significant works by Locke, Blow and Purcell.

BIBLIOGRAPHY Eleanore Boswell, *The Restoration Court Stage (1660–1702)*, Harvard University Press, 1932; George Allen and Unwin, *rp* 1966

P.H.

J. C. STANDFUSS

Johann C. Standfuss; *d* after *c*. 1759, ?Hamburg

Standfuss occupies a significant niche in musical history with his music for *Der Teufel ist los, oder Die verwandelten Weiber*, the prototype of the new German singspiel – a comic opera with spoken dialogue. The origin of the work was a one-act 'ballad farce' (similar to *The Beggar's Opera*) by Charles Coffey, entitled *The Devil to Pay, or The*

Wives Metamorphos'd (1731), with music provided by Seedo, the musical director at Drury Lane.

Subsequently, two German versions of the play appeared. One, by C. V. von Borck (a former Prussian ambassador to London), was presented in Berlin in 1743; and the other, by C. F. Weisse, provided the basis for Standfuss's setting, which was successfully performed in Leipzig in 1752 by G. H. Koch's company, for whom Standfuss was working as violinist and vocal coach. Despite objections about the dubious propriety of the form, the comic singspiel flourished. Standfuss produced two further examples in 1759, including a sequel to *Der Teufel ist los*. J. A. Hiller's enlarged version of the Standfuss comedy (1766) was the starting point for his own distinguished series of singspiels.

Operatic works: *Der Teufel ist los, oder Die verwandelten Weiber*, 1752; *Der lustige Schuster*, 1759; one lost singspiel
BIBLIOGRAPHY Thomas Bauman, *North German Opera in the Age of Goethe*, CUP, 1985

B.S.

CHARLES VILLIERS STANFORD

(Sir) Charles Villiers Stanford; *b* 30 September 1852, Dublin; *d* 29 March 1924, London

Although Stanford's name is often linked with that of Hubert Parry, mainly because they both taught at the Royal College of Music and wrote a number of oratorios, they were very different composers. Both had an academic education but in their musical outlook Stanford was the conservative, Parry the radical. Stanford studied in Leipzig with Reinecke in the 1870s. He showed more interest in opera than most of his contemporaries but realized the hopelessness of pursuing this line in Britain. Because of his connections with the Continent (where he was the friend of many musicians, including Brahms), he took his first opera, *The Veiled Prophet of Khorassan*, to the director of the Frankfurt Opera. But the first performance was given in Hanover, where the director had moved. Performances followed throughout Germany.

Stanford's second opera, *Savonarola*, was premiered in Hamburg (1884). After its single London performance under Hans Richter three months later, Stanford wrote: 'I scarcely recognized the opera I had seen in Hamburg.' Obstacles to a good performance had been created by the publisher, who was involved in a lawsuit over performing rights. While Professor of Composition at the Royal College of Music (1883–1924), Stanford encouraged opera and conducted many student performances.

Sadly his operas are rarely performed today, although his Shakespearean adaptation *Much Ado About Nothing* has much to commend it and a comparable case can be made for revival of *The Critic*, based on Sheridan's play. Stanford's gift for melody, as can be heard in his songs and such famous works as *Songs of the Fleet*, is fresh and lyrical and he was a deft, if unadventurous, orchestrator.

Operas: *The Veiled Prophet of Khorassan*, 1881; *Savonarola*, 1884; *The Canterbury Pilgrims*, 1884; *The Miner of Falun*, (1888); *Lorenza*, (1894); *Shamus O'Brien*, 1896; *Christopher Patch (The Barber of Bath)*, (1897); *Much Ado About Nothing (The Marriage of Hero)*, 1901; *The Critic (An Opera Rehearsed)*, 1916; *The Travelling Companion*, (1919), 1925
BIBLIOGRAPHY H. Plunket Greene, *Charles Villiers Stanford*, Arnold, 1935

M.K.

JOHN STANLEY

b 17 January 1712, London; *d* 19 May 1786, London

Stanley is an enigmatic figure: he may have been blind but is more likely to have been partially sighted; he may have set Henry Carey's *Teraminta* though this has also been ascribed to J. C. Smith. His incidental music to Hawkesworth's adaptation of Southerne's *Oroonoko* (1759) does not survive, nor does his setting of the stage masque *The Tears and Triumphs of Parnassus*, which commemorated the death of George II. But his dramatic pastoral *Arcadia, or The Shepherd's Wedding* (1761), a celebration of George III's marriage, reveals that he could command the lively *galant* style of his *Six Concertos in Seven Parts* (1742) when writing for the stage, even if he could not overcome the problems posed by Robert Lloyd's wooden libretto. Nevertheless, his real interest was in solo cantatas, oratorio, and instrumental music, along with the court odes he composed after his appointment as Master of the King's Musick in 1779.

BIBLIOGRAPHY Roger Fiske, *English Theatre Music in the Eighteenth Century*, OUP, 1973, 2nd edn, 1986; A. G. Williams, 'Stanley, Smith and Teraminta', *ML*, vol. 60 (1979), p. 312

R.Lu.

ROMAN STATKOWSKI

b 5 January 1859, Szczypiórno, near Kalisz; *d* 12 November 1925, Warsaw

A late developer, Statkowski studied in Warsaw with Żeleński and at the St Petersburg Conservatory with Solovyov and Rubinstein, completing his studies in 1890. He was influenced by Russian and German music, and the bulk of his work is instrumental. Although he wrote only two operas, they are the major successes of his early maturity. *Philaenis* won the International Opera Competition in London in 1903, and *Maria* the Warsaw Opera Competition in 1904. The operas occupy a place between those of Moniuszko and Szymanowski. They are Wagnerian in structure, with no separate numbers, leitmotifs, and duets in dialogue form. But the musical language is more traditional, dominated by *cantabile* melody with a Polish folk colouring, especially in the case of *Maria*. Its overture is often played in Poland as a separate concert piece.

BIBLIOGRAPHY J. W. Reiss, *Statkowski–Melcer–Młynarski–Stojowski*, Warsaw, 1949

Z.C.

JAN STEFANI

b 1746, Prague; *d* 24 February 1829, Warsaw

Stefani's *The Supposed Miracle* was the most popular Polish opera of the early 19th century. After studying in Italy, Stefani worked as conductor and violinist for the court orchestra in Vienna and from 1779 at the court in Warsaw as well as in churches and at the opera house. His own operas sprang directly from this last connection. They are vaudeville-like works, with songs rather than arias, which assign a limited role to a small orchestra. The only one to have survived complete is *The Supposed Miracle*, which is still performed in Poland. Stefani also wrote a ballet, cantatas, Masses, a large number of orchestral polonaises, chamber and piano music, but most of his music is lost.

Operas: *Król w kraju rozkoszy* (*The King of Cockaigne*), 1787; *Cud mniemany, czyli Krakowiacy i Górale* (*The Supposed Miracle, or Krakovians and Highlanders*), 1794; *Wdzięczni poddani Panu, czyli Wiejskie wesele* (*Thankful Serfs, or The Country Wedding*), 1796; *Drzewo zaczarowane* (*The Magic Tree*), 1796; *Frozyna, czyli Siedem razy jedna* (*Frozine, or Seven Times Dressed Up*), 1806; *Rotmistrz Górecki, czyli oswobodzenie* (*Captain Górecki, or The Liberation*), 1807; *Polka, czyli oblężenie Trembowli* (*The Polish Woman, or The Siege of Trembowla*), 1807; *Stary myśliwy* (*The Old Huntsman*), 1808; *Papirus, czyli ciekawość dawnych kobiet* (*Papyrus, or The Curiosity of Women in Ancient Times*), 1808

BIBLIOGRAPHY A. Nowak-Romanowicz, 'Muzyka polskiego Oświecenia i wczesnego Romantyzmu' ('The Music of Enlightenment and Early Romanticism in Poland'), in *Z dziejów polskiej kultury muzycznej*, vol. 2, Polskie Wydawnictwo Muzyczne, 1966

Z.C.

AGOSTINO STEFFANI

Agostino Steffani [Staffani, Steffano, Stefani, Stephani]; *b* 25 July, 1643, Castelfranco Véneto, Venice; *d* 12 February 1728, Frankfurt

Steffani was not only a composer, but also a churchman and a distinguished diplomat. Today he is remembered principally for his chamber duets, which had a strong influence on Handel. His operas reveal a highly developed dramatic sense, great lyric gifts, an exceptional ear for orchestral colour, and a striking skill for inventive harmonic line.

Steffani was brought to Munich in 1667 where he was to serve at the Electoral Court for 21 years. In 1672 he went to Rome for further study, under

Ercole Bernabei, returning to Munich in 1674. By 1678 he had been appointed Court and Chamber organist. A year after the accession of Maximilian II Emanuel he was made Director of Chamber Music (1681) and by 1688 he had supplied the Munich Court Theatre with five operas. He left Munich in that year, presumably because, with Bernabei firmly entrenched at court, he saw no chance of advancement. He obtained employment readily at the court of Duke Ernst August of Hanover, where he remained for 15 years, and wrote eight operas. In 1703 he moved to Düsseldorf, serving the Elector Johann Wilhelm for 6 years. He produced three operas (two completely new ones, and an earlier one dating from his Hanover period). In 1709 he returned to Hanover, where he remained for the rest of his life, absenting himself only on short trips. In 1727 he went to London where he had been elected President of the Academy of Vocal Music. His health was failing, and on his way from London to Italy he stopped at Frankfurt, where he suffered a stroke and died.

Niobe, regina di Tebe

Niobe, Queen of Thebes
Dramma per musica in three acts (4h 15m)
Libretto by Luigi Orlandi, after Book VI of Ovid's *Metamorphoses*
PREMIERES 5 January 1688, Hoftheater, Munich: modern revivals: 31 August 1977, Teatro Accademico Castelfranco Véneto; US: 9 November 1977, Alice Tully Hall, New York (concert)

The opera relates the story of Niobe, wife of Anfione (Amphion) ruler of Thebes, and beloved of Clearte. In her arrogance she overturns statues of the goddess Latona (Leto), demanding that her own children be proclaimed gods: instead, they are struck down by thunderbolts and Niobe herself is turned to stone. Orlandi manufactured the motivation of Creonte and Polifermo for their attack on Thebes – involving Creonte's abduction (disguised as Mars) of Niobe. He also invented the love story of Tiberino and Manto, daughter of the seer Tiresias (Teiresias) and the figure of Clearte.

The opera was composed for the opening of the remodelled Munich Hoftheater, and was presumably designed to show off all of its newest theatrical possibilities. The machinery of the theatre must have been remarkable. There are earthquakes, thunderbolts, clouds descending, transformations, dragons ascending, stones flying through the air and planets moving in harmonic procession across the sky.

RECORDING Zornig, Bonazzi, Belling, Collins, Murcell, Antonio Vivaldi O of Venice, Jenkins, Voce, 1977
EDITIONS manuscript score and parts, N. Jenkins (ed.), unpublished; sinfonia, eight arias with recitatives, one accompanied recitative, ed., in *DTB*, vol. 23

Le rivali concordi (Atalanta)

The Rivals Agreed (Atalanta)
Drama in a prologue and three acts (3h 30m)
Libretto by Ortensio Mauro

PREMIERES 20 February 1692, Schlosstheater, Hanover;
US: 7 May 1987, Alice Tully Hall, New York (concert)

Le rivali concordi was the fifth of eight operas that
Steffani wrote to texts by Mauro for Hanover, where
Duke Ernst August boasted a fine French orchestra
and leading Italian singers. The story is loosely based
on Greek mythology.

King Meleager of Calydon has offended the
goddess Diana. In revenge she has sent a boar to
devastate the countryside and cause famine.
Meleager's friends, Theseus, Jason and the Arcadian
huntress Atalanta, help him to slay the beast, and he
offers its head as a prize to Atalanta. Jason and
Theseus are furious, and plot to overthrow Meleager.
The story is further complicated by the fact that both
Jason and Theseus are in love with Atalanta. Their
respective wives, Medea and Ariadne, intervene to
frustrate their plans. Jason and Theseus eventually
succeed in defeating Meleager but, as they argue
over who shall have the huntress's hand, their wives
appear and Atalanta is left with Meleager, as she
always wanted.

The comedy was a success, with performances in
Hamburg (1698) and Stuttgart (1699 and 1701), both
in German. As with *Niobe* this score is written in the
French style. There is extensive use of dance forms
and movements throughout, indicating that ballet
played an important role.

EDITIONS manuscript score and parts, N. Jenkins (ed.),
unpublished; facsimile *rp*, Howard Mayer Brown and Eric
Eiers (eds), Garland, 1978

La libertà contenta
The Joy of Freedom
Drama in three acts (3h)
Libretto by Ortensio Mauro
PREMIERES 3 February 1693, Schlosstheater, Hanover; US:
31 October 1979, Alice Tully Hall, New York (concert)

This opera is peripherally associated with the so-
called Königsmark Affair. Count Phillipp Christoph
Königsmark, a Swedish aristocrat, the alleged lover
of Sophia Dorothea, wife of the Elector George of
Hanover (later King George I of England) assisted
her in one or two futile attempts to escape from
Hanover. Königsmark was seized and mysteriously
disappeared one year after the premiere of this
opera. The princess was known to have communicated her feelings to him in quotations from
La libertà contenta, whose very title she felt revealed
her plight. One quotation was taken from an aria in
Act III in which Timea sings, 'Whom should I love?
Should I rule with a king or suffer without a lover?'

The plot deals with the amorous escapades of five
men and two women. Princess Timea, engaged to
King Agi of Sparta, is also loved by both Alcibiade
and Lisandro. Aspasia, an Athenian betrothed to
Pericle, is the object of three men – King Agi,
Alcibiade and the philosopher Telamide. Aspasia and
Pericle are disguised as slaves. The principal figure is
Alcibiade, exiled from Athens for profligacy, and
unable to make up his mind which lady to marry. At
the end of the opera Agi announces that freedom's

joy is worth more than a kingdom. The garden scene
in Act II is a worthy precursor of the finale of the last
act of Mozart's *Figaro*. The opera was highly popular
in its day; it was later presented in German in
Hamburg, Stuttgart and Brunswick.

RECORDING Zornig, Fortunato, Hardesty, White, Aler,
Glaze, Murcell, Clarion Concerts O, Jenkins, Voce, 1970s
EDITIONS manuscript score and parts, N. Jenkins (ed.),
unpublished; overture and dance music in *Sonate da Camera*,
Amsterdam, *c*. 1705; duet in *Meslanges de musique latine,
française et italienne*, Paris, 1725; overture and two arias, ed.,
in *DTB*, vol. 23

Amor vien dal destino (Il Turno)
Love Comes from Destiny
Drama in a prologue and three acts (4h 15m)
Libretto by ?Ortensio Mauro
PREMIERES January 1709, Düsseldorf; US: 13 January
1982, Alice Tully Hall, New York (concert)

Although composed in 1694 during Steffani's
Hanover period, there exists no proof of a production at that time. This opera, one of Steffani's
richest scores, is one of three Steffani composed
for Düsseldorf and one of two staged for the
celebrations surrounding the elevation of Johann
Wilhelm of the Palatinate to the electoral honour in
Bavaria.

Lavinia, daughter of Latino (Latinus) is betrothed
to Turno (Turnus), a Latian prince, but loves
Aeneas. Her sister, Giuturna, loves Turno, who,
however, is determined to marry Lavinia. In a
complicated plot, Giuturna disguises herself as her
sister in order to be abducted by Turno. Latino
learns from his father, the forest god Fauno
(Faunus), that the union of Aeneas and Lavinia will
produce the Roman nation. Turno is defeated by
Aeneas, who spares his rival's life. All ends happily
as Turno accepts Giuturna's hand.

EDITIONS manuscript score and parts, N. Jenkins (ed.),
unpublished; introduction and five arias with recitatives, ed.,
in *DTB*, vol. 23

Tassilone
Tragedia per musica in five acts (4h)
Libretto by Stefano Benedetto Pallavicini
PREMIERES January 1709, Corte Elettorale Palatina,
Düsseldorf; US: 13 November 1973, Alice Tully Hall, New
York (concert)

Tassilone was the chief opera produced in Düsseldorf
in honour of the Elector Johann Wilhelm (see *Amor
vien dal destino*, above). The subject matter of the
opera, while dealing with events during the reign of
Charlemagne, reflects the political situation at the
Bavarian and Palatinate courts during the War of
the Spanish Succession, with the German Emperor
Joseph I represented as Charlemagne, Max Emanuel
of Bavaria as Tassilone (Tassilo), and Johann Wilhelm as Gheroldo. Although the events in each
case are not completely analogous, there is sufficient
similarity for parallels to be drawn. Pallavicini, as
secretary to Johann Wilhelm, surely had privy

knowledge of the Elector's political plans, and his scholarship and historical knowledge did the rest.

Tassilone, wedded to Gismonda, is under indictment for treason against the Emperor Charlemagne. He demands the right to a duel of divine judgement with the Emperor's champion. There are two possible champions: Gheroldo, Prince of Swabia, in love with the Emperor's daughter Rotrude, and Sigardo, who loves Rotrude's sister Teodata. Teodata is suspicious that Sigardo may also be courting Gismonda and reveals this to Tassilone, who swears revenge. In the duel against Sigardo, Tassilone is victorious but, on confronting Gismonda with her infidelity, his suspicions are proved wrong and he dies in her arms. Gheroldo finally wins Rotrude's hand, and the opera ends with a chorus of praise to virtue.

RECORDING Zornig, von Reichenbach, Bonazzi, Messana, Collins, White, Johnson, Corrado, Murcell, Antonio Vivaldi O of Venice, Jenkins, Città di Castelfranco, 1975: somewhat cut
EDITIONS f.s., Gerhard Croll (ed.), *Denkmäler Rheinischer Musik*, band 8, Musikverlag Schwann, 1958; five arias, ed., in *DTB*, vol. 23

Other operatic works: *Marco Aurelio*, 1681; *Servio Tullio*, 1686; *Alarico il Baltha*, 1687; *Henrico Leone*, 1689; *La lotta d'Hercole con Achelao* (divertimento drammatico), 1689; *La superbia d'Alessandro*, 1690; *Orlando Generoso*, 1691; *Baccanali*, 1695; *I trionfi del fato (Enea in Italia)*, 1695; *Briseide*, 1696; *Arminio*, 1707; 2 lost operas
BIBLIOGRAPHY G. Croll, *Agostino Steffani (1654–1728): Studien zur Biographie, Bibliographie der Opern und Turnierspiele*, dissertation, University of Munster, 1960

N.J.

CARL DAVID STEGMANN
b 1751, Stauchsa, nr Meissen; *d* 27 May 1826, Bonn

Stegmann's diverse talents enabled him to pursue parallel careers as a singer, actor, conductor, harpsichordist and composer. Following musical study at Dresden, he became renowned for his performances of tenor operatic roles, including an appearance in the first German version of Mozart's *Don Giovanni* at Mainz in 1789. But he also found success through the brilliance of his keyboard-playing, and the German operas he composed for the theatrical troupes to which he was attached, at Breslau, Königsberg, Danzig and elsewhere. His principal operatic achievement was the allegorical singspiel *Heinrich der Löwe*, written to commemorate the coronation of the Emperor Franz II in 1792. Richly scored and skilfully organized, it reflects his close knowledge of the operas of Gluck and Mozart and displays interesting anticipations of the use of leitmotif as a means of achieving dramatic unity.

Operatic works: *Der Kaufmann von Smirna*, 1773; *Der Deserteur*, 1775; *Die Rekruten auf dem Lande*, 1775; *Das redende Gemählde*, 1775; *Sultan Wampum, oder Die*

Wünsche, 1791; *Heinrich der Löwe*, 1792; *Der Triumph der Liebe, oder Das kühne Abentheuer*, 1796; *Die Roseninsel*, 1806; one lost opera
BIBLIOGRAPHY E. Metzel, 'Karl David Stegmann: aus dem Leben eines Bühnenkünstlers des 18. Jahrhunderts', *Archiv für Theatergeschichte*, vol. 1, Berlin, 1904, p. 129

B.S.

DANIEL STEIBELT
b 22 October 1765, Berlin; *d* 20 September 1823, St Petersburg

A brilliant pianist and composer, Steibelt had a mixed reputation. He deserted from the Prussian army in 1784, and settled in Paris from 1790. From there he travelled to many parts of Europe, rapidly establishing a reputation for the showy, colourful type of piano music in which he excelled. His first opera was a setting of a libretto by J. A. P. de Ségur based on Shakespeare's *Romeo and Juliet*. Rejected by the Paris Opéra, it was redesigned with spoken dialogue in place of the original recitative and eventually produced with considerable success at the Théâtre Feydeau. He had to leave Paris temporarily because of financial problems and travelled to London where he produced a pasticcio opera, *Albert and Adelaide* (1798). On his return to Paris he directed (in the presence of Napoleon) one of the earliest performances of Haydn's *The Creation*. In 1808, under pressure from his creditors in Paris, Steibelt moved to St Petersburg where he remained for the rest of his life, as director of the Opéra Français and, eventually, as maître de chapelle to the tsar. During this period he composed his last three piano concertos and several stage works, including the notable three-act opera, *Cendrillon*.

Operatic works: *Roméo et Juliette*, 1793; *Albert and Adelaide*, 1798; *La fête de Mars*, 1806; *La princesse de Babylone*, 1812; *Sargines*, c. 1810; *Les folies amoureuses*, c. 1810; *Cendrillon*, 1810; *Le jugement de Midas* (inc.), c. 1823
BIBLIOGRAPHY K. A. Hagberg, *Daniel Steibelt's Cendrillon: A Critical Edition with Notes on Steibelt's Life and Works*, dissertation, Eastman School of Music, 1975; E. Prout, 'Some Forgotten Operas, III: Steibelt's *Roméo et Juliette*', *MMR*, vol. 34 (1904), nos 9–11

B.S.

WILHELM STENHAMMAR
Karl Wilhelm Eugen Stenhammar; *b* 7 February 1871, Stockholm; *d* 20 November 1927, Stockholm

Stenhammar was undoubtedly the most important Swedish composer after Berwald. He occupied a rather similar position in Sweden to Elgar in the UK. He came from a musical family: his father was himself a composer of sorts but died when Wilhelm was only four. After his studies in Stockholm, Stenhammar went to Berlin in the 1890s, where he made something of a name for himself – he gave the first performance of his own First Piano Concerto in

Berlin with Richard Strauss conducting, and his overture *Excelsior* was premiered by Hans Richter and the Berlin Philharmonic.

Stenhammar's early music was much influenced by both Brahms and Wagner. Wagner's influence is most striking in the orchestral song *Florez och Blanzeflor* (*Flower and Whiteflower*) and the opera *Tirfing* (1897–8). During the first decade of the century, he was much in demand as a conductor both of the Gothenburg Symphony Orchestra (1906–22) and the Royal Opera, Stockholm. Today he is best known for his orchestral music and quartets.

Operas: *Tirfing*, 1898; *Das Fest auf Solhaug*, 1899, as *Gildet på Solhaug*, 1902

R.La.

WILLIAM GRANT STILL
b 11 May 1895, Woodville, Mississippi, US; *d* 3 December 1978, Los Angeles, US

Still has been called 'the Dean of Afro-American composers'. After service in the US navy he worked as a jazz musician and studied for two years with Varèse, as well as with Chadwick. In 1931 his *Afro-American Symphony* was played by the Rochester Philharmonic Symphony, a breakthrough for a black American: it was widely performed throughout America and Europe and established Still's reputation as a serious composer.

In 1934 he received a Guggenheim fellowship, moved to Los Angeles, and decided to concentrate on opera. *Blue Steel* uses jazz and spirituals, while *Troubled Island*, premiered by the New York City Opera in 1949, but composed in 1938, includes topical, Haitian traditional melodies. *A Bayou Legend*, premiered by Opera South in 1974, is perhaps the best known of the remainder of Still's operas (it was seen on television in 1981), all of which have libretti by his wife, Verna Arvey. A simple story of witchcraft set on the Mississippi Gulf coast in the early 19th century, the opera's unsophisticated narrative is appropriately matched by uncomplicated singable melodies, typical of Still's operatic style.

Operas: *Blue Steel*, (1935); *Troubled Island*, (1938), 1949; *A Bayou Legend*, (1940), 1974; *A Southern Interlude*, (1942); *Costaso*, (1949); *Mota*, (1951); *The Pillar*, (1956); *Minette Fontaine*, (1958); *Highway 1, USA*, 1963
BIBLIOGRAPHY   E. Southern, *The Music of Black Americans: A History*, W. W. Norton, 1971, *rp*, 1983

P.D.

KARLHEINZ STOCKHAUSEN
b 22 August 1928, Mödrath, nr Cologne

Stockhausen had no professional contact with opera throughout the first quarter-century of his composing life. Many of his works from the 1950s and 1960s have a strong element of spectacle – the concourse of three orchestras in *Gruppen* (1955–7), the response of a pianist and a percussionist to electronic sounds arriving from a tape in *Kontakte* (1959–60), the operation of six performers to extract vibrations from an amplified giant tam-tam in *Mikrophonie I* (1964), the chanting of a circle of six vocalists in *Stimmung* (1968) – but always the dramatic gesture arises from the musical practicality. The only two pieces with a distinct theatrical dimension – *Originale* (1961, a 'happening' with *Kontakte*) and *Oben und Unten* (a 'text composition' of 1968) – are among the few works the composer has not chosen to promote, and were marginal to his main endeavour, which was to conceive and exemplify new systems of composition based on what was known of the nature of sound.

But at the start of the 1970s this changed. Henceforth the rarity is the work that fails to present a dramatic illusion, though Stockhausen's background in instrumental and electronic music, coupled with his experience of Asian theatre as a widely travelling musician in the 1960s, made his approach to the lyric stage unusual. Perhaps his principal innovation was putting instrumentalists on stage as embodiments of dramatic characters, even to the extent that singers are secondary. Also, the lack of a consecutive narrative or of dialogue makes his theatrical works more like ceremonials or dream transcriptions than European plays and operas. Examples include *Trans* (1971) for an orchestra bathed in magenta light, *Harlekin* (1975) for a clarinettist who acts the part of a comic–didactic virtuoso, and *Sirius* (1975–7), where four soloists (trumpeter, soprano, bass clarinettist and bass singer) appear as visitors from another planet to play to the accompaniment of synthesized music. Since this, nearly all his works have been parts of *Licht*, a cycle of seven works with which he is making his operatic début.

Licht: Die sieben Tage der Woche
Light: The Seven Days of the Week
Cycle of seven operas
Libretto by the composer
Composed 1977–

The cycle has three principal characters, each of whom may be interpreted by one or more singers, instrumentalists and dancers: Michael, the hero figure, has his avatars in trumpet, tenor and dancer; Eva, the mother and lover, has hers in basset horn, soprano and dancer; and Luzifer, the father and antagonist, has his in trombone, bass and dancer (the overlap with *Sirius* comes about because since the mid-1970s Stockhausen has worked most regularly with members of his family and entourage, including his trumpeter son Markus and the clarinettist Suzanne Stephens). Each of the characters is also associated with a melodic formula, and the three formulae function partly as leitmotifs (because they, and different segments and superpositions of them, are linked with characters and events), partly as series (because all the music is notionally extrapolated from them) and partly as ragas (because they provide material for melodic elaboration).

The formulae ensure a certain consistency, and sometimes much more than that: whole sections of the score (e.g. *Luzifers Traum*) echo and re-echo the same harmonies, as if in minute examination of a brief instant of more normal musical time. This extremely static character goes along with the ceremonial nature of the enterprise, and also with the cycle's didactic intentions. Stockhausen works on his audience (and indeed on his performers) as a teacher, come to explain, slowly and steadily, how to listen to this music of melodic extrapolation: the performers, too, are asked to present themselves as instructors, especially in crucial scenes where education through and in music is what happens (*Michaels Reise*, *Kathinkas Gesang*, *Evas Lied*). However, the general solemnity and slowness is offset by a robust humour and by the great variety of means and forms. Each opera is a sequence of acts, scenes and vignettes which are highly diverse in scoring (drawing on a range of instrumental, vocal and electronic resources) and can be performed separately. The major divisions within each opera are indicated below.

When complete, the cycle will consist of an opera for each day of the week, with different arrangements of the characters dominant in each: *Montag* (Eva: birth), *Dienstag* (Michael–Luzifer: war), *Mittwoch* (Eva–Luzifer: consolidation), *Donnerstag* (Michael: learning), *Freitag* (Michael–Eva: Eva's temptation), *Samstag* (Luzifer: death), *Sonntag* (Michael–Eva–Luzifer: mystic union of Eva and Michael).

Donnerstag aus Licht
Thursday from Light
Opera in a greeting, three acts and a farewell (3h 45m)
Composed 1978–80
PREMIERES   15 March 1981, La Scala, Milan; UK: 16 September 1985, Covent Garden, London
PERFORMERS   Michael *t*/tpt/*dancer*, Eva *s*/basset hn/*speaking dancer*, Luzifer *b*/trbn/*speaking mime–dancer*, Michael's Accompanist pf, Clownesque Pair of Swallows cl, cl/basset hn, 2 Youths 2 soprano sax, old woman *actress*; satb chorus
FULL ORCHESTRA   tapes

SYNOPSIS
Donnerstag-Gruss (*Michaels-Gruss*), No. 48½ (composer's numbering)
Thursday Greeting (*Michael's Greeting*)
brass octet, pf, 3 perc-players
A slow fanfare–prelude designed to be played in the foyer as the audience assembles.

Act I   *Michaels Jugend*, No. 49
Michael's Youth
Scene 1   *Kindheit*, No. 49½
Childhood
for the 6 principal singers and instrumentalists, plus the Eva dancer and tapes
Michael is awakened musically, sexually and comically by his mother, while his father introduces him to prayer, hunting and theatre. The parents argue;

the mother is taken to an asylum, and the father goes off to war (here, as in other details, the opera follows the story of the composer's own formation). The musical atmosphere is static, soft and slow, sustained on the sounds of invisible choirs, trumpets and trombones.
Scene 2   *Mondeva*, No. 49Å
Moon-Eve
for t, basset hn
The instrumentalist – half bird, half woman – appears as a celestial visitor; Michael joins with her in an erotic duet.
Scene 3   *Examen*, No. 49¾
Examination
for the Michael performers, pf, basset hn and tapes, with a 'jury' of the Eva and Luzifer singers and dancers
Michael, accompanied by the pianist, playing what can be separately performed as *Klavierstück XII*, is brought before the jury to be examined in all three guises, encouraged by Mondeva. The jury enthusiastically admits him to the conservatory.

Act II   *Michaels Reise um die Erde*, No. 48
Michael's Journey around the Earth
for Michael as tpt, Eva as basset hn, the 2 clowning cl, small orchestra
This act is a single scene, a trumpet concerto for Michael as cosmic hero. He climbs into a globe on stage, and plays conversations with seven different locations on the earth, represented by the orchestra. He then hears a basset horn and steps out; Eva appears, and the two play a duet as they leave, while the globe is taken over by the two clowns, mocking the principal couple.

Act III   *Michaels Heimkehr*, No. 50
Michael's Homecoming
Scene 1   *Festival*, No. 50½
for full cast except pf and clowns
Michael, now threefold, returns to celestial realms and is welcomed by Eva, also threefold, with a choral–orchestral hymn. Michael thanks her, and she gives him gifts. An old woman interrupts the celebrations, and later Luzifer appears to battle with Michael in a trombone–trumpet duet. The playing of the two saxophonist boys restores the tone of celebration, but Luzifer storms on in his bass form to scoff, until Michael persuades him to leave so that the festival can be completed.
Scene 2   *Vision*, No. 50Å
for the Michael performers, Hammond organ and tape
After the immensities of the preceding scene, the opera returns to the long, quiet expanses of Act I. The tenor Michael sings throughout a recitative on his formula, explaining the meaning of what has been shown: how he, an angel of light at war with Luzifer, assumed the form of a man in order to teach humanity about God and music. Meanwhile the trumpeter Michael plays and the dancer Michael dances. In the middle of the scene he has a vision of shadow plays recalling seven stages of his life, accompanied by recordings of relevant passages from

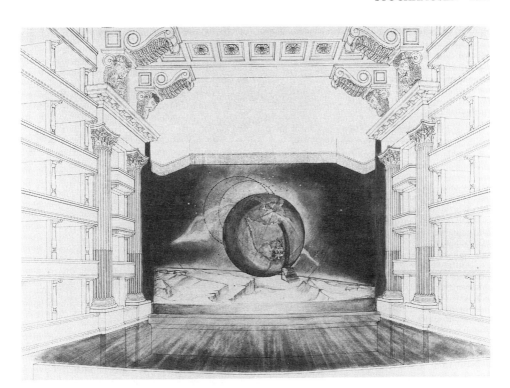

Design for Michael's Homecoming, Act III of Donnerstag aus Licht *(Milan, 1981)*

the opera. Finally the threefold being takes his leave of the audience.

Donnerstags-Abschied (*Michaels-Abschied*),
No. 50¾
*Thursday Farewell (*Michael's Farewell*)*
Five trumpet players, stationed on balconies or rooftops around the theatre as the audience leaves, play segments of the Michael melody as signals.

RECORDING Meriweather, Gambill, Hölle, Stephens, Markus Stockhausen, Majella Stockhausen, Ensemble InterContemporain, Stockhausen and Eötvös, DG, 1983
EDITION f.s., Stockhausen-Verlag, 1978–80

Samstag aus Licht
Saturday from Light
Opera in a greeting and four scenes (3h)
Composed 1981–3
PREMIERE 25 May 1984, Palazzo dello Sport, Milan
CAST Luzifer *b/stilt dancer*, Luzifer's Dream Player pf, Black Cat Kathinka fl, The Six Mortal Senses perc, Giant Human Face wind band, Michael tpt, 3 × 13 Monks *male chorus*, a Diabolical Wind Player trbn, Hammond organ, dancers/mimes

SYNOPSIS
*Samstags-Gruss (*Luzifers-Gruss*),* No. 53½
*Saturday Greeting (*Lucifer's Greeting*)*
for 26 brass and 2 perc-players
Four groups of musicians, placed at the points of the compass, intone a slow fanfare–prelude

Scene 1 *Luzifers Traum,* No. 51
Lucifer's Dream
for *b* and pf
Luzifer as bass dreams a piano piece, *Klavierstück XIII*, and chants. At the end he seems to be dead, but he is only play-acting. Nevertheless, the work proceeds as a huge funeral.
Scene 2 *Kathinkas Gesang als Luzifers Requiem,* No. 52
Kathinka's Song as Lucifer's Requiem
for fl and 6 perc-players
Kathinka, a flautist in cat costume, salutes the audience and plays a sequence of 22 exercises, accompanied by the percussionists playing bell plates and 'magic instruments' attached to their clothing. The senses (represented by the percussionists) are released; Kathinka then plays 11 'trombone tones' and cries out. The whole piece 'leads the souls of the dead through listening to clear consciousness'.
Scene 3 *Luzifers Tanz,* No. 53
Lucifer's Dance
for *b*, wind band, tpt, picc and dancers
Luzifer as bass is in control of an enormous human face, a vertical framework in which groups of wind and percussion-players sit, representing the features. He causes them to play in turn, also appearing as a dancer on high stilts. Eventually Michael as trumpeter comes on to protest, and there is a dance of tears. The mouth opens and the tongue comes out, bearing a piccolo-player (Kathinka), who plays for a dancer tearing bands from his body. The scene ends

with the orchestra going on strike and pandemonium ensuing.

Scene 4   *Luzifers Abschied*, No. 54
Lucifer's Farewell
for *tb* chorus, organ, 7 trbn
Taking place either in the theatre or in a church near by, this scene is a ceremony for a monastic chorus singing St Francis's *Lodi delle virtù* in the manner of a Japanese ritual. A Luciferian trombonist interrupts at one point, and the work ends with bells, the release of a wild bird, and the monks hurling coconuts on to a stone floor.

RECORDING   Hölle, Majella Stockhausen, Markus Stockhausen, Pasveer, etc., DG, 1988
EDITION   f.s., Stockhausen-Verlag, 1981–3

Montag aus Licht
Monday from Light
Opera in a greeting, three acts and a farewell (4h 30m)
Composed 1984–8
PREMIERE   7 May 1988, La Scala, Milan
PERFORMERS   Eva 3 *s*, Luzifer *b/actor*, 3 Sailors 3 *t*, Seven Boys of the Days 7 *child s*, Coeur de Basset basset hn, 3 Bassetesses 2 basset hn, *vocalist*, The Childcatcher fl, Wave Parrot pf; *satb* chorus, children's chorus, 'modern' orchestra of 3 synthesizer-players (one also playing trbn), perc (one player)

SYNOPSIS
Montags-Gruss (*Evas Gruss*), No. 55
Monday Greeting (*Eva's Greeting*)
for basset hn, orchestra and synthesizers
Replayed on tape in the foyer, with green lighting, the greeting is meant to suggest an arrival under water, ready for the gestatory nature of the opera.

Act I   *Evas Erstgeburt*, No. 56
Eve's First Birth
for the Eva and Luzifer performers, *t* sailors, choruses and 'modern' orchestra
The basset-horn music of the greeting continues; it is night, and a gigantic female statue is dimly visible. Women come to bring offerings, and the three Eva sopranos sing, as if in glossolalia, a hymn of the nine months of pregnancy. The statue gives birth to various creatures, and the sopranos sing a First Birth Aria, being joined in their Second Birth Aria by the sailors. Then the sopranos and choruses sing for a ballet of women pushing baby buggies. Luzifer, as bass and dancer tied together in their costuming, enters to mock, and the three sopranos sing a lament. Now as bass alone, Luzifer returns to suggest a break.

Act II   *Evas Zweitgeburt*, No. 57
Eve's Second Birth
Scene 1   *Mädchenprozession*, No. 57½
Girls' Procession
for girls' chorus
The girls enter singing a hymn to Eva.
Scene 2   *Befruchtung mit Klavierstück*, No. 57Å
Impregnation with Piano Piece
for pf, girls' chorus and 'modern' orchestra
An extended piano arrives from the wings to impregnate the Eva statue with *Klavierstück XIV*,

played by the Wave Parrot who was one of the creatures born in Act I.
Scene 3   *Wiedergeburt*
Further Birth
for choruses and 'modern' orchestra
The seven Boys of the Days are born from the statue, and greeted by the women and girls of the choruses.
Scene 4   *Evas Lied*, No. 57¾
Eva's Song
for the boys, 3 basset hn and 'modern' orchestra
Coeur de Basset emerges from the breast of the statue and teaches the boys their respective songs as representatives of the days. The three other 'bassetesses' come out of the statue, and all four lure the boys away. One of the boys calls for the lights to be put out, and they are.

Act III   *Evas Zauber*, No. 58
Eve's Magic
Scene 1   *Botschaft*, No. 58½
Message
for basset hn, alto fl, chorus and 'modern' orchestra
Coeur de Basset plays to the chorus, who brings news that a wonderful musician has arrived: he does so in the form of a flautist, who plays a duet with Coeur de Basset, with choral commentary.
Scene 2   *Der Kinderfänger*, No. 58Å
The Childcatcher
for fl, children's chorus and 'modern' orchestra
The magic flautist of the previous scene teaches the children a song.
Scene 3   *Entführung*
Abduction
for picc, children's chorus and 'modern' orchestra
The Childcatcher leads the children away to the clouds.

Montags-Abschied (*Evas-Abschied*), No. 59
Monday Farewell (*Eve's Farewell*)
for picc, 'modern' orchestra, voices and synthesizers
The audience departs through the foyer as if into the clouds, hearing a recorded extension of the last scene.

EDITION   f.s., Stockhausen-Verlag

Dienstag aus Licht
Tuesday from Light
Opera in a greeting and two acts (2h 30m)
Composed 1977–91
PREMIERE   10 May 1992, Gulbenkian Foundation, Lisbon
CAST   Eva *s*, Michael *t*/tpt, Luzifer *b*/trbn, Synthi-Fou synthesizer, chorus, instrumental groups, tape, dancers

SYNOPSIS
Dienstags-Gruss, No. 60
Tuesday Greeting
for chorus, *s*, 9 tpt, 9 trbn, 2 synthesizers
The war between Michael and Luzifer begins as a battle between rival masses, each supported by a synthesizer: sopranos and tenors with the trumpets on the side of Michael, altos and basses with the trombones taking Luzifer's part. The music is dense, clogged. A solo soprano as Eva keeps intervening to call for peace.

Act I *Der Jahreslauf*, No. 61
The Course of the Years
for *t*, *b*, 14 instrumentalists, dancers
The first part of *Licht* to be composed, this is a dance of unfolding time, in which the millennia, centuries, decades and years are represented by different groups of instruments and dancers. Luzifer tries to interrupt events, but is foiled by Michael: the two characters are present in their solo vocal personae, as if observing the action, and the act ends with them agreeing to go on a more testing combat. Without these sung additions the work was written for the Imperial Gagaku Ensemble of Tokyo, though the parts may also be played on Western instruments: flutes, soprano saxophones, synthesizers, guitar and percussion.

Act II *Invasion–Explosion mit Abschied*, No. 62
Invasion–Explosion with Farewell
for *s*, *t*, *b*, chorus, 3 tpts, 3 trbns, 2 synthesizers, 2 perc-players
The second contest between Michael and Luzifer directly engages the principals, and the imagery turns to that of military conflict. Octophonic electronic music surrounds the audience in the fire of aural shells and tracers, while the auditorium is invaded by platoons of Michael and Luzifer interpreters: a singer, three brass-players and two electric artists for each, firing off bursts of music at each other. The leading trumpeter Michael is killed, and there follows a 'Pietà' which he plays on the flugelhorn in a duet with the soprano Eva. Finally the chorus return, and then Synthi-Fou arrives to play a comic virtuoso solo to them.

RECORDING *Der Jahreslauf* only, no singers: Orchestral Ensemble, Stockhausen, DG, 1981
EDITION f.s., Stockhausen-Verlag, forthcoming

BIBLIOGRAPHY Michael Kurtz, trans. Richard Toop, *Stockhausen: A Biography*, Faber, 1992; Robin Maconie, *The Works of Karlheinz Stockhausen*, OUP, 2nd edn, 1990; Karlheinz Stockhausen, *Texte zur Musik*, vols 5 and 6, DuMont, 1989; Mya Tannenbaum, trans. David Butchart, *Conversations with Stockhausen*, Clarendon Press, 1987

P.A.G.

ROBERT STOLZ

Robert Elisabeth Stolz; *b* 25 August 1880, Graz; *d* 27 June 1975, Berlin

The son of a prominent music teacher and a concert pianist, Stolz was immersed in music from his earliest days. By remaining active as composer and conductor right up to the end of an exceptionally long life, he formed a unique link between the era of Brahms and Johann Strauss II, both of whom he knew, and the era of jet aeroplanes and stereo recordings. After studies with Fuchs and Humperdinck he held several posts as répétiteur and kapellmeister in provincial opera houses before turning exclusively to the lighter genre of operetta, and subsequently to film music. His total of well over 60 operettas may not include a single one of *Merry Widow* status, but several of them enjoyed considerable international success, and dozens of his individual songs have become 'evergreens' of the German-language world, comparable in popularity with the 'standards' of Kern, Gershwin or Berlin. His film scores, starting with the first German sound film, *Zwei Herzen im Dreivierteltakt* (Berlin, 1930), extended after his voluntary emigration to America in the Second World War to such notable Hollywood successes as *Spring Parade* (1941) and *It Happened Tomorrow* (1944). His numerous operetta recordings as conductor, made in the 1960s and 1970s, provide fascinating evidence of how such composers as Lehár, Fall and Kálmán wanted their music to sound, since Stolz had conducted the world premieres of many of their works 40 or 50 years earlier.

Opera: *Die Rosen der Madonna*, 1920 (RECORDING BASF, 1973)
Operettas and musicals: *Studentenulke*, 1901; *Schön Lorchen*, 1903; *Manöverliebe*, 1906; *Die lustigen Weiber von Wien*, 1908; *Der grosse Name*, 1909; *Das Glücksmädel*, 1910; *Der Minenkönig*, 1911; *Die eiserne Jungfrau*, 1911; *Du liebes Wien*, 1913; *Das Lumperl*, 1915; *Die Varietédiva*, 1915; *Der Favorit*, 1916; *Mädel, küsse mich*, 1916; *Die Bauernprinzessin*, 1916; *Eine einzige Nacht*, 1917, rev. 1927; *Lang, lang ist's her*, 1917; *Das Sperrsechserl*, 1920; *Der Tanz ins Glück*, 1920; *Die Tanzgräfin*, 1921; *Eine Sommernacht*, 1921; *Die Liebe geht um*, 1922; *Mädi*, 1923; *Der Hampelmann*, 1923; *Der Kavalier von zehn bis vier*, 1924; *Ein Rivieratraum*, 1924; *Due Baci*, 1925; *Märchen im Schnee*, 1927; *Der Mitternachtswalzer*, 1926; *Prinzessin Ti-Ti-Pa*, 1928; *Gloria und der Clown*, 1929; *Peppina*, 1930; two numbers for *Im weissen Rössl*, 1930; *Wenn die kleinen Veilchen blühen*, 1932 (RECORDING excerpts: Eurodisc, 1960s); *Venus in Seide*, 1932 (RECORDING excerpts: Eurodisc, 1960s); *Der verlorene Walzer, oder Zwei Herzen im Dreivierteltakt*, 1933 (RECORDING excerpts: Eurodisc, 1960s); *Gruez i, oder Himmelblaue Träume*, 1934 (RECORDING excerpts: Eurodisc, 1960s); *Ein Mädel hat sich verlaufen*, 1934; *Zum goldenen Halbmond*, 1935; *Rise and Shine*, 1936; *Der süsseste Schwindel der Welt*, 1937; *Die Reise um die Erde in 80 Minuten*, 1937; *Balalaika* (with Bernard Grun), 1938; *One Night of Love*, or *Tonight or Never*, 1942; *Mr Strauss Goes to Boston*, 1945; *Schicksal mit Musik*, 1946; *Drei von der Donau*, 1947; six numbers for *Ein Lied aus der Vorstadt*, 1948; *Frühling im Prater*, 1949; *Fest in Casablanca*, 1949; *Das Glücksrezept*, 1951; *Rainbow Square*, 1951; *Ballade vom lieben Augustin*, 1953; *Signorina*, 1955; *Behalt mich lieb, Cherie*, 1955; *Kleiner Schwindel in Paris* (rev. of *Der süsseste Schwindel der Welt*), 1956; *Hallo, das ist die Liebe* (rev. of *Der Tanz ins Glück*), 1958; *Kitty und die Weltkonferenz*, 1959; *Joie de vivre*, 1960; *Trauminsel* (rev. of *Signorina*), 1962 (RECORDING Amadeo, 1960s); *Ein schöner Herbst*, 1963 (RECORDING excerpts, Ariola, 1960s); *Die kleine und die grosse Welt* (rev. of *Kitty und die Weltkonferenz*), 1963; *Frühjahrsparade*, 1964 (RECORDING excerpts: Eurodisc, 1960s); *Wiener Café* (rev. of *Zum goldenen Halbmond*), 1965; *Hochzeit am Bodensee* (rev. of *Gruez i, oder Himmelblaue Träume*), 1969

BIBLIOGRAPHY Othmar Herbrich, *Robert Stolz, König der Melodie*, Amalthea, 1975; *rp*, Wilhelm Heyne, 1977

N.D.

STEPHEN STORACE

Stephen John Seymour Storace; *b* 4 April 1762, London;
d 19 March 1796, London

Storace was the son of an Italian double-bass-player
who emigrated to Dublin and from there to London.
He was a prodigy on the violin and an accomplished
amateur painter. His sister Nancy was a notable
comic soprano, the original Susanna in Mozart's
Figaro. Both received their musical education in
Italy. Nancy moved to Vienna in 1783 and became a
favourite of Joseph II, as a result of which Stephen
received commissions for two operas, *Gli sposi
malcontenti* and *Gli Equivoci*. Mozart was a friend, as
was the Irish tenor Michael Kelly. Storace played a
significant part in popularizing Mozart's music in
London and in his own operas employed a number
of Mozartian devices, notably ensembles which
continue to advance or complete the action. His
works come much nearer than those of his English
contemporaries to the ideal of music drama, though
only one of them, *Dido, Queen of Carthage* (music
lost), was all sung, and all contain music borrowed
from other pieces.

Given the quality of Storace's musical and
dramatic imagination it is unfortunate that *No Song,
No Supper* is his only English opera for which
orchestral parts survive. He had a gift for choosing
striking and topical subjects: *The Haunted Tower*
(1789) anticipates the Gothic novel and was an
enormous popular success; *The Cherokee* (1794)
anticipates Fennimore Cooper and the romance of
the western frontier; *The Iron Chest* (1796) derives
from William Godwin's *Caleb Williams*, a social
novel intended to demonstrate 'the tyranny and
perfidiousness exercised by the powerful members of
the community against those who are less privileged
than themselves'. *The Pirates* (1792) is Storace's most
accomplished work, and the first English example of
an escape opera, set in the Bay of Naples; it contains,
incidentally, the first known English waltz and what
may be the first use of a magic lantern on the English
stage. Storace's admirers included Hazlitt and Leigh
Hunt, who called him the only composer in whose
work 'English accentuation and Italian flow were
ever truly amalgamated'.

Gli Equivoci

Drama buffo in two acts (2h 45m)
Libretto by Lorenzo da Ponte, after *The Comedy of
Errors* by Shakespeare (*c.* 1594)
PREMIERES   27 December 1786, Burgtheater, Vienna; UK:
20 February 1974, Collegiate Theatre, London

Despite the relative success of his first opera, *Gli
sposi malcontenti*, Storace was dissatisfied with
Gaetano Brunati's libretto. He therefore turned to
Lorenzo da Ponte, who had succeeded so brilliantly
with Mozart's *Le nozze di Figaro* (in which Storace's
sister Nancy had played Susanna) in May 1786.
Da Ponte, who was secretly planning to write a libretto for Vicente Martín y Soler, had to accept
this commission since it came with the emperor's

approval and he was the court poet. To save time he
decided to adapt Shakespeare's *The Comedy of
Errors*. He reduced the First Folio's five acts to two,
renamed Antipholus Eufemio, excised Emilia (the
Abbess), and gave the Courtesan, and gave Dromio of
Syracuse a son, Dromincino. Otherwise the plot
remains Shakespeare's and the story of two pairs of
identical twins, masters and servants, provided da
Ponte and Storace with ample opportunities for the
ensemble numbers that had been such a feature of
Figaro, though here they serve farce rather than
comedy.

The overture represents the storm that casts
Euphemio and Dromio ashore at Ephesus and is
remarkable for its special effects; the orchestration
throughout the opera is subtle and unusual; the
ensemble writing is witty and accomplished. Da
Ponte eliminated the darker tones of Shakespeare's
play, but Storace still achieves pathos and tenderness, particularly in the finale of Act II. The
opera enjoyed a considerable success in Vienna and
elsewhere; Sheridan promised a production at Drury
Lane; it never materialized, and Storace cannibalized
parts of *Gli Equivoci* for *No Song, No Supper* and
The Pirates.

EDITIONS   f.s./v.s., Richard Platt (ed.), Stainer and Bell (on
hire), 1973

No Song, No Supper

Afterpiece in two acts with spoken dialogue (1h 15m)
Libretto by Prince Hoare
PREMIERE   16 April 1790, London

The characters are jovial tars, country bumpkins, and
Frederick, the local squire, new to his Cornish
inheritance, and shipwrecked on the borders of his
own estate where, disguised as a poor scholar, he has
courted Louisa, the most beautiful girl in England
and daughter of a wealthy farmer. Incognito, he is
too poor for her; as squire he is too rich. A sub-plot
concerns the wooing of Robin, the sailor who has
saved Frederick from drowning. All ends happily.
There are good ensembles and a number of *faux-naïf*
ballad-like songs. Sheridan, as manager of the Drury
Lane Theatre, originally rejected the piece, but
staged it for Michael Kelly's benefit ('this charming
and popular opera') after the success of *The Haunted
Tower* in which Kelly sang Lord William. The storm
overture, which was encored, comes from *Gli
equivoci*.

EDITIONS   f.s., Roger Fiske (ed.), *Musica Britannica*, vol. 16
(1959)

Works surviving: *Gli sposi malcontenti*, 1785; *Gli equivoci*,
1786; *La cameriera astuta* (fragments), 1788; *The Doctor and
the Apothecary* (after Dittersdorf), 1788; *The Haunted
Tower*, 1789; *The Siege of Belgrade* (after Martín y Soler),
1791; *The Pirates*, 1792; *The Prize*, 1793; *My Grandmother*,
1793; *The Cherokee*, 1794; *The Three and the Deuce*, 1795;
The Iron Chest, 1796, *Mahmoud* (inc.; completed by Nancy
Storace), 1796
BIBLIOGRAPHY   Roger Fiske, 'The Operas of Stephen
Storace', *PRMA*, vol. 86 (1959–60), pp. 15ff.; Roger Fiske,

English Theatre Music in the Eighteenth Century, OUP, 1973; 2nd edn, 1986; Michael Kelly, *Reminiscences*, 2 vols, London, 1826

R.Lu.

ALESSANDRO STRADELLA

b 3 April 1639, Nepi, nr Viterbo; *d* 25 February 1682, Genoa

Stradella was born into a noble family and seems to have acquired his earliest musical training in Bologna: he spent a good deal of time there before 1664, and is referred to in legal documents as 'Signor Bolognese'. The earliest document attesting his presence in Rome dates from 1667, when he composed a Latin oratorio for the Arciconfraternita del SS. Crocifisso. For the next decade Stradella was extremely busy in Rome, producing a large number of oratorios, serenatas, prologues and intermezzi.

There seems to have been a shady side to Stradella's character: in 1669 he attempted to embezzle church money and was forced to leave Rome for a while; and his final departure from the city in 1677 was precipitated by another scandal involving money and a contract of marriage. For the rest of his life Stradella was hounded by assassins: he moved to Venice where he became involved with the fiancée of Alvise Contarini. The couple fled to Turin with representatives of the Contarini in pursuit, and there was an unsuccessful attempt on his life. He moved to Genoa at the beginning of 1678; there his music was well received, and he composed three operas for the 1678–9 season: *La forza dell'amor paterno*, *Il Trespolo tutore* and *Le gare dell'amor eroico*. In 1681 he wrote a serenata, *Il barcheggio*, to celebrate the marriage that joined the Spinola and Brignole families; it was performed in the Bay of Genoa. The following year another romantic attachment caused the Lomellini family to hire an assassin, and Stradella's life ended in the Piazza Bianchi in Genoa. His music continued to be performed at the court in Modena for some years, and also in Roman theatres.

Stradella was, along with Alessandro Scarlatti and Bernardo Pasquini, one of the principal opera composers in Rome in the 1670s. The relatively limited size of his operatic output there can probably be attributed to his social standing and to his numerous escapades, but in Genoa, where he was able to establish his position, his rate of composition was greater. Stradella's musical style is characterized by fluent melodic lines and occasionally startling harmonic progressions. A notable attention to word-setting is apparent in his recitatives (which, following modern developments, were often accompanied by strings as well as the usual continuo group), while his arias, cast in a wide variety of forms, are frequently based on melodic or rhythmic ostinati. His later works, notably *Moro per amore*, show a shift in emphasis to the solo aria, at the expense of dramatic recitative and arioso passages, and a consequent increase in *da capo* form. Also, the instrumental parts are more integrated, alternating with the frequently demanding vocal line.

La forza dell'amor paterno

The Power of Paternal Love
Opera in three acts (1h 45m)
Libretto: an adaptation by an unknown author of Nicolo Minato's *Seleuco* (1666)
PREMIERE 10 November 1678, Teatro Falcone, Genoa

In *La forza dell'amor paterno*, both father and son (Seleuco and Antioco) are in love with the same woman (Lucinda). She is intended for Seleuco, but she loves his son. Eventually Seleuco renounces his claim to Lucinda out of paternal love.

The fashion for vocal virtuosity is reflected in the music, which includes some demanding *fioriture* passages, especially for Antioco. Nevertheless, the proportion of arias to recitative and arioso passages is small and many are extremely short and simple in style.

EDITION v.s., Alberto Gentili (ed.), Ricordi, 1930

Il Trespolo tutore

Trespolo the Tutor
Commedia in three acts
Libretto by Giovanni Cosimo Villifranchi after the play by G. B. Ricciardi (1669) previously set by Pasquini (1677)
PREMIERE 30 or 31 January 1679, Teatro Falcone, Genoa

Il Trespolo tutore is Stradella's only truly comic opera. It presents the drama of Artemisia, who has a dull and possessive tutor, Trespolo. Two brothers, Nino and Ciro, are both in love with her, but she loves her tutor. Trespolo's stupidity causes the drama to progress through a series of unexpected and humorous situations.

Comic opera was still in its infancy when *Il Trespolo tutore* was composed and the part of the tutor can be counted among the earliest basso buffo roles, a 'type' that was to become a regular feature of Italian opera buffa. Rapid recitatives, often scored in quavers or semiquavers rather than the more usual crotchets, help convey the comedy generated by situations that are clearly indebted to the popular *commedia dell'arte* tradition. Villifranchi's libretto also added two 'mad' scenes for Nina not present in Ricciardi's play.

EDITION excerpts (7 arias), in Heinz Hess (ed.), *Die Opern Alessandro Stradellas*, Breitkopf und Härtel, 1906
MANUSCRIPT Biblioteca Estense, Modena

Other operatic works: *Le gare dell'amor eroico* (also known as *L'Oratio*, or *Cocle sul Ponte*) 1679; *Moro per amore* (also known as *Il Floridoro*), (*c.* 1682), 1695 (EDITION facsimile, H. M. Brown (ed.), Garland, 1979); 2 lost operas
BIBLIOGRAPHY Carolyn Gianturco, 'Evidence for a Late Roman School of Opera', *ML*, vol. 56 (1975), pp. 4–17

G.D.

I L
TRESPOLO

TVTORE BALORDO

OPERA DRAMMATICA

Per Mufica

Da recitarfi nel Teatro Fontanelli
l' Anno 1686.

CONSECRATO

All' Altezza Sereniffima

DI FRANCESCO II.

Duca di Modona, Reggio &c.

IN MODONA;

Per gli Eredi Soliani Stamp. Duc. 1686.
Con Licenza de' Superiori.

Il Trespolo tutore; title page of the libretto, published in Modona, 1686

OSCAR STRAUS
Oscar Strauss; *b* 6 March 1870, Vienna; *d* 11 January 1954, Bad Ischl, Austria

Enchanted by a performance of Gilbert's and Sullivan's *The Mikado*, given by the D'Oyly Carte in Vienna (1886), Straus had operetta yearnings from an early age. Instead of taking the advice of Brahms and Max Bruch, with whom he studied in Berlin, about pursuing a classical career, Straus listened to Johann Strauss II, who advised him to conduct operettas provincially for experience. He did, in Pressburg (Bratislava) and Brünn (Brno), among other cities, and returned to Berlin at the end of the century, where he contributed humorous, satirical, and romantic songs to the Secession-Theater *Überbrettl* cabaret. In Vienna his first operetta was a burlesque after Wagner entitled *Die lustige Nibelungen* (1904), which was better liked in more liberal Berlin. The satire that so appealed to Straus

was not welcome in Vienna, where more sentimental tastes prevailed.

Following Lehár's lead with *Die lustige Witwe*, Straus supplied the Carltheater with a fabulous 'silver-age' triumph, *Ein Walzertraum*, later seen all over the world (and filmed memorably twice). Even more daring was *Der tapfere Soldat* (1908) – Shaw's *Arms and the Man* cunningly adapted. Subsequent operettas were not as widely popular, though *Der letzte Walzer* (1920) and *Mariette* (1928) deserve revivals. Also successful were *Eine Frau, die weiss was sie will* (1932), like *Mariette* basically a comedy with songs, and a 1937 Parisian production of *Trois valses*, an effective pasticcio based on the Johann Strausses I and II, with a third act by Oscar Straus. Straus's later, intimate, 1930s-boudoir style was particularly suited to film, especially Lubitsch's *One Hour with You* (1932). His last memorable work was the superlatively catchy waltz for the 1950 Ophuls film *La ronde*.

Straus's work does not bear the consistent signature that one so easily discovers in operettas by Lehár, or Kálmán, or Fall, possibly because they had distinctly inbred regional colorations that Straus, the Viennese cosmopolitan, did not. Yet Straus was able to achieve moments of intense, rhapsodic beauty, not to mention an idiomatically Viennese soulfulness – particularly in *Ein Walzertraum*. He was perhaps happiest with light-hearted comic songs or ensembles, a memory of his cabaret past. *Trois valses* is a clever amalgam of his contrasting styles, but it is in works such as *Der tapfere Soldat* that Straus's real melodic and structural brilliance appears.

Ein Walzertraum
A Waltz Dream
Operetta in three acts
Libretto by Felix Dormann and Leopold Jacobson, after a story from Hans Muller's *Buch der Abenteuer*
Composed 1907
PREMIERES 2 March 1907, Carltheater, Vienna; US: 27 January 1908, Broadway Theater, New York; UK: 28 March 1908, Hick's Theatre, London

The bittersweet story of Lieutenant Niki of the Hussars, just married to Princess Helene of Flausenthurm but in love with Franzi, the leader of an all-girl orchestra, was a sensation, vying in popularity in Vienna with *Die lustige Witwe*. The plot was romantically satisfying and humorous, and the score's canny mixture of frivolity and poignancy ensured the operetta's worldwide success.

Particularly noteworthy are the title waltz duet for Niki and his military friend in Act I, 'Leise, ganz leise', which has become almost as much of an anthem of 20th-century Viennese operetta as the *Merry Widow* waltz, the glittering Act II 'Temperament' female trio, and, in the same act, the immensely silly but catchy buffo–soubrette duet, 'Piccolo! Piccolo! Tsin-tsin-tsin'.

The sense of nostalgia for old Vienna that pervades the operetta intensified its popularity after the First World War, the collapse of the Habsburg empire, and the Nazi years: it is a period piece in the best (and most commercially valuable) sense of the term. But modern productions offer corrupt versions of the original score and libretto.

RECORDING Rothenberger, Moser, Fassbaender, Gedda, Brokmeier, Anheisser, Bavarian State Opera Ch, Munich, Graunke SO, Mattes, EMI Electrola, 1970s
FILM as *The Smiling Lieutenant*, Lubitsch (dir.), Paramount, 1931
EDITIONS v.ss., Ludwig Doblinger, 1908; as *A Waltz Dream*: Basil Hood and Adrian Ross (eds), J. B. Cramer, 1934

Der tapfere Soldat

The Chocolate Soldier (literally, *The Brave Soldier*)
Operetta in three acts
Libretto by Rudolf Bernauer and Leopold Jacobson, freely based on George Bernard Shaw's play *Arms and the Man* (1898)
PREMIERES 14 November 1908, Theater an der Wien, Vienna; US: 13 September 1909, Lyric Theatre, New York (trans. Stanislaus Stange as *The Chocolate Soldier*); UK: 10 September 1910, Lyric Theatre, London

The Chocolate Soldier has been more popular in English than in the German original, thanks to successful original runs on Broadway and in the West End, a popular revival in America in the 1940s, concert and radio versions, and Hollywood's bastardized film version. This substituted the plot of Molnár's *The Guardsman* for the Shaw story, after the dramatist refused to license his property to MGM.

During the Serbo-Bulgarian war the Popoff household gives shelter to a Serbian soldier whom they nickname 'The Chocolate Soldier' because he carries chocolate drops in his cartridge box instead of ammunition. After the war he returns and, having declared his love for Nadina Popoff, prepares to fight a duel with her betrothed, Alexius. But her father intervenes to prevent injury and declares, to Nadina's satisfaction, that she should marry her chocolate soldier.

If it were heard today in its original format, this might be considered Straus's finest operetta. Besides containing what is probably the most revered waltz in any 20th-century Viennese operetta, 'Komm, komm, Held meiner Träume' ('My Hero'), the score is brilliant and unusual, with Straus again excelling in comic ensembles, particularly the Act I finale, 'Tiralala!', and the Act II 'Song of the Coat'. There is also a wealth of glittering duets (notably the title song) and judicious sprinklings of Balkan coloration.

RECORDING Ayars, Carrol, Fredericks, Percival, The Guild Choristers, Al Goodman O, Goodman, RCA, 1959
FILM del Ruth (dir.), MGM, 1941
EDITIONS v.ss., Ludwig Doblinger, 1908; trans. S. Stange, Jerome H. Remick, 1919

Other operettas: *Der Weise von Cordova*, 1894; *Die Schweden vor Brünn*, 1895; *Der schwarze Mann*, 1900; *Colombine*, 1901; *Lolotte*, 1903; *Die lustigen Nibelungen*, 1904; *Zur indischen Witwe*, 1905; *Hugdietrichs Brautfahrt*, 1906; *Didi*, 1909; *Das Tal der Liebe*, 1909; *Venus im Grünen*, 1910; *Mein junger Herr*, 1910; *Die kleine Freundin*, 1911; *Der tapfere Cassian*, 1912; *Die Prinzessin von Tragant*, 1912; *The Dancing Viennese*, 1912; *Love and Laughter*, 1913; *Die himmelblaue Zeit*, 1914; *Rund um die Liebe*, 1914; *Die schöne*

Unbekannte, 1915; *Liebeszauber*, 1916; *Nachtfalter*, 1917; *Niobe*, 1917; *Eine Ballnacht*, 1918; *Dorfmusikanten*, 1919; *Der letzte Walzer*, 1920; *Nixchen*, 1921; *Die törichte Jungfrau*, 1922; *Die Perlen der Cleopatra*, 1923; *Tanz um die Liebe*, 1924; *La Teresina*, 1925; *Riquette*, 1925; *Die Königin*, 1926; *Mariette*, 1928; *Hochzeit in Hollywood*, 1928; *Die erst Beste*, 1929; *Der Bauerngeneral*, 1931; *Eine Frau, die weiss was sie will*, 1932; *Zwei lachende Augen*, 1933; *Liebelei*, 1933; *Walzerparadies*, 1935; *Drei Walzer*, 1935, rev. as *Trois valses; Mes amours*, 1940; *Die Musik kommt*, 1948; *Ihr erster Walzer*, 1950; *Bozena*, 1952
BIBLIOGRAPHY Bernard Grun, *Prince of Vienna: The Life, the Times, and the Melodies of Oscar Straus*, W. H. Allen, 1955

R.T.

JOHANN STRAUSS II

Johann Baptist Strauss; *b* 25 October 1825, Vienna; *d* 3 June 1899, Vienna

Johann Strauss II, the celebrated waltz king, was also the composer of the greatest of all Viennese operettas, *Die Fledermaus*, and a few others which still hold the stage. Although he chose his libretti foolishly and often set them mindlessly, the charge that Strauss had no theatrical instinct remains patently false. His music remains for millions the

Johann Strauss II

chief embodiment of the last glittering years of the Austro-Hungarian Empire.

Johann Strauss (the first waltz king) discouraged his son from becoming a professional musician. However, after his father left the family in 1842, the younger Strauss took a thorough musical training and his persistence soon paid off among the Viennese music publishers and dance halls, where he conducted his own orchestra. Soon Strauss II was as famous a composer, violinist and conductor as his father, and by the mid-1860s, when the huge success of Offenbach's operettas in Vienna aroused his interest, had also built up an international reputation through concert tours.

Strauss's first wife, Jetty Treffz, had taken some musical sketches to the director of the Theater an der Wien, Maximilian Steiner, who was able to convince the composer that his music was stageworthy. In 1869 Strauss composed *Die lustigen Weiber von Wien*, which was never produced, but his next operetta, *Indigo und die vierzig Räuber* (1871), was staged at the Theater an der Wien, conducted by the composer. Wags discussing the uncredited, unoriginal libretto referred to the '40 librettists'. But the public went crazy. There were productions abroad. The Paris version included the 'Blue Danube' waltz, whose phenomenal popularity is paralleled in the influence Strauss exerted not only on two generations of Viennese operetta, but on 'serious' composers. Brahms wrote of it, 'Not, unfortunately, by Johannes Brahms.' Wagner was an admirer, and among those who felt the influence of Strauss *fils* were Richard Strauss (no relation) and Maurice Ravel.

Der Karneval in Rom, the first of Strauss's operettas with an Italian setting, was an even bigger critical and commercial success in 1873. Both works were revised and remounted early in the 20th century, but have rarely been seen again. Not so the next work, *Die Fledermaus*. Though not an immediate triumph, it would become the most celebrated operetta of all time, performed not only in the popular theatre but also in the temples of high art, rubbing shoulders with the works of Mozart, Verdi and Wagner.

Thereafter *Cagliostro in Wien* (1875) wedded Italian and Austrian elements, but was distinguished – like its successors – mainly for its principal waltz. For *Prinz Methusalem* (1877), Strauss did not even wait for the German translation of the original French libretto he was setting. This did not prevent the work from doing quite well in Austria and in the US. The next work was even more popular with American audiences: *Das Spitzentuch der Königin* (1880), with a libretto Suppé had declined which had as its principal characters Cervantes and the Queen of Portugal. For every operetta Strauss composed, he also wrote various dance arrangements of their tunes, the sales of which were hugely lucrative for him and his publishers, and which served as publicity for the stage productions. Out of motifs from *Das Spitzentuch* came one of Strauss's greatest waltzes, 'Rosen aus dem Süden'. In the mid-1880s Strauss scored two of his greatest triumphs with *Eine Nacht in Venedig* and *Der Zigeunerbaron*; the latter is, after *Die Fledermaus*, the composer's most successful stage work.

None of Strauss's later operettas enjoyed the same acclaim, however, and despite sporadic attempts to revive them these works have for the most part passed into theatrical oblivion. In 1892 there were nine performances at the Hofoper of *Ritter Pázmán*, a through-composed work, set once again in Hungary. The *Waldmeister* overture is still occasionally aired, but little if anything is heard today from *Simplicius*, *Fürstin Ninetta*, *Jabuka*, or *Die Göttin der Vernunft*. In recent years, an authoritative edition of Strauss's autograph scores has shed new light on the major operettas and it is hoped that the minor works will be re-examined on stage as well as in print.

Textual deviations must be tolerated; certainly, all manner of pasticcios using Strauss's tunes appeared after the composer's death. The most famous was *Wiener Blut* (1899), which has been accepted as a genuine Strauss operetta because Strauss authorized its composition and vetted the music chosen before he died. It remains popular as a kitsch paean to early 19th-century Vienna, despite a tiresome book, insipid characters, and lyrics that are often ill-fitted to the music. *Walzer aus Wien* was a barely biographical study of the Strausses, father and son. A worldwide hit from 1931, it has usually been produced with great splendour. In New York it was *The Great Waltz*; in Paris, *Valses de Vienne*; in London, *Waltzes from Vienna*, where it was unimaginatively filmed by Alfred Hitchcock. A Hollywood spin-off entitled *The Great Waltz* (1938) was more popular.

Die Fledermaus

The Bat

Comic operetta in three acts (2h 15m)
Libretto by Carl Haffner and Richard Genée, based on the vaudeville *Le réveillon* by Henri Meilhac and Ludovic Halévy (1872)
Composed 1873–4
PREMIERES 5 April 1874, Theater an der Wien; US: 21 November 1874, Stadt Theater, New York; UK: 18 December 1876, Alhambra Theatre, London
CAST Gabriel von Eisenstein *t*, Alfred *t*, Dr Falke *bar*, Frank *bar*, Dr Blind *t*, Frosch *spoken role*, Rosalinde von Eisenstein *s*, Adele *s*, Prince Orlofsky *ms*; *satb* chorus of party guests, servants
ORCHESTRATION 2 fl/picc, 2 ob, 2 cl, 2 bsn, 4 hn, 2 tpt, 3 trbn, timp, bd, sd, bells, str

Strauss's most brilliant stage work is universally regarded as the Austrian operetta *in excelsis*. Originally planned for the Carltheater in Vienna as a strict translation of the play *Le réveillon*, it was then proposed by a publisher–agent as an operetta with music by Strauss for the rival Theater an der Wien. The play's more *risqué* elements – consorting with a prostitute, for one – were eliminated and most of the original names changed. The initial reception was quite favourable, but by 1880 the work had been seen in over 170 German-language theatres and after the Vienna Opera admitted it into its repertoire in the 1890s it was performed all over the world.

Curiously, *Die Fledermaus* was not at first as popular in the US as some other Strauss operettas.

SYNOPSIS

Act I In a spa near a large city (Vienna), Eisenstein has been sentenced to prison for a minor offence. Rosalinde, his wife, is serenaded by a singing teacher, Alfred ('Täubchen, das entflattert ist'), who promises to return after Eisenstein has begun his sentence. Adele, Rosalinde's maid, discloses to the audience that she wants to attend a party that evening given by the young Russian prince, Orlofsky. She tells her mistress she wants the night off to visit her sick aunt, but Rosalinde refuses. Eisenstein enters, furious with his inept lawyer, Dr Blind, for extending his gaol sentence ('Nein, mit solchen Advokaten'), but his friend Dr Falke cheers him up by recalling the time Eisenstein left him to walk home from a party in broad daylight in a bat costume. He then mentions the ball to be held at Prince Orlofsky's. If Eisenstein turns up at the prison at six the following morning, after the ball, the governor won't mind. Eisenstein agrees, and dresses for the evening, but tells his wife that he is about to begin his sentence. They bid one another an ironically tearful farewell. Rosalinde, who has dismissed her maid for the night after all, looks forward to her tryst with Alfred. The singing teacher arrives and they settle down to a cosy supper ('Trinke, Liebchen, trinke schnell'), but are interrupted by the arrival of the prison governor, Frank, who, assuming Rosalinde's companion to be her husband, takes Alfred off to prison. Rosalinde, not wishing to be compromised, encourages this misunderstanding ('Mein Herr, was dachten Sie von mir?'): who else but her husband would be in his dressing-gown?

Act II At Orlofsky's, the prince exhorts his guests to enjoy themselves ('Ich lade gern mir Gäste ein'); Dr Falke explains to the bored prince that he has created 'The bat's revenge' – a scheme to embarrass Eisenstein, who has just arrived in the guise of the Marquis Renard. Eisenstein recognizes Adele, who laughingly denies to the guests that she resembles his chambermaid ('Mein Herr Marquis'). Eisenstein is introduced first to a 'compatriot', 'Chevalier Chagrin' (Frank), and then to a mysterious, masked Hungarian countess; he flirts with her using his repeater watch, little realizing she is his own wife ('Dieser Anstand, so manierlich'). The 'countess' sings of her Magyar homeland to the party guests ('Klänge der Heimat'), and Eisenstein boasts of his practical joke years before which had had Dr Falke walking home from a ball in a bat costume, to the derision of the townsfolk. Orlofsky proposes a toast to King Champagne the First ('Im Feuerstrom der Reben'), and as the guests become more and more mellow, Dr Falke praises the spirit of brotherly (and sisterly) love that has come over them ('Brüderlein und Schwesterlein'). A ballet display (in many productions, a small gala performance with guest stars and interpolated numbers) is followed by a general waltz. As the clock strikes six, Eisenstein – and Frank – hurriedly depart.

Act III At the gaol, Alfred sings in his cell. The

C. A. Friese (Frank) and Alfred Schreiber (Frosch) in Die Fledermaus

gaoler, Frosch, tries to keep him quiet. In a melodrama, Frank, thoroughly drunk, sits at his desk and falls asleep. Adele and her sister enter in search of the 'Chevalier Chagrin'; Adele is sure he can help her become an actress ('Spiel' ich die Unschuld vom Lande'). Eisenstein arrives to serve his sentence. He is surprised to see his party friend as the prison warden, and more surprised to hear that this man personally arrested Eisenstein the previous evening, and that the prisoner has already begun serving his sentence. Determined to find out who the culprit cavorting with his wife is, Eisenstein disguises himself as Blind, and questions both Alfred and Rosalinde – who has come to the gaol – about their evening together. In a fury, he reveals himself, but is confronted with his own wife's fake Hungarian accent and the watch she cleverly snatched from him. The other party-goers enter the gaol, and Falke admits the whole set-up. Rather than pursue the evening's indiscretions, the principals decide to blame everything on the champagne ('O Fledermaus, o Fledermaus').

In *Die Fledermaus* Strauss couples the Parisian tendency to parody with a Viennese charm that never lapses into sentimentality. The libretto inspired a succession of happy ideas: Adele's high-spirited laughter becomes one of the great soubrette arias, 'Mein Herr Marquis', while the subterfuges of the various characters result, as in Mozart's *Le nozze di Figaro*, in some brilliant ensembles, notably the ironic farewells in Act I ('So muss allein ich bleiben . . . o je, o je, wie rührt mich dies!') and the finales to Acts I and II. Rosalinde's Hungarian disguise provides the excuse for the spirited csárdás 'Klänge der Heimat', while the original ballet sequence comprised a sequence of national dances (now usually replaced by a popular Strauss polka). Alfred's transformation from the orchestra leader of the French original to singing teacher made possible the curtain-raising serenade. Productions that preserve the role of Eisenstein as a tenor further lift the flavour of the piece. Only in Act III do the exuberant pacing and invention seem momentarily to falter; here the antics of the drunken Frosch can form an embarrassing weak link, though a skilled performance can equally provide the icing on the cake, as interpreters such as Franz Muxeneder and Frankie Howerd have proved.

Quite how Strauss himself saw the work within the tradition of great opera is uncertain, though the stuttering Dr Blind is a clear descendant of Mozart's Don Curzio, as also is Eisenstein of Count Almaviva; and the Act III melodrama in the gaol recalls comically (and surely unconsciously) *Fidelio*. But ever since Max Reinhardt's Berlin production of 1928, *Die Fledermaus* has been a fully-fledged member of the operatic repertoire, with memorable interpretations from such distinguished names as Krauss, Karajan and Carlos Kleiber.

RECORDINGS   1. Gueden, Lipp, Wagner, Patzak, Dermota, Poell, Vienna State Opera Ch, Vienna PO, Krauss, Decca, 1950; 2. Schwarzkopf, Streich, Gedda, Krebs, Kunz, Philharmonia Ch and O, Karajan, EMI, 1955; 3. Gueden, Köth, Resnik, Kmentt, Zampieri, Waechter, Vienna State Opera Ch, Vienna PO, Karajan, Decca, 1960; 4. Varady, Popp, Rebroff, Prey, Kollo, Weikl, Bavarian State Opera Ch and O, C. Kleiber, DG, 1976: the 1950 Decca version remains a classic with an ideal cast, but it omits dialogue, as does the ebullient Karajan set of 1955. His 1960 remake is complete with the bonus of a Gala Concert featuring most of the famous artists of the day. The Kleiber is an enjoyable, relatively recent set marred by a falsetto Orlofsky [A.B.]
FILMS   German versions in 1923, 1931, 1937, 1945, 1962; as *Oh! Rosalinda!!*, Powell and Pressburger (dirs), LABP, 1955
VIDEO   Coburn, Perry, Fassbaender, Waechter, Hopferwieser, Brendel, Bavarian State Opera Ch, Bavarian State O, C. Kleiber, United 1985/DG 1988: unevenly cast recording of Otto Schenk's sumptuous Munich production, featuring Fassbaender's fine Orlofsky
EDITIONS   f.s., *Johann Strauss Gesamtausgabe*, series 2, vol. 3, Doblinger/Universal, 1974; v.s., Eulenberg, 1968

Eine Nacht in Venedig

A Night in Venice
Operetta in three acts (2h)
Libretto by 'F. Zell' (Camillo Walzel) and Richard Genée, after the comedy *Le Château-Trompette*, by Jules Cormon and Michel Carré (1860)
Composed 1883
PREMIERES   3 October 1883, Friedrich-Wilhelmstädtisches Theater, Berlin; US: 19 April 1884, Daly's Theater, New York; UK: 25 May 1944, Cambridge Theatre, London

After the Berlin premiere of *Eine Nacht in Venedig* was greeted with howls of derision, the dialogue (which Strauss had not seen prior to the Berlin fiasco) was hastily revised for its Vienna premiere six days later. *Eine Nacht in Venedig* has been a popular

favourite since those Viennese revisions. Various other revisions and new versions have been tried since, the most successful being the one produced in Vienna in 1923, with a new book by Ernst Marschka and a revised score by Korngold.

During Carnival time in 18th-century Venice, the Duke of Urbino asks his barber, Caramello, to procure for him the aged Senator Delacqua's comely wife, Barbara. The barber, disguised as a gondolier, delivers his own girlfriend, Annina, who has disguised herself as Barbara. Other characters are similarly disguised in the incredibly complicated plot.

Though the libretto has never been deemed satisfactory, the music is simply, romantically, gorgeous – one of the most opulent of all Viennese operetta scores and the one in which Strauss most artfully melded Italian and Austrian elements. It has been successfully performed at the Viennese Staatsoper and other international opera houses and lends itself exceedingly well to *al fresco* presentation.

RECORDINGS   1. Korngold edition: Schwarzkopf, Loose, Gedda, Kunz, Philharmonia Ch and O, Ackermann, EMI, 1954; 2. Korngold edition: Streich, Görner, Gedda, Curzi, Bavarian Radio Symphony Ch and O, Graunke, EMI Electrola, 1969; 3. original edition: Schary, Scovotti, Bini, Brendel, Hungarian Radio Ch, State Opera O, Märzendorfer, Acanta, 1976: the 1954 is a classic version of the Korngold edition, not superseded by the stereo remake. The 'original' version includes music actually rejected by Strauss [A.B.]
EDITIONS   f.s., *Johann Strauss Gesamtausgabe*, series 2, vol. 9, Doblinger/Universal, 1970; v.ss., Aug. Cranz, 1967; arr. Korngold: Aug. Cranz, 1924

Der Zigeunerbaron

The Gypsy Baron
Comic opera in three acts (2h)
Libretto by Ignaz Schnitzer, after the novella *Sáffi* by Mor Jokai (1883)
PREMIERES   24 October 1885, Theater an der Wien; US: 15 February 1886, Casino Theater, New York; UK: 12 February 1935, Rudolf Steiner Theatre, London (amateur); 9 June 1964, Sadler's Wells, London
CAST   Sándor Barinkay *t*, Kálmán Zsupán *bar*, Ottokar *t*, Count Peter Homonay *bar*, Conte Carnero *bar*, Sáffi *s*, Czipra *ms*, Arsena *s*, Mirabella *a*, Pali *b*; *satb* chorus of gypsies, soldiers, pages, nobles, boatmen, Hungarian peasants, Viennese townspeople
FULL ORCHESTRA

Almost a musical *rapprochement* between the often-feuding dual monarchies of Austria and Hungary, *Der Zigeunerbaron* was received with enormous acclaim in both Vienna and Budapest and probably helped smooth any political friction until the end of the empire.

SYNOPSIS

Act I   In the mid-18th century, the young, exiled Barinkay returns to his estate, accompanied by the Royal Commissioner, Carnero ('Als flotter Geist'). The old gypsy Czipra reads Barinkay's hand and predicts he will find treasure, as well as a wife. The pig-breeder Zsupán, wealthy but illiterate ('Ja, das Schreiben und das Lesen'), proposes that the young man marry his daughter, Arsena. The girl is produced, but she is already in love with Ottokar, the son of her governess, Mirabella. Arsena proudly informs Barinkay that she cannot marry him, and wouldn't do so in any event unless he had the title of baron. Czipra's daughter Sáffi enters singing a native song ('So elend und so treu') that Barinkay seems to remember from childhood. When the other gypsies proclaim him as their long-lost master, Barinkay, now declaring himself a 'gypsy baron', again asks for Arsena's hand. When she refuses, he asks Sáffi for her hand, and insults Arsena, Zsupán, and Ottokar – who is in love with Arsena.

Act II Barinkay and Sáffi declare their love for each other ('Mein Aug' bewacht'), and Czipra helps Barinkay locate the site of the buried treasure ('Ha, seht es winkt'). When the injured parties from Act I turn up with a morality commissioner to protest the Barinkay and Sáffi match, the pair declare ('Wer uns getraut?') that they were married by a bullfinch and serenaded at their nuptials by a nightingale. The provincial governor, Count Homonay, rides in with his hussars to recruit patriots for the war against Spain ('Her die Hand, es muss ja sein'). Zsupán and Ottokar are drafted, and Barinkay joins up when he finds out to his surprise that Sáffi is in fact of noble birth – a Turkish pasha's daughter.

Act III The war is over, and Homonay's regiment is being fêted in Vienna ('Freuet Euch'). Zsupán, who managed to keep away from the fighting and who has picked the pockets of its victims, is applauded by the crowds. They also cheer Barinkay, whom Homonay creates a real baron. Despite Zsupán's entreaties, Barinkay declares his love for Sáffi and allows Arsena and Ottokar to be wed.

The romantic weight of the libretto drew from Strauss a more intensely emotional score than usual, its impressive Magyar colorations mixed in with his customarily lush and exuberant Viennese style. Outstanding are, in Act I, Barinkay's entrance song, with its lilting waltz refrain ('Ja, das alles auf Ehr!'), Zsupán's descriptive 'Ja, das Schreiben und das Lesen', and Sáffi's moody gypsy aria, 'So elend und so treu'; in Act II, the ebullient treasure waltz 'Ha! seht es winkt', the natural-marriage duet 'Wer uns getraut?', and Homonay's recruiting song 'Her die Hand, es muss ja sein'.

RECORDINGS 1. Zadek, Loose, Patzak, Poell, Preger, Vienna State Opera Ch, Vienna PO, Krauss, Decca, 1951; 2. Schwarzkopf, Köth, Gedda, Prey, Kunz, Philharmonia Ch and O, Ackermann, EMI, 1955; 3. Házy, Schädle, Schock, Waechter, Kusche, Ch and O of Deutsche Oper, Berlin, Stolz, Eurodisc, 1965: the first version, thoroughly authentic in style, is cut; the second is a classic and the third (though hardly new) is the only acceptable stereo version [A.B.]
EDITION v.s., Cranz, 1885

Other operatic works: *Indigo und die vierzig Räuber*, 1871; *Der Carneval in Rom*, 1873; *Cagliostro in Wien*, 1875; *Prinz Methusalem*, 1875; *Blindekuh*, 1878; *Das Spitzentuch der Königin*, 1880; *Der lustige Krieg*, 1881; *Simplicius*, 1887; *Ritter Pázmán*, 1892; *Fürstin Ninetta*, 1893; *Jabuka*, 1894;

Waldmeister, 1895; *Die Göttin der Vernunft*, 1897; *Wiener Blut*, 1899 (RECORDING Columbia, 1954)
BIBLIOGRAPHY Egon Gartenberg, *Johann Strauss: The End of an Era*, Pennsylvania State University Press, 1974; Marcel Prawy, *Johann Strauss: Weltgeschichte im Walzertakt*, Verlag Fritz Molden, 1975

R.T.

RICHARD STRAUSS

Richard Georg Strauss; *b* 11 June 1864, Munich, Bavaria; *d* 8 September 1949, Garmisch-Partenkirchen

Strauss achieved mastery in three musical genres: opera, of which he composed 15, orchestral tone poems and lieder. He was also one of the great conductors of his day, not only of his own works but also of those by Mozart, Wagner, Beethoven and many others. His father was the principal horn-player in the Bavarian Court Opera orchestra for nearly half a century and his mother was a member of the wealthy brewing family of Pschorr. His childhood, therefore, was comfortable and he grew up in a household devoted to music. He composed copiously from the age of six; by the time he was 16 he had heard his first symphony played by his father's orchestra conducted by Hermann Levi. His music attracted the attention of Hans von Bülow who, in 1885, offered Strauss a post as his assistant at Meiningen. There he met Alexander Ritter, a passionate Wagnerian, who persuaded the younger man, brought up on a rigid classical diet, to become a follower of the 'music of the future'. In 1886 Strauss was appointed third conductor at the Munich opera house and moved to the Weimar Court Opera in 1889, where his adventurous choice of repertoire brought him much publicity. Meanwhile the success of his tone poems *Don Juan* and *Tod und Verklärung* had led Bülow to dub him 'Richard the Third' (since, he said, after Wagner there could be no 'Richard the Second').

While at Weimar, he conducted the world premieres of Humperdinck's *Hänsel und Gretel* (1893) and of his own first opera *Guntram* (1894). In the latter the principal soprano role was sung by Pauline de Ahna who had been Strauss's pupil for several years; they were married in September 1894. He portrayed her capricious, tempestuous nature in several of his works, notably *Intermezzo* (Christine) and *Die Frau ohne Schatten* (the Dyer's Wife). She was a fine interpreter of his lieder, and Strauss's special sympathy for the female voice undoubtedly owes much to her influence and example. Strauss returned to the Munich Opera in 1894, becoming chief conductor there in 1896, and in 1898 was appointed chief conductor of the Royal Opera in Berlin, where he remained until 1908, a tenure almost exactly parallel with his friend Mahler's directorship of the Vienna Court Opera. Strauss was chief guest conductor at Berlin until 1919, when he agreed to be co-director at Vienna with Franz Schalk. He also played a leading part in 1920 in establishing the Salzburg Festival. Like many before and after him, Strauss fell foul of Viennese Opera politics and resigned in 1924. But in his five years there, with some legendary singers, he conducted important new productions of his own and others' operas. Those who heard him conduct *Così fan tutte*, *Fidelio* and *Tristan und Isolde* counted those performances among the great musical experiences of a lifetime.

Guntram, composed during the first rapture of Wagner-worship, was not a success and seven years passed before Strauss embarked on another opera. It is significant that *Feuersnot*, *Salome* and *Elektra* were one-act operas, stage equivalents of the tone poems with which, between 1888 and 1898, Strauss had established himself among the leaders of contemporary orchestral music. With *Salome* and *Elektra*, emotional blockbusters, he triumphed equally in the opera house, the former encountering resistance in some cities on moral grounds but winning public favour whenever it was performed. *Elektra* is a setting of the version of Sophocles' play by the Austrian poet and playwright Hugo von Hofmannsthal. Thus began the long and fruitful collaboration between composer and librettist which posterity can vicariously share through their absorbingly frank and detailed correspondence – 'We were born for one another,' Strauss wrote.

In *Elektra* Strauss went, in a few passages, as near to the frontier of atonality as he was ever to go in the name of Expressionism. But to interpret the subsequent operas as a retreat from modernism is seriously to misjudge and misunderstand Strauss's achievement. He and Hofmannsthal followed *Elektra* with their biggest popular success, *Der Rosenkavalier*, a Viennese comedy of 18th-century manners. But for all its waltzes and luscious melodies, it also has harmonic progressions as advanced as any in *Elektra*. Strauss's principal operatic ambition, evolved through his experience as a conductor, was for a perfect and democratic fusion of words and music. With this in mind he strove to develop an endless melodic recitative which flowed as naturally as conversation. The beginnings of this style can be detected in *Feuersnot* and throughout much of Act I of *Der Rosenkavalier*.

Indeed Strauss and Hofmannsthal wanted to break fresh ground in the opera house. 'New ideas must search for new forms,' Strauss wrote, and in *Ariadne auf Naxos* they attempted a bold marriage between straight theatre and chamber opera. But on practical and economic grounds alone, this was doomed to failure and, in a revised version, they substituted a short operatic prologue for the play. In this form, the opera has become firmly established. They followed it with their most ambitious venture, the fairy-tale cum allegory *Die Frau ohne Schatten*, in which Hofmannsthal's verbose flights of fancy were matched by music of outstanding intensity and opulence.

Strauss wrote his own libretto for *Intermezzo*, his dramatization of an episode in his married life, in which the melodic recitative style, developed in the prologue to *Ariadne*, fits the narrative like a glove. The fluidity of this style also ensured the success of *Arabella*, a return to romantic period comedy and the last collaboration with Hofmannsthal (who died before it was complete). Strauss could scarcely envisage the continuation of his operatic career without Hofmannsthal, but by a stroke of luck he met the novelist Stefan Zweig. Their opera buffa *Die schweigsame Frau*, based on Ben Jonson, is one of Strauss's happiest scores, a celebration of his delight in finding a new and congenial partner. But the advent of the Nazis meant the end of Strauss's collaboration with a Jew. On his next three operas he worked, grudgingly, with the Viennese theatre historian Joseph Gregor. In *Friedenstag* and *Daphne* he reverted to the one-act form. For the former, an anti-war opera banned in Germany after 1939, he forged a new and tougher style, while in the pastoral lyricism of *Daphne* can be heard the beginning of his last phase, the so-called 'Indian Summer', in which his music combined richness and simplicity. The autumnal splendour continued in *Die Liebe der Danae*, based on a discarded Hofmannsthal sketch, but achieved its operatic apogee in *Capriccio*. Here, in collaboration with the conductor Clemens Krauss, Strauss used the conflict between words and music as the theme of the opera itself. With its aristocratic 18th-century setting, its adorable heroine, its touches of broad comedy and its undercurrent of valediction, *Capriccio* was the perfect vehicle for all the best of Strauss to come together in the last chapter of his important contribution to the development of opera as a vital and progressive form.

Richard Strauss (right) and Hugo von Hofmannsthal, c. 1912

Guntram

Opera in three acts, Op. 25 (3h 15m; rev. version: 2h 30m)
Libretto by the composer
Composed February 1892–September 1893; rev. (cut) 1934
PREMIERES 10 May 1894, Hoftheater, Weimar; rev.
version: 29 October 1940, Nationaltheater, Weimar; US: 19
January 1983, Carnegie Hall, New York (concert)
CAST Guntram *t*, Freihild *s*, The Old Duke *b*, Duke Robert
b, Duke's Jester *t*, Old Man *t*, Old Woman *a*, Friedhold *b*,
Messenger *bar*, 2 Young Men 2 *b*, 3 Vassals 3 *b*, 4
Minnesingers 2 *t*, 2 *b*; *satb* chorus of ducal vassals,
Minnesingers, 4 monks, servants and vagrants
VERY LARGE ORCHESTRA including lute; onstage: 4 hn, 4
tenor hn, 4 tpt, 3 trbn, 4 sd

The subject of *Guntram* was suggested to Strauss by
Alexander Ritter, a violinist in the Meiningen Court
Orchestra while Strauss was its assistant conductor in
1885. He urged Strauss to emulate Wagner and write
his own libretto. Strauss began this task in August
1887. He later rewrote several sections and altered
the ending, to the intense dismay of the Roman
Catholic Ritter. But Strauss was an atheist and,
under the influence of Nietzsche, opted for an ending
in which his hero renounced his religious order and
walked away. He completed the composition sketch
in Cairo on Christmas Eve 1892, inscribing the
manuscript 'Deo gratia! Und dem heiligen Wagner'.
When the score was published, he sent a copy to
Verdi.

Felix Mottl wanted to conduct the first performance in Carlsruhe, but the tenor there declared the
title role to be unsingable. So Strauss conducted
the premiere at Weimar, with his fiancée Pauline
de Ahna as Freihild. A second performance, also
conducted by Strauss, was given in Munich on 16
November 1895. The critics savaged it and the tenor
and the orchestra protested so strongly that the
planned further two performances were cancelled.
Strauss never forgave Munich and had revenge on
the critics in the *Adversaries* section of his tone poem
Ein Heldenleben three years later and in his next
opera, *Feuersnot*. In 1934 Strauss cut *Guntram* (but
did not revise the orchestration) and this version was
performed in Weimar in 1940.

SYNOPSIS
Act I A forest clearing in 13th-century Germany.
Guntram and his mentor Friedhold, troubadours
belonging to a secret band of Minnesingers called the
Champions of Love, have been sent to succour
refugees from the tyranny of Duke Robert, whose
wife Freihild has been forbidden by her cruel
husband to help the poor. Guntram prevents a
woman from drowning herself in a lake and learns
that she is Freihild; he falls in love with her. Her
father, the Old Duke, and Duke Robert invite him to
their court to take part in a singing contest.

Act II At the court feast, Guntram hymns the
virtues of peace under a benevolent ruler. He is
interrupted by a messenger bringing news of an
invading army. Guntram incites the court against
Robert and kills him in a sword fight. The Old Duke
imprisons Guntram, but Freihild vows to free him.

Act III Guntram, in his dungeon, hears monks
singing requiems for Robert's soul. Freihild comes to
free him and to avow her love. When Friedhold also
arrives to bring Guntram to trial before the elders of
the guild, Guntram explains that he must expiate his
guilt in solitude, far away. Friedhold accepts this
reasoning 'in sad amazement'. Guntram asks Freihild
to let him go, much as he loves her, and walks out of
her life.

It is customary to regard *Guntram* as wholly influenced by Wagner, as the names of the characters
imply. But although there are obvious echoes of
Wagner in the score, much of it is mature Strauss: it
was, after all, composed immediately before the tone
poems *Till Eulenspiegel* and *Also sprach Zarathustra*.
It has not held the stage because of the weakness of
the plot, and the difficulty of the role of Guntram.
The love duet and the solo arias for Guntram and
Freihild are characteristic of Strauss's developing
vocal style. In the *Works of Peace* section of *Ein
Heldenleben*, there are more quotations from
Guntram than from any of his other works.

RECORDING Tokody, Takács, Goldberg, Hungarian Army
Ch, Hungarian State O, Queler, Hungaroton/CBS 1985: 1934
revision
EDITIONS f.s./v.s., Aibl, 1894–5; rev. version: f.s./v.s.,
Fürstner, 1934

Feuersnot

Fire Famine
Poem for singing in one act, Op. 50 (1h 30m)
Libretto by Ernst von Wolzogen, after an old Flemish legend,
The Extinguished Fires of Audenaarde
Composed October 1900–May 1901
PREMIERES 21 November 1901, Semper Opernhaus,
Dresden; UK: 9 July 1910, His Majesty's Theatre, London;
US: 1 December 1927, Civic Opera, Philadelphia
(Metropolitan Opera Company)
CAST Schweiker von Gundelfingen, the Bailiff *t*, Ortolf
Sentlinger *b*, Diemut, *s*, Elsbeth, Wigelis, Margret, her
friends *ms*, *a*, *s*, Kunrad the Leveller *bar*, Jörg Pöschel, the
Innkeeper *b*, Hämerlein, the Haberdasher *bar*, Kofel, the
Blacksmith *b*, Kunz Gilgenstock, the Baker and Brewer *b*,
Ortlieb Tulbeck, the Cooper *t*, Ursula, his wife *a*, Ruger
Aspeck, the Potter *t*, Walpurg, his wife *s*, a Maiden *s*;
children's chorus, *satb* chorus of citizens and servants
VERY LARGE ORCHESTRA onstage: glock, hp, harmonium,
vn, vc, 2 sd

The failure of *Guntram* in his native Munich
wounded Strauss, who planned revenge. In 1898
he met Baron Ernst von Wolzogen, a writer who
had founded the *Überbrettl*, a satirical cabaret. His
attempt to establish this entertainment in Munich
failed, so he was ready and willing to co-operate with
Strauss in 'wreaking vengeance' on these philistine
attitudes. Strauss found an old Flemish legend, *The
Extinguished Fires of Audenaarde*. Wolzogen toned
down its impropriety (though still not enough for
some opera managements), transferred the action to
medieval Munich, and made it obvious that Kunrad,
the sorcerer's apprentice, represented Strauss, with
the sorcerer (who does not appear) being Wagner.

The libretto contains puns on the names Strauss, Wagner and Wolzogen.

The opera had its first performance in Dresden, conducted by Ernst von Schuch. Strauss was so delighted that over the next 37 years he awarded eight more premieres to Dresden. In Vienna it was conducted by Mahler, and in London by Thomas Beecham. Munich did not hear it until 1905, when it saw the joke and enjoyed it. Ironically, it is the only city where *Feuersnot* can still regularly be heard.

SYNOPSIS

Midsummer's Eve in 12th-century Munich. Children are collecting wood for the traditional bonfires. Diemut, daughter of Sentlinger, the burgomaster, lets down a basketful on a block-and-tackle from her balcony. In the house opposite lives a young sorcerer, Kunrad, a stranger in the town. He encourages the children to help him pull his wooden house apart as he needs it no more. He sees Diemut, falls in love with her and kisses her. When the crowd has dispersed, she invites him to get into the basket, pulls it halfway to her balcony and leaves him there. The children and citizens return to jeer at him, but Kunrad utters a magic spell which puts out all the fires in the town. He leaps up to Diemut's balcony and harangues the crowd, telling them that the fires will remain extinguished until Diemut acknowledges the power of love. They implore her to yield and as she willingly does so, the fires are relit.

Feuersnot is a major advance on *Guntram*. The score is as light and witty as *Till Eulenspiegel* and packed with musical quotations. Its waltz themes anticipate *Der Rosenkavalier*, and Munich folksongs are cunningly embedded in the texture. Delightful use is made of the children's chorus. While *Guntram* was essentially an old-fashioned opera on Wagnerian lines, with long solo narrations, *Feuersnot* moves radically towards the conversational style Strauss was to develop in later years. Even in the long narration by Kunrad from Diemut's balcony, the style is altogether freer and more flexible. This narration is the core of the opera. In it Kunrad reminds Munich of his master, the old sorcerer, 'Meister Reichhart' (i.e. Wagner), whom they had driven out of town. The opera ends with an impassioned love scene for the orchestra alone which is sometimes heard as a concert-hall item.

RECORDING   Varady, Weikl, Schenk, Bavarian Radio Ch, Tolzer Knabenchor, Munich Radio O, Fricke, Acanta, 1984
EDITIONS   f.s./v.s., Fürstner, 1901

Salome

Drama in one act, Op. 54 (1h 45m)
Libretto by the composer from Hedwig Lachmann's German translation of the tragedy by Oscar Wilde (1893)
Composed November 1904–June 1905
PREMIERES   9 December 1905, Semper Opernhaus, Dresden; US: 22 January 1907, Metropolitan, New York; UK: 8 December 1910, Covent Garden, London
CAST   Herod *t*, Herodias *ms*, Salome *s*, Jokanaan *bar*, Narraboth *t*, page to Herodias *a*, 5 Jews 4 *t, b*,

First Nazarene *t*, Second Nazarene *b*, 2 soldiers 2 *b*, a Cappadocian *b*
ORCHESTRATION   picc, 3 fl, 2 ob, ca, heckelphone, E♭ cl, 2 B♭ cl, 2 A cl, B♭ b cl, 3 bsn, dbsn, 6 hn, 4 tpt, 4 trbn, b tuba, 4 timp, small timp, perc (t-t, cym, bd, sd, tambourine, triangle, xyl, castanets, glock), cel, 2 hp, organ, harmonium, str (16.16.10–12.10.8); reduced 1930 scoring: 3 fl, 3 ob, 3 cl, 3 bsn, 4 hn, 3 tpt, 3 trbn, tuba, timp, perc (4 players), cel, hp, str

Strauss saw Max Reinhardt's production of Wilde's French play *Salomé* (in a German translation) in Berlin in November 1902, with Gertrud Eysoldt in the title role. He was already sketching themes for an operatic setting, having been sent the play by Austrian poet Anton Lindner, who offered to fashion a verse libretto for him. But Strauss was not impressed by the first few scenes and decided that he himself would adapt Hedwig Lachmann's translation, which he shortened by about a third.

Strauss offered the first performance to Ernst von Schuch at Dresden. Some of the singers at first read-through wanted to return their parts as too difficult, but the Czech tenor Karel Burian (uncle of the composer Emil Burian), who created Herod, already knew his by heart. The Salome, Marie Wittich, regarded the opera as improper and refused to perform the Dance of the Seven Veils – 'I won't do it, I'm a respectable woman.' A dancer stood in for her in this scene (a solution sometimes adopted since). In spite of moralistic objections, *Salome* was a sensational success at Dresden (except with the critics) and was performed at 50 other opera houses within two years.

But the Church's and others' objections to the work were still strong. At the Berlin Court Opera, where Strauss was employed as chief conductor, the Kaiser would allow it to be performed only if the Star of Bethlehem was shown in the sky (even though Christ's birth took place 30 years before the action of the opera). After its Metropolitan premiere in New York, there was such an outcry, led by the daughter of the financier J. Pierpont Morgan, that further performances were cancelled. Mahler, who regarded it as 'one of the greatest masterpieces of our time', was only dissuaded by Strauss from resigning his directorship of the Vienna Court Opera after the censor refused to allow him to stage it (and it was not performed in Vienna until October 1918). The Kaiser said, 'I like this fellow Strauss, but *Salome* will do him a lot of damage.' Strauss's retort was: 'The damage enabled me to build my house in Garmisch.'

After completing the full score of *Salome*, Strauss also worked on a version with Wilde's original French text. In order to adapt his music to this text, he consulted his friend the novelist and poet Romain Rolland. This version (1930) is rarely performed, but was revived at Lyons in 1990 and subsequently recorded.

SYNOPSIS

On the terrace of the palace of the tetrarch Herod Antipas, the Syrian captain of the guard, Narraboth, is looking into the banqueting hall, captivated by the beauty of the 16-year-old Salome, daughter of

The first production of Salome *(Dresden, 1905)*

Herod's second wife Herodias by her first marriage ('Wie schön ist die Prinzessin Salome heute Nacht!'). Herodias's page warns him that something terrible may happen if he looks at Salome too much. The page has been alarmed by how strange the moon seems, 'like a woman rising from a tomb'. Two soldiers are guarding the cistern beneath the terrace where Jokanaan (John the Baptist) is imprisoned for denunciation of Herodias' marriage to her husband's brother. They hear his voice uttering prophecies. Salome leaves the banquet to evade her stepfather's lascivious glances and to escape from the religious arguments among the Jews, and from the Roman soldiers whom she hates. She hears Jokanaan and wheedles Narraboth into defying Herod's orders and bringing the prophet to meet her.

Jokanaan launches into a tirade against Herod and his wife. When Salome tells him she is the daughter of Herodias, he rails at her ('Zurück, Tochter Babylons!'), but she is fascinated by his voice and longs to touch his body and his hair and to kiss his mouth. At this point, Narraboth, horrified by her conduct, kills himself, but she hardly notices. Jokanaan tells her to seek salvation from the Son of Man and retreats into the cistern, cursing her as he goes.

Herod, Herodias and their attendants come on to the terrace. Herod, too, is disturbed by the strangeness of the moon. He slips in Narraboth's blood and orders the body to be removed. He feels a cold wind blowing and 'the beating of vast wings', but Herodias tells him he is ill. Herod offers Salome wine and fruit but she refuses. Jokanaan's voice is heard again. Herodias urges that he be handed over to the Jews, but Herod says, 'He is a holy man who has seen God.' This prompts a heated argument among the five Jews over the question of whether anyone has seen God. After Jokanaan's reference to the 'Saviour of the world' the two Nazarenes tell Herod of the Messiah's miracles, including raising a woman from the dead. This alarms Herod ('I will not allow him to raise the dead') but when Herodias complains that Jokanaan is reviling her, Herod replies, 'He did not speak your name.'

Herod commands Salome to dance for him. She refuses, despite promises of lavish gifts, but agrees when he says she can have whatever she desires. After the dance she claims her reward – Jokanaan's head on a silver charger. Herodias is delighted, but Salome says she wants it for her own pleasure, not to please her mother. Herod tries everything to dissuade her but she obsessively repeats her demand ('Gib mir den Kopf des Jokanaan!'). Eventually Herod gives in, saying, 'Truly she is her mother's child.' The executioner descends into the cistern and returns with the prophet's head on a silver shield. Salome seizes it and sings a long aria to it, taunting it for being unable to reply to her. 'If you had seen me, you would have loved me. I am hungry for your body.' Herod refuses to stay and as he climbs the staircase looks back to see Salome lost in ecstasy as she kisses Jokanaan's mouth. Horrified, he orders the soldiers to kill her ('Man töte dieses Weib!'). They crush her beneath their shields.

Salome is a study in obsessions, wrought by a composer whose powers of description in his orchestral tone poems had equipped him to depict in the theatre the strangeness of the happenings on this oriental night, with the moon lighting the scene and inducing an atmosphere of impending violence and madness. There is no overture. A rising arpeggio on the clarinet launches Narraboth into his rapturous vision of Salome and, from then to the end, there is no let-up in the intensity and tension of the score. The 105-strong orchestra is used with an imaginative power that was new to opera in 1905, the exotic tone colours reflecting the action on the stage both graphically and psychologically. The passage of nearly a century has not diminished the startling novelty of the sound as Salome awaits Jokanaan's execution, an effect created by four double-basses 'pinching' the string with thumb and forefinger and striking it with the bow. There are many other equally dramatic moments, with dissonances no less far-reaching in their tendency towards atonality than those that were to follow in *Elektra*.

The role of Salome is a tremendous challenge for a soprano, who ideally should combine a Wagnerian weight of tone with a girlish quality. In 1930 Strauss reduced the orchestration so that a light soprano could sing the part. The 20-minute final aria moves from animal frenzy to a demented erotic yearning. Yet it is not only Salome's obsession that Strauss presents with such calculated vividness. The religious zeal of Jokanaan is equally obsessive and is conveyed in music of lofty and noble quality. The music for Herod also brilliantly delineates the tetrarch's personality: neurotic, superstitious, lascivious – a gift of a part for a character tenor. Whatever the mood in this opera, whether it be sultry, savage, sadistic or sensuous, Strauss finds the orchestral colours to convey it to the listener with overwhelming intensity.

RECORDINGS 1. Nilsson, Hoffman, Stolze, Waechter, Vienna PO, Solti, Decca, 1961: uncut and vivid performance, magnificently recorded; 2. Final scene: Welitsch, Matačić, EMI, 1944: recorded during the celebrations of Strauss's 80th birthday, an unsurpassed performance; 3. Studer, Rysanek, Hiestermann, Terfel, O of Deutsche Oper, Berlin, Sinopoli, DG, 1991: vivid set, with Studer the best Salome since Welitsch; 4. Huffstodt, Jossoud, Dupouy, van Dam, Lyon Opera O, Nagano, Virgin, 1991: interesting set in Wilde's original French; 5. Goltz, Kenney, Patzak, Braun, Vienna PO, Krauss, Decca, 1954
VIDEOS 1. Malfitano, Rysanek, Hiestermann, Estes, O of Deutsche Oper, Berlin, Sinopoli, Teldec, 1992: Peter Wiegl's spare stage production, acutely filmed by Brian Large with Malfitano as a lascivious princess; 2. Stratas, Varnay, Beirer, Weikl, Vienna PO, Böhm, DG, 1980: notable for Stratas's spoilt-child Salome and Böhm's authentic conducting [A.B.]
EDITIONS f.s./v.s., Fürstner, 1905

Elektra

Tragedy in one act, Op. 58 (1h 45m)
Libretto by Hugo von Hofmannsthal, based on his own play after the tragedy by Sophocles (411 or 410 BC)
Composed June 1906–September 1908

PREMIERES 25 January 1909, Semper Opernhaus, Dresden; US: 1 February 1910, Manhattan Opera, New York; UK: 19 February 1910, Covent Garden, London
CAST Elektra *s*, Klytemnästra *ms*, Chrysothemis *s*, Aegisth *t*, Orest *bar*, Tutor to Orest *b*, Confidante *s*, Trainbearer *s*, Young Servant *t*, Old Servant *b*, Overseer *s*, First Maid *a*, Second and Third Maids 2 *ms*, Fourth and Fifth Maids 2 *s*; *satb* chorus of servants
ORCHESTRATION 3 fl/picc, 3 ob/ca, heckelphone, E♭ cl, 4 cl, b cl, 2 basset hn, 3 bsn, dbsn, 8 hn, B♭ tubas/2 F tubas, 6 tpt, bass tpt, 3 trbn, contrabass trbn, contrabass tuba, timp (2 players), perc (bd, sd, t-t, triangle, tambourine, cym, glock), cel, 2 hp, str (8 first vn, 8 second vn, 8 third vn, 6 va (also 4 vn), 6 first vc, 6 second vc, 8 db)

Hugo von Hofmannsthal wrote his play *Elektra*, an adaptation of Sophocles, in three weeks in August 1903, when he was 28. It was produced in Berlin the following October by Max Reinhardt and was a major success. Strauss probably saw it there or a few years later and recognized its potential as an operatic subject. He and Hofmannsthal met in November 1905, and the poet gave him a free hand to cut the play to make a libretto. Hofmannsthal wrote new lines for two episodes, the recognition scene and the duet between Elektra and Chrysothemis after the murders.

Strauss was at first wary of setting *Elektra* immediately after *Salome*, feeling (not unjustifiably) that the emotional contents were similar. But Hofmannsthal pressed him, and the opera was performed at Dresden early in 1909. There and elsewhere it enjoyed a *succès d'estime* rather than a popular success, but its title role was soon to attract a series of superb dramatic sopranos, while the role of Klytemnästra was also to become a favourite. *Elektra* is often spoken of in Freudian terms, but it is by no means certain that Hofmannsthal had read Freud at the time he wrote his play. His main source was Sophocles and the strength of the work is in its modern adaptation of Greek tragedy to which Strauss's music added a fearful strength.

SYNOPSIS

The courtyard of the royal palace at Mycenae, where Clytemnestra lives with Aegisthus. Serving women, drawing water from a well, are discussing Electra, daughter of King Agamemnon and Clytemnestra, who lives like a wild, unkempt animal. They all mock her, except one who is whipped for her loyalty. Electra, left alone, laments her loneliness ('Allein! Weh, ganz allein') and recalls the murder of her father Agamemnon by Aegisthus and Clytemnestra. Calling on her father's spirit to help her, Electra dreams of vengeance after which she will dance for joy. Her reverie is interrupted by her younger sister, Chrysothemis, with news that Clytemnestra and Aegisthus plan to imprison Electra in a tower. She sings of her own longing for a husband and children ('Ich hab's wie Feuer in der Brust').

A procession approaches; Clytemnestra and her entertainers are on their way to the ritual altar. The queen, bedecked with jewels and amulets, decides to consult Electra about how she can stop the horrible nightmares that disrupt her sleep. Electra brings the

Advance publicity for the UK premiere of Elektra *(London, 1912)*

From the opening onomatopoeic fanfare, 'Agamemnon', it becomes plain that the dead king is the opera's principal leitmotif. *Elektra* is a huge crescendo from start to finish, less lyrical and tonal than *Salome*. The work sounds better organized than its predecessor, probably because the libretto is tauter and less rhapsodic than Wilde's play. It is feasible to regard *Elektra* as a symphonic structure and it is firmly based on a tonal plan presenting each of the characters and their emotional states in a particular key. Both Electra and Clytemnestra, the most obsessive characters in the opera, are projected bitonally. Clytemnestra relates her dream in near-atonal harmonies as a kind of psychodrama, but it is inaccurate to describe *Elektra* in terms of the Schoenbergian Expressionism of *Erwartung* (1924). *Elektra* is near to being a number opera, with formal introductions to the arias. Although the level of dissonance is higher in *Elektra* than in *Feuersnot* or *Der Rosenkavalier*, it has many points of contact with these works, not least in its use of the waltz in various guises. The music to which Electra leads Aegisthus to his doom might have been written for Baron Ochs in *Der Rosenkavalier*.

If Strauss wrote nothing again like *Elektra*, it was not because he had consciously retreated from avant-garde procedures. He instinctively knew that, with this work and *Salome*, he had gone as far as he could in depicting obsessed heroines of this kind. To have continued would have been to invite the charge of repeating himself which had at first deterred him from setting *Elektra*.

Another important point to note about *Elektra* is that Strauss uses the orchestra to provide the opera with a wordless climax. Not until *Daphne*, nearly 30 years later, was he again to give the orchestra its head so completely. Music here triumphs over words, echoing Electra's opening of her final dance (a waltz) with the words 'Ob ich die Musik nicht höre? Sie kommt doch aus mir' ('You ask if I hear the music? It comes from me.').

RECORDINGS 1. Nilsson, Collier, Resnik, Krause, Vienna PO, Solti, Decca, 1967: uncut performance, technically superb, with a towering performance by Nilsson in the title role; 2. Marton, Studer, Lipovšek, Weikl, Bavarian Radio SO, Sawallisch, EMI, 1990: also uncut, with marvellous orchestral playing
VIDEOS 1. Rysanek, Ligendza, Varnay, Fischer-Dieskau, Vienna PO, Böhm, Decca, 1981: a memorably melodramatic staging by Götz Friedrich with Rysanek adding a new laurel to her long career and Böhm ending his with a classic reading; 2. Marton, Studer, Fassbaender, Grundheber, Vienna State Opera Ch and O, Abbado, Pioneer (laserdisc only), 1989: Harry Kupfer's melodramatic 1989 Vienna State Opera staging [A.B.]
EDITIONS f.s./v.s., Fürstner, 1908–9

subject round to her brother Orestes. She does not believe reports that he has gone mad. Electra tells her mother that a sacrificial victim will stop her dreams – Clytemnestra herself. The queen's terror gives way to maniacal laughter when her confidante whispers to her that Orestes is dead.

The same news is given to Electra by Chrysothemis, who refuses to join Electra in killing Aegisthus and their mother. Electra resolves she must act alone ('Nun denn, allein!') and digs frantically for the axe with which Agamemnon was killed and which he has buried in the courtyard. As she digs, a man enters the courtyard. He says he awaits a summons to bring news of Orestes' death. Electra berates him for being alive while a better man is dead. When he discovers who she is, he whispers, 'Orestes lives.' She does not recognize her questioner until servants kiss his garments: 'The dogs in the courtyard know me, but my sister does not.' After the powerful recognition scene that follows, she impresses on him what must be done. He enters the palace and Electra realizes that she has not given him the axe. But screams from the palace indicate Clytemnestra's death. These bring Aegisthus into the courtyard. Electra, chillingly amiable to him, lights him to the palace door. He shouts for help, to which Electra replies, 'Agamemnon hears you!' Electra begins her dance of joy, dropping dead at its climax. Chrysothemis beats vainly on the doors of the palace for admission, crying, 'Orest.' But Orestes is already being pursued by the Furies.

Der Rosenkavalier
The Knight of the Rose
Comedy for music in three acts, Op. 59 (3h 15m)
Libretto by Hugo von Hofmannsthal
Composed April 1909–September 1910
PREMIERES 26 January 1911, Hofoper, Dresden; UK: 29 January 1913, Covent Garden, London; US: 9 December 1913, Metropolitan, New York

CAST   Feldmarschallin, Princess Werdenberg *s*, Octavian, Count Rofrano *s*, Baron Ochs auf Lerchenau *b*, Herr von Faninal *bar*, Sophie *s*, Marianne Leitmetzerin, Sophie's duenna *s*, Valzacchi *t*, Annina *a*, Police Commissioner *b*, Marschallin's Major-domo (Struhan) *t*, Faninal's Major-domo *t*, Notary *b*, Innkeeper *t*, Italian Singer *t*, 3 Noble Orphans *s*, *ms*, *a*, Dressmaker *s*, Pet-seller *t*, 4 Marschallin's footmen 2 *t*, 2 *b*, 4 waiters *t*, 3 *b*, Mahomet *mime*; *silent*: scholar flautist, hairdresser, hairdresser's assistant, widow of noble family; *satb* chorus of footmen, couriers, heyducks, cookboys, guests, musicians, 2 watchmen, 4 little children, various personages of suspicious appearance
ORCHESTRATION   3 fl/picc, 3 ob/ca, cl in A, B♭, C, D, E♭ (3 players), b cl/basset hn, 3 bsn/dbsn, 4 hn, 3 tpt, 3 trbn, b tuba, timp, perc (3 players: bd, military d, cym, tambourine, triangle, glock, bells, castanets), 2 hp, cel, str (16.16.12.10.8); off-stage orchestra: (Act III) 2 fl, ob, 3 cl, 2 bsn, 2 hn, tpt, sd, harmonium, pf, 2 vn, va, vc, db (5 or 10 players)

The plot of *Der Rosenkavalier* was concocted within a few days in February 1909 by Hofmannsthal and his friend Count Harry Kessler. They borrowed ideas from many literary sources, including Molière, based some of the characters on operatic prototypes (Mozart's Countess and Cherubino in *Le nozze di Figaro* and Verdi's *Falstaff*) and also drew inspiration from the graphic arts (Hogarth's *Mariage à la mode*). Strauss was delighted by the resulting libretto for Act I and set it page by page as he received it. He was highly critical of parts of the plot in Acts II and III and these were adjusted to accommodate his ideas. Hofmannsthal created a mid-18th-century Vienna in considerable detail, but many of the customs (including the crucial idea of the presentation of a silver rose to the bride-to-be) were his own invention. The sense of class distinction and the subtlety of the language are prime features of the work's 'realism'.

The opera ran into censor trouble in Dresden and Berlin, but the principal threat to the Dresden premiere came from the inadequacy of the producer there. Strauss sent Max Reinhardt to supervise the carrying out of his own ideas, which he did without any credit in the programme. The opera was a huge success, with special trains being run to Dresden from various parts of Germany. The stage designs and production book prepared by Alfred Roller, who had been Mahler's scenic artist in Vienna, played a large part in the success and were used for several decades. London, Vienna, New York, Milan and many other operatic centres were quick to take up a work that remains in the repertoire of every major opera house and shows no sign of losing its popular appeal.

SYNOPSIS

Act I Vienna, during the reign of the Empress Maria Theresa. The bedroom of the Princess Werdenberg, wife of the Field Marshal (hence 'Marschallin'). She has spent the night with her 17-year-old lover Count Octavian. Their breakfast is interrupted by her cousin, Baron Ochs auf Lerchenau, described by Strauss as a 'rural Don Juan'. Octavian disguises himself as a chambermaid ('Mariandel'), with whom Ochs flirts. The baron has

come to ask the Marschallin to recommend a young nobleman as bearer of the traditional silver rose – a *Rosenkavalier* – to his fiancée, Sophie von Faninal, daughter of a recently ennobled arms dealer. It is then time for the Marschallin's *levée*. The stage is filled with tradesmen, various petitioners, a widow and her three daughters, a hairdresser, two intriguers (Valzacchi and Annina) and an Italian tenor who sings an aria ('Di rigori armato il seno') which is a pastiche of Mozart's Italian song settings. The song is cut short by an argument over dowry between Ochs and a lawyer. Valzacchi and Annina offer Ochs their services and Leopold, Ochs's bastard son (a non-speaking part), hands the silver rose to the Marschallin. Left alone, the Marschallin reflects on Ochs's conceit ('Da geht er hin') and compares herself when young with Sophie. At 32 she is acutely conscious of growing old and when Octavian returns he finds her in a melancholy mood, aware that he will soon leave her for a younger woman. She tells him that time ('Die Zeit, die ist ein sonderbar Ding') slips by so quickly that she often gets up in the night and stops the clocks. When Octavian leaves her, the Marschallin realizes they have not even kissed goodbye. She sends her little black page Mahomet to him with the casket containing the silver rose.

Act II In Herr von Faninal's palatial home Sophie, Faninal and her duenna are awaiting the rose-bearer's arrival by coach. Octavian ceremoniously presents her with the rose and they are mutually attracted at first sight. Ochs is ushered in by Faninal and fondles Sophie lecherously. Meanwhile his disreputable bodyguard causes chaos in the household. Sophie is appalled and Octavian vows to prevent the marriage. Their love duet ('Mit Ihren Augen voll Tränen') is abruptly ended when they are apprehended by Valzacchi and Annina, who send for Ochs. Octavian challenges Ochs to a duel and wounds him slightly. Ochs acts as if he has been severely injured and Sophie tells Faninal she refuses to marry this oaf. Octavian has meanwhile won over Valzacchi and Annina. While Ochs, bandaged, is left alone, Annina brings him a message from the Marschallin's chambermaid 'Mariandel' agreeing to a meeting. Ochs, delighted, sings his favourite waltz ('Ohne mich').

Act III In a private room at an inn Valzacchi, Annina and others, under Octavian's supervision, rehearse the opening of trapdoors and other devices with which they plan to scare Ochs. Octavian dons his disguise as 'Mariandel' and goes to meet the baron. They sit down to supper, served by Leopold. To the music of an offstage band's waltzes, Ochs tries vainly to seduce the 'girl', who refuses wine and his advances ('Nein, nein! Ich trink kein Wein'). Every time he approaches her, apparitions appear at windows or through trapdoors. Annina, dressed in black as a widow, enters to claim Ochs as her husband and father of her children, who burst in noisily shouting 'Papa!' Ochs calls the police and tells the suspicious commissioner that he is dining with his fiancée Sophie. Octavian has ordered Valzacchi to send for Faninal and Sophie, who refute Ochs's story. Octavian tells the commissioner the truth and

VERLAG UND EIGENTUM FÜR ALLE LÄNDER VON ADOLPH FÜRSTNER BERLIN W.
COPYRIGHT 1910 BY ADOLPH FÜRSTNER

Design by Alfred Roller for Baron Ochs's costume in Act II of Der Rosenkavalier *(Dresden, 1911)*

sheds his female attire. Meanwhile the Marschallin (summoned by Leopold) enters, recognizes the police commissioner as her husband's ex-orderly, and assures him that the affair was 'just a masquerade'. She advises Ochs to leave, which he does, pursued by creditors, children and tavern staff. In the sublime trio for the three soprano voices ('Hab mir's gelobt'), the young lovers sing of their delight and the Marschallin accepts the situation with a good grace. She leaves them together ('Ist ein Traum') while she invites Faninal to ride home with her. The stage is empty, but Mahomet runs in to search for a hand-kerchief Sophie has dropped. Waving it above his head, he rejoins them and the curtain falls.

Although Hofmannsthal imagined *Der Rosenkavalier* as a neo-Mozartian opera in the *Figaro* mould, Strauss's music is post-Wagnerian in its subtle symphonic development of leitmotifs and its use of

the orchestra in a richly allusive fashion. The score is both heavy and light and the vocal writing carries a stage further Strauss's development of a lyrical con-versational style that is neither aria nor recitative. The exquisite illustrative detail – whether it be the high polytonal chords for flutes, harps, celesta and three violins which depict the silver rose, the fast movement of the hairdresser's hands as he adjusts the Marschallin's coiffure or the graphic love-making of the prelude to Act I – shows Strauss the tone poet at the height of his creative powers.

All three leading female roles reveal Strauss's extraordinary musical affinity with the soprano voice – the Act III trio is one of the finest ensemble pieces in all opera – while the bass and baritone roles of Ochs and Faninal are also richly rewarding. The role of the Marschallin is one of the greatest of all operatic creations and has attracted a line of distinguished interpreters. Strauss bound the whole work together with a string of memorable waltz tunes (which he later arranged in two sequences for concert performance) and although both he and Hofmannsthal admitted in later years that there were *longueurs* in *Der Rosenkavalier*, they never quite recaptured its lyrical *élan*. With its perennial themes of melancholy at growing old, love at first sight and nostalgia for a vanishing age threatened by social upheaval, *Der Rosenkavalier* had every ingredient for a lasting popular success. But what has ensured that success is the matchless blend between a mar-vellous libretto and the music it called into being.

RECORDINGS 1. Reining, Jurinac, Gueden, Weber, Vienna PO, E. Kleiber, Decca, 1954: splendid uncut performance by a vintage Viennese cast, including Weber's memorable Ochs, under inspired direction of Kleiber; 2. Schumann, Lehmann, Olczewska, Mayr, Vienna PO, Heger, EMI, 1933: extracts only, but enshrining one of the finest casts ever to sing *Der Rosenkavalier*; 3. Stich-Randall, Schwarzkopf, Ludwig, Edelmann, Philharmonia O, Karajan, EMI, 1957: slightly cut, this is a favourite version in which Schwarzkopf's Marschallin is dominant; 4. Donath, Crespin, Minton, Jungwirth, Vienna PO, Solti, Decca, 1969: complete and superbly sung; 5. Te Kanawa, von Otter, Hendricks, Rydl, Staatskapelle Dresden, Haitink, EMI, 1991
VIDEOS 1. Popp, Jones, Fassbaender, Jungwirth, Ch and O of Bavarian State Opera, C. Kleiber, DG, 1979: an off-the-stage film of Otto Schenk's famous Munich production with a near-ideal cast and conductor; 2. Bonney, Te Kanawa, Baltsa, Haugland, Ch and O of Covent Garden, Solti, Castle, 1984: film of John Schlesinger's conventional staging [A.B.]
EDITIONS f.s./v.s., Fürstner, 1910

Ariadne auf Naxos

(Second version)
Ariadne on Naxos
Opera in one act, with prologue, Op. 60 (2h)
Libretto by Hugo von Hofmannsthal
Prologue composed 1911–July 1912; second version, May–June 1916
PREMIERES first version: 25 October 1912, Hoftheater, Stuttgart; UK: 27 May 1913, His Majesty's Theatre, Haymarket, London; second version: 4 October 1916, Hofoper, Vienna; UK: 27 May 1912, Covent Garden, London; US: 1 November 1928, Civic Opera, Philadelphia
CAST Composer *s*, Music Master *bar*, Dancing Master *t*, Wig-maker *b*, Lackey *b*, Prima Donna/Ariadne *s*,

Tenor/Bacchus *t*, Zerbinetta *s*, Harlequin *bar*, Scaramuccio *t*, Truffaldino *b*, Brighella *t*, Officer *t*, Naiad *s*, Dryad *a*, Echo *s*, Major-domo *spoken role*
ORCHESTRATION   picc, 2 fl, 2 ob, 2 cl, 2 bsn, 2 hn, tpt, trbn, str (6 vn, 4 va, 4 vc, 2 db), pf, 2 hp, harmonium, cel, timp, perc (glock, tambourine, triangle, cym, sd)

Both Hofmannsthal and Strauss were indebted to the producer Max Reinhardt who, without official credit, had transformed the Dresden production of *Der Rosenkavalier*. As a thank-offering, Hofmannsthal devised a novel combination of play and 30-minute opera, the former to be his adaptation of Molière's *Le bourgeois gentilhomme*, with incidental music for the dances, the latter *Ariadne auf Naxos*, with Strauss's music, which would interweave elements of opera seria with those of the *commedia dell'arte*. The opera was conceived as a divertissement after the dinner that concludes the play and was to be performed in the presence of Monsieur Jourdain, the 'bourgeois gentilhomme'. Between the play and opera came a short scene in prose in which those responsible for arranging the entertainments for Jourdain – the Composer and the Dancing Master – were told by Jourdain's footman that the two pieces must be performed simultaneously. This first version was performed in Stuttgart on 25 October 1912, but the evening lasted over six hours (the '30-minute opera' had become a 90-minute opera) and it was obvious to composer and librettist that in this form the work was impracticable, requiring both a drama company and an opera company to perform it.

In 1913 Hofmannsthal hit on a new version, with the opera preceded by a short sung prologue based on the linking scene. He eliminated Monsieur Jourdain and transferred the action of the prologue from 17th-century Paris to the 19th-century house of 'the richest man in Vienna'. Strauss at first was not interested, but in 1916 he composed the prologue. At the Vienna premiere the *travesti* role of the young Composer was sung by Lotte Lehmann, her first outstanding success. Although the original version is occasionally revived, it is the second version that has become part of the international repertoire.

SYNOPSIS (second version)
Prologue   In the house of the richest man in Vienna, where a sumptuous banquet is to be held in the evening, two theatrical groups are busy preparing their entertainments. The Music Master protests to the Major-domo about the decision to follow his pupil's opera seria, *Ariadne auf Naxos*, with 'vulgar buffoonery'. The Major-domo makes it plain that he who pays the piper calls the tune and that the fireworks display will begin at nine o'clock. The Composer wants a last-minute rehearsal with the violinists, but they are playing during dinner. The soprano who is to sing Ariadne is not available to go through her aria; the tenor cast as Bacchus objects to his wig. There is typical backstage chaos. Seeing the attractive Zerbinetta and inquiring who she is, the Composer is told by the Music Master that she is leader of the *commedia dell'arte* group which is to perform after the opera. Outraged, the Composer's

wrath is turned aside when a new melody occurs to him ('Du, Venus' Sohn'). The Major-domo returns to announce that his master now requires both entertainments to be performed simultaneously and still to end at nine o'clock sharp. More uproar, during which the Dancing Master suggests that the Composer should cut his opera to accommodate the harlequinade's dances.

The plot of *Ariadne* is explained to Zerbinetta, who mocks the idea of 'languishing in passionate longing and praying for death'. To her, another lover is the answer. Zerbinetta and the Composer find they have something in common when Zerbinetta tells him 'A moment is nothing – a glance is much' ('Ein Augenblick ist wenig – ein Blick ist viel'). 'Who can say that my heart is in the part I play?' Heartened, the Composer sings of music's power ('Musik ist eine heilige Kunst'). But when he sees the comedians scampering about, he cries, 'I should not have allowed it.'

Opera   On the island of Naxos, where Ariadne has been abandoned by Theseus, who took her with him from Crete after she had helped him to kill the Minotaur. Ariadne is asleep, watched over by three nymphs, Naiad, Dryad and Echo. They describe her perpetual, inconsolable weeping. Ariadne wakes. She can think of nothing except her betrayal by Theseus and she wants death to end her suffering. Zerbinetta and the comedians cannot believe in her desperation and Harlequin vainly tries to cheer her with a song about the joys of life. She sings of the purity of the kingdom of death ('Es gibt ein Reich') and longs for Hermes to lead her there. The comedians again try to cheer her up with singing and dancing, but to no avail. Zerbinetta sends them away and tries on her own, with her long coloratura aria ('Grossmächtige Prinzessin'), the gist of which is that there are plenty of other men besides Theseus. In the middle of the aria, Ariadne goes into her cave. Zerbinetta and her troupe then enact their entertainment in which the four comedians court her.

The three nymphs excitedly announce the arrival of the young god Bacchus, who has just escaped from the sorceress Circe. At first he mistakes Ariadne for another Circe, while she mistakes him for Theseus and then Hermes. But in the duet that follows, reality takes over and Ariadne's longing for death becomes a longing for love as Bacchus becomes aware of his divinity. As passion enfolds them, Zerbinetta comments that she was right all along: 'Off with the old, on with the new.'

The second version necessitated considerable revision of the score. Comments on the action by M. Jourdain and others, characters now eliminated, had to be deleted. Zerbinetta's aria was eased by dropping its pitch a whole tone for most of its duration: two major cuts amounting to about 80 bars of music were made, although Strauss replaced the second cut (in the closing section of the aria) by a new coda less than half as long, which contains a duet for voice and flute. A scene just before Bacchus' arrival, in which Zerbinetta interrupts Ariadne's address to her as yet invisible liberator, was deleted.

But the biggest alteration was the ending. In the first version, after the Ariadne–Bacchus love duet, the comedians return and Jourdain's guests depart. Part of Zerbinetta's aria is recapitulated as she points out that what has just occurred supports her view of life and love. The comedians' waltz returns as the four clowns and Zerbinetta sing and dance. Jourdain, who has been asleep, is wakened by a servant who asks if the firework display should begin. Jourdain ignores him and repeats his admiration for the true nobility. His trumpet tune ends the opera.

In *Ariadne auf Naxos*, the two contrasting elements in Strauss's musical personality – the rococo and the heroic – are interwoven much as the opera seria and the harlequinade are intermingled or, more accurately, juxtaposed, in the plot of the opera itself. It represents a major step forward in Strauss's defence of the musical territory he had mapped out for himself, the antithesis of the Schoenbergian revolution. Yet it is no backward step. The neo-baroque music of the harlequinade belongs as inescapably to the 20th century as does Stravinsky's *Pulcinella*.

A virtuoso feature of the work is Strauss's use of a small orchestra (36 players). So skilful is his scoring that in the passionate final duet for Ariadne and Bacchus it is rich enough to give the impression of a large orchestra. Part of the unique flavour of the second version of *Ariadne auf Naxos* derives from Strauss's brilliant juxtaposition of low comedy and high tragedy. In the prologue, where he made a spectacular advance in his development of a melodic conversational recitative, he is at home depicting the quarrels and chaos of backstage theatrical life. In the opera, he slips easily from the heroic style in which Ariadne's part is composed to the buffooning of the *commedia dell'arte* characters.

RECORDINGS 1. Streich, Schwarzkopf, Seefried, Schock, Philharmonia O, Karajan, EMI, 1954; 2. Gruberova, Norman, Varady, Frey, Fischer-Dieskau, Leipzig Gewandhaus O, Masur, Philips, 1988: the Masur is stylish and well recorded, but the Karajan recording with Schwarzkopf is a classic. There is also a marvellous 1944 performance, conducted by Böhm for Strauss's 80th birthday, with Irmgard Seefried as the Composer and Maria Reining as Ariadne (Acanta)
VIDEO Battle, Norman, Troyanos, King, O of the Metropolitan, New York, Levine, DG, 1991
EDITIONS first version: f.s./v.s., Fürstner, 1912; second version: f.s./v.s., Fürstner, 1916

Die Frau ohne Schatten

The Woman Without a Shadow
Opera in three acts, Op. 65 (3h 30m)
Libretto by Hugo von Hofmannsthal
Composed July 1914–June 1917
PREMIERES 10 October 1919, Staatsoper, Vienna; US: 18 September 1959, War Memorial Theatre, San Francisco; UK: 2 May 1966, Sadler's Wells, London (Hamburg Opera)
CAST Emperor *t*, Empress *s*, Nurse *ms*, Spirit Messenger *bar*, Guardian of the Threshold of the Temple *s* or *ct*, Apparition of a Youth *t*, Voice of the Falcon *s*, Voice from Above *a*, Barak the Dyer *bar*, Dyer's Wife *s*, Barak's brothers: One-Eyed *b*, One-Armed *b*, Hunchback *t*,

children's voices 3 *s*, 3 *a*, voices of the nightwatchmen 3 *b*; *satb* chorus of imperial servants, children, attendant spirits, spirit voices
ORCHESTRATION 4 fl/2 picc, 3 ob/ca, 2 B♭ cl/C cl, E♭/D cl, b cl/C cl, basset hn/C cl, 4 bsn/dbsn, 4 hn, 4 tpt, 4 trbn, 4 B♭/F tubas/4 hn, b tuba, glass harmonica, 2 cel, glock, 5 Chinese gongs, timp, perc (cymbals, sd, whip, xyl, bells, bd, large tenor drum, tambourine, triangle, 2 pairs castanets, t-t), 2 hp, str (16 first vn, 16 second vn, 6 first va, 6 second va, 6 first vc, 6 second vc, 8 db); offstage: 2 fl, ob, 2 C cl, bsn, hn, 6 tpt, 6 trbn, wind-machine, thunder-machine, organ, 4 t-t

Hofmannsthal first outlined his idea for a 'magic fairy-tale' in March 1911. He told Strauss that in it two men would confront two women and 'for one of the women your wife might well, in all discretion, be taken as a model'. Progress on the libretto was slow and was interrupted by the composition of the first version of *Ariadne auf Naxos*. Composer and librettist discussed the project in detail during a trip to Italy in the spring of 1913. Hofmannsthal explained that *Die Frau ohne Schatten* would veer between the world of spirits and the world of humans with an intermediate plane inhabited by the Emperor and Empress. He described it as standing 'in general terms, to *Zauberflöte* as *Rosenkavalier* does to *Figaro*'. Although the principal subject of the opera is infertility – the 'shadow' is the symbol of parenthood – its main dramatic interest is in the Empress's development from a fairy-tale creature into a human being through her realization that other people matter. She is prepared to sacrifice her own and her husband's life rather than allow the humble Barak and his shrewish wife to be forced apart. The libretto is heavy with symbolism and has often been dismissed as pretentious and incomprehensible, but Strauss himself had no difficulty with it and regarded it as Hofmannsthal's masterpiece. The outbreak of the First World War caused further delays, with Hofmannsthal unable to complete the third act until the spring of 1915.

In March 1919 Strauss became joint director of the post-war Vienna State Opera with Franz Schalk. He gave the first performance of the new opera to Vienna, but later admitted that it was a mistake in spite of a cast headed by Maria Jeritza, Lotte Lehmann and Richard Mayr. With the poverty and hunger attendant upon the end of hostilities, this was no time for such a difficult and complicated work to be performed. In addition, Alfred Roller, the director and set designer, surprisingly failed to realize some of the magical effects that were required. Few German theatres were equipped to stage it satisfactorily (the Dresden premiere was a disaster). Consequently the opera made its way slowly and was not staged in New York and London, for example, until 1966. Even in Munich, it is still cut in performance, but it has gradually come to be regarded by many Strauss enthusiasts as his greatest opera.

SYNOPSIS
Before the action of the opera begins, the Emperor of the South Eastern Islands was hunting with his

Set design by Alfred Roller for the falcon house in Die Frau
ohne Schatten *(Vienna, 1919)*

falcon and pursued a gazelle. Just as he was about to
kill it, it resumed its real form as the daughter of
Keikobad, master of the spirit world. The Emperor
married her, but she has remained neither spirit nor
human and has borne no children.

Act I   The Nurse is guarding the room where the
royal couple are sleeping. Keikobad's messenger
appears to tell her that if the Empress does not cast a
shadow (i.e. become pregnant) within three days, the
Emperor will be turned to stone and the Empress be
reclaimed by her father. The Emperor goes hunting
for three days to try to find his falcon. In his absence,
the falcon comes to the Empress and tells her what
Keikobad has threatened. She knows she can obtain
a shadow only from a human woman and forces the
Nurse to help her find one. They fly down to the
earth and go to the impoverished home of the Dyer
Barak, whose Wife is quarrelling with her husband's
deformed brothers. She is discontented and knows
that Barak wants children. The Nurse plans to turn
the Wife's unhappiness to her advantage. She tries to
buy her shadow, promising a life of luxury in return.
The Wife agrees to refuse her husband's advances for
three days, during which time the Empress and Nurse
will be her servants. Barak returns from market to
find he has been provided with a single bed.

Act II   While Barak is at work, the Nurse continues her temptation of his Wife, conjuring up the
young man of her dreams. But the Dyer's Wife
pushes the youth away when he tries to touch her.
Barak returns with a huge bowl of food for his
brothers and the beggar children who have followed
him home. His Wife refuses to eat. In his falcon-
house, the Emperor awaits the Empress, having been
told she will be there. He sees her and the Nurse slip
secretly into the house, senses they have been in the
world of humans and decides to kill the Empress. But
he cannot bring himself to do it and flees. Before
Barak leaves for work, the Nurse gives him a
sleeping draught. She again causes the young man to
appear. But the Wife takes fright and wakens Barak,
rebuking him for sleeping in the daytime and leaving
her a prey to robbers. The Empress, asleep in the

falcon-house, is overcome with remorse for Barak.
She hears the falcon's cry: 'The woman casts no
shadow! The Emperor must turn to stone!' She
laments: 'Whatever I touch I kill!' Barak's Wife
taunts him by telling him she was unfaithful while he
slept and has sold her shadow. Barak wants to kill
her and the Nurse provides a sword. The Wife
realizes that she loves him and the Empress
repudiates the shadow bargain. Barak lifts the sword
but it is snatched from him. The earth swallows him
and his Wife while the Nurse leads the Empress to
safety.

Act III   Imprisoned in separate cells, Barak and
his Wife realize that they belong together. They are
freed by servants of the spirit world to seek one
another. The Empress and the Nurse go by boat to
Keikobad's temple. The Empress recognizes its door
from a dream. The Nurse tries to dissuade her from
entering, warning her that she will be punished. But
the Empress dismisses the Nurse – 'I part from you
for ever' – and enters the temple. The voices of
Barak and his Wife are heard as they search for each
other. The Nurse says she hates all mankind and
deliberately misleads the couple, sending them in
opposite directions. She then tries to enter the
temple but Keikobad's messenger bars her way and
throws her into the boat, condemning her to wander
henceforth among those she hates. In the temple, the
Empress wants to face Keikobad. The Keeper of the
Threshold tempts her with a drink from the water of
life, after which the Dyer's Wife's shadow will be
hers. She can hear the voices of Barak and his Wife.
She refuses to drink and is shown the Emperor
turned to stone, only his terrified eyes remaining
alive. She offers to die with him and still refuses to
drink. The stage goes dark and when the light returns
the Empress is seen to cast a shadow and the
Emperor is restored to life. Because the Empress has
learned human feeling, Keikobad has forgiven her.
Emperor and Empress, Barak and Wife are reunited
while the voices of their unborn children sing their
praises.

Die Frau ohne Schatten is Strauss's largest and most
ambitious opera and the one in which the genius he
lavished on description and characterization in his
tone poems is most literally applied to the stage.
The composer of the opening horn-call of *Till
Eulenspiegel* is very obviously the same composer
who invented the haunting and unforgettable cry of
the falcon in this opera; and there are other striking
instrumental effects, such as the use of a glass
harmonica to depict the Empress's acquisition of a
shadow. While some passages are on an opulent,
Wagnerian scale, much of the score has the delicacy
of chamber music. In this respect it closely resembles
the Mahler of the Eighth Symphony and *Das Lied
von der Erde* (of all his scores it comes closest to a
homage to his colleague and friend). The exotic,
oriental flavour is a further link with *Das Lied von
der Erde*.

The score is another refutation of the widespread
allegation that Strauss 'went soft' after *Elektra*.
While there are such exquisite diatonic episodes as

the orchestral interlude in the first scene between Barak and his Wife – a simple melodizing around the chord of D♭ to illustrate the Dyer's compassionate and loving nature – there are also any number of examples of rootless harmony and near atonality. The Empress's dream, for instance, ends with an orchestral epilogue in which nightmarish harmonies sum up the anguish she has expressed.

Like *Der Rosenkavalier* the opera contains three great roles for women – the Empress, Barak's Wife and the Nurse – and a typically fine Strauss baritone part for Barak. We may wonder if Strauss's supposed hostility to the tenor voice was anything more than a joke on his part when we hear the magnificent music he wrote for the Emperor, notably his Act II aria in the hunting-lodge. Although Strauss told Hofmannsthal that he found it difficult to fill the Emperor, Empress and Nurse with musical red corpuscles as he had the characters in *Der Rosenkavalier*, he nevertheless gave all three characters some of the most powerful and elevated music he ever composed.

RECORDINGS 1. Behrens, Varady, Runkel, Domingo, van Dam, Vienna State Opera Ch, Vienna PO, Solti, Decca, 1992; 2. Studer, Vinzing, Schwarz, Kollo, Muff, Bavarian Radio SO, Sawallisch, EMI, 1988; both are uncut and highly recommended; 3. Rysanek, Ludwig, Thomas, Berry, Vienna PO, Karajan, Nuova Era, 1989: superb orchestral playing in recording of 1964 Vienna live performance; 4. Rysanek, Nilsson, King, Berry, Vienna PO, Böhm: splendid live 1977 performance, DG, 1986
EDITIONS f.s./v.s., Fürstner, 1919

Intermezzo

Bourgeois comedy with symphonic interludes in two acts, Op. 72 (2h 15m)
Libretto by the composer
Composed 1919–August 1923
PREMIERES 4 November 1924, Schauspielhaus of Dresden Staatsoper; US: 11 February 1963, Lincoln Center, New York; UK: 9 September 1965, King's Theatre, Edinburgh (Bavarian State Opera)
CAST Christine *s*, Robert Storch *bar*, Anna *s*, Baron Lummer *t*, Notary *bar*, Notary's Wife *s*, Conductor *t*, Commissioner *bar*, Lawyer *bar*, Opera Singer *b*, Franzl, boy *spoken role*; *silent*: young girl, chambermaid, housemaid, the Storchs' cook
ORCHESTRATION 2 fl/picc, 2 ob/ca, 2 cl/b cl, 2 bsn, 3 hn, 2 tpt, 2 trbn, pf, hp, timp, perc (cym, sd, bd, triangle, pair bells), harmonium, str (11.9.5.5.3)

After the heady brew of *Die Frau ohne Schatten*, Strauss yearned to write a work in a lighter vein. His ideas were contemptuously rejected by Hofmannsthal, who advised him to approach the Austrian dramatist Hermann Bahr. At a meeting in Salzburg in August 1916, Strauss outlined to Bahr an idea he had for an opera based on an incident in his marriage in May 1902 when Pauline had opened a letter mistakenly addressed to Strauss in which a woman named Mieze Mücke had asked for some opera tickets in Berlin. The actual letter contains no endearments – it begins 'Dear Herr Strauss' and ends 'Yours sincerely' – but Pauline evidently suspected the worst and sent a telegram to Strauss, who was

staying in the Isle of Wight after a tour of England, announcing their divorce. The matter was cleared up when it was established that Fräulein Mücke had confused Strauss with Josef Stransky.

After some months, Bahr withdrew, saying that the subject could be satisfactorily handled only by Strauss himself. So Strauss wrote the libretto, a brilliant one, based almost exclusively on real exchanges between Pauline and himself. The opera was first performed at Dresden, the sets being replicas of the Strausses' home at Garmisch. The baritone playing Storch (Josef Correck) wore a mask to make him resemble the composer as closely as possible. Christine was sung (at the first performance only) by Lotte Lehmann. Because the opera was felt to be in dubious taste, it soon dropped out of the repertoire. Pauline herself did not appreciate the joke. But after Strauss's death it was frequently performed in Munich and has gradually become more popular. In Britain, a particularly fine Glyndebourne production, with Elisabeth Söderström, and later Felicity Lott, as Christine, won it many admirers.

Sketch of the accident on the sledge run in Intermezzo *by Adolf Mahnke, who designed the first production (Dresden, 1924)*

SYNOPSIS

Act I At his home on the Grundlsee, the composer Robert Storch is preparing to leave for Vienna, where he is to conduct opera. His wife Christine is helping him pack. She'll be glad to have him out of the way for a while – why can't he have a job like other men that takes him out of the house every day? Composing isn't work compared with her household duties. Before he leaves, they have another quarrel, about the publicity attendant upon his career, and she refuses to kiss him goodbye until he says he might be in a train crash for all she knows. Left alone with her maid Anna, Christine bemoans being left to deal with the tax-collector and to look after her little son. She cheers up when a friend telephones to invite her to go tobogganning. On the sledge-run she collides with a young man who introduces himself as Baron Lummer. Her parents knew his family, so she arranges to meet him. They go to a dance in the inn on the Grundlsee. She takes him under her wing and rents a room for him in the house of the local notary, fussing about cleanliness and her protégé's migraines. Christine writes to Robert to tell him about Lummer, who then arrives. Conversation is fitful and Christine is reduced to reading him extracts from the newspaper. He sounds her out on how far she is prepared to help him in his career as a naturalist. Her husband – whom she now praises to the skies – will help him when he returns, she parries. After Lummer has left, she meditates on her love for her husband.

In his room, Lummer vents his feelings about the boring Christine. His girlfriend Resi arrives in skiing clothes but he sends her away for fear his landlady might see her and tell Christine. He writes to Christine, who explodes in anger when she reads his request for 1000 marks. He arrives at the Storch residence, to be given a stern lecture, which is interrupted by the arrival of a letter addressed to Robert. Christine opens it and, horrified, reads: 'Dear Sweetheart, send me two more tickets for the opera tomorrow. Afterwards in the bar as usual. Your Mieze Meier.' Christine at once sends a telegram: 'You know Mieze Meier. Your faithlessness proven, this is goodbye for ever.' She orders Anna to pack all the bags and wakes her child, who says he loves his father and doesn't want to go away.

Act II   In Vienna, the Lawyer, the Singer, the conductor Stroh and the Business Man are playing the card-game Skat and discussing Christine – 'A frightful woman, how does he put up with her?' When Storch joins them, they continue the banter and tease him about Christine's letter about Lummer. Nothing to worry about, says Storch, we understand one another. Christine's telegram is then delivered. Stroh shows surprise that Storch also knows Mieze Meier. Christine asks the Notary to represent her in divorce proceedings, which he assumes, to her annoyance, involve Lummer. She is even more annoyed when he refuses to act without consulting Storch, whom she respects. Storch, pacing agitatedly up and down in the rain in the Prater, is joined by Stroh, who says that Mieze has told him she intended her letter for him (Stroh) but confused the names. Then you must go to Grundlsee and explain it to my wife, Storch replies. At Grundlsee all is chaos as the packing proceeds. Stroh arrives to explain the confusion; later Storch himself returns, to be received coldly because, Christine says, he has not realized how much pain he has caused her. Robert admits he returned because the Notary had written to him about Lummer. But he believes in her innocence – and roars with laughter over the 1000 marks. The opera ends with loving reconciliation.

The fact that *Intermezzo* was a slice of Strauss's everyday life for too long obscured its importance, a pioneering opera in which everyday events – e.g. telephone conversations – became operatic fare. Thanks to Strauss's libretto, the action moves swiftly, with a cinematic flowing of one scene into the next. The symphonic interludes, miniature tone poems, sum up and add a dimension to the action. *Intermezzo* is also important as a further and major step in Strauss's lifelong quest for a viable marriage of words and music, in which the words are audible but the music paramount. In a long and fascinating preface to the published score, he warned conductors to pay particular attention to his dynamics, designed to ensure audibility of the text.

The libretto is in everyday conversational prose, which is set to a most subtle melodic recitative, both *secco* and *accompagnato*. The characters' inner feelings are delineated in the orchestral accompaniment, which is witty, allusive and graphic. There is much humour, but also a deep-lying seriousness. Strauss's own agony of mind at the thought of a divorce from his Pauline is starkly evoked in the scene in the Prater; and although the shrewish side of Pauline/Christine provides the audience with many laughs, her lovable side – and the tenderness her husband felt for her – is very evident. Although he could never have brought himself to treat such a subject, Hofmannsthal went to see *Intermezzo* and perspicaciously wrote to Strauss about its essential seriousness. Schoenberg too, as early as the 1920s, accounted it among Strauss's best and most enduring compositions.

RECORDING   Popp, Dallapozza, Fischer-Dieskau, Bavarian Radio SO, Sawallisch, EMI, 1980
VIDEO   Lott, Pringle, Caley, Glyndebourne Festival Ch, LPO, Kühn, Castle, 1983: straightforward film of excellent Glyndebourne performance [A.B.]
EDITIONS   f.s./v.s., Fürstner, 1924

Die ägyptische Helen

The Egyptian Helen
Opera in two acts, Op. 75 (2h 15m)
Libretto by Hugo von Hofmannsthal
Composed 1923–October 1927, rev. 1932–January 1933
PREMIERES   6 June 1928, Staatsoper, Dresden; rev. version: 14 August 1933, Festspielhaus, Salzburg; US: 6 November 1928, Metropolitan, New York
CAST   Helen *s*, Menelaus *t*, Hermione *s*, Aithra *s*, Altair *bar*, Da-ud *t*, 2 servants of Aithra *s*, *ms*, 3 elves 2 *s*, *a*, omniscient sea-shell *a*; *satb* chorus of elves, male and female warriors, slaves, eunuchs
LARGE ORCHESTRA including cel, organ, 2 hp; offstage: 6 ob, 6 cl, 4 hn, 2 tpt, 4 trbn, timp, 4 triangle, 2 tambourine, wind-machine

Hofmannsthal resumed his collaboration with Strauss in 1922 when they devised a ballet to Beethoven's incidental music for *The Ruins of Athens*. The poet suggested an opera about Helen of Troy. He had for some time been pondering how it was that Menelaus took back Helen as his wife after the Trojan War, which had been caused by her adultery with Paris. Strauss was hoping for a light-hearted piece on the lines of Offenbach's *La belle Hélène*. What he got, as so often from Hofmannsthal, began lightly but gradually acquired all kinds of psychological and symbolical nuances.

Nevertheless he was delighted with the libretto for Act I and Hofmannsthal, on hearing the music, declared it to be 'light and transparent, for all its high, noble seriousness'. Strauss had realized that the lightness of form at which Hofmannsthal was aiming did not require 'operetta' treatment. *Helena* became a romantic opera. As Strauss said in an interview before the premiere: 'I am afraid this music is melodious, sounds beautiful and unfortunately presents no problems to ears which have developed beyond the 19th century.'

Problems arose over the casting of Helen. The role was conceived for Maria Jeritza, whose physical beauty was a major asset, but Dresden could not afford her enormous fee. When Strauss agreed to the substitution of Elisabeth Rethberg, a good singer but not such a beauty, he was fiercely attacked by Hofmannsthal: 'This will ruin Helena, completely ruin her.' Jeritza sang the role in Vienna. The opera was not a success, nor has it been since, in spite of Strauss's revisions to Act II in 1933 at the request of Clemens Krauss.

SYNOPSIS

Act I In the palace of the sea-god Poseidon, the enchantress Aithra possesses a sea-shell (Mussel) which sees and knows everything and can report it. The Mussel says that in a ship off the coast Menelaus is about to kill his sleeping wife Helen of Troy. Aithra wrecks the ship and Menelaus and Helen take refuge in the palace. Helen now wants to regain Menelaus' love, even though he still plans to kill her for her adultery with Paris. Aithra restores Helen's youthful beauty and gives Menelaus a magic potion to make him believe that Helen was never in Troy with Paris but in an enchanted sleep in the palace of Aithra's father. She promises to build them a magic pavilion on the slopes of the Atlas Mountains and gives Helen a phial of lotus juice which will make them forget the past.

Act II After a passionate 'second wedding night', Menelaus thinks Helen is a phantom and wants to abandon her. The lotus juice doesn't work. Desert warriors, led by Altair, arrive (at Aithra's command). Menelaus mistakes Altair's son Da-ud for Paris and kills him while out hunting. Aithra discovers that Helen was mistakenly given the antidote to the lotus juice, but Helen offers it to Menelaus because she wants to restore his memory. He accepts her for what she is. Altair tries to seize Helen, but Aithra's warriors defeat him.

Die ägyptische Helena is the least performed and the least highly regarded of the Strauss–Hofmannsthal operas. Yet Hofmannsthal believed it was the best thing he had done and Strauss described the music as 'Greek Wagner'. Undoubtedly the libretto presents difficulties. The plot is confused and contrived in Act II and the characters have little life of their own. But the music has much to commend it. The *cantabile* style of the third act of *Die Frau ohne Schatten*, which gave rise to Barak's great aria 'Mir anvertraut', is here followed up. *Helena* is Strauss's *bel canto* opera, with arias, ensembles and other set pieces in profusion. Helen herself is a fully developed role, warm and sensuous, with Menelaus a more interesting vocal character than Bacchus in *Ariadne auf Naxos*. Some of the writing for the voice foreshadows the pure, serene style of his later works, notably *Daphne*. The orchestration is rich and bright, with a diamond-like hardness in the harmony.

RECORDING Jones, Hendricks, Kastu, White, Detroit SO, Dorati, Decca, 1979
EDITIONS f.s./v.s., Fürstner, 1928/33

Arabella

Lyric comedy in three acts, Op. 79 (2h 30m)
Libretto by Hugo von Hofmannsthal
Composed 1930–October 1932
PREMIERES 1 July 1933, Staatsoper, Dresden: UK: 17 May 1934, Covent Garden, London (Dresden Opera); US: 10 February 1955, Metropolitan, New York
CAST Count Waldner *b*, Adelaide, his wife *ms*, Arabella *s*, Zdenka *s*, Mandryka *bar*, Matteo *t*, Count Elemer *t*, Count Dominik *bar*, Count Lamoral *b*, Fiakermilli *s*, Fortune-teller *s*, 3 players 3 *b*; *spoken roles*: Welko, Djura, Jankel, hotel porter; *silent*: Arabella's companion, a doctor, groom; *satb* chorus of cabmen, ball guests, hotel guests, waiters
ORCHESTRATION 3 fl/picc, 2 ob, ca, 2 cl, cl in C, b cl, 3 bsn/dbsn, 4 hn, 3 tpt, 3 trbn, tuba, timp, hp, str

Hofmannsthal based his last libretto for Strauss on his novel *Lucidor* (1910), with some elements added from a proposed comedy, *Fiaker als Graf* ('Cabbie as Count'). Strauss had been pressing him for some time for 'a second *Rosenkavalier* without its mistakes and *longueurs*'. In what became *Arabella*, Hofmannsthal believed he had found the formula his collaborator required – a Viennese setting with a background of waltzes and a plot based on his favourite theme of love at first sight. He sent the libretto of Act I to Strauss in May 1928. Adjustments were made and the complete libretto was ready by Christmas 1928. Further revisions were delayed by Hofmannsthal's illness. Strauss wanted a substantial monologue for Arabella with which to end Act I and 'Mein Elemer!' was supplied on 10 July 1929. Strauss telegraphed his thanks and congratulations from Garmisch to Rodaun. But the telegram was not opened. It arrived on 15 July, the day of the funeral of Hofmannsthal's son Franz, who had committed suicide. An hour or so before the service, Hofmannsthal had a stroke and died.

Strauss began to compose *Arabella* in 1930. He dedicated it to Alfred Reucker and Fritz Busch, intendant and conductor of the Dresden State Opera where it was to be premiered. But in March 1933 the Nazis dismissed both men. Strauss withdrew the score, but Dresden held him to his contract and Clemens Krauss conducted the first performance with Viorica Ursuleac (who later became his wife) as Arabella. In Vienna Lotte Lehmann sang the title role. The critical response was cool, the general attitude being that it was an attempt to imitate *Rosenkavalier*, and was not as good. This attitude gradually given way to admiration for the opera on its own terms and it has become one of the best loved of Strauss's stage works. It is generally performed in the original three-act version, but Munich favours the producer Rudolf Hartmann's 1939 device of linking Acts II and III by omitting the final waltz and chorus of Act II.

SYNOPSIS

Act I Count Waldner, a retired cavalry officer, and his wife live in a slightly seedy Vienna hotel. They

Viorica Ursuleac (Arabella) and Martin Kremer (Matteo) (Dresden, 1933)

are hard up. Waldner gambles at the card table but rarely wins. They have two daughters, Arabella and Zdenka, but the latter is passed off as a boy because they cannot afford to bring out both girls in Vienna society. It is Carnival Day (Shrove Tuesday) 1860, and Countess Waldner (Adelaide) is consulting a fortune-teller who says that Arabella's successful suitor will be a foreigner, summoned by letter. Left alone, Zdenka admits an army officer, Matteo. He believes Arabella loves him because of the letters he receives from her. But these are written by Zdenka, who adores him. He leaves, threatening suicide or exile. When Arabella enters, Zdenka quarrels with her about her coldness to Matteo. Arabella says she will know the right man when she meets him. In fact she saw a stranger looking at her in the street that morning and wishes he would send her flowers. Count Elemer, one of three suitors, arrives to escort Arabella for a drive. She tells him she must choose a husband before the night is out while she is queen of the Cabbies' Ball. Before they leave, Arabella sees her stranger in the street outside. Waldner tells Adelaide he's been hoping for a letter from a former army comrade, Mandryka, a Croatian. He has sent the rich old man a portrait of Arabella. Sure enough, a waiter says a Mandryka is waiting to see him. But this is a tall, handsome young man, nephew of Waldner's friend, who is now dead. He has inherited his uncle's lands and wealth and, having seen her

portrait, has come to woo Arabella. He shows his bulging wallet to Waldner and tells him to help himself. After he has left, Arabella sings of the impossibility of marriage with Elemer ('Mein Elemer!').

Act II At the Cabbies' Ball, Arabella is presented to Mandryka, whom she recognizes as her stranger in the street. They declare their love and Mandryka tells her of the custom in his village whereby betrothed girls present a cup of clear Danube water to their fiancé as a token of chastity and allegiance. Arabella says she will dance farewell to her girlhood. The cabbies' mascot, the Fiakermilli, hails Arabella as the queen of the ball. Arabella has a final dance with each of her three suitors, Elemer, Dominik and Lamoral. Matteo has been hovering nearby and is assured by Zdenka of Arabella's love. She gives him a letter, supposedly from Arabella. This exchange is overheard by Mandryka. In the letter, Zdenka says, is the key to Arabella's bedroom (in reality, her own). Mandryka cannot believe this deception, but when he is given a letter from Arabella excusing herself from the remainder of the evening, he gets drunk, flirts with the Fiakermilli and insults the Waldners.

Act III From the main hall of the Waldners' hotel we see Matteo on the landing at the top of the staircase, emerging from what he believes to be Arabella's room. He cannot believe his eyes when he sees Arabella, in her ball gown, in the lobby. He tells her he cannot understand how she can be so distant after what has just passed between them. Arabella is mystified and annoyed. She denies she was upstairs 15 minutes ago. The Waldners and Mandryka arrive. Seeing Matteo, Mandryka is convinced of Arabella's fickleness and orders his servants to pack for departure. Arabella denies that Matteo is her lover. The silence is broken by a cry as Zdenka, in a nightdress, runs downstairs to say farewell to her family before she jumps into the river. She tells Arabella what has happened and reveals to Matteo that she is a girl and that it was her to whom he has just made love. Mandryka, ashamed, asks Waldner to accept Matteo as a son-in-law. Everyone disperses, leaving Arabella with Mandryka. She asks that his servant should bring her a glass of water to her room to quench her thirst. Mandryka soliloquizes on his stupidity. Then he sees Arabella descending the stairs bringing him the glass of water as in his village custom. 'Take me as I am!' she declares.

Arabella is Strauss's most romantic opera. For their last collaboration, Hofmannsthal eschewed his tendency to overload his libretti with symbols, mysticism and psychological insights. Instead he was content with a tale of love at first sight involving a strange and eccentric but very human group of characters. Just as *Die ägyptische Helena* seemed to reflect the cinema's preoccupation in the 1920s with sheikhs and desert songs, so in *Arabella* there is suggestion of a cinematic plot – awaiting Mr Right. But Strauss's music is of such charm and warmth that the improbabilities of the plot as they involve Matteo and Zdenka in Act III are of no account – one accepts it all. The scoring has a transparency and sweetness rare in 20th-century opera.

In setting the libretto, Strauss continued the *parlando* style he had been developing so successfully since the *Ariadne* prelude (though it can be found in *Feuersnot* in an embryonic state). *Arabella* created a new kind of music-theatre, combining the finest qualities of opera, operetta and musical.

Too much is made of the fact that Hofmannsthal died before he could revise Acts II and III. Although there are dramatic weaknesses in Act II, they are not fatal – and the Munich habit of running the last two acts together is no improvement in any respect. The comparison with *Der Rosenkavalier* is also overworked. Vienna and waltzes are about the only genuine similarities, both treated in very different ways in *Arabella*.

A feature of the score is Strauss's use of Slavonic folk music to give special flavour to the music for Mandryka. Lyricism is all in *Arabella*, both in the libretto and the music. If it is not Strauss's most profound opera, it is in many ways the most uncomplicatedly enjoyable, which is not to say that it lacks complexities. The heroine herself is a fascinating figure, as Strauss realized when he demanded a big aria for her to end Act I. In 'Mein Elemer!', he and Hofmannsthal provide a character study of Arabella that is the key to the whole opera.

RECORDINGS 1. Donath, Varady, Dallapozza, Fischer-Dieskau, Berry, Bavarian State Opera O, Sawallisch, EMI, 1981: complete and well sung; 2. Gueden, Della Casa, Dermota, London, Edelmann, Vienna PO, Solti, Decca, 1958: valuable for Della Casa's portrayal of title role
VIDEOS 1. Rolandi, Putnam, K. Lewis, Bröcheler, Glyndebourne Festival Ch, LPO, Haitink, Castle, 1984: film of John Cox's lively staging; 2. Ghazarian, Janowitz, Kollo, Weikl, Vienna PO, Solti, Decca, 1977: well-made version of Schenk staging [A.B.]
EDITIONS f.s./v.s., Fürstner, 1933

Die schweigsame Frau

The Silent Woman
Comic opera in three acts, Op. 80 (3h)
Libretto by Stefan Zweig, freely adapted from Ben Jonson's comedy *Epicoene, or The Silent Woman* (1609)
Composed October 1932–October 1934 (overture, January 1935)
PREMIERES 24 June 1935, Staatsoper, Dresden; US: 7 October 1958, City Center, New York; UK: 20 November 1961, Covent Garden, London
CAST Sir Morosus *b*, Housekeeper *a*, Barber *bar*, Henry *t*, Aminta *s*, Isotta *s*, Carlotta *ms*, Morbio *bar*, Vanuzzi *b*, Farfallo *b*; *satb* chorus of actors and neighbours
LARGE ORCHESTRA including large perc (3/4 players), cel, hp; offstage: organ, cembalo, tpts, bagpipe, drums

After Hofmannsthal's death, Strauss was introduced to the novelist and playwright Stefan Zweig (1881–1942), who suggested a collaboration. When he received the draft of Act I in the summer of 1932, Strauss was overjoyed: 'The born comic opera – more suited to music than either *Figaro* or *The Barber of Seville*.' The libretto was completed by mid-January 1933. Strauss completed the composition sketch in November 1933 and the full score in October 1934. The Nazis were now in power in Germany and had introduced their anti-Semitic legislation. Zweig, an Austrian, was Jewish, but his libretto for *Die schweigsame Frau* was personally approved by Hitler, who did not wish to attract unfavourable international publicity by acting against Strauss.

While at Dresden for the premiere, Strauss discovered that Zweig's name had been omitted from the programme. He demanded its restoration, threatening to leave if this was not done. He got his way, but meanwhile a letter he had written to Zweig criticizing the regime had been intercepted by the Gestapo and sent to Hitler. After four performances, the opera was banned throughout Germany. Karl Böhm conducted these performances, in which one of the great Strauss sopranos, Maria Cebotari, sang the role of Aminta.

SYNOPSIS

Act I The garrulous housekeeper to Sir Morosus, a retired 17th-century British admiral, tells the barber who comes to shave him every day that the lonely old man needs a wife and she would like this chance. The barber says her constant prattling would drive the old man mad, for an explosion on board ship had damaged the admiral's hearing, leaving him extremely sensitive to noise. However, while shaving Morosus, the barber suggests he should take a young, silent wife. Morosus denies that such a woman exists. Morosus's nephew Henry, whom the old man believed to be lost in Italy, arrives. What need has he now of a wife when he has an heir to whom to leave his treasures? Henry says he has a troupe of friends with him. Morosus thinks he means 'troops' and is horrified to discover that the 'soldiers' are an opera company. Moreover, the prima donna is Henry's wife, Aminta. Morosus disinherits Henry and orders the barber to find him a silent young woman. The barber hatches a plot.

Act II The barber tells Morosus he has found three girls from whom he can choose a wife. They are all impersonated by members of Henry's troupe. Morosus chooses 'Timidia' (in reality Aminta) because she is quiet and meek. A clergyman and lawyer (also disguised actors) perform a wedding ceremony. When Morosus and his 'wife' are left alone, Aminta sees that he is a fine man and wishes she had not become involved. But she plays her part and suddenly turns into a shrieking virago, breaking up his house. Henry promises that he will free Morosus from this dreadful woman next day.

Act III Aminta is supervising a noisy refurbishment of Morosus's living room. Henry, disguised as a music teacher, arrives to give her a singing lesson (Monteverdi and Legrenzi). The noise is driving Morosus mad, until the barber ushers in the Lord Chief Justice and two lawyers (actors, of course). But they cannot find a reason for divorce. However, the barber suggests that 'Lady Morosus' has slept with someone else before marriage. A disguised Henry confirms this. But one of the 'lawyers' rules that it was not stipulated that Timidia should be a virgin. Case dismissed. Morosus is distraught and at this point Henry and Aminta remove their disguises. Morosus sees the joke, congratulates the actors and calls for wine and music. He reflects on how wonderful a silent wife is when she is married to somebody else.

Strauss's delight in Zweig's libretto undoubtedly arose principally from the fact that at last he had been provided with a light comedy. It offered plenty of opportunities for parody. Like the *Ariadne* prologue, it gave him as characters members of an opera company, a world in which he felt at ease; and, in Aminta, he yet again had a heroine some of whose characteristics resembled those of his wife Pauline and who was also a reincarnation of Zerbinetta.

Several episodes in a work that partially reverts to the format of number opera have a Rossinian sparkle and there are lyrical interludes of considerable charm. Morosus, another Strauss self-portrait, is vividly drawn and the opera company roles – all musical descendants of the comedians in *Ariadne auf Naxos* – are effective in a well-produced staging. Perhaps the finest music comes at the start of Act II, with the touching duet for Aminta and Morosus followed by the bogus wedding ceremony, in which Strauss quotes from the Fitzwilliam Virginal Book.

Somewhere behind it all lurks the shade of Verdi's *Falstaff*. But Strauss does not keep the top spinning as effortlessly as Verdi, mainly because the quality of his melodic invention falls below his best. Even so, *Die schweigsame Frau* does not deserve the neglect into which it has fallen.

RECORDINGS 1. Scovotti, Büchner, Schöne, Adam, Staatskapelle Dresden, Janowski, EMI, 1979; 2. Gueden, Wunderlich, Prey, Hotter, Vienna PO, Böhm, EJS, 1959: a recording of a Salzburg Festival performance in 1959, with cuts, but worth tracking down
EDITIONS f.s./v.s., Fürstner, 1935

Friedenstag
Peace Day

Opera in one act, Op. 81 (1h 15m)
Libretto by Joseph Gregor
Composed October 1935–June 1936
PREMIERES 24 July 1938, Nationaltheater, Munich; US: 2 April 1967, University of Southern California, Los Angeles; UK: 28 March 1985, Logan Hall, London (concert)
CAST Commandant *bar*, Maria *s*, Sergeant-Major *b*, Corporal *bar*, Private Soldier *t*, Musketeer *b*, Bugler *b*, Officer *bar*, Front-Line Officer *bar*, Piedmontese *t*, Holsteiner *b*, Mayor *t*, Prelate *bar*, Woman *s*; *satb* chorus of soldiers of the garrison and of the besieging army, elders of the town, women of the deputation to the Commandant, townspeople
LARGE ORCHESTRA offstage: organ, signal tpt, bells

Among projects suggested to Strauss by Zweig before political considerations ended their collaboration was an opera tentatively called *24 October 1648*, about the end of the Thirty Years War and based partly on Calderón's play *La Redención de Breda* (1625). Strauss proposed that Zweig should supply him secretly with libretti and he would compose the operas and hide them until better times. Zweig realized the impracticability of such a scheme and urged the claims of the Viennese theatrical historian and archivist, Joseph Gregor (1888–1960). Strauss grudgingly accepted Gregor but savagely criticized the draft libretto for *Friedenstag*, as the *1648* opera became, and was grateful to Zweig for his amendments and revisions.

Friedenstag seems an unlikely choice of subject for Strauss – 'military matters just do not excite me,' said the composer of the battle scene in *Ein Heldenleben* – so one presumes that its anti-war message appealed to him as topical. It makes Hitler's attendance at the first Vienna performance an act of hypocrisy (or calculated deceit). At the Munich premiere, the part of the Commandant was sung by Hans Hotter, with Ludwig Weber as the Holsteiner and Ursuleac as Maria.

SYNOPSIS
It is the last day of the Thirty Years War, 24 October 1648. The besieged city is near to surrender. The inhabitants are starving and the soldiers in the fortress are near to breaking-point. Even the arrival of an Italian messenger, who sings a love song, does not lift their spirits. A deputation, headed by the Mayor, begs the Commandant to surrender to save their lives. He refuses; his orders are to fight to the last. But he tells them to await a signal at noon. They leave hopefully, but he tells his soldiers that he intends to blow up the fortress. He gives them the choice of staying or leaving. Those who decide to stay go to the cellars to prepare the gunpowder. The Commandant's wife, Maria, senses impending disaster. She knows her husband's inflexible resolve. He tells her of his plan and urges her to go, but she wants to die in his arms. The fuse is about to be lit when shots are heard, followed by bells. Maria realizes that these mean a proclamation of peace. The enemy forces approach the fortress with cannons bedecked with flowers. The Commandant believes this is a ruse and when his Holstein opponent arrives seeking reconciliation, he quarrels with him and both men draw their swords. Maria interposes herself between them and, after hesitation, they embrace. The people flood into the fortress and sing jubilantly of peace and brotherhood.

Even if the subject of *Friedenstag* was uncongenial to him, it nevertheless drew from Strauss some of his strongest diatonic music. The chorus has a larger part than in most of his operas. Although the role of Maria enabled him to compose two lyrical soprano arias, male voices predominate. We must be grateful to Gregor for his invention of the Piedmontese messenger whose Italianate song of happiness provides the required contrast during the sombre opening scene.

Strauss's most characteristic music occurs in Maria's second aria and in her impassioned duet with her husband, the Commandant. But more impressive, perhaps because rarer in this composer's work, is the stark and despairing music for the starving townspeople's delegation. The role of the

Commandant, too, with its inflexibility, irony and eventual thaw, gives splendid opportunities to the voice, as might have been expected from some of Strauss's *Lieder*. The final C major hymn to peace perhaps invites comparison with the finale of Beethoven's *Fidelio*; the same ideal and idealism inspired both composers.

EDITIONS f.s./v.s., Oertel, 1938

Daphne

Bucolic tragedy in one act, Op. 82 (1h 45m)
Libretto by Joseph Gregor
Composed summer 1936–December 1937
PREMIERES 15 October 1938, Staatsoper, Dresden; US: 7 October 1960, Brooklyn, New York (concert); 29 July 1964, Santa Fe; UK: 2 May 1987, Grand Theatre, Leeds
CAST Daphne *s*, Peneios *b*, Gaea *a*, Leukippos *t*, Apollo *t*, 4 shepherds *t*, *bar*, 2 *b*, 2 maids 2 *s*; *tb* chorus of shepherds, maskers; maids *silent*; dancers
ORCHESTRATION 3 fl/picc, 2 ob, ca, 2 A cl, C cl, b cl, basset hn, 3 bsn, dbsn, 4 hn, 3 tpt, 3 trbn, tuba, timp, perc (bd, cym, triangle, tambourine, t-t), 2 hp, str (16.16.12.10.8); offstage: organ, Alphorn

The subject of *Daphne* was offered by Gregor to Strauss at their first meeting in 1935. A libretto, revised and approved by Zweig, reached the composer in September of that year. Strauss was severely critical and two more versions were written before he began to compose any music. Gregor's original idea for the finale – Daphne's metamorphosis into a laurel tree – was choral. Strauss was dubious about it and discussed it with the conductor Clemens Krauss, with whom he had become increasingly friendly since the *Arabella* premiere in 1933. Krauss suggested that the transformation should be described by the orchestra, with Daphne singing wordlessly from within the tree when the change was completed.

Karl Böhm, to whom the opera was dedicated, conducted the first performance, the ninth premiere of a Strauss opera in Dresden. It was played in tandem with *Friedenstag*, as Gregor had intended, but Strauss then decided that the two one-act operas succeeded better separately. Performances throughout Germany and Austria then followed, but the Second World War held up its introduction elsewhere. However, there was a famous production in 1948 in Buenos Aires conducted by Erich Kleiber.

SYNOPSIS
On the slopes of Mount Olympus, Peneios summons his shepherds to bring their flocks and herds from the fields so that they can join in the feast of Dionysus. His daughter Daphne sings of her love of nature and of her longing for sunlight when she feels at one with the trees and birds. Leukippos, her friend since childhood, declares his love for her, but sexual passion has no meaning for her. Daphne's mother, Gaea, tells her to be ready for the feast, but she will not wear the dress provided. Her maids suggest to Leukippos that he should disguise himself as a woman to gain Daphne's love. Peneios senses some-

thing divine in the air and tells the shepherds to expect a godly visitation. As the thunderstorm rages, a young cowherd arrives – Apollo in disguise. He is entranced by Daphne and woos her, but she recoils from his passionate kiss, while realizing that this man is no ordinary mortal. The rites of the Dionysian feast begin. Leukippos, in girl's clothes, dances with Daphne but the jealous Apollo gives the masquerade away and hurls thunderbolts to halt the festivities. Leukippos accuses Apollo of also wooing Daphne in a disguise. The enraged god kills him. Daphne, too late, is heartbroken and refuses to go with Apollo. For his part, Apollo recognizes that he has gone too far. He asks pardon of Dionysus and asks Zeus to grant Daphne her wishes. In the moonlight, Daphne is transformed into a laurel, her wordless song calling from its branches.

Daphne is Strauss's pastoral symphony for the stage, chamber music composed for a large orchestra. The music, pentatonic and diatonic, is intensely lyrical, the scoring pure in texture, with a shining transparency which derives from passages in *Die Frau ohne Schatten* and foreshadows the so-called 'Indian summer' in which he composed the Oboe Concerto, the Second Horn Concerto and the sublime *Metamorphosen*.

The title role requires a lyric soprano capable also of intensity in the post-Romantic duet with Apollo. She sings her first long aria, a hymn to nature, 'O bleib, geliebter Tag', to the departing sun in one of the most glorious outbursts for female voice that Strauss ever wrote. The terror that Daphne experiences at the moment when Apollo kisses her is memorably conveyed in music of an unearthly hue. As for Strauss's supposed aversion to tenors, both Leukippos and Apollo are tenors, the first light and boyish, the second heroic. A final feature is Strauss's superb writing for woodwind, from the oboe solo with which the opera magically begins to the final transformation scene.

RECORDINGS 1. Popp, Wenkel, Goldberg, Schreier, Moll, Bavarian Radio SO, Haitink, EMI, 1983; 2. Gueden, Little, King, Wunderlich, Schoeffler, Vienna SO, Böhm, DG, 1964: outstanding cast and conducted by the opera's dedicatee, some cuts, recorded live at 1964 Vienna Festival; 3. Bampton, Dermota, Svanholm, L. Weber, O of Teatro Colón, Buenos Aires, E. Kleiber, Recital, 1948: a superb cast recorded live
EDITIONS f.s./v.s., Oertel, 1938

Die Liebe der Danae

Cheerful mythology in three acts, Op. 83 (2h 30m)
Libretto by Joseph Gregor, from a scenario by Hugo von Hofmannsthal
Composed February 1938–28 June 1940
PREMIERES 16 August 1944, Festspielhaus, Salzburg (dress rehearsal only); 14 August 1952, Festspielhaus, Salzburg; UK: 16 September 1953, Covent Garden, London (Vienna State Opera); US: 10 April 1964, University of Southern California, Los Angeles
CAST Jupiter *bar*, Mercury *t*, King Pollux *t*, Danae *s*, Xanthe *s*, Midas *t*, 4 kings 2 *t*, 2 *b*, 4 queens: Semele *s*, Europa *s*, Alkmene *ms*, Leda *a*, watchmen 4 *b*
LARGE ORCHESTRA including basset hn, 2 hp, cel, pf

In April 1920 Hofmannsthal sent Strauss a scenario in three acts called *Danae, oder die Vernunftheirat* (*Danae, or The Marriage of Convenience*). Perhaps because he was immersed in the affairs of the Vienna Opera and in composing *Intermezzo*, Strauss did not react to it and claimed to have forgotten it when Willi Schuh drew it to his attention in 1936. He was delighted, for it exactly met his wishes for a light, operetta-like piece with which to follow *Friedenstag* and *Daphne*. Coincidentally, Gregor had also sketched a scenario for a *Danae* opera, which he sent to Strauss, who thought it too serious and urged him to adhere to Hofmannsthal's treatment. By the end of June 1940, the opera was finished. Strauss decreed that it should not be performed until at least two years after the end of the war. But Krauss, who became artistic director of the Salzburg Festival in 1941, persuaded him to allow it to be performed at the 1944 Festival in honour of his 80th birthday. Six performances were planned. But the Allied invasion of Europe in June 1944 and the bomb plot against Hitler the following month resulted in a ban on all festivals. Salzburg, by special dispensation, was reduced to one concert and a dress rehearsal of *Die Liebe der Danae*, which Strauss attended. Ursuleac was Danae, Hotter sang Jupiter and Krauss conducted. The official first performance, with Annelies Kupper as Danae, was at the 1952 Saltzburg Festival, three years after Strauss's death. Since then performances have been intermittent.

SYNOPSIS

Act I   On the isle of Eos, King Pollux is warding off his creditors. Wait another day, he pleads: the four kings, his royal nephews by marriage, are seeking a rich husband for his beautiful daughter Danae, and the richest man in the world, King Midas of Lydia, has shown interest. Danae tells her servant Xanthe that she has dreamed she was covered by a shower of gold, which embraced her like a lover. She says she's interested only in a suitor who brings as much gold as she has just dreamed about. Midas, simply dressed, joins her but says he is Chrysopher, who has come to prepare her for the arrival of his friend Midas. They go to the harbour to await the arrival of 'Midas', who is Jupiter in disguise. Danae recognizes him as the visitor in her dream.

Act II   The four queens are decorating Danae's marriage bed. They recognize Jupiter when he walks in. He has been the lover of each of them in different guises, and they grill him about his pursuit of Danae. He confesses to Midas that he finds his four former conquests unattractively middle-aged and is worried that Danae prefers the real Midas to him. He warns Midas that he will return him to his former life as a donkey-driver if he attempts to win Danae's love. The four queens boast to Danae of their previous intimacy with her elderly bridegroom and advise her to stick to his younger companion. Midas/Chrysopher tells her he is Midas and to prove it turns the contents of the room to gold. When they embrace, there is a clap of thunder and Danae turns into a golden statue. Jupiter asks the statue to choose

between him and Midas. She chooses Midas. Restored to life, she and Midas disappear.

Act III   Midas and Danae are in the desert. Danae realizes that Midas has forfeited his golden touch as the price of loving her. He tells her of his past life and explains how Jupiter had taken his place when the four kings and queens arrived in Lydia with Danae's portrait. Danae, moved, forgets her passion for gold and remembers that she chose a life of poverty with Midas instead of luxury with Jupiter. In a forest landscape, Mercury appears to Jupiter to tell him that everyone on Olympus is laughing at his failure to win Danae. The four queens comfort him, but he bids them farewell. They are followed by Pollux, his creditors and the four kings, all furious with Jupiter for different reasons. Mercury suggests he should placate them with a shower of gold and advises him to pursue Danae. In Midas's hut Danae sings of her new happiness. Jupiter enters, tries to make Danae discontented but acknowledges defeat.

It is impossible when hearing *Die Liebe der Danae* not to wonder what Strauss and Hofmannsthal might have made of it in 1920. Some of Gregor's libretto is lame, and neither he nor Strauss seems to have been sure whether the opera was to be a 'cheerful mythology', with a touch of operetta, or something more serious. Through self-identification with the role of Jupiter, Strauss – increasingly conscious of his own isolation in Nazi Germany – created a moving character, based on Wotan but with a sense of humour. There are other Wagnerian allusions – one may identify Mercury with Loge and the four queens with the Rhinemaidens – but the music is mainly light in texture. In the last act Strauss regains the warmth and richness of his noontide in the noble pathos of the orchestral interlude, known as *Jupiter's Renunciation*, and all through the last scene in which Danae's big aria and her duet with Jupiter point forward to the autumnal profusion of his last works.

In spite of the uneven quality of the first two acts, they contain some of Strauss's wittiest music. The thematic material is on a high level, inventive and strongly characterized, while the orchestration throughout is apt, skilful and glowing with colour. It is unusual among Strauss operas in that, for all the beautiful music given to Danae, it is a male character, Jupiter, who is dominant.

RECORDING   Kupper, Traxel, Gostic, Szemere, Schoeffler, Vienna State Opera Ch, Vienna PO, Krauss, Melodram, 1952: a recording of the broadcast of the premiere, worth having for the incandescence of Clemens Krauss's conducting. A CD reissue (Melodram, 1989) also includes selections conducted by Kempe in 1953, with Rysanek and Frantz
EDITIONS   f.s./v.s., Oertel, 1944

Capriccio

Conversation piece for music in one act, Op. 85 (2h 15m)
Libretto by Clemens Krauss and the composer
Composed July 1940–August 1941
PREMIERES   28 October 1942, Nationaltheater, Munich; UK: 22 September 1953, Covent Garden, London (Bavarian

State Opera); US: 2 April 1954, Juilliard School of Music, New York

CAST Countess *s*, Count *bar*, Flamand *t*, Olivier *bar*, La Roche *b*, Clairon *a*, M. Taupe *t*, Italian Singer *s*, Italian tenor *t*, Major-domo *b*, 8 servants 4 *t*, 4 *b*, ballet dancer
ORCHESTRATION 3 fl/picc, 2 ob, ca, 2 B♭ cl, C cl, b cl, basset hn, 3 bsn/dbsn, 4 hn, 2 tpt, 3 trbn, timp, cym, bd, 2 hp, hpd, str (16.16.10.10.6); offstage: str sextet (2 vn, 2 va, 2 vc); onstage: vn, vc, hpd

Strauss's last opera was on the subject that had exercised him for most of his life: the relationship between words and music in opera. In 1935 Zweig had suggested reshaping Casti's comedy *Prima la musica, poi le parole* which had been set by Salieri (1786). Zweig passed on his idea to Gregor and together they devised a scenario. Over the next four years Strauss rejected two libretti by Gregor and consulted Clemens Krauss, who wrote a scenario but suggested Strauss should write the text himself. Gregor was dismissed and together Strauss and Krauss completed *Capriccio*. Although Krauss is credited with the libretto in the printed score, much of it is by Strauss. The first performance was given in Munich with Ursuleac as the Countess, Hotter as Olivier and Georg Hann as La Roche. In spite of the nightly air raids, each performance was fully attended and enthusiastically received. Krauss made several attempts to interest Strauss in writing another opera, but he replied 'One can only leave one testament.' At Hamburg in 1957, Rudolf Hartmann, the producer of the Munich premiere, divided the opera into two acts, making a break at the point where the Countess orders chocolate in the drawing room. This version has been widely adopted elsewhere, including at Glyndebourne.

SYNOPSIS
In a château near Paris *c.* 1775, the young widowed Countess Madeleine, with her brother the Count, is listening to a string sextet written in honour of her forthcoming birthday by the composer Flamand. Other members of the house party are the poet Olivier, who has written a play for the occasion, and

Reception after the world premiere of Capriccio *(Munich, 1942); from left to right: Viorica Ursuleac (Countess), Rudolf Hartmann (producer), Richard Strauss, Clemens Krauss (conductor and librettist) and Hildegard Ranczak (Clairon)*

the theatrical director La Roche, who is to produce it. The Count is to act in the play mainly because he is infatuated with the Parisian actress Clairon, who has recently broken off her affair with Olivier and is expected at any moment. On arrival, she inquires pointedly if Olivier has yet written the love scene. He has that morning written a sonnet as its climax and this is declaimed from manuscript by the Count and Clairon. While a rehearsal of his play begins, from which La Roche excludes him, Olivier reads the sonnet to the Countess, for whom it is intended ('Kein Andres, das mir so im Herzen loht'). Flamand, to Olivier's annoyance, promptly sets it to music and sings it to Madeleine and Olivier. Poet and composer quarrel over whose work it now is – the Countess says it is hers, a present from them both. Olivier is summoned by La Roche, and Flamand declares his love to the Countess. He demands an answer from her. She says she will meet him next morning at eleven, in the library. Chocolate is now served and La Roche introduces a young ballerina to entertain the company. After the dances (imitations of Couperin), fugal discussion of the relative merits of words and music begins. La Roche then introduces an Italian soprano and tenor, who sing a duet, after which La Roche describes the lavish entertainment he plans for the Countess's birthday. This is received with ribald comments which lead to two octets, the first a laughing ensemble, the second a quarrel (during which the Italian soprano eats too many cakes and drinks too much wine). La Roche replies with a long monologue in which he defines the work of a director and asks where the great artists of today are (the text was written by Strauss and its sentiments are obviously his). The Countess suggests Flamand and Olivier should collaborate on an opera for La Roche to direct. Various subjects (*Ariadne* and *Daphne* among them) are rejected. The Count suggests it should be 'about all of us and the events of today'. This is agreed and the company disperses to return to Paris. The servants tidy the salon and discuss what has been happening. The Major-domo gives them the evening off after they have prepared the Countess's supper. A voice is heard – it is the prompter, M. Taupe, who had fallen asleep and has been left behind. As he is led off to be given a meal, the Countess enters, dressed for supper, and stands on the terrace in the moonlight. The Major-domo gives her a message from Olivier – he will be in the library at eleven next morning to learn how the opera should end. 'How should it end?' she ponders. Is she more moved by words or music, does she love Olivier or Flamand? Can there be an ending that is not trivial? She curtsies to her reflection in a mirror and goes into supper – humming the melody of the sonnet.

In what he expected to be a dry, academic subject for opera, written for his own amusement – a theatrical fugue, as he described it to Krauss – and unlikely to appeal to a wide audience, Strauss paradoxically found in *Capriccio* a libretto to suit all that he did best. It drew from him a fresh fount of inspiration and has become one of his most popular works. His technical virtuosity is demonstrated in three vocal octets, the laughing and quarrelling ensembles and the servants' scherzo-like commentary on the day's proceedings. In the music for the Italian singers and the ballerina, his gift for parody is at its keenest and most affectionate. In the strange, half-lit scene for the prompter and the Major-domo, with its shifting harmonies and air of mystery, he recaptured something of the poetic fantasy of his *Don Quixote* variations (1897). The instrumental sextet that opens the opera and the scoring throughout the rest of the work are examples of Strauss at his most lyrical and sensitive, but suffused with autumnal melancholy, and in the role of the Countess he created one of his most adorable heroines and wrote for her music of intense melodic beauty in which the finest qualities of his *Lieder* and arias are combined to provide the ideal final 20 minutes for a last opera by Strauss.

The Strauss who was able to cut his musical cloth as the dramatic situation dictated is perfectly accommodated in *Capriccio*. Like *Der Rosenkavalier*, the work is gorgeously anachronistic. Although it is set in the late 18th century and a mock-rococo style is sometimes affected, the music belongs inescapably to Strauss's own era, which is one reason why productions updated to the 1920s and 1930s are successful, give or take the resulting ludicrousness of the libretto's references to Goldoni and Gluck as contemporary figures. As in the prologue to *Ariadne auf Naxos* and in *Intermezzo* and *Arabella*, the continuously melodic conversational recitative is here raised to a fine art. All the greatest features of his operas from *Der Rosenkavalier* onwards were filtered through the experience and wisdom gained over 30 years to find their apogee in *Capriccio*. Its resonances and delights increase at each hearing.

RECORDINGS   1. Janowitz, Fischer-Dieskau, Schreier, Prey, Ridderbusch, Troyanos, Bavarian Radio SO, Böhm, DG, 1972; 2. Schwarzkopf, Waechter, Gedda, Fischer-Dieskau, Hotter, Ludwig, Philharmonia O, Sawallisch, EMI, 1957–8: both fine performances, the latter in mono
EDITIONS   f.s./v.s., Oertel, 1942

BIBLIOGRAPHY   Kenneth Birkin, *Arabella*, CUP, 1989; Norman Del Mar, *Richard Strauss: A Critical Commentary on his Life and Works*, Barrie and Jenkins, 3 vols, 1962, 1969, 1972; B. Gilliam, *Elektra*, OUP, 1991; R. Hartmann, trans. G. Davis, *Richard Strauss: The Staging of his Operas and Ballets*, OUP, 1982; Nicholas John (ed.), ENO Opera Guides: *Arabella*, 1985; *Der Rosenkavalier*, 1981; *Salome/Elektra*, 1988, all published by John Calder; Michael Kennedy, *Richard Strauss*, Dent (Master Musicians series); 1976; rev. edn, 1988; William Mann, *Richard Strauss: A Critical Study of the Operas*, Cassell, 1964; Charles Osborne, *The Complete Operas of Richard Strauss*, Michael O'Mara, 1988; Derrick Puffett, *Elektra*, CUP, 1989; Derrick Puffett, *Salome*, CUP, 1989; *Richard Strauss and Hugo von Hofmannsthal*, *Correspondence*, Atlantis, 1952; trans. H. Hammelmann and E. Osers, Collins, 1961; *rp*, CUP, 1980; K. Wilhelm, trans. M. Whittall, *Richard Strauss: An Intimate Portrait*, Thames and Hudson, 1989

M.K.

IGOR STRAVINSKY

Igor Fyodorovich Stravinsky; *b* 17 June 1882, Oranienbaum (now Lomonosov), Russia; *d* 6 April 1971, New York

Of Stravinsky's twenty or so works for the theatre, perhaps four are definitely operas: *The Nightingale*, *Mavra*, *Oedipus Rex* and *The Rake's Progress*. But many of his best works are hard to categorize, since it was an essential part of his genius to invent genres to suit his subject matter. In 1913 he told a reporter: 'I dislike opera. Music can be married to gesture or to words – not to both without bigamy.' Yet between 'pure' ballet like *Petrushka* and 'pure' opera like *The Rake's Progress* are several works that combine dance with speech and/or singing, with or without narrative in the conventional sense. In such matters Stravinsky was evidently influenced by his compatriot Meyerhold, the theatre director, who rejected the 19th-century notion of stage realism in favour of an open-ended theatre where any resource is legitimate if it serves the central idea of the action. The use of masks (in *Pulcinella*, *Renard* and *Oedipus Rex*), ritualized action (*The Rite of Spring*, *Les Noces*, *Oedipus Rex*), deliberate breaks in style (*Petrushka*, *The Soldier's Tale*, *Persephone*), objectivization in the form of spoken or sung commentaries (*Renard*, *The Soldier's Tale*, *Oedipus Rex*), and other such devices, all originate in the Symbolist techniques of Meyerhold.

The Nightingale (begun 1908 or 1909) already suggests how a magical story can best be presented theatrically by creating a wholly artificial world with its own conventions of time and space. Many of Stravinsky's ballets are enactments of ritual, and some of the late ones tend towards abstraction. But he mostly favoured story works with a ritualistic or symbolic undertone and a free mixture of genres. Of these *The Wedding* (1914–17, 1921–3) and *Pulcinella* (1919) are ballets enriched by singing, while *Renard* (1915–16) and *The Soldier's Tale* (1918) are fables told through mime, dance and song or speech. Their informal style owes something to the antique Russian travelling theatre of the *skomorokhi* (minstrel buffoons), and they are prototypes of the later genre of music-theatre. Stravinsky returned to this genre in 1961–2 in *The Flood*, a modern miracle play written for television. In the 1920s, however, he reacted against popular theatre and evolved in its place a synthetic ('neo-classical') style based on art models and preferring subjects from classical literature or mythology. The stage works of this period have a certain Homeric grandeur combined with a strong religious symbolism. Nevertheless their treatment is at bottom similar to that of the earlier works, with an essentially simple action gaining depth and complexity through a variety of stage devices and stylistic allusions.

Stravinsky owed his meteoric early success to his association with Diaghilev and the Paris-based Ballets Russes. His upbringing might well have directed him more readily towards opera. His father was leading bass at the Mariinsky Theatre in St Petersburg, and his teacher was Rimsky-Korsakov, at the time when the master was writing his last operas. But Diaghilev wanted a ballet score (for *The Firebird*, 1910) and the result was so brilliant in its vitality of movement and fantastic orchestral colouring that Stravinsky was diverted into a genre that Diaghilev was busy pushing to the forefront of the modern aesthetic movement. Between then and his death in 1929, Diaghilev put on nine further stage works by Stravinsky, six of them ballets. For much of this period Stravinsky was a leading light of the Paris artistic scene (after spending the war years in Switzerland, he settled in France in 1920); and, while often on bad terms with Diaghilev, he numbered many of the prominent artists and thinkers of the day among his friends, including Debussy (until his death in 1918), Picasso, Cocteau, Valéry and Maritain. *Persephone* was the climax of this French stage of Stravinsky's life, completed in the year he became a French citizen (1934). His subsequent theatre works were nearly all written for the US, where he settled in 1940.

In trying to form a picture of Stravinsky's contribution to opera, it is obvious that one cannot wholly isolate his works in that form from his ballets and mixed-media pieces. His whole approach to opera was nourished by the spirit of magic and the intimate artifice he found in the ballets of Tchaikovsky, and *The Nightingale* is much closer in spirit to *The Nutcracker* than to *The Queen of Spades* or even the late magical operas of Rimsky-Korsakov (to which, however, it owes something musically). *Renard* is only a vocal piece in the sense that *The Wedding*, on which Stravinsky was stuck at the time, is a vocal piece; and *The Wedding* is vocal because the idea for it came from a reading of Kireyevsky's collection of folk verse and is inextricably bound up with the verbal exchanges, the risqué jokes and ritual sayings of the traditional peasant wedding. This is Stravinsky at his most drily economical; pithy modal tunes in folk style are given acid, wheezing harmonies and incisive but unpredictable rhythms like those in *The Rite of Spring* (1913), but without that work's primitive violence.

Later, however, after the end of the war and the Russian revolution, which cut him off from his home and roots, he turned against this ethnic strain. The songs in *Pulcinella* (1919), a Stravinsky-ization of music by, or at that time attributed to, Pergolesi, are in a courtly musical and linguistic Italian. *Mavra* (1921–2), though it has a Russian story, studiously avoids peasant types and instead takes as its subject a comic bourgeois tale by Pushkin, and for its musical models Glinka and Tchaikovsky. This is the real start of Stravinsky's neo-classical phase. Now his music is tonal, formal and vocally ornate. *Mavra* is a number opera, like Mozart's or Weber's. The instrumental works of the time allude to Bach, Haydn and Beethoven. In *Oedipus Rex* (1926–7) Handelian choruses and Verdian or Bellinian arias serve to dramatize a bookish and statuesque presentation of Sophocles, with a Latin text (explained somewhat patronizingly by a narrator in evening dress), immobile characters in masks and a two-dimensional set. For some reason this unpromising mixture produces one of the most powerful and moving operas in the history of the genre.

After emigrating to America, Stravinsky fell temporarily into a rut in which his neo-classicism became somewhat routine and predictable. *The Rake's Progress* (1947–51), for all its wit and polished craftsmanship, is conventional in a way no previous Stravinsky theatre piece had been; and, according to his new associate Robert Craft, it was partly out of depression at the lack of newness in his work that Stravinsky let himself be persuaded to study the music of the serial composers Schoenberg and Webern. The vitality of Stravinsky's own serial period (roughly from 1952) is one of the most startling aspects of a career marked by almost continuous renewal. The main thrust of these late works is religious, and it is symptomatic that the one sung drama of the period, *The Flood* – a typically geometric, diamantine piece of writing – should be on a biblical subject.

Categorical agreement about which Stravinsky works are and are not operas will never be reached. The following are those in which stage action is articulated wholly or partly by singing. But *The Wedding* and *Pulcinella* are omitted on the ground that they are undeniably ballets, in which dance is accompanied by singing as an additional resource.

The Nightingale

Solovyei

Le Rossignol

Conte lyrique in three acts (45m)

Libretto (in Russian) by the composer and Stepan Mitussov, after the story *The Emperor's Nightingale* by Hans Andersen
Composed 1908–9, 1913–14
PREMIERES 26 May 1914, Opéra, Paris; UK: 18 June 1914, Drury Lane, London; US: 6 March 1926, Metropolitan, New York
CAST Nightingale *s*, Cook *s*, Fisherman *t*, Emperor of China *bar*, Chamberlain *b*, Bonze *b*, Death *a*, 2 Japanese envoys *t*, *b*; *satb* chorus of courtiers and ghosts
LARGE ORCHESTRA including pf and cel, optional gtr and mand

In his autobiography, Stravinsky implies that Act I of *The Nightingale* was begun during the winter of 1907–8, and the sketches shown to Rimsky (died June 1908). Other evidence is that only the libretto was drafted by then, and the music composed between November (or possibly August) 1908 and November 1909, when the completed act was put aside in favour of *The Firebird*. After the premiere of *Petrushka* (13 June 1911), Stravinsky wrote to Benois (the scenarist and designer of that ballet), proposing a collaboration on *The Nightingale* for 1913, when he envisaged having completed *The Rite of Spring*. His letter clearly implies that he was already (in July 1911) starting Act II, though he must have shelved it at once to write the Balmont songs and *Zvyezdoliki*, before getting down to *The Rite* in September.

In February 1913 Alexander Sanine, a chief stage director of the newly founded Moscow Free Theatre, commissioned a three-act work from Stravinsky. Stravinsky responded by offering the existing act of

The Nightingale, but soon afterwards agreed to Sanine's suggestion that he complete the work for what he later called an 'unrefusable fee' of 10,000 roubles. The final two acts were composed, and the first act revised, by March 1914, and the first performance given by Diaghilev in Paris two months later (the MFT having meanwhile folded), with production by Sanine, and designs by Benois which Stravinsky later described as 'the most beautiful of all my early Diaghilev works'.

Stravinsky would probably never have written the last two acts but for the MFT fee. Even in 1911 he told Benois he had cooled towards the work, and by early 1913 Act I was about to be published as it stood. His style had changed drastically in three years during which he had written *The Firebird*, *Petrushka* and *The Rite of Spring*. Act I is in a late-Romantic manner indebted to Rimsky-Korsakov and Debussy, while in March 1913 he was completing *The Rite*, and already thinking about the austerities of *The Wedding*. He partly disguised the problem by revising Act I, sharpening up its orchestration and simplifying its harmony. He was also able to hide behind the *chinoiserie* of the later scenes, with their artificial and mechanistic detailing which permitted a contrast with the more sumptuous forest music of Act I. Meanwhile this mood could be called up by simple reprises of the Fisherman's Song. In practice, the change of style is unobtrusive.

For the Paris production, Diaghilev adopted the idea of double casting, with dancers onstage and singers in the pit. Stravinsky later extracted from the opera a symphonic poem, *The Song of the Nightingale* (1917) (drawing mainly on the later acts), and this was presented as a ballet by Diaghilev in Paris in February 1920.

SYNOPSIS

Act I The fame of the nightingale has reached the Emperor of China, who sends his chamberlain to the forest by the sea to invite her to sing at court. At first the chamberlain and courtiers mistake the bellowing of a forest cow and the croaking of the frogs for the nightingale's song, but with the help of the cook the invitation is at last delivered.

Act II At the Emperor's porcelain palace, the nightingale sings to the delight of all; but when envoys arrive from Japan with a mechanical nightingale, the real nightingale flies away. The Emperor, furious, banishes her and appoints the mechanical nightingale First Singer of the Bedside Table on the Left.

Act III The Emperor lies dying and is visited by the ghosts of his past deeds, and by Death herself, wearing the imperial crown. The nightingale sings once more, and Death is so entranced that she agrees to give the Emperor back his crown if only the song can continue. At dawn Death departs; the emperor again offers the nightingale a position at court, but she will agree only to come and sing to him each night.

RECORDINGS 1. Grist, Driscoll, Gramm, Washington Opera Society Ch and O, Stravinsky, CBS, 1961; 2. Bryn-

Costume design by Alexander Benois for the Emperor in The Nightingale *(Paris, 1914)*

Julson, Palmer, Caley, Howlett, Tomlinson, BBC Singers and SO, Boulez, Erato, 1991
EDITIONS f.s./v.s., Edition Russe de Musique, 1923, now Boosey & Hawkes (rev. 1962); the revisions are minor

Renard

Baika
Histoire burlesque chantée et jouée in one scene (16m)
Libretto (in Russian) by the composer, after Afanassyev's *Russian Folk Tales*
Composed 1916
PREMIERES 18 May 1922, Opéra, Paris; US: 25 January 1924, Aeolian Hall, New York (concert); UK: 15 July 1929, Covent Garden, London
CAST The Fox, the Cock, the Cat, the Ram, 2 *t*, 2 *b*, without fixed correlation with the dramatis personae
INSTRUMENTATION picc/fl, ob/ca, cl, bsn, 2 hn, tpt, cimbalom (or pf), timp, perc, 2 vn, va, vc, db

The commission for *Renard* goes back to 1912, when the Princesse Edmond de Polignac had asked Stravinsky for a 15-minute concerto for some 30 instruments. Work on this was delayed by the completion of *The Rite of Spring* and *The Nightingale*, and the composition of the first version of *The Wedding* (substantially written by December 1915). At this point, effectively exiled in Switzerland and needing to capitalize on the commission, Stravinsky took up his existing (1915) sketches for *Renard*, and composed the entire work between January and early August 1916.

In genre, *Renard* is hybrid. The stage action is performed entirely in mime, while, as in *The Wed-*

ding, the dialogue is presented by four singers placed among the instruments and only loosely attached to the characters onstage. Stravinsky seems to have had in the back of his mind the performing style of the Russian minstrel players (*skomorokhi*), while his wheezing and scraping 15-piece band, complete with the cimbalom, which he heard in a Geneva café in January 1915 and on which (he tells us) he composed *Renard*, is obviously suggestive of a peasant orchestra.

SYNOPSIS

The cock, after boasting of his prowess with his hens, is twice tempted down from his perch by the fox, initially disguised as a nun, then in her own person (the Russian word for fox is feminine). Each time the cock is rescued at the last minute by his friends, the cat and the ram, who chase away the fox and then, the second time, strangle her.

The *skomorokhi* were the descendants of pagan priests who were persecuted by the Christian Church but survived as strolling players presenting plays that were often anti-clerical. The idea of the nun as a fox in disguise is picked up in the music by a suggestion of plainsong as the fox tries to persuade the cock to come down and confess his sins (which naturally include polygamy).

But Stravinsky's own intention is not so much satirical as re-creative. The many levels of the play, from fable to social satire, simply lend vitality to the comedy, which, meanwhile, he modernizes through his typically astringent and ebullient music. Moreover, for all its apparent easy-goingness, *Renard* is a distinctly formal piece of work. The whole piece is framed by a march, to which the players enter and exit, and the central action of the comedy – the double enticement and rescue – is braced by wild ritualistic choruses the words of which include a substantial quantity of sheer nonsense, in the manner of other Russian verse Stravinsky set at the time. The sense of a re-enactment whose original meaning has somehow got lost down the years is a crucial element in much of Stravinsky's music of this period, and anticipates the symbolic use of forms and languages in his so-called neo-classical works.

RECORDINGS Shirley, Driscoll, Murphy, Gramm, Columbia SO Ensemble, Stravinsky, CBS, 1962: in English; in Russian: 1. Langridge, Jenkins, Hammond-Stroud, Lloyd, London Sinfonietta, Chailly, Decca, 1985; 2. Hetherington, Harrhy, Donnelly, Cavallier, Matrix Ensemble, Ziegler, ASV, 1991
EDITIONS f.s./v.s., Adolphe Henn (now J. & W. Chester), 1917

Mavra

Opera in one act (28m)
Libretto (in Russian) by Boris Kochno, after the poem 'The Little House at Kolomna' by Aleksandr Pushkin
Composed 1921–2
PREMIERES 3 June 1922, Opéra, Paris; UK: 27 April 1934 (broadcast); 21 August 1956, Edinburgh; US: 28 December 1934, Academy of Music, Philadelphia
CAST Parasha *s*, the Neighbour *ms*, the Mother *a*, the Hussar *t*

STANDARD ORCHESTRA but with solo vns and va only

Stravinsky's use of Russian folk sources and materials continued spasmodically until the *Symphonies of Wind Instruments* (1920). But in 1921 he made orchestrations for Diaghilev's London revival of Tchaikovsky's *The Sleeping Beauty*, and soon afterwards he composed *Mavra*, an opera buffa, which studiously distances itself from the Russian ethnic tradition and instead argues polemically for the cosmopolitan Russianism of Pushkin, Glinka and Tchaikovsky – to which three artists the score is dedicated.

Mavra is Stravinsky's first important synthetic work, in the sense that its whole style and subject matter are taken over consciously, like 'found objects' which the artist then proceeds to work on in his own way for his own ends. For the first time he published articles defending his aesthetic position. Tchaikovsky and Glinka were now in, Musorgsky and the rest of the Russian nationalists were out. Having come to live in Paris in 1920, Stravinsky may well have been more alert than before to the sharp movement of aesthetic and intellectual fashion in post-war France, and sensed that the most piquant way of shocking the Parisian trendsetters of 1921 was to align himself, intellectually, with a sophisticated Russian art that was unknown in Paris (Pushkin and Glinka) and an equally sophisticated one (Tchaikovsky) that smart Parisians regarded as vulgar. In keeping with this posture, he abandoned his folk-tale sources in favour of a *petit-bourgeois* satire set in suburban 19th-century St Petersburg,

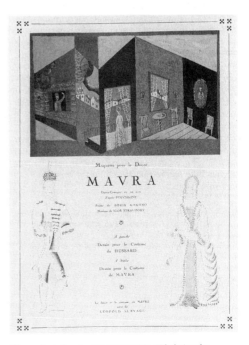

Mavra: *from the souvenir programme, with designs by Léopold Sauvage (Paris, 1922)*

and used the heightened and somewhat formal style-types of his models to parody the emotional triviality of that world.

SYNOPSIS

After a short overture, the curtain rises on Parasha at her embroidery, singing a lament for her absent lover (Parasha's Song). The hussar appears at the window twirling his moustache, and they sing a duet ending (after the hussar's departure) with a short reprise of Parasha's Song. Enter Parasha's mother, also singing a lament (for her dead cook, Phiocla), after which comes an elaborate duet with the neighbour, mainly on the subject of the weather and the cost of living. Next Parasha comes back with a new cook 'Mavra' (the hussar in disguise), and the ensuing dialogue leads to a formal quartet on the virtues of loyal servants. Exeunt the mother and the neighbour, leaving Parasha and Mavra to sing a brilliant love duet. Parasha then leaves with her mother, and Mavra, after yet another lament, decides the time has come for a shave, in the middle of which operation the mother comes back, and, mistaking the shaving 'cook' for a burglar, faints away. The hussar escapes through the window.

As with *Renard*, the flippancy of the plot conceals a strict and essentially formal musical design. The dialogues and laments are all traceable to models in Glinka or Tchaikovsky and are so written as to remain slightly detached from their trivial context and to retain the dignity and style of the models. *Mavra* marks the re-adoption by Stravinsky of the formulae of tonal music: cadences, definite keys (Parasha's Song is in B flat minor, the ensuing duet in B minor, etc.), and regular periodic barring. On the other hand Stravinsky refracts these techniques through cross-rhythmic patterns, subtle harmonic blurrings, and a highly unorthodox orchestral texture, dominated by wind and with prominent family groupings, as in Glinka.

Mavra flopped in Paris in 1922 and has been staged relatively little since. Certainly its satire is esoteric. But Stravinsky always thought highly of it and resented its failure. It is the only work of his own that he discusses in any detail in the lectures that became *The Poetics of Music* (1939), and recent revivals have shown that his faith in it may not have been misplaced.

RECORDING Belinck, Simmons, Rideout, Kolk, Columbia SO, Stravinsky, CBS, 1964: in Russian, with a feeling of authenticity but little real fluency
EDITIONS f.s./v.s., Edition Russe de Musique (now Boosey & Hawkes), 1925

Oedipus Rex

King Oedipus
Opera–oratorio in two acts (50m)
Libretto (in French) by Jean Cocteau (Latin sections translated by Jean Daniélou), after the play *Oedipus Tyrannus* by Sophocles
Composed 1926–7, rev. 1948
PREMIERES 30 May 1927, Théâtre Sarah-Bernhardt, Paris (concert); 23 February 1928, Staatsoper, Vienna; US: 24 April 1928, Boston (concert); 21 April 1931, New York; UK: 12 May 1928 (broadcast); 12 February 1936, London (concert); 21 August 1956, Edinburgh
CAST Oedipus *t*, Jocasta *ms*, Creon *b-bar*, Tiresias *b*, the Shepherd *t*, the Messenger *b-bar*, Speaker *spoken role*; *tb* chorus
ORCHESTRATION 3 fl, picc, 2 ob, ca, 3 E♭ cl, 2 bsn, dbsn, 4 hn, 4 tpt, 3 trbn, tuba, timp, perc, hp, pf, str

The idea for 'an opera in Latin on the subject of a tragedy of the ancient world, with which everyone would be familiar' was Stravinsky's own, as a letter to Cocteau of 11 October 1925 proves. He himself dated the inspiration for *Oedipus Rex* to the chance discovery of Joergenson's *Life of St Francis* on a Genoa bookstall in September of that year. On the other hand, the device of a spoken narration in the language of the audience (for which Stravinsky later 'blamed' Cocteau) was probably worked out between them, as was the intended visual handling, with the main characters immobile, like statues, able to gesture only with head and hands, within a monumental, tableau-like two-dimensional setting (a style that goes back to Cocteau's 1922 version of Sophocles' *Antigone*). The conception of a heroic tragedy immured within an antique convention is obviously fundamental, as is the idea of enriching such a conception from various heroic traditions: not only Greek, but Handelian and even Verdian–Bellinian. In one sense, this is no more than the translation into the theatre of the synthetic techniques of early neo-classicism; in another sense it updates the idea of symbolic re-enactment already present in *Renard* and *The Wedding*. The argument over whether *Oedipus* is opera or oratorio is thus specious. The subtitle merely refers to the various elements in the work as a whole, while it was first performed in concert because money could not be found in time for a stage version to be prepared.

SYNOPSIS

The speaker introduces each scene, describing the events we are about to witness. He 'is in a black suit . . . [and] expresses himself like a lecturer, presenting the story with a detached voice.'

Stravinsky with Ewald Dülberg and Otto Klemperer, designer and conductor of the Krolloper Oedipus Rex *(Berlin, 1928)*

Act I The Thebans implore their King Oedipus, who vanquished the Sphinx, to rescue them from the plague ('Liberi, vos liberabo'); Oedipus boastfully promises to do so. He reports that Creon, his brother-in-law, has been sent to consult the Delphic Oracle ('Respondit deus'); Creon arrives and announces that the murderer of King Laius is hiding in Thebes and must be hunted out before the plague will go. Oedipus undertakes to find the murderer ('Non reperias vetus scelas'). The people implore the blind seer, Tiresias, to tell what he knows ('Delie, exspectamus'). Tiresias refuses ('Dicere non possum'), but when Oedipus accuses him directly of the murder, he retorts that Laius' murderer is another king, now hiding in Thebes. Oedipus angrily accuses both Tiresias and Creon of plotting to seize the throne. At this moment the people hail the arrival of Oedipus' wife, Queen Jocasta.

Act II The final 'Gloria' chorus of Act I is repeated; the score indicates this before the speaker's introduction, but Stravinsky stated in Dialogues that he preferred the reprise to follow the introduction and lead straight into Jocasta's aria. Jocasta rebukes the princes for quarrelling ('Non erubescite, reges'). The oracle, she says, is a liar. It prophesied that Laius would be killed by her son, but in fact he was killed at a crossroads by thieves. Suddenly afraid, Oedipus tells Jocasta that once he killed an old man at a crossroads ('Pavesco subito'). He determines to find out the truth. The chorus greets the arrival of the shepherd and the messenger from Corinth ('Adest ominiscius pastor'). The messenger announces the death of King Polybus of Corinth. Oedipus, he reports, was not Polybus' son, but a foundling, discovered on a mountainside and brought up by a shepherd. Jocasta understands and tries to draw Oedipus away. Oedipus accuses her of shame at the discovery that he is not the son of a king ('Nonne monstrum rescituri'), but the shepherd and messenger spell out the truth: that Oedipus was the son of Laius and Jocasta, abandoned to die. Oedipus acknowledges the truth, that he has killed his father and married his mother ('Natus sum quo nefastum est'). The messenger, helped by the chorus, relates the death of Jocasta and Oedipus' self-blinding with her golden brooch ('Divum Jocastae caput mortuum'). Oedipus appears, a figure of revulsion. He is firmly but gently expelled from Thebes by the people.

Cocteau's treatment of the story assumes a knowledge of Sophocles, and cannot be properly understood without it. Here is the essential outline. The oracle warned King Laius that, as a punishment for stealing Pelops' son, Chrysippus, he would be killed by his own son; so, when Oedipus was born, Laius and Jocasta exposed him on a mountainside, piercing his feet with leather thongs. There he was found and brought up by a shepherd of the Corinthian King Polybus. Polybus, being childless, adopted (and named) Oedipus; later, Oedipus was taunted about his parentage, and, when he consulted the oracle, was told that he would kill his father and marry his mother. To avoid these crimes, and naturally supposing them to refer to Polybus and his wife, he left Corinth for Thebes, and on the way killed an old man he met at a crossroads, not recognizing him, of course, as King Laius. At Thebes he solved the riddle of the Sphinx, winning the hand of the now-widowed Queen Jocasta. It is crucial that, even when he begins to suspect that he is the murderer of King Laius and thus the cause of the plague in Thebes, Oedipus still does not realize that he is Laius' son. He simply believes his crime to be usurping the marital bed of a man he has killed. One other obscurity is his accusation of Tiresias' complicity with Creon, which is explained by the fact that, in Sophocles, it is Creon who first suggests consulting Tiresias.

Oedipus Rex is one of Stravinsky's greatest works and a climax both of his early synthetic (neoclassical) style and of his lifelong experimentation with theatrical technique. Like Mavra, it is a number opera in the classical tradition, though the numbers often evolve into substantial scenes, separated by the narration. The monumental character of each scene goes with the statuesque, sculptural design idea and with the impersonal grandeur of the Latin text. But many details of style break into this monumentality. The most obvious is the spoken narration, which is at first strictly separate from the music, but later intrudes into it to some limited extent. Stravinsky makes rich use of the ironic possibilities of this device. For instance, when (in the narration) Tiresias reveals that 'the murderer of the king is a king', the last four words are set rhythmically to the motif of the chorus's anxious anticipation of the seer's arrival, in which they do not, of course, yet know what he will reveal.

Another obvious 'break' is the mixture of musical styles. Handel seems to have been a conscious influence; but that of Italian opera is more striking, because more surprising. There are clear reminiscences of Verdi, Bellini, and even Puccini, and Stravinsky uses the idea of operatic vocalism itself to a dramatic end. Oedipus' coloratura diminishes with his self-confidence, and his last utterances, when the truth has struck him, are unadorned. These and other associative devices seem to act as a bridge between modern perception and the musically disembodied world of Greek tragedy: through what they sing and what accompanies them, the characters take on an extra dimension of humanity, like statues whose heads turn at the sound of music that is, so to speak, ours rather than theirs.

Both tonally and rhythmically, Oedipus Rex contains some of the plainest music Stravinsky ever wrote. The squarely cut choral ostinati (with their persistent minor-third motif) are worlds away from the subtleties of Mavra. Much of the score uses fixed tonal centres, contrasted by terracing rather than classical modulation. Moreover the work marks Stravinsky's use of a 'standard' symphony orchestra for the first time since The Rite of Spring and The Nightingale.

Stravinsky and Cocteau planned to stage Oedipus Rex in 1927 in honour of Diaghilev's 20th season, but the financial arrangements became immersed in

Parisian social politics, and in the end the premiere was given in concert form. The first stagings were in February the following year in Vienna and Berlin (Kroll Opera, under Klemperer). In the 1950s Stravinsky came to favour omitting the speaker altogether. But one of the most famous post-war (concert) performances, by Stravinsky in London's Festival Hall in 1959, had Cocteau as the speaker.

RECORDINGS 1. Mödl, Pears, Rehfuss, Cocteau, Cologne Radio Ch and O, Stravinsky, CBS, 1951: narration in French, musically brilliant as well as obviously historic; 2. Verrett, Shirley, Gramm, Westbrook, Washington Opera Society Ch and O, Stravinsky, CBS, 1962: narration in English; 3. Troyanos, Kollo, Krause, Wager, Harvard Glee Club, Boston SO, Bernstein, CBS, 1975: heavier than either of Stravinsky's recordings but powerful in its way
EDITIONS v.s., Edition Russe de Musique, 1927; rev. version: f.s./v.s., Boosey & Hawkes, 1949

Persephone

Mélodrame in three tableaux (56m)
Libretto by André Gide, after the Homeric hymn to Demeter
Composed 1933–4
PREMIERES 30 April 1934, Opéra, Paris; UK: 28 November 1934, Queen's Hall, London (concert); 12 December 1961, Covent Garden; US: 15 March 1935, Boston (concert); 15 July 1961, Santa Fe
CAST Eumolpus t, Persephone spoken role; satb chorus and children's choir
LARGE ORCHESTRA including pf

Commissioned by the dancer Ida Rubinstein, *Persephone* is the most hybrid of Stravinsky's works in the present listing. Unlike *The Wedding*, it requires the principal dancer to speak, while, for the chorus parts, the idea of dual characterization is taken over from that earlier work: dancers on-stage are roughly paralleled by singers who stand apart (onstage or offstage). There is admittedly more specific vocal characterization than in the earlier ballet. But the use of the speaker is more lyrical and less dramatic than in *Oedipus Rex*; there is no irony and only a very loose relation between the speech and the music, as in the French tradition of mélodrame – poetry recited with musical accompaniment.

Gide adapted an early poem of his own, in which the Greek legend of Persephone is Christianized by making her descent into the underworld a voluntary act of self-sacrifice. This links the early fertility myth with the Christian idea of renewal through atonement, and here Gide's ideas chimed splendidly with Stravinsky's. But over details, such as the correct treatment of French accentuation and the function of music in the whole scheme, they fell out. In the end, relations were so soured that Gide absented himself from the final rehearsals and premiere. Stravinsky later turned against the text altogether and waspishly suggested that it be replaced by a completely new one by Auden.

SYNOPSIS

Part I (Persephone's Abduction) After the opening invocation by the priest Eumolpus, nymphs sing in praise of the meadow flowers, but warn Persephone

not to pick the narcissus, whose perfume will give her a vision of the underworld. She bends over the flower, and seeing an image of the hopeless shades, picks it voluntarily and descends to them.

Part II (Persephone in the Underworld) Persephone is wooed by Pluto, Mercury and the shades, but she rejects everything except the pomergranate, which makes her long to return home (in Homer, however, eating the pomegranate would consign her to a perpetuity in the underworld). Gazing again into the narcissus, she sees a vision of winter on earth and her mother Demeter wandering in search of her.

Part III (Persephone Reborn) Invoked by the Greeks at the temple of Demeter, Persephone returns to earth. Roses sprout where her feet touch the soil. She accepts Triptolemus, the tiller of the soil, as her husband, but nevertheless resigns herself to spending half of each year in the underworld.

Persephone is the feminine side of the Stravinsky of *Oedipus Rex*. Like *Oedipus* it offers an oblique view of an ancient myth through modern eyes. The form is likewise that of a number opera, with musical set pieces linked by speech. But *Persephone* differs from *Oedipus* in its persistent sensuous delicacy and fragrance of style, symptomatized by the many female choruses (in *Oedipus* the chorus is entirely male). Even more than in *Oedipus*, the music is dominated by the interval of a third; and the extensive chromatic dissonance of so much of Stravinsky's earlier music is here confined to the underworld scenes, and even there is by his standards restrained.

RECORDING Zorina, Molese, Columbia Symphony Ch and O, Stravinsky, CBS, 1966: the later and more polished of Stravinsky's two recordings
EDITIONS f.s./v.s., Edition Russe de Musique (now Boosey & Hawkes), 1934; the rev. version of 1949 contains only trivial changes

The Rake's Progress

Opera in three acts (2h 15m)
Libretto by W. H. Auden and Chester Kallman after the cycle *A Rake's Progress* by William Hogarth (1735)
Composed 1947–51
PREMIERES 11 September 1951, La Fenice, Venice; UK: 2: January 1953 (radio); 25 August 1953, Edinburgh Festival; US: 14 February 1953, Metropolitan, New York
CAST Trulove b, Anne Trulove s, Tom Rakewell t, Nick Shadow bar, Mother Goose ms, Baba the Turk ms, Sellem t, Keeper of the Madhouse b; satb chorus of whores, roaring boys, servants, citizens, madmen
ORCHESTRATION 2 fl/picc, 2 ob/ca, 2 cl, 2 bsn, 2 hn, 2 tpt, timp, hpd (or pf), str

After settling in the US in 1940, Stravinsky went through an uneasy time in which the pressure to fulfil commissions of a 'typically' American, commercial sort went hand in hand with changes in style that were to lead to a complete new direction in his work of the 1950s. One important catalyst of change was his growing interest in pre-classical music. This is the period of the Mass (1944–8), and of the ballet *Orpheus* (1947), with its mixture of neo-classical

The opening scene of The Rake's Progress *(Venice, 1951)*

mannerisms and contrapuntal austerities. *The Rake's Progress*, which looks like a summation, is therefore also partly a work of transition.

Stravinsky saw the Hogarth prints at an exhibition in Chicago in May 1947. Later that year, he contacted W. H. Auden and proposed a collaboration (Auden soon brought in Chester Kallman as co-author). Auden was to prove a brilliant collaborator. His gift for investing verse in simple metres with rich meanings perfectly suited Stravinsky's need for variable patterns and a clear ethical thrust, and Auden's virtuosity made him uniquely quick at responding to specific requirements. Beyond question the libretto is one of the best ever written.

Although the work seems at first sight like a straight 18th-century pastiche, complete with *secco* recitative accompanied by harpsichord, it is one of Stravinsky's most complex and many-tiered scores. The influence of Mozart is obvious and well documented. But the actual subject is quite un-Mozartian; it rather suggests the urban world of *The Beggar's Opera*, as do the plain, lilting cut of its melodies, and its preference for strophic or verse-and-refrain forms. But while the dramatic setting of *The Beggar's Opera* clearly has a lot in common with Hogarth, the verse-and-refrain idea also recalls Stravinsky's lifelong interest in ritual forms where repetition and recurrence are more in evidence than organic development in the classical sense. That this was hardly a limitation is shown by the fact that the longest and most serious of the three acts, the third, proceeds almost entirely by interlocking verse forms. Here *The Rake* anticipates the proto-serial works of the 1950s, where the refrain form is ubiquitous.

Auden's view of the subject fitted this aspect of Stravinsky like a glove. Starting with the idea that Tom's downfall comes from his denial of Nature (Anne and ordered country life), he constructed a moving allegory in which the gruesome materialism of the city increasingly usurps the natural virtues – love, marriage, procreation, the ordinary rhythm of life. The opera begins and ends in spring; against Hogarth's London, Auden set up a pastoral idyll in the tradition of Theocritus. Tom is Adonis, who comes to a bad end for disobeying the command of his goddess lover, Venus. Cut off from his moral roots, he falls prey to philosophies of despair – existentialism, moral nihilism – and is about to succumb when the still small voice of love brings him back to his senses, or at least to life (since he does in fact lose his senses). Thus a mixture of antique conventions provides a frame for a strictly modern fable, just as in the music.

SYNOPSIS
'The action takes place in 18th-century England.'

Act I Scene 1 (The garden of Trulove's home in the country): A short prelude leads into a duet for Anne and Tom about the joys of spring ('The woods are green'). Later it becomes a trio, with Trulove voicing his fears about the marriage. Trulove suggests that Tom take a job, but Tom has other plans ('Here I stand' and 'Since it is not by merit'). At his words 'I wish I had money', a messenger (Nick Shadow) appears with news that he has inherited a fortune (quartet: 'I wished but once'). Tom agrees to go to London to settle his affairs, with Shadow as his servant. In a trio, Tom, Anne and Trulove voice their respective attitudes to easy money ('Laughter and light'); Scene 2 (Mother Goose's brothel, London): Roaring boys and whores sing of the joys of debauchery ('With air commanding'). Shadow and Mother Goose rehearse Tom in the catechism of vice. Only when love is mentioned does he falter and beg to be released. Shadow now introduces Tom as a would-be initiate, though Tom's cavatina ('Love, too frequently betrayed' with obbligato clarinet) sustains his regret at betraying true love, to the delight of the sentimental whores. As Mother Goose takes Tom off to her bed, the chorus sings the Lanterloo Chorus; Scene 3 (as Scene 1): Anne laments Tom's infidelity but makes up her mind to rescue him ('I go to him').

Act II Scene 1 (Rakewell's house in London): Tom, at breakfast, is already bored with fashionable life ('Vary the song'). Shadow enters with a newspaper report about the bearded lady, Baba the Turk, whom he proposes Tom should marry in order to demonstrate his freedom from 'those twin tyrants of appetite and conscience' ('In youth the panting slave pursues'). They sing of appetite and coming notoriety ('My tale shall be told'); Scene 2 (street in front of Rakewell's house): Anne has found Tom's house, but falters in front of the door. Tom enters in a sedan chair, preceded by servants. He presses Anne to leave him to his fate. From the sedan chair Baba demands to be handed down, and when Tom introduces her as his wife, Anne turns away (trio: 'Could it then have been known'). To the strains of a sarabande, Baba descends from the chair, and briefly gratifies the assembled crowd with a sight of her flowing black beard; Scene 3 (as Act II, Scene 1, but the room now cluttered with Baba's possessions): Baba chatters away about her life ('As I was saying'), ending with a lyrical appeal to Tom's finer feelings. Rebuffed, she breaks into a classic rage aria ('Scorned! Abused!'), smashing the china as she sings, until Tom silences her by putting his wig over her face, then himself falls asleep. Enter Shadow with a 'bread-making machine', which he demonstrates to the audience. Tom wakes up, having dreamt of just such a machine, which he imagines will abolish misery in the world (duet: 'Thanks to this excellent device').

Act III Scene 1 (the same, but covered with cobwebs and dust; Baba still where she was left): The populace has gathered for the sale of Tom's property. Anne also arrives, looking for Tom. Sellem, the auctioneer, begins ('Who hears me, knows me') with the sale of various curios, culminating in Baba herself, who, as the wig is removed, continues her rage aria where it left off. Offstage, Tom and Shadow are heard in a ballad song ('Old wives for sale!'). The sale grinds to a halt, as Baba advises Anne to go to Tom; Scene 2 (a churchyard; night): A short prelude for string quartet (the first music to be composed) leads to the final confrontation between Tom and Shadow. Shadow claims Tom's soul as wages. He proposes suicide on the stroke of twelve, but relents on the ninth stroke, and instead suggests a game of cards to decide Tom's fate. Unexpectedly Tom wins, by trusting the voice of love (that is, Anne, heard offstage). Shadow departs in a fury but condemns

Tom to insanity; Scene 3 (Bedlam): Tom, now insane, imagines himself as Adonis soon to be visited by Venus ('Prepare yourselves, heroic shades'), but the other inmates refuse to participate ('Leave all love and hope behind'). But Anne does come, sings him to sleep ('Gently, little boat'), and then departs with her father ('Every wearied body must'). Waking to find her gone, Tom seems to die of grief ('Mourn for Adonis'). Like Mozart's *Don Giovanni*, the opera ends with a moralistic epilogue ensemble ('Good people, just a moment').

The Rake's Progress is generally considered the culminating work of Stravinsky's neo-classicism. Its use of a standard 18th-century orchestra and of various operatic formal conventions, of clear tonal schemes and rhythmic periods, perpetuates the tradition of the Symphony in C and the Concerto in D. The formal schemes, and some of its instrumental textures, anticipate the *Cantata*, but there is no trace of serialism or any other conscious modernism. *The Rake* was Stravinsky's first setting of an English text (apart from the short cantata *Babel*). As with *Persephone*, its eccentric prosody has been criticized. But Auden himself pointedly defended it. The fact is that Stravinsky saw words as an element of rhythm, and was always ready to distort natural accentual patterns to enrich the musical movement. His *Rake* technique is essentially no different from his earlier handling of Russian, French or Latin.

Stravinsky worked on the opera for three years, to the exclusion of all else (except negotiations as to where it should be premiered and for how much money). The Venice premiere was fixed up by him over everyone's head and with disastrous consequences in Italian musical politics. (La Scala, Milan, had to be placated by a shared role in the production.) It was a *succès d'estime*, but artistically uneven. Stravinsky conducted effectively, but the cast was variable and Carl Ebert's production pleased neither the composer nor the librettists.

RECORDINGS 1. Schwarzkopf, Tourel, Rounseville, Cuenod, Kraus, Arié, Ch and O of La Fenice, Venice, Stravinsky, Cetra, 1951: taken live from the premiere; 2. Raskin, Sarfaty, Young, Miller, Reardon, Garrard, Sadler's Wells Ch, RPO, Stravinsky, CBS, 1964: the later and on the whole more polished of the composer's two studio recordings; 3. Pope, Walker, Varnay, Langridge, Dobson, Ramey, Dean, Best, London Sinfonietta Ch and O, Chailly, Decca, 1983
EDITIONS f.s./v.s., Boosey & Hawkes, 1951

The Flood

Musical play in one scene (23m)
Libretto by Robert Craft, from the Book of Genesis and the York and Chester miracle plays
Composed 1961–2
PREMIERES 14 June 1962, CBS TV, US; 30 April 1963, Staatsoper, Hamburg; UK: 2 October 1963, Royal Festival Hall, London (concert)
CAST Lucifer *t*, God 2 *b*; Narrator, Noah, Noah's wife and sons, Caller, *spoken roles; sat* chorus
LARGE ORCHESTRA including contrabass cl and contrabass tuba

After the ballet *Agon* (1953–7), Stravinsky wrote nothing directly for the theatre. *The Flood*, written for television, was nevertheless effectively conceived in terms of a practicable, workshop type of music-theatre, and this may partly explain the failure of the original television production, though the Hamburg staging is said to have been unsuccessful too. Compared with Britten's children's opera, *Noye's Fludde*, *The Flood* is exceptionally compressed and lacking in anecdote. As with other hybrid Stravinsky works, the action is articulated mainly through dance, and the narrator's role is more explanatory than (for example) alienatory, a fact that tends to dilute the dramatic effect of the whole.

The action consists of a series of tableaux, some orchestral, some vocal: 1. Prelude (orchestra: representation of chaos); 2. Te Deum (chorus and orchestra: a kind of serial chant – Stravinsky dubbed it 'Igorian chant'); 3. Narration: Creation, Expulsion of Lucifer, Temptation of Eve, Warning of the Flood (narrator and orchestra, interspersed with vocal 'solos' for Lucifer and God, and speeches for Noah); 4. The Building of the Ark (orchestra); 5. The Catalogue of the Animals (Noah and the Caller with orchestra); 6. The Comedy (Noah, his wife and sons, with orchestra); 7. The Flood (orchestra: a musical palindrome); 8. The Covenant of the Rainbow (God, Noah, with orchestra); 9. [Epilogue: described by Stravinsky as 'Prolepsis of Christianity'] (Lucifer, Narrator, then chorus, with orchestra). This final section opens with a reprise of the prelude (added after the first performance), and ends with a continuation of the *Te Deum*, also from the first part of the work. The idea is of a continuing cycle of sin and redemption – a new, pessimistic slant on Stravinsky's lifelong preoccupation with cyclic recurrence.

The Flood belongs to Stravinsky's advanced serial period, and is rich in the hidden constructivist devices that stimulated so much of his late work. For the listener, such issues are not important. What is obvious is the richness of musical idea, in a work completed when Stravinsky was 79. A certain shortwindedness is apparent, and the score is somewhat episodic in effect. But, as with *Persephone*, its main weakness is that the relation between speech and song is arbitrary. Why does Lucifer sing but Noah speak? Why narrate action that could be depicted and dramatized, when narration as such casts no particular light on that action, as it does in *The Soldier's Tale* or *Oedipus Rex*?

RECORDING   Harvey, Cabot, Lanchester, Reardon, Oliver, Tripp, Robinson, Columbia Symphony Ch and O, Stravinsky, CBS, 1962
EDITIONS   f.s./v.s., Boosey & Hawkes, 1963

BIBLIOGRAPHY   Robert Craft (ed.), *Stravinsky: Selected Correspondence*, 3 vols., Faber, 1982, 1984, 1985; Paul Griffiths, *Igor Stravinsky: The Rake's Progress*, CUP, 1982; Igor Stravinsky, *An Autobiography*, Gollancz, 1936; Igor Stravinsky and Robert Craft, *Conversations with Stravinsky*, Faber, 1959; also the later conversations, *Memories and Commentaries* (1960), *Expositions and Developments* (1962), *Dialogues and a Diary* (1968), rev. as *Dialogues* (1982); Vera Stravinsky and Robert Craft, *Stravinsky in Pictures and Documents*, Simon and Schuster, 1979; Stephen Walsh, *The Music of Stravinsky*, Routledge, 1988; Stephen Walsh, *Stravinsky: Oedipus Rex*, CUP, 1993

S.W.

CHARLES STROUSE
Charles Louis Strouse; *b* 7 June 1928, New York

Having studied with Aaron Copand and Nadia Boulanger, Strouse had the training to be a serious composer, but instead chose to concentrate on the popular field, notwithstanding the appearance in the 1980s of two operas based on children's stories. His meeting with lyricist Lee Adams in 1949 inaugurated a partnership that contributed to many revues before achieving considerable success with its first book musical, *Bye Bye Birdie*. Though holding an uneven commercial track record since, Strouse (usually with Adams) has several times achieved distinctive results: *Golden Boy* was one of the first Broadway scores to use jazz references effectively just as *Birdie* introduced some of the sounds of rock-and-roll.

Bye Bye Birdie
Musical comedy in two acts
Libretto by Michael Stewart; lyrics by Lee Adams
PREMIERES   14 April 1960, Martin Beck Theatre, New York; UK: 15 June 1961, Her Majesty's Theatre, London

This satire of the publicity generated by exploiting the drafting of a rock star into the US army made Strouse and Adams overnight successes. It introduced Gower Champion as an important director of musicals, and contained the hit 'Put on a Happy Face' and the comic *fugato* for teenagers, 'The Telephone Hour'.

RECORDING   Van Dyke, Rivera, Watson, Gautier, Lynde, Lawrence, CBS, 1960
FILM   Sidney (dir.), Kohlmar-Sydney/Columbia, 1963
EDITION   v.s., Edwin H. Morris, 1962

Applause
Musical comedy in two acts
Libretto by Betty Comden and Adolph Green, based on the film *All About Eve* and the original story by Mary Orr; lyrics by Lee Adams
PREMIERES   30 March 1970, Palace Theater, New York; UK: 16 November 1972, Her Majesty's Theatre, London

The familiar story of the eager, secretly ambitious young fan superseding the star she admired was given an updating by Comden and Green.

RECORDING   Bacall, Fuller, Cariou, Franklin, Pippin, ABC, 1970
EDITION   v.s., Edwin H. Morris, 1970

Annie

Musical comedy in two acts (2h)
Libretto by Thomas Meehan, based on the comic strip *Little Orphan Annie*; lyrics by Martin Charnin
PREMIERES   21 April 1977, Alvin Theater, New York; UK: 3 May 1978, Victoria Palace Theatre, London

Relentlessly cheerful orphan Annie, her dog Sandy, and wealthy guardian are the main protagonists in this musical that was in advance thought to be hopelessly corny for Broadway, yet turned into a long-running hit.

RECORDING   Loudon, McArdle, Shelton, Howard, CBS, 1977
FILM   Huston (dir.), Columbia, 1982
EDITION   v.s., Edwin H. Morris, 1977

Other musicals: *All American*, 1962; *Golden Boy*, 1964; *It's a Bird, It's a Plane, It's Superman*, 1966; *Six*, 1971; *I and Albert*, 1972; *A Broadway Musical*, 1978; *Flowers for Algernon*, 1979, as *Charlie and Algernon*, 1980; *Bring Back Birdie*, 1981; *Dance a Little Closer*, 1983; *Rags*, 1986; *Annie 2: Miss Hannigan's Revenge*, 1990, rev. as *Annie Warbucks*, 1992; *Nick & Nora*, 1991
Operas: *Nightingale*, 1982; *Charlotte's Web*, 1989
BIBLIOGRAPHY   David Ewen, *American Songwriters*, H. W. Wilson, 1987

J.A.C.

LESLIE STUART

Thomas Augustine Barrett; *b* 15 March 1864, Southport, Lancashire, England; *d* 27 March 1928, Richmond, Surrey, England

A cathedral organist appointment in Salford clearly served Stuart excellently as preparation for a career in popular music. He first made his name with music-hall songs such as 'Lily of Laguna', and until late in life continued to appear on the variety stage performing his own songs.

Florodora

Musical comedy in two acts
Book by Owen Hall; lyrics by Ernest Boyd-Jones and Paul Rubens
PREMIERES   11 November 1899, Lyric Theatre, London; US: 12 November 1900, Casino Theater, New York

This was Stuart's first complete work for the theatre; it traded in an exotic setting (the plot concerns a secret perfume manufactured in the Philippines) and alluring chorus girls ('Florodora girls' became a social phenomenon in the US). Stuart's musical gift was unusually highly developed and manifested itself in extended melodies with broad tonal structures (often mirroring chorus routines), of which the most famous is the double sextet 'Tell me, pretty maiden'.

RECORDING   excerpts: studio cast, HMV, 1931
EDITION   v.s., Francis, Day and Hunter, 1899

Other musical comedies: *The Silver Slipper*, 1901; *The School*

Girl, 1903; *The Belles of Mayfair*, 1906; *Havana*, 1908; *Captain Kidd*, 1910; *The Slim Princess*, 1910; *Peggy*, 1911; *Midnight Frolic*, 1917
BIBLIOGRAPHY   Kurt Gänzl, *The British Musical Theatre*, Macmillan, 1986

S.B.

JULE STYNE

Julius Kerwin Stein; *b* 31 December 1905, London

Taken by his family to Chicago aged eight, Styne studied the piano and became known as a child prodigy. He turned his talents to bandleading and arranging, and became a sought-after writer of hit songs for films and recordings. He ultimately established himself as a prolific Broadway composer, capably creating a varied body of work with a succession of collaborators. His ability to serve the special qualities of his leading performers has sometimes backfired, for most of his musicals have become so indelibly associated with their original stars that revivals are seldom considered feasible. *Gypsy* has been a notable exception.

Gypsy

Musical play in two acts (2h 45m)
Libretto by Arthur Laurents, based on the memoirs of Gypsy Rose Lee; lyrics by Stephen Sondheim
PREMIERES   21 May 1959, Broadway Theater, New York; UK: 29 May 1973, Piccadilly Theatre, London

Gypsy combines a flavourful backstage look at the vaudeville and burlesque circuits with a character study of a 'stage mother' who ultimately must face her own frustrated hopes. *Gypsy* ranks among the most distinguished work of all three of its authors, and among the best-written musical plays. Characterization through song has seldom been accomplished so effectively in a musical as with the series of solo opportunities given to the central character of Mama Rose, a role created by Ethel Merman.

RECORDINGS   1. Merman, Church, Klugman, Rosenstock, CBS, 1959; 2. Lansbury, Z. Charisse, Ingham, Leonard, RCA, 1973
FILM   Le Roy (dir.), Warner, 1962
EDITION   v.s., Williamson and Stratford, 1960

Other musicals: *Glad to See You*, 1944; *High Button Shoes*, 1947; *Gentlemen Prefer Blondes*, 1949, rev. as *Lorelei*, 1974; *Hazel Flagg*, 1953; *Peter Pan* (with M. Charlap), 1954; *Bells are Ringing*, 1956; *Say, Darling*, 1958; *Do Re Mi*, 1960; *Subways are for Sleeping*, 1961; *Funny Girl*, 1964; *Fade Out–Fade In*, 1964; *Hallelujah, Baby!*, 1967; *Darling of the Day*, 1968; *Look to the Lilies*, 1970; *Prettybelle*, 1971; *Sugar*, 1972; *Bar Mitzvah Boy*, 1978; *One Night Stand*, 1980; *Pieces of Eight*, 1985
BIBLIOGRAPHY   Theodore Taylor, *Jule: The Story of Composer Jule Styne*, Random House, 1979

J.A.C.

EUGEN SUCHOŇ

b 25 September 1908, Pezinok, Slovakia

Suchoň studied composition in Bratislava and then (1931–3) in Prague with Novák. On his return to Slovakia he held teaching appointments in music theory and music education at the Bratislava Academy (from 1933), High School of Education (from 1950) and finally at the University (1959–74). Suchoň has completed only two operas, but his first, *The Whirlpool*, achieved a success unparalleled in post-war Czechoslovak opera and was the first Slovak opera to establish itself firmly in the repertoire. A third opera, *Hannibal in Television* (*Hanibal v televízii*), from the early 1970s has not been completed.

The Whirlpool

Krútňava
Opera in six scenes (1h 45m)
Libretto by the composer and Števan Hoza, after the novel by Milo Urban
Composed 1941–9
PREMIERES 10 December 1949, National Theatre, Bratislava; US: 12 January 1979, Lansing, Michigan; UK: 27 August 1990, King's Theatre, Edinburgh (Slovak National Opera)

The Whirlpool has received more productions outside Czechoslovakia than any other post-war Czech or Slovak opera. Its appeal lies in a confidently large-scale, unashamed treatment of folk material subtly inflecting an accessible musical style, and a feeling for effective stage drama. The plot is a drama from country life (a jealous suitor murders his rival and marries his bride, but later repents). In this respect it owes something to Suchoň's Czech predecessors, Janáček, Foerster and Burian, whose *Jenůfa*, *Eva* and *Maryša* respectively are all set in neighbouring Moravia. Slovak folksong plays a decisive role in determining the opera's character, with colourful folk elements providing the core of two of the scenes. The work was long in gestation, and prepared for by Suchoň's choral settings of Slovak folksongs.

RECORDING Beňačková, Kopačka, Malachovský, Slovak Philharmonic Ch, Bratislava Radio SO, Frešo, Opus, 1973
EDITIONS v.ss., Slovenské hudobné vydavatel'stvo, 1951; Štátne hudobné vydavatel'stvo, 2nd edn, 1961

Svätopluk

Music drama in three acts (2h 30m)
Libretto by the composer, Ivan Stodola and Jela Krčméryová
Composed 1951–9
PREMIERE 10 March 1960, Slovak National Opera, Bratislava

Czech nationalist opera of the 19th century cultivated two main genres: folk and monumental history. After *The Whirlpool*, Suchoň followed this model by writing a *Libuše*-like pageant opera that looks back to the Great Moravian Empire of the 9th century.

This time saw the coming of Christianity to the region and the first political union of the present-day Czech- and Slovak-speaking regions. The folksong idiom of *The Whirlpool* gives way to a grander style, with large-scale choruses and a rather static though complicated action which deals with the death of the first king, Svätopluk, and the division of his kingdom between his three sons. Although finely crafted, the work is rather old-fashioned, and its nationalist concerns have meant that, unlike *The Whirlpool*, it has not crossed the borders of Czechoslovakia.

RECORDING Tikalová, Podvalová, Krásová, Žídek, Kočí, Haken, Prague NT Ch and O, Chalabala, Supraphon, 1961
EDITION v.s., Štátne hudobné vydavatel'stvo, 1963

BIBLIOGRAPHY Igor Vajda, *Slovenská opera*, Opus, 1988

J.T.

ARTHUR SULLIVAN

(Sir) Arthur Seymour Sullivan; *b* 13 May 1842, London; *d* 22 November 1900, London

Until the advent of Andrew Lloyd Webber, Arthur Sullivan was by far the most performed and internationally the best-known British composer for the theatre. In his early professional life he was an all-rounder, winning fame before he was 20 with his incidental music to *The Tempest* (1861) and proceeding to a symphony, a cello concerto, etc. But the financial rewards to be reaped from operetta, as well as his own proven mastery of it, led him later to concentrate almost entirely on the theatre and on large-scale choral works. Operetta is the internationally recognized term for the type of work on which William Schwenck Gilbert and Sullivan collaborated under Richard D'Oyly Carte's management (1875–96), but they themselves used the term 'comic opera'.

Carte built the Savoy Theatre in 1882 to house Gilbert's and Sullivan's chain of successes, though he himself did not confine the term 'Savoy Opera' to their works. In early days, and later during and after a period of personal estrangement from Gilbert, Sullivan worked with other librettists, notably Francis Cowley Burnand and Basil Hood, later the librettist of Edward German's *Merrie England* (1902). He used the term 'light opera' for *Haddon Hall* (libretto by Sydney Grundy). But his sole venture into what was then called grand opera was *Ivanhoe*, for which Carte built the Royal English Opera House (now the Palace Theatre) in 1891. For Carte, who failed to profit from his investment and had to sell the theatre, *Ivanhoe* spelt failure despite an initial run of 160 consecutive performances unrivalled for a 'serious' work. The music and libretto received weighty adverse criticism and it has not been successfully revived.

Curiously the operettas, though so often tied to satire on British social life of their own day (the 'aesthetic' craze in *Patience*, parliamentary anomalies in *Iolanthe*), have maintained a perennial life quite unparalleled by any other body of work from the Victorian theatre. They were original works, not adaptations from others. If Gilbert's extraordinary dexterity of language did much for these works, and added not a few proverbial phrases in doing so, Sullivan's scores likewise caught popular taste – and exhibited musical subtleties as well. In every one of the operettas there are numbers that, in contrapuntal wit or harmonic subtlety or musical allusiveness, have continued to make their appeal to sophisticated taste. The contrapuntal yoking of two apparently unrelated tunes became a Sullivan trademark while his patter songs, extended in *Ruddigore* to a patter trio, are no less effective than their predecessors in Rossini and Donizetti.

Recurrence of a musical motif as a dramatic indicator to the audience is rare; where found, it corresponds more to Bizet's and Gounod's usage than to Wagner's. A deeper level of musical linking has been demonstrated for *The Mikado* (see *Jacobs, 1986*) and is perhaps waiting to be discovered in others of the operetta scores. The fact that, in the non-English-speaking world, *The Mikado* has been the most widely performed of the operettas (with many translations) is puzzling. The butt of its satire

is Britain, not Japan, yet its musical and costumed orientalisms seem to have exerted their own attraction and gained it a place in that special sequence of operatic exotica which ranges from *L'Africaine* to *Madama Butterfly*.

NOTE

Voices: voice-types are not specified in the original published scores or libretti of Sullivan's stage works but are here given as usually allotted. A spoken role indicates a chorus performer who has individual speech but no solo singing.

Recordings: except for the all-sung *Trial by Jury*, *The Zoo* and *Ivanhoe*, a recording with dialogue is first selected if available, followed by one or two of the best recent non-dialogue recordings. A number of pre-1914 recordings, giving a clue to early performing styles, have been transferred to LP, tape and CD, two notable selections being *Gilbert and Sullivan: The Early Records (1898–1912)*, EMI, 1985, and *Sir Arthur Sullivan*, Symposium, 1992.

Cox and Box, or The Long-lost Brothers

Triumviretta in one act (original version: 1h; Savoy (1921) version: 30m)
Libretto by Francis Cowley Burnand, after John Maddison Morton's farce *Box and Cox* (1847)
PREMIERES 26 May 1866 (private performance with pf); 11 May 1867, Adelphi Theatre, London; US: 13 August 1875, New York

Vanity Fair *cartoon of Sullivan*

The farcical interaction of two lodgers, one occupying the accommodation by day and the other by night, provides a framework for the only non-Gilbert operetta of Sullivan's to have survived into the modern repertoire (though *The Zoo* has been broadcast and recorded). The only other character is the landlord, Bouncer (Mrs Bouncer in the original play), whose military posturings allow Sullivan to parody the operatic military manner with a repeated drum figure of 'rat-a-plan, rat-a-plan', best known at that time from Donizetti's *La fille du régiment*. The threesome gives rise to the playful designation of the work as a triumviretta, from *triumviri* (the group of three magistrates governing Ancient Rome) and *operetta*.

Sullivan's 'straight' setting of an absurd lyric ('Hushed is the bacon'), was to be a characteristic of his comic style. The composer sanctioned the separate publication of the song with different words as drawing-room fare. Of a similar comic absurdity is the vocalized 'instrumental' accompaniment to the duet serenade, 'The buttercup dwells on the lowly mead'. The resolution of the plot when the two lodgers discover they are brothers, though carried out in speech and drawn directly from the play, mocks operatic coincidence (as in *The Marriage of Figaro*, Act III):

BOX   Tell me – in mercy tell me – have you a
           strawberry mark on your left arm?
COX   No.
BOX   Then it is he!

Originally in ten numbers including the overture, it

Cover of Charles Coote's Cox and Box *quadrille*

is now commonly performed in a curtailed 'Savoy' version of nine numbers.

RECORDING   abbreviated 'Savoy' version: Styler, Riordan, Adams, New SO, Godfrey, Decca, 1962
VIDEO   Fryatt, Smythe, Marks, Drower, LSO, Faris, Video Gems, 1982
EDITION   original version: v.s., Metzler, 1869; Savoy version: v.s., Boosey, 1921

The Contrabandista, or The Law of the Ladrones

Comic opera in two acts (1h 15m)
Libretto by Francis Cowley Burnand
PREMIERES   18 December 1867, St George's Hall, London; US: 1879, Philadelphia (with additional music by Sousa)

Sullivan's first opera in more than one act shows many features of his later works, though in an undeveloped form. Particularly characteristic is the contrapuntal harnessing of two tunes representing different characters. A cachucha (as in *The Gondoliers*) and a bolero serve to illustrate the Spanish location. The hero is a camera-carrying tourist in Spain, Mr Grigg (baritone), who is chosen against his will as the leader of a robber band ('From rock to rock').

Grigg undergoes a comic mock-coronation ceremony ('Hail to the ancient hat') and faces the alarming prospect of being burdened with Inez, the formidable chieftainess of the robbers (alto), but eventually wins his freedom to return to 'my spouse, my cows and my sows'. Burnand's jocular word-play

does not always register in singing and the dramatic structure is not strong, but the music is lively enough, and prompted an expansion in 1894 into the full-length opera *The Chieftain*.

EDITION   v.s., Metzler, 1867

Thespis, or The Gods Grown Old

Operatic extravaganza in two acts (2h)
Libretto by W. S. Gilbert
PREMIERE   26 December 1871, Gaiety Theatre, London

Apart from the Act II ballet music which was reconstructed from manuscript sources in 1990, the original score does not survive. But *Thespis* is historically famous as the first collaboration of Gilbert and Sullivan. It was not so much a forerunner of the later collaborations under Richard D'Oyly Carte's management (tailored for a consciously respectable audience) as a contribution to the Gaiety Theatre tradition of burlesque. Unlike most of those burlesques it did not set new words to existing tunes, but its comedy was broad and parodistic: in the theatrical troupe which is temporarily entrusted with the functions of the gods of Olympus, Bacchus is replaced by an ex-drunkard wearing a medal to signify his recent conversion to teetotalism. Thespis, manager of the troupe, was played by the famous comedian Joe Toole.

Though never revived (presumably for reasons of taste), it was never disowned by the collaborators and the text was included by Gilbert (unfortunately with mistakes surviving from the 1871 libretto) in the complete edition of his plays. One number, 'Little maid of Arcadee', was published as a drawing-room ballad with the words modified to suit decorum. A chorus, 'Climbing over rocky mountain', was apparently the source of the chorus beginning with the same words in *The Pirates of Penzance*.

RECORDINGS   1. Fulham Light Opera Society, Spencer, RRE, 1970s; 2. ballet: D'Oyly Carte O, Pryce-Jones, TER, 1991; 3. ballet: RTE CO, Penny, Marco Polo, 1992
EDITION   f.s., Sir Arthur Sullivan Society (on hire)

Trial by Jury

Comic opera (originally dramatic cantata) in one act (45m)
Libretto by W. S. Gilbert
Composed 1875
PREMIERES   25 March 1875, Royalty Theatre, London; US: 15 November 1875, Eagle Theater, New York
CAST   Plaintiff *s*, Defendant *t*, Learned Judge *bar*, Usher *b*, Counsel for the Plaintiff *bar*, Foreman of the Jury *bar*; *satb* chorus of jurymen and bridesmaids

The first time Gilbert and Sullivan collaborated under Richard D'Oyly Carte's management (though Carte had not yet set up his own company) produced an all-sung work, oddly designated in the score as a dramatic cantata. In no subsequent collaboration with Gilbert did Sullivan retain the all-sung form (but see *The Zoo*). It is based on the comical extravagance of setting a court action to verse and to music, the action being that of breach of promise of marriage, a type of legal case that was already liable to ridicule. In addition to the impassioned statements of the point at issue, even routine matters such as the swearing in of the (all-male) jury are subjected to full musical treatment. The character of the Learned Judge (originally taken with much success by Sullivan's brother Fred, who was to die young) is the first of a famous line of comic parts with self-descriptive songs which often reveal moral ambiguities.

SYNOPSIS
The jury is waiting to try the case of 'Edwin, sued by Angelina'. The jurymen are addressed by the Usher: he and the jurors are already prejudiced against the Defendant, who enters and states his case to guitar accompaniment. The Learned Judge enters, is greeted, and gives an account of himself ('When I, good friends, was called to the Bar'). The Plaintiff enters in bridal dress and attended by bridesmaids. Her Counsel tells how she was courted, then jilted for another. The Defendant offers, 'I'll marry this lady today, and marry the other tomorrow.' The Judge is disposed to agree until reminded that such a step would constitute 'burglaree' ('A nice dilemma we have here'). No solution emerging to satisfy both sides, the Judge (who has taken a fancy to the Plaintiff from her first entrance) dismisses the court: 'Put your briefs upon the shelf: I will marry her myself!'

In the choral greeting to the Judge before his self-revelatory song, Sullivan parodies Handel's grandest oratorio manner, complete with word-repetition. A more specific parody, not merely of a composer but of an actual operatic number, is the climactic ensemble, 'A nice dilemma': in its imitative vocal entries, in general style, and even key, it is directly modelled on 'D'un pensiero', the Act I finale to Bellini's La sonnambula.

RECORDINGS   Hood, Round, Sandford, Reed, Adams, Raffell, D'Oyly Carte Ch, Royal Opera House O, Godfrey, Decca, 1964; Morison, R. Lewis, G. Baker, Glyndebourne Ch, Pro Arte O, Sargent, EMI, 1961
VIDEO   Howerd, Flowers, McDonnell, Bryson, LSO, Faris, Brent Walker, 1982
EDITION   v.s., Metzler, 1875

The Zoo
Musical folly in one act (40m)
Libretto by Bolton Rowe (pseudonym of Benjamin Charles Stephenson)
PREMIERE   5 June 1875, St James's Theatre, London

This brief, all-sung piece in 13 numbers is a minor but still attractive specimen of Sullivan's early stage work. Despite some weakness in dramatic construction it has won occasional revival since its modern republication. Its setting is the Zoological Gardens in London, where a chorus of members of the public finds itself the witness to two love affairs. Aesculapius Carboy, a chemist, is in love with Laetitia; Thomas Brown, really the Duke of Islington in disguise, loves the coquettish Eliza, an attendant at the refreshment stall of the Zoo.

Notable in comic musicality are Thomas's nervously stuttering oration, prompted by the sympathetic crowd, and a quartet ('Once more the face I loved so well') when the two pairs of lovers sing entirely different strains which are then neatly combined in counterpoint. Also amusingly done is the parody of operatic repetition: 'I will – I fly'; 'She will – she flies'; 'I fly . . .', etc.

RECORDING   Reid, Sandford, Ayldon, Goss, Metcalfe, D'Oyly Carte Ch, RPO, Nash, Decca, 1978
EDITIONS   v.ss., Garth Morton (ed.), Terence Rees, 1969; Cramer, 1975; R. Clyde, 1991

The Sorcerer
Comic opera in two acts (1h 45m)
Libretto by W. S. Gilbert
Composed 1877, rev. 1884
PREMIERES   17 November 1877, Opéra-Comique, London; rev. version: 11 October 1884, Savoy Theatre, London; US: 21 February 1879, Broadway Theater, New York
CAST   Sir Marmaduke Poindextre b, Alexis t, Aline s, John Wellington Wells bar, Lady Sangazure a, Dr Daly b-bar, a, b; satb chorus of villagers

Sullivan's first full-length work with Gilbert establishes what was to be their usual formal pattern – two acts, the first ending with a complex finale in several sections, the second with the reprise of some previous number. The element of the love philtre in the plot took up a motif already familiar in Victorian times with Donizetti's L'elisir d'amore (on which Gilbert had written a burlesque, Dulcamara, or The Little Duck and the Great Quack). Here, however, the framework is that of the theatrically conventional English village with gentlefolk, vicar, pew-opener (a female verger), and rather cloddish lower-class villagers. The disruptive element is incarnated in the tradesman–sorcerer Mr Wells, who lists his wares in the first of the great Gilbert and Sullivan patter songs ('My name is John Wellington Wells,/I'm a dealer in magic and spells'). He is unique among Gilbert's operatic characters in being allowed to die (supernaturally) in action.

SYNOPSIS
Act I Alexis, a Grenadier Guards officer and the son of Sir Marmaduke Poindextre, is betrothed to Aline, daughter of Lady Sangazure. Constance, however, is unhappy: daughter of the pew-opener Mrs Partlet, she loves the elderly vicar, Dr Daly, unaware that he loves her in return. Sir Marmaduke and Lady Sangazure exchange courtly compliments while (aside) confessing an intense passion for each other. Alexis is so convinced of love as a universal panacea that he has summoned a sorcerer, John Wellington Wells, to devise a philtre that will make everyone fall in love with the first individual to meet the eye. Wells brews his potion, to be administered in tea at a village merry-making: married people will naturally be immune from its effects.

The tea-party begins as Act I ends; at the beginning of Act II the effects of the potion have become visible, but have gone awry. Constance finds herself in love with a notary, Sir Marmaduke with

Mrs Partlet, Lady Sangazure with the Sorcerer himself (to his consternation) and Aline with Dr Daly. The misplaced magic is expunged when the Sorcerer volunteers to die. He descends into the earth and the merry-making resumes with all lovers rightfully paired.

The military-sounding music appropriate for Alexis as a Guards officer, the 'eerie' orchestral sounds accompanying Mr Wells's incantation, and the amiable sentiments of the Revd Dr Daly (who played the flageolet in the opening production) – all these serve to vary a score of considerable verve, though the ballads allotted to Alexis and Aline now seem too obviously destined to be excerpted for the drawing room. The duet of the two old people, Sir Marmaduke and Lady Sangazure, is particularly resourceful. It is set to one of the old dances to which Sullivan was attracted (a gavotte), and displays both the combination of two dissimilar tunes and the interpolation of asides into normal conversation.

For the 1884 revival Sullivan made changes including a significant shortening of the Act I finale: a formal return to the key of the opening of that finale (adhering to the practice of Mozart's or Rossini's finales) is sacrificed for greater dramatic tautness. He also rewrote the opening of Act II.

RECORDING (omitting dialogue) Reed, Adams, C. Palmer, D. Palmer, Masterson, Allister, Hood, D'Oyly Carte Ch, RPO, Godfrey, Decca, 1967
VIDEO Revill, Adams, Oliver, LSO, Faris, Brent Walker, 1982
EDITIONS v.s., Metzler, 1877; rev. version: v.s., Metzler, 1884

HMS Pinafore, or The Lass that Loved a Sailor

Comic opera in two acts (1h 45m)
Libretto by W. S. Gilbert
Composed 1878
PREMIERES 25 May 1878, Opéra-Comique, London; US: 25 November 1878, The Boston Museum, Boston
CAST Sir Joseph Porter *bar*, Captain Corcoran *b-bar*, Ralph Rackstraw *t*, Josephine *s*, Dick Deadeye *b*, Mrs Cripps (Little Buttercup) *a*, *ms*, *bar*, *b*, *silent; satb* chorus of Sir Joseph's relatives, sailors, marines, etc.

Although both of Gilbert's and Sullivan's previous collaborations had been given present-day settings, only with *HMS Pinafore* was a pronounced note of political and social satire introduced. Class relations within the navy (and outside it) and the dubious machinations of political appointments are set forth. The character of Sir Joseph Porter was inevitably taken, despite Gilbert's (perhaps ironic) denials, as being aimed at W. H. Smith, the actual First Lord of the Admiralty. All this was set within a highly traditional theatrical frame featuring the upright sailor lad, his faithful sweetheart, and the black-hearted villain (Dick Deadeye: 'It's a beast of a name, ain't it?').

After an initially cautious reception at the box office, *HMS Pinafore* grew into Gilbert's and Sullivan's first major success and has remained one of their most popular and frequently revived works,

the mock-patriotism of 'For he is an Englishman' becoming proverbial. This work too was the start of Gilbert's and Sullivan's North American (and wider) reputation: pirated performances of *HMS Pinafore* were so successful in Boston, New York and elsewhere that Carte decided to take the composer and librettist and their company across the Atlantic to present the work in authentic form (at the same time launching *The Pirates of Penzance*).

SYNOPSIS
Act I A happy regime is maintained aboard HMS *Pinafore*, now anchored at Portsmouth. The bumboat woman Mrs Cripps with her stock of useful and tasty wares is welcomed on board ('I'm called Little Buttercup'). To his sympathetic messmates, Ralph as a humble sailor discloses his audacity in his love for his captain's daughter Josephine. Captain Corcoran, the ship's commander, declares in a self-introductory song that he never uses bad language to his crew ('What, never?'/'Hardly ever!'). But he is worried that Josephine is disinclined to accept a proposal of marriage from an exalted quarter, the First Lord of the Admiralty, Sir Joseph Porter. Sir Joseph arrives, escorted by sisters, cousins and aunts. An autobiographical song recounts his rise to Cabinet minister ('When I was a lad I served a term/As office boy to an attorney's firm'). He has composed a three-part glee which is performed. Josephine, at first acting her rank, spurns Ralph's love, but after he threatens suicide she joyfully admits she loves him. All his mates, except the malevolent Deadeye, will help the pair get ashore that night to be married.

Act II In the evening Captain Corcoran sings to the moon of his worry about Josephine. Mrs Cripps tries to warn him of some mystery, but he does not comprehend. Josephine herself is doubtful of the hardships that confront her. But Sir Joseph, thinking to promote his own case in condescending to marry a captain's daughter, tells her that 'Love levels all ranks'. She takes that as arguing Ralph's case and is ready to proceed with the elopement. Warned by Dick Deadeye, her father steps in to prevent it. Ralph speaks up for his rights: 'I am an Englishman' (echoed by the chorus, 'For he himself has said it,/And it's greatly to his credit,/That he is an Englishman'). In reprimanding Ralph, Captain Corcoran says, 'Damme, it's too bad!', a profanity for which Sir Joseph confines him to his cabin while the presumptuous Ralph is taken off to the ship's dungeon.

Mrs Cripps makes a dramatic declaration in song: a former baby-farmer, she had both Ralph and Corcoran in her care as infants and mixed them up. They now re-emerge: Ralph as a captain, Corcoran as an able seaman. All is now serene for the lovers, Corcoran at the same time pairing off with Mrs Cripps and Sir Joseph with Hebe, one of his cousins.

Gilbert's strong characterization is so well fulfilled in Sullivan's music as to override the occasional weakness. The Act I finale, though it gathers a splendid momentum (with a remarkable artifice of rhythmical structure), does not get two opposing sides into dramatic and musical conflict as most of its successors do. The 'Buttercup' waltz is tediously plugged as an entr'acte and a mere medley of previous tunes serves to end Act II. But Ralph, Captain Corcoran, Sir Joseph and Josephine all live in their interactive music (particularly 'Never mind the why and wherefore') and almost as much musical resource is lavished on two characters parodied from opera or melodrama, Little Buttercup with 'gypsy blood in her veins' and the heavy-treading Dick Deadeye.

RECORDINGS   1. (with dialogue) Knight, Reed, D. Adams, Round, Skitch, Hindmarsh, Wright, D'Oyly Carte Ch, New SO, Godfrey, Decca, 1960; 2. (omitting dialogue) Ritchie, Ormiston, Sandison, Grace, Gillett, New Sadler's Wells Ch and O, Phipps, TER, 1987
VIDEOS   Marshall, Howerd, Drower, LSO, Faris, Brent Walker, 1982; D'Oyly Carte, Nash, Precision, 1980
EDITION   v.s., Metzler, 1878

The Pirates of Penzance, or The Slave of Duty

Comic opera in two acts (1h 45m)
Libretto by W. S. Gilbert
Composed 1879
PREMIERES   in skeleton form: 30 December 1879, Royal Bijou Theatre, Paignton; 3 April 1880, Opéra-Comique, London; US: 31 December 1879, New Fifth Avenue Theater, New York
CAST   Major-General Stanley *bar*, Pirate King *b*, Frederic *t*, Mabel *s*, Ruth *a*, Sergeant of Police *b-bar*, *s*, *ms*, *b*; *satb* chorus of pirates, police and General Stanley's daughters

Very much in the pattern of its highly successful predecessor, *The Pirates of Penzance* satirized not naval but military anomalies (in the person of the Major-General) and the police as well. Mock-patriotism is also invoked once again. The mainspring of the plot, however, arises from a recurrent target of Gilbert's satire, the idiocy and sometimes the hypocrisy of a literal-minded devotion to duty: here the knife is artfully twisted, with Frederic rigorously functioning as the 'slave of duty' of the opera's subtitle.

The piece received its formal premiere at the hands of the British company brought by Carte to New York, a mere token staging having been previously given at Paignton, Devon, to establish British copyright. After the American performances Gilbert and Sullivan made several alterations which bore fruit in the London production.

SYNOPSIS

Act I   Frederic, apprenticed to the pirate band as a boy, has reached the age of 21 and is congratulated: his apprenticeship over, he can be considered a full member of the band. But, though loyal while he had to be, he has decided to leave and oppose the Pirate King and his followers. Ruth, his former nursery-maid, who had led him to the apprenticeship through mishearing 'pilot' as 'pirate' and had herself become a maid-of-all-work to the pirates, hopes to persuade Frederic to marry her. (He has seen no other females to make comparison.) But to his

enraptured view a group of young women appears, the daughters of the Major-General, on an outing to the beach. To prevent their unknowingly exposing as much as a leg, Frederic announces his presence. He begs any one of them to accept him in marriage – and Mabel, considering it her duty, accepts ('Poor wand'ring one'). Suddenly the pirates appear and are about to abduct the young women when the Major-General himself arrives. He persuades them not to rob him, an orphan, of his daughters. Their better nature is touched. Only in an aside does the Major-General confess his fib – he is no orphan.

Frederic confronted by the Pirate King and Ruth in Act II of The Pirates of Penzance *(April 1880)*

Act II   That night, the Major-General is not abed as usual; his conscience is tormented by his fib. Under Frederic's command the police are now to take the vengeance of the law on the pirates. The Sergeant of Police and his men are disquieted by Mabel's fervent exhortation ('Go, ye heroes, go and die!'). Frederic is confronted by the Pirate King and Ruth who explain 'a most ingenious paradox': having been born on 29 February in leap year, and apprenticed not for 21 years but until his 21st birthday (which will not arrive till 1940) he is still bound to them. Frederic switches his 'duty' and bids a tearful farewell to Mabel. The police re-enter, the Sergeant proclaiming that 'A policeman's lot is not a happy one'. The pirates, now informed by Frederic of the Major-General's deception, are intent on revenge. The Major-General, still conscience-ridden, sings a song ('Softly sighing to the river') accompanied by the police and pirates of whose presence he is ignorant. The pirates overpower the police but yield when challenged 'in Queen Victoria's name'. The pirates themselves are revealed to be all 'noblemen who have gone wrong'; their crimes are forgiven, since 'peers will be peers', and they can marry the Major-General's daughters while Frederic and Mabel can get married too.

Musically *The Pirates* is, as Sullivan himself recognized, stronger than *Pinafore*. Nowhere in the whole Gilbert and Sullivan canon is anything more deft than the dovetailing of the love duet in waltz time into the chattering 2/4 women's chorus, 'How beautifully blue the sky' in Act I, the whole modulating from B to G and back again. The Major-

General's song in Act II, with its Schubertian water-rippling accompaniment, is placed as an absolutely straight number within a hilarious comic context – the Major-General's unawareness of the male choruses surely parodying a similar situation in *Il trovatore*. The process by which, some time after 1900, the melody of 'Come, friends, who plough the sea' was metamorphosed into the American song 'Hail, hail, the gang's all here' has still not been clarified.

RECORDINGS 1. (with dialogue) Reed, Adams, Potter, Masterson, C. Palmer, Brannigan, D'Oyly Carte Ch, RPO, Godfrey, Decca, 1968; 2. (omitting dialogue) Morison, Lewis, Brannigan, Milligan, Cameron, G. Baker, Glyndebourne Ch, Pro Arte O, Sargent, EMI, 1961; 3. Hill Smith, Rivers, Roberts, Creasy, D'Oyly Carte Opera Ch and O, Pryce-Jones, TER, 1990
VIDEO Allen, Michell, Oliver, Knight, LSO, Faris, Brent Walker, 1982
EDITION v.s., Chappell, 1880

Patience, or Bunthorne's Bride

Comic opera in two acts (2h)
Libretto by W. S. Gilbert
Composed 1880–81
PREMIERES 23 April 1881, Opéra-Comique, London; US: 22 September 1881, Standard Theater, New York
CAST Colonel Calverley *b*, Lieutenant the Duke of Dunstable *t*, Reginald Bunthorne, a fleshly poet *bar*, Archibald Grosvenor, an idyllic poet *b-bar*, Lady Jane *a*, Patience *s*, *s*, 2 *ms*, *bar*, *silent*; *satb* chorus of rapturous maidens and officers of Dragoon Guards

One of Gilbert's early *Bab Ballads*, entitled *The Rival Curates* and mocking clerical behaviour, was the original inspiration for *Patience*. A few clerical references survive ('Your style is much too sanctified, your cut is too canonical'). But, happily for posterity, Gilbert redirected his satire and made a butt of the 'aesthetic movement', associated with various writers and artists but particularly Oscar Wilde (then in his early twenties). The innocent dairymaid heroine and the swaggering soldiers come from established theatrical convention but the juxtaposition of different worlds is brilliantly brought off in musical as well as theatrical terms, with the bevy of love-languishing females forming a sharply individualized chorus. The puncturing of the pretensions of artistic poseurs, and the triumph of everyday common sense, has continued to make its point long after the fading of once-topical references ('greenery-yallery, Grosvenor Gallery'). The subtitle is a joke: nobody becomes Bunthorne's bride.

SYNOPSIS
Act I 'Twenty love-sick maidens' of high degree adore the pretentious poet Bunthorne – but the dairymaid Patience, whom he loves, is indifferent. Following an aesthetic ideal the maidens now have no time for their former lovers, the officers of the 35th Dragoon Guards, whose pride is declared by their Colonel. Alone, Bunthorne confesses he is 'an aesthetic sham', posing only to win admiration. Patience is approached by her long-lost childhood playmate, Grosvenor, also a poet; she is attracted by

Leonora Braham as Patience (London, 1881)

him but for that very reason, having been told that love must be unselfish, she rejects him. Bunthorne, convinced he will never win Patience, puts himself up for raffle. Patience intervenes: since love is unselfish, it becomes her duty to love and wed Bunthorne! The love-sick maidens return to their officers. But the sight of Grosvenor rekindles their aesthetic flame: they cluster round him as they once had round Bunthorne, leaving the officers dismayed.

Act II Stout, elderly Lady Jane laments her passing charms. Grosvenor, who loves Patience, vainly tries to put off the high-born maidens with 'the fable of the magnet and the churn'. Jane encourages Bunthorne, who feels snubbed by the maidens' desertion, to challenge Grosvenor directly. To win back their loves, the Colonel, Major and Lieutenant reappear in what they believe to be aesthetic dress and strike poses accordingly. Two of the maidens, Angela and Saphir, are smitten by them. Bunthorne challenges Grosvenor to abandon the aesthetic field: since he can say he did so on compulsion, Grosvenor is delighted to comply and become an ordinary person. Patience can now marry Grosvenor, the Lieutenant unexpectedly proposes to Jane, and everyone is satisfactorily paired except the posing Bunthorne.

Although the once-admired Act I sextet ('I hear the soft note') may now seem over-sentimental, the bounce of the military music and the simple melodiousness of several songs retain their appeal. The quintet with dance in Act II ('If Saphir I choose to marry') has a special exuberance, its 6/8 rhythm pointed by a syncopated high woodwind counterpoint: this music makes a happy return as the very last number of the operetta. Lady Jane's soliloquy at the beginning of Act II is punctuated by a comically grotesque recitative on the double-bass – an instrument the soloist usually pretends to play. But some gifted interpreters actually have played either cello or double-bass on stage.

RECORDINGS   1. (with dialogue) Adams, Potter, Reed, Sandford, New SO, Godfrey, Decca, 1961; 2. (omitting dialogue) Morison, Young, G. Baker, Cameron, M. Thomas, Sinclair, Harper, Harwood, Glyndebourne Ch, Pro Arte O, Sargent, EMI, 1962
VIDEO   Adams, Kennedy, Jenkins, LSO, Faris, Brent Walker, 1982
EDITION   v.s., Chappell, 1881

Iolanthe, or The Peer and the Peri

Comic opera in two acts (2h)
Libretto by W. S. Gilbert
Composed 1882
PREMIERES   25 November 1882, Savoy Theatre, London; US: 25 November 1882, Standard Theater, New York
CAST   Lord Chancellor *bar*, Earl of Mountararat *b*, Earl Tolloller *t*, Private Willis *b*, Strephon *bar*, Queen of the Fairies *a*, Iolanthe *ms*, Phyllis *s*, 2 *s*, *ms*; *satb* chorus of dukes, marquises, earls, viscounts, barons and fairies

Iolanthe was the first of the operettas written expressly for the Savoy Theatre (though Carte had moved his company there in the middle of the run of *Patience*) and it is hard to resist the idea that Sullivan found a new musical stimulus in the prospect. Gilbert's dramaturgical scheme is exceptionally strong, especially the counter-marching and conflict of peers and fairies at the end of Act I; an unusual richness of characterization invests the Lord Chancellor (in other respects the successor of mere patter-song professionals such as Sir Joseph Porter and the Major-General) with real pathos at the climax of the plot. The initial staging of the work displayed a helmeted, spear-carrying Queen of the Fairies as a kind of parodied Brünnhilde, but allegations of Wagnerism in Sullivan's music for the scene of Iolanthe's pardon should be met with scepticism.

SYNOPSIS

Act I   For the chorus of fairies there is little gaiety in life because one of their number, Iolanthe, was banished 25 years ago for marrying a mortal, a crime normally punished by death. The Queen of the Fairies is persuaded to pardon her, on condition that she does not communicate with her husband. Iolanthe appears, followed by her 24-year-old son, Strephon, who is a fairy only 'down to the waist'. He earns the approval of the Queen. His beloved Phyllis, a shepherdess and a ward of Chancery, enters with a solo, followed by a duet with Strephon ('None shall part us from each other'). They leave. Preceded with military pomp by a chorus of peers ('Loudly let the trumpet bray'), the Lord Chancellor introduces himself ('The law is the true embodiment'). All the peers are smitten with love for Phyllis, and Lords Tolloller and Mountararat in particular lay suit to her. Her declaration that she loves Strephon causes anger: his application to marry a ward in Chancery has already been dismissed. Distraught, Strephon

Cover of Charles d'Albert's Iolanthe *quadrille (1882)*

consults his young-looking fairy mother; Phyllis takes Iolanthe for a rival and, thinking Strephon unfaithful, declares her willingness to wed a peer. The Queen of the Fairies, summoned by Strephon and insulted by the Lord Chancellor, announces vengeance: Strephon shall go into Parliament and upset its cherished institutions. Fairies and peers exchange defiance.

Act II opens to display the Palace of Westminster: on sentry duty, Private Willis ponders the strange fact of 'ev'ry boy and ev'ry gal' becoming 'either a little Liberal or else a little Conservative' ('When all night long a chap remains'). The fairies are delighted at the legislative havoc being caused now that 'Strephon's a Member of Parliament', but Mountararat points out the dangers of the House of Lords becoming a house of intellectuals ('When Britain really rul'd the waves'). The fairies having begun to love the peers, their Queen endeavours to steady them by pointing out ('Oh, foolish fay') how she resists the 'simply godlike' charms of Private Willis. The Lord Chancellor discloses in a nightmare song ('When you're lying awake with a dismal headache') how his love for Phyllis – a ward of his own court – is upsetting him. Tolloller and Mountararat embolden him, so although Phyllis and Strephon have removed their mutual misunderstanding, the Lord Chancellor now decides to claim Phyllis for himself. The only one who can stop him is his former wife Iolanthe (whom he believes dead). She declares herself, thus inviting her own death sentence from the Queen. The Lord

Chancellor persuades the Queen to alter fairy law so that every fairy shall die 'who don't marry a mortal': she engages herself to Private Willis and all depart for fairyland.

Instead of being a mere medley of tunes (often assembled by one of Sullivan's musical assistants) the overture here is an accomplished sonata-type movement in which the tune of 'Oh, foolish fay' is combined by Sullivan with another tune of Mendelssohnian grace which does not occur in the operetta itself. And so the richness of this score continues, with a romantic pathos for Iolanthe's pardon and her later danger, and with a tiny, changing motif for the Lord Chancellor. The military strains, though they belong to peers rather than soldiers, are even more imposing than those in *Patience*. The sweetest and subtlest of all Sullivan's love duets (a soprano heroine paired with a baritone rather than a tenor hero) is 'None shall part us', its on-running melody underpinned by delicate harmonic progression.

RECORDINGS 1. (with dialogue) Reed, Adams, Round, Sandford, Styler, Knight, Newman, Sansom, D'Oyly Carte Ch, New SO, Godfrey, Decca, 1960; 2. (omitting dialogue) Morison, Thomas, Cameron, Brannigan, Wallace, G. Baker, Glyndebourne Ch, Pro Arte O, Sargent, EMI, 1960; 3. Suart, Creasy, Rath, Richard, Pert, D'Oyly Carte Ch and O, Pryce-Jones, TER, 1991
VIDEO Flowers, Hemsley, Hammond-Stroud, Van Allan, LSO, Faris, Brent Walker, 1982
EDITION v.s., Chappell, 1883

Princess Ida, or Castle Adamant

Comic opera in three acts (2h)
Libretto by W. S. Gilbert, after the poem *The Princess* by Alfred, Lord Tennyson (1847)
Composed 1883–4
PREMIERES 5 January 1884, Savoy Theatre, London; US: 11 February 1884, Fifth Avenue Theater, New York
CAST King Hildebrand *b-bar*, Hilarion *t*, Cyril *t*, Florian *bar*, King Gama *bar*, Arac *b*, Princess Ida *s*, Lady Blanche *a*, Psyche *s*, Melissa *ms*, *s*, *bar*, *b*, 3 *spoken roles*; *satb* chorus of soldiers, courtiers, girl graduates, Daughters of the Plough, etc.

Gilbert's and Sullivan's only three-act collaboration is also the only one with the dialogue in blank verse, a survival from *The Princess*, Gilbert's spoken play of 1870, itself a burlesque of Tennyson's long narrative poem of that name. Tennyson had prophesied and welcomed the emancipation of women; Gilbert ridiculed it. The satire of the opera ('A women's college? Maddest folly going!') was already out of date when it appeared. Sullivan's score nevertheless has borne regular revival for its mock-military fun and lyrical graces.

SYNOPSIS
Act I Princess Ida, daughter of King Gama, was betrothed at the age of one to Prince Hilarion, son of King Hildebrand, but 20 years later her father fails to produce her as promised for the marriage. Instead he arrives accompanied only by his three brainless

warrior sons. Ida has immured herself at a women's university where men are banned. Hilarion, with his friends Cyril and Florian, decides to go and hunt them out – using only the means of love ('Expressive glances/Shall be our lances').

Act II discloses Castle Adamant, site of the university. Unlike the hypocritical second-in-command, Lady Blanche, Princess Ida voices genuine aspiration in her invocation to Minerva, goddess of wisdom. Cyril and his friends enter, having scaled the walls. Seeing some robes they put them on and play at being females. The princess fails to detect them but Florian is recognized by his sister Psyche; she and her friend Melissa will support the men. Still in female dress they join the others for lunch, but Cyril gets tipsy and all three men are discovered and seized. Hildebrand's forces arrive outside and begin a siege of the castle.

Act III sees the collapse of Ida's dreams as her female force refuses to fight. She admits her mistakes and lovingly accepts Hilarion.

Gilbert's libretto gave Sullivan the opportunity to recapture the gracefulness of line and harmony to which he had risen in *Iolanthe*, and also to excel in martial patter and in the caricatured portrait of the sharp-tongued King Gama and his three oafish sons. One of the sons, Arac, has a splendid mock-Handelian song when deciding that it would be easier to fight by taking off his armour than keeping it on ('This helmet, I suppose'). It is hardly the composer's fault if the story fails to convince even on its own fable-like terms.

RECORDING (omitting dialogue) C. Palmer, D. Palmer, Potter, Raffell, Cook, Hood, Masterson, Harwood, Sandford, Adams, Skitch, Reed, D'Oyly Carte Ch, RPO, Sargent, Decca, 1965
VIDEO Gorshin, Howlett, Dale, LSO, Faris, Brent Walker, 1982
EDITION v.s., Chappell, 1884

The Mikado, or The Town of Titipu

Comic opera in two acts (2h 15m)
Libretto by W. S. Gilbert
Composed 1884–5
PREMIERES 14 March 1885, Savoy Theatre, London; US: 6 July 1885, Chicago (unauthorized); 19 August 1885, Fifth Avenue Theater, New York (D'Oyly Carte)
CAST The Mikado *b*, Nanki-Poo *t*, Ko-Ko *bar*, Pooh-Bah *b-bar*, Pish-Tush *bar*, Yum-Yum *s*, Pitti-Sing *ms*, Peep-Bo *ms*, Katisha *a*, (Go-To *b* sometimes added); *satb* chorus of schoolgirls, nobles, guards and coolies

The Mikado was the collaborators' longest-running work (672 performances) and, on its revival in 1896, became the first to achieve 1000 performances at the Savoy. Praised by the Viennese critic Hanslick, translated into many languages including Russian (for a performance under Stanislavsky's auspices), it is often considered Sullivan's masterpiece. Perhaps Gilbert's too: characters such as Pooh-Bah, phrases such as 'modified rapture!' and 'let the punishment fit the crime' became proverbial.

It was the first Gilbert and Sullivan piece set in a

Photograph of Sibyl Grey, Leonora Braham and Jessica Bond, the original three little maids in The Mikado *(London, 1885)*

recognized and strongly identified foreign location, but the 'Japanese' names are all English, obviously in cases such as Ko-Ko, less obviously with Pitti-Sing (baby talk for 'pretty thing'). Through the Japanese mask Gilbert satirized English abuses or absurdities, the more effectively because Sullivan's music is (typically of him) straight and not grotesque. Seemingly perfect in balance, the score has come down to us in a form not exactly that of the original. Shortly after the opening night the author and composer made two important structural changes, advancing Ko-Ko's 'little list' song within Act I and moving Yum-Yum's 'The sun, whose rays' from Act I to Act II.

SYNOPSIS
Act I Nanki-Poo, a wandering minstrel arriving in the town of Titipu ('A wand'ring minstrel I'), learns from Pish-Tush that Yum-Yum, whom he hoped to marry, is engaged to her guardian, Ko-Ko, a tailor who has become Lord High Executioner. Ko-Ko expounds his 'little list' of 'society offenders' who could usefully be decapitated. Yum-Yum and her friends Pitti-Sing and Peep-Bo ('Three little maids from school') are cheeky towards the colossal dignity of Pooh-Bah, 'Lord High Everything Else'. Nanki-Poo reveals to Yum-Yum that he is really the son of the Mikado, fleeing the amorous attentions of the elderly Katisha. After an edict from the Mikado Ko-Ko nerves himself to begin decapitations. Since Nanki-Poo is about to commit a love-sick suicide, a bargain is drawn: he will be permitted to marry Yum-Yum on condition of consenting to be beheaded in a month's time. Rejoicing is in order, and even the terrifying appearance of Katisha is defied ('For he's going to marry Yum-Yum'). She threatens the Mikado's vengeance.
Act II Yum-Yum, decked for her wedding, sings naïvely of her own beauty ('The sun, whose rays are

all ablaze'). Joined in a madrigal by Pitti-Sing and Pish-Tush the lovers rejoice ('Brightly dawns our wedding day'). But expectations are dampened when Ko-Ko discovers a law by which, when a man is executed, his bride is buried alive. The Mikado's arrival is announced: he identifies himself ('A more humane Mikado never did in Japan exist') and catalogues his own system of justice: 'to let the punishment fit the crime'. Ko-Ko, Pooh-Bah and Pitti-Sing regale him with an account of a supposed recent execution. But the Mikado learns that the 'victim' was Nanki-Poo, his own son: the penalty for encompassing the death of the heir apparent is 'something lingering, with boiling oil in it'. Nanki-Poo refuses to come back to life to exonerate his 'executioners' unless Katisha's amorous attentions can be diverted by Ko-Ko's marrying her, a prospect Ko-Ko views with the utmost distaste (duet: 'The flowers that bloom in the spring, tra-la'). Katisha enters ('Alone, and yet alive!'). By a cunning fable ('Tit-willow') Ko-Ko persuades her to accept him, on the supposition that Nanki-Poo has indeed been executed. When Nanki-Poo appears, now married to Yum-Yum, rejoicing is resumed and even the Mikado is pacified.

The interplay between the supposed Japanese scene and the real England satirized by Gilbert is kept up not merely in words ('The Japanese equivalent for "Hear, hear, hear!"') but in music. The score finds place for a madrigal in Sullivan's 'old English' style, and also for a glee ('See how the Fates their gifts allot'), as well as an authentic Japanese tune for the entrance of the Mikado. Its immediately captivating aspects, from patter to love duet, are underpinned by musical subtleties. In a trio for Pooh-Bah ('I am so proud'), Ko-Ko and Pish-Tush three dissimilar tunes are deftly counterpointed (the suggestion for such treatment came from Gilbert), and later a Bach fugue is cross-rhythmically quoted with the Mikado's reference to 'masses and fugues and ops,/By Bach, interwoven/With Spohr and Beethoven'.

RECORDINGS 1. (omitting dialogue) Morison, M. Sinclair, R. Lewis, G. Evans, Glyndebourne Ch, Pro Arte O, Sargent, EMI, 1958; 2. (slightly cut, omitting dialogue) Garrett, Bottone, Palmer, Idle, Angas, Van Allan, Richardson, Bullock, ENO Ch and O, Robinson, TER, 1987; 3. (omitting dialogue) McLaughlin, Palmer, Rolfe Johnson, Suart, Adams, Van Allan, Ch and O of WNO, Mackerras, Telarc, 1991; 4. Rees, Bottone, Roberts, Ker, Rivers, D'Oyly Carte Opera Ch and O, Pryce-Jones, TER, 1990; 5. Passmore, Dearth, Hyde, Pearl, 1980: 1908 recording, slightly cut
VIDEOS 1. Conrad, Revill, Dean, Flowers, LSO, Faris, Brent Walker, 1982; 2. Adams, Masterson, Palmer, Reed, Potter, City of Birmingham SO, Godfrey, 1965
EDITIONS v.s., Chappell, 1885; f.s., facsimile, G. Jacob (ed.), Gregg, 1968

Ruddigore, or The Witch's Curse

originally *Ruddygore*, but re-spelt within two weeks of the opening
Comic opera in two acts (2h 15m)
Libretto by W. S. Gilbert
Composed 1886–7

PREMIERES   22 January 1887, Savoy Theatre, London; US: 21 February 1887, Fifth Avenue Theatre, New York
CAST   Sir Ruthven Murgatroyd (disguised as Robin Oakapple) *bar*, Richard Dauntless *t*, Sir Despard Murgatroyd *b-bar*, Old Adam Goodheart *b*, Rose Maybud *s*, Mad Margaret *ms*, Dame Hannah *a*, Sir Roderic Murgatroyd *b*, *s*, 4 ghosts *spoken roles*; *satb* chorus of officers, ancestors, villagers and professional bridesmaids

Relying much on the spirit of the old burlesque – with the bold and cheerful sailor, over-modest village maiden, and bad baronet – *Ruddigore* was regarded as out of date in its satire and gained only modest success when first produced. It was not revived until December 1920 (in Glasgow) in a somewhat altered version sacrificing the original finale to Act II. Recent performances, live and recorded, have had recourse to some elements of the original version. The coming to life of an ancestral picture gallery had already been used by Gilbert (in *Ages Ago*, 1870, with music by Frederic Clay); there was originally a second coming to life, at the end of Act II, which was soon wisely replaced. The highly original character of Mad Margaret, probably intended by Gilbert mainly to guy the madness of Shakespeare's Ophelia, gained extra effectiveness from its relevance to the crazed heroines of such operas as *Lucia di Lammermoor*.

SYNOPSIS

Act I In the 18th-century village of Rederring in Cornwall with its corps of professional bridesmaids, Rose remains unwed. She is courted by Robin, but her primness and his shyness stand in the way. Richard, a sailor and Robin's foster-brother, volunteers to commend Robin's suit to Rose. Instead, he successfully proposes to her on his own behalf – only to see her change her mind again and embrace Robin. Mad Margaret enters, her madness induced by love for Sir Despard, the current 'bad baronet of Ruddigore': each successive holder of the title is condemned by a curse to commit a crime a day. The entry of Sir Despard terrifies all, but Despard hates his role and is delighted when Richard (claiming to act from a sense of duty, but really anxious to prise Rose from Robin) reveals that Robin is in fact Sir Ruthven, an elder brother who should have inherited the baronetcy and its curse. Rose returns to Richard and Despard to Margaret.

Act II Robin, now the villainous Sir Ruthven, faces the judgement of his ancestors for failing to commit his daily crime. The ancestors rise from their pictured images. They live a merry life (the resurrected Sir Roderic tells of their festival, 'the ghosts' high noon') but now sternly compel Robin to 'carry off a lady'. Despard and Margaret enter as reformed characters: any reversion to madness on her part can be cured by the word 'Basingstoke'. Robin's servant Adam, dispatched to abduct a lady, brings back Dame Hannah, who draws a dagger and has Robin at her mercy when the ghostly Sir Roderic intervenes. Hannah and he recognize each other as old lovers. Robin argues that to fail to commit a crime is, for a bad baronet, tantamount to suicide; but suicide is a crime, so Sir Roderic should never

have died at all! Roderic embraces Hannah, Robin (no longer villainous) embraces Rose, and Richard is content with the principal bridesmaid.

Such powerful music was contributed by Sullivan to the ghost scene that the bounds of comic artificiality are almost burst. There are other features of very strong individuality in the score, notably an unparalleled patter trio for Margaret, Robin and Despard in Act II and a sprightly 'old English' dance in 9/8 time ('Oh, happy the lily that's kissed by the bee') in Act I. Richard's 'nautical' music, sung and danced, freshens an old tradition, while Mad Margaret, whether accompanied by a Lucia-like flute on her first entrance or by comically wooden dance music in her reformed state, is a superb musical as well as dramatic creation.

RECORDINGS   1. (omitting dialogue, 1920 version) G. Baker, Lewis, Brannigan, Blackburn, Morison, Bowden, M. Sinclair, Glyndebourne Ch, Pro Arte O, Sargent, EMI, 1963; 2. (omitting dialogue, original version) Hill Smith, Ormiston, Hillman, J. Davies, Ayldon, Innocent, Lawlor, New Sadler's Wells Ch and O, Phipps, TER, 1987
VIDEO   V. Price, Adams, Oliver, LSO, Faris, Brent Walker, 1982
EDITIONS   v.s., Chappell, 1887; rev. version: v.s., Chappell, 1921

The Yeomen of the Guard, or The Merryman and his Maid

Comic opera in two acts (2h 15m)
Libretto by W. S. Gilbert
Composed 1888
PREMIERES   3 October 1888, Savoy Theatre, London; US: 17 October 1888, Casino Theater, New York
CAST   Colonel Fairfax *t*, Sergeant Meryll *bar*, Jack Point *bar*, Wilfred Shadbolt *bar*, Elsie Maynard *s*, Phoebe Meryll *ms*, Dame Carruthers *a*, 3 *t*, 3 *bar*, 2 spoken roles, silent; *satb* chorus of Yeomen of the Guard, gentlemen, citizens, etc.

With *The Yeomen of the Guard* Sullivan came as near as he could to a serious opera within what had been established as the Savoy convention. At the end the jester Jack Point, disappointed in love, falls 'insensible' amid the merry-making of the rest. Gilbert's plot, though originally criticized as uncomfortably close to that of William Vincent Wallace's opera *Maritana* (1845), achieves force as a serious drama in which comic elements are kept subordinate and not allowed to break from the Tudor period to introduce modern satire. None the less the comic juxtaposition of the quick-witted jester and the slow, would-be-funny Shadbolt ('Head Gaoler and Assistant Tormentor' at the Tower of London) gives brilliant contrast to the pathos of the rest. The opening is, for once, not an assertive chorus but a gentle soliloquy in song.

SYNOPSIS

Act I Phoebe, daughter of Sergeant Meryll of the Yeomen of the Guard at the Tower of London, sings at her spinning-wheel ('When maiden loves'). Secretly in love with the unjustly imprisoned Colonel Fairfax, she repulses the clumsy advances of the gaoler Shadbolt. Dame Carruthers, housekeeper of

Phœbe Meryll (Miss Jessie Bond) and
Wilfred Shadbolt (Mr. W. H. Denny)
'Were I thy Bride.'

Phœbe Meryll
(Miss Jessie Bond)

Sergeant Meryll
(Mr. Richard Temple)

Two scenes from The Yeomen of the Guard *(The Graphic, October 1888)*

the Tower, sings of its valiant history ('When our gallant Norman foes'). Anxious to rescue Fairfax (who once saved his life) from execution, Meryll plans with Phoebe to release him from his cell and pass him off as Phoebe's brother Leonard, himself due to join the Yeomen. Fairfax appears, reconciled to his fate ('Is life a boon?'), but asks the Lieutenant of the Tower to procure him a blindfold bride so that his possessions do not fall into the hands of his persecuting relatives. The arrival of two strolling players, Jack Point and Elsie ('I have a song to sing, O'), is auspicious; Elsie consents to be the blindfold bride. Phoebe wheedles the keys of the cells from Shadbolt ('Were I thy bride'); Fairfax is released and introduced as Leonard. When the time for the execution arrives there is uproar; Fairfax has vanished. Point, loving Elsie, now cannot court her since her husband Fairfax has not been executed.

Act II Point persuades Shadbolt to say he saw Fairfax in the river and shot him, in return for which Point will teach Shadbolt the jester's art. A quartet 'Strange adventure!' for Fairfax, Sergeant Meryll, Dame Carruthers and her niece Kate, discloses that Elsie (who has been heard talking in her sleep) was the mysterious blindfold bride. Elsie herself, still not

realizing whom she has married, has fallen in love with the supposed 'Leonard' but may not permit his advances because she must keep her wifely duty to Fairfax. A shot rings out and Shadbolt and Point tell their cooked-up story. Fairfax now being assumed dead, Point courts Elsie – clumsily; Fairfax offers to show him how – but makes the proposal on his own account as 'Leonard' and is accepted. Phoebe, still in love with Fairfax, shows her annoyance – and Shadbolt, realizing that this can be no brother of Phoebe's, sees the extent of the deception. Phoebe is obliged to promise to marry Shadbolt as the price of his silence; similarly Sergeant Meryll buys Dame Hannah's silence by ending his long resistance to marrying her. A reprieve for Fairfax arrives: he claims his bride, and only after an anguished moment does Elsie realize that her beloved 'Leonard' and her hitherto unseen husband Fairfax are the same. The jester Point, broken-hearted, falls insensible.

A formally unified sonata-type overture (as in the case of *Iolanthe* but not of most of the Savoy pieces) opens with a rising, fanfare-like figure which intermittently serves as a kind of representational theme for the stern Tower of London itself. The strolling players' ballad, 'I have a song to sing, O' is a cumulative structure (like that of the folksong 'Green grow the rushes, O'), a pattern that seems exceptionally to have been suggested by Gilbert himself, though the 'archaic' drone effect of the harmony is a brilliant touch of Sullivan's own. There is not a weak number in *The Yeomen*, and the Act II duet for Dame Carruthers and Sergeant Meryll (omitted in some performances and recordings) is a perfect comic foil to the prevailing seriousness: note the introduction of the lugubrious bassoon when her 'Rapture, rapture!' is replaced by his 'Doleful, doleful!'

RECORDINGS 1. (omitting dialogue) Hood, Harwood, Reed, Potter, Sandford, Adams, Knight, D'Oyly Carte Ch, RPO, Sargent, Decca, 1964; 2. (omitting dialogue) R. Lewis, G. Evans, Cameron, Brannigan, Morison, Sinclair, Case, Glyndebourne Ch, Pro Arte O, Sargent, EMI, 1960
VIDEOS 1. Grey, Marks, Gale, LSO, Faris, Brent Walker, 1982; 2. Steele (City of London Festival), New World Philharmonic Ch and O, Lloyd-Jones, 1977
EDITION v.s., Chappell, 1888

The Gondoliers, or The King of Barataria

Comic opera in two acts (2h 15m)
Libretto by W. S. Gilbert
Composed 1889
PREMIERES 7 December 1889, Savoy Theatre, London; US: 7 January 1890, New Park Theater, New York
CAST Duke of Plaza-Toro *bar*, Luiz *t*, Don Alhambra del Bolero *b-bar*, Marco Palmieri *t*, Giuseppe Palmieri *bar*, Duchess of Plaza-Toro *a*, Casilda *s*, Tessa *ms*, Gianetta *s*, 2 *ms*, *a*, *t*, *bar*, *b*, *spoken role*; *satb* chorus of gondoliers and contadine, men-at-arms, heralds and pages

The Gondoliers marks a reversion, after *The Yeomen of the Guard*, to the fully comic work with topical references introduced into the supposedly 18th-century setting in Venice and the island of Barataria (a location mentioned in *Don Quixote*). The plot treads some old ground, notably in the baby-swapping and the revelation of a secret at the end, but the satire on ultra-democratic sentiments (with the implication of hypocrisy thrown in) marked a subtly fresh turn of the Gilbertian knife. Sullivan rose to the opportunity to impart first an Italian, then a Spanish, flavour. By the design of Gilbert himself, responding to what he knew Sullivan craved in musical autonomy, the piece begins with about 18 minutes of music uninterrupted by speech.

SYNOPSIS
Act I The gondoliers Marco and Giuseppe choose their brides by a game of blind man's buff; by judicious cheating Giuseppe catches Tessa and Marco, Gianetta. The impoverished Duke of Plaza-Toro, 'that celebrated, cultivated, underrated nobleman', arrives accompanied by his overweening Duchess, his loyal drummer Luiz, and his daughter Casilda who was married in infancy to the heir of the throne of Barataria. Where is that husband now? Don Alhambra the Grand Inquisitor knows him well ('no possible doubt whatever') – he is one of two gondoliers. Luiz's mother, who was their nurse, will

declare which. This brings consternation to Luiz and Casilda, secretly in love. Marco and Giuseppe return with their new wives: learning that one of them is King of Barataria, they find it easy to drop their republican principles. Reigning jointly as an interim arrangement, they will set sail for Barataria forthwith, leaving their wives behind.

Act II In Barataria the court is said to display 'a despotism strict, combined with absolute equality': in fact the new monarchs are slaves to their courtiers. They pine for their wives (Marco: 'Take a pair of sparkling eyes'), who unexpectedly arrive from Venice. Celebrations are interrupted by the arrival of the Grand Inquisitor who criticizes their egalitarian regime ('When everyone is somebodee, then no one's anybody!'). Only now do Marco and Giuseppe learn to their dismay that one of them had contracted a marriage in infancy (quartet with Tessa and Gianetta: 'In a contemplative fashion'). The Duke of Plaza-Toro arrives with his usual entourage; the Duchess gives her recipe for duke-taming ('On the day when I was wedded to your admirable sire'). The embarrassment of the three young women (Casilda, Tessa, Gianetta) *vis-à-vis* the two young gondoliers is evident. At last Luiz's mother is shown in and recounts the deft interchange of babies by which her own son now emerges as the true king. Luiz re-enters, crowned. All is now disentangled and Venetian music recurs to end the opera.

If 'Take a pair of sparkling eyes' has by sheer lyrical grace become the most famous number of the opera, Sullivan's cleverest contribution was the Act II quartet, where individual voices break out furiously from the artificial calm. Gilbert himself in a letter had modestly suggested some elements of the musical treatment. The Italian and Spanish touches in songs and dances are enhanced by particularly brilliant orchestration, the quick repeated notes on the cornet (at that time used in the theatre in place of trumpets) giving extra excitement to 'Dance a cachucha' (the celebration of the wives' arrival in Barataria).

RECORDINGS 1. (with dialogue) Reed, Skitch, Sandford, Round, Styler, Knight, Toye, Sansom, Wright, D'Oyly Carte Ch, New SO, Godfrey, Decca, 1961; 2. (omitting dialogue) Morison, Lewis, G. Evans, Brannigan, Young, Graham, Cameron, M. Thomas, Glyndebourne Ch, Pro Arte O, Sargent, EMI, 1959
VIDEOS 1. Michell, Shilling, Egerton, LSO, Faris, Brent Walker, 1982; 2. Pert, Suart, Creasy, Olle, Rath, D'Oyly Carte Ch and O, Pryce-Jones, TER, 1991
EDITIONS f.s. David Lloyd-Jones (ed.), Eulenburg, 1984; v.s., Chappell, 1889

Ivanhoe

Romantic opera in three acts (3h)
Libretto by Julian Sturgis, after the novel by Sir Walter Scott (1820)
Composed 1890–91
PREMIERES 31 January 1891, Royal English Opera House, London; rev. version: 14 February 1895, Court Theatre, Liverpool; US: 23 November 1991, Jordan Hall, Boston
CAST Richard I *b*, Sir Brian de Bois-Guilbert, the Templar *bar*, De Bracy *t*, Cedric *bar*, Wilfred, Knight of Ivanhoe *t*,

Friar Tuck *b*, Isaac of York *b*, Rowena *s*, Ulrica *a*, Rebecca *s*, Grand Master of the Templars *b*, Prince John *bar*, 2 *bar*, 2 *silent*; *satb* chorus of knights, outlaws, crowd

Probably no previous English opera had been launched with such artistic expectation and such carefully nurtured publicity as *Ivanhoe*. 'I am endeavouring to establish English Grand Opera at the new theatre which I have built,' declared Richard D'Oyly Carte, intending other new works to follow if *Ivanhoe* should be a financial success. It was not, though it ran for 160 initial consecutive performances, and the enterprise collapsed.

Scott's novel has been dramatized in an old-fashioned way – evidently with some indebtedness to a previous operatic version, Marschner's *Der Templer und die Jüdin* (1829). An awkward dramatic scheme failed to highlight the love of hero and heroine, and the (divinely caused?) sudden death of the villain at the end is very weak. Sullivan's setting was similarly old-fashioned in its reliance on self-contained numbers, which sometimes end with an implied cue for a stop and applause. Occasionally, however, like *The Golden Legend* (the last of his cantatas, 1886), it shows that Sullivan really had something to say in vocal melody when it was not constrained by Gilbert's metre and rhyme.

SYNOPSIS

Act I Cedric, the Saxon thane, living under the rule of 'these thieving Normans', regrets having driven out his son Ivanhoe for daring to love Rowena, to whom Cedric is guardian. To Cedric's house, begging shelter for the night, come the Jew Isaac of York, and then a group of Norman knights including De Bracy and Sir Brian de Bois-Guilbert, commander of the Order of Knights Templar. Rowena appears, her beauty prompting Bois-Guilbert and De Bracy to plan to abduct her at the coming tournament. Alone, Rowena declares her love for Ivanhoe ('O moon, art thou clad in silver mail, like armour of my true knight?'). She receives a travelling palmer, not recognizing him as Ivanhoe in disguise. At the tournament the usurper Prince John presides, but the rightful King Richard appears in disguise as the Black Knight. Ivanhoe defeats Sir Brian in combat, shows his identity and is acclaimed by the Saxon crowd.

Act II King Richard, still in disguise, joins Friar Tuck and his fellow outlaws in the forest. The friar sings his drinking song, 'Hey, jolly Jenkin'. On news that Cedric, Rowena and Ivanhoe have been abducted, the king hurries to rescue them. At Torquilstone Castle, to which Isaac's daughter Rebecca has also been abducted, the captors are revealed as De Bracy, intent on wooing Rowena, and Sir Brian, who declares a fierce passion for Rebecca ('her southern splendour, like the Syrian moon'). Ulrica, a Saxon woman long ago taken and ravished by the Normans, warns Rebecca of her peril. Rebecca prays for rescue ('Lord of our chosen race') and resists Sir Brian's advances. A bugle call summons him away before he can ravish her.

Act III Still at Torquilstone, the wounded

Ivanhoe is nursed by Rebecca, who has fallen in love with him. There is fighting outside; Sir Brian enters and tears Rebecca away. King Richard is seen and recognized. Ulrica, avenging her shame of long ago, leaps to suicide. King Richard, in jovial mood, returns to the forest ('O, I would be an outlaw bold') and joins Cedric and Rowena; Cedric and Ivanhoe are reconciled. Ivanhoe leaves suddenly on the news that Rebecca has been taken to a stronghold of the Templars and has asked for a champion. Rebecca has been condemned to death for witchcraft. Ivanhoe as her champion confronts Sir Brian who miraculously dies. King Richard expels the Templars from England. With Ivanhoe and Rowena united, Rebecca is safe but heartbroken.

Strong choral writing frames the opera, but the interest of the solo parts is not always convincingly distributed. The part of Ulrica, though too obviously based on that of the baleful and mysterious Azucena of *Il trovatore*, is strong in itself but she hardly touches the action. Rowena, the nominal heroine, is a pale creation beside the Jewess, Rebecca. Rebecca's prayer in the face of likely ravishment, 'Guard me, Jehovah, guard me', has always been highly regarded, with its anxiously throbbing viola part and a peculiarly Eastern phrase in the vocal line which Sullivan said he drew from a synagogue service he had attended in his student days at Leipzig. The whole musical sequence (Act II, Scene 3) that embraces this number has a notable sweep, though weakened as drama by the villain's departure. The 'Savoy' element represented by Friar Tuck's drinking song might today be accepted as not such an unwelcome intrusion as it seemed to some of the original reviewers.

RECORDINGS amateur: Prince Consort, Lyle, Pearl, 1989
EDITIONS f.s./v.s., Chappell, 1891

Haddon Hall

Light opera in three acts (2h 30m)
Libretto by Sydney Grundy
Composed 1892
PREMIERE 24 September 1892, Savoy Theatre, London

In its basic dramatic action *Haddon Hall* is comic romance rather than comic satire, though there is rather crude fun poked at the excesses of Puritanism in both its supposed English and Scottish forms. The performer originally playing the McCrankie added a piece called 'Cock of the North', not of Sullivan's composition, on the bagpipes. The quasi-historical tale of the elopement of Dorothy Vernon with her lover from Haddon Hall in Derbyshire was pushed forward by the librettist from 1561 to the time of the Commonwealth. In order to secure his land, the royalist Sir George Vernon wishes his daughter Dorothy to marry her Puritan cousin Rupert. Her elopement with the royalist John Manners outrages Sir George, but the restoration of Charles II to the throne overturns the political situation and enables Sir George to accept Dorothy's choice. The political conflicts yield musical gains, especially when a unison hymnlike chant for the Puritans is set in counterpoint with a jolly choral patter in 6/8 time.

One of Sullivan's quasi-madrigals, with the refrain 'Earth was made for man's delight', is among his best and has since been separately published, but loses some effect through occurring too early in the opera (it is part of the opening number). Uniquely in his works for the Savoy, Sullivan wrote (as the finale of Act II) a very long number that begins in the middle of one scene, stretches through storm music during a scene change, and extends to cover the whole of the next scene – all this without the interruption of speech. Despite weaknesses, the total result may be claimed as a better stage work than *Ivanhoe* and Bernard Shaw's view was: 'I contend that Savoy Opera is a genre in itself, and that *Haddon Hall* is the highest and most consistent expression it has yet attained.'

RECORDING   amateur: Parish of Cheam Operatic Society, Harding, Pearl, 1981
EDITION   v.s., Chappell, 1892

Utopia Limited, or The Flowers of Progress

Comic opera in two acts (2h 30m)
Libretto by W. S. Gilbert
Composed 1893
PREMIERES   7 October 1893, Savoy Theatre, London; US: 26 March 1894, Broadway Theater, New York
CAST   King Paramount I *bar*, Scaphio *bar*, Phantis *bar*, Tarara *bar*, Captain Fitzbattleaxe *t*, Captain Sir Edward Corcoran *bar*, Mr Goldbury *bar*, Princess Zara *s*, Lady Sophy *a*, 3 *s*, 2 *t*, *bar*, 3 spoken roles; *satb* chorus of Utopian Islanders

In 1890 an astonished British public saw the partnership of Gilbert and Sullivan split apart. Gilbert accused Carte, their impresario, of improperly charging to the partnership an item of expense (a carpet) attributable to the Savoy Theatre itself. In what became publicly known as 'the carpet quarrel' Sullivan sided with Carte, with the consequence that Gilbert and Sullivan appeared on opposite sides of a court case. The legal action was inconclusive but the damage to the artistic partnership was grave. Even when eventually reconciled and reunited, Gilbert and Sullivan never recaptured public taste to quite the old extent.

In satirical audacity of plot, nevertheless, *Utopia Limited* showed Gilbert back on form. His mockery

of British institutions climaxed with the ceremony of an English court presentation readapted to 'the court of James's Hall', i.e. in the manner of a blackfaced minstrel show. It happens in 'Utopia', redefined as a South Sea island state. The importation of British 'improvements' includes the turning of the whole kingdom into a limited company under 'the Joint Stock Companies Act of '62', a phrase Sullivan actually set to music.

SYNOPSIS
Act I In the South Sea island of Utopia, King Paramount is the prey of his elderly and corrupt ministers Scaphio and Phantis, who are empowered to denounce him for any offence to Tarara, the Public Exploder. Zara, the King's elder daughter, is due to return from Girton College, Cambridge, with English accomplishments. Similarly his younger daughters, Nekaya and Kalyba, are under the charge of an English governess, Lady Sophy, who now demonstrates in a waltz song the formalities of proper courtship ('Bold-faced ranger – (perfect stranger) – meets two well-behaved young ladies'). She is attracted to the king and he to her but she is mystified by his refusal to deal with the anonymous journalist who writes scandalously of the king in the *Palace Peeper*. Zara arrives to choral acclaim ('O maiden rich in Girton lore . . .'). She has fallen in mutual love with her British military escort Captain Fitzbattleaxe, one of the 'Flowers of Progress' who will reform Utopia on British lines. Phantis and Scaphio are themselves in love with Zara but are persuaded that Fitzbattleaxe should hold her in trust pending a decision. The Flowers of Progress, introduced to the people, undertake to reform the army, navy, municipal services and theatrical morality. Mr Goldbury, a company promoter, will supervise a conversion of the country to a limited company. He explains the mysteries of company law ('Some seven men form an association . . .'). Scaphio, Phantis and Tarara express their alarm.

Act II Zara's and Fitzbattleaxe's expression of their love is marred only by the harmful effect of emotion on the tenor voice. The king conducts what he supposes an English-style court drawing-room ceremony ('Society has quite forsaken all her wicked courses'). Scaphio, Phantis and Tarara hatch a plot against the king (which eventually collapses). Mr Goldbury assures the two younger princesses that to

A sketch of Utopia Limited *(London, 1893)*

be 'a bright and beautiful English girl' requires no such primness as their governess suggests. The king confesses to Lady Sophy that he was compelled to write those salacious paragraphs about himself, and a duet clarifies their bliss ('Oh the rapture unrestrained of a candid retractation!'). An unexpected chorus of 'Down with the Flowers of Progress' reveals that the reforms are disliked because everything is now too perfect. But one English attribute has been forgotten – government by party. That will be added, confusion will return and prosperity with it, to the satisfaction of all.

Dance takes on a new role for Sullivan in this score. In Act I, a duet for Scaphio and Phantis involves each of them in a dance in quick 6/8 to express an emotion that the other has to guess. (In one case it is 'unselfishness'.) There is a reprise of the music with further dancing in Act II, followed by a no less novel use of whispering in song (likewise in a quick 6/8) so that the audience does not actually hear what plans are being made by Scaphio, Phantis and Tarara. Later the king and Lady Sophy express the final removal of their misunderstanding in a 'Graceful Dance' and then are joined by three other couples – Zara with Fitzbattleaxe, the younger daughters with two others of the Flowers of Progress – in the exhilaration of a tarantella. Most striking to the original audiences, however, and quite capable of making an effect even today, is Sullivan's bouncy imitation of blackfaced minstrel music for the 'drawing-room' scene, with tambourine: the tune, a relation of 'The keel row', was apparently a minstrel-show favourite as 'Johnny get your gun'.

RECORDING (omitting dialogue) Field, Holland, Ayldon, Reed, Sandford, Ellison, Buchan, Conroy-Ward, D'Oyly Carte Ch, RPO, Nash, Decca, 1976
EDITION v.s., Chappell, 1893

The Chieftain

Comic opera in two acts (2h)
Libretto by Francis Cowley Burnand
Composed 1894
PREMIERES 12 December 1894, Savoy Theatre, London; US: 9 September 1895, Abbey's Theater, New York

Sullivan and Burnand so extensively reworked their early operetta *The Contrabandista* as to justify its new title. The original Act I is largely retained, but with a new and better finale; Act II is quite new, bringing Dolly Grigg (soprano) to Spain on the track of her camera-carrying husband who has willy-nilly been installed as chief of a band of robbers. After the initial box-office takings quickly fell off, Sullivan supplied new songs and some dance music, duly incorporated in a new published edition. But the show closed after 97 performances (as compared with 245 for *Utopia Limited*, itself considered barely a satisfactory total).

Among the new material is a song for Inez (the bandit chieftainess, alto) beginning 'My parents were of great gentility', catching a Spanish flavour in a habanera rhythm which Sullivan had laid down in

advance to the librettist and which was new for him. There is also a lively love duet in French and English ('Ah, oui, j'étais une pensionnaire'), in which the performers imitate French operetta style.

RECORDING amateur: Sawston Light Opera Group, Pearl, 1978
EDITION v.s., Chappell, 1894; rev. edn, 1895

The Grand Duke, or The Statutory Duel

Comic opera in two acts (2h 30m)
Libretto by W. S. Gilbert
Composed 1895–6
PREMIERES 7 March 1896, Savoy Theatre, London; US: 7 April 1937, New York (amateur)
CAST Grand Duke Rudolph *bar*, Ernest Dummkopf *t*, Ludwig *b-bar*, Dr Tannhauser *bar*, Herald *bar*, Lisa *s*, Princess of Monte Carlo *s*, Prince of Monte Carlo *bar*, Julia Jellicoe *s*, Baroness von Krakenfeldt *a*, 5 *s or ms*, *bar*, *spoken role*; *satb* chorus of chamberlains, nobles, actors, actresses, etc.

Uniquely ending with the same wedding chorus with which it began, *The Grand Duke* has several items of musical interest but founders on the longest, wordiest and worst of all the libretti Gilbert wrote for Sullivan. A very large cast helps the plot to attain a baffling perplexity. Even Gilbert himself appears to have forgotten, by the end, the initial importance of the political conspiracy and the conspirators' mutual recognition by the eating of a sausage roll. By a pleasant paradox a new recruit to Carte's company, Ilka von Palmay, displayed her Hungarian accent as the English actress Julia Jellicoe in the otherwise stage-German setting. After an initial run of only 123 performances (about half as long as *Utopia Limited*), the operetta appears never to have been professionally revived except for a D'Oyly Carte concert performance in 1975 (giving rise to the recording cited below) and BBC broadcasts in 1966 and 1989.

SYNOPSIS
Act I In the Grand Duchy of Pfennig Halbpfennig (penny-halfpenny) the theatrical company is celebrating the marriage of two of its members, Lisa and Ludwig, and is also involved in a conspiracy to dethrone the Grand Duke. Ernest, the company manager, will take the Grand Duke's place and the haughty English actress, Julia Jellicoe, will condescend to be the new ruler's bride. But since the present Grand Duke has been apprised of the plot, the conspirators resort to 'a statutory duel' as explained by the notary. The duel is fought with cards, he who draws the lower card becoming legally dead and the winner taking the loser's rights. Ernest 'duels' with Ludwig: the latter draws an ace and is deemed the winner. He will go to the Grand Duke and denounce the 'dead' man as responsible for the conspiracy. The Grand Duke himself enters, miserable ('When you find you're a broken-down critter') but finds consolation with his fiancée, Baroness von Krakenfeldt, in their common devotion to parsimonious living ('As o'er our penny roll we sing'). Alarmed by talk of conspiracy, he is persuaded

to take part in another statutory duel; by pre-agreed cheating, Ludwig will win, become grand duke and take the unpleasant consequences. But since the legal provision for such duels is due to expire next day the true grand duke may then resume power. They 'duel' and Ludwig duly draws the ace. He looks forward to his reign ('Oh, a monarch who boasts intellectual graces . . .'). So Ludwig (and not Ernest) is grand duke, yet Julia still insists on her theatrical right to play the leading lady's role of grand duchess. She brushes aside Ludwig's recent bride, Lisa. Ludwig promises the troupe a jolly reign ('Sing hey, the jolly jinks of Pfennig Halbpfennig!').

Act II The reign is duly inaugurated with stage-Athenian celebrations. Julia outlines the fiercely dramatic way she will play her part as duchess. But the Baroness von Krakenfeldt, discovering that her grand duke is legally dead, insists that she has the right to his successor. Now it is Julia's turn to be ousted. Nor can she go back to marrying Ernest because, as Ludwig while grand duke has prolonged the law of the statutory duel for another century, Ernest is still legally dead. Set to marry Ludwig, the baroness rejoices at the prospect of feasting ('Come, bumpers aye, ever so many') all at public expense! But yet another candidate for grand duchess appears: the Princess of Monte Carlo, to whom the (real) grand duke was betrothed in infancy. Her father, the prince, presses her claim and tells how he became wealthy by acting as banker at roulette ('Take my advice, when deep in debt . . .'). But the notary upsets everything, revealing that in statutory duels the ace is properly the lowest, not the highest card. So Ludwig was never grand duke, nor had he the power to prolong the law of statutory duels – which is indeed on the point of expiry. Ludwig can be reunited with Lisa, Ernest with Julia. As for the real grand duke, the baroness, the princess, the conspiracy . . . who knows?

As a musical self-portrait of a comically worried man, the Grand Duke's 'When you find you're a broken-down critter' (Act I) can match the Lord Chancellor's nightmare song in *Iolanthe* and the peevish complaints of King Gama in *Princess Ida*. At such moments Sullivan showed that his fancy was by no means played out (and his harmonic boldness was increasing). He could also muster a delightful descant to accompany the notary's song (Act I) and gave the baroness a marvellously energetic second entrance (Act II), followed by a swaggering and catchy drinking song, very unusual for a middle-aged female character! But the note of lyrical pathos is missing from the score as it is from the heartless, mechanical libretto.

RECORDING (omitting dialogue) Goss, Holland, Reed, Reid, Rayner, Lilley, Conroy-Ward, Metcalfe, Ellison, Sandford, Ayldon, D'Oyly Carte Ch, RPO, Nash, Decca, 1976
EDITION v.s., Chappell, 1896

The Beauty Stone

Comic opera in three acts (2h 30m)
Libretto by Arthur Wing Pinero and J. Comyns Carr
Composed 1897–8
PREMIERE 28 May 1898, Savoy Theatre, London

Although presented by Carte at the Savoy, and using the regulars of Carte's company, *The Beauty Stone* does not belong to the Gilbertian mode. It is lightly romantic and displays no fewer than 21 characters in a tale of magic and chivalry in medieval Flanders – with the Devil as a comic character, as in Sullivan's cantata *The Golden Legend*. *The Beauty Stone* is a charm by which Laine, a young crippled woman of plain appearance, is able to transform herself into a beauty and captivate a noble lover. When she loses that magical power she no longer needs it, as the Lord of Mirlemont (tenor) has been blinded in battle and loves her for her own sake. The vocal character of Laine (soprano) is contrasted with those of the hero's Moorish mistress and a roguish village wench. Despite the eminence of Pinero as a playwright the libretto was greeted coolly and the music springs rarely to independent life.

RECORDING amateur: The Prince Consort O, Lyle, Pearl, 1984
EDITION v.s., Chappell, 1898

The Rose of Persia, or The Story-teller and the Slave

Comic opera in two acts (2h 15m)
Libretto by Basil Hood, after *The Arabian Nights*
Composed 1899
PREMIERES 29 November 1899, Savoy Theatre, London; US: 6 September 1900, Daly's Theater, New York

Alone of Sullivan's later librettists, Hood dared to write in Gilbertian style. The tale of mixed identities is presented with much ingenious, polysyllabic word-play (and even, after *The Mikado*, a further rhyme for 'executioner': 'the royal retributioner').

Hassan, a philanthropist, relieves the boredom of having 25 wives by nightly entertaining a crowd of beggars at his house, but is compromised by the visit of the sultana, disguised as a dancing girl. In Act II the sultan has the whim of taking the drugged Hassan home and parading him as the sultan himself.

The texture and sequence of musical numbers is very much in the old Savoy pattern of varied songs, forthright choruses, and light concerted pieces, including an amusingly cumulative male quartet. Even the disagreeable and hypocritical priest Abdallah is endowed with the fine, firm bass solo, 'When Islam first arose'. Well received at first, the work has merited occasional revival.

RECORDING amateur: The Prince Consort, Consort O, Lyle, Pearl, 1986
EDITION v.s., Chappell, 1900

The Emerald Isle, or The Caves of Carrig-Cleena

Comic opera in two acts (2h 15m)
Libretto by Basil Hood
Composed 1900, completed by Edward German
PREMIERES 27 April 1901, Savoy Theatre, London; US: 1 September 1902, Herald Square Theater, New York

Sullivan worked on *The Emerald Isle* at least up to October 1900, a month before his death, and the published score particularizes the first nine numbers as his own, with a few of the later ones (out of 30 in all). Edward German, who completed it, caught the style of deliberate Irishism – happily exploited in Stanford's recent *Shamus O'Brien* (1896) and taken up by Sullivan with rather too much enthusiasm for jigs in 6/8. In a different kind of 6/8, with a happier touch quite in his characteristic style, Sullivan wrote an entry for the Lord Lieutenant (representing English rule in Ireland) that conceals the opening notes of 'God Save the Queen' in the bass line.

Unfortunately Hood did not provide such a strong narrative as in *The Rose of Persia*. The British soldiers are scared from their duty by the subterfuge of Molly pretending to be the fairy Cleena. Finally 'Professor' Bunn ('Mesmerist, Ventriloquist, Humorist and General Illusionist') saves the rebels by persuading the Lord Lieutenant that as an English nobleman he must be 'more than half American' and therefore a friend of Ireland.

RECORDING amateur: Prince Consort, Lyle, Pearl, 1983
EDITION v.s., Chappell, 1901

Other operas: *The Sapphire Necklace* (inc.) (later *The False Heiress*), (1864), overture, 1866 (RECORDING Marco Polo, 1992), one further number published 1898 (lost)
BIBLIOGRAPHY I. Bradley, *The Annotated Gilbert and Sullivan*, Penguin, 1982; G. Hughes, *The Music of Arthur Sullivan*, Macmillan, 1962; Arthur Jacobs, *Arthur Sullivan: A Victorian Musician*, OUP, 1984; 2nd rev. edn, Scolar Press, 1992; Arthur Jacobs, 'The Mask of *The Mikado*', *Opera*, vol. 37 (1986), pp. 882–6; T. Rees, *Thespis: A Gilbert and Sullivan Enigma*, Dillons University Bookshop, 1964; P. M. Young, *Sir Arthur Sullivan*, Dent, 1971

A.J.

FRANZ VON SUPPÉ

Francesco Ezechiele Ermenegildo Cavaliere de Suppé-Demelli; *b* 18 April 1819, Spalato (now Split), Dalmatia; *d* 21 May 1895, Vienna

The creator of Viennese operetta came from a Belgian, Czech, Polish, Italian and Austro-Hungarian background, and, although he became one of Vienna's most illustrious sons, he never fully mastered the German language. He showed early promise on the flute, but his father wanted him to study law. On his father's death, Francesco accompanied his family to Vienna, where he studied at the Polytechnic Institute with a former pupil of Mozart, Ignaz von Seyfried.

Suppé played the flute in theatre orchestras, and by 1841 was a volunteer assistant conductor at the Theater in der Josefstadt. There, his first farce with songs (*Posse mit Gesang*), *Jung lustig, im Alter traurig*, was performed. Many other farces followed; today only their overtures are remembered. Grander operas also stem from this period, the earliest modelled after Donizetti.

Suppé varied his output of incidental music with a Wagner parody, *Der Tannenhäuser* (1852), and a 'life-portrait', *Mozart* (1854). Later in the 1850s, when the vogue for Offenbach's one-act operettas was at its height, the Theater an der Wien, unable to buy the rights to one of Offenbach's works, commissioned *Das Pensionat* (1860) from Suppé. Written in the Parisian style, this is generally regarded as the first important Viennese operetta.

Short operettas continued in the 1860s, notably *Die schöne Galathée* and *Die leichte Kavallerie*, and there was the well-regarded three-act *Banditenstreiche*, but the following decade was dominated at first by the operettas of Johann Strauss II at the Theater an der Wien. In 1876 Suppé led a full-fledged counter-attack at the rival Carltheater, armed with Strauss's own librettists, Zell and Genée. *Fatinitza* (based on a Scribe libretto set earlier by Auber) was a success, mainly through a supremely catchy march that was hummed throughout Europe and the US.

Three years later, the Carltheater saw the premiere of another worldwide success, *Boccaccio*. *Donna Juanita* continued the lucky streak of Suppé–Zell–Genée hits. But little after that has endured. Nevertheless, in their day, works such as *Die Afrikareise* and *Die Jagd nach dem Glück* played quite profitably not only in European but in American theatres.

Throughout his career Suppé continued to write weightier works, including the dramatic romantic opera *Des Matrosens Heimkehr*, the opéra comique *Bellmann*, and a Requiem Mass. If he was best exemplified by the jolly spirits of his comic operettas, he was plagued near the end of his life by the prospect of a gruesome death. He concentrated on religious music by day and occasionally slept in a coffin at night. His death was from starvation due to a horribly painful stomach cancer.

Die schöne Galathée
Beautiful Galatea

Comic–mythological opera in one act
Libretto by Poly Henrion (Leopold Kohl von Kohlenegg)
PREMIERES 30 June 1865, Meysels Theatre, Berlin; 9 September 1865, Carltheater, Vienna; UK: 6 November 1871, Opéra-Comique, London; US: 6 September 1867, Stadt Theater, New York

Pygmalion has fallen in love with a statue he has fashioned of the nymph Galatea. Aphrodite answers his prayers and brings her to life. She is, however, all too real, flirting with both Midas, Pygmalion's friend, and Ganymede, his assistant. In exasperation, Pygmalion asks Aphrodite to make the beautiful Galatea a statue once more, which he promptly sells to Midas.

This delightful operetta is the earliest Viennese work to remain in the Viennese repertoire – despite its Berlin premiere. Following the first productions of *La belle Hélène* (*Die schöne Helena*) it happily betrays the influence of Offenbach, and features a sensational overture that ends with a magnificent waltz. Other delightful moments include elaborately Italianate ensembles such as the spectacular trio

'Seht den Schmuck, den ich für Euch gebracht' and the subsequent drinking quintet, 'Hell im Glas', as well as a kiss duet with a distinctly Austrian piquancy. There are also couplets in the formula French style that were to persist throughout the course of Viennese operetta. The work is often given today in a revised format, often in more than one act.

RECORDINGS 1. Moffo, Kollo, Gruber, Wagemann, Bavarian Radio Ch and O, Eichhorn, 1974; 2. Roon, Kmentt, Preger, Wiener, Vienna State Opera Ch and O, Paulik, Saga, 1976
EDITIONS f.ss., manuscript facsimile, Im Selbst-Verlag des Verfassers (Vienna), 1865; arr. Isy Geiger, Bosworth, 1957; v.s., A. Cranz, [c. 1930]

Boccaccio

Comic opera in three acts
Libretto by F. Zell and Richard Genée, based on the play *Boccace, ou Le Décaméron* (1853), by Bayard, Leuven, Lhérie, and de Beauplan
PREMIERES 1 February 1879, Carltheater, Vienna; US: 23 April 1880, Thalia Theater, New York; UK: 22 April 1882, Comedy Theatre, London

The title shrewdly titillated, but the clever libretto is merely an innocent conceit woven about the poet Giovanni Boccaccio's romantic adventures in 14th-century Florence, surrounded by student friends. The amorous escapades they encounter during the course of the operetta come from Boccaccio's famous tales. These excite the women of Florence and scandalize their husbands. The principal love interest is the rivalry between Boccaccio and Pietro, the Prince of Palermo, for the hand of Fiametta, a grocer's daughter, which ends happily when the prince withdraws.

A brilliant overture prefaces what is considered Suppé's greatest (and certainly his most performed) full-length score. A rather heavy opening section soon gives way to a succession of spirited, Italianate ensembles, swaggering solos, bumptious choruses, and enchanting love duets, with the composer's assertive melodies and theatrically charged orchestrations giving the score enormous gusto. Among the best numbers are Boccaccio's first solo, 'Ich sehe einen jungen Mann dort stehn', the romantic duets 'Hab' ich nur deine Liebe' and 'Florenz hat schöne Frauen' (or 'Ma bella fiorentina'), and the spectacular, toe-tapping march, 'Der Witz, die Laune', which was obviously intended to repeat the success of the march from *Fatinitza* – and did.

RECORDING Rothenberger, Moser, Dallapozza, Prey, Berry, Bavarian State Opera Ch, Bavarian SO, Boskovsky, Electrola, 1974
FILM 1936, with Willy Fritsch as Boccaccio
EDITIONS f.s., Aug. Cranz, c. 1880; v.s., Aug. Cranz, 1879

Other operatic works: *Virginia*, (1837); *Gertrude della valle*, (1841); *Das Mädchen vom Lande*, 1847; *Dame Valentine, oder Frauenräuber und Wanderbursche*, 1851; *Paragraph 3*, 1858; *Das Pensionat*, 1860; *Die Kartenschlägerin*, 1862; *Zehn Mädchen und kein Mann*, 1862; *Die flotten Burschen*, 1863; *Das Corps der Rache*, 1864; *Dinorah, oder Die Turnerfahrt nach Hütteldorf*, 1865; *Die leichte Kavallerie*, 1866; *Die*

Tochter der Puszta, 1866; *Die Freigeister*, 1866; *Die Banditenstreiche*, 1867; *Die Frau Meisterin*, 1868; *Isabella*, 1869; *Tantalusqualen*, 1868; *Lohengelb, oder Die Jungfrau von Dragant*, 1870; *Canebas*, 1872; *Fatinitza*, 1876; *Der Teufel auf Erden*, 1878; *Donna Juanita*, 1880; *Der Gascogner*, 1881; *Das Herzblättchen*, 1882; *Die Afrikareise*, 1883; *Des Matrosens Heimkehr*, 1885; *Bellman*, 1887; *Die Jagd nach dem Glück*, 1888; *Das Modell*, 1895; *Die Pariserin, oder Das heimliche Bild*, 1898; music for c. 200 other farces, vaudevilles, etc.
BIBLIOGRAPHY Gervase Hughes, *Composers of Operettas*, Macmillan, 1962; Otto Schneidereit, *Franz von Suppé, Ein Wiener aus Dalmatien*, VEB Lied der Zeit, 1982

R.T.

CONRAD SUSA

b 26 April 1935, Springdale, Pennsylvania, US

Conrad Susa studied composition at Juilliard with Bergsma and Persichetti. His experience with public school systems, theatre (including musical directorship of the Stratford (Ontario) Shakespeare Festival), films and television has produced over a hundred scores. His operas, which have often evolved in close collaboration with a director and singers, have benefited from such a wide-ranging practical background. Their music displays an eclectic tonal style with quotation or near-quotation of familiar music, some reference to popular idioms when appropriate, and a clarity of expression united with considerable subtlety.

Transformations

Entertainment in two acts (2h)
Libretto from the book of poems by Anne Sexton (1971)
PREMIERES 5 May 1973, Cedar Village Theater, Minneapolis; UK: 8 September 1978, Young Vic, London (English Music Theatre)

Inspired by familiar fairy-tales (mostly their darker implications), *Transformations* characterizes its ten episodes in part by referring to various recent musical styles: singers are asked to evoke such performers as Bing Crosby and even the Andrews Sisters. The cast of eight (the same size as the orchestra) assumes different roles in each story.

EDITION v.s., E. C. Schirmer, 1973

Operas: *Black River*, 1975, rev. 1981; *The Love of Don Perlimplin*, 1984
BIBLIOGRAPHY Andrew Porter, *Music of Three Seasons: 1974–1977*, Farrar Straus Giroux, 1978

J.A.C.

FRANZ XAVER SÜSSMAYR

b 1766, Schwanenstadt; *d* 17 September 1803, Vienna

Süssmayr is remembered mainly for having completed Mozart's *Requiem* and for his collaboration with Mozart in the *secco* recitatives of *La clemenza di Tito*. But he was also a versatile composer in his own right, famous above all for his operas. In 1788 he became a private music teacher in Vienna, and also studied composition with Mozart (1791) and with Salieri (1792). From 1794 he was kapellmeister of the German opera at the National Theatre in Vienna, a post he held until his death.

The style of Süssmayr's operas is linked to the South-German and Austrian branch of singspiel. They promote a fantastic, idyllic and trivial view of life at the expense of dramatic probability and musical unity. His two most successful operas were *Der Spiegel von Arkadien*, with a text by Schikaneder, and *Soliman der Zweite*. *Der Spiegel von Arkadien* successfully attempted to imitate the style of *Die Zauberflöte* and was performed all over Europe and in Vienna until 1826. *Soliman der Zweite*, popular in Germany until 1828, is a crude adaptation of a play by C. S. Favart, set in a Turkish harem Süssmayr reduced the dramatic tension of the plot and only the eunuch Osmin's misogyny is musically characterized. Apart from the setting (Turkish themes were popular in Vienna at the time) there are similarities to Mozart's *Die Entführung aus dem Serail* in some of the arias, while – like Mozart – Süssmayr introduces 'oriental' motifs and instrumentation. Though evidently familiar with both the style of opéra comique and opera buffa, Süssmayr's short songlike arias abound in repetitions which made them both popular and easily memorable. The orchestral accompaniment merely provides a harmonic foundation for the vocal melody.

Operatic works: *Die Liebe für den König*, 1785; *Der Bürgermeister*, 1786; *Moses, oder Der Auszug aus Ägypten*, 1792; *L'incanto superato* (*Der besiegte Zauber*), 1793; *Piramo e Tisbe*, c. 1793; *Meister Schnaps, oder Er führt ihm's Mädchen selbst zu* (inc.), (c. 1793); *Il turco in Italia*, 1794; *Der Spiegel von Arkadien*, 1794 (EDITION facsimile, T. Bauman (ed.), *German Opera 1770–1800*, vol. 17, Garland, 1986); *Die edle Rache*, 1795; *Der Wildfang*, 1797; *Liebe macht kurzen Prozess, oder Heirat auf gewisse Art*, 1798; *Der Marktschreyer*, 1799; *Soliman der Zweite, oder Die drei Sultaninnen*, 1799; *Gülnare, oder Die persische Sklavin*, 1800; *Phasma, oder Die Erscheinung im Tempel der Verschwiegenheit*, 1801; *Das Hausgesinde*, (1802); *Gl'uccellatori* (inc.), (n.d.); *Alcidoro e Dalisa*, n.d.; 10 lost operatic works

BIBLIOGRAPHY H. H. Hausner, *Franz Xaver Süssmayr*, Bergland, 1964

M.F.

HEINRICH SUTERMEISTER

b 12 August 1910, Feuerthalen, canton of Schaffhausen, Switzerland

Sutermeister was inspired to embark on a musical career by the music of Honegger. After studying in Basle and Paris, he completed his musical education in Munich (1931–4), partly under the aegis of Walter Courvoisier, and then spent a year working as a répétiteur in Berne. Thereafter he devoted himself to composition, though he also taught at the

Hochschule in Hanover (1963–75). Orff and Egk were other formative influences of his youth, his music maintaining a broadly diatonic and easily accessible approach. Apart from a radio opera, *Die schwarze Spinne*, his first great success was *Romeo und Julia*, which, conducted by Karl Böhm, was premiered in Dresden in 1940. The composer defined the style of the work as 'late Verdi in modern guise'. In 1942 Böhm also conducted the first performance of *Die Zauberinsel*, in which Sutermeister sought to utilize certain aspects of baroque opera. Sutermeister's penchant for literaturoper comes out in *Raskolnikoff* and *Madame Bovary*. Works in a lighter vein include *Der rote Stiefel*, based on Hauff's tale *Das kalte Herz*; *Titus Feuerfuchs*, a burlesque opera; and *Seraphine*, an opera buffa based on Rabelais. Some of Sutermeister's operas exist in both stage and radio or television versions.

Operas: *Die schwarze Spinne*, 1936 (radio broadcast), 1949 (RECORDING Communauté de Travail, 1970s); *Romeo und Julia*, 1940; *Die Zauberinsel*, 1942; *Niobe*, 1946; *Raskolnikoff*, 1948; *Der rote Stiefel*, 1951; *Titus Feuerfuchs, oder 'Liebe, Tücke und Perücke'*, 1958; *Seraphine, oder 'Die stumme Apothekerin'*, 1960; *Das Gespenst von Canterville*, 1964; *Madame Bovary*, 1967; *Der Flaschenteufel*, (1971); *Le roi Bérenger*, 1985

BIBLIOGRAPHY Günter Birkner, *Heinrich Sutermeister. Der Weg des Bühnenkomponisten*, Hug, 1985

A.C.

MARGARET SUTHERLAND

Margaret Ada Sutherland; *b* 20 November 1897, Adelaide, Australia; *d* 12 August 1984, Melbourne, Australia

As a woman composer in early 20th-century Australia Sutherland had great difficulty in being accepted. From 1914 she studied piano and composition at the Melbourne Conservatorium. In 1923 she went overseas, studying in Paris, Vienna and London, where she worked with Arnold Bax before returning to Australia in 1925. The first Australian composer to adopt 20th-century composition styles, she achieved recognition only with the performance of her opera, *The Young Kabbarli*, in 1965.

The Young Kabbarli

Chamber opera in one act (35m)
Libretto by Maie Casey
PREMIERE 19 August 1965, Hobart

The libretto is based on an incident in the life of Daisy Bates, who spent most of her life with the Australian Aborigines, and concerns a cultural clash between Aboriginal and white cultures. The music juxtaposes Aboriginal music (including use of a didjeridu) and Irish folktunes. It was the first Australian opera to be recorded.

RECORDING Stevens, McKenzie, Patterson, Kohler, Gulpilil, New Opera of South Australia, Thomas, EMI, 1979
EDITION J. Albert, 1964

BIBLIOGRAPHY Jane Weiner LePage, *Women Composers, Conductors and Musicians of the 20th Century*, vol. 3, Scarecrow Press, 1988

A.I.G.

TADEUSZ SZELIGOWSKI
b 15 September 1896, Lvov; *d* 10 January 1963, Poznań

Szeligowski studied in Lvov, then in Cracow and in Paris with Nadia Boulanger (from 1929) where he belonged to the Association of Young Polish Musicians. Before Paris he taught at the conservatory in Vilnius and returned there in 1931. After the war Szeligowski was director of the music school in Lublin, then of the State Higher Opera School and Philharmonic in Poznań. He also taught composition there and, from 1951, at the State Higher Music School in Warsaw.

Szeligowski began composing operas after the Second World War and his highly differentiated compositional means are mainly the result of the variety of his libretti. In *Bunt żaków*, based on historical events in Cracow in 1549, harmony and texture are enriched with elements of old music, while *Krakatuk*, based on E. T. A. Hoffmann, remains neo-Romantic. The last operas are much more modern in language, although here too an emotional world of late Romanticism is combined with a simplicity derived from an underlying classical tendency.

Operas: *Bunt żaków* (*The Revolt of the Scholars*), 1951; *Krakatuk*, 1955; *Teodor Gentleman* (*Theodore, Gentleman*), 1963; *Odys płaczący i opuszczony* (*Odysseus Weeping and Abandoned*), radio opera–oratorio, 1961, 1973 (stage)
BIBLIOGRAPHY Z. Lissa, '*Bunt żaków*' *Tadeusza Szeligowskiego*, PWM, 1955, 2nd edn, 1957; F. Wozniak (ed.), *Tadeusz Szeligowski, Studia i wspomnienia* (*Tadeusz Szeligowski, Studies and Recollections*), Wydawnictwo Pomorze, 1987

J.M.

SÁNDOR SZOKOLAY
b 30 March 1931, Kúnágota, Hungary

Szokolay studied at the specialist Békéstarhos Music School in Budapest, and at the Budapest Academy, where he was taught by Ferenc Szábo and Ferenc Farkas. He quickly established credentials as a vocal writer, especially of choral music and music for children, but it was only with his first opera, *Vérnász* (1966), that he achieved a national, and later international, reputation, through productions in France, Germany and at the Edinburgh Festival. Szokolay has continued to write for the stage, though none of his subsequent six operas has enjoyed comparable success abroad. In Hungary he remains well known also for his choral cantatas, whose popularist cut suggests a somewhat different stance from that of his dramatic works.

Blood Wedding
Vérnász
Opera in three acts, Op. 26 (1h 45m)
Libretto: a condensed translation by Gyula Illyés of the play *Bodas de sangre* by Federico García Lorca
Composed 1962–4
PREMIERES 31 October 1964, Magyar Allami Operaház, Budapest; US: 19 May 1973, Columbus, Ohio; UK: 27 August 1973, King's Theatre, Edinburgh (Hungarian State Opera)

Lorca's powerful poetic drama deals with the violent collision of passion and honour at a rustic Spanish wedding. The Bride is preparing for her wedding to the Bridegroom, but is still under the spell of a former lover, Leonardo (himself now married), whose family were years ago responsible for the killing, in a family feud, of the Bridegroom's father and brothers. The wedding takes place, but Leonardo is present, and immediately afterwards he and the Bride ride away on horseback. In the pursuit that follows, both the Bridegroom and Leonardo are killed, leaving the Bridegroom's Mother to mourn that both fear and revenge are now past.

The success of Szokolay's first opera hinges on its clever fusion of an almost ritualistic symbolic intensity appropriate to Lorca's exalted poetic language and treatment, and a directness of musical utterance based on fairly uncomplicated vocal melody, somewhat in the *verismo* manner. Szokolay uses modern techniques such as serialism and sprechgesang within a style that is ultimately tonal, with vivid orchestral colouring. Conventional operatic elements include a passionate love duet and the Mother's lament; symbolism is embodied in parts for Death and the Moon, and there is a discreet Spanish flavour in certain rhythms, vocal inflexions, and the sound of castanets.

RECORDING Hazy, Komlóssy, Szönyi, Faragó, Hungarian State Opera Ch and O, Kórodi, Qualiton, 1966
EDITION v.s., Artisjus, 1964

Hamlet
Opera in three acts, Op. 31
Libretto by the composer, taken from János Arany's translation of the play by William Shakespeare (1601)
Composed 1965–8
PREMIERE 19 October 1968, Magyar Allami Operaház, Budapest

Szokolay's Hungarian-language setting, like Humphrey Searle's English one of the same period, is serial, but more freely so. Also like Searle's, it treats the text respectfully, though several scenes are omitted, and others (including the play within the play) expanded in the interests of operatic melodrama. There is a Ghost, but no Fortinbras. Szokolay's Hamlet is a nervous, unstable figure in keeping with the heightened, quasi-Expressionist atmosphere of the work as a whole.

EDITION v.s., Artisjus, 1968

Samson

Opera in two acts, Op. 31 (1h 30m)
Libretto by the composer, after the play by László Németh
Composed 1971–3
PREMIERE 26 October 1973, Magyar Allami Operaház, Budapest

Between *Hamlet* and *Samson*, Szokolay wrote a one-act 'fairy-tale' opera, *The Spring-bearing Maiden*, and a so-called ballet–oratorio called *The Victim*. *Samson*, too, like other Hungarian biblical operas (such as Durkó's *Mozsés*), has elements of oratorio. The chorus is important, but its role is static and descriptive, except in the spectacular final scene in the Temple of Dagon. A central part of the drama concerns the character development of Samson between his blinding and the eventual destruction of the temple. As before Szokolay reveals a gift for expressing drama through the voice, and the orchestral writing is bold but spare, colouring and reinforcing the singers but seldom stepping in front of them.

RECORDING Hazy, Melis, Palcsó, Nagy, Hungarian State Opera Ch and O, Korody, Hungaroton, 1975
EDITIONS f.s./v.s., Artisjus (on hire), 1973

Other operatic works: *A tavaszhozó kisleány* (*The Spring-bearing Maiden*), (1967); *Csalóka Péter* (*Sly Peter*), (1977); *Ecce homo* ('passion-opera'), (1984); *Szávitri*, (1988)
BIBLIOGRAPHY Imre Fábián, 'Two Opera Composers', *Tempo*, no. 88 (spring 1969), pp. 10–19; Stephen Walsh, 'Two Hamlets', *Tempo*, no. 89 (summer 1969), pp. 6–12

S.W.

KAROL SZYMANOWSKI

Karol Maciej Szymanowski; *b* 6 October 1882, Tymoszówka, Ukraine; *d* 29 March 1937, Lausanne, Switzerland

Szymanowski was the most important Polish composer to follow Chopin and Moniuszko. He was taught music by his father, then later by Gustav Neuhaus and finally by Zygmunt Noskowski in Warsaw. From 1911 to 1914 he lived mainly in Vienna where he made contact with Universal Edition, who became his main publishers.

Szymanowski was an energetic traveller. Before the First World War he visited Sicily and North Africa, and these journeys stimulated the interest in ancient and oriental cultures that was to colour works such as the opera *King Roger*, the Third Symphony, *Myths* and *Songs of an Infatuated Muezzin*. Szymanowski also wrote poems, and left sketches and fragments of six novels. The libretto for *King Roger*, written in collaboration with Jarosław Iwaszkiewicz, is derived from his novel *Ephebos*. From 1930 his home was at Zakopane in the Tatra Mountains, and the local folk music influenced his late compositions. At this time, he was also rector of the Warsaw Conservatory (1927–9, 1930–32), and from 1933 to 1936 he worked as a touring musician, playing his own piano music all over Europe. Apart from these episodes, Szymanowski devoted himself wholly to composition and writing.

He wrote music in many genres: four symphonies, two violin concertos, two string quartets, music for violin and for piano, operas, incidental music, a ballet-pantomime, vocal and choral music and many songs. They display a variety of influences and tendencies easily divisible into three periods. Up to 1914, Chopin and Skryabin are strong influences, but most obviously Richard Strauss – and later Reger. With the late-Romantic strain there is also a classical tendency which is manifested in his fascination with counterpoint and the use of dances such as the gavotte and minuet (in the Second Symphony) or the sarabande and minuet (in the Second Piano Sonata). The one-act *Hagith* derives from the spirit of German Expressionism as manifested in Strauss's *Salome*, though Szymanowski's harmony and texture are denser than Strauss's, and his emotional tension even more unrelenting.

In his middle period (1914–20) colour assumed greater importance, and Szymanowski's music became more impressionistic, reflecting his interest in oriental and ancient cultures. His most important opera, *King Roger*, belongs to this period. While working on it, Szymanowski was also composing works, such as the song-cycle *Słopiewnie*, that anticipate his so-called 'national' last period, when his music became simpler in structure and texture, with harmony that uses folk modes and is less chromatic. The major works of this final period are the Fourth Symphony, the Second Violin Concerto and the ballet *Harnasie*, whose Paris performance in 1936 was the composer's last great international success.

Through all his apparent changes of style, Szymanowski's attitude remained Romantic. Emotion is central to his music. As a composer he was prolific, but he was also an influential writer on music, touching on crucial contemporary musical issues and expressing strong views on, for example, the social role of music and on Chopin as a living musical tradition for the 20th century.

King Roger

(*The Shepherd*)
Król Roger
(*Pasterz*)
Opera in three acts, Op. 46 (1h 45m)
Libretto by Jarosław Iwaszkiewicz and the composer, after the composer's novel *Ephebos*
Composed 1918–24
PREMIERES 19 June 1926, Wielki Theatre, Warsaw; UK: 14 May 1975, Sadler's Wells, London
CAST King Roger II *bar*, Roxana *s*, Shepherd *t*, *a*, *t*, *b*; children's choir of acolytes; *satb* chorus of priests, monks, nuns, king's guard, Norman knights
ORCHESTRATION 3 fl/picc, 3 ob/ca, 3 cl/E♭ cl, b cl, 3 bsn/dbsn, 4 hn, 3 B♭ tpt, 3 trbn, tuba, timp, perc (sd, timbrel, bd, triangle, cym, xyl, bells) cel, 2 hp, pf, organ, str; onstage: 4 C tpt, t-t

Scene from Act II of King Roger *(Warsaw, 1926)*

In *King Roger* Szymanowski planned an integrated musical spectacle in which music, words and design would form part of a single concept in the manner of the Wagnerian ideal. The composer not only collaborated on the libretto but also gave detailed instructions for the sets. The drama is symbolic: the characters represent ideals, and the dramatic conflict is between the Pagan (personified by the Shepherd) and the Christian (personified by Roger).

SYNOPSIS
Act I Twelfth-century Sicily. In the cathedral at Palermo, the priests ask King Roger to imprison an unknown Shepherd, who has proclaimed a philosophy of beauty and pleasure which they see as threatening Christianity. The king is willing to comply, but his beloved wife Roxana begs him to hear the Shepherd before deciding. Roger agrees, and invites the Shepherd to his castle.

Act II The Shepherd, who comes from India, enters the castle with a group of disciples. They begin to dance. Roxana and the courtiers are won over by the Shepherd's charismatic personality and teaching, and when he leaves they follow.

Act III In the ruins of an ancient theatre Roger searches for Roxana and the Shepherd. Soon they appear, and he follows them like a pilgrim. Suddenly the Shepherd becomes Dionysus and his disciples bacchantes and maenads. They dance ecstatically, and then depart with Roxana. Roger remains alone, singing a hymn to the rising sun. He has resisted a powerful temptation, and has thereby achieved wholeness.

King Roger combines elements of opera and oratorio. Its statuesque action and important choral part suggest Stravinsky's *Oedipus Rex* or Schoenberg's *Moses and Aaron*. But the music itself has little in common with those works. Each act presents a different world: the first Byzantine, the second Arabic–Indian, the third Ancient Greek; and these characteristics determine the musical stylizations, which are not historically or geographically exact, but amount rather to suggestions of old church or oriental music (such as antiphonal psalmody or organum) in Act I; asymmetry of phrase, irregular metre, a narrow melodic range but with much ornamentation and free use of percussion in Act II. There are no quotations and no authentic scales. In Act III the stylization is achieved mainly through the scenery. There is some flavour of Tatra folksong, a symptom of Szymanowski's growing interest in folklore.

The music is extremely varied in texture. Though much of the choral music is archaic in character, the orchestra is sometimes treated as one vast instrument in the late-Romantic manner, offering dense textures and complex modern harmony. It is sometimes divided into smaller chamber ensembles, or there are instrumental solos, in the style of French Impressionism. The dense chromatic harmony is contrasted with the sound of parallel fifths and plain common chords, sometimes in order to differentiate character (King Roger – chromatic; Roxana – modal). This combination of styles produced a work with a unique atmosphere which has no real parallel in either earlier or contemporary music. The best-known number in the opera is Roxana's Act II aria, which is often performed as a violin solo in a transcription by Paweł Kochański.

RECORDING Rumowska, Hiolski, Nikodem, Pustelak, Dabrowski, Warsaw State Opera Ch and O, Mierzejewski, Polskie Nagrania, 1965
EDITIONS f.s., PWM/Universal, 1973; v.s., Universal, 1926

Other operatic works: *Loteria na mężów* (*Lottery for a Husband*) (operetta), (1909); *Hagith*, (1913), 1922; 2 lost operas

BIBLIOGRAPHY   Kornal Michałowski, *Karol Szymanowski, Katalog tematyczny dzieł i bibliografia* (*Karol Szymanowski, Thematic Catalogue of Works and Bibliography*), PWM, 1967; Jim Samson, *The Music of Szymanowski*, Kahn and Averill, 1980

Z.C.

OTAR TAKTAKISHVILI

Otar Vasilevich Taktakishvili; *b* 27 July 1924, Tbilisi, Georgia

Composer, choirmaster, conductor and a member of the Presidium of the International Music Council of UNESCO, Taktakishvili became from a very young age the most prominent Georgian composer. Unusually, he never studied in Moscow. His work is eclectic in the extreme and can show great vitality. His early works are all instrumental and unremarkable compared with the range of his theatrical work. *Mindiya* (1961), a slightly Symbolist man-versus-nature tale which relies heavily on folk material and the operas of Paliashvili, has music of an appealing lyricism. *Three Novellas* (1967), a theatrical *tour de force*, attempts to show the fate of the Georgian people in all walks of life and in various periods, using popular song, parody, folksong and band music woven into a lively patchwork. His later works develop this poster-like musical technique.

Operatic works: *Mindiya*, 1961 (RECORDING Melodiya, 1960s); *Sami novela* (*Three Novellas*), 1967, rev. as *Tri zhizni* (*Three Lives*), 1972 (RECORDING Melodiya, 1974); *Mtvaris Motatseba* (*The Abduction of the Moon*), 1976
BIBLIOGRAPHY S. D. Krebs, *Soviet Composers*, George Allen and Unwin, 1970

J.G.

JOSEF TAL

Joseph Gruenthal; *b* 18 September 1910, Pinne, nr Poznań

Tal studied at the Berlin Hochschule – where his teachers included Hindemith – but in 1934 emigrated to Palestine. He worked on a kibbutz, then later taught at the Jerusalem Conservatory, and became the first director of the new Israel Academy of Music in 1948.

Tal has been one of the most influential figures on the Israeli musical scene since the state was founded. But he has also dominated it creatively, and is widely regarded as the leading Israeli composer. His music is wide-ranging. It includes a large number of instrumental and orchestral scores, including many with pre-recorded electronic tape. These works show Tal to be a true eclectic, both technically and

stylistically, which partly accounts for his reputation in international circles such as the ISCM, as well as the success of his music outside Israel, especially in Germany. A confirmed serialist, he has also combined aleatoricism and electronics in music of a powerful dramatic and rhetorical thrust – as befits the central European artist who brings his consciousness of suffering humanity back to the nation that perhaps today most sharply symbolizes that condition.

Tal's eight operas nearly all embody that consciousness. At their best they express it directly and powerfully; at their worst they can seem laboured and pretentious. Biblical subjects abound. His first opera – really a concert or radio piece, subtitled 'opera-concertante' – is a 25-minute chamber setting of the story of Saul and the Witch of Endor, while his two most recent operas take us back to the Tower of Babel and the Garden of Eden respectively. By far his most successful opera has been *Ashmedai*. But *Massada 967* also made a real impact, and only its successor, *Die Versuchung*, was a complete failure, with its weary parable of a random group of explorers who find a 'natural' in the mountains, educate him with their values, and are (of course) finally destroyed by him. After this setback, Tal avoided opera for more than a decade.

Ashmedai
Opera in two acts
Libretto by Israel Eliraz, from the Talmud
Composed 1968–9
PREMIERES 9 November 1971, Städtische Oper, Hamburg (in a German version by Jacob Mittelmann); US: April 1976, City Opera, New York

Tal's first full-length opera, *Ashmedai*, aroused mixed reactions between those who found it a powerfully dramatic treatment of a complex and resonant subject, and those who found it too lightweight by half. The plot imagines that the demon Ashmedai challenges the king of a peaceable and somewhat depressed land to allow him to take over as king for a year. During his reign Ashmedai transforms the people into a warlike and aggressive nation while eating away their moral core. When the old king returns he is lynched.

Tal's score shows impressive mastery of a range of avant-garde techniques, and is certainly never less than accomplished. In Germany, where politically motivated drama always has a head start, the work was an instant success.

EDITION v.s., Israeli Music Institute, 1971

Masada 967

Opera in 15 scenes (1h 15m)
Libretto by Israel Eliraz
Composed 1971–2
PREMIERE 17 July 1973, Jerusalem (Israel Festival)

Masada is the great Jewish fortress which fell to the Romans in AD 73. Of its 967 inhabitants, 960 committed suicide.

In certain dramatic respects this work also disappoints. But the score, in which the voices are accompanied exclusively by a pre-recorded tape, is both intriguing and at times very impressive. *Masada*'s successor, *Die Versuchung* (commissioned by the Munich Festival on the strength of the earlier piece), also uses electronics.

EDITIONS f.s./v.s., Israeli Music Institute, 1973

Other operas: *Saul at Endor*, 1955; *Amnon and Tamar*, 1960; *Die Versuchung*, 1976; *Else*, 1975; *Der Turm*, 1987; *Der Garten*, 1988
BIBLIOGRAPHY Peter Gradenwitz, *Music and Musicians in Israel: A Comprehensive Guide to Modern Israeli Music*, Israeli Music Publications, 1951; 3rd edn, 1978

S.W.

SERGEI TANEYEV

Sergei Ivanovich Taneyev; *b* 25 November 1856, Vladimir-na-Klyaz'me, Russia; *d* 19 June 1915, Dyud'kovo, nr Moscow

Taneyev was an infant prodigy, entering the Moscow Conservatory when he was barely ten. He was to study both piano and composition, the latter with Tchaikovsky. This contact developed into a close and lifelong friendship. When Tchaikovsky resigned from the conservatory in 1878 Taneyev replaced him, becoming its director from 1885 to 1889. His remaining years were devoted to composition, to writing a definitive book on counterpoint and, after his final break with the conservatory during the 1905 revolutionary disturbances, to concert-giving.

Taneyev was a solitary among Russian composers. He had none of his contemporaries' interest in musical nationalism, realism, or fairy-tale fantasy. A slow and painstaking worker, he was at heart an 'absolute' composer, devoted to counterpoint (both baroque and Renaissance). It is no surprise that chamber music became his central creative interest in his later years, nor that he should have composed only one opera.

The Oresteia

Oresteya
A musical trilogy in three parts (eight scenes) (3h)
Libretto by Alexey Alexeyevich Venkstern, after the trilogy by Aeschylus

Composed 1887–94
PREMIERE 29 October 1895, Mariinsky Theatre, St Petersburg

Though Taneyev described *The Oresteia* as a trilogy, it is in fact an opera in three acts.

SYNOPSIS
Act I (*Agamemnon*) tells how, after the victorious outcome of the 10-year siege of Troy, Agamemnon returns with the captive Trojan princess Cassandra to Greece, where his wife, Clytemnestra, who has sent their son Orestes away, has taken a lover, Aegisthus. Cassandra predicts her own and Agamemnon's murders by Clytemnestra, and also the vengeance that Orestes will take on his mother for the death of his father. Clytemnestra kills Cassandra and Agamemnon.

Act II (*The Choephorae*) Agamemnon's ghost tells Clytemnestra of the fate that awaits her. Orestes returns to avenge his father. After being reunited with his sister Electra at their father's tomb, he kills first Aegisthus, then his mother. But he is appalled at what he has done, and flees in terror from the pursuing Furies.

Act III (*The Eumenides*) finds Orestes on the brink of madness. In the temple of Apollo the god protects him, then orders him back to Athens to await the verdict of Pallas Athene. Orestes is penitent, and Pallas releases him from guilt; all praise the goddess, praying that truth and happiness may reign in the world.

A subject from Greek mythology was an unusual choice for a Russian composer, but Taneyev had no interest in the plot's actual incidents (for instance, all the murders take place offstage, as in Aeschylus); instead he was moved by the themes of fate, revenge and expiation that underlie Aeschylus' tragedy. Though *The Oresteia* is a most carefully wrought and sometimes impressive score (especially in passages where Taneyev could capitalize on his formidable contrapuntal and harmonic resourcefulness), the invention lacks personality and real dramatic flair; too often its second-hand lyricism envelops rather than projects the characters and their feelings.

The Oresteia was performed eight times in its first two seasons, was revived in 1915, but then disappeared from the Russian repertoire until the Byelorussian State Opera revived it in 1964.

RECORDING Galushkina, Tkachenko, Chernobayev, Byelorussian State Opera, Kolomijzeva, DG, 1979: from Soviet tapes of 1966; heavily cut
EDITION v.s., State Music Publishers, 1970

D.B.

ANGELO TARCHI

b c. 1760, Naples; *d* 19 August 1814, Paris

Tarchi was a popular and prolific composer, at times

writing six operas in a year. He is now remembered for one dubious service to music – a shortened version of Acts III and IV of Mozart's *Le nozze di Figaro*, given at Monza in 1787 in honour of the Habsburgs. But his operas deserve re-evaluation.

His musical career began in 1771, when he entered the Neapolitan conservatory of the Pietà dei Turchini. At Carnival in 1778, Tarchi's first comic opera, *L'archetiello*, was staged at the conservatory; it so pleased King Ferdinand IV that he had it repeated in his palace at Caserta. This success immediately opened the doors of the Neapolitan opera houses specializing in opera buffa and commissions for Roman theatres followed. His operas then spread to northern Italy and finally reached the Saxon court at Dresden.

His first serious opera was produced at La Scala, Milan, during the 1784 Carnival. In May 1786 his contribution to a pasticcio for London, *La Virginia*, successfully launched the castrato Rubinelli in the city. Referring to this occasion, Charles Burney eulogized the young composer. In 1787 Tarchi took charge of the music of the King's Theatre in the Haymarket, but in 1790 was called to Paris, where he introduced himself with a revival of his best work, the tragedy *Il conte di Saldagna*. He cleverly oriented his writing towards Parisian taste, blending elements of his youthful efforts in the comic style with heroic opera to create *Il cavaliere errante* (1790) and *Don Quichotte* (1791). Tarchi's experience in France left its mark even after his return to Italy; comic and dramatic elements became intertwined in his works, giving rise to a kind of Italian opéra comique. He returned to Paris for good in 1797, composing solely operas in French. In 1802 he retired from the theatre and devoted the rest of his life to the teaching of singing.

Surviving operas: *Ademira*, 1783; *Bacco ed Arianna*, 1784; *L'Arminio*, 1785; *Ifigenia in Aulide*, 1785; *Ifigenia in Tauride*, 1785; *Ariarate*, 1786; *Il trionfo di Clelia*, 1786; *Il conte di Saldagna*, 1787; *Antioco*, 1787; *Alessandro nelle Indie*, 1788, rev. as *La generosità d'Alessandro*, 1789; *Artaserse*, 1788; *Il disertore francese*, 1789, rev. as *Il disertore*, 1791; *Ezio*, 1789, rev. 1792; *Giulio Sabino*, 1790; *Lo spazzacamino principe*, 1790; *L'impostura poco dura*, 1795; *Le cabriolet jaune, ou Le phénix d'Angoulême*, 1798; *Le trente et quarante*, 1799; *D'auberge en auberge, ou Les préventions*, 1800; *Une aventure de M. de Saint Foix, ou Le coup d'épée*, 1802; 33 lost operas

BIBLIOGRAPHY   Alfred Einstein, 'Mozart and Tarchi', in *MMR*, 1935; *rp* in *Essays on Music*, New York, 1956

D.A.D'A.

PHYLLIS TATE

Phyllis Margaret Duncan Tate; *b* 6 April 1911, Gerrards Cross, England; *d* 27 May 1987, London

Phyllis Tate, a daughter of the architect Duncan Tate, studied composition at the Royal Academy of Music with Herbert Farjeon. She is known for a variety of scores in smaller forms, including many vocal works and music for young performers. Her first stage work was the operetta *The Policeman's Serenade*, to a libretto by A. P. Herbert, successfully premiered at the RAM in 1932 but later disowned by its composer. Her first mature opera was *The Lodger*, commissioned by the RAM. Based by David Franklin on a novel by Mrs Belloc Lowndes, it is set in London at the time of Jack the Ripper (the 1890s). Dramatically the piece is effective, with its fog-and-gaslight atmosphere, and a divided set showing two rooms simultaneously. All this is lightened by a series of jolly choruses and the idiosyncratic use of polkas and waltzes. It remains the composer's most considerable operatic achievement.

Her later stage works include a comic opera based on John Gay's *The What D'Ye Call It* (Cheltenham, 1966), and several effective children's operas.

Operatic works: *The Lodger*, 1960; *Dark Pilgrimage* (television opera), 1963; *The What D'Ye Call It*, 1966; *The Story of Lieutenant Cockatoo* (television opera), 1968; *Twice in a Blue Moon*, 1969; *A Pride of Lions*, 1971; *St Martha and the Dragon*, 1978

BIBLIOGRAPHY   Martin Cooper, 'Phyllis Tate's *The Lodger*', *Listener*, 30 January 1964, p. 213

L.F.

JOHN TAVENER

John Kenneth Tavener; *b* 28 January 1944, London

Tavener, a pupil of Lennox Berkeley and David Lumsdaine at the Royal Academy of Music, shot to fame with his dramatic cantata *The Whale*, premiered by the London Sinfonietta in their inaugural concert in January 1968. In its ritualistic and 'naïvely' graphic treatment of a religious subject (from the Book of Jonah), as well as in its main musical influences (late Stravinsky, Messiaen), *The Whale* set the tone for much of Tavener's subsequent work, the bulk of which is vocal and/or choral. Catholic influences (with both a big and a small 'c') gradually give way to Orthodoxy and works with Greek or Russian associations, often on a large scale, nearly always with much repetition, an intensely contemplative atmosphere, and a much more unified – less freely associative – style than before.

Tavener's music is dramatic only in the sense that it refers (often graphically) to overwhelming events – in other words, in the sense that a church service is dramatic. He has, nevertheless, written with some success for the stage. Two early 'music dramas' – *The Cappemakers* (1964, rev. 1965) and *Cain and Abel* (1965), both based on the York Mystery Plays – were followed by the operas *Thérèse* and *A Gentle Spirit*. More recently he wrote a quasi-dramatic setting, in Greek, of a ritual poem by Andreas Kalvos, *Eis Thanaton* (1987), and a chamber opera, *Mary of Egypt* (1992).

Thérèse

Opera in one act (1h 45m)
Libretto by Gerard McLarnon
Composed 1973–6
PREMIERE 1 October 1979, Covent Garden, London

Thérèse is a kind of operatic *Dream of Gerontius* cum *Inferno* on the death agonies of Ste Thérèse de Lisieux, who is led Dante-like through hell towards heaven by her older contemporary the poet Rimbaud. The work is inherently no more dramatic than Tavener's concert works. Rather, it resembles his big stylized church ceremonials, such as *Ultimos ritos* (1972). The score is notable for its imposing spatial effects, and for its textual ecumenicism (with passages in Church Slavonic, Latin and Aramaic, among other languages). Thérèse's visions offer plenty of scope for imaginative staging and choreography. But the vocal writing, especially for the title soprano role, is taxing to an extent not always obviously justified by the dramatic exigencies of the opera.

EDITION v.s., Chester, 1977

A Gentle Spirit

Chamber opera in one act (45m)
Libretto by Gerard McLarnon, after the short story by Dostoevsky (1876)
Composed 1976–7
PREMIERE 6 June 1977, Theatre Royal, Bath

In St Petersburg in 1876, a pawnbroker contemplates the body of his young wife, who has killed herself by jumping from an upstairs window, and tries through a process of remembering to come to terms with the reasons for her suicide (an incident Dostoevsky took from a newspaper report). Like *Thérèse* the work proceeds mainly in flashback, and like that work it is stronger on theatrical effect than on drama. The chamber orchestra (14 players) includes much percussion and a pre-recorded tape.

EDITION v.s., Chester, 1978

Mary of Egypt

Chamber opera ('Moving Icon') in one act (1h 45m)
Libretto by Mother Thekla, after *The Account of the Life of Hallowed Mother Mary of Egypt*
Composed 1991
PREMIERE 19 June 1992, The Maltings, Snape

The prostitute Mary of Egypt encounters the holy man Zossima in the desert: the woman in adultery and the learned Pharisee. But her generosity in love waters his intellectual desert, and in the end it is she who redeems him.

This 'stained-glass' treatment of a subject previously made into more conventional operas by Massenet (*Thaïs*) and Respighi (*Maria egiziaca*), takes to an extreme Tavener's idea of theatre as a devotional ritual. The music is almost entirely slow and repetitive, with motionless pedal harmony over which two or three melodic figures of the most

elemental simplicity rotate in a manner perhaps dangerously redolent of minimalism. 'The whole piece', Tavener says, 'is loosely based on the ancient Byzantine hymn "Awed by the Beauty".' The sense of a ritual enactment is enhanced by the identification of the two main characters with obbligato instruments: Mary with a flute, Zossima with a trombone and the gong-like semantron.

RECORDING Rozario, Varcoe, Goodchild, Britten–Pears Chamber Ch, Ely Cathedral Choristers, Aldeburgh Festival Ensemble, Friend, Collins Classics, 1992
EDITIONS f.s./v.s., Chester, 1992

BIBLIOGRAPHY John Tavener, '*Thérèse*', *Opera*, vol. 30 (1979), pp. 944–7; Paul Griffiths, *New Sounds, New Personalities: British Composers of the 1980s*, Faber, 1985, pp. 106–12

S.W.

DEEMS TAYLOR

Joseph Deems Taylor; *b* 22 December 1885, New York; *d* 3 July 1966, New York

Taylor was a conservative American composer and critic whose operas were extremely successful in their day. As a young man he wrote musical comedies and was encouraged by Victor Herbert: after graduating from New York University he continued his studies while working in musical journalism. His music-appreciation talks on national radio made Taylor's name widely known and his writings were published.

His first grand opera, *The King's Henchman* (1927), close to *Tristan und Isolde* in plot, was commissioned by the Metropolitan in New York. The premiere was a major event and Lawrence Gilman called it 'the best American opera we have ever heard'. Wagnerian overtones extend to the music which includes leitmotifs and much chromatic writing. The opera remained in the Met's repertoire for three years and its success prompted the commission of *Peter Ibbetson* (1931), based on Constance Collier's theatrical adaptation of George du Maurier's novel. While critical response to *Ibbetson* was less enthusiastic (critics found the music far from original – 'old wine in bottles that are none too new' wrote one), it surpassed *The King's Henchman* as a popular success. The score echoes Wagner, Debussy and Puccini and also includes traditional waltzes and French folksongs.

Operatic works: *Cap'n Kidd & Co.*, 1908; *The Echo*, 1910; *The Breath of Scandal*, 1916; *The King's Henchman*, 1927 (RECORDING excerpts: New World, 1928); *Peter Ibbetson*, 1931 (RECORDING excerpts: Columbia, c. 1931); *Ramuntcho*, 1942; *The Dragon*, 1958
BIBLIOGRAPHY J. T. Howard, 'Deems Taylor', in *Studies of Contemporary American Composers*, vol. 4, J. Fischer & Bros., 1925, *rp*, 1940

P.D.

PYOTR TCHAIKOVSKY

Pyotr Ilyich Tchaikovsky; *b* 7 May 1840, Kamsko-Votkinsk
(Vyatka Province), Russia; *d* 6 November 1893, St Petersburg

Though only two of his operas, *Eugene Onegin* and
The Queen of Spades, are regularly performed
outside Russia, Tchaikovsky occupied himself more
with opera than with any other musical genre. He
wrote operas at every stage of his career, and they
were invariably given productions within a reasonably short time. Much more than ballet, opera charts
his development as a composer, even where it does
not represent his very best work.

The son of a mining engineer in Votkinsk, some
600 miles east of Moscow, Tchaikovsky moved with
his family to St Petersburg when he was eight. As a
child, he was almost excessively attached to his
mother, and when she died in 1854 he suffered an
emotional trauma from which he never completely
recovered. Relations with women were a problem for
the rest of his life. In 1868 it seems he came close to
marrying the Belgian opera singer, Désirée Artôt,
and in 1877 he allowed himself to be drawn into a
disastrous marriage by the desperation of the girl and
by his own feelings of guilt. These and his curious
epistolary friendship with his patroness Nadezhda
von Meck, whom he never met in person, were his
only attempts at close relationships with the female
sex outside his own family. But as a homosexual, he
suffered still greater agonies of guilt and self-
loathing; and eventually the strain was too much and
there can be no reasonable doubt that he committed
suicide.

There is little sign that Tchaikovsky's student years
under Anton Rubinstein at the St Petersburg
Conservatory (1862–5) prepared him for operatic
composition, and the Russian repertoire in the 1860s
offered few models by native composers. Not
surprisingly, Tchaikovsky's first experiment with the
form, *The Voyevoda* (1867–8), was unsuccessful,
while *Undine* (1869) was rejected outright by the
Imperial Theatre, and the composer subsequently
destroyed it. But he had a good dramatic instinct
which could rise to greatness when his personal
sympathies were fully engaged, and by the time he
tackled his third subject, *The Oprichnik*, he had
greatly developed his craft in instrumental music, and
had magnificently revealed a highly personal style in
his fantasy overture, *Romeo and Juliet* (1869, revised
1870 and 1880). In fact, *The Oprichnik* (1870–72) was
not only a great audience success, but a notable
achievement (though Tchaikovsky's own hostility to
it came to exceed even what he felt for its two
predecessors). Its individuality was reinforced by its
very pronounced Russianness, and in the old
Boyarina he created the first of those 'suffering
women' who were to prove the most memorable
characters in his operas.

But already he was being drawn towards his
nationalist contemporaries, led by Balakirev, and
the Second ('Little Russian') Symphony (1872)
especially revealed a radical shift in manner which
was confirmed in his fourth opera, *Vakula the Smith*
(1874), in which the score's four identified folksongs
are supplemented with passages of folksong pastiche.
With *Vakula*, however, Tchaikovsky's nationalist
phase came to an abrupt end. While the First Piano

Pyotr Tchaikovsky and his brothers, photographed in 1890: Nikolai and Pyotr (seated); Modest, Ippolit and Anatoli (standing)

Concerto (1874–5) signalled a return towards his earlier manner, the heightened turbulence and pathos of the symphonic fantasy *Francesca da Rimini* (1876) seemed almost to foretell the disastrous events of the following year.

Eugene Onegin (1877–8) is inextricably entangled with that traumatic episode: its story had uncanny parallels with Tchaikovsky's own life. It is undoubtedly his greatest opera and also his most characteristic, both in its content and its musico-dramatic technique. Composed under the impression of Bizet's *Carmen*, which Tchaikovsky saw in Paris in 1876 and adored, his handling of Pushkin's ironic verse tale also projects Bizet's concept of happy domesticity and social virtue undermined by inexorable personal tragedy. Especially crucial is the design of its scenario. Three of Tchaikovsky's last six operas are Pushkin-based, and it is in these that the episodic structure to which Russian libretti incline becomes most explicit. It was perhaps because *Eugene Onegin*, *Mazepa* and *The Queen of Spades* were literary classics, known to all educated Russians, that their scenarios could be more selective, relying on the listener's knowledge to fill any gaps in the plots. Be that as it may, all three (like Musorgsky's *Boris Godunov*, also drawn from Pushkin) use a 'strip cartoon' structure, each scene dwelling on a crucial incident in the story, thus giving the composer time to explore in depth the psychological states of his characters. In *Onegin* Tchaikovsky rose to such opportunities magnificently – above all in Tatyana's letter monologue, the finest scene in all his operas. Some consider *Onegin* his masterpiece.

No such claim could be made for *The Maid of Orleans* (1878–9; rev. 1882). *The Maid* suffered from Tchaikovsky's clear determination to compose a grandiose, Meyerbeerish work that would appeal to the taste of Western operatic audiences. But it was not only that 'commercial' considerations seem to have shaped *The Maid*; the traumatic events of 1877 had stunned his creative individuality. He shrank from society as far as possible to live mostly abroad or with his sister in the Ukraine, and few of the compositions of the next seven years are among his most powerful or characteristic. He attempted no symphony, turning instead to the freer form of the suite and serenade, and only two works are truly outstanding: the Piano Trio (1881–2) and the opera *Mazepa* (1881–3).

In the *Manfred Symphony* of 1885 Tchaikovsky rediscovered his full, most individual powers, and it might have been hoped that his next opera, *The Enchantress* (1885–7), would be a masterpiece matching *Onegin*. But for all its undeniable fluency and stretches of excellent music, it was crippled by its implausibly melodramatic subject. The Fifth Symphony (1888) and especially the great ballet *The Sleeping Beauty* (1888–9) are on a very different plane, and completely at one stylistically. Yet the most striking feature of *The Queen of Spades* (1890), Tchaikovsky's third Pushkin opera, is the savage stylistic dichotomy between the sombre, sometimes menacing music prompted by the remorseless

obsession of the main character, and the bright, cheerful music of the elegant society within which events are set. In several earlier works (most notably the *Rococo Variations* for cello and orchestra (1876)) Tchaikovsky had allowed 'Mozartean' style to mate with his own; now he himself confessed that some music in this opera was no more than 18th-century pastiche. Elsewhere, in the darker scenes and passages, the tragic pessimism of the Sixth Symphony (1893) is anticipated. For the three years after *The Queen of Spades* it seems that Tchaikovsky's creative resources were husbanding themselves for the stupendous achievement of this final symphony. Certainly all the intervening compositions are relatively relaxed, and his last opera, *Iolanta* (1891), is little more than a charming, though at times very affecting, piece.

The Voyevoda

Voyevoda

Opera in three acts (14 scenes), Op. 3 (2h 30m)
Libretto by Aleksandr Nikolaevich Ostrovsky and the composer, after *Son po Volge* (*A Dream on the Volga*) by Ostrovsky
Composed March 1867–August 1868
PREMIERE 11 February 1869, Bolshoi Theatre, Moscow

The Voyevoda is set in a town on the river Volga in the mid-17th century. Praskovya, daughter of a wealthy merchant, Dyuzhoy, is to be the arranged bride of the elderly Voyevoda (provincial governor), Shaligin, and this marriage could prove an obstacle to the union of Praskovya's sister, Mariya, with the Voyevoda's enemy, Bastryukov. However, when the Voyevoda sees Mariya he demands to marry her instead, and Bastryukov makes an unsuccessful attempt to rescue his beloved. Bastryukov and a fugitive, Dubrovin, whose wife had been abducted by the Voyevoda two years before, plan to rescue Mariya and Dubrovin's wife while the Voyevoda is away. Though the rescue attempt is thwarted by the unexpected return of the Voyevoda, the two couples are saved by the sudden appearance of a new Voyevoda sent to replace Shaligin.

Tchaikovsky's first opera ran for only five nights, and he later destroyed the score, though after his death it was reconstructed from the performing materials. *The Voyevoda* is an insecure piece, both stylistically and dramatically, but intermittently it comes to life, especially when Tchaikovsky allows his lyrical gift full rein. He thought well enough of some of the music to incorporate it into his third opera, *The Oprichnik*, and the ballet *Swan Lake* (in the entr'acte to Act IV and the opening of the *Scène finale*).

RECORDING abridged: Rozhdestvenskaya, Orfenov, Korolev, Demyanov, Moscow Radio Ch and SO, Kovalev, Melodiya, 1952
EDITIONS f.s., P. I. Tchaikovsky, *Polnoye sobraniye sochinenii* (complete edition), Izdatelstvo Muzïka, 1940–71 (hereafter abbreviated to *PSS*), vols 1A, B and V, 1953; v.s., *PSS*, vol. 1 (supplement), 1953

Undine

Undina

Opera in three acts
Libretto by Vladimir Sollogub, after Vasily Zhukovsky's translation of the tale *Undine* by Friedrich de la Motte Fouqué (1811)
Composed January–July 1869
Unperformed

Undine was rejected by the Imperial Opera in St Petersburg in 1869 and Tchaikovsky later destroyed the score. Three excerpts from Act I (the introduction, Undine's aria, and the chorus, duet and finale) have been restored from the performing material made for a concert in Moscow on 28 March 1870; subsequently the first two of these extracts were adapted for use in the incidental music to *The Snow Maiden* (1873), becoming the introduction and Lel's first song respectively. According to the composer's brother Modest, the wedding march was reused in the slow movement of the Second Symphony ('Little Russian', 1872) and the final duet was reworked into the celebrated *Pas d'action* with violin and cello obbligati in *Swan Lake* (1875–6).

EDITIONS f.s./v.s., *PSS*, vol. 2, 1953

The Oprichnik

Oprichnik

Opera in four acts (3h)
Libretto by the composer, after *The Oprichniks* by Ivan Lazhechnikov (1840s; published 1867)
Composed February 1870–April 1872
PREMIERES 24 April 1874, Mariinsky Theatre, St Petersburg; UK: 20 August 1992, Usher Hall, Edinburgh (concert)
CAST Prince Zhemchuzhny *b*, Natalya *s*, Molchan Mitkov *b*, Boyarina Morozova *ms*, Andrey Morozov *t*, Basmanov *a*, Prince Vyazminsky *bar*, a nurse *s*; *satb* chorus of oprichniks, peasants, girls and wedding guests
FULL ORCHESTRA

The Oprichnik was Tchaikovsky's first public triumph. But for the composer himself its success was double-edged, since during rehearsals he took an increasing dislike to it. The opera ran for 14 performances and was soon produced in Odessa, Kiev, then Moscow. Towards the end of his life Tchaikovsky tried to ward off revivals by pleading that he planned to revise the piece, though he clearly had no such intention.

SYNOPSIS

Act I Zhemchuzhny agrees to marry his daughter, Natalya, to the elderly Mitkov. Natalya is dismayed, for she loves Andrey, whose family has been dispossessed by her father. Andrey informs his friend Basmanov that he has decided to join the oprichniks, the personal bodyguard of Tsar Ivan the Terrible, in the hope of getting justice through the tsar.

Act II Andrey's mother, the Boyarina, worries over her son's association with Basmanov, who is already an oprichnik. Andrey remains silent about his intention. At the tsar's mansion Vyazminsky, who was a deadly enemy of Andrey's father, is furious when he hears that Ivan has agreed to take Andrey as an oprichnik; nevertheless he sees in this new turn of events hope of revenge. Vyazminsky administers the oath to Andrey; the latter knows if he breaks it he will die, but is especially appalled to discover he must renounce even his mother and Natalya.

Act III Unaware of all this, the Boyarina intercedes with Zhemchuzhny on her son's and Natalya's behalf. The prince remains adamant, but as he is removing his daughter, Andrey, Basmanov and the oprichniks enter. Learning her son is now an oprichnik the Boyarina curses him. Basmanov urges Andrey to beg the tsar to release him from his vow.

Act IV The tsar agrees to Andrey's request, but as his and Natalya's impending wedding is being celebrated at the tsar's mansion, a message arrives that Ivan wants to see the bride – alone. Andrey will not agree and curses the tsar. He is arrested, and Vyazminsky sends for the Boyarina. She witnesses her son's execution and falls lifeless.

Tchaikovsky was determined to reuse whatever music he could from his first opera, *The Voyevoda*, which he had now disowned, and Act I of *The Oprichnik* was designed specially to accommodate this. As a result it is dramatically malformed, and the weakest part of the opera, even though some of the music was worth salvaging. Elsewhere there is less alien material (though, curiously, Tchaikovsky allowed his close friend, Vladimir Shilovsky, to compose the *entr'acte* before Act II), and the musical matching of the melodrama is often very impressive; the second scene of Act II, where Andrey takes the oprichniks' oath, is particularly taut. Add to this the attractive national colouring of some movements (at least nine folksongs have been identified), the nobility of others (especially some of the choruses which clearly echo the idiom of Russian Orthodox Church music), the effective use of reminiscence themes, the avoidance of the elephantine ensembles that had done so much to engulf the characters of *The Voyevoda*, and the simple but clear musical delineation of Andrey, Basmanov and Natalya, and *The Oprichnik* shows itself to be an impressive achievement. Yet the opera is memorable above all perhaps for the secure and moving musical projection of the old Boyarina. *The Oprichnik* is not a great opera, but it is better than Tchaikovsky himself believed it to be.

RECORDING Rozhdestvenskaya, Legostayeva, Dolukhanova, Tarkhov, Korolev, Moscow Radio Ch and SO, Orlov, Melodiya, 1948
EDITIONS f.ss., Bessel, 1896; *PSS*, vols. 3A and B, 1959; v.ss., Bessel, 1874; *PSS*, vol. 34, 1959

Vakula the Smith

(rev. as *The Slippers*)

Kuznets Vakula (rev. as *Cherevichki*)

Opera in three acts, Op. 14 (rev. in four acts (eight scenes)) (2h 45m)
Libretto by Yakov Polonsky, after *Noch' pered rozhdestvom* (*Christmas Eve*) by Nikolay Gogol (1832); additional libretto in rev. version for Vakula's arioso in Act III by the composer and Nikolay Chayev
Composed June–September 1874; rev. February–April 1885, and late 1886

PREMIERES 6 December 1876, Mariinsky Theatre, St Petersburg; rev. version: 31 January 1887, Bolshoi Theatre, Moscow; UK: 17 May 1984, London University; US: 26 May 1922, Metropolitan, New York
CAST Vakula *t*, Solokha *ms*, the Devil *bar*, Chub *b*, Oxana *s*, Pan Golova, the mayor *b*, Panas *t*, Schoolteacher *t*, Prince *b-bar*, Orderly *t*, Old Peasant *b*, Woodgoblin *bar*; *satb* chorus of peasants, kobza players, rusalki (woodsprites), courtiers
FULL ORCHESTRA onstage: banda

Gogol's *Christmas Eve* is a wonderfully vivid, colourful, sometimes very funny tale of Ukrainian village life, blending the real world with that of enchantment and mixing peasant characters with supernatural beings. A libretto based on it, and renamed *Vakula the Smith*, had been intended for Aleksandr Serov, but two years after his death in 1871 it was made the basis of a competition, with performance by the Imperial Opera guaranteed for the winner. Tchaikovsky thought the closing date was in January 1875 (actually it was seven months later), and since it was June 1874 before he could begin work, he felt under great pressure. Nevertheless Gogol's tale so fired his imagination that within little more than six weeks the opera was composed; another three, and it was scored. On discovering his error and realizing preparation for production would not begin for over a year, he attempted to withdraw from the competition, being confident his work would be accepted independently by the Imperial Opera. Inevitably he was reprimanded when this manoeuvre came to light. Yet even this could not restrain him, and though all entries had been submitted under pseudonyms to ensure impartiality, he arranged for the overture to be performed (though withholding its title), then proposed to play the opera through to one of the judges, Rimsky-Korsakov. Despite all these glaring improprieties Tchaikovsky was not disqualified, and his opera was awarded the prize.

Tchaikovsky was delighted with the enthusiasm the performers showed for *Vakula* when rehearsals began, but he felt the audience's response at the premiere was disappointing (in fact, the opera was revived in each of the next three seasons). Perceiving what he felt to be the work's shortcomings, he thoroughly revised it in 1885, cutting about one-eighth but adding about twice as much new music, and simplifying some of the remainder to make it more effective in the theatre. Tchaikovsky himself conducted the five performances of *Cherevichki*, as the revised opera was called, but again success was limited, and it was never revived in his lifetime.

SYNOPSIS (revised version)

Act I Solokha, Vakula's mother and a witch, comes out into the moonlit village street in Dikanka. The Devil is smitten with her and joins in a comic love scene. However, he is furious with her son, who has painted him in the village church to look so ridiculous that all the other devils are laughing at him. Wanting revenge, the Devil plans to steal the moon and raise a snowstorm so that Oxana's father, Chub, will stay at home, and Vakula will not find his beloved alone. However, Chub and his friend, Panas, emerge into the storm, and decide to seek the inn. By now Oxana is admiring herself in front of her mirror. When Vakula creeps in and confesses his love she treats him ungraciously. Chub reappears so covered with snow that Vakula fails to recognize him and throws him back into the street. Oxana upbraids Vakula and pretends she loves someone else. He rushes out distraught before other young villagers arrive to begin celebrating Christmas. When they have left Oxana privately confesses her love for Vakula.

Act II Back in her cottage Solokha flirts again with the Devil until knocking is heard and the Devil jumps into a sack. The mayor enters and flirts with Solokha before there is another knocking and he too hides in a sack. This is repeated after first the schoolteacher, then Chub (whom Solokha favours) enter. On Vakula's approach Solokha and her four 'lovers' (whose heads appear from the sacks) join in an alarmed quintet. To leave the cottage free for Christmas festivities, Vakula decides to remove all the sacks. Meanwhile the villagers, young and old, have gathered in the village street. Oxana torments Vakula when he appears with the sacks; then she admires another girl's new shoes and promises that if Vakula will get the shoes worn by the empress herself, she will marry him. After a despairing Vakula has left with one of the sacks the villagers notice wriggling in the remaining ones, and they release the mayor, the schoolteacher and Chub. Only Chub can see a joke in what has happened, and the crowd joins in his laughter.

Act III Rusalki disturb a woodgoblin. Vakula sings of his sorrow. The Devil jumps out of the sack, but Vakula tricks him and makes him promise to take him to St Petersburg. On the Devil's back he is borne through the air to a reception room in the imperial palace. With the Devil's aid, he joins a group of Cossacks and reaches the great hall, where a polonaise is in progress. The prince announces a great victory. Vakula's strange request is sympathetically received, a splendid pair of high-heeled leather boots (the *cherevichki* of the title) is given him, and he again jumps on the Devil's back.

Act IV Oxana and Solokha are bewailing Vakula's disappearance. Oxana is now thoroughly contrite, will not join in the festivities, and leaves. Vakula enters, begs Chub's forgiveness for ejecting him, and asks for Oxana's hand. Chub agrees as Oxana reappears. Vakula offers her the boots. 'I don't want them. Without them I'm . . .' she stutters. Chub gives the couple his blessing and the *kobza*-players lead the general rejoicing.

'I believe unreservedly in *Cherevichki*'s future as a repertoire piece, and I consider it musically wellnigh my best opera,' Tchaikovsky wrote in 1890. His confidence in its quality was well placed. The subject was an excellent one, ideal for that self-consciously Russian idiom which he was currently anxious to exploit, and which is evident especially in the gopak rhythms in which the opera abounds. Yet it is far from just a folky opera; it exploits fully the resources of more traditional operatic lyricism (though these are always kept within bounds and the pacing is generally excellent) as well as the descriptive and atmospheric potential of the orchestra. However, it is as much to the rich variety of Gogol's characters as to the tale's pervading Russianness that Tchaikovsky responded, whether it was to the fresh young lovers (Vakula manly and strong, Oxana wilful yet lovable), the archly spirited Solokha, still capable of tempting the Devil himself – or to the latter, something of a buffoon and capable of being outwitted, but with the forces of nature at his command. Nor in any other opera did Tchaikovsky realize more fully the cameo characters, projecting them mainly by the vivid musical suggestions of their physical demeanour and movements (foretelling the great ballet composer). Solokha's scenes with the Devil and, above all, that in which she received her succession of suitors reveal Tchaikovsky's formidable comic gift. *Vakula the Smith/Cherevichki* is unique among Tchaikovsky's operas – the most heart-warming, the most unclouded, and still the most sadly neglected.

RECORDING Fomina, Simonova, Lisovsky, Klenov, Krivchenya, Moscow Radio Ch and SO, Fedoseyev, Melodiya, 1970s
EDITIONS *Vakula*: v.ss., Jurgenson, 1876; *PSS*, vol. 35, 1956; *Cherevichki*: f.ss., Jurgenson, 1898; *PSS*, vols. 7A and B, 1951; v.ss., Jurgenson, 1885; *PSS*, vol. 29, 1951

Eugene Onegin

Yevgenii Onegin
Lyrical scenes in three acts (seven scenes), Op. 24 (2h 30m)
Libretto by the composer, after the verse novel by Aleksandr Pushkin (1831); Triquet's couplets by Konstantin Shilovsky
Composed May 1877–February 1878; *écossaise* added 1885
PREMIERES 29 March 1879, Maly Theatre, Moscow Conservatory; UK: 17 October 1892, Olympic Theatre, London; US: 24 March 1920, Metropolitan, New York
CAST Larina *ms*, Tatyana *s*, Olga *a*, Filippevna *ms*, Eugene Onegin *bar*, Lensky *t*, Prince Gremin *b*, Captain *b*, Zaretsky *b*, Triquet *t*, Guillot *silent*; *satb* chorus of peasants, fruit-pickers (female) and ball guests
ORCHESTRATION picc, 2 fl, 2 ob, 2 cl, 2 bsn, 4 hn, 2 tpt, 3 trbn, timp, hp, str

In May 1877 Tchaikovsky had received a letter from a former Moscow Conservatory student, Antonina Milyukova, who was quite unknown to him, claiming she had been secretly in love with him for some years. Then on 25 May the singer Elizaveta Lavrovskaya suggested to him Pushkin's novel in verse, *Eugene Onegin*, as the subject for an opera. After initial hesitation Tchaikovsky's enthusiasm was aroused, and working from his own scenario and libretto (using Pushkin's lines as far as possible), he set to work on the scene that he had always found the most compelling; that in which the inexperienced Tatyana writes to Onegin confessing her love (which he rejects). While engaged on this he received a second letter from Antonina. Determined not to play Onegin to her Tatyana, he agreed to meet her, proposed marriage, and on 10 June left for a friend's country estate. When he returned five weeks later for

the wedding, he had already composed two-thirds of the opera.

His appalling marital situation drove him to attempt suicide, and in early October he fled from Antonina and was taken abroad by his brother, Anatoly, to recover. At first he was capable only of scoring what he had composed, and in November he proposed to his friend and the head of the Moscow Conservatory, Nikolay Rubinstein, that students should perform the first four scenes. A year later, in December 1878, these scenes were presented at a dress rehearsal, and three months later the entire opera was premiered.

It was Tchaikovsky's express wish that conservatory students should give the first performance, for he feared that the work's special qualities would be smothered by the habits and routine of the professional opera houses. Though a minority immediately perceived the work's rare qualities (Tchaikovsky insisted it should be published as 'lyrical scenes'), and though it received a number of modest productions in Russia during the early 1880s, it was not until the Imperial Opera produced it in St Petersburg in 1884 that it suddenly began to enjoy the success that has made it the most popular of all Russian operas. (In 1885, during this production's run, Tchaikovsky added the *écossaise* in the ballroom scene.) The opera reached Prague in 1888, and in 1892 Tchaikovsky himself was much impressed by a performance in Hamburg conducted by the young Gustav Mahler.

SYNOPSIS
Act I Scene 1: In the garden of her country house Mrs Larina gossips with the old nurse, Filippevna, as she listens to her daughters, Tatyana and Olga, singing a sentimental duet inside the house. A group of peasants approaches, bringing in the last of the harvest. They perform a choral dance for Mrs Larina, who orders them be given wine. Meanwhile Tatyana and Olga have entered. Olga draws attention to Tatyana's pallor; she herself, she observes, is always carefree. But Tatyana attributes her own condition to the romantic novel she is reading. Suddenly their neighbour, Lensky, and his friend, Onegin, are seen approaching. Mrs Larina receives them, then withdraws. The young people join in a quartet, Onegin comparing Olga unfavourably with Tatyana, Tatyana seeing in Onegin the man fate has chosen for her. Onegin comments patronizingly to Tatyana on the limitations of the world she inhabits; then they retire, leaving Lensky to voice his happiness with Olga. Mrs Larina and the nurse return to invite everybody indoors, and notice that Onegin and Tatyana are missing. As the couple re-enter, the nurse sees that Tatyana is under Onegin's spell. Scene 2: That night, as Filippevna helps her prepare for bed, Tatyana asks about the nurse's past, then suddenly confesses she is in love. Requesting writing material and dismissing the nurse, she writes to Onegin declaring her love. By the time she has finished it is morning, and she begs the nurse to send her grandson to deliver the letter. Scene 3: A few days later Onegin returns to give his reply; Tatyana

Illustration by M. V. Dobwinsky of the duel in Eugene Onegin

flees into the garden, where he rejects her confession with appalling, if unintended, condescension, telling her, in effect, to grow up. Tatyana is humiliated.

Act II Scene 1: Mrs Larina is holding a name-day party for Tatyana. A number of military men are present, as well as Lensky and Onegin. The latter is bored with the occasion, annoyed with Lensky for having brought him, and to get his revenge flirts with Olga by dancing with her. Olga abets him. Triquet, a Frenchman, sings some couplets he has written in Tatyana's honour, to her great embarrassment. During the following mazurka Onegin continues his flirtation with Olga; subsequently the two men exchange words, Lensky becoming increasingly heated until he loses his self-control and denounces Onegin. The guests have to separate them. Lensky rushes out, bidding farewell for ever to Olga, who faints. Scene 2: Next morning on a riverbank Lensky and his second, Zaretsky, are awaiting Onegin. Lensky sings of his love for Olga. Onegin arrives late, bringing his valet, Guillot, as his second. Lensky and Onegin reflect separately on the situation in which they are caught. Preparations for the duel are completed; Onegin fires and Lensky falls dead. Onegin is horrified at what he has done.

Act III Scene 1: In a splendid St Petersburg mansion Onegin is watching other guests dance a polonaise. After the duel he had left the area and some years have passed, but he remains troubled by what he has done, and bored with the society he finds himself in. An *écossaise* is danced; the arrival of Princess Gremina is announced. When she enters on her elderly husband's arm Onegin recognizes Tatyana. Prince Gremin tells Onegin of his love for Tatyana, then introduces his wife to him. Tatyana cuts short the meeting by pleading fatigue, and she and Gremin leave. Onegin confesses his love for Tatyana and leaves as the *écossaise* is resumed. Scene 2: The last encounter between Onegin and Tatyana takes place at her home. She enters distraught, holding the most recent of his letters. Onegin rushes in and falls on his knees. She reminds him how he had rejected her, and asks bitterly whether it is her new status that has induced Onegin to lay siege to her now. She reflects how close happiness had once been for both of them, but says firmly she will remain faithful to her husband. Telling him to go, she confesses she still loves him. He embraces her, but she orders him out. In despair he leaves.

Pushkin's verse novel had concerned itself with the clash between the decadent mores of an opulent St Petersburg society and the simple, wholesome ways of a rural family. However, though the dance scenes (the rural 'hop' of Tatyana's name-day party with its boisterous, unsophisticated dances, and the ballroom scene with its grand polonaise) define this social divide, Tchaikovsky's attention was focused implacably on the pain and suffering endured by individuals whose relationships are twisted or destroyed by the differences of these worlds. The opera's greatest riches lie not in these two tableaux nor in the slightly rambling first scene which establishes both the base for later events and, in the peasant choruses, the thoroughly Russian milieu, but in the intimate encounters of the remaining four scenes, where Tchaikovsky realizes with supreme sensitivity the inner worlds of his characters.

Though Lensky is simply a country squire who has been to university, and his music has at first no more than youthful freshness, when he is about to face Onegin's pistol a depth of pain is revealed that is deeply affecting. Much of Onegin himself remains concealed behind a mask of aloof sophistication until the belated awakening of his love for Tatyana suddenly exposes his helplessness when he becomes the victim of an irrepressible and truthful emotion. Tatyana's transformation, from the ingenuous but deeply serious adolescent of her great letter scene into the mature yet desperately unhappy woman who finally dismisses the man she loves, is disclosed with supreme mastery. The creation of Tatyana is the greatest single achievement of all Tchaikovsky's operas.

Nor should his deft handling of lesser roles be overlooked; the old nurse, Filippevna, the adoring husband, Gremin, and the 'very insipid' (Tachaikovsky's own words) Olga are all very clearly projected.

RECORDINGS 1. Kruglikova, Antonova, Kozlovsky, Nortzov, Mikhailov, Bolshoi Theatre Ch and O, Melik-Pashayev, Melodiya, 1948; 2. Vishnevskaya, Avdeyeva, Lemeshev, Belov, Petrov, Bolshoi Theatre Ch and O, Khaikin, Melodiya/Parlophone, 1956; 3. Kubiak, Hamari,

Burrows, Weikl, Ghiaurov, Covent Garden Ch and O, Solti, Decca, 1970: the two Russian sets present idiomatic, ensemble performance. The 1956 is a classic version, now on CD, superbly conducted by Khaikin with the young Vishnevskaya an ideal Tatyana. The Decca version is only for those who must have a stereo recording. (It is also available as a soundtrack for a Decca video in Peter Weigl's film.) [A.B.]

VIDEO   Freni, Dvorsky, Brendel, Ghiaurov, Chicago Lyric Opera Ch and O, Bartoletti, Castle, 1985

EDITIONS   f.ss., Jurgenson, 1880; *PSS*, vol. 4, 1948; v.ss., Jurgenson, 1880; (with libretto in English by David Lloyd-Jones), Schauer and May, 1971

The Maid of Orleans

Orleanskaya Dyeva

Opera in four acts (six scenes) (3h)

Libretto by the composer, after the translation by Vasily Zhukovsky of the tragedy *Die Jungfrau von Orleans* by Johann Christoph Friedrich von Schiller (1801)

Composed December 1878–September 1879; rev. 1882

PREMIERES   25 February 1881, Mariinsky Theatre, St Petersburg; UK: 22 February 1978, Collegiate Theatre, London; US: 2 July 1991, Metropolitan, New York (Bolshoi Opera)

CAST   Joan of Arc *s* or *ms*, Charles VII *t*, Agnès Sorel *s*, Dunois *bar*, Lionel *bar*, *s*, *t*, 5 *b*; *satb* chorus of young girls, angels, French folk, minstrels, courtiers; ballet

FULL ORCHESTRA including organ and banda

Tchaikovsky started work on *The Maid of Orleans* in December 1878 in Florence, beginning with the scene of Joan's recognition towards the end of Act II. Though Schiller was his main source (and where possible he used lines taken directly from Zhukovsky's translation), Tchaikovsky incorporated ideas from other writers, added some elements of his own (most of the choruses, for instance), then wrote his own libretto just ahead of composition. He completed the sketches in Paris less than three months later, though the scoring took a further four months: feeling that some of his earlier orchestration had been too detailed to be telling in the opera house, Tchaikovsky conducted a thorough review of his methods before scoring this opera.

Because of financial constraints the staging of the opera was totally inadequate, though a good musical performance ensured the work a warm reception. But despite revival in the following two seasons and revision (notably cuts) by Tchaikovsky, it was never given again in Russia during the composer's lifetime. The Prague performances of 1882 marked its only contemporary production abroad and the first production of a Tchaikovsky opera outside Russia.

SYNOPSIS

Act I   Joan is torn between the rival claims of a normal life and a sense of divine mission. But news of two French defeats and the siege of Orleans by the English decides her; she foretells the death of the English leader, Salisbury, which is forthwith confirmed, then leads the people in a prayer for victory and peace. Alone, she sadly bids farewell to her familiar world. A heavenly choir confirms her calling and predicts that she will save France.

Act II   At Chinon King Charles has been demoralized by the disasters that are facing France, and, despite the knight Dunois's exhortation, wishes for nothing except the love of his mistress, Agnès Sorel. By now Joan has led the French army to a great victory, and she comes before the king. Having observed further evidence of Joan's powers of second sight, and heard from her of her past – of how the Virgin had appeared and revealed to her her destiny to free France and crown him in Rheims the king entrusts his armies to her leadership and she receives the archbishop's blessing.

Act III   Scene 1: On the battlefield Joan encounters and vanquishes a Burgundian knight, Lionel, who has changed sides, but who now falls in love with her and rejoins the French. Joan reciprocates his feelings. Scene 2: Joan leads the king to his coronation in Rheims Cathedral, but her own father denounces her as an agent of the devil. Since she refuses to answer his question – 'Is she pure and holy?' – all turn against her, and she recoils from Lionel. She is banished.

Act IV   Scene 1: Still torn between her love for Lionel and her mission, Joan meets him, but their rapture is shattered by the heavenly choir condemning her. They are discovered by a group of English soldiers. Lionel dies defending Joan, and she allows herself to be taken. Scene 2: In Rouen Joan is led to the stake.

The Maid of Orleans is the dullest of Tchaikovsky's surviving operas; it is also one of the most flawed dramatically. Its problems stem partly from Tchaikovsky's determination to adopt the overblown manners of French grand opera, partly from the numbed condition of his creative faculties after the traumatic events of 1877, but also from his debasement of the character of Joan. Schiller had seen her as an innocent, momentarily tempted by love for Lionel, but expiating this by self-denial and death on the battlefield; Tchaikovsky permits her to indulge her love, then die in religious ecstasy. But if the tasteless sentimentality of this final view of his heroine sits easily with the equally contrived (though skilfully executed) attempt to rouse the spectator with orchestral tumult, grandiose choruses, and lavish spectacle (especially in the coronation scene), the opera has some worthwhile passages: the charming – and very Russian – girls' chorus that opens Act I, and Joan's farewell aria near its end, some of the ballet music (especially the tumblers' dance) and some portions of the king's and (especially) Agnès Sorel's music in Act II (above all, their united G flat conclusion), and portions of the extensive scenes for Joan and Lionel. The finest music is unquestionably Joan's unaffected, yet at times visionary, narration in Act II, even though here she seems less close, perhaps, to the historical Joan than to Tatyana in *Eugene Onegin*. It confirms that Tchaikovsky saw this heroine less as a figure of destiny than a victim of fate.

RECORDING   Arkhipova, Radchenko, Makhov, Yakovenko, Valaitis, Moscow Radio Ch and O, Rozhdestvensky, Melodiya/HMV, 1971

EDITIONS f.ss., Jurgenson, 1902; *PSS*, vols 5A and B, 1964; v.ss., Jurgenson, 1880; *PSS*, vol. 37, 1963

Mazepa
Mazepa

Opera in three acts (six scenes) (2h 45m)
Libretto by the composer and Viktor Burenin, after the epic poem *Poltava* by Aleksandr Pushkin (1829)
Composed summer 1881–April 1883
PREMIERES 15 February 1884, Bolshoi Theatre, Moscow; UK: 6 August 1888, Liverpool (Russian touring company); US: 14 December 1922, Boston Opera House (Ukrainian touring company)
CAST Mazepa *bar*, Kochubei *b*, Lyubov Kochubei *ms*, Mariya *s*, Andrei *t*, Orlik *b*, Iskra *t*, Drunken Cossack *t*; *satb* chorus of young girls, Cossacks, guests, Kochubei's servants, Mazepa's bodyguards, monks, executioners
ORCHESTRATION picc, 3 fl, 2 ob, ca, 2 cl, 2 bsn, 4 hn, 2 cornets, 2 tpt, 3 trbn, tuba, timp, perc, hp, str; onstage: banda

In 1709 the bid of the Cossack hetman, Mazepa, to gain Ukrainian independence from Russia ended in the defeat of himself and Charles XII of Sweden by Peter the Great at Poltava. This was one theme of Pushkin's *Poltava*; the other was the romantic relationship, also based on fact, of the elderly Mazepa with his own goddaughter, Mariya (Mazepa's apocryphal ride bound to a wild horse is ignored by Pushkin, though it conditioned part of Tchaikovsky's orchestral introduction). Viktor Burenin's libretto, drawn from Pushkin's epic poem, had been prepared for Karl Davidov, but he had made little progress and in 1881 Tchaikovsky asked Davidov to assign it to him. Over the next year he composed a few numbers, but systematic composition did not begin until an enforced seven-week stay on a friend's country estate in the summer of 1882. The sketches were completed in late September, but because of the extra attention Tchaikovsky had been giving to the special problems of scoring for the opera house, this operation was protracted, and it was April the following year before the opera was ready. By now Tchaikovsky's reputation in his native Russia was such that the Imperial Theatres in both Russia's leading cities competed for the piece, and it opened in St Petersburg only three days after its Moscow premiere. In both productions the staging was excellent, the performance at least adequate, and the opera enjoyed some success. But though it was also produced in Tiflis in 1885, *Mazepa* failed to secure a place in the repertoire.

SYNOPSIS

Act I Scene 1: Mariya, Kochubei's daughter, is in love with Mazepa and gently rejects the advances of Andrei. Meanwhile Kochubei is entertaining Mazepa, who asks for Mariya's hand. Kochubei is horrified because of their difference in age, but Mazepa protests his love – and he knows Mariya shares his feelings. A quarrel grows. Mariya agonizes over the choice she will have to make between her parents and her beloved. But when finally Mazepa demands she choose, in terrible agitation she leaves with him. Scene 2: Lyubov, Mariya's mother, exhorts her husband to move directly against Mazepa, but

Kochubei has a better plan. Mazepa has confided to him his scheme to join the Swedish king against Peter the Great in the cause of Ukrainian independence; now Kochubei will inform the tsar. Andrei begs to be sent as messenger, despite all the risks. All join in a chorus of hate against Mazepa.

Act II Scene 1: In a dungeon beneath Mazepa's castle Kochubei is chained to the wall. The tsar has not believed his accusations against Mazepa, and has delivered him and his associate, Iskra, into Mazepa's hands. He is to be executed the next day. Mazepa's henchman, Orlik, enters to interrogate him further, for he has not disclosed where his secret treasure is. Bitterly Kochubei tells Orlik to ask Mariya; she will show him everything. Orlik summons the torturer. Scene 2: In the castle Mazepa is comparing the calm of the night with the turmoil within his own soul. Kochubei must die – but how will Mariya react when she discovers all that has happened? Orlik enters to tell him Kochubei will not give away, and Mazepa confirms the execution. Mariya appears and reproaches him for being so preoccupied. Pressed by her, he reveals his plans for a free Ukraine; soon, he says, he could occupy a throne. Mariya is excited at the prospect and vows she will die with him if necessary. He then asks how she would act if required to choose between her husband and father. Totally ignorant of her father's plight, she affirms her choice would be for Mazepa. Mazepa leaves, deeply troubled. Lyubov quietly slips in. When she realizes her daughter knows nothing of what has happened, she discloses the situation. As the appalling truth dawns upon Mariya a march is heard offstage; the execution is already beginning. The two women rush out to try to prevent it. Scene 3: At the place of execution a crowd has gathered; a drunken Cossack is reproved for untimely merriment. The execution procession enters. Kochubei and Iskra kneel to pray, then mount the scaffold. The people crowd round, and the axes fall as Mariya and Lyubov rush in.

Act III The Battle of Poltava (depicted in a symphonic tableau using the well-known 'Slava' folktune) has been fought. Andrei enters the ruined garden of Kochubei's house. He had been searching for Mazepa; now, painfully, he recognizes where he is. Mazepa and Orlik enter as fugitives, and Andrei confronts Mazepa, but is fatally wounded. Mariya, now demented, emerges into the moonlight. There follows a mad scene. Finally Orlik persuades Mazepa to leave without her. Mariya perceives the dying Andrei, thinking he is a child, and cradling his head in her lap, sings him to sleep, staring blankly in front of her.

Though uneven and unashamedly melodramatic, *Mazepa* is one of Tchaikovsky's best operas. As in the Pushkin-based *Eugene Onegin*, its finest passages are those which focus on the predicaments and feelings of one or two characters; like Tatyana and Onegin in the earlier opera, Mariya and Mazepa are seen as victims of fate. Especially impressive is the dungeon scene at the opening of Act II, virtually a grim monologue for Kochubei which drew from

Tchaikovsky some of the darkest music he ever wrote. In complete contrast Mazepa's musings on the night and his love aria in the next scene are remarkably beautiful, while the ensuing love duet is tender, yet reveals much of the other emotions that affect the spirited Mariya and tormented Mazepa. The following encounter between Mariya and her mother is also admirably handled. Though the first scene sprawls, the full choral sections in this and the following scene being no more than efficiently conventional, the execution scene is splendidly taut and as fine as any of Tchaikovsky's crowd scenes (its first part, using two folksongs and labelled 'folk scene', is self-consciously national in flavour). The characters of Kochubei and Lyubov are well projected, but as in *Onegin*, it is the young tragic heroine who most engaged Tchaikovsky's creative sympathies, while Mazepa fades in interest. The final mad scene for Mariya is deeply affecting. The opera had originally concluded with Mariya's suicide and a crowded stage, but for the 1885 revival Tchaikovsky cut this, extending Mariya's lullaby instead. It is an ending whose pathos is absolutely right.

RECORDING Milashkina, Arkhipova, Mazurok, Atlantov, Eizen, Bolshoi Ch and O, Zhuraitis, Melodiya, 1970s
EDITIONS f.ss., Jurgenson, 1899; *PSS*, vols 6A and B, 1969; v.ss., Jurgenson, 1883; *PSS*, vol. 38, 1968

The Enchantress

Charodeika
Opera in four acts (3h)
Libretto by Ippolit Vasilevich Shpazhinsky after his own play (1885)
Composed October 1885–May 1887
PREMIERE 1 November 1887, Mariinsky Theatre, St Petersburg
CAST Prince Nikita *bar*, Princess Evpraksiya *ms*, Prince Yuri *t*, Mamïrov *b*, Nenila *ms*, Nastasya ('Kuma') *s*, Kudma *bar*, *s*, 3 *t*, *bar*, 2 *b-bar*, *b*; *satb* chorus of guests, male peasants, young girls, servants, huntsmen; ballet
FULL ORCHESTRA onstage: 4 hn

Early in 1885 Tchaikovsky's brother Modest directed his attention to a new play, *The Enchantress*, by Ippolit Shpazhinsky. Tchaikovsky read it and promptly requested its author to prepare a libretto. Shpazhinsky proved dilatory, however, and it was the autumn before Tchaikovsky could start composition. His enthusiasm for the subject remained and mostly the music came easily, though there were delays, partly because Tchaikovsky soon realized the projected five-act structure would be overlong and required revision. The sketches were completed on 30 August 1886, but when Tchaikovsky began scoring he realized it was still too long. Further cuts proved necessary during rehearsals. Though the premiere seemed a success, by the seventh performance the house was only half full, the audiences' disappointment was reflected in the press, and the opera was dropped after 12 performances. It was mounted in Tiflis in 1887, and given once in Moscow in 1890; otherwise it was not heard again in the composer's lifetime.

SYNOPSIS
Act I Guests are enjoying themselves in the courtyard of the inn of Nastasya, known as 'Kuma' ('Gossip'), on the banks of the river Oka near Nizhni-Novgorod. Yuri and huntsmen pass along the river – and it is clear Kuma is already secretly in love with the young prince. Yuri's father, the severe Prince Nikita, comes to investigate for himself the iniquities said to take place at Kuma's hostelry. But when he arrives with the puritanical old deacon, Mamïrov, he falls under the spell of the 'enchantress'. Kuma orders a tumbler's dance to entertain the prince and, at Kuma's suggestion, the prince compels an enraged Mamïrov to join in.

Act II In the garden of Nikita's house Mamïrov, wanting revenge for his humiliation, tells Princess Evpraksiya, Nikita's wife, that Kuma has bewitched her husband and become his mistress. The princess swears to be rid of Kuma. Yuri is upset at the discord he sees between his parents, and Nikita is torn between the distress he is causing his wife and his feelings for Kuma. When his wife attacks him for his relationship with Kuma, a furious quarrel develops. After Yuri has calmed a crowd that alleges his father's servants have robbed them, the princess reappears, and Yuri learns of his father's visits to Kuma. Now knowing the cause of dissension between his parents, he swears to kill Kuma.

Act III In Kuma's cottage Nikita tries to woo her, but she avoids his advances and finally confesses she loves another. He attempts to force himself on her, but she snatches a knife, saying she would rather die than submit. In rage he leaves. Kuma is warned of Yuri's vow. Left alone, she sees Yuri in the courtyard. But when he enters the house and discovers her, he is stopped short by her beauty. Using all her human charms, she works upon him. Gradually he feels pity for her, then passion. Their duet ends in mutual commitment.

Act IV On the banks of the Oka Yuri is to meet Kuma with whom he plans to elope. His mother, who believes Kuma has bewitched her son, comes disguised as a pilgrim to get from the wizard, Kudma, a deadly poison to kill the 'enchantress'. Kuma arrives in a boat with friends, bids them farewell, and sings of her love for Yuri. The princess tricks Kuma into drinking the poison. Soon after Yuri re-enters Kuma feels faint, the princess throws off her disguise, Kuma dies, and Yuri denounces his mother. Nikita appears, having heard of the intended elopement. Yuri accuses him of causing Kuma's death, and Nikita stabs him. The princess throws herself on Yuri's body, and is borne away with it. To the sound of the rising storm and the wizard's laughter, the prince goes mad.

One reading of the plot is sufficient to show why *The Enchantress* could never be a success; it is the more ironic, therefore, that this was the first libretto that Tchaikovsky ever commissioned himself and even more sad, considering he expended so much worthwhile music on it. He seems to have been attracted to the subject because he saw it as proclaiming the redeeming power of love; Kuma is

Set design by Viktor Vasnetsov for The Enchantress *(Moscow, 1890)*

transformed into a higher being by her love for Yuri. In addition he clearly detected parallels between *The Enchantress* and Bizet's *Carmen* (after *Don Giovanni* his favourite Western opera). *The Enchantress* is most notable for two scenes: the colourful opening, in which there is a splendid resurgence of Tchaikovsky's most national vein, and the extensive love scene in Act III, where the slowly changing relationship of Kuma and Yuri is charted in music that is as psychologically illuminating as it is beautiful. As in Tchaikovsky's three previous operas, it is the young, tragic heroine who has most engaged his creative sympathies.

RECORDING Glushkova, Simonova, Klenov, Kuznetsov, Ch and O of Moscow Radio, Provatorov, Melodiya, 1970s
EDITIONS f.ss., Jurgenson, 1901; *PSS*, vols 8A and B, 1949; v.ss., Jurgenson, 1887; *PSS*, vol. 40, 1949

The Queen of Spades

Pikovaya dama
Opera in three acts (seven scenes), Op. 68 (2h 45m)
Libretto by Modest Tchaikovsky and the composer, after the novel by Aleksandr Pushkin (1834); with incorporations from Pyotr Karabanov (the pastoral interlude in Scene 3), Vasily Zhukovsky and Konstantin Batyushkov
Composed January–June 1890
PREMIERES 19 December 1890, Mariinsky Theatre, St Petersburg; US: 5 March 1910, Metropolitan, New York (in German); UK: 29 May 1915, London Opera House, London

CAST Herman *t*, Count Tomsky (also Zlatogor) *bar*, Prince Eletsky *bar*, Chekalinsky *t*, Surin *b*, Chaplitsky *t*, Narumov *b*, Master of Ceremonies *t*, the Countess *ms*, Liza *s*, Polina (also Milovzor) *a*, Governess *ms*, Masha *s*, Prilepa *s*, Child-commander *spoken role*; *satb* chorus of nurses and governesses, boys, promenaders, girls, guests and gamblers; offstage: church choir
ORCHESTRATION picc, 2 fl, 2 ob, ca, 2 cl, b cl, 2 bsn, 4 hn, 2 tpt, 3 trbn, tuba, hp, pf, timp, perc, str; onstage: tpt, sd, children's tpts and drums

Pushkin's ironic, yet chilling short novel, *The Queen of Spades*, is a masterpiece of clarity and conciseness, and an almost ideal basis for a libretto. In fact, Tchaikovsky had disclaimed any interest in the subject when in 1887 his brother, Modest, had started drawing from it a libretto for Nikolay Klenovsky. But Modest had turned the piece into a romantic melodrama, and in the autumn of 1889, after Klenovsky had made little or no progress, Tchaikovsky himself was attracted to it. Because it was hoped to produce the opera during the following season, in January 1890 he settled in Florence where he could work undisturbed; the only problem was delays occasioned by Modest, who was completing the libretto back in Russia. The sketches were finished on 15 March and the scoring was begun in Rome on 9 April. So close was Tchaikovsky's identification with his central character, Herman, that he confessed he had wept while composing his death scene, and he was pleased with his friends' enthusiasm when he played the opera through to some of them on his return to Russia. Even more was he delighted with the response of Nikolay Figner, then the darling of the St Petersburg operatic public, who was to create the role of Herman. The premiere was splendidly mounted and performed, and was highly successful, though critical reaction was less approving, and the pregnancy of Medea Figner, Nikolay's wife, who created the part of Liza, meant the opera was suspended from the repertoire two months later.

The Queen of Spades was first produced in Kiev only 12 days after the St Petersburg premiere, and in Moscow on 16 November 1891. By this time critical reaction was becoming more favourable; in 1892 it was mounted in Odessa and Saratov and also in Prague.

SYNOPSIS

Act I The opera is set in St Petersburg in the late 18th century. Scene 1: In the Summer Garden, while others stroll and children play at soldiers, Chekalinsky, a gambler, and Surin, an officer, discuss Herman; this officer of German extraction obsessively watches others gamble, but will not join in. To a third officer, Tomsky, Herman confesses he is in love, though he does not know the lady's name. Eletsky is congratulated by Chekalinsky and Surin on his engagement. Asked who his fiancée is, the prince points to Liza, who has just entered with her grandmother, the old Countess. Herman is in despair, for Liza is his secret beloved. Tomsky tells how in her youth in Paris the old Countess had lost heavily at cards. To restore her fortune St Germain, at the price of a 'rendezvous', had given her the secret of three cards that would always win. She had confided the secret to her husband and one of her lovers, but then a ghost had appeared to her, telling her she would die at the hand of a third man who would come as a lover to wring it from her. Herman rejects the temptation this offers. He vows Eletsky shall never have Liza. Scene 2: In her room Liza and her friend Polina are entertaining some other girls. Liza, however, is very preoccupied. The others try to raise her spirits, but the governess bustles in to reprove them for unbecoming merriment. Left alone Liza reflects on her secret obsession. And suddenly that obsession is standing before her: Herman has entered through the balcony's open door. Liza is confused, but Herman begins to plead with her. He is interrupted when the Countess is heard outside, and he hides. The old woman wants to know why Liza is still dressed; she orders her to bed, then leaves. Herman emerges muttering the ghost's words, then resumes his declaration of love. Liza finally yields.

Act II Scene 1: In a great hall a masked ball is in progress. After the others have withdrawn while the room is prepared for the interlude, the prince asks Liza why she is out of spirits, and reaffirms his love. Herman enters carrying a letter from Liza: he is to meet her after the interlude. The guests are invited to witness the story of Prilepa and her rival lovers, the poor Milovzor and the wealthy Zlatogor. When this pastoral interlude is over Liza slips Herman a key; next day he is to come to her room where everything

will be settled. But Herman insists he will come that night. The master of ceremonies suddenly announces the empress herself is approaching. All line up to receive her. Scene 2: Herman surveys the Countess's empty bedroom. Midnight strikes. On hearing footsteps he hides. The Countess's maids lead their mistress through into her dressing room and Liza passes on to her own room. Prepared for bed, the old woman chooses to sit in a chair, muses to herself, then dismisses her maids. Herman emerges and tries to persuade her to reveal her secret, then draws a pistol and threatens her. She dies of fright. Liza returns from her room, and realizes how Herman has been using her. Desperately hurt and enraged, she dismisses him.

Act III Scene 1: In his room, to the distant sounds of trumpet calls and a church choir, Herman recalls with horror how he had gone to gaze on the Countess's body in her open coffin – and how the corpse had winked at him. Suddenly there is a noise outside, and the Countess's ghost enters. She has come to give him the secret of the three cards: 'Three . . . seven . . . ace!' Scene 2: Liza, still in love with Herman, has begged him to meet her beside the Winter Canal at midnight. Finally he appears, and they sing of their mutual love. But when she asks him to leave with her, he wants only to go to the gambling table. She realizes that he no longer recognizes her, and throws herself into the canal. Scene 3: In a gambling house, Eletsky has joined the others. Tomsky entertains the company with a song, and as play resumes Herman appears, announcing he wants to play for a very high stake. Choosing three, he wins, then stakes his winnings. Playing on seven, he wins again. When he insists on playing a third time, Eletsky demands to play against him. Herman stakes on ace, but when he picks up his card it is the queen of spades – and the Countess's ghost passes across the stage, smiling. Herman stabs himself, and begs Eletsky's forgiveness. The male chorus prays for the peace of his soul.

Tchaikovsky himself invented the sixth (Winter Canal) scene of *The Queen of Spades*, arguing that the audience would need to know what had happened to Liza. In fact, his decision was also a measure of how completely Modest's libretto had transformed Pushkin's objectively observed characters into hot-blooded mortals. Pushkin had been able to let Liza slip away almost casually, but the opera's audience was bound to identify closely with her and demand to know her destiny. There can be no doubt that it was this 'humanizing' of Pushkin's tale that made it attractive to Tchaikovsky.

The opera uniquely reverses Tchaikovsky's normal preference, for this time it is Herman, a male character, who gripped him. Nor among the female characters is his chief fascination with the young doomed woman, but rather with the aged and totally unsympathetic Countess whose presence, because she is not only a victim but also the agent of fate (for by her own death she achieves fate's purpose), looms over them all. The work is also unique for its extreme stylistic dichotomy, for it incorporates a very large

The Countess, played by Mariya Slavina, and her maids in The Queen of Spades *(St Petersburg, 1890)*

element of rococo pastiche (there are even two substantial quotations from other composers – the aria the Countess sings to herself in Act II from Grétry's *Richard Coeur-de-lion* (1784), and a polonaise by Jósef Kozlowski (1791) to end the ballroom scene) – which contrasts savagely with the dark, mysterious, sometimes sinister music to which the tragic destinies of the three main characters run their course. Even more, perhaps, than in *Eugene Onegin* it is the more intimate scenes that make this opera memorable, especially the scene in the Countess's bedroom; only the dungeon scene in *Mazepa* can match this for its harrowing intensity. But that had had a single dramatic concern – the suffering of Kochubei; this one manifests a complete mastery in projecting a changing dramatic and psychological situation. If Tatyana's letter scene in *Eugene Onegin* is the most moving scene in all Tchaikovsky's operas, this one is the most totally gripping.

RECORDINGS   1. Smolenskaya, Borisenko, Verbitskaya, Nelepp, Lisitsian, Ivanov, Bolshoi Ch and O, Melik-Pashayev, Melodiya, 1957; 2. Milashkina, Arkhipova, Levko, Andzhaparidzye, Mazurok, Kiselev, Bolshoi Ch and O, Khaikin, Melodiya, 1967; 3. Vishnevskaya, Schwarz, Resnik, Gougaloff, Weikl, Iordachescu, Tchaikovsky and French Women's Ch, ORTF O, Rostropovich, DG, 1976; 4. Evstatieva, Dilova, Ochman, Konsulov, Mazurok, Obretenov National Ch, Sofia Festival O, Tchakarov, Sony, 1990; 5. Freni, Ciesinski, Atlantov, Leiferkus, Hvorostovsky, Tanglewood Festival Ch, Boston SO, Ozawa, RCA, 1992: although a great rarity, the Melik-Pashayev set is the most exciting and most authentically performed version. The Khaikin maintains the Bolshoi tradition but is not as well performed. The Rostropovich version, in stereo, is vividly conducted but erratically sung. The Tchakarov and Ozawa

sets are both rewarding, thoughtful performances in excellent sound [A.B.]

EDITIONS   f.ss., Jurgenson, 1891; *PSS*, vol. 10, 1953; v.ss., Jurgenson, 1890; *PSS*, vol. 42, 1953; (with English libretto by Rosa Newmarch), Schirmer [n.d.]

Iolanthe
Iolanta

Lyric opera in one act, Op. 69 (1h 30m)
Libretto by Modest Tchaikovsky, after the translation by Vladimir Zotov of the play *Kong Renés datter* (*King René's Daughter*) by Henrik Hertz (1864)
Composed July–December 1891
PREMIERES   18 December 1892, Mariinsky Theatre, St Petersburg; UK: 20 March 1968, St Pancras Town Hall, London; US: 10 September 1933, Garden Theatre, Scarborough-on-Hudson
CAST   King René of Provence *b*, Robert *bar*, Vaudemont *t*, Ebn-Hakir *bar*, Iolanta *s, s, ms, a, t, b*; *satb* chorus of Iolanta's friends and attendants, king's entourage, Robert's followers
FULL ORCHESTRA

Tchaikovsky had first read Hertz's one-act play in 1883, but his decision that he would some time make an opera out of it seems to date from five years later, when he saw it staged. Then in 1890 the Imperial Theatres commissioned a two-act ballet (*Nutcracker*) and a one-act opera to make a double-bill. Having first sketched the ballet, he initially felt some ambivalence when he set about *Iolanta*, though subsequently he warmed to it. As in *The Queen of Spades*, the Figners were to sing leading roles, and by now it was certain that the premiere would be at least a *succès d'estime*. But the press bluntly judged the music weak, mauled Modest's libretto, and the double-bill survived only 11 performances. However the first foreign production of *Iolanta* by itself (in Hamburg) opened only 16 days after the Russian premiere, and the work has enjoyed some success abroad.

SYNOPSIS
In 15th-century Provence Iolanta, the daughter of King René, is blind, but does not know she is different from other people. Her attendants are forbidden to mention light, nor is any outsider to enter the garden on pain of death. Iolanta is betrothed to Robert, Duke of Burgundy, and by keeping her from the outside world her father has hoped to hide her disability from him until she is cured. A great Moorish physician, Ebn-Hakir, examines her, but tells René a cure is possible only if his daughter longs to see the light – and for this to happen she must be told of her blindness. Robert arrives with his friend Vaudemont, a Burgundian knight. Robert loves another, but when Vaudemont sees Iolanta he is entranced by her. When she is unable to tell red roses from white, he realizes the truth – and Iolanta is now also aware she is not as others are. 'What is light?' she asks. 'The creator's first gift to his world,' Vaudemont replies. When René returns he is appalled, but Ebn-Hakir perceives that the condition for cure now exists. Suddenly René himself sees how he can rouse his daughter's will to see; Vaudemont has entered the garden without permission, and if Iolanta is not cured, he will die, the king declares. At this Iolanta goes off with Ebn-Hakir. When she returns she can see; meanwhile Robert has admitted that his affections really lie elsewhere, and Vaudemont is discovered to be a suitable match for Iolanta. All rejoice.

The refinement and craft displayed in *Iolanta* is very high; its prime weakness lies in the quality of its musical materials. Yet it is not a work that should be lightly rejected any more than *The Enchantress*. This alone among Tchaikovsky's previous operas had been concerned with something more than human drama, and *Iolanta* also has a message. In *The Enchantress* it had been 'love is the redeeming power'; in *Iolanta* it is 'love is the healing power'. Dramatically the fatal flaw of the latter is that Iolanta is not truly driven by an ideal but by the fright her father gives her, while musically Tchaikovsky failed to catch the transcendent tone of this message. He is more successful with the human elements in the story, and his portrayal of the king and Ebn-Hakir is good. But it is Iolanta – yet another of his young, vulnerable heroines – who really captured his creative heart. As in his five previous operas, the scene with which he had started composition drew the best music from him, and the love duet, shorter but as carefully designed as that of *The Enchantress*, contains the opera's best – sometimes excellent – music.

RECORDING Sorokina, Nesterenko, Mazurok, Atlantov, Valaitis, Bolshoi Ch and O, Ermler, Melodiya/HMV, 1978
EDITIONS f.ss., Jurgenson, 1892; *PSS*, vol. 10, 1953; v.ss., Jurgenson, 1892; *PSS*, vol. 42, 1953

BIBLIOGRAPHY Gerald Abraham, 'Tchaikovsky's Operas', in Gerald Abraham (ed.), *Tchaikovsky: A Symposium*, Drummond, 1945; rev. reprint in Gerald Abraham, *Slavonic and Romantic Music*, Faber, 1968; David Brown, *Tchaikovsky: A Biographical and Critical Study*, 4 vols, Gollancz, 1978–91; Edward Garden, *Tchaikovsky*, Dent (Master Musicians series), 1973; John Warrack, *Tchaikovsky*, Hamilton, 1973; *rp*, 1989

D.B.

ALEKSANDR TCHEREPNIN
Aleksandr Nikolayevich Tcherepnin; *b* 21 January 1899, St Petersburg; *d* 29 September 1977, Paris

Son of Nikolay, Aleksandr Tcherepnin was an infant prodigy. A modernist who defied classification, his First Symphony caused a scandal in Paris in 1926. He devised new modes and a system of counterpoint, and has a scale named after him. He wrote a completion of Musorgsky's *The Marriage*. He taught and travelled in the Far East and started a publishing house in Tokyo. In 1948 he settled in America. His musical language combines Eastern and Western elements; his last opera, *The Farmer and the Nymph*, even employs Chinese folksongs and traditional instruments.

Operatic works: *01-01*, 1928, rev. 1934; *Die Hochzeit der Sobeide*, 1933; *Die Heirat* (completion of Musorgsky), 1937; *The Farmer and the Nymph*, 1952
BIBLIOGRAPHY W. Reich, *A. Tcherepnin*, Felix Alcan, 1970

J.G.

NIKOLAY TCHEREPNIN
Nikolay Nikolayevich Tcherepnin; *b* 15 May 1873, St Petersburg; *d* 26 June 1945, Issy-les-Moulineaux, nr Paris

Tcherepnin was strongly influenced by his teacher Rimsky-Korsakov and supervised the Parisian premiere of *The Golden Cockerel*. Diaghilev engaged him to conduct the first season of the Ballets Russes, for which he wrote the successful ballets, *Le pavillon d'Armide* and *Narcisse et Echo*. In 1918, Tcherepnin directed the conservatory in Tbilisi, but soon settled in Paris, where Pavlova commissioned more ballet scores from him. In 1923, he made the first completion of Musorgsky's *Sorochintsy Fair*, though this has been superseded by Shebalin's more authentic treatment. His music is of the Franco-Russian tradition, drawing on Rimsky, Debussy and Ravel, though his operas, *Swat* (1930), after Ostrovsky, and *Vanka* (1935), written in exile, are the most nostalgically nationalist of all his works.

BIBLIOGRAPHY M. D. Calvocoressi, *Tcherepnin*, Herbert Jenkins, 1929

J.G.

GEORG PHILIPP TELEMANN
b 14 March 1681, Magdeburg; *d* 25 June 1767, Hamburg

Telemann was the most prolific composer of the first half of the 18th century, and in his day his fame eclipsed all other German composers. His career was centred in Leipzig, Frankfurt am Main, and Hamburg, and generated an enormous catalogue of music in all forms and styles of the period. In addition he was active in these cities as a director of collegia musica and in organizing public concerts. Before commencing his studies (initially in law) at Leipzig University in 1701, Telemann had already advanced far in his knowledge of the theoretical and practical aspects of music, composing his first opera, *Sigismundus*, at the age of 12. His unusual musical talents were soon discovered. The mayor of Leipzig asked Telemann to compose a new cantata every second week for performances in St Thomas's Church. In 1702 Telemann founded a student collegium musicum, which was probably the first to be organized for the purpose of giving public concerts and which remained a distinguishing feature of musical life in Leipzig through most of the century.

The same year Telemann became director of the Leipzig Opera (established in 1693), for which he composed four operas in this period. (According to his autobiography, Telemann continued to compose operas for Leipzig – as many as 20 – sending them from other cities; none of these scores has been preserved.) Between 1705 and 1712 he held court positions at Sorau and later (probably from 1708) at Eisenach. In 1712 Telemann took the position of kantor at the Barfüsskirche in Frankfurt am Main, and soon also accepted a similar position at the Katharinenkirche there.

In 1721 Telemann became kantor of the Johanneum (a distinguished Latin school) in Hamburg, with the attendant responsibility of supplying music for the services of the five main churches: from 1722 he was also music director of the famous Hamburg Opera. Although frequently offered major musical positions elsewhere, he lived in Hamburg for the rest of his life. However, his fame spread throughout Europe and he corresponded with most of the important composers and music theorists of his time. His international reputation was further confirmed by a visit in 1737 to Paris, where his music was performed at court and at the Concerts Spirituels. In Hamburg, in addition to directing the Opera, Telemann also re-established the collegium musicum as a public concert organization.

By the time the Hamburg Opera was forced to close in 1738 Telemann had written at least 20 new scores for the theatre in addition to arranging, adapting, and often composing new music for revivals of operas by Keiser and Handel. Thereafter he wrote no further operas, devoting the remainder of his prolific career to sacred works and, notably, oratorios.

Regrettably Telemann's contribution to opera cannot be fully assessed since few remain out of the more than 40 he composed. The extant scores show Telemann to have left behind the compositional methods associated with the Baroque. There is an intentional shift of style to the popular, and a continuation of the Hamburg composers' tendency towards writing folksong-like tunes. Telemann developed further the innovative writing for orchestra that had already characterized the music of other Hamburg composers, especially Keiser and Graupner. Had more of his operas survived, Telemann would undoubtedly be viewed today as one of the major opera composers of the first half of the 18th century.

Der geduldige Socrates
The Patient Socrates
Comic opera in three acts (4h)
Libretto by Nicolò Minato, translated and adapted by Johann Ulrich von König
PREMIERE 28 January 1721, Theater am Gänsemarkt, Hamburg

Der geduldige Socrates was staged in Hamburg before Telemann had taken up his appointment at the Johanneum. His decision to move there was probably influenced by the city's operatic reputation, established by Keiser, in which he would have been keen to participate.

The central plot concerns Socrates' inability to solve his marital problems with his two wives, Xantippe and Amitta. There is a secondary plot in which an Athenian prince, Melito, is pursued by two young ladies, Rodisette and Edronica, and cannot decide between them for his wife. He comes to Socrates for advice. In Act II, Pitho, a student, brings Socrates a lampoon written against him by Aristophanes, but this leaves Socrates undisturbed. Finally, Socrates solves Melito's problem, pointing to Rodisette as the truer in love, but has still not been able to stop the constant quarrelling between his own wives.

Telemann by G. Lichtensteger

With its combination of serious and comic elements, the opera appealed to contemporary Hamburg taste and was a great success. Duets and ensembles appear alongside solo arias in conventional *da capo* form, and additional variety is provided by the inclusion of a number of German lieder. This contrast permitted sharper characterization of secondary characters (e.g. the inebriated Pitho's drinking songs) while still allowing the principal singers to shine in virtuoso arias.

RECORDING Vámossy, Farkas, Pászthy, Bártfai-Barta, Esswood, de Mey, Gregor, Savaria Vocal Ensemble, Capella Savaria, McGegan, Hungaroton, 1987
EDITIONS f.s., Bernd Baselt (ed.), *G. P. Telemann: Musikalische Werke*, vol. 20, Bärenreiter, 1967; v.s., Deutscher Verlag für Musik, 1966

Pimpinone, oder Die ungleiche Heirat, oder Das herrsch-süchtige Camer-Magden Pimpinone

Pimpinone, or The Unequal Marriage, or The Tyrannical Chambermaid Pimpinone
Lustiges zwischenspiel in three parts (1h 15m)
Libretto by Pietro Pariati, translated and adapted by Johann Philipp Praetorius
PREMIERES 27 September 1725, Theater am Gänsemarkt, Hamburg (between the acts of Telemann's version of Handel's opera, *Tamerlano*); US: 16 April 1939, University of Chicago

The plot of this simple comic intermezzo much resembles the text of Pergolesi's famous intermezzo *La serva padrona*, written eight years later. In Telemann's work Vespetta persuades the rich old Pimpinone to hire her as his maid. She immediately becomes the shrewish wife, while enjoying for herself total freedom from Pimpinone. The music is decidedly Italian in the new buffo style, though, as was the custom, the recitative and some of the arias and duets are in German. There are mock serious arias, highly amusing duets with short phrases, interrupted by rests, and short intrusions of violins. The vocal style often demands changes of register and comic repetitions of single syllables. The work had considerable popularity and a long performance history in Hamburg, and as a result Telemann wrote a sequel, *Die amours der Vespetta* (1727), which is unfortunately lost.

RECORDING Spreckelsen, Nimsgern, Ensemble Florilegium Musicum, Hirsch, Teldec, 1975
EDITIONS f.s., *Das Erber Deutsche Musik*, first series, vol. vi, 1936; v.s., Walter Bergmann (ed.), Schott, 1955

Other surviving operatic works: *Sieg der Schönheit*, 1722 (rev. 1725 and 1732 as *Genserich*); *Der neu-modische Liebhaber Damon*, 1724 (rev. of *Die Satyren in Arcadien*, 1719, lost), (EDITION Bernd Baselt (ed.), *G. P. Telemann: Musikalische Werke*, vol. 21, Bärenreiter); *Miriways*, 1728; *Emma und Eginhard*, 1728; *Flavius Bertaridus, König der Langobarden*, 1729; *Don Quichotte der Löwenritter*, 1761; excerpts only: *Adonis*, 1708; *Narcissus*, 1709; *Mario*, 1709; *Belsazar*, 1723; *Omphale*, 1724; *Adelheid*, 1724 or 1725; *La capricciosa e il credulo*, 1725; *Sancio*, 1727; *Calypso* (one chorus), 1727; *Die verkehrte Welt*, 1728; *Aesopus bei Hofe*, 1729; *Adam und Eva*,

n.d.; *Hercules und Alceste*, n.d.; *Herodes und Marianne*, n.d.; several lost operas
BIBLIOGRAPHY Richard Petzoldt, trans. Horace Fitzpatrick, *Georg Philipp Telemann*, Ernest Benn, 1974

G.J.B.

DOMINGO TERRADELLAS

Domingo [Domènec] Miguel Bernabé Terradellas [Domenico Terradeglas]; *baptized* 13 February 1713, Barcelona, Spain; *d* 25 May 1751, Rome

Like Vicente Martín y Soler and other Spanish composers in the 18th century, Domingo Terradellas decided at 19 to further his career abroad, writing some 12 operas to Italian libretti and in Italian style. The first of these was *Giuseppe riconosciuto*, with no less a distingushed librettist than Metastasio, produced in Rome in 1736. Again like Martín, by 1746 his fame as a composer of opere serie and buffe was such that he was to be found in London, rubbing shoulders with Handel; here, two new operas (*Annibale in Capua* and *Mitridate*) were put on at the King's Theatre; a second performance of *Mitridate* was given in 1747. The legend that, following the relative failure in Rome of his last opera, *Sesostri, re d'Egitto*, he threw himself into – or was murdered and thrown into – the Tiber, has more to do with his colourful reputation than with fact. However, Burney's crediting to him certain innovations in pianoforte and crescendo techniques is at least partly justified.

Operatic works: *Astarto*, 1739; *Cerere*, 1740; *Gli intrighi delle cantarine*, 1740; *Issipile*, 1741 or 1742; *Merope*, 1743; *Artaserse*, 1744; *Semiramide riconosciuta*, 1746; *Annibale in Capua* (coll.), 1746; *Mitridate*, 1746; *Bellerofonte*, 1747; *Didone abbandonata*, 1750; *Imeneo in Atene*, 1750; *Sesostri, re d'Egitto*, 1751
BIBLIOGRAPHY Antonio Martín Moreno, *Historia de la música española*, vol. 4: *Siglo XVIII*, Alianza, 1985; J. Roca, 'La producción musical de Domènec Terradellas ... ', *Revista musical catalana*, vol. 31 (1934), p. 305

J.W.S.

JOHANN THEILE

b 29 July 1646, Naumburg; *buried* 24 June 1724, Naumburg

Theile, a student of Schütz, is known particularly as a composer of sacred music as well as the author of treatises on contrapuntal practice. In 1673 Duke Christian Albrecht appointed him kapellmeister at Gottorf (Holstein), where he may have written his first operatic works. When the duke fled to Hamburg for political reasons, Theile accompanied him. Here in 1678 he participated in establishing the first public opera house outside Venice, the famous Oper am Gänsemarkt (it stood adjacent to the present-day Staatsoper). On 2 January 1678 the theatre opened with Theile's *Der erschaffene, gefallene und auffgerichtetet Mensch*. The libretto is based on the biblical story of Adam and Eve, and it established a trend towards sacred plots for operas during the early years of opera in Hamburg. This resulted from an attempt to deflect the vociferous criticism from the pietist ministers of the city who objected to opera on moral grounds. Also in 1679 Theile presented a second opera, *Orontes*, and in 1681 the sacred opera *Die Geburth Christi*. These works are lost except for a few arias from *Orontes*.

BIBLIOGRAPHY   G. J. Buelow 'Opera in Hamburg 300 Years Ago', *MT*, vol. 119 (1978), pp. 26–8

G.J.B.

AMBROISE THOMAS

Charles Louis Ambroise Thomas; *b* 5 August 1811, Metz, France; *d* 12 February 1896, Paris

The career of Ambroise Thomas mingled success and failure to a remarkable degree over a long period of time. His fame as an opera composer and his status as an Establishment figure, apparently unassailable, were not proof against reaction, neglect and indifference lasting long after his death. A Conservatoire pupil of Le Sueur, Thomas won the Prix de Rome in 1832. A series of mainly comic operas, including notably *Le Caïd*, *Le songe d'une nuit d'été* (not after Shakespeare but about him) and *Psyché*, was followed by a pause before the resounding achievements of *Mignon* and *Hamlet*. Those triumphs were not repeated. After becoming director of the Conservatoire in 1871 Thomas wrote only one major opera, *Françoise de Rimini*. Years later, in honour of the 1000th performance of *Mignon* in 1894, Thomas became the first composer to receive the Grand Cross of the Légion d'honneur. By then, while the public stayed faithful to *Mignon* and *Hamlet*, his reputation, whether with Wagnerites and Debussyists or the merely fashionable, was extinguished. Chabrier's remark about 'three kinds of music – good, bad and Ambroise Thomas' contains a gleam of truth. He was more follower than originator. There is in Thomas a deeper vein of lyrical sentiment than can be found in the comic operas of the first half of the century, but he did little to expand the genre. Gounod, Saint-Saëns and Bizet had more personal styles, yet Thomas possessed an amount of skill in writing opera from which they and others after them profited. His melodic gift went with a kind of inspired ordinariness to the heart of the public. For that he was not quickly forgiven.

Mignon

Opéra comique in three acts (five tableaux) (3h)
Libretto by Michel Carré and Jules Barbier after the novel *Wilhelm Meisters Lehrjahre* by Johann Wolfgang von Goethe (1796)
PREMIERES   17 November 1866, Opéra-Comique, Paris; UK: 5 July 1870, Drury Lane, London; US: 9 May 1871, French Opera House, New Orleans

An illustrated supplement of Le Petit Journal *celebrating the 1,000th performance of* Mignon *(Paris, 1894)*

CAST   Mignon *ms*, Philine *s*, Wilhelm *t*, Lothario *b* or *bar*, Laërte *t*, Frédérick *t* or *ms*, 1 *b*, 1 *spoken role*; *satb* chorus of gypsies, peasants, comedians, guests
FULL ORCHESTRA

The sequence of events is taken from the parts of Goethe's novel dealing with Wilhelm Meister and the old harper, the girl Mignon and the actress Philine. Except for the title role, characterization is rudimentary, but something remains of the atmosphere of theatrical vagabondage in the 18th century. Thomas, whose early good fortune at the Opéra-Comique had declined, waited some years before producing *Mignon* and was surprised by the warm welcome it received. The popularity of the work, with singers as well as public, never entirely faded even when the composer's reputation was at a low ebb. From the first interpreter, Galli-Marie, onwards mezzo-sopranos have been understandably attracted to the role of Mignon.

SYNOPSIS
Act I Wilhelm, a student, and the half-crazy Lothario, searching for his long-lost daughter, rescue a shy young girl called Mignon from a band of gypsies. They are observed by Philine and Laërte, strolling players. Mignon sings of her childhood in a land of golden memories. Philine's interest in Wilhelm arouses Mignon's jealousy. Wilhelm buys Mignon's liberty and offers his protection.
Act II The players are invited to perform in the theatre of Rosenberg castle. Frédérick, nephew of

the owner and in love with Philine, quarrels with Wilhelm. Mignon changes from servant boy's clothes into theatrical costume. Wilhelm is struck by her beauty. Meanwhile, in the palace theatre a play is being given. When it is over Philine celebrates her triumph in the role of Titania. She asks Mignon to fetch her a bouquet from the theatre. Laërte brings news that the theatre is in flames. Wilhelm rushes out and returns carrying Mignon.

Act III In an Italian country palazzo Lothario prays for Mignon's recovery. A servant tells Wilhelm the family history: the owner, Marquis Cypriani, left Italy after his wife died, believing their small daughter to have drowned. The name Cypriani stirs something in Lothario's mind. Wilhelm, now aware that he loves Mignon, hopes for a word from her. She comes in as if in a dream – she feels she has known the palace and its grounds before. Wilhelm assures her that her past sorrows are over. Their mutual confession of love is interrupted by the distant voice of Philine, reawakening Mignon's fears. Lothario, now richly clad, brings them a casket full of childish mementoes which Mignon recognizes. Lothario explains that he is the Marquis Cypriani and that Mignon is Sperata his daughter, not drowned but abducted. Philine, volatile but kind-hearted, offers the hand of friendship. She will bestow herself on the delighted Frédérick: Wilhelm is free. General rejoicing.

For London, Thomas made a shorter, alternative conclusion. Philine is heard but not seen, Mignon faints but recovers and is joined in a final trio of thanksgiving by Wilhelm and Lothario. For German audiences who might disapprove of the happy ending, Thomas provided a further alternative in which the reappearance of Philine causes a mortal shock to Mignon. Like *Faust* and *Carmen*, *Mignon* was written as an opéra comique with spoken dialogue. Also for London, Thomas substituted recitatives (in Italian) and made other alterations and additions. Frédérick was promoted from a *Trial* tenor to a *travesti* mezzo. The additions, which include a sung version of the Act II gavotte interlude for Frédérick, are a bonus; the recitatives are not.

RECORDING Welting, Von Stade, Horne, Vanzo, Zaccaria, Ambrosian Opera Ch, Philharmonia O, De Almeida, CBS, 1978: in French with recitatives and appendices
EDITIONS f.s., Heugel, [c. 1880]; v.s., Heugel, [1867]

Hamlet

Opera in five acts (seven tableaux) (2h 45m)
Libretto by Michel Carré and Jules Barbier after the play by William Shakespeare (1600–1601)
PREMIERES 9 March 1868, Opéra, Paris; UK: 19 June 1869, Covent Garden, London; US: 22 March 1872, Academy of Music, New York
CAST Hamlet *bar*, Claudius *b*, Gertrude *ms*, Ophélie *s*, Laërte *t*, Le spectre *b*, 2 *t*, 3 *b*; *satb* chorus of courtiers, soldiers, players, peasants
FULL ORCHESTRA including sax

Expectations of the poetic and philosophical richness and dramatic scope of Shakespeare must be

disappointed by Carré's and Barbier's drastic but ingenious reduction, from which familiar characters and incidents are omitted. Thomas's *Hamlet* obeys the laws not of Elizabethan tragedy but of French 19th-century opera. In many ways it is a model of its kind, combining powerful drama (the scene on the battlements and the confrontation between Hamlet and his mother) with more conventionally conceived episodes. Ophélie's mad scene may be 'floridly inconsequential' (Philip Robinson) by later standards, but it is an effective and affecting example of the genre. The first interpreters of Hamlet and Ophélie, Jean-Baptiste Faure and Christine Nilsson, had many distinguished successors. *Hamlet*, the composer's single great success at the Opéra, remained in the repertoire until 1938: it has recently been revived in Buxton, New York and Sydney.

SYNOPSIS

Act I Elsinore (Denmark). Prince Hamlet is shocked by the unseemly haste of the marriage, just celebrated, of his mother Gertrude, widow of the late king, to his brother and successor, Claudius. Hamlet affirms his love for Ophélie, whom her brother Laërte, about to leave for Norway, entrusts to Hamlet's care. Hamlet learns that his father's ghost has been seen. On the battlements. The ghost appears to Hamlet and reveals that he was murdered by Claudius. Hamlet swears vengeance.

Act II Hamlet's strange behaviour alarms Ophélie. The queen tries to comfort her. Hamlet has invited strolling players to entertain the court. He instructs them to perform a play about the murder of a king. Hamlet and the players carouse together. During the performance the king rises in confusion. In a frenzy Hamlet snatches the crown.

Act III Hamlet broods over his inability to take action. He overhears the prayers of the guilt-stricken king. The queen implores Hamlet to marry Ophélie, but he cruelly rejects her. She returns his ring. Hamlet forces his mother to consider the portraits of her two husbands and reveals that he knows the truth. The ghost materializes, urging Hamlet to slay the king but spare his mother.

Act IV Peasants dancing by a lake are joined by Ophélie, her reason gone, distributing flowers from a garland. After singing a melancholy ballad she subsides gently into the water.

Act V Hamlet muses in the cemetery on Ophélie's madness. He is still unaware of her death: the gravediggers do not know whose grave they are preparing. Laërte, returned from his journey, reproaches Hamlet. As they prepare to fight a procession appears, headed by the king and queen, with Ophélie's bier. Hamlet is commanded by the ghost to kill Claudius forthwith and assume the crown. Hamlet does his bidding and is acclaimed king.

For English audiences the original ending, which follows a French version of Shakespeare by Dumas *père* and Paul Maurice, was revised for Covent Garden. The ghost does not return: Hamlet kills the king and then kills himself. Richard Bonynge devised a compromise for Sydney (1982, later recorded) in which Hamlet, mortally wounded by Laërte, is reminded by the ghost of his vow, kills the king and dies on Ophélie's body.

RECORDING Sutherland, Winbergh, Milnes, Morris, WNO Ch and O, Bonynge, Decca, 1984
EDITIONS f.s., Heugel, [1900]; v.s., Heugel, [1868]

Other operas: *La double échelle*, 1837; *Le perruquier de la Régence*, 1838; *Le panier fleuri*, 1839; *Carline*, 1840; *Le Comte de Carmagnola*, 1841; *Le Guerrillero*, 1842; *Angélique et Médor*, 1843; *Mina*, 1843; *Le Caïd*, 1849; *Le songe d'une nuit d'été*, 1850; *Raymond*, 1851; *La Tonelli*, 1853; *La cour de Célimène*, 1855; *Psyché*, 1857; *Le carnaval de Venise*, 1857; *Le roman d'Elvire*, 1860; *Gille et Gillotin*, (1859) 1874; *Françoise de Rimini*, 1882
BIBLIOGRAPHY Max Loppert, '*Mignon*, opéra-comique, and Ambroise Thomas', Wexford Festival programme book, 1986

R.H.C.

VIRGIL THOMSON

Virgil Garnett Thomson; *b* 25 November 1896, Kansas City, US; *d* 30 September 1989, New York

As both composer and critic, Virgil Thomson was one of the most original figures in 20th-century American music. His important contribution to opera resulted from his collaboration with Gertrude Stein (1874–1946), whose techniques of verbal abstraction Thomson was able to translate into music; *Four Saints in Three Acts* and *The Mother of us all* have become classics of so-called 'non-narrative' opera.

Thomson's childhood gave him roots in an American vernacular – hymns, popular songs and parlour music – which is embedded in his compositions. When, after a period in the US army, he

American composers at the home of Virgil Thomson. From left to right: Samuel Barber, Virgil Thomson, Gian Carlo Menotti, William Schuman, Aaron Copland

went to Harvard, he found a more cosmopolitan cultural context. One of his teachers, S. Foster Damon, introduced him to the writings of Stein and the music of Erik Satie. He learned about vocal music through assisting Archibald T. Davison at the Harvard Glee Club and he joined their European tour in 1921. Thomson's link with Paris was inevitable: 'I came in my Harvard years to identify with France virtually all of music's recent glorious past, most of its acceptable present, and a large part of its future.' After 1923 Thomson spent most of his time in Paris until he became critic of the *New York Herald Tribune* in 1940. His voluminous writings have been influential – he had a rare gift for combining spontaneity and provocation; these qualities also inform his music. Though he studied with Nadia Boulanger, he remained independent of both neo-classicism and serialism. The straightforwardness of his music was controversial; as Thomson wrote in *The State of Music* (1939): 'When we made music that was simple, melodic and harmonious, the fury of the vested interests of modernism flared up like a gas-tank . . . I am considered a graceless whelp, a frivolous mountebank, an unfair competitor, and a dangerous character.'

Thomson's first Stein setting was a song with piano, 'Susie Asado' (1926). After he met Stein, in 1926, their collaboration developed, and *Capital Capitals* (1928) for four male voices and piano is confidently written in the style of the first opera, *Four Saints in Three Acts*.

Four Saints in Three Acts

Opera in four (sic) acts with prologue (1h 30m)
Libretto by Gertrude Stein
Composed 1927–8, orch. 1933
PREMIERES 20 May 1933, Ann Arbor (concert); 8 February 1934, auditorium of Avery Memorial, Hartford; France: May 1952, Théâtre des Champs-Elysées, Paris; UK: 27 April 1983, Almeida Theatre, London (semi-staged)

In his first opera Thomson set out to achieve the 'discipline of spontaneity', which he had recognized in the writings of Stein. His working method was to put the text on the piano and improvise, singing and playing. He did this for several days and only when he began to repeat himself did he know it was finished. He then wrote it down. Thomson wondered 'whether a piece so drenched in Anglican chant (running from Gilbert and Sullivan to Morning Prayer and back) could rise and sail'. Private performances in Paris convinced him that it could long before he orchestrated *Four Saints* for the Hartford production.

Thomson pointed out that *Four Saints* made theatrical history in several ways: it had an all-black cast (a year before Gershwin's *Porgy and Bess*); it was choreographed by the young Frederick Ashton and John Houseman and the Cellophane sets were by Florine Stettheimer; also, it ran for 60 performances on Broadway following the Hartford opening.

Since *Four Saints* is not a conventional narrative opera, there can be no description of the plot.

Thomson set everything Stein provided, even the stage directions where the scenes are not even numbered in consecutive order. This all adds to the sense of fun and to the opportunities for production. The scenario, written after the completion of both text and music, is the work of Maurice Grosser, the original producer, who calls *Four Saints* 'both an opera and a choreographic spectacle'. The setting is 16th-century Spain and the principal characters are St Teresa of Avila, St Ignatius Loyola and their confidants, St Settlement and St Chavez (there are 16 named saints in all, again contradicting the title). A compère and a commère comment on the action with studied illogicality. St Teresa is represented by two singers dressed alike. Stein intended St Ignatius' aria 'Pigeons on the Grass Alas' to reflect a vision of the Holy Ghost and specified a procession at the end of Act III but otherwise, as Grosser puts it, 'One should not try to interpret too literally the words of this opera, nor should one fall into the opposite error of thinking that they mean nothing at all.'

Despite its initial reception *Four Saints* has rarely been professionally staged – it offers few opportunities for vocal display. Thomson set Stein's surrealist text in a manner that defies stylistic categorization; extended monophonic linear passages are juxtaposed with quotations from religious music of all periods and references to nursery rhymes.

RECORDING Dale, Bradley, Allen, Quivar, Matthews, Brown, Thompson, Ch and O of our Time, Thome, Nonesuch, 1982
EDITION v.s., New York Music Press, 1947

The Mother of us all

Opera in two acts (1h 45m)
Libretto by Gertrude Stein
Composed 1946–7
PREMIERES 7 May 1947, Brander Matthews Hall, Columbia University, New York; UK: 26 June 1979, Kensington Town Hall, London (Abbey Opera)

After the Second World War Thomson returned to Paris to discuss a new opera with Stein. When Thomson suggested a subject from 19th-century American political life she proposed Susan B. Anthony, the pioneer of women's rights, and immediately began research. The libretto was the last thing she wrote.

Thomson's working method was similar to that employed in *Four Saints*, but this time he had to move faster: the premiere took place seven months after he began work. The cast, of students and young professionals, was directed by two composers – Jack Beeson, as répétiteur, and Otto Luening as conductor. *The Mother of us all* was well received, although some disadvantages were evident in the student cast and orchestra. However, the work's future lay mostly in such university settings – in the last 30 years *The Mother* has been given over 1000 times in some 200 productions.

The Mother of us all is based on the winning of votes for women in the US through the activities of Susan B. Anthony (1820–1906). The action, as well as the music, is more continuous than that of *Four Saints*, something Thomson may have learned from his film writing. Thomson once described the score as a 'musical memory' book, referring to his inclusion of 19th-century American ballads, hymns, songs and marches. Stein's licence with time brings together characters who could never have met: the cast also includes the composer and librettist themselves as narrators. A plot is hardly discernible, but in Act I there are political meetings where men in various responsible positions obstruct the progress of Susan B. Anthony's reforming zeal. Sub-plots, such as the relationship between Jo the Loiterer and Indiana Elliot, are used to attack the institution of marriage from the woman's point of view. In Act II the struggle continues – the word 'male' is inserted into the American constitution to hold up women's suffrage. In a moving epilogue a statue of Susan B. Anthony is unveiled in the Halls of Congress some years after her death when her cause has been achieved. In her final aria, suffused with hymnody, her ghost haunts the scene wondering if the struggle was worth it: 'But do we want what we have got . . . I was a martyr all my life not to what I won but to what was done.'

RECORDING Dunn, Godfrey, Lewis, Atherton, Booth, Santa Fe Opera Ch and O, Leppard, New World Records, 1976
EDITION v.s., New York Music Press, 1947

Lord Byron

Opera in three acts (1h 30m)
Libretto by Jack Larson
Composed 1961–8
PREMIERE 20 April 1972, Juilliard Theater, Lincoln Center, New York

Lord Byron was commissioned for the Metropolitan Opera by the Koussevitzky Foundation but has not been staged there. This fact indicates the ambitious scale on which Thomson was working. In contrast to Thomson's earlier operas *Lord Byron* has a definite plot, with a libretto that uses episodes from Byron's works. The opera opens when the poet's body has been brought back to London from Greece. His friends try to obtain burial in Westminster Abbey but finally fail because of the objections of the bureaucratic Dean. At the final curtain, however, Byron takes his place among the ghosts of Shelley, Jonson, Milton, etc., in Poet's Corner. Several scenes provide flashbacks to Byron's earlier life and loves, including his frustrated marriage and his love affair with his half-sister. The musical language of Lord Byron shows a further step away from the simplicity of *Four Saints*. More conservative and decidedly melodic, it includes a number of pastiche elements and cites well-known tunes such as 'Auld Lang Syne' and 'Ach du lieber Augustine'.

EDITION v.s., Southern, 1975

BIBLIOGRAPHY Virgil Thomson, *Virgil Thomson*, Weidenfeld and Nicolson, 1967; Virgil Thomson, *Music with*

Words, Yale, 1989; Victor F. Yellin, 'The Operas of Virgil Thomson', in Virgil Thomson, *American Music since 1910*, Weidenfeld and Nicolson, 1971

P.D.

MICHAEL TIPPETT
(Sir) Michael Kemp Tippett; *b* 2 January 1905, London

Tippett was brought up in the Suffolk countryside and educated at first privately and then, from the age of nine, at various boarding schools. His father was a lawyer who became the proprietor of a hotel in the south of France, his mother a nurse who became a novelist and a suffragette. After the First World War his parents lived abroad and from the age of 14 he had no real home, spending the holidays in those parts of southern Europe where his parents had temporarily settled. From this unusual and stimulating background, coloured not least by his parents' agnosticism, he gained a marked independence of outlook which was to stand him in good stead. He was expected to become a lawyer but even at preparatory school he had decided to become a composer. Apart from piano lessons he had no formal training until he went to the Royal College of Music in London in 1923. From then on he developed not only a passionate interest in music of all kinds but also the patience to accept that his compositional apprenticeship would take a long time. He was 30 when he completed his first characteristic work, his String Quartet No. 1 (1934–5), before which he had returned to the RCM for a second period of study, this time with R. O. Morris.

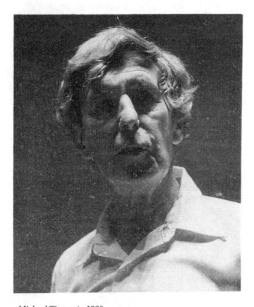

Michael Tippett in 1980

During the 1930s Tippett experimented with opera composition in four unpublished stage works. While these reveal little evidence of his mature style, they none the less show how he had been testing his ability to apply operatic techniques. His concert music from 1935 until 1946, when he started composing his first opera, *The Midsummer Marriage*, likewise shows him experimenting within the other principal musical genres. He wrote a Second String Quartet, a First Sonata for Piano, his well-known Concerto for Double String Orchestra, his oratorio *A Child of Our Time* and his First Symphony. *The Midsummer Marriage*, completed in 1952, can be seen therefore as the culmination of an extended compositional programme.

This very deliberate approach to composition shows how important the acquisition of technical skill was to him at a time when, in his opinion, English music was suffering from a lack of it. His early works also reveal his attitude towards the force of tradition. In this respect he was greatly influenced by the theoretical writings of T. S. Eliot. In 1937 Tippett met Eliot, who for a while became his 'spiritual and artistic mentor'. It was Eliot who advised him to write his own text for what became *A Child of Our Time*: having seen Tippett's draft he thought it was already a text in embryo, and that any 'poetry' he wrote would be obtrusive and impede the music. Eliot was thus largely responsible for Tippett's subsequent decision to write his own libretti. This has aroused criticism, though Tippett's operatic subject matter, as well as his writing style, is so individual that collaboration could only have resulted in damaging compromises.

Tippett's five operas offer a very distinctive interpretation of the nature of opera, in general proposing that the genre should explore deeper layers of human understanding than can be revealed through the interactions of a conventional plot. His characters may be sharply defined, but they tend towards the representational rather than the individual; while two of his operas, *King Priam* and *The Ice Break*, do have strong 'story lines', these are ultimately no less symbolic than the others. Tippett's prime justification for this approach is that if dramatic music is poorly equipped to conduct narrative, it is peculiarly well equipped to give perceptible shape to the emotional feelings, forces, intuitions that prompt human behaviour. It follows that opera might also have a socially therapeutic role to play, in enabling its listeners to discover more about their own psychology.

Tippett's commitment to this idea took root in 1938, when, as a result of the break-up of a tumultuous love affair, of problems with his homosexuality, as well as his disillusionment at the menacing political situation in Europe, he undertook a course of Jungian self-analysis. The result of this was not only that he felt better balanced as a person but also that he drew back from his involvement in the left-wing politics of the 1930s (when he had been a Trotskyist sympathizer) and devoted himself to his fundamental vocation as composer. The work in which his new-found attitude is most explicit is *A*

Child of Our Time, when he first showed his readiness to address in music large and seemingly intractable problems, here man's inhumanity to man. What gave him the confidence to do so – and also to become a pacifist and a conscientious objector during the Second World War (he was imprisoned in 1943 for refusing to comply with the conditions imposed by a tribunal) – was his Jungian understanding of the 'shadow' and 'light', reflected in the text of the penultimate section of the oratorio: 'I would know my shadow and my light,/so shall I at last be whole./Then courage, brother, dare the grave passage.' These lines enabled him to reach a characteristically affirmative, if in this case restrained, conclusion to the oratorio, even though it was written in wartime (1939–41). They provide the key to much of his subsequent output. *The Midsummer Marriage* is, in effect, a dramatization of them.

From 1940 until 1951 Tippett achieved prominence as director of music at Morley College, where his concert programmes proved to be the most adventurous heard in London during the war and for some years after. He then devoted himself almost entirely to composition.

Not until the 1960s did his music achieve proper recognition, having been frequently dismissed as the product of an impractical, if occasionally inspired, dilettante. This may be ascribed to the originality and complexity of his thought in general (as can also be seen in his published essays and his libretti), as well as to the fact that his musical language seemed to have been overtaken by post-war styles. But from the successful premiere of his second opera, *King Priam*, in 1962, and a BBC broadcast in 1963 of *The Midsummer Marriage*, a reassessment began, and it became apparent that here was a composer of international stature, a judgement reinforced by the inexhaustible invention of those major works that have flowed from his creativity ever since – symphonies, concertos, sonatas, quartets, not to mention operas, which remain at the core of his output.

The Midsummer Marriage

Opera in three acts (2h 30m)
Libretto by the composer
Composed 1946–52
PREMIERES 27 January 1955, Covent Garden, London; US: 15 October 1983, War Memorial Opera House, San Francisco
CAST Mark *t*, Jenifer *s*, King Fisher *bar*, Bella *s*, Jack *t*, Sosostris *a*, The Ancients *b*, *ms*, Strephon *dancer*; *satb* chorus of Mark's and Jenifer's friends; dancers
ORCHESTRATION 2 fl/picc, 2 ob, 2 cl, 2 bsn, 4 hn, 2 tpt, 3 trbn, timp, perc (2 players: sd, bd, cym, gong, triangle, tubular bells), hp, cel, str

The first performance of *The Midsummer Marriage* has acquired legendary status. Conducted by John Pritchard, produced by Christopher West, with scenery and costumes by Barbara Hepworth and choreography by John Cranko, it also had a strong cast, including Joan Sutherland, Richard Lewis and Otakar Kraus. Yet most press notices were violently

The Midsummer Marriage; *set design by Barbara Hepworth (London, 1955)*

hostile, at least to the libretto. This was dismissed variously as meaningless, amateurish or absurdly self-indulgent: Tippett, cripplingly inexperienced as an opera composer, paying the price for an ill-considered pursuit of the vogue for British opera that had followed the success of Britten's *Peter Grimes* in 1945. *The Midsummer Marriage*'s music, however, had not failed to win its admirers, and after a second Covent Garden production in 1968 conducted by Colin Davis, the opera rapidly gained ground and entered the international repertoire.

The opera is closely related to Mozart's *Die Zauberflöte*, having two pairs of lovers, one more elevated than the other but both in quest of enlightenment. Further correspondences are less clear for, in essence, Tippett's libretto comprises a journey into the world of Jungian archetypes, a dreamlike, imaginative realm where a mythological ritual of sacrifice and rebirth can be enacted, and the hero and heroine undergo the experiences that enable them to understand their full selves and embark on a true marriage. As such, it sets out an abiding theme in Tippett's output, which is the power of music to overcome ignorance and illusion about the human psyche and so effect a better understanding of human relationships. In tone the opera is exuberant, lyrical and emphatically affirmative throughout, even though written during the austere post-war years. In this respect it can be seen as Tippett's compensating message of vitality and rejuvenation – against the general character of the period and much of its music.

SYNOPSIS

Act I Dawn on Midsummer's Day, the scene a clearing on a wooded hilltop. The chorus is arriving for the runaway marriage of Mark and Jenifer. They notice a strange temple, at the centre of which sounds strange music. They hide, as dancers, led by Strephon (Mark's *alter ego*) and followed by the Ancients, emerge. Mark interrupts their dance, demanding a new one for his wedding day. The Ancients order a repeat of the old dance, during which the He-Ancient trips Strephon, demonstrating that change can be destructive and painful. The dancers and Ancients return to the temple. Mark puts the whole episode aside, settling down to wait for Jenifer. When she arrives, she announces there will be no wedding: 'It isn't love I want, but truth.' Their quarrel is cut short when she notices a spiral staircase by the temple and makes her decision: 'For me, the light! for you, the shadow!' She climbs the staircase and disappears from sight. Distraught, Mark plunges into a hillside cave. As its gates close, King Fisher, the businessman, with Bella his secretary, arrives in pursuit of his absconding daughter, Jenifer. He agrees to Bella's suggestion that Jack, her boyfriend who is a mechanic, should be asked to help open the gates. King Fisher bribes the men of the chorus to search for Mark. The women are not to be bought off. Jack's first attempt to open the gates fails and with King Fisher and then with Bella he prepares for a second attempt. As he raises his hammer a warning voice (Sosostris) tells King Fisher not to interfere. At the height of his frustration, Jenifer is revealed at the top of the staircase, then Mark at the mouth of the cave. The Ancients appear, with the dancers, to announce a contest: the two will sing of their experiences. Jenifer sings of the spiritual purity of hers, Mark of the bodily abandon of his. Jenifer, convinced of her moral superiority, holds up a mirror to Mark so he can see the beast he has become. But his gaze shatters her mirror and she now enters the cave to seek what has given him such power. In turn Mark decides to share Jenifer's experience, and while King Fisher is left nonplussed, the chorus happliy leaves spiritual journeys to Mark and Jenifer.

Act II Afternoon. Strephon at the temple, listening. He is frightened by distant voices and hides. Among the voices are Jack and Bella. It being Midsummer's Day, Bella proposes to Jack, and the two sing about their future life together. Three ritual dances follow, in which Strephon in various transformations is pursued by a female dancer similarly transformed. In the first (*The Earth in Autumn*) Strephon is a hare, hunted by a hound; he escapes. In the second (*The Waters in Winter*) he is a fish, is nearly caught by an otter and is injured. In the third (*The Air in Spring*) he is a bird with a broken wing and cannot escape the swooping hawk. At this point Bella cries out in terror, not knowing whether what she has seen is real or her own dreams. The dancers vanish. Jack comforts her and, her composure regained, she leaves with him, while the chorus is again heard singing behind the hill.

Act III Evening and night. The chorus is enjoying a party. King Fisher sends them away to collect Sosostris, his private clairvoyante, who will outwit the Ancients and restore Jenifer to him. The chorus reappears, not however with Sosostris but with a figure dressed as a jester and carrying a crystal bowl. The impostor turns out to be Jack. In the ensuing confusion the veiled figure of the real Sosostris appears. Jack places the bowl before her. She summons up her oracular powers and describes a vision of Mark and Jenifer making love. King Fisher is incensed, smashes the bowl and commands Jack to unveil Sosostris. Jack defies him, choosing instead to go off with Bella. King Fisher is left to unveil Sosostris himself. What emerges is not Sosostris but a lotus flower, whose petals unfold to reveal the transfigured Mark and Jenifer in mutual embrace. King Fisher aims a pistol at Mark. Mark and Jenifer turn their gaze towards him and he falls, dead. King Fisher's body is carried into the temple. Strephon and his dancers perform the fourth ritual dance (*Fire in Summer*) before the transfigured couple. Strephon sinks at their feet and is absorbed into the flower which closes and bursts into flame. The scene becomes dark and cold. Dawn breaks. Mark and Jenifer enter. She accepts the wedding ring and, as they disappear into the distance, the sun rises.

The Midsummer Marriage presents Tippett's 'early', tonal style at its most developed – irrepressibly vital and inventive, lyrical, richly textured and with light-footed rhythmic momentum. The opera's relatively traditional design, separate numbers linked in a continuous flow, disguises a very original dramaturgy, in which the action proceeds to the point of Jenifer's arrival and then shifts into a dream realm, not broken until the lovers reappear a few minutes from the end. So the bulk of the opera takes place in a period 'out of time'. This is a context in which Tippett can plausibly delve into the purely imaginative, the mythological and psychological, and in which another individual feature of the work, the integral use of dance, can find its place. The opera is not however entirely set in a fantasy world, for the chorus, as well as some other characters, notably Jack and Bella but including King Fisher, continually relate the action to the everyday.

Among the musical high points are the Act I arias of Jenifer and Mark, in which they sing respectively of their experiences of the Jungian animus and anima, the enchanting Act II duets of Bella and Jack and the extended Act III aria of Sosostris, a rare instance of an operatic aria for alto and remarkable evidence of the workings of the creative process. The *Ritual Dances* (the first three linked to the fourth) have become one of Tippett's most frequently performed works as a concert suite, and if in this guise their operatic function as further projections of the animus and anima is lost, their brilliant narrative imagery and their culminating expression, in the fourth dance, of ecstatic sexual and psychological fulfilment is amply realized, even when the last dance is performed without the voices and chorus.

RECORDING Carlyle, Harwood, Watts, Remedios,

Burrows, Herincx, Ch and O of Covent Garden, C. Davis, Philips, 1971
EDITIONS   v.s., Schott, 1954; study s., Schott, 1976

King Priam

Opera in three acts (2h)
Libretto by the composer
Composed 1958–61
PREMIERE   29 May 1962, Coventry Theatre, Coventry (Covent Garden Opera)
CAST   Priam *b-bar*, Hecuba *s*, Hector *bar*, Andromache *s*, Paris (as boy) *treble*, Paris (as man) *t*, Helen *ms*, Achilles *t*, Patroclus *bar*, Nurse *ms*, Old Man *b*, Young Guard *t*, Hermes *t*; *satb* chorus of hunters, wedding guests, serving women, etc.
ORCHESTRATION   2 fl/2 picc, ob, ca, cl, E♭ cl, b cl, bsn, dbsn, 4 hn, 4 tpt, 2 trbn, tuba, timp, perc (3 players: sd, bd, cym, t-t, triangle, wb, tambourine, xyl), hp, pf, gtr, str

King Priam is exceptional in Tippett's output, not so much because it marked a more radical break with his previous music than at any subsequent stage in his career, or even because its story is traditional, but because it is a tragedy. As such it can be seen as a critique of or a reaction to *The Midsummer Marriage*. Now it is shown that however honourable, human and deeply self-aware someone's actions might be, they may still lead to catastrophe. This is the essential message of an opera that on the surface seems a straightforward, if selective retelling of Homer's story of how Priam, King of Troy, reversed his decision to have his son Paris killed and thereby set in motion the Trojan War. The death of Priam may be cathartic, in the Aristotelian sense described by Hermes in the opera's last interlude, but it is final: it releases no possibility of life recharged or reborn, as with the endings of his other operas. It remains a profoundly inspiriting work however, because Tippett lights up the opera's mounting sequence of violence with moments of human insight and passion. Its accent on violence and brutality can be seen therefore not only as a means by which human values can be dramatized and upheld at times when the gods are at their most capricious, but also as a challenge to the mood of reconciliation that characterized the 1960s. Tippett's attitude in this latter respect was set in sharp relief at the opera's first performance, which took place just one day before that of Britten's *War Requiem*.

SYNOPSIS
Act I   Scene 1: Priam's palace. The birth of Paris. The baby is restless, as is Hecuba, his mother and queen of Troy. The Old Man interprets Hecuba's dream: Paris will cause his father's death. Hecuba's reaction is immediate. The young Priam hesitates, troubled by his conflicting responsibilities as father and king, before commanding that the child be killed. Interlude: The Nurse, Old Man and Young Guard comment on Priam's decision and introduce the course of the opera. Scene 2: Paris was not killed but given to a shepherd. As a young boy he meets his father and brother Hector while they are on a bull hunt. At the moment of recognition, Priam hesitates again, and then reverses his decision. He

takes Paris to Troy. Interlude: Further comment. Wedding guests announce Hector's marriage with Andromache and report of friction between the brothers and of Paris' departure for Greece, where he falls in love with Helen, wife of Menelaus of Sparta. Scene 3: Paris and Helen. The answer to Paris' dilemma – whether to provoke war by abducting Helen – is given in a vision (*The Judgement of Paris*). The god Hermes tells him to give the apple to the most beautiful of three goddesses. Two, Athene and Hera, remind him of his mother and sister-in-law: he gives it to Aphrodite. Despite the curses of Athene and Hera, he takes Helen to Troy.

Act II   Scene 1: Hector taunts his brother for not fighting the Greeks. Priam encourages both his sons and, separately, they rush off to battle. Interlude: Through the agency of Hermes, the Old Man is taken to the Greek camp to gloat over the inertia of Achilles. Scene 2: Achilles, refusing to fight because of a quarrel with Agamemnon, his chief, sings nostalgically of his homeland. His friend Patroclus persuades him of the desperate situation on the battlefield and Achilles allows Patroclus to fight Hector wearing Achilles' armour. Interlude: The Old Man asks Hermes to tell Priam of the danger. Scene 3: Hector has killed Patroclus and, with his father and brother, sings a hymn of thanksgiving, interrupted by the war cries of Achilles, who has been roused to action.

Act III   Scene 1: The war causes antagonism between the three women, but they are powerless and pray to their tutelary goddesses. Andromache senses the death of Hector. Interlude: Serving women comment on the impending collapse of Troy, and on the condition of Priam, who has been shielded from news of the war. Scene 2: Paris tells Priam of Hector's death. In torment, Priam relives his decision of the first scene. He begins to accept his own death. Interlude: instrumental. Scene 3: Priam visits the Greek camp to beg the body of Hector from Achilles, who feels pity for the old man and grants him his wish. They drink to their own deaths at the hands of their respective sons. Interlude: Hermes announces the imminent death of Priam and sings of the power of music to express cathartic experience. Scene 4: Paris tells Priam he has killed Achilles. Priam is unmoved. He dismisses everyone and speaks only to the mysterious Helen. Before he is killed by Neoptolemus, he has a momentary vision.

King Priam rejects the burgeoning tonal paragraphs of *The Midsummer Marriage* and is constructed in a series of short scenes and sung interludes (a method owing something to Brecht); in these the orchestra is split up into small ensembles, each character (and many of the concepts) has its own immediately recognizable sound quality and the musical language is more taut and dissonant. Only once, in the penultimate interlude, does Tippett treat his full orchestra as a unit. So there is little of the carefully modulated textures of *The Midsummer Marriage*, rather a rapid shifting of sound spectrum, between, for example, the horns and piano of Priam and the violins of Hecuba, or between the trumpets and percussion representing war, and the guitar of Achilles. Some of the characters – Hecuba and Andromache (cellos) for instance – are always represented by the same instruments. But Tippett does not stick rigidly to his methods and others, notably Priam and the semi-divine Helen and Achilles, also have a rich variety of associated instrumentation.

While there is no lack of lyrical music, Tippett's writing for voices in *King Priam* is typically declamatory in style, especially in the questing monologues which are a feature of the work and which emphasize the characters' individual predicaments and their isolation from one another. The moments of human compassion, between Achilles and Patroclus, or between Priam and Achilles, are correspondingly more poignant, their dramatic impact nicely counterpointed against the stark momentum of the rest of the opera and against its more obviously theatrical (and masterly) moments – such as the ends of Act I and Act II. Tippett's methods in *King Priam* became the source of much, if not all, of his subsequent output, both for the theatre and the concert hall.

RECORDING Harper, Palmer, Minton, Murray, Langridge, Tear, Bowen, Allen, Roberts, Wilson-Johnson, Bailey, London Sinfonietta Ch and O, Atherton, Argo, 1981
VIDEO J. Price, Walker, Mason, Curtis, Haskin, Jenkins, Suart, Kent Opera Ch and O, Norrington, Virgin, 1980: Nicholas Hytner's arresting production for Kent Opera, well filmed [A.B.]
EDITION v.s., Schott, 1962

The Knot Garden

Opera in three acts (1h 30m)
Libretto by the composer
Composed 1966–9
PREMIERES 2 December 1970, Covent Garden, London; US: 22 February 1974, Northwestern University Opera Theater, Cahn Auditorium, Evanston, Illinois
CAST Faber *bar*, Thea *ms*, Flora *s*, Denise *s*, Mel *b-bar*, Dov *t*, Mangus *t-bar*
ORCHESTRATION 2 fl/2 picc, ob, ca, 2 cl/2 b cl, E♭ cl, bsn, dbsn, 4 hn, 4 tpt, 2 trbn, tuba, timp, perc (3 players: sd, tenor d, bd, cym, suspended cym, t-t, tambourine, tubular bells, wbs, temple blocks, metal bar, claves, whip, castanets, small rattle, xyl, vib, glock, jazz kit), hp, pf, cel, electric gtr, str; reduced orchestration (Meirion Bowen): fl/picc, ob/ca, cl/E♭ cl/b cl, bsn/dbsn, 3 hn, 2 tpt, 2 trbn, perc (2 players), hp, pf/cel, electric gtr, 3 vn/3 va, va, vc, db

Between *King Priam* and *The Knot Garden* Tippett wrote three important concert works, of which the first two, his Piano Sonata No. 2 (1962) and Concerto for Orchestra (1963), explore the style, structural methods and even some of the material of *King Priam*. The third, *The Vision of Saint Augustine* (1965), ventures into realms of mystical experience and the perception of time. With *The Knot Garden* Tippett abruptly returned to earth. It is set in 'the present' and deals with directly contemporary problems – those stemming from a lifeless marriage and touching also on race relations, homosexuality and the torture of political prisoners, while in general

exploring the inner as opposed to the public lives of its seven characters. If this bold subject matter was perhaps not unexpected of Tippett, and the brilliantly faceted musical language, its rapid sequence of short scenes and its gritty style a natural development from *King Priam*, the opera's intimate yet intensely concentrated dramaturgy shows him at his most original. Its speed of movement is a product of his adaptation of television techniques (notably the little 'dissolve' sections which break up one scene in preparation for the next) and of contemporary stage lighting techniques; its essential substance is a product of contemporary psychotherapeutic techniques and of Shakespeare's *The Tempest*, this latter a conspicuous instance of his instinct to draw on cultural tradition while shaping it to his own purposes. Of all Tippett's operas, *The Knot Garden* is the most radical in its rejection of conventional narrative explanation. The whys and wherefores of the 'plot' have therefore to be deduced from what hints the libretto does provide. For all these reasons the opera was immediately recognized as strikingly original in conception and execution.

SYNOPSIS
Thea, a gardener, and Faber, a civil engineer, are a married couple in their mid-thirties. They have a ward, Flora. Thea has asked Mangus, a psychoanalyst, to stay with them so that he can help with Flora's adolescent problems. Mangus realizes, however, that it is the marriage that needs attention and he plans a therapy in which his charges will be persuaded to project their feelings on to characters from *The Tempest* and act them out in a series of 'charades' he has derived from the play. Faber will be Ferdinand and Flora Miranda. He has asked Thea to invite two friends to be Ariel and Caliban. These are a homosexual couple, Dov, a composer, and Mel, a black writer. Mangus himself will be Prospero, who with his 'magic art' will solve the opera. Thea, tactfully, will not be included. The scene is a high-walled house garden shutting out an industrial city. The garden changes shape metaphorically according to the situations – from a boxed-in knot garden to a tangled labyrinth or to a rose garden.

Act I The characters are introduced, Mangus testing his ability to summon up a tempest and a magic island, Thea and Faber locked in bitter confrontation, Flora neurotic, Dov and Mel ready to play-act though unsure of themselves. Thea's attempt to attract Mel begins to break open the entrenched positions but what really does so is the unexpected arrival of Denise, Thea's sister and a 'dedicated freedom fighter'. Disfigured from torture, she denounces them all.

Act II Mangus is understood to be manipulating a nightmarish tempest, in which the characters, in a series of duets, give vent to their suppressed desires and antagonisms. Eventually the two most hurt, Flora and Dov, are left to console each other.

Act III Before an audience of Thea and Denise, Mangus now masterminds four charades. The characters, including Thea and Denise, are able to some extent to come to terms with themselves –

Robert Tear, Jill Gomez, Thomas Hemsley and Josephine Barstow in The Knot Garden *(London, 1970)*

except Dov, who is isolated, and Mangus himself, who suddenly discovers that his behaviour has been grossly presumptuous. He stops the proceedings, all the cast comes forward and tentatively sings of the human qualities that, after all, can bind them, and the audience, together. In an epilogue Thea and Faber are about to embrace.

The emotional drama of *The Knot Garden* is dynamic and fast-moving, but within its pattern of little arias and ensembles Tippett also leaves room for large set pieces. Act I is geared to lead up to the first of them, a harrowing aria for Denise ('O you may stare in horror'), answered by the second, a septet for the whole cast, which since it is set in motion by Mel, is a blues, with a boogie-woogie middle section. Although some of Tippett's early music, notably his Concerto for Double String Orchestra, absorbs jazz into his style, this was the first time his interest in popular culture had been shown so directly in one of his operas. Naturally it also affected *The Knot Garden*'s instrumentation, which includes jazz kit and electric guitar. The guitar features prominently in the song Dov sings to Flora at the end of Act II, one of the most conspicuous moments of lyric warmth Tippett places in an otherwise sharp-edged and even astringent score. Flora's song to Dov, immediately before, is another

such moment, an exquisitely orchestrated version of Schubert's 'Die liebe Farbe'. Of all the solos in the opera Thea's Act III aria ('Now I am no longer afraid') is the most beautiful, and of all the ensembles the concluding quintet the most typical of the opera's intrinsic irony: a humanistic statement ('If for a timid moment we submit to love') punctuated by mocking quotations from some songs for Ariel Tippett had himself written for an earlier Old Vic production of *The Tempest*.

RECORDING Gomez, Barstow, Minton, Tear, Carey, Herincx, Hemsley, Ch and O of Covent Garden, C. Davis, Philips, 1974
EDITION v.s., Schott, 1970

The Ice Break

Opera in three acts (1h 15m)
Libretto by the composer
Composed 1973–6
PREMIERES 7 July 1977, Covent Garden, London; US: 18 May 1979, Savoy Theater, Boston (Opera Company of Boston)
CAST Lev *b*, Nadia *s*, Yuri *bar*, Gayle *s*, Hannah *ms*, Olympion *t*, Luke *t*, Lieutenant *bar*, Astron *ms* and *t* (or *ct*); *satb* chorus of blacks, whites, hippies
LARGE ORCHESTRA including vast perc section (5 players), electric organ, electric gtr and bass gtr

Immediately after *The Knot Garden* Tippett wrote his *Songs for Dov*, a parable explaining what happened to the character, and his Symphony No. 3, whose vocal second part includes a sequence of blues. By the time he wrote his next major work, *The Ice Break*, he therefore had explored some important resonances of *The Knot Garden* and was ready to confront the broad question set out at the end of the opera, and indeed of the symphony too. Left alone in the universe can mankind entrust its survival to its own capacity for love and mutual healing? Tippett himself has more starkly described the new opera's theme as a question of 'whether or not we can be reborn from the stereotypes we live in'. *The Ice Break* puts this to the test in an uncompromising way. It is more realistic, even surrealistic, than symbolic, and while it does have a moving and encouraging ending, this cannot be regarded as an entirely convincing outcome of the plot. As in most of his work the opera confronts a very large problem without presuming to offer a tidy solution.

SYNOPSIS

When Lev, a Soviet dissident, was sentenced, his wife Nadia with their baby son Yuri emigrated to the US. After 20 years of prison, labour camps and internal exile Lev has been released and also allowed to emigrate.

Act I In an airport lounge Nadia and Yuri await Lev's arrival. They encounter Gayle, Yuri's girlfriend, and Hannah, her black friend, a nurse, who have come to welcome Olympion, Hannah's boyfriend and a 'black champion'. Olympion eventually arrives surrounded by his adoring fans and plays the part expected of him. Nadia suddenly realizes that the soberly dressed man watching her is her husband. In Nadia's apartment they converse. In the airport Olympion, provoked by the sullen behaviour of Yuri, delivers his creed of black power. Gayle delivers hers of white liberalism and falls on her knees in front of him. Yuri is incensed. Olympion knocks him down and the fans divide into hostile factions of black and white. In the apartment Nadia tells Lev about the disturbing behaviour of Yuri, who now bursts in, dragging Gayle with him. He greets his father venomously.

Act II Intimate scenes – within the tensions of Lev's family, between Olympion and Hannah, and for Hannah alone – are set against scenes of mounting violence, which eventually reach confrontation and erupt in a race riot. Gayle and Olympion are killed, Yuri terribly injured. As the bodies are taken away, Lev turns to Hannah for comfort.

Act III Nadia is unable to struggle with life any more. Lev reads to her on her deathbed. They are assured by Luke, a young doctor, and Hannah that Yuri will recover, but Lev asks himself why he has come to this new country just to watch his wife's death and his son's hatred. Nadia lapses into childhood memories. As she dies Lev cries out for her to wait for him in Paradise. There is now an interlude in the 'Paradise Garden', where 'seekers of all kinds' await the appearance of Astron, a

'psychedelic messenger'. He enunciates some cryptic messages but, when treated too reverently, evaporates. The scene changes to the hospital where Yuri's bones have been set and his whole body encased in plaster. The plaster is cut away. As Yuri rejoices in his recovery, the stage is filled with revellers. Hannah wheels Yuri to his father. Father and son embrace.

The opera's title refers to the 'frightening but exhilarating sound of the ice breaking on the great northern rivers in the spring'. As a musical motif it appears several times, notably when Lev meets his wife and is reconciled with his son. Another striking motif is that associated with Lev's recollections of the poetry that sustained him in Russia and now does so again. It concludes the opera as he completes a passage from Goethe begun while Nadia was on her deathbed. A characteristic sound (rather than motif) is that of the chanting crowds who periodically overwhelm the stage. The chorus sings in a variety of ways, including one akin to rock, and forms a crucial part of the opera's very original dramatic design: anonymous mass behaviour in unpredictable invasions of a continuing domestic narrative. This latter proceeds as best it can and contains several beautiful numbers, which contrast poignantly with the bold and often garish music around them: the Act II duet for Olympion and Hannah, Nadia's death song and especially the long aria for Hannah placed at the centre of the whole opera.

RECORDING Harper, Clarey, Sylvan, Page, Walker, C. Robson, Randle, Bottone, Maxwell, Wilson-Johnson, London Sinfonietta Ch and O, Atherton, Virgin Classics, 1991
EDITION v.s., Schott, 1977

New Year

Opera in three acts (1h 30m)
Libretto by the composer
Composed 1986–8
PREMIERES 27 October 1989, Cullen Theater, Wortham Centre, Houston, Texas; UK: 1 July 1990, Glyndebourne, Sussex
CAST Presenter *male voice*, Jo Ann *s*, Donny *bar*, Nan *ms*, Merlin *bar*, Pelegrin *t*, Regan *s*; *satb* chorus of singers and dancers
LARGE ORCHESTRA including 3 sax (s, a, t, bar, b), vast perc. section (5 players), hp, electric gtr, bass gtr, small str section (4.4.4.4.2)

Tippett thought *The Ice Break* would be his last opera. He had already embarked on a series of major concert works (his Fourth Symphony and Fourth String Quartet, and Triple Concerto) and was pondering another which would sum up the experience of a lifetime. When the massive *The Mask of Time* was completed in late 1982, however, he began to change his mind about writing for the theatre again. *New Year* was completed when he was 83.

In some ways this last opera marks a return to the preoccupations of Tippett's first. After the rite of midsummer, there is the rite of midwinter; reality (urban violence) and fantasy (dream figures from a spaceship in the future) again interact, and again time is suspended. The new opera relates closely to the stage musical. There is a chorus of singers and dancers, dance being an integral element: there are solo song and dance numbers, some memorable tunes and Tippett continues his alliance with popular culture, here Afro-Caribbean music. Significantly, he relies on new lighting and staging techniques from the musical theatre to realize his visual conception of two distinct realms of experience. Television has again been a major stimulus to his imagination, particularly in the idea of the Presenter, a 'voice-over', the opera's link with the audience.

SYNOPSIS
Act I Prelude. Scene 1 – 'Somewhere': Jo Ann, an orphan and a trainee children's doctor, dreams of overcoming her fear of the violent world outside. Her foster brother, Donny, bursts in, teasing her and strutting about. Their foster mother Nan comes in search of him. Donny performs his 'Skarade', a song and dance number. Interlude – 'Nowhere': Merlin the computer wizard who has built a spaceship is showing Pelegrin, the navigator, his new computer. When it shows pictures of the past but not of the future, Merlin tries again and gets a picture of the anguished face of Jo Ann. Pelegrin is fascinated, but Regan, their boss, is concerned only with their voyage into the future at New Year. Alone, Pelegrin finds the picture of Jo Ann and sets off in his spaceship. Interlude. Scene 3: Pelegrin and Jo Ann meet but Pelegrin flies off before they can touch. Postlude.
     Act II Prelude. Scene 1: The crowd is preparing for the new year ritual. Nan, Jo Ann and Donny join in. A shaman materializes, dances himself into a trance, and hunts out the scapegoat of the old year – Donny, who is ritually beaten out. At the first stroke of midnight, the spaceship lands. Scene 2: Pelegrin seeks out Jo Ann. Regan demands an explanation of where she is. Donny steps forward and reveals that she is in the past. Regan quickly grasps that Pelegrin has deceived her and berates him and Jo Ann. Donny wants all attention directed on himself. Regan cuts matters short and the spaceship flies off. Scene 3: The crowd is furious, and turns on Donny, who is now really beaten up. As the midnight bell strikes 12 and the crowd sings 'Auld Lang Syne', Jo Ann drags her brother away.
     Act III Prelude. Scene 1: Nan has come again to fetch Donny. Before he is taken away he gives his sister a 'magic video' of his dreams. Pelegrin arrives to fetch Jo Ann. Interlude. Scene 2: Pelegrin takes Jo Ann to drink at the 'fountain of forgetting' or the 'lake of remembering'. She chooses to drink of the lake. They confess love for each other and Pelegrin now takes her to the Paradise Garden where she dances a ritual of inner peace and he picks a rose. Interlude. Scene 3: Pelegrin gives Jo Ann the rose and flies away. She dances, holding the rose. Merlin and Regan are seen cursing Pelegrin. When he returns he holds his hand up and the rose appears in it. Then Jo Ann is seen, wondering at her empty hand. The Presenter explains that she is ready to

open her door and go into the outside world. She does so encouraged by the Presenter, who now proclaims the 'universal dream': 'one humanity, one justice'.

Whatever the correspondences in dramatic conception between *New Year* and *The Midsummer Marriage,* the operas' music is very different. *New Year's* sound-world includes taped music for the spaceship but is epitomized by the saxophones, electric guitars and percussion associated with the singing and dancing of Donny – as in his Act I 'Skarade' and the Act II rap music with percussion only. Yet there is also an abundance of lyrical music, as in Jo Ann's Dreamsong ('Children of the terror town'), which acts as a kind of signature tune, and in that associated with Pelegrin. All the characters have music as vividly individualized as before, exemplifying Tippett's ability to conceive motifs that condense dramatic situations into the shortest of spaces. The opera is thus rich in incident, while at the same time having an easier flow than previously. In general it is laid out traditionally and each act has an extended ensemble: a trio, quartet and duet. The Act III duet also includes a notable example of Tippett's penchant for self-quotation in his late music: Jo Ann's dance is taken from the Paradise Garden scene in *The Mask of Time.*

EDITION v.s., Schott, 1989

Unpublished works: *The Village Opera* (ballad opera, 1729), performing arr., 1928; *Robin Hood* (folksong opera), 1934; *Robert of Sicily* (play for children), 1938; *Seven at One Stroke* (play for children), 1939
BIBLIOGRAPHY Meirion Bowen, *Michael Tippett*, Robson, 1982; Nicholas John (ed.), *The Operas of Michael Tippett*, Calder, 1985; Ian Kemp, *Tippett: The Composer and His Music*, Eulenburg, 1984; 2nd edn, OUP, 1987; Geraint Lewis (ed.), *Michael Tippett O.M.: A Celebration*, Baton, 1985; Michael Tippett, *Moving into Aquarius*, Routledge, 1959; 2nd edn, Paladin, 1974; Michael Tippett, ed. Meirion Bowen, *Music of the Angels*, Eulenburg, 1980; Michael Tippett, *Those Twentieth-Century Blues*, Weidenfeld, 1991; Arnold Whittall, *The Music of Britten and Tippett*, CUP, 1982; 2nd edn, 1990

I.K.

CAMILLO TOGNI
b 18 October 1922, Gussago, Brescia, Italy

Deeply influenced by the example of Schoenberg, whose music he studied intensively in the early 1940s, Togni evolved a distinctive style with strong roots in the Expressionist tradition. Along with Nono, he was one of the first Italian composers to respond to the new directions explored at the Darmstadt summer schools of the early 1950s, but his more recent works reconfirm a Schoenbergian filiation. Since the 1950s he has evolved a peculiarly sensitive and vivid vocal style, in repeatedly setting the poetry of 15th-century France and, crucially, that of Georg Trakl (1887–1914).

Blaubart

Bluebeard
Opera in one act (30m)
Libretto by the composer, after the puppet play by Georg
Trakl with a poem by Vaillant
Composed 1972–5
PREMIERE 14 December 1977, La Fenice, Venice

Togni first encountered Trakl's *Blaubart* in 1956.
Although he considered many subsequent works as
studies for an operatic setting of the text, the project
was not achieved until two decades later. Four
protagonists act out this brutal anatomization of
sexual violence. A boy and an old man watch from
afar as Bluebeard and Elizabeth come from their
marriage service. Overwhelmed by forebodings, the
boy kills himself. Bluebeard dismisses the weeping
old man and finally turns to the seduction of
Elizabeth. When she gives in she discovers the
putrefying secrets of Bluebeard's marriage chamber.
Bluebeard drags her out; he returns covered with
blood and collapses before a crucifix.

EDITIONS f.s., Ricordi, 1979; v.s., Ricordi (on hire), 1979

Barrabas

Opera in one act
Libretto by the composer , after *Aus goldenem Kelch:
Barrabas, eine Phantasie* by Georg Trakl
Composed 1981–5
PREMIERES 30 April 1981, RAI, Turin (sections I, III and
V; concert); 26 September 1985 (sections III and IV), La
Fenice, Venice

In this second Trakl-derived setting Togni explores
the triumph of vice. As the Son of Man is taken to
Golgotha, the freed Barrabas is hailed by a crowd of
prostitutes and thieves, and invited by a young man,
oiled and perfumed, to a luxurious party. As they
drink to the death of the Nazarene, the sun darkens
and the earth shakes: the work of Redemption is
done. *Blaubart* and *Barrabas* constitute the first two
parts of an intended trilogy.

D.O.-S.

TOMMASO TRAETTA

Tommaso Michele Francesco Saverio Traetta [Trajetta]; *b* 30
March 1727, Bitonto, near Bari; *d* 6 April 1779, Venice

Traetta is prominent among those composers who
brought French elements into Italian opera and
helped to break down Italian dramaturgical conventions in the second half of the 18th century. A
product of the Neapolitan conservatories, Traetta
studied with Porpora and Durante at the Conservatorio di S. Maria di Loreto between 1738 and
1748. Comic operas for local theatres may have
preceded his first commission, the opera seria *Il
Farnace*, for the Teatro San Carlo in Naples (1751).
Both comic and serious operas for Rome and several
northern Italian cities followed. In 1758 he became

court composer at Parma where he remained until
1765.

In Parma, Traetta became involved with Du
Tillot's efforts to combine elements from both
French tragédie lyrique and Italian opera seria in
response to opera criticism in both France and Italy.
The court poet Frugoni translated and adapted Pellegrin's libretto for Rameau's *Hippolyte et Aricie*
as *Ippolito ed Aricia* (1759) and Bernard's for his
Castor et Pollux as *I Tintaridi* (1760). The results
amounted to Italian aria opera on mythological,
rather than historical subject matter, embellished
with French choruses, programmatic orchestral music,
and spectacle. Traetta's settings of these works,
though scarcely revolutionary, show Rameau's
influence.

Commissions soon followed for Turin and German-
speaking centres where the fusion of French and
Italian styles was favoured. Cigna-Santi's reworking
of Verazi's libretto *Enea nel Lazio*, which Traetta set
for Turin in 1760, was no more than an Italian piece
with lavish spectacle. Meanwhile in Vienna, Count
Durazzo's efforts at a marriage of the two national
styles was biased towards French models. In 1761,
Traetta was commissioned to provide music for a
joint effort with Durazzo and Migliavacca, producing
an azione teatrale, *Armida*, based on Quinault's
libretto for Lully.

In Mannheim, Holzbauer produced *Ippolito* (1759)
probably using mainly Traetta's music. The court
poet Verazi then wrote a libretto, *Sofonisba*, for
Traetta in 1762, which initiated a series of operas
based on traditional historical texts but incorporating
various dramaturgical innovations and fused with
French elements such as chorus and spectacle.
Finally, in 1763, Traetta was commissioned to write a
full-length opera for Vienna based on the classical
subject of *Ifigenia in Tauride*.

In 1765, Traetta became musical director at the
Conservatorio dell'Ospedaletto in Venice. A year
later he wrote his most successful comic opera, *Le
serve rivali*, for the San Moisè in Venice. Traetta
accepted a court position at St Petersburg in 1768.
After adapting a number of earlier works to the
Russian taste (which was also heavily French), he
again collaborated with Coltellini in their masterpiece, *Antigona*, the culmination of both men's
efforts to revitalize opera seria. In 1775, Traetta
returned to Italy in ill health but was soon called
to London for the 1776–7 season. Here he produced an unsuccessful setting of *Germondo*, one
of Goldoni's few serious libretti. Settling in Venice in
1777, he continued to compose both serious and
comic works until his death.

Ippolito ed Aricia

Hippolytus and Aricia
Tragedia in five acts
Libretto by Carlo Innocenzo Frugoni, after *Hippolyte et
Aricie* by Simon-Joseph Pellegrin (1733)
PREMIERE 9 May 1759, Teatro Ducale, Parma

The libretto is based on Pellegrin's text for Rameau's
opera with some scenes taken from Racine's drama.

Count Francesco Algarotti, who had advocated a new kind of Italian opera using French models, had advised on its form.

Hippolytus, son of the Athenian ruler Theseus, is in love with Aricia, daughter of Theseus' dead rival. Theseus' wife, Phaedra, is also in love with Hippolytus, her stepson. Believing that Hippolytus has betrayed him, Theseus orders the gods to destroy him. Only after a sea monster causes Hippolytus' death does Theseus learn the truth. In order to achieve a happy ending, Phaedra takes poison, Theseus makes his peace with the sorrowing Aricia, and the goddess Diana restores Hippolytus to life, thus reuniting the young couple.

The opera takes from its French model the five-act format, the extraneous underworld scene and the many choruses, dances and sinfonias accompanying the appearances of deities in machines. Such spectacle had been purged from Italian opera in the late 17th century. But the piece is Italianate in its formal outline, since each scene contains a fixed number of characters, and the formal exit aria serves to stop the action for extended periods of vocal display. Most of the choruses and dances serve as entr'actes rather than occurring within the action according to the French manner.

EDITION   facsimile of manuscript, Garland, 1982

Armida

Azione teatrale in one act
Libretto by Giannambrogio Migliavacca and Giacomo Durazzo, after *Armide* by Philippe Quinault
Composed 1760, rev. 1767
PREMIERES   3 January 1761, Burgtheater, Vienna; rev. version: 27 May 1767, Teatro San Salvatore, Venice

This work closely follows Quinault's *Armide*, but the original five acts are contained within a single act of twenty scenes. The story begins as the witch Armida and a band of Saracens prepare to capture a group of crusaders with Rinaldo among them. In a confrontation the two fall in love. The crusaders bring Rinaldo back to his senses, and he abandons her. Armida falls into a rage, calls for her chariot drawn by dragons and leaves the scene in flames and smoke.

The work is significant in that it appeared in Vienna a year before a similar French-inspired azione teatrale, Gluck's *Orfeo*. Like its French model, *Armida* incorporates chorus, dance and pantomime, and the inclusion of several duets is unusual for an Italian piece.

MANUSCRIPT   Österreichische Nationalbibliothek, Musiksammlung, Vienna (four other manuscripts extant in other libraries)

Sofonisba

Dramma per musica in three acts
Libretto by Mattia Verazi, after *Scipione nelle Spagne* by Apostolo Zeno

PREMIERE   4 November 1762, Hoftheater, Mannheim

The opera is notable for its tragic ending, which represented a flagrant departure from the precept of 18th-century dramaturgy that an ending must represent what should have happened rather than what actually did happen. The plot is also unusual: rather than centring on a betrothed pair, it involves a married couple, Sofonisba and Siface, and a child. When Siface is believed dead in battle, Sofonisba's former betrothed, Massinissa, renews his suit. Siface reappears among the captives and reclaims his wife. Together they escape from their Roman captors but are soon retaken. Alone and fearful of being paraded in chains through the streets of Rome, Sofonisba takes the poison Massinissa has provided and is dying when the glad news of freedom arrives.

Verazi, a long-time collaborator with Jommelli in Stuttgart, took advantage of Traetta's experience with French opera and spectacle to initiate some radical departures from Italian practice. A programmatic overture accompanies the successful besieging of a city wall. Act I contains a pantomime ballet and chorus to accompany gladiatorial games. The lines between aria and recitative are blurred, expressive recitatives offer ample opportunities for orchestral effects, and arias are declamatory. In the striking trio finale of Act II, Sofonisba and Siface leave Massinissa to conclude the ensemble alone in frustrated rage.

EDITIONS   f.s., Hugo Goldschmidt (ed.), in *DTB*, xxv, Jg. xiv/1 (1914); xxix, Jg. xvii (1916); v.s. in Byron Cantrell, *Tommaso Traetta and his Opera 'Sofonisba'*, dissertation, University of California, 1957

Ifigenia in Tauride

Iphigenia in Tauris
Dramma per musica in three acts
Libretto by Marco Coltellini
PREMIERE   4 October 1763, Schloss Schönbrunn, Vienna

Orestes and Pylades are captured on the shores of Tauris while seeking the stolen image of Artemis. The high priestess Iphigenia is drawn to the strangers, and her confidant Dori aids them in their quest. The tyrant Toante then orders Iphigenia to sacrifice Dori as a means of appeasing the gods. The captured Pylades soon takes her place, but is saved when Orestes appears. When Pylades reveals that Orestes is the son of Agamemnon, Iphigenia recognizes her own brother. In order to save him from the angry tyrant, she stabs Toante, proclaiming to the people that with his death the gods have been appeased.

Ifigenia was the first full-length Viennese production incorporating French elements predating Gluck's *Alceste* by four years. The opera is outstanding for its extensive use of chorus, either alone or in combination with solos or ballet. Scenes combine chorus, dance, accompanied recitative, ensemble, cavatina and aria; there is French-inspired spectacle which includes a ghost scene containing a chorus and dance of the Furies, and a chorus interrupted by a storm realized in programmatic accompanied recitative. In 1767 Gluck contributed an overture and three numbers to precede the work.

EDITION facsimile of manuscript, Garland, 1978

Le serve rivali
The Rival Servants
Burletta in three acts
Libretto by Pietro Chiari
PREMIERE autumn 1766, Teatro San Moisè, Venice

A typical Italian web of amorous intrigue surrounds the lovers Giacinta and Giannino. Letanzio is also wooing Giacinta, while Palmetta is aggressively pursuing Giannino. Furthermore, Carlina, who is promised to Don Pipo, seeks permission to marry Don Grillo. After many plots and much masquerading, all ends satisfactorily.

Also typically, the opera consists of exit arias, cavatinas, and simple recitative with a duet for the principal couple, finales to each act and an introductory action ensemble. Both charming and amusing, the score is a masterful representation of Traetta's mature style. Giannino has a scena with orchestral storm effects. The duet contains some action and moves through several tempi.

RECORDING Dessì, Nazario, Mattiucci, Barbacini, Raffanti, Corbelli, San Remo SO, Mainardi, Bongiovanni, 1979
EDITION v.s., Edizioni Musicali OTOS, 1971

Antigona
Antigone
Tragedia per musica in three acts (1h 45m)
Libretto by Marco Coltellini, after Sophocles
PREMIERE 11 November 1772, Imperial Theatre, St Petersburg

The plot tells of the fortunes of the children of Oedipus and Jocasta. In the opening scenes, Polyneices challenges his brother Eteocles for the throne of Thebes. They die at each other's hands, and their maternal uncle Creon becomes king. He forbids the burial of the disturber Polyneices. In defiance of their uncle, Polyneices' sisters Antigone and Ismene prepare a funeral pyre. Dismayed at what has transpired, Haemon, the king's son and Antigone's betrothed, implicates himself by bearing the funeral urn to the vault. Antigone is condemned and Haemon disowned. The couple have resolved to die together when Creon at last relents and forgives them.

Radical departures from Italian dramaturgical practice include the spectacular introductory scenes, freely combining pantomime, dance, chorus and recitative, that open each act. Equally radical are the trios in Acts I and II, the arias that become ensembles, and the duet for the hero and the heroine's sister closing Act I. The many choruses and dances incorporated into the action and the arias with chorus are French-inspired. The music is particularly rich in the expressive use of wind instruments, including the clarinet, a recent addition to orchestral forces, and Traetta's orchestrally

accompanied recitatives contain passages of powerful dramatic effect.

EDITION f.s., Maggio Musicale Fiorentino, 1962

Other operas: Buovo d'Antona, 1750; Il Farnace, 1751; La costanza, 1752; I pastori felici, (?)1751, 1753; Le nozze contrastate, (?)1753, 1755; Ezio, (?)1754, 1757; L'incredulo, 1755; La fante furba, 1756; Nitteti, 1757; Didone abbandonata, 1757; Olimpiade, 1758, rev. 1769; Demofoonte, 1758; Solimano, 1759; Enea nel Lazio (Enea e Lavinia), 1760; I Tintaridi (Tindaridi), 1760; Le feste d'Imeneo, 1760; Stordilano, principe di Granata 1760, rev. as Il cavaliero errante, 1778; Zenobia, 1761; Alessandro nell'Indie, 1762; La francese a Malghera, 1764; Antigono, 1764; Semiramide, 1765; Siroe, re di Persia, 1767; Amore in trappola, 1768; L'isola disabitata, 1768; Il tributo campestra, 1768; Fetonte, 1768; Astrea placata, 1770; Amore e Psiche, 1773; Lucio Vero, 1774; Le quattro stagioni e i dodici mesi dell'anno (Le kalmouk), 1776; Germondo, 1776; La Merope, 1776; La disfatta di Dario, 1778; Gli eroi dei Campi Elisi (completed by G. Astaritta), 1779; Artenice (inc.)

BIBLIOGRAPHY H. Bloch, 'Tommaso Traetta's Reform of Italian Opera', Collectanea historiae musicae, vol. 3, Florence, 1963, p. 5; B. Cantrell, Tommaso Traetta and His Opera 'Sofonisba', diss., University of California, 1957; Daniel Heartz, 'Operatic Reform at Parma: Ippolito ed Aricia', Convegno sul settecento parmense nel 2o centenario della morte di C. I. Frugoni, Parma, 1968, p. 271

M.P.M.

EDUARD TUBIN
b 18 June 1905, Kallaste; d 17 November 1982, Stockholm

Tubin was born in the village of Kallaste on Lake Peipus in Estonia. In 1919, after the First World War, Estonia achieved independence and a music school was established in the university town of Tartu, where Tubin became a pupil of Heino Eller, the first Estonian composer of real quality and substance. Tubin attracted attention before the war with his first two symphonies. Following Estonia's incorporation into the Soviet Union by Stalin in 1940, and its occupation by the Nazis the following year, Tubin fled to Sweden in 1944 and made his home there. His music excited some interest and, in 1947, his Fifth Symphony was performed and published.

Tubin's music is tonal and his idiom was very much out of step with the more radical climate of Sweden during the 1950s, when musical life was dominated by figures such as Karl-Birger Blomdahl and Ingvar Lidholm. His neglect did not prevent him from composing ten symphonies, all of which have been recorded. They reveal him as a composer of real stature with a strong sense of form and momentum. He wrote relatively little for the stage; his full-length ballet, Kratt, has been produced in Gothenburg (1983) but in 1991 neither of his operas had been heard outside Estonia. The first, Barbara von Tisenhusen, was staged in Tartu in 1969. The second, Prosten von Reigi (The Parson from Reigi, 1971), draws on a Finnish–Estonian novel by Aino Kallas which tells of a 17th-century pastor whose wife elopes with his newly appointed deacon; the two adulterers are tried and condemned to death. It was revived in Tallinn in 1990.

RECORDINGS *Barbara von Tisenhusen*, Ondine, 1991; *The Parson from Reigi*, Ondine, 1991

R.La.

JOAQUÍN TURINA

b 9 December 1882, Seville, Spain; *d* 14 January 1949, Madrid

Turina's works reveal a French charm in his many piano pieces on Spanish subjects, a deftness of orchestral technique in his *Danzas fantásticas* and *Sinfonía sevillana*, and a sure command of form, deriving mainly from a thorough study of d'Indy's 'cyclical' theories. Despite a constant attempt to accommodate his works within traditional European forms, his music always retained a rich flavour of his native Andalusia.

Although Chase correctly declared that Turina achieved no conspicuous success with his stage works, his statement that Turina's style was 'not an organic growth, but a series of mannerisms that he repeats *ad infinitum*' seems unjust. The score of the biblical *La sulamita* impressed Falla, whom the young Turina met in Madrid in 1902, but the work was never performed. His zarzuela *Fea y con gracia* was considered derivative, though its spontaneous use of popular melody is pleasing. Turina's subsequent operas demonstrate his eclecticism both in their broad choice of subject matter, and in their almost naïve mix of musical styles. The charming *Navidad* opens in a cathedral on Christmas Eve, at the exact moment of the Adoration of the Christ Child, and tells how the entire array of statues at the altar comes to life, while *Jardín de oriente* was inspired by a visit to Morocco, and is set in a harem. *Navidad* contrasts a popular Andalusian with a religious style; *Jardín de oriente* is strongly balletic and stylizes Arabian music in the way fashionable in Europe at the time.

Operatic works: *La sulamita*, (1900); *Fea y con gracia* (zarzuela), 1904; *Margot*, 1914; *Navidad*, 1916; *Jardín de oriente*, 1923; *La anunciación*, 1924
BIBLIOGRAPHY Gilbert Chase, *The Music of Spain*, Dover, 1941; *rp*, 1959; Federico Sopeña, *Joaquín Turina*, Editora Nacional (Madrid), 1943; 2nd edn, 1956

S.J.W.

MARK-ANTHONY TURNAGE

b 10 June 1960, Grays, Essex, England

Turnage came to prominence in the 1980s with a sequence of instrumental and vocal pieces that culminated in his first opera, *Greek*. Its outstanding success earned him international acclaim, and a unique position among composers of his generation

for his distinctly lyrical voice, skill at creating complex yet lucid textures, and innate dramatic flair.

Night Dances, winner of the 1982 Guinness Composition Prize, had already presented these qualities in embryonic form. The work's skill and professionalism owed something to a series of distinguished teachers – including Knussen (at the Royal College of Music), and Henze and Schuller (at Tanglewood). But its musical essence derived from a personal vision encompassing the work of 20th-century masters from Stravinsky to Miles Davis and John Coltrane. Subsequent compositions, including *Lament for a Hanging Man* (1983), *On All Fours* (1985) and *Release* (1987), extended the range and accomplishment of this unusual synthesis. Meanwhile, the challenge of setting verses by Steven Berkoff in the unaccompanied chorus *One Hand in Brooklyn Heights* (1986) was influential in the genesis of *Greek* itself, as were *Beating about the Bush* (1987) for mezzo-soprano and ensemble, and *Gross Intrusion* for strings (1987). Subsequent offshoots include *Greek Suite* for mezzo, tenor and large ensemble (1989) and *Greek Songs* for mezzo, viola and ensemble (1990).

Quentin Hayes (Eddy) and Helen Charnock and Fiona Kimm (the two sphinxes) in Greek *(London, 1990)*

With the orchestral piece *Three Screaming Popes* (1989), Turnage began a fruitful period as Composer in Association with the City of Birmingham Symphony Orchestra, a collaboration that also resulted in *Momentum* (1991), written for the opening of Birmingham's Symphony Hall. *Killing Time* (1992), a half-hour dramatic piece for BBC Television, contains elements of opera, scena and dramatic song-cycle. Forthcoming major projects include a new opera for English National Opera's 1996–7 season.

Greek

Opera in two acts (1h 30m)
Libretto by the composer and Jonathan Moore, based on the play by Steven Berkoff (1980)
Composed 1987–8
PREMIERES 17 June 1988, Carl-Orff-Saal, Munich; UK: 25 August 1988, Leith Theatre, Edinburgh

Though the themes of *Greek* are universal, they acquire a topical status in the charged atmosphere of the late 1980s. Berkoff's play retells the Oedipus story in the context of a contemporary metropolis in which racism, violence and mass unemployment appear as metaphors for the plague blighting the city.

Written for four singers and a large instrumental ensemble (all doubling on percussion), the music matches the fast-moving stage events with a flexible, wide-ranging style, juxtaposing the hard-hitting vernacular of football chants with episodes of passionately lyrical beauty for Eddy (high baritone), the opera's tragic hero.

RECORDING Decca, 1993
EDITION v.s., Schott, 1988

BIBLIOGRAPHY 'Composer and Critic', *Royal College of Music Magazine*, summer 1991

N.W.

ROMUALD TWARDOWSKI
b 17 June 1930, Vilnius, Poland (now Lithuania)

Twardowski studied at the Lithuanian State Conservatory in Vilnius and later at the Warsaw Music Academy and in Paris with Nadia Boulanger. He wrote his first operas while a lecturer at the music school in Katowice before moving to Warsaw in 1967, where he has been a lecturer at the Music Academy since 1972. His compositions have won several prizes, including the Grand Prix at the Prince Rainier Competition (twice, for the ballet-pantomime *The Sorcerer's Statues* in 1965, and in 1973 for the music drama *Lord Jim*), and at the Tribune Internationale des Compositeurs UNESCO (1963).

His widely varied compositions combine neoclassical and modern styles and techniques. His operas are characterized by a concern for the dramatic structure of the libretto, and display unusual feeling for the stage and a powerful emotional directness. The relationship between structure and plasticity of expression may be brought out by exploiting contrasts in emotional tension (*Lord Jim, Maria Stuart*) or by linking reminiscences of medieval and Renaissance mystery and morality plays with the techniques of the modern stage (*The Tragedy, The History of St Catherine*). The radio (*The Fall of Father Suryn*) and television (*A Song Without Words*) operas form a special group.

Operas: *Cyrano de Bergerac*, 1963; *Tragedyja albo rzecz, o Janie i Herodzie* (*The Tragedy, or The Story of John and Herod*), 1969; *Upadek Ojca Suryna* (*The Fall of Father Suryn*), radio opera, 1969; *Lord Jim*, 1973; *Pieśń bez słów* (*A Song Without Words*), television opera, 1976; *Maria Stuart*, 1981; *Historia o św. Katarzynie* (*The History of St Catherine*), 1986

BIBLIOGRAPHY *Kto jest kim w Polsce* (*Who's Who in Poland*), Wydawnictwo Interpress, 1984; 2nd edn, 1989

J.M.

U

VIKTOR ULLMANN
b 1 January 1898, Prague; *d* 18 October 1944, ?Auschwitz

Ullmann studied with Schoenberg in Vienna and later in Prague with Alois Hába in the quarter-tone department of the Prague Musikhochschule. He also worked under Zemlinsky on the music staff of the Deutsches Theater, Prague, and was a member of Schoenberg's Society for Private Musical Performances (two of his song-cycles were performed by the Society in 1924). Like Hába, he was greatly interested in the teachings of Rudolf Steiner. In 1942 he was arrested by the Nazis and interned in Theresienstadt; on 16 October 1944 he was transferred to Auschwitz.

Der Kaiser von Atlantis, oder Die Tod-Verweigerung
The Emperor of Atlantis, or The Refusal to Die
Legend in four scenes, Op. 49 (1h)
Libretto by Peter Kien
Composed *c.* 1943
PREMIERES 16 December 1975, Bellevue Centre, Amsterdam; US: 21 April 1977, San Francisco Opera; UK: 7 May 1985, Imperial War Museum, London

The precise circumstances under which *Der Kaiser von Atlantis* was composed are uncertain. In Theresienstadt a fellow prisoner was the poet and painter Peter Kien. He and Ullmann set out to write an opera, drawing on the limited resources available (some distinguished singers and an orchestra of 13 players, including banjo, harpsichord and harmonium). Evidently the work was rehearsed, but the text was interpreted by the authorities as being anti-Hitler and its performance prohibited. Ullmann and Kien were both subsequently transferred to Auschwitz and met their deaths in the gas chamber. In 1972 an exhibition was devoted to Ullmann in Prague. Documents came to light which suggested that autograph material had by some miracle survived the Holocaust. Two years later, while working on Theresienstadt documentation, H. G. Adler discovered the performing materials, the manuscript score as well as a handwritten and a typed copy of the libretto in London. Kerry Woodward collated the diverse sources, completing sketchy or illegible passages to produce a performing edition of the score which he himself conducted at the world premiere.

The Kaiser of Atlantis has proclaimed a 'holy war'. Death abdicates his duties in protest, and the Kaiser's authority is further undermined by a rebellion. A girl and a soldier from opposing sides fall in love. Finally Death agrees to return to work, but only on condition that the Kaiser should be his first victim. During the course of the action the Kaiser loses touch with reality and becomes an almost sympathetic figure. The supposed analogy to contemporary events is shown to be superficial: anyway, it is Death who dominates the entire action.

The dramatic circumstances under which *Der Kaiser von Atlantis* was composed were an obvious bonus for the work's posthumous promoters. However, the powerful libretto needs no special pleading and, despite stylistic allegiances to Eisler and Weill, moments of Straussian harmony and jazz influence, Ullmann's score has sufficient individuality to stand on its own. Since its rediscovery it has been widely performed, recorded and televised.

EDITION Schott, 1992

Other works: *Peer Gynt*, (1928); *Der Sturz des Antichrist*, (1936); *Der zerbrochene Krug*, 1942
BIBLIOGRAPHY J. Karas, *Music in Terez in 1941–1945*, Beaufort Books, 1985

A.C.W.B.

IGNAZ UMLAUF
b 1746, Vienna; *d* 8 June 1796, Meidling, nr Vienna

Umlauf was the principal viola-player in the Viennese German Theatre orchestra when, in 1778, Joseph II asked him to compose *Die Bergknappen* as the opening work for the newly founded German National-Singspiel. As a result of its success he became kapellmeister of the ensemble and received five further commissions for singspiels before the theatre was disbanded in 1783. *Die schöne Schusterin* was Umlauf's greatest popular success and was performed extensively abroad and revived until 1825. Beethoven composed two replacement arias for it in 1791.

The stylistic inconsistency of Umlauf's singspiels bears witness to the difficulty in establishing a new genre of musical theatre which until then had only existed in contemporary music theory. While simple folklike songs predominate, accompanied recitatives and coloratura arias are borrowed from opera seria and the spoken dialogues and vaudevilles at the end resemble forms encountered in opéra comique. In the finale of some operas, however, Umlauf broke out of such a restrictive scheme, mingling recitatives, dialogues, arias and choral passages effectively.

Operatic works: *Die Insel der Liebe*, 1772; *Die Bergknappen*, 1778 (EDITION f.s., Robert Haas (ed.), *DTÖ*, vol. 36, 1911; *rp*, 1959); *Die Apotheke*, 1778; *Die schöne Schusterin, oder Die pücefarbenen Schuhe*, 1779 (EDITION facsimile, T. Bauman (ed.), *German Opera 1770–1800*, vol. 13, Garland, 1986); *Das Irrlicht* [*Der Irrwisch*], *oder Endlich fand er sie*, 1782, rev. 1796; *Welche*[*s*] *ist die beste Nation?*, 1782; *Die glücklichen Jäger*, 1786; *Der Ring der Liebe, oder Zemirens und Azors Ehestand*, 1786; *Melide*, (n.d.)
BIBLIOGRAPHY   Franz Hadamowsky, *Das Wiener Hoftheater (1776–1966)*, vol. 1, 1966; H. A. Koch, *Das Deutsche Singspiel*, Metzler, 1974

M.F.

FRANCESCO ANTONIO BALDASSARE UTTINI
b 1723, Bologna; *d* 25 October 1795, Stockholm

Uttini's principal claim to fame is that he composed the first opera in Swedish, *Thetis och Pelée*, for the Royal Opera established by King Gustav III. From his arrival in Sweden in 1755 until his retirement in 1788, Uttini was the driving force behind Stockholm's musical life.

Uttini studied in Bologna under Padre Martini. In 1743 he was received into the famed Accademica Filarmonica and was also employed by Pietro Mingotti's travelling opera troupe, with which he toured to Madrid and later to Copenhagen in the company of Gluck. Queen Louisa Ulrike, sister of Frederick the Great and consort of King Adolphus Frederick, persuaded Uttini to form his own theatre company and bring it to Stockholm. He performed his Italian operas at the Court Theatre in Drottningholm and his French opéras comiques in Stockholm. In 1767 he was appointed court kapellmeister, a position he held until 1782.

Operas surviving in whole or in part: *Demofoonte* (one aria), *c.* 1750; *L'Olimpiade* (one aria), 1753; *Armida* (pasticcio; coll. with Sarti and others), 1754; *Il rè pastore*, 1755; *L'eroe cinese*, 1757; *Thetis och Pelée* (arias only), 1773; *Aline, drottning uti Golcanda*, 1776; 14 lost operas
BIBLIOGRAPHY   E. Sundström, 'Francesco Antonio Uttini som musik-dramatiker', *STMf*, vol 45 (1963), pp. 33–93

N.J.

JÁNOS VAJDA
b 8 October 1949, Miskolc, Hungary

A composition pupil of Petrovics in Budapest, Vajda also studied in Amsterdam. He worked for some years as a répétiteur for Hungarian Radio and Television and since 1981 has taught composition at the Budapest Academy.

Vajda's best works are mostly choral or for the stage, and include several ballets as well as two operas. Of the operas, *Barabbás* (1977) is a rather conventionally Expressionistic treatment of a short story by Frigyes Karinthy. The one-act opera *Mario and the Magician* (*Mario és a varászló*, 1985), based on the story by Thomas Mann, is in a sense more individual. It marks (with Bozay's *Csongor és Tünde*) the arrival of post-modernism on the Hungarian musical stage, and makes considerable use of quotation (from Richard Strauss, Puccini, Berg). Commissioned by Hungarian Television, it was also staged with success at the Hungarian State Opera House in 1988, and subsequently recorded by Hungaroton.

BIBLIOGRAPHY Péter Halász, 'A New Hungarian Opera', and Paul Griffiths, 'Vajda's *Mario and the Magician*: The Score', *New Hungarian Quarterly*, no. 114 (summer 1989), vol. 30, pp. 224–8

S.W.

RALPH VAUGHAN WILLIAMS
b 12 October 1872, Down Ampney, Gloucestershire, England; *d* 26 August 1958, London

With his friend Gustav Holst, Vaughan Williams was one of the architects of the so-called English musical renaissance at the start of the 20th century. They deliberately turned away from continental influences – as far as that was ever possible – to become 'English' composers. The son of a clergyman and descended on his mother's side from Darwins and Wedgwoods, Vaughan Williams was educated at Charterhouse, the Royal College of Music and Trinity College, Cambridge. At the RCM he was a composition pupil of both Parry and Stanford. His earliest compositions were chamber music and songs, the latter including the popular *Linden Lea* (1901) and *Songs of Travel* (1904). At this time he became deeply involved in collecting folksongs, following the example of Cecil Sharp. From 1904 to 1906 he also edited the music of a new hymn book, *The English Hymnal*.

Although his choral setting of Walt Whitman, *Toward the Unknown Region*, was a success at the 1907 Leeds Festival, he was dissatisfied with his progress and in 1908 went to Paris for a period of intensive study with Ravel. Ironically, it was this foreign influence, rather than folksong, that released his creative originality. In the three years after his return from France he composed his First String Quartet, a song-cycle (*On Wenlock Edge*) based on Housman's *A Shropshire Lad* poems and the *Fantasia on a Theme by Thomas Tallis* for strings, and completed his large-scale *Sea Symphony* (Whitman again), which was the outstanding success at the 1910 Leeds Festival and placed him in the vanguard of his generation of British composers.

Primarily associated with choral and orchestral works (nine symphonies), Vaughan Williams wanted to succeed as an opera composer. In 1913, he was director of music to Sir Frank Benson's Shakespeare company at Stratford-upon-Avon. At this time he was completing his first opera, *Hugh the Drover*. After four years' active war service in 1914–18, he revised it for its first performance in 1924. Five operas followed, but apart from the short *Riders to the Sea*, none has won a regular place in the repertoire. On the day he died he was working on a seventh opera, *Thomas the Rhymer*.

Hugh the Drover, or Love in the Stocks
Romantic ballad opera in two acts (2h)
Libretto by Harold Child
Composed 1910–14; rev. 1924 and 1955; optional extra scene added, 1933
PREMIERES 4 July 1924, Parry Opera Theatre, Royal College of Music, London; first public performance: 14 July 1924, His Majesty's Theatre, Haymarket, London; US: 21 February 1928, Washington DC
CAST Hugh *t*, Mary *s*, John *b-bar*, Aunt Jane *a*, Constable *b*, 2 *t*, 2 *bar*; 9 smaller roles taken by chorus members; *satb* chorus of inhabitants of the town, toy-lamb sellers, primrose sellers, village boys, soldiers
MEDIUM ORCHESTRA including perc (4 players) and hp; on-and offstage: brass and perc

Vaughan Williams (top left) with his first wife Adeline, Gustav Holst and (seated) Dorothy Longman (an amateur violinist), Vally Lasker and Nora Day, both music teachers at St Paul's Girls School and colleagues of Holst

In writing *Hugh the Drover*, Vaughan Williams once said jocularly that his ambition was to put a boxing match on the stage of Covent Garden, an ambition still unfulfilled. In first approaching his librettist (a leader writer on *The Times*), he wrote, 'I see hardly any chance of an opera by an English composer ever being produced, at all events in our lifetime.' That was in 1909 or 1910, when he was 37. The remark is important in showing how composers of his generation felt the lack of an English operatic tradition.

SYNOPSIS
Act I The scene is set in a small Cotswold market-town (Northleach was in the composer's mind) during the Napoleonic wars (about 1812). A fair is in progress. Mary sings unenthusiastically of her forthcoming marriage to wealthy John the Butcher. A stranger, a drover named Hugh, falls in love with her at first sight and invites her to share his life on the open road. She agrees. Hugh proposes to fight John, with Mary as the stake. John loses and accuses Hugh of being a French spy. The crowd turns against him and the Constable (Mary's father) puts Hugh in the stocks.

Act II Early next morning. Mary has stolen the keys from her father. She and Hugh are about to run away when voices are heard and the alarm is raised. Hugh hides Mary under his cloak and suspicions are allayed. But John has brought Mary a spray of mayflowers and has discovered she is not at home. The Constable and Aunt Jane find her sitting in the stocks next to Hugh and refusing to be freed. The Constable and John disown her. At this point soldiers arrive and John urges the instant arrest and trial of Hugh. But the sergeant recognizes Hugh as an old friend and a loyal Englishman. He press-gangs

John 'to make a soldier of him'. In spite of pleas to them to stay, Hugh and Mary leave the town for their life of adventure.

Vaughan Williams used several folksongs in the score but his own tunes are what gives the opera, for all its dramatic weaknesses, its charm and appeal. The love duet between Hugh and Mary has a Puccinian warmth and lyricism and the choral episodes are attractive. For a production conducted by Sir Thomas Beecham in 1933, Vaughan Williams inserted a new scene at the beginning of Act II which includes three arias for John the Butcher and an extra one of considerable beauty for Mary. He later said he thought the scene was 'poor, musically and dramatically', but when he finally revised the opera in 1955 he left it as an option. Without it, the opera makes a short evening.

RECORDINGS 1. excerpts: Lewis, Willis, Davies, Collier, Dawson, unnamed O, Sargent, HMV, 1924: pre-electrically recorded by some of the cast from the first RCM and first professional (BNOC) performances; 2. Armstrong, Watts, Tear, Lloyd, Rippon, Ambrosian O Ch, RPO, Groves, EMI, 1979: the only complete recording
EDITIONS v.s., Curwen, 1924; rev. version (with extra 1933 scene): v.s., Curwen, 1959; final rev. version (lacks extra 1933 scene): v.s., Curwen, 1977

The Shepherds of the Delectable Mountains

Pastoral episode in one act (23m)
Libretto by the composer based on *The Pilgrim's Progress* (1674–9, 1684) by John Bunyan
Composed 1921–2
PREMIERE 11 June 1922, Parry Opera Theatre, Royal College of Music, London

CAST Pilgrim* *bar*, Knowledge* (First Shepherd) *bar*, Watchful (Second Shepherd) *t*, Sincere (Third Shepherd) *bar*, Celestial Messenger *t*, Voice of a Bird *s* (*written in treble clef); offstage *sa* chorus of celestial voices
SMALL ORCHESTRA of ww and str; offstage: tpt, hp, 3 bells

This was one of three compositions that occupied Vaughan Williams immediately after the First World War. The others were the Mass in G minor and *A Pastoral Symphony*. All contain music in which an ecstatic visionary rapture was the main emotional state rather than any angry or bitter reaction to the events of 1914–18. Vaughan Williams was an agnostic; his recourse to religious texts and subjects was both an acknowledgement of the important part played by religion in his countrymen's lives and of the inspiration he himself drew from the beauty of English prose.

SYNOPSIS
Three shepherds are kneeling in prayer before sunset. Pilgrim enters (Vaughan Williams did not adhere to Bunyan's name for his hero – Christian – because he wanted his opera to be an allegory suitable for any religious creed). He inquires if he is on the correct road for the Celestial City. On being reassured, he stays with them a while for solace. A bird sings Psalm 23 and the shepherds join in. A celestial messenger summons Pilgrim and ceremonially pierces his heart with an arrow. The shepherds anoint Pilgrim and as he enters the water of the River of Death, they sing and are joined by an offstage chorus.

The setting of 'Whoso dwelleth under the defence of the Most High' is an expansion of an alto solo in the incidental music Vaughan Williams wrote for a dramatization of *The Pilgrim's Progress* in 1906. Much of the counterpoint in the opera is triadic, but as in other works of this period, there is a strong flavour of bitonality.

EDITIONS f.s./v.s., OUP, 1925

Sir John in Love

Opera in four acts (2h)
Libretto by the composer based on *The Merry Wives of Windsor* by Shakespeare (1600–1601) and several other sources
Composed 1924–8, with *Prologue, Episode and Interlude* added in 1933 (*Prologue* later withdrawn)
PREMIERES 21 March 1929, Parry Opera Theatre, Royal College of Music, London; *Prologue, Episode and Interlude*: 30 October 1933, Victoria Rooms, Clifton, Bristol; US: 20 January 1949, Columbia University, New York
CAST Sir John Falstaff *bar*, Bardolph *t*, Nym *bar*, Pistol *b*, Mrs Page *s*, Mrs Ford *ms*, Anne Page *s*, Fenton *t*, Mrs Quickly *ms/a*, Ford *b*, *s*, *t*, 2 *t/bar*, 6 *bar*, 1 *b*, 4 *non-singing roles*; *satb* chorus of girl friends of Anne Page, women servants of Ford, citizens of Windsor, servants of Ford and Page; boy friends of William Page *non-singing*; dancers
MEDIUM ORCHESTRA with rattle, bells, hp

Vaughan Williams had wanted to compose a Shakespeare opera ever since his experience as music

director at Stratford-upon-Avon in 1913. It was then he first arranged 'Greensleeves', for *The Merry Wives* and for *Richard II*. Its use in *Sir John in Love* led to its being extracted as the popular *Fantasia on Greensleeves*. In compiling the libretto, Vaughan Williams used poems from other Shakespeare plays and from other authors such as Jonson, Middleton and Marlowe. He also incorporated into the score nine folksongs besides 'Greensleeves', pointing out in a preface that 'out of a total of 120 minutes' music, the folktunes occupy less than 15'. Of the 1933 additions, the *Interlude* contains the best music and strengthens the opera dramatically. It is customary to incorporate it as Scene 1 of Act III.

SYNOPSIS
Act I A substantial part of the act is occupied with Anne Page's rebellion against her mother's wish that she should marry Dr Caius. She is in love with Fenton, but Justice Shallow and Sir Hugh Evans want her to marry Shallow's cousin Slender. Towards the end of the act, Falstaff reveals to his cronies that he has written identical love letters to Mrs Ford and Mrs Page. Pistol and Nym refuse to deliver them and inform Ford, whose jealousy aria is the climax of the first act.

Act II Mrs Ford and Mrs Page read the letters to each other and plan revenge. Mrs Quickly delivers to Falstaff an invitation from Mrs Ford to call on her that morning. Ford (disguised as 'Brook') offers Falstaff money to seduce Mrs Ford in order to prove whether rumours of her easy virtue are true or false.

Act III Anne Page explains to the Host of the Garter Inn how she plans to deceive her parents and marry Fenton. The Host promises to find a priest to marry them next day. Falstaff calls on Mrs Ford, who is singing 'Greensleeves' when he arrives. He is wooing her when Mrs Quickly interrupts to say Mrs Page is coming. Falstaff hides in the laundry basket which, as planned, is carted off to be ditched in the Thames.

Act IV Ford asks his wife's pardon and they plot Falstaff's humiliation at Herne the Hunter's oak in Windsor Forest at midnight. There, as in Verdi,

Falstaff being teased in Act IV of Sir John in Love *(London, 1946)*

Falstaff is pinched by the village children disguised as fairies, after which Anne turns the tables on the Pages who think Anne has married Slender. But Anne and Fenton ride in, married, on a flower-decked cart and the opera ends with forgiveness all round.

Vaughan Williams wrote *Sir John in Love* for his own pleasure and poured into it some of his most lyrical music. Falstaff as lover is not guyed and is given some attractive love songs. There is variety of mood, from broad comedy to romance, and the subsidiary characters are well defined. The wedding chorus in the final scene, a setting of Ben Jonson's 'See the chariot at hand', is a highlight of a high-spirited score. Inevitably the opera suffers from comparison with Verdi, but in its more modest way it offers pleasures that have not yet been fully exploited by any professional company. Five choral extracts were converted into the cantata *In Windsor Forest* (1931).

RECORDING   Palmer, Eathorne, Bainbridge, Tear, Noble, Herincx, Lloyd, John Alldis Ch, New Philharmonia O, M. Davies, EMI, 1975
EDITIONS   v.s., OUP, 1930; corrected, 1971; *Prologue, Episode and Interlude*: v.s., OUP, 1936

The Poisoned Kiss, or The Empress and the Necromancer

Romantic extravaganza, with spoken dialogue, in three acts (2h)
Libretto by Evelyn Sharp, adapted from the story *The Poison Maid* by Richard Garnett (1888) and the story *Rapaccini's Daughter* by Nathaniel Hawthorne
Composed 1927–9; rev. 1934–5, 1936–7, 1956–7 (with new spoken dialogue by Ursula Vaughan Williams)
PREMIERES   12 May 1936, Arts Theatre, Cambridge; US: 21 April 1937, New York City Opera, New York
CAST   Angelica *s*, Tormentilla *s*, Gallanthus *bar*, Dipsacus *b*, Empress *a*, Amaryllus *t*, *s*, 2 *ms*; *satb* chorus
MEDIUM ORCHESTRA

Vaughan Williams confessed that *The Poisoned Kiss* was the only score he had never shown to Holst 'because he would never have understood how I considered it unimportant and yet wanted to write it'. He wanted to write a comic opera and agreed to collaborate with Cecil Sharp's sister Evelyn. The libretto's rather undergraduate humour has been part of the work's undoing in spite of delightful music. In the late 1920s, Vaughan Williams was working on three operas simultaneously – *Sir John in Love*, *Riders to the Sea* and *The Poisoned Kiss* – and at the same time began work on his large-scale ballet *Job*, a remarkable achievement for one not normally regarded principally as a dramatic composer.

SYNOPSIS
Act I   All the characters have botanical names. The magician Dipsacus was jilted when a young man by the Empress Persicaria. In revenge he plans to kill her son, Prince Amaryllus. He has brought up his daughter Tormentilla on a diet of poison so that when, as Dipsacus intends, the two young people

meet and fall in love, her first kiss will prove fatal to Amaryllus. As it happens, Amaryllus and his attendant Gallanthus have already seen Tormentilla and the prince declares that it is 'the real thing' this time and strikes her pet cobra, not realizing she is in no danger from it. Dipsacus keeps the lovers apart by a spell. Tormentilla demands to know what he is up to and, when he tells her, she says she will have no part in his death plot. She and her maid Angelica leave for Golden Town.
Act II   After various complications, Amaryllus and Tormentilla meet again and kiss, the Prince falling unconscious.
Act III   The cause is not poison (he has been fed on antidotes all his life) but a spell laid on him by Dipsacus. A doctor says that the only way to cure him is by summoning Tormentilla whose name Amaryllus keeps uttering. Dipsacus arrives to gloat over the Empress, but after quarrelling they rekindle their former love and the opera ends with three couples united – the Empress and Dipsacus, Tormentilla and Amaryllus, and Angelica and Gallanthus.

The Poisoned Kiss is midway between operetta and musical but its music does not wholeheartedly embrace those genres in spite of delicious waltzes, tangos and mock-jazz numbers. Such songs as 'Who would be unhappy me' and 'Blue larkspur in a garden' are happy inventions, and the visionary Vaughan Williams of the symphonies makes an appearance when the Empress conjures up a vision of the young lovers for Dipsacus. But for those who regard Vaughan Williams as mainly a composer of austere symphonies – a misleading view in any case – the music of this opera will come as a surprise. The pity is that, often being at odds with the libretto, it cannot overcome the defects of the text in the theatre.

EDITION   v.s., OUP, 1936

Riders to the Sea

Opera in one act (40m)
Libretto: an almost verbatim setting of the play *Riders to the Sea* by John Millington Synge (1902)
Composed 1925–32
PREMIERES   1 December 1937, Parry Opera Theatre, Royal College of Music, London; US: 26 February 1950, Cleveland, Ohio
CAST   Maurya *a*, Bartley *bar*, Cathleen *s*, Nora *s*, woman *ms*; women's chorus; men and women, *non-singing*
SMALL ORCHESTRA with ca, b cl, bd and sea machine

The play and opera deal with the lives of fisherfolk on the Isle of Arran.

SYNOPSIS
After a short prelude, Nora asks her sister Cathleen to help her identify clothes taken off a drowned corpse. She believes they belonged to their brother Michael, lost at sea like his father and four of his brothers. They hide the clothes in the loft so that their mother Maurya will not see them. She enters, worried that her last living son Bartley is to take horses to Galway Fair, which involves a sea crossing.

Bartley arrives to fetch a rope. Rejecting their pleas to him to stay, he says he will ride the red mare, with the grey pony following. The sisters reproach Maurya for not giving Bartley her blessing and force her to take him some food for the journey. While she is away, they identify the clothes as Michael's. Maurya returns, distressed. She has seen Bartley riding to the sea on the mare with Michael, wearing new clothes, on the pony. Cathleen tells her Michael is dead, and Maurya realizes her vision means Bartley will die. As she sings of the deaths of her menfolk, Bartley's dripping body is carried in. Maurya, almost relieved, sings that the sea can hurt her no more. 'No man at all can be living for ever, and we must be satisfied.'

This is Vaughan Williams's most successful opera and in every respect a key work in his output. Notwithstanding the depressing story, the subject of man against nature was one that always inspired strong music from him. The score is organized almost symphonically, much of the thematic material being derived from the short prelude. Also, the character of Maurya is fully developed, her final aria being Purcellian in its elegiac simplicity. The orchestration is subtle and evocative, with foreshadowings of the bleak and ghostly finale of the Sixth Symphony (1944–7). The keening of the women's voices as Bartley's body is taken into the house and the constant sound of the sea also anticipate the *Sinfonia Antartica* of 1952.

RECORDING   Burrowes, Watts, Price, Luxon, O Nova, M. Davies, EMI, 1970
EDITIONS   f.s., OUP, 1972; v.s., OUP, 1936

The Pilgrim's Progress

Morality in a prologue, four acts and an epilogue (2h)
Libretto by the composer founded on *The Pilgrim's Progress* (Part I, 1674–9; Part II, 1684) by John Bunyan, with interpolations from the Bible and verse by Ursula Vaughan Williams
Composed 1925–36; rev. 1942, 1944–9, 1951–2 (*The Shepherds of the Delectable Mountains* episode was composed in 1921; first sketches for a *Pilgrim* opera date from 1906.)
PREMIERES   26 April 1951, Covent Garden, London; US: 28 April 1968, Brigham Young University, Provo, Utah
CAST   Bunyan *b-bar*, Pilgrim *bar*, Evangelist *b*, Watchful *high bar*, Herald *bar*, Apollyon *b*, Lord Lechery *t buffo*, Lord Hate-Good *b*, Woodcutter's Boy *s* or *boy s*, Mr By-Ends *t buffo*, Mrs By-Ends *a*, 3 shepherds *t*, *bar*, *b*, Voice of a Bird *s*, 4 *s*, 2 *ms*, 3 *a*, 6 *t*, 4 *bar*, 4 *b* (many parts are doubled, and 11 singers are sufficient); *satb* chorus of men and women of the House Beautiful, 'certain persons clothed in gold', Doleful Creatures, Traders in Vanity Fair, chorus in the Celestial City, chorus on Earth; dancers
LARGE ORCHESTRA with perc, including gong, triangle, xyl, glock, bells, cel; onstage: tpt

This ambitious work was the culmination of Vaughan Williams's lifelong belief that Bunyan's allegory could form the basis of an opera. It preoccupied him for over forty years. In 1906 he wrote incidental music for a semi-amateur stage adaptation in Reigate, Surrey. In 1921 he composed the one-act episode *The Shepherds of the Delectable Mountains*

(see above), now incorporated into the larger work as Act IV, Scene 2, with an altered ending. He worked sporadically on Acts I and II from 1925 to 1936, when he abandoned the project and used some of the themes in his Fifth Symphony, begun in 1938 and first performed in 1943. His enthusiasm was rekindled in 1942 when he composed 38 sections of incidental music for a BBC dramatization by Edward Sackville-West. Some of this was incorporated into the final operatic version, on which he worked from 1944 to 1949.

SYNOPSIS
In a prologue, Bunyan is seen in Bedford Gaol writing the last words of his book. As he reads, Act I begins and Pilgrim is seen with a burden on his back. He is directed by the Evangelist to the Wicket Gate where his neighbours fail to persuade him to turn back. He kneels in front of the Cross. Three Shining Ones take his burden and lead him to the gate of the House Beautiful, where he is robed.

At the start of Act II, Pilgrim takes to the King's Highway. He is given armour. In the Valley of Humiliation he hears the howling of the Doleful Creatures and defeats Apollyon in a fight but is wounded. Two Heavenly Beings revive him and the Evangelist invests him with the Staff of Salvation, the Roll of the Word and the Key of Promise.

The first scene of Act III is Vanity Fair where Pilgrim rejects the seductive pleasures on offer. He is taken before Lord Hate-Good and condemned to death. In prison he bewails his fate until he remembers the Key of Promise. He unlocks the gates and walks to freedom.

In Act IV a Woodcutter's Boy directs Pilgrim to the Delectable Mountains. On the way he encounters Mr and Mrs By-Ends who decline to accompany him. Then follows the scene with the Shepherds. A Celestial Messenger summons him to the Celestial City and pierces his heart with an arrow. A trumpet sounds as Pilgrim passes through the River of Death and ascends to the gates of the city. In an epilogue, Bunyan offers his book to the audience.

Although criticized for its lack of dramatic action and for the leisurely tempo of much of the music, *The Pilgrim's Progress* can be a most affecting and impressive theatrical experience. The howling of the Doleful Creatures and the bustle of Vanity Fair are effectively represented; and the music for Pilgrim's arming, much of it familiar from the Fifth Symphony, and for his sojourn in prison is Vaughan Williams at the height of his powers, as is the uplifting penultimate scene when the Celestial City is reached. Having been composed over so long a period, the opera forms a synthesis of Vaughan Williams's stylistic progress over the years, from the pastoral meditation of the 1920s to the angry music of the middle symphonies and eventually the more experimental phase of the *Sinfonia Antartica* in his last decade. The composer's summing-up of its failure in 1951 was: 'It's not like the operas they are used to, but it's the sort of opera I wanted to write, and there it is.'

RECORDINGS   1. Armstrong, Partridge, English, Noble,
Shirley-Quirk, Carol Case, Herincx, London Philharmonic
Ch and O, Boult, EMI, 1972; 2. Whitehouse, Neale, Lloyd-
Roberts, Snell, Marsden, Taylor, Jackson, Chaundy, Ch and
O of Royal Northern College of Music, Manchester,
Kennaway, RNCM, 1992
EDITION   v.s., OUP, 1952

BIBLIOGRAPHY   Michael Kennedy, *The Works of Ralph
Vaughan Williams*, OUP, 1964; rev. edn, 1980; 2nd edn, 1992;
Wilfrid Mellers, *Vaughan Williams and the Vision of Albion*,
Barrie and Jenkins, 1989; Ursula Vaughan Williams, *R.V.W.:
A Biography*, OUP, 1964; rev. edn, 1985

M.K.

Woodcut from the prologue of L'Amfiparnaso *(1597)*

ORAZIO VECCHI

baptized 6 December 1550, Modena; *d* 19 February 1605,
Modena

Vecchi received an ecclesiastical training in Modena
and also studied with the madrigalist Salvatore
Essenga. He held cathedral appointments in Salò,
Modena, Reggio Emilia and Correggio before
returning to Modena as choirmaster of the Cathedral
in 1593 (and of Duke Cesare d'Este's court from
1598). Despite his ecclesiastical career and numerous
sacred publications, he was famed more for his
secular canzonets, madrigals and, in particular,
madrigal-comedies.

The madrigal-comedy was a loosely defined genre
rooted in the increasingly common tendency to
group polyphonic madrigals into cycles linked by
theme and by dramatic or emotional effect. First
Alessandro Striggio (with the chattering washerwomen of his *Il cicalamento delle donne al bucato,
1567),* and then Vecchi and his contemporary,
Adriano Banchieri, evoked the high spirits of the
commedia dell'arte, with dialect texts and nonsense
rhymes, overtly 'popular' musical styles and
humorous effects, often involving parody. Vecchi
published four such works in Venice: *Selva di varia
ricreatione* (1590); *L'Amfiparnaso* (1597); *Il convito
musicale* (1597), and *Le veglie di Siena* (1604).
But only *L'Amfiparnaso* has the thematic
coherence to be more than just a loose succession of
madrigals. The madrigal-comedy might be seen as
part of the search for new dramatic effects in late
16th-century music (and Vecchi himself is said to
have approved of Jacopo Peri's *Euridice*, which he
saw in 1600), but it is scarcely the important forerunner of opera that has often been assumed.

L'Amfiparnaso

Madrigal-comedy in three acts (55m)
Text possibly by Giulio Cesare Croce
PREMIERE   1594, Modena

The plot of this comedia harmonica, such as it is,
deals with the lives and loves of stock *commedia
dell'arte* characters (the old lecher Pantalone, the
pompous Dr Gratiano, the braggart Spanish Captain,
star-crossed young lovers and comic servants).

Vecchi provides a chain of five-part madrigals – some
serious, some light-hearted – with characters
represented by contrasted voice-groupings within the
texture. Although the work could conceivably be
acted and/or mimed, Vecchi's prologue makes it
clear that the comedy is for the ear rather than the
eye, and it is through his witty, delightful music that
the piece makes its effect.

RECORDINGS   1. Beltrani, Biolchini, Malacarne, Malaguti,
Nuovo Madrigaletto Italiano, Giani, Record Society, *c.* 1960;
2. Deller Consort, Collegium Aureum, Deller, Harmonia
Mundi, 1962
EDITIONS   Venice, 1597; C. Adkins (ed.), Chapel Hill, 1977

BIBLIOGRAPHY   Alfred Einstein, *The Italian Madrigal*,
Princeton University Press, 1949, vol. 2, pp. 772–98

T.C.

MATTIA VENTO

b 1735, Naples; *d* 22 November 1776, London

Vento studied in Naples and spent the years 1756–9
in Rome. His opera *L'egiziana* (1763) was done at
Venice and Milan, and was taken up by Gassmann in
Vienna and extensively revised as *Zingara*.

Late in 1763 Giordani invited Vento to London.
Burney described the music of his *Demofoonte* as
'natural, graceful and pleasing, always free from
vulgarity, but never very new or learned'. Vento was
a prolific contributor to the pasticcios popular in
London during the 1760s and 1770s. His opera *La
vestale* was criticized for its failure to exploit the
virtuosic talents of the great singers of the day. Vento
is said to have replied, 'God forbid I should ever
compose difficult music.'

Operatic works: *Le deluse accortezze*, 1756; *La finta semplice*,
1759; *L'egiziana*, 1763; *Leucippo*, 1764; *Demofoonte*, 1765;
Sofonisba, 1766; *La conquista del Messico*, 1767; *Artaserse*,
1771; *Il bacio*, 1776; *La vestale*, 1776

BIBLIOGRAPHY W. van Lennep *et al.* (eds), *The London Stage, 1764–89*, 5 pts, South Illinois Press, 1960–68

T.T.C.

GIUSEPPE VERDI

Giuseppe Fortunino Francesco Verdi; *b* 9/10 October 1813, Roncole, nr Busseto; *d* 27 January 1901, Milan

Giuseppe Verdi is one of a tiny group of composers who set the supreme standards by which the art of opera is judged; of his 28 operas – several of which exist in more than one version – about a dozen form the backbone of the standard operatic repertoire. He was the dominant figure in Italian opera for 50 years, and was largely responsible for a radical transformation of its character. But in many ways his revolution was a deeply conservative one, and he carried popular audiences with him almost to the end.

Born in a village in the rural depths of what is now the province of Parma, Verdi received his earliest musical education from church organists in Roncole and Busseto. His gifts made a deep impression on local music-lovers, and in 1832 one of them, a merchant named Antonio Barezzi, undertook to finance a year of study for him at the Milan Conservatory. Though Verdi did sit an entrance examination he was in fact too old to be admitted, and had to study privately instead, working under Vincenzo Lavigna. Lavigna was, Verdi recounted many years later, 'very good at counterpoint, a little pedantic, and didn't care for any music but Paisiello'.

Having completed his studies Verdi returned to Busseto to take up a position as director of music in the commune and marry Barezzi's daughter Margherita. Three years later he was back in Milan with his family, for he had been able to arrange for his first opera, *Oberto*, to be staged at La Scala. The premiere, in November 1839, was successful enough for the publisher Giovanni Ricordi to want to purchase it, and for Bartolomeo Merelli, impresario of La Scala, to offer Verdi a contract for three further operas. Between August 1838 and June 1840, however, both his two children and his wife died; in September 1840, his second opera, *Un giorno di regno*, was an inglorious fiasco, and Verdi's life, personal and professional, lay in ruins. Merelli's confidence in him did not falter, and his faith was rewarded when *Nabucco* triumphed in March 1842. This third opera established Verdi as a national figure; it also marked the beginning of what he was to call his *anni di galera* (years in the galleys) for impresarios from all over Italy were now eager to engage the rising star, and he was inescapably drawn into a life of grinding routine, composing, rehearsing and staging operas all over Italy and sometimes further afield. In the 17 years from *Nabucco* to *Un ballo in maschera* he composed 20 operas.

With its central theme of a chosen nation dreaming of deliverance from foreign bondage, *Nabucco* had a certain topicality in Risorgimento Italy; and the eloquence with which Verdi's music expressed moods of religious and national fervour played no small part in its success. Such Risorgimento overtones recur again and again during the *anni di galera*. Fastidious music-lovers of an older generation were sometimes repelled by the violence and noisiness of the young Verdi, but the majority of his operas enjoyed huge popular success, and made an important contribution to Italian national self-awareness. It was a providential coincidence that the name Verdi formed an acronym for 'Vittorio Emanuele, Re D'Italia'; and during the 1850s, as the Savoy monarchy became the focus for Italian national aspirations, the commonplace acclamation 'Viva Verdi' acquired a thrilling patriotic resonance.

This nationalist dimension contributed little, however, to the deepening of his art that took place between *Nabucco* and the so-called 'popular trilogy' – *Rigoletto*, *Il trovatore* and *La traviata* – of the early 1850s. *Nabucco* had given Verdi entrée to the best social and artistic circles: among the friends he made were Andrea Maffei, whose wife Clara was hostess of Milan's most cultivated salon, and Giulio Carcano, Italian translators of, respectively, Schiller and Shakespeare. During the 1840s Verdi developed into something of a literary connoisseur, an avid reader of dramatic literature from all over Europe. Inspired by this reading, his dramatic vision deepened; he acquired a sense of the potentialities of poetic drama, and hence of musical drama, that extended far beyond the conventions of Romantic opera. In his Hugo operas – *Ernani* (1844) and *Rigoletto* (1851) – his Schiller operas – particularly *Luisa Miller* (1850) – and his Shakespeare opera – *Macbeth* (1847) – we find Verdi stretching and bending the conventions inherited from his predecessors to give his operas an expressive range and a uniqueness of characterization and atmosphere that matched that of the greatest dramatists. Another Shakespearean project, *Re Lear* (*King Lear*), had first attracted Verdi as early as 1843. A libretto was written (by Somma, based on preliminary work by Cammarano); but though Verdi returned to the subject frequently and sketched much music for it, the scheme remained unrealized.

The repertoire of opera on which Verdi had been brought up as a student in the 1830s had been almost exclusively Italian. It was, however, infiltrated by French elements, mediated primarily through the operas written by Rossini in the late 1820s. It was Verdi's emulation of such models that gave both *Nabucco* and *I lombardi* something of the cut of French grand operas. As his reputation spread and invitations took him to London and Paris, he had the opportunity to experience grand opera at first hand, and made his first attempt at composing it himself – significantly *Jérusalem* (1847) is a revised version of *I lombardi*. His attitude to Parisian grand opera proved to be ambivalent; but the genre, and its greatest exponent, Giacomo Meyerbeer, certainly exerted a profound influence on his music in the 1850s and 1860s. After *Jérusalem* he composed two more French grand operas, *Les vêpres siciliennes* (1855) and *Don Carlos* (1867), and two of his Italian operas are based either on grand opera libretti (*Un ballo in maschera*, 1859) or on French scenarios in the grand opera manner (*Aida*, 1871). It was while he was in Paris in 1847 that he met up again with Giuseppina Strepponi, who had sung in the first performances of *Nabucco*, and who in due course (1859) was to become his second wife.

With *Un ballo in maschera* the *anni di galera* came to an end. Verdi was world famous and very wealthy, and had begun to enjoy the life of a country gentleman. In 1848 he had bought, in an 'unimproved' state, a property (Sant'Agata) near Busseto; he moved there in 1851, and worked for decades developing and beautifying it. Since he had by now earned an outstandingly honourable place in the life of his resurgent nation, Cavour – prime minister of the united Italy that finally materialized in 1860 – persuaded him to become a deputy in the Turin parliament: he represented his local district, Borgo San Donnino (now Fidenza), from 1861 to 1865. Verdi was now less productive as a composer, accepting new commissions only when they really interested him. Between 1860 and 1870 he wrote three operas; their performance venues – St Petersburg, Paris, Cairo – vividly express the reach of his reputation. Each opera is on a huge scale, and the last of them, *Aida*, achieves to perfection that fusion of the Italian and French traditions of opera that Verdi had long pursued. He was by now nearly 60, and many assumed that *Aida* marked the end of his operatic career. In 1874 he produced the *Messa da Requiem* in memory of Alessandro Manzoni.

Unlike Wagner, Verdi left no theoretical writings. But from his vast correspondence, particularly from his letters to his librettists and his publishers, it is not difficult to extract a Verdian 'aesthetics of opera' that rivals Wagner's in comprehensiveness and perhaps surpasses it in clarity. He never wavered in his loyalty to values inherited in his youth: a good opera was an opera that was acclaimed all over Italy by enthusiastic audiences in packed theatres; its object was the exploration of human passions and human behaviour in situations of extreme dramatic tension, and its principal means of expression was the fusion of poetry and music in dramatic song. He sought out subjects bolder than anything an earlier generation would have dared, and characters became more idiosyncratic, but his sense of values was in the classical Italian tradition. In rehearsal he was a rigorous disciplinarian, demanding absolute compliance with his demands; and these extended beyond the music to virtually every element of the staging. From *Les vêpres siciliennes* onward, his publisher Ricordi issued production books – *disposizioni sceniche* – which record how his operas were staged.

The 1870s were, for the most part, years of disillusion. The reality of the new Italian state did not match up to the dreams of those who had come to maturity in the heroic decades of the Risorgimento; its chronic financial difficulties had plunged opera houses into crisis, and many were closing. Worst of all for Verdi was his feeling that a younger generation was abandoning the traditions of Italian civilization to pursue fashions or ideals emanating from France and Germany. Wagner had become a major force among the avant garde, and though there was much in Wagner that Verdi admired, he did not see him as a good model for Italian composers. The primacy of song, the clarity of form and luminosity of sound to which Italian art had always aspired, a firm basis in humanist ethics – all seemed under threat.

His friendship with two remarkable men a generation younger than himself – the publisher Giulio Ricordi and the poet and composer Arrigo Boito – did much to draw Verdi out of this unhappy phase and make possible the glorious Indian summer of the 1880s and 1890s. He composed three operas in collaboration with Boito, to each of which Ricordi served as a kind of midwife – a second version of *Simon Boccanegra* (1881), and the two operas that stand as the most eloquent testimony to his lifelong veneration of Shakespeare, *Otello* (1887) and *Falstaff* (1893). None was to rival *Rigoletto*, *Il trovatore* or *La traviata* in popularity. But the very sophistication (especially in matters of harmony and instrumentation) that popular audiences sometimes found a little taxing appealed deeply to those educated in the the German musical tradition, and many musicians came to love and admire *Ernani* and *Nabucco* via an enthusiasm for the late Verdi.

By the 1890s Verdi had, in the words of Giuseppe

Souvenir print of Verdi at the time of the world premiere of Otello *with the conductor Franco Faccio, Romilda Pantaleoni (Desdemona), Francesco Navarini (Lodovico), Francesco Tamagno (Otello) and Victor Maurel (Iago); (Milan 1887)*

Depanis, a Turin journalist, come to be seen as 'the patriarch, the guardian deity of the fatherland'. His rare public appearances were occasions of astonishing demonstrations of affection and veneration; at his funeral, close on 30,000 people are reported to have lined the streets of Milan and to have joined spontaneously in singing 'Va pensiero' from *Nabucco*.

Oberto, conte di San Bonifacio

Oberto, Count of San Bonifacio
Opera (dramma) in two acts (2h 15m)
Libretto by Temistocle Solera, rev. from a libretto by Antonio Piazza, probably called *Rocester*
Composed summer 1835–summer 1839, rev. October 1840 and January 1841
PREMIERES 17 November 1839, La Scala, Milan; UK: 8 April 1965, St Pancras Town Hall, London (concert); 17 February 1982, Collegiate Theatre, London; US: 18 February 1978, Amato Theater, New York
CAST Cuniza *ms*, Riccardo, conte di Salinguerra *t*, Oberto, conte di San Bonifacio *b*, Leonora *s*, Imelda *ms*; *satb* chorus of knights, ladies, vassals
FULL ORCHESTRA

Verdi's first opera emerged from a complicated process of composing and rewriting that stretched over four years. During this time, the opera went under two, perhaps three different names – (?*Lord Hamilton*), *Rocester* and *Oberto*; at least two librettists worked on the text, and the action was moved from, presumably, 17th-century Britain to 13th-century Italy. However frustrating for the composer, this long gestation did give him time to impress influential friends with his music, notably the impresario Bartolomeo Merelli, who accepted the work for La Scala – a remarkable theatre in which to make an operatic début – and whose advice affected the opera's final form. *Oberto* enjoyed a fair success, prompting Merelli to commission more operas from the young composer, and encouraging Giovanni Ricordi, Milan's leading music publisher, to enter into a business relationship with him that was to prove uniquely advantageous to both parties.

SYNOPSIS
The scene is set in Bassano, in Ezzelino's castle and the vicinity in 1228. Defeated in battle by Ezzelino da Romano, Oberto has taken refuge in Mantua, leaving his daughter Leonora in the care of an aunt. She has been seduced by Riccardo and then abandoned, for he is to marry Cuniza, Ezzelino's sister.

Act I While Riccardo is escorted into Bassano by a welcoming party of courtiers, Leonora and Oberto make their way thither secretly, bent on revenge. Cuniza's reputation for magnanimity encourages Leonora to confide in her, and the noble lady does indeed take the wronged girl's part against the man who was about to become her own husband.

Act II Cuniza insists that Riccardo should keep faith with Leonora, and under her sponsorship their vows of love are renewed. But Oberto, believing that a duel to the death is the only way of satisfying family

honour, will have no part in any reconciliation. He is fatally wounded; a remorseful Riccardo flees into exile, and Leonora looks forward to an early death in a cloister.

Verdi made his début at a time when the leading composers of Italian opera, Donizetti and Mercadante, were becoming rather self-conscious about their native traditions, and attempting various types of 'reform', often French or German in inspiration. But Verdi seems quite at ease in the world of Italian Romantic melodrama. The sensation-packed, pseudo-historical libretto is typical of the earlier Donizetti; the musical architecture, formalized and often symmetrical, is modelled on Bellini; there is no questioning the primacy of the singing voice and the purely secondary role that refinements of instrumentation or harmony played in the young composer's scheme of things. Nevertheless a distinct musical personality is already emerging. There is a vehement and propulsive energy in the score, and a keen sense of what matters dramatically. Recitatives are carefully and expressively composed; characters are vividly brought to life, particularly in the ensembles, where Verdi is already adept at a kind of psychological counterpoint (cf. the Leonora–Oberto duet 'Del tuo favor' in Act I); and the austerity and formal freedom of Leonora's rondo finale shows the young composer unafraid to discard convention in the cause of dramatic verisimilitude.

RECORDING Dimitrova, Baldani, Bergonzi, Panerai, Bavarian Radio Ch, Munich Radio O, Gardelli, Orfeo, 1983
EDITIONS v.s., Ricordi, [1842]; later edns and *rps*

Un giorno di regno/Il finto Stanislao

King for a Day/The False Stanislas
Melodramma giocoso in two acts (2h)
Libretto by Felice Romani, a revision of his earlier libretto for Adalbert Gyrowetz, *Il finto Stanislao* (1818), in turn based on the comedy *Le faux Stanislas* by Alexandre Vincent Pineu-Duval (1808)
Composed spring–summer 1840
PREMIERES 5 September 1840, La Scala, Milan; 11 October 1845, Teatro San Benedetto, Venice (as *Il finto Stanislao*); US: 18 June 1960, Town Hall, New York; UK: 21 March 1961, St Pancras Town Hall, London
CAST Cavaliere di Belfiore *bar*, Barone di Kelbar *b buffo*, Marchesa del Poggio *s*, Giulietta di Kelbar *s*, Edoardo di Sanval *t*, La Rocca *b buffo*, Ivrea *t*, Delmonte *b*; *satb* chorus of the Baron's servants and vassals

The premiere of *Un giorno di regno*, the first of the three operas commissioned by the impresario Merelli after the success of *Oberto*, marked the lowest ebb of Verdi's career. Composed to an old-fashioned libretto, during a period of great personal distress – Verdi's wife Margherita died in June 1840 – and feebly performed by artists most of whom were ill at ease in the comic style, *Un giorno di regno* was hissed ignominiously from the stage and very rarely revived. At the first of the few revivals (Venice, 1845), Romani's original title, *Il finto Stanislao*, was restored.

SYNOPSIS

During the political crisis of 1733, the Cavaliere di Belfiore has, to distract attention from the genuine monarch, assumed the identity of King Stanislas of Poland, and arrived with much pomp at the castle of Baron Kelbar near Brest. There he finds himself in the middle of preparations for two weddings: the baron's daughter Giulietta is, most unwillingly, to marry the elderly La Rocca, while a local military official is hoping for the hand of the Marchesa del Poggio. This news astonishes Belfiore and makes his task more complicated, because he himself is the marchesa's lover. 'Stanislas' resourcefully uses his supposed regal authority to rescue Giulietta from marriage to La Rocca. Eventually a messenger arrives with news that the Polish crisis is resolved; Belfiore casts off his disguise, and claims the marchesa's hand.

Opera buffa in the Rossinian manner was in terminal decline by 1840, and it needed a composer with a lighter touch than Verdi's to derive much fun from its ageing mannerisms. *Un giorno di regno* demands exceptional tact from its performers; for instead of sparkle, the orchestral colouring has a monochrome stridency, and rhythms that might have danced are merely galumphing. But composing it did give Verdi the chance to practise his hand at a more flexible and conversational style of ensemble, an experience that was to pay off magnificently in *Nabucco* and the operas that followed.

RECORDING Norman, Cossotto, Carreras, Wixell, Sardinero, Ganzarolli, Ambrosian Singers, RPO, Gardelli, Philips, 1974
EDITIONS v.s., Ricordi, *c.* 1845; later edns and *rps*.

Nabucodonosor (Nabucco)

Nebuchadnezzar
Dramma lirico in four parts (2h 15m)
Libretto by Temistocle Solera, after the play *Nabucodonosor* (1836) by Anicet-Bourgeois and Francis Cornue, and the scenario of the ballet *Nabucodonosor* by Antonio Cortesi (1838)
Composed 1841; rev. August and December 1842
PREMIERES 9 March 1842, La Scala, Milan; UK: 3 March 1846, Her Majesty's Theatre, London (as *Nino*); US: 4 April 1848, Astor Opera House, New York
CAST Nabucodonosor (Nabucco), King of Babylon *bar*, Ismaele *t*, Zaccaria *b*, Abigaille *s*, Fenena *s*, High Priest of Baal, Abdallo *t*; *satb* chorus of Babylonian and Hebrew soldiers, Levites, Hebrew virgins, Babylonian women, magi, grandees of the Kingdom of Babylon, populace, etc.
ORCHESTRATION 2 fl/picc, 2 ob, ca, 2 cl, 2 bsn, 4 hn, 2 tpt, 3 trbn, cimbasso, timp, perc (bd, sd, triangle), 2 hp, str; onstage band

Nabucco occupies in Verdi's career very much the position that *Der fliegende Holländer* occupies in Wagner's: 'With this opera', he remarked, in the *Autobiographical Sketch* dictated to Giulio Ricordi in 1879, 'it is fair to say my career began.' After the humiliation of *Un giorno di regno* Verdi seriously considered giving up all ambitions for a career in opera. But Merelli, the impresario of La Scala, did

not lose faith in his talent. Early in 1841 he brought off a psychological masterstroke by suddenly thrusting a new libretto into the unsuspecting composer's hand, and bundling him out of his office. Verdi later insisted that he read Solera's libretto very reluctantly; but its biblical grandeur and pathos moved him deeply, haunted and finally obsessed him. By the autumn the opera was finished.

After the premiere, Milan's leading newspaper acclaimed a 'clamorous and total success'; *Nabucco* revealed Verdi as a major new force in the Italian theatre, and gave the rather gauche young provincial entrée into the best social and artistic circles in the city. By the end of the year it had enjoyed 65 performances at La Scala, and within two years had been sung all over north and central Italy, and as far afield as Vienna, Cagliari, Barcelona and Lisbon. More than any other Verdi opera, *Nabucco* – by virtue of its great central theme of national humiliation and renewal – was to prove a major spiritual experience for Italians during the Risorgimento era; in later decades it became an indispensable element of Risorgimento mythology.

SYNOPSIS

The scene is set in Jerusalem (Part I) and Babylon (Parts II, III and IV) in 587 BC.

Part I Jerusalem. Inside Solomon's Temple. As Nabucco's Assyrian hordes press upon Jerusalem, the Hebrews take refuge in the temple. Zaccaria, the high priest, has taken hostage Nabucco's daughter, Fenena; he urges the Hebrews to trust God and fight bravely ('D'Egitto là sui lidi' – 'Come notte a sol fulgente'). Fenena is left in the care of Ismaele; they have been lovers since he once led an embassage to Babylon, and she has become sympathetic to the Hebrew god. A group of soldiers bursts into the temple, led by the warlike Abigaille, Nabucco's elder daughter. She too loves Ismaele, and tries to woo him away from Fenena, promising to spare the otherwise doomed Jewish people. These now stream back into the temple, and Nabucco rides triumphantly in on horseback. Zaccaria threatens to kill Fenena ('Tremin gl'insani'), but Ismaele saves her from the high priest's sword, and she flees to the arms of her father. Nabucco and Abigaille shout for plunder and slaughter, while Zaccaria and the Hebrews anathematize Ismaele ('Mio furor, non più costretto' – 'Dalle genti sii reietto').

Part II The Wicked Man. Scene 1: Apartments in the palace. It has emerged that Abigaille is the offspring of slaves, and in the king's absence it is Fenena who is invested with his authority. But Abigaille has stolen the document that betrays her secret; moreover she has an ally in the High Priest of Baal, who circulates a rumour that Nabucco has died in battle and leads demands for Abigaille to become queen ('Anch'io dischiuso un giorno' – 'Salgo già del trono aurato'). Scene 2: Another room in the palace. Zaccaria reads holy scripture and prays for the gift of prophecy ('Tu sul labbro dei reggenti'). He reveals that Fenena has embraced the faith, and is now a fellow Jew. Rumour of Nabucco's death reaches them, but when Abigaille and her priests arrive and dispute Fenena's authority, they are confounded by the return of the king himself ('S'appressan gl'istanti'). Nabucco orders Babylonians and Jews alike to worship him as god, and is struck mad by a thunderbolt. He querulously calls for help ('Chi mi toglie il regio scettro?'), but Abigaille snatches up his fallen crown and reaffirms the glory of Baal.

Part III The Prophecy. Scene 1: The Hanging Gardens. Babylonians acclaim Abigaille; the High Priest demands that all Jews be killed, beginning with the traitorous Fenena. Nabucco appears, unkempt and still out of his wits, and attempts to reimpose his authority. But alone with Abigaille ('Donna, chi sei?'), he is tricked into putting his seal to the death warrant; when he realizes what he has done, and then sees Abigaille destroy the proof of her lowly birth, he pathetically, but fruitlessly, appeals for compassion ('O di qual'onta aggravasi' – 'Deh perdona, deh perdona'). Scene 2: The banks of the Euphrates. The Hebrews dream nostalgically of their distant homeland ('Va, pensiero, sull'ali dorate'). Zaccaria prophesies the downfall of Babylon.

Part IV The Broken Idol. Scene 1: An apartment in the palace. Nabucco awakes from his deranged slumbers (portrayed in an extended orchestral prelude) to hear the sounds of the procession conducting Fenena to her death. In a flash of inspiration he recognizes that Jehovah is the one omnipotent god, and kneels in prayer ('Dio di Giuda!'); then, his reason restored, he summons his warriors ('O prodi miei, seguitemi'). Scene 2: The Hanging Gardens. Fenena and the condemned Hebrews seek strength in prayer ('Oh, dischiuso è il firmamento!'). When Nabucco arrives the statue of Baal crumbles to dust. All join in worship of Jehovah ('Immenso Jehova'). Meanwhile Abigaille has taken poison; she begs forgiveness from Fenena, and dies in the fear of the Lord ('Su me . . . morente . . . esanime . . .'). (After the first two performances the closing scene was regularly cut, presumably with Verdi's authorization, to finish with 'Immenso Jehova'.)

Nabucco is a thrilling opera, but it has little of the urgent theatrical *élan* that was soon to become a hallmark of Verdi's style; its musical structure is altogether more massive than that of most of the operas he wrote in the 1840s, owing something to French grand opera, especially Rossini's *Moïse*. Each act contains at least one substantial tableau, and it is in these that the typical Risorgimento intermingling of religion and nationhood is clearest. Part I, for example, begins with a huge choral movement in which the Jews bewail the desecration of their land by Nabucco, and are exhorted by their high priest to remain true to the faith. The preoccupation with nationhood in Solera's text is matched in Verdi's music by the emphasis laid on the chorus which, whether in lament, denunciation or worship, represents the whole national and religious community. Early Milanese audiences were so enthusiastic about the choral music in *Nabucco* and its successor *I lombardi*, that they styled Verdi *'il padre del coro'*. Much of it, including the greater part of 'Va pensiero', is in unison and, in view

of its dramatic and expressive function, might appropriately be described as community singing.

Contemporaries were also struck – sometimes disconcerted – by the brassiness of Verdi's orchestral palette. A stage band appears for no fewer than four formal marches, and choral melodies and even solo arias are often doubled on trumpet and/or trombone; like those of Moses in Rossini's opera, many of Zaccaria's recitatives are accompanied by brass. At the same time *Nabucco* is the first of Verdi's operas in which certain scenes – Abigaille's death scene for example – are given a more intimate intensity by being accompanied by a small ensemble of instruments. Verdi's genius for musical characterization comes to a first climax in the turbulent rhythms and the vaulting and plunging melodies of Abigaille's music, and in its radical contrast with the bland cantabiles of Fenena.

RECORDINGS 1. Suliotis, Prevedi, Gobbi, Cava, Vienna State Opera Ch and O, Gardelli, Decca, 1965: notable for Gobbi's moving portrayal of the title part and Suliotis's fiery Abigaille; 2. Dimitrova, Domingo, Cappuccilli, Nesterenko, Ch and O of Berlin Deutsche Oper, Sinopoli, DG, 1984: erratic but exciting [A.B.]
VIDEO Dimitrova, Garaventa, Bruson, Petykov, Verona Arena Ch and O, Arena, Castle, 1981
EDITIONS f.s., R. Parker (ed.), *The Works of Giuseppe Verdi*, vol. 3, Chicago University Press/Ricordi, 1987; v.s., Ricordi, 1842; later edns and rps

I lombardi alla prima crociata

The Lombards at the First Crusade
Dramma lirico in four acts (2h 15m)
Libretto by Temistocle Solera, after the epic poem *I lombardi alla prima crociata* by Tommaso Grossi (1826)
Composed 1842–3, rev. July 1843; rev., as *Jérusalem*, 1847, see below
PREMIERES 11 February 1843, La Scala, Milan; UK: 12 May 1846, Her Majesty's Theatre, Haymarket, London; US: 3 March 1847, Palmo's Opera House, New York
CAST Arvino *t*, Pagano *b*, Giselda *s*, Oronte *t*, 2 *s*, *t*, 2 *b*; *satb* chorus of nuns, city fathers, hired ruffians, armed retainers in Folco's palace, ambassadors from Persia, Media, Damascus and Chaldea, knights and soldiers of the crusade, pilgrims, Lombard women, women of the harem, celestial virgins
FULL ORCHESTRA including onstage band

When Bartolomeo Merelli, impresario of La Scala, saw the effect of *Nabucco* on his customers, he boldly presented Verdi with a blank cheque for the third of the commissions he was to write for the theatre. After consulting Giuseppina Strepponi, his prima donna and later his second wife, the composer demanded, and received, the same fee that Bellini earned for *Norma*. Solera, who this time chose to model his text on one of the most admired works of Milanese literary Romanticism, designed *I lombardi* as a kind of companion piece to *Nabucco*, providing ample scope for marches, hymns and grandiose tableaux. With its baptism scene and an 'Ave Maria' aria – which had to be altered to 'Salve Maria' – *I lombardi* brought Verdi his first brush with the censors. The opera's premiere was as triumphant as that of *Nabucco*, and for many years it rivalled its predecessor in popularity; it was the first Verdi opera to be performed in America.

SYNOPSIS

The action takes place in 1096–7; Act I is set in Milan, Act II in and around Antioch, Acts III and IV near to Jerusalem.

Act I Vengeance. Pagano, one of the sons of Folco, Lord of Ro, returns from a pilgrimage undertaken to atone for his attempt on the life of his brother Arvino, whose wife he loves. But his passion is unassuaged, and at the very ceremony of reconciliation he is again plotting Arvino's death with a servant he has suborned. In error, Pagano kills not his brother but his aged father, Folco, and is overcome with remorse.

Act II The Man in the Cavern. Arvino is leading the Lombard forces on the Crusade, and at Antioch his daughter Giselda is captured by the Muslims. In despair, he consults a local hermit, who proves to be – though Arvino does not recognize him – the penitent Pagano. The two brothers lead an assault on the city, and Giselda is freed. But she denounces them for the un-Christian slaughter they have encouraged, and mourns the supposed death of the Muslim prince, Oronte, whom she loves.

Act III The Conversion. As the Crusaders advance on Jerusalem they are overtaken by Oronte, who has recovered from his wounds; Giselda flees with him from the camp. They are pursued by Arvino's soldiers, and Oronte is wounded again, this time fatally. Before dying he is baptized in the Jordan by the hermit (Pagano).

Act IV The Holy Sepulchre. The Crusaders are tormented by weariness and thirst; but a vision, vouchsafed to Giselda, leads them to the brook of Siloam, where they refresh themselves for the final, victorious assault on Jerusalem. In the battle the hermit is mortally wounded; at last he reveals his identity and the brothers are reconciled.

Episodic, even ramshackle in structure, *I lombardi* lacks the spiritual unity of *Nabucco*. But in certain respects it is the bolder work: the studied effects of harmonic and instrumental colour, for example in Giselda's 'Salve Maria!', the bold refashioning of conventions, as in her *cabaletta* 'No! . . . giusta causa', and many other passages testify to Verdi's unwillingness simply to repeat himself. For the first time he abandons the full-length overture in favour of a brief preludio, whose solemn strains are surely designed to set the keynote for the whole opera. The Act IV chorus, 'O Signore, dal tetto natio' – one of the movements that does seem to aim at replicating a *Nabucco* model ('Va pensiero') – became one of Verdi's best-loved pieces; its citation in Giuseppe Giusti's poem 'Sant'Ambrogio' is the most notable reference to Verdi's music in contemporary Italian literature.

RECORDING Deutekom, Domingo, Lo Monaco, Raimondi, Ambrosian Singers, RPO, Gardelli, Philips, 1972
EDITIONS f.s., Ricordi, [1957]; v.s., Ricordi, [1843]; later edns and *rps*

Ernani

Dramma lirico in four acts (parts) (2h 15m)
Libretto by Francesco Maria Piave, after the tragedy *Hernani* by Victor Hugo (1830)
Composed November 1843–February 1844, rev. September and December 1844
PREMIERES 9 March 1844, La Fenice, Venice; UK: 8 March 1845, Her Majesty's Theatre, Haymarket, London; US: 13 April 1847, Park Theater, New York
CAST Ernani *t*, Don Carlo, King of Spain *bar*, Don Ruy Gomez de Silva *b*, Elvira *s*, Giovanna *s*, Don Riccardo *t*, Jago *b*; *satb* chorus of rebel highlanders and bandits, knights and members of Silva's household, maids in attendance on Elvira, knights in attendance on Don Carlo, Spanish and German noblemen and their ladies; extras: highlanders and bandits, electors and grandees of the imperial court, pages of the imperial court, German soldiers, ladies, male and female followers
ORCHESTRATION picc, fl, 2 ob, 2 cl, b cl, 2 bsn, 4 hn, 2 tpt, 3 trbn, cimbasso, timp, perc (bd, sd), hp, str; onstage: band including bd; offstage: hn, 6 tpt ('interna')

By now theatres all over Italy were keen to engage Verdi. Having seen his first four operas staged at La Scala, he decided the time had come to accept an invitation from La Fenice, Venice, next to La Scala the leading opera house in northern Italy. And since much of the correspondence that now began to flow between Milan and Venice survives, *Ernani* provides us with a vivid picture of how the young Verdi went about his work. It is not surprising to find that he expects to be well paid; he insists on selecting his own singers, and on having time to rehearse thoroughly; he explains – and this was rare in Italy at the time – that he began to compose only when the libretto was completed to his satisfaction, because 'when I have a general conception of the whole poem the music always comes of its own accord'.

After the grandiosities of *Nabucco* and *I lombardi* Verdi was looking for a different kind of drama, faster moving and more fiery in its passions. And he embarked on what was to become a typical procedure, reading widely in Byron and Dumas and other heroes of Romanticism, until he came across something – in this case one of the landmarks of French Romantic theatre – in which, in a flash of intuition, he sensed an opera was latent. The librettist for *Ernani*, the Venetian poetaster Francesco Maria Piave, whom Verdi did not yet know personally, was soon to become his most trusted collaborator; not because he had more talent than Solera or Cammarano, but because he was so compliant. Already Verdi had very precise ideas about what he wanted from his librettist; and in his letters about *Ernani* we find him emphasizing two issues that were to remain obsessions for the rest of his life: the poet must be as concise as possible, and he must remain as faithful as possible to the situations and the words of the original play. Despite *Hernani*'s notoriety, it was possible, thanks to the comparatively liberal censorship in Venice, to get the libretto approved without too much aggravation. The censors were exercised by a few passages, notably the conspiracy scene. They insisted that this should be as brief as possible, that the conspirators should not draw their swords, that the king's words of pardon should be 'liberal and impressive'; and they drew something of the republican sting from Piave's text 'Si ridesti il Leon di Castiglia', which, however, was still able to inspire one of the most spine-tingling of the hymns to liberty that stud Verdi's early operas.

Verdi arrived in Venice at the start of December, allowing himself three months to compose, orchestrate and rehearse the opera, as well as supervising a revival of *I lombardi*. It was a trying winter: there were acute difficulties over assembling A suitable cast; *I lombardi* flopped, and Verdi became increasingly apprehensive as the Venetians hissed two more operas off the stage; last-minute hitches meant that neither sets nor costumes were quite ready for the premiere.

Nevertheless, *Ernani* was an immediate and lasting triumph. The first Verdi opera to be performed in Britain, it did more than any other to spread his reputation internationally during the 1840s, and remained a repertoire work for half a century. In the post-war Verdi renaissance it has proved to be, with *Nabucco*, the most resilient of his pre-*Macbeth* scores.

SYNOPSIS

The action takes place in 1519.

Act I (Part I: The Bandit) Scene 1: The mountains of Aragon; Don Ruy Gomez de Silva's Moorish castle is visible in the distance. Ernani joins his roistering company of outlaws. He loves Elvira, and has just heard that her guardian, Silva, is to marry her himself on the morrow; the outlaws plan to abduct her ('Come rugiada al cespite' – 'O tu, che l'alma adora'). Scene 2: Elvira's richly appointed room in Silva's castle. Night. Elvira fears and detests Silva; his gifts serve only to sharpen her longing for Ernani ('Ernani! . . . Ernani, involami' – 'Tutto sprezzo che d'Ernani'). Don Carlo also loves Elvira, and in Silva's absence makes one last attempt to persuade her to elope with him ('Da quel dì che t'ho veduta'/'Fiero sangue d'Aragona'). They are interrupted by Ernani, the king's deadly enemy in politics as in love. As Elvira struggles to keep them from one another's throats ('Tu se' Ernani!'), Silva returns. Finding his bride-to-be in the company of two strange men, he bewails his shame and prepares to avenge himself ('Infelice! e tu credevi': the *cabaletta* 'Infin che un brando vindice' is a later addition). When the king's identity is revealed, however, Silva changes his tone ('Oh cielo! è desso il re!!!'). Quixotically moved to help Ernani escape, Carlo describes him as one of his own servants; then in an ensemble, as Ernani and Elvira plan their elopement, and Ernani vows to avenge his father's death (for which Carlo was responsible), the king and Silva discuss political affairs.

Act II (Part II: The Guest) A magnificent hall in Don Ruy Gomez de Silva's castle. Rumours of Ernani's death are rife; Elvira has despaired of delaying her marriage any longer, and Silva's household is celebrating the wedding day. Ernani has, however, escaped; disguised as a pilgrim, he gains admission to the castle, where he hears that Silva and Elvira are to be married. Once alone

with him, Elvira persuades him of her undying love, and Silva returns to find them embracing passionately; the arrival of the king delays the execution of his vengeance ('Ah morir potessi adesso' – 'No . . . vendetta più tremenda'). Carlo has come in pursuit of Ernani, but Silva, ever punctilious in the laws of hospitality, refuses to surrender him. The king orders his men to search the castle; as they find nothing, he takes Elvira hostage ('Lo vedremo, o veglio audace' – 'Vieni meco, sol di rose'). Silva releases Ernani from his hiding place, presents him with a sword and demands the instant satisfaction of honour. Ernani refuses to fight an old man, and points out what Silva had not previously realized: that the king is their rival for Elvira's love. Silva agrees to let Ernani help him rescue Elvira, but only on the grimmest condition: Ernani gives him a hunting horn, and pledges that if he wishes him dead, he need only sound it; they ride off in pursuit ('Ecco il pegno: nel momento' – 'In arcione, in arcion, cavalieri').

Act III (Part III: Clemency) Subterranean vaults enclosing the tomb of Charlemagne at Aquisgrana (Aachen). The new Holy Roman Emperor is about to be named. Carlo, knowing that a group of conspirators is to meet in the vaults by Charlemagne's tomb, hides himself. Ambitious now for eternal glory, he bids farewell to the follies of youth ('Oh de' verd'anni miei'). The conspirators assemble – Ernani and Silva among them; Ernani is chosen to kill Carlo, and refuses, even when offered his own life in exchange, to yield the privilege to Silva; all conspirators join in a hymn to freedom ('Si ridesti il Leon di Castiglia'). Then as three cannon shots announce Carlo's election, he steps from Charlemagne's tomb and denounces the conspirators. Electors, nobles and soldiers stream into the vaults; Carlo condemns the rebels to condign punishment, but Elvira persuades him to emulate the clemency of Charlemagne ('Oh sommo Carlo').

Act IV (Part IV: The Mask) The terrace of Don Giovanni d'Aragona's (Ernani's) palace in Saragossa. A crowd of guests, momentarily troubled by a masked figure in black, celebrates the wedding of Ernani and Elvira. Hardly are the lovers left alone before a horn is heard in the distance; the mask approaches and reveals himself as Silva, come to demand the honouring of the pledge; unable to soften his obduracy, Ernani stabs himself and Elvira swoons ('Cessaro i suoni, disparì ogni face' – 'Solingo, errante e misero' – 'Ferma . . . crudele, estinguere').

With *Ernani* Verdi moved from the high-minded communal concerns of *Nabucco* and *I lombardi* to a world of passionate individualism. His attention focuses on the possibilities of musical characterization, and in particular – given a dramatic situation in which three men pay court to one woman – the expressive qualities of the three types of male voice. *Ernani* provides the archetypal pattern for a whole tradition of opera: the tenor, a youthful, suffering lover; the bass, an elderly ruthless egotist; and, most distinctively, the baritone, a psychologically more complex type, torn between tenderness and violence, self-indulgence and idealism.

Ernani is not a sophisticated work, but in scene after scene it shows the young Verdi at his most effective. The magnificent breadth of conception of the conspiracy scene (despite the censors), and its evocative orchestral colouring; the lyrical fervour of the arias ('Ernani! . . . Ernani involami', 'Vieni meco, sol di rose', etc.), and the enthralling expressive details of the recitatives (especially in Act IV) set standards that he was not to surpass for some years. And if the prelude that henceforth generally takes the place of the overture is intended to act as a microcosm of the drama, no later example does it more effectively than *Ernani*'s, with its juxtaposition of tender lyricism and tragic solemnity (the motif associated with Ernani's oath).

RECORDINGS 1. Price, Bergonzi, Sereni, Flagello, RCA Italiana Ch and O, Schippers, RCA, 1967: vital performance, notable for singing of Leontyne Price and Carlo Bergonzi; 2. Freni, Domingo, Bruson, Ghiaurov, La Scala Ch and O, Muti, HMV, 1977: excitingly conducted, eloquently sung (also on video, Castle) [A.B.]
EDITIONS f.s., C. Gallico (ed.), *The Works of Giuseppe Verdi*, v, Chicago University Press/Ricordi, 1985; v.s., Ricordi, [1844]; rev. edn, 1867

I due Foscari

The Two Foscari

Tragedia lirica in three acts (1h 45m)
Libretto by Francesco Maria Piave, after the historical tragedy *The Two Foscari* by Lord Byron (1821)
Composed May–October 1844; rev. March 1845; additional aria: December 1846
PREMIERES 3 November 1844, Teatro Argentina, Rome; UK: 10 April 1847, Her Majesty's Theatre, Haymarket, London; US: 10 May 1847, Boston
CAST Francesco Foscari *bar*, Jacopo Foscari *t*, Lucrezia Contarini *s*, Jacopo Loredano *b*, *s*, 2 *t*, *b*; *satb* chorus of Members of the Council of Ten and the Giunta, maidservants of Lucrezia, Venetian ladies, crowd, masked men and women; extras: Il Messer Grande (Chief of Police), 2 small sons of Jacopo Foscari, Comandadori, prison warders, gondoliers, sailors, crowd, masquers, pages of the Doge
FULL ORCHESTRA including onstage band and bell

I due Foscari was a subject for which Verdi had already sketched out a synopsis in the summer of 1843, when he was pondering his Venice commission. Unacceptable to the authorities there because of its unflattering portraits of some distinguished Venetian families, *I due Foscari* was temporarily shelved, only to be taken up a year later for Verdi's first Roman commission. It soon became clear that Byron's play was lacking in 'theatrical grandeur' (letter to Piave), and in making the operatic adaptation much of Verdi's care was devoted to the question of how best to enliven the spectacle and to make the hero Jacopo a more energetic figure. The premiere, by all accounts abysmally sung, was felt by the composer to have been a 'mezzo-fiasco'; as the singers settled into their roles audiences enjoyed the opera much more, but it never shared the popularity of its three predecessors.

SYNOPSIS

Act I Venice, 1457. The Foscari family is implacably hated by Loredano. Jacopo Foscari, exiled and homesick, is discovered to have been engaged in forbidden correspondence with another state; charged also with complicity in a murder, he is brought back to Venice for interrogation; his octogenarian father Francesco, though doge, is powerless to intervene on his behalf.

Act II Jacopo's wife Lucrezia and the doge visit Jacopo in prison, to warn him that he will again be exiled. Swayed by Loredano, the Council of Ten confirms the sentence, despite the sensational appearance at their deliberations of Lucrezia and her children, whose appeal for clemency comes close to moving many of them.

Act III Amid scenes of popular revelry, Jacopo is brought to the ship and bids Lucrezia farewell. Meanwhile, in the doge's palace, the charge of murder has been proved false. The doge's joy is short-lived, however, for Lucrezia returns to tell him that, weakened by torture and broken-hearted, Jacopo died as he boarded the ship. The Council of Ten, led by Loredano, now comes to demand Foscari's resignation; he resists them indignantly for a while, but finally succumbs, falling dead as the great bell of San Marco acclaims his successor.

In *I due Foscari*, Verdi's growing interest in musical characterization takes an unexpected form: each of the principals – the doge, Jacopo and Lucrezia – is given a distinctive orchestral theme, which accompanies them at each of their more important appearances on stage. A fourth recurring theme, this time vocal in origin ('Silenzio, mistero'), is associated with the Council of Ten. Despite the attempts of Verdi and Piave to enliven the drama, this opera remains one of the composer's most intimate and introspective scores; in 1848 he was to describe it as 'a funeral [with] too uniform an atmosphere and colour from beginning to end'. But that is to overlook many admirable qualities, among which one may mention a new refinement of craftsmanship, and a real attempt to match the 'delicacy and pathos' Verdi had admired in Byron's poem.

RECORDING Ricciarelli, Carreras, Cappuccilli, Ramey, Austrian Radio Ch and SO, Gardelli, Philips, 1977
VIDEO Ruark-Strummer, Cupido, Bruson, Roni, Ch and O of La Scala, Milan, Gavazzeni, Castle, 1988
EDITIONS f.s., Ricordi, [1951]; v.s., Ricordi, [1845]

Giovanna d'Arco

Joan of Arc

Dramma lirico in a prologue and three acts (2h)
Libretto by Temistocle Solera, in part after the 'Romantic tragedy' *Die Jungfrau von Orleans* by Johann Christoph Friedrich von Schiller (1801)
Composed November 1844–January 1845, rev. December 1845
PREMIERES 15 February 1845, La Scala, Milan; US: 1 March 1966, Carnegie Hall, New York (concert); UK: 23 May 1966, Royal Academy of Music, London
CAST Carlo (King Charles VII of France) *t*, Giovanna *s*, Giacomo *bar*, *t*, *b*; *satb* chorus of officers of the king,

villagers, people of Rheims, French and English soldiers, blessed spirits, evil spirits, grandees of the realm, heralds, pages, children, marshals, deputies, knights and ladies, magistrates, halberdiers, guards of honour
FULL ORCHESTRA including harmonium, fisarmonica and band

After *I lombardi*, the impresario Merelli tried, but failed, to persuade Verdi to write yet another opera for La Scala; before the composer went to Venice to produce *Ernani*, however, he did agree to come back to La Scala the following year with a new work. Sadly, during the 1844–5 season, the deteriorating standards of Merelli's productions soured relationships between impresario and composer, and after *Giovanna d'Arco* it was 36 years before another Verdi premiere was staged at La Scala. Despite frictions in the company, between Verdi and Merelli and among the singers, *Giovanna* was well performed and ecstatically received; for a time its popularity rivalled that of Verdi's earlier collaborations with Solera. In Rome and southern Italy, for reasons of religious susceptibility, it was for many years supplied with an amended text entitled *Orietta di Lesbo*.

SYNOPSIS
The action takes place in France, in Dom-Rémy, Rheims and near Rouen in 1429.

Prologue On the point of surrendering to the English, Carlo is inspired by a dream to visit a sanctuary in the forest near Dom-Rémy. There he meets Giovanna, the very incarnation of his dream, who prophesies that France's travail will soon be at an end.

Act I Giovanna's appearance in the French ranks has transformed the course of the war and the English are close to defeat. But Giovanna's father, Giacomo, a clergyman who fears that she is in the grip of demonic powers, believes it his duty to deliver her into the hands of the English. The inner voices that have always troubled Giovanna become more insistent as she acknowledges that she loves Carlo.

Act II As Carlo, Giovanna and the people stream out of the cathedral after the coronation, they are accosted by Giacomo, who challenges his daughter to deny that she is possessed by devils. She remains speechless, and he leads her away, hoping to save her immortal soul by having her burned at the stake.

Act III Giacomo realizes the terrible mistake he has made when he finds Giovanna, now a prisoner in the English camp, at prayer. He releases her, and watches as she leads the French forces to victory on the battlefield. Mortally wounded, Giovanna is reverently borne back to camp, where she dies.

For modern ears no opera illustrates more disconcertingly than *Giovanna d'Arco* the chasm between Verdi's best and worst music. While some of the solo and ensemble writing, particularly that for Giovanna and Carlo, is as fine as anything the young composer did, his mystic choruses – variously accompanied by harmonium and triangle (demons) and harp and fisarmonica (angels) – are likely to be felt to embody 19th-century taste at its most abysmal. But they are certainly, as Verdi's young composition pupil, Emanuele Muzio, enthusiastically declared, 'popular, truly Italian . . . full of seductive ideas that can be sung straightaway after a couple of hearings'; and when we read that within a few weeks of the premiere the favourite melodies of *Giovanna* were being ground out on the barrel organs on the streets of Milan, we may be confident that the choruses were among them. An oft-noted curiosity in the score is the resemblance to 'Hearts of Oak' of the chorus 'O duce, noi sempre mirasti' sung in Act I by the English soldiers.

RECORDING Caballé, Domingo, Milnes, Ambrosian Opera Ch, LSO, Levine, HMV, 1972
EDITIONS f.s., Ricordi, [?1951]; v.s., Ricordi, [1845]; later edns and *rps*

Alzira

Tragedia lirica in a prologue and two acts (1h 30m)
Libretto by Salvatore Cammarano, after the tragedy *Alzire, ou Les Américains* by Voltaire (1736)
Composed May–July 1845
PREMIERES 12 August 1845, Teatro San Carlo, Naples; US: 17 January 1968, Carnegie Hall, New York (concert); UK: 10 February 1970, Collegiate Theatre, London

In the earlier part of Verdi's career La Scala and La Fenice in the north of Italy and the San Carlo, Naples, in the south were the leading opera houses in the peninsula; and when the opportunity of composing for Naples arose, he seized it eagerly. Why *Alzira* turned out so poorly – 'a really ugly one' was the composer's own final assessment – is not easy to explain. One factor was certainly that, because of an exaggerated respect for his librettist's long stage experience, he took a less active role than usual in fashioning the libretto to his own needs. An inability to identify himself with the subject and an ominous dependence on routine is suggested in a remark made to a Milan friend, that he wrote the opera 'almost without noticing and with no trouble at all'. In only a handful of scenes – notably the Act I finale, where memories of the Act II finale of *Lucia di Lammermoor* are in the air – did Verdi's imagination really catch fire. The full-length sinfonia was commissioned separately, during rehearsals, when the theatre management found the opera too short. Enthusiastically received at the dress rehearsal, *Alzira* was already on the wane by the second night; it has only occasionally been revived.

SYNOPSIS
Gusmano, Spanish governor of Peru, and Zamoro, an Indian chieftain, are rivals for the love of the Inca princess Alzira. For most of the drama the Spaniard's ruthlessness is ironically contrasted with the magnanimity of the 'savages'. But when Zamoro stabs him as he is about to marry Alzira, he undergoes a deathbed enlightenment, pardons his rival, and restores Alzira to his arms.

RECORDING Cotrubas, Araiza, Bruson, Rootering, Bavarian Radio Ch, Munich Radio O, Gardelli, Orfeo, 1983
EDITIONS v.s., Ricordi, [1846]; later edns and rps

Attila

Dramma lirico in a prologue and three acts (1h 45m)
Libretto by Temistocle Solera with alterations by Francesco Maria Piave, after the tragedy *Attila, König der Hunnen* by Zacharias Werner (1808)
Composed September 1845–March 1846; substitute arias (both to replace 'Chi non avrebbe il misero') for later revivals, composed September and December 1846
PREMIERES 17 March 1846, La Fenice, Venice; UK: 14 March 1848, Her Majesty's Theatre, Haymarket, London; US: 15 April 1850, New York
CAST Attila, King of the Huns *b*, Ezio *bar*, Odabella *s*, Foresto *t*, *t*, *b*; *satb* chorus of chieftains, Hun king and soldiers, Huns, Gepids, Ostrogoths, Heruls, Thuringians, Quadi, Druids, priestesses, populace, men and women of Aquileia, maidens of Aquileia in martial dress, Roman officers and soldiers, Roman virgins and children, hermits, slaves
FULL ORCHESTRA including 4 tpt, bells; onstage 6 tpt, thunder-machine

The composition of *Attila* was bedevilled by problems. The original plan was for the Venetian librettist Piave to write the libretto, on the basis of a synopsis provided by Andrea Maffei – poet, translator and connoisseur of German literature – a close friend of Verdi, who was probably responsible for interesting him in Werner's play in the first instance. Having offered Piave a great deal of advice on the treatment of the subject, Verdi – for reasons unknown, but perhaps because he was beginning to think of *Attila* as a potential grand opera in the French style – decided that it would be preferable to entrust the text to the flamboyant Solera. But Solera disappeared to Spain just when he was most needed, and it was Piave who came to the rescue – if that is the apt phrase – by completing and revising Solera's unfinished text to Verdi's specifications. Verdi was ill for virtually the whole of the time he was composing the opera and, after the equivocally successful premiere, was ordered to take a six-month rest cure.

SYNOPSIS
Aquileia and the Adriatic lagoons, and near Rome, about the middle of the 5th century.
Prologue As Attila and his hordes advance into Italy, Odabella and a group of women who have escaped the slaughter impress him by their courage; he presents her with his sword and takes her into his entourage. Ezio, a Roman general, comes to parley, but Attila rejects his proposal that they share out the world between them. Meanwhile Foresto, Odabella's betrothed, arrives at Rio-Alto and urges the other Aquileian refugees to build a new city there – the future Venice.
Act I Meeting Foresto, Odabella denies betraying the Italian cause; rather she awaits an opportunity to kill the tyrant. Meanwhile Attila is trying to shake off the memory of an awe-inspiring dream. But his courage fails when the vision becomes a reality: Pope Leo (disguised for reasons of censor-

ship as an 'aged Roman') and attendants process into his camp to bar his way to Rome.
Act II Foresto and Ezio (who has been invited to one of Attila's banquets) lay plans for the defeat of the Huns. Sinister omens darken the atmosphere at the feast, and the king is saved from poisoning only by the intervention of Odabella. As her reward, Attila declares that she shall be his bride.
Act III During the wedding, the Romans surround the Huns' camp; as they attack, Odabella stabs Attila.

Perhaps from force of circumstance, *Attila* was to emerge as one of the crasser products of Verdi's 'galley years', which is sad, for he began the opera determined that he would not relapse into routine. There was to be no onstage band, he declared, because that was a piece of nonsensical provincialism that Italian theatres should be growing out of; nor was he going to compose lots of marches that might make the opera sound like a pale imitation of *Nabucco* or *Giovanna d'Arco*; as for the finale, that would be unlike anything anyone had ever written before. The positive fruit of these aspirations is not much in evidence, and the sheer noisiness of *Attila* made it a *bête noire* of fastidious critics. Verdi's interpretation of the subject was coloured by Madame de Staël's celebrated book *De l'Allemagne* (1810), which he urged Piave to read: in the rabid tones of Odabella's cavatina (prologue), for example, we may surely sense Verdi's desire to portray his heroine as, in Madame de Staël's words, 'a goddess of war'.

RECORDINGS 1. Deutekom, Bergonzi, Milnes, Raimondi, Ambrosian Singers, RPO, Gardelli, Philips, 1972; 2. Studer, Shicoff, Zancanaro, Ramey, Ch and O of La Scala, Milan, Muti, EMI, 1990: the Muti version is the more viscerally exciting account [A.B.]
VIDEO Chiara, Luchetti, Carroli, Nesterenko, Verona Arena Ch and O, Santi, Castle, 1985
EDITIONS f.s., Ricordi, [?1963]; v.ss., Lucca, [c.1846]; Ricordi, [c.1888]; and rps
MANUSCRIPT British Library, London

Macbeth

Opera (melodramma) in four acts (2h 30m)
Original version: libretto by Francesco Maria Piave (with additions by Andrea Maffei), after the tragedy by William Shakespeare (1605–6)
Revised version: French text translated from Piave (who revised the 1847 text himself) and Maffei by Charles Nuittier Alexandre Beaumont
Composed September 1846–February 1847, rev. November 1864–February 1865
PREMIERES original version: 14 March 1847, Teatro della Pergola, Florence; US: 24 April 1850, Niblo's Garden, New York; Ireland: 30 March 1859, Theatre Royal, Dublin; UK: 2 October 1860, Theatre Royal, Manchester; revised version: 21 April 1865, Théâtre-Lyrique, Paris; UK: 21 May 1938, Glyndebourne, Sussex; US: 24 October 1941, 44th Street Theater, New York
CAST Duncan, King of Scotland *silent*, Macbeth *bar*, Banco *b*, Lady Macbeth *s*, Lady Macbeth's lady-in-waiting *ms*, Macduff *t*, Malcolm *t*, Fleanzio *silent*, Doctor *b*, Macbeth's servant *b*, assassin *b*, 3 apparitions 2 *s*, *b*, (rev. version: herald *b*, Hecate, goddess of the night *silent*); *satb* chorus of witches,

Frontispiece from the first vocal score of Macbeth *(Ricordi, 1847)*

king's messengers, Scottish noblemen and exiles, assassins, English soldiers, bards, aerial spirits; (rev. version: ballet) ORCHESTRA picc, fl, 2 ob/ca, 2 cl/b cl, 2 bsn, 4 hn, 2 tpt, 3 trbn, cimbasso, timp, perc (bd, sd, cym, t-t), hp, str; onstage band; understage: 2 ob, 6 cl, 2 bsn, dbsn

The breakdown of Verdi's health at the time of *Attila* was a blessing in disguise: during the six-month convalescence that followed he was able to recover an artistic idealism he had been in danger of losing in the relentless routine of the previous two years. *Macbeth*, conceived at this time, was the boldest, the most consistently inventive and the most idealistic opera he had yet written. Verdi was already an ardent Shakespearean and was determined to do all he could to make his opera worthy of its model; sending Piave a first synopsis he described *Macbeth* as 'one of mankind's grandest creations', and demanded from the librettist 'extravagance and originality . . . brevity and sublimity'.

Macbeth is the first of Verdi's operas in which we find him taking as minute an interest in the staging as in the text and music. He would not commit himself to writing it until he knew he could have Felice Varesi – a supremely intelligent singer and actor – for the title role; he warned the Florence impresario, Alessandro Lanari, that no production expenses could be spared, since chorus and stage machinery were so important; he paid scrupulous attention to such details as lighting, the historical accuracy of the settings, the gestures and movements of the singers. In her memoirs, Marianna Barbieri-Nini, the first Lady Macbeth, described the unprecedented demands Verdi made on his performers: working on the sleep-walking scene, she found herself 'for three months, morning and evening, attempting to impersonate someone who speaks in her sleep, who (as the maestro put it) utters words . . . almost without moving her lips, the rest of the face motionless, the eyes shut'.

At the Florence premiere *Macbeth* was very warmly received. There was some critical unease that an Italian artist should have invested such enthusiasm in a subject in the *genere fantastico* – a transalpine aberration of taste, to the minds of many Italians; but the extraordinary quality of Verdi's dramatic vision was recognized and admired on all sides. The special place the opera held in his own affections is shown, first, in his dedication of it to Antonio Barezzi, the father-in-law to whom he owed so much; and, second, in the fact that it was the first opera for which he refused to provide *puntature* (adaptations of the arias for singers with different types of voice).

In 1863 Léon Carvalho, director of the Théâtre-Lyrique in Paris, asked Verdi to compose a ballet and a new choral finale for *Macbeth*. Returning to the score, Verdi found himself being drawn into a more radical revision than either he or Carvalho had anticipated. Despite the fine quality of this new music, the Paris *Macbeth* was relatively unsuccessful and has established itself as a repertoire work only during the last half-century.

SYNOPSIS
The scene is Scotland, principally Macbeth's castle.

Act I   Scene 1: A wood. As Macbeth and Banquo, two generals in Duncan's army, make their way home from battle, they come across a coven of witches. The witches foretell, among other prophecies, that Macbeth will be king of Scotland and Banquo the father of future kings – prophecies that chime strangely with Macbeth's own secret ambitions ('Due vaticini compiuti or sono'/'Oh, come s'empie costui d'orgoglio'). The witches disperse ('S'allontanarono!'). Scene 2: A hall in Macbeth's castle. Lady Macbeth reads a letter telling of her husband's military successes and of the witches' prophecy. She doubts if, without her prompting, he is ruthless enough to attain his ambitions. When a messenger announces that Duncan is accompanying Macbeth to the castle that night, she realizes that the time has come to act ('Vieni! t'affretta!'/'Or tutti sorgete, ministri infernali'); and on Macbeth's return, he is soon persuaded that Duncan must be killed. After nightfall, the vision of a bloody dagger leads him on to the murder ('Mi si affaccia un pugnal?!'). He returns, already racked by conscience; his wife chides him for his faint-heartedness and goes to Duncan's chamber to incriminate the guards ('Fatal mia donna! un murmure'). Macduff, a Scottish nobleman, and Banquo come to attend on the king; the murder is discovered ('Schiudi, inferno, la bocca ed inghiotti').

Act II Scene 1: A room in the castle. Macbeth is now king of Scotland, and Duncan's son Malcolm has taken refuge in England. Since the witches have prophesied that Banquo's sons will succeed to the throne, Macbeth and his wife resolve that they too must be killed (1847: 'Trionfai! securi alfine'; 1865: 'La luce langue, il faro spegnesi'). Scene 2: A park. Banquo and his son, Fleance, make their way towards Macbeth's castle ('Come dal ciel precipita'); they are attacked by assassins, but Fleance escapes. Scene 3: A magnificent hall. Macbeth and his queen welcome their guests, and the wine is soon flowing ('Si colmi il calice'). An assassin enters to tell Macbeth what happened in the park. As the king rejoins the banquet he is appalled to see the figure of Banquo sitting in his appointed place. Lady Macbeth tries to dispel the gathering shadows, but the ghost of Banquo returns. By now Macbeth's behaviour is filling his guests with suspicion; Macduff decides to join the exiles ('Sangue a me quell'ombra chiede').

Act III A gloomy cavern. The witches are brewing potions and casting spells. (In the 1865 version there follows a ballet of spirits, devils and witches, in honour of Hecate.) Macbeth enters, and in response to his questioning the witches conjure up a series of visions. These warn him to beware Macduff, but assure him that he need fear no man born of woman, and that he will be invincible until Birnam Wood (sic) moves against him. But then, terrified by the apparition of eight kings, followed by Banquo carrying a mirror ('Fuggi, regal fantasima'), Macbeth swoons, and the witches dance around him. When he recovers, he determines to exterminate Macduff and his family (1847: 'Vada in fiamme, e in polve cada'; 1865: 'Ora di morte e di vendetta').

Act IV Scene 1: A deserted place on the borders of Scotland and England; in the distance Birnam Wood. Scottish refugees bewail the plight of their country under Macbeth's rule ('Patria oppressa! il dolce nome'). Macduff, heartbroken to hear of the deaths of his wife and children, is urged by Malcolm to seek comfort in revenge ('Ah, la paterna mano'/'La patria tradita'). Plucking branches from the trees, they advance towards Macbeth's castle. Scene 2: A room in Macbeth's castle. A doctor and lady-in-waiting watch in horror as the sleep-walking Lady Macbeth muses over the murders she and her husband have committed ('Una macchia è qui tuttora'). Scene 3: A room in the castle. Macbeth is already so overwhelmed with melancholy ('Pietà, rispetto, amore') that the news of his wife's death leaves him unaffected. When his men report the moving of Birnam Wood, however, and when later, on the battlefield, Macduff tells how he was 'from his mother's womb untimely ripp'd', Macbeth realizes that he is doomed. 1847: he dies at Macduff's hands, cursing the ambition that he had delivered his soul to the powers of Hell ('Mal per me che m'affidai'); 1865: Macbeth and Macduff exeunt fighting; a few minutes later Malcolm's victorious troops enter, rejoicing in the liberation of their country ('Macbeth, Macbeth ov'è?').

Verdi's insistence that as much as possible of the quality of Shakespeare's tragedy should be preserved in the libretto had a transfiguring effect on his music, most clearly in what he called 'the two most important pieces in the opera'. In the great duet that follows the murder of Duncan in Act I, a densely packed sequence of poetic images taken from the play inspires a matching sequence of musical images, creating an exceptionally flexible operatic design, whose dramatic intensity never flags. And in the sleep-walking scene, where Shakespeare writes a highly charged prose, periodically lit up with phrases of shocking expressive power, Verdi contrives to match him by composing an orchestral backcloth packed with mysterious patterings and sighs, against which Lady Macbeth sings broken declamatory phrases, periodically opening up into great arches of cantabile melody. Both scenes are landmarks in Verdi's development as a master of dramatic orchestration, the broad daubs of his early style giving way to a more scrupulous selection and blending of colours.

A criticism sometimes directed at the 1865 revision is that the greater sophistication of the new music makes it impossible for the climactic scenes of the original to stand out as the dramatic peaks they were obviously intended to be. The greatest gains from a musical point of view are, first, Lady Macbeth's 'La luce langue', an aria of gloomy magnificence replacing an icily virtuosic cabaletta; and, second, the rewritten scene of the apparitions (Act III) where, with subtler phrasing, harmony and instrumentation, the strangeness of atmosphere is sustained with fewer lapses into the commonplace. The magnificent choral music in the last act is also largely a result of the Paris revision.

RECORDINGS 1. Cossotto, Carreras, Milnes, Raimondi, Ambrosian Opera Ch, Philharmonia O, Muti, EMI, 1976:

notable, accurate, well-cast set; 2. Verrett, Domingo, Cappuccilli, Ghiaurov, La Scala Ch and O, Abbado, DG, 1976: much admired by some critics; subtler, more intimate performance than Muti, with less idiomatic Lady Macbeth [A.B.]
VIDEO   Verrett, Luchetti, Nucci, Ramey, Ch and O of Teatro Comunale, Bologna, Chailly, 1987: Claude D'Anna's imaginative film takes some liberties and uses actors in two cases to mime for singers [A.B.]
EDITIONS   f.s., Ricordi, [n.d.]; *rp*, Kalmus, 1977; v.ss., original version: Ricordi, [1847]; rev. version: (French), Escudier, [1865]; (Italian), Ricordi, [1865]; new edn., 1883; *rps*
MANUSCRIPT   Bibliothèque Nationale, Paris

I masnadieri

The Brigands
Melodramma in four parts (2h 15m)
Libretto by Andrea Maffei after the drama *Die Räuber* by Johann Christoph Friedrich von Schiller (1781)
Composed (?)September–November 1846, March–July 1847
PREMIERES   22 July 1847, Her Majesty's Theatre, Haymarket, London; Italy: 12 February 1848, Teatro Apollo, Rome; US: 31 May 1860, Winter Gardens, New York
CAST   Massimiliano, Count Moor *b*, Carlo *t*, Francesco *bar*, Amalia *s*, 2 *t*, *b*; *satb* chorus of erring youths (later brigands), women, children, servants
FULL ORCHESTRA

Like *Macbeth*, *I masnadieri* was conceived during Verdi's convalescence in the summer of 1846, when Maffei was a constant companion; if his imagination was less challenged in this opera, it was probably because of the old-fashioned cut of his friend's libretto. For a composer with so keen a business sense as Verdi, the prospect of a London commission was enticing. But though he earned considerably more for *I masnadieri* than for any earlier opera, his hopes of further lucrative commissions foundered with the failure of the opera. Arbiters of taste in London still found Verdi's music disagreeably violent, and in making the tenor the focus of dramatic interest he failed to exploit the unique popularity enjoyed in the city by Jenny Lind, the original Amalia. *I masnadieri* was performed only four times and rarely revived even in Italy.

SYNOPSIS
The action is set in Germany, at the beginning of the 18th century, and covers a period of about three years.
    Part I Francesco Moor, having sown bitter dissension between his brother Carlo and their father Massimiliano, employs the vilest machinations to prevent reconciliation. In the meantime Carlo, driven to despair by what he believes to be his father's rejection, becomes the leader of a gang of outlaws. When Massimiliano is told, falsely, that Carlo is dead, he apparently dies of shock.
    Part II Francesco has installed himself as the new Count Moor. But his attempts to win the orphaned Amalia, Massimiliano's ward and Carlo's beloved, are vain.
    Part III A chance encounter with Amalia brings Carlo a momentary and illusive glimpse of happiness. But he relapses into despair and later, when he learns

that Massimiliano is imprisoned in a nearby ruin, violence. The old man is released, and the outlaws vow to wreak terrible vengeance on Francesco.
    Part IV After the outlaws have destroyed Francesco's castle, Amalia is carried off to their camp. Despite Amalia's love for him, Carlo relapses into blasphemous despair, stabs her, and goes off to deliver himself into the hands of the law.

One wonders how far it was the circumstance of composing for an unfamiliar audience that prompted Verdi to fashion his music as much to match the talents of his performers as the requirements of his dramatic theme: a prelude consisting largely of an eloquent solo for the principal cellist of the theatre orchestra, Alfredo Piatti; choruses of unusual length and sophistication of texture; above all, music for Amalia, the rather cool elegance and floridity of which were clearly inspired by the peculiar and, as Verdi felt, slightly anachronistic gifts of Jenny Lind. *I masnadieri* contains much more fine music than is commonly supposed; but it has an unusually high proportion of solo arias, and a correspondingly small number of the dramatic ensembles and confrontational duets that commonly generate so much of the theatrical voltage in Verdi; and he seems ill at ease with the Teutonic metaphysics with which Maffei occasionally (as in the Act III finale) loads the libretto.

RECORDINGS   1. Caballé, Bergonzi, Cappuccilli, Raimondi, Ambrosian Singers, New Philharmonia O, Gardelli, Philips, 1975: strong Verdi singing and conducting; 2. Sutherland, Bonisolli, Manuguerra, Ramey, WNO Ch and O, Bonynge, Decca, 1982: worth hearing for Sutherland and Ramey, but 1. preferable as a whole [A.B.]
EDITIONS   f.s., Ricordi, [c. 1950]; v.ss., Lucca, [1847]; Ricordi, [c. 1897]; *rps*

Jérusalem

Jerusalem
Opera in four acts (2h 30m)
Libretto by Alphonse Royer and Gustave Vaëz (pseudonym of Jean Nicolas Gustave van Nieuwenhuysen), a translation and adaptation of *I lombardi alla prima crociata*.
Composed August–October 1847
PREMIERES   26 November 1847, Opéra, Paris; Italy: 26 December 1850, La Scala, Milan; US: 24 January 1850, Théâtre d'Orléans, New Orleans; UK: 31 March 1990, Grand Theatre, Leeds
CAST   Gaston *t*, Le Comte de Toulouse *bar*, Roger *b*, Hélène *s*, *s*, 2 *t*, 3 *b*; *satb* chorus of knights, ladies, pages, soldiers, pilgrims, penitents, Arabs, sheiks, women of the harem, people of Ramla; ballet
FULL ORCHESTRA including organ, cornets; band of cornets, saxhorns and saxtrombas

There is something of the flavour of French grand opera in all the works Verdi composed in collaboration with Solera, and since 1845 he had from time to time considered adapting one of them for production at the Paris Opéra. When he arrived in Paris on his way back from London after the production of *I masnadieri* he was offered an attractive contract which provided the opportunity to try his hand at grand opera without the risk involved in composing an entirely new work (cf. Rossini's *Le siège de Corinth* and *Moïse et Pharaon*): *I lombardi* was to be radically revised and supplied with the obligatory ballet, and Verdi would be paid as for a new opera. Typically for an Italian, his attitude to the Opéra was equivocal: astonishment at the magnificence of the spectacle failed to alleviate a certain boredom with the total musico-dramatic experience; and by the time he had rehearsed *Jérusalem* for twice as long as even *Macbeth* had needed in Italy, he was rather bored with his 'new' opera too. For Paris, it proved a useful rather than indispensable addition to the repertoire; feebly translated by Calisto Bassi as *Gerusalemme*, it failed to supersede *I lombardi* in the affections of Italian audiences.

SYNOPSIS
The scene is set in Toulouse and Palestine; the period is 1095–9.

Act I On the eve of their departure for the Crusade, the betrothal of Gaston, Vicomte de Béarne, and Hélène, daughter of the Comte de Toulouse, seals the reconciliation between the two families. But Roger, the comte's brother, also loves Hélène and engages an assassin to kill Gaston. In error it is the comte who is attacked, and Gaston on whom the blame for the murder attempt – which is bungled – is laid.

Act II The Crusaders pass the Saracen city of Ramla, near which the penitent Roger lives as a hermit; he begs to be allowed to join them in their battle against the infidel. Meanwhile Hélène has learned that Gaston, who has been driven into exile, is a prisoner in Ramla; she too is captured as she searches for him.

Act III Hélène is immured in the harem, where the ballet takes place (no scenario for it has survived); Ramla is captured by the Crusaders and Hélène is rescued; but Gaston is dragged away to the public square and stripped of his accoutrements of nobility in readiness for execution on the morrow.

Act IV While the Crusaders advance on Jerusalem, the hermit (Roger) is asked to administer the last rites to the condemned Gaston. Recognizing him, he absolves him and gives him a sword. In the battle for Jerusalem, Gaston covers himself in glory, while Roger is mortally wounded; on his deathbed he reveals his identity, confesses his guilt and is reconciled with his brother.

Royer's and Vaëz's radical rewriting of the libretto of *I lombardi* clarifies the dramatic action considerably, reducing the number of scenes and eliminating otiose characters, while at the same time providing full scope for stage spectacle in the Parisian manner. In reworking his opera Verdi availed himself of the more ample choral and instrumental resources in Paris (several moments feature the cornets); but for the most part it is in the new fastidiousness of the craftsmanship – notably the carefully wrought linking passages between one movement and another – rather than in the inherent musical inventiveness that

Jérusalem scores over *I lombardi*. Of the newly composed music, the Act III finale – the scene of Gaston's public humiliation – is outstanding; magnificently performed at the premiere by Gilbert Duprez, it occasioned, according to Théophile Gautier, 'shudders of admiration' in the audience.

RECORDINGS *Jérusalem*: Ricciarelli, Carreras, Nimsgern, Rome Ch and SO of Italian Radio, Gavazzeni, Unique Opera, 1975; *Gerusalemme*: Gencer, Aragall, Guelfi, Zerbini, La Fenice Ch and O, Gavazzeni, MRF, 1963
EDITIONS   v.ss., (French), Bureau Central de Musique, [1847]; (Italian), Ricordi, [?1848]
MANUSCRIPT   Bibliothèque Nationale, Paris

Il corsaro
The Corsair
Melodramma tragico in three acts (1h 30m)
Libretto by Francesco Maria Piave, after the poem *The Corsair* by Lord Byron (1814)
Composed November 1847–February 1848 (partly sketched in 1846)
PREMIERES   25 October 1848, Teatro Grande, Trieste; UK: 15 March 1966, Camden Town Hall, London; US: 12 December 1981, Main Theater, Stony Brook, New York
CAST   Corrado *t*, Medora *s*, Gulnara *s*, Pasha Seid *bar*, 3 *t*, *b*, Anselmo (a corsair) *silent*; *satb* chorus of corsairs, guards, Turks, slaves, odalisques, Medora's handmaidens, FULL ORCHESTRA including band

The origins of *Il corsaro* go back to 1843–4, a period of Byronic enthusiasm which produced *I due Foscari* and plans for operas on *The Bride of Abydos* and *Cain*; by the summer of 1846 the libretto was written and several scenes fully sketched. There is no reason to doubt that Verdi composed the opera with as much conscientiousness as anything else he wrote, but the dislike he came to feel for Lucca, the publisher who commissioned it, soured his attitude to it. And as he was in Paris at the time of the premiere he made, most exceptionally, no attempt to take an active part in its production. He did, however, send a long letter to Marianna Barbieri-Nini, the original Gulnara, in which he offered much advice on the interpretation of her role: at the same time he suggested that the opera should be performed as if it had only two acts, the first two acts of the published score being run together without interval: 'The whole opera will thus gain in brevity and interest.'

SYNOPSIS
The scene is set on an island in the Aegean Sea and in the city of Coron. The period is the beginning of the 19th century.

Act I Despite the forebodings of his beloved, Medora, Corrado prepares to embark with his corsairs on a mysterious mission against the Turks.

Act II While his men set fire to Pasha Seid's fleet, Corrado gains admission to his palace disguised as a dervish. The fire threatens to engulf the seraglio, and as Corrado organizes the rescue of the women, he is captured. Gulnara, the Pasha's favourite, but a reluctant inmate of his harem, leads the women's appeals for mercy for the prisoner.

Act III Having failed to save Corrado, Gulnara

resolves to release him from prison herself, even though she has first to kill Seid. Corrado and Gulnara return to the corsairs' island only to find Medora on the point of death, for, believing Corrado dead, she had taken poison; in despair Corrado hurls himself into the sea.

What to Verdi seemed the most interesting scenes in *Il corsaro*, the prison scene and the final trio, were sketched as early as 1846, and when he returned to the opera nothing else stirred him quite so much. After the comparative weightiness of the previous three operas (each in its different way) *Il corsaro* seems a slight, even sketchy piece: the interest of the choral music is negligible, and there are few signs of Verdi's new-found orchestral sophistication. The attentive listener will, however, often be rewarded: there is, for example, no doubt that, even in something less than his best form, the composer is designing his arias more imaginatively (cf. the treatment of the reprises in 'Tutto parea sorridere' in Act I and 'Cento leggiadre vergini' in Act III); and both the *andante* and *allegro* movements in the Act II finale are as finely crafted and as imaginatively sustained as any comparable movements in Verdi's earlier works.

RECORDING Caballé, Norman, Carreras, Mastromei, Ambrosian Singers, New Philharmonia O, Gardelli, Philips, 1975
EDITIONS v.ss., Lucca, [1848]; Ricordi, [1902]; *rps*

La battaglia di Legnano
The Battle of Legnano
Tragedia lirica in four acts (1h 45m)
Libretto by Salvatore Cammarano, after the play *La bataille de Toulouse* by Joseph Méry (1828)
Composed November 1848–January 1849
PREMIERES 27 January 1849, Teatro Argentina, Rome; UK: 31 October 1960, Cardiff; US: 28 February 1976, Amato Theater, New York
CAST Rolando *bar*, Lida *s*, Arrigo *t, ms*, 2 *t, bar*, 4 *b*; *satb* chorus of Cavaliers of Death, magistrates and leaders of the people of Como, Lida's serving maids, people of Milan, senators of Milan, soldiers from Verona, Novara, Piacenza and Milan, German army
FULL ORCHESTRA including organ and bells; on/backstage: 6 tpt, 4 trbn, 2 sd

By 1848, the year of revolutions, virtually the whole of the Italian peninsula was simmering with liberal and patriotic enthusiasms. It was the librettist Cammarano who suggested the subject of *La battaglia di Legnano* to Verdi, because he supposed that at such a time 'there burns in you as in me the desire to evoke the most glorious episode of Italian history, that of the Lombard League'. He was right: Verdi, now resident primarily in Paris, was eager to make some artistic contribution to the pan-Italian cause in which he believed so fervently – it was during a lull in work on the opera that he composed the patriotic song 'Suona la tromba', and sent it to the republican leader Mazzini, expressing the hope that 'it might soon be sung amid the music of the cannon on the Lombardy plain'. The performance of

so flagrantly political an opera in Rome was possible only because, the Pope having fled the city late in 1848, it was temporarily governed by a republican triumvirate. Once the revolutionary upheavals of 1848–9 were quelled *La battaglia di Legnano* was doomed; it was occasionally revived in sober Flemish disguise as *L'assedio di Arlem*.

SYNOPSIS
Acts I, III and IV take place in Milan; Act II in Como. The period is 1176.
Act I (He is Alive!) During the wars between the Italian communes and the German emperor, Frederick Barbarossa, Arrigo, a warrior from Verona, is gravely wounded and reported dead. Returning to Milan after a long convalescence, he finds his fiancée Lida married to his own closest friend, Rolando, a Milanese duke.
Act II (Barbarossa!) Rolando and Arrigo try to persuade the citizens of Como to ally themselves with the Lombard League, but their conference is interrupted by the arrival of Barbarossa and his army.
Act III (Infamy) Arrigo is sworn in as one of the 'Cavaliers of Death'. The hour of the decisive battle with Barbarossa approaches, and Rolando bids his wife and child farewell. When the secret of Lida's and Arrigo's love is betrayed to him, he takes the cruellest revenge he can conceive: he locks up Arrigo, so that, unable to fight with the Cavaliers of Death, he will be an object of eternal infamy; but Arrigo manages to escape.
Act IV (To Die for the Fatherland) Barbarossa's army has been routed; but as Milan celebrates the Lombard victory, Arrigo is borne in mortally wounded. He solemnly testifies to Lida's innocence, is reconciled with Rolando, and dies embracing the Italian banner.

Verdi's most explicitly patriotic opera is, as far as its musical style is concerned, one of his most Parisian: alongside movements in the traditional Italian forms, one finds a three-part (ABA) 'romanza' in the French manner ('Ah! m'abbraccia d'esultanza'), and a duet ('È ver? . . . Sei d'altri?') in something resembling a classical sonata form; instrumental marches and grandiose choruses, generally more hymnic now than in *Nabucco*, provide much of the musical colouring. It is pageant as much as it is drama, a cunningly ordered sequence of processions and tableaux. The opening chorus, 'Viva Italia', is conceived as a kind of hypothetical national anthem, and recurs at strategic moments throughout the opera as the musical emblem of the Italian patriots. This opera closes a phase of Verdi's career: as an ideological testament it is unequivocal, and once it had been composed he felt no further need to burden his works with the Risorgimento overtones that are periodically to be detected in the operas of the 1840s.

RECORDING Ricciarelli, Carreras, Manuguerra, Ghiuselev, Austrian Radio Ch and SO, Gardelli, Philips, 1978
EDITIONS f.s., Ricordi, [?1961]; v.s. Ricordi, [?1850]; later edns and *rps*

Luisa Miller

Melodramma tragico in three acts (2h 15m)
Libretto by Salvatore Cammarano, after the 'bourgeois
tragedy' *Kabale und Liebe* by Johann Christoph Friedrich
von Schiller (1784)
Composed August–October 1849
PREMIERES 8 December 1849, Teatro San Carlo, Naples;
US: 27 October 1852, Philadelphia; UK: 3 June 1858, Her
Majesty's Theatre, Haymarket, London
CAST   Count Walter *b*, Rodolfo *t*, Federica, Duchess of
Ostheim *a*, Wurm *b*, Miller *bar*, Luisa *s*, Laura *ms*, peasant *t*;
satb chorus of maids-in-waiting to Federica, pages, members
of the household, bowmen (bodyguards), villagers
ORCHESTRATION   picc, 2 fl, 2 ob, 2 cl, 2 bsn, 4 hn, 2 tpt,
3 trbn, cimbasso, timp, bd, hp, str; onstage: 2 hn, bell, organ

The idea of composing an opera based on *Kabale
und Liebe* originated in the summer of 1846, when
Verdi was convalescing at Recoaro, and much in
the company of Andrea Maffei, Schiller's Italian
translator. As usual when he found a subject that
excited him, he at first imagined an opera that would
follow closely in the steps of its literary model. But
the opera was intended for Naples, the most old-
fashioned of the major operatic centres of Italy, and
Cammarano recognized at once that they would
never get it past the censors without eliminating
some episodes and raising some of the characters 'to
a nobler plane'. There is no doubt the composer
would have been more completely happy about
Luisa Miller had it proved possible to keep closer to
Schiller: he particularly regretted the sacrifice of
Lady Milford, the prince's mistress (replaced by
Federica, a 'respectable' widow), but Cammarano
explained that, quite apart from the problem of
censorship, no leading singer in Naples would be
prepared to undertake such a role.

The opera was warmly received at its premiere,
and has always been admired without ever quite
gaining for itself the central place in the repertoire
that most Verdians feel it deserves.

SYNOPSIS
The action takes place in the Tyrol, in the first half of
the 17th century.

Act I Love. Scene 1: A pleasant village. Luisa
Miller, daughter of a retired and widowed soldier, is
touched by the birthday greetings of the villagers, but
no longer feels truly happy when separated from
her beloved 'Carlo'. She assures Miller that there
never was a more honourable young man ('Lo vidi,
e'l primo palpito'); and when 'Carlo' joins the
celebrations her happiness is complete ('T'amo
d'amor ch'esprimere'). In conversation with Wurm,
castellan to Count Walter, and another admirer of
Luisa, Miller insists that his daughter must choose for
herself whom she will marry; but he is dismayed to
learn that 'Carlo' is in fact Rodolfo, Walter's son
('Sacra la scelta è d'un consorte' – 'Ah! fu giusto il
mio sospetto!'). Scene 2: A room in Count Walter's
castle. Walter, musing over his tormented relationship with Rodolfo ('Il mio sangue, la vita darei'),
hears of his love for Luisa, and insists that the

wedding planned for him with Federica, a young
widow, must go ahead without delay. Left alone with
Federica, a friend since childhood, Rodolfo decides
to confess the truth; but she loves him too much
to react with anything but indignation ('Dall'aule
raggianti di vano splendor'/'Deh! la parola amara'
'Arma, se vuoi, la mano'). Scene 3: Inside Miller's
house. As Miller is telling Luisa what he has learned
from Wurm, Rodolfo enters, and swears that he
he will keep faith with her. Walter himself now
appears; his insults prompt Miller to draw his sword
on him, and Walter's bodyguard takes both Miller
and Luisa prisoner. Rodolfo tries every means to
persuade his father to release them; finally, vowing
that he will make known to all the world how Walter
came to his title, he hurries away; the count orders
the Millers to be freed.

Act II Intrigue. Scene 1: Inside Miller's house.
Wurm tells Luisa that her father, a prisoner in
Walter's castle, will die unless she does exactly what
she is told. At his dictation she writes a letter,
professing that she has always known who Rodolfo
was, and that ambition prompted her association
with him. Initially she recoils from the task ('Tu
puniscimi, o Signore'); but when Wurm reminds her
of the consequences, she completes and signs the
letter ('A brani, a brani, o perfido'). She is then made
to swear that, when necessary, she will publicly
proclaim her love for Wurm. Scene 2: The castle –
Walter's apartment. Walter promises Wurm that he
has nothing to fear, even though Rodolfo has found
out about the murder they plotted together to seize
the title ('L'alto retaggio non ho bramato'). Federica
enters, and Luisa is brought in to confirm that there
are no longer any ties between herself and Rodolfo.
Finally, she professes to love Wurm ('Come celar le
smanie'). Scene 3: Hanging gardens in the castle.
Luisa's letter has destroyed all Rodolfo's hopes of
happiness ('Quando le sere al placido'). Wurm is
challenged to a duel, but by discharging his pistol
into the air he brings Walter and attendants rushing
to the scene. Rodolfo is persuaded that the fittest
way to be revenged is to marry Federica ('L'ara o
l'avello apprestami').

Act III Poison. Inside Miller's house. Resolved
to take her life, Luisa is writing a last letter to
Rodolfo when her father enters, released from
prison. She confesses what she intends to do; but
such is the old man's despair that she relents, and
agrees to join him in a life of exile from their old
home ('La tomba è un letto'/'Andrem, raminghi e
poveri'). Music sounds from the church where
Rodolfo and Federica are about to be married; but a
moment later Rodolfo appears, brandishing Luisa's
letter. As he questions her, he contrives for both of
them to drink poison. Via accusations, tears and
solemn warnings the ghastly truth emerges ('Piangi,
piangi il tuo dolore' – 'Maledetto, maledetto il dì
ch'io nacqui'). Miller returns to the scene only to
receive the embraces of his dying daughter, and
Rodolfo's prayers for forgiveness ('Padre ricevi
l'estremo addio'). By now all have assembled;
Rodolfo, with one last effort, runs Wurm through
with his sword, then falls dead beside Luisa.

After the stylistic adventures of *Macbeth* and the French-inspired operas of the late 1840s, Verdi returns to the mainstream of Italian melodrama, but at a higher level of sophistication and expressiveness. The music is more consistently inventive, such purely conventional elements as formal introductions and cadences are pared away or given expressive meaning, and the structures of aria and ensemble become more various and flexible. The wonderful duets in Act III best illustrate Verdi's habit of fashioning the musical forms to match the dramatic purpose: in the final section of 'Andrem, raminghi e poveri', Luisa does not, in the customary fashion, sing on equal terms with Miller; instead, in an ethereal, 'barely perceptible' descant, she hovers over him, guardian-angel-like; in 'Piangi, piangi il tuo dolore' no musical reconciliation is brought about between the pure-heartedness of Luisa and the blasphemous despair of Rodolfo: to the bitter end, the music of each remains distinct in melodic style, in colour and texture.

The opera owes much of its distinctive ethos to the simple eloquence of its choruses, notably those that open each of the three acts. In using the chorus so charmingly to evoke a vision of an idyllic and harmonious community Verdi was surely remembering Bellini's *La sonnambula*.

The full-length overture, one of Verdi's finest, is a monothematic sonata movement, based on a theme that recurs in various guises throughout the opera – but especially in Act III – as a symbol of the malign fate that destroys the lovers' happiness.

RECORDINGS 1. Caballé, Pavarotti, Milnes, Giaiotti, London Opera Ch, National PO, Maag, Decca, 1975: evenly cast, eloquent set; 2. Ricciarelli, Domingo, Bruson, Howell, Royal Opera House Ch and O, Maazel, DG, 1979: notable for Ricciarelli's exquisite account of title role; 3. Millo, Domingo, Chernov, Plishka, Ch and O of Metropolitan, New York, Levine, RCA, 1992: strong-limned performance, notable for Chernov's Miller [A.B.]
EDITIONS f.s., Ricordi, [?1937]; v.s., Ricordi, [1850]

Stiffelio

Stiffelius

Dramma lirico in three acts (1h 45m)
Libretto by Francesco Maria Piave, after the play *Le pasteur, ou L'évangile et le foyer* (1849), by Emile Souvestre and Eugène Bourgeois
Composed July–November 1850
PREMIERES 16 November 1850, Teatro Grande, Trieste; 26 December 1968, Teatro Regio, Parma (uncensored); UK: 14 February 1973, Collegiate Theatre, London; US: 17 February 1978, Boston
CAST Stiffelio *t*, Lina *s*, Stankar *bar*, Raffaele *t*, Jorg *b profondo, ms, t, spoken role; satb* chorus of members of Stankar's household, friends and followers of Stiffelio
FULL ORCHESTRA including organ

Of all Verdi's many bold choices of subject, that of *Stiffelio*, a tale of treachery and adultery, revenge and forgiveness among the members of an extreme Protestant sect, is surely the most unusual. The opera's viability was utterly destroyed when, at the last moment, the ecclesiastical censor in Trieste inflicted a series of bowdlerizations – notably in the final church scene – that made it dramatically pointless and in large measure unintelligible. Not surprisingly, it was coolly received, and it fared little better with a rewritten libretto (which incurred the composer's grave displeasure) in which the problematic central character became a German politician, Guglielmo Wellingrode. Fond of *Stiffelio* as Verdi was, it soon became clear that it had no future in the censor-ridden Italy of the 1850s, and by 1854 he had decided that the only way to salvage its remarkable music was by adapting it to a new libretto (see *Aroldo*, below). As a consequence of this rewriting, *Stiffelio* disappeared from view entirely; a full score was discovered only in the 1960s, and the opera received its belated uncensored Italian premiere in 1968.

SYNOPSIS
The scene is set in and near to Count Stankar's castle in Germany on the banks of the river Salzbach (*sic*) at the beginning of the 19th century.

Act I While Stiffelio is away on a preaching mission, his wife Lina is lured into an adulterous liaison with Raffaele. On Stiffelio's return, Lina's father, Stankar, prevents her from confessing her wrong-doing; he does, however, challenge Raffaele to a duel.

Act II The duel is interrupted by Stiffelio; but when he hears what is at issue, he insists on fighting Raffaele himself. Psalm-singing from the nearby church, and the solemn words of Jorg, an elderly minister, recall him to his duty as a man of God.

Act III Stiffelio offers Lina the chance of a divorce; she persuades him that she has always loved him, but had been treacherously seduced. When he goes to administer condign punishment on Raffaele, Stiffelio finds that Stankar has already killed him. Joining his flock in church he tries to recover his serenity of mind by reading from the Bible. It falls open at the story of the woman taken in adultery.

Verdi's music, in keeping with the dramatic theme, is as boldly unconventional as anything he had yet composed. Typical of the opera are movements in which the overall musical effect seems less important than a profusion of expressive detail designed to heighten the tensions of the moment. Stiffelio's Act I aria 'Vidi dovunque gemere' is so sensitive to the changing moods of the troubled Lina, to whom it is addressed, that it has the effect of a whole series of sharply contrasting ariosi. The finale, the Bible-reading scene so mauled by the censor, marks the most radical break with the stylistic conventions of the day: its single lyrical phrase, the climactic 'Perdonata! Iddio lo pronunziò', stands out electrifyingly from an austere context of recitative intonation and quietly reiterated instrumental ostinati. Such textural bleakness marks only one extreme of a wide spectrum of colours, some of which – the elaborately subdivided string patterns in Lina's Act II aria 'Ah, dagli scanni eterei', for example – are exceptionally rich.

RECORDING   Sass, Carreras, Manuguerra, Ganzarolli, Austrian Radio Ch and SO, Gardelli, Philips, 1979
EDITIONS   v.ss., Blanchet, [1850]; Ricordi, [1852]

Rigoletto

Melodramma in three acts (2h)
Libretto by Francesco Maria Piave, after the tragedy *Le roi s'amuse* by Victor Hugo (1832)
Composed November 1850–March 1851
PREMIERES   11 March 1851, La Fenice, Venice; UK: 14 May 1853, Covent Garden, London; US: 19 February 1855, Academy of Music, New York
CAST   Duke of Mantua *t*, Rigoletto *bar*, Gilda *s*, Sparafucile *b*, Maddalena *a*, Giovanna *ms*, Count Monterone *bar*, Marullo *bar*, Matteo Borsa *t*, Count Ceprano *b*, Countess Ceprano *ms*, court usher *t*, Duchess's page *ms*; *tb* chorus of gentlemen of the court; extras: ladies, pages, halberdiers
ORCHESTRATION   picc, 2 fl, 2 ob/ca, 2 cl, 2 bsn, 4 hn, 2 tpt, 3 trbn, cimbasso, timp, perc (bd, bells), str; onstage: band, bd, thunder-machine, str

If the ruination of *Stiffelio* was the most crushing blow Verdi ever received at the hands of the censors, the triumph of *Rigoletto* marked his most famous victory over them. In this instance problems were anticipated from the start – even in liberal Paris *Le roi s'amuse* had been banned after a single performance – and Verdi's determination to produce a worthy operatic version of Hugo's notorious play was resourcefully abetted by the Venetian theatre management. *Le roi s'amuse* thrilled him as no other subject since *Macbeth* had done; he found it 'the greatest subject and perhaps the greatest drama of modern times', and deemed Triboulet (who became Rigoletto) 'a creation worthy of Shakespeare'. Recognizing that the motif of the curse was both the seed and the moral of the drama, Verdi proposed to call the opera *La maledizione*, and probably during November 1850 it was fully sketched under that title, using the setting and the names of Hugo's play. Despite earlier assurances that the subject was acceptable, when the censors read Piave's libretto they were appalled, expressed their regrets that he and the 'celebrated maestro' had squandered their talents on a subject of 'such repellent immorality and obscene triviality', and forbade absolutely the performance of such an opera in Venice. Only after two rewritings was Piave able to produce a libretto that satisfied both Verdi and the censors: the first, *Il Duca di Vendome*, though acceptable to the censors, was dismissed out of hand by the composer because it eliminated everything that was original and powerful; the second, however – *Rigoletto* – satisfied both parties. By such ruses as shifting the action from the French court of François I to the court of an anonymous duke, and by eliminating some of the more flagrantly libertine passages, Piave soothed the political and moral sensibilities of the censors; but in all essentials Hugo's grotesque and macabre drama emerged unscathed. After his experience with *Stiffelio* Verdi would have accepted nothing less.
The premiere was a brilliant popular success, and within ten years *Rigoletto* had been staged in some 250 opera houses all over the world. But its early history was more problematic than that might

suggest. Not all censors were as accommodating as those in Venice, and for a decade and more a number of alternative versions of the opera – *Viscardello, Lionello, Clara di Perth* – were all that could be seen in many theatres. Sometimes the ending had to be altered, and Gilda emerged from her sack in good health to join Rigoletto in giving thanks for the 'clemenza del cielo'. Nor was censorship always the problem. In Bergamo, in September 1851, it was withdrawn from the repertoire after only one and a half performances, because of audience protests. Nevertheless, *Rigoletto* is the earliest of Verdi's operas whose popularity has survived essentially unimpaired from its first performance to the present.

SYNOPSIS
The scene is set in and near Mantua during the 16th century.
Act I   Scene 1: A magnificent hall in the ducal palace. A party is in progress. The libertine Duke proclaims his philosophy of taking his pleasure where he finds it ('Questa o quella per me pari sono'); he flirts with the Countess Ceprano, a sardonic commentary being provided by his jester, the hunchback Rigoletto. Enraged by Rigoletto's insults, Ceprano arranges for a group of courtiers to meet at his palace that night. The revelry is interrupted by Monterone, a political opponent whose daughter has been ravished by the Duke; mocked by Rigoletto, he lays a solemn curse on the Duke and his jester. Scene 2: The end of a blind alley. Rigoletto, haunted by Monterone's curse ('Quel vecchio maledivami!'), is accosted by Sparafucile, a professional assassin; he converses long with him, then compares his own way of life with that of his new acquaintance ('Pari siamo! io la lingua, egli ha il pugnale'). Unknown to the world at large, Rigoletto is a widower, who, all too familiar with the vices of the court, keeps his daughter Gilda in the strictest seclusion. He tells her of her mother, and solemnly enjoins the duenna Giovanna to guard her vigilantly ('Deh, non parlare al misero' – 'Veglia, o donna, questo fiore'). As they are speaking, the Duke (in disguise – he later introduces himself as a poor student, Gualtier Maldè) creeps into the courtyard, and is astonished to learn that his new flame is Rigoletto's daughter. When Rigoletto has gone indoors, he steps forward with a passionate avowal of love ('È il sol dell' anima'). Sounds of footsteps in the street disturb them, and the Duke bids a hasty farewell, leaving Gilda in ecstatic reverie ('Caro nome'). The footsteps were those of the courtiers gathering at Ceprano's house. They trick Rigoletto into allowing himself to be blindfolded; then he unwittingly helps them ransack his own house ('Zitti, zitti, moviamo a vendetta'), carrying off Gilda; Rigoletto hears her cries in the distance, tears off his blindfold, and recognizes in what has happened the force of Monterone's curse.
Act II   A reception room in the ducal palace. The Duke fears he has lost Gilda: returning to her house shortly after their parting he had found it deserted ('Ella mi fu rapita!' – 'Parmi veder le lagrime'). But

when the courtiers tell him of their night's exploits, he realizes that she is in his power, and hastens away to take his pleasure ('Possente amor mi chiama'). Rigoletto enters, searching anxiously for Gilda. Overhearing the courtiers' evasive replies when a page asks for the Duke, he realizes that she must be with him; he turns on them, denouncing them as contemptible hirelings ('Cortigiani, vil razza dannata'). Gilda appears, burning with shame; Rigoletto drives out the courtiers, and weeps as he hears her story ('Tutte le feste al tempio'). Monterone is escorted through the room on his way to prison; to Gilda's horror, Rigoletto assures the departing figure that he will soon be avenged ('Sì, vendetta, tremenda vendetta').

Act III The right bank of the Mincio. Having engaged the services of Sparafucile, Rigoletto brings Gilda to a half-ruined tavern where they observe the Duke settling down for an evening's drinking and whoring ('La donna è mobile'). He has been lured there by Maddalena, Sparafucile's sister, and now begins to make love to her; Gilda despairs, while Rigoletto meditates revenge ('Bella figlia dell' amore'). Rigoletto sends his daughter home, then arranges with Sparafucile to return at midnight for the Duke's body. A storm rises. Gilda returns in disguise, and hears Sparafucile and Maddalena arguing: Maddalena has fallen for the young man, now asleep upstairs, and wants to spare him. Sparafucile agrees that if someone else calls at the inn before Rigoletto's return, he can be murdered instead. With a short prayer, Gilda resolves to sacrifice herself; as the storm reaches its height, she enters the tavern ('Se pria ch'abbia il mezzo la notte toccato'). Rigoletto returns for the body, which is handed over in a sack. The sound of the Duke's singing in the distance arouses him from his meditations; he tears open the sack and discovers Gilda, still just alive. As she dies, she tries to comfort her distraught father ('V'ho ingannato! colpevole fui'); Monterone's curse is fulfilled.

Rigoletto marks Verdi's most radical break yet with the conventions of *ottocento* opera: there are no formal entrance arias (*sortite*) for the principal characters and no ensemble finales; for long stretches

there is no conventional recitative; and – part of its unique colouring – female voices are excluded from the chorus. Perhaps the most Verdian touch of all is that this revolutionary opera is, on the surface, simpler, more tuneful and popular than anything he had written before.

The key to *Rigoletto* is to be found in the characterization in Hugo's play, and Verdi's attempt to re-create it in musical terms. The split personality of the central character – 'grossly deformed and absurd but inwardly passionate and full of love', as Verdi put it – is the source of those veerings of tone, from darkness to light, from comedy to tragedy, which give *Rigoletto* an almost Shakespearean expressive range and a breadth of sympathy typical of all Verdi's greatest operas from this time forward. The hedonistic Duke makes his entry, not with the customary formal aria, but with a *ballata* (dance song) that falls naturally into place as part of the festivities of the opening scene, and follows this with a duet, accompanied by an instrumental minuet whose echoes of *Don Giovanni* are unlikely to be accidental. Gilda, a girl wholly lacking in prima donna-ish egotism, finds her proper medium of expression in a series of duets with the two men she loves. Her only aria, 'Caro nome', is a single movement in a unique form: a series of delicately musing variations on a theme, first played by the flutes, that serves as an emblem of her lover's (pretended) name. The Act III quartet, 'Bella figlia dell'amore' is one of Verdi's greatest and most characteristic achievements, resolving a situation of excruciating emotional complexity into a torrent of passionate but exquisitely shaped song.

The impression of some early critics that the vocal writing in *Rigoletto* was 'less splendid' than the orchestration seems largely unintelligible today. But it does highlight the remarkable originality of Verdi's score, and the freedom with which he avails himself of colouristic and harmonic resources rarely accorded high priority in the Italian tradition. The Rigoletto–Sparafucile dialogue in Act I, probably inspired by the duettino 'Qui che fai?' from Donizetti's *Lucrezia Borgia*, demonstrates his art of conjuring atmospheric colours from the orchestra and underlining certain phrases ('Sparafucil mi nomino') with harmonic progressions of rare audacity.

The quartet in Act III of Rigoletto; *illustration from an early vocal score*

RECORDINGS 1. Callas, di Stefano, Gobbi, Zaccaria, La Scala Ch and O, Serafin, EMI, 1955: classic mono recording with principals unsurpassed for subtlety and eloquence of phrasing; 2. Cotrubas, Domingo, Cappuccilli, Ghiaurov, Ch and O of Vienna Staatsoper, Giulini, DG, 1981: sensitive, securely cast stereo set conducted with strength and eloquence [A.B.]
VIDEO Gruberova, Pavarotti, Wixell, Furlanetto, Vienna State Opera Ch, Vienna PO, Chailly, Decca, 1983: Ponnelle's richly imagined film, splendidly sung [A.B.]
EDITIONS v.ss., Blanchet [1850]; Ricordi, 1852; Escudier, [1855]; Edward Downes (ed.), Royal Opera, Covent Garden (limited edn), 1993
AUTOGRAPH MANUSCRIPT copies: Conservatorio di Musica S. Pietro a Majella, Naples (two copies); Musiksammlung, Österreichische Nationalbibliothek, Vienna

Il trovatore

The Troubadour

Dramma in four parts (2h 15m)

Libretto by Salvatore Cammarano and Leone Emanuele
Bardare, after the play *El trovador* by Antonio García
Gutiérrez (1836)

Composed ?September 1851–January 1853; rev. for Paris 1856
PREMIERES 19 January 1853, Teatro Apollo, Rome; US: 2
May 1855, Academy of Music, New York; UK: 10 May 1855,
Covent Garden, London

CAST Il Conte di Luna *bar*, Leonora *s*, Azucena *ms*,
Manrico *t*, Ferrando *b profondo*, Ines *s*, Ruiz *t*, old gypsy *b*,
messenger *t*; *satb* chorus of companions of Leonora, nuns,
members of the count's household, men-at-arms, gypsies
ORCHESTRATION picc, fl, 2 ob, 2 cl, 2 bsn, 4 hn, 2 tpt, 3
trbn, cimbasso, timp, perc (bd, triangle, hammers and anvils),
str; onstage: hp, organ, hn, bells, sd

When Verdi first read García Gutiérrez's play it was,
as usual, the strong situations and the characters,
especially the gypsy Azucena, that fired his
imagination: he saw in the bizarre plot and the insane
passions of the protagonists a pretext for more
operatic boldness along the lines of *Rigoletto*. He
wrote to a friend, 'The more Cammarano provides
me with originality and freedom of form, the better I
shall be able to do.' And he went on to speculate
about an operatic ideal 'in which there were neither
cavatinas, nor duets, nor trios, nor choruses . . . and
the whole opera was (if I might express it this
way) one single piece'. Cammarano had his usual
sobering effect on Verdi's revolutionary impulses,
but the collaboration on *Il trovatore* was singularly
harmonious, and it was tragic that the librettist died
in July 1852, when composition was still at an early
stage. He had completed a first version of the libretto
virtually on his deathbed, but all revisions and
additions that Verdi later found necessary were made
by a young friend of Cammarano, Leone Emanuele
Bardare: they include several of the best-loved
numbers, including 'Stride la vampa!', 'Il balen del
suo sorriso' and 'D'amor sull'ali rosee'.

The success of the premiere surpassed even that of
Rigoletto, and the speed with which *Il trovatore* swept
the world, literally from Scotland to the South
Pacific, was even more sensational: street-theatre
parodies were widely enjoyed (by Verdi as much as
anyone) for decades. Despite, indeed in part because
of, its demotic tone, *Il trovatore* has come to be seen
as one of the composer's supreme achievements,
and the Verdian critic – especially if he is Italian
– is likely to extol its sublime vulgarity with
an enthusiasm that soars to mystic heights: 'the
definitive melodrama . . . the Via Crucis of Italian
song . . . this is where Verdi's art, which is all in
subversion, deformation, sublime caricature, sets the
four corners of the world on fire' (B. Barilli). The
opera's irrational magical power is encapsulated in a
familiar anecdote told of the first Italian prime
minister, the utterly unmusical Count Cavour, who,
on receiving the Austrian ultimatum that was to
bring France into alliance with Piedmont in the War
of Italian Unity, could find no more effective way of
expressing his excitement than throwing open the

window and singing 'Di quella pira' at the top of his
voice.

In 1856 Verdi was commissioned to adapt *Il
trovatore* for the Paris Opéra by adding an extended
ballet to the third act; this version, *La trouvère*, which
included a number of other revisions, was staged
under the composer's direction in January 1857.

SYNOPSIS

The action takes place partly in Biscay, partly in
Aragon, during the early 15th century.

Part I The Duel. Scene 1: A hall in the palace of
Aliaferia. Ferrando tells the story of Azucena,
daughter of a woman who, 20 years before, had been
burned for witchcraft because she cast the 'evil eye'
on Luna's infant brother; to avenge her, Azucena
allegedly threw the infant on the embers of the pyre
('Di due figli vivea padre beato'). **Scene 2:** The
gardens of the palace. In the days before the civil war
began, an unknown knight won Leonora's love by
his bravery at a tournament. Since then he has
sometimes returned in the guise of a troubadour to
serenade her ('Tacea la notte placida' – 'Di tale amor
che dirsi'). Through the garden her two admirers
approach: Luna (quietly) and Manrico (in full-
throated song – 'Deserta sulla terra'). Hastening to
greet Manrico, Leonora blunders into the arms of
Luna. The count is enraged to discover that his rival
is Manrico, a rebel in the civil war; the men rush
away to duel ('Di geloso amor sprezzato').

Part II The Gypsy. Scene 1: A ruined hovel at
the foot of a mountain in Biscay. Manrico has
defeated Luna in the duel, but spared his life; in turn
wounded by Luna in the wars, he has been nursed
back to health by Azucena, supposedly his mother.
She sings a ballad about a woman – it proves to be
her mother – who was burnt at the stake ('Stride la
vampa!') and goes on to tell the ghastly story of how,
seeking to avenge her, she had thrown into the
flames not the infant Luna but her own baby son
('Condotta ell'era in ceppi'). Then, confused, she
tries to reassure Manrico: of course he is her son. A
messenger brings news that Leonora, believing her
beloved dead, is about to take the veil; Manrico
hastens away ('Perigliarti ancor languente'). **Scene 2:**
The porch of a place of retreat near Castellor. Luna
has also heard of Leonora's intention and plans to
abduct her ('Il balen del suo sorriso' – 'Per me, ora
fatale'). As Leonora bids farewell to her companions,
Luna steps from the shadows; but he is confounded
by the appearance of Manrico ('E deggio . . . e posso
crederlo?'), who with his own followers hurries
Leonora away.

Part III The Gypsy's Son. Scene 1: An encampment. Luna's troops prepare to assault Manrico's
stronghold ('Squilli, echeggi la tromba guerriera').
Some soldiers have arrested a gypsy on suspicion
of spying, and Ferrando recognizes her as Azucena;
in terror she calls out for Manrico, so revealing
that he is her son ('Giorni poveri vivea'). Luna
is exultant: by burning her before the walls of
Manrico's fortress, he can torment his rival and at
the same time avenge his brother's death ('Deh,

rallentate, o barbari'). Scene 2: A room adjacent to the chapel at Castellor. In the beleaguered castle Manrico and Leonora are about to be married ('Ah! sì, ben mio'). Ruiz reports that a pyre has been erected outside the walls, and that Azucena is being dragged towards it in chains. Manrico leads off his men to the rescue ('Di quella pira').

Part IV The Execution. Scene 1: A wing of the palace of Aliaferia. Leonora comes, armed with a phial of poison, to rescue Manrico, who is now imprisoned with his mother; from the castle she hears monkish chants of death and Manrico's own singing (the so-called 'Miserere' scene: 'D'amor sull'ali rosee' – 'Miserere d'un alma già vicina' – 'Ah, che la morte ognora' – 'Tu vedrai che amore in terra'). She accosts Luna. At first deaf to her appeal, he assents when she offers herself as the price for Manrico's freedom; she takes the poison ('Mira, di acerbe lagrime' – 'Vivrà! . . . contende il giubilo'). Scene 2: A horrid dungeon. Manrico comforts the fearful Azucena, and she sleeps ('Sì, la stanchezza m'opprime, o figlio' – 'Ai nostri monti . . . ritorneremo'). Leonora comes to free Manrico; refusing to leave without her, he begins to suspect the bargain she may have made with Luna and, since she makes no denial, denounces her ('Parlar non vuoi? . . . Balen tremenda!'). When she sinks dying at his feet, he is overcome with remorse; Luna enters ('Prima che d'altri vivere') and consigns Manrico to immediate execution, forcing Azucena to watch from her prison window. As Manrico dies, she reveals to Luna that he has killed his own brother; her mother is avenged!

Despite Verdi's first thoughts on the subject, *Il trovatore* is an opera that rejoices unashamedly in the peculiar strengths of traditional Romantic melodrama, and generally makes fewer demands of the singers' acting skills or intelligence than does *Rigoletto*: Caruso once famously, if discouragingly, remarked that all one needed for a good performance were the four greatest singers in the world. In most scenes the traditional forms are clearly audible, contributing much to the sense of concentrated emotional intensity so characteristic of the score. Many numbers owe much of their expressive force to a style of melody that the composer had been developing from his earliest years, and which in *Il trovatore* reaches full maturity: typically the arias start from quiet, sometimes even unremarkable openings, gradually unfolding in mounting waves of melody to culminate in grand engulfing phrases employing the full extension of the voice. The opera's extraordinary range of scenic, psychological and musical expression is best seen in the so-called 'Miserere' scene, where the customary ingredients of *scena*, *cantabile* and *cabaletta* are enriched by episodes of ecclesiastical chanting, by a declamatory soliloquy for Leonora accompanied by shuddering ostinato rhythms for the full orchestra, and by the heart-broken ecstasy of Manrico's off-stage troubadour song. The masterly juxtaposition and combination of these elements make the 'Miserere' scene a supreme moment not only of Italian Romantic melodrama, but of the whole art of opera.

For some years the rebel, the non-conformist and the outcast had been a favourite figure in Verdi's operas: in *Il trovatore* a matching sense of alienation is vividly expressed in the music. The finely nuanced *cantabiles* of Leonora and Luna leave no doubt of their aristocratic breeding; but the music of Azucena and (more equivocally) Manrico is popular and balladesque in manner – particularly distinctive are the pervasive strumming rhythms in 3/8 metre.

RECORDINGS 1. Callas, Barbieri, Di Stefano, Panerai, Zaccaria, La Scala Ch and O, Karajan, EMI, 1956: unbeatable cast superbly conducted in slightly abridged mono version; 2. Price, Cossotto, Domingo, Milnes, Giaiotti, Ambrosian Opera Ch, New Philharmonia O, Mehta, RCA, 1969: glowingly sung and conducted, resplendent cast; 3. Plowright, Fassbaender, Domingo, Zancanaro, Nesterenko, Santa Cecilia Academy Ch and O, Giulini, DG, 1984: most successful modern set with strong cast welded into satisfying ensemble by Giulini [A.B.]
VIDEOS 1. Plowright, Cossotto, Bonisolli, Zancanaro, Ch and O of Verona Arena, Giovaninetti, Castle, 1985; 2. Marton, Zajick, Pavarotti, Milnes, Ch and O of Metropolitan, New York, Levine, DG, 1989: both powerful, unsubtle, off-the-stage performances; the first is better sung, tenor excepted [A.B.]
EDITIONS f.ss., Ricordi, 1913; new edn rev. and corrected, 1955; v.s., Ricordi, [1853]

La traviata
The Fallen Woman
Melodramma in three acts (2h)
Libretto by Francesco Maria Piave, after the play *La dame aux camélias* by Alexandre Dumas *fils* (1852)
Composed January–February 1853, rev. March–April 1854
PREMIERES 6 March 1853, La Fenice, Venice; rev. version: 6 May 1854, Teatro Gallo di San Benedetto, Venice; UK: 24 May 1856, Her Majesty's Theatre, Haymarket, London; US: 3 December 1856, Academy of Music, New York
CAST Violetta Valéry s, Flora Bervoix ms, Annina s, Alfredo Germont t, Giorgio Germont bar, Gastone, Viscomte de Letorières t, Baron Douphol bar, Marquis d'Obigny b, Doctor Grenvil b, Giuseppe t, Flora's servant b, messenger b; satb chorus of ladies and gentlemen, friends of Violetta and Flora, matadors, picadors, gypsies, servants of Violetta and Flora, masquers; dancers
ORCHESTRATION 2 fl/picc, 2 ob, 2 cl, 2 bsn, 4 hn, 2 tpt, 3 trbn, cimbasso, timp, perc (bd, triangle), str; backstage: band, hp; onstage: 2 picc, 4 cl, 2 hn, 2 trbn, castanets, picche, tambourines

For extended periods between August 1847 and March 1852, Verdi lived in Paris; it was the time when the new artistic vogue of realism was emerging, and *La traviata* is the most eloquent witness to the movement's influence on him. He may well have seen Dumas's *La dame aux camélias* when it was first staged in February 1852; but it was not until October, when he eventually acquired a copy of the play, that he decided to make an opera of it.

Warm memories of the *Rigoletto* premiere made it easy for the management of the Fenice theatre in Venice to engage Verdi for another opera. In addition to its high musical standards, Venice had the advantage of an unusually liberal censorship, without which *La traviata* would hardly have been possible at all. Nevertheless, despite the fact that this opera is

Fanny Salvini-Donatelli, the first Violetta

one of his most intimate and personal creations, Verdi, having heard bad reports of the singers, approached its premiere with less eagerness than might have been expected.

There is no truth in the oft-repeated tale that the opera's initial failure was due to its contemporary setting; in fact, despite Verdi's wish to have it performed in modern dress, it was set '*c*. 1700', and it was not until the 1880s – by which time, of course, the 1850s were a generation distant – that 'realistic' productions were attempted. Nor is there anything to support the claim that the plump Fanny Salvini-Donatelli made a laughably inept consumptive heroine: her performance in the role of Violetta was one of the few things at the premiere that met with general approval. The root of the problem, according to Felice Varesi, the distinguished baritone for whom Verdi had already composed the roles of Macbeth and Rigoletto, and who now appeared as the first Giorgio Germont, was that Verdi had composed the opera with sublime disregard for the vocal capabilities of his principals, and that 'this caused much strong feeling among the Venetian public'. After the premiere, Verdi withdrew the opera until the opportunity arose to stage it with an ideal cast and/or to revise it.

Antonio Gallo, impresario of the Teatro San Benedetto, had meanwhile been impressed with

La traviata, and bombarded the publisher, Ricordi, with requests to stage the work in his own theatre. Eventually Verdi consented, and took back five movements of his autograph score for revision (all from Acts II and III: the Violetta–Germont duet, the *cabaletta* of Germont's aria, the *largo* of the Act II finale, the Violetta–Alfredo duet, and the Act III finale). In this revised form *La traviata* was enthusiastically received; it soon rivalled *Il trovatore* in popularity, even in Victorian England, where its premiere had been greeted by a denunciatory leading article in *The Times* and where early Covent Garden productions refrained from supplying translations, out of consideration – it was implied – for patrons' moral well-being.

SYNOPSIS

The scene is set in Paris and its vicinity in about 1850.

Act I   A salon in Violetta's house: August. At a party given by the notorious courtesan, Violetta Valéry, Alfredo is introduced as an admirer. After a *brindisi* ('Libiam ne' lieti calici'), the guests move to an adjoining room for dancing. Violetta, afflicted by a fit of consumptive coughing, remains behind, and finds herself attended by a solicitous Alfredo. He urges her to abandon a way of life that can lead only to an early grave ('Un dì felice'). The party guests leave, and Violetta muses: could Alfredo really be the redeemer of whom she has dreamed ('È strano! . . . è strano!' – 'Ah, fors'è lui')? She shrugs off her foolish fancy ('Sempre libera degg'io').

Act II   Scene 1: A country house near Paris: January. For three months Alfredo and Violetta have lived together in the country. But Alfredo's happiness turns to shame when by chance he learns that Violetta has been selling her possessions to maintain them ('De' miei bollenti spiriti' – 'O mio rimorso! o infamia!'), and he hastens away to Paris to rearrange his affairs. Violetta is visited by an elderly gentleman, who proves to be Germont senior. He begs her to leave Alfredo for the sake of a younger daughter, whose prospects are threatened by her brother's liaison ('Pura siccome un angelo'); he dismisses all Violetta's hopes of happiness as delusions, transient as youth and beauty ('Non sapete quale affetto' – 'Un dì, quando le veneri'); finally he extracts from her a promise to renounce Alfredo for ever ('Dite alla giovine' – 'Morrò! . . . la mia memoria'). When Alfredo returns, Violetta bids him a passionate farewell, pretending that she is absenting herself only for a few hours. A little later he is brought a letter telling the truth: she is returning to a former protector, Baron Douphol. While Germont tries to comfort him ('Di Provenza il mar, il suol' – 'No, non udrai rimproveri'), Alfredo broods on vengeance. Scene 2: A gallery in Flora's palace. Flora's guests are entertained with masquerades of gypsies and bullfighters. Alfredo arrives, followed by Violetta and Douphol, and wins large sums of money at cards. The guests are summoned to dinner, but a moment later Violetta and Alfredo return alone: fearing for his life, she urges him to leave the party. Instead, he summons the revellers, and, announcing that he is paying off

Violetta for services rendered, hurls the money he has just won at her feet. At that moment his father arrives. In the finale the multitude of different passions provoked by Alfredo's insult are expressed.

Act III Violetta's bedroom: February. Despite Dr Grenvil's encouraging words, Violetta knows that she has only a few hours to live. She reads over a letter from Germont: Alfredo, who fled abroad after wounding Douphol in a duel, has been told of her sacrifice, and is hurrying back to Paris for her forgiveness. But alone and dying, Violetta has, realistically, only God's mercy to depend upon ('Addio, del passato'). The sound of Shrove Tuesday revels in the street contrasts ironically with the desolation within. Alfredo does return, however, and the lovers dream of escape from Paris, of health and happiness; but as Violetta tries to dress she collapses, and both realize she is on the point of death ('Parigi, o cara, noi lasceremo' – 'Gran Dio! morir sì giovane'). Grenvil returns, and Germont too arrives, anxious to make amends for the suffering he has caused; giving Alfredo a medallion to remember her by, and praying that he will find a wife more worthy of him, Violetta dies ('Prendi; quest'è l'immagine').

La traviata shares with *Rigoletto* and *Il trovatore* a magnificent directness of utterance: the three operas embody the principles of *ottocento* opera with sovereign mastery and freedom, and an unerring sense of dramatic purpose, and popular opinion is not deceived in seeing in them the ripest harvest of Italian Romantic melodrama. *La traviata* is the most elegant and refined of the three: typically its profusion of 3/8 rhythms – as common here as in *Il trovatore* – are evocative less of the primitive strummings of popular music than of the sensual swaying of the waltz. Its scoring is also the most delicate, its translucence serving in part (in the prelude and in much of Act III) as a musical symbol of the consumptive Violetta.

The clarity of the plot, and the overwhelming presence of a single moral idea – that of an ideal of love which survives all man's attempts to exploit and corrupt it – prompts Verdi to make fuller use than in any earlier opera of a single recurring theme. In the *cantabile* of the Act I duet, Alfredo and Violetta are characteristically contrasted, the hesitant phrases of the shy idealist being juxtaposed and later counterpointed with the fickle brilliance of the 'woman of pleasure'. Alfredo's solo rises to a magnificent climactic hymn to love ('Di quell'amor'), and in Violetta's great solo *scena* at the close of Act I, she takes up the same theme at the climax to the *cantabile* ('Ah, fors'è lui'), where she dreams of the true love that might one day redeem her. Between the two statements of her *cabaletta* ('Sempre libera'), it returns again, sung by Alfredo from the street below her window; and this is a masterstroke of dramatic psychology as well as a *coup de théâtre*, for to remind Violetta of Alfredo's love as she is in the midst of reasserting her philosophy of pleasure is to turn what might have been merely a brilliant *cabaletta* into a conflict of hedonism and idealism. In Act III the same theme recurs twice more, now in

purely orchestral form; for all illusory hope has vanished, and Violetta cherishes only the memory of what might have been.

Germont is as vividly characterized as the two lovers, his music made up in part of nostalgic Bellinian memories ('Pura siccome un angelo', 'Di Provenza il mar, il suol'), in part of songs in which his didactic manner is suggested by downbeats heavy with flurries of short notes ('Un dì, quando le veneri', 'No, non udrai rimproveri'). His Act II duet with Violetta is as magnificent a musico-dramatic achievement as anything Verdi ever wrote: the inexorable tragic thrust of the argument is embodied with rare finesse in a seemingly kaleidoscopic, but in fact masterfully controlled, sequence of short movements.

RECORDINGS 1. Callas, Kraus, Sereni, San Carlo (Lisbon) Ch and O, Ghione, EMI, 1958 live performance, issued 1980: Callas in her greatest role, unsurpassed for dramatic truth, and Alfredo Kraus is most stylish of Alfredos (slightly cut); 2. Cotrubas, Domingo, Milnes, Bavarian State Opera Ch and O, C. Kleiber, DG, 1977: vital, moving performance, vividly conducted (slightly cut); 3. Scotto, Kraus, Bruson, Ambrosian Opera Ch, Philharmonia O, Muti, EMI, 1982: complete version, authentically conducted, well sung though not so memorably as above versions; 4. Studer, Pavarotti, Pons, Ch and O of Metropolitan, New York, Levine, DG, 1992: not as inspired as the earlier three, but notable for Studer's gloriously sung Violetta [A.B.]
VIDEO McLaughlin, MacNeil, Ellis, Glyndebourne Festival Ch, LPO, Haitink, Pioneer (laserdisc)/Pickwick (VHS), 1987: McLaughlin proves a deeply moving, vulnerable Violetta in this satisfying ensemble performance [A.B.]
EDITIONS f.ss., Ricordi, 1914; rev. and corrected, edn 1955; v.ss. Ricordi, [c.1855]; later edns and *rps*

Les vêpres siciliennes

The Sicilian Vespers

Dramma in five acts (3h, including Act III ballet of *c.* 25m)
Libretto by Auguste Eugène Scribe and Charles Duveyrier, adapted from Scribe's earlier libretto *Le duc d'Albe* (1838)
Composed January 1854 – ?April 1855; one substitute aria, 'O toi che j'ai chéri', ?summer 1863
PREMIERES 13 June 1855, Opéra, Paris; UK: 27 July 1859, Drury Lane, London; US: 7 November 1859, Academy of Music, New York
CAST Guy de Montfort *bar*, Henri *t*, Jean Procida *b*, La Duchesse Hélène *s*, *a*, 3 *t*, *bar*, 2 *b*; *satb* chorus of Sicilian men and women, French soldiers, monks, etc.; extras and corps de ballet: French soldiers, betrothed couples, pages, nobles, officials, penitents, executioner, Sicilians, zephyrs, naiads, fauns, Bacchantes
FULL ORCHESTRA

Since his Parisian début with *Jérusalem* Verdi's international reputation had continued to grow; on his return to the Opéra he was able to insist that the great Scribe himself should be the librettist, that he should be allowed a three-month rehearsal period and guaranteed 40 performances within ten months of the premiere. The libretto was adapted from a text on which both Halévy (briefly in 1838) and Donizetti (intermittently, but at length, from 1839) had laboured in vain; and it was transformed into *Les vêpres siciliennes* by the fashionable device of 'anatopism', transferring the action from Flanders to 'a climate full of warmth and music' (Scribe). Warmly received at first – Berlioz found in it 'a grandeur, a sovereign mastery more marked than in the composer's previous creations' – *Les vêpres siciliennes* soon lost its hold on the repertoire and was not revived at the Opéra after 1865.

In Italy it was quite impossible to stage it under its original title until the relaxation of censorship that followed the Unification of 1861. In the Italian translation the action was shifted to 17th-century Portugal, and the opera became *Giovanna da Guzman*. Its vogue was restricted by the Act III ballet (which had been much admired in Paris, but was beyond the resources of most Italian theatres) and, probably in 1856, Verdi authorized its removal in Italian productions.

Les vêpres siciliennes is the earliest of Verdi's operas for which there survives a production book (a *mise-en-scène*, or detailed account of the original production). Verdi's Italian publisher, Ricordi, had this translated for *Giovanna da Guzman* and issued similar *disposizioni sceniche* for most of Verdi's later operas; they afford fascinating insights into the style of 19th-century opera production.

SYNOPSIS
The scene is set in and around Palermo; 1282.

Act I Sicilian resentment against the occupying French is fanned by Hélène, sister of the late Duke Frederick of Austria; the appearance of the hated viceroy Guy de Montfort rapidly disperses the crowd. Henri, a loyal follower of Frederick, refuses Montfort's offer of employment, and defies his warning to keep away from Hélène.

Act II Procida tells Henri and Hélène that he has failed to win foreign support for the Sicilians. Their cause receives a further setback when Henri is arrested for declining an invitation to a vice-regal ball. At the festival of Santa Rosalia, Procida deliberately inflames anti-French feeling by encouraging French soldiers to carry off a group of peasant girls.

Act III Henri, whom Montfort has discovered to be his own illegitimate son, spurns his father's affection. But at the ball, where his guests are entertained by a ballet, he frustrates an assassination attempt by Procida and Hélène. As they are dragged away to prison, the Sicilian conspirators curse Henri as a traitor.

Act IV Learning why Henri saved Montfort, Hélène readily forgives him: and he, having paid his father the debt of life, is ready to die with the conspirators if he cannot obtain a pardon for them. On condition that Henri will acknowledge him as his father, Montfort does issue a pardon; he further decrees that his son and Hélène shall marry without delay, to seal the new Franco-Sicilian amity.

Act V As the approaching marriage is celebrated, Hélène is appalled to learn from Procida that the wedding bells are to serve as a signal for a massacre. Her despairing attempts to stop the marriage are vain; bells ring out, and the Sicilians fall murderously upon the unsuspecting French.

What to Berlioz seemed 'grandeur and sovereign mastery' has sounded to many modern critics more like self-conscious and contrived artifice. *Les vêpres siciliennes* conspicuously lacks the seemingly effortless flow of invention, and the perfect matching of musical means to dramatic ends that distinguished its three predecessors. But Verdi was now looking to enlarge his range, and in that sense the opera was enormously fruitful. At this period Meyerbeer, the master of Parisian grand opera, was the contemporary Verdi most admired, and much of the music seems an attempt to lay hold on the resources of Meyerbeer's style for Verdi's own purposes: grandiose 'stereophonic' effects, the bold exploration of new vocal and instrumental textures in new lyrical designs, and everywhere an unprecedented flexibility in the handling of rhythm. But Verdi was not slavish in his emulation. It is typical of his more urgent sense of theatre that after the intimate scenes of Act IV (traditional in grand opera), he refused to allow Scribe to dissipate the dramatic tension by the usual return to grandiosity in Act V; instead the spectators' attention is held firmly focused on the plight of his central characters.

RECORDINGS 1. Callas, Kokolios Bardi, Mascherini, Christoff, Florence Festival Ch and O, E. Kleiber, Cetra, 1951: poorly recorded but historically important live performance; 2. Arroyo, Domingo, Milnes, Raimondi, Alldis Ch, New Philharmonia O, Levine, RCA, 1973: standard – and excellent – version [A.B.]
VIDEOS 1. Dunn, Luchetti, Nucci, Giaiotti, Ch and O of Teatro Comunale, Bologna, Chailly, Castle, 1986: film of Ronconi's staging; 2. Studer, Merritt, Zancanaro, Furlanetto, Ch and O of La Scala, Milan, Muti: same performance as on CD [A.B.]
EDITIONS f.s., Ricordi, [?1896], 5 vols; v.ss., (French), Escudier, [1855], rev. 1856; (Italian: *Giovanna da Guzman*), Ricordi, [c. 1858]; (Italian), Ricordi, 1944
MANUSCRIPT Bibliothèque Nationale, Paris

Simon Boccanegra (I)

Opera in a prologue and three acts
Libretto by Francesco Maria Piave, with additions by Giuseppe Montanelli, after Antonio García Gutiérrez's drama *Simón Bocanegra* (1843)
Composed Autumn 1856–early 1857
PREMIERE 12 March 1857, La Fenice, Venice

As work on *Les vêpres siciliennes* drew to a close, Verdi was planning to go on to revise *La battaglia di Legnano* and *Stiffelio* so that they would get past the censors; and he still longed to create a *King Lear*. It was not until the summer of 1856, when he signed another contract for Venice, that he started to think about quite new projects. He chose as a subject García Gutiérrez's *Simón Bocanegra*, perhaps hoping it would capture the public imagination as *Il trovatore* had done. Piave was nominally the librettist, but with Verdi now so much in Paris close collaboration was difficult, and much of the revising and polishing was done by Giuseppe Montanelli, an Italian poet in exile in Paris. García Gutiérrez's play is a rambling historical chronicle set at a period of political turmoil in 14th-century Genoa; Piave found it beyond his powers to make a lucid reduction of it, and the libretto was generally condemned as one of the most unintelligible ever to have reached the stage. Verdi's music was admired by some connoisseurs for its expressive and dramatic 'conscientiousness'; but the overriding impression it made on contemporaries was of gloomy and sometimes recondite experimentation, in which declamation had very much the upper hand over song: 'Not even Wagner would have ventured so far along this road,' declared one bemused critic. Revivals were few and rarely successful. In due course Verdi came to feel that the opera, quite apart from the incoherence of its plot, was 'too sad, too depressing', and in 1880 he agreed to make a radical revision in collaboration with Arrigo Boito. (See *Simon Boccanegra (II)*, below)

EDITION v.s., Ricordi, [1857]

Aroldo
Harold

Melodramma in four acts (2h)
Libretto by Francesco Maria Piave, adapted from his and Verdi's 1850 opera *Stiffelio*, borrowing names from Bulwer-Lytton's novel *Harold, the Last of the Saxon Kings* (1843), and with hints from Sir Walter Scott's *The Betrothed* (1825) and *The Lady of the Lake* (1810)
Composed spring 1856–summer 1857
PREMIERES 16 August 1857, Teatro Nuovo, Rimini; Ireland: 1959, Theatre Royal, Wexford; US: 4 May 1963, Academy of Music, New York; UK: 25 February 1964, St Pancras Town Hall, London
CAST Aroldo *t*, Mina *s*, Egberto *bar*, Briano *b profondo*, Godvino *t*, *ms*, *t*, silent role; *satb* chorus of Crusader knights, gentlemen and ladies of Kent, esquires, pages, heralds, huntsmen, Saxons, Scottish peasants
FULL ORCHESTRA offstage: band

Having given up all hope of seeing *Stiffelio* performed as he conceived it, Verdi transformed it into *Aroldo* during 1856–7, and the opera was staged to mark the opening of a new Teatro Comunale at Rimini. It was the first collaboration between Verdi and one of the rising stars of Italian music, Angelo Mariani, the outstanding conductor of his generation, and the first Italian – unless one counts Spontini – to abandon the traditional manner of directing performances from the first violin desk and to conduct with a baton. The premiere caused enormous excitement in Rimini, but in the greater operatic centres audiences were less easily persuaded of *Aroldo*'s merits: the opera was widely performed for a few years, but never established itself as a repertoire item.

SYNOPSIS

The scene is set, for the first three acts, in Egbert's castle near Kent (*sic*); for Act IV on the shores of Loch Lomond in Scotland; *c.* 1200.

Act I While Harold, a Saxon knight, is away at the Crusades, his wife Mina enters into an adulterous liaison with Godwin, a soldier of fortune. When Harold returns, accompanied by Brian,a hermit he has met in Palestine, she is prevented from confessing her wrong-doing by her father Egbert who, however, challenges Godwin to a duel to avenge the family honour.

Act II The duel is interrupted by Harold. When he realizes the matter at issue, he insists on fighting Godwin himself; but sacred songs from a nearby church remind him of his religious oaths as a Crusader, and dissolve his sanguinary mood.

Act III Having concealed Godwin in an adjoining room to overhear the conversation, Harold offers Mina the chance of a divorce. She persuades him that she had always loved him, but had been treacherously seduced. Harold goes to avenge himself on Godwin, but finds that Egbert has already killed him.

Act IV Still tormented by jealousy, Harold has withdrawn from the world in company with Brian. Mina and her father, outlaws from England because of Egbert's killing of Godwin, are providentially led to Harold's hut; and there the estranged husband and wife are reconciled.

Most of the new music in *Aroldo* is found in the first and last acts; the comparative sophistication of the newly composed choruses – the drinking song in Act I, the pastoral introductory scene and the *preghiera* in Act IV – and the orchestral virtuosity of the *burrasca* (storm) in Act IV show Verdi taking advantage of the new discipline that Mariani was instilling into Italian singers and players. Everywhere in the opera one may admire the mellowing sensibility and the shrewder craftsmanship of Verdi's middle years. The rewriting gives *Aroldo* an appropriate, warrior-like vigour, and Mina is a more fully realized figure than her Stiffelian prototype. But *Stiffelio* had been one of the most ethically 'advanced' dramas Verdi ever set; shifting its subject matter backwards from the 19th century to the Middle Ages undermined its psychological plausibility entirely.

RECORDING Caballé, Cecchele, Pons, Westminster Ch Soc, Opera O of New York, Queler, CBS, 1979
EDITIONS f.s., Ricordi, 1941; v.ss., Ricordi, [1858]; later edns and *rps*

Un ballo in maschera
A Masked Ball

Melodramma in three acts (2h 15m)
Libretto by Antonio Somma, after the libretto *Gustave III* by Augustin Eugène Scribe (1833)
Composed autumn 1857–early 1858
PREMIERES 17 February 1859, Teatro Apollo, Rome; US: 11 February 1861, Academy of Music, New York; UK: 15 June 1861, Lyceum (English Opera House), London
CAST 'American' version: Riccardo, Count of Warwick *t*, Renato *bar*, Amelia *s*, Ulrica *a*, Oscar *s*, Silvano *b*, Samuel *b*, Tom *b*, judge *t*, Amelia's servant *t*; 'Swedish' version: Gustavus III *t*, Count Anckarstroem *bar*, Amelia *s*, Mademoiselle Arvidson *a*, Oscar *s*, Christian *b*, Count Ribbing *b*, Count Horn *b*, judge *t*, Amelia's servant *t*; *satb* chorus of deputies, officers, sailors, guards, men, women and children of the populace, gentlemen, followers of Samuel/Ribbing and Tom/Horn, servants, masquers and dancing couples

ORCHESTRATION picc, fl, 2 ob, ca, 2 cl, 2 bsn, 4 hn, 2 tpt, 3 trbn, cimbasso, timp, perc (bd, cym), hp, str; onstage: band, small str orch, bell

While in Venice in 1853 for the production of *La traviata*, Verdi became friendly with the lawyer and playwright Antonio Somma; and he was delighted when Somma, a poet of some distinction in his day, volunteered to write a libretto for him. But the subject proposed did not, Verdi explained, have 'the variety my crazy brain would like'. And therefore, though the poet knew next to nothing about the technicalities of libretto-writing and needed a great deal of detailed advice, Verdi put him to work on *King Lear*, the libretto of which he managed to complete to the composer's satisfaction. Having signed a contract with the San Carlo at Naples early in 1857, Verdi spent several months negotiating with the theatre with a view to producing an opera on this theme; the plan eventually foundered, ostensibly because of his lack of confidence in the cast. With time running out, he now resorted to desperate measures, abandoning the search for a new subject and taking up an old libretto by Scribe, *Gustave III, ou Le bal masqué*, first set by Auber in 1833.

First approaches to the Neapolitan censors resulted in a crop of irritating demands: the king must become a duke, resident anywhere in the north 'except Norway or Sweden'; the action must be set in an age that believed in witchcraft; the hero must be tormented by remorse, etc. So when Verdi arrived in Naples early in 1858 to start rehearsals, the libretto, now called *Una Vendetta in Domino*, was set in 17th-century Pomerania; but the prospects of even this version being permitted vanished on 13 January, when an assassination attempt was made on the life of Napoleon III. The censors now demanded more fundamental alterations, and engaged a Neapolitan poet to rewrite the libretto (*Adelia degli Adimari*, set in 14th-century Florence). When the composer refused to have anything to do with a text that was quite alien to the spirit of his music, he was sued for breach of contract. The case was eventually settled out of court, but meanwhile Verdi had been in touch with the impresario Jacovacci about the possibility of staging the opera in Rome. Here, after some preliminary skirmishing, the censors agreed to let the subject stand, provided only that the hero be downgraded to a count, and the action removed from Europe altogether. It was Somma who, from the alternatives offered, chose colonial Boston; but he remained piqued with the indignities to which his libretto had been subjected, and refused to let his name appear on it.

Despite some shortcomings in the casting, *Un ballo in maschera* was an immediate triumph; though it was too sophisticated a score to find ready acceptance in smaller or provincial theatres, it is the only Verdi opera between *La traviata* and *Aida* to have been regularly performed and consistently admired through all changes of taste and fashion. Among the more 'interesting' revivals may be mentioned the opera's Boston premiere, when patrons were invited to join in the masked ball, extended for the occasion by a specially composed galop by the conductor, Verdi's pupil and friend, Emanuele Muzio. Verdi was quite happy with the Americanization of his opera, and never expressed any desire to transfer it back to Sweden; but, since a Danish production in Copenhagen in 1935, there has been an increasing tendency to restore the opera to its original setting.

SYNOPSIS ('American' version)

The action takes place in Boston and its vicinity at the end of the 17th century.

Act I Scene 1: A hall in the governor's residence. Officials attend on Riccardo, the easy-going governor of Boston; most are devoted to him, but there are among them some conspirators, led by Samuel and Tom. Riccardo's chief concern is the guest list for a forthcoming ball; the name of Amelia plunges him into romantic reverie ('La rivedrà nell'estasi'), and he is embarrassed to be interrupted by her husband Renato, his friend and secretary. Renato brings news of a conspiracy, and reminds him that his people's destiny depends upon him ('Alla vita che t'arride'). A judge demands an order of banishment on the enchantress Ulrica, but Riccardo heeds rather the pleas for clemency voiced by the page-boy Oscar ('Volta la terrea'). He proposes that he and his officials disguise themselves and visit Ulrica to discover what she really does ('Ogni cura si doni al diletto'). Scene 2: The enchantress's dwelling. Disguised as a fisherman, Riccardo enters Ulrica's hovel and finds her at her conjuring watched by a throng of women and children ('Re dell'abisso, affrettati'). She prophesies wealth for Silvano, a sailor, and Riccardo drops a commission into his pocket. One of Amelia's servants requests a private audience for his mistress: she seeks a cure for a guilty love that torments her; Ulrica's remedy involves picking herbs at midnight at the foot of the gallows; Amelia is determined to do what duty demands ('Segreta, acerba cura' – 'Della città all'occaso' – 'Consentimi, o Signore'), and the eavesdropping Riccardo resolves to join her; Amelia departs. Court officials now crowd into the cave, and Riccardo asks to be told his fortune ('Dì tu se fedele'). When Ulrica warns of imminent death at the hands of the man who first shakes his hand, Riccardo laughs it off ('È scherzo od è follia'); Renato joins them, and is greeted by a handshake. Riccardo's identity is revealed, and Silvano leads an anthem in his praise ('O figlio d'Inghilterra').

Act II A solitary field on the outskirts of Boston. Amelia is terrified by spectral imaginings, and tormented by the conflict of love and duty ('Ecco l'orrido campo' – 'Ma dall'arido stelo divulsa'). When Riccardo appears, she repulses him: let him spare her good name and keep faith with his friend, but he presses her to confess her love ('Non sai tu che se l'anima mia' – 'Oh, qual soave brivido'). Renato arrives to warn Riccardo that conspirators are closing an ambush round him. Seconded by Amelia, who has veiled herself at her husband's approach, he persuades Riccardo to take an indirect route to the city; meanwhile, he will escort the veiled lady back without speaking to her ('Odi tu come fremono cupi'). But they are waylaid by the conspirators, and in the ensuing argument Amelia lets fall her veil. Renato's humiliation is a source of ribald mirth ('Ve', se di notte qui colla sposa'); determined to avenge himself, he invites Samuel and Tom to his house on the morrow; then he leads his wife home.

Act III Scene 1: A study in Renato's house. Finding Renato determined to kill her, Amelia begs to be allowed to bid their son farewell ('Morrò, ma prima in grazia'). Left alone, Renato reflects that death is too severe a fate for her; but not for Riccardo who has poisoned every source of his friend's happiness ('Eri tu'). When Samuel and Tom arrive, he demands to join in their conspiracy ('Dunque l'onta di tutti sol una'); an argument about who should kill Riccardo is resolved in Renato's favour by the drawing of lots. Oscar brings an invitation to a masked ball at the governor's residence, and Amelia is filled with foreboding ('Di che fulgor, che musiche'). The conspirators agree on costumes and a password. Scene 2: A sumptuous small apartment in Riccardo's residence. Riccardo is resolved to send Amelia and Renato back to England ('Ma se m'è forza perderti'). Oscar brings a letter warning him that an assassination attempt will be made during the evening; but, as this will be his last farewell to Amelia, he hastens recklessly to the ball. Scene 3: A huge and richly decorated ball-room, splendidly illuminated and adorned for the ball. The conspirators despair of finding Riccardo; but Renato detects Oscar who, after some teasing ('Saper vorreste'), unwittingly betrays his disguise. Amelia urges Riccardo to escape; he tells her his plans, and is bidding farewell when Renato stabs him. In the finale, the dying Riccardo swears that Amelia is chaste; Renato is overcome with remorse, and all mourn the death of their beloved governor.

The central moment in any Italian Romantic opera was the ensemble – the *pezzo concertato* – at the heart of its Act I or Act II finale: some revelation or confrontation freezes the action, and the tension is discharged in ecstatic song. What is extraordinary in *Un ballo in maschera* is that in both *pezzi concertati* – that in Act I prompted by Ulrica's prophecy that Riccardo is soon to die; and that in Act II occurring when the veiled lady escorted by Renato proves to be his own wife – the tension is resolved not merely in song, but in laughter too: nervous in Act I, mocking in Act II. This is Verdi's most successful essay in the blending of tragedy and comedy in Shakespeare's manner; the sombre tale of guilty passion and murderous jealousy is lit up by flashes of 'brilliance and chivalry', and by an all-pervasive 'aura of gaiety' (Verdi).

This distinctive chiaroscuro is already unmistakable in the prelude and introduction; in both movements a darkly muttering theme, associated throughout the opera with the conspirators, casts its shadow over the otherwise serene harmonies and impulsive lyricism. The opera's ambivalent tone owes much to the blending of Verdi's native style with traits borrowed from French opera, such as the rhythmic *élan* of the galop-like Act I ensemble 'Ogni cura si doni al diletto'. French influence is particularly clear in the music of the page-boy, Oscar – a projection of the insouciant gaiety of Riccardo's own character – whose arias are in the French couplet form (strophes with refrain); both numbers, like several others in the opera, seem to borrow hints from Auber's setting of the text.

If the opera has nevertheless sometimes been described as Verdi's *Tristan* it is because no other of his mature operas places the love duet so centrally, or makes of it the dramatic fulcrum of the score, or invests it with such flaming incandescence. The transfiguring of the link between *cantabile* and *cabaletta* ('La mia vita . . . l'universo' etc.) into an ecstatic lyrical climax, and the subtly transformed recurrence of this before the duet verse of the *cabaletta* help ensure that the emotional exaltation achieved in the early part of the scene is sustained to the close, without interruption or anticlimax.

RECORDINGS 1. Milanov, Andreva, Castagna, Björling, Sved, Metropolitan Opera Ch and O, Panizza (1940 live performance), Myto, [1989]: treasurable for Milanov and Björling at their grandest and for Panizza's conducting; 2. Nelli, Haskins, Turner, Peerce, Merrill, Shaw Ch, NBC SO, Toscanini, RCA, 1954: Toscanini's classic interpretation recorded for posterity with reasonable cast; 3. Callas, Ratti, Barbieri, di Stefano, Gobbi, La Scala Ch and O, Votto, EMI, 1956: notable cast in vivid reading; 4. Arroyo, Grist, Cossotto, Domingo, Cappuccilli, Royal Opera House Ch and O, Muti, EMI, 1975: most satisfying of modern, stereo versions [A.B.]
EDITIONS f.ss., Ricordi, 1914; rev. and corrected edn, 1959; v.ss., Ricordi, [1860]; later edns and *rps*

Illustration from the first published score of Un ballo in maschera; *the assassination scene*

La forza del destino
The Force of Destiny
Opera in four acts (3h 15m)
Libretto by Francesco Maria Piave, based on the drama *Don*

Alvaro, o La fuerza del sino (1835) by Angel de Saavedra,
Duke of Rivas, and incorporating material adapted from
Wallensteins Lager (1799) by Johann Christoph Friedrich von
Schiller, translated by Andrea Maffei (1869 revisions by
Antonio Ghislanzoni)
Composed, but not fully orchestrated, August–November
1861; rev. autumn 1868–early 1869
PREMIERES   22 November 1862, Imperial (Bolshoi)
Theatre, St Petersburg; US: 24 February 1865, Academy of
Music, New York; UK: 22 June 1867, Her Majesty's Theatre,
Haymarket, London; rev. version: 27 February 1869, La
Scala, Milan
CAST   Il Marchese di Calatrava *b*, Leonora *s*, Don Carlo di
Vargas *bar*, Don Alvaro *t*, Preziosilla *ms*, Father Superior
(Padre Guardiano) *b*, Fra Melitone *bar*, Curra *s*, Alcalde *b*,
Mastro Trabuco *t*, Spanish military surgeon *t*; *satb* chorus of
muleteers, Spanish and Italian peasants, Spanish and Italian
soldiers of various ranks and their orderlies, Italian recruits,
Franciscan friars, peasant girls, *vivandières*; ballet: Spanish
and Italian peasant women and *vivandières*, Spanish and
Italian soldiers; extras: host, hostess, inn servants, muleteers,
Italian and Spanish soldiers of all ranks, drummers, buglers,
peasants, peasant women and girls of both nations, tumbler,
various pedlars
ORCHESTRATION   2 fl/picc, 2 ob, 2 cl/b cl, 2 bsn, 4 hn, 2 tpt,
3 trbn, cimbasso, timp, perc (sd, bd), 2 hp, str; onstage: organ,
6 tpt, 4 sd

The 'sixteen years in the galleys' had ended with *Un
ballo in maschera*; by the close of the 1850s Verdi
was leading the life of a country gentleman,
prosperous, world famous, with no obligation to
compose operas except on his own terms, when a
commission really interested him. *La forza del
destino* resulted from the first such commission: an
invitation from the Imperial Theatre of St Petersburg
for the 1861–2 season. Verdi was in theory given a
free hand over the choice of subject, though in fact
his first proposal, Victor Hugo's *Ruy Blas*, was
unceremoniously rejected by the censor. His choice
eventually alighted on *Don Alvaro* by one of Hugo's
Spanish imitators, the Duke of Rivas – an already
rambling play, which Verdi elaborated further by
incorporating into the encampment scene episodes
from Schiller's *Wallensteins Lager*. The premiere was
delayed by almost a year; for when Verdi arrived in
Russia late in 1861, he found the prima donna
unsatisfactory, and refused to proceed if she could
not be replaced.

The opera stands alone in the Verdi canon in
having an abstract idea for its title. By now, Verdi
was more insistent than ever that the age of 'operas
of cavatinas, duets, etc.' was past, and that the future
belonged to 'operas of ideas'. *La forza del destino*,
inspired by what he called a 'powerful, singular, and
truly vast' play, is one of the clearest demonstrations
of this conviction. And because the 'idea' concerns
chance – the sheer random fortuitousness with which
fate chooses its victims – the normal cut of a Verdian
opera, which is concentrated, concise and thrusting,
is replaced by a vast, shambling panorama of loosely
related episodes during which the principals disappear from the scene for whole acts at a time.

Staged at a period when Russian musical life was
in ferment, *La forza del destino* met with a confused
reception. It earned the composer the Order of St
Stanislas, but most critics found it wearisomely long,

and it did not escape a hostile demonstration –
apparently from a nationalist faction – at the third
performance. Nevertheless it is tempting to see in
its chronicle-like panorama of life in time of war
one of the prototypes of *Boris Godunov*, and thus
of a whole tradition of Russian opera. Early
performances in Italy were also only equivocally
successful, largely because of dissatisfaction with the
carnage at the opera's blasphemous and nihilistic
close. After much thought, Verdi and the librettist
Ghislanzoni (Piave had been incapacitated by a
stroke in 1867) arrived at a visually more discreet and
spiritually more resigned *dénouement*, in which the
influence of Alessandro Manzoni, the revered grand
old man of Italian literature, has plausibly been
detected. At the same time the events in Act III were
reordered; many scenes were revised in detail, and
the familiar full-length overture was composed to
replace the original prelude. Even in revised form,
the opera established itself slowly, probably because
it needed a first-rate conductor to co-ordinate it
successfully. A famous production at Dresden in
1926 under Fritz Busch was a milestone in the 20th-
century Verdi renaissance. By the early 1990s some
interest was being shown in reintroducing the
original St Petersburg version.

SYNOPSIS
The scene is set in Spain and Italy towards the
middle of the 18th century.

Act I   Seville. Leonora, daughter of the Marchese
di Calatrava, has agreed to elope with Alvaro, a
South American half-caste prince. The thought of
abandoning her home fills her with remorse ('Me
pellegrina ed orfana'), but when Alvaro arrives, she
soon declares herself ready to follow him to the
ends of the earth ('Seguirti fino agli ultimi'/'Sospiro,
luce ed anima'). They are interrupted by her father.
Alvaro throws his pistol at the Marchese's feet as
a gesture of surrender; the gun goes off, fatally
wounding the old man, who dies cursing his daughter.

Act II   The village of Hornachuelos and vicinity.
Scene 1: Large kitchen in the inn. The muleteer
Trabuco arrives with an unknown youth (Leonora in
disguise). Among the crowd is her brother Carlo,
who is pursuing Leonora and Alvaro, intent on
avenging his father's death; he too is disguised, as a
student. The gypsy girl Preziosilla tells of the wars in
Italy, singing the praises of military life ('Al suon del
tamburo'). Pilgrims pass by, and those in the inn join
in their prayer ('Su noi prostrati e supplici'). The
Alcalde now suggests that the student tell them who
he is; posing as one Pereda, Carlo claims to have left
university to help a friend hunt down his sister and
her seducer; the villain has however escaped across
the seas ('Son Pereda, son ricco d'onore'). Scene 2:
The monastery of Our Lady of the Angels, outside
Hornachuelos. Having overheard her brother's story
Leonora feels betrayed by Alvaro's flight; she prays
for forgiveness and a quiet mind ('Madre, pietosa
Vergine'). The Father Superior (Padre Guardiano)
has been forewarned of her visit, and after
questioning her ('Più tranquilla l'alma sento') agrees
to help her live as an anchorite in a nearby cave

('Sull'alba il piede all'eremo' – 'Tua grazia, o Dio'). The friars vow to respect the young penitent's solitude; the Father Superior leads them in prayer ('La Vergine degli Angeli') and Leonora hastens to her hiding place.

Act III In Italy, near to Velletri. Scene 1: A wood; night. Alvaro, now in the Spanish army, muses on the harshness of destiny and, believing Leonora to be dead, prays to her ('O tu che in seno agl'angeli'). Cries for help send him hurrying to the rescue; he returns with Carlo; they introduce themselves (using false names), and vow eternal comradeship. A surgeon and some orderlies watch the battle: the Italian–Spanish forces carry the day, but they are dismayed to see 'Don Federico Herreros' (Alvaro) fall injured. He is borne in, attended by Carlo, who is astonished by his violent reaction to the name Calatrava. Before Alvaro receives medical attention, he entrusts to Carlo some papers, to be destroyed in the event of his death ('Solenne in quest'ora'). The suspicion dawns on Carlo that his new friend is the long-pursued Alvaro; he resists the temptation to read the papers ('Urna fatale del mio destino'), but looking through Alvaro's other belongings finds a portrait of his sister, Leonora. When the surgeon pronounces Alvaro safe, Carlo exults: now for revenge! ('Egli è salvo! oh gioia immenso'). Scene 2: A military encampment near Velletri. Carlo challenges Alvaro to a duel. Reminding Carlo of their oath of friendship, Alvaro protests his innocence; he learns that Leonora is alive, and joyfully imagines that all may yet be well. But Carlo is adamant: both Alvaro and Leonora must die to satisfy family honour; the two men are soon fighting furiously ('No, d'un imene il vincolo' – 'Stolto! fra noi dischiudesi'). They are separated by a patrol, and Alvaro decides to retreat to a monastery. As reveille sounds, the camp comes to life: Preziosilla is telling fortunes ('Venite all'indovina'), and Trabuco bargaining with some soldiers; peasants are begging for food, and new recruits are consoled by the *vivandières* (Tarantella). The merry-making is interrupted by Melitone's 'sermon' ('Toh, toh! . . . Poffare il mondo!') which incenses the soldiers. Preziosilla beats the drum to turn their thoughts to serious business ('Rataplan, rataplan, della gloria'). [1862: the scene between Alvaro and Carlo follows the encampment scene and ends differently. They fight their duel to the bitter end, Alvaro, as he imagines, killing his adversary; in despair he returns to the battlefield to seek death ('S'affronti la morte').]

Act IV In the vicinity of Hornachuelos. Scene 1: A courtyard inside the monastery of Our Lady of the Angels. Five years have elapsed. Melitone is serving soup to the poor; as he and the Father Superior talk of one 'Padre Rafaello', we realize that this mysterious friar must be Alvaro ('Del mondo i disinganni'). The bell rings and Carlo enters. He demands to see 'Rafaello', and brusquely announces his intention of killing him. Alvaro's saintly behaviour provokes only insult; finally he snatches the sword Carlo offers and they hasten away to duel. Scene 2: A gorge between precipitous rocks. Leonora

has found no peace of mind ('Pace, pace, mio Dio!'). She hears the sound of fighting, and Alvaro rushes in, entreating the hermit to give absolution to a dying man. As Leonora rings the bell to summon the Father Superior, she and Alvaro recognize one another; he speeds her away to comfort her brother. A moment later a scream is heard: Carlo, even as he died, could not forgive Leonora, and stabbed her as she bent over him. Alvaro's blasphemous despair is softened by her prayers and the grave words of the Father Superior ('Non imprecare; umiliati'); and as Leonora dies Alvaro too glimpses some hope of redemption. [1862: the duel and the stabbing of Leonora take place on stage; the opera ends with Alvaro throwing himself into a ravine as the Father Superior and monks approach.]

The nature of the subject means that in *La forza del destino* episodic genre scenes and 'character songs' play a more conspicuous part than in any other Verdi opera. At the same time the overriding dramatic idea of a malevolent destiny is embodied in a theme – often described as the leitmotif of Destiny – that pervades much of the opera: it launches the overture, is heard at the tragic climax of Act I when Calatrava disturbs the eloping lovers and is accidentally killed, and recurs in several later scenes, particularly those in which Leonora is haunted by a pursuing nemesis. No other theme is used as extensively; but the long clarinet concertino that prefaces Act III and punctuates its opening scene – it was composed for St Petersburg's star clarinettist, Ernesto Cavallini, an old acquaintance from Verdi's student days – is a remarkable example of a thematic reminiscence (from the Act I duet, where Alvaro dreams of a happy future with Leonora) developed into an independent movement (in a context of heart-broken memories).

For all the novelty of the overall design, the familiar Verdi is present in every scene, and his musical language is developing in the most idiosyncratic ways. Act I, one of the fastest-moving and most densely packed acts in all Verdi, is full of such individual touches. Its opening scene, pitching the spectator into the middle of the dramatic action, is a casual dialogue set against a quietly sustained orchestral backcloth, and marks the composer's final rejection of the formal, decorative introductions of operatic tradition. Even when he does use traditional forms, his fast-developing musical language transfigures them; this is especially the case with the *cabalettas*: where once they derived their energy from pounding rhythmic repetitions, most of them now acquire their urgency from the fleetly moving basses and rapidly changing harmonies. Leonora's Act I aria 'Me pellegrina ed orfana' is one of the few pieces that has tangible links with the long-pondered *King Lear*; the text is taken directly from Somma's *Lear* libretto, though obviously that does not prove that the music was intended for *Lear*. In the improvisatory freedom of form, the chromatic nuances of the harmony and the flexibility of the instrumentation, it encapsulates much of Verdi's mature lyrical style.

RECORDINGS   1. Tebaldi, Barbieri, Del Monaco, Protti, Siepi, Florence Festival Ch and O, Mitropoulos, Cetra, 1953: memorable live performance (abridged) catching Tebaldi at her best under Mitropoulos's arresting conducting; 2. Callas, Nicolai, Tucker, Tagliabue, Rossi-Lemeni, La Scala Ch and O, Serafin, EMI, 1954: unevenly cast version (slightly cut) notable for Callas's Leonora; 3. Price, Verrett, Tucker, Merrill, Tozzi, RCA Italiana Ch and O, Schippers, RCA, 1964: strongly cast and conducted (complete); 4. Freni, Zajic, Domingo, Zancanaro, Plishka, La Scala Ch and O, Muti, EMI, 1987: most successful of modern, complete sets, fierily conducted [A.B.]
VIDEO   L. Price, I. Jones, Giacomini, Nucci, Giaiotti, Ch and O of the Metropolitan, New York, Levine, DG, 1984: staid production (Dexter) but some authentically Verdian singing of the old school from the principals [A.B.]
EDITIONS   f.ss., Ricordi, [c.1895]; later edns; Peters, [c. 1960]; v.ss., Ricordi, [1863]; rev. version, [1869]; later edns and *rps*

Don Carlos/Don Carlo

Grand opera in five acts (3h 30m)/Opera in four acts (3h)
French libretto by Joseph Méry and Camille du Locle, based on the dramatic poem *Don Carlos, Infant von Spanien* by Johann Christoph Friedrich von Schiller (1787) and on the play *Philippe II, roi d'Espagne* by Eugène Cormon (1846); Libretto of four-act version rev. du Locle; Italian translation by Angelo Zanardini, based on Achille de Lauzières's translation of the original five-act opera
Composed early 1866–February 1867, rev. November–December 1872; rev. (four-act) version June 1882–March 1883
PREMIERES   11 March 1867, Opéra, Paris; UK: 4 June 1867, Covent Garden, London; US: 12 April 1877, Academy of Music, New York; four-act version: 10 January 1884, La

Scala, Milan; hybrid five-act version: 29 December 1886, Modena
CAST   Philip II *b*, Don Carlos *t*, Rodrigo, Marquis of Posa *bar*, Grand Inquisitor *b*, monk *b*, Elisabeth de Valois *s*, Princess Eboli *ms*, Thibault *s*, voice from Heaven *s*, Countess d'Aremberg *silent role*, woman in mourning *silent role*, Count de Lerma *t*, royal herald *t*, 6 Flemish Deputies 6 *b*, 6 Inquisitors 6 *b*; *satb* chorus of lords and ladies of the French and Spanish courts, woodcutters, populace, pages, guards of Henri II and Philip II, monks, officers of the Inquisition, soldiers
ORCHESTRATION   picc, 3 fl, 2 ob, ca, 2 cl, 4 bsn, dbsn, 4 hn, 2 cornets, 2 tpt, 3 trbn, ophicleide, timp, perc (bd, triangle, bells, tambour basque, castanets), hp, harmonium, str; onstage: band; offstage: cannon

Together with Shakespeare and Hugo, Schiller was the playwright Verdi most revered. But the size and ideological complexity of his plays made operatic adaptation difficult and, *I masnadieri* and *Luisa Miller* notwithstanding, it is not until *Don Carlos* that we find Verdi getting to grips with the great German dramatist in all his rambling magnificence. The death of Meyerbeer in 1864 prompted the management of the Opéra to approach Verdi with a libretto found among Meyerbeer's papers, in the hope of persuading him to make a return to Paris. He dismissed the libretto out of hand, but when they returned to the charge the following year and offered him a scenario for *Don Carlos*, it 'really thrilled him'. He went to Paris in November 1865, signed a contract, and spent some four months there, hammering out a libretto with Méry and du Locle,

The first London production of Don Carlos *(Illustrated London News, July 1867)*

before returning to Busseto in the spring to complete the composition. The Fontainebleau scene and the *auto da fé* were the most substantial of several incidents borrowed from a contemporary play on Philip II by Eugène Cormon.

In its stirring depiction of the conflict between libertarianism and dogmatism Schiller's play appealed to some of Verdi's deepest convictions. Every scene of the opera breathes a passionate high-mindedness that makes it, for many listeners, the most inspiring of all his works. Sadly, as in the past, the Paris Opéra disappointed the composer's hopes: the endless tedium of the rehearsals, the lack of spontaneity and enthusiasm in the performance, the multitude of opinionated busybodies who hung about the place, were to provide him with material for satirical reflection for many a year.

No other Verdi opera has so complicated a stage history, and none survives in so many different forms: the *edizione integrale* distinguishes eight 'authentic' versions of the score. For all practical purposes these may be reduced to three, all of which now have a place in the repertoire: the five-act French grand opera (1867), the four-act Italian *Don Carlo* (1884), and the hybrid 'Modena version' (1886) which, broadly speaking, reinstates the original Act I while leaving the remaining acts in their revised 1884 form. What exactly constitutes the 1867 score is a complicated question. The immense length of the opera led to cuts being made during rehearsals, and when at the first dress rehearsal it was found to be still well over three and a half hours long (excluding intervals) it was cut more drastically (it had to finish before midnight, as the last trains to the Paris suburbs left at 12.35). The most ruthless excisions involved the opening chorus of Act I, and the duet in Act IV in which Philip and Carlos mourn the dead Posa. (Some of the deleted material from this served as the seed for the 'Lacrymosa' in the Requiem; and all the abandoned material was recovered and reconstructed by Verdi scholars in the 1960s and 1970s.) Cuts continued to be made, especially when the opera began to appear in Italy, and for a Naples production in 1872–3, Verdi himself revised and abbreviated several scenes. But *Don Carlos* stubbornly resisted popular success and in 1882 the composer embarked on a more drastic rewriting. Only Carlos's romance 'Je l'ai vu' (revised) survives from the original Act I, and much else – notably the Philip–Posa duet in Act II and the closing scene of the opera – was radically revised; in the process the opera draws closer to its Schiller model. This 1884 version is certainly 'more concise and vigorous' (Verdi); but the desire to reinstate the Fontainebleau act, which led to the hybrid 'Modena version' of 1886, is understandable. It restores much superb music (some of it drawn on in episodes of reminiscence later in the opera) and it makes plot and motivation much clearer.

Perhaps not surprisingly, despite the passionate admiration of some connoisseurs, *Don Carlos* was for long regarded as a 'problem opera'. In Paris it disappeared completely from the repertoire after 1869; even during the Verdi renaissance between the wars – indeed as late as the 1950s and 1960s – many opera houses felt it necessary to stage adaptations that 'improved' it in some way or another. It was not until well into the second half of the 20th century that *Don Carlos* came to be recognized, not only as Verdi's most ambitious opera, but as one of his supreme achievements.

SYNOPSIS
Act I takes place in France, Acts II–V in Spain; the period is *c.* 1560.

Act I The forest of Fontainebleau. France and Spain have long been at war. Carlos has come to France, impatient to be with Elisabeth, to whom he is betrothed ('Je l'ai vu et dans son sourire'). Elisabeth has lost her way in the forest during a hunt, and Carlos, introducing himself as a member of the Spanish diplomatic mission – for Elisabeth does not yet know him – undertakes to protect her while Thibault goes for help. He produces a portrait that shows that he is the man she is to marry; when the sound of cannon from the palace confirms that a peace has been concluded, their joy is complete ('De quels transports poignants et doux'). Thibault returns, followed by courtiers and people: as a pledge of the peace Elisabeth is to marry Carlos's widowed father, the great King Philip himself; recognizing that the well-being of her people depends upon her, Elisabeth assents ('L'heure fatale est sonnée' – 'O chants de fête').

Act II Scene 1: The cloisters at the monastery of Saint-Just. Monks meditate by the tomb of the Emperor Charles V ('Charles-Quint, l'auguste Empereur'); Carlos is startled by the resemblance of one of the monks to his late grandfather; he is joined by his dearest friend, Rodrigo, Marquis of Posa. Just returned from the Netherlands, Posa paints a grim picture of the oppression it suffers. And when he hears of Carlos's hopeless passion for Elisabeth, he urges him to go to Flanders and learn there to be a king: they renew their vows of fellowship in the service of liberty ('Mon compagnon, mon ami' – 'Dieu, tu semas dans nos âmes'). Scene 2: A pleasant spot by the gates of the monastery of Saint-Just. Thibault, Eboli and the ladies of the court shelter from the heat ('Sous ces bois au feuillage immense') and pass the time with song ('Au palais des fées' – the so-called 'Song of the Veil'). The queen joins them, then Posa, who delivers two letters, one from her father, the other, which she reads while he engages Eboli in gallantries, from Carlos. Posa requests an audience for Carlos ('L'Infant Carlos, notre espérance') for Philip is unsympathetic to his troubles; Eboli imagines Carlos may be in love with her. Carlos appears and, dismissing her attendants, Elisabeth struggles to remain calm; she agrees to help persuade Philip to send him to Flanders, but, to her distress, he swoons and raves ('O bien perdu . . . Trésor sans prix') then hurries away. Philip is angry to find his queen unattended and orders the guilty lady-in-waiting, Countess D'Aremberg, back to France; Elisabeth bids her farewell ('O ma chère compagne'). Posa is detained by the king and seizes the opportunity to protest about the plight of

Flanders ('O Roi! j'arrive de Flandre'); he urges him to give his people freedom. Impressed by Posa's integrity, Philip warns him to beware the Grand Inquisitor and confides his worries about Carlos and Elisabeth, and asks him to keep a watch on them. (The Philip–Posa scene is always performed in the 1884 form.)

Act III Scene 1: The Queen's Gardens. An enclosed grove. Festivities have been arranged for the eve of Philip's coronation. But Elisabeth wishes to spend the night in prayer, and entrusting Eboli with her mantilla, necklace and mask, asks her to stand in for her. Eboli, seeing the chance to make sure of Carlos's love ('Pour une nuit me voilà reine'), writes him a hasty note. A sumptuous ballet ('La Peregrina') is staged. (This opening scene is commonly omitted in favour of the Act II preludio of the 1884 version.) Mistaking Eboli for Elisabeth, Carlos declares his love ('C'est vous, c'est vous! ma bien-aimée'). When she unmasks, his confusion perplexes her: she warns him that Posa is now a confidant of the king, and that only she can protect him ('Hélas! votre jeunesse ignore'). Suddenly it dawns on her that Carlos and Elisabeth are lovers; at the same moment Posa appears. Despite his threats, she is determined to exact revenge by exposing the queen's liaison with her stepson ('Malheur sur toi, fils adultère'). Scene 2: A large piazza in front of the cathedral at Valladolid. A throng of people, gathered for an *auto da fé*, sings the king's praises ('Ce jour heureux'); Philip's coronation oath requires him to act as God's avenger with sword and fire. Carlos presents a group of deputies from Flanders and Brabant: they beg Philip to show clemency, a prayer in which the queen, Posa and most of the crowd join; but Philip's persecuting obduracy is encouraged by the monks ('Sire, la dernière heure'). Carlos now demands that his father entrust to him the regency of Flanders; when Philip dismisses the request, he draws his sword and vows to be the saviour of that unhappy land. All are scandalized by this breach of etiquette; Posa disarms Carlos, and is elevated to a dukedom by Philip. The *auto da fé* continues: an angelic voice is heard comforting the dying.

Act IV Scene 1: The king's cabinet at Valladolid. Philip muses wretchedly over his failure to win Elisabeth's love ('Elle ne m'aime pas!' – 'Je dormirais dans mon manteau royal'). The Grand Inquisitor is led in; he assures Philip that, if it is for the good of the faith, there can be no objection to having Carlos killed. But Posa represents a greater danger; and if Philip persists in protecting a heretic, he will have to answer for it to the Holy Office ('Dans ce beau pays'). Elisabeth is indignant to find her jewel box stolen; Philip has it on his table, and when she refuses to open it, forces it himself; a portrait of Carlos is found among her treasures. When he denounces her as an adulteress, she faints. At the king's summons, Eboli and Posa enter; he realizes that immediate action must be taken to save Carlos ('Maudit soit le soupçon infame'). Left alone with the queen, Eboli begs forgiveness: she stole the casket; what is worse, she is herself guilty of the sin of which Elisabeth stands suspected. The queen

banishes her from the court: she must choose exile or the cloister. Eboli curses her own beauty; before taking leave of the world she resolves to save Carlos ('O don fatal et détesté'). (The original French version makes no mention of the fact that Eboli is the king's mistress.) Scene 2: Carlos's prison. Posa comes to bid Carlos farewell and encourage him in his great libertarian mission. Two men appear at the cell door and Posa is shot. As he dies, he tells Carlos that Elisabeth will be at Saint-Just the next day ('Ah! je meurs, l'âme joyeuse'). The king enters and returns Carlos's sword; but his son repulses him. (Omitted before the Paris premiere: Philip and Carlos mourn Posa ('Qui me rendra ce mort').) The clanging of the tocsin signals a popular uprising; for a moment Philip seems in danger, but the appearance of the Grand Inquisitor reduces the mob to submission. Meanwhile Eboli enables Carlos to make his escape. (The whole scene following the death of Posa is normally performed in the shorter 1884 version.)

Act V The monastery of Saint-Just. Elisabeth recognizes that her earthly task will soon be done ('Toi qui sus le néant'). Carlos comes to bid farewell: Elisabeth blesses his Flanders mission, and they look forward to meeting again in a better world ('Oui, voilà l'héroïsme' – 'Au revoir dans un monde'). The king appears, attended by the Grand Inquisitor, and his officers; Carlos is anathematized. As he tries to evade the inquisitors he retreats towards Charles V's tomb, which suddenly opens; the monk from Act II reappears and is recognized as Charles V himself; Carlos is hurried away into the monastery. (The whole scene from Carlos's arrival is normally performed in the revised 1884 version, which does not include the anathematizing of Carlos by the inquisitors.)

'Severe and terrible like the savage monarch who built it,' wrote Verdi of the Escurial on a visit to Spain in 1863. As a dramatic character Philip enthralled Verdi, and it was at his insistence that *Don Carlos* included two of the king's great scenes of confrontation – with Posa in Act II, with the Grand Inquisitor in Act IV – that offered negligible scope for the conventionally operatic. The confidence that he could hold an audience spellbound with a scene of ideological debate was amply justified in the latter case: the fearsome clash of private sorrow and ruthless dogmatism, the whole expressed in vocal and orchestral colours of a chilling blackness, is one of the things in opera that, once heard, is never likely to be forgotten. The Philip–Posa scene, on the other hand, cost Verdi endless trouble (its alternative forms occupy almost 90 pages of vocal score in the *edizione integrale*); but every revision had the effect of eliminating relics of traditional lyricism, and bringing the scene closer to Schiller's thrilling dialectic.

Not only in the Grand Inquisitor scene but throughout *Don Carlos* Verdi's genius for the dramatic exploitation of colour, which had appeared fitfully as early as *Macbeth*, even *Ernani*, is revealed in full splendour: colours of garish magnificence in the *auto da fé*, other-worldly colours like the mysterious chords (high woodwind and deep horn pedal note) set against male voices in the prayer at the start of Act II, colours of desolating melancholy in Philip's incomparable 'Elle ne m'aime pas'. Nothing, however, contributes more to the dramatic colouring than the fact that the opera is, or should be, sung in French (even the 1884 version was conceived with a French text, then translated into Italian). Of course it is not Verdi's first French opera, but never before has it seemed so to matter that French imposes certain constraints on the manner of singing, which in turn make possible an inwardness and a type of sensibility new to Italian opera. The consequences are particularly remarkable in Carlos's music – far less extrovert, far more delicate in nuance than that of any earlier Verdi tenor.

All of which is not to imply any lack of lyrical abundance: on the contrary, what has been called Verdi's '*Aida* manner' (Budden) might with equal justice be called his '*Don Carlos* manner'. The nervous sensibility of the principal characters is expressed in a lyrical style of exceptional richness; for in arias and ensembles alike every nuance of every experience calls forth its own melody.

RECORDINGS 1. Caballé, Verrett, Domingo, Milnes, Raimondi, Foiani, Ambrosian Opera Ch, Royal Opera House O, Giulini, EMI, 1970: central performance of five-act

1886 Italian version, splendidly cast; 2. Ricciarelli, Valentini Terrani, Domingo, Nucci, Raimondi, Ghiaurov, La Scala Ch and O, Abbado, DG, 1985: composite 1886 version recorded in original French, also including – as an appendix – passages cut by Verdi before 1867 premiere [A.B.]
VIDEO Cotrubas, Baglioni, Lima, Zancanaro, Lloyd, Ch and O of Covent Garden, Haitink, Castle, 1985: fine performance of Visconti's famous staging [A.B.]
EDITIONS f.s., Ricordi, [n.d.]; v.s., Ursula Gunther (ed.), *Edizione integrale*, Ricordi, 1980 (2 vols)

Aida

Opera (melodramma) in four acts (2h 15m)
Libretto by Antonio Ghislanzoni, after a scenario by Auguste Mariette and a French prose version by Camille du Locle
Composed July 1870–after November 1870 (rev. continued until December 1871)
PREMIERES 24 December 1871, Opera House, Cairo; Italy: 8 February 1872, La Scala, Milan; US: 26 November 1873, Academy of Music, New York; UK: 22 June 1876, Covent Garden, London
CAST The King *b*, Amneris *ms*, Aida *s*, Radamès *t*, Ramfis *b*, Amonasro *bar*, High Priestess *s*, messenger *t*; *satb* chorus of priests, priestesses, ministers, captains, soldiers, functionaries, slaves and Ethiopian prisoners, Egyptian people
ORCHESTRATION picc, 3 fl, 2 ob, ca, 2 cl, b cl, 2 bsn, 4 hn, 2 tpt, 3 trbn, cimbasso, timp, perc (bd, cym, triangle, t-t), (2) hp, str; onstage: 3 'Egyptian' tpt in A♭, 3 'Egyptian' tpt in B, 4 tpt, 4 trbn, bd, hp

Philippe Chaperon's set design, modelled on the Amon-Ra temple in Karnak, for the world premiere of Aida *(Cairo, 1871)*

In November 1869, during celebrations to mark the completion of the Suez canal, a new opera house was opened in Cairo with a performance of *Rigoletto*. But the Khedive of Egypt, abetted by the distinguished French Egyptologist Auguste Mariette, was also determined to commission a specially composed opera for his theatre; since Mariette was a friend of Camille du Locle, one of the *Don Carlos* librettists, it was through him that Verdi was approached. In April 1870 Mariette sent du Locle a scenario he had written; though conventional in plot, it was rich in local colour and scenic detail, and Verdi liked it. In fact he was to show an almost Puccinian curiosity about the ambience of this drama, seeking advice on Egyptian religion, music, history and geography, and experimenting with flutes and trumpets specially constructed in a spurious ancient Egyptian style, for the scenes of ritual and celebration. Du Locle, working under Verdi's supervision, elaborated Mariette's synopsis into a French prose libretto, which in turn was rendered into Italian verse by Ghislanzoni. Dozens of letters between composer and librettist show Verdi taking as full a part as ever in planning the text: conceiving certain scenes himself (Amneris and her attendants and slaves in Act II Scene 1); urging Ghislanzoni boldly to cast away convention when it did not serve the dramatic purpose (Aida–Amonasro duet in Act III); dictating the metrical details in arias and ensembles (Act IV finale: 'You can't imagine what a beautiful melody can be written in so strange a form.').

Originally scheduled for January 1871, the premiere had to be delayed until the following season. For Mariette – who had gone to Paris in July 1870 to advise du Locle and the designers, so that the opera would be 'composed and executed in a strictly Egyptian style' – found himself immured in the city when the Franco-Prussian War broke out a few days later. The Prussian victory at Sedan (Verdi contributed part of his fee for *Aida* for the benefit of the French wounded) formed a suggestive background for the composition of the 'Triumph' scene (Act II Scene 2): with some distaste, Verdi referred Ghislanzoni to King Wilhelm's victory telegram as a suitable model for the priests' chorus!

Both in Cairo, where it was conducted by the double-bass virtuoso Giovanni Bottesini, and Milan, where it was in the trusty hands of Franco Faccio, *Aida* was enthusiastically received. It has remained one of Verdi's most popular operas, and in particular a natural first choice for open-air festival performances such as those that began at Verona in the early 20th century. For the Paris Opéra premiere (in French) in 1880, the Act II ballet was extended by some 90 bars; this expanded version of the scene at once became the standard form. On the other hand, the full-length overture written at Ricordi's suggestion for the Milan premiere was discarded before the performance even took place, and was first heard under Toscanini in 1940. Another abandoned movement was a chorus 'alla Palestrina', placed at the start of Act III; the definitive Act III *introduzione* was composed only in August 1871.

SYNOPSIS

The action takes place in Memphis and Thebes, in the time of the Pharaohs.

Act I   Scene 1: A hall in the Royal Palace at Memphis. In the wars with Ethiopia, Aida has been captured and brought to Memphis as a slave for Amneris, daughter of the Egyptian king: her father, the Ethiopian king Amonasro, has launched an invasion to rescue her. The young captain Radamès dreams of being chosen to lead the Egyptian forces; ironically, his longing for glory is inspired by Aida, whom he loves ('Celeste Aida'). Radamès in turn is loved by Amneris, who suspects that Aida may be her rival. The Egyptian king receives a report on the invasion; he announces that Isis has declared Radamès commander of the army, and leads the assembly in patriotic song ('Su! del Nilo al sacro lido'). Aida is torn between love of Radamès and love of her homeland ('Ritorna vincitor!'). Scene 2: The interior of the Temple of Vulcan at Memphis. The divinity is invoked with mystic song and dance, and the high priest Ramfis consecrates Radamès for his mission.

Act II   Scene 1: A room in Amneris' apartments. Amneris is arrayed for the triumphal return of the Egyptian army ('Chi mai fra gl'inni e i plausi'). In a long dialogue ('Fu la sorte dell'armi a' tuoi funesta') she poses as Aida's friend, tricks her into admitting her love for Radamès, and finally exults arrogantly over her. Scene 2: One of the gateways into the city of Thebes. The victorious host passes before the king ('Gloria all'Egitto, ad Iside'); Radamès is crowned with the victor's wreath, and offered any gift he chooses. The Ethiopian prisoners are led in, and though Amonasro is disguised as a common soldier Aida at once recognizes him. He tells the Egyptian king a false tale about his own death, and begs him to show magnanimity and release the prisoners ('Ma tu, Re, tu signore possente'). Despite the warnings of the priests, the crowd takes up his plea, and the issue is settled when Radamès adds his voice. The king bestows Amneris' hand on the young warrior, and the scene ends with a resumption of the triumphal anthems with which it commenced.

Act III   The banks of the Nile. Ramfis escorts Amneris to the temple where she is to spend the night before her marriage in prayer. Aida comes down to the river to meet Radamès; she fears she will never see her homeland again ('O patria mia'). To her astonishment, Amonasro suddenly appears. Once more he has invaded Egypt; this time, with Aida's help, the Ethiopians can win; and with a relentless barrage of moral blackmail, he forces her to agree to get Radamès to reveal the Egyptians' military plans ('Rivedrai le foreste imbalsamate'). Amonasro hides, and Aida sets about persuading her lover to elope with her. Reluctantly, he accepts her argument ('Pur ti riveggo, mia dolce Aida' – 'Fuggiam gli arbori inospiti' – 'Sì, fuggiam da queste mura'): if they make their getaway tonight, they will be able to pass the Napata gorges before the army moves into them. When he realizes that Amonasro has overheard him, Radamès is overcome with shame. Amneris and Ramfis re-emerge from the temple; Radamès saves Amneris from a murderous attack by Amonasro, then surrenders himself as Aida and her father escape.

Act IV Scene 1: A hall in the royal palace. The Ethiopians have been routed again and Amonasro killed; Aida has disappeared. Amneris halts the procession escorting Radamès to his trial: if only he will make some effort to explain himself, she will plead for mercy; but Radamès has lost all he values in life, and is resolved to die ('Già i sacerdoti adunansi' – 'Chi ti salva, sciagurato'). Amneris listens in mounting anguish to the progress of the trial; Radamès is sentenced to be buried alive under the altar of the god he has offended. Scene 2: The Temple of Vulcan. Anticipating Radamès' fate, Aida has hidden herself in the vault, and as he is entombed there, she emerges from the shadows. She consoles him with her vision of a paradise where love will be unalloyed ('Morir! sì pura e bella' – 'Vedi? di morte l'angelo'); and as priestesses perform a sacred dance in the temple above and Amneris prays for Radamès, they die in one another's arms ('O terra addio, addio o valle di pianti').

Aida is a summation of all that Verdi had hitherto achieved, brilliantly combining the strengths of Italian Romantic melodrama with those of French grand opera. No work epitomizes more splendidly the qualities the world admires in grand opera. But its dramatic pace belongs to his native tradition; so does its sense of priorities, for in Acts III and IV the external splendours recede, and we have to concern ourselves solely with the tormented humanity of the protagonists. Contemporaries saw signs of Wagner's influence too, probably in the comparatively superficial fact that recurring themes play a large part in the score. Both Aida and Amneris have their identifying themes – each in its own way sensuous and alluring – and another theme, severe and contrapuntal in character, is associated with Ramfis and the priests. A more distinctive feature of the opera is its uniquely powerful sense of time and place: the prominence of flutes, trumpets and harps helps evoke a world of bardic antiquity, while modal inflexions (most evident in the scene of Radamès' consecration) often colour the harmony.

The interaction of tradition and innovation that perplexed some early critics is best seen in the magnificent series of duets that runs through the opera, in all of which the starting point was a text in basically conventional form. It is fascinating to see how Verdi elaborated and varied this, sometimes playing up to, sometimes frustrating the audience's expectations. In the Aida–Amneris duet, for example (Act II, Scene 1), the '*cabaletta*' is in large part a kind of descant set against an offstage reprise of the chorus 'Su! del Nilo'; while in the duet finale of Act IV the (slow) *cabaletta* is provided with a supremely ironic commentary from Amneris. This closing scene occasioned Verdi some anxiety: he questioned Bottesini closely about the effect of what he described as an experiment in the 'ethereal genre'. Thomas Mann, using Hans Castorp in *The Magic Mountain* as his mouthpiece, saw it as a supreme

instance of music's idealizing tendency, its power to transfigure and beautify even the harshest realities.

RECORDINGS 1. Giannini, Minghini-Cattaneo, Pertile, Inghilleri, Manfrini, La Scala Ch and O, Sabajno, HMV, 1928; Pearl, 1990: historic version with four superb Italian-speaking principals, including Pertile's unsurpassed Radamès – now on CD; 2. Callas, Barbieri, Tucker, Gobbi, Modesti, La Scala Ch and O, Serafin, EMI, 1955: cast of all-round excellence, authoritatively conducted; 3. Milanov, Barbieri, Björling, Warren, Christoff, Rome Opera Ch and O, Perlea, RCA, 1955: Milanov and Björling giving lessons in Verdi style; 4. Caballé, Cossotto, Domingo, Cappuccilli, Ghiaurov, Royal Opera House O, New Philharmonia O, Muti, EMI, 1974: sensitively conducted, vividly cast modern performance; 5. Nelli, Gustavson, Tucker, Valdengo, Scott, Robert Shaw Chorale, NBC SO, Toscanini, RCA, 1949: historic performance now on video [A.B.]
VIDEOS 1. RCA, 1949 (see the final recording above); 2. Chiara, Cossotto, Martinucci, Scandola, Ch and O of the Verona Arena, Guadagno, Castle, 1981; 3. Chiara, Dimitrova, Pavarotti, Pons, Ghiaurov, Ch and O of Rome Opera, Maazel, 1985: the second is a typical Verona stand-and-sing effort; the third offers Ronconi's eccentric production. Both versions are stronger on power than on subtlety [A.B.]
EDITIONS f.ss., Ricordi, [1913]; rev. and corrected edn, 1953; v.ss., Ricordi, [1872]; 1880 *rps* incorporate the expanded ballet

Simon Boccanegra (II)

Melodramma in a prologue and three acts (2h 15m)
Libretto by Francesco Maria Piave and Arrigo Boito (a rewriting by Boito of Piave's 1857 libretto of the same name)
Composed December 1880–February 1881
PREMIERES 24 March 1881, La Scala, Milan; US: 28 January 1932, Metropolitan, New York; UK: 27 October 1948, Sadler's Wells, London
CAST Simon Boccanegra *bar*, Jacopo Fiesco *b*, Paolo Albiani *b*, Pietro *bar*, Maria Boccanegra (under the name of Amelia Grimaldi) *s*, Gabriele Adorno *t*, captain of the crossbowmen *t*, Amelia's maidservant *ms*; *satb* chorus of soldiers, sailors, people, Fiesco's servants, senators, the doge's court
ORCHESTRATION picc, fl, 2 ob, 2 cl, b cl, 2 bsn, 4 hn, 2 tpt, 3 trbn, cimbasso, timp, bd, str; onstage: hp, 4 tpt, 4 trbn, sd, bell

In November 1880 Verdi's publisher Giulio Ricordi raised the question of reviving *Simon Boccanegra*. Verdi was interested, but the opera would need revision; it was 'too sad, too desolate' as it stood; and he went on to mention, as a means of lightening the gloom, 'two stupendous letters' by the 14th-century poet, Petrarch. Addressing himself to the doges of Genoa and Venice, Petrarch had rebuked them for embarking on a fratricidal war, when they were 'both born of the same mother, Italy . . . how wonderful' – remarked Verdi – 'this feeling for an Italian fatherland at that time!' Boito, already well advanced on a libretto for *Otello*, was at first reluctant to undertake the revision; but Verdi had not yet committed himself to *Otello*, and almost certainly the shrewd Ricordi encouraged the *Simon Boccanegra* collaboration so that the two men could have the experience of working together on something slightly less momentous than a new opera. Verdi was not prepared to contemplate rewriting on the scale Boito suggested; so apart from a number of comparatively minor revisions, the librettist had to limit himself to creating a new second scene for Act I – the great council chamber scene. But the admiration Verdi felt for the way he did that – the general conception, the distinction of the verses, the ingenuity in solving niggling little problems of detail – was a major factor in persuading the composer that Boito was an ideal colleague. The poet himself 'attributed no artistic or literary merit to the patchwork I have made from poor Piave's libretto', and refused to allow his name to be publicly linked with the revised *Simon Boccanegra*.

Except for Act II, the least revised and therefore the most old-fashioned in style, the new *Simon Boccanegra* was warmly received. But for all Boito's ingenuity, and for all the magnificence of the 'late Verdi' style that here emerges for the first time, it remains a perplexing and sombre drama – an opera for connoisseurs rather than a popular favourite. Brahms, who saw it in Vienna in 1882, spoke for many: he found 'something talented and gripping everywhere, but after a while . . . ceased all investigations into the meaning of the libretto'.

SYNOPSIS
The action takes place in Genoa and its vicinity, about the middle of the 14th century. Twenty-five years elapse between the prologue and the drama.

Prologue A piazza in Genoa. A new doge is about to be elected; the goldsmith Paolo persuades Pietro, leader of the plebeian party, to vote for Simon Boccanegra, a corsair in the service of the republic. The sight of the darkened Fiesco palace prompts speculation on the fate of the unhappy Maria ('L'atra magion vedete?'), incarcerated here because her father disapproves of her love for Simon. Fiesco emerges from the palace: Maria has died ('Il lacerato spirito'); but his pride is unbroken, and he scorns Simon's offer of reconciliation. Only if he entrusts to Fiesco the daughter Maria has borne to Simon will he be forgiven; but the young Maria has disappeared without trace ('Del mar sul lido'). Simon enters the palace determined to see Maria once more; he discovers her corpse just as a throng of plebeians proclaims him doge.

Act I Scene 1: The garden of the Grimaldi palace outside Genoa. Amelia impatiently awaits her beloved, Gabriele Adorno ('Come in quest'ora bruna' – 'Cielo di stelle orbato'). She is worried at the dangers he and her guardian Andrea – in fact Fiesco – are running by conspiring against Boccanegra. Learning that the doge (Simon), whose visit is now announced, is likely to seek her hand for Paolo, Gabriele agrees to ask Andrea to bless them as man and wife ('Vieni a mirar la cerula' – 'Sì, sì, dell'ara il giubilo'). His love is unshaken when the supposed Amelia Grimaldi proves to be an orphan girl, and Andrea blesses him ('Vieni a me, ti benedico'). Greeting the doge, Amelia tells him her heart is already engaged; as Simon questions her, he recognizes her as his long-lost daughter Maria ('Orfanella il tetto umile' – 'Figlia! a tal nome io palpito'). The spurned Paolo plots to abduct Amelia.

Scene 2: The council chamber in the Palazzo degli Abati. A council meeting is interrupted by the sound of a brawl; a mob of plebeians drags in Gabriele and Fiesco. Gabriele tells the doge that Amelia has been abducted; he has killed the man who did it, but believes the abductor was acting on Simon's instructions. He now tries to kill Simon, but is prevented by the appearance of Amelia. Simmering hostility between patricians and plebeians threatens to break out into open fighting; appealing to ideals of brotherhood and patriotism, Simon re-establishes his authority ('Plebe! Patrizi! Popolo'); then he compels Paolo to anathematize the traitor in their midst.

Act II The doge's room in the ducal palace in Genoa. Paolo puts poison in Simon's water jug; he fails to enlist Fiesco in his plan to murder Simon, but enrages Gabriele by claiming that Amelia is the plaything of the doge's lust. Meeting Amelia, Gabriele denounces her bitterly; but she cannot yet explain her feelings for Simon ('Parla, in tuo cor virgineo'). As Simon approaches, Gabriele hides. Despite new evidence of Gabriele's plots, Amelia persuades her father to forgive him; he insists on being left alone, drinks from the poisoned water, and falls asleep. Amelia, fearful of what might happen, has only pretended to leave, and when her lover emerges bent on murder, she intervenes. Their argument wakens the doge; his relationship to Amelia can be concealed no longer, and Gabriele is appalled by what he has tried to do ('Perdon, perdon, Amelia'). Again insurrection is heard in the streets, and Simon is determined to seek reconciliation. If Gabriele can negotiate a peace, Amelia shall be his reward.

Act III Within the doge's palace. The Guelphs have been routed, and Paolo captured. As he is led to execution he meets Fiesco, who expresses his loathing of the poisoner and abductor. The sounds of the wedding of Amelia and Gabriele are heard from a distant part of the palace. Simon enters, the effects of the poison already far advanced; as he gazes out to sea, Fiesco emerges from the shadows. When Simon recognizes the old man, he surprises him by claiming the reconciliation that had been offered 25 years before; now he can fulfil the conditions: Amelia Grimaldi is Fiesco's long-lost granddaughter, and he gladly restores her to him. Fiesco's pride is broken at last, and, weeping, he embraces the dying Simon ('Piango, perchè mi parla'). The doge blesses the newly married couple and nominates Gabriele his successor ('Gran Dio, ti benedici').

Once Verdi had Boito's revised text, he composed/revised 'everything in sequence, just as if it were a matter of a new opera'. The more mechanical conventions of the 1850s now seemed intolerable to him, and there were few scenes – even where the libretto remained unaltered – that he did not scrutinize rigorously and, where necessary, rewrite. In the broadest terms the musical continuity is more skilfully sustained (thanks particularly to a more sophisticated use of the orchestra); the new material is of course in a riper and richer style, and the dramatic characterization is more interesting. Fiesco, through his Act I duet with Gabriele, acquires a warmer humanity, and Paolo becomes one of Boito's mephisophelean villains. Good examples of Verdi's musical transformation of an unaltered text are to be found in the first scene of the prologue, where the dialogue, instead of being punctuated by the customary figurations of accompanied recitative, is set against a gravely flowing orchestral theme (made much of in Liszt's *Réminiscences de Boccanegra*, 1882); and in the duet 'Orfanella il tetto umile', where the conventional cadenza is replaced by an exquisitely tender and poetic coda. Nevertheless discrepancies between Verdi's 1857 manner and his 1880 manner are an inescapable feature of the opera and have a singular effect; for Verdi, we must suppose, was moved to revise most radically those scenes he felt most deeply. At such critical moments, the characters might be said to rise to the occasion, and express themselves with a subtlety and power unknown in the 1857 score.

The most substantial new number is the Act I finale – the council chamber scene. Inspired by those Petrarch letters, Verdi, who as a young composer had had a positive genius for music in the most demotic manner, finds a voice worthy of his by now patriarchal status in Italian society. The magnificent declamatory fervour of Simon's solo, the radiance of Amelia's lyricism, the searching harmonies, the consummate craftsmanship of the whole ensemble combine to make the scene one of the noblest visions of social idealism in music.

RECORDINGS 1. de los Angeles, Campora, Gobbi, Christoff, Rome Opera Ch and O, Santini, EMI, 1957: classic mono version with characterful cast; 2. Ricciarelli, Domingo, Cappuccilli, Raimondi, RCA Italiana Ch and O, Gavazzeni, RCA, 1973: movingly enacted version not entirely superseded by 3; 3. Freni, Carreras, Cappuccilli, Ghiaurov, La Scala Ch and O, Abbado, DG, 1977: faithful recording of famous La Scala cast that sang in Strehler's memorable staging [A.B.]
VIDEO Te Kanawa, Sylvester, Agache, Scandiuzzi, Ch and O of Covent Garden, Solti, Decca, 1991: Moshinsky's illuminating production, stylishly sung, dully conducted [A.B.]
EDITIONS f.s., Ricordi, [c. 1955]; v.ss., Ricordi, [1881]; *rps*

Otello

Othello
Dramma lirico in four acts (2h 15m)
Libretto by Arrigo Boito, after the tragedy *Othello* by Shakespeare (1604–5)
Composed December 1884–November 1886; rev. April 1887
PREMIERES 5 February 1887, La Scala, Milan; US: 16 April 1888, Academy of Music, New York; UK: 5 July 1889, Lyceum, London
CAST Otello *t*, Iago *bar*, Cassio *t*, Roderigo *t*, Lodovico *b*, Montano *b*, herald *b*, Desdemona *s*, Emilia *ms*; *satb* chorus of soldiers and sailors of the Venetian Republic, Venetian ladies and gentlemen, Cypriot people, Greek men-at-arms, Dalmatians, Albanians, children of the island *trebles*; an innkeeper, 4 inn servants, ship's crew
ORCHESTRATION 3 fl/picc, 2 ob, ca, 2 cl, b cl, 4 bsn, 4 hn, 2 cornet, 2 tpt, 3 trbn, bass trbn, 2 hp, timp, perc (2 bd, cym, t-t), str; offstage: organ, cannon; onstage: 2 pistons in E♭, 6 cornets in B♭, 2 tpts in B♭, 3 tenor hn in E♭, 3 trbn, cornamusa, 2 mand, 2 gtr, tamburelli; lightning, thunder and thunderclaps

During the last 20 years of Verdi's life, Arrigo Boito was to become one of his closest friends, and their working relationship was one of the most remarkable in the history of opera. It was a position he did not win easily: almost 30 years Verdi's junior, he had deeply offended him with a foolish poem published in the 1860s, and it took all his generosity of spirit and all Ricordi's diplomacy to bring about a reconciliation. Their two Shakespearean operas, *Otello* and *Falstaff*, are widely regarded as the twin peaks of the whole Italian tradition of opera; a few critics, however, judge the collaboration more captiously, and deplore what they see as the artificiality and self-conscious intellectualism of Verdi's last last operas.

In adapting *Otello*, Boito omitted the first, Venetian act – save for a number of hints that are ingeniously recapitulated later, notably in the love duet in Act I; otherwise he follows the play closely. But his understanding of Shakespeare's characters had its roots in Continental sources – in the writings of August Wilhelm von Schlegel and François-Victor Hugo (whose French translation was his primary source), and in the style of Shakespeare performance growing up in Italy around the actors Ernesto Rossi and Tommaso Salvini. With *Otello*, Boito's emphasis lies on the 'Ethiopian' core of savage passion only fragilely contained beneath a veneer of Mediterranean civility; Desdemona, on the other hand, is a saintly idealization, 'a type of goodness, of resignation, of self-sacrifice' (Verdi). For Iago too, Boito and Verdi draw on this interpretative tradition; but, equally, his diabolical cynicism makes him one with a whole family of mephistophelean villains conceived by Boito for his opera libretti. The peculiar fascination Iago exerted over both men is seen from one of Boito's additions to Shakespeare's play, the 'Credo' in Act II – which Verdi found 'most beautiful and wholly Shakespearean'; and from the fact that for years they were disposed to call the opera *Jago*. They finally resolved to challenge comparison with Shakespeare by using his title only in January 1886, not much more than a year before the premiere.

No other opera, if one excepts *King Lear*, occupied Verdi so long. The possibility of composing *Otello* had first been put to him in earnest during a visit to Milan in June 1879, and a first draft of Boito's libretto was written during the summer and autumn; but it was not until November 1886 that Verdi was ready to declare the opera finished, and he continued to tinker with details even during the rehearsals. Faccio rehearsed his cast with exemplary zeal, and no detail of casting, *mise-en-scène* or general organization was too tiny for Ricordi's attention; even so, to the last moment Verdi reserved the right to withdraw the opera if anything failed to satisfy him. In the event he was not pleased with the premiere, but it was recognized internationally as an artistic occasion of the first importance, and prompted scenes of wild enthusiasm: the *Times* critic reported that at one o'clock in the morning the streets outside Verdi's hotel were still full of 'an eager multitude . . . shouting and yelling'.

Francesco Tamagno as Otello (Milan, 1887)

For the first performance at the Paris Opéra in October 1894, Verdi composed a short ballet; it forms part of the ceremony of welcome for the Venetian ambassadors in the Act III finale.

SYNOPSIS
The scene is set in a maritime city on the island of Cyprus at the end of the 15th century.

Act I   Outside the castle. A crowd watches as the ship bearing Otello, the new governor, battles into harbour through a hurricane; the Venetians have routed the Turks, and a celebratory bonfire is prepared. Otello's ensign, Iago, who hates both Otello and the young officer Cassio, promises to help Roderigo enjoy the love of Otello's wife, Desdemona; and, as the bonfire dies down ('Fuoco di gioia!'), sets his plan in motion. Wine flows freely in honour of the nuptials of Otello and Desdemona ('Inaffia l'ugola!'), Cassio is soon drunk; when Montano, the retiring governor, orders him to the ramparts, Roderigo and Iago easily provoke a brawl. Roderigo goes to raise havoc through the city, alarm bells clang, and Otello reappears, roused from his bed. Furious to find Montano wounded, and believing what 'honest Iago' tells him, he dismisses Cassio, appoints Iago in his stead, and sends him to re-establish order in the streets. Desdemona has also been roused by the pandemonium; the lovers are left alone, to recall the strange chances of fortune that brought them together ('Già nella notte densa').

Act II   A hall on the ground floor of the castle.

Having advised Cassio to ask Desdemona to intercede for him with Otello, Iago confesses his nihilistic creed ('Credo in un Dio crudel'). He urges Otello to watch Desdemona's behaviour with Cassio: it may be less innocent than he supposes. Otello is disturbed, but when he sees the islanders paying homage to his wife in the garden ('Dove guardi splendono'), his suspicions are disarmed. When Desdemona pleads with him for Cassio, he is reminded of Iago's warning, becomes irritable, and throws down the handkerchief she offers him; Emilia picks it up. In the quartet ('Dammi la dolce e lieta parola del perdono') Desdemona beseeches Otello to forgive her for any offence given; he muses gloomily; Iago snatches Desdemona's handkerchief from Emilia. Otello's dreams of love and glory are fast evaporating ('Nell'ore arcane della sua lussuria' – 'Ora è per sempre addio'), and he demands proof of his wife's guilt. Iago recounts how he had recently slept with Cassio, who, in his dreams, had unmistakably been making love to Desdemona ('Era la notte'); what is more, only the day before, he was carrying the handkerchief Otello had once given her. Otello swears to exact bloody vengeance ('Sì, pel ciel marmoreo giuro!').

Act III   The great hall of the castle. Iago outlines a plan to make Cassio chatter about Desdemona while Otello eavesdrops. Otello greets Desdemona with elaborate courtesy ('Dio ti giocondi, o sposo'); but as soon as she mentions Cassio, he becomes agitated, and after an argument about her handkerchief, drives her away; the grief occasioned BY her falseness is unendurable ('Dio! mi potevi scagliar'). Iago re-enters, followed by Cassio, who is soon talking about his mistress Bianca ('Essa t'avvince coi vaghi rai'). Otello, unable to catch Bianca's name, imagines the ribald laughter to be about Desdemona, and when Cassio produces the handkerchief, no further proof is required. While a distant chorus is heard greeting ambassadors from Venice, Otello and Iago plan how to kill the guilty pair. The ambassadors have come to recall Otello; Cassio is appointed his successor. But affairs of state are overshadowed by Otello's behaviour ('A terra! . . . sì . . .'); soon he is delirious; he drives everyone but Iago from the scene, curses Desdemona, and swoons. Cries of 'Viva Otello!' resound in the distance, while Iago spurns the prostrate figure with his heel.

Act IV   Desdemona's bedroom. While she prepares for bed, Desdemona sings the willow song ('Piangea cantando nell'erma landa') she once learned from her mother's maid. She bids Emilia goodnight, and having said her prayers ('Ave Maria') lies down to sleep. Otello enters, extinguishes the lamp, and kisses Desdemona; she realizes that he has come to kill her. Her entreaties are in vain, and he smothers her just as Emilia comes hammering at the door to announce that Cassio has killed Roderigo. Aghast to find Desdemona dying, she raises the alarm: Cassio, Iago, Lodovico and later Montano enter. As the truth emerges, Iago makes his escape, and Otello is disarmed. But he has a dagger hidden in his robes, and having bidden a solemn farewell to his comrades and a heart-broken one to the dead Desdemona, he stabs himself, and falls dying beside her.

As so often in Verdi the musical characterization is the key to the opera's individuality. Otello, he remarked, 'now the warrior, now the passionate lover, now crushed to the point of baseness, now ferocious like a savage, must sing and shout'; Desdemona 'must always, always sing'; but Iago 'has only to declaim and mock'. Again and again in *Otello*, Desdemona's pure-hearted and passionate lyricism, an expression of all that love and idealism the art of opera had been invented to express, is juxtaposed with, counterpointed against and undermined by Iago's nonchalant *parlando*, which is graced only with a few slithering and trilling touches of arioso, and which could, Verdi noted, 'with the exception of a few outbursts, be sung *mezza voce* throughout' – an unforgettable musical image of the mephistophelean 'spirit of denial'.

In 1882, when work on the opera was still at an early stage, Verdi predicted that *Otello* would be 'Italian in scale and Italian in who knows how many other ways . . . Perhaps a few melodies . . . (if I can find any) . . . and melody is always Italian . . .'. A few critics were deluded by the opera's seamless continuity, the sumptuousness of the orchestral writing and the sophistication of the harmony into imagining that he was at last coming round to a Wagnerian ideal of music drama. But the essence of his art remained the wedding of poetry and song in balanced lyrical forms; what is different in the later Verdi is that these forms are not confined to arias and ensembles, but blossom wherever poetry and the spirit of the drama suggests. In the opening scene, for example, two distinct musical shapes – one a prayer ('Dio, fulgor della bufera'), one an exclamation of joy ('Vittoria! vittoria!') – materialize out of the orchestral turmoil of the hurricane. Conversely, it is out of the songs and celebrations marking Otello's safe arrival that the dramatic action re-emerges: Iago's *brindisi* is the source of the musical figures that propel the brawl, just as the wine he sings of is the source of the drunkenness that causes it.

Many sections of the score draw inspiration directly from Shakespeare's poetry: for example, Otello's two great solos, 'Nell'ore arcane' in Act II ('What sense had I of her stol'n hours of lust?') and 'Dio! mi potevi scagliar' in Act III ('Had it pleas'd heaven to try me with affliction'). No Shakespeare-inspired detail is more telling than the threefold recurrence – at the close of the Act I love duet; when Otello enters Desdemona's bedchamber to kill her; and at the end of the opera – of the so-called 'kiss' motif: 'I kiss'd thee ere I kill'd thee; no way but this, killing myself to die upon a kiss.'

RECORDINGS 1. Nelli, Vinay, Valdengo, NBC Ch and SO, Toscanini, RCA, 1947: interpretation of authoritative power from Toscanini with sound, though not uniformly excellent, cast; 2. Rysanek, Vickers, Gobbi, Rome Opera Ch and O, Serafin, RCA, 1960: moving performance with most notable Otello and Iago of 1950s and 1960s; 3. Scotto, Domingo,

Milnes, Ambrosian Opera Ch, National PO, Levine, RCA, 1978: the most satisfactory of reasonably modern sets [A.B.]
VIDEO Freni, Vickers, Glossop, Deutsche Oper Ch, Berlin PO, Karajan, DG, 1974
EDITIONS f.ss., Ricordi, 1913; rev. edn (contains ballet music as appendix), 1958; v.ss., Ricordi, [1887]; later edns and *rp*s; rev. edn, 1944; (French – contains the 1894 ballet music, and certain other revisions made at the same time), Ricordi (Paris), [1894]

Falstaff

Commedia lirica in three acts (2h)
Libretto by Arrigo Boito, after the comedy *The Merry Wives of Windsor* by Shakespeare (1600–1601) and incorporating material from the histories *Henry IV, Parts I and II* (1597–8)
Composed ?August 1889; March 1890–December 1892; major revs March 1893 and January 1894
PREMIERES 9 February 1893, La Scala, Milan; UK: 19 May 1894, Covent Garden, London; US: 4 February 1895, Metropolitan, New York
CAST Sir John Falstaff *bar*, Ford *bar*, Fenton *t*, Dr Caius *t*, Bardolph *t*, Pistol *b*, Mrs Alice Ford *s*, Nannetta *s*, Mrs Quickly *ms*, Mrs Meg Page *ms*, Host of the Garter Inn *silent role*; Robin, Falstaff's page *silent role*; Ford's little pageboy *silent role*; *satb* chorus of burghers and commoners, Ford's servants, masquerade of elves, fairies, witches, etc.
ORCHESTRATION 3 fl/picc, 2 ob, ca, 2 cl, b cl, 2 bsn, 4 hn, 3 tpt, 3 trbn, bass trbn, timp, perc (triangle, cym, bd), hp, str; onstage: gtr; offstage: natural hn in A♭ *basso*, bell in F

Falstaff was Verdi's first comic opera since *Un giorno di regno*. There were those who felt, as Rossini did, that he was 'too melancholy and serious' to compose a successful one; but since *Luisa Miller* he had used elements of comedy to set off the prevailing tragic mood in his operas, and at various times since the 1860s he had considered making another attempt at comedy, if a suitable subject could be found. He was not interested in buffoonery: for all its Latin spirit, *Falstaff* was not an opera buffa, Verdi insisted, but a depiction of character.

As a result of their collaboration on *Otello*, Verdi now had complete trust in Boito, and embarked on this new enterprise – at first a secret between the two of them – with much zest. Shortly after receiving a first draft of the plot (summer 1889) he was experimenting with 'comic fugues' (it is likely that the opera's finale was conceived at this time), and when he received the complete libretto (March 1890) he drafted the whole of Act I in little more than a week. Such bursts of intense activity were to recur throughout the three and a half years he worked on *Falstaff*; but there were distractions and sorrows too (particularly the deaths of several of his closest friends) that drove music out of his head for months on end. It is obvious from the manuscripts and early printed sources that Verdi worked over every scene again and again, refining the craftsmanship, enriching the musical fabric, sharpening the wit. The process of revision continued while the score was being printed, throughout the period of rehearsals, and even during the first run of performances. Further rewriting, sometimes quite substantial, took place before the Rome performances in April 1893, and before the French premiere the following year.

Falstaff had long been one of Verdi's favourite characters – a supreme embodiment of Shakespeare's genius for 'inventing truth' – and Boito's libretto is the most brilliant of all operatic adaptations of Shakespeare. He adroitly condenses and clarifies the plot of *The Merry Wives*, while drawing freely on the two parts of *Henry IV* to give us a Falstaff in all his prodigious abundance of personality; at the same time Shakespeare's quintessential Englishness is translated to 'the gardens of the *Decameron*', the verse given an antique tang and raciness with vocabulary drawn from Boccaccio and the satirists of the Italian Renaissance. The libretto is beautifully formed: each act subdivided into one scene of character depiction for a small group of soloists and one of teeming action and elaborate ensembles.

No production book for *Falstaff* survives, but there is plenty of evidence that Verdi, who supervised a huge number of rehearsals in January and February 1893, insisted on a more naturalistic style of performance than in his tragic operas (a newspaper account survives of him demonstrating to Fenton how to kiss Nannetta with suitable ardour); and the designer Adolph Hohenstein was sent off to London and Windsor to ensure that sets and costumes were as authentic as possible. The premiere was a brilliant occasion, and aroused worldwide excitement. But a high proportion of opera-lovers, especially perhaps in Italy, were frankly bewildered, and the admiration of connoisseurs was not matched by the kind of popular enthusiasm that had attended the greater part of Verdi's career. It was in large part due to Toscanini, who made his superlatively drilled performances cornerstones of the repertoire in every opera house he directed, that *Falstaff* came to be regarded as a national classic rather than an object of bewildered admiration.

SYNOPSIS

The scene is set in Windsor, in the reign of Henry IV of England.

Act I Part 1: Inside the Garter Inn. Falstaff's carousing is interrupted by Dr Caius, who threatens to report him to the Star Chamber. Unable to ruffle Falstaff's bibulous calm, Caius turns on Bardolph and Pistol who, the previous night, had made him drunk and emptied his purse; the charges are denied, and Caius storms out. Finding they have no money to pay the bill, Falstaff blames his companions. Bardolph's glowing nose means they can economize on lanterns, but the savings are more than consumed in wine bills. He outlines a new enterprise: two wealthy citizens, Ford and Page, have beautiful wives; he will lay siege to their virtue as a means of getting at their husbands' money ('V'è noto un tal'). Bardolph and Pistol refuse to assist so dishonourable an enterprise; Falstaff harangues them on the subject of Honour ('L'Onore! Ladri!' – 'Puo l'onore riempirvi la pancia?'), before kicking them out. Part 2: The garden by Ford's house. Alice and Meg have received identical love letters from Falstaff ('Fulgida Alice! amor t'offro'), and decide he must be taught a lesson. Ford enters with Fenton and Caius (rivals for

Nannetta's hand), and Bardolph and Pistol, from whom he learns that Falstaff is bent on seducing his wife and emptying his money bags. While the women engage Mistress Quickly to lure Falstaff to an assignation, Ford plans to visit the Garter Inn in disguise to investigate these tales. Twice Nannetta and Fenton break away from their companions to kiss in the shadow of the trees ('Labbra di foco!').

Act II Part 1: Inside the Garter Inn. Mistress Quickly arrives with the answer to Falstaff's letters ('Reverenza!'): both wives love him, but only Alice is able to receive him – any day between two and three, when her husband is always out. Bardolph announces 'Mastro Fontana' ('Master Brook'): 'Fontana' introduces himself as a wealthy man accustomed to want for nothing; but he has fallen in love with, Ford's wife and all his wooing has been in vain ('C'è a Windsor una dama'). The gold he has brought with him is Falstaff's if he can seduce her; for once she has fallen to a man of the world like Sir John, she is more likely to listen to his own suit. Falstaff accepts the challenge; indeed it is almost won already, for he has an assignation with the lady in half an hour. He excuses himself a moment, and Ford is left alone, a prey to jealousy ('E sogno? o realtà?' – 'L'ora è fissata'). Falstaff returns, dressed to kill, and they go out together. Part 2: A room in Ford's house. Mistress Quickly reports on the success of her mission ('Giunta all'Albergo della *Giarrettiera*'). A screen is set up, a lute laid ready, and servants carry in a laundry basket; they all look forward to the adventure ('Gaie comari di Windsor'). Falstaff arrives, woos Alice ardently, and recalls the days of his slender youth ('Quand'ero paggio'). But Ford is heard approaching; Falstaff hides behind the screen, while Ford, assisted by Caius, Bardolph and Pistol, seeks high and low for the intruder. He soon rushes off to another part of the house, Falstaff is bundled into the laundry basket, and Fenton and Nannetta retreat behind the screen. While Ford closes in on – as he supposes – his wife and Falstaff, Nannetta and Fenton continue their romantic *tête-à-tête*. The screen is snatched away, to reveal only the young lovers, and a new hunt for Falstaff begins on a false scent laid by Bardolph. The laundry basket is hauled to the window, and as soon as Ford returns Falstaff is tipped into the river.

Act III Part 1: A courtyard outside the Garter Inn. Falstaff broods over his humiliation ('Mondo ladro'); but the consolations of steaming wine are infallible. Mistress Quickly brings a letter inviting him to a midnight assignation in Windsor Park; but he must come disguised as the 'Black Huntsman' who haunts the forest. The conversation is overheard by the other wives, by Ford, Caius and Fenton; and while Falstaff accompanies Mistress Quickly into the inn they plan the details of the midnight masquerade. Mistress Quickly reappears to hear Ford plotting Nannetta's marriage with Caius. Part 2: Windsor Great Park. Fenton's musings ('Dal labbro il canto estasiato vola') are interrupted by the wives: to outwit Ford and Caius last-minute changes of mask and costume are necessary. As midnight strikes, Falstaff enters; but his wooing of Alice is interrupted by the approach of a horde of spirits. With Falstaff prostrate on the ground in terror, Nannetta, disguised as the queen of the fairies, and her attendants weave a spell in solemn song and dance ('Sul fil d'un soffio etesio'). Then, while she and Fenton are hurried away, fantastically garbed figures torment Falstaff and conduct him through a litany of repentance. In the excitement Bardolph loses his hood; further unmaskings follow, and Falstaff realizes he has been made an ass of. Ford proposes that the betrothal of the queen of the fairies be celebrated: Caius's bride proves, when unveiled, to be Bardolph, while another masked couple brought forward for blessing are revealed as Nannetta and Fenton. Ford accepts the situation philosophically, and Falstaff leads the company in a fugal chorus celebrating the absurdity of the human condition ('Tutto nel mondo è burla').

It is not difficult to see why early audiences were sometimes bemused. By far the greater part of *Falstaff* moves at such a giddy pace that only the most fleeting glimpses of musical forms are perceived: the choicest melodies are come and gone with teasing rapidity, giving an effect that is at once virtuosic and tender, and beautifully suggestive of the spirit of Shakespearean comedy. Only in the final scene, as order returns and reconciliation is achieved, does the musical pace broaden out into a sequence of

Drawing by A. Ferraguti of the final scene of Falstaff *(Milan, 1893)*

almost ceremonial movements: serenade, dance, litany, fugue. In many passages musical continuity is achieved by the orchestral development of short melodic and rhythmic figures, a procedure more 'symphonic' than anything heard in Verdi's operas hitherto. Some of these symphonic passages are based on trenchant vocal phrases – 'dalle due alle tre' and 'te lo cornifico' in Act II, Part 1 for example – in which Verdi shows that his vaunted *parola scenica* – the 'theatrical word' that 'carves out a situation or a character' – can be as brilliantly apt in the comic vein as in the heroic or tragic.

With the passage for muted double-basses in the final scene of *Otello*, Verdi had become the first Italian since Spontini to earn a place in Berlioz's *Treatise on Orchestration*, as revised by Richard Strauss. Many an episode in *Falstaff* – Falstaff's self-portraits in the opening scene; his ruminations on his ducking in the river, culminating in the celebrated trill cum tremolo for virtually every instrument in the orchestra; the fairy music in the last act – demonstrates that, for sheer virtuosity in tone-painting the elderly Verdi rivalled Strauss himself. But it is orchestration of exquisite translucency: instruments are virtually never used simply to reinforce the voices. To sing unsupported by the orchestra was only one of the unfamiliar demands Verdi made on his performers; he knew that Italian singers in particular would be severely tested, for there was, he declared, no room in *Falstaff* for 'artists who want to sing too much . . . and fall asleep on the notes'; above all they would need to 'loosen up their tongues and clarify their pronunciation'.

RECORDINGS 1. Nelli, Stich-Randall, Merriman, Elmo, Madasi, Guerrera, Valdengo, Robert Shaw Ch, NBC SO, Toscanini, RCA, 1950: still the most vital performance ever recorded and one of the best casts, headed by Valdengo's vivid Falstaff; 2. Schwarzkopf, Moffo, Merriman, Barbieri, Alva, Panerai, Gobbi, Philharmonia Ch and O, Karajan, EMI, 1956: a reading notable for Gobbi's all-engrossing performance of the title role and Karajan's lithe conducting; 3. Ricciarelli, Hendricks, Boozer, Valentini Terrani, D. González, Nucci, Bruson, Los Angeles Master Ch and PO, Giulini, DG, 1983 (same cast and conductor at Covent Garden on video, Castle): serious but convincing view with Bruson as a dignified Falstaff; 4. Somigli, Oltrabella, Vasari, Cravcenko, Borgioli, Biasini, Stabile, Vienna State Opera Ch and O, Toscanini, Cetra, 1937: poorly recorded but historic live performance (Salzburg) of the Rome version, with Stabile's peerless Falstaff [A.B.]

EDITIONS f.ss., Ricordi, [1912]; rev. and corrected edn, [1959]; v.ss., Ricordi, [1893]; 2nd edn (Rome version), June [1893]; 3rd edn (includes Paris revisions and simplifications), [1897]; many rps; facsimile of autograph, Ricordi, (1951)

BIBLIOGRAPHY Julian Budden, *The Operas of Verdi*, 3 vols, Cassell, 1973, 1978, 1981; Julian Budden, *Verdi*, Dent (Master Musicians series), 1985; M. Conati (R. Stokes, trans.), *Interviews and Encounters with Verdi*, Gollancz, 1984; James Hepokoski, *Giuseppe Verdi: Falstaff*, CUP, 1983; James Hepokoski, *Giuseppe Verdi: Otello*, CUP, 1987; David Kimbell, *Verdi in the Age of Italian Romanticism*, CUP, 1981; Andrew Porter, 'Verdi', in *The New Grove Masters of Italian Opera*, Macmillan, 1983; the ENO/Covent Garden Opera Guides series (edited by Nicholas John and published by

John Calder) contains volumes on the following Verdi operas: *Macbeth*, 1990; *Rigoletto*, 1982; *Il trovatore*, 1983; *La traviata*, 1981; *Un ballo in maschera*, 1989; *La forza del destino*, 1983; *Don Carlos*, 1992; *Aida*, 1980; *Simon Boccanegra*, 1985; *Otello*, 1981; *Falstaff*, 1982

D.K.

ALEKSEI VERSTOVSKY
Aleksei Nikolayevich Verstovsky; *b* 1 March 1799, Seliverstovo, Tambov; *d* 17 November 1862, Moscow

Verstovsky was educated in St Petersburg as a civil engineer while also studying piano with John Field. He was soon drawn into aristocratic theatrical circles and made his composing début, writing couplets for a vaudeville, *Les perroquets de la mère Philippe*, in 1819. He moved to Moscow and was made inspector of theatres. At this time he became familiar with the works of Méhul, Cherubini and Weber, and under the spell of *Der Freischütz* wrote *Pan Twardowski*, enthusiastically claimed as 'the first Russian opera'. There is no trace of Weber in the musical style; it is a collection of couplets, songs and dances linked by dialogue – a singspiel, in fact. *Vadim* repeated this formula with some success, but with *Askold's Tomb* Verstovsky wrote what was probably the most widely performed Russian opera of the 19th century, drawing audiences until the Revolution; it was also the first Russian opera to be performed in the US. Verstovsky's later operas show more advanced features, including the replacement of dialogue by recitatives, but they were all failures. Despite the perennial popularity of *Askold's Tomb*, he died a neglected man, embittered by the fact that, in musical circles, the birth of Russian opera was attributed to Glinka, and not to him.

Askold's Tomb
Askol'dova mogila
Opera in four acts (2h 15m)
Libretto by Mikhail Nikolayevich Zagorskin, after his own novel (1833)
PREMIERES   28 September 1835, Bolshoi Theatre, Moscow; US: 1869, New York

The action takes place in Kiev, in pre-Christian times. It concerns the fate of Vseslav, an orphan adopted by Prince Svyatoslav. The Unknown, a charismatic and devilish figure, disapproves of the prince's dissolute regime and hankers for the past days of Askold. He attempts to turn Vseslav against his benefactor the Prince by abducting Vseslav's fiancée Nadezha and attributing this act to the prince. The tangled plot concludes with the Unknown perishing in the river Dnieper.

Some of the music is culled from old vaudevilles and romances, though generally the level of invention is superior to that in Verstovsky's other works, and some of the choral writing has an authentic folk tang that is prophetic. There was a rumour current in the 1870s that Verstovsky had won the opera from another composer, Varlamov, in a card game, but this was disproved. The most prominent critic of the early 19th century in Russia, Findeisen, wrote: 'If *A Life for the Tsar* outstripped its contemporaries, then *Askold's Tomb* captured their understanding, opinions and sympathies.'

RECORDING   excerpts: Kiselyeva, Nelepp, Al. Ivanov, USSR Radio Ch and SO, Smirnov, Melodiya, 1948 and 1951
EDITION   A. Gutheil, 1840

Other operas: *Pan Twardowski*, 1828; *Vadim*, 1832; *Toska po rodine* (*Longing for the Homeland*), 1839; *Churova Dolina* (*Chur Valley*), 1841; *Gromoboy*, 1858
BIBLIOGRAPHY   R. Newmarch, *Russian Opera*, Jenkins, 1914

J.G.

HEITOR VILLA-LOBOS
b 5 March 1887, Rio de Janeiro, Brazil; *d* 17 November 1959, Rio de Janeiro

Villa-Lobos emerged in the early 20th century as Brazil's most influential composer. Born when Brazil's colonial dependence on Europe was crumbling, as a young man he responded to the growing nationalism in literature and politics by embarking on the study and collection of his country's folk music. As a largely self-taught composer, guitarist and cellist he worked in street groups in Rio, as well as playing in theatre and opera orchestras. He wrote a vast amount of chamber and orchestral music and several operas, the earliest inspired by the music of Puccini, Wagner and others. His own first opera, *Femina*, was scheduled for performance at the Teatro Trianon, where he played in the orchestra, but the company went bankrupt and the production was cancelled.

Involvement with the Brazilian modernists and sojourns in Paris resulted in the consolidation of a remarkable and recognizably Brazilian style. Though musically an explorer (his folklorist style was widely attacked in Brazil), Villa-Lobos was never at his best in large-scale composition. His *Chôros*, piano

Heitor Villa-Lobos

miniatures and the famous *Bachianas brasileiras* are successful, but the symphonies and concertos fail. His operas were further beset by unstageable ideas and a piecemeal method of compilation.

Undaunted by his limited operatic success, Villa-Lobos continued to write or plan operas with characteristic aplomb. Most of them are now forgotten and have rarely been staged.

Izaht (or Enith-Izaht)

Opera in four acts (1h 30m)
Libretto by Azevedo Junior and the composer (using the pseudonym of E. Villalba Filho)
Composed 1912–14
PREMIERES 6 April 1940, Municipal Theatre, Rio de Janeiro (concert); 13 December 1958, Municipal Theatre, Rio de Janeiro

Izaht is a fantastic and complicated story of gypsies, criminals, street urchins and nobility, in a Poe-like Parisian setting. It involves huge numbers of soloists, chorus and dancers. Musically, it combines Puccinian lyricism with nationalist elements, together with certain bizarre touches of orchestration that point towards Villa-Lobos's mature style. It is typical of his often cavalier, approach to his work that the score combines material from two unpublished operas, *Aglaia* and *Elisa*. Its *Prelúdio sinfonico* remains a popular concert item in Brazil.

Yerma

Opera in three acts (1h 30m)
Libretto by the composer, after the play by Federico García Lorca (1934)
Composed 1955–6
PREMIERES 12 August 1971, Santa Fe; UK: 12 July 1989, Queen Elizabeth Hall, London (semi-staged)

Yerma is a late consolidation of Villa-Lobos's love for the Hispanic scene. Lorca's great Spanish tragedy is dressed in vivid orchestral colours which emphasize flamenco sounds and exotic percussion. The frustrated and repressed Yerma, unable to bear a child, becomes obsessed with fertility and conception. Eventually, when she realizes her hopes are in vain, she murders her husband. The vocal writing is declamatory and flamboyant, and often verges on the hysterical, underlining superbly the character of the tragic heroine.

EDITION Eschig (on hire)

Magdalena

Musical adventure in two acts (1h 30m)
Libretto by Robert Wright and George Forrest (lyrics), Frederick Hazlitt Brennan and Homer Curran (book)
Composed 1947
PREMIERE 26 July 1947, Los Angeles

Magdalena – a pot-pourri of familiar Villa-Lobos melodies – is centred around the Rio Magdalena in Colombia, and peopled by Latin stereotypes: a happy-go-lucky bus driver, Major Blanco, General Carabaña and a devout, simple girl called Maria. Villa-Lobos wrote the work while ill in New York,

and drew heavily on previously composed material, all of it unconnected with the opera's unlikely plot.

RECORDING Kaye, Esham, Gray, Hadley, Rose, O New England, Haile, CBS, 1989

Other operas: *Femina*, (*c.* 1908); *Aglaia*, (1909); *Elisa* (inc.), (1910); *Jésus*, (1918); *Zoé*, (1919); *Malazarte*, (1921); *A menina das nuvens*, (1958), 1960
BIBLIOGRAPHY Simon Wright, *Villa-Lobos*, OUP, 1992

S.J.W.

LEONARDO VINCI

b c. 1696, Strongoli, Calabria; *d* 27 or 28 May 1730, Naples

In a short but highly productive career spanning the years 1719 to 1730, Vinci established himself as one of the leading composers both of comic and serious operas in Naples and other Italian cities. A serious rival to Alessandro Scarlatti for the leadership of the so-called Neapolitan school, Vinci was also Pergolesi's teacher and enjoyed a considerable posthumous reputation: several of his operas were revived in the 1730s and 1740s.

Trained under Gaetano Greco at the Conservatorio dei Poveri di Gesù Cristo from 1708, Vinci gained his first position as maestro di cappella to the Prince of Sansevero. From 1725, following Scarlatti's death, he became pro-vicemaestro di cappella at the royal chapel in Naples and in 1728 was appointed maestro di cappella at the Conservatory where he had been taught.

He began his career with a series of eleven comic operas, many of them written in Neapolitan dialect and all of them premiered at the Teatro dei Fiorentini in Naples. Only one survives, *Le zite 'ngalera* (1722), described at the end of the 19th century by the Italian writer on music Nicola D'Arienzo as 'a continual hotch-potch of characters in a series of hilarious and equivocal scenes'. The freshness and originality of Vinci's style was recognized by contemporaries and well summed up by Burney, who wrote of his 'simplifying and polishing [the] melody, and calling the attention of the audience chiefly to the voice part, by disentangling it from fugue, complication and laboured contrivance'. Arias formed the focus of his operas. Rhythmically buoyant and elegant in shape, they reveal a strong tendency towards periodic melody, using balanced phrases, often three bars long. The same features, important for the development of aria forms, are in fact discernible in the work of Alessandro Scarlatti, who likewise simplified textures and put greater emphasis on melodic lines.

After 1722 Vinci turned his attention more to opera seria, writing two or three operas a year until his early death. Their style, influenced by his experience as a comic opera composer, marks a further extension of musical characteristics found in Scarlatti, including less active bass lines and a slower rate of harmonic change. Although Vinci's role as an innovator may have been exaggerated, his settings of texts by Metastasio for Naples, starting with *Didone abbandonata* in 1725 and ending with *Artaserse*, composed shortly before his death, were extremely influential. He generally kept his recitative simple, although the final act of *Didone*, with its orchestrally accompanied recitative, was much praised by the 18th-century Italian writer and connoisseur Francesco Algarotti. Vinci's posthumous fame rested above all on his setting of Metastasio's *Artaserse*, which was performed in repertoire in Naples, Ferrara and Macerata, and revived in London in 1734 in a production where at least five of the original arias were retained. It was also given at a gala performance in Naples in 1738 at the Teatro San Carlo and it inaugurated the first public opera house in Dresden in 1746.

Operas: *Le doje lettere*, 1719; *Lo cecato fauzo*, 1719; *Lo scagno*, 1720; *Lo scassone*, 1720; *Lo Barone di Trocchia*, 1721; *Don Ciccio*, 1721; *Le z ite 'ngalera*, 1722 (EDITION facsimile, Garland, 1979); *La festa di Bacco*, 1722; *Lo castiello sacchiato*, 1722; *Publio Cornelio Scipione*, 1722; *Lo labberinto*, 1723; *Semiramide*, 1723; *Silla dittatore*, 1723; *Farnace*, 1724; *La mogliera fedele*, 1724; *Turno Aricino*, 1724; *Ifigenia in Tauride*, 1725; *La Rosmira fedele*, 1725; *Il trionfo di Camilla*, 1725; *Didone abbandonata*, 1726 (EDITION facsimile, Garland, 1977); *Siroe, Re di Persia*, 1726; *L'asteria*, 1726; *Ernelinda*, 1726; *Gismondo*, 1727; *La caduta dei Decemviri*, 1727; *Catone in Utica*, 1728; *Medo*, 1728; *Flavio Anicio Olibrio*, 1728; *La Semiramide riconosciuta*, 1729; *Alessandro nell'Indie*, 1729; *Farnace*, 1729; *Artaserse*, 1730
BIBLIOGRAPHY   Robert B. Meikle, *Leonardo Vinci's Artaserse: An Edition with an Editorial and Critical Commentary*, dissertation, Cornell University, 1970; Michael F. Robinson, *Naples and Neapolitan Opera*, OUP, 1972

D.S.B.

FILIPPO VITALI
b c. 1590, Florence; *d* after March 1653, ?Florence

Vitali divided his career between Florence and Rome. He worked as a priest and freelance musician until the 1630s, when he entered the papal choir. In 1642 he became choirmaster of S. Lorenzo, Florence, and may have been in Bergamo in 1648–9, although he was back in Florence in the early 1650s.

Vitali's *Aretusa*, to a libretto by Ottavio Corsini, was the first favola in musica to be staged in Rome – on 8 February 1620. It was composed and rehearsed in 44 days. The preface to the score (Rome, 1620) cites the influence of Jacopo Peri and Giulio Caccini – Caccini's son, Pompeo, also painted the scenery – and the uninspired work exploits the typical, now archaic, Florentine recitative. The chorus scenes with interpolated solos, duets and trios over a repeating bass also appear old-fashioned.

In the 1620s, Vitali was associated with two Florentine academies: he published his intermedi for Jacopo Cicognini's *La finta mora* (performed by the Accademici Incostanti on 6 February 1623) and a serenata for the Accademici Rugginosi (performed on 20 August 1628). His works suggest that the

Florentine style urgently needed an injection of new ideas.

T.C.

ANTONIO VIVALDI
Antonio Lucio Vivaldi; *b* 4 March 1678, Venice; *d* 27 or 28 July 1741, Vienna

Vivaldi's importance as a composer of opera rests on several factors: his high productivity (nearly 50 operas are known); the high rate of their survival (16 complete works are preserved in scores, mostly autograph, in the Biblioteca Nazionale, Turin); their musical qualities, which not only reflect his expertise in the instrumental domain through their elaborate accompaniments and advanced sense of colour and texture but also show that he could handle the human voice with flair and sensitivity; and his parallel activity as an impresario, comparable in its day only to that of Handel. Despite this, in modern times his fame has rested almost entirely on his instrumental music.

Vivaldi's father was a violinist who frequently played in the Venetian theatre orchestras and must have introduced him early to opera. Although he was writing dramatic music by 1708, the year of his lost serenata, *Le gare del dovere*, his first opera, *Ottone in villa*, did not appear until 1713, when he

Caricature by Pier Leone Ghezzi of Vivaldi, the only authenticated portrait of the composer

already enjoyed a reputation as a formidable violinist and Italy's foremost composer of concertos. In the next five years he concentrated his operatic endeavours on his native city, producing five new scores and turning his hand to the management of the Sant'Angelo (1713–17) and San Moisè (1717–18) theatres. As commissioner, so to speak, of his own works, Vivaldi had the artistic latitude in which to forge a distinctive style that was vocally unpretentious but inventive in its instrumentation.

He spent a period in Mantua (1718–20) as director of secular music to its governor and composed three more operas there. Returning to Venice in 1720, he found that his style of opera had come under attack in Benedetto Marcello's satire *Il teatro alla moda* (1720) and at first had difficulty in re-establishing himself. However, commissions were now arriving in increasing number from outside Venice; he spent the 1723 and 1724 carnival seasons in Rome. From 1725 to 1728 he stood once more at the helm of Sant'Angelo. In the next decade, following his return from a visit to Bohemia in 1729–30, he extended his impresarial activity to the Italian mainland, taking his operas to a number of provincial centres. His correspondence with Guido Bentivoglio d'Aragona from 1736 to 1739 gives a vivid impression of the frequent frustrations that attended these enterprises. During two further seasons he had control of Sant'Angelo and he also continued to receive commissions, though fewer than before.

From the Roman operas onwards he bowed to the new fashions introduced by composers of the Neapolitan school. His vocal writing became more elaborate and his orchestral writing, though still resourceful, receded a little into the background. The late operas occasionally lack the stylistic assurance of those composed before 1730.

Vivaldi hardly ever departed from the principle universally accepted in the Italy of his time that music should be a simple ornament of the text rather than an equal partner in the dramatic discourse. Nevertheless, the musical distinction of his scores offers ample compensation.

RV numbers refer to P. Ryom, *Verzeichnis der Werke Antonio Vivaldis: kleine Ausgabe*, Leipzig, 1974, 2nd edn, 1979.

Ottone in villa
Ottone [Otho] in the Country
Dramma per musica in three acts, RV 729
Libretto by Domenico Lalli
PREMIERE May 1713, Teatro di Piazza, Vicenza

This first opera of Vivaldi is more erotic and pastoral than heroic in content. The plot revolves around the amours of Cleonilla, mistress of the Roman emperor Ottone. Caio, a handsome youth, courts Cleonilla to the dismay of his lover Tullia, who, disguised as a man under the name of Ostilio, attempts to win him back by herself conquering Cleonilla's heart under her feigned masculine identity. Tullia's efforts are finally rewarded, and Ottone commands Caio to marry her, but Cleonilla's infidelity goes unpunished.

Much of the musical interest in Vivaldi's score centres on the lively instrumental figurations and sensitive scoring. One especially attractive aria, Caio's 'L'ombre, l'aure, e ancora il rio', had two violins and two recorders concealed on stage to evoke the breezes and the brook respectively.

EDITION facsimile of the autograph score, Ricordi, 1983

L'incoronazione di Dario
The Coronation of Dario [Darius]
Dramma per musica in three acts, RV 719 (3h)
Libretto by Adriano Morselli
PREMIERE Carnival 1717, Teatro Sant'Angelo, Venice

The plot of the opera, one of Vivaldi's most colourful scores, concerns the successful efforts of Dario to win the hand of Statira, elder daughter of Ciro, and with it the crown of Persia. Statira is feeble-minded, and Dario's quest is almost thwarted by the machinations of Arpago and Oronte (two rival suitors), Statira's ambitious younger sister Argene, and the princesses' crotchety tutor Nicena. The role of Nicena, a basso buffo, provides an opportunity for Vivaldi to show his gift for comic writing. Morselli's libretto, set to music first in 1684, prescribes numerous short arias rather than the fewer but longer ones typical of opera after 1700; Vivaldi responds with a wealth of miniature but sharply characterized numbers. The good dramatic pacing of this work and its musical variety make it one of the most suited to modern revival of all Vivaldi's operas.

RECORDING Poulenard, Mellon, Ledroit, Lesne, Visse, Elwes, Verschaeve, Ensemble Baroque de Nice, Bezzina, Harmonia Mundi France, 1986: the best recording of a Vivaldi opera to date
MANUSCRIPT Biblioteca Nazionale, Turin

Tito Manlio
Titus Manlius
Dramma per musica in three acts, RV 738 (4h)
Libretto by Matteo Noris
PREMIERE Carnival 1719, Teatro Arciducale, Mantua

The most sumptuous of Vivaldi's Mantuan scores, this opera was written (in only five days, according to a note on the composer's autograph manuscript) to celebrate the wedding of the governor of Mantua, Prince Philip of Hesse-Darmstadt. Since the wedding was called off, the opera may have remained unperformed.

The central theme of the complex plot is the rivalry of Romans and Latins in the days of the Roman Republic, an opposition complicated by romantic attachments between individuals from both sides. The Roman consul Tito Manlio condemns his son Manlio to death for disobeying an order not to become involved in combat during a reconnaissance, a lapse of discipline that results in the death of Geminio, leader of the Latins; however, Manlio, who fully accepts his fate and nobly spurns an opportunity to save his life through treachery, is finally reprieved at the insistence of the legions. Vivaldi's score preserves an admirable balance between vocal and instrumental demands. The prominence of wind instruments in the orchestra, appropriate to the festive character of the opera, adds to the brilliance of the music.

RECORDING   Marshall, Wagemann, Finnilä, Hamari, Lerer, Luccardi, Berlin Radio Ch, Berlin CO, Negri, Philips, 1977
MANUSCRIPT   Biblioteca Nazionale, Turin

Il Giustino

Giustino [Justin]
Dramma per musica in three acts, RV 717
Libretto by Nicolo Beregani, revised by Pietro Pariati
PREMIERES   Carnival 1724, Teatro Capranica, Rome; US: October 1986, Houston, Texas

Of the two complete operas written by Vivaldi for Rome (he contributed one act to a third opera, Il Tigrane) only Il Giustino survives complete. It relates the appearance of the goddess Fortune to the peasant Giustino, his rise to leadership of the Byzantine army and the defeat of a Scythian army under Vitaliano, and the jealousy of the emperor Anastasio, who suspects Giustino of having designs on his wife Arianna and on the throne itself. Finally, all intrigues are foiled, all misunderstandings banished: Giustino is made emperor to general acclaim.

Vivaldi's score is full of picturesque detail; a sinfonia accompanying the descent of Fortune in a chariot emphasizes the rustic nature of the setting by borrowing the refrain theme of the Spring concerto from his own Four Seasons. The final chorus, an extended chaconne, is the most elaborate piece of its kind in any Vivaldi opera.

EDITION   f.s., Reinhard Strohm (ed.), Ricordi, 1990

Farnace

Dramma per musica in three acts, RV 711
Libretto by Antonio Maria Lucchini
PREMIERE   Carnival 1727, Teatro Sant'Angelo, Venice

This opera became one of Vivaldi's warhorses during the later part of his career. After being staged at Sant'Angelo in both the Carnival and the autumn of 1727, it travelled to Livorno in 1729, to Prague in 1730, to Pavia in 1731 (one of the two extant scores is for the last-named production), to Mantua in 1732, and to Treviso in 1737; Vivaldi planned to present it in Ferrara in 1739 (for which production the second score, of which only Acts I and II survive, was prepared), but to his great mortification it was withdrawn by the management. Vivaldi's protégée, Anna Girò, specialized in the role of Tamiri (alto), and the composer's nephew Pietro Mauro took the title role (tenor) in two productions. The central theme is the hatred of Berenice, Queen of Cappadocia, for Farnace, King of Pontus, and his wife Tamiri (who happens to be Berenice's own daughter). With the help of Roman soldiers Berenice almost succeeds in destroying Farnace and his family but is deflected from her cruel purpose at the last moment by the return of her maternal affections.

Vivaldi's rich and varied score includes an aria featuring a long, unbroken pedal note on the two horns ('Nell'intimo del petto'), another aria evoking iciness in a manner recalling the Winter concerto from The Four Seasons ('Gelido in ogni vena'), and a superb vocal quartet ('Io crudel? Giusto rigore') in which the four characters are skilfully differentiated.

RECORDING   Dessì, Gamberucci, Rizzi, Angeloni, Dupuy, Garazioti, Malakova, O Sinfonica di San Remo, de Bernart, Arkadia, 1982
MANUSCRIPTS   Biblioteca Nazionale, Turin

Orlando

Dramma per musica in three acts, RV 728 (4h)
Libretto by Grazio Braccioli after the epic poem Orlando Furioso by Ludovico Ariosto (1516)
PREMIERES   Autumn 1727, Teatro Sant'Angelo, Venice; US: 28 November 1980, Civic Opera, Dallas, Texas
CAST   Orlando a, Alcina a, Medoro a, Angelica s, Ruggiero a or male a, Bradamante a, Astolfo t
ORCHESTRATION   fl, 2 hn, str, cont

This opera had an unusual genesis. In autumn 1713, newly installed as impresario at Sant'Angelo, Vivaldi presented Orlando furioso, a composition by the minor composer Giovanni Alberto Ristori on a libretto by Grazio Braccioli, who during this period served the theatre as a kind of house librettist. Ristori's score, to which Vivaldi himself added a few numbers, proved immensely successful, running for over 40 performances. The following autumn, a companion piece, Orlando finto pazzo, for which Vivaldi wrote all the music, was staged at Sant'Angelo; however, it was unsuccessful and was soon taken off, being replaced by a revised Orlando furioso (RV Anh. 84) to which Vivaldi added some fresh numbers. He returned to the libretto in 1727, producing an almost entirely new setting of Braccioli's drama, this time entitled simply Orlando.

The libretto is based very loosely on Ariosto. Braccioli classicizes the dramatic treatment by observing the Aristotelian unities of time, place and action; but the genre remains, as in the original, an extraordinary mixture of the pastoral, the heroic and the comic.

SYNOPSIS

To elucidate the extremely intricate plot, one may first quote from Braccioli's own foreword: 'At the beginning, middle and end stand the love, madness and recovery of Orlando. The amours of Bradamante and Ruggiero, Angelica and Medoro, the changing moods of Alcina and the diverse passions of Astolfo, serve to embellish this story and bring it to its conclusion.'

The events all take place on the island of the evil enchantress Alcina.

Act I   Orlando, madly in love with Angelica, is persuaded not to kill his rival Medoro only when convinced by Alcina that the latter is Angelica's brother.

Act II   Ruggiero's lover Bradamante releases him from the spell and eventually forgives him his involuntary infidelity. Angelica and Medoro trick

Orlando into falling into one of Alcina's magic traps and celebrate their marriage in his absence. Orlando escapes and is driven insane when confronted with the proof of their mutual love.

Act III After further outbursts, the paladin finally recovers his senses, destroys Alcina's magic kingdom and magnanimously pardons Angelica and Medoro.

Vivaldi was a highly competent composer of recitative, but in no other opera by him does recitative – which includes many orchestrally accompanied passages and arioso episodes – become such a prominent and impressive part of the dramatic experience. Orlando has two long, expressive monologues in Act II, first when he breaks out of the cave in which Alcina has imprisoned him, and later when he is infuriated by the protestations of love carved on treebark by Angelica and Medoro. In Act III we see him at the height of his delirium, by turns pathetic and destructively demonic. The work also boasts some notable arias. In Act I Orlando's 'Nel profondo cieco mondo' conveys the same sense of mystery as the opening of the flute concerto *La notte*, which it resembles thematically; and the aria 'Sol da te, mio dolce amore', in which Ruggiero sings of his love for Alcina, has a splendidly elaborate flute obbligato that is one of the first known instances of this instrument's use in a Venetian score.

RECORDING de los Angeles, Gonzales, Horne, Valentini Terrani, Kozma, Bruscantini, Zaccaria, I Solisti Veneti, Scimone, Erato, 1977
MANUSCRIPT Biblioteca Nazionale, Turin

La fida ninfa
The Faithful Nymph
Dramma per musica in three acts, RV 714 (rev. as *Il giorno felice*, RV 777)
Libretto by Scipione Maffei
PREMIERE 6 January 1732, Teatro Filarmonico, Verona

Vivaldi's setting of Maffei's celebrated libretto inaugurated Verona's magnificent Teatro Filarmonico. The action takes place on the island of Naxos. The faithful nymph of the title is Licori, who remains true to her childhood sweetheart Osmino despite the attentions of her captor, the pirate Oralto, and other tests of her fidelity arising from mistaken identity. The score includes a storm sinfonia related to the first movement of the violin concerto *La tempesta di mare*, and an elaborately contrapuntal

The interior of the Teatro Filarmonico, Verona, during a performance of La fida ninfa

terzet, 'S'egli è ver che sua rota', closely related to a movement in one of the composer's sacred compositions, the *Confitebor* (RV 596).

RECORDING Falachi, Repetto, Calma, Constantino, Giacomotti, Chamber O, Monterosso, Vox, 1964
EDITION f.s., Ateneo Cremonese, 1964

L'Olimpiade
The Olympiad
Dramma per musica in three acts, RV 725 (3h 30m)
Libretto by Pietro Metastasio
PREMIERE Carnival 1734, Teatro Sant'Angelo, Venice

L'Olimpiade was one of only two libretti by Metastasio that Vivaldi set (the other was *Catone in Utica*); in general the philosophical, high-minded tone of the Roman poet seems not to have appealed to him. The plot hinges on a typically Metastasian piece of dramatic irony: in order to repay a debt of gratitude Megacle has to compete in the Olympic Games under the feigned identity of his friend Licida so that the latter may gain the victor's prize, which is the hand of Princess Aristea – but this Aristea is none other than Megacle's sweetheart, whom he would earlier have married but for the opposition of her father Clistene. All contradictions are eventually resolved when Licida is revealed to be Aristea's twin brother, thought to have been abandoned at birth.

Vivaldi's score contains several numbers of great lyrical beauty, notably the duet for Megacle and Aristea closing Act I and the Act III aria 'Non so donde viene' for Clistene, in which the king, who has condemned Licida to death, senses the latter's consanguinity; this aria is in a modified *da capo* form that anticipates formal developments in the second half of the century in a remarkable way.

RECORDING Kovács, Zempléni, Takács, Horváth, Káplán, Gáti, Miller, Budapest Madrigalists, Hungarian State O, Szekeres, Hungaroton, 1977
EDITION f.s., Ricordi, forthcoming

La Griselda
Griselda
Dramma per musica in three acts, RV 718
Libretto by Apostolo Zeno, revised by Carlo Goldoni, after *Il decamerone* by Boccaccio
PREMIERES May 1735, Teatro San Samuele, Venice; UK: 1 July 1983, Buxton

The particular fame of this opera arises from the fact that it involved a collaboration with Goldoni that is vividly recalled in the dramatist's published memoirs. It took all Goldoni's tact and patience to convince Vivaldi that he was no tyro in the art of revising old libretti for the convenience of singers, but a fluent exponent of this dubious practice. The essence of the operation was to devise new texts for the arias of Anna Girò (in the title role) that would allow her to show off her acting abilities but conceal her vocal deficiencies. The two men finally reached a perfect understanding, and the opera was a great success.

Zeno based his drama on a tale that was later taken up by several authors. Griselda is the humble-born wife of Gualtiero, King of Thessaly. To placate his subjects, angered by the misalliance, the king has secretly sent away his daughter Costanza, believed dead by everyone else, to be brought up at a foreign court. In order to demonstrate Griselda's fidelity and obedience Gualtiero pretends to repudiate her and declares his intention to marry Costanza. The queen emerges from this and other trials as a woman of almost superhuman loyalty and endurance, for which she is finally rewarded by her subjects' devotion.

La Griselda exemplifies the finely nuanced but rather heterogeneous style of Vivaldi's late operas. Outside their ritornellos the instruments rarely come into prominence, but in compensation the vocal lines have acquired greater presence. The musical characterization still aims to express affections of an abstract, general nature rather than unique personal qualities, but within that convention it is skilfully realized. Act II contains a very fine trio for Griselda, Gualtiero and Costanza, 'Non più regina ma pastorella'.

EDITION facsimile of the partly autograph score, Garland, 1978

Other operas: *Orlando finto pazzo*, 1714; *Arsilda regina di Ponto*, 1716; *Armida al campo d'Egitto* (Act II missing), 1718, as *Gl'inganni per vendetta*, 1720; *Il Teuzzone*, 1719; *La verità in cimento*, 1720; *Ercole su'l Termodonte*, 1723; *La virtù trionfante dell'amore e dell'odio, overo Il Tigrane* (Act II only; coll.), 1724; *Dorilla in Tempe*, 1726; *L'Atenaide*, 1728; *Bajazet (Tamerlano)* (coll.), 1735; *Catone in Utica* (Act I missing), 1737; *Rosmira* (pasticcio), 1738
Surviving short dramatic works: *Mio cor, povero cor* (serenata a tre), c. 1719; *Dall'eccelsa mia reggia*, 1725; *La Senna festeggiante*, c. 1726; 27 lost operatic works
BIBLIOGRAPHY M. Collins and E. K. Kirk (eds), *Opera and Vivaldi*, University of Texas Press, 1984; E. Cross, *The Late Operas of Antonio Vivaldi, 1727–1738*, UMI Research Press, 1981; Michael Talbot, *Vivaldi*, Dent, 1978, rev. edns, 1984, 1993

M.T.

AMADEO VIVES
b 18 November 1871, Collbató, Spain; *d* 1 December 1932, Madrid

Vives began his career as a successful choir trainer and a convent organist, but he is best remembered as the composer of almost 100 tuneful and amusing zarzuelas, of which *Doña Francisquita* (1923), based on Lope de Vega, was the most popular, commanding over 5000 performances in the 20 years after its premiere. His opera *Artus* (1897), based on Arthurian legend, is typical of the 'heroic' operatic subjects chosen by Vives before he finally decided to turn to the more accessible and more lucrative form of zarzuela. *Artus* had but fleeting success. Vives's deft orchestrations and informed literary tastes raise the level of his works well above those of his contemporaries, such as Jimenez and Valverde, whose music rivalled his at the time.

Operatic works: *L'emigrant*, 1894; *Artus*, 1897; *Don Lucas del Cigarral*, 1899; *La preciosilla*, 1899; *La luz verde*, 1899; *La fruta del tiempo*, 1899; *El rey de la Alpujarra*, 1899; *Campanas y cornetas*, 1900; *El escalo*, 1900; *Viaje de instrucción*, 1900; *La balada de la luz*, 1900; *Euda d'Uriac*, 1900; *Polvorilla*, 1900; *La buenaventura*, 1901; *A estudiar a Salamanca*, 1901; *Doloretes*, 1901; *El coco*, 1901; *La nube*, 1902; *El tirador de palomas*, 1902; *Sueño de invierno*, 1902; *El curita*, 1902; *La caprichosa*, 1902; *Lola Montes*, 1902; *El ramo de azahar*, 1903; *Su Alteza Imperial*, 1903; *El parador de las Golondrinas*, 1903; *Patria nueva*, 1903; *La vendimia*, 1904; *Bohemios*, 1904 (RECORDING Hispavox, 1966); *El húsar de la guardia*, 1904 (RECORDING Alhambra, 1971); *La familia de son Saturio, o el Salvador y los Evangelistas*, 1904; *El cochero*, 1905; *Sangre roja*, 1905; *La máscara duende*, 1905; *El dinero y el trabajo*, 1905; *El príncipe ruso*, 1905; *La favorita del rey*, 1905; *El arte de ser bonita*, 1905; *Las granadinas*, 1905; *El amigo del alma*, 1905; *La gatita blanca*, 1905; *Libertad*, 1905; *La Marcha Real*, 1906; *El golpe de Estado*, 1906; *La Machaquito*, 1906; *El guante amarillo*, 1906; *El diablo verde*, 1906; *Sangre torera*, 1906; *La chipén*, 1907; *Las tres cosas de Jerez*, 1907; *La rabalera*, 1907; *Pepe Botellas*, 1908; *Episodios nacionales*, 1908; *El talismán prodigioso*, 1908; *El becerro de oro*, 1909; *Viva la libertad!*, 1909; *A la vera der queré*, 1909; *La viuda mucho más alegre*, 1909; *Abreme la puerta*, 1909; *La muela del rey Farfán*, 1909; *Colomba*, 1910; *Juegos malabares*, 1910; *Así son todas*, 1910; *La fresa*, 1910; *La reina Mimí*, 1910; *El alma del querer*, 1910; *Gloria in excelsis*, 1910; *El palacio de los duendes*, 1910; *La casa de los enredos*, 1911; *Los viajes de Gulliver*, 1911; *Agua de noria*, 1911; *La canción española*, 1911; *La gallina de los huevos de oro*, 1911; *Anita la risueña*, 1911; *La generala*, 1912 (RECORDING Zafiro, c. 1976); *La veda del amor*, 1912; *El pretendiente*, 1913; *El gran simpático*, 1913; *Miss Australia*, 1914; *Maruxa*, 1914 (RECORDING Alhambra, 1974); *La cena de los húsares*, 1915; *Canciones epigramáticas*, 1915; *La ley del embudo*, 1916; *Los pendientes de la Trini o no hay mal que por bien no venga*, 1916; *La guitarra del amor*, 1916; *El señor Pandolfo*, 1916; *La mujer de Boliché*, 1917; *El tesoro*, 1917; *Todo el mundo en contra mía*, 1918; *Trianerías*, 1919; *Las Verónicas*, 1919; *Balada de carnaval*, 1919; *Pepe Conde o el mentir de las estrellas*, 1920; *El duquesito*, 1920; *El parque de Sevilla*, 1921; *El sinvergüenza en Palacio*, 1921; *El ministro Giroflar*, 1922; *Doña Francisquita*, 1923 (RECORDING Alhambra, c. 1953); *Sofía*, 1923; *Cuatro sardanas*, 1926; *La villana*, 1927 (RECORDING Alhambra, 1973); *L'entusiasme es la sal de l'ánima*, 1928; *Follies i paisatges*, 1928; *Los flamencos*, 1928; *Jo no sabía que el món era eixi*, 1929; *Noche de verbena*, 1929; *Talismán*, 1932; *El abanico* (inc.)

BIBLIOGRAPHY Angel Sagardia, *Amadeo Vives: vida y obra*, Editora Nacional, 1971

S.J.W.

CLAUDE VIVIER

b 14 April 1940, Montreal, Canada; *d* 7 March 1983, Paris

Vivier studied at the Montreal Conservatory with Gilles Tremblay (1967–70), and electronic music with Stockhausen in Cologne. He also undertook studies in non-Western music, travelling to the Far East in 1976. His only completed opera was the music drama *Kopernikus* (1980), subtitled *Rituel de mort*. Scored for seven soloists, instrumental

ensemble and tape, it reflects Vivier's obsession with death – treated often in his other works – as it follows the journey of a dead soul through the Kingdom of the Shades. References to Hinduism and Christianity, and use of invented language, create a multi-layered work with mystic resonances.

Vivier was in Paris working on a second opera on the death of Tchaikovsky, *Crois-tu en l'immortalité de l'âme*, when he was murdered in his apartment.

BIBLIOGRAPHY Max Loppert, review of *Kopernikus*, *Opera*, vol. 36 (1985), p. 1084

M.A.

GEORG JOSEPH VOGLER

Georg Joseph Vogler (Abbé Vogler); *b* 15 June 1749, Pleinach, nr Würzburg; *d* 6 May 1814, Darmstadt

Vogler studied at Würzburg and Bamberg, and was appointed first as almoner and then as chaplain at the court of the Elector Palatine, Carl Theodor, in Mannheim. Subsequently he was enabled to visit Italy for study with such teachers as Padre Martini in Bologna and Padre Francesco Vallotti in Padua. On his return to Mannheim, in 1775, he founded the important Mannheim Tonschule, and began an active career as teacher, historian, theorist, musicologist and composer. Most notable among his pupils at Darmstadt, where he became hofkapellmeister (1807), were Carl Maria von Weber and Giacomo Meyerbeer. As a teacher he was influential; as a composer immensely productive, but his music lacked the individuality necessary to ensure its survival. His numerous compositions for the stage include operas, melodramas and singspiels, to Italian, French, Swedish and German texts, and an overture and incidental music for *Hamlet*.

Gustav Adolph och Ebba Brahe

Gustavus Adolphus and Ebba Brahe
Lyric drama in three acts
Libretto by Johan Henrik Kellgren
PREMIERE 24 January 1788, Stockholm

Following his appointment in 1786 as kapellmeister to Gustavus III, King of Sweden (nominally for a period of 11 years, though European travel occupied much of his time), Vogler produced two stage works in Stockholm: music for a performance of Racine's *Athalie*, and this full-length patriotic opera to a Swedish text, which continued the tradition established by J. G. Naumann with his lyric tragedy *Gustav Wasa* (performed at Stockholm in January 1786). Ebba Brahe was one of the ladies at the court of Gustavus Adolphus.

RECORDING Andersson, Hallin, Blanc, R. Björling, Johansson, Ch and O of Royal Opera, Stockholm, Farncombe, MRF, 1973
EDITION *Monumenta musicae Svecicae*, vol. 7, Stockholm Nordiska, 1973

Other stage works: *Der Kaufmann von Smyrna*, 1771; *Lampedo*, 1779; *Erwin und Elmire*, 1781; *Albert der Dritte von Bayern*, 1781; *Le patriotisme*, 1783; *Le kermesse, ou La fête flamande*, 1783; *Athalie*, 1786; *Castore e Polluce*, 1787; *Zoroastre*, c. 1796; *Samori*, 1804; *Epimenides*, (c. 1806); *Der Admiral*, 1811

BIBLIOGRAPHY   W. Reckziegel: 'Georg Joseph Vogler', in *MGG*; H. Schweiger, 'Abt Vogler', *MQ*, vol. 25 (1939), p. 156

B.S.

RICHARD WAGNER

Wilhelm Richard Wagner; *b* 22 May 1813, Leipzig;
d 13 February 1883, Venice

Wagner is a major figure in the history of opera and
one of the most controversial (and written about)
figures of the 19th century. Late photographs of him
show an expensively dressed man wearing a velvet
beret whose calm and stately expression is that of a
prince among artists. The carefully nurtured image of
the distinguished 'reformer', however, disguises his
mercurial nature and nervous disposition (though
they were noticed by Renoir in a startling portrait
sketched as late as 1882) and above all gives the lie to
a turbulent career marked almost from the start by
radical ideas and actions.

No detail of Wagner's life was too sordid to be
aired in public in the 19th century (his liking for silk
underwear and supposedly homosexual relations
with his patron Ludwig II of Bavaria were two
favourites). Yet this lurid fascination would have
been unthinkable without the two things that will
always be most important about him: the power of
his music and the ambitious artistic claim he made
for opera. In a sense, he marks a return to the noble
spirit of court opera in the 17th century – opera, that
is, as a festive, unique and spectacular event. Seen in
this light, his sheer good luck in finding in Ludwig II
a modern royal patron prepared to sponsor him on
a reasonably lavish scale seems only logical given
the nature of the Wagnerian enterprise. Through
the agency of history and myth and the universal
humanity he saw in them, the 'extraordinary' operatic occasion, as opposed to the day-to-day opera
routinely organized in the public sphere according
to market demands, was to be a celebration not
so much of royal dynasties as of a notion of art
as redemption and catharsis addressed to the entire
human race. Drama on the highest level and music
aspiring to the condition of the symphony combined
with a passion for allegory in a bid to reconcile
the modern age of science with some highly ambivalent feelings about it. In other words, a performance of a Wagner 'drama' (posterity is still
oblivious to the fact that he rejected the term 'music
drama') was not just a special occasion transcending
the everyday commercial success of 'modern' opera
by, for example, Rossini or Meyerbeer. It was also
intended as a drastic form of cultural therapy.

Wagner's worldly polemics (which he set down in
16 substantial volumes of prose works) look clumsy
now next to the unshakeable distinction of his art.
His defence of the *Gesamtkunstwerk* – a utopian idea
adapted from Herder and the early Romantics
proposing the inherent unity of all the arts – and his
crusade against opera-as-a-business and the decline
of German culture pale before the intoxicating
effects of his music and his daring modernity. That
he discovered the world of dreams and the unconscious long before Freud, or that he is 'indisputably
the father of the structural analysis of myth' (Lévi-
Strauss), are claims that have long since been
inscribed in tablets of stone in some areas of
modernist lore. The German philosopher Adorno
even spoke of 'the birth of film out of the spirit of
[Wagner's] music', though the remark was intended
more as a polemical paradox than as a compliment.
(Adorno meant that the seamless musical continuity
of Wagner's works, each seductively flaunting their
unique identity and the artistic individuality of their
creator, had actually anticipated a technological art
and subtle means of persuasion that is essentially
anonymous and mass produced.)

Wagner's influence both on the development of
opera and on purely instrumental music is immense.
He began writing operas in the early 1830s. The
bloated dimensions of his early efforts (which are
often explained away as youthful inexperience) are
already a sign of an attempt to push opera to its
limits. The decisive breakthrough came with the huge
local success of *Rienzi* in Dresden in 1842 (in a
heavily cut version), though it was Wagner's fourth
opera, *Der fliegende Holländer*, first performed to
less enthusiastic audiences a few months later in the
same city, that marked his break with provincialism
and the real beginning of his distinctive style.

Wagner's greatest musical hero was unquestionably Beethoven, and especially the Beethoven
of the symphonies. Wagner emulated him in parts
of his operas up to *Lohengrin* (and in many early
instrumental works now mercifully forgotten), but
developed a large-scale quasi-symphonic style of
his own only by the time he began work on the music
of the *Ring*. The symphonic element in Wagner's
operas is said to have ensured their international
success because it was 'the essence of what had been

An engraving of the interior of the Bayreuth Opera House

expected of German music since the time of Haydn and Beethoven' (Carl Dahlhaus). But arguably the much vaunted symphonic 'unity' of Wagner's famous system of leitmotifs was less crucial than the way has leitmotifs imprinted themselves on the memory (Adorno likened them to advertising jingles). Indeed, his uncanny sense of musical metaphor, which he refined through an intense study of early Romantic lieder and then applied on a much larger and hence more public scale in his stage works, probably did more than anything else to establish his enormous fame by attracting ears previously deaf to opera and the classical style.

One of Wagner's principal aims was to make music come of age, so to speak, by proceeding from the notion of the sublime (as opposed to the beautiful) and by fusing music in an unprecedented way with literary and philosophical ideas. For Wagner this meant nothing less than the end of opera with its schematic sequence of set pieces (during the first stages of writing the *Ring* he declared publicly that he was going to write 'no more operas') and a widening of tonality and thematic continuity. To put it another way, Wagner found a cogent justification for taking music beyond its perceived limits of expression by cutting opera loose from its traditional moorings. Whatever the validity of his rationale now, the historical impact of the music that resulted from it is undeniable. He was able to organize vast tracts of continuously flowing music in which swift changes

in stylistic level and syntax were possible – a bold adventure in harmony and large-scale structure that left an indelible mark on the late 19th-century symphony. On a subjective level, his musical innovations led to new extremes of sensibility, and for many a dangerous feeling of disorientation that Nietzsche likened to the sense of losing one's depth in a large ocean. Others have simply compared his music to a drug.

In almost every respect Wagner's most radical work is *Tristan und Isolde*. Based on a medieval source noted for its vivid depiction of existential love and 'eternal death', and overlaid with a provocative interpretation of Schopenhauer's 'Metaphysics of Sexual Love', it was a *cause célèbre* by the end of the 19th century mainly on account of the explicit eroticism of its music. It is still Wagner's most incandescent work, standing on the threshold of musical modernity with its daring harmonies and open-ended musical syntax. At the same time its stubborn individuality and hot-house aestheticism – the sensual yearning for death and nothingness that has prompted its critics to accuse Wagner of cultural exhaustion and a pernicious nihilism – are at odds with Wagner's ideal of opera as a unique and revitalizing communal experience. Not surprisingly Wagner retreated from the extreme position of *Tristan*. Schopenhauer's negation of the will and denial of life (or rather Wagner's version of them) are transformed in subsequent works into a more conciliatory and beguiling form of world-sorrow by the inclusion of more obviously humanistic themes such as the popularity of art and the principle of nation (*Die Meistersinger*) and the conquering of sensuality by a divine moral code (*Parsifal*). Wagner's music became more accessible after *Tristan* too, but paradoxically also much richer and more refined than before.

Wagner was an outstanding performer and producer of his own works as well as those of others, including Gluck, Mozart and Beethoven. He influenced a whole generation in the art of conducting. But perhaps the most significant thing he did, apart from composing several masterpieces, was to organize the building of the Bayreuth Festival Theatre. It was constructed according to his specifications with an auditorium in the form of an amphitheatre (the opposite of the hierarchical seating arrangement in the Court Theatres with their tiers of boxes), a sunken and invisible orchestra, and a double proscenium which creates an illusion of perspective concentrating attention on to the stage image. It was an experiment in what Wagner called 'public art' that attempted to evade the then prevailing social and commercial conditions of opera in order to turn each performance of his works into something 'special' and available to all. From the first it could never be entirely independent of the conditions it sought to escape, as Wagner himself came to realize. But it still stands as a monument to that ideal.

Wagner's description of vocal parts is sometimes confusing and frequently inconsistent. Wotan in *Die Walküre* is a 'high bass', for instance, although now he would be called a 'bass baritone' or even a 'heroic baritone'. Alberich, Fasolt and Gunther in the *Ring* are also each described as a 'high bass'. This does not mean of course that they are to be cast with the same kind of voice. Wagner's descriptions usually refer to the vocal range, as opposed to the character, of a role. In *Siegfried* the Wanderer (Wotan) is thus a straightforward bass, as the tessitura of the part is lower than the Wotan in *Die Walküre*. In the following entries the voice specifications used by Wagner in his manuscript scores and first printed editions have been retained without further comment.

Die Feen

The Fairies

Grand romantic opera in three acts (3h)
Libretto by the composer, after the play *La donna serpente* by Carlo Gozzi (1762)
Composed 1833–4, rev. 1834
PREMIERES 10 January 1835, Magdeburg (overture; concert); 29 June 1888, Royal Court and National Theatre, Munich; UK: 17 May 1969, Birmingham (Midland Music Makers)
CAST King of the Fairies *b*, Ada *s*, Zemina and Farzana 2 *s*, Arindal *t*, Lora *s*, Morald *bar*, Gernot *b*, Drolla *s*, Gunther *t*, Harald *b*, voice of Groma *b*, a messenger *t*, Arindal's and Ada's 2 children *silent; satb* chorus of fairies, Morald's companions, men and women, soldiers, earth spirits, men of iron, Groma's invisible spirits
FULL ORCHESTRA onstage: 10 players including 4 trbn

Wagner tried his hand at opera twice before embarking on *Die Feen*. In 1830 he began a *Schäferoper* (pastorale) modelled on Goethe's singspiel *Die Laune des Verliebten* and in 1832 he started composing *Die Hochzeit* based on J. G. G. Büsching's book about medieval chivalry, *Ritterzeit und Ritterwesen* (1823). *Die Feen* was the first opera he actually completed. It was inspired by one of Carlo Gozzi's theatrical fairy-tales, *La donna serpente*, and also absorbed something of the chivalric atmosphere of *Die Hochzeit*, as well as including the names of four of its characters. The mixture of legend and medieval manners with oriental atmosphere and *commedia dell'arte* in Gozzi's fiabe teatrali (some of which Busoni, Prokofiev, Puccini and Henze also later drew on) is the first sign of Wagner's eclectic and little-noticed cosmopolitan view of opera and its possible sources. The strange amalgam of myth, history and fairy-tale is a striking premonition of Wagner's future works, especially *Lohengrin* and the *Ring*.

SYNOPSIS

Act I Ada, daughter of the king of the fairies, has fallen in love with Arindal, a mortal king. She is prepared to sacrifice her immortality, but only on condition that for eight years Arindal refrain from asking who she is. The eight years have nearly elapsed when Arindal succumbs to temptation. He loses Ada and is transported back to the mortal world where he is found by two knights, Gunther and Morald. They tell him that his kingdom is besieged and persuade him to return to lead the battle against the invaders. Arindal swears that he will never curse Ada whatever the circumstances.

Act II In order to join Arindal in the mortal world Ada is forced to put him to a terrible test. She appears to throw their children into a fire and to let it be known that she has led the battle against Arindal's people. Arindal curses her, not realizing that he has fallen prey to an illusion. Ada is turned into stone for a hundred years.

Act III Filled with remorse, Arindal wins Ada back with the help of a shield, a sword and a lyre given to him by Groma, a friendly magician. To the accompaniment of the lyre, Arindal sings a passionate song which melts the stone and Ada is reunited forever with Arindal who, through the power of music and love, has himself become immortal.

Looking back on his early works, the mature Wagner once pointed out that he changed the outcome of the Gozzi fable, in which the hero and heroine remain in the mortal world, to create a new ending more in keeping with the notion of redemption that dominates his later works. He also said several times that his models for *Die Feen* were Beethoven, Weber and Marschner, although there are French and Italian elements in the work as well, not to say borrowings from Mozart and Schikaneder's *Die Zauberflöte*. In reality Wagner's first 'grand romantic opera' is a compendium of the dominant operatic genres of the day (grand opera, opéra comique, opera seria and semiseria) but taken to an unusual extreme that is again a foretaste of his mature music dramas. He revised the opera in 1834 for a production planned for Leipzig which never took place. (Among other things he completely rewrote Ada's scene and aria in Act II and replaced several scenes with spoken dialogue.) Apart from the overture, *Die Feen* was not performed in Wagner's lifetime. The success of the posthumous premiere in Munich in 1888 was considerable, due in no small measure to the spectacular scenic effects created by Karl Lautenschläger.

RECORDING   Gray, Studer, Laki, Alexander, Hermann, Moll, Ch and SO, Bavarian Radio/Sawallisch, Orfeo, 1984
EDITIONS   f.ss., M. Balling (ed.), critical edn, Breitkopf und Härtel, 1912; critical edn, B. Schott's Söhne, in preparation; v.s., K. Ferd. Heckel, 1888

Das Liebesverbot, oder Die Novize von Palermo

The Ban on Love, or The Novice of Palermo
Grand comic opera in two acts
Libretto by the composer, after the play *Measure for Measure* by William Shakespeare (1604)
Composed: libretto 1834; music 1835–6
PREMIERES   6 April 1835, Civic Theatre, Magdeburg (Nos 3 and 4 only); 29 March 1836, Civic Theatre, Magdeburg; UK: 15 February 1965, University College, London
CAST   Friedrich *b*, Luzio *t*, Claudio *t*, Antonio *t*, Angelo *b*, Isabella *s*, Mariana *s*, Brighella *b buffo*, Danieli *b*, Dorella *s*, Pontio Pilato *t buffo*; *satb* chorus of nuns, supreme justices, guards, residents of Palermo, people, masked figures; band of musicians
FULL ORCHESTRA including ophicleide; onstage: bells, military band

Das Liebesverbot was Wagner's least favourite early opera. Yet in many ways it is his most significant. As a rebellion against the Biedermeier restoration and everything German, the opera is a self-conscious 'coming of age' that celebrates opéra comique, opera semiseria, Italian melody, boisterous freedom, lightness and clarity – in short, every non-German characteristic that Wagner (who was just 21 when he began the opera) could think of. In its sheer thoroughness, the deliberate reversal of Germanness in *Das Liebesverbot* is not without a certain heavy-handed quality that betrays its origin in the Young German movement of the 1830s. The paradoxical strategy smacks of the reaction against Hegel fashionable among the intellectuals of Wagner's generation who used Hegelian methods to promote ideas that Hegel would never have taken seriously. The glorification of instinct over reason, the rejection of property and the vilification of abstract thought are just three items of the anti-Hegelian agenda behind the apparent frivolity of *Das Liebesverbot* that left their mark on later works such as the *Ring*.

Wagner moved the action from the Vienna of Shakespeare's *Measure for Measure* to the headier atmosphere of Palermo. Instead of weighing human hypocrisy on the scales of justice as in the play, he introduced a comedy of intrigue and a licentious carnival that gives free rein to the senses, as opposed to the law of the state which represses them.

SYNOPSIS
Act I   A German called Friedrich rules temporarily as viceroy of Sicily in the absence of the king. He forbids all pleasure and has even banished his own wife Mariana to a convent. In private he craves for Isabella, another novice in the convent, who pretends to agree to sleep with him if he releases her brother Claudio, imprisoned for resisting the 'ban on love'.

Act II   At their rendezvous, Friedrich discovers his wife behind the carnival mask instead of Isabella (a situation borrowed from Mozart's and Da Ponte's *Le nozze di Figaro*, though the idea in another form had its origin in Shakespeare's play as well). In the presence of those he has persecuted, Friedrich is doubly exposed as an unfaithful husband and a hypocrite who cannot even obey the laws he has himself decreed.

After offering the opera to Leipzig, Berlin (Königstädter Theatre) and the Opéra-Comique in Paris, Wagner decided to take the more modest option of a premiere in Magdeburg, where he was then employed as a conductor. Two performances on 29 and 30 March 1836 were announced, the second of which had to be cancelled at the last minute because of a fist-fight between some of the singers. With Meyerbeer's help, Wagner attempted to arrange for the opera to be performed in Paris, and translated the libretto into French himself. Having repeatedly failed to secure a performance, he finally gave up his plans for the opera. *Das Liebesverbot* was not performed again in Wagner's lifetime. Wagner gave the manuscript of the full score to Ludwig II of Bavaria in 1866 with a dedication describing it as a 'sin of my youth'. From 1939 to 1945 the document was in the possession of Adolf Hitler. Its whereabouts now are unknown.

RECORDING   Warncke, Watts, Soffel, Lorig, Gelling, Ch and O of Bayreuth International Youth Festival, Bell, Mixtur, 1972
EDITIONS   f.ss., Breitkopf und Härtel, 1923; critical edn, B. Schott's Söhne, in preparation; v.s., Breitkopf und Härtel, 1923

Rienzi, der Letzte der Tribunen

Rienzi, the Last of the Tribunes
Grand tragic opera in five acts (4h 45m)
Libretto by the composer, after the novel *Rienzi, the Last of the Roman Tribunes* by Edward Bulwer-Lytton (1834)
Composed: libretto 1837–8, French translation 1839–40; music 1838–40
PREMIERES   20 October 1842, Royal Saxon Court Theatre, Dresden; US: 4 March 1878, Academy of Music, New York; UK: 27 January 1879, Her Majesty's Theatre, Haymarket, London
CAST   Cola Rienzi *t*, Irene *s*, Steffano Colonna *b*, Adriano *s*, Paolo Orsini *b*, Raimondo *b*, Baroncelli *t*, Cecco del Vecchio *b*, messenger of peace *s*, herald *t*, ambassador of Milan *b*, ambassadors of the Lombard cities *t*, *b*, ambassador of Naples *t*, ambassadors of Bohemia and Bavaria 2 *b*; *satb* chorus of Roman nobles and guardsmen, followers of the Colonna and Orsini families, priests and monks of all religious orders, senators, Roman men and women,

messengers of peace; pantomime (Act II): Collatinus, Lucretia, Virginia, Lucretia's virgins, Tarquinius, Tarquinius' warriors, Brutus, friends of Collatinus, young Romans, knights, the goddess of peace
ORCHESTRATION 3 fl/picc, 2 ob, 3 cl, 3 bsn, serpent, 4 hn, 4 tpt, 3 trbn, ophicleide, timp, bd, sd, tenor d, cym, triangle, t-t, hp, str; onstage: tpt, organ, bells; military bands (Act III): 12 tpt, 6 trbn, 4 ophicleide, 10 sd, 4 tenor d

According to Wagner's autobiography, he first had the idea for *Rienzi* in the summer of 1837 when, at an almost disastrously low point in his relations with his first wife Minna, he read Bulwer-Lytton's novel *Rienzi, the Last of the Roman Tribunes* (1834; German translation, 1836). In contemporary letters and an account of his life written in the early 1840s, however, he refers to a 'favourite idea' he had 'already been considering'. Before he read the novel, therefore, he could already have been acquainted with the subject from a different source. The version Wagner is most likely to have known is Mary Mitford's successful 'tragedy' *Rienzi* (1828). Unlike Bulwer, Mitford condensed Rienzi's two careers as tribune and senator into one, just as Wagner was to do in his opera. Other similarities, too, suggest that Wagner may have been acquainted with the play, though there is no doubt that Bulwer's more epic account was his main source.

The earliest known document for the opera (which in its complete form turned out to be Wagner's longest work) is a short prose sketch written in the summer of 1837 in Blasewitz or Travemünde outlining the entire action in just thirteen lines. Serious work on the project did not begin until June 1838 in Riga. By April 1839 the full score of Act I and a draft of Act II were finished. Now reunited with his wife, Wagner undertook with her a perilous and illegal journey without passports to escape from creditors via Norway to England, and eventually to Paris. He finished the full score of Act II on 12 September 1839 in Boulogne-sur-Mer, where he also met Meyerbeer for the first time. After a break of a few months, during which he tried unsuccessfully to gain a foothold in Paris with a number of works (including an aria for the High Priest to be inserted in Bellini's *Norma* and the first version of his *Faust* overture), he began composing Act III in February 1840. By November of the same year the full score of the entire opera was complete.

Contrary to a widely held belief, Wagner did not conceive *Rienzi* solely with a Paris production in mind. A letter of November 1838 to August Lewald clearly states his intention of producing the opera 'in German', preferably at the Court Opera in Berlin. Paris was not excluded as a possibility from the start; but only after Wagner's decision to flee Riga in 1839 did it become his principal goal. He translated the libretto into French himself. During 1840, however, as the prospect of a Paris premiere grew increasingly dim, he quickly reverted to his original idea of a performance in Germany, not even bothering to adjust the French translation to changes in the libretto made during the composition of the last three acts. With the help of a recommendation from Meyerbeer and the active support of friends in

Saxony, the opera was accepted for performance by the Dresden Royal Court Opera in June 1841. The premiere was conducted by Wagner in Gottfried Semper's new opera house on 20 October 1842 with Joseph Tichatschek as Rienzi and Wilhelmine Schröder-Devrient in the *travesti* role of Adriano. Despite the length of the performance (it lasted until past midnight) the occasion was one of the greatest public triumphs of Wagner's entire career, surpassed not even by the success of *Die Meistersinger* in 1868.

SYNOPSIS
Act I Rome in the mid-14th century. The Pope has fled to Avignon. His departure has fanned the flames of a feud between the noble houses of Orsini and Colonna. Anarchy prevails. It is night. Paolo Orsini and his followers try to abduct Irene, the sister of Rienzi. They are interrupted by the Colonnas. Adriano, the son of Steffano Colonna, frees Irene, but without managing to separate the warring factions. Only at the entrance of Rienzi is order restored. The nobles, intimidated by Rienzi's charisma, unwillingly agree to retire to continue their fight outside the city gates. Baroncelli and Cecco, representing the people, urge Rienzi to seize power. Assured of the support of Raimondo, the papal legate, Rienzi promises to act, urging the populace to gather at dawn when they hear the signal of revolution (already heard at the beginning of the overture): a long-held note played on a single trumpet. Adriano sharply criticizes Rienzi's political methods. But his heart has been softened by his love for Irene and Rienzi has little trouble in winning him over. In full armour in front of the Lateran Church, Rienzi proclaims the freedom of Rome ('Erstehe, hohe Roma, neu!'), but refuses to be made king. Shrewdly, he accepts the more modest, and in the long run more popular, title of tribune.

Act II A large hall in the Capitol. Rienzi has defeated the nobles who appear to submit to his command. In reality they are secretly planning to kill him. Adriano overhears the plot and threatens to betray them. Betrayal would be tantamount to patricide, Steffano Colonna retorts, since he, as leader of the conspiracy, would certainly be executed if it failed. After an inner struggle, Adriano decides to warn Rienzi. Peace celebrations are in progress. Towards the end of a pantomime presenting the rape of Lucretia (an allegorical mirror of the 'rape' of Rome by the nobles) Orsini tries to stab Rienzi, but his dagger cannot penetrate the chain-mail vest Rienzi is wearing under his robe for protection. The conspirators are condemned to death. Adriano and Irene beseech Rienzi to pardon them. To everyone's surprise, he yields to their demands on condition that the nobles swear a new oath of allegiance to the law of Rome. Rienzi manages to convince his bewildered followers of his magnanimity. In a jubilant chorus ('Rienzi, dir sei Preis'), they praise him once more as a hero of peace.

Act III A square in the old Forum. The nobles have broken their oath and are gathering forces outside the city for a march against Rienzi. The people are outraged. Rienzi inspires them to rise up without mercy against the traitors. Adriano is torn between his allegiance to Rienzi and loyalty to his father and expresses the hope that the two will be reconciled ('Gerechter Gott, so ist's entschieden schon'). Rienzi enters on horseback to intone the battle hymn 'Santo spirito cavaliere'. Adriano tries to intercept him, but in vain. The warriors march out accompanied by the priests, while the women, Irene and Adriano remain behind, calling on the Holy Virgin to protect the sons of Rome. The warriors, sadly depleted, return victorious. Among the enemy dead carried in is Steffano Colonna. Adriano throws himself on to his father's body swearing revenge against Rienzi. The people uneasily acclaim Rienzi victor and liberator.

Act IV The square in front of the Lateran Church. In disguise, Adriano has called Baroncelli, Cecco and their followers to a secret council. Baroncelli accuses Rienzi of complicity with the nobles. When the others demand proof, Adriano reveals his true identity and offers himself as a witness. All resolve to kill Rienzi. Intimidated by the power of the church, the new conspirators have to be goaded on by Adriano to stand in front of the Lateran to await the arrival of their victim. Rienzi arrives at the head of a procession. The conspirators try to block his way. Noticing their uncertainty, he chides them for their lack of idealism. Crushed with embarrassment (to the annoyance of Adriano), they are about to give way to Rienzi when Raimondo and the priests come forward to announce that he has been excommunicated. Rienzi is abandoned by everyone except Irene, who remains in a long embrace with her brother.

Act V A hall in the Capitol. Rienzi fervently implores God not to jeopardize his mission ('Allmächt'ger Vater, blick' herab'). Irene is ready to stand by her brother to the death. Not even Adriano can shake her resolve. A square in front of the Capitol. The people are setting the Capitol on fire. Rienzi delivers a terrible curse on Rome and its citizens, declaring them to be degenerate (*entartet*) and unworthy of his ideals. He remains in an embrace with Irene on the balcony. As Adriano enters the burning Capitol, the tower with the balcony collapses, burying all three. The nobles are seen returning to begin a violent attack on the people.

Charles Rosen has called *Rienzi* 'Meyerbeer's worst opera'. The clever reversal of Hans von Bülow's *bonmot* (he sardonically referred to the opera as Meyerbeer's best) is wide of the mark, both in terms of the quality of *Rienzi* and its historical significance. For one thing the opera owes more to Spontini and the Auber of *La muette de Portici* than it does to Meyerbeer. Wagner's revolutionary hero is also not unrelated to Rossini's *Guillaume Tell* – a grand opera that continued to exert an influence on Wagner (which he never properly acknowledged) long after he had repudiated the genre. For another thing Wagner's declared ambition to 'outdo' grand opera included such a reckless appropriation of other styles ranging from the operas of Bellini and Weber to

The final scene of Act IV of Rienzi *(Leipziger Illustrirte Zeitung, August 1843)*

Beethoven's symphonies that to call *Rienzi* a grand opera at all is to ignore its peculiarities and unique historical position. Not only is *Rienzi* the first of a notable line of Wagnerian heroes portraying the lonely idealist and would-be saviour of humanity, the utopian dimensions and diverse style of the opera also clearly point to (even if they do not match) the daring large-scale vision and wide-ranging musical ambition of Wagner's mature dramas.

Despite the overwhelming success of the Dresden premiere, *Rienzi* was taken up only slowly by other theatres. Wagner began to make cuts before the premiere and with the five following performances (until the end of November 1842) continued to experiment with further excisions and alternative versions of certain passages. At the beginning of 1843 he tried to avoid cuts by allowing the opera to be performed in two halves on successive evenings. The public complained bitterly (among other things because they were in effect paying twice for one opera) and Wagner was forced to revert to another one-evening version on 19 November 1843. With further cuts it was this version that was produced in Hamburg in March 1844 and again in Berlin in October 1847 (the latter with a new, more euphoric version of Rienzi's last words written with the volatile political climate that eventually led to the revolution of 1848/9 in mind). After Wagner's death, Cosima Wagner instigated a version supposedly 'according to the wishes of the Master' with drastic cuts and distortions that tried to obliterate all 'operatic' features from the work. It was published in 1899 and frequently performed, despite the protests of Richard Strauss and the prominent musical scholar Guido Adler. Apart from the critical edition begun in 1974, the most complete published scores are based on the much shortened Dresden version of 1843. However, as the original manuscript score is missing (it was in the possession of Adolf Hitler until the end of the Second World War), even the critical edition is incomplete. Performances since the Second World War have all been heavily cut. The studio performance broadcast by the BBC on 27 June 1976 was a notional reconstruction of the work as Wagner originally conceived it, part of which had to be orchestrated from sketches and other supplementary sources published in the critical edition.

RECORDINGS Martin, Wennberg, Kollo, Schreier, Adam, Hillebrand, Leipzig Radio Ch, Dresden State Opera Ch, Staatskapelle, Dresden, Hollreiser, EMI, 1976: based on the one-evening 1843 Dresden version, but with the revised ending composed for Berlin in 1847
EDITIONS f.ss., lithograph, Fürstenau, 1846; so-called 'Cosima version' (566 pp.), Adolph Fürstner, 1899; Adolph Fürstner, c. 1900; Reinhard Strohm and Egon Voss (eds), critical edn, 5 vols, B. Schott's Söhne, 1974; v.ss., C. F. Meser, 1844; Schott, 1911; Breitkopf und Härtel, 1914; after critical edn, B. Schott's Söhne, 1982; study s., Adolph Fürstner (later Eulenburg), 1911

Der fliegende Holländer

The Flying Dutchman
Romantic opera in three acts (2h 15m)
Libretto by the composer
Composed: libretto 1840, 1841; music 1840, 1841, rev. 1842, 1846, 1852, 1860
PREMIERES 2 January 1843, Royal Saxon Court Theatre, Dresden; UK: 23 July 1870, London (in Italian); US: 8 November 1876, Philadelphia (in Italian)
CAST Daland *b*, Senta *s*, Erik *t*, Mary *a*, Daland's steersman *t*, the Dutchman *high b*; *tb* choruses of sailors from the Norwegian ship, the Flying Dutchman's crew, *sa* chorus of young women
ORCHESTRATION picc, 2 fl, 2 ob, ca, 2 cl, 2 bsn, 4 hn, 2 tpt, 3 trbn, ophicleide, timp, str; end of overture 1860 (Paris version): 3 tpt (not 2), 2 hp; end of overture (printed version from 1860) and conclusion of Act III 1860: b tuba (not ophicleide), hp; onstage: 3 picc (if possible several players to each part), 6 hn, t-t, wind-machine

It is not certain when Wagner decided to turn the subject of the Flying Dutchman into an opera. However there is no doubt that his chief model was Heinrich Heine's *Memoirs of Herr von Schnabelewopski*, though he could have been acquainted with other sources such as Wilhelm Hauff's fairy-tale *Geschichte vom Gespensterschiff* (1825). The first surviving document is a prose scenario in French written during May 1840. Wagner's intention was to offer it to Meyerbeer's librettist Eugène Scribe, who would turn it into a libretto for a one-act curtain-raiser to a larger ballet (a practice then in vogue in Paris) which he, Wagner, would then be commissioned by the Opéra to compose. The plan was not new. Indeed, with a similar goal in mind Wagner had already sent Scribe a detailed scenario for a projected opera, *Die hohe Braut*, from Königsberg as early as 1836. But like practically all Wagner's Paris plans, this one fell on stony ground. Wagner received promises from the Opéra for an audition of three numbers (Senta's ballad, and the two sailors' songs in what is now Act III), which he composed between May and July 1840. The audition, however, never took place.

In 1841 Wagner sold the original scenario to the Paris Opéra for 500 francs. The Opéra then commissioned two librettists and the composer Pierre-Louis-Philippe Dietsch, later the conductor of the ill-fated Paris *Tannhäuser* performances in 1861, to turn Wagner's draft into *Le vaisseau fantôme*. which after only 11 performances sank, like the ship of its title, into eternal oblivion. According to Wagner's biography, he was forced to sell the scenario in order to rent the piano he needed to compose the opera himself. Much has been made of Wagner's 'humiliation' at having to do this. But the French prose scenario and the opera he eventually made out of it are actually very different. Wagner not only expanded the scale of the work, but also altered its 'tone' in order to introduce, or to elaborate on, several literary motifs in a way that went far beyond the scope of the first version, not to say notions of opera current at the time. The Dutchman's nihilism and yearning for death; the quasi-Christian idea of redemption; Senta's preoccupation with dreams and folly or illusion (*Wahn*); the transformation of Senta's suitor into a hunter whose humble profession and clumsy demeanour serve as a foil to her utopian release (in effect a *Liebestod à la Tristan*) from the narrow world he represents: all these elements meant that by the time Wagner had finished the libretto of *Holländer* in May 1841 he had included, at least in embryo, many of the major themes that were to dominate his later works.

The new version was so much more ambitious than the first that Wagner had no hesitation in offering it to the Court Opera in Berlin as a fully-fledged opera that could fill an entire evening. With Meyerbeer's help, it was accepted in March 1842. But delays, and a counter-offer from Dresden following the huge success of *Rienzi* there in October 1842, prompted Wagner to withdraw it. The opera was eventually given four performances in Dresden under Wagner's direction with Johann Michael Wächter as the Dutchman and Wilhelmine Schröder-Devrient in the role of Senta. It was only a moderate success. A few performances followed in 1843 in Riga and Kassel (where it was conducted by Spohr), and then in Berlin in 1844. The opera quickly disappeared from the repertoire before Wagner himself revived it in Zurich in April and May 1852.

SYNOPSIS
Act I The Norwegian coast. A steep cliff. Forced by fierce weather to cast anchor, Daland has gone ashore to reconnoitre. He recognizes Sandwike, a bay just seven miles from his home. He curses the wind – 'blowing out of the devil's crevice' – that prevents him from seeing Senta, his daughter. He returns on board and retires to his cabin, assuring his crew that all is well. The steersman is left on watch. He too sings of a loved one tantalizingly close. As he falls asleep, the storm revives and the Flying Dutchman's ship appears. The Dutchman, dressed in black Spanish costume, comes ashore. He is condemned to travel the seas for ever, returning to land every seven years in a hopeless search for salvation ('Die Frist ist um'). Only the Day of

Judgment can save him, when the world will shatter and eternal oblivion will be his. Daland returns on deck and shakes his steersman awake. He catches sight of the Dutchman, who asks him for hospitality and the hand of his daughter in return for unimaginable riches. Daland readily agrees. The steersman announces a favourable wind from the south and the rest of the Norwegian crew join in a jubilant final verse of his song.

Act II   A large room in Daland's house. A picture of a pale, bearded man wearing a black Spanish costume hangs on the wall. Senta is transfixed by it. Her governess Mary and the other women sit round a fire, spinning. The women sing of their spinning wheels creating enough wind to bring their lovers home. They mock Senta for falling in love with the old picture. She retorts by singing the ballad of the legendary Dutchman ('Traft ihr das Schiff im Meere an'). Salvation awaits him only if he can find a woman faithful unto death. 'I am that woman,' Senta declares, to the consternation of all. Only Erik's announcement of Daland's return brings her to her senses. Erik and Senta are alone. Erik is convinced that his hunter's livelihood will not qualify him in Daland's eyes as Senta's suitor and begs her to persuade her father otherwise. She feels more for the picture than for him, he complains. When she leads him close to the portrait to convey her feelings, he is certain that the devil has taken possession of her. He tells her of his dream ('Auf hohem Felsen lag ich träumend'). Senta listens enraptured: a strange ship; two men, one Senta's father, the other pale, wearing a black cloak; she kisses the stranger wildly; they both flee out to sea. Senta knows the dream is true. Daland and the stranger arrive. As Senta now gazes on the real Dutchman, Daland formally introduces them ('Mögst du, mein Kind'), but they ignore his banal speech about marriage and wealth. After Daland has discreetly withdrawn in amazement, the Dutchman expresses his mixed feelings about Senta ('Wie aus der Ferne'). Is she a long-lost dream come true? Or one of Satan's tricks? Senta asks if this is folly, an illusion ('ist's ein Wahn?'). She is deeply moved by the Dutchman's suffering. In turn, the Dutchman is touched by her compassion. She is an angel. He warns her of the terrible sacrifices she must make if she promises eternal faithfulness ('Ach! könntest das Geschick du ahnen'). But Senta is overcome by a powerful magic and does not flinch from her resolve to save him. Daland returns with a curious crowd. They are delighted at what they think is going to be a successful marriage.

Act III   A bay on a rocky shore. In the foreground to one side is Daland's house. The Norwegian ship, light and festive, is in the background with the Dutchman's vessel, shrouded in darkness, anchored nearby. The sailors celebrate ('Steuermann, lass' die Wacht!') and joke that the crew of the other ship are either all dead or like dragons guarding their hoard. Despite the Norwegian sailors' taunts, the strange vessel stays silent. Suddenly a fierce storm flares up around the Dutchman's ship and its crew sing that Satan has charmed it so that it will sail until eternity. The Norwegians flee in terror. Erik is horrified that Senta has agreed to marry the Dutchman. Does she not remember embracing him, as if to confess her love? ('Willst jenes Tag's du nicht dich mehr entsinnen'). The Dutchman overhears the conversation and misinterprets it. As he suspected, Senta is unfaithful: he will never find salvation. Senta frantically tries to convince him that he is wrong. Erik calls for help. The Dutchman reveals his true identity and in ecstasy Senta cries out to him as he departs ('Preis deinen Engel'). She leaps into the ocean and immediately the Dutchman's ship sinks. Against the rising sun, Senta and the Dutchman appear transfigured, soaring upwards hand in hand above the wreck of the vessel.

Wagner always insisted that *Der fliegende Holländer* was the opera that marked the real beginning of his career. From a critical point of view he was undoubtedly right. Historians have protested that *Rienzi* (in which the sublime and the unspeakably banal are disconcertingly entwined) has been seriously misjudged largely because of Wagner's overnegative and highly influential critique of it. Yet despite the magnificent moments in *Rienzi* and the fact that it is close to *Holländer* chronologically (at one point Wagner was working on both operas simultaneously) there is no denying that *Holländer* is in almost every respect a superior work.

Exactly how Wagner turned virtually overnight into a composer of genius is not an easy question to answer. The change from the historical subject matter of *Rienzi* to the more suggestive, and for Wagner always more sympathetic, world of myth and legend in *Holländer* clearly made a difference. So, too, did the dire circumstances of his life. An exile in Paris suffering endless setbacks in the fight for recognition, Wagner was arguably more deeply touched by the image of 'the Wandering Jew of the ocean' (Heine) than he ever had been by Rienzi's grandiose idealism. To see experience in life as sources of artistic inspiration may no longer be fashionable. But it would be a cold critic who ignored a possible connection between Wagner's serious existential doubts in his early Paris years and the bleak intensity of some of the best music in *Holländer*. The words 'in need and care' (*in Noth und Sorgen*) written at the end of the composition draft on 22 August 1841 meant exactly what they said.

Wagner was preoccupied at regular intervals with the Dutchman throughout a major period of his life. For the first performances he transposed Senta's ballad from A minor into G minor and relinquished his original idea of playing the three acts as one without an interval. (The current fashion for producing the opera in its original, supposedly 'authentic' one-act version should be weighed against the fact that Wagner never conducted, or encouraged, a performance of the opera in this form.) He undertook major revisions of the orchestration in 1846, and again in 1852 when he retouched the instrumentation of the ending of the overture. For a performance in Weimar in 1853, he expressly asked Liszt, who was to conduct the opera, to change the orchestration of a single chord: the accompaniment of Senta's cry at the start of the Act II finale. For his Paris concerts in 1860 he made two major additions to the ending of the overture and added a trumpet and two harps to its orchestration. He even began a completely new version of Senta's ballad (a sketch of which has survived) for a model performance of *Holländer* in Munich commissioned in 1864 by King Ludwig. Cosima von Bülow (later Wagner) reported to Ludwig in 1866 that Wagner was intending to revise *Holländer* so that it would be 'worthy to stand alongside *Tannhäuser* and *Lohengrin*'. During Wagner's last years, she noted in her diary (9 April 1880) that he 'wants to postpone the dictation of the autobiography until after the performance of *Parsifal* when he also wants to revise *Der fliegende Holländer*'. Not long afterwards, Cosima recorded one of his most famous remarks: 'He says that he still owes the world *Tannhäuser*' (23 January 1883). Wagner might have added that he still owed the world *Der fliegende Holländer* as well.

RECORDINGS   1. Ursuleac, Ostertag, Klarwein, Hotter, Hann, Bavarian State Opera Ch and O, Krauss, Acanta, 1944; 2. Varnay, Svanholm, Hayward, Hotter, S. Nilsson, Metropolitan Opera Ch and O, Reiner, OPR, 1950; 3. Varnay, Lustig, Traxel, Uhde, Weber, Bayreuth Festival Ch and O, Keilberth, Decca, 1955: another performance from the same year, conducted by Knappertsbusch, with the same cast, is also worth seeking out; 4. Silja, Uhl, Paskuda, Crass, Greindl, Bayreuth Festival Ch and O, Sawallisch, Philips, 1961; 5. Silja, Kozub, Unger, Adam, Talvela, BBC Ch, New Philharmonia O, Klemperer, EMI, 1968; 6. Balslev, Schunk, Clark, Estes, Salminen, Bayreuth Festival Ch and O, Nelsson, Philips, 1985. The first two performances, in indifferent sound, enshrine Hotter's haunted, unforgettable Dutchman. The first is better conducted and played; the second has much the preferable Senta in the young Varnay, who is also an asset in the 1955 Bayreuth account, a thrilling performance with Uhde as a tense, anguished Dutchman. The fourth recording, the original Dresden version in three acts, is another exciting Bayreuth reading with Silja and Crass almost equalling their predecessors while the fifth is a mixture of the Dresden version and Paris additions (despite the booklet saying Sawallisch reverts to the Dresden version). This recording features Adam's moving Dutchman and Klemperer's granite conducting. None of the more recent sets matches any of the first five, though the sixth is a vital recording [A.B.]
VIDEOS   1. Balslev, Schunk, Clark, Estes, Salminen, Bayreuth Festival Ch and O, Nielsson, Philips, 1985; 2. Behrens, Sirkiä, Silvasti, Grundheber, Salminen, Savonlinna Opera Festival Ch and O, Segerstam, Teldec, 1990; 3. Varady, Seiffert, Ress, Hale, Ryhänen, Bavarian State Opera Ch and O, Sawallisch, EMI, 1992: all three sets derive from performances in the opera house, but are different in character. The first is Kupfer's highly idiosyncratic interpretation. The second and third are conventional; they also have stronger Sentas and Dutchmen than the first. All are dramatically conducted [A.B.]
EDITIONS   f.ss., lithograph, self-published, 1845; F. Weingartner (ed.), Fürstner, 1897; Isolde Vetter (ed.), critical edn, 2 vols, B. Schott's Söhne, 1983; v.ss., C. F. Meser, 1844; Boosey, 1876; Novello, Ewer, 1877; Schott, 1912; Breitkopf und Härtel, 1914; Peters, 1914; study s., Weingartner edn, Fürstner (later Eulenburg), 1907

Tannhäuser und der Sängerkrieg auf Wartburg

Tannhäuser and the Song Contest on the Wartburg
Grand romantic opera in three acts; from 1859/60 onwards: *Handlung* in three acts (c. 3h; so-called Paris version: 3h 15m)
Libretto by the composer
The genesis and revisions of the work (libretto and music) have been divided into four stages as follows: Stage 1 (June 1842–premiere (19 October 1845)): libretto June 1842–April 1843; music July 1843–October 1845. Stage 2 (the preparations for the second performance (27 October 1845)– the first engraved f.s. (June 1860)): libretto spring 1847; music October 1845–May 1847, September 1851. Stage 3 (the preparations for staging the work in Paris (from autumn 1859) – the Paris performances (13, 18, 24 March 1861)): Wagner translates libretto into French September 1859– March 1861; music August/September 1860–March 1861. Stage 4 (August 1861 – the Vienna premiere (22 November 1875)): Wagner reworks libretto into German August/September 1861–spring 1865; music from summer/autumn 1861 (the so-called Paris version played today is actually this version)
PREMIERES   19 October 1845, Royal Saxon Court Theatre, Dresden; US: 4 April 1859, Stadt Theater, New York; UK: 6 May 1876, Covent Garden, London (in Italian)
CAST   Herrmann *deep b*, Tannhäuser *t*, Wolfram von Eschinbach *high b*, Walther von der Vogelweide *t*, Biterolf *b*, Heinrich der Schreiber *t*, Reinmar von Zweter *b*, Elisabeth *s*, Venus *s*, a young shepherd *s*, 4 pages *2 s, 2 a*; *satb* chorus of Thuringian knights, counts and nobles, noblewomen, older and younger pilgrims, sirens, naiads, nymphs, maenads; in stages 3 and 4 also: the three Graces, young men, cupids, satyrs, fauns

ORCHESTRATION   3 fl/picc, 2 ob, 2 cl, b cl, 2 bsn, 2 hn, 2 hand hn, 3 tpt, 3 trbn, b tuba, timp, bd, cym, triangle, tambourine, castanets (stages 3, 4), hp (stages 1, 2, 4), 4 hp (stage 3), str; onstage: Act I: Scene 1 (stages 1, 2): 4 fl, 4 cl, 4 bsn, 4 hn; Scene 1 (stages 3, 4): 2 fl, 2 ob, 2 cl, 2 bsn, 4 hn, hp; Scene 2 (stages 1, 2): 2 fl, 2 cl, 2 bsn, 2 hn; Scene 2 (stages 3, 4): 2 fl, 2 ob, 2 cl, 4 hn, hp; Scene 3: ca, 12 hand hn; Scene 4: 12 hand hn; Act II: Scene 3: 3 tpt; Scene 4: 12 tpt; Act III: Scene 3 (stage 1): 2 picc, 4 fl, 4 ob, 6 cl, 4 bsn, 4 hn, 2 tpt, triangle, cym, tambourine, 4 trbn; Scene 3 (stage 3): picc, 2 fl, 2 ob, 3 cl, 2 bsn, 2 hn, triangle, cym, tambourine; Scene 3 (stages 2, 4): 2 picc, 4 fl, 4 ob, 6 cl, 4 bsn, 4 hn, triangle, cym, tambourine (divided into two orchestras of equal size on the left and right beneath the stage), 4 trbn

According to Wagner's autobiography he was already making plans for *Tannhäuser* in 1841–2 during his first sojourn in Paris. The earliest surviving document is a prose scenario begun on 28 June 1842 after he had returned to Dresden. Here, and in the first libretto (completed in April 1843), the opera is called *Der Venusberg*. Wagner appears to have changed the title soon after finishing the libretto. In a letter to Schumann of 13 June 1843 he referred to the project as *Tannhäuser und der Wartburgkrieg* and in a letter written to his brother the next day simply as *Tannhäuser*.

The word 'and' (as opposed to the conventional 'or') in the opera's final title reflects its derivation from two separate legends: the theme of Tannhäuser and Venus on the one hand and Heinrich von Ofterdinger's defeat in the Wartburg song contest on the other. Wagner was less interested in the epic accounts of the two stories he found in his sources (of which there are more for *Tannhäuser* than any of his previous works) than in bringing them into dramatic conflict with one another. Two key texts were Heine's *Tannhäuser: A Legend* in the *Salon* (1837) – the same collection in which Wagner found the tale of *Der fliegende Holländer* – and Tieck's story *Der getreue Eckart und der Tannenhäuser* from the *Phantasus* collection (1812–17). Wagner never acknowledged his debt to Heine, though he does mention Tieck and E. T. A. Hoffmann's *Der Kampf der Sänger* from *Die Serapionsbrüder* of 1819. But he is disparaging about them and silent, too, about another source he must have known: Ludwig Bechstein's *Sagenschatz des Thüringerlandes* (a 'treasury of tales from Thuringia') of 1835 in which the song contest on the Wartburg and its hero Heinrich von Ofterdingen and the legend of Tannhäuser and the Venusberg are loosely connected. In his Paris years Wagner came across an obscure monograph, *Der Krieg von Wartburg* by C. T. L. Lucas (1838), which boldly claimed that Ofterdingen and Tannhäuser were one and the same person. The bizarre notion was immediately pilloried by the academic establishment. But for Wagner (as he more or less admitted in his autobiography) it was the key to a brilliant idea: the antithesis of two worlds dividing the hero against himself in a tragic conflict between sensuality and asceticism.

Tannhäuser has been described as Wagner's 'most medieval work' (Volker Mertens). This may be true in the sense that Wagner returned via German Romanticism to the spirit of the medieval tale of penance with (for instance) the idea of redemption through love in an afterlife that is deemed to be real, and with the image of the burgeoning staff as a symbol of God's grace for all mankind (including the worst of sinners). Yet Wagner's synthesis of his materials is so strikingly original and modern (the fear that it would be perceived otherwise may have been one reason why he was so coy in acknowledging some of his sources) that to see the opera as medieval at all is to miss its point. The pre-modern world of miracles and burning Christian faith becomes in Wagner's hands an allegory of a modern society impoverished by precisely those Christian values it claims to represent. The dialectical strategy (which Wagner later perfected in *Parsifal*) embraced other modernist issues, including the alienated artist who yearns for the world of the imagination, yet is fatally attracted to the real world as well. For the first time, the opera also betrays Wagner's uninhibited (and masochistic) attitude to sex, especially in his portrayal of Venus, whom he made even more explicit by contrasting her with Elisabeth, her exact opposite. Elisabeth is remotely related to a real historical character, the wife of Landgrave Ludwig IV (1200–1227). But as a virgin and quasi-Christian antithesis to Venus, the pagan goddess of love, she is entirely Wagner's invention.

SYNOPSIS

The action takes place in Thuringia and the Wartburg at the beginning of the 13th century.

Act I   A subterranean grotto inside the Venus-

Drawing by Th. Tischbein of Wilhelmine Schröder-Devrient (Venus) and Joseph Tichatschek (Tannhäuser) (Dresden, 1845)

berg (Horselberg, near Eisenach). Sirens, naiads, nymphs and bacchantes dance ecstatically. The song of the sirens ('Naht euch dem Strande') interrupts the wild movement at its orgiastic climax, and exhaustion and calm ensue. (In the Paris–Vienna versions, stages 3 and 4, Wagner added satyrs, fauns, young men, and an allegory in which the three Graces, with the help of cupids, quell the orgy. An image of the 'rape of Europe', riding on a white bull drawn through a blue sea by tritons and nereids, emerges through the mist at the end.) Tannhäuser, half kneeling before Venus, his harp at his side, yearns for release from the endlessly pleasurable, artificial world of the Venusberg. Human society and death, measured by real time and marked by pain and freedom, are drawing him away. Full of burning admiration for Venus and her charms ('Dir töne Lob!'), he begs her to let him leave. In despair, she curses him and the cold humans tempting him to abscond. Death will rebuff him, she warns; but he may return when it does. Invoking the Virgin Mary, Tannhäuser breaks away from the magic of the Venusberg. He finds himself at the foot of the Wartburg. A shepherd is singing and playing a pipe in praise of spring. A chorale sung by passing pilgrims moves Tannhäuser to kneel in prayer, as if to atone for his sins. Hunting horns are heard and the Landgrave appears with a large retinue. Astonished, the knights recognize Tannhäuser, who long ago parted from their company. He refuses their invitation to rejoin them. Only when Wolfram mentions the name of Elisabeth and tells of how much she misses him does he change his mind.

Act II Elisabeth greets the hall in the Wartburg where at last she is to see Tannhäuser again ('Dich, teure Halle, grüss' ich wieder'). Tannhäuser is led by Wolfram to Elisabeth. They rejoice at their reunion while Wolfram remains in the background, convinced that he has lost Elisabeth's love. The Landgrave sees that Elisabeth is perturbed. He tells her to keep her feelings to herself, at the same time announcing the forthcoming song contest in which Tannhäuser will once again participate. The power of song, he suggests, may offer a solution. The local nobles with their wives arrive at the Wartburg for the contest. The Landgrave gives the competing singers the task of defining the essence of love in song. Elisabeth will give the winner as his prize whatever he is bold enough to demand. The contest begins. Wolfram, Walther and Biterolf conceive love as something abstract and moral, while Tannhäuser, with increasing vehemence, opposes them with an image of love as a joyous, sensual experience. A fight nearly ensues, prevented only by a pious and conciliatory song from Wolfram ('O Himmel, lass dich jetzt erflehen'). But this merely goads Tannhäuser into singing a fourth verse of the song he sang to Venus at the beginning of the opera, this time with words praising the lusts of the flesh, and culminating in the demand that all should hasten to the Venusberg to learn the real meaning of love. The assembled company is scandalized. In the ensuing tumult, Elisabeth shields Tannhäuser from the knights rushing forward to kill him ('Zurück von ihm! Nicht Ihr seid seine Richter'). She implores the Landgrave to pardon the sinner, for whose salvation she is prepared to offer her life. Tannhäuser is expelled and ordered to go to Rome to seek forgiveness. As the hymn of the young pilgrims on their way to Rome sounds in the distance, Tannhäuser kisses the hem of Elisabeth's robe, and rushes out to join them.

Act III The Wartburg valley. It is autumn; evening is approaching. Elisabeth looks in vain for Tannhäuser among the pilgrims returning from Rome. She prays to the Virgin to take her from this earth ('Allmächt'ge Jungfrau, hör mein Flehen'), insisting to Wolfram that she must go her way alone. Wolfram is distraught at Elisabeth's decision to sacrifice her life. To calm himself, he begs the evening star to greet Elisabeth as she ascends to heaven ('O du, mein holder Abendstern'). Night has fallen. Tannhäuser, his pilgrim's garb torn, enters with faltering steps. He tells Wolfram of his journey to Rome ('Inbrunst im Herzen') and in particular of the Pope's harsh words to him: 'Just as this staff in my hand can never blossom, so can you never be redeemed from the flames of hell.' Tannhäuser is convinced he is damned and seeks to return to the Venusberg. In the first Dresden version (stage 1) his 'Rome narration' gradually turns into a delirious vision of the Venusberg. In desperation, Wolfram invokes the name of Elisabeth, at which point a chorus behind the scenes announces her blessed martyrdom. Tannhäuser has found salvation through

her death and expires in Wolfram's arms. In the revised Dresden version and all later versions (stages 2, 3 and 4) Venus appears in person and calls Tannhäuser to her. At Wolfram's naming of Elisabeth, a funeral procession with chorus appears from the direction of the Wartburg carrying her body on an open bier. Tannhäuser is transfixed at the sound of her name, whereupon Venus vanishes, lamenting that she has lost him. No longer spurned by death and redeemed at last, Tannhäuser sinks down dying over Elisabeth's body. The younger pilgrims enter with a staff that has put forth leaves, celebrating God's miracle with hallelujahs as the rising sun bathes the scene in the morning light.

Wagner did not break entirely with operatic convention in Tannhäuser; but by building the opera out of complex scenic units (which often resemble jumbled baroque allegories) he did move several steps beyond it. The richly suggestive dramaturgy, however, was not easy to translate into music. Already in 1843 Wagner hinted to friends that he was having difficulties with the composition of the opera. Considering the musical demands placed on him by the dialectical structure of the action this was hardly surprising. (Tannhäuser's song to Venus, for instance, not only had to sound noble and earnest as he longs for the real world in Act I, but also deliriously sensual when he yearns again for Venus in Act II.) The full score was completed in April 1845 and the first performance took place in Dresden in the following October under Wagner's baton with Joseph Tichatschek in the title role and Wilhelmine Schröder-Devrient as Venus. Audience reaction to the premiere was lukewarm and Wagner immediately began to revise the score with cuts in the finales of Acts I and II and a new orchestral introduction to Act III. Other alterations followed with the revival in Dresden on 1 August 1847, including a radical recomposition of the ending. Following Liszt's lead in Weimar in 1849, the opera was taken up in the 1850s by nearly every theatre in Germany, which prompted an unceasing flow of instructions and interpretations from Wagner's pen, and still more changes to the score. Wagner reserved his most drastic revisions for the three notorious Paris performances of 1861 in French (which were all different from each other) and still persisted in tinkering with the opera for the productions he supervised in Munich (1 August 1867) and Vienna (22 November 1875). The Paris revisions included the expansion and recomposition of the opening bacchanal and the second scene, as well as extensive modifications to the song contest. Except for the Vienna production, the overture was played in full by popular demand in the Paris and Munich performances, even though Wagner had insisted on cutting it and merging it without a break into the bacchanal (ironically a practice now familiar from the so-called Paris version). The version known today as the Paris version is in fact the Vienna version of 1875.

To the end of Wagner's life the preoccupation with the music of Tannhäuser never left him, as numerous remarks in Cosima's diaries prove. With the possible exception of *Der fliegende Holländer*, it is his only major score, in a sense, he never finished composing.

RECORDINGS   1. Silja, Bumbry, Windgassen, Waechter, Greindl, Bayreuth Festival Ch and O, Sawallisch, Philips, 1964; 2. Grümmer, Schech, Hopf, Fischer-Dieskau, Frick, Berlin State Opera Ch and O, Konwitschny, EMI, 1961; 3. Dernesch, Ludwig, Kollo, Braun, Sotin, Vienna State Opera Ch, Vienna PO, Solti, Decca, 1971: the Philips set recalls an exciting night at Bayreuth with Sawallisch choosing a conflation of the Dresden and Paris versions. Konwitschny's is the best reading of the Dresden version, and is well conducted, played and sung, although the Tannhäuser is a trial. Solti's set, pure Paris, is perhaps the best of his Wagner on disc and sports the most even cast [A.B.]
VIDEO   Jones (Venus and Elisabeth), Wenkoff, Weikl, Sotin, Bayreuth Festival Ch and O, C. Davis, Philips, 1978: features Götz Friedrich's highly personal, dark view of the work, excellently conducted [A.B.]
EDITIONS   f.ss., stage 1, lithograph, self-published, 1845; stage 2, C. F. Meser (Hermann Müller), 1860; later Boosey & Hawkes, 1973 ('Dresden version'); stage 4, C. F. Meser (Fürstner), 1888; later Boosey & Hawkes, 1973 (incorrectly described as the 'Paris version'); stage 4, A. Durand et fils, 1891; stages 2, 4 with additions by F. Mottl based on Wagner's directions for 1875 Vienna production, C. F. Peters, 1924; stages 1–4 with omissions, Balling (ed.), critical edn, Breitkopf und Härtel, 1929; Dresden version, stages 1 and 2, Reinhard Strohm (ed.), critical edn, 3 vols, B. Schott's Söhne, in preparation; v.ss., stage 1, C. F. Meser, 1846; stage 2, C. F. Meser, 1852; stage 3, G. Flaxland, 1861; stage 4, Breitkopf und Härtel, 1910; stages 4, 2 in appendix, Schott, 1912; stages 2 and 4, C. F. Peters, 1974; study s., stages 2, 3 and 4, Eulenburg, 1929

Lohengrin

Romantic opera in three acts (3h 30m)
Libretto by the composer
Composed: libretto 1845; music 1846–8
PREMIERES   28 August 1850, Grand Ducal Court Theatre, Weimar; US: 3 April 1871, Stadt Theater, New York; UK: 8 May 1875, Covent Garden, London (in Italian)
CAST   Heinrich der Vogler, deutscher König *b*, Lohengrin *t*, Elsa von Brabant *s*, Duke Gottfried *silent*, Friedrich von Telramund *bar*, Ortrud *s*, king's herald *b*, 4 Brabantine nobles 2 *t*, 2 *b*, 4 pages 2 *s*, 2 *a*; *satb* chorus of Saxon and Thuringian counts and nobles, Brabantine counts and nobles, noblewomen, pages, vassals, women, servants
ORCHESTRATION   3 fl/picc, 2 ob/ca, 3 cl/b cl, 3 bsn, 4 hn, 3 tpt, 3 trbn, b tuba, timp, perc (cym, triangle, tambourine), hp, str; onstage: 4 tpt (Act I), picc, 2 fl, 3 ob, 3 cl, 2 bsn, 3 hn, 3 tpt, 3 trbn, timp, cym (Act II, Scene 1), 4 tpt (Act II, Scenes 3, 4), 10 tpt, organ (Act II, Scene 5), 3 fl, 2 ob, 2 cl, 3 bsn, 4 hn, 2 tpt, triangle, hp (Act III, Scene 1), 4 tpt, 4 trbn (Act III, Scene 2), 12 tpt, tenor d (Act III, Scene 3)

Written between summer 1845 and April 1848, *Lohengrin* was intended originally for Dresden. To prepare the way for the premiere, Wagner conducted a concert performance of the finale of Act I at the Royal Saxon Court Theatre on 22 September 1848. The scenery was duly commissioned and a full-scale production announced to the press in January 1849. Wagner's involvement in the events leading to the ill-fated Dresden revolution of May 1849 prevented the project from going ahead. The eventual first performance in Weimar was conducted by Liszt, the opera's dedicatee, on the 101st anniversary of

Goethe's birth. The place and date were symbolic. After the failed revolutions of 1848/9, increasing nostalgia for Weimar's former cultural glory and Wagner's burgeoning reputation as the radically new hope of German art both focused critical attention on the event. The authorities inadvertently played their part by refusing to grant Wagner clemency. He was in political exile in Switzerland and in the eyes of Germany's cultural vanguard his conspicuous absence only made the premiere yet more significant. (According to Wagner's autobiography, he spent the evening in Lucerne in a tavern called the Swan 'watching the clock and closely following the hour of the opera's beginning and its presumed end'.) Though Wagner conducted excerpts in concerts in Zurich (1853), London (1855), Paris (1860) and Brussels (1860), nearly 11 years elapsed before a partial amnesty enabled him to hear the whole opera for the first time in a dress rehearsal in Vienna in May 1861.

In contrast to the idealism symbolized by the place and date of the premiere of *Lohengrin*, Wagner found its subsequent popularity irksome, especially the fame of its most celebrated item, the Bridal Chorus. Wagner introduced it to English audiences in his London concerts in 1855. Three years later at the marriage of Queen Victoria's daughter, Princess Victoria, to Frederick Wilhelm of Prussia it earned a permanent place in the history of popular culture when it was coupled for the first time with the Wedding March from Mendelssohn's *A Midsummer Night's Dream*. In its original context the Bridal Chorus is a masterpiece of sweet foreboding and a prelude to marital disaster. The irony of its transformation into a much-loved public symbol of faith in the institution of marriage was not lost on Wagner who sensed almost from the start that undue focus of attention on the best-known 'numbers' in *Lohengrin* left it open to serious misinterpretation. In 1853 when the opera was taken up by several German houses (and not long after by several foreign companies as well) he persuaded Breitkopf und Härtel to publish a brochure with production details and illustrations of scenery and costumes, which he described as 'according to my wishes'. Perhaps rightly resisting this somewhat peremptory authorial vigilance, hardly a single producer responded. Wagner continued to complain of inadequate performances and publicly expressed his dissatisfaction in an open letter of 7 November 1871 to Boito. Though Wagner conducted the opera several times, he personally supervised only two productions of it. The first (conducted by Hans von Bülow) was given on 16 June 1867 in Munich and the second (conducted by Hans Richter) took place in Vienna on 15 December 1875. The Munich production, Wagner told Boito, was the first time the work had been rehearsed according to its 'rhythmic–architectonic structure'.

SYNOPSIS

Act I   The first half of the tenth century. A meadow on the bank of the river Scheldt near Antwerp. After a nine-year truce, the Hungarians are again

Portrait by Karl Schweninger of Richard Wagner at Wahnfried, with a wealth of characters from Wagner's operas; the knight in the centre is Lohengrin

threatening to attack Germany. King Heinrich I of Saxony (Heinrich der Vogler) has come to Brabant to recruit men to help fend off an attack from the east. He finds the country in disarray and demands to know what is wrong. Friedrich von Telramund explains that he was granted the right to care for Elsa and her younger brother Gottfried, the children of the deceased Duke of Brabant. Gottfried has disappeared and Friedrich now formally accuses Elsa of murdering him at the instigation of a secret lover. Friedrich is so convinced that Elsa has lost her heart to another man that he has renounced his right to her and married Ortrud instead, the daughter of Radbod, Prince of Friesland. Elsa is guilty of fratricide, Friedrich argues, and as he is himself next of kin to the dead duke, he has a legitimate claim to be ruler of Brabant in her stead. Elsa is summoned and declares with a powerful radiance that she has dreamed of a knight who will come to protect her. Friedrich, certain that the knight is Elsa's secret lover, agrees to a trial by combat. In the distance a swan is seen drawing a boat carrying a knight in shining armour. The swan appears accompanied by the growing excitement of the onlookers. Lohengrin steps on to shore and Elsa, at first spellbound by his presence, throws herself enraptured at his feet. He asks her whether she will marry him if he wins on her behalf and lays down his conditions: never is she to ask about, or brood upon, his origin, his lineage, or his name. Heinrich leads a prayer ('Mein Herr und Gott'): may God weaken the strength of the liar and give power to the true hero. Lohengrin wins the fight and magnanimously spares Friedrich's life.

All rejoice while Ortrud broods ominously on the mysterious knight who is thwarting her plans.

Act II The citadel of Antwerp. Night. Friedrich and Ortrud, both shabbily dressed, are sitting on the steps of the minster in the foreground. The windows of the knights' dwelling at the back are brightly lit as the celebrations continue. Friedrich accuses Ortrud of lying to him about Elsa's supposed murder of Gottfried. Ortrud retaliates by calling Friedrich a coward. To regain his honour he must sow doubts in Elsa's mind by accusing Lohengrin of sorcery. If that fails, force must be used: those made strong by magic lose their strength merely by losing the smallest limb. Elsa appears on a balcony and tells the breezes of her happiness ('Euch, Lüften, die mein Klagen'). Her pity is cunningly aroused by Ortrud. As Elsa retires for a moment to let Ortrud inside, Ortrud's false pathos rapidly disappears in an abrupt and violent passage during which she invokes the pagan gods to help her regain power ('Entweihte Götter'). Elsa returns and Ortrud begins to insinuate doubt into her mind with the almost casual warning that her nameless protector could one day leave her just as mysteriously as he came. As day breaks the herald makes four announcements: Friedrich is banished; Brabant is given to Lohengrin who has relinquished the title of duke for that of 'protector'; the wedding between Lohengrin and Elsa is to take place that day; on the next, Lohengrin will lead the men of Brabant into battle. A small group of four nobles dissents. As Elsa approaches the minster where she is to marry her protector, Ortrud interrupts the procession to demand the revelation of Lohengrin's identity. No sooner has Lohengrin tried to comfort Elsa when Friedrich steps forward as well to accuse him of sorcery. Elsa manages to suppress her darkening dismay, but not before she receives unwelcome attention from Friedrich. He whispers to her that he can enter the bridal chamber that night to remove a fingertip from Lohengrin, which would break his magic strength. Lohengrin intervenes: he leads his bride solemnly into the minster and, as they reach the highest step, Elsa turns to him in deep emotion, only to catch a glimpse of Ortrud, her arm raised, as if certain of victory.

Act III The bridal chamber. An exuberant orchestral introduction leads into the gentle Bridal Chorus ('Treulich geführt'). It reflects the transition from highly public events to an intimate space where, after the wedding trains have left, the sense of claustrophobia increases as Elsa's doubts gain control. Nuptial bliss gradually turns insidiously into marital trauma. Elsa finally asks Lohengrin his name and origin, at which point Friedrich and the four disaffected nobles burst in to attack him. Lohengrin kills Friedrich and orders the four nobles to carry the body before Heinrich where, in front of the people of Brabant, Elsa's questions will be answered. Day breaks as the scene changes to the meadow as in Act I. Lohengrin announces that he cannot now lead the Brabantines into battle. He justifies the slaying of Friedrich and announces that Elsa, poisoned by treachery, has broken her vow. He reveals that in a wondrous castle in a faraway place is the holy cup carried to earth by an angel host ('In fernem Land'). Once a year a dove is sent to renew its strength: it is the Grail and it imparts supernatural power to the knights it selects. The Grail sends the knights to distant lands on errands of chivalry, but only on condition that they depart once their identity is known. Lohengrin announces that he is the son of Parsifal, King of the Grail, and utters his own name. The swan is seen returning. Lohengrin tells Elsa that had he been able to stay for only one year at her side the power of the Grail would have returned her brother to her. Lohengrin gives Elsa three objects to pass on to her brother if he ever returns: a horn to assist him in danger, a sword to make him victorious in battle and a ring to remind him of his sister's protector. Ortrud gloats on her apparent triumph ('Fahr' heim, du stolzer Helde!'), bragging that it was she who made Gottfried disappear by using a magic chain to turn him into a swan. Lohengrin answers her with a prayer. The white dove of the Grail hovers over the boat and the swan is miraculously transformed into Gottfried, a beautiful youth in gleaming silver apparel. As Lohengrin proclaims him leader of Brabant, Ortrud sinks powerless to the ground. Gottfried bows to Heinrich and rushes into the arms of his sister, while Lohengrin, standing with head bowed in the boat now being drawn by the dove, recedes into the distance. Elsa's soul leaves her body as she gradually collapses in her brother's arms.

The music of *Lohengrin* is hard to describe as forward-looking, yet equally difficult to dismiss as reactionary. In the first editions of the libretto and full score Wagner called *Lohengrin* a romantic opera, though he later withdrew the designation. The aura of chivalrous romance in *Lohengrin* notwithstanding, the opera also has an oddly 'classical' air about it. The polyphonic orchestral writing much admired by Richard Strauss, the close motivic relationships and above all the neat, often uncomfortably schematic dramatic and musical symmetries (the recapitulation of the Grail music in Act III for instance) are all evidence of Wagner's ambition to inject into the medium of opera something of the spirit of the great classical symphonists.

The musical details of *Lohengrin*, however, are rarely judged properly, mainly because Wagner's progressive tendencies, usually traced by historians with depressing regularity exclusively to *Tristan* and *Parsifal*, are said to consist of near-atonal chromaticism and irregular phrase structure. In fact, the anti-chromatic moments of *Lohengrin* are often the most striking (the opening of the prelude for instance) and even the regular phrases of the Bridal Chorus can seem daring and ambivalent in context. In a sense, *Lohengrin* is a contradiction in terms: it mixes genres that do not mix (fairy-tale opera and grand historical drama) and its music can still sound original precisely where, according to the conventional view of musical progress, it is least avant-garde.

With the exception of the Prelude, which was written last, *Lohengrin* is the first work Wagner composed systematically from beginning to end with almost polemical disregard for clear demarcations between operatic set pieces. (Ernest Newman's statement that the last act was composed first and the second act last is contradicted by the sketches.) The new method added irony to the initial success of the opera as a series of popular concert pieces, though it must be pointed out that Wagner's indulgence in allowing its large-scale formal rhythm (more akin to a symphony than an opera) to co-exist with more short-winded 'numbers' that could satisfy the most conservative of operatic tastes was part and parcel of his aesthetic strategy from the start. Wagner always rightly insisted, however, that *Lohengrin* is closer to the grand designs and seamless continuity of his later music dramas than it is usually thought to be. This may account for the fact that, in contrast to his other early operas, he was never tempted to revise it. The only substantial change he made was a cut in Lohengrin's Grail narration in Act III which he communicated to Liszt shortly before the first performance.

RECORDINGS 1. Steber, Varnay, Windgassen, Uhde, Greindl, Bayreuth Festival Ch and O, Keilberth, Decca, 1953; 2. Grümmer, Ludwig, Thomas, Fischer-Dieskau, Frick, Vienna State Opera Ch, Vienna PO, Kempe, EMI, 1963: the live Bayreuth performance has great presence and fine singing, the Kempe set has a formidable cast and superb conducting. There is also a Philips laserdisc of the 1982 Bayreuth staging, produced by Götz Friedrich [A.B.]
VIDEOS 1. Armstrong, Connell, Hofmann, Roar, Weikl, Vogel, Bayreuth Festival Opera Ch and O, Nielsson, Philips, 1980s: Friedrich's personal view of the work, sharply executed, variably sung; 2. Studer, Vejzovic, Domingo,

Walker, Lloyd, Vienna State Opera Ch and O, Abbado, Virgin, 1990: more orthodox staging, well sung and conducted [A.B.]

EDITIONS f.ss., lithograph, Breitkopf und Härtel, 1852; engraved, Breitkopf und Härtel, 1887; Durand and Schoenewerk, 1892; Balling (ed.), critical edn, Breitkopf und Härtel, 1914; with additions by Felix Mottl supposedly based on Wagner's directions for the 1875 Vienna production, C. F. Peters, 1917; John Deathridge (ed.), critical edn, 3 vols, B. Schott's Söhne, in preparation; v.ss., Breitkopf und Härtel, 1851; study s., Breitkopf und Härtel, 1906

Der Ring des Nibelungen

Ein Bühnenfestspiel für drei Tage und einen Vorabend
The Ring of the Nibelung
A stage festival play for three days and a preliminary evening
Libretto by the composer
PREMIERES as a cycle: 13–17 August 1876, Festspielhaus, Bayreuth; UK: 5–9 May 1882, Her Majesty's Theatre, London; US: 4–11 March 1889, Metropolitan, New York

Der Ring des Nibelungen is the biggest work in the history of Western music. It took 28 years to write, rewrite, rehearse, and finally to perform in its entirety at the first Bayreuth Festival in 1876. Wagner conceived it initially as an allegory of the social unrest in Europe that began with the Paris uprisings in February 1848. (The first documented reference to the project is 1 April of that year.) It soon turned into a parable of riddles and emotional conflict that dissolved politics into philosophical poetry, as it were, and reached far beyond the political upheavals that first inspired it. Even before the revolutions of 1848/9 Wagner's political views had been part of a utopian quest for a new kind of theatre that could reflect different truths about society that were less acute and yet – clouded by paradox and contradiction as they often were – more suggestive than politics or philosophy ever could be. Wagner saw the *Ring* as his *summum opus* that represented this ideal in its most radical form.

The *Ring* began relatively simply as the libretto of a single work, *Siegfrieds Tod* (later revised and retitled *Götterdämmerung*), which was first sketched in October 1848. Wagner's main source was the Middle High German *Nibelungenlied*, though he was by no means the first to consider its operatic possibilities. The philosopher F. T. Vischer had already published an essay in 1844 suggesting that the epic poem – regarded since its discovery in the mid-1700s as a kind of German *Iliad* – could be used as the subject of a new kind of musical drama which he called 'a grand heroic opera'. Probably following Vischer's example, Wagner designated *Siegfrieds Tod* in the same way and based the opera mainly on the first half of the *Nibelungenlied*, amplifying it with details from the second and from other versions of the legend.

In 1851 Wagner made the momentous decision to expand *Siegfrieds Tod* into a cycle of four dramas, which he called collectively *Der Ring des Nibelungen*. By this time he had undertaken a much more thorough study of the older oral tradition of the Nibelung myth. Among the works he examined and re-examined were the Old Norse Eddic poems, the

so-called *Poetic Edda*, Snorri Sturluson's 13th-century explanatory account of Scandinavian myth known as the *Prose Edda*, and the ancient narrative accounts in the *Völsunga Saga* and *Thidreks Saga*. From the *Poetic Edda* Wagner adapted the technique of *Stabreim* (the linking of words and lines by alliteration instead of end rhyme) as a new way of writing the texts for the additional dramas *Das Rheingold*, *Die Walküre* and *Der junge Siegfried* (as *Siegfried* was then called). The wealth of mythical situations that Wagner found in the older sources – the trials, contracts, riddles, prophecies, to name only a few – were also bound to tempt him to try something more than just another series of operas in the German Romantic tradition. His utopian journey from 'grand heroic opera' to a complex world myth or 'drama of the future', as he liked to refer to the new project, was inseparable from his discovery of the Nibelung myth in what he believed to be its most archaic form.

Another reason for Wagner's decision to write a four-part cycle (or more precisely a trilogy with a preliminary evening) was his conception of the project as a festival event. Here his model was the ancient Greek festival of Dionysus at Athens. His intention was not to imitate the awesome Athenian spectacles, but rather to revive their sense of communal celebration (as opposed to art as mere entertainment) which in his view the modern theatre totally lacked. Certain dramatic techniques, however, and even the idea of a thematically related cycle of festival dramas itself, were borrowed directly from Aeschylus. The blending of politics and myth; the interplay of gods and humans; the curse that drives the action forward with the oppressive memories of past events; the rule of law and the resolution of guilt; the cosmic mythical presentation of nature: the shaping of the *Ring* drama clearly owed a good deal to the *Oresteia* and to *Prometheus Bound*.

Almost from the start, the idea of the *Ring* project as a festival occasion went hand in hand with the notion of a theatre built specially for its performance. Two years after writing the libretto of *Siegfrieds Tod*, Wagner was already seriously thinking of designing and building a temporary theatre for it outside Zurich to which he would 'invite the most suitable singers, and organize everything necessary for a special event' (letter to E. B. Kietz, 14 September 1850). The idea was not carried out; nor did a later, far more ambitious, project fare much better when Ludwig II placed Wagner under contract in the mid-1860s to complete the *Ring* and ordered plans to proceed for a festival theatre to be built on the Gasteig in Munich, only to see the scheme aborted through political intrigue. The realization of this, for its creator extremely important, aspect of the *Ring* had to wait until the building of the Bayreuth Festival Theatre in the 1870s, which Wagner managed to bring about largely through private initiative and the co-operation of the Bayreuth authorities. Ludwig II, irritated that Wagner had relinquished Munich as a festival site, was eventually persuaded to support the project.

In many other respects, however, the *Ring* is not at

all like Greek drama. Nor in the course of its history has it ever really been dependent on Wagner's original festival concept. In a sense it is a return to the detailed scenic images of nature and mythological symbolism characteristic of 17th-century opera and also to what Walter Benjamin has called the 'allegorical drapery' of the baroque trauerspiele (literally 'sorrow-plays') to which the *Ring* text, richly embroidered as it is with powerfully suggestive icons, is by no means unrelated. (Wagner was a great admirer, for instance, of the allegorical plays of the Spanish dramatist Calderón.) The *Ring* is also a strange amalgam of poetic and musical imagery borrowed from the early Romantic lied, techniques indebted to Beethoven's monumental symphonic style, modernist ideas about politics and myth inherited mainly from Hegel's critics (the so-called Young Hegelians), the world of fairy-tale and, last but not least, a wonderfully inventive harmonic language indebted in part to the works of Franz Liszt.

Wagner published the *Ring* libretto in a private edition early in 1853, several months before he began composing the music for it. He read the entire text several times to groups of friends and acquaintances (many of whom later reported on the riveting power of his delivery) and published it again in revised form in 1863, this time with a preface containing an appeal to a 'princely patron' who might be found to help finance the project. It was this first public edition of the *Ring* text that drew the attention of the young Ludwig II and led to the famous association between the two men that changed the course of Wagner's life. Repercussions from the earlier private edition, however, had not been so positive. Without music, the words of the *Ring* on their own either seemed gratuitously artificial and inept (even to some of Wagner's friends) or gave the impression of an arcane, neo-gothic disinterment of medieval legend that was merely of academic interest. Indeed, a not insignificant detail in the history of the *Ring* is the fact that the first book about it to appear (by Franz Müller) was not so much about the cycle and its wider implications, but rather an introduction to its medieval sources, and moreover one published as early as 1862 before a note of the music had been performed in public. It is true that not long afterwards Wagner conducted excerpts from the music he had composed so far in two concerts in Vienna. But misunderstanding – and ridicule – of the *Ring* libretto persisted and was certainly a factor in Wagner's negative reaction to the premieres of *Das Rheingold* and *Die Walküre* ordered to take place by Ludwig II and conducted by Franz Wüllner in Munich in 1869 and 1870. Wagner did not attend the performances (though a large portion of Europe's musical intelligentsia did) partly on the reasonable grounds that an incomplete production of the cycle, which he had not even finished composing, could only lead to further misapprehension. He refused access to the full score of the third act of *Siegfried*, without which the premiere of the third drama in the cycle planned by the king for 1871 could not take place. And in blatant breach of his 1864 contract with the king, he undermined all attempts by Munich to

procure *Götterdämmerung*, the full score of which was finally finished on 21 November 1874.

Eventually, after superhuman efforts on Wagner's part, the first performance of all four dramas as a cycle took place under his direction in the newly built Festival Theatre in Bayreuth in August 1876 with a cast that included Amalie Materna as Brünnhilde, Franz Betz as Wotan and Albert Niemann as Siegmund. Wagner entrusted the conducting to his protégé Hans Richter, among other reasons because of his immense knowledge of instruments that proved invaluable in helping the orchestral musicians to solve some formidable technical problems in a score that at the time counted as one of the most modern and sophisticated in existence. Financially, the event was so disastrous that Wagner had to close the Festival Theatre for the next six years. The performances themselves were a different matter. Uneven as they were, they convinced many critics and observers that, far from simply resurrecting an archaic legend that for years had been the preserve of university professors, Wagner had successfully created, largely through the power of his music, a completely new myth that could provide a key to an interpretation and deeper understanding of the contemporary world for a wider audience.

Preliminary Evening: Das Rheingold
The Rhinegold
In one act (2h 30m)
Composed: libretto 1851–2; music 1853–4
PREMIERES 26 December 1862, Theater an der Wien, Vienna (excerpts from Scenes 1, 2 and 4; concert); 22 September 1869, Royal Court and National Theatre, Munich; 13 August 1876, Festspielhaus, Bayreuth (as part of the *Ring* cycle); UK: 5 May 1882, Her Majesty's Theatre, Haymarket, London; US: 4 January 1889, Metropolitan, New York
CAST Gods: Wotan *high b*, Donner *high b*, Froh *t*, Loge *t*; Goddesses: Fricka *low s*, Freia *high s*, Erda *low s*; Nibelungs: Alberich *high b*, Mime *t*; Giants: Fasolt *high b*, Fafner *low b*; Rhinedaughters: Woglinde *high s*, Wellgunde *high s*, Flosshilde *low s*; *tb* chorus of Nibelungs
ORCHESTRATION picc, 3 fl, 3 ob, ca, 3 cl, b cl, 3 bsn, 8 hn/4 tubas, 3 tpt, b tpt, 4 trbn/contrabass trbn, contrabass tuba, timp, perc (cym, triangle, t-t), 6 hp, str (16.16.12.12.8); onstage: 18 anvils of different sizes, hammer, hp

SYNOPSIS
Scene 1 At the bottom of the Rhine. In greenish twilight steep rocks are visible. Water swirls around them at the top while the waves dissolve into a damp mist lower down. The Rhinedaughters circle round the central reef which points upward to the brighter light above. Alberich comes out of a cleft in the rocks and makes advances to the Rhinedaughters who cruelly lead him on. Alberich eventually realizes that he is being ridiculed. Silenced by anger, he catches sight of the gleaming Rhinegold high on the central reef. Wellgunde imprudently reveals that whoever can fashion an all-powerful ring from the gold will inherit the world ('Der Welt Erbe gewänne zu eigen'). To the accompaniment of the famous Wagner tubas (sounding here for the first time), Woglinde adds that the required magic can be attained only by renouncing love ('Nur wer der

The trolleys carrying the 'swimming' Rhinemaidens in Das Rheingold *(Bayreuth, 1876)*

Minne Macht entsagt'). Alberich curses love with hideous passion and snatches the gold before vanishing into the depths.

Scene 2 An open space high in the mountains. The light of dawn reflects off the battlements of a magnificent castle. Wotan dreams of eternal power and a fortress for the gods. His wife Fricka rudely awakens him. While Wotan gazes enraptured at the magnificent edifice he has just been dreaming about, Fricka bluntly reminds him of its price. Built by the giant brothers Fasolt and Fafner, the fortress is to be paid for by giving them Freia, keeper of the golden apples of eternal youth. Freia rushes in, complaining that she has been threatened by Fasolt. The giants enter and Fasolt proceeds to lecture Wotan on the significance of contracts. The more pragmatic Fafner, however, knowing that Freia is indispensable to the gods, proposes to abduct her by force. Donner and Froh, Freia's brothers, hurry in to protect their sister, but the giants invoke their contract. The long-awaited god of fire, Loge, on whom Wotan is relying to find a way out of the dilemma, joins the gods at last and tells of many things ('So weit Leben und Weben'), including Alberich's theft of the gold and the mighty ring he has fashioned from it. The giants agree to take Freia away as a provisional hostage until evening, and then to hand her over in exchange for the gold. A pallid mist fills the stage. The gods begin to age, fearfully looking to Wotan for a way out of their plight. Wotan decides to travel with Loge to Nibelheim to take possession of the gold.

Scene 3 A subterranean cavern. Tormented in the first scene, Alberich is now the tormenter. With great skill, his brother Mime has created the Tarnhelm, a magic helmet which enables its wearer to assume any form at will. Alberich takes it from him by force and vanishes in a column of mist. Mime writhes in agony from Alberich's invisible whiplashes. Alberich takes off the Tarnhelm and drives a pack of Nibelung dwarfs laden with treasure before him. Eventually he notices Wotan and Loge.

Unable to resist a demonstration of his power, he kisses the ring on his finger, causing the screaming Nibelungs to scatter, and dons the Tarnhelm again to turn himself into a monstrous dragon. Loge cunningly suggests to Alberich that a small creature would better escape danger, but that the transformation would probably be too hard to accomplish. Alberich rises to the challenge and turns himself into a toad. Loge and Wotan easily capture him and drag him away.

Scene 4 An open space high in the mountains. Alberich is forced to give up the hoard which is dragged up through a cleft by the Nibelungs. Already humiliated in front of his own slaves, Alberich is completely ruined when Wotan violently takes the ring from him. Driven to confront Wotan, among other things with the telling argument that his own theft of the gold was a peccadillo compared with Wotan's present betrayal of the laws he supposedly upholds, Alberich curses the ring just as he cursed love in order to create it ('Wie durch Fluch er mir geriet, verflucht sei dieser Ring'). Henceforth no one who possesses the ring will escape death. The giants enter with Freia and plant two stakes in the ground on either side of her. They demand that the hoard be piled up until her shape is concealed. Now it is Wotan's turn to be humiliated: to fill the final crack the giants demand the ring. Wotan refuses until Erda, the goddess of earth, intervenes to deliver a sphinx-like warning about the end of the gods ('Ein düstrer Tag dämmert den Göttern'), advising him to discard the prize. With sudden resolve he throws the ring on to the pile. Freia is free and the gods return to their immortal state, at least for the moment. But to their horror they witness the first effects of the curse as Fafner kills Fasolt in the ensuing struggle for the ring. Donner conjures up a storm to clear the sultry air. Valhalla lies gleaming in the evening sun at the end of a rainbow bridge which the gods begin to cross in triumph. Diffidently joining the procession, Loge remarks that the gods are really hastening to their end ('Ihrem Ende eilen sie zu'). Their refurbished glory is also dimmed momentarily by the Rhinedaughters, who lament from the depths that their demand that the gold be returned to its original purity has gone unheeded.

EDITIONS f.ss., B. Schott's Söhne, 1873; Egon Voss (ed.), critical edn, 2 vols, B. Schott's Söhne, 1988; v.ss., B. Schott's Söhne, 1861; B. Schott's Söhne, 1899; Breitkopf und Hartel, 1914; C. F. Peters, 1914; study s., B. Schott's Söhne (later Eulenburg), 1901

First Day: Die Walküre
The Valkyrie
In three acts (3h 45m)
Composed: libretto 1851–2; music 1854–6
PREMIERES 26 December 1862, Theater an der Wien, Vienna (excerpts from Acts I and III; concert); 26 June 1870, Royal Court and National Theatre, Munich; 14 August 1876, Festspielhaus, Bayreuth (as part of the *Ring* cycle); US: 2 April 1877, Academy of Music, New York; UK: 6 May 1882, Her Majesty's Theatre, Haymarket, London
CAST Siegmund *t*, Hunding *b*, Wotan *high b*, Sieglinde *s*, Brünnhilde *s*, Fricka *s*, Valkyries: Gerhilde, Ortlinde, Waltraute, Schwertleite, Helmwige, Siegrune, Grimgerde, Rossweisse *s* and *a*
ORCHESTRATION as *Das Rheingold* (see above) plus 2nd picc/3rd fl, tenor d, glock; onstage: cow horn, thunder-machine

SYNOPSIS
Act I The interior of a house at the centre of which stands the trunk of a huge ash tree. A man is being pursued. He enters the house and staggers towards the hearth. The wife of Hunding, the absent master of the house, gives him water. The stranger explains that a storm has driven him there and prepares to leave. But the woman begs him to stay. A secret bond begins to grow between them. Hunding returns from combat. He is instinctively distrustful of the stranger, but reluctantly grants him hospitality for the night. Hunding insists on knowing his guest's name. The stranger says he calls himself 'Woeful' (*Wehwalt*) and explains by telling the story of his childhood. He and his father Wolf returned one day from the hunt to find his mother murdered and his twin sister abducted. He eventually lost track of his father and has been cursed with bad luck ever since, hence his name. A woman forced to marry someone she did not love had asked him for help, whereupon he killed her brothers whose kinsmen are now hunting him. Hunding, realizing that 'Woeful' is the killer, reveals that he is one of the hunters and challenges the stranger to combat the next day. Only the laws of hospitality protect him for the moment. Hunding's wife has tried to intervene, but Hunding orders her to leave to prepare his nightly drink. Alone, the stranger recalls his father's promise to provide him with a sword when in direst need ('Ein Schwert verhiess mir der Vater'). The woman returns. She has put a sleeping draught in Hunding's drink and proceeds to show the stranger a sword thrust into the tree. It was put there by a one-eyed man during her wedding to Hunding. None of the guests, nor anyone since, has had the strength to draw it out. She believes that the hero who can will more than make up for the shame she has had to

endure since robbers forced her to marry Hunding. She embraces the stranger passionately as the great door opens to let in a beautiful spring night. The stranger sings in praise of spring which, like a brother, has freed love, its sister, from the storms of winter ('Winterstürme wichen dem Wonnemond'). The metaphor soon turns into a reality. The woman knew from the single eye of the old man who planted the sword that she was his daughter. Seeing the same look in the stranger's eyes, she suspects that she is related to him too. The stranger asks her to give him a name she loves. When he tells her that his father's name was not Wolf, but Wälse, she knows for certain that he is the Wälsung for whom the sword is intended. She calls him Siegmund. Revelling in his name ('Siegmund heiss ich und Siegmund bin ich') Siegmund pulls the sword from the tree with a mighty wrench. Rapt with wonder and delight, the woman tells him that she is his twin sister Sieglinde. They embrace in ecstasy as Siegmund calls for the blossoming of the Wälsung race.

Act II A wild and rocky mountainside. Wotan knows that Siegmund and Sieglinde are fleeing from Hunding and that Hunding will eventually overtake them. He charges his favourite daughter Brünnhilde (borne to him by the earth goddess Erda) with the task of ensuring Siegmund's victory in his forthcoming duel with Hunding. Brünnhilde warns Wotan of the 'violent storm' in store for him from his wife Fricka, the guardian of marriage, who is approaching in a chariot drawn by a pair of rams. Fricka insists that Hunding has a right to vengeance. She upholds the law in the face of Wotan's advocacy of nature. The power of spring may have brought the twins together, but their incestuous union is a monstrous affront to reason. As for Wotan's grand idea of a free hero who would allow the gods to escape their guilty complicity in the theft of the Rhinegold, this is just false: Siegmund is not free, but merely a pawn in a game invented by Wotan, who is himself severely compromised by his promiscuity. Humbled by the sheer force of Fricka's reasoning, Wotan agrees to forbid Brünnhilde to let Siegmund win the battle against Hunding. The hero must be sacrificed to preserve the divine law. Alone with Brünnhilde, Wotan confesses that all along he has been deceiving himself. Master of the laws of the universe, he is also their victim. Only the end of everything he has built will cleanse the guilt of the gods ('Auf geb' ich mein Werk: nur eines will ich noch: das Ende!'). And for that end Alberich is working. He has created a son whom Wotan now blesses: may the hate of Alberich's child feed on the empty glory of the gods' divinity. Brünnhilde cannot accept Wotan's bleak nihilism and argues to protect Siegmund. Wotan threatens her with the direst consequences if she rebels. Siegmund and Sieglinde enter. Sieglinde is haunted by nightmarish visions of Hunding and his dogs in pursuit of them. She faints in Siegmund's arms. Brünnhilde appears to Siegmund and announces his impending death ('Siegmund! Sieh auf mich!'). But he refuses to go to Valhalla if Sieglinde cannot join him. Rather than put her and their unborn child at the mercy of a hostile world, he threatens to kill them. Brünnhilde is overcome by this display of human emotion and promises to defy her father's command. Hunding's horn is heard summoning Siegmund to battle. Sieglinde's nightmare is now a reality. Brünnhilde protects Siegmund with her shield. But Wotan intervenes and forces Siegmund's sword to shatter on his spear. Hunding drives his spear into the breast of the unarmed Siegmund. Wotan looks in anguish at Siegmund's body and with a dismissive wave of the hand causes Hunding to fall down dead. Meanwhile Brünnhilde has fled with Sieglinde on horseback after gathering up the pieces of the broken sword. In a thunderous rage Wotan storms off in pursuit of them.

Act III On the summit of a rocky mountain. The Valkyries gather together with warlike exuberance, each with a slain hero destined for Valhalla on the saddle of her horse. To their astonishment Brünnhilde arrives with a woman. The Valkyrie sisters, fearful of Wotan's wrath, refuse to protect them. Brünnhilde tells Sieglinde to flee to a forest in the east where she will be safe. There she will give birth to the noblest hero of the world ('den hehrsten Helden der Welt'). Brünnhilde gives her the shattered pieces of the sword and names the hero Siegfried, one joyous in victory, predicting that he will one day forge the fragments anew. Sieglinde sings a striking motif in reply ('O hehrstes Wunder! Herrlichste Maid!') which Wagner called the 'Glorification of Brünnhilde'. Brünnhilde faces Wotan without the protection of her sisters. To their horror, he condemns her to lie defenceless in a magic sleep, vulnerable to the first man who finds her. The Valkyries gallop away wildly. Left alone with Wotan, Brünnhilde justifies her actions. Although she is not wise, she knew in her heart that Wotan loved Siegmund ('Nicht weise bin ich, doch wusst'ich das eine, dass den Wälsung du liebst') which is why she disobeyed his order. Wotan is moved against his better judgement by her courage. Reluctantly he grants her only request. She is to be surrounded by a magic fire which only the freest hero who knows no fear can penetrate. With great emotion, Wotan bids farewell to his daughter and summons Loge to encircle her with fire: only one freer than himself will be able to win her.

EDITIONS f.ss., B. Schott's Söhne, 1874; Felix Mottl (ed.), C. F. Peters, 1921; Christa Jost (ed.), critical edn, 3 vols, B. Schott's Söhne, in preparation; v.ss., B. Schott's Söhne, 1865; B. Schott's Söhne, 1899; Breitkopf und Härtel, 1914; Felix Mottl (ed.), C. F. Peters, 1914; study s., B. Schott's Söhne (later Eulenburg), 1901

Second Day: Siegfried
In three acts (4h 15m)
Composed: libretto 1851–2; music 1856–7 (–end Act II in second draft), 1864–5 (orchestration of Act II), 1869–71 (Act III)
PREMIERES 1 January 1863, Theater an der Wien, Vienna (excerpts from Act I; concert); 16 August 1876, Festspielhaus, Bayreuth (as part of the *Ring* cycle); UK: 8 May 1882, Her Majesty's Theatre, Haymarket, London; US: 9 November 1887, Metropolitan, New York
CAST Siegfried *t*, Mime *t*, the Wanderer (Wotan) *b*, Fafner *b*, Erda *a*, Brünnhilde *s*, Woodbird *boy s*
ORCHESTRATION as *Das Rheingold* (see above) plus 2nd picc/3rd fl, 4th fl/picc, 4th ob/ca, 4th cl/b cl, glock; onstage: ca, hn, forging hammer, thunder-machine

SYNOPSIS
Act I The opening of a cave in the forest. Mime is frustrated that he can forge neither a sword strong enough for Siegfried nor piece together the shattered fragments of Notung ('Zwangvolle Plage'). Notung is the only weapon adequate for the task Mime has in mind for his powerful charge: the killing of the dragon Fafner in order to win back the ring. Siegfried enters boisterously from the forest. He has no respect for the puny dwarf who pretends to be his father. Siegfried forces him to confess the truth. A dying woman emerged from the forest to give birth in the cave. She entrusted the child to Mime, insisting that he should be called Siegfried, and gave him the fragments of Notung which had been shattered when the child's father was slain. Siegfried is thrilled by the story and, before racing back into the forest from which he senses freedom at last ('Aus dem Wald fort in die Welt ziehn'), orders Mime to mend the sword. The Wanderer, dressed in a dark blue-grey cloak, appears uninvited at Mime's hearth. Mime can be rid of him only by agreeing to a game of riddles. The Wanderer stakes his head on three questions from his unwilling host who, over-confident in his own cunning, agrees to ask them ('Drei der Fragen stell' ich mir frei'). The unwanted guest answers correctly and insists that Mime stake his own head on three questions in turn. But Mime, panic-stricken, cannot solve the third riddle: who will weld Notung together

Illustration by Theodore Pixis of Wotan's farewell to Brünnhilde in Act III of Die Walküre *(Munich, 1872)*

again? The Wanderer solves it for him: 'only one who has never felt fear' and the one to whom, he adds casually, Mime's head is now forfeit. Mime promises to take Siegfried to Fafner's lair to teach him fear. Disconcertingly for Mime, Siegfried is only too willing to co-operate. Siegfried starts to forge Notung himself, deliberately ignoring Mime's expertise. Dimly aware of Siegfried's destiny, Mime brews a poison to kill him once he has slain the dragon. Siegfried sings lustily of Notung as he forges ('Notung! Notung! Neidliches Schwert') and Mime skips around the cave in delight at the secret plan he has concocted to save his head. With the finished sword, Siegfried cuts the anvil in two and exultantly lifts Notung high in the air as Mime falls to the ground in fright.

Act II Deep in the forest at night. Alberich is on watch outside Fafner's cave. The Wanderer enters and stops to face Alberich who, as a shaft of moonlight illuminates the scene, quickly recognizes his adversary. Alberich, suspicious of the Wanderer's nonchalance, confronts him with his main weakness: his inability to steal the hoard yet again – an act that would shatter the rule of law once and for all. As if to prove his indifference, the Wanderer generously tells Alberich of Mime's plans to get the hoard for himself, and suggests warning Fafner who, to avoid being murdered, might relinquish the ring to Alberich before Mime arrives. The Wanderer even offers to waken the dragon himself. He knows full well, however, that everything is set on a course that no one, not even Alberich, can alter ('Alles ist nach seiner Art, an ihr wirst du nichts ändern'). Predictably the dragon refuses to listen and goes back to sleep. Siegfried and Mime arrive as day breaks. Mime conjures up threatening images of Fafner. But Siegfried is more intent on ridding himself of his guardian, whom he finds increasingly repulsive. Mime leaves Siegfried beneath a linden tree to muse on his origins. Siegfried cuts a reed pipe and tries to play it in order to converse with the birds. He loses patience and instead uses his silver horn. As the sounds of the horn grow faster and louder, Fafner begins to stir. Spewing venom out of its nostrils, the dragon heaves itself up to crush the interloper, only to expose its heart into which Siegfried swiftly plunges his sword. Realizing that his killer is only a naïve boy being used by someone more sinister, the dying Fafner warns Siegfried of Mime's true plans. Some of the dragon's blood spills on to Siegfried's hand. After involuntarily licking it, Siegfried can at last understand the song of one of the birds, who tells him that the hoard is now his ('Hei! Siegfried gehört nun der Niblungen Hort!'). After Siegfried has gone into the cave to look for the treasure, Mime and Alberich scuttle into sight, quarrelling about their right to the hoard. Siegfried emerges from the cave looking thoughtfully at the ring and the Tarnhelm he is carrying. Alberich withdraws as Mime persuades Siegfried to take the poisonous drink. But the dragon's blood also enables Siegfried to hear the murderous intent beneath Mime's ingratiating phrases. In a moment of disgust Siegfried kills Mime with a single stroke of his sword.

Alberich's mocking laughter echoes in the background, but Siegfried, oblivious, simply asks the Woodbird for a new and preferably more congenial companion. The Woodbird obliges by telling him of Brünnhilde who, asleep on a high rock and imprisoned by a magic fire, awaits a fearless hero to set her free. The Woodbird flies off to show Siegfried the way.

Act III A wild region at the foot of a rocky mountain. The Wanderer arouses Erda from a deep sleep. Bleakly observing that nothing can change the destiny of the world, he still wants her advice on 'how to slow down a rolling wheel' ('wie zu hemmen ein rollendes Rad?'). She replies that her mind is growing 'misty with the deeds of men' ('Männertaten umdämmern mir den Mut'). She was raped by Wotan and bore him Brünnhilde. She is confused and not even clear who her rude awakener is. Irritated but not surprised, the Wanderer announces the coming end of her wisdom, and the triumph of his will: the fall of the gods. The Wanderer awaits Siegfried who enters in high spirits. Their banter is good-humoured until the old man asks the young hero who it was who created Notung. The Wanderer laughs at Siegfried's ignorance and Siegfried, hurt by the condescension, in turn pours scorn on the Wanderer. With a single blow Siegfried cuts the Wanderer's spear in two. The Wanderer picks up the pieces and disappears in total darkness. Siegfried puts his horn to his lips and plunges into the billowing fire spreading down from the mountain. On the tip of Brünnhilde's rock, Siegfried has reached the sleeping Brünnhilde whom he mistakes at first for a male warrior. He cuts away the armour to discover a feminine form that fills him with a strange emotion that he knows is fear. He sinks down, as if he were about to die ('wie ersterbend'), and with closed eyes places a kiss on Brünnhilde's lips. She awakens slowly from the darkness of sleep, sitting up gradually to praise the sun and the earth. Siegfried and Brünnhilde are lost in delight, until she realizes that his love for her (not to mention his destruction of her armour) will impede the fierce independence she knew as a Valkyrie. Miraculously regaining his fearlessness, Siegfried overcomes Brünnhilde's qualms. Together they become ecstatically blind to the world, welcoming its destruction and the death of the gods with the delirium of 'radiant love, laughing death' ('leuchtende Liebe, lachender Tod').

EDITIONS   f.ss., B. Schott's Söhne, 1875; critical edn, B. Schott's Söhne, in preparation; v.ss., B. Schott's Söhne, 1871; B. Schott's Söhne, 1899; Breitkopf und Härtel, 1914; Felix Mottl (ed.), C. F. Peters, 1914; study s., B. Schott's Söhne (later Eulenburg), 1901

Third Day: Götterdämmerung

Twilight of the Gods
Prologue and three acts (4h 15m)
Composed: libretto 1848–52; music (sketches for *Siegfrieds Tod* 1850) 1869–74
PREMIERES   1 March and 6 May 1876, Musikvereinssaal, Vienna (excerpts from Prologue and Acts I and III; concerts); 17 August 1876, Festspielhaus, Bayreuth (as part of the *Ring*

cycle); UK: 9 May 1882, Her Majesty's Theatre, Haymarket, London; US: 25 January 1888, Metropolitan, New York
CAST Siegfried *t*, Gunther *high b*, Alberich *high b*, Hagen *low b*, Brünnhilde *s*, Gutrune *s*, Waltraute *low s*, First Norn *a*, Second Norn *s*, Third Norn *s*; Rhinedaughters: Woglinde *s*, Wellgunde *s*, Flosshilde *a*; *tb* chorus of vassals, *s* chorus of women
ORCHESTRATION as *Das Rheingold* (see above) plus tenor d, glock; onstage: cow horns, hns, 4 hp

SYNOPSIS
Prologue On the Valkyries' rock. The three Norns, daughters of Erda, spin the golden rope of world knowledge that binds past, present and future. The rope was once tied to the World Ash Tree until Wotan desecrated the Tree to create his spear and establish his rule of order over the universe. The Norns try to keep the rope taut. But the threads tangle and it snaps. The continuum between past and future is broken: the Norns' primeval wisdom is at an end. Outside a cave, Brünnhilde and Siegfried emerge with the rising of the sun, he in full armour, she leading her horse Grane. Brünnhilde sings that her love for Siegfried would not be true if she refused to let him go forth and to perform new deeds ('Zu neuen Taten'). Siegfried leaves Brünnhilde the ring as a token, and she in turn gives him Grane. Carrying his sword, he begins his descent from the rock and vanishes with the horse. His horn is heard from below as Brünnhilde bids him farewell.

Act I The hall of Gunther's court on the Rhine. Hagen, the illegitimate son of Alberich and Grimhild, is plotting to regain the ring for his father. His legitimate half-siblings Gunther and Gutrune, who have inherited their kingdom from their dead parents Gibich and Grimhild, sit on a throne to one side. Hagen gives them some (seemingly) sensible advice. If they are to retain the respect of their subjects, they must marry without delay. Hagen suggests Siegfried for Gutrune and Brünnhilde for Gunther. The lacklustre Gibichungs are overwhelmed with the thought, but sceptical until Hagen suggests a way of attracting their powerful partners-to-be. Gutrune is to give Siegfried a potion that will erase his memory of all other women. Once Gutrune has captured his heart, it will be easy for her brother to persuade him to woo Brünnhilde. Siegfried's horn sounds from his boat on the Rhine. Hagen calls out to him to come ashore. Siegfried steps on to land with his sword and Grane. He tells Gunther of the Tarnhelm and the ring. As planned, Gutrune offers him the potion of forgetfulness which he unwittingly accepts, dedicating his first drink to Brünnhilde and faithful love. Its effect is immediate: spellbound by Gutrune, he hears Gunther talk of the woman Gunther desires, but cannot win because she lives on a high mountain surrounded by a fire. Siegfried shows no sign of recognition. Knowing that he can penetrate the fire, he offers to woo the woman, using the Tarnhelm to disguise himself as his host. After sealing his promise with an oath of blood brotherhood, he sets off with Gunther for Brünnhilde's rock, leaving Hagen to guard the hall. Hagen savours the plot he has set in motion ('Hier sitz' ich zur Wacht'). On the Valkyries' rock,

Brünnhilde sits in front of the cave gazing rapturously at the ring. Dark storm clouds appear as Waltraute, one of the Valkyries, arrives to tell her of Wotan seated morosely in Valhalla, waiting passively for the end of the gods ('Höre mit Sinn, was ich dir sage'). Despite Waltraute's pleading, Brünnhilde refuses Wotan's only remaining wish: to free the gods from the curse by returning the ring to the Rhinedaughters. Brünnhilde vows never to renounce the ring, or the love it supposedly symbolizes ('Die Liebe liesse ich nie'). Waltraute hastens away, distraught. The brightening flames and the sound of a horn herald the arrival of Siegfried. But to Brünnhilde's horror a different figure steps out of the fire. In Gunther's shape, Siegfried wrestles with her and wrenches the ring from her finger. He forces her into the cave and lays his sword between them as witness that his wooing of Gunther's bride is chaste.

Act II In front of the hall of Gunther's court, Hagen is asleep. As the moon suddenly appears, Alberich can be seen in front of him, resting his arms on his son's knees. He exhorts Hagen to keep faith with their plan to ruin Siegfried and win back the ring ('Sei treu, Hagen, mein Sohn! Trauter Helde!'). With the help of the Tarnhelm, Siegfried arrives at the Gibichungs' court ahead of Gunther and Brünnhilde. In a detailed dialogue with Hagen and Gutrune, he describes his successsful wooing of Brünnhilde for Gunther and announces their imminent arrival. As if calling the Gibichung vassals to battle, Hagen summons them to greet Gunther and his bride. The vassals do not understand Hagen's warlike tone, or the need for the sharp weapons and bellowing horns. Hagen explains by proposing a barbaric feast, including the slaughter of animals for the gods, and uninhibited drunkenness. Solemnly, the vassals greet Gunther and Brünnhilde as they disembark. Brünnhilde appears crushed and humiliated until she sees the ring on Siegfried's finger. Roused to furious anger, she declares that Siegfried is her husband and flings desperate charges at him. To clear his name Siegfried swears an oath on Hagen's spear that its point may pierce his body if he is lying about who he is. Brünnhilde dedicates the sharp blade to Siegfried's downfall. After Siegfried has left to prepare for his marriage, Brünnhilde tells Hagen that she did not protect Siegfried's back with her magic as he would never have turned it towards an enemy. Now his enemy, she reveals that his back is the only place where he can be mortally wounded. Gunther, the deceived deceiver, is convinced of Siegfried's treachery by Hagen, but worried about the effect Siegfried's death will have on Gutrune. Hagen decides to make it look like a hunting accident. All are now dedicated to Siegfried's death. Calling on Wotan, guardian of vows, Brünnhilde and Gunther swear an oath of vengeance. Hagen in turn invokes the spirit of his father, Alberich, lord of the ring ('des Ringes Herrn'). Siegfried returns with Gutrune and the bridal procession, while Hagen forces Brünnhilde to join Gunther to prepare for a double wedding they know will never take place.

Act III A forest area on the banks of the Rhine. An elf has lured Siegfried away from his hunting companions to the riverbank where the Rhine-daughters are playing. They tell him he will die later that day if he keeps the ring. Laughing, he ignores them. They lament his blindness and swim away to 'a proud woman' ('ein stolzes Weib') who will soon inherit his treasure and give them a better hearing. Siegfried has rejoined his hunting companions who sit down to rest and drink. At Hagen's prompting he regales them with stories of Mime and Notung, of Fafner and the Woodbird. But Hagen has a servant slip an antidote into Siegfried's drink that enables him to tell the true story of Brünnhilde as well. Siegfried gives a rapturous account of how he learned about her from the Woodbird and how passionately she embraced him after his bold kiss. Wotan's two ravens fly up out of a bush. Hagen asks Siegfried if he can understand them too. Siegfried turns, and immediately Hagen thrusts his spear into Siegfried's back. Perjury is avenged, Hagen gloats to the horrified onlookers. The vassals take up Siegfried's body to form a solemn cortège as the magnificent funeral march recollects and reflects on the hero's life. In the hall of Gunther's court, Gutrune has been plagued by disturbing dreams and the sight of Brünnhilde walking to the banks of the Rhine. When she discovers Siegfried's body, brought back by the hunters, she nearly faints with shock. Hagen freely admits the murder and kills Gunther in a fight over the ring. But when Hagen reaches for the ring, the dead Siegfried's hand rises menacingly to prevent him from taking it. Brünnhilde comes forward to silence Gutrune's lament and to contemplate the dead Siegfried. She orders his body to be placed on a funeral pyre ('Starke Scheite schichtet mir dort am Rande des Rheines zuhauf'). Now, after talking to the Rhinedaughters, she understands Wotan's will to end the gods, to rid them of the curse that also ensnared her innocent lover. She takes the ring, puts it on her finger and casts a torch on the pyre. To cleanse the ring from the curse with fire before it is returned to the Rhinedaughters, she leaps with her horse into the burning pyre, united with Siegfried in death. The Rhine overflows its banks and pours over the flames. As the Rhinedaughters appear on the waves, Hagen rushes headlong into the flood to demand the return of the ring. Woglinde and Wellgunde draw him into the depths, while Flosshilde holds up the ring in triumph. The hall has collapsed, and in its ruins the men and women watch apprehensively as an increasingly bright glow appears in the sky. Gradually the hall of Valhalla becomes visible, filled with gods and heroes just as Waltraute described it in Act I. As the orchestra recalls Erda's prophecy in *Das Rheingold* of the end of the gods ('Ein düstrer Tag dämmert den Göttern'), the hall appears to be completely consumed by bright flames.

EDITIONS f.ss., B. Schott's Söhne, 1876; Hartmut Fladt (ed.), critical edn, 3 vols, B. Schott's Söhne, 1980–82; v.ss., B. Schott's Söhne, 1875; B. Schott's Söhne, 1900; Breitkopf und Härtel, 1914; Felix Mottl (ed.), C. F. Peters, 1914; study s., B. Schott's Söhne (later Eulenburg), 1901

Wagner's *Ring* has been interpreted in so many wildly contradictory ways that it probably counts as the most ingratiating work ever written for the operatic stage. Yet the fact that it has far transcended its original destiny as a 'stage festival play' and German national epic is testimony not only to the potency of Wagner's self-made myth, but also to the consistently superior quality of his music. The search for archetypal images and mythical heroes in the forging of the *Ring* libretto would have been unthinkable without the assistance of pioneering works such as Jacob Grimm's *German Mythology* (1835) and Karl Simrock's *Lay of the Amelungs* (1843–9), which provided the building blocks of, and methods of linking, the various stories and legends Wagner needed to create his own myth. But for the composition of the music there was no such help. Wagner's five-and-a-half-year musical silence between the completion of *Lohengrin* in April 1848 and the start of work on the *Ring* in November 1853 suggests that the difficulties were formidable: at no other point in his life was Wagner musically silent for so long.

Once a start had been made on the music, however, the composition proceeded so rapidly that it is hard to believe that Wagner had no premeditated strategy in mind. Astonishingly, he finished the first drafts of *Das Rheingold* and *Die Walküre* in (respectively) only two and a half and six months. Wagner himself, and most of his biographers since, have explained this rush of invention with certain events in his (usually turbulent) private life. Seventeen coded messages to Mathilde Wesendonck, for instance, the wife of a rich friend and benefactor, with whom he fell in love in 1854, were inserted into the first draft of Act I of *Die Walküre*. But Wagner surely must have used some of his long musical silence to think out, at least in broad terms, strategies that were determined to a large extent by the interaction of the different levels of his myth. The network of leitmotifs, the highly original use of keys and form that usurps all sense of traditional operatic set numbers, not to mention the mirroring of the drama through extremely differentiated orchestration, are worked out too carefully and consistently (at least in the first half of the cycle) for anything else to seem possible.

Alone the sheer quantity of motifs (there are over a hundred) Wagner needed to fill out about 15 hours of music suggests an important difference between the leitmotif system he invented specifically for the *Ring* and the well-tried operatic device of the so-called reminiscence motif he had used, albeit with great originality, in his earlier operas. (In *Lohengrin*, for instance, there are only six main motifs in the entire opera, fewer than in the first scene of *Das Rheingold* alone.) In short, the necessity of another kind of motivic network arose because of Wagner's decision in the *Ring* finally to abolish the contrast between unstructured recitative and musically highly organized 'set pieces' typical of conventional opera. Usually for reasons of dramatic irony, Wagner reinvented the contrast at certain places in the *Ring* (the start of Loge's laconic narration to the gods in the second scene of *Das Rheingold* for instance) but basically set out to create a continuous musical–dramatic dialogue that relies for its coherence not on predictable stylistic changes but on a steady interchange of related motifs that can be joined, combined and varied in countless ways without loss of identity. The technique is fundamentally an extension of Berlioz's *idée fixe* (a resilient theme symbolizing a central figure in a story that returns in different shapes and sizes during the course of the narrative). This is not to deny the originality of Wagner's daring concept of motifs in series that not only represent significant aspects of the unfolding drama but also relate to each other to provide the narrative with a semblance of logic and a scaffold for its monumental structure on a musical level.

Contrary to a widely held belief, Wagner named a few of the leitmotifs in the *Ring* in his sketches and occasionally to friends. The practice, usually thought to be the invention of Hans von Wolzogen, the compiler of the first leitmotif guides, has often been misused and misunderstood. Wagner called the motif sung by Alberich when he renounces love to steal the gold in the opening scene of *Das Rheingold* the 'curse on love' (*Liebesfluch*). But he did not intend to suggest (and arguably neither did Wolzogen) that the meaning of the motif stays literally the same later in the cycle. Avid leitmotif watchers have all noticed Wagner's 'inconsistency' and apparently lamentable lack of rigour in Act I of *Die Walküre* when he allows Siegmund to sing the motif in its original key of C minor as he pulls the sword out of the ash tree – a moment leading to a triumphant announcement of the so-called 'sword' motif in C major when Siegmund, far from having cursed love, seems to have discovered it for the first time. Few have considered the reverse parallel (of which there are many in the *Ring*) with the opening scene of *Das Rheingold* when, after the dazzling presentation of the gold in C major by the Rhinedaughters, the music shifts gradually to C minor and Alberich's snatching of the treasure. By moving emphatically in the opposite direction, Siegmund's music in *Die Walküre* promises to negate the consequences of Alberich's primal crime – a possible reading that suggests that Siegmund's singing of the motif is not a 'mistake', but an attempt to exorcize its original meaning. That Siegmund turns out to be the wrong hero for the task and the promise a false one only adds irony to the moment in retrospect. Indeed, after Siegmund is killed, the memory of the past weighs so oppressively on the motif that Wagner can use it again to great ironic effect in Act I of *Götterdämmerung* when Brünnhilde tells Waltraute in all sincerity that she will never renounce her love for Siegfried, only to do just that at the end of Act II. Nearly all the motifs in the *Ring* resonate similarly with memories of past events which, though the actual notes of the motifs may stay exactly the same, never cease to accumulate and hence to be gradually transformed as the tragedy unfolds.

Wagner deliberately used one motif so sparingly that there could be no mistake about it. Bernard Shaw was puzzled by it (as many later commentators

have been), calling it 'the most trumpery phrase in the entire tetralogy', the sole valuable quality of which was its 'gushing effect'. He was referring to the motif that, 'since it undoubtedly does gush very emphatically', dominates the concluding moments of the cycle. In effect the ending of the *Ring* is a vast musical recapitulation. Salient motifs, cadences, keys, fragments of form and even details of orchestration return from earlier parts of the tetralogy to sum up a great parable of human existence. The feeling of circular movement, of going back over the whole cycle to the beginning, could be seen as a metaphor for Wotan's pessimism – a static, spatial image that is filled with what Walter Benjamin called 'the disconsolate chronicle of world history'. At the same time the motif Wagner chose to end the *Ring* has been heard only once before when Sieglinde sings it to Brünnhilde in Act III of *Die Walküre* after Brünnhilde has alluded to Siegfried's future destiny. The last-minute development of it in the final moments of the *Ring* is so unexpected that it appears to cut across the feeling of endless return, as if to break the circle of history, by celebrating instead Siegfried's victory in reconciling, through his death, the conflict between nature and society at the root of the myth. The motif is certainly triumphant, as Wagner stressed when, in contrast to the leitmotif guides, he called it not the 'redemption through love' but the 'glorification of Brünnhilde' – a perfectly logical description since it is Brünnhilde who successfully brings the story to an end by announcing that its true hero has completed his task.

RECORDINGS 1. Flagstad, Konetzni, Höngen, Treptow, Lorenz, Suthaus, Sattler, Markwort, Frantz, Pernersdorfer, Weber, La Scala Ch and O, Furtwängler, Hunt, 1950; 2. Mödl, Konetzni, Cavelti, Klose, Malaniuk, Windgassen, Suthaus, Patzak, Frantz, Neidlinger, Frick, Greindl, Rome Radio Ch and O, Furtwängler, EMI, 1953; 3. Varnay, Resnik, Malaniuk, Vinay, Windgassen, Witte, Kuén, Hotter, Neidlinger, Weber, Greindl, Bayreuth Festival Ch and O, Krauss, Foyer, 1953; 4. Nilsson, Crespin, Flagstad/Ludwig, Windgassen, King, Svanholm, Stolze, London/Hotter, Frick, Böhme, Vienna State Opera Ch, Vienna PO, Solti, Decca, 1957–66; 5. Nilsson, Rysanek, Burmeister, Mödl, Windgassen, Wohlfahrt, Adam, Neidlinger, Talvela, Böhme, Greindl, Bayreuth Festival Ch and O, Böhm, Philips, 1966–7: no one performance will be satisfying in every respect though the 1950 Furtwängler/La Scala comes close to it, apart from the inferior recording. It also preserves for posterity Flagstad's unforgettable Brünnhilde. The Furtwängler/Rome is in vastly better sound, but hasn't quite the same eloquence or such satisfying playing, but it again proves the conductor supreme in the cycle. Krauss's more dramatic and highly characterized reading enshrines Varnay's Brünnhilde and Hotter's Wotan at their considerable best, none to compare since. Böhm's account catches the *frisson* of real evenings at Bayreuth and catches Nilsson at her peak. She sings with just as much strength and gleam for Solti, but his cycle – for all its sonic power as a recording – is inconsistent, having been recorded over such a long spell of years. It is heard at its most potent in the outer works, which can be acquired separately. This set can claim historical importance as the first studio recording of the *Ring* ever to appear complete on disc. Besides these, there is Janowski's Eurodisc from the 1980s, notable for the playing of the Dresden Staatskapelle but too lightweight as an interpretation and with an uneven cast.

Karajan's chamber-music-like cycle should be avoided: as a whole it is too self-conscious. The cycles conducted by Levine and Haitink are variable in quality, the Haitink preferable in the two later works [A.B.]

VIDEOS 1. Boulez/Chéreau, Bayreuth, Philips, 1980; 2. Sawallisch/Lehnhoff, Bavarian State Opera, 1989; 3. Levine/Schenk, Metropolitan, DG, 1990: these three cycles are complementary. The mould-breaking Chéreau concept looks well on video and hasn't dated. Schenk's Met effort does the conventional very well. The Lehnhoff interpretation is eccentric, enlivened by inspirational strokes of genius. Musically, the first is well unified, dedicated and concentrated. The third is heavyweight and variably sung. The second is superbly conducted and distinguished by the partnership of Behrens as Brünnhilde with Robert Hale, best of recent Wotans [A.B.]

Tristan und Isolde

Handlung in three acts (3h 45m)
Libretto by the composer
Composed: libretto 1857; music 1856–9
PREMIERES 12 March 1859, Prague (Prelude with concert ending by Hans von Bülow; concert); 25 January 1860, Théâtre Italien, Paris (Prelude with concert ending by Wagner; concert); 10 March 1863, St Petersburg (Prelude and Transfiguration; concert); 10 June 1865, Royal Court and National Theatre, Munich; UK: 20 June 1882, Drury Lane, London; US: 1 December 1886, Metropolitan, New York
CAST Tristan *t*, King Marke *b*, Isolde *s*, Kurwenal *bar*, Melot *t*, Brangäne *s*, shepherd *t*, steersman *bar*, voice of young sailor *t*; *tb* chorus of ship's crew, knights and pages
ORCHESTRATION 3 fl/picc, 2 ob, ca, 2 cl, b cl, 3 bsn, 4 hn, 3 tpt, 3 trbn, b tuba, timp, cym, triangle, hp, str; onstage: ca, 6 hn (Act II, Scene 1: 'the horns are to be doubled in strength if possible, or better still there should be several players to a part'), 3 tpt, 3 trbn

Inspired by his reading of the philosopher Arthur Schopenhauer, Wagner first conceived *Tristan und Isolde* in the autumn of 1854. Another immediate stimulus was a dramatization of the story by his friend Karl Ritter of which he was extremely critical, calling it too elaborate and packed with 'adventurous incidents'. One of two operatic foretastes of Wagner's masterpiece is the famous light-hearted account of Tristan and Isolde in Donizetti's opera *L'elisir d'amore*, the title of which is itself an allusion to the tale. (Wagner probably knew the opera, as it was in the repertoire of the Dresden Court Opera when he was conductor there in the 1840s.) The other is a scenario of an opera *Tristan und Isolde* in five acts written by the poet Robert Reinick for Schumann in 1846, who eventually decided not to compose it. (In all likelihood Wagner knew this too since he conversed regularly with Schumann in 1845 and 1846 at the Engelklub in Dresden about their respective artistic plans.) As an operatic venture and in terms of its sheer rigour and boldness, however, Wagner's *Tristan* is without precedent, even when compared with his previous works.

Wagner's main source was Gottfried von Strassburg's medieval epic *Tristan* (*c.* 1215) – in the 19th century a work admired for its style and pilloried for its suspect morality in about equal measure. There were several reasons for Wagner's sudden decision to adapt it, including its (for medieval texts) unusual subject of fated and enchanted, as opposed to courtly, love that leads to physical destruction and 'eternal death' (êweclîchez sterben). The idea was in tune not only with Wagner's newly awakened interest in Schopenhauer, who believed that the preconscious Will was an expression of the sexual drive and the road to salvation its negation, but also with his increasing love for Mathilde Wesendonck, the wife of his long-suffering patron Otto Wesendonck – a love that Wagner knew, because of his dependency on the latter, would be unlikely to become a reality. This interpretation is at least not hard to read into a famous letter about *Tristan* he wrote to Liszt in December 1854: 'Since I have never enjoyed the real happiness of love in my life, I want to erect another monument to this most beautiful of dreams in which love will be properly sated from beginning to end.'

Wagner called *Tristan* 'the most full-blooded musical conception'. In the end the musical challenge was perhaps his most important reason for writing it. (His wife Cosima later wrote in her diaries on 11 December 1878 – carefully omitting to mention the role of Mathilde Wesendonck – that 'he had felt the urge to express himself symphonically for once, and that led to *Tristan*'.) In 1857 Wagner interrupted work on the *Ring* at the end of *Siegfried* Act II and finished *Tristan* two years later, often working at breakneck speed to deliver each act to the printer on time before moving on to the next. Indeed, half the score was already in print before he finished composing it – an odd situation that had to do with the comical fact that he was desperate for cash from the publisher who would pay him only an act at a time. After its publication in 1860 the work was widely regarded as unperformable. The first performance was planned for the Vienna Court Opera in 1861, but abandoned after 77 rehearsals. The premiere eventually took place in Munich in 1865, conducted by Hans von Bülow with Ludwig Schnorr von Carolsfeld and his wife Malwina in the leading roles. Nine years elapsed before a second production was attempted in Weimar.

SYNOPSIS

Act I An awning on board Tristan's ship during a crossing from Ireland to Cornwall. Isolde is being taken to Cornwall against her will to marry King Marke. Resolved to die, she tells her confidante Brangäne to call Tristan to speak to her. Tristan is politely evasive and, when Brangäne insists, his trusted companion Kurwenal leaps up to sing a mocking song about Morald, a knight of Ireland who came to Cornwall to claim its tribute, only to be killed by Tristan. Now Morald's head hangs in Ireland as payment. The knights and the ship's crew join lustily in the refrain. A furious Isolde confides to Brangäne her version of the story ('Wie lachend sie mir Lieder singen'). Morald was her fiancé who in his fatal battle with Tristan seriously wounded him. Sick and dying, Tristan returned to Ireland in a small boat, where he was found by Isolde and nursed back to health. Disguised as 'Tantris', he went unrecognized by her until she noticed a notch in his sword that perfectly matched a splinter extracted

Ludwig and Malwina Schnorr von Carolsfeld as Tristan and Isolde (Munich, 1865)

from Morald's body. She raised a sword to kill him, but as he looked longingly into her eyes she let it fall. Now he has repaid her kindness by returning to claim her as a bride in a loveless marriage. Brangäne tries to calm her by reminding her of her mother's elixir of love. But Isolde will hear of only one of her mother's magic potions: the elixir of death. Kurwenal enters to announce their imminent landing and the approach of Tristan. Isolde demands vengeance for the death of Morald and offers Tristan a drink of atonement. Recognizing the elixir of death, Tristan drinks to Isolde. She wrenches the cup from his hand and drains it herself. Grimly expecting to die, they are overcome by passionate love instead, oblivious to the cries of the knights and the sailors as the ship prepares to land. Brangäne confesses in despair that she has substituted the elixir of love. Isolde, dismayed that she is now condemned to live, falls unconscious on to Tristan's breast.

Act II A garden with tall trees in front of Isolde's apartment in King Marke's royal fortress in Cornwall. It is a summer night and the king's hunting party can be heard setting out. Isolde is impatiently waiting for Brangäne to extinguish the torch burning by the door as a signal to Tristan that he can come to her safely. But Brangäne is hesitant, believing that Tristan's best friend Melot, who has arranged the hunt so that the lovers can meet, has actually set a trap. Isolde is scornful, impatiently putting out the torch herself and ordering Brangäne to stand watch in the tower. Tristan enters and the lovers fall passionately into each other's arms. Both deliver a curse on 'the spiteful day' ('dem tückischen Tage')

that has bedazzled them, and a hymn to the night, a symbol of death that will ensure the eternal existence of their love ('O sink hernieder, Nacht der Liebe'). They ignore Brangäne's warnings about the imminent break of day and enter into an ecstatic duet which is brutally interrupted at its climax by the sudden entrance of Kurwenal who warns of King Marke's approach. Marke enters with Melot and the hunting party. In an extended monologue, the bewildered king asks in vain how his faithful nephew could betray him ('Dies, Tristan, mir?'). Tristan yearns for the night. As he bends down to kiss Isolde, Melot draws his sword. Instead of defending himself, Tristan lets his guard fall and sinks wounded into the arms of Kurwenal.

Act III Tristan's fortress in Brittany. The sound of a melancholy tune played by an old shepherd awakes Tristan from a deep coma. Overjoyed, Kurwenal tells how he brought Tristan back to his homeland to recover. Kurwenal is hourly awaiting Isolde's ship and the shepherd will play a joyful melody when it is sighted. In demented excitement Tristan curses the terrible elixir of love ('verflucht sei, furchtbarer Trank!') and imagines he sees the ship approaching with Isolde on it transfigured and full of grace. Suddenly the shepherd sounds his joyful melody. Tristan rips the bandages off his wound and leaps from the sickbed to struggle forward to meet Isolde as she enters, only to die in her arms with her name on his lips. A second ship arrives, and King Marke, Melot and their retinue pour into the castle. In a rage Kurwenal kills Melot, but collapses seriously wounded, dying at the feet of the dead Tristan. Brangäne tells Isolde that she has explained everything about the fatal elixir of love to the king who has come to Brittany to forgive Tristan. But Isolde is deaf to her words. She sees Tristan awakened to new life in eternal death ('Mild und leise, wie er lächelt') and falls, as if transfigured, into Brangäne's arms.

Bernard Shaw once admitted that Wagner had retraced 'poetic love' to its 'alleged origin in sexual passion, the emotional phenomena of which he has expressed in music with a frankness and forcible naturalism which would possibly have scandalized Shelley'. Shaw was thinking especially of *Tristan und Isolde*, which from the first, with its graphic 'translation into music of the emotions which accompany the union of a pair of lovers', posed a moral as well as a musical challenge to 19th-century audiences. That Duchess Sophie of Bavaria was not allowed to attend the first performance of *Tristan* in 1865 out of moral considerations, despite the fact that she was a mature 20-year-old woman married to Duke Carl Theodor of Bavaria, is only one historical detail illustrating the point. Wagner's need to present unquenchable yearning and sexual passion in a convincing way, however, led him to widen the scope of his musical resources so drastically that *Tristan* almost inevitably soon became one of the most important musical works of the 19th century. In 1878 he explained to Cosima his need at the time of *Tristan* 'to push himself to the limit musically'. And indeed the unprecedented expansion of harmonic possibilities audible in the very first chord of the work (the so-called 'Tristan chord' is by far the most widely analysed collection of four notes in Western music) and the sheer freedom and invention in the handling of individual chromatic lines mean that it is quite justifiable to speak of the music of *Tristan* as a harbinger of the new music of the 20th century. (The music of *Tristan* is never actually atonal, though it energizes the tonal system from within to near breaking-point.) Composers have frequently acknowledged and parodied the modernist ambition of *Tristan* by using its opening phrase in their own works, including Wagner himself who, in Act III of *Die Meistersinger*, was the first to cite it. Perhaps the subtlest use of it is in the final movement of Alban Berg's *Lyric Suite* where it recalls not only the avant-garde aspect of *Tristan*, but also its erotic *raison d'être*. Berg blended Wagner's music into a 12-note movement in such a way that it can be explained, as Berg himself pointed out, in terms of the working of the 12-note row. At the same time it was intended as part of a secret programme referring to his affair with Hanna Fuchs-Robettin, the sister of Franz Werfel and wife of a rich industrialist. The parallel with Wagner's infatuation with Mathilde Wesendonck, one of the inspirations behind *Tristan* and also the wife of a wealthy businessman, was obviously not a coincidence.

RECORDINGS 1. Flagstad, Thebom, Suthaus, Fischer-Dieskau, Greindl, Covent Garden Ch, Philharmonia O, Furtwängler, HMV, 1952; 2. Mödl, Malaniuk, Vinay, Hotter, Weber, Bayreuth Festival Ch and O, Karajan, Cetra, 1952; 3. Nilsson, Ludwig, Windgassen, Waechter, Talvela, Bayreuth Festival Ch and O, Böhm, DG, 1966; 4. Behrens, Minton, Hofmann, Weikl, Sotin, Bavarian Radio Ch and SO, Bernstein, Philips, 1983: the Furtwängler set is an all-time classic with an unsurpassable cast and conductor. The 1952 live account from Bayreuth runs it close, a more dramatic, visceral account, almost as well sung. The 1966 Bayreuth set is still more thrilling as a live encounter with the work, movingly sung by Nilsson and Windgassen. The combination of such spontaneous artists as Behrens and Bernstein recommends the 1983 version, also recorded live [A.B.]
VIDEO J. Meier, Schwarz, Kollo, Becht, Salminen, Bayreuth Festival Ch and O, Barenboim, Philips (laserdisc only), 1983: Ponnelle's beautifully designed, individual interpretation, awkwardly conducted, moderately sung [A.B.]
EDITIONS f.ss., Breitkopf und Härtel, 1860; Felix Mottl (ed.), C. F. Peters, 1914; Balling (ed.), critical edn, Breitkopf und Härtel, 1925; Isolde Vetter (ed.), critical edn, 3 vols, B. Schott's Söhne, Mainz, in preparation; v.ss., Breitkopf und Härtel, 1860; Schott, 1906; study s., Breitkopf und Härtel (later Eulenburg), 1911

Die Meistersinger von Nürnberg

The Mastersingers of Nuremberg
In three acts (4h 15m)
Libretto by the composer
Composed: libretto 1845, 1861–2, 1866–7; music 1862–4, 1866–7
PREMIERES 1 November 1862, Gewandhaus, Leipzig (Prelude; concert); 26 December 1862, Theater an der Wien, Vienna (excerpts from Act I, Scene 3 Assembly of the Mastersinger Guild for orchestra alone and Pogner's address; concert); 5 November 1863, Prague (Sachs's Shoemaker Song

from Act II; concert); 12 July 1865, Residenztheater, Munich (excerpts from Act I, Scene 3, including Walther's Trial Song; concert); 4 April 1868, Liedertafel Frohsinn, Linz (Sachs's closing address and final chorus from Act III; concert, conducted Anton Bruckner); 21 June 1868, Royal Court and National Theatre, Munich; UK: 30 May 1882, Drury Lane, London; US: 4 January 1886, Metropolitan, New York
CAST Mastersingers: Hans Sachs (shoemaker) *b*, Veit Pogner (goldsmith) *b*, Kunz Vogelgesang (furrier) *t*, Konrad Nachtigall (tinsmith) *b*, Sixtus Beckmesser (town clerk) *b*, Fritz Kothner (baker) *b*, Balthasar Zorn (pewterer) *t*, Ulrich Eisslinger (grocer) *t*, Augustin Moser (tailor) *t*, Hermann Ortel (soap-boiler) *b*, Hans Schwarz (stocking weaver) *b*, Hans Foltz (coppersmith) *b*; Walther von Stolzing *t*, David *t*, Eva *s*, Magdalene *s*, night-watchman *b*; *satb* chorus of men and women from every guild, journeymen, apprentices, young women, populace
ORCHESTRATION 3 fl/picc, 2 ob, 2 cl, 2 bsn, 4 hn, 3 tpt, 3 trbn, bass tuba, timp, bd, cym, triangle, glock, hp, lute, str; onstage: organ, a nightwatchman's cow horn (F♯), hns, tpts 'in different keys with as many players as needed', tenor ds

Die Meistersinger is an exception among Wagner's works in that it is not substantially based on any narrative source, though no end of literary and historical detail was lavished on it. Characterizations of its main figure, Hans Sachs, and other background material were provided by Goethe's poem 'An Account of an Old Woodcut Showing Hans Sachs's Poetic Calling' and Gervinus's influential *History of German Literature*, as well as Lortzing's 1840 opera *Hans Sachs* (an adaptation of a play written in 1827 by the Viennese court dramatist J. L. F. Deinhardstein). Ironically, Wagner had no hesitation in resorting to the well-known methods of his arch-rival Meyerbeer with some painstaking research into into local colour, including details of medieval Nuremberg, various folk traditions, and the doctrine and practices of the historical mastersingers, which he gleaned mostly from J. C. Wagenseil's *Book of the Master-Singers' Gracious Art* (1687). But apart from some ideas taken from E. T. A. Hoffmann's *Master Martin the Cooper and His Apprentices* (1819) and a few other sources, the story of the opera is largely Wagner's own invention.

Wagner first sketched out a scenario for *Die Meistersinger* in 1845. He wrote later that he conceived it then as a work that stood in relation to the song contest on the Wartburg in *Tannhäuser* 'like a richly textured satyr play', just as in ancient Athens 'a comic satyr play would follow a tragedy'. Not long after the fiasco of the revised Paris *Tannhäuser* in 1861 the idea reasserted itself, but with the key difference that it took its bearings this time from *Tristan* and the philosophy of Schopenhauer. The passion of the young nobleman for the woman he wins in the singing competition in the first version became a blind urge driven by fate in the second (at one point Eva explains to Sachs that she did not choose to love Walther, rather her love 'chose' her and became an 'unheard-of torment') and Sachs was transformed into a far more substantial figure who beneath his jovial appearance is himself distracted by irrational feelings for the same woman. But Wagner also deliberately turned the tables on *Tristan* and Schopenhauer's pessimism by (among other things) fleshing out the conclusion of *Die Meistersinger* until it glowed with robust health and life. Sachs announces warmly that Walther's prize song has 'strength to live', resigning himself cheerfully to his loss of Eva with noble thoughts on the 'folly' (*Wahn*) of the world at the mercy of the blind Will. Despite their compulsive attraction to one another, Walther and Eva are prevented from renouncing society (that is – in the language of *Tristan* – from experiencing an inevitable love-death) and live happily ever after. The 'richly textured satyr play' to *Tannhäuser*, in other words, became a richly ironic counterpart to *Tristan* instead.

The premiere in Munich of *Die Meistersinger* was conducted by Hans von Bülow with a cast including Franz Betz (Sachs), Gustav Hölzel (Beckmesser), Franz Nachbaur (Walther) and Mathilde Mallinger (Eva). It was a resounding triumph comparable only to the first performance of *Rienzi* in Dresden in 1842. Over the years the mellow irony of the 'internal' drama of *Die Meistersinger* has proved to be its most enduring quality. But its immediate success was due more to its extrovert nationalism which found enormous resonance in the years leading up to the 1870 Franco-Prussian War. There is a world of difference between this and Hitler's misappropriation of *Die Meistersinger* as the official opera of the Nuremberg party congresses during the Nazi period. Even though the sheer genius of the work transcends that part of it that has its origins in the growing nationalist fervour in Germany in the 1860s, its concluding propaganda on behalf of the hegemony of German art is for some still hard to accept, despite efforts to see it in historical perspective.

SYNOPSIS

Act I Nuremberg; the mid-16th century. St Catherine's Church. Walther von Stolzing, a young Franconian knight who has sold his estate with the help of the goldsmith Veit Pogner, has made his home in Nuremberg and fallen in love with Pogner's daughter Eva. After the afternoon service on the eve of Midsummer's Day, Eva and her nurse Magdalene tell Walther that Pogner has promised the hand of his daughter to the mastersinger who wins the singing competition due to take place on the morrow. Walther has no alternative but to join the mastersingers' guild. An examination for membership is about to take place and Magdalene persuades her sweetheart David to initiate Walther into the mastersingers' rules and regulations without delay. Pogner is flattered that a nobleman wishes to join the guild and lends Walther his support. Walther tells the assembled masters that his singing teacher was an ancient book by Walther von der Vogelweide and his school the depths of the forest ('Am stillen Herd in Winterszeit'). But the reaction is sceptical: only Hans Sachs senses something out of the ordinary. Walther is allowed to proceed to a formal trial song and the town clerk Sixtus Beckmesser, a mastersinger who is just as determined to win Eva's hand, acts as marker to note each fault. Out of Beckmesser's formal invitation to begin ('Fanget an')

Walther improvises a dithyramb in praise of nature and love. But Beckmesser soon chalks up enough mistakes to exceed the statutory limit. Sachs's admiration for the boldness and originality of the candidate falls on deaf ears. Walther is declared by the majority to have failed the test.

Act II A street with the houses of Pogner and Sachs. Eva hears the bad news about Walther from Magdalene. Snatches of Walther's trial song continue to haunt Sachs, who cannot grasp how the song could sound old, yet at the same time so new ('Es klang so alt, und war doch so neu'). Walther and Eva decide to flee, only to find their escape thwarted by Sachs. Beckmesser appears with his lute, ready to try out his prize song on Eva who, already forewarned, has asked Magdalene to take her place at her window. Sachs constantly interrupts Beckmesser with a deliberately coarse shoemaker's song (a delicious parody of Siegfried's forging songs in the *Ring*) and finally agrees to listen only if Beckmesser lets him act as marker. Sachs strikes the soles of the shoes he is making every time Beckmesser makes a mistake. Beckmesser tries to drown the blows by singing louder, only to wake the neighbours, including David who, at the sight of Beckmesser apparently serenading Magdalene, becomes furiously jealous. David attacks Beckmesser and their fight quickly escalates into a violent free-for-all during which Walther and Eva again try to escape. Sachs intervenes to separate them, giving the half-swooning Eva into the protection of her father, while he quickly leads Walther into his workshop. At the sound of the approaching night-watchman's horn, the tumult ends almost as suddenly as it began.

Act III Sachs's workshop the next morning. David comes to offer his apologies for the night before. Left alone, Sachs continues reading a large folio, musing on the folly he sees everywhere beneath the self-torment of the human race ('Wahn, Wahn! Überall Wahn!'). Walther enters and sings Sachs a song that has just come to him in a dream. Sachs helps him to shape the first two verses, sensing something new at last that can be reconciled with the mastersingers' rules. After they have left Beckmesser limps into the workshop and discovers a sheet of paper on which Sachs has written the song. He immediately takes it to be a prize song by Sachs, who suddenly looks like yet another dangerous rival. On his return Sachs calms Beckmesser's fears and generously gives him the manuscript, though cannily forgetting to mention its real author. Eva enters and Walther, transfixed by the sight of her, improvises the third verse of his song. Sachs knows he will never realize his love for Eva, but prefers to be nobly cheerful about it. The woes of King Marke in the sad story of Tristan and Isolde, he tells Eva, are not for him (at which point Wagner cites his own *Tristan*). After a moving quintet in celebration of the 'baptism' of Walther's prize song by Sachs ('Selig, wie die Sonne'), the scene changes to the festival meadow outside Nuremberg where the singing competition is to take place. The first candidate is Beckmesser who proceeds to bowdlerize the words of the song given to him by Sachs ('Morgen ich

Engraving by Theodore Pixis of Act II of Die Meistersinger von Nürnberg *(Munich, 1868)*

leuchte in rosigem Schein'). He is ridiculed by the townspeople and in a rage declares that Sachs is the author of the poem. But this only gives Sachs an ideal opportunity to call on the true author. Walther delivers an impassioned rendering of his song ('Morgenlich leuchtend im rosigen Schein') which wins unanimous approval from populace and mastersingers alike. The prize and Eva's hand are Walther's, though he instinctively recoils from accepting the guild's chain of honour. After Sachs voices his opinion about the importance of the masters and their art for Germany ('Verachtet mir die Meister nicht'), Walther changes his mind and joins in the celebration of Sachs as the embodiment of 'holy German art'.

Wagner's original intention in 1861 after the famous *Tannhäuser* débâcle in Paris was to complete the *Ring*, which he had abandoned four years before to write *Tristan*. Suddenly in October he wrote to his publisher that he had decided instead to cheer himself up with 'something lighter' that would be finished much faster, in a year. That year turned into six – the last note of the score of *Die Meistersinger* was written on 24 October 1867 at eight o'clock in the evening – and probably no other single fact about the opera is more eloquent than this about the difficulties Wagner had in composing it. Finding a musical style for *Die Meistersinger* that stood in the same relation to *Tristan* as its libretto – a style that is which would turn the earlier work on its head

without letting the ironic reversal descend into emptiness or banality – proved to be a trickier task than Wagner had anticipated.

Simplicity was hard for Wagner. The overture and Act I of *Die Meistersinger* took *four-and-a-half* years to complete which, even accounting for interruptions, was for him a surprisingly long time. If he found it difficult at first to write music that concealed its highly advanced technique so well that the most distinctive thing about it would be its apparent lack of sophistication, once he had discovered the right stylistic balance for the work (or – in the language of the mastersingers – its correct 'tone') it took him only another year and a half to finish it. One of the results of this hard thinking is that large sections of *Die Meistersinger* are written in inverted commas, so to speak, yet retain a powerful semblance of immediacy in spite of – or perhaps even because of – the fact that they are historical stylizations. The music of *Tristan* is placed inside the robust diatonicism of Lutheran chorales and quasi-baroque counterpoint which become richly tinged with chromatic harmony as a result. The new is passed through the filter of the old, just as Walther's prize song in the last act is subjected by Sachs to the rules of the mastersingers' guild. Though he took longer than usual to do it, Wagner had once more discovered an ingenious musical metaphor that mirrored a central concern of the drama: the widening divide between high art and popular culture and the fracturing of tradition by the radically new.

RECORDINGS 1. Schwarzkopf, Malaniuk, Hopf, Unger, Edelmann, Kunz, Dalberg, Bayreuth Festival Ch and O, Karajan, EMI, 1951; 2. Grümmer, Höffgen, Hopf, Unger, Frantz, Kusche, Frick, St Hedwig's Cathedral Ch, O of Deutsche Oper, Berlin, Kempe, EMI, 1956; 3. Donath, Hesse, Kollo, Schreier, Adam, G. Evans, Moll, Leipzig Radio Ch, Dresden Staatskapelle, Karajan, EMI, 1970: Karajan's Bayreuth set is a loving, lively account, soundly cast. Kempe's version is just as warm and possibly even better sung. The later Karajan in stereo has the most refined playing, from the Dresden orchestra, on any version, and another excellent cast. All these readings are worthy of the opera [A.B.]
VIDEO Höggarden, Schiml, Jerusalem, Clark, Weikl, Schenk, Bayreuth Festival Ch and O, Stein, Philips (laserdisc only), 1984: rather ordinary staging (Wolfgang Wagner) and performance [A.B.]
EDITIONS f.ss., B. Schott's Söhne, 1868; C. F. Peters, 1914; Egon Voss (ed.), critical edn, 3 vols, B. Schott's Söhne, 1979; v.ss., B. Schott's Söhne, 1868; B. Schott's Söhne, 1903; Breitkopf und Härtel, 1914; C. F. Peters, 1914; study s., B. Schott's Söhne (later Eulenburg), 1904

Parsifal

Bühnenweihfestspiel ('stage dedication play') in three acts (4h–4h 30m)
Libretto by the composer
Composed: libretto 1865, 1877; music 1877–82
PREMIERES 25 December 1878, Haus Wahnfried, Bayreuth (Prelude; concert); 12 November 1880, Royal Court and National Theatre, Munich (Prelude; concert); 26 July 1882, Festspielhaus, Bayreuth; UK: 10 November 1884, London (concert); 2 February 1914, Covent Garden, London; US: 3 March 1886, New York (concert); 24 December 1903, Metropolitan New York;
CAST Amfortas *bar*, Titurel *b*, Gurnemanz *b*, Parsifal *t*, Klingsor *b*, Kundry *s*, First and Second Knights of the Grail *t*, *b*, First and Second Squires 2 *s*, Third and Fourth Squires 2 *t*, an *a* voice, Klingsor's flower maidens: 6 *s*, 2 *sa* choruses; *tb* brotherhood of the knights of the Grail, *at* young men, *sa* boys
ORCHESTRATION 3 fl/picc, 3 ob, ca, 3 cl, b cl, 3 bsn, dbsn, 4 hn, 3 tpt, 3 trbn, b tuba, timp, 2 hp, str; onstage: 6 tpt, 6 trbn, tenor d, glock, thunder-machine

Parsifal has never been a work to attract moderate comment. Variously described as sublime, vicious or merely decadent, it has always fascinated critics who have seen it as a 'superior magic opera' which 'revels in the wondrous' (Eduard Hanslick) or as a 'profoundly inhuman spectacle, glorifying a barren masculine world whose ideals are a combination of militarism and monasticism' (Peter Wapnewski). Given the suggestive allegory Wagner designed for what he called his 'last card' and 'farewell to the world', the controversy is hardly surprising. However, whether *Parsifal* is a sinister millenarianist fantasy about the redemption of an Aryan Jesus from Judaism (as Germany's most vociferous post-war anti-Wagnerite Hartmut Zelinsky seems to think) or just a feeble Armageddon cocktail with large twists of Schopenhauer, critics of its supposed inhumanity will always find it hard to account for the fascinating beauty of its score and the inconvenient fact that militancy and aggression could not be further removed from its central idea.

Parsifal is based on the notion of compassion (*Mitleid*) borrowed from the philosophy of Schopenhauer and subjected to some characteristically Wagnerian variations. Schopenhauer and

Wagner saw compassion as a specific moral response to the violent chaos of the world – a beatific annihilation of the Will, so to speak, achieved through a denial of Eros and (in Wagner's personal version of the doctrine) a deep sympathy with the suffering in others caused by the torment of sexual desire. *Parsifal* has been called anti-*Tristan* (where salvation depends on the opposite notion of consummated sexual longing) though it is probably best understood as a dialectical counterpart offering a different solution to the same, and for Wagner always extremely important, problem of blind carnality and the pain it inflicts. In fact, Wagner's first idea in 1856 had been to introduce Parsifal into Act III of *Tristan* where, during his wanderings in search of the Grail, he visits Tristan on his sickbed. But Parsifal's compassionate response to Tristan's suffering had so many implications of its own (at one point in the early *Tristan* sketches he asks whether the whole world is not just 'unquenchable longing' and how it can ever be 'stilled') that Wagner decided to drop the plan and to make Parsifal the subject of a separate work.

The idea of compassion also influenced Wagner's radical treatment of his main literary source, Wolfram von Eschenbach's early 13th-century romance *Parzival*. Wagner discussed Wolfram and sexual asceticism at length in his letters to Mathilde Wesendonck in the late 1850s (in view of his rapidly cooling feelings towards her after finishing *Tristan* this was perhaps to be expected) and came to the conclusion that he would have to compress the enormous 24,810-line poem into just 'three climactic situations'. In the final work these have been turned in effect into three successive stages of compassion (a concept foreign to Wolfram's poem, incidentally, at least as Schopenhauer and Wagner understood it) which begins as a vague and unformed feeling in Parsifal's response to the Grail ceremony in Act I, progresses to a burning insight into Amfortas's suffering at the moment of Kundry's kiss in Act II, and with the baptism of Kundry and the healing of Amfortas's wound in Act III, is finally and miraculously transformed into an act of redemption. *Parsifal* is fundamentally a cathartic ritual that unfolds in three cycles, each more intense than the last. The melancholy history of the Grail community, however, which has taken place before the action begins, slowly asserts itself too as the work progresses. *Parsifal* is by no means just a comforting vision of a possible future state of grace. The gradual fulfilment of the prophecy announced at the start – the coming of the redeemer made wise through compassion – is also precariously balanced against irrevocably painful memories of the past. It is therefore important first to explain the past events weighing on the action of the drama.

The action takes place in Spain in two contrasting worlds on the same mountain range. To the north on the Christian side lies Monsalvat, the castle of the knights of the Grail. It was built by Titurel as a shrine for the chalice used at the Last Supper in which Joseph of Arimathea caught the blood of Christ on the cross, and for the spear that pierced Christ's side.

Set design by Paul von Joukowsky for the Temple of the Holy Grail in the first production of Parsifal *(Bayreuth, 1882)*

Only those who are chaste through spiritual self-examination may take part in the life-giving ritual of the unveiling of the Grail (i.e. the chalice) by Titurel's son Amfortas, the present king. On the southern slope facing Moorish (i.e. heathen) Spain is Klingsor's castle. Klingsor, once a pious hermit unable to suppress sinful desire through reflection, castrated himself and was spurned by the Grail community. Determined to possess the chalice and the spear for himself, he turned to paganism and magic in order to lure the Grail knights into his magic garden where his seductive flower maidens trap them with the very power they have learned to repress.

Linking the two worlds is Kundry, who once laughed at Christ on the cross and is condemned to live for eternity, both as a decoy and prostitute in Klingsor's castle, and as a repentant slave in the kingdom of the Grail. Klingsor has absolute power over her, as only he knows of her history and her tormented double existence, from which she seeks in vain to be delivered through death. On his orders she once seduced Amfortas, who had set out with the holy spear to put an end to Klingsor's threat. Klingsor stole the spear with which he seriously wounded Amfortas in the side. Amfortas was led home by his trusty knight Gurnemanz to administer the unveiling of the Grail. But his wound refuses to heal with the consequence that the ritual has become a torture and his kingdom increasingly desolate.

SYNOPSIS

Act I A shady forest in the region of the Grail castle. After recounting the oppressive past weighing on the Grail community to some of its younger members, Gurnemanz tells of a prophetic saying that came to Amfortas in a vision: a blameless fool made wise through compassion ('durch Mitleid wissend, der reine Tor') will one day redeem him and become king of the Grail. The young knights are disturbed by the arrival of a youth who has killed a swan. Gurnemanz questions him, but the intruder is aware of nothing, not even his name: only Kundry knows he is an orphan. Gurnemanz thinks he may have found the innocent fool who will redeem Amfortas. During a long transformation scene he leads him into the castle of the Grail. They witness Amfortas's torment as, under pressure from his father Titurel, he unwillingly unveils the Grail. The stranger is moved by the event, but cannot grasp its deeper meaning.

Act II Klingsor's magic castle. Klingsor wakes Kundry and commands her to trap the simple youth approaching his domain, against whom he will again wield the holy spear. After easily resisting the flower maidens, the youth is transfixed when Kundry calls out 'Parsifal' – the name his mother once gave him in a dream. Kundry inveigles him with her charm, cleverly exploiting his deep feelings of guilt about his mother's death. She gives him a long kiss on the mouth. He jumps up in shock: now he senses the terrible consequences of sinful longing, the torment of Amfortas's wound that burns in his own heart ('Amfortas! – Die Wunde!'). Furious that he continues to reject her sensual allure, Kundry summons Klingsor. But Parsifal regains the spear and Klingsor's castle crumbles to dust.

Act III In the region of the Grail castle. Years have passed. Amfortas has refused to unveil the Grail and the knights, debilitated and distressed, await their deliverer. Gurnemanz is an old man living as a hermit on the edge of the forest. He discovers Kundry again, almost dead. Parsifal enters in black armour with the holy spear sunken at his side. Gurnemanz knows that the moment of salvation has come: he anoints Parsifal as the new king of the Grail while Kundry washes the feet of the new king and receives from him the baptism of absolution. It is the magic of Good Friday: nature has regained its lost innocence. Kundry's tears of repentance are tears of benediction, Parsifal tells her gently, and the meadow smiles ('du weinest – sieh! es lacht die Aue'). The scene changes gradually into the castle of the Grail, as in Act I. The knights urge Amfortas to unveil the Grail; but he refuses and demands that they kill him. This time Parsifal understands: he takes the spear and places its tip on Amfortas's side. The wound heals and the power of the holy spear is restored (the spear was deconsecrated the moment it pierced Amfortas, who had sullied the purity of Christ through his transgression in Kundry's arms). Now the taint of sin has been removed from the spear, the symbol of Christ's sacrifice. Parsifal orders the unveiling of the Grail. Kundry dies and the chorus quietly intones a new saying: 'Redemption to the Redeemer' ('Erlösung dem Erlöser').

Although the first performance of *Parsifal*, conducted by Hermann Levi, made a profound impression, Wagner insisted, as he had already agreed with Ludwig II in 1880, that the work be performed only in Bayreuth. Ironically, the first to ignore the stipulation was Ludwig himself, who ordered three performances of the Bayreuth production to take place in the Munich Court Opera in 1884 and 1885. The whole work was occasionally given in concert in countries that were not signatories to the Bern Convention (London 1884, New York 1886, Boston 1891, Amsterdam 1896) and there were unauthorized productions at the New York Metropolitan on 24 December 1903 and in Amsterdam on 20 June 1905 respectively. (The New York production was also taken on tour throughout the United States when it was performed no fewer than 130 times.) As the full score of *Parsifal* had been widely available since 1883, however, it is actually more surprising that the 'rape of the Grail' (as the New York production became known to the Bayreuth faithful) had not already happened much sooner. Cosima Wagner petitioned the Reichstag twice to extend the copyright beyond the statutory 30 years after the composer's death, first in 1901 and again in 1912, this time armed with 18,000 signatures. But her efforts were unsuccessful. When the copyright lapsed in 1914 nearly every major opera house rushed to mount its own production: *Parsifal* was deconsecrated and its secular existence began.

Before 1914 modern composers who wanted to hear *Parsifal* (and most of them did) had to make the pilgrimage to the Bayreuth shrine to witness its yearly unveiling. Debussy went in 1888, Berg in 1909, and Stravinsky was easily tempted by Diaghilev to go with him in 1912, even though it meant interrupting work on *Le sacre du printemps*. Berg complained of the 'empty-headed folly' (*leerer Wahn*) of Bayreuth and Stravinsky noted in dismay that the inside of the theatre was like a crematorium (and a very old one at that). Indeed, the fading iconic world of the German Empire the Festival Theatre represented seems to have been repellent to many of Europe's visiting intelligentsia. For Berg, however, the sophisticated refinement and sheer loveliness of the music of *Parsifal* was worth the trip. Stravinsky, who is wrongly supposed to have rejected *Parsifal* out of hand during his visit, deliberately stayed silent about the music, preferring to lambast the audience and the cult-like atmosphere of the performance. Debussy saw the gulf between Wagner's musical genius and the rest of his Bayreuth legacy in the work itself. The score is 'one of the most beautiful monuments ever raised to music', he wrote a few years after his visit, while the 'moral and religious ideas' represented by the allegory 'are completely false'. The startling volte-face is a suspect critical strategy, though it has been used by other prominent critics, including Nietzsche and Adorno, and tends to reflect modern opinion. The baroque-like rhetorical figures and highly intricate musical textures in *Parsifal*, however, are metaphorical reflections on its supposedly creaky allegory which are arguably still only imperfectly understood.

RECORDINGS 1. Mödl, Windgassen, London, Uhde, Weber, Bayreuth Festival Ch and O, Knappertsbusch, Decca, 1951; 2. Dalis, Thomas, London, Neidlinger, Hotter, Bayreuth Festival Ch and O, Knappertsbusch, Philips, 1962; 3. Ludwig, Kollo, Fischer-Dieskau, Kelemen, Frick, Vienna Boys' Choir, Vienna State Opera Ch, Vienna PO, Solti, Decca, 1972; 4. Vejzovic, Hofmann, Van Dam, Nimsgern, Moll, Ch of Deutsche Oper, Berlin, Berlin PO, Karajan, DG, 1983; 5. Meier, Jerusalem, Van Dam, von Kannen, Hölle, Berlin State Opera Ch, Berlin PO, Barenboim, Teldec, 1991: both of the Bayreuth/Knappertsbusch performances are classics with little to choose between them though the second is the more accurate and has Hotter's marvellous Gurnemanz. The Solti set is a model of accuracy and recording but a shade dull. The Karajan version has great intensity and a splendid cast. The most recent Barenboim is a deeply considered, marvellously sung and recorded version, marred only by an indifferent Gurnemanz. All are interpretations worthy, in their several ways, of the work [A.B.]

VIDEO Randová, Jerusalem, Weikl, Roar, Sotin, Bayreuth Festival Ch and O, Stein: reverential but dullish production (Wolfgang Wagner) and performance [A.B.]

EDITIONS f.ss., B. Schott's Söhne, 1883; Felix Mottl (ed.), C. F. Peters, 1921; G. Ricordi, Milan, 1928; Martin Geck and Egon Voss (eds), critical edn, 3 vols, B. Schott's Söhne, 1972–3; v.ss., B. Schott's Söhne, 1882; B. Schott's Söhne, 1902; Felix Mottl (ed.), C. F. Peters, 1914; Breitkopf und Härtel, 1914; study s., B. Schott's Söhne (later Eulenburg), 1904

BIBLIOGRAPHY Theodor W. Adorno, *In Search of Wagner*, NLB, 1981; *rp*, [n.d.]; Carl Dahlhaus, *Richard Wagner's Music*

Dramas, CUP, 1979; rp, 1992; John Deathridge and Carl Dahlhaus, The New Grove Wagner, Macmillan, 1984; John Deathridge, Martin Geck and Egon Voss (eds), Wagner Werk-Verzeichnis, Schott, 1986; Barry Millington, Wagner, Dent, 1984; Ulrich Müller and Peter Wapnewski (eds), Wagner Handbook, Harvard, 1992; Ernest Newman, Wagner Nights, Putnam, 1949; rp, 1991; Ernest Newman, The Life of Richard Wagner, 4 vols, CUP, 1976

BIBLIOGRAPHY Peter P. Pachl, Siegfried Wagner: Genie im Schatten, Nymphenburger, 1988; Geoffrey Skelton, Wagner at Bayreuth: Experiment and Tradition, Barrie and Rockliff, 1965

J.W.D.

J.W.D.

SIEGFRIED WAGNER

Siegfried Helferich Richard Wagner; b 6 June 1869, Tribschen, nr Lucerne, Switzerland; d 4 August 1930, Bayreuth

Siegfried was the only son of Richard and Cosima Wagner. He studied music with Humperdinck, but decided in 1890 on a career in architecture instead. After studies in Berlin and Karlsruhe, he was won back to music largely by the conductor Felix Mottl. His subsequent career as conductor, producer and administrator was centred around the Bayreuth Festival founded by his father. He first conducted the Ring cycle there in 1896 and took over the direction of the festival from his mother in 1906. As a composer he was more widely active. Apart from vocal and instrumental works, including the symphonic poem Sehnsucht, premiered in London (1895), he completed fourteen full-length operas, finished two others except for the orchestration and left two more as fragments. He wrote all his libretti himself.

The 'official' Bayreuth view was that music drama based on mythology had been brought to perfection by his father. For the most part, therefore, Siegfried deliberately tried to avoid it. He developed a highly eclectic musical style that drew on early-Romantic and folk as well as modern idioms. For his operas he showed a preference for historical subjects and folklore and looked more to the late-Romantic fairy-tale operas written by his father's brother-in-law Alexander Ritter and his old teacher Humperdinck, than to his father's music dramas, as models. Between 1899 and 1923 eleven of Siegfried Wagner's operas were premiered, many of them at leading German opera houses, and two others, Der Heidenkönig and Das Flüchlein, das Jeder mitbekam, were produced posthumously (in 1933 and 1984 respectively). Only Der Bärenhäuter (1899) and An allem ist Hütchen schuld (1917) – were ever more than moderately successful.

Operas: Der Bärenhäuter, 1899; Herzog Wildfang, 1901; Der Kobold, 1904; Bruder Lustig, 1905; Sternengebot, 1908; Banadietrich, 1910; Schwarzschwanenreich, (1910), 1918; Sonnenflammen, (1912), 1918; Der Heidenkönig, (1913), 1933; Der Friedensengel, (1914), 1926; An allem ist Hütchen schuld, 1917; Das Liebesopfer (inc.), (1917); Der Schmied von Marienburg, (1920), 1923; Rainulf und Adelasia, (1922), Prelude, 1923; Die heilige Linde, (1927), Prelude, 1924, some scenes, 1933; Wahnopfer (inc.), (1928); Walamund (not orch.), (1929); Das Flüchlein, das Jeder mitbekam, (1929), orch. Hans Peter Mohr 1984

RUDOLF WAGNER-RÉGENY

b 28 August 1903, Szász-Régen, Romania; d 18 September 1969, Berlin, Germany

Wagner-Régeny had a fitful career. He studied with Schreker in Berlin and came briefly to prominence at the end of the Weimar Republic when some small theatre pieces were staged. In 1935 the Nazis championed Der Günstling as a model of their new opera style and his next opera, Die Bürger von Calais, despite its anti-militarist story, was eagerly awaited. Its similarity to the last European music of Kurt Weill (in particular Die Bürgschaft, which had been banned by the Nazis immediately they came to power) raised official eyebrows and his next opera, Johanna Balk, brought him disgrace and conscription. He recovered from a nervous break-down and after 1945 settled in East Germany where he won official favour and recognition. He evolved a personalized 12-note serial technique in orchestral pieces such as Mythologische Figurinen (1951) as well as in chamber works and songs, but he was not doctrinaire, reverting to non-serial methods for two biblical works, Cantica Davidi regis (1954) and Genesis (1955–6), and his last opera, Das Bergwerk zu Falun.

Der Günstling, oder Die letzten Tage des grossen Herrn Fabiano

The Favourite, or The Last Days of the Great Fabiano
Opera in three acts (four scenes) (2h)
Libretto by Caspar Neher, after the German version by Georg Büchner of the prose drama Marie Tudor by Victor Hugo (1833)
Composed 1932–4
PREMIERE 20 February 1935, Semper Oper, Dresden

The Nazis championed this opera as a model for German composers, with its traditional historical plot, which would not have disgraced Donizetti or Verdi, and its effective, tuneful music. Curiously it was born of a potentially dangerous collaboration: out his librettist Caspar Neher was one of the standing figures of the reviled Weimar Republic. Essentially a designer, he had worked with such artists as Max Reinhardt and Carl Ebert, at Otto Klemperer's Kroll Theater in Berlin, and particularly with Brecht and Weill on The Threepenny Opera and The Rise and Fall of the City of Mahagonny. He had also written the libretto for Weill's last European opera, Die Bürgschaft.

Mary Tudor is required to execute her favourite, an Italian accused of being a spy. Her Council of State has him arrested in a compromising situation with another woman and although Mary signs the death warrant, too late she regrets it.

The music employs a neo-modal style with simple harmonies and syllabic word-setting. There is frequent use of recorders as period colour. There are several set pieces, including duets for the Italian spy and Mary, the Italian and his mistress, and a major concluding aria for Mary.

RECORDING excerpts: Dvořáková, Geszty, Kachel, Kreyssig, Rössler, Berlin Radio Ch and SO, Masur, Eterna, 1964
EDITIONS f.s./v.s., Universal, 1934

Die Bürger von Calais
The Burghers of Calais
Opera in three acts (2h)
Libretto by Caspar Neher, after Georg Kaiser's play (1917), itself based on the account of the Siege of Calais (1346–7) in Jean Froissart's *Chroniques*, Book I (1369–73)
Composed 1936–8
PREMIERES 28 January 1939, Staatsoper, Berlin; UK: 21 June 1987, BBC Radio 3 (studio recording)
CAST Cornelia *s*, English Queen *s*, Peter Wissant *t*, Josef Wissant *t*, Burgomaster *b*, 4 *s*, 3 *a*, 2 *t*, 4 *bar*, 2 *b*; *satb* chorus of washerwomen and other citizens of Calais
FULL ORCHESTRA including 2 sax

Der Günstling had placed Wagner-Régeny among Nazi Germany's most favoured artists. This opera compromised that. Again his librettist was Neher and they deliberately used the title of an anti-militarist play, now banned by the Nazis, by the Expressionist playwright Georg Kaiser. The opera faces the conflict of individual responsibility in society: is it better that for the collective good others should be sacrificed? Is individual sacrifice in the larger cause futile? Who decides the sacrificial victim? Despite these concerns, and with Europe accelerating towards war, the Nazis gave it a prestige premiere in Berlin under another of their musical heroes, Herbert von Karajan.

SYNOPSIS
Act I After a year's deprivation, the starving citizens of Calais are advised by their burgomaster to surrender to the English. One citizen, Josef, has disappeared rather than accept the disgrace of surrender. The burgomaster's wife, Cornelia, decides

Caspar Neher's stage design for Act III of Die Bürger von Calais *(Berlin, 1939)*

to appeal personally to the English Queen as woman and mother.

Act II The appeal fails; the encounter is outside the city walls, Cornelia having been protected by some English washerwomen and having protected Josef from capture. The Queen refuses to intercede but orders their safe conduct back to the city.

Act III At first the citizens reject the English surrender terms but Josef's voice persuades them – only six burghers need die to save six thousand. The chosen six leave, but as the citizens pack their belongings an English officer announces their reprieve.

Wagner-Régeny's music is dispassionate, mainly observing the action rather than illustrating it. Its effectiveness lies in its handling of simple tunes and forms. The outer acts are monumental, with large, massed choruses moving in simple, austere harmonies. The climax, a long, slow chorale as the citizens realize that they were prepared to sacrifice their friends for their own salvation, is particularly harrowing. Act II is more intimate, with the confrontation of the Queen and Cornelia in an affecting duet, a folksong-like number for the six washerwomen and a rumbustious song for two English soldiers.

RECORDING excerpts (coupled with excerpts from *Johanna Balk*): Breul, Weimann, Hellmich, Leipzig Radio Ch and SO, Kegel, Eterna, 1973
EDITIONS f.s., Universal, 1939; v.s., Universal, 1938

Johanna Balk
Opera in three acts
Libretto by Caspar Neher, after Transylvanian chronicles
Composed 1938–40
PREMIERE 4 April 1941, Staatsoper, Vienna

Wagner-Régeny paid dearly for this work. It was banned from performance within 500 kilometres of Berlin and its composer was conscripted. Both its music, suggesting the manner of Kurt Weill's *The Threepenny Opera* (long since banned), and its plot, parodying a political tyrant, were found unacceptable.

RECORDING excerpts (coupled with excerpts from *Die Bürger von Calais*): Bolkestein, Büchner, Hellmich, Thomaschke, Nau, Leipzig Radio Ch and SO, Kegel, Eterna, 1973
EDITIONS f.s., Universal, [n.d.]; v.s., Universal, 1941

Das Bergwerk zu Falun
The Mine at Falun
Opera in eight scenes
Libretto by the composer, after the play by Hugo von Hofmannsthal (1899)
Composed 1958–60
PREMIERE 16 August 1961, Old Festspielhaus, Salzburg

Elis, a seaman, is lured by the Mine Queen and a 200-year-old ghost to abandon his father's sea-faring career and adopt his mother's, in the mine. He falls in love with the queen's daughter and then jilts her on their wedding day. The story explores the psychology of archetypal father–mother relationships.

EDITION v.s., Bote und Bock, 1960

Other operatic works: *Sganarelle, oder Der Schein trügt*, (1923), 1929; *Moschopulos*, 1928; *Der nackte König*, (1928), 1930; *Esau und Jacob (biblische Szene)*, 1930; *La sainte courtisane (musikalische Szene for four speakers and chamber orchestra)*, 1930; *Die Fabel vom seiligen Schlächtermeister (Stück für die Musikbühne in three scenes)*, (1932), 1964; *Persische Episode (Stück für die Musikbühne in four acts)*, (1950), 1963; *Prometheus (szenisches Oratorium)*, 1959
BIBLIOGRAPHY D. Härtwig, *Rudolf Wagner-Régeny*, Henschel, 1965

C.B.

VINCENT WALLACE
William Vincent Wallace; *b* 11 March 1812, Waterford, Ireland; *d* 12 October 1865, Vieuzos, Hautes-Pyrénées, France

Wallace's career concedes little in flamboyance to that of any other composer. The details are sometimes hazy, thanks to a truth-embroidering imagination that enthralled Berlioz but renders biographical details unreliable. As a young man in Dublin he was recognized as a talented pianist and violinist. A restless traveller (and probably a bigamist), Wallace went to Tasmania in 1835 and to Australia in 1836, giving concerts and possibly beginning operatic composition. In 1838 he left Sydney – heavily in debt, and deserting his wife and son – and established himself in Valparaiso, Chile. In 1841 he conducted Italian opera in Mexico City. He then moved north, concluding this phase of his travels in New York in 1843.

Before long he moved to Europe. *Maritana*, his first and most famous opera, was produced in London in 1845. Wallace's second opera, *Matilda of Hungary* (1847), is, like its predecessor, Italianate but less convincing; in particular it suffers from a weak libretto by Alfred Bunn, whose management of Drury Lane, then the main venue for English opera, was shortly to collapse.

After further travels in North and South America (and another 'marriage' in New York), Wallace moved to Germany in 1858 and to London the following year. The different styles of *Lurline* (1860) and *The Amber Witch* (1861) may reflect his operatic experiences while travelling in Germany. Italian elements are less prominent, the orchestral writing is more substantial, and the characterization, aided by more sophisticated use of recurrent material, is of a higher quality. *Lurline* is indebted to Weber in various regards, and, appropriately for an opera set in and alongside the river Rhine, the orchestral episodes encourage speculation as to Wagner's influence too.

Wallace's last two operas are again different. The light-hearted *Love's Triumph* (1862), set in France,

brings together ballad, glee, waltz, minuet, and polonaise rhythms, a sparkling *mélange* that epitomizes Wallace's colourful and versatile contribution to English opera, while *The Desert Flower* (1863) includes modal writing to characterize American Indians.

Maritana
Opera in three acts (3h)
Libretto by Edward Fitzball, after the play *Don César de Bazan* by d'Ennery and Pinel Dumanoir
PREMIERES 15 November 1845, Drury Lane, London; US: 9 November 1846, Philadelphia

The plot concerns the eponymous heroine and Don Caesar de Bazan, who emerge safely from the intrigues of the Spanish court, having saved the king's honour and ensured lifelong happiness for themselves. The opera's musical style was much influenced by Italian opera: various passages recall Rossini and Bellini. The Act II finale, with its canonic 'ensemble of perplexity', is a case in point. Wallace also included three ballads, which approach those of Balfe, the master of this characteristically English element, in their lyricism.

RECORDINGS 1. Licette, Serena, Nash, Noble, 'Grand Opera Company' Ch and O, Raybould, Columbia, 1931; 2. Strathdee, Mason, Byles, Davies, Allen, Beaufort Opera Ch and O, Vandernoot, RRE, 1973
EDITION f.s./v.s., Boosey & Co., 1888

Other operas: *Matilda of Hungary*, 1847; *Lurline*, 1860; *The Amber Witch*, 1861; *Love's Triumph*, 1862; *The Desert Flower*, 1863
Unperformed operas (n.dd.): *The Maid of Zurich*, *The King's Page*, *Estrella* (inc.), *Gulnare*, *Olga*
BIBLIOGRAPHY Hector Berlioz, *Evenings in the Orchestra*, trans. C. R. Fortescue, Penguin, 1963, pp. 310–20

G.B.

MARIA ANTONIA WALPURGIS
Maria Antonia Walpurgis, Electress of Saxony; *b* 18 July 1724, Munich; *d* 23 April 1780, Dresden

The remarkable talents of Maria Antonia Walpurgis, eldest daughter of the Elector Karl Albert of Bavaria, were shown in music, painting and literature. Her self-portrait was engraved on the title page of her first opera, and a number of her literary works, including poems in French and Italian, were published after 1747 when she became a member of the Arcadian Academy in Rome. Although remembered chiefly for her liberal support of leading artists of the time, her own music is significant. Her two opere serie, *Il trionfo della fedeltà* (1754) and *Talestri, regina delle amazoni* (1760), for which she wrote both texts and music, were mounted with success, not only in her own court circles but also in many principal European cities, and published by Breitkopf. Metastasio and Hasse, both of whom may have assisted her with the composition of her first opera, were particularly influential on her work. As a singer of distinction, she herself took leading roles in the performances at court. However, in later life her activities lessened as she found herself increasingly alienated by the introduction of new Neapolitan styles in opera at the expense of the older ideals of Hasse and Metastasio.

BIBLIOGRAPHY H. Drewes, *Maria Antonia Walpurgis als Komponistin*, dissertation, University of Cologne, 1933; Noske, 1934; F. M. Rudhart, *Geschichte der Oper am Hofe zu München*, Freising, 1865

B.S.

IGNAZ WALTER

Johann Ignaz Walter [Walderth]; *b* 31 August 1755, Radonitz [now Radonice], Bohemia; *d* 22 February 1822, Regensburg

During a lengthy career in the German musical theatre, Walter made contributions as a composer, music director and singer. His many successes in tenor operatic roles at the Nationaltheater in Vienna brought him to the notice of Mozart, who proposed him for the part of Pasha Selim in *Die Entführung aus dem Serail* – originally planned as a sung role. Among his singspiels, special interest attaches to his *Doctor Faust* (to a libretto compiled by H. G. Schmieder), the earliest operatic work based on Goethe's dramatic poem. This was first performed in 1797 at Bremen, where Walter was opera director. Revised for a further performance at Hanover in the following year it created a strong initial impression, but was overshadowed by later masterpieces based on the same subject.

Operatic works: *Der Aepfeldieb, c.* 1781; *Peter, du bleibst, oder Der Hausfreund auf dem Lande*, 1781; *Die 25,000 Gulden, oder Im Dunkeln ist nicht gut munkeln*, 1783; *Der Kaufmann von Smyrna*, 1783; *Der Trank der Unsterblichkeit*, 1783; *Der Graf von Walltron, oder Die Subordination*, 1784; *Des Teufels Lustschloss*, 1787; *Der ausgeprügelte Teufel*, 1790; *Der gerade Weg ist der beste*, 1790; *Der Spiegel-Ritter*, 1791; *Die Hirtin der Alpen*, 1792; *Die [Zauber] Harfe*, 1793; *Die böse Frau*, 1794; *Doctor Faust*, 1797; *Das Wildpret*, 1799; *Die Weinlese*, 1799; *Löwensteins Geist, oder Die Teufelsmühle am Wienerberg, zweyter Theil*, 1809; *Hass und Liebe, oder Das Fischermädchen*, 1815
BIBLIOGRAPHY K. M. Pisarowitz, 'Walter (Walderth), (Johann) Ignaz', in *MGG*

B.S.

HERMANN WOLFGANG VON WALTERSHAUSEN

Hermann Wolfgang Sartorius Freiherr von Waltershausen; *b* 12 October 1882, Göttingen; *d* 13 August 1954, Munich

Waltershausen is best known for his musical tragedy, *Oberst Chabert*. Neither his first opera, *Else Klapperzehen*, nor his later works for the stage captured the attention of the public. At the age of ten Waltershausen's right arm and leg were amputated, but this did not deter him from pursuing a career as a conductor, writer on music and educator. In 1901 he moved from Strasburg to Munich, where he studied composition with Ludwig Thuille. In 1917 he founded a private school for advanced musical studies, and in 1920 was appointed professor and assistant director of the State Academy of Music. In 1923 he became director of the Academy, holding the post until 1933. In 1948 he founded the private Waltershausen Seminar, and continued to teach in Munich until his death.

Oberst Chabert

Colonel Chabert
Musical tragedy in three acts, Op. 10
Libretto after the story *Comtesse à deux maris* by Honoré de Balzac (1832)
Composed 1910
PREMIERE 18 January 1912, Frankfurt am Main

Colonel Chabert, wrongly presumed to have died in action at the battle of Preussisch-Eylau in 1807, returns to Paris in disguise only to discover that his wife has remarried. The untenable situation leads inexorably to Chabert's suicide. A striking feature is the recurring use of a tritone to depict his predicament.

EDITION v.s., Drei-Masken-Verlag, 1911

Other operatic works: *Else Klapperzehen*, 1909; *Richardis*, 1915; *Die Rauensteiner Hochzeit*, 1919; *Die Gräfin von Tolosa*, (1936)
BIBLIOGRAPHY Karl-Robert Danler and Richard Mader, *Hermann Wolfgang Sartorius Freiherr von Waltershausen*, Schneider, 1984

A.C.

WILLIAM WALTON

(Sir) William Turner Walton; *b* 29 March 1902, Oldham, Lancashire, England; *d* 8 March 1983, Ischia, Italy

The son of an organist and choirmaster in industrial Lancashire, Walton won a choral scholarship to Christ Church Cathedral School, Oxford, in 1912. His early compositions (songs and anthems) date from about 1916 and won the interest of Hubert Parry. In 1919, while an undergraduate, he was 'adopted' by the Sitwells and first attracted attention in 1922 with his collaboration with Edith Sitwell in the entertainment *Façade*. From 1925, when he composed *Portsmouth Point*, until the outbreak of war in 1939, he was in the forefront of his generation with a succession of works – the Viola Concerto (1929), the cantata *Belshazzar's Feast* (1931), the First Symphony (1935) and the Violin Concerto written for Jascha Heifetz (1939).

In 1941 Walton and Cecil Gray pondered the possibility of an opera about the Italian composer Gesualdo. Gray completed a libretto, but no music was forthcoming. Six years later, the BBC commissioned an opera from Walton. He chose the subject *Troilus and Cressida* with Christopher Hassall as librettist. The opera was not completed until 1954, by which time Walton had settled permanently on the island of Ischia in the Bay of Naples. A Covent Garden premiere was only moderately successful and productions followed in Milan and San Francisco. Deeply wounded by failure, Walton for the next twenty years searched for singers and producers who would do justice to his opera and, with the promise of a Covent Garden revival in 1976, recast the role of Cressida for the mezzo-soprano Janet Baker.

Meanwhile in 1967 he had completed a short one-act opera, *The Bear*, based on a vaudeville by Chekhov. This had been commissioned by the Aldeburgh Festival at the suggestion of Peter Pears and was from the first a success. Walton's light touch and his gift for parody, evident as early as *Façade*, were admirably deployed in this sparkling piece and make it all the more regrettable that he never proceeded with a suggestion to base an opera on Wilde's *The Importance of Being Earnest*, a subject that would surely have suited him ideally. Walton undoubtedly had dramatic talents, as *Belshazzar's Feast* indicated early in his career, but they led him to the film studio more frequently than to the opera house.

He composed the music for Laurence Olivier's three Shakespeare films, *Henry V* (1944), *Hamlet* (1947) and *Richard III* (1955), and among the best known of his other film scores are those from *The First of the Few* (1942), about R. J. Mitchell, who designed the Spitfire fighter aircraft, and Bernard Shaw's *Major Barbara* (1941). Orchestral suites have been extracted from several of his film scores. The *Henry V* music, on a large and ambitious scale, is one of the finest examples of music inspired by the cinema.

Troilus and Cressida

Opera in three acts (2h)
Libretto by Christopher Hassall, after *Troilus and Criseyde* by Geoffrey Chaucer (c. 1380–82) and other sources
Composed 1948–54; rev. 1963, 1972–6
PREMIERES 3 December 1954, Covent Garden, London; US: 7 October 1955, War Memorial Opera House, San Francisco; rev. version: 12 November 1976, Covent Garden, London
CAST Troilus *t*, Cressida *ms* (originally *s*), Pandarus *t buffo*, Evadne *ms*, Calkas *b*, Antenor *bar*, Horaste *bar*, Diomede *bar*; *satb* chorus of priests and priestesses of Pallas, Trojans and Greeks
LARGE ORCHESTRA including perc (4–5 players), 2 hp, cel; offstage: brass and perc

Walton was spurred to compose *Troilus and Cressida* by the success of Britten's *Peter Grimes* in 1945. Rivalry had always encouraged his creativity. 'I thought it was not a good thing', he said, 'for British opera to have only one opera by one composer', a statement that took no account of Delius and Vaughan Williams. His intention was to write an English *bel canto* opera. The role of Cressida was written for the soprano Elisabeth Schwarzkopf, but she never sang it on stage and recorded only a few brief extracts. Walton was intensely disappointed by Sir Malcolm Sargent's conducting of the Covent Garden premiere.

SYNOPSIS
Act I The Trojan War has lasted ten years. The High Priest of Troy, Calkas, father of Cressida, says that the Delphic Oracle advises surrender to the Greeks. When the crowd turns on him he is defended by Prince Troilus, who is in love with Cressida. She is a war widow and tends the altar in the temple because she knows her father is preparing to desert, as he later does. Her dandyish uncle, Pandarus, encourages the relationship with Troilus and persuades Cressida to leave her crimson scarf as a love token.

Act II After a night of love in Pandarus' house, where they are marooned by a thunderstorm, the lovers are interrupted by the arrival of the Greek prince Diomede, who announces that Cressida must join Calkas as the price of her father's services in exchange for a Trojan prisoner. Diomede is attracted by Cressida's beauty. Troilus promises to send her daily messages and to bribe the Greek sentries to allow them to meet. He returns the scarf as a symbol of their love.

Act III Ten weeks later, Cressida has not heard from Troilus and agrees to marry Diomede, to whom she gives her scarf. Her servant Evadne has been intercepting and burning Troilus' messages on the orders of Calkas. Troilus, meanwhile, has arranged her ransom and visits the Greek camp during a truce. He sees the scarf on Diomede's helmet and claims Cressida as his own. He attacks Diomede, but is stabbed in the back by Calkas. Diomede, aghast, orders Calkas to be returned to the Trojans but

William Walton, c. 1972

insists that Cressida remain as a soldier's whore. She picks up Troilus' sword and stabs herself.

In spite of much beautiful and compelling music – such as the 'scarf' motif and several of Cressida's arias – *Troilus and Cressida* fails to fulfil its composer's ambitions for it. The libretto, too flowery and diffuse, is partly to blame, but the music is uneven in quality and does not achieve the heroic style that was needed to make *Troilus and Cressida* credible. The finest characterization in the opera is the tenor buffo role of Pandarus, sung originally by Peter Pears. It comes near to parody of Britten but it has its own elegant wit. The orchestral score, too, is consistently splendid. But the parts somehow do not add up to a whole, and it is arguable whether Walton improved matters by transposing the heroine's part for a mezzo.

RECORDINGS 1. Baker, Bainbridge, Cassilly, English, Van Allan, Luxon, Covent Garden Ch and O, Foster, EMI, 1976: a compilation (complete) from recordings made at the series of performances at Covent Garden at the end of 1976; 2. Schwarzkopf, Lewis, Philharmonia O, Walton, Columbia, 1955: excerpts, with the original Troilus and the intended Cressida
EDITIONS   v.s., OUP, 1954; rev. version: v.s., OUP, 1980

The Bear

Extravaganza in one act (50m)
Libretto by Paul Dehn and the composer, based on the vaudeville *Medved* by Anton Chekhov (1888)
Composed 1965–7
PREMIERES 3 June 1967, Jubilee Hall, Aldeburgh; US: 15 August 1968, Aspen Music Festival, Colorado
CAST Yeliena Ivanova Popova *ms*, Grigory Stepanovitch Smirnov *bar*, Luka *b*
SMALL ORCHESTRA with perc, hp, pf

Walton received a commission for an opera from the Koussevitzky Music Foundation in 1958, but did not undertake it until 1965, when the Aldeburgh Festival wanted a work from him for the English Opera Group. He had met and liked the writer Paul Dehn in Ischia and together they adapted the short Chekhov play.

SYNOPSIS
Madame Popova is an attractive young widow. She claims she will mourn for the rest of her life, but her manservant Luka urges her to start life again: her husband had been unfaithful and did not deserve her loyalty to his memory. They are interrupted by Smirnov, a huge bear of a man, who forces his way in to demand immediate payment of a debt incurred by her husband for oats for the horse Toby. Smirnov, too, urges her to put off her widow's weeds and unveil like Salome. They argue over whether men or women are more faithful in love. She calls him a boor and asks Luka to show him out. Smirnov challenges her to a duel – he is now attracted by her spirit. She fetches her husband's pistol, but Smirnov has to show her how to use it. She has fallen for him. There is no duel.

In *The Bear*, Walton at 65 recaptured something of the insouciance that marked *Façade* when he was 19. The score is full of affectionate and subtle parodies of, among others, Puccini, Richard Strauss, Britten and Offenbach. For instance, Smirnov's parody of the Russian aristocrat's use of French in 'Madame, je vous prie' and Popova's catalogue of her husband's infidelities in 'I was a constant, faithful wife'. The opera is a thoroughly effective caricature.

RECORDING Sinclair, Shaw, Lumsden, ECO, Lockhart, EMI, 1967: the original Aldeburgh cast
EDITION v.s., OUP, 1968

BIBLIOGRAPHY Frank Howes, *The Music of William Walton*, OUP, 1965; 2nd edn, 1974; Michael Kennedy, *Portrait of Walton*, OUP, 1989; Susana Walton, *Behind the Façade*, OUP, 1987

M.K.

ROBERT WARD

Robert Eugene Ward; *b* 13 September 1917, Cleveland, Ohio, US

Ward is a prolific American composer and a distinguished teacher, who has made his strongest impact through opera. His recognition as a composer of orchestral works, notably his Second Symphony (1947), led to the commission of *The Crucible* from the Ford Foundation. An earlier opera, *He Who Gets Slapped*, had been quite well received, but *The Crucible* secured his reputation.

Maintaining his accessible, eclectic style, Ward followed up his success with four further full-length operas. Of these, *The Lady from Colorado*, a 'Western' opera, which includes many singable tunes, and *Claudia Legare*, a transferral of Ibsen's *Hedda Gabler* to South Carolina, have been the best received.

The Crucible

Opera in four acts (2h)
Libretto by Bernard Stambler, after the play by Arthur Miller (1953)
PREMIERES 26 October 1961, New York City Opera; UK: 6 June 1984, Bloomsbury Theatre, London (Abbey Opera)

Miller's classic drama, in which the Salem witchcraft trials of 1692 were linked to the McCarthy era in the US, provided a strong subject. Ward and Stambler stuck closely to Miller's original five-scene version of the play and by use of an expressive *parlando* style of writing, Ward succeeds in sustaining the play's dramatic tension. Rather less effective is the mixture of American folk music with Puccinian lyricism.

RECORDING Brooks, Bible, Alberts, Ludgin, New York City Opera O, Buckley, CRI, 1963
EDITION v.s., Highgate Press, Galaxy Music Corp, 1962

Other operas: *He Who Gets Slapped* (originally *Pantaloon*), 1956; *The Lady from Colorado*, 1964; *Claudia Legare*, 1978; *Abelard and Heloise*, 1981; *Minutes till Midnight*, 1982

BIBLIOGRAPHY   D. Ewen, *American Composers: A Biographical Dictionary*, Hall, 1983

P.D.

CARL MARIA VON WEBER

Carl Maria Friedrich Ernst [von] Weber; *b* ?18 November 1786, Eutin; *d* 5 June 1826, London

Weber played a key role in the development of German Romantic opera. His most enduringly successful work, *Der Freischütz*, combines national characteristics in both plot and music with dramatic vitality, vivid musical imagery and appealing directness of style. These qualities ensured not only that it enjoyed extraordinary popularity in its own day, but also that, alone of early-Romantic German operas, it still retains a firm place in the standard operatic repertoire. Weber's later operas, *Euryanthe* and *Oberon*, though they contain some of his finest music, are, for very different reasons, flawed masterpieces.

Weber's childhood was spent in a theatrical environment, accompanying his father's touring theatre company as it travelled around Bavaria performing fashionable plays and singspiels. His education was haphazard; he received some instruction in music from his half-brother Fridolin and sporadic lessons from teachers in the various towns where the troupe performed. In Hildburghausen, J. P. Heuschkel laid the foundations of his later pianistic virtuosity; in Salzburg he took lessons from Michael Haydn, and in Munich he took singing and composition lessons. With the help of the Munich court organist, Johann Nepomuk Kalcher, the 13-year-old Weber composed his first opera, a singspiel, *Die Macht der Liebe und des Weins*, in 1798. The score was destroyed in a fire at Kalcher's house shortly after its composition. His second opera, *Das Waldmädchen*, was composed shortly afterwards in Freiberg, to a libretto by Carl von Steinsberg, by whose travelling company it was performed.

By 1801 Weber was back in Salzburg, continuing his studies with Michael Haydn, where he wrote his third opera, *Peter Schmoll und seine Nachbarn*. Early in 1803 it was staged in Augsburg, where his half-brother Edmund was conducting at the theatre. Later that year Weber moved to Vienna, intending to study with Joseph Haydn, but he came instead under the influence of the Abbé Vogler, whose impact on Weber's musical development was profound and lasting.

At Vogler's recommendation, the 17-year-old Weber was offered the post of kapellmeister at the Breslau theatre in 1804. During his two years in Breslau he attempted to reform the repertoire, but encountered considerable opposition. He began another opera, on a libretto based on Musäus's 'Rübezahl' story, but only three numbers, which show no perceptible advance in his creative power, survive. Weber's departure from Breslau was precipitated when he accidentally drank engraving

acid. Returning to work after a two-month convalescence, he found that most of his reforms had been undone, and he resigned.

After a sojourn in Carlsruhe where he composed his two symphonies, Weber moved in 1807 to Stuttgart as secretary to Duke Ludwig of Württemberg. Encouraged by the hofkapellmeister there, Franz Danzi, Weber continued to compose for the theatre, writing incidental music for Schiller's *Turandot* (1809) and working on the opera *Silvana*, which he completed after he had moved to Stuttgart in 1810. The first ideas for *Der Freischütz* came later that year in Darmstadt when, on a visit to Stift Neuberg, he and Alexander von Dusch got as far as sketching a scenario. But Dusch, an amateur cellist, had insufficient time to prepare a libretto and the project was postponed. Apart from the singspiel *Abu Hassan*, Weber composed no stage works during this period, turning his attention instead to instrumental works and to his own tours as a concert pianist. Early in 1813, however, he was persuaded to accept the post of kapellmeister at the Prague opera. Here, as earlier in Breslau, he immersed himself in his work of reforming the running of the opera house and its repertoire (basing it on the works of Mozart and on French opera), a task that left him little time to pursue his own compositions and which took its toll on his health. Disagreements with the opera's directors were constant, and in October 1816 he handed in his resignation and left for Berlin.

Within a few months he had secured himself a position as Royal Saxon kapellmeister in Dresden. While this gave him authority over the city's German opera, local taste favoured Italian opera so the challenge set Weber in fostering an indigenous opera was substantial. He set about the task with his customary diligence and enthusiasm, once again leaving himself little time for composition. But, meeting Friedrich Kind, the idea of an opera on the *Freischütz* story was rekindled. Work proceeded fitfully – interruptions included a royal commission for an opera *Alcidor* (later cancelled) – but by May 1820 *Der Freischütz*, Weber's first opera for nine years, was complete (except for one aria, added the following year). The premiere was a triumph and it was rapidly taken up throughout Europe, making Weber an international celebrity.

The success of *Der Freischütz* led to a commission for a new opera for the 1822–3 season at the Kärntnertortheater in Vienna. Weber embraced the project with enthusiasm and, laying aside his work on *Die drei Pintos* (a comic work he had begun in the summer of 1820), began seeking a suitable subject. Unfortunately, both his choice of Helmina von Chezy as librettist and *Euryanthe* as subject proved disastrous. Despite a respectfully received Vienna premiere, the opera's weaknesses soon became apparent, and it was withdrawn after 20 performances.

For more than a year after the premiere of *Euryanthe*, Weber composed almost nothing. But, in August 1824, he was invited by Charles Kemble to write a new opera for London and, persuaded that by this means he would be able to provide for his

Anonymous sketch of Weber; London, 1826

family's financial security after his death, he accepted the commission. Against his doctor's advice, he travelled to London in February 1826 for the production of *Oberon* and he died the day before he had planned to travel home.

J. numbers refer to F. W. Jahn, *Carl Maria von Weber in seinen Werken: Chronologisch-thematisches Verzeichniss seiner sämmtlichen Compositionen*, Berlin, 1871.

Silvana

Romantic opera in three acts, J. 87
Libretto by Franz Carl Hiemer, after Carl von Steinberg's libretto for Weber's earlier opera *Das Waldmädchen*
Composed 1808–10
PREMIERES 16 September 1810, Frankfurt am Main; UK: 2 September 1828, Surrey Theatre, London

The score contains some reused musical material from Weber's first opera, *Das Waldmädchen*. Although its premiere was not particularly promising, *Silvana* became Weber's first significant success when it was enthusiastically received in Berlin two years later (for this production numbers 4 and 10 were completely rewritten by the composer who considered the original version 'too long').

Count Rudolf falls in love with Silvana, the dumb heroine, after finding her living wild in the forest. He, however, is betrothed to Mechtilde whom he does not love and is unaware that Mechtilde is in love with Albert, son of an old enemy of her father. Years earlier, Albert's father had kidnapped Mechtilde's sister, Ottilie. When Silvana not only turns out to be

the lost Ottilie but also recovers her voice, everyone is happily reconciled.

The music combines simple folklike songs and ornate coloratura arias and, though evidently the work of an immature composer, contains elements that point to Weber's later mastery. His responsiveness to natural phenomena is shown in the forest scene at the beginning of Act I and the storm in Act III. The characterization of some of the principal figures in the drama is distinctive, as is his feeling for sensitive and colourful orchestration.

EDITIONS f.ss., H. J. Moser (ed.), *C. M. von Weber: Musikalische Werke: Erste Kritische Gesamtausgabe*; Willibald Kaehler (ed.), vol. 2, no. 2, Dr Benno Filser Verlag, 1928; *rp*, New York, 1977; v.s., Berlin, 1828

Abu Hassan

Singspiel in one act, J. 106 (50m)
Libretto by Franz Carl Hiemer, after the story *Le dormeur éveillé* by Antoine Galland, in *Mille et une nuits, Contes Arabes traduit en François* (1712)
Composed 1810–11
PREMIERES 4 June 1811, Residenztheater, Munich; UK: 4 April 1825, Drury Lane, London; US: 5 November 1827, Park Theater, New York
CAST Abu Hassan *t*, Fatime *s*, Omar *b*, Harun al Raschid, Zobeide, Mesru, Zemrude, *spoken roles; satb* chorus of Abu Hassan's creditors, followers of the Caliph
CLASSICAL ORCHESTRA plus 2 gtr and 'Turkish' perc (triangle, cym, bd, sd)

Weber began working seriously on *Abu Hassan* shortly before the premiere of *Silvana*. In August 1810 he wrote the chorus of creditors, 'Geld! geld! geld!', an appropriate choice in view of his own recent experiences with moneylenders (he and his father had been involved in some dubious financial transactions; Weber was arrested and, on his release, had to leave Württemberg hurriedly). The other seven numbers of the original version followed in haphazard succession during the remainder of the year, and on 12 January 1811 he completed the overture. For a performance in Gotha in 1813 he added a new duet for Abu Hassan and Fatime, and for a revival in Dresden in 1823 he composed Fatime's lament over the supposed death of Abu Hassan.

SYNOPSIS
Abu Hassan and his devoted wife, Fatime, are being pressed for payment of debts by the moneylender Omar who is also, unsuccessfully, making advances to Fatime. Abu Hassan, cup-bearer to the Caliph, decides to pretend that his wife has died and to claim the money for her funeral from the Caliph. Fatime plans to pretend the same about Abu Hassan with the Caliph's wife, Zobeide. They each succeed in obtaining the money. While Abu Hassan is away, Omar tries to make love to Fatime, but when he hears Abu Hassan returning he hides in a cupboard. Fatime tells Abu Hassan, in a whisper, about Omar and together they act out a charade to convince the terrified Omar that Abu Hassan is after his blood. When the Caliph sends his servant Mesru to discover

whether Abu Hassan or Fatime is really dead, Fatime feigns death, and when Zobeide sends Zemrude, Abu Hassan does the same. The Caliph and his wife then come in person and find both Abu Hassan and Fatime apparently dead. But when Abu Hassan hears the Caliph offer 10,000 gold dinars to anyone who can clear up the mystery he leaps up and reveals the subterfuge. The Caliph is so amused that he forgives Abu Hassan's impudence and when he hears of Omar's activities he orders the cupboard to be taken (with its contents) to the city prison.

Mozart's influence is clearly apparent in the music of *Abu Hassan*; the parallels with *Die Entführung aus dem Serail* are evident. Not only does Weber echo the then popular Turkish theme (there is a spirited Turkish march with 'oriental' percussion for the Caliph's entrance) but occasional turns of phrase are directly reminiscent of passages in Mozart's opera (e.g. the trio 'Ängstlich klopft es mir im Herzen' suggests Belmonte's aria 'O wie ängstlich' in *Die Entführung*). While conforming to the traditional outline of singspiel with its individual arias and spoken dialogue and general lightness of tone, Weber's music displays an inventiveness, particularly evident in the characterization, which transcends the bounds of the genre.

RECORDING Moser, Gedda, Moll, Bavarian State Opera Ch and O, Sawallisch, Electrola, 1975
EDITIONS f.s., Willy-Werner Göttig (ed.), Verlag der Seiboldschen Buchdruckerei Werner Dohany, Offenbach, 1925; *rp*, Gregg International, 1986; v.s., N. Simrock, *c.* 1819

Der Freischütz

The Free-Shooter
Romantic opera in three acts, J. 277 (2h 30m)
Libretto by Johann Friedrich Kind, after *Gespensterbuch* by Johann August Apel and Friedrich Laun (1811)
Composed 1817–21
PREMIERES 18 June 1821, Schauspielhaus, Berlin; UK: 22 July 1824, Lyceum, London; US: 2 March 1825, New York
CAST Max *t*, Kilian *bar*, Cuno *b*, Caspar *b*, Ännchen *s*, Agathe *s*, Samiel *spoken role*, 4 bridesmaids 4 *s*, Ottokar *bar*; *satb* chorus of hunters, peasants, spirits, bridesmaids, followers of the Prince
ORCHESTRATION picc, 2 fl, 2 ob, 2 cl, 2 bsn, 4 hn, 2 tpt, 3 trbn, timp, str

Weber considered writing an opera on the *Freischütz* story in 1811, after reading the tale in Apel's and Laun's newly published *Gespensterbuch*. When he became kapellmeister in Dresden in 1817, he revived the idea and discussed it with Friedrich Kind, who rapidly produced the draft of a libretto. At this stage it was entitled *Der Probeschuss* ('The Test Shot'). The story had already been used as the basis of a number of other theatrical pieces: by Franz Xaver von Caspar with music by Carl Neuner (1812); by Ferdinand Rosenau (1816); by Aloys Gleich with music by Franz Roser (1816). In 1818 Spohr, with the collaboration of Georg Doring, also began to compose an opera based on Apel's tale but, on hearing that Weber was working on the same subject, abandoned it in favour of *Zemire und Azor*.

Weber's poor health, his efforts on behalf of the German opera in Dresden, and the pressure of other commissions slowed down the composition of *Der Freischütz*. In 1819 he began to work more intensively on the score (by then known as *Die Jägersbraut* ('The Hunter's Bride')) after he had reached an agreement that it should open the newly rebuilt Schauspielhaus in Berlin. (In fact, the Schauspielhaus was opened with a Goethe play, but *Der Freischütz* was the first musical piece to be performed there.) The premiere was a triumph and the opera was soon being performed throughout Europe.

Der Freischütz was by far the most popular German opera of the first half of the 19th century. But its tremendous popularity is only partly explained by its musical and dramatic characteristics. It came at an opportune moment in German history, when the upsurge of patriotic feeling, following the defeat of Napoleon, was at its height. With its powerfully German character, in both drama and music, *Der Freischütz* seized the German imagination and remained a significant symbol of national identity throughout the difficult times that followed.

By 1830 *Der Freischütz* had been translated into Danish, Swedish, Czech, Russian, English, French, Hungarian, Polish and Dutch. It was also produced in many severely mutilated versions and its success led to a number of parodies. In 1824 a piece was published under the title *Samiel, oder Die Wunderpille* and in England 'Septimus Globus' issued '*Der Freischütz*, a new muse-sick-all and see-nick performance from the new German uproar. By the celebrated Funnybear'. In the same year Castil-Blaze also produced his French version as *Robin des Bois*, which infuriated the young Berlioz. But Berlioz was later persuaded, albeit reluctantly, to supply recitatives and a ballet for a Paris production of *Der Freischütz* in 1841.

SYNOPSIS

Act I In front of an inn in the Bohemian forest, peasants are congratulating Kilian on his victory over Max, a forester, in a shooting competition ('Victoria, victoria'). They taunt Max and only the arrival of Cuno, the head forester, prevents a fight. Caspar, another forester (who has made a compact with Samiel, the Black Huntsman), mockingly suggests that Max should call on the dark powers for assistance. Cuno rebukes Caspar, but warns Max that if he fails in the shooting test, he will not be allowed to marry his daughter Agathe. The peasants exit to a waltz; Max, alone, ponders his lack of success ('Durch die Wälder') while Samiel observes him. Caspar joins Max and insists on drinking several toasts with him; his coarse drinking song ('Hier im ird'schen Jammerthal') enrages Max. Caspar offers to help Max pass the test and proves the point by giving him his gun, with which he miraculously shoots an almost invisible eagle. Caspar explains that it was loaded with a magic bullet, and that seven more can be cast if he will come to the Wolf's Glen at midnight. Caspar plans to offer Max as a victim

The Wolf's Glen in Der Freischütz *(Weimar, 1822)*

to Samiel in place of himself and exults in Max's impending damnation ('Schweig, schweig').

Act II In Cuno's house, Ännchen is rehanging a portrait which had fallen down, hitting Agathe. She cheers her cousin in a lively arietta ('Kommt ein schlanker Bursch gegangen') and Agathe relates how, that morning, the Hermit, warning her of impending danger, gave her holy roses for her protection. Agathe's uneasiness gives way to joy when she hears Max approaching ('Leise, leise'). Her uneasiness returns, however, when Max explains that he must collect a stag which he has shot near the Wolf's Glen ('Wie? Was? Entsetzen!'). In the Wolf's Glen, as midnight strikes, Caspar summons Samiel who accepts the substitute victim. Max arrives and, together, they cast seven bullets. Between each of the castings there are increasingly horrific supernatural manifestations; finally Samiel himself appears. Caspar and Max fall unconscious and calm returns.

Act III The following day Max, out hunting, has made three magnificent shots and has only one magic bullet left; Caspar has used all his three. Agathe is praying ('Und ob die Wolke'). She dreamt that she was a white dove; when Max fired his gun she fell, but the dove vanished and she was Agathe again,

while a black bird lay bleeding at her feet. Ännchen tries to dispel Agathe's anxiety with a merry tale ('Einst träumte'). The bridesmaids arrive and sing a folksong ('Wir winden dir den Jungfernkranz'). Ännchen arrives with a box containing flowers, but a funeral wreath has been sent instead of a wedding wreath. They decide to make a new wreath from the Hermit's roses. The shooting test is about to begin. Prince Ottokar chooses a white dove as target. As Max takes aim Agathe enters and cries to him to hold fire since she is the dove. The Hermit causes the dove to fly off to another tree behind which Caspar is hiding. Max shoots, and both Agathe and Caspar fall. Everyone thinks Max has shot Agathe ('Schaut, o schaut'), but the bullet has hit Caspar; he dies cursing. Max makes a full confession and, after the intervention of the Hermit, the prince pardons him.

The overture sets the scene for the opera; its two principal tonalities – C minor and C major – represent the opposing forces of good and evil. The appearance of the diminished seventh chord, associated with Samiel (F♯, A, C, E♭) foreshadows the dark side of the drama. The *molto vivace* section is based on passages to come later in the opera: Max's

'Doch mich umgarnen finstre Mächte' (from 'Durch die Wälder'), full of foreboding, and Agathe's exultant 'Süss entzückt entgegen ihm' (from 'Leise, leise').

Throughout the opera, keys play an important part in underlining the conflict between good and evil. The major keys, particularly the sharp keys, are associated with simplicity and goodness, while the minor keys, especially C minor, characterize the dark powers. Samiel's diminished seventh chord appears periodically and acts as a leitmotif, warning of the approaching evil. The whole of the Wolf's Glen scene is built round tonalities based on the individual notes of this chord: the music begins in F♯ minor; at Samiel's appearance it moves to C minor; as Max arrives it modulates to E♭; it returns to C minor and they begin casting the bullets, then, as the bullets are cast, the music alternates between C minor and A minor with copious use of diminished sevenths; at the end, when Caspar and Max fall unconscious, the tonality returns to F♯ minor.

Weber's brilliant orchestration creates dramatic atmospheric effects. In the opening section of the overture horns conjure up a vision of forests and hunting, while low clarinets and timpani create a sense of foreboding. The shrill piccolo is used to give a devilish quality to the end of Caspar's aria and masterly orchestration plays a significant part in creating the powerful atmosphere of the Wolf's Glen scene, which was regarded as a *locus classicus* of German Romantic imagery and imagination during the 19th century. Perhaps the most important musical contribution to the enduring success of the opera, however, is the vigour of Weber's melodic invention. His handling of both the folksong-like choruses and solos and the weightier arias and ensembles is equally successful.

RECORDINGS 1. Grümmer, Otto, Schock, Kohn, Deutsche Oper Ch, Berlin PO, Keilberth, EMI, 1959: sound, central performance, particularly admired for Elisabeth Grümmer's Agathe; 2. Janowitz, Mathis, Schreier, Adam, Leipzig Radio Ch, Dresden Staatskapelle, C. Kleiber, DG, 1973: strongly cast, exuberantly conducted [A.B.]
EDITIONS f.ss., Schlesinger, 1843; *rp*, Gregg International, 1969; autograph facsimile, George Knepler (ed.), Peters, 1978; v.s., Schott, 1822

Die drei Pintos
The Three Pintos
Opera in three acts (inc.), J. Anh. 5
Libretto by Theodore Hell, after the story *Der Brautkampf* by Carl Seidel (1819)
Begun 1820, abandoned 1824, completed by Gustav Mahler, 1888, with new text by Carl von Weber
PREMIERES 20 January 1888, Neues Stadttheater, Leipzig; UK: 10 April 1962, John Lewis Theatre, London; US: 6 June 1979, Loretto-Hilton Center, St Louis, Missouri

While in the final stages of writing *Der Freischütz*, Weber began to consider a comic opera to Hell's libretto, *Die drei Pintos*, and started sketching it in the summer of 1820. He continued to work on it sporadically during 1821 until he began work on *Euryanthe*. Although his interest in *Die drei Pintos*

revived in the autumn of 1824, it was finally abandoned when he decided to compose *Oberon* for London.

Clarissa's lover Don Gomez, aided by the student Don Gaston, impersonates Don Pinto, the man whom Clarissa's father intends for her husband, but whom none of them have met. (The title *The Three Pintos* derives from the fact that Gaston and Gomez each impersonate Pinto in turn.) Their plans are disrupted by the arrival of the real Pinto, but matters are amicably resolved and Don Gomez is betrothed to Clarissa.

Weber sketched only the first seven of the 17 projected numbers (the whole of Act I, and the first number of Act II). After his death, his wife sent them to Meyerbeer, with a view to his completing the opera, but Meyerbeer returned them to the Weber family in 1847. Eventually, Weber's grandson, Carl, gave them to Mahler, who used them as a basis for his own completion. Mahler's first idea was to use Weber's music to create Acts I and II and have Act III spoken. But he soon decided against this course. His final version consists of 21 numbers; he used all of the Pinto sketches, though not in their original positions, and supplemented these with little-known pieces by Weber, mostly written for inclusion in other people's dramas or operas, which he arranged and rescored, producing much of the detail from his own imagination.

RECORDING Popp, Hollweg, Prey, Moll, Netherlands Vocal Ensemble, Munich PO, Bertini, RCA, 1976
EDITIONS f.s./v.s., C. F. Kahnt, 1888

Euryanthe
Grand heroic–romantic opera in three acts, J. 291 (2h 45m)
Libretto by Helmina von Chezy, after the 13th-century French romance, *L'histoire du très-noble et chevalereux prince Gérard, comte de Nevers, et de la très-virtueuse et très chaste princesse Euriant de Savoye, sa mye*
Composed 1822–3
PREMIERES 25 October 1823, Kärntnertortheater, Vienna; UK: 29 June 1833, Covent Garden, London; US: 23 December 1887, Metropolitan, New York
CAST King Louis VI *b*, Adolar *t*, Lysiart *b*, Euryanthe *s*, Eglantine *s*, Rudolf *t*, Bertha *s*; *satb* chorus of ladies, noblemen, knights, hunters, peasants
FULL ORCHESTRA

As a direct result of the success of *Der Freischütz* Weber was invited to compose an opera in the same style for Vienna. He decided, however, to write a very different kind of work. Like Spohr and Schubert, who were each working on through-composed operas (respectively *Jessonda* and *Alfonso und Estrella*) at about the same time, Weber decided to dispense with spoken dialogue in favour of continuous music.

The premiere, conducted by Weber, achieved a *succès d'estime*, but many found the plot confusing and the whole opera too long. Weber himself sanctioned cuts totalling 172 bars, and after his departure from Vienna a further 352 bars were excised. *Euryanthe* was subsequently staged in many theatres, but it has retained only a tenuous place in

Wilhelmine Schröder-Devrient as Euryanthe (Dresden, 1839)

the repertoire. Attempts to make it more viable through the production of new performing versions have not succeeded.

SYNOPSIS

Act I In King Louis VI's hall Adolar praises the virtue of his absent bride, Euryanthe. Lysiart wagers his lands against Adolar's that he can prove Euryanthe unfaithful. Meanwhile, in Adolar's castle, Eglantine, who is also in love with Adolar and who covertly hates Euryanthe, persuades her to reveal the secret of the ghost of Adolar's sister, Emma, who committed suicide with poison contained in her ring. Lysiart arrives at the castle and Euryanthe welcomes him.

Act II That night, Eglantine, coming out of Emma's tomb after removing the poisoned ring from the corpse, is surprised by Lysiart. They form an alliance. Back in the king's hall, Lysiart produces Emma's ring as proof of Euryanthe's love for him and claims victory in the wager. Adolar's estates are forfeit and he takes Euryanthe away, intending to kill her.

Act III Adolar and Euryanthe are in a mountain gorge. Suddenly a snake appears. Euryanthe tries to protect Adolar. He kills it, but touched by her offer of self-sacrifice he cannot bring himself to kill her and abandons her to the elements. She is found by the king and his hunting party; explaining Eglantine's deceit, she easily convinces the king of her innocence. Adolar returns to his castle and confronts Lysiart who is about to marry Eglantine. The king arrives and clears up the misunderstandings about Euryanthe. Eglantine pours scorn on Lysiart; he stabs her to death and is led away. The opera ends with Euryanthe and Adolar happily united.

Weber's aim in *Euryanthe* to show that he could write opera in a much grander style than *Der Freischütz* succeeded, as far as the music is concerned. However, *Euryanthe* is fatally marred by the weakness of its libretto; despite this and the dramatic deficiencies of the work as a whole, its

influence on later composers, notably Marschner, Schumann, Liszt and Wagner, was considerable.

RECORDING Norman, Hunter, Gedda, Krause, Vogel, Leipzig Radio Ch, Dresden Staatskapelle, Janowski, HMV, 1975
EDITIONS f.s., Schlesinger, 1866; *rp*, Gregg International, 1969; v.ss., Steiner, 1824; Robert Lienau, 1955

Oberon, or The Elf King's Oath

Romantic opera in three acts, J. 306
Libretto by James Robinson Planche, after *Oberon* by Christoph Martin Wieland (1780) and the 13th-century French romance *Huon de Bordeaux*
Composed 1825–6
PREMIERES 12 April 1826, Covent Garden, London; US: 20 September 1828, Park Theater, New York
CAST Oberon *t*, Puck *ms*, Reiza *s*, Sir Huon of Bordeaux *t*, Sherasmin *bar*, Fatima *ms*, 2 Mermaids 2 *ms*, Namouna, Haroun al Rachid, Babekan, Abdallah, Roshana, Almanzor, *spoken roles*; *satb* chorus of fairies, ladies, knights, slaves, mermaids, etc.
FULL ORCHESTRA

Weber was originally asked to write *Oberon* for the London season of 1825, but delays over the libretto led to a year's postponement. Weber quickly realized that he was dealing with a very different libretto from those he was used to, and he wrote to Planche in February 1825, 'The intermixing of so many principal actors who do not sing, the omission of the music in the most important moments – all these things deprive our *Oberon* the title of an Opera, and will make him unfit for all other Theatres in Europe; which is a very bad thing for me, but – *passons là dessus*.'

SYNOPSIS

Act I Oberon and Titania have quarrelled over whether man or woman is the more inconstant in love; they have vowed not to be reunited until they find a couple who are constant. Puck informs Oberon that Charlemagne has condemned Huon of Bordeaux to go to Baghdad, where he must kill the man on the Caliph's right hand, then kiss the Caliph's daughter and marry her. Oberon decides to use Huon as a means to win reconciliation with Titania. He conjures up a vision of the Caliph's daughter, Reiza, and Huon falls instantly in love. Reiza is similarly smitten with Huon. He gives Huon a fairy horn and a magic goblet. He then despatches Huon and his squire, Sherasmin, to Baghdad.

Act II After a number of adventures they manage, through the power of the horn, to carry off Reiza and her maid, Fatima, with whom Sherasmin has fallen in love; they escape by ship. Later, all except Huon are carried off to Tunis by pirates.

Act III With the help of Oberon and his horn, Huon succeeds in rescuing his companions. Oberon, reunited with Titania, transports the lovers to Charlemagne's palace where the opera ends in general rejoicing.

Despite the circumstances of its composition, *Oberon* contains some of Weber's most delightful music (best known is Reiza's scene and aria 'Ocean! thou mighty monster'). This has ensured it a permanent, if peripheral, place in the repertoire, even though its essentially undramatic structure is far from satisfactory. British audiences of the day were more anxious for spectacular stage effects (e.g. Oberon conjures up 'the interior of a Persian kiosk' to tempt Huon) and plentiful ballad-like songs than for the artistically unified concept that concerned Weber. To accommodate John Braham, the original Huon, the aria 'From boyhood trained' was replaced with 'Ah, 'tis a glorious sight to see', and an additional aria, 'Ruler of his awful hour', was inserted. Such practicalities meant that use of the unifying musical devices employed in Weber's earlier operas (tonalities, characterization through orchestral colouring, etc.) was impossible. However, Weber unified the opera by employing Oberon's horn call, which opens the overture, as a motif at various points in the work. Had he lived, he would certainly have revised *Oberon*, adding recitatives, to make it suitable for the German stage.

In 1860, Planche produced a revised version in Italian, which had recitatives by Weber's pupil Julius Benedict and incorporated some music from *Euryanthe*. There have been many other arrangements including one with recitative by Franz Wüllner, and one by Gustav Brecher with sections of instrumental music by Gustav Mahler (based on material from the opera) to accompany the dialogue.

RECORDINGS   1. Nilsson, Hamari, Domingo, Grobe, Prey, Bavarian Radio Ch and SO, Kubelik, DG, 1971; 2. Voigt, Ziegler, Heppner, Lakes, Croft, Cologne Opera Ch, Cologne PO, Gürzenich O, Conlon, EMI, 1992: both versions are well sung and conducted; the second benefits from better sound [A.B.]
EDITIONS   f.s., Schlesinger, 1874; *rp*, Gregg International, 1969; v.ss., Schlesinger, 1826; Schirmer, 1918

Other operas: *Das Waldmädchen* (fragments of 2 arias survive), 1800; *Peter Schmoll und seine Nachbarn*, 1803; *Rübezahl, oder Der Beherrscher der Geister* (3 numbers survive), (1805); 1 lost opera
BIBLIOGRAPHY   G. Jones, 'Weber's 'Secondary Worlds': The Later Operas of Carl Maria von Weber', *IRASM*, vol. 7 (1976), p. 219; Michael C. Tusa, *Euryanthe and Carl Maria von Weber's Dramaturgy of German Opera*, Clarendon Press, 1991; John Warrack, *Carl Maria von Weber*, Hamish Hamilton, 1968; *rp*, 1976; John Warrack (ed.), *Carl Maria von Weber: Writings on Music*, CUP, 1981

C.A.B.

JOSEPH WEIGL

b 28 March 1766, Eisenstadt; *d* 3 February 1846, Vienna

Weigl studied with Albrechtsberger (1776–1782) and in 1783 Gluck and Salieri promoted his first opera, *Die unnütze Vorsicht, oder Die betrogene Arglist*, at the Burgtheater. In 1784 Weigl began studying with Salieri. He was on the music staff of the court theatre during rehearsals of Mozart's *Le nozze di Figaro* and *Don Giovanni* and, in 1790, became deputy

kapellmeister at the court theatre. In 1792 he received a permanent contract there as kapellmeister and composer.

Weigl remained in Vienna all his life, declining offers from the Stuttgart Opera (1802) and from the Milan Conservatory (1808) following the successful staging there of two of his operas. Weigl is particularly remembered for his singspiels, *Das Waisenhaus* and *Die Schweizerfamilie*. *Die Schweizerfamilie*, widely performed during the 19th century, follows a fashion for sentimental plots set in a peaceful natural surrounding. Conflicts between protagonists are reduced to a minimum and the main singers lack individual characterization. But Weigl uses certain motifs in the manner of recollection motifs to create a musical continuity, and he had a gift for writing singable tunes which probably accounts for his popularity.

Operatic works: *Die unnütze Vorsicht, oder Die betrogene Arglist*, 1783; *Il pazzo per forza*, 1788; *La caffettiera bizzarra*, 1790; *Der Strassensammler (Lumpensammler)*, 1792; *La principessa d'Amalfi*, 1794; *Das Petermännchen*, 1794; *Giulietta e Pierotto*, 1794; *I solitari*, 1797; *L'amor marinaro, ossia Il corsaro*, 1797; *Das Dorf im Gebirge*, 1798; *L'accademia del maestro Cisolfaut*, 1798; *L'uniforme*, 1800; *Die Herrenhuterin*, 1804; *Vestas Feuer*, 1805; *Il principe invisibile*, 1806; *Kaiser Hadrian*, 1807; *Ostade, oder Adrian von Ostade*, 1807; *Il rivale di se stesso*, 1808; *Das Waisenhaus*, 1808; *Die Schweizerfamilie*, 1809; *Die Verwandlungen*, 1810; *Der Einsiedler auf den Alpen*, 1810; *Franciska von Foix*, 1812; *Der Bergsturz*, 1813; *Die Jugend Peter des Grossen*, 1814; *L'imboscata*, 1815; *Margaritta d'Anjou, ossia L'orfano d'Inghilterra*, 1816; *Die Nachtigall und der Rabe*, 1818; *Daniel in der Löwengrube, oder Baals Sturz*, 1820; *König Waldemar, oder Die dänischen Fischer*, 1821; *Edmund und Caroline*, 1821; *Die eiserne Pforte*, 1823; one lost opera
BIBLIOGRAPHY   Rudolph Angermüller, 'Zwei Selbstbiographien von Joseph Weigl (1766–1846)', *DJbM*, vol. 16 (1973), p. 46; C. M. v. Weber, *Writings on Music*, CUP, 1981

M.F.

KURT WEILL

Kurt Julian Weill; *b* 2 March 1900, Dessau, Saxony; *d* 3 April 1950, New York

Weill was the third child of the chief cantor at the Dessau synagogue. He received his musical education first from the conductor Albert Bing (a pupil of Pfitzner) in Dessau and in 1918 from Humperdinck at the Berlin Hochschule für Musik. After a year's practical work at the opera house in his home town (where Hans Knappertsbusch was the music director) and as staff conductor at the Lüdenscheid opera in Westphalia, he returned to Berlin in 1920 to join Busoni's composition masterclass.

By the time he started to collaborate with Bertolt Brecht in 1927, Weill was established as one of the leading composers in Weimar Germany, with four successful stage works under his belt; it was indeed Weill who gave the unknown writer his first chance of fame with the sensational premiere of the *Mahagonny Songspiel* at Baden-Baden. Brecht continued to ride on Weill's coat-tails with *Die Dreigroschenoper* (1928), *Aufstieg und Fall der Stadt Mahagonny* (1930), *Happy End* (1929) and *Der Jasager* (1930), after which they drifted apart; as Lotte Lenya, whom the composer had married in 1926, was to put it later, her husband was not interested in setting the Communist manifesto to music, and Weill resumed collaboration with the Expressionist playwright Georg Kaiser in *Der Silbersee* (February 1933). This was simultaneously premiered in three cities (which gives some idea of the composer's status), but was to be the last Weill premiere in Germany. Nazi thugs disrupted early performances, and nine days after the first night the Reichstag fire gave them the opportunity to assume power. Weill fled precipitately from Berlin to Paris in March, with few belongings and none of his music.

The Nazis seem to have feared him more than any other composer, and for years went to inordinate lengths through diplomatic channels worldwide to have his scores, orchestral parts and records destroyed. Weill himself believed that all his German works save for *Dreigroschenoper* were irretrievably lost, and reused some of the music in later pieces.

Weill spent 18 months in Paris, which saw a brief reunion with Brecht for *Die sieben Todsünden* and the incidental music for Jacques Deval's play *Marie Galante* (which included one of his greatest songs, 'J'attends un navire', later used as a signal by the French resistance), and went to the US in 1935 to complete the score for the Franz Werfel–Max Reinhardt pageant of Jewish history, *Der Weg der Verheissung*, eventually staged as *The Eternal Road* (New York, 1937). He remained in the States for the rest of his life, composing for Broadway and Hollywood, and died from a heart condition in 1950 while embarking on a musical version of *Huckleberry Finn*.

Weill is beyond any doubt one of the most important composers for the theatre – a more accurate designation than 'opera composer' – of the 20th century. His precise place in the history of Western music in general and opera in particular is still impossible to assess. The cultural upheaval caused by the short-lived but still reverberating Nazi tyranny in the very heartland of European music; a generally left-wing political and critical stance, allied to knee-jerk anti-American sentiment in post-war Europe that bolstered accusations of a progressive composer 'selling out' to Broadway commercialism (his US works are loathed in Germany); Weill's tragically premature death aged only 50: all contribute to clouding a highly complex issue.

At the time, the end of the First World War seemed like a watershed, though today we may see it as only the first act of a European drama that is still being played out. But it afforded an opportunity for composers to grapple with the post-Wagnerian legacy. Wagner had pushed tonality as far as it could go: what next? Strauss largely wrote neo-Wagnerian operas; Schoenberg devised a new musical language, dodecaphony; Stravinsky and Busoni advanced – or

retreated – into neo-classicism; Schreker, Zemlinsky and others nudged Wagnerianism over the edge into no-holds-barred Expressionism. Most composers embraced without question an aesthetic of linear progress: music could only get more complicated, more demanding, more remote from everyday audiences, more dependent on a state-subsidized system of presentation. The artificial separation of high art and popular art is still a very real problem, and it seems to be only in music that this linear progress has been accepted virtually without question: few would regard the path in painting from, say, Giotto to Raphael, as one of smooth, uninterrupted progress.

Weill's early works are conventionally Expressionist; there is a vitally important neo-classical element in *Dreigroschenoper* and *Mahagonny*. The latter was rejected by Otto Klemperer – later a leading exponent of the 'sell-out' school of Weill criticism – at the Krolloper, and Weill took it instead to Berlin's equivalent of Broadway, the Kurfürstendamm, for a commercial run. *Dreigroschenoper* and *Happy End* were commercial ventures, and although there were still projects for subsidized theatres (*Die Bürgschaft* and *Der Silbersee*) he had taken the basic decision to write for a mass audience long before he went to America. In Germany he transformed into high art familiar song and dance idioms of the time and place, and the mass popularity of *Dreigroschenoper* cannot be overstressed. In America he naturally turned to the popular and folk idioms of his new homeland – to have done otherwise would have been senseless – and it is this that has stuck in sensitive European throats. But as Weill wrote in 1949, 'The American popular song, growing out of American folk music, is the basis of the American musical theatre, just as the Italian song was the basis of Italian opera.'

The notion that a radical, left-wing composer 'sold out' to naked commerce does not bear serious examination. The people Weill collaborated with in the US were for the main part committed radicals of the kind who got into serious trouble in the McCarthy era, and *Johnny Johnson*, *Knickerbocker Holiday*, *Street Scene*, *Love Life* and *Lost in the Stars* are works brimming over with political and social concern. The collaboration with Brecht cannot be taken as evidence that Weill was in any sense a conventional left-winger: the break coincided with the playwright's conversion to orthodox communism. Weill, on the evidence in particular of his US output as well as his later German works, could best be described as a militant humanist, a man set on using popular theatre to combat intolerance, prejudice, deprivation and injustice wherever they were to be found.

His compositional aesthetic is neatly summed up in an interview he gave to the *New York Sun* in 1940. 'I have never acknowledged the difference between "serious" music and "light" music. There is only good music and bad music,' he said, and continued with a direct challenge to critical orthodoxy: 'Schoenberg has said he is writing for a time 50 years after his death. But the great classical composers wrote for their contemporary audiences. They wanted those who heard their music to understand it, and they did. For myself, I write for today. I don't give a damn about writing for posterity.'

Weill was above all a great writer of tunes: the Ballad of Mack the Knife has become an authentic 20th-century folksong, and he composed many others worthy of that status. He was a tirelessly inventive orchestrator, varying the accompaniments to each verse of his songs and, almost uniquely on Broadway, insisted on scoring every bar of his works and writing his own dance sequences. Yet his melodic genius should not be taken to imply the smallest degree of facileness: David Drew's analysis of *Dreigroschen-oper* in the Cambridge Opera Handbook (see BIBLIOGRAPHY) suggests a personal, highly complex serialist technique.

An of necessity interim report must credit Weill with at least four masterpieces: *Dreigroschenoper, Mahagonny*, and *Die sieben Todsünden* have never lost their hold on the repertoire, and after regular revival *Street Scene* has now been accepted as one of the great American operas, a work to set beside *Porgy and Bess* and one he considered to be his first complete technical success. A pleasing new critical stance holds that it was with *Street Scene* that he reached full maturity as a composer for the theatre.

When the rest of his output is investigated now that prejudice against his later works is fading, other masterpieces may emerge. As it is, his importance in having shown that popular theatre can – or rather must – be serious is now generally accepted, and his influence on later Broadway composers, from Bernstein to Sondheim, is incalculable.

Der Protagonist

Opera in one act, Op. 14 (1h 15m)
Libretto by Georg Kaiser
PREMIERES   27 March 1926, Dresden State Opera; UK: 12 March 1986, Bloomsbury Theatre, London (Camden Festival); US: 1993, Santa Fe

The fact that the 26-year-old composer collaborated on his first opera with one of the leading playwrights of the day bears witness to the reputation he had already established for himself in Germany, and the success of the premiere, conducted by Fritz Busch, both confirmed and greatly strengthened his position with his publishers, Universal Edition.

A theatrical troupe in Shakespearean England rehearses a mildly licentious pantomime farce, to be performed before the Duke. The eponymous leader of the troupe (tenor) has an unhealthily intense relationship with his sister, who reveals to him that she has a lover of long standing, news he takes with a mixture of incredulousness and surprising equanimity. As she leaves to fetch her Young Lord, the Duke's Major-domo announces that a Bishop is joining the party, and the farce must be replaced by something more suitable. The Protagonist orders his troupe to repeat the same action as tragedy, and at the climax of the re-rehearsal the sister returns with her Young Lord. The Protagonist, confusing stage action with reality, stabs his sister, but asks the authorities to delay his arrest until after the evening's performance, since this is the best role he has ever played.

Der Protagonist has been neatly described as *Pagliacci* for grown-ups. The score is Hindemithian in its atonal spikiness, the vocal writing somewhat angular. The first mime sequence is written with virtuoso dash for wind alone.

EDITIONS   f.s., Universal (on hire); v.s., Universal, 1926

Der Zar läßt sich photographieren

The Tsar has his Photograph Taken
Opera buffa in one act, Op. 21 (45m)
Libretto by Georg Kaiser
Composed 1927
PREMIERES   18 February 1928, Leipzig Opera; US: 27 October 1949, Juilliard School of Music, New York; UK: 12 March 1986, Bloomsbury Theatre, London (Camden Festival)

Der Zar was composed as a companion piece for *Der Protagonist*, the original pairing (*Royal Palace*, to a libretto by Iwan Goll) not having been a success. By contrast, Weill's first comedy was performed more often in Germany than any of his works other than *Dreigroschenoper*.

The setting is a fashionable photographic studio in Paris in 1914. Angèle, the proprietress, is told that the Tsar is on his way for a portrait session. A revolutionary gang led by a woman bursts in, binds and gags the studio staff and fits a revolver into the camera. The Tsar, an informal and relaxed autocrat with normal appetites, arrives and is immediately attracted by the False Angèle. He dismisses his entourage and a game of cat and mouse, of love and death, ensues with ironic comments from a male chorus. The amorous Tsar insists on taking the False Angèle's photograph first, and she escapes this only by pretending to succumb to his advances. When warning is brought of an assassination attempt, she plays for time by putting on a record of the smoochy *Tango Angèle* and, pretending to undress while the Tsar waits with his eyes covered, makes good her and her gang's escape. The real Angèle returns, and the Tsar, disappointed at her comparative plainness, nevertheless has his photograph taken.

This smart, witty and sophisticated little comedy deserved its success by not outstaying its welcome beyond 45 minutes, and it has more to say about illusion and reality, about love and death, than is immediately apparent. The *Tango Angèle* became Weill's first best-selling record.

RECORDING   Napier, Pohl, McDaniel, Cologne Radio O, Latham-Koenig, Capriccio, 1984
EDITIONS   f.s./v.s., Universal, 1927

Die Dreigroschenoper

The Threepenny Opera
Play with music in three acts (music: 1h 15m; full-length play)
Libretto and play text by Bertolt Brecht, based on the translation by Elisabeth Hauptmann of *The Beggar's Opera* by John Gay (1728), with interpolated ballads by François Villon and Rudyard Kipling

PREMIERES 31 August 1928, Theater am Schiffbauerdamm, Berlin; US: 13 April 1933, Empire Theater, New York; UK: 9 February 1956, Royal Court Theatre, London
CAST Jonathan Jeremiah Peachum *bar*, Mrs Peachum *ms*, Polly Peachum *s*, Macheath *t*, Tiger Brown/Streetsinger *bar*, Lucy *s*, Jenny Diver *s*, Macheath's gang; *satb* chorus of whores, beggars and police
ORCHESTRATION 10 players: tenor sax/sop sax/bsn/2nd cl, alto sax/fl/1st cl, 2 tpt, trbn/db, banjo/vc/gtr/bandoneon, timp, perc, harmonium/cel, pf/conductor

Weill composed the score of *Die Dreigroschenoper* in the spring and summer of 1928 for the impresario J. E. Aufricht, who had unexpectedly come into money and taken a lease of the Theater am Schiffbauerdamm. Final rehearsals were chaotic – the piece did not find its final form until well after the premiere – and the theatre was not full on the first night. Those involved were half expecting a flop. But despite mixed notices word of mouth ensured a hit of near-unprecedented proportions (the triumph of *The Merry Widow* a quarter of a century earlier provides a nicely ironic parallel) and the piece was soon staged throughout Europe (save for Britain) and in the US. Only the advent of the Nazis in 1933 interrupted its near continuous run in Berlin and countless productions all over Germany.

Roma Bahn (Polly) and Harald Paulsen (Macheath) in Die Dreigroschenoper *(Berlin, 1928)*

SYNOPSIS

Act I In a prologue set in London's Soho, the Streetsinger sings the Ballad of Mack the Knife, admiringly cataloguing the petty criminal's crimes. Mr and Mrs Peachum briefly interrupt the businesslike organization of the band of beggars and thieves they control to note the absence of their daughter Polly. It emerges that she has eloped with Mack, a highly unsuitable son-in-law. In the second scene Polly and Mack celebrate their wedding in a stable surrounded by stolen goods and the gang. Polly entertains the company with a song she recently heard a bedraggled hotel chambermaid singing (Pirate Jenny). Among the guests is the police chief Tiger Brown, Mack's old school friend. They reminisce over happy days in the Indian Army (Canon Song). Left alone, the newly-weds sing a love duet of sickly sentimentality. Back with her parents, Polly seeks to explain her new liaison via the Barbara Song, but they are determined to force Brown to arrest Mack. In the First Threepenny Finale, the three comment on the intractability of human existence.

Act II In the stable, Mack and Polly sing a duet of farewell: he has 'business' to attend to. Meanwhile, Mrs Peachum bribes the whore Jenny to betray Mack to the police (Song of Sexual Dependency), which Jenny duly does in a brothel in Turnbridge, having first joined with him in the Tango Ballad, in which they remember affectionately the good old days when he was her pimp. In the Old Bailey, Mack sings the Ballad of the Good Life (based on Villon). Brown's daughter Lucy, feigning pregnancy, reproaches Mack and sings a furious Jealousy Duet with Polly, but nevertheless helps her seducer to escape. The Second Threepenny Finale, sung by the entire company, returns to the problems of human existence: man survives only by suppressing his humanity and exploiting his fellow man.

Act III Peachum blackmails Brown: if Mack is not rearrested, his army of beggars will disrupt the forthcoming coronation. Mack is found with another whore and returned to the Old Bailey. Polly and his gang are unable, or unwilling, to come up with the necessary bribe to prevent his hanging. He takes bitter farewell of the world. But Peachum announces that the company has thought up a different ending (Third Threepenny Finale): the King's Messenger (Brown) brings news that in honour of the coronation the queen grants Mack a reprieve, a peerage, a grace-and-favour castle and a pension. The company sings a mock-Bach chorale of ironic relief: 'Don't prosecute crime: it will die out of its own accord.'

The action was never intended to be in any way naturalistic: décor and acting style were non-representational, and the plot came to a halt for the musical numbers, which were differently lit. This was 'epic theatre' after the manner of the day and, in Weill's words, 'the most consistent reaction to Wagner . . . the complete destruction of the concept of music drama'. *The Beggar's Opera* satirized the 18th-century ruling classes by putting them in a low-life setting (Hogarth's painting shows the original cast still very grandly dressed); *The Threepenny Opera*'s target is the solid bourgeoisie of post-war Europe. It has become customary to play both works as low-life extravaganzas, which weakens their impact: the characters should be instantly, inescapably recognizable as, and to, the audience.

Weill wrote the music not for opera singers, but for artists from the fields of cabaret, musical comedy and (in the case of Macheath) operetta. The dart of his satire is poisoned by the beauty and catchiness of the tunes. As you hum or listen to them, the cheerful, subversive obscenity of the words inevitably sinks in, nowhere more devastatingly than in the Tango Ballad, the Song of Sexual Dependency (which the first Mrs Peachum refused to sing), or – more pointfully – the finales. The songs nevertheless need to be sung properly, not snarled or shouted as has become the custom in low-life productions: early recordings (hoarded and secretly played by liberal Germans under Nazi rule) reveal a sweetness and innocence of approach that makes their appeal all the more insinuating.

Brecht revised both the libretto and the lyrics after the premiere, bringing them into line with his own growing Marxist convictions and by 1931 establishing the text as usually played today. The original is shorter, funnier, more anarchic and less didactic, but is unlikely to be revived before Brecht's copyright runs out.

The New York revival of 1954, which ran for 2,611 performances in Marc Blitzstein's translation, marked a significant stage in the revival of interest in Weill's work – revivals and recordings of his other European scores followed – and confirmed *Dreigroschenoper* as one of the most important (and in the right circumstances enjoyable) pieces of music theatre composed in the 20th century.

RECORDINGS 1. Koczian, Lenya, Wolffberg, Hesterburg, Schellow, Grunert, Trenk-Trebitsch, Neuss, Sender Freies Berlin O, Brückner-Rüggeberg, CBS, 1958; 2. Lemper, Milva, Tremper, Dernesch, Kollo, Reichmann, Adorf, Boysen, RIAS Berlin Sinfonietta, Mauceri, Decca, 1990
EDITIONS v.s., Universal, 1928; study s., Philharmonia/Universal, 1980

Happy End

Comedy with music in three acts (music: 40m; full-length play)
Book by 'Dorothy Lane' (Elisabeth Hauptmann); lyrics by Bertolt Brecht
PREMIERES 2 September 1929, Theater am Schiffbauerdamm, Berlin; UK: 14 August 1964, Traverse Theatre, Edinburgh; US: 6 April 1972, Yale Repertory Theater, New Haven, Connecticut
CAST Lilian Holliday *s*, Bill Cracker *t* or *bar*, Lady in Grey *s*, Dr Nakamura *bar*, Hannibal Jackson *t*, Sam Wurlitzer *bar*, spoken roles
BAND of 9 players

To cash in on the unprecedented success of *Die Dreigroschenoper*, the impresario Aufricht solicited another play with music from Weill and Brecht. Brecht subcontracted the book to Elisabeth Hauptmann, one of his many long-suffering mis-mistresses and collaborators (the true extent of her contribution to *Dreigroschenoper* is only now being established). During the run up to the premiere of *Happy End* she attempted suicide when Brecht suddenly married Helene Weigel; in the circum-

stances it is hardly surprising that the resulting text is less than coherent. Brecht wrote some new song texts and cannibalized others.

The cast, which included Carola Neher, Oskar Homolka, Helene Weigel, Peter Lorre and Kurt Gerron, was kept waiting until the last minute for the text of Act III, and one reason for this became obvious at the premiere: after two well-received acts, Weigel apparently stepped out of character to harangue the audience with socialist propaganda in the third, and the piece ended with an agitprop ensemble entitled 'Hosannah Rockefeller'. The evening was a fiasco, and there were only two further performances.

The action, loosely inspired by Shaw's *Major Barbara* and strikingly similar to Damon Runyon's *Guys and Dolls*, tells of a Salvation Army lass (Lilian) who falls for a criminal (Cracker); eventually Salvationists and criminals – in some versions the gang leader, the Lady in Grey, and the Salvationist General turn out to be the same – join forces in capitalist enterprise. The play is entertaining, if somewhat inconsequential; the 13 musical numbers, though, only loosely connected to it, mark the apogee of Weill's Berlin song style and a significant musical advance on *Dreigroschenoper*. The melodies are longer-breathed and the instrumentation more inventive and varied – each song verse is differently accompanied. The agitprop numbers are undeniably stirring, but it is the nostalgically sentimental songs that have entered the repertoire: the Bilbao Song, the Sailors' Tango and above all 'Surabaya Johnny'. The play has never enjoyed a commercial success, but a *Happy End Songspiel* devised by the Weill authority David Drew in 1975 has enjoyed wide currency.

RECORDINGS 1. Lenya, Brückner-Rüggeberg, Philips/CBS, 1960: with deletions from 'Hosannah Rockefeller'; 2. Thomas, Dickinson, Langridge, Partridge, Luxon, London Sinfonietta, Atherton, DG, 1975: minus Bilbao Song; 3. Ramm, Raffeiner, Ploog, Kimbrough, Koenig Ensemble, Latham-Koenig, Capriccio, 1988
EDITIONS v.s./study s., Universal, 1980

Aufstieg und Fall der Stadt Mahagonny

Rise and Fall of the City of Mahagonny
Opera in three acts (2h 15m)
Libretto by Bertolt Brecht
Composed 1927–9
PREMIERES 9 March 1930, Neues Theater, Leipzig; US: 23 February 1952, Town Hall, New York; UK: 16 January 1963, Sadler's Wells, London
CAST Leocadia Begbick *ms*, Fatty the Bookkeeper *t*, Trinity Moses *bar*, Jenny Smith *s*, Jim Mahoney *t*, Jakob Schmidt *t*, Bankroll Bill *bar*, Alaska Wolf Joe *b*, Tobby Higgins *t*; satb chorus of people of Mahagonny
ORCHESTRATION 2 fl, ob, cl, alto sax, tenor sax, 2 bsn/dbsn, 2 hn, 3 tpt, 2 trbn, tuba, timp, perc, pf, harmonium, banjo, b gtr, bandoneon, str; onstage band: 2 picc, 2 cl, 3 sax, 2 bsn, 2 hn, 2 tpt, 2 trbn, tuba, perc, pf, zither, banjo, bandoneon

The full-length *Mahagonny* opera, conceived early in 1927, received a preview in the form of the so-called

The boxing ring in The Rise and Fall of the City of Mahagonny *(Baden-Baden, 1927); in the photograph are Kurt Weill (second from left), Bertolt Brecht and Lotte Lenya (third and fourth from right)*

Mahagonny Songspiel, a music-theatre setting of a group of loosely linked poems from Brecht's *Hauspostille* about an imaginary US city. God consigns its licentious citizens to hell, but they truculently reply that they are there already. The *Songspiel* fulfilled a commission to Weill from the Baden-Baden Deutsche Kammermusik festival, and the premiere there on 17 July 1927 was an enormous *succès de scandale* – an audience expecting respectable avant-garde experiment was regaled with raucous music-hall songs set in a boxing ring.

SYNOPSIS

Act I   A desert in America. A battered truck drives on to the stage and breaks down. Its passengers are Begbick, Fatty and Trinity Moses, fugitives from justice on charges of white-slaving and fraud. Noting that it is easier to extract gold from men than from the dried-up riverbed they are stranded on, Begbick decides to found Mahagonny, a 'city of nets' given over to pleasure since life is so miserable everywhere else. Jenny and her friends – the first 'sharks' – enter: 'Oh show us the way to the next whisky bar' (Alabama Song). Fatty and Moses recruit emigrants from the industrial cities of the world, and Jimmy Mahoney and his friends Jake, Bill and Joe, four 'simple lumberjacks from Alaska', arrive to a sprightly parody of the Bridesmaids' Chorus from *Der Freischütz*. They are offered their choice of girls,

and Jimmy buys Jenny Smith for 30 dollars. She asks him whether or not he would like her to wear knickers. He answers in the negative. Mahagonny suffers a recession, and Jimmy is only just dissuaded from leaving by his friends. In the saloon he rails (to a parody of 'The Maiden's Prayer') against too much peace and quiet. An approaching typhoon is the answer to his prayer. As they await its arrival, Jimmy protests that the city is hemmed in by too many regulations: society should be founded on total permissiveness, on *laissez-faire* and each man for himself – 'as you make your bed, so you lie on it' ('Wie man sich bettet so liegt man').

Act II   Mahagonny is miraculously spared and its citizens follow Jimmy's precepts in four tableaux: gluttony, in which Jake eats himself to death; lechery, in which Begbick presides over a brothel; fighting, in which Jimmy puts all his money on Joe in a boxing match with Trinity Moses (Joe is killed); and drinking, in which Jimmy buys rounds of drinks for which he cannot pay. When Begbick demands payment, Jenny refuses his appeal for a loan and throws 'Wie man sich bettet' back at him. Imprisoned, he dreads the dawn of a new day.

Act III   In the courts, Tobby Higgins is cleared of murder after handing money over to the bench. Jimmy asks Bill for a loan so that his case may similarly be heard fairly; Bill replies that he is fond of him, but money is something else. So Jimmy has no defence against accusations of subversion, the violation of Jenny, the death of Joe for financial gain and – the most serious crime of all in Mahagonny – inability to pay, for which he is sentenced to death. The remaining principals dream of another city, Benares, only to hear that it has been destroyed by an earthquake. Jimmy bids farewell to Jenny and exhorts the citizens to continue living life to the full: there is no afterlife, and he has no regrets. As he is strapped into the electric chair, they enact God's visit to Mahagonny. Following his execution, there are mass demonstrations and counter-demonstrations against the rising cost of living while the city burns. Jimmy's relics are paraded, but there is no way of helping a dead man.

Following the Leipzig premiere and stagings in other German cities, *Mahagonny* was turned down by Klemperer at the Berlin Krolloper; Weill responded by organizing a commercial run on the Kurfürstendamm in December 1931 conducted by Zemlinsky. Revisions were made, and rehearsals saw the not-quite-final break with Brecht, who resented the dominance of the music and accused the composer of writing 'phoney Richard Strauss'. After the war Brecht supervised a drastically cut, ideologically more acceptable version for performance in the DDR. Weill himself allowed substantial cuts for a Vienna production in 1932, and had performances not been interrupted by the Nazi regime would surely have worked to tighten the action more systematically and resolve the conflict between the need for operatically trained voices and decidedly unoperatic material.

Nevertheless, *Mahagonny* as it stands remains one of the great 20th-century operas, a beguiling mixture of lively neo-classical formulae and music-hall songs, melodically prodigiously rich. The expressionistically grotesque trial scene builds up unstoppable dramatic momentum, and the finale with its marches and counter-marches, in which all the hit tunes are brought back, has a pole-axing effect. This is in a way a 20th-century equivalent to *Die Zauberflöte*, a journey not from darkness to light, but from darkness to even greater darkness, one in which the eternal truths proposed are distinctly less comfortable than Mozart's and Schikaneder's. No easy answers are given (Brecht had not yet quite embraced Marxist fundamentalism), which makes the work all the more disturbing. At the final curtain the cast is, as it were, addressing the audience with the title of Weill's lost musical of 1927, *Na und?* ('And so?'). The fact that that question remains unanswered 60 years later suggests that *Mahagonny* has by no means had its day.

RECORDING Lenya, Litz, Sauerbaum, Günter, Markwort, Mund, unnamed O, Brückner-Rüggeberg, CBS, 1956
EDITIONS f.s., Universal, 1929; v.s., David Drew (ed.), Universal, 1969

Der Jasager
He Who Says Yes
School opera in two acts (30m)

Libretto by Bertolt Brecht, after Elisabeth Hauptmann's translation of the 15th-century Japanese Noh play *Taniko* by Zenchiku
PREMIERES 24 June 1930, Radio Berlin (broadcast); 24 June 1930, Zentral Institut für Erziehung und Unterricht, Berlin

Der Jasager was commissioned by Neue Musik Berlin (successor to the Baden-Baden Contemporary Music Festival) from Weill in 1930. Following the management's rejection on political grounds of Hanns Eisler's *Die Massnahme*, also to a Brecht libretto, Weill withdrew his score out of solidarity; it was premiered shortly after the end of the festival. *Die Massnahme* is Brecht at his most Stalinist, and *Der Jasager* is scarcely less so. 'It is important above all to learn acquiescence,' runs the opening line. A boy begs to join a scientific expedition (a religious pilgrimage in the Japanese original) on a hazardous journey across the mountains in order to get medicine for his sick mother. On the journey he falls ill. According to ancient custom, rather than jeopardize the expedition as a whole, the sick individual is thrown over the precipice. The boy is asked if he acquiesces. He says yes. His companions throw him down collectively, so that no one will feel guiltier than his neighbour.

Weill's score is severely neo-classical and ice cold, as befits the subject; the text is written in an infuriating *faux-naïf* style, almost a parody of itself; the message is morally repulsive and, given the subsequent history of Russia and Eastern Europe, full of chilling foreboding. Apart from *The Seven Deadly Sins*, this was Weill's final collaboration with Brecht. Performances were intended to be followed by discussions among the performers; early reactions were so hostile that the surprised Brecht wrote an alternative version, *He Who Says No*, in which Weill played no part.

RECORDING Schmeisser, Helling, Schütte, Chamber Chorus of Dortmund University, Westphalia CO, Gundlach, Capriccio, 1990
EDITIONS f.s./v.s., Universal, 1930

Die Bürgschaft
The Surety
Opera in a prologue and three acts (3h)
Libretto by Caspar Neher and the composer, based on the story *Der Afrikanische Rechtspruch*, by the 18th-century philosopher and critic Johann Gottfried von Herder
Composed 1931
PREMIERE 10 March 1932, Städtische Oper, Berlin

For Weill *Die Bürgschaft* marked the end of a creative period that had started with the Baden-Baden *Mahagonny* of 1927 and embraced the four-year collaboration with Brecht; he had started work with the designer–librettist Neher long before the terminal row with the playwright over the Kurfürstendamm *Mahagonny* in December 1931. The premiere was conducted by Fritz Stiedry and produced by Carl Ebert.

The plot places Herder's parable in the context of the contemporary political situation.

SYNOPSIS

Prologue In the ideal, imaginary state of Urb the cattle farmer Matthes is saved from creditors when his friend Orth, a grain merchant, stands surety for him. The chorus remarks that man's natural goodness can be changed only by external circumstances.

Act I Six years later Matthes buys a sack of grain from Orth without knowing that his friend has out of generosity hidden gold in it; when he discovers the gold Matthes assumes this was a mistake and says nothing, but is forced to admit his chicanery when blackmailed by extortionists.

Act II The dispute over ownership is taken to court and the judge rules that the men's children should marry and have the gold as their wedding present. But an envoy from a neighbouring Great Power (in Herder, Alexander the Great) intervenes, arrests both men and confiscates the gold.

Act III A further six years later the state has been industrialized by the Great Power and suffered famine, plague, war and inflation, but Matthes has become rich. An angry mob, discovering him to have cheated them, pursues him to Orth's house, where he seeks sanctuary. Orth hands him over to be bludgeoned to death and delivers the moral: in the end, only power and money count. Urb society has been corrupted.

Die Bürgschaft inevitably became a political football. The liberal press hailed it as a highly topical allegory, but Nazi pressure meant there were only three performances in Berlin, and many planned provincial productions were cancelled. The song style that Weill developed in his Brecht period is here replaced by slightly uncompromising neo-classical patterns; the score is dry and, given its content, a little long. It has seldom been revived.

EDITIONS f.s./v.s., Universal (on hire), 1932

Der Silbersee

Ein Wintermärchen
The Silver Lake – A Winter's Tale
Play with music in three acts (music: 1h 15m; full-length play)
Libretto and play text by Georg Kaiser (1932)
PREMIERES 18 February 1933, simultaneously in three cities: Altes Theater, Leipzig; Stadttheater, Magdeburg, and Stadttheater, Erfurt; US: 20 March 1980, New York City Opera (radically revised version by Hugh Wheeler (play and lyrics) and Lys Simonette (musical arrangement)); UK: 17 June 1982, Manchester University Theatre (amateur); 30 March 1987, Bloomsbury Theatre, London (Abbey Opera)
CAST Fennimore *s*, Frau von Luber *ms*, 2 Shopgirls 2 *s*, Severin *t*, Lottery Agent *t*, Olim *bar*, Baron Laur *bar*, *spoken roles*; *satb* chorus
FULL ORCHESTRA

For his last theatre composition before being forced into exile Weill resumed collaboration with Europe's leading Expressionist playwright Georg Kaiser, and the result was, in the words of the original Leipzig director Detlef Sierck (reborn as the Hollywood movie director Douglas Sirk), 'ten times tougher than any Brecht play'. By the time of the successful

triple premiere Hitler was already chancellor, and Nazi thugs disrupted early performances. The Reichstag fire and suspension of civil liberties followed, and within a month Weill had fled to Paris.

SYNOPSIS

The allegorical action is clearly based on contemporary social and political circumstances.

Act I Severin and his comrades, unemployed and starving on the shores of the Silver Lake, raid a grocery store; while the comrades take bread, Severin steals a pineapple and is shot and wounded by the Policeman Olim. Olim's liberal conscience (offstage voices) pricks him: if he were rich, he would devote his life to caring for the wounded looter. A Lottery Agent answers his prayer to a smoochy tango. Confined to a wheelchair, Severin agrees to move in to the castle that his unknown benefactor has bought.

Act II Olim's housekeeper Frau von Luber and her seedy accomplice Baron Laur employ the former's niece Fennimore as a companion, and plot to reveal Olim's true identity to the vengeful Severin. But thanks to Fennimore, the men are reconciled.

Act III Cheated out of his property by his bourgeois employees, Olim leads Severin to joint death in the Silver Lake, but the waters miraculously freeze over and bear them to a new life on the other side.

A hauntingly atmospheric and suggestive work, *Der Silbersee* is arguably the masterpiece of Weill's German period. Yet it is fraught with performance problems, composed as it was for the sort of municipal theatrical ensemble of singers and actors that scarcely exists any more (it was conceived for the Deutsches Theater in Berlin, but political pressures necessitated provincial premieres). Kaiser's play demands virtuoso acting; the role of Severin needs a robust operatic tenor with dramatic ability to match, and the genre of play-with-music has anyway not prospered. Yet this is no excuse for the New York City Opera version, musically a well-meaning travesty of Weill's intentions, dramaturgically a betrayal of Kaiser (Hugh Wheeler, on adapting the play, professed himself 'bored with that 1930-ish play, pissy-assed socialism').

In contrast to the Brecht collaborations, the musical numbers are firmly integrated into the text rather than alienatory devices, save for the Ballad of Caesar's Death, a rousing march song sung by the mousy Fennimore and, with its message that those who live by the sword shall perish by it, aimed directly at Hitler. The despair of the starving workers, the prissiness of the shop assistants, the sleaze of the Lottery Agent, the cynical opportunism of the bourgeois intriguers, all are caught in music of spellbinding dramatic power.

Perhaps the main problem is the optimistic ending, in characteristically bittersweet waltz tempo: given the political situation of the time, the irony is hard to stomach – so much so that at the work's UK premiere it was set (not altogether convincingly) in the gas chamber of a concentration camp, just lest the audience miss the irony. Despite all its problems, *Der Silbersee*'s time will come.

RECORDING Heichele, Tamassy, Schmidt, Korte, Holdorf, Cologne Radio O, Latham-Koenig, Capriccio, 1989
EDITIONS manuscript f.s., Universal (on hire), 1933; v.s., Universal, 1933

Die sieben Todsünden

The Seven Deadly Sins
Ballet chanté in one act (35m)
Scenario by Edward James and Boris Kochno; choreography by George Balanchine; libretto by Bertolt Brecht
PREMIERES 7 June 1933, Théâtre des Champs-Elysées, Paris; UK: 28 June 1933, Savoy Theatre, London (as *Anna-Anna*); US: 4 December 1958, City Center, New York
CAST Anna I *s*, Anna II *dancer*, the Family 2 *t*, *bar*, *b*
MEDIUM-SIZED ORCHESTRA including banjo

Within a month of arriving in Paris in 1933 Weill had been commissioned to compose a ballet by the English philanthropist Edward James. He was funding the first season of Balanchine's and Kochno's dance company Les Ballets 1933, which had just broken away from Diaghilev's Ballets Russes. James insisted on a role for his estranged wife, the dancer Tilly Losch, in the hope that it would lead to a reconciliation (it didn't – they divorced spectacularly the following year), and when the basic idea of dividing a split personality between a dancer and a singer, between flesh and spirit, was established, James in turn suggested Lotte Lenya for the singing role, although Weill and Lenya were at the time in the middle of their own divorce proceedings (they remarried in the US in 1937). Lenya's lover at the time, Otto von Pasetti, was given one of the tenor roles in the family.

When Cocteau declined to write the libretto, James urged Brecht on a none-too-willing Weill: they had fallen out over the Kurfürstendamm *Mahagonny* 18 months earlier. Brecht was at first unenthusiastic about the scenario, but managed to feed enough social criticism into it to salve his conscience. When the libretto was included in his collected works after the war, he expanded the title to *Die sieben Todsünden der Kleinbürger* ('of the Petty-Bourgeois'), lest anyone miss the point.

SYNOPSIS
In the prologue the two Annas, sisters from Louisiana, introduce themselves. Anna I, the singer, is the practical, down-to-earth one; her dancing sister Anna II, she warns us, is a bit dizzy (*etwas verrückt*). 'But we're really one person, not two, with one past and one future, one heart and one savings bank account.' Their mission is to travel to seven cities in America to earn enough money for their family to build a little house back in Louisiana, and the voices of the family quartet (the mother sung by the bass) are throughout heard singing biblical bromides warning them not to fall into sin. The basic joke is that the instinctive dancer Anna is tempted to give in to sin at each turn, but is prevented by the singer Anna: sin compromises their earning power. Thus, Anna II is too proud to take her clothes off in a striptease cabaret ('Pride is only for rich people,' warns Anna I); too wrathful over cruelty to an animal when working as a movie extra, and risking dismissal; too prone to gluttony when agents want only slim dancers; too much given to lust (a toy-boy), which upsets her sugar-daddy (named 'Edward', an obvious in-joke); and so on. Bourgeois morality is wittily turned on its head. In the epilogue the sisters return to the little house in Louisiana, the practical Anna I triumphant, Anna II's human spirit utterly crushed.

Weill here achieved a perfect synthesis of popular form and weightiness of content. The tunes beguile, the dance rhythms sparkle, yet the score is rigorously organized along traditional symphonic lines. The sardonic musical wit balances that in the text, but the composer triumphs decisively over the detached librettist in the compassion he shows for human, instinctive, near-wordless Anna II. The final bars are heart-rending.

The premiere, attended by the Parisian *beau monde*, was an artistic triumph, but the season as a whole was a financial disaster. Among those who attended the first run was Lincoln Kirstein, who recognized Balanchine's genius and was to lure the choreographer to the US and found the New York City Ballet for him. The company gave the US premiere (and first post-war performance) of Weill's ballet in 1958, with Lenya. It has been given numerous productions since. When Lenya was engaged for the premiere, Weill sanctioned downward transpositions of parts of the score to accommodate her limited resources. It has been recorded mostly in that form.

RECORDINGS Lenya, NW German Radio O, Brückner-Rüggeberg, Philips/CBS, 1960: with transpositions; Ross, CBSO, Rattle, EMI, 1983: original pitch
EDITIONS f.s. (original version), Universal, 1968; v.s. (both versions), Universal, 1972

Der Kuhhandel

Horse-trading
Operetta in two acts (incomplete)
Libretto by Robert Vambery
Composed 1934

An American armaments executive tries to foment war between two states sharing a Caribbean island in order to profit from both sides. He overcomes the problems posed by the pacifist principles of one of the presidents by organizing a military coup against him. The cow of the title is owned by Juan, a villager, but is twice distrained in lieu of taxes imposed for military expenditure. All ends happily when the armaments supplied to both sides prove faulty and unusable.

As prospects of a European performance in German receded, Weill agreed to adapt and complete the material for performance in London (28 June 1935, Savoy Theatre) under the title of *A Kingdom for a Cow*. The adapter of the book was Reginald Arkell, then famous for his stage version of

1066 and All That, and the romantic lead was created by Webster Booth. Predictably, the anti-war, anti-capitalist satire with its echoes of German epic theatre was not to the taste of West End audiences: despite some favourable notices, the show flopped. Weill later reused much of the music in his US theatre pieces. The original *Kuhhandel* has, however, been reconstructed, and is the last Weill work awaiting its premiere.

RECORDING   Peacock, Büchner, Raffeiner, Ch and SO of West German Radio, Latham-Koenig, Capriccio, 1990
EDITION   f.s., Schott (on hire), 1978

Johnny Johnson
Musical play in three acts (music: 1h; full-length play)
Libretto by Paul Green
PREMIERES   19 November 1936, by Group Theatre at 44th Street Theater, New York; UK: 6 August 1986, Almeida Theatre, London (by Not the RSC)

Weill's first music-theatre work written wholly in the USA is apple-pie American in subject matter but distinctly German in musical outline. It gives the lie to the 'sell-out to Broadway' canard, being written near collectively at the left-wing Group Theatre's summer camp to a text by the pacifist southern writer Paul Green. The cast at the Broadway premiere, directed by Lee Strasberg, included Elia Kazan, Lee J. Cobb and John Garfield (the last-named was a victim of the McCarthy purges).

The action opens in 1917. A peace rally is interrupted by the announcement of President Wilson's declaration of war (the march 'Peace, peace, peace' is repeated note for note to the words 'War, war, war', a distinctly worrying example of music's non-specific power). Johnny joins up, converses with the Statue of Liberty as he sails for Europe, is horrified by what he witnesses in the trenches, befriends a German sniper, and out of naïve, very American idealism seeks to promote peace. He releases laughing gas at a High Command conference and, disguised as a general, declares an armistice. He is arrested and shipped home to an asylum for the criminally insane, where he sets up a League of Nations for the inmates. After ten years, lobotomized, he is deemed safe to be released, and becomes an itinerant toy-seller, refusing to stock military wares.

Many of the musical numbers are acid parodies, some recycled from earlier scores: the recruiting officer's tango, the sour romantic number for Johnny's perfidious girlfriend Minny-Belle, a Wild West pastiche and a satirical Psychiatry Song (one verse accompanied by celesta and trombone). But the dialogue for Johnny and the Statue of Liberty, the Lament of the Cannons over the sleeping GIs doomed to die the next day, and the prayers of the German and American Chaplains (words identical, languages different) have great theatrical power. Johnny's Song, heard in full only as the finale, is one of Weill's great tunes. While it is curious that Weill, who knew better than anyone the political horror engulfing Europe, should have subscribed to an idealist pacifist tract, this cannot diminish *Johnny Johnson*'s stark theatrical power. It demands revival.

RECORDING   Lear, Lenya, Meredith, Merrill, Stewart, unnamed O, Matlowsky, Heliodor, 1957
EDITION   v.s., Samuel French, 1940

The Eternal Road
Biblical drama in four parts (music: 2h 45m)
Text by Franz Werfel under the title *Der Weg der Verheissung* ('The Road of Promise'), translated and adapted by Ludwig Lewisohn, with extra lyrics by Charles Alan
PREMIERE   4 January 1937, Manhattan Opera House, New York

The music for this Franz Werfel–Max Reinhardt Old Testament pageant was Weill's passport to the US in 1935. A Jewish community at a time of persecution is inspired by a Rabbi's readings from the Torah and his answers to an Adversary, which are interspersed with biblical scenes. The Synagogue is raided by armed men, but the faith of the expelled community remains intact. The spectacular premiere production, for which the interior of the Manhattan Opera House was rebuilt in four levels with the Eternal Road climbing up them, was artistically successful but lost a great deal of money – running costs far exceeded takings from even full houses. It ran for 153 performances. The original cast included Lotte Lenya as Miriam and the Witch of Endor, and, in the crucial role of the youth who sees a vision of the Messiah, the future film director Sidney Lumet.

The fact that the score was substantially adapted from the original German setting, and later raided for fund-raising pageants during the war, has meant that what remains of *The Eternal Road* is a musicological quagmire. A staged revival is obviously out of the question on grounds of cost, but it is to be hoped that one of the repeatedly promised concert performances will one day materialize. It has been neither published nor recorded.

MANUSCRIPT   f.s., Kurt Weill Foundation, New York

Knickerbocker Holiday
Musical play (music: 1h; full-length play)
Libretto by Maxwell Anderson, based on *The History of New York by Diedrich Knickerbocker* by Washington Irving (1809)
PREMIERE   19 October 1938, Ethel Barrymore Theater, New York (Playwrights' Company)

It is still too early to come to terms with this astonishing political satire: the goal-posts have been moved too often. Anderson, a close friend and collaborator of Weill's throughout his life in America and an old-fashioned libertarian, uses Irving's history to attack Roosevelt's New Deal and equate him with Hitler. Other members of the co-operative Playwrights' Company tried to tone down the attack, but the associations remain crystal clear: the protagonist Peter Stuyvesant has one leg and Roosevelt was crippled with polio; Stuyvesant promises the citizens of New Amsterdam 'strength through joy'; there are countless other political cross-references.

Irving-as-narrator introduces Governor Stuyvesant as he sails to the New World in 1647 ('They've got two hours more of democracy and stupidity, and then I arrive'). Stuyvesant cuts a swathe through the corrupt New Amsterdam Council, institutionalizes the corruption, and plans to marry the Council President's daughter Tina. She prefers the all-American hero Brom Broek, and Stuyvesant sets about having him summarily hanged ('When a man's guilty, what the hell's the use of a trial?'). When the citizens intervene, Stuyvesant's troops turn their guns on them. Irving is forced to intervene – the parallel with *Threepenny Opera* is clear – to achieve an artificial Happy End.

Much pastiche Gilbert and Sullivan in the score is not out of place given the context; the Political Honeymoon chorus is bitterly acid; there is some vintage Weill love music ('It never was you'). Above all there is the September Song, another of Weill's great tunes and a sweetener to ensure that Walter Huston took the leading role; the quirky lyrics have been romanticized in nearly all the many recordings. The show ran for seven months on Broadway, made Weill's name, and was sold to Hollywood (only three of his numbers survive in the movie). There have been no major revivals: American audiences might find *Knickerbocker Holiday* too embarrassing, Europeans too obscure. But the music needs rescuing from undeserved neglect.

RECORDING Huston, Madden/Darling, Brooks, Shackelton, unnamed O, Abravanel/Levy, compilation recording, AEI, 1938/45
EDITION v.s., Chappell, 1938

Lady in the Dark
Play with music (music: 1h; full-length play)
Book by Moss Hart; lyrics by Ira Gershwin
PREMIERES 21 January 1941, Alvin Theater, New York; UK: 9 December 1981, Nottingham Playhouse

This was Weill's greatest commercial success on Broadway (as with *Knickerbocker Holiday*, though, the Hollywood movie was a travesty). Moss Hart's play deals creakily with the psychological problems of Liza Elliot, editor of a glossy New York fashion magazine, and the men in her life – the sugar-daddy who funds the magazine (but won't divorce his wife), a Hollywood film star (created on Broadway by Victor Mature), and the advertising manager with whom she has a sparky Beatrice-and-Benedick relationship. To decide which one she will marry – no prizes for guessing – she resorts to the psychiatrist's couch.

The piece is saved from triviality by the brilliance of the four extended, self-contained musical sequences, each covering a session with the shrink. Ira Gershwin's witty, intricately rhymed lyrics acted as a spur to Weill's invention. The score not only has a sophisticated glitter unmatched elsewhere in his output, but a truly nightmarish quality as well; the key to Liza's trauma lies in a half-remembered childhood song, fragments of which are heard in the

Gertrude Lawrence, the first Lady in the Dark (New York, 1941)

first three dream sequences and which is sung in full in the last.

Although through-composed, the dreams include separate songs: 'This is new', one of Weill's most silkily seductive melodies, 'The saga of Jenny', 'Tchaikovsky' (a tongue-twisting list of Russian composers first sung by Danny Kaye), and the key to the trauma, 'My ship'. The leading role was written for Gertrude Lawrence, and revivals of this unimportant but enormously accomplished and entertaining work depend on the presence of a star of equal magnetism.

RECORDING Stevens, Reardon, Green, Bridges, unnamed O, Engel, US Columbia, 1961
EDITIONS f.s., critical edn, David Loud (ed.), Kurt Weill Foundation, New York, 1991; v.s., Chappell, 1941

One Touch of Venus
Musical comedy in two acts (music: 1h; full-length play)
Book by S. J. Perelman and Ogden Nash, after the novel *The Tinted Venus* by 'F. J. Anstey' (T. A. Guthrie); lyrics by Ogden Nash
PREMIERES 7 October 1943, Imperial Theater, New York; UK: 16 August 1992, Barbican Centre, London (concert with pf)

The Victorian humorist Anstey's story, in turn surely inspired by Mérimée's *La Vénus d'Ille*, tells of a respectable London hairdresser inadvertently bringing a statue of Venus to life and his embarrassment in explaining her away to his equally respectable fiancée. Perelman and Nash updated the action to contemporary New York and made Venus a great deal more demanding than she would have been in Victorian London. This is the basic comic premiss: the roles of predatory male and coy female are reversed, and the suspense hinges on whether or not the goddess gets to lay the humble barber with the unlikely name of Rodney (she does).

This is the nearest Weill came to the Broadway of Cole Porter. Perelman's book is in delightfully dubious taste, and Nash's dazzlingly inventive lyrics even more so, cascading with *risqué* double meanings. The score includes one of Weill's greatest tunes ('Speak low') and much else of note: 'The trouble with women' (a barbershop quartet lifted from *Happy End*), 'Love shouldn't be serious' (a beguiling waltz), The Ballad of Dr Crippen (very Berlin, as the title would suggest) and two first-rate dance episodes. Marlene Dietrich turned down the title role on grounds of taste; the young Mary Martin took it on and established herself as a Broadway star. The premiere was directed by Elia Kazan and choreographed by Agnes de Mille, and the show ran for nearly two years. The movie version with Ava Gardner (1948) doesn't begin to do justice to the original. Why this dazzling *jeu d'esprit* has never been staged in Europe remains an unfathomable mystery.

RECORDING   Martin, Baker, unnamed Ch and O, Abravanel, AEI, 1943
EDITION   v.s., Chappell (on hire)

The Firebrand of Florence

Operetta in two acts
Book by Edwin Justus Mayer, based on his play *The Firebrand*; lyrics by Ira Gershwin
PREMIERE   22 March 1945, Alvin Theater, New York

Very loosely based on Benvenuto Cellini's auto-biography, Weill's attempt at a spectacular operetta (tried out in Boston under the title *Much Ado about Love*) flopped disastrously – it ran for only 43 performances. The plot centres on intertwined amorous intrigues: the Duke of Florence desires Cellini's model, Angela, and the Duchess lusts after Cellini, who enjoys both ladies and escapes the attention of the hangman. Had Ezio Pinza accepted the leading role things might have been different; it was suggested at the time that the uncertain English of Lotte Lenya, singing the role of the Duchess (one of the few occasions on which she appeared in one of her husband's US works during his lifetime), was no help. There are some good numbers in this rather overblown, hastily written work – the Duchess's 'Sing me not a ballad', 'There'll be life, there'll be love', 'A rhyme for Angela' – but (a rare occurrence) not all the orchestrations are by the composer. Ira Gershwin's lyrics, full of word-play and outrageous rhymes, are almost the work's strongest point. *Firebrand* was neither recorded nor published.

MANUSCRIPT   f.s., Kurt Weill Foundation, New York

Street Scene

'An American Opera' in two acts (2h 30m)

Book by Elmer Rice, based on his own play (1929); lyrics by Langston Hughes
Composed 1946
PREMIERES   9 January 1947, Adelphi Theater, New York; UK: 6 June 1983, Royal Academy of Music, London (semi-staged and much cut); 26 April 1987, Palace Theatre, London
CAST   Anna Maurrant *s*, Rose Maurrant *s*, Mrs Jones *ms*, Mrs Fiorentino *s*, Mrs Olsen *a*, Sam Kaplan *t*, Frank Maurrant *b*, Harry Easter *bar*, Willy Maurrant *boy s*, Henry Davis *bar*, Mr Buchanan *t*, Mr Fiorentino *t*, Jennie Hildebrand *ms*, Mrs Hildebrand *ms*, Mr Jones *bar*, Mr Kaplan *t*, 2 Nursemaids *s*, *ms*, *spoken roles*; *satb* chorus of neighbours
ORCHESTRATION   fl, ob, 2 cl, b cl, bsn, 2 hn, 2 tpt, 2 trbn, hp, pf, perc, str

Weill had known the playwright Elmer Rice since his earliest days in America – they met during rehearsals of *Johnny Johnson* in 1936, and he wrote incidental music for Rice's play *Two on an Island* in 1939 – and the possibility of turning Rice's social-realist study of life in a slum tenement block into an opera had been at the back of his mind since seeing a performance of *Street Scene* in Europe before being driven into exile. 'It seemed like a great challenge to me', he wrote later, 'to find the inherent poetry in these people and to blend my music with the stark realism of the play.'

Other composers had seen operatic possibilities in *Street Scene*, but Rice was fiercely protective of his material; he turned down Deems Taylor's pro-jected setting for the Met because it strayed too far from the original. Weill secured the playwright's agreement in 1945, and the result is remarkably faithful; the composer from the land of *Fidelio* and *Freischütz* saw no problem with long passages of spoken dialogue in serious music drama, and his use of Hollywood rather than Benda-inspired mélodrame helped bind music and speech into an indissoluble whole. 'Not until *Street Scene* did I achieve a real blending of drama and music,' wrote Weill at the time of the premiere.

The black poet Langston Hughes was engaged to supply the lyrics, and the collaboration was close if not always easy. Hughes took Weill to Harlem to gather material for the Janitor's Song, and together they roamed New York listening to vendors' cries and children's street games. After a less than suc-cessful try-out in Philadelphia, *Street Scene* ran in New York for 148 performances (a modest first run compared to *Lady in the Dark*, but not bad for an opera – Gershwin's *Porgy and Bess* managed only 126). The leading roles were taken by trained opera singers: Polyna Stoska of the City Opera as Anna, Norman Cordon of the Met as Frank, Anne Jeffreys as Rose and Brian Sullivan, a future Lohengrin, as Sam.

SYNOPSIS

Act I   The sidewalk outside a tenement block in New York City; early evening in June (the action is contained within 24 hours). The inhabitants of the block, half stifled by the humidity ('Ain't it awful, the heat'), are introduced: the black Janitor ('I got a marble and a star'); the tenement bitch, Mrs Jones, who leads the gossip about Anna Maurrant's affair

Poster for Street Scene *(New York, 1947)*

with the milk collector, Mr Sankey; Sam Kaplan, a shy, bookish boy in calf love with the Maurrant daughter, Rose; Sam's father Abraham, an elderly socialist firebrand, and his sister Shirley, a teacher; Mr Buchanan, whose wife is about to give birth for the first time; finally the Maurrants, Frank, an inarticulate, reactionary theatre electrician, and his wife Anna, who expresses her disillusion in the extended aria 'Somehow I never could believe' – she contrasts her romantic girlhood dreams with the bitter reality of life. The solace of her affair with Mr Sankey is known to all except her husband, who nevertheless starts to suspect something during the course of Act I. Mr Fiorentino – the block is authentically multiracial – leads the Ice Cream Sextet, likening a cone to the torch held by the Statue of Liberty glimpsed by all European immigrants as they sail into New York. Jennie Hildebrand returns from her graduation ceremony to general rejoicing ('Wrapped in a ribbon'); the cheerful optimism of the concerted number is tempered by the knowledge that the Hildebrand family, deserted by the father, is to be evicted for non-payment of rent the following day. Maurrant leaves for an evening's drinking; gossip resumes; Sam attacks the gossipers before singing of his misery in 'Lonely house'. Rose Maurrant enters with Harry Easter, a married man from her office with plans to set her up as his mistress. He tempts her with the

sleazy 'Wouldn't you like to be on Broadway'; she counters with 'What use would the moon be'; like her mother before her, she nurtures romantic ideals. Easter prudently withdraws when Maurrant returns drunk from the bar. Buchanan's wife goes into labour; Anna Maurrant runs to help her. Mrs Jones's daughter Mae enters with an admirer, Dick; their love is anything but romantic ('Moonfaced, starry eyed', an energetic jitterbug). In a long duet ('Pain! Nothing but pain') Rose and Sam sing of the possibility of escape to a better life, taking as a symbol Walt Whitman's Lilac Bush ('In the dooryard fronting an old farmhouse') before bidding each other a tender goodnight.

Act II   Early the next morning. Raucous children's street games carry a whiff of the class war. Buchanan thanks Anna, who has been up all night with his wife. Frank leaves for work, after gruffly rejecting Rose's plea to him to be kinder to her mother (trio: 'You've got no right'). Anna sends her son Willy off to school. Rose tells Sam about Harry Easter's importunings, and they sing of running away together. Easter arrives to accompany Rose to an office funeral. Anna Maurrant invites Mr Sankey up to her apartment. City marshalls start to put the Hildebrands' belongings out on the sidewalk. The suspicious Maurrant returns unexpectedly, and Sam's shouted warning to Anna is too late: shots ring out. Maurrant escapes, but Rose returns with an excited crowd to see her dying mother being carried out to the ambulance (ensemble: 'The woman who lived up there'). Sankey is dead. The eviction of the Hildebrands proceeds. Some hours later, Scene 2 is launched by two nursemaids from uptown gawking at the scene of the double murder with their charges ('Sleep, baby dear') – the other side of the class war. Maurrant is caught, and before being led away by the police tells Rose he killed her mother out of jealousy and panic at the thought of losing her. The crowd disperses, leaving Rose and Sam alone. She plans to go away to start a new life, and kindly but firmly refuses to let the lovelorn Sam go with her. The experience of her parents' tragedy makes her unwilling to enter any such commitment. She leaves. Two prospective tenants come to view the Hildebrands' empty apartment. The neighbours drift back to the sidewalk ('Ain't it awful, the heat'). Life goes on.

The technical brilliance of *Street Scene* cannot be overstressed, nor the way Weill sets Rice's intentionally flat prose to music of charm, colour and dramatic power. Some commentators have found Hughes's lyrics banal, but underprivileged, barely literate people tend to express themselves in cliché – they know no other way. To that extent, Hughes's verses are as social-realist as Rice's prose. The action is set among – to borrow a phrase from *Dreigroschenoper* – 'the poorest of the poor', which is rare enough in opera (Gustave Charpentier's *Louise* is one of the very few other operatic studies of working-class life). The tenement represents a trap, and the action examines various ways of coming to terms with or escaping from it. Mae and Dick resort to dope and sex; Anna to adultery; Sam to study and self-improvement; many of the others – including Frank Maurrant – to drink. For a moment Rose seriously considers Harry Easter's offer: anything to escape the grinding, cheerless spiritual and material poverty of the tenement. Otherwise Rose dreams with Sam of Whitman's Lilac Bush, which remains a dream, since *Street Scene*'s creators heroically declined to settle for the Broadway Happy End. The fact that it ends with two young lives irretrievably ruined – this is not a cheerful evening in the theatre – may account for its slow acceptance into the general operatic repertoire; Weill couldn't quite, like Janáček, turn physical disaster into spiritual triumph. On the other hand, Weill's musical treatment of all the inhabitants of the tenement trap (save perhaps for the monstrous Mrs Jones, a villain of Begbick or Frau von Luber proportions) is notable for its compassion, its anger and its total lack of condescension.

In *Mahagonny* Brecht's doggerel line 'Is here no telephone' has been proposed as the catch-phrase of 20th-century alienation; the last words of 'Ain't it awful, the heat', which opens and closes *Street Scene*, are 'Don't know what I'm gonna do' – just as powerful an image of the hopelessness of the 20th-century human condition. Nowhere else is the voice of Weill the militant humanist heard so clearly.

RECORDINGS 1. Ciesinski, Kelly, Bullock, Dickinson, Bottone, Bronder, Van Allan, ENO O, Carl Davis, That's Entertainment, 1991; 2. Barstow, Réaux, Mackillop, Dickinson, Hadley, Mee, Ramey, Scottish Opera O, Mauceri, Decca, 1991
EDITION v.s., Chappell, 1947

Down in the Valley

Folk opera in one act (40m)
Libretto by Arnold Sundgaard
PREMIERES 15 July 1948, Indiana University Auditorium, Bloomington; UK: 23 October 1957, Bristol Opera School

Down in the Valley was first conceived as an opera for radio in 1945, but withdrawn by the composer and revised at slightly greater length for performance by college and amateur groups. The form of the work, however, betrays its origins: chorus (with leader) providing the links between frequent changes of time and place. Brack Weaver, a wholesome all-American boy, escapes from prison on the eve of his execution to spend his last hours with Jennie Parsons and relive the story of their love. Brack got involved in a fight at a hoe-down with the drunken, knife-toting Thomas Bouché, a rival for Jennie who was killed in the struggle. Brack was sentenced to death. Their story ended, Brack gives himself up at dawn. The score is bound together by the eponymous folksong, much repeated by the chorus with harmonies of increasingly Deliusian tortuousness; in between, the flashback narrative is carried in mélodrame and dialogue, and there are set pieces in church and at the fatal hoe-down. The piece moves forward easily and – unashamedly sentimental, apple-pie American – is well aimed at its market.

RECORDINGS 1. Bell, McGraw, Smith, Jacquemot, RCA O, Adler, RCA, 1950; 2. Davidson, Acito, Collup, Mabry, mixed O, Gundlach, Capriccio, 1990
EDITION v.s., Schirmer, 1948

Love Life

Vaudeville in two acts (full-length)
Libretto by Alan Jay Lerner
PREMIERES 7 October 1948, 46th Street Theater, New York; UK: 17 November 1991, Theatre Museum, Covent Garden, London (concert with pf)

Weill's only collaboration with Lerner – temporarily separated from Loewe – dealt with the subject of an American marriage, but viewed each stage of its breakdown at a different moment in US history. Susan and Sam set up home in 1791, and their life progresses through leaps of 30 years at a time, through the Industrial Revolution and the Depression, to the 1940s. The various stages in the disintegration of their relationship are separated by vaudeville acts commenting sourly on the economic, materialistic and socio-cultural pressures on the marriage. The finale is an extended Minstrel Show at the end of which Susan and Sam edge towards reconciliation and understanding.

This ironic sideways glance at American values was years ahead of its time: as the outline suggests, it is much nearer the world of Sondheim than that of Rodgers and Hammerstein. There is a freshness and buoyancy to the score, as well as a mordant wit that harks back to the youthful Berlin Weill, though the musical idiom is pure Broadway – 'Susan's Dream', the soft-shoe shuffle 'Progress', 'Green-up Time' and the vaudeville chorus 'That's Economics (but awful bad for love)' are among the best numbers. The premiere was directed by Elia Kazan, but the respectable first run of 252 performances coincided with an ASCAP strike, which meant that the score was not published and no original-cast recording was made: this is one of the least known of Weill's Broadway shows and one whose full-scale revival is most eagerly awaited.

MANUSCRIPT f.s., Kurt Weill Foundation, New York

Lost in the Stars

A musical tragedy in two acts (music: 1h; full-length play)
Libretto by Maxwell Anderson, based on the novel *Cry the Beloved Country* by Alan Paton (1948)
PREMIERES 30 October 1949, Music Box Theater, New York (Playwrights' Company); UK: 23 May 1991, Brighton Festival (New Sussex Opera)

For his last completed work Weill resumed collaboration with his lifelong friend Maxwell Anderson in a faithful adaptation of Paton's popular novel set in South Africa. The Revd Stephen Kumalo goes to Johannesburg in search of his son Absalom, who has fallen into dubious company and become involved in the unpremeditated murder of a young, liberal white man. Absalom is given an unfair trial and executed, and the work ends with the black and white fathers reconciled and united by a vision of a new South Africa.

If good liberal intentions were all, *Lost in the Stars* could count as one of Weill's lasting successes, but time, not to mention South African history, has not been kind. Even at the start it was felt that the picture painted of racial conflict was too rosy, not to say tinged with Uncle Tom-ish condescension, one reason why Paul Robeson declined to sing the leading role. It was taken by Todd Duncan, the creator of Gershwin's Porgy, and the premiere was staged by *Porgy*'s original director, Rouben Mamoulian.

The only serious flaw in the work is the over-sentimental, much-recorded title song, which sticks out both musically and dramatically from all that surrounds it with near-embarrassing prominence, and is arguably the only instance in which the composer bowed to commercial pressures. The rest of the music, scored with the utmost ingenuity for a chamber orchestra of twelve (Virgil Thomson wrote that instrumentally this was the composer's masterpiece), is top-drawer Weill, especially the elaborate choruses 'Fear', 'Murder in Parkwold', 'Cry the Beloved Country' and 'Train to Johannesburg' (another, the cynical and rather essential 'Gold', was cut before the premiere but has since been restored). The musical underpinning of the dialogue is as faultlessly achieved as in *Street Scene*.

The time for *Lost in the Stars*, like that for *Silbersee*, may yet come, but so far revivals have been few and unmarked by success, for reasons that have little to do with the quality of the music.

RECORDING Matthews, Duncan, Roane, unnamed Ch and O, Levine, US Decca, 1949
EDITION v.s., Chappell, 1950

Other works: *Royal Palace*, 1927; *Na und?* (lost), (1927); *Davy Crockett* (inc.), (1938); *Ulysses Africanus* (inc.), (1939); *Huckleberry Finn* (unfinished at the composer's death), (1950)
BIBLIOGRAPHY David Drew, *Kurt Weill, A Handbook*, Faber and Faber, 1987; Stephen Hinton (ed.), *Kurt Weill: The Threepenny Opera*, CUP (Cambridge Opera Handbook), 1990; Kim H. Kowalke, *Kurt Weill in Europe*, Ann Arbor, 1979; Kim H. Kowalke (ed.), *A New Orpheus, Essays on Kurt Weill*, Yale University Press, 1986; Ronald Sanders, *The Days Grow Short, The Life and Music of Kurt Weill*, Weidenfeld and Nicolson, 1980

R.M.

JAROMÍR WEINBERGER

b 8 January 1896, Prague; *d* 8 August 1967, St Petersburg, Florida, US

A child prodigy who published his first piano pieces in his teens, Weinberger had private lessons with Křička and later with Karel and Talich before studying at the Prague Conservatory with Novák (1910–13, composition) and Hoffmeister (1910–15, piano). His traditional Czech schooling merged with elements of French Impressionism (from Novák) and was further enhanced through outstanding contra-

puntal skills when he later studied at the Leipzig Conservatory with Reger (1916).

Weinberger taught briefly at Ithaca (New York) Conservatory (1922–3), before returning to Czechoslovakia. At first he worked as dramaturg at the Slovak National Theatre in Bratislava (1923–4), then as head of a music school in Cheb before settling in Prague. The financial success of *Švanda the Bagpiper* enabled him to devote himself exclusively to composition: between its premiere in 1927 and 1931 the work was given some 2000 times in many different languages. But personal and artistic happiness was denied Weinberger. None of his later operas had anything like the same success, and his life became increasingly hazardous as a Jew in central Europe. He moved from Baden (near Vienna) at first to France and England, and finally to New York in January 1939. By then he considered his career to be over; he was, in his words, 'a composer of the past', and he wrote no more operas. His orchestral works petered out after the 1940s. In 1949 Weinberger and his wife settled in St Petersburg, Florida, where they lived in virtual isolation until his suicide in 1967.

Weinberger's first opera, *Kocúrkovo*, was written to a Slovak text: an attempt to promote Slovak by setting an existing Slovak stage play. It achieved one performance in Bratislava two years after Weinberger's stint there as dramaturg. After *Švanda* Weinberger wrote three more operas. *Die geliebte Stimme*, based on a German novel set in Yugoslavia, and *The Outcasts of Poker Flat*, based on the novel by Bret Harte, were given in Munich and Brno respectively in the early 1930s, but despite the initially favourable reception of the first, neither attracted any further attention. *Wallenstein*, after Schiller's tragedy, Weinberger's final and only serious opera, was given in Vienna under unfavourable circumstances shortly before the *Anschluss*. Thus it is that Weinberger is known for one opera alone, *Švanda the Bagpiper*.

Švanda [Schwanda] the Bagpiper
Švanda dudák

Folk opera in two acts (five scenes) (2h)
Libretto by Miloš Kareš after the folk-tale, with additions by Max Brod
Composed ?1924–6
PREMIERES 27 April 1927, National Theatre, Prague; US: 7 November 1931, Metropolitan, New York; UK: 11 May 1934, Covent Garden, London
CAST Švanda *bar*, Dorotka *s*, Babinský *t*, Queen *ms*, Devil *b*, 5 *t*, 2 *b*; *satb* chorus of Queen's retinue, people of all classes, doorkeeper, soldiers, lawcourt officials, trumpeters and drummers, hangman's assistants, devils, old crones, apparitions from hell, hell's soldiers and musicians, countryfolk
FULL ORCHESTRA

The legend of Švanda the bagpiper, one of the most resonant in Czech folk mythology, brings together the Czechs' reputation as musicians, the fine bagpipe tradition of southern Bohemia, and various folk-tales common to central Europe in which a bagpiper (or other musician) saves himself from various disasters

Costume design by Vladimir Hrska for the Devil in Švanda
the Bagpiper (*Prague, 1927*)

by the magic quality of his instrument. These tales
served as the basis for the play by Josef Kajetán
Tyl, *The Bagpiper of Strakonice* (1847), which itself
further popularized the legend and inspired the
operas by Hřímalý and Bendl. Weinberger's opera,
however, is based only loosely on Tyl's play. It has
in common the central characters of Švanda and
Dorotka and the idea of Švanda going off into the
world to seek his fortune with his magic instrument,
and instead learning a lesson and returning home to
live contentedly with his wife.

SYNOPSIS
Act I Babinský, a robber who has hidden himself
from his pursuers at Švanda's farm, persuades
Švanda to seek his fortune abroad with his bagpipes.
Švanda's first stop is in the neighbouring kingdom,
ruled by a queen with a heart of ice. Švanda plays
his famous polka; everyone begins dancing compulsively, even the Queen, who decides to marry
Švanda. The arrival of Švanda's wife Dorotka in hot
pursuit puts an end to the festivities and to Švanda's
good fortune: he and Dorotka are condemned to
death. At the scene of execution Švanda is saved
by Babinský, who steals the executioner's axe and
passes Švanda his bagpipes. Švanda plays, everyone
begins dancing, and Švanda, Babinský and Dorotka
escape. Dorotka, however, is jealous, and in seeking
to reassure her Švanda invokes the Devil and is
immediately transported to hell.
Act II Hell is boredom – Švanda and the Devil

pass the time playing cards. Babinský, an honoured
visitor, challenges the Devil to a game, staking
Švanda's bagpipes against Švanda's soul. The Devil
is revealed as a cheat, and Švanda regains his free
dom. Švanda and Dorotka are reunited, much to
Babinský's chagrin: he has had his eye on the
attractive Dorotka from the beginning.

While the Queen may have had some foundation in
Tyl's 'Sad Princess', Švanda's elaborate escape from
execution is new, as is the character of Babinský,
who engineers it. The hell scene, too, is not in Tyl,
though its provenance is not hard to find: in Dvořák's
The Devil and Kate, where there is an equally
musical hell, presided over by a Devil who is also
comic and incompetent rather than frightening.
Musically, the piece is equally indebted to Czech
tradition. Although Weinberger was capable of
modernistic gestures, as for instance in the effective
depiction of the Queen's court, much of the score
comes across as updated Smetana pastiche. The fugal
overture looks back to *The Bartered Bride* (though
the famous fugue seems weighed down with
contrapuntal learning rather than sparkling with *joie
de vivre*). Polka-like sections abound for the
obligatory dancing. The sentimental main tune, 'Na
tom našem dvoře' (the German words fit rather
better), is plugged relentlessly until the concluding
grandioso version for choir and the two main soloists.
There is no doubting the skill, particularly in the
orchestration, with which the piece is put together,
but from the start the Czechs regarded it as a
meretricious confection that played all the emotive
cards of Czech nationalism long after their currency
had expired. Significantly the opera achieved real
popularity only outside Czechoslovakia. The Polka
and Fugue survive independently as light concert
pieces.

RECORDING Popp, Killebrew, Jerusalem, Prey, Nimsgern,
Munich Radio O, Wallberg, CBS, 1981: in German
EDITION v.s., Universal, 1928

Other operas: *Kocúrkovo* (a fictitious place with quaint
inhabitants), 1925; *Die geliebte Stimme* (*Milovaný hlas*; *The
Beloved Voice*), 1931; *Lidé z Poker Flatu* (*The Outcasts of
Poker Flat*), 1932; *Wallenstein* (*Valdštejn*), 1937
Operettas: *Frühlingsstürme* (*Jarní bouře*; *Spring Storms*),
1933; *Na růžích ustláno* (*On a Bed of Roses*), 1933; *Apropos,
co dělá Andula?* (*Apropos, What is Andula up to?*), 1934;
Císař pan na třešních (*The Emperor in the Cherry Trees*), 1936
BIBLIOGRAPHY David Z. Kushner: 'Jaromír Weinberger
(1896–1967)', *From Bohemia to America*, fall 1988, pp. 293–
313

J.T.

JUDITH WEIR

b 11 May 1954, Cambridge

Weir first studied with John Tavener, then with
Robin Holloway at Cambridge and Gunther Schuller

at Tanglewood. *A Night at the Chinese Opera* (1987), her first full-length opera, put her firmly on the map as a composer with a distinct theatrical aptitude and an accessible yet individual musical language. These qualities had been discernible in a string of earlier concert works that perhaps could be termed 'concert-theatre' or opera-in-embryo: works that involve narrative and dramatic techniques of an operatic kind but, for reasons of scale, inhabit a concert hall rather than a theatre. The most reductionist of these is *King Harald's Saga* (1979), a ten-minute 'grand opera in three acts' for unaccompanied soprano singing eight solo roles and one representing the Norwegian army. In all her works, Weir uses her own texts derived from a variety of sources. In *Harald*, she uses an Icelandic saga, and something fundamental to all her texts is in the tone of this original source: a deadpan narrative style that enables fantastic and epic events to be recounted with economy and speed. *A Serbian Cabaret* (1984) intersperses improvisations on folksongs played by a piano quartet with the players narrating the song texts, presenting each as a tiny drama in its own right. In *The Consolations of Scholarship* (1985), described as a 'music drama' for mezzo-soprano and nine instruments, the Yüan dynasty tale (the same story as *A Night at the Chinese Opera*) unfolds through plain narration and relevant philosophical discourse. This work has been convincingly staged, further confounding any attempt to classify what counts as opera within her *oeuvre*.

Weir's musical language is aphoristic and under-stated, developing in early works from a quasiminimalist style to encompass more straightforwardly melodic ideas, that can assimilate all sorts of ethnic flavouring, whether Scottish (as Weir is herself), Chinese, Spanish or Serbian, without resorting to parody and pastiche. Weir has cited Stravinsky's *Oedipus Rex* as a major influence on her work. Also similar to Stravinsky in his neo-classical phase is her emotional detachment from her material: she always prefers to depict rather than psychologize. This has led her work to be dubbed witty and ironic, and while these qualities are present, dark and sinister elements are pervasive, particularly in *The Black Spider* (1984), a children's opera, and *HEAVEN ABLAZE in his Breast* (1989), a retelling of E. T. A. Hoffmann's *The Sandman* for eight dancers, six singers and two pianos – an experimental mixture of dance, opera, extended vocal techniques and spoken theatre.

A Night at the Chinese Opera

Opera in three acts (1h 45m)
Libretto by the composer, based on the 13th-century Yüan dynasty drama *The Chao Family Orphan* by Chi Chun-Hsiang
PREMIERES   8 July 1987, Everyman Theatre, Cheltenham; US: 29 July 1989, Santa Fe

The setting is late 13th-century China, under the military rule of Mongolia, the era of Khubilai Khan and of Marco Polo. It concerns Chao Lin, a Chinese collaborator with the Mongolian regime, who attends a performance of *The Chao Family Orphan*. He finds

Meryl Drower (Actor) in A Night at the Chinese Opera *(Cheltenham, 1987)*

that the first half of the play mirrors his own life and strives to take steps to avoid his surmised fate. Acts I and III tell his story and origin, and Act II is an interrupted performance of the play, accompanied by a reduced orchestra (predominately flutes, violas, basses and percussion) imitating traditional Chinese music. This act adheres closely to the traditional style of Yüan drama in its mixture of speech and sung rhythmic declamation, and in its fast and furious pace. The two narratives, that of Chao Lin and that of the play, essentially the same story, entwine in the final act with a double conclusion, one tragic and one more optimistic.

The music is economical, pictorial, spacious and brilliantly coloured. One instantly identifiable stylistic trait – a naturalistic speech rhythm duplicated simultaneously by the orchestra – aptly both supports and undermines the text – a fitting musical metaphor for a work where so much is double edged.

EDITIONS   f.s./v.s., Novello, 1987

The Vanishing Bridegroom

Opera in three parts (1h 30m)
Libretto by the composer, drawn from J. F. Campbell of Islay (ed.), *Popular Tales of the West Highlands*, vol. 2 (1860), and Alexander Carmichael (ed.), *Carmina Gadelica*, vol. 2 (1900)
PREMIERES   17 October 1990, Theatre Royal, Glasgow; US: 2 June 1992, Loretto-Hilton Center, St Louis, Missouri

Three separate Highland tales concerning bride-grooms who vanish in one way or another are linked to give the semblance of a family saga. In *The Inheritance* a man dies and, to discover which of his three sons has stolen his legacy, the doctor tells a parable (enacted) of a bride sent by her rich husband back to her former lover who then returns her; on her way home she is robbed. The doctor then asks the sons which man they most admire: the husband, the lover or the robbers. By admiring the robbers, the youngest gives himself away. In *The Disappearance*, the bride, now settled with her husband, has a child. On his way to fetch the priest for the christening, the husband is lured away by fairies. He reappears, still young, to find that 20 years have passed and his daughter has grown up. In *The Stranger*, the daughter is courted by a rich and handsome man, but she distrusts him. When the priest sanctifies the ground she stands on, the man is revealed as the devil. The sanctified ground blooms and the girl is left alone and independent.

The use of story within a story is characteristic of Weir's work, but here takes on a new simplicity and directness. The music is very different from that of her previous opera, darker, more contrapuntal and with a deepening vein of lyricism, particularly in the bride's lament in Part 1 – and the whole of Part 2. This opens with a fabulously rapt meditation on one chord, which flavours the entire act, culminating in a magical scene where 20 years pass in five minutes of stage time. The chorus has a major role throughout, most memorably as mourners in the first part and as Gaelic singing fairies in Part 2. This, her only stagework that is sung throughout, is the nearest to a conventional opera in Weir's output.

EDITIONS f.s./v.s., J. W. Chester, 1990

Other operatic works: *King Harald's Saga*, 1979; *The Black Spider* (children's opera), 1984; *The Consolations of Scholarship*, 1985; *HEAVEN ABLAZE in his Breast*, 1989; *Scipio's Dream* (Mozart adaptation; television), 1991
BIBLIOGRAPHY Tom Morgan, 'Judith Weir', *New Music*, OUP, 1988, pp. 22–50; Judith Weir, '*A Night at the Chinese Opera*: Libretto and a Note on the Opera', Novello, 1988; Judith Weir, 'On Stravinsky's *Oedipus Rex*', (in ENO Opera Guide no. 43: *Oedipus Rex/The Rake's Progress*), John Calder, 1991

J.G.

JOHN WELDON

b 19 January 1676, Chichester, England; *d* 7 May 1736, London

A chorister at Eton, a pupil of Henry Purcell and organist of New College, Oxford, Weldon unexpectedly sprang to prominence in 1701 when he won first prize in a competition to set Congreve's masque *The Judgement of Paris*. He beat John Eccles, Daniel Purcell, Gottfried Finger and Johann Franck, all older and better-established composers. The Musick Prize launched Weldon into London's musical society: soon after he joined the Chapel Royal, became organist of St Bride's, Fleet Street, and was patronized by the Duke of Bedford. Weldon contributed music to a number of plays before the Italian opera swept English theatre music from the stage a few years later. His subsequent career was taken up largely with church music, though he wrote incidental music for *The Tempest* around 1712, a score probably identical with the one long attributed to Purcell.

The Judgement of Paris

All-sung masque
Text by William Congreve
PREMIERE 6 May 1701, Dorset Garden Theatre, London

Congreve wrote *The Judgement of Paris* for the Musick Prize, the famous operatic competition unexpectedly won by Weldon. Though the settings are all-sung Congreve called it a masque because it is based on Classical myth and has elements of allegory: the shepherd Paris has to choose whether to award the golden apple of beauty (a symbol of the 'Musick Prize') to Juno, Pallas Athene or Venus: Venus wins. Weldon's setting probably won because it is a little more Italian in style than those by Eccles and Daniel Purcell; it has simple, tuneful songs and colourful orchestration. It is his only surviving all-sung dramatic work, though he collaborated with Charles Dieupart in *Britain's Happiness*, an 'entertainment . . . after the manner of an opera' (1704; lost).

EDITION facsimile: Curtis Price and Robert Hume (eds), *Music in London Entertainment*, series C, Stainer and Bell, forthcoming

BIBLIOGRAPHY Roger Fiske, *English Theatre Music in the Eighteenth Century*, OUP, 1973; 2nd edn, 1986

P.H.

EGON WELLESZ

Egon Joseph Wellesz; *b* 21 October 1885, Vienna; *d* 9 November 1974, Oxford, England

Egon Wellesz was both an eminent scholar (Byzantine music, hymnology, history of opera) and a composer; he was also a pupil of Schoenberg, whose first biographer he was. After the *Anschluss* he came to Oxford in 1938, where he established himself as a university reader, teacher and composer, but more of symphonies than stage works. Wellesz's music shows the impact of Schoenberg, but his operatic writing, though angular, is never doctrinally 12-note. He never set great store by harmonic effect as such, preferring the 'greater durability' of part-writing, with purposeful melody and well-defined rhythm. At its best his music has atmosphere and a firm response to dramatic mood.

It was a performance of *Der Freischütz* conducted by Mahler that determined Wellesz to become a composer and, although much of his early music is instrumental, opera was a dominant thread in the first half of his life. His first opera was *Die Prinzessin Girnara*, to a libretto by the poet Jakob Wassermann (drawing on an episode in his novel, *Christian Wahnschaffe* (1918)). Composed in the summer of 1919, it was successfully produced at Hanover and Frankfurt in 1921, and in a revised version at Mannheim in 1928. It was thanks to Wassermann that Wellesz met Hugo von Hofmannsthal on whose adaptations of Euripides he based his operas, *Alkestis* and *Die Bakchantinnen*. Hofmannsthal also

Design by Alfred Roller for Act II of Wellesz's Die Bakchantinnen *(Vienna, 1931)*

suggested the theme of the one-act ballet, *Alkestis auf Skyros* (composed in 1921) which includes a wordless melisma for two singers. Between the two Euripides operas came two short pieces: *Die Opferung des Gefangenen* (*The Sacrifice of the Prisoner*), a one-act 'kultisches drama', and a one-act singspiel cum chamber opera, *Scherz, List und Rache*, to a libretto by the composer after Goethe's singspiel for Philipp Christoph Kayser (1755–1823).

Incognita

Opera in three acts, Op. 69
Libretto by Elizabeth Mackenzie, after the novel *Incognita, or Love and Duty Reconciled* by William Congreve (1692)
Composed 1950
PREMIERE   5 December 1951, Town Hall, Oxford

Incognita marked Wellesz's return to opera after a break of 20 years. A full-scale work in the Straussian tradition, it is distinguished by much characteristic generosity of feeling and endearing charm. The plot hinges on disguise, mistaken identities and misunderstood intentions, all of which are happily resolved.

Other operatic works: *Die Prinzessin Girnara*, 1921, rev. 1928; *Alkestis*, 1924; *Die Opferung des Gefangenen*, 1926; *Scherz, List und Rache*, 1928; *Die Bakchantinnen*, 1931

BIBLIOGRAPHY   Caroline Benser, *Egon Wellesz (1885–1974) – Chronicle of a 20th-century Musician*, American University Press, 1985; Egon Wellesz, *Essays on Opera*, Dobson, 1950

R.La.

FELIX WERDER

b 24 February 1922, Berlin

On arrival in Australia in 1940 as refugees, Werder and his parents, who had been part of a cultured musical circle in Berlin, were interned, but the presence of many musicians in the camp led to the first performance of some of his work. A prolific but self-critical composer, Werder was encouraged by Eugene Goossens to continue composing at a time when many in Australia thought his work too avant garde. He is noted for his theoretical writings, having been for many years music critic of the *Melbourne Age* and a lecturer in adult education. In his operas, he rejected all 19th-century developments in favour of a Mozartian approach. His work also shows affinities with Kurt Weill as well as an inclination to explode operatic convention.

Stage works: *Kisses for a Quid*, 1961; *The General*, 1966; *Agamemnon*, 1967; *Private*, 1969; *The Affair*, 1969; *The Vicious Square*, 1971; *The Conversion*, 1973; *The Medea*, 1985; *Belsazar*, 1988; *Business Day*, 1989
BIBLIOGRAPHY   Essay by Maureen Therese Radic in Frank Callaway and David Tunley (eds), *Australian Composition in the 20th Century*, OUP, 1978

A.I.G.

LARS JOHAN WERLE

b 23 June 1926, Gävle, Sweden

Werle studied at Uppsala University. In 1958 he joined the music department of Swedish Radio and became head of its chamber music section in 1969. In 1970 he left to teach at the State Musical Drama School and in 1977 became composer in residence at the Gothenburg Opera. His operas make use of flashback, collage and film techniques, and include some aleatoric elements.

Werle first came to wider attention with his chamber opera, *Drömmen om Therese*. Its success prompted a commission from the Hamburg Staatsoper. This was *Resan*, to a libretto by Lars Runsten based on P. C. Jersild's novel, *Till varmare Länder (To Warmer Countries)*. *Tintomara*, to a libretto by Leif Söderström, based on a Swedish classic (Almqvist's *Drottningens juvelsmycke (The Queen's Jewel)*), was commissioned by the Stockholm Royal Opera for its bicentenary in 1973. The opera is set in 1792 at the time of the assassination of King Gustav III and quotes from, among other things, Joseph Martin Kraus's *Funeral Music for Gustav III* (1792) and *Così fan tutte*. Originally in three acts, it was revised and given in its two-act form in both Gothenburg and Stockholm (1981). Much of the invention is imaginative and the idiom accessible, with moments that recall Ravel and Puccini.

Drömmen om Therese

The Dream about Therese
Chamber opera in two acts
Libretto by Lars Runsten, after the short story *Pour une nuit d'amour* by Emile Zola
Composed 1960–64
PREMIERES 26 May 1964, Rotunda, Royal Opera, Stockholm; UK: 2 September 1974, Gateway Theatre, Edinburgh (Stockholm Royal Opera)

Drömmen om Therese inaugurated the newly built Rotunda at the Royal Opera in Stockholm. The orchestra is placed in a circle behind the audience and the performers on a round stage in the middle of the hall. The work makes use of a wide variety of post-Expressionistic techniques including aleatoric elements and electronic tape, but its dramatic flair is not matched by consistently sustained musical invention.

RECORDING excerpts: Hallin, af Malmborg, Jehrlander, Saedén, CO, Gielen, Telefunken, c. 1970

Other operatic works: *Resan (The Journey)*, 1969; *En saga om sinnen (A story of the senses)*, (television opera), 1971; *Tintomara*, 1973; *Medusan och djävelun (The Medusa and the Devil)*, 1973; *Animalen (The Animals' Conference)*, 1979

R.La.

THE WHO

Roger Harry Daltrey, *b* 1 March 1945, Hammersmith, England; John Alec Entwistle, *b* 9 October 1946, Chiswick, England; Keith Moon, *b* 23 August 1947, Wembley, England, *d* 7 September 1978, London; Peter Dennis Blandford Townshend, *b* 19 May 1945, Chiswick, England

The Who was one of the most celebrated British rock groups of the 1960s. In their music, rooted in rhythm-and-blues, they broke new ground and more with the use of powerful amplification and destructive stage antics. In 1968, following a succession of hit singles including 'My Generation' – an anthem for 1960s youth – the group's leading light, Townshend, created the classic rock opera, *Tommy*, an early extension of the 'concept album', years before the advent of pop videos. The story of a blind, deaf and dumb boy who grows up to be a pinball champ and guru provided a loose narrative, but the work was a phenomenal success, with live performances at the Coliseum, London (1969), and the Metropolitan, New York (1971). An orchestrated version, with the London Symphony Orchestra, Rod Stewart, *et al.*, appeared in 1972, and the first full stage production, by Lou Reizner, came in 1973. Ken Russell's film version (1975) starred Daltrey (as Tommy), Ann-Margret, Tina Turner and Elton John. Memorable numbers included 'Pinball Wizard' and 'See me, feel me'.

Inevitably *Tommy* spawned a number of less successful imitations. Townshend and the group abandoned a further project (*Lifehouse*) before recording the more complex *Quadrophenia* (1973) which looked at 'Mod' life in the early 1960s through the eyes of a young Londoner. The 1979 film and soundtrack were made with the group's new drummer, Kenny Jones.

BIBLIOGRAPHY Gary Herman, *The Who*, November Books, 1971

M.A.

HEALEY WILLAN

James Healey Willan; *b* 12 October 1880, Balham, London; *d* 16 February 1968, Toronto, Canada

Born and educated in England, Willan went to Canada in 1913 to teach at the Toronto Royal Conservatory. He was Vice Principal there (1920–36) and Professor of Music at Toronto University (1936–50). He became known in the UK after his anthem 'O Lord, our Governor' was sung at the 1953 Coronation.

Though he is known principally as a composer of church music, he also wrote six ballad operas, much incidental music, an arrangement of *The Beggar's Opera* by John Gay and two operas. Both operas are to libretti by the Irish-Canadian poet John Coulter (1888–1980): *Transit through Fire* (the first CBC commission for a radio opera) and *Deirdre of the Sorrows*, probably the first full-length opera written in Canada. Originally for radio, it was drastically revised for the stage and produced in Toronto in 1965. The opera tells the tragic Irish legend of Conochar, High King of Ullah, and of his unrequited love for Deirdre, who finally dies.

Willan declared that he 'believed strongly in the leitmotif principle', but he did not apply the principle rigorously. His romantic idiom, despite more than passing resemblances to Delius, Boughton and possibly Holbrooke, has a wholly personal vigour.

Operatic works: *L'ordre du bon temps*, 1928; *Prince Charlie and Flora*, 1929; *The Ayrshire Ploughman*, n.d.; *Transit through Fire* (radio opera), (1942); *Deirdre of the Sorrows* (radio opera), 1946, rev. as *Deirdre*, 1965; 2 lost ballad operas
BIBLIOGRAPHY F. R. C. Clarke, *Healey Willan: Life and Music*, University of Toronto Press, 1983

L.F.

GRACE WILLIAMS

Grace Mary Williams; *b* 19 February 1906, Barry, Wales; *d* 10 February 1977, Barry

Grace Williams developed an interest in opera as a student in London and Vienna. In the 1930s she was friendly with Benjamin Britten, who was able to get her commissions for film music. From this period date also two ballets which were her first works for the theatre. Britten was later a major influence on Williams's only opera.

The Parlour

Comedy in one act (1h 15m)
Libretto by the composer, after the story *En famille* by Guy de Maupassant (1881)
Completed 25 August 1961
PREMIERE 5 May 1966, New Theatre, Cardiff

Set in a British seaside town in 1870, the action centres on a cantankerous old grandmother and the immediate disposal of her goods and chattels by the family after her apparent sudden death. But Grandmama's death has been no more than a coma, through which she has heard everything ...

MANUSCRIPT Welsh Music Information Centre

BIBLIOGRAPHY Malcolm Boyd, *Grace Williams*, University of Wales Press, 1980

M.B.

MALCOLM WILLIAMSON

Malcolm Benjamin Graham Christopher Williamson;
b 21 November 1931, Sydney, Australia

Although he has lived in England since the age of 22 and has made only occasional visits to his home country, Malcolm Williamson still considers himself an Australian composer. One of his most recent works is Australian in content: *The Dawn is at Hand*, a choral work to words by Australian Aboriginal poet Oodgeroo Noonuccal, performed in Brisbane in 1989. Williamson studied composition at the New South Wales Conservatorium with Eugene Goossens and then in London with Elisabeth Lutyens and Erwin Stein. He is an accomplished pianist and organist. Among his theatre works, a ballet score, *The Display* (1962), which was performed to

choreography by Robert Helpmann and designs by Sidney Nolan, was an important milestone in the development of Australian dance. His operas not only cover a wide range of styles, but envisage a wide range of performing capabilities, many of them (such as *Dunstan and the Devil*) being written for children or amateur performing forces. His 'cassations' are simple but effective choral works (miniature operas) for audience participation, in which the audience is coached on the spot.

He is also interested in music as therapy for handicapped children. On the borderline of classification as opera is *The Brilliant and the Dark* (1969), an 'operatic sequence' to words by Ursula Vaughan Williams, a collection of women's words from the Middle Ages to the present. While the children's operas have been performed in Australia with reasonable frequency, particularly *The Happy Prince*, the major operas have been staged only in England, although *The Violins of St Jacques* received a television production from the Australian Broadcasting Commission (shown in 1975). Williamson was appointed Master of the Queen's Music in 1975 and was awarded a CBE in 1976.

Our Man in Havana

Opera in three acts (2h 30m)
Libretto by Sidney Gilliat, after the novel by Graham Greene (1958)
PREMIERE 2 July 1963, Sadler's Wells, London

Williamson's earliest stage works were musical comedies written in the late 1950s, of which *No Bed for Bacon* was produced in Bristol (1958). But *Our Man in Havana* was his first true opera, and it was the comparative success of this tragi-comedy that launched him on the string of theatrical works that followed. The setting of Greene's 'entertainment', about a vacuum-cleaner salesman in Cuba who becomes an unwilling British agent, is eclectic, as are all Williamson's early works, combining the vitality and punchiness of Rodgers and Hammerstein with parodies of more esoteric modern models such as Stravinsky, Berg and Britten – a not always

A scene from Malcolm Williamson's Our Man in Havana *(London, 1963)*

convincing mix. Good tunes alternate with weird avant-garde noises, song-and-dialogue with longer stretches of through-composition. The pacing is uneven. But an essential energy and some excellent melodic invention keep the work afloat.

EDITION v.s., Weinberger, 1964

English Eccentrics

Chamber opera in two acts (1h 45m)
Libretto by Geoffrey Dunn, after the book by Edith Sitwell (1933)
PREMIERE 11 June 1964, Jubilee Hall, Aldeburgh

Williamson's second opera, again a comedy but this time for chamber forces (six singers, seven players, no chorus), is more concise but also more esoteric than his first. Sitwell's book is more of a procession than a narrative, and the opera's staging depends on brisk production, since each member of the cast plays several characters, with quick costume changes. But the eclectic elements in Williamson's style fit together more persuasively here than before.

EDITION v.s., Chappell, 1964

The Happy Prince

Children's opera in one act (40m)
Libretto by the composer, after the fairy-tale by Oscar Wilde (1888)
PREMIERE 22 May 1965, Farnham Parish Church

The first of Williamson's operas for children remains his best, despite the rather cloying sentimentality of the story, about a statue driven by pity to give the gold and precious stones with which he is covered to the poor and starving. It calls for a large children's choir, (young) female voices, and a small band of piano duet, four percussionists, and optional string quintet.

RECORDING Cantelo, Stevens, Lehane, Rex, Guildhall School Chamber Ch, str quintet and perc., Williamson and Bennett (pf duet), Dods, Argo, 1966
EDITION v.s., Weinberger, 1965

Julius Caesar Jones

Children's opera in two acts (1h)
Libretto by Geoffrey Dunn
PREMIERE 4 January 1966, Jeanetta Cochrane Theatre, London

Based on an original (and, Williamson has said, partly autobiographical) story about the children of a London family whose garden games become dangerously and nearly fatally real, *Julius Caesar Jones* combines a number of strong parts for children with three adult voices, cast more as parental stereotypes. The accompanying ensemble uses the same forces as Britten's *The Turn of the Screw*.

RECORDING Cantelo, Procter, Maurel, Finchley Children's Music Group, Andrewes, Argo, 1967
EDITIONS v.s./choral s., Weinberger, 1966

The Violins of Saint-Jacques

Opera in three acts (2h 15m)
Libretto by William Chappell, after the novel by Patrick Leigh Fermor (1953)
PREMIERE 29 November 1966, Sadler's Wells, London

This full-scale romantic opera sets a patchwork of emotional, sexual and social dramas on a French Caribbean volcanic island (originally Martinique, 1902) which is about to erupt, and does so, with rather obvious symbolic effect, towards the end of the work.

EDITION v.s., Weinberger, 1972

Other operatic works: *Dunstan and the Devil* (chamber opera), 1967; *The Growing Castle* (chamber opera), 1968; *Lucky Peter's Journey*, 1969; *The Red Sea*, 1972
BIBLIOGRAPHY Essay by Brian Chatterton in Frank Callaway and David Tunley (eds), *Australian Composition in the 20th Century*, OUP, 1978

A.I.G./S.W.

MEREDITH WILLSON

Robert Reiniger Meredith Willson; *b* 18 May 1902, Mason City, Iowa, US; *d* 15 June 1984, Santa Monica, California, US

Meredith Willson's first musical career was as a flautist in the Sousa Band and the New York Philharmonic. Later an orchestral composer, song-writer and radio personality, he turned to his native Iowa for the subject matter of his highly successful first musical, *The Music Man*. His subsequent shows never matched this achievement, but they all display a distinctive blend of sentiment, nostalgia and show-biz sparkle.

The Music Man

Musical comedy in two acts (film: 2h 30m)
Libretto by Meredith Willson (story by Meredith Willson and Franklin Lacey)
PREMIERES 19 December 1957, Majestic Theater, New York; UK: 16 March 1961, Adelphi Theatre, London

'Professor' Harold Hill, a specialist in raising money for non-existent boys' bands, comes to River City, Iowa, in 1912. He ultimately stays, changed by the love of the town librarian and saved by the genuine vitality and joy he has brought to River City. The score features period re-creations such as barbershop quartets, extended novelties such as train imitations, unrhymed spoken patter, and two songs that became standards: '76 Trombones' and 'Till there was you'.

RECORDING Preston, Cook, Greene, Capitol, 1957
FILM da Costa (dir.), Warner, 1962
EDITION v.s., Frank Music and Rinimer, 1958

Other musicals: *The Unsinkable Molly Brown*, 1960; *Here's Love*, 1963; *1491*, 1969
BIBLIOGRAPHY Meredith Willson, *But He Doesn't Know the Territory*, Putnam, 1959

J.A.C.

PETER WINTER

Peter Winter [von Winter]; *baptized* 28 August 1754, Mannheim; *d* 17 October 1825, Munich

After early experience with the court orchestra at Mannheim (in which he was a violinist at the age of ten), and in the stimulating artistic milieu of Munich, where the court moved in 1778, Winter embarked on an active professional life which led to his appointment as vice-kapellmeister in 1787 and court kapellmeister 11 years later. His first major stage composition for Munich, *Helena und Paris* (1782), an attempt to continue the serious German opera style of Holzbauer's *Gunther von Schwarzburg*, was not a success. Undeterred he continued to produce theatrical works in a variety of forms, not only singspiels and melodramas for Munich and Vienna – including *Das Labyrinth*, designed as a sequel to Mozart's *Die Zauberflöte*, and *Der Sturm*, a comedy loosely based on Shakespeare's *The Tempest* – but also Italian seria and buffa works for Naples and Venice, and tragédies lyriques for Paris. Although he never visited England a number of his stage works were successfully produced at the Haymarket Theatre in London, including *La grotta di Calipso* (1803) to a libretto by Lorenzo da Ponte. However, his greatest success was with *Das unterbrochene Opferfest* (Vienna, 1796), to a libretto by F. X. Huber, which won him widespread fame across central Europe. In this work, as in several of his later German operas, he achieved convincing music drama on a large scale, creating an attractive melodic style in his arias, enriched by colourful harmonic schemes, effective handling of the chorus and varied patterns of instrumentation. The influence of Gluck and Mozart is apparent, but it is distilled into a personal mode of expression which, although modest in scope, points forward interestingly towards the world of Weber and his contemporaries.

Operatic works: *Cora und Alonso*, 1778; *Lenardo und Blandine*, 1779; *Reinold und Armida*, 1780; *Helena und Paris*, 1782; *Das Hirtenmädchen*, 1784; *Der Bettelstudent, oder Das Donnerwetter*, 1785; *Bellerophon*, 1785; *Circe*, 1788; *Medea und Jason*, 1789; *Jery und Bäteli*, 1790; *Scherz, List und Rache*, 1790; *Das Lindenfest, oder Das Fest der Freundschaft*, (1790); *Psyche*, 1790; *Catone in Utica*, 1791; *Antigona*, 1791; *Il sacrifizio di Creta, ossia Arianna e Teseo*, 1792; *La mort d'Orphée et d'Euridice*, 1792; *I fratelli rivali*, 1793; *Belisa, ossia La fedeltà riconosciuta*, 1794; *Ogus, ossia Il trionfo del bel sesso*, 1795; *I due vedovi*, 1796; *Das unterbrochene Opferfest*, 1796; *Babylons Pyramiden*, 1797; *Elise, Gräfin von Hilburg*, 1798; *Das Labyrinth, oder Der Kampf mit den Elementen*, 1798; *Der Sturm*, 1798; *Marie von Montalban*, 1800; *Tamerlan*, 1802; *La grotta di Calipso*, 1803; *Il trionfo dell'amor fraterno*, 1804; *Il ratto di Proserpina*, 1804; *Zaira*, 1805; *Der Frauenbund*, 1805; *Die beiden Blinden*, 1810; *Colmal*, 1809; *Die Pantoffeln*, 1811; *Maometto II*, 1817; *Il due Valdomiri*, 1817; *Etelinda*, 1818; *Der Sänger und der Schneider*, 1820

BIBLIOGRAPHY   L. Kuckuk, *Peter Winter als deutscher Opernkomponist*, dissertation, University of Heidelberg, 1923; Anna Amalie Abert, 'Peter Winter (von Winter)', in *Grove*, Macmillan, 1980

B.S.

ERNST WILHELM WOLF

baptized 25 February 1735, Grossen Behringen; *d* 29 or 30 November 1792, Weimar

After early experience at the University of Jena, where he directed the collegium musicum, and in teaching at Leipzig and Naumburg, Wolf settled in Weimar, from *c.* 1760, and remained in service there for the rest of his career – as konzertmeister, organist, and eventually, from 1772, kapellmeister. He wrote some 20 singspiels, many of a comic or sentimental character, which though mainly conventional in style were widely admired during his lifetime. Particularly appealing are his arias and ensembles in folksong style, evident in *Die Dorf- deputierten*. In the early 1770s Wolf received an attractive offer from Frederick the Great to succeed C. P. E. Bach at his court in Potsdam; but he refused it, preferring to remain within the circle of generous patronage provided at Weimar by the Duchess Anna Amalia.

Surviving operatic works: *Das Gärtnermädchen*, 1769; *Das Rosenfest*, 1772; *Die Dorfdeputierten*, 1772; *Die treuen Köhler*, 1772; *Der Abend im Walde*, 1773; *Das grosse Los*, 1774; *Le monde de la lune*, (unperformed); *Alceste*, 1780; 10 lost

BIBLIOGRAPHY   D. Hartwig, 'Ernst Wilhelm Wolf', in *MGG*

B.S.

HUGO WOLF

Hugo Filipp Jakob Wolf; *b* 13 March 1860, Windischgraz, Styria (now Slovenj Gradec, Slovenia); *d* 22 February 1903, Vienna

Encouraged by his first public successes with lieder, of which he became the acknowledged master of his time, Wolf rekindled an interest in opera first prompted by his brief experience as kapellmeister at Salzburg (1881–2). Early in 1890 he completed his 44 settings of the *Spanisches Liederbuch* and, with his mind on Spanish subjects, he considered and rejected a draft libretto on Alarcón's *El sombrero de tres picos* (1874), sent to him by Rosa Mayreder, a friend of a friend. Other ideas, on *The Tempest*, Pocahontas, Buddha, Apuleis and much else, were toyed with to no avail, including Alarcón's *El niño de la bola*, to which he also later returned.

A change of heart on the Mayreder libretto in preference to another on the same subject by Franz Schumann set him to work and, in a typical creative burst of composition, the four-act *Der Corregidor* was completed in piano score by July 1894 and orchestrated by the end of the year. Offered in turn to Vienna, Berlin and Prague, it was successively turned down until accepted for Mannheim, where its premiere in 1896 was a distinctive success. The interest was not maintained but, after some revisions by Wolf the next year, it was given productions in various cities, including a reduction to three acts for

A Hugo Wolf evening at the Vienna Wagner Verein; the composer is at the piano

Vienna (1904). Some 35 productions have been listed up to the mid-1970s.

In 1897, already a sick man mentally and with the symptoms of his terminal illness, Wolf began setting another Alarcón libretto by Moritz Hoernes (again having first rejected one by Rosa Mayreder) on *El niño* retitled *Manuel Venegas*. After he had composed some 60 pages of piano score Wolf's mind gave way and he wrote no more music. The fragment is credited in some sources with a performance at Mannheim in 1903, but was more recently heard at the Stuttgart Liederhalle on 5 July 1989. It was described as having ravishing chorus writing, richly seasoned melodic *parlando* for solo singers and soaring melody for Manuel.

Der Corregidor
The Corregidor
Opera in four acts
Libretto by Rosa Mayreder-Obermayer, after the short story *El sombrero de tres picos* by Pedro de Alarcón (1874)
Composed April–December 1894, rev. 1897
PREMIERES   7 June 1896, Mannheim Theatre; UK: 13 July 1934, Royal Academy of Music, London; US: 5 January 1959, Carnegie Hall, New York (concert)

The story is best known on the musical stage as Léonide Massine's ballet, *The Three-cornered Hat*, with music by Manuel de Falla (1919). In an Andalucian town the elderly *corregidor* (regional and judicial governor) amorously pursues Frasquita, wife of the miller Tío Lucas; she uses the advances for her own ends but retains her virtue, while the *corregidor* has Lucas arrested on a trumped-up charge. Arriving, in the miller's absence, wet from a fall into the millstream, the *corregidor* is put to bed by Frasquita while his clothes are dried; these are found and put on by a returning Lucas. In the ensuing confusion of identities both men are soundly thrashed and the moral is pointed.

An admirer of Wagner, Wolf employed Wagnerian texture and orchestral scale, but structured his opera less as a musical drama than as a sequence of song forms, in solos, duets and ensembles. Many of these are considered to reflect Wolf's mature lyrical invention at its best, but they express the inward thoughts or feelings of characters rather than the characters themselves. The score includes two songs from the *Spanisches Liederbuch* newly orchestrated: 'In dem Schatten meiner Locken' and 'Herz, verzage nicht geschwind'. The lyrical passages are linked on a lower level of invention arising from a lack of interest in stagecraft, and with some over-reliance on repeated motifs such as that associated with the *corregidor*.

RECORDINGS 1. Teschemacher, Fuchs, Erb, Herrmann, Böhme, Frick, Dresden Opera Ch and O, Elmendorff, Urania, 1944; 2. Donath, Soffel, Hollweg, Fischer-Dieskau, Moll, von Halem, Berlin RIAS Chamber Ch, Berlin Radio SO, Albrecht, Schwann, 1986: the early recording is historic and keenly characterized, but the more recent one is the more accurate [A.B.]
EDITIONS   f.s., Peters, 1904; v.s., Peters, 1896

BIBLIOGRAPHY   Peter Cook, *Hugo Wolf's 'Corregidor': A Study of the Opera and its Origins*, private publication, London, 1976; Horst Koegler, review of Stuttgart performance of *Manuel Venegas*, *Opera*, vol. 40 (1989), pp. 1478–9

N.G.

ERMANNO WOLF-FERRARI
Ermanno Wolf; *b* 12 January 1876, Venice; *d* 21 January 1948, Venice

The surname that Wolf-Ferrari used after about 1895 brought together those of his Bavarian father and Venetian mother – neatly symbolizing the uncertainty about his nationality that persistently haunted him. Born in Italy, he studied in Munich and spent much of his adult life in the German-speaking world. Moreover, his works were at first much more successful north of the Alps than in his native land. A crucial factor underlying this was his failure, until well after the First World War, to be taken up by an Italian publisher.

After initially concentrating mainly on instrumental music, Wolf-Ferrari first came before the opera public with *Cenerentola* (1900), which won success in Bremen after a disastrous premiere in Venice. Though eclectic, the work shows a promising inventiveness in (for example) its sometimes unexpectedly bold harmonies. It was, however, in his next two operas that Wolf-Ferrari created that special type of graceful, gently satirical comedy which was to become distinctively his own: though first performed in German, *Le donne curiose* and *I quatro rusteghi* were originally composed to Italian libretti based on Goldoni. *I quatro rusteghi* in particular recaptures the spirit, rather than the letter, of 18th-century opera buffa with a charm and subtlety that place it among the best Italian operatic comedies since Verdi's *Falstaff*. *Il segreto di Susanna*, though slighter, has won even wider success, thanks partly to its conveniently small cast.

I gioielli della Madonna, by contrast, shows Wolf-Ferrari trying his hand at post-Mascagnian *verismo*, a genre to which his talents were ill suited. Then, after the unjustly neglected little Molière opera *L'amore medico* (1913), he went through a prolonged crisis under the impact of the First World War, during which he took refuge in Zurich. Since Italy and Germany were fighting on opposite sides, his mixed blood and background proved particularly problematical for someone of his hypersensitive yet childlike temperament: small wonder that he composed little during the war and the immediately post-war years. However, *Sly* has recently resurfaced after decades of neglect.

In the 1930s Wolf-Ferrari wrote three further comic operas, including two more adaptations of Goldoni. Of these, *Il campiello* is regarded by many in both Italy and Germany as fully equal to *I quatro rusteghi*. After 1940 only one more opera followed, and Wolf-Ferrari again became prolific in the field of instrumental music.

I quatro rusteghi

(*Die vier Grobiane*)

School for Fathers (literally, *The Four Curmudgeons*)

Comic opera in three acts (four scenes) (2h 15m)

Libretto by [Luigi Sugana and] Giuseppe Pizzolato, based on the play *I rusteghi* by Carlo Goldoni (1760)

Composed *c.* 1904–5

PREMIERES   19 March 1906, Hoftheater, Munich; UK: 7 June 1946, Sadler's Wells, London; US: 18 October 1951, City Center, New York

Although the librettists made appropriate changes, they skilfully retained important features of Goldoni's famous comedy. Here as there, most of the

I quatro rusteghi (Munich, 1939)

characters use Venetian dialect: only Count Riccardo speaks standard Italian, thus identifying himself as an outsider and an aristocrat. The spirit of Wolf-Ferrari's music indeed seems so closely bound up with the racy idiosyncrasies of Venetian speech that something essential is inevitably lost in translation.

The *rusteghi* of the title (the Venetian word has very different overtones from its Italian counterpart) are crusty old pedants, hidebound by the mores of the society in which they live. One of them, Lunardo, has arranged for his daughter Lucieta to marry his friend Maurizio's son Filipeto; but custom dictates that the young couple may not see each other before their wedding. Naturally both youngsters rebel fiercely and, with the help of the older female characters and of Count Riccardo, Filipeto is smuggled into Lunardo's house disguised as a woman. The couple fall for each other at once. But, having discovered that Filipeto has anticipated marriage to the extent of actually meeting his bride-to-be, Lunardo decrees that the wedding must now be cancelled. Only after determined persuasion by the more enlightened characters – including a formidable tirade by Felice, the wife of one of the other *rusteghi* – do Lunardo and his friends relent.

This slender plot provides ample scope both for memorable comic characterization and for deft evocation of the 18th-century setting; and the music rises delightfully to the occasion. Using the old opera buffa tradition as a creative starting point rather than a rigid model, Wolf-Ferrari finds room for passing allusions to Wagner and Verdi, for mildly 'modern' touches of dissonance, and even for a Venetian popular melody which figures prominently in all three acts. Yet, far from being merely eclectic, the total effect is surprisingly unified and personal, so spontaneous is the melodic invention, so individual the delicately imaginative orchestration. An immediate success in Germany, *I quatro rusteghi* took considerably longer to convince the Italians, and reached the English-speaking world only after the Second World War. Edward Dent's witty translation contributed significantly to the opera's great success at its British premiere in 1946.

RECORDING Carteri, Ligabue, Elmo, Valletti, Rossi-Lemeni, Maionica, Stefanoni, Luise, La Scala O, Votto, Fonit Cetra, 1992 (recorded 1954)
EDITION v.s., Josef Weinberger, 1906

Il segreto di Susanna

(*Susannens Geheimnis*)
Susanna's Secret
Intermezzo in one act (45m)
Libretto by Enrico Golisciani
Composed ?1909
PREMIERES 4 December 1909, Hoftheater, Munich; US: 14 March 1911, Metropolitan, New York; UK: 11 July 1911, Covent Garden, London

Though too slight and eclectic to show Wolf-Ferrari's full stature as a composer, this amiable *jeu d'esprit* deserves its popularity. Not only is it cheap to produce (having only two singing characters), but its unaffected tunefulness, and the disarmingly simple idea of the libretto, have an immediate, undemanding appeal. Count Gil suspects that his young wife Susanna has a lover. How else can he explain the smell of tobacco smoke that pervades the house? Why else did he catch sight of her out and about without his permission? It eventually emerges – after a sustained build-up of misunderstanding – that Susanna herself is the smoker and that the purpose of her furtive outing was to buy more cigarettes. Relieved, Gil agrees to take up smoking too, to keep her company.

The music's allusions range from almost literal pastiche of opera buffa in the vivacious little overture to free yet unmistakable references to Debussy's *Prélude à l'après-midi d'un faune* in the woodwind phrases representing cigarette smoke. Such stylistic waverings matter little in so unpretentious a piece; but the distinctive personal 'voice' of Wolf-Ferrari's best comic style, which was all-pervading in *I quatro rusteghi*, is here only intermittently audible.

RECORDING 1. Chiara, Weikl, O of Covent Garden, Gardelli, Decca, 1976; 2. Scotto, Bruson, Philharmonia O, Pritchard, CBS, 1981
EDITION v.s., Josef Weinberger, 1911

I gioielli della Madonna

(*Der Schmuck der Madonna*)
The Jewels of the Madonna
Opera in three acts (2h 15m)
Libretto by Carlo Zangarini and Enrico Golisciani (text rev. 1933)
Composed *c.* 1910–11
PREMIERES 23 December 1911, Kurfürstenoper, Berlin; US: 16 January 1912, Auditorium, Chicago; UK: 30 May 1912, Covent Garden, London

Wolf-Ferrari's sudden turn to crude post-Mascagnian *verismo* must have startled many after the preceding elegant comedies. His motivation was probably partly opportunistic: hoping to break down Italian resistance to his music, he evidently thought it prudent to follow current Italian fashions. Ironically, the opera attracted even less attention in Italy than its predecessors, and instead won disproportionate success in the English-speaking world.

Although in three acts, *I gioielli* recalls *Cavalleria rusticana* in its violent story of jealousy and revenge in a southern Italian community. The scene is Naples on the feast day of the Madonna. Gennaro, a blacksmith, loves his foster-sister Maliella, who prefers the romantic charms of Rafaele, leader of a group of Camorristi (the Neapolitan equivalent of the Mafia). Rafaele tells Maliella that to prove his love he would even steal the jewels from the statue of the Madonna which is being carried past in a procession. On hearing of this boast, Gennaro steals the jewels himself as proof that his love is the stronger. Maliella yields to him (but with Rafaele always in mind), and then adorns herself in the jewels, thus adding to the sacrilege and deeply shocking everyone – including the Camorristi. The upshot is that Maliella drowns herself in the sea and Gennaro stabs himself.

Wolf-Ferrari clothed this melodramatic story in abundant local colour, prominently using at least one real Neapolitan melody. The result has a certain raw exuberance, but too often lapses into a vulgarity wholly absent from his comedies. The latter part of Gennaro's duet with his mother in Act I stands out as an oasis of profoundly Wolf-Ferrarian lyricism.

RECORDING Tinsley, Turp, Glossop, King, BBC Singers and SO, Erede, MRF, 1976
EDITION v.s., Josef Weinberger, 1911

Sly, ovvero La leggenda del dormiente risvegliato

Sly, or The Legend of the Awakened Sleeper
Opera in three acts (four scenes) (2h)
Libretto by Giovacchino Forzano, taking the idea of the prologue to Shakespeare's *The Taming of the Shrew* as its starting-point
Composed 1920s
PREMIERE 29 December 1927, La Scala, Milan

The three operas that Wolf-Ferrari completed during his crisis years have seldom been staged, and some might regard them as psychological documents rather than balanced works of art. However, the recent revival of interest in *Sly* has resulted in successful productions and an impressive German recording. The libretto, in which the opening of *The Taming of the Shrew* is adapted so as to lead into a grim tragic drama, is admittedly strange: one can see why it had been turned down by Puccini, but one can also understand its special appeal to Wolf-Ferrari after his recent troubles.

Christopher Sly, who in the opera is a vagabond–poet rather than a tinker, meets the Earl of Westmorland in a tavern. Like Shakespeare's anonymous 'lord', the earl decides to amuse himself at Sly's expense by transporting him, in a drunken stupor, to his own castle, dressing him up in magnificent clothes, and deceiving him into thinking that he is an aristocrat. When he awakes, the earl's friends convince the poet that he has just recovered after ten years of loss of memory. As part of the charade, Dolly (the earl's mistress, who was also present in the tavern scene) plays the role of Sly's 'wife'. Gradually she realizes that she is genuinely in love with the poet. But at a certain point in the game, Sly is rudely made aware that he is the victim of a hoax: being in fact deeply in debt, he is 'arrested' and locked in the castle cellar. In despair, he slashes his wrists and bleeds to death: Dolly, who comes to assure him of her love, arrives too late to save him.

On paper the music of *Sly* may seem excessively eclectic, alluding to styles that range from Wagner (especially in Dolly's scenes with Sly) to something surprisingly akin to Kurt Weill in parts of the tavern scene. A good performance, however, can convey an extraordinary, relentless sense of a vulnerable individual being bullied by the vagaries of fortune, so that the impact of Sly's desperate monologue in Act III becomes profoundly moving.

RECORDING Polaski, Bader, Reeh, Haertel, Ch and O of the Niedersächsischen Staatsoper, Hanover, Maxym, Acanta, 1983
EDITION v.s., Casa Musicale Sonzogno, 1927

Il campiello
The Little Square in Venice
Comic opera in three acts (1h 45m)
Libretto by Mario Ghisalberti, based on the play by Carlo Goldoni (1756)
Composed ?c. 1934
PREMIERE 12 February 1936, La Scala, Milan

Wolf-Ferrari's operas of the 1930s show signs of a new serenity. It may be relevant that he wrote *Il campiello* for the principal Italian publisher (Ricordi) and opera house (La Scala): thus the long period when his works were largely ignored in Italy was now truly past.

In *Il campiello* Wolf-Ferrari returned to Goldoni for his subject matter, thus renewing contact with a world which in *I quatro rusteghi* had brought out his best qualities. The adaptation of Goldoni is even more faithful in this case, for the original is itself in verse, as well as being largely (like *I quatro rusteghi*) in Venetian dialect.

Throughout, the scene remains the 'little square' of the title. The people who frequent it include Gasparina, an affected, slightly snobbish young lady with a lisp; Cavaliere Astolfi, an aristocratic (but penniless) 'outsider' speaking standard Italian, who courts Gasparina and eventually takes her away with him to Naples; Lucieta and Gnese, working-class girls whose local boyfriends do not prevent the cavaliere from taking an interest in them too; and some older women – notably Dona Cate Panciana and Dona Pasqua Polegana (both sung by tenors) – who try to worm their own grotesque ways into the tangled love affairs. The total effect is a richly satirical evocation of a close-knit (but quarrelsome), mainly working-class community.

Wolf-Ferrari's music successfully revives most of the best characteristics already encountered in *I quatro rusteghi*, and reaches out into bolder realms of 20th-century dissonance in the formidable quarrel scene that erupts in the final act. On the whole, however, the underlying mood (beneath the satirical surface) is of a childlike simplicity and a seraphic calm, which many find deeply touching.

RECORDING Rizzieri, Zanolli, Meneguzzer, Savio, Guggia, Mercuriali, Borriello, Milan Ch and SO of Italian Radio, Gracis, MRF, 1963
EDITION v.s., Ricordi, 1935

Other operas: *Irene*, (1896); *La Camargo* (inc.), (c. 1897); *Cenerentola* (*Aschenbrödel*), 1900, rev. 1902; *Le donne curiose* (*Die neugierigen Frauen*), 1903 (RECORDING Micheluzzi, Ratti, Franzini, Capecchi, Pedani, Maionica, Badioli, Milan Ch and SO of Italian Radio, Simonetto, MRF, 1958); *L'amore medico* (*Der Liebhaber als Arzt*), 1913; *Gli amanti sposi*, (mainly 1914–16), 1925; *Das Himmelskleid* (*La veste del cielo*), (c. 1917–25), 1927; *La vedova scaltra*, 1931 (RECORDING Noni, Gatta, Lazzari, Blaffard, Capecchi, Cassinelli, Milan Ch and SO of Italian Radio, Sanzogno, MRF, 1955); *La dama boba*, 1939; *Gli dei a Tebe* (*Der Kuckuck von Theben*), 1943
BIBLIOGRAPHY Raffaello de Rensis, *Ermanno Wolf-Ferrari: la sua vita d'artista*, Fratelli Treves, 1937; James Ringo, 'Ermanno Wolf-Ferrari, an Appreciation of his Work', *RMI*, vol. 51 (1949), pp. 224–47

J.C.G.W.

PAUL WRANITZKY
Paul [Pavel] Wranitzky [Vranický, Wraniczky, Wranizky]; *b* 30 December 1756, Nová Říše, Moravia; *d* 26 September 1808, Vienna

After a sound musical training in Moravia, Wranitzky went to Vienna at 20 to continue his musical studies, notably with Haydn. In 1785 he was appointed music director to Count Johann Nepomuk Esterházy and in 1790 he became chief orchestral director of the Viennese court theatres. Wranitzky was friendly with Beethoven (he conducted the premiere of his First Symphony) and with Haydn (he conducted the Vienna performances of *The Creation* in 1799 and 1800) and was a member of the same Freemasons' lodge as Mozart. His music, which includes 51 symphonies and much chamber music, is solidly and unremarkably in the Viennese classical mould, though folklike elements in some of the slighter pieces are sometimes said to stem from his Moravian upbringing. Unlike his brother Anton, who was also active in Viennese theatres, he was a prolific composer of singspiels and ballets. He is remembered chiefly for his singspiel *Oberon*, a precursor of *Die Zauberflöte*.

Oberon, König der Elfen
Oberon, King of the Fairies
Romantic singspiel in three acts
Libretto by Frederike Sophie Seyler, after Wieland, arranged by J. G. K. Giesecke
PREMIERE 7 November 1789, Theater auf der Wieden, Vienna

Oberon was produced two years before *Die Zauberflöte* and its success prompted Schikaneder to conceive *Die Zauberflöte* for Mozart at the same theatre, using many of the same ingredients. The two plots have striking similarities, involving a hero and his quest in a foreign setting (the knight Huon in Baghdad and Tunis; the prince Tamino in Egypt) and aided by magic instruments (a magic horn; a magic flute) and beneficent supernatural powers (Oberon; Sarastro). Both pairs of lovers (Huon and Amanda; Tamino and Pamina) have to overcome many obstacles before they achieve happiness. This was all familiar material of the Viennese popular stage; where Mozart's opera differs is in the Masonic and humanitarian ideas which transform the plot to something altogether more serious, and in the stature of the music. Wranitzky's *Oberon* is simpler in this respect, with ensembles confined to the finales, though much the same range of genres is apparent: simple song forms for Scherazmin (the Papageno figure), deeply felt arias and duets for the central pair, and coloratura for the supernatural (Oberon).

After its Vienna premiere, *Oberon* was given in Frankfurt on the occasion of the Emperor Leopold II's coronation in October 1790, and had a run of 35 performances there. It was performed all over Germany and in several other countries. In Vienna it formed part of the standard repertoire until 1826, when it was ousted by Weber's *Oberon*. Goethe thought highly of the work and in a letter written in 1796 invited Wranitzky to set his continuation of *Die Zauberflöte*.

EDITION   v.s., J. H. Gotz, 1795

Operatic works: *Merkur, der Heiratsstifter, oder Der Geiz im Geldkasten* (one aria only), 1793; *Das Fest der Lazaronen*, 1795; *Das Maroccanische Reich*, 1795; *Die gute Mutter*, 1795; *Der Schreiner*, 1799; *Das Picknick der Götter*, 1804; *Das Mitgefühl*, 1805; 3 lost operas

BIBLIOGRAPHY   Petra Heerenová, 'Zpěvohra Oberon Pavla Vranického a její libreto' ('Wranitzky's Opera *Oberon* and Its Libretto'), *Opus musicum*, vol. 4, Brno, 1972, pp. 73–8

J.T.

IANNIS XENAKIS

b 29 May 1922, Braila, Romania

The Greek composer Xenakis's early training was as an engineer and architect, and he worked for Le Corbusier on a number of projects. Spatial elements have played an important part in many of his compositions, and his score for Aeschylus' *Oresteia* (1965–6) involved all aspects of theatre, including acting and singing, stage sets and visual spectacle. His most ambitious multi-media compositions have been a series of *Polytopes* mounted mainly at important historical sites, such as Persepolis in Iran, the Roman baths of Cluny in Paris and Mycenae in Greece. In the Paris *Polytope* (1972), in parallel with the electronic music on tape, there is a lighting score for 600 strobe lights, and for 400 mirrors reflecting the beams from three lasers, all mounted on metal scaffolding covering the surfaces of the building. The Mycenae event (1978), designed to illustrate the continuity of Greek language and culture and performed to an audience of over 10,000 per night, involved soloists, choirs, orchestra and electronic music broadcast across the landscape, processions of peasants, children and soldiers, anti-aircraft searchlights illuminating the mountains and clouds, fires, enormous cinema projections, and a flock of hundreds of goats with lamps and specially manufactured bells.

BIBLIOGRAPHY   Nouritza Matossian, *Xenakis*, Kahn and Averill, 19 86

G.C.P.

The Polytope *at the Thermes de Cluny near Paris (December 1973)*

VINCENT YOUMANS

Vincent Millie Youmans; *b* 27 September 1898, New York; *d* 5 April 1946, Denver, US

Vincent Youmans turned to music only after working on Wall Street and in the navy. George Gershwin's support secured him co-composer status for the musical *Three Little Girls in Blue*, and the success of that show paved the way for his three hits of the 1920s: *Wildflower*, *No! No! Nanette!*, and *Hit the Deck*. Though his ventures thereafter encompassed some ambitious experimental work, none met with any great success. After one well-received film score (*Flying Down to Rio*) Youmans retired suffering from tuberculosis in 1934. In the 1920s he was respected as much as any of the great Broadway composers, but is now remembered principally for the fine individual songs he wrote during his brief career rather than for complete scores – with one exception.

No! No! Nanette!

Musical comedy in three acts
Libretto by Otto Harbach and Frank Mandel, based on *My Lady Friends* by Emil Nyitray and Mandel; lyrics by Irving Caesar and Otto Harbach
PREMIERES 23 April 1923, Garrick Theatre, Detroit; UK: 11 March 1925, Palace Theatre, London

So popular during its try-out period that it had enjoyed two touring companies and a London production by the time it opened in New York in September 1925, *No! No! Nanette!* (shorn of its exclamation marks in revival) tells a simple story of family misunderstandings and resolutions in New York and Atlantic City. Two of its songs rank among the most infectiously familiar of the musical theatre: 'I want to be happy' and 'Tea for Two'.

RECORDING Gallagher, Keeler, Watson, Gilford, Van Davis, CBS, 1971: recording of a completely revised and reconceived version which has become the standard performing edition
EDITIONS v.s., Chappell/Harms, 1925; rev. version, v.s., Warner Bros, 1972

Other musicals include: *Two Little Girls in Blue* (with Paul Lannin), 1921; *Wildflower* (with Herbert Stothart), 1923; *Mary Jane McKane* (with Stothart), 1923; *Lollipop*, 1924; *Oh, Please!*, 1926; *Hit the Deck*, 1927; *Rainbow*, 1928; *Great Day*, 1929; *Smiles*, 1930; *Through the Years*, 1932
BIBLIOGRAPHY Gerald Bordman, *Days to be Happy, Years to be Sad: The Life and Music of Vincent Youmans*, OUP, 1982

J.A.C.

MAURICE YVAIN

b 12 February, 1891, Paris; *d* 28 July 1965, Suresnes, France

Yvain studied formally at the Paris Conservatoire but found his *métier* writing popular songs for the cabaret and café-concert. His numbers were later used in music-hall and revue, by singers such as Maurice Chevalier and Mistinguett ('Mon homme'). *Ta bouche* (1922) was an opérette in the new, comédie-musicale style: intimate, saucy, rapidly paced, and comparatively jazzy (though not yet quite in the truly American manner). *Là-haut* (1923), starring Chevalier, was a heavenly fantasy that reminded some of Offenbach, though the score was resolutely of the 1920s. Subsequent successes included *Bouche à bouche* and *Pas sur la bouche!* (both 1925) and other racily titled works. Later operettas were of the grand spectacle variety, including *Au soleil du Mexique* (1935) and *Chanson gitane* (1946), and there were several film scores. Recent revivals have revealed the infectious gaiety of the 'bouche' operettas.

Operettas: *Ta bouche*, 1921; *Là-haut*, 1923 (RECORDING Decca, 1960s); *Toutes les femmes*, 1923; *La dame en décolleté*, 1924; *Gosse de riche*, 1924; *Bouche à bouche*, 1925; *Pas sur la bouche!*, 1925; *Un bon garçon*, 1926; *Yes*, 1928; *Kadubec*, 1929; *Elle est à vous*, 1929; *Miami*, 1930; *Encore cinquante centimes*, 1931; *Paris qui brille*, 1931; *Vacances*, 1935; *Au soleil du Mexique*, 1935; *Chanson gitane*, 1947 (RECORDING Pathé, 1950s); *Le corsaire noir*, 1958
BIBLIOGRAPHY Maurice Yvain, *Ma belle opérette*, La Table Ronde, 1962

R.T.

IVAN ZAJC

Ivan Zajc [Giovanni von Zaytz]; *b* 3 August 1832, Rijeka;
d 16 December 1914, Zagreb

An extraordinarily prolific composer, with more than
1000 works to his name, Zajc dominated Croatian
music in the generation after Lisinski and effectively
re-created Croatian opera following the demise of
the Illyrian movement. He first studied music with
his father. In 1850 he enrolled at the Milan conservatory where his teachers included Lauro Rossi
and Mazzucato. In his final examinations he won
first prize with his opera *La Tirolese*. The death of
his parents forced him to return home, but in 1862
he moved to Vienna where he soon became a
celebrated composer and conductor of operettas,
alongside Suppé and Millöcker. In 1870 he returned
to Zagreb, where he was opera director until 1889
and director of the music school until his retirement
in 1908.

Zajc's operatic works are far more cosmopolitan
than those of his predecessors, their nationalism
more akin to Verdi's Risorgimento operas than to
the folk-based idioms of Glinka and Lisinski. His
most important opera, *Nikola Šubić Zrinjski*, is a
historical tragedy set during the years of Ottoman
domination, and successfully employs lyric and
heroic styles.

Operas: *La Tirolese*, 1855; *Amelia, ossia Il bandito*, 1860; *Die
Braut von Messina*, (*c.* 1860); *Die Hexe von Boissy*, 1866;
Mislav, 1870; *Ban Leget*, 1872; *Nicola Šubić Zrinjski*, 1876
(RECORDING Jugoton, 1960s); *Lizinka*, 1878; *Pan
Tvardovski*, 1880; *Zlatka*, 1885; *Gospoote i husari* (*Ladies and
Hussars*), 1886; *Kraljev hir* (*The King's Whim*), 1889; *Armida*,
1896; *I minatori*, (1899); *Postolar i vrag* (*The Cobbler and the
Devil*; concert opera), 1901; *Primorka*, 1901; *Oče naš* (*Our
Father*), 1911; *Prvi grijeh* (*Original Sin*), 1912
Operettas: 26 including: *Mannschaft an Bord*, 1863;
Fitzliputzli, 1864; *Die Lazzaroni von Neapel*, 1865;
Nachtschwärmer, 1866; *Das Rendezvous in der Schweiz*, 1867;
Das Gaugericht, 1867; *Nach Mekka*, 1868; *Somnambule*, 1868;
Der Meisterschuss von Pottenstein, 1868; *Meister Puff*, 1869;
Der gefangene Amor, 1874; *Afrodita*, 1888; *Noć u Kairu* (*A
Night in Cairo*), 1904; *Der Wilding*, 1905; *Nihilistica*, 1906
BIBLIOGRAPHY   Josip Andreis, trans. Vladimir Ivin, *Music
in Croatia*, Institute of Musicology/Academy of Music,
Zagreb, 1973, *rp*, 1982

M.A.

EVŽEN ZÁMEČNÍK

b 5 February 1939, Frýdek-Místek

After studies in Brno, Munich (1968–70), and as an
external student at the Prague Academy (1974–8),
Zámečník earned his living as a violinist in Brno
at the opera orchestra (1963–71) and in the State
Philharmonic (1971–81). In 1982 he became conductor and artistic director of the ensemble Brno
Brass-Band, and in 1989 dramaturg at the Brno
Opera. His accessible musical style is an amalgam of
essentially neo-classical and avant-garde techniques.
His works are mostly instrumental (including a
number for brass band), but his stage works, written
primarily with children in mind, have achieved
particular success and have been widely performed in
Czechoslovakia.

Ferdie the Ant

Ferda Mravenec
Children's opera in two parts (eight scenes)
Libretto by the composer, after Ondřej Sekora
Composed 1971
PREMIERE   1 June 1977, Janáček Opera House, Brno

Based on a popular Czech children's story (with a
cast of anthropomorphic insects), this is an opera
within an opera. The action takes place backstage
and the work has the didactic aim of introducing
children to the craft and poetics of opera, parading
a large vocabulary of operatic devices and styles.
The chief characters (including a pretty but rather
boastful ladybird) recur in an independent sequel,
Bag the Beetle.

Other operas: *Fraška o kádi* (*The Comedy of the Tub*), 1968;
Brouk Pytlík (*Bag the Beetle*), (1982), 1988
BIBLIOGRAPHY   Alena Martínková *et al.* (eds), *Čeští
skladatelé současnosti* (*Czech Composers of Today*), Panton,
1985

J.T.

RICCARDO ZANDONAI

Riccardo Antonio Francesco Zandonai; *b* 28 May 1883, Sacco
di Rovereto, Trentino, Italy; *d* 5 June 1944, Pesaro, Italy

Among the Italian composers born around 1880, Zandonai can on the whole be ranked as a traditionalist (he had studied for a time under Mascagni). However, he was never a mere imitator of his famous predecessors: he showed considerable enterprise in grafting aptly colourful details and piquant harmonic enrichments on to basically traditional stems.

His first opera to attract much attention was *Il grillo del focolare* (1908), which was well enough received to persuade Ricordi's publishing house to give him preferential treatment during the next few years – evidently regarding him as Puccini's natural successor. The firm even sent him to Spain to 'collect material' for his next opera, *Conchita*, which confirmed their hopes by gaining him his first major success. The peak of his operatic achievement was reached when *Francesca da Rimini* was launched in 1914, quickly winning worldwide fame.

None of Zandonai's later works succeeded in matching *Francesca*'s lasting popularity, and before long he showed dangerous signs of repeating himself: this is notably the case in *Giulietta e Romeo*, his second most frequently performed opera. *I cavalieri di Ekebù* is more interesting; and Zandonai's last completed opera, *La farsa amorosa* (1933), based on the same story as Falla's *The Three-Cornered Hat*, also deserves attention at its modest level: with two donkeys among its principal characters, the work revives aspects of the spirit of the old opera-buffa tradition.

Conchita

Opera in four acts (six scenes) (*c.* 1h 45m)
Libretto by Maurice Vaucaire and Carlo Zangarini, based on the novel *La femme et le pantin* Pierre Louÿs (1898)
Composed 1909–10
PREMIERES 14 October 1911, Teatro dal Verme, Milan; UK: 3 July 1912, Covent Garden, London; US: 28 September 1912, San Francisco

Vaucaire's adaptation of Louÿs's decadent novel was originally offered as the basis of a libretto for Puccini, who rejected it in 1907. That his doubts were well founded remains clear in the modified version set by Zandonai: for one thing, the partial parallels with *Carmen* are inescapable.

Initially Conchita, too, is a flirtatious worker in a cigarette factory in Seville; later she works as an erotic dancer. She differs from Carmen, however, in that she never fully yields to the men whom she brazenly leads on. Her main victim is Mateo, a rich young man who offers financial help to her and her mother, only to be rewarded by a series of cruel games in which Conchita's attitude to him seems to change capriciously. Yet the opera, unlike Louÿs's novel, has a wholly unconvincing happy ending, comparable, perhaps, to that of Puccini's *Turandot*.

By the time he wrote *Conchita*, Zandonai's basically Italian style was already being skilfully enriched by apt borrowings from Debussy and Strauss. The orchestration is colourful, the ensemble scenes vivacious, whereas the would-be passionate

music tends to seem more self-conscious. The score's principal virtue is its strong sense of the picturesque, with many Spanish touches which at times parallel Falla rather than recalling Bizet. The work is still occasionally heard in Italy.

RECORDING excerpts: Davy, Campora, Ch of Teatro Comunale, Bologna, San Remo SO, Gavarini, Cetra, 1961
EDITION v.s., Ricordi, 1911

Francesca da Rimini

Opera in four acts (five scenes) (2h 15m)
Libretto by Tito Ricordi, a shortened version of the play by Gabriele d'Annunzio (1901)
Composed 1912–13
PREMIERES 19 February 1914, Teatro Regio, Turin; UK: 16 July 1914, Covent Garden, London; US: 22 December 1916, Metropolitan, New York

Poster design by G. Palanti for Francesca da Rimini *(Milan, 1914)*

D'Annunzio's ornately colourful dramatic elaboration of the story from Dante's *Inferno* was heavily
cut for operatic purposes. The resultant work captured the popular imagination to a greater extent
than any other D'Annunzio opera: by 1976 it had
been produced (or revived) well over 200 times in
more than 20 countries.

Francesca has been promised in marriage to the
lame and brutal lord of Rimini, Gianciotto
Malatesta, whom she has never seen. To overcome
her expected resistance to the idea, her family tricks
her into thinking that Gianciotto's handsome
younger brother Paolo – who arrives as ambassador
from the Malatestas – is her husband-to-be: she falls
in love with him in a remarkable 'silent love duet',
which forms the serenely beautiful culmination of
Act I. Their love develops throughout the opera,
although the marriage to Gianciotto takes place: at
first the lovers keep their emotions to themselves;
but when Francesca finds Paolo slightly wounded
while the castle of Rimini is being attacked, she
reveals her feelings to him and finds them recip-
rocated. Their love bursts fully into flower while they
are reading together from a book about the love of
Lancelot and Guinevere. But Paolo's evil, one-
eyed younger brother Malatestino, also in love with
Francesca, becomes aware of what is going on and
arranges for Gianciotto to catch the pair together,
killing them on the spot.

As in *Conchita*, Zandonai's flair for picturesque
colour is much in evidence: his wish to create a
suitably 'medieval' atmosphere even led him to
feature a lute in the orchestra. The ensembles of
female voices include some of his most radiantly
beautiful inventions; whereas the Act II battle music,
though exciting enough, is undeniably crude in its
unbridled rhetoric. The characterization is on the
whole less original or persuasive than the evocation
of context. But despite the work's uneven quality, its
merits are more than sufficient to justify its lasting
success.

RECORDING   Kabaivanska, Matteuzzi, De Palma,
Manuguerra, Bulgarian Television and Radio Ch and SO,
Arena, RCA, 1988
EDITION   v.s., Ricordi, 1914

Giulietta e Romeo

Opera in three acts (four scenes) (1h 45m)
Libretto by Arturo Rossato [and Nicola d'Atri], freely based
on the stories by Luigi da Porto and Matteo Bandello from
which Shakespeare's play was partly derived
Composed 1920–21
PREMIERE   14 February 1922, Teatro Costanzi, Rome

Since the libretto was based mainly on Shakespeare's
sources, many well-known Shakespearean features
are disconcertingly absent. Apart from Romeo and
Giulietta themselves, Tebaldo (equivalent to, but
more important than, Tybalt) is the only named
member of either of the warring families who
appears. Friar Lawrence, too, is missing, and the
lovers die simultaneously. Though sharing some of
Francesca da Rimini's best qualities, the musical
invention of *Giulietta* is significantly less memorable.

Yet the work has been frequently revived in Italy,
and the vivid *Danza del torchio* and *Cavalcata di
Romeo* have a regular place in the Italian orchestral
repertoire.

RECORDING   Mazza-Medici, Lo Forese, Zanasi, Ch of the
Teatro Comunale, Bologna, San Remo SO, Gavarini, Cetra,
1961
EDITIONS   v.s., Ricordi, 1922

I cavalieri di Ekebù

The Cavaliers of Ekeby
Opera in four acts (1h 45m)
Libretto by Arturo Rossato, freely based on the novel *Gösta
Berlings Saga* by Selma Lagerlöf (1891)
Composed 1923–4
PREMIERES   7 March 1925, La Scala, Milan

A knowledge of the original novel is necessary if
one is fully to understand the strange plot of this
opera, which consequently won particular success in
Scandinavia, where *Gösta Berlings Saga* has enjoyed
lasting popularity.

Gösta Berling, a drunken unfrocked priest,
becomes a member of a band of former drop-outs
(the 'cavaliers' of the title) who have been given
protection and purpose by the lady of the Castle
of Ekeby, in western Sweden. Known as 'la
Comandante', she is the owner of some flourishing
ironworks, which are the mainstay of the local
economy; but when one of the cavaliers reveals to
her husband a sin from her past life, she is ruthlessly
driven from home. In her absence the management
of the ironworks passes to the cavaliers, who neglect
them until the starving local people compel them to
beg the Comandante to return. By now she is near to
death; but as she dies, she has the joy of seeing the
ironworks getting back into action, with the cavaliers
singing in praise of the work ethic.

Though eclectic as ever, Zandonai's music contains
new departures. The Scandinavian atmosphere is
evoked in dark, shadowy sonorities and occasional
echoes of Grieg, while the harmonic vocabulary sometimes reaches out at least as far into dissonance as
Puccini's *Turandot*.

RECORDINGS   Malatrasi, Barbieri, Picchi, Malaspina,
Zaccaria, Milan Ch and SO of Italian Radio, Simonetto,
MRF, 1958; excerpts: Hertzberg, Thorborg, Beyron, Larson,
O of Royal Theatre of Stockholm, Grevillius, Swedish EMI,
1974 (recorded 1928)
EDITION   v.s., Ricordi, 1925

Other operas: *La coppa del re*, (before 1907); *L'uccellino
d'oro* ('fiaba musicale'), 1907; *Il grillo del focolare*, 1908;
Melenis, 1912; *La via della finestra*, 1919, rev. 1923; *Giuliano*,
1928; *Una partita*, 1933; *La farsa amorosa*, 1933; *Il bacio*
(inc.), (1944), RAI 1954

BIBLIOGRAPHY   Bruno Cagnoli, *Riccardo Zandonai*,
Società di Studi Trentini di Scienze Storiche, Trent, 1978;
Renato Chiesa (ed.), *Riccardo Zandonai*, Unicopli, 1984

J.C.G.W.

WŁADYSŁAW ŻELEŃSKI
b 6 June 1837, Grodkowice, near Cracow; *d* 23 January 1921, Cracow

After Moniuszko, Żeleński was the most outstanding Polish opera composer of the late 19th century. He was also a pianist and teacher. In the years 1850–57 he studied at the Nowodworski College in Cracow and then in Prague and in Paris (1866–70). From 1872 Żeleński taught at the Musical Institute in Warsaw and from 1878 he was the artistic director of the Warsaw Musical Society. In 1881 he moved to Cracow where he founded the Conservatory of the Musical Society and wrote symphonies, chamber music, piano, organ and vocal works.

Żeleński continued the national current in music but with distinct classicist tendencies, modelled on German music. His first works, whose vocal writing is closely linked with song style, are lyrical operas, devoid of strong dramatic tension. The intensification of dramatic force in his later operas is influenced by Wagner.

Operas: *Konrad Wallenrod*, 1885; *Goplana*, 1896; *Janek*, 1900; *Stara baśń* (*The Ancient Tale*), 1907
BIBLIOGRAPHY   Z. Jachimecki, *Władysław Żeleński*, PWM, 1959

J.M.

CARL ZELLER
Carl Johann Adam Zeller; *b* 19 June 1842, St Peter in der Au; *d* 17 August 1898, Baden, nr Vienna

Zeller mastered several instruments as a child and his fine boy soprano voice took him into the Vienna Boys' Choir. He later studied law and music and went into the civil service, rising prominently in the Ministry of Arts and Education. His first comic opera, *Joconde* (1876), set in Scotland, attracted scant attention. But 15 years later *Der Vogelhändler* was a world hit, with its folksy Tyrolean setting (moved to the German Rhine Palatinate to avoid censorship problems), charming melodies and rich ensembles – plus a choice dialect part for its adored star, Alexander Girardi. *Der Obersteiger* (1894) carefully repeated the volksoperette formula and succeeded, in its day. Zeller's final years were clouded by a spinal injury and a resulting lawsuit, during which he was convicted of perjury. He suffered a stroke before his humiliating prison sentence was due to begin.

Operatic works: *Joconde*, 1876; *Die Fornarina*, 1878; *Capitän Nicoll*, 1880; *Der Vagabund*, 1886; *Der Vogelhändler*, 1891 (RECORDINGS Electrola, 1974; excerpts: Philips, *c.* 1954); *Der Obersteiger*, 1894; *Der Kellermeister* (completed Johann Brandl), 1901
BIBLIOGRAPHY   Otto Schneidereit, *Operette A–Z*, Henschelverlag, 1971; C. W. Zeller, *Mein Vater Carl Zeller*, St Pölten, 1942

R.T.

ALEXANDER ZEMLINSKY
Alexander [von] Zemlinsky [Zemlinszky]; *b* 14 October 1871, Vienna; *d* 15 March 1942, Larchmont, New York

Zemlinsky was a child of his time, his music eclectically reflecting the worlds in which he lived. He reached adulthood in Brahms-dominated Vienna and maturity during the turbulent *fin-de-siècle* period when *art nouveau* was the all-pervading artistic ambience, when Mahler (the greatest influence on his music) was director of the Vienna Court Opera and Viennese operetta was at its best. He reached his zenith during the First World War and the period of cultural turmoil that followed, and shared in the reaction against Expressionism and the demand for a 'new objectivity' characterized by Kurt Weill.

Alexander Zemlinsky

Zemlinsky was better known in his lifetime as a conductor than as a composer. In his early career the two paths ran parallel. He became conductor of Vienna's Carltheater in 1900 and the same year Mahler staged his second opera, *Es war einmal*, at the Vienna Court Opera, after advising the young composer on revising it and indeed composing 50 bars himself. In 1904 Zemlinsky moved to the newly opened Jubiläumtheater (later to become the Volksoper) and the same year launched a society to foster new music in Vienna with his brother-in-law and one-time pupil, Schoenberg. Three years later he joined Mahler at the Vienna Court Opera as a conductor, but after Mahler's resignation later that season his successor, Felix Weingartner, cancelled plans to produce Zemlinsky's third opera, *Der Traumgörge*, although it was already in rehearsal, and Zemlinsky resigned too. He returned to the Volksoper where he emulated Mahler's innovative repertoire planning, conducting the Viennese premieres of Dukas's *Ariane et Barbe-Bleue* and Strauss's *Salome*. From 1911 to 1927 Zemlinsky was opera director at the Neues Deutsches Theater in

Prague and it was here that he wrote his most significant works, while continuing his championship of modern music – including the world premiere of Schoenberg's *Erwartung* and employing members of the Schoenberg circle on his staff – as well as conducting much of the standard repertoire. Stravinsky praised his Mozart conducting (some of Zemlinsky's 1920s performances have been reissued on CD). In 1927 he moved to Berlin to be Klemperer's deputy at the Kroll Opera and stayed there until its closure in 1930. However he continued teaching at the Musikhochschule until 1933 when, in the wake of the Nazi takeover, he moved back to Vienna where he had no permanent post. In 1938 Hitler's *Anschluss* drove Zemlinsky, at 67, out of Europe. He settled in the United States but made little impact. Zemlinsky's music was virtually ignored from 1934 until the late 1970s when German and British radio stations and a handful of German opera houses began reviving it. He suffered from being closely connected with three major figures, Mahler, Schoenberg and Klemperer; but his posthumous recognition has benefited from these connections.

Sarema

Opera in three acts
Libretto by the composer after the play *Die Rose vom Kaukasus* by R. von Gottschall
Composed 1894–6
PREMIERE   10 October 1897, Hofoper, Munich

Zemlinsky's first opera won him the Luitpold Prize from Munich in 1896. The vocal score was partly prepared by his pupil Arnold Schoenberg.

EDITION   v.s., Berté, 1899

Es war einmal

Once Upon a Time
Opera in a prologue and three acts (five scenes) (1h 45m)
Libretto by Maximilian Singer after the triptych of Danish folk-tales by Holger Drachmann
Composed and revised 1897–9
PREMIERES   22 January 1900, Hofoper, Vienna; UK: 1 June 1989, BBC Radio 3 (studio co-production by members of the European Broadcasting Union)

This fairy-story opera is a cross between *Turandot* and *The Taming of the Shrew*. A princess spurns all noble suitors until her father, the king, banishes her for publicly kissing a gypsy, his prize for telling her a secret. In Act II she becomes his wife and gradually falls in love with him, becoming his helpmate too. In Act III a handsome prince is jilted by his bride but, Cinderella-like, the girl who fits her wedding dress will become his wife. It fits the gypsy/princess perfectly. She protests in vain; only then does she realize that her gypsy husband is the prince in disguise. He has won her heart and they live happily ever after.

The music is dramatically effective; it contains some folklike melodies, others with Brahmsian textures and others with Wagnerian heroic harmonies. At Mahler's suggestion Zemlinsky revised the score, thinning some of the orchestral textures and making some of the vocal lines more effective. He expanded the orchestral interlude between the Prologue and Act I and made cuts, including tightening the opening and closing of Act III. He completely rewrote the ending of Act I, using thematic material from the next act, to make more of this pivotal moment in which the change from near-operetta to darker matters heralds the deeper exploration of the princess's psychology.

RECORDING   Johansson, Westi, Haugland, Danish Radio SO, Graf, Largo, 1987: the EBU performance of the revised version
MANUSCRIPTS   Library of Congress, Washington, and Stadtbibliothek, Vienna
EDITION   rev. version: J. Maegaard (ed.), Ricordi, 1990

Der Traumgörge

Görge the Dreamer
Opera in two acts and an epilogue (2h 15m)
Libretto by Leo Feld, rev. Johannes Wattke
Composed 1903–6
PREMIERE   11 October 1980, Nuremberg Music Theatre

Zemlinsky's third opera sets another fairy-story; its underlying message reflects Zemlinsky's obsessive concern with the hero as outsider coupled with the conflict between 'art for the artist's sake' and 'art as an expression of reality'.

SYNOPSIS
Act I   Görge, an aesthetic daydreamer, prefers the beautiful fantasies of his books to reality. His fiancée, Grete, wants him to be more practical, like the down-to-earth Hans. On their betrothal day Görge imagines a princess calling him to go out and conquer the world. He follows this call and abandons Grete. The vision is illusory.

Act II   Several years later he has become an outcast, loved only by Gertrude, another outsider, widely held to be a witch. But when Görge has a chance to lead a revolution (his gift for words makes him the peasants' natural leader) his followers cannot accept his relationship with Gertrude. He abandons them.

Epilogue   He returns with Gertrude to his village where he uses his inheritance for good works and settles into a conventional existence. He realizes that Gertrude is his visionary princess and through her his dreams have come true.

Zemlinsky never heard this opera. It was in rehearsal at the Vienna Court Opera in 1907 but after Mahler's resignation the production was cancelled and Zemlinsky seems not to have promoted it further. The complete performance material lay forgotten in the Opera's archives until the late 1970s.

RECORDING   Martin, Coburn, Protschka, Frankfurt Radio SO, Albrecht, Capriccio, 1987: a live performance of a heavily cut concert version (omitting 30m of music) but it gives a flavour of the score
EDITIONS   v.ss., limited edition, Karzcag und Wallner, *c.* 1907; Ricordi, 1990

Kleider machen Leute

Clothes Make the Man

Musical comedy in a prologue and two acts (1h 45m)
Libretto by Leo Feld after the novella by Gottfried Keller
(1860)
Composed 1907–10 (in a prologue and three acts), rev. 1922
PREMIERES 2 October 1910, Volksoper, Vienna; rev.
version: 20 April 1922, Neues Deutsches Theater, Prague;
UK: 5 May 1989, BBC Radio 3 (recording from Vienna
Volksoper, June 1985)
CAST Wenzel Strapinski *t*, Nettchen *s*, Melchior Bohni *bar*,
5 *s*, 4 *t*, 4 *bar*, 2 *b*, 1 *spoken role* (male); *satb* chorus of men
and women from Goldach and Seldwyla
LARGE ORCHESTRA onstage: band (8 players), pf

This was the only Zemlinsky opera premiered under
his own baton. Its musical style is closer to the
Viennese operetta tradition of Lehár than to the
intensity of Richard Strauss but the humour lacks the
lightness of either.

SYNOPSIS (revised version)
Prologue In mid-19th-century Seldwyla, Switzerland, Wenzel Strapinski, a Polish tailor, decides to
leave and seek his fortune. He is offered a lift to
Goldach, the neighbouring town, in a splendid
stagecoach.
    Act I The coach rolls into Goldach and the
coachman starts a rumour that his passenger is a
count. The citizens are respectful, entertaining him
lavishly and even replacing the luggage he claims to
have lost. The daughter of one of them, Nettchen,
already engaged to a boring older man, finds the
'count' very attractive, and he her. However, the
jealous fiancé is suspicious of the needle marks on
the tailor's fingers and decides to investigate.
    Act II The next day the romance between
Strapinski and Nettchen develops. Their love duet is
overheard by her fiancé but when faced with his
accusation of infidelity Nettchen, to both men's
dismay, announces that she and Strapinski are to
marry. Her father invites everyone to a celebration
that evening. By then her former fiancé has traced
Strapinski's humble origins and unmasks him in a
masque of 'costumes through the ages' which
climaxes in another tailor donning a grand coat
identical to Strapinski's. But Strapinski reminds them
that he made no claim for himself; it was the
townsfolk who treated him like an aristocrat. The
only person he has deceived was Nettchen. She stops
him leaving, saying that even if she can't be a
countess, she can still be the wife of a master tailor.

The music illustrates the characters rather than
develops their personalities – the pompous *petit-
bourgeois* town merchants, with their propensity for
cheap waltzes; the fiancé's malicious jealousy,
displayed in an orchestral interlude in Act II; the
folklike innocence of the tailor, and the harmonically
freer music of the love between him and Nettchen.
The emotional language is restrained – Lehár shorn
of the overblown sentiments – and the sound and
shape of the music redolent of Mahler's *Des Knaben
Wunderhorn*.

RECORDING Mathis, Winkler, Slabbert, Ch and O of
Zurich Opera, Weikert, Koch-Schwann, 1991
EDITIONS v.ss., original version, Bote und Bock, 1911; rev.
version, Universal, 1922

Eine florentinische Tragödie

A Florentine Tragedy

Opera in one act, Op. 16 (55m)
Libretto: the play by Oscar Wilde (1894), trans. Max
Meyerfeld
Composed 1915–14 March 1916
PREMIERES 30 January 1917, Württembergisches
Staatstheater, Stuttgart; US: 22 April 1982, Manhattan School
of Music, New York; UK: 22 August 1983, King's Theatre,
Edinburgh (Hamburg Staatsoper)
CAST Bianca *ms*, Guido Bardi *t*, Simone *b*
FULL ORCHESTRA

With this opera, premiered by his fellow composer
and opera-house director Max von Schillings,
Zemlinsky achieved a modest international success
and, together with his other Wilde opera (*Der
Zwerg*), it re-established his reputation in the 1980s.
The emotionally ambiguous plot is typically *fin de
siècle*, the music capturing the hot-house atmosphere
of the lovers' ardour. Zemlinsky stipulated that the
opera be illuminated only by shadowy moonlight.

SYNOPSIS
Simone, a merchant in 16th-century Florence, returns
home early and finds his wife, Bianca, with Guido,
the Duke of Florence's son. Initially he feigns
innocence and fawningly tries to sell the aristocrat
some of his fabulous fabrics and drinks with him.
Gradually Simone's comments become more barbed,
Guido's less circumspect and Bianca's more reckless.
When it becomes clear that Simone knows that they
are having an affair the two men duel, Bianca at first
urging on Guido to kill her husband and liberate her
love for him; but after Guido falls mortally wounded
Bianca realizes that what she really needed was
for her husband to assert himself. The couple are
reconciled over the corpse of her lover.

The opera is dominated by Simone. Zemlinsky's
edgy, atmospheric music heightens his barely repressed fury, the malevolence behind the volubility and
the apparent sincerity of Wilde's character. Bianca
and Guido are given few words but her hatred
for Simone and the contempt in which Guido holds
him are portrayed through iridescent colours and
searing nervous energy. As in Richard Strauss's
Der Rosenkavalier (1911), their passionate love-
making is depicted exhilaratingly in the orchestral
prelude before the curtain rises, and its music returns
briefly as part of their later love duet; Zemlinsky
places this for maximum dramatic effect at the
moment of maximum danger, as the likelihood of
Simone discovering their affair increases with the
lovers' every heedless moment. Guido's death occurs
over a desperate, violent, descending scale – a simple
device but here dramatically convincing and
musically cathartic.

RECORDING   Soffel, Riegel, Sarabia, Berlin Radio SO, Albrecht, Schwann, 1985
EDITION   v.s., Universal, 1916

Der Zwerg
The Dwarf
Ein tragisches Märchen für Musik in one act, Op. 17 (1h 30m)
Libretto by Georg C. Klaren, after the story *The Birthday of the Infanta* by Oscar Wilde (1888)
Composed 1920–4 January 1921
PREMIERES   28 May 1922, Theater am Habsburger Ring, Cologne; UK: 22 August 1983, King's Theatre, Edinburgh (Hamburg Staatsoper)
CAST   Donna Clara, the Infanta *s*, Dwarf *t*, Ghita *s*, Don Estoban *b*, 3 ladies-in-waiting 3 *s*; *sa* chorus of the Infanta's entourage (playmates, maids and ladies); beggars *silent*
FULL ORCHESTRA   small offstage band

With this opera Zemlinsky returned to a subject he had considered a decade earlier, the explosion that can result when physical deformity becomes a barrier to emotional fulfilment. *Der Zwerg* might sum up the predicament of Zemlinsky himself: a short, unattractive man who never recovered from the ending of his relationship with Alma Mahler and who constantly sought the company of young women. *Der Zwerg* was his most successful opera with performances in Vienna, Prague and Berlin. It has been at the forefront of the Zemlinsky revival.

SYNOPSIS
The Spanish Infanta's best birthday present is a proud but melancholy dwarf who is entirely unaware of his grotesque appearance. The Infanta and her friends are ordered to cover the mirrors so he cannot see himself; the truth would kill him. He mournfully explains that he was an orphan, sold to a sultan, knowing neither mother nor homeland; everyone laughs at him and only God loves him. Although he is a court singer he wants to sing only sad songs when he sees the Infanta. They play together. In her childish way, she tells him she loves him and he realizes he truly loves her. His passion grows; she is the first person not to mock him and she gives him a present of a white rose. But the Infanta selfishly remarks that he is different from her and orders her maid Ghita to show him a mirror. The kindly Ghita refuses but eventually the dwarf sees his reflection and realizes the truth. He begs the Infanta to tell him the image is not him. She cruelly tells him she will still play with him but only as one would with an animal; one must love people. As the dwarf dies, his heart broken, he begs for the white rose.

This tragic story is matched by a characteristically eclectic score. The dance rhythms have a Spanish flavour and the orchestration accompanying the girls is iridescent with clear, neo-classical textures. The Infanta's music underlines her treatment of the dwarf as a toy. Her emotion is synthetic; whenever the games cease her music matches her brittle, spoilt personality. The dwarf, however, is real. Growling, jerky trombones and tuba characterize his ugliness

while his claim to be the princess's knight in shining armour is set to Wagnerian mock heroics. But his love music has a radiant innocence and the anguish of his self-awakening, his rejection and death have a shattering, Mahlerian melancholy intensified at its catharsis by echoes of the rest of the world, unconcerned, outside.

For the production that relaunched the work, by the Hamburg State Opera in 1982, the text was rewritten by Adolf Dresen to correspond more closely to the original Oscar Wilde story, making the dwarf an abducted, uneducated and absurd peasant, not an innocent courtier used to royal palaces, and making several cuts. This version significantly changes the relationship between text and music.

RECORDING   as *Der Geburtstag der Infantin*, using the rev. version of the text: Nielsen, Riegel, Berlin Radio SO, Albrecht, Schwann, 1984
EDITIONS   f.s., Universal, 1923; v.s., Universal, 1921

Der Kreidekreis
The Chalk Circle
Opera in three acts (seven scenes) (2h 30m)
Libretto after the play by Klabund (pseudonym for Alfred Henschke) (1923)
Composed 1930–8 October 1932
PREMIERES   14 October 1933, Stadttheater, Zurich; US: 12 May 1988, Cincinnati University, Ohio
CAST   Tschang-Haitang *s*, Tschang-Ling *bar*, Pao *t*, Ma *bar*, Yu-Pei *s*, *a*, *t*, *bar*, *spoken role*, several *silent*
LARGE ORCHESTRA including 2 sax and banjo

In the decade between *Der Zwerg* and *Der Kreidekreis* Zemlinsky composed only three works. Two of them later formed the cornerstones of his posthumous rehabilitation, the Third String Quartet (1924) and the Lyric Symphony (1922), a setting for soprano, baritone and orchestra of poems by the Indian writer Rabindranath Tagore. (The third work, unperformed until 1965, was the seven Symphonic Songs, Op. 20 (1929), settings of German translations of poems by Afro-Americans – Langston Hughes, Countee Cullen, Frank Horne and Jean Toomer.) In choosing a Chinese setting for his next opera Zemlinsky again looked outside Europe, widening still further his literary sources. The 1920s also saw a profound change of taste in Germany, to the *Neue Sachlichkeit* ('new objectivity') exemplified musically by Weill, Hindemith and Krenek. Composers who did not change their style accordingly generally found opera-house doors closed to them or publishers uncooperative. Although the rise of the Nazis further complicated matters for Jewish composers such as Zemlinsky, *Der Kreiderkreis* was performed in 1934 in Nazi Germany. But in *Der Kreidekreis* Zemlinsky had paid 'objectivity' lip-service by parodying different styles to characterize his somewhat cardboard characters and situations.

SYNOPSIS
In ancient China a husband has committed suicide, provoked by the mandarin Ma's inhumane taxes; his son, Tschang-Ling, has become a revolutionary

dreamer while his penniless widow is reduced to selling their daughter, Tschang-Haitang, to a bordello.

Act I   In the bordello Haitang has two suitors, Prince Pao and Ma himself. Ma wins her.

Act II   Haitang's beautiful nature transforms the cruel mandarin. She persuades her brother to postpone his plan to assassinate him and Ma, now in love with Haitang, abandons his childless first wife, Yu-Pei, for her and their newborn son. He proposes changing his will in their favour but Yu-Pei hears about it, poisons the mandarin and accuses Haitang of the murder.

Act III   Yu-Pei bribes the judge and produces perjured evidence that Haitang was the murderer and that Haitang's son is actually Yu-Pei's, in which case Yu-Pei will inherit the mandarin's estate. But before the judge's death sentence can be effected news comes that the old emperor has died and his successor, Prince Pao, is reviewing all capital sentences. On their way to Peking Haitang and her brother are trapped in a blizzard when they encounter some coarse soldiers (who arrest the brother for observing that the new emperor will be as corrupt as any other ruler). In Peking Pao draws a chalk circle around the baby; whoever pulls him out of the circle is the real mother. Yu-Pei wins easily but Pao declares that Haitang has proved her motherhood by refusing a tug-of-war which would risk hurting her child. Pao then confesses that he had secretly gained access to Haitang's bedroom on the first night she spent at Ma's (she had believed their love-making was just a beautiful dream) and that the boy is their son. Haitang becomes empress.

Der Kreidekreis contains spoken dialogue, melodrama and singing. The vocal writing is frequently declamatory arioso. Only for the good characters, Haitang, Pao and Ma (but only in Act II), does Zemlinsky write with his own voice – exuberant, red-blooded and intensely lyrical. For his evil characters he uses a variety of parodies: pastiche Kurt Weill, with prominent saxophones and characteristically sinuous melodies, for the opening scene in the bordello from which Haitang is sold; complicated Stravinskian rhythms with strong, declamatory writing for the brutal mandarin Ma in Act I before Haitang transforms him; a Mahlerian military march when the soldiers arrive in the blizzard. Oriental colour is simulated through occasional pentatonic melodies and harmonies based on fourths.

RECORDING   Behle, Ottenthal, Goldberg, Peper, Hermann, Helm, Berlin Radio SO, Soltesz, Capriccio, 1990
EDITIONS   f.s., Universal, 1933; v.s., Universal, 1932

Der König Kandaules
King Candaules
Opera in three acts
Libretto by the composer after the German adaptation by Franz Blei of the play *Le roi Candaule* by André Gide (1901)
Composed 14 May 1935–29 December 1936 (short score, 137 pages orchestrated), orch. completed by Antony Beaumont
PREMIERE   scheduled for autumn 1996, Staatsoper, Hamburg

CAST   König Kandaules *dramatic t*, Gyges *dramatic bar*, Nyssia *dramatic s*, 3 *t*, 2 *bar*, 4 *b*, *silent*; *tb* chorus of guests, offstage voices; servants *silent*
LARGE ORCHESTRA including hp, cel; onstage: 2 fl, hp, vla, tambourine

In 1933, on leaving Nazi Germany, Zemlinsky decided to abandon his career as an opera conductor and return to his native Vienna to devote the greater part of his energies to composition. Works dating from this period include the Fourth String Quartet (1936) and *Der König Kandaules*. After Zemlinsky's death the manuscript remained in the Library of Congress, Washington DC, until Antony Beaumont began work on it in 1989.

In ancient Lydia, the king, Kandaules, throws a banquet at which his queen, Nyssia, is to appear for the first time in public unveiled. A magic ring is found embedded in the flesh of a fish that is served at the royal table. Gyges, an uncouth but honest fisherman, is called before the king to account for his catch. Kandaules is fascinated by Gyges, dressing him in fine clothes and heaping riches upon him. Gyges unwillingly takes the magic ring, later exploiting its powers not only to see Nyssia naked but also to spend a night in her arms. Finally he murders Kandaules and orders Nyssia to resume the veil; she refuses, saying, 'Kandaules has torn it to shreds.'

In the death of the king, the opera can be seen as an allegory of the end of an epoch of Western music; the new dynasty founded by Gyges symbolizes the new music as advocated by Zemlinsky's friend Schoenberg. Zemlinsky himself described the music of this opera as 'ultra-modern': it moves logically and boldly from pentatonicism and diatonicism through bitonality and polytonality to the very threshold of atonality. The composer never previously achieved proportions so perfect, nor demonstrated his sense of theatre so tellingly, as in *Der König Kandaules*.

RECORDING   Prelude to Act III and monologue: Grundheber, Hamburg State SO, Albrecht, Capriccio, 1993
EDITION   v.s., Ricordi, 1993

Incomplete operas: (all manuscripts in the Library of Congress, Washington DC) *Malwa*, (1913); *Der heilige Vitalis*, 1915; *Raphael, oder Das Chagrinleder*, (1918); *Circe*, (1939)
BIBLIOGRAPHY   R. Stephan, *Alexander Zemlinsky: ein unbekannter Meister der Wiener Schule*, Kieler Beitrage zur Musikwissenschaft, 1978; Horst Weber, *Alexander Zemlinsky, Österreichische Komponisten des XX. Jahrhunderts*, vol. 23, Verlag Elisabeth Lafite/Österreichischer Bundesverlag fur Unterricht, Vienna, 1977

C.B. and A.C.W.B.

MARC'ANTONIO ZIANI
b c. 1653, Venice; *d* 22 January 1715, Vienna

Ziani's earliest Venetian productions were adaptations of operas composed for Vienna by Cesti and

Draghi. Between 1679 and the end of the century Ziani was active as an opera composer in Venice, while also maintaining links with the Mantuan court in the capacity of maestro at S. Barbara. His first opera, *Alessandro Magno in Sidone* (1679), was repeated in the same year in Naples, perhaps thanks to his uncle's influence there. With the Gonzaga line in Mantua coming to an end, Ziani made approaches to Leopold I, for instance in the dedication of his oratorio *Il giudizio di Salamone*. The emperor employed him and in 1700 Ziani became vice-hofkapellmeister (and later hofkapellmeister) in Vienna, thus following his uncle Pietro Andrea in taking the Venetian operatic tradition across the Alps. In the following 15 years he composed 20 stage works for the court theatre. Ziani has been criticized for a tendency to neglect overall structure, but his instrumental writing is particularly colourful and makes notable use of solo obbligati. He shared with his uncle a lightness of touch and an ability to delineate character which ensured the popularity of their operas on both sides of the Alps.

Extant operas: *Alessandro Magno in Sidone*, 1679; *L'Alcibiade*, 1680; *Damira placata*, 1680; *La Flora* (coll. with A. Sartorio), 1681; *Tullo Ostilio*, 1685; *La Rosalinda*, 1692; *La Costanza in trionfo* (only arias survive), 1696; *Il Gordiano Pio*, 1700; *L'Esopo* (only Act III survives), 1702; *Caio Popilio*, 1704; *L'Ercole vincitor dell'invidia*, 1706; *La Flora*, 1706; *Il Meleagro*, 1706; *Introduzione per musica al problema della prima accademia . . . se si possi trovare un'amore senza speranza*, 1706; *Introduzione per musica al problema della seconda accademia . . . sè più innamori bella donna che pianga overo bella donna, che canti*, 1706; *Alboino* (only Act III survives), 1707; *Il Campidoglio ricuperato*, 1709; *Chilonida*, 1709; *L'Atenaide* (coll. with Negri, Caldara and Conti), 1711 or 1714; *Andromeda*, 1714; 27 lost operas

G.D.

PIETRO ANDREA ZIANI

b ?before 21 December 1616, Venice; *d* 12 February 1684, Naples

Ziani was a member of the community of S. Salvatore in Venice and its organist, but even his earliest music from the 1640s – including madrigals and canzonette – shows a preference for secular forms. From the mid-1650s, probably having left the order, he composed a number of operas for Venice, and for two years from 1657 he directed the music at the prestigious church of S. Maria Maggiore in Bergamo. Associations with noble patrons in the 1660s took him further north, and he worked in Innsbruck, Vienna and Dresden. In 1669 he succeeded Cavalli as first organist at St Mark's, Venice, and seven years later followed him as maestro. He attended performances of his own works in Naples in 1677, and never returned to Venice, accepting instead appointments at court and the Conservatorio S. Onofrio there.

Ziani was one of the leading Venetian opera composers of the generation of Cavalli; through his influence opera gained in popularity north of the

Alps. Eight of his operas from the 1660s were performed in Vienna, and he was a regular provider of works for the Venetian, and later the Neapolitan, stage. The characterization in Ziani's operas is notable, as is his emphasis on comic scenes with fast-moving recitative, reminiscent of the exchanges of real speech. He felt that the public had lost the appetite for serious opera, and was happy to provide them with farce and satire, even parodying the major figures of Classical history to achieve his ends. He contributed to the establishment of elements such as the use of *siciliano* rhythm and string accompaniments to arias, but perhaps his greatest contribution lay in the creation of a favourable climate for opera in Vienna, and in influencing his nephew, Marc'Antonio, to take advantage of it.

Extant operas: *Le fortune di Rodope e di Damira*, 1657; *L'Antigona delusa da Alceste*, 1660; *L'Annibale in Capua*, 1661; *Gli scherzi di Fortuna subordinato al Pirro*, 1662; *Le fatiche d'Ercole per Deianira*, 1662; *La ricreazione burlesca*, 1663 or 1668; *L'Amor guerriero*, 1663; *L'Invidia conculcata dalla Virtù, Merito, Valore della S.C. Mta di Leopoldo imperatore*, 1664; *Cloridea*, 1665; *La Circe*, 1665; *L'Elice*, 1666; *La Galatea*, 1667; *La Semiramide*, 1670; *L'Ippolita Reina delle amazzoni* (coll. with Busca and Agostini), 1670; *L'Heraclio*, 1671; *Attila*, 1672; *Candaule*, 1679; *L'innocenza risorta, overo Etio*, 1683, rev. as *Il Talano preservato*, 1683 (EDITION H. M. Brown (ed.), Garland, 1978); 10 lost operas

G.D.

CARL MICHAEL ZIEHRER

b 2 May 1843, Vienna; *d* 14 November 1922, Vienna

The son of a prosperous hatter, Ziehrer was sent to the Vienna Conservatory. In 1863, with help from a Viennese music publisher, and financing from his father, he conducted his own dance orchestra. He composed dance music, while at the same time becoming a top military bandmaster, eventually leading the prestigious *Hoch und Deutschmeister* Nr 4 regiment band. Not surprisingly, it is the waltzes and marches that provide the most memorable passages in his operettas.

Operettas appeared from 1866, including one with an American Indian setting, *Der bleiche Zauberer* (after James Fenimore Cooper), but Ziehrer's first notable success was with *Die Landstreicher* (1899). It had several long summertime runs, but is seldom revived today. Of Ziehrer's other operettas only *Der Fremdenführer* (1902) still reappears occasionally in Vienna, but his marches are still Austrian national treasures. In 1908 he became the last imperial and royal hofballmusikdirektor, succeeding the Johann Strausses.

Operettas: *Das Orakel zu Delphi*, 1872; *König Jerome*, 1878; *Alexander der Grosse*, 1879; *Ein kleiner Don Juan*, 1879; *Wiener Kinder*, 1881; *Ein Deutschmeister*, 1888; *Die schöne Rigo*, 1898; *Die Landstreicher*, 1899; *Die drei Wünsche*, 1901; *Der Fremdenführer*, 1902; *Der Schätzmeister*, 1904; *Fesche Geister*, 1905; *Ein tolles Mädel*, 1907; *Am Lido*, 1907; *Der Liebeswalzer*, 1908; *Herr und Frau Biedermeier*, 1909; *Der*

Gaukler, 1909; *In fünfz ig Jahren*, 1911; *Ball bei Hof*, 1911; *Manöverkinder*, 1912; *Fürst Casimir*, 1913; *Das dumme Herz*, 1914; *Es war ein schöne Zeit*, 1918
BIBLIOGRAPHY Max Schönherr, *C. M. Ziehrer: sein Werk, sein Leben, seine Zeit*, Österreichischer Bundesverlag, 1974

R.T.

BERND ALOIS ZIMMERMANN
b 20 March 1918, Bliesheim, Cologne; *d* 10 August 1970, Königsdorf, Cologne

Brought up under the Nazis, Zimmermann is the classic instance in music of the psychological instabilities of post-war Germany. A pupil of Philipp Jarnach during the war, and of Wolfgang Fortner and René Leibowitz after it, he emerged as a composer at a time when a slightly younger generation of new composers was adopting extreme solutions to the problems of recent European history. Zimmermann was trained in serial method. He attended the Darmstadt Ferienkursen in 1948–50, and much of his early music shares the angular lines and intellectual schemes cultivated there. But there is always a feeling in these instrumental works that a tortured spirit is fighting to escape from mental prison. In his only opera, *Die Soldaten*, the spirit finally breaks out, and on its many levels this work is one of the most characteristic products of early 1960s Germany, with its desperate need to reject its own intellectual and military history while rummaging in that history for causes, explanations and scapegoats.

Die Soldaten established a pluralist, associative style which was to become Zimmermann's trademark, and was to serve him in several striking works during the last decade of his life. These works show increasing intellectual as well as stylistic anxiety. It could well be that the generous use of quotation in the *Requiem für einen jungen Dichter* shows too much faith in the artistic power of good credentials. It certainly looks, in any case, as if Zimmerman was personally overtaken by the menace of history. In August 1970 he took his own life, apparently in blank despair at the state of the world.

Die Soldaten
The Soldiers
Opera in four acts (1hr 45m)
Libretto by the composer, after the play by Jakob Michael Reinold Lenz (1776)
Composed 1958–60, rev. 1963–4
PREMIERES 15 February 1965, Cologne Opera House; UK: 21 August 1972, King's Theatre, Edinburgh (Deutsche Oper am Rhein); US: 22 January 1982, Boston
CAST Wesener *b*, Marie *very dramatic coloratura s*, Charlotte *ms*, Wesener's Old Mother *low a*, Stolzius *youthful high bar*, Stolzius's Mother *very dramatic a*, Obrist *b*, Desportes *very high t*, Pirzel *high t*, Eisenhardt *heroic bar*, Haudy *heroic bar*, Mary *bar*, Countess de la Roche *ms*, Her Son *very high lyrical t*, 3 *very high t* (or *dramatic s*), 4 *actors, dancers*, 18 officers and cadets *spoken roles*, and stage percussion
VERY LARGE ORCHESTRA including 5 Wagner tubas, 8/9 perc-players, gtr, hpd, pf, organ duet; separate stage perc and jazz combo; 3 film screens, 3 film projectors, loudspeakers

Edith Gabry (Marie) in Die Soldaten *(Cologne, 1965)*

Lenz's play was based on an incident he himself had witnessed in Strasburg. A friend – an aristocratic soldier in the French garrison – had failed to honour a marriage contract with the daughter of a Strasburg jeweller. The play is a bitter attack on the tendency of an idle and peripatetic soldiery to ruin local girls in this way, but attributes the problem partly to the fact that the soldiers were on oath to remain unmarried. Zimmermann characteristically generalizes this plot into a rambling attack on soldiers everywhere, with the setting transferred to French Flanders.

SYNOPSIS
Act I Scene 1 (Strofe): After a long opening prelude, the curtain rises on the house of the fancy-goods dealer, Wesener, in Lille. His daughter Marie is writing to the mother of her fiancé, the draper Stolzius, in Armentières. Scene 2 (Ciacona I), the letter is received and Stolzius is teased by his mother. Scene 3 (Ricercari I): Back in Lille, Marie is courted by Desportes, a French officer. But Wesener refuses him permission to take Marie to the theatre. Later he lectures her on the dubious morals of soldiers. Scene 4 (Toccata I): On the old town moat in Armentières, French officers discuss their leisure activities. Captain Haudy defends the theatre and its attendant debauchery against the disapproval of the chaplain Eisenhardt. Scene 5 (Nocturno I) returns us to Lille, where Wesener advises Marie to discourage neither the aristocratic Desportes nor Stolzius.

Act II Scene 1 (Toccata II): In the crowded Armentières coffee house, Eisenhardt deplores Haudy's plot to lure Marie away from Stolzius. The officers tease Stolzius about Desportes's designs on his fiancée. Scene 2 (Capriccio, Corale and Ciacona II) has three simultaneous settings. In Lille Desportes seduces Marie, who has received a scolding letter from Stolzius; in the same place, but on a darkened stage, Marie's grandmother sings of her coming ruin; in Armentières Stolzius and his mother receive Marie's reply, written with Desportes's help.

Act III   Scene 1 (Rondino): Eisenhardt remarks with concern to Captain Pirzel that Captain Mary has also taken lodgings in Lille. Scene 2 (Rappresentazione): Meanwhile, in Lille, Stolzius takes a post as Mary's batman. Scene 3 (Ricercari II): Mary arrives with Stolzius to take Marie for a drive. She only half-recognizes Stolzius. Scene 4 (Nocturno II) introduces the Countess de la Roche, a philanthropic aristocrat. Her son, too, is involved with Marie, and the Countess determines to save her. In Scene 5 (Tropi) she visits Marie and engages her as companion.

Act IV   Scene 1 (Toccata III): Marie has run away and threatens to rejoin Desportes (who is now in prison); wanting to be rid of her, he offers Marie to his gamekeeper, who rapes her. This is shown on film, while a complex stage action, in the Armentières coffee house, suggests various levels of interpretation, culminating in the question, 'Must those who suffer evil be afraid?' Scene 2 (Ciacona III): Mary and Desportes are at dinner, waited on by Stolzius. They discuss Marie contemptuously, but Stolzius has poisoned Desportes. As he dies, Stolzius walks on to Mary's sword. Scene 3 (Nocturno III): Wesener is accosted by a beggarwoman by the river Lys. He fails to recognize his own daughter. As he hands her a coin she sinks to the ground.

In its montage of short scenes and savage anti-military satire, the play looks forward half a century to *Woyzeck* (whose author, Georg Büchner, wrote a novel about Lenz). Zimmermann took the hint, and the Berg of *Wozzeck* (as well as of *Lulu*) is an obvious father figure of *Die Soldaten*. Zimmermann not only uses film, but also various musical layering techniques. Berg's associative methods (dance music in *Wozzeck*, film in *Lulu*) are greatly extended, while his touches of quasi-cinematic montage become a standard device. Zimmermann uses actual film, both to extend the scope of Lenz's action and to bring in newsreel associations. More interestingly, he has multi-level scenes depicting simultaneous or non-sequential actions. Finally he adopts Berg's device of associating each scene with a musical genre (chaconne, toccata, ricercar, etc.); moreover by giving different scenes the same generic name, he suggests connections between them, a procedure not found in Berg. Bach chorales pop up in more or less straightforward arrangements to suggest an apocalyptic view of the action. Pop music and jazz accompany a ballet sequence in Act II Scene 1. The dense overlaying of styles and texts comes to a climax in the final act, where Eisenhardt's voice intones the Lord's Prayer in Latin to the accompaniment of tapes of military commands, the sound of 'unrestrained weeping', 'hopeless moaning', and so forth. Pop music emanates (along with a crowd of drunken soldiers) from a dance hall, while film of military equipment, tanks, etc., reminds us that all evil is ultimately one: a valid if not startling observation.

Is *Die Soldaten* more than the sum of its parts? It hardly seems so now that its early vogue (especially in Germany) has subsided. Dramatically it is one-paced, and Zimmermann's own angular vocal style and undifferentiated orchestral textures convey little interest in the human significance of the actual plot. In a review of the British premiere, Winton Dean compared the work with Meyerbeer, quoting Wagner's dictum: 'effects without causes'. As a document of its time it certainly has importance, but that is unlikely to guarantee it a permanent place in the repertoire.

RECORDING   1. Gabry, de Ridder, Nicolai, Cologne Opera Ch, Gürzenich O, Gielen, Wergo, 1965; 2. Vargas, Shade, Ebbecke, Cochran, Munkittrick, Wolansky, Ch and O of Stuttgart State Opera, Kontarsky, Teldec, 1989
EDITIONS   f.s., Schott, 1975; v.s., Schott, 1966

BIBLIOGRAPHY   Hans Heinsheimer, 'The Soldiers is Coming', *Opera News*, January 1982, pp. 18–19, 36; Heinz Joseph Herbort, 'B. A. Zimmermann: *Die Soldaten*', booklet with Wergo recording, 1965

S.W.

UDO ZIMMERMANN
b 6 October 1943, Dresden

In 1967, while studying in Dresden, Udo Zimmermann presented his much praised opera *Weisse Rose*. In eight scenes and seven flashbacks the work retells the story of Sophie and Hans Scholl, their plan to assassinate Hitler and their brutal execution. Zimmermann's personal style was initially influenced by Henze (particularly *Elegy for Young Lovers*) and Lutosławski. 'I experiment gladly and frequently,' he later wrote, 'but I take no pleasure in a boldness whose only virtue is a palpable lack of good sense.' With *Mutazioni* for orchestra (1972) he won international recognition. *Der Schuhu* (1975), a brilliant and subtle score, testifies to Zimmermann's striking theatrical talent.

His next opera, *Die wundersame Schustersfrau*, received its first performance in Western Germany, where it aroused only moderate enthusiasm. In 1986 the Hamburg Opera presented a new work based on *Weisse Rose*, this time in the form of scenes for two singers and 15 instruments. The text (by Wolfgang Willaschek) and the composer's Expressionist score were not well received.

Zimmermann's combined musical and diplomatic talents have since led to his appointment as artistic director of the Leipzig Opera.

Der Schuhu und die fliegende Prinzessin
The Schuhu and the Flying Princess
Opera in three parts (2h 30m)
Libretto by Peter Hacks
Composed 1974–5
PREMIERE   30 December 1976, Dresden

The imaginative libretto tells the tale of the Schuhu, a fantasy creature born out of an egg. Zimmermann uses an ensemble of 12 singers in multiple roles who also form a chorus; the orchestra, two identical groups of 17 players, sits on stage and takes an active part in the drama. The composer explains: 'It's a play about the meaning of life, the search for happiness and perfect harmony.'

EDITION v.s., Deutsche Verlag für Musik, 1977

Other operatic works: *Die Weisse Rose* (opera), 1967; *Die zweite Entscheidung*, 1970; *Levins Mühle*, 1972; *Die wundersame Schustersfrau*, 1979; *Weisse Rose* (scenes), 1985
BIBLIOGRAPHY U. Stürzbecher, *Komponisten in der DDR*, Hildesheim, 1979

A.C.W.B.

NICCOLÒ ANTONIO ZINGARELLI
b 4 April 1752, Naples; *d* 5 May 1837, Torre del Greco-Napoli

Zingarelli began his musical studies at the age of seven at the Conservatory of S. Maria di Loreto where Cimarosa was a fellow student. In 1781 he made his operatic début with an opera seria, *Montezuma*, which despite being found too 'learned' by the Neapolitan public aroused interest. Zingarelli soon received several commissions from theatres in northern and central Italy, notably Milan. In 1785 Haydn revived *Montezuma* at the Eszterháza theatre, and chose his *Alsinda* for the following season. In 1790 he visited Paris where his *Antigone*, adopting some of the reform principles of French opera, won little favour. Thereafter he shunned novelty and contented himself with tried and tested formulae.

With the revolution in Paris Zingarelli fled to Milan where he was briefly musical director at the cathedral, and later maestro of the prestigious cappella of the Santa Casa in Loreto. In addition to producing a great quantity of sacred works, Zingarelli wrote comic operas, achieving immediate success with *Il mercato di Monfregoso* (1792) and *La secchia rapita* (1793). The former was admired by Stendhal when he heard it in 1811.

On Guglielmi's death in 1804 Zingarelli became the musical director of St Peter's in Rome – the summit of a Catholic composer's aspirations. In 1813, he returned to Naples to become principal of its royal music college and to succeed Paisiello as director of the cathedral cappella. Though he was essentially a backward-looking composer of the

Neapolitan school, one of the last inheritors of the opera-seria tradition, the seeds of Bellini and Mercadante, who were both his students, can be discerned in his works.

Surviving operas: *Montezuma*, 1781; *Alsinda*, 1785; *Ifigenia in Aulide*, 1787; *Artaserse*, 1789; *Antigone*, 1790; *La morte di Cesare*, 1790; *Pirro re di Epiro*, 1791; *Annibale in Torino*, 1792; *L'oracolo sannita*, 1792; *Il mercato di Monfregoso*, 1792; *Apelle*, 1793, rev. as *Apelle e Campaspe*, 1795; *Quinto Fabio*, 1794; *Il conte di Saldagna*, 1794; *Gli Orazi e i Curiazi*, 1795; *Giulietta e Romeo*, 1796; *La morte di Mitridate*, 1797; *Ines de Castro*, 1798; *Carolina e Mexicow*, 1798; *Meleagro*, 1798; *Il ritratto*, 1799; *Il ratto delle Sabine*, 1799; *Clitennestra*, 1800; *Edipo a Colono*, 1802; *Il bevitore fortunato*, 1803; *Berenice regina d'Armenia*, 1811; 4 doubtful works; 17 lost
BIBLIOGRAPHY Maria Caraci, 'Niccolò Zingarelli tra mito e critica' in *NRMI*, vol. 22 (1988), pp. 375–422

D.A.D'A.

JOHANN RUDOLPH ZUMSTEEG
Johann Rudolph Zumsteeg [Zum Steeg]; *b* 10 January 1760, Sachsenflur, nr Mergentheim; *d* 27 January 1802, Stuttgart

Although remembered chiefly for his large output of lieder and ballads, which were especially influential on the young Schubert, Zumsteeg also wrote singspiels, Italian operas, melodramas and incidental music. His most important stage work is *Die Geisterinsel*, a singspiel based on F. W. Gotter's German translation of Shakespeare's *The Tempest*, which was first performed at the court theatre in Stuttgart in November 1798. In style Zumsteeg's work betrays the general influence of Jommelli, and reflects his interest in the melodrama techniques developed by Benda; but clearly evident also – particularly in his melodic writing and instrumentation – is his love for, and profound knowledge of, the operas of Mozart, several of which he was the first to present in Stuttgart.

Operatic works: *Des tartarische Gesetz*, 1780; *Der Schuss von Gänzewiz, oder Der Betrug aus Liebe*, 1781; *Le feste della Tessaglia*, 1782; *Le delizie campestri, o Ippolito e Aricia*, 1782; *Armide*, 1785; *Zalaor*, 1787; *Tamira*, 1788; *Airs de divertissement*, 1796; *Le chant de parens éloignés de leurs enfants*, 1796; *Die Geisterinsel*, 1798; *Das Pfauenfest*, 1801; *Elbondocani*, 1803
BIBLIOGRAPHY K. Haering, 'Johann Rudolph Zumsteeg: Opern-, Balladen- und Liederkomponist, Konzertmeister, 1760–1802', *Schwabische Lebensbilder*, vol. 2, Stuttgart, 1941, p. 545

B.S.

List of Contributors

G.A.
Gerald Abraham (1904–1988) was a musicologist of wide-ranging sympathies and interests, perhaps best remembered for his extensive work on Slavonic music. He was associated with the BBC from 1935, first as assistant editor of *Radio Times*, and helped to launch the Third Programme (now Radio 3); he took up his last appointment there, as Assistant Controller of Music, in 1962. In 1947 he became the first Professor of Music at Liverpool University. A leading light in numerous important musical organizations, his appointments included Chairman of the editorial board of the *New Grove Dictionary of Music* and President of the Royal Musical Association.

D.A.D'A.
Domenico Antonio d'Alessandro, born in Naples in 1960, studied musicology at the University of Bologna. He began researching early and has broadcast and published on various aspects of music in 17th- and 18th-century Naples. Since 1987 he has been cataloguing the manuscripts at the library of the Conservatory S. Pietro a Majella, Naples. Publications include: *Music in Naples during the 17th century through notices and newspapers* (1983), *Opera in Naples from 1650–1670* (1984) and *Mozart in Naples: an iconographic testimonial* (1993).

F.A.
Felix Aprahamian (born 1914, London), British music critic, writer and broadcaster, has been a familiar figure on the London scene since 1931, when he began his career as a musical journalist. He was deputy music critic of the *Sunday Times* (1948–89), and has also been for many years a leading reviewer for the *Gramophone*. He even appeared in a film (Schlesinger's *Darling*, 1965) in the role of a critic. An authority on French music, he has also been adviser to the Delius Trust since 1961, and is Vice President of the Delius Society. He edited the essays of Ernest Newman, and was co-editor of the 20th-century volume of *The Heritage of Music* (1989).

J.A.
John D. Arnn (1943–1992) received his college education at Denison University (Granville, Ohio), and his Ph.D. from Rutgers University (New Brunswick, New Jersey) in 1987, with a dissertation entitled *Text, Music, and Drama in Three Operas by Reinhard Keiser*.

W.A.
William Ashbrook (born 28 January 1922, Philadelphia) was educated at the University of Pennsylvania and at Harvard. After a 40-year career of teaching humanities, mostly at Indiana State University, he is Distinguished Professor Emeritus of Humanities. He continues to teach part-time, to lecture, and to write copiously on the subject of Italian opera of the Ottocento. His studies of Donizetti and Puccini are well known. He is currently engaged on a critical bio-graphy of Arrigo Boito.

M.A.
Mark Audus studied at the University of Nottingham where his teachers included Nigel Osborne and John Tyrrell. Following postgraduate studies at King's College, London, he became editor at Universal Edition, London, working particularly closely on scores by Birtwistle. More recently, he has worked with John Tyrrell and Charles Mackerras on editions of Janáček's operas. Freelance writer since 1989 (Bach, Bruckner, Erich Kleiber, etc.). Since 1987 conductor, Bern Bach Soloists and, since 1991, music director of St Catherine's, Hatcham.

S.B.
Stephen Banfield is best known for his work on 19th- and 20th-century British music, in particular his book *Sensibility and English Song*. He is also the author of *Sondheim's Broadway Musicals* (forthcoming). After 14 years on the academic staff of Keele University he is now Elgar Professor of Music and Head of the School of Performance Studies in the University of Birmingham.

A.C.W.B.
Antony Beaumont, a Londoner (born 1949), read music at Cambridge. Since 1972 he has been resident in Germany, where he is active as a conductor but also broadcasts, lectures and writes about music. After several years of intensive research he wrote two books about Busoni and reconstructed the closing scene of the unfinished opera *Doktor Faust*. He has now turned his attention to Zemlinsky and is preparing several publications devoted to him.

C.B.
Clive Bennett is Editor of Opera at BBC Radio 3.

G.B.
George Biddlecombe studied at the Royal Academy
of Music and at Oxford University. He teaches at the
Royal Academy of Music and specializes in 19th-
century opera, particularly with regard to feminist
aspects.

A.B.
Alan Blyth writes reviews of opera recordings for the
Daily Telegraph, has edited three volumes of *Opera
on Record* and written a guide entitled *Opera on CD*.
He has contributed for 25 years to Radio 3's *Record
Review* and to *Gramophone* on vocal issues. From
1966 to 1983 he was associate editor of *Opera*, and
remains on the editorial board of the magazine, to
which he has regularly contributed profiles and
reviews.

M.B.
Malcolm Boyd (born 1932) studied music at Durham
University. He taught for several years at the Welsh
College of Music and Drama in Cardiff, and then at
the University of Wales College of Cardiff. He retired
in 1992. His writings have included books on Bach
and Domenico Scarlatti, and he worked on the
editorial staff of the *New Grove Dictionary of Music*.

S.S.V.B.
Sally Bradshaw read English at Cambridge and
studied singing at the Guildhall School of Music,
then with Régine Crespin in Paris and Myra Ross in
London. She has a special interest in Handel (sharing his birthdate) and has recorded the roles of
Agrippina (Harmonia Mundi) and Alcina (Capriccio). She wrote, acted and sang the title role in the
award-winning play *Maria Malibran*, premiered at
the Edinburgh Festival (1990). In 1991 she starred
in Kurt Weill's *Love Life* in London and in 1992 was
vocal soloist on Mike Oldfield's *Tubular Bells 2*.

V.B.
Volkmar Braunbehrens lives in Freiburg (where he
was born in 1941). He studied German literature,
history of art and history of music at the universities
of Munich, Heidelberg and Berlin (FU) and taught
history of literature in Berlin and Osnabruck. Writings
include: *Mozart in Vienna* (Munich, 1986; New
York/London, 1990); *Maligned Master – The Life of
Antonio Salieri* (Munich, 1989; New York, 1992).

P.B.B.
Patricia B. Brauner (Ph.D., Yale University, 1970) is a
member of the editorial committee of the *Edizione
critica della Opere di Gioachino Rossini* (Fondazione
Rossini and G. Ricordi) and Coordinator of the Center
for Italian Opera Studies at the University of Chicago.
She was a contributor to the *New Grove Dictionary of
Music* and editor of Rossini's *Ermione* (with Philip
Gossett), *Armida* (with Charles S. Brauner), and *La
riconoscenza* for the critical edition.

M.C.B.
Manuel Carlos de Brito (born 26 April 1945). He
graduated in Germanic philology at Lisbon Univer-

sity and obtained his M.Mus. and Ph.D. degrees at
London University (King's College). He is at present
a lecturer at the Musicology Department of the Uni-
versidade Nova de Lisboa. He has published many
articles on Portuguese music history and is also the
author of *Opera in Portugal in the Eighteenth Century* (CUP, 1989) and *Estudos de História da Música
em Portugal* (Editorial Estampa, 1989), as well as
editor-in-chief of a *Dicionário de Música e Músicos
Portugueses* to be published by the Gulbenkian Foundation.

C.A.B.
Clive Brown studied at Cambridge (M.A.) and
Oxford (D.Phil.), and was Lecturer in Music at The
Queen's College, Oxford (1981–9). He is at present
Senior Lecturer in Performance Studies at Bretton
Hall College, University of Leeds. Publications
include a critical biography of Spohr (CUP), articles
on performing practice, opera and early Romantic
music, as well as critical editions of Beethoven and
Weber; he is preparing a book on classical and
Romantic performing practice for OUP. He has con-
ducted revivals of operas by Schubert, Mendelssohn,
Spohr and Haydn.

D.B.
David Brown was, after five years' school-
mastering, music librarian of London University for
three years before joining the music staff of
Southampton University in 1962. He retired as
Professor of Musicology there in 1989. He has
published books on Thomas Weelkes, John Wilbye
and Glinka; his four-volume study of Tchaikovsky
was completed in 1990. He has also edited numerous editions of English Renaissance music,
contributed many articles to periodicals, and has
broadcast frequently.

J.W.B.
Jennifer   Williams   Brown   (Ph.D.,   musicology,
Cornell, 1992) specializes in 17th-century Venetian
opera. Her dissertation examines the problems of aria
borrowing, revivals, and revisions in the late 17th century; she has also presented papers on 17th-century
source studies, opera production, and harmonic organization. From 1987 to 1990 she taught part-time at the
Eastman School of Music, where she prepared an edition of Cavalli's *La Calisto* for productions at Eastman
and in New York. She is currently Assistant Professor
of Musicology at Louisiana State University.

I.B.
Ian Brunskill is a former editor of *Opera Now* who
now works for *The Times*. He has also written on
music and opera for the *Guardian*, *The Times
Literary Supplement*, *Opera*, *Classic CD* and the
Musical Times.

G.J.B.
George   J.   Buelow,   Professor   of   Musicology
at Indiana University, Bloomington, has research
interests focused on the history of baroque music
and the history of opera. He is Past-President of

the American Bach Society, board member of the International Musicological Society, and former editor of *Studies in Musicology*, published by UMI Research Press. He is the author of the forthcoming *History of Baroque Music* (W. W. Norton), and editor and contributing author of volume 4 of the series *Man and Music, The Late Baroque* (Macmillan).

D.J.B.
Donald Burrows is a Senior Lecturer in Music at the Open University, and an internationally known Handel scholar, being a member of the Vorstand of the Händel-Gesellschaft and a member of the Advisory Board for the Maryland Handel Festival (USA) as well as a founding Council member of the Handel Institute. He is co-author of a forthcoming *Catalogue of Handel's Musical Autographs* (OUP) and has written on many aspects of Handel's music, as well as editing *Messiah, Alexander's Feast* and Handel's violin sonatas for publication.

D.S.B.
David Butchart was born in Paisley in 1952 and studied at Glasgow and Oxford, completing his doctoral dissertation in 1979. He has written a study of the madrigals of Marco da Gagliano, published several articles on Alessandro Striggio snr, and edited books of madrigals by Striggio and Andrea Gabrieli. Since 1986 he has been English-language editor at Deutsche Grammophon in Hamburg.

D.A.C.
David Cairns (born 1926) took a (first-class) degree in history at Oxford (1948). In 1950, with Stephen Gray, he founded the Chelsea Opera Group, singing in early performances (Leporello, Dr Bartolo) conducted by Colin Davis. He has worked at the House of Commons (as library clerk, 1951–3), *The Times Educational Supplement* (1955–8) and since 1958 as music critic on the *Spectator*, the *Financial Times*, the *Sunday Times*, etc. He was Classical Programme Co-ordinator, Philips Records (1967–72), is founder/conductor of The Thorington Players (1983–), and, since 1985, Distinguished Visiting Professor, University of California, Davis. He became Officier de l'Ordre des Arts et des Lettres in 1991. Publications include: as translator, Berlioz's *Memoirs* (1969); *Responses: Musical Essays and Reviews* (1973); *Berlioz: The Making of an Artist* (1989); contributions to ENO Opera Guides on *Die Zauberflöte* (1980) and *Falstaff* (1982).

T.C.
Tim Carter has worked extensively on early baroque opera – his doctoral dissertation was on Jacopo Peri – and on music in Florence over the 1600s, as well as being the author of the Cambridge Opera Handbook on Mozart's *Le nozze di Figaro* and *Music in Late Renaissance and Early Baroque Italy* (Batsford). He is currently Reader in Music at Royal Holloway and Bedford New College, University of London.

D.P.C.
David Charlton was educated at Ealing Grammar School, the Royal Academy of Music, and the universities of Nottingham and Cambridge. His teachers included John Railton, Lois Phillips and Arnold Whittall. A lecturer (now Reader) at the University of East Anglia, he has published first modern editions of the symphonies of Méhul, and books on Grétry and E. T. A. Hoffmann. He has written for the *New Oxford History of Music*, the *New Grove Dictionary of Music*, and many other books and journals.

Z.C.
Zofia Chechlinska is a musicologist, and the author of books on Polish 19th-century music, including Chopin. She is head of the Music Department of the Institute of Art in Warsaw, the editor of a series devoted to 19th-century musical culture and the editor of *Chopin Studies*, published by the Chopin Society in Warsaw. She contributed to the *New Grove Dictionary of Music*. She is currently preparing a book on the history of 19th-century musical culture in Poland.

A.C.
Alfred Clayton read music at the universities of Oxford, Cambridge, Hamburg and Vienna. He has written articles and reviews and published numerous translations. These include Carl Dahlhaus, *Schoenberg and the New Music* (1987; translated jointly with Derek Puffett) and Paul Badura-Skoda, *Interpreting Bach at the Keyboard* (1992).

J.A.C.
Jon Alan Conrad teaches music theory and literature at the University of Delaware. He has been a contributing editor of *Opus* magazine, and has written articles and reviews for the *Kurt Weill Newsletter*, *Opera Quarterly* and the *New York Times*. He is a contributor to the *New Grove Dictionary of Opera* and the *Metropolitan Opera Guide to Recorded Opera*.

E.C.
Elisabeth Cook took her doctorate at the University of East Anglia, researching into aspects of the 18th-century opéra comique. She combines a full-time career in teaching with freelance editing and has contributed articles to a number of dictionaries of music and of opera.

T.T.C.
Tim Crawford (born 1948) studied lute at the Royal College of Music and worked for 15 years as a professional lutenist. He has wide musical interests, but his extensive musicological research has concentrated on lute music. He worked on *Early Music* magazine for a year (1984–5), and continues to contribute reviews. Since 1989 he has worked at King's College, London, researching into computers and lute music. He is editing the works of S. L. Weiss, the great 18th-century lutenist and friend of Bach, for *Das Erbe deutscher Musik* (Peters edition).

R.H.C.
Ronald Henry Crichton (born 1913) was educated at
Radley College and Christ Church, Oxford. Before
the Second World War he worked in London on
Anglo-French cultural relations. After army service
(1940–46) and work for the British Council (Greece,
Belgium, W. Germany, London) 1946–67 he joined
the *Financial Times* as music critic 1967. Since
reaching retirement age in 1978 he has been an independent contributor to the *Financial Times*, *Opera*
and other publications; joint editor with Mary Clarke
of *Dictionary of Modern Ballet* (1959); contributor to
the *New Grove Dictionary of Music* (1980), *Opera on
Record* (1983), *New Grove History of Opera* (1989),
The Heritage of Music (1989). Publications include:
*Manuel de Falla – A Descriptive Catalogue of his
Works* (1976), *Falla* (BBC Music Guides, 1982) and
the abridged edition of *The Memoirs of Ethel Smyth*
(1987).

B.D.
Basil Deane was born and educated in Northern
Ireland. He has been Professor of Music in the universities of Sheffield, Manchester and Birmingham, and
has held the posts of Music Director at the Arts Council of Great Britain and Foundation Director of the
Hong Kong Academy for Performing Arts. His principal research interests are in French music, and
music of the classical period. He has published books
on Roussel, Cherubini and Hoddinott, and is currently
working on a study of the French theatre from 1789 to
1815.

J.W.D.
John Deathridge (born in 1944) is a Fellow and
Director of Studies in Music at King's College, Uni-
versity of Cambridge. He has also been Visiting
Professor at the universities of Princeton and Chicago
and is an editor of the *Richard Wagner-Gesamtaus-
gabe* in Munich. His recent publications include an
enlarged edition of *The Family Letters of Richard
Wagner* (1991), the English-language edition of
Ulrich Müller's and Peter Wapnewski's *Wagner
Handbook* (1992) and an article on Wagner and the
post-modern (1992).

P.D.
Peter Dickinson is a composer, writer, broadcaster
and pianist. An Emeritus Professor of Keele University, where he started the Music Department with its
Centre for American Music in 1974, he is now Professor at Goldsmiths' College of the University of
London. His recorded compositions involve some of
the leading performers and include the concertos for
organ and for piano; a series of song-cycles with
piano and choral works such as *Outcry* and the *Mass
of the Apocalypse*. His book, *The Music of Lennox
Berkeley*, was published in 1989.

G.D.
Graham Dixon is a Senior Producer at BBC Radio 3
specializing in early music programmes. Since completing his doctorate on music in baroque Rome, he
has written extensively on Italian music, and has con-

tributed substantially to Monteverdi and Handel
research, as well as writing a monograph on Carissimi
for OUP. He is in demand as a lecturer throughout
Europe, and contributes reviews to many journals; he
is actively involved with the promotion of early
music in the UK, and is Musicological Adviser to the
York Early Music Festival.

N.D.
Nigel Douglas studied at the Vienna Musikakademie
and has appeared worldwide in a repertoire of over
80 principal tenor roles, his special areas being
20th-century opera and Viennese operetta. He has
directed productions for Sadler's Wells, the Royal
Flemish Opera and the Australian Opera; he has
presented some 300 programmes on opera and
operetta for BBC Radio, and his first book, *Legendary Voices*, was published in London by André
Deutsch in 1992.

J.D.
Jonathan Dove was born in 1959. His operas include
Hastings Spring (Glyndebourne's first community
opera); *Music for Drowning*; *Pig* (for English National Opera Contemporary Opera Studio). Other works
include a wind serenade based on Mozart's *Le nozze
di Figaro* for Glyndebourne's Mozart celebrations,
and he has composed several scores for dance, theatre
and film. For City of Birmingham Touring Opera
he has orchestrated *La Cenerentola*, *La Bohème*, *Falstaff*, *Die Zauberflöte* and *The Ring Saga* (which he
also adapted for performances over two evenings
with Graham Vick).

J.E.
Julia Engelhardt (MA Heidelberg) is a freelance picture editor (with a passion for classical music),
exhibition researcher and writer specializing in art,
architecture and design. She has worked on numerous
exhibitions at the Hayward Gallery, London. Her
work has been published by OUP (The Heritage of
Music Series), the Arts Council/South Bank Centre,
Thames and Hudson, and the Victoria and Albert
Museum.

M.F.
Michael Fend was awarded a Ph.D. at Berlin's Technical University in 1983. Publications include:
Gioseffo Zarlino, *Theorie des Tonsystems, übersetzt,
kommentiert und eingeleitet* (Bern, 1989), and C.
Burnett, M. Fend and P. Gouk (eds), *The Second
Sense, Studies in Hearing and Musical Judgement
from Antiquity to the Seventeenth Century* (The Warburg Institute Surveys and Text, vol. 22, London
1991).

C.F.
Christopher Fifield is a conductor, author and broadcaster. For many years he was on the staff at
Glyndebourne and, for a decade, Director of Music at
University College, London. He wrote the first biography of the composer Max Bruch, and of Wagner's
amanuensis, the conductor Hans Richter. He is

preparing biographies of Anton Bruckner and Hans von Bülow.

E.F.
Elizabeth Forbes, an autodidact, is a musical journalist who specializes in opera. She has contributed to many encyclopedias, including the *New Grove Dictionary of Music* (1980) and the *New Grove Dictionary of Opera* (1992) and has published the following books: *Opera from A to Z* (1977), *The Observer's Book of Opera* and *Mario and Grisi: A Biography* (1985). She also works as a translator and has translated opera libretti from French, German and Swedish.

L.F.
Lewis Foreman is known for his biography of Sir Arnold Bax, and books on Rubbra, Grainger, Havergal Brian, Sir Arthur Bliss, and a chronological anthology of British composers' letters, *From Parry to Britten*. For over 20 years he has worked to devise enterprising concerts, typical being a historical conspectus of 'British Opera 1876–1916' at St John's, Smith Square, in 1982, issued on two LPs. Music Trustee of the Sir Arnold Bax Trust, for 15 years he was a member of the City of Westminster Arts Council Music Committee.

E.G.
Edward Garden is Professor of Music at Sheffield University. He has written many articles on Russian music. His books include the definitive one in English on Balakirev, and the volume on Tchaikovsky in Dent's Master Musicians series, which has been revised and reprinted many times and translated into German and Spanish. He has co-edited for OUP an edition of correspondence between Tchaikovsky and Nadezhda von Meck (1876–8).

N.G.
Noël Goodwin is a member of the editorial board of *Opera* and regular critic for *The Times*. He was music critic of the *Daily Express* 1956–78, London correspondent *Opera News* (New York) 1975–90 and a Council Member and Deputy Chairman of the Music Advisory Panel, Arts Council of Great Britain 1979–81. He collaborated with Sir Geraint Evans on *A Knight at the Opera* (1984), was editor of the *Royal Yearbooks* 1978–80 and has contributed to the *New Grove Dictionary of Music* and the *New Grove Dictionary of Opera, Enzyklopädie des Musiktheaters* (Munich), *Encyclopaedia Britannica* and other works of reference.

P.G.
Philip Gossett (Ph.D., Princeton University, 1970) is Robert W. Reneker Distinguished Service Professor in the Department of Music and Dean of the Division of Humanities of the University of Chicago. He is general editor of *The Works of Giuseppe Verdi* (University of Chicago Press and G. Ricordi) and Direttore dell'edizione of the *Edizione critica delle Opere di Gioachino Rossini* (Fondazione Rossini and G. Ricordi). He is the author of *'Anna Bolena' and the Maturity of Gaetano Donizetti* (OUP, 1985) and

of numerous studies, articles and reviews, as well as the critical editions of Rossini's *Tancredi, Ermione* (with Patricia Brauner), and *Semiramide* (with Alberto Zedda).

J.G.
Julian Grant lives and works in London. Writings include 'A Foot in Bluebeard's Door' for ENO's Bartók opera guide and various articles on Russian music. Operas staged in London have been *The Skin Drum* (1990, ENO Studio), *Out of Season* (1991, Royal Opera House Garden Venture), *The Queen of Sheba's Legs* (1991, ENO Baylis programme) and *A Family Affair* (1993, Almeida Opera).

P.A.G.
Paul Griffiths (born 1947) was educated in Birmingham and at Oxford. In the 1970s he worked on the *New Grove Dictionary of Music* while also writing music criticism for the *Financial Times, The Times* and other papers. He was chief music critic of *The Times* 1982–92. His publications include several books on music (including studies of Boulez, Cage, Bartók, Davies, Ligeti, Messiaen and Stravinsky), two novels and a libretto for Mozart, *The Jewel Box*.

A.I.G.
Alison Gyger was born Alison Jones in Newcastle, New South Wales, 1933. Studies at the universities of Sydney and New England (Ph.D. 1969) were followed by lecturing in early English language and literature at these universities and the Australian National University. She has written for *Opera Australia* – background and historical articles – translated libretti and written a book, *Opera for the Antipodes*, on the early history of opera in Australia.

R.L.H.
Robert Henderson is the music critic of the *Daily Telegraph*. He studied at the universities of Durham and Oxford (with Egon Wellesz, the medievalist Frank Harrison and the art historian Edgar Wind). After graduating he worked for several years as a freelance writer and broadcaster, specializing in medieval and 20th-century music. He has written extensively on the music of Henze, is a regular contributor to *Opera*, and wrote the chapters on Monteverdi and Offenbach in Alan Blyth's *Opera on Record*.

AF.H.
Amanda Holden, a Londoner from a medical/musical background, studied at Oxford University with Egon Wellesz and (piano) at the Guildhall School of Music with James Gibb. After several years (as Amanda Warren) as a freelance recital accompanist, a music therapist (she began the department at Charing Cross Hospital's Child Development Research Centre) and a teacher at the Guildhall, she began (in 1985) planning *The Viking Opera Guide* and translating opera libretti. Her translations include several operas by Mozart, Rameau's *Les Boréades*, Verdi's *Falstaff* and Wagner's *Lohengrin*.

R.G.H.
Robin Holloway was born in 1943 in the Midlands, but brought up in London as a chorister at St Paul's Cathedral, then as a schoolboy at King's, Wimbledon. At Cambridge he read English then music – the dual preoccupations of a lifetime. He has held a fellowship at Caius College since 1969 and a university lectureship since 1975. Compositions include two operas – *Clarissa* (1976, ENO 1990) and its buffa complement, inspired by the life and work of Cynthia Payne (1991) – and numerous orchestral works, ensemble pieces, concertos, songs, etc. He also contributes many articles to books and journals, most regularly a monthly music review in the *Spectator*.

P.H.
Peter Holman, born 1946, studied at London University. He has a busy performing career as director of The Parley of Instruments, Opera Restor'd and the Suffolk Villages Festival, and as a tutor on early music courses. He contributes regularly to scholarly journals and conferences, and has taught at many colleges and universities in England and abroad; he is Senior Lecturer at Colchester Institute Music School. His book *Four and Twenty Fiddlers: The Violin at the English Court 1540–1690* will be published by OUP in 1993.

W.C.H.
William C. Holmes is Professor of Music at the University of California at Irvine. He has published articles on 17th- and 18th-century opera and a book on Alessandro Scarlatti. Holmes has recently finished a book-length study on opera in early 18th-century Florence, and is presently completing the critical edition of *La forza del destino* for *The Operas of Giuseppe Verdi*.

L.H.
Leslie Howard, the British composer, pianist and musicologist (born in Melbourne in 1948) is himself the composer of the operas *Hreidar the Fool* (Melbourne, 1975) and *Prague Spring* (in progress), as well as a good deal of chamber music. He is a regular writer and broadcaster on music, and especially the music of Liszt. He is President of the British Liszt Society, and is currently engaged in the mammoth project of recording that composer's complete piano music for Hyperion – some 70 compact discs in all. His repertoire includes over 80 concertos, and his recital programmes cover an enormous range of rare and familiar works, with special emphasis on Russian music and the complete works of Beethoven and Liszt.

E.H.
Elizabeth Hudson teaches at the University of Virginia. She is an editor of the *Cambridge Opera Journal* and is preparing a book on Verdi and narrative.

S.H.
Steven Huebner holds a Ph.D. degree from Princeton University and is currently Associate Professor of Music at McGill University in Montreal, Canada. His

first book, *The Operas of Charles Gounod*, published in 1990, will be followed by a second – on *fin-de-siècle* French opera.

G.H.
Gwen Hughes is a former assistant editor of *Opera Now*. She is now a producer at BBC Radio 3, working principally in opera.

J.T.H.
John Hughes has been a collector of vocal recordings for 40 years. He is chairman of the Recorded Vocal Art Society, deputy editor of *The Record Collector* (a magazine devoted to recordings of singers), has contributed to *Opera on Record* and wrote the biographical notes for EMI's *Record of Singing*, vol. 4.

A.J.
Arthur Jacobs lectured at the Royal Academy of Music 1965–79, was Head of the Department of Music at Huddersfield Polytechnic 1979–84, and has lectured at various US, Canadian and Australian universities. A member of the editorial board of *Opera* since 1962 and a translator of many operas for performance, his books include *Arthur Sullivan: A Victorian Musician* and the *Penguin Dictionary of Music* (five editions).

N.J.
Newell Jenkins, conductor, musicologist, writer. Education 1932–9, Germany; 1939–41, Yale. American Field Service, 1942–5. Military Government, Württemberg-Baden, 1945–7. Fulbright Fellowship, Florence, 1948–9. Founder Director, Piccola Accademia Musicale, 1952. Founder Director, Clarion Music Society, 1957–present. Founder Director, Castelfranco Veneto Festival, 1975–8. Edited music of Sammartini, Brunetti, Vivaldi, Steffani, Kraus, etc. Teacher: New York University, Cornell, Grinell, University of California, Irvine, etc. Guest conductor: Stockholm Philharmonic, Drottningholm and Wexford Festivals, etc. Honours: Italy, Sweden, New York City, Lincoln Center, Yale University. Many publications and recordings.

P.J.
Peter Jonas is General Director of the Bavarian State Opera. Previously, he was General Director, English National Opera (1985–93); Director of Artistic Administration, Chicago Symphony Orchestra and Orchestral Association of Chicago (1976–85); Assistant to Music Director, Chicago Symphony Orchestra (1974–6). He has been a Fellow of the Royal College of Music since 1990 and a Member of the Council there since 1988. He was educated at the University of Sussex, the Royal Northern College of Music (Northern School of Music) and the Royal College of Music.

B.L.K.
Barbara L. Kelly is a Scottish musicologist specializing in French music of the early 20th century. After

graduating from the University of Glasgow, she studied in America at the University of Illinois with Professor Alexander Ringer and is now at Liverpool University. She has written on Maeterlinck and French opera, and Milhaud and his collaboration with Paul Claudel. Her present research is focused on Milhaud and the concept of the French musical tradition.

I.K.
Ian Kemp recently retired as Professor of Music at the University of Manchester, having previously held appointments at the universities of Aberdeen, Cambridge and Leeds. In 1965 he edited the first book to be published on Tippett, and is author of a major study, *Tippett: The Composer and his Music*. He has also written on Berlioz, Hindemith and Weill.

M.K.
Michael Kennedy, born in Manchester in 1926, has been a music critic for the *Daily Telegraph* and latterly the *Sunday Telegraph* since 1950. He has written biographical studies of Elgar, Vaughan Williams, Britten, Walton, Mahler and Strauss, histories of the Hallé Orchestra and the Royal Manchester College of Music, biographies of Sir John Barbirolli and Sir Adrian Boult, and the *Oxford Dictionary of Music*. He is a regular broadcaster and contributor to *Opera*, *Gramophone*, and other periodicals. He is the author of the Strauss entry in the *New Grove Dictionary of Music* and of a BBC music guide to the Strauss tone-poems. He was appointed OBE in 1981 for services to music.

N.K.
Nicholas Kenyon is Controller, BBC Radio 3. He was born in Cheshire and read Modern History at Balliol College, Oxford. He worked for the English Bach Festival and the BBC before becoming a music critic of the *New Yorker*, 1979–82. He returned to London as a music critic of *The Times* and Music Editor of the *Listener*; he joined the *Observer* in 1986 and was also Editor of *Early Music*, 1983–92. He has been a member of the Music Advisory Panels of the Arts Council and the South Bank Centre, and he is author of *The BBC Symphony Orchestra, 1930–80*, and *Simon Rattle: The Making of a Conductor*; and editor of *Authenticity and Early Music*.

D.K.
David Kimbell, by birth a Man of Kent, has spent the whole of his professional life in Scotland; he is currently Professor of Music and Dean of the Faculty of Music at the University of Edinburgh. Author of *Verdi in the Age of Italian Romanticism* and *Italian Opera* (both CUP); he is also a contributor to the *New Oxford History of Music* and the Halle edition of the collected works of Handel.

R.La.
Robert Layton studied at Oxford with Edmund Rubbra and Egon Wellesz. He spent two years in Sweden at the universities of Uppsala and Stockholm. He joined the BBC Music Division in 1959 and retired as Senior Music Producer in 1990. He has been responsible for

such programmes as *Interpretations on Record*. He has contributed a quarterly 'Retrospect' to *Gramophone* for a number of years and has written books on Berwald and Sibelius. In 1987 he was awarded the Sibelius Medal and in the following year was made a Knight of the Order of the White Rose of Finland.

L.E.L.
Lowell Lindgren is Professor of Music at Massachusetts Institute of Technology. He is the author of 'Musicians and Librettists in the Correspondence of Gio. Giacomo Zamboni', *RMA Research Chronicle*, vol. 24 (1991), and 'The Accomplishments of the Learned and Ingenious Nicola Francesco Haym', *Studi Musicali*, vol. 16 (1987), pp. 247–380. He is also editor of 'Bits and Pieces: Music for Theater', *Harvard Library Bulletin*, vol. 2, no. 1 (winter 1991), 'Camilla by Giovanni Bononcini', *Music for London Entertainment*, E/2 (1990), and 'Cantatas by Giovanni Bononcini', *The Italian Cantata*, vol 10 (1985).

R.Lu.
Richard Luckett is Pepys Librarian and Precentor of Magdalene College, Cambridge, and a University Lecturer in English. H e has published *Handel's Messiah: A Celebration* (1992), and has edited, with Christopher Hogwood, *English Music in the Eighteenth Century*, a collection of essays; his contributions to *The Companion* to the Latham and Matthews edition of Pepys's *Diary* include the article on music and the biographies of musicians.

D.L.-J.
David Lloyd-Jones has conducted over 100 different operas in Great Britain and abroad in his career as freelance conductor, Assistant Music Director of English National Opera (1972–8) and Artistic Director of Opera North (1978–90). He has made critical editions of *Boris Godunov* (OUP and Muzika), *The Gondoliers* (Eulenberg) and *La jolie fille de Perth* (UMP). He is an acknowledged authority on Russian music and has made widely used singing translations of operas by Musorgsky, Borodin, Tchaikovsky and Prokofiev.

H.M.
Hugh Macdonald is Avis Blewett Professor of Music at Washington University, St Louis. He has taught at Cambridge, Oxford and Glasgow, where he was Professor of Music, 1980–87. He has been General Editor of the *New Berlioz Edition* since its inception in 1967 and has published books on Berlioz and Skryabin. He has edited Berlioz's three operas and has made a number of opera translations, including Debussy's *Pelléas et Mélisande*.

N.M.
Noel Malcolm studied at Cambridge University, where he was awarded a starred first in English and a doctorate in History. From 1981 to 1988 he was a Fellow of Gonville and Caius College. He was Political Correspondent of the *Spectator* from 1987 to 1991,

when he became that paper's Foreign Editor. He has published a biography of Marc'Antonio de Dominis (1984), a study of the life and music of George Enescu (1990), and an edition of the complete correspondence of Thomas Hobbes (1993).

I.J.M.
Jonathan Mantle was born in England in 1954 and educated at Cambridge University. He is the author of several books, including a biography of Andrew Lloyd Webber.

M.McC.
Marita P. McClymonds, Ph.D., University of California, Berkeley, 1978, is Associate Professor and Chair of the Department of Music, University of Virginia, where she also serves as Principal Investigator for the US–RISM Libretto Cataloguing Project. Publications include her dissertation, *Niccolò Jommelli: The Last Years, 1769–1774* and numerous journal articles, dictionary entries and reviews. She is currently completing a monograph, *Innovations and Modifications in Italian Opera Seria, 1750 to 1800*, partially funded by a fellowship from the American Council of Learned Societies.

R.M.
Rodney Milnes read history at Oxford, and after a short career in publishing moved into musical journalism. He has been associated with *Opera* magazine since 1971, and became editor in 1986. He was opera critic of the *Spectator* from 1970 to 1990, and after two years with the London *Evening Standard* was appointed chief opera critic of *The Times* in 1992. He has translated many operas, including *Rusalka (Dvořák)*, *Osud* (Janáček) and *Tannhäuser* (Wagner). He was appointed Knight of the Order of the White Rose of Finland in 1987.

J.M.
Jerzy Morawski, born 1932, Warsaw. Polish musicologist. Education: musicology with J. Chominski at Warsaw University (1951–8), theory of music and piano at the Academy of Music in Warsaw (1953–61). Since 1956 he has worked in the Institute of the Arts of the Polish Academy of Sciences, where in 1970 he took a doctorate. Author of several publications and source editions, mainly on medieval music; editor of the series *Monumenta Musicae in Polonia* and *Musica Medii Aevi*; member of the Union of Polish Composers and International Musicological Society.

D.M.
David Murray was born in Halifax, Nova Scotia. He studied music and philosophy in Canada (and played the piano professionally), then studied more philosophy at Oxford. He wrote many scores for radio plays and theatre and now lectures in philosophy at Birkbeck College, University of London, and reviews music for the *Financial Times*, the BBC and various journals. He has also contributed to several books about music.

M.N.
Martin Neary, born in 1940, is half French. Organist and Master of the Choristers at Westminster Abbey since 1988, he was previously Organist of St Margaret's, Westminster (1965–71) and of Winchester Cathedral (1972–87). An innovative choir trainer and conductor of numerous baroque and contemporary performances, he has made many recordings and worldwide foreign tours both as recital organist and as choir conductor. He has commissioned many new works, notably from Jonathan Harvey and John Tavener; he has edited *Early French Organ Music* for OUP; his compositions include responses, descants and numerous carol arrangements. He was President of the Royal College of Organists (1988–90).

D.O.-S.
David Osmond-Smith, born in 1946, completed his education at the universities of Cambridge and York. In 1970 he went to Milan to study with Umberto Eco, but also worked with Cathy Berberian and with Luciano Berio, of whose music he has made a special study. Since 1973 he has taught at the University of Sussex, where he is now Reader in Music. He has published two books on Berio, plus numerous other essays and translations. He broadcasts regularly, and lectures in Italy, Norway and France.

R.P.
Roger Parker teaches music at Cornell University. He has written numerous articles on 19th-century Italian opera, and is co-author (with Arthur Groos) of *Giacomo Puccini: La bohème* (CUP, 1986). He is the editor of *Nabucco* in the *Verdi Critical Edition*, and is co-editor of the *Cambridge Opera Journal*.

M.E.P.
Marvin E. Paymer received his Ph.D. from the City University of New York, where he has taught at York and Hunter Colleges. His interests have centred on the authenticity of the hundreds of works attributed to Giovanni Battista Pergolesi and to this end he has received fellowships from the Andrew Melon Foundation and the National Endowment for the Humanities. Paymer is co-founder of the Pergolesi Research Center and of the new Pergolesi complete works.

K.P.
Keith Potter is Lecturer in Music, Goldsmiths' College, University of London, and writer on many aspects of contemporary music. He has particular interests in American and British composition since 1945, including John Cage, Morton Feldman, Philip Glass and Steve Reich, and the younger generation of British composers. From 1971 to 1988 he was Founding and Chief Editor of *Contact,* a journal of contemporary music; for eight years he wrote a regular new music column and many reviews for *Classical Music* magazine. He is a regular contributor to the *Independent, The Times Literary Supplement* and the *BBC Music Magazine.*

C.A.P.
Curtis Price is a specialist on baroque and classical music and opera. He is the author of *Music in the Restoration Theatre*, *Henry Purcell and the London Stage*, the Norton Critical Score of *Dido and Aeneas* and numerous articles on English and Italian music. In 1985 he received the Dent Medal of the Royal Musical Association. Among his other scholarly interests are the music of Handel and the history of theatre architecture. He is King Edward Professor and Head of the Department of Music at King's College, London, and a Director of the Royal Academy of Music.

G.C.P.
Guy Protheroe is a freelance conductor and writer working equally in classical and commercial music. Among his specializations is Greek music: he has conducted and recorded much modern Greek music, including most of the ensemble music of Xenakis, particularly with Spectrum and the Xenakis Ensemble (Holland). In parallel he has worked for many years internationally with Vangelis as conductor and arranger for concerts, recordings, film and television performances. He was Artistic Director of the Greek Festival in London 1989 and of the Festival of Byzantine Music in London in 1990, and also lectures on Greek music.

C.I.P.
Charlotte Purkis graduated in music from Leeds University in 1982, became a tutor for the Open University and a junior research fellow in literature at Wolfson College, Oxford. Currently Lecturer in Performing Arts at the University of Southampton, she has written on Krenek and Max Brand for the *New Grove Dictionary of Opera* and published elsewhere on Rutland Boughton and Rudolf Laban, as well as on erotic literature and theatre in the 1890s.

M.F.R.
Michael Robinson, born in Gloucester in 1933, is Professor of Music and Head of Department at the University of Wales, Cardiff, Chairman of the University of Wales Creative Arts subject panel, and Chairman of the Welsh Music Information Centre. He is the author of *Opera Before Mozart* (Hutchinson, 1966), *Naples and Neapolitan Opera* (Clarendon Press, 1972), *A Thematic Catalogue of the Works of Giovanni Paisiello* (Pendragon Press, 1991), and numerous articles on opera. He is also a composer of chamber music and conductor of the Cardiff University chamber orchestra.

S.R.
Stephen Roe's *The Keyboard Music of J. C. Bach* was published in 1989 (Garland, NY). He has written on J. S., C. P. E., and J. C. Bach, has edited Johann Christian's Vauxhall songs and the keyboard music. He is Director of the Manuscript Department at Sotheby's, where he specializes in music manuscripts.

M.R.
Michael Rose, born in 1926, was educated at Marlborough and Magdalen College, Oxford, and did

military service, 1944–8. A writer and broadcaster, he was co-author, with the late Hanna Hammelmann, of the radio series *The Birth of an Opera* (1955–76) and of the libretto for a version of Mozart's *Der Schauspieldirektor* (Glyndebourne, 1957); with John Amis he was co-author of *Words about Music* (1989). He has contributed articles and editorial advice to the *New Grove Dictionary of Music* and all the musical articles to the *Oxford Companion to English Literature* (new edn, 1985). In Italy, he co-directed, and provided scripts and music for, documentary films on Fra Angelico, Raphael and Goya for US television. He is currently a director of A. Zwemmer Ltd, art booksellers, and music consultant to Zwemmer/OUP Music and Books.

J.R.
Julian Rushton took his Mus.B. at Cambridge and D.Phil. at Oxford, his thesis being *Music and Drama at the Académie royale de musique, Paris, 1774–1789* (1969). He taught at the universities of East Anglia and Cambridge until 1982 when he became Professor of Music at the University of Leeds. He has taught and lectured in Canada, the United States, and Israel. Publications include Cambridge Opera Handbooks on *Don Giovanni* (1981) and *Idomeneo* (1993); *The Musical Language of Berlioz* (1983); four volumes of the New Berlioz Edition (including *La damnation de Faust*) and two prefaces for the Pendragon French Opera edition. He is general editor of Cambridge Music Handbooks and serves on the editorial boards of *Music Analysis* and *Musica Britannica*.

G.S.
Graham Sadler was educated at the universities of Nottingham and London. Senior Lecturer in Music at the University of Hull, recordings reviews editor of *Early Music*, co-author of the *New Grove French Baroque Masters* (1986), and area adviser to the *New Grove Dictionary of Opera*, he has written numerous articles and broadcasts on Rameau and his period. Editions include music by Campra, Leclair, Lully and Rameau, many of which have been recorded and/or broadcast.

J.W.S.
Jack Sage was a student, lecturer and latterly Head of the Department of Spanish at King's College, London, with spells at Birkbeck College and the universities of Pittsburgh and Austin, Texas. His special areas of research are Spanish Renaissance and baroque song, opera and zarzuela, drama and poetry. He is now Emeritus Professor of the University of London.

J.C.S.
Jeremy Sams is a freelance accordionist, composer, translator and director.

R.J.S.
Robert Samuels studied English and music at Robinson College, Cambridge, including electronic music with Peter Zinovieff and a Ph.D. with Derrick

Puffett. Interests include the works of Mahler, music analysis, and contemporary theory. He is currently on the staff of the Music Department at Lancaster University.

L.S.
Lionel Sawkins, formerly Principal Lecturer in Music, Roehampton Institute, London, and Visiting Professor, Groupe de Formation Doctorale (Musique et Musicologie) at the Ecole Normale Supérieure, Paris, has contributed many articles on French baroque music to books, journals and dictionaries in France and Britain, and edited works by Lully, Lalande, Rameau and Royer. He is currently preparing the *Catalogue raisonné* of Lalande's works, to be published by OUP under the auspices of the Centre de Musique Baroque de Versailles.

R.L.S.
Robert Saxton (born 1953), began composing aged six and, after early advice from Benjamin Britten, studied for four years with Elisabeth Lutyens. He read music at Cambridge (1972–5, with Robin Holloway) and as a postgraduate at Oxford (1975–6, with Robert Sherlaw Johnson); he also had lessons with Luciano Berio. He has fulfilled commissions from the BBC (radio and television), LSO, ECO, LPO, London Sinfonietta, Fires of London, the Aldeburgh, Cheltenham, City of London, Glyndebourne, Huddersfield Festivals, etc. He is Head of Composition at the Guildhall School, London. Recent commissions include an opera, *Caritas*, and a cello concerto (for Rostropovich). Several of his works are available on CD. He was awarded a D.Mus. (Oxon) in 1992.

J.A.S.
Jan Smaczny studied at Oxford University and the Charles University in Prague. A specialist in the operas of Dvořák, he has written and broadcast on many aspects of Czech music. Since 1983 he has been a lecturer in music at the University of Birmingham. He also writes frequently for the *Independent*, *Opera* and the *BBC Music Magazine*.

B.S.
Frederic Basil Rowley Smallman has been Emeritus Professor of Music, University of Liverpool, since 1985. He was educated at Cranleigh School, the Royal College of Music and New College, Oxford, and was Lecturer and Senior Lecturer, the University of Nottingham, 1950–64. He was then James and Constance Alsop Professor of Music, Dean of the Arts Faculty, and Pro-Vice-Chancellor, University of Liverpool, 1965–85. He was also Accompanist (part-time), Midland Region BBC, 1955–64, and a director of Phoenix Opera, 1967–70. He has conducted several operas. He is the author of books on Passion music, Schütz, and the piano trio, and of numerous articles, particularly on 17th-century German music.

E.S.
Erik Smith (M.A. Cantab, 1954) is the son of German conductor Hans Schmidt-Isserstedt but grew up in England. He has worked for Universal Edition

(Vienna, 1957), as record producer for Decca (1968), Head of A. & R. (until 1989) and record producer for Philips: his many recordings include 80 operas. He was musical organizer of the 1991 Philips Complete Mozart Edition, for which he also orchestrated several sketches. His publications include many record-sleeve notes and articles (mainly on Mozart), BBC Music Guide on Mozart serenades and dances and the music section of the CUP guide to *Die Zauberflöte*.

M.T.
Michael Talbot, born in Luton in 1943, is Professor of Music at the University of Liverpool, where he has taught for over 20 years. He is known internationally for his work on Italian, particularly Venetian, music of the late Baroque, and his publications include numerous books (on Albinoni and Vivaldi), articles, reviews, and musical editions. He is a Fellow of the British Academy.

R.T.
Richard Traubner is the author of *Operetta: A Theatrical History* (Gollancz) and a frequent contributor to the *New York Times*, *Opera News*, *The Economist*, *Stagebill*, *American Record Guide*, and other publications. He has lectured and broadcast on operetta and film throughout the US and the UK, and has written notes for many opera and record companies. His four Offenbach translations have been produced around the US, and he has directed and designed several operettas. He restored material for the New York Shakespeare Festival *Pirates of Penzance*, and wrote new lyrics for the 1991 Houston Grand Opera production of *Babes in Toyland*.

C.T.
Carol Traupman teaches at Moravian College, Bethlehem, Pennsylvania, and is completing a dissertation at Cornell University on Verdi's mid-century contemporaries. She has written numerous articles for the forthcoming *Harvard Dictionary of Musicians*.

J.T.
John Tyrrell was born in Harare, Zimbabwe, and studied at the universities of Cape Town, Oxford and Brno. He worked at the *New Grove Dictionary of Music* and the *Musical Times*, and since 1976 has taught at the University of Nottingham, where in 1989 he became Reader in Opera Studies. His books include *Leoš Janáček: Káťa Kabanová* (1982), *Czech Opera* (1988), which has also been published in Czech (1992), and *Janáček's Operas: A Documentary Account* (1992).

S.W.
Stephen Walsh was born in 1942 and educated at St Paul's School, London, and Gonville and Caius College, Cambridge. From 1963 to 1976 he worked as a music critic and broadcaster in London, writing regularly for *The Times*, *Daily Telegraph* and *Financial*

Times. He was deputy music critic of the *Observer* from 1966 to 1985. Since 1976 he has been Senior Lecturer in Music at Cardiff University. He is the author of several books on music, including *Bartók Chamber Music* (BBC, 1982), and *The Music of Stravinsky* (Routledge/OUP, 1988/1993); he is now at work on a biography of Stravinsky.

J.W.

John Warrack studied at the Royal College of Music and played in various opera orchestras before turning to research and criticism. He was music critic of the *Sunday Telegraph*, then Director of the Leeds Festival, and University Lecturer in Music and Fellow of St Hugh's College, Oxford, until 1993. His books include *Carl Maria von Weber*, *Tchaikovsky*, and (with Ewan West) the *Oxford Dictionary of Opera*. Oxford conferred the degree of D.Litt. on him in 1989.

J.C.G.W.

John C. G. Waterhouse (born 1939) studied at the University of Oxford, where in 1969 he was awarded a D.Phil. for his thesis *The Emergence of Modern Italian Music* (up to 1940). He has been a lecturer in music in the extramural departments of the universities of Belfast (1966–72) and Birmingham (from 1973), and has also spent much time in Italy. His many publications on 20th-century Italian music include the book *La musica di Gian Francesco Malipiero* (1990); an English version is in preparation.

N.W.

Nicholas Williams studied at Cambridge University with Alexander Goehr. He works in music publishing and as a music critic for the *Independent*.

C.W.

Caroline Wood's doctoral thesis was entitled *J.-B. Lully and His Successors: Music and Drama in the Tragédie en musique, 1673–1715.* She has made a special study of scene types in the operas of this period. She lectures in the Department of Music at the University of Hull.

L.A.W.

Lesley A. Wright is currently an Associate Professor of Musicology at the University of Hawaii. After her doctoral dissertation on Bizet's compositional process (Princeton University), she has continued her research on Bizet and his contemporaries. She has prepared editions of Bizet's letters and musical works and has published articles both in dictionaries and in such journals as *19th-Century Music*, *Studies in Music* and *Current Musicology*.

S.J.W.

Simon Wright, born in 1956, read music at University College, Cardiff, and then went to Brazil to research the life and music of Heitor Villa-Lobos for a doctoral dissertation. He has written, lectured and broadcast on Brazilian music and has recently published a book on Villa-Lobos. He combines his post as orchestral hire librarian for OUP with freelance music criticism and research.

D.W.-J.

David Wyn-Jones is a lecturer in the Department of Music, University of Wales College of Cardiff. He is the author with H. C. Robbins Landon of *Haydn, His Life and Music.* He has prepared critical editions of music by J. C. Bach, Haydn and Vanhal, and contributed to the *Heritage of Music* and *The Mozart Compendium.*

Picture Credits

Picture editor: Julia Engelhardt

Agence de Presse Bernand, Paris: 1244
Archive Photos, New York: 349
Archiv für Kunst und Geschichte, Berlin: 584
Archives nationales, Paris: 206
Ashmolean Museum, Oxford: 1046
The Australian Opera, Sydney – photo John C,
  Walsh: 973
Bachrušin Museum, Moscow: 1091
Clive Barda, Performing Arts Library, London: 110,
  1102, 1208
Bartók Archives, Magyar Tudományos Akadémia,
  Budapest: 56
Bayerische Staatoper, Archive, Munich: 1043 – photo
  © Anne Kirchbach: 323, 344
Biblioteca Apostolica Vaticana, Rome: 765, 1166
Biblioteca del Conservatorio, Milan – photo
  Giancarlo Costa: 1149
Biblioteca Nazionale, Centrale, Florence: 4, 339
Bibliothèque et Musée de l'Opéra, Paris: 39, 94, 118,
  284, 382, 558, 573, 596, 654, 659, 830, 833, 850,
  1003, 1155
Bibliothèque municipale, Besançon: 383
Bibliothèque nationale, Paris: 115, 119, 130, 180,
  199, 250, 318, 370, 376, 379, 381, 396, 398, 411,
  588, 832, 835, 837, 838, 844, 851, 920, 930
© Bildarchiv Preussischer Kulturbesitz, Berlin:
  endpapers, 1215, 1219
Bodleian Library, Oxford 576
Boosey & Hawkes Music Publishers, New York:
  1052
Boston Public Library: 175
The British Library, London: 178, 179, 188, 209, 235,
  241, 262, 280, 406, 455, 525, 552, 616, 681, 708,
  711, 735, 754, 769, 777, 780, 795, 927, 933, 970,
  1122, 1133, 1141; Newspaper Library: 252, 394,
  412, 626, 664, 931
British Museum, Department of Prints and Drawings
  © Trustees of the British Museum: 5, 416
The Britten-Pears Library, Aldeburgh: 143, 148;
  photo Nigel Luckhurst: 145
Bundesarchiv, Koblenz: 1048
Collection David Cairns, London: 92
© Jim Caldwell, Houston: 19
By permission of the Syndics of the Cambridge
  University Library: 126
Chester Music, London: 728

Civico Museo Bibliografico Musicale, Bologna –
  photo Scala, Florence: 133
Giancarlo Costa, Milan: 218, 288, 641, 652, 749,
  808, 811, 817, 884, 890, 892, 900, 903, 1011,
  1124
Culver Pictures, New York: 501
Czech Centre of the International Theatre Institute,
  Prague: 214, 614, 1231
Denis de Marney/Boosey & Hawkes, London: 153
Deutsche Oper, Berlin – photo Ilse Buhs: 238 photo
  Ilse Buhs, Jürgen Remler: 464
Deutsche Staatsoper, Berlin: 259, 1205
Deutsches Theatermuseum, Munich: 190, 266, 476,
  609, 643, 694, 774, 795, 1178, 1197, 1240
Devonshire Collection, Chatsworth, reproduced by
  permission of the Chatsworth Settlement Trustees
  – photo Courtauld Institute of Art: 320
Dominic Photography, London – photo Zoë Dominic:
  78, 107, 158, 1107, photo Catherine Ashmore:
  1232
Dumont-Lindemann-Archiv, Theatermuseum,
  Düsseldorf – photo Fred Kliché: 480
© English National Opera, London – photo Bill
  Rafferty: 12; photo Michael le Poer Trench: 1113
Esterhazy Archive, Budapest – photo H.C. Robbins
  Landon: 459
Ralph Fassey, Villemomble: 1013
Finnish National Opera, Helsinki: 653
Gerald Fitzgerald, New York: 648
Forschungsinstitut für Musiktheater, Universität
  Bayreuth, Schloss Thurnau: 48, 140, 211, 266,
  369, 479
Fotomas Index, London: 446, 763, 1097
Collection Anthony Gasson, London: 67, 100, 112,
  131, 273, 564, 617, 631, 815, 1056, 1098, 1160
Gemäeldegalerie Alte Meister, Dresden – photo
  Sächsische Landesbibliothek, Deutsche Fotothek:
  430
Gesellschaft der Musikfreunde, Vienna: 751
Gloucestershire Eche, Cheltenham: 231
Glyndebourne Festival Opera, Lewes – photo Guy
  Gravett: 639
Bob Golby, New York: 878
Graphische Sammlung Albertina, Vienna – photo
  Österreichische Nationalbibliothek, Bildarchiv und
  Porträtsammlung: 452, 963
Historisches Museum der Stadt Wien, Vienna: 703,
  966, 1239
Horst Huber, Stuttgart: 363

Hulton/The Bettmann Archive, New York: 80, 314, 1100

The Hulton-Deutsch Collection, London: 90, 177, 462, 795, 1164

Internationale Stiftung Mozarteum, Salzburg: 700; photo H.C Robbins Landon: 685

Collection Peter Joslin, Wokingham: 1050, 1060, 1061, 1062, 1064, 1066, 1067, 1069

© Anne Kirchbach, Starnberg: 854

Peter Krupeneye, New Rochelle:13

Kungl. Teatern, Stockholm – photo Enar Merkel Rydberg: 570

Kupferstichkabinett, Dresden – photo Sächsische Landesbibliothek, Deutsche Fotothek: 587, 942

Library of Congress, Washington DC : 677

G. Magrini, Viareggio: 806

Mander & Mitcheson Theatre Collection, London: 425

Colette Masson/Enguérand, Paris: 656

The Metropolitan Opera Archives, New York: 293, 494

The Metropolitan Opera Association – photo Winnie Klotz: 362, 365

Collection Madeleine Darius Milhaud, Paris: 668

The Minnesota Opera, Minneapolis: 30

Arnoldo Mondador Editore, Milan: 358, 566

Moravské Muzeum v Brno, Brno: 498, 508, 511

© Munch Museum, Oslo: 254

Musée d'Orsay – photo Lauros Giraudon: 198

Musée du Louvre, Collection Rothschild, Paris – photo Réunion des Musees nationaux: 591

Museo Teatrale alla Scala, Milan: 62, 69, 783, 810; photo Giancarlo Costa: 788, 1247; photo Scala, Florence: 267

Museum für Hamburgische Geschichte, Hamburg: 426

Museum of Czech Music, Prague – photo Olga Hilmerová: 299, 302, 987, 988, 989, 993

Musikbibliothek der Stadt Leipzig: 1006

courtesy of John Napier, London: 575

Národní Muzeum v Praze Theatre Department, Prague: 22; photo Olga Hilmerova: 507

© The Trustees of the National Library of Scotland, Edinburgh: 96

National Film Archive © Turner Home Entertainment: 791

National-Galerie, Sammlung der Zeichnungen, Staatliche Museen zu Berlin: 483

National Portrait Gallery, London: 403, 822

Nederlands Theater Institute, Amsterdam – photo Maria Austria/Particam Foundation: 601

The New York Public Library: 225, 523, 580; Vandamm Collection, Theater Collection: 91, 102, 352, 876, 1226

The New York Times; photo Sam Ialk: 798

© 1993 Novosti (London): 1083

Opera Rara, London: 64, 290

Opera Society of Washington – photo George de Vincent: 356

Oper der Stadt Köln, Cologne – photo Doenitz: 332; photo Stefan Odry: 1255

Opernhaus Zürich: 84

Országos Széchényi Könyvtár, Special Collections Department, Budapest: 311

Österreichische Nationalbibliothek, Bildarchiv und Porträtsammlung, Vienna: 10, 60, 197, 216, 297, 337, 341, 454, 471, 560, 657, 706, 883, 947, 1019, 1021, 1249

Österreochisches TheaterMuseum, Vienna: 329, 390, 1002, 1234

Private Collection – photo Bridgeman Art Library, London: 418

Raccolta delle Stampe Achille Bertarelli, Milan: 275, 688

Rainsville Archive, London: 16, 82, 92, 247, 344, 366, 534, 619, 867, 870, 873, 953, 981, 1174, 1182

G. Ricordi & C., Milan: 731

© Stuart Robinson/Aquarius Picture Library, Hastings: 244

Roger-Viollet, Paris: 489 – Collection Viollet: frontispiece, 203; photo Lipnitzki-Viollet: 921; photo N.D.Roger-Viollet: 8

Collection Michael Rose: 72

Royal Academy of Music Library, London – photo Rita Castle: 825

Royal College of Music: 882; Department of Portraits: 32, 44, 165, 968, 1118, 1211

Royal Opera House Archives, London: 6, 628, 630, 820, 899, 1029, 1144, 1152, 1163, 1191, 1200, 1202

Sächsische Landesbibliothek Abteilung Deutsche Fotothek, Dresden: 928

Salzburger Festspiele, Salzburg: 89

Arnold Schoenberg Institute, University of Southern California, Los Angeles – photo Allan Dean Walker: 955

B. Schott's Söhne, Mainz: 535, 743

Society for Cooperation in Russian and Soviet Studies, London: 135, 799, 827, 864, 925, 980

Donald Southern, London: 1236

Elisabeth Speidel, Obereistedt: 761

Staatliche Kunstsammlungen, Weimar: 1213

Staatsbibliothek zu Berlin, Preussischer Kulturbesitz, Musikabteilung, Berlin: 170

Staatsoper Hamburg – photo Fritz Peyer: 387

Stadt -und Universitätsbibliothek Frankfurt am Main: 492, 959, 961

Statens Kunstmuseer, Stockholm – photo Åsa Lundén: 540

Stiftung Weimarer Klassik, Herzogin Anna Amalia Bibliothek, Weimar: 75, 528

Collection Richard Strauss, Grünwald: 1024, 1038

Richard Strauss Insitut, Munich; by permission of the publishers, B.Schott's Söhne, Mainz: 1031, 1034

Archives Théodore Stravinsky, Geneva: 866

Jaromir Svoboda, Prague: 757

© 1993 Martha Swope, New York: 415, 998

Teatro alla Scala photo Ezio Piccaglani: 801

Theatermuseum, Universität zu Köln, Cologne: 554, 739, 742, 1035

Theatre Museum, Warsaw – photo CAF Press-Photo Agency: 673, 1077

Courtesy of Carl Toms: 156

Rauno Traeskelin, Helsinki: 936

Ullstein Bilderdienst, Berlin: 1027

Collection Ursula Vaughan Williams, © Angus McBean Estate, Debenham: 1119

1272   *Picture Credits*

Courtesy of the Board of Trustees of the Victoria &
   Albert Museum, London: 221, 1094; – Theatre
   Museum: 137, 635, 1047, 1648; – photo Houston
   Rogers: 1103
Virginia Opera Association, Norfolk, Virginia: 715
Richard-Wagner-Museum, Bayreuth: 1185, 1189
Courtesy of the Weill-Lenya Research Center, Kurt
   Weill Foundation for Music, New York: 167, 1221,
   1228
Windsor Castle, Royal Library © 1993 Her Majesty
   The Queen: 1169

Roger Wood, Deal: 151
Zentralbibliothek Zürich: 951

*We would like to thank Heritage of Music, The
Herbert Press and Prof. H. C. Robbins Landon for
their help.*

*Every effort has been made to find the copyright
holders. If any copyright holders have not been
contacted, the publisher will be pleased to hear from
them.*

Index of Librettists

Index of Titles

WATERFORD CITY AND COUNTY

WITHDRAWN

LIBRARIES

Flintshire Library Services

C29 0000 1209 455

MEDDYGINIAETHAU
GWERIN CYMRU

Cyflwynedig i Howard, Alun, Xanthe ac Alys

ac Er Cof am fy Rhieni
David ac Elizabeth Jones
(1896-1971) (1913-1981)